Encyclopedia of Cold War Espionage, Spies, and Secret Operations

Encyclopedia of Cold War Espionage, Spies, and Secret Operations

RICHARD C.S. TRAHAIR

GREENWOOD PRESS
Westport, Connecticut • London

Library of Congress Cataloging-in-Publication Data

Trahair, R.C.S.
    Encyclopedia of Cold War espionage, spies, and secret operations / Richard C.S.
Trahair.
        p. cm.
    Includes bibliographical references and index.
    ISBN 0–313–31955–3 (alk. paper)
    1. Espionage—History—20th century—Dictionaries. 2. Spies—Biography—
Dictionaries. 3. Cold War—Dictionaries. I. Title.
    UB270.T73   2004
    327.12′09′04503—dc22   2004043644

British Library Cataloguing in Publication Data is available.

Library of Congress Catalog Card Number: 2004043644
ISBN: 0–313–31955–3

First published in 2004

Greenwood Press, 88 Post Road West, Westport, CT 06881
An imprint of Greenwood Publishing Group, Inc.
www.greenwood.com

Printed in the United States of America

The paper used in this book complies with the
Permanent Paper Standard issued by the National
Information Standards Organization (Z39.48–1984).

10 9 8 7 6 5 4 3 2 1

Contents

List of Entries

Guide to Related Topics

AFFAIRS, CRISES, DISASTERS, HOAXES, AND SCANDALS

Amerasia Case
Berlin Spy Carousel
Bloch Affair
Brandt Resignation
Brown Affair
Burchett Interview
Crabb Affair
Cuban Missile Crisis
Daniloff Affair
Favaro Affair
Fletcher Murder
Gouzenko Defection
Heath Caper
Hitler Diaries
Holt Hoax
Irangate/Iran–Contra Affair
Israel and the Nuclear Weapons Crisis
KAL 007 Tragedy
Keeler, Christine
Kennedy Assassination and the KGB
Kilim Affair
Kuzmich Episode
Munsinger, Gerda
Oatis Affair
Oswald, Lee Harvey
Pentagon Papers
Petrov Affair
Powers, Francis Garry
Rebet and Bandera Wet Affairs
Rosenberg, Ethel, and Rosenberg, Julius
Sheraton Raid
Sobell, Morton
Spycatcher Affair
Trevor-Roper, Hugh Redwald
Vogeler, Robert A.
Volkov Incident
Ward, Stephen
Wright, Peter

AGENTS OF INFLUENCE

Agent DAN
Burchett, Wilfred Graham
Burgess, Guy Francis de Moncey
Currie, Lauchlin
Driberg, Tom
Ellsberg, Daniel
Favaro, Frank
Hill, John Edward Christopher
Hinton, Joan Chase
Klugmann, Norman John "James"
Service, John Stewart

AMERICAN SPIES AND INFORMANTS

Bentley, Elizabeth Terrill
Calomiris, Angela
Chambers, Whittaker
Childs, Jack, and Childs, Morris
Lovestone, Jay
Matusow, Harvey Marshall

Preface

The *Encyclopedia of Cold War Espionage, Spies, and Secret Operations* provides information about individuals who were involved in espionage during the Cold War, the circumstances that gave rise to their exploits, and the results of what they did. The book invites readers who are unfamiliar with the work of Cold War spies and secret agents to begin a study of them and their activities.

The *Encyclopedia* is written from a humanities and social science viewpoint and has three main parts. The heart of the book consists of over 300 entries that include accounts of the lives of Cold War spies and secret agents and descriptions of important Cold War intelligence operations. The entries are supported by the other main parts of the volume: a chronology of significant espionage activities relating to the Cold War and a glossary of important terms and figures that provides and elucidates the background for the entries. Each entry concludes with at least one reference to another source of information, whether print or electronic, that will help readers find more on the subject in any public or university library.

Entries are extensively cross-referenced both to other entries and to terms appearing in the glossary. In the entries, terms that are set in **boldface** type appear in the glossary with a detailed description. At the end of an entry, "See also" cross-references draw the reader's attention to related entries. Biographical entries provide information on the subject's life and background as well as on his or her espionage activities. Whenever known, life dates are provided for biographical entries; when such dates vary in different sources, "c." will appear before the date, indicating that the date is approximate and cannot be established exactly from the secondary literature. When dates are unknown or highly uncertain, "fl." is used to indicate the period when the event occurred or the individual flourished.

The second part of the *Encyclopedia* is a detailed chronology of Cold War espionage, which will lead readers through the main espionage-related events of the Cold War period. The chronology is based on the entries included in this work, on the work of prominent writers on espionage, and primarily on the research of Richard Aldrich (2002), Christopher Andrew and Oleg Gordievsky (1990), and Jeffrey

Richelson (1995). It provides dates of activities back to 1917 to show clearly that the practice of espionage between the world powers was well established before the end of World War II and the commencement of the international hostilities now known as the Cold War.

The third part of the *Encyclopedia* is a glossary of some important technical terms used by spies and secret agents, such as "dead drop" and "sheep-dipping"; organizations and agencies involved in espionage; important political events that occurred during or before the Cold War era; and people who were involved to a minor degree in secret activities.

Because it would require many volumes to provide comprehensive coverage of all the spies, agents, operations, and agencies involved in Cold War espionage, the *Encyclopedia*'s entries offer only an illustrative selection of the most important of these figures and topics. The glossary and chronology supplement the information provided in the entries and offset the disadvantage inherent in an illustrative approach, and also serve to encourage further encyclopedic work in this field of study.

The *Encyclopedia* also includes a guide to related topics, which will allow readers to trace broad themes throughout the book; an introduction, which reviews the secondary literature on Cold War espionage and includes a reference list of the important secondary sources of information currently available; and a detailed subject index, which will allow users to access important information in the entries not otherwise reachable through the cross-references or the topic guide.

The main entries were selected in the belief that the Cold War, usually thought to have begun in 1946 and to have ended in about 1990, centered on conflict between two superpowers—the Soviet Union (U.S.S.R.) and the United States. The Soviet Union was supported by its satellite nations in Eastern Europe and elsewhere, while the United States was supported by the United Kingdom and the countries of the British Commonwealth, and the other members of the North Atlantic Treaty Organization (NATO) and their supporters. The conflict between the two superpowers, which was often perceived as an ideological war between communism and capitalism (Walker, 1993), arose from attempts by each country to combat the expanding international influence of the other after 1945. However, both Soviet and Western Cold War espionage began well before the end of World War II and appears to have continued well into the 1990s. For this reason, the *Encyclopedia* includes spies and their secret work before and after World War II. Also, the book assumes that Cold War espionage, which appears to have begun in Europe, extended well beyond that continent and involved nations and regions that have so far been given little attention in the literature of Cold War espionage.

The entries have been selected to illustrate broadly the range of espionage activity and its human characteristics, rather than its technical aspects, during the Cold War. Among the entries the reader will find spies and secret agents of both sexes from different backgrounds, social classes, and cultures, as well as espionage in many nations around the world, including Albania, Argentina, Australia, the Balkan countries, the Baltic states, Canada, Chile, Congo, Czechoslovakia, the Dutch East Indies, East Germany, Ethiopia, Finland, France, Great Britain, Hungary, Indonesia, Iran, Iraq, Israel, Italy, Korea, Lebanon, Libya, Malta, Mexico, New Zealand, Norway, Romania, South Africa, Spain, Sweden, Switzerland, the United States, the U.S.S.R., Venezuela, West Germany, and Yugoslavia.

In addition to showing that Cold War espionage began before 1946 and extended beyond 1990, and was conducted well beyond the European continent, the *Encyclopedia* illustrates other far-reaching implications of Cold War spying and secret paramilitary operations. In this broad view of Cold War espionage, spies and secret agents play many social roles, acting, at various times, as academics, agents of influence, authors, assassins, bankers, bureaucrats, charmers, confidence tricksters, defectors, diplomats, double agents, engineers, economists, heroes (both real and imagined), ideologues, innocents, enemies (both real and imagined), journalists, liars, mistaken identities, nonexistent characters, novelists, osteopaths, pilots, prostitutes, romantics, sex workers, scholars, scientists, spymasters, theorists, thieves, traitors, and victims. Espionage operations involve affairs (political and sexual), blackmail, corruption, entrapment, debacles, disinformation, diplomatic scandals, family businesses, front organizations, myth-making activities, mass emigration, mass and individual murder, publishing hoaxes, recruitment and training programs, and technological advances.

The reader will also find among the entries two characters and two operations from spy fiction. The characters are Magnus Pym, the perfect spy in John le Carré's autobiographical novel, *A Perfect Spy* (1986), and James Bond, the perfect secret agent, in the books of Ian Fleming. Both writers stand out for their contributions to popular espionage literature between 1946 and 1990, both worked in espionage, and both attracted the deep and lasting resentment and disdain of professionals in the intelligence community (Rimington, 2001).

The two fictional operations concern the efforts of Magnus Pym in Le Carré's *A Perfect Spy* and the KGB's OPERATION KHOLSTOMER in Robert Littell's fictional history of the CIA, *The Company: A Novel of the CIA* (2002). In Littell's work, the U.S.S.R. attempts to win the Cold War quickly by extirpating Western capitalism from the world economy; in Le Carré's book, two spies, one from each side of the Cold War, tell how they cooperated in Operation GREENSLEEVES to feed the Cold War antagonists with information that was intended to maintain a balance of power between the two and prevent an apocalyptic war.

REFERENCES

Aldrich, Richard J., *The Hidden Hand: Britain, America and Cold War Secret Intelligence* (New York: Overlook Press, 2002).

Andrew, Christopher, and Oleg Gordievsky, *KGB: The Inside Story of Its Foreign Operations from Lenin to Gorbachev* (London: Hodder and Stoughton, 1990).

Le Carré, John, *A Perfect Spy* (London: Hodder and Stoughton, 1986).

Littell, Robert, *The Company: A Novel of the CIA* (New York: Overlook Press, 2002).

Richelson, Jeffrey T., *A Century of Spies: Intelligence in the Twentieth Century* (New York: Oxford University Press, 1995).

Rimington, Stella, *Open Secret: The Autobiography of the Former Director-General of MI5* (London: Hutchinson, 2001).

Walker, Martin, *The Cold War: A History* (New York: Henry Holt, 1993).

Acknowledgments

I had considerable help from many friends and academic colleagues who supported this work with information, discussions, and advice.

At La Trobe University's Borchardt Library, I was fortunate to have the guidance of Eva Fisch, Val Forbes, Julie Marshall, Max Smith, and their helpers. Staff at the Victorian State Library provided valuable help also. Funds for the work came from La Trobe University's School of Social Sciences. I am grateful to the office staff in the Department of Sociology for help with typing the manuscript.

Among those who helped me in Australia were Annie Bobeff, Ian Boyle, Alfred Clark, Diana Howell and her family, Heather Eather, Beatrice Meadowcroft, and M. I. Severn; in England, Anthony Grey and his staff; in the United States, Casey Brown, Steven Brown, Cynthia Harris, Lloyd DeMause, Gillian Trahair, Eric Trist, and John Wagner.

The work is based entirely on secondary sources; I did not seek help or support from any members of the intelligence community or their associates, although it would have been very helpful. I was offered names of retired members of the secret services, but decided to use only published material for this book. Three times, I found much later, I had been in deep discussion with individuals whose experiences in the intelligence community far exceeded my own. Some of these discussions were of considerable help in extending my understanding of some issues that professionals in intelligence must face.

At the end of the introduction there appears a short discussion of the information that the public has had on espionage and secret political work during the Cold War. Such information can lead a scholar into error. In this work, errors of fact and interpretation may emerge; I would be pleased to know them and will acknowledge their source in the hope that an encyclopedic work like this can be clarified, extended, and refined in future.

Richard C.S. Trahair
School of Social Sciences
La Trobe University, Melbourne

Introduction: Reviewing the Literature on Cold War Espionage

HISTORY OF COLD WAR ESPIONAGE

The *Encyclopedia of Cold War Espionage, Spies, and Secret Operations* draws heavily upon the work of numerous scholars currently engaged in writing the history of the Cold War. Prominent among these scholars are Christopher Andrew of Cambridge University and Richard Aldrich of the University of Nottingham, whose works were particularly helpful in compiling the chronology of Cold War espionage that follows the *Encyclopedia*'s A–Z. Of special interest are Andrew and Oleg Gordievsky's *The KGB* (1990) and the first volume of Andrew and Vasili Mitrokhin's *The Mitrokhin Archive* (1999). In these two volumes, the reader will find an account of how Russia's secret services, which were eventually known as the KGB, evolved in name, structure, and function between 1917 and 1990. Readers will also learn who ran these organizations, both in the Soviet Union and in major world capitals. Both books include a list of acronyms and abbreviations for major Soviet espionage organizations and related institutions that thrived during the Cold War. A note on how Russian names can be consistently transliterated is also provided. *The Mitrokhin Archive* also includes new discoveries made in the KGB archives and provides access to KGB secrets that had been unavailable until recently.

The reader will also benefit greatly from *Battleground Berlin* (1997), by David Murphy et al., an account of secret operations conducted by both sides in the Cold War after World War II. The work also provides access to authoritative accounts of operations and individuals that are incompletely recorded elsewhere and to details of American and British CIA/SIS operations, such as the Berlin tunnel, which were known to the KGB.

Richard Aldrich's *The Hidden Hand* (2002), like his earlier research on intelligence in the Pacific in World War II, includes studies on the secret politics, both personal and institutional, that occurred between 1941, when Russia became an ally of Great Britain, to the Profumo scandal in Britain in 1963. Stephen Dorril, a frequent writer on espionage in Britain, published a comprehensive study titled *MI6* (2000), which is another essential source on Cold War espionage in the Special Intelligence Services of Britain.

In the United States, many books on the Cold War have been published, and at Harvard University a special Cold War history project is underway. David Wise (1968, 1979, 1988, 1992) devoted his writing career to Cold War politics and espionage, regularly publishing on the CIA and the lives of spies. In *A Century of Spies* (1995), Jeffrey Richelson emphasizes the technological aspects of spying and covers the main spy scandals of the period. Recently, Lori Bogle (2001) collected 20 contemporary essays on Cold War espionage; these essays are valuable for their details of operations and government policies during the first 15 years after World War II.

In the history of Cold War espionage in the United States, the atom bomb spies hold a premier place. In *Bombshell: The Secret Story of America's Unknown Spy Conspiracy* (1997), Joseph Albright and Marcia Kunstel tell how Soviet spies worked inside the Manhattan Project; in *Red Spy Queen* (2002), Kathryn Olmstead presents a fine biography of Elizabeth Bentley and those around her, who penetrated many U.S. government agencies and sent much information to the Soviets. Her work has been augmented by Lauren Kessler's 2003 biography of Bentley and her role in McCarthy era politics.

In the national interest, all parties to the Cold War keep information about Cold War espionage secret. In the United Kingdom, Nigel West (1987, 1991, 1993, 2000) and Chapman Pincher (1984, 1987) are two prolific writers on Cold War espionage. Their work shaped the first stages of the history of Cold War espionage because they had privileged access to people inside the intelligence services and had the sensitivity and astuteness to be careful about what they sent to their publishers.

Richard Aldrich (2002) writes that the first historians of Cold War espionage were shown information by the intelligence community and were given only material that the community believed would not endanger national security if made public. If Aldrich is right, and most documentation on Cold War espionage operations involving Great Britain has been destroyed, we must not expect more than 2 to 3 percent of our knowledge about Cold War espionage to be reliable and based on documents. Also, we now know that British intelligence authorities allowed publication of *The Mitrokhin Archive* (1999) largely because the material was being edited by Professor Christopher Andrew, a noted Cambridge historian who was trusted by the intelligence community. Furthermore, in April 1995, U.S. President Bill Clinton required U.S. government agencies, with few exceptions, to release documentation that had been held for more than 25 years. Aldrich (2002, p. 7) reports that the U.S. Army complied with the request, but the CIA held back 93 million exempt pages, 66 million of which still had not been processed in 1998. When it comes to Cold War espionage, much will probably never be known. That we shall not know much of what happened in Cold War espionage is both frustrating and appropriate. Although there are strong arguments against secret service agencies in democracies, there will always be secrets to keep and expose, unless basic mistrust among humans can somehow be eliminated.

The systematic weeding of the archives in the secret services is common. To some, it is decent and proper, a protection to the family and associates of spies and secret agents, and something that is morally and ethically required. Few people would work in the secret services unless they could be assured that what they do is kept secret long enough for them to pass out of danger. Whenever national secrets are made public, morale falls in the secret services, as occurred in the CIA in the mid-1970s when the *New York Times*, the President, and the U.S. Congress investigated and revealed secret and sometimes illegal activities. Also, in the early 1990s, research into the history of Cold War espionage was impaired when the KGB archives were opened to historians—access was limited, carefully controlled, and then closed to only a few (Aldrich, 2002).

The work of writers who make a point of exposing espionage indicates that secrets and secret-keeping have both moral and psychological interest, which study of the Cold War can augment and clarify. While Philip Agee (1975) and Victor Marchetti (1974) aimed to demoralize the U.S. intelligence community with their writings, Phillip Knightley (1987) reviewed espionage in *The Second Oldest Profession* and cataloged and moralized over the achievements of various secret services. His criticism centered on the value of the organizations and the competence of their administrators and managers and showed that in most secret services there was considerable room for improvement and cost-cutting. Knightley's view was shared by Chapman Pincher in *Too Secret Too Long* (1984), and more recently was taken up by Arthur Hulnick in *Fixing the Spy Machine* (1999).

MOTIVATION AND ESPIONAGE

Knowing what spies and secret agents do, and how they perform their work, is not sufficient for understanding or explaining Cold War espionage; one must also consider why some people choose to be spies and secret agents, while others prefer open, public political activity.

Biographies have been used to criticize the intelligence services in Great Britain and to examine how well those services are run. Anthony Masters published *The Man Who Was M* (1984), a biography of Maxwell Knight, code-named M; Richard Deacon, a historian who, like Chapman Pincher and Nigel West, reported for many years on Cold War espionage and diplomacy, published a biography of Sir Maurice Oldfield in 1984. Other biographies followed, including Anthony Brown's *"C": The Secret Life of Sir Stewart Menzies* (1987) and Tom Bower's *The Perfect English Spy* (1995), on the life of Sir Dick White. These works are complemented in their analysis of the personal impact of espionage by Tom Mangold's *Cold Warrior* (1991), a powerful study of the CIA's counterintelligence chief, James J. Angleton. Mangold describes the psychological cost of an espionage service that asks far too much of its staff. The same price was paid by Frank Wisner, the intensely anticommunist CIA agent who committed suicide in 1965.

Through the study of biographies and autobiographies it may be possible to answer the question: What motivates people to undertake espionage? In the 1980s, the answer to that question was that spies turned from ideological spying to spying for money. The Permanent Select Committee on Intelligence of the U.S. House of Representatives and the Select Committee on Intelligence of the U.S. Senate suggested that financial pressure, not ideology, was the primary motivation of many spies (Stone, 1989). This answer is attractive because it is simple, clear, understandable, and straightforward; it requires little or no further thought or research. However, it is also largely unsatisfying because it is widely accepted that the pursuit of money and wealth is often a cover story that conceals motives behind much human behavior and experience.

Rejecting that kind of answer, Chapman Pincher, in *Traitors: The Anatomy of Treason* (1987), offered a theory researched during 1985, the "Year of the Spy" (see Richelson, 1995). Pincher examined the lives of many traitors who had been caught and suggested that their motivation for treachery could be understood with a theory that added feelings of resentment and a high "blackmailability" (for persons with access to secret information) to the desire for money. He then augmented this list of three with other possible motivations, including sexual amorality, lying, arrogance and boastfulness, excessive drug and alcohol use, a sense of power, the need for adventure and excitement, greed, a love of foreign travel, and, finally, ideology. In such an explanation, the concepts for the theory and the observations of motives are the same and are reduced to a mere list of attributes and activities that describe, rather than explain, what feelings impel human action.

In "A Q-Method Study in Espionage: George Blake, Superspy" (1997), Richard Trahair examined the case of George Blake by examining Blake's autobiography—*No Other Choice* (1990)—for what Blake felt about himself and the importance of those feelings for what he did at different points in his life. When the data were systematically analyzed, results showed a person who enjoyed deception believed he was superior to most others he knew, liked taking risks and being adventurous, and placed much explanatory importance on childhood experiences. His colleagues were blind to these patterns of feeling and saw him merely as a divided character who felt disrespected because of his Jewish father and his lack of established connections within the British old-boy network. Blake recalled feeling joy as he concentrated on the technical procedures of spying and felt divorced from everyday life while he did his spying. His autobiography provides a rich list of these divisive feelings from childhood and adolescence, and it appears that many of these feelings were restaged in Blake's outstanding achievements as a double agent.

The three elements—feelings of arrogance, a sense of risk-taking, and the joy of deceiving others with conscious duplicity—also comprise the motives that lie behind Chapman Pincher's theory; they are evident as well in John Costello's *Mask of Treachery* (1988) and Barry Penrose and Simon Freeman's *Conspiracy of Silence* (1986), two studies of the life of British spy Anthony Blunt. In his *A Divided Life* (1989), a biography of Donald Maclean, Robert Cecil shows that Maclean's duplicity and arrogance were well established in early childhood, as was his high anxiety over risking his welfare. As Pincher remarks in *Traitors: The Anatomy of Treason* (1987), the factors that are basic to the personality of a spy are evident in life histories, and the individuals differ only in the factor pattern or the balance between the relevant elements of personality.

In *The Emotional Life of Nations* (2002), Lloyd DeMause examines the idea of the divided self—a common theme in writing about spies—and suggests that duplicity, a sense of being divided, and compartmentalized thinking, which the spy Klaus Fuchs admitted to, are evidence of emotional dissociation (see also Greenacre, 1969; Williams, 1987; and Trahair, 1994). DeMause indicates that some origins of nondemocratic politics can be found in how individuals think, and he concludes that the personal origins of nondemocratic politics involve dissociative thinking to resolve conflict.

Dissociative thought can be used as a defense in espionage; for example, it helps individuals to win over and extract information from their enemies by using charm on persons they hate; it supports the "need-to-know" techniques for controlling the work of one's agents and exercising authority over them; and it can be used to compartmentalize information to limit the costs of being caught by one's enemies. These processes are well known in the control of espionage systems and in the management of the psychological state of dissociation; at the same time, they are costly and, as Mangold (1991) shows in the case of James Angleton, illustrate this organizational and personality process superbly.

PROFESSIONALISM IN ESPIONAGE

It is not possible for readers to have an intimate familiarity with Cold War espionage unless they work for their country's spy system. How is this possible? In the late 1970s, I had students who showed an interest in becoming intelligence analysts; so, over lunch with the former head of an espionage agency, I asked him how he chose his colleagues. He said he never employed individuals who applied for work in his organization. In the late 1980s, I met a young man who had recently quit an intelligence agency. He had left his university course for a year and applied to be a chauffer to senior government figures. Not long after he began driving, he was approached to become an intelligence analyst. He took the work and later found that his new employer had learned more about his life than he could recall. As the entries in this book show, the intelligence community and its organizations have changed since the beginning of the Cold War and now approach a level of professionalism that was not so evident at the end of World War II.

During the Cold War, the occupation of spies became the profession of espionage. An occupation becomes a profession when it develops a theoretical perspective on its work; promotes a moral justification for its activities and how those activities serve the community or nation; allows entry to its ranks through special selection and training; employs the methods of professionally trained historians and scientists to establish reliable knowledge among its members; and publishes the reliable knowledge of its activities in learned journals and books. A theoretical justification for knowing the secrets of foreign powers, and for never passing one's own secrets to them, appears among the justifications of modern espionage in the *Encyclopedia*'s entries on George Young, Stella Rimington, Richard Bissell, Jr., William Colby, and Markus Wolf. Questions about personal morals and social ethics are the concern of the novelist John Le Carré (see entry and his 1986 novel, *A Perfect Spy*) and are taken up by Myron Aronoff (1999).

In the new profession of espionage, entrants are selected and specially trained for espionage by unique technical procedures, some of which were taken from the rough-and-tumble of clandestine work in World War II, honed by scientific research and technology, and then applied in many secret operations since 1945. After the flight to Moscow by the British spies Guy Burgess and Donald Maclean in 1951, rationalized personnel selection and vetting procedures were developed to restrict entry into the intelligence profession and to retrain and evaluate agents to see if they were still fit for their work. The technical procedures for spying and clandestine operations, known as tradecraft, have acquired much from the science laboratory and the fieldwork of anthropology and other social sciences, as well as from drug research and the psychological warfare methods of social psychology. Also, small groups formed in the Cold War intelligence services began to override the adventurousness of the old guard from World War II; the old-boy networks began to give way to the professional association of former espionage agents and to young, ambitious intelligence experts. Today on the Internet, the reader can find associations of former agents joining with writers of espionage books to offer expert advice on intelligence matters for the corporate world (CiCentre, 2003).

Universities offer courses in intelligence studies and strategic defense, and they encourage political scientists to work on the history of espionage and to publish biographies of intelligence officers and accounts of their work. Also, the ethics of espionage and the morality of spies in the advise-and-consent process of democratically elected governments and totalitarian regimes are under consideration. The intelligence community now publishes its research, and more secrets are becoming available to the public. The *Encyclopedia*'s entries illustrate the professionalization of espionage in these ways.

Among the professional publications in espionage, the reader will find two journals that regularly review books and publish research on espionage: the *Journal of Intelligence and Counter Intelligence* and *Intelligence and National Security*. Apart from these two, other professional journals in politics and law publish research closely related to espionage and raise discussion of the professionalization of espionage. These journals include the *American Historical Review*, the *American Political Science Review*, *Stanford Law Review*, *Foreign Affairs*, *Foreign Politics*, and the British journal *International Affairs*. Newspapers and newsmagazines that can be relied on for accounts of espionage are, in the United States, the *New York Times*, the *Washington Post*, and *Time* and, in Britain, the *Guardian*, the *Times*, and the *Observer*.

For the advanced study of espionage, a valuable source is the annotated bibliography of magazine and journal articles from 1844 to 1998 in James Calder's *Intelligence, Espionage and Related Topics* (1999). Calder's work also includes an informative introductory essay that lists all major journals in the field, a brief but valuable list of early espionage literature, and the journals and other publications available only to professionals in the intelligence community. For the technical language and procedures of espionage, a good introduction is *Brassey's Book of Espionage* (1996) by John Laffin, an author with firsthand expertise in the military aspects of intelligence and the strategy and tactics of counterintelligence.

Recently, four important books have appeared for general readers and students with a serious interest in the field. In *The Puzzle Palace* (1982) and *Body of Secrets* (2001), James Bamford describes how the United States established its security organizations. In *The Haunted Wood: Soviet Espionage in America—The Stalin Era* (1999), Allen Weinstein and Alexander Vassiliev published a gripping account of the origins of Soviet espionage in the United States during Josef Stalin's regime; and John Earl Haynes and Harvey Klehr, in *Venona: Decoding Soviet Espionage in America* (1999), provides one of the more detailed and readable accounts of the VENONA material, showing how the decoding of that data changed the history of Cold War espionage.

ESPIONAGE AND RELIABLE KNOWLEDGE

The history of Cold War espionage has become a legitimate field of professional inquiry, but it is at present severely hampered by its secondary literature (Aldrich, 2002). The *Encyclopedia of Cold War Espionage, Spies, and Secret Operations* is based entirely on secondary literature, the only source the everyday reader may use when looking for information on the subject. In that literature, many problems arise, and some will infuriate those approaching the subject for the first time.

First, individuals who spy often do so under more than one name and code name. This is common practice in tradecraft. The reader will also find authors spelling even the simplest names differently; for example, Lionel Crabb, the underwater expert who disappeared during a Soviet official visit to England in May 1956, is sometimes spelled Crabbe. Second, there is much confusion in the literature as to when spies and agents were born and died or when various events occurred in their lives; for example, when were the Rosenbergs caught, tried, and found guilty, and for how long were they imprisoned? Third, the names of operations may change during the operation itself; the Bay of Pigs operation, for instance, underwent several name changes; and some names will differ according to which agency—usually the CIA or the SIS—or which author—British or American—is reporting the operation; an example is the Berlin tunnel. Fourth, Russian names will often have different spellings, depending upon which author is reporting the agent's activities. The reader is advised to consult Andrew and Gordievsky (1990) or Andrew and Mitrokhin (1999) for the Russian transliteration. Fifth, some operations are couched in a myth or a curious metaphor, such as the Mossad myth, and this metaphor promotes different accounts of the operation at different times during the Cold War. The VENONA project was subject to this practice for more than 40 years in the national interest, despite the Soviets being informed of the project early in its existence. Sixth, authors who are critical of their government, and want to expose the incompetence of the secret services and make secret information public, sometimes humiliate other authors by accusing them of errors of fact when the "facts" are not securely known. They often attribute to others malicious intentions to mislead the public or, worse, intentions to serve the public with amazing revelations to which the people should have had access beforehand; examples are the hunt in Britain for the third, fourth, and fifth men in the group of Cambridge spies known as the Magnificent Five and the mole who allegedly ran the British secret services and who might have been none other than the British Prime Minister! The psychology of revealing and keeping secrets may help the reader to understand this interest in generally exposing the truth, especially among those who pursue secret political work (see Berggren, 1975; Greenacre, 1969; Jones, 1941; Margolis, 1966, 1974; Sulzberger, 1953).

Finally, some of the secondary sources are deliberately misleading propaganda or self-serving, or both (see, for example, Blake, 1990; Philby, 1968; Lonsdale, 1965); but, like Peter Wright's *Spy Catcher: The Candid Autobiography of a Senior Intelligence Officer* (1987), they all give the reader something of the culture and feeling of Cold War espionage, if not reliable knowledge of material facts.

In the *Encyclopedia*, I have checked facts closely. I would be grateful to know of any errors of fact or interpretation. In those instances where reliable knowledge is weak, I have used tentative language on the subject and have tried to show that even reliable knowledge may not be accurate, but is, for the time being, only true enough.

Readers need not be anguished by the challenges to reliable knowledge in the secondary literature on Cold War espionage. Instead, they should accept the invitation to enter the field, consider carefully what they read, and enjoy it. They should also recognize the shortcomings of information is subject to the internal principle of "need-to-know" among secret security organizations and the external practice of "plausible deniability" for public relations (see Hulnick, 1999; Rimington, 2001; Saunders, 2000).

The *Encyclopedia* is intended to support espionage studies and asks for the extension of their recognition. It also aims to arouse, encourage, and inform curiosity about espionage and those who practice it; the entries tend to illuminate the human side of espionage rather than focus precisely on its technical features. The *Encyclopedia* draws on a wide range of sources from academic to popular and welcomes the reader to study a new profession that serves the reliable interdisciplinary knowledge.

REFERENCES

Agee, Philip, *Inside the Company: CIA Diary* (London: Allen Lane, 1975).

Albright, Joseph, and Marcia Kunstel, *Bombshell: The Secret Story of America's Unknown Spy Conspiracy* (New York: Times Books/Random House, 1997).

Aldrich, Richard J., *The Hidden Hand: Britain, America and Cold War Secret Intelligence* (New York: Overlook Press, 2002).

Andrew, Christopher, and Oleg Gordievsky, *KGB: The Inside Story of Its Foreign Operations from Lenin to Gorbachev* (London: Hodder and Stoughton, 1990).

Andrew, Christopher, and Vasili Mitrokhin, *The Mitrokhin Archive: The KGB in Europe and the West* (London: Lane, 1999).

Aronoff, Myron J., *The Spy Novels of John Le Carré: Balancing Ethics and Politics* (New York: St. Martin's Press, 1999).

Bamford, James, *The Puzzle Palace: A Report on America's Most Secret Agency* (Boston: Houghton Mifflin, 1982).

Bamford, James, *Body of Secrets: How America's NSA and Britain's GCHQ Eavesdrop on the World* (London: Century, 2001).

Berggren, Erik, *The Psychology of Confession* (Leiden: Brill, 1975).

Blake, George, *No Other Choice: An Autobiography* (London: Jonathan Cape, 1990).

Bogle, Lori L., ed., *The Cold War*, vol. 4 (New York: Garland, 2001).

Bower, Tom, *The Perfect English Spy: Sir Dick White and the Secret War 1935–90* (London: Heinemann, 1995).

Brown, Anthony Cave, *"C": The Secret Life of Sir Stewart Menzies, Spymaster to Winston Churchill* (New York: Macmillan, 1987).

Calder, James D., *Intelligence, Espionage and Related Topics: An Annotated Bibliography of Serial Journal and Magazine Scholarship, 1844–1998* (Westport, CT: Greenwood Press, 1999).

Cecil, Robert, *A Divided Life: A Personal Portrait of the Spy Donald Maclean* (New York: William Morrow, 1989).

CiCentre, The Centre for Counterintelligence and Security Studies, http://www.cicentre.com, 2003.

Costello, John, *Mask of Treachery: Spies, Lies, Buggery and Betrayal: The First Documented Dossier on Anthony Blunt's Cambridge Spy Ring* (New York: William Morrow, 1988).

Deacon, Richard, *C: A Biography of Sir Maurice Oldfield* (London: Macdonald, 1984).

DeMause, Lloyd, *The Emotional Life of Nations* (New York: Karmac, 2002).

Dorril, Stephen, *MI6: Inside the Covert World of Her Majesty's Secret Intelligence Service* (New York: The Free Press, 2000).

Greenacre, Phyllis, "Treason and the Traitor," *American Imago* 26 (1969): 199–232.

Haynes, John Earl, and Harvey Klehr, *Venona: Decoding Soviet Espionage in America* (New Haven, CT: Yale University Press, 1999).

Hulnick, Arthur S., *Fixing the Spy Machine: Preparing American Intelligence for the Twenty-first Century* (Westport, CT: Praeger/Greenwood, 1999).

Jones, E., "The Psychology of Quislingism," *International Journal of Psychoanalysis* 35 (1941): 27–33.

Kessler, Lauren. *Clever Girl. Elizabeth Bentley, The Spy who Ushered in the McCarthy Era* (New York: HarperCollins, 2003).

Knightley, Phillip, *The Second Oldest Profession: Spies and Spying in the Twentieth Century* (New York: W.W. Norton, 1987).

Laffin, John, *Brassey's Book of Espionage* (Dulles, VA: Brassey's, 1996).

Le Carré, John, *A Perfect Spy* (London: Hodder and Stoughton, 1986).

Littlell, Robert, *The Company: A Novel of the CIA* (New York: Overlook Press, 2002).

Lonsdale, Gordon, *Spy: Twenty Years in Soviet Secret Service. The Memoirs of Gordon Lonsdale* (New York: Hawthorn Books, 1965).

Mangold, Tom, *Cold Warrior: James Jesus Angleton, The CIA Master Spy Hunter* (New York: Simon & Schuster, 1991).

Marchetti, Victor, *The CIA and the Cult of Intelligence* (New York: Alfred A. Knopf, 1974).

Margolis, Gerald J., "Secrecy and Identity," *International Journal of Psycho-Analysis* 47 (1966): 517–522.

Margolis, Jerald J., "The Psychology of Keeping Secrets," *International Review of Psycho-Analysis* 1 (1974): 291–296.

Masters, Anthony, *The Man Who Was M* (Oxford: Blackwell, 1984).

Murphy, David E., Sergei A. Kondrashev, and George Bailey, *Battleground Berlin: CIA vs. KGB in the Cold War* (New Haven, CT: Yale University Press, 1997).

Olmstead, Kathryn, *Red Spy Queen: A Biography of Elizabeth Bentley* (Chapel Hill: University of North Carolina Press, 2002).

Penrose, Barry, and Simon Freeman, *Conspiracy of Silence: The Secret Life of Anthony Blunt*, updated ed. (London: Grafton, 1986).

Philby, Kim, *My Secret War* (London: MacGibbon and Kee, 1968).

Pincher, Chapman, *Too Secret Too Long* (London: Sidgwick & Jackson, 1984).

Pincher, Chapman, *Traitors: The Anatomy of Treason* (New York: St. Martin's Press, 1987).

Richelson, Jeffrey T., *A Century of Spies: Intelligence in the Twentieth Century* (New York: Oxford University Press, 1995).

Rimington, Stella, *Open Secret: The Autobiography of the Former Director-General of MI5* (London: Hutchinson, 2001).

Saunders, Francis, *The Cultural Cold War: The CIA and the World of Arts and Letters* (New York: The New Press, 2000).

Stone, L. A., "On the Psychological Makeup of a Spy," *Forensic Reports* 2 (1989): 215–221.

Sulzberger, C. F., "Why Is It Hard to Keep Secrets?" *Psychoanalysis: Journal of the Psycho-analytic Society* 2 (1953): 37–43.

Trahair, Richard C. S., "A Psycho Historical Approach to Espionage: Klaus Fuchs (1911–1988)," *Mentalities* 9 (1994): 28–49.

Trahair, Richard C. S., "A Q-Method Study in Espionage: George Blake, Superspy," *Mentalities* 12 (1997): 1–15.

Weinstein, Allen, and Alexander Vassiliev, *The Haunted Wood: Soviet Espionage in America—The Stalin Era* (New York: Modern Library, 1999).

West, Nigel, *Molehunt: The Full Story of the Soviet Spy in MI5* (Sevenoaks, UK: Hodder and Stoughton, 1987).

West, Nigel, *Seven Spies Who Changed the World* (London: Secker & Warburg, 1991).

West, Nigel, *The Illegals: The Double Lives of the Cold War's Most Secret Agents* (London: Hodder and Stoughton, 1993).

West, Nigel, *The Third Secret: The CIA, Solidarity, and the KGB Plot to Kill the Pope* (New York: HarperCollins, 2000).

Williams, Robert C., *Klaus Fuchs, Atom Spy* (Cambridge, MA: Harvard University Press, 1987).

Wise, David, *The Espionage Establishment* (London: Cape, 1968).

Wise, David, *The American Police State: The Government Against the People* (New York: Vintage Books, 1979).

Wise, David, *The Spy Who Got Away: The Inside Story of the CIA Agent Who Betrayed His Country* (London: Fontana/Collins, 1988).

Wise, David, *Molehunt: The Secret Search for Traitors in the Shattered CIA* (New York: Random House, 1992).

Wright, Peter, *Spy Catcher: The Candid Autobiography of a Senior Intelligence Officer* (New York: Viking Press, 1987).

Encyclopedia of Cold War Espionage, Spies, and Secret Operations

A

ABEL, RUDOLPH IVANOVICH (1903–1971). Rudolph Ivanovich Abel was the final identity used by Vilyam Genrikhovich Fisher, known as "Willie Fisher," the Russian spy who was exchanged for American pilot Gary Powers (1930–1977) on February 10, 1962.

The much celebrated arrest of Rudolph Abel occurred in a New York hotel on June 21, 1956. Willie Fisher would not give his name to his interrogators at the Alien Detention Facility in Texas, where he was flown immediately after being caught. After a few days, he admitted to being Rudolph Ivanovich Abel, the name of a dead friend with whom he had a close connection. In this way, Fisher concealed his identity, and at the same time indicated to **Moscow Center** that the man whom the newspapers announced had been caught for espionage was in fact himself.

See also FISHER, VILYAM (WILLIE) GENRIKHOVICH; HAYHANEN, REINO; OPERATION LYUTENTSIA; POWERS, FRANCIS GARY

Source: Andrew, Christopher, and Vasili Mitrokhin, *The Mitrokhin Archive: The KGB in Europe and the West* (London: Lane, 1999).

AGEE, PHILIP BURNETT FRANKLIN (1935–). Philip Agee, a former **Central Intelligence Agency (CIA)** officer, quit the CIA in 1969, claiming to be disillusioned by its organization, and became, according to Pincher (1987), an **agent of influence**. Others suggest he was fired. He disseminated disinformation in the Soviet interest, and exploited the Western freedoms of expression. He decided to expose all he could of the CIA because he did not like its methods.

After leaving the CIA, Agee went to the National University of Mexico and enrolled in Latin American studies. He quit his studies to go to Cuba, where he began writing on the CIA. He may have become a member of the **DGI,** and had its research assistance for his work. In January 1975 Agee published his book in Britain, *Inside the Company: CIA Diary*. The work was supported by the **KGB** with great interest and some information. The book made public the names of approximately

250 CIA operatives, and claimed the CIA had destroyed many institutions and millions of lives around the world. The publication had exactly the impact that the KGB wanted, under its **"active measures"** program of influential acts or operations designed to discredit the United States. Prestigious newspapers and magazines wrote of the CIA corruption, assassinations, and unrelenting espionage.

Richard S. Welch (1929–1975), a U.S. diplomat in Greece, was murdered in December 1975, possibly as a consequence of Agee's revelations and other information printed in a magazine, *Counterspy*. The CIA became the world's laughingstock, and it was necessary to move its employees from their duties and otherwise to avoid the damage to the CIA's work, especially in Latin America. In May 1976 Agee, code-named PONT, informed the KGB that a **walk-in,** code-named MAREK, a master sergeant of Czechoslovakian origins at Fort Bliss, Texas, who approached the Soviet embassy in Mexico City in December 1966 and was recruited in June 1968, had been for the next eight years a CIA **"dangle."** Later in 1976 Agee was ordered out of Britain, which gave rise to great public debate and even greater publicity for his work. Eventually he was forced to quit Britain for Holland in June 1977.

The KGB congratulated itself on its secret efforts to bolster Agee's success, and provided him with ever more information that could be used to discredit the secret CIA work. In 1978 Agee began publishing *Covert Action Information Bulletin* to undermine further the CIA worldwide operations. Again help came from the KGB and also the DGI. Agee's next book was *Dirty Work: The CIA in Western Europe,* in which he named over 700 CIA employees in Western Europe. Meanwhile, the *Bulletin* published a secret CIA document on its plans for the period 1976–1981. Then came *Dirty Work: The CIA in Africa*. Agee had to conceal his authorship of this work for fear of losing his right to reside in Germany. By this stage Agee had made public the names of over 2,000 CIA employees.

In 1980 the U.S. Senate Intelligence Committee described the impact of activities like Agee's as follows: they broke links with covert sources that were costly to replace, especially where foreign languages were necessary; reduced the number of agents who could be assigned as replacements for blown colleagues; lost agents to the CIA who had irreplaceable skills and experience. Agee lost his U.S. passport, but was granted one from Grenada and one from Nicaragua. The U.S. Senate Intelligence Committee proposed an "Anti-Agee Bill," and it became law in June 1981. By 1983 Agee's influence had declined. Agee now lives in Cuba.

See also WELCH, RICHARD

Sources: Agee, Philip, *On the Run* (London: Bloomsbury, 1987); Agee, Philip, *Inside the Company: CIA Diary* (London: Allen Lane, 1975); Agee, Philip, and Louis Wolf, *Dirty Work: The CIA in Western Europe* (London: Zed Press, 1978); Andrew, Christopher, and Vasili Mitrokhin, *The Mitrokhin Archive: The KGB in Europe and the West* (London: Lane, 1999); Mahoney, Harry T., and Marjorie L. Mahoney, *Biographic Dictionary of Espionage* (San Francisco: Austin & Winfield, 1998); Payne, Ronald, and Christopher Dobson, *Who's Who in Espionage* (New York: St Martin's Press, 1984); Pincher, Chapman, *Traitors: The Anatomy of Treason* (New York: St. Martin's Press, 1987); Turner, Stansfield, *Secrecy and Democracy* (London: Sidgwick & Jackson, 1985).

AGENT DAN (fl. 1960–1985). Agent DAN was an anonymous **agent of influence** in Britain, who had a U.S. connection and who was to be greeted in London with the **password phrase** "Didn't I meet you at Vick's restaurant on Connecticut Avenue?"

In the 1950s the KGB aimed to recruit British agents with political influence to get inside information and to promote **"active measures,"** such as propaganda favorable to the Soviets in newspaper reports. Agent DAN was a journalist who was alleged to have served the **KGB** in this way, but his identity is not securely known. The KGB's **resident** recruited Agent DAN in 1959 and gave him the task of writing prepared essays for a left-wing weekly, *Tribune*.

Vasili Mitrokhin (1941–) recorded that £200 was paid in early 1967 to an Agent DAN; and an Agent DAN, a British engineer, was working for an American company, and had been recruited in 1969, but he was not the same person as Agent DAN the journalist, although he had the same **code name**. The journalist was the most reliable of KGB agents who aimed to influence the British public's views of the Soviets in the 1960s.

In the 1970s contact with him ceased, and by the early 1980s he was no longer giving active service. But in 1999, when *The Mitrokhin Archive* was published, Agent DAN became a topic of anger among journalists and others when it was alleged that Agent DAN had been working inside Britain's Labour Party during the **Cold War**. One person cited was the editor of the *Tribune*, Dick Clements, and he was named in the *Sunday Times,* where it was alleged that he was recruited by the KGB and the East German **STASI**. Oleg Gordievsky (1938–) said Clements had been an agent of influence, and so had Michael Foot (1913–), the Labour Party leader from 1980 to 1983. Foot took the *Sunday Times* to court for libel and won. In September 1999 Clements considered doing the same.

Others who might have been Agent DAN were a former lecturer at Leeds University and well-known **Campaign for Nuclear Disarmament** member, Vic Allen; Gwyneth Edwards, a former lecturer and professor of German Studies at Loughborough University, was also named. Fiona Houlding scorned a similar accusation that she had been Agent DAN. She had been an English-language assistant at Karl-Marx University in Leipzig, and the STASI eyed her as a possible **agent**. The fallout from the ignorance of who was a spy fueled much contempt at the time.

Sources: Aitken, Ian, "Spies You Can't Believe In," *Guardian Weekly*, September 23–29, 1999, p.13; Andrew, Christopher, and Vasili Mitrokhin, *The Mitrokhin Archive: The KGB in Europe and the West* (London: Lane, 1999); Andrew, Christopher, and Vasili Mitrokhin, *The Mitrokhin Archive: The KGB in Europe and the West* (London: Lane, 1999); Gillan, Audrey, "Former Labour Leaders Scorn Spy Claims," *Guardian,* September 21, 1999, www.guardian.co.uk/Archive/Article/0,4273,3903987,000.html; Haynes, John Earl, and Harvey Klehr, *Venona: Decoding Soviet Espionage in America* (New Haven, CT: Yale University Press, 1999).

AKHMEROV, ISKHAK ABDULOVICH (1901–1975). Akhmerov was an important **KGB** officer who controlled Soviet **agents** in the United States in the late 1940s.

Akhmerov was a Tartar and joined the Bolshevik Party (1919), graduated from Moscow State University with a diploma in international relations in 1930, and joined the **OGPU** that year. He helped suppress anti-Soviet activities in the Bukhara, joined the Foreign Intelligence Section, and served in Turkey. In 1934 he was a field officer in China, and probably in the following year entered the United States illegally; he ran the Soviet station (1942–1945) without diplomatic cover.

Akhmerov used the cover of a successful furrier and was also known as Michael Green, Michael Adamec, and Bill Greinke; his **code name** was YUNG. He married

Earl Browder's niece, Helen Lowry, and she joined him in espionage work. Elizabeth Bentley (1908–1963) knew him simply as Bill.

One of Akhmerov's major tasks was to oversee the group of U.S. government agents serving Nathan Gregory Silvermaster (fl. 1899–1964). Elizabeth Bentley eventually found him to be an obnoxious supervisor and he grew to dislike her, after attempts to placate her obvious dislike of him and how he operated.

On returning to the U.S.S.R., Akhmerov was made deputy head of the KGB's Illegal Division, was promoted to colonel, and was awarded several honors.

See also BENTLEY, ELIZABETH; SILVERMASTER, NATHAN

Sources: Andrew, Christopher, and Vasili Mitrokhin, *The Mitrokhin Archive: The KGB in Europe and the West* (London: Lane, 1999); Haynes, John Earl, and Harvey Klehr, *Venona: Decoding Soviet Espionage in America* (New Haven, CT: Yale University Press, 1999); Olmstead, Kathryn, *Red Spy Queen: A Biography of Elizabeth Bentley* (Chapel Hill: University of North Carolina Press, 2002); Weinstein, Allen, and Alexander Vassiliev, *The Haunted Wood: Soviet Espionage in America—The Stalin Era* (New York: Random House, 1999).

ALBANIAN PROJECT. The Albanian Project or Albanian Affair, also known as Operation VALUABLE, was one of the first attempts by Western intelligence agencies to curb the perceived expansion of Russia into Europe during the **Cold War**. After a long period of planning, it began in October 1949 and was over in November 1951, when the last attempt failed and the secret operation was well known to the enemy.

In April 1943 two British **agents** from the **SOE** secretly entered Albania with gold and equipment to establish a resistance force against the Italian invaders. The Communist resistance group, led by Enver Hoxha (1908–1985), benefited from six months of training. In July 1943 after the fall of Italy's Fascist leader, Albania was invaded by German troops, who harshly brought the nation under their control. One result of the second brutal invasion was to strengthen the resolve of the partisans, especially the Communist group.

By April 1944, British SOE operatives were back in Albania and found themselves in an ambivalent relationship with Hoxha and his followers. In November 1944, Hoxha established control in Albania, and by January 1946 had outlawed anti-Communist political groups and leaders, Catholics, merchants, and foreigners in general. In the channel between the island of Corfu and Greece, Hoxha's Albanian government fired on two British cruisers in May 1946; the government apologized to the British, closed the narrow international waterway, and thereby precipitated the Corfu channel case. In October that year British ships were mined in the channel; in November a U.S. mission was charged with espionage. Both the American and British governments were appalled at Hoxha's brutal dictatorship in Albania. By January 1949, after the International Court of Justice had reported on its investigation of the Corfu channel case, a Swedish official who had been involved in the investigation likened a visit to Albania to a glimpse into hell.

In Britain, the Foreign Office had established in 1946 the **Russia Committee**—a group that included government defense representatives and delegates from the secret services—to make a policy in opposition to Russia's extension of control over nations on its western borders. The committee's Cold War Subcommittee aimed to loosen Russia's grip on its satellite nations by promoting in each one civil discontent, internal confusion, and political and economic strife. It was agreed this would drain Russia of economic resources, require vast expenditure on her militias, and weaken her control in Eastern Europe. Albania was considered to be one of the first nations—the others would fall like dominoes—to be freed from Russian domination. This was expected to happen within the next five years.

In November 1948 Albania was selected because this policy had worked in Greece, it was financially affordable for Great Britain, and enough of the Albanian people seemed opposed to Enver Hoxha. Also, an officially sanctioned, secret, politico-military operation to overthrow Hoxha would punish Albania for its role in the Corfu channel case and for harboring Greek Communists, and turn a small, weak pro-Soviet state into pro-Western democracy. The scheme would be carried out with U.S. support and without consulting Britain's European allies.

The idea was immediately embraced by Frank Wisner (1909–1965). America and Britain would secretly sponsor a rebellion in Albania and pay for, train, and equip Albanian exiles to effect the rebellion, afterward disclaiming all knowledge of the operation.

By May 1949 the British agents who had originally supported Albanians during **World War II** were managing Operation VALUABLE. In mid-July 1949 the Albanian exiles—to be known as "the pixies"—were arriving in Malta from Italy for training. In October 1949 nine agents landed in Albania, but were ambushed; only four escaped. A second group arrived, only to be temporarily imprisoned by Greek border guards. In July 1950, SIS agents were infiltrated but were caught. After a modest success the training was completely reorganized, and U.S. plans and controls were enlarged.

In November 1950 four émigrés were caught by Albanian security forces. In July 1951 12 men were caught or either killed or tortured and prepared for show trials in October 1951 with other prisoners. While the show trials were being broadcast, another U.S. paratroop mission was undertaken, and failed, in November 1951.

Operation VALUABLE's failure has been largely attributed to Kim Philby (1912–1988), who alerted the **MGB**/KI through his Soviet handler in London in September 1949, when he was on the way from Istanbul to his new **MI6** posting in Washington. But why did some agents, and not others, escape the Albanian authorities? Bethell (1984) suggests that the operation was Philby's greatest coup. West (1988) suggests that two agents were tortured, and probably told more to their interrogators than Philby could have known; that the divided émigré community in Malta or Athens could have leaked information; that "the pixies" themselves were not an entirely cohesive band, and some may have talked; that betrayal was a way of life among Balkan families; and that Albanian Communist agents in Italy may have pressured exiles who had family left in Albania.

See also PHILBY, HAROLD "KIM"; WISNER, FRANK

Sources: Andrew, Christopher, and Oleg Gordievsky, *KGB: The Inside Story of Its Foreign Operations from Lenin to Gorbachev* (London: Hodder and Stoughton, 1990); Aldrich, Richard J., *The Hidden Hand: Britain, America and Cold War Secret Intelligence* (New York: Overlook Press, 2002); Bethell, Nicholas, *The Great Betrayal: The Untold Story of Kim Philby's Biggest Coup* (London: Hodder and Stoughton, 1994); Hoxha, Enver, *The Anglo-American Threat to Albania: Memoirs of the National Liberation War* (Tirana: 8 Nentori, 1982); Knightley, Phillip, *Philby: The Life and Views of the KGB Masterspy* (London: Pan, 1988); Philby, Kim, *My Secret War* (London: MacGibbon and Kee, 1968); Smiley, David, *The Albanian Assignment* (London: Chatto and Windus, 1984); West, Nigel, *The Friends: Britain's Post-War Secret Operations* (London: Weidenfeld and Nicolson, 1988; Coronet ed., 1990).

ALLENDE GOSSENS, SALVADOR (1908–1973). Salvador Allende Gossens, the Chilean Marxist leader, allegedly fell victim to American imperialism by way of the **Cental Intelligence Agency (CIA)** intervention in the politics of Chile, and died a hero during an attack on his government.

Allende four times sought the presidency of Chile and finally won in 1970 by a narrow majority, representing a left-wing coalition, the Alliance of Popular Liberty. He introduced measures to transform Chile into a socialist state, the first time a Marxist nation would be established in South America. This alarmed President Richard Nixon (1913–1994), especially when Allende and Fidel Castro (1927–), Cuba's Communist leader, appeared to hold similar political ideologies.

Nixon pursued a clandestine economic policy to destabilize the Chilean government and, in September 1973, with support from the CIA, General Augusto Pinochet (1915–) seized power, and attacked the presidential palace with tanks, bombs, and rockets. Allende refused to resign. He was supported by the police and the presidential guard, and while he held out for two hours, the palace was set ablaze around him. His doctor said he appeared to have committed suicide; others are certain he died at the hands of Pinochet's soldiers

See also HELMS, RICHARD; OPERATION TRACK TWO

Sources: Falcoff, Mark, *Modern Chile, 1970–1989: A Critical History* (New Brunswick, NJ: Transaction Publishers, 1989); Kornbluh, Peter, *The Pinochet File* (Washington, DC: National Security Archives, 2003); Rojas, Róbinson, *The Murder of Allende and the End of the Chilean Way to Socialism,* trans. Andree Conrad (New York: Harper & Row, 1976); Sifakis, Carl, *Encyclopedia of Assassinations: A Compendium of Attempted and Successful Assassinations Throughout History* (New York: Facts on File, 1993).

AMERASIA **CASE (1945).** A long-standing case of supposed espionage in the United States that was never prosecuted, and involved *Amerasia,* a fortnightly magazine about Asia; the beginnings of the **Red Scare** that dominated foreign policy in the early stages of the **Cold War** in the United States; and the destruction of the careers of noted American experts on China.

In the January 1945 issue of *Amerasia,* a pro-Communist magazine with its head office in New York City, appeared an article "British Imperial Policy in Asia," which included a report on British activity in Thailand. The article used information taken from a classified report by the **OSS** chief of Southern Asia, Kenneth Wells. The original report—not the article in *Amerasia*—described secret Thai resistence forces in action against Japanese invaders. Clearly, the author of the article must have seen the classified report, and by publishing some of its content in *Amerasia* may have put the Thai resistance in peril.

On March 11, OSS agents secretly entered the *Amerasia* head office and found photographs of top-secret documents from the British and U.S. navies, the U.S. State Department, and the OSS and files from the U.S. Office of Censorship. Information on the whereabouts of Japanese ships and secret plans for the bombing of Japan lay on the table. The agents took a small sample of the documents so that the *Amerasia* staff would not suspect a breakin.

For over two months the FBI watched the *Amerasia* staff, and found that most of the U.S. government departments that held classified documents had been penetrated. Investigators believed the origins of the penetration to be pro-Communist, not pro-Axis (Germany, Japan, Italy). At the time there was little public awareness of espionage against the United States. On June 7 Emmanuel Larsen and John Stewart Service (U.S. State Department), Lieutenant Andrew Roth (U.S. Navy Reserve), Philip Jaffe and Kate Mitchell (editors of *Amerasia*), and Mark Gayn (a journalist) were arrested for conspiracy to commit espionage.

With the arrest of the *Amerasia* group, a trial of alleged spies was widely anticipated. But no trial took place, and as time went by, the people arrested became the victims of allegations that they were either Communists or Communist sympathizers, and a threat to the United States.

Nothing happened to the *Amerasia* group in 1945. It was agreed by the prosecution that compulsive zeal and whim among journalists who collected and leaked government documents, and not the intention to spy on the government, was the primary motive for publishing the offending article. Soon this agreement was seen by some as a whitewash of people who were believed to be driven by Communist ideology; others thought the whitewash was a Communist conspiracy in itself.

Years later the Tydings Committee, established to investigated the efforts of Joseph McCarthy (1908–1957), disagreed with those beliefs; others refused to believe any conspiracy theories emanating from Joseph McCarthy. For years the *Amerasia* case was a subject of frequent controversy whenever U.S. policy toward Communist China was debated. Whether or not the *Amerasia* case involved treasonous espionage was never settled.

Observers at that time were suspicious of the agreement between the defense and prosecuting lawyers when the prosecutor got a job with a law firm that had been established by a member of the family of one of the possible defendants in the *Amerasia* case; when a possible defendant in the case quit the United States amid publicity that he was a Soviet **agent**; and when the U.S. Justice Department did not see that a crime had taken place or that its staff had made a mistake.

A close study of the *Amerasia* case showed that respected U.S. citizens had spied for communism; had laid the groundwork for **McCarthyism** and affected the loyalty and security of government employees; had begun debate on the China question; had caused government officials to lie; had revealed turf wars among members of major government agencies; and had destroyed the reputations of valuable experts.

See also SERVICE, JOHN STEWART

Sources: Haynes, John Earl, and Harvey Klehr, *Venona: Decoding Soviet Espionage in America* (New Haven, CT: Yale University Press, 1999); Klehr, Harvey, and Ronald Radosh, *The Amerasia Spy Case: Prelude to McCarthyism* (Chapel Hill: University of North Carolina Press, 1996).

AMES, ALDRICH HAZEN "RICK" (1941–). Ames was a **Central Intelligence Agency (CIA)** officer for many years before he offered classified information to the Soviets in April 1985 for money. By 1994 he had became one of the richest known U.S. spies for the Soviets, and was caught largely because he displayed expenses far beyond what his salary would allow.

Rick Ames was raised in River Forth, Wisconsin, the son of Carlton Ames, a CIA counterintelligence official. He signed on as a CIA trainee in 1962, two years after his father died. Ames studied history at George Washington University for five years;

and, after two years CIA training, he and his wife were posted to Ankara, Turkey (1969–1972).

After five years Ames was posted back at CIA headquarters; his task was to analyze top-secret material. Next he was sent to New York City to spot potential Russian **recruits** at the United Nations. In New York he was unhappy with his work and found he had insufficient money, and his marriage was distressing.

In 1981, without his wife, Ames went to Mexico to recruit agents. He found Mariadel Rosario Casas Dupuy, highly intelligent and well connected, a cultural attaché at the Colombian embassy. By April 1983 she was his mistress and a paid CIA **agent** until December, when Ames was posted back to CIA headquarters and its Soviet Counterintelligence Branch for Southeastern Europe.

He worked at Langley for two years and was authorized to phone and meet with Russian embassy officials in an effort to find possible defectors. In April 1985 he was a **walk-in** who offered his services to the **KGB** in a one-off scam, as he put it, for U.S.$50,000. Instead, for almost nine years he became a Soviet spy, and gave the KGB the names of over 20 Western agents, including Dimitri Polyakov (c. 1921–1985), Adolf Tolkachev (d. 1985), and Oleg Gordievsky (1938–). The first two were executed, and the last managed to escape with help from the British **SIS** through Finland. Most of the others were shot.

In August 1985 Ames divorced his wife and married his mistress. In February 1986 he began meeting Russian agents without making this known to his superiors. That July he was assigned to work in Rome until 1989, and while there he secretly deposited large sums of money into personal accounts in Colombia, Italy, and Switzerland.

Ames was among Russia's CIA **moles** who passed the five-year **polygraph test**. But his high living was noticed in the local press when he was in Italy. In 1989 he said he had married wealthy woman. One female CIA agent did not believe this, but did not have adequate staff to investigate Ames fully. She noted that a day after reporting a meeting with a KGB agent, Ames made a large deposit in his second bank account.

In 1990 when a valuable CIA agent code-named PROLOGUE disappeared, Ames fell again under suspicion, and was moved to another section. Not until October 1993 did investigators have good evidence of his treason; the FBI waited until February 1994, when Ames was due to visit Moscow, before trapping him.

Ames was found to be the most senior known source recruited by the KGB in America; his efforts led to the death of many CIA agents in Russia; and before he was caught, Ames received close to U.S.$3 million with another $2 million on the way.

His wife was jailed for five years; Ames himself, for life; the woman whistle-blower took early retirement; and Ames was regarded by the Russian authorities as being as valuable to them as Kim Philby (1912–1988) had been.

Ames's feelings about his escapades—as he told them in a CNN interview (1998)—were "shock, depression, horror, instant recognition, one's life flashed before me . . . not a sense of relief, something more painful than that." In 1985, so he said, the motivation involved was "personal, banal, greed, folly, simple as that." Others suggested that maybe he wanted to buy his wife's love. He said, "I was exposing [American agents] to the full machinery of Communism, the Law, prosecution and capital punishment . . . certainly I felt I could enure myself against a reaction." Of

Dimitri Polyakov, Ames said, "Many spies like Dimitri F. Polyakov gave up names . . . secrets . . . and I did the same thing, for reasons that I considered sufficient to myself. I gave up the names of some of the same people who had earlier given up others. [Espionage is] a nasty kind of circle with terrible human costs."

See also PHILBY, HAROLD "KIM"; POLYAKOV, DIMITRI

Sources: Adams, James, *Sellout: Aldrich Ames and the Corruptions of the CIA* (New York: Viking Press, 1995); Andrew, Christopher, and Vasili Mitrokhin, *The Mitrokhin Archive: The KGB in Europe and the West* (London: Lane, 1999); Anon., "Rationalizing Treason: Interview with Aldrich Ames," wwwcnn.com/specials/cold.war/experience/spies/interview/ ames, 1998; Bowman, M. E., "The 'Worst Spy': Perceptions of Espionage," *American Intelligence Journal* 18 (1990): 57–62; Carr, Caleb, "Aldrich Ames and the Conduct of American Intelligence," *World Policy Journal* 11 (1994): 19–28; Earley, Pete, *Confessions of a Spy: The Real Story of Aldrich Ames* (London: Hodder and Stoughton, 1997); Laffin, John, *Brassey's Book of Espionage* (London: Brassey's, 1996); Maas, Peter, *Killer Spy: The Inside Story of the FBI Pursuit and Capture of Aldrich Ames, America's Deadliest Spy* (New York: Warner Books, 1995); Mahoney, Harry T., and Marjorie L. Mahoney, *Biographic Dictionary of Espionage* (San Francisco: Austin & Winfield, 1998); Weiner, Tim, David Johnson, and Neil A. Lewis, *Betrayal: The Story of Aldrich Ames, an American Spy* (New York: Random House, 1995).

ANGLETON, JAMES JESUS (1917–1987). James Jesus Angleton was the secretive counterintelligence head of the **Central Intelligence Agency (CIA)** from 1951 to 1973. He was noted for his chain-smoking, deviousness, and obsessive pursuit of **KGB** spies in the West's intelligence agencies.

James Angleton was born in Boise, Idaho, and was buried there 70 years later, having died of lung cancer. His father was a military man who married a Mexican beauty in Nogales, and worked all his life for the National Cash Register Company (NCR) in Boise until 1927, and later in Dayton, Ohio, before becoming its owner. In 1931 the family went to Milan, Italy, where Angleton's father ran National Cash Register as a private concern before selling it back to the original firm in 1964, upon his retirement.

Angleton was educated at private schools in England, where he acquired a deep appreciation for all things British and mastered a charming Old World courtesy. He went to Yale (1937–1941), a tall, intelligent, gracious fellow noted for his English accent and Mexican good looks. Although he was knowledgeable and maintained an unshakable respect for the poetry of T. S. Eliot, Angleton was a poor student and suffered from insomnia. He married in July 1943, and at the age of 25 joined the **Office of Strategic Services (OSS)**; he was a second lieutenant in six months and a first lieutenant by March 1945. During **World War II** he served in Italy, and worked assiduously.

Angleton joined the CIA in December 1947, but took leave for seven months before beginning his first assignment. In September 1948 he joined the CIA's Office of Special Operations, responsible for studying espionage and counterespionage everywhere there was a CIA station. He was consumed by work and a hatred of his middle name, Jesus, which his mother had given him.

In 1951 Angleton became the head of the CIA Israeli desk and, under the regime and patronage of Allen Welsh Dulles (1893–1969), later was made the first head of counterintelligence in the CIA. He was appointed in response to the **Doolittle Report**. For 20 years Angleton and Dulles had a close working relationship, which established for Angleton a profound power base. Angleton broadened it with clever administrative skills and practices that no one could shake. His other patron was Richard Helms (1913–2002), Angleton's superior from 1962 to 1973. His relations with these two gave Angleton vast personal influence inside and outside the CIA, which he combined with his experience, obsessive secrecy, cleverness, and tightly controlled, unaudited, secret slush funds. Impossible to undermine, Angleton became a CIA legend.

In 1962 Angleton moved to a large office in the new CIA building in Langley, Virginia, and ran an empire of CIA counterintelligence staff, the Special Investigation Group (SIG). The task of the SIG was to seek evidence for the KGB penetration of the CIA, and other secret services in the West. Around himself Angleton built a special informal group of colleagues known as **intelligence fundamentalists.**

One of Angleton's closest friends and professional associates was the British agent in Washington who acted as a liaison officer between the **SIS (MI6)** and the CIA, Kim Philby (1912–1988). Often they were seen lunching together, deep in their own worlds of espionage. Trouble was that Angleton's trusted British pal was a KGB spy. In January 1963 Philby, who had worked assiduously for the Soviet cause since 1934, would be forced to flee to Moscow. From that time Angleton was obsessed by this betrayal, and it appears to have destroyed all trust he had in any person thereafter, and profoundly distorted his sense of reality.

In December 1961 Anatoli Golitsyn (1926–), a KGB officer, defected to the West and came to Washington, where he alleged that in the CIA had been penetrated by a KGB mole, code-named SASHA. Angleton worked closely with Golitsyn and, much to the distress of other CIA officials outside Angleton's circle, made Golitsyn a CIA consultant, paid him handsomely, and allowed him access to information normally denied others.

Anatoli Golitsyn convinced Angleton that all political differences between the Soviets and their satellite countries were part of a grand scheme—as was the Sino–Soviet split (1960–1971)—to fool the West; that the KGB was working effectively to take over all the secret services of the West, including **NATO** and the French secret service; that U.S. moles working for the West inside the KGB were being played back against the West; that KGB agents headed the British intelligence services and its Labour government. In fact Golitsyn was mentally unstable, deluded about his own importance, and highly unreliable. Only two of the more than 170 pieces of information he gave the West were of any value.

Angleton spent the final years of his career—and his life—in a passionate, deep pursuit of KGB agents inside the CIA; a serious result was the ruin of innocent employees inside the CIA. In 1973 the senior management of the CIA underwent considerable change, and in 1974 the organization came under close scrutiny, rid itself of Angleton, and was able to examine a catalog of false trails along which his operations had swept agents of goodwill, whose careers had been destroyed.

William Egan Colby (1920–1996), former OSS member and colleague of Richard Helms (1913–2002), became the Director of Central Intelligence, and disagreed with Angleton's personal views on counterintelligence. Under Angleton no spies had ever been caught, so Colby thought. He fired Angleton in December 1974, shortly before the publication of an article in the *New York Times* that drew attention to possible violations of the CIA charter, due in part to dubious operations under Angleton's control.

To Angleton the changes that followed his forced retirement were like watching 200 years of counterintelligence being thrown away. At his retirement celebration he gave a rambling speech that summarized his beliefs about the great Soviet threat. His listeners were greatly embarrassed at the obvious paranoia that had beset the man. A dramatic reconstruction of the speech appears in Littell's (2002) novel about the CIA.

See also COLBY, WILLIAM; DULLES, ALLEN; GOLITSYN, ANATOLI; HELMS, RICHARD; OPERATION CHAOS; OPERATION HT-LINGUAL; OPERATION KHOLSTOMER; OPERATION SAPPHIRE; PHILBY, HAROLD "KIM"

Sources: Littell, Robert, *The Company: A Novel of the CIA* (Woodstock and New York: Overlook Press, 2002); Mahoney, Harry T., and Marjorie L. Mahoney, *Biographic Dictionary of Espionage* (San Francisco: Austin & Winfield, 1998); Mangold, Tom, *Cold Warrior: James Jesus Angleton, the CIA Master Spy Hunter* (New York: Simon & Schuster, 1991); Volkman, Ernest, *Espionage: The Greatest Spy Operations of the 20th Century* (New York: Wiley, 1995); Wise, David, *Molehunt* (New York: Random House, 1992).

ARBENZ GUZMAN, JACOBO (1913–1971). Jacabo Arbenz Guzman came from a Salvadoran family, and was an army officer and later Defense Minister (1945–1950) in the Guatemalan government before being elected President (1950). He was overthrown in a **Central Intelligence Agency (CIA)**–directed coup.

In a bitter electoral contest in Guatemala, Guzman's opponent was assassinated. Arbenz campaign manager was the founder of the Guatemalan Communist Party and an editor of the party's newspaper. After taking up the presidency in March 1951, he continued the agrarian reforms (1952) of the Guatemalan revolution, and expropriated 240,000 acres of the United Fruit Company of Boston's Pacific coast holdings. The company had connections with the U.S. Secretary of State and the director of the CIA. In Guatemala the U.S. ambassador reported that in his opinion the new Guatemalan leader was too closely linked with communism. A CIA agent in Mexico City who knew Guatemala well asserted that Arbenz's wife had a powerful hold over him, and believed that Arbenz was a Communist puppet.

President **Dwight D. Eisenhower** (1890–1969), who had recently outlawed the **CPUSA** (1954), had the CIA overthrow Guzman's government by secretly organizing a military coup in June 1954. Guzman lived in exile. He died by drowning in scalding water in his bathtub, which suggests he could have been murdered.

See also OPERATION PBSUCCESS

Sources: Ambrose, Stephen E., *Ike's Spies: Eisenhower and the Espionage Establishment.* 2nd ed. (Jackson: University Press of Mississippi, 1999); Sifakis, Carl, *Encyclopedia of Assassinations: A Compendium of Attempted and Successful Assassinations Throughout History* (New York: Facts on File, 1993); Smith, Joseph, and Simon Davis, *Historical Dictionary of the Cold War* (New York: Scarecrow Press, 2000).

ATRAKCHI ASSASSINATION (1985). Albert Atrakchi (1955–1985) was a young administrative attaché at the Israeli embassy in Egypt. He was killed by submachine gun on August 20, 1985 in a Cairo suburb. His wife and another embassy employee were wounded. The assassination was the first such death in the six years after Israel and Egypt resumed diplomatic relations following their hostilities. Four years earlier Anwar Sadat (1918–1981), Egypt's President who had helped arrange the resumption of diplomatic ties between the two countries, had been assassinated. Both Israel and Egypt condemned the assassination of Atrakchi. An unknown organization, Egypt's Revolution, claimed responsibility, announcing that it had been necessary to attack members of Israeli intelligence and that further attacks would be carried out until Israel quit the Middle East.

Source: Sifakis, Carl, *Encyclopedia of Assassinations: A Compendium of Attempted and Successful Assassinations Throughout History* (New York: Facts on File, 1993).

B

BANDA, GERTRUDE (fl. 1905–1950). Gertrude Banda was an Indonesian who spied for her country during **World War II** against Japan, and for a brief period during the **Cold War** was a double agent serving the Indonesians against Communists in her homeland.

Banda's origins are obscure. An unlikely story is that she may have been the daughter of Mata Hari (1876–1917); but she would have been 17 and living in Batavia when her mother was executed. Probably her father was an Indonesian and her mother was a white woman.

Banda became a teacher. It has been rumored that she was the mistress of a rich Dutchman who died in 1935, leaving her well off.

During World War II Banda's comfortable home was occupied by the Japanese invaders. She would listen to them and glean information to pass on to the Indonesian underground forces about Eurasians who supported the Japanese, and then give disinformation to the Japanese.

Banda worked for **Achmed Sukarno** (1901–1970), who opposed the return to Dutch colonial rule over Indonesia (Dutch East Indies) after World War II. She supplied him with the secret plans for the restoration of Dutch colonial supremacy, and thereby helped him to counter the efforts of the Netherlands.

Banda married an Indonesian Communist guerrilla, and persuaded him to turn against the Communists and support the U.K. and U.S. policies in Southeast Asia rather than the aims of the Indonesian and Chinese Communists. The British sent her to Washington to get U.S. aid for the British plan to establish an Indonesian republic free of Dutch domination. Her husband was murdered while she was in America. She was recruited by the **Central Intelligence Agency (CIA).**

Sukarno was elected Indonesia's first President in 1949, and would remain in office until removed by a military rebellion in 1966. At the same time, in China, **Mao Zedong** (1893–1976) had established the People's Republic of China. Banda was sent to Communist China to get information on the Red Chinese Army and Soviet views on the new Chinese regime. In March 1950 she went to North Korea; when she got there, she was recognized by a former Indonesian contact, and was immediately arrested and shot.

Source: Mahoney, M. H., *Women in Espionage* (Santa Barbara, CA: ABC-CLIO, 1993).

BARNETT, DAVID HENRY (fl. 1940–1978). David Barnett was a failed American businessman and former **Central Intelligence Agency (CIA)** operative who sold CIA secrets for over U.S.$92,000.

In Jakarta, Indonesia, David Barnett had an exporting business that was unsuccessful. He was recruited by the **KGB** in 1956. Then he was a CIA employee from 1958 to 1970. He contacted a Soviet officer and demanded U.S.$75,000 for the names of over 30 CIA officers and overseas **agents**, but he was prepared to accept U.S.$25,000. He gave the names and personal details of CIA officers who might be turned by the KGB, as well as the names of Soviet diplomats whom the CIA had plans to turn into their own spies.

Barnett was able to inform the Soviets that the surface-to-air missiles being used against the U.S. aircraft in the **Vietnam War** (1964–1975) were not accurate because a CIA secret operation had earlier penetrated the Indonesian navy, which also used the same weapons, and found that their electronics could be jammed. This information was sent to the Americans, and they managed to render the surface-to-air missiles inadequate.

Because his information was not current, Barnett's handler wanted him to get closer to the U.S. Senate Committee on Intelligence; if this was not possible, then he should establish himself inside either the U.S. State Department's Bureau of Intelligence and Research or the CIA. He was not able to achieve the first two goals, but did manage to get rehired on a contract basis by the CIA in 1979, to teach recruits the skills of coping with hostile interrogation.

In 1980, Barnett was caught communicating with his handler at the Soviet embassy, and finally admitted what he had done. The CIA did not want Barnett to be tried, and recommended the U.S. Department of Justice make a private deal with him so that at the trial any adverse publicity about the CIA would be avoided.

The case against Barnett was so strong that he pleaded guilty, and the trial judge received evidence under seal, so little became known to the public. Barnett was sentenced to 18 years in jail.

Sources: Allen, Thomas B., and Norman Polmar, *Merchants of Treason: America's Secrets for Sale* (New York: Delacorte Press, 1988); Bell, Griffin B., and Ronald J. Ostrow, *Taking Care of the Law* (New York: Morrow, 1982); Mahoney, Harry T., and Marjorie L. Mahoney, *Biographic Dictionary of Espionage* (San Francisco: Austin & Winfield, 1998).

BELL, WILLIAM HOLDEN (fl. 1920–1980). William Bell, an engineer with Hughes Aircraft Corporation, sold secrets to a Polish intelligence officer, Marion Zacharski (fl. 1947–1986) for over U.S.$100,000 in cash and U.S.$60,000 in gold. His case is sometimes used to illustrate how easy it is to attract a citizen to espionage when life is difficult to bear.

In 1952 Bell graduated from the University of California at Los Angeles and joined Hughes Aircraft Corporation, where he eventually held top-secret defense contract status.

At the age of 28 he married, and he and his wife had son about 10 years later. Their son died when he was 19, and Holden and his wife were divorced. In 1977, while recovering from the shock of these two events, Bell became friends with a neighbor who had recently settled in America and managed the local branch of a Polish–American engineering company.

Bell's new friend was a salesman for the company, which sold industrial equipment to the aerospace industry. His neighbor was also a secret recruiting **agent** for the Polish intelligence secret services.

In July 1976, Bell, beset with financial problems, had to file for bankruptcy. The Polish agent paid him U.S.$5,000 for the names of potential customers at Hughes Aircraft and two other aerospace companies that were involved in top-secret military projects.

Next, Bell's neighbor sought unclassified literature from Bell about his own work. Bell was paid well for this "consulting" work. Before long he was a committed spy for the Polish intelligence service.

Bell married a flight attendant who had a six-year-old son. He had expenses that his neighbor was helping him to meet and knew that he was doing wrong, but allowed the friendly business relationship to continue.

Bell gave the neighbor a secret proposal that he had been preparing on sophisticated, undetectable radar intended for tanks under attack. At the time he needed U.S.$12,000 for a deposit on a new apartment; his neighbor had the money ready, and provided Bell with a camera with which he was to film secret documents.

Next, Bell was in Innsbruck, Austria, with a camera and plenty of money for expenses. In Austria he learned from an associate of his neighbor that if he did not do as expected, his new wife could be in peril; he received another U.S.$7,000 in cash to help ease this unpleasantness.

In 1980 to 1981 Bell was in Europe three times, working for his neighbor and being well paid. In June 1981 he was caught, largely due to a Polish defector at the United Nations who provided information on the Polish intelligence officers operating in the United States. Bell confessed, and agreed to help have his neighbor caught. Both were found guilty of espionage; the neighbor got life in prison, while Bell was sentenced to eight years jail.

See also ZACHARSKI, MARION

Sources: Allen, Thomas B., and Norman Polmar, *Merchants of Treason: America's Secrets for Sale* (New York: Delacorte Press, 1988); Barron, John, *The KGB Today: The Hidden Hand* (New York: Reader's Digest Press, 1983); Richelson, Jeffrey T., *A Century of Spies: Intelligence in the Twentieth Century* (New York: Oxford University Press, 1995).

BENNETT, LESLIE JAMES "JIM" (1920–). Jim Bennett was a career **agent** and bureaucrat in the British and Canadian secret services who became a victim of James J. Angleton's (1917–1987) search for **moles** in the West's intelligence services.

Born in South Wales, Bennett was raised in working-class poverty at Penrhiwceiber, a village in the Aberdare Valley overlooking a quarry and train line, where his father, a union miner, helped maintain a socialist community in the mid-1920s while other nearby villages idealized and supported communism.

In May 1940 Bennett joined the British army, served in the Signal Corps in the Mediterranean, and after **World War II** entered secret service for the British government's communications headquarters (**GCHQ**). He was posted to Istanbul, where he met the young and ambitious Kim Philby (1912–1988); by 1950 Bennett was working in Melbourne, Australia.

Bennett married an Australian woman, and after further service in Hong Kong and Britain he went to Canada in July 1950 to serve in the **Royal Canadian Mounted Police Force (RCMP)** in Ottawa, in "B" Branch, working in counter-espionage. By the late 1960s Bennett was the deputy chief of the branch. He was never popular for both personal and career reasons, and seemed an outsider to many. During the 1950s and 1960s Bennett was embarrassed by a series of operational failures that he thought were due to inexperienced operatives, the superior training of Soviet spies, and a **KGB** spy in the RCMP.

In 1962 Bennett was invited by James J. Angleton to interrogate the Soviet defector Anatoli Golitsyn (1926–), who gave enough information for the detection of two minor Russian spies in the Canadian intelligence services.

Bennett himself became a possible spy suspect, and this was exacerbated when he came into conflict with Angleton and his supporters in 1964. In 1967 Angleton opened a file on Bennett in the belief he really was a KGB spy. Allegations mounted, and by July 1972 Bennett was forced to resign quietly. He protested his innocence.

Bennett's wife and children left him, and, long unemployed, he finally found menial work, first in South Africa and later in Australia. The intelligence communities in Canada, Australia, New Zealand, Britain, and America were informed of his alleged guilt.

In 1974, when James Angleton was forced to retire from the **Central Intelligence Agency (CIA)** and inquiry was made into Bennett, it was found that there was no evidence that he had ever been a mole for the KGB and that his loyalty to Canada was secure and always had been.

In August 1985, Vitaly Sergeyevich Yurchenko (1936–), an unstable defector to the West, said that it was true there had been a mole in the Canadian Security Service during Bennett's tenure, but that it had certainly not been him; rather, it was Gilles G. Brunet, whose father had been the first director of the security service in the mid-1950s.

Bennett had been one of the victims of James Angleton's unrelenting and at times irrational pursuit of Russian spies in counterintelligence services outside the **U.S.S.R.** When last seen, during the late 1980s, he was living alone, in relative poverty, in a suburb of Adelaide, South Australia.

See also ANGLETON, JAMES; GOLITSYN, ANATOLI; OPERATION GRIDIRON; PHILBY, HAROLD "KIM"; YURCHENKO, VITALY

Sources: Mangold, Tom, *Cold Warrior: James Jesus Angleton, the CIA Master Spy Hunter* (New York: Simon & Schuster, 1991); Richelson, Jeffrey T., *A Century of Spies: Intelligence in the Twentieth Century* (New York: Oxford University Press, 1995); Sawatsky, John, *For Services Rendered: Leslie James Bennett and the RCMP Security Service* (Garden City, NY: Doubleday, 1982); West, Nigel, *The Circus: MI5 Operations 1945–1972* (New York: Stein and Day, 1983); Wright, Peter, with Paul Greengrass, *Spycatcher: The Candid Autobiography of a Senior Intelligence Officer* (Melbourne: William Heinemann Australia, 1987).

BENTLEY, ELIZABETH TERRILL (1908–1963). Elizabeth Bentley was one of the most noted U.S. citizens to spy for the Soviets, change allegiances, and name over 50 Americans who, she said, helped her spy for the Soviets. Her efforts initiated the case of Alger Hiss (1904–1996), the denunciations by Joseph McCarthy (1908–1957) of Communists in U.S. government agencies, and the prosecution under the **Smith Act (1940)** of America's Communist leaders during the late 1940s and early 1950s.

Elizabeth Bentley, an only child, was born in New Milford, Connecticut. Her mother was a schoolteacher, and her father a dry-goods merchant and manager of a newspaper dedicated to checking excessive alcohol consumption. She claimed descent from a framer of the U.S. Declaration of Independence and creator of the U.S. Constitution. She was raised in a strict household whose members often moved around in New York State and to Pennsylvania.

After graduation from Rochester East High School in Rochester, New York, Bentley studied English on a scholarship at Vassar College (A.B. 1930), and graduated, a lonely, friendless, and sad character. With money she inherited after her mother's death, she traveled in Europe and returned to teach languages at Foxcroft, a finishing school for young women in Virginia.

In 1932 Bentley enrolled for graduate studies at Columbia University and went to Florence in 1933, following her father's death. In Italy she became promiscuous, lived a high life, and drank to excess.

Bentley completed the thesis for her M.A., but what she submitted in Europe was the work of another. She failed her exams, and attempted suicide. The U.S. consul in Florence hushed up the incident, and she returned in 1934 to the United States—an alcoholic, a deceiver, and sexually experienced—and was awarded an M.A. in languages from Columbia University (1935). For the rest of her life she suffered from alcoholism and depression.

Unable to find teaching work, Bentley took a secretarial course, worked for the Home Relief Bureau in New York (1935–1938), and later became a secretary at the Italian Library of Information in New York. In need of companionship and claiming to uphold humanitarian ideals, she had already joined the **Communist Party of the United States of America (CPUSA)** at the suggestion of a friend at Columbia University, and thought she would use her job to campaign against Benito Mussolini's (1883–1945) Fascist nation and serve Russia.

Bentley befriended and became the lover of Jacob Golos (1890–1943), an **NKVD** secret police **agent,** who induced her to quit the CPUSA and, after teaching her how to spy, made her his **cutout** with other agents. She used her job as a cover for espionage for the CPUSA.

By June 1941 Bentley had become a fortnightly courier between groups of Communist agents in U.S. government departments in Washington and the secret Soviet agency in New York. She collected information, relayed instructions on what data Russia needed, delivered Communist Party news, and collected party dues.

Because Jacob Golos was overworked, it was Bentley who brought to New York microfilms of documents from the White House, the Pentagon, the **OSS**, and the departments of State, Treasury, and Justice. Such work made her familiar with the George A. Silverman's group of agents in Washington.

After the death of Jacob Golos in November 1943, Bentley felt isolated from the Communist espionage community, depressed, alone, and alienated. At first she took over their espionage network, learned identities of other American subversives, and reported to Anatoli Gromov (a.k.a. GORSKY, fl. 1908–1946), who had been Donald Maclean's (1913–1983) Soviet controller in London and was now in Washington. In time she would find Gromov obnoxious.

Bentley quit communism in 1945, disillusioned by the Soviet exploitation of the U.S., and in August went to the **Federal Bureau of Investigation (FBI)** and agreed to become a double agent for the agency within the CPUSA. In fact, she had been under FBI surveillance as a suspected Communist since May 1941. At the end of 1946 she appeared before a grand jury, and ended her career as a double agent.

In 1948, Bentley converted to Catholicism, and in the summer of that year helped identify over 35 people in U.S. government departments who had supplied her with secret military and political information. Each one either denied her allegations, as did Harry Dexter White (1892–1948), or invoked the **Fifth Amendment**.

Later Bentley's testimony helped convict Julius and Ethel Rosenberg, who were executed for treason in 1953; the economist William W. Remington, who was murdered in prison in 1954; and Morton Sobell (1917–).

Bentley became a lecturer and consultant on communism for the FBI. Recent research (Wilson, 1999; Olmstead, 2002) shows that after she had given her evidence, she endured many personal and financial difficulties, and became an unemployable, abusive alcoholic. She blackmailed the FBI into paying her expenses to assure her testimony at William Remington's trials in 1951 and 1952. Her autobiography is a self-congratulatory tribute, contains evidence of lying and deception, and was largely the work of two men.

Her embarrassment to the FBI and her financial difficulties continued until Bentley found work as a teacher on the faculty of a Catholic college in Louisiana, where she taught from 1958 to her death.

After 1956 Bentley was no longer news. Although she was a plain woman, during the **Cold War** newspapers depicted her as "a spy queen."

See also CHAMBERS, WHITTAKER; HISS, ALGER; ROSENBERG, ETHEL, AND ROSENBERG, JULIUS; SILVERMAN, A. GEORGE; SOBELL, MORTON; WHITE, HARRY

Sources: Andrew, Christopher, and Vasili Mitrokhin, *The Mitrokhin Archive: The KGB in Europe and the West* (London: Lane, 1999); Bentley, Elizabeth, *Out of Bondage* (New York: Devin-Adair, 1951; New York: Ballantine Books, 1988); Garraty, John A., ed., *Dictionary of American Biography,* supplement 7 (1961–1965) (New York: Scribner's, 1981); Haynes, John Earl, and Harvey Klehr, *Venona: Decoding Soviet Espionage in America* (New Haven, CT: Yale University Press, 1999); Hyde, Earl M., Jr., "Bernard Shuster and Joseph Katz: KGB Master Spies in the United States," *International Journal of Intelligence and Counterintelligence* 12 (1999): 35–57; Klehr, Harvey, John Earl Haynes, and Fredrikh Igorevich Firsov, *The Secret World of American Communism* (New Haven, CT: Yale University Press, 1998); Mahoney, Harry T., and Marjorie L. Mahoney, *Biographic Dictionary of Espionage* (San Francisco: Austin & Winfield, 1998); Olmstead, Kathryn S., *Red Spy Queen: A Biography of Elizabeth Bentley* (Chapel Hill: University of North Carolina Press, 2002); Pincher, Chapman, *Traitors: The Anatomy of Treason* (New York: St. Martin's Press, 1987); Weinstein, Allen, and Alexander Vassiliev, *The Haunted Wood: Soviet Espionage in America—The Stalin Era* (New York: Random House, 1999); Wilson, Veronica A., "Elizabeth Bentley and Cold War Representation: Some Masks Not Dropped," *Intelligence and National Security* 14 (1999): 49–69.

BERIA, LAVRENTI PAVLOVICH (1899–1953).

Lavrenti Pavlovich Beria was a Soviet political leader and head of the secret police.

Born in Georgia, Beria joined with **Josef Stalin** (1879–1953) in the brutal treatment of Russians during the 1930s and became head of the **NKVD** in August 1938. He was responsible for many of Stalin's purges and exterminations in the Baltic states and Poland in **World War II**. He organized labor camps, border guards, counterintelligence operations, and the security of the state. He wiped out resistance early in World War II in the Baltic states and Poland.

At the **Tehran Conference** (November–December 1943) and the **Yalta Conference** (February 1945) Beria supervised the bugging of President Franklin

D. Roosevelt's (1882–1945) accommodations in an effort to establish the true intentions of the West in their discussion about what to do after World War II. In 1946 he sought severe reparations from Germany and the support of aggressive policies in Turkey, and was antagonistic to the policies of both the United States and the United Kingdom. At this stage of his career he was the third most powerful Russian leader, behind only Stalin and his Foreign Minister.

On August 29, 1949, Beria was a witness at the early morning detonation of the first Russian **atom bomb**. A few minutes later he phoned Stalin, who told Beria that he already knew about the blast. Beria's immediate response was to promise his colleagues that he would grind into the dirt anyone he found spying on him. He appeared to seek Stalin's post, and in 1952 his envied position in Soviet politics was undermined and his power base began to shrink. Nevertheless, he aimed to rule the **U.S.S.R.** when Stalin died, March 5, 1953. Three other men also sought Stalin's place: in order of influence they were **Georgi Malenkov** (1902–1988), **Vyacheslav Mikhailovich Molotov** (1890–1986), and **Nikita Khrushchev** (1894–1971). Ten days after Stalin's death Beria merged the **MGB** into the **Soviet Ministry of Internal Affairs (MVD)** and took over both departments. In the place of many officials he put men loyal to his interests. He increased his authority by offering to relax the strict domestic and foreign policies he had once supported; dallied with the Yugoslav leader, **Josip Tito** (1892–1980), an avowed personal enemy of Stalin's; and suggested there be a cease-fire in the **Korean War** (1950–1953).

In June 1953 Beria's reforms were discredited during the East Berlin workers' uprising. This was enough to cause Beria to appear to be an ally of the West, and a traitor to the U.S.S.R. At a Politburo meeting early in July 1953, on a prearranged signal from Malenkov, Beria was arrested at gunpoint; the meeting called for his resignation and he was charged with being a Western agent. While his MVD endured a more or less bloodless purge, Beria was tried in secret, and shot with six of his close allies in late December.

Sources: Andrew, Christopher, and Oleg Gordievsky, *KGB: The Inside Story of Its Foreign Operations from Lenin to Gorbachev* (London: Hodder and Stoughton, 1990); Andrew, Christopher, and Vasili Mitrokhin, *The Mitrokhin Archive: The KGB in Europe and the West* (London: Lane, 1999); Mahoney, Harry T., and Marjorie L. Mahoney, *Biographic Dictionary of Espionage* (San Francisco: Austin & Winfield, 1998); Richelson, Jeffrey T., *A Century of Spies: Intelligence in the Twentieth Century* (New York: Oxford University Press, 1995).

BERLIN SPY CAROUSEL (1966–1989). A complex espionage operation run by two young scholars in Berlin who managed to work for three spy agencies at the same time, on both sides of the **Cold War.**

At the University of Beijing in 1966, Hu Simeng (1936–), a graduate student in Western languages, married Horst Gasde, an East German graduate student studying Chinese. After completing their studies the couple went to East Germany, where Horst taught at Humbolt University. He joined the East Germany intelligence services and began to recruit foreign students, especially Chinese, to spy on their homeland when they returned. He recommended his wife to the intelligence services; she agreed to spy on the East German Chinese community, especially its diplomats. Unknown to the East German intelligence and the **KGB**, she had already been recruited by Chinese intelligence to spy on East Germans. Horst knew.

At that time the Sino–Soviet split allowed Hu Simeng, with impunity, to inform East Germans that she would betray her homeland, China, because of its brutal

Cultural Revolution, and to tell the Chinese that she would betray her East German hosts because they were weak and poor Communists who worked closely with un-trustworthy Russians.

Hu Simeng was paid well by both the Chinese and the East Germans. Together, she and her husband enjoyed an immensely high living standard, and were permit-ted to travel freely from the East to the West. To ensure that this utopian arrange-ment lasted, Hu Simeng told her Chinese and Russian handlers that each had approached her to spy on the other. Delighted with this news, both separately en-couraged her to take up the offer.

The couple revealed Chinese spies to the East Germans and East German spies to the Chinese. Knowing this, each side gave them disinfromation to pass on to the other. Then the Gasdes told each side about the disinformation, thereby creating a carousel driven by worthless but fascinating intelligence lies. From 1967 to 1977 tale-spinning made the Gasdes very rich, and provided worthless information for both the East Germans and the Chinese.

In 1978 the East Germans decided to penetrate the Berlin station of the **Central Intelligence Agency (CIA),** which had earned a poor reputation, especially from its clumsy attempt to recruit Chinese spies living in East Germany. Directed by the East Germans, Hu Simeng would spend time flipping through magazines at a kiosk in West Berlin. As expected, she was approached by a CIA operative from a research institute; she told him she was unhappy with life in China and her living conditions in East Germany. He offered her a job writing reports on political life in China for his bogus research institute; she wanted to consider the offer; they met again, and in a week she became a CIA spy!

Regularly Hu took disinformation from her East German handler, itself based largely on disinformation from her Chinese handler, to a safe house in West Berlin, and gave the mishmash to her CIA handler. To add to this bewildering carousel of lie-spinning, she recommended to the CIA that they recruit her husband, who, she said, was no longer content with his East German espionage supervisors. Thus Hu Simeng and her husband were recruited to the CIA.

The last recruitment produced an amazingly complex set of deceptions. Hu Simeng was a triple agent. She worked for the Chinese, who did not know she also worked for the East Germans; the East Germans did not know she also worked for the Chi-nese; the East Germans did know she worked for the CIA; the CIA did not know she worked for both the Chinese and the East Germans. She gave the Chinese disinformation from the KGB and East Germans; knowing this, the Chinese gave her disinformation to pass on to the East Germans; the East Germans took this dis-information and distorted it further before it was given to the CIA; the CIA did not know that the Chinese, East Germans, and KGB intelligence services were produc-ing this mixture of disinformation for its agents.

At the same time her husband, Horst, was working for the CIA; the CIA did not know that he was working for the East Germans or that the East Germans were mak-ing up disinformation for him to give to the CIA; the CIA did not know that the Chinese knew what the East Germans were doing (because he told Hu, and she told the Chinese after she told the East Germans).

The Berlin Carousel turned on its axis of disinformation until 1989, when the Cold War ended. When East and West German governments united, the West Germans discovered the carousel. The CIA agents were told, and they told the Chinese that

Hu had deceived them. When her husband went to his CIA contact to collect his $300 monthly retainer, he was dismissed.

Finally, in 1990 one of his East German contacts tried to recruit Horst and Hu into the KGB. They refused. The carousel had stopped.

Source: Volkman, Ernest, *Espionage: The Greatest Spy Operations of the 20th Century* (New York: Wiley, 1995).

BETTANEY, MICHAEL (1950–). Michael Bettaney was one of the first British intelligence officers to offer his services to the **KGB** in many years after 1954.

Bettaney joined **MI5** in 1975, and was assigned to Soviet counterespionage. His alcoholism was becoming known in MI5, and should have been noted; perhaps he should have been moved from counterintelligence activities.

Bettaney volunteered as a Soviet **agent** in 1983. At Eastertime he put through the letterbox of Arkadi Vasilyevich Guk, the newly appointed London **resident**—an alcoholic and a highly suspicious character—a letter outlining the reasons why MI5 wanted three Soviet intelligence officers expelled from England, with details of how they had been detected, and offering further information. So suspicious was Guk that he saw this offer as a British ploy, a **coattail operation**.

Oleg Gordievsky (1938–), the **SIS**'s spy inside the KGB since 1974, informed the British when Guk stated his suspicions. Bettaney tried again later in the summer, but Guk, suspicious as ever, considered the offer as another British ploy. In despair, Bettaney tried the KGB in Vienna. Arrested on September 16, 1983, he was jailed for 23 years for his efforts on April 16, 1984.

Only a few inside MI5 knew of Gordievsky's position, illustrating the importance of the **need-to-know principle**: had Bettaney been among those who did know of Gordievsky's role, he would probably not have been caught. Also, after his discovery and conviction, the U.K. Security Commission, which exists to report on violations of the **Official Secrets Act**, issued a highly critical report on the management of MI5.

See also GORDIEVSKY, OLEG

Sources: Andrew, Christopher, and Oleg Gordievsky, *KGB: The Inside Story of Its Foreign Operations from Lenin to Gorbachev* (London: Hodder and Stoughton, 1990); Andrew, Christopher, and Vasili Mitrokhin, *The Mitrokhin Archive: The KGB in Europe and the West* (London: Lane, 1999); Laffin, John, *Brassey's Book of Espionage* (London: Brassey's, 1996); Pincher, Chapman, *Too Secret Too Long* (London: Sidgwick & Jackson, 1984); Pincher, Chapman, *Traitors: The Anatomy of Treason* (New York: St. Martin's Press, 1987); Rimington, Stella, *Open Secret: The Autobiography of the Former Director-General of MI5* (London: Hutchinson, 2001).

BIALOGUSKI, MICHAEL (1917–1984). Michael Bialoguski was an important link between the **Australian Security Intelligence Organization (ASIO)** and the Russian defector Vladimir Petrov (1907–1991) in the early 1950s, and helped Petrov come to a decision about his defection.

Bialoguski was born in Kiev, Ukraine, of Polish parents. His father was a veterinarian and his mother a dentist. When Poland became a state (1920), his father took the family to live in the eastern provinces. Michael went to school in Vilna, northeast Poland, and studied music at the Vilna Conservatory, receiving a diploma in the violin (1935) before beginning a medical course. When he was a fourth-year medical student, he was charged in November 1939 with possessing illegal weapons and imprisoned. After his release he worked in a collective theater. The **NKVD** arrested him, but in 1940 he escaped the Russian occupation and fled to Dutch Curacao.

Bialoguski married Irena Vandos, and divorced her in February 1941. Afterward he crossed the U.S.S.R. to Vladivostok, and then to Japan. By June 1941 he had reached Sydney, Australia. Early in 1942 he was called up by the Australian army, but after five months was advised to further his medical studies (1943).

In May 1943 Bialoguski he married Patricia Ryan, and was discharged from the army toward the end of 1944. By early 1945 he was a fourth-year medical student at the University of Sydney and an occasional violinist.

Bialoguski became aware of Communist political groups in Australia, and was convinced that most Australians had little understanding of the brutal methods used by Communist leaders in the **U.S.S.R.** To him Australian authorities were ignorant of and complacent toward Russian communism; he decided to see if this were true, and approached the **Commonwealth Investigation Service (CIS)** to establish for himself their awareness of a Communist fifth column in Australia. The CIS employed him to join Russian clubs, make friends, and spy on them. His contacts among Communist sympathizers extended, and the CIS was pleased with his work.

Bialoguski improved his English enough to obtain his medical degree by October 1947, worked for various employers as a medical officer, and in early 1948 joined a medical practice at Thirroul, south of Sydney. He extended his contacts with Russian immigrants, and made friends easily, presenting himself as interested in cultural and scientific matters. He held an anti-Fascist position in politics.

Bialoguski quit the practice in 1949 to return to Sydney, and joined the Sydney Symphony Orchestra. Also, he found the CIS had been superseded by the ASIO, answerable to the Australian Prime Minister.

After establishing himself in Macquarie Street, the fashionable medical center of Sydney, Bialoguski renewed his contacts at Russian social clubs and in Communist front organizations with an apparent interest in cultural and intellectual pursuits. He was a charming, young divorced man.

At the end of 1949 Bialoguski learned his mother was dead; his father had died earlier in a concentration camp; his brother, Stefan, had escaped to the Middle East, and reached Australia. Now Bialoguski knew that if he were found to be a secret agent for the West, no reprisals could be taken against his family in Russian-occupied Poland. He joined local Communist front organizations that claimed to be pursuing peace, became well acquainted with local **TASS** officials, prospered in his medical practice, enlarged his network among Australian and Russian intellectuals, and at the end of July 1951 met Vladimir Petrov (1907–1991), the newly appointed Soviet consul, Third Secretary of the Soviet embassy, and secret head of the MVD in Australia.

During the next three years Bialoguski became a close confidante and a friend of Petrov and his wife "Dusya." In time Petrov's superiors in Russia and their minions sent to Australia offended him deeply, and his work and his relations with Russian officials became unbearable. He began to think of staying in Australia.

Bialoguski fed Petrov's discontent and eventually helped bring about a quiet defection; later he saw the dramatically publicized escape, through kidnapping, of Petrov's wife in April 1954.

In January 1956 Bialoguski married again, and that year his book *The Petrov Story* (1955) was made into a U.S. TV documentary. Although he earned AUS$18,000 from the book, he had financial problems, failed to pay his second wife's alimony, and in 1957 spent a short period in jail.

Bialoguski went to England, where he established a medical practice near Epsom. He had one daughter and two sons. In 1961 he returned to Australia for a libel suit against his second wife.

In 1967 Bialoguski studied music in Siena, Italy; two years later he made his debut with the New Philharmonic Orchestra at Royal Albert Hall in London. He continued his career as a conductor in Germany and England, and appeared on television in West Germany. In 1974 he was in the Commonwealth Orchestra, and made a vanity recording with the New Philharmonic Orchestra. Living with his family in England, Bialoguski ensured his role in the Petrov affair had been forgotten (Kay, 1985). He died in 1984.

See also PETROV AFFAIR; PETROV, EVDOKIA; PETROV, VLADIMIR

Sources: Bialoguski, Michael, *The Petrov Story* (London: William Heinemann, 1955); Frank, Cain, *The Australian Security Intelligence Organization: An Unofficial History* (Ilford, Essex, UK: Frank Cass, 1994); Hall, Richard, *The Secret State: Australia's Spy Industry* (Stanmore, NSW: Cassell, 1978); Kay, Ernest., ed., *International Who's Who in Music and Musicians' Directory* (Cambridge: International Who's Who in Music, 1985); Manne, Robert, *The Petrov Affair: Politics and Espionage* (Sydney: Pergamon, 1987); McKnight, David, *Australia's Spies and Their Secrets* (St. Leonards, NSW: Allen and Unwin, 1994).

BINGHAM, DAVID (fl. 1945–1982). David Bingham was a British naval sub-lieutenant who was jailed for 21 years in the early 1970s for selling information on submarines to the Soviets.

Bingham and his wife, Maureen, were unsophisticated British spies who tried to manage their debts by giving information for money to Russians in the early 1970s.

Maureen Bingham was a spendthrift who could not properly care for her family. She offered to supply the Russians with information that her husband, a Royal Navy officer, could provide early in 1970. **MI5** was aware of their activity immediately because Maureen walked into the Soviet embassy quite openly. MI5 hoped that if it took no notice of the Binghams' spying, the Soviet controllers would think that the Binghams' work had gone unnoticed. Nikolai Kuzmin, the Soviet controller, gave £600 to Bingham and said some of it was for his wife.

Bingham learned to photograph information at the Portland Naval Base. His espionage lasted two years, until the **GRU** came to believe that Maureen's ineptitude was so gross that MI5 must be using the Binghams to provide poor or misleading information. The Binghams were **dropped dead.** Harassed by his wife's debtors and fearing he may have been found out, Bingham confessed to his naval superiors. Consequently MI5 never had to reveal that they knew about the Binghams' espionage.

Although MI5 had carefully managed the information that Bingham gave the Russians to ensure little harm was done, his treachery attracted a jail term of 21 years in 1972 (Laffin, 1996, p. 60) or 1974 (Pincher, 1987 p. 84) or 1975 (Pincher, 1987 p. 240).

In spite of the wildly variable secondary information on when Bingham was sentenced—it was probably 1972—it seems clear he was released, probably on parole, in July 1982. Maureen was given a suspended sentence.

Sources: Andrew, Christopher, and Oleg Gordievsky, *KGB: The Inside Story of Its Foreign Operations from Lenin to Gorbachev* (London: Hodder and Stoughton, 1990); Laffin, John, *Brassey's Book of Espionage* (London: Brassey's, 1996); Pincher, Chapman, *Traitors: The Anatomy of Treason* (New York: St. Martin's Press, 1987).

BISSELL, RICHARD MERVIN, JR. (1909–1994). In the **Cold War,** Richard Bissell, Jr., was noted for directing plans for the **Central Intelligence Agency (CIA)** between 1959 and 1962, and for his presidency of the Institute for Defense Analysis (1962–1964). He assisted in the **U-2 spy flights program,** was the operational chief of the **Bay of Pigs invasion** of Cuba in April 1961, and worked briefly on policy making for the U.S. secret involvement in the **Vietnam War.** After leaving the CIA, and shortly before he died, Bissell wrote his memoirs and concluded them with a coherent philosophy for covert operations.

Bissell came from an early, well-established American family; his father was a notable East Coast insurance executive. Richard was born and raised in the Mark Twain House in Hartford, Connecticut; the family spent summers in Maine, and would travel often in Europe. Bissell was educated at Kingswood, a school that took over the house in which he had been raised. Later he went to Groton, a preparatory school in Massachusetts. He became well-connected through his associations at school, and went to Yale to study history (1928–1932).

Later Bissell studied in Europe for a year, then returned to Yale to study economics for his Ph.D. (May 1939). A year later he married Ann Bushnell.

In 1941 Bissell and his wife went to live in Washington, where he worked in the Department of Commerce. He attended the **Yalta Conference** (1945) and left it feeling **Josef Stalin** (1879–1953) would make no ally. After the **Potsdam Conference** (July 1945) he began to sense Soviet–U.S. tension. He joined the Office of War Mobilization and Reconversion, and when the **Marshall Plan** (1947–1952) was announced, he served on committees to realize the aims of the plan, and finally served as a senior officer in the Economic Cooperation Administration (ECA).

When the **Korean War** (1950–1953) came, Bissell saw problems of national security and rearmament emerge. These problems led to the abolition of the ECA, and in 1952 Bissell joined the **Ford Foundation**. But by the middle of 1953 Allen Dulles (1893–1969) wanted him to work for the CIA. Bissell agreed, and in February 1954 joined the agency, becoming familiar with its clandestine operations (e.g., in Guatemala, 1954), the development and use of the U-2 spy plane and the scandal surrounding Francis Gary Powers (1960), crises in the Congo (1959–1960), counterinsurgency in Vietnam (1961), the Bay of Pigs fiasco (April 1961), and Operation MONGOOSE (1962). He was greatly disappointed with President **John F. Kennedy**'s (1917–1963) handling of the Bay of Pigs invasion, and later published his views on Kennedy in his memoirs.

Bissell left the CIA when removed from the influential post he had held for years, and was appointed to its Science and Technology Directorate in March 1962. In recognition of his efforts he was awarded a National Security Medal. By the middle of 1962 he was President of the Institute for Defense Analysis, an organization for the recruitment of university personnel for the testing of weapons.

Bissell died in February 1994 from heart disease.

He wrote his memoirs, and concluded them with an essay on the philosophy of covert action, which states why it is necessary for an organization like the CIA to undertake secret operations that intervene in the affairs of other countries. He argued that democracy requires secret operations, and that they must be controlled by the proper authority, be legal, and be in the national interest. Authority should always rest *not* with the elected members of the U.S. Congress, but with the executive branch. To Bissell secrecy did not conflict with the openness of a democracy.

He believed that in a democracy all organizations must be protected and be able to act in private to allow for careful deliberation and decision making before acting. For this reason democracy is compatible with secrecy.

The secret operations that center on the involvement in the affairs of other nations, Bissell felt, can be justified where the broad interests of the United States are concerned. He did not believe that there would be unanimity on the question: Should the United States intervene in the affairs of other nations to protect its broad interests?

Bissell identified the main reason given for accepting such activities. The first concerned military security; he believed that under any circumstances the United States must be able to influence the balance of power in a conflict that threatened its national interest. The second concerned economic interest: for the United States to be economically strong, it must have unlimited access to all needed resources, and be able to go evade and circumvent the efforts of other nations to prevent this. The third reason concerned international order: since the United States aims for democracy to be upheld in a*ll* nations, the forces of communism, totalitarianism, and fascism must be seen as threats to democracy and contained, if necessary, through intervention. Finally, Bissell had a humanitarian concern: it is the duty of the United States to reduce the gap between the rich and the poor, so as to bring stability to the world. For these four sets of reasons **covert actions**—the secret means of influencing people, organizations, and events in other countries, and the concealment of sponsorship— are frequently necessary. He outlines the major means, procedures, and policies underlying his philosophy in the final pages of his memoirs.

See also DULLES, ALLEN; OPERATION PLUTO AND OPERATION ZAPATA; POWERS, FRANCIS GARY

Sources: Bissell, Richard M., Jr., "Response to Lucien S. Vandenbroucke, the 'Confessions' of Allen Dulles: New Evidence on the Bay of Pigs," *Diplomatic History* 8 (1984): 377–380; Bissell, Richard M., Jr., "Reflections on the Bay of Pigs: Operation Zapata," *Strategic Review* 8 (1984): 66–70; Bissell, Richard M., Jr., "Origins of the U-2: Interview with Richard M. Bissell," *Air Power History* 36 (1984): 15–23; Bissell, Richard Mervin, Jr., with Jonathan E. Lewis and Frances T. Pudio, *Reflections of a Cold Warrior: From Yalta to the Bay of Pigs* (New Haven, CT: Yale University Press, 1996).

BLAKE, GEORGE (1922–). George Blake was a **double agent** employed by the British secret service **SIS**, and in 1954 turned to the Soviet cause and spied for Russia until he was caught in 1961. His major achievements were to inform the Russians of hundreds of spies who served Britain—many died as a result—and to keep the **KGB** up to date on Operation GOLD, the Berlin tunnel (1954–1955).

Blake was born November 11, 1922, in Rotterdam, the eldest child and only son of Albert William Behar (1889–1935) and Catherine Beijderwetten (fl. 1895–1990). Beher, a successful Jewish businessman, died when Blake was 13. Blake was sent to Cairo to be raised by his aunt and uncle; he returned to Holland in 1938.

In **World War II**, Blake was caught by the Nazis but eluded them, and with help from the British, reached England, where he joined his family. In November 1943 he joined the Royal Navy and was sent on an officer training course; in the spring of 1944 he became a sublieutenant.

After a short period with submarines, Blake was posted to Naval Intelligence, and was seconded to the Dutch Section of the **Special Operations Executive (SOE)**. He became an interpreter for the Supreme Headquarters of the Allied Expeditionary Forces (**SHAEF**), and later was at General Bernard Montgomery's headquarters when the German Northwest Army Corps surrendered. In Hamburg, he was promoted to intelligence officer, was later awarded the Dutch equivalent of the **MBE**, and for the Nazi war crimes trials helped collect information on German submarine activities.

In 1947, aged 24, Blake returned to England, where he received a scholarship to study Russian at Cambridge. By Easter 1948 his Russian was good enough for him to be employed in the U.K. Foreign Office, and to work in **MI6** under Sir **Stewart Menzies** (1890–1968) as "C," who was chief of the SIS from 1939 to 1952. As a temporary vice consul in the Far Eastern Department, he went to serve at the British Legation in Seoul, South Korea.

In June 1950, during the **Korean War** (1950–1953), Blake was made a prisoner of war in Pyongyang, North Korea, and was taken to Hadjang, where brainwashing techniques had been introduced. He was held captive until April 1953, shortly before the Korean War armistice. He was rewarded with a letter of thanks from **Anthony Eden** (1897–1977)—the equivalent of an OBE—for his outstanding work in Korea.

Blake returned to MI6 as assistant chief of Department Y, and, with **Central Intelligence Agency (CIA)** help, secretly investigated commercial legations of Russian and Eastern Bloc countries in England, Europe, and Egypt. In September 1954, Blake married Gillian Allen, daughter of a Russian expert in the Foreign Office. They were sent to Berlin, where he worked on Operation STOPWATCH/GOLD, known also as the Berlin tunnel, a CIA/SIS operation. Like the Vienna tunnel earlier, the Berlin tunnel tapped the phone connection between Moscow and the Russian military headquarters in Berlin. The Russians discovered the tunnel in 1956.

After five years Blake applied to be posted back to London, and in September 1960 he and his family were sent to Lebanon, where for his next assignment Blake studied Arabic. Before Easter 1961, MI6 recalled Blake; he was accused of offenses against the **Official Secrets Act** on the basis of Russian defector Michal Goleniewski's information. At first he denied the accusations, but later broke down and confessed. The confession was made either in response to the strain of three days of interrogation and being insulted, yet again, by his interrogators stating they knew he had been brainwashed into working for the Communists while imprisoned in Korea, or in response to being told that he had been closely watched during a lunch break from interrogation, and seen pondering over making a phone call, presumably to his Russian handlers. Early in May 1961, Blake, 39, was charged and pleaded guilty to five violations of the Official Secrets Act.

As he would write in his autobiography, by the autumn of 1951 Blake had become strongly convinced of the virtues of communism and had resolved to join the Communist cause to establish a more balanced and just world society; and to this end, during his capture in Korea he had approached Russian authorities and volunteered to make available whatever information he could. So for seven years he betrayed the British government.

Prime Minister Harold Macmillan (1894–1986) was opposed to putting Blake on trial, but was persuaded otherwise by the head of MI6, who thought George Blake was as bad as, if not worse than, Kim Philby (1912–1988). Macmillan agreed, providing that the sentence could be arranged so that Blake served more than 14 years in prison. He was given the longest sentence in British criminal history, 42 years. The story was put about that each year was one for every British agent he had betrayed.

But as Blake concluded accurately, he got one 14-year sentence for each of the three charges of which he was found guilty, and they were to be served consecutively.

Blake divorced, and in October 1966 he escaped from Wormwood Scrubs Prison to Moscow, where he eventually remarried. His escape was difficult to believe at the time: some thought it was due to a deal between the KGB and MI6 officers who thought the 42-year sentence too long and to certain deter other suspected spies from confessing if caught.

A month after reaching Moscow Blake was given the Order of Lenin. He met Kim Philby (1912–1988) and Donald Maclean (1913–1983). In 1990 he published his autobiography. He wrote that he had turned against the West after witnessing the U.S. bombing of civilians in Seoul, and felt he had to do something about it. He was due royalties from his autobiography, but in 1997 the Appeal Court prevented him from collecting them.

Blake always denied that his betrayal of Western spies led to the execution of over 400 individuals, and said that he was told they would not be killed. They were, according to Oleg Kalugin (1934–). While he was night duty officer he copied Peter Lunn's (1914–) card index of agents used by the SIS station in Berlin.

In 1991 Blake said in an ABC News report that he had made a mistake in his support for the **U.S.S.R.**

See also GOLENIEWSKI, MICHAL; LUNN, PETER; MACLEAN, DONALD; OPERATION STOPWATCH; PHILBY, HAROLD "KIM"

Sources: Andrew, Christopher, and Oleg Gordievsky, *KGB: The Inside Story of Its Foreign Operations* (London: Hodder and Stoughton, 1990); Andrew, Christopher, and Vasili Mitrokhin, *The Mitrokhin Archive: The KGB in Europe and the West* (London: Lane, 1999); Blake, George, *No Other Choice: An Autobiography* (London: Jonathan Cape, 1990); Bourke, Séan, *The Springing of George Blake*, Mayflower, 1971 ed. (London: Cassell, 1970; London: Mayflower, 1971); Ford, Richard, "Double Agent Blake Forced to Forfeit Royalties," *The Times*, December 17, 1971, p. 1; Höhne, Heinz, and Herman Zolling, *Network: The Truth about General Gehlen and His Spy Ring,* trans. Richard Barry (London: Secker and Warburg, 1971); Hyde, H. Montgomery, *George Blake: Superspy* (London: Constable, 1987); Kalugin, Oleg, and Fen Montaigne, *Spymaster: My 32 Years in Intelligence and Espionage Against the West* (London: Smith Gryphon, 1994); Laffin, John, *Brassey's Book of Espionage* (London: Brassey's, 1996); Penrose, Barry, "Vicar Who Hid Blake Quizzed," *Sunday Times*, May 25, 1997, Home News; Randle, Michael, and Pat Pottle, *The Blake Escape*, rev. ed. (London: Sphere, 1990); Richelson, Jeffrey T., *A Century of Spies: Intelligence in the Twentieth Century* (New York: Oxford University Press, 1995), pp. 263, 273, 278, 286; Shaw, Terence, "Blake's Spy Book Profit Is Blocked," *The Daily Telegraph*, December 17, 1997, p. 9; Stafford, David, *Spies Beneath Berlin* (London: John Murray, 2002); West, Nigel, and Oleg Tsarev, *The Crown Jewels: The British Secrets at the Heart of the KGB Archives* (New Haven, CT: Yale University Press, 1999).

BLOCH AFFAIR (1989–1990). The Bloch Affair was a scandal that centered on Felix Bloch (1935–) and was brought into public awareness by a TV news reporter in 1989.

Bloch had been deputy chief of station in Vienna (1980–1987) with access to a vast array of U.S. secret documents. A stamp collector, he was introduced by an Englishman to a fellow collector, Pierre Bart; the Englishman's identity is obscure, but he was probably William Lomax or Richard Lomas (d. 1985), who had worked for the American embassy after coming to Vienna in 1945 until his retirement in 1978.

Bloch met Pierre Bart in three different European cities in 1989, and gave him stamps on approval. The **Federal Bureau of Investigation (FBI)** believed that Bloch was passing secrets, not giving stamps, to a **KGB** officer.

In May 1989 Bloch was in Washington, as director of regional economic and political affairs, European desk, and felt at that the time that his career was no longer promising. Pierre Bart phoned him and arranged a meeting. At the time Bart was under surveillance, suspected of using the name of another man as a cover for his own, which was Reino Gikman (c. 1930–). At the time Bloch was about to leave for official business in France.

On May 14, 1989, Bloch went to a bar at the Hotel Meurice in Paris to meet Bart. Later they seated themselves in the restaurant, where Bloch placed his black airline bag beneath the table. After the meal he left without the bag. Later Bart paid the check and, carrying the bag, headed for his hotel. These events were videorecorded by the **Direction de la Surveillance du Territoire (DST)**, France's counterintelligence agency. Bloch did not appear to know that his companion was a KGB **agent** posing as a Parisian. Reino Gikman was a Finn who had lived in Vienna since 1948.

Bloch would later tell the FBI that he had brought a bag containing albums of stamps on approval for his dinner companion, whom he knew only vaguely as a man from Vienna, named Pierre Bart. After passing the stamps to Bart/Gikman, Bloch attended his appointed meetings, and flew to Madrid for further meetings before returning to Washington. He went to Brussels in late May 1989, to be available for a meeting he had earlier arranged between President **George H. W. Bush** (1924–) and the European Community President.

While in Brussels, Bloch went to dinner with Bart/Gikman and again handed him stamps. The **Central Intelligence Agency (CIA)** observed this rendezvous. Bloch returned to Washington, where in late June he had a phone call from Bart/Gikman that seemed to the FBI listeners to be in code. The listeners concluded that the So-viets now knew Bloch and Bart/Gikman were under U.S. surveillance, and prob-ably had been informed of this by a **mole** inside the U.S. intelligence community. Later this mole was found to be Robert Hanssen (1944–). Immediately the FBI interrogated Bloch, showed him surveillance photos of the meetings with Bart/Gikman, took his passport, and kept him under continuous surveillance.

All this information was secret until an ABC News journalist concocted a grainy film of a bogus simulated meeting, presumably between Bloch and Bart/Gikman, for a TV news broadcast that many people later thought had been leaked by the FBI to help them get a confession out of Bloch. Minutes after John McWethy, the TV correspondent, broke the story on July 21, 1989, the State Department confirmed its content; Bloch was denied access to his workplace, and he was put on leave. He appeared to be on trial for treason, and the Bloch Affair was securely established and running in many newspapers.

The FBI discovered that during the time Bloch was in Vienna, he had befriended a young Viennese prostitute. She was brought to Washington to testify before a grand jury. The public learned that in 1980 Bloch had answered her advertisement in Viennese newspaper and had visited her weekly; she provided him with sado-masochistic sex. While in the United States she was under constant FBI guard. From her evidence the FBI assumed that the KGB had learned of Bloch's sexual prefer-ence and had blackmailed him, perhaps from his earliest days in Berlin. At one time the FBI assumed Bloch had sold secrets to pay for sex, but later it was found his financial position was secure and there was no evidence to support the assumption.

Early in December 1989 the FBI surveillance appeared to cease. The Bloch Affair could not be supported because he would not confess, and had never been caught in active espionage. Probably the French DST officers had had no reason to arrest him because he had not broken French law. No one knows for certain what was in the bag he left for Reino Gikman. Bloch said stamps; no one else said anything.

The FBI left the case open, and was shamed for having promoted a massive, pointless surveillance of a man on whom they could not find evidence of guilt. The FBI stoutly denied that it had leaked its suspicions to the ABC reporter who fabricated the TV film. Bloch was free, but he was taken off the State Department payroll and moves were made to have him dismissed. He refused to resign for fear of putting his pension at risk. He started looking for another job because he felt he could never prove his innocence. His only crimes were disrespect for his ambassador and exposing himself to public blackmail. Reino Gikman vanished after June 11, 1989.

To rekindle public interest in the Bloch affair in 1993, ABC Television put together an account of his case; the program was judged tasteless and embarrassing, and a public apology was made next day.

See also BLOCH, FELIX; GIKMAN, REINO; HANSSEN, ROBERT

Source: Wise, David, "The Felix Bloch Affair," *New York Times Magazine,* May 13, 1990, p. 28.

BLOCH, FELIX (1935–). Felix Bloch was at the center of a spy scandal in the United States, beginning in July 1989 to December 1989, which led to the disgrace of both Bloch and the **Federal Bureau of Investigation (FBI).**

Felix Bloch was born in Vienna. He escaped Nazi-occupied Austria with his Jewish parents and twin sister in April 1939, and the children were raised in New York City as Presbyterians—his mother converted, his father did not—and attended the Brick Presbyterian Church on Park Avenue, the church of the Rockefeller family.

In 1957 Bloch graduated from the University of Pennsylvania, then studied for a year in Italy, and returned to the United States to study international relations at Johns Hopkins University. He married the daughter of a state senator in 1959, and joined the Intelligence Division of the U.S. State Department. In Düsseldorf, Germany, in 1960 they had their first daughter; two years later they had another. The family was subsequently stationed for two years in Caracas, Venezuela.

On returning to the United States, Bloch completed an M.A. in international relations; he was posted in 1970 to West Berlin and later to East Berlin. He was then transferred to Singapore, and in 1980 to Vienna. By May 1983 he had become the ambassador's Deputy Chief of Mission. He worked assiduously, in the hope that he would become the U.S. ambassador in Vienna, a city he fully enjoyed.

In May 1986 the newly appointed ambassador and Bloch were at sword's points over many matters, often arguing; the ambassador suspected Bloch had been breaching security, and Bloch thought the ambassador was a fool. By the summer of 1987 Bloch has been withdrawn from Vienna and posted back to Washington. He was suspected of spying for Russia because of inexplicable meetings with Reino Gikman. When questioned, Bloch said he and Gikman were stamp collectors, and he gave Gikman stamps to examine on approval. The FBI kept Bloch under constant secret surveillance, but he would not confess.

When the secret surveillance was made public in July 1989, the media as well the FBI harassed him, and he was virtually on public trial in the media for treason. He would not confess. The FBI did not have secure evidence that he had spied for the Russians. Nevertheless, he was fired on security grounds because he had lied to his interrogators, and the State Department canceled his $57,000 pension.

Bloch found it hard to get employment. In North Carolina he became a bus driver for the Chapel Hill Transit Service in July 1992, and was there still in early 2001. He has been arrested for shoplifting three times and pleaded guilty. He was fined $60 and agreed to do community service.

When Robert Hanssen (1944–) was caught and imprisoned for spying, his interrogation revealed that he had warned Bloch about the investigation by the FBI into the phone call of June 22, 1989, the last time Bloch spoke with Gikman. The FBI interviewed Bloch; he again denied having been a spy, and refused further questioning. The case remains open, and the FBI continues to investigate.

See also BLOCH AFFAIR; GIKMAN, REINO

Sources: Mahoney, Harry T., and Marjorie L. Mahoney, *Biographic Dictionary of Espionage* (San Francisco: Austin & Winfield, 1998); Robinson, Bryan, "From Alleged Spy to Bus Driver: Whatever Happened to Felix Bloch?" abcnews.com, February 21, 2001; Wise, David, "The Felix Bloch Affair," *New York Times Magazine,* May 13, 1990, p. 28.

BLUNT, ANTHONY FREDERICK (1907–1983).

Anthony Blunt was a Soviet **agent**, first of the **KGB**'s Magnificent Five; a self-possessed, cool, aloof, high-flying intellectual with a grudge against the British Establishment.

Anthony Blunt was the third son of a Bournemouth clergyman; his mother was connected to Britain's royal family, and lived as a patriotic, puritanical teetotaler. All his life Anthony loved her.

In 1911 the family was in Paris, where Reverend Blunt served as chaplain to the British embassy. Anthony attended preparatory school in Paris, and was educated for five years at Marlborough College (1921–1926). Later, at Trinity College, Cambridge, he failed to achieve a first in mathematics and, driven by his failure, undertook the study of modern languages, beginning in October 1927. He traveled to Bavaria and Austria in 1928, and on his return began to advance his career as an expert in European art and as an art critic.

In May 1928 Blunt was elected to the Society of Apostles, a secret intellectual society at Cambridge, where he gained important friends and personal influence. The membership later helped him find people who would be well suited to high office in Britain's civil service. The seeds of Marxism spread among the Apostles and others among the elite intellectuals of Cambridge. Blunt played bridge well; shared a close friendship with Andrew Gow; and loved Julian Bell, who had early adopted socialism. In the autumn of 1928 Blunt founded *Venture,* a magazine that introduced left-wing writers; by now he was clearly a supporter of international communism.

In 1930, a year after his father died, Blunt took a first-class degree in modern languages and was awarded a senior scholarship. In October 1932, he was elected a fellow of Trinity College, Cambridge.

By 1932 Blunt was a political agent for the Soviets; in 1935 he was **talent spotting** for them; in 1937 he was supervising Michael Straight (1916–2004). Thus, in 1963, when he confessed secretly to **MI5** that he became a Communist in the mid-

1930s, when Marxism was spreading rapidly through Cambridge undergraduates, he was a telling a lie. Later he would lie often in his public statements.

MI5 had an active interest in young scholars with Communist preferences in the mid-1920s, and the **GRU** had an undercover agent in Cambridge in the early 1930s. In 1935 Blunt went to the Soviet Union and he contributed to the *Left Review*.

In 1940 Blunt, 33, was recruited as a military liaison officer into MI5 to deal with routine matters of security. From this post he was well established to serve his Soviet handlers.

In 1944 Blunt is reported as moving to **SHAEF**, where he may have been able to keep the Soviets informed on the West's invasion of Europe. In 1945 he quit espionage for the Soviets, who accepted his decision, and in November was the Surveyor of the King's Pictures.

Blunt did not come under suspicion until 1951, when, under pressure from the Soviets, Donald Maclean (1913–1983) and Guy Burgess (1911–1963) defected. Because he was not under suspicion immediately, Blunt was able to get a key to Burgess's flat, and ensure there was little or no incriminating evidence around for MI5, including Kim Philby's (1912–1988) warnings to Burgess. Blunt was almost pushed into defection at the same time as Burgess and Maclean, but declined, probably because he had such a privileged life in British society and at the Courtauld Institute. It took 13 years before Anthony Blunt confessed to MI5 that he had been a Soviet agent.

On April 2, 1964, Sir Anthony Blunt, now the Surveyor of the Queen's Pictures, confessed falsely to having been recruited to the Soviet cause by Guy Burgess while at Trinity College, Cambridge. The confession was kept secret; it was expected that he would identify fellow traitors. He named John Cairncross (1913–1995) but did not identify any currently active spies. Blunt's **code name** was JOHNSON.

In November 1979 Blunt was exposed publicly as a Soviet spy but not charged, in the belief that he would give much more information on Soviet spies. However, his listing of pro-Soviet notables and **agents of influence** was more a case of expedience than a genuine change of heart.

Blunt said he had been was surprised when Burgess told him that the Soviets would allow him to leave their service in 1945. It was possible, if not likely, that the KGB already had a well-placed **mole** in MI5, and did not need Blunt any more. But in 1963 Blunt could not say who the mole might be. Internal secret investigations were made, but there was no evidence to support any charges against the many names that arose.

Also, Blunt did not identify the eight Russian spies who had been identified from another source. In fact, a study of Blunt's efforts for MI5 after being caught showed that he said nothing of value about GRU networks, and seemed to reveal too little about his final connection with the KGB. Today the reliability of his information is in doubt. He died in disgrace.

See also BURGESS, GUY; DRIBERG, TOM; LIDDELL, GUY; MACLEAN, DONALD; MAGNIFICENT FIVE; REES, GORONWY

Sources: Andrew, Christopher, and Oleg Gordievsky, *KGB: The Inside Story of Its Foreign Operations* (London: Hodder and Stoughton, 1990); Carter, Miranda, *Anthony Blunt: His Lives* (London: Macmillan, 2001); Costello, John, *Mask of Treachery: Spies, Lies, Buggery and Betrayal. The First Documented Dossier on Anthony Blunt's Cambridge Spy Ring* (New York: William Morrow, 1988); Costello, John, and Oleg Tsarev, *Deadly Illusions* (New York: Crown, 1993); Deacon, Richard, *The Cambridge Apostles: A History of Cambridge University's Elite*

Intellectual Secret Society (New York: Farrar, Straus and Giroux, 1986); Knightley, Phillip, *The Second Oldest Profession: The Spy as Bureaucrat, Patriot, Fantasist and Whore* (London: Andre Deutsch, 1986); Laffin, John, *Brassey's Book of Espionage* (London: Brassey's, 1996); Mahoney, Harry T., and Marjorie L. Mahoney, *Biographic Dictionary of Espionage* (San Francisco: Austin & Winfield, 1998); Pincher, Chapman, *Traitors: The Anatomy of Treason* (New York: St. Martin's Press, 1987).

BOND, JAMES (c. 1924–). Since 1953, when he first appeared, James Bond, a fictional secret **agent,** has captured the popular imagination of espionage buffs and dominated cinema fantasies of the **Cold War**.

James Bond was introduced to the public by Ian Fleming (1908–1964), himself a secret service employee during **World War II**, and in the late 1950s taken up by filmmakers and turned into a heroic image that romanticized clandestine Cold War operations.

From the novels and short stories by Ian Fleming, it is possible to reconstruct the biography of James Bond. He was the son of Andrew Bond, a Scot of Glencoe, who married a Swiss, Monique Delacroix, a few years after **World War I**. They lived on the European continent, where Andrew represented the Vickers armaments firm. When James was born, Andrew put down his name for Eton. For 11 years, James, an only child, lived with his parents on the Continent and became fluent in French and German. His parents were ardent skiers, and were killed in a skiing accident.

James Bond was placed in the hands of an erudite and accomplished aunt, presumably his father's sister, who lived at Pett Bottom, near Canterbury in Kent, and prepared the lad for entry to Eton. Unfortunately, after two halves, James's aunt was asked to remove the youth from Eton; he was transferred to his father's old school, Fettes. Although James did not have the opportunities that flow from an education at Eton, he developed the bearing of a natural aristocrat.

James entered "government service," a euphemism for the British secret services, after World War II. His career was a cover story for the autobiography of Ian Fleming, author of 12 novels and many short stories about James Bond's adventures. When he was 43, Fleming married, and said he used the James Bond novels to take his mind away from the traumas of the marriage.

Fleming's novels about Bond resonated well with more or less unconscious child-like wishes that centered on the daily restaging of ambivalent events in the readers' upbringing.

The first of Bond's operations took place early in 1946, shortly before the last days of **SMERSH** (*smyert shpionam*, Russian for "death to all spies") and is recorded in the 1953 novel *Casino Royale*. In this book, Le Chiffre, a high ranking SMERSH operative, absconds with SMERSH funds for a business venture that fails. At a French casino he tries to recoup his losses by gambling at chemin de fer. Bond is sent by his boss, "M," to gamble against Le Chiffre and win. Bond loses. A **Central Intelligence Agency (CIA)** officer stakes Bond, and he wins. In anger Le Chiffre captures Bond and his woman assistant, Vesper Lynd. Bond suffers near-castration and death when Le Chiffre tortures him; SMERSH operatives find Le Chiffre, execute him, and ignore Bond. Vesper takes James to a hospital, where he recovers his health; together they spend 10 days in a small hotel where he recovers his virility. They fall in love. She commits suicide. Why? She was a counterspy.

All Bond's adventures follow the same theme. Three novels—*Dr. No* (1958), *From Russia with Love* (1957), and *Goldfinger* (1959)—were filmed, and made James Bond a household name for his romantic and innocently amusing espionage. More than 20 Bond films have been made, most of them emphasizing the combined use of fast cars and elaborate weaponry for murder and wild sexual promiscuity during secret operations. These two themes were not evident in the novels, and intelligence experts use every opportunity to state they are rare in nonfictional covert operations.

The name of James Bond was taken from that of a naturalist, and the exploits were drawn partly from the activities of a secret agent in the British navy in Norway during World War II, Lieutenant Commander Patrick Dalzel-Job (1913–2003). Dalzel-Job never claimed to be the model, but Fleming told him he was. In World War II, Dalzel-Job's most daring exploit was in 1940; he disobeyed orders, and rescued all the women and children in Narvik, Norway, shortly before the Germans bombed the township. The King of Norway awarded Dalzel-Job Norway's Knight's Cross of St. Olav for his bravery.

Sources: Amis, Kingsley, *The James Bond Dossier* (London: Cape, 1965); Anonymous, "War Hero Was Model for James Bond," *The Age* (Melbourne), October 16, 2003, p. 10 (first published in *The Guardian* [London]); Boyd, Ann S., *The Devil with James Bond* (Richmond, VA: John Knox Press, 1967); McCormick, Donald, *17F: The Life of Ian Fleming* (London: Peter Owen, 1993); Pearson, John, *The Life of Ian Fleming* (London: Cape, 1966); Trahair, Richard C. S., "A Contribution to the Psychological Study of the Modern Hero: The Case of James Bond," *The Australian and New Zealand Journal of Psychiatry* 8 (1974): 155–165.

BOSSARD, FRANK (1912–). Frank Bossard, a projects officer at the British Ministry of Aviation, was caught photographing secret documents for sale to the Soviets, and became one of only two successful prosecutions of Soviet spies in Britain in the late 1960s.

Bossard was sentenced to six months' hard labor for uttering false checks in 1934. He joined the Royal Air Force (RAF) in December 1940, and used forged documents in his application. During the war he was in the Radar Branch in the Middle East, and was demobilized with the rank of flight lieutenant.

Bossard was seconded to the Scientific and Technical Intelligence Branch and served in Germany, interviewing people who might have some useful technical experience. He returned to London in 1958 to continue his intelligence work, and after being promoted he was placed in the British embassy in Bonn as a Second Secretary.

In 1954, while completing the required **positive vetting** form, Bossard omitted mention of his criminal record, and when discovered, he said he had a lapse of memory about his 1934 criminal convictions.

In 1960 Bossard was transferred to guided weapons work in the Aviation Ministry. Beginning in 1961, he supplied the Russians with photographs of classified material from his work in the Guided Weapons Research and Development Division.

Bossard kept his espionage equipment in the Left Luggage Office at London's Waterloo Station. He checked into a nearby hotel as John Hathaway, and photographed the files he had taken from his office earlier in the day. At **dead letter boxes** he collected his money and left the material for the **GRU**. He was betrayed by Dimitri F. Polyakov (c. 1921–1988). He was caught on March 15, 1965, as he was leaving a hotel room in Bloomsbury. On May 10, 1965, he was jailed for 21 years.

Sources: Laffin, John, *Brassey's Book of Espionage* (London: Brassey's 1996); Pincher, Chapman, *Too Secret Too Long* (London: Sidgwick & Jackson, 1984); Pincher, Chapman, *Traitors: The Anatomy of Treason* (New York: St. Martin's Press, 1987); Volkman, Ernest, *Espionage: The Greatest Spy Operations of the 20th Century* (New York: Wiley, 1995).

BOYCE, CHRISTOPHER JOHN (1953–). With his close friend Andrew Daulton Lee (1952–), Christopher Boyce spied for the Soviets; together they received a large amount of money, which was used partly to support Lee's drug habit.

Christopher Boyce was born in Colorado, son of a **Federal Bureau of Investigation (FBI)** officer. Christopher had a boyhood friend, Andrew Daulton Lee, with whom he attended church and school, sang in the church choir, and shared an interest in falconry.

After dropping out of college, in 1970 Boyce secured, with his father's help, poorly paid clerical work in a highly secret department of TRW Corporation in Redondo Beach, California. TRW operated reconnaissance spy satellites for the **Central Intelligence Agency (CIA).**

Boyce was one of only five who worked in the "black vault," a 5-foot by 15-foot room that housed equipment to encode secret communications for the CIA headquarters in Langley, Virginia. Every day he would change the cipher on each machine that tapped out messages among the CIA, other ground stations, and the U.S. spy satellites. Also, he was one of only a few who had access to the highly secret SIGNET satellite projects, Rhyolite and Argus.

Boyce began selling to the Soviets the secrets in the "black vault." Lee agreed to become Boyce's courier, and would take the Russians' tiny photos of the codes. Their work began in March 1976.

Boyce suspected that Lee, a drug user and peddler, was giving him only part of what the Russians were paying them. So, in October 1976, Boyce flew to Mexico City and met his Russian contact, Boris Alexei Grishin, who, recognizing Boyce's intelligence, suggested he return to the university and study Chinese or Russian, and with these qualifications seek employment with the U.S. government. Expenses would be paid by the **KGB.** Boyce agreed to do this, but only after he'd done one last job scheduled for January 5, 1977, and worth U.S.$75,000.

Lee bungled the delivery, and next day foolishly tried to attract the attention of the Russian embassy. He was arrested by the Mexican police, to whom he appeared to be a terrorist. When they found the secret negatives, the police called in the FBI, and by mid-January, Lee and Boyce were imprisoned. Boyce was sentenced to 40 years in prison.

Boyce escaped in 1980, and, after robbing 17 banks, was captured a year later. These adventures appeared in two books by Robert Lindsey, and the film *The Falcon and the Snowman* (1985).

See also LEE, ANDREW DAULTON

Sources: Andrew, Christopher, and Vasili Mitrokhin *The Mitrokhin Archive: The KGB in Europe and the West* (London: Lane, 1999); Bamford, James, *The Puzzle Palace: A Report on America's Most Secret Agency*, Penguin with new Afterword, 1983 ed. (Boston: Houghton Mifflin, 1982; with a new Afterword, New York: Penguin, 1983); Lindsey, Robert, *The Falcon and the Snowman* (New York: Simon & Schuster, 1979); Lindsey, Robert, *The Flight of the Falcon* (New York: Simon & Schuster, 1983); Mahoney, Harry T., and Marjorie L. Mahoney, *Biographic Dictionary of Espionage* (San Francisco: Austin & Winfield, 1998); Pincher, Chapman, *Traitors: The Anatomy of Treason* (New York: St. Martin's Press, 1987); Richelson, Jeffrey T., *A Century of Spies: Intelligence in the Twentieth Century* (New York: Oxford University Press, 1995), pp. 338–346.

BRANDT RESIGNATION (1974). Willy Brandt (1913–1992), the name taken by Karl Herbert Frahm, was West Germany's noted socialist politician, who became federal Chancellor of West Germany (1969–1974). He had to resign in 1974 when it was found that one of his advisers was a Russian spy.

During the Nazi regime Brandt had lived in exile in Norway. As a moderate socialist after **World War II**, he became Berlin's mayor (1957–1966), helped shape the policy and structure of the Social Democratic Party (1964–1987), and became an international figure during the **Berlin Wall** crisis in August 1961, when he strongly resisted its being built. He was Foreign Minister in 1966, and became West Germany's Chancellor in 1969.

Brandt advocated Ostpolitik, an attitude that would develop into a policy of reconciliation between East and West Germany, and would lead to the signing of the Basic Treaty with East Germany. He signed the Nuclear Non-proliferation Treaty, and concluded treaties with Poland and the Soviet Union. These efforts put paid to the idea that Germany would seek to reestablish its hopes to dominate Europe and regain territory lost after World War II.

For his sincere work toward peace in Europe through the policy of détente, Brandt was awarded the Nobel Peace Prize (1971). Suddenly he was forced to resign as Chancellor of West Germany in May 1974, when it was found that one of his top aides, Günther Guillaume (1927–), was a spy working for the German Democratic Republic's foreign intelligence service.

After the scandal Brandt chaired the North–South Commission of the United Nations (1979) and produced the Brandt Report, recommending greater aid to Third World nations.

See also GUILLAUME, GÜNTHER

Sources: Andrew, Christopher, and Vasili Mitrokhin, *The Mitrokhin Archive: The KGB in Europe and the West* (London: Lane, 1999); Deacon, Richard, *Spyclopedia: The Comprehensive Handbook of Espionage* (New York: William Morrow, 1987).

BRITTEN, DOUGLAS (1931–). Douglas Britten, a Royal Air Force (RAF) technician, was a Russian spy for six years while being blackmailed by the Soviets.

Britten entered the RAF in 1949 and trained as a radio operator. His interest in amateur radio reception and transmission had attracted the attention of the Soviets, and he was recruited when ambling through the Science Museum in London in 1962.

Britten's first task was to get a transmitter and sell it to his Russian contact, YURI. Knowing it was outdated and available on the open market, Britten got one easily and sold it for a handsome profit to YURI, who, it seems, also knew it was far from useful to the RAF.

Shortly afterward Britten was sent to serve in Cyprus until October 1966 as a non-commissioned officer. While there he was photographed taking cash from his Soviet case officer. Thereafter blackmail determined his services to the **U.S.S.R.**

Britten would do most of his work for the Soviets when he was serving in Cyprus, at one of Great Britain's most important listening stations. Beginning early in 1967, he was under constant pressure in England to provide the Russians with more information. This ceased in February 1968, when the British secret services photographed him delivering a message to the Soviet consulate in London's Kensington Palace Gardens after his Soviet contact had not kept their appointment. He was arrested in September and tried in November.

When caught, Britten cooperated with British security and pleaded guilty, but there was no chance to use him as a **double agent** for providing the Russians with

disinformation. Also, inquiries in 1965 and in 1968 showed he had been in financial difficulties and was a capable liar.

Sources: Andrew, Christopher, and Vasili Mitrokhin, *The Mitrokhin Archive: The KGB in Europe and the West* (London: Lane, 1999); Laffin, John, *Brassey's Book of Espionage* (London: Brassey's, 1996); Pincher, Chapman, *Too Secret Too Long* (London: Sidgwick & Jackson, 1984); Pincher, Chapman, *Traitors: The Anatomy of Treason* (New York: St. Martin's Press, 1987); West, Nigel, *The Circus: MI5 Operations 1945–1972* (New York: Stein and Day, 1983).

BROWN AFFAIR (1958). A political scandal in Australia involving an unknown man, named only Brown, who had access to secret documents that he should never have seen.

Secret papers in Britain show that in 1958, Prime Ministers **Harold Macmillan** (1894–1986) and Sir **Robert Menzies** (1894–1978) were terrified the Americans would discover a major security lapse had occurred at the **Woomera rocket range** in South Australia. Australia and Britain feared that America would no longer trust them if it discovered that a Royal Australian Air Force trainee had sold secrets to the Communists about the joint guided-missile trials at the Woomera base.

Menzies was infuriated by what he saw as British bungling that allowed the suspect, known only as Brown, to escape briefly from custody, thereby threatening to reveal the whole affair. The main concern was that a National Service trainee, without rank and with an appalling personal history in England, appeared to have been in a position where he had access to secret documents.

If normal procedures had been followed, Brown would have been prosecuted in the Australian court and the disclosures, according to Menzies, would have been devastating to Australian–American relations. Macmillan agreed that Brown should be flown back to Britain, where a court-martial would be held behind closed doors. Macmillan urged Menzies not to risk publicity by prosecuting the Ukrainian recipient of the information.

Two weeks later, Menzies cabled Macmillan with the bad news that not only had Brown escaped from British military custody after acquiring a key to let himself out, but also that a newspaper in Adelaide, South Australia, had apparently picked up the story. Menzies intervened by approaching the editor with an appeal to his patriotism. Meanwhile, back in Woomera, Brown was quickly recaptured, and nothing more of his fate is known.

Sources: Debelle, Penelope, "Who Agreed to 'an Appeal to Patriotism'?" *The Age*, January 22, 2000, p. 4; Debelle, Penelope, "Murdoch Denies That He Stifled Spy Story," *The Age*, January 24, 2000.

BUCKLEY ASSASSINATION (1985). William Buckley (1928–1985), **Central Intelligence Agency (CIA)** chief of station in Beirut, was probably tortured to death or left to die in June 1985 after being kidnapped by Islamic terrorists in Lebanon in March 1984. His capture and death over a year later were central to the arms-for-hostages scandal toward the end of President Ronald Reagan's (1911–2004) tenure.

In his attempt to free Buckley, William Casey (1913–1987), the CIA director, violated the administration's policy on how to deal with hostage takers. Lieutenant Colonel Oliver North (1943–) planned to use a Middle East informant to pay for Buckley's freedom. North told the U.S. National Security Adviser that $200,000 would be sufficient to free three U.S. hostages, including Buckley. President Reagan agreed to the plan, providing the money came from private sources; a Texas billionaire agreed to provide the money. However, early in June 1985, North found that the sum agreed on would be only a down payment; the new price would be $1 million for each of the three hostages. The plan was approved, and the down payment was delivered.

On October 4, 1985, Buckley's execution was publicized by the Islamic Jihad, Shiite extremists, who had exploded a car bomb in September that killed 40 people at the U.S. embassy in East Beirut. A photograph of what was alleged to be Buckley's corpse appeared in a Beirut newspaper in mid-October. The Islamic Jihad announced the execution of Buckley was in response to the Israeli bombing of the **PLO** base in Tunisia.

Sources: Sifakis, Carl, *Encyclopedia of Assassinations: A Compendium of Attempted and Successful Assassinations Throughout History* (New York: Facts on File, 1993); West, Nigel, *Seven Spies Who Changed the World* (London: Secker & Warburg, 1991); Woodward, Bob, *Veil: The Secret Wars of the CIA, 1981–87* (New York: Simon & Schuster, 1987).

BURCHETT INTERVIEW (1967). An interview conducted in 1967 by the controversial Australian journalist Wilfred Burchett (1911–1983) with Vietnam's Foreign Minister, Nguyen Duy Trinh, in which the latter challenged U.S. President **Lyndon B. Johnson** (1908–1973) to peace talks on Vietnam. In 1967 Aleksey Kosygin (1904–1980), the Russian leader, used the interview as a basis for suggesting peace negotiations over the **Vietnam War**. Through Mai Van Bo, the Hanoi government called the event "the Burchett interview."

Burchett was known as a prominent Communist journalist, an **agent of influence**, and an alleged spy who used propaganda in support of the North Koreans in their conflict with the United Nations forces in the **Korean War** (1950–1953).

See also BURCHETT, WILFRED GRAHAM

Sources: Manne, Robert, *Agent of Influence: The Life and Times of Wilfred Burchett* (Toronto: Mackenzie Institute 1989); Perry, Roland, *The Exile: Burchett, Reporter of Conflict* (Richmond: Heinemann Australia, 1988).

BURCHETT, WILFRED GRAHAM (1911–1983). Wilfred Burchett was a notable journalist and **agent of influence** for the Soviets, and considered by the West to be a Soviet asset.

Burchett was the son of a Gippsland house builder and was raised in Victoria, Australia. He left his homeland for England in 1936, and in 1937 joined the Society for Cultural Relations with Russia; he worked for Russia's Intourist for a year in 1938.

Before **World War II**, Burchett worked to have Jews released from Germany, and returned to Australia (1939), where he became a war correspondent for the *Daily Express* in Chungking, reporting on the Pacific and Asia. His great scoop was a fine eyewitness account of Hiroshima in 1945; it got him a post in London on the *Daily Express*, and later as a Berlin correspondent for *The Times*.

Burchett established contacts with the **MGB**, and by 1948 was providing it with valuable information. As a reporter of the London *Times* he wrote on the show trial of Robert A. Vogeler (1911–). He worked diligently for Russia's supporters in Korea, China, and Vietnam, and became an excellent contact for Western journalists, introducing them to the right people and providing them with information useful to the Soviet aims.

Burchett was well acquainted with the defecting British spies, and had excellent relations with high officials in the Soviet government and the **KGB**, although at times they saw him as a loose cannon.

Burchett returned to Australia in 1950 and spoke against the Australian Liberal government's attempts to ban the **CPA**, and nuclear armament. During the **Korean War** (1950–1953) he went to China to report on cease-fire talks, visited allied POW camps, and is alleged to have used POWs for propaganda interviews against the West. He was later based in Moscow and Eastern Europe, and reported for pro-Soviet radical newspapers and London's *Financial Times*. **ASIO** sought information on Burchett that would prove he had committed treason, but its officers were unable to find sufficient evidence.

Instead, in 1955 Burchett lost his right to an Australian passport, and, for his alleged handling of POWs, was refused another for over 20 years. He was even denied entry to Australia for his father's funeral. His reputation was in tatters from regular attacks by anti-Communists in Australia. Burchett reported on the **Vietnam War**, made movies for the **Viet Cong** cause, and in 1967 arranged for a leading New York journalist to visit Hanoi, and subsequently conducted the interview that bears his name.

In 1968 Burchett obtained a Cuban passport. Two years later he defied the ban on his entry to Australia and flew into Brisbane in the private plane of a millionaire. He was not prosecuted. This meant he had a temporary entry permit, and he spoke to the National Press Club, denying he had been involved in brainwashing POW soldiers during the Korean War.

Burchett visited President Richard Nixon (1913–1994) and Henry Kissinger in 1971 to tell them that Hanoi would not negotiate peace terms, and arranged for Jane Fonda (1937–) to visit Hanoi and scripted her 1972 talks.

Burchett returned to Australia after Gough Whitlam (1916–) and the **Australian Labor Party** came to power (1972); to supplement his income, which had seriously diminished after the Vietnam War, he brought a defamation case against an Australian Roman Catholic politician who had said Burchett was a KGB **agent** (1974). Burchett lost. Deeper in debt, he fled Australia immediately.

Burchett continued to work for the Soviets in Africa. Late in 1977 he went on a fund-raising lecture tour of United States, defending all aspects of Communist rule in many lands. In 1982, still in debt, and warned about his excessive use of alcohol, he left his comfortable life in Paris for Sofia. In 1983 he was a central figure in reports on Bulgarian connections with an attempted assassination of the Pope. He published many books reflecting a strong interest in communism in many countries, and attracted much criticism for his cause.

Sources: Burchett, Wilfred G., *Passport: An Autobiography* (Melbourne: Nelson, 1969); Burchett, Wilfred G., *Memoirs of a Rebel Journalist: At the Barricades* (South Melbourne: Macmillan, 1981); Manne, Robert, *Agent of Influence: The Life and Times of Wilfred Burchett* (Toronto: The Mackenzie Institute, 1989); McKnight, David, *Australia's Spies and Their Secrets* (St. Leonards, NSW: Allen and Unwin, 1984); Perry, Roland, *The Exile: Burchett, Reporter of Conflict* (Richmond, VIC: Heinemann Australia, 1988); Perry, Roland, "How the KGB Used Wilfred Burchett," *The Age*, March 6, 1993, Extra, p. 5; Perry, Roland, "Burchett Through David Irving Glasses," *The Age*, May 15, 2000, p. 9; Sekuless, Peter, *A Handful of Hacks* (St. Leonards, NSW: Allen and Unwin,1999); Smith, Wayne "The Truth That Came in from the Cold" *The Weekend Australian* (Canberra), 3–4 April (2004), p. 31; Wilde,

William H., Joy Hooton, and Barry Andrew, eds., *The Oxford Companion to Australian Literature,* 2nd ed. (Melbourne: Oxford University Press, 1994).

BURGESS, GUY FRANCIS DE MONCEY (1911–1963). Guy Burgess was one of the Magnificent Five, the Soviets' best-known group of British **Cold War** agents.

Burgess, the son of a British naval officer, was educated at Eton and became a history scholar at Trinity College, Cambridge, where in the mid-1930s he was drawn to communism. At Cambridge he was elected in November 1932 to the secret society of the intellectual elite, the Apostles In December 1934, through an introduction from Donald Maclean (1913–1983), he was recruited to the Soviet cause by Arnold Deutsch (1904–1942), code-named OTTO. Burgess, code-named MÄCHEN, made many friends and an untold number of close contacts in high places, and presented himself as a dissolute, disheveled, seductive, and drunken homosexual with wildly offensive manners and a brilliant intellect. He seemed the last person the Soviets would want as a secret **agent.**

In 1935 Burgess left Cambridge, and by November that year was secretary to a pro-German conservative, Jack MacNamara—probably early cover for Burgess's commitment to the Soviets. For brief period in the middle of 1936 he worked on *The Times,* and that October joined the BBC as a talks producer for three years, then moved on to the News Department of the Foreign Office. It is surprising to some that he was ever employed, since he made obvious his drunkenness, homosexuality, and love of the Communist cause.

At this time Burgess's friendship with the author Gronowy Rees (1909–1979) was securely established. He was the godfather to one of Rees's children.

By 1938, however, Burgess appeared to have turned to Fascism. He had been instructed earlier by his Soviet handler to do so, and to keep his preference for communism concealed. This way he could more easily penetrate Fascist organizations and groups in Britain and report on them to the Soviets.

In November 1937 Burgess was much taken with Rees's review of a book *Grey Children*, about economic misery in South Wales. During an evening of heavy drinking, a discussion of the review led Burgess to tell Rees that he had worked for the **COMINTERN** after graduating from Cambridge; he also mentioned the name of Anthony Blunt (1907–1983) and quickly insisted Rees forget what he had said.

In 1944 Burgess got a temporary job in the U.K. Foreign Office and took the opportunity to pass copies of thousands of secret documents to the Soviets. By 1947 he had a permanent post in the Foreign Office, and his drug abuse and homosexuality were established securely and publicly. He was first the private secretary to the Minister of State, and then was moved to the Information Research Department to manage the effects of Soviet propaganda. In November 1948 he was put in the Far Eastern Department of the Foreign Office. In August 1950 he was sent to the British embassy in Washington as Second Secretary for Far Eastern Affairs, working with and living briefly in the same house as Kim Philby (1912–1988).

By 1951 the VENONA material had indicated Donald Maclean (1913–1983) was probably the Soviet spy code-named HOMER. Having heard this from Kim Philby, Maclean was anxious about the future. Burgess, who had been virtually expelled from Washington in April 1951 for his obnoxious behavior, told Maclean that the Soviets had plans to get him to Moscow. Together they fled at the end of May in 1951.

Burgess found Moscow depressing until the **KGB** was able to further his debauched career with sufficient alcohol and attractive homosexual company. He died of heart disease, aged 52, in a Moscow hospital. A few years later, his life was recounted in a misleading biography written by a close associate, Tom Driberg (1905–1976).

See also BLUNT, ANTHONY; MACLEAN, DONALD; MAGNIFICENT FIVE; PHILBY, HAROLD "KIM"; REES, GORONWY

Sources: Andrew, Christopher, and Vasili Mitrokhin, *The Mitrokhin Archive: The KGB in Europe and the West* (London: Lane, 1999); Boyle, Andrew, *The Fourth Man: The Definitive Account of Philby, Guy Burgess, Donald Maclean and Who Recruited Them to Spy for Russia* (New York: Dial Press, 1979); Costello, John, *Mask of Treachery: Spies, Lies, Buggery and Betrayal. The First Documented Dossier on Anthony Blunt's Cambridge Spy Ring* (New York: William Morrow, 1988); Costello, John, and Oleg Tsarev, *Deadly Illusions* (New York: Crown, 1993); Driberg, Tom, *Guy Burgess: A Portrait with Background* (London: Weidenfeld and Nicolson, 1956); Laffin, John, *Brassey's Book of Espionage* (London: Brassey's, 1996); Mahoney, Harry T., and Marjorie L. Mahoney, *Biographic Dictionary of Espionage* (San Francisco: Austin & Winfield, 1998); Richelson, Jeffrey T., *A Century of Spies: Intelligence in the Twentieth Century* (New York: Oxford University Press, 1995).

C

CAIRNCROSS, JOHN (1913–1995). John Cairncross was one of the **KGB's** Magnificent Five, the Cambridge group of spies that included Anthony Blunt (1907– 1983), Guy Burgess (1911–1963), Donald Maclean (1913–1983), and Kim Philby (1912–1988). Cairncross was the outsider of the group.

Cairncross was born in Scotland and educated at Glasgow University and Trinity College, Cambridge, where he studied modern languages and was recruited to the Soviet cause. When Cairncross was introduced to communism, he became attracted to it, so he said, solely because of its opposition to Nazism, and rejected its Marxist philosophy and economics.

Cairncross spent two years at the Sorbonne in Paris (1932–1934); visited Spain in April 1936; and received outstanding marks on the entrance examinations for the U.K. Foreign, Office, which he joined in November 1936. He became friendly with Donald Maclean and Guy Burgess. In May 1937 he was recruited to the Soviet cause when James Klugmann (1912–1977) introduced him to Arnold Deutsch (1904– 1942). Cairncross'ss **code name** was MOLIERE, and later LISZT and MER. He was moved to the German Department of the Foreign Office at the end of the year.

In December 1938 Cairncross was moved to the U.K. Treasury, and then to be the private secretary of a cabinet minister toward the end of 1940. At the end of 1942 he was in the **Secret Intelligence Service (SIS), MI6,** and working at the **Government Code & Cipher School (GCCS),** which had moved from London to **Bletchley Park** shortly before the war began. While there, he worked on the ENIGMA project and had access to Foreign Office files with information on British policy, which he passed to the **NKVD** by way of Burgess and James Klugmann.

Cairncross decided in the summer of 1943 that Winston Churchill (1874–1965) was wrongly denying the Soviet Union critical information about the Wehrmacht's imminent tank attack in Kursk. He passed the appropriate secret documents to a Soviet officer in London. He communicated to the Soviets the GCCS decrypts of German coded messages about the thickness of the armor of the new German Tiger tank, and information about the movements of hundreds of Luftwaffe aircraft on the eve of the battle of Kursk in the summer of 1943. Kursk was one of the Soviet Union's most important military successes. For this crucial information Cairncross was awarded the **Order of the Red Banner**. After Germany's defeat, he specialized in defense expenditure at the U.K. Treasury.

In 1951, following Guy Burgess's and Donald Maclean's disappearance, Cairncross came under suspicion as a Soviet **agent.** When ridding Burgess's apartment of incriminating evidence, Anthony Blunt left behind notes about British economic policy that had been written by Cairncross. Government officials told him to say nothing, and resign. Cairncross said only some of his efforts were for the Soviets, resigned in 1952, and went to teach in the United States. In 1964 he agreed with **MI5** to be silent about his connections with the secret services.

Cairncross joined the United Nations Food and Agriculture Organization in Rome, and returned to studying French literature, translating for Penguin Classics, and writing books on the French actor and playwright Jean Molière and a social history of Christian polygamy.

Cairncross moved to France and lived with his woman friend, an opera singer, for many years.

In 1990 his work for the Soviets was made public, and he was named as the "fifth man" in Britain's famous Cambridge spy ring. His accuser was Oleg Gordievsky (1938–). The accusation angered Cairncross, and he attacked it as misinformation, denying that he was the "fifth man." He asserted that what he gave the Soviets over 14 years was largely worthless information, that he was no traitor, and that after 1945 his contact with the KGB was only formal.

Cairncross returned to Britain earlier in 1995, rented a house in the West Country, and married a month after the death of his first wife, Gabriella. He wrote his memoirs, and although he was seriously ill, completed most of the work with help from Rupert Allason, Tory MP for Torbay known as Nigel West, a prolific writer of espionage books.

Several times Cairncross was invited to return to Britain by MI5, notably by Stella Rimington, its head, which suggests MI5 had more questions on allegations about Soviet efforts to get access to Western intelligence.

Evidence about John Cairncross remains in the KGB's archives; in the opinion of his case officer, a KGB specialist, Yuri Modin, speaking in 1991, Cairncross was among the KGB's highly valued British informants. All of Modin's claims have been denied by Cairncross, but he was never well enough to face the criticism that his autobiographical study raised. He always denied he was a spy.

The KGB archives indicate that Cairncross's account of his life is largely a denial of the work that he actually did for the Soviets.

See also BLUNT, ANTHONY; BURGESS, GUY; GORDIEVSKY, OLEG; MACLEAN, DONALD; MAGNIFICENT FIVE; PHILBY, HAROLD "KIM"

Sources: Andrew, Christopher, and Oleg Gordievsky, *KGB: The Inside Story of Its Foreign Operations* (London: Hodder and Stoughton, 1990); Andrew, Christopher, and Vasili Mitrokhin, *The Mitrokhin Archive: The KGB in Europe and the West* (London: Lane, 1999); Anonymous, "And Now There Are Five: John Cairncross Implicated as 'Fifth Man' in British Spy Ring," *Time*, October 29, 1990, p. 64; Bower, Tom, "Still Battling for Kursk," *The Guardian*, October 9, 1997, p. T11; Cairncross, John, *The Enigma Spy: An Autobiography. The Story of a Man Who Changed the Course of World War Two* (London: Century, 1997);

Laffin, John, *Brassey's Book of Espionage* (London: Brassey's, 1996); Pincher, Chapman, *Traitors: The Anatomy of Treason* (New York: St. Martin's Press, 1987).

CALOMIRIS, ANGELA (1916–). Angela Calomiris worked inside the **Communist Party of the United States of America (CPUSA),** for the **Federal Bureau of Investigation (FBI),** and in 1949 identified party leaders who were later found guilty under the **Smith Act** (1940).

Calomiris was born of immigrant Greek parents in New York City and raised in poverty; she moved to Greenwich Village to study photography. She became a qualified playground supervisor at various schools in the city, and joined the Photo League to learn more about photography. In the League she met Communists, but their attempts to interest her in communism did not succeed.

In February 1942 the FBI asked Calomiris to join the CPUSA and spy on Communists in the League. She agreed. The FBI taught her basic **tradecraft.** Shortly afterward she was invited to join the CPUSA, and for party reasons, she named herself Angela Cole.

Members of the CPUSA trusted Calomiris, and she eventually rose in the party ranks to financial secretary of the New York branch. In this position she had access to an array of information on the party and its membership.

In April 1949 Calomiris was a witness at the Department of Justice inquiry into the CPUSA leadership. She provided full details on top Communist leaders, and their influence on party members. The prosecution claimed leaders were acting seditiously, and the jury agreed.

Calomiris went back to photojournalism and was no longer a public figure.

Sources: Calomiris, Angela, *Red Masquerade: Undercover for the FBI* (New York: J.B. Lippincott, 1950); Mahoney, M. H., *Women in Espionage* (Santa Barbara, CA: ABC-CLIO, 1993); Powers, Richard Gid, *Secrecy and Power: The Life of J. Edgar Hoover* (London: Hutchinson, 1987).

CANADIAN SPIES (1946–1947). After Igor Sergeyevich Gouzenko (1919–1982) defected in September 1945, he presented the Canadian government with the documents he had taken from the Russian embassy in Ottawa. In March 1946 the **Royal Canadian Mounted Police** (RCMP) reported on a network of undercover agents who had been working at the Soviet embassy in Ottawa; the report listed the technical equipment that had interested the members of the network and their names. Among the people investigated, charged, and tried were the following:

Eric Adams, an engineer and member of a Communist group in Ottawa since 1936, served many Soviet agencies; he was acquitted in 1946.

James Scotland Benning, code-named BENSON, was in the Department of Munitions and Supply; he was imprisoned for five years in 1946, but the sentence was quashed on appeal in 1947.

Dr. Raymond Boyer, a professor of chemistry at McGill University, gave the Soviets information on explosives research, and was found guilty in 1947; in 1948 he was sentenced to two years in prison.

Agatha Chapman was acquitted in 1946 of conspiring to divulge confidential information.

Harold Samuel Gerson, a geological engineer, gave the Soviets information on the testing of projectiles, and was jailed for five years in 1946; on appeal he was tried again in 1947 and sentenced to four years.

Professor Israel Halperin, code-named BACON, worked in the Mathematics Department at Queen's University, and gave Russia secret technical information on his research into the highly devastating military equipment used against Japan; he was acquitted in 1947.

Harry Harris was charged in 1947 with providing false a passport to a Russian **agent**, and was sentenced to five years in prison.

Captain Gordon Lunan of the Canadian Information Service led a spy ring, the Lunan Group, which reported to Lieutenant Colonel Rogov, assistant military attaché in the Soviet embassy. In 1946 he admitted the charge and was sentenced to five years in jail for espionage, plus one more year for contempt of court in 1947.

Edward Wilfred Mazerall was an electrical engineer who gave the Soviets research information on radar; he admitted the charges and was sentenced to four years in prison.

Squadron Leader Matt Simons Nightingale, an RCAF engineer, was acquitted in 1946.

Squadron-leader Poland, Secretary of the Psychological Warfare Committee of the Wartime Information Board, and a member of the Intelligence Unit in the Royal Canadian Air Force, provided the Russians with maps and other documents; his case was dropped for lack of evidence.

Fred Rose, elected to the Canadian House of Representatives, was a member of the Labour Progressives (Communists). He was arrested in 1946 for giving plans and documents to the Soviets and conspiring with members of the Lunan Group. He was found guilty and imprisoned for six years; in 1947 he was expelled from the Canadian Parliament.

Dr. David Shugar, of Polish origin, was in the Royal Canadian Navy and conspired to inform the Russians on special equipment for submarine detection. His case was dropped in 1947.

Durnford Smith, code-named BADEAU, worked in the Radio Branch of the National Research Council, and was sentenced to five years in jail in 1946.

Kathleen Mary Willsher worked for the British High Commission, admitted the charges, and was sentenced to three years in prison.

Emma Woikin, of Russian origin, a cypher clerk in the Department of External Affairs, gave the Russians the contents of secret telegrams. She admitted the charges and was sentenced to prison for two and a half years.

William Pappin was acquitted of the charge of issuing false passports for Russians in 1946.

See also GOUZENKO, IGOR

Source: Rosenberger, Walter, and Herbert C. Tonin, "Canada—Disclosures of Soviet Espionage Organization," *Keesing's Contemporary Archives* 6 (London: Longman, 1948): 7939–7941, 9289.

CASEY, WILLIAM JOSEPH (1913–1987). William Casey, raised a Catholic and educated by Jesuits, became a millionaire, a New York tax lawyer, a businessman, and an **OSS** officer. He is noted for expanding the operations and staff of the **Central Intelligence Agency (CIA)** after lean years in the late 1970s; for his dogged attempts to rescue William Buckley (1928–1985), his CIA chief of station in Beirut who had been kidnapped, and his role in the Irangate scandal, which disgraced the U.S. president in the late 1980s.

During **World War II,** Casey, then a wealthy New York tax attorney, joined the OSS, but was not suited to direct operations because of poor eyesight. He became OSS station chief in London toward the end of the war, and planned an operation that parachuted 150 Polish, Belgian, and French **agents** into Europe to undermine the Germans in the major cities, and help the Allied forces advance.

Between 1954 and 1971 Casey's firm, Institute for Business Planning, was a considerable success. In 1981 he became **Ronald Reagan**'s (1911–2004) campaign manager.

Casey was made the director of the CIA from 1981 to 1987. Under him, the first CIA director to have cabinet rank, there was a five-fold expansion of the CIA operations in three years. In 1982 the budget of the CIA was increased 15 percent; in 1983 it rose another 25 percent. By 1985 it was spending U.S.$1.5 billion per year, and was the fastest-growing government agency in the United States.

Casey sought to give his agents unrestricted authority to spy on U.S. citizens abroad and at home; to use break-ins, physical surveillance, infiltration of domestic organizations, and otherwise overcome many restrictions on the CIA in the late 1970s. Also, he wanted to raise the staffing and the morale of counterintelligence agents who had been distressed at the treatment given to James J. Angleton (1917– 1987).

Shortly after taking over the CIA, Casey was briefed on the Russian invasion of Afghanistan, and decided that through CIA intervention the Russians must be attacked, so that they would soon be forced to the negotiating table. Also, he demanded greater funding for the CIA in its support for the mujahideen. By 1985 support for this resistance movement in Afghanistan was U.S.$250 million per year. At the time the CIA also supplied the resistance in Afghanistan with over U.S.$2 billion in counterfeit Afghan currency to pay the exorbitant costs of transport and bribery inside Afghanistan.

In 1984 Casey became deeply involved with Oliver North (1934–) in the Irangate scandal to sell arms to Iran for the release of U.S. hostages—among whom was William Buckley, a much-favored CIA official—and then use the profit to distribute funds to the Nicaraguan Contras, who had been cut off from U.S. funding by the 1984 **Boland Amendments**. It appears that between 1984 and 1986 Robert C. McFarlane and Vice Admiral John M. Poindexter violated the Boland Amendments by approving support for the Nicaraguan Contras and for having these operations conducted out of the authority of the National Security Council staff with Oliver North as the action officer, assisted by Major General Richard V. Secord. When the Irangate scandal erupted, Casey appears to have tried to distance himself and the CIA from illegal activities, and he may have attempted to keep evidence of his and alleged CIA involvement concealed from the U.S. Congress.

Casey was always supportive of the President, and in November 1985 went to London to talk in secret with the defector Oleg Gordievsky (1938–), to get firsthand the best information he could on Russia's new leader, Mikhail Gorbachev, before his November 1985 summit meeting with Ronald Reagan.

Casey was incapacitated by a brain tumor late in 1986. He resigned after undergoing an operation in February 1987. He died in May. At his funeral a Catholic bishop denounced Casey's policies.

See also BUCKLEY ASSASSINATION; IRANGATE/IRAN–CONTRA AFFAIR
Sources: Deacon, Richard, *Spyclopedia: The Comprehensive Handbook of Espionage* (New York: William Morrow, 1987); Persico, Joseph E., *William Casey (1913–87): From the OSS to the CIA* (New York: Viking, 1990); Persico, Joseph E., *William Casey (1913–87): The Lives and Secrets of William Casey* (Toronto: Penguin Books of Canada, 1991); Richelson, Jeffrey T., *A Century of Spies: Intelligence in the Twentieth Century* (New York: Oxford University Press, 1995); Woodward, Bob, *Veil: The Secret Wars of the CIA, 1981–87* (New York: Simon & Schuster, 1997).

CHAMBERS, WHITTAKER (1901–1961). Jay Vivian Chambers, known also as David Breen, Charles Adams, Lloyd Cantwell, Carl, and, notoriously, as Whittaker Chambers, gave evidence at the **House Un-American Activities Committee (HUAC)** inquiry that brought down Alger Hiss (1904–1996), and helped begin the witch-hunt for Communists in the United States in the early 1950s.

Chambers was one of two sons born to a newspaperman and a former actress. He was raised in Lynbrook, Long Island, then a fishing village surrounded by farms. He was a bookish lad, and recognized as a talented writer by his professors at Columbia University. He was also an alcoholic tending toward bisexuality, a womanizer, and a writer of blasphemous plays, activities that led to his being banned from Columbia University.

A lost soul in his early twenties, Chambers could not be adequately guided by family, religion, and education. He joined the Communist Party in 1925, reported until 1929 for *The Daily Worker*, and was a fine propagandist, poet, and translator of German texts. After drifting briefly away from the Communist Party, he rejoined it in 1931. In 1932 the party ordered him to work underground, and he became a paid Soviet secret police **agent** in New York, and later in Washington. His aim was to cultivate Marxist thinkers in U.S. government departments. In the Agricultural Adjustment Administration he found such a thinker, Alger Hiss, in 1934.

By 1936 Chambers began to doubt his allegiance to communism, due largely to **Josef Stalin**'s (1879–1953) murderous purges in Russia during the 1930s. He was distressed deeply when a Russian associate disappeared in the United States, presumably assassinated.

Chambers had been to Moscow to learn his craft for the Communists, and when ordered again to go to Moscow, he refused. He began to keep copies of information that he had collected, so as not to be left without something to protect himself and his family should he ever decide to defect from the party. Frighted by what he was learning about Russia and its efforts to penetrate the United States, in April 1938 he took his family into hiding. With his information in a safe place, he broke contact with the **NKVD**.

Chambers befriended the Russian defector Walter Krivitsky (c. 1900–1941), and began to think of defection himself. In 1939 he felt that the Nazis would use the spy ring he had served, because Russia and Germany were invading together. So he went to speak with the Secretary of State and chief intelligence adviser to the President **Adolf A. Berle** (1895–1971). Chambers gave a list of people he had received information from; among them were Alger Hiss and Lauchlin Currie (1900–1993).

After Krivitsky's body was found in February 1941, Berle warned the **Federal Bureau of Investigation (FBI)** that the Soviets might assassinate Chambers. Not until November 1945, when the FBI had information from Elizabeth Bentley (1908–

1963), did it examine closely what Chambers had said. It seemed his allegations had become relevant.

On August 2, 1948, by now a senior editor for *Time*, Chambers was called to appear before the HUAC. On August 4, he stated that he had overseen a group of Communists among the staffs of U.S. government agencies; among others he named Harry Dexter White (1892–1948) and Alger Hiss. At the time he did not charge his former friends with treason. Next day, Hiss appeared before the HUAC and denied Chambers's allegation. In his second testimony on August 7, Chambers gave three more items of evidence pointing to Hiss's guilt. On August 17 Hiss admitted that he once knew Chambers as George Crossly, and that two of the items of evidence that Chambers mentioned were true. On September 27 Hiss filed a suit against Chambers for slander.

On November 17 Chambers gave the HUAC over 60 pages of U.S. State Department documents that were copied by Hiss on a Woodstock typewriter, and four pages in Hiss's handwriting. All these were said to have been given to Chambers in 1938. The papers had been hidden in Chambers's Maryland garden, and included five rolls of microfilm and two rolls with confidential government documents. They became known as the "Pumpkin Papers" because they had been concealed in a vegetable patch.

Hiss was later tried and found guilty of perjury, and jailed in March 1951 for 44 months. Chambers published his view of the case in 1952.

When Chambers died, the *National Review* published a memorial issue, *Time* celebrated his life with a two-page obituary. In 1984 President **Ronald Reagan** (1911–2004) awarded Chambers the highest honor that a U.S. citizen can receive, the Medal of Freedom, and over the objections of the U.S. National Park Service, had the area where the "Pumpkin Papers" had been concealed, declared a historic landmark.

See also BENTLEY, ELIZABETH; HISS, ALGER

Sources: Andrew, Christopher, and Vasili Mitrokhin, *The Mitrokhin Archive: The KGB in Europe and the West* (London: Lane, 1999); Chambers, Whittaker, *Witness* (New York: Random House, 1952); Hyde, Earl M., Jr., "Bernard Shuster and Joseph Katz: KGB Master Spies in the United States," *International Journal of Intelligence and Counterintelligence* 12 (1999): 35–57; Lowenthal, John, "Venona and Alger Hiss," *Intelligence and National Security* 15 (2000): 98-130; Mahoney, Harry T., and Marjorie L. Mahoney, *Biographic Dictionary of Espionage* (San Francisco: Austin & Winfield, 1998); Olmstead, Kathryn, *Red Spy Queen: A Biography of Elizabeth Bentley* (Chapel Hill: University of North Carolina Press, 2002); Tanenhaus, Sam, *Whittaker Chambers: A Biography* (New York: Random House, 1997).

CHILDS, JACK (d. 1980), AND CHILDS, MORRIS (fl. 1935–1980). Jack and Morris were brothers born in Chilovsky, Kiev, and raised as Jack and Morris Childs in Chicago. They became **Federal Bureau of Investigation (FBI)** agents (1954) and worked against the **Kremlin**, to which they had owed allegiance when they were members of the **Communist Party of the United States of America (CPUSA)**.

Jack, a self-designated con man, was the party's bagman, and for over 20 years smuggled millions of dollars from Moscow to the United States. Morris was a well-educated man who in 1929 had been invited to attend a school for revolutionaries, the Lenin School of Moscow, where he became acquainted with **Walter Ulbricht**

(1893–1973), **Yuri Vladimorovich Andropov** (1914–1984), Mikhail Suslov (1902–1982), and Josip Broz, the young **Josip Tito** (1892–1980).

Morris, code-named KHAB, was also known as Morris Summers, Ramsey Kemp Martin, and D. Douglas Mozart. In April 1958 he was invited to Moscow to discuss funding of the moribund CPUSA, a victim of the McCarthy era (1952–1954) and its aftermath. He received $270,000 and promptly channeled it through the Canadian Communist Party; during the next 19 years, while working for the FBI, the brothers conned $30 million out of Moscow into New York. Morris would annually go with his budget to Russia until the late 1970s, while Jack handled the transfer of funds at the New York end. The transfer, code-named VALDAY, occurred at four different places in Manhattan, each with several exits in case the operation was detected.

Jack Childs, who was also known as D. Brooks and code-named MARAT, admitted to skimming 5 percent of the money. He not only collected money, but also exchanged written messages at **dead drops** and through **brush contacts**. The men became rich, especially since the FBI paid them $30,000 a year, a large salary for the 1950s and 1960s. Morris lived in luxury, with apartments in Manhattan, Moscow, and Chicago.

By 1974 the **KGB** was suspicious, wondering how the brothers could travel so easily on false passports, and keep up their work with known prewar contacts within Soviet intelligence. Because Jack appeared to be in bad health, the KGB suggested that he be replaced by another **agent**. This was not done. In 1975 the brothers were awarded the **Order of the Red Banner**. Again in 1977 the KGB thought Jack should be replaced due to illness. Again this was not done. The brothers were still highly active during 1978.

In May 1980 Morris feared he might be arrested, so he gave the cash he had been hiding to an associate. That August Jack died, and later Morris retired to Florida.

In 1987 the brothers became the first spies to be decorated by both the Soviets and the United States, when **Ronald Reagan** (1911–2004) awarded them the Presidential Medal of Freedom.

See also OPERATION SOLO

Sources: Andrew, Christopher, and Vasili Mitrokhin, *The Mitrokhin Archive: The KGB in Europe and the West* (London: Lane, 1999); Barron, John, *Operation Solo: The FBI Man in the Kremlin* (Washington, DC: Regnery, 1996); Klehr, Harvey, John Earl Haynes, and Fridrikh Igorevich Firsov, *The Soviet World of American Communism* (New Haven, CT: Yale University Press, 1998).

CHISHOLM, JANET ANNE (1932–).

Mrs. Janet Chisholm was an **MI6** spy whose task was to meet Oleg Penkovsky (1919–1963) to collect secret information on the Soviets in 1962.

Chisholm was the wife of Roderick Chisholm, an MI6 officer at the British embassy in Moscow. On Oleg Penkovsky's second journey to London, he met her and learned how he should contact her and pass on what secret information he had collected. He used a small candy box that held exactly four rolls of film.

In January 1962 Chisholm took her children for a walk in a park in Moscow. She met a Russian who gave the children a candy box. The **brush contact** was observed by **KGB** watchers. Oleg Penkovsky saw he was under surveillance, and planned that future meetings with her would take place at receptions in March 1962, in the British embassy, and in July at the U.S. embassy.

After Penkovsky was caught, the Chisholms were sent to a new embassy, and Roger became a declared or legitimate employee in the Foreign Office instead of a covert spy.

See also PENKOVSKY, OLEG

Sources: Andrew, Christopher, and Oleg Gordievsky, *KGB: The Inside Story of Its Foreign Operations from Lenin to Gorbachev* (London: Hodder and Stoughton, 1990); Gibney, Frank, ed., *The Penkovsky Papers: The Russian Who Spied for the West* (London: Collins, 1965).

CLAYTON, WALTER SEDDON (1906–1997). Walter Clayton, a committed Communist, was a main organizer of the **Communist Party of Australia (CPA)**, and **ASIO**'s major target in counterintelligence for many years. Australia's Petrov Royal Commission on Espionage (1954) named him a Soviet **agent**, code-named KLOD or CLODE. When he defected in April 1954, Vladimir Petrov (1907–1991) stated the CPA had a group of members in the Australian government's Department of External Affairs who gave documents on Australian, British, and U.S. foreign policy to Mr. Markov at the Soviet embassy. Petrov knew the major contact as K, or KLOD/CLODE.

Clayton was born in New Zealand and in 1931 settled in Melbourne, Australia. He sold bags and travel goods wholesale. He was much impressed with the widespread misery accompanying the 1930s Great Depression, and joined the CPA.

A regular soapbox speaker in public, Clayton was arrested in 1938 for protesting against the politics of allowing the visit to Australia of a Nazi yachtsman. In 1939 he traveled north to live in Sydney, where he helped distribute the *Workers Weekly*. Those who knew him saw a ruthless, dogmatic, puzzling, and secretive character.

In June 1940 the National Security Act in Australia banned the Communist and Fascist parties. Clayton was nabbed immediately in a police raid and was kept under investigation, but he was rarely seen again because he went underground to protect himself and to further the party's interests. He married Helen Lane, a descendant of William Lane, who in June 1893 had led the Australian group seeking to establish a socialist utopia in Paraguay. She divorced Clayton in 1945, and he cared for Shirley Hallett, Clayton's best friend, until her death in February 1946.

Clayton went underground again in 1947 to organize the CPA apparatus, for fear that rampant anti-Communism would again ensure the party was banned. Investigation of him continued, and it was found that he was a member of the CPA's Central Control Commission, the internal guardian of the CPA.

Underground, Clayton drew together a small group of CPA members who could provide accommodations, false addresses, cars, **dead-letter boxes, safe houses**, concealed tunnels and similar places, and transmitters and other items and services needed to run a clandestine operation. At one point the group had two small cells in the local police force and the Australian army. One of the members gave Clayton a copy of a report on his secret investigations, thereby revealing the person inside the CPA who was an informer. By 1950 Clayton, like Ian Milner (1911–1991) and Jim Hall, was suspected by ASIO of helping Soviet espionage.

In May 1954 Clayton came out of hiding and appeared at the Royal Commission on Espionage, the Australian government's response to Vladimir Petrov's defection in April. Clayton could not be easily found because he was hiding on a farm near Milton in New South Wales. At the inquiry Clayton was asked only nine questions; he carefully denied he had ever met anyone at the Russian embassy. He agreed that in the past he had used different addresses, but only for lawful activities. He claimed that he could not recall ever having met either Jim Hill (Ted Hill's brother) or Ian Milner. Afterward Clayton disappeared again.

In 1956 Clayton married Peace Gowland. In the following year he was ill, and was apparently becoming an alcoholic. He had dwindling support in the CPA, and to ASIO it appeared the Soviets might want him out of Australia, for fear that he might expose the network of spies which ASIO suspected still operated in the government's External Affairs Department. ASIO then began Operation PIGEON to find and convict Clayton.

See also OPERATION PIGEON

Sources: Barnett, Harvey, *Tale of the Scorpion: The World of Spies and Terrorists in Australia—An Intelligence Officer's Candid Story* (South Melbourne: Sun Books, 1989); Fitzgerald, Ross, "Disillusion with Life under the Hammer and Sickle," *The Weekend Australian* (Canberra), 3–4 April (2004); Inquirer 31; Manne, Robert, *The Petrov Affair: Politics and Espionage* (Sydney: Pergamon, 1987); McKnight, David, *Australia's Spies and Their Secrets* (St. Leonards, NSW: Allen and Unwin, 1994); Smith, Wayne "The Truth That Came in from the Cold," *The Weekend Australian* (Canberra), 3–4 April (2004), p. 31.

COHEN, LEONTINA (1913–1992), AND COHEN, MORRIS (1905–1995).

Morris Cohen and his wife, Leontina ("Lona"), were also known in Britain as Peter Kroger (1910–1995) and his wife, Helen (1913–1992). They were two of the most important North American–born **illegals** to serve the **U.S.S.R.** in both the United States and Great Britain.

Morris Cohen became a Soviet **agent** while serving the International Brigades during the **Spanish Civil War** (1936–1939). After marrying Leontina, he persuaded her to serve the Communist cause as well. Their work was interrupted in 1942, when Morris was conscripted; it began again in 1945, when Lona worked as a Soviet courier, passing to her handlers in New York **atom bomb** secrets from Ted Hall (1925–1999) in **Los Alamos**, New Mexico, and from agents in the Canadian Chalk River atomic research center.

In 1946, following the defection of Elizabeth Bentley (1908–1963), Moscow broke with the Cohens; later they were reactivated after their visits to Paris. In 1949, Morris and Lona became members of William Fisher's (1902–1971) group. It included Ted Hall, by now a Ph.D. student at the University of Chicago. He was planning to break with Moscow and to work for the Progressive Party's presidential hopeful, **Henry A. Wallace** (1882–1965). The Cohens persuaded Hall to stay with the U.S.S.R.

When Julius Rosenberg (1918–1953) and his wife, Ethel (1916–1953), were caught and convicted in 1951 for conspiracy to commit espionage in wartime, the Cohens were sent to safety in Mexico, where they were cared for by Spanish Communists and had their identities changed before being sent to Britain.

In 1954 a Soviet agent at the New Zealand consulate in Paris, Paddy Costello, who had been recruited at Cambridge University, and would later become a professor of Russian at Manchester University, provided the Cohens with New Zealand passports: Morris Cohen would be Peter Kroger, from Gisborne, New Zealand; Lona would be Helen Kroger, from Boyle, Alberta. Peter's cover was that of an antiquarian book dealer.

When they reached Britain, the Cohens established themselves as a convivial pair, well-liked and highly amusing company. For Russia they were radio operators; they secreted their equipment in a bungalow in Ruislip, Middlesex.

The Cohens were members of what later became known as the Portland spy group, headed by Gordon Arthur Lonsdale (1922–1970), the Russian agent born Konon Molody. When Lonsdale was caught and imprisoned in 1961, after four years of successful espionage, the Krogers got 20 years each; their accomplices Harry Houghton (1905–) and his mistress, Ethel Gee (1915–), got 15 years each. They were caught after being informed on by the Polish defector Michal Goleniewski (fl. 1922–1972).

The Cohens were freed in a 1969 spy exchange for the British lecturer Gerald Brooke. For services to the U.S.S.R. the Cohens were awarded the Order of the Red Star, a well-furnished apartment in Moscow, and the enduring respect of the **KGB**.

The KGB spread the rumor that the Krogers were Poles and had returned to Poland, where Peter was an academic in a university English department. In 1971 on the street in Moscow, George Blake (1922–) met Peter briefly. They had known each other in Wormwood Scrubs Prison in the early 1960s. In 1992, Lona died, aged 80; in 1995 Morris, aged 90, died. President **Boris Yeltsin** (1931–) made Morris a Hero of the Russian Federation.

See also BENTLEY, ELIZABETH; FISHER, VILYAM; GEE, ELIZABETH ETHEL; HALL, THEODORE; HOUGHTON, HARRY; MOLODY, KONON

Sources: Albright, Joseph, and Marcia Kunstel, *Bombshell: The Secret Story of America's Unknown Atomic Spy Conspiracy* (New York: Times Books, 1997); Andrew, Christopher, and Vasili Mitrokhin, *The Mitrokhin Archive: The KGB in Europe and the West* (London: Lane, 1999); Deacon, Richard, *Spyclopedia: The Comprehensive Handbook of Espionage* (New York: William Morrow, 1987); Frolik, Joseph, *The Frolik Defection* (London: Leo Cooper, 1975).

COLBY, WILLIAM E. (1920–1996). William Egan Colby was the head of the **Central Intelligence Agency (CIA)** in the mid-1970s, and for a short time endured the disgrace attaching to the U.S. Congress's investigations of the alleged inappropriateness and possible illegality of the CIA's past activities.

Colby graduated from Princeton in 1940, and during **World War II** served in the **OSS**, and in 1944 was parachuted into German-occupied France, where he commanded a group of saboteurs. The OSS was disbanded in December 1945.

In 1947 Colby finished his postgraduate degree in law at Columbia University, and in 1950 joined the CIA. He served the CIA in the U.S. embassies in Sweden (1951–1953), Italy (1953–1958), and South Vietnam (1959–1962).

In 1962 he was recalled to Washington, where as chief of the Far East Division of the CIA, he helped control Operation PHOENIX, which aimed at pacification in the **Vietnam War** from 1962 through 1967. In September 1973 Colby was appointed director of the CIA.

As head of the CIA, Colby's career was dominated by allegations in the *New York Times*, in December 1974, that in the past the CIA had probably conducted illegal activities. Inside the CIA these were known as the "**family jewels.**" Colby studied evidence for them carefully, and then cooperated with the U.S. Congressional enquiries into the appropriateness and possible illegality of CIA clandestine operations, such as its apparent intrusion into domestic espionage, and assassinations of foreign leaders. As a result the CIA was brought under greater government control, and many conservative political leaders criticized Colby for allowing this to happen.

In 1976 President **Gerald Ford** (1913–) replaced Colby with **George W. H. Bush** (1924–), who later became Vice President under **Ronald Reagan** (1911–2004), and President for one term.

After leaving the CIA, Colby worked actively on arms reduction around the world. His memoirs were published as *Honorable Men* (1978) and *Lost Victory* (1989).

Sources: Colby, William, with and Peter Forbath, *Honorable Men: My Life in the CIA* (New York: Simon & Schuster, 1978); Prados, John, *Lost Crusader: The Secret Wars of CIA Director William Colby* (London: Oxford University Press, 2003).

CONNOCK, MICHAEL (1934–). Michael Connock was a British journalist who almost became a spy.

Connock graduated from Oxford University; failed, due to intense competition, to secure employment in the British foreign service; and in 1957 joined the *Financial Times* (his first job), and later the *Daily Express;* and returned to the *Financial Times* to write a diary column in 1961. When it became clear to his employers that he was familiar with Russian, he was offered the job of Soviet and East European correspondent for the *Financial Times*. He made many contacts in East Europe and became fond of a married woman, Anna Kowalska, and once was in Russia with her. His wife said that she feared he would find someone in Poland, and finish like Greville Wynn (1919–1990), the businessman spy. Curiously enough, in November 1962 Connock was staying in the same hotel in Budapest as Wynn on the night he was arrested.

For eight years Connock was a correspondent; early in 1969 he went to Poland to collect political and economic information, and to study the country's Jewish problem. His main contact was with the Polish Chamber of Commerce, where three men arranged to discuss his writing a newspaper article on Polish fishing trawlers. They met, and took a train for the coastal town of Sopot, where he was to stay at the Grand Hotel. He was met there by two men, driven to the hotel, and, finding it overbooked, was driven toward Gydnia. The car stopped, and the men told him they were from the "security apparatus" took him to a nearby office. He feared that he might be imprisoned. However, he was brought food and drink, was addressed as "Panie Connock," was interrogated as to his identity and background, and was promised no harm would come to him. They were from the Polish Secret Service. They wanted to know how he had learned Polish and Russian. Was he in contact with the British intelligence services? While Connock was being plied with more food and brandy, they questioned him further and promised help if he helped them. It seemed they already knew much about him, and were preparing to blackmail him. He told them of his contacts, and his affection for Anna Kowalski. Recently he had seen her, but could do so no longer because her husband told him that any association she had with a foreigner would put her in hazard with Polish authorities.

Connock's interrogators didn't believe the details of his story and accused him of breaking up families, and produced letters from Anna's family asking the Polish Ministry of Foreign Affairs to stop him from visiting Poland. If they were acted upon, he was told, he would lose his right to visit Poland. Clearly blackmail was central to this interrogation. Connock decided that he would do whatever he was asked, then return to Britain and make a pubic statement about how he had been blackmailed into espionage.

Connock signed an agreement to cooperate on many matters, including counterintelligence. In return some expenses would be paid, and he was given an envelope of innocuous photographs of himself and Anna as tourists.

Returning to the Grand Hotel, Connock found it now had a room for him. He worried that the Polish secret service might think that he was attempting trick them and imagined the trouble he would have to endure on his return home. His employers dismissed him and gave him 16 months salary due under terms of his contract. Connock wrote the story of how he almost became a spy and had it published around the world.

Source: Connock, Michael, "They Tried to Make Me Spy," *The Age* (Melbourne), March 17, 1969, p. 6.

COPLON, JUDITH (1921–). Shortly after **World War II,** Judith Coplon worked for the Soviets while an employee of the **Federal Bureau of Investigation (FBI).** Twice she was caught and tried, and both times she was set free.

Coplon was born into an old American-Jewish family, and was recruited by the Soviets when she became a Communist while at Barnard College in 1944. She was made a political analyst in the New York office of the U.S. Justice Department (May 1948). She worked so well in the Foreign Agents Registration Section that she was promoted to the Washington office.

In December 1949, a secret source, probably VENONA, found that the Soviets were getting secret information from the Justice Department. It seems the information came from a woman who until recently had worked in New York and now was in Washington. Coplon was suspected immediately.

A tap was put on Coplon's phone at home and in her office; all mail to and from her was examined; all visitors she met were photographed, and all people she spoke with were checked out; she was followed closely, and she may have had her home bugged as well as her office. She was under full surveillance by Robert Lamphere (1918–2002), who was responsible for catching her.

Coplon gave her neighbors the impression she was a quiet and refined young woman who had no men friends. In fact, FBI surveillance showed she did have men come to her apartment.

Once Coplon asked her supervisor to show her the list of Soviet **agents** operating in the United States. He reported the request to the FBI and managed to put her off for the time being.

Walter Lamphere decided set Coplon up by producing a fake letter that appeared to be highly secret. When given the assignment to check out people whose names appeared in the fake letter, she asked for leave over a long weekend, and her supervisor agreed. She was followed closely. She tried to ensure she was not being followed, and when satisfied she was not, she met her handler, Valentine Gubitchev, an engineer who was employed in the Architectural Department of the United Nations, at a jewelry shop. He worked for the Soviet consulate. When they parted, the FBI followed him and observed his regular use of counterespionage techniques normally employed to prevent being observed and followed.

At work Judith Coplon was moved to another office: she asked why, and was assured she was the best person for the new tasks allocated to her position. Nevertheless, she still appeared in her original office in Washington.

A month later Coplon asked for time off for another long weekend. She was granted permission and she followed the same procedure, meeting her handler, who once again appeared to be using countersurveillance techniques. Another month later, with another fake document, she followed the same procedure; this time the FBI arrested her and her Soviet handler.

Nothing incriminating was found on the Soviet handler, but in Coplon's purse there were copies of many secret documents, including the fake document used to trap her. Both defendants said they had had evidence planted on them by the FBI. Nevertheless, Coplon was found guilty of espionage, and her handler was declared persona non grata.

Apparently Coplon was in love with her handler, and he had promised to marry her when he got his divorce. She was released on bail pending her appeal. Immediately she married her lawyer!

Coplon was tried twice; once in New York and once in Washington. The New York conviction was overturned because there had been no warrant for her arrest. The other conviction was reversed because a conversation between her and her lawyer had been unlawfully recorded. Thereby she avoided a jail term of 15 years and settled down to the life of a suburban housewife.

Later, J. Edgar Hoover would call this case one of the biggest disasters in the history of the FBI. The case was known in FBI circles as "the Punch-and-Judy Show."

See also LAMPHERE, ROBERT

Sources: Anonymous, "A Spy Catcher Who Broke the Soviet Codes: Robert Joseph Lamphere, Spy Catcher, 14-2-1918–7-1-2002," *The Age* (Melbourne), February 2, 2002, Obituaries, p. 9 (first published in *New York Times*); Cook, Fred J., *The FBI Nobody Knows* (New York: Macmillan, 1964); Gentry, Curt, *J. Edgar Hoover: The Man and His Secrets* (New York: Norton, 1991); Mahoney, Harry T., and Marjorie L. Mahoney, *Biographic Dictionary of Espionage* (San Francisco: Austin & Winfield, 1998); Mitchell, Marcia, and Thomas Mitchell, *The Spy Who Seduced America: The Judith Coplon Story* (Montpelier, VT: Invisible Cities Press, 2002); Pincher, Chapman, *Traitors: The Anatomy of Treason* (New York: St. Martin's Press, 1987); Whitehead, Donald, *The FBI Story* (New York: Random House, 1956).

CRABB AFFAIR (1956–1957). The Crabb Affair was a British political-intelligence scandal involving the disappearance of an expert underwater saboteur, Commander Lionel Phillip Kenneth "Buster" Crabb (sometimes spelled Crabbe) (1909–1956), whose services were eagerly sought for salvaging sunken vessels in the 1950s.

Nicholas Elliott (1916–1994), a long-serving **MI6** officer who headed a special naval section of Britain's Naval Intelligence Division (NID), agreed to discover, for Rear Admiral John Inglis, information about the propeller design of the very fast Russian cruiser *Ordzhonikidze*. It had brought **Nikita Khrushchev** (1894–1971) and **Nikolai Bulganin** (1895–1975) to the United Kingdom on a friendly state visit.

The new British Prime Minister, Sir Anthony Eden (1897–1977), was eager to reduce the hostility between Britain and Russia, and forbade both **MI5** and MI6 to undertake any intelligence operations against the Russians. Neither intelligence agency took him seriously. They had already bugged the visitors' accommodation at Claridges Hotel, and would discover whatever they could about the very fast cruiser.

The British Admiralty wanted to know if the Soviet ship was fitted with an anti-sonar device (AGOUTI) that reduced underwater noise. For the job Nicholas Elliott decided to use a freelance frogman—in case anything went wrong—and chose the retired Royal Navy commander "Buster" Crabb. MI5 and MI6 officers planned the operation.

On April 19, 1956, Crabb dived, and never returned. The Soviets on board the cruiser reported a frogman wearing a diving suit near the ship. Before any cover story could be prepared, the rear admiral from the *Ordzhonikidze* asked Britain's Rear Admiral Philip Burnett for an explanation.

The Russians knew what had happened and spent the day asking unanswerable questions, enjoying the embarrassment of the British naval chiefs who had not been told of the operation. Quickly the MI6 officers went to Crabb's hotel, paid his bill, and collected his belongings. Two days later a policeman went back to the hotel and tore out the registration pages relating to Crabb. At a press conference shortly afterward, Khrushchev alluded amusingly to underwater problems, and soon the story was in the newspapers.

The British secret services tried to conceal the truth with a lie about Crabb's work in a bay three miles away. This **disinformation** led to embarrassing questions in Parliament. The Russians lost interest in the affair after Anthony Eden was forced to admit that without official approval an underwater operation had been conducted against the Russian ship.

What happened is not securely known. It is likely that the Russians had been informed well before they got to England, and Russian frogmen were waiting for Crabb, caught him, and took him on board the *Ordzhonikidze*. One story is that after he was caught, Crabb died in the ship's sick bay. Others stories suggest that Crabb was alive for months afterward. In June 1957 a fisherman found a body with no hands or head. It was not Crabb's. Security officers forced a man who knew Crabb to say it was his body. The body was then officially buried as Crabb's.

But the story that he was alive would not die. Was it true that he was seen in Russia, living under another name and training frogmen for the Russian navy? A Russian sea captain said that Crabb had given him a message for his fiancée. This story came from Captain R. Melkov, master of the Russian vessel *Kolpino*, then at dock in London. In May 1968 Melkov was found shot dead in his cabin—verdict, suicide.

The Crabb Affair caused dissension between the Prime Minister and the MI6 chief, Major General Sir John Sinclair, who was forced to resign. Also, the scandal so affected the special relationship between the **Central Intelligence Agency (CIA)** and MI6, that the planned **U-2 spy flights** that were to originate from Lakenheath, England, under cover as weather reconnaissance flights, had to be moved to Wiesbaden in West Germany.

See also CRABB, LIONEL; ELLIOTT, JOHN NICHOLAS

Sources: Deacon, Richard, *Spyclopedia: The Comprehensive Handbook of Espionage* (New York: William Morrow, 1987); Pincher, Chapman, *Too Secret Too Long* (London: Sidgwick & Jackson, 1984); Richelson, Jeffrey T., *A Century of Spies: Intelligence in the Twentieth Century* (New York: Oxford University Press, 1995); Rusbridger, James, *The Intelligence Game: The Illusions and Delusions of International Espionage* (London: Bodley Head, 1989); West, Nigel, *A Matter of Trust* (London: Weidenfeld and Nicolson, 1982); Wright, Peter, with Paul Greengrass, *Spycatcher: The Candid Autobiography of a Senior Intelligence Officer* (Melbourne: William Heinemann Australia, 1987).

CRABB, LIONEL PHILLIP "BUSTER" (1910–1956). "Buster Crabb" was an expert underwater saboteur and an outstanding frogman; he was allegedly found headless after a failed attempt to examine a Soviet vessel while it was in a British harbor.

Crabb (sometimes spelled Crabbe) was born into a poor family and received little education. At the age of eight years he became interested in the navy and longed to go to sea; a few years later he joined the British merchant marine. He traveled the Far East and at one time spied for **Chiang Kai-shek** (1887–1975).

In 1940 Crabb attempted to enlist in the Royal Navy, but was rejected because of his poor eyesight. However, he managed to convince the recruitment officers that he would make a good underwater bomb disposal officer, and he was accepted and commissioned in 1941. Off Gibralter he cleared delayed-action limpet mines from the hulls of British warships. He became the Royal Navy's most notable frogman, and received the George Medal and an **OBE.** On Italy's surrender, its frogmen refused to comply with the conventions of war unless they surrendered to Lieutenant Commander Lionel Crabb. He had helped salvage the submarines *H.M.S. Affray* and *H.M.S. Truculent.*

According to one report Crabb secretly examined the hull of a Soviet cruiser that was in Portsmouth harbor at the time of the coronation of Queen Elizabeth II (June 1953).

Crabb retired from the Royal Navy in 1955, a heavy drinker and smoker. He found few underwater jobs. He was a consultant to the makers of the film *Cockleshell Heroes.* In April 1956 he went to Portsmouth with his fiancée, Patricia Rose (d. 1987), whom he had told about his next mission. When they returned to London, Crabb was met by two MI6 officers, and plans were made for him to visit the *H.M.S. Vernon*, the Royal Navy's diving center. There he made plans to use oxygen equipment to examine underwater the special propeller design of the very fast visiting Russian cruiser, *Ordzhonikidze.* Such equipment would leave no trail of bubbles to disclose its presence underwater.

On April 19 Crabb set off for the Russian cruiser, and was never seen alive again. The Naval Intelligence Division (NID) searched for him unsuccessfully, and in the middle of May a scandal surrounded his disappearance. In June 1957 a headless body, with no hands, was found near Chichester harbor, and it was stated officially that the corpse was that of Crabb.

In 1972 Harry Houghton (1905–) wrote that Crabb got into difficulties underwater; was captured by the Russians and brought unconscious, due to lack of oxygen, on board the Russian cruiser; and died shortly afterward, on April 19.

See also CRABB AFFAIR

Sources: Deacon, Richard, *Spyclopedia: The Comprehensive Handbook of Espionage* (New York: William Morrow, 1987); Houghton, Harry, *Operation Portland: The Autobiography of a Spy* (London: Rupert Hart-Davis, 1972); Pincher, Chapman, *Too Secret Too Long* (London: Sidgwick & Jackson, 1984); Rusbridger, James, *The Intelligence Game: The Illusions and Delusions of International Espionage* (London: Bodley Head, 1989).

CUBAN MISSILE CRISIS (1962). For two weeks in October 1962, the world appeared to be at the edge of another world war when the United States found clear evidence of Russian intercontinental ballistic missiles in Cuba, 90 miles from the coast of the United States.

In March 1962 Fidel Castro Ruz (1927–), the dictator of Cuba, had the **KGB** begin to establish revolutions in Latin America from a base in Havana. In May, **Nikita Khrushchev** (1894–1971) decided to establish a missile base in Cuba, which he thought would impress the United States with the Soviets' missile power, deter the United States from aiming a first strike, and, at the same time, make a dramatic gesture in support of Cuba's Communist dictator.

Russia assumed the United States could not detect a missile base until it was too late to do anything. This was false, because **U-2 spy flights** could photograph and identify military installations, and because Oleg Penkovsky (1919–1963) had given the United States the Russian plans of missile bases that eliminated any doubts about the precision of U-2 spy plane photography.

In May 1961, the President's brother, Robert Kennedy (1925–1968), and Georgi Bolshakov, a KGB **agent** working as a journalist, began regular meetings. Robert Kennedy, impressed by the Russian's honesty, probably did not know he was dealing with a KGB agent. Bolshakov persuaded Robert Kennedy that President **John F. Kennedy** (1917–1963) and Nikita Khrushchev should speak frankly to each other through Robert and himself. In this way a back channel was established between the two leaders.

In October 1962, the U-2 spy planes revealed the presence of the Cuban missile bases. Robert Kennedy felt sure that Bolshakov knew of the missiles, but Bolshakov denied any knowledge of them. It appears the back channel was being used to conceal the arming of Cuba and not to extend a cooperative relationship between the **Cold War** adversaries. And when President Kennedy found in fact that missiles *were* in Cuba, he felt personally deceived by the Russian leader and his go-between. The contact was ended, Bolshakov was replaced, and the crisis worsened. A war seemed imminent.

On October 28, after last-minute negotiations and a secret deal, Khrushchev announced that all missile bases in Cuba would be closed. This made it appeard to the Americans and their allies that President Kennedy was a strong leader who had outsmarted Khrushchev.

In fact, the Russians maintained a spy base outside Havana, which they used to monitor U.S. communications until it was dismantled in 2002.

In 1978, for the first time, details became known of the 1962 deal between Kennedy and Khrushchev: the latter would cease arming Cuba if Kennedy took the U.S. missiles out of Turkey. This appeared in Arthur Schlesinger, Jr.'s, book on Robert Kennedy.

In 1998 Robert MacNamara, a leading adviser to John F. Kennedy in 1962, and Schlesinger met the Russian general who had been in charge at the time of the Cuban missile crisis, and they learned that there had been far more deadly warheads established in Cuba than the Americans had known about in 1962.

See also PENKOVSKY, OLEG

Sources: Andrew, Christopher, and Oleg Gordievsky, *KGB: The Inside Story of Its Foreign Operations from Lenin to Gorbachev* (London: Hodder and Stoughton, 1990); Andrew, Christopher, and Vasili Mitrokhin, *The Mitrokhin Archive: The KGB in Europe and the West* (London: Lane, 1999); Ashby, Timothy Garton, *The Bear in the Backyard: Moscow's Caribbean Strategy* (Lexington, MA: Lexington Books, 1987); Brugioni, Dino, *Eyeball to Eyeball: The Inside Story of the Cuban Missile Crisis* (New York: Random House, 1991); Eubank, Keith, *The Missile Crisis in Cuba* (New York: Krieger, 2000); Frankel, Max, "Learning from the Missile Crisis," *Smithsonian* 33 (October 2002): 52–56, 57, 61–62; Nathan, James A., *Anatomy of the Cuban Missile Crisis* (Westport, CT: Greenwood, 2000); Reuters, "Russian Spy Base Closes in Cuba After 40 Years," *The Age*, January 28, 2002, p. 7; Scott, Len, "Espionage and the Cold War: Oleg Penkovsky and the Cuban Missile Crisis," *Intelligence and National Security* 14 (1999): 23–47; Usowski, Peter S., "John McCone and the Cuban Missile Crisis: A Persistent Approach to the Intelligence Policy Relationship," *International Journal of Intelligence* 2 (1989): 547–576.

CURRIE, LAUCHLIN (1900–1993). Lauchlin Currie, a high-ranking adviser in the White House during Franklin D. Roosevelt's (1882–1945) administration, was named as a Soviet spy by Elizabeth Bentley (1908–1963). He denied this, and dismissed all further allegations for the rest of his life. Recent evidence suggests that at best he carefully selected what he thought the Soviets might want to know and, at the beginning of the **Cold War,** for which he had his own agenda of personal diplomacy, provided information to three friends he knew were Soviet **agents.**

Lauchlin Currie was born in Nova Scotia, was educated at the London School of Economics, and as a postgraduate scholar studied economics at Harvard. He became a U.S. citizen in 1934, and worked with Harry Dexter White (1892–1948) at the U.S. Treasury in the Department of Research and Statistics; later he moved to the Federal Reserve Board. In 1939 Currie joined the Roosevelt administration as an economic adviser. He was an eclectic, liberal planner, and anticipated John Maynard Keynes's (1883–1946) contributions to economics.

In September 1939, after the Russians and Nazis had signed their nonaggression treaty in August, Whittaker Chambers (1901–1961) gave a list of people to the anti-Communist intelligence adviser to the U.S. President and Secretary of State Adolf A. Berle (1895–1971). The people on the list had supplied information for the Soviets over the previous 10 years. Currie's name was on that list, along with Alger Hiss (1904–1996) and Harry Dexter White.

In 1940 Currie met and worked with Nathan Silvermaster (fl. 1899–1957) on a labor problem; both knew George Silverman (fl. 1930–1955). In January 1942 the **NKGB** leadership wanted both Lud Ullman (fl. 1930–1950) and Nathan Silvermaster to continue their efforts to recruit their colleague Currie, who at this time was an adviser to the White House. That year he defended the character of Nathan Silvermaster, whose loyalty was being investigated by the **Federal Bureau of Investigation (FBI);** he also went to China as Franklin Roosevelt's personal representative to discuss China's economy with the Nationalist government. Some scholars asked whether or not he knew Silvermaster and Silverman were spies. He did; and he informed Silverman of the U.S. attempts to break a Soviet code, though he did not say which one.

In October 1943 Currie, who was by this time an influential figure in the White House, managed to get another investigation of Silvermaster stopped. In the summer of 1944 he informed his Soviet contacts of the differing views held by Charles de Gaulle (1890–1970) and Franklin D. Roosevelt over the international status of France's colonies, which included Indochina, after Japan was defeated; also, he said Roosevelt would find the Soviet conditions regarding the Polish–Soviet border acceptable. In 1945 **Harry S. Truman** (1884–1972) had Currie removed as a presidential adviser.

When Kim Philby (1912–1988) informed his Soviet masters of Elizabeth Bentley's betrayal in November 1945, the NKGB froze all contact with her, and among the code names they listed was PAGE, Currie's **code name.**

Currie appeared voluntarily in 1948 before the **House Un-American Activities Committee (HUAC),** and impressed **Richard Nixon** (1913–1994) with his fervent loyalty to the United States and his dignified denial of Elizabeth Bentley's assertions that he had spied for the Soviets. He said he never knew anyone had taken his statements and provided them to a foreign power. For some years the FBI had a minor interest in following him.

In the middle of 1949, after his appearance before the HUAC, Currie went to Colombia and reported on the economy for the International Bank for Reconstruction and Development (World Bank). Later, outside Bogotá, Colombia, he bought a cattle ranch, and in 1953 divorced his wife and married a Colombian. He took out Colombian citizenship in 1958, and in 1986 again dismissed statements that he had ever been a spy for the Soviets.

Recent evidence shows that Currie told the Soviets about the U.S. code-breaking, sought to prevent U.S.-Soviet conflict, and had his own agenda of personal diplomacy. Carefully selecting what he thought the Soviets might want to know, he provided information to friends whom he knew to be Soviet agents. After **World War II** these liberally motivated actions brought him down.

See also BENTLEY, ELIZABETH; CHAMBERS, WHITTAKER; HISS, ALGER; SILVERMAN, A. GEORGE; SILVERMASTER, NATHAN; WHITE, HARRY DEXTER

Sources: Benson, Robert Louis, and Michael Warner, eds., *Venona: Soviet Espionage and the American Response, 1939–1957* (Washington, DC: National Security Agency and Central Intelligence Agency, 1996); Haynes, John Earl, and Harvey Klehr, *Venona: Decoding Soviet Espionage in America* (New Haven, CT: Yale University Press, 1999); Olmstead, Kathryn, *Red Spy Queen: A Biography of Elizabeth Bentley* (Chapel Hill: University of North Carolina Press, 2002); Sandilands, Roger, *The Life and Political Economy of Lauchlin Currie: New Dealer and Development Economist* (Durham, NC: Duke University Press, 1990); Sandilands, Roger, "Guilt by Association? Lauchlin Currie's Alleged Involvement with Washington Economists in Soviet Espionage," *History of Political Economy* 32 (2000): 473–515; Weinstein, Allen, and Alexander Vassiliev, *The Haunted Wood: Soviet Espionage in America—The Stalin Era* (New York: Random House, 1999).

D

DANILOFF AFFAIR (1985). The Daniloff Affair involved the secret **tit-for-tat** exchange between the United States and the **U.S.S.R.** of alleged spies and dissidents, the possibility of canceling the first summit involving U.S. President **Ronald Reagan** (1911–2004) and Mikhail Gorbachev (1931–), and the U.S. allegations that too many of the Soviet UN delegates were engaging in espionage.

In January 1985 Nicholas Daniloff, a U.S. *News & World Report* correspondent in Moscow, found a letter in his mailbox from a dissident Roman Catholic priest, Father Roman. Inside the letter was a message to William Casey (1913–1987), which Daniloff took to the U.S. embassy and gave to the Second Secretary—who was also a **Central Intelligence Agency (CIA)** officer—along with the phone number of the priest.

In May 1986 Daniloff was arrested by the **KGB** and charged with espionage. He was chosen in response to the arrest in New York of Gennardi Zakharov, a Soviet spy with the cover of a UN officer.

Father Roman was a KGB plant. The CIA officer at the U.S. embassy made an error when he mentioned that a journalist had brought the letter to the embassy. This error had identified Daniloff.

If Nicholas Daniloff were to be tried, it would appear at the trial that he had known a CIA officer and had worked with him, and this would damage the reputation of the United States.

The United States and the U.S.S.R. bargained, and finally struck a deal. Daniloff was set free; the next day Zakharov was freed in an exchange that the U.S. President denied was a trade; and the dissident Yuri Orlov and his wife were permitted to leave the U.S.S.R.

Source: Wise, David, *The Spy Who Got Away: The Inside Story of the CIA Agent Who Betrayed His Country* (London: Fontana/Collins, 1988).

DAWE, AMOS (fl. 1970–1982). Amos Dawe was an unwilling **KGB** agent and clever Hong Kong businessman who was drawn into a KGB plan to get control of U.S. technology in **Silicon Valley**, California.

Dawe's origins are obscure. As a young man he had a sharp eye, and rose rapidly from poverty to enormous wealth. It was widely held that he controlled 200 companies in six Asian nations, but in truth he had bribed his auditors, and only a few people knew that he was almost bankrupt in the early 1970s. Among those people were Vachislav Rhyhov (fl. 1974–1975), who managed the Singapore branch of Moscow's Narodny Bank.

Rhyhov secretly agreed to support Dawe, and finance his future commercial plans, but only if Dawe would go to the United States and, as an individual, purchase banks in Silicon Valley. Dawe reluctantly agreed.

Dawe's work began in 1974, when he negotiated the purchase of three banks. He was about to acquire his fourth when the U.S. banking community turned away from him. Unknown to him, the **Central Intelligence Agency (CIA)** had discovered the scheme and, through a Honk Kong journalist, had informed all America's bankers of a KGB plan, headed by Dawe, to control international commerce.

Dawe returned to Asia and disappeared, and later was found close to death after a beating by Thai gangsters. In 1978 he fled Asia for California and, expecting the Americans would prosecute him, gave himself up to the **Federal Bureau of Investigation (FBI).** The U.S. government did not charge him, but many wanted to sue him. Hong Kong friends rescued him by way of extradition. In retaliation, the U.S. government insisted Dawe be convicted in Hong Kong for embezzlement, and jailed for five years. In 1982, before being indicted, for that charge, Dawe disappeared in Hong Kong and has not been seen since.

The KGB might have killed Dawe as an example to others seeking to swindle it; perhaps Dawe had banked vast sums in Europe, and after changes in his appearance and living standards, settled comfortably in Canada.

Source: Laffin, John, *Brassey's Book of Espionage* (London: Brassey's, 1996).

DE VOSJOLI, PHILIPPE THYRAUD (fl. 1922–1991).

Philippe De Vosjoli was born in Romorantin, France, and as a youth fought with the Resistance, headed by Charles de Gaulle (1890–1970); later he worked as an intelligence officer in French Indochina (later Vietnam), Algeria, and Cuba. In 1951 he was the first of the liaison officers appointed to Washington, DC, by the **SDECE**. He associated closely with James Angleton (1917–1987) until seriously threatened with dismissal, and resumed the friendship shortly before Angleton died.

Angleton had allowed the Soviet defector Anatoli Golitsyn (1926–) to become as familiar with **Central Intelligence Agency (CIA)** records as **MI5** and **MI6** had allowed him to become with theirs. This meant that Golitsyn saw what the French intelligence service was sending Angleton. It was not long before Golitsyn was able to convince Angleton that inside the French secret service there was a **mole**, code-named SAPPHIRE.

Although De Vosjoli never dealt with Golitsyn directly, he found that he could not answer convincingly the suggestions that came to him—via Angleton—about suspected moles in the French secret services. He had no way of denying or confirming Angleton's growing suspicions.

When De Vosjoli informed his colleagues at home, and asked them for information, they became concerned about his fitness for the job. To them he appeared to be witch-hunting at Golitsyn's behest. By December 1962, Golitsyn's charges were so erratic and numerous that De Vosjoli himself came under suspicion as disloyal to French intelligence interests in Washington. He was ordered to spy on the Americans, recruit a clandestine intelligence network in the United States in order to penetrate the American nuclear research laboratories, and establish the extent of U.S. nuclear power and weapons. What was expected seemed madness to De Vosjoli, and he told his superiors so; they replied that it was Anatoli Golitsyn who was insane, not themselves.

Nevertheless, in time De Vosjoli came to accept the Angleton—Golitsyn thesis that U.S. secrets were flowing freely out of France to the **KGB**. At the same time he felt his superiors believed deeply that he was no longer loyal to France. Foolishly, he drew closer to Angleton, and was recruited to the CIA on the assumption he would spy on the French for the Americans, and report how much the French were spying on the United States and the extent to which the KGB had penetrated French intelligence. This operation was cleared right up to the President.

Although De Vosjoli denied that he had ever been recruited to the CIA, suspicions that he had been were not dying. Also, a story was put about that he and Angleton together had raided the French embassy in Washington sometime in mid-1963. Twenty-six years later De Vosjoli would deny that the event had occurred.

Suspicious of his waning loyalty, the French authorities recalled De Vosjoli. Fearing he would be murdered if he returned to France, he resigned. After a party that was given him by the CIA, and receiving gifts from the CIA chief and Angleton, he disappeared. In fact he went to be with his mistress in New York, where he also met an important French nuclear spy who was running the French scheme to penetrate the U.S. nuclear program.

Shortly after meeting the spy, De Vosjoli saw a senior French espionage officer of the SDECE meeting with the French nuclear spy, and immediately concluded the former had been sent to the United States to assassinate him. He immediately took his mistress with him, in a camper van, to Mexico. He could not be found.

De Vosjoli relaxed in Mexico, awaiting permission to reenter the United States to work legally as a civilian. In 1965 he met the American novelist Leon Uris, who decided, on hearing De Vosjoli's story, that they should write a novel; they did, and *Topaz* became a best-seller and was filmed by Alfred Hitchcock.

De Vosjoli prospered as an investment consultant. In 1970 he published his memoirs, and later visited France on an American passport. He concluded that his 12 years in the intelligence services had shown him that the world of intelligence had a lot of sick people in it.

See also ANGLETON, JAMES; GOLITSYN, ANATOLI; OPERATION SAPPHIRE

Sources: De Vosjoli, Philippe Thyraud, *Lamia* (Boston: Little, Brown, 1970); Frolik, Joseph, *The Frolik Defection* (London: Leo Cooper, 1975); Mangold, Tom, *Cold Warrior: James Jesus Angleton, the CIA Master Spy Hunter* (New York: Simon & Schuster, 1991).

DEFENSE SUPPORT PROGRAM—SATELLITES (1958).

The DSP (Defense Support Program) is the second—the first was CORONA—in the United States to provide instant warnings of Russian airborne attacks on the United States and Europe. The programs used radar and other intelligence sources and secret devices. For 30 years this program operated secretly, and detected infrared plumes from their satellite stations over 20,000 miles into space.

The program began late in 1958 after the testing of the Missile Defense Alarm System (MIDAS), and eventually came under the control of the U.S. Air Force. There were many expensive failures with MIDAS, and the program was often redeveloped;

in 1966 it became known as Program 461. Satellite lifetimes were improved, and results began to be more and more successful.

The program required ground stations around the world to be sure of a continuous cover over China and the **U.S.S.R.** In 1968 the U.S. Air Force Defense System Office chose **Woomera** in South Australia, which had been as used as a missile testing ground by the British. At Woomera the United States and Australia established a joint defense communications station named Nurrungar, Aboriginal for "to hear." By 1970 it was operational with 250–300 U.S. personnel.

A ground station free of coastal strip interference, yet able to detect missiles shot from the U.S.S.R., was established at Aurora, Colorado, at the Buckley Air National Guard Base. Later the DSP established a ground station in West Germany.

In Australia the resistance to the program presented security problems. The Nurrungar and CIA signals intelligence station RHYOLITE, at Pine Gap, were criticized in the *New York Times, Aviation Week and Space Technology, Aerospace Daily*, and *Space News.*

In 1971 some Australian members of Parliament demanded the U.S. military close its installations in Australia; news stories appeared about U.S. spy stations; and critics argued that their presence violated Australia's sovereignty and, in the event of a nuclear war, would be attacked first. The **Australian Labor Party** (ALP) declared its policy would ensure that if the U.S. bases at Pine Gap and Woomera violated Australian sovereignty, their closure would be demanded.

In 1988, after almost 18 months of public discussion, protests, and charges of government duplicity and secret policies about Woomera and Pine Gap, and amid growing fears among Australians that they would be wiped out first in a nuclear war, the United States and Australia signed a 10-year agreement on operations at the two stations.

The program detected launches of intercontinental ballistic missiles, medium-to-intermediate-range missiles, and submarine-launched missiles; planes flying on afterburners; nuclear testing programs in China and by France in the Pacific; surface-to-air and Scud missiles fired during the Yom Kippur War; infrared intelligence from Soviet naval weapons depots, Soviet propellant plants, and a munitions dump, and a gasoline supply center; and the explosion of TWA 810 over Scotland and a plane collision off the Atlantic coast of Africa. It also monitored missile firing during the war between Iran and Iraq (1980–1988); the Soviet Scud firings during the Afghanistan War; the Israeli secret test of its Jericho missile; India's missile firing; South Africa's Arnston missile tests; and many missile tests conducted by the Chinese, as well as missiles fired during the Gulf War (1990). The program informed the United States more recently that India, Pakistan, Iran, Iraq, Israel, and North Korea had medium-to-intermediate-range missiles, and that both China and North Korea have been helping other nations to acquire these arms.

The DSP has established a relatively new program: FEWS, or Follow-on Early Warning Detection System. This development means the Woomera and the West German ground stations can be closed down, and all satellite information will be collected, collated, and processed at the U.S. ground station.

The DSP arose in response to fears that soon after the end of **World War II,** Russia would attack Europe and the United States. Today Russia and the United States share the information collected by the DSP satellites. The fear of attack comes today from "rogue states" and terrorists who have acquired nuclear missiles and the means to fire them toward the United States and her allies.

Source: Richelson, Jeffrey, *America's Space Sentinels: DSP Satellites* (Lawrence: University Press of Kansas, 1999).

DRIBERG, TOM (1905–1976). Tom Driberg was a Soviet **agent of influence** and a **double agent.**

Driberg was educated at Lancing College and Christ Church, Oxford; while still a schoolboy, he was recruited to **MI5** by Maxwell Knight (1900–1968) and, being both charming and intelligent, penetrated the Young Communist League, and eventually the Communist Party. He was much admired by the bisexual Knight, to whom he gave excellent information.

At the age of 28, Driberg joined the *Daily Express.* In 1941 he was expelled from the Communist Party when a close friend exposed his duplicity, In 1942 he was an Independent MP for Malden in Essex, and a Labour MP in 1945. Iinvited to rejoin the Communist Party, he agreed. Thereafter Driberg was double agent, working for both MI5 and the **NKGB**, largely for money. He also worked as an agent for Czechoslovakia's security services.

From Driberg both the **KGB** and MI5 learned much about the personal life of British members of Parliament, so that both could use blackmail to further their secret aims. The information he gave to the KGB was so useful that some of it got as far as the Politburo. He published a sanitized biography of Guy Burgess (1911–1963), in 1956, stating Burgess was neither a spy nor an alcoholic.

Driberg was Chairman of the Labour Party in Britain in 1957–1958. By then the KGB was using him as both a propagandist and an agent of influence; he appeared to enjoy his role as a double agent. Even so, he often wrote what he wanted, especially about Vietnam and nuclear deterrence policies.

In 1964 Driberg was regarded as too untrustworthy to be in Labour Prime Minister **Harold Wilson**'s (1916–1995) ministry. By 1968 he seemed to have broken from the KGB. He had a heart attack early in 1968. After losing the sight of one eye, he retired in 1970. He was elevated to Lord Bradwell (1975) as a Labour peer, and was known both affectionately and cynically as "Lord of the Spies." His blatant homosexuality led to only one prosecution, but he was quickly acquitted. Perhaps it was part of his espionage duties.

Driberg published books dealing with Lord Beaverbrook (1879–1964), moral rearmament, and himself. After his death in 1976, MI5 was convinced that he had been controlled more by the KGB than MI5, and that he had moved ideologically further to the left than had been suspected. To some colleagues he was delightful character: amusing, entertaining, and witty, a veritable prankster of espionage.

See also BURGESS, GUY

Sources: Abse, Leo, *Margaret, Daughter of Beatrice: A Politician's Psycho-Biography of Margaret Thatcher* (London: Cape, 1989); Andrew, Christopher, and Oleg Gordievsky, *KGB: The Inside Story of Its Foreign Operations from Lenin to Gorbachev* (London: Hodder and Stoughton, 1990); Andrew, Christopher, and Vasili Mitrokhin, *The Mitrokhin Archive: The KGB in Europe and the West* (London: Lane, 1999); Driberg, Tom, *The Best of Both Worlds: A Personal Diary* (London: Phoenix House, 1953); Driberg, Tom, *Guy Burgess: A Portrait with Background* (London: Weidenfeld and Nicolson, 1956); Driberg, Tom, *Beaverbrook: A Study in Power and Frustration* (London: Weidenfeld and Nicolson, 1956); Driberg, Tom, *The Mystery of Moral Re-Armament: A Study of Frank Buchman and His Movement* (London: Secker & Warburg, 1964); Driberg, Tom, *Ruling Passions: The Autobiography of Tom Driberg* (London: Quartet, 1978); Masters, Anthony, *The Man Who Was M* (Oxford: Blackwell, 1984);

Pincher, Chapman, *Their Trade Is Treachery* (London: Sidgwick & Jackson, 1981; rev. ed., New York: Bantam, 1982); Pincher, Chapman, *Too Secret Too Long* (London: Sidgwick & Jackson, 1984); Pincher, Chapman, *Traitors: The Anatomy of Treason* (New York: St. Martin's Press, 1987).

DULLES, ALLEN WELSH (1893–1969). Allen Dulles was an outstanding diplomat and senior member of the U.S. intelligence community who helped established the early **Cold War** policy of the United States, and led the **Central Intelligence Agency (CIA)** for many years, until he was disgraced by the unsuccessful invasion of Cuba in April 1961.

Dulles was born in Washington, DC, studied at Princeton, and served in the U.S. diplomatic corps in Vienna, Bern, Paris, Berlin, and Istanbul. After being chief of the Division of Near Eastern Affairs in the Department of State (1922–1926), he was a member of a law firm until 1942.

In April 1942 the temporary organization of eight intelligence agencies under the direction of **William J. Donvan** (1883–1959) was renamed **Office of Strategic Services (OSS)**; Switzerland, neutral during **World War II**, was chosen as the major outpost for OSS penetration of Nazi Germany.

Dulles, a man of personal quality, was to mingle freely with important businesspeople in Switzerland and with the nation's intellectuals; tap the information flow from Germany and Italy; and report his findings through the U.S. office of the financial attaché. In November 1942 he slipped into Switzerland and began his work.

Dulles's valuable reports warned the Allies about the V-2 rockets that were to be used to bomb London; described the German resistance movements and troop relocation at the time of the Normandy invasion in June 1944; reported on Benito Mussolini's fall (1943) and the mass murder of Jews; and warned early of the **U.S.S.R.**'s postwar intentions. He prepared documents for the Nuremberg Trials (1945); he anticipated George Kennan's containment policy (1946); developed plans for the reconstruction of postwar Europe; and helped to establish the Marshall Plan (1947).

In 1948 Dulles was appointed to head a committee to reconstruct the Central Intelligence Agency, and became the Director of Central Intelligence (DCI) and head of the CIA by 1953. In the course of his work he enhanced the National Intelligence Estimates (NIE) by avoiding excessive interference in their presentation, and helped in establishing their validity and reliability by calling on outside consultants, such as George Kennan (1904–).

Dulles was brought down by the failed **Bay of Pigs invasion** in 1961. It was condemned for many reasons, the most salient being that no prior estimates had been made—other than by the officers in the CIA who were passionately committed to the ill-fated operation—of the likelihood of a spontaneous uprising among unarmed Cubans in a revolt against the Cuban government.

On the death of President **John F. Kennedy** (1917–1963) in 1963, the incoming president, **Lyndon B. Johnson** (1908–1973), insisted that Dulles be appointed to the Warren Commission to inquire into the Kennedy assassination.

Dulles's biographers saw him as man who held the values of President Woodrow Wilson (1856–1924), a man who put aside the pursuit of wealth and the thrill of power for the pursuit of utopian ideals. Dulles's claim to authority inspired confidence among his followers, but too often he tended to miss crucial details in his work, which proved him to be a better operator than an administrator; also, he was thought to be too self-indulgent, as shown in his womanizing, keeping of mistresses, and inconsiderate attitude to his wife.

See also ABEL, RUDOLPH; OPERATION AJAX; OPERATION PLUTO AND OPERATION ZAPATA

Sources: Mahoney, Harry T., and Marjorie L. Mahoney, *Biographic Dictionary of Espionage* (San Francisco: Austin & Winfield, 1998); Grose, Peter, *Gentleman Spy: The Life of Allen Dulles* (Boston: Houghton Mifflin, 1994); Srodes, James, *Allen Dulles: Master of Spies* (Washington, DC: Regnery, 1999).

DUNLAP, JACK E. (fl. 1935–1963). Jack E. Dunlap, a **Korean War** (1950–1953) hero who was awarded the Purple Heart and Bronze Star, spied for the Soviets in the early 1960s while working as a staff sergeant at the National Security Agency (NSA), Fort Meade, Maryland.

Dunlap might have been recruited to the **GRU** when he was in Turkey in 1957. In 1960 he was chauffeur for the chief of staff, Major General Coverdale, at the NSA headquarters, Fort Meade, where he was entrusted with the job of taking secret documents from one office to another.

Dunlap had a large family, and it was observed—but not given much notice—that on his U.S.$500 a week wages he had several expensive automobiles, a cabin cruiser, a drinking problem, a mistress, and the reputation of womanizer.

It seems that at the time Dunlap needed more money, so in the spring or summer of 1960 he went to the Soviet embassy in Washington, offering secret documents for money. For over two and half years he gave his GRU case officer many manuals, books, plans, and details of cipher machines at NSA. He may have given them **Central Intelligence Agency (CIA)** estimates of Soviet forces in Eastern Europe. His GRU case officer photographed the documents and returned them without delay to Dunlap, so as to preserve his courier schedule.

In March 1963, while taking a **polygraph test,** Dunlap admitted to petty theft. Six members of the NSA staff had used him to smuggle home office equipment and furniture. Over the years this activity had probably extended his access to NSA documents. He was moved in May to an orderly room job.

Dunlap was betrayed by Dimitri F. Polyakov (c. 1921–1988). In June 1963, he attempted suicide by poisoning, and with a pistol, but was found in time by friends. In July, Dunlap asphyxiated himself with the exhaust from his car, and was buried with full military honors in Arlington National Cemetery.

See also POLYAKOV, DIMITRI

Sources: Andrew, Christopher, and Oleg Gordievsky, *KGB: The Inside Story of Its Foreign Operations from Lenin to Gorbachev* (London: Hodder and Stoughton, 1990); Bamford, James, *The Puzzle Palace: A Report on America's Most Secret Agency* (Boston: Houghton Mifflin, 1982); Epstein, Edward Jay, *Deception: The War Between the KGB and the CIA* (New York: Simon & Schuster, 1989); Oberdorfer, Don, "The Playboy Sergeant," in Allen Dulles, ed., *Great True Spy Stories* (Secaucus, NJ: Castle, 1968), pp. 65–72; Volkman, Ernest, *Espionage: The Greatest Spy Operations of the 20th Century* (New York: Wiley, 1995).

E

EARLY SOVIET SPIES IN BRITAIN BEFORE THE COLD WAR. George Armstrong (fl. 1920–1941) was a member of the **Communist Party of Great Britain (CPGB)** and was hanged for treason in July 1941.

Cedric Belfrage (fl. 1940–1990), code-named CHARLIE, was a British journalist and member of the CPGB and the British Security Coordination in New York immediately after the United States entered **World War II.** He offered his services to the Soviet intelligence by approaching **Earl Browder** (1891–1973), who sent him to Jacob Golos (1890–1943), a Soviet secret police **agent** of the **NKVD.** Belfrage had access to a great range of intelligence information that went between Britain and the United States. At the end of the war he was controlled in the United States by Vasili Zarubin, whose cover was blown when he was denounced to the **Federal Bureau of Investigation (FBI)** by Vasili Mironov in the summer of 1943. Belfrage escaped prosecution because he was detected after the end of World War II, and was a permanent resident in the United States. He was identified by Elizabeth Bentley (1908–1963) and died in June 1990.

Douglas Springhall (1901–1953) was a member of the CPGB. In 1924 he attended the Communist Congress in Moscow, and in 1926 was sent to prison for two months for his support of the general strike in Great Britain, serving as an agitator in the Young Communist League. He recruited Alexander Foote (fl. 1905–1956) into the British Battalion of the International Brigades in the **Spanish Civil War.** After visiting Moscow on **GRU** business in 1939, he became an illegal agent runner for the GRU in Britain. He was jailed after having been charged with receiving secrets from the Air Ministry (1943).

Also jailed in 1943 was Ormond Uren (fl. 1920–1943), a Scottish junior officer in the Highland Light Infantry, who had been seconded to **SOE**'s Hungarian sabotage and resistance organization at its headquarters in London. He was arrested in June 1943 after a clandestine meeting with Douglas Springhall. Both were GRU agents. He had passed Springhall information on the SOE policy and communications on Eastern Europe, in order to indicate that his commitment to communism was sincere. He was a secret member of the CPGB, which he had joined in 1940. In October 1943 he was court-martialed, lost his commission, and received a sentence of seven years in jail. He commented that he might not have been caught and tried had he gone to Cambridge University instead of the University in Edinburgh.

In 1944, shortly after the imprisonment of Springhall and Uren, the **SIS** established a section to look closely into communism in Britain and related Soviet activities. On discovering this, Kim Philby (1912–1988), by clever means, managed to get himself appointed head of that part of the SIS organization, Section IX.

See also PHILBY, HAROLD "KIM"

Sources: Andrew, Christopher, and Oleg Gordievsky, *KGB: The Inside Story of Its Foreign Operations from Lenin to Gorbachev* (London: Hodder and Stoughton, 1990); Andrew, Christopher, and Vasili Mitrokhin, *The Mitrokhin Archive: The KGB in Europe and the West* (London: Lane, 1999); Dorril, Stephen, *MI6: Inside the Covert World of Her Majesty's Secret Intelligence Service* (New York: The Free Press, 2000); Bentley, Elizabeth, *Out of Bondage* (New York: Ballantine Books, 1988); Foot, M.R.D., *SOE* (London: BBC, 1984); Pincher, Chapman, *Too Secret Too Long* (London: Sidgwick & Jackson, 1984); West, Nigel, *Seven Spies Who Changed the World* (London: Secker & Warburg, 1991).

ELLIOTT, JOHN NICHOLAS REDE (1916–1994). Nicholas Elliott, **CBE**, was a leader of British **Cold War** espionage, a director of **MI6**, and is noted for his embarrassing association with the scandal and disappearance of Lionel "Buster" Crabb (1910–1956) and the attempt to get Kim Philby (1912–1988) to confess.

Elliott was the only son of Sir Claude Elliott, who in 1933 became the headmaster of Eton College. Nicholas was born in the Belgravia district of London, where his father worked at the British Admiralty during **World War I**. At the age of five he was taken by his parents to live in Cambridge, where he was raised in comfort while his father researched history. Four years later he was sent to Durnford Preparatory School in Langton Matravers, a village on the Isle of Purbeck in Dorset, where life was such a health hazard, and so unpleasantly rigorous, that he left after a few years. Later he would compare the school to a vile doss house. He was at Eton from 1930 to 1933, before his father's appointment as headmaster.

Elliott graduated from Trinity College, Cambridge, with a third-class degree, and in October 1938 was offered an honorary attaché post at the British embassy in the Netherlands. In the summer of 1940, when the Germans invaded the Netherlands, Nicholas was evacuated; he sought a post in the Scots Guards, was commissioned into the intelligence unit, and had the task later of looking after **double agents** for **MI5**.

On his way to Cairo in May 1942, the ship on which Elliott was traveling was attacked by a German U-boat; in Cairo he met a woman ambulance driver, who later became his wife. Together they were posted to Istanbul, where he worked as a counterintelligence officer and managed to get a senior **Abwehr** officer to defect, much to the chagrin of Adolf Hitler (1889–1945), who immediately had the German Army's secret services completely reorganized under Heinrich Himmler (1900–1945), the Nazi Gestapo chief.

In January 1945 Elliott was posted to Bern, Switzerland, as **SIS** head of station; during the 1950s he was head of station in Vienna, and after a short time in London, became station head in Beirut from 1960 to 1962.

While in London in 1956, Elliott was involved in the failed espionage operation by Commander "Buster" Crabb. The operation did not have government authorization, and when discovered, it was most embarrassing to Prime Minister **Anthony Eden** (1897–1977), who was entertaining Russian leaders **Nikita Khrushchev** (1894–1973) and **Nikolai Bulganin** (1895–1975) at the time, and led the Russians to make a formal protest. Fourteen months after the scandal, Crabb's alleged corpse, handless and decapitated, was found in June 1957. Elliott's career was tarnished, but he survived when sufficient evidence was found that the Foreign Office official had approved the operation.

In the early 1960s it was clear to many in the U.K. secret services that Kim Philby was a double agent. To catch him, it was necessary to induce him to confess. Because he had been close to Elliott, who had often supported Philby when under deep suspicion, Elliott agreed to go to Beirut to see if he could get the required confession. He did. But when Elliott returned to Britain, Philby fled to Moscow in January 1963. Philby later reported that Elliott, an old friend, tried to push him into defection, not a confession.

In 1969 it was clear to Elliott, who had been a director of MI6 for six years, and was responsible for the evaluation of MI6 intelligence for use by other sections of government, that he was never going to get the top MI6 job. He retired at the age of 52, and became an executive director of a large company, Lonhro; his work required much travel in Europe, the Middle East, and Africa. In March 1973 he lost his job in a boardroom dispute that would lead to inquiries for years afterward, and for which he had to give evidence. He took a job in Hong Kong with an international stockbroker for a firm who valued his international contacts. After four years he left the firm, and established his own consultancy, specializing in foreign affairs and counterterrorism.

Elliott died in April 1994, leaving a widow and a son; his daughter died earlier. He published two volumes of memoirs, *Never Judge a Man by His Umbrella* (1991) and *With My Little Eye* (1994), shortly before he died.

See also CRABB AFFAIR; CRABB, LIONEL; PHILBY, HAROLD "KIM"

Sources: Anonymous, "Nicholas Elliott, CBE: Obituary," *The Times* (London), April 14, 1994, Features; Borovik, Genrikh, *The Philby Files: The Secret Life of Master Spy Kim Philby,* trans. Antonina W. Bouis (Boston: Little, Brown, 1994); Bower, Tom, *The Perfect English Spy: Sir Dick White and the Secret War 1935–90* (London: Heinemann, 1995); Wright, Peter, with Paul Greengrass, *Spycatcher: The Candid Autobiography of a Senior Intelligence Officer* (Melbourne: William Heinemann Australia, 1987).

ELLIS, CHARLES HOWARD "DICK" (1895–1975). Dick Ellis was a suspected Soviet **agent** who served in **MI6** and other branches of the British secret services for a lifetime, and came under suspicion only after the defection of Guy Burgess and Donald Maclean in May 1951.

Ellis was born in Sydney, Australia, studied modern languages, served in **World War I,** and in Transcaspia took part in British operations against the Bolsheviks. In 1921 he returned to studies at Oxford, perfected his French at the Sorbonne in Paris, improved his Russian, and married a Russian woman from an émigré family.

In 1924 his expert linguistic skills got him a post in MI6 as agent working undercover in the British passport control office in Berlin, and later in Paris. In Paris he worked among the White Russian émigré community, some members of which were spies for both Russia and Germany. For further cover and more income, he wrote for newspapers and a recruited his brother-in-law Alexander Zilenski (1914–) as an agent.

By 1938 Ellis had divorced his wife and married an English woman; in 1940 he was sent to New York as a colonel, and deputy head of British Security Coordination; he worked under William Stephenson, code-named INTREPID. Recent evidence indicates that in the United States Ellis used the cover name "Howard," and the author Chapman Pincher (1984) hints that his work in the United States was sometimes for the Germans.

In 1944 Ellis returned to London headquarters of MI6 and received many wartime honors, and in 1946 was promoted to MI6 controller for Southeast Asia, based in Singapore. In 1950 he was sent to Australia to help establish **ASIS**. Also he became controller of North and South American affairs.

In 1951, after the defection of Guy Burgess (1911–1963) and Donald Maclean (1913–1983), Ellis came under suspicion. Some information showed he had given the German **Abwehr** the **order of battle** from MI6, and that before **World War II** he had warned Germany that the British had tapped the telephone line between the German embassy and Adolf Hitler (1889–1945) in Berlin. He may have been protected from further investigation by the efforts of Kim Philby (1912–1988). By 1953 the possibility had emerged of a political scandal, and in the national interest it was agreed to go no further with this line of investigation. In June 1953 Ellis retired from MI6, apparently for reasons of ill health.

Ellis retired to Australia, traveling there alone, having divorced again. Despite his alleged ill health he took a two-year contract with ASIS. After two months he broke the contract and returned to England early in 1954.

After Kim Philby defected in January 1963, the question was again asked whether Philby had covered for Ellis years before, and if so, perhaps Ellis had spied not only for the Germans in World War II but also for the Soviets.

During his short stay in Australia, Ellis had learned of the imminent defection off Vladimir Petrov (1907–1991). Perhaps he feared Petrov would name him as a **KGB** agent, and, since he was under contract to ASIS, if he was arrested, he might be tried in Australia.

In March 1954 Ellis was back in London; in April 1954 Petrov defected. Ellis reported to MI6 leadership about Petrov in Australia, and was told that because Philby was still under suspicion, he should not be seen with Philby. In fact Ellis did contact Philby. Later, Anthony Blunt (1907–1983) would tell his interrogators that Philby had known that Petrov would defect before April 1954. Perhaps Ellis had warned Philby.

Between 1953 and 1965 Ellis worked in MI6 archives, removing files of no further use.

Early in 1966 the FLUENCY Committee, a joint MI5–MI6 high-level investigating group, sought reliable knowledge of Soviet penetration in Britain's security service and **SIS**. It investigated Ellis to discover if he might have been a Soviet spy. The committee concluded Ellis had been a paid agent of the Germans up to 1940, and that he might have served the Soviets from as early as 1920. To test their conclusions, the committee need a confession from him.

Aged 71, Ellis was brought in for interrogation. He denied spying for Germany and Russia; later he admitted he had helped the Germans in the 1939 Venlo Incident, and had given information to the Russians in 1939. He said he hardly knew Kim Philby, which was false; that he had hurried back from Australia to marry, which also was false; and denied he had met Philby and had been warned against meeting him—another lie.

The FLUENCY Committee concluded Ellis had been as Soviet agent for about 30 years—first **GRU**, later **KGB**—and that he had spied for Germany. Later investigation by the **Central Intelligence Agency (CIA)** suggested that there is circumstantial evidence for the FLUENCY Committee's findings.

In 1981, U.K. Prime Minister **Margaret Thatcher** (1925–) declined to state that Ellis was not guilty after having been advised that the information on him was accurate in many details.

See also FLUENCY COMMITTEE; PETROV, VLADIMIR; PHILBY, HAROLD "KIM"

Sources: Knightley, Phillip, *The Second Oldest Profession: The Spy as Bureaucrat, Patriot, Fantasist and Whore* (London: Andre Deutsch, 1986); Pincher, Chapman, *Too Secret Too Long* (London: Sidgwick & Jackson, 1984); Pincher, Chapman, *Traitors: The Anatomy of Treason* (New York: St. Martin's Press, 1987); West, Nigel, *The Friends: Britain's Post-War Secret Operations* (London: Weidenfeld and Nicolson, 1988; Coronet ed., 1990).

ELLSBERG, DANIEL (1931–). Appalled by the private and illegal use of secrecy among U.S. presidents, Daniel Ellsberg produced the "Pentagon Papers," which revealed the practices of two U.S. presidents during the **Vietnam War.**

Ellsberg's parents were of Russian–Jewish ancestry, but born in America, and became devout Christian Scientists. On a scholarship Ellsberg studied at Harvard University and spent a year in the U.S. Marine Corps, serving as a platoon leader in the 3rd Battalion, Second Marine Division.

Ellsberg completed his economics Ph.D. in game theory at Harvard, and later joined the Economics Department at the Rand Corporation, working on the control issues involved in nuclear war.

In 1961, after reading highly secret information in the National Intelligence Estimate (NIE), Ellsberg found that **John F. Kennedy**'s presidential campaign had played upon public anxiety about the "**missile gap**"—Russia had more and better nuclear missiles than the United States—and that at the time of the presidential campaign in 1960, the gap was secretly known to be in the U.S.'s favor, not Russia's. This falsehood bothered Ellsberg, who had visited Saigon in 1960.

In the summer of 1964, Ellsberg took a post in the **Pentagon**, doing a job that gave him unrestricted access to highly secret information. That year he learned firsthand about the extraordinary difference between what President **Lyndon B. Johnson** (1908–1973) told the U.S. Congress in secret, and what was made available to the U.S. public. The subject matter concerned hostilities involving the U.S.S. *Maddox* and what happened in the Gulf of Tonkin early in August 1964, and the falsehoods which the President told the U.S. Senate Foreign Relations Committee to ensure its chairman sponsored the Tonkin Gulf Resolution. The resolution was the nearest the United States came to declaring war in Vietnam.

In 1965, much impressed by a talk given by Major General Edward G. Lansdale (1908–1987), Ellsberg arranged to be transferred from the Department of Defense to the Department of State, and was sent to Saigon to report on the U.S. village pacification scheme. He found no evidence of pacification, and concluded that United States should not have been involved in the Vietnam conflict.

In January 1968, when the **Tet Offensive** showed the **Viet Cong** could attack every province of South Vietnam simultaneously, many questions were raised about America's leadership in the Vietnam War. On March 10, the *New York Times* published leaked information from the Pentagon showing that over 200,000 U.S. combat troops were needed urgently in Vietnam. The U.S. Congress was shocked and American citizens were angered, because both had been assured the Vietnam War was progressing as planned. From this Ellsberg concluded that the U.S. President could get Americans to support their country's commitment to the Vietnam conflict only by lies and having the truth withheld from government officials. Ellsberg decided this could not be tolerated, but had no means to do anything about it.

An opportunity came his way when Ellsberg was recalled to Washington, and given the task of writing for the Secretary of Defense, Clark McAdams Clifford, a volume of the history of American involvement in Vietnam from 1945 to the present, using highly secret information. He chose the year 1961 and the role of John F. Kennedy. He found support for the general conclusion that all post–World War II U.S. presidents had falsely informed the U.S. Congress and the American people about U.S. activities in Indochina, and that the source of this false information was *not* advisers and subordinates who had misled or deceived their presidents.

Ellsberg arranged to have a full set of the top-secret documents held in his safe in the Rand Corporation. He found that 7,000 pages of documents showed four presidents and their administrations had lied for 23 years to conceal plans and actions relating to mass murders. In October 1967, Ellsberg and his friends copied all 47 volumes of classified material. He gave full sets of these "Pentagon Papers," as they would be called later, to senior U.S. senators, with the suggestion that they be printed in the *Congressional Record*. No one accepted his suggestion.

In March 1971, Ellsberg called the *New York Times*. It was interested, but would not guarantee publication, and demanded a full set of the documents. Ellsberg felt this might lead to his arrest by the **Federal Bureau of Investigation (FBI)** before full publication of the material could be achieved.

Ellsberg's personal contact inside the *New York Times* managed to steal a copy of the "Pentagon Papers," and arranged their publication, but did not tell Ellsberg what he had done. By chance, one day before the publication Ellsberg learned what was to happen. Immediately he removed to a friend's apartment his own copy of the material, and went into hiding for two weeks before being arrested.

On June 12, 1971, the "Pentagon Papers" became public. The White House got an injunction to cease publication, but it was voided by the U.S. Supreme Court. Meanwhile Ellsberg sent copies of the material to other newspapers. On June 28 he gave himself up, and was charged with 12 felonies, and could face up to 115 years in jail.

Although the "Pentagon Papers" did not go beyond 1968, and were not directly relevant to the current U.S. administration, President **Richard Nixon** (1913–1994) suspected Ellsberg had further information that it might undermine *his* presidency, and wanted Ellsberg neutralized. First, the files of Ellsberg's psychiatrist were burglarized for information that could be used to blackmail or otherwise discredit Ellsberg; when that failed, a plan was hatched to have Ellsberg's legs broken. Then the judge involved in charges against Ellsberg was offered the directorship of the FBI if he would incarcerate Ellsberg. At the same time the **Watergate** scandal was indicating that the White House was deeply involved in illegal activities. On May 11, 1973, the judge accepted a motion to dismiss all charges against Daniel Ellsberg.

Ellsberg's efforts showed Presidents Lyndon B. Johnson and John F. Kennedy had knowingly deceived the American public; that their subordinates had not deceived the presidents; and that procedures, practices, and career incentives in U.S. government agencies build an apparatus of secrecy that helps concentrate power in the executive branch, and subvert the checks and balances in the U.S. Constitution.

Ellsberg's memoirs fill gaps that were evident but could not be filled at the time of his trial, and dismissal of the charges, when it became known that the judge, who had coveted the directorship of the FBI, had been secretly offered the post.

Ellsberg gave many lectures on his views about secret services in a democracy, and reviewed his life in a recent memoir. He believes that today things have not changed.

See also LANSDALE, EDWARD; PENTAGON PAPERS

Sources: Campbell, Duncan, "It's Time to Take Big Risks. Interview with Daniel Ellsberg," *Guardian Weekly* (London), December 26, 2002, p. 11; Ellsberg, Daniel, *Secrets: A Memoir of Vietnam and the Pentagon Papers* (New York: Viking, 2002); Kreisler, Harry, "Presidential Decisions and Public Dissent: Conversation with Daniel Ellsberg,"1998, http://globetrotter.berkeley.edu/people/Ellsberg/ellsberg98-1.html.

F

FAVARO AFFAIR (1975). In October 1975, the Favaro Affair, named after Frank Favaro (1935–2000), forced the Australian Prime Minister Gough Whitlam (1916–) into a conflict with **ASIS** (Australian Secret Intelligence Service) and the control of its activities.

Frank Favaro was an Australian landowner and hotelier in Portuguese Timor. Early in 1975 he was recruited by MO9, a section of ASIS, to seek information on local political groups. He appeared to favor the policies of the UDT (Timorese Democratic Union), a right-of-center group in Timor that sought integration with Indonesia. The UDT failed to seize power in Timor during an attempted coup on August 11, 1975.

Frank Favaro, a touchy man given to grievances, wanted to be paid more for work he had done for ASIS (MO9). He wrote a demanding letter to Australia's Prime Minister and the Minister for Foreign Affairs. The letter drew Whitlam's attention to what MO9 was doing in East Timor. Whitlam immediately got the resignation of the head of ASIS William T. Robertson because, without notifying the Australian government, ASIS had apparently employed an Australian **agent** in Timor who could have been involved in the failed coup, and might have appeared to be interfering in East Timor's internal affairs. At a more important level, this raised the question of whether or not the government had executive power over Australia's security services. In Whitlam's view it did.

The Whitlam government was dismissed shortly afterward, amid speculation that the dismissal had been influenced partly by **Central Intelligence Agency (CIA)** activities in Australia. Whitlam denied this until 1988, when he said he thought the CIA had probably been involved in the dismissal of his government.

See also FAVARO, FRANK; WHITLAM COUP

Sources: Barnett, Harvey, *Tale of the Scorpion: The World of Spies and Terrorists in Australia—An Intelligence Officer's Candid Story* (South Melbourne: Sun, 1989); Hall, Richard, *The Secret State: Australia's Spy Industry* (Stanmore, NSW: Cassell, 1978); Toohey, Brian, and Brian Pinwell, *Oyster: The Story of the Australian Secret Intelligence Services* (Port Melbourne: William Heinemann Australia, 1989).

FAVARO, FRANK (1935–2000). Frank Favaro was an Australian businessman in Portuguese Timor who was recruited by **ASIS** to collect information on local politics; his work inadvertently led to changes in Australian government policy on secret services. He may have been a **double agent.**

Born in Innisfail, Queensland, Favaro was the son of Italian immigrants; the family drifted, penniless, when Frank's father was interned from 1939 to 1943 with many other Italians during **World War II.**

Favaro was educated at a primary school in Darwin, and began work as a mechanic. In 1955 he married, and became a successful Fiat automobile dealer. In 1971 he went to Dili in East Timor, and bought Hotel Dili; although he was color-blind, he managed to secure a pilot's license and bought a light aircraft to commute between Darwin and Dili. His family was living in Dili when a revolution in Portugal helped bring about the decolonization of Timor.

Favaro was a prominent figure in Timor when the civil war began in August 1975. His plane's radio was a major communication channel with the outside world during hostilities between the Indonesians, who were fighting communism, and their enemy, the Fretilin nationalists.

ASIS recruited Favaro in March 1975. He was later judged unsuitable for such employment, being highly talkative, earthy, rambunctious, and gregarious; and his ownership of Hotel Dili raised a problem of whose interests he might be supporting.

To most people Favaro appeared to be a loyal Australian. With Timor's Fretilin nationalists he negotiated the safe passage by RAAF (Royal Australian Air Force) aircraft of endangered Australian citizens from Dili, and had ready access to Indonesian naval officers. He visited Fretilin prisons and tried to get the guards to cease beating the prisoners so brutally. Once, when under siege, he advocated using Molotov cocktails to get rid of what he called the "bloody natives."

In September 1975 ASIS fired Favaro. Accused of being a spy for both the Indonesians and the Australians, he left Timor in November 1975. He took the legal right to the name of the hotel with him. In October his ASIS file was leaked to the press. When the Australian Foreign Minister denied that Favaro had been a paid intelligence agent, Prime Minister Gough Whitlam (1916–) found that this was untrue. The Prime Minister blamed William T. Robertson, the head of ASIS at the time, and fired him.

Favaro always maintained that at the time of his ASIS recruitment, he was told he answered directly to the Prime Minister.

Today in East Timor, now a separate nation, the Hotel Dili thrives under the ownership of Favaro's son.

See also FAVARO AFFAIR

Sources: Barnett, Harvey, *Tale of the Scorpion: The World of Spies and Terrorists in Australia—An Intelligence Officer's Candid Story* (South Melbourne: Sun Books, 1989); Jollife, Jill, "Obituaries: Frank Favaro," *The Age*, October 10, 2000, p. 7; Toohey, Brian, and Brian Pinwell, *Oyster: The Story of the Australian Secret Intelligence Services* (Port Melbourne: William Heinemann Australia, 1989).

FELFE, HEINZ (fl. 1950–1963). Heinz Felfe was Soviet **double agent** who seriously compromised the **Gehlen organization**.

Felfe was a lieutenant in the SD (the Nazi SS Security Service) during **World War II**, and worked for the British **SIS** after the war. He was dismissed because he sold information to both sides in the late 1940s.

In April 1950 Felfe, now a retired police officer, told the German Federal Minister of the Interior and later the head of the **BfV** (West Germany's Internal Security Office) that he knew of people who had been approached by the Russians to recruit wartime friends and have them penetrate the Gehlen organization. He suggested passing **disinformation** to the Russians to gain their confidence and learn something of the Russian spy networks in West Germany. His impressions were noted and filed.

In September 1951, Felfe signed on with the Soviet secret service; in November joined the Gehlen organization. His becoming a double agent was helped by a contact in the Gehlen organization's old-boy network of the Nazi secret service members who had survived the war.

Felfe had a notable career in the **BND**. He impressed Reinhard Gehlen (1902–1979) when they first met. By 1958 Gehlen was fascinated with the intelligence Felfe could produce and promoted him to the Soviet desk in the Counterespionage Section, where Felfe enjoyed the salary of a senior civil servant. He could get the secret minutes of the East German Politburo. On his wall he had an elaborate and detailed map of Karlshorst, the Soviet **KGB** headquarters, and used it as a showpiece of efficiency. Gehlen would often show it to visitors, and took a copy with him when traveling.

Some staff members were suspicious of Felfe and his remarkable efficiency. Gehlen dismissed this as envy. By the autumn of 1961 support for the suspicion had spread, but no material proof of treason was available. In October 1961 Felfe was identified by Michal Goleniewski (fl. 1922–1972) and arrested, as were his accomplices from the Nazi days. Gehlen's lifework was totally compromised.

Felfe was tried in July 1963, found guilty, and sentenced to 15 years' hard labor.

Sources: Andrew, Christopher, and Oleg Gordievsky, *KGB: The Inside Story of Its Foreign Operations from Lenin to Gorbachev* (London: Hodder and Stoughton, 1990); Cookridge, E. H., *Gehlen: Spy of the Century* (London: Hodder and Stoughton, 1971); Höhne, Heinz, and Herman Zolling, *Network: The Truth About General Gehlen and His Spy Ring*, trans. Richard Barry (London: Secker & Warburg, 1971).

FIELD, NOEL HAVILAND (fl. 1913–1970). Noel Field was a well-intentioned, romantic, Communist sympathizer, and former American diplomat who was accused by **Moscow Center** in 1949 of being a bogus Communist working for Western intelligence and for the Yugoslav leader **Josip Tito** (1892–1980).

Noel Field did his Ph.D. in political science at Harvard, and joined the European Division of the U.S. State Department. In 1934 he was recruited to the **NKVD** and code-named ERNST. While he worked in the department, the European Division would become important to the Soviets (until the mid-1940s); a coworker was Alger Hiss (1904–1996), and the two became close friends. In 1936 Field, much conflicted by demands of his Soviet case handlers to steal government documents and his desire *not* to betray anyone, moved to the Disarmament Secretariat of the League of Nations in Geneva. Then he began actively spying for Russia. His first two Soviet case officers defected to the West; one was murdered by the Soviets for doing so, and Field was blackmailed by two others.

In 1937 Field went briefly to Moscow for information on what he might do. At the time the Soviet purges were peaking, and he was suspected of being a **double agent**.

During **World War II** (1939–1945) Field organized welfare and relief work, and tried to have the **OSS** head in Switzerland, Allen Dulles (1893–1969), join with the German Communists to undermine the Nazis. At the time this policy was cognate with his Communist sympathies. Dulles did not agree to Field's suggestion.

Field was fired from his relief work in 1947, and in 1948 he feared that he might be questioned about his relations with Alger Hiss. He and his family fled to Europe, where he was used by the West to place individuals sympathetic to the West in the Communist parties of Central Europe.

Field attempted to find work as a journalist or academic in Eastern Europe, but was always suspected of being a spy for the West. This was largely because in 1941 he had helped Laszlo Radjk, who became a popular Hungarian postwar leader, get out of a French internment camp and return to Hungary. Radjk was executed by the Soviets during **Josef Stalin**'s (1879–1953) purges of the leadership in Russian satellites (1949–1952).

In 1949 Field, who had had no job for two years, was encouraged to visit Prague for an academic post. At the time Field was tall, gaunt, and stooped; spoke in a soft voice; had a shambling gait and neatly combed gray hair; and seem gently cultured. He appeared to be the sort of man you trusted and respected. Nevertheless, Field and his family were arrested and interrogated; his connection with Radjk was used to build a conspiracy involving Radjk and the main Western espionage agencies against Russia and her satellites. Field was held by the Hungarians and interrogated until 1954. Field's brother vanished in Poland.

In 1954 a Polish intelligence officer, Joseph Swiatlo, who had interrogated Field's brother, defected to the West, and told of what the Fields had endured.

It appears that the Soviet purges of 1949–1952 in Eastern Europe could well have been an attempt to smear the local Communist parties in Eastern Europe; an alternative view is that the purges, and the dreadful publicity they received, were political windfalls for the West.

Field was released and rehabilitated after the death of Stalin, but never to returned to the United States. He died in Hungary in 1970.

See also DULLES, ALLEN; HISS, ALGER

Sources: Andrew, Christopher, and Oleg Gordievsky, *KGB: The Inside Story of Its Foreign Operations from Lenin to Gorbachev* (London: Hodder and Stoughton, 1990); Aldrich, Richard J., *The Hidden Hand: Britain, America and Cold War Secret Intelligence* (New York: Overlook Press, 2002); Haynes, John Earl, and Harvey Klehr, *Venona: Decoding Soviet Espionage in America* (New Haven, CT: Yale University Press, 1999); Lewis, Flora, *The Man Who Disappeared: The Strange History of Noel Field* (London: Arthur Barker, 1965); Weinstein, Allen, *Perjury: The Hiss–Chambers Case*, rev. ed. (New York: Random House, 1997); Weinstein, Allen, and Alexander Vassiliev, *The Haunted Wood: Soviet Espionage in America—The Stalin Era* (New York: Random House, 1999).

FISHER, VILYAM (WILLIE) GENRIKHOVICH (1903–1971). Vilyam Genrikhovich Fisher, code-named MARK, was a Russian **agent** with many names. His last name was Rudolph Abel. He was captured in 1956 and exchanged for the American U-2 spy plane pilot Francis Gary Powers (1930–1977) in 1962.

Fisher was born in Newcastle-on-Tyne, England. His father was of German origin, but both parents were Russian citizens who supported the Bolshevik cause. Little is known about Fisher's early life. One source suggests his father was a clerk at a newspaper edited by Lenin and Trotsky, and that as a lad William sold the paper on the streets of London. In 1921 the Fisher family returned to Russia, where Fisher was a **COMINTERN** translator; later he trained in the army and served in the foreign intelligence agency in Norway, Turkey, Britain, and France. Although he had lived in Britain, he was never suspected of treason during the Great Terror in Russia, and in 1936 became head of a school for training radio operators for illegal work. In 1938 he was ousted from the **NKVD**, but returned to serve in intelligence operations against German invaders during the **Great Patriotic War.**

In 1946 Fisher began training for illegal residency, and was given the identity of Andrei Kayotis, an artist, born in Lithuania in 1895. He went to the United States and returned briefly to Europe and Russia, maintaining the identities of Fisher and Kayotis. In 1948, in New York, he was given papers establishing his identity as Emil Goldfus, and maintained the identities of Goldfus and Kayotis. The genuine Goldfus, had been born in 1902, had died at 14 months of age. Fisher's identity as Goldfus made him out to be the son of a German house painter, raised in New York and educated until he was 14, when Goldfus supposedly went to work in Detroit until 1926, and then in Grand Rapids, Michigan, and Chicago. **Moscow Center** instructed him to be a self-employed artist.

In 1949 Fisher headed a group of agents that included Morris Cohen (1905–1995) and his wife, Lona (1913–1993); Ted Hall (1925–1999), the young **atom bomb spy,** and two nuclear physicists; the group was code-named VOLUNTEER. For his work Fisher received the **Order of the Red Banner** (1949).

In New York an incompetent controller of Kim Philby (1912–1988) was transferred to work under Fisher's expert supervision. One story is that this man had lost a hollowed-out coin that was used to hide microfilm. For this mistake his work was terminated in 1951. While Klaus Fuchs (1911–1988), Alger Hiss (1904–1996), and Julius (1917–1953) and Ethel (1916–1953) Rosenberg were being tried for espionage, and Senator Joseph McCarthy (1908–1957) was conducting his rampage against the **Red Menace,** Fisher went unnoticed until the failure of his assistant Reino Hayhanen (fl. 1945–1971) put Fisher's work in hazard. Hayhanen was incompetent, an alcoholic, a liar, and a convicted drunken driver. His wife also was an alcoholic. In May 1956 he was recalled to Moscow, but on the way defected to the West. Fisher was told only of Hayhanen's disappearance, and was ordered to leave New York immediately. Fisher disobeyed this instruction.

In 1957 Fisher got a new identity, Robert Callow, but before he could use it, he was arrested in a New York hotel on June 21 and flown to the Alien Detention Facility in McAllen, Texas. After a few days he admitted to being a Russian spy; newspapers covered the story vividly. To add to the publicity, he would not give his name. Finally he gave his name as Rudolph Ivanovich Abel, which was an old friend who had died. By naming himself thus, he was using the U.S. newspaper publicity to tell Moscow Center that it was Willie Fisher who had been caught.

Fisher was tried and imprisoned for 30 years. His embittered wife complained to the **KGB**, but instead of receiving sympathy, was fired from her job as a harp player in a circus orchestra, and given a paltry pension. At the penitentiary Fisher befriended the convicted Soviet spy Morton Sobell (1917–). On February 10, 1962, he was exchanged at **Glienicke Bridge**, the link between Potsdam and West Berlin, for the American U-2 pilot Francis Gary Powers (1930–1977).

In Russia, Abel was portrayed as a heroic missionary and given the Order of Lenin. Some sources say he taught at the KGB spy school and wrote an autobiography. No mention was made of his failure to follow orders; instead, he was said to have been caught through the treachery of others.

The Americans reported Abel as a heroic spymaster, not as a plain little gray man who did his dreary work so throughly. Later in Russia, Fisher was ignored, and he once likened himself to an exhibit in a museum.

In the United States the Soviet defector Anatoli Golitsyn (1926–) tried to convince intelligence authorities that Rudolf Abel returned to Russia as an agent for the **Federal Bureau of Investigation (FBI).** He later changed his view and said that Abel had become a KGB agent again. It was many years before the KGB found capable replacements for Fisher's illegal American residency. His monument is in Moscow's Donskoy Monastery.

See also ABEL, RUDOLPH IVANOVICH; COHEN, LEONTINA AND COHEN, MORRIS; FUCHS, EMIL JULIUS KLAUS; GOLITSYN, ANATOLI; HALL, THEODORE; HISS, ALGER

Sources: Andrew, Christopher, and Vasili Mitrokhin, *The Mitrokhin Archive: The KGB in Europe and the West* (London: Lane, 1999); Berkinow, Louise, *Abel*, rev. ed. (New York: Ballantine, 1982); Deacon, Richard, *Spyclopedia: The Comprehensive Handbook of Espionage* (New York: William Morrow, 1987); Donovan, James B., *Strangers on a Bridge: The Case of Colonel Abel* (London: Secker & Warburg, 1964); Mangold, Tom, *Cold Warrior: James Jesus Angleton, the CIA Master Spy Hunter* (New York: Simon & Schuster, 1991); Rositzke, Harry, *The KGB: The Eyes of Russia* (Garden City, NY: Doubleday, 1981); Whitney, Craig R., *Spy Trader: Germany's Devil's Advocate and the Darkest Secret of the Cold War* (New York: Random House, 1993).

FLETCHER MURDER (1984). The Fletcher murder in London, outside the Libyan People's Bureau, in April 1984 illustrates the problems faced when secret information becomes public, and embarrasses several police and secret services involved in demonstrations, the curtailment of terrorist activities, and the public images of the agencies involved.

Outside the Libyan People's Bureau, on St. James's Square, on April 17, 1984, a policewoman, Yvonne Fletcher, 25, was murdered and 11 were injured when gunshots were fired from within the Bureau at a crowd of anti-Gaddafi demonstrators. The protest was against the use of the Libyan embassy as a base for terrorist attacks. At the time Great Britain's diplomatic relations with Libya had been broken, and the Libyan diplomats and others had seven days in which to leave the country.

Hollingsworth and Fielding (1999) claim that in its attempt to get control of other terrorist activities in the U.K., the police blamed **MI5** for Fletcher's death. It was alleged that Muammar al-Gaddafi (1942–) had ordered the embassy staff to use hostile action against demonstrators, and this directive had been intercepted by MI5 but not passed on.

It seems the telegram giving the instructions was intercepted by **GCHQ** but not passed on in time. The special police branch, the secret services, MI5 and **MI6**, and Britain's Home Office all became embroiled in the conflict, and much was made of turf wars between them relating to terrorist threats in the U.K.

The secret information about Gaddafi's telegram from Libya became available through David Shayler, a former MI5 officer who was making many disclosures about the secret services in Britain; he had had to leave England and live in Paris because, in late 1999, if he were to return to England, he would be arrested and probably prosecuted under Britain's **Official Secrets Act**.

Sources: Hollingsworth, Mark, and Nick Fielding, *Defending the Realm: MI5 and the Shayler Affair* (London: Andre Deutsch, 2000); Norton-Taylor, Richard, "Shayler Book Blames MI5 for PC Fletcher's Death," *Guardian Weekly* (London), September 30, 1999, p. 9.

FLUENCY COMMITTEE (1964–1967). The FLUENCY Committee was a high-level group of members of Britain's secret services charged with investigating Soviet penetration of Britain's intelligence community.

After the discovery in April 1961 of George Blake's (1922–) penetration of the **SIS** and Kim Philby's (1912–1988) escape to Moscow in January 1963, the need arose for a departmental investigation to show whether or not there were other Soviet agents undermining the British secret services from within.

In November 1964 a joint committee of **MI6** and **MI5** officers was agreed to, and code-named FLUENCY—the next name on the operations list—and the chairmanship would be rotated every six months between MI6 and MI5. The committee's aim was to investigate all allegations of penetration of SIS (MI6) and the Security Service (MI5), and recommend any further inquiries if needed.

Although the purpose of the committee seemed urgent at the time, its members were to continue with tasks normally allocated to their positions. This indicated to some observers that there was neither the time nor the money available to do the work immediately and thoroughly. Roger Hollis (1905–1973), head of MI5, thought the committee was unnecessary and believed it would undermine morale; others thought it was a Gestapo-like proposal; and others quickly found 40 suspicious cases and were certain that there were **moles** in Great Britain's secret services.

The main reason for the establishment of the committee was probably the work of Kim Philby. Early in 1966 the committee provided a list of 200 instances of possible Soviet penetration. The investigations centered on Dick Ellis (1895–1975), Roger Hollis, and Graham Mitchell. Members of the committee included Arthur Martin, Geoffrey Hinton, Terence Lecky, Christopher Phillpotts, and Stephen Mowbray.

Peter Wright (1916–1995) was on the committee and made a mission out of doggedly pursuing Roger Hollis as the major Soviet **agent**; and in 1984, well after the committee was beginning to wind up its activities, Wright declared he was certain that Hollis was the man! Little credence was given to his assertions because inside the **KGB**, Britain had its own mole, Oleg Gordievsky (1938–), who knew that Hollis was not a Soviet agent.

See also ELLIS, CHARLES DICK; GORDIEVSKY, OLEG; HOLLIS, ROGER; WRIGHT, PETER

Sources: Andrew, Christopher, and Oleg Gordievsky, *KGB: The Inside Story of Its Foreign Operations from Lenin to Gorbachev* (London: Hodder and Stoughton, 1990); Pincher, Chapman, *Their Trade Is Treachery* (London: Sidgwick & Jackson, 1981; rev. ed., New York: Bantam, 1982); Pincher, Chapman, *Too Secret Too Long* (London: Sidgwick & Jackson, 1984); West, Nigel, *The Friends: Britain's Post-War Secret Operations* (London: Weidenfeld and Nicolson, 1988; Coronet ed., 1990); Wright, Peter, with Paul Greengrass, *Spycatcher: The Candid Autobiography of a Senior Intelligence Officer* (Melbourne: William Heinemann Australia, 1987).

FOOTE, ALEXANDER ALLAN (fl. 1905–1956). Alexander Allan Foote was a British supporter of the Communist cause and a Communist Party member in the 1930s; fought in the **Spanish Civil War** and **World War II;** defected to the West in 1947; informed the British of his work during World War II; and, as a public servant, published a well-received book on espionage.

Alexander Foote was born in Liverpool, left school to be apprenticed to an automobile mechanic, and in 1936 went to Spain, looking for some new, exciting experiences. In 1937 he was recruited into Soviet intelligence while a member of the British Battalion of the International Brigades, having been drawn to the Soviet cause when he learned of the death of his friend John Cornford in Spain.

Foote was courier for the Communist Party in Britain, and was recruited to the **Lucy Ring** by Ursula (Ruth) Kuczynski (fl. 1907–1992) as a wireless operator. In the World War II he spied against the Nazis, but for the first six months was not sure who he was working for, or who was directing his work. He was arrested by the Swiss Security Service (Bundespolizei) in November 1943, released in September 1944, and went to Paris to work in the Soviet embassy. Later, in Moscow, he was trained for missions in the United States.

In 1947 the **GRU** returned Foote to fieldwork and posted him to Washington, but, disillusioned with the Soviet system, he defected when he was in Berlin.

Foote cooperated with interrogators in the British secret services in return for the promise of a government post. He told about a Soviet **agent** in the United Kingdom, Ursula (Ruth) Kuczynski, living in Chipping Norton, near Harwell, the atomic research center; that some years before, he had gone to fight for the Communists; about his service in Germany, and how he had been recruited and trained to work in Switzerland for the Lucy Ring; that in 1943 he was imprisoned by the Swiss, was later released, and, posing as a Soviet citizen, had traveled to Moscow.

Foote eventually got a position in the Ministry of Agriculture and Fisheries, and wrote a book that was ghosted by **MI5**. He died in 1956 (Pincher, 1987) or 1958 (Mahoney and Mahoney, 1998).

Sources: Foote, Alexander, *Handbook for Spies* (Garden City, NY: Doubleday, 1949); Foote, Alexander, "The Tell-Tale Air," in Allen Dulles, ed., *Great True Spy Stories* (Secaucus, NJ: Castle, 1968), pp. 173–180; Knightley, Phillip, *The Second Oldest Profession: The Spy as Bureaucrat, Patriot, Fantasist and Whore* (London: Andre Deutsch, 1986); Mahoney, Harry T., and Marjorie L. Mahoney, *Biographic Dictionary of Espionage* (San Francisco: Austin & Winfield, 1998); Pincher, Chapman, *Traitors: The Anatomy of Treason* (New York: St. Martin's Press, 1987).

FROLIK, JOSEF (c. 1925–). Josef Frolik was a Czechoslovakian defector who believed his country had been ruined by the Russia invasion in 1968 and wanted to tell the West what misery lay behind the **Iron Curtain**.

Frolik was the illegitimate son of an unknown father and a seamstress who married when Josef was about seven years old, then abandoned him to be reared by his grandfather, a retired, lung-damaged miner. His stepfather, whose name Josef would take, was a member of the then illegal Communist Party of Czechoslovakia, and was imprisoned after the Nazi invasion. He committed suicide rather then betray his political colleagues.

After **World War II,** Frolik studied accountancy and, aged 21, became chief administrator of *Rude Pravo,* a Communist newspaper. In 1949 he entred military service, and in December 1952 went into the Czechoslovakian secret service's Finance Directorate. The 1953 he was put into the main Accounts Department. He saw much brutal treatment of the Czechoslovakian people, many of whom considered the Russians to be invaders, and he also saw widespread corruption, alcoholism, theft, power abuse, self-aggrandizement, and sexual perversion among Czechoslovakian supporters of their Russian masters. In 1960, after many failed attempts to enter the counterintelligence service, Frolik's application finally succeeded when he got support from a childhood friend.

From 1960 to 1964 Frolik worked in Czechoslovakia on the British desk, where his first task was to help Konon Molody (Gordon Lonsdale) (1922–1970) escape from prison in England. In 1962, after four months of training—the only espionage training he claimed to have received—he was sent to London for four years as a labor attaché in the Czech embassy. He found the Czech diplomats to be corrupt, drunken lechers who failed consistently in their operations.

After a year's initiation into the routines of counterintelligence work in Britain, Frolik began seeking recruits from among British trade unionists, especially older members who felt the British authorities had sacrificed Czechoslovakia to Adolf Hitler in 1938 and 1939.Often he sought to recruit officials whom later he discovered were already being run by the **KGB**; he was immediately banned from such work. Frolik was one of 30 **agents** in the Czechoslovakian intelligence services in London; in the mid-1960s they had agents in Parliament, the cabinet, trade unions, the police, the Treasury, government research, and business. Each officer had about 20 agents to supervise.

In part this success was due to an appallingly underfunded and undermanned **MI5**. At the same time the Czech secret service was well-funded and its agents well-trained. They used blackmail to trap journalists and members of **Harold Wilson**'s (1916–1995) government who would deliver military secrets to the Czechoslovakian intelligence services. (After Frolik's defection these members of Parliament were investigated, and 18 years later one of them was still in Parliament.)

By the middle of 1965 Prague thought Frolik was a security risk because of his alleged contacts with MI5. By the end of 1965 he felt he must defect. After being caught by a **Warsaw Pact** intelligence service scheme to test his allegiance, he was recalled to Prague in 1966; he found his **NATO** assignment canceled and himself under close surveillance by the Russians. He established a link between the **IRA** and the Czech military intelligence, and he ran black African students as counterintelligence agents, work for which he was awarded the Order of Merit.

Twenty-four hours after Czechoslovakia was invaded by the Russians in the spring of 1968, Frolik was arrested and later released. In October 1968, much impressed by the defection of Major Ladislav Bittman (alias Brychta), Frolik decided that he, too, would defect. He contacted a **Cental Intelligence Agency (CIA)** official, and they planned his escape.

Frolik felt that he would probably be dismissed in August 1969. Completely lacking trust in the Czechoslovakian authorities, and fearing for his life, he collected many secret documents and took a vacation in the Czech holiday camp for secret agents in Bulgaria. There, CIA agents helped him find his way into Turkey with his secret cache of papers. He arrived in Washington on July 21, 1969. By 1974 two attempts had been made to kill Frolik. He was given a new job and a new identity. He published his memoirs as a defector in 1975, saying that he did this as a warning to the

West and its associates that the Soviets would never cease their attempt to rule the world by military force, subversion, corruption, blackmail, and bribery of those who were vulnerable to their methods. Frolik's attitude toward Czechoslovakia under Russian domination was like that of other defectors, and at the time ran contrary to the attitude of détente (1972). First, his homeland resembled a concentration camp, maintained by armed guards and surrounded with barbed wire and personnel mines; second, its citizens experienced nothing of the consumer society and felt terrorized by secret police; third, those in authority were bloodthirsty monsters who stole from the state treasury and corrupted all other state agencies. Frolik came to hate his invaded and corrupted homeland, and felt his personal debt to the Czech people, whom he loved, could be met by defecting to the free world and telling the Western democracies the truth about his occupied homeland.

See also MOLODY, KONON

Sources: Frolik, Joseph, *The Frolik Defection* (London: Leo Cooper, 1975); Knightley, Phillip, *The Second Oldest Profession: The Spy as Bureaucrat, Patriot, Fantasist and Whore* (London: Andre Deutsch, 1986).

FUCHS, EMIL JULIUS KLAUS (1911–1988). Klaus Fuchs was the second of the **atom spies** to be caught in Britain and imprisoned after **World War II**.

Fuchs was born in Rüsselsheim, near Frankfurt, the son of the village clergyman. His family moved to Eisenbach, Thuringia (eastern Germany), where, aged 17, he was an outstanding student in mathematics and physics. He studied at the University of Leipzig, became an active member of the Social Democratic Party, and opposed both Communist and Nazi student organizations.

The family moved to Kiel, where Klaus continued university studies and his active interest in student politics. He broke with the Social Democratic Party in 1931, during the presidential election, when he offered to speak for the Communist Party candidate. He joined the German Communist Party, and in 1933, after Adolf Hitler (1889–1945) came to power, he fled Kiel for Berlin, went to Paris, and finally settled in Bristol.

At Bristol University, Fuchs worked as a research assistant in physics (1934), maintained contact with the Communist Party, and completed his Ph.D. (1937) before becoming a research physicist at Edinburgh University (D.Sc., 1939). In 1939, because he was a German citizen in the United Kingdom, Fuchs was investigated and classified, at first, as unlikely to be a security risk. However, in June 1940 he was interned on the Isle of Man, and in July was shipped to Sherbrooke Camp, Quebec. He maintained his open support for the Communist Party while in Canada, and six months later he was released and shipped back to Scotland, where he resumed his work at Edinburgh University (January 1941). In May 1941 he went to Birmingham. He was hired by Marcus Oliphant, but banned by the British government from working on Oliphant's radar project, and was put onto the less important project of the development of atomic physics. Soon he was recruited by the Russians. He signed the **Official Secrets Act**, which prevented him from communicating anything of his work to foreigners. In August 1942, Fuchs became a British citizen and Oliphant recommended him for work on the **Manhattan Project**.

In December 1943 Fuchs went to the East Coast of the United States to continue work on the **atom bomb**. In August 1944 he left the East Coast for Los Alamos, New Mexico, to work further on the bomb. In 1946 Fuchs returned to

England, where he took a post at the Atomic Energy Research Establishment, Harwell, in August. Fuchs headed a division, earned respect of his colleagues, and made a few friends.

In January 1947, Prime Minister **Clement Attlee** (1883–1967) decided Britain herself would produce an atomic (plutonium) bomb, and because Fuchs had special knowledge of plutonium, he was assigned to the project's theoretical work. In November 1947 Fuchs attended meetings in Washington on the declassification of wartime secrets, and renewed contacts with his Los Alamos colleagues and friends. The British atomic bomb project became public in May 1948.

In September 1949 an atomic explosion occurred in Kazakhstan in the **U.S.S.R.** Believing he could come under suspicion as a possible security risk, Fuchs approached the Harwell security officer, who suggested that he discuss questions of security with **MI5.** Late in January 1950, Fuchs confessed to having informed the Russians about his research on the atomic bomb between 1942 and March 1949. On February 28, 1950, he was charged with having "for a purpose prejudicial to the safety and interests of the State . . . communicated to a person unknown information relating to atomic research which was calculated to be . . . might have been, or was intended to be . . . useful to an enemy" in Birmingham (1943), New York (1943 and 1944), Boston (1945), and Berkshire (1947).

At his trial Fuch's prime motives for betrayal were stated to be communism, self-deception, and an unusual working of his mind. He was sentenced to 14 years' imprisonment, most of which was spent in Wakefield Prison, Yorkshire.

The Soviet government announced it never had any contact whatsoever with Fuchs. He served nine years and four months of his sentence, and was released early for good conduct on June 23, 1959. On leaving prison he went immediately to East Germany and became deputy director of the Institute of Nuclear Research, Rossendorf, near Dresden, and lectured at the local academy. He often traveled within Communist bloc countries, attending conferences and giving seminars. He joined the German Communist Party and married Margaret Keilson, a fellow student in his days at Kiel University. After retiring in 1979, he worked for peace movements and for nuclear disarmament. He was honored by East Germany with the Order of Merit of the Fatherland and the Order of Karl Marx. His secret political activities during the 1940s were estimated to have saved the Russian scientists about two years of research work on the atomic bomb. He died January 28, 1988.

See also MAY, ALLAN NUNN; PONTECORVO, BRUNO

Sources: Andrew, Christopher, and Vasili Mitrokhin, *The Mitrokhin Archive: The KGB in Europe and the West* (London: Lane, 1999); Laffin, John, *Brassey's Book of Espionage* (London: Brassey's, 1996); Mahoney, Harry T., and Marjorie L. Mahoney, *Biographic Dictionary of Espionage* (San Francisco: Austin & Winfield, 1998); Moorehead, Alan, *The Traitors: The Double Life of Fuchs, Pontecorvo and Nunn May* (London: Hamish Hamilton, 1952); Moss, Norman, *Klaus Fuchs: The Man Who Stole the Atom Bomb* (London: Grafton, 1987); Sillitoe, Percy, *Cloak Without Dagger* (London: Cassell, 1955); Trahair, Richard C. S., "A Psycho Historical Approach to Espionage: Klaus Fuchs (1911–1988)," *Mentalities* 9 (2) (1994): 28–49; Williams, Robert C., *Klaus Fuchs, Atom Spy* (Cambridge, MA: Harvard University Press, 1987).

G

GARBER, JOY ANN (fl. 1919–1963). Joy Ann Garber was a Russian spy, a **sleeper**, who worked in the United States with her husband from late 1958 to October 1968.

Joy Garber, also known as Ann Baltch and Bertha Rosalie Jackson, was born in Poland. Trained as a hairdresser, she married Alexander Sokolov (1919–) in Germany. He had been raised in Paris and become fluent in European languages as well as Russian. He was trained as a Communist spy in Moscow. They went to Russia, and Joy was trained in preparation for their espionage work in Central America and Europe.

At the end of 1958 they went to the United States and lived separate lives, in separate apartments, in New York City. Sokolov took the identity of Robert Baltch, born in 1924 and raised in Pennsylvania. The two staged a meeting, at which Joy Garber decided to date Robert Baltch regularly, and in April 1959 she "married" him. Now she was Ann Baltch, who worked as a hairdresser, and had a husband, Robert, who was a language teacher.

For seven years the two lived in the Bronx as sleepers. Ann took a beautician's course. After April 1960 the couple moved to Baltimore, Maryland, where Robert again taught languages and Ann was a beautician.

During those seven years, a shipyard worker who spied for the Soviets, Kaarlo Toumi, was recruited to be a **double agent** for the **Central Intelligence Agency (CIA)** while continuing with his work for the Soviets.

The Baltches were seen by **Federal Bureau of Investigation (FBI)** agents at one of Toumi's **dead drops**. Thereafter they were kept under surveillance; they were found to have changed their residence more frequently than expected, and they bought a cabin in the countryside where they kept a transmitter for sending information to Moscow.

In November 1962 the couple moved to an apartment in Washington, where Robert continued teaching languages. By now the FBI was monitoring the Baltches closely. In May 1963 it was clear that they were using a dead drop beneath a Long Island railway bridge for contacting the Soviet personnel officer of the Soviet UN delegates. By June the Baltches knew they were being watched. They prepared to leave, but were arrested and tried for espionage. The Soviets claimed never to have heard of them.

The Baltches were released on a legal technicality. Evidence from eavesdropping was not admissible in court. They were swapped for two Americans in a Soviet prison. In 1963 they flew Air India to Prague, and disappeared.

Sources: Cookridge, E. H., *Spy Trade* (New York: Walker, 1971); Mahoney, Harry T., and Marjorie L. Mahoney, *Biographic Dictionary of Espionage* (San Francisco: Austin & Winfield, 1998); Mahoney, M. H., *Women in Espionage* (Santa Barbara, CA: ABC-CLIO, 1993).

GARDNER, MEREDITH KNOX (1913–2002). Meredith Gardner broke the cipher in the VENONA material that led to the identification of Judith Coplon (1921–); Julius (1918–1953) and Ethel (1916–1953) Rosenberg; Donald Maclean (1913–1983), one of the **Magnificent Five KGB agents** in the Cambridge spy ring; and Ted Hall (1925–1999) and Klaus Fuchs (1911–1988), who worked on the Manhattan Project.

Gardner was born in Okolona, Mississippi. He was a student at the University of Texas, and afterward at the University of Wisconsin. He became fluent in many European languages as well as Japanese. Early in **World War II** he joined the U.S. Army's Security Agency. His first work was on German codes; later he worked on Japanese messages.

At the time the **SIS** was faced with the Russian problem, the decoding of Russian diplomatic cables. Since the beginning of World War II the U.S. government had collected copies of these cables, and, suspicious of **Josef Stalin**'s (1879–1953) intentions, Colonel Carter Clark, a military intelligence expert, decided in February 1943 he would get them decoded. Gardner began working on the Russian problem in 1945.

At first, code-breaking was very difficult because, unlike the Japanese, who frequently used the same sequence of additives in their codes, the Russians used a **one-time pad**. Gardner was helped when, in the rush to meet wartime demands, a KGB agent in Moscow made the error of using the one-time pad more than once. Also, Gardner was aided by a set of secret cables that were taken from the Soviet Purchasing Commission in New York during a raid.

In 1948 Gardner managed to break the code of the 1944–1945 messages, and among them were messages sent from Winston Churchill (1874–1965) to the new U.S. President, Harry Truman (1884–1972). Eventually he decoded a message indicating that in Washington there probably were spies connected with the British embassy, one of whom who was sending the Soviets reports on the process for producing uranium-235, information available only from those working on the Manhattan Project. They were Klaus Fuchs, code-named REST, Donald Maclean, code-named HOMER, and Ted Hall, code-named MLAD. Late in 1948 Gardner was able to help Robert Lamphere (1918–2002) in the **Federal Bureau of Investigation (FBI)** case of Judith Coplon.

Late in 1949, when he came to Washington, Kim Philby (1912–1988) acquainted himself with Gardner and his work, and actually looked over his shoulder while he decoded Soviet cables in **Arlington Hall**. Philby tipped off Donald Maclean and Guy Burgess (1911–1963), who escaped to Moscow in May 1951.

Gardner retired from the National Security Agency in 1972, and spent much time on cryptic crosswords and tracing his Scottish ancestry.

See also COPLON, JUDITH; FUCHS, EMIL JULIUS KLAUS; MACLEAN, DONALD; PHILBY, HAROLD "KIM"

Sources: Anonymous, "Codebreaker Who Solved 'Crosswords' of Nuclear Spies: Meredith Gardner, Cryptanalyst, 1913-9-8-2002," *The Age* (Melbourne), September 11, 2002, Obituaries, p.11 (first published in the *London Telegraph*); Gentry, Curt, *J. Edgar Hoover: The Man and His Secrets* (New York: Norton, 1991); Haynes, John Earl, and Harvey Klehr, *Venona: Decoding Soviet Espionage in America* (New Haven, CT: Yale University Press, 1999); Weinstein, Allen, and Alexander Vassiliev, *The Haunted Wood: Soviet Espionage in America—The Stalin Era* (New York: Random House, 1999).

GEE, ELIZABETH ETHEL (1915–). Elizabeth "Bunty" Gee was a member of the Portland spy ring, headed by Konon Molody, also known as Gordon Lonsdale (1922–1970), and served by Morris (1905–1995) and Lona (1913–1993) Cohen, also known as Peter and Helen Kroger.

Ethel's father was a blacksmith in Hampshire, England; she had a private school education, and in her forties was still living with her elderly parents when she fell in love with a **KGB** spy, Harry F. Houghton (1905–).

In 1959 a **Central Intelligence Agency (CIA)** agent working in Polish intelligence identified two spies inside British intelligence services, and one of them had a name that sounded like Houghton's.

Houghton had been recruited into the KGB after **World War II** in Warsaw, and reactivated by the Soviets when he was posted to England. In 1958 he met Ethel Gee. She worked in the records office at Great Britain's Portland Naval Base. In 1959 he bought a cottage and she helped him to decorate it, in the hope that they would marry. Houghton introduced Gee to Gordon Lonsdale, also known at the time as Alex Johnson, who persuaded her to work on espionage with Houghton. Codenamed ASYA, she brought documents from the record office to her home on Friday evenings; Houghton photographed them, and she returned them on Monday morning.

Houghton's estranged wife reported to **MI5** that her husband, employed in Dorset at Portland's Underwater Weapons Research Establishment, had run off with a woman at the base. MI5 officers watched Houghton as he went every month to Gee in London; at a rail station each the time he gave Gordon Lonsdale, a Canadian businessman, a bag in return for an envelope.

Outside the Old Vic Theatre in London, in January 1961, Houghton, Gee, and Lonsdale were arrested. In Gee's shopping bag were many secret documents from Portland. At her home more evidence of espionage was found.

A CIA **mole** in the Polish UB, Michal Goleniewski (fl. 1922–1972), had led MI5 to Gordon Lonsdale. Houghton and Gee got 15 years each in prison. When released, they were married.

See also COHEN, LEONTINA, AND COHEN, MORRIS; GOLENIEWSKI, MICHAL; HOUGHTON, HARRY; MOLODY, KONON

Sources: Andrew, Christopher, and Oleg Gordievsky, *KGB: The Inside Story of Its Foreign Operations from Lenin to Gorbachev* (London: Hodder and Stoughton, 1990); Andrew, Christopher, and Vasili Mitrokhin, *The Mitrokhin Archive: The KGB in Europe and the West* (London: Lane, 1999); Mahoney, M. H., *Women in Espionage* (Santa Barbara, CA: ABC-CLIO,

1993); West, Rebecca, *The New Meaning of Treason* (New York: Viking, 1964); Wright, Peter, with Paul Greengrass, *Spycatcher: The Candid Autobiography of a Senior Intelligence Officer* (Melbourne: William Heinemann Australia, 1987).

GEHLEN, REINHARD (1902–1979). Reinhard Gehlen was a German military officer who provided the West with valuable information on Russian military resources and personnel at the end of **World War II**; the information was held and controlled by the **Central Intelligence Agency (CIA)** until **Gehlen's organization** became the core of the secret services of West Germany.

Reinhard Gehlen was born in Erfurt; his father, Walther Gehlen, was a lieutenant in the Thuringian Field Artillery; his mother, Katharina, was descended from an aristocratic Flemish family named Van Vaernewyck. Walther became a bookseller in 1908 in Breslau; Reinhard attended Koenig Wilhelm High School and was outstanding in class, a capable debater, and a lone wolf socially.

In 1918 Gehlen he joined his father's old regiment, and in 1921 was transferred to a Silesian unit in Schweidnitz. He was promoted to second lieutenant in 1923 and full lieutenant in 1928; he was married in September 1931 to a daughter of a lieutenant colonel distantly related to one of Frederick the Great's generals. In 1935 Gehlen joined the General Staff of the German army and in 1936 was sent to the General Staff Operations Section.

By the beginning of World War II, Gehlen was senior staff officer of the 213th Infantry Division. As a major he was an important aide to the Chief of Staff of the army, and within two years was an expert on the Eastern Front. He was influential in shaping Operation BARBAROSSA, the Nazi invasion of Russia, in July 1941.

In April 1942 Gehlen was head of the Foreign Armies East, and thoroughly reorganized the section of the German army that dealt with intelligence on the Russian front. He was head until dismissed by Adolf Hitler (1889–1945) in April 1945.

At the time Gehlen had plans to take his whole intelligence organization over to the Americans. During the Russian advance on Germany he preserved his archives and kept them in a mine shaft in Bavaria, hidden from the Russians, until he negotiated their use by the **Central Intelligence Agency (CIA).** He believed, even before war ended, that the alliance between the United States and the **U.S.S.R.** would not last, and afterward **Josef Stalin** (1879–1953) would never allow Russian-occupied East European countries their independence would risk war with the West over Germany.

In 1945, after the defeat of Hitler, Brigadier General Edwin L. Sibert (1897–), chief of the U.S. Intelligence Forces of Occupation, had Gehlen taken out of a prisoner-of-war camp. He did not inform his superiors until August 1945, when he had tangible evidence of the information Gehlen had secreted. It was not until February 1946 that the Americans agreed to use Gehlen to work for them against the Soviets.

In May 1949 the newly formed CIA made a secret agreement with Gehlen's secret service. It was to be a German organization, not a part of the CIA, with contact through liaison officers. Its aim was to collect intelligence on the nations in the Eastern bloc; once a government was established in Germany, Gehlen's secret service would be the responsibility of that government, and all previous agreements with the United States would be canceled. No secret service missions were to run contrary to Germany's national interest. Gehlen's organization received its first funding, U.S.$3.4 million. Gehlen's first task was to move his agents into the Eastern bloc nations and establish his organization inside the U.S.S.R. The organization grew and contributed much to the U.S. foreign policy in Europe.

Until 1956 Gehlen and his "Gehlen Org"—his organization's informal title—were funded by and under the control of the CIA. The Gehlen Org served and created espionage organizations around the world: Egypt, Israel, Britain, the United States, South America, the Congo, Tanzania, Afghanistan, and France.

When his organization became the West German Secret Service, the **BND**, Gehlen was its president (1956–1968). During this time he conducted espionage operations against the West as well as the Communists. Many scandals reduced the influence of his work and lowered his respect among those who believed he was their ally. While Allen Dulles (1893–1969), head of the CIA, praised Gehlen's work, U.S. Army chiefs decried his activities.

Gehlen's influence was greatly undermined by the Felfe Affair, in which it became evident in 1961 that Heinz Felfe (fl. 1950–1963), who carved out his career in the BND, was a **double agent** working for the Russians. Gehlen's recruitment policies came under fire. He had trusted his intuition; had insisted he knew staff better than did other security experts; and had followed an elitist policy of recruitment and prevented security control that would have identified Soviet penetration of his organization.

Felfe was tried in July 1963, found guilty, and sentenced to 15 years' hard labor. Gehlen was not asked to retire prematurely from the BND. Another case showed Gehlen's leadership to be faulty, and he suffered several setbacks in his administration. On the other hand, in June 1967 it was the BND information which assured the CIA chief, Richard Helms (1913–2002), shortly before the Six-Day War in the Middle East that Israel would certainly attack, a view not shared by Dean Rusk, U.S. Secretary of State.

In April 1968, Gehlen was invested with the Grand Cross of the Federal Republic's Order of Merit with star and sash, and said not a word in reply at the ceremony.

In 1971 Gehlen published his memoirs. In Germany they were met with considerable hostility; in the United States they aroused anxiety among members of the intelligence community.

See also FELFE, HEINZ

Sources: Cookridge, E. H., *Gehlen: Spy of the Century* (New York: Pyramid, 1971); Gehlen, Reinhard, *Der Dienst* (Mainz and Wiesbaden: Von Hase & Koehelr, 1971), trans as *The Gehlen Memoirs* (New York: Collins, 1972); Höhne, Heinz, and Herman Zolling, *Network: The Truth About General Gehlen and His Spy Ring*, trans Richard Barry (London. Secker & Warburg, 1972); Mahoney, Harry T., and Marjorie L. Mahoney, *Biographic Dictionary of Espionage* (San Francisco: Austin & Winfield, 1998); Trevor-Roper, Hugh R., Introduction, in Heinz Höhne and Hermann Zolling, *Network: The Truth About General Gehlen and His Spy Ring* (London: Secker & Warburg, 1972), pp. xi–xvi.

GERHARDT, DIETER FELIX (c. 1935–). Dieter Felix Gerhardt was a South African naval officer who spied for the Soviets for 20 years, probably for money and also to take revenge for the treatment of his father during **World War II.**

Gerhardt, born in Germany, was the son of a German architect who immigrated to South Africa shortly before World War II. The old man held such extreme right-wing views that the pro-British government of South Africa interned him in a detention camp during World War II. Dieter felt that South Africa's treatment of his father was unfair. His childhood generally seems to have been unhappy, and at school he was called "Jumbo" because he was so fat, tall, uncoordinated, and ungainly.

Gerhardt joined the South African navy, and in his early twenties, after successfully completing his initial training, he went to England about 1962 to train in new weapons at the Manadon Royal Naval Engineering College, Plymouth. While there, he went to London for a day's leave and immediately offered his services to the **GRU**. Also, in England he met the woman who was to become his wife.

After serving in various places around the world, Gerhardt brought his new wife to live in Simonstown, a small township where the South African navy had an important shipyard. A popular fellow, he was welcomed warmly on his return to South Africa. He introduced his wife to colleagues, saying that she was Danish.

In time the couple moved into the residential area of the naval community, and Gerhardt gave his colleagues the impression that he had to move largely because his wife felt that she was socially above community members.

Gerhardt told his wife that he felt he wanted to avenge the South African government's treatment of his father. He had access to the Silvermines maritime tracking station, operated by the South African navy.

The facility monitored sea traffic in the southern Atlantic and the Indian Ocean to the coast of Western Australia. Gerhardt became a commodore in the South African navy, in command of Simonstown Naval Station.

During the Falklands War (April–June 1982), the Royal Navy used the station for refueling. Gerhardt may have sent the Soviets information on the British Polaris submarine, and helped inform the Argentines on Royal Navy shipping during the Falklands War. He was observed at Gibraltar by **MI5** agents before the Falklands War, and may have given the Soviets information on antiaircraft missiles.

From 1964 until his arrest in 1983, Gerhardt provided ever more valuable information to the Soviets as he rose in the ranks of the South African navy.

As a result of his espionage, Gerhardt became wealthy, divorced his British wife, and married Ruth Johr, a GRU **agent** who helped him maintain regular contact with the Soviets. He was captured in New York as a result of Operation FAREWELL, involving the Soviet defector Vladimir Vetrov (1928–1983), who reported Gerhardt's work to the **Central Intelligence Agency (CIA).**

Gerhardt pleaded guilty, confessed, and with his wife was found guilty of high treason; he was jailed for life instead of being executed, the usual fate of traitors in South Africa.

It was assumed that the South African government expected to trade Gerhardt for one of their Moscow spies. In prison he enjoyed access to whatever books and facilities for study he seemed to want while his lawyers pursued various means for his release. In the early 1990s the political systems in Russia and South Africa had changed so much that it seemed appropriate to the leaders of both nations, Boris Yeltsin (1931–) and F. W. de Klerk (1936–), that Gerhardt should be released, since there no longer appeared to be any good reason to keep him in prison.

See OPERATION FAREWELL; VETROV, VLADIMIR

Sources: Anonymous, "South African Officer Guilty of Spying," *New York Times,* October 30, 1983, p. A3; Coggin, Janet. *The Spy's Wife: A True Account of Marriage to a KGB Master Spy.* (London: Constable, 1999); Deacon, Richard, *Spyclopedia: The Comprehensive Handbook of Espionage* (New York: William Morrow, 1987); Mahoney, Harry T., and Marjorie L. Mahoney, *Biographic Dictionary of Espionage* (San Francisco: Austin & Winfield, 1998);

O' Toole, Thomas, "South Africa's Spying Seen as a Painful Blow to the West," *Washington Post*, June 11, 1984, p. A10; Richelson, Jeffrey T., *A Century of Spies: Intelligence in the Twentieth Century* (New York: Oxford University Press, 1995); Rusbridger, James, *The Intelligence Game: The Illusions and Delusions of International Espionage* (London: Bodley Head, 1989).

GIKMAN, REINO (c. 1930–). Reino Gikman was the alleged **KGB** controller of Felix Bloch (1935–), a high ranking U.S. State Department official who was thought to have given secrets, concealed as stamps, to the Russians, and who became the center of the Bloch Affair (1989–1990) in the United States.

Gikman was born in Ino, Karelia, in part of Soviet-dominated Finland. After **World War II** Gikman lived in Bremen, West Germany, and may have became a computer expert with IBM. In 1966 he moved to Finland; married in 1968; and with his wife, Martta, moved a year later to Düsseldorf, where their son was born. In the 1970s Martta and their son disappeared. Gikman went alone to Vienna in 1979, lived for five years in the Hotel Post, and then with a woman named Helga Hobart. For his dealings with Felix Bloch, Gikman assumed the identity of Pierre Bart, the name of a man known to the French secret services.

The **Federal Bureau of Investigation (FBI)** investigated the connection between Bloch and Gikman, and assumed that in 1980, after Bloch came to Vienna, Gikman was made his KGB controller, though there was no definite evidence for this.

Gikman met Bloch three times, then disappeared in June 1989. Later Helga Hobart told a reporter that Gikman had worked for IBM, specializing in computers; she would not say if she knew anything about stamps.

See also BLOCH AFFAIR; BLOCH, FELIX

Source: Wise, David, "The Felix Bloch Affair," *New York Times Magazine,* May 13, 1990, p. 28.

GOLD, HARRY (1910–1972). Harry Gold was one of the **atom spies** whose main function was to be a courier between the **Manhattan Project** spies and the Russians who wanted information on the U.S. Army's development of the **atom bomb**.

Gold, a Russian Jew, was born Heinrich Golodnitsky in Bern, Switzerland; his parents, Samuel and Celia Golodnitsky had fled from Kiev in 1907. They immigrated to America in 1914, and on Ellis Island their family name was changed to Gold. The family searched for regular work in Arkansas, Minnesota, and Illinois, then finally settled in Philadelphia, where in 1917 the Golds had another son, Joseph. Heinrich's name was changed to Harry in 1922, when his parents became U.S. citizens. Gold's father was a cabinetmaker.

Gold attended the George Sharswood Public School, and got his high school diploma from South Philadelphia High School in the summer of 1928.

Gold worked briefly at cabinetmaking until he got a job in the Pennsylvania Sugar Company's chemistry department. While there he saved his pay and, at the University of Pennsylvania, studied chemistry in the Towne Scientific School. When his father was unemployed in the 1930s, Gold supported the family. In 1932 he was laid off, and found work with a soap maker in 1933.

Gold's friend in the **Federation of Architects, Engineers, Chemists and Technicians (FAECT)** converted him to communism. By April 1935 Gold was looking for chemical technology that could be passed on to the Russians. He met an **NKVD**

agent, who instructed him to leave the FAECT and work underground for the Communist cause.

Harry completed his B.S. degree at Xavier University in Cincinnati—with financial help from the Soviets—by mid-1940 and gained a secure position as an analytical chemist. He lived at home and spied under the direction of Jacob Golos (1890–1943) and later for Semon Semonov, known to him as Sam, and for Anatoli Yakovlev, known to him as John. Yakovlev, who was the Soviet Vice Consul and NKVD controller, also controlled Julius Rosenberg (1918–1953).

Gold's major work as courier for the Soviets involved getting information from Klaus Fuchs (1911–1988), an important scientist in the Manhattan Project, the U.S. Army research for producing an atom bomb.

In 1944 Gold met Fuchs in New York. He identified Fuchs as a man carrying a handball; Fuchs identified Gold as man carrying a green covered book and a pair of gloves. Gold introduced himself as Raymond, while Fuchs used his real name. They met seven times in the winter, spring, and summer of 1944; and once in Boston, in January 1945, after Fuchs had been assigned to **Los Alamos** for his work on the Manhattan Project. It was difficult for them to meet at Los Alamos, so they arranged to meet in Santa Fe. In New Mexico they met in June and September 1945. Fuchs would give Gold packages containing details on the atom bomb; also, he described the explosion of the Los Alamos bomb of the type that was later dropped on Hiroshima.

Gold liked his secret political work; it made him feel important. He also obtained and delivered secrets from Morton Sobell (1917–), who worked at General Electric Laboratories, and from David Greenglass (1922–), an army machinist at Los Alamos.

By 1946 the **Federal Bureau of Investigation (FBI)** had found that Gold was part of a spy network, and had him under surveillance. At the time Gold was a biochemist at Philadelphia General Hospital. In 1947 he and Elizabeth Bentley (1908–1963) appeared before a grand jury on charges of espionage. There was insufficient evidence to warrant an indictment. Early in 1950 Klaus Fuchs confessed in England to espionage for Russia; when he was shown a movie of Gold, Fuchs stated that Gold was his American contact.

Gold confessed in May and July 1950 and named David Greenglass, Morton Sobell, and the Rosenbergs as atom spies. Although Gold never met the Rosenbergs, he said that he knew about them, which helped convict the Rosenbergs at their trial.

Gold was convicted and given a sentence of 30 years. He claimed he only wanted to help the Soviet Union to become an industrial nation. He was paroled in 1965 and moved back to Philadelphia, where he died in poverty. The **Kremlin** awarded him the Order of the Red Star.

See also BENTLEY, ELIZABETH; FUCHS, EMIL JULIUS KLAUS; GREENGLASS, DAVID, AND GREENGLASS, RUTH; ROSENBERG, ETHEL, AND ROSENBERG, JULIUS; SOBELL, MORTON

Sources: Allen, Thomas B., and Norman Polmar, *Merchants of Treason: America's Secrets for Sale* (New York: Delacorte Press, 1988); Mahoney, Harry T., and Marjorie L. Mahoney, *Biographic Dictionary of Espionage* (San Francisco: Austin & Winfield, 1998); Pilat, Oliver, *The Atom Spies* (New York: Putnam, 1952); Pincher, Chapman, *Traitors: The Anatomy of Treason* (New York: St. Martin's Press, 1987); Radosh, Ronald, and Joyce Milton, *The Rosenberg File: A Search for the Truth* (New York: Holt, Rinehart and Winston, 1983); Weinstein, Allen, and Alexander Vassiliev, *The Haunted Wood: Soviet Espionage in America—*

The Stalin Era (New York: Random House, 1999); Williams, Robert C., *Klaus Fuchs, Atom Spy* (Cambridge, MA: Harvard University Press, 1987).

GOLENIEWSKI, MICHAL (1922–1972). Goleniewski was a defector to the West who named George Blake (1922–), the members of the Portland spy ring, and others when he crossed over to the West in January 1959.

Michal Goleniewski was born in 1922 in Nieswiere, once a part of Russia. He was a **KGB agent** inside the Polish security service intelligence (UB, predecessor of the **SB**). A powerfully built man with blue eyes and a commanding presence, he was, until January 1958, deputy chief of Polish military intelligence. In 1958 he began sending information to the **Central Intelligence Agency (CIA),** in letters to U.S. embassies in Europe. His identity was unknown to the CIA, which code-named him SNIPER, until he presented himself in the West.

In 1960, when a colleague told him that the KGB had found a spy in the UB, Goleniewski immediately concluded he was in danger, phoned the emergency number that the CIA had given him, and with his East German mistress, who knew him as Roman Kowalski, a Polish journalist, escaped to the West on January 5, 1961.

Goleniewski feared assassination so greatly that when the British secret service questioned him about a KGB spy code-named DIAMOND/DIOMID, he demanded that he be interviewed in a separate room for fear that his interrogator might be DIAMOND/DIOMID, and murder him on the spot.

Goleniewski identified George Blake, code-named DIOMID, the man he feared, and held the British authorities in contempt for not finding Blake sooner from the leads he had already given. Also he identified Heinz Felfe (fl. 1950–1963), the KGB's man in the West German Intelligence Service (**BND**), responsible for Karlshorst operations. He also identified Harry Frederick Houghton (1905–), which helped break the Portland spy ring run by Konon Molody (Gordon Lonsdale) (1922–1970). He identified hundreds of other Polish and Soviet intelligence officers.

Goleniewski said that the KGB's attempt to coordinate East German intelligence services had not been successful because most members of the services believed that such coordination would expose their sources.

In 1972 Goleniewski indicated to intelligence officers in England that he had seen documents dated 1959 indicating that Henri Kissinger (1923–) was a Soviet spy. At that time Goleniewski's information was regarded with suspicion: Why had he revealed it in 1972 so long after his defection? Nevertheless, James Angleton (1917– 1987) was given the information.

Goleniewski's curious unreliability extended to his claim to be a descendent of Tsar Nicholas II.

See also BLAKE, GEORGE; FELFE, HEINZ; HOUGHTON, HARRY; MOLODY, KONON

Sources: Andrew, Christopher, and Oleg Gordievsky, *KGB: The Inside Story of Its Foreign Operations* (London: Hodder and Stoughton, 1990); Andrew, Christopher, and Vasili Mitrokhin, *The Mitrokhin Archive: The KGB in Europe and the West* (London: Lane, 1999); Mangold, Tom, *Cold Warrior: James Jesus Angleton, the CIA Master Spy Hunter* (New York: Simon & Schuster, 1991); Murphy, David E., Sergei A. Kondrashev, and George Bailey, *Battleground Berlin: CIA vs KGB in the Cold War* (New Haven, CT: Yale University Press,

1997); Pincher, Chapman, *Traitors: The Anatomy of Treason* (New York: St. Martin's Press, 1987); Wright, Peter, with Paul Greengrass, *Spycatcher: The Candid Autobiography of a Senior Intelligence Officer* (Melbourne: William Heinemann Australia, 1987).

GOLITSYN, ANATOLI MIKHAILOVICH (1926–). Golitsyn defected to the West in December 1961 and informed the **Central Intelligence Agency (CIA)** of important intelligence on the **KGB**'s methods, gave information that led to discovery of a few Soviet **agents**, presented conspiracy theories that attracted the attention of James Angleton (1917–1987), and illustrated Golitsyn's paranoia more than genuine threats to the West.

At the age of 18, Golitsyn was transferred from military duties to counterintelligence school, and a year later joined the KGB (1945). He was responsible for the security of Soviet citizens living overseas. For two years he was trained in further counterintelligence, and by 1951 was a KGB case officer in the Anglo–American Department; he married and was posted to Vienna (1953–1955). First he was on surveillance of Soviet émigrés, and later of British authorities. On returning to Moscow, he studied at the KGB Higher Intelligence School until 1959, and was briefly posted to KGB headquarters to work on American and **NATO** matters. Finally, he was posted to Finland (1960) to control Western counterintelligence work. From there he defected to the West in December 1961 by walking into the American embassy in Helsinki. He was taken secretly to Washington.

Golitsyn was a loner, had few friends, was a perpetual student and arrogant theoretician, and believed he was well-connected among his colleagues. He loved to devise new schemes to reorganize his work, especially in the First Directorate of the KGB, and would argue with superiors about their work organization, and even report their inadequacies to superiors at **Moscow Center**. A professional troublemaker, he knew that he was not going to be promoted; also, he was aware his seven-year marriage was failing. Some observers believed that he committed to both communism and the comforts of Western life; that he had a duty to tell the world where it had gone wrong.

Immediately after his defection the KGB put it about that Golitsyn was morally weak, a careerist, vain, and a victim of the West's exploitation. The KGB also defamed him as a smuggler, and code-named him GORBATY, meaning "hunchback."

When he defected, Golitsyn provided little specific material other than the name of Elsie Mai, a Finn who had penetrated the British consulate in Helsinki. He named five **agents of influence** who were at that time of very little value, and identified a spy at NATO headhunters, George Pâques (1914–), who would later confess to having given the KGB the Anglo–French plan to attack the Suez Canal in 1956, and NATO strategy to defend Western Europe should the Soviets invade. Also, Golitsyn identified a Canadian, Professor Hugh Hambleton (1922–), a KGB recruit from the 1950s who was once a NATO economic analyst.

Golitsyn refused to speak Russian with his interrogators, and firmly suspected that the KGB had penetrated all corners of Western intelligence, especially the CIA and **MI6**. To him, any Russian-speaking employee in these two agencies was a KGB agent. Consequently, interviews with him in broken English were time-consuming and laced with misunderstandings. This, combined with his personal arrogance and vagueness about details—and his failure to bring with him documented proof of what he asserted—created much doubt about the clarity and truth of his statements, and clouded the credibility of his claim that he had been planning his defection for over five years.

Before Golisyn would answer questions clearly, he demanded to see Western documents relating to them. Even so, he did provide sufficient proof to end Kim Philby's (1912–1988) career as a **double agent** when he recalled having heard reference to a phrase "The Ring of Five" (*Pyatyorka*) well before he defected. He identified one or two spies in the British Admiralty, including John Vassall (1924–1996).

In March 1963, Golitsyn was interviewed in London, and concluded from poor but fascinating information on the illness that killed Hugh Gaitskill (1906–1963) that he had probably been poisoned by the KGB to hasten the opportunity for its man **Harold Wilson** (1916–1995) to become Prime Minister. This was quite improbable on medical grounds; and for political reasons it was quite foolish, because the policy of using political assassination had been dropped by the KGB by then, and their man would have been George Brown (1914–1985), who was more likely at that time to follow Hugh Gaitskill.

Also, George Blake (1922–) had given British intelligence greater details on many of Golitsyn's assertions many months earlier when he was interrogated. Finally, Golitsyn was incorrect when he said that the KGB in London had no department that attended to the security of Soviet nationals in Great Britain.

In July 1963 Golitsyn left Britain after a failed attempt to keep his visit secret. On returning to his Washington **safe house**, enjoying a regular stipend and false identity, Golitsyn began to allege vaguely that Soviet defectors and Soviet informants to the **Federal Bureau of Investigation (FBI)** were nothing but **Kremlin** plants who aimed to discredit him and undermine his utopian plans for a better world.

Assuming the KGB had agents in all Western intelligence services, and noting that Harold Wilson had often visited Moscow on business in the 1950s, Golitsyn asserted that Wilson had been seduced into serving the KGB. In this fantasy he gained support from James Jesus Angleton (1917–1987), head of CIA counterintelligence, and his deputy Ramond Rocca.

Angleton inflated his suspicions in line with Golitsyn's primary beliefs and assumed that there was a **mole** called SASHA central to KGB operations in West and East Germany. Golitsyn had said it was man called K____, and could not recall his name. There had been a SASHA in the German spy world—Alexsandr ("Sasha") Kopatzky, alias Igor Orlov. But he was never code-named SASHA. A **molehunt** was driven by Angleton's obsessive suspicions and Golitsyn's maddening vagueness and passionate disillusionment; nothing came of it except the name of a corrupt officer who stole CIA funds. Angleton and Golitsyn operated together in a folie à deux and conducted molehunt that turned the CIA upside down and inside out, but found no mole.

Next Golitsyn advanced the view that the KGB had begun to pretend that Russia's unity and politico-economic power had waned so that it could induce the West to drop its guard against Russian espionage and find itself off balance in reaction to the Communist bloc of nations in Eastern Europe. To support this view, Golitsyn pointed—without evidence—to the use of Soviet **disinformation;** this, he indicated, was evident from the Soviet conflict with the Yugoslav leader **Josip Tito** (1892–1980), events surrounding the **Prague Spring** invasion of Czechoslovakia, the Sino–**Soviet split** (1960–1971), and the **Solidarity** uprising in Poland. They were nothing but tricks of KGB propaganda and disinformation, and had no basis in reality. The Golitsyn–Angleton relationship began to ruin careers in the CIA, especially with the hunt for the imagined assassins of President **John F. Kennedy** (1917–1963). Further, the British intelligence community became divided over the controversial charge that Sir Roger Hollis (1905–1973) and Harold Wilson were KGB puppets. These fantasies became known as the "Golitsyn Syndrome."

Golitsyn even believed that Svetlana Stalin, the Soviet dictator's daughter, had come to the United States to see him, and to lead him into a KGB assassination trap; and that when she left the United States a year later, the KGB had dropped the idea of killing him. In 1986, when she returned as Lana Peters, the assassination plot was revived in Golitsyn's mind. Finally, Golitsyn asserted that the policy of **glasnost** was a secret display of a KGB Department D **"active measure."**

With a pistol at his bedside, Golitsyn would write memos to the White House, arguing that he alone could adequately warn the United States against the Kremlin, and for this reason he was the main enemy that the Kremlin was planning to kill.

See also ANGLETON, JAMES; BLAKE, GEORGE; HOLLIS, ROGER; PHILBY, HAROLD "KIM"

Sources: Andrew, Christopher, and Vasili Mitrokhin, *The Mitrokhin Archive: The KGB in Europe and the West* (London: Lane, 1999); Barry, John, "Broad Impact of 'Martel' Everywhere but France," *Life*, April 29, 1968, pp. 60–61; Brook-Shepherd, Gordon, *The Storm Birds. Soviet Post War Defectors: The Dramatic True Stories 1945–1985* (New York: Henry Holt, 1989); De Vosjoli, Philippe T., "A Head That Holds Sinister Secrets," *Life*, April 29, 1968, pp. 53–59; Mangold, Tom, *Cold Warrior: James Jesus Angleton, the CIA Master Spy Hunter* (New York: Simon & Schuster, 1991); Martin, David, *Wilderness of Mirrors* (New York: Ballantine, 1981).

GORDIEVSKY, OLEG (1938–). Gordievsky was a notable spy for the **SIS** while inside the **KGB** during the period from immediately after the invasion of Czechoslovakia, the end of the Prague Spring (August 1968) until July 1985, when he escaped to the West.

Oleg Gordievsky's father was an official in the **NKVD.** Oleg entered the Moscow Institute of International Relations in 1956 and was trained for work in the KGB and to be a diplomat. About August 1961 he went to East Berlin to train for another year at the Soviet embassy, and was then sent to Moscow for four more years of training, including work in Department S for **illegals,** and the **FCD.** His first overseas assignment was in Copenhagen (1966–1970); then he went back to **Moscow Center** (1970–1972), returned to Copenhagen (1973–1978), worked again in Moscow Center (1978–1982), and then was posted to London (1982–1985).

Gordievsky turned to the West in 1968 mainly in response to the repression of the Prague Spring, in much the same frame of mind as as those, like Oleg Kalugin (1934–), who saw the end of the Communist state in the **U.S.S.R.** at the end of 1989. In 1973, much concerned about how to promote democracy in a system opposed to it, Gordievsky looked for contacts in the West. Late in 1974 he began his collaboration with the West.

Among the valuable information Gordievsky gave the West was an assurance that the "fifth man" was not Sir Roger Hollis (1905–1973), former head of **MI5,** but John Cairncross (1913–1995). In December 1984 he briefed Mikhail Gorbachev for his successful visit with **Margaret Thatcher** (1925–), and in January 1985, after a brilliant career in the KGB, he was told he was the London **resident.**

In May 1985 Gordievsky was summoned back to Moscow to confirm his new appointment, but he had an uncanny feeling that all was not well. In Moscow, late in May, it became clear that he would be kept waiting for an unusually long time,

underwent an interview at which he thought he had been drugged, and believed that he had enemies at Moscow Center who were waiting for him to make an error and be found wanting. He played for time, took leave until early August, and while on leave escaped in July, through Finland, to the West.

When he joined the KGB Gordievsky thought that British spies were among the most competent. This was based on a myth that the British Consul in Moscow was had been plotting a coup against Lenin that was almost a success. Later, when the KGB had to work with the British secret services during **World War II,** they found the British impressive, attractive, dedicated, intelligent, and imaginative, especially when they learned from Kim Philby (1912–1988) that there were fewer than 10 British agents operating in the Soviet Section. This showed him how much talent the Soviets were up against.

In the summer of 1986, Gordievsky read Christopher Andrew's work on espionage, and together they found enough common ground to collaborate on a history of the KGB, which they published in 1990. In 1990 Gordievsky was a consulting editor for *Intelligence and National Security,* a leading academic journal in intelligence research.

"Charm is the key qualification for a successful agent," wrote Gordievsky in 2000. To him charm was what makes it possible for a person to use good arguments effectively and persuade others to give him what he seeks. This skill is acquired, so Gordievsky believes, at British schools and universities. John Le Carré (David Cornwell, the British espionage novelist) also agrees that charm is an essential feature of a perfect spy.

In contrast to other agencies, the CIA is too large to do its job, states Gordievsky. Its departments overlap, and, especially in Latin America, agents are tripping over one another. In the United States the best and brightest are recruited into large corporations and paid well; the CIA has to take second-rate material. He found that in the British secret services, nine out of ten officers are clever and charming; in the CIA it is only one in ten.

To Gordievsky the French are the most incompetent **agents**, as was shown by Operation SATANIC (1986), also known as the "the *Rainbow Warrior* affair." Nevertheless, Gordievsky found the French to have a competent counterintelligence service, though it is held in contempt by the military because technically the counterintelligence staff members are policemen.

See also CAIRNCROSS, JOHN; HOLLIS, ROGER; OPERATION SATANIC

Sources: Andrew, Christopher, and Oleg Gordievsky, *KGB: The Inside Story of Its Foreign Operations* (London: Hodder and Stoughton, 1990); Earley, Pete, *Confessions of a Spy: The Real Story of Aldrich Ames* (London: Hodder and Stoughton, 1997); Gordievsky, Oleg, "Good Spies, Bad Spies," *The Guardian Weekly*, May 4–10, 2000, p. 13;. Richelson, Jeffrey T., *A Century of Spies: Intelligence in the Twentieth Century* (New York: Oxford University Press, 1995).

GORDON, BETTY (1927–). Betty Gordon was a British spy who worked undercover against members of the Communist Party of Great Britain (CPGB) from 1947 to 1962.

Betty Gordon trained as a stenographer and, aged about 20, after being employed by several British firms, joined the office staff at **MI5**. When it was clear to her employer that she would be capable of carrying out undercover work, she was given the training for and the task of penetrating the CPGB and reporting on its members' alleged policy of getting control of British industry.

Gordon took a temporary job with the CPGB, and in time was accepted within the party and given responsibilities for its organization. She worked on the *Soviet Weekly*, and taught English to Chinese diplomats at London's Communist Chinese embassy.

Gordon lived as a part-time nanny with two important British Communist leaders, Betty Reid and John Lewis. She had a baby at their home. In their household she heard discussions of CPGB policy and met many visitors and Communist sympathizers.

In 1958 Gordon worked for an English-language magazine in East Berlin, and had access to policies and schemes of Germany's Communists; these were reported to **MI6** officials in West Berlin.

In 1962 Gordon retired on a pension to care for her child. All her Communist friends deserted her when they learned what she had done. Later she had a nervous breakdown, which was attributed to the strain of leading a double life.

Sources: Mahoney, M. H., *Women in Espionage* (Santa Barbara, CA: ABC-CLIO, 1993); Payne, Ronald, and Christopher Dobson, *Who's Who in Espionage* (New York: St. Martin's Press, 1984).

GOUZENKO DEFECTION (1945). On September 5, 1945, Igor S. Gouzenko (c. 1919–1982), a cypher clerk in the Soviet embassy in Ottawa, Canada, defected to the West, his clothing stuffed with secret documents. This is often taken to be the first major espionage event of the **Cold War.**

Shortly before he was to return to Moscow, and precisely when his embassy replacement was in conference with a superior and his colleagues were at the movies, Gouzenko gathered the secret material and left his office at 8 P.M. First he approached the *Ottawa Journal,* without success, then the **Royal Canadian Mounted Police,** but no one could understand what he had done and, naive about defections, failed to see his motives or the value of what he was offering.

World War II had just ended, and Canada had no reason to be wary of Russian policies, since **Josef Stalin** (1879–1953) had for years been working with the Western allies to defeat Germany.

Soon the **NKVD** was after Gouzenko, and to avoid capture, he was forced to seek help from a neighbor who worked in the Royal Canadian Air Force, who quickly brought in the local police. Next day little was done by either the *Ottawa Journal* or employees at the Ministry of Justice until Sir William Stephenson, a wartime **agent** known as "Intrepid," who by chance happened to be in Ottawa at the time, heard what Gouzenko had done, and strongly recommended that the information be accepted and his case be considered. Even so, the Prime Minister of Canada was cautious until his security authorities had advised him on the value of Gouzenko's material. In an inquiry it became clear that many Canadians had secretly and actively placed their interest in communism well above Canada's national interest; that, as a result, Canadian citizens had become vulnerable to the activities of these Communists; that Gouzenko's defection showed clearly how Soviet espionage in Canada was being used to collect estimates of U.S. troop movements from Europe to the Pacific; that Britain had harbored spies in the British High Commission in Ottawa and in the research laboratories that worked to perfect the **atom bomb**; and that Russia, far from having a general grasp of the atom bomb, enjoyed considerable knowledge of its development from its agents in the **Manhattan Project**.

As result of this defection, a Soviet spy ring in Canada was discovered and disbanded; nine members were put in prison; a Canadian member of Parliament, Fred Rose, was jailed; Alan Nunn May was exposed; and the network in the United States including Harry Gold, David Greenglass, and Julius and Ethel Rosenberg was uncovered.

See also: CANADIAN SPIES; FUCHS, EMIL JULIUS KLAUS; GOUZENKO, IGOR; MAY, ALAN NUNN

Sources: Andrew, Christopher, and Vasili Mitrokhin, *The Mitrokhin Archive: The KGB in Europe and the West* (London: Lane, 1999); Bothwell, Robert, and J. L. Granatstein, eds., *The Gouzenko Transcripts* (Ottawa: Deneau, 1985); Brook-Shepherd, Gordon, *The Storm Birds. Soviet Post War Defectors: The Dramatic True Stories 1945–1985* (New York: Henry Holt, 1989); Canadian Royal Commission, *The Defection of Igor Gouzenko,* 3 vols. (Laguna Hills, CA: Aegean Park Press, 1984; reprint of 1948 ed.); Granatstein, J. L., and David Stafford, *Spy Wars: Espionage and Canada from Gouzenko to Glasnost* (Toronto: Key Porter, 1990).

GOUZENKO, IGOR SERGEYEVICH (fl. 1919–1985). Gouzenko, a **GRU** cipher clerk in the Soviet embassy in Ottawa, Canada, defected with hundreds of documents, and with difficulty managed to get protection from the Canadian authorities. The documents are often regarded as the first information the West had of Russian duplicity after **World War II.**

Igor Sergeyevich Gouzenko was born between 1919 and 1922 in the **U.S.S.R.**, and at the age of 17 he joined the Young Communist League, **Komsomol**; studied engineering; and in July 1941 was drafted into military intelligence with the **NKVD**, coding and decoding as a cipher clerk at the military headquarters of the Red Army in Moscow. After some experience in battle and further training as a cipher expert, in 1942 he was made a lieutenant in the **GRU,** the main intelligence directorate for the General Staff, and in the summer of 1943 was sent with his wife, Anna, to the Soviet embassy in Ottawa, where he was given the **code name** KLERK.

Gouzenko was much impressed by the friendliness of Canadian citizens, and their high standard of living. For 15 months he worked in a high-security office that seemed more like a prison than a workplace, coding and decoding messages to and from Moscow. He lived in an apartment with his wife, had a child, befriended his Canadian neighbors, and was quickly drawn to the comforts of Canadian suburban life. In September 1944 Gouzenko was ordered to return to Moscow, but his superiors persuaded the Moscow authorities to allow him to remain at his Canadian post, where the workload had become heavy and his skills were much needed. About one year later he was recalled to Moscow again, probably because it had been discovered that he inadvertently left a secret document on his desk overnight. Other clerks had been punished severely for such errors. Knowing this, and feeling concerned for the future of his pregnant wife, who was carrying their second child, and impressed by the Canadian way of life, he decided to stay in Canada.

Carefully Gouzenko selected secret documents that related to Canadian affairs specifically and to some Western countries generally. The documents showed there were Communist spies in British establishments in Canada and Britain, and gave information on Communists working in the United States. This was the first clear proof Soviet duplicity, and an early indication that espionage was to become a central tool in **Cold War** diplomacy and conflict. Gouzenko had to lead a secret life thereafter.

Without revealing his whereabouts, Gouzenko published his autobiography, *This Was My Choice* (1948), which was later filmed as *The Iron Curtain*. In May 1952, a year after the flight of Guy Burgess (1911–1963) and Donald Maclean (1913–1983), Gouzenko wrote to the Canadian government to say that he had heard years before that someone with a Russian background had held high office in Britain's wartime intelligence services. Rumor and hearsay indicated that that person might have been Roger Hollis (1905–1973), the **MI5** official sent to interrogate Gouzenko in 1945, who would later become MI5's Director General from 1956 to 1965.

Gouzenko published a modern view of Russia in a novel, *The Fall of a Titan* (1954). For the information he provided on Allan Nunn May (1911–2003), Gouzenko was given British citizenship. He developed diabetes and became blind; he had very little money, was given a modest annuity that was eroded by inflation, and died, aged 63, in Canada.

The **KGB** tried unsuccessfully to find him for many years.

See also CANADIAN SPIES; GOUZENKO DEFECTION

Sources: Bothwell, Robert, "Gouzenko: The Untold Story," *Canadian Historical Review* 66 (2) (1985): 9 (book review); Bothwell, Robert, and J. L. Granatstein, eds., *The Gouzenko Transcripts* (Ottawa: Deneau, 1985); Brook-Shepherd, Gordon, *The Storm Birds. Soviet Post War Defectors: The Dramatic True Stories 1945–1985* (New York: Henry Holt, 1989); Bryden, J., *Best Kept Secret: Canadian Intelligence in the Second World War* (Toronto: Lester, 1993); Dallin, David, *Soviet Espionage* (New Haven, CT: Yale University Press, 1995); Deacon, Richard, *Spyclopedia: The Comprehensive Handbook of Espionage* (New York: William Morrow, 1987); Gouzenko, Igor, *This Was My Choice* (London: Eyre and Spottiswoode, 1948); Gouzenko, Igor, *The Fall of a Titan,* trans. Mervyn Black (London: Cassell, 1954); Gouzenko, Igor, "The Clerk They Wouldn't Believe," in Allen Dulles, ed., *Great True Spy Stories* (Secaucus, NJ: Castle, 1968), pp. 219–232; Hyde, Earl M., Jr., Bernard Shuster, and Joseph Katz, "KGB Master Spies in the United States," *International Journal of Intelligence and Counterintelligence* 12 (1999): 35–57; Mahoney, Harry T., and Marjorie L. Mahoney, *Biographic Dictionary of Espionage* (San Francisco: Austin & Winfield, 1998); Pincher, Chapman, *Traitors: The Anatomy of Treason* (New York: St. Martin's Press, 1987); Sawatsky, John, *Gouzenko: The Untold Story* (Toronto: Macmillan, 1985); Taschereau, Robert, and R. L. Kellock, *Report of the Royal Commission to Investigate Facts Relating to the Communication of Secret and Confidential Information to Agents of a Foreign Power* (Ottawa: Government Publisher, 1946); West, Nigel, "Canadian Intelligence Literature: Gouzenko and the RCMP," *Intelligence Quarterly* 2 (1986): 15–16; Whitaker, R., and G. Marcuse, *Cold War Canada: The Making of a National Insecurity State 1845–1957* (Toronto: University of Toronto Press, 1994).

GREENGLASS, DAVID (1922–), AND GREENGLASS, RUTH (1925–).

David and Ruth Greenglass worked for Julius Rosenberg (1918–1953) to provide the Soviets with information on the construction of the **atom bomb** in the mid-1940s.

David Greenglass, the fourth child in the family of a Russian machinist with an Austrian wife, was raised on New York's Lower East Side. He knew young Ruth Prinz, who idealized him; and as a teenager he made the acquaintance of Julius Rosenberg, who would later marry his older sister Ethel (1916–1953). Ethel drew him into joining the Young Communist League, and he developed an active interest in communism. He neglected his studies at the Brooklyn Polytechnic Institute, and later at the Pratt Institute; had a job with a telephone company; and spent much time as a union organizer. He married Ruth Prinz in December 1942; she was 18 and he was 20.

Greenglass dropped out of college and became a machinist. Shortly after the marriage he was drafted into the U.S. Army (1943), and Ruth had to move to wherever he was stationed, living in a rented apartment. He would preach his political ideals to fellow soldiers. He became a capable wood machinist, and was stationed at Oak Ridge, Tennessee, and later at **Los Alamos** with the **Manhattan Project** (July 1944), where he worked for 18 months on the atom bomb. Wives were not permitted to visit during the first period of employment at Los Alamos, so Ruth went back to New York to live, and saved up for their second wedding anniversary in November 1944.

In November 1944 Greenglass was working on a project but did not know exactly what it was. It was the atom bomb, and he worked on the lens system and devices that focused the explosion to concentrate radioactive matter.

The security system at Los Alamos allowed workers to leave their workplaces and circulate information. Consequently Greenglass was in a position to pick up information on the bomb from conversations with coworkers.

When he heard about his brother-in-law David's assignment to Los Alamos, Julius Rosenberg persuaded Ruth to ask her husband about supplying Russia with information on the atomic research. Greenglass had a memory for blueprints, and could lead people into conversations that provided details. Julius's wife, Ethel, insisted that Ruth do what Julius wanted. Ruth resisted. To help her decision, Julius gave Ruth money for the fare to New Mexico.

Ruth visited David in Albuquerque, New Mexico; told him what Julius wanted; and asked David to forward information on the project to Julius. He refused; Ruth told him how low their finances were, and that Julius had given her money to travel to be with him. Next day Greenglass changed his mind, and thereafter supplied the information until he left the U.S. Army in 1946.

Greenglass was neither a clever nor an ambitious man, and would often tell the story that he had slept through the first atomic test rather than get up to see if the bomb worked.

After **World War II** the Rosenbergs and Greenglasses pursued failed joint business ventures (1946–1950), and the families became hostile toward one another over money problems.

In November 1949, after news of Klaus Fuchs's (1911–1988) espionage had appeared in the newspapers, a **Federal Bureau of Investigation (FBI) agent** talked with Greenglass about who he might have known at Los Alamos; he said that he had heard of Fuchs, but knew nothing more.

In the first half of 1950, Julius Rosenberg, much agitated by the effects of Fuchs's trial, the confession of Elizabeth Bentley, and the efforts of the FBI to find Communists among American citizens, came with money and plans for the Greenglass family to flee to Mexico in June. Ruth and David would not go. On June 15 FBI agents came to see Greenglass, and the following day he told the full story.

In exchange for immunity from prosecution, Greenglass decided to be a witness against the Rosenbergs. The investigating agents sought ever more information from him, always using the threat that if he did not help, they would charge Ruth with espionage.

Greenglass admitted giving secret information to the Russians but refused to implicate his sister Ethel Rosenberg, saying she knew nothing of what was going on. Ruth, who did not like the Rosenbergs, said that Ethel not only knew what was going on, but that she had typed up David's notes. This extended the bitter family conflict.

When he heard of the discrepancy, what was Greenglass to do? Call his wife a liar? He quickly changed his story to corroborate that of Ruth, and gave false evidence to prevent his wife's being charged. Also, the prosecution encouraged him to lie. The evidence he gave was that his sister Ethel had typed up his espionage notes on a Remington typewriter, and that the notes were intended to be sent to Moscow.

Ruth Greenglass was not charged, and David Greenglass was sentenced to 15 years jail for passing on information. In 1960 he was released, and lived under an assumed name with Ruth. He worked at inventing the waterproof electrical outlet. In 1990 he was living in Queens, New York, when he was interviewed for the *New York Times* by Sam Roberts.

In 2001, with the publication of Sam Roberts's *The Brother*, Greenglass stated that he had lied at the trial of the Rosenbergs. He recalled that in June 1953 he would not sacrifice his wife and children for his sister Ethel's sake. In 2001 he said he does not know who did the typing. He believed the Rosenbergs went to their death not admitting to espionage because they were stupid. He now believes Ethel was responsible for her own death by electrocution.

At the time, Greenglass recalled, he did not think the Rosenbergs would be given a death sentence. The notes, typed or handwritten, he thought, were of very little value. But to the prosecution the Remington typewriter was like a smoking gun. In 2001 Greenglass also admitted that he had lied to a U.S. Congressional committee.

See also BENTLEY, ELIZABETH; FUCHS, EMIL JULIUS KLAUS; ROSENBERG, ETHEL, AND ROSENBERG, JULIUS

Sources: Allen, Thomas B., and Norman Polmar, *Merchants of Treason: America's Secrets for Sale* (New York: Delacorte Press, 1988); Ellison, Michael, "Spy's Brother Drops a Bombshell," *The Age*, December 7, 2001, p. 11; Hyde, Earl M., Jr., Bernard Shuster, and Joseph Katz, "KGB Master Spies in the United States," *International Journal of Intelligence and Counterintelligence* 12 (1999): 35–57; Mahoney, Harry T., and Marjorie L. Mahoney, *Biographic Dictionary of Espionage* (San Francisco: Austin & Winfield, 1998); Pilat, Oliver, *The Atom Spies* (New York: Putnam, 1952); Roberts, Sam, *The Brother: The Untold Story of Atomic Spy David Greenglass and How He Sent His Sister, Ethel Rosenberg, to the Electric Chair* (New York: Random House, 2001).

GUILLAUME, GÜNTHER (c. 1927–). Günther Guillaume was an important asistant to Willy Brandt (1913–1992), the West German statesman and Chancellor. At the same time, Guillaume was a master spy for East Germany's Main Department of Intelligence of the Ministry for State Security under the direction of Markus Wolf (1923–). Guillaume's work for the Soviets was one of the most highly regarded intelligence coups of the **Cold War** between 1970 and 1974.

Günther was the son of a doctor, Ernst Guillaume, who had once saved Willy Brandt from capture, and by the 1950s had himself become a dependent invalid. Günther helped support his father with a job that entailed coming daily from East Germany to work in West Berlin.

Aware that Guillaume had developed a loathing for the West, the **KGB** recruited him with an eye to using old family connections to place him close to Willy Brandt. For a time he had been in the Nazi Party, which may have helped the KGB to blackmail him.

Coden-amed HANSEN, Guillaume, with his wife Kristal, faked an escape from East Germany to Frankfurt, West Germany, and opened a shop as a cover for their intelligence work (1956). Presenting themselves as strong supporters of anti-Communism, they joined and worked for the Social Democratic Party. In the 1960s Guillaume had little access to valuable secrets. But in twelve years of assiduous work under Markus Wolf's direction, he was elected to the Frankfurt city council (1968), and from this post applied successfully to work for Willy Brandt's office dealing with political organizations and trade union affairs.

Efficient, hardworking, and outwardly cheerful, Guillaume was noticed, and in 1972 was promoted to a position where he handled Brandt's travel arrangements. From Guillaume's reports the Russians could evaluate the public's views of the changing policies on East–West relations advocated by Brandt, West Germany's popular socialist politician and Chancellor (1969).

After Brandt's election as Chancellor in November 1972, Guillaume was well established as one of his most trusted aides, free to attend party leadership discussions and parliamentary meetings. In May 1973 he was suspected of espionage; but the allegations were not taken seriously. In fact he gave sensitive material to Russians sent from President **Richard Nixon** (1913–1994) to Brandt, as well as passing on **NATO** material.

On April 24, 1974, Guillaume and his wife were arrested; he quickly confessed his loyalty to East Germany. The scandal forced Brandt to resign in May.

At the trial in Düsseldorf (1993) of Markus Wolf, Guillaume described how he had infiltrated the office of Willy Brandt, but could not recall details of his work, saying that it had already appeared in his memoirs, published in East Germany (1988). In his political memoirs Brandt (1992) wrote that he had not taken seriously the suspicions about Guillaume because he, Brandt, had overestimated his knowledge of human nature. Wolf regarded the Brandt Affair as a disaster for East–West relations.

Guillaume was imprisoned for 15 years, but was freed in 1981 in an exchange with East Germany for 30 political prisoners. His wife had been freed in another spy exchange a few months earlier. Guillaume was awarded the Order of Lenin, given a villa, and received a doctorate of law for his outstanding work. He defended his espionage as a "partisan for peace."

See also BRANDT RESIGNATION

Sources: Andrew, Christopher, and Vasili Mitrokhin, *The Mitrokhin Archive: The KGB in Europe and the West* (London: Lane, 1999); Pincher, Chapman, *Traitors: The Anatomy of Treason* (New York: St. Martin's Press, 1987); Richelson, Jeffrey T., *A Century of Spies: Intelligence in the Twentieth Century* (New York: Oxford University Press, 1995); Rositzke, Harry, *The KGB: The Eyes of Russia* (Garden City, NY: Doubleday, 1981); Vogel, Steve, "Mole Who Doomed Brandt Tells How He Spied," *Washington Post*, July 1, 1993, p. A16; Wolf, Markus, *Man Without a Face: The Autobiography of Communism's Greatest Spymaster* (New York: Times Books, 1997).

H

HALL, THEODORE ALVIN (1925–1999). Hall was the youngest scientist at **Los Alamos** to provide information to the Soviets on his work for the **Manhattan Project.**

Theodore Alvin "Ted" Hall, an American Jew, son of a furrier, was a brilliant student who was educated in physics at Harvard University. There he befriended Saville Savoy Sax (1924–1980), a year older than Ted, and a member of the Young Communist League. Sax's mother worked for the Russian War Relief, and probably through her Hall joined the League.

After graduation Hall worked at the Steel Founders' Union, then got a job as the youngest physicist to work on the Los Alamos **atom bomb** project, where he witnessed the first atom bomb explosion in July 1945.

Sax introduced Hall to the Soviet cause, and he began to idealize Russia as a simple worker–peasant state. Also he was religious, regularly attended synagogue, and would spend hours in meditation. In November 1944, when his Russian handler considered him suitable for espionage, Hall was working at a camp in Los Alamos.

On the advice of Saville Sax, Hall decided to provide his Soviet contact with a report on the group he worked with, and names of important personnel he knew at Los Alamos. Later he decided to give the Russians what he could so, that there would be no nation with a monopoly of nuclear power. He would pass information to Lona Cohen (1913–1993), who gave it to her Russian contacts in New York.

The U.S. atom bomb was detonated by implosion, a term unfamiliar to the Russians, and in 1949 they detonated their own bomb this way, probably because of the role Hall played in getting information on the atom bomb so promptly to them.

In 1948 Hall was working for a Ph.D. at the University of Chicago; there he and his wife, both members of the Communist Party, decided to change their allegiance. He wanted to join the presidential campaign of Henry A. Wallace (1882–1965), the pro-Soviet leader of the Progressive Party. Morris Cohen (1905–1995) persuaded

Hall to stay with the Soviet cause, and remain a member of the group, code-named, VOLUNTEER, which he headed.

In March 1951 Hall was suspected of espionage and interrogated by the **Federal Bureau of Investigation (FBI),** but was not charged for a lack of evidence. In 1962 he settled in England. He would never confirm accusations of espionage. But after the public release in 1995 of the VENONA cables between the Russian spymasters and their spies during World War II, Hall issued a written statement indicating he might have been a spy for Russia, and that as a young man he had felt it was dangerous if America alone were to have nuclear weapons. Also, he said that he felt he might have helped prevent the dropping of an atom bomb on China in 1949 or the early 1950s.

Hall had Parkinson's disease, and died of kidney cancer in Cambridge, England, where he was a leading but diffident pioneer in biological research.

Authorities in the West's secret services believe that Hall and Klaus Fuchs (1911–1988) provided enough for the Russians to detonate an exact copy of the Los Alamos explosion four years afterward.

See also COHEN, LEONTINA, AND COHEN, MORRIS; FUCHS, EMIL JULIUS KLAUS

Sources: Albright, Joseph, and Marcia Kunstel, *Bombshell: The Secret Story of America's Unknown Spy Conspiracy* (New York: Times Books/Random House, 1997); Andrew, Christopher, and Vasili Mitrokhin, *The Mitrokhin Archive: The KGB in Europe and the West* (London: Lane, 1999); Cohen, Sam, "Ted Hall: A Soldier from Venona," *International Journal of Intelligence and CounterIntelligence* 11 (1998): 351–365; Cowell, Alan, "Obituary: Theodore Alvin Hall: Physicist and Spy," *The Age*, November 16, 1999, p. 7 (first published in *New York Times*); Haynes, John Earl, and Harvey Klehr, *Venona: Decoding Soviet Espionage in America* (New Haven, CT: Yale University Press, 1999); Weinstein, Allen, and Alexander Vassiliev, *The Haunted Wood: Soviet Espionage in America—The Stalin Era* (New York: Random House, 1999).

HAMBLETON, HUGH (1922–). For over 30 years Hambleton passed secrets to the Soviets; he was sentenced to 10 years in jail in 1982, but released after less than eight.

Hambleton was born in Ottawa, Canada. His father was English, and Hugh held dual citizenship of Canada and Britain. He was educated in both Britain and Canada, and spent some of his childhood in France, where his father was a press correspondent.

From 1944 to 1945 Hambleton served in the Free French Army in Algiers, and was a French liaison officer with the U.S. Army's 103rd Division in Europe. In 1945 he joined the Intelligence Section of the Canadian army, and was in Strasbourg, France, as an intelligence officer who interviewed German prisoners of war. Of himself he said that he felt a need to be important enough to have people pay attention to him.

Hambleton came out of the war a committed Communist, was **talent-spotted** by a Canadian Communist leader, and in 1952 was recruited as a Soviet **agent** code-named RIMEN, later changed to RADOV. He was in Paris two years later, studying economics at the Sorbonne. In 1956 he began work for **NATO,** and for five years provided valuable material to his Russian handler. After a security check he lost his job at NATO, but was not charged with any wrongdoing.

In 1961 Hambleton studied at the London School of Economics, where he completed a Ph.D., and in 1964 he was made a professor of economics at Laval

University in Quebec. He disliked his Soviet handler in Canada, and his contact with the **KGB** diminished after his handler tried to get him to take a job with the government's External Affairs Department. Hambleton later resumed relations with the KGB, traveling in Canada, the United States, and the Caribbean. In 1978 his handler, who had been arrested by the **Federal Bureau of Investigation (FBI)** in May 1977, was turned, and Hambleton was one of his victims.

In 1979 the KGB warned Hambleton to destroy all compromising material in his possession, and to escape to East Germany. He chose not to follow these instructions, and in 1980 was the center of speculation and questions in the Canadian Parliament. Hambleton appeared to enjoy the publicity, and denied that he had ever spied. It appears the KGB had paid him U.S.$18,000. Speculation subsided, and Hambleton visited London two years later.

Information from Anatoli Golitsyn (1926–) and others led to Hambleton's arrest in June 1982. He was tried under the Official Secrets Act, and jailed for 10 years. He appeared to believe that he had been given immunity from prosecution. In June 1986 he was put into a Canadian jail, and in March 1989 was released under supervision.

See also GOLITSYN, ANATOLI

Sources: Andrew, Christopher, and Vasili Mitrokhin, *The Mitrokhin Archive: The KGB in Europe and the West* (London: Lane, 1999); Barron, John, *The KGB Today: The Hidden Hand* (New York: Reader's Digest Press, 1983); Brook-Shepherd, Gordon, *The Storm Birds. Soviet Post War Defectors: The Dramatic True Stories 1945–1985* (New York: Henry Holt, 1989); Deacon, Richard, *Spyclopedia: The Comprehensive Handbook of Espionage* (New York: William Morrow, 1987); Granatstein, J. L., and David Stafford, *Spy Wars: Espionage and Canada from Gouzenko to Glasnost* (Toronto: Key Porter, 1990); Heaps, Leo, *Hugh Hambleton, Spy: Thirty Years with the KGB* (Toronto: Methuen, 1983); Laffin, John, *Brassey's Book of Espionage* (London: Brassey's, 1986).

HAMILTON, VICTOR NORRIS (fl. 1950–1960). Victor N. Hamilton worked as a cryptanalyst for the U.S. National Security Agency (NSA), and after quitting made public the efforts of the NSA to break codes and analyze communications between Arab countries and their communications with the **U.S.S.R.** in the 1960s.

Hamilton, an Arab, graduated from the American University in Beirut, and was eager to get a university teaching post in America. This was difficult, so he worked as a doorman until an American colonel recruited him to the NSA. His task was to break codes for the NSA's Production Organization. He met an American woman, whom he married in the 1950s while he was in Libya. After he changed his name to Hamilton from Hindali, he and his wife settled in the United States, in the state of Georgia. He was naturalized as an American citizen.

In June 1957 Hamilton was a research analyst in the Near East Division of the Production Organization's All Other Countries section. It was dealing with information flowing between Egypt, Syria, Iraq, Jordan, Lebanon, Saudi Arabia, Yemen, Libya, Morocco, Tunisia, Turkey, Iran, Greece, and Ethiopia.

The task was to study and break the codes in the communications made from Arab countries to any part of the world. This included communications between, for example, the United Arab Republic (Egypt and Syria) and the U.S.S.R., and concerned the U.S.S.R.'s petroleum needs; it also included government as well as commercial instructions of every government in the Middle East.

In February 1959 Hamilton had a mental breakdown, but was kept on by NSA because it had few employees competent in Arabic. A few months later he was forced to resign, showing symptoms of schizophrenia. He claimed he faked the symptoms so that he could leave, and he did so. Four years later, in July 1963, in Moscow, Hamilton published in *Izvestia* an account of his work and secrets of the NSA.

For 30 years Hamilton was in a Russian hospital, diagnosed with schizophrenia.

Sources: Andrew, Christopher, and Oleg Gordievsky, *KGB: The Inside Story of Its Foreign Operations from Lenin to Gorbachev* (London: Hodder and Stoughton, 1990); Bamford, James, *The Puzzle Palace: A Report on America's Most Secret Agency* (Boston: Houghton Mifflin, 1982); Shane, Scott, and Tom Bowman, "Some at NSA Betrayed Country," *Baltimore Sun*, December: 3–15, 1995, p. 6.

HANSSEN, ROBERT PHILIP (1944–). For 21 years, the **Federal Bureau of Investigation (FBI) agent** Robert Philip Hanssen spied for the Soviets, until he was caught in 2000.

Hanssen was born in Chicago. His father was a veteran policeman who worked for 30 years in local anti-Communist intelligence. Philip was raised a Lutheran in a middle-class suburb of Chicago. He seemed a polite, well-behaved boy who did well at school and pleased his teachers. As an adolescent, aged about 15, he said he wanted to be another Kim Philby (1912–1988), and from then on, aimed to undermine his father's anti-Communist work. At Knox College he studied chemistry, and kept a secret from his mother—he was also studying Russian.

At Northwestern University, Hanssen studied dentistry and accounting. He worked for the Chicago police force until he was 32, and then joined the FBI. Between 1978 and 1981 he was a field officer in the FBI Soviet Division in New York.

Hanssen was noticed for being highly religious and believing that he was mentally superior to his peers and leaders. He showed subtle arrogance, and was nicknamed "Dr. Death" for his sallow complexion, dark hair, black suits, and humorlessness. He had no interpersonal skills, and was therefore not used to recruit Soviet turncoats.

At work Hanssen developed skill in the use of computers for investigative systems, which gave him access to the true names of all FBI intelligence sources in New York; he knew where all the bugs were in the Soviet offices; he was always asking questions. At some time in 1979 he began spying for the Soviets.

Between January 1981 and November 1985 Hanssen and his family lived in their own house in Vienna, Virginia. Robert was given various assignments in the FBI offices in Washington, DC and in New York. In New York he stayed at the YMCA. In August 1983 he was assigned from a budget unit to the Soviet Analytical Unit in Washington, which gave him access to much government-classified information. In October 1984 he signed a classified information nondisclosure agreement.

In early October 1985, through a minor KGB officer, Hanssen contacted Viktor I. Cherkashin, a **KGB** colonel and chief of counterespionage in the Soviet embassy, with the reputation of being skilled in handling **double agents**. Hanssen offered the services of "B"—no-name—for $100,000, and gave the names of three KGB agents who had been working for the FBI. Two of them were tried and executed; the other was jailed, and now lives in California. In 1991 Hanssen was paid $100,000 and given diamonds. The KGB reported to him that it had put $600,000 in a Moscow bank, but he believed this to be a lie. His contacts with the Russians ceased in 1991.

Hanssen was married with six children, and lived in a modest home in a modest suburb; on a government salary he educated his children at a Catholic schools and had three aging cars. He was often seen walking the dog, rarely stopped to chat with neighbors, attended Sunday mass with the family at the same church as his boss, and belonged to a conservative religious society. He had a supportive wife and was admired by the neighbors; together they appeared to enjoy a sunny optimism, seemed skilled at child-rearing, and were reserved, aloof, and generally well-regarded. He was seen as a good father and son, a capable professional in his work, and an honest, loyal, upright citizen.

In Hanssen's career the circumstances were favourable for his work and betrayal. In the FBI's National Security Division, he worked on the intellectually demanding case-building tasks of counterintelligence. He was a voracious reader of spy novels, Marxist tomes, and log reports. Hanssen had access to invaluable U.S. secrets and gave over 6,000 pages of them to Russia, endangering all U.S. attempts at penetration of Russia in the 1980s. He got away with this for 15 years because his cover was so good.

In 1992 the FBI investigated why so many operations had been blown in the last five years of the 1980s. From this investigation they caught Rick Ames (1941–) in 1994, Harold Nicholson (fl. 1950–1997) in 1996, and the FBI's Earl Edwin Pitts (fl. 1987–1997).

After these discoveries Hanssen put his name through the FBI database and found he was not under suspicion, so he returned to his espionage for the Russians. Meanwhile, the FBI continued searching for a **mole**.

By autumn 2000 the FBI was certain it had found a mole. Hanssen's name came up on a list of suspects, but no evidence indicated he was spying or would be motivated to be a spy for Russia. Three clues helped identify him: the final one was a KGB dossier revealing that he was "B." On February 12, 2000, he was caught red-handed. On being captured, he asked, "What took you so long?"

The U.S. experts in intelligence believe that they do not have a system that can prevent the type of action in which Hanssen engaged. They asked what makes a man betray, and why he got away with it for so long.

Answers: Hanssen had been humiliated by his father, a Chicago policeman. He had no male role model for authority with whom he could readily identify; in 1976 he adopted the FBI, and later the Catholic Church's Opus Dei movement with its unrelenting, unambiguous mission. He was the ideal choice for a Soviet double agent, because he was insecure, needed to impress those in authority, and had access to high levels of government secrets. Although he showed outwardly that his inner life was highly moral, he felt the only sin he committed was getting caught. In fact, a helpful KGB source exposed him. His Christian veneer was hiding his lust for a sex worker girlfriend, the use of sex videos and adult sex Web sites, and even sexual involvement with his sister-in-law.

In July 2001 Hanssen accepted a plea agreement that spared him the death penalty. Early in May 2002 he was jailed for life. Norman Mailer and Lawrence Schiller made a film of his life from an investigation of the case in 2002.

After months studying the documents that helped identify Hanssen, the FBI investigators were convinced he could not have done the work alone, and began suspect that in the FBI there was another mole during the **Cold War.**

See also AMES, ALDRICH "RICK"; BLOCH, FELIX

Sources: Anonymous, "U.S. Spycatchers Hunt for Second Russian Mole," *The Age*, March 27, 2001, p. 9; Masters, Brook A., "FBI Spy Is Jailed for Life Without Parole," *Guardian Weekly*, May 16, 2002, p. 28; McGeary, Johanna, "The FBI Spy," *Time*, March 5, 2001, pp. 24–30; Mailer, Norman. *Master Spy: The Robert Hanssen Story*. Film by Oakdale Productions (Oakdale, CA: 2002); Risen, James, "Soviet Spy Jailed After Costing U.S. Millions," *The Sunday Age*, May 12, 2002, World, p. 1; Schiller, Lawrence, *Into the Mirror: The Life of Masterspy Robert P. Hanssen* (New York: HarperCollins, 2001); Wise, David A., *The Bureau and the Mole: Unmasking of Robert Philip Hanssen, the Most Dangerous Double Agent in FBI History* (New York: Schwarz, 2002).

HAREL, ISSER (1912–2003). During the **Cold War**, Isser Harel was the hard, ambitious, and unorthodox Israeli spymaster who organized the capture in 1961 of Adolf Eichmann, the Nazi SS officer responsible for administering the **"Final Solution."**

Harel was born Isser Halperin in Vitebsk, Russia, and by 1922 had moved to Dvinsk in Latvia, when the Russian revolutionaries confiscated his father's successful vinegar factory. His father reestablished the firm, and six years later Isser left for Riga, where he prepared to immigrate to Palestine. With forged documents he went via Warsaw, Vienna, and Rome to Genoa, where he boarded a ship to British-mandated Palestine in 1930. He brought with him, illegally, a disassembled pistol concealed in a loaf of bread.

In Palestine, Harel worked as a laborer; helped found Kibbutz Shefaim; and joined Hagana, the large clandestine organization, and eventually the Jewish Settlement Police. In 1944 he was in Hagana's intelligence service, Shai. Inarticulate and a poor writer, he was ambitious, so he adopted a powerful authoritarian style and earned the name "Isser the Terrible," among other titles, for his efficiency as a soldier.

By 1947 Harel was leading the Shai espionage on the Stern Gang and Irgun terrorists, as well as spying on the British. He became a close confidant and supporter of David Ben-Gurion (1886–1973), the Jews' leader in Palestine.

In September 1948, following the assassination of the UN negotiator Count Folke Bernadotte (1895–1948), and under instructions from David Ben-Gurion, Harel rounded up the Israeli terrorists in the Stern Gang and Irgun. Also, he arranged for his spies to infiltrate Communist groups and the right-wing opposition Herut Party of Menachem Begin (1913–1992).

In September 1952 Harel became the **Mossad** chief, and recruited former members of the Stern Gang and Irgun. Among them was Yitzhak Shamir, who was for 10 years the head of Mossad operations in Europe. In October 1956, Harel, head of both Mossad and **Shin Bet**, used a deceptive operation to keep away the Egyptian bombers in the Sinai War.

For several years Harel's personal political ambitions were frustrated, and he attracted much criticism for his broad suspicions of both Arabs and Israel's Western allies.

In 1960 Harel commanded the operation that captured "Ricardo Klement," the name taken by Adolf Eichmann (1906–1962), a resident of Buenos Aires, who was spirited away on the midnight plane to Israel on May 20. Eichmann was tried and sentenced to hang; after his appeal the sentence was carried out in May 1962. That year Harel learned of Germans who were developing unconventional weapons for

Egypt, and, without permission from Ben-Gurion, immediately launched a secret letter bomb campaign against families of those he suspected. Also he arranged the publication of newspaper stories in Israel about the weapons Egypt was developing. In a confrontation with Ben-Gurion, Harel resigned, and shortly after, Ben-Gurion was out of office.

In 1965–1966 Harel returned to intelligence work as an adviser to the government, but left when he found information was being kept from him. He was elected to the Knesset as a member of the newly established Ha'reshima Ha'mamlachtit Party three years later.

Harel published several books, including the account of Eichmann's capture; was married; and had one daughter.

Sources: Anonymous, "Spymaster Found Final Solution for Eichmann," *The Age* (Melbourne), February 25, 2003, p. 9 (first published in *Daily Telegraph* [London]); Black, Ian, and Benny Morris, *Israel's Secret Wars: The Untold History of Israeli Intelligence* (London: Hamish Hamilton, 1991); Deacon, Richard, *Spyclopedia: The Comprehensive Handbook of Espionage* (New York: William Morrow, 1987); Eisenberg, Dennis, Uri Dan, and Eli Landau, *The Mossad Inside Stories: Israel's Secret Intelligence Service* (London: Paddington Press, 1978); Harel, Isser, *The House on Garibaldi Street* (New York: Viking, 1975).

HARPER, JAMES DURWOOD (c. 1934–). James Harper provided secrets to the Russians in the 1980s for enormous sums of money, without any ideological interest in who got the information.

James Durwood Harper was an electrical engineer in **Silicon Valley**. From his girlfriend, a defense contractor's employee, he got a hundred pounds of classified documents on the Minuteman missile in June 1980.

The **KGB** gave $100,000 for the documents; they were delivered to the **SB** (Polish Security Services) and then to the KGB. This indicated how well the KGB was integrated with the East German intelligence community as well as those in Czechoslovakia, Poland, Hungary, and Bulgaria. In September 1980 Harper got more documents, for which he received $20,000, and still more in February 1981 ($70,000) and a year later ($50,000).

Anxious not to be punished when caught, Harper tried through his lawyer to negotiate immunity with the **Central Intelligence Agency (CIA),** but failed to so. A CIA agent in the SB established his identity, and he was arrested in October 1983.

Sources: Allen, Thomas B., and Norman Polmar, *Merchants of Treason: America's Secrets for Sale* (New York: Delacorte Press, 1988); Richelson, Jeffrey T., *A Century of Spies: Intelligence in the Twentieth Century* (New York: Oxford University Press, 1995).

HART, EDITH TUDOR (1908–1973). Edith Hart was a Communist sympathizer and a photographer with a wide range of contacts in Great Britain who helped her find recruits to the Soviet cause.

Edith Tudor Hart was born Edith Suschitsky in Vienna, daughter of a radical socialist who ran a bookshop. After training to be a Montessori teacher, she went to work in England. Two years later she returned to Vienna to study photography. She was a member of the illegal Austrian Communist Party, and completed undercover missions as a Soviet **agent** in Paris in 1929.

In 1933 she married the medical practitioner working at the British consulate, Dr. Alex Tudor Hart, and together they returned to England. As a surgeon her husband joined the Republican forces in Spain, while she maintained a photographic studio in Brixton. She knew Arnold Deutsch (1904–1942), who recruited her to the Soviet cause with the **code name** of EDITH. The Harts were code-named STRELA (arrow).

Litzi Friedmann, code-named MARY, the first wife of Kim Philby (1912–1988), was Hart's close friend in Vienna. The Philbys returned to London in May 1934. Litzi introduced Kim Philby to Edith, who took him to meet Arnold Deutsch in June 1934.

Hart had a son in 1936, and specialized in child photography. Her photography gave her a wide range of contacts in British society, where she proved to be an excellent recruiter for the Soviets. Also, she was active in the Workers Camera Club, contributed to *Picture Post*, and helped artists to fight Fascism and oppose the imminent European war. She maintained regular contact with Litzi Friedmann and helped further understanding between the Communist Party of Great Britain and the Soviet embassy.

The Harts were divorced after Alex returned from Spain.

In 1938–1939 Edith and Litzi were used by Guy Burgess (1911–1963) as couriers to make contact with the **NKVD** in Paris, where Litzi had a large apartment.

Once Hart lost her diary, which contained the details of Arnold Deutsch's activities. Consequently her name was associated with the police raid on the home of the leader of the Woolwich Arsenal spy ring, Peter Glading.

After **World War II**, Hart was employed as a commercial photographer for the Ministry of Education. She continued her work for the Soviets for a short period, and later ran a small antiques store in Brighton. Her mental health was not stable, however; and her son was in special care. She died of liver cancer.

See also BURGESS, GUY; PHILBY, HAROLD "KIM"

Sources: Andrew, Christopher, and Oleg Gordievsky, *KGB: The Inside Story of Its Foreign Operations from Lenin to Gorbachev* (London: Hodder and Stoughton, 1990); Andrew, Christopher, and Vasili Mitrokhin, *The Mitrokhin Archive: The KGB in Europe and the West* (London: Lane, 1999); West, Nigel, and Oleg Tsarev, *The Crown Jewels: The British Secrets at the Heart of the KGB Archives* (New Haven, CT: Yale University Press, 1999).

HAYHANEN, REINO (fl. 1918–1971). Reino Hayhanen was the name used by an incompetent Soviet **agent** who did not follow orders, abused alcohol, in desperation defected to the West with his wife, and died in what may have been an automobile accident.

Hayhanen was sent to New York to be Willie Fisher's (a.k.a. Rudolph Abel) (1903–1971) assistant. Hayhanen had several identities. The first was that of Eugene Nikolai Maki, allegedly born in 1919 in the United States to a Finnish father and an American mother, and who, as an eight-year old, went to Karelia, a region of Finnish Russia.

In 1949 Hayhanen had a new birth certificate that made him out to be Reino Hayhanen, who in 1952, now code-named VIK, sailed on the *Queen Mary* to New York, where he established himself with his Finnish wife, Hannah. A story is told that for his efforts **Moscow Center** mailed him a hollowed-out nickel containing a microfilm message congratulating him on his safe arrival in New York. He mislaid the nickel, and later used it to buy a newspaper. A newsboy passed the nickel to the **Federal Bureau of Investigation (FBI),** which years later decoded the message and with it was able to catch a Soviet **illegal.**

In the summer of 1954 Hayhanen worked as Willie Fisher's assistant. He was incompetent in matters of security, and a serious alcoholic. So was his wife. Also, he was probably a fraud. In 1955 he stole $5,000 put aside to help Morton Sobell's wife, and claimed that he had given it to her.

In 1956 Hayhanen was convicted of drunken driving. He was recalled to Moscow in 1957. Before he left, he lied to Willie Fisher about his espionage efforts; in Paris, late in April, he collected his travel money from the **KGB** at the Soviet embassy, and a few days later went to the American embassy and defected.

He was taken to America, denounced Rudolf Abel, and was settled comfortably. He died in a automobile accident on the Pennsylvania Turnpike. At first it was believed that his death had been contrived by the KGB's Thirteenth Department, but this was found to be KGB **disinformation.**

See also FISHER, VILYAM (WILLIE); SOBELL, MORTON

Sources: Andrew, Christopher, and Vasili Mitrokhin, *The Mitrokhin Archive: The KGB in Europe and the West* (London: Lane, 1999); Deacon, Richard, *Spyclopedia: The Comprehensive Handbook of Espionage* (New York: William Morrow, 1987).

HEATH CAPER (c. 1966). The Heath Caper was a failed but amusing **KGB–** Czechoslovakian operation to discredit a noted British Conservative politician.

Edward Richard George Heath (1916–) was a rising star in Britain's Conservative Party in the 1960s, and became its leader from 1965 to 1975, during which period he brought the United Kingdom into the European Community. The Heath Caper began when he was about 50, was unmarried and had no known mistress, and was judged by the KGB to be a possible target for blackmail as a homosexual, if only he could be caught in the appropriate circumstances.

A Czechoslovakian diplomat and spy with impeccable connections in Britain, Jan Mrazek was acquainted with some well-known homosexuals in Britain, but had no evidence connecting them to Heath. So, Jan—"John," as he was known in Britain— aimed to snare Heath by enticing him to Czechoslovakia, trapping him with homosexuals, and forcing him through blackmail to feed the Soviets information from the top level of Britain's Conservative Party.

The Czechoslovakian Secret Service had staff well-trained in all forms of sexual seduction. Heath was gifted player of at the organ. The Czechoslovakian Secret Service got help from Jaroslav Reinberger, a handsome bisexual organist who knew Heath. Two recitals by Reinberger were arranged in Britain, and Heath attended both. At the second he mentioned how much he would like to play the renowned organ in Prague's Church of St James. Delighted, the Czechoslovakian Secret Service arranged for Heath to get an invitation to play, and he accepted. The stage was set for one of the greatest blackmailing successes of the Czechoslovakian Secret Service. But at the last moment Heath could not come to Czechoslovakia; British counter-intelligence had warned of the possibility of blackmail. Two years in the planning, the Heath Caper came to nothing.

Sources: Andrew, Christopher, and Oleg Gordievsky, *KGB: The Inside Story of Its Foreign Operations from Lenin to Gorbachev* (London: Hodder and Stoughton, 1990); Deacon, Richard, *Spyclopedia: The Comprehensive Handbook of Espionage* (New York: William Morrow, 1987); Frolik, Joseph, *The Frolik Defection* (London: Leo Cooper, 1975).

HELMS, RICHARD McGARRAH (1913–2002). Richard Helms, a highly professional espionage officer, was the first head of the **Central Intelligence Agency (CIA)** (1966–1973) to come up through the ranks, the first insider to get the top job since Allen W. Dulles (1893–1969), and the first to be prosecuted, found guilty, and punished for lying to the U.S. Congress about CIA activities.

Richard Helms was born in St. Davids, Pennsylvania, the son of an Alcoa executive. He was raised in New Jersey; at a high school in Switzerland, studied French and German; and graduated from Williams College in Massachusetts (1935). He wanted to own a daily newspaper.

Helms joined the United Press International (UPI) staff in Berlin in 1935. In 1936 he covered the Berlin Olympic Games, and with other journalists interviewed the German dictator, Adolf Hitler (1889–1945).

In 1938, Helms returned to the United States to be advertising manager for an Indianapolis newspaper. In 1942 he served the U.S. Navy in New York as a fundraiser for the Naval Relief Society. He was then reassigned to antisubmarine operations. In August 1943 he began to use his German language skills to work for the **OSS** on covert activities.

Helms learned to value highly both secrecy and the gathering of reliable information. He worked for the OSS in England and France and, unlike many other OSS **agents**, stayed on after VE (Victory in Europe) Day. He held desk jobs in New York, Washington, and London. In 1946 he led the counterintelligence activities of the Office of Special Operation (OSO) in Switzerland, Austria, and Germany. In July of the following year, when the OSO became a division of the newly established CIA and was integrated with the Office of Policy Coordination (OPC)—together they were renamed the Directorate of Plans—Helms undertook CIA's black operations. These centered on anti-Communist activities, and aimed to undermine left-wing political parties and governments abroad (e.g., the Italian elections in the late 1940s and 1950s).

During the **Red Scare** of the early 1950s, when Senator Joseph McCarthy (1908–1957) was hunting down Communists in U.S. government departments, Helms chaired a committee in the CIA to protect it from McCarthy's efforts to infiltrate the organization with his own informers. And during his directorship, the CIA launched Operation CHAOS, a secret, and highly questionable, domestic surveillance in the United States that was not revealed until 1975.

Helms worked with Reinhard Gehlen's (1902–1979) West German espionage operations and advised Washington in the early stages of the **Cold War** that the Russians had established a worldwide espionage network and were intent on using covert operations to accomplish world domination through communism.

On returning to Washington, Helms served in CIA middle management, watching his superiors fall by the wayside: Lyman Kirkpatrick from polio, Frank Wisner (1909–1965) from a nervous breakdown, and Allen Dulles from the **Bay of Pigs** disaster (April 1961).

After the Bay of Pigs invasion failed, Helms replaced Richard Bissell, Jr. (1909–1994), in the CIA in 1962. President **John F. Kennedy** (1917–1963) and his brother Robert gave Helms, among others, that of ridding Cuba of Fidel Castro (1927–) and his Communist regime.

In October 1962, following the **Cuban missile crisis**, Helms was sent to Vietnam, where he carried out President Kennedy's directive to have the South Vietnam regime overthrown. Less than a month later, Kennedy was assassinated. President **Lyndon B. Johnson** (1908–1973) made Helms deputy head of the CIA, then head in 1966. He was the first CIA man to have risen to the top.

In Vietnam and neighboring Laos, Helms helped organize operations to curb North Vietnam's military supply lines, and to support South Vietnam's secret counterterrorist groups. When Helms informed the president how badly the U.S. Army was conducting the **Vietnam War** (1964–1975), a conflict arose between the CIA and the **Pentagon** chiefs. Military information on the North Vietnamese was distorted, and as a result the U.S. military was surprised by the size of the enemy's forces in the **Tet Offensive** (1968).

When **Richard Nixon** (1913–1994) became U.S. President, Helms, although quite accurate in his evaluation of Soviet missile strength, came into conflict with the White House's policy and that of its advisers. In September 1970, President Richard Nixon told Helms that a regime headed by Salvador Allende (1908–1973) in Chile would be unacceptable, and instructed the CIA to work to prevent it. The task was *not* to include the U.S. Embassy, was *not* to worry about the risks of the operation, and it should *seriously* damage the Chilean economy. He could draw on U.S.$10 million if necessary.

Despite the CIA's efforts Allende was elected in. October 1970. The CIA then worked harder to cause turmoil in Chile, and perhaps organized the crippling transport strikes of 1972 and 1973, which seriously damaged the economy. The problem was finally settled on September 11, 1973, with a coup led by General Augusto Pinochet (1915–) and the death of Allende.

Meanwhile, Helms was at pains to ensure that the scandal surrounding the **Watergate** break-in of June 1972—a former CIA officer, Howard Hunt, was involved—was kept at arm's length from the CIA. Notwithstanding, it appears that the White House launched a rumor that the CIA had been close to the Watergate break-in. In December 1972 Helms was summoned to Camp David, where he refused President Richard Nixon's requests to have the CIA help cover up the scandal and the facts about the Watergate break-in. In February 1973 Nixon fired Helms, replaced him with James Schlesinger, and made Helms the U.S. ambassador to Iran.

Often Helms had to return to the United States to appear before Congressional investigations of the CIA. To these investigators it became clear, in March 1973, from statements by William Merriam, Vice President of International Telephone and Telegraph, that the CIA had been deeply involved in efforts to bring down Allende's regime in Chile. In support of both the national interest and the secret promises made to the president at the time, Helms denied that the CIA had been in any way part of Allende's downfall.

Also, it was rumored that Helms had had a role in the assassination of Patrice Lumumba (1925–1961) in the Congo, and at home had supported suspected illegal domestic surveillance, Operation CHAOS, by the CIA.

Helms was charged with perjury for his denial of the CIA involvement in Chile, found guilty, fined $2,000, and given a two-year suspended sentence (1977). The fine was paid by full-time CIA officers.

To CIA officers and commentators who knew well the culture of the intelligence community, Helms, an experienced spymaster, was found guilty of doing what he had been told to do, doing it very well indeed, and maintaining an unremiting allegiance to his profession. In 1983, President **Ronald Reagan** (1911–2004) praised Helms for his services, and awarded him the National Security Medal. At the time, Helms, a consultant on Middle East investments, was reported to have remarked, "I have no feelings about remorse or exoneration"; another source reports that he actually said he considered the reward "an exoneration."

In Helms's view, the CIA worked only for the U.S. President, and he, like other heads of the CIA, did not welcome Congressional investigations of the CIA, much less Congressional oversight of CIA operations.

See also ALLENDE GOSSENS, SALVADOR; BISSELL, RICHARD; DULLES, ALLEN; LUMUMBA, PATRICE; OPERATION CHAOS; OPERATION MONGOOSE; WISNER, FRANK

Sources: Barnes, Bart, "Richard Helms: Obituary," *Guardian Weekly* (London), October 31, 2002, p. 32 (originally published in the *Washington Post*); Colby, William, with Peter Forbath, *Honorable Men: My Life in the CIA* (New York: Simon & Schuster, 1978); Jackson, Harold, "CIA Chief Who Lied to Congress over Chile: Richard McGarrah Helms 30-3-1913–22-10-2002," *The Age* (Melbourne), October 29, 2002, Obituaries, p. 9 (originally published in *The Guardian*); Powers, Thomas, *The Man Who Kept the Secrets: Richard Helms and the CIA* (New York: Knopf, 1979); Richelson, Jeffrey T., *A Century of Spies: Intelligence in the Twentieth Century* (New York: Oxford University Press, 1995).

HILL, JAMES "JIM" FREDERICK (fl. 1918–1954). Jim Hill, code-named TOURIST by the **MVD,** was an alleged Australian spy, one of group of 12, who gave information to the Russians. This was asserted publicly during the Petrov Affair (1954–1955).

Jim Hill, born in Australia, worked as a bank clerk after leaving school, and studied law at night. In 1938 it appears that he had joined the **Communist Party of Australia (CPA),** but may have been an undercover member for some time before that. He studied at the University of Melbourne, and, had he been a Communist Party member, he would probably have known Walter Seddon Clayton (c. 1906–), code-named KLOD, who was in charge of party affairs and knew Jim's brother, Ted Hill, who would become a CPA leader.

In 1941 Jim Hill joined the Australian army, and to his associates showed notable left-wing views. He moved to Canberra in June 1945 to take a position in the Department of External Affairs. At the time Ian Milner (1911–1991) was also in the department, having joined in February. It appears that neither Milner nor Hill was a CPA member, but both could have been under instructions of Communist officials. In those days it was not uncommon for CPA sympathizers to become active nonparty members for the Communist cause.

Evidence appeared later that Jim Hill became valuable contact for Walter Clayton. When they met late in 1945, Hill gave Clayton communications originating at the British Foreign Office and a report to the Australian External Affairs Minister on activities in Bulgaria, Greece, and Romania.

In response to Igor Gouzenko's (1919–1982) defection in September 1945, Hill and his associates were instructed by Soviet intelligence to be cautious in their work. In 1949 Hill was secretly investigated by **ASIO** after the nervous breakdown of a leading member of the CPA, who stated that Hill was an undercover **agent** for the party.

Roger Hollis (1905–1973), who came to Australia to help establish ASIO, believed that Hill, who was working in the United Nations Division of the Department of External Affairs at the time, had given a Soviet agent a copy of a cable received in Australia from the British. Apparently the information in the cable was not classified, and passing it on to the Soviet diplomat was congruent with the open diplomatic policy of the Australian government, which wanted to help Soviet diplomats who were interested in Australia's policies.

In June 1950 Hill was transferred to London, where he met Jim Skardon. Skardon had interrogated Klaus Fuchs (1911–1988) and had encouraged him to confess. He mentioned to Hill the names of Allan Nunn May (1911–2003) and Klaus Fuchs, told Hill that his espionage was well known in Britain, and that suggested that, like May and Fuchs, he should come clean. Later Hill's colleagues assumed that **MI5** was intending to frame Hill for espionage, because Hill's name was among 12 listed by MI5 and ASIO as being Soviet agents.

In September 1950 Hill left London for Australia, certain his career in the External Affairs Department was over. On arrival he was transferred, then quit the public service and became a lawyer with his own practice. ASIO kept him under surveillance, and found that all he had were left-wing friends and ideas.

By June 1953 the 12 suspected Soviet spies—now known as "The Case"—had dropped to four, including Jim Hill. Prime Minster **Robert Menzies** (1894–1978) was informed. In April 1954, the Prime Minster announced the defection of Vladimir Petrov, and that a Royal Commission on Espionage would begin in May.

The view that Hill was a Soviet spy became weak when Petrov said that he had no knowledge of Hill being a Soviet agent in Australia. Also, at the inquiry Hill denied having passed information to the Soviets.

See also CLAYTON, WALTER SEDDON; MILNER, IAN; PETROV AFFAIR

Sources: Hall, Richard, *The Rhodes Scholar Spy* (Sydney: Random House Australia, 1991); Manne, Robert, *The Petrov Affair: Politics and Espionage* (Sydney: Pergamon, 1987); McKnight, David, *Australia's Spies and Their Secrets* (St. Leonards, NSW: Allen and Unwin, 1994); McQueen, Humphrey, "The Code of Silence," *The Weekend Australian* (Canberra), April 3–4 (2004), pp. 30–31. Smith, Wayne "The Truth That Came in from the Cold" *The Weekend Australian* (Canberra), 3–4 April (2004), p. 31

HILL, JOHN EDWARD CHRISTOPHER (1912–2003).

Christopher Hill was a notable British historian and Master of Balliol College, Oxford, and has been accused recently of being a Soviet **agent of influence** during the early part of the **Cold War.**

Christopher Hill was born in York, England, in 1912. His father was a wealthy solicitor and devoted Methodist; Christopher's mother, who influenced him much, had a fine sense of humanity and a good humor. They were not happy with his Communist sympathies, which were evident even during his high school days at St Peter's School, York.

Hill was persuaded to enter Oxford University rather than Cambridge. He was an outstanding scholar, won many prizes, and was a fine sportsman. In 1934 he spent 10 months in the Soviet Union, and probably then joined the CPGB. In 1936 Hill lectured at University College, Cardiff, and in 1938 he became a fellow and tutor at his Oxford College, Balliol. He was always at Balliol except for his service in **World War II.**

In 1940, Hill was a private in the security police, then a lieutenant in the Oxford and Buckinghamshire Light Infantry; in 1943 he was a major in the Intelligence Corps, and later was seconded to the Foreign Office.

Sometimes using a pseudonym, Hill wrote for left-wing publications, and his *The English Revolution, 1640* (1940) became the standard Marxist interpretation of the English Civil Wars (1642–1648). Frequently he lectured for the Workers' Educational Association and to trade union students at Ruskin College, Oxford. In 1957, after the Hungarian revolution, he resigned from the Communist Party, but maintained his Marxist view that economic forces and class conflicts were the most important of all historical forces, and he sought a world dominated by socialist democracy. His earliest work argued that the English Civil Wars (1642–1648) were not only an interregnum forced on the nation with a revolution justified by the ideology of Puritanism, but also a great change in the life and beliefs of common English people at the time.

Although his political views were never hidden, Hill's membership of the CPGB was. So as a Communist he served in the Foreign Office; during World War II he was head of the Russian desk, and may have used his post to promote Soviet policy with others who had the same sympathies.

In 1985 Anthony Glees, a British historian, approached Hill for information; they met; Hill told Glees that he hoped Glees would not expose him for his Communist sympathies and activities, and that he had assumed **MI5** had cleared him of all suspicion before recruiting him to military intelligence in 1940, and for his secondment to the Foreign Office. Hill appears to have escaped identification as a Communist by not mentioning his party membership.

Glees learned Hill had worked with a group of Russian engineers examining tanks in England, and was seconded to the Northern department of the Foreign Office in1943 because he was fluent in Russian. And later, as head of the Russian desk, it appears Hill had recommended all White Russians who taught Russian at British universities be replaced with Soviet-approved staff, and that after World War II, all Polish exiles be treated similarly.

Also, Hill was friends with Peter Smollett, head of the Russian desk at the Ministry of Information, and the two sought to advance what they believed was an appropriate British foreign policy toward the Soviets. Smollett was a friend of Kim Philby (1912–1988), and persuaded British publishers to reject *Animal Farm* by George Orwell. At the same time Hill's department maintained it was convinced **Josef Stalin** (1879–1953) had no plans to extend the **U.S.S.R.** after the war, a view that contradicted the later **containment** policy dominant in early Cold War politics in the West.

While in the Foreign Office, Hill published *The Soviets and Ourselves: Two Commonwealths*, under the pseudonym K. E. Holme; the work idealized Lenin, stated all Soviet citizens had the right to vote, and that Stalin's purges in the 1930s were not violent, but instead were similar to the ideas of the Chartist movement.

Hill's first marriage, to Inez Waugh in 1944, was dissolved. They had one daughter, deceased; in 1956 he married Bridget Sutton, who died in 2002. They had one son, Andrew, and one daughter. Andrew said recently that his father never discussed the time he was in the Communist Party of Great Britain.

Sources: Andrew, Christopher, and Oleg Gordievsky, *KGB: The Inside Story of Its Foreign Operations from Lenin to Gorbachev* (London: Hodder and Stoughton, 1990); Anonymous, "Obituary: Christopher Hill," *The Times* (London), February 26, 2003, Features, p. 30;

Cobain, Ian, "Was Oxford's Most Famous Marxist a Soviet Mole?" *The Times* (London), March 5, 2003, p. 3.

HINTON, JOAN CHASE (c. 1918–). Joan Chase Hinton loathed the United States so much that she worked assiduously to provide the Chinese Communist government with scientific information about the **Manhattan Project.**

Joan Hinton's mother ran an experimental school, Putney School, whose faculty included Communists; among her friends were Elizabeth Bentley's (1908–1963) espionage informants, including Alger (1904–1996) and Priscilla Hiss and Harry Dexter White (1892–1948).

Hinton attended Bennington College and devoted herself to the study of science. She also attended Cornell University and the University of Wisconsin, and appeared to be a brilliant scholar. She sought work at the Manhattan Project, and through her mother's friend J. Robert Oppenheimer (1904–1967) was given a research assistantship at **Los Alamos,** with top-secret clearance.

At the end of **World War II,** Hinton left the project in shame, she would later assert, because of the U.S. President's decision in August 1945 to drop **atom bombs** on Japan. After leaving the project—contrary to her Communist friends' advice—she got a research assistantship with a fellowship from the University of Chicago to work with Enrico Fermi at the Arogonne National Laboratories.

In December 1947, in the wake of publicity about the September anti-Communist investigations of the Hollywood Ten in New York, Hinton got a passport to go China. She was toting a suitcase full of information from her work in Los Alamos and the Arogonne Laboratories.

In Shanghai, Hinton married a U.S. agriculturist; her brother William and his wife, staunch supporters of the Communist cause, accompanied her and her husband to Communist-dominated areas of China.

In September 1951, well after the People's Republic of China was established, at a peace conference Joan spoke vehemently against America's germ warfare in Korea. She followed that with propaganda broadcasts from Peking on U.S. Fascist foreign policy, and its effect on the United Nations troops in Korea, and became known in the United States as "Peking Joan."

Sources: Burnham, James, *The Web of Subversion* (New York: John Day, 1954); De Toledano, Ralph, *The Greatest Plot in History* (New York: Duell, Sloan & Pearce, 1963); Mahoney, M. H., *Women in Espionage* (Santa Barbara, CA: ABC-CLIO, 1993).

HISS, ALGER (1904–1996). Alger Hiss was a former American diplomat, well-connected to the American establishment, who was accused of perjury in 1950, during the early investigations of government agencies and their Communist employees in the United States. At the inquiries he was accused of being a spy for the Soviets, and had he been tried on that charge, might well have been found guilty and executed. He served four years for perjury.

Alger Hiss was the fourth of five children. His father, a manager of a dry goods company, committed suicide when Alger was two years old. Alger was raised by his mother and an unmarried aunt. He attended Johns Hopkins University and completed a law degree at Harvard (1929). He became clerk to the U.S. Supreme Court judge Oliver Wendell Holmes (1841–1935). In 1933 he joined the administration of President Franklin D. Roosevelt (1882–1945), worked on New Deal programs, and later directed the Office of Special Political Affairs.

In 1945, at the **Dumbarton Oaks** Conference, he helped establish the United Nations, and was among Roosevelt's staff at the **Yalta Conference** in February 1945.

At the first meeting of the United Nations, Hiss was temporary Secretary-General. In 1946 he was a senior adviser to the U.S. delegation at the first session of the United Nations, in London.

Hiss's politics were humanitarian and liberal. In 1946 he left a distinguished government career to be President of the Carnegie Endowment for International Peace, an organization that sought the elimination of war as a mode of settling international conflict. His directed its funds toward UN projects.

In August 1948, a senior editor at *Time*, Whittaker Chambers (1901–1961), alleged at a **House Un-American Activities Committee (HUAC)** inquiry that Hiss was one of several New Deal government officers who belonged to a secret group of Communists, and passed on information to Soviet **agents** who sent it to Moscow. Hiss denied the accusation. Before a TV audience Chambers accused Hiss of lying; Hiss called Chambers a liar, spy, and traitor and dared him to make the allegations in public. When Chambers did, Hiss sued for slander and U.S.$75,000 recompense.

During the slander trial, Chambers tried to show he was telling the truth, and produced retyped government documents that he alleged Hiss had given him in 1938. Dubbed the "Pumpkin Papers," they had been on rolls of microfilm and had been hidden in a hollowed-out pumpkin on a Maryland farm.

A grand jury summoned Hiss, who again denied seeing Chambers after 1937, and charged him with perjury. The trial began May 31, 1949, and Hiss's lawyer excoriated Whittaker Chambers's reputation; he was depicted as an unreliable witness, overweight, and untrustworthy. Hiss was a slim patrician by comparison. After two weeks the jury was split, eight to four in favor of conviction. A second trial produced a witness who named Hiss a Communist from the 1930s. He was found guilty and sentenced to five years in prison. His appeal failed; he was disbarred from practicing law; and in March 1951 he went to jail for 44 months.

In 1952 Whittaker Chambers published his views of the case; in 1957 and 1988, Hiss published his memoirs. On leaving jail, Hiss worked for 15 years in a factory, and then as a salesperson. Between 1958 and 1960 **Richard Nixon** (1913–1994) used Hiss's case to help him launch a political career partly based on the U.S. public anxiety aroused in the early 1950s **Red Menace,** which had been led largely by the work of Joseph McCarthy (1908–1957).

When Whittaker Chambers was dead, and Richard Nixon had resigned the U.S. presidency in disgrace, Hiss was reinstated as a lawyer. He worked assiduously to retrieve his reputation by asserting that the evidence used to convict him was not authentic. Weinstein (1978) examined the evidence and concluded Hiss had been guilty. Many noted U.S. scholars were impressed by the finding. Hiss appealed his conviction, tried to get it overturned, but did not succeed.

In 1984 President **Ronald Reagan** (1911–2004) awarded Whittaker Chambers a Medal of Freedom, and the farm where the "Pumpkin Papers" were found was declared a historic landmark.

Hiss was given great hope in 1992 when the chairman of Russia's military intelligence archives announced that the charges against Hiss had no foundations. This was countered by the discovery that a deceased American spy, Noel Field (fl. 1934–1954) had confessed earlier in Hungary that Hiss was a spy.

In 1996 the NSA released information showing Hiss was probably a Russian agent, code-named ALES, and had flown to Moscow shortly after the Yalta Conference

(February 4–11, 1945). Hiss, by now in his nineties, recalled the Moscow visit; he said that he had visited Moscow for one night only, with the intention of studying the city's subway. The NSA statement was taken by many liberal-minded intellectuals to be the document needed to established Hiss's guilt.

Hiss died two days after his ninety-second birthday, protesting his innocence.

In May 1999 a judge in New York ruled that the public's right to know outweighed the government's interest in keeping secret the proceedings of the grand jury investigations involving Hiss, and that the relevant papers indicated the role Richard Nixon played in baiting supporters of communism in the early 1950s.

Olmstead (2002) lists the writers for and against Hiss at various times between his trial and his death. Weinstein and Vassiliev (1999) provide details of the groups, including Hiss's contemporaries, in the U.S. government who served Soviet interests in the 1930s.

See also CHAMBERS, WHITTAKER

Sources: Alterman, Eric, "I Spy with One Little Eye . . . Spotting Cold War Espionage Has Turned into a Journalistic Game Without Rules," *The Nation*, April 29, 1996, pp. 20–24; Andrew, Christopher, and Vasili Mitrokhin, *The Mitrokhin Archive: The KGB in Europe and the West* (London: Lane, 1999); Anonymous, "Alger Hiss: Obituary," *The Times* (London), November 18, 1996, p. 23; Bone, James, "Judge Releases Papers in Hiss Spy Case," *The Times* (London), May 15, 1999, p. 20; Buckley, William F., Jr., "Alger Hiss, R.I.P (Doubt Unexplainably Remains About the Guilt of the Late Spy)," *National Review*, December 9, 1996, pp. 22–25, 65; Chambers, Whittaker, *Witness* (New York: Random House, 1952); Hiss, Alger, *In the Court of Public Opinion* (New York: Knopf, 1957); Hiss, Alger, *Recollections of a Life* (New York: Henry Holt, 1988); Hiss, Tony, *The View from Alger's Window: A Son's Memoir* (New York: Knopf, 1999); Lowenthal, John, "Venona and Alger Hiss," *Intelligence and National Security* 15 (2000): 98–130; Mahoney, Harry T., and Marjorie L. Mahoney, *Biographic Dictionary of Espionage* (San Francisco: Austin & Winfield, 1998); Olmstead, Kathryn, *Red Spy Queen: A Biography of Elizabeth Bentley* (Chapel Hill: University of North Carolina Press, 2002); Schumpeter, Peter, "Obituary: Spy Charge Outraged a Nation: Alger Hiss," *The Age* (Melbourne), November 20, 1996, p. B2; Tannenhaus, Sam, "New Reasons to Doubt Hiss," *Wall Street Journal*, November 18, 1993, p. A-20; Weinstein, Allen, *Perjury: The Hiss-Chambers Case*, rev. ed. (New York: Random House, 1997); Weinstein, Allen, and Alexander Vassiliev, *The Haunted Wood: Soviet Espionage in America—The Stalin Era* (New York: Random House, 1999); Zeligs, Meyer A., *Friendship and Fratricide: An Analysis of Whittaker Chambers and Alger Hiss* (New York: Viking, 1967).

HITLER DIARIES (1983). The Hitler Diaries, discovered late in April 1983, were found to be a fraud early in May 1983; many years later, they were found to have been part of a **STASI/KGB** operation to discredit and confuse historians in the West.

In April 1983 *Stern* magazine published extracts from 60 volumes of diaries that the magazine had been assured came from the pen of Adolf Hitler (1889–1945) between 1933 and 1945. Before the first excerpts were published, *Stern* paid about 10 million marks to a "Dr. Fischer" through a photographer-journalist, Gerd Heidemann. While Heidemann was taking some of the money for himself, the man known as Dr. Fischer was having the diaries smuggled out of East Germany inside pianos.

When the diaries were discovered, experts were sought to verify their authenticity, and the outstanding British historian Hugh Trevor-Roper (1914–2003)—raised to Lord Dacre of Glanton in 1979—believed them to be authentic. He was well-known for many historical studies, including *The Philby Affair* (1968), and had served as an intelligence officer during **World War II.** He argued, using the criterion of internal consistency, that although signatures could be forged easily, a large and well-integrated archive was less easily produced and that the archive cohered as a whole in itself. Some experts were unsure of the diaries' authenticity, and others thought they were a hoax. David Irving, a conservative historian, who at first denounced the diaries as a hoax—shortly before they were found to be so—supported the view of Lord Dacre.

The *Sunday Times* bought the rights to publish the diaries. After the *Times* had published Lord Dacre's article endorsing their authenticity, on April 24 it published the first installment, "The Secrets of Hitler's War," and billed it as a "world exclusive"—running a front-page news story and four pages inside, with the promise of more extracts to come. Lord Dacre was a director of *Times* Newspapers at the time.

Early in May 1983 it was clear the diaries were indeed a fake. They were books of postwar manufacture with thread not made before 1950; a plastic monogram on the cover of one diary was FH instead of AH; the texts were occasionally inaccurate and anachronistic; the ink was too modern, and had recently been applied to paper; and on May 14 the author of the diaries, the unknown "Dr. Fischer," Konrad Kujau (d. 2000), an excellent forger from Stuttgart, was arrested. Gerd Heidemann, who "discovered" the diaries, was arrested a few days later. Heidemann said that Kujau duped him, but Kujau always claimed that he had informed Heidemann all along that the diaries were fakes.

The *Sunday Times* serialization was called off. Lord Dacre made a fine and gracious apology for having been hoaxed. The West German government declared the 60-volume work counterfeit. Heidemann and Kujau were jailed in July 1985 for four and a half years. Kujau died shortly after his release, but not before he had begun selling other forgeries successfully. At his release, Heidemann turned his back on the industry of collecting Nazi memorabilia.

In July 2002 it was revealed that Heidemann was a **double** agent working for East Germany's intelligence service, STASI. Part of his STASI file was published in *Der Spiegel,* and stated that he had claimed to have handed over his payments from the East Germans to West Germany's counterintelligence service. It appears that the "Hitler Diaries" was not a failed hoax, but instead a deliberate Soviet operation in **disinformation.**

As a successful operation in KGB disinformation at the time, the revelation that the diaries were a hoax embarrassed the *Sunday Times*, owned by the Australian–American media proprietor, Rupert Murdoch (1931–), and undermined the high reputation of one of England's leading historians, Lord Dacre.

The STASI documents recently published stated that Heidemann had joined the STASI in 1953 as a photographer and journalist whose main task was to photograph military targets and the premises of secret service organizations in Germany, especially those of the British. He photographed sites throughout Germany for this purpose and was well paid. He felt he never had enough money, always wanting to be paid more; it seems the "Hitler Diaries" were too good an opportunity for him to miss.

Der Spiegel said Heidemann wrote to the STASI in 1955, withdrawing his services. But the files revealed that in 1978, he was handed over by the department that had recruited him to the STASI's Foreign Espionage Department under Markus Wolf (1923–). In 1986 Heidemann's file was archived, indicating that he was no longer considered an employable **agent**.

See also TREVOR-ROPER, HUGH

Sources: Anonymous, "Scholar with an Appetite for Historical Debate," *The Age* (Melbourne), January 20, 2003, Obituaries, p. 11; Hooper, John, "Stasi Link Adds New Twist to Hitler Diaries Hoax," *The Age* (Melbourne), July 30, 2002, World, p. 7 (originally published in *The Guardian,* July 29, 2002, and followed the next day with a correction).

HOLLIS, ROGER (1905–1973). Roger Hollis became the head of **MI5** and was thought to be a Soviet **agent** while in that position. An investigation of him did not reveal sufficient reliable evidence that he had been a Russian spy and his name was cleared, but deep suspicions remain, although there is little to support them.

Roger Hollis was born at Wells, Somerset, the third of four sons of the vice principal of the local theological college. Later his father was a cleric in Leeds, then Headingly, before returning to Wells as principal of the college; eventually he became bishop of Taunton. Hollis did not complete his degree at of Oxford University, worked in a bank to save money to go to China in 1927, and later was a journalist. Finally he took a job with the British American Tobacco Company.

Hollis made friends with leading Chinese Communists. In 1936, after contracting tuberculosis, he returned to Britain; joined MI5 in 1938; and eventually served as its Director-General until he retired in 1965.

Hollis was under suspicion as a Soviet agent from 1965 until 1970. Britain's closest allies were warned of his possible treachery in 1974, and several MI5 and **MI6** officers who investigated him were certain that he was a spy for Russia.

In March 1981, U.K. Prime Minister **Margaret Thatcher** (1925–), told the U.K. House of Commons that from two investigations into the work and the duties of the late Sir Roger Hollis, head of MI5 from 1956 to 1965, there was no conclusive proof of Sir Roger's innocence, and no evidence was found that incriminated him.

Suspicion rested on many impressions. After the conviction of John Vassall (1924–1996) in 1962 for his work as a Soviet agent, another suspect, an admiral, was thought to be a valuable informant, but Hollis twice refused to allow MI5 officials to interrogate him. Also, Hollis ordered the destruction of many documents that some thought would be valuable evidence of Russian espionage.

Those people who accepted Mrs. Thatcher's final conclusion, but still suspected Hollis, concluded that he was more incompetent than treacherous. For example, he did not report adequately to the Prime Minister over a period of two years during the course of the affair involving **John Profumo**.

Chapman Pincher, the British espionage writer, and Peter Wright were convinced that Hollis was a Soviet agent in the mid-1980s. Andrew and Gordievsky (1990) have shown that in the Soviet London **residency** the **KGB** had had no source inside MI5 or MI6 since 1961. At the time one reason why the British government dismissed charges against Hollis was that MI6 had its own high-ranking source inside the KGB.

Today Christine Keeler (1942–) still believes Hollis, whom she saw often between 1959 and 1962 in conversation with Stephen Ward (1912–1963), was a Soviet agent.

See also GORDIEVSKY, OLEG; KEELER, CHRISTINE; VASSALL, WILLIAM JOHN CHRISTOPHER; WARD, STEPHEN; WRIGHT, PETER

Sources: Andrew, Christopher, and Oleg Gordievsky, *KGB: The Inside Story of Its Foreign Operations* (London: Hodder and Stoughton, 1990); Brook-Shepherd, Gordon, *The*

Storm Birds. Soviet Post War Defectors: The Dramatic True Stories 1945–1985 (New York: Henry Holt, 1989); Keeler, Christine, *The Truth at Last: My Story* (London: Sidgwick & Jackson, 2000); McQueen, Humphrey, "The Code of Silence," *The Weekend Australian* (Canberra), April 3–4 (2004), pp. 30–31; Pincher, Chapman, *Too Secret Too Long* (London: Sidgwick & Jackson, 1984); Pincher, Chapman, *Traitors: The Anatomy of Treason* (New York: St. Martin's Press, 1987); West, William John, *The Truth About Hollis: An Investigation* (London: Duckworth, 1989); Wright, Peter, with Paul Greengrass, *Spycatcher: The Candid Autobiography of a Senior Intelligence Officer* (Melbourne: William Heinemann Australia, 1988).

HOLT, HAROLD EDWARD (1908–1967). Harold Holt was a member of the Australian House of Representatives from 1935 to 1967, and Prime Minister of Australia in 1966–1967. He served under the leadership of Sir **Robert Menzies** (1894–1978) before being appointed by Menzies as his successor early in 1966. In 1983 a book was published that alleged Holt had been a Chinese intelligence **agent** since 1929.

Harold Holt was born in Sydney. At the age of six he was left in the care of his uncle and aunt in Canberra while his parents went to England. His parents divorced when he was 10 years old, and a year later he was sent to a private school in Melbourne, where he was a good sportsman and was made school prefect. He studied law at the University of Melbourne, and was a charming, handsome, impecunious undergraduate, one for the ladies, and always at the center of a fast life. He was a skilled orator and debater who advanced socialist ideas. He graduated in law in 1930, and undertook a commerce degree in the next year. He won a prize for a critical essay on socialism, and began writing articles for the Chinese consulate in Melbourne.

In 1983, the noted British author Anthony Grey published *The Prime Minister Was a Spy*. In the book he set out the information that had been given to him indicating Holt had spied for China for many years, beginning about 1929. The following account is based on that book.

In July 1929, Holt, aged 20, debated at the University of Melbourne on the value of trade with China; three months later he was paid for a copy of his views, and urged to write more by the Chinese Consul-General. By March 1931 Holt was receiving £100 sterling for each essay he presented to the Chinese consulate.

In March 1932 Holt established a law practice in Melbourne, joined the United Australia Party, and became a paid after-dinner speaker. He maintained intermittent contact with the Chinese consulate officials, and continued to write articles for them on the Australian viewpoint; in the articles he tended to take a socialist position.

In September 1935 Holt became a federal member of Parliament for the United Australia Party. In his parliamentary debates he supported the public ownership of major public utilities and services, constraints on private enterprise in the interests of the nation, and non-Communist attitudes.

At about this time Holt was becoming an **agent of influence** for the Chinese cause. He had the **code name** H. K. BORS, and was taught **tradecraft** during the next two years. He was given questions to raise in Parliament that, when answered, would help China better understand Australia's relations with the United States, its policies regarding the British navy and air force, and internal methods to be adopted in Australia to curb civil disturbances.

By 1940 Holt was a government minister. After the 1942 election, when his party lost power, he was to be a **sleeper** in his role as Chinese agent of influence. He learned that he would remain as sleeper until the Chinese government was stabilized after the civil war in China.

In 1946 Holt married Zara Fell (née Dickens) and cared for her three sons.

Holt's attitude to communism was always strongly negative, but he held that from 1950 Australia was an Asian nation, and he wanted a balance in the influx of immigrants from Asia and Europe.

In 1952 Holt's services were sought again for China. His political work required considerable international travel. While traveling, how was he to report regularly to his Chinese handler? He was to write extensive letters to his friends on what he did each day and what impressions he had of the leaders he met and the conferences he attended. The letters were typed with several carbon copies. An extra copy was made and sent to his handler.

The information in the letters was in a strange pattern; although the letters read as if they constituted a travel diary; discussions with international leaders, politicians, generals, bankers, and other important officials were accompanied by elaborately described theater visits, almost as if they were intended for show-business people rather than the folks at home. They contained much confidential information in the form—so it appeared—of a code related to room decor, clothing, menus, theater programs, and betting information on racehorses.

In this way Holt's alleged provision of secret information to the Chinese government continued well into the 1960s. One story is that on August 24, 1965, Prime Minister Robert Menzies informed his cabinet that Australia's commitment of troops to South Vietnam would be doubled. The decision took the cabinet by surprise. Immediately, the Australian government sent a secret coded message to the governments of South Vietnam, New Zealand, and the United States. Menzies said he would make a public announcement about the decision in two days, when the Australian Parliament met. But the next day, 24 hours before Menzies was to speak in Parliament, Australian newspapers, radio, and television reported Menzies's decision.

How did this happen? According to the information provided to Holt's biographer, Holt had left the cabinet meeting for 10 minutes immediately after Menzies had told them his news, and, from a public phone, informed his Chinese handler of Menzies's secret decision; the handler immediately informed Peking, and Peking leaked the information to foreign correspondents in South Vietnam. At the time, **ASIO** officials were certain that there had been a cabinet leak.

Holt became Australia's Prime Minister on January 26, 1966. For some months he was obviously anxious and under strain. In June 1966 he is reported to have stopped in San Francisco and disappeared for two days. During that time, so the story goes, he consulted a senior Chinese official, from whom he discovered that a safe escape route was available should he ever need one. Holt then visited U.S. President **Lyndon B. Johnson** and the Prime Minister of Great Britain before coming home. By October that year Holt had increased the number of Australians serving in the **Vietnam War** (1964–1973) to 8,000. In November 1966, following a visit to Australia from the U.S. President, Holt ran in an election and won handsomely.

In 1967 Holt faced many difficult political and personal problems, some of which were raised by his own colleagues. He seemed to be losing his grasp of procedural matters in Parliament. He could not conceal the strain he was under. In May 1967

ASIO delivered a file to his desk that indicated to him that he was suspected of having contacted Soviet secret agents. Further information brought up the code name H. K. BORS.

Holt met with his handler, claimed he was losing his grip, and stated that he wanted to give up the prime ministership and leave by the safe escape route promised to him the previous June with Chinese officials in San Francisco. In November 1967 he learned that a plan was in place, and that the first date available for departure would be December 17. That day, at 12:15 P.M., Holt defected with the aid of two Chinese frogmen who took him underwater to a Chinese submarine off the coast near his summer house.

The official and accepted account makes this story above seem utterly bizarre. On December 17, 1967, the official account goes, the seventeenth Prime Minister of Australia, Harold Holt, disappeared in the surf near his holiday home, Portsea. His body was not found; he was presumed to have drowned. Some people suggested he was shot, and others that he had committed suicide; in 1983 it was declared he had been the highest-placed spy the Communists had ever had in the West. This final thesis has been dismissed as bizarre, but never been investigated because, for one thing, a body has never been found, and in Victoria, where Holt disappeared, no inquest is possible without a body. On January 5, 1968, the Commonwealth of Australia Police reported that there was no indication that the disappearance of the Prime Minister was anything other than accidental.

In 2003 plans were announced to make it possible for a coroner's inquiry to be made into Holt's death.

See also HOLT HOAX

Sources: Anonymous, "Holt Family Denounces Book's Spy Claims," *The Australian*, November 21, 1983, p. 1; Darrich, Robert, "Ten Years Afterwards . . . Had Harold Holt Lost the Will to Live?" *The Bulletin*, December 24–31, 1977, pp. 36–41; Faligot, Roger, and Remi Kauffer, *The Chinese Secret Service* (London: Headline, 1989); Grey, Anthony, *The Prime Minister Was a Spy* (London: Hodder and Stoughton, 1983); Larkin, John, and Geoffrey Barker, *The Holt Report* (Melbourne: The Age, 1968); Rusbridger, James, *The Intelligence Game: The Illusions and Delusions of International Espionage* (London: Bodley Head, 1989).

HOLT HOAX (1983). In the 1930s, Harold Holt (1908–1967), a conservative politician during **World War II** who became Australia's Prime Minister in 1966–1967, believed that Australia's future lay with Asia, and that China would soon become the major power in the Pacific. This view was contrary to the prevailing attitudes among political leaders in the British Commonwealth. Holt disappeared in the surf at Portsea, south of Melbourne, on December 17, 1967, and his body was never recovered. One bizarre explanation for his disappearance was that he had been a spy for China, and had been whisked away to China after entering the surf.

In 1983, a noted British author, Anthony Grey, was given information from Chinese sources by a retired naval intelligence officer, and later copies of Holt's personal diaries, which led him to investigate the most unlikely suggestion that since 1929, Holt had been informing the Chinese governments, both Nationalist and Communist, about international affairs relating to the British Commonwealth and matters internal to Australia. In his book on the allegations, Grey showed that Holt was run by a Chinese **agent** in Australia who changed sides when the Communists defeated the Nationalists in 1946.

In 1966 Holt was made Prime Minister on the retirement of Sir **Robert Menzies** (1894–1978). Grey states that **ASIO** had doubts about Holt. Holt discovered this, and fearing for his safety, arranged to be taken to China. He went into the sea on December 17, 1967, and was helped by Chinese frogmen to board a submarine.

The book presenting this incredible tale aimed to force the Australian government to hold a Royal Commission of Inquiry into the allegation that the Prime Minister was a spy for China. On publication, the book was denounced, and Grey and his main source for the book were humiliated in many newspapers and on TV.

The book was made to look like a hoax very quickly. It was to appear first as several articles in *The Observer* (London), and a few days later, in Australia, was to be released in its entirety. The identity of the main source of the work was to be kept secret, and revealed later.

Unknown to the author, and in violation of his agreement with *The Observer*, copies of the book were sent secretly to Australia, where a few days before it was to be released, the work was ridiculed in *The Age* (Melbourne). Although many of the criticisms were unfounded, and many political commentators were available to denounce the book as a hoax—without having the opportunity to read it—the ridicule was so effective that a proper inquiry was never held, and the idea was spread that the author and the publisher had been hoaxed.

Had an official inquiry been conducted, it would have revealed many matters embarrassing to the Australian secret services, and their relations with U.S. and British colleagues, and would have damaged the reputations of several politicians and notables at the time of Holt's disappearance. The attack on the reputation of the author and his source was met with legal charges for defamation in which the two were successful.

Among the criticisms of the book were charges that most of the checkable facts were false; that the recall of facts of 30 years earlier is suspect; the major British source was indiscreet, and only briefly held his last position; that a claim about Holt's qualifications was false; that it was "far-fetched" to say Holt made an important phone call in only 10 minutes to his Melbourne contact after learning that Menzies had decided to increase the Australian forces in Vietnam; that because his travel diaries were written jointly with his wife, Zara, the suggestion that they were written in code is not convincing; that his private secretary denied that he disappeared for 48 hours in San Francisco in 1967; that ASIO would have caught Holt if he had been a spy; that there is an error in stating his age at a certain time in the story; that the author misspelled a word; that the author did not find out what happened to Holt after December 17, 1967; and, finally, that Holt could never have been a spy for the Chinese or gone to live in China because he did not like Chinese food!

Shortly after the first attack on the book in *The Age*, several of the checkable facts about Holt's activities at university—alleged by the early critics to be to be false— were found to be true.

See also HOLT, HAROLD

Sources: Anonymous, "China Denies Holt Spy Story," *The Australian* (Canberra), November 24, 1983, p. 2; Faligot, Roger, and Remi Kauffer, *The Chinese Secret Service* (London: Headline, 1989); Grey, Anthony, *The Prime Minister Was a Spy* (London: Hodder and Stoughton, 1983); Holt, Zara, *My Life and Harry* (Melbourne: The Herald and Weekly Times, 1968); Larkin, John, and Geoffrey Barker, *The Holt Report* (Melbourne: The Age, 1968); Rusbridger, James, *The Intelligence Game: The Illusions and Delusions of International*

Espionage (London: Bodley Head, 1989); Shepherd, Alex, "The Incredible Submarine: Book Review of Grey, Anthony (1983), The Prime Minister Was a Spy" *Australian Book Review* 61 (1984): 33–34.

HONEYTRAP OPERATIONS. A honeytrap is an operation aiming to recruit **agents** to the secret service with threats to expose their romantic or illicit sexual intimacies and thereby wreck reputations; it is also a means of getting intelligence on foreign nationals by using prostitutes instructed to inform on their customers. After the end of **World War II** the practice became so prevalent in occupied Europe that the U.S. government demanded its employees abroad inform their superiors of any romantic and sexually intimate relationship with a foreigner whose country posed an exceptional intelligence threat to the United States. Russia was such a country.

KGB officers were trained to instruct prostitutes to offer sex to foreigners in exchange for intelligence. Such KGB officers were usually colonels, and known as "uncles." They would instruct a prostitute to find out what was in a foreigner's suitcase, or go as far as maintaining a long-term relationship with the foreigner so as to trap him into counterintelligence work. Such women were known as "swallows," and were chosen for their youth and good looks. Many would do the work voluntarily, and some who felt guilty about this activity would rationalize their feelings by denying that they had studied their victims' papers or personal property closely, but merely looked for suspicious activities and items, which was a quite natural thing for Russians to do with strangers.

Although some KGB officials felt guilty about forcing women into the role of a swallow, they did not feel guilty as professional espionage agents. They simply split or dissociated their selves from their role. Also, KGB agents would rationalize the honeytrap by stating that the swallows felt they were serving their country, and that there were plenty of volunteers for the work.

The KGB would have women work the streets to entrap business visitors. Some of the women were criminals who could be blackmailed into honeytrap work for the police militia. Most of these women came from the provinces.

The KGB and the police officials would sometimes conflict over their turf, and over the prostitutes themselves. Some KGB would kill women if they did not cooperate.

Take the case of Monica. She is approached by a KGB officer after she has been seen in the company of a foreign businessman. The police call her and take her to a city hotel. There she is told that the Japanese, Germans, and Americans are enemies of Russia. Fearful that she might be sent back to her home in the provinces, she agrees to cooperate. A KGB controller picks her up, gives her a key to an apartment. The apartment has been bugged for KGB espionage operations. She feels very guilty. She picks up a German, takes him to the flat; there they talk about **NATO,** and what they say is recorded.

Many women were encouraged to form large groups and work the hotels where foreigners stayed. Most were good-looking, clever, patriotic women who were not paid, but were given presents for their work. The women had to do anything their clients wanted.

The women were sometimes in danger from their KGB controllers. After the swallows had entrapped their victims, their superiors would reckon that if the swallows were willing to sleep with the enemy, they should be expected to sleep with their bosses as well.

Some women were blackmailed by the KGB so that they would become swallows. Usually the KGB agent would threaten to bring suffering to a young woman's family if she did not inform on her victim/lover. When the lover left the town, often the swallow would turn to alcohol and other drugs for solace, and become deeply depressed. One woman lost her lover because the KGB threatened her family if she were to accept the man's marriage proposal. Later she was forced into regular prostitution.

Many swallows were murdered. At a major Moscow hotel about 20 attractive young women worked for the KGB, and seduced visiting businessmen. One group was rounded up, charged with being spies themselves; some were jailed and most were shot.

One notable swallow was an attractive actress who was often on the arm of **Josip Tito** (1892–1980). She was asked by the KGB to divulge intimacies but she would not do so; the Soviet agents threatened the lives of her family, but she continued to refuse; even after an attempt to murder her by poisoning, she still would not speak.

There were national differences between victims of the honeytrap. The Italians, being open and passionate, were regarded as easy prey; the Germans and Americans were not difficult to recruit with the honeytrap; the British provided some successful cases; but the Swedes, Danes, and especially the Dutch were the most difficult to recruit with the honeytrap.

The **Central Intelligence Agency (CIA)** tends to deny that it ever use the honeytrap for espionage; there is some evidence that the case of Vitaly Yurchenko refutes this denial, because he was entrapped by a woman and she later published the details.

In London **MI5** used the honeytrap. The venue was the Eve Club on Regent Street, where call girls were available to Soviet bloc businessmen and diplomats, The Eve Club was established from the time of Queen Elizabeth II's coronation in June 1953 to Valentine's Day 1994. It was closed because of high rents. The Eve Club was run by Helen Constantinescu, a Belgian refugee who told the British press she had literally hundreds of stories to tell about MI5's exploitation of her girls.

The French ambassador and the air attaché in Moscow from 1956 to 1968 were both seduced by swallows. The ambassador was beaten up by his swallow's bogus husband, a hard-working KGB officer. Both victims were photographed, and blackmail was planned. The air attaché committed suicide, while the ambassador was brought home to France to endure a short period of disgrace.

Men who are used as agents to seduce women, especially secretaries of political figures, are known as **Romeo spies.**

See also KEELER, CHRISTINE; LONETREE, CLAYTON; MILLER, RICHARD; MUNSINGER, GERDA; OGORODNIKOV, SVETLANA; OPERATION DEJEAN; RITCHIE, RHONA; STONEHOUSE, JOHN; SYMONDS, JOHN; VANUNU, MORDECAI; YURCHENKO, VITALY

Sources: Andrew, Christopher, and Oleg Gordievsky, *KGB: The Inside Story of Its Foreign Operations* (London: Hodder and Stoughton, 1990); Bower, Donald E., *Sex Espionage* (New York: Knightsbridge, 1990); Doran, Jamie, *Honeytrap* (London: Atlantic Celtic Films, 1997); Lewis, David, *Sexpionage: The Exploitation of Sex by Soviet Intelligence* (London: Heinrich Hanau, 1976); Mahoney, Harry T., and Marjorie L. Mahoney, *Biographic Dictionary of Espionage* (San Francisco: Austin & Winfield, 1998).

HORAKOVA, MILADA (1901–1950). Milada Horakova was Czechoslovakian spy who worked against the Soviet domination of her homeland.

Milada Horakova was born at Christmas in Prague, the daughter of pencil factory worker. Her mother was a housewife. As young woman during **World War I,** Horakova tended to wounded soldiers, and after her high school studies began a medical degree, but later changed to law. On graduation she began to work for the leader of the Czechoslovakian Women's Movement in 1923. Four years later she married an editor at Prague's radio station, and had daughter in 1933.

In March 1939 Horakova joined the Czechoslovakia underground resistance against the Nazi invaders. She was caught by the Nazis, gave false information to her interrogator, was tortured mercilessly, and sent to a prison near Dachau. When the war ended, American forces freed her and her husband, and she returned to Prague.

Horakova worked to organize the women's resistance to the Soviet invasion of her country, and helped establish the anti-Communist Women's Council. Her organization was penetrated by Soviet spies. She and her husband gave valuable intelligence to the United States until September 1949, when the **MGB** caught them. Again she was brutally interrogated. Her husband escaped, but she was tried for treason and hanged in June 1950.

Sources: Hoehling, A. A., *Women Who Spied* (New York: Dodd, Mead, 1967); Mahoney, M. H., *Women in Espionage* (Santa Barbara, CA: ABC-CLIO, 1993).

HOUGHTON, HARRY FREDERICK (1905–). Harry Houghton was born in Lincoln, England, where he went to school until he was 14; next he worked for two years before signing on for 12 years' service in the Royal Navy. In 1945 he quit the navy to work as a clerk for the Civil Service at the Portsmouth dockyard.

Houghton married, and was assigned to the naval attaché's office in the British embassy in Warsaw, where he entered the black market with some success. He met an attractive Polish woman who was pleased to offer herself to him for black market goods. After 15 months he was sent back to Great Britain, where he was given a responsible job with the Underwater Weapons Establishment at Portland in November 1952.

Houghton took a mistress, Ethel "Bunty" Gee (1915–), and his wife divorced him after 17 years of marriage.

Four years later a friend of his Polish girlfriend contacted Houghton with a plan to make money by exporting penicillin to Poland The scheme failed, and it was suggested he might sell information easily obtainable from his workplace. He agreed, and Konon Molody (1922–1970) became his case officer.

Houghton had little access to files he might sell, but Ethel Gee could get almost any information because she worked in the Records Office. She agreed to spy for Houghton, because he convinced her that the files were being made available to an American naval officer who needed them for a British ally. Molody used the name of Gordon Lonsdale, and also had the services of Morris and Lona Cohen, who were using the names Peter and Helen Kroger. The group constituted the Portland spy ring. Houghton was code-named SHAH; Ethel was ASYA.

They were exposed by the Polish defector Michal Goleniewski (fl. 1922–1964). In London, near the Old Vic Theatre, they were caught, and charged with espionage in February 1961. In 1962 Houghton and Ethel Gee were given 15 years in prison, but were released on parole on May 12, 1970, after nine years of exemplary conduct in prison. Molody had been exchanged for Greville Wynne, and the Krogers for Gerald Brooke.

Houghton and Ethel were married, and lived in Dorset. He published his autobiography in 1972.

See also COHEN, LEONTINA, AND COHEN, MORRIS; GEE, ELIZABETH ETHEL; GOLENIEWSKI, MICHAL; MOLODY, KONON

Sources: Andrew, Christopher, and Oleg Gordievsky, *KGB: The Inside Story of Its Foreign Operations from Lenin to Gorbachev* (London: Hodder and Stoughton, 1990); Andrew, Christopher, and Vasili Mitrokhin, *The Mitrokhin Archive: The KGB in Europe and the West* (London: Lane, 1999); Houghton, Harry, *Operation Portland: The Autobiography of a Spy* (London: Rupert Hart-Davis, 1972); Laffin, John, *Brassey's Book of Espionage* (London: Brassey's, 1996); Mahoney, Harry T., and Marjorie L. Mahoney, *Biographic Dictionary of Espionage* (San Francisco: Austin & Winfield, 1998); Rusbridger, James, *The Intelligence Game: The Illusions and Delusions of International Espionage* (London: Bodley Head, 1989); West, Nigel, and Oleg Tsarev, *The Crown Jewels: The British Secrets at the Heart of the KGB Archives* (New Haven, CT: Yale University Press, 1999).

HOWARD, EDWARD LEE (1951–). Edward Howard was the first **Central Intelligence Agency (CIA) agent** to escape from the United States and defect to the Soviet Union. He appears to have done so out of a profound sense of injustice at being unfairly dismissed from the CIA.

Howard was born in Alamogordo, New Mexico. His father was an air force sergeant who worked on various bases in the United States and abroad. While in Germany, Howard learned German, made friends, and became an altar boy. He lived in England in 1969 and attended boarding school.

On returning to the United States, Howard studied at the University of Texas, and in 1970 was completing extramural studies in Germany. In 1972 he graduated with a degree in business studies and joined the U.S. Peace Corps, after having been rejected by the CIA because he was too young. In 1975 he attended the American University in Washington, graduated in 1976, and married a woman he had met while in the Peace Corps.

After working successfully with several different firms, Howard managed to join the CIA. He was trained in 1981 at Camp Peary, the **Farm,** in **tradecraft,** and made it through to the elite **SE,** a CIA unit concerned with clandestine services.

Howard had a habit of consuming too much alcohol, and in 1981, being under pressure, sought medical help.

Howard was chosen to go to Moscow, where, after further training, both he and his wife would be spies. Howard worked for 15 months on the Soviet desk, saw much of the secret information involving U.S. agents, and was informed of the essential secrets of the CIA's operations in the **U.S.S.R.** Although Howard established several good covers for his Moscow assignment, he acquired all the skills needed to be able to use a position in the U.S. Foreign Service for his main cover by acquiring documents signed by the U.S. President that made him out to be a consular officer.

Howard's final step before going to Moscow was to take his last **polygraph test.** It was a disaster. The data were so bad, he was dismissed from the CIA. Howard was devastated and his colleagues were amazed.

Howard got a job as an economic analyst in Santa Fe, New Mexico. In October 1983 he came to Washington and, hurt by his dismissal from the CIA, sat outside the Soviet embassy, thinking of taking revenge for what had been done to him. Later, he said that he had considered going into the embassy and offering to give the Soviets what he knew about the CIA, but he could not go through with it. When he later admitted to sitting and contemplating the act, but not doing anything about it, others only half-believed him. In fact he did offer to serve the Soviets, and kept this secret.

On returning to Sante Fe, Howard was involved in a serious and violent brawl; in April 1984 he agreed to plead guilty to a charge of aggravated battery, was fined, and was put on probation for five years. This meant he could not leave the United States without permission.

In September 1984 Howard and his family went to Europe. A year later, a Soviet defector, Vitaly Yurchenko (1936–), informed the **Federal Bureau of Investigation (FBI)** that while in Europe, an ex-CIA employee, code-named ROBERT, had given the **KGB** classified documents and had been well paid. Howard denied ever being in Vienna during the 1984 trip.

In April 1985 Howard went secretly to Vienna, thereby violating his probation. He said he went to sell some unusual antiques. Later in 1985, when Vitaly Yurchenko defected and told the FBI about ROBERT—the spy whom the CIA had prepared for Moscow but never permitted to go—the FBI interrogated Howard and kept him under close surveillance. He always denied that he had approached the Soviets or that he had spied for them. But by this time he feared the FBI would find he had been abroad illegally. With his wife, Mary, he planned an escape, which was helped largely by the failure of the FBI's surveillance officers.

Howard flew to Copenhagen and then to Frankfurt, where for U.S.$2,000 he bought a new passport, and used it when he flew on to Helsinki. For nine months he traveled to Canada and Latin America. He got various jobs in Europe (e.g., he taught English and was chauffeur to a businessman). Also, he grew a beard. He phoned his wife in March 1986, and that June was in Vienna.

Shortly after Howard's escape his wife told the FBI that she now knew he had gone to Vienna in 1984, and been paid for classified documents. It appears that he probably did leave a note at the Soviet embassy in 1983; in 1984, probably in July, the Soviets had accepted him as a possible defector, funded his flight to Europe, and received valuable documents. His reward was money put into a Swiss bank account. The CIA found that it contained possibly U.S.$150,000. Also, his wife took the FBI to a small box of gold and money hidden in the desert near their home.

The U.S. Senate Intelligence Committee inquired into the Howard case; privately one of the members admitted that the committee would never find the truth, and observed that the CIA was limiting the information it was prepared to give. Inside the CIA at least two investigations were made.

In June 1986, after spending nine months traveling, Howard turned up at the Soviet embassy in Budapest. A week later he was sent to Moscow, where he was given an apartment, and a dacha on the city's outskirts. He found the KGB did not use polygraphs, much to his relief. Nineteen months later he and his wife were reunited in a Moscow guesthouse.

The consequences of his defection were disastrous for the CIA, whose head, William Casey (1913–1987), admitted at the time in a secret enquiry, "We screwed up."

Sources: Pincher, Chapman, *Traitors: The Anatomy of Treason* (New York: St. Martin's Press, 1987); Wise, David, *The Spy Who Got Away: The Inside Story of the CIA Agent Who Betrayed His Country* (London: Fontana/Collins, 1988).

I

IRANGATE/IRAN–CONTRA AFFAIR (1985–1989). The Iran–Contra Affair involved a secret deal between the United States and Iran that was handled in part by the **Central Intelligence Agency (CIA)** head, William Casey (1913–1987), who doggedly sought the release of a CIA hostage, William Buckley (1928–1985), among others. Casey did so with a secret deal that involved a U.S. Army lieutenant, Oliver North (1943–); a British citizen, Terry Waite; and others, and provided arms to the Iranians in return for the release of U.S. hostages taken during the civil war in Lebanon. The deal made a profit. With secret White House approval, the profit was used to fund the U.S.-backed Contras in Nicaragua, to whom U.S. Congress had banned legitimate funds. President **Ronald Reagan**'s (1911–2004) good name was involved, heads rolled in in the White House, and the scandal almost matched the **Watergate** scandal of 1974.

In 1979 the Sandinista National Liberation Front (FSLN), or Sandinistas, ended the dictatorship of the Somoza family in a revolution in Nicaragua. On May 4, 1983, President Reagan announced that the United States backed the Contras, a terrorist group of counterrevolutionaries, against the Marxist government of the Sandinistas. Previously the United States had been helping the Contras covertly with a flow of weapons. It became U.S. policy that the Sandinistas had betrayed their original revolutionary principles and ruled only with a gun.

Having established a reputation for a unexpectedly pluralistic political agenda by 1984, the Sandinistas held an election and got 67 percent of the vote. The United States refused to accept the outcome and instead continued its policy of supporting the Contras.

In April 1985 the U.S. Congress rejected President Reagan's request for support to the Contras. In June 1986, in The Hague, the World Court stated that President Reagan had broken international law by supporting the Contras.

Earlier, in Beirut, during the summer of 1984, the Shia supporters of Iran had captured a U.S. citizen, David Jacobsen; 18 months later, on November 2, 1986, he was freed following the intervention of Terry Waite, a representative of Great Britain's Archbishop of Canterbury. It was stated at the time that the United States had not been involved in the release, but a Beirut magazine reported that Lieutenant Oliver North, a member of the National Security Council staff, had made a deal with the Iranians and used Terry Waite as a pawn. The scandal to be known as "Irangate" had begun.

Late in November 1986, President Reagan admitted that for 18 months secret diplomacy had helped to free U.S. hostages and had involved a deal that provided small amounts of arms to the Iranians. However, it was known that the deal had produced a large profit and that the money was secretly given to the Contras. At the same time Admiral John Poindexter, the President's National Security Adviser, resigned, as did Oliver North, and President Reagan announced a review of the National Security Council, stating that he had not been fully informed that a deal had in fact been arranged. "Irangate" was well underway.

In January 1987, President Reagan expressed regret that there had been an arms-for-hostages deal. At the time, in Beirut, Terry Waite had disappeared while negotiating with Hezbollah, the "Party of God" militant supporters of the Iranian ruler, Ayatollah Khomeini (1902–1989). Was Terry Waite being an effective negotiator, or was he deeply tainted by the association he had inadvertently had with the CIA and Irangate?

In February 1987, an inquiry headed by Senator John Tower, the Tower Commission, investigated the Iran–Contra deal and suggested that President Reagan had made a mistake and should have monitored the operation more closely. It also criticized Donald T. Regan (1918–2003), the White House chief of staff, for allowing such chaos to take place in the White House, and Oliver North for concealing the facts about a scheme he had hatched.

In July 1987, John Poindexter told the U.S. Congress that it was he who had authorized the diversion of money made from the arms sale with Iran to the Contras. Also, he admitted that he had shredded a document, bearing President Reagan's signature, authorizing the Iran–Contra deal. Poindexter was convicted but later won an appeal on a technicality. Oliver North said he assumed, but did not know for certain, that President Reagan was aware of the deal. Afterward, North became a U.S. hero, regarded as a great patriot for, as his secretary said, going "above the written law." The U.S. Congress reported in November 1987 that the ultimate responsibility for the deceit and corruption in Irangate lay with President Reagan, and stressed that he should have known fully about the Iran–Contra deal.

In August 1987 the presidents of Costa Rica, El Salvador, Guatemala, Honduras, and Nicaragua signed an accord to declare an amnesty, restore freedom of the press, restore freedom of political association, hold internationally monitored elections, arrange a cease-fire with guerrilla forces, and stop rebels from using bases in one another's countries to mount cross-border attacks. They set November 7, 1987, as the date for these changes.

In May 1989 Oliver North, who had testified that he did not plan the Irangate scheme, but merely followed orders, was found guilty of three of the 12 counts with which he was charged.

Meanwhile, in the ensuing civil war 50,000 Nicaraguans died. By 1990, wearied by the dread of further war, the electorate voted for Violeta Chamorro, whom the

United States supported. The Sandinistas' leader, Daniel Ortega (1945–), gave way to the newly elected head of state, the first leader to do so in Nicaragua's history.

See also BUCKLEY ASSASSINATION; CASEY, WILLIAM JOSEPH

Sources: Campbell, Duncan, "Getting the Right Result: Nicaragua's Election Showed the U.S. Still Won't Allow a Free Vote," *The Guardian* (London), November 7, 2001, www.guardian.co.uk/comment/story; Godson, Roy, *Dirty Tricks or Trump Cards: U.S. Covert Action and Counterintelligence* (Washington, DC: Brassey's, 1995); Prados, John, *Presidents' Secret Wars: CIA and Pentagon Covert Operations from World War II Through Iranscam* (New York: William Morrow, 1986); Rositzke, Harry A., *CIA's Secret Operations: Espionage and Counterespionage and Covert Action* (Boulder, CO: Westview Press, 1988); Woodward, Bob, *Veil: The Secret Wars of the CIA, 1981–87* (New York: Simon & Schuster, 1987).

ISRAEL AND THE NUCLEAR WEAPONS CRISIS (1950–1998). Israel is the only nuclear power that refuses, for security reasons, to admit is has nuclear weapons; it will not allow international inspections. The Federation of American Scientists has concluded that Internet photographs of a secret Israeli reactor in the 36-square-mile site in the Negev Desert at Dimona show Israel could have produced enough plutonium for up to 200 nuclear weapons.

When Israel was founded in 1948, the director of its atomic energy research argued that nuclear energy should augment Israel's poor natural resources and its small military forces. In 1950 low-grade uranium had been found and heavy water production had begun. In 1952, Israel established its Atomic Energy Commission; it was secret and controlled by the Defense Ministry.

In 1953 Israel began developing nuclear weapons; in 1956, after the Suez crisis, when Israel occupied the Sinai Peninsula, the Russians threatened a nuclear attack on Israel if she did not withdraw.

In secret, France agreed to help Israel develop a nuclear deterrent; the United States had not helped France to obtain a nuclear bomb; so, through Israel, France believed it could access U.S. technology, especially heavy water. To strengthen their bargaining position with France, Israel could gently blackmail the French into cooperating as compensation for the Vichy French brutalities during **World War II** toward Jews, and France's use of former Nazi collaborators in its intelligence community.

The French experts helped build an Israeli reactor underground at Dimona in the Negev desert, near Beersheba. The Israelis said it was a manganese plant, or sometimes a textile plant, to conceal the nuclear complex. In 1956, **U-2 spy flights** identified it, and December 16, 1960, its presence was reported in the *New York Times*. The U.S. inspection teams observed some parts of the nuclear installation (1962–1969), which officially was to be used for peaceful purposes.

After 10 years the French–Israeli cooperation ended, and Israel sought to complete its nuclear program independently. Only the United States, the **U.S.S.R.**, the U.K., France, and China had uranium enrichment facilities. By the late 1960s Israel probably became the sixth nation to be able to make nuclear weapons. She got the heavy water needed from the United States, France, and Norway; and Operation PLUMBAT yielded the uranium. Various reports indicated that Israel had between two and 13 atomic bombs in 1967 and over 400 by 1997, with missile systems to deliver them. By 1974 Israel's **atomic bomb** was no secret, but Israel would not divulge the presence of nuclear weapons. In 1998 the Israeli nuclear military resources were openly discussed by Shimon Peres (1923–), who claimed the nuclear power was to be used only for peace.

See also OPERATION PLUMBAT; POLLARD, JONATHAN; VANUNU, MORDECAI
Sources: Anonymous, "Revealed: The Secrets of Israel's Nuclear Arsenal," *Sunday Times* (London), October 5, 1986, pp. 1, 4–5; Farr, Warner D., *The Third Temple's Holy of Holies: Israel's Nuclear Weapons* (Maxwell, AL: USAF Counterproliferation Center, Air War College, Air University, 1999); Toscano, Louis, *Triple Cross: Israel, the Atomic Bomb and the Man Who Spilled the Secrets* (New York: Carol Publishing Group, 1990); Whitaker, Brian, and Richard Norton-Taylor, "Israeli Nuclear Site Revealed," *Guardian Weekly*, August 31, 2000, p. 4.

IVANOV, EUGENE Y. M. (1926–1994). Eugene Yevgeny M. Ivanov was an assistant naval attaché and lieutenant commander stationed in London at the Russian embassy (1960–1963). He became involved in the Profumo Affair (1963), a political scandal named after the British politician **John Profumo** (1915–).

Eugene Ivanov arrived in London on March 27, 1960, to take up his duties as a **GRU** officer. His English was quite competent. In January he met and lunched with Stephen Ward (1912–1963), a portraitist, osteopath, and committed Communist sympathizer, whose friend, the editor of the *Daily Telegraph*, wanted Ward to go to Moscow to sketch **Nikita Khrushchev** (1894–1971) for his newspaper.

Ivanov and Ward became friends. On at least one occasion Ivanov slept with Christine Keeler (1942–), a British sex worker to whom he had been introduced by Ward. That one *certain* occasion was on the night of the day after a poolside party at Cliveden, Lord's Astor's retreat, when Keeler first met John Profumo, Secretary for War in the British cabinet. Others suggest Keeler and Ivanov were lovers more than once. Keeler herself claimed in her memoirs, and earlier to Chapman Pincher (1984), that she slept with him only once.

Their affair may have been part of a plan by Ward, working with **MI5**, to trap Ivanov and blackmail him into defecting to the British. Another, less naïve, plan was perhaps that Ward, under instructions from the **Kremlin**, was to entrap John Profumo. Christine Keeler asserts that this was the case, and that Ward was either controlling or working with Ivanov to this end. Ward was given small sums of money for documents delivered to Ivanov at least once by Keeler. Ward encouraged Keeler to have an affair with Profumo, which she did until October 1961. It appears that Ivanov may have been instructed to use his relations with Keeler and Ward to find out when certain atomic warheads would be delivered to West Germany. Keeler wrote that she had been asked to spy, through pillow talk, on Profumo and find the date for delivery of those arms. In the Denning Report, an inquiry into the scandal, and in the then Prime Minister's memoirs, the idea that Ivanov sought help from Christine Keeler in this way was discounted.

In April 1962 Ward suggested to the head of Britain's Foreign Office that Ivanov could be helpful in a discussion of U.K.–Soviet interests. When MI5 learned this, it warned the Foreign Office that Ivanov was a GRU spy. In October 1962, at the height of the **Cuban missile crisis**, Ward again tried to have Ivanov used to recommend that the crisis be solved with a summit conference. Nothing came of this. In late January 1963, seven days after Christine Keeler had signed a contract with a British Sunday paper to tell her story—someone had attempted to kill her in December 1962—Ivanov left Britain, or, as Keeler would write 40 years later, "escaped" home to Moscow.

Why Ivanov left is not yet clear, although MI5 knew a week beforehand that he was to leave. When he left, it seemed to the head of MI5 that the Profumo Affair no longer had any security interest. On the other hand, others argue that Ivanov's departure could have indicated that his intelligence functions were most important. His diplomatic status meant he could not have been prosecuted in Great Britain, and all he did was seek information about weapons from the United States, which was not a crime. But he could have been questioned; because of that his superiors were probably concerned, and bundled him out of England as fast as possible.

Later a false trail of Ivanov's activities was laid, probably to confuse the **Federal Bureau of Investigation (FBI)**. A Russian **agent** informed the FBI that he had met Ivanov, saying he had boasted of placing a hidden microphone in Keeler's bedroom. MI5 found this could not have been so; the same source told the FBI that it was not the **KGB** but the French intelligence service that had engineered the Profumo Affair. This was either more **disinformation** or mindless gossip.

Shortly before he died, Ivanov met Keeler in Moscow, and told her that long ago, when they had been together, he had felt guilty, embarrassed, and ashamed of his affair with her, and that when his wife learned that he had betrayed her, she left him.

In Russia, Ivanov was awarded the Order of Lenin. He never remarried, and, according to Christine Keeler, lived a sad, lonely life in Moscow.

See also KEELER, CHRISTINE; WARD, STEPHEN

Sources: Bower, Tom, *The Perfect English Spy: Sir Dick White and the Secret War 1935–90* (London: Heinemann, 1995); Keeler, Christine, *The Truth at Last: My Story* (London: Sidgwick & Jackson, 2000); Pincher, Chapman, *Too Secret Too Long* (London: Sidgwick & Jackson, 1984); West, Nigel, *The Circus: MI5 Operations 1945–1972* (New York: Stein and Day, 1983).

IVANOV, VALERI (1948–). Valeri Ivanov was a Russian **agent** who tried to establish a close relationship with David Combe, an ambitious **Australian Labor Party** member who wanted to advance his career as a political lobbyist. In April 1983 **ASIO** informed the Australian government that the relationship between Ivanov and Combe posed a threat to Australia's national security, and Ivanov was expelled from Australia immediately.

Source: Marr, David, *The Ivanov Trail* (Melbourne: Thomas Nelson, 1984).

J

JOHN, OTTO (fl. 1939–1997). Otto John defected from West to East Germany in July 1954 and returned to West Germany in December 1955; even today it is a mystery as to why and how this happened.

Otto John was a lawyer for the German airline Lufthansa. In 1939 he associated with the chief of German intelligence, who saw John's travel to Lisbon and Madrid—the capitals of two neutral countries during **World War II**—as a useful means of keeping in touch with various nations. One of the links was through an American reporter who was familiar with the U.S. president.

In 1942 and 1943 John was in Lisbon concerning himself, as he always claimed, with anti-Nazi resistance. But at the time Kim Philby (1912–1988) suspected that John was probably under Gestapo control. In 1944, after the July 20 plot to kill Hitler failed, John escaped to Lisbon, went to England, was interned briefly, and by December 1944 had become a British collaborator. He worked in psychological propaganda and made radio broadcasts. Later he worked on the problems of war crimes, and went to live in the Federal Republic of Germany (FRG).

John befriended a playboy gynecologist, Wolfgang Wohlgemuth, a pseudo-Communist. According to Soviet records, Wohlgemuth suggested the **KGB** could meet with John, and in July 1954—the tenth anniversary of the failed attempt to kill Hitler—John rode in Wohlgemuth's car into East Berlin, and was taken to a **safe house** near Karlshorst, the KGB headquarters. The Soviets always insisted that the trip was voluntary.

Another account suggests that John was plied with alcohol until drunk, and largely due to encouragement by Wolfgang Wohlgemuth—he was either a guide or an abductor—staggered into East Berlin. In an effort to recruit him, the Soviets drugged his coffee, and when he woke 30 hours later, heard a faked Western broadcast saying that he had defected to the German Democratic Republic. Three weeks later John had a press interview in which he said he wanted to have a united Germany; that West Germany's leader, Konrad Adenauer (1876–1967), was a committed separatist and tolerated too many ex-Nazis in government; and that he, Otto John, had crossed the border voluntarily. At the time John was the first head of the Federal Office for the Protection of the Constitution, West Germany's counterintelligence agency (**BfV**). British and American intelligence officers were in shock at his defection.

For almost a year John toured East Germany, stating publicly his wish for a unified Germany, free of all Nazi taint. On December 15, 1955, in the late afternoon he suddenly appeared in West Berlin. A friend had helped him elude his East German bodyguards and take a plane to Cologne. He was interrogated, arrested as a traitor, and jailed for four years. He spent only 18 months in prison.

John had been the British favorite to head the BfV, but when he defected and returned, the organization was all but useless.

On entering prison, John tried to clear his name. His story was that Wohlgemuth had drugged and kidnapped him, had taken him to East Berlin, and under duress he had been forced to talk with the KGB, but had given away no secrets.

Was he drugged and kidnaped and taken unwillingly to East Germany? Or was he a propagandist promoting anti-Nazism and a unified Germany? The mystery remains. In December 1995 it was decided by the highest court in Germany that there was insufficient new evidence to alter the original verdict. He died on March 26, 1997.

Sources: Aldrich, Richard J., *The Hidden Hand: Britain, America and Cold War Secret Intelligence* (New York: Overlook Press, 2002); Andrew, Christopher, and Vasili Mitrokhin, *The Mitrokhin Archive: The KGB in Europe and the West* (London: Lane, 1999); Frischauer, Willi, *The Man Who Came Back: The Story of Otto John* (London: Frederick Mullet, 1958); John, Otto, *Twice Through the Lines* (New York: Harper & Row, 1972); Knightley, Phillip, *Philby: The Life and Views of the KGB Masterspy* (London: Pan, 1988); Murphy, David E., Sergei A. Kondrashev, and George Bailey, *Battleground Berlin: CIA vs KGB in the Cold War* (New Haven, CT: Yale University Press, 1997).

JOHNSON, ROBERT LEE (fl. 1923–1972). Robert Lee Johnson spied for the Soviets from the mid-1950s until 1964, and is reputed to have been the most damaging of U.S. Army spies in the early stages of the **Cold War**.

Johnson was stationed in Berlin, where in 1953 he sought political asylum for himself and his fiancée, Hedy, a prostitute. The Soviets convinced him to stay as an agent-in-place in the West, and draw wages from each employer, which he did. He found homosexuals among his military acquaintances who were prepared to spy for the Soviets.

Johnson's own work for the **KGB** was of little significance. With Hedy he left Europe for Las Vegas, where he hoped to be a successful gambler and writer. Instead he became an alcoholic, and Hedy returned to prostitution.

In January 1959 the KGB contacted Johnson through a homosexual acquaintance he had made in Europe, and he began work for the KGB again, this time on a U.S. Army post as a guard for the missile sites. For the KGB he photographed plans and other documents; next he was posted to France, where he worked as guard at the Armed Forces Courier Center at Orly Airport, and was able to get valuable classified material in 1961. For that information **Nikita Khrushchev** (1894–1971) rewarded him with money, a holiday in Monte Carlo, and a high rank in the Red Army (1962).

After supplying bags of documents on U.S. codes and secret locations of nuclear warheads in Europe, Johnson was transferred again. He disappeared in 1964, and was eventually caught in 1965 with information from the defector Yuri Nosenko (fl. 1927–1987). Johnson was jailed for 25 years and died in prison.

See also NOSENKO, YURI

Sources: Andrew, Christopher, and Oleg Gordievsky, *KGB: The Inside Story of Its Foreign Operations from Lenin to Gorbachev* (London: Hodder and Stoughton, 1990); Andrew, Christopher, and Vasili Mitrokhin, *The Mitrokhin Archive: The KGB in Europe and the West* (London: Lane, 1999); Barron, John, "The Sergeant Who Opened the Door," *Reader's Digest,* January 1974, pp. 187–194; Barron, John, *KGB: The Secret Work of Soviet Agents* (New York: Reader's Digest Press, 1974); Campbell, Kenneth J., "Robert L. Johnson: The Army Johnnie Walker," *American Intelligence Journal* 11 (1990): 5–10; Mahoney, Harry T., and Marjorie L. Mahoney, *Biographic Dictionary of Espionage* (San Francisco: Austin & Winfield, 1998); Mangold, Tom, *Cold Warrior: James Jesus Angleton (1917–87), the CIA Master Spy Hunter* (New York: Simon & Schuster, 1991); Pincher, Chapman, *Traitors: The Anatomy of Treason* (New York: St. Martin's Press, 1987).

JORDAN MURDER (1967). The apparent, and official, suicide of the director-general of the Zionist Joint Distribution Committee for Jewish Relief.

In the evening of August 16, not long after the Six-Day War in the Middle East (June 5–10, 1967), Charles Jordan (fl. 1967), director-general of the Zionist Joint Distribution Committee for Jewish Relief, left his hotel in Prague to buy cigarettes.

Jordan was abducted by four Egyptian guerrillas, in the presence of Czechoslovakian security officers, who suspected Jordan of spying, and was taken to the Egyptian embassy. The abductors were followed by the security officers, who, with added forces, surrounded the embassy. About 3 A.M., Jordan's body was dropped into the Vltava River. In the embassy, Jordan had been injected with scopolamine, a sedative and alleged "truth drug," and interrogated before being murdered.

Next day Vladimir Kouchy, Secretary of the Central Committee of the Czechoslovakian Communist Party, told the Egyptian ambassador to have the murderers leave Czechoslovakia. Three days later three Palestinian students left for the German Democratic Republic to continue their studies. After the postmortem, the Czech government announced that Jordan had committed suicide by drowning.

The Americans were outraged, and asked why Jordan had traveled thousands of miles merely to drown himself in an obscure European river. An independent Swiss pathologist, Ernst Harmeier, repeated the postmortem and found the drug in Jordan's pancreas. Later, in Switzerland, Harmeier appeared to have lain down in the snow near his car and froze to death.

It seems the Russian-dominated Czech government, not wishing to spoil relations with Egypt or engender sympathy for the Jews, decided that the deaths of Charles Jordan and of the independent examiner of Jordan's body were suicides.

Source: Frolik, Joseph, *The Frolik Defection* (London: Leo Cooper, 1975).

K

KADAR, JANOS (1912–1989). Janos Kadar was an alleged spy in Hungary who suffered, and eventually benefited, from the many changes of policy in both Russia and Hungary during the **Cold War**.

In Hungary, Kadar joined the illegal Communist Party in 1932, served the Hungarian underground during **World War II,** and, when the party took over Hungary after the war, sided with those in opposition to the interests of the underground supporters. He became the Minister for Home Affairs. He was a follower of Laszlo Radjk, and avoided the early Stalinist purges in Hungary by persuading Radjk to admit support for **Josip Tito** (1892–1980). However, in 1951 Kadar was found guilty of treason, Titoism, and spying; he was sentenced to four years in prison. After much torture he was released in 1954, and eventually worked his way back into power, becoming a Politburo member of the Hungarian Workers' Party in July 1956.

Kadar became First Secretary in late October 1956; however, he went to the Ukraine secretly; formed a government in opposition to that in power in Hungary; and after the Soviet invasion of Hungary early in November, and its crushing of the October revolution, took control of Hungary's government and presided over 30 years of reform. He was deposed in 1988 after having initially followed Soviet policies and later allowing some liberal reforms.

Sources: Kovrig, B., *Communism in Hungary from Kun to Kadar* (Stanford, CA: Hoover Institution Press, 1979); Smith, Joseph, and Simon Davis, *Historical Dictionary of the Cold War* (New York: Scarecrow Press, 2000).

KAL 007 TRAGEDY (1983). The KAL 007 (Korean Air Lines flight 007) tragedy was presumed in the United States to be a brutal attack by the Soviets on an unarmed passenger aircraft flying from the United States to Asia; the Soviets saw it as a U.S. spy plane. The difference in viewpoint made for an international incident that threatened world peace and escalated public irrationalities during the **Cold War**.

KAL 007 crashed, killing 269 passengers, during the night of August 31, 1983, on its flight from New York to Seoul, South Korea.

During refueling at Anchorage, Alaska, the plane's captain, Chun Byung-in, a veteran of the **Korean War** (1950–1953), took on more fuel than needed. The flight began to drift off course as if its highly sophisticated navigation system were badly programmed, or simply turned off. The flight was hundreds of miles from its planned flight path, but the captain reported that it was on track.

Navigation computers should have caught the error. It was highly unlikely that all the radar navigation systems would separately fail to note the flight's route. The plane flew over dangerous regions.

Cold War tension was high: the Soviet Pacific Fleet had grown enormously, and included several large submarines, each of which carried 80 nuclear warheads. There were 2,400 Soviet combat aircraft in the region, and nearly half a million soldiers along the Chinese border; in addition, America's Seventh Fleet patrolled the western Pacific with four large aircraft carriers. They were supported by U.S. naval bases in the Aleutian Islands, Japan, South Korea, and several Pacific islands. The latest F-16 bombers were readily available.

Earlier in 1983 large Russian naval exercises had been held in the area, and the commander in chief of the U.S. Pacific forces was convinced the Pacific was where a confrontation with Russia was likely. Both sides used various surveillance systems: ground listening stations, reconnaissance ships, planes, and satellites. On the night of August 31, over the Kamchatka Peninsula, KAL 007 passed near U.S. surveillance aircraft that were there to monitor new Soviet missiles due to be fired that night.

One explanation for the crash is that the Soviet radar controllers confused the two aircraft, and as the civilian airliner, KAL 007, crossed Soviet airspace, they scrambled their defenses. Others have suggested that the civilian flight was on a secret **CIA** operation. Unanswered questions include: Was the flight off course due to many coincidental navigational errors? Was the pilot taking a shortcut? If so, why didn't he take care not to go into Russian airspace? Had the Soviets jammed the navigation system deliberately? Why did KAL 007 not respond to the Soviet plane's wing-waggling and firing of tracers? The Russian pilot thought the plane was a civilian jet, so why shoot it down?

Russia thought the flight was on an espionage operation that aimed to provoke the Soviets to reveal their secret new defense systems. This has not been proved conclusively. A Russian investigation concluded, over nine years after the tragedy, that it was an accident caused by incompetent Soviet operators.

Another report says, contrary to official reports, that KAL 007 was not shot down over Sakhalin, but was destroyed off Honshu, nearly an hour later than the report claimed.

Both sides in the Cold War became ever more suspicious of the other; President **Ronald Reagan** exploited the anti-Soviet sentiment growing in the United States to increase military spending.

A psychiatric analysis was made of the public and political outrage over the tragic "accident" by Luhrmann (1984).

Sources: Brun, Michel, *Incident at Sakhalin: The True Mission of Flight 007* (New York: Four Worlds Eight Windows, 1995); Dallin, Alexander, *Black Box: KAL 007 and the Superpowers* (Berkeley: University of California Press, 1985); Johnson, Richard William, *Shootdown: The Verdict on KAL 007* (London: Chatto and Windus, 1986); Luhrmann, George W., "The KAL Shootdown: A Symbol in the Search for Evil," *Journal of Psychohistory* 12 (1984): 79–120; Richelson, Jeffrey T., *A Century of Spies: Intelligence in the Twentieth Century* (New York: Oxford University Press, 1995).

KAMPILES, WILLIAM PETER (1954–). William Kampiles was discontented with the work he did for the **Central Intelligence Agency (CIA),** stole some of its valuable manuals, sold them to the **GRU,** bragged about his success to a friend, and was caught by the **Federal Bureau of Investigation (FBI).**

Raised in Greek-speaking family, William Kampiles graduated from Indiana University (1976) and, aged 23, was made a junior watch officer at Washington's CIA operations in March 1977. He found the work tedious. In a single room he sat through boring, long shifts, frequently sought a transfer, and every time was unsuccessful. He felt that he did not seem to be what the CIA wanted, and was disappointed that his fluent Greek was unlikely to bring him an overseas posting he hoped for.

After eight months Kampiles resigned. In November 1977 he took with him a letter showing how dissatisfied the CIA was with his performance and a copy of a manual for a spying satellite, KH-11.

In late February 1978, on a trip to Greece, Kampiles went into the Russian embassy in Athens, and told an official he could provided the embassy with valuable information on U.S. satellites for a long time. The next day when he met a military attaché (GRU), he showed him a few pages from the manual on the KH-11. The pages comprised a table of contents, a picture of what the satellite looked like, and a summary of the handbook. For the complete manual he wanted U.S.$10,000. He got U.S.$3,000.

The manual described characteristics of the satellite's system, its limitations, and its capabilities and illustrated the quality of its photos and the processing of photographs. With the manual at hand, the Soviets could arrange to have their aircraft hidden on the ground when the U.S. satellite was overhead, or put into place effective camouflage that would make the satellite photos useless.

The Russians were interested in more information from Kampiles, primarily on America's own military, not American information on the Russian military. Shortly after his return home from Athens, Kampiles bragged to a CIA friend that he'd been to Greece and fooled the Russians into giving him $3,000. The FBI was informed, and he finally admitted to selling the KH-11 manual. In 1978 he received a sentence of 40 years in jail.

Sources: Laffin, John, *Brassey's Book of Espionage* (London: Brassey's, 1996); Pincher, Chapman, *Traitors: The Anatomy of Treason* (New York: St. Martin's Press, 1987); Richelson, Jeffrey T., *A Century of Spies: Intelligence in the Twentieth Century* (New York: Oxford University Press, 1995).

KATKOV ASSASSINATION (1985). In 1985 the Islamic Jihad assassinated a popular **KGB** officer, one of four Soviet hostages they had recently taken; the KGB quickly mounted a successful operation to get the assassins to release the remaining hostages.

In September 1985 the Islamic Jihad took hostage three Russian diplomats—Arkadi Katkov, Oleg Spirine, and Valeri Kornev—and the embassy doctor, Nikolai Versky. This was the first time that Russians had been kidnapped in the 10 years of the civil war in Lebanon.

The reason for this change of policy was that Russia was supporting Syria, and Syria was attacking the besieged Sunni militia in Tripoli. The implication was that if the Russians were to cease their support of Syria, the three diplomats and the doctor would be freed. In the belief that the Syrians would solve the problem, the Soviets ignored the kidnappers' demands.

Early in October, near the destroyed sports stadium in Beirut, Katkov's corpse was found. He had been one of the KGB's favored officers. The KGB found a family member of one of the people they thought had abducted the Russians. He was tortured, and his penis was delivered to the Hezbollah with the threat that all the kidnappers' families would endure similar treatment unless the hostages were released. At the same time nearly all Soviet personnel in Beirut were evacuated. The hostages were returned promptly.

Source: West, Nigel, *Seven Spies Who Changed the World* (London: Secker & Warburg, 1991).

KATYN MASSACRE (1940–1990). The Katyn Massacre was a Russian operation by the **NKVD** during **World War II** that became an important secret during the **Cold War** and was not made public until the Cold War had ended.

In April 1940, when Russia and Nazi Germany were allies, over 14,000 Polish officers and 7,000 landowners in Poland were captured and massacred in the Katyn Forest near Smolensk in the western **U.S.S.R.**

After World War II many Poles hated deeply what the Soviets had done, and it was rumored that it had been done under a secret order by **Josef Stalin** (1879–1953).

The secret massacre became known gradually. In April 1943 the Polish leader told the British Prime Minister that he had evidence of the massacre; at the same time the Germans broadcast that they had found the graves, accused the Soviets of the massacre, and proposed an international inquiry. The Nazis had invaded in the middle of 1941, so Russia was on the side of the Western Allies by April 1943.

The Soviets first declared that the executions had been performed on construction workers, and that it was the Germans who had committed the massacre; second, that the 1943 announcement by the Germans showed that the Poles were now collaborating with the Nazis, and for that reason Russia had ended diplomatic relations with the Polish government in exile led by General Wladyskaw Sikorski (1881–1943) in London, and had turned to the Communist Polish government in exile, led by Boleslaw Bierut (1892–1956). The breach in relations between Russia and Poland also led to the agreement—achieved largely by Winston Churchill (1874–1965)—at the **Tehran conference (1943)** that the postwar Soviet–Polish border would revert to the so-called **Curzon Line** of 1920.

The details of the massacre remained a secret until 1988, when clear evidence appeared that indicated what might have happened. Mikhail Gorbachev (1931–) announced a commission of Polish and Soviet historians would study the massacre as part of the new **glasnost** policy of the Soviet Union; in April 1990 the Soviets admitted to the massacre, and in May 1990 Gorbachev apologized to the Polish premier; later Boris Yeltsin (1931–) gave Lech Walesa (1943–) a copy of a document signed by Stalin ordering the NKVD execution.

Sources: Andrew, Christopher, and Oleg Gordievsky, *KGB: The Inside Story of Its Foreign Operations from Lenin to Gorbachev* (London: Hodder and Stoughton, 1990); Andrew, Christopher, and Vasili Mitrokhin, *The Mitrokhin Archive: The KGB in Europe and the West* (London: Lane, 1999); Arms, Thomas S., *Encyclopedia of the Cold War* (New York: Facts on File, 1994).

KEELER, CHRISTINE (1942–). Christine Keeler was a British sex worker, model, and showgirl who allegedly was involved in espionage operations for the

British, and whose exploits were partly responsible for bringing down the Conservative British Prime Minister **Harold Macmillan** (1894–1986) in October 1963, and the Conservative government a year later by scandalizing the reputation of the nation's Secretary of State for War, **John Profumo** (1915–).

Christine Keeler was born into a broken, poor family; at the age of four she was raised in a railway carriage at Wraybury, Berkshire. Her father had left her mother, and she lived with a man for 30 years before marrying him. Christine was unhappy at school, but, as would become known later, was highly intelligent and a capable sportswoman. At the age of 15 she went to work as an office worker, loathed it, became ill, and left home to live with relatives; she left them in 1957 to live in London.

Keeler had a beautiful body, and got work as a dancer at the Cabaret Club. The club had 20,000 members on the books; she was expected to dance for whoever wanted her, and sleep with wealthy customers whom she liked and trusted. Among the visitors were members of royalty in Britain and from abroad. She was raped, became pregnant, and induced an abortion. In June 1959 she met Stephen Ward (1912–1963), an osteopath and portraitist, who charmed her into becoming his housemate; he became her confidant, father figure, and guide. She claimed they were never lovers; others claim she was his mistress.

Keeler lived in Stephen Ward's London apartment for several years, and was supported by him and her sex work, as well as club dancing and a little modeling. Ward introduced her to many highly regarded members of British society, and into work at their orgies, where she became well-known as an attractive sex partner. She occasionally found a man she loved. As a procurer who planned sexual orgies, and a notable portraitist, Stephen Ward was, so she claimed, in a fine position to exploit the sexual needs of foreign diplomats whom **MI5** may have wanted to blackmail into being informants or **defectors-in-place.**

Stephen Ward, a Communist sympathizer who may have become a Communist in 1956, befriended a Russian naval attaché, who was a **GRU** officer, at the Soviet embassy, Eugene Ivanov (1926–1994). In July 1961, Ward brought Christine to a party of Lord Astor's friends and introduced her to Britain's Secretary of State for War, John Profumo. She became Profumo's lover, and the sex partner of Ivanov. He and Stephen Ward required Keeler to see whether or not she could get secret military information from John Profumo.

MI5 warned Profumo, Ward, Keeler, and Ivanov. Profumo promptly ended his affair with Keeler in October 1961. Keeler told Ward that Profumo had been warned. Ward then offered to help MI5 to persuade the naval attaché to defect. MI5 did not trust Ward. Ward continued his efforts as a **double agent** and **agent of influence.**

Keeler was also the mistress of a Jamaican drug dealer who was arrested and tried after attacking Stephen Ward's home. At the trial she told of her sexual relations with Profumo, the Russian attaché, and the Jamaican; that Profumo had been foolish to have her as a sex partner; and that Stephen Ward was indiscreet in his efforts to procure sex workers for people high in British society.

In 1963 the opposition spokesman for security suggested in the British House of Commons that Keeler's affair with Profumo could have affected the nation's security. Profumo had denied all allegations made against him, but the damage to his reputation had been great by June 1963, and he resigned. In July, Ward was tried for living off earnings of prostitutes, including Christine Keeler. Ward had no adequate defense, and committed suicide in August 1963. Keeler was briefly imprisoned on related charges.

Keeler wrote of her career, and a film, *Scandal* (1989), was made about her and others in Britain at the time. After her autobiography was published and the film was made, many aspects of her trial were questioned. Years later, she published another autobiography that mentions many figures in Britain's **Cold War** intelligence community.

After the scandal Keeler changed her name in an effort to get rid of the identity that dogged her, but she failed. She worked under a different name in a laundry business, and in a school, until her true identity became known. In her life after the Profumo affair she also remained in the sex industry and knew intimately, among others, such notables as Douglas Fairbanks, Jr., Peter Lawford, and Ringo Starr. For a short time she earned money from telling her story to newspapers, and making public appearances.

In her colorful memoirs Keeler tells all: she worked daily on cryptic crosswords; played bridge with Yehudi Menuhin; was threatened by Lord Denning (1899–1999), whose inquiries provided an official view of the Profumo affair; learned of threats to the life of President **John F. Kennedy** (1917–1963) *before* he was assassinated; saw photos of double agents she would not identify; admitted she was a spy for Stephen Ward and Roger Hollis (1905–1973); married unsuccessfully; had two children; and gave up men in 1978.

Keeler's later memoirs are a sad catalog of information that is difficult to check. Also, in them she maintains that Sir Roger Hollis was without doubt, and contrary to **Margaret Thatcher's** (1925–) assertions to the House of Commons, a Soviet agent who worked with Stephen Ward, her erstwhile mentor and procurer.

See also HOLLIS, ROGER; IVANOV, EUGENE; WARD, STEPHEN

Sources: Keeler, Christine, with Douglas Thompson, *The Truth at Last: My Story* (London: Sidgwick & Jackson, 2000); Mahoney, M. H., *Women in Espionage* (Santa Barbara, CA: ABC-CLIO, 1993); Pincher, Chapman, *Too Secret Too Long* (London: Sidgwick & Jackson, 1984).

KEENAN, HELEN (1945–). Working in London, Helen Keenan passed secret documents to a Rhodesian businessman; later her efforts influenced the review of the British government's requirements for vetting its employees in secret government work.

Helen Keenan was born into a middle-class family in Canada. In 1967 she was a highly regarded employee in the office of Great Britain's Prime Minister. Her work centered on interesting current affairs, but she quit unexpectedly because, so she said, the work was boring. **MI5** monitored her activities and found that she had befriended Norman Blackburn, a Rhodesian businessman, who wanted to know the U.K. government policy on Rhodesia's future. She stole for him copies of secret documents from British cabinet meetings. MI5 found Blackburn was a spy for South Africa's Bureau of State Security. He admitted that he had received cabinet material from Helen Keenan, and had given it to Rhodesian intelligence officers based in Ireland.

In July 1967, Keenan was tried, found guilty, and given six months in prison; Norman Blackburn was sentenced to five years' imprisonment.

Sources: Laffin, John, *Brassey's Book of Espionage* (London: Brassey's, 1996); Leigh, David, *The Wilson Plot* (New York: Pantheon, 1988); Mahoney, M. H., *Women in Espionage* (Santa Barbara, CA: ABC-CLIO, 1993).

KENNAN, GEORGE FROST (1904–). George F. Kennan was a notable American diplomat and adviser on secret operations whose ideas were largely the origin of the U.S. foreign policy of **containment** in the early stages of the **Cold War.**

Born into a middle-class family in Milwaukee, Wisconsin, George Kennan was educated at St. John's Military Academy in Delafield. As a teenager he was much impressed by the writings of F. Scott Fitzgerald (1896–1940), who depicted the cynicism, gaiety, dissipation, and confusion among young Americans after **World War I** and during the Jazz Age, especially in his *This Side of Paradise* (1920). He decided to go, as Fitzgerald had, to Princeton University. Little traveled, Kennan was periodically depressed and socially diffident, but intellectually gifted. He entered the U.S. Foreign Service and served in Germany (1928), Estonia, Latvia, Lithuania, and other "listening posts" for information on the Soviet Union. He marred a Norwegian, Annelise Soerensen, in 1931.

Kennan became an expert on Russia. From 1933 to 1935 he was posted to the reopened embassy in Moscow, accompanying Ambassador William C. Bullitt. Kennan observed the Soviet show trials. Between 1935 and 1939 he served in Vienna, Moscow, and Prague.

Kennan became self-confident and developed a clear personal view toward totalitarian regimes. After two years in the U.S. embassy in Berlin at the beginning of **World War II** he was interned by the Nazis at Bad Neuheim, was repatriated in May 1942, was sent to Lisbon, and later acted as counselor of the U.S. delegation to the European Advisory Commission to prepare for the Allies' policy in Europe. He became the senior career diplomat in Moscow in the late 1940s, and gave a public speech on V-E Day in Moscow. He worked with Franklin D. Roosevelt (1882–1945), Harry S. Truman (1884–1972), and **Josef Stalin** (1879–1953), Dean Acheson (1893–1971), and George C. Marshall (1880–1959).

Kennan disagreed with the friendly approach to the **U.S.S.R.** of the Secretary of State, James F. Byrnes (1879–1972), and on February 22, 1946, he sent the "long telegram" or "Kennan telegram," as it is often known. It advocated taking a hard line against the U.S.S.R. and found a good reception in Washington. The policy recommended was a long-term, patient, firm, and vigilant containment of Russian expansive tendencies; it also cataloged the eternally mournful and suspicious character of Russians and the dangers of Stalin's regime, born as it was in revolution, a form of social change that Kennan thought most offensive to human civilization.

After being read widely by political commentators in Washington, the contents of Kennan's telegram appeared in *Foreign Affairs* under the pseudonym of "X," and titled "The Sources of Soviet Conduct."

The policy of containment toward the U.S.S.R. never lost favor among ambitious U.S. politicians who were deeply opposed to communism, and today many believe it was the unrelenting pursuit of this policy that ended the Cold War in the West's favor.

However acceptable the policy of containment was to politicians, Kennan's ideas were criticized strongly by the notable political columnist Walter Lippman (1889–1974) in 1947, in a series of articles in the *New York Herald Tribune*. Lippmann wrote that he believed that containment would make conflict with the Soviets worse, and fuel what he called the "Cold War" and never reduce international tension.

In 1952 Kennan was ambassador to the Soviet Union, but became persona non grata after making unflattering comments about Stalin, and comparing the U.S.S.R.

to Nazi Germany, during a short visit to Berlin. He was eased out of the high office he had achieved so quickly, and retired from the U.S. Foreign Service in July 1953. He became a professor of history for almost 20 years before being appointed by President **John F. Kennedy** (1917–1963) to be ambassador to Yugoslavia in the 1960s.

During his academic career Kennan gave the Reith Lectures for the BBC and recommended the withdrawal of troops from Germany, arguing that until the United States stopped pushing the Russians against a closed door, it would not be known if they would be prepared to go through an open one. He returned to academic life, retired in 1974, and furthered his prolific scholarly career at Princeton's Institute for Advanced Studies.

Kennan might have been conservative, but he was not a hawk in his international policies; he opposed the formation of **NATO**, objected to the United States entering the **Vietnam War**, was greatly displeased at the **arms race**, and did not want President **Ronald Reagan**'s (1911–2004) buildup of arms. On the other hand, he doubted that political independence was appropriate for Afghanistan; he doubted the soundness of U.S. policy to intervene for humanitarian reasons in Somalia, Bosnia, and Kosovo; he was not a strong supporter of U.S. policy that insisted on advancing human rights in foreign countries. Better, he thought, to avoid trying to solve the world's problems, unless they were of an immediate threat to the United States.

At the end of his career Kennan was opposed to U.S. expansionism. He lacked any confidence in massive nations because their leaders, he observed, lose realistic contact with their peoples, and for this reason he advocated the decentralization of the United States.

See also LIPPMANN, WALTER

Sources: Gaddis, John L., *The United States and the Origins of the Cold War, 1941–1947* (New York: Columbia University Press, 1972); Kennan, George F., *Memoirs: 1925–1950* (Boston: Atlantic/Little, Brown, 1967); Kennan, George F., and John Lukacs, *George F. Kennan and the Origins of Containment, 1944–1946* (Columbia: University of Missouri Press, 1997); Lemann, Nicholas, "The Provocateur," *The New Yorker,* November 13, 2000, pp. 94–95, 97–98, 100; Lippmann, Walter, *The Cold War: A Study in U.S. Foreign Policy* (New York: Harper, 1947; New York: Harper & Row, 1972); Smith, Joseph, and Simon Davis, *Historical Dictionary of the Cold War* (New York: Scarecrow Press, 2000); Walker, Martin, *The Cold War: A History* (New York: Henry Holt, 1993).

KENNEDY ASSASSINATION AND THE KGB (1964–1974). The **KGB** used the Kennedy assassination (1963) to further its program of **active measures** designed to discredit the United States. The active measure involving the Kennedy assassination was the perpetration of a conspiracy theory that assumed Kennedy had been assassinated by a group of racist, fascist industrialists in the U.S. oil industry. Another view was that **John F. Kennedy**'s (1917–1963) death was a successful KGB assassination, but this was roundly denied by all but Anatoli Golitsyn (1926–).

The KGB not only interpreted and assessed intelligence, but also aimed to change world situations more or less violently. "Active measures" were the KGB's more or less violent means of doing this; they used conspiracy theories, well supported by lies, **disinformation,** and propaganda, to discredit and undermine the reputation of their "main adversary," the United States. The KGB used the 1963 Kennedy assassination to promote a **Cold War** conspiracy theory that discredited the United States generally, and its political economy in particular. This active measure lasted longer than other KGB distortions of political reality.

The accepted evidence was that President John F. Kennedy died November 22, 1963; he was shot by Lee Harvey Oswald (1939–1963), who was caught and, while in custody, was murdered publicly by Jack Ruby (1911–1967).

The KGB conspiracy theory was as follows. In December 1963, shortly after the assassination, the KGB reported having learned from Polish informants and a U.S. industrialist that Kennedy's assassination had been plotted and executed by H. L. Hunt and two racist colleagues, all three of whom were fascist oil magnates. At the time Hunt enjoyed a reputation for trumpeting wild statements about who was a Communist in America, and on his list was President Kennedy.

The KGB asserted that shortly before the assassination, Jack Ruby, a close acquaintance of Hunt, had offered Lee Harvey Oswald a large sum of money to kill the President. The well-planned scheme looked like a failure when Oswald was caught and claimed to be innocent. He appeared ready to tell how he had been made the fall guy for the President's murder. So, discovering this, at his first opportunity Ruby shot Oswald to prevent the truth about the conspiracy from becoming known.

The KGB conspiracy theory refined some features of the main story. First, Hunt's cabal had chosen Oswald so as to deflect public attention away from itself, because he had seemed once to have held Communist sympathies. Oswald had recently spent time living and working in the Soviet Union. Second, the KGB had been embarrassed by Oswald's apparent defection from the United States to the Soviets, and then from the Soviets to the United States, between 1961 and 1962. During that time the KGB had suspected Oswald first of being a **Central Intelligence Agency (CIA) agent**, and later of being an unstable character. The KGB was happy to be rid of him. He became a further embarrassment to the KGB when, on his return to the United States, he wrote to get Soviet permission to work underground against the government of the United States by joining the **CPUSA**. By that time the KGB had concluded that Oswald was probably a **Federal Bureau of Investigation (FBI)** agent. This remarkably strained pattern of second-guessing and double-thinking was conveniently contained by the KGB assertion that Oswald's murder was an essential part of H. L. Hunt's plot.

When the **Warren Commission** (1964) concluded that, on balance, Lee Harvey Oswald had acted alone in the murder of John F. Kennedy, the KGB fueled the conspiracy theory by supporting a well-established view among U.S. citizens that the President had been assassinated not by a deranged, lone killer but by a shady group of Americans with powerful support from a political force originating from America's military–industrial interests.

In support of this development a KGB agent in New York, the publisher Carlo A. Marzani, was paid well to publish *Oswald: Assassin or Fall Guy?* (1964). The book's thesis was a conspiracy theory: the U.S. "military–industrial complex," which **Dwight D. Eisenhower** (1890–1969) had identified in the final days of his presidency, was led by H. L. Hunt, and plotted Kennedy's death because the young President sought a test-ban treaty, curtailment of U.S.-supported Latin American militias, and an end to the Cold War. This policy would weaken the military–industrial complex. In this version of the conspiracy, Lee Harvey Oswald was expendable, an insignificant agent of the U.S. secret services, and could be conveniently murdered when necessary and without loss. The book went unnoticed because of the great public attention given to the Warren Commission's report. Also, the author was thought to be biased because he was both a German and a Communist.

The KGB then turned its attention toward an American author who, like many others, found it hard to accept the conclusion that a deranged, lone assassin had killed John F. Kennedy. Mark Lane published *Rush to Judgment* (1966). Although the New York Soviet **residency** never contacted Mark Lane, it arranged for his travel and research funds to be augmented with U.S.$1,500. His book, like early conspiracy theses, argued that high-level U.S. government and industrial complicity lay behind the death of John F. Kennedy.

Over the next five or so years the KGB believed that this conspiracy theory was a great benefit to the Soviet cause, and they took many opportunities to augment it with disinformation suggesting that the CIA had conspired in the assassination of the President. The KGB pointed to E. Howard Hunt, a **Watergate** conspirator with CIA connections, confusing him with H. L. Hunt; and it forged a letter, long thought to be genuine by high U.S. authorities, that gave the false impression that shortly before Kennedy's assassination, Lee Harvey Oswald and E. Howard Hunt met. The disinformation was not successful, and, to add more confusion to the tangle of deceptions, the KGB announced that the CIA had plotted to undermine the KGB's efforts to bring forth the truth!

This wildly confusing disinformation ended, partly, when E. Howard Hunt complained that he felt many U.S. citizens believed he had been a party to Kennedy's assassination.

Finally, a scandal arose that centered on high authorities who had in 1964 withheld information from the Warren Commission; this scandal combined with the Watergate scandal (1974), which accused the CIA of playing a role in misleading the U.S. public about the President.

So, between 1964 and 1974 the KGB could argue that however shadowed and distorted its evidence, U.S. capitalists had hired Lee Harvey Oswald to murder John F. Kennedy, and then murdered Oswald to keep him quiet, and that in a hidden way the CIA had been clearly involved.

See also OSWALD, LEE HARVEY

Sources: Andrew, Christopher, and Vasili Mitrokhin, *The Mitrokhin Archive: The KGB in Europe and the West* (London: Lane, 1999); Goldberg, Robert, *Enemies Within—The Culture of Conspiracy in Modern America* (New Haven CT: Yale University Press, 2001); Joesten, Joachim, *Oswald: Assassin or Fall Guy?* (New York: Marzani & Munsell, 1964); Lane, Mark, *Rush to Judgment* (New York: Holt, Rinehart and Winston, 1966); Mailer, Norman, *Oswald's Tale: An American Mystery* (New York: Random House, 1995); Mangold, Tom, *Cold Warrior: James Jesus Angleton, the CIA Master Spy Hunter* (New York: Simon & Schuster, 1991).

KILIM AFFAIR (1984). A little-known but embarrassing fiasco for **ASIS** and the Australian government in 1984, involving the recruitment of a Russian spy or an Australian **agent.**

Early in 1984, ASIS sought to recruit a member of the Soviet embassy staff in Bangkok, Thailand. On April 6, the Soviet embassy called a press conference to state that Ron Ford, counselor at the Australian embassy, had, in league with the **Central Intelligence Agency (CIA),** offered Alexandre Kilim, a Soviet official, money and the choice of living in Australia or the United States if he provided ASIS with secret Russian documents.

The Australian government replied immediately that in fact Kilim had tried to cultivate a Third Secretary in the Australian embassy, Paul Bernard; and following

Kilim's request for information, the embassy had decided that Ron Ford, senior to Bernard, must take his place at a lunch, and warn the Russians that their approaches were not accepted. The Australian government also denied any connection with any security agency in Bangkok, which was an unusual assertion, given the well-known fact that ASIS, the CIA, and **MI6** had a well-established special relationship in most of the world's capitals.

Unsourced information indicated that Kilim was about to accept the ASIS offer, but the **KGB** sensed this, and set up the public conference to trap ASIS, give it bad publicity, and reveal its agents. Since it is an important rule that Australian ministerial approval has to be given to ASIS before it tries to recruit agents from inside a foreign service, the Kilim fiasco embarrassed not only ASIS but also the Australian government in Canberra.

Source: Toohey, Brian, and Brian Pinwell, *Oyster: The Story of the Australian Secret Intelligence Services* (Port Melbourne: William Heinemann Australia, 1989).

KIM SUIM (1924–1950). Kim Suim spied for the Chinese Communists against the United States before the outbreak of the **Korean War** (1950–1953).

Kim Suim was born into an impoverished Korean peasant family, and educated by U.S. missionaries. In 1942 she met a Communist agitator; he seduced her, and from him she learned some Communist beliefs and basic **tradecraft**. He got her work in the dental clinic of a missionary college, and she attended evening classes in communism.

After **World War II,** Kim worked under cover for the Communists as a hostess to American troops who were in Korea eradicating the last of the Japanese militia. She worked also as a prostitute for high-ranking U.S. officers. Next, she became a telephone operator at the Korean headquarters of the U.S. military, and from monitoring military phone calls collected useful information for the Chinese Communists.

A U.S. colonel fell in love with Kim, and from him she learned much about relations between the U.S. President and America's military chiefs. Kim was then given a position in U.S. counterintelligence, and had access to top-secret reports on investigations into Chinese Communists and intelligence work in Korea. In the American colonel's house Kim established her transmitter, receiver, and other espionage equipment.

The American colonel returned to the United States without Kim, so her Communist case officer assigned her next to the Korean President, Syngman Rhee (1875–1965).

Before she could begin her project, Kim was arrested by the intelligence services in South Korea. They had known of her espionage activities for years. She was tried in June 1950 for many crimes against the Republic of Korea. Thirty days after the Korean War began in June 1950, she was executed by firing squad at Kimpo Airport.

Sources: Mahoney, M. H., *Women in Espionage* (Santa Barbara, CA: ABC-CLIO, 1993); Singer, Kurt, *Spy Stories from Asia* (New York: Wilfred Funk, 1955).

KLUGMANN, NORMAN JOHN "JAMES" (1912–1977). James Klugmann was a Soviet **agent** in Britain from the time he was recruited in 1937 to the beginning of the **Cold War**. He helped recruit people who were drawn to the Soviet cause; passed information to the Soviets, especially on problems in the **Balkan states,** and was a staunch supporter of the Communist Party of Great Britain.

James Klugmann, a Jew whose prosperous family lived in the Hampstead district of London, entered Trinity College, Cambridge, on a modern languages scholarship from Gresham's School, as did Donald Maclean (1913–1983). Klugmann was remarkably clever and charming, with a deep and interesting command of politics. Early in his youth he announced he was a Marxist, and that he had taken up the Communist cause to annoy the authorities at his old school. During holidays he was often seen with Donald Maclean in pubs and cinemas.

In the middle of 1933 Klugmann met Guy Burgess (1911–1963), and through him got to know Anthony Blunt (1907–1983). Klugmann introduced Maclean to Burgess. He also set himself the task of recruiting people to the Communist cause and the Cambridge Union Socialist Society, which was dominated by a Marxist core. In 1937 Klugmann introduced John Cairncross to **Arnold Deutsch** (1904–1942).

In February 1942 Klugmann was assigned to the **SOE** in Cairo. Fluent in Serbo-Croatian, he was most useful in briefing Allied officers who were to be assigned to operations in Yugoslavia. Also Klugmann informed the **NKGB** of Britain's secret operations and policy for Yugoslavia. In his position he was able to advance the interests of **Josip Tito** (1892–1980), and Tito's conversations, indicating Klugmann had done so, were later recorded by **MI5** spies who had penetrated the British headquarters of the British Communist Party.

In the middle of 1945 Klugmann was with Tito's military mission in Yugoslavia. After the hostilites he was removed from any position of influence, and went back to his career as an active Communist. Later he would be a member of the British Communist Party's Political Committee, and in 1968 he published the history of the party. Apart from his wartime experience Klugmann was not a valuable spy for Russia because he did not have access to secrets after the war.

Later, John Cairncross said that Klugmann had been his recruiter, and wanted him, now he was no longer part of the intelligence community, to indicate what he had done for the Soviets before the Cold War. Cairncross believed if Klugmann were to do so, then he (Cairncross) would be able to return to Britain from his self-imposed exile without being charged for his past espionage. Klugmann treated the suggestion with contempt, and this was one reason Cairncross spent the rest of his life outside Britain.

Sources: Andrew, Christopher, and Oleg Gordievsky, *KGB: The Inside Story of Its Foreign Operations from Lenin to Gorbachev* (London: Hodder and Stoughton, 1990); Andrew, Christopher, and Vasili Mitrokhin, *The Mitrokhin Archive: The KGB in Europe and the West* (London: Lane, 1999); Cairncross, John, *The Enigma Spy: An Autobiography. The Story of a Man Who Changed the Course of World War Two* (London: Century, 1997); Klugmann, James, *History of the Communist Party of Great Britian* (London: Lawrence and Wishart, 1968); Martin, David, "James Klugmann, SOE-Cairo and the Mihailovich Deception," in David Charters and Maurice Tugwell, eds., *Deception in East–West Relations* (London: Pergamon-Brassey's, 1990); Pincher, Chapman, *Traitors: The Anatomy of Treason* (New York: St. Martin's Press, 1987); West, Nigel, *Seven Spies Who Changed the World* (London: Secker & Warburg, 1991).

KOENIG, ROBERTA (1939–). Roberta Koenig was an East German spy who was a **sleeper** in West Germany.

Koenig was born in Dresden, Germany. In 1967 she was pregnant and wanted an **abortion,** an illegal act in East Germany at the time. Her doctor was an East

German police informant. Some weeks after the abortion, an East German intelligence officer asked her to spy for East Germany. Because she had no choice, she agreed.

Koenig's task was to learn the customs of West German women well enough to be able to pass herself off as coming from West Germany, and with this skill get a position in the West German Ministry of Defense. After taking several jobs to acquire an intimate familiarity with the office methods used in the West, she succeeded in getting the position.

To indicate to her intermediary that the reports on the Ministry of Defense were available, she would place a mark on a certain tree in a local park, then go to lunch nearby at her favorite restaurant. In the women's lavatory at the restaurant she would leave the reports for the intermediary. After lunch, she would return to the park to see if there was a mark on another tree, to indicate that the intermediary had collected the material from the **dead drop** in the lavatory. The intermediary would take the material to her case officer.

Koenig's procedures were effective until the West German security police noted how regularly she would go to lunch in the same restaurant, and then return to the park to look at the trees once more. She and her case officer were arrested; he was sentenced to five years in prison, and she to four.

Sources: Altavilla, Enrico, *The Art of Spying* (Englewood Cliffs, NJ: Prentice-Hall, 1967); Mahoney, M. H., *Women in Espionage* (Santa Barbara, CA: ABC-CLIO, 1993).

KOMER, ROBERT WILLIAM (1922–2000). Komer was noted for the effort he put into the village pacification scheme, Operation PHOENIX, supported by President **Lyndon B. Johnson** (1908–1973) during the **Vietnam War.**

Robert Komer lived in Arlington, Virginia. He was born in Chicago, raised in St. Louis, and educated at Harvard University, where he earned a degree in business administration.

During **World War II,** Komer was a lieutenant in army intelligence in Europe and was awarded the Bronze Star. One of the first to join the **Central Intelligence Agency (CIA)** in 1947, he analyzed and interpreted data for recommendations on problems in the Middle East, and became the expert on that area for the National Security Council staff in the White House. Also he provided background advice for the negotiations between the Dutch and the Indonesians over the latter's control of West Irian.

In March 1966, Komer was used by the White House as a troubleshooter in Vietnam, and his brash and abrasive style was valuable in getting the White House staff to understand and accept the village pacification program for winning the war. He wanted a solution to the problem of how the military and the civilians in the war could cooperate.

A hard-driving army man and CIA veteran, Komer was sent to Saigon in 1967 to run the pacification program. The assignment, close to President Johnson's heart, was to parallel the strictly military effort of the United States. "He was about the best thing that had happened to the Vietnam War (1964–73) at that date," former CIA director William Colby (1920–1996) wrote in his 1978 memoirs.

Komer's work for **CORDS** during his tenure in Vietnam included modernizing and preparing South Vietnamese territorial forces, and repairing the destruction left by the enemy's **Tet Offensive** (1968).

In much commentary on Vietnam, CORDS has been associated with one of the most controversial programs of the war. In addition to winning popular loyalty to the United States and its South Vietnamese ally, officials wished also to root out the **Viet Cong** loyalists. A secret plan for this, Operation PHOENIX, was put into effect after Komer had left, and questions were later raised about whether assassination was or was not among its tactics.

During President Jimmy Carter's (1924–) administration, Komer helped frame policy in the **Pentagon** as an Undersecretary of Defense.

See also COLBY, WILLIAM; OPERATION PHOENIX

Sources: Colby, William, with Peter Forbath, *Honorable Men: My Life in the CIA* (New York: Simon & Schuster, 1978); Weil, Robert, "Obituary: Robert W. Komer: CIA Agent, 1922–9/4/2000," *The Age*, April 13, 2001, p. 7.

KOPATZKY, ALEKSANDR ("SASHA") GRIGORYEVICH (1923–1981).

Kopatzky was a **double agent** who probably was more inclined to serve the Soviets than the West. His nickname was confused by the **FBI** with the **code name** of a much sought-after double agent.

Aleksandr ("Sasha") Grigoryevich Kopatzky was born in Suroch, Bryansk Oblast, or, as he once said, he was born in 1922 in Kiev. In August 1941 he was a Russian intelligence officer. The Germans captured him in 1943, and, while he was recovering from injury, persuaded him to join German intelligence.

Early in 1945 Kopatzky served the anti-Soviet Russian Army of Liberation with the German Wehrmacht as it fought against the Red Army. Imprisoned after hostilities in the former Dachau concentration camp, Kopatzky was asked to work for the American–German Intelligence Unit that had been established under the former Wehrmacht intelligence head in the East, Reinhard Gehlen (1902–1979) in 1946.

Two years later Kopatzky married the daughter of a former SS officer, and in 1949 visited the Soviet military center in Baden-Baden. He was taken in secret to East Berlin, and from then on, undertook espionage for the Soviets. He penetrated an anti-Soviet immigrants' organization in Munich that was linked with the **Central Intelligence Agency (CIA)**. He was recruited into the CIA in 1951.

Moscow Center code-named Kopatzky ERWIN, HERBERT, and later RICHARD, and augmented his CIA salary generously. In one operation he personally arranged for an Estonian CIA **agent** to be handed over to Soviet intelligence, and for 10 years endangered other CIA intelligence operations in Germany.

Kopatzky was rewarded well with money and gold watches. He worked at the CIA's West Berlin station, and sought women sex workers to become CIA agents and spy on Soviet soldiers. This work gave him many chances to sabotage CIA operations, to identify many U.S. intelligence agents and East German agents, and to mislead the CIA as to who was and was not an agent working for Russia. Once he organized the defection of a fraud who worked for the Voice of America.

Kopatzky's name was changed to Igor Orlov to conceal his identity after charges of drunken driving, and to make it easier for him to get American citizenship. Three years later his CIA cover was blown in Berlin, so he was shipped to Washington for more training, and returned to operations in Austria.

In the 1960s the CIA suspected Kopatzky of being a Soviet double agent; and early in 1961 he was put under close investigation. He appeared to quit espionage, and started a gallery for framing pictures in Alexandria, Virginia.

In 1965 the **Federal Bureau of Investigation (FBI)** was searching for secure evidence to convict Kopatzky. He was observed entering Washington's Soviet embassy. Apparently the Soviet plan was to make a hero of him in Moscow, like Rudolph Abel (1903–1971), but his wife would not leave America.

The FBI never had any secure evidence for conviction, and when given a good lead by Anatoli Golitsyn (1926–), it incorrectly assumed that Orlov was code-named SASHA; however, that was merely his nickname.

In 1978 the **KGB** ceased communicating with Kopatzky. He died in 1982.

While she was watching an adaptation of a Le Carré novel on TV, Kopatzky's wife suspected that her husband had married her to deepen his cover as a spy.

Ten years later his widow, who ran Gallery Orlov in Washington, considered the gallery to be an espionage writers' haven. Many tourists visit today with that in mind.

Sources: Andrew, Christopher, and Vasili Mitrokhin, *The Mitrokhin Archive: The KGB in Europe and the West* (London: Lane, 1999); Murphy, David E., Sergei A. Kondrashev, and George Bailey, *Battleground Berlin: CIA vs KGB in the Cold War* (New Haven, CT: Yale University Press, 1997); Wise, David, *Molehunt: The Secret Search for Traitors in the Shattered CIA* (New York: Random House, 1992).

KRÖTENSCHIELD, BORIS MIKHAILOVICH (fl. 1910–1957).

Boris Mikhailovich Krötenschield, also known as Krotov and code-amed KRETCHIN, was a workaholic who was noted for being an energetic, talented, and efficient Soviet controller of the Magnificent Five—Kim Philby (1912–1988), Donald Maclean (1913–1983), Guy Burgess (1911–1963), John Cairncross (1913–1995), and Anthony Blunt (1907–1983)—from late 1944 to late 1947.

Boris Krötenschield was in England when the **SIS**, which had established its Section IX for the examination of Soviet and Communist activities, expanded to consolidate work on Soviet espionage and subversion under Kim Philby's guidance. In the countryside near London, Krötenschield would collect bags full of Foreign Office documents delivered by Guy Burgess.

It was Anthony Blunt who warned Krötenschield that **MI5** had placed listening devices in the British Communist Party's headquarters in London; and he had the pleasure of informing John Cairncross that for the delivery of ULTRA decrypts he had been awarded the **Order of the Red Banner**. The award was held, as a matter of course, by the Soviets for safekeeping.

In 1945 Krötenschield noticed Blunt was under considerable stress while providing thousands of documents for the Soviets. After the end of **World War II**, Blunt was given permission by the Soviets to leave MI5, which he did in November 1945, for five to ten years. Once he had secured an academic post, in which demands on him were much less, he became composed, found life easier, and could continue his efforts for Russia.

Krötenschield was Jew, and this later militated against his deserved promotion in the **KGB**.

See also CAIRNCROSS, JOHN

Sources: Andrew, Christopher, and Oleg Gordievsky, *KGB: The Inside Story of Its Foreign Operations* (London: Hodder and Stoughton, 1990); Andrew, Christopher, and Vasili Mitrokhin, *The Mitrokhin Archive: The KGB in Europe and the West* (London: Lane, 1999); Weinstein, Allen, and Alexander Vassiliev, *The Haunted Wood: Soviet Espionage in America—The Stalin Era* (New York: Random House, 1999).

KUCZYNSKI, JUERGEN (fl. 1905–1945). Juergen Kuczynski was born in Germany, the elder brother of Sonia Kuczynski (fl. 1907–1992). He became a dedicated Communist. Like other Jews who were dedicated to communism, and appalled by Hitler's anti-Semitic policies, he used his cover for pro-Communist work. He joined Germany's Communist Party in 1930, was recruited into the **GRU**, and in 1936 under cover as a Jewish refugee, worked in Britain, supplying Moscow with economic intelligence and helping other Soviet **agents.**

In exile in the United Kingdom, Kuczynski maintained his membership in the German Socialist Democratic Party, and was interned in January 1940 for three months; on his release he made friends with the Soviet ambassador, who controlled four of the Soviets' Magnificent Five.

In 1941 Kuczynski was approached by Klaus Fuchs (1911–1988), and recruited him to Soviet espionage. He gave the headquarters of the **OSS** a list of seven Soviet secret **agents** in Britain who were suited to fight in anti-Nazi operations in Germany. Also he worked for the OSS in evaluating the impact of bombing on German industry, and was made a lieutenant colonel in the U.S. Army while sending much information to Moscow.

In November 1945, Kuczynski returned to Germany to help establish a Communist state.

See also FUCHS, EMIL JULIUS KLAUS; KUCZYNSKI, URSULA RUTH

Sources: Mahoney, Harry T., and Marjorie L. Mahoney, *Biographic Dictionary of Espionage* (San Francisco: Austin & Winfield, 1998); Pincher, Chapman, *Traitors: The Anatomy of Treason* (New York: St. Martin's Press, 1987); Werner, Ruth, *Sonya's Report* (London: Chatto and Windus, 1991).

KUCZYNSKI, URSULA RUTH (fl. 1907–1992). Ursula Ruth Kuczynski was also known as Sonya or Sonia, and code-named SONIA and SONYA; she also used the names Ruth Werner, AZ, Ruth Beurton, and Ursula Beurton. Her life was devoted to communism in Europe and Asia.

Kuczynski, born in Berlin, the daughter of Rene Kuczynski, a famous German refugee who once taught at Oxford University. She came from a middle-class Jewish family and followed the Communist cause that her father espoused; at the age of 17, in 1924, she led the propaganda arm of the Communist Party in Germany.

With her father and brother Kuczynski worked in the United States during the late 1920s for the **GRU** while employed in a New York bookshop. In 1929 she returned Germany, married her childhood sweetheart, Rudolf Hamburger, an architect, and went to Shanghai, where they both were Soviet **agents.**

In Shanghai, Kuczynski worked for the Soviet agent Richard Sorge (1895–1944), recruiting agents and writing as AZ. She became Sorge's secret lover. She returned to Moscow for training, and afterward she and her husband were assigned to work in Manchuria under cover as a bookseller for an American firm. In 1935 she and husband went to Britain, where her father was teaching at the London School of Economics.

In 1937 Kuczynski was awarded the **Order of the Red Banner** in Moscow for her Shanghai work, and was sent in September 1938 to establish the GRU unit known as the **Lucy Ring** in Switzerland. She and her husband separated.

Her sister recruited Alexander Foote (1905–1956) to Sonia's network, and he came to live with her. Leon Charles Beurton joined the network in August 1939.

Immediately after the **Ribbentrop–Molotov Pact**, late in August 1939, Kuczynski denounced her work for Russia publicly, dissociated herself from the **U.S.S.R.**, and went into deep cover to improve her work for the GRU. At its direction she divorced her husband and married Leon Charles Beurton, so as to get a British passport.

Early in 1941 Kuczynski and her children went to Britain, unaware that the children's nurse, bitterly upset at being left without anyone to care for, had earlier denounced her as a Soviet spy to the British. Living safely in Britain, Kuczynski played the role of a persecuted Jew named Mrs. Brewer while she put together a network of agents and acquired a transmitter to keep in touch with Moscow.

Beurton joined Kuczynski in July 1942 and was drafted into the army. Juergen Kuczynski (fl. 1905–1945), her brother, helped her to recruit agents, including Klaus Fuchs (1911–1988). While in Britain she informed Moscow that it was British policy not to give military aid to the Soviet Union. MI5 found her, apparently while the agency was seeking information on her. Shortly afterward she and husband went to East Berlin, and in 1977 she published *Sonia's Report* in East Germany. She was made an honorary colonel in the Red Army. In 1992 she was living in East Germany.

See also FOOTE, ALEXANDER; KUCZYNSKI, JUERGEN

Sources: Andrew, Christopher, and Vasili Mitrokhin, *The Mitrokhin Archive: The KGB in Europe and the West* (London: Lane, 1999); Foote, Alexander, *Handbook for Spies* (New York: Doubleday, 1949); Mahoney, Harry T., and Marjorie L. Mahoney, *Biographic Dictionary of Espionage* (San Francisco: Austin & Winfield, 1998); Werner, Ruth, *Sonia's Report* (London: Chatto and Windus, 1991); West, Nigel, *The Circus: MI5 Operations 1945–1972* (New York: Stein and Day, 1983).

KUZMICH EPISODE (1954–1990). A curious episode the history of the **Cold War** that illustrates one problem that writers and scholars have in establishing reliable knowledge in the field of espionage.

Kuzma Kuzmich was a fictional character, a convert to communism who still adhered to vestiges of capitalism and often appeared in Russian novels. This name was given to a young **KGB** officer with pleasant, open features who sat in on George Blake's (1922–) initial interviews with his KGB contact, a stocky, bald fellow. Kuzmich was tall, aristocratic, university trained, and spoke fluent English. He did not interview Blake, but did interview Blake's companions. He got the name Kuzma Kuzmich from one of those companions, Philip Dean.

Dean's true name was Gerassimos Gigantes. He wrote his account of the experiences of those who were captured by the North Koreans, and had accompanied Blake on a death march in Korea.

The young man nicknamed Kuzmich was a White Russian from Harbin who had accepted communism in 1945, but was not a fanatic neophyte because he longed to be in business, and to enjoy the fleshpots of Beirut and Alexandria.

Espionage writers on Blake's activities mistook his name for that of a real person, and believed he had been Blake's first interrogator. These two errors were due to Blake's leaving the false impression that his interrogator had been the tall young man with open features, rather than a stocky, bald fellow. Later research by these same writers established, again falsely, but in good faith, that the *true* name of the young interrogator was probably Gregory Kuzmitch, an official in the Political Education Section of the **MGB** (Ministry of State Security). With a "t" now inserted in his name, his tasks were thought to be serving **TASS** journalists and ballet companies, and preventing their members' defection when visiting the West.

This growing error multiplied itself when Kuzmitch's diplomatic career was researched *before* his falsely asserted work in Korea. Kuzmitch served the Soviet ambassador in Canada until 1947; next he was in London until 1952, and later in Washington. He was an attaché whose *real* name was Kuznetsov when in London. In 1950 he was recalled to Moscow, and later was sent to Korea to turn American and British prisoners. Furthermore, at the end of the **Korean War** (1950–1953) he defected to the United States and worked for the **CIA**!

Be it ever so plausible, this career, like the person who was supposed to have followed it, is *totally* false! No one on the Russian embassy's Ottawa staff in 1945 was transferred to London, because the British would not accept diplomats tainted with an espionage affair like that involving Igor Gouzenko (fl. 1919–1985); no one called Kuznetsov was in the Soviet embassy in London from 1945 to 1950; there is no defector with the name of Kuzmitch on the defectors' list in the Central Intelligence Agency (CIA) in 1953–1954. All those who defected between 1948 and 1957 have been listed, and none were in Korea. Also, this name is not on the KGB's traitors list from 1945 to 1969.

Finally, it is unlikely that the KGB defector who had changed allegiances *before* Blake was known to be a Soviet agent would have failed to mention Blake's work to his CIA interrogators. Such a valuable piece of information would be enough to set the defector up for life in the United States, for having Blake caught well before he was, and for saving both the cost and the embarrassment of a failed operation, the Berlin tunnel (1954–1955).

Kuzmitch was referred to in other expert writings, in which, to overcome the hurdle of incredibility, Blake's confession was recorded as having occurred *after* Easter 1961.

The fiction of the Kuzmich episode was further elaborated after 1985 with Oleg Gordievsky's defection and publication of the book *KGB: The Inside Story*, where he is named Grigori Kuzmich. This is notable because Gordievsky had been entrusted to write a history of the KGB's work in Britain, and was helped in this work after his defection by a highly regarded British scholar in the history of espionage. The Kuzmich episode, named as such by the military historian Nigel West (1991), shows that with the best intentions, reliable knowledge in espionage research on the Cold War can be flawed by diligent and competent researchers who work assiduously to increase its accuracy.

Sources: Andrew, Christopher, and Oleg Gordievsky, *KGB: The Inside Story of Its Foreign Operations from Lenin to Gorbachev* (London: Hodder and Stoughton, 1990); Blake, George, *No Other Choice: An Autobiography* (London: Jonathan Cape, 1990); West, Nigel, *Seven Spies Who Changed the World* (London: Secker & Warburg, 1991).

L

LABOR ATTACHÉS' OPERATIONS. Recent U.S. State Department documents released to the Australian academic David Knight (2003) show that U.S. embassies employed labor attachés as well as cultural and defense attachés during the **Cold War**. The labor attaché would become acquainted with leaders in trade unions and labor/socialist political parties, and report on them to the U.S. State Department. They would work covertly with anti-Communist organizations in activities that interfered with Australia's political life, and they may have served the interests of U.S. intelligence agencies.

U.S. labor attachés in Australia betweeen 1966 and 1969 were Bob Walkinshaw, Emil Lindahl, and Doyle Martin. They watched closely the political struggle in the Australian Council of Trade Unions; sent records of anti-Communist sources to the State Department; cultivated such labor leaders as the ambitions and charismatic Robert Hawke (1929–), the left-wing leader Jim Cairns (1914–2003), and the anti-Communist leader Bob A. Santamaria (1915–1998); reported on labor leaders' attitudes toward the United States; sent evidence of foreign policy views in conflict with those of the United States; and became aware of the **Australian Labor Party**'s aim to inquire into **Central Intelligence Agency (CIA)** activities in Australia.

Recent records show that the CIA received reports from the U.S. labor attachés in Australia, and that the CIA funded trips to the United States for Australian union leaders who had been chosen for this privilege by the labor attachés. It is well known that the Soviets funded similar trips to Russia. It is assumed by many writers that both sides in the Cold War used labor attachés to spot talented and useful **agents**. This was the task of Josef Frolik (c. 1925–).

Sources: Frolik, Joseph, *The Frolik Defection* (London: Leo Cooper, 1975); McKnight, David, "Labor and the Quiet Americans," *The Age* (Melbourne), February 20, 2003, p. 15.

LAMPHERE, ROBERT JOSEPH (1918–2002). Robert Lamphere supervised important espionage cases for the **Federal Bureau of Investigation (FBI)** in its

Espionage Section during the **Cold War**, using decoded material from the VENONA project.

Robert Lamphere was born at Wardner, Idaho, and after graduating from the University of Idaho he began studying law and completed the degree at the National Law School in Washington, DC. He was employed at the FBI and is remembered for having made over 400 arrests in his first four years. He was transferred to the Soviet Espionage Section, and learned of the secret **Manhattan Project** and that Soviet **agents** were spying on the project and getting information on its research.

Lamphere became aware of the National Security Agency's code-breaking project. In his autobiography he never mentions the sources, but it was clearly the VENONA project, which began in February 1943 when Colonel Carter Clark, whose Special Branch supervised the Signals Intelligence Service and set out to study encoded Soviet diplomatic cables.

In 1943 the director of the FBI, J. Edgar Hoover (1895–1972), received an anonymous letter that reported that Soviet agents were spying on Americans, and he assigned Lamphere to breaking the Soviet code. The 1944–1945 code information was first deciphered in 1948 by Meredith Gardner (1913–2002). Late that year he gave Lamphere information that helped him identify Judith Coplon (1921–).

Lamphere used the decoded material from the VENONA project to construct case studies of espionage. He built the cases and followed them from Klaus Fuchs (1911–1988), to Harry Gold (1910–1972) and Ruth (1925–) and David (1922–) Greenglass, and finally to Julius (1918–1953) and Ethel (1916–1953) Rosenberg. In this work he got much help again from his friend Meredith Gardner.

Lamphere hoped that the Rosenbergs would not be put to death, but be given the opportunity to talk about their crimes; he was very angry when their deaths were announced. Also, he felt that the efforts of Joseph McCarthy (1908–1957) hurt the anti-Communist cause in the United States, and turned many liberals against the legitimate curtailment of Communist activities in U.S. government agencies.

See also COPLON, JUDITH; FUCHS, EMIL JULIUS KLAUS; GREENGLASS, DAVID, AND GREENGLASS, RUTH; ROSENBERG, ETHEL, AND ROSENBERG, JULIUS; VENONA PROJECT

Sources: Anonymous, "A Spy Catcher Who Broke the Soviet Codes. Robert Joseph Lamphere, Spy Catcher 14-2-1918–7-1-2002," *The Age* (Melbourne), February 2, 2002, Obituaries, p. 9 (originally published in the *New York Times*); Gentry, Curt, *J. Edgar Hoover: The Man and His Secrets* (New York: Norton, 1991); Haynes, John Earl, and Harvey Klehr, *Venona: Decoding Soviet Espionage in America* (New Haven, CT: Yale University Press, 1999); Lamphere, Robert J., and Tom Schactman, *The FBI–KGB War: A Special Agent's Story* (New York: Random House, 1986).

LANSDALE, EDWARD G. (1908–1987). Major General Edward G. Lansdale became a noted expert on unconventional warfare. He was deeply interested in the application of psychological methods not only to warfare but also to civilian operations and the rehabilitation of rnrmy guerrilla fighters. He consistently recommended the use of strong actions during the **Cold War,** and his imaginative ideas and talks on counterinsurgency, psychological operations, and civic programs have drawn much attention.

Edward Lansdale was born in Detroit, Michigan, the second of four sons of Henry Lansdale of Virginia and Sara Philips of California. He was raised and educated in Michigan, New York, and California; as a young man wrote for newspapers and magazines, and later entered the advertising industry in Los Angeles. In **World War II** he was brought into the **OSS**, and in 1943 was a lieutenant in the U.S. Army, specializing in intelligence work.

Lansdale was posted to headquarters of the U.S. Air force in the western Pacific in 1945, and was promoted to major and head of the Intelligence Division. For three years he helped the Philippine Army establish and build its intelligence service, and resolved many problems arising among the prisoners of war of many nationalities.

In 1948 Lansdale left the Philippines to be an instructor at the Strategic Intelligence School, at Lowry Air Force Base in Colorado. After being promoted to lieutenant colonel in 1949, he was sent to the Joint U.S. Military Assistance Group in the Philippines to help with intelligence services needed to combat the Communist-led **Hukbalahap** guerrilla fighters. He believed that a good intelligence officer was one who could live the life of those on whom he sought intelligence. Following the field research methods of anthropologists and social psychologists, he created special techniques to achieve his aims, and supported the use of civic reforms and the rehabilitation of Hukbalahap prisoners.

In 1953 Lansdale was in French Indochina, supporting the French forces by advising on special counterguerrilla operations. After another period working the Philippines he was called to serve in Saigon for two years. As head of the **Central Intelligence Agency (CIA)** military mission in Saigon, he advised the Vietnamese army and government on internal security problems, pacification campaigns, and related psychological operations, and used intelligence for the integration of small armies, civic actions, and refugee schemes.

By 1959 Lansdale was serving the U.S. President's Committee on Military Assistance, and was made a brigadier general in 1961. President **John F. Kennedy** (1917–1963) called on him to complete Operation MONGOOSE, a secret scheme of sabotage to bring down Fidel Castro (1927–) and rid Cuba of Communists. From this strange and unfulfilled project, and his imaginative ways of planning unusual warfare procedures, Lansdale's reputation grew into a legend. He became known as the "Ugly American," and was a model for the main character in a novel of that name by William J. Lederer and Eugene Burdick.

Excerpts from Lansdale's early report to President Kennedy on Vietnam appeared in the *New York Times* publication of the "Pentagon Papers"; Lansdale's own papers and tapes are kept in the Library of Congress.

See also PENTAGON PAPERS

Sources: Ambrose, Stephen E., *Ike's Spies: Eisenhower and the Espionage Establishment,* 2nd ed. (Jackson: University Press of Mississippi, 1999); Colby, William, with Peter Forbath, *Honorable Men: My Life in the CIA* (New York: Simon & Schuster, 1978); Currey, Cecil Barr, *Edward Lansdale: The Unquiet American* (Boston: Houghton Mifflin, 1989); Ellsberg, Daniel, *Secrets: A Memoir of Vietnam and the Pentagon Papers* (New York: Viking, 2002); Fish, Lydia M., "Edward G. Lansdale and the Folksongs of Americans in the Vietnam War," *Journal of the American Folklore Society* 102 (1989): 1–23; Marchetti, Victor, and John Marks, *The CIA and the Cult of Intelligence* (New York: Knopf, 1964); Smith, Joseph, and Simon Davis, *Historical Dictionary of the Cold War* (New York: Scarecrow Press, 2000); Wise, David, and Thomas B. Ross, *The Invisible Government* (New York: Random House, 1964).

LE CARRÉ, JOHN (1931–). John Le Carré is the name used by David Cornwell, an outstanding British writer of spy novels during the **Cold War**. He chose his nom de plume when he passed a shop front displaying the name, but later remarked that this was lie that he had learned to believe. His life as spy appears in his fictional autobiography, *A Perfect Spy* (1986), which describes the hero Magnus Pym and captures the essentials of decadence in British espionage.

David Cornwell was born in Poole, Dorset, the younger son in a Protestant family. His father, Ronnie, was a crook, and deserted his mother, Olive. She died in 1975. During Ronnie's first jail term for fraud (1934–1935), Olive left her children. Not until he was 18 did David learn of his father's crimes, and not until he was 21 did he see his mother again.

Cornwell attended St. Andrew's Prep School and Sherborne School. In 1948 he went to study German for year at the University of Bern. While in Bern he was recruited into the secret services. He served British military intelligence in Austria (1950–1952).

Cornwell entered Lincoln College, Oxford (1952–1956), read modern languages, and taught German for two years at Eton College (1956–1958). While he was at Oxford, his father was declared bankrupt, and David withdrew from studies for a year to earn money teaching at Millfield. Later he graduated with first-class honors.

In 1954 Cornwell's father, now married a second time and with two more children, endured another brilliant bankruptcy. That year David married Ann Sharp; and they would have three sons before divorcing in 1971.

After teaching at Eton College, Cornwell worked as a freelance illustrator for the next two years, completed the illustrations for *Talking Birds* (1961), by Maxwell Knight (1900–1968)—Ian Fleming's (1908–1964) model for "M"—and probably worked for **MI5**. Until 1966 he was a spy and, as Second Secretary at Britain's embassy in Bonn, saw the building of the Berlin Wall.

Cornwell remarried in 1972 and had another son. He wrote spy novels that have attracted much attention and been filmed, and remarked that it was probably his way to express his revenge against society.

Cornwell's espionage novels, and much of his writing after he turned to broader political issues in 1989, use the British and American intelligence organizations and their centralist authorities as models for the moral decline of Western civilization during his lifetime.

Cornwell felt that he had deserted a lifetime of responsibilities, as had his mother and father. His mother ran away from home to marry; his father rejected his repressive upbringing for a life of petty crime. Cornwell claims he left school prematurely at 16, married to escape being a bachelor when he was 23, quit the secret services aged 33, left his first marriage at 36, and deserted the real world for that of the author for the rest of his life.

In 1963, his novel *The Spy Who Came in from the Cold* brought Cornwell wealth and security. In his early novels (1961–1979) he uses a character named George Smiley as the center for his stories and his own moral discourse. From *The Little Drummer Girl* (1983) to *The Constant Gardener* (2001) Cornwell has kept the espionage establishment in the shadows of his novels while he explores broad themes in international politics and commerce that center on moral questions central to Middle East conflicts, the arms trade, illicit manipulation of local politics, and the commercial misuse of medical research.

See also OPERATION GREENSLEEVES; PYM, MAGNUS

Sources: Aronoff, Myron J.,"Intelligence and the Dilemma of Democracy: Themes in the Work of John Le Carré," paper presented at the Annual Meeting of the American Political Science Association, New York, September 1–4, 1994; Aronoff, Myron J., *The Spy Novels of John Le Carré* (New York: St. Martin's Press, 1999); Beene, Lynn D., *John Le Carré* (New York: Twayne, 1992); Bold, Alan E., ed., *The Quest for Le Carré* (New York: St. Martin's Press, 1988); Cooper, Andrew, "Dreaming the Other: Ideology and Character in John Le Carré's Novels," *Free Associations* 5 (1995): 303–325; Laity, Susan, "The Second Burden of a Former Child: Doubling and Repetition in 'A Perfect Spy,'" in Harold Bloom, ed., *John Le Carré* (New York: Chelsea House, 1987), pp. 137–164; Le Carré, John, *A Perfect Spy* (London: Hodder and Stoughton, 1986); Lewis, Peter, *John Le Carré* (New York: Frederick Ungar, 1985).

LEE, ANDREW DAULTON (1952–). Andrew Lee was an American drug dealer who became a messenger for the spy Christopher Boyce (1953–) and was caught in Mexico City.

Lee was adopted. His father was born in the countryside of Illinois, served in the U.S. Air Force during **World War II**, and after being demobilized studied medicine and eventually became a wealthy pathologist. Lee was short and stocky, and walked with a swagger.

Lee graduated from St. John Fisher Grade School in 1966, and went on to Palos Verdes High School. He appeared to be deeply affected by the pupils who teased him about his height, and the nickname they gave him, "Mickey Rooney." On the other hand, because his parents were wealthy, he lacked for nothing. At school and in college, he befriended Christopher John Boyce, and they found common interest in falconry.

Lee graduated from high school in 1970, and that September he enrolled in Allan Hancock Junior College in Santa Maria, north of Los Angeles. But he dropped out. He had been drawn to taking drugs taking while in high school, and continued with the habit in junior college. To conceal his failing grades, he would tamper with his report card before bringing it home.

In time Lee found it necessary to peddle drugs to ensure he could afford his habit. In October 1971 he was arrested for selling drugs to high school students. He received a suspended sentence and promised to return to college. He attended Whittaker College; again he dropped out. He failed to quit taking drugs, could not get a job to help him pay for the habit, and returned to drug dealing for U.S.$1,500 a week. In 1974 he was arrested, jailed, and after a year he was released for good behavior.

In January 1975, Lee's boyhood friend Christopher Boyce suggested that Andrew sell secret documents, which Christopher could photocopy at his workplace, to the Soviets at their Mexico City embassy. Lee contacted the officials at the Soviet embassy, offered them valuable information that would ensure they could read **Central Intelligence Agency (CIA)** communications between its various stations and headquarters. The material would lay bare the vital daily code systems of the CIA activities worldwide. For over a year Boyce and Lee profited from providing a vast array of classified information to the Soviets.

On March 15, 1976, Lee went to Vienna, taking a roll of film containing cipher messages between CIA headquarters and its receiving stations around the world, as well as the technical record describing secret plans for the new Argus communications system.

For U.S.$75,000 Boyce agreed to make a final delivery of secret plans on the CIA satellite network for its spy program over China and the **U.S.S.R.** before beginning another project with the Soviets. On January 5, 1977, Lee landed in Mexico City on his last courier mission, carrying an envelope containing the Pyramider documents with more than 415 film negatives. But he was late with the delivery in Mexico City, and to finalize the operation, broke fundamental **tradecraft** rules.

Next day he went to the Soviet embassy and attracted attention by tossing a book jacket marked **"KGB"** into the embassy. Mexican police thought he was a terrorist, arrested him, and discovered the negatives. The Mexico City police interrogated him brutally until he confessed, and informed the **Federal Bureau of Investigation (FBI).** The FBI caught Boyce and Lee, and had them in jail by the middle of January. They were tried, and Lee was sentenced to life imprisonment on July 18, 1977.

See also BOYCE, CHRISTOPHER

Sources: Bamford, James, *The Puzzle Palace: A Report on America's Most Secret Agency* (Boston: Houghton Mifflin, 1982; New York: Penguin, 1983); Lindsey, Robert, *The Falcon and the Snowman* (New York: Simon & Schuster, 1979); Lindsey, Robert, *The Flight of the Falcon* (New York: Simon & Schuster, 1983); Mahoney, Harry T., and Marjorie L. Mahoney, *Biographic Dictionary of Espionage* (San Francisco: Austin & Winfield, 1998); Pincher, Chapman, *Traitors: The Anatomy of Treason* (New York: St. Martin's Press, 1987).

LEOPOLD, JOHN (1890–1958). John Leopold spied during the 1930s for the **Royal Canadian Mounted Police (RCMP),** and in the **Cold War** became Canada's leading anti-Communist expert and head of research in the intelligence division of the RCMP. He died under mysterious circumstances.

Johan Leopold was a Jew born in Bohemia, and came to Canada in 1913. Once there, he changed his name and described himself as a Roman Catholic. In Bohemia he had had a college education, and worked as a forester and estate manger. In 1914 he became a homesteader in western Alberta, but found farming too difficult, and appllied to enter the RCMP in September 1918.

Leopold's application would not have normally been accepted for several reasons: he was not tall enough and his chest was too narrow for RCMP service; he came from Eastern Europe, obviously did not have a British background, looked like a foreigner, and was a Jew. But the RCMP needed men to infiltrate the radical groups in Canada's working class, and to spy on people who obviously came from non-English-speaking countries where radicalism and ethnicity were thought to be linked. Leopold spoke Polish, German, Ukrainian, Czech, and English. He was given a dual role, on a three-year contract, as both policeman and secret **agent**.

Canada had participated in the Allied intervention force in the Russian Civil War (1918–1920), so spying on new immigrants was an essential part of Canadian internal security. Leopold lived in a **safe house** and operated from Regina, a main stop on the national rail line. He took the name Jack Esselwein, a house painter, and posed as a political radical. He joined the One Big Union, a radical labor organization, and was an official in the Workers' Party of Canada, a public arm of the Communist Party of Canada (CPC). As "Number 30" he reported secretly on Communist affairs to the RCMP. He was one of several men employed this way. When his contract ended, it was found that Leopold/Esselwein was wholly trusted by the Communist Party in Regina, so his employer decided to use him as a penetration agent. He was such a capable **double agent** that in 1925 he was elected President of the Regina branch of the CPC.

Under great pressure as a double agent, Leopold turned to alcohol to help him cope with the strain, and became an alcoholic. He was exposed as a spy and expelled from the Communist Party in 1928. The RCMP wanted to keep him, so he was sent to the Yukon as a regular member of the RCMP, a "Mountie."

Throughout the 1930s, in the Canadian government's battle with communism, Leopold's expertise was regularly called on: he was involved in the 1931 trial of Communists as criminals in Canada, and he worked undercover to break up a narcotics ring operating over the border in the United States. Although his alcohol problem remained and he contracted syphilis, his status in the RCMP grew, and by 1938 he was promoted.

Leopold wanted to retire during **World War II**, but was refused, and in 1942 was made an inspector. In October 1945, following the defection of Igor Gouzenko (fl. 1919–1982), Leopold was made the head of Special Section, and was sent to help analyze the information that Gouzenko had brought with him. Later he worked on policies regarding the security clearances for civil servants, incoming intelligence, and the penetration of Canadian universities by Communists. By 1951 he had become the RCMP's chief Communist expert and head of its Intelligence Research Section. He retired in 1952 and died of heart failure in 1958; beside him in his bed was an unregistered pistol, which left his death a mystery. His obituary in the *Ottawa Journal* noted that he was dedicated to fighting the menace of communism.

Source: Hewitt, Steve, "Royal Canadian Mounted Spy: The Secret Life of John Leopold/ Jack Esselwein," *Intelligence and National Security* 15 (2000): 144–168.

LEUNG, KATRINA (1954–). Katrina Leung was arrested in April 2003 after it had been found that for at least 20 years she had been a **double agent** for China.

In 1983 Leung, a naturalized U.S. citizen, began an affair with James Smith, who had been a **Federal Bureau of Investigation (FBI)** agent since 1970 and would retire in 2000. The FBI said Smith recruited her in the early 1980s as an **agent** and became her handler, seeking information from her about China. She was code-named PARLOR MAID. Meanwhile, she secretly photocopied classified documents that he brought to her house, and passed on copies to China.

At dinners for visiting Chinese notables Leung would introduce FBI agents; she became indispensable at Chinese–American functions, a strong, popular, attractive, and colorful character who lived in a wealthy suburb of Los Angeles, San Marino. Whenever she was photographed with dignitaries, she would be at the center of the photo; she was a translator, and spoke fluent English, Cantonese, and Mandarin; formed her own consulting company; and would work for both sides of U.S. politics.

Leung was denied bail because she was thought to be flight risk and a potential theat to national security. Her lawyers announced that she was innocent, and a loyal U.S. citizen.

Leung was charged with illegally obtaining classified material from her FBI handler. She had copied two national security documents and three times had illegal possession of secret papers. James Smith was arrested and charged with wire fraud and gross negligence in handling of national security document, and was freed on a U.S.$250,000 bond after their arrest on April 9, 2003.

In April, Leung's lawyers insisted that she was more deserving of bail than James Smith, and suggested that perhaps sexism or racism might be the reason for the decision to keep in jail until her trial.

In May 2003 Leung's lawyers argued that she was being offered up as a sacrifice by the FBI in order to cover its tracks. She had been stabbed in the back, they claimed, by the same bureaucrats who had benefited from her service. Her husband, Kam, said she was being treated so harshly because she was not born in the United States, and that if she were in China, she would be cleared of espionage.

James Smith's prosecutors asserted that he had taken classified material to meetings with Ms. Leung and allowed it to remain in an unlocked briefcase.

The FBI claimed it paid Leung U.S.$1.7 million over 20 years for her information. It seems one of the documents she took was an electronic communication about Chinese fugitives, and another was about an FBI investigation, ROYAL TOURIST.

If convicted, Leung could be jailed for 50 years.

Sources: Anonymous, "United States: Suspected Double Agent Refused Bail," *The Age* (Melbourne), April 17, 2003, World, p. 15; Murphy, Dean, and Calvin Sims, "The Spy Who Never Forgot," *The Age* (Melbourne), April 12, 2003, World, p. 24; Whitcomb, Dan, "Two-Timing American Spy Faces Five Charges," *The Age* (Melbourne), May 10, 2003, p. 17.

LEVCHENKO, STANISLAV (1941–). Levchenko defected to the West from Tokyo in October 1979, after serving Soviet interests with sophisticated and effective "**active measures**" in Japan for many years.

Stanislav Levchenko was born into a military family in Moscow. His father was a research chemist who headed a department in a military institution; his mother, a pediatrician, was a Jew who died when Stanislav was three. After leaving high school in 1958, he studied Japanese and English at Moscow University's Institute of Asian and African Studies, and became an expert on Japan.

Levchenko married twice: first, when he was 18, and again, a few years later, to an architecture student. From both sets of in-laws he learned of the brutal excesses of **Josef Stalin**'s (1879–1953) rule, and the corruption of the Communist regime generally. This information impressed him and would later help to explain his defection.

Levchenko graduated in 1964, and for the next 15 years served the Soviet interests in matters to do with Japan. In 1965 he was a Japanese interpreter with the Soviet Peace Committee, which controlled the World Peace Council, a Communist front. He worked for some years manipulating world opinion against the **Vietnam War** (1964–1973) and America's role in it. But Soviet subversion and propaganda centering on activities in Japan became Levchenko's specialty.

In 1966 Levchenko was trained to infiltrate Britain to study how prepared her nuclear forces were; later that year he was in Japan, interpreting for a Soviet trade delegation and making contact with Japan's peace movement leaders. After another year's training in espionage **tradecraft** at the Foreign Intelligence School in Yurlovo, he became a senior **KGB** officer assigned to the Japanese desk in the KGB First Directorate, at Moscow headquarters. He had reached the privileged level of a Russian military careerist. By 1974 he and his wife had paid many visits to Japan, and seen several world capitals.

Levchenko studied journalism, and in 1975 was sent to Tokyo to work on the staff of Russia's *New Times*. He was one of a dozen KGB spies.

However successful he had been, Levchenko's employment conditions in Japan were far from what he expected. His housing was poor; his superior was an inept, vulgar workaholic who worked behind his subordinates' backs.

Soon Levchenko managed to regain the privileges he and his wife once enjoyed, but he had to appear to have earned them. First he managed to cultivate a Japanese socialist politician, and blackmailed him into serving Soviet plans for Japan for four years. Later, after his unpleasant superior had returned to Moscow, Levchenko was given the task of handling a Japanese journalist who, 10 years before, had been recruited to the Soviet cause. They became close friends.

As result of his fine work, Levchenko was promoted to major early in 1979. But he was thinking of defection. He had been back in Moscow six months earlier, and found it disgusted him with its corruption and cynicism. Also, his career seemed to have halted, and his former superior was now even more powerful and obnoxious. He was tiring of the intrigue needed to get his work done; his future appeared to lie in corrupt Moscow; and his marriage was not happy.

In September 1979 Levchenko was expected to hand over his Japanese contacts and leave for Moscow in a month. He had been a great success, having had put into operation many "active measures"—KGB activities to strengthen Soviet influence and weaken Western influence—in the Far East. In late October, his last task was to provide the KGB with a list of all Japanese security officers. His journalist friend helped him do this in a few hours.

Next day, after losing anyone who might be following him, Levchenko approached a U.S. naval commander in the Sanno Hotel and defected. He was granted political asylum in the United States. Moments before he left the airport for the United States, he had the opportunity to name his obnoxious former superior as the top KGB officer who has working against Japanese interests.

In the U.S., after interrogation to ensure he was not a KGB plant, Levchenko was disguised, and lived in hiding. The KGB has long sought to assassinate him.

See also WORLD PEACE COUNCIL

Sources: Brook-Shepherd, Gordon, *The Storm Birds. Soviet Post War Defectors: The Dramatic True Stories 1945–1985* (New York: Henry Holt, 1989); Laffin, John, *Brassey's Book of Espionage* (London: Brassey's, 1996); Levchenko, Stanislav, *On the Wrong Side: My Life in the KGB* (Washington, DC: Pergamon-Brassey's International Defense Publishers, 1988).

LIDDELL, GUY MAYNARD (1892–1958). Guy Liddell, a major **MI5** leader in wartime, was a popular, admired, and capable officer in espionage and counterespionage, but toward the end of his career his reputation was irrevocably harmed by his unwise choice of friends from among those who worked with him.

Liddell was the son of an army captain, and as youngster was interested in a career in music. He studied in Germany, but was drawn into action in **World War I** in the Royal Field Artillery (1914–1919), for which he earned a Military Cross. In 1919 he joined Scotland Yard, and became the liaison officer between Scotland Yard and MI5.

By 1927 Liddell had learned much about the Russians and communism from intercepts of Russian cables between Moscow and the Soviet headquarters in London at Arcos House. In May that year he led a raid on Arcos House, expecting to find evidence of espionage against Great Britain among documents in Russian hands. All that was found was three people and a stack of burned documents. Liddell believed the Foreign Office had tipped off Arcos House, but a taint of suspicion established itself on his name for years.

In 1931 Liddell was counterintelligence expert, and the link between the police **Special Branch** and MI5; that year he was transferred to MI5, and controlled 30 employees. Among them was Dick White (1906–1993), the only university man in the organization. Liddell hired White to act as his private secretary while learning the new profession of espionage. At the time the armed services were much opposed to intelligence work, and regarded it as a career suitable only for those who studied foreign languages and had no ability to command men in the field.

In August 1940, when Liddell was director of Division B (counterespionage) for MI5, Victor Rothschild introduced him to Anthony Blunt (1907–1983), who had been discharged in October 1939 from an intelligence course because of his Marxist beliefs. Despite many objections from others, Liddell recruited Blunt into MI5 and briefly had him as his personal assistant. Shortly afterward Blunt took charge of the surveillance of neutral embassies that could become the target of enemy recruiters.

Early in the war Liddell sent Dusko Popov to inform J. Edgar Hoover (1895–1972) of the attack on Pearl Harbor. Hoover considered Popov unreliable; and Liddell was frowned upon for not informing the U.S. Office of Naval Intelligence of the impending Japanese attack. Also, he made a secret visit to Canada in 1944. As the war was brought to an end, he became better acquainted with Anthony Blunt and Kim Philby (1912–1988), and they enjoyed his personal support.

Liddell was considered, but rejected, for the position of head of MI5. His reputation was not spotless, so the Prime Minister did not support him. In May 1946, when Percy Sillitoe became head of MI5, Liddell was bitter; and to some observers it seemed that he, Roger Hollis (1905–1973), and Dick White (1906–1993) isolated Sillitoe and turned his staff against him.

After the war Liddell was well known as a friend of Kim Philby, Guy Burgess (1911–1963), and Anthony Blunt, and he would visit Blunt and Burgess when they shared a London flat. Soon his friendship with Burgess would reflect badly on his reputation.

When Guy Burgess and Donald Maclean defected in May 1951, Liddell came under suspicion. Apparently he had been advised that Maclean was a suspected Soviet spy two days before the pair fled to Moscow.

In June 1951 Liddell gave his support to Operation POST REPORT, which aimed to screen the thousands of displaced persons from the European continent who were seeking to enter Great Britain. It was successful for MI5 and **MI6**, but added nothing to Liddell's reputation because of his known association with Guy Burgess.

In fact, Liddell's view of Burgess was ambivalent. He would not have Burgess in the office at MI5; at the same time he was an open friend of Burgess, and it was noted he attended the wild, drunken gathering at Burgess's flat in October 1950 to celebrate his appointment to Washington.

After the flight of Burgess and Maclean, and well before it was securely known that they were in Moscow, Liddell met with Goronwy Rees (1909–1979), who told Liddell that in 1937 Burgess had admitted to being a servant of the **COMINTERN**, and had suggested Rees be one, too. At the meeting Liddell seemed more interested in where Maclean was than in Burgess's earlier comments. Anthony Blunt attended this meeting with Rees, and both he and Liddell advised Rees against making a formal statement on the matter; further, Liddell insisted that if Rees were to do so, he could become a suspected Soviet spy for not having revealed the information on Burgess years before.

When details of the flight of the two **double agents** became known, an investigation was held into MI5's functioning, and Liddell was placed under suspicion. Why had he commented on Donald Maclean when told about Guy Burgess's early Soviet activities? Had he, perhaps, at the October 1950 party told Burgess to warn Maclean he was being investigated? Had Liddell perhaps had intimate sexual relations with Burgess? As the search for the truth progressed, Liddell's reputation was more deeply stained.

Liddell remained nominally in MI5 for two more years. In 1953 he was awarded a **CB**, having retired too old to be Percy Sillitoe's successor, and too discredited by his connection with Burgess for continued employment. A capable and popular servant of the secret services, he was sidelined, and effectively demoted by being made the Chief of Security for the British Atomic Energy Authority at Harwell.

In 1956 Liddell proposed Roger Hollis, who was already a member of the **Reform Club**, to membership of the club next door, the Travellers' Club, in the Pall Mall section of London. Two years later Liddell died, and Anthony Blunt was in tears at the funeral.

In 1979, with the exposure of Anthony Blunt's career as a Soviet spy, Liddell's reputation came under attack again. He was among the many names of imagined—and deceased—**moles** who had either been in the British secret service or closely aligned to it. Just before his death in November 1979, Goronwy Rees denounced Liddell as a traitor and one of Guy Burgess's lovers.

Liddell's diaries, code-named WALLFLOWERS, were saved from destruction by Peter Wright (1916–1995), who found that Rees was correct about Anthony Blunt, but that the denunciation of Liddell as a servant of the Soviet cause was groundless.

Costello (1988) presents a comprehensive argument for questioning Liddell's career, concluding that he was either incompetent, plagued by bad luck, or the grandfather of Soviet moles. Andrew and Gordievsky (1990) show that suspicions of Liddell as a Soviet mole in the British security services are in error.

See also BLUNT, ANTHONY; BURGESS, GUY; HOLLIS, ROGER; MACLEAN, DONALD; OPERATION POST REPORT; PHILBY, HAROLD "KIM"; REES, GORONWY

Sources: Andrew, Christopher, and Oleg Gordievsky, *KGB: The Inside Story of Its Foreign Operations from Lenin to Gorbachev* (London: Hodder and Stoughton, 1990); Bower, Tom, *The Perfect English Spy: Sir Dick White and the Secret War 1935–90* (London: Heinemann, 1995); Costello, John, *Mask of Treachery: Spies, Lies, Buggery and Betrayal. The First Documented Dossier on Anthony Blunt's Cambridge Spy Ring* (New York: William Morrow, 1988); Deacon, Richard, *Spyclopedia: The Comprehensive Handbook of Espionage* (New York: William Morrow, 1987); Pincher, Chapman, *Too Secret Too Long* (London: Sidgwick & Jackson, 1984); Rees, Jenny, *Looking for Mr. Nobody: The Secret Life of Goronwy Rees* (London: Weidenfeld and Nicolson, 1994); Wright, Peter, with Paul Greengrass, *Spycatcher: The Candid Autobiography of a Senior Intelligence Officer* (Melbourne: William Heinemann Australia, 1987).

LIPKA, ROBERT STEPHAN (fl. 1945–1997). Lipka is an example of the ideology-free, money-hungry spy who illustrates the pattern of materialist motivation among later **Cold War** spies.

Robert Lipka enlisted in the U.S. Army and, between the ages of 19 and 22 (1964–1967), worked in the National Security Agency (NSA) as a clerk in the central communications room. Lipka provided highly secret information to the **KGB,** and he may have been responsible for the loss of American lives during the **Vietnam War.** While the government was aware of a major security breach in the 1960s, it had not been able to identify Lipka as a suspect. He used **dead drops** along the Potomac River, and was paid U.S.$500–$1,000 for each delivery.

Lipka was probably the young soldier described in the autobiography of former KGB Major General Oleg Kalugin, who reported on a **walk-in** during the 1960s who was interested only in money. According to Kalugin, the documents that the soldier provided were top secret NSA reports to the White House and copies of communications on units and movements around the world. The Soviets apparently paid Lipka a total of U.S.$27,000. In 1967 he left the NSA, and stopped meeting his KGB handlers in 1974.

In 1993 his ex-wife informed the **Federal Bureau of Investigation (FBI)** about Lipka's espionage. FBI **agents** posing as Russian contacts caught him. He was arrested on February 23, 1996, at his home in Millersville, Pennsylvania. To avoid a sentence of more than 18 years, he pleaded guilty to one count of espionage, and on September 24, 1997, he was sentenced to serve 18 years in federal prison.

Sources: Andrew, Christopher, and Vasili Mitrokhin, *The Mitrokhin Archive: The KGB in Europe and the West* (London: Lane, 1999); Anonymous, "Ex-Clerk at NSA Is Guilty of Spying," *Baltimore Sun,* May 24, 1997, p. 13; Kalugin, Oleg, and Fen Montaigne, *Spymaster: My 32 Years in Intelligence and Espionage Against the West* (London: SmithGryphon, 1994).

LIPPMANN, WALTER (1889–1974). Walter Lippmann was not a spy, but a critic of U.S. foreign policy that was adopted to manage the **Cold War**—including the use of espionage—and is regarded as the person who coined the term "Cold War." His views were contrary to those of George Kennan (1904–) and his supporters, who advocated the first U.S. Cold War policy of **containment.**

Lippmann graduated from Harvard University in 1914, became an assistant to President Woodrow Wilson (1856–1924), and helped to draft his international policy. After working for government he returned to journalism in 1931, and became a noted liberal humanist, and a political writer for the *New York Herald Tribune.* He won two Pulitzer Prizes. His column was syndicated in 250 U.S. newspapers and 50 overseas press publications.

Lippmann's view was that foreign policy should be pragmatic and realistic rather than advocate high principles and morals, and that the United States should not challenge or confront the **U.S.S.R.** in Europe. A practical man, he wanted Turkey and Greece protected to safeguard the U.S. oil interests in the Middle East.

Lippmann thought President **Harry Truman's** (1884–1972) support in the fight against communism overseas was a wrongheaded crusade; containing Soviet expansion would support not curb Soviet imperialism; he preferred to settle relations between East and West rather than contain the West's opponent, the U.S.S.R.

Lippmann coined the term "Cold War " for a book, published in November 1947, based on articles in the *New York Herald Tribune* that he had written in response to George Kennan's foreign policy outlined in the "long telegram." Lippman wanted the nuclear policy of the United States defined clearly, and objected to an alliance between the Nationalist Chinese leadership and the United States because of the hostility it would arouse with Communist China; he advocated the neutralization, demilitarization, and unification of Germany; and to counter communism, he believed the United States should encourage the growth of democracy in the Third World.

Although he supported **John F. Kennedy** (1917–1963) as a charismatic leader for the U.S. people, Lippmann found Kennedy's economic and foreign policies inadequate, and he strongly criticized the U.S. involvement in Vietnam.

See also KENNAN, GEORGE

Sources: Blum, D. Steven, *Walter Lippmann: Cosmopolitanism in the Century of Total Wars* (Ithaca, NY: Cornell University Press, 1984); Lippmann, Walter, *The Cold War: A Study in U.S. Foreign Policy* (New York: Harper, 1947; New York: Harper & Row, 1972); Smith, Joseph, and Simon Davis, *Historical Dictionary of the Cold War* (New York: Scarecrow Press, 2000).

LONETREE, CLAYTON J. (1961–). Clayton Lonetree was caught in a **KGB** honeytrap, and became the first U.S. Marine found guilty of spying for the Soviets while guarding the U.S. embassy in Moscow (1985).

Marine Sergeant Clayton J. Lonetree was a Navaho whose great uncle had been awarded a Congressional Medal of Honor. Lonetree wanted to continue the family tradition with valorous service in the U.S. Marines. His exam results were poor, yet he did get into the Marines and was given a post in Moscow. He was an alcoholic and not very bright, and had had to take tests over and over to get the post of Marine security guard.

In Moscow the Marines were not allowed to bring their wives, so they would smuggle women into their sleeping quarters at the barracks—the "Animal House"— or sometimes meet them at a dance held at the residence of the American ambassador.

Lonetree was lonely in Moscow, and he did not get much mail. He tried writing to a former girlfriend, only to learn she had married. He met Violetta in the fall of 1985. She was a tall, fair-skinned, and beautiful translator/receptionist who had studied English at the Institute of Foreign Languages in Moscow. She had been placed at the U.S. embassy by the KGB.

Although Lonetree had been warned about fraternizing with Soviets, he had seen enough friends and superiors date Russian women to feel comfortable doing the same. He and Violetta took long walks in the park, had tea, and were alone in her apartment. Lonetree fell in love with her.

Violetta introduced Lonetree to her Uncle Sasha—a KGB **agent**, Alexei G. Yefimov—who asked about Lonetree's life in the United States, his political views, his activities in Moscow, and his life in the embassy. Lonetree enjoyed the older man's attention. One day Sasha pulled a prepared list of questions from his pocket, and Lonetree finally realized that Violetta's uncle worked for the KGB.

Lonetree kept meeting with Violetta and Sasha for six months, and he used elaborate techniques to make sure he was not being followed when he went to see them. In this way he felt life became more interesting and began to resemble the spy novels he liked to read. He thought that Violetta loved him, and probably did not see what was going to happen.

Lonetree's Moscow sojourn came to an end, and rather than leave Europe and his love, he sought reassignment to guard duty at the U.S. embassy in Vienna. But there he was lonely again. Uncle Sasha arrived with photographs and a letter from

Violetta. Lonetree wanted to return to Moscow and marry Violetta. Sasha could see he was probably ready for something more than avuncular talk.

The first item Lonetree delivered to the KGB agent was an old embassy phone book. The second was a map of the embassy interior, its alarm systems and floor plans, for which he received U.S.$1,800. He used most of the money to buy Violetta a handmade Viennese gown. Next came three photographs of embassy employees thought to be CIA agents, rewarded with another U.S.$1,800.

Sasha proposed an undercover trip back to Moscow, where Lonetree could visit Violetta and undergo KGB training. Lonetree arranged for vacation leave from the embassy. But he became anxious, and started to drink more than usual and to lie awake at nights thinking of how he could get out of providing Sasha with information. Lonetree now felt that Sasha was not Violetta's uncle.

In December 1986 Lonetree approached a **Central Intelligence Agency (CIA)** officer at the U.S. embassy's Christmas party in Vienna and, quite drunk, he said he was in trouble and blurted a story of his dealings with the Soviets while he was in Moscow. Later he told of his love affair with Violetta and that he had met her uncle. Then he confessed to giving the uncle information, and was arrested and tried. At the time he was suspected of being responsible for the deaths of 20 CIA operatives he had identified. Later it was found that it was Aldrich H. Ames (1941–) who had been giving the KGB names of CIA operatives. Lonetree had been used as KGB cover for Ames.

In August 1987 Lonetree was sentenced to 30 years in a military prison at Leavenworth, Kansas; fined U.S.$5,000; given a dishonorable discharge without benefits; and reduced to the rank of private. His defense had been that he was working to lure and capture Edward Lee Howard (1951–), and have him returned to the United States.

For 10 years Violetta was depressed at not being with Lonetree, and rejected the advances of other men. In 1997 his sentence was reduced to nine years, and he was permitted to go home and live with his people. It appears from Doran (1997) that he and Violetta still loved one another. But Violetta was a KGB agent, though she always denied it. Lonetree has taken up with another woman.

By 1990 it appears that the KGB benefited little from Lonetree's information.

See also HOWARD, EDWARD

Sources: Allen, Thomas B., and Norman Polmar, *Merchants of Treason: America's Secrets for Sale* (New York: Delacorte Press, 1988); Andrew, Christopher, and Oleg Gordievsky, *KGB: The Inside Story of Its Foreign Operations from Lenin to Gorbachev* (London: Hodder and Stoughton, 1990); Barker, Rodney, *Dancing with the Devil: Sex, Espionage, and the U.S. Marines. The Clayton Lonetree Story* (New York: Simon & Schuster, 1996); Bowman, M. E., "The 'Worst Spy': Perceptions of Espionage," *American Intelligence Journal* 18 (1998): 57–62; Doran, Jamie, *Honeytrap* (London: Atlantic Celtic Films, 1997); Earley, Pete, *Confessions of a Spy: The Real Story of Aldrich Ames* (London: Hodder and Stoughton, 1997); Kessler, Ronald, *Moscow Station: How the KGB Penetrated the American Embassy* (New York: Scribner's, 1989); Wise, David, *The Spy Who Got Away: The Inside Story of the CIA Agent Who Betrayed His Country* (London: Fontana/Collins, 1988); Zak, William, Jr., "Sixth Amendment Issues Posed by the Court-Martial of Clayton Lonetree," *American Criminal Law Review* 30 (1992): 187–214.

LONG, LEONARD "LEO" HENRY (fl. 1917–1985). Leo Long spied for the Soviets until 1952, having been recruited to the Communist cause by Anthony Blunt (1907–1983) at Cambridge in the late 1930s.

Leo Long came from the working class, son of an unemployed carpenter, and held deep convictions about the inequities of British society. On a scholarship, he went up to Trinity College, Cambridge, in October 1935. He was a Marxist and a committed Communist. Anthony Blunt supervised Long's studies, and probably had him elected to the **Apostles** in May 1937, at much the same time as he recruited him to the **NKVD**, code-named RALPH (West and Tsarev, 1998, p. 133).

In 1938 Long graduated, but the NKVD did not indicate what he should do. So he went to Europe and taught in Frankfurt. When **World War II** began, he joined the Oxford and Bucks Light Infantry, and, being fluent in German, was made a lieutenant in the Intelligence Corps.

In 1941 Long was in MI-14 (War Office), a section that collected information on the German **order of battle.** From **Bletchley Park** he had access to ULTRA intelligence, and the breaking of the varieties of Enigma codes.

During World War II, Anthony Blunt ran Long personally as an NKVD/**NKGB** subagent for the Soviets. In Blunt's absence, Guy Burgess (1911–1963) was his handler (West and Tsarev, 1998, p. 144). Long would meet weekly with Blunt, and provided a précis of what he had come to know that week. Long's deep commitment to the Soviet cause led him to provide Blunt with everything he could to help Russians, who valued highly the information they received, especially the relayed ULTRA decrypts.

At the end of World War II, Long joined the British Control Commission in Germany and became its deputy head of intelligence. He had married, was divorced, and was raising his children. In the last months of 1946 Anthony Blunt was sending the Russians Long's information from the Commission. Long's contact with the Soviets broke when Blunt was no longer active, although Long would always be deeply impressed by Blunt for his mentoring in Cambridge.

When Kim Philby (1912–1988) fled to Moscow and published his own account of what he had done, and when Anthony Blunt was interrogated in April 1964, Long was in jeopardy.

Michael Straight (1916–2004) told the **Federal Bureau of Investigation (FBI)** in June 1963 that Leo Long might have been recruited to the Soviets. Long was advised by Blunt to come clean; if he did, he would probably not be prosecuted. He was interrogated later in 1964 and asked for immunity; it was not granted, but he was advised that if he were to cooperate with the authorities, prosecution would be unlikely. Long admitted that he was still providing the Russians with secret material up to 1952.

Long's interrogation was secret, and not made public until the appearance of Chapman Pincher's *Their Trade Is Treachery* in 1981. Pincher noted that Long had been recruited in the 1930s, and ceased to help the Russians when he married, to ensure his family was not in danger.

The **code name** ELLI was a mystery to the West, and many in the British secret services thought it could have been Graham Mitchell, Guy Liddell (1892–1958), or Roger Hollis (1905–1973). In 1981, so Gordievsky reported, he saw Long's **KGB** file and discovered his code name was ELLI.

In 1981 Long he was working for a commercial firm. In November 1981 **Margaret Thatcher** (1925–) was reported to have named him, and Long appeared on television, showing remorse for his activities. He was never charged. In 1981 and

1985 he gave full interviews for the book by Penrose and Simon, *Conspiracy of Silence* (1986).

Later, Long said his wartime espionage was treasonable.

See also BLUNT, ANTHONY; BURGESS, GUY; HOLLIS, ROGER; LIDDELL, GUY; PHILBY, HAROLD "KIM"; STRAIGHT, MICHAEL

Sources: Andrew, Christopher, and Oleg Gordievsky, *KGB: The Inside Story of Its Foreign Operations from Lenin to Gorbachev* (London: Hodder and Stoughton, 1990); Deacon, Richard, *The Cambridge Apostles: A History of Cambridge University's Elite Intellectual Secret Society* (New York: Farrar, Straus & Giroux, 1986); Laffin, John, *Brassey's Book of Espionage* (London: Brassey's, 1996); Penrose, Barry, and Simon Freeman, *Conspiracy of Silence: The Secret Life of Anthony Blunt,* updated ed. (London: Grafton, 1986); Pincher, Chapman, *Too Secret Too Long* (London: Sidgwick & Jackson, 1984); Pincher, Chapman, *Traitors: The Anatomy of Treason* (New York: St. Martin's Press, 1987).

LONSDALE, GORDON (1922–1970). See MOLODY, KONON

LOVESTONE, JAY (fl. 1899–1990). Jay Lovestone was a shadowy character and a **Central Intelligence Agency (CIA) agent** within the personal world of James Angleton (1917–1987), head of the CIA counterintelligence operations.

Lovestone was a Communist until he underwent a political epiphany and became an anti-Communist zealot after **World War II**. In the late 1940s he began running the AFL–CIO's Department of International Affairs, and would secretly identify Communists among the union members and report on them to the CIA.

Beginning in 1955, James Angleton used Lovestone as a paid CIA agent; he was controlled by Angleton via the head of the Israel desk in the CIA. Lovestone would give the CIA information about trade union affairs worldwide, and be paid for that information through Angleton's lawyer in New York. Lovestone received not only a salary from the CIA, but also subsidies for his New York office from secret funds under Angleton's control. Lovestone would also distribute CIA funds for Angleton around the world.

Angleton received Lovestone's reports, marked them "JX," numbered them, and from time to time read amusing parts to his colleagues. Angleton had deep, secure confidence in Lovestone's work.

The two were united in their beliefs about Russia's great Communist threat to the West. To others in the CIA it became evident the Lovestone reports were overvalued, tending to gossip more than valuable intelligence, and often reported on people who were unimportant. William Colby (1920–1996) felt ambivalent about the reports, so their contribution was closely investigated and they were found seriously wanting. Colby ended the Angleton–Lovestone connection, much to Angleton's distress, not long before he forced Angleton to retire.

See also ANGLETON, JAMES; COLBY, WILLIAM

Source: Mangold, Tom, *Cold Warrior: James Jesus Angleton, the CIA Master Spy Hunter* (New York: Simon & Schuster, 1991).

LUMUMBA, PATRICE (1925–1961). Patrice Lumumba was the first Prime Minister of the independent Republic of the Congo in Africa; he was killed six months after becoming the nation's head, and his death was linked to the **Cold War** policy makers and intelligence community of the United States, including President **Dwight D. Eisenhower** (1890–1969).

Lumumba was born in Katako Kombe, and became a trade unionist and postal clerk in the colonial civil service of the Belgian Congo. In 1958 he established the Mouvement National Congolais, whose goal was based on the "self-government now" politics of Ghana's leader Kwame Nkrumah (1909–1972).

On June 20, 1960, as soon as the Belgian Congo was declared a republic, internal political strife began. At the independence ceremony King Baudouin (1930–1993) of Belgium celebrated the granting of his colony's independence with a catalog of Belgium's contributions to the Congo over the last 80 years of colonial government, and presented the Prime Minister, Patrice Lumumba, age 34, with Belgium's Order of Leopold. In reply Lumumba denounced the 80 years of Belgian colonial domination as unrelenting, insulting, and naked racism.

Eleven days later a civil war began as the army mutinied, Lumumba appealed for help from the United Nations, and the Congo's copper-rich Katanga Province seceded from the republic under the control of a thrice-declared bankrupt businessman, Moïse Tshombe (1917–1969). Riots, raping, and looting spread. Belgian troops were parachuted in to establish control. UN soldiers arrived in mid-July, and Lumumba declared martial law.

In late July, Lumumba went to the United States to seek economic aid, but undermined what appeared to be successful discussions by suggesting that he invite Soviet troops to force the Belgian troops to withdraw. In early August civil war began in earnest between Tshombe's soldiers and the UN troops. The crisis deepened. More UN troops arrived in the Congo, and Swedish soldiers replaced the Belgian troops by mid-August.

Meanwhile, in the United States, the President and a special group that authorized covert operations agreed that in their plans for the Congo, getting rid of Lumumba would be an option. Why? Since he appeared unable to quell the chaos in the new republic, there was a strong possibility of a Communist takeover. For many years this would be interpreted as a high-level directive from the United States to assassinate Lumumba.

Early in September the Soviets promised help to the Congo, and Lumumba dismissed the new President, Joseph Kasavubu (1913–1969), whose military leader, Joseph Mobutu (1930–1997), had the support of the **Central Intelligence Agency (CIA).** Joseph Kasavubu immediately fired Lumumba; he refused to leave, and ordered his troops to invade Katanga. The tension was felt in the United Nations, and the Russians demanded the Secretary-General of the United Nations resign.

The CIA prepared to deal with Lumumba. Apparently this was not necessary, or so some critics have argued. For 40 years it was believed that in the Congo, Lumumba lost control of the armed forces, and fled to Leopoldville for protection by the UN troops. In December, Mobutu's forces captured Lumumba while he was trying to reach his stronghold in Stanleyville. He was imprisoned, and murdered on January 17, 1961. His body was never found. There was certainly a plot to have him killed, but whether or not he was killed on orders from the CIA was not securely known.

In September 1960 a CIA operative came to the Congo with a vial of poison that was to be placed on Lumumba's toothbrush (Whitlelaw, 2000); Bissell (1996) says he was killed by his own people; De Witte (2000) writes that the CIA knew of Lumumba's transfer to Katanga, and Belgian authorities arranged for the assassination, the dismemberment of the corpse, and its disposal in sulfuric acid. In May 2000 the Belgian Parliament opened an investigation into the murder (Lister, 2000).

Recently it was alleged that the Belgians called their role in the death of Lumumba Operation BARRACUDA.

Sources: Bissell, Richard Mervin, Jr., with Jonathan E. Lewis and Frances T. Pudio, *Reflections of a Cold Warrior: From Yalta to the Bay of Pigs* (New Haven, CT: Yale University Press, 1996); Black, Ian, "Files Show U.K. Backed Murder Plot," *Guardian*, June 28, 2001, Guardian Unlimited Archive, www.guardian.co.uk/Archive/Article/0,4273,4211887,00.html; De Witte, Ludo, *The Assassination of Lumumba* (London: Verso, 2000); De Witte, Ludo, Colin Legum, and Brian Urqhuart, "The Tragedy of Lumumba: An Exchange," *New York Review of Books*, December 20, 2001, pp. 103–105; Lister, David, "1961 Congo Murder File Reopened," *The Times* (London), May 3, 2000, p. 17; Smith, Joseph, and Simon Davis, *Historical Dictionary of the Cold War* (New York: Scarecrow Press, 2000); U.S. Senate, *Alleged Assassination Plots Involving Foreign Leaders* (Washington, DC: Government Printing Office, 1975); Whitelaw, Kevin, "A Killing in the Congo: Lumumba's Death No Longer Seems a CIA Plot," *U.S. News & World Report*, July 24, 2000, www.usnews.com.

LUNN, PETER NORTHCOTE (1914–). Peter Lunn was one of the British spymasters early in the **Cold War**. He is noted for his unusual methods of espionage, especially telephone tapping, and his passion for high-speed skiing.

Peter Lunn is the son of Sir Arnold Lunn, founder of Lunn's Travel Agency, and himself an early member of Britain's secret services. Peter was educated at Eton before entering government service in 1939. He had a slight build and blue eyes, spoke in a soft voice with a lisp, and appeared to be a quiet, gentle fellow. However benign in appearance, he was a forceful man of strong will, hardworking, a devout Roman Catholic, and militant anti-Communist.

Prior to his government work, Lunn was a member of the British international ski team from 1931 to 1937; from 1934 to 1937 he was the team's captain, and he led the British Olympic ski team in 1936 in Garmisch. In 1939 he married the daughter of Viscount Gormanstan; they had two sons and two daughters.

Lunn's "government service" mentioned in Black and Black (2003) was largely in the British secret services. He joined the **SIS** in 1941, at much the same time as Kim Philby (1912–1988). A Royal Artillery officer, Lunn was seconded to **MI6**, and supervised secret operations for 30 years. He worked in Malta (1939–1944), Italy (1944–1945), West Germany (1945–1946), London (1946–1948), Vienna (1948–1950), Bern (1950–1953), Berlin (1953–1956), London again (1956–1957), Bonn (1957–1962), Beirut (1962–1967), and London for a third time (1967–1968).

In 1947 Lunn was in command of Hamburg station, and in 1950 headed the SIS Vienna station as Second Secretary. His main problem was: how to penetrate the Soviet bloc, mainly Czechoslovakia and Hungary, and establish what was happening inside the Russian military, whose headquarters was in the Russian sector of Vienna.

Lunn discovered that beneath the French and British sectors of Vienna there were telephone cables that linked field units and airports of the Russian army with its headquarters. He got expert advice on tapping those lines, and a private mining consultant agreed to construct a tunnel from the basement of a police post to the main phone cable between the Soviet headquarters in the Imperial Hotel and Schwechat, the Russian military airfield (Operation CONFLICT).

In the early 1950s Lunn was in charge of London's efforts to recruit large numbers of members of the National Union of Students to act as **agents** for **MI6** while they traveled on the European continent.

In 1954 Lunn was head of station in Berlin, and cooperated with his opposite number in the **Central Intelligence Agency (CIA)** to bring about work on the Berlin tunnel (Operation STOPWATCH/GOLD). Most of the manpower and funds were provided by the Americans, while the technical skills and experience from the Vienna tunnel came from Lunn's officers. Unknown to either the SIS or the CIA, the tunnel was revealed to the Soviets by George Blake (1922–) from its beginning.

While Lunn was station chief Berlin, he introduced a card index of agents. In the event of an alert or arrest, the duty officer would pull out the card index and see which of 50 MI6 officers should be summoned. Occasionally George Blake was the night duty officer. He copied the names of all the service's agents and, at regular meetings in East Berlin, passed the contents of SIS's whole structure to his **KGB** controller, Nikolai Rodin.

On the night the Soviet soldiers "'discovered" the tunnel, **Nikita Khrushchev** (1894–1973) was at **Chequers**, a guest of the British Prime Minister. Khrushchev had been fully briefed about the tunnel and the propaganda, and was prepared to avoid implicating the British at this time because détente policies were emerging internationally after **Josef Stalin**'s (1879–1953) death. So, to ensure good Anglo–Soviet relations, all press accusations about the tunnel were directed against the Americans. Lunn was forced to watch as the CIA took the credit for what had been his idea. For his efforts he was awarded the **CMG**.

Skiing was Lunn's lifetime activity. In 1935 and in 1947 he published books on high-speed skiing, a skier's primer in 1948, and the *Guinness Book of Skiing* in 1983. He competed in the Inferno downhill ski race from 1978 to 1986, in 1988 and 1989, and from 1995 to 2002. He loved skiing for its combination of thrills and technical demands, the kind of experiences readily found in espionage.

Lunn's wife died in 1976, and he retired from government service in 1986.

See also BLAKE, GEORGE; OPERATIONS CONFLICT, LORD, AND SUGAR; OPERATION STOPWATCH

Sources: Andrew, Christopher, and Vasili Mitrokhin, *The Mitrokhin Archive: The KGB in Europe and the West* (London: Lane, 1999); Black, A., and C. Black, *Who's Who: An Annual Biographical Dictionary* (London: A. & C. Black, 2003); Blake, George, *No Other Choice: An Autobiography* (London: Jonathan Cape, 1990); Dorril, Stephen, *MI6: Inside the Covert World of Her Majesty's Secret Intelligence Service* (New York: The Free Press, 2000); Stafford, David, *Spies Beneath Berlin* (London: John Murray, 2000).

LYALIN, OLEG ADOLFOVICH (fl. 1937–1972).

Oleg Lyalin, a **KGB** expert in terrorist tactics, was skillfully blackmailed by **MI5** into serving the interests of the West.

Oleg Lyalin was born in the **U.S.S.R.** In 1970 he used the cover of a Soviet trade mission member. He was an outstanding KGB saboteur who planned **active measures**, a KGB policy of mounting terrorist attacks in many Western countries.

In February 1971 Lyalin was having an affair with his secretary, Irina Teplyakova. MI5 used this to threaten blackmail and to **recruit** him; he agreed to cooperate with MI5, providing that he could have access to a **safe house** where he could continue his affair.

Early in the morning of August 31, 1971, Lyalin was arrested on a drunk-driving charge, and because he refused to cooperate with police and did not have diplomatic immunity, he was put in jail, and might well have been tried and given a short prison sentence. MI5 moved swiftly. Before they knew it, Lyalin wanted to defect. His drunk-driving case was dropped, and he began to tell what he knew.

Lyalin was the first intelligence officer to defect to the British since the end of **World War II,** and the first to have been recruited by MI5. His main task had been to find British targets for Soviet terrorist acts, mainly the sabotage of public services and the assassination of political and other important figures. A special department, Department V, had been established in the KGB to organize these activities in major Western capitals.

Lyalin told of his tasks, but more important, he gave the British secret services a list of KGB **agents** who were working on the Department V active measures. MI5 suspected many of the individuals were spies, and had their suspicions confirmed by Lyalin's statements as well as learning of some new cases. Altogether 105 Soviet agents were made persona non grata following Lyalin's disclosures. This was a great shock to the Soviet embassy in London.

Sources: Andrew, Christopher, and Oleg Gordievsky, *KGB: The Inside Story of Its Foreign Operations from Lenin to Gorbachev* (London: Hodder and Stoughton, 1990); Andrew, Christopher, and Vasili Mitrokhin, *The Mitrokhin Archive: The KGB in Europe and the West* (London: Lane, 1999); Brook-Shepherd, Gordon, *The Storm Birds. Soviet Post War Defectors: The Dramatic True Stories 1945–1985* (New York: Henry Holt, 1989); Pincher, Chapman, *Traitors: The Anatomy of Treason* (New York: St. Martin's Press, 1987).

M

MACLEAN, DONALD DUART (1913–1983). Donald Maclean was one of the Magnificent Five, a group of British citizens who spied for the Soviets before and during the **Cold War.**

Donald Maclean was the third son of five children of Sir Donald Maclean, a lawyer and Liberal member of Parliament, and Gwendolyn Devitt. Aged 12, in 1925, Donald went to Gresham's School, where he became a prefect in the headmaster's house in 1928.

The school had an ambivalent system of personal control that advocated the "honor system" of discipline, yet insisted the boys have their pockets sewed closed. Maclean paid lip service to the conformity required at school, and developed a strong belief in the power of his own judgment, a staunch grasp of the truth, and little concern for the foolishness of others. Also, he would mock higher authorities by appearing to conform to their requests and practicing duplicity to undermine their influence.

Maclean radiated charm to cover his deep loathing for most authority, and added to that charm clever skills he needed to lead a double life. His tendency to lead a double life was evident at home and at school, and would become central to his work in the British Foreign Office.

In October 1931, on a scholarship, Maclean went up to Trinity College to study modern languages; his father died in the following year; and in 1933 Maclean moved out of the college into his own accommodations. At the time Cambridge had about 7,000 undergraduates, and about 1,000 were members of the Cambridge University Socialist Society. In his politics Maclean sought participant democracy for undergraduates and staff, equality for women students, and the right of students to use university property for political meetings.

Maclean graduated with first-class honors in modern languages in June 1934, and in August 1934 he was recruited to the Communist cause by Theodore Maly, a Soviet **illegal.** Maclean's **code names** were WAIS (German) and SIROTA (Russian), both meaning "orphan" (probably because of his father's recent death).

In October 1935, after cramming for the entrance exam, Maclean was successful in his application to enter the British Foreign Office. He worked in the League of Nations and Western Department, and in September 1938 was appointed Third Secretary in Great Britain's Paris embassy. In Paris he began drinking to excess. He told his mistress, an American named Melinda Marley, that he worked for Soviet intelligence. In June 1940 he married Melinda, and they quickly returned to Britain following the fall of France to Nazi Germany.

A few weeks later Maclean met Kim Philby (1912–1988) for the first time since the mid-1930s. By 1941 Maclean was supplying large numbers of documents to the Soviets.

In May 1944 the Macleans were sent to New York, and in January 1945 they were living in Washington. Donald was assigned to work on the secret development of the **atom bomb**, known as the **Tube Alloys Project** in Britain and the **Manhattan Project** in the United States. For two years before he was made the Joint Secretary of the Combined Policy Committee (CPC) in February 1947, Maclean had access to most of the valuable material on the atom bomb projects, and could ensure that his Russian handlers got what the Soviets needed to advance their own development of an atom bomb.

Maclean worked long hours on other matters, and managed to gain membership on committees and in informal groups that held information valuable for the **NKVD.** He was in contact with Alger Hiss (1904–1996), and provided the Soviets with advance information on the U.S. position in various UN debates.

In May 1945 Maclean defended the Russian position on its veto in the Security Council, and on its demand for UN membership for several of its satellite nations. In August that year Elizabeth Bentley (1908–1963) defected to the **Federal Bureau of Investigation (FBI),** and in September Igor Gouzenko (c. 1919–1982) defected to the West in Canada.

In July 1946 Maclean visited his wife in a New York hospital, where she was giving birth to their second son. This was recorded in the VENONA material, and when decoded would firmly establish that he was a Soviet **agent**, now code-named HOMER. However, this did not become securely known to Western authorities until April 1951.

Meanwhile, Maclean was acting head of Chancery until November 1946; in February 1947 he was the British cosecretary of the CPC. This gave him improved access to the documents that the NKVD wanted. He was at a special conference in November 1947 on the declassification of weapons technology. There he was able to learn what was still regarded as secret, such as the technology for detecting nuclear explosions at a distance; uranium requirements and supply; how many nuclear bombs the United States had; how were they stored; and how much processed uranium was available. In November 1947 Maclean had a pass that allowed him on 20 occasions to enter the **Atomic Energy Commission** building.

In September 1948 Maclean returned to London, and was to go to Cairo as counselor and head of Chancery in October. The British were resented in Egypt; Maclean and his wife were growing apart; his workload was getting very heavy; and he was becoming addicted to alcohol. He sent a note to his Soviet handler, saying he wanted to be relieved of working for Soviet intelligence due to the strain of work.

After several distressing incidents, Maclean became no longer fit for service, was sent on a six-month leave from Cairo to London in May 1950, and underwent psychiatric therapy for alcoholism and homosexuality. He also sought the company and help of friends in England. But nothing was of much help to him: political idealism, alcohol, or psychotherapy.

By September 1949, Kim Philby, who had been briefed about HOMER, was certain that Maclean must be the man; by the end of 1950 the number of suspects for the identity of HOMER was reduced to 50.

Melinda joined Donald, who had returned to work in London at the Foreign Office, and by January 1951 they had bought a house. But late in January, after the conviction of Alger Hiss, Maclean, rather drunk, muttered to a friend, "I am the English Hiss." With his high consumption of alcohol he was becoming ever more unstable.

Moscow Center agreed to exfiltrate Maclean because they knew that under interrogation he was likely to break down and put the other members of the Magnificent Five in hazard. Melinda agreed with this decision. At the end of May he and Guy Burgess (1911–1963) secretly left England for Moscow.

After his defection to Russia, Maclean became a Soviet citizen, Mark Petrovich Fraser, and, working as a foreign policy analyst, taught at the Knibyshev Pedagogical Institute, where he was paid twice the pension that Guy Burgess was receiving. In September 1953 Melinda and the children were exfiltrated to Moscow.

In September 1956, Maclean gave his first press conference, saying that he had gone to Moscow to work for a better understanding between the Soviets and the West.

Later Melinda left Maclean for Kim Philby, eventually abandoned him as well, and returned to the United States, where she died of cancer.

See also BLUNT, ANTHONY; BURGESS, GUY; CAIRNCROSS, JOHN; MAGNIFICENT FIVE; PHILBY, HAROLD "KIM"

Sources: Andrew, Christopher, and Vasili Mitrokhin, *The Mitrokhin Archive: The KGB in Europe and the West* (London: Lane, 1999); Boyle, Andrew, *The Fourth Man: The Definitive Account of Philby (1912–88), Guy Burgess, Donald Maclean and Who Recruited Them to Spy for Russia* (New York: Dial Press, 1979); Cecil, Robert, *A Divided Life: A Personal Portrait of the Spy Donald Maclean* (New York: William Morrow, 1989); Costello, John, and Oleg Tsarev, *Deadly Illusions* (New York: Crown, 1993); Hoare, Geoffrey, *The Missing Macleans* (New York: Viking, 1955); Laffin, John, *Brassey's Book of Espionage* (London: Brassey's, 1996); Mahoney, Harry T., and Marjorie L. Mahoney, *Biographic Dictionary of Espionage* (San Francisco: Austin & Winfield, 1998); Volkman, Ernest, *Espionage: The Greatest Spy Operations of the 20th Century* (New York: Wiley, 1995).

MAGNIFICENT FIVE. The Magnificent Five is a **KGB** name for five British spies, all of whom were at Cambridge University in the late 1920s and early 1930s.

The five were Anthony Frederick Blunt (1907–1983), Guy Francis de Moncey Burgess (1911–1963), Harold Adrian Russell "Kim" Philby (1912–1988), Donald Duart Maclean (1913–1983), and John Cairncross (1913–1995).

During **World War II** they were known as "the London Five" because they were all run by the KGB from the London **residency.** They were dubbed the "Magnificent Five" by the First Chief Directorate after the movie *The Magnificent Seven* (1960), inspired by a Japanese movie, *The Seven Samurai* (1954).

The 1960 movie was a rousing Hollywood western adventure in which the American film stars Yul Brynner, Steve McQueen, Charles Bronson, James Coburn, Eli Wallach, and Robert Vaughan, all gunfighters, come to the aid of a village of Mexican farmers plagued by bandits. The 1954 film involved seven Japanese swordsmen who had much the same task.

In Britain, writers, historians, and journalists would call the five the "Cambridge spies" and the "Cambridge spy ring." This gave the impression that they were recruited as a team and worked together. In fact they were recruited at different times and worked in different places, but, when possible, they would help each other to secure places where they could work effectively. They rarely communicated with each other, and often were not working in the same country. Their main common factor was motivation: they have been labeled "ideological" spies, and contrasted with spies who provided secrets merely for money. Their glory days ended in May 1951 with the flight to Moscow of Burgess and Maclean, and the failure of Blunt to completely sanitize Burgess's apartment after the flight.

They began their careers as Soviet **agents** in the 1930s. John Cairncross denied he was one of them, which throws into question the KGB concept of a working group of five, or cell. Also, some officials in **Moscow Center** held the view that the Magnificent Five was a false conception because all five were **double agents**, working for the British rather than the Soviets, passing some false and some true information to their Soviet handlers in a grand British **Cold War** conspiracy. Many commentators regard this as fanciful.

See also BLUNT, ANTHONY; BURGESS, GUY; CAIRNCROSS, JOHN; MACLEAN, DONALD; PHILBY, HAROLD "KIM"

Sources: Andrew, Christopher, and Oleg Gordievsky, *KGB: The Inside Story of Its Foreign Operations from Lenin to Gorbachev* (London: Hodder and Stoughton, 1990); Andrew, Christopher, and Vasili Mitrokhin, *The Mitrokhin Archive: The KGB in Europe and the West* (London: Lane, 1999); Borovik, Genrikh, *The Philby Files: The Secret Life of Master Spy Kim Philby (1912–88)* (Boston: Little, Brown, 1994); Cairncross, John, *The Enigma Spy: An Autobiography. The Story of a Man Who Changed the Course of World War Two* (London: Century, 1997); Costello, John, and Oleg Tsarev, *Deadly Illusions* (New York: Crown, 1993); Kerr, Sheila, "Review Article. KGB Sources on the Cambridge Network of Soviet Spies: True or False?" *Intelligence and National Security* 11 (1996): 561–585; Modin, Yuri, *My Five Cambridge Friends* (London: Headline, 1994); Sudoplatov, Pavel, and Anatoli Sudoplatov, *Special Tasks: The Memoirs of an Unwanted Witness, a Soviet Spymaster* (Boston: Little, Brown, 1994).

MARKOV ASSASSINATION (1978). Georgi Markov (1929–1978) was a a handsome, gray-haired Bulgarian dissident. Early in his career he was a close associate of Bulgaria's President Todor Zhivkov (1911–), but turned against communism and fled to England, where in BBC broadcasts he criticized the Bulgarian government and leadership.

In the belief that Bulgarian citizens were offended by the broadcasts, President Zhivkov said he wanted Markov "physically removed"—the President's words—from London. **Yuri Andropov** (1914–1984) agreed, but was not pleased to be associated with this request.

Sergei Golubev, head of security for the Intelligence Directorate, was given the task of murdering Markov without leaving a trace of what had killed him. On advice from the laboratories of the Operational and Technical Directorate of the **KGB**, he chose a poison pellet, rather than poisoned jelly to rub on his skin or poison to put in his food. The pellet would contain ricin, a poison derived from castor plant seeds.

The poison pellet was tested successfully on a horse, and then on a prisoner who had been sentenced to death. The experimenters used an umbrella tip; the unsuspecting prisoner thought he had been stung by a bee, but he did not die! Nevertheless, the plan was to be carried out on Markov.

On September 7, 1978, while Markov was waiting on Waterloo Bridge for a bus, the killer prodded him with the poisoned umbrella tip. Later, in hospital, Markov recounted that he had felt a sudden sting in his right thigh, and, turning, saw a man who had apparently dropped his umbrella; the stranger picked up the umbrella, apologized, and got into a taxi. Doctors could not determine the cause of Markov's illness. He died September 11.

Vladimir Kostov, a Bulgarian defector, was alerted by this episode to an attack on himself in Paris the previous August; the following month a steel pellet, still intact, had been found in his back. In his case, the poison had been ineffective because it either was too old or was not released.

Markov's body was exhumed, and an autopsy revealed a small pellet in a wound on his right thigh. In his case the ricin had decomposed, and entered his body.

Sources: Andrew, Christopher, and Oleg Gordievsky, *KGB: The Inside Story of Its Foreign Operations from Lenin to Gorbachev* (London: Hodder and Stoughton, 1990); Andrew, Christopher, and Vasili Mitrokhin, *The Mitrokhin Archive: The KGB in Europe and the West* (London: Lane, 1990); Kalugin, Oleg, and Fen Montaigne, *Spymaster: My 32 Years in Intelligence and Espionage Against the West* (London: Smith Gryphon, 1994); Sifakis, Carl, *Encyclopedia of Assassinations: A Compendium of Attempted and Successful Assassinations Throughout History* (New York: Facts on File, 1993).

MARSHALL, KAY (fl. 1926–1963). Kay Marshall, an Englishwoman who had come to New Zealand to marry a serviceman during **World War II,** was recruited into Soviet intelligence, and worked as a **double agent** for **ASIO.**

An attractive and independent brunette, Kay Marshall worked in Wellington, New Zealand, in the late 1950s. She was personally charming, and had worked in many countries. She had a son, and her marriage had ended. By 1956 she was working in the passport office of the British High Commission in New Zealand.

In September 1960 Marshall had been recruited to Soviet intelligence, but acted as a double agent for the New Zealand security service.

The Soviet press attaché, an intelligence **agent,** approached Marshall, gave her presents, and asked for several documents that were publicly available. Apparently he was planning to have her give him the public documents, and then ask her later for secret material. Recognizing this commonly used Soviet ploy, Marshall immediately told her case officer, and in time handed the Russian **disinformation** in the form of false documents marked "confidential."

In September 1960, when Moscow recalled the agent, he was replaced with a rude vulgarian whom Marshall would no longer work with. She told him she wanted to go to Australia. He advised her that she would be met by his counterpart in Sydney. In December 1960 she came to Australia, where ASIO was much interested in finding Soviet intelligence agents after the defection of Vladimir Petrov (1907–1991).

In Australia, ASIO gave Marshall the **code name** SYLVIA. Eventually she met the Soviet agent, as the Russian in New Zealand had told her she would. At all of their meetings she wore a concealed microphone and transmitter. The Russian agent was a spy known to ASIO as Ivan Skripov (fl. 1960–1963), but Marshall knew him as

"John." He gave her several tasks to see whether or not she would make a good secret agent. Some of their meetings were filmed, and would be used later by ASIO for training.

Two years after her arrival in Sydney and work as a double agent, in December 1962 Ivan Skripov gave Marshall a package to deliver; it was opened first by ASIO, and found to contain a valuable and unusual transmitter. It was resealed. ASIO planned to observe her giving the package to the person it was intended for, and then have the police arrest him when he passed it on to another person. The agent for whom the package was intended did not appear at the planned meeting with Marshall. Possibly the people for whom the package was intended could see they were under surveillance.

Six days later Marshall met Skripov, and he demanded the transmitter. She managed to keep it for four weeks by failing to keep later appointments. On February 7, 1963, Skripov was declared persona non grata and had to leave Australia within a week. Her work with him ended.

See also SKRIPOV, IVAN

Sources: Laffin, John, *Brassey's Book of Espionage* (London: Brassey's, 1996); McKnight, David, *Australia's Spies and Their Secrets* (St. Leonards, NSW: Allen and Unwin, 1994).

MARSHALL, WILLIAM MARTIN (fl. 1927–1960). William Marshall was a naïve young British wireless operator who was caught in the early 1950s and charged under the Official Secrets Act, but may have been part of a clever Soviet scheme to draw attention away from a valuable **agent** who was under **MI5**'s suspicion.

William Marshall was the son of a London bus driver and, aged 14, joined the U.K. Sea Cadets, where he learned Morse code. When he was called up for military service in 1945, he served in Palestine and Egypt in the Royal Signal Corps and was trained in radio operations; he was demobilized in 1948. He joined the Diplomatic Wireless Service in Britain's Foreign Office and was posted to the Middle East, and later to the British embassy in Moscow.

A shy and awkward young man, Marshall felt that in his lowly position at the embassy it was difficult to find companions. He liked movies, but found he would have to learn Russian to understand them, so he made a few Russian contacts. The Russian intelligence services noticed him. In December 1951 he was returned to London.

Late in April 1952 Marshall was seen talking with Pavel Kuznetsov, a Soviet diplomat. In May 1952 he met Kuznetsov again, and in June 1952 attended the British-Soviet Friendship Society meeting in Holborn Hall. Often he had lunch with his new friend, and they would meet in various public places, to sit and talk. The two were frequently under observation by MI5 officers.

In June 1952, as the two were leaving a London park, where they had been talking and apparently sharing notes, Marshall was arrested and the Soviet official was quickly searched to see if he had secret British documents that Marshall was suspected of passing to him. No documents were found on the Soviet official, but in Marshall's wallet was a copy of a secret document that later was shown by a handwriting expert to have been transcribed by Marshall himself. Under Britain's **Official Secrets Act**, Marshall was charged with unlawfully obtaining information for the benefit of a foreign power.

Sillitoe (1955), former Director-General of MI5, wrote that the Soviet official had blundered in not teaching Marshall basic **tradecraft**, and was returned to Moscow in disgrace. While Marshall had distinguished himself as a fantasist spy, the British secret services had effectively neutralized, once again, the Soviets in their attempts to turn a British citizen into a Soviet asset.

On the other hand, Rebecca West (1953, 1968) reported from her observations at Marshall's trial on July 9–10, 1952, that Marshall had not *obtained* information, but had it normally in his possession through his duties at work, so the charge of obtaining was not viable; second, she noted that he was charged with recording information for the benefit of a foreign power. Although he had transcribed the secret document, and it was clearly in his own handwriting, there was no evidence that he had taken it from his wallet and handed it to his Soviet friend. Nobody had overheard their conversation; nobody had seen them exchanging notes or other items. In short, Marshal was not guilty as charged on both counts.

Marshall answered questions in a naïve, simpleminded manner, and offered a vague and improbable account of his activities involving his failure to return a diplomatic pass to the Soviets in Moscow, meeting with an official at a time that was difficult to believe, becoming petulant about his being a misfit in the embassy in Moscow, and complaining that he did not agree with his parents' anti-Communist views. In addition to these self-defeating statements, he said he and his Soviet friend talked politics—Korea, Malaysia, and divided Germany—and shared news summaries, maps, and cultural information on Moscow. Even this was not sufficient to establish his guilt in the jury's mind.

Finally, Marshall said petulantly that he knew nothing at all about the transcribed copy of the document that the police found in his wallet. As far as he could see, the only explanation was that *the police* must have somehow gotten a copy of the original document, had it transcribed into Marshall's hand by a *brilliant graphologist*, and secretly *planted it* in Marshall's wallet without his knowing! The jury found him guilty of having copied the secret document, and he was sentenced to five years in prison.

While Sir Percy Sillitoe suggested that the Soviet official bungled the handling of his young agent, and MI5 had neutralized yet another Soviet attempt to have British citizens become Soviet spies, Rebecca West argued the opposite. She wrote that the awkward, gullible, inept, and naïve Marshall was selected by the Soviet official to attend regular, publicly observable meetings with him. No meeting had much of a clandestine character; every one was in an open place where everything could be seen, but nothing could be heard. These were excellent circumstances to fuel suspicion among intelligence operatives. But why do this?

West suggested that Marshall was duped into regular meetings that he imagined were clandestine, and then served up to British intelligence to direct attention from a valuable asset who was working for the Soviets. Who might that have been? The Magnificent Five were no longer what they had been; the Russians knew that the West had the VENONA material and were decoding it; Donald Maclean (1913–1983) and Guy Burgess (1911–1963) were safe in Moscow; Anthony Blunt (1907–1983) had become less active as a secret agent. Their replacements had not been chosen, and their work was certainly not finished. Who, then? Kim Philby (1912–1988)? He was in danger during 1952.

After the trial, the Soviet Chargé d'Affaires protested Pavel Kuznetsov's being searched by the police, claiming it had been illegal. The Foreign Office replied by requesting he be withdrawn, and he left Great Britain in mid-July.

See also BLUNT, ANTHONY; MAGNIFICENT FIVE; PHILBY, HAROLD "KIM"

Sources: Sillitoe, Percy, *Cloak Without Dagger* (London: Cassell, 1955); West, Nigel, *The Circus: MI5 Operations 1945–1972* (New York: Stein and Day, 1983); West, Rebecca, *A Train of Powder* (London: Viking Press, 1953); West, Rebecca, "The Agent the Soviets Wanted Caught," in Allen Dulles, ed., *Great True Spy Stories* (Secaucus, NJ: Castle, 1968), pp. 145–157.

MATUSOW, HARVEY MARSHALL (1926–2002). Harvey Marshall Matusow was a notorious liar who was paid by the **Federal Bureau of Investigation (FBI)** for spying on Communists; he testified before the **House Un-American Activities Commission (HUAC)** largely to advance his sense of self-worth. He was jailed for almost three years for perjury. He lived in England for many years afterward, before returning to the United States as a writer and entertainer.

Harvey Matusow, the younger son of a New York cigar store owner, lived a comfortable middle-class life in the Bronx. At school and in family life he was an over-achiever, and always felt he could and should do better, to please himself and others. He failed in his attempt to join the Royal Canadian Air Force, but in 1943 he proudly became a U.S. Air Force cadet in training. At the time his brother was a bombardier, and was shot down over Germany. Matusow transferred to the U.S. Army and was stationed in Mainz, Germany, where, he promised his mother, he would find his brother, a presumed prisoner of war. Instead he found his brother's grave and sufficient information to date his death.

In 1946 Matusow was discharged, joined the Air Force Reserve, and went to college for a semester. He joined American Youth for Democracy, then the **CPUSA** (1947) as part of a search for an identity he could be proud of. He found the party organization inept but nevertheless worked hard for the party, and was rewarded with a trip to Puerto Rico.

In time Matusow felt the party leadership to be too authoritarian, and was hurt by what he felt was unjustified criticism of his work for the party. His resentment turned to bitterness toward party members. In 1950 he contacted the FBI, and joined what he would later call a bandwagon of heroic informants like Elizabeth Bentley (1908–1963). He attended Communist Party meetings as a secret FBI **agent**, and for U.S.$70–75 a month informed on party members.

Matusow left New York for New Mexico because he felt so bad about betraying his party friends; however, he was willing to report to the FBI on the other persons at a guest house where he was staying, because he said, those whom he betrayed in New Mexico were hardly known to him. On returning to New York he was expelled from the party in December 1950.

Matusow joined the U.S. Air Force, but found he would never be sent to Korea because it became known that he had been a member of the CPUSA. To clear his name, he sought help from friends who knew the investigator for HUAC. Matusow was subpoenaed to appear before HUAC in late November 1951, and he was well-coached for his replies; he left the Air Force in December 1951.

Matusow went to Dayton, Ohio, where he worked with an anti-Communist magazine, *Counterattack* and found Communists for the Ohio Un-American Activities

Commission, which made him a paid informer. Also he spied for the Dayton Police Force and worked as an **agent provocateur** under various identities. In February 1952 he again appeared before HUAC, and so enjoyed the publicity he received that he decided to be a professional witness/informant for educational and law enforcement agencies in New York. In his short career he named over 200 people as Communists or sympathizers of communism. He married Arvilla Peterson Bentley, a notable supporter of Joseph McCarthy (1908–1957) and his efforts to rid the United States of communism.

In 1955 Matusow published *False Witness,* an autobiography that raised much controversy. The book told of his lies in naming as Communists nearly all the 200 people he mentioned before HUAC. He was sentenced to five years jail for perjury, and served 44 months. At the time some observers believed the book brilliantly exposed the questionable tactics of Joseph McCarthy and other American anti-Communists, while others felt Matusow had been telling the truth before HUAC; Matusow himself believed his life was a three-ring circus. His claims that McCarthy and his associates encouraged him to lie helped to undermine **McCarthyism.**

On being released from prison, Matusow was blacklisted, and moved to the United Kingdom; in 1966 he founded the London Film Makers Cooperative and produced avant-garde films and organized film festivals. He was an interviewer for the BBC (1966–1972) and New Zealand Broadcasting, as well as Swedish Radio. He wrote for the *Sunday Times,* the *International Times,* and *Oz;* he also edited *The American.* In the 1990s he returned to the United States to live in Utah and run the state's first public access TV program. He had appeared in off-Broadway theater (1948–1949), and later was on *The Mike Douglas Show* and *Magic Mouse Theater* (1978–1996).

Matusow married more than 11 times—he married his first wife twice—and raised many children, some of them adopted. He considered himself, for facing his life's many problems, to be another Job; he joined a series of communes that offered a variety of religions. He had several names, including Harvey Job Matusow and Omar Muldoon. He died from complications following a car accident in January 2002.

The University of Sussex houses the Matusow Archive.

Sources: Anonymous, "Magic Mouse: Remembering Harvey Matusow" (2002), www.magicmouse.org; Anonymous, "Obituary: Harvey Marshall Matusow, Anti-Communist Informer: The Man Who Cried Wolf and Paid with His Liberty," *The Age,* February 13, 2002, p. 11 (originally published in the *New York Times*); Fried, Albert, ed., *McCarthyism: The Great American Red Scare. A Documentary History* (New York: Oxford University Press, 1997); Kahn, Albert Eugene, *The Matusow Affair: Memoir of a National Scandal* (Mount Kisco, NY: Moyer Bell, 1987); Matusow, Harvey Marshall, *False Witness* (New York: Cameron and Kahn, 1955).

MAY, ALLAN NUNN (1911–2003). Allan Nunn May was the first of the British **atom spies** to provide the Soviets with information on the research done in England and the United States that led to the use of the **atom bomb** on Hiroshima in August 1945. He believed that the United States should not have a monopoly on atomic energy, and acted at first to ensure that Russia had nuclear resources similar to those in Germany in **World War II.**

Allan Nunn May was born at King's Norton, near Birmingham, Worcestershire. He was the youngest child in his family (he had a sister and two brothers), and his father was a brass founder. At age 13 he was Foundation's Scholar at King Edward's School in Birmingham, and later won a scholarship to Trinity College, Cambridge (1930). He was a contemporary of Donald Maclean (1913–1983). May had a brilliant record at in mathematics and the natural sciences, and got his Ph.D. in 1936, the year he visited Leningrad. In Leningrad he was much impressed by what he saw; he had been born in a district of England hit by economic depression and had developed left-wing sympathies.

Soon after his visit to Russia, May joined the editorial board of the *Scientific Worker*, the official journal of the National Association of Scientific Workers, which included many Communists, and joined a Communist Party cell. Before World War II he taught at London University as a member of King's College. In 1939 he was working on a secret project involving radar, and at the time allowed his membership in the Communist Party to lapse.

A noted young experimental physicist, May was invited by James Chadwick to join Britain's atomic bomb project, **Tube Alloys**, in April 1942, and signed the **Official Secrets Act**. Evidence indicates he had made contact with the Russians around this time, which was not unusual because Russia had become an ally of Great Britain. At the time he believed that the Germans had a working reactor that could use a nuclear weapon against the Russians. This was later shown to be false.

In January 1943 May went to Canada to work on the Anglo–Canadian nuclear research project. The research team was headed by John Douglas Cockroft (1897–1967), director of the Atomic Energy Division at the Canadian National Research Council, Montreal. May was one of the first to be recruited to the **GRU**. He was a secret Communist, apparently a loner, and to him the business of espionage was painful, but necessary, for a real contribution to mankind.

By late in 1944 May had a case officer, Pavel Angelo, of the GRU in Ottawa. His **code names** were ALEK and PRIMROSE. Three days after Hiroshima, he provided Pavel Angelo with a detailed research report on the atomic bomb dropped on Hiroshima, and with samples of U-235 and U-233 from the Arogonne National Laboratory in Chicago. He was given a few hundred dollars and some whisky as a token payment, but when this became known later, he said that it was used to trick him, and that he had burned the money. This evidence helped to convict him.

After Igor Sergeyevich Gouzenko (c. 1919–1982) defected with much information on the atom spies, May was permitted by Britain's secret services to return to King's College, London, because it was hoped that he would reveal his secret Communist contacts in 1945. In February 1946 May was asked about possible leaks of information concerning his work in Canada. He denied there had been leaks, but on February 20 changed his story and confessed to providing Russian **agents** with some uranium samples in the belief that the Soviets had a right to share in the secret information.

On Gouzenko's information given to Canadian authorities, May was arrested, and made a written confession that he had decided to provide Russia with the information to ensure the development of atomic energy was not confined to the United States. He felt that this was his contribution to the safety of humankind, just as doctors felt about their research.

On the day of his trial May changed his plea from "not guilty" to "guilty." The judge thought May to be a conceited, wicked, and arrogant character, and promptly sentenced him to 10 years in prison. During his sentence in jail his colleagues ensured that his research was published and kept up their friendship with him. He was released for being model prisoner at the end of 1952.

May had married a Viennese woman, Dr. Hildegarde Broda, who had a medical post at Cambridge, and they had a son, who was aged 17 when his father rejoined the family early in 1953. May was blacklisted until 1962. Meanwhile he studied modern theoretical physics, and was probably supported with funds from a private laboratory that made scientific equipment for research.

After failing for years to find an academic post abroad, May eventually accepted a professorship of physics at the University of Ghana in 1962. The post was made available largely because the nation needed his wife's medical services. In 1978 he returned to Cambridge, where he did research in solid-state physics and established a science museum. Otherwise he lived in obscurity, and may have been the author of a letter to the editor in the *Peking Daily* (1982).

See also FUCHS, EMIL JULIUS KLAUS; GOUZENKO, IGOR

Sources: Brook-Shepherd, Gordon, *The Storm Birds. Soviet Post War Defectors: The Dramatic True Stories 1945–1985* (New York: Henry Holt, 1989); Canadian Royal Commission, *The Defection of Igor Gouzenko*, 3 vols. (repr. Laguna Hills, CA: Aegean Park Press, 1984); Fountain, Nigel, and Richard Norton-Taylor, "Physicist Who Began the Atomic Spy Era," *The Age* (Melbourne), January 27, 2003, Obituaries, p. 11 (originally published in *The Guardian*); Laffin, John, *Brassey's Book of Espionage* (London: Brassey's, 1996); Rositzke, Harry, *The KGB: The Story of the Sorge Spy Ring* (New York: McGraw-Hill, 1985); Sudoplatov, Pavel, and Anatoli Sudoplatov, *Special Tasks: The Memoirs of an Unwanted Witness, a Soviet Spymaster* (Boston: Little, Brown, 1994).

McCARTHY, JOSEPH R. (1908–1957).

McCarthy was leader of the hunt for Communists in U.S. government agencies early in the 1950s.

Joseph Raymond McCarthy was born at Grand Chute, Wisconsin, and died at Bethesda, Maryland. Aged 16, he left school to work on his father's farm; he went to night school, and graduated in law from Marquette University (1935). After practicing law he was elected circuit judge in Wisconsin.

During **World War II**, McCarthy took temporary leave from judicial duties, was commissioned as a lieutenant, and served in the Marines as an intelligence officer, returning to the United States in 1944. He resigned in March 1945, and later claimed falsely that he had risen from private to captain, won a Distinguished Flying Cross and Air Medal, and been wounded in action.

In 1946 McCarthy was elected to the U.S. Senate. On February 9, 1950, he made his celebrated speech in Wheeling, West Virginia, fulminating against the U.S. State Department's harboring of Communists. For three years he pursued communism in America. In 1953, as chairman of the Permanent Subcommittee on Investigations, he began inquiries into the Voice of America and the Army Signal Corps at Fort Monmouth, New Jersey. The latter brought him down. His search for subversive and un-American and Communist activities in the U.S. Army was not acceptable, and after it had led to the destruction of many careers, McCarthy was censured for violation of democratic procedures. His name is now associated with **McCarthyism,** a witch-hunting practice and ideology.

See also MATUSOW, HARVEY

Sources: Caute, David, *The Great Fear: The Anti-communism Purge Under Truman and Eisenhower* (New York: Simon & Schuster, 1978); Ewald, William Bragg, Jr., *Who Killed Joe McCarthy?* (New York: Simon & Schuster, 1984); Fried, Albert, ed., *McCarthyism: The Great*

American Red Scare. A Documentary History (New York: Oxford University Press, 1997); Garraty, John A., ed., *Dictionary of American Biography,* supp. 6 (New York: Scribner's, 1980); Latham, Earl, *The Meaning of McCarthyism,* 2nd ed. (Lexington, MA: D.C. Heath, 1973); Oshinsky, David M., *A Conspiracy So Immense: The World of Joe McCarthy* (New York: Free Press, 1983); Reeves, Thomas C., *The Life and Times of Joe McCarthy* (New York: Stein and Day, 1982); Riff, Michael A., *Dictionary of Modern Political Ideologies* (Manchester: Manchester University Press, 1987); Rovere, Richard H., *Senator Joe McCarthy* (Cleveland, OH: World, 1959).

MILLER, RICHARD (1937–). Richard Miller was a **Federal Bureau of Investigation (FBI) agent** who claimed to be a **double agent** for the FBI inside the **KGB.** He was caught—through his ineptitude and a need for money and sex—and tried twice for espionage.

Miller became an FBI agent in the early 1960s. He was not highly regarded, and seemed to blunder in his work. Also he sold Amway products from his car, cadged from stores with his FBI badge, and stole and sold FBI information. He was unkempt, disheveled, and grossly overweight. He was short of money, and although he worked hard to support his wife and eight children, he was far from successful. He lived away from his family during the week, and spent weekends trying to make something of their miserable avocado farm.

In 1982 Miller was transferred from important routine activities to counter-intelligence, an activity in which the FBI at Los Angeles had little interest. But in May 1984 he met a Russian émigré, Svetlana Ogorodnikov (c. 1950–), a low-level KGB worker, who had a 13-year-old son and whose husband was meatpacker. Earlier she had attempted unsuccessfully to be a spy, using honeytrap procedures, became pregnant, and had an **abortion.** The FBI knew of her, and when she and Miller began their affair, kept both under surveillance.

In August 1984 Ogorodnikov took evidence of Miller's FBI status to the Soviet consulate in San Francisco, showed she had a hold over him, and stated she might be able to get him to be a KGB **mole** inside the FBI. She had told Miller that she could get him gold and money if he were to spy for her. First she wanted him to find the whereabouts of the Soviet defector Stanislav Levchenko (1941–), who had defected to the West from Tokyo. Miller was not able to do this, but he did pass on an important FBI manual. At the time the FBI decided it was now appropriate to establish Operation WHIPWORM. The FBI officers would watch Miller closely and see if it were possible to turn him into a double agent for the FBI.

Shortly afterward it appeared that Ogorodnikov was planning to get Miller to defect to the **U.S.S.R.,** a scheme that would not fit with the FBI plans. Meanwhile, in September 1984 Miller approached his superiors with a scheme to become a double agent inside the KGB for the FBI! He wanted to do this well, and thereby dispel the reputation he had as an incompetent within the FBI. To the FBI this seemed to be an attempt by Miller to turn himself in because he had found out that he was under FBI surveillance.

To save face, the FBI dismissed Miller, and immediately arrested him for espionage, thereby appearing to have caught a felon who was a *former* FBI employee. At the same time Ogorodnikov and her husband were arrested, and much evidence of espionage activities was found in their apartment. Both pleaded guilty, and made a deal. Ogorodnikov also agreed to testify at Miller's trial.

At Miller's trial in November 1984 the evidence against him was strong, and his lawyers claimed that he has been on a mission as a double agent inside the KGB for the FBI. The jury was deadlocked, and a mistrial was declared. Early in 1985, at the second trial, Ogorodnikov appeared for the defense, but her contribution was shredded into nothing of value and the jury found Miller guilty. He was sentenced to two life terms, plus 50 years, in prison, and fined U.S.$60,000.

See also OGORODNIKOV, SVETLANA

Sources: Allen, Thomas B., and Norman Polmar, *Merchants of Treason: America's Secrets for Sale* (New York: Delacorte Press, 1988); Pincher, Chapman, *Traitors: The Anatomy of Treason* (New York: St. Martin's Press, 1987).

MILNER, IAN FRANCIS GEORGE (1911–1991). In 1954 Ian Milner was identified as one of three Soviet **agents** who passed information to Russia while working in the Australian government's Foreign Service.

Ian Milner was born in New Zealand, the son of a prominent and traditional headmaster and educator; he was educated at his father's school and, in his final year was the top academic prize-winner of the school and an outstanding sportsman. He entered Canterbury University College; rejected his father's conservative views; became a noted debater and poet; and published and wrote for a local political and literary journal. He was a fine scholar, won a Rhodes Scholarship to Oxford University, and became a dedicated dialectical materialist.

Milner wrote articles that idealized life in the **U.S.S.R.**, which he saw briefly in 1934 on his travels from New Zealand to Oxford. He graduated with first-class honors in philosophy, politics, and economics; joined the Essay Society, the Oxford equivalent of the **Apostles** at Cambridge University; and often argued, in a self-sacrificing, compassionate style, that the future lay with communism and Russia.

In October 1937 Milner imagined a worker's revolution would take hold in Britain once fascism had been defeated in the imminent European war. To complete his scholarship requirements, he traveled through the East, and across the Pacific to California, where at the University of California he planned to study political science.

Unhappy with his studies in California, Milner went to Columbia University in New York, and wrote on New Zealand's policies and interests in the Far East for the Institute of Pacific Relations. In 1939 he returned home and found a job in education; when war was declared, he spoke at public meetings as a member of the Wellington Peace and Anticonscription Committee.

In January 1940 Milner was made a lecturer in political science at the University of Melbourne, where the local Commonwealth Investigation Branch (CIB) opened a file on him. He joined the **Communist Party (CPA)** branch in Melbourne—it was declared illegal in June 1940—which held the hard core of the University Labor Party. Milner worked in clandestine study groups, married his New Zealand sweetheart, became an executive member of the Australian Council for Civil Liberties, and addressed peace movement meetings, the Australian–Soviet Friendship League, and the Free Thought Society.

In 1943, when the CPA was legalized, Milner did not admit to being a member, and explained this by saying the origin of his Marxist views had emerged in Britain when he witnessed objectors being bashed at one of Oswald Mosley's (1896–1980) prewar meetings of his British Union of Fascists; probably earlier, in New Zealand, he had been drawn to the policies of the U.S.S.R. Late in 1944 he was appointed to the Post-Hostilities Division (P-HD) of the Australian government's Department of External Affairs, and took the oath of allegiance.

In 1945 Milner stole classified documents, copied them, and passed the copies to the Soviet embassy by way of a New Zealand-born **cutout**, Walter Seddon Clayton (c. 1906–1997), code-named KLOD/CLODE. The P-HD files that Milner could so easily obtain and copy held information on British relations with the Polish and the Czech governments, Anglo–American policies on Eastern Europe, British plans for the Middle East, views on Russia's attempts to get access for its navy to the Mediterranean, plans for Japan's surrender, trade with Russia, and worldwide reports by Britain's High Commissioners.

A victim of departmental politics, Milner was maneuvered into the Australian contingent in the Political Office of the UN Security Council (1947–1949), where he worked assiduously on problems in the **Balkan states**, the Middle East, and especially Korea. It appears that he was recruited securely into Soviet intelligence while working at the United Nations. By this time he had a security file in the United States. He and his wife had deeply anti-American attitudes.

After a short vacation in Australia, Milner returned to work in New York, and in June 1950 planned short holiday in Switzerland. While there, he was probably warned that the colleague in Australia's External Affairs Department who shared his views on Russia, Jim Hill (1918–), had been interrogated in London, and although not charged with treason, had been moved to a job where he no longer had access to material of value to the U.S.S.R.

In October 1950 Milner was teaching English at Charles University in Prague, a position he could not have been given without special local influence. He lived in a small expatriate community; in the late 1950s his marriage broke up; over the years he was contacted by Australian diplomats, and could visit London and New Zealand, where he insisted he had never been a Communist Party member.

Sources: Hall, Richard, *The Rhodes Scholar Spy* (Milson's Point: Random House Australia, 1991); McKnight, David, *Australia's Spies and Their Secrets* (St. Leonards, NSW: Allen and Unwin, 1994); McKnight, David, *Espionage and the Roots of the Cold War* (London: Frank Cass, 2001); McQueen, Humphrey, "The Code of Silence," *The Weekend Australian* (Canberra), April 3–4, 2004, pp. 30–31; O'Sullivan, Vincent, ed., *Interesting Lines: The Memoirs of Ian Milner* (Wellington, NZ: Victoria University Press, 1993).

MITROKHIN ARCHIVE (1992–1999). The Mitrokhin Archive was brought to the West in 1992 by a Soviet defector, and published in 1999 with the help of a British scholar, Professor Christopher Andrew (1941–). The archive contains much information that the **KGB** wanted to be secret, and had suppressed. It is a most valuable source for the history of espionage during the **Cold War.**

Colonel Vasili Mitrokhin (c. 1928–) failed his superiors in 1953 while in Tel Aviv, Israel, and was sent to work in the KGB archives in 1956.

For 10 years Mitrokhin made notes of classified files, and in 1984, after his retirement, concealed the notes in milk churns buried under his country dacha. Eight years later he offered them to the **Central Intelligence Agency (CIA),** but it refused them.

A British spy officer helped Mitrokhin. The **SIS** approached Professor Christopher Andrew in 1995 to participate in the publication project. Professor Andrew had worked previously on the Oleg Gordievsky books and had the necessary security clearance. He agreed to complete the project, knowing that ministerial approval would be required before the book could be published. The SIS named Andrew as the editor for the book in March 1996.

The former U.K. Defense Minister Tom King reported to the British Parliament's Intelligence and Security Committee that Mitrokhin was not content with the way in which the book was published, felt that he failed in what he had hoped to achieve, and wanted full control over the handling of his material. The report goes on to say that Christopher Andrew was chosen by the SIS to edit and collate the Mitrokhin Archive because "the SIS regarded Professor Andrew as a safe pair of hands." A second volume was to have appeared in 2001.

The work led to 50 investigations in Germany, and will be most valuable to writing the history of the KGB. A government inquiry into the origins of the publication has probably held up publication of the second volume.

Criticism of the book was both slim and predictable. One view suggests that the book is what the SIS wanted; another states the work does not praise the KGB enough for its outstanding efforts; a third says that although the work is overlaid with Western interests, the Russian viewpoint is clearly evident.

For historians the archive is an essential and rare primary source largely because it combines the opportunity to know something reliable about the KGB over 12 years with an interpretation of the KGB by a Russian citizen who wanted to see Soviet socialism reformed.

Source: Andrew, Christopher, and Vasili Mitrokhin, *The Mitrokhin Archive: The KGB in Europe and the West* (London: Lane, 1999).

MOLODY, KONON TROFIMOVICH (1922–1970). Konon Molody, better known as Gordon Lonsdale, was a Soviet **agent** who used the cover of a successful businessman while heading the Portland spy ring in Britain.

Konon Trofimovich Molody was the son of two Soviet scientists. At the age of 10, he was sent to live with an aunt in California. He was educated in San Francisco and returned to Russia in 1938.

During the **World War II** (Russia's **Great Patriotic War**) Molody worked for the **NKVD** and afterward studied Chinese; he began his training as an **illegal** agent in 1951. He was posted to Canada (1954) with a false passport which he used to get another passport as Gordon Arnold Lonsdale (**code name** KIZH).

In March 1955 Lonsdale was sent to London to establish a spy network; he used the cover of a student of Chinese, and later became a businessman. He operated jukeboxes and vending and gaming machines, and years later claimed to have made a fortune. In his support group were radio operators Morris Cohen (1905–1995) and his wife, Leonita, also known as Lona (1913–1993), who were known as Peter and Helen Kroger. In 1958 Lonsdale's control extended briefly to include Melita Norwood (1912–). He also ran Harry Houghton (1905–) and his mistress, Ethel Gee (1915–). Houghton kept Lonsdale informed on underwater weapons at the Portland Naval Base.

During 1960 security officials at Portland and **MI5** observed Houghton spending more money than he earned, and he was frequently seen giving packages to Lonsdale. A **CIA mole** in the Polish **UB**, Michal Goleniewski (fl. 1922–1972), had defected and identified them.

In January 1961 the Special Branch apprehended Lonsdale. To the public Lonsdale became known as the Portland spy, and his group, as the Portland spy ring. He was sentenced to 25 years in prison. The Krogers got 20 years each, and Houghton and Gee got 15 years each.

In 1964 Lonsdale was freed in a spy exchange for a British businessmen, Greville Wynne (1919–1990), who had served 11 months of eight-year sentence for spying on the Soviet Union.

Back in Moscow, Lonsdale/Molody became depressed at the widespread inefficiency and incompetency he saw in the Soviet Union's industry, and was highly critical of it; and his outspoken views made him friendless. He turned to alcohol.

One day after suffering a stroke while collecting mushrooms, Molody died, on October 14, 1970. A monument to him was erected in 1976 beside that of Vilyam Fisher (alias Rudolph Abel) in Donskoy Monastery in Moscow.

See also COHEN, LEONTINA, AND COHEN, MORRIS; FISHER, VILYAM; GEE, ELIZABETH ETHEL; GOLENIEWSKI, MICHAL; HOUGHTON, HARRY; WYNNE, GREVILLE

Sources: Andrew, Christopher, and Vasili Mitrokhin, *The Mitrokhin Archive: The KGB in Europe and the West* (London: Lane, 1999); Frolik, Joseph, *The Frolik Defection* (London: Leo Cooper, 1975); Houghton, Harry, *Operation Portland: The Autobiography of a Spy* (London: Rupert Hart-Davis, 1972); Lonsdale, Gordon, *Spy: Twenty Years in Soviet Secret Service. The Memoirs of Gordon Lonsdale* (New York: Hawthorn Books, 1965); Mahoney, Harry T., and Marjorie L. Mahoney, *Biographic Dictionary of Espionage* (San Francisco: Austin & Winfield, 1998); Wright, Peter, with Paul Greengrass, *Spycatcher: The Candid Autobiography of a Senior Intelligence Officer* (Melbourne: William Heinemann, 1987).

MOSSAD MYTH (1956). The Mossad myth states that the Israeli secret service, Mossad, is capable of *any* kind of covert intelligence mission.

In 1948 the newly established **Central Intelligence Agency (CIA)** faced the growing power of communism in Western Europe and China, as well as the crisis in Berlin, and it appeared to the CIA that the socialist basis of the new nation of Israel—it celebrated May Day, it recognized Communist China, and its citizens sang the "Internationale"—was inimical to Western interests. Israel wanted cooperation with the United States, and showed it could provide information on all aspects of life in Russia and its satellites, largely through reports from Russian immigrants to Israel.

The two nations made haste slowly until the Mossad myth was well established. In February 1956, at the 20th Soviet Communist Party Congress, **Nikita Khrushchev** (1894–1973) denounced **Josef Stalin** (1879–1953) for the horrors of his totalitarian regime. The CIA wanted a copy of this secret speech to show the world and discredit Stalin for his general disregard of human rights and his specific crimes against humanity. In June 1956 the *New York Times* published the speech without revealing its source.

The CIA claimed it had obtained the copy, but would not disclose how. Back in February both **MI6** and the CIA knew Khrushchev was going to speak disparagingly of Stalin's regime, but neither could not get a copy. The CIA secretly offered $1 million for a copy. Mossad gave the CIA a copy, but would not reveal its source, arguing that the content was more important than the source. The CIA was much impressed.

How did Mossad do it? The only answer was to believe Mossad capable of any kind of covert intelligence mission! The Mossad myth had emerged. In fact, Victor

Gregevsky, a young Jewish journalist in the Polish news agency, discovered the speech by chance. He believed deeply in Marx until he lost faith when he learned of Stalin's totalitarianism in the early 1950s. His family immigrated to Israel; he considered going with them, but decided to wait. Also, he decided that he would never inform against the **U.S.S.R.**

Forty years later, in an interview on Israeli television, Gregevsky told how he got a copy of the speech. He noticed it on the desk of a woman friend in Warsaw; she allowed him to borrow it; he copied it, and after examining its details, gave it to an Israeli embassy officer in Warsaw. On arriving in Tel Aviv, the speech attracted the attention of Israel's leaders; they saw it as an opportunity to promote the value of Israeli intelligence in the eyes of the CIA. At first the CIA thought it was a fraud, but it was leaked to the *New York Times*. Israel's Foreign Minister read it for the first time in the newspaper.

The CIA was still hesitant to show or develop a working relationship with Israel for fear of damaging contacts with Arab intelligence. It took years for the CIA to reciprocate, and eventually it bypassed President **Dwight D. Eisenhower's** (1890–1969) publicly stated restriction on selling Middle East nations military equipment. Secretly at first, and publicly later, Mossad and the CIA cooperated, but always pragmatically—for example, in the Iran–Contra deal (1985).

Source: Kahana, Ephaim, "Mossad–CIA Cooperation," *International Journal of Intelligence and Counterintelligence* 14 (2001): 409–420.

MUNSINGER, GERDA (1929–). Gerda Munsinger was a German prostitute who became the center of Canada's Munsinger Affair (1966), though no evidence was found that she had ever been a Soviet spy. The Munsinger Affair centered on the fear that something threatening could have taken place, though it actually did not, and involved the **RCMP**, a Royal Commission of Inquiry, and defamatory and scandalous charges and countercharges about her as the Mata Hari of the **Cold War**.

Between 1947 and 1949 there appeared to Western intelligence officers some indications that Gerda Heseler had spied for the Russians, had stolen transit passes and currency, and was a prostitute who once lived with a Soviet intelligence colonel.

Gerda Heseler tried unsuccessfully to emigrate to Canada in 1952. Shortly afterward she married Mike Munsinger, a U.S. citizen who had been demobilized in Germany and was returning to the United States. She was refused entry to the United States in 1953.

In 1955 Munsinger managed to get into Canada by using her married name of Gerda Munsinger. She settled in Montreal, worked as a prostitute and call girl, and associated with well-known criminals.

In November 1960 Munsinger was interrogated by the RCMP, and indicated casually that she was the mistress of Pierre Sévigny, the Associate Minister of National Defense, and was friendly with George Hees, Minister for Transport (later the Trade and Commerce Minister). She was kept under RCMP surveillance and her phone was tapped. To the RCMP she was a successful prostitute whose professional opportunities gained much ground in leading government circles.

By December 1960 the RCMP investigators were convinced that Munsinger was a threat to the national security. When the Canadian Prime Minister learned this, he asked Pierre Sévigny to break his relations with her, but not to resign. In February

1961 Munsinger was caught passing bad checks. An unknown source applied sufficient pressure to have her not charged for her crimes. On the day after she left jail, she traveled to Germany.

On March 10, 1966, Canada's Justice Minister, Lucien Cardin, confirmed rumors then circulating that a woman known as Olga Munsinger had had relationships with ministers in the Canadian government some years before, and that at the time was probably a Soviet spy. She had died of cancer in Germany.

Suddenly, Munsinger was found in Munich by a *Toronto Daily* reporter. In the Canadian media fascination rose in what looked like a sex-spy scandal. In Parliament details were collected of sexual indiscretions among government officials and ministers.

In their testimony, several high-ranking government ministers described Munsinger as a respectable and attractive woman, like many other ladies of distinction who commanded respect in Canadian high society. None knew she was a prostitute.

In its testimony the RCMP showed from extensive phone tapping and constant surveillance that Munsinger was not only a prostitute, and well-known as such to many high-ranking government officials and ministers, but also a threat to national security because she could be blackmailed by the Soviets into telling what she had learned from pillow talk. From this it was argued that as a spy for the Soviets in Canada she had potential; that potential was based solely on alleged espionage when she was in Germany many years before. It was then alleged that, as a sophisticated espionage **agent**, she had infiltrated Canadian government circles, and could be blackmailed not only by the Soviets but also by the Canadian criminal underworld.

Munsinger was now presented in the press as a female foreign agent, similar to Christine Keeler (1941–), who got information from government officials by using her feminine wiles. The Munsinger Affair was made to seem worse than the Profumo Affair.

After the Toronto *Daily Star* published an interview with Munsinger, Igor Gouzenko (c. 1919–1982) appeared on televison in March 1966, a bag over his head, saying that the Munsinger Affair was like the usual Soviet **active measures** to discredit an established Western government and its officeholders.

Later in March 1966 a member of the Canadian underworld alleged that Munsinger, who was well known to him, had never been a spy, but was a name-dropper; and, if she were a spy, then her training had been inept. Later accounts suggested that Munsinger had worked for **NATO**, and in April 1966 the *Daily Star* suggested she had been a spy, but based its claim on RCMP evidence that she had lived in 1949 with a Russian intelligence colonel. Further articles suggested that she was like the actresses Bridget Bardot and Sophia Loren, and in fact she was the Mata Hari of the Cold War.

In the United States there appeared an article that stated America's female spies were not German barmaids, as was Gerda Munsinger, but talented, attractive, college graduates who spoke at least five languages. In time she was presented as trollop, a cheap tramp, and a blonde playgirl.

In time the Canadian media rejected the idea that Munsinger had posed a security risk simply because of her relations with a government minister; and that government ministers, like other men, had the right to personal life. In this vein the Munsinger Affair petered out.

A Royal Commission of Inquiry was conducted into the Munsinger Affair from April 6 to May 24, 1966. In September the commission's report criticized both Pierre Sévigny and the Prime Minister.

In 1992 a film, *Gerda*, presented the different images of Gerda Munsinger during the Munsinger Affair.

Source: Van Seters, Deborah, "The Munsinger Affair: Images of Espionage and Security in 1960s Canada," *Intelligence and National Security* 13 (1998): 71–84.

N

NECHIPORENKO, OLEG MAKSIMOVICH (1932–). Although Oleg Nechiporenko served the **KGB** around the world, his notable work was done for 10 years in Mexico, where he recruited young Mexicans to undermine the government and worked to turn Mexico into a Soviet-dominated nation like Cuba, and to ensure it became a threat to the United States.

Oleg Nechiporenko claimed to have come on his mother's side from gypsy stock in central Russia, and on his father's side from the Ukraine. He was married, had two children, and, after being trained for KGB work, came to Mexico with his family in 1961. His Spanish was faultless, and his task was to infiltrate the Mexican civil service with Russian **agents**, primarily women secretaries. He was also a KGB spy who spied on Russians for Department SK. In 1970 one of the women secretaries in the Russian embassy defected to the Mexicans and told much about his operations. Consequently, he made it his goal to discredit her account of his clandestine work in Mexico.

Nechiporenko's main interest was to recruit Americans who had fled the McCarthy investigations (1951–1953) and young Mexican citizens who belonged to the Partido Comunista Mexicano, the Communist Party of Mexico. Some young people would be offered a university scholarship to go to Moscow. Others were supported in their attempts to found and operate a subversive group, Movimiento de Acción Revolucionario (MAR). When MAR started robbing banks, the KGB supported it in an effort to make Mexico another Soviet satellite country. The MAR terrorists were arrested in March 1971, and two days later Nechiporenko and other Russian diplomats were ordered to leave Mexico.

Until 1985 Nechiporenko served the Soviets in Central America and North Vietnam, and taught at Moscow's **Andropov Institute**. He gave Philip Agee (1935–) a list of CIA officers who worked in Africa. He and the head of the **DGI**, Pedro Pupo Perez, decided that the publication of Agee's *Dirty Work II* should take place in

September 1979, when the heads of nonaligned countries were attending a conference in Havana, and Fidel Castro (1927–) was the conference president.

In May 1991, with the **Cold War** over, Nechiporenko retired from the KGB, and in the following year helped with a U.S. Senate inquiry into Americans who had been prisoners of war, or were missing in action, in Southeast Asia.

See also AGEE, PHILIP

Sources: Andrew, Christopher, and Vasili Mitrokhin, *The Mitrokhin Archive: The KGB in Europe and the West* (London: Lane, 1999); Mahoney, Harry T., and Marjorie L. Mahoney, *Biographic Dictionary of Espionage* (San Francisco: Austin & Winfield, 1998); Nechiporenko, Oleg Maksimovich, *Passport to Assassination* (New York: Carol Publishing, 1993); Smith, Joseph B., *Portrait of a Cold Warrior* (New York: Ballantine, 1976).

NICHOLSON, HAROLD JAMES (fl. 1950–1997). Harold Nicholson was one of the last spies of the **Cold War.** He passed U.S. secrets to the Russians, but unlike the ideologues who appeared to justify their actions as support for the Communist cause in the early stages of the Cold War, he and such contemporaries as Aldrich Hazen Ames and Earl Pitts sold secrets to the Russians for money.

Harold Nicholson was the son of a U.S. Air Force master sergeant whose career moved him from base to base. Harold became a conceited, ambitious, and intelligent man who seemed to know everything. He graduated from Oregon State University in 1973 with a BA in geography; entered the U.S. Army and fulfilled his ROTC requirements; and married Laura, his college sweetheart that year.

In his work Nicholson, like his father, was moved from one military base to another, serving in both the United States and Japan as an intelligence captain. He and Laura had three children. In 1978 he was awarded an MA in counseling and education from the University of Maryland, and in 1980 joined the **Central Intelligence Agency (CIA).** After basic training he was a case officer in Manila, Bangkok, and Tokyo between 1982 and 1989, and then was sent to Romania.

Nicholson was chief of station in Romania, and deputy chief of station in Malaysia before becoming an instructor for two years at the **Farm**, a CIA training facility at **Camp Peary** in Virginia. His final appointment was to the Counterterrorism Section at CIA headquarters.

Personal and family difficulties arose for Nicholson in Romania. He would often have to leave the family for a few days, and Laura would feel abandoned. To some people he appeared intensely ambitions and overeager in his work, and they would notice his wife was seldom present at U.S. embassy social functions that she was expected to attend as a matter of routine.

In June 1992 Laura fled Romania with the children, and in 1994, after a 21-year marriage, they were divorced. Nicholson was granted primary custody of the children, but frequently found the costs of raising the family burdensome.

In 1995 Nicholson's **polygraph test** showed he might be lying, so his superiors gave immediate attention his to travel patterns and his bank deposits. Inexplicable deposits were found in his bank accounts. He had deposited U.S.$120,000 after a trip to London, New Delhi, Bangkok, and Kuala Lumpur. He pleaded guilty to accepting U.S.$180,000 worth of goods and services from the Russians.

In 1994, while in Kuala Lumpur, Nicholson offered to help the Soviets, and made no effort to cover his tracks. Between 1994 and 1996 he gave the Soviets the identities of **recruits** he helped train at the Farm. For this help—at about the time of his divorce settlement—Nicholson may have received U.S.$12,000 from the Russians.

Nicholson took a Thai mistress, and stayed with her in Phuket, Thailand, in Hawaii, and in a luxury hotel in Singapore. He was once seen meeting a Russian contact on a crowded rail platform. After failing to get a posting that he had sought closer to Russia, he informed the Russians of this news by sending them a postcard from a fake address. On November 16, 1996, while preparing to leave for Switzerland with more U.S. secrets for the Russians, he was arrested.

In March 1997, Nicholson pleaded guilty to the single charge of selling secrets to the Russians, and faced a fine of U.S.$250,000. The judge said that Nicholson's sentence could be reduced to between 21 and 27 years, and by another 15 percent for good behavior, thereby reducing imprisonment to 20 years. His lawyer would only say that Nicholson had been a patriot for 20 years, and had put his life in hazard to serve his country.

Nicholson's case was like that of Earl Pitts (fl. 1987–1997), who admitted to spying for Russia since 1987. Both men sold secrets for money and sought to avoid a life sentence by pleading guilty.

See also AMES, ALDRICH; PITTS, EARL

Sources: Abrams, Jim, "CIA Man Confesses to Selling Secrets to Russia," *The Age*, November 20, 1997, p. 3; Anonymous, "Amorous Entanglement Tripped Up CIA Spy," *The Age*, November 21, 1997, p. 3; Bowman, M. E., "The 'Worst Spy': Perceptions of Espionage," *American Intelligence Journal* 18 (1998): 57–62; Mahoney, Harry T., and Marjorie L. Mahoney, *Biographic Dictionary of Espionage* (San Francisco: Austin & Winfield, 1998); Wolf, Jim, "Agent Sold Secrets to Russia: CIA," *The Age*, November 20, 1996, p. A10.

NORWOOD, MELITA STEDMAN (1912–). Melita Norwood was a British spy who served the Soviets in Great Britain and was not revealed to the public until the publication of the Mitrokhin archives in 1999. She was a most important woman **NKVD agent** and the longest-serving of the British spies.

Melita Sinus had a Latvian father and a British mother. She worked for the British Non-Ferrous Metals Research Association (1932–1972) and was a secret member of the Communist Party of Great Britain. She was recruited to the NKVD in 1937, a committed ideological agent. She was involved with the **Woolwich Arsenal** spy case and was almost caught in January 1938. Her work was discontinued, and she was reactivated in May 1938.

The Russians valued her work was highly, and in 1941 she was put under control of the **GRU** agent Ursula Ruth Kuczynski (fl. 1907–1992), who also ran Klaus Fuchs (1911–1988). She married a fellow Communist, a mathematician, and became Melita Stedman Norwood. She was instructed never to tell her husband of her espionage.

A committed, reliable, and disciplined agent, Norwood provided information in March 1945 on **Tube Alloys,** thereby making a great contribution to Russia's atomic intelligence. She also recruited at least one agent. After the capture and trial of Klaus Fuchs, Norwood was again put on ice again for fear of her being caught. She was reactivated in October 1952.

For the next 20 years Norwood had seven different controllers in England, and saw each of them only four to five times a year to provide them with documents. **Moscow Center** and the GRU fought jealously for the control of Norwood.

In 1999, when her identity became known, Norwood was called the "Red Granny." She confessed in September 1999 that she had begun a secret life spying for the Russians shortly after **World War II**, and served Moscow Center for 40 years. For her work the Russians gave her the **Order of the Red Banner** and a pension of £20 a month.

Norwood's case was reviewed by Britain's Home Secretary, who concluded that the evidence of her treachery was too slim to justify charging her. Apparently **MI5** had long suspected her treason but never had sufficient evidence on which to act.

See also FUCHS, EMIL JULIUS KLAUS; KUCZYNSKI, URSULA RUTH

Sources: Andrew, Christopher, and Vasili Mitrokhin, *The Mitrokhin Archive: The KGB in Europe and the West* (London: Lane, 1999); Honigsbaum, Mark, and Antony Barnett, "Cold War's Secret Lives Emerge from Shadows," *The Guardian,* September 19, 1999, www.guardian.co.uk/Archive/Article/0,4237,3903494,00html; Mann, Simon, "'Red Granny' Escapes Court," *The Age,* December 22, 1999, p.12.

NOSENKO, YURI IVANOVICH (fl. 1927–1987). Nosenko was a noted **Cold War** defector to the West who spent over four years in prison in the United States while James Angleton (1917–1987) and his counterintelligence associates worked to establish whether the Russian was a Soviet spy sent to undermine the **Central Intelligence Agency (CIA)** or a genuine defector.

Yuri Nosenko's father was an engineer who had labored in the Odessa shipyards and educated himself; and his mother was the daughter of an architect. In 1934 the family moved to Leningrad; at out the outbreak of **World War II,** in September 1939, the family was in Moscow. Yuri's father became a high government official, and died in 1956 as Minister of Shipping.

At the age of 14, Nosenko was sent to a naval preparatory school (1942). Later he turned to diplomacy rather than going to sea, and his family had him enrolled in the State Institute of International Relations. After two years he was drafted into the **GRU**, and served for three years in naval intelligence. In Vladivostok, he analyzed U.S. radio signals and the military information found in U.S. public records.

In 1953 Noseko was sent back to Moscow, and he married. That year he was drafted into the **MVD/KGB**'s Second Chief Directorate, which concerned itself with foreign intelligence. For 10 years he attended to the recruitment of **agents** from among Western tourists who came to see Russia, and among them he found Lee Harvey Oswald (1939–1963).

In 1957 Nosenko began considering defection to the West. He was in England, serving as a security officer for Russian athletes, and was drawn to the high living standards that the British enjoyed. Also, that year he found the KGB had a dossier on his late father. In 1960, following a trip to Cuba, he made an unsuccessful attempt to contact a Western intelligence officer. In Geneva in June 1962, while at a disarmament conference, he offered to spy for the West.

The CIA offered Nosenko the usual terms: act as a **defector-in-place** until he and his family were helped to leave the Soviet Union when the time was right, and he would be paid a pension for life. He was code-named AE/EA FOXTROT. He informed on John William C. Vassall (1924–1996), the spy in the British Admiralty; gave some information on the Soviet discovery of Pyotr Popov's (c. 1920–1959) betrayal; and betrayed Robert Lee Johnson (fl. 1923–1972); he also told about the 40 tiny microphones built into the walls of the U.S. embassy in Moscow.

Nosenko decided to defect without his family in February 1964 because he was under suspicion by the KGB. He dressed in a U.S. Army uniform, was taken to the CIA's camp for defectors north of Frankfurt for two weeks, and then was flown to

Washington. After the defection the KGB code-named him IDOL, and declared him a womanizer and an ambitious careerist. In March 1964 one of the first plots to murder Nosenko was hatched. During a projected interview between Nosenko and some U.S. State Department officials and their Russian counterparts, Oleg Kalugin (1934–) would shoot Nosenko, and be freed later in a Western spy swap. The interview did not take place.

But earlier, in 1962, a CIA officer had had doubts about Nosenko's genuineness, and had queried inconsistencies in his account of himself. So, unknown to him in 1964, Nosenko was defecting into an environment prejudiced against what he believed he had to offer and highly suspicious of his motives. It seemed to the CIA that he might be a KGB plant, and that he had been party to an imagined KGB plot to have Lee Harvey Oswald assassinate U.S. President **John F. Kennedy** (1917–1963) in November 1963.

James Angleton managed to convince others of this view after having consulted with Anatoli Golitsyn (1926–), who claimed, after reading the Nosenko file, that he had been sent by the KGB to the United States to mislead the CIA and to discredit Golitsyn.

For four years and three months Nosenko was held in a CIA cell that was not unlike a bank vault, and interrogated for almost 300 days. This was done largely because Angleton and his coworkers believed Nosenko was a KGB spy and not a genuine defector; that inside the CIA was a **mole** called SASHA, whom Nosenko must have known; and that Nosenko knew about the KGB's alleged use of Oswald in the killing of President Kennedy. Later, some of Angleton's supporters would deny that he had had a central role in Nosenko's imprisonment.

In April 1969 Nosenko was cleared of suspicion and received a regular salary as a CIA adviser, as well as some lump-sum payments. It had become was clear from independent evidence in the case of Yuri Loginov (1933–1969) that Nosenko was genuine.

In 1975 a KGB agent in the Russian Orthodox Church hired a professional killer to murder Nosenko for U.S.$100,000, but the hit man was arrested before he could complete the KGB contract.

See also ANGLETON, JAMES; GOLITSYN, ANATOLI; OSWALD, LEE HARVEY; VASSALL, WILLIAM JOHN

Sources: Andrew, Christopher, and Vasili Mitrokhin, *The Mitrokhin Archive: The KGB in Europe and the West* (London: Lane, 1999); Brook-Shepherd, Gordon, *The Storm Birds. Soviet Post War Defectors: The Dramatic True Stories 1945–1985* (New York: Henry Holt, 1989); Halpern, Samuel, and Hayden Peake, "Did Angleton (1917–87) Jail Nosenko?" *International Journal of Intelligence and Counterintelligence* 3 (1989): 457–464; Kalugin, Oleg, and Fen Montaigne, *Spymaster: My 32 Years in Intelligence and Espionage Against the West* (London: Smith Gryphon, 1994); Mangold, Tom, *Cold Warrior: James Jesus Angleton, the CIA Master Spy Hunter* (New York: Simon & Schuster, 1991); Martin, David, *Wilderness of Mirrors* (New York: Ballantine, 1981); Volkman, Ernest, *Espionage: The Greatest Spy Operations of the 20th Century* (New York: Wiley, 1995); West, Nigel, *The Circus: MI5 Operations 1945–1972* (New York: Stein and Day, 1983).

NUREYEV, RUDOLF (1938–1993). Rudolf Nureyev, an outstanding Russian ballet dancer, was the victim of **KGB special actions** after he defected in Paris in June 1961. He was accused by the Soviets of having betrayed his country, and was put on on the KGB list of **wet affairs**.

Rudolf Nureyev was born in Silesia, trained in folk dancing, and later attended the Leningrad Choreographic School. In June 1961, while on tour with the Kirov Ballet Company, he defected to the West at Le Bourget Airport by calling to the French police to protect him. At the time, newspapers reported that Soviet officials knew of Nureyev's intentions, and failed to persuade him not to defect.

The KGB tried to intimidate Nureyev by undermining his performance on the first night he appeared with a Western company. In February 1962 he performed at Covent Garden with Margot Fonteyn (1919–1991) in *Giselle*, and received 23 curtain calls. A few months later he embarrassed the **Kremlin** further with his "leap to the West," as he put it, in his memoirs. The KGB explained his betrayal by reference to his immorality and immaturity, and in revenge planned to sprinkle glass on the stage where he was to dance, and also threatened to break his legs.

Nureyev performed in many countries, produced ballets, and appeared in movies of *Swan Lake* (1966), *Don Quixote* (1974), and *Valentino* (1977). He was highly promiscuous and had many intimate companions, the last being Robert Tracey (1979–1993). Nureyev enjoyed both men and women as lovers.

Nureyev died of AIDS, a secret kept until after his death, and left U.S.$33 million for a foundation in his name.

Sources: Andrew, Christopher, and Vasili Mitrokhin, *The Mitrokhin Archive: The KGB in Europe and the West* (London: Lane, 1999); Ezard, John, "Nureyev, My Lover," *The Age* (Melbourne), February 4, 2003, Culture, pp. 1, 3 (originally published in *The Guardian*); Nureyev, Rudolf, *Nureyev: An Autobiography with Pictures* (London: Hodder and Stoughton, 1962); Percival, John, *Nureyev: Aspects of the Dancer* (London: Faber and Faber, 1976); Sheymov, Victor, *Tower of Secrets: A Real Life Spy Thriller* (Annapolis, MD: Naval Institute Press, 1993).

O

OATIS AFFAIR (1951–1953). The Oatis Affair was one of the first Soviet attempts to capture and try U.S. reporters as spies after **World War II**. William N. Oatis (1914–1997) was the bureau chief for the Associated Press in Czechoslovakia when he was imprisoned and tried as a spy in an alleged war between the United States and Czechoslovakia.

Oatis was born in Marion, Indiana, and studied at De Pauw University (1932–1933). Before World War II he was a reporter on the *Leader-Tribune* in Marion (1933–1937) and worked as a rewrite man in Indianapolis, New York, and London. He served in the U.S. Army (1942–1946) and studied at the universities of Minnesota (1943–1944) and Michigan (1945). After the war he was in Prague and served as bureau chief for the Associated Press from 1950 to 1952.

Following the Communist coup in Czechoslovakia (March 1948), foreign publications (except technical information) were banned, and listening to foreign broadcasts was a crime. Foreign journalists were either expelled for inaccurate reporting or arrested as spies and imprisoned. When he got to Czechoslovakia, one of Oatis's first assignments was to find out if **Josef Stalin**'s (1879–1953) foreign minister Andrei Vyshinsky (1883–1954), who had replaced **Vyacheslav M. Molotov** (1890–1986) in March 1949, had really been sent to Carlsbad for medical treatment. Oatis found that the minister had instead attended a secret meeting of COMINFORM delegates from many Communist countries.

After being accused earlier of "unobjective reporting," Oatis was detained in April 1951 by the Czechoslovakian government—at the time under Russian domination—and charged with espionage. Espionage was defined as attempts to obtain state secrets with the intention of betraying them to a foreign power; and a state secret was anything that should be kept secret from unauthorized authorities in Czechoslovakia. He was tried, found guilty, and imprisoned.

Oatis was forced to confess. He was one of the first journalists to be indicted after a false confession of espionage when in fact he had accurately reported news. From the Czech government's point of view, laid down by the **U.S.S.R.,** he was employed by the United States in its undeclared war against Czechoslovakia.

In court Oatis was not allowed to wear his glasses while being cross-examined, and could not see his questioners. In addition to being charged with espionage, he was implicated in a murder. Using his false confession as evidence, Czechoslovakia found Oatis guilty of espionage and sentenced him to 10 years in prison.

During Oatis's trial the *Editor and Publisher* in America took up his cause, ridiculed the charge that he could have been a U.S. spy, and put much political pressure on the U.S. government to get his release. The Communist authorities made it clear that they expected to be paid a ransom for Oatis's release.

At the time, many observers expected that America would get Oatis back if Radio Free Europe's broadcasts to Czechoslovakia from Germany were stopped. He was released to the U.S. government, returned to the United States in 1953, and was exonerated in a judicial review (1969).

Back in the United States, Oatis became a reporter at the United Nations bureau of Associated Press. He received the William the Silent Award (1954), and became the president of the United Nations Correspondents' Association (1970).

By 1963 in Czechoslovakia the regulations were relaxed, and after Alexander Dubcek (1921–1992) took power in January 1966, most bans on journalism were lifted until the Russians again took charge.

Oatis's case was similar to that of the American communications engineer Robert Vogeler (1911–), who also had been forced to falsely confess to espionage by his captors in Hungary.

See also VOGELER, ROBERT

Sources: Kurian, George T., *World Press Encyclopedia,* vol. 1 (New York: Facts on File, 1982); Oatis, William N., "Why I Confessed," *Life,* September 21, 1953, p. 35; Vogeler, Robert A., *I Was Stalin's Prisoner* (London: W.H. Allen, 1952); *Who's Who in America, 1980–81* (Chicago: Marquis Who's Who, 1982).

OGORODNIKOV, SVETLANA (c. 1950–).

Svetlana Ogorodnikov, an inexperienced Russian spy, was caught in a honeytrap of her own making, and failed to avoid a long jail sentence.

Svetlana was born and raised in Russia, married Nikolai Ogorodnikov, and in 1973 immigrated with him to the United States as a **KGB** clerk. The **Federal Bureau of Investigation (FBI)** kept them under surveillance and concluded that neither was a threat to the national security of the United States.

Although Svetlana presented herself as a senior KGB officer, she was not competent to hold such a position, and with her husband became involved unwittingly in an espionage operation.

During an investigation she met an experienced but maladroit FBI **agent,** Richard Miller (1937–), and cultivated him to no clear purpose, other than to listen to him and his personal problems (e.g., he complained he had a job with insufficient pay and was overweight). In 1984 they became lovers, apparently on the understanding that she would be sexually available if he were to provide her with classified FBI documents. At the time she was still under FBI surveillance. When the relationship was discovered in 1985, Svetlana, her husband, and Miller were arrested.

At the time the motivation for their relationship was obscure. Miller stated that he used Ogorodnikov to discover KGB operations on the West Coast of the United

States, and did not know that she was a KGB agent; Svetlana and her husband pleaded guilty to conspiring to commit espionage.

Svetlana was sentenced to jail for 18 years, and her husband for eight; their son was sent home to be raised in Moscow.

See also MILLER, RICHARD

Sources: Allen, Thomas B., and Norman Polmar, *Merchants of Treason: America's Secrets for Sale* (New York: Delacorte Press, 1988); Corson, William R., and Robert T. Crowley, *The New KGB: Engine of Soviet Power* (New York: William Morrow, 1985); Mahoney, M. H., *Women in Espionage* (Santa Barbara, CA: ABC-CLIO, 1993).

OLSEN, FRANK (1910–1953). Frank Olsen was a **Central Intelligence Agency (CIA)** scientist who died when his body fell onto the pavement outside the Hotel Pennsylvania in New York early one morning in late November 1953. Olsen's death was determined to be an accident in 1953, a suicide in 1975, and a murder in 2002. The case has implications for the secret use of murder to uphold the national interest during the **Cold War.**

Olsen was a U.S. Army captain and senior scientist at the U.S. Army's biological weapons research center, which had been established in 1943 at Fort Detrick, Maryland. As a hobby he took home movies of his family and of his travels overseas. In the late 1940s he told a very close friend and colleague that he was about to begin research on "hot stuff," their term for anthrax and similar agents. Although Olsen was recognized and regarded as a loyal U.S. patriot, and was most enthusiastic about his work, he became distressed when he saw what the experimental use of "hot stuff" did to animals.

Olsen was known to have little interest in following regulations, for being open, and for not worrying about speaking his mind. In October 1949 he was suspected of disclosing government secrets; four years later the accusation was unproven.

In April 1950 Olsen was given a diplomatic passport, which indicated to his close friend that Olsen was not only a U.S. Army captain but also a CIA **agent.** He traveled to Europe and filmed where he had been for the family. At one point he was at CIA headquarters in Frankfurt, in the I.G. Farben building. In June 1950, while in Germany, he became aware of Operation ARTICHOKE, a secret CIA project that used drugs during the interrogation and torture of individuals thought to be Communist spies.

In June 1951 Olsen was in Frankfurt again. He witnessed individuals being brainwashed, tortured, and being made to talk. At the same time, in the U.S., the U.S. Army was experimenting on its own troops with **LSD** and similar drugs to see if it were possible to use them in battle to overwhelm an enemy and conquer it without killing.

Olsen traveled to London, Paris, and Stockholm in 1953, and in early August was in Berlin with a CIA agent watching top-level Russian agents being interrogated with Operation ARTICHOKE techniques. When he returned home, he told his close friend and colleague that he was much troubled to have been where he knew interrogations had led to the suspect's death. He wanted to leave a CIA.

At that time U.S. prisoners of war during the Korean conflict were coming home, and among them were soldiers who had "confessed" in Korean prison camps that the U.S. Army was using techniques of biological warfare against its enemy. To his close friend Olsen appeared to know that the U.S. Army was using Operation AR-

TICHOKE techniques with these war veterans to have them state that they had made the Korean "confessions" under duress, and to deny that the U.S. Army had ever used biological warfare methods in Korea. Olsen appeared shocked to find out for himself that the United States was using such techniques on repatriated American soldiers, just as it was in Berlin on captured Russian spies.

In November 1953 Olsen attended a bogus meeting of sports analysts. In reality it was a conference run for 10 top scientists by Operation ARTICHOKE, where the CIA operatives spiked the attendees' drinks with LSD, without their knowledge. Later Olsen learned that the participants had been interrogated using Operation ARTI-CHOKE techniques, and he believed that he had been drugged because he talked too much. That weekend he went home, much distressed, and told his wife he had made a terrible mistake. On vacation in the summer of 1953 he had wanted to speak intimately with his brother-in-law—an unusual request, his brother-in-law recalled—appeared agitated, short-tempered, and anxious, and began talking seriously of leaving his job and retraining as a dentist.

On November 28, 1953, Olsen was with a CIA agent in the Hotel Pennsylvania in New York. He died early that morning, having fallen onto the pavement from the window in a room on the thirteenth floor. The autopsy showed his body was lacerated by glass, and it was decided he had fallen by accident. The CIA agent who was with Olsen said he had been asleep during the catastrophe, heard nothing, and gave no reason for their visit to New York. Olsen was buried, and the family was informed.

Twenty years later, after the publication of the **Rockefeller Commission**'s (1975) findings regarding CIA activities, it was found that Olsen had died differently. He had been depressed due to a dose of drugs that he did not know he had been given, and had flung himself out the window of the hotel. His family was shocked. The head of the CIA apologized to them, as did President **Gerald Ford** (1913–). The matter was dropped until the early 1990s.

Olsen's son was never satisfied with the explanation of his father's death, and moved to have his body exhumed for reexamination in the early 1990s. Results showed no evidence of any lacerations to the body, and that Olsen had probably been knocked unconscious by a blow to his forehead with a heavy object before he went out the window. The hotel manager recalled that after the fall, a phone call had been made from the room to say, "Well, he's gone," and the person who was called replied to the caller, "Well, that's too bad." The method of murder was a technique recommended for assassination without leaving clues in a CIA manual used at the time of Olsen's death.

From this it appears reasonable to conclude that Frank Olsen was murdered, probably to prevent him from endangering the nation's security.

See also OPERATION ARTICHOKE

Sources: Colby, William, *Honorable Men: My Life in the CIA* (New York: Simon & Schuster, 1978); Hulnick, Arthur S., *Fixing the Spy Machine: Preparing American Intelligence for the Twenty-first Century* (Westport, CT: Praeger/Greenwood, 1999); Koch, Egmont R., and Michael Wech, *The Secret War: Bio-Weapons and the CIA*, Gert Monheim, ed. (Film-production WDR, 2002).

OPERATION ABLE ARCHER 83 (1983). ABLE ARCHER 83 was a short, secret **NATO** operation that raised the level of anxiety among Soviet leaders that the West might begin a nuclear attack on Russia or its satellites.

From November 2 to November 11, 1983, a NATO exercise to practice the use of nuclear weapons in wartime was undertaken. At different levels of threat it simulated the commands made to launch nuclear weapons and the attendant deployment of military forces. No action was taken, and no troops were moved.

As a general procedure ABLE ARCHER was a precaution employed regularly, but on this occasion the specific procedure, ABLE ARCHER 83, used a new form of communication, one more appropriate to nuclear than to conventional warfare. The operation was monitored by the **U.S.S.R.,** and the West monitored the U.S.S.R.'s monitoring. The West discovered that **Warsaw Pact** communications suddenly increased at the time, indicating a rise in Soviet anxiety about the West's intentions.

Weeks later, Soviet concern during ABLE ARCHER 83 became more clearly known to the West when a **KGB** officer who spied for the **SIS** reported that Soviet leaders were anxious about a possible U.S. nuclear attack that November. When ABEL ARCHER 83 ended on November 11, anxiety dropped in the **Kremlin**, but rose again in January 1984 with the establishment of new U.S. Pershing II missiles in Britain. The West failed to see from its monitoring that in response to the possible threat of ABLE ARCHER 83, the level of alert of Soviet fighters in East Germany was raised.

By the summer of 1984 of the Russian anxiety level had fallen. The main events in 1983 and 1984 were as follows: the shooting down of KAL 007 on August 31, 1983; ABLE ARCHER; and the arrival of U.S. missiles in Britain. In sequence they seriously drew the two parties toward a nuclear **Cold War**, but both human and technical intelligence showed the fears were not high enough to begin serious hostilities.

The seriousness of the operation and the tension relating to it are captured well in Littell's (2002) fictional Operation KHOLSTOMER.

See Also KAL 007 TRAGEDY; OPERATION KHOLSTOMER; OPERATION RYAN

Sources: Littell, Robert, *The Company: A Novel of the CIA* (New York: Overlook Press, 2002); Richelson, Jeffrey T., *A Century of Spies: Intelligence in the Twentieth Century* (New York: Oxford University Press, 1995).

OPERATION AJAX (1953). Operation AJAX (Richelson, 1995) or TAPJAX/ BOOT (Deacon 1988) was a secret **SIS/Central Intelligence Agency (CIA)** operation that secured power for the Shah of Iran when the country's popular nationalist government was dominated by the Prime Minister, Mohammed Mossadegh (1880–1967).

Mohammed Mossadegh was born in Tehran, was educated in law at Lausanne University, and held several posts in Iranian government ministries in the 1920s. In 1925 he retired, but returned to politics in 1944. He was a devoted nationalist who directed his attacks at the Anglo–Iranian Oil Company (AIOC), which he believed had exploited the Iranian economy for 50 years.

When he became Prime Minister of Iran, Mossadegh nationalized the oil industry, a monopoly largely owned by British Petroleum (BP), and prepared a plan to compensate the previous owners with funds from the profits of the oil sales. Both the Conservative and non-Conservative governments in Great Britian wanted BP, one of seven oil companies that controlled the world's oil industry, to maintain its monopoly and feared the loss would cripple British prestige in the Middle East at a time when Arab nationalism ran high. The British took their case to the United Nations and the International Court of Justice, and lost. Russia hailed Mossadegh's success and urged the Iranian Tudeh Party (Communist) to support him.

The British Foreign Secretary, the Minister of Defense, and the BP chairman proposed military intervention. Britain's Prime Minister, **Clement Attlee** (1883-1967), would not agree; instead, an embargo was put on Iranian oil and Iranian funds in British banks were frozen.

At first the United States wanted little to do with the problem in Iran, experiencing problems itself at the time with oil industry cartels. President **Dwight D. Eisenhower** (1890–1969) supported Mossadegh's attempt to make his country independent politically and economically in 1953. In time the British embargo crippled the Iranian economy, and the Americans feared the Soviets would seek further influence in Iran.

The CIA, with support from the British SIS, planned to support the Shah and undermine Mossadegh's weakening control of the Iranian government. On August 8, 1953, Eisenhower gave the CIA permission to bring about the downfall of Mossadegh. With help from the U.S. embassy in Tehran, nonpartisans were brought to the city and encouraged to riot by liberally distributing $100,000 in cash among them, and the Shah's loyal general, Fazlollah Zahedi, arrived to manage the coup, arrested Mossadegh—who appeared to have escaped—and had him jailed.

The most important U.S. actors in the coup were Allen Dulles (1893–1969), CIA head; Kermit Roosevelt (1916–2000), chief of the CIA Plans Directorate's Near East and Africa Division; the American ambassador in Tehran; and the former chief of the New Jersey State Police, H. Norman Schwarzkopf (1896–1958), a CIA military specialist attached to the American embassy, who from 1942 to 1948 served the internal security needs of the Shah.

Under Kermit Roosevelt's direction the CIA arranged for Iran's newspapers to publish pro-Shah and anti-Mossadegh articles; to print "true" stories that had been fabricated, with cartoons and interviews that had never taken place; to brib members of the Iranian militia; to spread false rumors about Mossadegh's government; to produce fake documentation of secret agreements between the Iranian Communist party and Mossadegh; to find individuals who pretended to be Communists and behaved accordingly; to mislead Iranian religious officials into believing their lives were in danger and their homes were to be torched; to incite rioters to burn down newspaper offices that supported Mossadegh; and to bribe the army chief to take over from Mossadegh.

After his arrest Mossadegh was condemned by the Shah for supporting communism, committing treason, and pursuing a doctrine of negative equilibrium for Iran's economy. He was jailed for three years, and in 1956 was placed under house arrest until he died in 1967.

See also DULLES, ALLEN; ROOSEVELT, KERMIT

Sources: Ambrose, Stephen E., *Ike's Spies: Eisenhower and the Espionage Establishment*, 2nd ed. (Jackson: University Press of Mississippi, 1999); Barlett, Donald L., and James B. Steele, "The Oily Americans," *Time*, May 19, 2003, pp. 37–38; Prados, John, *Presidents' Secret Wars: CIA and Pentagon Covert Operations from World War II Through Iranscam* (New York: Quill, 1988); Richelson, Jeffrey T., *A Century of Spies: Intelligence in the Twentieth Century* (New York: Oxford University Press, 1995); Saikal, Amin, *The Rise and Fall of the Shah* (Princeton, NJ: Princeton University Press, 1980).

OPERATION ARTICHOKE (fl. 1951–1972?). Operation ARTICHOKE was a secret **Central Intelligence Agency (CIA)** operation that centred on the possible use on humans of biological warfare weapons, drugs, hypnosis, brainwashing, and torture to get accurate information from enemy suspects. Fragments of its history became public in the case of Frank Olsen (1910–1953).

In 1945 concentration camp survivors in occupied Nazi Germany told the United States and its allies about the camp doctors' experiments with drugs on fellow inmates. Operation DUSTBIN was the U.S. operation conducted for the purpose of establishing what the camp doctors had found in their experiments. One leading Nazi camp doctor was Kurt Blome. At the Nuremberg trials (1945–1946) he was found guilty and condemned to death, but was spared and taken by the U.S. secret services to help in Operation DUSTBIN.

The United States was concerned that the **U.S.S.R.** might use biological warfare weapons like anthrax, and wanted to be prepared for their use and to have an adequate supply of them. An American biochemist, Frank Olsen, worked on the project at Fort Detrick, Maryland, monitoring the experimental use of such weapons in Antigua, Alaska, and even San Francisco.

In October 1951 at the CIA's secret Camp King, near Oberursal, Germany, Operation ARTICHOKE was well established. It used cruel interrogation techniques including drugs, hypnosis, and torture techniques that in a short time became accepted. CIA interrogators sought to manipulate the minds of Russian spies they had captured so as to get top secret material, and then to erase the memory of what had happened to them. In Camp King one of the doctors was Karl Blome.

The CIA was experimenting with drugs not only on Army personnel but also on regular citizens. One of its dirty tricks performed as part of Operation ARTICHOKE was to establish a bogus brothel on Bedford Street in Greenwich Village in New York City; get men into it; and hire real prostitutes to join them, spike the men's drinks with **LSD**, and then talk with them about drugs, security, or crime. The experimental subjects were never informed, nor was their consent obtained.

The secrecy of Operation ARTICHOKE was broken, but without a full public exposure, by Seymour Hersch, a prominent journalist with the *New York Times.* In December 1974, he told the CIA director, William Colby (1920–1996), that he had information on the highly secret "**Family Jewels**" of the CIA, especially Operation CHAOS. On December 22 the *New York Times* published Hersch's article claiming the CIA had violated its charter, and had conducted illegal domestic intelligence operations against antiwar protesters (Operation CHAOS) and other dissidents during **Richard Nixon**'s administration. In response to President **Gerald Ford**'s questions on the article, Colby prepared a statement on the "Family Jewels." At the same time the retirement of James Jesus Angleton (1917–1987) became public, which added to the interest in CIA activities.

Early in January 1975 President Ford established a commission to inquire into the *New York Times*'s charges, the **Rockefeller Commission,** named after Vice President **Nelson Rockefeller**. In five months its report was released, and concluded that the CIA had kept within its statutory authority, but had undertaken some activities it should not undertake again; some of the activities had actually been at the behest of presidents; some activities were dubious, others unlawful, and in 1973 and 1974 the CIA had taken action to end such activities.

In early 1975, around the CIA there whorled a public outrage, and the U.S. Congress decided it, too, would investigate the CIA, and did so under the chairmanship of Frank Church (1924–1984). Late in January 1975 President Gerald Ford (1913–) admitted, off the record and in strict confidence, to the senior editors of the *New York Times* that among the "Family Jewels" were sensitive items including top-secret assassinations. By late February this secret had been leaked. Hysteria in the press mounted. In 1973 the CIA stated assassinations had been banned in 1972. The Rockefeller Commission looked into the question immediately, but it did not finish its work on the issue, and all CIA documents relating to it went to the **Church Committee**. For months the CIA's reputation was battered in the press. Out of this sensational reporting came the case of Frank Olsen, which until then had been secret.

The Rockefeller Commission's report embarrassed the CIA when it told the circumstances surrounding Frank Olsen's suicide. It reported Frank Olsen had been administered LSD without his knowledge in 1953 during a test program conducted by the CIA and the U.S. Army. William Colby had been told that a death in the line of duty had occurred in the program. Olsen's death was now declared a suicide while in a depressed state, possibly if not certainly, due to the drugs he had been given without his consent or knowledge. The CIA records stated, Colby wrote, that "to ensure that Olsen's suicide was treated as the line-of-duty death . . . appropriate arrangements were made to take care of the family."

The Olsen family was shocked at the commission's reporting of Frank Olsen's death. At the time they understood, so Olsen's son stated in 2001, that their father had fallen to his death and that it had been an accident.

What was done to allay the distress of the family? Two different stories have been told. In the White House, in July 1975, Richard Cheney and Donald Rumsfeld recommended to President Ford that, in the government's name, he should officially apologize to Olsen's family for Frank's death. The President took this advice because he was warned that should the Olsen case ever go to court, it might be necessary to make public government secrets whose revelation could imperil the national interest. Ford hosted the Olsen family and apologized, and the state secrets were no longer in hazard.

In his memoirs, former CIA Director William Colby recalls having been given a 693-page report of possible violations or of questionable activities in regard to the CIA's legislative charter. Some called them the CIA's Family Jewels: Among them were "some of the bizarre and tragic cases where the Agency experimented with mind-control drugs, including one of a CIA officer who, without his knowledge, was given LSD, which caused a deep depression and eventually his death." Colby wrote that he apologized to the Olsens, and met them personally, "to discuss how to give them the CIA records and thus open up and overcome a twenty year secret. . . . (The list in the drug area, however, was far from comprehensive, since the records had been destroyed in 1972.)" (Colby, 1978, pp. 340, 426).

Olsen's son was never satisfied with the account of his father's death. During the 1990s he had it investigated; brought to light, in the report of the the investigation, the existence of Operation ARTICHOKE; and came to the conclusion on the evidence, none of which had been available at the time of his father's death, that Frank Olsen had been murdered by the CIA to protect the secrecy of Operation ARTICHOKE.

In a recent book on planning changes to the CIA, Hulnick (1999, p. 74) wrote, "The CIA's involvement in drug experimentation, in which mind-altering drugs were administered to unwitting victims, one of whom subsequently committed suicide might lead today to an indictment for criminal behavior."

Olsen's son said he does not plan to let the matter rest (Koch, 2002).

See also OLSEN, FRANK

Sources: Colby, William, *Honorable Men: My Life in the CIA* (New York: Simon & Schuster, 1978); Hulnick, Arthur S., *Fixing the Spy Machine: Preparing American Intelligence for the Twenty-first Century* (Westport, CT: Praeger/Greenwood, 1999); Koch, Egmont R., and Michael Wech, *The Secret War: Bio-Weapons and the CIA,* Gert Monheim, ed. (Film-production WDR, 2002).

OPERATION CHAOS (1967–1973). Operation CHAOS (formally MH-CHAOS) was a huge mail-opening scheme, similar to Operation HT-LINGUAL, which originated from the request of President **Lyndon B. Johnson** (1908–1973), who wanted to know if the anti–**Vietnam War** (1964–1973) movement in the United States was being manipulated by Communists. At the time the **Federal Bureau of Investigation (FBI)** was gathering information on protest groups, and frequently doing so by having its **agents** secretly join them. Since the **CIA** was not permitted to operate inside the United States, Operation CHAOS was strictly outside its charter, yet quite reasonably within aspects of its domain.

To ensure the secrecy of this project, like Operation HT-LINGUAL it was run by James Angleton (1917–1987), and free of the usual restraints of approval, methods, record keeping, and budget and review procedures. Angleton's counterintelligence staff collected thousands of documents on U.S. peace movements, members of the New Left, university radicals, and black nationalists. Overseas stations were told the project had top priority. It was found that there was no foreign involvement in the protests, and this was reported to Presidents Lyndon B. Johnson and **Richard Nixon** (1913–1994).

It was a politically dangerous operation because if it were leaked, it could easily be argued that the CIA was acting outside its charter by investigating domestic activities. Essentially the aim of Operation CHAOS was to find foreign links to U.S. dissidents.

After four years, when William Colby (1920–1996) was heading the CIA, secrecy about the operation within the agency was low and many of the young staff members were gossiping about Operation CHAOS, and some began to suspect that it was possibly illegal. Colby decided to reduce the anxiety attaching to the operation by having a thorough investigation of it, and informally stating the operation's purpose and procedures.

In 1972 Richard Helms (1913–2002) had turned the operation away from the study of dissenters and toward the investigation of international terrorism, a legal pursuit of the CIA. However, after a year people suspected that his efforts were merely a cover for Operation CHAOS. Colby found the practices of the secret service poisoned the people who were rendering the best service they could; high secrecy and compartmentation of activities made it impossible to allay anxieties among the young staff.

After the publication in December 1973 of an article about the illegalities of CIA projects, Operation CHAOS came to an end. Early in 1974 the **Rockefeller Commission** found the operation was carried well beyond its brief. How? First, the CIA sought personal files on U.S. citizens that were held by the FBI; second, to find foreign groups having contacts with members of dissident groups, it was necessary to put undercover agents into those dissident groups to establish the activities of the foreigners. Altogether, only three agents reported improperly on U.S. dissidents in the United States.

In 1973, when James Schlesinger became, for five months, the new Director of Central Intelligence (DCI), he asked James Angleton what had been achieved by the operation and learned that, like Operation HT-LINGUAL, it had yielded very little. He immediately closed it down internally. Later it was formally ended by William Colby, the new DCI.

See also ANGLETON, JAMES; COLBY, WILLIAM; HELMS, RICHARD; OPERATION HT-LINGUAL

Sources: Borosage, Robert L., "Secrecy vs. the Constitution," *Society* 12 (1975): 71–75; Colby, William, with Peter Forbath, *Honorable Men: My Life in the CIA* (New York: Simon & Schuster, 1978); Mangold, Tom, *Cold Warrior: James Jesus Angleton, the CIA Master Spy Hunter* (New York: Simon & Schuster, 1991); Rositzke, Harry, *The CIA's Secret Operations* (New York: Reader's Digest Press, 1977); U.S. Commission on CIA Activities Within the United States, *Report to the President* (Washington, DC: Government Printing Office, June 1975), the Rockefeller Commission report U.S. Senate, *Select Committee to Study Government Operations with Respect to Intelligence Activities,* 6 vols. (Washington, DC: Government Printing Office, 1975–1976), the Church Committee report.

OPERATION COINTELPRO (1956–1971). After **World War II** membership of the **CPUSA** was declining, and in 1956 the head of the **Federal Bureau of Investigation (FBI)**, J. Edgar Hoover (1895–1972) approved a domestic security scheme to weaken the party further. Called COINTELPRO, it would use any methods that were available to disgrace Communists. In the 1960s such programs were applied to many other groups in the United States.

The COINTELPRO programs would spread rumors and use deception, place informants in the CPUSA, and arrest homosexual party members in order to humiliate all other members. Also they would frame some party members by announcing, falsely, that they were paid FBI informants. The FBI **agents** would prevent meetings from being held by making anonymous phone calls. They would plant stories in the newspapers about party officials who had just bought a new automobile, saying they did so with party funds. By December 1957 there were about only 3,500 members in the CPUSA.

A U.S. House of Representative intelligence study found that as a result of this domestic espionage, harassment, and counterintelligence, careers were ruined, friendships were broke off, reputations were blackened, businesses were destroyed, lives were put in hazard, marriages were ended, people were fired from jobs, and violence was fomented.

In this covert series of operations an FBI informant would play at being an **agent provocateur,** and teach selected activists how to use explosives and commit crimes. On occasion, an FBI agent would behave as a violent, irrational, embarrassing, or crazy member of a left-wing group, and instruct unstable or naïve group members to commit criminal or ill-conceived acts; for instance, university students would be encouraged to set a dog on fire to demonstrate on campus what life in Vietnam was *really* like, and one agent–informant led students in a criminal raid on a draft board in Camden, New Jersey, teaching them how to break noiselessly into an office and to open filing cabinets without keys.

Among the groups that were harassed in the program were black nationalists and civil rights workers in the 1960s; any radical arm of any group was fair game, especially members of the New Left. Some of Lee Harvey Oswald's (1939–1963) activities have the mark of this program, and he may well have been secretly funded through it.

In April 1971 J. Edgar Hoover ended all COINTELPRO activities that were the basis of the FBI's domestic security operations.

Sources: Gentry, Curt, *J. Edgar Hoover: The Man and His Secrets* (New York: Norton, 1991); Mailer, Norman, *Oswald's Tale: An American Mystery* (New York: Random House, 1995); Power, Richard Gid, *Secrecy and Power: The Life of J. Edgar Hoover* (London: Hutchinson, 1987); Wise, David, *The American Police State: The Government Against the People* (New York: Vintage Books, 1979).

OPERATIONS CONFLICT, LORD, AND SUGAR (1952–1955). Operation CONFLICT and its suboperations, Operations LORD and SUGAR, involved tapping the phone lines between Moscow and Russian military centers in Vienna. After **World War II**, Vienna, like Berlin, was divided into four militarized zones: British, French, Soviet, and American. In 1955 the four agreed to withdraw troops from Vienna, and to guarantee Austria's neutrality.

Before 1955 the West's main problem was how to penetrate the Soviet-controlled East European nations, mainly Czechoslovakia and Hungary, and to learn what was happening inside the Russian military headquarters in the Hotel Imperial in the Russian sector of Vienna.

The British had established Section Y, an especially secret section of the **SIS**, to exploit special technical information sources by using sophisticated listening devices. The head of the section was Peter Lunn (1914–). Lunn discovered that beneath the French and British sectors of Vienna lay telephone cables that linked field units and airports of the Russian army with its headquarters. Lunn planned to tap and record conversations on the lines, and he devised and ran Operations CONFLICT, LORD, and SUGAR.

At the time tapping lines for intelligence, in addition to information on individual suspects and for security purposes, was relatively new. The first tapping was to be done at a British military police station, six meters from a cable that linked the Soviet headquarters in Vienna with the Schwechat military airport. Peter Lunn worked hard to get approval for the operation; when money became available, military authorities cooperated, and a short tunnel was dug from the basement of the police station, a tap was put in place, and a listening post set up with recording apparatus. It was so successful that in December 1952 two more taps were established; one, called Operation SUGAR, ran from a British business that traded in jewelry, and was funded by SIS; the other, Operation LORD, was run from a fashionable suburb of Vienna in a villa owned by a former Dutch intelligence officer.

The information from these taps was of enormous value for three years. After the taps were made, the main problem was to find people who knew Russian so well that they would have little trouble translating the information into English. For security reasons the recruitment of translators and the information processing were done in London. Some of its staff members were flown in from Vienna. Other transcribers were "St. Petersburg English," émigrés to England who had had a history in the timber and fur trade with Russia or had once established factories in Russia. After the Russian Revolution in 1917, such merchants and industrialists had settled in England. Other transcribers were daughters of Russian émigrés and former Polish army officers.

By October 1953 the facts about these operations were made available to the Soviets by their **double agent** in the SIS, George Blake (1922–).

The work was successful until a streetcar going over the tunnel caused it to collapse (Cavendish, 1990). Although that ended the Vienna tunnel, it inspired a similar operation in Berlin, Operation GOLD.

See also LUNN, PETER; OPERATION STOPWATCH

Sources: Blake, George, *No Other Choice: An Autobiography* (London: Jonathan Cape, 1990); Cavendish, Anthony, *Inside Intelligence* (London: Collins, 1990); Dorril, Stephen, *MI6: Inside the Covert World of Her Majesty's Secret Intelligence Service* (New York: The Free Press, 2000); Murphy, David E., Sergei A. Kondrashev, and George Bailey, *Battleground Berlin: CIA vs KGB in the Cold War* (New Haven, CT: Yale University Press, 1997).

OPERATION CONGRESS (1950–1979). Operation CONGRESS, so named in Saunders (1999), was a **Central Intelligence Agency (CIA)**–funded series of projects that centered on many artistic and cultural activities around the world during the **Cold War.** Funding was secret, and after it was discovered in 1967, the organization for funding was renamed and otherwise changed, but by 1979 it was no longer viable.

Late in June 1950, days before the **Korean War** (1950–1953) began, 4,000 people were invited to meet in Berlin to hear some of the West's noted intellectuals speak. Among them were James T. Farrell (1904–1979), Tennessee Williams (1911–1983), Carson McCullers (1917–1967), Arthur Schlesinger, Jr. (1917–), Sidney Hook (1902–1989), Hugh. R. Trevor-Roper (1914–2003), and Jules Romains (1885–1972). Two intellectuals who chose not to attend were Jean-Paul Sartre (1905–1980) and Maurice Merleau-Ponty (1908–1961).

Berlin's mayor opened the conference, and the attendees worked in groups, went on guided tours, appeared at press conferences, and attended cocktail parties and concerts. They discussed art, artists, citizenship, peace, freedom, science, totalitarianism, and the relations between these activities and systems of thought. Opposition to communism became central to their discussions.

Arthur Koestler (1905–1983) called for fighting groups to topple communism; others spoke of the difference between good **atom bombs** and bad atom bombs, criticized intellectuals who chose not to attend the conference, and declared freedom could never be neutral. At the end of the conference Koestler cried out, "Friends, freedom has seized the offensive," and produced a 14-point manifesto for the constitution of a Congress for Cultural Freedom. Years later, Hugh Trevor-Roper recalled that the meeting was like a Nazi Party rally, and remembered observing the sense of guilt that appeared to drive Koestler.

The conference arose from Western opinion that the Soviets were generously funding their intellectuals, and that the West should do the same. Only the United States had the funds to pursue this policy. The Berlin conference was funded by the CIA; and in 1951, through the **Marshall Plan**, the CIA arranged to set aside U.S.$200,000—equivalent to U.S.$1.5 million in 2003—for the administration of the Congress for Cultural Freedom. The Congress headquarters was on the Boulevarde Haussman in Paris.

The Congress's policy was to support left-wing views and activities that were not based on, or supportive of, communism as an alternative to non-pro-Western or non-anti-American viewpoints. Eventually this policy would fail, because the non-Communist left (NCL) members were not reliable supporters of any accepted or correct political cause. They could soften their resistance to pro-Soviet interests and attitudes, especially those involving selected humanitarian issues, and still be taking a view opposed to that of the United States. This political error appears to have partly arisen from the personal views of Allen Dulles (1893–1969), CIA head at the time, that the world's struggle against communism should fund institutions that provided a useful non-Communist ideology. In time this would lead the CIA to nurture non-Communist left-wing activists who sabotaged the U.S. activities against Cuba, and in Latin America and Vietnam.

In April 1967, a U.S. magazine, *Ramparts,* published the results of its investigation into CIA covert activities and revealed the CIA's role in funding the Congress; shortly afterward many U.S. societies, trusts, fraternities, and other groups that had benefited from CIA funding were perceived to be possible CIA fronts and organizations.

The CIA had sponsored the Congress for Cultural Freedom from its beginning, and subsidized many learned and intellectual magazines around the globe, such as *Encounter* in Britain and *Quadrant* in Australia. Editors and trustees who controlled the magazines were not always aware that funds came to them from the CIA, probably because the **Ford Foundation** and other philanthropic organizations would channel CIA funds where they could be used. Because some trustees knew the CIA's role, and others did not, control of the publications split, and many editors and trustees resigned when they learned that they had been unwittingly serving the CIA.

Late in April 1967 the General Assembly of the Congress confirmed reports that the CIA had funded the work of the Congress; said it was proud of its own achievements since 1950; claimed its activities had been free of any CIA influence and that its members' intellectual integrity had not been impaired; and condemned the CIA for its deceptions in general and for its poisoning of intellectual discussion in particular. At the time a vast array of the world's intelligentsia whose careers had benefited from the Congress for Cultural Freedom knew that it was a CIA-funded organization.

Arthur Koestler was among many intellectuals who said it did not matter where the money came from; Lionel Trilling (1905–1975) and Mary McCarthy (1912–1989) merely accepted the money, while others asserted that the CIA's activities were a benign necessity of the Cold War, and by comparison with its military coups, the CIA's intellectual coups were rarely effective in changing people's minds. Hanna Arendt (1906–1975) and Angus Wilson (1913–1991) believed the CIA had discredited intellectuals with its deceptions and secrecy.

After 1967 the CIA continued to fund associations and forums that were once connected with the Congress. However well the funding source was hidden, the Congress's international influence rapidly declined. It was renamed the International Association for Cultural Freedom, and the Ford Foundation, which had earlier brokered millions of dollars for philanthropic funds for the Congress, provided all financing and gave intellectuals the perceived independence they believed their organization had once held. Even so, in January 1979, the Association dissolved itself, and one of the CIA's means of providing intellectual's with cultural freedom disappeared.

An outstanding opportunity for the CIA to provide cultural freedom had appeared in 1950 after the death of George Orwell (1903–1950). Two officers from Frank Wisner's (1909–1965) **OPC** promised Orwell's widow that they would arrange for her to meet Clark Gable (1901–1960), her favorite actor, in return for her signing over the film rights of *Animal Farm.* The film was financed and distributed globally by the

CIA in 1956. Back in 1952 the screen play was not thought to follow the U.S. **Psychological Strategy Board's (PSB)** aims closely enough, so the ending of the story was changed. Instead of closing the film with Communist pigs and capitalist men being indistinguishable in their foul pursuits, the animals on the farm rose up, stormed the farmhouse, banished the farmers, and left the pigs wallowing in their own cesspool of corruption. Typical Communists! In this way the natural corruption of communism was easily distinguished from the incidental waywardness of capitalism.

In 1956, Orwell's *Nineteen Eighty-four*, required reading for CIA and PSB members, was similarly prepared for distribution as a film. In the novel the universal misery and ignorance, which had been induced by bland ignorance of worldwide slavery and manipulation of mass culture, had grown to be a feature of the two world groups—Them and Us. In the film version the hero appears to have overcome his broken spirit and to be able to think, be it ever so tentatively, for himself. Natural triumph of the Western individual over Communist totalitarianism!

In her account of the CIA's influence on intellectuals, Saunders (1999) writes, with irony, that it was the same set of people who had been raised on classical literature and educated at America's foremost universities who, after **World War II**, recruited Nazis, manipulated democratic elections in foreign lands, administered **LSD** to subjects without their informed consent, opened their citizens' mail illegally, funded dictatorships, and plotted assassinations—all in the interest of securing an empire for the United States. This use of irony for criticism meets resistence in the work of CIA apologists Richard Bissell (1996) and William Colby (1987).

See also BISSELL, RICHARD, JR.; COLBY, WILLIAM

Sources: Bissell, Richard Mervin, Jr., with Jonathan E. Lewis and Frances T. Pudio, *Reflections of a Cold Warrior: From Yalta to the Bay of Pigs* (New Haven, CT: Yale University Press, 1996); Colby, William, with Peter Forbath, *Honorable Men: My Life in the CIA* (New York: Simon & Schuster, 1978); Miller, Arthur, *Timebends: A Life* (London: Methuen, 1987); Saunders, Francis S., *Who Paid the Piper? The CIA and the Cultural Cold War* (London: Granta, 1999), also published as *The Cultural Cold War: The CIA and the World of Arts and Letters* (New York: The New Press, 2000).

OPERATION CORONA (1960). An expensive and frustrating operation funded largely by the **Central Intelligence Agency (CIA)** that sought to employ reconnaissance flights by satellites rather than piloted planes, and was rejected in principle by the U.S. Air Force as unworkable.

Operation CORONA aimed to launch a satellite, take photographs, and fire a capsule out of the satellite's orbit to bring the film back to earth. It was publically known as DISCOVERER, but to those working on its espionage function, it was known as Operation CORONA. It was undertaken in response to the successful launch of the Russian satellite, *Sputnik*, in October 1957. At the time the **Cold War** turned into a conflict over supremacy in space, and whether or not the United States had the advantage over the **U.S.S.R.** in being able to fire intercontinental missiles with nuclear warheads.

For 18 months CORONA was a frustrating failure, and information collected by satellite had an impact on the rhetoric of the Democrats' presidential candidate, Senator **John F. Kennedy** (1917–1963), in the 1960 election.

The operators aimed to have an exposed film capsule drop by parachute—thereby making its descent into the atmosphere slow—then fall into the ocean and be picked up. Operation CORONA was not as successful as the **U-2 spy flights** because of frequent technical errors. The stabilizing system failed and satellite would fall out of orbit; sometimes the film would be ejected and be lost; on other occasions the vehicle would not get into orbit; sometimes capsule would fail to send out a signal so that it could be found (on one occasion a plane was sent to find it, but without success); another launch simply crashed to earth. The researchers found a satellite would spin out of control, burn up in the atmosphere, get lost in the ocean, or even blow up.

At the tenth attempt—and these were highly expensive—in February 1960, CORONA did not get into orbit; the next CORONA was lost by the tracking stations; the twelfth simply fell off its launching pad.

In August 1960 the lucky thirteenth CORONA succeeded. On this occasion everything worked, but bad weather made it impossible to find the ejected capsule. Attempt 14 was a complete success, and the ejected film was caught in midair.

Information gleaned from satellite reconnaissance showed that, contrary to the speeches during the 1960 election campaign between **Richard M. Nixon** (1913–1994) and John F. Kennedy, the supposed **missile gap** between the United States and the U.S.S.R. was *not* in favor of the U.S.S.R. The Soviets had about 50 missiles that could reach the United States; the United States had 250 that could reach the U.S.S.R. This became public in September 1961, well after John Kennedy had been narrowly elected President.

Sources: Bissell, Richard Mervin, Jr., with Jonathan E. Lewis and Frances T. Pudio, *Reflections of a Cold Warrior: From Yalta to the Bay of Pigs* (New Haven, CT: Yale University Press, 1996); Burrows, William E., *Deep Black: Space Espionage and National Security* (New York: Random House, 1986); McDougall, Walter A., *The Heavens and the Earth: A Political History of the Space Age* (New York: Basic Books, 1985); Richelson, Jeffrey T., *A Century of Spies: Intelligence in the Twentieth Century* (New York: Oxford University Press, 1995).

OPERATION DEJEAN (1962). Maurice Dejean, the French ambassador to Moscow between 1956 and 1962, was caught in a honeytrap.

Maurice Dejean was known to adore young women. **Nikita Khrushchev** (1894–1973) supported a **KGB** plot to entrap Dejean using a swallow (a woman sex worker). The KGB usually recruited honeytrap victims by photographing them making love with the swallow, and then using blackmail to get the information they wanted. But in this case the operation, taken over by Oleg Mikhailovich Gribanov, was handled more delicately.

Gribanov arranged for Dejean's wife to be occupied elsewhere with young artists, while lascivious beauties, sometimes from among the Bolshoi ballerinas, were drafted to tempt Dejean. He was caught in bed with Laura, who had told him her husband was abroad. Pretending to be her husband, a KGB **agent** burst in, started beating Dejean, and shouted to his "wife" that he did not care who the man was. Dejean confided in his close Russian associate, who also was KGB, and asked him to calm down the enraged "husband." This was done. Thereafter, the ambassador would occasionally discuss with this close Russian friend details of French policy that were secret. In this operation blackmail was not appropriate, but it could be called upon if necessary.

At the same time, the French air attaché, Colonel Louis Guibaud, was caught in a similar honeytrap. He committed suicide rather than be blackmailed.

After his air attaché's suicide, Dejean had to leave for Paris, where he was welcomed publicly by De Gaulle with "Alors, Dejean, on couche!" Details of the story were covered up, and Dejean went to work quietly in the diplomatic service elsewhere.

One of the KGB agents who helped organize the seduction of Dejean defected, and revealed the operation before blackmail had been contemplated.

Recent information shows that at much the same time, a third French member of the diplomatic service in Moscow, a woman, was seduced by a male swallow, and, after seeing her photographs, was persuaded to serve the KGB. Back in Paris in the early 1960s, she broke her connections with the KGB.

See also HONEYTRAP OPERATIONS

Sources: Andrew, Christopher, and Oleg Gordievsky, *KGB: The Inside Story of Its Foreign Operations* (London: Hodder and Stoughton, 1990); Barron, John, *The KGB Today: The Hidden Hand* (New York: Reader's Digest Press, 1983); Lewis, David, *Sexpionage: The Exploitation of Sex by Soviet Intelligence* (London: Heinrich Hanau Publications, 1976).

OPERATION EAGLE CLAW (1980). A failed secret operation in April 1980, involving America's Delta Force, to rescue 52 diplomats held hostage by Iranians in the U.S. embassy in Tehran.

In early November 1979, fanatical supporters, called "students," of the Iranian leader Ayatollah Khomeini (1900–1989), who earlier that year had replaced the Shah of Iran, Mohamed Reza Pahlavi (1919–1980), stormed the U.S. embassy in Tehran and took nearly 100 hostages. Outside the embassy thousands chanted anti-American slogans and constructed a gibbet from which to hang the exiled Shah should the United States allow him to return to Iran.

At first the Ayatollah's role was unclear, but later he would support the "students." Meanwhile, until the end of January 1980, six U.S. diplomats hid in the Canadian embassy. They managed to escape when the **CIA** forged Iranian visa stamps and had them put into Canadian passports, thereby enabling Americans to leave Iran. Furious, the Iranian Foreign Minister vowed revenge on the Canadians.

In March the Secretary-General of the United Nations ordered a UN commission to solve the crisis. However, before the commission could see the hostages, the Ayatollah demanded that its members express their views on the "crimes of the Shah" and that "Great Satan," the United States. This demand indicated publicly, for the first time, that the "students" were indeed acting in accordance with the policies of the Iranian government.

Publicly, President **Jimmy Carter** (1924–) stated that it seemed the Iranian government was not in adequate control of the situation. In secret he agreed to Operation EAGLE CLAW, in which Delta Force would rescue the remaining 52 hostages from its secret base in the Iranian desert. In the early hours of April 25, 1980, Operation EAGLE CLAW was aborted because of technical problem associated with getting sufficient helicopters ready to complete the mission. The mission was secret until a refueling problem arose with one of the helicopters when it collided with a tanker. The explosion killed eight men, and the mission was known around the world.

Later it would be argued that the mission failed because there had been too many U.S. agencies involved in the planning and execution of Operation EAGLE CLAW, and that their coordination had never been achieved adequately. The hostage takers threatened to kill the captives if another attempt were made. President Carter took responsibility for the fiasco.

This failure, and the success two weeks later, in London, of the British **SAS** in a raid on Iranian terrorists in London, contributed much to the humiliation of Carter's administration and his failure at the next presidential election. Christopher Warren, a leading White House official during the Carter administration, arranged for the hostages to be freed. However, to humiliate President Carter as much as possible, the Iranians would not allow them to go free until after the U.S. presidential election.

Shortly after the inauguration of President **Ronald Reagan** (1911–2004), in January 1981, he announced that the 52 hostages were free after 444 days in captivity. In secret, it appears, the hostage takers had received $3 billion and a planeload of paramilitary spare parts which were seen being delivered just as the hostages' plane left Iranian airspace.

Sources: Fraser, Robert, "Occupation of U.S. Embassy in Tehran by Islamic Revolutionary 'Students,'" *Keesings Contemporary Archives*, 26 (March 21, 1980), 30150; Smith, Joseph, and Simon Davis, *Historical Dictionary of the Cold War* (New York: Scarecrow Press, 2000); Walker, Martin, *The Cold War: A History* (New York: Henry Holt, 1993).

OPERATION FOOT (1972). Operation FOOT was a British response to the general Soviet plan to advance terrorist activities in the West.

Secret **KGB** plans to advance terrorism against the West lay behind the Soviet policy to normalize international relations in the early 1970s. The policy was undermined by defectors, among whom was Oleg Adolfovich Lyalin (fl. 1937–1972) a capable saboteur, hand-to-hand fighter, and parachutist.

In London, Lyalin was recruited to **MI5** in the spring of 1971. For six months beforehand he had told MI5 about plans for terrorist attacks in London, America, West Germany, France, and Italy. The terrorism and sabotage involved poisoning the public water supply, assassinating political leaders, flooding underground railways, bombing early-warning systems and airfields, and gassing office workers.

In September 1971 the Soviet chargé d'affaires was told that 105 KGB and **GRU** officers, all posing as diplomatic staff, would be expelled. **Whitehall** called this massive expulsion policy Operation FOOT, and argued that there were far more KGB and GRU **agents** in Britain than MI5 and other British secret services could manage. It had become clear that agents were planning to mount terrorist attacks in England, and Oleg Lyalin's revelations about the details made it all the more important that the agents be immediately expelled. This decision crippled the KGB plans.

The Russians promptly denounced Lyalin as morally depraved, and many KGB officers were fired or demoted for having allowed such a disgrace. The KGB's peacetime sabotage plans evaporated. Oleg Gordievsky (1938–) regarded Operation FOOT as an expulsion without precedent, and one that deeply shocked **Moscow Center**.

To manage the Soviet public relations disaster, in Russia that October, Kim Philby (1912–1988), a confirmed alcoholic by this time, was dried out and given the tasks of denouncing the British government for fabricating slander about the Soviets and of claiming the massive expulsion was in fear of Russia's attempt to achieve international peace through normalizing international relations.

See also LYALIN, OLEG; PHILBY, HAROLD "KIM"

Sources: Andrew, Christopher, and Vasili Mitrokhin, *The Mitrokhin Archive: The KGB in Europe and the West* (London: Lane, 1999); Brook-Shepherd, Gordon, *The Storm Birds. Soviet Post War Defectors: The Dramatic True Stories 1945–1985* (New York: Henry Holt, 1989).

OPERATION GRAIL (1945–1947). Operation GRAIL was one of the earliest American espionage operations in Berlin after the end of **World War II**. The operation centered on discovering the extent of Soviet military intentions and resources in East Germany. Its success appears to have been limited.

Berlin Operations Base (BOB) was the Berlin base of the U.S. War Department's Strategic Service Unit, a unit of the **OSS**. Its mission was to provide the U.S. military in occupied Germany, and especially in Berlin, with intelligence needed to understand and cope with the Soviet intentions and operations in Germany.

Late in the summer of 1945 it became clear to the U.S. military that the Soviets were intruding vigorously into many aspects of German life, such as transportation, food supply, industrial organization, political organization, and the considerable dismantling of German military–industrial organizations, especially those relating to the production of an **atom bomb**.

A Soviet corporation was established to mine uranium for Russia's atom bomb, process uranium, produce distilled calcium and nickel wire mesh, and provide forced labor to work on Soviet atom bomb projects. In June 1945 the U.S. forces withdrew from their front position in East Germany; BOB, which relied heavily on army intelligence, had to collect its own intelligence after January 1946. The new BOB program was Operation GRAIL. Its main task was to discover the Soviet army's **order of battle**. To do this, BOB had to find German **agents** who would contact old friends near Russian military garrisons and airports. Over 250 agents observed and photographed Soviet installations and activities; those who were detained were readily replaced; a few were doubled back to spy against the West. Often those whom the Russians arrested were tried and eventually sent to the **Gulag.**

Training of the BOB agents was not sophisticated, and through socializing with one another they became readily identifiable. **Safe houses** were not always used properly, and standards of safety and reporting varied. But overall the operation was successful enough, and provided the U.S. military high command with much information on airfields, troop movements, training, ammunition supplies, and garrison security.

The operation was ended in the autumn of 1946 when strings of secret agents were arrested. The agents had formed a chain or network of former military officers of the German army; they would be controlled by an American case officer and would find 20 or so local agents. From these agents the officer would gather their reports and take them to a safe house in West Berlin, where he would type up the results for the U.S. case officer.

Sometimes the agents would be approached by a Soviet security official who would ask them to find information on public attitudes to Soviet policy. After serving the Soviet officer for a short time, the agents would be arrested, interrogated, and shown photos of his presemce and activity near a safe house.

The Soviets were well-informed about the spy networks of BOB. Operation GRAIL was formally terminated in March 1947.

Source: Murphy, David E., Sergei A. Kondrashev, and George Bailey, *Battleground Berlin: CIA vs KGB in the Cold War* (New Haven, CT: Yale University Press, 1997).

OPERATION GRAND SLAM (1960). Operation GRAND SLAM was the name given to the first flight scheduled over the *entire* **U.S.S.R.** Before this flight the U-2 spy planes had not flown more than halfway across Soviet territory. This would be the longest **U-2 spy flight** to date, and president **Dwight D. Eisenhower** (1890–

1969) forbade any further flights after May 1, 1960; he was anxious that nothing should endanger the summit meeting he was about to have with **Nikita Khrushchev** (1894–1971). The pilot, Francis Gary Powers (1929–1977), and the U-2 spy plane were shot down on May 1, 1960.

See also POWERS, FRANCIS GARY

Sources: Ambrose, Stephen E., *Ike's Spies: Eisenhower and the Espionage Establishment,* 2nd ed. (Jackson: University Press of Mississippi, 1999); Bissell, Richard Mervin, Jr., with Jonathan E. Lewis and Frances T. Pudio, *Reflections of a Cold Warrior: From Yalta to the Bay of Pigs* (New Haven, CT: Yale University Press, 1996).

OPERATION GREENSLEEVES. A fictional operation that appeared in *A Perfect Spy* (1986), the autobiographical novel by David Cornwell, who wrote **Cold War** spy novels under the name of John Le Carré. Operation GREENSLEEVES is the operation of perfect spies.

In Operation GREENSLEEVES, Magnus Pym befriends Axel H., a Carlsbad refugee and illegal immigrant in Switzerland, whose origins are obscure and whose intellect and learning Pym admires. Nevertheless, Magus betrays Axel to the British Secret service, which informs the American Secret Service; and Axel disappears.

Years later, after his recruitment into the British secret services and promotion to lieutenant, Pym meets Axel in a remote Czech farmhouse. Pym learns that Axel had been taken into custody constantly and severely beaten for being an **illegal** by various authorities—American, West German, Czech—presumably for having been a Nazi.

The Czech authorities discovered that Axel's father had been a socialist hero during the **Spanish Civil War** (1935–1938), and that Axel was intelligent enough for a technical education. Axel did well, rose in the Communist Party hierarchy, and secured his place among the Communist elite.

When he meets Axel again, Pym expects his old friend to defect to the West, but instead Axel proposes that Pym take him in as a **defector-in-place** and that together he and Pym, being reasonable men who do not want another world war and who are tired of heroics, can, through their well-founded friendship, become influences for the good of humanity.

Axel gives Magnus Pym secret information for the West to evaluate, and insists that Pym say it comes from a lonely Sergeant Pavel in Czech Army intelligence. The material is so impressive that the British secret services **code name** its source GREENSLEEVES, and authorize the operation. When Axel and Magnus meet a second time, Pym has many questions, but Axel says the British must starve, thus giving them a better appetite for the next meeting. So Pym tells his superiors that Sergeant Pavel is ill with remorse and casts a veil of reasons over the silence, hinting that future information may include material on rocket weaponry. At the third meeting Pym gets a clearer view of what was previously obscure; a complete account of Soviet air forces in Czechoslovakia!

This information secures Magnus Pym's career, and the British require that he work alone with Axel and deify Operation Greensleeves in their intelligence community. At the next meeting Axel seeks Pym's help. In a purge of Titoists from the Soviet-dominated Czech government, the lives of its senior bureaucrats and their families have been ruined, and now Axel has been chosen for interrogation. To secure his future, Axel says he told his interrogators that he was cultivating a British traitor, a big fish in the British army. Now Axel must give some proof of this big fish, some information perhaps of a British traitor who is being blackmailed—high-level information, deeply secret, and of such quality that it would impress Axel's superiors and secure his position in the purge.

This creates a turning point in Pym's career. After much thought he decides, "The loyal attacher would never again betray his friend in exchange for the illusion of being a servant of national security." His loves, duties, and allegiances have never been clearer. "Together we [Axel and Magnus] can change the world." Pym does not go to his superior to seek valuable information to pass on to Axel, and thereby preserve Axel's security as a defector-in-place. Why? Pym reasons to himself that his superiors would no longer trust him to work alone with Axel in the interests of Operation GREENSLEEVES; his immediate superior would lose face and be demoted for running a **double agent** with out permission; since Pym's compulsory military service would expire soon anyway, and a turf struggle inside the British secret services to control GREENSLEEVES would erupt, Axel would be put in hazard again; and Pym's successor would find the deception immediately. So with goodwill, faith in himself, great courage, and a strong desire to help Axel and himself to win a "great victory," Pym photographs secret documents in his superior's files, saying to himself, "Axel, I've done it! We're free. We've put the world to rights . . . we are the men of the middle ground—we have founded our own country with a population of two!"

After Pym's return to England, the source of GREENSLEEVES does not show up, and reports coming in to Pym's former superior, who immediately took over Pym's role, show that the material that once appeared valuable was, on close scrutiny, already known. As for Pym and Axel, they work as double agents in a relationship that ensures the security of their own utopian nation of two and protects the whole world from destruction by keeping both sides in the Cold War fully informed on each other's military resources and political intentions.

See also LE CARRÉ, JOHN

Source: Le Carré, John, *A Perfect Spy* (London: Hodder and Stoughton, 1986).

OPERATION GRIDIRON (1969). Sometimes called the Bennett Case, Operation GRIDIRON was a secret inquiry, begun late in 1969, into the reasons for the high failure rate of counterintelligence work done in Canada while Leslie James Bennett (1920–) was deputy chief of B Branch (Counterintelligence) of the **RCMP.** The question was: Could Bennett have sabotaged his own operations because he was a **KGB mole?**

See also BENNETT, LESLIE JAMES "JIM"

Sources: Mangold, Tom, *Cold Warrior: James Jesus Angleton, the CIA Master Spy Hunter* (New York: Simon & Schuster, 1991); Sawatsky, John, *For Services Rendered: Leslie James Bennett and the RCMP Security Service* (Garden City, NY: Doubleday, 1982); Wise, David, *Molehunt: The Secret Search for Traitors the Shattered the CIA* (New York: Random House, 1992).

OPERATION HT-LINGUAL (1955–1973). Operation HT-LINGUAL began in 1955 to find whether or not **illegal** Soviet **agents** in the United States were communicating with the **U.S.S.R.** through the U.S. mail, and to find among Soviet citizens nuclear scientists and military officers whose letters to the United States might reveal useful information or show they might be recruitable into U.S. espionage.

The operation was, like Operation CHAOS, kept under the control of James Angleton (1917–1987), who ran it quietly until 1973, when William Colby (1920–1996) was appointed DCI. At that time a *New York Times* journalist, Seymour Hersh, warned Colby that he had detected the secret operations CHAOS and HT-LINGUAL, which Angleton ran, and would publish what he knew in December 1973, declaring it a massive espionage program directed against U.S. citizens, and therefore a violation of the **CIA** charter.

When the news broke, Angleton and his loyal followers said that William Colby had fed the story to Hersh. Shortly after, Angleton was forced to retire. Later it was found that Angleton had mislaid or misappropriated some of the mail collected during this program.

Like CHAOS, HT-LINGUAL was investigated by the U.S. Congress in the summer of 1975 by the **Church Committee**, a special U.S. Senate committee headed by Senator Frank Church, a Democrat from Idaho.

See also ANGLETON, JAMES; OPERATION CHAOS

Sources: Colby, William, with Peter Forbath, *Honorable Men: My Life in the CIA* (New York: Simon & Schuster, 1978); Mangold, Tom, *Cold Warrior: James Jesus Angleton, the CIA Master Spy Hunter* (New York: Simon & Schuster, 1991); Rositzke, Harry, *The CIA's Secret Operations* (New York: Reader's Digest Press, 1977); U.S. Senate, *Select Committee to Study Government Operations with Respect to Intelligence Activities,* 6 vols. (Washington, DC: Government Printing Office, 1975–1976), the Church Committee report.

OPERATION KAMEN (c. 1948–1958). Operation KAMEN was a secret Soviet operation that aimed to find traitors in Czechoslovakia after the Russian invasion in February 1948.

Many Czechoslovakians were prepared to pay 25,000 to 30,000 crowns to escape Russian-occupied Czechoslovakia after **World War II**. They would pay a professional people-smuggler to help them cross into West Germany, where, much relieved, they would reveal details of life in Czechoslovakia under Russian rule. When he discovered this illegal practice, Colonel Antonin Prchal used the information to find Czechoslovakian dissidents. He recruited the people-smugglers, knowing they got their clients through the Czechoslovakian resistance movement; and through them he would catch many would-be escapees.

To extend his operation, Prchal established a fake West Germany forest in Czechoslovakia where unwitting would-be escapees were taken by a corrupt people-smuggler whom they had paid and trusted and were welcomed by Colonel Prchal's men, masquerading as agents of the United States. To these men the escapees would give details of how they had planned to escape Czechoslovakia, and the names of their supporters among the resistance units and of dissidents. Shortly afterward the fake agents would reveal themselves as members of the Czechoslovakian secret service. Later these **agents** would search Czechoslovakia for the dissidents, and eventually have them tried for treason.

Other would-be escapees were murdered by their people-smuggler, who chose to pervert the corrupt operation for their own ends. Eventually Operation KAMEN was so corrupted that it had to be stopped in the late 1950s by the Minister for State Security, Rudolf Barak, who reorganized the Czechoslovakian secret service and became a popular figure in his country.

Source: Frolik, Joseph, *The Frolik Defection* (London: Leo Cooper, 1975).

OPERATION KHOLSTOMER (fl. 1955–1984). Operation KHOLSTOMER was a fictional **KGB** operation to overthrow Western capitalism and win the **Cold War**. Although the plot is fictional, it is quite plausible, and was devised by Robert Littell (2002), who links it with the U.S. Operation ABLE ARCHER in 1983 and with the obsessions of James Angleton (1917–1987) about the Soviets' aim to dominate Western society through getting control of its secret services by means of **moles** in the major banking and government organizations.

An experienced KGB **agent**, STARIK (Russian for "old man"), directed KHOLSTOMER between 1974 and 1984; earlier he directed Kim Philby (1912–1988), and now controlled SASHA, a Russian mole inside the **CIA**, who was an obsession with James Angleton.

Since the mid-1950s the KGB has been planning KHOLSTOMER. It was to be financed by syphoning off funds from sales of oil, gas, and armaments and putting the money into tax havens in the Channel Islands, Switzerland, and the Caribbean. It operated through shell companies that were owned by two other companies, which in turn were owned by one or more companies based in Geneva or Bermuda, which in turn were owned by other companies. The KHOLSTOMER/KGB owned shell companies controlling U.S.$63 billion, and the money was held in New York banks that could not identify the ultimate owners of the money. On any day U.S.$500–$600 billion dollars changes hands in New York on the spot market, where sales are executed immediately.

The plan was first to plant articles in the world's newspapers stating how weak the U.S. dollar was, then suddenly sell U.S.$63 billion. Speculators, insurance companies, private banks, retirement funds, and the Europan and Asian Central banks would be sucked in by the general panic of the moment. Panic money would flow at a rate 10 times that of the original U.S.$63 billion. Thus, U.S.$600 billion would be dumped suddenly into the spot market, *in addition to* the regular daily sale of U.S. dollars.

The U.S. Federal Reserve Bank would intervene and buy up the dollars to stabilize the U.S. currency. But this would come too late and be too little to prevent the downward spiral of the dollar. Seventy percent of the foreign currency holdings in the central banks of Japan, Hong Kong, Taiwan, and Malaysia was in U.S. dollars, a total of U.S.$1 trillion. Ninety percent of the U.S.$1 trillion was held in U.S. Treasury bonds and bills. The KGB had agents in those central banks, who, at the first sign of the fall in the American dollar, would push their bank to hedge against further deterioration in their holdings, and to sell 20 percent of their Treasury bond assets. At the same time the U.S. dollar declined, the American bond market would collapse, and then a panic would follow in Wall Street, the Dow Jones index would fall suddenly, and European stock markets would plunge. Europeans with U.S. dollars would panic, sell their U.S. holdings, and switch to gold.

In America, Europe, and Asia interest rates would climb as the bond market fell. American companies would sell less at home and abroad, and America's trade deficit would rise. Inflation also would rise, the U.S. economy would slow down, and unemployment would increase.

The failure of the U.S. economy, and its chaos, would affect France and Italy, where powerful Communist parties could offer an alternative policy to free their people from U.S. economic domination; this would lead to a closer alignment of those countries with the Soviet bloc. West Germany, Spain, and Scandinavia would slowly follow suit.

It remained for STARIK to find the right time to bring KHOLSTOMER to the attention of the Russian leadership, and set the plan in operation.

In 1974 the American economy was in recession and inflation was soaring. STARIK intended to present KHOLSTOMER to **Yuri Andropov** (1914–1984), KGB Chairman, and if he approved, then to the Politburo Committee of Three, who decided on international intelligence operations; if they approved, then **Leonid Brezhnev** (1906–1982) could be approached.

STARIK found that Brezhnev was fascinated by the planning of the scheme, but was not ready to agree. Brezhnev saw the scheme would destroy capitalist democracies and make him a greater Russian ruler than Lenin, and lead the Soviets to victory in the Cold War. Andropov and the Committee of Three had cleared the plot. American inflation was soaring; the Dow Jones had fallen to 570 from 1003 two years previously; the rise of oil prices from $2.50 per barrel to $11.25 after the Middle East War in 1973 weakened the American dollar. If the attack on the American dollar were to begin in 1974, there was a good chance the U.S. economy would go into a recessionary spiral from which it would never recover. The only American who understood this was James Angleton; he had tracked down the plan, and then been discredited and sent into retirement. It seemed the time was right.

Brezhnev shook his head, and reminded STARIK of what happened in the Cuban missile crisis. If KHOLSTOMER were to be followed, Brezhnev warned, the United States would provoke a war against the Soviet Union. The **Great Patriotic War** had saved the United States from the Great Depression after 1929. Capitalists always turned to war when a depression occurred. Perhaps, advised Brezhnev, in seven years KHOLSTOMER would be appropriate.

Meanwhile, at his final speech to his colleagues at the end of 1974, Angleton listed the following as Soviet agents in place: Harold Wilson (1916–1995), Olaf Palme, Willy Brandt, Lester Pearson, Roger Hollis, Averell Harriman, and Henry Kissinger. His colleagues had heard it all before. Angleton insisted, as he always did, that they helped the KGB orchestrate détente, the **Prague Spring**, the illusion of a **Sino–Soviet split,** the Albanian defection, and the independence of the Italian Communists from Moscow. These deceptions were practiced to destabilize the West by luring it into believing the Cold War was over. Further, inside the CIA, Soviet agent SASHA was still twisting information about these matters to ensure the CIA overlooked the threats and menaces. The listeners rolled their eyes as Angleton continued: STARIK, Kim Philby's former handler, was now directing KHOLSTOMER, the greatest of all Soviet plots to ravage the economies of the Western industrial nations. The colleagues left the room, except for SASHA. Angleton attacked SASHA, and claimed that out of the **wilderness of mirrors** he had teased the plot from tiny pieces of information others had ignored.

Years later, in October 1983, Yuri Andropov, who succeeded Leonid Brezhnev, was dying from kidney disease. STARIK visited him to discuss KHOLSTOMER, which had divided the Committee of Three, Gorbachev being against it. Andropov stated that **Ronald Reagan**'s (1911–2004) Star Wars **(SDI)** project, if followed, could not be matched by the Soviets because it would bankrupt the Soviet economy; ABLE ARCHER was about to begin, allegedly a practice run for a nuclear first strike on the Soviet Union, and could easily be a cover for the imperialist powers to wipe out the Soviets; and Reagan's "evil empire" speech suggested he had grand ambitions to destroy the Soviets. For these reasons, Andropov approved KHOLSTOMER, and instructed STARIK that it should begin before the end of November.

On November 12, 1983, alone again with Andropov for the final KHOLSTOMER briefing, STARIK reported that the accounts in offshore banks were set to dump the U.S.$63 billion onto the spot market; at the first sign of the downturn the Soviet **agents of influence** in Japan, Hong Kong, and Malaysia, and the economist close to Chancellor Helmut Kohl would press the central banks to sell off Treasury bonds to protect their holdings, and the bond market would fall. But Andropov began to wonder if ABLE ARCHER was *really* intended to cover a preemptive strike. To sway his judgment, STARIK told two lies: that the **Pentagon** is seeking CIA information on the Soviet movement of ICBM trains, and that ABLE ARCHER would now be held in December. These false threats affected the dying man; Andropov agreed that KHOLSTOMER was the Soviet's last hope!

Meanwhile, SASHA had qualms about KHOLSTOMER, and became aware that his reports had been falsified by STARIK. SASHA believed that KHOLSTOMER was the Soviets' answer to ABLE ARCHER. He knew exactly what STARIK was about to do, and saw the Cold War winding down and KHOLSTOMER pushing the world into an economic recession. Millions would suffer for no reason.

Later that day CIA head William Colby met with President Reagan to describe KHOLSTOMER, the Soviet plot to undermine the U.S. currency and destabilize the economy. The CIA had already informed the Federal Reserve; it was ready for D-Day and would support the dollar as soon as there was a sell-off on the spot market. Also, the CIA had flooded the media with inside stories of the Federal Reserve's policy to support the dollar. Thus the panic money would never materialize. The CIA had neutralized the Soviet agents of influence; one was arrested on charges of molesting a minor, and the others were encouraged to take a vacation. The CIA had undermined KHOLSTOMER.

Shortly afterward, Angleton had a visitor at his Arlington, Virginia, home. The visitor briefed Angleton on KHOLSTOMER. He told Angleton that the KGB *did* have a mole inside the CIA after all, that Angleton had identified him accurately, and that because of Angleton's warnings KHOLSTOMER has been stalled.

See also ANGLETON, JAMES; OPERATION ABLE ARCHER 83

Sources: Littell, Robert, *The Company: A Novel of the CIA* (Woodstock and New York: Overlook Press, 2002); Mangold, Tom, *Cold Warrior: James Jesus Angleton, the CIA Master Spy Hunter* (New York: Simon & Schuster, 1991).

OPERATION LIGHTHOUSE (1959). In September and October 1959 the British government planned to test **atom bombs** at Maralinga in central Australia. The top-secret operation, named Operation LIGHTHOUSE, was called off when the British, U.S., and Soviet governments agreed to a moratorium on nuclear testing in October 1958.

The operation was to place over 500 troops in networks of trenches around the sites of four nuclear tests in the Maralinga Desert. This became known in May 2001 when the British Ministry of Information confirmed that about 24 British and New Zealand soldiers tested protective clothing by crawling through a fallout zone after a test at Maralinga in 1956. A controversy arose when the British Nuclear Test Veterans Association indicated that the British government had been acting immorally when it planned to use soldiers as guinea pigs.

In the test the soldiers were to have their blood count measured before they arrived at the site, to provide a baseline for checks on the effect of radiation from nuclear blasts. This documentary evidence flies in the face of statements made over many years by Defense Ministers in all governments that soldiers were never intended to be the subject of radiation experiments.

Sources: Forbes, Mark, "Nuclear Test Inquiry Ordered," *The Age*, May 23, 2001, p. 4; Hawthorne, Maria, "'Ground Zero' Plan for N-Troops," *The Age*, May 22, 2001, p. 3.

OPERATION LUCH (fl. c. 1973–1990). Operation LUCH (Russian for "sunbeam") was the **code name** of a **Cold War** operation that established a network of spies across divided Germany to supply **Moscow Center** with intelligence should the German Democratic Republic collapse.

The **KGB**'s main concern was the growing impact on citizens of East Germany of the Western ideology beamed through Western broadcasts and visits by West Germans. Moscow Center calculated in the mid-1970s that 500,000 citizens were hostile to the existing political system, and thought the West would for a long time retain a solid base of support in the German Democratic Republic.

A long-running KGB operation, LUCH monitored public opinion within the East German population and the Communist Party, contacts between East and West Germans, and alleged attempts by the United States and the Federal Republic of Germany to undermine socialism in the German Democratic Republic. By 1974 the section of the **Karlshorst** KGB responsible for Operation LUCH was elevated to directorate status.

During Vladimir Putin's posting in Germany (1984–1989) he worked in a unit called "the friends," who aimed to recruit **agents** across West and East Germany and who would report to the KGB in Berlin and to Moscow.

The Russians were also using the LUCH network for another purpose. Because East Germans did not have the money or resources to compete with the West in the field of technological research, they would wait until the scientists in the West had done the research and then use secret agents to steal the results and copy the technology without having to bear the high development costs. Today German authorities suspect some agents recruited for this purpose by Putin and the KGB are still active. From LUCH and other KGB operations Putin gained much respect, and this helped him to power in Russia.

Sources: Andrew, Christopher, and Vasili Mitrokhin, *The Mitrokhin Archive: The KGB in Europe and the West* (London: Lane, 1999); Franchetti, Mark, "Spycatchers Hunt for Putin's Puppets," *The Australian*, January 17, 2000, p. 13.

OPERATION LYUTENTSIA (1962). The operation was a major **KGB** exercise, handled by the former Soviet **resident** in Ottawa, Vladimir Pavlovich Burdin. In the West the operation was known simply as the exchange of Francis Gary Powers (1929–1977) for "Willie Fisher" (1903–1971), better known as Rudolph Abel.

The exchange was made possible when Rudolph Abel's counsel, James B. Donovan, pleaded that an exchange of prisoners through diplomatic channels could be to the benefit of the United States in the future when an American of a rank similar to Abel's was captured by the Soviets.

Two year later, in the spring of 1959, Wolfgang Vogel (1925–), an East German lawyer, was chosen to represent the Soviets in the exchange. In July a "Frau Abel" wrote to Vogel, asking him to represent her interests. Later, in his office, she was accompanied by a woman who appeared to be Abel's "daughter" and an "interpreter" who claimed he was a family cousin. The daughter had written to James Donovan, Abel's U.S. representative, and had given him Vogel's address.

Also "Frau Abel" wrote to Donovan, asking if she could be of any help to her husband, and when he replied that his fee of U.S.$10,000 would have to be paid first—and then be given to charity—she replied saying this amount of money would be difficult for her to find. This exchange allowed Vogel to write to Donovan, claiming he was representing her interests, and that from now on Donovan should contact him alone. By September, Donovan had been paid from the money in the **STASI**'s foreign currency accounts; he donated it to three American universities.

In May 1960 the Soviets had a person to trade for Abel who was similar in importance: Francis Gary Powers. But before Vogel had been introduced to the exchange, Powers's father, Oliver, had written to Rudolph Abel, suggesting the exchange.

Powers got a 10-year jail sentence for espionage. Meanwhile, Vogel got the money to pay Rudolph Abel's lawyer, and money to pay Abel's U.S.$3,000 fine. In May 1961, "Frau Abel" sent a letter to Donovan saying that she had heard of Oliver Powers's suggestion and that her husband had written to her to say it had nothing to do with him; she now wondered what could be done. Immediately, Donovan contacted the **Central Intelligence Agency (CIA),** saying he thought this looked like an offer from the Soviets to exchange Abel for Powers. He also wrote to "Frau Abel" to suggest that she get her government to show some interest and good faith in arranging the exchange.

In June, "Frau Abel" replied, saying that the East German embassy had assured her that if her husband were pardoned, then Powers would also be amnestied. In mid-August, Donovan received a letter for Abel and one for himself, suggesting that Powers and Abel be released simultaneously. At the same time this deal was being planned, the **Berlin Wall** was going up.

In February, Donovan went to Berlin—a city now under much tension—to arrange the exchange. He had been informed by Vogel that if Abel were released, then Powers and two other minor offenders would be released in return. He was introduced to "Frau Abel," the "daughter," and the "interpreter," but was told by a Soviet authority that the three-for-one deal was no longer on.

Donovan then met Vogel, and learned the Russians sought to change the original deal; now they would exchange Abel for one of the two other minor offenders. Donovan was angered—as was Vogel—and indicated secretly to Vogel that he would not retreat from the original deal. This put Vogel in an awkward position, professionally. He went to his Soviet superiors and told them the new deal would not be accepted. So the Soviet superior spoke alone with Donovan, and claimed that Powers now was of less importance as a bargaining chip than Abel; henceforth the deal was Abel for one of the other minor offenders—an unknown student.

Exasperated, Donovan said he would return to America unless he got the deal they had planned earlier, a swap of Powers and one of the minor offenders for Abel.

Next day a deal was made to release Abel, Powers, and another offender—at the same time, but in different places. While Abel and Powers would be exchanged at **Glienicke Bridge**, at the same time the other minor offender would be released at **Checkpoint Charlie**. This last arrangement was made to appease the East German authorities, who had been kept out of the deal.

The exchange was made on the bridge linking Potsdam with West Berlin (Glienicke Bridge), later known as the "Bridge of Spies." The KGB had hidden groups watching for U.S. militia, and an armed KGB operational group was ready in the East German Customs Service. Powers was accompanied by another armed group from Potsdam. The U.S. guard with Abel was close to six and a half feet tall and weighed 300 pounds. Another group of soldiers was armed with submachine guns, and the East Germans had a group of 20 army reservists with machine guns and grenades.

The exchange procedure was held up at first by the failure of the Soviets to assure Donovan that the other offender had been released at Checkpoint Charlie when Abel and Powers were being swapped. Eventually the Abel–Powers exchange was made, and Donovan noticed that the U.S. Air Force crew who had taken Powers into their custody, and was about to fly him to Washington, looked at him like he was a pariah.

Although **Moscow Center** was pleased with the exchange, leaders of East Germany were insulted that they had not been fully involved in the details of the exchange. After the exchange, Robert Kennedy (1925–1968) asked the Soviet embassy for the portrait of his brother that Abel had painted while in prison. Moscow Center thought the request was a provocation, and refused.

See also ABEL, RUDOLPH; POWERS, FRANCIS GARY

Sources: Andrew, Christopher, and Vasili Mitrokhin, *The Mitrokhin Archive: The KGB in Europe and the West* (London: Lane, 1999); Donovan, James B., *Strangers on a Bridge: The Case of Colonel Abel* (London: Secker & Warburg, 1964); Whitney, Craig R., *Spy Trader: Germany's Devil's Advocate and the Darkest Secret of the Cold War* (New York: Random House, 1993).

OPERATION MOSES (fl. c. 1984–1985). Operation MOSES was a secret **Mossad** operation to help the black Jews, known as Falashas, to leave Ethiopia and settle in Israel, where they could begin a new life free of oppression.

By the mid-1950s the 20,000 Ethiopian Jews were prevented from purchasing land in Ethiopia, were known by Christian Ethiopians as Falashas (meaning "bastard strangers"), and were kept in a hostile environment in the northern Ethiopian mountains.

At that time, for Haile Selassie (1891–1975), who had been Ethiopia's Emperor since 1930—except for a period between Italy's 1935 invasion of Ethiopia (Abyssinia) and the end of **World War II**—it was a matter of pride that no Jews in his country be allowed to emigrate to Israel.

The Israeli government did not encourage Ethiopia's Jews to come to Israel until 1977, after Haile Selassie had been overthrown and died. Ethiopia then had a Marxist government and was supported by the **U.S.S.R.**, East Germany, and Israel; its neighbor, Somalia, had the support of the United States, Saudi Arabia and Egypt. Suddenly, a diplomatic error by Israel led the Ethiopian leadership once again to prevent its Jews from emigrating to Israel. This error by Israel and the new decision by Ethiopia gave rise to Operation MOSES.

First, young Ethiopians who had managed to reach Israel were trained by Mossad **agents** and sent back to Ethiopia to encourage the Falashas to come to Israel via the Sudan. But too many died on the way. Next, a camp was established clandestinely in the Sudan as a safe haven for the travelers. That was achieved by bribing the Sudan government and its security services, getting help from the United Nations, and the formation of a Kenyan escape route. This procedure was effective until the government in Nairobi shut down the flow of Falashas for fear of hostility from other Arab and Africa nations.

So Mossad and the **Central Intelligene Agency (CIA)** established a dummy travel company, Navco, with a village for scuba diving tourists. The Falashas came to the village as bogus tourists; frogmen would take them to boats offshore; then they sailed up the coast to an airport and were then flown to Israel. The local officials decided that the secret emigration would have to be curtailed.

Operation MOSES was reborn in 1984. A small Sudanese airport was refurbished, and unmarked Hercules transports would pick up 200 Ethiopians at a time. The passengers were careful to leave no trace of their presence behind. Khartoum airport was similarly used when U.S.$200 million was secretly made available from the United States and Mossad placed U.S.$600 million in Swiss and London bank accounts for the Sudanese president.

Also, a religious Jew from Brussels, who owned an airline, was persuaded to put his fleet secretly at Mossad's disposal. Between November 1984 and January 1985 about 7,000 Ethiopian Jews flew secretly to Brussels from Khartoum, and on to Israel.

Operation MOSES ended in January 1985 when an official mistakenly let newspapers know about the successful scheme. The secret became an embarrassment when public, and the Ethiopian and Sudanese governments saved face by promptly declaring that Israel had been kidnapping Ethiopian citizens! So in March, the Vice President of the United States, George H. W. Bush (1924–), arranged with the President of Ethiopia to fly the remaining young Ethiopians to Israel. This left 10,000 in Ethiopia, much to Israel's displeasure.

Source: Raviv, Dan, and Yossi Melman, *Every Spy a Prince* (Boston: Houghton Mifflin, 1990).

OPERATION PBSUCCESS (1952–1954). Operation PBSUCCESS was a **Central Intelligence Agency (CIA)** covert operation against the government of Guatemala in 1954 because it was seen as a Communist threat to the United States and Latin America.

In October 1944 military officers overthrew the 13-year dictatorship of Jorge Ubico in Guatemala. Juan José Arévalo, an educator, was then elected President, and he introduced reforms tending strongly to a social democracy or "spiritual socialism," as he called it; the landed aristocracy was anxious as it watched him rely on the outlawed Communist Party for support. He was known as "Sandia" ("the watermelon"), green on the outside and red on the inside.

In 1950 the presidential election was between a conservative, the armed forces chief, Francisco Javier Arana, and a liberal with Communist supporters, the Minister of Defense, Jacobo Arbenz Guzman (1913–1971). The campaign was bitter. Arana was assassinated—probably by a young army lieutenant—and Arbenz, whose campaign director edited the local Communist Party's newspaper, was elected. In mid-1953 the U.S. State Department was warned that communism was rife in Guatemala. as evidenced by the new Guatemalan Congress's grave respect for the death of **Josef Stalin** (1879–1953), and later in 1954 by the evidence that Czechoslovakia was exporting arms to the Arbenz government, a direct violation of the **Monroe Doctrine**.

The United States decided to take covert action against what it believed was a threatening Communist-dominated regime, and chose Carlos Enrique Castillo Armas (1914–1957), a counterrevolutionary hero trained by the U.S. military and a Central American hero with considerable charisma, to lead a coup with rebels who were being trained in Honduras. The CIA officers who oversaw the operation were Frank

Wisner (1909–1965) and Richard Bissell, Jr. (1909–1994); the operation's headquarters were at Opa-Locka, outside Miami, Florida; the funding was U.S.$5–7 million.

In May the CIA began using psychological warfare techniques—the radio station Voice of Liberation—to tell the Guatemalan population that a massive force, led by Castillo Armas was heading for the capital, Guatemalan City. In mid-June 1954 Castillo Armas crossed into Guatemala with his 150 rebels, traveled six miles, and settled down in a church, awaiting the fall of the government. It appeared the operation would fail.

However, the propaganda convinced many to defect, including an air force pilot, whom a CIA **agent** got drunk and induced to persuade his fellow pilots to desert the government's air force and join the rebels. This new "rebel air force" bombed Guatemala at random, sometimes using empty Coca-Cola bottles that whistled down like bombs, as well as packets of dynamite with grenades. Finally they bombed a munitions supply with dramatic effect on the people below. This rebel air force was immediately disbanded to make possible the covert operation principle of plausible denial, but shortly afterward, the United States helped through supplying planes by way of the Nicaraguan air force.

Then Arbenz failed in his own defense of Guatemala's government. He distributed weapons to what were in effect Communist-supported militias. The conservative leaders of the army disapproved, and declared that they would no longer support him. He resigned, and fled to Mexico.

The operation was a success for many reasons: the U.S. President agreed to provide planes; the **disinformation** program and black propaganda helped to spread dissent in Guatemala and defections from Arbenz's air force and government; the nationalization of parts of the United Fruit Company's holdings, which had links with the Dulles family; and the enormous power, albeit hidden, of U.S. policy to see Arbenz brought down.

The success of PBSUCCESS, and the CIA's clandestine operations in Iran and Italy, would be used to illustrate the agency's capacity to effect regime change in nations where the rise of communism was perceived to be a threat to the United States.

Castillo Armas reversed many of his predecessor's agrarian reforms, and had left-wing workers purged from both unions and government. He was assassinated in July 1957 by a Guatemalan palace guard who until two years before had been in the regular army and was discharged for left-wing leanings. Apparently the assassin acted alone, because other guards who were jailed as accomplices were later released.

See also ARBENZ GUZMAN, JACOBO; BISSELL, RICHARD, JR.; WISNER, FRANK

Sources: Ambrose, Stephen E., *Ike's Spies: Eisenhower and the Espionage Establishment,* 2nd ed. (Jackson: University Press of Mississippi, 1999); Bissell, Richard Mervin, Jr., with Jonathan E. Lewis and Frances T. Pudio, *Reflections of a Cold Warrior: From Yalta to the Bay of Pigs* (New Haven, CT: Yale University Press, 1996); Blasier, Cole, *The Hovering Giant: U.S. Responses to Revolutionary Change in Latin America* (Pittsburgh, PA: University of Pittsburgh Press, 1985); Callather, Nick, *Secret History: The CIA Account of Its Operations in Guatemala, 1952–1954* (Stanford, CA: Stanford University Press, 1999); Immerman, Richard H., *The CIA in Guatemala* (Austin: University of Texas Press, 1982); Johnson, Harold, "Obituary: William Bundy," *Guardian Weekly,* October 12–18, 2000, p. 13; Sifakis, Carl, *Encyclopedia of Assassinations: A Compendium of Attempted and Successful Assassinations Throughout History* (New York: Facts on File, 1993); Smith, Joseph, and Simon Davis, *Historical Dictionary of* *the Cold War* (New York: Scarecrow Press, 2000); Thomas, Stafford T., "A Political Theory of the CIA," *International Journal of Intelligence and Counterintelligence* 11 (1998): 57–72.

OPERATION PHOENIX (1968–1973). During the **Vietnam War** (1964–1973) the United States and its South Vietnam allies devised a plan to root out **Viet Cong** loyalists at the same time it tried to win the loyalty of the Vietnamese by a program known as **CORDS** (Civil Operations and Revolutionary Development Support). The aim was to reequip the South Vietnamese forces, and at the same time repair the destruction left by the **Tet Offensive** (1968). In the program the attempt to find the Viet Cong loyalists among the Vietnamese in South Vietnam was known as Operation PHOENIX, and William Colby (1920–1996) headed the operation.

In Operation PHOENIX, its critics allege, 20,000–60,000 Viet Cong and suspected Communist sympathizers died and uncivilized practices were employed to destroy the Viet Cong infrastructure between 1968 and 1973. Work was done by "black teams." The team would be given a person to kill: someone suspected of selling out to the enemy, a **double agent**, a black marketeer suspected of affecting the community's war effort. When identified, the target would be sought by black team members masquerading as the enemy, so that the Viet Cong would be blamed for the murder. They would disseminate propaganda, collect intelligence, establish cells and networks among the Montagnard villages, disrupt Viet Cong infiltration groups and way stations, make small raids, kidnap, ambush, kill Viet Cong **agents**, destroy rice crops, rescue Montagnard slaves who served the Viet Cong, and use the Montagnards to sabotage Viet Cong efforts. This view is presented by Valentine (1990), who describes the operation as incompetently managed and encouraging horrifying abuses; McGehee (1996) catalogs the major allegations against the **Central Intelligence Agency (CIA)** and the U.S. military.

William Colby's reputation was greatly damaged by investigations that followed the allegations about Operation PHOENIX. In his memoirs he gave an account of the operation and the reason for it. He describes how the VCI (Viet Cong infrastructure) assassinated village chiefs, mined roads on which busloads of civilians died, taxed the villages to fund VCI activities, and held threatening propaganda sessions to influence the villagers. In the operation against these daily attacks on Vietnamese citizens, the U.S. forces would ensure their intelligence was accurate, provide advisers to support the operation against the VCI, seek out suspected leaders of the VCI in villages, and check carefully the accuracy of information on them. Colby stated that Operation PHOENIX had no forces of its own, and therefore did not conduct operations against the VCI.

Moyer (1997) wrote a balanced account of the operation, avoided propaganda about the purpose of the program, and carefully examined the claims about atrocities on both sides of the Vietnam conflict.

See also COLBY, WILLIAM

Sources: McGehee, Ralph, "CIA Operation Phoenix in Vietnam" (1996), www.serendipity.li/cia/operation_phoenix.htm.; McNeill, Ian, *The Team: Australian Army Advisers on Vietnam 1962–1972* (Canberra: Australian War Memorial, 1984); Moyer, Mark, *Phoenix and the Birds of Prey: The CIA's Secret Campaign to Destroy the Viet Cong* (Annapolis, MD: Naval Institute Press, 1997); Toohey, Brian, and Brian Pinwell, *Oyster: The Story of the Australian Secret Intelligence Services* (Port Melbourne: William Heinemann Australia, 1989); Valentine, Douglas, *The Phoenix Program* (New York: William Morris, 1990); Weil,

Robert, "Obituary: Robert W. Komer, CIA Agent, 1922–9/4/2000," *The Age*, April 13, 2000, p. 7.

OPERATION PIGEON (1957–1970). Operation PIGEON was run by **ASIO** in an effort to get information from Walter Seddon Clayton (1906–1997), the organizer of the **CPA**, who allegedly masterminded a Soviet spy ring in Australia after **World War II.**

Since 1948 Walter Clayton had organized underground printers, **safe houses**, meeting places, and all the accoutrements of espionage **tradecraft** to provide a secure place for Australia's Communists should the government ban the CPA. It had been banned from 1940 to 1942, when the **U.S.S.R.** was Australia's enemy; now, as the **Red Scare** established itself in the United States and in Great Britain, the party would be outlawed once more. Attempts by **Robert Menzies** (1894–1978) to achieve this failed in Australia.

Walter Clayton had kept away from the public eye since the end of World War II, and had emerged to appear before the Royal Commission on Espionage in 1954, following the defection of Vladimir Petrov (1907–1991) and his assertion that a spy ring had existed in Australia, and that "K" had been a major contact between the Soviet embassy and Australian Communist spies. At the commission's hearings Clayton appeared to answer only nine questions, and told nothing of such a spy ring.

For six months, beginning in 1957, ASIO put pressure on Clayton to confess that he had run a spy network in Australia. In February, Clayton had sought a passport for travel outside Australia. ASIO thought their "pigeon," as they called him, might fly. In March he was forcibly interviewed but had nothing to say. He was warned that if he offered nothing, he would never again get back into Australia. He had a reservation to leave by ship on March 31.

To prevent Clayton from leaving easily, the head of ASIO told the Australian Taxation Department that Clayton had paid no tax while working under an assumed name. The CPA got him a bodyguard, who was confronted and bullied by ASIO officers when Clayton went to pay this tax prior to leaving. On the day before he was to leave, Clayton's passport was canceled, with the Australian Prime Minister's agreement.

Still Clayton would reveal nothing of the spy network that ASIO was certain operated in Australia. Therefore ASIO sought former CPA members who would inform on him. Operation PIGEON continued relentlessly, but little happened over the next 12 months.

In November 1957, Clayton, who by now had fallen out with the leaders of the CPA, needed to find employment, so he bought a boat to work as a fisherman. He was always kept under surveillance by ASIO because it was feared he would leave Australia, and end ASIO's hopes to discover the long-suspected spy network. In October 1962, with ASIO's assent, Clayton's home was bugged. His file was still open in the 1970s, but Operation PIGEON probably faded away and disappeared after 1990.

See also CLAYTON, WALTER SEDDON

Source: McKnight, David, *Australia's Spies and Their Secrets* (St. Leonards, NSW: Allen and Unwin, 1994).

OPERATION PLUMBAT (c. 1965). Operation PLUMBAT was a combined **LAKAM–Mossad** secret operation in the mid-1960s, undertaken in support of the Israeli nuclear weapons policy; it did not become known until 1973.

In the summer of 1973 a Moroccan waiter working in Lillehammer, Norway, was mistaken for Ali Salemeh, a noted terrorist who had planned the killing of the Israeli Olympic athletes in September 1972. He was assassinated by a Mossad hit team led by Dan Aerbel (fl. 1965–1975), who had been hunting for Ali Salemeh. Aerbel's men were arrested for murder. To be considered for a milder sentence, Aerbel offered to tell the story of Operation PLUMBAT and mysterious disappearance some years earlier of 200 tons of uranium.

In 1965 the Israelis decided on a policy that became known as the "Samson option," the possession of nuclear weapons to deter the threat of Arab invasion. First it was necessary to get enriched uranium, the supply and distribution of which were controlled largely by America, through the International Atomic Energy Agency (IAEA). America had decided no uranium oxide of bomb-making proportions would ever be available in the Middle East. To circumvent U.S. policy, Mossad decided to penetrate companies that mined and processed uranium, and direct enough of it secretly to Israel.

To do this Dan Aerbel, a Danish businessman whose family members had died in the Holocaust, befriended Herbert Schulzen, a former German pilot who felt remorse for his nation's contribution to the Holocaust. He was a partner in a small German chemical firm. He was invited to Israel, entertained by disguised Mossad **agents**, learned much of how Jews were suffering at Arab hands, and was deeply affected by the stories he was told.

On returning to Germany, Schulzen received many business contracts from Israel, and his small firm prospered immensely. Next, he was asked to supply 200 tons of uranium oxide for Israel's nuclear research. It was ordered from a Belgian firm. The International Atomic Energy Agency examined all contracts involving uranium that could be used for nuclear bombs, and found the small firm held sufficient funds with a Swiss bank and was prospering, and that the planned shipment—from Antwerp to Milan and from Milan to the firm's plant—was in accord with IAEA rules.

The deposit in the Swiss bank and all the details and plans had been prepared by Mossad, which had established its own shipping company in Switzerland and had bought a vessel to sail under the Liberian flag. The ship's crew was hired, and the vessel sailed in November to Antwerp; the uranium was loaded in drums marked "plumbat." But instead of heading for Italy, the ship docked at Hamburg, the crew was paid off, and a new crew was taken on. On November 17 the ship departed Hamburg for Genoa, but was reported lost when it failed to reach port.

Fifteen days later the apparently lost ship docked at a port in Turkey. Again the vessel acquired a fresh crew, and a new captain. Weeks later the ship docked at Palermo, where the captain and crew deserted the ship. A new captain and crew were found, and the ship sailed to Antwerp. All the uranium—enough for 15 nuclear bombs—had disappeared.

Was it was stolen? Was it in the hands of international terrorists? The question was not answered until Dan Aerbel offered the Danish authorities an account of Operation PLUMBAT so as to lessen the sentence that his murder charge had brought.

It seems that the substituted crews had been Israeli soldiers who, using a fleet of small boats, stole the uranium in the middle of the Mediterranean.

In Norway the Mossad team received a milder sentence than expected, and disappeared when released from jail. Herbert Schulzen was not charged, and the ship was sold to a company in Cyprus and renamed. Mossad did not officially acknowledge the operation.

See also ISRAEL AND THE NUCLEAR WEAPONS CRISIS; RAFAEL, SYLVIA

Sources: Davenport, Elaine, Paul Eddy, and Peter Gillman, *The Plumbat Affair* (Philadelphia: J.B. Lippincott, 1978); Deacon, Richard, *Spyclopedia: The Comprehensive Handbook of Espionage* (New York: Silver Arrow Books/William Morrow, 1987); Eisenberg, Dennis, Eli Landau, and Menaham Portugali, *Operation Uranium Ship* (New York: Signet, 1978); Volkman, Ernest, *Espionage: The Greatest Spy Operations of the 20th Century* (New York: Wiley, 1995).

OPERATION PLUTO AND OPERATION ZAPATA (1961). Operation PLUTO, named after the god of the underworld, was a secret operation sought by President **Dwight D. Eisenhower** (1890–1969) to rid Cuba of communism under the control of Fidel Castro (1927–). It was desired greatly by Vice President **Richard M. Nixon** (1913–1994), who wanted Castro out by October 1960, so that the Cuban leader did not become an election issue when Nixon vied for the presidency with **John F. Kennedy** (1917–1963). Although privately Nixon would claim that Operation PLUTO was his, he was not its only planner. After various schemes had failed to kill Castro, it was decided to have anti-Castro Cuban exiles invade Cuba.

Seven days before President Kennedy came to power, January 10, 1961, the United States had severed diplomatic relations with Cuba, and the **Central Intelligence Agency (CIA),** which had been preparing the assassination of Fidel Castro, presented the Eisenhower administration and the new President with an overview of the situation as follows:

> Moscow had put in power a puppet ruler who rigged elections, nationalized the American-owned sugar plantations and industry, controlled the press, jailed thousands of political opponents, killed about 500 other political adversaries, sought weapons from the Soviets, adopted Marxist ideology, sent pilots to Czechoslovakia for training on MiGs, and promoted dissent in Nicaragua, Haiti, Panama, and the Dominican Republic in order to surround the southern United States with Communist satellites. Further, CIA operatives, under Richard Bissell, Jr., planned for Cuban exiles opposed to Castro to head a brigade of 500 to 1,500 troops to land near Trinidad, in southern Cuba, where anti-Castro groups could be found. Cuban pilots, trained to fly old B-26s, would conduct an air strike from a training camp in Guatemala. The landing at Trinidad would coincide with the establishment of a provisional Cuban government, and set off an uprising against Castro. Most of Castro's 280,000-man army were not in sympathy with his regime; many army officers were ready to the rebel; the peasantry in western Cuba would rise up immediately. The brigade would be joined by Castro's political prisoners. The ship carrying the anti-Castro Cuban exiles to the beachhead would have enough arms and equipment aboard for twice that number of fighters. If the campaign were to fail within a week, the troops would adopt guerrilla tactics, and lead the regime change from the mountains.

President Kennedy did not want the invasion to appear to have U.S. origins, and demanded that the anti-Castro Cuban exiles should land at Bahía de Cochinos (the Bay of Pigs), 100 miles west of Trinidad and 80 miles across swamps from the mountains. Also, Kennedy was concerned that the air strikes would make it obvious that the United States was involved, and although he did not want them at all, he was prepared to allow for about half the number of air strikes proposed; further he did not want a dawn invasion, but a night-time invasion, so that all ships would be clear of the invasion site by first light. Even with these changes he was still not satisfied, and reserved the right to cancel the operation up to 24 hours before the landing. The revised operation was named Operation ZAPATA and was under the control of the CIA's Deputy Director of Plans, Richard M. Bissell, Jr. (1909–1994).

Bissell pointed out that these changes would make the guerrilla warfare plan less likely to succeed. Nevertheless, more influential U.S. authorities believed that a U.S. hand in the invasion could be plausibly denied; but the Secretary of State, Dean Rusk, would not give his views on the new plan.

Further, the President wanted the initial air strike cut, thereby reducing the air support for the invasion by half, which put the anticipated results of the invasion in the balance. Kennedy then postponed the second of two planned air strikes until it was clear that the invasion had been a success. This meant that 80 percent of the planned air support for the invaders was cut.

The plan was put into operation on April 17, 1960, and from the beginning it was a disaster. In the end 114 invaders died and 1,189 were captured.

Why did it fail? Views critical of the CIA strategy were established: Castro was too firmly in power for a spontaneous uprising of unarmed Cubans to dislodge him; there were not enough outraged Cubans to support the small group of invaders; the exercise went beyond the CIA charter; there was too great a lack of understanding between President Kennedy and Allen Dulles (1893–1969) and between their respective staffs; some CIA staff members erroneously believed that if the operation were ever in trouble, it would be bailed out by the U.S. military; Dulles delegated far too much to Bissell; at all key junctures it seemed that Dulles was absent; the great enthusiasm for the scheme was combined with its amazing secrecy to put into operation a plan that in too many ways the senior intelligence officers were not familiar with; the scheme violated Dulles's dictum that the slapdash cloak-and-dagger methods of the **OSS** are not suited to war; Bissell, who had directed the U-2 spy plane program, knew too little about the form of covert operations; no prior estimates had been made—other than by officers involved in the operation—of the likelihood that, spontaneously, unarmed Cubans would revolt against the government.

The disaster was examined formally by a senior military officer, who concluded the CIA did not have the staff or the logistics to support or complete such a complex paramilitary operation on a hostile beach, and that, if necessary, such operations in future should be handled by the U.S. Department of Defense.

The U.S. public was angry because an operation that might not have been necessary was carried out with such inadequate U.S. support, and that the Bay of Pigs invasion became a total victory for Castro.

Adlai Stevenson, the U.S. ambassador to the United Nations, was embarrassed to find he had been duped into thinking the United States had no hand in the invasion. The CIA head, Allen Dulles, offered his resignation; it was accepted. Richard Bissell, Jr., was forced to resign.

Bissell believed that the invasion failed because the time and place of landing were changed; the guerrilla forces on Cuba were not as strong as he had been believed; Castro's forces were much stronger than previously estimated; and the United States could not plausibly deny that it had instigated the invasion because rumors of the invasion had been widely rumored weeks before the invasion.

In March 2001 Cuban documents on the failed invasion were made public.

See also BISSELL, RICHARD, JR.; DULLES, ALLEN

Sources: Bissell, Richard, Jr., with Jonathan E. Lewis and Frances T. Pudio, *Reflections of a Cold Warrior: From Yalta to the Bay of Pigs* (New Haven, CT: Yale University Press, 1996); Kesaris, Paul, ed., *Operation Zapata: The "Ultrasensitive" Report and Testimony of the Board of Inquiry on the Bay of Pigs* (Frederick, MD: University Publications of America, 1981); Rostow, Walter W., *The Diffusion of Power: An Essay in Recent History* (New York: Macmillan, 1972); Summers, Anthony, and Robbyn Swann, *The Arrogance of Power: The Secret World of Richard Nixon* (London: Orion, 2000); Weiner, Tim, "Files Reveal Secrets of Cuban Invasion Fiasco," *The Age* (Melbourne), March 24, 2001, p. 19 (originally published in the *New York Times*).

OPERATION POOR RICHARD (1958). When U.S. Vice President **Richard M. Nixon** (1913–1994) visited Latin America in May 1958, he was met with hostility and violence in Peru and Venezuela. The hostility was so threatening that President **Dwight D. Eisenhower** (1890–1969) ordered Operation POOR RICHARD, the movement of thousands of Marines, paratroops, six destroyers, a cruiser, and an aircraft carrier toward Venezuela. The protesters were anti-U.S. demonstrators. Nixon and his wife were spat upon, stoned, and heckled with death chants and placards stating "Muera Nixon." Nixon recalled that the crowds called for blood.

Sources: Nixon, Richard M., *The Memoirs of Richard Nixon* (London: Macmillan, 1978); Summers, Anthony, and Robbyn Swann, *The Arrogance of Power: The Secret World of Richard Nixon* (London: Orion, 2000).

OPERATION POST REPORT (1951). A British operation, supported by both **MI5** and **MI6,** to survey displaced persons from Europe as they came to Great Britain after **World War II,** so as to identify undesirable aliens.

Both the Soviets and the British were concerned about the émigré movements in Europe after World War II and to what extent displaced individuals had been involved in war crimes or other undesirable activities.

In England, the Home Office supported an operation to screen 200,000 foreign workers who, according to Guy Liddell (1892–1958), Deputy Director of MI5, could establish a fifth column inside the United Kingdom. The operation was not aimed at war criminals so much as displaced persons who might be serving Soviet interests. Also, Liddell wanted the operation to identify anti-Communists, fluent speakers of Russian, and people aware of Soviet policies and practices who might be induced to serve the British secret services.

In June 1951 the operation, approved by the U.K. Joint Intelligence Committee, carried out a massive survey of displaced Albanians, Balts, Hungarians, Poles, Russians, Romanians, and Yugoslavs. The officers were looking for those who denounced or circulated Russian propaganda, had embassy contacts, had served in the Red Army, and could make contacts inside the Russian satellite countries.

The results of the survey were valuable primarily in serving the interests of MI5 and MI6, not for finding war criminals or other undesirables. Intelligence rather than security was the purpose of the operation, although at the time it was not presented that way.

See also LIDDELL, GUY

Source: Dorril, Stephen, *MI6: Inside the Covert World of Her Majesty's Secret Intelligence Service* (New York: The Free Press, 2000).

OPERATION RHINE (1954). Operation RHINE was a failed Soviet assassination. In Frankfurt the mission was to kill the Ukranian National Labor Alliance leader, George Sergeevich Okolovich. Because the operation was to be carried out in West Germany, it had to approved by the Soviet Presidium. The procedure was supervised by the newly appointed Aleksandr Semyonovich Panyushkin; the assassin, Nikolai Khokhlov, was instructed by a Soviet expert in judo and the use of pistols. The pistol operated electrically, had a silencer, was hidden in packet of cigarettes, and fired cyanide bullets. The assassin called on his intended victim, announced his mission, and said he would not carry it out. He defected to the **Central Intelligence Agency (CIA),** and revealed the story in April 1954 at a special press conference where the weapon was displayed and photographed.

Source: Andrew, Christopher, and Oleg Gordievsky, *KGB: The Inside Story of Its Foreign Operations from Lenin to Gorbachev* (London: Hodder and Stoughton, 1990).

OPERATION RYAN (1981–1983). In May 1981 Leonid Brezhnev (1906–1982) announced that the United States was preparing for a nuclear war. This came as the consequence of a deterioration in U.S.–Soviet relations that resulted from the Soviet invasion of Afghanistan (1979) and the U.S. boycott of the Moscow Olympic Games (1980). Since it appeared that the alleged U.S. preparation for nuclear war was a major threat to the **U.S.S.R.**, in Russia the **KGB** and the **GRU** would work together. Their project was named Raketno Yadernoye Napdenie ("nuclear missile attack") and code-named RYAN.

RYAN was to monitor all U.S. activities, using the COSMOS satellite, which would make daily photographs of military installations; the SIGNET network would note any increases in radar activities in the United States; equipment at Lourdes would monitor U.S. military and civilian activities outside the United States; in Europe 300 ground stations would monitor **NATO** activities; COMINT installations inside the United States and in the Scandinavian countries and in Southern Europe would monitor and intercept phone calls and microwave transmissions. Spies and secret **agents** would be alert for signs of crises and unusual movements and evacuations around embassies and military posts, and would gather information relating to a possible nuclear war.

New, precise instructions on Operation RYAN went to all KGB **residences** early in 1983. Frequently in Russia alarm about U.S. policy was evident; this was especially so when President **Ronald Reagan** (1911–2004) declared the U.S.S.R. to be an "Evil Empire" (March 23, 1983) and advanced a **Strategic Defense Initiative (SDI),** known as "Star Wars," the title of a popular film released in 1977.

In Russia fears rose further, and were reinforced after the landslide victory in Great Britain of **Margaret Thatcher** (1925–) in June 1983. Many political intelligence officers and experts in the U.S.S.R. did not believe in the policy of Operation RYAN, and thought the fear on which it was based fed upon itself. By November 1983 Soviet fears had peaked with the rumor that the **Warsaw Pact** countries had been penetrated and that an attack using nuclear, chemical, and biological weapons was imminent.

In January 1984 the fear heightened further, and the risk of a nuclear war was felt to be dangerously high, but by June 1984 the U.S.S.R. Foreign Ministry officials had all but dropped their concern about a nuclear onslaught from the United States.

During the next year, priority attaching to Operation RYAN diminished, and seemed to evaporate with the death or dismissal of some leading military and defense officials.

See also OPERATION ABLE ARCHER 83

Sources: Andrew, Christopher, and Oleg Gordievsky, *KGB: The Inside Story of Its Foreign Operations* (London: Hodder and Stoughton, 1990); Andrew, Christopher, and Vasili Mitrokhin, *The Mitrokhin Archive: The KGB in Europe and the West* (London: Lane, 1999); Richelson, Jeffrey T., *A Century of Spies: Intelligence in the Twentieth Century* (New York: Oxford University Press, 1995).

OPERATION SAPPHIRE (1962). SAPPHIRE was an informal title given by the Soviets to a group of many **moles** whom the **KGB** had recruited in France and valued as much as precious jewels of that name.

In April–May 1962 President **John Kennedy** (1917–1963) was persuaded by information from James Angleton (1917–1987) to offer his personal guarantee on the credibility of Anatoli Golitsyn's (1926–) views that there was a KGB mole in the French intelligence services. A French intelligence officer was sent to Washington to investigate MARTEL, as the French code-named Golitsyn. His investigation led to the arrest of Georges Pâques (1914–), a spy in **NATO,** who was caught, tried, and put in jail. Curiously enough, Pâques was caught on a charge that Golitsyn could not have been able to make, because Golitsyn was not on the spot until several years after Pâques's treason had been committed.

SAPPHIRE became an enormous network of imagined spies that the KGB was thought to have inside the French intelligence community, but nothing came of the time-wasting and reputation-destroying investigations that occurred under its name. Its major victim was Philippe de Vosjoli, who eventually survived, and the publication and production of *Topaz,* a novel and and a film based lightly on his experiences.

See also DE VOSJOLI, PHILIPPE; PÂQUES, GEORGES

Sources: Barry, John, "Broad Impact of 'Martel' Everywhere but France," *Life* (Australia), April 29, 1968, pp. 44, 60–61; De Vosjoli, Philippe T., "A Head That Holds Sinister Secrets," *Life* (Australia), April 29, 1968, pp. 44, 53–59; De Vosjoli, Philippe L. Thyraud, *Lamia* (Boston: Little, Brown, 1970); Mangold, Tom, *Cold Warrior: James Jesus Angleton, the CIA Master Spy Hunter* (New York: Simon & Schuster, 1991).

OPERATION SATANIC (1986). Operation SATANIC was a French secret operation to prevent Greenpeace's vessel, the *Rainbow Warrior,* from disrupting the French nuclear testing program in the Pacific. It is known also as the *Rainbow Warrior* Affair.

Before midnight on July 10, 1985, the *Rainbow Warrior's* engine room exploded while the vessel was docked in Auckland, New Zealand. Shortly afterward an explosion destroyed the propulsion machinery, thereby making it impossible for the craft's owner, Greenpeace, to use the vessel in its protest against the French plans to detonate underground nuclear tests at Mururoa atoll in the Pacific Ocean. After the first explosion the 12 people on board fled; the ship's photographer, Fernando Pereira, returned to get his equipment and died in the second explosion. At first it was decided that the explosions were accidental. Soon a police investigation suspected the French secret service.

At the end of August 1985, an official French report declared the French government had not intended to damage the vessel; on September 17, *Le Monde* ridiculed the report and stated the French army had sunk the *Rainbow Warrior;* soon after, the head of the French secret service (**DGSE**) and the French Minister of Defense resigned.

Earlier in 1985, Christine Cabon, a French secret **agent** who had earlier had infiltrated the **PLO**, left New Zealand, having completed an assignment to penetrate Greenpeace and report to the DGSE the organization's plans to disrupt French nuclear testing in the Pacific. On June 22, Operation SATANIC began.

Three DGSE agents sailed to New Zealand on a chartered yacht, captained by a contractor who appeared to be a rich playboy. They were supported by Alain Mafart and Dominique Prieur, two supposed Swiss honeymooners; their mission was led by Louis-Pierre Dillias from his room on the seventh floor in the Hyatt hotel overlooking Auckland harbor. On July 7 the *Rainbow Warrior* docked, and the French saboteurs attached mines with delayed fuses to the craft. On July 10 the saboteurs were sailing to Norfolk Island when the mines exploded. Dillias and the bogus honeymooners continued their New Zealand vacation for another 10 days. The French team concealed its activities, but an observant New Zealander reported to the police having seen the saboteurs wearing wetsuits and loading apparently stolen equipment into a van, and noted its license number. The police found the van had been rented by two Swiss honeymooners. When questioned, the honeymooners had little to say. When Alain Mafart was asked why he had details of his honeymoon expenses, he indicated it was simply a habit. The police then asked why had he had deliberately overstated the expenses. As a honeymooner he had no reason to do so, because to whom would he submit his costs? Quickly he made a phone call to Paris. When the New Zealand police tried to trace the call, they found the number did not exist. The two were caught. The DGSE blundered its way through, lying unsuccessfully to conceal its agents.

The surveillance operation to protect French nuclear testing had been part of a long-term scheme, and the Greenpeace protests were one of many that had been investigated. The French used what became known as "dirty tricks" similar to those of the **Central Inteligence Agency (CIA).** The scandal provoked a formal inquiry, and raised doubts about how the French secret services used their budget. Nevertheless, almost everyone was exonerated, and the overriding principle of national interest was invoked.

While the New Zealand and Australian public were moved by the French action, the French public all but ignored the *Rainbow Warrior* Affair. However, the French secret services were reorganized, and heads rolled.

Alain Mafart and Dominique Prieur were tried, found guilty, and jailed early in July 1986 for 10 years. In response, France declared a trade war on New Zealand, which could not afford its economic impact. Thus, with France, New Zealand agreed to place the conflict before a UN arbitrator and to abide by the arbitrator's decision. The French had to pay compensation, and its two agents were placed, with their families, for three years in custody on Hao atoll in French Polynesia instead of spending 10 years alone in a New Zealand jail. The UN Secretary-General, Pérez de Cuéllar, ruled that France must pay New Zealand NZ$10 million and ensure the agents' detention was not relaxed.

In December 1987 Alain Mafart, complaining of a stomach ailment, was evacuated; and during the last stage of the French elections in 1988, Dominique Prieur, claiming to be pregnant, returned to France. The New Zealand Prime Minister said the French action was a breach of the agreement made with the United Nations. Furious, he sought an explanation. The French Prime Minister Jacques Chirac said in Tahiti that the two agents were not being detained, but were on a three-year posting.

In 1989 Dominique Prieur was promoted to major, and in 1994 Alain Mafart was promoted to lieutenant colonel. The New Zealand, Australian, and French intelligence communities were apparently pleased to see the matter laid to rest.

Sources: Dyson, John, *Sink the* Rainbow (London: Gollanz, 1986); Faligot, Roger, and Pascal Krop, *La Piscine: The French Secret Service Since 1944* (New York: Blackwell, 1989); King, Michael, *The Death of the* Rainbow Warrior (London: Penguin, 1986); Marenches, Count de, and Christine Ockrent, *The Evil Empire* (London: Sidgwick & Jackson, 1988); Morgan, Robin, Brian Whitaker, et al., *The Sunday Times Insight:* Rainbow Warrior (London: Arrow Books, 1986); Richelson, Jeffrey T., *A Century of Spies: Intelligence in the Twentieth Century* (New York: Oxford University Press, 1995); Sands, Alistair, "The *Rainbow Warrior* Affair and Realism: A Critique," working paper 113 (Canberra: Peace Research Center, Research School of Pacific Studies, Australian National University, 1991); Toohey, Brian, and Brian Pinwell, *Oyster: The Story of the Australian Secret Intelligence Services* (Port Melbourne: William Heinemann Australia, 1989).

OPERATION SHRAPNEL (1954–1955). Operation SHRAPNEL was joint operation run by the **SIS** and the **Central Intelligence Agency (CIA)** in the early 1950s. The aim was to support anti-Soviet émigré organizations such as NTS (the National Labor Alliance, an alliance of social-democratic movements in Soviet Russia). It was an expensive operation, and proved ineffective largely because the NTS organizations inside Russia had become dominated by the Soviets.

In 1954 a **STASI** officer operating undercover in West Germany had Aleksandr Trushnovich, the West Berlin leader of the NTS kidnapped, and turned him over to the **KGB** at Karlshorst. The KGB had further successes in October 1957, when the NTS ideologue Lev Rebet was assassinated, and in October 1959, with the murder of Stepan Bandera. By that time the SIS had quit the operation and left the work of helping anti-Soviet émigré organizations to the Americans.

See also REBET AND BANDERA WET AFFAIRS

Sources: Andrew, Christopher, and Vasili Mitrokhin, *The Mitrokhin Archive: The KGB in Europe and the West* (London: Lane, 1999); Blake, George, *No Other Choice: An Autobiography* (London: Jonathan Cape, 1990).

OPERATION SILICON VALLEY (1975). A successful **Central Intelligence Agency (CIA)** operation that wrecked a simple and outrageous plan of the **KGB** to control information technology secrets destined for the U.S. military.

During the early stages of the **Vietnam War** (1964–1973) the Russians had acquired U.S. computerized armaments. In the late 1960s they wanted more. In 1969 the KGB chief, **Yuri V. Andropov** (1914–1984) established Department T in the KGB with the mission of stealing American technology and, if possible, recruiting outstanding technical staff, from Silicon Valley.

In early 1973, Amos Dawe (fl. 1970–1982), a wealthy Hong Kong businessman, was commissioned by the manager of the Singapore branch of Moscow's Narodny Bank to collect information technology by purchasing 20 U.S. banks, each worth $100 million, in Silicon Valley. Dawe was chosen because, unknown to most of his creditors, he was in financial trouble. If he agreed, Dawe would avoid personal financial problems and Russia would get financial control of the majority of Silicon Valley banking, and thus be able to spy on corporations that were developing and selling advanced information technology to the U.S. military. At the time, in America, international companies were banned from such purchases, but individuals were not.

With the source of funds well concealed, Dawe began work in 1974, and entered many American company boardrooms and learned their secrets. Late in 1975, when the CIA was told what Dawe was doing, it countered with an equally clever scheme, Operation SILICON VALLEY. In October 1975 the CIA leaked what they knew to a Hong Kong journalist; in his newsletter he told how the Narodny Bank was secretly attempting to bring down international commerce with the help of Amos Dawe and a Singapore bank manager. Immediately U.S. bankers were alarmed.

Suddenly, Amos Dawe, who was at the time negotiating to buy his fourth bank, found no one would talk business with him. Narodny Bank lost the money it had acquired for the venture; the Singapore branch manager was brought home to Moscow for discipline; and Dawe disappeared.

With help from Hong Kong friends, Dawe was extradited to Hong Kong to avoid being sued in the United States; in retaliation the U.S. government tried to have him charged with fraud and embezzlement, and put in jail for five years. But early in 1982 Dawe disappeared once more.

See also DAWE, AMOS

Source: Laffin, John, *Brassey's Book of Espionage* (London: Brassey's, 1996).

OPERATION SILVER (1948–1952). After **World War II**, Vienna, like Berlin, was divided into four militarized zones: British, French, Soviet, and U.S. Sir **Stewart Menzies** (1890–1968), chief of the **SIS**, and known as "C," was familiar with the secret VENONA material. He sent Peter Lunn (1914–) to Vienna to look into intercepting Russian communications between Vienna and Moscow.

Lunn found that the Russians were using the Austrian telephone trunk lines that connected the Red Army with Moscow and other large capital cities in Europe. He discovered all calls from the **Kremlin** in Moscow to the headquarters of the Red Army in Austria, at the Imperial Hotel, came through those trunk lines, which were buried beside a road though the Vienna suburb of Schwechet, in the Anglo–French zone of Vienna.

"C" authorized the purchase of a shop near the highway, and had it sell goods that the Austrians loved. It became a profitable commercial venture and a fine cover for Operation SILVER. Next, the SIS bought a private house, dug a 70-foot tunnel to the trunk line, and put a tap on it. The intercepted material helped assessments in London of Soviet military preparations to resolve **Cold War** problems, and the U.K. defense intelligence staff soon had the Soviet **order of battle** and the locations of all military services. One story suggests that the operation was successful until a streetcar going over the tunnel caused it to collapse. Another says the Vienna tunnel, as it is sometimes called, was a secret until discovered by the Americans; then it became useful to them, too, well into the period of the **Korean War** (1950–1953). The Vienna tunnel inspired a similar operation in Berlin, Operation GOLD, in 1955.

See also BLAKE, GEORGE; LUNN, PETER

Sources: Blake, George, *No Other Choice: An Autobiography* (London: Jonathan Cape, 1990); Brown, Anthony Cave, *"C": The Secret Life of Sir Stewart Menzies, Spymaster to Winston Churchill* (New York: Macmillan, 1987); Cavendish, Anthony, *Inside Intelligence* (London: Collins, 1990); Laffin, John, *Brassey's Book of Espionage* (London: Brassey's, 1996).

OPERATION SOLO (1954–1978?). Operation SOLO was an extraordinary espionage program carried out by two brothers, Morris and Jack Childs, who worked as informants for the **Federal Bureau of Investigation (FBI)** while members of the **CPUSA.**

As the CPUSA's bagman, Jack Childs smuggled about $30 million from Moscow to the United States while he was in charge of relations with the Communist Party of the Soviet Union, acted as the American branch's foreign minister, and influenced other groups of Communists in the United States Between 1958 and 1978 he traveled 50 times between Moscow and America, reporting to his FBI handlers each time. The brothers were joined by Morris's wife, Eva Lieb Childs, who was an FBI **recruit** as well.

The operation received high praise in 1996, but the report of their activities is not as accurate as historians would want. It seems that in 1954, when the CPUSA had been all but destroyed by prosecutions under the McCarran Act (1950) and the **Smith Act** (1940), the FBI approached Jack Childs to be its **mole** in the CPUSA. Jack was a con man, but Morris was well connected with the Russian Communist elite. The FBI secured Jack's recruitment through payment for a serious heart operation. Thereafter it appears the two men set out to make a fortune as **double agents.**

Claims were made that their secret work for America was brilliant, legendary, and fundamental in preventing uncontrollable hostilities during the **Cold War**; every president from **John F. Kennedy** (1917–1963) to **Ronald Reagan** (1911–2004) based important decisions on data from Operation SOLO, including exploitation of the **Sino–Soviet split** (1960–1971), détente with **Leonid Brezhnev** (1906–1982) in the early 1970s, and **Richard M. Nixon**'s (1913–1994) relations with China. However brilliant these accomplishments, the story of Operation SOLO seemed implausible, looked impossible, and was not confirmable, because evidence was based on the stories of FBI **agents** who handled Operation SOLO, and there were no documents to support the recollections.

But with the publication of the Mitrokhin archive much evidence appeared that corroborates the activities of the Childs brothers, although the archive does not identify the operation as SOLO, no doubt because it was an unknown FBI scam against the **KGB**. The FBI archives will be a major source on this operation.

See also CHILDS, JACK, AND CHILDS, MORRIS

Sources: Andrew, Christopher, and Vasili Mitrokhin, *The Mitrokhin Archive: The KGB in Europe and the West* (London: Lane, 1999); Barron, John, *Operation Solo: The FBI Man in the Kremlin* (Washington, DC: Regnery, 1996); Fischer, Ben B., "The Big Con Game: Review of Barron, John. 1996. Operation Solo: The FBI Man in the Kremlin," *International Journal of Intelligence and Counterintelligence* 10 (4) (1998): 473–478; DeLoach, Cartha D. "Deke," *Hoover's FBI: The Inside Story of Hoover's Trusted Lieutenant* (Washington, DC: Regnery, 1995); Garrow, David J., *The FBI and Martin Luther King, Jr.: From Solo to Memphis* (New York: Penguin, 1981); Klehr, Harvey, John Earl Haynes, and Fridrikh Igorevich Firsov, *The Soviet World of American Communism* (New Haven, CT: Yale University Press, 1998).

OPERATION SPANDAU (1948). Operation SPANDAU was an imagined British operation that arose from secret fears following the **Berlin blockade.**

In July 1948, a few months after the **U.S.S.R.** imposed the Berlin blockade, it became the Soviet Union's turn to supervise the Nazi war criminals prisoners in Spandau Prison. Major General E. O. Herbert, the officer commanding British troops in Berlin, informed the British government in **Whitehall** that since there were 40 to 50 Russian soldiers in Spandau, and Soviet military personnel were stationed nearby, it would be easy for Russia to seize any prisoners they wanted and take them to the U.S.S.R.

British officials in Germany became alarmed that the Soviet Union might want to seize Albert Speer (1905–1981), Rudolf Hess (1894–1987), and Karl Doenitz (1891–1980) for their propaganda value and technical knowledge. Whitehall was not troubled by the personal fate of the prisoners, but it was alarmed at the prospect of losing Speer and Doenitz, who, if they escaped or fell into Russian hands, would be useful if they could be compelled or induced to work for Russia. For example, to the end of his life, Doenitz had the loyalty of many submarines crews, and with his knowledge at the disposal of the Russians, British authorities worried about the way in which the Russians would use his expertise on submarines. From the British viewpoint, it would be most unfortunate if the Russians were ever to get exclusive control of the top Nazis in Spandau. The British anxiety about the possible seizure receded by December 1948.

Source: Travis, Alan, "Britain Feared Soviet Plot to Kidnap Nazis, Papers Reveal," *The Age*, March 24, 2000, p. 6.

OPERATION STOPWATCH (1954–1956). The operation, variously called Operation STOPWATCH (**SIS**), Operation GOLD (**Central Intelligence Agency, [CIA]**), and Operation PRINCE (West, 1991), and the Berlin Tunnel in most reports, was an attempt by the CIA and the SIS to tap the phone lines between the Russian military headquarters in Berlin and Moscow. From the beginning the Russians knew of the operation because inside the SIS a British spy serving Russia took minutes of the meetings of the committee that ran the operation. The operation's military effectiveness has been long debated.

George Blake (1922–) kept the minutes for meetings of the project, which he called Operation STOPWATCH/GOLD. It was inaugurated in February 1954, and aimed to build a 600-yard tunnel at Alt Glienicke, on the border of the Russian and American zones in Berlin, so as to tap Soviet communication cables. A copy of Blake's notes appears in Murphy et al. (1997, Appendix 9).

The tunnel, to be about half a mile long, was a response to the fear that Russia would invade West Germany and to the knowledge that it would take over 2,000 well-placed **agents** to keep the West adequately informed on Soviet military intentions and resources. A similar venture had been successful in Vienna.

The Americans financed and built the Berlin tunnel, and the British supplied the technical tapping equipment. For 13 months the CIA and **MI6** intercepted telephone land lines in East Berlin with this tunnel. The tunnel was 1,476 feet and involved moving 3,100 tons of dirt; the tapping of 172 land lines required hundreds of tape recorders.

There was a myth that the tunnel was the brainchild of Reinhard Gehlen (1902–1979), but this is not true; it was a scheme developed by the CIA and the SIS after the success of the Vienna tunnel, the idea of "C" and of Peter Lunn (1914–), who had been head of station in Vienna. The Berlin tunnel was built by the CIA's Berlin Operations Base (**BOB**), and nicknamed "Harvey's Hole," after Bill Harvey. Peter Lunn returned to Berlin in 1953 as head of the SIS station.

The listeners collected 443,000 conversations on the military in the U.S.S.R.; East Germany; and Poland. Information covered Soviet forces' training exercises; biographical information on high and low defense officers and politicians; the introduction of special tanks; radio codes used by the Soviet air defense; reports on declining morale and poor discipline; the motivation and training of Soviet army personnel; the gossip, lies, and duplicity of army officers; gossip about corruption at all levels; and the perks and secretly held attitudes of Soviet policy makers. The tunnel was made known to the Soviets by George Blake before the digging began. Much was made of the Soviets' use of the tunnel for **KGB disinformation** before the timed "discovery" in April 1956.

At the time of the discovery **Nikita Khrushchev** (1894–1971) was a guest of the British Prime Minister in England, and aware the discovery was imminent. He insisted the blame for the tunnel not be directed to the British, but only to the Americans. This would help improve Anglo–Soviet relations, and damage the special relationship the Americans and British enjoyed. So Peter Lunn, whose idea it was primarily, watched the CIA get the all the credit for the enterprise.

The KGB did surprisingly little about the use of the tunnel, and let it be used because the information that the West was collecting was of little value to the CIA/SIS, because there were bureaucratic errors made in communicating between KGB departments and because it was necessary not to imperil Blake's position as a **double agent** for the KGB. Sensitive Soviet material was sent routinely by overhead lines.

McEwen (1990) wrote a novel using the Berlin tunnel as a backdrop; the operation has appeared in other novels and many films (Murphy et al., 1997).

See also BLAKE, GEORGE; LUNN, PETER; YOUNG, GEORGE

Sources: Blake, George, *No Other Choice: An Autobiography* (London: Jonathan Cape, 1990); Bower, Tom, *The Perfect English Spy: Sir Dick White and the Secret War 1935–90* (London: Heinemann, 1995), pp. 259–269; Deacon, Richard, *Spyclopedia: The Comprehensive Handbook of Espionage* (New York: Silver Arrow Books/William Morrow, 1987); Evans, Joseph, "Berlin Tunnel Intelligence: A Bumbling KGB," *International Journal of Intelligence and Counterintelligence* 9 (1) (1996): 43–50; Feifer, George, "The Berlin Tunnel," *MHQ: The Quarterly Journal of Military History* 10 (1998): 62–71; Höhne, Heinz, and Herman Zolling, *Network: The Truth About General Gehlen and His Spy Ring,* Richard Barry, trans. (London: Secker & Warburg, 1971); Knopp, Guido, *Top Spies: Traitors in the Secret War* (Munich: C. Bertlesmann, 1994); Laffin, John, *Brassey's Book of Espionage* (London: Brassey's, 1996); McEwan, Ian, *The Innocent or the Special Relationship* (London: Jonathan Cape, 1990; New York: Vintage, 2001); Murphy, David E., Sergei A. Kondrashev, and George Bailey, *Battleground Berlin: CIA vs KGB in the Cold War* (New Haven, CT: Yale University Press, 1997); Nechiporenko, Oleg M., *Passport to Assassination* (New York: Birch Lane Press, 1993); Stafford, David, *Spies Beneath Berlin* (London: John Murray, 2002).

OPERATION TOP HAT (1959–1985). Operation TOP HAT was a **Federal Bureau of Investigation (FBI)** and **Central Intelligence Agency (CIA)** operation involving a Russian spy who defected and served the agencies until he was identified and shot by the Soviets.

By October 1959, the **KGB** and the **GRU** were using the UN headquarters in New York for training ambitious intelligence **agents** for their first overseas appointment. In 1951 the GRU had sent Dimitri F. Polyakov (c. 1921–1988) to the UN as one of Russia's young diplomats: his task was to acquire secret American technology. He returned to Moscow in 1956, and was again posted to the United Nations in 1959. At the time the FBI learned that although he was a colonel, Polyakov was apparently unhappy with his lowly position in Russia's military intelligence bureaucracy.

The FBI contacted Polyakov—dropped the handkerchief—and he approached them later. He said he was betraying Russia for his own interests. At one time the FBI rewarded him with what he really wanted, antique, handmade guns.

In a New York **safe house** Polyakov informed the FBI of American traitors and the FBI arranged to keep him a secret from those he was betraying. In 1962 TOP HAT came under CIA control, was renamed BOURBON and GT/ACCORD, and served the CIA admirably. In return the CIA protected Polyakov very well. However, in January 1985 TOPHAT was blown by Aldrich H. Ames (1941–), and in 1988 Polyakov was executed.

See also AMES, ALDRICH HAZEN; POLYAKOV, DIMITRI

Sources: Earley, Pete, *Confessions of a Spy: The Real Story of Aldrich Ames* (London: Hodder and Stoughton, 1997); Mangold, Tom, *Cold Warrior: James Jesus Angleton, the CIA Master Spy Hunter* (New York: Simon & Schuster, 1991); Volkman, Ernest, *Espionage: The Greatest Spy Operations of the 20th Century* (New York: Wiley, 1995).

OPERATION TRACK TWO. Operation TRACK TWO was a U.S. government operation, using the **Central Intelligence Agency (CIA)** to overthrow the President of Chile, Salvador Allende Gossens (1908–1973).

The goal took longer to achieve than expected. In September 1970 Allende was elected with a 36 percent majority to the presidency of Chile. The Army Chief of Staff, Rene Schneider, gave Allende support, as did the parliamentary opposition. Allende had to wait 60 days before he took office. U.S. President **Richard Nixon** (1913–1994) and his national security adviser Henry Kissinger (1923–) wanted Allende ousted because of his left-wing policies, and his electoral victory was seen as a geopolitical move by the **U.S.S.R.** in the **Cold War**. At the time it was compared to the **Bay of Pigs** disaster of April 1961.

Nixon and Kissinger decided that Schneider should be kidnapped; this, they thought, would lead to a coup; their preferred military leader, Augusto Pinochet (1915–), would then be in power. It would be a CIA operation named Operation TRACK TWO, and would effectively end the alleged Communist domination of Chile.

Behind the back of the United States ambassador, Edward Korrey, who believed Allende was no threat to the United States, the CIA officers in Santiago were ordered to overthrow Allende and ensure the American hand was hidden. From among Chile's right-wing army officers, Colonel Paul Wimert, the U.S. military attaché, drew a hit squad. General Roberto Viaux was one of the leading plotters. On October 15, so Kissinger would later claim, he gave the order to abort the Viaux coup because of its unlikely success and turned off Operation TRACK TWO. But the following day the CIA telexed its men in Santiago, insisting that Allende must be overthrown in a coup. Arms and ammunition were sent by diplomatic pouch to Santiago on October 19, 1970. On October 22 Schneider was killed; the hit squad was paid with the U.S.$250,000 that Wimert had been given. Although the plan misfired, largely because Allende's support from the army and the opposition Christian Democratic Party rose after Schneider's death, U.S. policy on Allende's regime held firm. In various ways the United States arranged economic chaos and social disorder among citizens of Chile for several years.

By September 1973, with strong support from high levels of the Catholic Church, conservative politicians and army generals headed by Pinochet, law and order were brought to the streets of Santiago. Allende died in the presidential palace. His death was by suicide, according to Allende's personal surgeon, Dr. Patricio Guijon Klein; others suggest it was murder.

Augusto Pinochet became Chile's President, and his government was marked by violation of human rights, especially in 1975–1976. From the West's point of view Pinochet, was Chile's heroic savior. Kissinger went to Chile to speak at a conference on Chile's human rights violations in June 1976; but when he spoke secretly with Pinochet, he said that he had been obliged to take a public stand on human rights violations that would mollify the U.S. Congress, so that the level of aid the United States provided for Chile under Pinochet's rule would not be cut.

See also ALLENDE GOSSENS, SALVADOR

Sources: Franklin, Jonathan, "CIA 'Helped' Set Up Pinochet's Secret Police," *Guardian Weekly*, September 28–October 4, 2000, p. 5; Franklin, Jonathan, "U.S. Agencies Paid Millions to Back Pinochet," *Guardian Weekly*, November 22, 2000, p. 4; Henderson, Robert D. A., "Project Rodriquista: Opposing Pinochet's Regime in Chile," *International Journal of Intelligence and Counterintelligence* 13 (2000): 438–489; Hilton, Isabel, and Jeevan Vasagar, "Pinochet to Stand Trial in Chile," *Guardian Weekly*, December 7–13, 2000, p. 4; Huismann, Wilfred, *Der Fall Kissinger (the Kissinger Case)* (WDR, 2001), a film; Loeb, Vernon, "Top CIA Officials Refuse to Declassify Chile Files," *Guardian Weekly*, August 17–23, 2000, p. 28; O'Shaughnessy, Hugh, "Pinochet's Drug Link Comes to Light: For Years Chile Has Been Supplying Drugs to Europe," *Guardian Weekly*, December 14–20, 2000, p. 5; Porteous, Clinton, "Pinochet Declared Unfit to Stand Trial," *The Age*, July 11, 2001, p. 4; Sifakis, Carl, *Encyclopedia of Assassinations: A Compendium of Attempted and Successful Assassinations Throughout History* (New York: Facts on File, 1993).

OPERATION VALUABLE. See ALBANIAN PROJECT

OPPENHEIMER, JULIUS ROBERT (1904–1967). Julius Robert Oppenheimer, an American Jew, headed scientific research on the **atom bomb** in the United States; in 1954 he lost his security clearance and was forced out of the U.S. Atomic Energy Commission for past associations with Communists.

J. Robert Oppenheimer was a professor of physics at the University of California (1936–1947) and directed the construction of the university's cyclotron. He was an expert on nuclear disintegration, relativity, and cosmic radiation. From 1947 to 1967 he was a director of the Institute for Advanced Studies at Princeton University.

Between the late 1930s and 1942 he had supported the U.S. Popular Front; allied himself with the **CPUSA** between the late 1930s and 1942; indicated he was not concerned about the **Ribbentrop-Molotov Pact** (1939); given money to the CPUSA; and, shortly before starting on the **Manhattan Project** in 1943, had associated with known Soviet contacts and Communist leaders. The **NKGB** urged its agents in the United States to cultivate him and recruit him to the Soviet cause. He was code-named CHESTER for this purpose.

Oppenheimer's brother and sister-in-law were underground CPUSA members; his wife had been a Communist and married an official of the CPUSA who had died in the **Spanish Civil War.** Recruiting Oppenheimer to the Soviet cause was hardly possible because of the security established around him.

In August 1943 Oppenheimer told security officers that he knew one of his staff had been approached to give sensitive information to the Soviets, then changed his story to say that he was the one who had been approached. He provided other information, and again revised his statements.

In 1945 Oppenheimer was approached by an NKGB informant in Washington, who later informed his handler that Oppenheimer wanted international agreement on the development and use of nuclear energy, that he would not be an **agent**, and that atom secrets would not be revealed until the countries involved enjoyed full political cooperation. In short, he was a liberal, not a Communist political man. Between 1946 and 1953 he was the chairman of the U.S. Atomic Energy Commission. He opposed the development of the **hydrogen bomb**, an idea that Sudoplatov (1994) claims was Soviet propaganda that he had introduced through Klaus Fuchs (1911–1983) in 1946.

In 1954 Oppenheimer's security clearance was canceled. VENONA material suggests that the reports about him show that he did not provide Soviet agents with information, that his ties to the Communist Party had been strong until 1941, and that he appeared to have been indifferent to the question of whether or not the Soviets were spying on the Manhattan Project.

After being found a security risk, Oppenheimer returned to Princeton University, where he had directed the Institute for Advanced Studies. In 1963 he was given the Fermi Award.

Sources: Alterman, Eric, "I Spy with One Little Eye . . . Spotting Cold War Espionage Has Turned into a Journalistic Game Without Rules," *The Nation*, April 29, 1996, pp. 20–24; Ambrose, Stephen E., *Ike's Spies: Eisenhower and the Espionage Establishment*, 2nd ed. (Jackson: University Press of Mississippi, 1999); Haynes, John Earl, and Harvey Klehr, *Venona: Decoding Soviet Espionage in America* (New Haven, CT: Yale University Press, 1999); Smith, Alice, and Charles Weiner, eds., *Robert Oppenheimer: Letters and Recollections* (Stanford, CA: Stanford University Press, 1980); Sudoplatov, Pavel, and Anatoli Sudoplatov, *Special Tasks: The Memoirs of an Unwanted Witness, a Soviet Spymaster* (Boston: Little, Brown, 1994); Weinstein, Allen, and Alexander Vassiliev, *The Haunted Wood: Soviet Espionage in America— The Stalin Era* (New York: Random House, 1999).

ORLOV, ALEKSANDR MIKHAILOVICH (1895–1973).

An important Soviet **defector**, code-named SCHWED, who came to the United States in the late 1930s and provided valuable information on the Soviets after **Josef Stalin**'s death in 1953.

Orlov (originally Leon Felbin) was a Jew who studied law, turned to Bolshevism in 1917, and took the name of Lev Nikolsky. In 1920, having joined the Red Army, he came to the attention of Felix Dzerzhinski (1877–1926) for his abilities in counterintelligence in Poland.

Orlov was assistant prosecutor at the Supreme Court and later an economic adviser, and then was made the **OGPU resident** in Paris. In 1928 he was head of Soviet intelligence in Berlin as a member of the Soviet trade delegation, and by now was using the name Aleksandr Orlov.

In 1931 Orlov returned to Moscow, to the headquarters of OGPU, to head the unit concerned with economic intelligence. He also evaluated secret reports of OGPU's Foreign Department espionage networks, produced a training manual on espionage, and until 1936 directed the counterintelligence activities of the Central Military School.

Orlov was in London in July 1934 and from September 1934 to October 1935. He was partly involved in Arnold Deutsch's (1904–1942) recruitment of Kim Philby

(1912–1988). Then Orlov was sent to Spain to control undercover operations and the training of saboteurs and guerrillas to work against the nationalists. He also was to build a secret **NKVD** force to bring about the Stalinization of Spain. In the belief that he was about to be killed by the NKVD, he defected when suddenly recalled to Moscow.

By the summer of 1938 Orlov and his wife had escaped through France and Canada to the United States. At the time he sent a letter to Leon Trotsky (1879–1940), warning him that an NKVD assassin named Mark was about to murder him.

The Orlovs hid for 15 years in Cleveland, Ohio. Orlov feared the Russians would catch him, and he changed his name and address often to elude capture. In 1953, when Josef Stalin died, Orlov wrote articles for *Life* magazine cataloging the horrors of Stalinism in the Soviet Union. He published a book based on the articles in 1954. The **Federal Bureau of Investigation (FBI)** investigated him, and he was debriefed thoroughly, revealing much that was previously unknown about Soviet spy rings and their recruiting methods in the United States when he appeared in September 1955 and February 1957 before the U.S. Senate's Internal Security Subcommittee of the Judiciary Committee.

Orlov published a valuable account of Soviet intelligence in *Handbook of Intelligence and Guerilla Warfare* (1963). For some time before he died the Soviets tried to get him to return to Russia, offering him a generous pension and housing. He declined the offer.

Sources: Andrew, Christopher, and Vasili Mitrokhin, *The Mitrokhin Archive: The KGB in Europe and the West* (London: Lane, 1999); Corson, William R., and Robert T. Crowley, *The New KGB: Engine of Soviet Power* (New York: William Morrow, 1985); Costello, John, *Mask of Treachery: Spies, Lies, Buggery and Betrayal. The First Documented Dossier on Anthony Blunt's Cambridge Spy Ring* (New York: William Morrow, 1988); Costello, John, and Oleg Tsarev, *Deadly Illusions* (New York: Crown, 1993); Orlov, Aleksandr, *The Secret History of Stalin's Crimes* (London: Jarrold's, 1954); Orlov, Aleksandr, *A Handbook of Intelligence and Guerrilla Warfare* (Ann Arbor: University of Michigan Press, 1963).

OSWALD, LEE HARVEY (1939–1963).

Lee Harvey Oswald was, officially, the lone and deranged assassin of U.S. President **John F. Kennedy** (1917–1963). In the **Cold War** he was suspected for a time of being an **agent** of the **KGB** because, prior to the assassination, he had lived in Russia and had left with a Russian wife.

Lee Harvey Oswald was born in New Orleans two months after his father's death. His widowed mother already had two sons. He was raised in relative poverty, and placed frequently in an orphanage until his mother remarried. They lived in Fort Worth, Texas.

This marriage ended in divorce, and when his brothers grew up, Oswald lived with his mother. In 1952 they moved to New York. Oswald was dyslexic and a poor student, and played truant from high school. He read some Marx, and all of the U.S. Marines manual; eventually he joined the Marines after his mother had moved, via New Orleans, back to Fort Worth.

Oswald served in Japan, met some Japanese Communists, and lost any affection he might have had for the United States Three days after his discharge in 1958 he went to Moscow, intending to become a Russian citizen. He succeeded in finding work in a Minsk radio factory; was well supported by his Russian hosts; and, after dallying with a few young Russian women, in April 1961 married Marina Prusakova (1941–).

Before marrying, Oswald planned to return to the United States. After surmounting many U.S. and **U.S.S.R.** bureaucratic hurdles, he, Marina, and their daughter, June, arrived in New York in the summer of 1962. Throughout his stay in Russia, Oswald had been under KGB surveillance, suspected of espionage for the United States; the rest of his life in the United States, he was under **Central Intelligence Agency (CIA)** and **Federal Bureau of Investigation (FBI)** surveillance, suspected of espionage for Russia.

The Oswalds lived in Dallas with relatives, were welcomed into the local Russian émigré community, and were supported by Oswald's family. Although their marriage began a long, slow, but clear disintegration, Oswald was always an attentive husband and supportive father. He appeared to have a double life and an almost dissociated identity, and was often regarded as a divided character. They separated often, until Marina had had enough.

Oswald developed socialist political beliefs, and he appeared to offer humane support for Cubans. He attempted to murder an elderly right-wing U.S. general; he decried both Russian and U.S. economic systems; and he was suspected of being part of a Russian plot to undermine the U.S. political system.

Oswald shot President John F. Kennedy in Dallas, November 22, 1963, and, while under police protection, was himself murdered two days later by Jack Ruby (1911–1967), a small-time nightclub owner with criminal associations. Oswald's murder seen on television and sent around the world.

The U.S. inquiry into the President's death, the **Warren Commission**, made no attempt to establish fully Oswald's motives and concluded that he was the lone, deranged killer of the President.

For over 35 years many writers believed that various groups had conspired to kill President Kennedy—the military–industrial complex, overseas and domestic secret service groups, crime syndicates, right-wing extremists, pro- and anti-Cuban groups— that Oswald was indirectly involved with them to an unknown degree and that he may well have been chosen as a sacrifice in one or more schemes to cover the truth. This view is advanced in Oliver Stone's film *JFK* (1991).

Most of the reliable knowledge about Oswald and those who knew him appears in Mailer's (1995) literary inquiry into Oswald's mysterious life. The book, like the film *JFK*, illustrates well the spirit and psychology of Cold War espionage; but, while the film is directed to a fixed conclusion on Oswald's guilt and the role of conspiracy, the book offers no fixed conclusion on either.

At present we are left with the explanation that Lee Harvey Oswald, the lone, deranged killer of John F. Kennedy, played the role of a Cold War nihilist, a man who bent on changing the world—not only the two parties to the Cold War, the "superpowers"—by upholding the dystopian principle that all things must get a lot worse before any one thing can get better. He was driven by a missionary's zeal, gross deceit, and the dreams of a frustrated narcissist.

See also KENNEDY ASSASSINATION; OPERATION COINTELPRO

Sources: Andrew, Christopher, and Vasili Mitrokhin, *The Mitrokhin Archive: The KGB in Europe and the West* (London: Lane, 1999); Epstein, Edward Jay, *Legend: The Secret World of Lee Harvey Oswald* (New York: Reader's Digest and McGraw-Hill, 1978); Fonzi, Gaeton, *The Last Investigation* (New York: Thunder's Mouth Press, 1993); Mailer, Norman, *Oswald's Tale: An American Mystery* (New York: Random House, 1995); McMillan, Priscilla J., *Marina and Lee* (New York: Harper & Row, 1977); Posner, Gerald, *Case Closed: Lee Harvey Oswald* *and the Assassination of JFK* (New York: Random House, 1994); Summers, Anthony, *Conspiracy* (New York: McGraw-Hill, 1980).

OWEN, WILL (1901–1980). Will Owen, a British member of Parliament (MP), spied for the Czechoslovakian government, was paid generously, and had lavish vacations. He was never caught.

Will Owen, a miner's son, oldest of 10 children from an impoverished home—which he disparaged for never providing him with sufficient comfort—was the Labour MP for Morpeth. He was recruited in his mid-fifties to the Czechoslovakian security services after the November 1954 election, code-named LEE, and known informally as "Greedy Bastard." For £500 every month and free vacations in Czechoslovakia, for 15 years he gave the Czech security services top-secret data about the British army and Britain's contributions to **NATO**. The information was based partly on what he learned as a member of the House of Commons Defense Estimates Committee.

Owen's espionage was discovered after the defection of Joseph Frolik (c. 1925–) in the summer of 1969. Frolik said Owen had passed on a vast array of valuable information on military matters. Owen resigned in April 1970. He had large sums in his bank account, paid no taxes on them, and had to admit he had lied about the amounts and their source. He was tried in May 1970, and, to his surprise, was acquitted because the information against him was hearsay and it could not be otherwise proved that he had actually transmitted secrets.

After his acquittal it was clear that Owen had lied about the amount of money he had received. He agreed to interrogation by **MI5,** providing Leo Abse, a lawyer, an independent parliamentarian, and a psychoanalytic scholar, could be present to prevent him from further investigation and prosecution. He confessed more to MI5, but little could be done with the information.

See also FROLIK, JOSEF

Sources: Abse, Leo, *Margaret, Daughter of Beatrice: A Politician's Psycho-biography of Margaret Thatcher* (London: Cape, 1989); Andrew, Christopher, and Oleg Gordievsky, *KGB: The Inside Story of Its Foreign Operations from Lenin to Gorbachev* (London: Hodder and Stoughton, 1990); Frolik, Joseph, *The Frolik Defection* (London: Leo Cooper, 1975); Pincher, Chapman, *Too Secret Too Long* (London: Sidgwick & Jackson, 1984); West, Nigel, *The Circus: MI5 Operations 1945–1972* (New York: Stein and Day, 1983).

OXFORD SPY RING. Little is securely known about the Oxford spy ring, but much about it was expected to appear with the publication of the Mitrokhin Archive (1999).

The **code name** of the chief organizer of the Oxford spy ring was SCOTT, but the person's identity is unknown. By 1937 it was certain that he had a secure foundation for a secret organization of **talent spotters** and recruiters for the Soviet cause in Britain. Peter Wright (1916–1995) of **MI5** identified some members of the group, with help from Anthony Blunt (1907–1983); among them was Phoebe Pool, who committed suicide after naming Jenifer Fischer Williams, who had married an Oxford professor, Herbert Hart.

In the late 1930s Jenifer Hart told she would be more effective as a Communist if she quit the British Communist Party, joined the civil service and maintained a secret membership in the party. She became the private secretary to Sir Alexander Maxwell, the Permanent Secretary to the Home Office. She publicly dropped her membership in the Communist Party, went underground, and met "Otto."

"Otto" was identified early by Pierre de Villemarest (De Villemarest, 2000) and later by Peter Wright as Arnold Deutsch (1904–1942), the successful Soviet **illegal** who worked closely with Edith Tudor Hart (1908–1973) to recruit Kim Philby (1912–1988) and would later run Philby, Guy Burgess (1911–1963), and Edith Tudor Hart herself.

Jenifer Hart named Bernard Floud, the Labour MP in Harold Wilson's first government (1964–1970), who committed suicide in October 1967; also she named Arthur Wynn, Sir Andrew Cohen (who died before he could be interviewed), and Sir Denis Proctor, all of whom were sympathetic to the Soviet cause in the 1930s. Those living were interviewed a generation later to establish whether or not they had served **Moscow Center**. All denied treachery.

Moscow Center boasted that this Oxford spy network operated in tandem with the Magnificent Five, the Cambridge spies. However, nothing of this appeared in the Mitrokhin Archive.

See also MAGNIFICENT FIVE; PHILBY, HAROLD "KIM"; WRIGHT, PETER

Sources: Andrew, Christopher, and Vasili Mitrokhin, *The Mitrokhin Archive: The KGB in Europe and the West* (London: Lane, 1999); Costello, John, *Mask of Treachery: Spies, Lies, Buggery and Betrayal. The First Documented Dossier on Anthony Blunt's Cambridge Spy Ring* (New York: William Morrow, 1988); De Villemarest, Pierre, "The Mysterious 'Otto,'" *International Journal of Intelligence and Counterintelligence* 15 (2000): 520; Hart, Jenifer, *Ask Me No More* (London: Peter Halborn, 1998); West, Nigel, "The Oxford Spy Ring. Review of Hart, Jenifer. 1998. Ask Me No More," *International Journal of Intelligence and Counterintelligence* 12 (2) (2000): 233–236.

P

PÂQUES, GEORGES (1914–). Georges Pâques, a French spy for the Soviets for 20 years, was found almost by accident, apparently a victim of his own vanity.

Georges Pâques was born in France, had an outstanding academic record, and in 1943, aged 29, was recruited by the **NKVD**. He was passing information to the Soviets when he was in Algiers in 1944, as head of the Political Affairs Section of the Free French Broadcasting Service of the French provisional government, headed by Charles de Gaulle.

After **World War II** ended, Pâques served the French cabinet and was an adviser to various ministers. He wanted to play an important part in France's international relations, and aimed to produce a balance in international relations between the **U.S.S.R.** and the powerful United States. He liked to think that he could make a difference, and that both **Josef Stalin** (1879–1953) and **Nikita Khrushchev** (1894–1971) admired his work.

After 1958, when Charles de Gaulle (1890–1970) returned to power, Pâques was permitted to see major defense documents. During for four years of access to them, he learned much about the French general military staff, its training for high-level operations, and its role at **NATO** headquarters. In 1962 Pâques was working at NATO. Every two weeks he met his Soviet handlers in a forest near Paris and would pass on information that, at one point, included the complete defense plan that NATO had for Europe. Pâques liked to hear from the Soviets that he was having an effect on high level decision making and came to believe that he contributed significantly to the peaceful end of the **Berlin crisis** (1958–1961) and to the subsequent decision to construct the **Berlin Wall**.

When he defected in 1961, Anatoli Golitsyn (1926–) provided some sketchy information to start an investigation that resulted in Pâques's arrest, confession, and conviction in 1963. Pâques was imprisoned for life in 1964, but the sentence was later reduced to 20 years. At the time France was a full military member of NATO and Pâques was the deputy chief of the French section of NATO's Press and Information Department.

The French took Golitsyn's vague information, refined and clarified it, and began to suspect Pâques, but in the end he was identified clearly by the senior official in the **DST**, Marcel Chalet. Also, the information Golitsyn gave could never have been directly relevant to Pâques; Golitsyn could refer only to information available to him before his defection in 1961, and Pâques did not enter NATO until 1962. It took a year for the Pâques investigation to be concluded. In fact, apart from Pâques, no one was identified from Golitsyn's material between 1962 and the end of the **Cold War.**

See also GOLITSYN, ANATOLI

Sources: Andrew, Christopher, and Oleg Gordievsky, *KGB: The Inside Story of Its Foreign Operations from Lenin to Gorbachev* (London: Hodder and Stoughton, 1990); Mangold, Tom, *Cold Warrior: James Jesus Angleton, the CIA Master Spy Hunter* (New York: Simon & Schuster, 1991); Pincher, Chapman, *Traitors: The Anatomy of Treason* (New York: St. Martin's Press, 1987); Wolton, Thierry, *Le KGB en France* (Paris: Bernard Grase, 1986).

PELTON, RONALD W. (1931–). Ronald Pelton, one of the U.S. spies caught in the "**Year of the Spy,**" took up espionage because he needed money. He received about U.S.$35,000 for five years of spying.

Pelton was raised in Benton Harbor, Michigan; joined the U.S. Air Force, where he learned Russian; and was posted to Pakistan to work as a spy using electronic equipment. In 1965 he joined the National Security Agency (NSA). A religious man, he was married and had four children.

In his late forties, Pelton began building a home for his family, but got into financial difficulties. He decided to declare bankruptcy in 1979 because he feared his top-secret security clearance would be threatened by his mounting debts. He left the NSA and worked as a salesman for a boatbuilder.

In need of money in January 1980, Pelton phoned the Soviet embassy, seeking to offer valuable material. The **Federal Bureau of Investigation (FBI)** recorded the phone call, and he was seen entering the embassy the next afternoon. He took with him a document showing he had passed NSA training requirements. He could not supply documents, but only evidence from his remarkably accurate memory. He was greeted at the embassy by Vitaly Yurchenko (1936–), the security officer. After they had talked a little, he had Pelton shave off his beard and leave with a group of workers so as not to be identified by any watchers.

In the spring of 1984 Pelton met Ann Barry, fell in love, and began using drugs. In April 1985 he left his wife.

In 1985 Yurchenko defected to the West for about two months, and one item he brought with him was about MR. LONG, a valuable spy who came into the embassy in the late seventies or early eighties. Pelton was identified as that spy from Yurchenko's comment that the suspect had given some information to the Soviets on Operation IVY BELLS, a valuable underwater operation. The investigators eliminated those who were *not* involved in the operation; among those remaining was Pelton.

Pelton was arrested November 24, 1985, and admitted his crimes to the FBI after an ingenious trap had been set and carefully sprung by two FBI **agents.** They encouraged him to talk, and to imagine he could be a **double agent** for the FBI. Pelton might well have gone free had he said nothing, because the FBI had evidence of only one phone call to a secret Soviet operative, and no evidence of his having observed passing items to a foreign power. They got him to say that he did spy and that what he did might well have endangered America's national interest.

He was accused of exposing Operation IVY BELLS, an offshoot of a **Central Intelligence Agency (CIA)** project that the U.S. Navy and the NSA had taken over; of possibly exposing Operation CHALET/VORTEX (1978); and of revealing an operation involving the U.S. embassy in Moscow, a joint operation with the British, and other operations involving Soviet signals and intercepted communications.

Pelton was convicted on June 5, 1986, and sentenced to life in prison.

Sources: Allen, Thomas B., and Norman Polmar, *Merchants of Treason: America's Secrets for Sale* (New York: Delacorte Press, 1988); Bowman, M. E., "The 'Worst Spy': Perceptions of Espionage," *American Intelligence Journal* 18 (1998): 57–62; Richelson, Jeffrey T., *A Century of Spies: Intelligence in the Twentieth Century* (New York: Oxford University Press, 1995); Woodward, Bob, *Veil: The Secret Wars of the CIA, 1981–87* (New York: Simon & Schuster, 1987).

PENKOVSKY, OLEG VLADIMIROVICH (1919–1963). Penkovsky was a high-ranking Soviet military figure who, for a brief period in the early 1960s, informed the West on many aspects of Soviet military strengths and weaknesses, and is believed to have contributed much to the ending of the Cuban missile crisis (1962).

Penkovsky was born into a respected Russian family; his father was an engineer and a lieutenant in Russia's White Army. He died in the Russian Civil War (1918–1920), when Oleg was only four months old. Family members included a judge, military officers, and politicians.

An only child, Penkovsky started school at age eight, became an outstanding student, and in 1939 graduated from the Kiev Military School. In **World War II** he held both political and military posts, became a member of the Communist Party, and was wounded in 1944. He married Vera Gapanovich (1930–), and in 1946 they had a daughter, Galina.

Penkovsky studied at a military academy (1945–1948), and by 1953 was a senior intelligence officer in the Soviet army. In Ankara, Turkey, he was a **GRU agent** and assistant military attaché (1955–1956) when first noticed by Western intelligence as a possible defector.

In 1960 Penkovsky tried, through students, to make an offer to American authorities in Moscow shortly after the trial of Francis Gary Powers (1930–1977). The offer was regarded as a provocative move by a plant. In November 1960, in Moscow, Greville Wynne (1919–1990), a British businessman who planned to enter into trading relations with Russia and had close ties to the British intelligence community, met Penkovsky. In time they became close friends. In April 1961 Penkovsky gave Greville a package containing information on his career and valuable secret information that showed he would be of great value to the West's intelligence community.

Two weeks later Penkovsky came to London with six colleagues, apparently on a trade mission. After working all day with the trade organization, at night he met **Central Intelligence Agency (CIA)** and **SIS** officials; he told them what he knew of Russian missiles, and passed more documents on many Soviet secrets to the West. In October 1961 he returned to Moscow, and in November he and Vera, who was pregnant with their second daughter, took a vacation. He began his espionage activities again in December 1961.

On July 2, 1962, Greville Wynne flew to Moscow to see Penkovsky, who said he felt that the **KGB** was watching him. However, he dismissed the feeling because as a high-ranking GRU officer he was virtually untouchable.

Penkovsky was able to tell the United States of the limits of Russian power, and to give **John F. Kennedy** (1917–1963) three days grace in which to decide what to do in the Cuban missile crisis (October 1962). Penkovsky revealed the Soviet's lack of warheads and a guidance system, and showed that **Nikita Khrushchev** (1894–1971) was bluffing. He gave the United States the operating manual for the equipment that the Russians were taking to Cuba. His espionage for the West ended in August 1962.

Penkovsky was arrested October 22, 1962, and in May 1963, with Greville Wynne, was found guilty of treason. He was shot five days later.

Penkovsky's personal motivation has always been questionable. Views include that he hated Nikita Khrushchev; perhaps he sought to avenge the death of his father, who died while serving in Russia's White Army in its conflict with the Communists; he hated the Communist system; he had deep religious convictions; he was vain; he was deeply angered at the slow rise he had endured in the Soviet bureaucracy; he suffered from bipolar disorder; and his morals were corrupt.

Others believe that Penkovsky was the channel through which the interests of the anti-Khrushchev faction, comprising influential Russians who believed him to be too hard on the new U.S. President, could flow. Central to these views was the firm belief that Khrushchev could threaten the United States, but did not have the resources to follow up the threats, much less to undertake a nuclear first strike.

Another opinion suggests that Penkovsky was earlier drawn to a better life in the West; and when this was known, he was used by the KGB until he was no longer necessary (i.e., when the Cuban missile crisis ended).

Greville Wynne, a far from reliable source, wrote that Penkovsky was astonished at the personal freedoms he saw in Britain, and he made it clear he needed women, as he said, "to help me forget myself." Also, Penkovsky told Wynne that he felt guilty at being a poor father and husband, and believed "I am something else as well. I'm really two people." When he collected girls around him in Paris, Penkovsky pretended he was an actor and that Wynne was a filmmaker; together they would entertain women lavishly in restaurants. Recent research suggests that during the Cuban missile crisis Penkovsky's intelligence was distorted because opinion leaders and scholars had no access to archives which have recently been made available (Scott, 1999).

See also POWERS, FRANCIS GARY; WYNNE, GREVILLE

Sources: Andrew, Christopher, *For the President's Eyes Only: Secret Intelligence and the American Presidency from Washington to Bush* (London: HarperCollins, 1995); Andrew, Christopher, and Oleg Gordievsky, *KGB: The Inside Story of Its Foreign Operations from Lenin to Gorbachev* (London: Hodder and Stoughton, 1990); Andrew, Christopher, and Vasili Mitrokhin, *The Mitrokhin Archive: The KGB in Europe and the West* (London: Lane, 1999); Brook-Shepherd, Gordon, *The Storm Birds. Soviet Post War Defectors: The Dramatic True Stories 1945–1985* (New York: Henry Holt, 1989); Gibney, Frank, ed., *The Penkovsky Papers: The Russian Who Spied for the West*, Pyotr Deryabin, trans. (London: Collins 1965); Knightley, Phillip, *The Second Oldest Profession: The Spy as Bureaucrat, Patriot, Fantasist and Whore* (London: Andre Deutsch, 1986); Mahoney, Harry T., and Marjorie L. Mahoney, *Biographic Dictionary of Espionage* (San Francisco: Austin & Winfield, 1998); Schechter, Jerrold L., and Peter S. Deriabin, *The Spy Who Saved the World: How a Secret Colonel Changed the Course of the*

Cold War (New York: Scribner's, 1992); Scott, Len, "Espionage and the Cold War: Oleg Penkovsky and the Cuban Missile Crisis," *Intelligence and National Security* 14 (1999): 23–47; West, Nigel, *Seven Spies Who Changed the World* (London: Secker & Warburg, 1991); Wright, Peter, with Paul Greengrass, *Spycatcher: The Candid Autobiography of a Senior Intelligence Officer* (Melbourne: William Heinemann Australia, 1987); Wynne, Greville, *The Man from Moscow*, Arrow ed. 1968 ed. (London: Hutchinson, 1967; Arrow ed., 1968).

PENTAGON PAPERS (1971). The publication of the Pentagon Papers was the result of one man's secret mission against corruption of presidential power in the United States between 1945 and 1968.

The Pentagon Papers contain secret information and have the formal title *History of U.S. Decision-making in Vietnam, 1945–68;* they were first printed primarily in the *New York Times*, beginning June 13, 1971. The publication of the secrets was the result of a personal and secret mission of Daniel Ellsberg (1931–) to undermine the misrepresentations and lies told to the U.S. Congress and the American people by U.S. presidents.

The U.S. Department of Justice attempted to prevent the publication of the material, but on June 30, 1971, the U.S. Supreme Court decided the *New York Times* and the *Washington Post* were free to publish the Pentagon Papers. The Court reminded the U.S. Justice Department that it was forbidden to violate the U.S. Constitution's First Amendment by restraining material before publication.

See also ELLSBERG, DANIEL

Sources: Anonymous, *The Pentagon Papers* (Gravel ed.; Boston: Beacon Press, 1971); Ellsberg, Daniel, *Secrets: A Memoir of Vietnam and the Pentagon Papers* (New York: Viking, 2002); Johnson, Chalmers, "Who's in Charge? Review of Ellsberg, Daniel. 2002. Secrets: A Memoir of Vietnam and the Pentagon Papers," *London Review of Books*, February 6, 2003, pp. 7–9.

PERLO, VICTOR (fl. 1915–1992). Victor Perlo was the leader of a group of U.S. government employees who served the interests of the Soviet Union during the latter stages of **World War II** and in the first year of the **Cold War.**

Victor Perlo was born of Russian Jewish parents who had fled to the United States. He earned an M.A. in mathematics at Columba University, then joined the National Recovery Administration and later the Federal Home Loan Bank Board in 1935. He developed his grasp of economics during two years at the Brookings Institution, and in 1939 joined the Commerce Department. By this time he was an underground member of the **CPUSA.** Three years later he was senior economist at the U.S. War Production Board (WPB). As a Soviet **agent** he was code-named RAIDER.

Perlo was among those who were providing intelligence to the Soviets in the late 1930s, and curtailed their activities after the 1938 defection of Whittaker Chambers (1901–1961).

By early 1944 a group had formed around Perlo, and he saw to it that Elizabeth Bentley (1908–1963) received their material. She was at first their coordinator, and later their courier. The group was amateurish in their **tradecraft**, and internally was subject to personal distress and conflict.

Perlo had become chief of the Aviation Section of the WPB. He and his wife, Katherine, who also worked for the Soviets, were divorced, and Perlo remarried. His former wife had symptoms of schizophrenia. She failed to get custody of their daughter and was living in Texas when she wrote to President Franklin D. Roosevelt (1882–1945) in April 1944, naming her former husband and others as spies for the **U.S.S.R.** The letter was not taken seriously by those in the White House who were responsible for security.

Late in 1945 the work of Perlo's group spying for the Soviets was ending. Between February and October 1945 many U.S. documents were sent by the group to Moscow: these included WPB memoranda concerning aircraft to be sent to Russia if she were to declare war on Japan; WPB reports on aluminum supplies to the U.S.S.R.; production of B-29 bombers; use of Saudi Arabian oil; secret production data on aircraft; data on the Export–Import Bank; the industrial capacities of industrial areas of Western-occupied Germany; and acquisition of bases in Europe for building missiles.

Following the revelations by Elizabeth Bentley, the **Federal Bureau of Investigation (FBI)** hoped to find enough information to prosecute Perlo, who had, with most others, taken the **Fifth Amendment**, when pressed by investigators regarding their association with the Communist cause. In 1947 the FBI had decided it could not prosecute Perlo, and instead arranged to have him, and others, removed from employment where they might be able to continue to serve Russia's interests. Perlo was removed from the Division of Monetary Research.

For many years Perlo denied he was a Communist, saying that all he did was try to help the New Deal become a reality during the Roosevelt presidency. In 1981 he became an open member of the CPUSA. In 1991, when the Party split over Russia's reforms he denounced them as treachery and betrayal. All his life he revered the old leaders of the U.S.S.R.

None of Perlo's group were prosecuted for espionage; it is clear now from the VENONA material that they were working for the Soviets. The group, sometimes called the Perlo/Kramer group, included Edward Joseph Fitzgerald (WPB), who gave information on the specifications of guns, and tanks; Harold Glasser (U.S. Treasury Department), who gave information on economic plans, and was the group's choice to replace Secretary of the Treasury Harry Dexter White (1892–1948); Allan Rosenberg of the Foreign Economic Administration, who gave information on U.S. plans for Germany after **World War II**; Charles Kramer, code-named LOT, an economist who worked for the Kilgore Committee in the U.S. Congress (Senate Committee on War Mobilization); Solomon Aaron Leschinsky and Henry Samuel Magdoff, both of whom worked for the WPB; Alger Hiss (1904–1996) of the State Department; John Abt, who worked on labor and education issues for the La Follette Committee of the U.S. Congress; and David Niven Wheeler, who was on the editorial board of the Research and Analysis Division of the **OSS**.

Sources: Andrew, Christopher, and Vasili Mitrokhin, *The Mitrokhin Archive: The KGB in Europe and the West* (London: Lane, 1999); Bentley, Elizabeth, *Out of Bondage* (New York: Ballantine Books, 1988); Haynes, John Earl, and Harvey Klehr, *Venona: Decoding Soviet Espionage in America* (New Haven, CT: Yale University Press, 1999); Hyde, Earl M., Jr., "Bernard Shuster and Joseph Katz: KGB Master Spies in the United States," *International Journal of Intelligence and Counterintelligence* 12 (1999): 35–57; Klehr, Harvey, John Earl Haynes, and Fredrikh Igorevich Firsov, *The Secret World of American Communism* (New Haven, CT: Yale University Press, 1998); Olmstead, Kathryn, *Red Spy Queen: A Biography of Elizabeth Bentley* (Chapel Hill: University of North Carolina Press, 2002); Perlo, Victor, "Reply to Herbert Aptheker," *Political Affairs* 71 (1992): 25–29; Weinstein, Allen, and Alexander

Vassiliev, *The Haunted Wood: Soviet Espionage in America—The Stalin Era* (New York: Random House, 1999).

PERRY, GEOFFREY E. (1927–2000). Geoffrey Perry was an amateur **Cold War** spy for Britain. While he was a schoolteacher he used rudimentary equipment to uncover secret details of the Soviet space program, and later became a trusted consultant to U.S. government agencies.

At the Kettering Grammar School, Perry and students whom he had trained to interpret satellite signals from a simple radio receiver caused an international concern in 1966, when he announced that the Soviet Union and had begun using a third launching site, whose existence was then secret. The amateur monitoring program, which eventually outgrew the school, and is now an international collaboration called the Kettering Group, became one of the best sources of public information on Soviet satellites as they malfunctioned, fell out of the sky, or simply went about their business routinely.

Perry was first interested in emissions from satellites by a German V-2 rocket that landed near his home during **World War II.** By the early 1960s, with amateur radio equipment, he was monitoring the radio transmissions of telemetry from Soviet satellites.

Perry's methods centered on the Doppler effect, which is based on the observed rising and falling of train whistles as they approach. The effect has a similar consequences for the observation of radio emissions from satellites. The degree and timing of the rise and fall allowed Perry to deduce changes in satellites' altitudes as well as other aspects of their movement.

In 1966, Perry noticed that the Soviet satellites were in a new orbit and were communicating to a new place on the ground. He concluded that the Soviets had begun using a new launching site. In 1978, after a student pointed out irregularities in the motions of the satellites he had been assigned, Perry predicted the crash of the Soviet nuclear-powered satellite. It crashed to earth in Canada.

Source: Anonymous, "Obituary: Geoffrey E. Perry Amateur 'Spy'" 4-8-1927–18-1-2000," *The Age*, January 27, 2000, p. 7.

PETERSON, MARTHA D. (c. 1947–). Martha Peterson was the chance victim of a simple **KGB active measure** in the late 1970s.

Peterson, a widow whose husband had been shot down over Laos in 1973, was posted to the U.S. consulate in Moscow in 1977, and became skilled in Russian. She interviewed Soviet citizens who wanted to immigrate to the United States. A fair-haired, attractive woman with a green belt in tae kwon do, "Mrs. Peterson," as she was known, was a **Central Intelligence Agency (CIA) agent** who worked undercover as a vice consul.

On July 15, 1977, Peterson dressed as a poor Moscow inhabitant and, after shedding her Soviet surveillance agents, was found, by chance, placing a hollowed-out rock in a bridge over the Moscow River in the Lenin Hills. The bridge was being watched for another reason. The KGB claimed that the rock contained poison capsules, a tiny radio and camera, gold, and a microphone. She was accused of servicing a **dead drop** that was to be retrieved by a Russian who worked for the United States. Consequently, she was expelled from the **U.S.S.R.** for espionage.

Izvestia, the Soviet government's newspaper, reported that she was expelled because she had intended to poison a Soviet citizen. The **KGB** claimed that she left
poison for an agent to use against a Russian citizen, and wanted to know who was
to be killed that way.

On June 12, 1978, *Izvestia* published a photo of Peterson; the alleged contents
of the rock appeared on a table before her. At that time two Soviet spies were on
trial for having stolen U.S. naval secrets, and the KGB used what it alleged she was
hiding to retaliate with propaganda to discredit the United States. Her story was
reported in *Newsweek* two weeks later.

Sources: Mahoney, Harry T., and Marjorie L. Mahoney, *Biographic Dictionary of Espionage* (San Francisco: Austin & Winfield, 1998); Richelson, Jeffrey T., *American Espionage
and the Soviet Target* (New York: William Morrow, 1987); Wise, David, *The Spy Who Got
Away: The Inside Story of the CIA Agent Who Betrayed His Country* (London: Fontana/Collins,
1988).

PETROV AFFAIR (1954–1956). The Petrov Affair was one of the early Soviet
spy dramas of the **Cold War.** A Russian spy, Vladimir Petrov (1907–1991) and his
wife, Evdokia (1914–2002), defected to the West via **ASIO.**

In Australia the defection became an important political event when it was said
that the Australian Prime Minister at the time, **Robert Gordon Menzies** (1894–
1978), had conspired with ASIO officers to use the defection and the publicity surrounding it in a political campaign against the **Australian Labor Party (ALP)** and
its leader, Dr. Herbert V. Evatt (1894–1965). The Petrov Affair split the ALP, and
many of its supporters formed the Democratic Labor Party (DLP), a strongly anti-
Communist group supported by many Catholic intellectuals.

The defection provided information on Soviet penetration of British intelligence
agencies, but the alleged conspiracy theory has little support. The character of the
alleged spy ring around Petrov was exaggerated at the time; it was primarily a local
group of amateurs rather than a sophisticated espionage unit. In 1996 Evdokia Petrov
gave interviews to ASIO officials for the Oral History Section of the National Library
in Canberra. The interviews became public only after her death.

Evdokia died in July 2002, and many points relating to the Petrov Affair were cleared
up. Did the Soviet Union provide funds for the Australian Communist Party (**CPA**)?
She said she saw a suitcase containing U.S.$25,000 marked for delivery to the Austra-
lian Communist Party boss; the Petrovs' defection was in response to an accusation
that they were disloyal shortly after Vladimir Petrov had been promoted to colonel in
the **KGB**; there was no conspiracy with Prime Minister Menzies, who had no part in
their defection; she indicated her wish to defect with a wink to a senior Australian official in Darwin; Rupert Lockwood had composed the infamous document "J," despite denials before a royal commission inquiring into the Petrov defection, and the
ALP and CPA assertion that it was a fabrication by a secret police organization.

As a result of the Petrov Affair the prestige of ASIO rose in the eyes of the **Federal
Bureau of Investigation (FBI), MI5, MI6,** and the **Central Intelligence Agency
(CIA),** which in 1954 stationed an officer permanently in Australia. Intelligence from
the Petrovs identified more than 500 Soviet intelligence operatives, and helped the
career of Charles Spry, head of ASIO. Petrov's memoirs, ghost-written by a former poet
and ASIO officer, Michael Thwaites, appeared as *Empire of Fear* in 1956.

See also PETROV, EVDOKIA; PETROV, VLADIMIR MIKHAILOVICH

Sources: Bialoguski, Michael, *The Petrov Story* (London: William Heinemann, 1955); McKnight, David, *Australia's Spies and Their Secrets* (St. Leonards, NSW: Allen and Unwin, 1994); McKnight, David, "The Moscow–Canberra Cables: How Soviet Intelligence Obtained British Secrets Through the Back Door," *Intelligence and National Security* 13 (1998): 159–170; McQueen, Humphrey, "The Code of Silence," *The Weekend Australian* (Canberra), April 3–4, 2004, pp. 30–31; Manne, Robert, *The Petrov Affair: Politics and Espionage* (Sydney: Pergamon, 1987); Petrov, Vladimir, and Evdokia Petrov, *Empire of Fear* (New York: Praeger, 1956); Koutsoukis, Jason, "Fifty Years on, the Spy Scandal That Heated up the Cold War." *The Age* (Melbourne), April 3, 2004, p. 9.

PETROV, EVDOKIA (1914–2002). Evdokia Petrov was a Soviet **agent** in the Russian embassy in Canberra, Australia, when her husband decided to defect. She, too, defected under highly dramatic circumstances in 1954.

Evdokia "Dusya" Petrov, née Kartsev, was five years old when she and her family left the village of Lipsky, near Moscow, in search of food. In 1924 they settled in Moscow, where she studied English, and at 19 she was encouraged to join the **OGPU.**

By 1934 Petrov was a code breaker and a student of Japanese. Within eight years she became a specialist in these activities, and was promoted. She married in 1936, but her husband fell immediately under suspicion and was banished to a labor camp. In 1938 she married V. Protelarsky and traveled with him as an intelligence officer and cipher expert in her own right.

In Australia, Petrov worked for the Russian embassy, and she and her husband lived in Canberra. When her husband defected on April 3, 1954, she was put under house arrest by the Russians and led to believe her husband had died. She had to decide whether to stay in Australia alone or return to her family in Russia. Her Russian controllers intended that she go back to Russia, where she would meet the fate she deserved as the widow of a would-be enemy of the state.

Petrov was confused, depressed, and anxious when her husband's defection was made public. If she stayed in Australia with him, her family in Russia would probably be murdered; if she returned to Russia, she would lose her freedom and perhaps her life. Her plight became a public calamity, because it appeared Australia had abandoned her. She flew to Darwin on her way to Russia, but on the plane an **ASIO** officer discussed options. During the stopover she still maintained she should return to Russia, even after speaking with her husband on the phone. She went for a moment into the office of an Australian official, and promptly disappeared. The Russians believed she had been kidnapped. This was exactly what ASIO had arranged.

Under the name of Maria Anna Allyson, Petrov lived with her husband in secrecy, in the Melbourne suburb of Bentleigh. She died in July 2002. She had given interviews to ASIO officials in 1996, for the Oral History Section of the National Library in Canberra, on how and why she and her husband had defected.

See also BIALOGUSKI, MICHAEL; PETROV AFFAIR; PETROV, VLADIMIR MIKHAILOVICH

Sources: Bialoguski, Michael, *The Petrov Story* (London: William Heinemann, 1955); Miller, Beverly, and Alan Thornhill, "Secrets of Defection: Petrov, Her Last Interview," *The Herald-Sun* (Melbourne), August 29, 2002, pp. 1, 4; Smith, Wayne, "The Truth That Came in from the Cold," *The Weekend Australian* (Canberra), April 3–4, 2004, p. 31.

PETROV, VLADIMIR MIKHAILOVICH (1907–1991). Vladimir Petrov defected to the West in Sydney, Australia, in April 1954 and provided information on Russian espionage around the world.

Vladimir Mikhailovich Petrov was born Anafasy Mikhailovich Shorokhov in Siberia. His parents were illiterate peasants. When he was seven, his father was killed by lightning. He had two years of schooling (1915–1917) before the Russian Revolution closed the schools.

At the age of 12, Petrov worked to keep the family from starvation. He lived with his mother and two brothers in poverty, and worked as a blacksmith's apprentice for eight years, until a Bolshevik agitator encouraged him to establish a **Komsomol** cell in his village.

After being sent to train in the industrial town of Sverdlovsk, Siberia, in 1927, Petrov became a member of the Communist Party. Two years later, renamed Protelarsky, he organized young factory workers in northern Siberia, and beginning in 1930 served three years in the navy, where he learned cipher operations. By 1933 he was recruited to the Moscow State Security Service, where he became a cipher expert for the **NKVD** under diplomatic cover. He attended the Moscow **show trials** during the late 1930s.

As a major in the NKVD, Petrov maintained communications between concentration camps and the NKVD. When Germany invaded Russia in July 1941, he was renamed Petrov and sent to Sweden. In 1947 he and his wife, Evdokia (1914–2002), returned to Moscow, and three years later where he worked on security matters in the MGB and was promoted to colonel. His cover was an official who worked for the Third Secretary concerned with cultural and consular matters.

On arriving in Australia, Petrov was befriended by a man he thought was a pro-Soviet **mole**, Dr. Michael Bialoguski (1917–1985), a charming, fashionable Sydney doctor worked for **ASIO**, spying on Russians in Australia. They became friends, each apparently trying to engage the other as a **double agent**.

On April 3, 1954, Petrov, much disaffected by political changes in Moscow and also drawn to the comfortable life available in Australia, was persuaded to defect in Sydney; two weeks later his wife followed him, amid much drama and unsuccessful attempts by Russian **agents** to abduct her in Darwin. They were kept in a **safe house** in Palm Beach, where for 18 months Michael Thwaites (1915–), head of ASIO counterespionage and well-known poet, helped the Petrovs write their memoirs. Later, Petrov, who was given £5000 by ASIO, purchased a house for £3500.

Petrov died as Sven Allyson, in secrecy, in the Melbourne suburb of Bentleigh. According to his wife, he had an unhappy life after becoming disenchanted with the way Russia was administered after the death of **Josef Stalin** (1879–1953). He was accused, she said, of establishing a pro-Beria faction within the Communist Party.

See also BERIA, LAVRENTI; BIALOGUSKI, MICHAEL; PETROV AFFAIR; PETROV, EVDOKIA

Sources: Bialoguski, Michael, *The Petrov Story* (London: William Heinemann, 1955); Guilliatt, Richard, "Two of Us: Michael Thwaites and Penelope Thwaites," *The Age Good Weekend* (Melbourne), September 26, 2002, p. 12; McQueen, Humphrey, "The Code of Silence," *The Weekend Australian* (Canberra), April 3–4, 2004, pp. 30–31; Mahoney, Harry T., and Marjorie L. Mahoney, *Biographic Dictionary of Espionage* (San Francisco: Austin & Winfield, 1998); Manne, Robert, *The Petrov Affair: Politics and Espionage* (Sydney: Pergamon, 1987); Miller, Beverly, and Alan Thornhill, "Secrets of Defection: Petrov, Her Last Interview," *The Herald-Sun*, April 29, 2002, pp. 1, 4; Petrov, Vladimir, and Evdokia Petrov, *Empire* *of Fear* (New York: Praeger, 1956); Whitlam, Nicholas, and John Stubbs, *Nest of Traitors: The Petrov Affair* (St Lucia: University of Queensland Press, 1985).

PHILBY, HAROLD ADRIAN RUSSELL "KIM" (1912–1988). Harold Adrian Russell Philby was the most outstanding of the British traitors among the Magnificent Five, and spied for Russia for almost 30 years from the time he was recruited to the Soviet cause at Cambridge in 1934.

Harold Philby was born in the Punjab; his mother was the daughter of a Eurasian public servant, and his father was an eccentric, antiestablishment employee in the Indian Civil Service. Nicknamed "Kim," Philby was educated at Westminster School and Trinity College, Cambridge. While at Cambridge he approached Donald Maclean (1913–1983) and asked him to break with the Communist Party in Britain and begin to work for the **NKVD.**

After graduation Philby married a Jewish Communist in Vienna (1933); they returned to England, and separated in 1937. Philby went to Paris, and then Spain, where he wrote about the **Spanish Civil War** (1937–1939) for *The Times.* At the end of 1940 he was an instructor in the Special Operations Executive (**SOE**); by September 1941 he had joined Section V of **SIS (MI6)** as a counterintelligence expert. In 1943 he was responsible for Section V, and late in 1944 headed the anti-Soviet unit, Section IX. When the SIS was reorganized, Philby became head of both Section V and Section IX.

Philby married again, and in 1947 the family went to Istanbul, where he was head of station. After two years he was posted to Washington, in August 1949. He was there until May 1951, when Guy Burgess (1911–1963) and Donald Maclean (1913–1983) defected. Philby immediately came under suspicion as a Soviet **agent**. It was known that he had been a member of the Communist Party of Great Britain, that his first wife was a Communist; and that his father had a prison record and a reputation for being anti-British. Furthermore, Philby could not expect promotion within the SIS.

The **Central Intelligence Agency (CIA)** decided that since he had been a friend of Guy Burgess, Philby would no longer be accepted in the United States as a liaison officer between the SIS and the CIA. While in Washington he had become one of James J. Angleton's (1917–1987) close friends, and learned much from him about CIA activities.

Following the defection of his colleagues, Philby became known as the "**third man**," the person who had probably tipped off Donald Maclean that he was about to be brought in for interrogation. In November 1951 Philby, no longer accepted in the United States, was forced to resign from the SIS and given a small payout. He had satisfied the SIS authorities that he was not a Communist agent operating as a **mole** inside the SIS; but among members of **MI5** the suspicion remained.

In truth, since recruitment in June 1934, Philby had worked for the Communist cause effectively, providing Moscow with what it wanted to know, especially when he was a close colleague of James Angleton.

Philby's passport, withdrawn when he was interrogated during 1951, was returned in May 1952. Briefly he worked as a freelance journalist, and for 18 months with an import–export firm in London. Family life was difficult because back in 1950, while still in Washington, Philby and his wife Aileen had separated but kept up the appearance of being married. After four years she became psychiatrically ill: depressed, deluded, highly suspicious, and suicidal.

Philby's contact with the **MGB** was broken in 1951 because he would no longer be able to inform Moscow of SIS secrets. In 1954 he met Anthony Blunt (1907–1983), who may have tried to have Philby given financial support by the Soviets.

In 1955, a year after the Petrov defection (April 1954), the press again linked Philby's name to the "third man." British libel laws prevented publication of anything that said Philby had been the man who warned Donald Maclean to leave. But in the U.K. Parliament a member is protected from such laws, and could announce that Philby was in fact the "third man," and he was quoted in the press. This happened, and the statement was quoted in London's *Evening Standard*.

Philby was interrogated once more by the SIS, which again concluded that he was innocent, and sent that finding to the British government. The SIS also said that if Philby had been guilty, as MI5 colleagues still maintained, he would not have behaved the way he did over the last four years (1951–1955).

Victorious, Philby called a press conference in December 1955, after Prime Minister **Harold Macmillan** (1894–1986) had spoken in support of him in Parliament, and deftly fended off any further accusations from the press. In the summer of 1956 he was asked to serve the SIS in the Middle East, under journalistic cover. He would be paid by both the SIS and the newspaper. He agreed immediately.

Philby's mother died early in 1957; his second wife, Aileen, died in December of that year. In 1958 he married his third wife in Beirut, and went through the ceremony again in London in 1959. His father died in 1960.

In Beirut, Philby was under SIS instructions to get information on Arab nationalist leaders, most of whom were known personally to his late father. His information satisfied the SIS. Now a spy for only the SIS in Beirut, Philby had no contact with the **KGB**. In 1958 **Moscow Center** called him back into the fold.

Philby served the Soviets again until 1963, when Nicholas Elliott (1916–1994), an old friend and the Beirut head of station, told him that the British now knew Philby always had been a Soviet agent. Philby was offered the chance to retire from the SIS and live incognito in Britain, without being charged with treason, provided he told the SIS everything.

In January 1963 Philby crossed the border into the **U.S.S.R.**, and lived there until he died in 1988. In Moscow he married again, and his Russian wife, Rufina, wrote that at the end of his life he was depressed and alcoholic.

Philby was never wholly trusted by the KGB, which opened his mail and bugged his phone. Films, novels, and TV programs were made about him and his career, and he published his memoirs.

See also ANGLETON, JAMES; BLUNT, ANTHONY; BURGESS, GUY; CAIRNCROSS, JOHN; MACLEAN, DONALD; MAGNIFICENT FIVE; PETROV, VLADIMIR

Sources: Andrew, Christopher, and Oleg Gordievsky, *KGB: The Inside Story of Its Foreign Operations from Lenin to Gorbachev* (London: Hodder and Stoughton, 1990); Andrew, Christopher, and Vasili Mitrokhin, *The Mitrokhin Archive: The KGB in Europe and the West* (London: Lane, 1999); Borovik, Genrikh, *The Philby Files: The Secret Life of Master Spy Philby (1912–88)*, Antonina W. Bouis, trans. (Boston: Little, Brown, 1994); Bower, Tom, *The Perfect English Spy: Sir Dick White and the Secret War 1935–90* (London: Heinemann, 1995); Boyle, Andrew, *The Fourth Man: The Definitive Account of Kim Philby, Guy Burgess, Donald Maclean and Who Recruited Them to Spy for Russia* (New York: Dial Press, 1979); Brown,

Anthony Cave, *Treason in the Blood: H. St. John Philby, Kim Philby, and the Spy Case of the Century* (London: Robert Hale 1994); Costello, John, and Oleg Tsarev, *Deadly Illusions* (New York: Crown, 1993); Knightley, Phillip, *Philby: The Life and Views of the KGB Masterspy* (London: Pan, 1988); Philby, Kim, *My Secret War* (London: MacGibbon and Kee, 1968); Philby, Rufina, *The Private Life of Kim Philby: The Moscow Years* (London: St. Ermin's, 1999); Sheehan, Edward R. F., "The Rise and Fall of a Soviet Agent," in Allen Dulles, ed., *Great True Spy Stories* (Secaucus, NJ: Castle, 1968), pp. 49–72; Volkman, Ernest, *Espionage: The Greatest Spy Operations of the 20th Century* (New York: Wiley, 1995); West, Nigel, *The Friends: Britain's Post-War Secret Operations* (London: Weidenfeld and Nicolson, 1988).

PITTS, EARL EDWIN (fl. 1987–1997). Earl Pitts was a senior **Federal Bureau of Investigation (FBI) agent,** who received U.S.\$224,000 from Russian intelligence for providing top-secret documents to the **KGB/SVR,** including a list of FBI personnel who were providing intelligence on Russia.

In July 1987 Pitts, a new agent in the FBI's New York City field office, wrote to an officer in the Soviet mission at the United Nations and asked to see a KGB officer. Nine times between 1988 and 1992 Pitts provided documents to his KGB/SVR handler, Aleksandr Karpov. After each meeting there was a deposit in one of Pitts's bank accounts scattered around Washington. After 1992 Pitts ceased his spying for Russia.

Pitts was named as a secret agent by his Soviet handler, Aleksandr Karpov, when he became a **double agent** for the FBI. The FBI set a trap for Pitts, using FBI agents posing as Russians. Without any trouble they got him to agree to return to espionage. For 15 months Pitts provided these bogus agents with classified documents and received $65,000. Pitts's wife told the FBI that she suspected her husband of espionage.

Pitts was arrested in December 1996 at the FBI Academy in Quantico, Virginia, and charged with providing classified information to the Russian intelligence services from 1987 to 1992. Following the discovery of a computer disk with a letter to his supposed Russian handler, Pitts decided to plead guilty. He explained that he held many grievances against the FBI and had spied in revenge against the organization. He was sentenced to 27 years in prison in June 1997.

Sources: Bowman, M. E., "The 'Worst Spy': Perceptions of Espionage," *American Intelligence Journal* 18 (1998): 57–62; Mahoney, Harry T., and Marjorie L. Mahoney, *Biographic Dictionary of Espionage* (San Francisco: Austin & Winfield, 1998).

POLLARD, ANNE HENDERSON (1960–). Anne Pollard helped her husband, Jonathan Jay Pollard (1954–) spy for Israel and conceal his espionage activities.

Anne Henderson Pollard took night in classes in the University of Maryland while a secretary at Washington's American Institute of Architects. She met and married Jonathan J. Pollard, an intelligence officer in the U.S. Navy. After their marriage she worked in public relations with the National Rifle Association.

Pollard became aware of her husband's espionage for Israel. He stole documents from his workplace and held them in their apartment for copying. He warned her that if he should be in trouble, he would telephone her and say a code word, "cactus"; and this would be her instruction to get rid of the documents in their apartment.

In November 1985 Jonathan Pollard made such a call and said the code word; Anne Pollard took a suitcase filled with documents to a neighbor's house. On returning to their apartment she found her husband with naval security agents who had boxes of documents she had failed to notice.

Jonathan Pollard contacted the Israeli embassy and was assured by his case officer that the Israeli government would help him and his wife to leave the United States and live in Israel. A few days later the Pollards prepared to leave the United States via the Israeli embassy, but they were not allowed into the embassy compound.

The Pollards were arrested and charged with espionage. Jonathan was sentenced to life imprisonment. Anne defended herself by stating she acted out of love and duty to her husband, and she believed she was helping him and doing no harm to the country. She was sentenced to five years in prison.

See also POLLARD, JONATHAN JAY

Sources: Blitzer, Wolf, *Territory of Lies: The Exclusive Story of Jonathan Jay Pollard, the American Who Spied on His Country for Israel, and How He Was Betrayed* (New York: Harper & Row, 1989); Mahoney, M. H., *Women in Espionage* (Santa Barbara, CA: ABC-CLIO, 1993); Raviv, Dan, and Yossi Melman, *Every Spy a Prince* (Boston: Houghton Mifflin, 1990).

POLLARD, JONATHAN JAY (1954–). Jonathan Jay Pollard was an ideological, peace-loving American and a Zionist zealot who appeared to be unstable and egocentric. He spied for the Israeli government, was caught, and was sentenced to life imprisonment. His long sentence appears to be related to the presence of several Israeli spies who sought U.S. technology in the early 1980s.

Jonathan Pollard was born into a Jewish family in Galveston, Texas, and raised in South Bend, Indiana. He went to Tufts University, and was remembered as being emotionally troubled, having a powerful a imagination, and later as making false claims that he held a high military post in the Israeli army and was being trained in intelligence. Once he apparently claimed to have killed an Arab while on active duty in the Israeli army.

After graduating from Stanford in 1977, Pollard applied for, and was rejected by, the **Central Intelligence Agency (CIA)**, on the grounds of occasional drug use. He studied law at Tufts University, but in 1979, before completing the degree, he began to work for U.S. Navy as an intelligence analyst, and later was assigned to the antiterrorism center in the Naval Investigative Service. In this position he saw much classified information.

In 1981 Pollard's security clearance was taken away because he appeared to have emotional problems and to behave strangely; it was suggested he get treatment, but instead he found a way to have the decision reversed and have his security clearance reestablished.

In May 1984 Pollard made friends with an officer in the Israeli air force, and said that the United States did not properly share its intelligence with Israel. These conversations led to Pollard's being approached by the Israeli Bureau of Scientific Liaisons (**LAKAM**) to provide Israel with satellite photos of the Middle East, especially Iraq.

The Israelis found Pollard's information very valuable. The data related to new weapons systems in Egypt, Jordan, and Saudi Arabia. Photos of **PLO** residences were provided, too. The data helped in the September 1985 Israeli attack on the PLO. Pollard became engaged to Anne Henderson.

The Israelis flew the couple to Paris and gave them U.S.$10,000, jewelry, and a monthly stipend of U.S.$1,500. In August, they were wed and spent their honeymoon in Venice, paid for by Israel. Jonathan Pollard was given a false passport in the name of Danny Cohen, and a Swiss bank account was opened for him to receive his expenses and a regular salary. Pollard provided the Israelis with suitcases of documents and aerial photographs. The Israelis got U.S. military plans, maps, and reconnaissance photographs taken all over the Middle East. He was the best asset that the Israelis ever had.

In time Pollard's tasks at work began to overwhelm him, and his supervisor noticed he had on his desk files that were unrelated to his work; later a colleague saw him leaving work with packages of material, and it was found that his computer had recently accessed secret files and Middle East messages that were not related to his everyday duties. Navy counterintelligence **agents** installed TV monitors at Pollard's workplace, and learned he was amassing a vast store of secret material for his personal use.

On November 18, 1985, Pollard was arrested and interrogated; during a break in questioning, he phoned his wife, Anne, and, in code, told her to take away the cases of documents at his home. Anne took them to a woman friend at a neighboring home, but the friend, the daughter of a Navy officer, telephoned the Naval Intelligence Service after looking in the suitcases.

Pollard contacted his Israeli handler, who said he should come to the Israeli embassy, and they would help. Imagining that the Israelis would give him and his wife political asylum and safe transit to Israel, Pollard went to the embassy, was turned away, and was immediately arrested by the **Federal Bureau of Investigation (FBI).**

Pollard, 32, was sentenced to life in prison, and his wife served three years of a five-year sentence.

In the late 1980s in Washington there were many pro-Jewish lobbyists who were suspected of serving **Mossad** illegally, and the U.S.–Israeli intelligence alliance fell to a low point.

In 1993 President Bill Clinton (1946–) refused to cut Pollard's sentence after a request from Yitzhak Rabin (1922–1995). Reasons were the government's need to maintain control over the distribution of classified information to a foreign power; the damaging effect of Pollard's disclosures; and Pollard's inclusion of classified material in letters he sent from prison

In 1994, with the support of the Israeli government, Pollard sought to have his sentence commuted, but President Clinton and Congress refused. Rumors indicated that one reason for the refusal was the convincing evidence that other Americans were spying for Israel. The rumors were not substantiated, and the Israelis offered to turn over documents that allegedly had been obtained through Pollard's efforts so the United States might assess the alleged damage Pollard's work had caused. The Israelis mistakenly included among the returned data a classified document from their archives that could never been supplied to them by Pollard, thereby supporting the U.S. suspicion that other Americans were working for Israel within the U.S. government.

In July 1995 Pollard tried again, and was again turned down. Laffin (1996) writes that in 1995 Israel and the United States made a deal to free Pollard and that he went to live in Israel. The deal did not go through.

An organization established to get Pollard's release (Anonymous, 2003) has argued vehemently that the United States had made frequent commitments to Israel that Pollard would be released. In November 2001 Pollard was still serving a life sentence. The organization maintains that his sentence was disproportionate to the admissions he made—he was never tried; the plea bargain was not honored; secret evidence was used; the charge of treason was technically false; the sentencing judge communicated inappropriately with the prosecutors; and the sentencing procedure was based on false allegations.

The final argument advanced to support Pollard's release, was that President Clinton, who pardoned many lawbreakers just before he left office, promised clemency for Pollard. But Clinton would not allow the release of Pollard to the Israelis in return for concessions from Israel in its conflict with and incarceration of Palestinians.

Supporters of Pollard argue that his sentence was not due to the crime he committed, but to his stumbling on dealings between the White House and Saddam Hussein during the presidency of **Ronald Reagan** (1911–2004).

See also POLLARD, ANNE HENDERSON

Sources: Anonymous, "The Facts of the Pollard Case" (2003), www.jonathanpollard org/facts.htm; Black, Ian, and Benny Morris, *Israel's Secret Wars: The Untold History of Israeli Intelligence* (London: Hamish Hamilton, 1991); Bowman, M. E., "The 'Worst Spy': Perceptions of Espionage," *American Intelligence Journal* 18 (1998): 57–62; Deacon, Richard, *Spyclopedia: The Comprehensive Handbook of Espionage* (New York: Silver Arrow Books/William Morrow, 1987); Goldenberg, Elliot, *The Hunting Horse: The Truth Behind the Jonathon Pollard Spy Case* (New York: Prometheus Books, 2000); Hersh, Seymour M., *The Samson Option: Israel's Nuclear Arsenal and American Foreign Policy* (New York: Random House, 1991); Kahana, Ephraim, "Mossad–CIA Cooperation," *International Journal of Intelligence and Counterintelligence* 14 (2001): 409–420; Mahoney, Harry T., and Marjorie L. Mahoney, *Biographic Dictionary of Espionage* (San Francisco: Austin & Winfield, 1998); Raviv, Dan, and Yossi Melman, *Every Spy a Prince* (Boston: Houghton Mifflin, 1990); Raviv, Dan, and Yossi Melman, *Friends Indeed: Inside the U.S.–Israel Alliance* (New York: Hyperion, 1994); Yaniv, Avner, *Politics and Strategy in Israel* (Tel Aviv: Sifryat Poalim, 1994).

POLYAKOV, DIMITRI FEDOROVICH (1921–1988). Beginning in the early 1960s, Dimitri Polyakov was one of the most valuable **GRU** spies to provide material for the United States for over 20 years.

Dimitri Polyakov was the son of a Ukrainian bookkeeper, served as an artillery officer in **World War II**, and afterward was sent to the prestigious Frunze Military Academy, where after graduation he was recruited into the GRU. He was posted to New York in 1951 as a member of the UN mission. His task was to steal technological secrets.

Polyakov returned to Moscow in 1956; was posted to Berlin, where he ran **illegals** into West Germany; and was promoted to colonel. By 1959 he was becoming disillusioned with the Russian system and the inadequate salary he received. He came to the attention of two **Federal Bureau of Investigation (FBI) agents** in 1961. Later he approached an American diplomat and for 25 years worked as a **double agent** until he was betrayed by another traitor.

Code-named TOP HAT, Polyakov was recruited to the **Central Intelligence Agency (CIA)** in New York, when he was about to return to Russia in 1962. He worked for the CIA for many years while holding the highest rank within the **GRU.**

Polyakov was dissatisfied not only with the system that did not pay him enough, but also with U.S.S.R. government, because it did not look after its people, intended to go into a war against the United States that it was unable to win, and would lead the Russian people into great suffering. He told the FBI about many traitors in the

United States who were working for the Russians, including Jack E. Dunlap (fl. 1935–1963) and the British researcher Frank Bossard (1912–).

When assigned to Rangoon, Burma, Polyakov provided the CIA with GRU details on Chinese and Vietnamese military forces, and internal data on the **Sino–Soviet split** (1960–1971), which immeasurably helped the administration of President **Richard Nixon** (1913–1994) to secure relations with to China and to end the **Vietnam War.**

Polyakov was made a general by 1974, and in 1978 was reassigned to Moscow. As such he was one of the most highly valued agents working for the CIA by 1980. From his reports the CIA learned that Russia had concluded she was unable to win a nuclear war.

In January 1985 Polyakov was betrayed by Rick Ames (1941–), a CIA officer who had approached the KGB with the promise of obtaining anything they wanted to know. Polyakov was tried in secret, and at his trial said he was critical of the Russian leadership, its nuclear missile strategy, and its use of chemical and biological warfare. After he was caught, he spent three years expecting to die. He was executed with a bullet to the back of the head, and buried in an unmarked grave.

See also AMES, ALDRICH HAZEN; OPERATION TOP HAT

Sources: Earley, Pete, *Confessions of a Spy: The Real Story of Aldrich Ames* (London: Hodder and Stoughton, 1997); Mangold, Tom, *Cold Warrior: James Jesus Angleton, the CIA Master Spy Hunter* (New York: Simon & Schuster, 1991); Volkman, Ernest, *Espionage: The Greatest Spy Operations of the 20th Century* (New York: Wiley, 1995).

PONTECORVO, BRUNO (1913–1993). Bruno Pontecorvo was one of the **atom spies** who served Soviet interests while working on the **atom bomb** in the United States.

A Jew, Bruno Pontecorvo was born August 22, 1913, and raised amid wartime uncertainties. The family comprised eight children and lived in a two-story house in Pisa.

In 1938, under Adolf Hitler's (1889–1945) influence, Benito Mussolini (1883–1945) came down heavily on Jews in Italy. The family business faltered, and its members divided; one group went to England and the other, including Bruno, Paul, and Gilberto, to other nations in Europe or North America. The most able of all the family, Bruno went to university, where he studied math and physics, and in Rome took a doctorate in physics (1934).

Pontecorvo worked under Enrico Fermi (1901–1954) and won a national fellowship (1936) to study in Paris, where he met and married Hellene Marianne Nordblum, a Swedish student; on July 30, 1938, their first child was born. Pontecorvo worked under Frédéric Joliot-Curie at the Institute of Radium in Paris, and in 1939 toured laboratories in Scandinavia, the Netherlands, and Switzerland. He married Hellene in January 1940.

The family escaped from Europe through Spain and Portugal to the United States. On the way they declared to different authorities that they were variously medical doctors or had commercial interests. Pontecorvo got a job in Tulsa, Oklahoma, doing radiographic oil-well logging, and filed for a patent for an invention had devised for this process. In 1943, it was suggested that, with others, he join the Anglo–Canadian research group in Montreal doing atomic energy research. He still had an Italian passport, but had filed for U.S. citizenship in 1941.

For the next nine years Pontecorvo was often undecided about his preferred nationality and occupation. For six years he worked on the Chalk River heavy water project near the Deep River settlement. After the war he was asked by the British Ministry of Supply to stay on and conduct further experiments in Canada.

Twice Pontecorvo was investigated for security reasons, and at no time was he found to be a security risk. He never talked politics, and associated with men who were loyal to their scientific work in North America.

Pontecorvo was offered many jobs at American universities, and had to decide whether to be an American citizen or a British subject, an academic or a civil servant.

In December 1947 a trip to Europe decided him. Pontecorvo went alone to England and secured an offer to work at the British nuclear research center at Harwell; he went next to Milan and planned to return by ship to New York in January 1948. But he left from Italy by train, met friends in Paris over New Year, missed the boat, and flew to America on January 6. He was due to complete naturalization papers for his American citizenship by mid-April, but changed his mind; and in February 1948, while visiting Canada, he took out British citizenship, and the next year set out for Harwell as Senior Principal Scientific Officer.

At Harwell, while Klaus Fuchs's (1911–1988) trial was pending in February 1950, Pontecorvo spoke on personal matters with the security officer at Harwell, Henry Arnold.

Pontecorvo was buoyant and likable, dark, handsome, well-mannered, and charming. He was a flirt, and an asset at a cocktail party. Because he was so generous and careless with his money, he was often broke. Artless, frank and genuine, he was unlike what one would expect a spy to be. He seemed lazy and irresponsible, was a good tennis player, and loved to drive about England. A respected and able scientist, he was creative and thought to be an original thinker.

Pontecorvo's wife rarely attended the parties and tennis groups that her husband loved. She was shy, blonde, pretty, and without friends; those who knew her thought that she had become anxious and shy as she aged. She stayed at home and cared for their three children. She did all the housework, although on his salary of £1,300 a year she could have employed help. They never entertained. Their house was cheerless and bare, more like a camp than a home.

In 1950 Pontecorvo's problem was that his brother, Gilberto, was a Communist living in Italy. Bruno was hoping for a post at Liverpool University, and his brother's politics might affect his chances of being appointed. In May 1950 he was even more restless, even though he and the family had settled down in England. He tried to find academic positions in Italy and America. That month he lectured in Paris, visited Brussels, negotiated for work with the Anglo–Iranian Oil Company, and in September went with several Harwell scientists to a conference at Lake Como in Italy. He was still looking for a high academic post, and was interested in applying for positions in physics at universities in Rome and Pisa.

In further discussions with Henry Arnold at Harwell, Pontecorvo said that if he were successful in his academic applications, he would revert to Italian citizenship. But his application to Pisa arrived too late, and he abandoned his proposal to go to Paris when he was offered a job at Liverpool. Distressed at what was happening at the trial of Klaus Fuchs, Pontecorvo spoke further with Henry Arnold.

Pontecorvo admitted to having met Gilberto at Lake Como, and he added that others in his family had Communist sympathies. The lighthearted side of Pontecorvo's character was absent, and he seemed to feel that he was under close surveillance.

Aware of a report from Sweden that stated Pontecorvo and his wife were Communists, Henry Arnold watched and listened to Pontecorvo even more closely. Pontecorvo went to Liverpool to see about the job there, but appeared reluctant to go; the research technology was outstanding, but he was unsure about the work. Finally, he accepted the position and decided to begin on January 1, 1951. In June 1950, the family went to Cornwall briefly, then planned a camping trip in Italy beginning July 25, 1950; they would take their new car, visit family members, and camp out on the way with new equipment. But at a party before they left Pontecorvo's wife was seen crying.

The trip across Europe was both haphazard and joyful. But on August 22, Pontecorvo's thirty-seventh birthday, things started to go wrong. His car collided with a cyclist, and later the children suffered sunstroke; he cabled his family to say he could not meet them in France because of car trouble and the children's illness. Five days later he took the family to Rome, but their family in Rome was not able to accommodate all of them. On August 29 he and his wife booked tickets for Stockholm. He sent a postcard to Harwell saying goodbye. On September 2 they flew from Stockholm to Helsinki, Finland. They were met at the airport, and taken away with their luggage by car.

Apparently, **Moscow Center** decided no longer to risk their **agents**, and evacuated Pontecorvo and his family through Finland by a well-tried route. Subsequently, Pontecorvo worked in physics, was honored frequently—the Order of Lenin twice—and always denied being an atom spy. According to Pavel and Anatoli Sudoplatov (1994), he acted as a conduit for atomic secrets to the Russians from Enrico Fermi.

Late in 1942 Pontecorvo had provided information on the first nuclear chain reaction; in 1943 he told his Russian contacts that Enrico Fermi was willing to provide even more information, and he met with Russian **illegals** in the United States and Mexico to further this work. In September 1945 he had provided a report on the atomic bomb detonated in July 1945. In 1946, when he was in Italy and Switzerland, he had met an agent who planned his escape route. The escape was regarded as a success because it prevented the **Federal Bureau of Investigation (FBI)** and **MI5** from finding other sources of atomic secrets.

On March 1, 1965, Pontecorvo published an article in *Pravda*, and later held an interview in which he said that he had worked on atomic projects of a nonmilitary kind, and praised the efforts of the U.S.S.R. for international peace. He died in Dubna, the nuclear research center outside Moscow, in 1993. His **code name** may have been HURON, MLAD, or YOUNGSTER.

See also FUCHS, EMIL JULIUS KLAUS

Sources: Andrew, Christopher, and Oleg Gordievsky, *KGB: The Inside Story of Its Foreign Operations* (London: Hodder and Stoughton, 1990); Hyde, H. Montgomery, *The Atom Bomb Spies* (London: Hamish Hamilton, 1980); Moorehead, Alan, *The Traitors: The Double Life of Fuchs, Pontecorvo and Nunn May* (London: Hamish Hamilton, 1952); Pilat, Oliver, *The Atom Spies* (London: Allen, 1954); Sudoplatov, Pavel, and Anatoli Sudoplatov, *Special Tasks: The Memoirs of an Unwanted Witness, a Soviet Spymaster* (Boston: Little, Brown, 1994).

POPOV, PYOTR SEMYONOVICH (1922–1960). Pyotr Popov, a Russian infantry officer who had transferred to the **GRU**, volunteered his services to the **Central Intelligence Agency (CIA)** in 1952; he was arrested and executed in 1959.

Pyotr Popov was born in 1922 and raised in a poor district a few kilometers southeast of Khady, near the Volga River. When he was eight, a commissar came to turn the local farms into a collective farm. His father objected, and the family was taken away next day to Khady, to await further orders. The family was ultimately pardoned.

In 1935, when Popov was 13, his father died. In 1938, aged 16, Popov was transferred to a middle school in Tula, 300 miles from his village; in September 1939, after the Nazi invasion of Poland, Russian forces occupied some parts of the land. In April 1940, at 18, Popov found his school had been made into a military academy; by September 1941, he was a junior lieutenant assigned to an ammunition train to service the front line against Nazi armies. After four years on the central front, and being twice wounded, in 1943 he was, as a matter of course, accepted into the Communist Party.

In December 1944, Popov was interviewed for entrance to the Frunze Military Academy, the Soviet command's staff college. In March 1945, at the academy he began a three-year course to become an officer and eventually a general.

Popov fell in love with a woman named Galina, and they married in December 1945. They were given a two-bedroom flat with a shared bathroom, which at that time was a luxury apartment in Moscow. They had a son and a daughter, and in 1948, without choice, Popov was assigned to the Chief Intelligence Directorate of the Soviet General Staff, and attended a military intelligence school. In June 1951 he graduated, and was posted to Vienna in 1952. Popov had battled his way into a high level of Soviet society.

Nothing could erase Popov's memory of his family's early years of misery. He considered **Josef Stalin** (1879–1953) a maniacal tyrant, and his successors to be henchmen. Popov wanted to smash the Soviet Union and allow Russian peasants to become farmers, occupy their own land, and live without the presence of secret police.

In January 1953, in Vienna, Popov dropped a letter into the automobile of a U.S. Foreign Service official. Once Popov's information had squared with what the CIA knew, the next question they had to ask him was why he would risk his life as a spy. The CIA learned that Popov loathed the secret police and all the trappings of state security, and he was tired of duplicity and half-truths, and the relegation of the individual to nothing in the Soviet system.

When Popov approached the CIA, he had a mistress whom he had recruited. He found that he did not have enough money to keep both her and his family. And if his boss, whom Popov hated, found out that Popov had a mistress, he would be deported to Siberia.

Popov supplied information to the CIA, but he took too many risks, drank too much, and would not always follow directions. He identified over 650 GRU officers, and provided many leads to their **agents.**

A rumor spread that in 1956 George Blake (1922–) had read a letter written by Popov to his CIA case officer. Blake saw that there was a **mole** inside the GRU, and that was a threat to him. Blake informed the Russians. Later it was found that a case that involved Russian **illegals** was compromised, and Popov was the only GRU case officer who had known the details of the case.

When the **KGB** was sure it had its man, it carefully had Popov's wife and children moved, and tried to ensure there was no suspicion that their agent had been identified. Some KGB officials hoped they could turn Popov around, and play him against the West. Later it appeared that George Blake had not been involved in finding Popov's treachery.

Popov was arrested in October 1959 and was tried on January 6–7, 1960. He was found guilty and sentenced to death. He was executed by firing squad in June 1960. No public statements about him were made until March 1963, when suspicious activities attributed to "P" were described in *Izvestia*. The articles read like KGB propaganda, and "P" appeared to be Popov.

Unlike other sources on Popov, Murphy et al. (1997) provide information from both sides in the **Cold War.**

Sources: Hood, William, *Mole: The True Story of the First Russian Intelligence Officer Recruited by the CIA* (New York: Norton, 1982); Hyde, H. Montgomery, *George Blake: Superspy* (London: Constable, 1987); Murphy, David E., Sergei A. Kondrashev, and George Bailey, *Battleground Berlin: CIA vs KGB in the Cold War* (New Haven, CT: Yale University Press, 1997); Pincher, Chapman, *Traitors: The Anatomy of Treason* (New York: St. Martin's Press, 1987).

POWERS, FRANCIS GARY (1929–1977). Francis Gary Powers, a U-2 spy plane pilot downed over Russia on May 1 1960, was captured, tried, and given 10 years in a Russian prison. Powers had made **U-2 spy flights** along the borders of Turkey, Afghanistan, the southern Caspian Sea, the Black Sea, and the Soviet Union between 1956 and May 1, 1960. Assured that Powers's plane could not be recovered, President **Dwight D. Eisenhower** (1890–1969) issued the usual plausible denial. But later that May it was obvious that America was using U-2 aircraft to spy on Russia, much to America's embarrassment.

Francis Gary Powers was born into a working-class family in Burdine, Kentucky; his father had been a pit miner, was injured, and began a small shoe repair business. His mother was a housewife and helped on their tiny farm. Powers was educated at Milligan College; he married and had no children.

In 1950 Powers volunteered for the U.S. Air Force, and was trained in Greenwich, Missouri, and Phoenix, Arizona. After graduating, he was made a first lieutenant. His task was to fly along the **U.S.S.R.** border, seeking information on radar and radio stations.

Powers was recruited into the U-2 spy plane program, trained for seven months, and was **sheep-dipped** to provide the plausible deniability that a government needs if its clandestine missions fail. He signed with the **Central Intelligence Agency (CIA)** and was sworn to secrecy; the penalty for breaking the secrecy was a fine of U.S.$10,000. He was paid U.S.$2,500 a month for intelligence work, U.S.$1,800 more than his normal salary. He was sent for training for U-2 flights in Nevada, and given the name of Palmer. He was in the "10-10," the CIA **code name** for his reconnaissance unit; to the public he was apparently employed by **NASA** to conduct high-altitude aerial reconnaissance.

The flights would go east from Incirlik, Turkey, on to Tehran, south of the Caspian Sea, north to Afghanistan, on to Afghanistan's eastern border with Pakistan, then return to Incirlik. Emergency airfields were at Meshed and Tehran.

In April 1960 Powers was at Peshawar airport in Pakistan, preparing for a flight on May 1. For this flight he was ordered to fly from Peshawar over the Aral Sea,

Sverdlovsk, Kirov, Archangel, Murmansk, and land at Bodø, Norway. When crossing the U.S.S.R. he would photograph missile-launching sites and other important military establishments.

Powers flew to 65,000 feet (20,000 meters) and then into Soviet airspace. While he was plotting his course, his plane was hit; its wings and tail fell off, landing south-southeast of Sverdlovsk. He parachuted to safety.

Powers had facilities to destroy both the plane and the intelligence he had collected if forced to land. He also had a lethal dose of curare for suicide if tortured, a silenced pistol, cartridges, a dagger, an inflatable rubber boat, maps of Eastern Europe, signal flares, kindling, a flashlight, a compass, a saw, fishing tackle, Russian money, rings, and wristwatches.

Powers was captured at about 11 A.M., 150 meters away from where he had landed. He was helped out of his parachute, detained as a foreigner, and disarmed. The plane was scattered over 20 square kilometers (nine square miles). Powers would later identify the crashed plane as the one he had been flying.

Powers was tried for espionage on August 17, 1960. He gave personal information to the presiding judge, said he understood his rights and did not challenge the court as established, and had no objections to make and nothing to say. He said he understood the charge and pleaded guilty. Under examination he told about his work, denied having been tortured, and said, in his own words, that he had been well treated.

Powers gave many details of how he had been recruited and trained, his contract with the CIA, and conditions of employment. He was held in prison for two years, and on February 10, 1962, was exchanged for Rudolph Abel (1903–1971).

On his return to the United States, Powers gave an account of his trial. Unlike the crew of a U.S. reconnaissance aircraft downed in July 1949 over the Bering Sea, Powers was not met as a hero by the U.S. President.

After the exchange Powers was taken to Andrews Air Force Base and then to Ashford Farm, in Maryland, for debriefing in. The interviewers concluded that Powers had tried to mislead his Russian interrogators, acquitted himself appropriately, and made a reasonable effort to destroy his aircraft. No agreement was reached on the altitude at which his craft had been damaged. Some people concluded that Powers had lost control of the aircraft, and others believed he had fallen asleep, but now it appears his plane was hit by a Soviet missile and/or some part of the plane fell off.

It was not until March 1962 that Powers's freedom was celebrated, doubts about his skills and capacities as a pilot were put aside, and he was made an American hero.

In January 1963 Powers and his wife were divorced; Powers married a CIA colleague, left the CIA for California, and worked for the Lockheed Aircraft Corporation as a test pilot. Five years later he published his *Operation Overflight,* and Lockheed fired him. He had written that the public had not known how high he had been was flying in May 1960; he also said he would never have committed suicide, and that his critics did not accept the apology he gave in Moscow for having made the flight.

A Los Angeles radio station employed Powers to fly Cessnas—and later a helicopter—and report on weather and traffic. On August 1, 1977, his craft ran out of fuel, and he and his crew died in the crash. The crash again raised the question of his competence as a flyer. President Jimmy Carter (1924–) allowed Powers to be buried at Arlington National Cemetery, with CIA approval.

In May 2000 Powers was posthumously awarded military honors, exactly 40 years after his capture. The Powers family was presented with his Prisoner-of-War Medal, Distinguished Flying Cross, and National Defense Service Medal during a 30-minute ceremony at an Air Force base north of Sacramento.

Sources: Ambrose, Stephen E., *Ike's Spies: Eisenhower and the Espionage Establishment,* 2nd ed. (Jackson: University Press of Mississippi, 1999); Anonymous, *The Trial of the U-2: Exclusive Authorized Account of the Court Proceedings of the Case of Francis Gary Powers Heard before the Military Division of the Supreme Court of the U.S.S.R., Moscow 17-19 1960* (Chicago: World Publishing, 1960); Bissell, Richard Mervin, Jr., with Jonathan E. Lewis and Frances T. Pudio, *Reflections of a Cold Warrior: From Yalta to the Bay of Pigs* (New Haven, CT: Yale University Press, 1996), ch. 5; Smith, Joseph, and Simon Davis, *Historical Dictionary of the Cold War* (New York: Scarecrow Press, 2000); West, Nigel, *Seven Spies Who Changed the World* (London: Secker & Warburg, 1991).

PRAEGER, NICHOLAS (1928–1981). Nicholas Praeger was the son of a long-serving clerk in the British consulate in Prague who was also a Czechoslovakian intelligence **agent**. Before his retirement in 1948, Nicholas's father was naturalized as a British subject. This meant his son, who was born in Czechoslovakia, could claim British citizenship. In 1949 Praeger and his wife, Jana, brought their baby to live with them in England.

Aged 21, Praeger joined the Royal Air Force (RAF), claiming to have been born in England and to have lived there all his life with his father, whom he also claimed was born in England. He made no mention of being married.

By 1956 Praeger was a well-trained radar technician with access to top-secret information, first at Fighter Command's headquarters at Stanmore and later at the RAF base at Wittering. He was also a committed Communist. In 1959 he applied for a passport to go to Hawaii. Instead he went to Czechoslovakia, using a visa stamped by a known Czechoslovakian intelligence agent. While there he was easily recruited to the Czechoslovakian security services (StB), and code-named MARCONI. He and his wife returned to England, and he began spying diligently for his new employers.

In 1961 Praeger left the RAF and joined the English Electric Company. Little that he gleaned was of value until he produced details of radar-jamming equipment on the British nuclear strike bombers. This information was of value to the Russians because it greatly deterred Britain's power to effect a nuclear attack. Over the next 10 years Praeger was often in Czechoslovakia, and on one visit helped to install a British computer in a steel factory. Until 1969 he worked for English Electric.

In January 1971, acting on information from the Josef Frolik (1925–) and the defection of an agent posing as a visa officer at the London embassy, the British police searched Praeger's house and found espionage equipment. Praeger was questioned, and his trial began in June 1971. At the trial all the offenses he was charged with were alleged to have been committed 10 years before. Praeger's defense was that he was blackmailed into spying in order to protect his wife's family in Czechoslovakia. Later he said his wife was a spy, and that she was responsible for the espionage he was charged with. She had disappeared, but her lover gave evidence against her.

Praeger was found guilty of espionage and sentenced to 12 years in prison. His sentence was reduced when it became clear that his treatment was far more severe than that given to others who had committed worse offenses.

Praeger died in 1981 after spending some time under the threat of deportation. See also FROLIK, JOSEF

Sources: Andrew, Christopher, and Oleg Gordievsky, *KGB: The Inside Story of Its Foreign Operations from Lenin to Gorbachev* (London: Hodder and Stoughton, 1990); Frolik, Joseph, *The Frolik Defection* (London: Leo Cooper, 1975); Laffin, John, *Brassey's Book of Espionage* (London: Brassey's, 1996); Pincher, Chapman, *Too Secret Too Long* (London: Sidgwick & Jackson, 1984); West, Nigel, *The Circus: MI5 Operations 1945–1972* (New York: Stein and Day, 1983).

PRIME, GEOFFREY ARTHUR (c. 1937–). Geoffrey Prime worked in **GCHQ** as a civilian (1968–1977) and resigned after providing the **KGB** with much valuable information. He was arrested on sex charges, and his espionage work for the Russians was discovered. In November 1982 he was sentenced to 35 years in prison.

After leaving school, Prime in worked in a copper factory, and in August 1956 began his national service with the Royal Air Force (RAF); he later studied Russian and German at the RAF school. In 1964 was posted to an RAF facility in West Berlin, where he spied on Russian pilots and listened to Radio Moscow. He gave the impression that his character was weak, that he was sexually inadequate, and that he wanted to improve his life.

In January 1968, when passing through the East Berlin checkpoint, Prime gave a note to a guard offering his services to the **U.S.S.R.** After being welcomed, he established contact with the KGB. After returning to London he sent information regularly to his Soviet handlers by using invisible ink letters that he either posted to East Berlin or put in a **dead drop.**

In 1973 Prime lost his code pads; he informed his handlers, and they did not contact him for a year. Depressed by the end of his four-year marriage, he went to see a psychiatrist. Later, by way of his sister, he was sent a suitcase of espionage equipment and money. The KGB had reactivated him.

In 1974 Prime was vetted, and promoted to the point where he dealt with highly sensitive material. Much pleased with this new status, the KGB handlers arranged to meet him in Vienna in September 1975, praised him, and gave him £750.

Prime was posted to GCHQ, in Cheltenham, where the technology was available to spy on the political and commercial life of most nations, and on the military resources of Russia, America, China, and Ireland. GCHQ was the center of information on nuclear resources. Also through GCHQ, **MI6** communicated with its agents around the world and eavesdropped on its enemies, its allies, and local citizens. It was supported by funds from America, Australia, Britain, and Canada.

Prime flew to Vienna again with a cache of valuable material for his KGB handlers. By November 1976 he had been promoted to section chief and had access to even more highly sensitive material. But the work was so much of strain that, aged 39, he resigned from GCHQ. The KGB still wanted information from him. In Vienna they gave him another £4,000 for his services.

In Britain, during the summer of 1982 Prime began to commit sexual offenses, confessed his assaults to his wife, and eventually spoke of his espionage activities. She reported him to the police. In November 1982 he was found guilty of spying and sexual assaults, and given a 35-year sentence.

The **Central Intelligence Agency (CIA)** was never given information about Prime until well after his arrest, and the agency estimated he had cost the United States many millions of dollars and many lost **agents**. He is noted not only for being a social misfit and sexual pervert but also for being recruited and passing all the British vetting checks.

Sources: Andrew, Christopher, and Oleg Gordievsky, *KGB: The Inside Story of Its Foreign Operations from Lenin to Gorbachev* (London: Hodder and Stoughton, 1990); Bamford, James, *The Puzzle Palace: A Report on America's Most Secret Agency* (New York: Penguin, 1983); Deacon, Richard, *Spyclopedia: The Comprehensive Handbook of Espionage* (New York: Silver Arrow/William Morrow, 1987); Laffin, John, *Brassey's Book of Espionage* (London: Brassey's, 1996); Mahoney, Harry T., and Marjorie L. Mahoney, *Biographic Dictionary of Espionage* (San Francisco: Austin & Winfield, 1998); Payne, Ronald, and Christopher Dobson, *Who's Who in Espionage* (New York: St. Martin's Press, 1984); Pincher, Chapman, *Too Secret Too Long* (New York: St. Martin's Press, 1984); Pincher, Chapman, *Traitors: The Anatomy of Treason* (New York: St. Martin's Press, 1987); Prime, Rona, and Jean Watson, *Time of Trial: The Personal Story Behind the Cheltenham Spy Scandal* (London: Hodder and Stoughton, 1984).

PYM, MAGNUS (fl. 1931–1985). Magnus Pym is the perfect British **Cold War** spy in the autobiographical novel *A Perfect Spy* (1986) by John Le Carré, the pseudonym of David J. M. Cornwell (1931–). He came to literary fame in September 1963 with the publication of his novel *The Spy Who Came In from the Cold,* which describes the chilling hell of the triple-cross in Cold War espionage; *A Perfect Spy* depicts the upbringing, occupation, and motivation of a perfect Cold War spy.

Magnus Pym's father, Rick (fl. 1910–1985), is an English confidence trickster, and his mother is an abused depressive who is institutionalized when Magnus, her only son, is a little fellow. Rick is jailed, and afterward, in his career of petty crime, only just manages to keep a step ahead of the law; teaches his son the value of deception and betraying trusted friends; and otherwise prepares the lad for an empty emotional life. For Rick sincerity and gratitude are founded on the finely honed and superficial skills of a charmer, and elaborate intrigue is the main source of joy in all interpersonal relations, especially those involving the love of women.

After **World War II**, one of Rick's failed scams leaves Magnus abandoned in Bern, Switzerland, where he befriends Axel H., an illegal immigrant raised in Carlsbad. Their friendship becomes close; but guided by a British intelligence officer, Magnus betrays Axel; returns to England to study law at Oxford; reads modern languages instead; completes his national service in the army; joins military intelligence; and is drawn into an unexpected meeting with Axel in Europe.

So far Manus's upbringing and training have prepared him well for the life of a perfect spy. All that is now required is a moral justification for betraying those you love and are loyal to, and who believe in you. With Axel, Magnus makes a deal to perfect their work as spies by becoming **defectors-in-place** together. This work becomes their vocation for almost 25 years. While Axel endures the brutal purges of Russian-dominated Czechoslovakia, Pym claws his way to the top of Britain's establishment-run intelligence world. They achieve a perfect moral, almost utopian, relationship: each provides the other with highly valuable secret information that they vow contributes to diminishing the likelihood of a third world war by ensuring that neither side in the Cold War has an intelligence advantage over the other. Their arrangement is dubbed Operation GREENSLEEVES by the British intelligence community, which, for a time, believe it has a defector-in-place.

Pym marries twice; has a son, Tom, by his second wife; and holds important espionage posts in British embassies in various European capitals. His diplomatic career and his work with Axel peak when the two celebrate their success at a July 4 party in Washington, where Pym is deputy head of station.

When the **Central Intelligence Agency (CIA)** uses computers to correlate the delivery of rich Czechoslovakian intelligence with the fact that Axel and Pym are often together when the intelligence becomes known, American intelligence officers suspect a **mole** in Britain's secret service. Pym is interrogated by his superiors and, of course, is found loyal to the service.

Meanwhile, Rick, an established jailbird, is beseeching Magnus for money and restricting his sense of freedom. Rick dies, and Magnus is elated by a deep feeling of freedom; he hurries to the funeral, flees his family and colleagues, and disappears. He rents a room in a seaside boardinghouse so that, alone, he can write his autobiography for Tom, his son. On completing the work—the novel itself—Magnus achieves nirvana by shooting himself with a stolen pistol.

At the time of publication the novel attracted over 20 laudatory reviews from the world's most influential newspapers and magazines, and later was made into a BBCTV film. A fine study of the morality of Le Carré's spy novels, with a full reading list, appears in Aronoff (1999).

See also LE CARRÉ, JOHN; OPERATION GREENSLEEVES

Sources: Aronoff, Myron J., *The Spy Novels of John Le Carré: Balancing Ethics and Politics* (New York: St. Martin's Press, 1999); Cooper, Andrew, "Dreaming the Other: Ideology and Character in John Le Carré's Novels," *Free Associations* 5 (1995): 303–325; Laity, Susan, "The Second Burden of a Former Child: Doubling and Repetition in 'A Perfect Spy,'" in Harold Bloom, ed., *John Le Carré* (New York: Chelsea House, 1987), pp. 137–164; Le Carré, John, *A Perfect Spy* (London: Hodder and Stoughton, 1986).

R

RAFAEL, SYLVIA (fl. 1960–1985). Sylvia Rafael was an Israeli assassin. Born in South Africa, she went to Israel as a volunteer in a kibbutz. She was recruited by **Mossad** and became a most capable member of an Israeli hit team that was sent in 1973 to Norway. Her cover name was Patricia Roxborough, and she traveled as a newspaper photographer from Canada.

Assisted by Norwegian intelligence services, the hit team aimed to find and assassinate Ali Hassan Salameh, a leading member of the Palestine Liberation Organization's (**PLO**) **Black September** gang who had assassinated the Israeli Olympic athletes at Munich in September 1972.

In July 1973, in Lillehammer, a small Norwegian town, the Israeli team murdered a Moroccan waiter by mistake. The error may have been due to a misidentification of Salameh by an Algerian Black September courier who had been intimidated into becoming a **double agent** for Mossad. The Norwegian intelligence services tried to help most of the team to escape, but six members were caught. Sylvia Rafael and Abraham Gehmer were found by police as they were trying to leave Norway disguised as a Canadian married couple.

Consequently, the secret relationship between Mossad and Norway's intelligence services was exposed, and it was believed that the fiasco would put an end to the Israeli scheme to eliminate the Black September gang. Many had already been murdered by Mossad in what was known as Operation SPRINGTIME OF YOUTH. By January 1979 the real Ali Hassan Salameh had been murdered.

The two assassins were found guilty of complicity in the waiter's assassination, and sentenced to prison for five and a half years.

Rafael kept a diary and published it. After almost two years in prison she was released, and returned to Israel, where a heroine's welcome awaited her. In September 1985, according to the *Daily Telegraph,* she was reported to have been murdered in the marina at Larnaca, Cyprus, on Yom Kippur; in fact, however, she was living in Norway (Black and Morris, 1991), where she had fallen in love with her lawyer and married him.

The Lillehammer error was an embarrassment to Mossad, which referred to it as "Ley-ha-Mar," meaning "The Night of Bitterness."

See also ISRAEL AND THE NUCLEAR WEAPONS CRISIS

Sources: Black, Ian, and Benny Morris, *Israel's Secret Wars: The Untold History of Israeli Intelligence* (London: Hamish Hamilton, 1991); Mahoney, M. H., *Women in Espionage* (Santa Barbara, CA: ABC-CLIO, 1993); Payne, Ronald, and Christopher Dobson, *Who's Who in Espionage* (New York: St. Martin's Press, 1984); Raviv, Dan, and Yossi Melman, *Every Spy a Prince* (Boston: Houghton Mifflin, 1990).

REBET AND BANDERA WET AFFAIRS. Two assassinations ordered by the **KGB** in its attempt to prevent attempts by Ukrainian exiles to undermine Soviet control of their country.

In October 1957, exiled Ukrainian politician and editor Lev Rebet, and in October 1959, Ukrainian nationalist Stephan Bandera, were murdered by a KGB **agent.** They were exiles and hostile to the **U.S.S.R.** occupation of their country.

Lev Rebet lived in Munich and edited the *Ukrainski Samostinik.* The assassination was ordered by the KGB's Department 13 of the First Chief Directorate, as a matter of U.S.S.R. international policy. Both murders employed the same technique and the same murderer, Bogdan Stashinsky (1931–). He used a pistol-like weapon that fires a vapor at the face of the victim, 18 inches away. The victim inhales the vapor and dies quickly, as if from a heart attack. The vapor, which leaves no trace, may have been prussic acid.

To ensure he does not also succumb to the lethal vapor, the assassin first takes an antidote, and after killing the victim inhales the vapor from a crushed ampule of sodium thiosulphate and amyl nitrate.

See also OPERATION RHINE; STASHINSKY, BOGDAN

Sources: Aldrich, Richard J., *The Hidden Hand: Britain, America and Cold War Secret Intelligence* (New York: Overlook Press, 2002); Andrew, Christopher, and Oleg Gordievsky, *KGB: The Inside Story of Its Foreign Operations from Lenin to Gorbachev* (London: Hodder and Stoughton, 1990); Andrew, Christopher, and Vasili Mitrokhin, *The Mitrokhin Archive: The KGB in Europe and the West* (London: Lane, 1999); Deacon, Richard, with Nigel West, *Spy! Six Stories of Modern Espionage* (London: BBC, 1980); Frolik, Joseph, *The Frolik Defection* (London: Leo Cooper, 1975).

REES, GORONWY (1909–1979). Rees was a **Cold War** warrior and author who as a young man held a romantic and sentimental view of the Communist cause, and appeared to have given it up shortly before **World War II**. After the war he became conflicted when in 1951 he revealed an espionage secret he had promised not to tell. The revelation plagued his literary career, and eventually condemned him to distort his knowledge of Cold War spies, and to have his life judged as a cautionary tale in espionage.

Goronwy Rees was born in November 1909 in Aberystwyth, Wales, the youngest child of a Calvinist Methodist minister. He idealized his father and hoped to please him; his father infused a strong social conscience into the boy. Rees matured as a sensitive romantic, and was often spoiled by his mother.

In 1923 the family moved to Cardiff, where Rees attended the high school, worked hard, and studied history. He won a scholarship to New College, Oxford, in October 1928.

At university Rees enjoyed the social life, loved German, wrote poems, and pretended Oxford was Paris. He felt drawn to socialism and Marxism. His studies were a success, and he was awarded a senior scholarship in October 1931.

At Oxford, Rees begun his career as an author and developed his passion for Germany. In November 1931, All Souls College elected him a fellow, one of 40, because he had great potential as a historian and scholar.

In the spiring of 1932 Rees went to Freiburg, Vienna, and Berlin; worked in a film; and did a little research. He loved Berlin, but when he returned in 1934, he found it had changed so much under Adolf Hitler (1889–1945), that he and his socialist friends were appalled.

On his return to Oxford, Rees met Guy Burgess (1911–1963) who was visiting briefly, and their close friendship began after Rees rejected Burgess's homosexual advances.

Rees wrote novels and articles for newspapers, and formed an ambivalent position in his politics. In 1935 he was assistant editor of *The Spectator* and was living in London near Burgess, with whom he would discuss the **Spanish Civil War** (1936–1939). As he gathered around him many noted members of London's literary circle, Rees began to drink too much alcohol, and developed a reputation for womanizing.

In 1936 Rees, who was on the Executive Committee of the British Section of the International Association of Writers for the Defense of Culture—a Communist front organization—went to the Association's conference in Paris with Burgess. In November 1937, while Rees and Burgess talked about Rees's book review of *Grey Children*, a study of economic depression in South Wales, Burgess told Rees that he worked for the **COMINTERN**. He wanted Rees to help him, and gave him the name of Anthony Blunt (1907–1983); he made Rees promise not to reveal to anyone the substance of their conversation. At the time Rees could not see how he could help Burgess in his work.

In April 1939 Rees joined the Royal Territorial Army Artillery; and after the **Ribbentrop–Molotov Pact** in late August of that year, gave up his sympathy for the Soviet cause and his acceptance of Marxist thinking. He probably maintained an unconscious feeling for Marxist ideas.

Rees was commissioned in 1940 into the Royal Welsh Fusiliers, and by August 1940 was appointed to the intelligence unit. He married in December 1940, and was reelected as a fellow of All Souls College for another seven years.

He maintained his reputation for chasing women and was often unfaithful to his wife, and in the intelligence unit he was interested in the morality and reliability of much of the intelligence he saw. He also was concerned about Guy Burgess's activities.

After World War II, Rees was a lieutenant colonel, and worked in the political division of the Allied Control Commission. He saw a lot of Burgess, who visited the Rees family in London. In 1946 he became a director of an engineering firm, and also worked part-time in the **SIS** Political Section, evaluating secret information from **agents** and concerning himself with the problem of the spreading influence of the Soviet Union.

Rees saw Guy Burgess frequently, and was so concerned, it appears, about Burgess's telling him of the COMINTERN in 1937 that he told Burgess that he had written down their 1937 talk and left a copy with his lawyer. This distressed Burgess. Apparently Rees was lying. Nevertheless, the two often drank together and talked politics, showing evident differences in their views. In 1950 Rees published his third novel, *Where No Wounds Were.*

In April 1951 Rees became Estate Bursar of All Souls College. In May of that year, at dinner with his wife in his club, Donald Maclean (1913–1983), whom Rees had not seen for 15 years, lurched drunkenly up to Rees's table and said that he (Rees) had ratted on those who had thought he was a friend and political supporter. Rees wrote later, disingenuously, that from this outburst he immediately concluded that Maclean and Burgess were Communists. In May, Burgess, much agitated, came to see Rees and talked about the policies he seen in place in the United States Shortly afterward Burgess disappeared, and Rees suspected he had gone to Moscow.

With this suspicion in mind, Rees had lunch with Guy Liddell (1892–1958) and Anthony Blunt. He told them informally what he knew of Burgess, but said nothing about what Burgess had said about Blunt. Later, Rees was interviewed formally by Liddell and Dick White (1906–1993); he realized that he had given them the impression that he himself was a Soviet spy, then told them all he knew about Burgess and mentioned Blunt's name.

Years later Dick White said he had never trusted Rees, and he hated Blunt. He thought Rees was a liar; if he'd known about all these things then, why had he not revealed them earlier? To White, it seemed Rees believed **MI5** knew about Burgess, and did nothing.

After the meeting with White and Liddell, Rees became obsessed with revealing Anthony Blunt as a Soviet spy: he believed that Blunt knew that Rees knew the truth, and that Blunt knew that Rees had told MI5.

When it was obvious that Burgess and Maclean had flown to Moscow, newspapers described the close friendship between Rees and Burgess, and from that time, June 18, 1951, Rees's reputation was tainted by the suspicion that he, too, had been a Soviet **agent**.

In October 1953 Rees was inaugurated as the principal of University College, Wales. In February 1956, after Burgess and Maclean made public their flight to Moscow, Rees published articles about Burgess in *People*. They caused Rees to be ostracized. He resigned from the university in March 1957, his reputation utterly destroyed.

The most convincing explanation of Rees's extraordinary action was that he had expected Burgess to implicate him in espionage, and wanted to strike first, to cripple Burgess's credibility. In his articles, Rees stated that Burgess was a blackmailer protected by his homosexual pals in MI5, and that he was so incompetent he should have been expelled. The destructive force in Rees's articles bounced off the implacable walls around the British establishment, and wounded him hideously.

After his resignation Rees was struck by a car and spent six months in hospital. He had no job and no money, did a little work with BBC-TV, became depressed and was placed in psychiatric care. His illness worsened in 1963 after his father's death. Over the next 10 years, always short of money, Rees wrote for *Encounter* and published four books.

In 1972 Rees published *A Chapter of Accidents,* which provides his explanation for the decision to write the self-destructive articles in *People*. It was reviewed widely and raised interesting controversy. In June 1972 his wife died. He died in December 1979, not long after seeing, to his delight, that Anthony Blunt had been caught.

One account says that on his deathbed Rees repeated the claim that the late Guy Liddell was a Soviet agent; no independent evidence supported Rees' deathbed statement.

Shortly before Anthony Blunt died in March 1983, he accused Rees of being a Soviet agent in the 1930s, and said that he had quit work for the Soviet secret services when the Ribbentrop–Molotov Pact (1939) was signed.

Andrew and Mitrokhin (1999) state that early in 1938, Burgess had approached Rees and recruited him, but later Rees would have others believe that this was not so. He was code-named FLEET and later GROSS. His potential as an agent was important to **Moscow Center.** When Rees told Burgess that he would no longer serve the Soviet cause, Burgess had asked the **NKVD** to assassinate Rees, but the request was refused.

Sources: Andrew, Christopher, and Vasili Mitrokhin, *The Mitrokhin Archive: The KGB in Europe and the West* (London: Lane, 1999); Annan, Noel, *Our Age: Portrait of a Generation* (London: Weidenfeld and Nicolson, 1990); Rees, Goronwy, *A Chapter of Accidents* (London: Chatto and Windus, 1971); Rees, Jenny, *Looking for Mr. Nobody: The Secret Life of Goronwy Rees* (London: Weidenfeld and Nicolson, 1994); Wright, Peter, with Paul Greengrass, *Spycatcher: The Candid Autobiography of a Senior Intelligence Officer* (Melbourne: William Heinemann Australia, 1987).

RIMINGTON, STELLA (1935–). Stella Rimington was head of **MI5** from December 1991 to April 1996, having been the protégée of the preceding Director-General. She assumed her duties in February 1992, and was one of the first women to head an intelligence agency in Britain.

Stella was born in London, the only daughter of David Whitehouse, an engineer. In Barrow-in-Furness she attended Crosslands Convent; when she was 12, the family moved to Nottinghamshire, where her father was chief draftsman for the Staunton Ironworks. She attended Nottingham High School for Girls, and was not an outstanding pupil; she was elected head girl, but her teachers thought her unsuited for the post, since she was rather radical. She failed to enter Newnham College, Oxford, and went to read English at Edinburgh University; later she trained as an archivist in Liverpool. As a young girl she was anxious, frightened of lightning, claustrophobic, and socially insecure.

In 1963, aged 28, Stella married John Rimington, a senior diplomat in Delhi. This led to her being approached by MI5. They had two daughters. When they returned to England, she got a job at MI5, apparently because she told the interviewers what they wanted to hear; at the time, she was interested only in the pay and how it could be used to refurbish her home.

After 10 years Rimington decided to quit MI5 and sought the headship of the elite girl's school Roedean. Her application was unsuccessful, but in MI5 she was made supervisor of recruitment. This gave her the opportunity to study the reasons people take up secret political work. She concluded that the motivations to work in espionage were interest in the task; loyalty to colleagues, the organization, and the nation; and the feeling that the job was worthwhile.

Rimington's husband supported her in her career and cooperated with the press on many items relating to her activities, particularly the denigration of Peter Wright (1916–1995), a retired MI5 officer who wrote *Spy Catcher*, an unflattering account of his employer.

Rimington was promoted to direct MI5's Counterterrorism Branch in the late 1980s. Together with Scotland Yard, she had the chief responsibility for combating terrorism of the Irish Republican Army (**IRA**). Before being made head of MI5 she supervised several of its branches responsible for monitoring subversives, including trade unions and certain members of Parliament. In April and May 1984 she helped monitor the miners' strike through infiltration of unions and technical surveillance. She was blamed for improper monitoring of several British labor leaders. She was in charge of Operation FLAVIUS, better known as "Death on the Roads," in which three IRA members were killed in Gibraltar on MI5's orders.

Aged 56 years, Rimington separated from her husband and became a single mother of two children. Her husband, John, headed the Health and Safety Executive of the British government. At home her neighbors knew her as a soberly dressed civil servant; and at work she was known as "Remington Stella," after the TV private eye program *Remington Steele*.

In her autobiography Rimington claims to have dragged MI5 out of its old-fashioned gentlemen's club style of organization into a better focused security service. Her managerial style seems to have been ambiguous: she valued creativity and imagination, but saw herself as successful because she was not interested in theory and was practical; she thought MI5 was inward-looking in its choice of recruits, but praised it for its individualism, diversity, and eccentricity; she admired strong, bullying leaders, but claims to have preferred a collegial style, which she thought was because she was a woman; she believed she got to the top without conforming her thinking to the ideas of others, but many saw her as a close follower of Prime Minister **Margaret Thatcher**'s (1925–) ideologies.

Before Rimington's rise in authority, other women held high positions in MI5. Ann Orr-Ewing was in charge of the investigation of Roger Hollis (1905–1973) to determine if he were the "fifth man." Before Remington was named as MI5 head, there was speculation that Margaret Ramsey would be considered, because she was known to have close contact with the Labour Party.

Rimington rose to the top of the traditionally male-dominated hierarchy, whose top personnel would humorously describe the women staff as consisting of middle-class, twin-set-and-pearls ladies who spent their time ironing copies of the left-wing *Morning Star* and other similar publications for their superiors to analyze. Her autobiography claims that she shook the organization of MI5 from this mold forever.

Sources: Mahoney, Harry T., and Marjorie L. Mahoney, *Biographic Dictionary of Espionage* (San Francisco: Austin & Winfield, 1998); Porter, Bernard, "More Interesting Than Learning How to Make Brandy Snaps. Review of Rimington, Stella. 2001. The Autobiography of the Former Director-General of MI5," *London Review of Books*, October 18, 2001, pp. 8–9; Rimington, Stella, *Open Secret: The Autobiography of the Former Director-General of MI5* (London: Hutchinson, 2001).

RITCHIE, RHONA (fl. 1953–1982). Rhona Ritchie, a Scottish lawyer, was used for espionage by her Egyptian lover and came very close to not being a **Cold War** spy because of her inaccurate information.

After a strict upbringing in a Scottish middle-class family and being head prefect at her school, Ritchie became an outstanding graduate in law and a fine university lecturer. She gave the impression of being cultured, elegant, honest, intelligent, loyal, reliable, and stylish.

Following a year of teaching at Glasgow University, Ritchie joined the U.K. Foreign Office. At a London party she met an Egyptian embassy official, and they became lovers. In 1981 she was posted to the British embassy in Tel Aviv as a Second Secretary. She added Hebrew to her French and German, and after the **Camp David Accords** (March 1979) she renewed the relationship with her Egyptian lover, Riffaat El-Ansarry.

Ritchie began to leak the contents of official telegrams to him, such as cables from Lord Carrington (1919–), the U.K. Foreign Secretary, to U.S. Secretary of State Alexander M. Haigh, Jr. (1924–). She was caught; and in November 1982 she was charged under Section 2 of Britain's Official Secrets Act with an unusual crime: *the wrongful combination of information.* Found guilty, she was given a suspended sentence of nine months, and her career ended in disgrace. Her lover was promoted, posted to Vienna, and continued his work.

Whether on not Rhona Ritchie was a Cold War spy is not clear. Her lover had told her that he wanted to know the contents of the telegrams to improve his grasp of current international issues; she gave them to him, knowing that they would be public within 24 hours.

Ritchie's lawyer argued that she was no spy, had pleaded guilty, and in innocence had displayed openly what she had done. The prosecutor argued that her guilt centered on whether or not she had the authority to hand on the information that had come to her; in her defense against that argument, her lawyer indicated that it was common practice among diplomats to disclose sensitive material informally, especially since it would very soon become public.

Finally, it was clear to the judge that Ritchie was "guilty enough": guilty of foolishness and of trusting a lover whose profession it was to betray love whenever necessary.

Source: Laffin, John, *Brassey's Book of Espionage* (London: Brassey's, 1996).

ROOSEVELT, KERMIT "KIM" (1916–2000).

Kermit Roosevelt was the secret organizer behind the **Central Intelligence Agency (CIA)–SIS** coup to bring down the Prime Minister of Iran and support the Shah in August 1953. This was known as Operation AJAX, one of the first espionage operations conducted by the CIA during the presidency of **Dwight D. Eisenhower** (1890–1969).

Kermit "Kim" Roosevelt was born in Buenos Aires. His father was in the shipping and banking industry. Kermit was the grandson of President Theodore Roosevelt (1858–1919) and a distant cousin of Franklin D. Roosevelt (1882–1945). Kermit graduated from Harvard University and, after teaching for a short period, served in the Middle East with the **OSS** during **World War II**. Roosevelt headed the CIA Plans Directorate, Near East and Africa Division. In the late 1940s he met Kim Philby (1912–1988), whom he considered to be urbane, courteous, and most unlikely to be a treacherous Soviet spy. Roosevelt married, and had three sons.

The British **MI6** approached Roosevelt to join Operation AJAX. He was to be in charge. The operation aimed to restore the power of the Shah of Iran by toppling

Prime Minister Mohammed Mossadegh (1880–1967), who had the support of the Tudeh (Communist) Party in the Iranian Parliament.

The successful coup was Roosevelt's responsibility. He had the support of the U.S. President; the CIA head, Allen W. Dulles (1893–1969); the U.S. ambassador in Tehran; and the former chief of the New Jersey State Police, General H. Norman Schwarzkopf (1896–1958), who was then a CIA military specialist attached to the American embassy. The latter brought the CIA money with him to pay hired rioters in the streets of Tehran in August 1953.

Years later a myth grew that Roosevelt, behaving just like his grandfather, had led the way to Mossadegh's capture and downfall in a grand and heroic manner. In fact, however, he kept out of sight and waited until the coup was a success; later, when the time came for celebrations, he was thanked personally by the sobbing Shah, who said, "I owe my throne to God, my people, my army and to you."

On his way back to the United States, Roosevelt visited Winston Churchill (1874–1965), Prime Minister of Great Britain, and after regaling him with the story, went on to Washington to report on the coup to the Dulles brothers and the Secretary of Defense. President Eisenhower, on vacation at the time, never allowed his name to be associated with Roosevelt's operation. For 25 years Roosevelt's work was kept as secret as possible.

In 1958 Roosevelt left the CIA, worked for about six years for Gulf Oil, and then was a consultant to U.S. companies in the Middle East and to Middle East government officials in the United States.

In 1979 Roosevelt published his memoir of the operation. The publishers withdrew the book from circulation for a time, apparently at the request of the Anglo–Iranian Oil Company's successor, British Petroleum, which objected to having its predecessor's name and its own associated with the secret decision to bring about the clandestine coup (Ambrose, 1999).

Sources: Ambrose, Stephen E., *Ike's Spies: Eisenhower and the Espionage Establishment,* 2nd ed. (Jackson: University Press of Mississippi, 1999); Molotsky, Irvin, "Director of CIA's 1953 Coup in Iran," *The Age,* June 14, 2000, p. 7 (obituary originally published in the *New York Times*); Roosevelt, Kermit, *Countercoup: The Struggle for Control of Iran* (New York: McGraw-Hill, 1979); Saikal, Amin, *The Rise and Fall of the Shah* (Princeton, NJ: Princeton University Press, 1980).

ROSENBERG, ETHEL (c. 1915–1953), AND ROSENBERG, JULIUS (c. 1918–1953).

Ethel and Julius Rosenberg were American Communists who spied for Russia and were discovered in the United States after the trial in England of Klaus Fuchs (1911–1988). Amid worldwide controversy they were put to death for their crimes in June 1953.

Julius Rosenberg was the son of a religious civic leader in the Jewish community of New York City's East Side. His father was a union representative in the clothing industry, and hoped his son would be rabbi. Julius went to Seward Park High School, and at the end of each day went to Hebrew High School. But, aged 16, he turned away from his father's plans and, deciding to be an electrical engineer, entered the School of Technology at the City College of New York in June 1934. He also took to communism and became a proselytizer for the Communist cause. He would study by day, and often at night did his homework in the apartment of the Greenglass family.

Young Ethel Greenglass wanted to be a poet, an actress, a dancer, a singer, and a pianist. In 1931, aged 16, she graduated from high school and began work as a stenographer. She joined the Communist Party when she was a member of the United Retail and Wholesalers Union, and met Julius at a one of the party's gatherings. They became friends, and she would type up his engineering reports; Julius would bring gifts for Ethel's young brother, David Greenglass (1922–), who later joined the **CPUSA.**

At college Julius centered his political interest on the Young Communist League and the American Students Union. In 1939 he graduated with a B.Sc. in electrical engineering, and in June that year married Ethel. Shortly after, David joined the Young Communist League.

Julius worked as a tool designer, and with his friends strengthened and stimulated the membership and union activities of the **FAECT.** Ethel and Julius worked assiduously to raise funds for Communist causes and front organizations, such as the Joint Anti-Fascist Refugee Committee and the International Workers' Order.

In 1942 **Moscow Center** decided the controller of a U.S. espionage group, Jacob Golos (1890–1943), who delivered material directly to **NKGB** operatives, had insufficient technical knowledge for the task. Julius, code-named ANTENNA and later LIBERAL, was to take over. The task was to collect information on the U.S. Army's research on and development of an **atom bomb**, the **Manhattan Project**. By October 1942 Julius had been well trained, and was happy that in the future he could give information of the sort he had given to the NKGB New York station. By this time the Soviets were collecting information on scientists at Columbia University, MIT, and other research centers working on atomic energy.

In March 1943 the Rosenbergs had a son, Michael, and by then Julius had been promoted to associate engineering inspector in the Signal Corps. Julius was suspended in February 1945 and dismissed in March; he joined the Emerson Radio Company, one of the organizations that he had earlier been inspecting.

In June 1950 the **Federal Bureau of Investigation (FBI)** visited Julius and asked him whether or not it was true, as David Greenglass had told them, that he had been supplying secret information to Russia. In July he was arrested. In August, Ethel was arrested on charges of conspiracy to commit treason.

At the trial the following account of the Rosenbergs' activities emerged: David Greenglass had worked on the Manhattan Project and was induced to provide drawings to the Rosenbergs in January 1945, and later that year Harry Gold (1910–1972) gave the Rosenbergs more technical sketches from Greenglass. The Russians exploded their atomic bomb four years later; afterward, Klaus Fuchs confessed to espionage for the Soviets, and in doing so identified Harry Gold. In June, Greenglass confessed and named the Rosenbergs. The Rosenbergs were told by the Soviets to plead not guilty, which they did. At the trial David Greenglass changed his story to ensure his wife, Ruth, would not be indicted; in doing so, he made it certain that his sister, Ethel, would be found guilty. The Rosenbergs were found guilty and sentenced to death for, as the judge said, an act worse than murder, and for causing the Communist aggression in Korea. The **Korean War** (1950–1953) had begun in June 1950, the month they were arrested.

Although evidence against Ethel was threadbare—she had typed up her brother's reports for transmission to the Soviet embassy—secret VENONA traffic showed a man-and-wife team was serving the Soviet interests with information from the Manhattan Project.

Around the world the sentence was debated, and in the United States it was reviewed frequently, but the U.S. Supreme Court upheld the judge's decision. The public relations expert in the White House advised President **Dwight D. Eisenhower** (1890–1969) to consider clemency for the Rosenbergs because their execution would damage the reputation of the United States with its European allies, who wanted mercy to be shown to them; he also stated that Eisenhower's show of clemency would help check Joseph McCarthy's (1908–1957) witch-hunt. McCarthy heard of the plea and said the adviser was unpatriotic; McCarthy supporters called him a dangerous liberal. Ten months later the public relations adviser resigned and returned to his post at *Time* magazine in 1954.

It was argued at the time that, at worst, Ethel was a Communist married to a Communist spy and was a willing typist. President Eisenhower could have granted Ethel clemency, but he would not do so. He wrote privately to his son that because he felt Ethel was strong and recalcitrant, and had in fact had *led* the spy ring in every thing it did, he believed that if she, and not her husband, were to be given clemency, the Soviets would recruit their spies from among women.

The Rosenbergs were executed in June 1953. Many books were published about the Rosenbergs, their trial, and the controversy it raised. In one of the most recent books, Meeropol (2003), the Rosenberg's son, acknowledges that his father may have been a spy, but that in 1953 both parents died because they were framed by a political system that he will always oppose.

See also FUCHS, EMIL JULIUS KLAUS; GOLD, HARRY; GREENGLASS, DAVID, AND GREENGLASS, RUTH

Sources: Ambrose, Stephen E., *Ike's Spies: Eisenhower and the Espionage Establishment*, 2nd ed. (Jackson: University Press of Mississippi, 1999); Cook, Fred J., *The FBI Nobody Knows* (New York: Macmillan, 1964); Feklisov, Alexander, and Sergei Kostin, *The Man Behind the Rosenbergs*. Translated from the French 1999 editon by Catherine Dop (New York: Enigma, 2001); Fineberg, S. Andill, *The Rosenberg Case: Fact and Fiction* (New York: Oceana, 1953); Garber, Majorie, and Rebecca L. Walkowitz, eds., *Secret Agents: The Rosenberg Case, McCarthyism, and Fifties America* (New York: Routledge, 1995); Gentry, Curt, *J. Edgar Hoover: The Man and His Secrets* (New York: Norton, 1991); Haynes, John Earl, and Harvey Klehr, *Venona: Decoding Soviet Espionage in America* (New Haven, CT: Yale University Press, 1999); Hoover, J. Edgar, *Masters of Deceit* (New York: Henry Holt, 1958); Mahoney, Harry T., and Marjorie L. Mahoney, *Biographic Dictionary of Espionage* (San Francisco: Austin & Winfield, 1998); Meeropol, Robert, *An Execution in the Family: One Son's Journey* (New York: St. Martin's Press, 2003); Meeropol, Robert, and Michael Meeropol, *We Are Your Sons* (New York: Ballantine, 1975); Pilat, Oliver, *The Atom Spies* (London: Allen, 1954); Powers, Richard G., *The Life of J. Edgar Hoover: Secrecy and Power* (New York: Macmillan, 1987); Radosh, Ronald, and Joyce Milton, *The Rosenberg File: A Search for the Truth* (New York: Holt, Rinehart and Winston, 1983); Radosh, Ronald, and Joyce Milton, *The Rosenberg File*, rev. ed. (New Haven, CT: Yale University Press, 1997); Schneir, Walter, and Marion Schneir, *Invitation to an Inquest: Reopening the Rosenberg "Atom Spy" Case* (New York: Pantheon, 1965; Baltimore: Penguin, 1974); Weinstein, Allen, and Alexander Vassiliev, *The Haunted Wood: Soviet Espionage in America—The Stalin Era* (New York: Random House, 1999); Yalkowsky, Stanley, *The Murder of the Rosenbergs* (New York: Stanley Yalkowsky, 1990).

S

SERVICE, JOHN STEWART (1909–1999). John Service was a victim of the *Amerasia* spy case, and his experience illustrates the potency of fear as it surrounded false accusations of espionage in the United States during the **Cold War.**

John Service was born in Ch'ang-tu in Szechwan Province, China. His parents were graduates of the University of California at Berkeley. His father administered a YMCA program, and both parents admired and collected the fine arts of China and Tibet. Service was educated at home until 1915, when he was enrolled in a Cleveland, Ohio, school for a year; at age 11 he went to boarding school in Shanghai; and in 1924 he completed his schooling in Berkeley. He traveled to Asia, and later graduated in fine arts from Oberlin College, and became a distance runner; on returning to China, he worked in a bank and was married (1932) before entering the U.S. Foreign Service in 1935.

Service served in Peking (1936) and Shanghai (1938), and in 1941 he was a political officer in Chunking, the new Nationalist capital of China. He and his wife, Caroline, and two infants were evacuated to Chungking during **World War II.** He was a highly regarded member of the "China Hands," a group of respected experts on China among U.S. government advisers.

In August 1943 Service became chief political officer to the U.S. commander of Far East Operations. He thought Generalissimo **Chiang Kai-shek**'s (1887–1975) Kuomintang (KMT), a nationalist political party, was profoundly corrupt and disorganized, and saw that the Communists were managing well the village communes under Japanese control. To Service, Chiang was an old-fashioned warlord, so he recommended the United States send observers to Yunan to confer with Mao Zedong (1893–1976) because the Communist guerrillas in the north had the measure of the Japanese invaders. Service went to Yunan and praised what the Communists had achieved. He reported that Chinese Reds were Marxists, willing to work with the KMT to defeat Japan, and gradually lead China into socialism. Later, Service would be charged falsely with stating that the Chinese Reds were not real Communists but mere agrarian reformists.

Service's anti-Chiang views and intelligence information put him under suspicion from the KMT and its secret police, who found two items with which to discredit him. First, he became an acquaintance of the KMT Finance Minister, who in 1963, was revealed to be a Communist spying in Chungking; and second, in 1944 Service fell in love briefly with a young Chinese actress and had an affair with her. He returned to his wife and family in California later that year; they we expecting their third child.

In March 1945 Service was sent to observe the Communist Party's first congress in China, but was suddenly called back to Washington to examine a foreign policy conflict over China.

For two months the **Federal Bureau of Investigation (FBI)** kept the *Amerasia* magazine's staff under surveillance. Then they were arrested in June 1945. Service was one of the magazine's important contributors on China. It appeared to Service's critics—who saw him as an ambitious young man—that he had exposed the alleged corruption of Chiang Kai-shek's rule in China and had written for the magazine in the hope that Mao would take over China (he did in December 1949); when that happened, Service would have proved to his superiors that he was an appropriate candidate for the U.S. ambassadorship to Communist China.

Service's arrest centered not only a debate on U.S. policy for China, but also on the belief that a long trial would occur. But no trial occurred. However, in the press Service was involved in attacks on the reputation and reliability of political figures involved in the U.S. defense industry's relations with Nationalist China and on the U.S. government policy on Red China; there was a grand jury investigation related to *Amerasia*'s publishing of Service's ideas; and, toward the end of 1945, Elizabeth Bentley (1908–1963) revealed that Communists in government agencies were spying for the **U.S.S.R.**

In August 1945, on the day an **atom bomb** was dropped on Japan and his son was born, Service appeared before a grand jury and was exonerated. But the *Amerasia* case dogged him for years after.

In 1948 Service, recognized as one of the "China Hands," was promoted—the youngest ever—to class 2 in the U.S. Foreign Service. In August 1948 Service became the target of the "China Lobby" for his earlier reports that appeared in a U.S. State Department paper on U.S.–China relations. At the time Service was about to made consul general in Calcutta, and would require U.S. Senate approval. To avoid the process of Senate confirmation, the post was downgraded to a consular assistant-ship in Delhi.

Service had already been cleared three times by the U.S. State Department's **Loyalty–Security Board**. But in March 1950, after Service had set sail for India with his family, he was recalled immediately; the Loyalty–Security Board had reopened his case because Joseph McCarthy (1908–1957) alleged that Service was a known associate of and collaborator with Communists.

The Loyalty–Security Board wanted to know how much Service had passed to the *Amerasia* editors. Service denied being a source, but the FBI contradicted him. George Kennan (1904–   ) said that Service's reports had had no ideological content, and his criticism of Chiang Kai-shek was inconsequential. Others helped exonerate

Service, and in October 1950 he was reinstated, but now there was no hope that he would hold a diplomatic appointment that required U.S. Senate approval.

The Tydings Committee report of July 1950 led to yet another Loyalty–Security Board investigation of Service's file. The file contained a false allegation that Service had had as a lover a Chinese spy in the pay of the Soviets; and the board members were shown records of Service's praise for *Amerasia* magazine, his offhand comments made about his colleagues, and notes that alleged he had failed to criticize colleagues who had allegedly praised the Soviet Union. Dean Acheson (1893–1971) fired Service on December 12, 1951.

Service lost a brilliant career through false charges and leaked and inaccurate information, all supplied by political enemies. He was the first of the "China Hands" to be forced in this way from the U.S. Foreign Service. The others were John Carter Vincent, John Paton Davies, and Oliver Edmund Clubb. All were vindicated, but none recovered his lost reputation.

Disgraced and unemployed, Service took a job with a firm that made steam traps, and made enough with an export business to pay off his debts. By 1957 he managed to get his case heard by the U.S. Supreme Court, won, and was reinstated in the U.S. Foreign Service, but was denied a security clearance. He went to Liverpool, England, for three years, and in 1962 he began postgraduate studies at the University of California at Berkeley. He got a master's degree in political science and became library curator at the university's Center for Chinese Studies. In the 1970s he visited China, helped lay the basis for **Richard Nixon**'s (1913–1994) visit to China, was welcomed in the State Department at a reception for the "China Hands," and in 1984 returned to China to follow the path of the Long March made by Mao in the 1930s.

The *Amerasia* case remained alive as books were published containing false statements about Service. In 1971 he published *The Amerasia Papers,* and in 1974, a book of his dispatches, *Lost Chance in China.* He appeared before the U.S. Senate Foreign Relations Committee, and later was an honored guest in China. In 1986 the *Amerasia* case was still debated.

Service's wife died in 1997, and he died at age 89 two years later.

See also *AMERASIA* CASE

Sources: Anonymous, "John Service, 89, McCarthy Era Victim," *Chicago Tribune,* February 5, 1999, p. 12; Barnes, Bart, "Old China Hand Dies at 89: Foreign Service Officer Was Fired During Red Scare but Reinstated by Supreme Court," *Washington Post,* February 4, 1999, p. B6; Kahn, E. J., Jr., *The China Hands: America's Foreign Service Officers and What Befell Them* (New York: Viking, 1975); Kifner, John, "John Service, a Purged China Hand, Dies at 89," *New York Times,* February 4, 1999, p. B11; Klehr, Harvey, and Ronald Radosh, *The Amerasia Spy Case: Prelude to McCarthyism* (Chapel Hill: University of North Carolina Press, 1996); Latham, Earl, *The Communist Controversy in Washington: From the New Deal to McCarthy* (Cambridge, MA: Harvard University Press, 1966); Oshinsky, David M., *A Conspiracy So Immense: The World of Joe McCarthy* (New York: The Free Press, 1983); Service, John S., *The Amerasia Papers: Some Problems in the History of U.S.–China Relations* (Berkeley: University of California Press, 1971).

SHACKLEY, THEODORE G. "TED" (1927–2002). Ted Shackley was an expert in U.S. clandestine operations in Cuba, Chile, and Vietnam; following the government investigations of the **Central Intelligence Agency (CIA)** in the mid-seventies, he retired and established his own security consulting firm.

In 1945, aged 18, Ted Shackley was taken into in U.S. Army intelligence largely because his grandmother had made him relatively fluent in Polish. He worked in counterintelligence in Berlin and Nuremberg. After **World War II** he planned to become a lawyer, but instead was recruited to the CIA in 1951. He appeared to others to be cold, efficient, unusual in his manner, and self-centered; he was given the nickname "Blond Ghost."

In the late 1950s Shackley became chief of station in Miami, and his task was to undermine Fidel Castro's (1927–) newly established Communist regime in Cuba. He used sabotage, and tried to build a network of spies and informants. Neither affected the Castro regime greatly because the spies and **agents** employed were also working for the Cuban secret services, which had been well organized in the latter half of 1959, following their adoption of **KGB** espionage methods. Also, some of Shackley's recruits indicated that he had become involved in drug trafficking.

In 1966 Shackley was sent to Laos, where drug dealing was ever present in recruiting tribesman to attack the enemy supply lines. Heroin was the basic currency and also was being used by U.S. troops. When **Lyndon B. Johnson** (1908–1973) ceased using the Laotians, he sent Shackley to Saigon, where he was chief of station from 1968 to 1973.

The CIA had been disgraced when it did not predict the **Tet Offensive** (1968), so Shackley began to emphasize intelligence gathering as much as clandestine operations. But he preferred reports to be more positive than depressing, and this may have contributed to the failure of President **Richard Nixon**'s (1913–1994) administration to get accurate estimates of how the Vietnam military operations were progressing.

Shackley's term as chief of station coincided with the period when John A. Walker, Jr. (1937–), who worked for 17 years for the **KGB** (1968–1985), was so effective in keeping the North Vietnamese well informed about U.S. air strikes and naval movements. Shackley wrote of the enemy, "they were ready. It was uncanny. We never figured it out" (Andrew and Gordievsky, 1990, p. 442).

In the early 1970s, after his return to Washington, Shackley was made part of the operation that was to undermine the elected Chilean government and assist the military coup of 1973 that brought Augusto Pinochet (1915–) to power. Consequently, he was promoted to the third most powerful position in the CIA, Associate Deputy Director for Operations. But shortly afterward, he was involved in the investigations (such as those conducted by the **Rockefeller Commission** and the **Church Committee**) into the CIA under Presidents **Gerald Ford** (1913–) and **Jimmy Carter** (1924–).

President Carter had Stansfield Turner restructure the CIA, and Shackley was pushed aside; he left the CIA in 1979 and ran a security consulting firm. The Iran–Contra Affair led to the jailing of some of his closest associates, but he escaped all charges.

See also ALLENDE GOSSENS, SALVADOR; IRANGATE/IRAN–CONTRA AFFAIR; WALKER, JOHN ANTHONY JR.

Sources: Andrew, Christopher, and Oleg Gordievsky, *KGB: The Inside Story of Its Foreign Operations from Lenin to Gorbachev* (London: Hodder and Stoughton, 1990); Barron, John, *Breaking the Ring* (New York: Avon Books, 1988); Jackson, Harold, "CIA Mastermind of Clandestine Operations in Cuba, Chile and Vietnam," *The Age* (Melbourne), December 23, 2002, Obituaries, p. 9 (originally published in *The Guardian*); Volkman, Ernest, *Espionage: The Greatest Spy Operations of the 20th Century* (New York: Wiley, 1995).

SHADRIN, NICHOLAS (1928–1975). Shadrin was Soviet **defector** whose disappearance was puzzling; he was suspected of being a **double agent.**

Nicholas Shadrin was the **Central Intelligence Agency (CIA)** name given to Nikolai Fyodorovich Atramanov, born in Leningrad. He was in the Soviet navy and defected to the United States while in Sweden in 1959. He was sponsored by the U.S. Office of Naval Intelligence, and gave valuable information on Soviet nuclear plans and tactics dealing with submarines.

In the United States, Shadrin was made a translator in the U.S. Naval Scientific and Technical Center. In 1966 he was sent to the Defense Intelligence Agency, and a Soviet **agent** tried to recruit him. Reluctantly, he went to the **Federal Bureau of Investigation (FBI)** and became a double agent, feeding the Soviets **disinformation.** Shadrin was code-named LARK. The CIA had expected that Shadrin's case officer would also defect.

In 1974 Shadrin told his Russian case officer that he thought he could find Yuri Nosenko (fl. 1927–1987), who had defected to the West in 1964. By 1975 the Soviets were convinced Shadrin was a double agent. In December he was told to go to Vienna to meet his new controller. Soviet agents abducted him, and in an attempt of get him secretly from Vienna to Moscow, they accidentally injected him with a fatal dose of a drug. His disappearance was a mystery to the West's intelligence community. Some thought he had defected to Russia, others, that he had died.

Shadrin's fate became known to the West when Vitaly Yurchenko (1936–) informed the CIA during his brief defection to the West in 1985.

See also YURCHENKO, VITALY

Sources: Andrew, Christopher, and Vasili Mitrokhin, *The Mitrokhin Archive: The KGB in Europe and the West* (London: Lane, 1999); Hurt, Henry, *The Spy Who Never Came Back* (New York: McGraw-Hill, 1981); Pincher, Chapman, *Traitors: The Anatomy of Treason* (New York: St. Martin's Press, 1987); Richelson, Jeffrey T., *A Century of Spies: Intelligence in the Twentieth Century* (New York: Oxford University Press, 1995).

SHERATON RAID (1983–1984). An embarrassing fiasco, and perhaps the worst scandal in the history of **ASIS**, was the Sheraton Hotel raid in Melbourne.

Like the sinking of the *Rainbow Warrior* (1986) by the French and the downing of the **U-2 spy flight** (1960), the fiasco of the Sheraton raid arose from an effort by the government to deny involvement in a failed secret operation. The denial was shaped thus: if the operation is blown, the secret government agency that executed it does not exist; the names of the **agents** are unknown; and the offending government never supported the secret offenders.

On November 11, 1983, training began for an ASIS team in close-quarters combat, surveillance, illegal entry methods, and medical skills. On November 24, arms were removed from a secret armory, without authorization. On November 25 it was decided that in a training operation an armed rescue would take place. The team members were briefed on November 26 and November 27: their task was to observe "John," a **defector** living on a farm outside the city; his brother "Michael," a cipher clerk in a foreign embassy in Canberra, also "wanted to defect," but first would have to be sure "John" was safe.

The training operation began with the surveillance of "John," who then went to a nearby town to consult with "foreign intelligence officers." Those officers abducted "John" and drove him to the Sheraton Hotel in Melbourne. In the course of this exercise the six trainees lost "John" and his "abductors." This was the *first* error in the fiasco.

An army instruction team that was helping to conduct the training had to tell the trainees that "John" and his "captors" had gone to the Sheraton. For two days the trainees' only task was to observe the "foreign intelligence officers." On November 29 the trainees were instructed to capture "John," who was in a room on the tenth floor of the Sheraton, from the "foreign intelligence officers."

Dressed as a waiter, a trainee went to room on the tenth floor to ask for someone to sign for a parcel delivery; a "foreign intelligence officer" refused, so the other trainees broke down the door with a sledgehammer. The use of force was not expected, and had not been mentioned as a possibility to the authorities of the training operation. This was the *second* mistake; those in charge of all such operations should be fully informed on all details of a training operation.

The "foreign intelligence officers" who had refused entry to the room were handcuffed and "drugged"; the trainees removed "John," also "drugged," from the bathtub, dried and dressed him, and prepared to leave.

The hotel manager was alerted and went to investigate. He was about to step from the elevator when he was confronted by the trainee team leader; they fought in the elevator, and when the elevator reached the ground floor, the manager called the police.

The team leader returned to the room, removed the handcuffs from the "foreign intelligence officers," and ran downstairs to meet his team, which was leaving the hotel via a backdoor.

Meanwhile, the team with "John" had gone to the ground floor, only to be met by the angry manager and staff. The team explained that they were on an ASIS training exercise, escaped via the kitchen, and drove off in the getaway car. The hotel staff got the automobile's license number.

Within minutes the police stopped the car and took the occupants for questioning. On learning what had happened, the head of the operation went to the hotel, misrepresented himself, explained what had happened, and offered to pay for the damage.

In police custody the trainees seemed to be amused by the police concern that a crime had been committed, and on learning what had happened, several state and federal politicians began to squabble about this publicly.

The misadventure was fully and dramatically reported in the media, and a scandal developed involving the following issues: secret activities are beyond the law; thus, when caught, intelligence agents should not be punished like criminals; federal government politicians pressured the state politicians to drop the state police's charges; the federal government hinted it would make public the identity of the trainees to the state police; the head of the relevant section of the ASIS service was forced to retire; the federal government decided to keep secret the trainees' names; the federal government maintained it had nothing to do with the scandal; later a federal government spokesman denounced the secret service and insisted all costs be claimed from its budget; the federal government spokesman publicly stated how many people were involved in the secret training exercise and promised the state police he would provide the names, a promise he never kept; the federal government spokesman claimed in Parliament that the government did not know the organization that planned the training operation, and changed the final draft of *Hansard*, the official record of Parliament, to this effect, even though the actual words used had already appeared in newspaper reports.

To limit the public discussion, speculation, and scandal, and to examine the case further, the federal government established a royal commission to look into the Sheraton raid. The nation's Prime Minister and the state Premier conferred on national security issues raised by revealing the identities of the 12 people involved in the raid.

The scandal would not die. Then stories appeared about Australian spies and agents abroad having their identities revealed and their operations aborted if names were to be made public.

The royal commission ended in February 1984, found that the Sheraton raid had been an organizational error, and hoped the ensuing scandal would not endanger future ASIS operations or the reputation of its officers; it criticized ASIS management; and it absolved the federal government even though it appointed a person to head special operations who had no experience of a special operations.

Thus the Westminster Principle, that ministers are responsible for the activities of their departments, was effectively ignored; and the commission argued that the minister "should not have been informed."

In March 1984 the state and federal governments introduced legislation to enable the courts to conceal the identities of trainees, in the national interest. In November 1984 the federal High Court ruled the secret contract did not stop government from giving identities, but supported the nondisclosure of identities. Legal opinions agreed that in such cases counterespionage activities should attract legal sanctions; police officers ought not to be so zealous in dealing with minor offenses; discretion should be used in revealing information related to secret operations; it is illegal for a secret service officer to harm a citizen; blame might best be attributed to higher officers and managers; secrecy is no justification for taking illegal action; and government and Parliament should offer no dispensation from due legal process.

The scandal slowly died down, the training unit was quietly disbanded, and the Sheraton Hotel was compensated with over AUS$300,000; the government set up another inquiry that quietly recommended disciplinary action; and the project head was removed from office.

Source: Toohey, Brian, and Brian Pinwell, *Oyster: The Story of the Australian Secret Intelligence Services* (Port Melbourne: William Heinemann Australia, 1989).

SILVERMAN, A. GEORGE (fl. 1930–1955). George Silverman was a member of the group of U.S. government employees who provided information through various channels for the Soviets, beginning with the courier Whittaker Chambers (1901–1961), and later under the control of Nathan Gregory Silvermaster (fl. 1899–1964).

George Silverman was a Harvard graduate who became a U.S. Treasury statistician, and entered the network of informers around Whittaker Chambers from 1935 to 1936. He may have recruited Harry Dexter White (1892–1948). He worked for the Railway Retirement Board from the mid-1930s to 1942, and was a **CPUSA** underground supporter. He then got a position at the **Pentagon**, and while there helped William Ludwig Ullman to gain employment as well. Both supported the Russians with military secrets. Their motive seems to have been similar to that of the Magnificent Five: to support the **COMINTERN**'s secret war against fascism. His associates saw Silverman as brilliant, odd, offensive, indiscreet, dogmatic, and fearful of being caught by the **Federal Bureau of Investigation (FBI)**.

See also CHAMBERS, WHITTAKER; SILVERMASTER, NATHAN

Sources: Andrew, Christopher, and Oleg Gordievsky, *KGB: The Inside Story of Its Foreign Operations from Lenin to Gorbachev* (London: Hodder and Stoughton, 1990); Andrew, Christopher, and Vasili Mitrokhin, *The Mitrokhin Archive: The KGB in Europe and the West* (London: Lane, 1999); Olmstead, Kathryn, *Red Spy Queen: A Biography of Elizabeth Bentley* (Chapel Hill: University of North Carolina Press, 2002); Weinstein, Allen, and Alexander Vassiliev, *The Haunted Wood: Soviet Espionage in America—The Stalin Era* (New York: Random House, 1999).

SILVERMASTER, HELEN WITTE (fl. 1900–1948).

Helen Silvermaster, the wife of Nathan G. Silvermaster (fl. 1899–1957), helped her husband in his organization of the Silvermaster Group in Washington to ensure the **U.S.S.R.** had information from the United States that would help in negotiations for postwar Europe.

Helen Silvermaster, née Witte, was born into the aristocratic Russian Baltic family of Baron Witte and was distantly related to the czarist Prime Minister Count Witte. Her father had Communist leanings. She helped him to hide Communist sympathizers from the czarist police, and to distribute Bolshevik literature. She married a White Russian nobleman, but she divorced him shortly after the birth of their son.

Helen came to the United States, where she married Nathan Gregory Silvermaster, a Jew who had been persecuted in Russia and raised in China. They met while Nathan was a postgraduate student at the University of California (1927). Early in the 1930s he was an underground member of the **CPUSA** and probably an **OGPU agent**.

The Silvermasters went to Washington, DC, in 1935 to work in the administration of the New Deal. Nathan, an economist, became the coordinator of the Silvermaster Group, a number of Americans who had deep sympathy with the Soviet experiment and who, from their various government departments, would provide information for Silvermaster, who then passed it to the U.S.S.R.

Helen would photograph the documents at her home in Washington, help collate and maintain the classified information, and make it available to Elizabeth Bentley (1908–1963) every two weeks or so, when she came to collect it for her case officer (1941–1944).

In the household was a family friend, William Ludwig Ullman, who worked for the Division of Monetary Research in the U.S. Treasury and later at the **Pentagon**. He was an amateur photographer, and a member of the Silvermaster Group. Ullman and Helen were lovers, which, it appears, Nathan did not mind.

Shortly after meeting Elizabeth Bentley for the first time, Helen Silvermaster did not trust her, and believed she might be a **Federal Bureau of Investigation (FBI)** agent. She spoke her mind to Jacob Golos (1890–1943), Bentley's case officer, and was admonished for airing such suspicions. When Bentley did defect, she described Helen's activities in the Silvermaster Group, and in response Helen denied them all. The Silvermasters left Washington after Bentley's revelations and lived in New Jersey.

See also BENTLEY, ELIZABETH; SILVERMASTER, NATHAN

Sources: Haynes, John Earl, and Harvey Klehr, *Venona: Decoding Soviet Espionage in America* (New Haven, CT: Yale University Press, 1999); Mahoney, M. H., *Women in Espionage* (Santa Barbara, CA: ABC-CLIO, 1993); Olmstead, Kathryn, *Red Spy Queen: A Biography of Elizabeth Bentley* (Chapel Hill: University of North Carolina Press, 2002);

Weinstein, Allen, and Alexander Vassiliev, *The Haunted Wood: Soviet Espionage in America—The Stalin Era* (New York: Random House, 1999).

SILVERMASTER, NATHAN GREGORY (fl. 1899–1957). Nathan Gregory Silvermaster was the head of one of the pro-Soviet groups whose members worked in various U.S. government agencies in Washington and produced for the Soviets valuable information collected by such couriers as Whittaker Chambers (1901–1961) and Elizabeth Bentley (1908–1963). The Silvermaster Group members were not always clear as to who would get the information: the **NKGB** in Moscow, the **CPUSA**, or the **COMINTERN.**

Nathan Silvermaster was born in Odessa and came with his family to the United States in 1914. He spoke Russian, studied economics at college, and between 1920 and 1935 was a postgraduate student of economics at the University of California and an active Communist. He served as **Earl Browder**'s (1891–1973) courier in the 1934 strike in California. He married Helen Witte (**code name** DORA), a relative of the czarist Prime Minister Count Witte.

In 1935 the Silvermasters came to Washington, where Nathan worked in various government agencies, eventually joining the U.S. Treasury Department. William Ludwig Ullman, a friend and fellow Communist, lived in the Silvermasters' apartment. In 1940 he met Jacob Golos (1890–1943) through Earl Browder. Because Silvermaster spoke Russian, he was well-received among Soviet **agents.**

In June 1942 Silvermaster was discharged from the Treasury Department and hired by the Farm Security Administration. He had been investigated by the **Federal Bureau of Investigation (FBI),** but with Lauchlin Currie's (1900–1993) help and the support of Harry Dexter White (1892–1948) he managed to satisfy his investigators and keep his position.

Silvermaster was supplied with information by several members, known as the Silvermaster Group, including Solomon Adler, Frank Coe, William Taylor, Harry Dexter White, William Ludwig Ullman, David Silverman, and Lauchlin Currie. From the Foreign Economic Administration, Silvermaster got information for the Soviets from Sonia Gold (in Treasury) and Bella Gold (in Commerce). Helen Silvermaster collated the material brought to their apartment.

Valuable as it was, the information received did not always satisfy the leaders of the NKGB in Moscow, who wanted to know how leaders in the United States felt about the national borders in Europe that were to be established after **World War II,** and the independence of small nations on Russia's western border with Europe.

In time it was clear that Silvermaster was an autocratic taskmaster who did not want control of the Silvermaster Group taken from him. Not long before the war ended, his relations with his superior inside the United States—Silverman did not know the man was Itzhak Akhmerov—were in tatters, and those supplying the information were finding Silvermaster a difficult man to serve.

In 1944 the Soviets awarded Silvermaster the **Order of the Red Banner**, and his wife, the Order of the Red Star, in honor of their work. By 1945 his work for the Soviets was over.

In July 1947 Silvermaster was living with a Russian friend in New Jersey, and by 1951 he and William Ludwig Ullman had become wealthy house builders.

See also SILVERMASTER, HELEN WITTE

Sources: Andrew, Christopher, and Oleg Gordievsky, *KGB: The Inside Story of Its Foreign Operations from Lenin to Gorbachev* (London: Hodder and Stoughton, 1990); Andrew, Christopher, and Vasili Mitrokhin, *The Mitrokhin Archive: The KGB in Europe and the West* (London: Lane, 1999); Olmstead, Kathryn, *Red Spy Queen: A Biography of Elizabeth Bentley* (Chapel Hill: University of North Carolina Press, 2002); Weinstein, Allen, and Alexander Vassiliev, *The Haunted Wood: Soviet Espionage in America—The Stalin Era* (New York: Random House, 1999).

SKRIPOV, IVAN (fl. 1960–1963). Ivan Skripov, the First Secretary at the Soviet embassy in Canberra, Australia, was expelled for espionage on February 2, 1963. He had been set up by an **agent provocateur,** Kay Marshall (fl. 1935–1964).

The Australian intelligence community was proud of its achievement in catching Skripov, who had been filmed meeting with Kay Marshall in the Sydney Botanical Gardens. In response to Skripov's expulsion from Australia, in June 1963 an Australian diplomat, W. I. Morrison, was expelled from Moscow on charges of espionage. Morrison had been expelled once before, in 1954, after Vladimir Petrov (1907–1991) had defected. Skripov never held a diplomatic post again.

See also MARSHALL, KAY; PETROV, VLADIMIR

Sources: Hall, Richard, *The Secret State: Australia's Spy Industry* (Stanmore, NSW: Cassell, 1978); McKnight, David, *Australia's Spies and Their Secrets* (St. Leonards, NSW: Allen and Unwin, 1994).

SOBELL, MORTON (1917–). Morton Sobell was convicted of conspiracy to commit espionage with of the Rosenbergs in 1951, and sentenced to a jail for 30 years. His case was one of the most controversial in U.S. legal history because the charge against him involved questionable police procedures and was based largely on statements from a close friend, who perjured himself.

Son of a Bronx pharmacist, Morton Sobell was educated at Stuyvesant High School and the City College of New York. He completed a master's degree in electrical engineering at the University of Michigan, and worked briefly at the Naval Ordnance Bureau in Washington, and in Schenectady, New York, worked for General Electric. From 1939 to 1943 Sobell was involved with the Communist Party's activities.

In June 1950 Sobell and his wife, Helen, took a vacation to Mexico City, where they rented an apartment. He mailed some letters using unimaginative pseudonyms, which is surprising because he was well known to the local police, who reported on his movements to the **Federal Bureau of Investigation (FBI).** He inquired about traveling to Cuba, wandered the city, and befriended a neighbor who shared his liberal political views.

Sobell had wanted to go to Mexico sooner, but the job he was working on had to be finished; also, he wanted to leave the United States because he did not want to serve in the U.S. forces in Korea and felt that his country was tending toward dictatorship. In Mexico there were were many American citizens, political fugitives who did not want to be subpoenaed to appear before the **House Un-American Activities Committee** inquiries.

Sobell went to Vera Cruz and Tampico after cashing in his return tickets to New York. He used pseudonyms again when traveling. He then went back to Mexico City, and he and his wife prepared to return to New York.

In mid-August 1950, Sobell was kidnapped from Mexico City by men claiming to be police. He was put struggling into a taxi, and knocked unconscious. The family was driven to the border town of Laredo, Texas, where they were deported from Mexico and jailed for five days. They were then brought to the Rosenbergs' indictment and charged with having conspired to commit espionage from June 15, 1944, to August 3, 1950.

With Julius and Ethel Rosenberg, Anatoli A. Yakovlev, and David Greenglass, Morton Sobell went to trial on March 6, 1951, in New York. Sobell was charged with giving the Soviets information relating to national defense of the United States.

At first Sobell was not charged with any particular offense. Later an informant, his close friend and best man at Sobell's wedding, Max Elitcher, testified that Sobell was getting information for Russia from his work at General Electric in Schenectady. Elitcher was a perjurer. Sobell did not testify at the trial, choosing instead to assert his privilege under the **Fifth Amendment**. The prosecution presented no evidence that Sobell had anything to do with the **atom bomb** research; nevertheless he was connected with the Rosenbergs, and this gave the impression that an extensive spy ring had been operating. The Rosenbergs were sentenced to death, and Sobell was given 30 years in prison.

On appeal it was argued that Max Elitcher's evidence was inadmissible hearsay; that Sobell was never part of the conspiracy; and that he was illegally kidnapped by U.S. **agents** in a place outside their jurisdiction. A new trial was sought on these grounds, emphasizing that he should be tried by himself. The appeal failed.

Sobell was sent to Alcatraz for seven years. In late February 1958 he was moved from Alcatraz to Leavenworth, and later to the Atlanta Penitentiary. Alcatraz was disgusting, and had been chosen for Sobell because the FBI and U.S. Justice Department officials hoped the unpleasant prison conditions would induce him to confess to what the officials believed he had done. He was adamant that he would not rat on his fellow prisoners to save his own skin. He maintained that he would always be open and honest while in prison. Over the years many notables supported his cause, including Bertrand Russell (1872–1970).

In 1962 Sobell made his first application for parole; it failed. Thereafter his family picketed in front of the White House. His case is one of the most controversial in U.S. legal history. In 1966 Sobell petitioned the U.S. District Court for release from prison, on the assumption that the secrecy of Klaus Fuchs's (1911–1988) confession had prevented showing that Harry Gold (1912–1972) was not the courier for David Greenglass (1922–) or Fuchs, and that information from Greenglass was without any credence. His petition failed.

In 1969 Sobell was released from prison, and he published his autobiography in 1974 with considerable emphasis on his experiences in prison. He maintained the he was never involved in any spy ring, and claimed that he had fled to Mexico because he had earlier lied about his membership in the Communist Party. Within three weeks of being released he was back in school, studying electrical engineering and enjoying the challenge of understanding the great developments in the field since his incarceration.

Sobell wrote that he saw his case as an integral part of the "establishment's national policy," and that "Ethel and Julius could never have been executed in 1969. People could no longer be frightened with submission the way they had been in the 1950s . . . now [blacks] all rode head erect [on the subway] proudly looking ahead" (Sobell, 1974, pp. 522, 525).

In 1997 Sobell's letters to newspapers in New York showed how dissatisfied he was with the interpretations put on the VENONA material in regard to the Rosenberg case. In 2001 the Golden Gate National Park Association reprinted his autobiography, largely because it was written by a well-educated man and gave a remarkably accurate account of prison life in Alcatraz.

Recent studies suggest that the information that might have come to the Soviets from Sobell would not have been of much value to the development of the Soviet atom bomb; rather, it was the work of Ted Hall (1925–1999) and Klaus Fuchs that was of importance to the Russians. Also, if Sobell had been connected to a conspiracy, then it was probably not one involving the Rosenbergs.

See also FUCHS, EMIL JULIUS KLAUS; GOLD, HARRY; GREENGLASS, DAVID, AND GREENGLASS, RUTH; HALL, THEODORE; ROSENBERG, ETHEL, AND ROSENBERG, JULIUS

Sources: Allen, Thomas B., and Norman Polmar, *Merchants of Treason: America's Secrets for Sale* (New York: Delacorte Press, 1988); Radosh, Ronald, and Joyce Milton, *The Rosenberg File: A Search for the Truth* (New York: Holt, Rinehart and Winston, 1983); Root, Jonathan, *The Betrayers: The Rosenberg Case—A Reappraisal of an American Crisis* (New York: Coward-McCann, 1963); Sobell, Morton, *On Doing Time* (New York: Scribner's, 1974); Sobell, Morton, "Sobell on 'Venona and the Rosenbergs'" (1997), www2.h-net.msu.ed/~diplo/Sobell.htm; Sobell, Morton, *On Doing Time*, 2nd ed. (San Francisco: Golden Gate National Park Association, 2001); Williams, Robert C., *Klaus Fuchs, Atom Spy* (Cambridge, MA: Harvard University Press, 1987).

SPYCATCHER AFFAIR (1987). The Spycatcher Affair arose when Peter Wright (1916–1995), a retired **MI5** officer, published his memoirs outside Britain; the British government then banned the sale of the book and spent over a year attempting, without success, to make the ban legal. The affair shows that it is necessary to establish in Britain (if not elsewhere), as Rimington (2002, p. 287) states, "a properly run clearance procedure which people are encouraged to use instead of one that is . . . confusing to everyone."

In July 1984 Wright claimed, among other things, that Sir Roger Hollis (1905–1973), former head of MI5, had been a Soviet **agent**. Also, he told much about the activities of MI5, which did little to enhance the agency's reputation during the **Cold War.**

At the end of March 1987, the Supreme Court in Sydney, Australia, allowed publication of *Spycatcher* in Australia. The British government had spent 18 months trying to prevent its publication, claiming that it would endanger national security and encourage other former MI5 agents to publish confidential information.

A complete set of case reports from four jurisdictions appeared in the report by Fysh (1989); Chapman Pincher (1988), a popular espionage journalist whom Peter Wright informed about the British secret service, wrote to place his literary reputation in a good light and exonerate himself from illegal dealings.

Turnbull (1988) presents a full, well-written account of his relations with Peter Wright and the crossexamination he made of Sir Robert Armstrong, who, not fully aware of his role, came to Australia to put the case for Prime Minister **Margaret Thatcher (1925–).**

After the court's decision to allow publication of the book, the spokesperson for the U.K. government announced that the government had won the case. In fact it had lost.

Since the Spycatcher Affair, other cases have arisen, one of which involved Richard Tomlinson, recruited to **MI6** in 1991 while at Cambridge and jailed for a year for breaking a Cold War code that Peter Wright, and Stella Rimington, former head of MI5, violated.

See also RIMINGTON, STELLA; WRIGHT, PETER

Sources: Fysh, Michael, *The Spycatcher Cases* (London: Sweet and Maxwell, 1989); Hall, Richard V., *A Spy's Revenge* (Ringwood, VIC: Penguin, 1987); Pincher, Chapman, *The Spycatcher Affair* (New York: St. Martin's Press, 1988); Rimington, Stella, *Open Secret: The Autobiography of the Former Director-General of MI5* (London: Hutchinson, 2001; Arrow, 2002); Tomlinson, Richard, *The Big Breach: From Top Secret to Maximum Security* (New York: HarperCollins, 2001); Turnbull, Malcolm, *The Spycatcher Trial* (London: Heinemann, 1988); Wright, Peter, with Paul Greengrass, *Spycatcher: The Candid Autobiography of a Senior Intelligence Officer* (Melbourne: William Heinemann Australia, 1987).

STANLEY, JOHN (1916–2000). John Stanley managed the Prudential Assurance Company's office in Cairo, and became suspected of espionage.

Five weeks after President Gamal Abdel Nasser (1918–1970) of Egypt had nationalized the Suez Canal, John Stanley was arrested in Cairo and interrogated at 2:30 A.M. on September 3, 1956. With four other Britons and a dozen Egyptians he was accused of membership in an espionage ring, and was sent to a Cairo jail to await trial. Egyptian authorities could produce no convincing evidence that Stanley had ever been a spy, although they were interested in his index of phonograph records and the diagrams he had made about the rules of yacht races, which they probably suspected consisted of secret information in code.

For 10 months Stanley would often recite Psalms in his cell, smoke casually whenever in court, and write cheerful letters to his wife about the amusing handlebar mustache he was trying to grow. References to the mustache were considered to be a code. "The Moustache They Feared," as he was dubbed, was set free and arrived in London on July 1, 1957.

Source: Anonymous, "Obituary: John Stanley, Tried for Espionage During the Suez Crisis 9-5-1916–2000," *The Age*, September 12, 2000, Today, Life & Times, p. 7.

STASHINSKY, BOGDAN (1931–). Stashinsky was a **KGB** assassin who defected while the Berlin Wall was being erected, in August 1961.

Bogdan Stashinsky was born in a village near Limburg (Lvov) in West Ukraine, the third child in a peasant family of Greek Orthodox Church members. His youth was a confusion of national loyalties: Polish, Ukrainian, German, and Russian.

In 1948 Stashinsky graduated from the Lvov Gymnasium and, failing to gain entrance to a medical course, he studied mathematics at the Lvov Teachers' Training College. In mid-1950 he was caught traveling on a train without a ticket, and was interrogated by the Ministry of State Security (**MGB**), and it became clear to him that if his family were to be protected from prosecution for their resistance to Soviet rule in the Ukraine, then he should give the **U.S.S.R.** information on the Ukrainian underground. Aged 19, the frightened lad signed a declaration binding him to work for the MGB and pledging him to secrecy.

Fearing that if he did not agree he might find his studies canceled, Stashinsky penetrated the underground group, informed on it, and was then told that if he wanted to remain safe and free, he had to give up his studies and enter the MGB.

Stashinsky was sent to Kiev for two years of training and also learned German. The MGB then allowed him (in 1954) to see his parents and tell them where he worked. Drawn into espionage before he knew what was happening to him, he was given a new identity: Joseph Lehman, a look-alike from Poland, born in Germany in November 1930, one year before his own birth. Stashinsky established the Lehman

legend for himself, and, when handed over to a Soviet case officer in the Soviet-occupied zone of Germany, became highly regarded by the KGB.

Stashinsky was a press operator in a factory close to the Czech and East German borders. He then moved to East Berlin as a freelance interpreter in German and Polish at the East German Ministry for Home and Foreign Trade. In 1956 he started working solely for the KGB. As Joseph Lehman he had established contact with Ukrainian immigrants working in Munich, and began his watch on Lev Rebet, former Ukrainian politician and resistance leader. By now the West German secret police knew of Stashinsky, and he appears to have felt he was a true believer in the Communist cause.

Meanwhile, Stashinsky fell in love with a German woman, Inga Pohl, age 21, an apprentice hairdresser in West Berlin whose family was hostile to communism. He introduced himself to her as Joseph Lehman, a German national from Poland.

Following orders from the KGB, Stashinsky murdered Rebet in October 1957, found it hard to reconcile himself to the act, and became deeply worried about his relationship with Inga. In 1958 he was ordered to assassinate Stephan Bandera, a Ukrainian writer to be killed in the same way as Rebet. By now Stashinsky was torn among his life with the woman he loved, his Christian belief that he should not kill, the guilt at killing in a cowardly way, and the fear that if he did not do as the KGB ordered, he would never have a life with Inga. Also, he felt there was no possibility of escape from the KGB.

By April 1959 Stashinsky and Inga were secretly engaged, against the wishes of the KGB. The KGB gave him a weapon and instructions that would make it possible to complete a perfect murder of Stephan Bandera. His first attempt was a failure. In August 1959 he was given permission to visit his parents in the following October, but he must kill Bandera first. He was left in no doubt of what would happen if he failed a second time. He was successful, and when he reported his mission complete, he was awarded the **Order of the Red Banner,** to be presented to him in Moscow.

Stashinsky had to lie to Inga and pretend that he was not going to Moscow. He began to fret about how much he hated his job and decided never to kill again. He wanted to marry, and to tell Inga the truth about himself; so he told her that he was not an interpreter for the East German Trade Ministry but a member the KGB.

At Christmas 1959 Stashinsky returned to East Berlin, under orders not to go to West Germany or into West Berlin. He doubled back swiftly to be with Inga at the hairdresser's in West Berlin. There he told her everything except that he had murdered two men. They agreed to keep the full story from her parents, and to maintain his identity as Joseph Lehman. After much difficulty from the KGB they got permission to marry in a Protestant church, and in May 1960 were ordered back to Moscow, as a married couple, so he could improve his German.

Together they decided that life under Soviet domination was a living hell. Inga was pregnant in September; the KGB wanted her to abort. This determined their decision to defect to the West. They had their baby, but the child died. The KGB wanted to detain them, declaring the child had been poisoned by the Americans in an effort to have Stashinsky come over to the West.

On August 12, the day before the Berlin Wall was to become a reality, and the day of their baby's funeral, they escaped into West Berlin. They were taken to the West German police and then the U.S. Security Offices, where, after questioning,

Stashinsky was handed over to the police and made to stand trial in October 1962.

He told everything, and was sentenced to six years in prison for each murder and one year for espionage; and this was commuted to a total of eight years. In 1966 he was secretly released on New Year's Eve, and went to America.

Anatoli Golitsyn (1926–) defected four months after Stashinsky in 1960, and said that 17 KGB officers were fired or demoted after Stashinsky's trial and imprisonment.

See also GOLITSYN, ANATOLI; REBET AND BANDERA WET AFFAIRS

Sources: Anders, Karl, *Murder to Order* (London: Ampersand, 1965); Andrew, Christopher, and Vasili Mitrokhin, *The Mitrokhin Archive: The KGB in Europe and the West* (London: Lane, 1999); Deacon, Richard, with Nigel West, *Spy! Six Stories of Modern Espionage* (London: BBC, 1980); Steele, John L., "Assassin Disarmed by Love," in Allen Dulles, ed., *Great True Spy Stories* (Secaucus, NJ: Castle, 1966), pp. 337–350; Subcommittee to Investigate the Administration of the Internal Security Laws of the Committee of the Judiciary, United States Senate, *Murder and Kidnapping as an Instrument of Soviet Policy* (Washington, DC: Government Printing Office, 1965).

STERN, MARTHA DODD (1908–1990). With her husband, Alfred Kaufman Stern, Martha Dodd, a U.S. citizen and Soviet **agent,** was indicted for espionage against the United States; the charges were dropped in 1979 when it was clear that a prosecution would not be successful.

Martha Dodd was born into the family of an academic and diplomat. A popular and attractive young woman who would flirt relentlessly, she was once the poet Carl Sandburg's (1878–1967) lover, and he wrote poetry about his feelings for her. In 1932 she married a New York Banker on impulse. She got divorced of him, and in 1933 her father, a former professor of history at the University of Chicago, where she had studied, took her with him to Berlin. He had been appointed U.S. ambassador to Hitler's Germany.

While in Germany, Martha had an affair with the head of the Gestapo. Evidence recently appeared that she wanted sexual relations with many, many men whom she met. Once she tried to seduce Adolf Hitler (1889–1945), but he refused her. She became passionately opposed to Nazism. Possibly at about this time she was recruited to communism. In 1936 she began an affair with the First Secretary of the Soviet embassy. She stole some security documents from her father and gave them to her Soviet lover. She vowed to marry him, but he died in **Josef Stalin**'s (1879–1953) purge of his political enemies.

On her return to America in 1938, Martha married a wealthy man, Alfred Kaufman Stern (fl. 1896–1986), and they devoted their lives to left-wing causes. Alfred Stern had been married to a Sears Roebuck heiress. In 1939 Martha Stern published a memoir that exposed the horror of Nazism, *Through Embassy Eyes*. In the early 1940s, for a short period, the book was scheduled to be filmed by Darryl Zanuck.

Alfred Stern and his wife gave large sums to the **CPUSA** in the 1940s. Her brother, William Dodd, Jr., shared their views. They lived comfortably in an apartment on Central Park West in New York City, and lavishly entertained many artists and writers who shared their views at parties in their sumptuous home in Connecticut.

Recruited—perhaps by Martha—into Soviet espionage, Alfred used a bogus vice presidency of the Boris Morros Music Company as a cover for Soviet **illegals.** The company head was Boris Morros (1895–1963), a flamboyant Hollywood producer and music publisher who had earlier been recruited as a Russian spy. He introduced

Alfred Stern to the chief of Russian espionage in the United States. By December 1943 Alfred Stern had provided U.S.$130,000 capital for the company.

Unknown to his recruiter, and to the Sterns, Boris Morros was a **double agent** working for the **Federal Bureau of Investigation (FBI)**. Alfred Stern was suspicious of Morros, but his case officer dismissed the idea. Into their espionage group Martha introduced Jane Zlatovski (1912–1979) and others.

In December 1953 the Sterns fled the United States for Mexico to avoid being called as witnesses in the investigation into Soviet espionage in the United States. To stay in Mexico without the proper documents, the Sterns bribed Mexican officials. Also, they transferred money from the sale of stocks and securities in the United States to Mexico, and with the money established two mercantile companies.

In January 1957 the Sterns were subpoenaed to appear in New York before a grand jury, but with the help of a lawyer friend who had been a U.S. ambassador to Mexico, they avoided extradition, and paid a fine of U.S.$50,000 for contempt of court.

Mexican police agents, who had previously helped the FBI abduct suspected Communists seeking safe haven in Mexico, planned to kidnap the Sterns and informally deport them to a spot near Laredo, Texas. From that point the Sterns could be abducted by the FBI and taken to New York. The Sterns arranged with a **KGB** agent at the Soviet embassy in Mexico City to get fake passports from Paraguay, and then fly to Prague. Two days beforehand, their lawyer friend flew directly to Ireland. When the Paraguayan government learned of the corruption among its Mexican embassy staff, it canceled the passports.

The Sterns settled in Prague, and for most of 1957 lived in Russia. Between 1963 and 1970 they were in Cuba, until Martha Stern found the country too unpleasant for her taste and they returned to Prague.

Almost 20 years after the Sterns had been indicted for espionage against the United States in 1957, President **Jimmy Carter** (1924–) was petitioned to reconsider the indictments. In March 1979 the charges against the Sterns were dropped for lack of adequate information and evidence to ensure prosecution. A Democratic Congressman had taken up their cause, and managed to get them what they had wanted. Alfred Stern contributed generously to the Congressman's campaign.

Alfred died in Prague in July 1986, and Martha in August 1990.

Sources: Haynes, John Earl, and Harvey Klehr, *Venona: Decoding Soviet Espionage in America* (New Haven, CT: Yale University Press, 1999); Mahoney, Harry T., and Marjorie L. Mahoney, *Biographic Dictionary of Espionage* (San Francisco: Austin & Winfield, 1998); Mahoney, M. H., *Women in Espionage* (Santa Barbara, CA: ABC-CLIO, 1993); Morros, Boris, *My Ten Years as a Counterspy* (New York: Viking Press, 1959); Weinstein, Allen, and Alexander Vassiliev, *The Haunted Wood: Soviet Espionage in America—The Stalin Era* (New York: Random House, 1999).

STONEHOUSE, JOHN (1925–1988). Stonehouse, a British politician, was alleged to be a spy for the Czechoslovakian intelligence organization, StB, and appears to have been caught in a honeytrap operation.

John Stonehouse was a former British Labour minister in the Aviation and Technology ministries, later Postmaster-General and Minister for Posts and Telecommunications. He may have been enticed in a honeytrap operation in Czechoslovakia.

He entered Parliament in 1957 unsuspected of espionage for the Soviets. Later he led the life of a man unsatisfied with his identity. He faked a suicide in 1974 by leaving his clothes on the beach in Miami Beach. Later, using a false passport, he turned up in Australia, aiming to establish a new life and apparently seeking to avoid responsibilities as an alleged director of a bank in Bangladesh. Also, he was running away with his secretary. In December 1974, Prime Minister **Harold Wilson** (1916–1995) had announced that **MI5** had no evidence, other than two Czechoslovakian defectors' statements, that Stonehouse had been an StB spy.

Late in March 1975 Stonehouse and his secretary were charged with forging and uttering. A warrant was issued in London for their arrest, alleging that he had stolen over £22,000 and U.S.$12,000 with false traveler's checks, illegal overdrafts, false birth certificates, and false applications for passports. He tried to leave Australia while on bail in June 1975. He was sent to England, where he addressed the House of Commons in October that year.

Early in April 1976 Stonehouse quit the Labour Party, leaving it with a majority of only one; on April 14 he joined the English National Party. In August he was found guilty of fraud and theft, and sentenced to seven years in jail. His mistress got two years. He resigned as an MP on August 27, 1976, and was released from prison on August 14, 1979.

Stonehouse decided to be a novelist, and in 1983 he proposed writing a novel with Chapman Pincher. He published *Ralph* (1982). He died five years later. Although he was cleared of treachery, and the Czechs had apparently not succeeded in blackmailing him into espionage, MI5 officials believed otherwise.

See also HONEYTRAP OPERATIONS

Sources: Andrew, Christopher, and Oleg Gordievsky, *KGB: The Inside Story of Its Foreign Operations from Lenin to Gorbachev* (London: Hodder and Stoughton, 1990); Pincher, Chapman, *Their Trade Is Treachery* (London: Sidgwick & Jackson, 1981; rev. ed., New York: Bantam, 1982); Pincher, Chapman, *Too Secret Too Long* (London: Sidgwick & Jackson, 1984); Stonehouse, John, *Ralph* (London: Jonathan Cape, 1982); Wright, Peter, with Paul Greengrass, *Spycatcher: The Candid Autobiography of a Senior Intelligence Officer* (Melbourne: William Heinemann Australia, 1987).

STRAIGHT, MICHAEL WHITNEY (1916–2004). Michael Straight was a romantic Communist who gave large sums to the Communist cause and served the interests of the **U.S.S.R.** until **World War II** began and he joined the U.S. Air Force. He confessed to serving the Communists, and in doing so revealed Anthony Blunt (1907–1983).

Born in the United States to rich parents, Michael Straight was educated at Dartington Hall in Devon, England; attended the London School of Economics in 1933; and took up left-wing politics. In the autumn of 1934 he went to university in Cambridge to study economics, and moved into Trinity College in his second year. At Cambridge he joined a Communist cell, funded the *Daily Worker* for several years, and in 1936 he accepted the invitation to become a member of the elite intellectual group at Cambridge, the **Apostles**. Anthony Blunt recruited him into Soviet service in 1937. At the time Straight's income was about to rise from U.S.$50,000 to U.S.$75,000.

In July 1937 Straight sailed to America, and sought help from President Franklin Roosevelt (1882–1945) and his wife, who were family friends of the Straights, to find employment. He worked as a volunteer on temporary assignment in the Office of the Economic Adviser in the Department of State, and wrote a report about Europe.

In April 1938 Straight was contacted by his Soviet handler, Michael Green, the name used by Iskhak Akhmerov (1901–1975). In September 1938 he gave his handler a copy of the report. He was ordered to work for Moscow's cause in the United States, but did not do exactly what was needed by **Moscow Center**: **talent spotting** among high government officials, especially in the White House.

The **Ribbentrop–Molotov Pact** in late August 1939 shocked Straight, as it did other Communist intellectuals. He married. The two experiences, combined with "Michael Green's" departure from America, reduced Straight's interest in the Communist cause. By July 1941 he was working for the *New Republic*. In 1942, when "Michael Green" returned to America, Straight made it clear to him that he was not serving the Soviet cause any further. He joined the U.S. Air Force.

In London in 1946, Straight met once with Anthony Blunt, and in 1949 he met with Guy Burgess (1911–1963). In March 1951 he met Burgess in Washington. By 1956 Straight saw himself as a liberal, and committed to advance the conditions of the poor and minorities in the United States.

Straight became an author and published novels, and was always a patron of the arts. In June 1963 President **John F. Kennedy** (1917–1963) created the Advisory Council on the Arts, and Arthur Schlesinger, Jr., showed Straight a list of names selected by the President. Among the 30 members of the Council he found his own name. Also, Straight was expected to chair the Council. Before he could be appointed, he had to undergo vetting by the **Fedeal Bureau of Investigation (FBI)**. He did not want to face that, and asked Schlesinger to withdraw his name; the next day he began his 40 to 50 hours of confession to the FBI about his political past. He repeated what he had told British intelligence officers in January 1964. Anthony Blunt was now known to be a Soviet **agent.**

In September 1964 Straight met with Blunt in London. Blunt said he was grateful for what Straight had done, that the confession had lifted a great burden from his shoulders, and that he always wondered when Straight would confess.

For ten years afterward, Straight would be asked details about the work he did for the Soviets and those who worked with him. He spoke with them for the last time in the 1970s.

Early in 1999 Straight acknowledged to Allen Weinstein that the Soviet intelligence files confirmed what he had written in his autobiography, *After Long Silence* (1983). Straight left his archive to Cornell University in Ithaca, New York.

Sources: Anonymous, "Michael Straight: Millionaire Spy, Soviet Mole Who Told MI5 About Anthony Blunt," *The Age* (originally published in the *London Telgraph*) (Melbourne), January 23, 2004, p. 16; Costello, John, *Mask of Treachery: Spies, Lies, Buggery and Betrayal. The First Documented Dossier on Anthony Blunt's Cambridge Spy Ring* (New York: William Morrow, 1968); Deacon, Richard, *The Cambridge Apostles: A History of Cambridge University's Elite Intellectual Secret Society* (New York: Farrar, Straus & Giroux, 1986); Mahoney, Harry T., and Marjorie L. Mahoney, *Biographic Dictionary of Espionage* (San Francisco: Austin & Winfield, 1998); Pincher, Chapman, *Too Secret Too Long* (London: Sidgwick & Jackson, 1984); Straight, Michael, *After Long Silence* (New York: Norton, 1983); Weinstein, Allen, and Alexander Vassiliev, *The Haunted Wood: Soviet Espionage in America—The Stalin Era* (New York: Random House, 1999); Wright, Peter, with Paul Greengrass, *Spycatcher: The Candid Autobiography of a Senior Intelligence Officer* (Melbourne: William Heinemann Australia, 1987).

SYMONDS, JOHN (1936–). John Symonds was a former British policeman who served the **KGB** as a **Romeo spy** around the world for eight years, until he could no longer perform the tasks allocated to his position.

John Symonds, a detective sergeant, told reporters in September 1969 that he was among the group of corrupt detectives paid by a South London gang of criminals. In 1972, while awaiting trial, he fled on a false passport and, with money short, in August went to the Soviet embassy in Rabat, Morocco, and offered to serve the KGB. He said he was Special Branch, and claimed falsely that the British Secretary of State had bribed a corrupt police superintendent.

The KGB chose Symonds for his good looks to be a Romeo spy, and seduce women who had access to classified information. In the summer of 1973 he worked the Black Sea resorts to this end, and trapped the wife of a Federal Republic of Germany official. Their affair continued, and the information he secured was so important that it was sent to **Yuri Andropov** (1914–1984).

Symonds's efforts spread, and by the latter part of 1973 he had women in Bonn, and in British and American missions in Africa. In Moscow, posing as a French businessman, Symonds befriended yet another useful British target. In 1976 he traveled through Bulgaria, Africa, India, and Southeast Asia, where after several conquests for the KGB he feared being caught. Quickly he returned to Bulgaria.

With a new identity, that of a deceased Australian, Symonds went to Australia, via Tokyo and New Zealand, cultivating a **legend** for his false identity. He aimed to get an Australian passport. In Australia he fared well at first, but his money ran out, and he failed to get a passport in the name of his new identity.

Symonds returned to Vienna and then went to Moscow, where he was given the identity of a Canadian businessman, and was instructed to seduce an old lover once again. Again he failed. This was his swan song as a Romeo spy.

Symonds became emotionally unstable, left Europe, and in 1980 surrendered on the corruption charges from eight years earlier. He defended himself at his trial, mentioned nothing of his work for the KGB, and was imprisoned for two years.

In 1984 the British authorities granted Symonds immunity from prosecution as a spy for the help he gave in criminal matters earlier. As a KGB **agent** he was codenamed SCOT, and used the identities of Jean-Jacques Baudouin, Raymond Francis Everett, and John Frederick Freeman.

See also HONEYTRAP OPERATIONS

Sources: Andrew, Christopher, and Vasili Mitrokhin, *The Mitrokhin Archive: The KGB in Europe and the West* (London: Lane, 1999); Mann, Simon, "'Red Granny' Escapes Court," *The Age*, December 22, 1999, p. 12.

T

THEREMIN, LEON (1896–1993). Leon Theremin, Russian inventor of the etherphone, is reputed to be father of electronic music. He turned his inventive musical achievements to use for the Soviet secret services.

Leon Theremin was a flamboyant and prolific musical inventor who began the practice of electronic music with the instrument called a theremin. It is played without being touched, and is assumed to be the precursor of the modern synthesizer.

In the late 1920s and early 1930s Theremin worked in the United States, and his invention, an electroacoustic device, aroused much interest among New Yorkers. In 1930 Alexandra Stephanoff played the RCA Theremin on an NBC radio broadcast. In 1934 Clara Rockmore made her debut with Theremin's instrument. At the same time Theremin was passing on data about U.S. industrial technology to the Soviets.

In 1938 Theremin disappeared from New York. When he returned to the Soviet Union, he was arrested. He was presumed to have died in the Stalinist purges of the late 1930s. In fact he was sent to a Siberian labor camp for many years, survived the ordeal, and was taken eventually into the **KGB,** which employed his expertise to devise bugging technology for use in U.S. diplomatic offices and embassies.

In 1960 Robert Moog, who devised the Moog synthesizer, played a model transistorized theremin.

Using the technology that lay behind the theremin, Theremin developed early versions of television and multimedia devices, and his work anticipated the games in virtual reality that are played on TV screens today.

Source: Glinsky, Albert, *Theremin: Ethermusic and Espionage* (Champagne and Urbana: University of Illinois Press, 2001).

TREHOLT, ARNE (fl. 1943–1985). Arne Treholt was a Norwegian spy for the **KGB** and the Iraqi government while a senior officer in the Norwegian Ministry of Foreign Affairs, and was said to be the greatest traitor to Norway since Vidkun Quisling (1887–1945).

Treholt's father was the Minister of Agriculture in the Labor government of Norway. Arne studied political science at university, and was a student member of the Norwegian Labor Party. He protested vigorously against the **Vietnam War**, and worked as journalist. He was anti-American, befriended socialists in Greece, and in Norway organized efforts to discredit and otherwise oppose the repressive order of the Greek colonels.

Treholt became a member of the staff of Jens Evensen, Norway's noted expert in international law, and in the late 1960s, as a journalist for the Norwegian Labor Party journal, wrote attacks on the **Central Intelligence Agency (CIA).**

Noticed by the KGB, Treholt began to enjoy social contacts with members of the Soviet embassy. Over the next three years he met 15 times with a KGB official, thought he might help build bridges between East and West, took money from the KGB, and was snared into developing a clandestine relationship with a senior KGB case officer. Thus began his 16-year espionage career for the KGB. Using flattery and manipulation, the KGB worked to get information from him through his contact with individuals in the Foreign Policy Institute of Norway and the Norwegian Labor Party.

In 1973 Treholt became the personal assistant to the Minister for Trade, later moved to the Ministry for Law and the Sea, and soon after was a Deputy Minister with access to cabinet papers. Twice he visited Moscow, and appears to have fallen into a honeytrap that had been set for him by the KGB in 1975.

By 1977 Treholt had divorced his first wife, married an attractive TV personality, and become a potential candidate for high office in the Norwegian Labor Party. That year, he helped Jens Evensen, Minister of the Law and the Sea, negotiate with the Russians a controversial, sensitive treaty, the Barents Sea Agreement, and showed his case officer the notes he had made on those negotiations as well as some secret Norwegian state papers. When the negotiations on the Barents Sea Agreement finished, it appeared to be in Russia's favor. During that year his case officer was expelled from Norway for espionage involving Gunvor Galtung Haavik, an elderly secretary in the Norwegian Foreign Ministry, who had been recruited in 1950 to spy for the KGB.

In 1978 Treholt became a member of the Norwegian mission to the United Nations, where at the time Norway was a member of the Security Council. Before going to New York he met his old case officer in Helsinki to receive instructions on this great opportunity for the KGB, and to learn who would be his New York case officer.

Treholt stayed in New York until 1982 and enjoyed a good life, training for the New York marathon, speculating in precious metals, and racing a trotter he had bought. He saw his case officer three times in Helsinki and Vienna, locations favored by the KGB because Austria was neutral and Finland required no visas from Russian officials.

Treholt did not know he had been under surveillance by the **Federal Bureau of Investigation (FBI)** since 1980, due to information from Oleg Gordievsky (1938–), a KGB **agent** who had been working for the British since 1974. When Treholt returned to Norway, he applied to be the Ministry of Foreign Affairs nominee at the Norwegian Defense College (1982–1983). This post required a high-level security clearance because the nominee would have access to **NATO** documents. The FBI report showed he was probably a Soviet agent. The Norwegians kept him under surveillance, but at the time had no secure evidence of his espionage.

Treholt went to Helsinki to see his case officer. The Norwegian police photographed him in the company of his case officer and another KGB agent. At Oslo airport he was arrested, and his briefcase was found to contain many documents from the Foreign Affairs Ministry. When shown a photo of him with his case officer, he vomited.

Treholt was caught; to escape, he tried to get the police to join him to make a secret deal to undermine the KGB! After thousands of pages of documents had been found in his house, Treholt was charged and tried for treason. In his defense he gave wild rationalizations for what he had done, claimed to be carrying out what he called unorthodox diplomacy, and adopted a grand, vain, and superior attitude as to the importance of his clandestine activities.

Treholt was imprisoned for 20 years in 1985, and much of the money given him by the KGB was confiscated.

See also GORDIEVSKY, OLEG

Sources: Andrew, Christopher, and Oleg Gordievsky, *KGB: The Inside Story of Its Foreign Operations from Lenin to Gorbachev* (London: Hodder and Stoughton, 1990); Barnett, Harvey, *Tale of the Scorpion: The World of Spies and Terrorists in Australia—An Intelligence Officer's Candid Story* (South Melbourne: Sun Books, 1989); Pincher, Chapman, *Traitors: The Anatomy of Treason* (New York: St. Martin's Press, 1987); Tofte, Ornulf, *Spaneren* (Oslo: Gyldendal Norsk Forlag, 1987).

TREVOR-ROPER, HUGH REDWALD (1914–2003). Hugh Trevor-Roper was an eminent and colorful British historian who worked in British intelligence during **World War II** and afterward became an outstanding historian and masterly critic, though he was briefly duped by the faked "Hitler Diaries" in April 1983. It appears they were produced by a forger and peddled, probably, by a **double agent** for the East Germans.

Hugh Trevor-Roper was the son of a country doctor in Northumberland, and went to Charterhouse for his early education and to Christ Church, Oxford. He was a research fellow at Merton College, Oxford (1937–1939), studied classics, and then turned to modern history.

During World War II, Trevor-Roper served in the Radio Security Service and the **SIS**, working on the penetration and deception of the German secret service. After the war he was commissioned to establish securely whether or not Adolf Hitler (1889–1945) was actually dead, and wrote *The Last Days of Hitler* (1947). He married Alexandra, the eldest daughter of Field Marshall Earl Haigh, in 1954. She died in 1997.

In 1957 Trevor-Roper was appointed Regius Professor of modern history at Oxford University, a post he held until 1980, when he became master of Peterhouse, Cambridge University; he retired in 1987.

Trevor-Roper's intellectual interest in the **Cold War** was evident in his work *The Philby Affair* (1968) is a sensitive study of a man with whom he worked during the war. He defended espionage, but not the practice of it by British professionals, before 1950. He questioned the **Warren Commission**'s conclusion (1964) that Lee Harvey Oswald (1939–1963) was the lone assassin of U.S. President **John F. Kennedy** (1917–1963).

Hugh Trevor-Roper wrote prolifically, and disturbed many of his contemporaries whose intellectual achievements he would readily belittle. He was antagonistic to

Marxism and its intellectual sterility, and became a staunch supporter of Prime Minister **Margaret Thatcher** (1925–), who in 1979 made him a life peer, Lord Dacre of Glanton. Always interested in modern Germany, he produced *The Goebbels Diaries* (1978), and papers on Nazism. Neither a Tory nor a Conservative, Trevor-Roper held a liberal position in politics and believed fanatics were little more than persons who worked long and maliciously to overcome their lowly social origins. He had no elaborate utopian ideals other than to espouse a relaxed society free of the day's tensions, and without orthodox tenets.

In 1983 Trevor-Roper's reputation was severely damaged when he authenticated the fraudulent "Hitler Diaries" for the *Times* Newspapers, of which he was a director. In April he examined the 61 volumes of documents briefly in the vaults of a Swiss bank, felt they were genuine, and the *Times* Newspapers outbid *Newsweek* for first rights. Many experts did not agree with him. In May it was clear the documents were a fraud. He made a handsome apology for his mistake, and discovered that supposed many friends in the media were indeed his enemies.

See also HITLER DIARIES

Sources: Anonymous, "Lord Dacre of Glanton: Obituary," *The Times* (London), January 27, 2003, pp. 3, 8; Anonymous, "Scholar with an Appetite for Historical Debate," *The Age* (Melbourne), January 20, 2003, Obituaries, p. 11.

TROFIMOFF, GEORGE (c. 1927–). George Trofimoff, codenamed by the **KGB** as ANTEY, MARKIZ, and KONSUL, was a colonel in the U.S. Army who spied for the Soviets from 1969 until 1994.

George Trofimoff, was born in Germany to Russian immigrants. In 1948 he enlisted in the U.S. Army, became a naturalized U.S. citizen in 1951, was commissioned in the U.S. Army Reserves in 1953, honorably discharged in 1956, and retired as a colonel in 1987. From 1959 to 1994 he worked for the U.S. Army as a civilian in military intelligence and served primarily in Germany. He held secret and top-secret clearances throughout his career, with access to **NATO** member states' secret information.

According to a U.S. federal grand jury indictment, Trofimoff was recruited to the KGB by Igor Vladimirovich Susemihl (d. 1999), code-named ZUZEMIHL and IRINEY, who was a childhood friend in Germany and had become a priest in the Russian Orthodox Church. In his religious career, Susemihl was Archbishop of Vienna and Austria, temporary Archbishop of Baden and Bavaria, and afterward Metropolitan of Vienna and Austria. He lived near Munich until his death. The KGB regularly exploited the Church and its officials.

Trofimoff's recruitment to the Soviets occurred shortly after he was made chief of the U.S. Army contingent at the Joint Interrogations Center in Nuremberg, where Allied intelligence officers debriefed **Warsaw Pact** defectors from the Soviet bloc.

While Trofimoff rose through the ranks, becoming cleared for access to top-secret material in the Army Reserve, Susemihl climbed the ladder in the hierarchy of the Church. Arrested in 1994 by German officials on suspicion of espionage, both were released because of Germany's five-year statute of limitations on espionage.

Trofimoff would steal documents and photograph them; he was paid by the KGB through his boyhood friend and well as directly by the KGB. He received approximately 90,000 Deutsch marks. He used a parole—an oral recognition signal—when meeting with his KGB handler.

After seven years of investigation, in July 2002 the **Federal Bureau of Investigation (FBI)** arrested Trofimoff in Tampa, Florida, after he accepted payment from an FBI **agent** who posed as a Russian agent. He was charged with passing secret documents to the KGB, and later to a Russian foreign espionage service, for 26 years.

For this work Trofimoff had been awarded the **Order of the Red Banner**. He was held without bail on a single count of espionage, which carries life sentence.

Sources: Loeb, Vernon, "Retired U.S. Army Colonel Accused as Russian Spy," *Guardian Weekly*, June 22–28, 2000, p. 28; Loeb, Vernon, "Retired U.S. Army Colonel Accused as Russian Spy," *Guardian Weekly*, June 22–28, 2000, p. 28; U.S. Attorney's Office, Middle District of Florida, "Retired Army Officer Arrested for Espionage" (2000), www.cicentre.com/Documents/DOC_Trofimoff_Press_Release (also Trofimoff_Affidavit.htm).

V

VANUNU, MORDECAI (1954–). Mordecai Vanunu was an Israeli whistle-blower who revealed that Israel had a nuclear arsenal; trapped by **Mossad,** he was sentenced to jail for 18 years. His sentence seems to some to be inappropriate for a prisoner of conscience.

Vanunu was the second child in a Jewish family who moved from Marrakech, Morocco, to Israel in the 1960s. The family settled in a poor desert town; his father made a living selling religious artifacts in a market freely operated by Arabs and Jews.

After serving as a corporal in the Israeli army, Vanunu failed in his study of physics at university, and became a trainee technician at Dimona, the Israeli Nuclear Research Center. He was to work on highly secret projects, and in February 1977 signed an official document never to reveal anything of his work. This meant he became a member of an elite group, was given special treatment, and was excused from further military service.

Vanunu became a left-wing radical, rejected Jewish orthodoxy, and sought membership in the Israeli Communist Party. Late in 1985 his behavior appeared quite odd, and he seemed to be a security risk. Presenting their decision as a cost-cutting measure at work, his employers chose to pay him off and have him leave.

With the money Vanunu traveled around the world, and while in Australia became a Christian. In Sydney he met an ambitious newspaperman from Colombia, who promised to turn him into a successful journalist.

Vanunu had two rolls of film taken clandestinely at his secret workplace in Dimona. The photographs showed the Israelis had nuclear devices with Jericho and F-16 warheads that could deliver a neutron bomb, and an underground facility to produce plutonium. The journalist tried to sell the photographs, failed at first, and finally got a $50,000 offer from London's *Sunday Times*, providing it did business with Vanunu alone.

Meanwhile, the Australian security services had learned that Vanunu had a story to sell about Israel's secret nuclear bomb program, and informed Mossad. Mossad sent agents to observe him in Australia, and to follow him to London. In London the experts who evaluated Vanunu's material agreed that Israel had considerable capacity to produce atomic bombs.

About this time the Colombian journalist sold a short article on Vanunu's material to the *Sunday Mirror*. The representatives from the *Sunday Times* were trying to ensure Vanunu was not going to be caught by Mossad. They moved him from one **safe house** to another, and gave him various disguises. But he was identified, and Mossad set a honeytrap for him named Cindy.

Cindy was an attractive American, the wife of a captain in Israeli intelligence, and she promised to have sex with him if they went to Rome. In late September 1986 Mossad trapped him in Rome. He was found guilty of treason in March 1988 and sentenced to 18 years jail.

The motive behind Israel's secret services is not clear. Recent research appears to show the Israelis were able to prevent publication of the photographs. Some observers argued that the Israelis allowed the photographs to be shown as a warning to Arab nations that Israel's rumored nuclear power was genuine. It was suspected that Israel had been working on its atomic arsenal for many years. In 1994 it was known that Israel had 200 nuclear warheads. Its Dimona nuclear factory is still not open to international inspection, as is the Israel chemical weapons factory in Nes Zion.

Similarly, Vanunu's motivation appears complicated: Did he act as a simple, genuine pacifist, protesting against the threat of war—accidental or otherwise—or did he use protest as a technique to publicize an imbalance in the nuclear weapons armories of Russia and the West? Was the 18-year sentence appropriate to the crime committed, or far too severe, considering the widely held views on Israel's nuclear arms? He has spent 12 of the last 16 or so years in solitary confinement in Israel's highest-security prison.

In the middle of April 2004 Vanunu was released from prison, but faced severe restrictions on his personal rights and freedoms. He was forbidden from traveling abroad, approaching international boundaries, and could not move about or contact foreigners personally or by e-mail.

See also HONEYTRAP OPERATIONS

Sources: Cohen, Yoel, *The Whistle Blower of Dimona: Israel, Vanunu and the Bomb* (New York: Holmes and Meier, 2002); Gaffney, Mark, *Dimona: The Third Temple. The Story Behind the Vanunu Revelation* (Brattleboro, VT: Amana Books, 1989); Mahoney, Harry T., and Marjorie L. Mahoney, *Biographic Dictionary of Espionage* (San Francisco: Austin & Winfield, 1998); O'Loughlin, Ed, "Vanunu Faces Severe Curbs after Jail," *The Age* (Melbourne), April 21, 2004, p. 15; Raviv, Dan, and Yossi Melman, *Every Spy a Prince* (Boston: Houghton Mifflin, 1990); Raviv, Dan, and Yossi Melman, *Friends Indeed: Inside the U.S.–Israel Alliance* (New York: Hyperion, 1994); Toscano, Louis, *Triple Cross: Isreal, the Atomic Bomb and the Man Who Spilled the Secrets* (New York: Carol Publishing Group, 1990); Wainwright, Hilary, "West Has Duty to Liberate This Prisoner of Conscience," *Guardian Weekly* (London), October 10, 2002, p. 12.

VASSALL, WILLIAM JOHN CHRISTOPHER (1924–1996).

John Vassall was a British serviceman who was blackmailed into serving the **KGB**, identified by a defector, and given a long prison sentence.

John Vassall was born in St. Bartholomew's Hospital in London, where his father was a Church of England chaplain, and his mother was a Catholic nurse. In boyhood he developed an interest in religious pageantry. At school in Monmouth he recognized his homosexuality and, a lonely and sad fellow, made an unsuccessful attempt to enter Keble College, Oxford.

In 1943 Vassall joined the Royal Air Force (RAF), where, after being turned down as a trainee pilot, he was given training in photography. At work he was known as "Auntie Vera" and thought to be insignificant. He joined the Admiralty as a junior clerk, and spent his free time recreation at the Bath Club in Mayfair, had many wealthy friends, and led a rather flamboyant life. He failed to get a posting to Washington. He converted to Catholicism in 1951, without his father's knowledge, in order to please his mother.

Vassall's career as a spy began when he was posted to Moscow in 1953, as a clerk to the naval attaché. Without being adequately vetted he was appointed to a junior attaché post in Moscow. After establishing his sexual preference, the Russians had him photographed naked with a Russian man and blackmailed him into espionage for the **U.S.S.R.** In 1955 homosexual behavior was a criminal offense in the United Kingdom and the Soviet Union. Sexual entrapment was such a danger to national security that any vulnerable person would be a threat if allowed access to sensitive information. Vassall was such a person. He did not support Communist ideology, and maintained that he was loyal to Great Britain.

His photography training helped Vassall to be a competent spy, and gave the Russians much material, little of which was of value. On returning to Britain to work in naval intelligence, he was transferred to the Military Branch of the Admiralty. His Russian handlers saw this as a great opportunity to get some valuable information. This time Vassall was vetted because he could access information about atomic weapons (1955). He became a personal assistant to the deputy director of naval intelligence.

His Russian handlers paid Vassall well for what he gave them. He spent the money lavishly on clothes and holidays, frequently to places where the rich were to be found. When friends noticed that the rent of his Dolphin Square apartment was almost equal to his salary before tax, he would remark that his wealth was based on private investments. The money paid for the decoration of his apartment and extended his homosexual contacts. In 1961, when the Portland spy case became public, Vassall's Russian case officer broke contact with him until after the Portland criminals were imprisoned. When he was back in contact with his Russian handlers, he gave them new information on submarines and sonar detection.

Vassall was arrested on September 12, 1962. He had been named by the defector Anatoli Golitsyn (1926–). When security officers searched his Dolphin Square home in London, they found a new Praktina document-copying camera.

Following Vassall's imprisonment, the British 10 years, he was put on parole and went to a monastery in Sussex. Vassall always maintained he had been blackmailed into espionage. He claimed in his autobiography that, being a somewhat minor figure in espionage, his sentence of 18 years was too great when one compared it with the 14-year sentence of the **atom spy** Klaus Fuchs (1911–1988). After changing his name to John Phillips, Vassall lived in obscurity in St. John's Wood, North London.

See also GOLITSYN, ANATOLI

Sources: Andrew, Christopher, and Oleg Gordievsky, *KGB: The Inside Story of Its Foreign Operations from Lenin to Gorbachev* (London: Hodder and Stoughton, 1990); Andrew, Christopher, and Vasili Mitrokhin, *The Mitrokhin Archive: The KGB in Europe and the West* (London: Lane, 1999); Brook-Shepherd, Gordon, *The Storm Birds. Soviet Post War Defectors: The Dramatic True Stories 1945–1985* (New York: Henry Holt, 1989); Deacon, Richard, with Nigel West, *Spy! Six Stories of Modern Espionage* (London: BBC, 1980); Laffin, John, *Brassey's Book of Espionage* (London: Brassey's, 1996); Leitch, David, "Obituary: John William Vassall," *The Independent*, December 9, 1996, p. 14; Pincher, Chapman, *Traitors: The Anatomy of Treason* (New York: St. Martin's Press, 1987); Thomas, Robert McG., Jr., "John Vassall, 71, Spy at Heart of Scandal That Shook Britain," *New York Times*, December 6, 1996, p. D17; Vassall, John, *Vassall* (London: Sidgwick & Jackson, 1975).

VENONA PROJECT (1943–1985). The VENONA project was a secret operation that aimed to decode encrypted cables sent between Moscow and Russia's military and diplomatic stations in the United States, beginning in 1943.

In 1943, Colonel Carter Clarke, head of the U.S. Army's Special Branch—a section of the U.S. War Department's Military Intelligence Division—wanted to know the intentions of the Soviet leadership, and whether or not the Soviets were negotiating a peace with Nazi Germany. In February, Clarke established a program to decipher Soviet diplomatic cables. The cables had been collected since the beginning of **World War II**; if the code could be broken, then the communications between Soviet leaders and their diplomats in the United States could become known, and these were bound to indicate **Josef Stalin**'s (1879–1953) intentions.

The code was difficult to break because it used a **one-time pad.** In 1946 the first messages became intelligible. They showed little of the Soviet leadership's intentions; instead, they showed that espionage was being conducted against the West.

An early VENONA cable showed clearly that the Soviet Union had spies inside the **Manhattan Project**. In 1948 the cables showed that the Soviets had spies in almost every U.S. government department, and they were sending the Soviets information of great diplomatic significance and military value. Furthermore, the people who were having the information sent to the Soviets were in high standing, close to the President, and of great influence in government planning. Among them were Lauchlin Currie (1900–1993), Alger Hiss (1904–1996), Nathan Gregory Silvermaster (fl. 1899–1964), William Perl, and Maurice Halperin. In the Manhattan Project were Klaus Fuchs (1911–1988), Theodore Hall (1925–1999), David Greenglass (1922–), and Julius Rosenberg (1918–1953).

In 1945 over 200,000 cables were available to decode. The program was secret from the beginning; few people in government knew of it; those who knew were senior Army officers who consulted with the **Federal Bureau of Investigation (FBI)** and the **Central Intelligence Agency (CIA).** President **Harry S. Truman** (1884–1972) did not have direct access to it, although he was informed about the material in the cables when it was relevant to espionage cases. At first the project was named BRIDE, and later was given the name VENONA. In 1952 the CIA became active in the program. The decoding was done near Washington, in Virginia at **Arlington Hall**, previously a girls' college.

Three thousand messages were decoded by the time the project became public in 1995. The collection includes 200,000 texts, in code, and refers to about 800 **code names** of Soviet **agents**. Many were difficult to identify. But when the Soviet Union collapsed, and the Soviet archives were opened, it was possible to compare their contents with what the VENONA project had found; as a result, the history of **Cold War** espionage began to change.

The most noted code breaker was Meredith Gardner (1913–2002). In 1948 a clerk, William Weisband (fl. 1920–1950), who worked in the U.S. precursor of the National Security Agency, informed the Soviets of VENONA data collection; the **KGB** changed its coding procedures immediately. Probably Kim Philby (1912–1988) had access to VENONA material when he looked over the shoulder of Meredith Gardner while he was decoding some material. Philby probably warned Donald Maclean of what he knew the VENONA material had yielded, and passed on fragments of it to his Soviet case officer.

To ensure the decoding was secret, a cover story was an established to hide the origins of the task; it was put about, cautiously, that in 1941, on the battlefield in Finland, a burned KGB code book had been discovered, which helped code breakers begin the massive task of decrypting VENONA data. In truth, sometime in 1944 a photographic copy of a complete code book had become available. Some of available information gleaned from the VENONA data in the latter part of 1945, when Igor Gouzenko (1919–1982) had defected, showed growing anxiety among KGB officials, and their warnings to important handlers of valuable agents.

In England VENONA revealed there were at least eight Russian agents in Britain, one of whom was working as a scientist in the defense industry. In Washington, the material helped narrow the field in the search for HOMER, a British diplomat who passed information on Churchill's secret telegrams to Roosevelt. In time it became clear that HOMER was Donald Maclean (1913–1983). **Code name** HICKS was found to be Guy Burgess (1911–1963). It was not until 1961 that STANLEY was found to be Kim Philby JOHNSON turned out to be Anthony Blunt (1907–1983).

See also FUCHS, EMIL JULIUS KLAUS; GARDNER, MEREDITH; MACLEAN, DONALD; WEISBAND, WILLIAM

Sources: Alvarez, D., "Behind Venona: American Signals Intelligence in the Early Cold War," *Intelligence and National Security* 14 (1999): 179–186; Andrew, Christopher M., "The Venona Secret," in K. G. Robertson, ed., *War, Resistance and Intelligence* (New York: Macmillan, 1999), pp. 203–225; Andrew, Christopher, and Oleg Gordievsky, *KGB: The Inside Story of Its Foreign Operations* (London: Hodder and Stoughton, 1990); Ball, Desmond, and David Horner, *Breaking the Codes: Australia's KGB Network, 1940–1950* (St. Leonards, NSW: Allen and Unwin, 1998); Haynes, John Earl, and Harvey Klehr, *Venona: Decoding Soviet Espionage in America* (New Haven, CT: Yale University Press, 1999); Lamphere, Robert J., and Tom Schactman, *The FBI–KGB War: A Special Agent's Story* (New York: Random House, 1986); Martin, David, *Wilderness of Mirrors* (New York: Ballantine, 1981); McKnight, David, "The Moscow–Canberra Cables: How Soviet Intelligence Obtained British Secrets Through the Back Door," *Intelligence and National Security* 13 (1998): 159–170; Pincher, Chapman, *Too Secret Too Long* (London: Sidgwick & Jackson, 1984); Weinstein, Allen, and Alexander Vassiliev, *The Haunted Wood: Soviet Espionage in America—The Stalin Era* (New York: Random House, 1999); West, Nigel, *Seven Spies Who Changed the World* (London: Secker & Warburg, 1991); West, Nigel, *Venona: The Greatest Secret of the Cold War* (London: HarperCollins, 1999); Wright, Peter, with Paul Greengrass, *Spycatcher: The Candid Autobiography of a Senior Intelligence Officer* (Melbourne: William Heinemann Australia, 1988); www.nsa.gov:8080/docs/Venona/monographs/monographs.html.

VETROV, VLADIMIR IPPOLITOVICH (1928–1983). Vladimir Ippolitovich Vetrov was a **KGB** official in Department T who defected to the West in 1980 and provided it with much information on the activities of Department T, the Soviet spy system that stole Western science and technology for use in Russian industry and the Soviet military.

Vladimir Vetrov was born into Russian nobility; was well educated, having studied automobile engineering, and was a widely read collector of fine art. In 1965 he was posted to Paris as a Department T officer. He had married the daughter of an admiral, and she appears to have had cultural interests similar to her husband's. For five years in France he cultivated French industrialists and scientists, and became a close friend of a leader in the French electronics industry. However cultured he appeared, Vetrov was unstable when he drank too much alcohol. One night, when drunk, he smashed his car. Knowing he would be in trouble with his KGB superiors, he begged for help from a business friend, who had the car repaired within hours and paid for it himself. Vetrov was profoundly grateful. In 1970 Vetrov left Paris to return to Moscow. He continued to see his friend every six weeks or so when the businessman visited Moscow.

Ten years passed. By now Vetrov was a high-ranking official with immediate access to Department T's information stolen from the West, especially military–industrial secrets and special data on nuclear research, computer technology, and space and missile programs. He wrote to his French business friend, suggesting they meet in Moscow. The businessman took the letter to the French counterintelligence service, **DST**, which agreed to follow up Vetrov's letter. In Moscow, Vetrov became an **agent** for the DST.

Code-named FAREWELL by the French, Vetrov passed thousands of documents to the West; consequently Western intelligence agents saw the extent of the successful Russian spy network that worked earlier so very effectively in stealing secret Western science and technology, and learned which Russian agencies were most active, how they operated and were staffed, and the value to Russian industry and the Soviet military of data and information that Department T had collected.

Further, Vetrov listed the KGB personnel whose expulsion from France would help curb the Soviet technical espionage. Also he provided a list of agents recruited to the Soviet cause in many countries, including West Germany and America. Among those recruits was Dieter Gerhardt (c. 1935–), the South African naval officer who had spied so effectively for the Soviets. Also from Vetrov the West learned what Soviet satellite countries had provided for Russian industry. Allied countries shared this information that the French had collected from Vetrov, and valued highly what he had provided about recruited agents.

In February 1982 Vetrov's espionage work ended. In a Moscow park he was in his automobile, drinking champagne with his mistress, a KGB office secretary. A stranger approached the car; Vetrov jumped out, panicked, and thinking the stranger suspected he was an agent of the West, stabbed him. Vetrov's mistress leaped out of the automobile and ran away. He chased her, caught her, and stabbed her, too. He drove off leaving both for dead. Later, Vetrov returned to the scene, where the police were gathering. His mistress was still alive, and pointed him out to the police. He was caught, tried for murder, and received a 12-year jail sentence.

While he was in jail Vetrov's letters to his wife were routinely opened by KGB inspectors. It seemed to them that the letters showed there was more to his life than previously thought. Under interrogation he confessed to being a **defector-in-place**. He was executed in 1983.

Vetrov, like many other Russian **defectors,** said he disdained the nation's Communist leadership for its vulgarity, corruption, brutality, unrelenting self-advancement, and failure to help the Russian people. At the end of his life he wished he had done more to undermine the leaders of Russia and to advance what he thought was the civilized life in the West.

See also GERHARDT, DIETER

Sources: Andrew, Christopher, and Vasili Mitrokhin, *The Mitrokhin Archive: The KGB in Europe and the West* (London: Lane, 1999); Brook-Shepherd, Gordon, *The Storm Birds. Soviet Post War Defectors: The Dramatic True Stories 1945–1985* (New York: Henry Holt, 1989); Richelson, Jeffrey T., *A Century of Spies: Intelligence in the Twentieth Century* (New York: Oxford University Press, 1995); West, Nigel, *Games of Intelligence: The Classified Conflict of International Espionage* (London: Weidenfeld and Nicolson, 1989).

VOGELER, ROBERT A. (1911–). Robert Vogeler was among several U.S. citizens arrested in Eastern Europe by authorities in nations newly under Russian control. Accused of espionage and subject to brainwashing during brutal interrogation, these persons were encouraged to confess to activities for which they were not responsible.

Robert Vogeler was born in New York. His father, an engineer, was German Lutheran and his mother a French Catholic. He was raised to speak both French and German, and later he became fluent in Flemish. Much of his early life was spent in Europe. He was educated in New York, New Jersey, Wiesbaden, Germany, and in a French school in Mainz, Germany. He completed his education at Peekskill Military Academy in New York, graduated from the U.S. Naval Academy, and resigned from the U.S. Navy at the end of 1931.

Vogeler married and settled in Mobile, Alabama, in a rubber and tire business. After an unsuccessful marriage, he divorced, and joined a firm of electrical engineers that sent him to Europe, where he was contracted to work with IT&T in Europe's growing communications industry. Vogeler married a Belgian woman, and after **World War II** worked in Austria and Hungary, during the early years of reconstruction of European industry.

In November 1949 the Hungarian police arrested Vogeler and put him on trial for espionage and sabotage against the economy of Communist-dominated Hungary. The conditions of imprisonment are described in his *I Was Stalin's Prisoner* (1952), which tells how he came to confess falsely to being the leader of a spy ring in Hungary, and gives details of the trial in February 1952.

While in prison Vogeler was reduced to exhaustion and despair from sleep deprivation and isolation from personal contacts. He felt his mind being split in two; one part would do what he wanted, and the other would do anything it was commanded to do. The splitting took place under brutal interrogation; finally he confessed to having been a spy, and gave his interrogators the "truth" they wanted to hear.

At the time, Eugene Karp (fl. 1920–1949), a close friend of Vogeler and U.S. naval attaché in Romania, was murdered on the Orient Express.

It was not until Vogeler's wife, Lucille, threatened to blackmail U.S. authorities that Dean Acheson (1893–1971) began negotiations for his release. On June 16, 1952, after putting great pressure on important U.S. figures, she was successful.

The Hungarian government agreed to Vogeler's release, and the United States allowed the Hungarian government to reopen consulates in the United States, rescinded travel bans on Hungarians in the United States, returned confiscated Hungarian property in the American zone of Germany, and ended Voice of America broadcasts from Germany to Hungary.

In July 1954, in Dallas, Texas, Vogeler protested against the life sentence given Corporal Claude Batchelor, a **Korean War** (1950–1953) veteran. Like Vogeler, Batchelor had been was subject to Communist brainwashing for two years while a prisoner of war. In this protest Vogeler was joined by Harvey Matusow (1926–2002) and H. W. Walker, the chairman of the U.S. draft board.

Similar treatment had been given to Cardinal Jozsef Mindszenty (1892–1975), primate of Hungary, who was charged with plotting against the Hungarian government (1948). Like Vogeler he had confessed to most charges, including treason, black market dealing, and conspiracy. Western observers believed he had been drugged and tortured into his confession, and Pope Pius XII announced that the Hungarians had used a "secret influence" on the cardinal (1949).

These cases illustrate the view in the 1950s that Communists were capable of a dramatic assault on the mind, and from this came the **Cold War** belief in political brainwashing.

Vogeler's experience became the basis of a fictional account of brainwashing in Paul Gallico's *Trial by Terror* (1952). Such control of the mind was further illustrated in the novel and the film *The Manchurian Candidate,* in which an imprisoned American soldier is brainwashed by Communists into becoming an assassin. The film was kept out of circulation for many years because it showed the murder of important U.S. political figures at the time of the Kennedy assassination (1963).

Recently it has become evident that after World War II the **Central Intelligence Agency (CIA)** and the U.S. Army had secretly experimented with the use of drugs to alter the mind for military reasons.

See also OATIS AFFAIR; OLSEN, FRANK

Sources: Condon, Richard, *The Manchurian Candidate* (New York: McGraw-Hill, 1959); Gallico, Paul, *Trial by Terror* (New York: Alfred A. Knopf, 1952); Hodos, George H., *Show Trials: Stalinist Purges in Eastern Europe* (New York: Praeger, 1987); Matusow, Harvey M., *False Witness* (Sydney: Current Book Distributers, 1955); Vogeler, Robert A., *I Was Stalin's Prisoner* (London: W.H. Allen, 1952).

VOLKOV INCIDENT (1945). The Volkov Incident was a brief event with enormous repercussions for Russian espionage efforts at the end of the **World War II** because, by a series of fortunate mishaps and clever delays, it helped protect centrally placed secret **agents** who had worked tirelessly inside the British intelligence community for the Communist cause since the late 1930s.

Konstantin Petrovich Volkov (c. 1912–1945) came with his wife from Moscow as vice consul at the Russian consulate in Istanbul in May 1945. He had decided to defect to the West, and put secret documents in suitcase in an empty Moscow apartment before leaving.

In August, Volkov wrote to C. H. Page, his opposite number in the British consulate, asking for an appointment to discuss urgent matters late that evening or early the following day, August 28. Volkov also requested that Page find an Englishman to act as interpreter, and that Page reply immediately with either his own visiting card or a phone message asking for a Soviet official to come and discuss matters regarding a Soviet citizen.

Page, who had nothing to do with British intelligence and no experience on defection by secret agents, was puzzled by the request and discussed it with a colleague. He decided it was a prank. Not having heard from Page, Volkov arrived at the British embassy on September 4, and declared to an interpreter that he had valuable information to give to the British, and wanted in return £50,000—some sources say it was only £27,000—political asylum, and safe passage to Cyprus for him and his wife. The information, in a suitcase in an empty Moscow apartment, included the names of hundreds of Soviet agents in Turkey and 250 in Britain. Also he said that in Britain two agents worked in the Foreign Office—probably he was referring to Guy Burgess (1911–1963) and Donald Maclean (1913–1983)—and seven in the intelligence services, one of whom was head of British counterintelligence relating to Russian affairs—probably Kim Philby (1912–1988). Further, he had a list of intelligence operatives in Moscow and the Middle East, as well as other official documents and procedures. Also, he said that the Russians had recorded all encrypted communications between London and the British embassy in Moscow for the last two years. This meant that the **Kremlin** must have known secret British and American views on what was to be done in Europe when the war ended, well before the conferences between leaders of the Western Allies at **Tehran** (1943), **Yalta** (1945), and **Potsdam** (1945).

Finally, to ensure he would not be caught by his colleagues before defecting, Volkov insisted that his offer be sent to Britain by diplomatic pouch because all telegrams from Istanbul to the Foreign Office in Britain were being tapped by the Russians.

Volkov left a written copy of his demands with Page and John L. Reed. There were many delays. First, because the British ambassador to Turkey was away, Page and Reed took Volkov's offer to Alexander Knox-Helms, the chargé d' affaires; he did not inform the head of British intelligence in Istanbul, Cyrl Machray, and sent a letter to the Assistant Undersecretary at the Foreign Office. The letter took two weeks to come to the attention of Sir **Stewart Menzies** (1890–1968), who then sought an opinion from Kim Philby, who had been head of the Russian Section IX since October 1944. Knowing that a similar defection—Igor Gouzenko (1919–1982)—had taken place in Ottawa, Philby immediately informed his Russian handler, who on September 19 sent the news to Moscow.

Two days later the Turkish consulate in Moscow issued two visas for agents posing as diplomats. On September 23 Philby, who had employed several strategies to block the speedy evaluation of Volkov's attractive demands, got permission to fly to Istanbul, with the task, as he would put it later, of ensuring Volkov and his wife were in safe hands.

On September 25 the two Russian agents arrived in Istanbul from Bulgaria, and left the next day with two drugged and heavily bandaged passengers on stretchers. A press counselor from the British consulate in Istanbul who happened to be at the airport saw that one of the passengers was Volkov, whom he knew well.

Philby continued on his way from England to Istanbul to help get Volkov away to safety, but when he arrived, he found that at the Russian consulate Volkov was not available, and, on October 1, that Volkov was in Moscow. Philby affected surprise, appeared unhappy at the failure of his efforts, concluded that Volkov had either betrayed himself or been trapped by a listening device in his own room, and surmised that the idea that the Russians had been tipped off was without reliable evidence, and therefore not worthy of including in his report.

However, the idea that someone had tipped off the Russians would not die. Philby, concerned that he might be considered the source of the suspected tip, learned that a Soviet citizen named Constantine Volkov had boarded a ship leaving Woolwich, the naval base near London, for the United States early in 1946. He had U.S. officials hastening to establish the identity of this Constantin Volkov in the false belief that it was the Konstantin Volkov he had missed in Istanbul. People were busy with this false lead for two years, checking and rechecking it, until it was clear there had been two different Russians with much the same name.

The Volkov Case, as Kim Philby called it, was one of his early achievements, and is recorded in all its duplicity and reverence for good luck in his *My Secret War* (1968) and Borovik's *The Philby Files* (1994).

See also PHILBY, HAROLD ADRIAN RUSSELL "KIM"

Sources: Andrew, Christopher, and Oleg Gordievsky, *KGB: The Inside Story of Its Foreign Operations* (London: Hodder and Stoughton, 1990); Andrew, Christopher, and Vasili Mitrokhin, *The Mitrokhin Archive: The KGB in Europe and the West* (London: Lane, 1999); Borovik, Genrikh, *The Philby Files: The Secret Life of Master Spy Kim Philby* (Boston: Little, Brown, 1994); Brook-Shepherd, Gordon, *The Storm Birds. Soviet Post War Defectors: The Dramatic True Stories 1945–1985* (New York: Henry Holt, 1989); Philby, Kim, *My Secret War* (London: MacGibbon and Kee, 1968; Panther ed., 1969); Pincher, Chapman, *Traitors: The Anatomy of Treason* (New York: St. Martin's Press, 1987).

VOLKOV, KONSTANTIN PETROVICH (c. 1912–1945). Konstantin Volkov was one of the first postwar defectors who planned to leave Russia for the West, but failed, probably because he was identified by Kim Philby (1912–1988).

Konstantin Volkov was in his early thirties when he and his wife, Zoya, arrived from Moscow in Istanbul, where he was to take up the post of vice consul at the Soviet embassy. Little is securely known about him.

Volkov was lieutenant in the **NKVD** intelligence services, and Istanbul was his first posting. Before leaving for Moscow he had planned to defect to the West. He packed a suitcase with documents that he knew would be valued by the British intelligence community, and kept them in an empty apartment in Moscow, from which he later said he would get them when he was assured the British would meet his demands.

Late in August 1945, before Igor Gouzenko (1919–1982) had fled the Russian embassy in Ottawa, his clothes stuffed with documents, Volkov contacted the British consulate in Istanbul with his proposal. Because his proposal met with much caution, and was delayed in reaching Britain, when it did come, it was drawn, fatefully, to the attention of Kim Philby. He probably made Volkov's plans to his superiors, and the Volkovs were promptly returned to Moscow.

Volkov confessed and was executed. His name was given to the celebrated Volkov Incident, an amazingly fortunate train of events for the **U.S.S.R.**, which saved the skin of Kim Philby and allowed him to work effectively for Russia inside the British intelligence community until the early 1950s.

See also PHILBY, HAROLD ADRIAN RUSSELL "KIM"; VOLKOV INCIDENT

Sources: Andrew, Christopher, and Vasili Mitrokhin, *The Mitrokhin Archive: The KGB in Europe and the West* (London: Lane, 1999); Brook-Shepherd, Gordon, *The Storm Birds. Soviet Post War Defectors: The Dramatic True Stories 1945–1985* (New York: Henry Holt, 1989).

W

WALESA AND KGB DISINFORMATION OPERATIONS (1980–1985).
During the 1980s the **KGB** set out to destroy the reputation of Lech Walesa (1943–),
who led Solidarity, an independent trade-union movement in Poland.

Solidarity arose from strikes at Gdansk in 1980, and under Walesa's leadership its
membership rapidly increased. Poles wanted political and economic concessions. In
1981 the President proclaimed martial law, arrested Solidarity leaders, and outlawed
the movement (1982). By 1989 the Polish government, pressured by both the right
and the left wings, established talks from which Solidarity emerged as the leading
organization. Walesa resigned in December 1990 after being elected President of
Poland.

During this time police used forged information to discredit Walesa. He was accused of spying on fellow dissidents as the KGB **agent** BOLEK, and of doing so in
collaboration with the Communist secret police. The information used against him
in a Warsaw court consisted of forgeries that had been produced by a special police
unit that had been established in the 1980s with the aim of discrediting him. In 1985
one false report made it appear that Walesa was a paid agent. Also, forged papers were
submitted to the Nobel committee in 1982 to prevent him from winning the Nobel
Peace Prize. He did win the next year. He thought that the attempts to discredit him
were a vendetta by his former political enemies.

Sources: Andrew, Christopher, and Vasili Mitrokhin, *The Mitrokhin Archive: The KGB in
Europe and the West* (London: Lane, 1999), pp. 695ff.; Connolly, Kate, "Walesa Cleared of
Spying for Communists," *Guardian Weekly*, August 17–23, 2000, p. 5; Smith, Joseph, and
Simon Davis, *Historical Dictionary of the Cold War* (New York: Scarecrow Press, 2000).

WALKER, JOHN ANTHONY, JR. (1937–). John Walker, Jr., was one of the
most valuable Soviet spies from 1968, when he was in the U.S. Navy, until 1985,
when he was enjoying retirement on the money he had made from the efforts of the
spy ring that he controlled. His abused wife informed on him to the **Federal Bureau
of Investigation (FBI).**

John's father, John Anthony Walker, Sr., often unemployed, worked as a publicity officer for Warner Brothers until he lost the job after a serious automobile accident in 1944. He became an alcoholic, and by 1947 the family was poor and John, Sr., was beating his wife. John, Jr., wanted to kill his father. As a teenager, he and some friends started committing petty thefts, and in June 1955 they confessed to the police. He joined the U.S. Navy to avoid going to jail.

From June 1956 Walker was stationed in Boston, and sailed from Canada down to Cuba. He met Barbara Crowley (1937–); they married in June 1957, and had their first child in December. By May 1960 they had three daughters. John Walker was promoted often, and in June 1960 he went to submarine school in New London, Connecticut. By 1962 he was stationed on the West Coast, and moved the family to California. His wife gave birth to their son.

Walker wanted to better himself, joined the John Birch Society, and began extensive reading courses. Also he began having extramarital affairs when away from home on naval exercises. His wife did the same, and the marriage began to deteriorate. Wanting to go into business and make money, Walker and his brother decided to open a bar, but the business was always close to bankruptcy. By November 1967 the Walkers were broke.

In December 1967 Walker's job was that of watch officer in the communication room for the U.S. Navy's submarine operations, and he was expected to read every message sent to or received from U.S. submarines in the Atlantic. He stole secret material from work and sold it to the Soviets. The first document he stole was a key list for an old cryptograph machine, and the money he received helped him and his wife enjoy Christmas that year.

Walker managed to steal regularly and get paid well for naval secrets. In February 1968 he received U.S.$5,000 for the cipher card he had given the **KGB**. From that time, he communicated only through **dead-letter boxes** and would have no direct personal contact with a KGB handler until August 1977 in Vienna. He would photograph documents and leave them where he was told. He retired from the navy in 1976, and used a friend as a subagent in espionage.

While becoming financially successful through the espionage, Walker abused his wife over many years. She decided she had had enough, and several times got almost to the point of telling the FBI about her husband. In the early 1980s Walker had recruited his son, Michael, into his lucrative espionage, and thereby gave birth to the Walker family spy ring. But he failed to recruit his daughters.

In November 1984 Barbara Walker told her daughter that she had turned her father in to the FBI. He owed her alimony. The FBI tapped Walker's phone, and by May 1985 he was caught. The rest of the family of spies were also caught. In November 1986 Walker went to prison for life; his older brother Arthur also got life imprisonment; his son, Michael, got three concurrent terms, and could be paroled in eight years; his friend Jerry A. Whitworth (1939–) got 365 years in prison, with the hope of parole at the age of 107.

Walker and his spy ring provided the KGB with information and manuals used by all the U.S. armed services, the **Central Intelligence Agency (CIA),** the State Department, and the FBI. Vitaly Yurchenko (1936–) believed the Walker spy ring was the most important Western spy group who worked for the KGB.

During the **Vietnam War** the CIA chief of station in Saigon could not understand how the **Viet Cong** had managed to learn beforehand when and where the U.S. air strikes were to be made. At the same time the U.S. Navy found that what it had believed were secret exercises were known to the enemy. The information that the Soviets received through Walker made it possible to anticipate military exercises and plans, as well the supplies needed from 1968 to 1973 for the Americans during that war.

Walker was so valuable to the Soviets that he was made an admiral in the Soviet navy for his outstanding contributions to cause of peace.

See also SHACKLEY, THEODORE; YURCHENKO, VITALY

Sources: Andrew, Christopher, and Oleg Gordievsky, *KGB: The Inside Story of Its Foreign Operations from Lenin to Gorbachev* (London: Hodder and Stoughton, 1990); Barron, John, *Breaking the Ring* (New York: Avon Books, 1988); Bowman, M. E., "The 'Worst Spy': Perceptions of Espionage," *American Intelligence Journal* 18 (1998): 57–62; Earley, Pete, *Family of Spies: Inside the John Walker Spy Ring* (New York: Bantam Books, 1988, 1989); Volkman, Ernest, *Espionage: The Greatest Spy Operations of the 20th Century* (New York: Wiley, 1995).

WALTERS, VERNON (1917–2002). Vernon Walters, a U.S. nationalist, and deputy director of the **Central Intelligence Agency (CIA),** was a shrewd judge of international relations and had a reputation for being in the right place at the wrong time. He contributed inadvertently to the efforts of conspiracy theorists during the **Cold War**, especially those whose attention had been drawn to the way President **John F. Kennedy** (1917–1963) was assassinated and the motive for his death.

Vernon Walters was born in New York City, the youngest son of a British insurance **agent** who brought the child to Europe from the United States when he was six. He studied at French and British schools, and by age 16 was fluent in most European languages.

Because his father's insurance business had been badly affected by the 1930s depression, Walters worked in New York as a claims adjuster.

In **World War II,** Walters was at first an army private (1941), but his language skills raised him to officer status quickly, and to the post of confidential aide to General Mark Clark. He served in North Africa and in Italy. This posting helped Walters later to become well-connected among important young people.

Walters joined General George C. Marshall (1880–1959) in negotiating the use of U.S. aid under the **Marshall Plan** for the reconstruction of Europe's economy. He was an interpreter for President **Harry S. Truman** (1884–1972) at international meetings, and later was one of Averell Harriman's (1891–1986) aides. Also he accompanied President Truman in 1950, and witnessed the President's views on General Douglas MacArthur's (1880–1964) insubordination over U.S. policy in the **Korean War** (1950–1953) in April 1951.

When **Dwight D. Eisenhower** (1890–1969) entered the White House as President in January 1953, Walters was there to assist. He became a military attaché, and performed the diplomatic tasks attaching to that position.

In 1956, Walters was there when Vice President **Richard Nixon**'s (1913–1994) car was stoned in Venezuela. Walters, but not the Vice President, was injured.

One of the conspiracy theories that Walters may have inadvertently promoted was begun when, at the autopsy of John Kennedy, an unidentified individual ordered Dr. Humes, the pathologist, not to dissect the neck wounds of the dead President. This allowed controversy to flourish about the direction of gunfire and the number of shots fired, as well as their timing. It helped establish the conspiracy theory that Kennedy was probably shot from the front rather than the side or behind, and that there were several shooters, probably located on a grassy knoll in front of the motorcade. That unidentified person was Walters.

In 1964, when he was military attaché in Rio de Janeiro, Walters may well have been involved in the plot to overcome the regime of João Goulart. In 1969, he helped smuggle Henry Kissinger (1923–), who was seeking peace with Vietnam, into France. Walters used the French President's special plane and leaked **disinformation** indicating the special plane was carrying the President's mistress. Walters had to apologize personally to the French President's wife.

Walters became involved in the **Watergate** scandal (1974) when he warned the **Federal Bureau of Investigation (FBI)** that a thorough investigation of the Watergate break-in would embarrass the CIA. This false claim was later withdrawn.

In 1972, President Nixon appointed Walters deputy director of the CIA. In April 1975, while William Colby (1920–1996) was conveniently unavailable, Walters undertook the embarrassing task of presenting a CIA medal—approved two years earlier—to James Jesus Angleton (1917–1987) for his contributions to the security of the United States. In the summer of 1975 he appeared before the **Church Committee**. He retired from the U.S. Army as a lieutenant general in 1976.

Walters endured close scrutiny during the various investigations of the CIA in the mid to late 1970s, and was awarded a CIA medal for his successful management of the political pressure on the CIA at that time. He was at the center of a scandal that indicated he had perhaps been involved in supporting visas for agents who murdered Chile's opposition leadership in Washington. No charges were filed.

Walters was sociable, garrulous, and usually careful in what he said. He is reported to have strongly warned Pakistan against building nuclear weapons, and to have advised Pope John Paul II to bring about the collapse in Poland of the regime that was resisting **Solidarity**.

In 1985 Walters was made U.S. ambassador to the United Nations, and instead of bringing it to its knees, as many UN officials expected, he became one of its respected supporters. He was named U.S. ambassador to Bonn not long before the Berlin Wall was torn down. He was popular on German TV shows for his fluency in German and his view—not shared at the time by the U.S. State Department—that Germany would probably be united in a few years.

See also KENNEDY ASSASSINATION AND THE KGB

Sources: Anonymous, "Interpreter to Five Presidents: Vernon A. Walters, Soldier, Diplomat and Deputy CIA Chief, 3-1-1917–10-2-2002," *The Age* (Melbourne), February 20, 2002, p. 11 (originally published in the *New York Times*); Colby, William, with Peter Forbath, *Honorable Men: My Life in the CIA* (New York: Simon & Schuster, 1978); Jackson, Harold, "Lieutenant General Vernon Walters," *The Guardian* (London), February 18, 2002, www.guardian.co.uk/obituaries; Longbottom, C., "Plot Thickens," *The Guardian* (London), February 21, 2002, www.guardian.co.uk/letters; Mangold, Tom, *Cold Warrior: James Jesus Angleton, the CIA Master Spy Hunter* (New York: Simon & Schuster, 1991).

WARD, STEPHEN (1912–1963). Stephen Ward was a committed Communist sympathizer, if not a Russian **agent**, in London who procured sex workers for members of Britain's high society. His efforts to spy on the British government of **Harold Macmillan** (1894–1986) by using call girls failed. He became central to the **John Profumo** (1915–) affair in 1963, was arrested, charged, and found guilty of procuring.

Stephen Ward's mother was from Ireland, and his father was a vicar who became the prebendary (honorary canon) of Exeter Cathedral in 1934. Educated at Canford in Dorset, he worked as a translator in Germany between the two world wars, visited Paris, and studied osteopathy in the United States.

In **World War II,** Ward served in the Royal Armoured Corps and, as skilled osteopath, would treat his fellow soldiers until the army doctors directed otherwise, and made him a stretcher bearer. He was well connected socially and regularly attended nightclubs with notables, including Prince Philip, who in 1947 would later marry Britain's future Queen Elizabeth II.

After World War II, Ward established himself as a fashionable London osteopath, cultivated the wealthy, and named among his patients Winston Churchill (1874–1965) Frank Sinatra, Elizabeth Taylor, Averall Harriman (1981–1986), and J. Paul Getty. He was married for one year (1949), and then became a charming ladies' man, so well known that he was capable of extending his circle of attractive, fast-living, and glamorous associates, acquaintances, and intimate friends into the highest places. Also, Ward was an able portraitist, and often was commissioned by the press to sketch members of important families, including royalty.

On the other side of his personality lay a powerful loathing for the rich, the famous, America, and Western capitalism. His osteopathy, massage therapy, and portraiture for the rich served as a cover for his work as a committed Soviet sympathizer, spy, and **agent of influence**. Keeler (2002) claims he became a Communist in 1956.

Ward collected attractive young women in the sex industry and made them available for the pleasure of members of Britain's high society; he did this by planning and arranging sex parties and orgies. He witnessed the wild sexual proceedings, photographed the events, and drew portraits of the guests. Among his finest contacts was his friend Lord Astor (1907–1966), whose sexual interests, preferences, and practices Ward found he could readily and profitably satisfy, and extend when called upon. He was in an excellent position to provide information for blackmailing important people into serving the Soviet cause.

One of the young women Ward used and employed was Christine Keeler (1942–), whom he met in June 1959. A lost soul, she readily agreed to live in his apartment as an alleged lover, if not a mistress, and accept employment as a sex worker. In the apartment she claims she witnessed Ward's meetings with Anthony Blunt (1907–1983), Roger Hollis (1905–1973), and Eugene Ivanov (1926–1994), a Russian spy who arrived in London as a naval attaché in March 1960. Keeler would always maintain, but with no secure evidence, that Hollis, the head of **MI5**, was without doubt a Soviet agent, and that he helped to conceal Ward's espionage.

Colin Coote, editor of the *Daily Telegraph* and golfing friend of Roger Hollis, may have arranged a meeting between Ward and Ivanov, in the hope that Ward could get a visa to Moscow and sketch **Nikita Khrushchev** (1894–1971) for the newspaper. Christine Keeler, who knew Ward well by this time, believed that the story was a cover for Ward to appear in public with Ivanov, who, she claimed, came to London to work for Ward.

Ward arranged for Keeler to meet John Profumo, a friend of Lord Astor and Secretary of State for War in Prime Minister Harold Macmillan's cabinet. Keeler and Profumo had an affair until October 1961. During that time she had spent at least one night with Ivanov.

Ward may have induced Keeler to seek—through pillow talk—secret information from Profumo on the movement of Western armaments in Europe. This he would pass to Moscow via Ivanov. Keeler asserted this to be true.

In May 1962 Ward approached **MI5** with a plan that it recruit him to serve the national interest. He also tried to have Ivanov help to advance the possibility of a summit conference between the Soviets and the United States to resolve the **Cuban missile crisis**. Both plans were unacceptable. MI5 already had grave doubts about Ward's motives, and had known of his Soviet sympathies for many years.

When relations between Keeler, Profumo, and Ivanov became public, and Profumo had to resign, Ward was arrested in June 1963 and charged with living off the earnings of prostitution and with procuring a girl under 21 to have unlawful sexual intercourse. He was tried in July 1963, but shortly before he was found guilty, he took a fatal overdose of Nembutal.

See also BLUNT, ANTHONY; HOLLIS, ROGER; IVANOV, EUGENE; KEELER, CHRISTINE

Sources: Astor, Bronwen, *Her Life and Times* (New York: HarperCollins, 2000; Booker, Christopher, *The Neophiliacs: A Study of the Revolution in English Life in the Fifties and Sixties* (London: Collins, 1969); Bower, Tom, *The Perfect English Spy: Sir Dick White and the Secret War 1935–90* (London: Heinemann, 1995); Charlton, Warwick, *Stephen Ward Speaks* (London: Today Magazine, Two-in-One Book, 1963); Dorril, Stephen, and Anthony Summers, *Honeytrap: The Secret Worlds of Stephen Ward* (London: Weidenfeld and Nicolson, 1987); Keeler, Christine, *The Truth at Last: My Story* (London: Sidgwick & Jackson, 2000); Kennedy, Ludovic Henry Coverley, *The Trial of Stephen Ward*, rev. ed. (London: Gollancz, 1987; 1st ed., 1964); Pincher, Chapman, *Too Secret Too Long* (London: Sidgwick & Jackson, 1984); West, Nigel, *The Circus: MI5 Operations 1945–1972* (New York: Stein and Day, 1983); West, Rebecca, "Doctor Stephen Ward Returns," *Esquire*, September 1964, p. 138.

WATSON, ALISTER GEORGE DOUGLAS (fl. 1907–1982). Alister Watson was a fellow of King's College, Cambridge, and a onetime secretary of the **Apostles;** he helped convert his classmate in first year, Anthony Blunt (1907–1983), to Marxism, and may have been a member of Guy Burgess's (1911–1963) Ring of Five. The Ring was modeled on the German Fünfergruppen, and its membership fluctuated, but probably included Watson and James Klugmann (1912–1977); neither carried the same level of importance as members of the Magnificent Five.

Alister Watson was elected to the Apostles in January 1927, became a first-class mathematician, and was a fellow of King's College from 1933 to 1939. He was a **talent spotter** for the Russians, a member of the British Communist Party, and an advocate of the genius Alan Turing (1912–1954), the inventor of the modern computer in Great Britain. Also, he felt that the British government did not, as a matter of policy, sufficiently respect those at university who were extending reliable knowledge and human understanding.

When **World War II** began, Watson joined the Admiralty as a scientific officer on radar and engineering projects, and after the war, in 1953, he became a principal scientific officer at the Admiralty's Teddington Research Laboratories, working on the detection of submarines with low-frequency equipment.

Watson shared accommodation with the brother of Peter Wright (1916–1995). Peter Wright disliked him personally. To some, Watson seemed eccentric and boorish. Peter Wright noted that he was head of one of the most important secret research jobs in the defense establishment, and had had the same sequence of case officers as the Magnificent Five: Anatoli Gorsky, Boris Krotov, and Yuri Modin.

After Anthony Blunt's secret 1964 confession, Watson was investigated by **MI5**, and consequently moved to a position involving nonsecret work at the National Institute of Oceanography in 1967. He retired in 1972 and died 10 years later, before any secure evidence of his espionage could be established.

Sources: Andrew, Christopher, and Oleg Gordievsky, *KGB: The Inside Story of Its Foreign Operations* (London: Hodder and Stoughton, 1990); Costello, John, *Mask of Treachery: Spies, Lies, Buggery and Betrayal. The First Documented Dossier on Anthony Blunt's Cambridge Spy Ring* (New York: William Morrow, 1988); Deacon, Richard, *The Cambridge Apostles: A History of Cambridge University's Elite Intellectual Secret Society* (New York: Farrar, Straus & Giroux, 1986).

WEISBAND, WILLIAM (fl. 1920–1950). William Weisband was a clerk in the U.S. Army who informed the Soviets that the Americans had the VENONA encrypts of Russian communications between Moscow and the major diplomatic and military stations.

William Weisband was born in Egypt of Russian parents who immigrated to the United States in the 1920s. In 1934 he was recruited to the Soviet cause in the **NKVD**. He became a U.S. citizen in 1938 and joined the U.S. Army in 1942; in **World War II** his language skills got him a commission at the Officers Candidate School. He was assigned to the Army's Signals Security Agency, the forerunner of the National Security Agency. He served in North Africa and Italy, then was posted back to the United States late in 1944. In 1945, with other Russian specialists, Weisband became a consultant on major security projects and was sent to Washington to help decode the VENONA material.

Being in a position to advise on problems with the Russian language, Weisband quickly learned of progress on decoding the VENONA material. Also he would cultivate the secretaries, sit beside them, and indirectly become aware of valuable information. In three VENONA messages the name LINK appreared, and the details seemed to fit Weisband. Other sources say he was code-named ZHORA

Weisband's contact with the Soviets was broken between 1945 and 1947, and restored early in 1948 when the VENONA information he was providing was so valuable. From his efforts the Soviets learned that American intelligence had acquired information on how the Russians had penetrated the **OSS**, Russia's military stations, its industrial productivity, and work on its **atom bomb** project. As a result the Soviets took action to defend future information sources and decrease the U.S. ability to decode secret messages.

From February to August 1948, Weisband passed documents to his **case officer**; but when Elizabeth Bentley (1908–1963) and Whittaker Chambers (1901–1961) started giving information to the American intelligence community, he began to use **dead drops.**

Weisband would put documents under his shirt, and at his lunch break smuggle them out of his office and put them in the trunk of his car. He was not permitted to photograph the documents for fear of being detected. From August 1948 he would meet his case officer every six to eight weeks until April 1950, when his concern about being caught was recognized. He received small sums of money for his services.

In December 1949 the **Federal Bureau of Investigation (FBI)** detected Weisband meeting one of his contacts. In April 1950 he received almost U.S.$1,700 in cash for his services, Soviet connections were severed again, and he was given a password should future contact ever be needed.

Weisband was arrested, but the government did not have adequate evidence to prosecute him for espionage; even so, because he failed to appear when called before a federal grand jury investigating the Communist Party in America, he was jailed for a year for contempt of court.

See also GARDNER, MEREDITH; VENONA PROJECT

Sources: Andrew, Christopher, and Vasili Mitrokhin, *The Mitrokhin Archive: The KGB in Europe and the West* (London: Lane, 1999); Haynes, John Earl, and Harvey Klehr, *Venona: Decoding Soviet Espionage in America* (New Haven, CT: Yale University Press, 1999); Weinstein, Allen, and Alexander Vassiliev, *The Haunted Wood: Soviet Espionage in America— The Stalin Era* (New York: Random House, 1999).

WELCH, RICHARD S. (1929–1975). Welch was the thirty-second **Central Intelligence Agency (CIA)** officer to be assassinated in the line of duty; the case became celebrated because of the way in which the assassins identified him.

Once chief of station in Lima, Peru, Welch was a senior executive in the CIA, working at a management level, which would normally have protected him against assassination.

Welch was working under light cover in Athens. His name had appeared in November 1975 in the English-language *Athens News*. The Committee of Greeks and Greek Americans had sent an open letter for publication in the newspaper. It named 10 CIA people and gave their addresses. The source of the information is not securely known. In *Counterspy* (1975), Philip Agee (1935–), a former employee of the CIA who believed the CIA should be neutralized, had mentioned Welch's name. It had already appeared in *Who's Who in the CIA* (1968), probably a **KGB** publication, by Julius Mader, and also in a Peruvian journal in 1974.

At the time bus tours of Athens would identify Welch's address. He was assassinated on his doorstep late at night, after attending a party at the U.S. ambassador's residence. In the United States he became a martyr and was given funeral with full military honors. Philip Agee was held responsible for his death.

In 1977 Agee learned that he was not party to any crime that would lead to his being charged in the United States; CIA officers were much grieved by this decision.

See also AGEE, PHILIP

Sources: Agee, Philip, *On the Run* (London: Bloomsbury, 1987); Colby, William, with Peter Forbath, *Honorable Men: My Life in the CIA* (New York: Simon & Schuster, 1978); Sifakis, Carl, *Encyclopedia of Assassinations: A Compendium of Attempted and Successful Assassinations Throughout History* (New York: Facts on File, 1993).

WHITE, HARRY DEXTER (1892–1948). Harry Dexter White was a leading U.S. government economist whose reports on the U.S. economy were regarded as treasonous by some, but of little significance by others. In the late 1940s, shortly before he died, he became an embarrassment to the U.S. government because of the charges of espionage that were leveled against him.

Harry Dexter White was born in the United States of Russian-Jewish immigrants, became an economist, and held important government posts. In 1934 he entered the U.S. Treasury Department, and by December 1941 was Assistant Secretary of the Treasury. From this powerful position he provided Russia with information on U.S. government fiscal policy.

In the 1930s, Russia's Fourth Department, later the **GRU,** ran **agents** in U.S. government departments in Washington. The most notable were young and ambitious idealists who believed they were fighting a secret war against fascism. Among them were Alger Hiss (1904–1996); Julian Eric Wadleigh (1916–), who entered the State Department in 1936; George Silverman (fl. 1916–1943), and White, whom Silverman probably recruited. The group of four was established loosely in 1935 by Whittaker Chambers (1901–1961), and resembled the Magnificent Five in Britain. Chambers was the courier between the Soviet espionage authorities in the United States and the group.

In 1938, disillusioned with Stalinism, Chambers broke with the **NKVD,** and in September 1939 gave a list of Soviet agents to **Adolf A. Berle** (1895–1971), the U.S. Assistant Secretary of State. Although the information was largely ignored until 1943, White, much disturbed by Chamber's defection, ceased giving information to the Soviets.

White seemed timid and divided in his loyalties; he suffered from heart trouble and appeared to have abandoned espionage to achieve personal calm and to placate his wife, whom he had promised he would spy no more. But shortly after Pearl Harbor, in December 1941, he was induced by Nathan Gregory Silvermaster (fl. 1899–1964) to supply Russia with more information. He agreed, but would give information to one member of the committee of the American Communist Party.

In 1942, with Lauchlin Currie (1900–1993), White defended Nathan Gregory Silvermaster when his loyalty was being investigated by the **Federal Bureau of Investigation (FBI).**

White was a leader in the postwar scheme to establish the **International Monetary Fund** and International Bank for Reconstruction and Development (July 1944). He supported the **U.S.S.R.** request for $20 billion in reparations from Germany, and a permanent ban of chemical, electrical, and related metal industries in Germany after the war. Also he helped to provide Russia with the means to print a postwar currency like that the United States had planned to use.

By March 1945 the Silvermaster group was known among Washington's Communists, as was White's connection to it; and by September 1945, after the defections of Elizabeth Bentley (1908–1963) and Igor Gouzenko (1919–1982), the **NKGB** was fearful for all its agents in North America.

The FBI told President **Harry Truman** (1884–1972) in January 1946 what they knew of White, and Truman tried unsuccessfully to withdraw his nomination of White to be the first American director of the International Monetary Fund. White accepted the position, and resigned 11 months later, in April 1947.

At the end of July 1948, testimony from Elizabeth Bentley, and later from Whittaker Chambers, was given before the **House Un-American Activities Committee (HUAC).** White was named as a Soviet sympathizer and agent. Consequently White, who at this time was a financial consultant, appeared before the committee and denied all the allegations. Three days later he died of a heart attack.

White was never indicted for or convicted of espionage. Later his most vehement critic was Herbert Brownell, Jr., the U.S. Attorney General, who denounced White in November 1953, creating a public relations problem for President **Dwight D. Eisenhower** (1890–1969) at a time when **McCarthyism** was rampant.

Recent research suggests Elizabeth Bentley's allegations and information on White were far from accurate, and concludes that White was a romantic idealist who passed his summaries of sensitive documents to the Soviets in the belief that his efforts did no harm to the United States, and would help further Soviet–U.S. cooperation. Others do not agree (Olmstead, 2002; Weinstein and Vassiliev, 1999).

See also BENTLEY, ELIZABETH; CHAMBERS, WHITTAKER; CURRIE, LAUCHLIN; HISS, ALGER; SILVERMAN, A. GEORGE; SILVERMASTER, NATHAN GREGORY

Sources: Andrew, Christopher, and Oleg Gordievsky, *KGB: The Inside Story of Its Foreign Operations from Lenin to Gorbachev* (London: Hodder and Stoughton, 1990); Andrew, Christopher, and Vasili Mitrokhin, *The Mitrokhin Archive: The KGB in Europe and the West* (London: Lane, 1999); Guth, David W., "Ike's Red Scare: The Harry Dexter White Crisis," *American Journalism* 13 (1996): 157–175; Olmstead, Kathryn, *Red Spy Queen: A Biography of Elizabeth Bentley* (Chapel Hill: University of North Carolina Press, 2002); Pincher, Chapman, *Traitors: The Anatomy of Treason* (New York: St Martin's Press, 1987); Rees, David, *Harry Dexter White: A Study in Paradox* (New York: Coward, McCann & Geoghegan, 1973); Weinstein, Allen, and Alexander Vassiliev, *The Haunted Wood: Soviet Espionage in America— The Stalin Era* (New York: Random House, 1999).

WHITLAM COUP (1975). An alleged coup involving the conspiracy theory that the **Central Intelligence Agency (CIA)** was involved, more or less directly, in the dismissal of the Australian Prime Minister in December 1975.

Edward Gough Whitlam (1916–) was the Prime Minister of Australia from 1972 to 1975. His federal government was the first Australian Labor Party (**ALP**) administration in over 25 years. A conspiracy theory states that the CIA played an important role in a coup to oust him. As one ex-CIA **agent** put it in 1980: "The CIA's aim in Australia was to get rid of a government they did not like and that was not cooperative . . . it's a Chile, but [in] a much more sophisticated and subtle form."

On being elected, Whitlam immediately ended military conscription, ordered Australian troops out of Vietnam, and freed imprisoned draft evaders; later he banned racially selected sporting teams from playing in Australia, introduced equal pay for women, raised welfare benefits, established a national health service, doubled spending on education, abolished university fees, ended censorship, reformed divorce laws, made legal aid a right, advanced the causes of Aborigines, women, and immigrants, set up ethnic radio networks, elevated the arts generally, furthered the film industry, scrapped royal patronage of public honors, and replaced the Australian anthem.

In international affairs Whitlam galled many conservative interests in the United States. He supported the Indian Ocean Zone of Peace; recognized China, Cuba, North Korea, and East Germany; condemned French nuclear testing in the Pacific; and welcomed Chilean refugees to Australia. Also he condemned the U.S. conduct of the **Vietnam War**, especially the November 1972 U.S. bombing of North Vietnam, and hinted at drawing both Japan and Indonesia into protests against the United States for that bombing. One of his leading ministers even called for boycotts of American goods.

Whitlam also said he wanted no further vetting or harassing of his staff by the Australian Security and Intelligence Organization (**ASIO**). ASIO's informal and powerful authority derived from a treaty between secret services in England and the United States, and involved a profound and secret pact of loyalty. Informally, so respected observers would say, Australia's intelligence agencies operated as if their headquarters were in Langley, Virginia, inside the CIA.

When he came to office in December 1972, Gough Whitlam found Australian intelligence agents had been involved in destabilizing the regime of Salvador Allende

(1908–1973) in Chile; he transferred the head of ASIO, and then dismissed the head of the Australian Secret Intelligence Service (**ASIS**) for its operations in East Timor.

In response to Whitlam's changes, a CIA agent in the U.S. embassy in Australia said the new Prime Minister had "just cut off one of his options," and later a CIA officer in Saigon said he was told by his authorities that "Australians might as well be regarded as North Vietnamese collaborators." Before Whitlam came to power, Australia was important to the CIA because, first, it was one of the stable political systems in Southeast Asia, and second, the United States had secret installations in Australia for monitoring Russian military activities. They were essential U.S. operations, and were top secret. These bases were put in jeopardy when Gough Whitlam indicated in 1974 that he wanted no foreign military bases in Australia.

Whitlam planned to reformulate Australia's alliance with the United States. To the U.S. ambassador, Australia no longer seemed as politically stable as before, and many joking but somewhat threatening allusions were made to what might happen if American–Australian relations were to unravel.

In April 1974 the leader of the left-wing faction in the ALP, Jim Cairns (1914–2003), became Deputy Prime Minister. The CIA heads were concerned that a Communist sympathizer was in high office in Australia. In July 1975, the deputy was fired, and the American President was informed in a CIA secret report that some of the documents used to discredit him had been forged by the CIA.

Earlier, in 1974, an office worker in a Californian aerospace company, Christopher Boyce (1953–), discovered that the CIA was not honoring agreements with Australia by concealing information available from the U.S. secret bases in Australia. When this was made public, it led to a scandal, which revealed that a high-ranking CIA officer referred to the Australian Governor-General as a pawn of the CIA.

The Australian Governor-General had once been a member of a CIA-funded cultural organization, and he entertained members of the defense and intelligence communities in Australia, but never allowed their names to appear on a formal guest list. He also had had briefings with the U.S. ambassador.

By October 1975 internal political scandals about Australia's budget put the government in jeopardy. To solve the problem, Australia's opposition leader in Parliament wanted an election, the third in three years. Whitlam refused.

According to the Whitlam Coup conspiracy theory, the CIA then acted quickly to bring Whitlam's government down so as to protect CIA interests. Why? Whitlam had threatened not to extend the leases on the U.S. secret bases; in response, the CIA worked to persuade others with vested interests to get rid of Whitlam.

The conspiracy theory suggests that in London the CIA chief discussed the problem with heads of the British secret services, and suggested the delicate alliance between Britain and the United States was in jeopardy, especially since **MI6** had secret bases in Australia, too. By November 10 Whitlam learned how concerned CIA chiefs were that Australia might damage the integrity of its relations with America and the United Kingdom. The CIA demands were sent to Australia's Governor-General, who would later falsely deny having had any contact with American or other secret services.

On the day Whitlam was to announce his policy on the CIA and the U.S. bases, the Governor-General fired Whitlam and appointed the opposition leader to form a caretaker government; the latter then called the general election he had wanted. Whitlam lost the election.

When the conspiracy theory was aired, it was derided vigorously as a paranoid, left-wing theory. Even Whitlam refused to accept the idea that the CIA might have had a hand in his downfall. William Colby (1920–1996), once the head of the CIA stated (1981), "We have never interfered in Australian politics."

By early 1988, after many investigative journalists had culled the information for its veracity—much of it from ex-CIA officers—Whitlam concluded that there was no doubt that the CIA had been involved in political events in Australia when he lost power. The information to support the conspiracy theory was drawn together and most persuasively presented in Pilger's *A Secret Country* (1989).

Source: Pilger, John, *A Secret Country* (London: Jonathan Cape, 1989; New York: Vintage, 1991).

WISNER, FRANK GARDINER (1909–1965). Frank Wisner was colorful and legendary character of American **Cold War** espionage, highly imaginative and devoted to the anti-Communist cause in Europe. An active patriot and a casualty of Cold War espionage, he committed suicide.

Frank Wisner was born in Mississippi, studied law at the University of Virginia, and joined a noted Wall Street law firm. He was a dashing young man with a glamorous set of well-born friends on America's East Coast. Among them were George F. Kennan (1904–) and future **OSS** chief **William J. Donovan** (1883–1959).

After serving in naval intelligence in **World War II**, Wisner was transferred to the OSS at Donovan's request. Early in 1944 he was appointed station director in Istanbul, and established a spy network which helped the U.S. Air Force find and bomb the Romanian oil fields. Also he operated in Africa, France, and Germany.

In September 1944, Wisner went to Bucharest to direct OSS operations, but when the Russians occupied the Romanian capital and claimed to have "liberated" it, Wisner and his OSS command were ousted from the city. Incensed, Wisner got a firsthand view of Soviet dictatorship, and was adamant that the Soviet Union was the world's next menace.

Returning to his legal practice, Wisner found his old way of life without purpose. He felt the threat to the United States of communism so deeply that he volunteered to combat it. He went back to Washington, where in 1945 he became Deputy Assistant Secretary of State for Occupied Areas. His job was to gather intelligence in war-ruined Europe, particularly in Berlin, which, following the collapse of Hitler's regime, had been divided into four separate military zones: American, British, French, and Soviet.

In June 1948 an Office of Special Projects was established within the **CIA**; later it was renamed the Office of Policy Coordination (OPC). Wisner was made its director in August, nominated by the Secretary of State. At the time the Soviets were preparing for the **Berlin blockade** (1948–1949).

The Office became active in September, and within a month Wisner had a catalog of projects involving propaganda, support for resistance movements, economic warfare, establishment of anti-Communist front organizations, and the founding of networks of stay behinds. These projects were to sabotage Soviet attempts to advance Russian expansion into Europe.

Wisner had a keen interest in using psychological, covert weapons in the Cold War. In his covert operations he helped to establish Radio Liberty and Radio Free Europe.

He made solidified U.S. relations with anti-Soviet resistance movements in Eastern Europe, and in the Baltic states he worked with the **Gehlen Org.** and the British **SIS.** The Gehlen Organization recruited thousands of émigrés from the Baltic States, and recommended some as recruits. The infiltration of Western spies into the Baltic states was ineffective in the long run, and by the mid-1950s had been abandoned.

Wisner became a colorful figure in the CIA between 1948 and 1958. He and his confreres would dream up and put into operation madcap schemes to undermine Communist activities. For example, at youth festivals they would set off stink bombs; in East Europe they had 300 million leaflets dropped from planes; and they dropped condoms labeled "medium" into Russia. Wisner behaved as if he were part of a young, invincible, and godlike group of amateurs with personal gifts for uncanny and contrarian larks that accomplished more than any ordinary, bureaucratically controlled plan could conceive of. He and his colleagues would brag about the CIA success in Latin America and Iran in the early 1950s like charmed pranksters.

With James Angleton (1917–1987), Wisner ran Operation RED SOX/RED CAP. It trained Hungarian, Polish, Romanian, and Czechoslovakian paramilitary operatives for covert projects to undermine the Soviet government in their homelands.

At the time the CIA had a copy of **Nikita Khrushchev's** (1894–1971) secret speech of 1956 denouncing **Josef Stalin's** (1879–1953) regime and personality. They wanted publication of the secret speech held back until the resistance fighters they were training in the Eastern bloc countries were able to bring disaster to Soviet rule, and support new governments.

The speech was made public at the behest of the CIA head, with presidential approval, on June 4, 1956. In Eastern Europe, the excitement created by the speech spread to Hungary, and in October the students took to the streets; Wisner's operations trainees joined them as freedom fighters in Budapest. Russia made concessions, and Wisner's Radio Free Europe encouraged the rebels to try to get more from Khrushchev. At the end of October the Hungarians vowed to withdraw from the **Warsaw Pact.** The Russian army invaded Hungary, and street fighting left 30,000 Hungarians dead. The United States would not send in troops. The Angleton–Wisner Operation RED SOX/RED CAP failed, and was stopped by President **Dwight D. Eisenhower** (1890–1969).

Wisner had expected widespread anti-Communist revolt in many Eastern bloc countries, and the Hungarian defeat appeared to affect him deeply. Also, it seems he contracted hepatitis. He left work to recover. He went to Vienna at the end of the Hungarian uprising in 1956 and later traveled to Rome. Close to a nervous breakdown, he withdrew from his post for health reasons, and Richard Bissell, Jr. (1909–1994), took over as Deputy Director for Plans. When Wisner returned to work he was made station chief in London, but he fell ill again and suffered serious nervous disorders. In 1958 he was committed to a private mental hospital and diagnosed as suffering from manic-depressive psychosis. His files in the CIA were destroyed because they appeared to be more like the rambling of a man out of his mind. In mental torment, he killed himself with a shotgun in 1965.

Like Secretary of Defense James V. Forrestal (1892–1949), Wisner was seen as a tragic casualty of the stress of the Cold War.

See also ANGLETON, JAMES

Sources: Ambrose, Stephen E., *Ike's Spies: Eisenhower and the Espionage Establishment,* 2nd ed. (Jackson: University Press of Mississippi, 1999); Colby, William, with Peter Forbath,

Honorable Men: My Life in the CIA (New York: Simon & Schuster, 1978); Dorril, Stephen, *MI6: Fifty Years of Special Operations* (London: Fourth Estate, 2000); Murphy, David E., Sergei A. Kondrashev, and George Bailey, *Battleground Berlin: CIA vs KGB in the Cold War* (New Haven, CT: Yale University Press, 1997); Prados, John, *Presidents' Secret Wars: CIA and Pentagon Covert Operations from World War II Through Iranscam* (New York: Quill, 1988); Richelson, Jeffrey T., *A Century of Spies: Intelligence in the Twentieth Century* (New York: Oxford University Press, 1995); Thomas, Evan, *The Very Best Men: Four Who Dared. The Early Years of the CIA* (New York: Simon & Schuster, 1995).

WOLF, MARKUS (1923–). Markus Wolf, aged 29, headed the international intelligence unit, **HVA** (Hauptverwaltung-Aufklärung), of East Germany's Ministry for State Security (MfS), or **STASI**. For 33 years he avoided being photographed, and consequently was given the sobriquet "The Man Without a Face." He controlled about 4,000 spies outside East Germany, and had them infiltrate **NATO** and even the administration of the West German Chancellor, Willi Brandt (1913–1992). He is noted for his ideology of espionage in the **Cold War.**

Markus Wolf was born in Germany, and when Hitler came to power, his parents took him to Moscow. The boy was raised in Russia, and worked for Deutscher Volksender, a Russian-controlled German radio station. In 1945 he returned to Berlin, and lived in a comfortable apartment near his workplace, Berliner Rundfunk, a Soviet-controlled radio station.

In November 1945 Wolf covered the trials of Nazi war criminals in Nuremberg, and returned to Berlin in 1946. He was a reliable young man, and fluent in German and Russian; for these reasons was appointed to an East German mission in Moscow, where he worked until August 1951, when he was appointed to work for the new Insitut für Wirshaftswissenschaftliche Forschung (IWF). This was the name given to the East German foreign intelligence service. It was officially known as the Aussenpolitische Nachrichtendienst of the G.D.R., and was under the control of Anton Ackermann. Its existence was never officially admitted.

Wolf was appointed to assist the chief of the Counterintelligence Section of IWF; in December 1952 he was made the chief of IWF, a surprising appointment for such a young man. In the 1950s he estimated that there were about 80 secret services operating in Berlin.

Immediately after **Stalin**'s death in March 1953, Wolf and his Soviet advisers were concerned that their leader's death might lead the West to launch military action against East Germany. A spy scandal—the Volcano Affair—at the time led to the public announcement in *Der Spiegel* that Wolf was the head of IWF. He deliberately kept a low profile while Lavrenti Beria (1899–1953) was visiting Berlin during the workers' strikes in the summer of 1953, and when Beria was arrested on his return to Moscow. Later Wolf's IWF was turned into Main Department 15 of the new Secretariat for State Security.

Wolf established a reputation for being decent, disciplined, and intelligent; his **agents** aimed to recruit spies from major government institutions in West Germany, and in NATO and its allies, especially the West German Foreign Office, and to do so through family contacts among people who were well educated and familiar with members of the diplomatic community. His intelligence group was the HVA. One of its celebrated successes was to have Günther Guillaume (1927–) work closely with to Willy Brandt and send details of political strategies in West Germany to the Soviets.

In 1968, student protests helped identify young dissidents who felt that they wanted to do something to undermine established and traditional means of government control. They were sought by Wolf's agents.

In discussing his work Wolf said that traditional ideological motives for recruiting agents were augmented by personal motives, social pressure, money, and sex.

Wolf used the honeytrap. He would employ young men who were meant for service in the West and advise them that when they needed sex, they should find a woman among government secretaries. In some cases the women's love was severely abused, and their lives became a tragedy when they were found, convicted, and punished. Others had happy relationships, and some even married their beloved agents and established families.

To Wolf romance and love were merely instruments of espionage, not ends in themselves. When an employee fell in love and provided a lover with information vital to the national interest, romance was secondary, and, as a rule death was the accepted sanction for those who betrayed the national interest.

This followed from Wolf's unshakable belief that Cold War espionage was the "invisible front"—Wolf's term—the equivalent of a wartime front where the militia is always on the alert, and death in the service of the national interest is a soldier's duty.

Wolf's experience showed that although high-ranking politicians, diplomats, and army officers could be valuable targets in the war that aimed to recruit informers and spies, low-level employees in the army and government were frequently more valuable.

Each agent had to be willing to collect and pass on information, accept the risks that such work involved, and be unscrupulous and capable of putting aside the guilt that people normally feel when betraying their country and those to whom they have promised loyalty and from whom they have gained absolute trust. No pressure to betray, Wolf asserted, can be effective if the individual is not willing to begin betraying trust, or to continue to provide secret information after having decided to cease doing so.

Because there are personal as well as ideological motives involved in betrayal, Wolf found that when choosing a target for recruitment, the whole person—problems, difficulties, likes, and dislikes—had to be discovered and evaluated. Homosexuality, sexual perversions, gambling, overextended debt are not by themselves always points of pressure that recruiters can play upon.

Wolf concluded that money is the most easily tapped motive among people raised in Western economies because they emphasize consumerism and place a high value on the possession of capital. Once this widely established attitude is discovered in the person being targeted, and the strength of his underlying feelings is clear, then resistance to recruitment is not hard to overcome.

In Wolf's view, once the value of money has been used to recruit an individual, the next step is to help him suppress the attendant feelings of guilt for having done something unclean, and to establish a positive attitude toward himself, by having him see that the work of espionage is actually good and useful, and will contribute to world stability and peace on earth.

Wolf's approach to espionage was a mixture of arrogance and humility: he believed, first, that it is not possible to evaluate accurately the contribution of the intelligence community to the prevention of a full-scale conflict; second, the knowledge gained through espionage probably did reduce the likelihood of adventurous actions during the Cold War, as well as the occurrence of military activity and the escalation of international tension; and third, that in the management of international tension, spies were far more realistic than diplomats, military officers, and politicians, especially in the assessment of the balance power between nations in any region where they had collected and distributed intelligence.

Wolf retired in 1986. After the reunification of Germany (1990) he was captured, tried for treason, and given six years in prison; the sentence was overturned, and he was convicted of lesser charges, and given a suspended sentence. In 1997 he published his memoirs.

Wolf came into spy literature as Karla in the novels of John Le Carré (1931–).

See also GUILLAME, GÜNTHER; HONEYTRAP OPERATIONS; LE CARRÉ, JOHN

Sources: Andrew, Christopher, and Vasili Mitrokhin, *The Mitrokhin Archive: The KGB in Europe and the West* (London: Lane, 1999); Anonymous, "The Man Without a Face: Interview with Markus Wolf," CNN (1998, 2000), www.cnn.com/specials/cold.war/experience/spies/-interview/wolf; Aronoff, Myron J., *The Spy Novels of John Le Carré: Balancing Ethics and Politics* (New York: St. Martin's Press, 1999); Ash, Timothy Garton, "The Imperfect Spy," *New York Review of Books,* June 26, 1997, pp. 12, 14, 16; Knightley, Phillip, "A Spymaster Recalls the Twists of the Game; This Man, Who May Have Been Le Carrés 'Karla,' Has Some Surprises to Share About the Heights of Cold War Espionage," *The Independent,* July 27, 1997, p. 17; Murphy, David E., Sergei A. Kondrashev, and George Bailey, *Battleground Berlin: CIA vs KGB in the Cold War* (New Haven, CT: Yale University Press, 1997); Wolf, Markus, and Anne McElvoy, *Man Without a Face: The Autobiography of Communism's Greatest Spymaster* (New York: Times Books, 1997).

WORLD PEACE COUNCIL (1954–1990). The World Peace Council (WPC) was one of the important Soviet front organizations.

The WPC was founded in Paris, but was expelled for supporting fifth column activities. It was moved to Prague. In 1954 it was established in Vienna, but in 1957 the Austrian government banned it for undermining the Austrian state. It established a headquarters in Helsinki in 1968, and later was again in Vienna until 1990 under the name Institute for Peace.

An Indian Communist, Romesh Chandra, headed the WPC and linked its aims with the needs of Third World countries; he also criticized **NATO** as a great threat to world peace in 1971. Late in the 1970s the Soviet was providing the WPC with U.S.$50 million.

Even though it was a Soviet front, the United Nations accredited the WPC, and it was supported by individuals who were unaware of or unconcerned by its Soviet sponsorship. The **KGB** arranged for the distribution of funds to the WPC through the **U.S.S.R.**'s International Department. The main Soviet aim seemed to be that the world should know the U.S.S.R. was no threat to peace.

During the later stages of the **Vietnam War** (1964–1973), the WPC worked to promote **active measures**, a prime propaganda policy of the KGB. In the 1980s its influence diminished, and in 1986 Romesh Chandra was replaced. By 1989 the WPC had lost its credibility, especially when it announced that 90 percent of its funds came from the U.S.S.R.

Sources: Andrew, Christopher, and Oleg Gordievsky, *KGB: The Inside Story of Its Foreign Operations from Lenin to Gorbachev* (London: Hodder and Stoughton, 1990); Brook-Shepherd, Gordon, *The Storm Birds. Soviet Post War Defectors: The Dramatic True Stories 1945–1985* (New York: Henry Holt, 1989).

WRAIGHT, ANTHONY (1934–). Anthony Wraight spied for the Russians while working for Britain's Royal Air Force (RAF); to avoid capture he defected to Moscow, but found life was not what he had hoped it would be.

Wraight was a flying officer in the RAF who noticed that he had trouble with his eyesight. For an alternative career he began film studies, which led him to meet members of the Soviet's Society for Cultural Relations. The society was a front for **talent spotting** and recruitment into the Soviet secret services. He was introduced to a Soviet state film administrator, a **GRU** officer undercover at the Soviet embassy, and was soon drawn enough to Communist ideology to want to study at the Soviet State Institute for Cinematography in Moscow.

British security officers were suspicious of Wraight's relations with the GRU officer and questioned him in March 1956. Without concealing his actions, Wraight immediately flew to Berlin, where he took the subway to the East Berlin, made a pro-Communist radio broadcast, and then went on to Moscow. In Moscow he gave the Soviets secrets about aircraft, planned troop movements, and American air force bases in Britain, among other classified material.

In 1959, dissatisfied with life in the **U.S.S.R.** and having nothing more to interest the Soviets, Wraight was allowed to return to Britain. He was immediately detained and tried to offer something of value in return for a lenient sentence. Young and apparently unstable, he was given only three years in jail.

Sources: Laffin, John, *Brassey's Book of Espionage* (London: Brassey's, 1996); Pincher, Chapman, *Too Secret Too Long* (London: Sidgwick & Jackson, 1984); Pincher, Chapman, *Traitors: The Anatomy of Treason* (New York: St. Martin's Press, 1987).

WRIGHT, PETER (1916–1995). Peter Wright was the author of *Spycatcher*, a book that claimed to reveal the workings of the British secret service; it embarrassed the British government when it was allowed to be published in Australia after 18 months of litigation.

Peter Wright was in born in Chesterfield, England, and entered the Admiralty Research Laboratory early in **World War II,** was transferred to **MI5** in September 1955, and worked in counterintelligence and developed techniques and devices for detecting **moles.** He became a close confidant of the **Central Intelligence Agency (CIA)** counterintelligence head, James Jesus Angleton (1917–1987) and helped form a faction inside MI5 whose members were certain that at high and middle levels their organization was run by Soviet moles. This fear, fueled by information from the defection in 1963 of Anatoli Golitsyn (1926–) to the West, spread to services in the United States.

Peter Wright became a member of the informal group of **intelligence fundamentalists** in the CIA who held Angleton in high regard, were much swayed by a deep belief in their professionalism, and were devoted to fighting communism and the U.S.S.R.'s attempt to dominate the world. Wright disclosed much of MI5's work on detecting who, among the British leaders, were suspected of being sympathetic to the Soviet cause, and told the writer Chapman Pincher (1914–) for his 1981 book *Their Trade Is Treachery.*

Inside the secret service Wright was moved out of the counterespionage field, and finally out of MI5 altogether, by Michael Hanley, Director General of MI5, in 1976. Wright went to live in Cygnet, Tasmania (1978), where the cost of daily life would be cheap, and wrote *Spycatcher* (1987).

In 1984 Wright had stated that Roger Hollis (1905–1973), who came to Australia at the beginning of the **Cold War** to help establish **ASIO**, was in fact a Soviet spy, and been able to plant **double agents** in ASIO in the 1950s. He added that these moles were probably still in place. In her book *Open Secret* (2001), MI5's former chief, Stella Rimington (1935–) admonishes Wright for telling Chapman Pincher all he could remember of code words and operations, for causing much harm and embarrassment to Britain's intelligence community, and for making misleading revelations.

Wright was apparently motivated by a grudge about an unfair calculation of his pension. He was not given credit for the years he had spent working for the Admiralty. His pension was reviewed by bodies inside and outside the secret services and, according to Stella Rimington, Wright was given his due, quite precisely.

In a TV interview Wright recanted what he had said and written about high-ranking people in MI5, but little public attention was paid to what he said.

The British government decided to do all it could to prevent the publication of Wright's book, without regard to cost. It lost the case because the outcome was probably a foregone conclusion, and because Wright's case was handled so well by his legal counsel, Malcolm Turnbull.

The popularity of Wright's erratic but fascinating book, and the result of the court case, solved the financial problem that his pension appears to have created. Despite its inaccuracies, Wright's autobiography presents the culture of the intelligence community in a vivid and useful manner.

See also ANGLETON, JAMES; SPYCATCHER AFFAIR

Sources: Hall, Richard V., *A Spy's Revenge* (Ringwood, VIC: Penguin Books, 1987); Mangold, Tom, *Cold Warrior: James Jesus Angleton, the CIA Master Spy Hunter* (New York: Simon & Schuster, 1991); Pincher, Chapman, *Their Trade Is Treachery* (London: Sidgwick & Jackson, 1981); Rimington, Stella, *Open Secret: The Autobiography of the Former Director-General of MI5* (London: Hutchinson, 2001; Arrow ed., 2002); Turnbull, Malcolm, *The Spycatcher Trial* (London: Heinemann, 1988); West, Nigel, *Seven Spies Who Changed the World* (London: Secker & Warburg, 1991); Wright, Peter, with Paul Greengrass, *Spycatcher: The Candid Autobiography of a Senior Intelligence Officer* (Melbourne: William Heinemann Australia, 1987).

WYNNE, GREVILLE MAYNARD (1919–1990). Greville Wynne was a British businessman who for 18 months served as a link between a Russian **defector-in-place**, Colonel Oleg Penkovsky (1919–1963), and the American and British secret services. In late 1962 they were discovered by Soviet espionage authorities, and were tried and found guilty in 1963.

Greville Wynne, born in a poor Welsh village, was the son of the foreman in an engineering workshop. Dyslexic, he quit school in 1933 to work, at the age of 14, for an electrical contractor, and later became an apprentice in a telephone factory. He claimed to have begun his career in the secret service in Britain when, in 1938, he reported to authorities on a suspected Nazi employee in a factory where he worked. This, he wrote, led to his secret work in the British army, where, he claimed, he was promoted to major and later to lieutenant colonel.

After **World War II,** Wynne traded in electrical equipment between India and Europe, and by 1955 he had been encouraged to enter the East European market by a colleague from his secret service days, and especially to seek trade with the Soviet bloc. In November 1960, after a trip to Moscow, he returned to London and learned that Colonel Oleg Penkovsky would be an important man to meet. On returning to Moscow, he met Oleg Penkovsky and a close friendship between them began. Wynne said he had taped all their conversations.

In April and May 1961, Penkovsky gave Wynne secret material when he was in Moscow. He was entertained in Penkovsky's home, where he learned Penkovsky's wife was ignorant of her husband's espionage and his status in the **GRU**, and believed he was merely a Red Army colonel. In July 1961 Wynne underwent a realistic and brutal initiation in Britain to see how well he could tolerate interrogation should he be caught. More exchanges with Penkovsky took place until Wynne was arrested November 2, 1962, in Budapest.

When caught, Wynne patiently confused his interrogators, as he had been taught, and was delighted at the effect the confusion had on them. Nevertheless, kept in filthy conditions, deprived of cigarettes, and starved, he was frightened and lonely and felt harassed. Sometimes he was interrogated gently and given access to a prison library, and some of his personal effects were returned. Wynne's wife was allowed to visit him. During his imprisonment, he said, he denied that he was a spy, and rationalized his contact with Penkovsky as innocent, involving nothing more than friendly favors. He made diagrams and drawings of electrical and mechanical devices instead of writing a confession, which was what his interrogators wanted. Also, when confronted with Penkovsky, who was much distressed from brutal interrogation, Wynne noted he always maintained that Wynne was never a spy, merely a businessman.

Wynne was in prison for five months before hearing a tape recording of the secret conversations he had had with Penkovsky. The conversations showed Wynne that he would have to confess to being involved in espionage if he wanted the interrogations to cease and a trial to be held. He and Penkovsky met, and it was agreed that Wynne, against his better judgment, would confess to being an unwitting spy, thereby discrediting **MI5**; perhaps this would lead to Penkovsky's being imprisoned rather than executed. Before the trial Wynne was harassed again by several prosecutors, was allowed only five minutes with a lawyer who was to defend him, and was instructed in what to say, what not to say, and shaved and dressed neatly. Rehearsals were held, false statements were signed as the truth, and the trial began May 7, 1963.

Penkovsky was accused of betraying his motherland by giving secret information to the British while he was in London in July and August 1961, and in Paris in September and October 1961. In his cross-examination Wynne differed little from Penkovsky in details of evidence. He said he helped Russians and found them always friendly, loving, and hospitable. He gave the impression that the British intelligence community was very powerful, and that he, a mere businessman, had been deceived by them into working for MI5. Both he and Penkovsky were found guilty; the latter was shot and all his personal property was confiscated, while Wynne was sentenced to three years in prison to be followed by another five in a correctional labor colony.

On April 22, 1964, Wynne was exchanged for Kolon Molody, known as Gordon Lonsdale (1922–1970), in Berlin, at Checkpoint Heerstrasse at dawn. When Wynne got home after his imprisonment, he was hailed as a hero. Later he and his wife were divorced, he lost contact with his son, and he became an alcoholic.

The media always presented Wynne as a hero, an innocent businessman trapped by the **KGB**. This fiction ended when he learned that Penkovsky's secret work was to be published. Apparently annoyed that no mention of him appeared in the forthcoming *The Penkovsky Papers*, Wynne demanded that he write the foreword; shortly after, Wynne had his own version of the events written by his brother-in-law. It was titled *The Man from Moscow* (1967) and showed that he had been no innocent businessman but instead a remarkably brave secret service operative.

Much of Wynne's biography is hard to believe (West, 1990). The rest of his life, like his distorted biography, was a catalog of differences between the real and the imagined world. At one point he became a real estate salesman, but by 1972 proved a failure at that. He lived in the Canary Islands, Malta, and Majorca. In 1980 he married a Dutch woman, but in time that marriage failed due to his alcoholism. In his later years he took to rose cultivation. Before he died, probably from throat cancer, he threatened to sue various media and publishers for defamation. Nothing came of it because the defendants would have shown convincingly that Wynne had left the army without a commission, and in many other regards was not what he seemed or made himself out to be.

Some people called Wynne a Walter Mitty character who craved publicity and excitement. His account of himself as a loyal British patriot and passionate supporter of the free enterprise system sits strangely with the evidence of his producing a neo-Marxist pamphlet after World War II denouncing capitalism to Britain's downtrodden workers, as does the transcript of the secret interview taped in 1962 in which he offered his services to the KGB. Finally, he admitted in a radio broadcast that it was hard for him to distinguish reality from fantasy, which indicates that his reported life and career was probably that of a man suffering from the strains of dyslexia, the duplicitous lifestyle of the espionage profession, and a form of disassociative identity disorder. He died in February 1990.

See also PENKOVSKY, OLEG

Sources: Andrew, Christopher, and Oleg Gordievsky, *KGB: The Inside Story of Its Foreign Operations from Lenin to Gorbachev* (London: Hodder and Stoughton, 1990); Deriabin, Piotr, and Frank Gibney, *The Penkovsky Papers: The Russian Who Spied for the West* (London: Collins, 1965; 2nd ed., 1966); West, Nigel, *Seven Spies Who Changed the World* (London: Secker & Warburg, 1991); Wynne, Greville, *The Man from Moscow* (London: Hutchinson, 1967; Arrow ed., 1968); Wynne, Greville, *The Man from Odessa* (London: Robert Hale, 1981).

Y

YOUNG, GEORGE KENNEDY (1911–1990). George Young, **CBE, CMG, MBE,** was the outspoken and unconventional vice chief of the U.K. Secret Intelligence Service (**MI6**) and an early chairman of the Berlin tunnel project, the joint **SIS–Central Intelligence Agency (CIA)** Operation STOPWATCH/GOLD.

George Young was a Scot, educated at Dumfries Academy and St. Andrew's University, where he studied modern languages; later he studied at the universities of Giessen and Dijon, and at Yale, where he graduated with an M.A. in political science. He became a journalist with the *Glasgow Herald* for three years. In 1939 he married Geryke Harthoorn, daughter of a noted Dutch lawyer.

Young was socialist reformer, opposed Neville Chamberlain's (1869–1940) policy of appeasing Adolf Hitler (1889–1945), and during **World War II** was in the King's Own Scottish Border Regiment before serving in army intelligence in 1943 and later in the British secret service.

Early in the war Young recruited **double agents** in East Africa, and later, with help from analysts at **Bletchley Park,** caught German **agents** in Italy. Also he worked to reduce Nazi extermination camps in Europe. At the end of the war he helped dismantle the German **Abwehr,** and found that much of the German army's intelligence was based on information from British newspapers. At the end of hostilities he returned to journalism and became the British United Press correspondent in Berlin, where he spied on the Russian army.

Young saw little public interest in serious reports on Europe, and was quickly and easily recruited into MI6 by John Bruce-Lockhart, a friend from his St. Andrews University days; he was made station head in Vienna after George Berry's tenure. In Vienna he established a spy network to assess the intentions of the Russian military, and tried to penetrate the Austrian Communist Party. In 1949 he returned to London, and Peter Lunn (1914–) took his place in Vienna.

In London, Young was certain that in Albania, Operation VALUABLE had failed because of **KGB** infiltrators. When he was deputy director of SIS, he dismantled the operation and spread the trainees around the world. Also, while in London he was frustrated to find that clandestine operations and establishment of reliable knowledge were not valued in the Foreign Office. He lost respect for the use of diplomacy against the spread of Soviet influence in Europe.

Young took charge of British side of Operation AJAX in the Middle East, and with the CIA helped to topple Mohammed Mossadegh in 1953, but could not persuade the Americans to help in getting rid of Gamal Abdel Nasser.

Young issued a circular, reproduced in part by Blake (1990, p. 168), which stated, "it is the spy who has been called upon to remedy the . . . deficiencies of ministers, diplomats, generals, and priests. . . . We spies . . . live closer to the realities and hard facts of international relations than other practitioners of governments. We are actively free of the problems of status, of precedence, departmental attitudes and evasions of personal responsibility, which create the official cast of mind. . . . It is not surprising . . . that the spy finds himself the main guardian of intellectual integrity."

Young opposed the handling of the **Suez crisis,** developed close relations with Israel's **Mossad,** and supported the Shah of Iran in establishing his secret police.

In 1961 it was made clear to Young that, largely because he was so outspoken, he would never reach the top of MI6, so he retired to become a banker with Kleinwort Benson. In 1962 he wrote *Masters of Indecision*, an attack on how **Whitehall** did its work, and later wrote a text on merchant banking.

In the mid-1970s Young joined Unison, a group of former admirals and army officers that aimed to curb industrial strikes and civil strife in Great Britain.

Young turned away from being an early Labour supporter, and ran unsuccessfully as the Conservative candidate for Brent East in the 1974 election. He worked vigorously for **Margaret Thatcher** (1925–) to be elected the leader of the Conservatives and held unflinching views on the effects of mass immigration on Britain's culture. Some thought him a racist and Fascist. In truth he was more a humanitarian individualist, who upheld the old Scottish standards of open dissent and independent free thought.

See also OPERATION AJAX; OPERATION STOPWATCH

Sources: Anonymous, "George Young: Obituary," *The Times* (London), May 11, 1990, Features; Bethell, Nicholas, *The Great Betrayal: The Untold Story of Kim Philby's Biggest Coup* (London: Hodder and Stoughton, 1984); Blake, George, *No Other Choice: An Autobiography* (London: Jonathan Cape, 1990); Bower, Tom, *The Perfect English Spy: Sir Dick White and the Secret War 1935–90* (London: Heinemann, 1995); Dorril, Stephen, *MI6: Inside the Covert World of Her Majesty's Secret Intelligence Service* (New York: The Free Press, 2000); Norton-Taylor, Richard, "MI6 Extremist and Tory Action Man: Obituary of George Kennedy Young," *The Guardian* (London), May 11, 1990, p. 10; Young, George K., *Masters of Indecision: An Enquiry into the Political Process* (London: Methuen, 1962); Young, George K., *Subversion and the British Riposte* (Glasgow: Osian, 1984).

YURCHENKO, VITALY SERGEYEVICH (1936–). Yurchenko defected to the **Central Intelligence Agency (CIA)** in September 1985 and shortly afterward defected back to the **KGB.** Why he did this is not fully understood.

Vitaly Yurchenko was the KGB officer in Moscow who was in charge of all clandestine operations in the United States and Canada (1975–1980). For the next five years he was the chief of a KGB counterintelligence directorate (1980–1985); its

purpose was to find **moles** inside the KGB. He worked with George Blake (1922–
) and Kim Philby (1912–1988).

In 1960 Yurchenko joined the KGB's Armed Forces Counterintelligence Directorate after having served in the Soviet navy. He was an operations officer and deputy
chief of the KGB's special department for the Black Sea fleet until December 1968,
and was then transferred to Egypt as the Soviet adviser to the Egyptian navy in
Alexandria. Afterward he spent three years as the deputy chief of the Third Chief
Directorate, and was responsible for recruiting foreigners to Soviet intelligence and
for putting Soviet spies into Western intelligence agencies.

In 1975, Yurchenko was security officer at the Soviet embassy in Washington. His
task was to ensure Soviet citizens and establishments in the United States were secure, and to find any vulnerable members of the Soviet staff who might be easily
exploited by the **Federal Bureau of Investigation (FBI)** and the CIA. He returned
to Moscow in 1980. In 1985 he was put in charge of legal KGB **residencies** in the
United States and Canada.

Yurchenko landed in Rome in July 1985, a well-dressed, athletic man who spoke
English very well. He probably came to Rome to deal with a contact or to prevent
Soviet scientists at a Rome conference from defecting. Early in August the CIA
learned that he wanted to defect. He stayed in Rome for eight days. As soon as he
defected, he was flown to Andrews Air Force Base, and then taken to a **safe house**
in northern Virginia, and finally to a comfortable home near Coventry.

Yurchenko warned the CIA that Oleg A. Gordievsky (1938–), who had been an
spy for England inside the KGB for many years, was in danger of being caught. This
helped the British to arrange the immediate exfiltration of Gordievsky in September. Yurchenko also identified Ronald Pelton (1931–), a KGB **agent** who had earlier worked in the Canadian Security Service. He warned the CIA about a chemical
dust that was being used to track CIA agents; and he gave information on Nicholas
Shadrin (1928–1975), a U.S. **double agent**, whose real name was Nikolai Artamonev
and who had died while being abducted by the KGB in 1975.

Yurchenko said a former CIA agent who had not been permitted to go to Moscow
due to drug abuse, and was code-named ROBERT, had been spying for the KGB.
It was obvious that he was talking about Edward Lee Howard (1951–), who,
Yurchenko said, had been to Vienna in 1984 with classified comments for the KGB.
Howard left the United States late in September. Also he told the CIA how valu-
able to the KGB the espionage of John A. Walker, Jr. (1937–), had been.

Yurchenko was offered a fine home, fully furnished, U.S.$1 million, and a salary
of over U.S.$60,000 a year, adjusted for inflation. He seemed uneasy; he missed his
teenage son; he showed little interest in or respect for his interrogators or guards;
and he appeared to have defected because the **U.S.S.R.** system exasperated him. Also,
he said he wanted to meet his former mistress, whom he had loved in Washington
in the late 1970s and now was in Canada with her husband.

The CIA arranged a secret meeting in September. The woman was the attractive
mother of two, and a qualified pediatrician. Yurchenko proposed that she defect with
him, and that they settle in the United States. She declined, and he seemed most
disappointed.

Yurchenko's stomach was ulcerated, and he was annoyed that his defection had
been leaked to the press along with most of the details of his interrogation.

To placate Yurchenko, it seems the CIA sent him to a physician for his stomach pains and arranged for him to have a private dinner with William Casey (1913–1987).

Early in November, Yurchenko contacted the Russian embassy, and at the end of the day, excused himself from the table at restaurant where he was eating with his American guard, and defected back to the Soviets. Shortly afterward he held a press conference and in accented English said he was kidnapped in Rome, abducted by the CIA, so heavily drugged he did not know what he had said to the CIA, and had never heard of Edward Lee Howard until he read his name in the papers. He said fat, stupid guards had violated his privacy, forced him to speak English, and prevented him from contacting his family. He mentioned a dinner with William Casey and the million-dollar job offer.

On November 6 Yurchenko flew back to Russia, and opinion was divided as to whether he had been a genuine **defector**. Was he sent to embarrass the CIA? To protect a senior mole inside the CIA by giving away Edward Lee Howard? Was he deeply upset because what he said had been leaked and he was made into a pawn in another person's greater and mysterious intelligence scheme?

The Soviet consul general in Montreal, husband of Yurchenko's former mistress, denied the affair and called it a dirty lie; his wife referred to it as dirty linen. When he got back to Moscow, Yurchenko told the press that the affair was a private matter; that he had been forced to play golf against his will and to entertain his hosts in costly restaurants; and that William Casey was rude and unkempt.

In March 1986 Yurchenko said he had returned to his old job, and in September 1987 mocked reports that he had been executed.

In 1993 the head of the CIA said he believed Yurchenko had been a genuine defector.

See also CASEY, WILLIAM; GORDIEVSKY, OLEG; HOWARD, EDWARD LEE; PELTON, RONALD; SHADRIN NICHOLAS

Sources: Andrew, Christopher, and Oleg Gordievsky, *KGB: The Inside Story of Its Foreign Operations from Lenin to Gorbachev* (London: Hodder and Stoughton, 1990); Brook-Shepherd, Gordon, *The Storm Birds. Soviet Post War Defectors: The Dramatic True Stories 1945–1985* (New York. Henry Holt, 1989); Earley, Pete, *Confessions of a Spy: The Real Story of Aldrich Ames* (London: Hodder and Stoughton, 1997); Kessler, Ronald, *Escape from the CIA: How the CIA Won and Lost the Most Important KGB Spy Ever to Defect to the U.S.* (New York: Pocket Books, 1991); Mangold, Tom, *Cold Warrior: James Jesus Angleton, the CIA Master Spy Hunter* (New York: Simon & Schuster, 1991); Pincher, Chapman, *Traitors: The Anatomy of Treason* (New York: St. Martin's Press, 1987); Richelson, Jeffrey T., *A Century of Spies: Intelligence in the Twentieth Century* (New York: Oxford University Press, 1995), pp. 390ff.; Wise, David, *The Spy Who Got Away: The Inside Story of the CIA Agent Who Betrayed His Country* (London: Fontana/Collins, 1988); Woodward, Bob, *Veil: The Secret Wars of the CIA, 1981–87* (New York: Simon & Schuster, 1987).

Z

ZACHARSKI, MARION W. (fl. 1947–1986). Zacharski was head of Polamco, the Polish-American Machinery Corporation, owned by the Polish government. It was controlled by **SB**, Polish intelligence. He masqueraded as an engineer and businessman in the United States, while buying stolen technology.

When Polamco was established in 1976, Zacharski came to the United States with Polish-made machine tools for installation in U.S. manufacturing equipment. While installing equipment in the United States, he and other engineers would steal valuable secret aircraft systems.

Zacharski befriended William Bell (fl. 1920–1980), an information technology consultant in the Hughes Corporation, lent Bell sufficient money to make Bell dependent on him, and then blackmailed Bell into providing documents on fighter aircraft and missiles from the Hughes Corporation. The **Federal Bureau of Investigation (FBI)** allowed the relationship between Bell and Zacharski to continue for two years, until Bell could be trapped in 1979. Bell was caught and jailed for eight years, in what became was known as the "Ding-Dong" Affair.

Bell betrayed Zacharski, who was arrested in California in 1981. He was charged with paying Bell $110,000 over four years for film of valuable documents on weaponry and radar. In 1984 he was in the federal penitentiary in Memphis, Tennessee. By the winter of 1985 he and three others were being bargained for 25 Soviets. He and the other three were exchanged on June 11, 1986.

See also BELL, WILLIAM

Sources: Laffin, John, *Brassey's Book of Espionage* (London: Brassey's, 1996); Whitney, Craig R., *Spy Trader: Germany's Devil's Advocate and the Darkest Secret of the Cold War* (New York: Random House, 1993).

ZBYTEK, CHARLES (fl. 1922–1962). Charles Zbytek was a Czechoslovakian **double agent** who served both sides successfully during the early part of the **Cold War.**

Charles Zbytek was singer from Moravia who had been in England during **World War II,** serving in the Free Czechoslovakian Army. In the early 1950s, with the Moravian choir traveling in Wales, he decided to defect to the West rather than continue to live in Soviet-dominated Czechoslovakia. He joined the Czechoslovakia Intelligence Office (CIO), an anti-Communist intelligence service based in Hampstead, London, which, with help from the British Secret Intelligence Service (**SIS**), penetrated Czechoslovakia.

The CIO was led by a dissident from the Czechoslovakian army, Colonel Prochazka, who in 1948 had decided against supporting the Communist invasion of his homeland and established the espionage service in Britain. Zbytek became a filing clerk for Colonel Prochazka; probably for money alone, he decided that here was an opportunity to spy for the Communists, who now dominated Czechoslovakia.

Zbytek knew the names of all Colnel Prochazka's CIO **agents** in Czechoslovakia; and for two years, while working as a double agent, he informed the Communists about the CIO agents. His efforts were so effective that in two years the CIO had failed, its financial support from Britain had evaporated, and its agents in Czechoslovakia were being imprisoned and killed. By this time Zbytek, code-named LIGHT, had been paid £40,000.

Among Czechoslovakian secret service officials Zbytek became known as the Czechoslovakian equivalent of Kim Philby (1912–1988). Semiretired as a boardinghouse keeper in Folkestone, Zbytek changed his name to Charlie Charles, and allegedly died of heart attack.

Source: Frolik, Joseph, *The Frolik Defection* (London: Leo Cooper, 1975).

ZLATOVSKI, JANE FOSTER (1912–1980). Jane Foster Zlatovski—sometimes spelled Zlatowski—spied for the Soviets in Indonesia and on U.S. Army **agents** in Europe, and later worked as a **double agent** for the French.

Jane Foster was born and educated in California. Her father was a rich businessman. She graduated from Mills College (1935), then traveled in Europe. She married a Dutchman, and they went to the Dutch East Indies in 1936. Two years later she visited her family in California, may have joined the Communist Party at that time, and divorced her husband. In 1941 she was introduced by her friends in New York to her second husband, George Zlatovski (fl. 1913–1957).

In 1942, while her husband was in the military, Zlatovski went to Washington. Much valued for her fluency in Malay and European languages, she worked in the Netherlands Study Unit, coordinating intelligence on the Dutch East Indies, and later as an analyst for the Federal Board of Economic Warfare. While in Washington she was acquainted with active **CPUSA** members and a close friend was an **NKVD** agent. By June 1942 she was mentioned in VENONA cables. In 1943 she was transferred to Salzburg, Austria, to work for the **OSS**. In July 1944 she was in Ceylon; after much travel around Southeast Asia she was sent back to Washington in December 1945.

In the early 1940s Martha Dodd Stern (1908–1990) recruited Zlatovski into a Soviet spy group run by Jack Soble, a former confidant of Leon Trotsky. She reported to the Soviets on Indonesia and on her work with the OSS, and provided biographical data on CIA spies in Europe.

Her American husband, George Zlatovski, was a Russian-born émigré who had come to the United States in 1922. During the 1930s he joined the Young Communist

League, and during the **Spanish Civil War** (1937–1939) served with the International Brigades. Shortly after they were married, he was drafted into the U.S. Army (1942), received intelligence training, provided the Soviets with valuable intelligence on the West, and left the army in 1948 as a lieutenant.

By 1957 the Zlatovskis were in France. The U.S. Federal Court indicted them for espionage and treason. The French would not allow them to be extradited to the United States for allegedly having committed political crimes; the U.S. government claimed that the Zlatovskis had committed criminal offenses as Communist agents; the French argued that as loyal Communists they had acted politically, not criminally.

Unknown to the U.S. Federal Court, the French counterintelligence forces had decided to use the Zlatovskis as double agents to work against known Communist spies in France.

See also STERN, MARTHA DODD

Sources: Haynes, John Earl, and Harvey Klehr, *Venona: Decoding Soviet Espionage in America* (New Haven, CT: Yale University Press, 1999); Mahoney, Harry T., and Marjorie L. Mahoney, *Biographic Dictionary of Espionage* (San Francisco: Austin & Winfield, 1998); Morros, Boris, *My Ten Years as a Counterspy* (New York: Viking Press, 1959); Zlatovski, Jane F., *An Un-American Lady* (London: Sidgwick & Jackson, 1980).

Chronology for
Cold War Espionage

1917

March
Following the abdication of Russia's Czar, the United States recognizes the new government in Russia led largely by Alexander Kerensky (1880–1970).

November
U.S. President Woodrow Wilson refuses to recognize the new, revolutionary Bolshevik Russian government lead by Vladimir Lenin (1870–1924).

December
The Russian government's secret service, Cheka, is established at first as a temporary measure, and headed by a workaholic, Felix E. Dzerzhinski (1877–1926), known as "Iron Feliks."

1918

March
Bolsheviks in Russia now call themselves the Russian Communist Party. British marines land at Murmansk.

April
British and Japanese expeditionary militia land in Vladivostok.

May
Civil War begins in Russia, and lasts two and half years. Robert Bruce Lockhart, former British Consul-General in Moscow, is conspiring with American and French diplomats to bring down the Russian government.

August
American sailors, a French battalion, and British marines land at Archangel to support a coup by anti-Bolsheviks. The Lockhardt conspiracy is progressing with the involvement of notorious British spy and secret agent Sidney Reilly (1874–1925).

1919

March
COMINTERN is created to control international communism—the Communist parties outside Russia—all of which are to act in accordance with the new Russian regime's policies.

June
Jacob Novosivitsky, a U.S. Bolshevik, is arrested in Liverpool and turned into a double agent to work against the COMINTERN and Ludwig Martens, a self-appointed Soviet representative in New York.

1920

January	At a secret meeting in Holland, Sylvia Pankhurst (1882–1960) seeks recognition from Lenin of her Workers Socialist Federation, a Communist party in Britain.
February	U.K. Special Branch's secret reports on revolutionaries in Great Britain are given to the U.S. embassy in London with Britain's emergency plans for combating Communist-led strikes.
August	The Communist Party of Great Britain (CPGB) is established in London, and MI5 is aware Theodore Rothenstein has been made CPGB chairman by Moscow.

1921

January	Based on secret reports from London, Ludwig Martens is deported from the United States, with 40 of his staff, for advocating the overthrow of the U.S. Congress.
March	Anglo–Soviet Trade Treaty is signed, and trade delegates from Russia aim to subvert British trade unions and conduct industrial espionage by the GRU.
June	Russia establishes its London headquarters at Soviet House, and its trade delegates have limited diplomatic immunity. Arcos Limited (All-Russian Co-operative Society) is established as a cover for GRU agents in London; by the end of the year Arcos has branches in most European capitals.

1922

February	The Russian Cheka is incorporated into the NKVD (as GPU).

1923

July	The Russian NKVD becomes the OGPU.

1924

By this time, MI5 has penetrated the Communist Party of Great Britain (CPGB).

June	The British government recognizes the Soviet government; in the United States, Amtorg—the American Trading Company—is formed to extend Soviet subversion of American industry under the cover of legitimate business.
October	The Labour government of Ramsay MacDonald, the United Kingdom's first socialist government, resigns after losing a vote of confidence; MI5 leaks the secret Zinoviev letter, allegedly from Moscow, urging revolution in Great Britain.
November	Great Britain's new Tory government, led by Stanley Baldwin, finds the Zinoviev letter to be genuine.

1925

October	Britain's Special Branch raids the headquarters of the CPGB.
December	British secret agent Sidney Reilly is put to death, a victim of a peacetime Cheka deception, "The Trust." A myth grows that Reilly was still alive in 1945.

1926

October Anthony Blunt, later one of a group of Soviet agents in Britain known as the Magnificent Five, arrives at Cambridge on a mathematics scholarship.

1927

May Looking for evidence of espionage, the Special Branch in London raids the Arcos premises housing 35 diplomatically accredited members of the Soviet trade delegation.

June Soviet diplomats are expelled from Great Britain during 1927, and in June, 20 people, among them two former Russian princes, are executed in the U.S.S.R. as British spies.

October Three British spies are condemned to death in the U.S.S.R.

1928

January Three Britons are sentenced to 10 years in jail for spying for the Soviet Union.
October The first five-year plan to change the Soviet economy begins.

1929

October Kim Philby, a future member of the Magnificent Five, a group of Soviet agents in Britain, goes up to Trinity College, Cambridge; joins the Cambridge University Socialist Society; and studies history (in 1931, he switches to economics). The COMINTERN portrays the October Wall Street crash as the final collapse of capitalism; the CPGB members and Marxist sympathizers among intellectuals in Europe and America believe the 1930s will begin the Communist millennium.

1930

June Josef Stalin justifies purges for cleansing Russia, collectivizing landownership, and establishing a new economic order.

October Guy Burgess, a later member of the Magnificent Five, a group of Soviet agents in Britain, goes up to Trinity College, Cambridge, on a history scholarship.

1931

The first cell of Communists is formed at Cambridge; it includes Maurice Dobb (CPGB), Roy Pascal (modern languages), Jim Lees (former miner), Clemens Palme Dutt (an associate of Harry Pollitt of the CPGB), and the psychologist Dennis H. Scott.

October Donald Maclean, another future member of the Magnificent Five, a group of Soviet agents in Britain, goes up to Trinity College, Cambridge.

1933

October Late in 1933 or early in 1934, Anthony Blunt comes under Soviet control.
November The U.S. establishes diplomatic and trade relations with the U.S.S.R., and an American embassy is to be in Moscow. The ambassador, William C. Bullitt believes no U.S. espionage will be necessary in Russia because of the nation's basic honesty. The NKVD uses attractive ballerinas for honeypot espionage.

1934

July   The Russian OGPU is incorporated again into the NKVD (as GUGB).
August   Donald Maclean is recruited to the Communist cause.
October   John Cairncross, a future member of the Magnificent Five, a group of Soviet
              agents in Britain, goes up to Trinity College, Cambridge.
December   Donald Maclean arranges for Guy Burgess to meet the Soviet agent Arnold
              Deutsch.

1935

October   Leo Long is at Cambridge University. Donald Maclean passes the British
              Foreign Office entrance exams.
              Benito Mussolini invades Ethiopia.

1936

July   The Spanish Civil War begins with an uprising of army generals led by Fran-
              cisco Franco.
November   John Cairncross joins the British Foreign Office.

1937

January   Anthony Blunt recruits Michael Straight to the Soviet cause.
May   About this time Anthony Blunt recruits Leo Long to the Soviet cause and has
              him elected to the Apostles, a secret society at Cambridge University. John
              Cairncross is recruited to the Soviet cause.
              Stanley Baldwin retires; Neville Chamberlain becomes Great Britain's Prime
              Minister and pursues his policy of appeasing Hitler.

1938

January   Percy Glading and two other Soviet agents of the COMINTERN are arrested
              for spying inside the Royal Arsenal at Woolwich, East London.
December   Guy Burgess enters the SIS, Section D, for sabotage and psychological war-
              fare.

1939

January   Spanish Civil war ends.
August   A nonaggression pact—the Ribbentrop–Molotov Pact—is signed between the
              Fascist state of Nazi Germany and the Communist state of the U.S.S.R.
              Outside Russia the pact turns away many ideological Communists from the
              U.S.S.R., Stalin, and communism.
September   Great Britain declares war on Nazi Germany after its invasion of Poland.
November   From now until 1952, Stewart Menzies, known to his subordinates as "C," is
              chief of the United Kingdom's Secret Intelligence Service (SIS), also known
              as MI6.

1940

July   Guy Burgess is partly responsible for Kim Philby being recruited into Section
              D of MI6, which soon after becomes the Special Operations Executive
              (SOE), with Philby as its propaganda expert.

September	Earl Browder is told that carefully selected members of the Communist Party of the United States (CPUSA) must work underground, and be not known as party members, thereby making it easier to penetrate U.S. government agencies and selected committees, and to serve as covert couriers of secret information for the U.S.S.R.

1941

January	Early in the year, Noel Field begins directing refugee services in Marseilles, France, for the national branches of the Communist Party on the European continent.
February	The NKVD becomes the NKGB. Lavrenti Beria heads the organization.
May	Rudolf Hess, Adolf Hitler's deputy, flies to England to meet with the Duke of Hamilton to plan peace; this exacerbates the fear at Moscow Center that a separate peace between Britain and Germany is being explored.
July	The NKGB is incorporated again into the NKVD (as GUGB).

1942

February	Angela Calomiris is employed by the FBI to join the CPUSA and spy on Communists.
April	Allan Nunn May joins Britain's atomic bomb project, Tube Alloys, and signs the Official Secrets Act.
October	Julius Rosenberg is now well-trained in providing technical information to the Soviets.

1943

From now until 1949, under the control of Semyon Markov, an NKGB official in the Soviet embassy in Canberra, Australia, at least two Soviet agents are operating in the Australian government's Ministry of Foreign Affairs. Later VENONA encrypts compromise Markov's agents.

January	Allan Nunn May goes to Canada to work on the Anglo–Canadian nuclear research project, and is recruited into the GRU.
	Under the supervision of Colonel Carter Clark, the U.S. Army Signal Intelligence Service begins a secret program, later code-named VENONA, to decode Soviet diplomatic communications collected since September 1939.
April	Douglas Springhall and Ormond Uren are watched by MI5 and arrested in June.
	Soviet and Polish governments in exile in London break relations over the Katyn Forest massacre, which is not acknowledged as a Soviet secret service operation until after 1990.
	The Russian NKVD is now the NKGB.
May	COMINTERN is dissolved and replaced by COMINFORM, which is intended to control the pursuit of communism outside Russia. NKGB and GRU, and army intelligence, assume all espionage activities for the U.S.S.R.
August	At their meeting in Quebec, Winston Churchill and Franklin Roosevelt agree on the establishment of the Combined Policy Committee, an Anglo–American–Canadian partnership for the development of the atom bomb. The agreement deliberately excludes the U.S.S.R.
	The FBI receives an anonymous letter from an apparently disaffected Soviet official, describing a network of spies in the United States and mentioning the name of the American Communist Party leader, Earl Browder.

J. Robert Oppenheimer, director of the Manhattan Project, tells security officers that one of his staff has been approached to give sensitive information to the Soviets, then changes his story to say that he is the one who has been approached.

The British minister responsible for MI6 is warned by MI5 that MI6 has Communists in its organization. After Douglas Springhall is caught, Stewart Menzies, head of MI6, reports to the British Foreign Office that Soviet Russia does not trust Great Britain and could turn out to be a dangerous, secret, and aggressive enemy.

October   For the second time, Lauchlin Currie, an influential adviser in the White House, manages to curtail an investigation into the loyalty of Nathan Silvermaster.

November   At the Allied leaders' conference in Tehran, Iran, Lavrenti Beria bugs the accommodations of the West's officials, and informs Stalin of the West's current policies relating to the outcome of World War II.

December   Klaus Fuchs goes to the East Coast of the United States to continue secret work on the atom bomb.

1944

A story is put about that the OSS obtained an NKVD/NKGB code book that will make it possible to decode the West's massive archive of communications between Moscow and its embassies and military stations. Only a few in the West are allowed to know of the material and the code book. It is called VENONA. The secrecy of VENONA is maintained until the 1980s.

Georges Pâques is recruited to the NKVD. In Charles de Gaulle's provisional government in Algiers, Major Ismail Akmedov seeks to defect to the United States; when he is rejected, he defects to the Turkish Security Services.

February   Josef Stalin creates Department S to use information from the West's scientists for atom bomb research.

April   In Washington, Victor Kravchenko defects to the West from the Soviet purchasing commission, AMTORG. At first an embarrassment to the West, in the late 1940s he became an asset. Wartime defectors before him were Walter Krivitsky and Grigory Dessedorsky.

Winston Churchill aims to purge all U.K. government departments of Communists because they are likely to betray U.K. secrets.

May   The U.K. Foreign Office sends Donald Maclean to New York.

June   Donald and Melinda Maclean arrive in New York; in January 1945 they settle in Washington.

July   Russia establishes the Polish National Committee of Liberation in Lubin.

August   Klaus Fuchs leaves New York for Los Alamos, New Mexico, to work further on the atom bomb for the Manhattan Project.

October   In Los Alamos, Ted Hall decides to serve the Soviet cause.

November   Enver Hoxha controls Albania, and by January 1946 outlaws anti-Communist political groups and their leaders, and Catholics.

1945

Taking over the U.K. Foreign Office, Ernest Bevin rationalizes its leadership base in Mediterranean and Middle East countries from that of aristocrats to progressive and capable administrators.

Harry Dexter White leaves the U.S. Treasury Department to head the International Monetary Fund.

John Cairncross moves from the SIS to the British Treasury, but still provides monthly reports to Boris Krotov.

The Intelligence Division of the British Control Commission in occupied Germany, created in 1944, now employs many SIS and MI5 staff members.

January   HUAC is made a permanent committee under John Rankin (D-Mississippi) until October 1946.

The Lubin Committee (1944) is recognized by the U.S.S.R. as the government of Poland, and by the West as a puppet of the U.S.S.R.

Donald Maclean is now in Washington, with access to the U.S. atomic bomb research.

Nicholas Elliott is head of the SIS station in Bern, Switzerland.

February   Leaders of the the Big Three Powers—Josef Stalin (U.S.S.R.), Winston Churchill (U.K.), and Franklin D. Roosevelt (U.S.)—meet at Yalta to confer on spheres of influence and where national borders might be drawn after the end of World War II. President Roosevelt is accompanied by Alger Hiss, a Soviet spy in the U.S. Department of State; Stalin, who had arranged with Lavrenti Beria for the British and American accommodations to be bugged, indicates an everlasting conflict between communism and capitalism.

March   OSS agents raid the head office of the *Amerasia* magazine New York City and find photographic evidence of classified files from many U.S. government agencies.

Melita Norwood is supplying the Soviets with information about Tube Alloys.

April   Alger Hiss is the chief organizer of the United Nations conference in San Francisco.

May   Harry Hopkins, close adviser to the late President Roosevelt, is Harry S. Truman's emissary to Josef Stalin; he displays pro-Soviet attitudes, which appear to NKVD personnel to indicate he is a true Soviet agent—which he is not.

Thirty German air force officers, captured by the British security forces, begin to produce the secret details of the Soviet air force, and during the next year many are sent to Washington to work for U.S. intelligence agencies.

The FBI counterintelligence unit tentatively identifies Ted Hall as Mlad in the VENONA cables.

June   FBI arrests *Amerasia* magazine editors Phil Jaffe and Kate Mitchell, State Department employees Emmanuel Larsen and John Stewart Service, Naval Intelligence officer Andrew Roth, and journalist Mark Gayn.

The U.S.S.R. says it intends to occupy fully half the area of the German Third Reich.

The first Soviet commander in Berlin is ambushed and murdered, probably by the former Nazi Werewolf Unit.

July   At a conference in Potsdam between the leaders of the Allies, Moscow Center has probably bugged the accommodations of the West's officials, and informs Josef Stalin of the West's secret policies on the outcome in the Pacific theater of World War II.

London Signals Intelligence Board convenes a special committee that decides to lock up secret records, recruit historians to write official histories that would not betray ULTRA, and create a review body to sanitize the wartime memoirs of those who worked in secret.

August   Elizabeth Bentley agrees to serve the FBI, and begins her denunciation of Soviet agents in the United States.

Konstantin Volkov, from the Soviet embassy in Istanbul, writes to the British Vice Consul, but gets no reply.

The United States drops two atom bombs on Japan to end World War II.

September   About this time Stalin gives control of the Soviet atom bomb project to Lavrenti Beria. With information from Kim Philby, Moscow Center learns that in Istanbul, Konstantin Volkov wants to defect to the West, and abducts him immediately. Philby reports to MI6 that Volkov is unreliable.

Igor Gouzenko defects to the West from the Soviet embassy in Ottawa, Canada, with incriminating documents about Soviet espionage in Canada and the United States.

In London the Foreign Ministers' Conference breaks down.

President Truman disbands the OSS; its functions are now under the U.S. Navy, and the War and State departments.

October   From now until October 1948 Guy Burgess supplies many Foreign Office documents to a Russian agent for photographing.

Allan Nunn May returns to London and is kept under surveillance.

SIS operations begin to support the anti-Soviet resistance movement in Latvia.

November   Kim Philby informs the NKGB of Elizabeth Bentley's betrayal, and the NKGB instructs all section chiefs to cease contacts with individuals known to her, thereby defeating the FBI attempts to use her as double agent. The U.S.S.R. begins to lose close contact with its Magnificent Five. Anthony Blunt leaves MI5.

Moscow learns of J. Robert Oppenheimer's view that international agreement is needed on atomic energy matters, and that atomic secrets will become available only when political cooperation is established around the world. He is no longer suited to the Soviet cause.

In Bulgaria the Communist-rigged elections are a success for the U.S.S.R.

Marshal Tito wins rigged elections in Yugoslavia.

Percy Sillitoe, Chief Constable of Kent, is to be made head of MI5; his deputy is Guy Liddell, whose division had worked on the Doublecross deception. Sillitoe's appointment is not welcome among top MI5 personnel.

December   Kim Philby is now the only member of the Magnificent Five to be inside MI6 in England. Anthony Blunt is the Surveyor of the King's Pictures.

1946

During this year the Gehlen Org is officially made part of the BND, and William Weisband is recruited to the MGB.

January   President Harry Truman establishes the U.S. National Intelligence Authority to coordinate federal intelligence operations through the Central Intelligence Group.

BOB, which relied heavily on U.S. Army intelligence in Berlin, now must collect its own intelligence, and begins Operation GRAIL.

February   David Greenglass leaves Los Alamos, New Mexico.

George Kennan sends his "long telegram" from Moscow to Washington, insisting on a policy of containment in dealing with the U.S.S.R. J. Parnell Thomas (R-New York) heads the House Un-American Activities Committee (HUAC) until January 1949.

Igor Gouzenko's story becomes public. Canada indicts 22 Communist agents. Allan Nunn May confesses to providing the Soviets with information on the atom bomb. Truman is told of Harry Dexter White's alleged relations with the Soviets.

March   About this time James Bond is on his first assignment, vividly described in Ian Fleming's *Casino Royale* (1953).

SMERSH's (Death to All Spies) work is over, and the organization is subsumed under the Third Directorate of the MGB. The NKVD and NKGB are raised in status to ministries: MVD and MGB, respectively. The NKGB is now known as the MGB.

The "Iron Curtain" speech by former British Prime Minister Winston Churchill warns the world that "from Stettin in the Baltic to Trieste in the Adriatic an Iron Curtain has descended across the continent" of Europe, separating Russian-occupied nations from the others.

In Indochina the French Foreign Legion secretly employs many former Nazi SS guards to hunt Communist guerrillas.

April   British operations to support Latvian partisans become a victim of Operations MAXIS and ROBERT, counterintelligence operations run by the U.S.S.R.

On the anniversary of Vladimir Lenin's death the Socialist Unity Party succeeds in suppressing social democracy in East Germany.

May   Alan Nunn May, the first of the atom spies to be caught, is charged in Great Britain with communicating information, in violation of the Official Secrets Act.

June   Klaus Fuchs leaves Los Alamos, New Mexico, for England, where he takes a post at the Atomic Energy Research Establishment, Harwell.

July   Jewish Resistance terrorists bomb the King David Hotel, headquarters of the British Palestine Army Command, in Jerusalem, leaving 42 dead and over 100 injured or missing. It is regarded as a British intelligence failure.

With the McCarran rider to the 1940 Smith Act, the U.S. State Department has the power to dismiss employees found to be Communists.

Meredith Gardner decodes VENONA material with clues from Igor Gouzenko and Elizabeth Bentley.

August   The U.S. Atomic Energy Commission (AEC) is established by the McMahon Act.

December Moscow Radio states that British spies are working to destabilize governments in Yugoslavia, Albania, and Greece.

1947

January   During this year Anthony Blunt is promoted from deputy director to director of the Courtauld Institute, a post he holds for 25 years. MGB and Polish UB wipe out WiN in Poland. Show trials in Yugoslavia reveal spies in the service of foreign imperialists, Chetniks, capitalists, Catholics, and the Soviet secret services.

Alger Hiss leaves the U.S. State Department for the presidency of the Carnegie Endowment.

British Prime Minister Clement Attlee (1883–1967) decides Britain will produce an atomic (plutonium) bomb. The decision is secret.

February Donald Maclean is Joint Secretary of the Combined Policy Committee, which coordinates the nuclear policy of the U.K., the United States, and Canada.

The Voice of America begins regular broadcasts to Russia from Munich, Manila, and Honolulu.

Richard Nixon (1913–1994) attacks Gerhard Eisler, a German Communist spy who escapes to East Germany as a stowaway.

The U.S. Senate is told that Soviet spies have infiltrated U.S. atomic plants in Canada and stolen secret information, but the Canadian government denies this.

Until 1948, Kim Philby is First Secretary at the British consulate in Istanbul and regularly betrays SIS and other agents who cross the border into Soviet satellite countries.

March	Operation GRAIL is formally terminated, after being recognized by BOB, in the autumn of 1946.
	The Truman Doctrine is declared as the U.S. President seeks U.S.$400 million for Turkey and Greece, to support the anti-Communist forces. Amid Republican victories in the U.S. Congress, President Harry Truman establishes a loyalty program; public anxiety grows in the United States that communism is expanding its influence abroad, and Communists are infiltrating the U.S. government.
May	GEN183, Committee of Subversive Activities, a secret group, is founded by Prime Minister Clement Attlee to uncover Soviet espionage inside the U.K. government.
June	Until he leaves the United States in 1951, Donald Maclean, First Secretary at the British embassy in Washington, has access to the AEC files and the estimates of uranium ore supply and other requirements. The Marshall Plan is announced at Harvard University.
	Werner von Braun and associates are secretly transferred to the United States with the agreement of British intelligence at about this time.
July	In the United States the CIA is established.
	George Kennan's "long telegram" advocating containment of the U.S.S.R. is published in *Foreign Affairs*. He is attacked by right-wing interests for advocating the United States as the best and most prepared nation to undertake and fund the fight against the expansion of communism. In reply to this article, the U.S. political commentator Walter Lippmann writes several newspaper articles and coins the term "Cold War."
	Raoul Wallenberg, the Swedish diplomat who helped Jews escape Hungary with Swedish passports, dies. He is murdered by the NKVD, and to conceal his murder, his death is listed as caused by a heart attack.
August	The COMINFORM succeeds the COMINTERN through August and September.
	The East German security police is created.
	The United States has the three pillars of its "containment" policy firmly established: the Truman Doctrine (March 12, 1947); the Marshall Plan (June 5, 1947); the National Security Act (July 28, 1947).
September	The U.S. National Security Act creates the National Security Council, the Department of Defense (Army, Navy, and Air Force), and the CIA.
	HUAC subpoenas 41 witnesses in an investigation of communism in Hollywood. The "Hollywood Ten" are jailed for contempt, and blacklisting of Hollywood writers and actors begins.
October	Russian foreign intelligence is transferred to KI until November 1951.
November	Walter Lippmann's book *The Cold War* is published, and the term is used to summarize hostile relations between the Soviets and their allies and the nations of the West.
December	Bulgaria becomes the staunchest satellite of the U.S.S.R.
	James J. Angleton joins the CIA.
	Joan Hinton gets a passport to go from the United States to China. She takes with her a suitcase of information from her nuclear research work in Los Alamos and other laboratories.

1948

In Poland the UB forms a false WiN (Polish anti-Soviet underground movement), and for four years stings the CIA's attempts to undermine the Soviets in Poland.

Meredith Gardner, of the U.S. Army Security Agency, breaks more of the VENONA codes material.

William Weisband informs the U.S.S.R. about VENONA. Over the next four years the CIA expenses for covert actions grow from U.S.$2 million to U.S.$200 million.

January	Czechoslovakia's security service is routinely spying on non-Communist government ministers while claiming to protect all politicians.
February	Sir Percy Sillitoe, head of MI5, and Roger Hollis visit Australia to help establish a secure secret service, and discuss a list of VENONA suspects indicating Russian spies and agents are working inside the Australian government's Foreign Affairs Department. They are Frances Bernie, an assistant to Dr. Evatt; Ian Milner (BURO); and Jim Hill (TOURIST). Nine others names appear in the VENONA material. In Canberra, Sillitoe gives the impression that MI5 has a mole inside the Russian secret service. ASIO is established by mid-1949.
	Russia begins jamming Voice of America broadcasts.
March	The CIA Special Procedures Group is established and later becomes Frank Wisner's Office of Policy Coordination (OPC).
	U.S. General Lucius Clay warns that in his view, war will begin in six months. Later, British General Bernard Montgomery agrees with him.
	Truman establishes the U.S. Federal Employee Loyalty Program.
	Following a coup in Czechoslovakia, Foreign Minister Jan Masaryk dies in an alleged fall from an office window.
	Military and civilian advisers from the U.S.S.R. quit Yugoslavia, denouncing the government as riddled with heresy and British spies. By June, Soviet agents are found among Josip Tito's cabinet, bodyguards, and other forces.
April	A U.S.-sponsored economic program, the Marshall Plan, begins to aid devastated European countries ravaged by World War II.
	In Italy the Christian Democrats win in an election that is also a victory for the CIA Office of Special Operations. George Kennan suggests the Office of Policy Coordination be established to carry out more successful covert actions like the Italian election.
May	For the next two years the U.S.S.R. recognizes the legality of the state of Israel, which is a blow to U.K. control in the Middle East.
	Rigged elections in Czechoslovakia complete Communist power gains.
	The state of Israel is proclaimed, with David Ben-Gurion as leader; President Harry Truman immediately recognizes the new nation, and Egypt masses its forces on the border as Britain withdraws its troops from its UN mandate in Palestine.
	The British atomic bomb project becomes public.
June	Crisis in Berlin. Soviet troops block all road, rail, and canal traffic between West Berlin and the West. America, Britain, and France fly in food and essential supplies to West Berliners for 15 months, the Berlin Airlift.
	The COMINFORM expels Yugoslavia and calls for the overthrow of Josip Tito.
	Isser Harel establishes Shin Bet, and leads it until 1963.
	The CIA is authorized by U.S. National Security Council Directive 10/2 to undertake political and paramilitary operations in the Office of Policy Coordination, under Frank Wisner. Wisner recruits Reinhard Gehlen, who exposes former Nazi officers and recruits underground groups to begin the covert war against the Soviets in occupied East Europe.
	Josip Tito splits from the Soviet bloc with impunity, showing the United Kingdom and the United States what can be hoped for in containing Soviet aspirations in Eastern Europe.

July   Fears regarding Operation SPANDAU are aroused; the operation itself never
                  takes place.

                  U.S. B-29 bombers arrive in Britain in anticipation of a crisis in Berlin.

                  The British SIS plans for a war with Russia.

August   Before HUAC, Whittaker Chambers testifies that he and Alger Hiss spied for
                  the U.S.S.R. in the 1930s. Hiss denies all allegations; later admits he knew
                  Chambers under another name.

                  Harry Dexter White dies shortly after giving evidence before HUAC.

September   Around this time James Angleton becomes chief of counterintelligence in the
                  United States.

                  U.K. chiefs of staff advocate weakening the Russian hold over Eastern Europe,
                  short of war, largely due to the Czechoslovakian coup in March, the Berlin
                  crisis, and the establishment of COMINFORM.

                  The UN negotiator in the Middle East conflict over Palestine, Count Folke
                  Bernadotte, is assassinated; Isser Harel rounds up the Stern Gang and Irgun,
                  Israeli terrorist groups.

October   Donald Maclean is posted to Cairo as counselor and head of the British
                  chancery.

                  George Blake is sent by MI6 to South Korea.

November   Harry S. Truman is elected U.S. President.

December   HUAC charges Alger Hiss with perjury for denying he had connections with
                  the U.S.S.R. in the 1930s.

1949

Early in 1949 OPC attempts, unsuccessfully, to overthrow Tito in Yugoslavia. MGB penetrates
the Ukraine anti-Soviet resistance movements, Organization of Ukrainian Nationalists (OUN)
and National Labor Alliance (NTS). MGB captures SIS agents who attempt to contact the
OUN.

In response to Josip Tito's split from the U.S.S.R., leaders in Hungary and Bulgaria are
arrested, tried, and executed by the Soviet-dominated governments. Many other leaders in
Soviet-dominated Eastern European countries (e.g., Czechoslovakia) are purged. This brutal
political change of regime continues until 1952, when the Soviet bloc appears to be stabilized, and many of the victims are denounced as being involved with Western intelligence
services.

January   Dwight Eisenhower notes in his diary that the world is threatened by a mono-
                  lithic mass of Communist imperialism, to which the United States must
                  respond with strength, serenity, and confidence.

                  Peking falls to the Chinese Communist forces of Mao Zedong.

March   Enver Hoxha, Albania's chief, visits Moscow to prepare for the Albanian show
                  trials in May of Koci Xoxe, Hoxa's rival, head of Sigurimi (Albania's secu-
                  rity services), and supporter of Josip Tito.

                  Judith Coplon is arrested for espionage in America.

April   Angela Calomiris, an FBI double agent, gives evidence on the Communist
                  Party leaders in the United States.

                  The North Atlantic Treaty Organization (NATO) establishes a common de-
                  fense alliance between nations of the West against the Soviet Union in East-
                  ern Europe.

May   Berlin Blockade of 11 months ends.

July   Russia secretly tests its first atom bomb.

                  Koci Xoxe is executed after "confessing" to being a wartime recruit to the
                  West's secret services, knowing that Josip Tito was a British secret agent,

and plotting with him and Britain's SIS to make Albania part of
Yugoslavia.

The first trial of Alger Hiss for perjury ends with a hung jury.

August   Konrad Adenauer, 73, leader of the Christian Democrats, wins the Federal
Republic of Germany (FRG) election for Chancellor.

September   Milada Horakova, a Czechoslovakian nationalist, is caught by the MGB, interrogated and tried for treason, and hanged in June 1950.

Kim Philby arrives in Washington to take over from Peter Dwyer as head of
station.

President Harry Truman announces that the U.S.S.R. detonated an atom bomb
in Kazakhstan.

Meredith Gardner finds the VENONA encrypts of 1944 include material revealing that Klaus Fuchs was a Soviet spy.

Russia announces it tested an atom bomb in July.

October   Guy Burgess is posted to the Far Eastern Department. Earlier, while drunk in
Gibralter and Tangiers, Burgess had identified U.K. secret agents. His Soviet
colleagues wonder if he is anxious about being revealed as spy by the
VENONA decrypts.

The German Democratic Republic is founded.

Operation VALUABLE begins with a failed SIS landing of 26 trained resistance supporters on the Albanian coast, probably blown by Kim Philby.

The People's Republic of China is founded, and under Mao Zedong's control, most of China turns to communism. Great Britain recognizes Communist China, but the United States does not.

Aware of the VENONA material, Kim Philby passes it on, and Donald Maclean
becomes anxious about the decrypts. Moscow fears a plethora of U.S. spy
trials.

In Washington, as SIS liaison officer, Philby is having regular lunches with
James Angleton (1917–1987) and using their close friendship to provide
his case officer with details of U.S. and U.K. secret operations.

November   John Drew's note to the SIS and chiefs of staff recommends the establishment
of a deception organization with the aim—not unlike the KGB's "active
measures" policy—of destroying Stalinism for fear of Russia's repeating the
purges of the 1930s.

Robert Vogeler is arrested by the Hungarian police and put on trial for espionage and sabotage against the economy.

December   Bruno Pontecorvo is working at Harwell with Klaus Fuchs and is found to
have Communist relatives.

Chiang Kai-shek flees to Formosa (Taiwan).

1950

During the year CIA policy is to support anti-Soviet underground movements in Eastern
Europe.

Early in the year Galtung Haavik, code-named VIKA and later GRETA, is blackmailed into
serving the Soviets and begins a 27-year career, handing her controllers thousands of classified documents from the Norwegian Foreign Ministry.

Harvey Matusow contacts the FBI, and becomes a paid spy.

January   Alger Hiss is sentenced to five years in jail for perjury.

Klaus Fuchs confesses to having informed the Russians about his research on
the atomic bomb between 1942 and March 1949; he is arrested in February,
tried, and sentenced in April.

February	A decrypted NKGB message of 1944 indicates that David Greenglass is spying for the U.S.S.R.
	Joseph McCarthy denounces 205 supposed Communists in U.S. government departments, and crusades against "Godless Communists" and the "Red Menace." A subcommittee of the Foreign Relations Committee is established to examine his allegations; it is chaired by Millard Tydings, a Democrat from Maryland.
March	Gertrude Banda, a CIA double agent in Indonesia, is arrested and shot while on a visit to North Korea.
	In her second trial Judith Coplon is found guilty and sentenced to 15 years in prison. Later her conviction is reversed on the grounds that the FBI wiretaps were illegal.
	Valentin Gubitchev is found guilty of espionage and leaves the United States with a suspended sentence, on the condition he never returns.
April	Guy Burgess reports to the U.S.S.R. on Western intelligence about Russian and Chinese forces in Korea.
	President Harry Truman begins the "Campaign of Truth," a psychological offensive against Soviet propaganda.
	William Weisband, who told the Soviets about VENONA, is jailed for failing to respond to a grand jury summons.
May	Donald Maclean breaks down in Cairo, and goes into psychiatric treatment for sexual and identity disorders.
	Harry Gold confesses to being a Soviet agent, and in July names David Greenglass, Morton Sobell, and Ethel and Julius Rosenberg as Soviet agents.
June	David Greenglass, Ethel Rosenberg's brother, implicates Julius Rosenberg in espionage for the U.S.S.R. To the FBI, Julius Rosenberg denies he had supplied the Soviets.
	The Korean War begins, and 16 UN countries fight alongside South Korea until the armistice in 1953.
	Moscow Center evacuates the Pontecorvo family to the U.S.S.R. via Finland.
	Questioned by Jim Skardon, top MI5 interrogator in London, Jim Hill is encouraged to confess to providing the Soviets with information from Australia.
July	Julius Rosenberg, 32, is arrested on charges of spying for Russia.
	The Tydings Committee Report denounces Joseph McCarthy, who immediately begins a public attack on the committee members standing for election to the U.S. Congress later in 1950.
August	Guy Burgess is Second Secretary in the U.K. embassy in Washington, and informs the U.S.S.R. of U.K. policy on the People's Republic of China and Korea.
	Morton Sobell is kidnapped in Mexico City; taken to the border; deported from Mexico as an undesirable alien, and then taken to the East Coast of the United States, to be charged with conspiring to commit espionage with Julius Rosenberg.
September	Donald Maclean recovers, and now heads the American desk in the Foreign Office in London.
	In the United States, the McCarran Internal Security Act states all Communist-front organizations must be registered with the U.S. Attorney General; all Communists are banned from national defense; members of all totalitarian organizations are banned from entering the United States; and if a national emergency is declared in the United States, all Communists are to be interned.

October	After watching Israel's links with the United States grow, the U.S.S.R. identifies a Zionist conspiracy, and gives support to Arab nations that are enemies of Israel.
	General Douglas MacArthur crosses the 38th parallel into North Korea; the Chinese army crosses the Yalu River and pushes him back.
	OPC becomes part of the CIA.
November	Kim Philby spends Thanksgiving with James Angleton.
	A CIA-supported landing in Albania is blown, probably by Philby.
December	Josef Stalin is convinced of the threat of World War III.
	The number of HOMER suspects is 35.
	Harvey Matusow is expelled from the CPUSA.

1951

During the year the CIA takes full responsibility for the disastrous Albanian project, Operation VALUABLE.

The MGB begins to recruit Hugh Hambleton, a Canadian economist.

Peter Lunn's Operation SILVER, the Vienna tunnel, is a success for the SIS.

January	For three months the United States and U.K. fear grows that that the war in Korea is part of the Soviet plan to expand the Russian empire. This fear is conveyed in reports to Moscow from Guy Burgess and Donald Maclean. Josef Stalin sees these fears as a cover for the West's plan for war.
	Guy Burgess crashes Kim Philby's dinner party for high-ranking FBI and CIA officers and insults the wife of a guest; her husband, William Harvey (CIA), begins next day to investigate the backgrounds of both Philby and Burgess.
February	Kim Philby regularly attends many Anglo–American intelligence conferences.
	Vladimir Petrov and his wife are appointed to the Soviet consulate in Canberra.
March	The trial of Julius and Ethel Rosenberg begins.
	Guy Burgess and Michael Straight meet in Washington.
	Ted Hall, former scientist at Los Alamos, is suspected of espionage and interrogated by the FBI, but not charged, for lack of evidence.
April	British commandos are behind enemy lines in the Korean War, demolishing railway lines.
	General Douglas MacArthur is relieved of his command in Korea by President Harry Truman when he calls for permission to bomb Chinese cities and invade China.
	HOMER suspects are reduced to only nine.
	Julius and Ethel Rosenberg are sentenced to death for espionage.
	At the behest of George Kennan, President Harry Truman signs the directive to establish the Psychological Strategy Board.
	Guy Burgess is ordered back to the U.K. in disgrace; before leaving, he plans with Kim Philby on how to help Donald Maclean, who is now aware he is under surveillance as HOMER, escape.
	William N. Oatis, U.S. newspaperman, is detained in Czechoslovakia and charged with espionage.
May	In the U.K., Guy Burgess informs Donald Maclean of their escape plan, and Kim Philby gives the vital tip-off. Under great stress Burgess and Maclean flee. Anthony Blunt refuses the offer to flee with them, and ineptly clears Burgess's flat of incriminating evidence. As far as the public knows, Burgess and Maclean have vanished without a trace, perhaps defected.
June	After the defection of Guy Burgess and Donald Maclean, Dick Ellis in MI6 comes under suspicion.

Frank Olsen becomes aware of Operation ARTICHOKE.

About now George Blake is recruited to the KGB and the Kuzmich confusion (1954–1990) begins.

Kim Philby, no longer permitted to stay in Washington, is recalled and officially retired. Burgess and Maclean are reported missing.

The head of StB reports on Jewish bourgeois internationalists whose espionage is subverting Soviet interests in Czechoslovakia.

Joseph McCarthy attacks Secretary of State George Marshall as an "instrument of a Soviet conspiracy."

Operation POST REPORT is approved by the U.K. Joint Intelligence Committee.

July	Michael Bialoguski meets Vladimir Petrov, the newly appointed Soviet consul, Third Secretary of the Soviet embassy, and secret head of the MVD in Australia.
September	At a peace conference Joan Hinton speaks out vehemently against American germ warfare in Korea, and later earns the sobriquet "Peking Joan."
	Heinz Felfe is recruited to the MGB.
October	George Blake recalls, perhaps falsely, that it was late in autumn that he passed a note to a North Korean guard to see an official at the Soviet embassy in Pyongyang, North Korea, for whom he had valuable information.
	Joseph McCarthy attacks Adlai Stevenson's reputation.
November	Heinz Felfe joins the Gehlen Org, as a double agent for the Soviets.
	Kim Philby is forced to resign from the SIS and given a small payout. He is tried informally by SIS, but there is insufficient evidence to charge him formally with espionage. Many MI5 officers believe Philby is guilty of treason, but only a few of his SIS colleagues feel the same.
December	A victim of the *Amerasia* case, John Service is the first of the old "China hands" to be falsely blamed for disloyalty and forced out of the U.S. Foreign Service.

1952

During the year Jews are purged from the list of MGB agents in the U.K. and United States George Kennan, U.S. ambassador in Moscow, finds the embassy thoroughly bugged. Inside the East German Ministry of State Security, Main Department XV—later called Main Department of Reconnaissance—is formed by Markus Wolf. John Sinclair takes over direction of the SIS in Great Britain.

February	The United Kingdom's secret Permanent Undersecretary's Department (PUSD) becomes operative.
	Bruno Pontecorvo announces he is working in the U.S.S.R.
April	With CIA support the final attempt to overthrow the Communist regime in Albania fails.
June	Robert Vogeler, a U.S. businessman, is to be released from prison in Hungary.
	William Marshall is arrested for passing secrets to a Soviet official in London, tried, and sentenced to five years in prison.
July	Gamal Abdel Nasser leads in a coup in Egypt.
	Harvey Matusow appears before the HUAC and decides to name people as Communists even though he knows they are not. Eventually he will name over 200.
September	Isser Harel becomes the Mossad chief.
October	At the first Communist Party conference since 1939, Josef Stalin has the Politburo of 10 men replaced with the 36-member Presidium.

Off the Monte Bello Islands near Western Australia's coast, Britain detonates its first atom bomb. News of the test is leaked to the press before the Australian Prime Minister informs his cabinet or the minister responsible.

November   Dwight Eisenhower, U.S. military leader in Europe during World War II, is elected to the U.S. presidency.

The U.S. National Security Agency is founded; its forerunner was the U.S. Army Forces Security Agency.

December   Allan Nunn May is released from prison for being a model prisoner.

The MGB exposes its WiN deception in Poland and humiliates the CIA.

In Vienna, the SIS's Operation CONFLICT is so successful it is followed by Operation SUGAR and Operation LORD.

1953

During the year Alister D. Watson, head of submarine detection at the U.K. Admiralty Research Laboratories, is spying for the MGB.

Heinz Felfe's bogus network for BND is established in Moscow.

The first head of station in Moscow for the CIA is seduced by a Soviet swallow and sent home in disgrace. Others are similarly caught.

Robert Bialek of the GDR's State Security Services (SSD) defects, and lives in West Berlin under an assumed name.

January   Pytor Popov, a GRU officer, becomes a CIA agent.

March   Josef Stalin dies, deeply suspicious that many of his senior, long-serving, loyal supporters are in fact spies for the West. Lavrenti Beria quickly integrates the MGB with the MVD (Ministry of Interior), places them under his control, and sets many supporters around him. With Georgi Malenkov and Nikita Khrushchev he ends the anti-Semitic witch-hunt in the U.S.S.R., but allows the Zionist conspiracy to continue. The MGB, transferred to the KI in 1947, is now combined with an enlarged MVD, with Beria at its head.

June   Dick Ellis retires from MI6 due to ill health.

Soviet troops put down anti-Communist revolts in East Germany.

The Rosenbergs are executed. They are noted for their courage, and there are deep suspicions that they suffered a miscarriage of justice. At every opportunity Moscow Center follows an active measures program in support of the Rosenbergs' innocence.

George Blake has returned home to England after imprisonment in North Korea, and decides secretly to serve Moscow Center.

July   George Kennan, father of the U.S. containment policy toward the U.S.S.R., returns to academe after becoming *persona non grata*. In 1952, while visiting Berlin as U.S. ambassador to the Soviet Union, he had made unflattering comments about Stalin, and compared the U.S.S.R. to Nazi Germany.

On his return from observing the East Berlin workers' riot being put down, Lavrenti Beria is arrested for his antiparty divisiveness, imperialist activities, treason, rape, and moral degradation; is tried; and is executed in December.

The Korean War armistice is announced.

Twelve Australians are believed to be Soviet agents, including Jim Hill and Ian Milner.

August   Sir Percy Sillitoe retires as head of MI5.

The Soviets test their hydrogen bomb.

A military coup staged by the CIA and the SIS, Operation AJAX, overthrows Dr. Mohammed Mossadegh and restores the Shah's power in Iran.

October   Allen Dulles approves the Berlin tunnel project, Operation STOPWATCH/
                  GOLD, and the SIS and CIA meet in London to discuss its construction,
                  with George Blake on the committee.
                  Petrov inquiry in Australia opens.
November   Frank Olsen, former CIA agent, dies in a fall from a hotel window in New
                  York.
December   Martha Dodd Stern and her husband flee the United States for Mexico to avoid
                  investigation as Soviet agents.

1954

January   Yuri Rastvorov defects to the CIA from the Soviets' Tokyo residency.
February   Operation RHINE is aborted by its hired assassin, who immediately defects
                  to the West; in April, at a Voice of America studio, he is photographed
                  shaking his intended victim's hand.
                  Pyotr Deryabin defects from the First Chief Directorate to the CIA in Vienna.
                  Richard Bissell, Jr., joins the CIA, and helps to administer many of its opera-
                  tions.
March   U.S. Army–McCarthy hearings begin, and are televised for over 180 hours.
                  The MGB is separated from the MVD and downgraded from a ministry to a
                  committee, Komitet Gosudarstvennoy Besopasnosti (KGB), and placed
                  under political control of the Council of Ministers. KGB will become the
                  widely used name for all Soviet state security organizations.
April   A show trial in Tirana, Albania, records the final disastrous attempt, with CIA
                  support, of the Albanian "pixies" to overthrow the Communist government
                  in Albania.
                  In Sydney, Australia, with help from Michael Bialoguski, Vladimir Petrov de-
                  fects to the West; his wife, Evdokia, defects at the Darwin airport. Petrov
                  provides clear evidence that Guy Burgess and Donald Maclean are in Mos-
                  cow. Yuri Modin, Kim Philby's case officer, assures him that Petrov knows
                  nothing of Philby's work. The Australian Prime Minister announces the
                  defection of Petrov and a Royal Commission on Espionage in Australia
                  (Petrov Inquiry).
                  George Blake is posted to Berlin.
                  President Dwight Eisenhower announces the "domino theory" in support of
                  U.S. support of the French in Indochina, which is approaching 80 percent
                  of France's war costs.
June   In Guatemala the CIA supports an invasion and military coup, Operation
                  PBSUCCESS, that overthrows Jacobo Arbenz Guzman's government.
July   Otto John, head of the FRG secret service, disappears—defects to East Ger-
                  many—and holds a conference to denounce the rise of Nazism in West
                  Germany.
                  At the Petrov Inquiry, Vladimir Petrov asserts that all TASS press agents are
                  Soviet spies. Evdokia Petrov states that the shocking "Document J" was
                  written by Rupert Lockwood.
                  The Indochina war ends, and Vietnam is divided at the 17th parallel.
August   President Dwight Eisenhower outlaws the Communist Party in the United
                  States.
September   In Australia the Prime Minister now has a bodyguard.
November   Alger Hiss is released after 44 months in prison, and spends the rest of his life
                  attempting to show he was never a Soviet agent.
December   Permission is given to Lockheed Aircraft to produce U-2 reconnaissance air-
                  craft, funded partly by the CIA.

Senator Joseph McCarthy is censured by the U.S. Senate for his allegations that there are Communists in the U.S. Army.

James Angleton becomes first CIA Chief of Counterintelligence, and the leader of Western counterintelligence.

1955

During the year Eisenhower's proposal to the U.S.S.R. for an "open skies" policy regarding the reconnaissance of all military establishments is rejected; it is secretly adopted anyway by the United States, which uses U-2 spy flights regularly thereafter.

Following the defection of Guy Burgess and Donald Maclean (1951) and the revelations of Igor Gouzenko (1945), Elizabeth Bentley (1945), and Whittaker Chambers, Moscow Center forbids the recruitment to espionage of Communist Party members.

Ignoring the Baghdad Pact, Gamal Abdel Nasser makes an arms deal with the Soviet Union through the Soviet satellite Czechoslovakia.

Peter Wright begins employment with MI5, and Gordon Lonsdale establishes a successful business with KGB funds in Great Britain.

Harvey Matusow publishes *False Witness*, admitting he lied to the HUAC because he was encouraged to do so by Joseph McCarthy.

Using photographs of John Vassall's homosexual activities in Moscow, the KGB blackmails him into its service.

February	Operation STOPWATCH/GOLD, the SIS/CIA's Berlin tunnel, is now operating.
March	The Petrov Inquiry ends after 126 days, spread over 11 months. Vladimir Petrov has secretly named 500 or more Soviet spies.
	Bruno Pontecorvo denies he is working on nuclear research projects for the Soviets.
May	Soviet Union and seven East European countries sign the Warsaw Pact to have a unified command against NATO. West Germany is a sovereign state.
August	First official flight of the U-2 spy plane.
December	Kim Philby is cleared publicly of being the "third man."
	Otto John returns to the West, is jailed for four years, and attributes his 1954 defection to excessive alcohol consumption and his colleagues' manipulative persuasion.

1956

U.S. Secretary of State John Foster Dulles declares that to be neutral in these times is obsolete, immoral, and shortsighted; Urho Kaleva Kekkonen becomes President of Finland (until 1981) and acts as an important Soviet agent of influence in Scandinavia.

February	At the Twentieth Soviet Communist Party Congress, Khrushchev makes a "secret speech" condemning Stalin. The CIA offers a large reward for a copy of the speech. It is published four months later in the *New York Times*.
	Guy Burgess and Donald Maclean surface in Moscow, announcing they had never been Communists, and had gone to Moscow to improve international relations.
	Robert Bialek, former SSD (The German Democratic Republic's Security Service, popularly known as the STASI) is betrayed by George Blake, abducted, and executed.
March	Anthony Wraight, an RAF officer, is questioned about his relations with a GRU officer in London; he defects to Berlin and later to Moscow.
	Writing anonymously, Goronwy Rees publishes the first of six articles in *People* telling all about Guy Burgess. Rees is identified two weeks after publication.
	Nikita Khrushchev's February speech denouncing Stalin is made public.

April	Buster Crabb disappears—in fact, dies—on a secret underwater mission to investigate a visiting Soviet vessel in Portsmouth. The KGB is secretly amused.
	The COMINFORM is dissolved by Nikita Khrushchev.
	The KGB stages the "discovery" of the Berlin tunnel when Nikita Khrushchev is visiting Great Britain. The tunnel is credited with being a CIA operation, and its British planner, Peter Lunn, receives no publicity.
June	John Vassall returns to London from Moscow, where he served as clerk to the naval attaché in the British embassy and was blackmailed into service by the KGB.
	Gamal Abdel Nasser, an Egyptian nationalist, is elected, unopposed, the President of Egypt.
July	First secret overflight of the U.S.S.R. by the U-2 spy plane.
	Egypt nationalizes the Paris-based Suez Canal Company, in response to the U.K. and the United States ceasing to provide aid to Egypt after she had done an arms deal with the Soviets through Czechoslovakia. The Suez crisis begins.
October	Operation MUSKETEER begins with the Israeli invasion of the Sinai Peninsula.
November	In Hungary a revolution is put down in six weeks when the Soviet militia and the KGB invade the nation. Many citizens flee to the West.
	President Dwight Eisenhower is ambivalent about U-2 flights; on one hand, he wants the United States to be more moral and correct than the U.S.S.R. in its standing in world affairs, but on the other hand, he allows the U-2 flights to continue even though they may be detected by the Soviets.
November	Operation MUSKETEER, a secret invasion of the Suez Canal Zone by French and British forces, is unknown to U.S. President Dwight Eisenhower.
December	Fidel Castro returns secretly to Cuba, and with a small armed group begins the fight against the dictator Fulgencio Batista.
	Suez Crisis ends: British and French forces quit the Suez Canal Zone; Nasser's prestige is enhanced; the Soviet Union appears a friend of Arab nations; the Western alliance appears split; Anthony Eden, Britain's Prime Minister, is embarrassed.

1957

Until 1961 Hugh Hambleton is working at NATO headquarters, and handing military and economic plans of NATO to the KGB.

January	The Eisenhower Doctrine pledges support to anti-Soviet and anti-Nasser regimes in the Middle East. Harold Macmillan replaces Anthony Eden as Britain's Prime Minister.
	Martha Dodd Stern, a former Soviet agent, and her husband are subpoenaed in Mexico to appear before a New York grand jury, but avoid being extradited from Mexico and pay a fine for contempt of court.
June	A body is found and identified, falsely, as that of Buster Crabb.
	Willie Fisher is arrested in a New York hotel, and in a few days declares he is Rudolph Abel.
July	Helen Keenan is found guilty of passing secret U.K. government documents to a South African spy, and sentenced to jail for six months.
	John Stanley, a U.K. businessman and alleged spy, is released from prison in Egypt.
September	KGB assassination attempt on Nikolai Khokhlov fails.
October	KGB assassin Bogan Stashinsky kills Lev Rebet, a prominent Ukrainian émigré, in West Germany.
	Russia launches *Sputnik*, and the United States seems behind in the space race.

1958

During this year the last of the Hungarian revolution (October–November 1956) leaders are tried and either executed or jailed.

Heinz Felfe, a Soviet agent, becomes head of Soviet counterintelligence inside the West German BND, and is able to reveal to the Soviets most plans of the West's intelligence services.

The "Red Casanova," Carl Helmers, is arrested.

February	A secret decision is made to complete Operation CORONA with a recoverable capsule for the U-2 spy plane.
March	Nikita Khrushchev is Soviet Premier as well as leader of the Soviet Communist Party.
April	Morris Childs, an FBI secret agent, is invited to Moscow to discuss funding for the moribund CPUSA; with his brother, he serves the KGB, but for 19 years is a double agent for the FBI.
May	Gamal Abdel Nasser makes a visit to Moscow.
	Vice President Richard Nixon breaks off his Latin American visit because of hostile demonstrations, and is protected by Operation POOR RICHARD.
October	The U.S. and Soviet governments agree to a moratorium on nuclear testing, and Operation LIGHTHOUSE is called off.
November	About this time the United States begins its satellite defense support program, which uses satellites and receiving stations in Australia and Europe to observe Soviet military activities.
	Pyotr Popov's espionage is securely known to the Soviets.

1959

Anthony Wraight returns to Great Britain, is caught, and is jailed for three years for defecting to the U.S.S.R. in 1956.

The Soviet embassy is reopened in Australia. A secret KGB agent becomes the head of Egyptian intelligence services, and close adviser to Gamal Abdel Nasser.

January	Fidel Castro overthrows Fulgencio Batista's dictatorship in Cuba and establishes a Marxist nation.
February	The first Operation CORONA flight occurs.
May	A large conference of senior Soviet politicians and the KGB plans to coordinate "active measures," "special actions," and "wet affairs" throughout the Soviet bloc in an effort to counter threats from Japan, NATO, and the United States.
June	After serving nine years and four months of his 14-year sentence, Klaus Fuchs is released from prison early for good conduct, and settles in East Germany.
	Stephen Ward and Christine Keeler become acquainted in London.
July	Fidel Castro's chief of intelligence meets in Mexico City with KGB officials to plan the reorganization of Cuba's secret services.
October	By now the KGB and the GRU are regularly using their delegation to the United Nations in New York for intelligence training.
	KGB assassin Bogan Stashinsky kills Stephan Bandera, a prominent Ukrainian émigré.
	In Moscow, Pyotr Popov, a valuable double agent for the West, is caught by the Soviets.
December	Bernon F. Mitchell and William H. Martin, mathematicians, are Soviet "walkins" at the U.S. National Security Agency.
	Fidel Castro expropriates plantations in Cuba that have U.S. owners.

1960

Over the next 10 years the KGB and GRU will more than double their number of agents in London.

January President Dwight Eisenhower and a special group in charge of U.S. covert operations decide that the regime in Cuba is a threat to the United States and must be changed.

Michal Goleniewski defects to the West and identifies Gordon Lonsdale (Konon Molody) and George Blake as spies.

Pyotr Popov is tried for espionage and found guilty.

March Eugene Ivanov arrives in London to take up his duties as a GRU officer.

May Isser Harel captures Adolf Eichmann.

Over Sverdlovsk, Russia, Francis Gary Powers's U-2 spy plane is downed. The Paris summit collapses when President Dwight Eisenhower refuses to apologize to Nikita Khrushchev for the U-2 espionage flight.

The U.S.S.R. and Cuba establish diplomatic relations.

June Jack Dunlap begins providing the Soviets with NSA secrets.

Pyotr Popov is executed by firing squad.

The mathematicians Bernon Mitchell and William Martin go to Moscow via Havana, and reveal the NSA decrypts communications between the U.S. allies. They have knowledge of secret U-2 flights.

July Nikita Khrushchev announces the U.S.S.R. supports Cuba fully.

August After 13 failures Operation CORONA succeeds.

The Soviets promise considerable aid to Patrice Lumumba in the Congo; civil war begins in the Congo; President Dwight Eisenhower and his special group may have secretly decided to get rid of Lumumba.

September Kay Marshall, a double agent for the New Zealand security service, is recruited to Soviet intelligence in New Zealand.

October The execution of 17 Cubans and 3 Americans in Cuba becomes known. The United States announces its trade embargo against Cuba.

November John F. Kennedy is elected President of the United States.

December In South Vietnam the Communists (Vietcong) establish the National Liberation Front against the rule of President Diem.

1961

January Gordon Lonsdale's (Konon Molody) group, the Portland spy ring, centering on the U.K. Underwater Weapons Establishment at Portland, England, is caught after being identified by the defector Michal Goleniewski; its members are sentenced to 18 to 25 years in prison.

Patrice Lumumba, deposed head of the Congo Republic, is assassinated; the CIA is implicated in his death for 40 years.

April George Blake is interrogated, confesses, and is sentenced to 42 years in prison.

The first man to travel in space is Yuri Gagarin, a Soviet astronaut.

The Bay of Pigs disaster, Operation PLUTO/ZAPATA, occurs.

In April and May, Oleg Penkovsky gives Greville Wynne secret material in Moscow.

May Robert Kennedy and Georgi N. Bolshakov, a Russian newspaperman, meet secretly every two weeks. Kennedy appears unaware that Bolshakov is a KGB agent.

June Rudolf Nureyev, an outstanding Russian ballet dancer, defects to the West at Le Bourget Airport, and thereafter becomes a target of KGB "special actions."

July	Christine Keeler meets Britain's Secretary of War, John Profumo; they become lovers at the same time she is the sex partner of the Soviet naval attaché. The attaché and Stephen Ward require Keeler to get secret military information from Profumo.
August	KGB assassin Bogan Stashinsky defects to the West.
	To stop the flow of East German citizens to the West, East Germany builds a wall in Berlin. The Berlin Wall becomes a stark symbol of the Cold War.
September	Oleg Penkovsky, a senior GRU officer, is recruited to the CIA and SIS for 18 months and provides highly valuable material to the West.
October	Heinz Felfe and his associates from the Nazi days are arrested after being identified by Michal Goleniewski. Reinhard Gehlen's lifework is compromised.
November	MI5 warns John Profumo about Christine Keeler and Eugene Ivanov. Profumo immediately ends his affair with Keeler.
December	Anatoli Mikhailovich Golitsyn defects to the West from Helsinki. He identifies the KGB's Operation SAPPHIRE in the French counterespionage agency, and contributes much to conspiratorial thought among French, British, and American counterintelligence officers. Later Georges Pâques is arrested, convicted, and sentenced to 20 years in prison on the information from Golitsyn.
	Robert Lee Johnson steals NATO and U.S. Sixth Fleet secret documents in France.

1962

January	In Beirut at about this time, Yuri Modin warns Kim Philby never to return to Britain because he may be arrested.
	While walking with her children in a Moscow park, Janet Ann Chisholm, wife of a British diplomat, meets a Russian, Oleg Penkovsky, who gives the children a candy box. The contact is observed by the KGB.
February	New Minutemen ICBM and medium-range missiles in Britain and Turkey put the United States ahead of the U.S.S.R. in the nuclear arms race.
	The Soviet Union announces that Francis Gary Powers has been pardoned and allowed to return to the United States. The United States exchanges Rudolph Abel for Powers and two others.
March	Richard Bissell, Jr., is removed from the influential post he had held in the CIA for years because of the Bay of Pigs disaster, and is appointed to the Science and Technology Directorate in the CIA shortly before leaving the agency.
June	Yuri Nosenko begins to negotiate his defection to the West.
September	John Vassall is caught in the U.K., and sentenced later in the year to 18 years in prison; he serves only 10.
October	Bogan Stashinsky is tried, and jailed for eight years. Later KGB policy on "wet affairs" is modified, KGB officers are demoted, and assassinations by the KGB become less frequent.
	U-2 spy planes detect ballistic missile sites under construction in Cuba, and a world war crisis begins; it ends in two weeks with a secret deal between Nikita Khrushchev and John F. Kennedy, details of which are not revealed until many years later. Kennedy appears to "win" the conflict and resolve the crisis, and embarrass Khrushchev.
November	Greville Wynne is arrested in Budapest.
December	Cuba begins to release prisoners captured at the Bay of Pigs disaster in exchange for food and medicine valued at $53 million.
	Nikita Khrushchev congratulates Robert L. Johnson, and makes him a major in the Red Army for espionage while a guard in France.

1963

January	Eugene Ivanov leaves Great Britain.
	Nicholas Elliott, former friend and SIS colleague, offers Kim Philby immunity from prosecution in return for a full confession; instead, Philby defects and later reports that Elliott, his old friend, tried to push him into defection rather than confession.
February	Ivan Skripov is declared *persona non grata* and leaves Australia within a week, following the work of ASIO and Kay Marshall in catching him committing espionage.
March	The Soviet ambassador to the United States, Anatoli F. Dobrynin, begins secret discussions with Henry Kissinger and thereby establishes the "back channel" between Moscow and Washington, helping to create détente policy.
April	Fidel Castro is feted as a hero in Moscow as he visits Nikita Khrushchev. Shortly after the visit, Cuba's DGI staff is being trained by the KGB.
May	The British government admits it carried out secret atomic tests at Maralinga in Australia, and adds later that its own soldiers were used a guinea pigs to test the effects of the explosions.
	Oleg Penkovsky and Greville Wynne are on trial in Moscow.
June	Both the United States and the U.S.S.R. use and accept the use of satellite surveillance and photograph reconnaissance for military espionage.
	Michael Straight is interviewed by the FBI and speaks of Anthony Blunt, Leo Long, and others he knew at Cambridge.
	Jack E. Dunlap, a U.S. war hero in Korea, is found to have been spying for the Soviets since about 1957.
	John Profumo resigns after having misled the British Parliament about his relations with Christine Keeler.
July	Jack E. Dunlap, a Soviet spy at the NSA, commits suicide, and is buried with U.S. military honors.
	Victor Hamilton, a former NSA cryptanalyst who suffered from schizophrenia, publishes in *Izvestia* an account of his work with the NSA in the Near East.
	Heinz Felfe is tried, found guilty, and sentenced to 15 years of hard labor. Reinhard Gehlen is not asked to retire prematurely from the BND.
	Dr. Giuseppe Martelli, an Italian physicist who was suspected of spying and arrested in 1962, is acquitted for lack of evidence.
August	Nuclear test ban treaty prohibits tests of nuclear weapons in the atmosphere, underwater, and in space.
	Stephen Ward commits suicide.
	Guy Burgess dies and is cremated.
September	*The Spy Who Came in from the Cold,* by John Le Carré, is published, is critically acclaimed, and goes through many printings; the modern spy novel is reshaped.
November	Lee Harvey Oswald assassinates President John Kennedy, and is later murdered by Jack Ruby.
December	The KGB reports having learned from Polish informants and a U.S. industrialist that John Kennedy's assassination had been plotted and executed by a leading American industrialist and two of his racist colleagues. In various forms this KGB disinformation is spread and maintained for 10 years.

1964

During this year Maurice Dejean's eight-year sojourn as French ambassador to Moscow ends when his relations with a KGB swallow become known. His air attaché is similarly caught, and commits suicide.

February	Yuri Nosenko defects, and the U.S. embassy learns of the many bugs in the new Moscow embassy.
April	Gordon Lonsdale (Konon Molody) is freed in a spy exchange with Greville Wynne.
	Anthony Blunt is interrogated by MI5 and confesses falsely to being recruited to the Soviet cause by Guy Burgess while at Trinity College, Cambridge.
	Josef Frolik of the StB is posted as a labor attaché to London.
August	About this time Daniel Ellsberg takes a job in the Pentagon and has unrestricted access to highly secret information from which he learns firsthand about the difference between what President Lyndon Johnson told the U.S. Congress in secret, and what was made available to the American public.
	The U.S. Congress permits the expansion of America's involvement in the Vietnam War following what were thought to be repeated acts of violence against the armed forces of the United States. It was alleged that North Vietnam had twice attacked two U.S. destroyers, the U.S.S. *Maddox* and the U.S.S. *Turner Joy,* in the Gulf of Tonkin. Later it appeared the repeated acts of violence and alleged attacks were merely one somewhat minor event.
October	China tests the atom bomb.
	KGB plotters help force Nikita Khrushchev's resignation.
November	The MI5/MI6 FLUENCY Committee is established to investigate Soviet penetration of Britain's secret services. One of its tasks is to establish the identity of ELLI, and consequently many senior members of Britain's intelligence community come under suspicion and investigation.

1965

For 11 years the KGB intensifies its espionage mission to acquire modern scientific and technological intelligence.

Gradually the last of the captured invaders of the Bay of Pigs disaster are released in an exchange with the United States for $53 million worth of food and medicine.

March	In London, Frank Bossard of the U.K. Ministry of Aviation is caught spying for the GRU, and in May he is jailed for 21 years.

1966

	Until 1969 China undergoes a full-scale revolution to establish a working-class culture across the nation—the Cultural Revolution.
March	The Munsinger Affair begins in Canada with the discovery of Gerda Munsinger in Munich.

1967

A clerk in the Greater London Council Motor Licensing Department is recruited to the KGB, and it learns the license plate numbers of all MI5 and SIS operatives, thereby regularly compromising British intelligence surveillance of Russian agents in England.

Over the next 20 years the U.S.S.R. puts over 130 SIGINT satellites into orbit for the GRU.

Leonore Sütterlein, a "secretary spy" who is run by Markus Wolf in the Bonn Foreign Ministry, is eventually found to be a KGB spy, and commits suicide.

March	Stalin's daughter, Svetlana, defects to the West while at the funeral of her third husband in India, and goes to the United States in April.
April	Yuri Andropov serves as KGB chief for the next 15 years, thereby facilitating Leonid Brezhnev's policy of building a close link between the KGB and the Communist Party's Central Committee.
	The KGB's attempted abduction of Stalin's daughter in New York fails.
June	The Israeli air force secretly disables the Egyptian air force, then devastates bases in Jordan, Syria, and Iraq, and within six days quadruples the land under Israel's control in the Six-Day War.
December	John A. Walker, Jr., of the U.S. Navy, sells his first set of documents to the Soviet embassy, celebrates Christmas happily, and begins a long, profitable career spying for the KGB.

1968

January	When passing through the East Berlin checkpoint, Geoffrey Prime offers his services to the U.S.S.R.
	Fidel Castro rebels against the Kremlin as 35 pro-Moscow Cubans are sentenced to prison for publishing anti-Castro propaganda.
February	Douglas Britten, an RAF technician, is photographed by MI5 delivering a message to the Soviet consulate in London.
March	A letter forged by the KGB, an "active measure," appears to be from the U.S. Office of Naval Research and reveals the existence of American bacteriological war weapons in Thailand and Vietnam.
April	The first indications appear in *Life* that the KGB mole, later to be called MARTEL, had penetrated France's intelligence agency. At that time the late President John Kennedy had warned Charles de Gaulle of a KGB mole—Operation SAPPHIRE—in the French secret services.
	Reinhard Gehlen is invested with the Grand Cross of the Federal Republic of Germany's Order of Merit with star and sash, and says not a word at the ceremony.
May	The "Prague Spring," a liberalization of government policy in Czecholslovakia, is clearly evident.
July	The KGB fabricates evidence of Western plots in Czechoslovakia with inflammatory posters in Prague calling for the overthrow of communism and withdrawal from the Warsaw Pact; the KGB plants and "discovers" arms caches to by used by the West to overthrow the Czechoslovakian government.
August	Fidel Castro's rebelliousness toward the Kremlin ceases, and he accuses U.S. spies of working with Czechoslovakian leaders, calling them Fascists and reactionaries; later, he endorses the Soviet invasion of Czechoslovakia.
	Alexander Dubcek is replaced as First Secretary of the Czech Communist Party, and the "Prague Spring" is over.
September	The British leave Aden; after a week on the throne, Iman Ahmad is assassinated; and the Marxist People's Democratic Republic of (South) Yemen (PDRY) is established. The KGB monitors the PDRY for internal political intrigues.
September	Kim Philby's stylish and provocative memoirs, *My Silent War,* are published.
	The World Peace Council, a Soviet front organization, moves its headquarters to Helsinki.
October	Hermann Lüdke of the FRG, head of NATO logistics, commits suicide after the discovery that he had photographed secret NATO documents. Horst

Wendland, deputy chief of the BND and StB agent, also commits suicide. In the next two weeks other Bonn civil servants also commit suicide.

November Douglas Britten, RAF technician, is jailed for 21 years, having been a spy for the Soviets for six years.

1969

March Yasser Arafat becomes head of the Palestine Liberation Organization, making Fatah, the military resistance movement, the dominant organ of the Palestinian government.

April Yuri Nosenko is cleared by the United States of being a Soviet agent, and begins to receive a salary and other benefits.

July Joseph Frolik defects to Washington.

September Muammar Gaddafi leads a military coup in Libya; the KGB considers him mentally unstable.

October A KGB journalist hints that the Soviet Union may consider a pre-emptive nuclear strike against China. The rumor is spread by the KGB around the world as an "active measure" to raise anxiety in China.

November Günter Guillaume, a Soviet agent, becomes a trusted secretary and confidant to Willy Brandt, Chancellor of West Germany.

1970

During this year China launches its own satellite.

The DGI is purged of anti-Soviet elements, and KGB advisers are placed beside the office of the head of the DGI; DGI membership at Cuba's embassy in London is expanded; in Chile, Savador Allende Gossens approves of Cuba's DGI using Chile as a base for training members of Latin American revolutionary movements.

Günter Guillaume, personal aide to Willy Brandt, keeps Markus Wolf informed on Bonn's policies toward East Germany and secrets of the BfV and NATO.

Irene Schultz, a "secretary spy" in the Science Ministry of the West German government, is convicted of working for HVA.

Between 1970 and 1975 the KGB doubles its staff in diplomatic offices in the United States and at the United Nations, while in the U.K. it is forced to cut back its staff.

May Will Owen is tried for espionage in Great Britain, and to his surprise is acquitted because information against him is found to be hearsay.

1971

January British police search Nicholas Praeger's house and find espionage equipment.

February Oleg Lyalin, a KGB saboteur, is blackmailed by MI5 into being an agent in place.

March After Movimiento de Acción Revolucionario members, revolutionary terrorists in Mexico, are arrested, Oleg Nechiporenko, a KGB agent, is ordered to leave Mexico with other Russian diplomats.

June Nicholas Praeger, a Czechoslovakian spy, is tried and found guilty of espionage, and sentenced to 12 years in jail.

The "Pentagon Papers" become public.

August A Treaty of Peace, Friendship and Cooperation is signed secretly by the Soviet Union and India; both countries demand that the United States withdraw from Vietnam. The KGB residency in New Delhi is upgraded, and its number of operations grows.

September   Nikita Khrushchev dies in obscurity, a mere pensioner.
              Oleg Lyalin defects from the London Soviet residency. Consequently, 105
                 Russian diplomats are expelled from Britain or prevented from reentering
                 the country for matters relating to espionage (Operation FOOT). Moscow
                 Center's long and effective influence in Great Britain ceases.
October   Gordon Lonsdale (Konon Molody) dies, aged 48, a KGB hero.
November   To the chagrin of the United States, Nationalist China is replaced on the UN
                 Security Council by Communist China.

1972

January   Early in 1972, Oleg Kalugin takes on the alcoholic Kim Philby as a consult-
                 ant, and he lectures for about eight months to young students at the KGB
                 Higher School.
February   President Richard Nixon visits China for 10 days and helps restore U.S. rela-
                 tions with Communist China.
May   President Richard Nixon makes the first official visit to the U.S.S.R. by a U.S.
                 president, and during the next two years more Soviet–U.S. treaties—includ-
                 ing ICBM and SALT I—are signed than in the period since 1933, when
                 diplomatic relations were established.
June   Strategic Arms Limitations Treaty I limits antiballistic missile systems in the
                 U.S.–Soviet arms race.
July   Jim Bennett is forced to resign from the Canadian secret services, suspected
                 falsely by James Angleton for some time of being a Soviet agent.
              About this time David Bingham is sentenced to 21 years for espionage in Great
                 Britain.
September   In the United States, John C. Masterman publishes *The Double-cross System
                 in the War of 1939 to 1945*.
              At the Olympic Games in Munich, Israeli athletes are assassinated by Black
                 September Arab guerrillas who demand the release of 200 Palestinians in
                 Israeli jails.
November   About November the DIE (Rumanian Intelligence Service) begins to supply
                 the PLO with weapons, false passports, and surveillance equipment.

1973

During this year, Gerda Schröder, a West German embassy secretary, is caught and convicted
of being an HVA spy.

February   Richard Helms, CIA head, is fired by President Richard Nixon and made the
                 U.S. ambassador in Tehran, Iran.
May   Günter Guillaume is suspected of espionage for Markus Wolf and put under
                 surveillance.
July   In Lillehammer, Norway, a Mossad hit squad assassinates the wrong man in
                 their attempt to kill a Black September terrorist leader.
September   Salvador Allende Gossens dies while being pursued by General Augusto
                 Pinochet's forces. For three years previously the Chilean economy had been
                 undermined by the CIA in accordance with White House policy.
October   Probably about September the Soviets cease shipping arms to the People's
                 Republic of China (PRC); the GRU notes that Soviet military equipment
                 already in China is being painted over to indicate that it came from North
                 Korea.

1974

During this year arms deals begin between Libya and the U.S.S.R.

April   Günther Guillaume and his wife are found to have been spying for the for-
             eign intelligence service of the German Democratic Republic. Willy Brandt
             resigns early in May.

June   After Arafat's visit to Moscow, the KGB begins training guerrilla fighters for
             the PLO at Balashika training school in Moscow. The Soviets agree to open
             a PLO office in Moscow.

August   President Richard M. Nixon resigns, and the KGB sees it as a great success
             for the enemies of détente, of the Zionists, and of the U.S. military–
             industrial complex.

December   Operations ARTICHOKE and CHAOS and the CIA "family jewels" become
             public in the United States through the efforts of Seymour Hersh, a promi-
             nent journalist with the *New York Times*. It appears that the CIA may have
             violated its charter and committed inappropriate, and possibly illegal, acts.
             About this time Oleg Gordievsky begins full-time work for the SIS, and the
             forced retirement of James J. Angleton becomes known.

1975

During this year the Rockefeller Commission and the Church Committee investigate allegations that the CIA has undertaken illegal activities.

January   In Great Britain, Philip Agee publishes his book *Inside the Company: CIA
             Diary*, and makes public the names of approximately 250 CIA operatives.

March   Frank Favaro is recruited into the ASIS to help resolve the conflict between
             the Indonesian government and the East Timor rebels.

April   Andrew Daulton Lee, a U.S. drug dealer, supplies the KGB in Mexico with
             technical data from Christopher Boyce concerning U.S. satellite systems.
             Without resistance the North Vietnamese enter Saigon, and the war in Vietnam
             ends.

August   The civil war in East Timor involves ASIS.
             Following the Helsinki Final Act, the "Helsinki Watch Groups" established
             in the U.S.S.R. to monitor human rights abuse are gradually closed down.

September   ASIS fires Frank Favaro.
             China establishes an embassy in the European Community.

October   Frank Favaro's ASIS files are leaked, the Favaro Affair emerges in the Austra-
             lian press, and the ASIS head is fired.
             The CIA puts into play Operation SILICON VALLEY against Amos Dawe.

November   Accused of being a double agent for both the Indonesians and the Australians,
             Frank Favaro leaves East Timor.

December   Ilich Ramírez, son of a Venezuelan millionaire and known as Carlos the Jackal,
             working for the PLO and Muammar Gaddafi, leads Palestinian and Ger-
             man terrorists in a kidnapping of OPEC oil ministers in Vienna. Carlos was
             trained in terrorist skills in Soviet and Cuban camps.
             Richard Welch is murdered in Greece, while on CIA duty, the thirty-second
             CIA officer to die this way.

1976

Peter Wright retires from MI5 on what he claims is a meager pension.

March   Christopher Boyce and Andrew Daulton Lee begin to sell secrets to the Soviets.
             Anwar Sadat, President of Egypt, denounces the Soviet–Egyptian friendship treaty.

May   Philip Agee informs the KGB that a "walk-in" recruited in June 1968 was a CIA "dangle."

June   The PLO hijacks an aircraft and lands it at Entebbe, Uganda.

July   In response to the Tindemans Report on the European Community (EU), the Soviets seek intelligence on the European Community's politicians, declaring them to be part of an anti-Soviet conspiracy, especially since China has established an embassy in the EU.

William Bell begins to sell classified information to the Soviets so as to cover his personal expenses.

November   After Syria invades Lebanon, the KGB fears that because the U.S.S.R. armed Syria, its agents' lives may be in jeopardy from PLO terrorists, and orders the agents to take special precautions. Quickly a PLO office is opened in Moscow to assuage PLO anger, and the KGB distances itself from Syria.

Moscow Center fears that Egypt's President, Anwar Sadat, will turn away from the Soviets and take support from the West.

1977

January   Christopher Boyce and Andrew Daulton Lee are caught.

Galtung Haavik is caught after 27 years of spying on Norway for Russia; she dies six months before her trial.

After the Haavik case Norway expels six Soviet intelligence officers, tit-for-tat, the Soviets expel three Norwegians.

May   In the spring, Goronwy Rees tells Andrew Boyle that Anthony Blunt was the "fourth man" in the Cambridge spy ring. In 1979 Boyle publishes his *The Climate of Treason*, which cites this information.

June   The PLO hijacks an aircraft at Mogadishu, Somalia.

July   Andrew Daulton Lee, a drug dealer and spy, is imprisoned for life.

Soviet agents in Moscow detect Martha Peterson, a CIA agent.

August   John A. Walker, Jr., meets his KGB controller in Casablanca for the first time since February 1968.

October   Admiral Stansfield Turner, President Carter's appointment to head the CIA, conducts the "Halloween Massacre" by eliminating 820 positions in the CIA's Clandestine Services.

December   The KGB celebrates its sixtieth anniversary with a monument to the "unknown intelligence officer."

1978

February   William Kampiles, a former CIA employee, walks into the Soviet residency in Greece and gives the KGB a manual on U.S. satellites.

April   A Communist coup in Afghanistan overthrows the republican regime, and the KGB supports Babrak Karmal, a KGB agent; however, his opponent, Noor Mohammed Taraki, wins the struggle for power.

An undersecretary to the United Nations, a Soviet agent named Arkadi N. Shevchenko, defects to the West.

June   U.S. officials announce they have again found KGB bugging devices in the U.S. embassy in Moscow.

September   Georgi Markov, a Bulgarian dissident, is murdered in London with a poisoned umbrella tip.

November   William Kampiles is caught.

1979

During this year a secret Libyan–Soviet agreement is signed on matters of intelligence and security. Libyan agents are trained by the KGB; the KGB receives intelligence on U.S. activities in the eastern Mediterranean. The KGB begins publishing error-filled pamphlets and falsehoods to undermine the election of Margaret Thatcher as Great Britain's Prime Minister. Robert Hanssen, an FBI agent, begins to spy for the Soviets.

April	Saddam Hussein begins murdering Iraqi Communists, and the KGB reactivates its former Iraqi agents and begins to collect SIGINT intelligence from Syria.
August	In Afghanistan, Taraki is murdered by Hafizullah Amin. The KGB plans to poison Amin to ensure anti-Soviet Islamic republicans do not overthrow the Communist regime.
October	Stanislav Levchenko defects to the West in Tokyo.
November	The U.S. government bans arms sales to Iran.
	Anthony Blunt is exposed formally as a Soviet agent, the "fourth man" among the Magnificent Five, and stripped of his knighthood.
December	KGB troops invade Afghanistan, murder Hafizullah Amin—and accidentally kill their own leader and a dozen other KGB troops. Babrak Karmal announces he rules Afghanistan, and that Amin was a bloodthirsty U.S. imperialist and a CIA agent. A nine-year guerrilla war begins.

1980

Secrecy surrounding VENONA is being gradually lifted.

January	A KGB general predicts the Afghanistan conflict will be "Russia's Vietnam." The KGB installs a tough new head of Afghanistan's secret services, and Afghans are brutalized and murdered under interrogation.
	Ronald W. Pelton, code-named MR. LONG, walks in to offer his services to the Soviet embassy.
April	Operation EAGLE CLAW, involving America's Delta Force, fails to rescue 52 diplomatic hostages held by Iranians in the U.S. embassy in Tehran.
September	Saddam Hussein invades Iran with secret backing from the U.S.S.R.
	Lech Walesa establishes Solidarity, a trade union independent of government control, in Poland on September 22.

1981

January	Hostages taken at the U.S. embassy in Iran are released, and the United States lifts some trade restrictions on Iran except for arms deals.
	William Casey is appointed head of the CIA.
February	The KGB chooses Wojciech Jaruzelski to effect a coup in Poland and overthrow the Solidarity movement.
March	British Prime Minister Margaret Thatcher announces that from two investigations into the work and the duties of the late Sir Roger Hollis, head of MI5 from 1956 to 1965, there was no conclusive proof of Sir Roger's innocence, and no evidence was found that incriminated him.
May	At a secret KGB conference in Moscow, Leonid Brezhnev states that the new President of the United States is preparing for a nuclear war. Yuri Andropov announces that to prepare for this war, the KGB and the GRU will work together on Operation RYAN to collect information on the expected plans for a U.S. nuclear missile attack. The operation continues until 1984.
June	Meat price rises in Poland spark a wave of industrial strikes that in time coalesce in the Solidarity movement among unions.

The United States Intelligence Committee's proposed "Anti-Agee Bill" becomes law.

William Bell is caught and sentenced to eight years jail for selling classified information to the Soviets.

July   Oleg Gordievsky escapes to the West and reveals that Leo Long was codenamed ELLI.

Urho Kaleva Kekkonen steps down as Finland's President due to ill health.

October   Jaruzelski becomes First Secretary of the Communist Party of Poland and plans a military coup.

Anwar Sadat is assassinated by Muslim extremists, and Moscow Center applauds; he had long been a target of KGB "active measures": he was touted by the KGB as a former Nazi, suffering from mental illness, dominated by his spouse, using a bodyguard from the CIA, and being a CIA agent, with a CIA villa waiting for him, should he live to retirement.

November   Arne H. Peterson, a Danish KGB agent of influence, is arrested and charged with collaborating with the KGB in publication of false information aimed to undermine Margaret Thatcher's leadership in Britain. Peterson is later released. British Prime Minister Thatcher names Leo Long as a Soviet spy, but he is not charged.

Operation RYAN continues as the KGB collects information on a presumed plan by the United States to use nuclear weapons to attack Russia.

December   In Poland the military takes control and appears to vanquish Solidarity.

1982

For some years, assistance in support of the Sandinistas' Nicaraguan Army by the Soviets and Cuba has gradually increased, and now agreements are made about the Soviet SIGINT bases, as well as plans for training of state security officers in Nicaragua.

February   Fear of a U.S. nuclear strike drives more feverish work on Operation RYAN, and KGB efforts in NATO countries expand to unrealistic extents.

April   Argentina invades the Falkland Islands, and the KGB resident in London reports that the ensuing brief conflict was a British colonial war aimed to shore up Prime Minister Margaret Thatcher's declining popularity, and to test new military equipment for NATO.

Dieter Gerhardt is observed in Gibralter by MI5, and later suspected of providing Soviets with information on antiaircraft missiles used against the British in the Falklands War in April or May.

June   On the basis of information from Anatoli Golitsyn and others, Hugh Hambleton is arrested, tried under the Official Secrets Act, and jailed for 10 years.

Oleg Gordievsky, a Russian spy for the SIS, arrives in London to find alarmism among KGB agents in their collection of information for Operation RYAN.

The KGB in London is used to provide funds secretly for the African National Congress and the South African Communist Party until January 1983.

July   David Bingham is released on parole after having been sentenced to 21 years in prison for espionage.

September With a forged letter that appears in London's *New Statesman,* the KGB uses Operation GOLF in Washington as an "active measure" to discredit the U.S. ambassador to the United Nations.

October   Vladimir Kuzichkin defects to the West and brings details of the Soviets' role in espionage and sabotage in Iran.

November   Leonid Brezhnev dies, and Yuri Andropov is the new Russian leader.
              Geoffrey Prime is found guilty of espionage and child molestation, and sen-
              tenced to 35 years in prison.

1983

During this year the KGB finds Yasser Arafat untrustworthy; despite Russia's continued support for him, the KGB anticipates a Marxist uprising inside the PLO may replace Arafat's leadership.

February   The KGB plans "active measures" worldwide to discredit Ronald Reagan in
              his run for reelection as President in November 1984.
March   Ronald Reagan denounces the U.S.S.R. as an "evil empire," and calls for a
              space-age shield to intercept missiles and replace the deterrent of instant
              retaliation. Named the Strategic Defence Initiative, it is immediately dubbed
              the "Star Wars" policy. Reagan's "Star Wars" speech indicates to the KGB
              that he believes the United States could enter a nuclear war and win.
April   ASIO informs the Australian government that the relationship between Valeri
              Ivanov, of the Soviet embassy in Canberra, and David Combe, a political
              lobbyist, poses a threat to Australia's national security. Ivanov is expelled,
              and Combe is not permitted to lobby cabinet members.
              The "Hitler Diaries" are authenticated by the noted historian Hugh Trevor-
              Roper, and will be published by Rupert Murdoch's London *Times.*
              Michael Bettaney is the first MI5 agent in many years to offer his services to
              the London KGB.
May   Edward Lee Howard is forced to leave his employment with the CIA after
              failing a polygraph test. He had been fully trained as a CIA agent to work
              under diplomatic cover in the U.S. embassy in Moscow.
              The "Hitler Diaries" are found to be a fake. The hoax embarrasses Trevor-
              Roper.
June   In June and July, Michael Bettaney gives more secrets to the KGB in Lon-
              don.
              Margaret Thatcher wins in a landslide; during her campaign the KGB residency
              and the GRU take no action on Moscow's plans to use Labour Party mem-
              bers to discredit her.
August   Edward Lee Howard, former CIA officer, contacts the KGB in Vienna.
              Instructions from Moscow to Russia's London residency on Operation RYAN
              become more urgent and frequent.
September   The KAL 007 tragedy kills 239 airline passengers due to an error by a So-
              viet fighter pilot. To cover the error, Moscow issues false allegations and
              information about the United States., South Korea, and Japan. KGB of-
              ficers are much amused by the nonsense in the cover stories. Also, the
              United States declares KAL 007 was shot down deliberately and in cold
              blood by a Soviet pilot, and that it illustrates the Soviets use only vio-
              lence and lies in their policy making.
              Operation RYAN is given even higher priority by the KGB.
              In England, Michael Bettaney is arrested for espionage and given a 23-year
              prison sentence in April 1984.
October   A CIA agent inside the Polish security services, the SB, establishes the iden-
              tity of the American spy James Harper, and he is arrested for espionage for
              the KGB and Poland since June 1980.

Dieter Gerhardt confesses and is found guilty of treason; he is jailed rather than being executed, as is usually the case in South Africa.

French and American soldiers are killed in terrorist attacks in Lebanon.

Lech Walesa is awarded the Nobel Peace Prize, but the KGB regards him as part of a Western–Jewish plot to destabilize Europe.

The United States declares that it will not invade Grenada, but does so the next day, and overthrows the Marxist–Leninist ruler, Maurice Bishop. The KGB concludes the United States will probably soon invade Nicaragua also, and destroy the Sandinista government.

November   The KGB is certain that Operation ABLE ARCHER 83 will trigger a nuclear attack on Russia within 10 days. Inside the KGB, anxiety over Operation RYAN peaks.

Over 240 U.S. Marines die in a Beirut bombing.

Cruise and Pershing II missiles begin to reach West Germany.

OPERATION ABLE ARCHER 83 is completed successfully, without realizing the KGB fears of a real nuclear attack on Russia.

Harold Holt, the Australian Prime Minister who disappeared into the sea in 1967, is identified in a biography as a spy for China; the book is immediately dismissed as a bizarre hoax, and the charge is never investigated.

The Sheridan raid, an ASIS fiasco, embarrasses the Australian government as it attempts to deny involvement in a failed training operation.

December   The French and U.S. embassies in Kuwait are bombed by al-Dawa (The Call) as part of a holy war.

1984

Despite Soviet journalists and diplomats declaring the Soviet influence in the Middle East is declining, the KGB maintains activities in Syria, Iraq, Libya, and South Yemen.

In the United States and Europe the KGB arranges with the South African government to regulate the price of gold, diamonds, and precious metals.

January   The KGB still fears the United States will launch a nuclear attack on Russia, and maintains Operation RYAN is still vital to Soviet interests.

The FCD of the KGB reaffirms its policy to frustrate U.S. intentions to dominate the world.

Arne Treholt, a member of the Norwegian UN mission, is arrested at Oslo airport with a briefcase of Foreign Ministry documents for his Soviet contact. He is sentenced to 25 years in jail in 1985.

February   Yuri Andropov dies, and Margaret Thatcher and Vice President George H. W. Bush attend the funeral.

March   The KGB still fears a U.S. nuclear attack on Russia.

April   Muammar Gaddafi is alleged to have called for violence against anti-Gaddafi demonstrators in London that led to the killing of a London policewoman. In its attempt to get control of other terrorist activities in Britain, the police allegedly blame MI5 for the woman's death because it did not pass on evidence it had at the time of Gaddafi's instructions. The Soviets turn against Gaddafi after the murder of the policewoman.

Michael Bettany is jailed for 23 years.

President Ronald Reagan signs National Security Decision Directive 138 to coordinate counterterrorist agencies in the United States.

The Soviet embassy calls a press conference in Bangkok to state that a counselor at the Australian embassy has, in league with the CIA, offered Alexandre Kilim, a Soviet official, money and sanctuary in Australia or the

<table>
<tr><td>May</td><td>United States if he provides ASIS with secret Russian documents. The public statement embarrasses both the Australian government and ASIS because it breaks the Australian government's diplomatic policy.</td></tr>
</table>

May	Arkady Guk, the KGB resident to whom Michael Bettaney had sent a letter in April 1983, is declared *persona non grata* and expelled; tit–for-tat, the security officer at the British embassy in Moscow is expelled.
	Jonathan Jay Pollard shows he is eager to spy for the Israelis, beginning in the summer.
	The Soviets elevate the European Community, NATO, and China to a threat level commensurate with that of its "Main Adversary," the United States.
June	Operation RYAN is still vital to Soviet interests.
August	The head of the First Chief Directorate, KGB, Vladimir Kryuchkov, suspects that unexplained explosions during August and September in Bulgaria are sophisticated Western secret service attempts to destabilize the Soviet bloc. The Soviets begin to fear the spread of international terrorism.
October	Mikhail Gorbachev appears to want negotiations with the West.
November	In the United States, Richard Miller is tried for espionage, but a mistrial is declared. In 1985 he is tried again, found guilty, and sentenced to two life terms, plus 50 years, and heavily fined.
December	After extensive briefing by Oleg Gordievsky, a double agent for the SIS inside the KGB, Mikhail Gorbachev visits successfully with Prime Minister Thatcher in London; the KGB's Operation RYAN no longer exists, and the KGB backs Gorbachev.
	The KGB has ordered "active measures" to discredit Pope John Paul II, an alleged "reactionary," during 1985.
	The KGB is delighted that New Zealand's Prime Minister will not allow U.S. nuclear-armed or -powered ships into New Zealand's waters.

1985

A number of high-profile spy cases become public, ensuring that 1985 will become known as the "Year of the Spy."

Following an inquiry into the management practices of MI5 by the Security Commission, a Foreign Office official, not a career member of the secret services, is made head of MI5.

January	Mossad's Operation MOSES ends.
March	Konstantin Chernenko, 73, dies; Mikhail Gorbachev becomes General Secretary of the Communist Party and Russia's new leader. Gorbachev begins an economic and political program of perestroika, aimed at restructuring the Soviet Union.
	In London *The Observer* prints the news that Peter Wright, a former MI5 employee, is about to publish his memoirs on his career in the British secret services.
April	Soviet fears are that "Star Wars" will affect the Soviet satellite communications; that the decline of the Soviet economy is becoming known to the CIA; and that the United States is using grain exports to the U.S.S.R. to infect (poison) Russians.
	In Washington, Aldrich Ames, a CIA officer, offers to spy for the Soviets. Among others, General Dimitri Polyakov, a Russian double agent for the CIA, is betrayed by Ames, who is not caught until early 1994.
	Barbara Walker, who by now has informed the FBI about her husband's, John Walker, espionage, works with the FBI to catch him.
	Egypt's Revolution assassinates Albert Atrakchi, who is allegedly a spy for Israel in Egypt.

May	The KGB orchestrates heckling, as an "active measure," at President Reagan's address to the European Parliament.
	Muammar Gaddafi announces his Mutararabbisoun (Always Ready) terrorist forces are prepared to assassinate anyone, anywhere.
	Sergei Bokhan, 49, deputy director of the GRU in Athens, defects to the West. His family is apparently returned to Moscow.
	John A. Walker, Jr., is arrested, and his family of spies is broken up.
June	The Israelis agree to free Shiites in return for for the release of hostages on a TWA flight with 135 U.S. citizens aboard, heading for Rome.
July	Greenpeace's *Rainbow Warrior* is sunk in the harbor of Auckland, New Zealand, and a photographer is dead. France denies any involvement, but recants later.
	Oleg Gordievsky, a double agent for the SIS, escapes from Russia to Britain.
August	Hans Tiedge, a senior West German counterintelligence officer, defects.
	Vitaly Yurchenko indicates he wants to defect to the West.
September	Edward Lee Howard, a disgraced CIA officer, escapes to Europe, and in June 1986 appears in Moscow.
	The Islamic Jihad takes a doctor and three Russian diplomats—one is a KGB officer, Arkadi Katkov—hostage and threaten their execution.
	Oleg Gordievsky's request for political asylum is announced in London and Washington.
	The United Kingdom expels 31 Soviet intelligence officers; in a tit-for-tat reaction, Russia expels 31 British embassy personnel.
October	Arkadi Katkov, a KGB officer, is found dead in Beirut.
	In the Russian *Literaturnaya Gazeta* a false report is published as a KGB "active measure"; it states that the AIDS virus had been developed at the U.S. Army's Fort Detrick, Maryland, from two naturally occurring viruses and then spread throughout the Third World.
	William Buckley's execution is announced.
	The *New York Times* announces that Edward Lee Howard has been identified by Vitaly Yurchenko, a Soviet defector.
November	Ronald Reagan and Mikhail Gorbachev meet in a summit conference.
	Vitaly Yurchenko redefects to Moscow after informing on Edward Lee Howard; Ronald W. Pelton, Leslie Bennett, Igor Orlov, Larry Wu-tai Chin, and Jonathan Jay Pollard are arrested.

1986

February	Larry Wu-tai Chin is found guilty of espionage, and commits suicide.
March	The U.S. State Department announces a reduction in the size of the Soviet delegation to the United Nations from 275 to 170 over two years, alleging some Soviet personnel are engaged in espionage.
April	Oleg Kalugin begins his a strong criticism of the KGB and the Communist Party; within a year, he is removed from the Leningrad KGB.
May	Nicholas Daniloff is arrested by the KGB in Moscow and charged with espionage.
June	Hugh Hambleton is put into a Canadian jail, and in March 1989 is released under supervision.
July	French secret agents involved in the *Rainbow Warrior* affair—the sinking of the Greenpeace vessel of that name—are caught, and jailed in New Zealand for 10 years.
August	Edward Lee Howard, the first CIA defector, is granted political asylum in the U.S.S.R.

September   Mordecai Vanunu is caught in a honeytrap by Mossad.

The KGB, which arrested Nicholas Daniloff for espionage, claims the CIA chief of station in Moscow had given Daniloff his instructions—but at the time that CIA head had been recalled!

In his address to the United Nations, President Reagan criticizes the Soviets for arresting Nicholas Daniloff, and accuses them of having members of their UN staff engage in espionage. Fifty-five Soviet diplomats— intelligence officers—are expelled from the United States; Nicholas Daniloff is released; and this ends the crisis and opens the way for the summit conference between Reagan and Gorbachev.

Edward Lee Howard appears on Soviet television.

October   Great Britain's *Sunday Express* reports on the United States secretly spreading AIDS, and over the next six months the report is widely published in the Third World.

Mikhail Gorbachev and Ronald Reagan meet at Reykjavik, Iceland, and "Star Wars" is their main point of difference.

The Boland Cutoff or Boland Amendment, signed into law by President Ronald Reagan as part of Public Law 98-473, prohibits the obligation or expenditure of appropriated funds in support of military or paramilitary operations in Nicaragua.

November   John A. Walker, Jr., is sentenced to life in prison for espionage.

December   Sergeant Clayton J. Lonetree approaches a CIA officer at the U.S. embassy's Christmas party in Vienna to confess to espionage resulting from a honeytrap operation.

1987

During the year, among the KGB's "active measures" is a forged letter by William Casey on CIA plans to destabilize the Prime Minister of India. The U.S. House of Representatives investigates the case of Edward Lee Howard.

March   The British government fails in its attempt to get a permanent injunction to prevent the publishing of Peter Wright's *Spycatcher*.

May   William Casey dies.

June   Jonathan Jay Pollard is sentenced to 27 years in prison for passing classified information to the Israelis.

July   An FBI agent, Earl Pitts, writes to an officer in the Soviet mission at the United Nations and asks to see a KGB officer. He becomes a Soviet spy from 1988 to 1996.

Admiral John Poindexter tells the U.S. Congress it was he who had authorized the diversion of money made from the arms sale to Iran to the Nicaraguan Contras.

August   Marine Sergeant Clayton J. Lonetree is demoted, fined, dishonorably discharged, and sentenced to 30 years in prison.

Moscow disowns the story that the United States developed AIDS and spread it around the Third World.

September   The British government decides to take its attempt to prevent *Spycatcher*'s publication to the Australian High Court. The book is available in Canada and the United States.

December   On his first visit to Washington to sign a treaty on the reduction of nuclear arsenals, Mikhail Gorbachev takes with him, for the first time ever, the head of the First Chief Directorate (Foreign Intelligence) of the KGB.

Using trade embargoes, a UN arbitrator, and a broken commitment to New Zealand, France gets its *Rainbow Warrior* agents released from custody and back to France.

1988

During the year, among the KGB "active measures" is a forged letter from President Ronald Reagan instructing the NSA to destabilize Panama.

May   Kim Philby dies; he was known to the KGB merely as AGENT TOM.

June   A false report, a KGB "active measure," states that body parts of butchered Latin American children are being used in the United States in organ transplant operations, and is known as "baby parts trafficking."

The High Court in Australia dismisses the British government's case against the publication of *Spycatcher,* on the grounds that it is attempting to enforce the British penal code in Australia. The British government's spokesman claims falsely that Britain *won* the case since the appeal had been dismissed on a technical point of law.

September   A French Communist member of the European Parliament condemns "baby parts trafficking."

The false story about the United States spreading AIDS ceases to be mentioned in the Soviet media.

October   Vladimir Aleksandrovich Kryuchkov becomes KGB chairman, and is noted for his adaptability, optimism, and awareness of change in the Soviet international image due to reforms in the U.S.S.R.; he calls for more objectivity from the West, and pursues a policy for Russian collaboration with the West against international terrorism.

December   In the Caucasus Mountains, Armenians hijack a transport plane in order to get to Israel; the KGB gives the group leader drugs to calm him, and encourages the flight in the belief that the Israelis can handle the crime peacefully and return the hijackers. This was done.

1989

During the year, for the first time a U.S. ambassador is received in the office of the KGB chief; the World Peace Council, a KGB front organization, loses its credibility when its funding is shown to be largely from the KGB.

February   The Russian army withdraws from Afghanistan, having failed to get control of the first Third World country it occupied. A million Afghans and 13,000 Soviet troops died.

April   In Poland, Solidarity is made legal, and later the Communist-led state is gone.

May   Colonel Oliver North, who had testified that he did not plan the Irangate scheme (the diversion of money made from an arms sale to Iran to the Nicaraguan Contras) but merely followed orders, was found guilty of 3 of the 12 counts with which he was charged.

June   Foreign visitors and journalists in Moscow are told the late Raoul Wallenberg, a Swedish diplomat, was a playboy and womanizer, a collaborator of Lavrenti Beria, and a friend of Adolf Eichmann and Heinrich Himmler in 1944. Reino Gikman, Felix Bloch's contact, disappears.

July   Vladimir Kryuchkov warns the world that nuclear terrorism is imminent. The secret investigation of Felix Bloch is made public on American TV, and the Bloch Affair begins.

October   The KGB Fifth Directorate, which monitors dissidents and intellectuals, is abolished; Vladimir Kryuchkov states the U.S.S.R. has identified over 1,500 terrorists in the last 20 years.

November   The Berlin Wall, potent symbol of the Cold War, is breached as the East German government opens its borders with West Germany.

1990

During the year, one of the KGB's "active measures" is a report stating that the United States has developed an "ethnic weapon," a paramilitary device that kills nonwhites only.

January	A false story about the United States developing and spreading the AIDS virus appears on British and German TV.
February	Oleg Kalugin leaves the KGB. The electoral defeat of the Sandinistas in Nicaragua puts the Soviet SIGINT station in peril.
April	The KGB accepts responsibility for the 1940 massacre of almost 15,000 Polish officers, plus thousands of others, in the Katyn Forest.
May	Boris Yeltsin is elected Chairman of the Russian Supreme Soviet, and in place of the KGB guard, he has his security given over to the Supreme Soviet secretariat.
June	Oleg Kalugin fights the KGB publicly, and becomes a consultant to Vadim Bakatin, former head of the Soviet Interior Ministry, who heads the KGB until December 1991, bringing many reforms.
October	With NATO and Soviet approval, East Germany and West Germany become united after the general collapse of communism in Eastern Europe.

1991

May	With the Cold War over, Oleg Nechiporenko retires from the KGB, and a year later helps the U.S. Senate inquire into Americans who had been prisoners of war, or were missing in action, in Southeast Asia.
December	Mikhail Gorbachev resigns, the Soviet Union collapses, and 74 years of Communist domination in Russia end. President Bill Clinton denies a clemency request from Yitzak Rabin, made in November, to reduce the sentence of Jonathan J. Pollard.

1994

February	Aldrich Ames, a CIA operative who served the KGB, is trapped.

1996

November	Harold Nicholson, one of the last Cold War U.S. spies for Russia, is arrested.

1997

June	Earl Pitts is sentenced to 27 years in prison.
September	Robert Lipka, a former U.S. NSA clerk, pleads guilty to espionage for the Soviets and is sentenced to 18 years in prison.

1999

September	In England, Melita Norwood is publicly acknowledged as a Soviet Cold War spy, and called the "Red Granny."

2000

February	Robert Hanssen, a former FBI agent, is caught after spying for the Soviets for 21 years.

May   The Belgian Parliament opens an investigation into the murder of Patrice
               Lumumba after evidence appears that states Lumumba was assassinated by
               Belgian forces in 1960.

July   George Trofimoff, a Soviet spy in the U.S. Army, is arrested in Tampa, Florida,
               by the FBI, after spying for the Soviets for over 20 years.

2001

July   The fake "Hitler Diaries" appear to have been handled by a STASI agent, and
               may have been part of a clever KGB disinformation program in April 1983.
               After the publication of a biography on himself, David Greenglass admits
               to lying at the Rosenberg trial and to the U.S. Congress in 1953.

2003

April   Katrina Leung is arrested and charged with being a Cold War double agent
               for China for 20 years.

Glossary

Boldfaced names and terms within entries are crossreferences to other Glossary entries.

ABM Treaty (1972). Anti-Ballistic Missile Treaty of 1972 was signed by the United States and the **U.S.S.R.**, and limited both to only 100 ABM launchers within 140 kilometers of an ICBM base.

ABM Treaty (1983). The Anti-Ballistic Missile Treaty of March 1983 appeared to the Soviets to be threatened by President Ronald Reagan's "Star Wars" vision, which was to be realized at the end of the century. In fact, it was 2002 before the vision reappeared with President George W. Bush's Strategic Defense Initiative (**SDI**).

Abortion. Because abortion was illegal in Germany in the 1950s and in Britain until 1967, it was possible to blackmail abortionists and the women who sought their help, and to endanger the welfare of women who sought an abortion at the hands of an unscrupulous abortionist. Blackmail was also used to secure the services of women spies in East Germany.

Abwehr. The German Army intelligence service throughout **World War II**.

Active Measures (*aktivinyye meropriatia*). The name given to the **KGB**'s attempts to change world events by using more or less violet means. The more violent means were "**special actions.**" Nonviolent "active measures" were aimed at discrediting the Soviets' "main adversary," the United States.

AEC. See **Atomic Energy Commission**

Afghan Coup (1979). In December 1979, the Soviets took over Afghanistan in an effort to ensure the Marxist, pro-Soviet People's Democratic Party of Afghanistan was secure under the rule of Babrak Karmal. By initiating the long and bloody Afghan War (1981–1988), the Soviet invasion proved to be a costly failure. About 13,000 Soviet troops and a million Afghans died in the war, and the Islamic mujahideen ruled the country thereafter. Some observers believed that the Afghan War was as disastrous for the Soviets as the **Vietnam War** was for the United States.

Agent. The term has several meanings. A Russian agent or "assistant" was first recruited by way of a **KGB** trap. In the beginning, the individual was often led to believe that the information he or she could make available to a resident (the KGB chief attached to the Soviet embassy in the agent's country) could be safely given and generously paid for. In fact, as soon as such persons were paid, they were trapped into becoming and remaining agents, since the acceptance of money opened them to blackmail should they attempt to stop working for the KGB. Possible recruits were carefully scouted. Potential agents displayed a number of common traits or situations: they were often middle-ranking members of an organization that offered them access to valuable information; they were not interested in promotion; or they were resentful of their failure to be recognized by their organization, because of poor health, excessive drinking, or a perception of incompetence. They might also have a reputation, whether deserved or not, for womanizing; they might be too critical of their government's policies or practices; they usually lacked any loyalty to an employer they perceived as ungrateful. Anyone who, for these or any other reasons, could be tempted to take money for passing information was a potential agent for the **U.S.S.R.**

In Western intelligence organizations, an agent is a person recruited to perform clandestine missions. In the U.S. **Federal Bureau of Investigation** (**FBI**), an agent is an employee of the organization; in the U.K., an agent is not an employee, but a person who has access to whatever the secret services want and who can be induced to provide it. (See **Farm** for the agents in the **CIA**.)

In most intelligence agencies the agents have **code names;** sometimes one agent will have different code names, and these may correspond to stages in their life or activities that are relevant to their character and work. For example, Kim Philby was SÖHNCHEN, STANLEY, SYNOK, and TOM; Victor Perlo was RAIDER; Aleksandr Orlov was SCHWED; and Alger Hiss was ALES.

Agent of Influence. For the **U.S.S.R.**, an **agent** of influence—in Russian, *agent vliyaniya*—was a reliable source in a foreign government, business, media, or academia who did not spy for money. In the West, the term referred to Communist or Marxist sympathizers who assisted the Soviet revolution, and were sometimes called fellow travelers. Many such people would decline to be Communist Party members to protect their careers. Wilfred Burchett and Christopher Hill had the reputation for being such agents. Agent DAN (1960–1985) was a supposed agent of influence serving the Soviets in Britain.

Agent Provocateur. An **agent** who joins an allegedly subversive group, spies on its members, and reports to his handler; the agent provocateur also incites the group members to act and put themselves in hazard, thereby destroying the group's standing and reputation.

ALP. See **Australian Labor Party**

Andropov Institute. A Soviet institute for the training of recruits to espionage. Courses ran for one to three years; students were given a **legend**, or false name and identity, and military rank, but wore civilian clothes. Students were given physical training and taught languages, intelligence operations, current affairs, and military skills and **tradecraft**. Their training was similar to that given **CIA** recruits at the **Farm**.

Andropov, Yuri Vladimorovich (1914–1984). Andropov was leader of the **U.S.S.R.** from 1982 to 1984. As Soviet ambassador to Hungary in 1956, he helped defeat the Hungarian Uprising, and thereafter his career blossomed. He also helped oust **Nikita Khrushchev** in October 1964, and was chairman of the **KGB** from April 1967 until April 1982, when he became general secretary of the Communist Party and Russia's leader. He responded to President **Ronald Reagan's** "Star Wars" (**SDI**) vision with costly support for Soviet military expansion against the West. Andropov died of kidney failure in February 1984.

Apostles. The Apostles was a secret society at Cambridge University, founded as a debating group, the Cambridge Conversazione Society, in 1820. It became known simply as the "Society," and was not especially secret. Its members were a few of the university's intellectual elite. It may have been named the Apostles at a time when there were 12 members, or perhaps because the members tended to be evangelists, and wanted to debate, propagate, and explain the Gospels. Anthony Blunt was elected to membership in May 1928, Julian Bell in November 1928, Guy Burgess in November 1932, Leo Long in May 1937, and Michael Straight in 1936.

Arlington Hall. In January 1942, a leading U.S. lawyer, Alfred McCormack, was made special assistant to the U.S. Secretary of War, and had as one of his tasks to present intelligence to responsible authorities in Washington. In the War Department, he formed the Military Intelligence Service, headed by Colonel Carter W. Clark. Clark extended the Signal Intelligence Service (SIGINT), and in doing so moved it to a secluded and spacious girls' college in Arlington, Virginia. Called Arlington Hall, it was surrounded by an attractive and quiet estate, with wooden and brick buildings, and was much suited to expansion without being noticed. It was here that the VENONA project received close attention and, at first, that all SIGINT operations were concentrated. In Great Britain code-breaking was housed at **Bletchley Park**, in a mansion 60 miles north of London.

Arms Control. The many attempts to reduce, manage, regulate, and otherwise defuse the arms race, especially in regard to nuclear weapons. During the **Cold War** the United Nations established a disarmament commission (1952) to help establish the Non-Proliferation Treaty (1968). The **U.S.S.R.,** the United States, and the U.K. negotiated a Nuclear Test-Ban Treaty (1963); direct talks between the U.S.S.R. and the United States produced the Strategic Arms Limitations Talks, or SALT (1969–1972); Mutual Balanced Force Reduction (MBFR) talks began in 1973 between **NATO** and **Warsaw Pact** countries; in 1982 the START (Strategic Arms Reduction Talks) began; in 1987 the superpowers—the United States and the U.S.S.R.—met, seeking to eliminate intermediate-range nuclear forces (INF). In 1990 treaties were signed on the reduction of chemical weaponry.

Arms Race. A competition, between the Western allies (the United States being the most powerful) and their opponents in the **Cold War** (the **U.S.S.R.** and her Communist satellites and allies), to achieve the advantage in armaments, so that the more powerful of the two would probably win World War III, should it ever take place.

ASIO (Australian Security Intelligence Organization). After its creation in 1948–1949, ASIO was established in March 1949 under Sir Charles Spry (1950–1970), and concerned itself with intelligence gathering and security inside Australia. Its head is responsible to the attorney general of Australia.

ASIS (Australian Secret Intelligence Service). Established in 1952, ASIS is modeled on **MI6**, the British Secret Intelligence Service (**SIS**). ASIS works outside Australia and is concerned with clandestine collection of information on the capabilities and intentions of foreign countries. Its staffing and functions are secret. It is part of the Department of Foreign Affairs and Trade. Today ASIS is assumed by intelligence experts to have a staff of 200; 72 are in the field at 18 Australian diplomatic missions. In each mission one ASIS member is declared to be such, and that official works with his counterpart in the host intelligence agency to exchange information as an overt spy; the others are not declared, and work secretly to find information, as does a conventional spy. In Bangkok (Thailand), Jakarta (Indonesia), and Tokyo (Japan), there are probably more than two ASIS officers. During the 1960s in ASIS, attention was given to Communist and military groups in Indonesia; today attention focuses on the politics of Indonesia and other Asian nations, terrorism, and weapons of mass destruction. ASIS became known publicly in the 1970s, and was acknowledged to exist in 1977. Recently ASIS was stripped of its paramilitary clandestine operations; they are now the tasks of the Australian army's special forces and counterterrorism units. ASIS's most recent success was the discovery of covert operations relating to the use of weapons of mass destruction by a rogue state. (For more information, see Hamish McDonald, "Puppet-Master Now Pulling the Strings at ASIS," *The Age* [Melbourne], February 15, 2003, p. 15.)

Atom Bomb. The first atom bomb was detonated near **Los Alamos** in the desert of New Mexico, July 15, 1945. Two atom bombs were then dropped by American planes on Japan early in August, bringing **World War II** to an end. The first Russian atom bomb was detonated in late August 1949. In September 1949, U.S. President **Harry S. Truman** announced the West had discovered the Russians had the atom bomb, and declared that it was now necessary to have a truly effective, enforceable international control of atomic energy. He was persuaded by **Edward Teller** (1908–2003) that a **hydrogen bomb** would be the best deterrent against the Soviets. In 1952 Great Britain detonated her first atom bomb, off the coast of West Australia at the Monte Bello Islands.

Atom Spies/Nuclear Spies. Among the major American and British scientists who were believed to have been persuaded by a network of Russian **illegals** to share atomic secrets with the Russians were Julius Robert Oppenheimer (1904–1963), Enrico Fermi (1901–1954), Leo Szilard (1898–1964), Bruno Pontecorvo (1913–1993), Alan Nunn May (1911–1985), and Emil Julius Klaus Fuchs (1911–1988).

Atomic Energy Commission (AEC). The U.S. Atomic Energy Commission was established by the McMahon Act in 1946, which forbade the transmission of any U.S. information on atomic energy to a foreign power. This bill ended the agreement in 1944 between Franklin D. Roosevelt (1882–1945) and Winston Churchill (1874–1965) to cooperate in the development of atomic energy for military and civil purposes. The act promoted some rivalry between the United States and the U.K. in the development of larger nuclear bombs and weapons.

Attlee, Clement Richard (1883–1967). The U.K. Labour politician, tough and shrewd as an administrator, who joined the coalition government of Winston Churchill (1874–1965) as Lord Privy Seal (1940–1942) and Deputy Prime Minister (1942–1945), and was elected Prime Minister in July 1945. During the **Cold War** he supported U.S. President **Harry S. Truman** in most matters, brought Great Britain into NATO, tried to reduce the rivalry between the **U.S.S.R.** and the United States, and sought nuclear cooperation with **Josef Stalin**; these actions caused him to lose much support from Great Britain's military leadership. He held the view that an atomic conflict was unwinnable, yet in January 1947 secretly began the British atomic bomb project. He had Great Britain withdraw from the civil war in Greece, and give up its control of Pakistan and India in August 1947, and kept British forces in the **Korean War** (1950–1953). He opposed America's views on the new Communist government in China, and refused to support a military attack on Iran over its nationalization of its oil industry. At home his government introduced the National Health Act, cut the power of the House of Lords, and nationalized many industries. Percy Sillitoe was an unpopular choice as head of **MI5** instead of his deputy, Guy Liddell; Allan Nunn May and Klaus Fuchs were found to have been prominent **atom bomb** spies during Attlee's tenure; and the career of the **KGB**'s Magnificent Five drew to an end with the defection of Guy Burgess and Donald Maclean in May 1951, shortly after the Rosenbergs were found guilty of spying in the United States. In November 1951 Attlee lost the election to Churchill, and Hugh Gaitskill succeeded Attlee as Britain's Labour Party leader in 1955.

Australian Labor Party (ALP). The Australian political party that tends to represent the interests of nonconservative citizens, and finds strong support among people with a preference for social democracy. During the early years of the **Cold War,** the party was attacked by its critics for harboring among its members supporters of communism. Its major opposition came from the Liberal Party of Australia, whose forerunner was the United Australia Party.

Australian Secret Intelligence Service. See **ASIS**

Australian Security Intelligence Organization. See **ASIO**

Axis. See **World War II**

Balance of Terror. The term "balance of terror" was used to describe the international tension, fear, and threats that arose whenever the **Cold War** appeared to be turning into a traditional war between the superpowers, Russia and the United States. This feeling was evident shortly before the **Korean War** (1950–1953), and especially during the **Cuban missile crisis** (1962) and following the speech made by President **Ronald Reagan** on his Strategic Defense Initiative (**SDI**) or "Star Wars" (1983).

Balkan States. The Balkans, meaning "mountains" in Turkish, are on the peninsula of Southeastern Europe between the Adriatic and Aegean Seas. The nations are Albania, Bosnia-Herzegovina, Bulgaria, Croatia, Greece, Romania, Slovenia, the part of Turkey in Europe, and Yugoslavia. An informal arrangement, the Balkans Percentage Deal, was made between Winston Churchill and **Josef Stalin** in October 1944 when they met in Moscow. The important question was: After the Nazis were beaten, who and how much would each of the victors have as a sphere of influence in Europe? Churchill sketched out the spheres and percentages as follows: Romania would be controlled 90 percent by Russia and 10 percent by the others; Greece would be 90 percent British and American, leaving 10 percent for Russia; Yugoslavia and Hungary would be divided equally; and Bulgaria would be 75 percent for Russia and 25 percent for the others.

Bay of Pigs Invasion (April 1961). Operation ZAPATA, which resulted in the invasion of the Bay of Pigs in Cuba by anti-Castro Cubans, was a covert **CIA** operation that aimed to overthrow the government of Fidel Castro. Although the operation was sanctioned by the administration of President **Dwight Eisenhower** (1890–1969), his successor, President **John Kennedy** had to support and take responsibility for it. According to his senior CIA staff, Kennedy so changed the operation that it was doomed to fail. When it did, Kennedy appeared weak and the CIA was deeply discredited. In October 1962, Soviet leader **Nikita Khrushchev**, taking advantage of the failed invasion, tried to establish Russian missiles in Cuba. Thanks to the Bay of Pigs, similar operations were in the future put into the hands of regular military forces rather than those of covert CIA operatives.

Berle, Adolf Augustus (1895–1971). Berle was a strong anti-Communist who served as U.S. President Franklin D. Roosevelt's (1882–1945) intelligence adviser and was U.S. Assistant Secretary of State from 1938 to 1944. In September 1939, Whittaker Chambers informed Berle of 18 U.S. government employees who were spies or Communist sympathizers. Most held minor jobs, except for Alger and Donald Hiss, who were middle-ranking and respected employees in Berle's department. Berle believed at the time that there was no substance to back up Chambers's allegations.

Berlin Blockade and Airlift (1948–1949). Although Berlin was itself occupied by all four Allied powers—Great Britain, France, the Soviet Union, and the United States—the city was surrounded by the Soviet zone of occupation in Germany. In 1948–1949, the city was blockaded by the Russians, and the Allies had to airlift supplies into their sectors of the city from late June 1948 to early May 1949.

Berlin Crisis (1958). A conflict between the Russians and the West arose over the Russian demand that the status of Berlin be settled in six months. After nine months of talks, many problems relating to Berlin were still not resolved.

Berlin Operations Base (BOB). The American Berlin Operations Base (BOB) was a section of the U.S. War Department's Strategic Service Unit, a unit of the **OSS**. It provided the

Glossary

U.S. Army in occupied Germany with intelligence on, for example, the **order of battle** of the **U.S.S.R.**

Berlin Wall (1961). In August 1961, the failure to resolve the problems over the status of Berlin, the division of Germany, and the exodus of East Germans to the West led **Nikita Khrushchev** to authorize the building of a wall between the Russian sector and the rest of the city. The wall was sealed off first with barbed wire, and later reinforced with concrete by the Russians. Escapers were shot—191 were killed—and about 5000 were captured by the East German authorities. The Berlin Wall was removed on the night of November 9, 1989. It had become the most potent physical representation of the **Cold War,** and its breaching was a tangible sign that the Cold War was concluding.

BfV (Bundesamt für Verfassungsschutz). The BfV was the Federal Internal Security Police of West Germany. Established in 1950 under Dr. Otto John, the BfV's main task was to watch for extremists of both the left and the right inside West Germany.

Black September. A splinter group of the Palestine Liberation Organization (**PLO**) formed in 1970, and operating from Syria and Lebanon. In 1972, at the Munich Olympics, the group slaughtered 11 Israelis, and were hunted down by **Mossad.** The name was taken from the month in which Palestinian guerrillas were expelled from Jordan by King Hussein.

Bletchley Park. The name used to designate the code-breaking division of the British secret services during **World War II.** Shortly before the war, the Government Code & Cipher School (**GCCS**) moved from the headquarters of the **SIS** in London to a small town, Bletchley, 60 miles north, and operated in a nineteenth-century mansion. Around it was a cluster of prefabricated huts. In Bletchley the GCCS was safe from German bombers. At Bletchley Park, the cracking of the ENIGMA cipher machine was achieved, using a model that had been provided to the British by Polish cryptographers who had worked for the Germans. ENIGMA was resolved by Alan M. Turing's (1912–1954) inventing the forerunner of the modern computer.

BND (Bundesnachrichtendienst). The BND was the Federal Republic of Germany's foreign intelligence agency, and the West German equivalent of the **CIA.**

BOB. See **Berlin Operations Base**

Boland Cutoff or Boland Amendments. The Boland Cutoff was signed into law by President **Ronald Reagan** as part of Public Law 98-473. It prohibited the obligation or expenditure of appropriated funds in support of military or paramilitary operations in Nicaragua. The amendments grew out of the fear that Reagan might pull the United States into another **Vietnam War** if he continued his secret war against communism in Nicaragua. They were attached to defense appropriations in December 1982 and October 1984. They were sponsored by Edward P. Boland, a Democratic congressman from Massachusetts. In part the amendments targeted funds available to the **CIA,** the Department of Defense, or any other agency of the U.S. involved in intelligence. Covert methods were used to get around the Boland Amendments, and this, when discovered, led to the **Iran–Contra Affair** and disgraced the U.S. presidency toward the end of Reagan's second term. Reagan stated he did not authorize anyone to violate the Boland Amendments.

BOSS. The South African Bureau for State Security.

Brezhnev, Leonid (1906–1982). During World War II, Brezhnev was a political commissar in the Ukraine, and rose to be chairman of the Moldavian Communist Party (1950–1954). When he entered the Politburo, he was loyal to **Nikita Khrushchev,** became Politburo chairman, then helped overthrow Khrushchev in October 1964. Brezhnev became Secretary of the Communist Party, with Alexei Kosygin as the nation's Prime Minister. Brezhnev was a consensus leader at home, and tended to blunt differences between opposing interests in Russia's politics and to promote a gerontocracy in his choice of supporters. He had **Yuri Andropov** (1914–1984) made head of the **KGB** in April 1967. After the third Israeli–Arab war in June 1967, Brezhnev chose to support rebuilding the Arabs' military, and had spies penetrate Egypt's government; the head of the KGB front organization the World Peace Council, Romesh Chandra, was a loyal Indian Communist who regularly denounced the United States. The Brezhnev Doctrine (1968–1989), established in September 1968, allowed Russian satellite nations to follow separate roads to socialism, providing their activities did no damage to socialism at home or abroad, and to a worldwide workers' movement for socialism. This policy led to five varieties of socialism: nationalist, revisionist, unpredictable, ineffective pro-Soviet, and effective pro-Soviet with little local support. The doctrine was abandoned in 1989.

By 1971 the Soviet embassy in New Delhi had a staff that included 150 KGB personnel. Under Brezhnev, Cuba's intelligence forces were purged of anti-Soviet officers, and with help from the KGB, the Cuban secret service was retrained. The KGB enlarged its recruitment of technologists for its London residency, which benefited enormously from the information provided by British spies including Frank Bossard, Douglas Britten, David Bingham, Nicholas Praeger, Geoffrey Prime, and John Stonehouse. In the United States, the KGB would benefit for years from the espionage of John A. Walker, Jr., and his family, beginning in December 1967, that led the United States into disaster during the **Vietnam War.** On the other hand, the KGB was frustrated by the defection in 1969 of Josef Frolik from Czechoslovakia to Great Britain and the defection in London of the professional assassin Oleg Lyalin, as well as the subsequent expulsion of 105 KGB and **GRU** staff from Great Britain. The Russian economy began its sharp decline under Brezhnev's regime; it could no longer support the demands of the military. Brezhnev's health began to fail after 1978; the international policy of détente collapsed; and the Soviets invaded Afghanistan in December 1979 without due thought about unintended consequences. While Brezhnev was dying, Yuri Andropov worked to ensure he would be Brezhnev's successor.

Browder, Earl (1891–1973). Earl Browder was leader of the American Communist Party. He and his sister Margaret both served the **KGB** and the various forms of the Soviet secret police that worked abroad.

Brush Contact. A secret form of communication between agents or an **agent** and a **case officer** when passing each other in the street or in a crowded place. In some cases it is possible for one person to give another an item—a note or microfilm—during the brush contact, and to do it so quickly that an observer does not know for certain that anything changed hands.

Bulganin, Nikolai (1895–1975). A Soviet political leader who aligned himself with **Nikita Khrushchev** after **Josef Stalin**'s death, and was made Soviet Prime Minister in 1955. He toured the world with Khrushchev, and was in Great Britain during the **Crabb Affair.** In March 1958 he was sent to Stavropol in a minor economic post, and retired to oblivion after 1960.

Bundesamt für Verfassungsschutz. See **BfV**

Bundesnachrichtendienst. See **BND**

Burned. A **case officer** or secret **agent** is burned when he or she is compromised, caught, or identified, and thus no longer useful.

Bush, George H. W. (1924–). Bush was U.S. President from 1989 to 1993. Educated at Yale, he served in the U.S. Navy in **World War II**, founded an oil company in 1953, and entered politics. He was Ambassador to the United Nations and headed the **CIA** (1975–

1976) before becoming **Ronald Reagan**'s Vice President. His most popular achievement was to lead America's Operation Desert Storm in February 1991, which quickly defeated Saddam Hussein's forces that earlier had invaded Kuwait. His notable effort was to oversee the final stages of the **Cold War,** in which he showed great skill in negotiations to advance cooperative and friendly relations with the changing political leaderships in Russia. His work was set back a little with the overthrow of Mikhail Gorbachev; nevertheless, Bush and **Boris Yeltsin** appeared to establish friendly relations. Bush lost the 1992 presidential election to Bill Clinton, apparently due to excessive indecisiveness and caution in his application of American foreign policies.

Camp David Accords. In March 1979 at Camp David, Maryland, the U.S. President's conference center for informal international negotiations, an agreement was signed by the Egyptian and Israeli leaders to end their war that had begun in 1948.

Camp Peary. See **Farm**

Campaign for Nuclear Disarmament (CND). Sometimes referred to as the Committee for Nuclear Disarmament, the CND is a British nonpolitical organization that seeks the worldwide abolition of nuclear weapons. It was launched in 1958 by Bertrand Russell (1872–1970) and Canon John Collins. Some of its members helped George Blake escape from prison.

Carter, Jimmy (1924–). A former Governor of Georgia who was elected to the U.S. presidency in November 1976, after the brief tenure and defeat at the polls of **Richard Nixon**'s (1913-1994) second Vice President, **Gerald R. Ford** (1913–). Carter's rise to power was helped by public feelings over the **Watergate** scandal, the end of the **Vietnam War**, and, partly, the disgracing of the **CIA** following the **Church Committee** inquires of 1975–1976. Carter put détente and human rights issues at sword's point; he formally recognized the People's Republic of China; and he established the **Camp David Accords** between Israel and Egypt. But the U.S. Congress considered his approach to the **U.S.S.R.** too soft, and saw the Soviets getting a stronger hold in Nicaragua, Africa, and the Middle East. The CIA, much demoralized, failed to assess accurately the pressure on America's ally, the Shah of Iran, and when he fled in January 1979, Carter's administration appeared weak.

In November 1979, when U.S. hostages were taken by revolutionaries in the Islamic Republic of Iran, under the leadership of Ayatollah Ruhollah Khomeini (1902–1989), the CIA managed to get some people out by deceptive means; nevertheless, Carter appeared to Americans to be weaker still, especially when a secret military attempt to release the hostages failed in April 1980. His Carter Doctrine of January 1980 attacked the Soviet invasion of Afghanistan a month earlier; had the United States boycott the Olympic Games in Moscow that year; and imposed trade sanctions. Nevertheless, although he increased U.S. military budgets, his image was not improved. The 1980 presidential election was won by the Republican, **Ronald Reagan**, a former Hollywood star and Governor of California. Carter's final humiliation came when Reagan, aged 70, announced the release of hostages in Iran after being inaugurated as President in January 1981. Carter's work since then has been to promote world peace.

Casablanca Conference (1943). The conference between Winston Churchill and Franklin D. Roosevelt in January 1943 at which they agreed that the surrender of Germany, Italy, and Japan must be unconditional.

Case Officer. An **SIS** or **CIA** employee who runs or directs an **agent** in the field.

CB. Companion of the Order of the Bath.

CBE. Commander of the Order of the British Empire, an award for service to the British nation.

Ceausescu, Nicolae (1918–1989). Ceausescu was the Communist dictator of Romania from 1975 to 1989. He became leader of the Romanian Communist Party in 1965, and in 1975, head of state, while his wife became First Deputy Prime Minister. The couple had a brutal security police that tolerated no dissent, especially in the media. Ceausescu presented himself as Romania's hero, but exported most of the nation's food production to pay its foreign debt, and created a polluting industrial wasteland. He lived in luxury and had begun building himself a palace. In December 1989, immediately after the fall of the **Berlin Wall**, ethnic Hungarians protested against Ceausescu's rule, and the Romanian troops loyal to him did not repress the uprising. When Ceausescu tried to rally support, he failed, was arrested by his own traffic police, and taken back to Bucharest, where he was tried and shot.

Cell of Five. The Fünfergruppen—groups or rings of five members—originated in 1869 with revolutionary underground organizations in tsarist Russia, and were taken up in principle by German workers who wanted to undermine Nazism and the German Communist Party early in 1932. The leader of the group was the only member supposed to know the whereabouts and identities of the other members, and he alone was allowed to contact the next level of the organization's hierarchy. Like the **need-to-know principle**, this was an efficient defense against the rigors of brutal interrogation and slips of the tongue. The efficacy of this technique for espionage is questionable, however, and has been confused with the grouping and organization of the five Cambridge spies, the Magnificent Five.

Central Intelligence Agency (CIA). The CIA is the American secret service organization that has as its aim the collecting of information and the protecting of its **agents,** irrespective of their nationality. The CIA may not operate, although it has done so, to defeat the enemy's intelligence services in the United States. That function is assigned to the **Federal Bureau of Investigation (FBI).**

Checkpoint Charlie. A crossing point for non-Germans from the American sector to the Russian sector of Berlin. It was dismantled in June 1990 as a symbol of the **Cold War**'s end. At the checkpoint, the West and the Soviets exchanged spies, as they also did at **Glienicke Bridge**.

Cheka or Vcheka. The Cheka, the All-Russian Extraordinary Commission for the Suppression of Counterrevolution and Sabotage, was established in December 1917 and run by an aristocratic Pole, Felix Dzerzhinski (1877–1926). It was the original Communist secret service, and became incorporated in the **NKVD** as the GPU, or secret police, in February 1922; in July 1923 it was the **OGPU**, an independent organization. In July 1934 it was reincorporated into the NKVD as GUGB. In February 1941 it was the independent **NKGB**; in July 1941 it was again reincorporated into the NKVD as GUGB. In April 1943 it again became the independent NKGB. In March 1946 it was named the **MGB.** From October 1947 to November 1951 foreign intelligence was transferred to KI (The Committee of Information). In March 1953 it was combined with the MVD, and in March 1954 it became the **KGB,** the State Security Service. It is common and accepted practice in writing about the Russian secret services to use the name KGB for the state security organization in the **U.S.S.R.** since its establishment as Cheka in 1917.

Chequers. A Tudor mansion in the Chiltern Hills of Buckinghamshire, England, presented to the nation by Lord and Lady Lee of Fareham to be used as the country seat of Great Britain's Prime Minister.

Chiang Kai-shek (1887–1975). Chiang Kai-shek, also known as Jiang Jieshi, was a Chinese militarist who turned to politics, helped overthrow the Chinese empire in 1911, and as a nationalist was China's major political leader until 1949. He was aligned with Western values: he married a woman educated in the United States, and he converted to Christianity. After the rise of communism in China, he was defeated in a civil war by **Mao Zedong** and sought refuge in Taiwan, where he managed to maintain power by changing the island into a fortress against communism in Southeast Asia.

Chief of Station. The individual usually in charge of foreign intelligence at a Western embassy overseas.

China Hands. The "old China Hands" was a group in the U.S. State Department who predicted the Communists would win control of China in the civil war between **Mao Zedong**'s Communists and **Chiang Kai-shek**'s Nationalists. The latter were seen as incompetent, selfish, and corrupt. The China Hands recommended that America pressure Chiang to reform his government and direct his troops against the Japanese in cooperation with Mao Zedong's Communists. In the early 1950s, after Mao won control of China, "Who Lost China?" became an American election slogan, to which the answer was the "old China Hands," according to the ambitious U.S. conservatives. All the "old China Hands" were purged from their jobs on the basis of false charges made by their political enemies. The first to go was John Stewart Service; he was followed by John Carter Vincent, John Paton Davies, Jr., and Oliver Edmund Clubb. All were vindicated, but none recovered. Their enemies were members of the **China Lobby**.

China Lobby. During and after **World War II**, American conservatives wanted to support **Chiang Kai-shek**, the leader of Nationalist China, against **Mao Zedong**, the Communist leader who won the civil war in China and ruled the country after 1949. Much of the blame for the Communist victory was attributed in the United States to a pro-Soviet conspiracy of the "old **China Hands**" who worked in the U.S. State Department. With help from Joseph McCarthy and false charges presented to the **loyalty–security board** in the U.S. State Department, the "old China Hands" were fired. The first to go was John S. Service, who was considered to have acted treasonably.

Chinese Cultural Revolution (1966–1968). The Cultural Revolution was a full-scale revolution to establish a working-class culture in the People's Republic of China (PRC) and restore the purity of the Communist movement. **Mao Zedong** released terror with the "Red Guard," consisting principally of students, who attacked anyone who could be seen as an enemy of Mao. Mao was deified, and factions competed for excellence in being Maoist. The Kremlin was denounced as a band of renegades and traitors, as were many major Chinese figures, and spy mania was rampant as foreigners were persecuted and imprisoned. Soviet diplomats were smuggled out to safety. Seeing China as chaotic and terror-stricken, the **KGB** was shocked at the brutality of the revolution and the varieties of torture employed. Possibly 30 million people were persecuted, and 1 million died.

Church Committee (1975–1976). A special U.S. Senate select committee established to study the past activities, especially those that might have been illegal or improper, of American intelligence agencies, especially the **Central Intelligence Agency (CIA)**. It was named after the Democratic senator from Idaho, Frank Forrester Church (1924–1984). At the time the public was aroused by Seymour Hersh's article in the *New York Times* (December 1974) that suggested that the CIA might have been secretly investigating U.S. citizens—which was illegal—and could have been involved in rigging elections or planning the assassinations of political figures in foreign nations, including Fidel Castro (Cuba), Salvador Allende (Chile), and Mohammed Mossadegh (Iran).

CIA. See **Central Intelligence Agency**

CIS. See **Commonwealth Investigation Service (CIS)**

Civil Operations and Revolutionary Development Support. See **CORDS**

CMG. The Companion of the Order of St. Michael and St. George is a British award for service to the nation.

CND. See **Campaign for Nuclear Disarmament**

Coattail Operation. An attempt to offer one's **Cold War** opponent information about one's own secret service that, in effect, is designed to catch the individual to whom the offer is made so that one's secret service has reason to expel him. When Michael Bettany offered his services, this was probably in the mind of the head of the Soviet residency in London (1983), who, like Bettany, was an alcoholic and concerned about his career.

Code Name. The name given to an **agent** or operation, usually printed in capitals, to hide the true name; for instance, Donald Maclean, the British **double agent** among the Cambridge Five, was code-named HOMER by the Russians.

Cold War. A remorseless, intense struggle for the upper hand, by all means short of actual fighting, by the superpowers between early 1946 and late 1989. Its origins are still debated, but it seems to have been identified by George Orwell, and was given its name by Walter Lippmann in a collection of articles he published in a critical review of George Kennan's "long telegram" of February 1946. Other events from the Cold War's origins are Churchill's **Iron Curtain** speech in March 1946, the withdrawal of the British from the politics of Greece in 1947, and the subsequent entry of the United States with its containment policy toward Russia and its **Marshall Plan** for the economic reconstruction of Europe. Most writers assume the Cold War ended when the **Berlin Wall** was breached at the end of 1989.

Combined Policy Committee. A committee agreed to by Winston Churchill (1874–1965) and Franklin Roosevelt (1882–1945) to oversee the Anglo–American–Canadian partnership in developing the **atom bomb**. No other countries were represented, especially the **U.S.S.R.**

COMINTERN. The COMINTERN was founded in 1919 and dissolved in September 1943. It was the main Russian system for controlling communism worldwide.

Commonwealth Investigation Service (CIS). An Australian security organization, established in December 1945, to watch for subversives in Australia, and especially to establish awareness of a Communist fifth column in Australia. The CIS employed **agents** to join Russian clubs, make friends, identify Communist sympathizers, and inform on them. In December 1948 an inquiry suggested it should investigate government employees who handled secret information.

Communist Bloc. The group of nations, especially in Europe, that supported or were dominated by the **U.S.S.R.**

Compromised. When an operation, asset, or bought **agent** is uncovered, it is said to be compromised.

Containment. The earliest of several **Cold War** policies adopted by the West to limit the expansion of the **U.S.S.R.** into Europe, Asia, Africa, and the Middle East. In July 1947 an anonymous article, "The Sources of Soviet Conduct," was published by "X" in the prestigious U.S. journal *Foreign Affairs*. In the article, the author emphasized the need for patient, firm, and vigilant "containment of Russian expansion" after **World War II**. This policy was taken up by the West as its first step in the Cold War. The author was George Frost Kennan, who had already put these ideas to his colleagues in the U.S. State Department in his long telegram to them early in 1946.

CORDS. Civil Operations and Revolutionary Development Support was a program of the **CIA** and the U.S. military during the **Vietnam War**. One of its major operations was Operation PHOENIX (1968–1973).

Courtauld Institute. The Courtauld Institute of Art houses the collection of paintings presented to the University of London by Samuel Courtauld (1876–1947). He also bequeathed to it his house in Portman Square. Courtauld, director of his family's silk firm, was one of the first British collectors of French impressionist paintings. From 1947 until 1972, Anthony Blunt was director of the Institute and ruled it like a medieval court; it became a notable postgraduate art center.

Covert Action. Hidden activities performed by an intelligence agency.

CPA. Communist Party of Australia.

CPUSA. Communist Party of the United States of America.

Crown Jewels. An informal term used by the **KGB** to identify the tangible results of successful espionage in Great Britain by Russian spies and secret **agents**.

Curzon Line. The Polish–Russian frontier proposed after **World War I**, in 1919. The British foreign secretary, Lord Curzon, recommended that the Poles who had invaded Russia should withdraw to this line, pending a peace conference. The 1945 frontier tends to follow this line.

Cutout. A go-between who serves as a contact between a spy's network chief and a source of supply.

Dangle. A dangle is a secret **agent** who presents himself as a **defector-in-place** to pass disinformation to the enemy's secret service. "Dangle" can also mean to display an attractive bait to lure a person to one's side in espionage. In Great Britain, the second meaning is sometimes referred to as "trailing one's coat."

Dead Drop/ Dead-Letter Box. A place where information is left to picked up later by either the **agent** or the agent's **case officer**. For example, one dead-letter box used by Konon Molody (also known as Gordon Lonsdale) was the men's lavatory at London's Classic Cinema in Baker Street. Material was hidden in a condom in the cistern. The advantage of the dead-letter box is that no physical contact can be observed between members of an intelligence network as they exchange information or items.

Defector-in-Place. A **defector** who continues to work, apparently as usual, after he has changed from serving his country to serving its enemy.

Defectors. Important Soviet defectors were Igor Gouzenko, Anatoli Golitsyn, Oleg Gordievsky, Pyotr Deryabin, Yuri Rastvorov, Vladimir and Evdokia Petrov, Reino Hayhanen, Nikolai Khokhlov, and Bogdan Stashinsky. Among the West's important defectors were George Blake, Anthony Blunt, Christopher Boyce, Guy Burgess, Heinz Felfe, Klaus Fuchs, Dieter Gerhardt, Günter Guillaume, Michal Goleniewski, Donald Maclean, George Pâques, Kim Philby, Geoffrey Prime, Julius Rosenberg, John A. Walker, Jr., and Aldrich Ames.

Deutsch, Arnold (1904–1942). Deutsch was known as one of the Soviets' great **illegals**. He was an Austrian, brilliantly educated, who turned to communism and went to England for three years; as an illegal he recruited Edith Tudor Hart, Kim Philby, Alexander Orlov, and Theodore Maly; approached Guy Burgess, Anthony Blunt, and John Cairncross; and ran the **Woolwich Arsenal** spy ring (1937–1938). Deutsch died trying to rescue fellow passengers of the S.S. *Donbass*, sunk by a U-boat in the Atlantic Ocean in November 1942.

DGI. Dirección General de Inteligencia, the Cuban foreign intelligence and security forces.

DGSE. Direction Générale de Securité Extérieure, the French foreign intelligence service.

Dirty Operations and Tricks. An operation discovered to be out of the control of one's secret agency, and being supervised clandestinely by the intelligence officers of one's enemy. Dirty tricks are the inhuman and dishonest practices used to achieve the clandestine goals of dirty operations, such as drugs, hypnosis, torture, kidnapping, assassination, murder, robbery, varieties of manipulation of information, countless dishonest practices, and illegal activities. As a rule "dirty" is applied to a person working for his enemies while serving his own secret services.

Disinformation. Carefully prepared lies, many of which are difficult to verify as such.

Donovan, William Joseph (1883–1959). Donovan was U.S. district attorney (1922–1924) and assistant to the U.S. Attorney General (1925–1929). He became national security adviser to U.S. Presidents Herbert C. Hoover (1874–1964) and Franklin D. Roosevelt (1882–1945). Donovan was head of the Office of Strategic Services (**OSS**) from 1942 to 1945, and was made a brigadier general in 1943.

Doolittle Report. A report on the **Central Intelligence Agency (CIA),** commissioned by Allen W. Dulles (1893–1969) in late 1954, and completed by Lieutenant General James Harold Doolittle (1896–1993), a famous **World War II** aviator. The report was requested by President **Dwight Eisenhower** in response to an attempt by Senator Mike Mansfield to have a joint committee of the U.S. Congress investigate America's clandestine services, primarily the CIA. The report resonated with Eisenhower's views. It found that the CIA was losing in the espionage war with its implacable enemy the **KGB**, which was highly dangerous because it played a game without rules; the CIA should be more ruthless, and develop espionage and counterespionage techniques to subvert and destroy the Soviets with methods cleverer than theirs; protect the CIA from penetration by the KGB; and keep the American public aware of Russia's aim to dominate the world. One result of the report was the creation of a counterintelligence staff run by James J. Angleton (1917–1987).

Double Agents. Spies who remain loyal to their nation's intelligence services while secretly working for its enemy. From their new masters the double agents provide a mixture of truth (pure gold, 25-carat gold) and **disinformation** (chicken shit) to their original masters. When the original masters find out they have been fooled or betrayed, the double agent is tried and shot or jailed. Examples are George Blake (for **MI6** but loyal to the **KGB**), Yuri Loginov (for the KGB but loyal to the **CIA**). Usually the discovered double agent is murdered before any inquiry, to ensure that no one else within the intelligence community copies him. When double agents stay in their official position and work both sides for their masters, then their masters have a **defector-in-place.**

Dropped Dead. To be dropped dead is to have one's communications cut, especially with Soviet **case officers.**

DST. Direction de la Surveillance du Territoire, France's counterintelligence agency.

Dumbarton Oaks. A mansion in Washington, DC, used for seminars; in 1944, a conference held there laid the foundation of the United Nations Conference.

Eden, Robert Anthony (1897–1977). Prime Minister of Great Britain and leader of the Conservative Party from 1955 to 1957. He entered Parliament in 1922, specialized in foreign affairs, and enjoyed a high reputation for diplomatic skill. He was Winston Churchill's (1874–1965) Foreign Secretary during **World War II**, and again from 1951 to 1955; he became Prime Minister when Churchill stood aside in April 1955, and promptly won a landslide victory in the general election in May. In July he sponsored the first summit meeting of the Big Four. In September it was announced officially that Guy Burgess and Donald Maclean had been Soviet spies. Two months later, Kim Philby, who had secretly helped the two men flee to Moscow in May, skillfully convinced the press he had not been involved.

In April 1956, during the visit of **Nikita Khrushchev** and **Nikolai Bulganin** to Great Britain, Eden's government was embarrassed by the death of the spy "Buster" Crabb while examining the hull of the Russian ship that brought the men on a peace visit. In July, Gamal

Abdel Nasser nationalized the Suez Canal, which Eden thought undermined Great Britain's security. With France and Israel, Britain secretly began an invasion of Egypt, without consulting President **Dwight Eisenhower**. It was Eden's most disastrous decision. Khrushchev supported Egypt, Britain suffered an oil embargo, Eisenhower would not help maintain Britain's alternative means of purchasing petroleum, and Eden was forced into a unilateral cease-fire without consulting France. In December, UN forces oversaw the end of the struggle, Nasser became a hero to Egypt's citizens, Russia became a welcome ally to Arab nations in the Middle East, and Eden's political career was ruined. Much of his brief tenure as Prime Minister was dominated by another crisis in Cyprus. Illness led to Eden to resign, and he was replaced as Prime Minister in mid-January 1957 by **Harold Macmillan** (1894–1986).

Eisenhower, Dwight D. (1890–1969). Eisenhower was President of the United States from January 1953 to January 1961; a Republican, he was preceded in office by Democrat **Harry Truman** and followed by Democrat **John F. Kennedy.** Eisenhower was a career soldier who was in charge of the invasion of the European continent that ended **World War II,** and thereafter was one of the world's most powerful international figures. In England, Winston Churchill (1874–1965) introduced Eisenhower, a skeptic as far as intelligence was concerned, to Operation ULTRA, the breaking of the Nazi wartime code by the British with the ENIGMA machine.

In June 1953 Eisenhower allowed the execution of Ethel Rosenberg to go ahead. He believed she had led the Rosenberg spy group, and felt that if she were not executed, the Russians would employ more women as spies; he directed that J. Robert Oppenheimer (1904–1967) be investigated for having been disloyal, which resulted in the scientist's never working for the U.S. government again; he called for a report on the Soviet Union's espionage, the **Doolittle Report**; he supported the clandestine operations that returned the Shah to Iran to powerand ended the rule of Mohammed Mossadegh (1880–1967), and helped end the rule in Guatemala of Jacobo Arbenz Guzman (1913–1971); refused the **CIA**'s request to support more effectively the Hungarian uprising in 1956, for fear of beginning World War III; he forced the British and the French to return the Suez Canal to Egyptian control, and would not follow a CIA request to get rid of Gamal Abdel Nasser; he established a board to advise him on intelligence activities (January 1956); and he gave personal support to Allen W. Dulles as head of the CIA.

Under Eisenhower the United States provided great financial support to the French in their conflict against Communist forces in Vietnam; on the advice of the CIA, Eisenhower backed the regime of Ngo Dinh Diem in Vietnam in 1954, but would not send in U.S. troops; suddenly he withdrew the CIA projects for Indonesia in 1958, and thereafter saw **Achmed Sukarno**'s (1901–1970) regime become unstable, and witnessed vast massacres in Southeast Asia; and he announced the United States was neutral during the Indonesian civil war in the 1960s, while the CIA secretly intervened because the Indonesian president was apparently accepting arms from the Soviets.

The Eisenhower Doctrine was a policy to provide economic, and possibly military, aid to Middle East nations threatened by communism. The policy was dropped late in 1958 when little support for it came from within America.

Eisenhower had great faith in aerial reconnaissance; he insisted that pilots of **U-2 spy flights** be Strategic Air Command pilots under secret contract to the CIA, to ensure they operated as civilian intelligence officers; he proposed an "Open Skies" policy to attract Soviet support for his peace plans, but the Russian leadership regarded this policy as part of an espionage plot. When Eisenhower refused to apologize to the Russians for using the U-2 spy plane over the **U.S.S.R.**, **Nikita Khrushchev** ended the Paris Summit Conference with Eisenhower, which had been called to help reduce the likelihood of war.

Eisenhower approved the ending of the rule of Patrice Lumumba (1925–1961) in the Belgian Congo in August 1960, but had left office by the time Lumumba was murdered.

Much has been made of the CIA's alleged role in Lumumba's death. Also before his leaving office, Eisenhower's regime saw may plots to end the life of Fidel Castro (1927–), and plans to invade Cuba to return non-Communist rule to Cuba. The plans for assassination were often bizarre, and the invasion was left to **John Kennedy**'s tenure as president.

Eisenhower Doctrine (January 1957). President **Dwight Eisenhower**'s policy to provide economic, and possibly military, aid to Middle East nations threatened by communism. The policy was dropped late in 1958 when little support for it came from within the United States.

FAECT. A Congress of Industrial Organizations (CIO) union, the Federation of Architects, Engineers, Chemists and Technicians, which had among its members U.S. **atom spies** who served the interests of the **U.S.S.R.**, such as Julius Rosenberg.

Family Jewels. A list of over 700 possibly illegal activities of the **Central Intelligence Agency (CIA).** The activities were made public in 1973 and included plans to assassinate Fidel Castro, and the experimental use of drugs without informed consent, as in the death of Frank Olsen.

Farm. The Farm is the informal name of the Camp Peary training facility for **Central Intelligence Agency (CIA) agents** who are to work in Clandestine Services. During the **Cold War** the Farm was not acknowledged even though former CIA employees wrote about it. It is a forested site, closed to outsiders, and not unlike a prisoner-of-war camp. Originally it was a training camp for the U.S. Navy. Aerial photographs show it has an airstrip, fishing lakes, deer, target ranges, accommodation barracks, a large warehouse, and a gymnasium. The yearlong course at the Farm teaches CIA staff the recruitment of agents in the field, communication with agents using radio, codes, secret writing techniques, microdots, **dead drops**, signals; surveillance and countersurveillance; methods of escape and evasion; weapons assembly and handling; explosives and their detonation; sabotage techniques; breaking and entering; locksmith skills; illegal mail and seal opening; photography; use of **one-time pads**; dissolving paper; border crossing in difficult terrain; infiltration by boat; obstacle climbing; use of hand grenades; snatching and exfiltration of agents; tailing others; drycleaning (shedding agents who follow you); long marches; tent erection in the dark; killing without weapons; disguises; false-flag recruitment by pretending to represent countries other than one's own; and diverse role-playing skills.

FBI. See **Federal Bureau of Investigation**

FCD. The First Chief (Foreign Intelligence) Directorate of the KGB.

Federal Bureau of Investigation (FBI). The federal agency responsible for the internal security of the United States.

Fifth Amendment. In the United States, to "take the Fifth Amendment" is to exercise the right guaranteed by the Fifth Amendment of the U.S. Constitution of refusing to answer questions in order to avoid incriminating oneself.

Fifth Man. In 1979 the "fourth man" in the **KGB**'s "Magnificent Five" was exposed as Anthony Blunt. This led to speculation as to who was the fifth man, on the false assumption that the Soviet Union always employed its **agents** in one place to work in groups of five, and no more. False trails led to the following candidates: Frank Birch, Sefton Delmer, Andrew Gow, Sir Roger Hollis, Guy Liddell, Graham Mitchell, Arthur Pigou, Sir Rudolf Peierls, Lord Rothschild, and Dr. Wilfred Mann. In 1981 Oleg Gordievsky knew who was the fifth man from his work on the **FCD**'s history and it was not Sir Roger Hollis. Peierls and Rothschild sued for libel, and Mann made a convincing case for his not being the fifth man. In 1984 Peter Wright nevertheless alleged it had been Sir Roger Hollis. In 2002 Christine Keeler added her voice to his view. In 1990 it was clear that John Cairncross was the fifth man in the KGB's Magnificent Five.

Final Solution. The shortened English translation of the Nazi euphemism *Endlosung de Judenfrage*—meaning the "final solution to the Jewish question," the extermination of all Jews. The policy was introduced by Heinrich Himmler (1900–1945), head of the Nazi SS elite corps since 1929; it was carried out notably by Karl Adolf Eichmann (1906–1962). He administered concentration camps where 6 million Jews were murdered between 1941 and 1945. After **World War II** he hid in Argentina, where many Nazis found safety, until he was found, abducted by the Israeli **agent** Isser Harel, and brought to trial and executed.

Fleming, Ian (1908–1964). The **Cold War** author of the James Bond adventures that glamorized the work of secret **agents** by blending sex with violence in an exciting lifestyle; Fleming was a dilettante, educated at Eton and two European universities, worked for Reuters, and served in British naval intelligence during **World War II**.

Ford, Gerald R. (1913–). Ford was appointed Vice President of the United States by **Richard Nixon** after Spiro T. Agnew (1919–1996) was forced to resign the position following charges of corruption in October 1973. Shortly after Ford became President and Nelson Rockefeller (1908–1979) became his Vice President, the **CIA** was demoralized late in December 1974 by Seymour Hersh's article in the *New York Times*. Although the **Rockefeller Commission** (1975) appointed by Ford to inquire into charges that the CIA might have operated illegally, found little reason to condemn the CIA, the results of the **Church Committee**'s investigation of the CIA during 1975–1976 were greatly demoralizing to the organization, its staff, its officers, and its future planning. Ford worked to promote closer relations with the **U.S.S.R.** through the efforts of Henry Kissinger (1923–) and also promoted arms limitation, but was weakened at home when his policies appeared to allow the Soviets to become superior to the United States in nuclear capability. His policy to support South Vietnamese, Cambodians, and Angolans further weakened his support at home, and he lost the presidential election to **Jimmy Carter** in 1976.

Ford Foundation. Founded in 1936 as a philanthropic and charitable trust, the Ford Foundation was used to distribute **Central Intelligence Agency (CIA)** funding for cultural purposes.

Franco, Franciso (1882–1975). Fascist head of state in Spain after the **Spanish Civil War** (1937–1939), from 1939 to 1975. Although Spain was neutral during **World War II**, Franco's sympathies lay with Nazi Germany and its leader, Adolf Hitler.

Fünfergruppen. See **Cell of Five**

GCCS. The British Government Code & Cipher School at **Bletchley Park**, 60 miles north of London.

GCHQ. Government Communications Headquarters was Great Britain's post–**World War II** name for **Bletchely Park**, where the ULTRA operation, which decoded German communications, was stationed. Its mission was to gather intelligence by technical means; **MI5** was the domestic secret service that aimed to protect Great Britain from threats to its national security; the Secret Intelligence Service (**SIS**), also known as **MI6**, continued to collect foreign intelligence related to defense and foreign affairs.

Gehlen Org. Gehlen Org was the name given informally to the Gehlen Organization. It was formed in 1946 under the command of the U.S. Army, and comprised what was left of Nazi Major General Reinhard Gehlen's **World War II** Foreign Armies intelligence network of spies who had managed to survive the Soviet occupation of Eastern Europe and function inside the **U.S.S.R.** When Gehlen showed there was a sound network that had penetrated the Soviets, he was able to convince the Americans that he had an organization of some value. The **Central Intelligence Agency (CIA)** was in nominal control, and it supported the idea that Gehlen should recruit members of the German army, the SS, and anti-

Soviet people whom he knew in Eastern Europe to penetrate the U.S.S.R. and conduct counterintelligence operations. In April 1956 Gehlen's organization became part of the Federal Republic of Germany, and was designated its intelligence and security service. The service was scandalized when it was alleged that its personnel had threatened members of the press and that **double agents** working for the Soviets had been working in the organization. In 1968 Gehlen retired.

Glasnost. The concept of glasnost (openness) led to changes in Soviet society when it was introduced into domestic politics in 1985 by Mikhail Gorbachev (1931–). It was accompanied by a policy of perestroika, which required restructuring Soviet society. The twin policies aimed to reduce corruption and increase efficiency in Soviet government and industry, and encourage liberal views in politics. In time it led to unrest, nationalist demands, and the destruction of the Soviet Union, the displacement of the Communist Party, and the formation of the Commonwealth of Independent States.

Glienicke Bridge. At the southwest entrance to Berlin, the **Berlin Wall** surrounded the East German side of the Glienicke Bridge, an elegant steel span across the Havel River where it grows wider toward Wannsee. The bridge stood in a forest park surrounding the Glienicke hunting lodge erected in the late seventeenth century. Spy exchanges were often made here, as well as at **Checkpoint Charlie.**

Government Communications Headquarters. See **GCHQ**

Great Patriotic War. The name given in Russia to **World War II**, which was fought between 1939 and 1945.

GRU. The Soviet military intelligence agency.

Gulag. The Gulag was a set of forced labor camps established in 1919, and flourished notably in the early 1930s under **Josef Stalin**'s rule; possibly millions of Russian died there. In 1955, following Stalin's death, the Gulag was disbanded, but a system of labor colonies was not. Among the inmates were criminals, dissident intellectuals, disloyal members of ethnic groups, and members of ousted political factions.

Hauptverwaltung-Aufklärung. See **HVA**

Heath, Edward Richard George (1916–). The British Conservative Prime Minister from June 1970 to 1974. He was committed to European unity, and Britain joined the European Community during Heath's tenure as Prime Minister. However, he was not able to curb rising inflation and widespread strikes that accompanied the escalation in the world's oil prices, and lost the election to **Harold Wilson** in 1974; he resigned as Tory leader in February 1975. Before he came to power he was the intended victim of a failed blackmail plan by the Czechoslovakian secret services. During Heath's tenure as Prime Minister, Nicholas Praeger, a Czechoslovakian spy, was tried and found guilty of espionage, and sentenced to 12 years in jail; also, David Bingham was sentenced to 21 years for espionage in Great Britain.

Hollywood Ten (September 1947). A group of Hollywood actors who wanted to support their colleagues who were being hounded by the **House Un-American Activities Committee (HUAC)** for having possible Communist sympathies. The Hollywood Ten—really 19—got much support from friends the film industry. Their number rose to 1,000; 28 of them—including John Huston, Humphrey Bogart, Lauren Bacall, Ira Gershwin, Sterling Hayden, June Havoc, Gene Kelly, and Danny Kaye—came to Washington for the HUAC hearings and brought a petition that was presented to the House. The petition stated that the HUAC investigation perverted fair and impartial procedures, and had besmirched the characters of many individuals. The petition went nowhere, and Bogart was heard to say that going to Washington was a mistake.

Home, Alec Douglas (1903–1995). Conservative Prime Minister of Great Britain for one year after the resignation of **Harold Macmillan** in October 1963. As Earl of Home, the Conservative Party's compromise choice for leader resigned six peerages a few days before becoming Prime Minister as Sir Alec Douglas Home, and was for 15 days a member of neither house of Parliament until he won a Scottish by-election. During his leadership of Great Britain, U.S. President **John F. Kennedy** was assassinated, the scandal of the Profumo Affair was raised again with the sentencing of Christine Keeler for perjury, and Greville Wynne was exchanged for the Russian **agent** Konon Molody (Gordon Lonsdale). Home honored the retirement from British politics of Winston Churchill (1874–1965); saw the passing of the espionage novelist who created James Bond, **Ian Fleming** (1908–1964); and, a day after **Nikita Khrushchev**'s fall from power in Russia, lost the British general election to the Labour leader **Harold Wilson** (1916–1995). See also **Profumo, John Dennis**.

House Un-American Activities Committee (HUAC). In 1938 the U.S. House of Representatives created the Special Committee on Un-American Activities under the conservative Martin Dies of Texas. That year it exposed Communists in government, trades unions, and Hollywood. During the war it was not prominent, but in January 1945 it came alive again under the aegis of a racist, John E. Rankin. It was given the task of investigating un-American propaganda in the United States, the diffusion of such propaganda from outside the United States, or from within, and any attack on the principles that were upheld by the U.S. Constitution. In the late 1940s the committee investigated alleged Communist interference with and penetration of the American film industry and government. In June 1957, after there had been obvious abuse of its powers of investigation, the Supreme Court curbed its punitive authority to some degree, for the first time, in the case of *Watkins v. United States*. In 1969 HUAC changed its name to the Committee on Internal Security, and it was abolished in 1975.

HUAC. See **House Un-American Activities Committee**

Hukbalahap Rebellion. The Hukbalahap was a Filipino peasant resistance movement, originating in central Luzon and aiming to free the Philippines from Japanese invaders during **World War II.** The Hukbalahap also opposed the U.S.-backed landlord elite in the Philippines. They rebelled against the Manila government in the early 1950s, and were not suppressed until 1954.

HUMINT. Human intelligence coming from espionage and individual activities.

HVA (Hauptverwaltung-Aufklärung). The international intelligence unit of East Germany's Ministerium für Staatssicherheit (MfS), or Ministry for State Security, known as the **STASI**. It was established securely in the early 1950s by Markus Wolf.

Hydrogen Bomb (1951). A thermonuclear bomb more powerful that the original **atom bomb**; it is based on the release of masses of energy through the fusion of lighter atoms (e.g., hydrogen or its isotope deuterium), rather than the splitting of heavier atoms. After the Soviets had exploded their first atom bomb in August 1949, **Edward Teller** (1908–2003) was able to persuade President **Harry Truman** that the international balance of power would be tipped in America's favor if it produced a hydrogen bomb. The bomb was at least 750 times more powerful than the atom bomb dropped in August 1945 on Japan, and would be the best available deterrent against Russia's feared expansionism. The first test was in the Pacific in May 1951. Such a bomb could be dropped from a plane by 1954. In the race to redress the perceived imbalance of nuclear power, Russia tested its first thermonuclear device in August 1954, and had a weapon ready by November 1955. Shortly before his withdrawal from the prime ministership in April 1955, Winston Churchill (1874–1965) argued that Great Britain's possession of the hydrogen bomb would compel peace, and therefore "safety would be the sturdy child of terror." The United Kingdom had its first such device tested in 1957.

Illegal. "Illegals" are the most sophisticated of **KGB** spies. They function outside the cover of journalist or a diplomat; are well trained; and may be either foreigners or professional **agents** sent to a country often with a false identity. On arrival they are hidden among the many immigrants. They are hard to find, and they keep in touch with their foreign administrators by means that are often unavailable to most people. Their training includes codes, cipher-breaking, radio transmission, **brush contacts**, special signaling locations, **dead-drop** operations, **cutout** contacts, microphotography, and secret writing with special inks. They are given a false identity or **legend**, rehearse it often, and learn a language to a proficient level, especially English. They enter a target country; complete a cover job; and, as citizens of that target country, are exemplary, honest, trustworthy, and hardworking; pay their taxes; and join community projects and parent groups at their children's schools. They are run by a field officer with whom they make regular contact by using dead drops or brush contacts or radio transmission. "Legals" is a term some writers use to refer to KGB spies who have the cover of a legitimate occupation, such as a diplomat or a journalist, in a foreign country.

Intelligence Fundamentalists. A special group in the **Central Intelligence Agency (CIA)** that James Angleton collected, comprising counterintelligence zealots from the CIA and other secret services, who believed they had been called to the vocation of professional intelligence, and knew best and understood exactly the threat that endangered them and the West generally. This intelligence brotherhood had a unique methodology to support its ideology. Peter Wright was a member.

International Monetary Fund (IMF) and World Bank. Proposed at the Bretton Woods conference in 1944, the IMF was based in Washington, DC in 1945. The World Bank is the common name for the World Bank for Reconstruction and Development, and was established also in Washington in 1945 by the United Nations. The two are closely allied; but unlike the World Bank, which invests capital for productive aims and encourages private foreign investment, the IMF is not a development agency; instead, it supports international monetary cooperation, stabilization of exchange rates, and aims to eliminate foreign-exchange restrictions.

IRA. Irish Republican Army.

Iron Curtain (1945–1946). A colloquial name for the **Cold War** frontier between Soviet-dominated countries in Eastern Europe and the non-Communist countries of Western Europe. In February 1945 Joseph Goebbels (1897–1945), the Nazi propagandist, wrote an article in *Das Reich* in which he designated the Soviet sphere of influence at the time; this idea appeared in the British press, and Winston Churchill (1874–1965) said he "viewed with profound misgiving the descent of an iron curtain between us and everything to the eastward." The idea that Russia sought a protective boundary between itself and Europe arose at the **Potsdam Conference** in August 1945. **Clement Attlee** (1883–1967) had replaced Churchill, and **Harry Truman** had replaced Franklin D. Roosevelt, as the West's representatives in the conference of the Big Three—Great Britain, the Soviet Union, and the United States. At the conference **Josef Stalin** suggested that the Soviet Union would regard all western Germany as being under the West's influence and all eastern Germany as being under Russia's influence. In reply to this suggestion, Truman asked whether Stalin aimed to establish a line down Europe from the Baltic Sea in the north to the Adriatic Sea in the south. Stalin said yes. In March 1946, Winston Churchill said in Fulton, Missouri, what the Kennan "long telegram" of February 1946 had placed in the minds of all U.S. State Department senior officers: "From Stettin in the Baltic to Trieste in the Adriatic, an iron curtain has descended across the continent." A cartoon appeared in the Soviet magazine

Krokodil depicting Winston Churchill, fully armed, ranting and waving two flags. One said "Iron Curtain Over Europe," and the other, "Anglo–Saxons Should Rule the World."

Izvestia. Russian for "news." The daily newspaper of the Soviet government, *Izvestia* was founded in 1917.

Johnson, Lyndon B. (1908–1973). Lyndon B. Johnson became Vice President of the United States in 1961, and U.S. President on the death of **John F. Kennedy** in November 1963. He withdrew as a candidate in the 1968 presidential election, and retired from public affairs in 1969. During his tenure as President, Johnson, an avowed anti-Communist, drew the United States deeply into the **Vietnam War**. He escalated hostilities to win the war until the **Vietcong** launched the unexpected **Tet Offensive** in January 1968, and changed his policy to negotiate an end to the conflict.

One of the most damaging espionage operations against the efforts of the U.S. in Vietnam at this time was the work of John A. Walker, Jr., and his spy ring, which over several years provided the **KGB** with information and technical manuals used by all the U.S. armed services, the **Central Intelligence Agency (CIA),** the State Department, and the **Federal Bureau of Investigation (FBI).** Information that the Soviets received through him made it possible to anticipate military operations toward the end of Johnson's tenure. Not until the mid-1980s did the United States learn how damaging Walker's espionage had been to its efforts in Vietnam.

Johnson's reputation in international matters became poorly regarded, and to some he seemed incompetent, especially to America's **NATO** allies, who were far from respectful toward him.

Karlshorst. The residency and headquarters of the Russian secret services in Russian-occupied Germany, located in Berlin after **World War II**. In June 1945, the Russian intelligence services were formed into a combined residency, subordinated to the **First Chief** (foreign intelligence) Directorate of the **NKGB** in Moscow. By August 1945, Karlshorst was operating, and its first head was Aleksandr Mikhailovich Korotkov, who had been deputy resident in Berlin in 1941. At Karlshorst the Soviet Military Administration was established, and Korotkov was its deputy political adviser. In time the term Karlshorst became synonymous with the **KGB** headquarters in Germany.

Kennedy, John F. (1917–1963). In 1960, Kennedy defeated Vice President **Richard Nixon** (1913–1994) in the U.S. presidential election, campaigning on the alleged weakness of President **Dwight Eisenhower**'s international policies in the **Cold War** and the fears at home associated with an alleged **missile gap** between the superpowers, a gap that had put the United States at a disadvantage in the international balance of power. Once elected, he spoke eloquently of his policy to win support of Third World nations and advanced a progressive policy on international development.

Kennedy opposed Communist expansion in Vietnam and sent in U.S. military advisers to support the South Vietnamese. He inherited the Eisenhower plan to support an invasion of Cuba and the overthrow of Fidel Castro (1927–), but did not fully support the **Central Intelligence Agency (CIA)** plan; the result was the **Bay of Pigs** disaster in April 1961. His relations with **Nikita Khrushchev** deteriorated, and his policy to defend West Germany was met with the construction of the **Berlin Wall** in August 1961, a powerful Cold War symbol of superpower antagonism. But in October 1962 Kennedy gained much international and domestic respect for facing the secret attempts by Russia to establish a missile base in Cuba, and became a hero to his fellow Americans. Some believed he exacerbated international conflict with the Soviets, while others concluded he aimed to reduce hostilities and withdraw military involvement in Southeast Asia. Nevertheless, the **Vietnam War,** which he partly encouraged, grew under his successor, **Lyndon B. Johnson**, after Kennedy's assassination in November 1963.

The assassination was used for almost 10 years by the **KGB** to perpetuate false and misleading explanations of the event, and to put out conspiracy theories that the assassination was a CIA plot, and a bold attempt by U.S. industrial interests to bring down the Kennedy presidency.

KGB. The Soviet Union's Komitet Gosudarstvennoy Bezopasnosti, the Committee of State Security, acted both abroad and within the Soviet Union to secure the nation, whereas, in the United States, the **CIA** is responsible for foreign security while the **Federal Bureau of Investigation (FBI)** attends to domestic security. In March 1954 the **MGB** was separated from the **MVD** and downgraded from a ministry to a committee, Komitet Gosudarstvennoy Besopasnosti, and placed under political control of the Council of Ministers. During the **Cold War**, the KGB operated in five divisions: overseas operations; counterintelligence and secret police work; border guard and KGB military corps; suppression of dissidents; and electronic espionage. The value attaching to each domain varied from time to time during the Cold War; under Mikhail Gorbachev, KGB officers became open to foreign and Soviet journalists who could interview staff for the media; also, the secret police work and suppression of dissidents was reduced; emphasis on industrial espionage rose; in the early 1990s powers were increased in the face of economic espionage to combat Russia's growing nationalism; in 1991 the KGB hard-liners, fearing a CIA plot to penetrate the KGB and the Soviet economy, and government generally, led a coup against Gorbachev that failed. After the coup failed, the KGB's image was much tarnished, its head was replaced, and the organization was purged of coup supporters.

In December 1991 the KGB became merely a part of Russia's government, and like Western secret services was split into international security, under a domestic government ministry, and the KGB, nominally a foreign espionage section. In 1992 the KGB (now concerned only with foreign espionage) was renamed the FIS, and its new head went so far as to suggest the FIS cooperated with the CIA. (The early evolution, structure, and leadership of the KGB are treated in Christopher Andrew and Oleg Gordievsky, *The KGB: Inside Story* [London: Hodder and Stoughton, 1990].) See also **Cheka** for a summary of the evolution.

Khrushchev, Nikita Sergeyevich (1894–1971). Khrushchev was born in the Ukraine, and during the 1930s was one of **Josef Stalin**'s supporters. In **World War II** he was First Secretary of the Ukrainian Communist Party, and in 1949 came back to Moscow to join Stalin's inner circle, which included **Nikolai Bulganin**, **Georgi Malenkov,** and Lavrenti Beria. After Stalin's death in 1953, Khrushchev had become Soviet leader by February 1955. He denounced Stalin in a secret speech in February 1956, at the Twentieth Congress of the Soviet Communist Party. With a colorful personal diplomacy, a conciliatory manner, and special foreign aid projects, he forged new Soviet foreign relations, especially with Cuba, Egypt, Indonesia, and India. At home he expanded the agrarian economy of the Soviet Union and directed funds away from industry and the military to housing and consumer goods, showing Russians they could perhaps have a living standard approaching that of the West. He weathered an attempted coup by the Politburo in 1957, and responded by getting closer control of the military and earning kudos from the *Sputnik* success. He appointed himself Premier, and began an unsuccessful scheme to advance agricultural and industrial development. He attempted to secure his weakening power base by taking a warlike approach to international relations; in 1960 he bullied President **Dwight Eisenhower** over the **U-2 spy flights;** had the **Berlin Wall** erected in 1961; and took the world in 1962 to the edge of existence with the **Cuban missile crisis**. At home he lost support after agricultural failures, giving too little support to the military, allowing high rises in the cost of living, and advocating a new plan for electing candidates to Communist Party positions. His relations with China became antagonistic, and some believed he was preparing to split from the Chinese

Communist policies. He was forced to retire in October 1964, and was replaced by **Leonid Brezhnev** and Alexei Kosygin. See also **Kennedy, John F.**

Komsomol. Membership and training in Komosol, the Young Communist League,was required before a young person could aspire to membership in the Communist Party in Soviet Russia.

Korean War (1950–1953). On June 25, 1950, war broke out between North and South Korea; the South Koreans were supported by the UN forces and the United States. The UN forces, under the command of General Douglas MacArthur (1880–1964), pushed the North Korean forces to the border with China. China entered the war on the North Korean side and pushed the UN forces back toward Seoul, the capital of South Korea. Eventually the fighting became deadlocked, and an armistice was called, with each side where it was at about the beginning of hostilities. The final battle line was accepted as the boundary between North and South Korea.

Kremlin. The Kremlin, a citadel in Moscow, is the center of administration of the Russian government and was once synonymous with the Soviet Communist government. It covers 28 hectares and includes palaces, monuments, and churches, which are surrounded by a wall 2,235 meters (7,333 feet) long. Its construction began in 1156 as a wooden fort. Later it became the residence of the grand dukes of Moscow, and the palace for the coronation of Russian emperors and empresses.

LAKAM. A Hebrew acronym for Science Liaison Bureau, a small and efficient division of the Israeli intelligence services. Established in the 1950s, LAKAM guarded the secrets of the Israeli nuclear capability. In time its activities involved the theft of advanced nuclear technology by espionage. The organization appointed the science attachés to the Israeli embassy in Washington.

Legend. A spy's fictional identity and a complete cover story developed for operatives.

Los Alamos. Los Alamos, a town in northern New Mexico, on the top of a broad mesa riven by canyons, near the Rio Grande. On the Pajarito Plateau, 7,200 feet above sea level, was the Los Alamos Ranch School, originally a preparatory school for boys from wealthy families, with cabins, barns, and an icehouse. It was chosen for the secret development of the U.S. **atom bomb**. Late in 1942 J. Robert Oppenheimer commandeered the site, and the laboratory was operational by March 1943. The name of the laboratory and its location were secrets because of the risk of Nazi sabotage. The U.S. Army's engineers knew the 54,000-acre site as Project Y, ZIA Project, and Area L. Others called it "the Hill." In internal documents only the name Los Alamos Laboratory was used. After the atom bomb had been detonated in July 1945, the laboratory's future was in doubt, so Los Alamos University was established, with a faculty of scientists that had made the bomb. It closed its doors in January 1946. Many of the Los Alamos alumni went to the University of Chicago by October 1946, to the new Institute for Nuclear Studies (later renamed for **Edward Teller** [1908–2003], who had been the assistant director of the Los Alamos Laboratory, and would later be known as the "father of the **hydrogen bomb**"). See also **Atom Spies/ Nuclear Spies.**

Loyalty–Security Board Investigations in the United States. In March 1947, President **Harry Truman** established loyalty–security boards. Every government agency in the United States had to convene a board to investigate charges of disloyalty and decide on their veracity. The accused were allowed to attend the hearing and respond to charges against them; they were not told the accuser's name; they were not permitted to question their accuser or others. If dismissed from government service, the accused could appeal, first to their agency chief, and next to the review board head. Loose standards were used of what was meant by treason, sabotage, or affiliation with a Fascist or Communist group. Disloyalty—

the grounds for dismissal—was to be based on reasonable grounds. Government employment was not a right, but a privilege; the proof of innocence was on the accused; any accuser had merely to make a charge, and an investigation would begin. Consequently, on the basis of civil liberty violations, many humanitarian anti-Communists were concerned to protect government employees from loyalty–security boards and their abuse.

LSD (Lysergic acid diethylamide). LSD is a hallucinogenic drug with unpredictable effects; it is illegal in most countries. It was once thought to have a military value, for it could distort the enemy's orientation in battle, and perhaps achieve a great advantage without having to kill enemy troops. American troops were used as experimental subjects, and the results were far from acceptable.

Lucy Ring. The Lucy Ring or **Ring of Three** was a Soviet operation in Switzerland during **World War II** that provided the Russians with operational information from military sources. It was called "Lucy" after the **code name** of its main informant, Karel Sedlacek, a Czechoslovakian military intelligence officer working in Switzerland as a journalist under cover as Thomas Selzinger.

Macmillan, Harold (1894–1986). Great Britain's Conservative Prime Minister from January 1957 until he resigned in October 1963. He worked closely with Presidents **Dwight Eisenhower** and **John Kennedy** to strengthen Anglo–American relations as Britain's colonial interests declined. During the period he was Prime Minister, a body identified as that of "Buster" Crabb was found; a British businessman jailed in Egypt for espionage was released; Anthony Wraight, a British **defector** who redefected, was caught and jailed, as were George Blake, John Vassall, and the Portland spy ring headed by Gordon Lonsdale (Konon Molody); Greville Wynne was caught and tried in Moscow; Kim Philby escaped in January 1963; and the Profumo Affair came to a head in the summer of 1963 with the resignation of **John Profumo** and the trial of Stephen Ward. In disarray after the Denning Report condemned his government over the Profumo Affair, Macmillan retired, and **Alec Douglas-Home** took his place.

Main adversary (*glavny protivnik*). Soviet secret services' term for the United States.

Malenkov, Georgi (1902–1988). Malenkov was a Soviet political leader, and a personal secretary to **Josef Stalin** during the purges in the mid-1930s. After Stalin's death he was briefly the Premier of the **U.S.S.R.**, then ceded power to **Nikita Khrushchev.** He supported the policy of peaceful coexistence with capitalism, felt war was futile, and became unpopular for his past relations with Stalin. He was demoted from the Politburo in 1957 after failing to remove Khrushchev, and in 1964 was expelled from the Communist Party and exiled.

Manhattan Project (1942–1947). The project aimed to provide the U.S. military with an **atom bomb** to bring **World War II** to a quick end. The project was named after the Manhattan Engineer District in New York and was started in June 1942 at the U.S. War Department. Most of the work on the project was done at **Los Alamos**, New Mexico; Oak Ridge, Tennessee; Hanford, Washington; the University of California at Berkeley; and the University of Chicago. In Project Y Division at Los Alamos, the weapon was designed by J. Robert Oppenheimer (1904–1967); the first experimental bomb was detonated near Alamogordo, New Mexico, on July 16, 1946. Control of nuclear and atomic energy and its military applications was taken from the War Department on January 1, 1947, and put in the hands of the U.S. **Atomic Energy Commission** (AEC). See also **Atom Spies/ Nuclear Spies**.

Mao Zedong (1893–1976). Sometimes known as Mao Tse-tung, Mao was a Chinese statesman. In 1921 he helped establish the Chinese Communist Party; in 1934–1935 he led Chinese Communists on a march of 6,000 miles, using guerrilla methods to attack the

Nationalists under **Chiang Kai-shek**. He won peasant support and defeated his opponents, and China became a Communist nation in October 1949.

Marshall Plan (1947–1952). The plan aimed to reconstruct Europe after the economic devastation of **World War II**. In March 1947, following a particularly severe European winter, an acute fuel and food shortage, and a financial crisis for the **International Monetary Fund** and the World Bank, Dean Acheson (1893–1971) suggested to President **Harry Truman** (1884–1972) that his policy to aid Greece and Turkey might be extended to other nations needing financial, technical, and military aid. Their committee, augmented by George C. Marshall (1880–1959), George Kennan (1904–), and William Clayton (1880–1986), decided that in order to avoid political extremism that might threaten U.S. security, and to aim for political and economic stability in the world, a plan was needed to give aid to all European nations, including Russia. Acheson aired the idea—with supporting arguments—as common sense, not charity, in May 1947; in June, Marshall briefly reiterated the main advantages of such a scheme, and it then became known as the Marshall Plan. The plan aimed to alleviate the pain, hunger, and poverty in Europe. The British and French press responded favorably.

The Soviets objected to Germany's being included, for fear it would become a powerful industrial nation again; wanted to know how much the United States would give; and insisted that each nation should be allowed to spend the aid in any way it chose without others, especially the United States, interfering. Because political strings were attached to the provision of funds, the Soviets did not want to accept the policy or the money of U.S. "imperialists"; Czechoslovakia and Poland accepted the plan until otherwise directed by the Soviets, who saw it as nothing but an extension of the Truman Doctrine. Funds were made available in 1947, and continued until 1952. The plan was a success, but widened the rift between the United States and the **U.S.S.R.**, which led to the formation of a distinct Eastern European economic domain and the Committee for Mutual Economic Assistance (COMECON), and to the **Berlin Blockade and Airlift** (1947–1948).

For its covert operations, the **Central Intelligence Agency (CIA)** sought funding by way of the Marshall Plan. For each U.S. dollar in aid received, the recipient country had to contribute an equal amount in local currency, 95 percent of which would be used in Marshall Plan programs and 5 percent, known as "counterpart funds," by the U.S. government through the Economic Cooperation Administration (ECA). The ECA was under the direction of the U.S. Secretary of State, and used the "counterpart funds" to finance administration and other miscellaneous costs. The definition of these costs was a gray area, and when the head of the **Office of Policy Coordination** (OPC), Frank Wisner, sought funds for his covert operations from Richard Bissell, Jr., head of ECA, he was looking at the "counterpart funds." Funds were made available to Wisner in the belief that W. Averell Harriman, Secretary of Commerce, had agreed to using the funds for this purpose. Later, the OPC operations would become part of the CIA activities to battle and contain the spread of communism in Europe.

MBE. In the U.K., the MBE is an award for service to the nation; it stands for Member of the Order of the British Empire.

McCarthyism. The second **Red Scare** in the United States was named after the junior Republican senator from Wisconsin, Joseph McCarthy (1908–1957). He spoke in February 1950 of many Communists in high places in the U.S. government agencies. He was unable to substantiate his allegations, but his inflammatory speeches had a deep and fearful impact on the American public. The fear was of Communist control over government in America, and it began when U.S. leaders were enjoined to consider George Kennan's "long telegram" (1946), Churchill's "**Iron Curtain**" speech (1946), Walter Lippmann's identification of a "**Cold War**" (1946–1947), the revelations by Elizabeth Bentley (1908–1963) and others in the late 1940s that Communist spies had helped provide Russia with information to detonate an **atom bomb** (1949), the **Korean War** (1950–1953), and the trial and execution of Ethel and Julius Rosenberg (1951—1953). Against this fear-ridden background, between 1950 and 1953 McCarthy became one of the most powerful shapers of U.S. foreign policy and furthered widespread anxieties about communism and its aim to dominate the world. He used his chairmanship of a Senate subcommittee to find and root out Communists from all government departments and prominent positions in the media. His bullying tactics were censured in 1954, and the irrational fear surrounding them dissipated. Nevertheless, many people could not regain their lost their careers and were condemned to suffer.

Menzies, Sir Robert Gordon (1894–1978). An Australian conservative politician and leader of the Liberal Party in Australia from 1944 to 1966. He was Australia's longest-serving Prime Minister—1944–1946 and 1949–1966—and held fast to a strong commitment to Great Britain and a close alliance with the United States. His long time in power was helped by a split in the **Australian Labor Party** over its attitude to communism during the **Cold War**. His secure leadership was assisted by the inquiry into the espionage and defection of Vladimir Petrov and his wife in 1954.

Menzies, Sir Stewart (1890–1968). Known by his subordinates as "C," and by his friends and equals as "Stewart," Menzies was chief of Great Britain's **SIS** (1939–1952), roughly equivalent to the American **Central Intelligence Agency (CIA).**

MfS. The East German Ministry of State Security, Ministerium für Staatssicherheit is known as **STASI,** the German Democratic Republic's internal security force.

MGB. Ministersvo Gosudarstvennoi Bezopastnosti was the Russian Ministry of State Security, 1946–1954.

MI5. Founded in 1909, MI5 was a paramilitary organization that aimed to defend the British Empire against subversion. In 1916 its name was changed to the Directorate of Military Intelligence, and its head was Vernon Kell. Into the **Cold War,** Britain's Joint Intelligence Organization (JIO) coordinated the efforts of Britain's various intelligence agencies and was responsible to the British cabinet. It provided intelligence assessments from reports and cables from military intelligence, counterintelligence (MI5), the **Secret Intelligence Service (MI6),** the British Foreign Office, and Government Communication Headquarters (**GCHQ**), as well as the intelligence from the **CIA, ASIO**, Canada, and New Zealand. The JIO is run by the Joint Intelligence Committee (JIC) and comprises the director of MI6, the director general of MI5, the director of GCHQ at Cheltenham, the Director of Intelligence in the Ministry of Defense, the Deputy Chief of Staff at the Ministry of Defense, the Coordinator of Intelligence and Security, Foreign Office officials, and intelligence representatives from the United States, Canada, Australia, and New Zealand.

MI6. The alternative name for the **SIS**, the Secret Intelligence Service in the United Kingdom. MI6 was formed in 1946 with the legacy of the Special Operations Executive (**SOE**). MI6 is a secret organization that concerns itself with military intelligence and is a cover name for what was originally the Secret Service Bureau, an organization that was taken into the British War Office (1909). At the end of 1915 the organization was renamed MI(1)C, and two years later was placed under the control of the Foreign Office. In 1919 the British cabinet allocated to the Secret Intelligence Service (SIS), yet another new name for the Secret Service Bureau, tasks associated with all intelligence matters outside Britain; to **MI5** it allocated the responsibility for counterespionage within the United Kingdom and Britain's overseas regions and interests. MI6 became better known as the Secret Intelligence Service (SIS) than as Military Intelligence, Section 6; it was referred to informally by those who were close to it or members of it as the Friends or the Firm. Members of the intelligence community outside MI6, especially those in MI5, referred to MI6 as the "people across the park." At the beginning of the **Cold War,** MI6 had Major General **Sir Stewart Menzies** as its head.

At that time MI6 had several units, each with a different task: R1 collected political intelligence and made it available to the Foreign Office; R2 was concerned with air information and served the interests of the Air Ministry; R3 acquired naval intelligence and provided it for the Admiralty; R5 dealt with counterespionage information and other matters dealing with subversion and communism—it had no one to serve but itself and MI5, and the foreign services of Britain's allies; R6 collected economic information and sent it to the Board of Trade, the Bank of England, and the Treasury; R7 was concerned with scientific information and was known as Tube Alloys Liaison, which worked on nuclear research; and R8 dealt with **GCHQ** at Cheltenham. Between MI6 and MI5 there was an unfriendly rivalry. Each thought it was superior to the other. Hostility arose over Kim Philby, who was in MI6. Members of MI5 thought that members of MI6 did not treat Philby severely enough, while members of MI6 loathed the acrimonious pursuit of Philby, whom they believed to be decent and trustworthy until the early 1960s. With the defection of Donald Maclean and Guy Burgess, all the British secret services were suspect in Washington, and tensions between the two groups extended and seriously affected MI6 morale.

Another conflict involving MI6 arose in its relations with the U.K. military leadership after **World War II**. Early in 1949 the secret Permanent Undersecretary's Department was established by Ernest Bevin (1881–1951). It was a secret superdepartment of the U.K. Foreign Office, and was given responsibility for intelligence and special operations; its name was often used to cover for the SIS. It was formed to prevent the British military leadership from running clandestine operations.

In Britain an important committee was established in the U.K. Foreign Office that had a bearing on MI6 activities to develop strategies to deal with Cold War relations with Russia, called the **Russia Committee**. It supervised the reestablishment of Great Britain's covert operations against the perceived threats from the **U.S.S.R.** It arose from the advice of the U.K. equivalent of George Kennan in the United States, Frank Roberts, an influential British diplomat in Moscow. The committee was under the control of diplomats, not the British military or the British cabinet. It was no longer British policy to work with the Soviets in 1946; at the first meeting of the Russia Committee, in April 1946, the members discussed how the Soviets, like Nazi leaders, were attacking Great Britain's policies that centered on social democracy.

Missile Gap. In 1957, the Gaither Report implied that the Soviets were superior to the United States in intercontinental ballistic missiles (ICBMs). This meant the Soviets could strike first and with greater effect, should the **Cold War** erupt in massive violence. In fear, U.S. policy makers wanted the missile gap closed. President **Dwight Eisenhower** (1890–1969) advanced the development of the Polaris missile, which would be fired from a submarine, and the Minuteman, to be fired from a hidden underground bunker. By 1961 satellite reconnaissance of the **U.S.S.R.** showed that it was the United States that had the advantage in the missile gap.

Mole. An **agent** who has penetrated a hostile intelligence service, has gained its trust, and works to keep his preferred service informed about the service he is betraying. In the 1930s the term referred to a Communist who worked underground, as moles do, for the Soviet cause, and especially to those Communists who publicly renounced membership in the Communist Party so as to appear to be non-Communists and become trusted by those who were being betrayed. In modern use the term "mole" applies to anyone who secretly penetrates an organization, gains its members' trust, and either steals its classified information and/or undermines it clandestinely. John Le Carré's novels brought the term into popular use. Some experienced intelligence officers claim the term was never used professionally in British and American operations; others disagree, and point to Kim Philby (1912–1988) as the prime example. An early use of the term in espionage appears in a note by the English philosopher, statesman, and scientific thinker Francis Bacon (1561–1626) in *The Historie of the Raigne of Henry VII* (1602).

Molehunt. The search for **moles** in one's own secret service.

Molotov, Vyacheslav Mikhailovich (1890–1986). Molotov was the Foreign Minister of the **U.S.S.R.**, and with Joachim von Ribbentrop (1893–1946) signed the nonaggression pact between Nazi Germany and the U.S.S.R. a few weeks before the beginning of **World War II**. Their pact is known as the **Ribbentrop–Molotov Pact** and the Molotov–Ribbentrop Pact.

Monroe Doctrine. The political principle that Europe must not intervene in the affairs of nations on the American continents. It arose when John Quincy Adams (1767–1848), U.S. Secretary of State, saw a threat from the Concert of Europe and the Holy alliance, and formulated the principle to resist attempts to reestablish European hegemony in the Americas. The doctrine was stated by President James Monroe (1758–1831) in his State of the Union address on December 2, 1823.

Moscow Center. Usually the term refers to the **KGB** headquarters on Dzerzhinsky Square in Moscow; more generally the term is used to refer to the highest authority in the Soviet secret services. Originally it was the Fifth Section of the **OGPU** Intelligence Division, which ran intelligence-gathering and counterintelligence of the Foreign Division. It was once one of the most powerful institutions in the U.S.S.R. It lay between Lubyanka and Srietenka, a spacious area with a notorious prison at its center, in the heart of Moscow. To Moscow Center were sent all data on an individual who was being selected, evaluated, developed, and recruited into the Soviet service. At one stage, for purposes of blackmail, Moscow Center held probably the most complete list of homosexuals in the British establishment.

Mossad. The Mossad is Israel's security service. In March 1951 Israel's Prime Minister established the Mossad ha'Merkazi Le Teum, the Central Institute for Coordination. The organization was under the Prime Minister's office, and given espionage tasks only; it could be involved in covert operations with the approval of the military. In September 1952, under its new head, Isser Harel, Mossad funding was greatly increased. The organization was renamed the Mossad Letafkidim Meouychadim, Cental Institute for Intelligence and Security. It was renamed again in 1963, Ha-Mossad le Modiin ule-Tafkidim Meyuhadim, Institute for Intelligence and Special Tasks. Its reputation for spying and secret operations worldwide is formidable.

Motivation to Be an Intelligence Officer. Stella Rimington, former head of **MI5**, suggests that to work in intelligence requires one to complete operations that are sometimes life-threatening; staff members work in small groups so their work can be supervised and secure. Money is not the main reason for working in intelligence: top executive pay, bonuses, and stock options are not available, as in industry; instead, people are intrinsically interested in their tasks and find them exciting, because they are painstaking or fast-moving or important to complete. Among the capable intelligence staff characteristics she emphasizes a strong sense of loyalty to the organization, colleagues, and the nation.

All intelligence officers deal with material that, if leaked, could have consequences for the national security. For this reason security checks are carried out regularly after the first checks at the time of recruitment and appointment. Such checks arouse suspicion within the organization. This suspicion has to be militated against, and loyalty and trust enhanced, so that the small groups, so frequently used in intelligence operations, can work together effectively. In communicating information to keep people properly informed on relevant operations, to maintain their support for change in management practices during times of organizational upheaval, and to keep them appreciative of the **need-to-know** principle, great care is need in interpersonal dealings with individuals. Why? Poorly managed suspicion can easily fuel resentment in an organization where money cannot be used to overwhelm the feeling among staff that they are insufficiently valued; some individuals may easily turn to spying for the enemy, or publishing their memoirs, to compensate for their resentment.

MVD. Soviet Ministry of Internal Affairs.

NASA. In 1958, President **Dwight Eisenhower** (1890–1969) established the National Aeronautics and Space Administration.

National Intelligence Estimates (NIE). National Intelligence Estimates are the predictive assessments, based on data from all agencies and all sources, and made by the **Central Intelligence Agency (CIA)** about important international issues.

National Security Act (1947). The U.S. National Security Act established the **Central Intelligence Agency (CIA),** its legality, and the restrictions on its activities. The CIA's main task was to correlate and evaluate all intelligence collected from other government departments, such as the military.

The National Security Council (NSC) convened for the first time in December 1947; under the National Security Act, it has the authority to establish national policy and commit federal funds without the knowledge of the U.S. Congress. It also has the authority to ensure its directives are not made public; some directives have been criticized as violations of the U.S. Constitution because they enable the executive branch of the U.S. government to make laws of its own. Examples of NSC directives are President **Harry Truman**'s order to use covert operations to cause unrest in Communist-dominated nations in Eastern Europe; President **John Kennedy**'s decision to invade Cuba in April 1961; President **Lyndon Johnson**'s decision to support military incursions into Laos during the **Vietnam War**; the invasion of Grenada; and the allocation of $19 million to train Contras in Central America. President **Ronald Reagan** signed over 300 directives; only about 50 were made public before 1995.

The National Security Agency was established in secrecy in November 1952, and was to be responsible for all intelligence activities of the U.S. government. It intercepts foreign communications and safeguards U.S. transmissions. It is located in Fort Meade, Maryland, and has a major center at Menwith Hill in England. In 1962 its existence was acknowledged; it functions outside normal channels of government accountability; its budget is secret and far larger than that of any other intelligence agency. In the early 1980s it appears there was no U.S. law that limited the NSA's activities, but there were laws to restrict information becoming known about its work. The NSA is free of legal restrictions, and also has the power to eavesdrop far more than any other U.S. agency.

NATO. The North Atlantic Treaty Organization, established in 1950 and dominated by the United States, presented a unified Western force in the face of the political threats to Europe posed by the **U.S.S.R.,** which responded with an alliance dominated by itself, the **Warsaw Pact.**

Need-to-Know Principle. In intelligence organizations, not everyone needs to know or should know everything; it is an effective security check. For instance, in the case of the **MI5** officer Michael Bettany, he did not know that **MI6** had a **double agent** in the **KGB**; however valuable the principle might be, it may lead to a duplication of work and misunderstandings, and can be used by incompetent managers to cover their shortcomings.

Nixon, Richard M. (1913–1994). The U.S. President from January 1969 to August 1974. He came to the public eye in the pursuit of Alger Hiss (1904–1996) when, as a congressman from California, he served on the **House Un-American Activities Committee (HUAC)**; he later served as President **Dwight Eisenhower**'s Vice President and sought the presidency in 1960 but was defeated by **John F. Kennedy.** Nixon won the presidency in 1968, when the Democrats were in great disarray over U.S. failures in Vietnam and in establishing a credible foreign policy. He had the United States withdraw from Vietnam, received much help in this from Henry Kissinger, presided over the policy of détente, established U.S. diplomatic relations with the People's Republic of China, and in 1972 was reelected in a landslide victory (in part because of his plans for having the U.S. troops leave Vietnam in March 1973). Nixon used clandestine means to destabilize and eventually bring down the government of Chile by September 1973, and precipitated a scandal when it became known he attempted to conceal the illegal **Watergate** break-in. He failed to get **Central Intelligence Agency (CIA)** support for his attempts to cover his tracks, and had to resign or face impeachment in 1974. He spent the remainder of his life attempting to shore up his self-defiled public image and overcome his political disgrace. See also **Vietnam War**.

NKGB. The Russian People's Commissariat of State Security (Soviet security service) in 1941 and between 1943 and 1946. It preceded the **MGB**.

NKVD. The Narodnyi Kommissariat Vnutrenniki Del is the People's Commissariat for Internal Affairs. It incorporated Soviet state security in 1922–1923 and 1934–1943. It was the predecessor of the **MVD**, succeeded the **OGPU**, and preceded the **KGB**.

North Atlantic Treaty Organization. See **NATO**

OBE. The Order of the British Empire is a reward for service to the United Kingdom.

Office of Policy Coordination (OPC). The OPC was approved on June 18, 1948, as the covert arm of the **CIA**, and its operations were kept secret so as to be plausibly deniable. The organization was under the direction of Frank Wisner (1900–1965). At first the organization and its functions were known as the Office of Special Projects. Wisner, formally with the **OSS**, had just returned to Washington from Europe, where he had been a deputy to the Assistant Secretary of State for Occupied Areas. He had worked undercover and had been well acquainted with leading foreign and American diplomats and military personnel, as well as senior administrators in the **Truman** White House. The OPC personnel were second in command in a U.S. embassy, and they aimed to be friendly with government heads and to cultivate informal relations with senior government officials. They went around rather than through diplomatic channels because they deemed diplomacy to be inefficient. The original OPC funds were obscure; its staff was not identifiable, and they reported to Wisner himself. In fact, their funds came in part from the **Marshall Plan**'s Economic Cooperation Administration, headed by Richard Bissell, Jr. (1909–1994). The U.S. State Department and Defense Department offered the OPC guidance on its policies and goals. These policies were economic, political, and psychological. Wisner often preferred psychological tactics, and believed pro-Western propaganda could manage and defeat pro-Communist propaganda. Others in the Central Intelligence Agency (CIA) preferred economic policies because they were rational, and they considered the psychological techniques of the OPC to be mere gimmickry. The Office of Policy Coordination had a system of projects in the media (especially radio), labor unions, and refugee groups. The projects were designed by men in the field, who also evaluated their results. Consequently this policy led to OPC field workers competing for their favorite projects.

Office of Strategic Services (OSS). The OSS was a U.S. organization in **World War II** formed for sabotage and intelligence purposes. In the summer of 1941 President Franklin Roosevelt (1882–1945) issued an executive decree that accepted the pressing argument of **William J. Donovan** (1883–1959) that the eight U.S. government intelligence agencies at that time be put under one organization with Donovan as its coordinator of information. In this organization he was joined by Allen W. Dulles (1893–1969). In April 1942 this organization was renamed Office of Strategic Services (OSS), and Switzerland, neutral during World War II, was chosen as the major outpost for OSS penetration of Hitler's

Germany. In 1945 the OSS was disbanded. By early 1948 the functions of the OSS were reconstructed and replaced on the recommendation of a committee headed by Allen Dulles, who became the head of the new **Central Intelligence Agency (CIA)** until 1963.

Official Secrets Act. Most nations have a law that is designed to prevent government employees from passing secret and classified information to a foreign power. Employees in the intelligence agencies sign an agreement not to disclose information that they know to be secret. This agreement is believed to be in the national interest. Many of these acts are constantly under review.

In 1989, the British Parliament passed the Official Secrets Act to replace section 2 of an act of 1911 that had been too wide-ranging. For example, under the 1911 act it would have been an offense to make public the number of cups of tea the Prime Minister had consumed! The 1989 act makes the disclosure of confidential material from government sources by employees subject to disciplinary procedures; also, it is an offense for a former member of the security and intelligence services, or those working closely with them, to make public information about their work. There is no public-interest defense, and disclosure of information already in the public domain is still a crime. Newspaper writers who repeat disclosures can be prosecuted.

The United States does not have an Official Secrets Act; the law that comes closest to one is an act that was signed into law by President Franklin Roosevelt in June 1933, the Act for the Preservation of Government Records (H.R. 4220, Public Law 37). It states that a government employee shall not give a foreign government or diplomatic mission a code or coded document. At the time the penalty was U.S.$10,000 or a jail term of 10 years, maximum. During the **Cold War** this law was slightly modified.

OGPU. The Unified State Political Directorate was the Soviet security service from 1923 to 1944.

One-Time Pad (OTP). The one-time pad is a pad of pages on which there are lists of random numbers, usually five in a group. They are used to decipher messages with the help of a grid of numbers used the way the margins are used on a road map. Only one other copy of the pad exists—the **agent**'s or the **case officer**'s. When the case officer sends a coded message, the agent uses his copy of the appropriate page to decipher the message. Once it has been used, the page is destroyed. Thus, the code cannot be broken unless, in error, the page is not destroyed and is used more than once. It was this error that led to the decoding of the VENONA material.

OPC. See **Office of Policy Coordination**

Order of Battle. The formal, hierarchical structure of an organization—usually military—and the names of the people assigned to each position in that structure; sometimes it includes the tasks allocated to the positions.

Order of the Red Banner. The oldest Soviet award presented to those who served the nation with bravery, self-sacrifice, and courage by defending it; accomplishing special assignments; and showing support for the state security of the Soviet Union.

OSS. See **Office of Strategic Services**

Password Phrase. A means of secretly identifying oneself to another; for example, "Didn't I meet you at Vick's restaurant on Connecticut Avenue?"

Pentagon. The Pentagon is the headquarters of the U.S. Department of Defense near Washington, DC. It was built in 1941–1943 in the shape of five concentric pentagons covering 34 acres (13.8 hectares), and is one of the largest buildings in the world.

Perestroika. See **Glasnost**

PLO. Palestine Liberation Organization.

Plumber. A **CIA** operative who, dressed as a tradesman on apparently legitimate business, enters a building, often legally, to install a surveillance device, such as a **teardrop** (a tiny microphone to transmit what is said in the room to a receiver far away).

Polygraph Test. A test that indicates physiological changes (pulse and breathing rates, blood pressure, galvanic skin response) in the body while an individual is answering questions. It is known as a lie detector test and was originally devised in 1892 by James Mackenzie. The test is applied in the belief that the physiological changes are out of a person's conscious control, and that they are indications of anxiety, tension, and stress associated, for that individual, with the immediate conditions under which the test is being conducted. Thus, when being given a test, if a person tells a lie, he is expected to feel anxious or guilty, and changes in his physiological state will give him away. Because this assumption is not supported in every instance for the same person, or for similar instances with different people, the test is notoriously unreliable. For this reason it is only one of several checks that are made regularly on employees of secret services.

For some testees, the polygraph seems to employ the "Pinocchio effect," a mythical bodily response to telling a lie. Some testers use this effect by frightening the testee into thinking that the polygraph will correctly detect a lie, when all the machine can do is assess bodily changes in blood pressure, heartbeat, breathing rate, and sweating.

Positive Vetting. Before and during the **Cold War** the selection of **recruits** to the secret services and checking on them were based on personal recommendations. This proved to be inadequate. One incompetent or untrustworthy spy could recommend another. In the early 1950s positive vetting was introduced; it required a full investigation of the individual: his background, his private life, and his political leanings. His employers and teachers were interviewed, and at least two character witnesses are called upon. They were expected to complete a form about the individual, and state weaknesses and habits that might make the person a security risk. This form of selection became practice in Great Britain after the spy scandals involving Klaus Fuchs, and the defections of Guy Burgess and Donald Maclean. At the time the new system met resistance on the grounds that it was too much like the activities of Joseph McCarthy. As originally applied, positive vetting rarely showed up unsuitable candidates, never pointed out a spy, and, because it was introduced too late, did little to unmask individuals in the 1960s who had already been cleared.

Potsdam Conference (July 1945). Two months after the end of **World War II**, President **Harry Truman**, Winston Churchill, and **Josef Stalin** met in Potsdam, Germany, to decide on how the policies outlined at the **Yalta Conference** would be implemented. Churchill was replaced by **Clement Attlee** (1883–1967), who won the British election in late July. Arrangements were made in friendly fashion on the partition of Germany, ridding the German government of Nazis, reparations, and the territorial boundaries of Poland. Truman mentioned indirectly to Stalin that the United States had a new, powerful weapon; Stalin knew he meant the **atom bomb** because of the Soviet spies' work at **Los Alamos**. Stalin said he hoped it would be used wisely, but secretly suspected Truman was raising the stakes for a conflict between the superpowers. The friendly feeling at the conference soon evaporated; conflict arose over Poland and the division of Germany.

Prague Spring. Liberal reforms introduced by Alexander Dubçek in Czechoslovakia during the spring of 1968. In August the Soviet-led **Warsaw Pact** forces invaded Czechoslovakia, and in 1969 the repressive power of the **U.S.S.R.** was established in Czechoslovakia.

Profumo, John Dennis (1915–). A British conservative politician, educated at Harrow and Oxford, Profumo held several government posts before 1960, when he became the Secretary for War. He resigned when his intimate relations with Christine Keeler (1942–), a sex worker who was also having relations with a Russian naval attaché, became undeniable. Thereafter, he spent his life working for charity, and in 1975 he was awarded a **CBE**. He was married to the beautiful English actress Valerie Hobson. She supported him throughout his disgrace in 1963, and followed his work with her charities for the mentally disabled and lepers. In 1989 a film, *Scandal*, made much use of the Profumo Affair in its story line.

PRC. People's Republic of China.

PSB. The Psychological Strategy Board was much favored by George Kennan, who persuaded President **Harry Truman** to sign a secret directive to establish the board: its aim was to interpose its views and doctrines secretly into whatever might endanger the nation, without appearing totalitarian.

Psychological Strategy Board. See **PSB**

RCMP Force (Royal Canadian Mounted Police Force). Based on the structure of the Royal Irish Constabulary, the North West Mounted Police, an armed paramilitary force in Canada's newly acquired western territory, was formed in 1873. In 1904 the word "Royal" was added to the name in recognition of its members' distinguished service for the British Empire in the Boer Wars (1880–1881 and 1899–1902). It brought law and order primarily to western provinces of Canada—Manitoba, Saskatchewan, and Alberta—which, following **World War I** (1914–1918), were attracting immigrants from Europe.

Reagan, Ronald W. (1911–2004). Former Hollywood film star, Republican, and governor of California who defeated **Jimmy Carter** in the U.S. presidential election in November 1980, and served for two terms. A vigorous anti-Communist, Reagan lowered federal taxes; stimulated the U.S. economy; and declared the Soviet Union to be an "evil empire," which provoked **Yuri Andropov** to propose Operation RYAN in March 1981; and blamed the Soviets for deliberately shooting down the KAL 007 flight. He took a strong, aggressive position against the **U.S.S.R.** and supported the reestablishment of the powers of the **Central Intelligence Agency** (**CIA**), which was well funded for many years. His campaign organizer, William Casey (1913–1987), headed the CIA from 1981 to 1987. The CIA went into Afghanistan and provided equipment and funds for anti-Communist fighters. In response to Reagan's warlike attitude to the Soviets, and his refusal to allow any nearby governments (such as those in Cuba, Nicaragua, and Grenada) to threaten the United States with their Communist policies, the **KGB** aimed to discredit Reagan when he sought reelection in November 1984. The scheme failed. During Reagan's second term, especially in 1985, many U.S. citizens were found to have spied for the Soviets during the **Cold War**. The U.S. Congress refused Reagan the funds to help the Nicaraguan Contras, recruited earlier by the CIA, so Reagan used covert techniques to support them, including the diversion of funds gained from the secret sale of arms to Iran to gain the freedom of U.S. hostages there. When this was exposed in the **Irangate Affair**, Reagan was disgraced a little, but others became the scapegoats (e.g., Oliver North and John Poindexter). Reagan chose **George H. W. Bush**, former head of the CIA, to be his Vice President; he continued, somewhat more cautiously, the bulk of Reagan's policies when he was elected to the U.S. presidency in 1988.

Recruit. A recruit is an American term for an individual, or "asset," who is persuaded to cooperate with American interests, and then come under the control of the **case officer** or handler who recruited him.

Red Menace. The fear that Russian communism will dominate one's national politics. See also **Red Scare.**

Red Scare. In the United States there have been two outstanding Red Scares, periods when the fear of communism was intense. The first followed the success of the Bolsheviks in the Russian Revolution of 1917; the United States, among others, sent troops to aid the White

Army against the Bolsheviks' Red Army in the Russian Civil War (1918–1920), and did not recognize the **U.S.S.R.** until 1933. In the United States, socialist admirers of the Russian Bolsheviks formed two small Communist parties and deserted the Socialist Party. The members were largely foreign-born. After **World War I,** in 1919, an anti-Communist move reduced the group membership by 80 percent. The attack was led by the U.S. Department of Justice and driven by Attorney General Mitchell A. Palmer (1872–1936), who was aiming to become President. As a matter of routine, federal officials arrested American Communists, would not allow them to get help from a lawyer, held them without trial, and ensured those born outside the United States were deported. These "Palmer Raids" were unconstitutional but effective. When the Red Scare ended in 1921, the Communist groups melded into the Communist Party of the United States of America (**CPUSA**). The second Red Scare is also known as **McCarthyism.** See also **Red Menace.**

Reform Club. A London men's club, established in 1836 for liberal-minded members, and almost as popular, so Chapman Pincher suggests, among the British "fifth estate" as its neighboring club, the Travelers'.

Resident. In Russian *rezident, rezidentura,* meant the chief of the **KGB** who was attached to the Soviet embassy in a foreign country.

Ribbentrop-Molotov Pact (1939). Another name for the nonaggression pact signed by Nazi Germany and the **U.S.S.R.** in late August 1939.

Ring of Three. See **Lucy Ring**

Rockefeller Commission (1975). A commission of inquiry, established by President **Gerald Ford** early in 1975, to investigate the charge that the **Central Intelligence Agency (CIA)** might have conducted illegal investigations in the United States. The need for such an inquiry arose after the publication in the *New York Times,* in December 1974, of an article that suggested the CIA had been conducting illegal activities. The Rockefeller Commission concluded its work in May 1975. Nelson Rockefeller (1908–1979), Vice President (1974–1978) under Ford, headed the commission.

Romeo Spies. Men whose task is to seduce women who have access to confidential material, in the hope that through pillow talk the women will reveal secrets.

ROTC. Reserve Officer Training Corps, a U.S. recruitment and training system, often found on U.S. university campuses, for staffing the U.S. military with well-educated officers.

Royal Canadian Mounted Police Force. See **RCMP Force**

Run. In intelligence parlance, "run" means to manage, control, supervise, or otherwise direct and handle the activities of a spy or **agent** in the field.

Russia Committee. A U.K. Foreign Office committee that supervised the reestablishment of Great Britain's covert operations against the perceived threats from the **U.S.S.R.** It arose from the advice of the British equivalent of George Kennan in the United States, Frank Roberts, an influential British diplomat in Moscow. The committee was under the control of diplomats, not the British military or the British cabinet. It was no longer British policy to work with the Soviets in 1946; at the first meeting of the Russia Committee, in April 1946, the members discussed how the Soviets, like Nazi leaders, were attacking Great Britain's policies that centered on social democracy.

Russian Civil War (1918–1920). A conflict between the anti-Communist White Army and the Red Army, led by Leon Trotsky (1879–1940). The Red Army was victorious. It is sometimes referred to as the War of Allied Intervention. Forces opposed to the Bolshevik takeover of Russia in October 1917 clashed with the Red Army hastily raised by Trotsky. In northern Russia, forces from France, Britain, Germany, and the United States landed at Murmansk and occupied Archangel (1918–1920). U.S. and Japanese forces in Siberia supported an anti-Communist, all-Russian government and, helped by Czechoslovakians, got control of the Trans-Siberian Railway. The counterrevolutionary forces failed to cooperate, and the efforts to prevent Russia from becoming a Communist nation collapsed.

Sadat, Anwar (1918–1981). Sadat was an Egyptian politician who succeeded Gamal Abdel Nasser, after his sudden death in September 1970, as president of Egypt. From the beginning he undermined the secure base of **KGB** espionage in Egypt. By the end of 1971, **Moscow Center** believed Sadat was a traitor. His head of intelligence was in contact with the **Central Intelligence Agency (CIA)**. In 1972 Sadat ordered Soviet advisers out of Egypt, and 21,000 left in seven days. Nevertheless, the Soviets continued to give Egypt military and political aid, for fear it would go over to the United States completely. In 1974 a referendum supported Sadat's plans to reform the Egyptian society, economy, and polity. In 1977 he reconciled his nation with the Israelis, and he and the Israeli prime minister shared the Nobel Peace Prize in 1978. Islamic fundamentalists assassinated him.

Safe House. A secret meeting place, often a house or an apartment, owned by the nation's secret services, where **agents** meet and exchange information, as if they were ordinary citizens going about their everyday life. Sometimes the safe house is used as a haven for agents who are being exfiltrated from some perilous location.

SAS. Special Air Service in the United Kingdom, which recruited from regiments throughout the army. It served in Malaysia, Oman, Yemen, the Falkland Islands, and Northern Ireland, and also in the Middle East during the 1991 Gulf War.

SB. Sluzba Bczvieczenstwa, the Polish intelligence service.

SDECE. Service de Documentation Extérieure de le Contre-Espionnage, the precursor to the **DGSE**, the Direction Générale de Securité Extérieure. The French Foreign Intelligence Agency. The name change was made in April 1982.

SDI. The Strategic Defense Initiative, popularly known as "Star Wars," was announced by President **Ronald Reagan** on March 23, 1983, in a television address to the American nation. On March 8, Reagan had declared the Soviet Union to be an "evil empire." The "Star Wars" address, which visualized a ballistic missile shield around the United States, provoked Soviet leaders to suspect more than usual that the United States intended to go to war with the Soviet Union.

SE. An elite **Central Intelligence Agency (CIA)** directorate, highly secret, and responsible for clandestine services in the Soviet Union and **Communist Bloc** countries.

SHAEF. Supreme Headquarters Allied Expeditionary Force on the European continent at the end of **Word War II**.

Shcharansky, Anatoli (1948–). A Russian dissident or refusnik, and loyal Communist, who was arrested in March 1977 for his efforts to bring to the fore human rights issues in the Soviet Union. He was sentenced to 13 years in prison; by the summer of 1985 he had served seven years, and was an international celebrity for his work and suffering. He was exchanged for five East Europeans in February 1986.

Sheep-dipped. An **agent** is sheep-dipped when he is withdrawn from an official public service that is lawful for civilians, such as the army, to serve in a secret agency like the **Central Intelligence Agency (CIA)**. He is given a new identity, and all records of his earlier, legal service are destroyed; they will be denied if they are ever alleged to have existed. The denial is plausible because there are no records to substantiate the allegations. Metaphorically speaking, this is what happens to sheep when they are dipped in a fluid that frees them from vermin or disease. For example, Francis Gary Powers was moved from his regular and legal Air Force service to the CIA to fly U-2 plane; the **U-2 spy flights** were secretly authorized by U.S. President **Dwight Eisenhower** (1890–1969), although publicly they were said to be illegal. The president would deny, as a matter of policy, ever giving permission for such illegal flights, especially if the pilot was caught. Powers was caught and his plane was confiscated, and there was plenty of tangible evidence that he was a CIA agent. In his case the sheep-dipping failed, and the U.S. President had to retract his denial. Also, in May 1958, during a CIA bombing mission in Indonesia, Allan L. Pope's plane was shot down, and the U.S ambassador did as President Eisenhower instructed, alleging Pope was U.S. citizen who worked as a mercenary.

Shin Bet. The Jewish organization (Sherut HaBitachon HaKlali in Hebrew) that spied on and took counterintelligence action against dangerous dissidents in the Jewish community in Israel.

Show Trial. A public and well-reported trial of individuals who have committed crimes against the state. In Russia, in the 1930s and 1940s, show trials were held to convict individuals who were economic traitors and saboteurs; they included Communist officials, army officers, and Bolshevik leaders. In many of the Soviet show trials of the 1930s Andrei Vyshinsky was the Soviet prosecutor. Show trials were used during the **Cold War** for propaganda against the West; for example, the trials of Robert Vogeler, Francis Gary Powers, and Greville Wynne.

Silicon Valley. Between San Jose and Palo Alto in California's Santa Clara County lies Silicon Valley, noted for computing and the manufacture of electronics, and named for the exensive use of silicon in the production of modern electronics.

Sino–Soviet Split (1960–1971). A split between the Soviet Union and the People's Republic of China (PRC) that probably began after **Josef Stalin**'s death, and was clear only when Soviet advisers were told to quit the PRC in July 1960, after the Soviets took away its aid to China following a Communist conference in Bucharest, Romania (June 1960). The PRC did not accept the peaceful coexistence of communism with the West and the overtures made to nationalist leaders following the withdrawal of colonial governments in Africa and Asia. The Chinese Communist leader, **Mao Zedong**, also known as Mao Tse-tung (1873–1976), rejected the anti-Stalinist views advocated by **Nikita Khrushchev**. China declared it was leading the worldwide Communist movement, and the Soviets ceased helping China with its nuclear program. In 1961 Mao supported Albania's withdrawal from the **Warsaw Pact**, and in 1968 he condemned the Soviet invasion of Czechoslovakia. In March 1969, China and the Soviet Union clashed along their border. In the **Central Intelligence Agency (CIA)**, a small group of counterintelligence agents around James J. Angleton (1917–1987) saw the split as a fable, part of a plot to mislead Western intelligence authorities.

SIS (MI6). The Secret Intelligence Service in Great Britain had plans ready in 1948 in case of a war with Russia after **World War II**. The main activities of the SIS in plans for war with Russia would have been to supply tactical, strategic, political, military, scientific, and economic information; to spread rumors and false information, and make black broadcasts; to organize safe houses and bases; to mark targets; to plan and organize escape routes; by air and sea, to send in and get out of enemy-occupied territory stores and personnel; to organize strikes in the enemy's industries, and sabotage industrial machinery and equipment; to stimulate, build, and maintain resistance groups and movements, and cooperate with clandestine and resistance groups; and to organize sudden attacks on, or secret demolition of, special targets. These plans could be in operation after at least three months preparation. See also **MI5; MI6**.

Six-Day War in the Middle East (June 5–10, 1967). On June 5, 1967, under the command of Mordechai Hod (1926–2003), the Israeli air force secretly disabled the Egyptian air force, and then devastated bases in Jordan, Syria, and Iraq; the preemptive strike took half a day, and within six days Israel had conquered the Gaza Strip, East Jerusalem, the Sinai Desert, and the Golan Heights, thereby quadrupling the land under its control.

Sleepers or Sleeper Agents. Agents who are sent into a foreign country, lie low, and become active—sometimes 20 years later—when needed. The practice was used more by the Russians than the British.

SMERSH. From Smert Shpionam, Russian for "death to all spies"; it was part of the Soviet secret services which in March 1946 was taken over by the Third Directorate of the MGB, the counter-espionage assassins.

Smith Act or U.S. Alien Registration Act (1940). This act required registration of aliens and forbade advocating the forcible overthrow of the U.S. government. It was aimed at both individuals and institutions, and specifically forbade undermining the loyalty of the armed forces, assassinations of public officeholders, and all violent public activities. The act intended to outlaw Fascist groups, such as Nazis and Communists. The act was used between the late 1940s and the mid-1950s during the **Red Scare**—the work of Joseph McCarthy and his supporters and colleagues—to rid the United States of alleged Communists, who, by the McCarthyites' definition, advocated the use of violence in the pursuit of their political aims. The act was disabled in June 1957, when the U.S. Supreme Court held, in the case of *Yates v. United States,* that the government must provide a much more precise definition of advocacy in trying Communists under the act. See also **McCarthyism**.

SOE. The Special Operations Executive, the paramilitary service of British intelligence in **World War II,** established in July 1940.

Solidarity. A trade union established in Poland in September 1980; it affirmed the right to strike in November by agreeing that the Communist United Workers' Party had a political monopoly of labor. During 1981 Solidarity sought relaxation of political censorship, independence of its management, and unions established outside heavy industry. At its first national congress, in September 1981, it sought to uphold democratic values, along with national and Christian principles of authority and control. In December the Polish prime minister established martial law and the union was crushed. Solidarity went underground, organized successful strikes in 1988, and negotiated political reforms early in 1989. By June 1989 in national elections Solidarity forced the establishment of a coalition government in which the Communists were in the minority. Its leader's reputation was subject to extensive misrepresentation by the **KGB**.

Spanish Civil War (1936–1939). The civil war began in 1936 when a group of army officers led by General **Francisco Franco** rose against the government; it had the support of the German Nazis and the Italian Fascists. Support for the government came from International Brigades with unofficial British and Soviet support. The militarists won.

Special Actions. KGB term for sabotage and assassination.

Special Branch. In the United Kingdom, the Special Branch is a section of the police force originally founded to deal with Irish Fenian activists in 1883. All the police forces in the United Kingsom have their Special Branch. Their task is to act as the executive branch of **MI5** to prevent or investigate espionage, sabotage, and subversion. Special Branch provides bodyguards for public figures, and performs immigration and naturalization duties at airports and seaports.

Special Operations Executive. See **SOE.**

Special Relationship. During the early stages of the **Cold War** a "special relationship" was developing between the United States and the British Commonwealth. The term was used by Foreign Secretary Ernest Bevin (1881–1951) early in 1946 when he described how Britain and the United States would work together on questions significant to peace in the Middle East. Early in 1945 Bevin had stated the political viewpoint central to this relationship: "The long-term advantage to Britain and the Commonwealth is to have our affairs so interwoven with those of the United States in external and strategic matters that any idea of war between the two countries is utterly impossible, and that in fact, however the matter may be worded, we all stand or fall together." Two important early developments were the establishment in Britain of U.S. air and naval bases, and the integration and co-ordination of military and intelligence operations. In the intelligence field this meant the exchange of sensitive secret information, and special operations like Operation STOP-WATCH/GOLD. Both were fraught with problems and failure, and much hostility arose between British and American members of the respective secret services.

Tension grew in this relationship that led, from time to time, to the belief among American intelligence experts that it was quite wrong to allow the British to have access to certain intelligence; on the other hand, members of the British intelligence community had little respect for their "American cousins," as they called them. In fact, the two countries had different versions of the Cold War from time to time. Nevertheless, the leaders of both countries would frequently repeat publicly that as the loathing for the Russians grew in the United States and Great Britain, those two nations "enjoyed" a "special relationship." In Canada and Australia different views of the "special relationship" waxed and waned. At first the Canadians were alarmed at the growing hostility between the United States and Russia, and considered taking a neutralist position, like Sweden. But once Russia had the nuclear bomb and the ability to send it over the North Pole, Canada found herself on the side of the United States. Australia once urged its citizens to fly the Union Jack and the Red Army flag together in celebrations. Also, the Communist Party of Australia (**CPA**) had grown during **World War II**.

Shortly after World War II, Australia's polices experienced a great upheaval, and, after 1945, extreme dependence in many economic and military matters; both Britain and the United States provided Australia with a strong anti-Soviet policy. In time Australia had a "special relationship" with the United States, which included Australia's secret American intelligence base at Pine Gap and the frequent exchange of intelligence personnel between the secret services of the two countries. In his novels, John le Carré often ridicules and satirizes the "special relationship" and those who tout it.

Sputnik. In October 1957 the Russians successfully launched the first satellite, *Sputnik* (fellow traveler), to investigate space.

Stalin, Josef (1879–1953). The name taken by Iosif Vissarionovich Dzhugashvili, the dictator of the Soviet Union from 1924 to his death in 1953. He was born near Tiflis, Georgia, the son of a shoemaker. He attended a nearby theological seminary but was expelled for spreading Marxist propaganda. In 1896 he joined the Social Democratic Party, and sided with the Bolsheviks after the party split in 1903; he was often exiled to Siberia for political activity (1904–1913), but always managed to escape. He took the name Stalin (Man of Steel) from activities before the Russian Revolution in 1913. A close associate of Lenin, Stalin took part in the 1917 Revolution and became a member of its military council (1920–1923). Following Lenin's death (1924), Stalin established himself as Russia's dictator, and is now held fully responsible for murderous purges in most aspects of Russian life during his rule. Following the Nazi invasion of Russia in 1941, he became commissar for defense and chairman of the Council of People's Commissars, thus taking over supreme direction of military operations. In 1943 he was created marshal of the Soviet Union. Until his death he held personal power over all Russia. Throughout his domination of the Soviet Union and his efforts to spread communism around the world, he promoted and employed espionage to establish *razvedka*, a Russian term for "truthful intelligence." Such intelligence could be obtained only from secret informants, undercover **agents**, and stolen documents. Stalin favored this as the best source of intelligence; his leading **Cold War** spymaster was Lavrenti Pavlovich Beria (1899–1953).

STASI or Stasi. The internal security force of the German Democratic Republic (GDR), titled Ministerium für Staatssicherheit (MfS) or Ministry for State Security. It was established securely in the early 1950s by Markus Wolf (1923–).

Suez Crisis. In July 1956, in response to the termination of discussions with Britain and the United States over aid for Egypt, Egypt's leader Gamal Abel Nasser nationalized the Suez Canal. This provoked Operation MUSKETEER, in which the Israeli, French, and British forces invaded the Suez Canal Zone. The operation was kept secret from U.S. President **Dwight Eisenhower**. The Soviet leader, **Nikita Khrushchev,** supported Nasser. British Prime Minister **Anthony Eden** was forced to accept a cease-fire in November, and did not consult the French. The United Nations supervised the end of the invasion. As a result Nasser's reputation was enhanced, the British prime minister resigned in January 1957, and the Soviets became an anti-imperialist friend of the Arab nations. After the Suez Crisis, the canal was closed for eight years (1967–1975).

Sukarno, Achmed (1901–1970). Sukarno was an Indonesian nationalist and political leader who opposed the attempt by the Dutch to reestablish its control over the Dutch East Indies after **World War II.** Sukarno favored a nonalignment policy in international relations, and the **Eisenhower** administration suspected he was a Communist supporter. In 1958, expecting it could get rid of Sukarno, the **Central Intelligence Agency (CIA)** secretly supported a military coup in Indonesia. The revolt failed. He was overthrown in 1966 by a military rebellion.

SVR (Sluzhba Vneshnei Razvedki). The SVR is the Russian Federation Foreign Intelligence Service, established after the fall of the Soviet Union.

Swiss Bank Account. It was possible until 1985 to have a secret bank account in Switzerland, where under clause 47(b) of the Swiss Banking Act, a bank employee who revealed confidential information could be fined 20,000 Swiss francs and put in jail for six months. Such bank accounts were used widely in the espionage community.

Talent spotting. Passing on to a higher authority the name of a capable individual who could be approached for membership in the intelligence community.

TASS. Acronym for the Telegrafnoya Agentstvo Sovyetkovo Soyuza, the official news agency of the former Soviet Union; it was established in 1925 in Leningrad (St. Petersburg), and was renamed ITAR/TASS in 1992.

Teardrops. Concealed microphones the size of the tip of a ballpoint pen, used to bug a source of information.

Tehran Conference (1943). A conference in November–December 1943 in Tehran, Iran, where Winston Churchill (1874–1965), Franklin Roosevelt (1882–1945), and **Josef Stalin** (1879–1953) met to plan the defeat of Nazi Germany and the settlement of Europe after hostilities ended. Stalin wanted, and got, the Baltic, Polish, and Romanian territories that he had previously overrun; the British and Americans agreed to invade the European continent; and the Soviets agreed to declare war on Japan three months after the Nazi government of Germany had been defeated. The Soviets agreed to the U.S. plans to extend its international controls in Europe, and mistakenly assumed that in return there would be no objection to the Soviets taking over more of Eastern Europe. Later, President **Harry**

Truman would strongly object to this Soviet policy and extension of control, and in one regard established a beginning to the **Cold War** and a policy of **containment** of the Soviet expansion to the east.

Teller, Edward (1908–2003). The assistant director of the **Los Alamos** Laboratory, where the first **atom bomb** was produced. He was born in Hungary, fled Nazi Germany, became a naturalized American citizen, and after **World War II** persuaded President **Harry Truman** of America's need to have a **hydrogen bomb** as a deterrent. It was 750 times more powerful than the original bombs dropped on Japan in August 1945, and was first detonated in the Pacific in May 1951.

Tet Offensive (1968). At the end of January 1968, the **Viet Cong** launched a surprise offensive on many American bases in Vietnam, which coincided with the New Year holiday. The **Central Intelligence Agency (CIA)** was held partly responsible for not warning the United States that such an offensive was being planned. This was a turning point in the **Vietnam War**, at a time when Americans were being told the Vietnam conflict was winnable. On American TV, Viet Cong forces were shown attacking the American embassy in Saigon. Confidence in the expected American success in Vietnam began to wane, and President **Lyndon Johnson** sought a different way to resolve the conflict. He had supported a village pacification scheme, and now he sought a negotiated settlement of hostilities.

Thatcher, Margaret H. (1925–). Great Britain's Conservative Prime Minister from 1979 until 1990. After being educated at Oxford University, she joined the Conservative Party, and in 1959 was elected to Parliament. She successfully challenged **Edward Heath** for the party's leadership in February 1975. She won the general election in 1983, and amid party discontent resigned the leadership in 1990. Her views were clearly right-wing; she was known as the "Iron Lady" and was respected for her strength in the U.S.S.R. She attended **Yuri Andropov**'s funeral with U.S. Vice President **George H. W. Bush**. Because her policies and leadership style were congruent with those of President **Ronald Reagan**, she influenced American **Cold War** attitudes to the new Soviet leader, Mikhail Gorbachev.

During Thatcher's leadership of Britain, the **KGB** published falsehoods to undermine her election campaign; Anthony Blunt was exposed as the "fourth man"; she announced that there was no evidence either way to substantiate any espionage charges against the late Sir Roger Hollis and his leadership of **MI5**; Oleg Gordievsky became a most valuable **defector-in-place** for the West; Hugh Hambleton was jailed for 10 years for violating the Official Secrets Act; Vladimir Kuzichkin defected to the West; Geoffrey Prime was found guilty of espionage; Michael Bettany of MI5 was caught and jailed for offering his services to the London KGB; the police blamed MI5 for a policewoman's death because it did not pass on secret evidence of Muamaar Gaddafi's instructions to his Libyan terrorists in London; Thatcher met and announced she could "do business" with Gorbachev, following his briefing with a Soviet **double agent** working for Britain's **SIS**; and she failed badly in her unrelenting efforts to prevent the distribution of Peter Wright's *Spycatcher* memoirs. After losing the leadership of her party, she published her memoirs and regularly toured the world, making speeches about international politics to conservative groups.

Third Man. The term was adopted by the press and was the title of a popular film which was made shortly after **World War II** from a short story by Graham Greene. In the film the "third man" was a mysterious figure whose identity was obscure. In May 1951, Guy Burgess and Donald Maclean fled to Moscow, and newspapermen wondered who had helped them. Often Kim Philby was suspected, and he was dubbed the "third man." He successfully denied the allegation. Eventually he *was* found to be the "third man"; while working for the **SIS**, he learned the game was up and fled Beirut for Moscow in January 1963.

Tit-for-Tat. Regularly during the **Cold War** each side would expel diplomats from its country in retaliation for discovering that bona fide diplomats had been caught spying. The sequence is illustrated well as follows: On March 7, 1986, the U.S. State Department announced a reduction in the size of the Soviet delegation to the United Nations from 272 to 170 over two years, alleging some Soviet personnel were spies; on August 23, 1986, the **FBI** arrested Gennady Zakharov, a Soviet UN delegate, for spying; on August 30, the **U.S.S.R.** arrested Nicholas Daniloff, a *U.S. News and World Report* journalist, and charged him with spying. President **Ronald Reagan** said he believed it was in retaliation for the arrest of Zakharov. On September 5, Reagan wrote to Mikhail Gorbachev, assuring him that Daniloff was no spy; Gorbachev rejected Reagan's assurance, thereby making Reagan out to be liar and putting the Reykjavik Summit at hazard; on September 13, Secretary of State George Schultz announced that Daniloff had been released into custody of the American embassy in Moscow, and the United States released Zakharov into the custody of the Soviet ambassador in Washington; the White House planned to discuss the issue of Daniloff's arrest as often as possible, which could adversely affect Soviet–American relations; on September 17, 25 members of the Soviet UN delegation were expected to leave because the delegation was too large and many members were spies; on September 20, Secretary of State Schultz announced that in two days of talks with the Soviet foreign minister in Washington, the Daniloff Affair was the major item on which no agreement was reached; on September 22, Reagan addressed the United Nations, criticizing the U.S.S.R. for arresting Daniloff and accusing the Soviets of using UN staff for spying; on September 30, Daniloff was released and the crisis ended, opening the way to the summit between Gorbachev and Reagan in Reykjavik; on October 19 the Soviet Union expelled five U.S. diplomats in retaliation for the U.S. expulsion of 25 Soviet diplomats on September 17; on October 21 the United States expelled 55 Soviet diplomats for the five Americans expelled on October 19; on October 22 the U.S.S.R. expelled five American diplomats and announced 260 Russian workers in the U.S. embassy would no longer be permitted to work there.

Tito/Broz, Josip (1892–1980). He was the ruler of Yugoslavia after **World War II** and had his own variety of communism, which angered **Josef Stalin**.

Tradecraft. Tradecraft comprises such espionage field techniques as the following:
1. *Meeting an **agent** or **case officer** on assignment:* Always arrive at a rendezvous on time; never late, never early. Before a meeting, inspect the rendezvous. If your contact is late or missing, never linger at the rendezvous; return there only at prearranged times. Always have a rendezvous alternative. On an assignment, avoid friends; if friends appear while you're on an assignment, break away as soon as possible. When meeting in public with colleagues, keep your hands, glass, or cup over your mouth to prevent lip-reading by strangers. Pass messages to your colleague when close to him, never at arm's length.
2. *Observation:* Observe the physical features of individuals, remember their names and occupations. Memorize photos and descriptions of enemy agents, and look out for them at a rendezvous.
3. *Dead-letter box:* Ensure that the location of a dead-letter box is where the receiver can be seen without suspicion, for example, in public places like gardens, graveyards, entrances to buildings. Change **dead drop** sites frequently.
4. *Interrogation:* If you are caught and subjected to investigation or interrogation, expect no food, light, water, or cigarettes; your clothes will be removed; you won't have a chance to go to the lavatory or to sleep. You will be shuffled from darkness into light and vice versa, dirty, stinking, very cold or very hot, stiff and bruised, and you will have no exercise. You'll be constantly interrogated and accused, and demands will be made on you constantly and without notice. You will be hit on the body where it won't show (e.g., the mouth, between the shoulder blades, above the liver). The pain will be great. The interrogator's procedure will be simply making a statement or an assertion, and your denial will lead to

assault. You will be starved, then fed later with a thin gruel; you will have a splitting head-ache; you will feel confused as your sense of time is lost and fantasies will begin to domi-nate your thoughts; you will have illogical streams of thought, feel angry, begin swearing, and this will lead to further beatings; in time you will lose your fear, feel like giving up, become apathetic, and be willing to do or say whatever is demanded of you.

Truman, Harry S. (1884–1972). U.S. president following the death of President Franklin Roosevelt in April 1945. Truman delayed the **Potsdam Conference** (July 1945) until af-ter the secret **atom bomb** test in the desert outside **Los Alamos**, and at the conference hinted to **Josef Stalin** that the United States had a new powerful weapon, a fact Stalin al-ready knew through the work of the **atom bomb spies**. Following a policy of reducing the postwar U.S. military forces, Truman had the **OSS** deactivated in September 1945; es-pionage was placed under control of the War Department; research and analysis were put into the State Department, and virtually evaporated. In January 1946, the Central Intelli-gence Group (CIG) was formed; it answered to the Secretary of Defense, and was to coor-dinate, plan, evaluate, and disseminate U.S. intelligence under the departments of War, Navy, and State. The new scheme failed, and in July 1947 the **National Security Act** led to the establishment of the National Security Council, directly responsible to President Truman. The CIG was called the **Central Intelligence Agency (CIA),** and was independent but responsible to the National Security Council (NSC). The CIA was to advise the NSC on national security matters; coordinate intelligence activities; collect, coordinate, evaluate, and appropriately disseminate intelligence; serve the common good; and perform other activi-ties relating to national security at the NSC's behest. The last of these tasks was to become the CIA's most controversial duty, and in 1963 Truman reflected that the CIA had gone well beyond its original brief, and had become a peacetime cloak-and-dagger department—and sometimes a powerful policy maker for the U.S. government after it began performing covert operations in 1947. George Kennan (1904–) would agree with this in 1975.

Like most U.S. Presidents, Truman upheld a political doctrine, the Truman Doctrine (1947). In response to the February 1947 announcement that Great Britain would shortly withdraw its military presence from Greece, the United States feared such action would lead to a Communist victory in the Greek civil war. Truman announced that the United States would give aid to Greece and Turkey to resist Communist expansion, and especially to prevent access by the Soviets to the Mediterranean. To ensure his policy would be accepted by Americans who could not see that their national interest was threatened, Truman exag-gerated the extent of the Soviet danger, and announced that if Greece and Turkey were not helped to the degree he wanted, then free people around the world would be placed under Communist threat. To some observers this doctrine began the **Cold War**, and gave purpose early to the CIA.

Under Truman the CIA pursued many goals, both successfully and badly. It intervened successfully in the election of the first Italian government after **World War II** (April 1948) and followed Truman's policy of **containment.** In 1949 the U.S. Congress passed the CIA Act, which exempted the CIA from disclosing anything about its officers and their use of funds; the CIA would use **Marshall Plan** funds for covert operations. The CIA parachuted troops into Hungary, Poland, and Czechoslovakia but failed to predict the onset of the **Korean War** (June 1950) and was shut out of the Far East by General Douglas MacArthur until he permitted them to operate in Korea.

Truman appointed an anti-Communist adviser, Walter Bedell Smith, to head the CIA as Director of Central Intelligence in 1950; this helped Truman appease Joseph McCarthy, and later Smith balanced this bias by appointing a more open-minded person, Allen W. Dulles, as his deputy in 1951. The CIA budget rose twenty-fold, to U.S.$82 million, by 1952, and its foreign stations multiplied seven times between 1949 and 1952. By then there were more than 40 operations underway in Central Europe, especially in Poland. The structure of the U.S. intelligence services under Truman changed little after November 1952, when **Dwight Eisenhower** (1890–1969) was elected President of the United States.

Tube Alloys Project. A secret British project for developing an **atom bomb** was discussed by the secret MAUD committee in mid-1941; its members believed an atom bomb could be produced by 1943. In the autumn of 1941, the Tube Alloys Consultative Committee was established to achieve this purpose. See also **Combined Policy Committee; Manhattan Project.**

U-2 Spy Flights. Utility 2 was the **code name** for the secret American spy plane. Between 1956 and 1960 the United States learned much about military activities in the U.S.S.R. and its satellites from U-2 photography flights. In 1950 the U.S. Strategic Air Command (SAC) began unauthorized espionage flights over the U.S.S.R., using modified B-29 bombers, until President **Harry Truman** (1884–1972) found out, and banned them. In 1956, when **Dwight Eisenhower** (1890–1969) was President, Lockheed U-2 reconnaissance jet planes were readily available for espionage. They were single-seated, high-altitude aircraft that flew at 75,000 feet, well away from Soviet missiles and fighters. Cameras on these planes could photograph everything the U.S. military needed.

In June 1956, U-2 flights over the Soviet Union began again, and from 90,000 feet Russian installations were photographed clearly. In 1957 photographs showed a Russian ICBM had been developed. It was tested in May and failed; another succeeded in August and flew 3,500 nautical miles. U-2 spy plane photos appeared to indicate considerable growth in Soviet military capability. It seemed a race was on between the Russians and the West to secure the most powerful way to deliver nuclear weapons against an enemy. Russia had intercontinental missiles by May 1957.

In 1958, President Eisenhower established the National Aeronautics and Space Administration, and some **Pentagon** funds were directed to producing a satellite that would replace the secret U-2 espionage flights. By the end of 1959, the U.S.S.R. had launched 40 missiles. Early in April 1960, Eisenhower authorized a resumption of the U-2 spy plane project, and a U-2 flight photographed what appeared to be four ICBMs.

In May 1960 a U-2 spy plane was shot down over Soviet territory. Immediately, the National Security Agency denied it was conducting U-2 flights over the Soviet Union, though in fact it had been doing so for four years. **Nikita Khrushchev** (1894–1971) produced the pilot, Francis Gary Powers (1929–1977), with cameras and all the technology of high-altitude espionage. U-2 cameras could, from 13 miles up, show the license plate number of an automobile in the street, and with later techniques could detect the make of the vehicle. Russian militia were observed in Cuba, and U-2 flights showed that in August 1962 there was clear evidence of sites for surface-to-air-missile batteries.

By October 14, 1962, it was evident from U-2 flight photographs that special ICBM launchers were among palm trees that partly concealed equipment normally found with ballistic missiles. U-2 flights established that the Russians were putting ICBMs into Cuba, and the **Cuban missile crisis** began that month.

UB. The Polish security service, predecessor of the **SB.**

Ulbricht, Walter (1893–1973). The East German Communist political leader was brought by Stalin into Berlin to reconstruct the German Communist Party in June 1945. He worked vigorously for the establishment of political organizations to support communism in East Germany, and was devoted to the Soviet cause. But when he opposed some of the Soviet policies for dealing with the West, he was removed as leader of the Socialist Unity Party in 1971.

Union of Soviet Socialist Republics (U.S.S.R., Soviet Union). The Union of Socialist Soviet Republics was established after the Communist revolution in 1917, and was frequently referred to as the Soviet Union. It comprised Russia, Belorussia, Ukraine, the three Baltic states of Estonia, Latvia, and Lithuania, Georgia, Armenia, Moldova (Moldavia), Azerbaijan, Kazakhstan, Kirghizia, Turkmenistan, Tajikistan, and Uzbekistan. It was dissolved in 1991 after a rise of local nationalist feeling and general unrest in some of the original nations, which began to secede.

Venlo Incident (1939). In November 1939 an attempt was made to end **World War II**. Two British officers in the secret services planned to meet an important German officer—possibly the head of the German secret service—who had indicated he wanted to defect and had a plan to oust Adolf Hitler and end hostilities between Germany and Great Britain. The meeting was to be at Venlo, on the border of Germany and Holland; the latter had been neutral during **World War I**. It was a trap: the two officers were kidnapped, and later they discovered their German contact was an **agent** for the Nazi Central Security Agency. In England the story was censored, and the incident was described as a Dutch escapade involving no Britons. The rumors that circulated about the Venlo incident aroused suspicions that the Germans were trying to make a separate peace with Britain.

Viet Cong or Vietcong. The Communist guerrilla organization in South Vietnam from 1960 to 1975, which joined with the opponents of the Saigon regime of Ngo Dinh Diem, and at the time was named the National Front for the Liberation of South Vietnam. When the United States became involved in the **Vietnam War** (1964–1975), the Viet Cong were supplied with arms and forces by North Vietnam by way of the Ho Chi Minh Trail through nearby Laos and Cambodia. The Viet Cong operations finally undermined the U.S. support for the South Vietnamese army and led to the reunification of Vietnam in 1975. The VCI, or Viet Cong Infrastructure, comprised the organizations and activities of the Viet Cong in South Vietnam.

Vietnam War (1964–1975). In 1964 the United States entered the civil war in Vietnam to shore up the non-Communist government of the country. Vietnam was divided into North Vietnam, under Communist rule, and South Vietnam, strongly supported by the United States. Massive hostilities began when President **Lyndon Johnson** persuaded the U.S. Congress to approve his policy following the attack on U.S. warships in the Gulf of Tonkin. Recent research concludes the attack was not what the U.S. Congress and public were led to believe. Also, since at least 1954, the United States had been intervening secretly in Vietnam by funding and providing military support for French attempts to ensure non-Communist rule in its colonies in Indochina. By the early 1970s it was clear the civil war could not be won, but a settlement between governments in the north and south was too difficult to secure militarily, especially with U.S. forces present. In January 1973, U.S. forces were withdrawn after the Paris Peace Accords were signed. North Vietnam triumphed early in 1975. Saigon was renamed Ho Chi Minh City in 1976. The United States lost more troops in the war than in its European campaigns during **World War II**. The Indochinese states were devastated, and Cambodia was destabilized.

Vogel, Wolfgang (1925–). Vogel, an East German lawyer, was a well-known **agent** who managed spy exchanges during the **Cold War**, notably the exchange of Francis Gary Powers for Rudolph Abel. See also **U-2 Spy Flights**.

Walk-in. An unexpected **agent**; one who presents himself at an embassy and states that he has documents or access to documents he is willing pass to the embassy. Such agents are looked upon with suspicion, and are at first considered to be plants. Some, like John A. Walker, Jr., have been extremely valuable to the Soviets.

Wallace, Henry Agard (1888–1965). Wallace was born in Adair County, Iowa, and educated at Iowa State College. In 1910 he had joined the family-owned periodical *Wallace's*

Farmer. He edited it from 1924 to 1933 and developed high-yielding strains of hybrid corn. His family was Republican, but Wallace joined the Democratic Party in 1928. He was Secretary of Agriculture (1933–1941) and Vice President (1941–1945); in 1944 he lost the vice presidential nomination to **Harry Truman**. While serving as Secretary of Commerce (1945–1948), he was dismissed by Truman for attacking the government's foreign policy. He was editor of the *New Republic* (1946–1947) and ran unsuccessfully for President in 1948 as a candidate of the Progressive Party, which was declared a Communist front.

Warren Commission. A commission appointed by President **Lyndon Johnson** immediately after the assassination of **John F. Kennedy** in 1963 to inquire into the President's death. It issued a controversial report (1964), *Report of the President's Commission on the Assassination of President John F. Kennedy*. It found Lee Harvey Oswald (1939–1963) acted alone in assassinating the President. The commission was discredited when it became clear that Kennedy might have died at the hands of several killers. By then it was too late to remedy the failures of the commission, and whoever murdered Kennedy is not securely known. Many books that have appeared on the matter focus on a possible conspiracy. However, a strong case can be made that the conspiracy theories are unsound and that Oswald alone assassinated Kennedy.

Warsaw Pact. The pact was formed in May 1955 among the Soviet Union, Albania, Bulgaria, Czechoslovakia, the German Democratic Republic, Hungary, Poland, and Romania. It was a politico-military pact, aiming to stand against **NATO**, into which the Federal Republic of Germany had been admitted. It was dissolved in July 1991.

Watergate. The name of the building into which five conspirators broke in June 1972 to find information that would be useful for the reelection of **Richard Nixon** (1913–1994) as U.S. President. E. Howard Hunt, one of the conspirators, had been an employee of the **Central Intelligence Agency (CIA)**. His surname was falsely used by the **KGB** to extend and refine its theory that a group headed by a man named Hunt had killed President **John Kennedy**. The Hunt with whom they confused E. Howard Hunt was H. L. Hunt, a U.S. oil magnate, whom the KGB had earlier asserted was the prime mover of Kennedy's assassination. This deliberate confusion allowed the KGB to link the assassination of Kennedy in 1963 with the policies of the CIA.

Wet Affairs. A **KGB** term for assassinations.

Whitehall. A street in central London between Trafalgar Square and the Houses of Parliament with many government offices. The term is synonymous with government authority in Britain.

Wilderness of Mirrors. The organizational culture of the secret services. In it deceptions are false, lies are truth, the reflections are illuminating and confusing. The phrase centers on the problem of the reliability of the secret information about espionage and the identity of spies. The mirrors comprise information from **defectors**, **disinformation** from the opposing sides in the **Cold War**, deviously covered false trails, and facts thought to be valid but incomplete (and later established as totally untrue). The phrase has been attributed to James J. Angleton, and to the title of the book by David Martin, *Wilderness of Mirrors* (New York: Ballantine Books, 1981).

Wilson, Harold (1916–1995). Wilson was a British Labour politician who was Prime Minister from 1964 to 1970, and again from 1974 to 1976. An outstanding student at Oxford University, he lectured in economics, and later was chosen by **Clement Attlee** to join the Ministry of Works; eventually he became President of the Board of Trade (1947–1951), and was named leader of the Labour Party in February 1963. He won four out of five elections for his party, and often reconciled extremist positions among its policy makers. He succeeded in establishing the Open University, but he failed to have Britain made a member of the European Community, to have his peace initiatives for the **Vietnam War** accepted by Peking in 1965, to induce Ian Smith to accept a legitimate basis for the Rhodesian government's authority, to have the steel industry nationalized, and to solve the bitter industrial strife that arose during Britain's economic malaise while he was the nation's leader. However, he did get the trade unions to accept a wage freeze in July 1966.

While he was the Prime Minister, the Queen canceled Kim Philby's **OBE** in August 1965, George Blake escaped from jail that October, and in the following year Kim Philby made his first public statements and showed that Russia regarded him as a hero. In 1968 Douglas Britten was jailed for espionage. In 1964 the FLUENCY Committee had begun its search for Soviet **moles** in **MI5** and **MI6;** years later Wilson was falsely touted as the **KGB**'s 1963 replacement for Hugh Gaitskill (1906–1963) and as the KGB's man in a high place— Prime Minister—by Anatoli Golitsyn (1926–), who had defected to the West in December 1961. This theory was supported by a wayward faction in the British intelligence community, as well as prominent members of the U.K. Establishment who wanted to smear Wilson's reputation. He retired unexpectedly in 1976, firmly claiming that he had made it clear years before that he would cease work at 60 years of age.

WiN or WIN. The term is is an acronym for the Polish for "Freedom and Independence" and was originally the name of the final vestige of the Polish Home Army, the last of the anti-Soviet underground movements. It was wiped out in 1947 by the MGB-controlled Polish Secret Service (UB), and set up falsely in 1948 to sting the **Central Intelligence Agency (CIA)** by making it believe that it was the original anti-Soviet underground movement.

Woolwich Arsenal Affair (1938). Woolwich, a district of East London on the south bank of the Thames River, was the site of the Royal Arsenal. Inside the arsenal, Percy Glading, a **COMINTERN agent**, headed a Soviet spy ring originally organized by Arnold Deutsch. An **MI5** agent, Olga Grey, won his confidence, and in February 1937 rented an apartment in Kensington as a **safe house**. Noted Soviet agents met there. MI5 waited until it could catch the members of the spy ring, and in January 1938 Glading and two other spies were arrested; they were jailed three months later.

Woomera Rocket Range. In 1947, about 175 kilometers northwest of Port Augusta in South Australia, Woomera township was established. For 10 years an American space-tracking station was nearby; it closed down in 1972. In addition a Joint Defense Space Communications Station was established by the defense authorities of the United States and Australia. In 1967 the Woomera rocket range was to be the site of tests of satellite launcher vehicles for the European Launcher Development Organization. During the **Cold War** many of the activities around Woomera were secret; the highway went through a prohibited area that travelers were not allowed to enter.

World War I (1914–1918). A European war fought between the Allied Powers—Britain, France, Russia, Japan, and Serbia, which were joined by Italy in 1915, Portugal and Romania in 1916, and the United States and Greece in 1917—against the Central Powers of Germany, the Austro-Hungarian Empire, Ottoman Turkey, and Bulgaria, which joined the hostilities in 1915. The traditional view is that the war was caused by a fear of Germany's colonial policies and shifting tensions emerging in the **Balkan states**. Ten million died, and 20 million were wounded. An armistice was signed and peace terms agreed to in the Versailles Peace Settlement (1919–1923).

World War II (1939–1945). A war between the Allies and the Axis Powers. The latter were a group of nations at first comprising Nazi Germany and Fascist Italy that agreed to proclaim the Rome–Berlin Axis in October 1936, around which all Europe might assemble; Japan joined Germany in the anti-**COMINTERN** pact—to collaborate against international communism—in November 1936; by 1939 the agreement had become a politico-military alliance or "pact of steel," and a tripartite pact in 1940, when Hungary, Romania, Bulgaria, and the Nazi-occupied states of Slovakia and Croatia joined. The Allies included Britain, which declared war on Germany after its invasion of Poland in September 1939; the U.S.S.R., which joined Britain in July 1941 after being suddenly invaded in June by its erstwhile ally, Nazi Germany; and the United States, which joined Britain and Russia after Japan bombed Pearl Harbor in December 1941. Hostilities in Europe ended in May 1945, after Hitler's suicide, and in the Pacific in August, after the United States dropped **atom bombs** on Hiroshima and Nagasaki in Japan. At least 55 million people died during the hostilities. Three years later the Allied alliance collapsed, and the **Cold War** securely established itself.

Yalta Conference (February 1945). Josef Stalin, Winston Churchill, and Franklin D. Roosevelt met at Yalta to discuss post–**World War II** issues. They decided Germany should surrender and be partitioned into four military zones—French, British, Russian, and American; that Germany should pay reparations for the destruction it had inflicted; democratic elections should be held in Europe; and the Soviets would keep a large portion of Poland. They endorsed the establishment of the United Nations, and the Soviets agreed to go to war against Japan after the fall of Germany. At the conference, Alger Hiss, a Soviet **agent,** was member of the U.S. delegation.

"Year of the Spy" (1985). The phrase, coined late in 1985, to summarize the activities among notable spies and **defectors** in the **Cold War**. In May, John A. Walker, Jr., was arrested in the United States, and so were his son Michael, his brother Arthur, and his friend Jerry Whitworth; in August Vitaly Yurchenko indicated he wanted to defect to the United States while in Italy; on September 12, the British government announced the request for political asylum by Oleg Gordievsky, a **double agent** for the **SIS** inside the **KGB**; later in September, Edward Lee Howard, a former **Central Intelligence Agency (CIA) agent**, escaped before the **Federal Bureau of Investigation (FBI)** could arrest him for espionage; early in November, Yurchenko redefected after informing the CIA about, among other things, Ronald Pelton, the structure of the KGB, the Canadian spy Leslie Bennett, Igor Orlov and SASHA, Nikolai Atramanov, and Nicholas Shadrin; later in November, Anne and Jonathon Jay Pollard, Ronald Pelton, and Larry Wu-tai Chin were arrested in the United States; Sharon Scrange, a CIA clerk in Ghana, gave her lover names of CIA operatives in Ghana; Randy M. Jeffries tried to sell a secret U.S. Congress transcript to the Soviets; Richard Miller was tried in the fall for giving his mistress, a KGB agent, secret documents in 1984, and was tried again in 1986.

Yeltsin, Boris (1931–). Yeltsin served Mikhail Gorbachev as Secretary of the Central Committee of the Soviet Communist Party. After his political disagreements with Gorbachev, he was demoted. But in March 1989, after the Soviet constitution had been reformed, he was elected to represent a Moscow constituency in the Congress of People's Deputies. In 1990, he resigned from the Communist Party, and that May, after the Soviet Union became a federal republic, Yeltsin was elected its president. After putting down a military coup in August 1991, he restructured the government, and was the leader of the new Russia.

Zhukov, Georgi Konstantinovich (1897–1974). The outstanding Russian Army leader who was made a Russian hero for the effective Red Army invasion of Nazi Germany in **World War II**. He and **Nikita Khrushchev** schemed successfully in 1953 to bring down Lavrenti

Beria after **Josef Stalin** had died. Zhukov was made the Defense Minister early in 1955; directed the details of the suppression of the Hungarian uprising in 1956; and saw to it that the Politburo did not manage to oust Khrushchev in 1957. Although a strong supporter of Khrushchev, Zhukov was dismissed late in October 1957 for his policies on the reform of the military and the part it ought to play in the politics of the U.S.S.R.

Index

Bold page numbers indicate location of main entries.

About the Author

RICHARD C.S. TRAHAIR is Social Research Advisor and Consulting Psychologist at La Trobe University, Bundoora, Victoria, Australia. He is the author of *From Aristotelian to Reaganomics: A Dictionary of Eponyms with Biographies in the Social Sciences* (Greenwood, 1994) and *Utopia and Utopians: An Historical Dictionary* (Greenwood, 1999).

Cost Accounting
A Managerial Emphasis

Fourteenth Edition

Charles T. Horngren
STANFORD UNIVERSITY

Srikant M. Datar
HARVARD UNIVERSITY

Madhav V. Rajan
STANFORD UNIVERSITY

Prentice Hall

Boston   Columbus   Indianapolis   New York   San Francisco   Upper Saddle River
Amsterdam   Cape Town   Dubai   London   Madrid   Milan   Munich   Paris   Montréal   Toronto
Delhi   Mexico City   São Paulo   Sydney   Hong Kong   Seoul   Singapore   Taipei   Tokyo

Editorial Director: Sally Yagan
Editor in Chief: Donna Battista
AVP/Executive Editor: Stephanie Wall
Editorial Project Manager: Christina Rumbaugh
Editorial Assistant: Brian Reilly
Director of Marketing: Patrice Jones
Senior Managing Editor: Cynthia Zonneveld
Senior Project Manager: Lynne Breitfeller
Operations Specialist: Natacha Moore
Senior Art Director: Anthony Gemmellaro
Text Designer: Rachael Cronin
Cover Designer: Anthony Gemmellaro
Manager, Rights and Permissions: Hessa Albader
Permission Coordinator: Tracy Metevier

Manager, Visual Research & Permissions:
  Karen Sanatar
Photo Researcher: Heather Kemp
Cover Photo: George Hammerstein/
  Corbis/Solus
Media Project Manager: Allison Longley
Production Media Project Manager: John Cassar
Full-Service Project Management:
  GEX Publishing Services
Composition: GEX Publishing Services
Printer/Binder: Webcrafters Inc.
Cover Printer: Lehigh-Phoenix
  Color/Hagerstown
Text Font: 10/12 Sabon

Credits and acknowledgments borrowed from other sources and reproduced, with permission, in this textbook appear on appropriate page within text (or on the copyright page).

Photo Credits: page 3 Oleksiy Maksymenko\Alamy Images; **page 15** BuildPix\Alamy Images Royalty Free; **page 27** DAVID SWANSON/STAFF PHOTOGRAPH/PHILADELPHIA INQUIRER/RAPPORT SYNDICATION; **page 33** Jim Wilson \Redux Pictures; **page 63** Getty Images, Inc.—Liaison; **page 78** Richard Drew \AP Wide World Photos; **page 99** Dana Hoff \Getty Images, Inc.—Liaison; **page 108** BRANDON THIBODEAUX/THE NEW YORK TIMES; **page 139** Ethan Miller \Getty Images, Inc.—Liaison; **page 160** James Leynse\CORBIS- NY; **page 183** Michael Blann \Getty Images, Inc.—Liaison; **page 198** Getty Images, Inc.; **page 227** Eric Gay \AP Wide World Photos; **page 237** Stephen Chernin\Newscom; **page 263** Jason Kempin \Redux Pictures; **page 280** Getty Images, Inc.—Liaison; **page 301** Erin Siegal \Redux Pictures; **page 319** DIANE COLLINS/JORDAN HOLLENDER/GETTY IMAGES; **page 341** Al Seib/Los Angeles Times/MCT/Newscom; **page 356** Kristoffer Tripplaar \Alamy Images; **page 391** © (JAMES LEYNSE) / CORBIS All Rights Reserved; **page 400** mediablitzimages limited \Alamy Images; **page 433** Ajit Solanki \AP Wide World Photos; **page 441** Steven Sheppard \AP Wide World Photos; **page 467** Namas Bhojani\Getty Images, Inc.—Bloomberg News; **page 484** Facebook, Inc.; **page 503** © (GUS RUELAS)/Reuters / CORBIS All Rights Reserved/; **page 518** Rich Schultz\AP Wide World Photos; **page 543** David Zalubowski\AP Wide World Photos; **page 560** Erik S. Lesser\AP Wide World Photos; **page 577** Jim West \Alamy Images; **page 590** Jay Laprete\Getty Images, Inc.—Bloomberg News; **page 607** Karen BLEIER\Newscom; **page 627** Adidas Americas; **page 645** Kevin P. Casey \Getty Images, Inc.—Bloomberg News; **page 659** Ed Andrieski\AP Wide World Photos; **page 684** Daniel Heighton\Alamy Images; **page 671** Steven Senne\AP Wide World Photos; **page 717** Diane Bondareff/Picture Group via AP IMAGES; **page 703** Newscom; **page 758** Yoshikazu Tsuno/AFP/Getty Images/Newscom; **page 739** Charles Krupa\AP Wide World Photos; **page 793** Lenscap \Alamy Images; **page 775** Symantec Corporation; **page 825** AFP Photo/Jim Watson/Newscom; **page 807** AFP Photo/Gabriel Bouys/Newscom

Microsoft® and Windows® are registered trademarks of the Microsoft Corporation in the U.S.A. and other countries. Screen shots and icons reprinted with permission from the Microsoft Corporation. This book is not sponsored or endorsed by or affiliated with the Microsoft Corporation.

Library of Congress Cataloging-in-Publication Data
Horngren, Charles T.,
 Cost accounting : a managerial emphasis / Charles T. Horngren, Srikant M. Datar, Madhav V. Rajan. -- 14th ed.
  p. cm.
 Includes bibliographical references and index.
 ISBN 978-0-13-210917-8 (hbk. : alk. paper) 1. Cost accounting. I. Datar, Srikant M. II. Rajan, Madhav V. III. Title.
 HF5686.C8H59 2012
 658.15'11--dc22   2010042908

10 9 8 7 6 5 4 3 2 1

Prentice Hall
is an imprint of

ISBN-13: 978-0-13-210917-8
ISBN-10: 0-13-210917-4

Brief Contents

Contents

About the Authors

Charles T. Horngren is the Edmund W. Littlefield Professor of Accounting, Emeritus, at Stanford University. A Graduate of Marquette University, he received his MBA from Harvard University and his PhD from the University of Chicago. He is also the recipient of honorary doctorates from Marquette University and DePaul University.

A certified public accountant, Horngren served on the Accounting Principles Board for six years, the Financial Accounting Standards Board Advisory Council for five years, and the Council of the American Institute of Certified Public Accountants for three years. For six years, he served as a trustee of the Financial Accounting Foundation, which oversees the Financial Accounting Standards Board and the Government Accounting Standards Board. Horngren is a member of the Accounting Hall of Fame.

A member of the American Accounting Association, Horngren has been its president and its director of research. He received its first Outstanding Accounting Educator Award. The California Certified Public Accountants Foundation gave Horngren its Faculty Excellence Award and its Distinguished Professor Award. He is the first person to have received both awards.

The American Institute of Certified Public Accountants presented its first Outstanding Educator Award to Horngren.

Horngren was named Accountant of the Year, Education, by the national professional accounting fraternity, Beta Alpha Psi.

Professor Horngren is also a member of the Institute of Management Accountants, from whom he received its Distinguished Service Award. He was also a member of the Institutes' Board of Regents, which administers the Certified Management Accountant examinations.

Horngren is the author of other accounting books published by Prentice Hall: *Introduction to Management Accounting*, 15th ed. (2011, with Sundem and Stratton); *Introduction to Financial Accounting*, 10th ed. (2011, with Sundem and Elliott); *Accounting*, 8th ed. (2010, with Harrison and Bamber); and *Financial Accounting*, 8th ed. (2010, with Harrison).

Horngren is the Consulting Editor for the Charles T. Horngren Series in Accounting.

Srikant M. Datar is the Arthur Lowes Dickinson Professor of Business Administration and Senior Associate Dean at Harvard University. A graduate with distinction from the University of Bombay, he received gold medals upon graduation from the Indian Institute of Management, Ahmedabad, and the Institute of Cost and Works Accountants of India. A chartered accountant, he holds two master's degrees and a PhD from Stanford University.

Cited by his students as a dedicated and innovative teacher, Datar received the George Leland Bach Award for Excellence in the Classroom at Carnegie Mellon University and the Distinguished Teaching Award at Stanford University.

Datar has published his research in leading accounting, marketing, and operations management journals, including *The Accounting Review, Contemporary Accounting Research, Journal of Accounting, Auditing and Finance, Journal of Accounting and Economics, Journal of Accounting Research*, and *Management Science*. He has also served on the editorial board of several journals and presented his research to corporate executives and academic audiences in North America, South America, Asia, Africa, Australia, and Europe.

Datar is a member of the board of directors of Novartis A.G., ICF International, KPIT Cummins Infosystems Ltd., Stryker Corporation, and Harvard Business Publishing, and has worked with many organizations, including Apple Computer, AT&T, Boeing, Du Pont, Ford, General Motors, HSBC, Hewlett-Packard, Morgan Stanley, PepsiCo, TRW,

Visa, and the World Bank. He is a member of the American Accounting Association and the Institute of Management Accountants.

Madhav V. Rajan is the Gregor G. Peterson Professor of Accounting and Senior Associate Dean at Stanford University. From 2002 to 2010, he was the area coordinator for accounting at Stanford's Graduate School of Business.

Rajan received his undergraduate degree in commerce from the University of Madras, India, and his MS in accounting, MBA, and PhD degrees from the Graduate School of Industrial Administration at Carnegie Mellon University. In 1990, his dissertation won the Alexander Henderson Award for Excellence in Economic Theory.

Rajan's primary area of research interest is the economics-based analysis of management accounting issues, especially as they relate to internal control cost allocation, capital budgeting, quality management, supply chain, and performance systems in firms. He has published his research in leading accounting and operations management journals including *The Accounting Review*, *Review of Financial Studies*, *Journal of Accounting Research*, and *Management Science*. In 2004, he received the Notable Contribution to Management Accounting Literature Award.

Rajan has served as the Departmental Editor for Accounting at *Management Science*, as well as associate editor for both the accounting and operations areas. From 2002 to 2008, Rajan served as an editor of *The Accounting Review*. He is also currently an associate editor for the *Journal of Accounting, Auditing and Finance*. Rajan is a member of the management accounting section of the American Accounting Association and has twice been a plenary speaker at the AAA Management Accounting Conference.

Rajan has won several teaching awards at Wharton and Stanford, including the David W. Hauck Award, the highest undergraduate teaching honor at Wharton. Rajan has taught in a variety of executive education programs including the Stanford Executive Program, the National Football League Program for Managers, and the National Basketball Players Association Program, as well as custom programs for firms including nVidia, Genentech, and Google.

Preface

Studying Cost Accounting is one of the best business investments a student can make. Why? Because success in any organization—from the smallest corner store to the largest multinational corporation—requires the use of cost accounting concepts and practices. Cost accounting provides key data to managers for planning and controlling, as well as costing products, services, even customers. This book focuses on how cost accounting helps managers make better decisions, as cost accountants are increasingly becoming integral members of their company's decision-making teams. In order to emphasize this prominence in decision-making, we use the "different costs for different purposes" theme throughout this book. By focusing on basic concepts, analyses, uses, and procedures instead of procedures alone, we recognize cost accounting as a managerial tool for business strategy and implementation.

We also prepare students for the rewards and challenges they face in the professional cost accounting world of today and tomorrow. For example, we emphasize both the development of analytical skills such as Excel to leverage available information technology and the values and behaviors that make cost accountants effective in the workplace.

Hallmark Features of *Cost Accounting*

- Exceptionally strong emphasis on managerial uses of cost information
- Clarity and understandability of the text
- Excellent balance in integrating modern topics with traditional coverage
- Emphasis on human behavior aspects
- Extensive use of real-world examples
- Ability to teach chapters in different sequences
- Excellent quantity, quality, and range of assignment material

The first thirteen chapters provide the essence of a one-term (quarter or semester) course. There is ample text and assignment material in the book's twenty-three chapters for a two-term course. This book can be used immediately after the student has had an introductory course in financial accounting. Alternatively, this book can build on an introductory course in managerial accounting.

Deciding on the sequence of chapters in a textbook is a challenge. Since every instructor has a unique way of organizing his or her course, we utilize a modular, flexible organization that permits a course to be custom tailored. *This organization facilitates diverse approaches to teaching and learning.*

As an example of the book's flexibility, consider our treatment of process costing. Process costing is described in Chapters 17 and 18. Instructors interested in filling out a student's perspective of costing systems can move directly from job-order costing described in Chapter 4 to Chapter 17 without interruption in the flow of material. Other instructors may want their students to delve into activity-based costing and budgeting and more decision-oriented topics early in the course. These instructors may prefer to postpone discussion of process costing.

New to This Edition
Greater Emphasis on Strategy

This edition deepens the book's emphasis on strategy development and execution. Several chapters build on the strategy theme introduced in Chapter 1. Chapter 13 has a greater discussion of strategy maps as a useful tool to implement the balanced scorecard and a simplified presentation of how income statements of companies can be analyzed from the strategic perspective of product differentiation or cost leadership. We also discuss strategy considerations in the design of activity-based costing systems in Chapter 5, the preparation of budgets in Chapter 6, and decision making in Chapters 11 and 12.

Deeper Consideration of Global Issues

Business is increasingly becoming more global. Even small and medium-sized companies across the manufacturing, merchandising, and service sectors are being forced to deal with the effects of globalization. Global considerations permeate many chapters. For example, Chapter 11 discusses the benefits and the challenges that arise when outsourcing products or services outside the United States. Chapter 22 examines the importance of transfer pricing in minimizing the tax burden faced by multinational companies. Several new examples of management accounting applications in companies are drawn from international settings.

Increased Focus on the Service Sector

In keeping with the shifts in the U.S. and world economy this edition makes greater use of service sector examples. For example, Chapter 2 discusses the concepts around the measurement of costs in a software development rather than a manufacturing setting. Chapter 6 provides several examples of the use of budgets and targets in service companies. Several concepts in action boxes focus on the service sector such as activity-based costing at Charles Schwab (Chapter 5) and managing wireless data bottlenecks (Chapter 19).

New Cutting Edge Topics

The pace of change in organizations continues to be rapid. The fourteenth edition of *Cost Accounting* reflects changes occurring in the role of cost accounting in organizations.

- We have introduced foreign currency and forward contract issues in the context of outsourcing decisions.
- We have added ideas based on Six Sigma to the discussion of quality.
- We have rewritten the chapter on strategy and the balanced scorecard and simplified the presentation to connect strategy development, strategy maps, balanced scorecard, and analysis of operating income.
- We discuss current trends towards Beyond Budgeting and the use of rolling forecasts.
- We develop the link between traditional forms of cost allocation and the nascent movement in Europe towards Resource Consumption Accounting.
- We focus more sharply on how companies are simplifying their costing systems with the presentation of value streams and lean accounting.

Opening Vignettes

Each chapter opens with a vignette on a real company situation. The vignettes engage the reader in a business situation, or dilemma, illustrating why and how the concepts in the chapter are relevant in business. For example, Chapter 1 describes how Apple uses cost accounting information to make decisions relating to how they price the most popular songs on iTunes. Chapter 3 explains how the band U2 paid for their extensive new stage by lowering ticket prices. Chapter 7 describes how even the NBA was forced to cut costs after over half of the league's franchises declared losses. Chapter 11 shows how JetBlue uses Twitter and e-mail to help their customers make better pricing decisions. Chapter 12 discusses how Tata Motors designed a car for the Indian masses, priced at only $2,500. Chapter 14 shows how Best Buy boosts profits by analyzing its customers and their buying habits. Chapter 18 describes how Boeing incurred great losses as it reworked its much-anticipated Dreamliner airplane.

Concepts in Action Boxes

Found in every chapter, these boxes cover real-world cost accounting issues across a variety of industries including automobile racing, defense contracting, entertainment, manufacturing, and retailing. New examples include

- How Zipcar Helps Reduce Business Transportation Costs p. 33
- Job Costing at Cowboys Stadium p. 108
- The "Death Spiral" and the End of Landline Telephone Service p. 319
- Transfer Pricing Dispute Temporarily Stops the Flow of Fiji Water p. 793

Streamlined Presentation

We continue to try to simplify and streamline our presentation of various topics to make it as easy as possible for a student to learn the concepts, tools, and frameworks introduced in different chapters. Examples of more streamlined presentations can be found in

- Chapter 3 on the discussion of target net income
- Chapter 5 on the core issues in activity-based costing (ABC)
- Chapter 8, which uses a single comprehensive example to illustrate the use of variance analysis in ABC systems
- Chapter 13, which has a much simpler presentation of the strategic analysis of operating income
- Chapter 15, which uses a simpler, unified framework to discuss various cost-allocation methods
- Chapters 17 and 18, where the material on standard costing has been moved to the appendix, allowing for smoother transitions through the sections in the body of the chapter

Selected Chapter-by-Chapter Content Changes

Thank you for your continued support of Cost Accounting. In every new edition, we strive to update this text thoroughly. To ease your transition from the thirteenth edition, here are selected highlights of chapter changes for the fourteenth edition.

Chapter 1 has been rewritten to focus on strategy, decision-making, and learning emphasizing the managerial issues that animate modern management accounting. It now emphasizes decision making instead of problem solving, performance evaluation instead of scorekeeping and learning instead of attention directing.

Chapter 2 has been rewritten to emphasize the service sector. For example, instead of a manufacturing company context, the chapter uses the software development setting at a company like Apple Inc. to discuss cost measurement. It also develops ideas related to risk when discussing fixed versus variable costs.

Chapter 3 has been rewritten to simplify the presentation of target net income by describing how target net income can be converted to target operating income. This allows students to use the equations already developed for target operating income when discussing target net income. We deleted the section on multiple cost drivers, because it is closely related to the multi-product example discussed in the chapter. The managerial and decision-making aspects of the chapter have also been strengthened.

Chapter 4 has been reorganized to first discuss normal costing and then actual costing because normal costing is much more prevalent in practice. As a result of this change the exhibits in the early part of the chapter tie in more closely to the detailed exhibits of normal job-costing systems in manufacturing later in the chapter. The presentation of actual costing has been retained to help students understand the benefits and challenges of actual costing systems. To focus on job costing, we moved the discussion of responsibility centers and departments to Chapter 6.

Chapter 5 has been reorganized to clearly distinguish design choices, implementation challenges, and managerial applications of ABC systems. The presentation of the ideas has been simplified and streamlined to focus on the core issues.

Chapter 6 now includes ideas from relevant applied research on the usefulness of budgets and the circumstances in which they add the greatest value, as well as the challenges in administering them. It incorporates new material on the Beyond Budgeting movement, and in particular the trend towards the use of rolling forecasts.

Chapters 7 and 8 present a streamlined discussion of direct-cost and overhead variances, respectively. The separate sections on ABC and variance analysis in Chapters 7 and 8 have now been combined into a single integrated example at the end of Chapter 8. A new appendix to Chapter 7 now addresses more detailed revenue variances using the existing Webb Company example. The use of potentially confusing terms such as 2-variance analysis and 1-variance analysis has been eliminated.

We have rewritten Chapter 9 as a single integrated chapter with the same running example rather than as two distinct sub-parts on inventory costing and capacity analysis. The material on the tax and financial reporting implications of various capacity concepts has also been fully revised.

Chapter 10 has been revised to provide a more linear progression through the ideas of cost estimation and the choice of cost drivers, culminating in the use of quantitative analysis (regression analysis, in particular) for managerial decision-making.

Chapter 11 now includes more discussion of global issues such as foreign currency considerations in international outsourcing decisions. There is also greater emphasis on strategy and decision-making.

Chapter 12 has been reorganized to more sharply delineate short-run from long-run costing and pricing and to bring together the various considerations other than costs that affect pricing decisions. This reorganization has helped streamline several sections in the chapter.

Chapter 13 has been substantially rewritten. Strategy maps are presented as a way to link strategic objectives and as a useful first step in developing balanced scorecard measures. The section on strategic analysis of operating income has been significantly simplified by focusing on only one indirect cost and eliminating most of the technical details. Finally, the section on engineered and discretionary costs has been considerably shortened to focus on only the key ideas.

Chapter 14 now discusses the use of "whale curves" to depict the outcome of customer profitability analysis. The last part of the chapter has been rationalized to focus on the decomposition of sales volume variances into quantity and mix variances; and the calculation of sales mix variances has also been simplified.

Chapter 15 has been completely revised and uses a simple, unified conceptual framework to discuss various cost allocation methods (single-rate versus dual-rate, actual costs versus budgeted costs, etc.).

Chapter 16 now provides a more in-depth discussion of the rationale underlying joint cost allocation as well as the reasons why some firms *do not* allocate costs (along with real-world examples).

Chapters 17 and 18 have been reorganized, with the material on standard costing moved to the appendix in both chapters. This reorganization has made the chapters easier to navigate and fully consistent (since all sections in the body of the chapter now use actual costing). The material on multiple inspection points from the appendix to Chapter 18 has been moved into the body of the chapter, but using a variant of the existing example involving Anzio Corp.

Chapter 19 introduces the idea of Six Sigma quality. It also integrates design quality, conformance quality, and financial and nonfinancial measures of quality. The discussion of queues, delays, and costs of time has been significantly streamlined.

Chapter 20's discussion of EOQ has been substantially revised and the ideas of lean accounting further developed. The section on backflush costing has been completely rewritten.

Chapter 21 has been revised to incorporate the payback period method with discounting, and also now includes survey evidence on the use of various capital budgeting methods. The discussion of goal congruence and performance measurement has been simplified and combined, making the latter half of the chapter easier to follow.

Chapter 22 has been fully rewritten with a new section on the use of hybrid pricing methods. The chapter also now includes a fuller description (and a variety of examples) of the use of transfer pricing for tax minimization, and incorporates such developments as the recent tax changes proposed by the Obama administration.

Chapter 23 includes a more thorough description of Residual Income and EVA, as well as a more streamlined discussion of the various choices of accounting-based perform-ance measures.

Resources

In addition to this textbook and MyAccountingLab, the following resources are available for students:

- Student Study Guide—self study aid full of review features.
- Student Solutions Manual—solutions and assistance for even numbered problems.
- Excel Manual—workbook designed for Excel practice.
- Companion website—www.pearsonhighered.com/horngren.

The following resources are available for Instructors:

- Solutions Manual
- Test Gen
- Instructors Manual
- PowerPoint Presentations
- Image Library
- Instructors Resource Center—www.pearsonhighered.com/horngren

Acknowledgments

We are indebted to many people for their ideas and assistance. Our primary thanks go to the many academics and practitioners who have advanced our knowledge of cost accounting. The package of teaching materials we present is the work of skillful and val-ued team members developing some excellent end-of-chapter assignment material. Tommy Goodwin, Ian Gow (Northwestern), Richard Saouma (UCLA) and Shalin Shah (Berkeley) provided outstanding research assistance on technical issues and current developments. We would also like to thank the dedicated and hard working supplement author team and GEX Publishing Services. The book is much better because of the efforts of these colleagues.

In shaping this edition, we would like to thank a group of colleagues who worked closely with us and the editorial team. This group provided detailed feedback and partic-ipated in focus groups that guided the direction of this edition:

Wagdy Abdallah
Seton Hall University
David Alldredge
Salt Lake Community College
Felicia Baldwin
Richard J. Daley College
Molly Brown
James Madison University
Shannon Charles
Brigham Young University

David Franz
San Francisco State University
Anna Jensen
Indiana University
Donna McGovern
Custom Business Results, Inc.
Cindy Nye
Bellevue University
Glenn Pate
Florida Atlantic University

Kelly Pope
DePaul University
Jenice Prather-Kinsey
University of Missouri
Melvin Roush
Pitt State University
Karen Shastri
Pitt University
Frank Stangota
Rutgers University
Patrick Stegman
College of Lake County

We would also like to extend our thanks to those professors who provided detailed written reviews or comments on drafts. These professors include the following:

Robyn Alcock
Central Queensland University

David S. Baglia
Grove City College

Charles Bailey
University of Central Florida

Robert Bauman
Allan Hancock Joint Community College

David Bilker
University of Maryland, University College

Marvin Bouillon
Iowa State University

Dennis Caplan
Columbia University

Donald W. Gribbin
Southern Illinois University

Rosalie Hallbauer
Florida International University

John Haverty
St. Joseph's University

Jean Hawkins
William Jewell College

Rodger Holland
Francis Marion University

Jiunn C. Huang
San Francisco State University

Zafar U. Khan
Eastern Michigan University

Larry N. Killough
Virginia Polytechnic Institute & State University

Keith Kramer
Southern Oregon University

Jay Law
Central Washington University

Sandra Lazzarini
University of Queensland

Gary J. Mann
University of Texas at El Paso

Ronald Marshall
Michigan State University

Maureen Mascha
Marquette University

Pam Meyer
University of Louisiana at Lafayette

Marjorie Platt
Northeastern University

Roy W. Regel
University of Montana

Pradyot K. Sen
University of Cincinnati

Gim S. Seow
University of Connecticut

Rebekah A. Sheely
Northeastern University

Robert J. Shepherd
University of California, Santa Cruz

Kenneth Sinclair
Lehigh University

Vic Stanton
California State University, Hayward

Carolyn Streuly
Marquette University

Gerald Thalmann
North Central College

Peter D. Woodlock
Youngstown State University

James Williamson
San Diego State University

Sung-Soo Yoon
UCLA at Los Angeles

Jennifer Dosch
Metro State University

Joe Dowd
Eastern Washington University

Leslie Kren
University of Wisconsin-Madison

Michele Matherly
Xavier University

Laurie Burney
Mississippi State University

Mike Morris
Notre Dame University

Cinthia Nye
Bellevue University

Roy Regel
University of Montana

Margaret Shackell-Dowel
Notre Dame University

Marvin Bouillon
Iowa State University

Kreag Danvers
Clarion University of Pennsylvania

A.J. Cataldo II
West Chester University

Kenneth Danko
San Francisco State University

T.S. Amer
Northern Arizona University

Robert Hartman
University of Iowa

Diane Satin
California State University East Bay

John Stancil
Florida Southern College

Michael Flores
Wichita University

Ralph Greenberg
Temple University

Paul Warrick
Westwood College

Karen Schoenebeck
Southwestern College

Thomas D. Fields
Washington University in St. Louis

Constance Hylton
George Mason University

Robert Alford
DePaul University

Michael Eames
Santa Clara University

We also would like to thank our colleagues who helped us greatly by accuracy checking the text and supplements including Molly Brown, Barbara Durham, and Anna Jensen.

We thank the people at Prentice Hall for their hard work and dedication, including Donna Battista, Stephanie Wall, Christina Rumbaugh, Brian Reilly, Cindy Zonneveld, Lynne Breitfeller, Natacha Moore, and Kate Thomas and Kelly Morrison at GEX Publishing Services. We must extend special thanks to Deepa Chungi, the development editor on this edition, who took charge of this project and directed it across the finish line. This book would not have been possible without her dedication and skill.

Alexandra Gural, Jacqueline Archer, and others expertly managed the production aspects of all the manuscript preparation with superb skill and tremendous dedication. We are deeply appreciative of their good spirits, loyalty, and ability to stay calm in the most hectic of times. The constant support of Bianca Baggio and Caroline Roop is greatly appreciated.

Appreciation also goes to the American Institute of Certified Public Accountants, the Institute of Management Accountants, the Society of Management Accountants of Canada, the Certified General Accountants Association of Canada, the Financial Executive Institute of America, and many other publishers and companies for their generous permission to quote from their publications. Problems from the Uniform CPA examinations are designated (CPA); problems from the Certified Management Accountant examination are designated (CMA); problems from the Canadian examinations administered by the Society of Management Accountants are designated (SMA); and problems from the Certified General Accountants Association are designated (CGA). Many of these problems are adapted to highlight particular points.

We are grateful to the professors who contributed assignment material for this edition. Their names are indicated in parentheses at the start of their specific problems. Comments from users are welcome.

CHARLES T. HORNGREN
SRIKANT M. DATAR
MADHAV V. RAJAN

To Our Families
The Horngren Family (CH)
Swati, Radhika, Gayatri, Sidharth (SD)
Gayathri, Sanjana, Anupama (MVR)

▶ Learning Objectives

1. Distinguish financial accounting from management accounting

2. Understand how management accountants affect strategic decisions

3. Describe the set of business functions in the value chain and identify the dimensions of performance that customers are expecting of companies

4. Explain the five-step decision-making process and its role in management accounting

5. Describe three guidelines management accountants follow in supporting managers

6. Understand how management accounting fits into an organization's structure

7. Understand what professional ethics mean to management accountants

All businesses are concerned about revenues and costs.

Whether their products are automobiles, fast food, or the latest designer fashions, managers must understand how revenues and costs behave or risk losing control. Managers use cost accounting information to make decisions related to strategy formulation, research and development, budgeting, production planning, and pricing, among others. Sometimes these decisions involve tradeoffs. The following article shows how companies like Apple make those tradeoffs to increase their profits.

iTunes Variable Pricing: Downloads Are Down, but Profits Are Up[1]

Can selling less of something be more profitable than selling more of it? In 2009, Apple changed the pricing structure for songs sold through iTunes from a flat fee of $0.99 to a three-tier price point system of $0.69, $0.99, and $1.29. The top 200 songs in any given week make up more than one-sixth of digital music sales. Apple now charges the higher price of $1.29 for these hit songs by artists like Taylor Swift and the Black Eyed Peas.

After the first six months of the new pricing model in the iTunes store, downloads of the top 200 tracks were down by about 6%. While the number of downloads dropped, the higher prices generated more revenue than before the new pricing structure was in place. Since Apple's iTunes costs—wholesale song costs, network and transaction fees, and other operating costs—do not vary based on the price of each download, the profits from the 30% increase in price more than made up for the losses from the 6% decrease in volume.

To increase profits beyond those created by higher prices, Apple also began to manage iTunes' costs. Transaction costs (what Apple pays credit-card processors like Visa and MasterCard) have decreased, and Apple has also reduced the number of people working in the iTunes store.

---

[1] *Sources:* Bruno, Anthony and Glenn Peoples. 2009. Variable iTunes pricing a moneymaker for artists. *Reuters*, June 21. http://www.reuters.com/article/idUSTRE55K0DJ20090621; Peoples, Glenn. 2009. The long tale? *Billboard*, November 14. http://www.billboard.biz/bbbiz/content_display/magazine/features/e3i35ed869fbd929ccdcca52ed7fd9262d3?imw=Y; Savitz, Eric. 2007. Apple: Turns out, iTunes makes money Pacific Crest says; subscription services seems inevitable. *Barron's* "Tech Trader Daily" blog, April 23. http://blogs.barrons.com/techtraderdaily/2007/04/23/apple-turns-out-itunes-makes-money-pacific-crest-says-subscription-service-seems-inevitable/

The study of modern cost accounting yields insights into how managers and accountants can contribute to successfully running their businesses. It also prepares them for leadership roles. Many large companies, such as Constellation Energy, Jones Soda, Nike, and the Pittsburgh Steelers, have senior executives with accounting backgrounds.

Financial Accounting, Management Accounting, and Cost Accounting

As many of you have already seen in your financial accounting class, accounting systems take economic events and transactions, such as sales and materials purchases, and process the data into information helpful to managers, sales representatives, production supervisors, and others. Processing any economic transaction means collecting, categorizing, summarizing, and analyzing. For example, costs are collected by category, such as materials, labor, and shipping. These costs are then summarized to determine total costs by month, quarter, or year. The results are analyzed to evaluate, say, how costs have changed relative to revenues from one period to the next. Accounting systems provide the information found in the income statement, the balance sheet, the statement of cash flow, and in performance reports, such as the cost of serving customers or running an advertising campaign. Managers use accounting information to administer the activities, businesses, or functional areas they oversee and to coordinate those activities, businesses, or functions within the framework of the organization. Understanding this information is essential for managers to do their jobs.

Individual managers often require the information in an accounting system to be presented or reported differently. Consider, for example, sales order information. A sales manager may be interested in the total dollar amount of sales to determine the commissions to be paid. A distribution manager may be interested in the sales order quantities by geographic region and by customer-requested delivery dates to ensure timely deliveries. A manufacturing manager may be interested in the quantities of various products and their desired delivery dates, so that he or she can develop an effective production schedule. To simultaneously serve the needs of all three managers, companies create a database—sometimes called a data warehouse or infobarn—consisting of small, detailed bits of information that can be used for multiple purposes. For instance, the sales order database will contain detailed information about product, quantity ordered, selling price, and delivery details (place and date) for each sales order. The database stores information in a way that allows different managers to access the information they need. Many companies are building their own Enterprise Resource Planning (ERP) systems, single databases that collect data and feed it into applications that support the company's business activities, such as purchasing, production, distribution, and sales.

Financial accounting and management accounting have different goals. As many of you know, **financial accounting** focuses on reporting to external parties such as investors, government agencies, banks, and suppliers. It measures and records business transactions and provides financial statements that are based on generally accepted accounting principles (GAAP). The most important way that financial accounting information affects managers' decisions and actions is through compensation, which is often, in part, based on numbers in financial statements.

Learning Objective 1

Distinguish financial accounting

. . . . reporting on past performance to external users

from management accounting

. . . helping managers make decisions

Management accounting measures, analyzes, and reports financial and nonfinancial information that helps managers make decisions to fulfill the goals of an organization. Managers use management accounting information to develop, communicate, and implement strategy. They also use management accounting information to coordinate product design, production, and marketing decisions and to evaluate performance. Management accounting information and reports do not have to follow set principles or rules. The key questions are always (1) how will this information help managers do their jobs better, and (2) do the benefits of producing this information exceed the costs?

Exhibit 1-1 summarizes the major differences between management accounting and financial accounting. Note, however, that reports such as balance sheets, income statements, and statements of cash flows are common to both management accounting and financial accounting.

Cost accounting provides information for management accounting and financial accounting. **Cost accounting** measures, analyzes, and reports financial and nonfinancial information relating to the costs of acquiring or using resources in an organization. For example, calculating the cost of a product is a cost accounting function that answers financial accounting's inventory-valuation needs and management accounting's decision-making needs (such as deciding how to price products and choosing which products to promote). Modern cost accounting takes the perspective that collecting cost information is a function of the management decisions being made. Thus, the distinction between management accounting and cost accounting is not so clear-cut, and we often use these terms interchangeably in the book.

We frequently hear business people use the term *cost management*. Unfortunately, that term has no uniform definition. We use **cost management** to describe the approaches and activities of managers to use resources to increase value to customers and to achieve organizational goals. Cost management decisions include decisions such as whether to enter new markets, implement new organizational processes, and change product designs. Information from accounting systems helps managers to manage costs, but the information and the accounting systems themselves are not cost management.

Cost management has a broad focus and is not only about reduction in costs. Cost management includes decisions to incur additional costs, for example to improve

Decision Point

How is management accounting different from financial accounting?

	Exhibit 1-1	Major Differences Between Management and Financial Accounting

	Management Accounting	Financial Accounting
Purpose of information	Help managers make decisions to fulfill an organization's goals	Communicate organization's financial position to investors, banks, regulators, and other outside parties
Primary users	Managers of the organization	External users such as investors, banks, regulators, and suppliers
Focus and emphasis	Future-oriented (budget for 2011 prepared in 2010)	Past-oriented (reports on 2010 performance prepared in 2011)
Rules of measurement and reporting	Internal measures and reports do not have to follow GAAP but are based on cost-benefit analysis	Financial statements must be prepared in accordance with GAAP and be certified by external, independent auditors
Time span and type of reports	Varies from hourly information to 15 to 20 years, with financial and nonfinancial reports on products, departments, territories, and strategies	Annual and quarterly financial reports, primarily on the company as a whole
Behavioral implications	Designed to influence the behavior of managers and other employees	Primarily reports economic events but also influences behavior because manager's compensation is often based on reported financial results

customer satisfaction and quality and to develop new products, with the goal of enhancing revenues and profits.

Strategic Decisions and the Management Accountant

Strategy specifies how an organization matches its own capabilities with the opportunities in the marketplace to accomplish its objectives. In other words, strategy describes how an organization will compete and the opportunities its managers should seek and pursue. Businesses follow one of two broad strategies. Some companies, such as Southwest Airlines and Vanguard (the mutual fund company) follow a cost leadership strategy. They have been profitable and have grown over the years on the basis of providing quality products or services at low prices by judiciously managing their costs. Other companies such as Apple Inc., the maker of iPods and iPhones, and Johnson & Johnson, the pharmaceutical giant, follow a product differentiation strategy. They generate their profits and growth on the basis of their ability to offer differentiated or unique products or services that appeal to their customers and are often priced higher than the less-popular products or services of their competitors.

Deciding between these strategies is a critical part of what managers do. Management accountants work closely with managers in formulating strategy by providing information about the sources of competitive advantage—for example, the cost, productivity, or efficiency advantage of their company relative to competitors or the premium prices a company can charge relative to the costs of adding features that make its products or services distinctive. **Strategic cost management** describes cost management that specifically focuses on strategic issues.

Management accounting information helps managers formulate strategy by answering questions such as the following:

- Who are our most important customers, and how can we be competitive and deliver value to them? After Amazon.com's success in selling books online, management accountants at Barnes and Noble presented senior executives with the costs and benefits of several alternative approaches for building its information technology infrastructure and developing the capabilities to also sell books online. A similar cost-benefit analysis led Toyota to build flexible computer-integrated manufacturing (CIM) plants that enable it to use the same equipment efficiently to produce a variety of cars in response to changing customer tastes.

- What substitute products exist in the marketplace, and how do they differ from our product in terms of price and quality? Hewlett-Packard, for example, designs and prices new printers after comparing the functionality and quality of its printers to other printers available in the marketplace.

- What is our most critical capability? Is it technology, production, or marketing? How can we leverage it for new strategic initiatives? Kellogg Company, for example, uses the reputation of its brand to introduce new types of cereal.

- Will adequate cash be available to fund the strategy, or will additional funds need to be raised? Proctor & Gamble, for example, issued new debt and equity to fund its strategic acquisition of Gillette, a maker of shaving products.

The best-designed strategies and the best-developed capabilities are useless unless they are effectively executed. In the next section, we describe how management accountants help managers take actions that create value for their customers.

Value Chain and Supply Chain Analysis and Key Success Factors

Customers demand much more than just a fair price; they expect quality products (goods or services) delivered in a timely way. These multiple factors drive how a customer experiences a product and the value or usefulness a customer derives from the product. How then does a company go about creating this value?

Learning Objective **2**

Understand how management accountants affect strategic decisions

. . . they provide information about the sources of competitive advantage

Decision Point

How do management accountants support strategic decisions?

Value-Chain Analysis

Learning Objective 3

Describe the set of business functions in the value chain and identify the dimensions of performance that customers are expecting of companies

. . . R&D, design, production, marketing, distribution, and customer service supported by administration to achieve cost and efficiency, quality, time, and innovation

Value chain is the sequence of business functions in which customer usefulness is added to products. Exhibit 1-2 shows six primary business functions: research and development, design, production, marketing, distribution, and customer service. We illustrate these business functions using Sony Corporation's television division.

1. **Research and development (R&D)**—Generating and experimenting with ideas related to new products, services, or processes. At Sony, this function includes research on alternative television signal transmission (analog, digital, and high-definition) and on the clarity of different shapes and thicknesses of television screens.

2. **Design of products and processes**—Detailed planning, engineering, and testing of products and processes. Design at Sony includes determining the number of component parts in a television set and the effect of alternative product designs on quality and manufacturing costs. Some representations of the value chain collectively refer to the first two steps as technology development.[2]

3. **Production**—Procuring, transporting and storing (also called inbound logistics), coordinating, and assembling (also called operations) resources to produce a product or deliver a service. Production of a Sony television set includes the procurement and assembly of the electronic parts, the cabinet, and the packaging used for shipping.

4. **Marketing (including sales)**—Promoting and selling products or services to customers or prospective customers. Sony markets its televisions at trade shows, via advertisements in newspapers and magazines, on the Internet, and through its sales force.

5. **Distribution**—Processing orders and shipping products or services to customers (also called outbound logistics). Distribution for Sony includes shipping to retail outlets, catalog vendors, direct sales via the Internet, and other channels through which customers purchase televisions.

6. **Customer service**—Providing after-sales service to customers. Sony provides customer service on its televisions in the form of customer-help telephone lines, support on the Internet, and warranty repair work.

In addition to the six primary business functions, Exhibit 1-2 shows an administrative function, which includes functions such as accounting and finance, human resource management, and information technology, that support the six primary business functions. When discussing the value chain in subsequent chapters of the book, we include the administrative support function within the primary functions. For example, included in the marketing function is the function of analyzing, reporting, and accounting for resources spent in different marketing channels, while the production function includes the human resource management function of training front-line workers.

Each of these business functions is essential to companies satisfying their customers and keeping them satisfied (and loyal) over time. Companies use the term *customer relationship management (CRM)* to describe a strategy that integrates people and technology in all business functions to deepen relationships with customers, partners, and distributors. CRM initiatives use technology to coordinate all customer-facing activities

Exhibit 1-2   Different Parts of the Value Chain

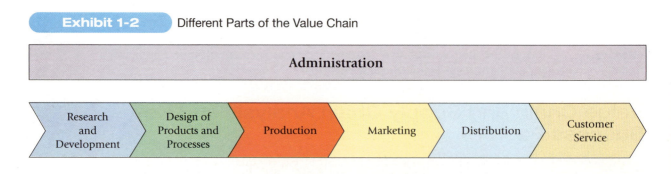

---

[2] M. Porter, *Competitive Advantage* (New York: Free Press, 1985).

(such as marketing, sales calls, distribution, and post sales support) and the design and production activities necessary to get products to customers.

At different times and in different industries, one or more of these functions is more critical than others. For example, a company developing an innovative new product or operating in the pharmaceutical industry, where innovation is the key to profitability, will emphasize R&D and design of products and processes. A company in the consumer goods industry will focus on marketing, distribution, and customer service to build its brand.

Exhibit 1-2 depicts the usual order in which different business-function activities physically occur. Do not, however, interpret Exhibit 1-2 as implying that managers should proceed sequentially through the value chain when planning and managing their activities. Companies gain (in terms of cost, quality, and the speed with which new products are developed) if two or more of the individual business functions of the value chain work concurrently as a team. For example, inputs into design decisions by production, marketing, distribution, and customer service managers often lead to design choices that reduce total costs of the company.

Managers track the costs incurred in each value-chain category. Their goal is to reduce costs and to improve efficiency. Management accounting information helps managers make cost-benefit tradeoffs. For example, is it cheaper to buy products from outside vendors or to do manufacturing in-house? How does investing resources in design and manufacturing reduce costs of marketing and customer service?

Supply-Chain Analysis

The parts of the value chain associated with producing and delivering a product or service—production and distribution—is referred to as the *supply chain*. **Supply chain** describes the flow of goods, services, and information from the initial sources of materials and services to the delivery of products to consumers, regardless of whether those activities occur in the same organization or in other organizations. Consider Coke and Pepsi, for example; many companies play a role in bringing these products to consumers. Exhibit 1-3 presents an overview of the supply chain. Cost management emphasizes integrating and coordinating activities across all companies in the supply chain, to improve performance and reduce costs. Both the Coca-Cola Company and Pepsi Bottling Group require their suppliers (such as plastic and aluminum companies and sugar refiners) to frequently deliver small quantities of materials directly to the production floor to reduce materials-handling costs. Similarly, to reduce inventory levels in the supply chain, Wal-Mart is asking its suppliers, such as Coca-Cola, to be responsible for and to manage inventory at both the Coca-Cola warehouse and Wal-Mart.

Key Success Factors

Customers want companies to use the value chain and supply chain to deliver ever improving levels of performance regarding several (or even all) of the following:

- **Cost and efficiency**—Companies face continuous pressure to reduce the cost of the products they sell. To calculate and manage the cost of products, managers must first understand the tasks or activities (such as setting up machines or distributing

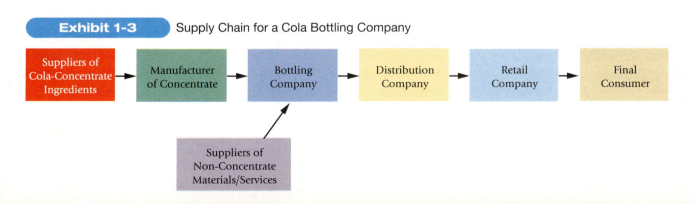

Exhibit 1-3 Supply Chain for a Cola Bottling Company

Suppliers of Cola-Concentrate Ingredients → Manufacturer of Concentrate → Bottling Company → Distribution Company → Retail Company → Final Consumer

Suppliers of Non-Concentrate Materials/Services

products) that cause costs to arise. They must also monitor the marketplace to determine prices that customers are willing to pay for products or services. Management accounting information helps managers calculate a target cost for a product by subtracting the operating income per unit of product that the company desires to earn from the "target price." To achieve the target cost, managers eliminate some activities (such as rework) and reduce the costs of performing activities in all value-chain functions—from initial R&D to customer service.

Increased global competition places ever-increasing pressure on companies to lower costs. Many U.S. companies have cut costs by outsourcing some of their business functions. Nike, for example, has moved its manufacturing operations to China and Mexico. Microsoft and IBM are increasingly doing their software development in Spain, eastern Europe, and India.

- **Quality**—Customers expect high levels of quality. Total quality management (TQM) aims to improve operations throughout the value chain and to deliver products and services that exceed customer expectations. Using TQM, companies design products or services to meet the needs and wants of customers and make these products with zero (or very few) defects and waste, and minimal inventories. Managers use management accounting information to evaluate the costs and revenue benefits of TQM initiatives.

- **Time**—Time has many dimensions. New-product development time is the time it takes for new products to be created and brought to market. The increasing pace of technological innovation has led to shorter product life cycles and more rapid introduction of new products. To make product and design decisions, managers need to understand the costs and benefits of a product over its life cycle.

  Customer-response time describes the speed at which an organization responds to customer requests. To increase customer satisfaction, organizations need to reduce delivery time and reliably meet promised delivery dates. The primary cause of delays is bottlenecks that occur when the work to be performed on a machine, for example, exceeds available capacity. To deliver the product on time, managers need to increase the capacity of the machine to produce more output. Management accounting information helps managers quantify the costs and benefits of relieving bottleneck constraints.

- **Innovation**—A constant flow of innovative products or services is the basis for ongoing company success. Managers rely on management accounting information to evaluate alternative investment and R&D decisions.

Companies are increasingly applying the key success factors of cost and efficiency, quality, time, and innovation to promote sustainability—the development and implementation of strategies to achieve long-term financial, social, and environmental performance. For example, the Japanese copier company Ricoh's sustainability efforts aggressively focus on energy conservation, resource conservation, product recycling, and pollution prevention. By designing products that can be easily recycled, Ricoh simultaneously improves efficiency, cost, and quality. Interest in sustainability appears to be intensifying. Already, government regulations, in countries such as China and India, are impelling companies to develop and report on their sustainability initiatives.

Management accountants help managers track performance of competitors on the key success factors. Competitive information serves as a *benchmark* and alerts managers to market changes. Companies are always seeking to *continuously improve* their operations. These improvements include on-time arrival for Southwest Airlines, customer access to online auctions at eBay, and cost reduction on housing products at Lowes. Sometimes, more-fundamental changes in operations, such as redesigning a manufacturing process to reduce costs, may be necessary. However, successful strategy implementation requires more than value-chain and supply-chain analysis and execution of key success factors. It is the decisions that managers make that help them to develop, integrate, and implement their strategies.

Decision Point ▶

How do companies add value, and what are the dimensions of performance that customers are expecting of companies?

Decision Making, Planning, and Control: The Five-Step Decision-Making Process

We illustrate a five-step decision-making process using the example of the *Daily News*, a newspaper in Boulder, Colorado. Subsequent chapters of the book describe how managers use this five-step decision-making process to make many different types of decisions.

The *Daily News* differentiates itself from its competitors based on in-depth analyses of news by its highly rated journalists, use of color to enhance attractiveness to readers and advertisers, and a Web site that delivers up-to-the-minute news, interviews, and analyses. It has substantial capabilities to deliver on this strategy, such as an automated, computer-integrated, state-of-the-art printing facility; a Web-based information technology infrastructure; and a distribution network that is one of the best in the newspaper industry.

To keep up with steadily increasing production costs, Naomi Crawford, the manager of the *Daily News*, needs to increase revenues. To decide what she should do, Naomi works through the five-step decision-making process.

1. **Identify the problem and uncertainties.** Naomi has two main choices:
   a. Increase the selling price of the newspaper, or
   b. increase the rate per page charged to advertisers.

   The key uncertainty is the effect on demand of any increase in prices or rates. A decrease in demand could offset any increase in prices or rates and lead to lower overall revenues.

2. **Obtain information.** Gathering information before making a decision helps managers gain a better understanding of the uncertainties. Naomi asks her marketing manager to talk to some representative readers to gauge their reaction to an increase in the newspaper's selling price. She asks her advertising sales manager to talk to current and potential advertisers to assess demand for advertising. She also reviews the effect that past price increases had on readership. Ramon Sandoval, the management accountant at the *Daily News*, presents information about the impact of past increases or decreases in advertising rates on advertising revenues. He also collects and analyzes information on advertising rates charged by competing newspapers and other media outlets.

3. **Make predictions about the future.** On the basis of this information, Naomi makes predictions about the future. She concludes that increasing prices would upset readers and decrease readership. She has a different view about advertising rates. She expects a market-wide increase in advertising rates and believes that increasing rates will have little effect on the number of advertising pages sold.

   Naomi recognizes that making predictions requires judgment. She looks for biases in her thinking. Has she correctly judged reader sentiment or is the negative publicity of a price increase overly influencing her decision making? How sure is she that competitors will increase advertising rates? Is her thinking in this respect biased by how competitors have responded in the past? Have circumstances changed? How confident is she that her sales representatives can convince advertisers to pay higher rates? Naomi retests her assumptions and reviews her thinking. She feels comfortable with her predictions and judgments.

4. **Make decisions by choosing among alternatives.** When making decisions, strategy is a vital guidepost; many individuals in different parts of the organization at different times make decisions. Consistency with strategy binds individuals and timelines together and provides a common purpose for disparate decisions. Aligning decisions with strategy enables an organization to implement its strategy and achieve its goals. Without this alignment, decisions will be uncoordinated, pull the organization in different directions, and produce inconsistent results.

   Consistent with the product differentiation strategy, Naomi decides to increase advertising rates by 4% to $5,200 per page in March 2011. She is confident that the *Daily News*'s distinctive style and Web presence will increase readership, creating value for advertisers. She communicates the new advertising rate schedule to the sales department. Ramon estimates advertising revenues of $4,160,000 ($5,200 per page × 800 pages predicted to be sold in March 2011).

Learning Objective 4

Explain the five-step decision-making process

. . . identify the problem and uncertainties, obtain information, make predictions about the future, make decisions by choosing among alternatives, implement the decision, evaluate performance, and learn

and its role in management accounting

. . . planning and control of operations and activities

Steps 1 through 4 are collectively referred to as *planning*. **Planning** comprises selecting organization goals and strategies, predicting results under various alternative ways of achieving those goals, deciding how to attain the desired goals, and communicating the goals and how to achieve them to the entire organization. Management accountants serve as business partners in these planning activities because of their understanding of what creates value and the key success factors.

The most important planning tool when implementing strategy is a budget. A **budget** is the quantitative expression of a proposed plan of action by management and is an aid to coordinating what needs to be done to execute that plan. For March 2011, budgeted advertising revenue equals $4,160,000. The full budget for March 2011 includes budgeted circulation revenue and the production, distribution, and customer-service costs to achieve sales goals; the anticipated cash flows; and the potential financing needs. Because the process of preparing a budget crosses business functions, it forces coordination and communication throughout the company, as well as with the company's suppliers and customers.

5. **Implement the decision, evaluate performance, and learn.** Managers at the *Daily News* take actions to implement the March 2011 budget. Management accountants collect information to follow through on how actual performance compares to planned or budgeted performance (also referred to as scorekeeping). Information on actual results is different from the *pre-decision* planning information Naomi collected in Step 2, which enabled her to better understand uncertainties, to make predictions, and to make a decision. The comparison of actual performance to budgeted performance is the *control* or *post-decision* role of information. **Control** comprises taking actions that implement the planning decisions, deciding how to evaluate performance, and providing feedback and learning to help future decision making.

   Measuring actual performance informs managers how well they and their subunits are doing. Linking rewards to performance helps motivate managers. These rewards are both intrinsic (recognition for a job well-done) and extrinsic (salary, bonuses, and promotions linked to performance). A budget serves as much as a control tool as a planning tool. Why? Because a budget is a benchmark against which actual performance can be compared.

Consider performance evaluation at the *Daily News*. During March 2011, the newspaper sold advertising, issued invoices, and received payments. These invoices and receipts were recorded in the accounting system. Exhibit 1-4 shows the *Daily News*'s performance report of advertising revenues for March 2011. This report indicates that 760 pages of advertising (40 pages fewer than the budgeted 800 pages) were sold. The average rate per page was $5,080, compared with the budgeted $5,200 rate, yielding actual advertising revenues of $3,860,800. The actual advertising revenues were $299,200 less than the budgeted $4,160,000. Observe how managers use both financial and nonfinancial information, such as pages of advertising, to evaluate performance.

The performance report in Exhibit 1-4 spurs investigation and learning. **Learning** is examining past performance (the control function) and systematically exploring alternative ways to make better-informed decisions and plans in the future. Learning can lead to changes in goals, changes in strategies, changes in the ways decision alternatives are identified,

			Difference:	**Difference as a**
	Actual	**Budgeted**	**(Actual Result −**	**Percentage of**
	Result	**Amount**	**Budgeted Amount)**	**Budgeted Amount**
	(1)	**(2)**	**(3) = (1) − (2)**	**(4) = (3) ÷ (2)**
Advertising pages sold	760 pages	800 pages	40 pages Unfavorable	5.0% Unfavorable
Average rate per page	$5,080	$5,200	$120 Unfavorable	2.3% Unfavorable
Advertising revenues	$3,860,800	$4,160,000	$299,200 Unfavorable	7.2% Unfavorable

Exhibit 1-4

Performance Report of Advertising Revenues at the *Daily News* for March 2011

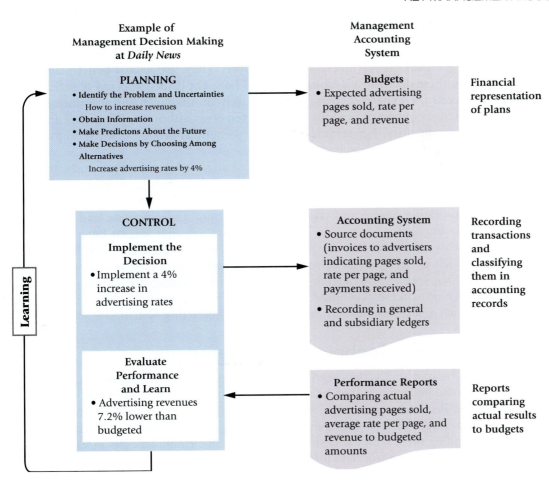

Exhibit 1-5

How Accounting Aids Decision Making, Planning, and Control at the *Daily News*

changes in the range of information collected when making predictions, and sometimes changes in managers.

The performance report in Exhibit 1-4 would prompt the management accountant to raise several questions directing the attention of managers to problems and opportunities. Is the strategy of differentiating the *Daily News* from other newspapers attracting more readers? In implementing the new advertising rates, did the marketing and sales department make sufficient efforts to convince advertisers that, even with the higher rate of $5,200 per page, advertising in the *Daily News* was a good buy? Why was the actual average rate per page $5,080 instead of the budgeted rate of $5,200? Did some sales representatives offer discounted rates? Did economic conditions cause the decline in advertising revenues? Are revenues falling because editorial and production standards have declined? Answers to these questions could prompt the newspaper's publisher to take subsequent actions, including, for example, adding more sales personnel or making changes in editorial policy. Good implementation requires the marketing, editorial, and production departments to work together and coordinate their actions.

The management accountant could go further by identifying the specific advertisers that cut back or stopped advertising after the rate increase went into effect. Managers could then decide when and how sales representatives should follow-up with these advertisers.

The left side of Exhibit 1-5 provides an overview of the decision-making processes at the *Daily News*. The right side of the exhibit highlights how the management accounting system aids in decision making.

Key Management Accounting Guidelines

Three guidelines help management accountants provide the most value to their companies in strategic and operational decision making: Employ a cost-benefit approach, give full recognition to behavioral and technical considerations, and use different costs for different purposes.

Decision Point

How do managers make decisions to implement strategy?

Learning Objective 5

Describe three guidelines management accountants follow in supporting managers

. . . employing a cost-benefit approach, recognizing behavioral as well as technical considerations, and calculating different costs for different purposes

Cost-Benefit Approach

Managers continually face resource-allocation decisions, such as whether to purchase a new software package or hire a new employee. They use a **cost-benefit approach** when making these decisions: Resources should be spent if the expected benefits to the company exceed the expected costs. Managers rely on management accounting information to quantify expected benefits and expected costs although all benefits and costs are not easy to quantify. Nevertheless, the cost-benefit approach is a useful guide for making resource-allocation decisions.

Consider the installation of a company's first budgeting system. Previously, the company used historical recordkeeping and little formal planning. A major benefit of installing a budgeting system is that it compels managers to plan ahead, compare actual to budgeted information, learn, and take corrective action. These actions lead to different decisions that improve performance relative to decisions that would have been made using the historical system, but the benefits are not easy to measure. On the cost side, some costs, such as investments in software and training are easier to quantify. Others, such as the time spent by managers on the budgeting process, are harder to quantify. Regardless, senior managers compare expected benefits and expected costs, exercise judgment, and reach a decision, in this case to install the budgeting system.

Behavioral and Technical Considerations

The cost-benefit approach is the criterion that assists managers in deciding whether, say, to install a proposed budgeting system instead of continuing to use an existing historical system. In making this decision senior managers consider two simultaneous missions: one technical and one behavioral. The technical considerations help managers make wise economic decisions by providing them with the desired information (for example, costs in various value-chain categories) in an appropriate format (such as actual results versus budgeted amounts) and at the preferred frequency. Now consider the human (the behavioral) side of why budgeting is used. Budgets induce a different set of decisions within an organization because of better collaboration, planning, and motivation. The behavioral considerations encourage managers and other employees to strive for achieving the goals of the organization.

Both managers and management accountants should always remember that management is not confined exclusively to technical matters. Management is primarily a human activity that should focus on how to help individuals do their jobs better—for example, by helping them to understand which of their activities adds value and which does not. Moreover, when workers underperform, behavioral considerations suggest that management systems and processes should cause managers to personally discuss with workers ways to improve performance rather than just sending them a report highlighting their underperformance.

Different Costs for Different Purposes

This book emphasizes that managers use alternative ways to compute costs in different decision-making situations, because there are different costs for different purposes. A cost concept used for the external-reporting purpose of accounting may not be an appropriate concept for internal, routine reporting to managers.

Consider the advertising costs associated with Microsoft Corporation's launch of a major product with a useful life of several years. For external reporting to shareholders, television advertising costs for this product are fully expensed in the income statement in the year they are incurred. GAAP requires this immediate expensing for external reporting. For internal purposes of evaluating management performance, however, the television advertising costs could be capitalized and then amortized or written off as expenses over several years. Microsoft could capitalize these advertising costs if it believes doing so results in a more accurate and fairer measure of the performance of the managers that launched the new product.

We now discuss the relationships and reporting responsibilities among managers and management accountants within a company's organization structure.

Decision Point ▶

What guidelines do management accountants use?

Organization Structure and the Management Accountant

We focus first on broad management functions and then look at how the management accounting and finance functions support managers.

Learning Objective 6

Understand how management accounting fits into an organization's structure

. . . for example, the responsibilities of the controller

Line and Staff Relationships

Organizations distinguish between line management and staff management. **Line management**, such as production, marketing, and distribution management, is directly responsible for attaining the goals of the organization. For example, managers of manufacturing divisions may target particular levels of budgeted operating income, certain levels of product quality and safety, and compliance with environmental laws. Similarly, the pediatrics department in a hospital is responsible for quality of service, costs, and patient billings. **Staff management**, such as management accountants and information technology and human-resources management, provides advice, support, and assistance to line management. A plant manager (a line function) may be responsible for investing in new equipment. A management accountant (a staff function) works as a business partner of the plant manager by preparing detailed operating-cost comparisons of alternative pieces of equipment.

Increasingly, organizations such as Honda and Dell are using teams to achieve their objectives. These teams include both line and staff management so that all inputs into a decision are available simultaneously.

The Chief Financial Officer and the Controller

The **chief financial officer (CFO)**—also called the **finance director** in many countries—is the executive responsible for overseeing the financial operations of an organization. The responsibilities of the CFO vary among organizations, but they usually include the following areas:

- **Controllership**—includes providing financial information for reports to managers and shareholders, and overseeing the overall operations of the accounting system
- **Treasury**—includes banking and short- and long-term financing, investments, and cash management
- **Risk management**—includes managing the financial risk of interest-rate and exchange-rate changes and derivatives management
- **Taxation**—includes income taxes, sales taxes, and international tax planning
- **Investor relations**—includes communicating with, responding to, and interacting with shareholders
- **Internal audit**—includes reviewing and analyzing financial and other records to attest to the integrity of the organization's financial reports and to adherence to its policies and procedures

The **controller** (also called the *chief accounting officer*) is the financial executive primarily responsible for management accounting and financial accounting. This book focuses on the controller as the chief management accounting executive. Modern controllers do not do any controlling in terms of line authority except over their own departments. Yet the modern concept of controllership maintains that the controller exercises control in a special sense. By reporting and interpreting relevant data, the controller influences the behavior of all employees and exerts a force that impels line managers toward making better-informed decisions as they implement their strategies.

Exhibit 1-6 is an organization chart of the CFO and the corporate controller at Nike, the leading footwear and apparel company. The CFO is a staff manager who reports to and supports the chief executive officer (CEO). As in most organizations, the corporate controller at Nike reports to the CFO. Nike also has regional controllers who support regional managers in the major geographic regions in which the company operates, such

Exhibit 1-6

Nike: Reporting
Relationship for the
CFO and the Corporate
Controller

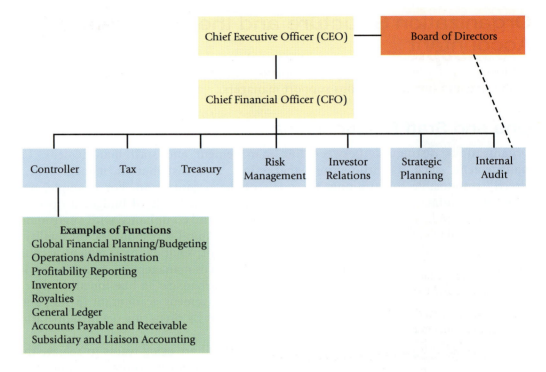

as the United States, Asia Pacific, Latin America, and Europe. Individual countries sometimes have a country controller. Organization charts such as the one in Exhibit 1-6 show formal reporting relationships. In most organizations, there also are informal relationships that must be understood when managers attempt to implement their decisions. Examples of informal relationships are friendships among managers (friendships of a professional or personal kind) and the personal preferences of top management about the managers they rely on in decision making.

Ponder what managers do to design and implement strategies and the organization structures within which they operate. Then think about the management accountants' and controllers' roles. It should be clear that the successful management accountant must have technical and analytical competence *as well as* behavioral and interpersonal skills. The Concepts in Action box on page 15 describes some desirable values and behaviors and why they are so critical to the partnership between management accountants and managers. We will refer to these values and behaviors as we discuss different topics in subsequent chapters of this book.

Decision Point ▶

Where does the
management
accounting function
fit into an
organization's
structure?

Professional Ethics

At no time has the focus on ethical conduct been sharper than it is today. Corporate scandals at Enron, WorldCom, and Arthur Andersen have seriously eroded the public's confidence in corporations. All employees in a company, whether in line management or staff management, must comply with the organization's—and more broadly, society's—expectations of ethical standards.

Learning Objective 7

Understand what
professional ethics
mean to management
accountants

. . . for example,
management
accountants must
maintain integrity and
credibility in every
aspect of their job

Institutional Support

Accountants have special obligations regarding ethics, given that they are responsible for the integrity of the financial information provided to internal and external parties. The Sarbanes–Oxley legislation in the United States, passed in 2002 in response to a series of corporate scandals, focuses on improving internal control, corporate governance, monitoring of managers, and disclosure practices of public corporations. These regulations call for tough ethical standards on managers and accountants and provide a process for employees to report violations of illegal and unethical acts.

Concepts in Action

Management Accounting Beyond the Numbers

When you hear the job title "accountant," what comes to mind? The CPA who does your tax return each year? Individuals who prepare budgets at Dell or Sony? To people outside the profession, it may seem like accountants are just "numbers people." It is true that most accountants are adept financial managers, yet their skills do not stop there. To be successful, management accountants must possess certain values and behaviors that reach well beyond basic analytical abilities.

Working in cross-functional teams and as a business partner of managers. It is not enough that management accountants simply be technically competent in their area of study. They also need to be able to work in teams, to learn about business issues, to understand the motivations of different individuals, to respect the views of their colleagues, and to show empathy and trust.

Promoting fact-based analysis and making tough-minded, critical judgments without being adversarial. Management accountants must raise tough questions for managers to consider, especially when preparing budgets. They must do so thoughtfully and with the intent of improving plans and decisions. In the case of Washington Mutual's bank failure, management accountants should have raised questions about whether the company's risky mortgage lending would be profitable if housing prices declined.

Leading and motivating people to change and be innovative. Implementing new ideas, however good they may be, is seldom easy. When the United States Department of Defense sought to consolidate more than 320 finance and accounting systems into a centralized platform, the accounting services director and his team of management accountants made sure that the vision for change was well understood throughout the agency. Ultimately, each individual's performance was aligned with the transformative change and incentive pay was introduced to promote adoption and drive innovation within this new framework.

Communicating clearly, openly, and candidly. Communicating information is a large part of a management accountant's job. A few years ago, Pitney Bowes Inc. (PBI), a $4 billion global provider of integrated mail and document management solutions, implemented a reporting initiative to give managers feedback in key areas. The initiative succeeded because it was clearly designed and openly communicated by PBI's team of management accountants.

Having a strong sense of integrity. Management accountants must never succumb to pressure from managers to manipulate financial information. They must always remember that their primary commitment is to the organization and its shareholders. At WorldCom, under pressure from senior managers, members of the accounting staff concealed billions of dollars in expenses. Because the accounting staff lacked the integrity and courage to stand up to and report corrupt senior managers, WorldCom landed in bankruptcy. Some members of the accounting staff and the senior executive team served prison terms for their actions.

Sources: Dash, Eric and Andrew Ross Sorkin. 2008. Government seizes WaMu and sells some assets. *New York Times,* September 25. http://www.nytimes.com/2008/09/26/business/26wamu.html; Garling, Wendy. 2007. Winning the Transformation Battle at the Defense Finance and Accounting Service. *Balanced Scorecard Report,* May–June. http://cb.hbsp.harvard.edu/cb/web/product_detail.seam?R=B0705C-PDF-ENG; Gollakota, Kamala and Vipin Gupta. 2009. *WorldCom Inc.: What went wrong.* Richard Ivey School of Business Case No. 905M43. London, ON: The University of Western Ontario. http://cb.hbsp.harvard.edu/cb/web/product_detail.seam?R=905M43-PDF-ENG; Green, Mark, Jeannine Garrity, Andrea Gumbus, and Bridget Lyons. 2002. Pitney Bowes Calls for New Metrics. *Strategic Finance,* May. http://www.allbusiness.com/accounting-reporting/reports-statements-profit/189988-1.html

Professional accounting organizations, which represent management accountants in many countries, promote high ethical standards.[3] Each of these organizations provides certification programs indicating that the holder has demonstrated the competency of technical knowledge required by that organization in management accounting and financial management, respectively.

In the United States, the Institute of Management Accountants (IMA) has also issued ethical guidelines. Exhibit 1-7 presents the IMA's guidance on issues relating to competence,

---

[3] See Appendix C: Cost Accounting in Professional Examinations in MyAccountingLab and at www.pearsonhighered.com/horngren for a list of professional management accounting organizations in the United States, Canada, Australia, Japan, and the United Kingdom.

Practitioners of management accounting and financial management have an obligation to the public, their profession, the organizations they serve, and themselves to maintain the highest standards of ethical conduct. In recognition of this obligation, the Institute of Management Accountants has promulgated the following standards of ethical professional practice. Adherence to these standards, both domestically and internationally, is integral to achieving the Objectives of Management Accounting. Practitioners of management accounting and financial management shall not commit acts contrary to these standards nor shall they condone the commission of such acts by others within their organizations.

IMA STATEMENT OF ETHICAL PROFESSIONAL PRACTICE

Practitioners of management accounting and financial management shall behave ethically. A commitment to ethical professional practice includes overarching principles that express our values and standards that guide our conduct.

PRINCIPLES

IMA's overarching ethical principles include: Honesty, Fairness, Objectivity, and Responsibility. Practitioners shall act in accordance with these principles and shall encourage others within their organizations to adhere to them.

STANDARDS

A practitioner's failure to comply with the following standards may result in disciplinary action.

COMPETENCE

Each practitioner has a responsibility to:
1. Maintain an appropriate level of professional expertise by continually developing knowledge and skills.
2. Perform professional duties in accordance with relevant laws, regulations, and technical standards.
3. Provide decision support information and recommendations that are accurate, clear, concise, and timely.
4. Recognize and communicate professional limitations or other constraints that would preclude responsible judgment or successful performance of an activity.

CONFIDENTIALITY

Each practitioner has a responsibility to:
1. Keep information confidential except when disclosure is authorized or legally required.
2. Inform all relevant parties regarding appropriate use of confidential information. Monitor subordinates' activities to ensure compliance.
3. Refrain from using confidential information for unethical or illegal advantage.

INTEGRITY

Each practitioner has a responsibility to:
1. Mitigate actual conflicts of interest. Regularly communicate with business associates to avoid apparent conflicts of interest. Advise all parties of any potential conflicts.
2. Refrain from engaging in any conduct that would prejudice carrying out duties ethically.
3. Abstain from engaging in or supporting any activity that might discredit the profession.

CREDIBILITY

Each practitioner has a responsibility to:
1. Communicate information fairly and objectively.
2. Disclose all relevant information that could reasonably be expected to influence an intended user's understanding of the reports, analyses, or recommendations.
3. Disclose delays or deficiencies in information, timeliness, processing, or internal controls in conformance with organization policy and/or applicable law.

Source: Statement on Management Accounting Number 1-C. 2005. *IMA Statement of Ethical Professional Practice.* Montvale, NJ: Institute of Management Accountants. Reprinted with permission from the Institute of Management Accountants, Montvale, NJ, www.imanet.org.

confidentiality, integrity, and credibility. To provide support to its members to act ethically at all times, the IMA runs an ethics hotline service. Members can call professional counselors at the IMA's Ethics Counseling Service to discuss their ethical dilemmas. The counselors help identify the key ethical issues and possible alternative ways of resolving them, and confidentiality is guaranteed. The IMA is just one of many institutions that help navigate management accountants through what could be turbulent ethical waters.

Typical Ethical Challenges

Ethical issues can confront management accountants in many ways. Here are two examples:

- **Case A:** A division manager has concerns about the commercial potential of a software product for which development costs are currently being capitalized as an asset rather than being shown as an expense for internal reporting purposes. The manager's bonus is based, in part, on division profits. The manager argues that showing development costs as an asset is justified because the new product will generate profits but presents little evidence to support his argument. The last two products from this division have been unsuccessful. The management accountant disagrees but wants to avoid a difficult personal confrontation with the boss, the division manager.

- **Case B:** A packaging supplier, bidding for a new contract, offers the management accountant of the purchasing company an all-expenses-paid weekend to the Super Bowl. The supplier does not mention the new contract when extending the invitation. The accountant is not a personal friend of the supplier. The accountant knows cost issues are critical in approving the new contract and is concerned that the supplier will ask for details about bids by competing packaging companies.

In each case the management accountant is faced with an ethical dilemma. Case A involves competence, credibility, and integrity. The management accountant should request that the division manager provide credible evidence that the new product is commercially viable. If the manager does not provide such evidence, expensing development costs in the current period is appropriate. Case B involves confidentiality and integrity.

Ethical issues are not always clear-cut. The supplier in Case B may have no intention of raising issues associated with the bid. However, the appearance of a conflict of interest in Case B is sufficient for many companies to prohibit employees from accepting "favors" from suppliers. Exhibit 1-8 presents the IMA's guidance on "Resolution of Ethical Conflict." The accountant in Case B should discuss the invitation with his or her immediate supervisor. If the visit is approved, the accountant should inform the supplier that the

Exhibit 1-8

Resolution of
Ethical Conflict

In applying the Standards of Ethical Professional Practice, you may encounter problems identifying unethical behavior or resolving an ethical conflict. When faced with ethical issues, you should follow your organization's established policies on the resolution of such conflict. If these policies do not resolve the ethical conflict, you should consider the following courses of action:

1. Discuss the issue with your immediate supervisor except when it appears that the supervisor is involved. In that case, present the issue to the next level. If you cannot achieve a satisfactory resolution, submit the issue to the next management level. If your immediate superior is the chief executive officer or equivalent, the acceptable reviewing authority may be a group such as the audit committee, executive committee, board of directors, board of trustees, or owners. Contact with levels above the immediate superior should be initiated only with your superior's knowledge, assuming he or she is not involved. Communication of such problems to authorities or individuals not employed or engaged by the organization is not considered appropriate, unless you believe there is a clear violation of the law.

2. Clarify relevant ethical issues by initiating a confidential discussion with an IMA Ethics Counselor or other impartial advisor to obtain a better understanding of possible courses of action.

3. Consult your own attorney as to legal obligations and rights concerning the ethical conflict.

Source: Statement on Management Accounting Number 1-C. 2005. *IMA Statement of Ethical Professional Practice.* Montvale, NJ: Institute of Management Accountants. Reprinted with permission from the Institute of Management Accountants, Montvale, NJ, www.imanet.org.

Johnson was new to the Controller's position and wanted to make sure that Clark's orders were followed. Johnson came up with the following ideas for making the third quarter budgeted targets:

a. Stop all research and development efforts on the drug Lyricon until after year-end. This change would delay the drug going to market by at least six months. It is also possible that in the meantime a PharmaCor competitor could make it to market with a similar drug.

b. Sell off rights to the drug, Markapro. The company had not planned on doing this because, under current market conditions, it would get less than fair value. It would, however, result in a onetime gain that could offset the budget short-fall. Of course, all future profits from Markapro would be lost.

c. Capitalize some of the company's R&D expenditures reducing R&D expense on the income statement. This transaction would not be in accordance with GAAP, but Johnson thought it was justifiable, since the Lyricon drug was going to market early next year. Johnson would argue that capitalizing R & D costs this year and expensing them next year would better match revenues and expenses.

Required

1. Referring to the "Standards of Ethical Behavior for Practitioners of Management Accounting and Financial Management," Exhibit 1-7 on page 16, which of the preceding items (**a–c**) are acceptable to use? Which are unacceptable?
2. What would you recommend Johnson do?

1-29 Professional ethics and end-of-year actions. Janet Taylor is the new division controller of the snack-foods division of Gourmet Foods. Gourmet Foods has reported a minimum 15% growth in annual earnings for each of the past five years. The snack-foods division has reported annual earnings growth of more than 20% each year in this same period. During the current year, the economy went into a recession. The corporate controller estimates a 10% annual earnings growth rate for Gourmet Foods this year. One month before the December 31 fiscal year-end of the current year, Taylor estimates the snack-foods division will report an annual earnings growth of only 8%. Warren Ryan, the snack-foods division president, is not happy, but he notes that "the end-of-year actions" still need to be taken.

Taylor makes some inquiries and is able to compile the following list of end-of-year actions that were more or less accepted by the previous division controller:

a. Deferring December's routine monthly maintenance on packaging equipment by an independent contractor until January of next year

b. Extending the close of the current fiscal year beyond December 31 so that some sales of next year are included in the current year

c. Altering dates of shipping documents of next January's sales to record them as sales in December of the current year

d. Giving salespeople a double bonus to exceed December sales targets

e. Deferring the current period's advertising by reducing the number of television spots run in December and running more than planned in January of next year

f. Deferring the current period's reported advertising costs by having Gourmet Foods' outside advertising agency delay billing December advertisements until January of next year or by having the agency alter invoices to conceal the December date

g. Persuading carriers to accept merchandise for shipment in December of the current year although they normally would not have done so

Required

1. Why might the snack-foods division president want to take these end-of-year actions?
2. Taylor is deeply troubled and reads the "Standards of Ethical Behavior for Practitioners of Management Accounting and Financial Management" in Exhibit 1-7 (p. 16). Classify each of the end-of-year actions (**a–g**) as acceptable or unacceptable according to that document.
3. What should Taylor do if Ryan suggests that these end-of-year actions are taken in every division of Gourmet Foods and that she will greatly harm the snack-foods division if she does not cooperate and paint the rosiest picture possible of the division's results?

1-30 Professional ethics and end-of-year actions. Deacon Publishing House is a publishing company that produces consumer magazines. The house and home division, which sells home-improvement and home-decorating magazines, has seen a 20% reduction in operating income over the past nine months, primarily due to the recent economic recession and the depressed consumer housing market. The division's Controller, Todd Allen, has felt pressure from the CFO to improve his division's operating results by the end of the year. Allen is considering the following options for improving the division's performance by year-end:

a. Cancelling two of the division's least profitable magazines, resulting in the layoff of twenty-five employees.

b. Selling the new printing equipment that was purchased in January and replacing it with discarded equipment from one of the company's other divisions. The previously discarded equipment no longer meets current safety standards.

c. Recognizing unearned subscription revenue (cash received in advance for magazines that will be delivered in the future) as revenue when cash is received in the current month (just before fiscal year end) instead of showing it as a liability.

d. Reducing the division's Allowance for Bad Debt Expense. This transaction alone would increase operating income by 5%.

e. Recognizing advertising revenues that relate to January in December.

f. Switching from declining balance to straight line depreciation to reduce depreciation expense in the current year.

Required

1. What are the motivations for Allen to improve the division's year-end operating earnings?

2. From the point of view of the "Standards of Ethical Behavior for Practitioners of Management Accounting and Financial Management," Exhibit 1-7 on page 16, which of the preceding items (**a–f**) are acceptable? Which are unacceptable?

3. What should Allen do about the pressure to improve performance?

Collaborative Learning Problem

1-31 **Global company, ethical challenges.** Bredahl Logistics, a U.S. shipping company, has just begun distributing goods across the Atlantic to Norway. The company began operations in 2010, transporting goods to South America. The company's earnings are currently trailing behind its competitors and Bredahl's investors are becoming anxious. Some of the company's largest investors are even talking of selling their interest in the shipping newcomer. Bredahl's CEO, Marcus Hamsen, calls an emergency meeting with his executive team. Hamsen needs a plan before his upcoming conference call with uneasy investors. Brehdal's executive staff make the following suggestions for salvaging the company's short-term operating results:

a. Stop all transatlantic shipping efforts. The start-up costs for the new operations are hurting current profit margins.

b. Make deep cuts in pricing through the end of the year to generate additional revenue.

c. Pressure current customers to take early delivery of goods before the end of the year so that more revenue can be reported in this year's financial statements.

d. Sell-off distribution equipment prior to year-end. The sale would result in one-time gains that could offset the company's lagging profits. The owned equipment could be replaced with leased equipment at a lower cost in the current year.

e. Record executive year-end bonus compensation for the current year in the next year when it is paid after the December fiscal year-end.

f. Recognize sales revenues on orders received, but not shipped as of the end of the year.

g. Establish corporate headquarters in Ireland before the end of the year, lowering the company's corporate tax rate from 28% to 12.5%.

Required

1. As the management accountant for Brehdahl, evaluate each of the preceding items (**a–g**) in the context of the "Standards of Ethical Behavior for Practitioners of Management Accounting and Financial Management," Exhibit 1-7 on page 16. Which of the items are in violation of these ethics standards and which are acceptable?

2. What should the management accountant do with respect to those items that are in violation of the ethical standards for management accountants?

An Introduction to Cost Terms and Purposes

What does the word cost mean to you?

Is it the price you pay for something of value? A cash outflow? Something that affects profitability? There are many different types of costs, and at different times organizations put more or less emphasis on them. When times are good companies often focus on selling as much as they can, with costs taking a backseat. But when times get tough, the emphasis usually shifts to costs and cutting them, as General Motors tried to do. Unfortunately, when times became really bad GM was unable to cut costs fast enough leading to Chapter 11 bankruptcy.

GM Collapses Under the Weight of its Fixed Costs[1]

After nearly 80 years as the world's largest automaker, General Motors (GM) was forced to file for bankruptcy protection in 2009. Declining sales and the rise of Japanese competitors, such as Toyota and Honda, affected GM's viability given its high fixed costs—costs that did not decrease as the number of cars that GM made and sold declined.

A decade of belt-tightening brought GM's variable costs—costs such as material costs that vary with the number of cars that GM makes—in line with those of the Japanese. Unfortunately for GM, a large percentage of its operating costs were fixed because union contracts made it difficult for the company to close its factories or reduce pensions and health benefits owed to retired workers.

To cover its high fixed costs, GM needed to sell a lot of cars. Starting in 2001, it began offering sales incentives and rebates, which for a few years were somewhat successful. GM also expanded aggressively into China and Europe.

But in 2005, growth efforts slowed, and GM lost $10.4 billion. As a result, GM embarked on a reorganization plan that closed more than a dozen plants, eliminated tens of thousands of jobs, slashed retirement plan benefits for its 40,000-plus salaried employees, and froze its pension program.

Despite these cuts, GM could not reduce its costs fast enough to keep up with the steadily declining market for new cars and trucks. In the United States, as gas prices rose above $4 a gallon, GM's product

---

[1] *Sources:* Loomis, Carol. 2006. The tragedy of General Motors. *Fortune*, February 6; *New York Times*. 2009. Times topics: Automotive industry crisis. December 6. http://topics.nytimes.com/top/reference/timestopics/subjects/c/credit_crisis/auto_industry/index.html; Taylor, III, Alex. 2005. GM hits the skids. *Fortune*, April 4; Vlasic, Bill and Nick Bunkley. 2008. G.M. says U.S. cash is its best hope. *New York Times*, November 8.

mix was too heavily weighted toward gas-guzzling trucks, pickup trucks, and sport utility vehicles, all of which were experiencing sharp decreases in sales.

In late 2008, as the economic crisis worsened, GM announced plans to cut $15 billion in costs and raise $5 billion through the sale of assets, like its Hummer brand of off-road vehicles. "We're cutting to the bone," said Fritz Henderson, GM's president. "But given the situation, we think that's appropriate."

It was appropriate, but it wasn't enough. By November 2008, GM had lost more than $18 billion for the year, and the government loaned the company $20 billion to continue operations. Ultimately, its restructuring efforts fell short, and the weight of GM's fixed costs drove the company into bankruptcy. In court papers, the company claimed $82.3 billion in assets and $172.8 billion in debt.

When it emerges from bankruptcy, GM will be a much smaller company with only four brands of cars (down from eight), more than 20,000 fewer hourly union workers, and as many as 20 additional shuttered factories.

As the story of General Motors illustrates, managers must understand costs in order to interpret and act on accounting information. Organizations as varied as as the United Way, the Mayo Clinic, and Sony generate reports containing a variety of cost concepts and terms that managers need to run their businesses. Managers must understand these concepts and terms to effectively use the information provided. This chapter discusses cost concepts and terms that are the basis of accounting information used for internal and external reporting.

Costs and Cost Terminology

Accountants define **cost** as a resource sacrificed or forgone to achieve a specific objective. A cost (such as direct materials or advertising) is usually measured as the monetary amount that must be paid to acquire goods or services. An **actual cost** is the cost incurred (a historical or past cost), as distinguished from a **budgeted cost**, which is a predicted or forecasted cost (a future cost).

When you think of cost, you invariably think of it in the context of finding the cost of a particular thing. We call this thing a **cost object**, which is anything for which a measurement of costs is desired. Suppose that you were a manager at BMW's Spartanburg, South Carolina, plant. BMW makes several different types of cars and sport activity vehicles (SAVs) at this plant. What cost objects can you think of? Now look at Exhibit 2-1.

You will see that BMW managers not only want to know the cost of various products, such as the BMW X5, but they also want to know the costs of things such as projects,

Learning Objective 1

Define and illustrate a cost object

. . . examples of cost objects are products, services, activities, processes, and customers

Cost Object	Illustration
Product	A BMW X5 sports activity vehicle
Service	Telephone hotline providing information and assistance to BMW dealers
Project	R&D project on enhancing the DVD system in BMW cars
Customer	Herb Chambers Motors, the BMW dealer that purchases a broad range of BMW vehicles
Activity	Setting up machines for production or maintaining production equipment
Department	Environmental, health, and safety department

services, and departments. Managers use their knowledge of these costs to guide decisions about, for example, product innovation, quality, and customer service.

Now think about whether a manager at BMW might want to know the *budgeted cost* of a cost object, or the *actual cost*. Managers almost always need to know both types of costs when making decisions. For example, comparing budgeted costs to actual costs helps managers evaluate how well they did and learn about how they can do better in the future.

How does a cost system determine the costs of various cost objects? Typically in two basic stages: accumulation, followed by assignment. **Cost accumulation** is the collection of cost data in some organized way by means of an accounting system. For example, at its Spartanburg plant, BMW collects (accumulates) costs in various categories such as different types of materials, different classifications of labor, and costs incurred for supervision. Managers and management accountants then *assign* these accumulated costs to designated cost objects, such as the different models of cars that BMW manufactures at the plant. BMW managers use this cost information in two main ways:

1. when *making* decisions, for instance, on how to price different models of cars or how much to invest in R&D and marketing and

2. for *implementing* decisions, by influencing and motivating employees to act and learn, for example, by rewarding employees for reducing costs.

Now that we know why it is useful to assign costs, we turn our attention to some concepts that will help us do it. Again, think of the different types of costs that we just discussed—materials, labor, and supervision. You are probably thinking that some costs, such as costs of materials, are easier to assign to a cost object than others, such as costs of supervision. As you will see, this is indeed the case.

Direct Costs and Indirect Costs

We now describe how costs are classified as direct and indirect costs and the methods used to assign these costs to cost objects.

- **Direct costs of a cost object** are related to the particular cost object and can be traced to it in an economically feasible (cost-effective) way. For example, the cost of steel or tires is a direct cost of BMW X5s. The cost of the steel or tires can be easily traced to or identified with the BMW X5. The workers on the BMW X5 line request materials from the warehouse and the material requisition document identifies the cost of the materials supplied to the X5. In a similar vein, individual workers record the time spent working on the X5 on time sheets. The cost of this labor can easily be traced to the X5 and is another example of a direct cost. The term **cost tracing** is used to describe the assignment of direct costs to a particular cost object.

- **Indirect costs of a cost object** are related to the particular cost object but cannot be traced to it in an economically feasible (cost-effective) way. For example, the salaries of plant administrators (including the plant manager) who oversee production of the many different types of cars produced at the Spartanburg plant are an indirect cost of the X5s. Plant administration costs are related to the cost object (X5s) because plant administration is necessary for managing the production of X5s. Plant administration costs are indirect costs because plant administrators also oversee the production of other

Exhibit 2-2

Cost Assignment to a
Cost Object

TYPE OF COST	COST ASSIGNMENT	COST OBJECT
Direct Costs Example: Cost of steel and tires for the BMW X5	**Cost Tracing** based on material requisition document →	**Example: BMW X5**
Indirect Costs Example: Lease cost for Spartanburg plant where BMW makes the X5 and other models of cars	**Cost Allocation** no requisition document →	

products, such as the Z4 Roadster. Unlike the cost of steel or tires, there is no requisition of plant administration services and it is virtually impossible to trace plant administration costs to the X5 line. The term **cost allocation** is used to describe the assignment of indirect costs to a particular cost object. **Cost assignment** is a general term that encompasses both (1) tracing direct costs to a cost object and (2) allocating indirect costs to a cost object. Exhibit 2-2 depicts direct costs and indirect costs and both forms of cost assignment—cost tracing and cost allocation—using the example of the BMW X5.

Challenges in Cost Allocation

Consider the cost to lease the Spartanburg plant. This cost is an indirect cost of the X5—there is no separate lease agreement for the area of the plant where the X5 is made. But BMW *allocates* to the X5 a part of the lease cost of the building—for example, on the basis of an estimate of the percentage of the building's floor space occupied for the production of the X5 relative to the total floor space used to produce all models of cars.

Managers want to assign costs accurately to cost objects. Inaccurate product costs will mislead managers about the profitability of different products and could cause managers to unknowingly promote unprofitable products while deemphasizing profitable products. Generally, managers are more confident about the accuracy of direct costs of cost objects, such as the cost of steel and tires of the X5.

Identifying indirect costs of cost objects, on the other hand, can be more challenging. Consider the lease. An intuitive method is to allocate lease costs on the basis of the total floor space occupied by each car model. This approach measures the building resources used by each car model reasonably and accurately. The more floor space that a car model occupies, the greater the lease costs assigned to it. Accurately allocating other indirect costs, such as plant administration to the X5, however, is more difficult. For example, should these costs be allocated on the basis of the number of workers working on each car model or the number of cars produced of each model? How to measure the share of plant administration used by each car model is not clear-cut.

Factors Affecting Direct/Indirect Cost Classifications

Several factors affect the classification of a cost as direct or indirect:

■ **The materiality of the cost in question.** The smaller the amount of a cost—that is, the more immaterial the cost is—the less likely that it is economically feasible to trace that cost to a particular cost object. Consider a mail-order catalog company such as Lands' End. It would be economically feasible to trace the courier charge for delivering a package to an individual customer as a direct cost. In contrast, the cost of the invoice paper included in the package would be classified as an indirect cost. Why? Although the cost of the paper can be traced to each customer, it is not cost-effective to do so. The benefits of knowing that, say, exactly 0.5¢ worth of paper is included in each package do not exceed the data processing and administrative costs of tracing the cost to each package. The time of the sales administrator, who earns a salary of $45,000 a year, is better spent organizing customer information to assist in focused marketing efforts than on tracking the cost of paper.

■ **Available information-gathering technology.** Improvements in information-gathering technology make it possible to consider more and more costs as direct costs. Bar codes, for example, allow manufacturing plants to treat certain low-cost materials such as clips and screws, which were previously classified as indirect costs, as direct costs of products. At Dell, component parts such as the computer chip and the CD-ROM drive display a bar code that can be scanned at every point in the production process. Bar codes can be read into a manufacturing cost file by waving a "wand" in the same quick and efficient way supermarket checkout clerks enter the cost of each item purchased by a customer.

■ **Design of operations.** Classifying a cost as direct is easier if a company's facility (or some part of it) is used exclusively for a specific cost object, such as a specific product or a particular customer. For example, the cost of the General Chemicals facility dedicated to manufacturing soda ash is a direct cost of soda ash.

Decision Point ▶

How do managers decide whether a cost is a direct or indirect cost?

Be aware that a specific cost may be both a direct cost of one cost object and an indirect cost of another cost object. *That is, the direct/indirect classification depends on the choice of the cost object.* For example, the salary of an assembly department supervisor at BMW is a direct cost if the cost object is the assembly department, but it is an indirect cost if the cost object is a product such as the BMW X5 SAV, because the assembly department assembles many different models. A useful rule to remember is that the broader the definition of the cost object—the assembly department rather than the X5 SAV—the higher the proportion of total costs that are direct costs and the more confidence a manager has in the accuracy of the resulting cost amounts.

Cost-Behavior Patterns: Variable Costs and Fixed Costs

Learning Objective 3

Explain variable costs and fixed costs

. . . the two basic ways in which costs behave

Costing systems record the cost of resources acquired, such as materials, labor, and equipment, and track how those resources are used to produce and sell products or services. Recording the costs of resources acquired and used allows managers to see how costs behave. Consider two basic types of cost-behavior patterns found in many accounting systems. A **variable cost** changes *in total* in proportion to changes in the related level of total activity or volume. A **fixed cost** remains unchanged *in total* for a given time period, despite wide changes in the related level of total activity or volume. Costs are defined as variable or fixed with respect to *a specific activity* and for *a given time period*. Surveys of practice repeatedly show that identifying a cost as variable or fixed provides valuable information for making many management decisions and is an important input when evaluating performance. To illustrate these two basic types of costs, again consider costs at the Spartanburg, South Carolina, plant of BMW.

1. **Variable Costs:** If BMW buys a steering wheel at $60 for each of its BMW X5 vehicles, then the total cost of steering wheels is $60 times the number of vehicles produced, as the following table illustrates.

Number of X5s Produced (1)	Variable Cost per Steering Wheel (2)	Total Variable Cost of Steering Wheels (3) = (1) × (2)
1	$60	$ 60
1,000	60	60,000
3,000	60	180,000

The steering wheel cost is an example of a variable cost because *total cost* changes in proportion to changes in the number of vehicles produced. The cost per unit of a variable cost is constant. It is precisely because the variable cost per steering wheel in column 2 is the same for each steering wheel that the total variable cost of steering wheels in column 3 changes proportionately with the number of X5s produced in column 1. When considering how variable costs behave, always focus on *total* costs.

Exhibit 2-3

Graphs of Variable and Fixed Costs

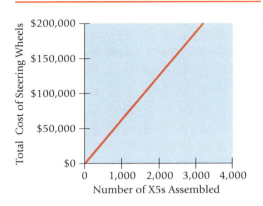

PANEL A: Variable Cost of Steering Wheels at $60 per BMW X5 Assembled

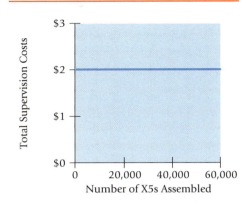

PANEL B: Supervision Costs for the BMW X5 assembly line (in millions)

Exhibit 2-3, Panel A, graphically illustrates the total variable cost of steering wheels. The cost is represented by a straight line that climbs from left to right. The phrases "strictly variable" and "proportionately variable" are sometimes used to describe the variable cost in Panel A.

Consider an example of a variable cost with respect to a different activity—the $20 hourly wage paid to each worker to set up machines at the Spartanburg plant. Setup labor cost is a variable cost with respect to setup hours because setup cost changes in total in proportion to the number of setup hours used.

2. **Fixed Costs:** Suppose BMW incurs a total cost of $2,000,000 per year for supervisors who work exclusively on the X5 line. These costs are unchanged in total over a designated range of the number of vehicles produced during a given time span (see Exhibit 2-3, Panel B). Fixed costs become smaller and smaller on a per unit basis as the number of vehicles assembled increases, as the following table shows.

Annual Total Fixed Supervision Costs for BMW X5 Assembly Line (1)	Number of X5s Produced (2)	Fixed Supervision Cost per X5 (3) = (1) ÷ (2)
$2,000,000	10,000	$200
$2,000,000	25,000	80
$2,000,000	50,000	40

It is precisely because *total* line supervision costs are fixed at $2,000,000 that fixed supervision cost per X5 decreases as the number of X5s produced increases; the same fixed cost is spread over a larger number of X5s. Do not be misled by the change in fixed cost per unit. Just as in the case of variable costs, when considering fixed costs, always focus on *total costs*. Costs are fixed when total costs remain unchanged despite significant changes in the level of total activity or volume.

Why are some costs variable and other costs fixed? Recall that a cost is usually measured as the amount of money that must be paid to acquire goods and services. Total cost of steering wheels is a variable cost because BMW buys the steering wheels only when they are needed. As more X5s are produced, proportionately more steering wheels are acquired and proportionately more costs are incurred.

Contrast the description of variable costs with the $2,000,000 of fixed costs per year incurred by BMW for supervision of the X5 assembly line. This level of supervision is acquired and put in place well before BMW uses it to produce X5s and before BMW even knows how many X5s it will produce. Suppose that BMW puts in place supervisors capable of supervising the production of 60,000 X5s each year. If the demand is for only 55,000 X5s, there will be idle capacity. Supervisors on the X5 line could have supervised the production of 60,000 X5s but will supervise only 55,000 X5s because of the lower demand. However, BMW must pay for the unused line supervision capacity because the cost of supervision cannot be reduced in the short run. If demand is even lower—say only 50,000 X5s—line supervision costs will still be the same $2,000,000, and idle capacity will increase.

Unlike variable costs, fixed costs of resources (such as for line supervision) cannot be quickly and easily changed to match the resources needed or used. Over time, however, managers can take actions to reduce fixed costs. For example, if the X5 line needs to be run for fewer hours because of low demand for X5s, BMW may lay off supervisors or move them to another production line. Unlike variable costs that go away automatically if the resources are not used, reducing fixed costs requires active intervention on the part of managers.

Do not assume that individual cost items are inherently variable or fixed. Consider labor costs. Labor costs can be purely variable with respect to units produced when workers are paid on a piece-unit (piece-rate) basis. For example, some garment workers are paid on a per-shirt-sewed basis. In contrast, labor costs at a plant in the coming year are sometimes appropriately classified as fixed.

For instance, a labor union agreement might set annual salaries and conditions, contain a no-layoff clause, and severely restrict a company's flexibility to assign workers to any other plant that has demand for labor. Japanese companies have for a long time had a policy of lifetime employment for their workers. Although such a policy entails higher fixed labor costs, the benefits are increased loyalty and dedication to the company and higher productivity. As the General Motors example in the chapter opener (p. 26) illustrated, such a policy increases the risk of losses during economic downturns as revenues decrease, while fixed costs remain unchanged. The recent global economic crisis has made companies very wary of locking-in fixed costs. The Concepts in Action box on page 33 describes how a car-sharing service offers companies the opportunity to convert the fixed costs of owning corporate cars into variable costs by renting cars on an as-needed basis.

A particular cost item could be variable with respect to one level of activity and fixed with respect to another. Consider annual registration and license costs for a fleet of planes owned by an airline company. Registration and license costs would be a variable cost with respect to the number of planes owned. But registration and license costs for a particular plane are fixed with respect to the miles flown by that plane during a year.

To focus on key concepts, we have classified the behavior of costs as variable or fixed. Some costs have both fixed and variable elements and are called *mixed* or *semivariable* costs. For example, a company's telephone costs may have a fixed monthly payment and a charge per phone-minute used. We discuss mixed costs and techniques to separate out their fixed and variable components in Chapter 10.

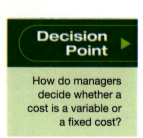

Decision Point

How do managers decide whether a cost is a variable or a fixed cost?

Cost Drivers

A **cost driver** is a variable, such as the level of activity or volume that causally affects costs over a given time span. An *activity* is an event, task, or unit of work with a specified purpose—for example, designing products, setting up machines, or testing products. The level of activity or volume is a cost driver if there is a cause-and-effect relationship between a change in the level of activity or volume and a change in the level of total costs. For example, if product-design costs change with the number of parts in a product, the number of parts is a cost driver of product-design costs. Similarly, miles driven is often a cost driver of distribution costs.

The cost driver of a variable cost is the level of activity or volume whose change causes proportionate changes in the variable cost. For example, the number of vehicles assembled is the cost driver of the total cost of steering wheels. If setup workers are paid an hourly wage, the number of setup hours is the cost driver of total (variable) setup costs.

Costs that are fixed in the short run have no cost driver in the short run but may have a cost driver in the long run. Consider the costs of testing, say, 0.1% of the color printers produced at a Hewlett-Packard plant. These costs consist of equipment and staff costs of the testing department that are difficult to change and, hence, are fixed in the short run with respect to changes in the volume of production. In this case, volume of production is not a cost driver of testing costs in the short run. In the long run, however, Hewlett-Packard will increase or decrease the testing department's equipment and staff to the levels needed to support future production volumes. In the long run, volume of production is a cost driver of testing costs. Costing systems that identify the cost of each activity such as testing, design, or set up are called *activity-based costing systems*.

Concepts in Action

How Zipcar Helps Reduce Twitter's Transportation Costs

Soaring gas prices, high insurance costs, and hefty parking fees have forced many businesses to reexamine whether owning corporate cars is economical. In some cities, Zipcar has emerged as an attractive alternative. Zipcar provides an "on demand" option for urban individuals and businesses to rent a car by the week, the day, or even the hour. Zipcar members make a reservation by phone or Internet, go to the parking lot where the car is located (usually by walking or public transportation), use an electronic card or iPhone application that unlocks the car door via a wireless sensor, and then simply climb in and drive away. Rental fees begin around $7 per hour and $66 per day, and include gas, insurance, and some mileage (usually around 180 miles per day). Currently, business customers account for 15% of Zipcar's revenues, but that number is expected to double in the coming years.

Let's think about what Zipcar means for companies. Many small businesses own a company car or two for getting to meetings, making deliveries, and running errands. Similarly, many large companies own a fleet of cars to shuttle visiting executives and clients back and forth from appointments, business lunches, and the airport. Traditionally, owning these cars has involved very high fixed costs, including buying the asset (car), costs of the maintenance department, and insurance for multiple drivers. Unfortunately, businesses had no other options.

Now, however, companies like Twitter can use Zipcar for on-demand mobility while reducing their transportation and overhead costs. Based in downtown San Francisco, Twitter managers use Zipcar's fleet of Mini Coopers and Toyota Priuses to meet venture capitalists and partners in Silicon Valley. "We would get in a Zipcar to drive down to San Jose to pitch investors or go across the city," says Jack Dorsey, the micro-blogging service's co-founder. "Taxis are hard to find and unreliable here." Twitter also uses Zipcar when traveling far away from its headquarters, like when visiting advertisers in New York and technology vendors in Boston, forgoing the traditional black sedans and long taxi rides from the airport.

From a business perspective, Zipcar allows companies to convert the fixed costs of owning a company car to variable costs. If business slows, or a car isn't required to visit a client, Zipcar customers are not saddled with the fixed costs of car ownership. Of course, if companies use Zipcar too frequently, they can end up paying more overall than they would have paid if they purchased and maintained the car themselves.

Along with cutting corporate spending, car sharing services like Zipcar reduce congestion on the road and promote environmental sustainability. Users report reducing their vehicle miles traveled by 44%, and surveys show CO_2 emissions are being cut by up to 50% per user. Beyond that, each shared car takes up to 20 cars off the road as members sell their cars or decide not to buy new ones—challenging the whole principle of owning a car. "The future of transportation will be a blend of things like Zipcar, public transportation, and private car ownership," says Bill Ford, Ford's executive chairman. But the automaker isn't worried. "Not only do I not fear that, but I think it's a great opportunity for us to participate in the changing nature of car ownership."

Sources: Keegan, Paul. 2009. Zipcar – the best new idea in business. *Fortune,* August 27. http://money.cnn.com/2009/08/26/news/companies/zipcar_car_rentals.fortune/; Olsen, Elizabeth. 2009. Car sharing reinvents the company wheels. *New York Times,* May 7. http://www.nytimes.com/2009/05/07/business/businessspecial/07CAR.html; Zipcar, Inc. Zipcar for business case studies. http://www.zipcar.com/business/is-it/case-studies (accessed October 8, 2009)

Relevant Range

Relevant range is the band of normal activity level or volume in which there is a specific relationship between the level of activity or volume and the cost in question. For example, a fixed cost is fixed only in relation to a given wide range of total activity or volume (at which the company is expected to operate) and only for a given time span (usually a particular budget period). Suppose that BMW contracts with Thomas Transport Company (TTC) to transport X5s to BMW dealers. TTC rents two trucks, and each truck has annual fixed rental costs of $40,000. The maximum annual usage of each truck is 120,000 miles. In the current year (2011), the predicted combined total hauling of the two trucks is 170,000 miles.

Exhibit 2-4 shows how annual fixed costs behave at different levels of miles of hauling. Up to 120,000 miles, TTC can operate with one truck; from 120,001 to 240,000 miles, it operates with two trucks; from 240,001 to 360,000 miles, it operates with three trucks. This

Exhibit 2-4

Fixed-Cost Behavior at
Thomas Transport
Company

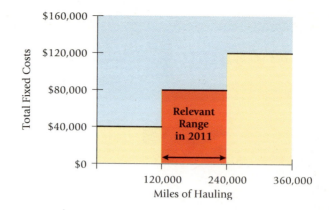

pattern will continue as TTC adds trucks to its fleet to provide more miles of hauling. Given the predicted 170,000-mile usage for 2011, the range from 120,001 to 240,000 miles hauled is the range in which TTC expects to operate, resulting in fixed rental costs of $80,000. Within this relevant range, changes in miles hauled will not affect the annual fixed costs.

Fixed costs may change from one year to the next. For example, if the total rental fee of the two trucks is increased by $2,000 for 2012, the total level of fixed costs will increase to $82,000 (all else remaining the same). If that increase occurs, total rental costs will be fixed at this new level of $82,000 for 2012 for miles hauled in the 120,001 to 240,000 range.

The basic assumption of the relevant range also applies to variable costs. That is, outside the relevant range, variable costs, such as direct materials, may not change proportionately with changes in production volume. For example, above a certain volume, direct material costs may increase at a lower rate because of price discounts on purchases greater than a certain quantity.

Relationships of Types of Costs

We have introduced two major classifications of costs: direct/indirect and variable/fixed. Costs may simultaneously be as follows:

- Direct and variable
- Direct and fixed
- Indirect and variable
- Indirect and fixed

Exhibit 2-5 shows examples of costs in each of these four cost classifications for the BMW X5.

Exhibit 2-5

Examples of Costs in
Combinations of the
Direct/Indirect and
Variable/Fixed Cost
Classifications for a Car
Manufacturer

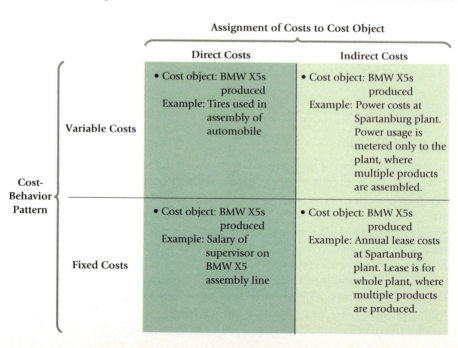

Total Costs and Unit Costs

The preceding section concentrated on the behavior patterns of total costs in relation to activity or volume levels. We now consider unit costs.

Learning Objective 4

Interpret unit costs cautiously

. . . for many decisions, managers should use total costs, not unit costs

Unit Costs

Generally, the decision maker should think in terms of total costs rather than unit costs. In many decision contexts, however, calculating a unit cost is essential. Consider the booking agent who has to make the decision to book Paul McCartney to play at Shea Stadium. She estimates the cost of the event to be $4,000,000. This knowledge is helpful for the decision, but it is not enough.

Before a decision can be reached, the booking agent also must predict the number of people who will attend. Without knowledge of both total cost and number of attendees, she cannot make an informed decision on a possible admission price to recover the cost of the event or even on whether to have the event at all. So she computes the unit cost of the event by dividing the total cost ($4,000,000) by the expected number of people who will attend. If 50,000 people attend, the unit cost is $80 ($4,000,000 ÷ 50,000) per person; if 20,000 attend, the unit cost increases to $200 ($4,000,000 ÷ 20,000).

Unless the total cost is "unitized" (that is, averaged with respect to the level of activity or volume), the $4,000,000 cost is difficult to interpret. The unit cost combines the total cost and the number of people in a handy, communicative way.

Accounting systems typically report both total-cost amounts and average-cost-per-unit amounts. A **unit cost**, also called an **average cost**, is calculated by dividing total cost by the related number of units. The units might be expressed in various ways. Examples are automobiles assembled, packages delivered, or hours worked. Suppose that, in 2011, its first year of operations, $40,000,000 of manufacturing costs are incurred to produce 500,000 speaker systems at the Memphis plant of Tennessee Products. Then the unit cost is $80:

$$\frac{\text{Total manufacturing costs}}{\text{Number of units manufactured}} = \frac{\$40,000,000}{500,000 \text{ units}} = \$80 \text{ per unit}$$

If 480,000 units are sold and 20,000 units remain in ending inventory, the unit-cost concept helps in the determination of total costs in the income statement and balance sheet and, hence, the financial results reported by Tennessee Products to shareholders, banks, and the government.

Cost of goods sold in the income statement, 480,000 units × $80 per unit	$38,400,000
Ending inventory in the balance sheet, 20,000 units × $80 per unit	1,600,000
Total manufacturing costs of 500,000 units	$40,000,000

Unit costs are found in all areas of the value chain—for example, unit cost of product design, of sales visits, and of customer-service calls. By summing unit costs throughout the value chain, managers calculate the unit cost of the different products or services they deliver and determine the profitability of each product or service. Managers use this information, for example, to decide the products in which they should invest more resources, such as R&D and marketing, and the prices they should charge.

Use Unit Costs Cautiously

Although unit costs are regularly used in financial reports and for making product mix and pricing decisions, *managers should think in terms of total costs rather than unit costs for many decisions.* Consider the manager of the Memphis plant of Tennessee Products. Assume the $40,000,000 in costs in 2011 consist of $10,000,000 of fixed costs and $30,000,000 of variable costs (at $60 variable cost per speaker system produced). Suppose the total fixed cost and the variable cost per speaker system in 2012 are expected to be unchanged from 2011. The budgeted costs for 2012 at different production levels, calculated on the basis of total variable costs, total fixed costs, and total costs, are as follows:

Units Produced (1)	Variable Cost per Unit (2)	Total Variable Costs (3) = (1) × (2)	Total Fixed Costs (4)	Total Costs (5) = (3) + (4)	Unit Cost (6) = (5) ÷ (1)
100,000	$60	$ 6,000,000	$10,000,000	$16,000,000	$160.00
200,000	$60	$12,000,000	$10,000,000	$22,000,000	$110.00
500,000	$60	$30,000,000	$10,000,000	$40,000,000	$ 80.00
800,000	$60	$48,000,000	$10,000,000	$58,000,000	$ 72.50
1,000,000	$60	$60,000,000	$10,000,000	$70,000,000	$ 70.00

A plant manager who uses the 2011 unit cost of $80 per unit will underestimate actual total costs if 2012 output is below the 2011 level of 500,000 units. If actual volume is 200,000 units due to, say, the presence of a new competitor, actual costs would be $22,000,000. The unit cost of $80 times 200,000 units equals $16,000,000, which underestimates the actual total costs by $6,000,000 ($22,000,000 – $16,000,000). *The unit cost of $80 applies only when 500,000 units are produced.*

An overreliance on unit cost in this situation could lead to insufficient cash being available to pay costs if volume declines to 200,000 units. As the table indicates, for making this decision, managers should think in terms of total variable costs, total fixed costs, and total costs rather than unit cost. As a general rule, first calculate total costs, then compute a unit cost, if it is needed for a particular decision.

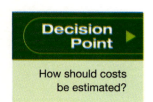

Decision Point ▶

How should costs be estimated?

Business Sectors, Types of Inventory, Inventoriable Costs, and Period Costs

In this section, we describe the different sectors of the economy, the different types of inventory that companies hold, and some commonly used classifications of manufacturing costs.

Manufacturing-, Merchandising-, and Service-Sector Companies

Learning Objective 5

Distinguish inventoriable costs

. . . assets when incurred, then cost of goods sold

from period costs

. . . expenses of the period when incurred

We define three sectors of the economy and provide examples of companies in each sector.

1. **Manufacturing-sector companies** purchase materials and components and convert them into various finished goods. Examples are automotive companies such as Jaguar, cellular phone producers such as Nokia, food-processing companies such as Heinz, and computer companies such as Toshiba.

2. **Merchandising-sector companies** purchase and then sell tangible products without changing their basic form. This sector includes companies engaged in retailing (for example, bookstores such as Barnes and Noble or department stores such as Target), distribution (for example, a supplier of hospital products, such as Owens and Minor), or wholesaling (for example, a supplier of electronic components, such as Arrow Electronics).

3. **Service-sector companies** provide services (intangible products)—for example, legal advice or audits—to their customers. Examples are law firms such as Wachtell, Lipton, Rosen & Katz, accounting firms such as Ernst and Young, banks such as Barclays, mutual fund companies such as Fidelity, insurance companies such as Aetna, transportation companies such as Singapore Airlines, advertising agencies such as Saatchi & Saatchi, television stations such as Turner Broadcasting, Internet service providers such as Comcast, travel agencies such as American Express, and brokerage firms such as Merrill Lynch.

Types of Inventory

Manufacturing-sector companies purchase materials and components and convert them into various finished goods. These companies typically have one or more of the following three types of inventory:

1. **Direct materials inventory.** Direct materials in stock and awaiting use in the manufacturing process (for example, computer chips and components needed to manufacture cellular phones).
2. **Work-in-process inventory.** Goods partially worked on but not yet completed (for example, cellular phones at various stages of completion in the manufacturing process). This is also called **work in progress**.
3. **Finished goods inventory.** Goods (for example, cellular phones) completed but not yet sold.

Merchandising-sector companies purchase tangible products and then sell them without changing their basic form. They hold only one type of inventory, which is products in their original purchased form, called *merchandise inventory*. Service-sector companies provide only services or intangible products and so do not hold inventories of tangible products.

Commonly Used Classifications of Manufacturing Costs

Three terms commonly used when describing manufacturing costs are direct material costs, direct manufacturing labor costs, and indirect manufacturing costs. These terms build on the direct versus indirect cost distinction we had described earlier, in the context of manufacturing costs.

1. **Direct material costs** are the acquisition costs of all materials that eventually become part of the cost object (work in process and then finished goods) and can be traced to the cost object in an economically feasible way. Acquisition costs of direct materials include freight-in (inward delivery) charges, sales taxes, and custom duties. Examples of direct material costs are the steel and tires used to make the BMW X5, and the computer chips used to make cellular phones.
2. **Direct manufacturing labor costs** include the compensation of all manufacturing labor that can be traced to the cost object (work in process and then finished goods) in an economically feasible way. Examples include wages and fringe benefits paid to machine operators and assembly-line workers who convert direct materials purchased to finished goods.
3. **Indirect manufacturing costs** are all manufacturing costs that are related to the cost object (work in process and then finished goods) but cannot be traced to that cost object in an economically feasible way. Examples include supplies, indirect materials such as lubricants, indirect manufacturing labor such as plant maintenance and cleaning labor, plant rent, plant insurance, property taxes on the plant, plant depreciation, and the compensation of plant managers. This cost category is also referred to as **manufacturing overhead costs** or **factory overhead costs**. We use *indirect manufacturing costs* and *manufacturing overhead costs* interchangeably in this book.

We now describe the distinction between inventoriable costs and period costs.

Inventoriable Costs

Inventoriable costs are all costs of a product that are considered as assets in the balance sheet when they are incurred and that become cost of goods sold only when the product is sold. For manufacturing-sector companies, all manufacturing costs are inventoriable costs. Consider Cellular Products, a manufacturer of cellular phones. Costs of direct materials, such as computer chips, issued to production (from direct material inventory), direct manufacturing labor costs, and manufacturing overhead costs create new assets, starting as work in process and becoming finished goods (the cellular phones). Hence, manufacturing costs are included in work-in-process inventory and in finished goods inventory (they are "inventoried") to accumulate the costs of creating these assets.

When the cellular phones are sold, the cost of manufacturing them is matched against **revenues**, which are inflows of assets (usually cash or accounts receivable) received for products or services provided to customers. The cost of goods sold includes all manufacturing costs (direct materials, direct manufacturing labor, and manufacturing overhead costs) incurred to produce them. The cellular phones may be sold during a different accounting period than the period in which they were manufactured. Thus, inventorying manufacturing costs in the balance sheet during the accounting period when goods are manufactured and expensing the manufacturing costs in a later income statement when the goods are sold matches revenues and expenses.

For merchandising-sector companies such as Wal-Mart, inventoriable costs are the costs of purchasing the goods that are resold in their same form. These costs comprise the costs of the goods themselves plus any incoming freight, insurance, and handling costs for those goods. Service-sector companies provide only services or intangible products. The absence of inventories of tangible products for sale means there are no inventoriable costs.

Period Costs

Period costs are all costs in the income statement other than cost of goods sold. Period costs, such as marketing, distribution and customer service costs, are treated as expenses of the accounting period in which they are incurred because they are expected to benefit revenues in that period and are not expected to benefit revenues in future periods. Some costs such as R&D costs are treated as period costs because, although these costs may benefit revenues in a future period if the R&D efforts are successful, it is highly uncertain if and when these benefits will occur. Expensing period costs as they are incurred best matches expenses to revenues.

For manufacturing-sector companies, period costs in the income statement are all nonmanufacturing costs (for example, design costs and costs of shipping products to customers). For merchandising-sector companies, period costs in the income statement are all costs not related to the cost of goods purchased for resale. Examples of these period costs are labor costs of sales floor personnel and advertising costs. Because there are no inventoriable costs for service-sector companies, all costs in the income statement are period costs.

Exhibit 2-5 showed examples of inventoriable costs in direct/indirect and variable/fixed cost classifications for a car manufacturer. Exhibit 2-6 shows examples of period costs in direct/indirect and variable/fixed cost classifications at a bank.

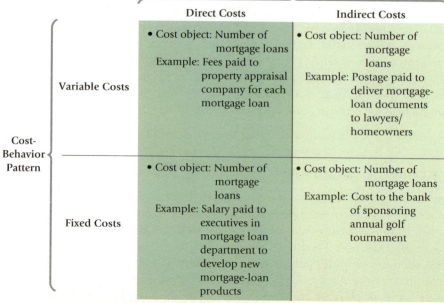

Exhibit 2-6

Examples of Period Costs in Combinations of the Direct/Indirect and Variable/Fixed Cost Classifications at a Bank

		Assignment of Costs to Cost Object	
		Direct Costs	Indirect Costs
Cost-Behavior Pattern	Variable Costs	● Cost object: Number of mortgage loans Example: Fees paid to property appraisal company for each mortgage loan	● Cost object: Number of mortgage loans Example: Postage paid to deliver mortgage-loan documents to lawyers/homeowners
	Fixed Costs	● Cost object: Number of mortgage loans Example: Salary paid to executives in mortgage loan department to develop new mortgage-loan products	● Cost object: Number of mortgage loans Example: Cost to the bank of sponsoring annual golf tournament

Illustrating the Flow of Inventoriable Costs and Period Costs

We illustrate the flow of inventoriable costs and period costs through the income statement of a manufacturing company, for which the distinction between inventoriable costs and period costs is most detailed.

Manufacturing-Sector Example

Follow the flow of costs for Cellular Products in Exhibit 2-7 and Exhibit 2-8. Exhibit 2-7 visually highlights the differences in the flow of inventoriable and period costs for a manufacturing-sector company. Note how, as described in the previous section, inventoriable costs go through the balance sheet accounts of work-in-process inventory and finished goods inventory before entering cost of goods sold in the income statement. Period costs are expensed directly in the income statement. Exhibit 2-8 takes the visual presentation in Exhibit 2-7 and shows how inventoriable costs and period expenses would appear in the income statement and schedule of cost of goods manufactured of a manufacturing company.

We start by tracking the flow of direct materials shown on the left of Exhibit 2-7 and in Panel B of Exhibit 2-8.

Step 1: Cost of direct materials used in 2011. Note how the arrows in Exhibit 2-7 for beginning inventory, $11,000 (all numbers in thousands), and direct material purchases, $73,000, "fill up" the direct material inventory box and how direct material used, $76,000 "empties out" direct material inventory leaving an ending inventory of direct materials of $8,000 that becomes the beginning inventory for the next year.

The cost of direct materials used is calculated in Exhibit 2-8, Panel B (light blue shaded area) as follows:

Beginning inventory of direct materials, January 1, 2011	$11,000
+ Purchases of direct materials in 2011	73,000
− Ending inventory of direct materials, December 31, 2011	8,000
= Direct materials used in 2011	$76,000

Exhibit 2-7 Flow of Revenue and Costs for a Manufacturing-Sector Company, Cellular Products (in thousands)

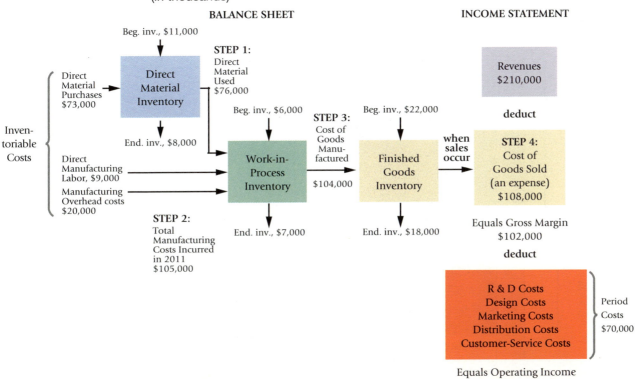

Exhibit 2-8   Income Statement and Schedule of Cost of Goods Manufactured of a Manufacturing-Sector Company, Cellular Products

	A	B	C	D
1	**PANEL A: INCOME STATEMENT**			
2	**Cellular Products**			
3	**Income Statement**			
4	**For the Year Ended December 31, 2011 (in thousands)**			
5	Revenues		$210,000	
6	Cost of goods sold:			
7	Beginning finished goods inventory, January 1, 2009	$ 22,000		
8	Cost of goods manufactured (see Panel B)	104,000	←	
9	Cost of goods available for sale	126,000		
10	Ending finished goods inventory, December 31, 2009	18,000		
11	Cost of goods sold		108,000	
12	Gross margin (or gross profit)		102,000	
13	Operating costs:			
14	R&D, design, mktg., dist., and cust.-service cost	70,000		
15	Total operating costs		70,000	
16	Operating income		$ 32,000	
17				
18	**PANEL B: COST OF GOODS MANUFACTURED**			
19	**Cellular Products**			
20	**Schedule of Cost of Goods Manufactured[a]**			
21	**For the Year Ended December 31, 2009 (in thousands)**			
22	Direct materials:			
23	Beginning inventory, January 1, 2009	$11,000		
24	Purchases of direct materials	73,000		
25	Cost of direct materials available for use	84,000		
26	Ending inventory, December 31, 2009	8,000		
27	Direct materials used		$ 76,000	
28	Direct manufacturing labor		9,000	
29	Manufacturing overhead costs:			
30	Indirect manufacturing labor	$ 7,000		
31	Supplies	2,000		
32	Heat, light, and power	5,000		
33	Depreciation—plant building	2,000		
34	Depreciation—plant equipment	3,000		
35	Miscellaneous	1,000		
36	Total manufacturing overhead costs		20,000	
37	Manufacturing costs incurred during 2009		105,000	
38	Beginning work-in-process inventory, January 1, 2009		6,000	
39	Total manufacturing costs to account for		111,000	
40	Ending work-in-process inventory, December 31, 2009		7,000	
41	Cost of goods manufactured (to income statement)		$104,000	
42	[a]Note that this schedule can become a schedule of cost of goods manufactured and sold simply by including the beginning and ending finished goods inventory figures in the supporting schedule rather than in the body of the income statement.			

STEP 4 (rows 7–11)
STEP 1 (rows 23–27)
STEP 2 (rows 28–36)
STEP 3 (rows 37–41)

Step 2: Total manufacturing costs incurred in 2011. Total manufacturing costs refers to all direct manufacturing costs and manufacturing overhead costs incurred during 2011 for all goods worked on during the year. Cellular Products classifies its manufacturing costs into the three categories described earlier.

(i) Direct materials used in 2011 (shaded light blue in Exhibit 2-8, Panel B)	$ 76,000
(ii) Direct manufacturing labor in 2011 (shaded blue in Exhibit 2-8, Panel B)	9,000
(iii) Manufacturing overhead costs in 2011 (shaded dark blue in Exhibit 2-8, Panel B)	20,000
Total manufacturing costs incurred in 2011	$105,000

Note how in Exhibit 2-7, these costs increase work-in-process inventory.

Step 3: Cost of goods manufactured in 2011. Cost of goods manufactured refers to the cost of goods brought to completion, whether they were started before or during the current accounting period.

Note how the work-in-process inventory box in Exhibit 2-7 has a very similar structure to the direct material inventory box described in Step 1. Beginning work-in-process inventory of $6,000 and total manufacturing costs incurred in 2011 of $105,000 "fill-up" the work-in-process inventory box. Some of the manufacturing costs incurred during 2011 are held back as the cost of the ending work-in-process inventory. The ending work-in-process inventory of $7,000 becomes the beginning inventory for the next year, and the cost of goods manufactured during 2011 of $104,000 "empties out" the work-in-process inventory while "filling up" the finished goods inventory box.

The cost of goods manufactured in 2011 (shaded green) is calculated in Exhibit 2-8, Panel B as follows:

Beginning work-in-process inventory, January 1, 2011	$ 6,000
+ Total manufacturing costs incurred in 2011	105,000
= Total manufacturing costs to account for	111,000
− Ending work-in-process inventory, December 31, 2011	7,000
= Cost of goods manufactured in 2011	$104,000

Step 4: Cost of goods sold in 2011. The cost of goods sold is the cost of finished goods inventory sold to customers during the current accounting period. Looking at the finished goods inventory box in Exhibit 2-7, we see that the beginning inventory of finished goods of $22,000 and cost of goods manufactured in 2011 of $104,000 "fill up" the finished goods inventory box. The ending inventory of finished goods of $18,000 becomes the beginning inventory for the next year, and the cost of goods sold during 2011 of $108,000 "empties out" the finished goods inventory.

This cost of goods sold is an expense that is matched against revenues. The cost of goods sold for Cellular Products (shaded brown) is computed in Exhibit 2-8, Panel A, as follows:

Beginning inventory of finished goods, January 1, 2011	$ 22,000
+ Cost of goods manufactured in 2011	104,000
− Ending inventory of finished goods, December 31, 2011	18,000
= Cost of goods sold in 2011	$108,000

Exhibit 2-9 shows related general ledger T-accounts for Cellular Products' manufacturing cost flow. Note how the cost of goods manufactured ($104,000) is the cost of all goods completed during the accounting period. These costs are all inventoriable costs. Goods completed during the period are transferred to finished goods inventory. These costs become cost of goods sold in the accounting period when the goods are sold. Also note that the direct materials, direct manufacturing labor, and manufacturing overhead costs of the units in work-in-process inventory ($7,000) and finished goods inventory ($18,000) as of December 31, 2011, will appear as an asset in the balance sheet. These costs will become expenses next year when these units are sold.

| Exhibit 2-9 | General Ledger T-Accounts for Cellular Products' Manufacturing Cost Flow (in thousands) |

Work-in-Process Inventory				Finished Goods Inventory				Cost of Goods Sold
Bal. Jan. 1, 2011	6,000	Cost of goods		Bal. Jan. 1, 2011	22,000	Cost of		108,000
Direct materials used	76,000	manufactured	104,000		104,000	goods sold	108,000	
Direct manuf. labor	9,000			Bal. Dec. 31, 2011	18,000			
Indirect manuf. costs	20,000							
Bal. Dec. 31, 2011	7,000							

We are now in a position to prepare Cellular Products' income statement for 2011. The income statement of Cellular Products is shown on the right-hand side of Exhibit 2-7 and in Exhibit 2-8, Panel A. Revenues of Cellular Products are (in thousands) $210,000. Inventoriable costs expensed during 2011 equal cost of goods sold of $108,000.

$$\text{Gross margin} = \text{Revenues} - \text{Cost of goods sold} = \$210,000 - \$108,000 = \$102,000.$$

The $70,000 of operating costs comprising R&D, design, marketing, distribution, and customer-service costs are period costs of Cellular Products. These period costs include, for example, salaries of salespersons, depreciation on computers and other equipment used in marketing, and the cost of leasing warehouse space for distribution. **Operating income** equals total revenues from operations minus cost of goods sold and operating (period) costs (excluding interest expense and income taxes) or equivalently, gross margin minus period costs. The operating income of Cellular Products is $32,000 (gross margin, $102,000 – period costs, $70,000). Those of you familiar with financial accounting will note that period costs are typically called selling, general, and administrative expenses in the income statement

Newcomers to cost accounting frequently assume that indirect costs such as rent, telephone, and depreciation are always costs of the period in which they are incurred and are not associated with inventories. When these costs are incurred in marketing or in corporate headquarters, they are period costs. However, when these costs are incurred in manufacturing, they are manufacturing overhead costs and are inventoriable.

Recap of Inventoriable Costs and Period Costs

Exhibit 2-7 highlights the differences between inventoriable costs and period costs for a manufacturing company. The manufacturing costs of finished goods include direct materials, other direct manufacturing costs such as direct manufacturing labor, and manufacturing overhead costs such as supervision, production control, and machine maintenance. All these costs are inventoriable: They are assigned to work-in-process inventory until the goods are completed and then to finished goods inventory until the goods are sold. All nonmanufacturing costs, such as R&D, design, and distribution costs, are period costs.

Inventoriable costs and period costs flow through the income statement at a merchandising company similar to the way costs flow at a manufacturing company. At a merchandising company, however, the flow of costs is much simpler to understand and track. Exhibit 2-10 shows the inventoriable costs and period costs for a retailer or wholesaler who buys goods for resale. The only inventoriable cost is the cost of merchandise. (This corresponds to the cost of finished goods manufactured for a manufacturing company.) Purchased goods are held as merchandise inventory, the cost of which is shown as an asset in the balance sheet. As the goods are sold, their costs are shown in the income statement as cost of goods sold. A retailer or wholesaler also has a variety of marketing, distribution, and customer-service costs, which are period costs. In the income statement, period costs are deducted from revenues without ever having been included as part of inventory.

> **Decision Point** ▶
>
> What are the differences in the accounting for inventoriable versus period costs?

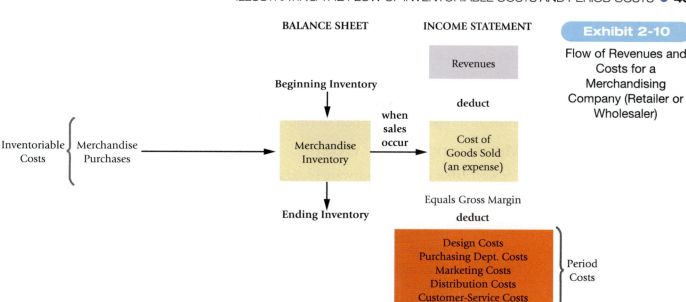

Exhibit 2-10

Flow of Revenues and Costs for a Merchandising Company (Retailer or Wholesaler)

Prime Costs and Conversion Costs

Two terms used to describe cost classifications in manufacturing costing systems are prime costs and conversion costs. **Prime costs** are all direct manufacturing costs. For Cellular Products,

$$\text{Prime costs} = \text{Direct material costs} + \text{Direct manufacturing labor costs} =$$
$$\$76{,}000 + \$9{,}000 = \$85{,}000$$

As we have already discussed, the greater the proportion of prime costs in a company's cost structure, the more confident managers can be about the accuracy of the costs of products. As information-gathering technology improves, companies can add more and more direct-cost categories. For example, power costs might be metered in specific areas of a plant and identified as a direct cost of specific products. Furthermore, if a production line were dedicated to the manufacture of a specific product, the depreciation on the production equipment would be a direct manufacturing cost and would be included in prime costs. Computer software companies often have a "purchased technology" direct manufacturing cost item. This item, which represents payments to suppliers who develop software algorithms for a product, is also included in prime costs. **Conversion costs** are all manufacturing costs other than direct material costs. Conversion costs represent all manufacturing costs incurred to convert direct materials into finished goods. For Cellular Products,

$$\text{Conversion costs} = \frac{\text{Direct manufacturing}}{\text{labor costs}} + \frac{\text{Manufacturing}}{\text{overhead costs}} = \$9{,}000 + \$20{,}000 = \$29{,}000$$

Note that direct manufacturing labor costs are a part of both prime costs and conversion costs.

Some manufacturing operations, such as computer-integrated manufacturing (CIM) plants, have very few workers. The workers' roles are to monitor the manufacturing process and to maintain the equipment that produces multiple products. Costing systems in CIM plants do not have a direct manufacturing labor cost category because direct manufacturing labor cost is relatively small and because it is difficult to trace this cost to products. In CIM plants, the only prime cost is direct material costs, and conversion costs consist only of manufacturing overhead costs.

Measuring Costs Requires Judgment

Measuring costs requires judgment. That's because there are alternative ways in which costs can be defined and classified. Different companies or sometimes even different subunits within the same company may define and classify costs differently. Be careful to define and understand the ways costs are measured in a company or situation. We first illustrate this point with respect to labor cost measurement.

Measuring Labor Costs

Consider labor costs for software programming at companies such as Apple where programmers work on different software applications for products like the iMac, the iPod, and the iPhone. Although labor cost classifications vary among companies, many companies use multiple labor cost categories:

- Direct programming labor costs that can be traced to individual products
- Overhead (examples of prominent labor components of overhead follow):
  - Indirect labor compensation for
    Office staff
    Office security
    Rework labor (time spent by direct laborers correcting software errors)
    Overtime premium paid to software programmers (explained next)
    Idle time (explained next)
  - Managers', department heads', and supervisors' salaries
  - Payroll fringe costs, for example, health care premiums and pension costs (explained later)

Note how *indirect labor costs* are commonly divided into many subclassifications, for example, office staff and idle time, to retain information on different categories of indirect labor. Note also that managers' salaries usually are not classified as indirect labor costs. Instead, the compensation of supervisors, department heads, and all others who are regarded as management is placed in a separate classification of labor-related overhead.

Overtime Premium and Idle Time

The purpose of classifying costs in detail is to associate an individual cost with a specific cause or reason for why it was incurred. Two classes of indirect labor—overtime premium and idle time—need special mention. **Overtime premium** is the wage rate paid to workers (for both direct labor and indirect labor) in *excess* of their straight-time wage rates. Overtime premium is usually considered to be a part of indirect costs or overhead. Consider the example of George Flexner, a junior software programmer who writes software for multiple products. He is paid $20 per hour for straight-time and $30 per hour (time and a half) for overtime. His overtime premium is $10 per overtime hour. If he works 44 hours, including 4 overtime hours, in one week, his gross compensation would be classified as follows:

Direct programming labor: 44 hours × $20 per hour	$880
Overtime premium: 4 hours × $10 per hour	40
Total compensation for 44 hours	$920

In this example, why is the overtime premium of direct programming labor usually considered an overhead cost rather than a direct cost? After all, it can be traced to specific products that George worked on while working overtime. Overtime premium is generally not considered a direct cost because the particular job that George worked on during the overtime hours is a matter of chance. For example, assume that George worked on two products for 5 hours each on a specific workday of 10 hours, including 2 overtime hours. Should the product George worked on during hours 9 and 10 be assigned the overtime premium? Or should the premium be prorated over both products? Prorating the overtime premium does not "penalize"—add to the cost of—a particular product solely because it happened to be worked on during the overtime hours. *Instead, the overtime premium is considered to be attributable to the heavy overall volume of work. Its cost is regarded as part of overhead, which is borne by both products.*

Sometimes overtime is not random. For example, a launch deadline for a particular product may clearly be the sole source of overtime. In such instances, the overtime premium is regarded as a direct cost of that product.

Another subclassification of indirect labor is the idle time of both direct and indirect labor. **Idle time** is wages paid for unproductive time caused by lack of orders, machine or computer breakdowns, work delays, poor scheduling, and the like. For example, if George had no work for 3 hours during that week while waiting to receive code from another colleague, George's earnings would be classified as follows:

Direct programming labor: 41 hours × $20/hour	$820
Idle time (overhead): 3 hours × $20/hour	60
Overtime premium (overhead): 4 hours × $10/hour	40
Total earnings for 44 hours	$920

Clearly, the idle time is not related to a particular product, nor, as we have already discussed, is the overtime premium. Both overtime premium and idle time are considered overhead costs.

Benefits of Defining Accounting Terms

Managers, accountants, suppliers, and others will avoid many problems if they thoroughly understand and agree on the classifications and meanings of the cost terms introduced in this chapter and later in this book.

Consider the classification of programming labor *payroll fringe costs* (for example, employer payments for employee benefits such as Social Security, life insurance, health insurance, and pensions). Consider, for example, a software programmer, who is paid a wage of $20 an hour with fringe benefits totaling, say, $5 per hour. Some companies classify the $20 as a direct programming labor cost of the product for which the software is being written and the $5 as overhead cost. Other companies classify the entire $25 as direct programming labor cost. The latter approach is preferable because the stated wage and the fringe benefit costs together are a fundamental part of acquiring direct software programming labor services.

Caution: In every situation, pinpoint clearly what direct labor includes and what direct labor excludes. Achieving clarity may prevent disputes regarding cost-reimbursement contracts, income tax payments, and labor union matters. Consider that some countries such as Costa Rica and Mauritius offer substantial income tax savings to foreign companies that generate employment within their borders. In some cases, to qualify for the tax benefits, the direct labor costs must at least equal a specified percentage of the total costs.

When direct labor costs are not precisely defined, disputes have arisen as to whether payroll fringe costs should be included as part of direct labor costs when calculating the direct labor percentage for qualifying for such tax benefits. Companies have sought to classify payroll fringe costs as part of direct labor costs to make direct labor costs a higher percentage of total costs. Tax authorities have argued that payroll fringe costs are part of overhead. In addition to fringe benefits, other debated items are compensation for training time, idle time, vacations, sick leave, and overtime premium. To prevent disputes, contracts and laws should be as specific as possible regarding definitions and measurements.

Different Meanings of Product Costs

Many cost terms found in practice have ambiguous meanings. Consider the term *product cost*. A **product cost** is the sum of the costs assigned to a product for a specific purpose. Different purposes can result in different measures of product cost, as the brackets on the value chain in Exhibit 2-11 illustrate:

- **Pricing and product-mix decisions.** For the purposes of making decisions about pricing and which products provide the most profits, the manager is interested in the overall (total) profitability of different products and, consequently, assigns costs incurred in all business functions of the value chain to the different products.

- **Contracting with government agencies.** Government contracts often reimburse contractors on the basis of the "cost of a product" plus a prespecified margin of profit. Because of the cost-plus profit margin nature of the contract, government agencies provide detailed guidelines on the cost items they will allow and disallow

Learning Objective 6

Explain why product costs are computed in different ways for different purposes

. . . examples are pricing and product-mix decisions, government contracts, and financial statements

Exhibit 2-11

Different Product Costs
for Different Purposes

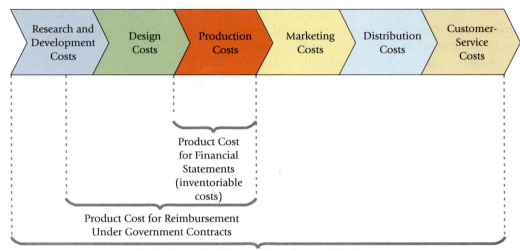

when calculating the cost of a product. For example, some government agencies explicitly exclude marketing, distribution, and customer-service costs from the product costs that qualify for reimbursement, and they may only partially reimburse R&D costs. These agencies want to reimburse contractors for only those costs most closely related to delivering products under the contract. The second bracket in Exhibit 2-11 shows how the product-cost calculations for a specific contract may allow for all design and production costs but only part of R&D costs.

- **Preparing financial statements for external reporting under generally accepted accounting principles (GAAP).** Under GAAP, only manufacturing costs can be assigned to inventories in the financial statements. For purposes of calculating inventory costs, product costs include only inventoriable (manufacturing) costs.

As Exhibit 2-11 illustrates, product-cost measures range from a narrow set of costs for financial statements—a set that includes only inventoriable costs—to a broader set of costs for reimbursement under a government contract to a still broader set of costs for pricing and product-mix decisions.

This section focused on how different purposes result in the inclusion of different cost items of the value chain of business functions when product costs are calculated. The same caution about the need to be clear and precise about cost concepts and their measurement applies to each cost classification introduced in this chapter. Exhibit 2-12 summarizes the key cost classifications.

Using the five-step process described in Chapter 1, think about how these different classifications of costs are helpful to managers when making decisions and evaluating performance.

1. *Identify the problem and uncertainties.* Consider a decision about how much to price a product. This decision often depends on how much it costs to make the product.
2. *Obtain information.* Managers identify direct and indirect costs of a product in each business function. Managers also gather other information about customers, competitors, and prices of substitute products.

Decision Point ▶

Why do managers assign different costs to the same cost object?

Exhibit 2-12

Alternative
Classifications of Costs

1. Business function
   a. Research and development
   b. Design of products and processes
   c. Production
   d. Marketing
   e. Distribution
   f. Customer service
2. Assignment to a cost object
   a. Direct cost
   b. Indirect cost

3. Behavior pattern in relation to the level of activity or volume
   a. Variable cost
   b. Fixed cost
4. Aggregate or average
   a. Total cost
   b. Unit cost
5. Assets or expenses
   a. Inventoriable cost
   b Period cost

3. *Make predictions about the future.* Managers estimate what it will cost to make the product in the future. This requires predictions about the quantity of product that managers expect to sell and an understanding of fixed and variable costs.

4. *Make decisions by choosing among alternatives.* Managers choose a price to charge based on a thorough understanding of costs and other information.

5. *Implement the decision, evaluate performance, and learn.* Managers control costs and learn by comparing actual total and unit costs against predicted amounts.

The next section describes how the basic concepts introduced in this chapter lead to a framework for understanding cost accounting and cost management that can then be applied to the study of many topics, such as strategy evaluation, quality, and investment decisions.

A Framework for Cost Accounting and Cost Management

Three features of cost accounting and cost management across a wide range of applications are as follows:

1. Calculating the cost of products, services, and other cost objects
2. Obtaining information for planning and control and performance evaluation
3. Analyzing the relevant information for making decisions

We develop these ideas in Chapters 3 through 12. The ideas also form the foundation for the study of various topics later in the book.

Learning Objective 7

Describe a framework for cost accounting and cost management

. . . three features that help managers make decisions

Calculating the Cost of Products, Services, and Other Cost Objects

We have already seen the different purposes and measures of product costs. Whatever the purpose, the costing system traces direct costs and allocates indirect costs to products. Chapters 4 and 5 describe systems, such as activity-based costing systems, used to calculate total costs and unit costs of products and services. The chapters also discuss how managers use this information to formulate strategy and make pricing, product-mix, and cost-management decisions.

Obtaining Information for Planning and Control and Performance Evaluation

Budgeting is the most commonly used tool for planning and control. A budget forces managers to look ahead, to translate strategy into plans, to coordinate and communicate within the organization, and to provide a benchmark for evaluating performance. Budgeting often plays a major role in affecting behavior and decisions because managers strive to meet budget targets. Chapter 6 describes budgeting systems.

At the end of a reporting period, managers compare actual results to planned performance. The manager's tasks are to understand why differences (called variances) between actual and planned performances arise and to use the information provided by these variances as feedback to promote learning and future improvement. Managers also use variances as well as nonfinancial measures, such as defect rates and customer satisfaction ratings, to control and evaluate the performance of various departments, divisions, and managers. Chapters 7 and 8 discuss variance analysis. Chapter 9 describes planning, control, and inventory-costing issues relating to capacity. Chapters 6, 7, 8, and 9 focus on the management accountant's role in implementing strategy.

Analyzing the Relevant Information for Making Decisions

When making decisions about strategy design and strategy implementation, managers must understand which revenues and costs to consider and which ones to ignore. Management accountants help managers identify what information is relevant and what information is irrelevant. Consider a decision about whether to buy a product from an outside vendor or to make it in-house. The costing system indicates that it costs $25 per unit to make the product in-house. A vendor offers the product for $22 per unit. At first glance, it seems it will cost less for the company to buy the product rather than make it. Suppose, however, that of the $25 to make the product in-house, $5 consists of plant lease costs that the company has already paid under the lease contract. Furthermore, if the product is bought, the plant will remain idle. That is, there is no opportunity to profit by putting the plant to some alternative use. Under these conditions, it will cost less to make the product than to buy it. That's because making the product costs only an *additional* $20 per unit ($25 − $5), compared with an *additional* $22 per unit if it is bought. The $5 per unit of lease cost is irrelevant to the decision because it is a *past* (or *sunk*) cost that has already been incurred regardless of whether the product is made or bought. Analyzing relevant information is a key aspect of making decisions.

When making strategic decisions about which products and how much to produce, managers must know how revenues and costs vary with changes in output levels. For this purpose, managers need to distinguish fixed costs from variable costs. Chapter 3 analyzes how operating income changes with changes in units sold and how managers use this information to make decisions such as how much to spend on advertising. Chapter 10 describes methods to estimate the fixed and variable components of costs. Chapter 11 applies the concept of relevance to decision making in many different situations and describes methods managers use to maximize income given the resource constraints they face. Chapter 12 describes how management accountants help managers determine prices and manage costs across the value chain and over a product's life cycle.

Later chapters in the book discuss topics such as strategy evaluation, customer profitability, quality, just-in-time systems, investment decisions, transfer pricing, and performance evaluation. Each of these topics invariably has product costing, planning and control, and decision-making perspectives. A command of the first 12 chapters will help you master these topics. For example, Chapter 13 on strategy describes the balanced scorecard, a set of financial and nonfinancial measures used to implement strategy that builds on the planning and control functions. The section on strategic analysis of operating income builds on ideas of product costing and variance analysis. The section on downsizing and managing capacity builds on ideas of relevant revenues and relevant costs.

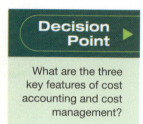

Decision Point ▶

What are the three key features of cost accounting and cost management?

Problem for Self-Study

Foxwood Company is a metal- and woodcutting manufacturer, selling products to the home construction market. Consider the following data for 2011:

Sandpaper	$ 2,000
Materials-handling costs	70,000
Lubricants and coolants	5,000
Miscellaneous indirect manufacturing labor	40,000
Direct manufacturing labor	300,000
Direct materials inventory Jan. 1, 2011	40,000
Direct materials inventory Dec. 31, 2011	50,000
Finished goods inventory Jan. 1, 2011	100,000
Finished goods inventory Dec. 31, 2011	150,000
Work-in-process inventory Jan. 1, 2011	10,000
Work-in-process inventory Dec. 31, 2011	14,000
Plant-leasing costs	54,000
Depreciation—plant equipment	36,000
Property taxes on plant equipment	4,000
Fire insurance on plant equipment	3,000
Direct materials purchased	460,000
Revenues	1,360,000
Marketing promotions	60,000
Marketing salaries	100,000
Distribution costs	70,000
Customer-service costs	100,000

1. Prepare an income statement with a separate supporting schedule of cost of goods manufactured. For all manufacturing items, classify costs as direct costs or indirect costs and indicate by V or F whether each is basically a variable cost or a fixed cost (when the cost object is a product unit). If in doubt, decide on the basis of whether the total cost will change substantially over a wide range of units produced.

2. Suppose that both the direct material costs and the plant-leasing costs are for the production of 900,000 units. What is the direct material cost of each unit produced? What is the plant-leasing cost per unit? Assume that the plant-leasing cost is a fixed cost.

3. Suppose Foxwood Company manufactures 1,000,000 units next year. Repeat the computation in requirement 2 for direct materials and plant-leasing costs. Assume the implied cost-behavior patterns persist.

4. As a management consultant, explain concisely to the company president why the unit cost for direct materials did not change in requirements 2 and 3 but the unit cost for plant-leasing costs did change.

Solution

1.

Foxwood Company
Income Statement
For the Year Ended December 31, 2011

Revenues		$1,360,000
Cost of goods sold		
Beginning finished goods inventory January 1, 2011	$ 100,000	
Cost of goods manufactured (see the following schedule)	960,000	
Cost of goods available for sale	1,060,000	
Deduct ending finished goods inventory		
December 31, 2011	150,000	910,000
Gross margin (or gross profit)		450,000
Operating costs		
Marketing promotions	60,000	
Marketing salaries	100,000	
Distribution costs	70,000	
Customer-service costs	100,000	330,000
Operating income		$ 120,000

Foxwood Company
Schedule of Cost of Goods Manufactured
For the Year Ended December 31, 2011

Direct materials		
Beginning inventory, January 1, 2011	$ 40,000	
Purchases of direct materials	460,000	
Cost of direct materials available for use	500,000	
Ending inventory, December 31, 2011	50,000	
Direct materials used	450,000 (V)	
Direct manufacturing labor	300,000 (V)	
Indirect manufacturing costs		
Sandpaper	$ 2,000 (V)	
Materials-handling costs	70,000 (V)	
Lubricants and coolants	5,000 (V)	
Miscellaneous indirect manufacturing labor	40,000 (V)	
Plant-leasing costs	54,000 (F)	
Depreciation—plant equipment	36,000 (F)	
Property taxes on plant equipment	4,000 (F)	
Fire insurance on plant equipment	3,000 (F)	214,000
Manufacturing costs incurred during 2011		964,000
Beginning work-in-process inventory, January 1, 2011		10,000
Total manufacturing costs to account for		974,000
Ending work-in-process inventory, December 31, 2011		14,000
Cost of goods manufactured (to income statement)		$ 960,000

2. Direct material unit cost = Direct materials used ÷ Units produced
= $450,000 ÷ 900,000 units = $0.50 per unit
   Plant-leasing unit cost = Plant-leasing costs ÷ Units produced
= $54,000 ÷ 900,000 units = $0.06 per unit

3. The direct material costs are variable, so they would increase in total from $450,000 to $500,000 (1,000,000 units × $0.50 per unit). However, their unit cost would be unaffected: $500,000 ÷ 1,000,000 units = $0.50 per unit.

   In contrast, the plant-leasing costs of $54,000 are fixed, so they would not increase in total. However, the plant-leasing cost per unit would decline from $0.060 to $0.054: $54,000 ÷ 1,000,000 units = $0.054 per unit.

4. The explanation would begin with the answer to requirement 3. As a consultant, you should stress that the unitizing (averaging) of costs that have different behavior patterns can be misleading. A common error is to assume that a total unit cost, which is often a sum of variable unit cost and fixed unit cost, is an indicator that total costs change in proportion to changes in production levels. The next chapter demonstrates the necessity for distinguishing between cost-behavior patterns. You must be wary, especially about average fixed cost per unit. Too often, unit fixed cost is erroneously regarded as being indistinguishable from unit variable cost.

Decision Points

The following question-and-answer format summarizes the chapter's learning objectives. Each decision presents a key question related to a learning objective. The guidelines are the answer to that question.

Decision	Guidelines
1. What is a cost object?	A cost object is anything for which a separate measurement of cost is needed. Examples include a product, a service, a project, a customer, a brand category, an activity, and a department.
2. How do managers decide whether a cost is a direct or an indirect cost?	A direct cost is any cost that is related to a particular cost object and can be traced to that cost object in an economically feasible way. Indirect costs are related to the particular cost object but cannot be traced to it in an economically feasible way. The same cost can be direct for one cost object and indirect for another cost object. This book uses *cost tracing* to describe the assignment of direct costs to a cost object and *cost allocation* to describe the assignment of indirect costs to a cost object.
3. How do managers decide whether a cost is a variable or a fixed cost?	A variable cost changes *in total* in proportion to changes in the related level of total activity or volume. A fixed cost remains unchanged *in total* for a given time period despite wide changes in the related level of total activity or volume.
4. How should costs be estimated?	In general, focus on total costs, not unit costs. When making total cost estimates, think of variable costs as an amount per unit and fixed costs as a total amount. The unit cost of a cost object should be interpreted cautiously when it includes a fixed-cost component.
5. What are the differences in the accounting for inventoriable versus period costs?	Inventoriable costs are all costs of a product that are regarded as an asset in the accounting period when they are incurred and become cost of goods sold in the accounting period when the product is sold. Period costs are expensed in the accounting period in which they are incurred and are all of the costs in an income statement other than cost of goods sold.

6. Why do managers assign different costs to the same cost objects?

Managers can assign different costs to the same cost object depending on the purpose. For example, for the external reporting purpose in a manufacturing company, the inventoriable cost of a product includes only manufacturing costs. In contrast, costs from all business functions of the value chain often are assigned to a product for pricing and product-mix decisions.

7. What are the three key features of cost accounting and cost management?

Three features of cost accounting and cost management are (1) calculating the cost of products, services, and other cost objects; (2) obtaining information for planning and control and performance evaluation; and (3) analyzing relevant information for making decisions.

Terms to Learn

This chapter contains more basic terms than any other in this book. Do not proceed before you check your understanding of the following terms. Both the chapter and the Glossary at the end of the book contain definitions.

actual cost (**p. 27**)
average cost (**p. 35**)
budgeted cost (**p. 27**)
conversion costs (**p. 43**)
cost (**p. 27**)
cost accumulation (**p. 28**)
cost allocation (**p. 29**)
cost assignment (**p. 29**)
cost driver (**p. 32**)
cost object (**p. 27**)
cost of goods manufactured (**p. 41**)
cost tracing (**p. 28**)
direct costs of a cost object (**p. 28**)

direct manufacturing labor costs (**p. 37**)
direct material costs (**p. 37**)
direct materials inventory (**p. 37**)
factory overhead costs (**p. 37**)
finished goods inventory (**p. 37**)
fixed cost (**p. 30**)
idle time (**p. 45**)
indirect costs of a cost object (**p. 28**)
indirect manufacturing costs (**p. 37**)
inventoriable costs (**p. 37**)
manufacturing overhead costs (**p. 37**)
manufacturing-sector companies (**p. 36**)

merchandising-sector companies (**p. 36**)
operating income (**p. 42**)
overtime premium (**p. 44**)
period costs (**p. 38**)
prime costs (**p. 43**)
product cost (**p. 45**)
relevant range (**p. 33**)
revenues (**p. 38**)
service-sector companies (**p. 36**)
unit cost (**p. 35**)
variable cost (**p. 30**)
work-in-process inventory (**p. 37**)
work in progress (**p. 37**)

Assignment Material

Questions

2-1 Define cost object and give three examples.
2-2 Define direct costs and indirect costs.
2-3 Why do managers consider direct costs to be more accurate than indirect costs?
2-4 Name three factors that will affect the classification of a cost as direct or indirect.
2-5 Define variable cost and fixed cost. Give an example of each.
2-6 What is a cost driver? Give one example.
2-7 What is the relevant range? What role does the relevant-range concept play in explaining how costs behave?
2-8 Explain why unit costs must often be interpreted with caution.
2-9 Describe how manufacturing-, merchandising-, and service-sector companies differ from each other.
2-10 What are three different types of inventory that manufacturing companies hold?
2-11 Distinguish between inventoriable costs and period costs.
2-12 Define the following: direct material costs, direct manufacturing-labor costs, manufacturing overhead costs, prime costs, and conversion costs.
2-13 Describe the overtime-premium and idle-time categories of indirect labor.
2-14 Define product cost. Describe three different purposes for computing product costs.
2-15 What are three common features of cost accounting and cost management?

MyAccountingLab ®

Exercises

2-16 **Computing and interpreting manufacturing unit costs.** Minnesota Office Products (MOP) produces three different paper products at its Vaasa lumber plant: Supreme, Deluxe, and Regular. Each product has its own dedicated production line at the plant. It currently uses the following three-part classification for its manufacturing costs: direct materials, direct manufacturing labor, and manufacturing overhead costs. Total manufacturing overhead costs of the plant in July 2011 are $150 million ($15 million of which are fixed). This total amount is allocated to each product line on the basis of the direct manufacturing labor costs of each line. Summary data (in millions) for July 2011 are as follows:

	Supreme	Deluxe	Regular
Direct material costs	$ 89	$ 57	$ 60
Direct manufacturing labor costs	$ 16	$ 26	$ 8
Manufacturing overhead costs	$ 48	$ 78	$ 24
Units produced	125	150	140

Required

1. Compute the manufacturing cost per unit for each product produced in July 2011.
2. Suppose that in August 2011, production was 150 million units of Supreme, 190 million units of Deluxe, and 220 million units of Regular. Why might the July 2011 information on manufacturing cost per unit be misleading when predicting total manufacturing costs in August 2011?

2-17 **Direct, indirect, fixed, and variable costs.** Best Breads manufactures two types of bread, which are sold as wholesale products to various specialty retail bakeries. Each loaf of bread requires a three-step process. The first step is mixing. The mixing department combines all of the necessary ingredients to create the dough and processes it through high speed mixers. The dough is then left to rise before baking. The second step is baking, which is an entirely automated process. The baking department molds the dough into its final shape and bakes each loaf of bread in a high temperature oven. The final step is finishing, which is an entirely manual process. The finishing department coats each loaf of bread with a special glaze, allows the bread to cool, and then carefully packages each loaf in a specialty carton for sale in retail bakeries.

Required

1. Costs involved in the process are listed next. For each cost, indicate whether it is a direct variable, direct fixed, indirect variable, or indirect fixed cost, assuming "units of production of each kind of bread" is the cost object.

Costs:
Yeast	Mixing department manager
Flour	Materials handlers in each department
Packaging materials	Custodian in factory
Depreciation on ovens	Night guard in factory
Depreciation on mixing machines	Machinist (running the mixing machine)
Rent on factory building	Machine maintenance personnel in each department
Fire insurance on factory building	Maintenance supplies for factory
Factory utilities	Cleaning supplies for factory
Finishing department hourly laborers	

2. If the cost object were the "mixing department" rather than units of production of each kind of bread, which preceding costs would now be direct instead of indirect costs?

2-18 **Classification of costs, service sector.** Consumer Focus is a marketing research firm that organizes focus groups for consumer-product companies. Each focus group has eight individuals who are paid $50 per session to provide comments on new products. These focus groups meet in hotels and are led by a trained, independent, marketing specialist hired by Consumer Focus. Each specialist is paid a fixed retainer to conduct a minimum number of sessions and a per session fee of $2,000. A Consumer Focus staff member attends each session to ensure that all the logistical aspects run smoothly.

Classify each cost item (**A–H**) as follows:

Required

  a. Direct or indirect (D or I) costs with respect to each individual focus group.

  b. Variable or fixed (V or F) costs with respect to how the total costs of Consumer Focus change as the number of focus groups conducted changes. (If in doubt, select on the basis of whether the total costs will change substantially if there is a large change in the number of groups conducted.)

You will have two answers (D or I; V or F) for each of the following items:

Cost Item	D or I	V or F
A. Payment to individuals in each focus group to provide comments on new products		
B. Annual subscription of Consumer Focus to *Consumer Reports* magazine		
C. Phone calls made by Consumer Focus staff member to confirm individuals will attend a focus group session (Records of individual calls are not kept.)		
D. Retainer paid to focus group leader to conduct 20 focus groups per year on new medical products		
E. Meals provided to participants in each focus group		
F. Lease payment by Consumer Focus for corporate office		
G. Cost of tapes used to record comments made by individuals in a focus group session (These tapes are sent to the company whose products are being tested.)		
H. Gasoline costs of Consumer Focus staff for company-owned vehicles (Staff members submit monthly bills with no mileage breakdowns.)		

2-19 **Classification of costs, merchandising sector.** Home Entertainment Center (HEC) operates a large store in San Francisco. The store has both a video section and a music (compact disks and tapes) section. HEC reports revenues for the video section separately from the music section.

Classify each cost item (**A–H**) as follows:

Required

  a. Direct or indirect (D or I) costs with respect to the total number of videos sold.

  b. Variable or fixed (V or F) costs with respect to how the total costs of the video section change as the total number of videos sold changes. (If in doubt, select on the basis of whether the total costs will change substantially if there is a large change in the total number of videos sold.)

You will have two answers (D or I; V or F) for each of the following items:

Cost Item	D or I	V or F
A. Annual retainer paid to a video distributor		
B. Electricity costs of the HEC store (single bill covers entire store)		
C. Costs of videos purchased for sale to customers		
D. Subscription to *Video Trends* magazine		
E. Leasing of computer software used for financial budgeting at the HEC store		
F. Cost of popcorn provided free to all customers of the HEC store		
G. Earthquake insurance policy for the HEC store		
H. Freight-in costs of videos purchased by HEC		

2-20 **Classification of costs, manufacturing sector.** The Fremont, California, plant of New United Motor Manufacturing, Inc. (NUMMI), a joint venture of General Motors and Toyota, assembles two types of cars (Corollas and Geo Prisms). Separate assembly lines are used for each type of car.

Classify each cost item (**A–H**) as follows:

Required

  a. Direct or indirect (D or I) costs with respect to the total number of cars of each type assembled (Corolla or Geo Prism).

  b. Variable or fixed (V or F) costs with respect to how the total costs of the plant change as the total number of cars of each type assembled changes. (If in doubt, select on the basis of whether the total costs will change substantially if there is a large change in the total number of cars of each type assembled.)

You will have two answers (D or I; V or F) for each of the following items:

Cost Item	D or I V or F
A. Cost of tires used on Geo Prisms	
B. Salary of public relations manager for NUMMI plant	
C. Annual awards dinner for Corolla suppliers	
D. Salary of engineer who monitors design changes on Geo Prism	
E. Freight costs of Corolla engines shipped from Toyota City, Japan, to Fremont, California	
F. Electricity costs for NUMMI plant (single bill covers entire plant)	
G. Wages paid to temporary assembly-line workers hired in periods of high production (paid on hourly basis)	
H. Annual fire-insurance policy cost for NUMMI plant	

2-21 Variable costs, fixed costs, total costs. Bridget Ashton is getting ready to open a small restaurant. She is on a tight budget and must choose between the following long-distance phone plans:

Plan A: Pay 10 cents per minute of long-distance calling.

Plan B: Pay a fixed monthly fee of $15 for up to 240 long-distance minutes, and 8 cents per minute thereafter (if she uses fewer than 240 minutes in any month, she still pays $15 for the month).

Plan C: Pay a fixed monthly fee of $22 for up to 510 long-distance minutes and 5 cents per minute thereafter (if she uses fewer than 510 minutes, she still pays $22 for the month).

Required

1. Draw a graph of the total monthly costs of the three plans for different levels of monthly long-distance calling.
2. Which plan should Ashton choose if she expects to make 100 minutes of long-distance calls? 240 minutes? 540 minutes?

2-22 Variable costs and fixed costs. Consolidated Minerals (CM) owns the rights to extract minerals from beach sands on Fraser Island. CM has costs in three areas:

a. Payment to a mining subcontractor who charges $80 per ton of beach sand mined and returned to the beach (after being processed on the mainland to extract three minerals: ilmenite, rutile, and zircon).

b. Payment of a government mining and environmental tax of $50 per ton of beach sand mined.

c. Payment to a barge operator. This operator charges $150,000 per month to transport each batch of beach sand—up to 100 tons per batch per day—to the mainland and then return to Fraser Island (that is, 0 to 100 tons per day = $150,000 per month; 101 to 200 tons per day = $300,000 per month, and so on).

  Each barge operates 25 days per month. The $150,000 monthly charge must be paid even if fewer than 100 tons are transported on any day and even if CM requires fewer than 25 days of barge transportation in that month.

CM is currently mining 180 tons of beach sands per day for 25 days per month.

Required

1. What is the variable cost per ton of beach sand mined? What is the fixed cost to CM per month?
2. Plot a graph of the variable costs and another graph of the fixed costs of CM. Your graphs should be similar to Exhibit 2-3, Panel A (p. 31), and Exhibit 2-4 (p. 34). Is the concept of relevant range applicable to your graphs? Explain.
3. What is the unit cost per ton of beach sand mined (a) if 180 tons are mined each day and (b) if 220 tons are mined each day? Explain the difference in the unit-cost figures.

2-23 Variable costs, fixed costs, relevant range. Sweetum Candies manufactures jaw-breaker candies in a fully automated process. The machine that produces candies was purchased recently and can make 4,100 per month. The machine costs $9,000 and is depreciated using straight line depreciation over 10 years assuming zero residual value. Rent for the factory space and warehouse, and other fixed manufacturing overhead costs total $1,200 per month.

  Sweetum currently makes and sells 3,800 jaw-breakers per month. Sweetum buys just enough materials each month to make the jaw-breakers it needs to sell. Materials cost 30 cents per jawbreaker.

  Next year Sweetum expects demand to increase by 100%. At this volume of materials purchased, it will get a 10% discount on price. Rent and other fixed manufacturing overhead costs will remain the same.

Required

1. What is Sweetum's current annual relevant range of output?
2. What is Sweetum's current annual fixed manufacturing cost within the relevant range? What is the annual variable manufacturing cost?
3. What will Sweetum's relevant range of output be next year? How if at all, will total annual fixed and variable manufacturing costs change next year? Assume that if it needs to Sweetum could buy an identical machine at the same cost as the one it already has.

2-24 Cost drivers and value chain. Helner Cell Phones (HCP) is developing a new touch screen smartphone to compete in the cellular phone industry. The phones will be sold at wholesale prices to cell phone companies, which will in turn sell them in retail stores to the final customer. HCP has undertaken the following activities in its value chain to bring its product to market:

Identify customer needs (What do smartphone users want?)
Perform market research on competing brands
Design a prototype of the HCP smartphone
Market the new design to cell phone companies
Manufacture the HCP smartphone
Process orders from cell phone companies
Package the HCP smartphones
Deliver the HCP smartphones to the cell phone companies
Provide online assistance to cell phone users for use of the HCP smartphone
Make design changes to the smartphone based on customer feedback

During the process of product development, production, marketing, distribution, and customer service, HCP has kept track of the following cost drivers:

Number of smartphones shipped by HCP
Number of design changes
Number of deliveries made to cell phone companies
Engineering hours spent on initial product design
Hours spent researching competing market brands
Customer-service hours
Number of smartphone orders processed
Number of cell phone companies purchasing the HCP smartphone
Machine hours required to run the production equipment
Number of surveys returned and processed from competing smartphone users

Required

1. Identify each value chain activity listed at the beginning of the exercise with one of the following value-chain categories:
   a. Design of products and processes
   b. Production
   c. Marketing
   d. Distribution
   e. Customer Service

2. Use the list of preceding cost drivers to find one or more reasonable cost drivers for each of the activities in HCP's value chain.

2-25 Cost drivers and functions. The list of representative cost drivers in the right column of this table are randomized with respect to the list of functions in the left column. That is, they do not match.

Function	Representative Cost Driver
1. Accounting	A. Number of invoices sent
2. Human resources	B. Number of purchase orders
3. Data processing	C. Number of research scientists
4. Research and development	D. Hours of computer processing unit (CPU)
5. Purchasing	E. Number of employees
6. Distribution	F. Number of transactions processed
7. Billing	G. Number of deliveries made

Required

1. Match each function with its representative cost driver.
2. Give a second example of a cost driver for each function.

2-26 Total costs and unit costs. A student association has hired a band and a caterer for a graduation party. The band will charge a fixed fee of $1,000 for an evening of music, and the caterer will charge a fixed fee of $600 for the party setup and an additional $9 per person who attends. Snacks and soft drinks will be provided by the caterer for the duration of the party. Students attending the party will pay $5 each at the door.

Required

1. Draw a graph depicting the fixed cost, the variable cost, and the total cost to the student association for different attendance levels.
2. Suppose 100 people attend the party. What is the total cost to the student association? What is the cost per person?

3. Suppose 500 people attend the party. What is the total cost to the student association and the cost per attendee?
4. Draw a graph depicting the cost per attendee for different attendance levels. As president of the student association, you want to request a grant to cover some of the party costs. Will you use the per attendee cost numbers to make your case? Why or why not?

2-27 **Total and unit cost, decision making.** Gayle's Glassworks makes glass flanges for scientific use. Materials cost $1 per flange, and the glass blowers are paid a wage rate of $28 per hour. A glass blower blows 10 flanges per hour. Fixed manufacturing costs for flanges are $28,000 per period. Period (nonmanufacturing) costs associated with flanges are $10,000 per period, and are fixed.

Required

1. Graph the fixed, variable, and total manufacturing cost for flanges, using units (number of flanges) on the *x*-axis.
2. Assume Gayle's Glassworks manufactures and sells 5,000 flanges this period. Its competitor, Flora's Flasks, sells flanges for $10 each. Can Gayle sell below Flora's price and still make a profit on the flanges?
3. How would your answer to requirement 2 differ if Gayle's Glassworks made and sold 10,000 flanges this period? Why? What does this indicate about the use of unit cost in decision making?

2-28 **Inventoriable costs versus period costs.** Each of the following cost items pertains to one of these companies: General Electric (a manufacturing-sector company), Safeway (a merchandising-sector company), and Google (a service-sector company):

a. Perrier mineral water purchased by Safeway for sale to its customers
b. Electricity used to provide lighting for assembly-line workers at a General Electric refrigerator-assembly plant
c. Depreciation on Google's computer equipment used to update directories of Web sites
d. Electricity used to provide lighting for Safeway's store aisles
e. Depreciation on General Electric's computer equipment used for quality testing of refrigerator components during the assembly process
f. Salaries of Safeway's marketing personnel planning local-newspaper advertising campaigns
g. Perrier mineral water purchased by Google for consumption by its software engineers
h. Salaries of Google's marketing personnel selling banner advertising

Required

1. Distinguish between manufacturing-, merchandising-, and service-sector companies.
2. Distinguish between inventoriable costs and period costs.
3. Classify each of the cost items (**a–h**) as an inventoriable cost or a period cost. Explain your answers.

MyAccountingLab

Problems

2-29 **Computing cost of goods purchased and cost of goods sold.** The following data are for Marvin Department Store. The account balances (in thousands) are for 2011.

Marketing, distribution, and customer-service costs	$ 37,000
Merchandise inventory, January 1, 2011	27,000
Utilities	17,000
General and administrative costs	43,000
Merchandise inventory, December 31, 2011	34,000
Purchases	155,000
Miscellaneous costs	4,000
Transportation-in	7,000
Purchase returns and allowances	4,000
Purchase discounts	6,000
Revenues	280,000

Required

1. Compute (**a**) the cost of goods purchased and (**b**) the cost of goods sold.
2. Prepare the income statement for 2011.

2-30 **Cost of goods purchased, cost of goods sold, and income statement.** The following data are for Montgomery Retail Outlet Stores. The account balances (in thousands) are for 2011.

Marketing and advertising costs	$ 24,000
Merchandise inventory, January 1, 2011	45,000
Shipping of merchandise to customers	2,000

Building depreciation	$ 4,200
Purchases	260,000
General and administrative costs	32,000
Merchandise inventory, December 31, 2011	52,000
Merchandise freight-in	10,000
Purchase returns and allowances	11,000
Purchase discounts	9,000
Revenues	320,000

Required

1. Compute (a) the cost of goods purchased and (b) the cost of goods sold.
2. Prepare the income statement for 2011.

2-31 Flow of Inventoriable Costs. Renka's Heaters selected data for October 2011 are presented here (in millions):

Direct materials inventory 10/1/2011	$ 105
Direct materials purchased	365
Direct materials used	385
Total manufacturing overhead costs	450
Variable manufacturing overhead costs	265
Total manufacturing costs incurred during October 2011	1,610
Work-in-process inventory 10/1/2011	230
Cost of goods manufactured	1,660
Finished goods inventory 10/1/2011	130
Cost of goods sold	1,770

Calculate the following costs:

Required

1. Direct materials inventory 10/31/2011
2. Fixed manufacturing overhead costs for October 2011
3. Direct manufacturing labor costs for October 2011
4. Work-in-process inventory 10/31/2011
5. Cost of finished goods available for sale in October 2011
6. Finished goods inventory 10/31/2011

2-32 Cost of finished goods manufactured, income statement, manufacturing company. Consider the following account balances (in thousands) for the Canseco Company:

	Home Insert Page Layout Formulas Data Review View		
	A	B	C
1	**Canseco Company**	**Beginning of**	**End of**
2		**2011**	**2011**
3	Direct materials inventory	$22,000	$26,000
4	Work-in-process inventory	21,000	20,000
5	Finished goods inventory	18,000	23,000
6	Purchases of direct materials		75,000
7	Direct manufacturing labor		25,000
8	Indirect manufacturing labor		15,000
9	Plant insurance		9,000
10	Depreciation—plant, building, and equipment		11,000
11	Repairs and maintenance—plant		4,000
12	Marketing, distribution, and customer-service costs		93,000
13	General and administrative costs		29,000

Required

1. Prepare a schedule for the cost of goods manufactured for 2011.
2. Revenues for 2011 were $300 million. Prepare the income statement for 2011.

2-33 Cost of goods manufactured, income statement, manufacturing company. Consider the following account balances (in thousands) for the Piedmont Corporation:

Piedmont Corporation	Beginning of 2011	End of 2011
Direct materials inventory	65,000	34,000
Work-in-process inventory	83,000	72,000
Finished goods inventory	123,000	102,000
Purchases of direct materials		128,000
Direct manufacturing labor		106,000
Indirect manufacturing labor		48,000
Indirect materials		14,000
Plant insurance		2,000
Depreciation—plant, building, and equipment		21,000
Plant utilities		12,000
Repairs and maintenance—plant		8,000
Equipment leasing costs		32,000
Marketing, distribution, and customer-service costs		62,000
General and administrative costs		34,000

Required

1. Prepare a schedule for the cost of goods manufactured for 2011.
2. Revenues for 2011 were $600 million. Prepare the income statement for 2011.

2-34 Income statement and schedule of cost of goods manufactured. The Howell Corporation has the following account balances (in millions):

For Specific Date		For Year 2011	
Direct materials inventory, Jan. 1, 2011	$15	Purchases of direct materials	$325
Work-in-process inventory, Jan. 1, 2011	10	Direct manufacturing labor	100
Finished goods inventory, Jan. 1, 2011	70	Depreciation—plant and equipment	80
Direct materials inventory, Dec. 31, 2011	20	Plant supervisory salaries	5
Work-in-process inventory, Dec. 31, 2011	5	Miscellaneous plant overhead	35
Finished goods inventory, Dec. 31, 2011	55	Revenues	950
		Marketing, distribution, and customer-service costs	240
		Plant supplies used	10
		Plant utilities	30
		Indirect manufacturing labor	60

Required

Prepare an income statement and a supporting schedule of cost of goods manufactured for the year ended December 31, 2011. (For additional questions regarding these facts, see the next problem.)

2-35 Interpretation of statements (continuation of 2-34).

Required

1. How would the answer to Problem 2-34 be modified if you were asked for a schedule of cost of goods manufactured and sold instead of a schedule of cost of goods manufactured? Be specific.
2. Would the sales manager's salary (included in marketing, distribution, and customer-service costs) be accounted for any differently if the Howell Corporation were a merchandising-sector company instead of a manufacturing-sector company? Using the flow of manufacturing costs outlined in Exhibit 2-9 (p. 42), describe how the wages of an assembler in the plant would be accounted for in this manufacturing company.
3. Plant supervisory salaries are usually regarded as manufacturing overhead costs. When might some of these costs be regarded as direct manufacturing costs? Give an example.
4. Suppose that both the direct materials used and the plant and equipment depreciation are related to the manufacture of 1 million units of product. What is the unit cost for the direct materials assigned to those units? What is the unit cost for plant and equipment depreciation? Assume that yearly plant and equipment depreciation is computed on a straight-line basis.
5. Assume that the implied cost-behavior patterns in requirement 4 persist. That is, direct material costs behave as a variable cost, and plant and equipment depreciation behaves as a fixed cost. Repeat the

computations in requirement 4, assuming that the costs are being predicted for the manufacture of 1.2 million units of product. How would the total costs be affected?

6. As a management accountant, explain concisely to the president why the unit costs differed in requirements 4 and 5.

2-36 **Income statement and schedule of cost of goods manufactured.** The following items (in millions) pertain to Calendar Corporation:

For Specific Date		For Year 2011	
Work-in-process inventory, Jan. 1, 2011	$18	Plant utilities	$ 9
Direct materials inventory, Dec. 31, 2011	8	Indirect manufacturing labor	27
Finished goods inventory, Dec. 31, 2011	11	Depreciation—plant and equipment	6
Accounts payable, Dec. 31, 2011	24	Revenues	355
Accounts receivable, Jan. 1, 2011	52	Miscellaneous manufacturing overhead	15
Work-in-process inventory, Dec. 31, 2011	3	Marketing, distribution, and customer-service costs	94
Finished goods inventory, Jan 1, 2011	47	Direct materials purchased	84
Accounts receivable, Dec. 31, 2011	38	Direct manufacturing labor	42
Accounts payable, Jan. 1, 2011	49	Plant supplies used	4
Direct materials inventory, Jan. 1, 2011	32	Property taxes on plant	2

Calendar's manufacturing costing system uses a three-part classification of direct materials, direct manufacturing labor, and manufacturing overhead costs.

Prepare an income statement and a supporting schedule of cost of goods manufactured. (For additional questions regarding these facts, see the next problem.)

Required

2-37 **Terminology, interpretation of statements (continuation of 2-36).**

1. Calculate total prime costs and total conversion costs.
2. Calculate total inventoriable costs and period costs.
3. Design costs and R&D costs are not considered product costs for financial statement purposes. When might some of these costs be regarded as product costs? Give an example.
4. Suppose that both the direct materials used and the depreciation on plant and equipment are related to the manufacture of 2 million units of product. Determine the unit cost for the direct materials assigned to those units and the unit cost for depreciation on plant and equipment. Assume that yearly depreciation is computed on a straight-line basis.
5. Assume that the implied cost-behavior patterns in requirement 4 persist. That is, direct material costs behave as a variable cost and depreciation on plant and equipment behaves as a fixed cost. Repeat the computations in requirement 4, assuming that the costs are being predicted for the manufacture of 3 million units of product. Determine the effect on total costs.
6. Assume that depreciation on the equipment (but not the plant) is computed based on the number of units produced because the equipment deteriorates with units produced. The depreciation rate on equipment is $1 per unit. Calculate the depreciation on equipment assuming (a) 2 million units of product are produced and (b) 3 million units of product are produced.

2-38 **Labor cost, overtime, and idle time.** Jim Anderson works in the production department of Midwest Steelworks as a machine operator. Jim, a long-time employee of Midwest, is paid on an hourly basis at a rate of $20 per hour. Jim works five 8-hour shifts per week Monday–Friday (40 hours). Any time Jim works over and above these 40 hours is considered overtime for which he is paid at a rate of time and a half ($30 per hour). If the overtime falls on weekends, Jim is paid at a rate of double time ($40 per hour). Jim is also paid an additional $20 per hour for any holidays worked, even if it is part of his regular 40 hours.

Jim is paid his regular wages even if the machines are down (not operating) due to regular machine maintenance, slow order periods, or unexpected mechanical problems. These hours are considered "idle time."

During December Jim worked the following hours:

	Hours worked including machine downtime	Machine downtime
Week 1	44	3.5
Week 2	43	6.4
Week 3	48	5.8
Week 4	46	2

Included in the total hours worked are two company holidays (Christmas Eve and Christmas Day) during Week 4. All overtime worked by Jim was Monday–Friday, except for the hours worked in Week 3. All of the Week 3 overtime hours were worked on a Saturday.

Required

1. Calculate (a) direct manufacturing labor, (b) idle time, (c) overtime and holiday premium, and (d) total earnings for Jim in December.
2. Is idle time and overtime premium a direct or indirect cost of the products that Jim worked on in December? Explain.

2-39 Missing records, computing inventory costs. Ron Williams recently took over as the controller of Johnson Brothers Manufacturing. Last month, the previous controller left the company with little notice and left the accounting records in disarray. Ron needs the ending inventory balances to report first quarter numbers.

For the previous month (March 2011) Ron was able to piece together the following information:

Direct materials purchased	$ 240,000
Work-in-process inventory, 3/1/2011	$ 70,000
Direct materials inventory, 3/1/2011	$ 25,000
Finished goods inventory, 3/1/2011	$ 320,000
Conversion Costs	$ 660,000
Total manufacturing costs added during the period	$ 840,000
Cost of goods manufactured	4 times direct materials used
Gross margin as a percentage of revenues	20%
Revenues	$1,037,500

Required

Calculate the cost of:

1. Finished goods inventory, 3/31/2011
2. Work-in-process inventory, 3/31/2011
3. Direct materials inventory, 3/31/2011

2-40 Comprehensive problem on unit costs, product costs. Denver Office Equipment manufactures and sells metal shelving. It began operations on January 1, 2011. Costs incurred for 2011 are as follows (V stands for variable; F stands for fixed):

Direct materials used	$147,600 V
Direct manufacturing labor costs	38,400 V
Plant energy costs	2,000 V
Indirect manufacturing labor costs	14,000 V
Indirect manufacturing labor costs	19,000 F
Other indirect manufacturing costs	11,000 V
Other indirect manufacturing costs	14,000 F
Marketing, distribution, and customer-service costs	128,000 V
Marketing, distribution, and customer-service costs	48,000 F
Administrative costs	56,000 F

Variable manufacturing costs are variable with respect to units produced. Variable marketing, distribution, and customer-service costs are variable with respect to units sold.

Inventory data are as follows:

	Beginning: January 1, 2011	Ending: December 31, 2011
Direct materials	0 lb	2,400 lbs
Work in process	0 units	0 units
Finished goods	0 units	? units

Production in 2011 was 123,000 units. Two pounds of direct materials are used to make one unit of finished product.

Revenues in 2011 were $594,000. The selling price per unit and the purchase price per pound of direct materials were stable throughout the year. The company's ending inventory of finished goods is carried at the average unit manufacturing cost for 2011. Finished-goods inventory at December 31, 2011, was $26,000.

1. Calculate direct materials inventory, total cost, December 31, 2011.
2. Calculate finished-goods inventory, total units, December 31, 2011.
3. Calculate selling price in 2011.
4. Calculate operating income for 2011.

Required

2-41 **Cost Classification; Ethics.** Scott Hewitt, the new Plant Manager of Old World Manufacturing Plant Number 7, has just reviewed a draft of his year-end financial statements. Hewitt receives a year-end bonus of 10% of the plant's operating income before tax. The year-end income statement provided by the plant's controller was disappointing to say the least. After reviewing the numbers, Hewitt demanded that his controller go back and "work the numbers" again. Hewitt insisted that if he didn't see a better operating income number the next time around he would be forced to look for a new controller.

Old World Manufacturing classifies all costs directly related to the manufacturing of its product as product costs. These costs are inventoried and later expensed as costs of goods sold when the product is sold. All other expenses, including finished goods warehousing costs of $3,250,000 are classified as period expenses. Hewitt had suggested that warehousing costs be included as product costs because they are "definitely related to our product." The company produced 200,000 units during the period and sold 180,000 units.

As the controller reworked the numbers he discovered that if he included warehousing costs as product costs, he could improve operating income by $325,000. He was also sure these new numbers would make Hewitt happy.

1. Show numerically how operating income would improve by $325,000 just by classifying the preceding costs as product costs instead of period expenses?
2. Is Hewitt correct in his justification that these costs "are definitely related to our product."
3. By how much will Hewitt profit personally if the controller makes the adjustments in requirement 1.
4. What should the plant controller do?

Required

Collaborative Learning Problem

2-42 **Finding unknown amounts.** An auditor for the Internal Revenue Service is trying to reconstruct some partially destroyed records of two taxpayers. For each of the cases in the accompanying list, find the unknowns designated by the letters A through D.

	Case 1	Case 2
	(in thousands)	
Accounts receivable, 12/31	$ 6,000	$ 2,100
Cost of goods sold	A	20,000
Accounts payable, 1/1	3,000	1,700
Accounts payable, 12/31	1,800	1,500
Finished goods inventory, 12/31	B	5,300
Gross margin	11,300	C
Work-in-process inventory, 1/1	0	800
Work-in-process inventory, 12/31	0	3,000
Finished goods inventory, 1/1	4,000	4,000
Direct materials used	8,000	12,000
Direct manufacturing labor	3,000	5,000
Manufacturing overhead costs	7,000	D
Purchases of direct materials	9,000	7,000
Revenues	32,000	31,800
Accounts receivable, 1/1	2,000	1,400

Cost-Volume-Profit Analysis

All managers want to know how profits will change as the units sold of a product or service change.

Home Depot managers, for example, might wonder how many units of a new product must be sold to break even or make a certain amount of profit. Procter & Gamble managers might ask themselves how expanding their business into a particular foreign market would affect costs, selling price, and profits. These questions have a common "what-if" theme. Examining the results of these what-if possibilities and alternatives helps managers make better decisions.

Managers must also decide how to price their products and understand the effect of their pricing decisions on revenues and profits. The following article explains how the Irish rock band U2 recently decided whether it should decrease the prices on some of its tickets during its recent world tour. Does lowering ticket price sound like a wise strategy to you?

How the "The Biggest Rock Show Ever" Turned a Big Profit[1]

When U2 embarked on its recent world tour, *Rolling Stone* magazine called it "the biggest rock show ever." Visiting large stadiums across the United States and Europe, the Irish quartet performed on an imposing 164-foot high stage that resembled a spaceship, complete with a massive video screen and footbridges leading to ringed catwalks.

With an ambitious 48-date trek planned, U2 actually had three separate stages leapfrogging its global itinerary—each one costing nearly $40 million dollars. As a result, the tour's success was dependent not only on each night's concert, but also recouping its tremendous fixed costs—costs that do not change with the number of fans in the audience.

To cover its high fixed costs and make a profit, U2 needed to sell a lot of tickets. To maximize revenue, the tour employed a unique in-the-round stage configuration, which boosted stadium capacity by roughly 20%, and sold tickets for as little as $30, far less than most large outdoor concerts.

The band's plan worked—despite a broader music industry slump and global recession, U2 shattered attendance records in most of the venues it played. By the end of the tour, the band played to over

---

[1] *Source*: Gundersen, Edna. 2009. U2 turns 360 stadium into attendance-shattering sellouts. *USA Today*, October 4. www.usatoday.com/life/music/news/2009-10-04-u2-stadium-tour_N.htm

3 million fans, racking up almost $300 million in ticket and merchandise sales and turning a profit. As you read this chapter, you will begin to understand how and why U2 made the decision to lower prices.

Many capital intensive companies, such as US Airways and United Airlines in the airlines industry and Global Crossing and WorldCom in the telecommunications industry, have high fixed costs. They must generate sufficient revenues to cover these costs and turn a profit. When revenues declined at these companies during 2001 and 2002 and fixed costs remained high, these companies declared bankruptcy. The methods of CVP analysis described in this chapter help managers minimize such risks.

Essentials of CVP Analysis

In Chapter 2, we discussed total revenues, total costs, and income. **Cost-volume-profit (CVP) analysis** studies the behavior and relationship among these elements as changes occur in the units sold, the selling price, the variable cost per unit, or the fixed costs of a product. Let's consider an example to illustrate CVP analysis.

> Example: Emma Frost is considering selling GMAT Success, a test prep book and software package for the business school admission test, at a college fair in Chicago. Emma knows she can purchase this package from a wholesaler at $120 per package, with the privilege of returning all unsold packages and receiving a full $120 refund per package. She also knows that she must pay $2,000 to the organizers for the booth rental at the fair. She will incur no other costs. She must decide whether she should rent a booth.

Emma, like most managers who face such a situation, works through a series of steps.

1. **Identify the problem and uncertainties.** The decision to rent the booth hinges critically on how Emma resolves two important uncertainties—the price she can charge and the number of packages she can sell at that price. Every decision deals with selecting a course of action. Emma must decide knowing that the outcome of the chosen action is uncertain and will only be known in the future. The more confident Emma is about selling a large number of packages at a good price, the more willing she will be to rent the booth.

2. **Obtain information.** When faced with uncertainty, managers obtain information that might help them understand the uncertainties better. For example, Emma gathers information about the type of individuals likely to attend the fair and other test-prep packages that might be sold at the fair. She also gathers data on her past experiences selling GMAT Success at fairs very much like the Chicago fair.

3. **Make predictions about the future.** Using all the information available to them, managers make predictions. Emma predicts that she can charge a price of $200 for GMAT Success. At that price she is reasonably confident that she will be able to sell at least 30 packages and possibly as many as 60. In making these predictions, Emma like most managers, must be realistic and exercise careful judgment. If her predictions are excessively optimistic, Emma will rent the booth when she should not. If they are unduly pessimistic, Emma will not rent the booth when she should.

Emma's predictions rest on the belief that her experience at the Chicago fair will be similar to her experience at the Boston fair four months earlier. Yet, Emma is uncertain about several aspects of her prediction. Is the comparison between Boston and Chicago appropriate? Have conditions and circumstances changed over the last four months? Are there any biases creeping into her thinking? She is keen on selling at the Chicago fair because sales in the last couple of months have been lower than expected. Is this experience making her predictions overly optimistic? Has she ignored some of the competitive risks? Will the other test prep vendors at the fair reduce their prices?

Emma reviews her thinking. She retests her assumptions. She also explores these questions with John Mills, a close friend, who has extensive experience selling test-prep packages like GMAT Success. In the end, she feels quite confident that her predictions are reasonable, accurate, and carefully thought through.

4. **Make decisions by choosing among alternatives.** Emma uses the CVP analysis that follows, and decides to rent the booth at the Chicago fair.

5. **Implement the decision, evaluate performance, and learn.** Thoughtful managers never stop learning. They compare their actual performance to predicted performance to understand why things worked out the way they did and what they might learn. At the end of the Chicago fair, for example, Emma would want to evaluate whether her predictions about price and the number of packages she could sell were correct. Such feedback would be very helpful to Emma as she makes decisions about renting booths at subsequent fairs.

How does Emma use CVP analysis in Step 4 to make her decision? Emma begins by identifying which costs are fixed and which costs are variable and then calculates *contribution margin.*

Contribution Margins

The booth-rental cost of $2,000 is a fixed cost because it will not change no matter how many packages Emma sells. The cost of the package itself is a variable cost because it increases in proportion to the number of packages sold. Emma will incur a cost of $120 for each package that she sells. To get an idea of how operating income will change as a result of selling different quantities of packages, Emma calculates operating income if sales are 5 packages and if sales are 40 packages.

	5 packages sold	**40 packages sold**
Revenues	$ 1,000 ($200 per package × 5 packages)	$8,000 ($200 per package × 40 packages)
Variable purchase costs	600 ($120 per package × 5 packages)	4,800 ($120 per package × 40 packages)
Fixed costs	2,000	2,000
Operating income	$(1,600)	$1,200

The only numbers that change from selling different quantities of packages are *total revenues* and *total variable costs.* The difference between total revenues and total variable costs is called **contribution margin.** That is,

Contribution margin = Total revenues − Total variable costs

Contribution margin indicates why operating income changes as the number of units sold changes. The contribution margin when Emma sells 5 packages is $400 ($1,000 in total revenues minus $600 in total variable costs); the contribution margin when Emma sells

40 packages is $3,200 ($8,000 in total revenues minus $4,800 in total variable costs). When calculating the contribution margin, be sure to subtract all variable costs. For example, if Emma had variable selling costs because she paid a commission to salespeople for each package they sold at the fair, variable costs would include the cost of each package plus the sales commission.

Contribution margin per unit is a useful tool for calculating contribution margin and operating income. It is defined as,

$$\text{Contribution margin per unit} = \text{Selling price} - \text{Variable cost per unit}$$

In the GMAT Success example, contribution margin per package, or per unit, is $200 − $120 = $80. Contribution margin per unit recognizes the tight coupling of selling price and variable cost per unit. Unlike fixed costs, Emma will only incur the variable cost per unit of $120 when she sells a unit of GMAT Success for $200.

Contribution margin per unit provides a second way to calculate contribution margin:

$$\text{Contribution margin} = \text{Contribution margin per unit} \times \text{Number of units sold}$$

For example, when 40 packages are sold, contribution margin = $80 per unit × 40 units = $3,200.

Even before she gets to the fair, Emma incurs $2,000 in fixed costs. Because the contribution margin per unit is $80, Emma will recover $80 for each package that she sells at the fair. Emma hopes to sell enough packages to fully recover the $2,000 she spent for renting the booth and to then start making a profit.

Exhibit 3-1 presents contribution margins for different quantities of packages sold. The income statement in Exhibit 3-1 is called a **contribution income statement** because it groups costs into variable costs and fixed costs to highlight contribution margin. Each additional package sold from 0 to 1 to 5 increases contribution margin by $80 per package, recovering more of the fixed costs and reducing the operating loss. If Emma sells 25 packages, contribution margin equals $2,000 ($80 per package × 25 packages), exactly recovering fixed costs and resulting in $0 operating income. If Emma sells 40 packages, contribution margin increases by another $1,200 ($3,200 − $2,000), all of which becomes operating income. As you look across Exhibit 3-1 from left to right, you see that the increase in contribution margin exactly equals the increase in operating income (or the decrease in operating loss).

Instead of expressing contribution margin as a dollar amount per unit, we can express it as a percentage called **contribution margin percentage** (or **contribution margin ratio**):

$$\text{Contribution margin percentage (or contribution margin ratio)} = \frac{\text{Contribution margin per unit}}{\text{Selling price}}$$

In our example,

$$\text{Contribution margin percentage} = \frac{\$80}{\$200} = 0.40, \text{ or } 40\%$$

Contribution margin percentage is the contribution margin per dollar of revenue. Emma earns 40% of each dollar of revenue (equal to 40 cents).

Exhibit 3-1

Contribution Income Statement for Different Quantities of GMAT Success Packages Sold

	A	B	C	D	E	F	G	H
	Home	Insert	Page Layout	Formulas	Data	Review	View	
1				Number of Packages Sold				
2				0	1	5	25	40
3	Revenues	$ 200	per package	$ 0	$ 200	$ 1,000	$5,000	$8,000
4	Variable costs	$ 120	per package	0	120	600	3,000	4,800
5	Contribution margin	$ 80	per package	0	80	400	2,000	3,200
6	Fixed costs	$2,000		2,000	2,000	2,000	2,000	2,000
7	Operating income			$(2,000)	$(1,920)	$(1,600)	$ 0	$1,200

Most companies have multiple products. As we shall see later in this chapter, calculating contribution margin per unit when there are multiple products is more cumbersome. In practice, companies routinely use contribution margin percentage as a handy way to calculate contribution margin for different dollar amounts of revenue:

$$\text{Contribution margin} = \text{Contribution margin percentage} \times \text{Revenues (in dollars)}$$

For example, in Exhibit 3-1, if Emma sells 40 packages, revenues will be $8,000 and contribution margin will equal 40% of $8,000, or 0.40 × $8,000 = $3,200. Emma earns operating income of $1,200 ($3,200 − Fixed costs, $2,000) by selling 40 packages for $8,000.

Expressing CVP Relationships

How was the Excel spreadsheet in Exhibit 3-1 constructed? Underlying the Exhibit are some equations that express the CVP relationships. To make good decisions using CVP analysis, we must understand these relationships and the structure of the contribution income statement in Exhibit 3-1. There are three related ways (we will call them methods) to think more deeply about and model CVP relationships:

1. The equation method
2. The contribution margin method
3. The graph method

The equation method and the contribution margin method are most useful when managers want to determine operating income at few specific levels of sales (for example 5, 15, 25, and 40 units sold). The graph method helps managers visualize the relationship between units sold and operating income over a wide range of quantities of units sold. As we shall see later in the chapter, different methods are useful for different decisions.

Equation Method

Each column in Exhibit 3-1 is expressed as an equation.

$$\text{Revenues} - \text{Variable costs} - \text{Fixed costs} = \text{Operating income}$$

How are revenues in each column calculated?

$$\text{Revenues} = \text{Selling price } (SP) \times \text{Quantity of units sold } (Q)$$

How are variable costs in each column calculated?

$$\text{Variable costs} = \text{Variable cost per unit } (VCU) \times \text{Quantity of units sold } (Q)$$

So,

$$\left[\left(\begin{array}{c} \text{Selling} \\ \text{price} \end{array} \times \begin{array}{c} \text{Quantity of} \\ \text{units sold} \end{array} \right) - \left(\begin{array}{c} \text{Variable cost} \\ \text{per unit} \end{array} \times \begin{array}{c} \text{Quantity of} \\ \text{units sold} \end{array} \right) \right] - \begin{array}{c} \text{Fixed} \\ \text{costs} \end{array} = \begin{array}{c} \text{Operating} \\ \text{income} \end{array} \quad \textbf{(Equation 1)}$$

Equation 1 becomes the basis for calculating operating income for different quantities of units sold. For example, if you go to cell F7 in Exhibit 3-1, the calculation of operating income when Emma sells 5 packages is

$$(\$200 \times 5) - (\$120 \times 5) - \$2,000 = \$1,000 - \$600 - \$2,000 = -\$1,600$$

Contribution Margin Method

Rearranging equation 1,

$$\left[\left(\begin{array}{c} \text{Selling} \\ \text{price} \end{array} - \begin{array}{c} \text{Variable cost} \\ \text{per unit} \end{array} \right) \times \left(\begin{array}{c} \text{Quantity of} \\ \text{units sold} \end{array} \right) \right] - \begin{array}{c} \text{Fixed} \\ \text{costs} \end{array} = \begin{array}{c} \text{Operating} \\ \text{income} \end{array}$$

$$\left(\begin{array}{c} \text{Contribution margin} \\ \text{per unit} \end{array} \times \begin{array}{c} \text{Quantity of} \\ \text{units sold} \end{array} \right) - \begin{array}{c} \text{Fixed} \\ \text{costs} \end{array} = \begin{array}{c} \text{Operating} \\ \text{income} \end{array} \quad \textbf{(Equation 2)}$$

In our GMAT Success example, contribution margin per unit is $80 ($200 − $120), so when Emma sells 5 packages,

$$\text{Operating income} = (\$80 \times 5) - \$2{,}000 = -\$1{,}600$$

Equation 2 expresses the basic idea we described earlier—each unit sold helps Emma recover $80 (in contribution margin) of the $2,000 in fixed costs.

Graph Method

In the graph method, we represent total costs and total revenues graphically. Each is shown as a line on a graph. Exhibit 3-2 illustrates the graph method for GMAT Success. Because we have assumed that total costs and total revenues behave in a linear fashion, we need only two points to plot the line representing each of them.

1. **Total costs line.** The total costs line is the sum of fixed costs and variable costs. Fixed costs are $2,000 for all quantities of units sold within the relevant range. To plot the total costs line, use as one point the $2,000 fixed costs at zero units sold (point A) because variable costs are $0 when no units are sold. Select a second point by choosing any other convenient output level (say, 40 units sold) and determine the corresponding total costs. Total variable costs at this output level are $4,800 (40 units × $120 per unit). Remember, fixed costs are $2,000 at all quantities of units sold within the relevant range, so total costs at 40 units sold equal $6,800 ($2,000 + $4,800), which is point B in Exhibit 3-2. The total costs line is the straight line from point A through point B.

2. **Total revenues line.** One convenient starting point is $0 revenues at 0 units sold, which is point C in Exhibit 3-2. Select a second point by choosing any other convenient output level and determining the corresponding total revenues. At 40 units sold, total revenues are $8,000 ($200 per unit × 40 units), which is point D in Exhibit 3-2. The total revenues line is the straight line from point C through point D.

   Profit or loss at any sales level can be determined by the vertical distance between the two lines at that level in Exhibit 3-2. For quantities fewer than 25 units sold, total costs exceed total revenues, and the purple area indicates operating losses. For quantities greater than 25 units sold, total revenues exceed total costs, and the blue-green area indicates operating incomes. At 25 units sold, total revenues equal total costs. Emma will break even by selling 25 packages.

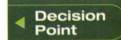

Decision Point

How can CVP analysis assist managers?

Exhibit 3-2

Cost-Volume Graph for GMAT Success

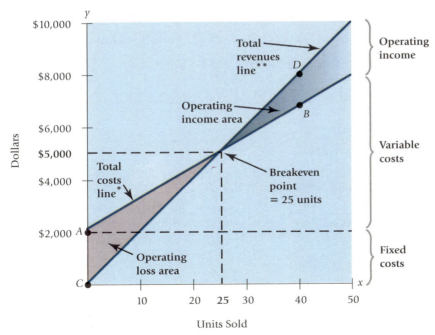

*Slope of the total costs line is the variable cost per unit = $120
**Slope of the total revenues line is the selling price = $200

Cost-Volume-Profit Assumptions

Now that you have seen how CVP analysis works, think about the following assumptions we made during the analysis:

1. Changes in the levels of revenues and costs arise only because of changes in the number of product (or service) units sold. The number of units sold is the only revenue driver and the only cost driver. Just as a cost driver is any factor that affects costs, a **revenue driver** is a variable, such as volume, that causally affects revenues.

2. Total costs can be separated into two components: a fixed component that does not vary with units sold and a variable component that changes with respect to units sold.

3. When represented graphically, the behaviors of total revenues and total costs are linear (meaning they can be represented as a straight line) in relation to units sold within a relevant range (and time period).

4. Selling price, variable cost per unit, and total fixed costs (within a relevant range and time period) are known and constant.

As the CVP assumptions make clear, an important feature of CVP analysis is distinguishing fixed from variable costs. Always keep in mind, however, that whether a cost is variable or fixed depends on the time period for a decision.

The shorter the time horizon, the higher the percentage of total costs considered fixed. For example, suppose an American Airlines plane will depart from its gate in the next hour and currently has 20 seats unsold. A potential passenger arrives with a transferable ticket from a competing airline. The variable costs (such as one more meal) to American of placing one more passenger in an otherwise empty seat is negligible At the time of this decision, with only an hour to go before the flight departs, virtually all costs (such as crew costs and baggage-handling costs) are fixed.

Alternatively, suppose American Airlines must decide whether to keep this flight in its flight schedule. This decision will have a one-year planning horizon. If American Airlines decides to cancel this flight because very few passengers during the last year have taken this flight, many more costs, including crew costs, baggage-handling costs, and airport fees, would be considered variable. That's because over this longer horizon, these costs would not have to be incurred if the flight were no longer operating. Always consider the relevant range, the length of the time horizon, and the specific decision situation when classifying costs as variable or fixed.

Breakeven Point and Target Operating Income

**Learning
Objective** **2**

Determine the
breakeven point and
output level needed to
achieve a target
operating income

. . . compare
contribution margin
and fixed costs

Managers and entrepreneurs like Emma always want to know how much they must sell to earn a given amount of income. Equally important, they want to know how much they must sell to avoid a loss.

Breakeven Point

The **breakeven point** (BEP) is that quantity of output sold at which total revenues equal total costs—that is, the quantity of output sold that results in $0 of operating income. We have already seen how to use the graph method to calculate the breakeven point. Recall from Exhibit 3-1 that operating income was $0 when Emma sold 25 units, the breakeven point. But by understanding the equations underlying the calculations in Exhibit 3-1, we can calculate the breakeven point directly for GMAT Success rather than trying out different quantities and checking when operating income equals $0.

Recall the equation method (equation 1):

$$\left(\begin{array}{c}\text{Selling}\\\text{price}\end{array} \times \begin{array}{c}\text{Quantity of}\\\text{units sold}\end{array}\right) - \left(\begin{array}{c}\text{Variable cost}\\\text{per unit}\end{array} \times \begin{array}{c}\text{Quantity of}\\\text{units sold}\end{array}\right) - \begin{array}{c}\text{Fixed}\\\text{costs}\end{array} = \begin{array}{c}\text{Operating}\\\text{income}\end{array}$$

Setting operating income equal to $0 and denoting quantity of output units that must be sold by Q,

$$(\$200 \times Q) - (\$120 \times Q) - \$2,000 = \$0$$
$$\$80 \times Q = \$2,000$$
$$Q = \$2,000 \div \$80 \text{ per unit } = 25 \text{ units}$$

If Emma sells fewer than 25 units, she will incur a loss; if she sells 25 units, she will break even; and if she sells more than 25 units, she will make a profit. While this breakeven point is expressed in units, it can also be expressed in revenues: 25 units × $200 selling price = $5,000.

Recall the contribution margin method (equation 2):

$$\left(\begin{array}{c} \text{Contribution} \\ \text{margin per unit} \end{array} \times \begin{array}{c} \text{Quantity of} \\ \text{units sold} \end{array} \right) - \text{Fixed costs} = \text{Operating income}$$

At the breakeven point, operating income is by definition $0 and so,

$$\text{Contribution margin per unit} \times \text{Breakeven number of units} = \text{Fixed cost} \quad \textbf{(Equation 3)}$$

Rearranging equation 3 and entering the data,

$$\frac{\text{Breakeven}}{\text{number of units}} = \frac{\text{Fixed costs}}{\text{Contribution margin per unit}} = \frac{\$2,000}{\$80 \text{ per unit}} = 25 \text{ units}$$

$$\text{Breakeven revenues} = \text{Breakeven number of units} \times \text{Selling price}$$
$$= 25 \text{ units} \times \$200 \text{ per unit} = \$5,000$$

In practice (because they have multiple products), companies usually calculate breakeven point directly in terms of revenues using contribution margin percentages. Recall that in the GMAT Success example,

$$\frac{\text{Contribution margin}}{\text{percentage}} = \frac{\text{Contribution margin per unit}}{\text{Selling price}} = \frac{\$80}{\$200} = 0.40, \text{ or } 40\%$$

That is, 40% of each dollar of revenue, or 40 cents, is contribution margin. To break even, contribution margin must equal fixed costs of $2,000. To earn $2,000 of contribution margin, when $1 of revenue earns $0.40 of contribution margin, revenues must equal $2,000 ÷ 0.40 = $5,000.

$$\frac{\text{Breakeven}}{\text{revenues}} = \frac{\text{Fixed costs}}{\text{Contribution margin \%}} = \frac{\$2,000}{0.40} = \$5,000$$

While the breakeven point tells managers how much they must sell to avoid a loss, managers are equally interested in how they will achieve the operating income targets underlying their strategies and plans. In our example, selling 25 units at a price of $200 assures Emma that she will not lose money if she rents the booth. This news is comforting, but we next describe how Emma determines how much she needs to sell to achieve a targeted amount of operating income.

Target Operating Income

We illustrate target operating income calculations by asking the following question: How many units must Emma sell to earn an operating income of $1,200? One approach is to keep plugging in different quantities into Exhibit 3-1 and check when operating income equals $1,200. Exhibit 3-1 shows that operating income is $1,200 when 40 packages are sold. A more convenient approach is to use equation 1 from page 66.

$$\left[\left(\begin{array}{c} \text{Selling} \\ \text{price} \end{array} \times \begin{array}{c} \text{Quantity of} \\ \text{units sold} \end{array} \right) - \left(\begin{array}{c} \text{Variable cost} \\ \text{per unit} \end{array} \times \begin{array}{c} \text{Quantity of} \\ \text{units sold} \end{array} \right) \right] - \begin{array}{c} \text{Fixed} \\ \text{costs} \end{array} = \begin{array}{c} \text{Operating} \\ \text{income} \end{array} \quad \textbf{(Equation 1)}$$

We denote by Q the unknown quantity of units Emma must sell to earn an operating income of $1,200. Selling price is $200, variable cost per package is $120, fixed costs are

$2,000, and target operating income is $1,200. Substituting these values into equation 1, we have

$$(\$200 \times Q) - (\$120 \times Q) - \$2{,}000 = \$1{,}200$$
$$\$80 \times Q = \$2{,}000 + \$1{,}200 = \$3{,}200$$
$$Q = \$3{,}200 \div \$80 \text{ per unit} = 40 \text{ units}$$

Alternatively, we could use equation 2,

$$\left(\begin{array}{c} \text{Contribution margin} \\ \text{per unit} \end{array} \times \begin{array}{c} \text{Quantity of} \\ \text{units sold} \end{array} \right) - \begin{array}{c} \text{Fixed} \\ \text{costs} \end{array} = \begin{array}{c} \text{Operating} \\ \text{income} \end{array} \qquad \textbf{(Equation 2)}$$

Given a target operating income ($1,200 in this case), we can rearrange terms to get equation 4.

$$\begin{array}{c} \text{Quantity of units} \\ \text{required to be sold} \end{array} = \frac{\text{Fixed costs + Target operating income}}{\text{Contribution margin per unit}} \qquad \textbf{(Equation 4)}$$

$$\begin{array}{c} \text{Quantity of units} \\ \text{required to be sold} \end{array} = \frac{\$2{,}000 + \$1{,}200}{\$80 \text{ per unit}} = 40 \text{ units}$$

Proof:

Revenues, $200 per unit × 40 units	$8,000
Variable costs, $120 per unit × 40 units	4,800
Contribution margin, $80 per unit × 40 units	3,200
Fixed costs	2,000
Operating income	$1,200

The revenues needed to earn an operating income of $1,200 can also be calculated directly by recognizing (1) that $3,200 of contribution margin must be earned (fixed costs of $2,000 plus operating income of $1,200) and (2) that $1 of revenue earns $0.40 (40 cents) of contribution margin. To earn $3,200 of contribution margin, revenues must equal $3,200 ÷ 0.40 = $8,000.

$$\text{Revenues needed to earn operating income of }\$1{,}200 = \frac{\$2{,}000 + \$1{,}200}{0.40} = \frac{\$3{,}200}{0.40} = \$8{,}000$$

The graph in Exhibit 3-2 is very difficult to use to answer the question: How many units must Emma sell to earn an operating income of $1,200? Why? Because it is not easy to determine from the graph the precise point at which the difference between the total revenues line and the total costs line equals $1,200. However, recasting Exhibit 3-2 in the form of a profit-volume (PV) graph makes it easier to answer this question.

A **PV graph** shows how changes in the quantity of units sold affect operating income. Exhibit 3-3 is the PV graph for GMAT Success (fixed costs, $2,000; selling price, $200; and variable cost per unit, $120). The PV line can be drawn using two points. One convenient point (M) is the operating loss at 0 units sold, which is equal to the fixed costs of $2,000, shown at –$2,000 on the vertical axis. A second convenient point (N) is the breakeven point, which is 25 units in our example (see p. 69). The PV line is the straight line from point M through point N. To find the number of units Emma must sell to earn an operating income of $1,200, draw a horizontal line parallel to the *x*-axis corresponding to $1,200 on the vertical axis (that's the *y*-axis). At the point where this line intersects the PV line, draw a vertical line down to the horizontal axis (that's the *x*-axis). The vertical line intersects the *x*-axis at 40 units, indicating that by selling 40 units Emma will earn an operating income of $1,200.

Target Net Income and Income Taxes

Net income is operating income plus nonoperating revenues (such as interest revenue) minus nonoperating costs (such as interest cost) minus income taxes. For simplicity, throughout this chapter we assume nonoperating revenues and nonoperating costs are zero. Thus,

$$\text{Net income} = \text{Operating income} - \text{Income taxes}$$

Until now, we have ignored the effect of income taxes in our CVP analysis. In many companies, the income targets for managers in their strategic plans are expressed in terms of

---

Decision Point ▶

How can managers determine the breakeven point or the output needed to achieve a target operating income?

Learning Objective 3

Understand how income taxes affect CVP analysis

. . . focus on net income

Exhibit 3-3

Profit-Volume Graph for
GMAT Success

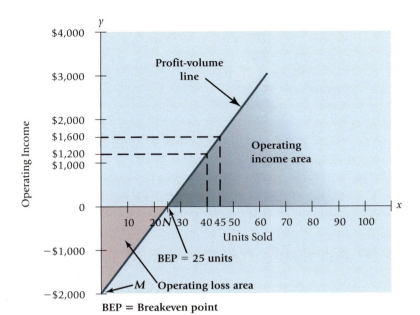

BEP = Breakeven point

net income. That's because top management wants subordinate managers to take into account the effects their decisions have on operating income after income taxes. Some decisions may not result in large operating incomes, but they may have favorable tax consequences, making them attractive on a net income basis—the measure that drives shareholders' dividends and returns.

To make net income evaluations, CVP calculations for target income must be stated in terms of target net income instead of target operating income. For example, Emma may be interested in knowing the quantity of units she must sell to earn a net income of $960, assuming an income tax rate of 40%.

$$\text{Target net income} = \left(\begin{array}{c}\text{Target}\\\text{operating income}\end{array}\right) - \left(\begin{array}{c}\text{Target}\\\text{operating income}\end{array} \times \text{Tax rate}\right)$$

$$\text{Target net income} = (\text{Target operating income}) \times (1 - \text{Tax rate})$$

$$\text{Target operating income} = \frac{\text{Target net income}}{1 - \text{Tax rate}} = \frac{\$960}{1 - 0.40} = \$1,600$$

In other words, to earn a target net income of $960, Emma's target operating income is $1,600.

Proof:

Target operating income	$1,600
Tax at 40% (0.40 × $1,600)	640
Target net income	$ 960

The key step is to take the target net income number and convert it into the corresponding target operating income number. We can then use equation 1 for target operating income and substitute numbers from our GMAT Success example.

$$\left[\left(\begin{array}{c}\text{Selling}\\\text{price}\end{array} \times \begin{array}{c}\text{Quantity of}\\\text{units sold}\end{array}\right) - \left(\begin{array}{c}\text{Variable cost}\\\text{per unit}\end{array} \times \begin{array}{c}\text{Quantity of}\\\text{units sold}\end{array}\right)\right] - \begin{array}{c}\text{Fixed}\\\text{costs}\end{array} = \begin{array}{c}\text{Operating}\\\text{income}\end{array} \quad \textbf{(Equation 1)}$$

$$(\$200 \times Q) - (\$120 \times Q) - \$2,000 = \$1,600$$
$$\$80 \times Q = \$3,600$$
$$Q = \$3,600 \div \$80 \text{ per unit} = 45 \text{ units}$$

Alternatively we can calculate the number of units Emma must sell by using the contribution margin method and equation 4:

$$\begin{array}{c}\text{Quantity of units}\\\text{required to be sold}\end{array} = \frac{\text{Fixed costs} + \text{Target operating income}}{\text{Contribution margin per unit}} \quad \textbf{(Equation 4)}$$

$$= \frac{\$2,000 + \$1,600}{\$80 \text{ per unit}} = 45 \text{ units}$$

Proof:

Revenues, $200 per unit × 45 units		$9,000
Variable costs, $120 per unit × 45 units		5,400
Contribution margin		3,600
Fixed costs		2,000
Operating income		1,600
Income taxes, $1,600 × 0.40		640
Net income		$ 960

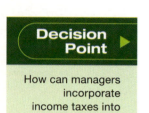

Decision Point ▶

How can managers incorporate income taxes into CVP analysis?

Learning Objective 4

Explain how managers use CVP analysis in decision making

. . . choose the alternative that maximizes operating income

Emma can also use the PV graph in Exhibit 3-3. To earn target operating income of $1,600, Emma needs to sell 45 units.

Focusing the analysis on target net income instead of target operating income will not change the breakeven point. That's because, by definition, operating income at the breakeven point is $0, and no income taxes are paid when there is no operating income.

Using CVP Analysis for Decision Making

We have seen how CVP analysis is useful for calculating the units that need to be sold to break even, or to achieve a target operating income or target net income. Managers also use CVP analysis to guide other decisions, many of them strategic decisions. Consider a decision about choosing additional features for an existing product. Different choices can affect selling prices, variable cost per unit, fixed costs, units sold, and operating income. CVP analysis helps managers make product decisions by estimating the expected profitability of these choices.

Strategic decisions invariably entail risk. CVP analysis can be used to evaluate how operating income will be affected if the original predicted data are not achieved—say, if sales are 10% lower than estimated. Evaluating this risk affects other strategic decisions a company might make. For example, if the probability of a decline in sales seems high, a manager may take actions to change the cost structure to have more variable costs and fewer fixed costs. We return to our GMAT Success example to illustrate how CVP analysis can be used for strategic decisions concerning advertising and selling price.

Decision to Advertise

Suppose Emma anticipates selling 40 units at the fair. Exhibit 3-3 indicates that Emma's operating income will be $1,200. Emma is considering placing an advertisement describing the product and its features in the fair brochure. The advertisement will be a fixed cost of $500. Emma thinks that advertising will increase sales by 10% to 44 packages. Should Emma advertise? The following table presents the CVP analysis.

	40 Packages Sold with No Advertising (1)	44 Packages Sold with Advertising (2)	Difference (3) = (2) − (1)
Revenues ($200 × 40; $200 × 44)	$8,000	$8,800	$ 800
Variable costs ($120 × 40; $120 × 44)	4,800	5,280	480
Contribution margin ($80 × 40; $80 × 44)	3,200	3,520	320
Fixed costs	2,000	2,500	500
Operating income	$1,200	$1,020	$(180)

Operating income will decrease from $1,200 to $1,020, so Emma should not advertise. Note that Emma could focus only on the difference column and come to the same conclusion: If Emma advertises, contribution margin will increase by $320 (revenues, $800 − variable costs, $480), and fixed costs will increase by $500, resulting in a $180 decrease in operating income.

As you become more familiar with CVP analysis, try evaluating decisions based on differences rather than mechanically working through the contribution income statement. Analyzing differences gets to the heart of CVP analysis and sharpens intuition by focusing only on the revenues and costs that will change as a result of a decision.

Decision to Reduce Selling Price

Having decided not to advertise, Emma is contemplating whether to reduce the selling price to $175. At this price, she thinks she will sell 50 units. At this quantity, the test-prep package wholesaler who supplies GMAT Success will sell the packages to Emma for $115 per unit instead of $120. Should Emma reduce the selling price?

Contribution margin from lowering price to $175: ($175 − $115) per unit × 50 units	$3,000
Contribution margin from maintaining price at $200: ($200 − $120) per unit × 40 units	3,200
Change in contribution margin from lowering price	$ (200)

Decreasing the price will reduce contribution margin by $200 and, because the fixed costs of $2,000 will not change, it will also reduce operating income by $200. Emma should not reduce the selling price.

Determining Target Prices

Emma could also ask "At what price can I sell 50 units (purchased at $115 per unit) and continue to earn an operating income of $1,200?" The answer is $179, as the following calculations show.

Target operating income	$1,200
Add fixed costs	2,000
Target contribution margin	$3,200
Divided by number of units sold	÷50 units
Target contribution margin per unit	$ 64
Add variable cost per unit	115
Target selling price	$ 179

Proof:	Revenues, $179 per unit × 50 units	$8,950
	Variable costs, $115 per unit × 50 units	5,750
	Contribution margin	3,200
	Fixed costs	2,000
	Operating income	$1,200

Emma should also examine the effects of other decisions, such as simultaneously increasing advertising costs and lowering prices. In each case, Emma will compare the changes in contribution margin (through the effects on selling prices, variable costs, and quantities of units sold) to the changes in fixed costs, and she will choose the alternative that provides the highest operating income.

Decision Point

How do managers use CVP analysis to make decisions?

Sensitivity Analysis and Margin of Safety

Before choosing strategies and plans about how to implement strategies, managers frequently analyze the sensitivity of their decisions to changes in underlying assumptions. **Sensitivity analysis** is a "what-if" technique that managers use to examine how an outcome will change if the original predicted data are not achieved or if an underlying assumption changes. In the context of CVP analysis, sensitivity analysis answers questions such as, "What will operating income be if the quantity of units sold decreases by 5% from the original prediction?" and "What will operating income be if variable cost per unit increases by 10%?" Sensitivity analysis broadens managers' perspectives to possible outcomes that might occur *before* costs are committed.

Electronic spreadsheets, such as Excel, enable managers to conduct CVP-based sensitivity analyses in a systematic and efficient way. Using spreadsheets, managers can conduct sensitivity analysis to examine the effect and interaction of changes in selling price, variable cost per unit, fixed costs, and target operating income. Exhibit 3-4 displays a spreadsheet for the GMAT Success example.

Using the spreadsheet, Emma can immediately see how many units she needs to sell to achieve particular operating-income levels, given alternative levels of fixed costs and variable cost per unit that she may face. For example, 32 units must be sold to earn an

Learning Objective 5

Explain how sensitivity analysis helps managers cope with uncertainty

. . . determine the effect on operating income of different assumptions

Exhibit 3-5

Profit-Volume Graph for
Alternative Rental
Options for GMAT
Success

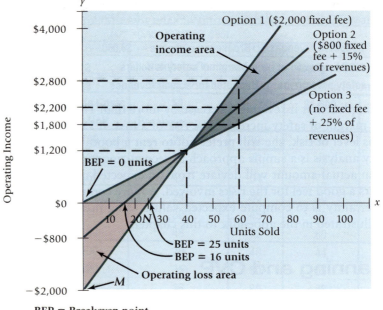

BEP = Breakeven point

income (or loss), depending on the demand for GMAT Success. Faced with this uncertainty, Emma's choice will be influenced by her confidence in the level of demand for GMAT Success and her willingness to risk losses if demand is low. For example, if Emma's tolerance for risk is high, she will choose Option 1 with its high potential rewards. If, however, Emma is averse to taking risk, she will prefer Option 3, where the rewards are smaller if sales are high but where she never suffers a loss if sales are low.

Operating Leverage

The risk-return trade-off across alternative cost structures can be measured as *operating leverage*. **Operating leverage** describes the effects that fixed costs have on changes in operating income as changes occur in units sold and contribution margin. Organizations with a high proportion of fixed costs in their cost structures, as is the case under Option 1, have high operating leverage. The line representing Option 1 in Exhibit 3-5 is the steepest of the three lines. Small increases in sales lead to large increases in operating income. Small decreases in sales result in relatively large decreases in operating income, leading to a greater risk of operating losses. *At any given level of sales,*

$$\text{Degree of operating leverage} = \frac{\text{Contribution margin}}{\text{Operating income}}$$

The following table shows the **degree of operating leverage** at sales of 40 units for the three rental options.

	Option 1	Option 2	Option 3
1. Contribution margin per unit (p. 75)	$ 80	$ 50	$ 30
2. Contribution margin (row 1 × 40 units)	$3,200	$2,000	$1,200
3. Operating income (from Exhibit 3-5)	$1,200	$1,200	$1,200
4. Degree of operating leverage (row 2 ÷ row 3)	$\frac{\$3,200}{\$1,200} = 2.67$	$\frac{\$2,000}{\$1,200} = 1.67$	$\frac{\$1,200}{\$1,200} = 1.00$

These results indicate that, when sales are 40 units, a percentage change in sales and contribution margin will result in 2.67 times that percentage change in operating income for Option 1, but the same percentage change (1.00) in operating income for Option 3. Consider, for example, a sales increase of 50% from 40 to 60 units. Contribution margin will increase by 50% under each option. Operating income, however, will increase by ⌐   × 50% = 133% from $1,200 to $2,800 in Option 1, but it will increase by only $1.00 \times 50\% = 50\%$ from \$1,200 to \$1,800 in Option 3 (see Exhibit 3-5). The degree of operating leverage at a given level of sales helps managers calculate the effect of sales fluctuations on operating income.

Keep in mind that, in the presence of fixed costs, the degree of operating leverage is different at different levels of sales. For example, at sales of 60 units, the degree of operating leverage under each of the three options is as follows:

	Option 1	Option 2	Option 3
1. Contribution margin per unit (p. 75)	$ 80	$ 50	$ 30
2. Contribution margin (row 1 $\times$ 60 units)	$4,800	$3,000	$1,800
3. Operating income (from Exhibit 3-5)	$2,800	$2,200	$1,800
4. Degree of operating leverage (row 2 ÷ row 3)	$\dfrac{\$4,800}{\$2,800} = 1.71$	$\dfrac{\$3,000}{\$2,200} = 1.36$	$\dfrac{\$1,800}{\$1,800} = 1.00$

The degree of operating leverage decreases from 2.67 (at sales of 40 units) to 1.71 (at sales of 60 units) under Option 1 and from 1.67 to 1.36 under Option 2. In general, whenever there are fixed costs, the degree of operating leverage decreases as the level of sales increases beyond the breakeven point. If fixed costs are \$0 as in Option 3, contribution margin equals operating income, and the degree of operating leverage equals 1.00 at all sales levels.

But why must managers monitor operating leverage carefully? Again, consider companies such as General Motors, Global Crossing, US Airways, United Airlines, and WorldCom. Their high operating leverage was a major reason for their financial problems. Anticipating high demand for their services, these companies borrowed money to acquire assets, resulting in high fixed costs. As sales declined, these companies suffered losses and could not generate sufficient cash to service their interest and debt, causing them to seek bankruptcy protection. Managers and management accountants should always evaluate how the level of fixed costs and variable costs they choose will affect the risk-return trade-off. See Concepts in Action, page 78, for another example of the risks of high fixed costs.

What actions are managers taking to reduce their fixed costs? Many companies are moving their manufacturing facilities from the United States to lower-cost countries, such as Mexico and China. To substitute high fixed costs with lower variable costs, companies are purchasing products from lower-cost suppliers instead of manufacturing products themselves. These actions reduce both costs and operating leverage. More recently, General Electric and Hewlett-Packard began outsourcing service functions, such as post-sales customer service, by shifting their customer call centers to countries, such as India, where costs are lower. These decisions by companies are not without controversy. Some economists argue that outsourcing helps to keep costs, and therefore prices, low and enables U.S. companies to remain globally competitive. Others argue that outsourcing reduces job opportunities in the United States and hurts working-class families.

◀ **Decision Point**

How should managers choose among different variable-cost/ fixed-cost structures?

Effects of Sales Mix on Income

Sales mix is the quantities (or proportion) of various products (or services) that constitute total unit sales of a company. Suppose Emma is now budgeting for a subsequent college fair in New York. She plans to sell two different test-prep packages—GMAT Success and GRE Guarantee—and budgets the following:

Learning Objective 7

Apply CVP analysis to a company producing multiple products

. . . assume sales mix of products remains constant as total units sold changes

	GMAT Success	GRE Guarantee	Total
Expected sales	60	40	100
Revenues, $200 and $100 per unit	$12,000	$4,000	$16,000
Variable costs, $120 and $70 per unit	7,200	2,800	10,000
Contribution margin, $80 and $30 per unit	$ 4,800	$1,200	6,000
Fixed costs			4,500
Operating income			$ 1,500

Of course, there are many different sales mixes (in units) that result in a contribution margin of $4,500 and cause Emma to break even, as the following table shows:

| Sales Mix (Units) | | Contribution Margin from | | |
GMAT Success (1)	GRE Guarantee (2)	GMAT Success (3) = $80 × (1)	GRE Guarantee (4) = $30 × (2)	Total Contribution Margin (5) = (3) + (4)
48	22	$3,840	$ 660	$4,500
36	54	2,880	1,620	4,500
30	70	2,400	2,100	4,500

If for example, the sales mix changes to 3 units of GMAT Success for every 7 units of GRE Guarantee, the breakeven point increases from 75 units to 100 units, comprising 30 units of GMAT Success and 70 units of GRE Guarantee. The breakeven quantity increases because the sales mix has shifted toward the lower-contribution-margin product, GRE Guarantee ($30 per unit compared to GMAT Success's $80 per unit). In general, for any given total quantity of units sold, as the sales mix shifts toward units with lower contribution margins (more units of GRE Guarantee compared to GMAT Success), operating income will be lower.

How do companies choose their sales mix? They adjust their mix to respond to demand changes. For example, as gasoline prices increase and customers want smaller cars, auto companies shift their production mix to produce smaller cars.

The multi-product case has two cost drivers, GMAT Success and GRE Guarantee. It shows how CVP and breakeven analysis can be adapted to the case of multiple cost drivers. The key point is that many different combinations of cost drivers can result in a given contribution margin.

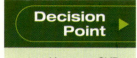

Decision Point ▶

How can CVP analysis be applied to a company producing multiple products?

CVP Analysis in Service and Nonprofit Organizations

Thus far, our CVP analysis has focused on a merchandising company. CVP can also be applied to decisions by manufacturing companies like BMW, service companies like Bank of America, and nonprofit organizations like the United Way. To apply CVP analysis in service and nonprofit organizations, we need to focus on measuring their output, which is different from the tangible units sold by manufacturing and merchandising companies. Examples of output measures in various service and nonprofit industries are as follows:

Industry	Measure of Output
Airlines	Passenger miles
Hotels/motels	Room-nights occupied
Hospitals	Patient days
Universities	Student credit-hours

Consider an agency of the Massachusetts Department of Social Welfare with a $900,000 budget appropriation (its revenues) for 2011. This nonprofit agency's purpose is to assist handicapped people seeking employment. On average, the agency supplements each person's income by $5,000 annually. The agency's only other costs are fixed costs of rent and administrative salaries equal to $270,000. The agency manager wants to know how many people could be assisted in 2011. We can use CVP analysis here by setting operating income to $0. Let Q be the number of handicapped people to be assisted:

$$\text{Revenues} - \text{Variable costs} - \text{Fixed costs} = 0$$
$$\$900,000 - \$5,000\,Q - \$270,000 = 0$$
$$\$5,000\,Q = \$900,000 - \$270,000 = \$630,000$$
$$Q = \$630,000 \div \$5,000 \text{ per person} = 126 \text{ people}$$

Suppose the manager is concerned that the total budget appropriation for 2012 will be reduced by 15% to $900,000 × (1 − 0.15) = $765,000. The manager wants to know how many handicapped people could be assisted with this reduced budget. Assume the same amount of monetary assistance per person:

$$\$765,000 - \$5,000\,Q - \$270,000 = 0$$
$$\$5,000\,Q = \$765,000 - \$270,000 = \$495,000$$
$$Q = \$495,000 \div \$5,000 \text{ per person} = 99 \text{ people}$$

Note the following two characteristics of the CVP relationships in this nonprofit situation:

1. The percentage drop in the number of people assisted, $(126 - 99) \div 126$, or 21.4%, is greater than the 15% reduction in the budget appropriation. It is greater because the $270,000 in fixed costs still must be paid, leaving a proportionately lower budget to assist people. The percentage drop in service exceeds the percentage drop in budget appropriation.

2. Given the reduced budget appropriation (revenues) of $765,000, the manager can adjust operations to stay within this appropriation in one or more of three basic ways: (a) reduce the number of people assisted from the current 126, (b) reduce the variable cost (the extent of assistance per person) from the current $5,000 per person, or (c) reduce the total fixed costs from the current $270,000.

Contribution Margin Versus Gross Margin

In the following equations, we clearly distinguish contribution margin, which provides information for CVP analysis, from gross margin, a measure of competitiveness, as defined in Chapter 2.

$$\text{Gross margin} = \text{Revenues} - \text{Cost of goods sold}$$
$$\text{Contribution margin} = \text{Revenues} - \text{All variable costs}$$

Gross margin measures how much a company can charge for its products over and above the cost of acquiring or producing them. Companies, such as branded pharmaceuticals, have high gross margins because their products provide unique and distinctive benefits to consumers. Products such as televisions that operate in competitive markets have low gross margins. Contribution margin indicates how much of a company's revenues are available to cover fixed costs. It helps in assessing risk of loss. Risk of loss is low (high) if, when sales are low, contribution margin exceeds (is less than) fixed costs. Gross margin and contribution margin are related but give different insights. For example, a company operating in a competitive market with a low gross margin will have a low risk of loss if its fixed costs are small.

Consider the distinction between gross margin and contribution margin in the context of manufacturing companies. In the manufacturing sector, contribution margin and gross margin differ in two respects: fixed manufacturing costs and variable nonmanufacturing costs. The following example (figures assumed) illustrates this difference:

Contribution Income Statement Emphasizing Contribution Margin (in 000s)			Financial Accounting Income Statement Emphasizing Gross Margin (in 000s)	
Revenues		$1,000	Revenues	$1,000
Variable manufacturing costs	$250		Cost of goods sold (variable manufacturing costs, $250 + fixed manufacturing costs, $160)	410
Variable nonmanufacturing costs	270	520		
Contribution margin		480	Gross margin	590
Fixed manufacturing costs	160		Nonmanufacturing costs	
Fixed nonmanufacturing costs	138	298	(variable, $270 + fixed $138)	408
Operating income		$ 182	Operating income	$ 182

Fixed manufacturing costs of $160,000 are not deducted from revenues when computing contribution margin but are deducted when computing gross margin. Cost of goods sold in a manufacturing company includes all variable manufacturing costs and

3-19 CVP exercises. The Super Donut owns and operates six doughnut outlets in and round Kansas City. You are given the following corporate budget data for next year:

Revenues	$10,000,000
Fixed costs	$ 1,800,000
Variable costs	$ 8,000,000

Variable costs change with respect to the number of doughnuts sold.

Required Compute the budgeted operating income for each of the following deviations from the original budget data. (Consider each case independently.)

1. A 10% increase in contribution margin, holding revenues constant
2. A 10% decrease in contribution margin, holding revenues constant
3. A 5% increase in fixed costs
4. A 5% decrease in fixed costs
5. An 8% increase in units sold
6. An 8% decrease in units sold
7. A 10% increase in fixed costs and a 10% increase in units sold
8. A 5% increase in fixed costs and a 5% decrease in variable costs

3-20 CVP exercises. The Doral Company manufactures and sells pens. Currently, 5,000,000 units are sold per year at $0.50 per unit. Fixed costs are $900,000 per year. Variable costs are $0.30 per unit.

Required Consider each case separately:
1a. What is the current annual operating income?
 b. What is the present breakeven point in revenues?

Compute the new operating income for each of the following changes:
2. A $0.04 per unit increase in variable costs
3. A 10% increase in fixed costs and a 10% increase in units sold
4. A 20% decrease in fixed costs, a 20% decrease in selling price, a 10% decrease in variable cost per unit, and a 40% increase in units sold

Compute the new breakeven point in units for each of the following changes:
5. A 10% increase in fixed costs
6. A 10% increase in selling price and a $20,000 increase in fixed costs

3-21 CVP analysis, income taxes. Brooke Motors is a small car dealership. On average, it sells a car for $27,000, which it purchases from the manufacturer for $23,000. Each month, Brooke Motors pays $48,200 in rent and utilities and $68,000 for salespeople's salaries. In addition to their salaries, salespeople are paid a commission of $600 for each car they sell. Brooke Motors also spends $13,000 each month for local advertisements. Its tax rate is 40%.

Required
1. How many cars must Brooke Motors sell each month to break even?
2. Brooke Motors has a target monthly net income of $51,000. What is its target monthly operating income? How many cars must be sold each month to reach the target monthly net income of $51,000?

3-22 CVP analysis, income taxes. The Express Banquet has two restaurants that are open 24-hours a day. Fixed costs for the two restaurants together total $459,000 per year. Service varies from a cup of coffee to full meals. The average sales check per customer is $8.50. The average cost of food and other variable costs for each customer is $3.40. The income tax rate is 30%. Target net income is $107,100.

Required
1. Compute the revenues needed to earn the target net income.
2. How many customers are needed to break even? To earn net income of $107,100?
3. Compute net income if the number of customers is 170,000.

3-23 CVP analysis, sensitivity analysis. Hoot Washington is the newly elected leader of the Republican Party. Media Publishers is negotiating to publish Hoot's Manifesto, a new book that promises to be an instant best-seller. The fixed costs of producing and marketing the book will be $500,000. The variable costs of producing and marketing will be $4.00 per copy sold. These costs are before any payments to Hoot. Hoot negotiates an up-front payment of $3 million, plus a 15% royalty rate on the net sales price of each book. The net sales price is the listed bookstore price of $30, minus the margin paid to the bookstore to sell the book. The normal bookstore margin of 30% of the listed bookstore price is expected to apply.

Required
1. Prepare a PV graph for Media Publishers.
2. How many copies must Media Publishers sell to (a) break even and (b) earn a target operating income of $2 million?
3. Examine the sensitivity of the breakeven point to the following changes:

   a. Decreasing the normal bookstore margin to 20% of the listed bookstore price of $30
   b. Increasing the listed bookstore price to $40 while keeping the bookstore margin at 30%
   c. Comment on the results

3-24 **CVP analysis, margin of safety.** Suppose Doral Corp.'s breakeven point is revenues of $1,100,000. Fixed costs are $660,000.

Required

1. Compute the contribution margin percentage.
2. Compute the selling price if variable costs are $16 per unit.
3. Suppose 95,000 units are sold. Compute the margin of safety in units and dollars.

3-25 **Operating leverage.** Color Rugs is holding a two-week carpet sale at Jerry's Club, a local warehouse store. Color Rugs plans to sell carpets for $500 each. The company will purchase the carpets from a local distributor for $350 each, with the privilege of returning any unsold units for a full refund. Jerry's Club has offered Color Rugs two payment alternatives for the use of space.

- Option 1: A fixed payment of $5,000 for the sale period
- Option 2: 10% of total revenues earned during the sale period

Assume Color Rugs will incur no other costs.

Required

1. Calculate the breakeven point in units for (a) option 1 and (b) option 2.
2. At what level of revenues will Color Rugs earn the same operating income under either option?
   a. For what range of unit sales will Color Rugs prefer option 1?
   b. For what range of unit sales will Color Rugs prefer option 2?
3. Calculate the degree of operating leverage at sales of 100 units for the two rental options.
4. Briefly explain and interpret your answer to requirement 3.

3-26 **CVP analysis, international cost structure differences.** Global Textiles, Inc., is considering three possible countries for the sole manufacturing site of its newest area rug: Singapore, Brazil, and the United States. All area rugs are to be sold to retail outlets in the United States for $250 per unit. These retail outlets add their own markup when selling to final customers. Fixed costs and variable cost per unit (area rug) differ in the three countries.

Country	Sales Price to Retail Outlets	Annual Fixed Costs	Variable Manufacturing Cost per Area Rug	Variable Marketing & Distribution Cost per Area Rug
Singapore	$250.00	$ 9,000,000	$75.00	$25.00
Brazil	250.00	8,400,000	60.00	15.00
United States	250.00	12,400,000	82.50	12.50

Required

1. Compute the breakeven point for Global Textiles, Inc., in each country in (a) units sold and (b) revenues.
2. If Global Textiles, Inc., plans to produce and sell 75,000 rugs in 2011, what is the budgeted operating income for each of the three manufacturing locations? Comment on the results.

3-27 **Sales mix, new and upgrade customers.** Data 1-2-3 is a top-selling electronic spreadsheet product. Data is about to release version 5.0. It divides its customers into two groups: new customers and upgrade customers (those who previously purchased Data 1-2-3, 4.0 or earlier versions). Although the same physical product is provided to each customer group, sizable differences exist in selling prices and variable marketing costs:

	New Customers		Upgrade Customers	
Selling price		$275		$100
Variable costs				
Manufacturing	$35		$35	
Marketing	65	100	15	50
Contribution margin		$175		$ 50

The fixed costs of Data 1-2-3, 5.0 are $15,000,000. The planned sales mix in units is 60% new customers and 40% upgrade customers.

Required

1. What is the Data 1-2-3, 5.0 breakeven point in units, assuming that the planned 60%:40% sales mix is attained?
2. If the sales mix is attained, what is the operating income when 220,000 total units are sold?
3. Show how the breakeven point in units changes with the following customer mixes:
   a. New 40% and Upgrade 60%
   b. New 80% and Upgrade 20%
   c. Comment on the results

3-28 **Sales mix, three products.** Bobbie's Bagel Shop sells only coffee and bagels. Bobbie estimates that every time she sells one bagel, she sells four cups of coffee. The budgeted cost information for Bobbie's products for 2011 follows:

	Coffee	Bagels
Selling Price	$2.50	$3.75
Product ingredients	$0.25	$0.50
Hourly sales staff (cost per unit)	$0.50	$1.00
Packaging	$0.50	$0.25
Fixed Costs		
Rent on store and equipment	$5,000	
Marketing and advertising cost	$2,000	

Required

1. How many cups of coffee and how many bagels must Bobbie sell in order to break even assuming the sales mix of four cups of coffee to one bagel, given previously?
2. If the sales mix is four cups of coffee to one bagel, how many units of each product does Bobbie need to sell to earn operating income before tax of $28,000?
3. Assume that Bobbie decides to add the sale of muffins to her product mix. The selling price for muffins is $3.00 and the related variable costs are $0.75. Assuming a sales mix of three cups of coffee to two bagels to one muffin, how many units of each product does Bobbie need to sell in order to break even? Comment on the results.

3-29 **CVP, Not for profit.** Monroe Classical Music Society is a not-for-profit organization that brings guest artists to the community's greater metropolitan area. The Music Society just bought a small concert hall in the center of town to house its performances. The mortgage payments on the concert hall are expected to be $2,000 per month. The organization pays its guest performers $1,000 per concert and anticipates corresponding ticket sales to be $2,500 per event. The Music Society also incurs costs of approximately $500 per concert for marketing and advertising. The organization pays its artistic director $50,000 per year and expects to receive $40,000 in donations in addition to its ticket sales.

Required

1. If the Monroe Classical Music Society just breaks even, how many concerts does it hold?
2. In addition to the organization's artistic director, the Music Society would like to hire a marketing director for $40,000 per year. What is the breakeven point? The Music Society anticipates that the addition of a marketing director would allow the organization to increase the number of concerts to 60 per year. What is the Music Society's operating income/(loss) if it hires the new marketing director?
3. The Music Society expects to receive a grant that would provide the organization with an additional $20,000 toward the payment of the marketing director's salary. What is the breakeven point if the Music Society hires the marketing director and receives the grant?

3-30 **Contribution margin, decision making.** Lurvey Men's Clothing's revenues and cost data for 2011 are as follows:

Revenues		$600,000
Cost of goods sold		300,000
Gross margin		300,000
Operating costs:		
Salaries fixed	$170,000	
Sales commissions (10% of sales)	60,000	
Depreciation of equipment and fixtures	20,000	
Store rent ($4,500 per month)	54,000	
Other operating costs	45,000	349,000
Operating income (loss)		$ (49,000)

Mr. Lurvey, the owner of the store, is unhappy with the operating results. An analysis of other operating costs reveals that it includes $30,000 variable costs, which vary with sales volume, and $15,000 (fixed) costs.

Required

1. Compute the contribution margin of Lurvey Men's Clothing.
2. Compute the contribution margin percentage.
3. Mr. Lurvey estimates that he can increase revenues by 15% by incurring additional advertising costs of $13,000. Calculate the impact of the additional advertising costs on operating income.

3-31 **Contribution margin, gross margin, and margin of safety.** Mirabella Cosmetics manufactures and sells a face cream to small ethnic stores in the greater New York area. It presents the monthly operating income statement shown here to George Lopez, a potential investor in the business. Help Mr. Lopez understand Mirabella's cost structure.

	A	B	C	D
1	Mirabella Cosmetics			
2	Operating Income Statement, June 2011			
3	Units sold			10,000
4	Revenues			$100,000
5	Cost of goods sold			
6	Variable manufacturing costs		$55,000	
7	Fixed manufacturing costs		20,000	
8	Total			75,000
9	Gross margin			25,000
10	Operating costs			
11	Variable marketing costs		$ 5,000	
12	Fixed marketing & administration costs		10,000	
13	Total operating costs			15,000
14	Operating income			$ 10,000

Required

1. Recast the income statement to emphasize contribution margin.
2. Calculate the contribution margin percentage and breakeven point in units and revenues for June 2011.
3. What is the margin of safety (in units) for June 2011?
4. If sales in June were only 8,000 units and Mirabella's tax rate is 30%, calculate its net income.

3-32 Uncertainty and expected costs. Foodmart Corp, an international retail giant, is considering implementing a new business to business (B2B) information system for processing purchase orders. The current system costs Foodmart $2,500,000 per month and $50 per order. Foodmart has two options, a partially automated B2B and a fully automated B2B system. The partially automated B2B system will have a fixed cost of $10,000,000 per month and a variable cost of $40 per order. The fully automated B2B system has a fixed cost of $20,000,000 per month and $25 per order.

Based on data from the last two years, Foodmart has determined the following distribution on monthly orders:

Monthly Number of Orders	Probability
350,000	0.15
450,000	0.20
550,000	0.35
650,000	0.20
750,000	0.10

Required

1. Prepare a table showing the cost of each plan for each quantity of monthly orders.
2. What is the expected cost of each plan?
3. In addition to the information systems costs, what other factors should Foodmart consider before deciding to implement a new B2B system?

Problems

3-33 CVP analysis, service firm. Lifetime Escapes generates average revenue of $5,000 per person on its five-day package tours to wildlife parks in Kenya. The variable costs per person are as follows:

Airfare	$1,400
Hotel accommodations	1,100
Meals	300
Ground transportation	100
Park tickets and other costs	800
Total	$3,700

Annual fixed costs total $520,000.

Required

1. Calculate the number of package tours that must be sold to break even.
2. Calculate the revenue needed to earn a target operating income of $91,000.
3. If fixed costs increase by $32,000, what decrease in variable cost per person must be achieved to maintain the breakeven point calculated in requirement 1?

3-34 **CVP, target operating income, service firm.** Snow Leopard Daycare provides daycare for children Mondays through Fridays. Its monthly variable costs per child are as follows:

Lunch and snacks	$150
Educational supplies	60
Other supplies (paper products, toiletries, etc.)	20
Total	$230

Monthly fixed costs consist of the following:

Rent	$2,150
Utilities	200
Insurance	250
Salaries	2,350
Miscellaneous	650
Total	$5,600

Snow Leopard charges each parent $580 per child.

Required

1. Calculate the breakeven point.
2. Snow Leopard's target operating income is $10,500 per month. Compute the number of children who must be enrolled to achieve the target operating income.
3. Snow Leopard lost its lease and had to move to another building. Monthly rent for the new building is $3,150. At the suggestion of parents, Snow Leopard plans to take children on field trips. Monthly costs of the field trips are $1,300. By how much should Snow Leopard increase fees per child to meet the target operating income of $10,500 per month, assuming the same number of children as in requirement 2?

3-35 **CVP analysis, margin of safety.** (CMA, adapted) Technology Solutions sells a ready-to-use software product for small businesses. The current selling price is $300. Projected operating income for 2011 is $490,000 based on a sales volume of 10,000 units. Variable costs of producing the software are $120 per unit sold plus an additional cost of $5 per unit for shipping and handling. Technology Solutions annual fixed costs are $1,260,000.

Required

1. Calculate Technology Solutions breakeven point and margin of safety in units.
2. Calculate the company's operating income for 2011 if there is a 10% increase in unit sales.
3. For 2012, management expects that the per unit production cost of the software will increase by 30%, but the shipping and handling costs per unit will decrease by 20%. Calculate the sales revenue Technology Solutions must generate for 2012 to maintain the current year's operating income if the selling price remains unchanged, assuming all other data as in the original problem.

3-36 **CVP analysis, income taxes.** (CMA, adapted) R. A. Ro and Company, a manufacturer of quality handmade walnut bowls, has had a steady growth in sales for the past five years. However, increased competition has led Mr. Ro, the president, to believe that an aggressive marketing campaign will be necessary next year to maintain the company's present growth. To prepare for next year's marketing campaign, the company's controller has prepared and presented Mr. Ro with the following data for the current year, 2011:

Variable cost (per bowl)		
Direct materials		$ 3.25
Direct manufacturing labor		8.00
Variable overhead (manufacturing, marketing, distribution, and customer service)		2.50
Total variable cost per bowl		$ 13.75
Fixed costs		
Manufacturing		$ 25,000
Marketing, distribution, and customer service		110,000
Total fixed costs		$135,000
Selling price		25.00
Expected sales, 20,000 units		$500,000
Income tax rate		40%

Required

1. What is the projected net income for 2011?
2. What is the breakeven point in units for 2011?
3. Mr. Ro has set the revenue target for 2012 at a level of $550,000 (or 22,000 bowls). He believes an additional marketing cost of $11,250 for advertising in 2012, with all other costs remaining constant, will be necessary to attain the revenue target. What is the net income for 2012 if the additional $11,250 is spent and the revenue target is met?
4. What is the breakeven point in revenues for 2012 if the additional $11,250 is spent for advertising?
5. If the additional $11,250 is spent, what are the required 2012 revenues for 2012 net income to equal 2011 net income?
6. At a sales level of 22,000 units, what maximum amount can be spent on advertising if a 2012 net income of $60,000 is desired?

3-37 CVP, sensitivity analysis. The Brown Shoe Company produces its famous shoe, the Divine Loafer that sells for $60 per pair. Operating income for 2011 is as follows:

Sales revenue ($60 per pair)	$300,000
Variable cost ($25 per pair)	125,000
Contribution margin	175,000
Fixed cost	100,000
Operating income	$ 75,000

Brown Shoe Company would like to increase its profitability over the next year by at least 25%. To do so, the company is considering the following options:

Required

1. Replace a portion of its variable labor with an automated machining process. This would result in a 20% decrease in variable cost per unit, but a 15% increase in fixed costs. Sales would remain the same.
2. Spend $30,000 on a new advertising campaign, which would increase sales by 20%.
3. Increase both selling price by $10 per unit and variable costs by $7 per unit by using a higher quality leather material in the production of its shoes. The higher priced shoe would cause demand to drop by approximately 10%.
4. Add a second manufacturing facility which would double Brown's fixed costs, but would increase sales by 60%.

Evaluate each of the alternatives considered by Brown Shoes. Do any of the options meet or exceed Brown's targeted increase in income of 25%? What should Brown do?

3-38 CVP analysis, shoe stores. The WalkRite Shoe Company operates a chain of shoe stores that sell 10 different styles of inexpensive men's shoes with identical unit costs and selling prices. A unit is defined as a pair of shoes. Each store has a store manager who is paid a fixed salary. Individual salespeople receive a fixed salary and a sales commission. WalkRite is considering opening another store that is expected to have the revenue and cost relationships shown here:

	Home	Insert	Page Layout	Formulas	Data	Review	View	
	A		B		C	D		E
1	Unit Variable Data (per pair of shoes)					Annual Fixed Costs		
2	Selling price		$30.00			Rent		$ 60,000
3	Cost of shoes		$19.50			Salaries		200,000
4	Sales commission		1.50			Advertising		80,000
5	Variable cost per unit		$21.00			Other fixed costs		20,000
6						Total fixed costs		$360,000

Consider each question independently:

Required

1. What is the annual breakeven point in (a) units sold and (b) revenues?
2. If 35,000 units are sold, what will be the store's operating income (loss)?
3. If sales commissions are discontinued and fixed salaries are raised by a total of $81,000, what would be the annual breakeven point in (a) units sold and (b) revenues?
4. Refer to the original data. If, in addition to his fixed salary, the store manager is paid a commission of $0.30 per unit sold, what would be the annual breakeven point in (a) units sold and (b) revenues?
5. Refer to the original data. If, in addition to his fixed salary, the store manager is paid a commission of $0.30 *per unit in excess of the breakeven point*, what would be the store's operating income if 50,000 units were sold?

monitoring actual costs of direct materials. Direct material usage can be reported hourly—if the benefits exceed the cost of such frequent reporting.

Similarly, information about direct manufacturing labor is obtained as employees log into computer terminals and key in the job numbers, their employee numbers, and start and end times of their work on different jobs. The computer automatically prints the labor time record and, using hourly rates stored for each employee, calculates the direct manufacturing labor costs of individual jobs. Information technology also provides managers with instantaneous feedback to help control manufacturing overhead costs, jobs in process, jobs completed, and jobs shipped and installed at customer sites.

Actual Costing

How would the cost of Job WPP 298 change if Robinson had used actual costing rather than normal costing? Both actual costing and normal costing trace direct costs to jobs in the same way because source documents identify the actual quantities and actual rates of direct materials and direct manufacturing labor for a job as the work is being done. The only difference between costing a job with normal costing and actual costing is that normal costing uses *budgeted* indirect-cost rates, whereas actual costing uses *actual* indirect-cost rates calculated annually at the end of the year. Exhibit 4-5 distinguishes actual costing from normal costing.

The following actual data for 2011 are for Robinson's manufacturing operations:

	Actual
Total manufacturing overhead costs	$1,215,000
Total direct manufacturing labor-hours	27,000

Steps 1 and 2 are exactly as before: Step 1 identifies WPP 298 as the cost object; Step 2 calculates actual direct material costs of $4,606, and actual direct manufacturing labor costs of $1,579. Recall from Step 3 that Robinson uses a single cost-allocation base, direct manufacturing labor-hours, to allocate all manufacturing overhead costs to jobs. The actual quantity of direct manufacturing labor-hours for 2011 is 27,000 hours. In Step 4, Robinson groups all actual indirect manufacturing costs of $1,215,000 into a single manufacturing overhead cost pool. In Step 5, the **actual indirect-cost rate** is calculated by dividing actual total indirect costs in the pool (determined in Step 4) by the actual total quantity of the cost-allocation base (determined in Step 3). Robinson calculates the actual manufacturing overhead rate in 2011 for its single manufacturing overhead cost pool as follows:

$$\begin{aligned}\text{Actual manufacturing overhead rate} &= \frac{\text{Actual annual manufacturing overhead costs}}{\text{Actual annual quantity of the cost-allocation base}}\\[2mm] &= \frac{\$1,215,000}{27,000 \text{ direct manufacturing labor-hours}}\\[2mm] &= \$45 \text{ per direct manufacturing labor-hour}\end{aligned}$$

In Step 6, under an actual-costing system,

$$\begin{aligned}\text{Manufacturing overhead costs allocated to WPP 298} &= \text{Actual manufacturing overhead rate} \times \text{Actual quantity of direct manufacturing labor-hours}\\[2mm] &= \$45 \text{ per direct manuf. labor-hour} \times 88 \text{ direct manufacturing labor-hours}\\[2mm] &= \$3,960\end{aligned}$$

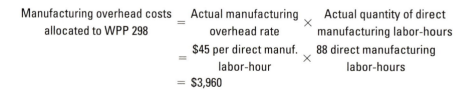

	Actual Costing	**Normal Costing**
Direct Costs	Actual direct-cost rates × actual quantities of direct-cost inputs	Actual direct-cost rates × actual quantities of direct-cost inputs
Indirect Costs	Actual indirect-cost rates × actual quantities of cost-allocation bases	Budgeted indirect-cost rates × actual quantities of cost-allocation bases

In Step 7, the cost of the job under actual costing is $10,145, calculated as follows:

Direct manufacturing costs		
Direct materials	$4,606	
Direct manufacturing labor	1,579	$ 6,185
Manufacturing overhead costs		
($45 per direct manufacturing labor-hour × 88 actual		
direct manufacturing labor-hours)		3,960
Total manufacturing costs of job		$10,145

The manufacturing cost of the WPP 298 job is higher by $440 under actual costing ($10,145) than it is under normal costing ($9,705) because the actual indirect-cost rate is $45 per hour, whereas the budgeted indirect-cost rate is $40 per hour. That is, ($45 − $40) × 88 actual direct manufacturing labor-hours = $440.

As we discussed previously, manufacturing costs of a job are available much earlier under a normal-costing system. Consequently, Robinson's manufacturing and sales managers can evaluate the profitability of different jobs, the efficiency with which the jobs are done, and the pricing of different jobs as soon as the jobs are completed, while the experience is still fresh in everyone's mind. Another advantage of normal costing is that corrective actions can be implemented much sooner. At the end of the year, though, costs allocated using normal costing will not, in general, equal actual costs incurred. If material, adjustments will need to be made so that the cost of jobs and the costs in various inventory accounts are based on actual rather that normal costing. We describe these adjustments later in the chapter.

> **◄ Decision Point**
>
> How do you distinguish actual costing from normal costing?

A Normal Job-Costing System in Manufacturing

We now explain how a normal job-costing system operates in manufacturing. Continuing with the Robinson Company example, the following illustration considers events that occurred in February 2011. Before getting into details, study Exhibit 4-6, which provides a broad framework for understanding the flow of costs in job costing.

The upper part of Exhibit 4-6 shows the flow of inventoriable costs from the purchase of materials and other manufacturing inputs, to their conversion into work-in-process and finished goods, to the sale of finished goods.

Direct materials used and direct manufacturing labor can be easily traced to jobs. They become part of work-in-process inventory on the balance sheet because direct manufacturing labor transforms direct materials into another asset, work-in-process inventory. Robinson also incurs manufacturing overhead costs (including indirect materials and indirect manufacturing labor) to convert direct materials into work-in-process inventory. The overhead (indirect) costs, however, cannot be easily traced to individual jobs.

> **Learning Objective 6**
>
> Track the flow of costs in a job-costing system
>
> . . . from purchase of materials to sale of finished goods

Exhibit 4-6 Flow of Costs in Job Costing

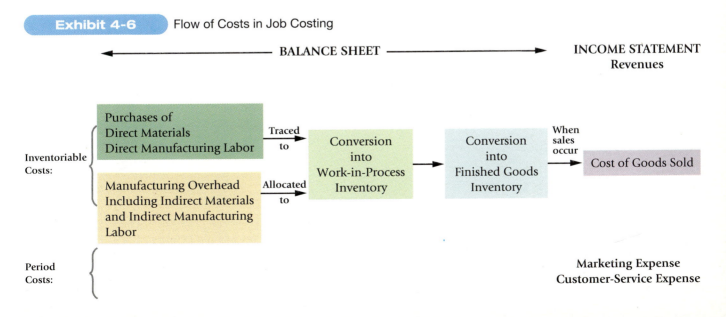

Manufacturing overhead costs, therefore, are first accumulated in a manufacturing overhead account and later allocated to individual jobs. As manufacturing overhead costs are allocated, they become part of work-in-process inventory.

As individual jobs are completed, work-in-process inventory becomes another balance sheet asset, finished goods inventory. Only when finished goods are sold is an expense, cost of goods sold, recognized in the income statement and matched against revenues earned.

The lower part of Exhibit 4-6 shows the period costs—marketing and customer-service costs. These costs do not create any assets on the balance sheet because they are not incurred to transform materials into a finished product. Instead, they are expensed in the income statement, as they are incurred, to best match revenues.

We next describe the entries made in the general ledger.

General Ledger

You know by this point that a job-costing system has a separate job-cost record for each job. A summary of the job-cost record is typically found in a subsidiary ledger. The general ledger account Work-in-Process Control presents the total of these separate job-cost records pertaining to all unfinished jobs. The job-cost records and Work-in-Process Control account track job costs from when jobs start until they are complete.

Exhibit 4-7 shows T-account relationships for Robinson Company's general ledger. The general ledger gives a "bird's-eye view" of the costing system. The amounts shown in

Exhibit 4-7	Manufacturing Job-Costing System Using Normal Costing: Diagram of General Ledger Relationships for February 2011

GENERAL LEDGER

① Purchase of direct and indirect materials, $89,000
② Usage of direct materials, $81,000, and indirect materials, $4,000

③ Cash paid for direct manufacturing labor, $39,000, and indirect manufacturing labor, $15,000

④ Incurrence of other manufacturing dept. overhead, $75,000
⑤ Allocation of manufacturing overhead, $80,000

⑥ Completion and transfer to finished goods, $188,800
⑦ Cost of goods sold, $180,000

⑧ Incurrence of marketing and customer-service costs, $60,000
⑨ Sales, $270,000

GENERAL LEDGER

MATERIALS CONTROL
① 89,000 | ② 85,000

MANUFACTURING OVERHEAD CONTROL
② 4,000 |
③ 15,000 |
④ 75,000 |

CASH CONTROL
| ③ 54,000
| ④ 57,000
| ⑧ 60,000

MANUFACTURING OVERHEAD ALLOCATED
| ⑤ 80,000

ACCOUNTS PAYABLE CONTROL
| ① 89,000

ACCUMULATED DEPRECIATION CONTROL
| ④ 18,000

WORK-IN-PROCESS CONTROL
② 81,000 | ⑥ 188,800
③ 39,000 |
⑤ 80,000 |
Bal. 11,200 |

FINISHED GOODS CONTROL
⑥ 188,800 | ⑦ 180,000
Bal. 8,800 |

ACCOUNTS RECEIVABLE CONTROL
⑨ 270,000 |

REVENUES
| ⑨ 270,000

COST OF GOODS SOLD
⑦ 180,000 |

MARKETING EXPENSES
⑧ 45,000 |

CUSTOMER-SERVICE EXPENSES
⑧ 15,000 |

The debit balance of $11,200 in the Work-in-Process Control account represents the total cost of all jobs that have not been completed as of the end of February 2011. There were no incomplete jobs as of the beginning of February 2011.

The debit balance of $8,800 in the Finished Goods Control account represents the cost of all jobs that have been completed but not sold as of the end of February 2011. There were no jobs completed but not sold as of the beginning of February 2011.

Exhibit 4-7 are based on the transactions and journal entries that follow. As you go through each journal entry, use Exhibit 4-7 to see how the various entries being made come together. General ledger accounts with "Control" in the titles (for example, Materials Control and Accounts Payable Control) have underlying subsidiary ledgers that contain additional details, such as each type of material in inventory and individual suppliers that Robinson must pay.

Some companies simultaneously make entries in the general ledger and subsidiary ledger accounts. Others, such as Robinson, make entries in the subsidiary ledger when transactions occur and entries in the general ledger less frequently, on a monthly basis.

A general ledger should be viewed as only one of many tools that assist management in planning and control. To control operations, managers rely on not only the source documents used to record amounts in the subsidiary ledgers, but also on nonfinancial information such as the percentage of jobs requiring rework.

Explanations of Transactions

We next look at a summary of Robinson Company's transactions for February 2011 and the corresponding journal entries for those transactions.

1. Purchases of materials (direct and indirect) on credit, $89,000

Materials Control	89,000	
Accounts Payable Control		89,000

2. Usage of direct materials, $81,000, and indirect materials, $4,000

Work-in-Process Control	81,000	
Manufacturing Overhead Control	4,000	
Materials Control		85,000

3. Manufacturing payroll for February: direct labor, $39,000, and indirect labor, $15,000, paid in cash

Work-in-Process Control	39,000	
Manufacturing Overhead Control	15,000	
Cash Control		54,000

4. Other manufacturing overhead costs incurred during February, $75,000, consisting of supervision and engineering salaries, $44,000 (paid in cash); plant utilities, repairs, and insurance, $13,000 (paid in cash); and plant depreciation, $18,000

Manufacturing Overhead Control	75,000	
Cash Control		57,000
Accumulated Depreciation Control		18,000

5. Allocation of manufacturing overhead to jobs, $80,000

Work-in-Process Control	80,000	
Manufacturing Overhead Allocated		80,000

Under normal costing, **manufacturing overhead allocated**—also called **manufacturing overhead applied**—is the amount of manufacturing overhead costs allocated to individual jobs based on the budgeted rate multiplied by actual quantity used of the allocation base. Keep in mind the distinct difference between transactions 4 and 5. In transaction 4, all actual overhead costs incurred throughout the month are added (debited) to the Manufacturing Overhead Control account. These costs are *not* debited to Work-in-Process Control because, unlike direct costs, they cannot be traced to individual jobs. Manufacturing overhead costs are added (debited) to individual jobs and to Work-in-Process Control *only when* manufacturing overhead costs are allocated in Transaction 5. At the time these costs are allocated, Manufacturing Overhead Control is, *in effect*, decreased (credited) via its contra account, Manufacturing Overhead Allocated. Recall that under normal costing, the budgeted manufacturing overhead rate of $40 per direct manufacturing labor-hour is calculated at the beginning of the year on the basis of predictions of annual manufacturing overhead costs and the annual quantity of the cost-allocation base. Almost certainly, the overhead allocated will differ from the actual overhead incurred. In a later section, we discuss what to do with this difference.

6. Completion and transfer of individual jobs to finished goods, $188,800

Finished Goods Control	188,800	
Work-in-Process Control		188,800

7. Cost of goods sold, $180,000

Cost of Goods Sold	180,000	
Finished Goods Control		180,000

8. Marketing costs for February, $45,000, and customer service costs for February, $15,000, paid in cash

Marketing Expenses	45,000	
Customer Service Expenses	15,000	
Cash Control		60,000

9. Sales revenues, all on credit, $270,000

Accounts Receivable Control	270,000	
Revenues		270,000

Subsidiary Ledgers

Exhibits 4-8 and 4-9 present subsidiary ledgers that contain the underlying details—the "worm's-eye view" that helps Robinson's managers keep track of the WPP 298 job, as opposed to the "bird's-eye view" of the general ledger. The sum of all entries in

Exhibit 4-8   Subsidiary Ledger for Materials, Labor, and Manufacturing Department Overhead[1]

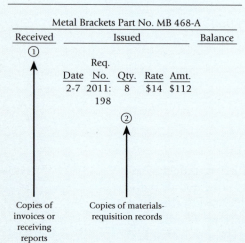

PANEL A: Materials Records by Type of Materials

Metal Brackets Part No. MB 468-A

Received	Issued				Balance
①	Req.				
	Date	No.	Qty.	Rate	Amt.
	2-7	2011: 198	8	$14	$112
		②			

Copies of invoices or receiving reports

Copies of materials-requisition records

Total cost of all types of materials received in February, $89,000

Total cost of all types of materials issued in February, $85,000

PANEL B: Labor Records by Employee

G. L. Cook Empl. No. 551-87-3076

Week Endg.	Job No.	Hours Worked	Rate	Amt.
2-13	WPP			
	298	25	$18	$450
	JL 256	12	18	216
	Mntnce.	3	18	54
				$720
2-20	③			

Copies of labor-time sheets

Total cost of all direct and indirect manufacturing labor incurred in February, $54,000 ($39,000 + $15,000)

PANEL C: Manufacturing Department Overhead Records by Month

February 2011

Indir. Matr. Issued	Indir. Manuf. Labor	Supervn. & Eng.	Plant Ins. & Utilities	Plant Deprn.
②	③	④	④	④
	Manuf. labor-time record or payroll analysis		Payroll analysis, invoices, special authorizations	
Copies of materials requisitions				
$4,000	$15,000	$44,000	$13,000	$18,000

Other manufacturing overhead costs incurred in February, $75,000

[1]The arrows show how the supporting documentation (for example, copies of materials requisition records) results in the journal entry number shown in circles (for example, journal entry number 2) that corresponds to the entries in Exhibit 4-7.

Exhibit 4-9 Subsidiary Ledger for Individual Jobs[1]

PANEL A: Work-in-Process Inventory Records by Jobs

Job No. WPP 298

	In-Process				Completed		Balance	
Date	Direct Materials	Direct Manuf. Labor	Allocated Manuf. Overhead	Total Cost	Date	Total Cost	Date	Total Cost
2-7	$ 112			$ 112				
2-13		$ 450		$ 450				
•	•	•		•				
2-28	$4,606 ②	$1,579 ③	$3,520 ⑤	$9,705	2-28	$9,705 ⑥	2-28	$0

↑ ② Copies of materials-requisition records

↑ ③ Copies of labor-time sheets

↑ ⑤ Budgeted rate × actual direct manuf. labor-hours

↑ ⑥ Completed job-cost record

Total cost of direct materials issued to all jobs in Feb., $81,000

Total cost of direct manuf. labor used on all jobs in Feb., $39,000

Total manuf. overhead allocated to all jobs in Feb., $80,000

Total cost of all jobs completed and transferred to finished goods in Feb., $188,800

PANEL B: Finished Goods Inventory Records by Job

Job No. WPP 298

Received		Issued		Balance	
Date	Amt.	Date	Amt.	Date	Amt.
2-28	$9,705 ⑥	2-28	$9,705 ⑦	2-28	$0

↑ ⑥ Completed job-cost record

↑ ⑦ Costed sales invoice

Total cost of all jobs transferred to finished goods in Feb., $188,800

Total cost of all jobs sold and invoiced in Feb., $180,000

[1]The arrows show how the supporting documentation (for example, copies of materials requisition records) results in the journal entry number shown in circles (for example, journal entry number 2) that corresponds to the entries in Exhibit 4-7.

underlying subsidiary ledgers equals the total amount in the corresponding general ledger control accounts.

Material Records by Type of Materials

The subsidiary ledger for materials at Robinson Company—called *Materials Records*—keeps a continuous record of quantity received, quantity issued to jobs, and inventory balances for each type of material. Panel A of Exhibit 4-8 shows the Materials Record for Metal Brackets (Part No. MB 468-A). In many companies, the source documents supporting the receipt and issue of materials (the material requisition record in Exhibit 4-3, Panel A, p. 106) are scanned into a computer. Software programs then automatically update the Materials Records and make all the necessary accounting entries in the subsidiary and general ledgers. The cost of materials received across all types of direct and indirect material records for February 2011 is $89,000 (Exhibit 4-8, Panel A). The cost of materials issued across all types of direct and indirect material records for February 2011 is $85,000 (Exhibit 4-8, Panel A).

As direct materials are used, they are recorded as issued in the Materials Records (see Exhibit 4-8, Panel A, for a record of the Metal Brackets issued for the WPP machine job). Direct materials are also charged to Work-in-Process Inventory Records for Jobs, which are the subsidiary ledger accounts for the Work-in-Process Control account in the general ledger. For example, the metal brackets used in the WPP machine job appear as direct material costs of $112 in the subsidiary ledger under the work-in-process inventory record for WPP 298 (Exhibit 4-9, Panel A, based on the job-cost record source document in Exhibit 4-2, p. 105.). The cost of direct materials used across all job-cost records for February 2011 is $81,000 (Exhibit 4-9, Panel A).

As indirect materials (for example, lubricants) are used, they are charged to the Manufacturing Department overhead records (Exhibit 4-8, Panel C), which comprise the subsidiary ledger for Manufacturing Overhead Control. The Manufacturing Department overhead records accumulate actual costs in individual overhead categories by each indirect-cost-pool account in the general ledger. Recall that Robinson has only one indirect-cost pool: Manufacturing Overhead. The cost of indirect materials used is not added directly to individual job records. Instead, the cost of these indirect materials is allocated to individual job records as a part of manufacturing overhead.

Labor Records by Employee

Labor records by employee (see Exhibit 4-8, Panel B for G. L. Cook) are used to trace direct manufacturing labor to individual jobs and to accumulate the indirect manufacturing labor in Manufacturing Department overhead records (Exhibit 4-8, Panel C). The labor records are based on the labor-time sheet source documents (see Exhibit 4-3, Panel B, p. 106). The subsidiary ledger for employee labor records shows the different jobs that G. L. Cook, Employee No. 551-87-3076 worked on and the $720 of wages owed to Cook, for the week ending February 13. The sum of total wages owed to all employees for February 2011 is $54,000. The job-cost record for WPP 298 shows direct manufacturing labor costs of $450 for the time Cook spent on the WPP machine job (Exhibit 4-9, Panel A). Total direct manufacturing labor costs recorded in all job-cost records (the subsidiary ledger for Work-in-Process Control) for February 2011 is $39,000.

G. L. Cook's employee record shows $54 for maintenance, which is an indirect manufacturing labor cost. The total indirect manufacturing labor costs of $15,000 for February 2011 appear in the Manufacturing Department overhead records in the subsidiary ledger (Exhibit 4-8, Panel C). These costs, by definition, cannot be traced to an individual job. Instead, they are allocated to individual jobs as a part of manufacturing overhead.

Manufacturing Department Overhead Records by Month

The Manufacturing Department overhead records (see Exhibit 4-8, Panel C) that make up the subsidiary ledger for Manufacturing Overhead Control show details of different categories of overhead costs such as indirect materials, indirect manufacturing labor, supervision and engineering, plant insurance and utilities, and plant depreciation. The source documents for these entries include invoices (for example, a utility bill) and special schedules (for example, a depreciation schedule) from the responsible accounting officer. Manufacturing department overhead for February 2011 is indirect materials, $4,000; indirect manufacturing labor, $15,000; and other manufacturing overhead, $75,000 (Exhibit 4-8, Panel C).

Work-in-Process Inventory Records by Jobs

As we have already discussed, the job-cost record for each individual job in the subsidiary ledger is debited by the actual cost of direct materials and direct manufacturing labor used by individual jobs. In Robinson's normal-costing system, the job-cost record for each individual job in the subsidiary ledger is also debited for manufacturing overhead allocated based on the budgeted manufacturing overhead rate times the actual direct manufacturing labor-hours used in that job. For example, the job-cost record for Job WPP 298 (Exhibit 4-9, Panel A) shows Manufacturing Overhead Allocated of $3,520 (budgeted rate of $40 per labor-hour × 88 actual direct manufacturing labor-hours used). For the 2,000 actual direct manufacturing labor-hours used for all jobs in February 2011, total manufacturing overhead allocated equals $40 per labor-hour × 2,000 direct manufacturing labor-hours = $80,000.

Finished Goods Inventory Records by Jobs

Exhibit 4-9, Panel A, shows that Job WPP 298 was completed at a cost of $9,705. Job WPP 298 also simultaneously appears in the finished goods records of the subsidiary ledger. The total cost of all jobs completed and transferred to finished goods in February 2011 is $188,800 (Exhibit 4-9, Panels A and B). Exhibit 4-9, Panel B, indicates that Job WPP 298 was sold and delivered to the customer on February 28, 2011, at which time $9,705 was transferred from finished goods to cost of goods sold. The total cost of all jobs sold and invoiced in February 2011 is $180,000 (Exhibit 4-9, Panel B).

Revenues		$270,000
Cost of goods sold ($180,000 + $14,000[1])		194,000
Gross margin		76,000
Operating costs		
Marketing costs	$45,000	
Customer-service costs	15,000	
Total operating costs		60,000
Operating income		$ 16,000

[1]Cost of goods sold has been increased by $14,000, the difference between the Manufacturing overhead control account ($94,000) and the Manufacturing overhead allocated ($80,000). In a later section of this chapter, we discuss this adjustment, which represents the amount by which actual manufacturing overhead cost exceeds the manufacturing overhead allocated to jobs during February 2011.

Other Subsidiary Records

Just as in manufacturing payroll, Robinson maintains employee labor records in subsidiary ledgers for marketing and customer service payroll as well as records for different types of advertising costs (print, television, and radio). An accounts receivable subsidiary ledger is also used to record the February 2011 amounts due from each customer, including the $15,000 due from the sale of Job WPP 298.

At this point, pause and review the nine entries in this illustration. Exhibit 4-7 is a handy summary of all nine general-ledger entries presented in T-account form. Be sure to trace each journal entry, step-by-step, to T-accounts in the general ledger presented in Exhibit 4-7.

Exhibit 4-10 provides Robinson's income statement for February 2011 using information from entries 7, 8, and 9. If desired, the cost of goods sold calculations can be further subdivided and presented in the format of Exhibit 2-8, page 40.

Nonmanufacturing Costs and Job Costing

Chapter 2 (pp. 45–47) pointed out that companies use product costs for different purposes. The product costs reported as inventoriable costs to shareholders may differ from product costs reported for government contracting and may also differ from product costs reported to managers for guiding pricing and product-mix decisions. We emphasize that even though marketing and customer-service costs are expensed when incurred for financial accounting purposes, companies often trace or allocate these costs to individual jobs for pricing, product-mix, and cost-management decisions.

To identify marketing and customer-service costs of individual jobs, Robinson can use the same approach to job costing described earlier in this chapter in the context of manufacturing. Robinson can trace the direct marketing costs and customer-service costs to jobs. Assume marketing and customer-service costs have the same cost-allocation base, revenues, and are included in a single cost pool. Robinson can then calculate a budgeted indirect-cost rate by dividing budgeted indirect marketing costs plus budgeted indirect customer-service costs by budgeted revenues. Robinson can use this rate to allocate these indirect costs to jobs. For example, if this rate were 15% of revenues, Robinson would allocate $2,250 to Job WPP 298 (0.15 × $15,000, the revenue from the job). By assigning both manufacturing costs and nonmanufacturing costs to jobs, Robinson can compare all costs against the revenues that different jobs generate.

◄ Decision Point

How are transactions recorded in a manufacturing job-costing system?

Budgeted Indirect Costs and End-of-Accounting-Year Adjustments

Using budgeted indirect-cost rates and normal costing instead of actual costing has the advantage that indirect costs can be assigned to individual jobs on an ongoing and timely basis, rather than only at the end of the fiscal year when actual costs are known. However, budgeted rates are unlikely to equal actual rates because they are based on estimates made up to 12 months before actual costs are incurred. We now consider adjustments that are needed when, at the end of the fiscal year, indirect costs allocated differ from actual indirect costs incurred. Recall that for the numerator and denominator reasons discussed earlier (pp. 103–104), we do *not* expect actual overhead costs incurred each month to equal overhead costs allocated each month.

Underallocated and Overallocated Direct Costs

Underallocated indirect costs occur when the allocated amount of indirect costs in an accounting period is less than the actual (incurred) amount. **Overallocated indirect costs** occur when the allocated amount of indirect costs in an accounting period is greater than the actual (incurred) amount.

$$\text{Underallocated (overallocated) indirect costs} =$$
$$\text{Actual indirect costs incurred} - \text{Indirect costs allocated}$$

Underallocated (overallocated) indirect costs are also called **underapplied (overapplied) indirect costs** and **underabsorbed (overabsorbed) indirect costs**.

Consider the manufacturing overhead cost pool at Robinson Company. There are two indirect-cost accounts in the general ledger that have to do with manufacturing overhead:

1. Manufacturing Overhead Control, the record of the actual costs in all the individual overhead categories (such as indirect materials, indirect manufacturing labor, supervision, engineering, utilities, and plant depreciation)

2. Manufacturing Overhead Allocated, the record of the manufacturing overhead allocated to individual jobs on the basis of the budgeted rate multiplied by actual direct manufacturing labor-hours

At the end of the year, the overhead accounts show the following amounts.

Manufacturing Overhead Control		Manufacturing Overhead Allocated	
Bal. Dec. 31, 2011	1,215,000	Bal. Dec. 31, 2011	1,080,000

The $1,080,000 credit balance in Manufacturing Overhead Allocated results from multiplying the 27,000 actual direct manufacturing labor-hours worked on all jobs in 2011 by the budgeted rate of $40 per direct manufacturing labor-hour.

The $135,000 ($1,215,000 – $1,080,000) difference (a net debit) is an underallocated amount because actual manufacturing overhead costs are greater than the allocated amount. This difference arises from two reasons related to the computation of the $40 budgeted hourly rate:

1. **Numerator reason (indirect-cost pool).** Actual manufacturing overhead costs of $1,215,000 are greater than the budgeted amount of $1,120,000.

2. **Denominator reason (quantity of allocation base).** Actual direct manufacturing labor-hours of 27,000 are fewer than the budgeted 28,000 hours.

There are three main approaches to accounting for the $135,000 underallocated manufacturing overhead caused by Robinson underestimating manufacturing overhead costs and overestimating the quantity of the cost-allocation base: (1) adjusted allocation-rate approach, (2) proration approach, and (3) write-off to cost of goods sold approach.

Adjusted Allocation-Rate Approach

The **adjusted allocation-rate approach** restates all overhead entries in the general ledger and subsidiary ledgers using actual cost rates rather than budgeted cost rates. First, the actual manufacturing overhead rate is computed at the end of the fiscal year. Then, the manufacturing overhead costs allocated to every job during the year are recomputed using the actual manufacturing overhead rate (rather than the budgeted manufacturing overhead rate). Finally, end-of-year closing entries are made. The result is that at year-end, every job-cost record and finished goods record—as well as the ending Work-in-Process Control, Finished Goods Control, and Cost of Goods Sold accounts—represent actual manufacturing overhead costs incurred.

The widespread adoption of computerized accounting systems has greatly reduced the cost of using the adjusted allocation-rate approach. In our Robinson example, the actual manufacturing overhead ($1,215,000) exceeds the manufacturing overhead allocated ($1,080,000) by 12.5% [($1,215,000 – $1,080,000) ÷ $1,080,000]. At year-end, Robinson could increase the manufacturing overhead allocated to each job in 2011 by 12.5% using a single software command. The command would adjust both the subsidiary ledgers and the general ledger.

Consider the Western Pulp and Paper machine job, WPP 298. Under normal costing, the manufacturing overhead allocated to the job is $3,520 (the budgeted rate of $40 per direct manufacturing labor-hour × 88 hours). Increasing the manufacturing overhead allocated by 12.5%, or $440 ($3,520 × 0.125), means the adjusted amount of manufacturing overhead allocated to Job WPP 298 equals $3,960 ($3,520 + $440). Note from page 110 that using actual costing, manufacturing overhead allocated to this job is $3,960 (the actual rate of $45 per direct manufacturing labor-hour × 88 hours). Making this adjustment under normal costing for each job in the subsidiary ledgers ensures that all $1,215,000 of manufacturing overhead is allocated to jobs.

The adjusted allocation-rate approach yields the benefits of both the *timeliness and convenience of normal costing during the year and the allocation of actual manufacturing overhead costs at year-end*. Each individual job-cost record and the end-of-year account balances for inventories and cost of goods sold are adjusted to actual costs. After-the-fact analysis of actual profitability of individual jobs provides managers with accurate and useful insights for future decisions about job pricing, which jobs to emphasize, and ways to manage job costs.

Proration Approach

Proration spreads underallocated overhead or overallocated overhead among ending work-in-process inventory, finished goods inventory, and cost of goods sold. Materials inventory is not included in this proration, because no manufacturing overhead costs have been allocated to it. In our Robinson example, end-of-year proration is made to the ending balances in Work-in-Process Control, Finished Goods Control, and Cost of Goods Sold. Assume the following actual results for Robinson Company in 2011:

Account	Account Balance (Before Proration)	Allocated Manufacturing Overhead Included in Each Account Balance (Before Proration)
Work-in-process control	$ 50,000	$ 16,200
Finished goods control	75,000	31,320
Cost of goods sold	2,375,000	1,032,480
	$2,500,000	$1,080,000

How should Robinson prorate the underallocated $135,000 of manufacturing overhead at the end of 2011?

Robinson prorates underallocated or overallocated amounts on the basis of the total amount of manufacturing overhead allocated in 2011 (before proration) in the ending balances of Work-in-Process Control, Finished Goods Control, and Cost of Goods Sold. The $135,000 underallocated overhead is prorated over the three affected accounts in proportion to the total amount of manufacturing overhead allocated (before proration) in column 2 of the following table, resulting in the ending balances (after proration) in column 5 at actual costs.

	A	B	C	D	E	F	G
10		Account Balance (Before Proration)	Allocated Manufacturing Overhead Included in Each Account Balance (Before Proration)	Allocated Manufacturing Overhead Included in Each Account Balance as a Percent of Total	Proration of $135,000 of Underallocated Manufacturing Overhead		Account Balance (After Proration)
11	**Account**	(1)	(2)	(3) = (2) / $1,080,000	(4) = (3) x $135,000		(5) = (1) + (4)
12	Work-in-process control	$ 50,000	$ 16,200	1.5%	0.015 x $135,000 =	$ 2,025	$ 52,025
13	Finished goods control	75,000	31,320	2.9%	0.029 x 135,000 =	3,915	78,915
14	Cost of goods sold	2,375,000	1,032,480	95.6%	0.956 x 135,000 =	129,060	2,504,060
15	Total	$2,500,000	$1,080,000	100.0%		$135,000	$2,635,000

Prorating on the basis of the manufacturing overhead allocated (before proration) results in allocating manufacturing overhead based on actual manufacturing overhead costs. Recall that the actual manufacturing overhead ($1,215,000) in 2011 exceeds the manufacturing overhead allocated ($1,080,000) in 2011 by 12.5%. The proration amounts in column 4 can also be derived by multiplying the balances in column 2 by 0.125. For example, the $3,915 proration to Finished Goods is 0.125 × $31,320. Adding these amounts effectively means allocating manufacturing overhead at 112.5% of what had been allocated before. The journal entry to record this proration is as follows:

Work-in-Process Control	2,025	
Finished Goods Control	3,915	
Cost of Goods Sold	129,060	
Manufacturing Overhead Allocated	1,080,000	
Manufacturing Overhead Control		1,215,000

If manufacturing overhead had been overallocated, the Work-in-Process Control, Finished Goods Control, and Cost of Goods Sold accounts would be decreased (credited) instead of increased (debited).

This journal entry closes (brings to zero) the manufacturing overhead-related accounts and restates the 2011 ending balances for Work-in-Process Control, Finished Goods Control, and Cost of Goods Sold to what they would have been if actual manufacturing overhead rates had been used rather than budgeted manufacturing overhead rates. This method reports the same 2011 ending balances in the general ledger as the adjusted allocation-rate approach. However, unlike the adjusted allocation-rate approach, the sum of the amounts shown in the subsidiary ledgers will not match the amounts shown in the general ledger after proration. That's because the amounts in the subsidiary ledgers will still show allocated overhead based on budgeted manufacturing overhead rates. The proration approach only adjusts the general ledger and not the subsidiary ledgers to actual manufacturing overhead rates.

Some companies use the proration approach but base it on the ending balances of Work-in-Process Control, Finished Goods Control, and Cost of Goods Sold before proration (column 1 of the preceding table). The following table shows that prorations based on ending account balances are not the same as the more accurate prorations calculated earlier based on the amount of manufacturing overhead allocated to the accounts because the proportions of manufacturing overhead costs to total costs in these accounts are not the same.

	Home	Insert	Page Layout	Formulas	Data	Review	View		

	A	B	C	D	E	F
1		**Account Balance (Before Proration)**	**Account Balance as a Percent of Total**	**Proration of $135,000 of Underallocated Manufacturing Overhead**		**Account Balance (After Proration)**
2	**Account**	**(1)**	**(2) = (1) / $2,500,000**	**(3) = (2) x $135,000**		**(4) = (1) + (3)**
3	Work-in-process control	$ 50,000	2.0%	0.02 x $135,000 =	$ 2,700	$ 52,700
4	Finished goods control	75,000	3.0%	0.03 x 135,000 =	4,050	79,050
5	Cost of goods sold	2,375,000	95.0%	0.95 x 135,000 =	128,250	2,503,250
6	Total	$2,500,000	100.0%		$135,000	$2,635,000

However, proration based on ending balances is frequently justified as being an expedient way of approximating the more accurate results from using manufacturing overhead costs allocated.

Write-Off to Cost of Goods Sold Approach

Under this approach, the total under- or overallocated manufacturing overhead is included in this year's Cost of Goods Sold. For Robinson, the journal entry would be as follows:

Cost of Goods Sold	135,000	
Manufacturing Overhead Allocated	1,080,000	
Manufacturing Overhead Control		1,215,000

Robinson's two Manufacturing Overhead accounts are closed with the difference between them included in cost of goods sold. The Cost of Goods Sold account after the write-off equals $2,510,000, the balance before the write-off of $2,375,000 *plus the underallocated* manufacturing overhead amount of $135,000.

Choice Among Approaches

Which of these three approaches is the best one to use? In making this decision, managers should be guided by the causes for underallocation or overallocation and the purpose of the adjustment. The most common purpose is to state the balance sheet and income statement amounts based on actual rather than budgeted manufacturing overhead rates.

Many management accountants, industrial engineers, and managers argue that to the extent that the under- or overallocated overhead cost measures inefficiency during the period, it should be written off to Cost of Goods Sold instead of being prorated. This line of reasoning argues for applying a combination of the write-off and proration methods. For example, the portion of the underallocated overhead cost that is due to inefficiency (say, because of excessive spending) and that could have been avoided should be written off to Cost of Goods Sold, whereas the portion that is unavoidable should be prorated. Unlike full proration, this approach avoids carrying the costs of inefficiency as part of inventory assets.

Proration should be based on the manufacturing overhead allocated component in the ending balances of Work-in-Process Control, Finished Goods Control, and Cost of Goods Sold. Prorating to each individual job (as in the adjusted allocation-rate approach) is only done if the goal is to develop the most accurate record of individual job costs for profitability analysis purposes.

For balance sheet and income statement reporting purposes, the write-off to Cost of Goods Sold is the simplest approach for dealing with under- or overallocated overhead. If the amount of under- or overallocated overhead is small—in comparison with total operating income or some other measure of materiality—the write-off to Cost of Goods Sold approach yields a good approximation to more accurate, but more complex, approaches. Companies are also becoming increasingly conscious of inventory control, and quantities of inventories are lower than they were in earlier years. As a result, cost of goods sold tends to be higher in relation to the dollar amount of work-in-process and finished goods inventories. Also, the inventory balances of job-costing companies are usually small

Decision Point

How should managers dispose of under- or overallocated manufacturing overhead costs at the end of the fiscal year?

because goods are often made in response to customer orders. Consequently, as is true in our Robinson example, writing off, instead of prorating, under- or overallocated overhead is unlikely to result in significant distortions in financial statements.

The Robinson Company illustration assumed that a single manufacturing overhead cost pool with direct manufacturing labor-hours as the cost-allocation base was appropriate for allocating all manufacturing overhead costs to jobs. Had Robinson used multiple cost-allocation bases, such as direct manufacturing labor-hours and machine-hours, it would have created two cost pools and calculated two budgeted overhead rates: one based on direct manufacturing labor-hours and the other based on machine-hours to allocate overhead costs to jobs. The general ledger would contain Manufacturing Overhead Control and Manufacturing Overhead Allocated amounts for each cost pool. End-of-year adjustments for under- or overallocated overhead costs would then be made separately for each cost pool.

Variations from Normal Costing: A Service-Sector Example

Job costing is also very useful in service industries such as accounting and consulting firms, advertising agencies, auto repair shops, and hospitals. In an accounting firm, each audit is a job. The costs of each audit are accumulated in a job-cost record, much like the document used by Robinson Company, based on the seven-step approach described earlier. On the basis of labor-time sheets, direct labor costs of the professional staff—audit partners, audit managers, and audit staff—are traced to individual jobs. Other direct costs, such as travel, out-of-town meals and lodging, phone, fax, and copying, are also traced to jobs. The costs of secretarial support, office staff, rent, and depreciation of furniture and equipment are indirect costs because these costs cannot be traced to jobs in an economically feasible way. Indirect costs are allocated to jobs, for example, using a cost-allocation base such as number of professional labor-hours.

In some service organizations, a variation from normal costing is helpful because actual direct-labor costs—the largest component of total costs—can be difficult to trace to jobs as they are completed. For example, in our audit illustration, the actual direct-labor costs may include bonuses that become known only at the end of the year (a numerator reason). Also, the hours worked each period might vary significantly depending on the number of working days each month and the demand from clients (a denominator reason). In situations like these, a company needing timely information during the progress of an audit (and not wanting to wait until the end of the fiscal year) will use budgeted rates for some direct costs and budgeted rates for indirect costs. All budgeted rates are calculated at the start of the fiscal year. In contrast, normal costing uses actual cost rates for all direct costs and budgeted cost rates only for indirect costs.

The mechanics of using budgeted rates for direct costs are similar to the methods employed when using budgeted rates for indirect costs in normal costing. We illustrate this for Donahue and Associates, a public accounting firm. For 2011, Donahue budgets total direct-labor costs of $14,400,000, total indirect costs of $12,960,000, and total direct (professional) labor-hours of 288,000. In this case,

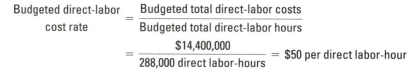

$$\frac{\text{Budgeted direct-labor}}{\text{cost rate}} = \frac{\text{Budgeted total direct-labor costs}}{\text{Budgeted total direct-labor hours}}$$

$$= \frac{\$14,400,000}{288,000 \text{ direct labor-hours}} = \$50 \text{ per direct labor-hour}$$

Assuming only one indirect-cost pool and total direct-labor costs as the cost-allocation base,

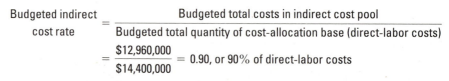

$$\frac{\text{Budgeted indirect}}{\text{cost rate}} = \frac{\text{Budgeted total costs in indirect cost pool}}{\text{Budgeted total quantity of cost-allocation base (direct-labor costs)}}$$

$$= \frac{\$12,960,000}{\$14,400,000} = 0.90, \text{ or } 90\% \text{ of direct-labor costs}$$

Suppose that in March 2011, an audit of Hanley Transport, a client of Donahue, uses 800 direct labor-hours. Donahue calculates the direct-labor costs of the Hanley Transport audit by multiplying the budgeted direct-labor cost rate, $50 per direct labor-hour, by

800, the actual quantity of direct labor-hours. The indirect costs allocated to the Hanley Transport audit are determined by multiplying the budgeted indirect-cost rate (90%) by the direct-labor costs assigned to the job ($40,000). Assuming no other direct costs for travel and the like, the cost of the Hanley Transport audit is as follows:

Direct-labor costs, $50 × 800	$40,000
Indirect costs allocated, 90% × $40,000	36,000
Total	$76,000

At the end of the fiscal year, the direct costs traced to jobs using budgeted rates will generally not equal actual direct costs because the actual rate and the budgeted rate are developed at different times using different information. End-of-year adjustments for under- or overallocated direct costs would need to be made in the same way that adjustments are made for under- or overallocated indirect costs.

The Donahue and Associates example illustrates that all costing systems do not exactly match either the actual-costing system or the normal-costing system described earlier in the chapter. As another example, engineering consulting firms often have some actual direct costs (cost of making blueprints or fees paid to outside experts), other direct costs (professional labor costs) assigned to jobs using a budgeted rate, and indirect costs (engineering and office-support costs) allocated to jobs using a budgeted rate. Therefore, users of costing systems should be aware of the different systems that they may encounter.

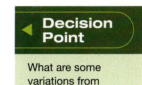

Decision Point

What are some variations from normal costing?

Problem for Self-Study

You are asked to bring the following incomplete accounts of Endeavor Printing, Inc., up-to-date through January 31, 2012. Consider the data that appear in the T-accounts as well as the following information in items (a) through (j).

Endeavor's normal-costing system has two direct-cost categories (direct material costs and direct manufacturing labor costs) and one indirect-cost pool (manufacturing overhead costs, which are allocated using direct manufacturing labor costs).

Materials Control		Wages Payable Control	
12-31-2011 Bal. 15,000			1-31-2012 Bal. 3,000

Work-in-Process Control		Manufacturing Overhead Control	
		1-31-2012 Bal. 57,000	

Finished Goods Control		Costs of Goods Sold	
12-31-2011 Bal. 20,000			

Additional information follows:

a. Manufacturing overhead is allocated using a budgeted rate that is set every December. Management forecasts next year's manufacturing overhead costs and next year's direct manufacturing labor costs. The budget for 2012 is $600,000 for manufacturing overhead costs and $400,000 for direct manufacturing labor costs.

b. The only job unfinished on January 31, 2012, is No. 419, on which direct manufacturing labor costs are $2,000 (125 direct manufacturing labor-hours) and direct material costs are $8,000.

c. Total direct materials issued to production during January 2012 are $90,000.

d. Cost of goods completed during January is $180,000.

e. Materials inventory as of January 31, 2012, is $20,000.

f. Finished goods inventory as of January 31, 2012, is $15,000.

g. All plant workers earn the same wage rate. Direct manufacturing labor-hours used for January total 2,500 hours. Other labor costs total $10,000.

h. The gross plant payroll paid in January equals $52,000. Ignore withholdings.

i. All "actual" manufacturing overhead incurred during January has already been posted.

j. All materials are direct materials.

Required Calculate the following:

1. Materials purchased during January
2. Cost of Goods Sold during January
3. Direct manufacturing labor costs incurred during January
4. Manufacturing Overhead Allocated during January
5. Balance, Wages Payable Control, December 31, 2011
6. Balance, Work-in-Process Control, January 31, 2012
7. Balance, Work-in-Process Control, December 31, 2011
8. Manufacturing Overhead Underallocated or Overallocated for January 2012

Solution

Amounts from the T-accounts are labeled "(T)."

1. From Materials Control T-account, Materials purchased: $90,000 (c) + $20,000 (e) − $15,000 (T) = $95,000
2. From Finished Goods Control T-account, Cost of Goods Sold: $20,000 (T) + $180,000 (d) − $15,000 (f) = $185,000
3. Direct manufacturing wage rate: $2,000 (b) ÷ 125 direct manufacturing labor-hours (b) = $16 per direct manufacturing labor-hour
   Direct manufacturing labor costs: 2,500 direct manufacturing labor-hours (g) × $16 per hour = $40,000
4. Manufacturing overhead rate: $600,000 (a) ÷ $400,000 (a) = 150%

Manufacturing Overhead Allocated: 150% of $40,000 = 1.50 × $40,000 (see 3) = $60,000

5. From Wages Payable Control T-account, Wages Payable Control, December 31, 2011: $52,000 (h) + $3,000 (T) − $40,000 (see 3) − $10,000 (g) = $5,000
6. Work-in-Process Control, January 31, 2012: $8,000 (b) + $2,000 (b) + 150% of $2,000 (b) = $13,000 (This answer is used in item 7.)
7. From Work-in-Process Control T-account, Work-in-Process Control, December 31, 2011: $180,000 (d) + $13,000 (see 6) − $90,000 (c) − $40,000 (see 3) − $60,000 (see 4) = $3,000
8. Manufacturing overhead overallocated: $60,000 (see 4) − $57,000 (T) = $3,000.

Letters alongside entries in T-accounts correspond to letters in the preceding additional information. Numbers alongside entries in T-accounts correspond to numbers in the preceding requirements.

Materials Control

December 31, 2011, Bal.	(given)	15,000			
	(1)	95,000*		(c)	90,000
January 31, 2012, Bal.	(e)	20,000			

Work-in-Process Control

December 31, 2011, Bal.	(7)	3,000		(d)	180,000
Direct materials	(c)	90,000			
Direct manufacturing labor	(b) (g) (3)	40,000			
Manufacturing overhead allocated	(3) (a) (4)	60,000			
January 31, 2012, Bal.	(b) (6)	13,000			

Finished Goods Control

December 31, 2011, Bal.	(given)	20,000		(2)	185,000
	(d)	180,000			
January 31, 2012, Bal.	(f)	15,000			

*Can be computed only after all other postings in the account have been made.

Wages Payable Control

(h)	52,000	December 31, 2011, Bal.	(5)	5,000
			(g) (3)	40,000
			(g)	10,000
		January 31, 2012	(given)	3,000

Manufacturing Overhead Control

Total January charges	(given)	57,000

Manufacturing Overhead Allocated

	(3) (a) (4)	60,000

Cost of Goods Sold

(d) (f) (2)	185,000	

Decision Points

The following question-and-answer format summarizes the chapter's learning objectives. Each decision presents a key question related to a learning objective. The guidelines are the answer to that question.

Decision	Guidelines
1. What are the building-block concepts of a costing system?	The building-block concepts of a costing system are cost object, direct costs of a cost object, indirect costs of a cost object, cost pool, and cost-allocation base. Costing-system overview diagrams represent these concepts in a systematic way. Costing systems aim to report cost numbers that reflect the way chosen cost objects (such as products or services) use the resources of an organization.
2. How do you distinguish job costing from process costing?	Job-costing systems assign costs to distinct units of a product or service. Process-costing systems assign costs to masses of identical or similar units and compute unit costs on an average basis. These two costing systems represent opposite ends of a continuum. The costing systems of many companies combine some elements of both job costing and process costing.
3. What is the main challenge of implementing job-costing systems?	The main challenge of implementing job-costing systems is estimating actual costs of jobs in a timely manner.
4. How do you implement a normal-costing system?	A general seven-step approach to normal costing requires identifying (1) the job, (2) the actual direct costs, (3) the budgeted cost-allocation bases, (4) the budgeted indirect cost pools, (5) the budgeted cost-allocation rates, (6) the allocated indirect costs (budgeted rate times actual quantity), and (7) the total direct and indirect costs of a job.
5. How do you distinguish actual costing from normal costing?	Actual costing and normal costing differ in the type of indirect-cost rates used:

	Actual Costing	Normal Costing
Direct-cost rates	Actual rates	Actual rates
Indirect-cost rates	Actual rates	Budgeted rates

Both systems use actual quantities of inputs for tracing direct costs and actual quantities of the allocation bases for allocating indirect costs.

6. How are transactions recorded in a manufacturing job-costing system?

A job-costing system in manufacturing records the flow of inventoriable costs in the general and subsidiary ledgers for (a) acquisition of materials and other manufacturing inputs, (b) their conversion into work in process, (c) their conversion into finished goods, and (d) the sale of finished goods. The job costing system also expenses period costs, such as marketing costs, as they are incurred.

7. How should managers dispose of under- or over-allocated manufacturing overhead costs at the end of the fiscal year?

The two theoretically correct approaches to disposing of under- or overallocated manufacturing overhead costs at the end of the fiscal year for correctly stating balance sheet and income statement amounts are (1) to adjust the allocation rate and (2) to prorate on the basis of the total amount of the allocated manufacturing overhead cost in the ending balances of Work-in-Process Control, Finished Goods Control, and Cost of Goods Sold. Many companies, however, simply write off amounts of under- or overallocated manufacturing overhead to Cost of Goods Sold when amounts are immaterial.

8. What are some variations from normal costing?

In some variations from normal costing, organizations use budgeted rates to assign direct costs, as well as indirect costs, to jobs.

Terms to Learn

This chapter and the Glossary at the end of the book contain definitions of the following important terms:

actual costing (**p. 102**)
actual indirect-cost rate (**p. 110**)
adjusted allocation-rate approach (**p. 118**)
budgeted indirect-cost rate (**p. 104**)
cost-allocation base (**p. 100**)
cost-application base (**p. 100**)
cost pool (**p. 100**)
job (**p. 100**)
job-cost record (**p. 104**)

job-cost sheet (**p. 104**)
job-costing system (**p. 100**)
labor-time sheet (**p. 106**)
manufacturing overhead allocated (**p. 113**)
manufacturing overhead applied (**p. 113**)
materials-requisition record (**p. 105**)
normal costing (**p. 104**)

overabsorbed indirect costs (**p. 118**)
overallocated indirect costs (**p. 118**)
overapplied indirect costs (**p. 118**)
process-costing system (**p. 101**)
proration (**p. 119**)
source document (**p. 104**)
underabsorbed indirect costs (**p. 118**)
underallocated indirect costs (**p. 118**)
underapplied indirect costs (**p. 118**)

Assignment Material

MyAccountingLab

Questions

4-1 Define cost pool, cost tracing, cost allocation, and cost-allocation base.

4-2 How does a job-costing system differ from a process-costing system?

4-3 Why might an advertising agency use job costing for an advertising campaign by Pepsi, whereas a bank might use process costing to determine the cost of checking account deposits?

4-4 Describe the seven steps in job costing.

4-5 Give examples of two cost objects in companies using job costing?

4-6 Describe three major source documents used in job-costing systems.

4-7 What is the advantage of using computerized source documents to prepare job-cost records?

4-8 Give two reasons why most organizations use an annual period rather than a weekly or monthly period to compute budgeted indirect-cost rates.

4-9 Distinguish between actual costing and normal costing.

4-10 Describe two ways in which a house construction company may use job-cost information.

4-11 Comment on the following statement: "In a normal-costing system, the amounts in the Manufacturing Overhead Control account will always equal the amounts in the Manufacturing Overhead Allocated account."

4-12 Describe three different debit entries to the Work-in-Process Control T-account under normal costing.

4-13 Describe three alternative ways to dispose of under- or overallocated overhead costs.

4-14 When might a company use budgeted costs rather than actual costs to compute direct-labor rates?

4-15 Describe briefly why Electronic Data Interchange (EDI) is helpful to managers.

Exercises

4-16 Job costing, process costing. In each of the following situations, determine whether job costing or process costing would be more appropriate.

a. A CPA firm
b. An oil refinery
c. A custom furniture manufacturer
d. A tire manufacturer
e. A textbook publisher
f. A pharmaceutical company
g. An advertising agency
h. An apparel manufacturing plant
i. A flour mill
j. A paint manufacturer
k. A medical care facility

l. A landscaping company
m. A cola-drink-concentrate producer
n. A movie studio
o. A law firm
p. A commercial aircraft manufacturer
q. A management consulting firm
r. A breakfast-cereal company
s. A catering service
t. A paper mill
u. An auto repair shop

4-17 Actual costing, normal costing, accounting for manufacturing overhead. Destin Products uses a job-costing system with two direct-cost categories (direct materials and direct manufacturing labor) and one manufacturing overhead cost pool. Destin allocates manufacturing overhead costs using direct manufacturing labor costs. Destin provides the following information:

	Budget for 2011	Actual Results for 2011
Direct material costs	$2,000,000	$1,900,000
Direct manufacturing labor costs	1,500,000	1,450,000
Manufacturing overhead costs	2,700,000	2,755,000

Required

1. Compute the actual and budgeted manufacturing overhead rates for 2011.
2. During March, the job-cost record for Job 626 contained the following information:

Direct materials used	$40,000
Direct manufacturing labor costs	$30,000

Compute the cost of Job 626 using (a) actual costing and (b) normal costing.
3. At the end of 2011, compute the under- or overallocated manufacturing overhead under normal costing. Why is there no under- or overallocated overhead under actual costing?

4-18 Job costing, normal and actual costing. Amesbury Construction assembles residential houses. It uses a job-costing system with two direct-cost categories (direct materials and direct labor) and one indirect-cost pool (assembly support). Direct labor-hours is the allocation base for assembly support costs. In December 2010, Amesbury budgets 2011 assembly-support costs to be $8,300,000 and 2011 direct labor-hours to be 166,000.

At the end of 2011, Amesbury is comparing the costs of several jobs that were started and completed in 2011.

	Laguna Model	Mission Model
Construction period	Feb–June 2011	May–Oct 2011
Direct material costs	$106,760	$127,550
Direct labor costs	$ 36,950	$ 41,320
Direct labor-hours	960	1,050

Direct materials and direct labor are paid for on a contract basis. The costs of each are known when direct materials are used or when direct labor-hours are worked. The 2011 actual assembly-support costs were $6,520,000, and the actual direct labor-hours were 163,000.

Required

1. Compute the (a) budgeted indirect-cost rate and (b) actual indirect-cost rate. Why do they differ?
2. What are the job costs of the Laguna Model and the Mission Model using (a) normal costing and (b) actual costing?
3. Why might Amesbury Construction prefer normal costing over actual costing?

4-19 Budgeted manufacturing overhead rate, allocated manufacturing overhead. Gammaro Company uses normal costing. It allocates manufacturing overhead costs using a budgeted rate per machine-hour. The following data are available for 2011:

Budgeted manufacturing overhead costs	$4,200,000
Budgeted machine-hours	175,000
Actual manufacturing overhead costs	$4,050,000
Actual machine-hours	170,000

1. Calculate the budgeted manufacturing overhead rate.
2. Calculate the manufacturing overhead allocated during 2011.
3. Calculate the amount of under- or overallocated manufacturing overhead.

4-20 Job costing, accounting for manufacturing overhead, budgeted rates. The Lynn Company uses a normal job-costing system at its Minneapolis plant. The plant has a machining department and an assembly department. Its job-costing system has two direct-cost categories (direct materials and direct manufacturing labor) and two manufacturing overhead cost pools (the machining department overhead, allocated to jobs based on actual machine-hours, and the assembly department overhead, allocated to jobs based on actual direct manufacturing labor costs). The 2011 budget for the plant is as follows:

	Machining Department	Assembly Department
Manufacturing overhead	$1,800,000	$3,600,000
Direct manufacturing labor costs	$1,400,000	$2,000,000
Direct manufacturing labor-hours	100,000	200,000
Machine-hours	50,000	200,000

1. Present an overview diagram of Lynn's job-costing system. Compute the budgeted manufacturing overhead rate for each department.
2. During February, the job-cost record for Job 494 contained the following:

	Machining Department	Assembly Department
Direct materials used	$45,000	$70,000
Direct manufacturing labor costs	$14,000	$15,000
Direct manufacturing labor-hours	1,000	1,500
Machine-hours	2,000	1,000

Compute the total manufacturing overhead costs allocated to Job 494.
3. At the end of 2011, the actual manufacturing overhead costs were $2,100,000 in machining and $3,700,000 in assembly. Assume that 55,000 actual machine-hours were used in machining and that actual direct manufacturing labor costs in assembly were $2,200,000. Compute the over- or underallocated manufacturing overhead for each department.

4-21 Job costing, consulting firm. Turner & Associates, a consulting firm, has the following condensed budget for 2011:

Revenues		$21,250,000
Total costs:		
Direct costs		
Professional Labor	$ 5,312,500	
Indirect costs		
Client support	13,600,000	18,912,500
Operating income		$ 2,337,500

Turner has a single direct-cost category (professional labor) and a single indirect-cost pool (client support). Indirect costs are allocated to jobs on the basis of professional labor costs.

1. Prepare an overview diagram of the job-costing system. Calculate the 2011 budgeted indirect-cost rate for Turner & Associates.
2. The markup rate for pricing jobs is intended to produce operating income equal to 11% of revenues. Calculate the markup rate as a percentage of professional labor costs.
3. Turner is bidding on a consulting job for Tasty Chicken, a fast-food chain specializing in poultry meats. The budgeted breakdown of professional labor on the job is as follows:

Professional Labor Category	Budgeted Rate per Hour	Budgeted Hours
Director	$198	4
Partner	101	17
Associate	49	42
Assistant	36	153

Calculate the budgeted cost of the Tasty Chicken job. How much will Turner bid for the job if it is to earn its target operating income of 11% of revenues?

4-22 Time period used to compute indirect cost rates. Splash Manufacturing produces outdoor wading and slide pools. The company uses a normal-costing system and allocates manufacturing overhead on the basis of direct manufacturing labor-hours. Most of the company's production and sales occur in the first and second quarters of the year. The company is in danger of losing one of its larger customers, Sotco Wholesale, due to large fluctuations in price. The owner of Splash has requested an analysis of the manufacturing cost per unit in the second and third quarters. You have been provided the following budgeted information for the coming year:

	Quarter			
	1	2	3	4
Pools manufactured and sold	700	500	150	150

It takes 0.5 direct manufacturing labor-hour to make each pool. The actual direct material cost is $7.50 per pool. The actual direct manufacturing labor rate is $16 per hour. The budgeted variable manufacturing overhead rate is $12 per direct manufacturing labor-hour. Budgeted fixed manufacturing overhead costs are $10,500 each quarter.

Required

1. Calculate the total manufacturing cost per unit for the second and third quarter assuming the company allocates manufacturing overhead costs based on the budgeted manufacturing overhead rate determined for each quarter.
2. Calculate the total manufacturing cost per unit for the second and third quarter assuming the company allocates manufacturing overhead costs based on an annual budgeted manufacturing overhead rate.
3. Splash Manufacturing prices its pools at manufacturing cost plus 30%. Why might Sotco Wholesale be seeing large fluctuations in the prices of pools? Which of the methods described in requirements 1 and 2 would you recommend Splash use? Explain.

4-23 Accounting for manufacturing overhead. Consider the following selected cost data for the Pittsburgh Forging Company for 2011.

Budgeted manufacturing overhead costs	$7,500,000
Budgeted machine-hours	250,000
Actual manufacturing overhead costs	$7,300,000
Actual machine-hours	245,000

The company uses normal costing. Its job-costing system has a single manufacturing overhead cost pool. Costs are allocated to jobs using a budgeted machine-hour rate. Any amount of under- or overallocation is written off to Cost of Goods Sold.

Required

1. Compute the budgeted manufacturing overhead rate.
2. Prepare the journal entries to record the allocation of manufacturing overhead.
3. Compute the amount of under- or overallocation of manufacturing overhead. Is the amount material? Prepare a journal entry to dispose of this amount.

4-24 Job costing, journal entries. The University of Chicago Press is wholly owned by the university. It performs the bulk of its work for other university departments, which pay as though the press were an outside business enterprise. The press also publishes and maintains a stock of books for general sale. The press uses normal costing to cost each job. Its job-costing system has two direct-cost categories (direct materials and direct manufacturing labor) and one indirect-cost pool (manufacturing overhead, allocated on the basis of direct manufacturing labor costs).

The following data (in thousands) pertain to 2011:

Direct materials and supplies purchased on credit	$ 800
Direct materials used	710
Indirect materials issued to various production departments	100
Direct manufacturing labor	1,300
Indirect manufacturing labor incurred by various production departments	900
Depreciation on building and manufacturing equipment	400
Miscellaneous manufacturing overhead* incurred by various production departments (ordinarily would be detailed as repairs, photocopying, utilities, etc.)	550
Manufacturing overhead allocated at 160% of direct manufacturing labor costs	?
Cost of goods manufactured	4,120
Revenues	8,000
Cost of goods sold (before adjustment for under- or overallocated manufacturing overhead)	4,020
Inventories, December 31, 2010 (not 2011):	

---

* The term manufacturing overhead is not used uniformly. Other terms that are often encountered in printing companies include job overhead and shop overhead.

Materials Control	100
Work-in-Process Control	60
Finished Goods Control	500

Required

1. Prepare an overview diagram of the job-costing system at the University of Chicago Press.
2. Prepare journal entries to summarize the 2011 transactions. As your final entry, dispose of the year-end under- or overallocated manufacturing overhead as a write-off to Cost of Goods Sold. Number your entries. Explanations for each entry may be omitted.
3. Show posted T-accounts for all inventories, Cost of Goods Sold, Manufacturing Overhead Control, and Manufacturing Overhead Allocated.

4-25 Journal entries, T-accounts, and source documents. Production Company produces gadgets for the coveted small appliance market. The following data reflect activity for the year 2011:

Costs incurred:	
Purchases of direct materials (net) on credit	$124,000
Direct manufacturing labor cost	80,000
Indirect labor	54,500
Depreciation, factory equipment	30,000
Depreciation, office equipment	7,000
Maintenance, factory equipment	20,000
Miscellaneous factory overhead	9,500
Rent, factory building	70,000
Advertising expense	90,000
Sales commissions	30,000
Inventories:	

	January 1, 2011	December 31, 2011
Direct materials	$ 9,000	$11,000
Work in process	6,000	21,000
Finished goods	69,000	24,000

Production Co. uses a normal costing system and allocates overhead to work in process at a rate of $2.50 per direct manufacturing labor dollar. Indirect materials are insignificant so there is no inventory account for indirect materials.

Required

1. Prepare journal entries to record the transactions for 2011 including an entry to close out over- or underallocated overhead to cost of goods sold. For each journal entry indicate the source document that would be used to authorize each entry. Also note which subsidiary ledger, if any, should be referenced as backup for the entry.
2. Post the journal entries to T-accounts for all of the inventories, Cost of Goods Sold, the Manufacturing Overhead Control Account, and the Manufacturing Overhead Allocated Account.

4-26 Job costing, journal entries. Donnell Transport assembles prestige manufactured homes. Its job costing system has two direct-cost categories (direct materials and direct manufacturing labor) and one indirect-cost pool (manufacturing overhead allocated at a budgeted $30 per machine-hour in 2011). The following data (in millions) pertain to operations for 2011:

Materials Control, beginning balance, January 1, 2011	$ 12
Work-in-Process Control, beginning balance, January 1, 2011	2
Finished Goods Control, beginning balance, January 1, 2011	6
Materials and supplies purchased on credit	150
Direct materials used	145
Indirect materials (supplies) issued to various production departments	10
Direct manufacturing labor	90
Indirect manufacturing labor incurred by various production departments	30
Depreciation on plant and manufacturing equipment	19
Miscellaneous manufacturing overhead incurred (ordinarily would be detailed as repairs, utilities, etc., with a corresponding credit to various liability accounts)	9
Manufacturing overhead allocated, 2,100,000 actual machine-hours	?
Cost of goods manufactured	294
Revenues	400
Cost of goods sold	292

1. Prepare an overview diagram of Donnell Transport's job-costing system.

2. Prepare journal entries. Number your entries. Explanations for each entry may be omitted. Post to T-accounts. What is the ending balance of Work-in-Process Control?

3. Show the journal entry for disposing of under- or overallocated manufacturing overhead directly as a year-end write-off to Cost of Goods Sold. Post the entry to T-accounts.

4-27 Job costing, unit cost, ending work in process. Rafael Company produces pipes for concert-quality organs. Each job is unique. In April 2011, it completed all outstanding orders, and then, in May 2011, it worked on only two jobs, M1 and M2:

	A	B	C
1	Rafael Company, May 2011	Job M1	Job M2
2	Direct materials	$ 78,000	$ 51,000
3	Direct manufacturing labor	273,000	208,000

Direct manufacturing labor is paid at the rate of $26 per hour. Manufacturing overhead costs are allocated at a budgeted rate of $20 per direct manufacturing labor-hour. Only Job M1 was completed in May.

1. Calculate the total cost for Job M1.

2. 1,100 pipes were produced for Job M1. Calculate the cost per pipe.

3. Prepare the journal entry transferring Job M1 to finished goods.

4. What is the ending balance in the Work-in-Process Control account?

4-28 Job costing; actual, normal, and variation from normal costing. Chico & Partners, a Quebec-based public accounting partnership, specializes in audit services. Its job-costing system has a single direct-cost category (professional labor) and a single indirect-cost pool (audit support, which contains all costs of the Audit Support Department). Audit support costs are allocated to individual jobs using actual professional labor-hours. Chico & Partners employs 10 professionals to perform audit services.

Budgeted and actual amounts for 2011 are as follows:

	A	B	C
1	Chico & Partners		
2	Budget for 2011		
3	Professional labor compensation	$990,000	
4	Audit support department costs	$774,000	
5	Professional labor-hours billed to clients	18,000	hours
6			
7	Actual results for 2011		
8	Audit support department costs	$735,000	
9	Professional labor-hours billed to clients	17,500	
10	Actual professional labor cost rate	$ 59	per hour

1. Compute the direct-cost rate and the indirect-cost rate per professional labor-hour for 2011 under (a) actual costing, (b) normal costing, and (c) the variation from normal costing that uses budgeted rates for direct costs.

2. Chico's 2011 audit of Pierre & Co. was budgeted to take 150 hours of professional labor time. The actual professional labor time spent on the audit was 160 hours. Compute the cost of the Pierre & Co. audit using (a) actual costing, (b) normal costing, and (c) the variation from normal costing that uses budgeted rates for direct costs. Explain any differences in the job cost.

4-29 Job costing; actual, normal, and variation from normal costing. Braden Brothers, Inc., is an architecture firm specializing in high-rise buildings. Its job-costing system has a single direct-cost category (architectural labor) and a single indirect-cost pool, which contains all costs of supporting the office. Support costs are allocated to individual jobs using architect labor-hours. Braden Brothers employs 15 architects.

Budgeted and actual amounts for 2010 are as follows:

Braden Brothers, Inc.

Budget for 2010	
Architect labor cost	$2,880,000
Office support costs	$1,728,000
Architect labor-hours billed to clients	32,000 hours
Actual results for 2010	
Office support costs	$1,729,500
Architect labor-hours billed to clients	34,590 hours
Actual architect labor cost rate	$ 92 per hour

Required

1. Compute the direct-cost rate and the indirect-cost rate per architectural labor-hour for 2010 under (a) actual costing, (b) normal costing, and (c) the variation from normal costing that uses budgeted rates for direct costs.
2. Braden Brother's architectural sketches for Champ Tower in Houston was budgeted to take 275 hours of architectural labor time. The actual architectural labor time spent on the job was 250 hours. Compute the cost of the Champ Tower sketches using (a) actual costing, (b) normal costing, and (c) the variation from normal costing that uses budgeted rates for direct costs.

4-30 Proration of overhead. The Ride-On-Wave Company (ROW) produces a line of non-motorized boats. ROW uses a normal-costing system and allocates manufacturing overhead using direct manufacturing labor cost. The following data are for 2011:

Budgeted manufacturing overhead cost	$125,000
Budgeted direct manufacturing labor cost	$250,000
Actual manufacturing overhead cost	$117,000
Actual direct manufacturing labor cost	$228,000

Inventory balances on December 31, 2011, were as follows:

Account	Ending balance	2011 direct manufacturing labor cost in ending balance
Work in process	$ 50,700	$ 20,520
Finished goods	245,050	59,280
Cost of goods sold	549,250	148,200

Required

1. Calculate the manufacturing overhead allocation rate.
2. Compute the amount of under- or overallocated manufacturing overhead.
3. Calculate the ending balances in work in process, finished goods, and cost of goods sold if under-overallocated manufacturing overhead is as follows:
   a. Written off to cost of goods sold
   b. Prorated based on ending balances (before proration) in each of the three accounts
   c. Prorated based on the overhead allocated in 2011 in the ending balances (before proration) in each of the three accounts
4. Which method makes the most sense? Justify your answer.

MyAccountingLab

Problems

4-31 Job costing, accounting for manufacturing overhead, budgeted rates. The Fasano Company uses a job-costing system at its Dover, Delaware, plant. The plant has a machining department and a finishing department. Fasano uses normal costing with two direct-cost categories (direct materials and direct manufacturing labor) and two manufacturing overhead cost pools (the machining department with machine-hours as the allocation base, and the finishing department with direct manufacturing labor costs as the allocation base). The 2011 budget for the plant is as follows:

	Machining Department	Finishing Department
Manufacturing overhead costs	$10,660,000	$7,372,000
Direct manufacturing labor costs	$ 940,000	$3,800,000
Direct manufacturing labor-hours	36,000	145,000
Machine-hours	205,000	32,000

Required

1. Prepare an overview diagram of Fasano's job-costing system.
2. What is the budgeted manufacturing overhead rate in the machining department? In the finishing department?
3. During the month of January, the job-cost record for Job 431 shows the following:

	Machining Department	Finishing Department
Direct materials used	$15,500	$ 5,000
Direct manufacturing labor costs	$ 400	$1,1,00
Direct manufacturing labor-hours	50	50
Machine-hours	130	20

Compute the total manufacturing overhead cost allocated to Job 431.
4. Assuming that Job 431 consisted of 400 units of product, what is the cost per unit?
5. Amounts at the end of 2011 are as follows:

	Machining Department	Finishing Department
Manufacturing overhead incurred	$11,070,000	$8,236,000
Direct manufacturing labor costs	$ 1,000,000	$4,400,000
Machine-hours	210,000	31,000

Compute the under- or overallocated manufacturing overhead for each department and for the Dover plant as a whole.
6. Why might Fasano use two different manufacturing overhead cost pools in its job-costing system?

4-32 Service industry, job costing, law firm. Keating & Associates is a law firm specializing in labor relations and employee-related work. It employs 25 professionals (5 partners and 20 associates) who work directly with its clients. The average budgeted total compensation per professional for 2011 is $104,000. Each professional is budgeted to have 1,600 billable hours to clients in 2011. All professionals work for clients to their maximum 1,600 billable hours available. All professional labor costs are included in a single direct-cost category and are traced to jobs on a per-hour basis. All costs of Keating & Associates other than professional labor costs are included in a single indirect-cost pool (legal support) and are allocated to jobs using professional labor-hours as the allocation base. The budgeted level of indirect costs in 2011 is $2,200,000.

Required

1. Prepare an overview diagram of Keating's job-costing system.
2. Compute the 2011 budgeted direct-cost rate per hour of professional labor.
3. Compute the 2011 budgeted indirect-cost rate per hour of professional labor.
4. Keating & Associates is considering bidding on two jobs:
   a. Litigation work for Richardson, Inc., which requires 100 budgeted hours of professional labor
   b. Labor contract work for Punch, Inc., which requires 150 budgeted hours of professional labor
   Prepare a cost estimate for each job.

4-33 Service industry, job costing, two direct- and two indirect-cost categories, law firm (continuation of 4-32). Keating has just completed a review of its job-costing system. This review included a detailed analysis of how past jobs used the firm's resources and interviews with personnel about what factors drive the level of indirect costs. Management concluded that a system with two direct-cost categories (professional partner labor and professional associate labor) and two indirect-cost categories (general support and secretarial support) would yield more accurate job costs. Budgeted information for 2011 related to the two direct-cost categories is as follows:

	Professional Partner Labor	Professional Associate Labor
Number of professionals	5	20
Hours of billable time per professional	1,600 per year	1,600 per year
Total compensation (average per professional)	$200,000	$80,000

Budgeted information for 2011 relating to the two indirect-cost categories is as follows:

	General Support	Secretarial Support
Total costs	$1,800,000	$400,000
Cost-allocation base	Professional labor-hours	Partner labor-hours

Required

1. Compute the 2011 budgeted direct-cost rates for (a) professional partners and (b) professional associates.
2. Compute the 2011 budgeted indirect-cost rates for (a) general support and (b) secretarial support.

3. Compute the budgeted costs for the Richardson and Punch jobs, given the following information:

	Richardson, Inc.	Punch, Inc.
Professional partners	60 hours	30 hours
Professional associates	40 hours	120 hours

4. Comment on the results in requirement 3. Why are the job costs different from those computed in Problem 4-32?

4-34 Proration of overhead. (Z. Iqbal, adapted) The Zaf Radiator Company uses a normal-costing system with a single manufacturing overhead cost pool and machine-hours as the cost-allocation base. The following data are for 2011:

Budgeted manufacturing overhead costs	$4,800,000
Overhead allocation base	Machine-hours
Budgeted machine-hours	80,000
Manufacturing overhead costs incurred	$4,900,000
Actual machine-hours	75,000

Machine-hours data and the ending balances (before proration of under- or overallocated overhead) are as follows:

	Actual Machine-Hours	2011 End-of-Year Balance
Cost of Goods Sold	60,000	$8,000,000
Finished Goods Control	11,000	1,250,000
Work-in-Process Control	4,000	750,000

Required

1. Compute the budgeted manufacturing overhead rate for 2011.
2. Compute the under- or overallocated manufacturing overhead of Zaf Radiator in 2011. Dispose of this amount using the following:
   a. Write-off to Cost of Goods Sold
   b. Proration based on ending balances (before proration) in Work-in-Process Control, Finished Goods Control, and Cost of Goods Sold
   c. Proration based on the overhead allocated in 2011 (before proration) in the ending balances of Work-in-Process Control, Finished Goods Control, and Cost of Goods Sold
3. Which method do you prefer in requirement 2? Explain.

4-35 Normal costing, overhead allocation, working backward. Gibson Manufacturing uses normal costing for its job-costing system, which has two direct-cost categories (direct materials and direct manufacturing labor) and one indirect-cost category (manufacturing overhead). The following information is obtained for 2011:

- Total manufacturing costs, $8,000,000
- Manufacturing overhead allocated, $3,600,000 (allocated at a rate of 200% of direct manufacturing labor costs)
- Work-in-process inventory on January 1, 2011, $320,000
- Cost of finished goods manufactured, $7,920,000

Required

1. Use information in the first two bullet points to calculate (a) direct manufacturing labor costs in 2011 and (b) cost of direct materials used in 2011.
2. Calculate the ending work-in-process inventory on December 31, 2011.

4-36 Proration of overhead with two indirect cost pools. New Rise, Inc., produces porcelain figurines. The production is semi-automated where the figurine is molded almost entirely by operator-less machines and then individually hand-painted. The overhead in the molding department is allocated based on machine-hours and the overhead in the painting department is allocated based on direct manufacturing labor-hours. New Rise, Inc., uses a normal-costing system and reported actual overhead for the month of May of $17,248 and $31,485 for the molding and painting departments, respectively. The company reported the following information related to its inventory accounts and cost of goods sold for the month of May:

	Work in Process	Finished Goods	Cost of Goods Sold
Balance before proration	$27,720	$15,523.20	$115,156.80
Molding Department Overhead Allocated	$ 4,602	$ 957.00	$ 12,489.00
Painting Department Overhead Allocated	$ 2,306	$ 1,897.00	$ 24,982.00

1. Calculate the over- or underallocated overhead for each of the Molding and Painting departments for May.
2. Calculate the ending balances in work in process, finished goods, and cost of goods sold if the under- or overallocated overhead amounts in *each* department are as follows:
   a. Written off to cost of goods sold
   b. Prorated based on the ending balance (before proration) in each of the three accounts
   c. Prorated based on the overhead allocated in May (before proration) in the ending balances in each of the three accounts
3. Which method would you choose? Explain.

4-37 General ledger relationships, under- and overallocation. (S. Sridhar, adapted) Needham Company uses normal costing in its job-costing system. Partially completed T-accounts and additional information for Needham for 2011 are as follows:

Direct Materials Control			Work-in-Process Control			Finished Goods Control		
1-1-2011	30,000	380,000	1-1-2011	20,000		1-1-2011	10,000	900,000
	400,000		Dir. manuf.				940,000	
			labor	360,000				

Manufacturing Overhead Control		Manufacturing Overhead Allocated		Cost of Goods Sold	
540,000					

Additional information follows:

a. Direct manufacturing labor wage rate was $15 per hour.
b. Manufacturing overhead was allocated at $20 per direct manufacturing labor-hour.
c. During the year, sales revenues were $1,090,000, and marketing and distribution costs were $140,000.

1. What was the amount of direct materials issued to production during 2011?
2. What was the amount of manufacturing overhead allocated to jobs during 2011?
3. What was the total cost of jobs completed during 2011?
4. What was the balance of work-in-process inventory on December 31, 2011?
5. What was the cost of goods sold before proration of under- or overallocated overhead?
6. What was the under- or overallocated manufacturing overhead in 2011?
7. Dispose of the under- or overallocated manufacturing overhead using the following:
   a. Write-off to Cost of Goods Sold
   b. Proration based on ending balances (before proration) in Work-in-Process Control, Finished Goods Control, and Cost of Goods Sold
8. Using each of the approaches in requirement 7, calculate Needham's operating income for 2011.
9. Which approach in requirement 7 do you recommend Needham use? Explain your answer briefly.

4-38 Overview of general ledger relationships. Brady Company uses normal costing in its job-costing system. The company produces custom bikes for toddlers. The beginning balances (December 1) and ending balances (as of December 30) in their inventory accounts are as follows:

	Beginning Balance 12/1	Ending Balance 12/30
Materials Control	$1,200	$ 7,600
Work-in-Process Control	5,800	8,100
Manufacturing Department Overhead Control	—	94,070
Finished Goods Control	3,500	18,500

Additional information follows:

a. Direct materials purchased during December were $65,400.
b. Cost of goods manufactured for December was $225,000.
c. No direct materials were returned to suppliers.
d. No units were started or completed on December 31.
e. The manufacturing labor costs for the December 31 working day: direct manufacturing labor, $3,850, and indirect manufacturing labor, $950.
f. Manufacturing overhead has been allocated at 120% of direct manufacturing labor costs through December 30.

Required

1. Prepare journal entries for the December 31 payroll.
2. Use T-accounts to compute the following:
   a. The total amount of materials requisitioned into work in process during December
   b. The total amount of direct manufacturing labor recorded in work in process during December (Hint: You have to solve requirements **2b** and **2c** simultaneously)
   c. The total amount of manufacturing overhead recorded in work in process during December
   d. Ending balance in work in process, December 31
   e. Cost of goods sold for December before adjustments for under- or overallocated manufacturing overhead
3. Prepare closing journal entries related to manufacturing overhead. Assume that all under- or overallocated manufacturing overhead is closed directly to Cost of Goods Sold.

4-39 **Allocation and proration of overhead.** Tamden, Inc., prints custom marketing materials. The business was started January 1, 2010. The company uses a normal-costing system. It has two direct cost pools, materials and labor and one indirect cost pool, overhead. Overhead is charged to printing jobs on the basis of direct labor cost. The following information is available for 2010.

Budgeted direct labor costs	$150,000
Budgeted overhead costs	$180,000
Costs of actual material used	$126,500
Actual direct labor costs	$148,750
Actual overhead costs	$176,000

There were two jobs in process on December 31, 2010: Job 11 and Job 12. Costs added to each job as of December 31 are as follows:

	Direct materials	Direct labor
Job 11	$3,620	$4,500
Job 12	$6,830	$7,250

Tamden, Inc., has no finished goods inventories because all printing jobs are transferred to cost of goods sold when completed.

Required

1. Compute the overhead allocation rate.
2. Calculate the balance in ending work in process and cost of goods sold before any adjustments for under- or overallocated overhead.
3. Calculate under- or overallocated overhead.
4. Calculate the ending balances in work in process and cost of goods sold if the under- or overallocated overhead amount is as follows:
   a. Written off to cost of goods sold
   b. Prorated using the ending balance (before proration) in cost of goods sold and work-in-process control accounts
5. Which of the methods in requirement 4 would you choose? Explain.

4-40 **Job costing, contracting, ethics.** Kingston Company manufactures modular homes. The company has two main products that it sells commercially: a 1,000 square foot, one-bedroom model and a 1,500 square foot, two-bedroom model. The company recently began providing emergency housing (huts) to FEMA. The emergency housing is similar to the 1,000 square foot model.

FEMA has requested Kingston to create a bid for 150 emergency huts to be sent for flood victims in the south. Your boss has asked that you prepare this bid. In preparing the bid, you find a recent invoice to FEMA for 200 huts provided after hurricane Katrina. You also have a standard cost sheet for the 1,000 square foot model sold commercially. Both are provided as follows:

Standard cost sheet: 1,000 sq. ft. one-bedroom model

Direct materials		$ 8,000
Direct manufacturing labor	30 hours	600
Manufacturing overhead*	$3 per direct labor dollar	1,800
Total cost		$10,400
Retail markup on total cost		20%
Retail price		$12,480

---

*Overhead cost pool includes inspection labor ($15 per hour), setup labor ($12 per hour), and other indirect costs associated with production.

INVOICE:
DATE: September 15, 2005
BILL TO: FEMA
FOR: 200 Emergency Huts
SHIP TO: New Orleans, Louisiana

Direct materials	$1,840,000
Direct manufacturing labor**	138,400
Manufacturing overhead	415,200
Total cost	2,393,600
Government contract markup on total cost	15%
Total due	$2,752,640

**Direct manufacturing labor includes 28 production hours per unit, 4 inspection hours per unit, and 6 setup hours per unit

1. Calculate the total bid if you base your calculations on the standard cost sheet assuming a cost plus 15% government contract.

Required

2. Calculate the total bid if you base your calculations on the September 15, 2005, invoice assuming a cost plus 15% government contract.
3. What are the main discrepancies between the bids you calculated in #1 and #2?
4. What bid should you present to your boss? What principles from the IMA *Standards of Ethical Conduct for Practitioners of Management Accounting and Financial Management* should guide your decision?

Collaborative Learning Problem

4-41 **Job costing—service industry.** Cam Cody schedules book signings for science fiction authors and creates e-books and books on CD to sell at each signing. Cody uses a normal-costing system with two direct cost pools, labor and materials, and one indirect cost pool, general overhead. General overhead is allocated to each signing based on 80% of labor cost. Actual overhead equaled allocated overhead in March 2010. Actual overhead in April was $1,980. All costs incurred during the planning stage for a signing and during the signing are gathered in a balance sheet account called "Signings in Progress (SIP)." When a signing is completed, the costs are transferred to an income statement account called "Cost of Completed Signings (CCS)." Following is cost information for April 2010:

Author	From Beginning SIP Materials	From Beginning SIP Labor	Incurred in April Materials	Incurred in April Labor
N. Asher	$425	$750	$ 90	$225
T. Bucknell	710	575	150	75
S. Brown	200	550	320	450
S. King	—	—	650	400
D. Sherman	—	—	150	200

The following information relates to April 2010.

As of April 1, there were three signings in progress, *N. Asher, T. Bucknell,* and *S. Brown.* Signings for *S. King* and *D. Sherman* were started during April. The signings for *T. Bucknell* and *S. King* were completed during April.

1. Calculate SIP at the end of April.

Required

2. Calculate CCS for April.
3. Calculate under/overallocated overhead at the end of April.
4. Calculate the ending balances in SIP and CCS if the under/overallocated overhead amount is as follows:
   a. Written off to CCS
   b. Prorated based on the ending balances (before proration) in SIP and CCS
   c. Prorated based on the overhead allocated in April in the ending balances of SIP and CCS (before proration)
5. Which of the methods in requirement 4 would you choose?

objects (such as products or services) when the individual products or services, may in fact, use those resources in nonuniform ways.

Undercosting and Overcosting

The following example illustrates how averaging can result in inaccurate and misleading cost data. Consider the cost of a restaurant bill for four colleagues who meet monthly to discuss business developments. Each diner orders separate entrees, desserts, and drinks. The restaurant bill for the most recent meeting is as follows:

	Emma	James	Jessica	Matthew	Total	Average
Entree	$11	$20	$15	$14	$ 60	$15
Dessert	0	8	4	4	16	4
Drinks	4	14	8	6	32	8
Total	$15	$42	$27	$24	$108	$27

If the $108 total restaurant bill is divided evenly, $27 is the average cost per diner. This cost-averaging approach treats each diner the same. Emma would probably object to paying $27 because her actual cost is only $15; she ordered the lowest-cost entree, had no dessert, and had the lowest-cost drink. When costs are averaged across all four diners, both Emma and Matthew are overcosted, James is undercosted, and Jessica is (by coincidence) accurately costed.

Broad averaging can lead to undercosting or overcosting of products or services:

- **Product undercosting**—a product consumes a high level of resources but is reported to have a low cost per unit (James's dinner).

- **Product overcosting**—a product consumes a low level of resources but is reported to have a high cost per unit (Emma's dinner).

What are the strategic consequences of product undercosting and overcosting? Think of a company that uses cost information about its products to guide pricing decisions. Undercosted products will be underpriced and may even lead to sales that actually result in losses—sales bring in less revenue than the cost of resources they use. Overcosted products lead to overpricing, causing these products to lose market share to competitors producing similar products. Worse still, product undercosting and overcosting causes managers to focus on the wrong products, drawing attention to overcosted products whose costs may in fact be perfectly reasonable and ignoring undercosted products that in fact consume large amounts of resources.

Product-Cost Cross-Subsidization

Product-cost cross-subsidization means that if a company undercosts one of its products, it will overcost at least one of its other products. Similarly, if a company overcosts one of its products, it will undercost at least one of its other products. Product-cost cross-subsidization is very common in situations in which a cost is uniformly spread—meaning it is broadly averaged—across multiple products without recognizing the amount of resources consumed by each product.

In the restaurant-bill example, the amount of cost cross-subsidization of each diner can be readily computed *because all cost items can be traced as direct costs to each diner*. If all diners pay $27, Emma is paying $12 more than her actual cost of $15. She is cross-subsidizing James who is paying $15 less than his actual cost of $42. Calculating the amount of cost cross-subsidization takes more work when there are indirect costs to be considered. Why? Because when the resources represented by indirect costs are used by two or more diners, we need to find a way to allocate costs to each diner. Consider, for example, a $40 bottle of wine whose cost is shared equally. Each diner would pay $10 ($40 ÷ 4). Suppose Matthew drinks 2 glasses of wine while Emma, James, and Jessica drink one glass each for a total of 5 glasses. Allocating the cost of the bottle of wine on the basis of the glasses of wine that each diner drinks would result in Matthew paying $16 ($40 × 2/5) and each of the others $8 ($40 × 1/5). In this case, by sharing the cost equally, Emma, James, and Jessica are each paying $2 ($10 – $8) more and are cross-subsidizing Matthew who is paying $6 ($16 – $10) less for the wine he consumes.

To see the effects of broad averaging on direct and indirect costs, we consider Plastim Corporation's costing system.

Decision Point

When does product undercosting or overcosting occur?

Simple Costing System at Plastim Corporation

Plastim Corporation manufactures lenses for the rear taillights of automobiles. A lens, made from black, red, orange, or white plastic, is the part of the lamp visible on the automobile's exterior. Lenses are made by injecting molten plastic into a mold to give the lamp its desired shape. The mold is cooled to allow the molten plastic to solidify, and the lens is removed.

Under its contract with Giovanni Motors, a major automobile manufacturer, Plastim makes two types of lenses: a complex lens, CL5, and a simple lens, S3. The complex lens is a large lens with special features, such as multicolor molding (when more than one color is injected into the mold) and a complex shape that wraps around the corner of the car. Manufacturing CL5 lenses is more complex because various parts in the mold must align and fit precisely. The S3 lens is simpler to make because it has a single color and few special features.

Design, Manufacturing, and Distribution Processes

The sequence of steps to design, produce, and distribute lenses, whether simple or complex, is as follows:

- **Design products and processes.** Each year Giovanni Motors specifies some modifications to the simple and complex lenses. Plastim's design department designs the molds from which the lenses will be made and specifies the processes needed (that is, details of the manufacturing operations).
- **Manufacture lenses.** The lenses are molded, finished, cleaned, and inspected.
- **Distribute lenses.** Finished lenses are packed and sent to Giovanni Motors.

Plastim is operating at capacity and incurs very low marketing costs. Because of its high-quality products, Plastim has minimal customer-service costs. Plastim's business environment is very competitive with respect to simple lenses. At a recent meeting, Giovanni's purchasing manager indicated that a new supplier, Bandix, which makes only simple lenses, is offering to supply the S3 lens to Giovanni at a price of $53, well below the $63 price that Plastim is currently projecting and budgeting for 2011. Unless Plastim can lower its selling price, it will lose the Giovanni business for the simple lens for the upcoming model year. Fortunately, the same competitive pressures do not exist for the complex lens, which Plastim currently sells to Giovanni at $137 per lens.

Plastim's management has two primary options:

- Plastim can give up the Giovanni business in simple lenses if selling simple lenses is unprofitable. Bandix makes only simple lenses and perhaps, therefore, uses simpler technology and processes than Plastim. The simpler operations may give Bandix a cost advantage that Plastim cannot match. If so, it is better for Plastim to not supply the S3 lens to Giovanni.
- Plastim can reduce the price of the simple lens and either accept a lower margin or aggressively seek to reduce costs.

To make these long-run strategic decisions, management needs to first understand the costs to design, make, and distribute the S3 and CL5 lenses.

While Bandix makes only simple lenses and can fairly accurately calculate the cost of a lens by dividing total costs by units produced, Plastim's costing environment is more challenging. The processes to make both simple and complex lenses are more complicated than the processes required to make only simple lenses. Plastim needs to find a way to allocate costs to each type of lens.

In computing costs, Plastim assigns both variable costs and costs that are fixed in the short run to the S3 and CL5 lenses. Managers cost products and services to guide long-run strategic decisions (for example, what mix of products and services to produce and sell and what prices to charge for them). In the long-run, managers want revenues to exceed total costs (variable and fixed) to design, make, and distribute the lenses.

To guide their pricing and cost-management decisions, Plastim's managers assign all costs, both manufacturing and nonmanufacturing, to the S3 and CL5 lenses. If managers had wanted to calculate the cost of inventory, Plastim's management accountants would have assigned only manufacturing costs to the lenses, as required by generally accepted accounting principles. Surveys of company practice across the globe overwhelmingly indicate that the vast majority of companies use costing systems not just for inventory costing but also for strategic purposes such as pricing and product-mix decisions and decisions about cost reduction, process improvement, design, and planning and budgeting. As a result, even merchandising-sector companies (for whom inventory costing is straight-forward) and service-sector companies (who have no inventory) expend considerable resources in designing and operating their costing systems. In this chapter, we take this more strategic focus and allocate costs in all functions of the value chain to the S3 and CL5 lenses.

Simple Costing System Using a Single Indirect-Cost Pool

Plastim has historically had a simple costing system that allocates indirect costs using a single indirect-cost rate, the type of system described in Chapter 4. We calculate budgeted costs for each type of lens in 2011 using Plastim's simple costing system and later contrast it with activity-based costing. (Note that instead of jobs, as in Chapter 4, we now have products as the cost objects.) Exhibit 5-1 shows an overview of Plastim's simple costing system. Use this exhibit as a guide as you study the following steps, each of which is marked in Exhibit 5-1.

Exhibit 5-1

Overview of Plastim's Simple Costing System

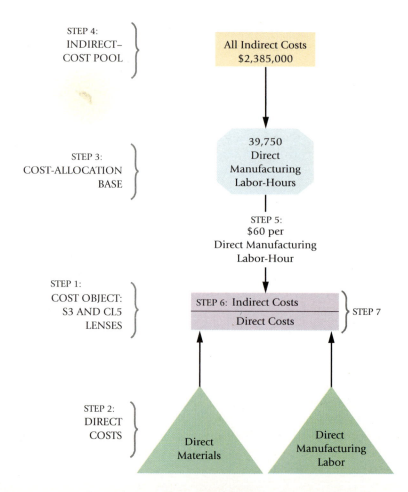

Step 1: Identify the Products That Are the Chosen Cost Objects. The cost objects are the 60,000 simple S3 lenses and the 15,000 complex CL5 lenses that Plastim will produce in 2011. Plastim's goal is to first calculate the total costs and then the unit cost of designing, manufacturing, and distributing these lenses.

Step 2: Identify the Direct Costs of the Products. Plastim identifies the direct costs—direct materials and direct manufacturing labor—of the lenses. Exhibit 5-2 shows the direct and indirect costs for the S3 and the CL5 lenses using the simple costing system. The direct cost calculations appear on lines 5, 6, and 7 of Exhibit 5-2. Plastim classifies all other costs as indirect costs.

Step 3: Select the Cost-Allocation Bases to Use for Allocating Indirect (or Overhead) Costs to the Products. A majority of the indirect costs consist of salaries paid to supervisors, engineers, manufacturing support, and maintenance staff, all supporting direct manufacturing labor. Plastim uses direct manufacturing labor-hours as the only allocation base to allocate all manufacturing and nonmanufacturing indirect costs to S3 and CL5. In 2011, Plastim plans to use 39,750 direct manufacturing labor-hours.

Step 4: Identify the Indirect Costs Associated with Each Cost-Allocation Base. Because Plastim uses only a single cost-allocation base, Plastim groups all budgeted indirect costs of $2,385,000 for 2011 into a single overhead cost pool.

Step 5: Compute the Rate per Unit of Each Cost-Allocation Base.

$$\text{Budgeted indirect-cost rate} = \frac{\text{Budgeted total costs in indirect-cost pool}}{\text{Budgeted total quantity of cost-allocation base}}$$

$$= \frac{\$2,385,000}{39,750 \text{ direct manufacturing labor-hours}}$$

$$= \$60 \text{ per direct manufacturing labor-hour}$$

Step 6: Compute the Indirect Costs Allocated to the Products. Plastim expects to use 30,000 total direct manufacturing labor-hours to make the 60,000 S3 lenses and 9,750 total direct manufacturing labor-hours to make the 15,000 CL5 lenses. Exhibit 5-2 shows indirect costs of $1,800,000 ($60 per direct manufacturing labor-hour × 30,000 direct manufacturing labor-hours) allocated to the simple lens and $585,000 ($60 per direct manufacturing labor-hour × 9,750 direct manufacturing labor-hours) allocated to the complex lens.

Step 7: Compute the Total Cost of the Products by Adding All Direct and Indirect Costs Assigned to the Products. Exhibit 5-2 presents the product costs for the simple and complex lenses. The direct costs are calculated in Step 2 and the indirect costs in Step 6. Be sure you see the parallel between the simple costing system overview diagram (Exhibit 5-1)

Exhibit 5-2 Plastim's Product Costs Using the Simple Costing System

	A	B	C	D	E	F	G
1		60,000			15,000		
2		Simple Lenses (S3)			Complex Lenses (CL5)		
3		Total	per Unit		Total	per Unit	Total
4		(1)	(2) = (1) ÷ 60,000		(3)	(4) = (3) ÷ 15,000	(5) = (1) + (3)
5	Direct materials	$1,125,000	$18.75		$ 675,000	$45.00	$1,800,000
6	Direct manufacturing labor	600,000	10.00		195,000	13.00	795,000
7	Total direct costs (Step 2)	1,725,000	28.75		870,000	58.00	2,595,000
8	Indirect costs allocated (Step 6)	1,800,000	30.00		585,000	39.00	2,385,000
9	Total costs (Step 7)	$3,525,000	$58.75		$1,455,000	$97.00	$4,980,000
10							

and the costs calculated in Step 7. Exhibit 5-1 shows two direct-cost categories and one indirect-cost category. Hence, the budgeted cost of each type of lens in Step 7 (Exhibit 5-2) has three line items: two for direct costs and one for allocated indirect costs. The budgeted cost per S3 lens is $58.75, well above the $53 selling price quoted by Bandix. The budgeted cost per CL5 lens is $97.

Applying the Five-Step Decision-Making Process at Plastim

To decide how it should respond to the threat that Bandix poses to its S3 lens business, Plastim's management works through the five-step decision-making process introduced in Chapter 1.

Step 1:   Identify the problem and uncertainties. The problem is clear: If Plastim wants to retain the Giovanni business for S3 lenses and make a profit, it must find a way to reduce the price and costs of the S3 lens. The two major uncertainties Plastim faces are (1) whether Plastim's technology and processes for the S3 lens are competitive with Bandix's and (2) whether the S3 lens is overcosted by the simple costing system.

Step 2:   Obtain information. Management asks a team of its design and process engineers to analyze and evaluate the design, manufacturing, and distribution operations for the S3 lens. The team is very confident that the technology and processes for the S3 lens are not inferior to those of Bandix and other competitors because Plastim has many years of experience in manufacturing and distributing the S3 with a history and culture of continuous process improvements. If anything, the team is less certain about Plastim's capabilities in manufacturing and distributing complex lenses, because it only recently started making this type of lens. Given these doubts, management is happy that Giovanni Motors considers the price of the CL5 lens to be competitive. It is somewhat of a puzzle, though, how at the currently budgeted prices, Plastim is expected to earn a very large profit margin percentage (operating income ÷ revenues) on the CL5 lenses and a small profit margin on the S3 lenses:

	60,000 Simple Lenses (S3) Total (1)	per Unit (2) = (1) ÷ 60,000	15,000 Complex Lenses (CL5) Total (3)	per Unit (4) = (3) ÷ 15,000	Total (5) = (1) + (3)
Revenues	$3,780,000	$63.00	$2,055,000	$137.00	$5,835,000
Total costs	3,525,000	58.75	1,455,000	97.00	4,980,000
Operating income	$ 255,000	$ 4.25	$ 600,000	$ 40.00	$ 855,000
Profit margin percentage		6.75%		29.20%	

As it continues to gather information, Plastim's management begins to ponder why the profit margins (and process) are under so much pressure for the S3 lens, where the company has strong capabilities, but high on the newer, less-established CL5 lens. Plastim is not deliberately charging a low price for S3, so management starts to believe that perhaps the problem lies with its costing system. Plastim's simple costing system may be overcosting the simple S3 lens (assigning too much cost to it) and undercosting the complex CL5 lens (assigning too little cost to it).

Step 3:   Make predictions about the future. Plastim's key challenge is to get a better estimate of what it will cost to design, make, and distribute the S3 and CL5 lenses. Management is fairly confident about the direct material and direct manufacturing labor costs of each lens because these costs are easily traced to the lenses. But management is quite concerned about how accurately the simple costing system measures the indirect resources used by each type of lens. It believes it can do much better.

At the same time, management wants to ensure that no biases enter its thinking. In particular, it wants to be careful that the desire to be competitive on the S3 lens should not lead to assumptions that bias in favor of lowering costs of the S3 lens.

Step 4: Make decisions by choosing among alternatives. On the basis of predicted costs, and taking into account how Bandix might respond, Plastim's managers must decide whether they should bid for Giovanni Motors' S3 lens business and if they do bid, what price they should offer.

Step 5: Implement the decision, evaluate performance, and learn. If Plastim bids and wins Giovanni's S3 lens business, it must compare actual costs, as it makes and ships S3 lenses, to predicted costs and learn why actual costs deviate from predicted costs. Such evaluation and learning form the basis for future improvements.

The next few sections focus on Steps 3, 4, and 5—how Plastim improves the allocation of indirect costs to the S3 and CL5 lenses, how it uses these predictions to bid for the S3 lens business, and how it makes product design and process improvements.

Refining a Costing System

A **refined costing system** reduces the use of broad averages for assigning the cost of resources to cost objects (such as jobs, products, and services) and provides better measurement of the costs of indirect resources used by different cost objects—no matter how differently various cost objects use indirect resources.

Reasons for Refining a Costing System

There are three principal reasons that have accelerated the demand for such refinements.

1. **Increase in product diversity.** The growing demand for customized products has led companies to increase the variety of products and services they offer. Kanthal, the Swedish manufacturer of heating elements, for example, produces more than 10,000 different types of electrical heating wires and thermostats. Banks, such as the Cooperative Bank in the United Kingdom, offer many different types of accounts and services: special passbook accounts, ATMs, credit cards, and electronic banking. These products differ in the demands they place on the resources needed to produce them, because of differences in volume, process, and complexity. The use of broad averages is likely to lead to distorted and inaccurate cost information.

2. **Increase in indirect costs.** The use of product and process technology such as computer-integrated manufacturing (CIM) and flexible manufacturing systems (FMS), has led to an increase in indirect costs and a decrease in direct costs, particularly direct manufacturing labor costs. In CIM and FMS, computers on the manufacturing floor give instructions to set up and run equipment quickly and automatically. The computers accurately measure hundreds of production parameters and directly control the manufacturing processes to achieve high-quality output. Managing more complex technology and producing very diverse products also requires committing an increasing amount of resources for various support functions, such as production scheduling, product and process design, and engineering. Because direct manufacturing labor is not a cost driver of these costs, allocating indirect costs on the basis of direct manufacturing labor (which was the common practice) does not accurately measure how resources are being used by different products.

3. **Competition in product markets.** As markets have become more competitive, managers have felt the need to obtain more accurate cost information to help them make important strategic decisions, such as how to price products and which products to sell. Making correct pricing and product mix decisions is critical in competitive markets because competitors quickly capitalize on a company's mistakes.

   Whereas the preceding factors point to reasons for the increase in *demand* for refined cost systems, *advances in information technology* have enabled companies to implement these refinements. Costing system refinements require more data gathering and more analysis, and improvements in information technology have drastically reduced the costs to gather, validate, store, and analyze vast quantities of data.

Learning Objective 2

Present three guidelines for refining a costing system

. . . classify more costs as direct costs, expand the number of indirect-cost pools, and identify cost drivers

Guidelines for Refining a Costing System

There are three main guidelines for refining a costing system. In the following sections, we delve more deeply into each in the context of the Plastim example.

1. **Direct-cost tracing.** Identify as many direct costs as is economically feasible. This guideline aims to reduce the amount of costs classified as indirect, thereby minimizing the extent to which costs have to be allocated, rather than traced.

2. **Indirect-cost pools.** Expand the number of indirect-cost pools until each pool is more homogeneous. All costs in a *homogeneous cost pool* have the same or a similar cause-and-effect (or benefits-received) relationship with a single cost driver that is used as the cost-allocation base. Consider, for example, a single indirect-cost pool containing both indirect machining costs and indirect distribution costs that are allocated to products using machine-hours. This pool is not homogeneous because machine-hours are a cost driver of machining costs but not of distribution costs, which has a different cost driver, number of shipments. If, instead, machining costs and distribution costs are separated into two indirect-cost pools (with machine-hours as the cost-allocation base for the machining cost pool and number of shipments as the cost-allocation base for the distribution cost pool), each indirect-cost pool would become homogeneous.

3. **Cost-allocation bases.** As we describe later in the chapter, whenever possible, use the cost driver (the cause of indirect costs) as the cost-allocation base for each homogenous indirect-cost pool (the effect).

Decision Point ▶

How do managers refine a costing system?

Learning Objective 3

Distinguish between simple and activity-based costing systems

. . . unlike simple systems, ABC systems calculate costs of individual activities to cost products

Activity-Based Costing Systems

One of the best tools for refining a costing system is activity-based costing. **Activity-based costing** (ABC) refines a costing system by identifying individual activities as the fundamental cost objects. An **activity** is an event, task, or unit of work with a specified purpose—for example, designing products, setting up machines, operating machines, and distributing products. More informally, activities are verbs; they are things that a firm does. To help make strategic decisions, ABC systems identify activities in all functions of the value chain, calculate costs of individual activities, and assign costs to cost objects such as products and services on the basis of the mix of activities needed to produce each product or service.[2]

Fundamental Cost Objects: Activities → Costs of Activities → **Assignment to Other Cost Objects**: Costs of • Products • Services • Customers

Plastim's ABC System

After reviewing its simple costing system and the potential miscosting of product costs, Plastim decides to implement an ABC system. Direct material costs and direct manufacturing labor costs can be traced to products easily, so the ABC system focuses on refining the assignment of indirect costs to departments, processes, products, or other cost objects. Plastim's ABC system identifies various activities that help explain why Plastim incurs the costs it currently classifies as indirect in its simple costing system. In other words, it breaks up the current indirect cost pool into finer pools of costs related to various activities. To identify these activities, Plastim organizes a team comprised of managers from design, manufacturing, distribution, accounting, and administration.

---

[2] For more details on ABC systems, see R. Cooper and R. S. Kaplan, *The Design of Cost Management Systems* (Upper Saddle River, NJ: Prentice Hall, 1999); G. Cokins, *Activity-Based Cost Management: An Executive's Guide* (Hoboken, NJ: John Wiley & Sons, 2001); and R. S. Kaplan and S. Anderson, *Time-Driven Activity-Based Costing: A Simpler and More Powerful Path to Higher Profits* (Boston: Harvard Business School Press, 2007).

Defining activities is not a simple matter. The team evaluates hundreds of tasks performed at Plastim before choosing the activities that form the basis of its ABC system. For example, it decides if maintenance of molding machines, operations of molding machines, and process control should each be regarded as a separate activity or should be combined into a single activity. An activity-based costing system with many activities becomes overly detailed and unwieldy to operate. An activity-based costing system with too few activities may not be refined enough to measure cause-and-effect relationships between cost drivers and various indirect costs. Plastim's team focuses on activities that account for a sizable fraction of indirect costs and combines activities that have the same cost driver into a single activity. For example, the team decides to combine maintenance of molding machines, operations of molding machines, and process control into a single activity—molding machine operations—because all these activities have the same cost driver: molding machine-hours.

The team identifies the following seven activities by developing a flowchart of all the steps and processes needed to design, manufacture, and distribute S3 and CL5 lenses.

a. Design products and processes

b. Set up molding machines to ensure that the molds are properly held in place and parts are properly aligned before manufacturing starts

c. Operate molding machines to manufacture lenses

d. Clean and maintain the molds after lenses are manufactured

e. Prepare batches of finished lenses for shipment

f. Distribute lenses to customers

g. Administer and manage all processes at Plastim

These activity descriptions form the basis of the activity-based costing system—sometimes called an *activity list* or *activity dictionary*. Compiling the list of tasks, however, is only the first step in implementing activity-based costing systems. Plastim must also identify the cost of each activity and the related cost driver. To do so, Plastim uses the three guidelines for refining a costing system described on page 146.

1. **Direct-cost tracing.** Plastim's ABC system subdivides the single indirect cost pool into seven smaller cost pools related to the different activities. The costs in the cleaning and maintenance activity cost pool (item d) consist of salaries and wages paid to workers who clean the mold. These costs are direct costs, because they can be economically traced to a specific mold and lens.

2. **Indirect-cost pools.** The remaining six activity cost pools are indirect cost pools. Unlike the single indirect cost pool of Plastim's simple costing system, each of the activity-related cost pools is homogeneous. That is, each activity cost pool includes only those narrow and focused set of costs that have the same cost driver. For example, the distribution cost pool includes only those costs (such as wages of truck drivers) that, over time, increase as the cost driver of distribution costs, cubic feet of packages delivered, increases. In the simple costing system, all indirect costs were lumped together and the cost-allocation base, direct manufacturing labor-hours, was not a cost driver of the indirect costs.

   Determining costs of activity pools requires assigning and reassigning costs accumulated in support departments, such as human resources and information systems, to each of the activity cost pools on the basis of how various activities use support department resources. This is commonly referred to as *first-stage allocation*, a topic which we discuss in detail in Chapters 14 and 15. We focus here on the *second-stage allocation*, the allocation of costs of activity cost pools to products.

3. **Cost-allocation bases.** For each activity cost pool, the cost driver is used (whenever possible) as the cost-allocation base. To identify cost drivers, Plastim's managers consider various alternatives and use their knowledge of operations to choose among them. For example, Plastim's managers choose setup-hours rather than the number of setups as the cost driver of setup costs, because Plastim's managers believe that more complex setups take more time and are more costly. Over time, Plastim's managers can use data to test their beliefs. (Chapter 10 discusses several methods to estimate the relationship between a cost driver and costs.)

The logic of ABC systems is twofold. First, structuring activity cost pools more finely with cost drivers for each activity cost pool as the cost-allocation base leads to more accurate costing of activities. Second, allocating these costs to products by measuring the cost-allocation bases of different activities used by different products leads to more accurate product costs. We illustrate this logic by focusing on the setup activity at Plastim.

Setting up molding machines frequently entails trial runs, fine-tuning, and adjustments. Improper setups cause quality problems such as scratches on the surface of the lens. The resources needed for each setup depend on the complexity of the manufacturing operation. Complex lenses require more setup resources (setup-hours) per setup than simple lenses. Furthermore, complex lenses can be produced only in small batches because the molds for complex lenses need to be cleaned more often than molds for simple lenses. Thus, relative to simple lenses, complex lenses not only use more setup-hours per setup, but they also require more frequent setups.

Setup data for the simple S3 lens and the complex CL5 lens are as follows:

		Simple S3 Lens	Complex CL5 Lens	Total
1	Quantity of lenses produced	60,000	15,000	
2	Number of lenses produced per batch	240	50	
3 = (1) ÷ (2)	Number of batches	250	300	
4	Setup time per batch	2 hours	5 hours	
5 = (3) × (4)	Total setup-hours	500 hours	1,500 hours	2,000 hours

Of the $2,385,000 in the total indirect-cost pool, Plastim identifies the total costs of setups (consisting mainly of depreciation on setup equipment and allocated costs of process engineers, quality engineers, and supervisors) to be $300,000. Recall that in its simple costing system, Plastim uses direct manufacturing labor-hours to allocate all indirect costs to products. The following table compares how setup costs allocated to simple and complex lenses will be different if Plastim allocates setup costs to lenses based on setup-hours rather than direct manufacturing labor-hours. Of the $60 total rate per direct manufacturing labor-hour (p. 143), the setup cost per direct manufacturing labor-hour amounts to $7.54717 ($300,000 ÷ 39,750 total direct manufacturing labor-hours). The setup cost per setup-hour equals $150 ($300,000 ÷ 2,000 total setup-hours).

	Simple S3 Lens	Complex CL5 Lens	Total
Setup cost allocated using direct manufacturing labor-hours:			
$7.54717 × 30,000; $7.54717 × 9,750	$226,415	$ 73,585	$300,000
Setup cost allocated using setup-hours:			
$150 × 500; $150 × 1,500	$ 75,000	$225,000	$300,000

As we have already discussed when presenting guidelines 2 and 3, setup-hours, not direct manufacturing labor-hours, are the cost driver of setup costs.. The CL5 lens uses substantially more setup-hours than the S3 lens (1,500 hours ÷ 2,000 hours = 75% of the total setup-hours) because the CL5 requires a greater number of setups (batches) and each setup is more challenging and requires more setup-hours.

The ABC system therefore allocates substantially more setup costs to CL5 than to S3. When direct manufacturing labor-hours rather than setup-hours are used to allocate setup costs in the simple costing system, it is the S3 lens that is allocated a very large share of the setup costs because the S3 lens uses a larger proportion of direct manufacturing labor-hours (30,000 ÷ 39,750 = 75.47%). As a result, the simple costing system overcosts the S3 lens with regard to setup costs.

Note that setup-hours are related to batches (or groups) of lenses made, not the number of individual lenses. Activity-based costing attempts to identify the most relevant cause-and-effect relationship for each activity pool, without restricting the cost driver to only units of output or variables related to units of output (such as direct manufacturing labor-hours). As our discussion of setups illustrates, limiting cost-allocation bases in this manner weakens the cause-and-effect relationship between the cost-allocation base and the costs in a cost pool.

Decision Point

What is the difference between the design of a simple costing system and an activity-based costing (ABC) system?

Cost Hierarchies

A **cost hierarchy** categorizes various activity cost pools on the basis of the different types of cost drivers, or cost-allocation bases, or different degrees of difficulty in determining cause-and-effect (or benefits-received) relationships. ABC systems commonly use a cost hierarchy with four levels—output unit-level costs, batch-level costs, product-sustaining costs, and facility-sustaining costs—to identify cost-allocation bases that are cost drivers of the activity cost pools.

Output unit-level costs are the costs of activities performed on each individual unit of a product or service. Machine operations costs (such as the cost of energy, machine depreciation, and repair) related to the activity of running the automated molding machines are output unit-level costs. They are output unit-level costs because, over time, the cost of this activity increases with additional units of output produced (or machine-hours used). Plastim's ABC system uses molding machine-hours—an output-unit level cost-allocation base—to allocate machine operations costs to products.

Batch-level costs are the costs of activities related to a group of units of a product or service rather than each individual unit of product or service. In the Plastim example, setup costs are batch-level costs because, over time, the cost of this setup activity increases with setup-hours needed to produce batches (groups) of lenses. As described in the table on page 148, the S3 lens requires 500 setup-hours (2 setup-hours per batch × 250 batches). The CL5 lens requires 1,500 setup-hours (5 setup-hours per batch × 300 batches). The total setup costs allocated to S3 and CL5 depend on the total setup-hours required by each type of lens, not on the number of units of S3 and CL5 produced. (Setup costs being a batch-level cost cannot be avoided by producing one less unit of S3 or CL5.) Plastim's ABC system uses setup-hours—a batch-level cost-allocation base—to allocate setup costs to products. Other examples of batch-level costs are material-handling and quality-inspection costs associated with batches (not the quantities) of products produced, and costs of placing purchase orders, receiving materials, and paying invoices related to the number of purchase orders placed rather than the quantity or value of materials purchased.

Product-sustaining costs (**service-sustaining costs**) are the costs of activities undertaken to support individual products or services regardless of the number of units or batches in which the units are produced. In the Plastim example, design costs are product-sustaining costs. Over time, design costs depend largely on the time designers spend on designing and modifying the product, the mold, and the process. These design costs are a function of the complexity of the mold, measured by the number of parts in the mold multiplied by the area (in square feet) over which the molten plastic must flow (12 parts × 2.5 square feet, or 30 parts-square feet for the S3 lens, and 14 parts × 5 square feet, or 70 parts-square feet for the CL5 lens). As a result, the total design costs allocated to S3 and CL5 depend on the complexity of the mold, regardless of the number of units or batches of production. Design costs cannot be avoided by producing fewer units or running fewer batches. Plastim's ABC system uses parts-square feet—a product-sustaining cost-allocation base—to allocate design costs to products. Other examples of product-sustaining costs are product research and development costs, costs of making engineering changes, and marketing costs to launch new products.

Facility-sustaining costs are the costs of activities that cannot be traced to individual products or services but that support the organization as a whole. In the Plastim example, the general administration costs (including top management compensation, rent, and building security) are facility-sustaining costs. It is usually difficult to find a good cause-and-effect relationship between these costs and the cost-allocation base. This lack of a cause-and-effect relationship causes some companies not to allocate these costs to products and instead to deduct them as a separate lump-sum amount from operating income. Other companies, such as Plastim, allocate facility-sustaining costs to products on some basis—for example, direct manufacturing labor-hours—because management believes all costs should be allocated to products. Allocating all costs to products or services becomes important when management wants to set selling prices on the basis of an amount of cost that includes all costs.

Learning Objective 4

Describe a four-part cost hierarchy

. . . a four-part cost hierarchy is used to categorize costs based on different types of cost drivers—for example, costs that vary with each unit of a product versus costs that vary with each batch of products

◄ **Decision Point**

What is a cost hierarchy?

Implementing Activity-Based Costing

Now that you understand the basic concepts of ABC, let's use it to refine Plastim's simple costing system, compare it to alternative costing systems, and examine what managers look for when deciding whether or not to develop ABC systems.

Implementing ABC at Plastim

In order to apply ABC to Plastim's costing system, we follow the seven-step approach to costing and the three guidelines for refining costing systems (increasing direct-cost tracing, creating homogeneous indirect-cost pools, and identifying cost-allocation bases that have cause-and-effect relationships with costs in the cost pool). Exhibit 5-3 shows an overview of Plastim's ABC system. Use this exhibit as a guide as you study the following steps, each of which is marked in Exhibit 5-3.

Step 1: Identify the Products That Are the Chosen Cost Objects. The cost objects are the 60,000 S3 and the 15,000 CL5 lenses that Plastim will produce in 2011. Plastim's goal is to first calculate the total costs and then the per-unit cost of designing, manufacturing, and distributing these lenses.

Step 2: Identify the Direct Costs of the Products. Plastim identifies as direct costs of the lenses: direct material costs, direct manufacturing labor costs, and mold cleaning and maintenance costs because these costs can be economically traced to a specific lens or mold.

Exhibit 5-5 shows the direct and indirect costs for the S3 and CL5 lenses using the ABC system. The direct costs calculations appear on lines 6, 7, 8, and 9 of Exhibit 5-5. Plastim classifies all other costs as indirect costs, as we will see in Exhibit 5-4.

Step 3: Select the Activities and Cost-Allocation Bases to Use for Allocating Indirect Costs to the Products. Following guidelines 2 and 3 for refining a costing system, Plastim identifies six activities—(a) design, (b) molding machine setups, (c) machine operations, (d) shipment setup, (e) distribution, and (f) administration—for allocating indirect costs to products. Exhibit 5-4, column 2, shows the cost hierarchy category, and column 4

Exhibit 5-3 Overview of Plastim's Activity-Based Costing System

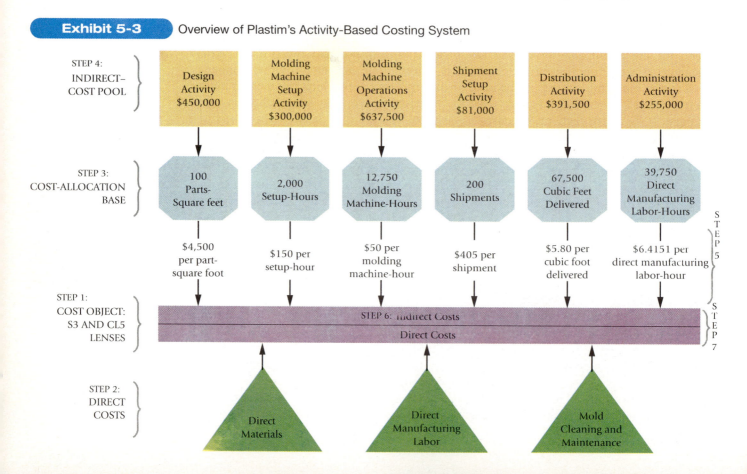

Exhibit 5-4   Activity-Cost Rates for Indirect-Cost Pools

	Home	Insert	Page Layout	Formulas	Data	Review	View	
	A	B	C	D	E	F	G	H
1			(Step 4)	(Step 3)		(Step 5)		
2	**Activity**	**Cost Hierarchy Category**	**Total Budgeted Indirect Costs**	**Budgeted Quantity of Cost-Allocation Base**		**Budgeted Indirect Cost Rate**		**Cause-and-Effect Relationship Between Allocation Base and Activity Cost**
3	(1)	(2)	(3)	(4)		(5) = (3) ÷ (4)		(6)
4	Design	Product-sustaining	$450,000	100	parts-square feet	$ 4,500	per part-square foot	Design Department indirect costs increase with more complex molds (more parts, larger surface area).
5	Setup molding machines	Batch-level	$300,000	2,000	setup-hours	$ 150	per setup-hour	Indirect setup costs increase with setup-hours.
6	Machine operations	Output unit-level	$637,500	12,750	molding machine-hours	$ 50	per molding machine-hour	Indirect costs of operating molding machines increases with molding machine-hours.
7	Shipment setup	Batch-level	$ 81,000	200	shipments	$ 405	per shipment	Shipping costs incurred to prepare batches for shipment increase with the number of shipments.
8	Distribution	Output-unit-level	$391,500	67,500	cubic feet delivered	$ 5.80	per cubic foot delivered	Distribution costs increase with the cubic feet of packages delivered.
9	Administration	Facility sustaining	$255,000	39,750	direct manuf. labor-hours	$6.4151	per direct manuf. labor-hour	The demand for administrative resources increases with direct manufacturing labor-hours.

shows the cost-allocation base and the budgeted quantity of the cost-allocation base for each activity described in column 1.

Identifying the cost-allocation bases defines the number of activity pools into which costs must be grouped in an ABC system. For example, rather than define the design activities of product design, process design, and prototyping as separate activities, Plastim defines these three activities together as a combined "design" activity and forms a homogeneous design cost pool. Why? Because the same cost driver, the complexity of the mold, drives costs of each design activity. A second consideration for choosing a cost-allocation base is the availability of reliable data and measures. For example, in its ABC system, Plastim measures mold complexity in terms of the number of parts in the mold and the surface area of the mold (parts-square feet). If these data are difficult to obtain or measure, Plastim may be forced to use some other measure of complexity, such as the amount of material flowing through the mold that may only be weakly related to the cost of the design activity.

Step 4: Identify the Indirect Costs Associated with Each Cost-Allocation Base. In this step, Plastim assigns budgeted indirect costs for 2011 to activities (see Exhibit 5-4, column 3), to the extent possible, on the basis of a cause-and-effect relationship between the cost-allocation base for an activity and the cost. For example, all costs that have a cause-and-effect relationship to cubic feet of packages moved are assigned to the distribution cost pool. Of course, the strength of the cause-and-effect relationship between the cost-allocation base and the cost of an activity varies across cost pools. For example, the cause-and-effect relationship between direct manufacturing labor-hours and administration activity costs is not as strong as the relationship between setup-hours and setup activity costs.

Some costs can be directly identified with a particular activity. For example, cost of materials used when designing products, salaries paid to design engineers, and depreciation of equipment used in the design department are directly identified with the design activity. Other costs need to be allocated across activities. For example, on the basis of interviews or time records, manufacturing engineers and supervisors estimate the time they will spend on design, molding machine setup, and machine operations. The time to be spent on these activities serves as a basis for allocating each manufacturing engineer's and supervisor's salary

Exhibit 5-5	Plastim's Product Costs Using Activity-Based Costing System

A	B	C	D	E	F	G
		60,000			15,000	
		Simple Lenses (S3)			Complex Lenses (CL5)	
	Total	per Unit		Total	per Unit	Total
4 Cost Description	(1)	(2) = (1) ÷ 60,000		(3)	(4) = (3) ÷ 15,000	(5) = (1) + (3)
5 Direct costs						
6 Direct materials	$1,125,000	$18.75		$ 675,000	$ 45.00	$1,800,000
7 Direct manufacturing labor	600,000	10.00		195,000	13.00	795,000
8 Direct mold cleaning and maintenance costs	120,000	2.00		150,000	10.00	270,000
9 Total direct costs (Step 2)	1,845,000	30.75		1,020,000	68.00	2,865,000
10 Indirect Costs of Activities						
11 Design						
12 S3, 30 parts-sq.ft. × $4,500	135,000	2.25				} 450,000
13 CL5, 70 parts-sq.ft. × $4,500				315,000	21.00	
14 Setup of molding machines						
15 S3, 500 setup-hours × $150	75,000	1.25				} 300,000
16 CL5, 1,500 setup-hours × $150				225,000	15.00	
17 Machine operations						
18 S3, 9,000 molding machine-hours × $50	450,000	7.50				} 637,500
19 CL5, 3,750 molding machine-hours × $50				187,500	12.50	
20 Shipment setup						
21 S3, 100 shipments × $405	40,500	0.67				} 81,000
22 CL5, 100 shipments × $405				40,500	2.70	
23 Distribution						
24 S3, 45,000 cubic feet delivered × $5.80	261,000	4.35				} 391,500
25 CL5, 22,500 cubic feet delivered × $5.80				130,500	8.70	
26 Administration						
27 S3, 30,000 dir. manuf. labor-hours × $6.4151	192,453	3.21				} 255,000
28 CL5, 9,750 dir. manuf. labor-hours × $6.4151				62,547	4.17	
29 Total indirect costs allocated (Step 6)	1,153,953	19.23		961,047	64.07	2,115,000
30 Total Costs (Step 7)	$2,998,953	$49.98		$1,981,047	$132.07	$4,980,000
31						

costs to various activities. Still other costs are allocated to activity-cost pools using allocation bases that measure how these costs support different activities. For example, rent costs are allocated to activity cost pools on the basis of square-feet area used by different activities.

The point here is that all costs do not fit neatly into activity categories. Often, costs may first need to be allocated to activities (Stage 1 of the 2-stage cost-allocation model) before the costs of the activities can be allocated to products (Stage 2).

Step 5: Compute the Rate per Unit of Each Cost-Allocation Base. Exhibit 5-4, column 5, summarizes the calculation of the budgeted indirect cost rates using the budgeted quantity of the cost-allocation base from Step 3 and the total budgeted indirect costs of each activity from Step 4.

Step 6: Compute the Indirect Costs Allocated to the Products. Exhibit 5-5 shows total budgeted indirect costs of $1,153,953 allocated to the simple lens and $961,047 allocated to the complex lens. Follow the budgeted indirect cost calculations for each lens in Exhibit 5-5. For each activity, Plastim's operations personnel indicate the total quantity of the cost-allocation base that will be used by each type of lens (recall that Plastim operates at capacity). For example, lines 15 and 16 of Exhibit 5-5 show that of the 2,000 total setup-hours, the S3 lens is budgeted to use 500 hours and the CL5 lens 1,500 hours. The budgeted indirect cost rate is $150 per setup-hour (Exhibit 5-4, column 5, line 5). Therefore, the total budgeted cost of the setup activity allocated to the S3 lens is $75,000 (500 setup-hours × $150 per setup-hour) and to the CL5 lens is $225,000 (1,500 setup-hours × $150 per setup-hour). Budgeted setup cost per unit equals $1.25 ($75,000 ÷ 60,000 units) for the S3 lens and $15 ($225,000 ÷ 15,000 units) for the CL5 lens.

Step 7: Compute the Total Cost of the Products by Adding All Direct and Indirect Costs Assigned to the Products. Exhibit 5-5 presents the product costs for the simple and complex lenses. The direct costs are calculated in Step 2, and the indirect costs are calculated in Step 6. The ABC system overview in Exhibit 5-3 shows three direct-cost categories and six indirect-cost categories. The budgeted cost of each lens type in Exhibit 5-5 has nine line items, three for direct costs and six for indirect costs. The differences between the ABC product costs of S3 and CL5 calculated in Exhibit 5-5 highlight how each of these products uses different amounts of direct and indirect costs in each activity area.

We emphasize two features of ABC systems. First, these systems identify all costs used by products, whether the costs are variable or fixed in the short run. When making long-run strategic decisions using ABC information, managers want revenues to exceed total costs. Second, recognizing the hierarchy of costs is critical when allocating costs to products. It is easiest to use the cost hierarchy to first calculate the total costs of each product. The per-unit costs can then be derived by dividing total costs by the number of units produced.

> **◄ Decision Point**
>
> How do managers cost products or services using ABC systems?

Comparing Alternative Costing Systems

Exhibit 5-6 compares the simple costing system using a single indirect-cost pool (Exhibit 5-1 and Exhibit 5-2) Plastim had been using and the ABC system (Exhibit 5-3 and Exhibit 5-5). Note three points in Exhibit 5-6, consistent with the guidelines for

> **Exhibit 5-6**
>
> Comparing Alternative Costing Systems

	Simple Costing System Using a Single Indirect-Cost Pool (1)	ABC System (2)	Difference (3) = (2) − (1)
Direct-cost categories	2	3	1
	Direct materials Direct manufacturing labor	Direct materials Direct manufacturing labor Direct mold cleaning and maintenance labor	
Total direct costs	$2,595,000	$2,865,000	$270,000
Indirect-cost pools	1	6	5
	Single indirect-cost pool allocated using direct manufacturing labor-hours	Design (parts-square feet)[1] Molding machine setup (setup-hours) Machine operations (molding machine-hours) Shipment setup (number of shipments) Distribution (cubic feet delivered) Administration (direct manufacturing labor-hours)	
Total indirect costs	$2,385,000	$2,115,000	($270,000)
Total costs assigned to simple (S3) lens	$3,525,000	$2,998,953	($526,047)
Cost per unit of simple (S3) lens	$58.75	$49.98	($8.77)
Total costs assigned to complex (CL5) lens	$1,455,000	$1,981,047	$526,047
Cost per unit of complex (CL5) lens	$97.00	$132.07	$35.07

[1]Cost drivers for the various indirect-cost pools are shown in parentheses.

refining a costing system: (1) ABC systems trace more costs as direct costs; (2) ABC systems create homogeneous cost pools linked to different activities; and (3) for each activity-cost pool, ABC systems seek a cost-allocation base that has a cause-and-effect relationship with costs in the cost pool.

The homogeneous cost pools and the choice of cost-allocation bases, tied to the cost hierarchy, give Plastim's managers greater confidence in the activity and product cost numbers from the ABC system. The bottom part of Exhibit 5-6 shows that allocating costs to lenses using only an output unit-level allocation base—direct manufacturing labor-hours, as in the single indirect-cost pool system used prior to ABC—overcosts the simple S3 lens by $8.77 per unit and undercosts the complex CL5 lens by $35.07 per unit. The CL5 lens uses a disproportionately larger amount of output unit-level, batch-level, and product-sustaining costs than is represented by the direct manufacturing labor-hour cost-allocation base. The S3 lens uses a disproportionately smaller amount of these costs.

The benefit of an ABC system is that it provides information to make better decisions. But this benefit must be weighed against the measurement and implementation costs of an ABC system.

Considerations in Implementing Activity-Based-Costing Systems

Learning Objective 6

Evaluate the costs and benefits of implementing activity-based costing systems

. . . measurement difficulties versus more accurate costs that aid in decision making

Managers choose the level of detail to use in a costing system by evaluating the expected costs of the system against the expected benefits that result from better decisions. There are telltale signs of when an ABC system is likely to provide the most benefits. Here are some of these signs:

- Significant amounts of indirect costs are allocated using only one or two cost pools.
- All or most indirect costs are identified as output unit-level costs (few indirect costs are described as batch-level costs, product-sustaining costs, or facility-sustaining costs).
- Products make diverse demands on resources because of differences in volume, process steps, batch size, or complexity.
- Products that a company is well-suited to make and sell show small profits; whereas products that a company is less suited to produce and sell show large profits.
- Operations staff has substantial disagreement with the reported costs of manufacturing and marketing products and services.

When a company decides to implement ABC, it must make important choices about the level of detail to use. Should it choose many finely specified activities, cost drivers, and cost pools, or would a few suffice? For example, Plastim could identify a different molding machine-hour rate for each different type of molding machine. In making such choices, managers weigh the benefits against the costs and limitations of implementing a more detailed costing system.

The main costs and limitations of an ABC system are the measurements necessary to implement it. ABC systems require management to estimate costs of activity pools and to identify and measure cost drivers for these pools to serve as cost-allocation bases. Even basic ABC systems require many calculations to determine costs of products and services. These measurements are costly. Activity cost rates also need to be updated regularly.

As ABC systems get very detailed and more cost pools are created, more allocations are necessary to calculate activity costs for each cost pool. This increases the chances of misidentifying the costs of different activity cost pools. For example, supervisors are more prone to incorrectly identify the time they spent on different activities if they have to allocate their time over five activities rather than only two activities.

At times, companies are also forced to use allocation bases for which data are readily available rather than allocation bases they would have liked to use. For example, a company might be forced to use the number of loads moved, instead of the degree of difficulty and distance of different loads moved, as the allocation base for

Concepts in Action   Successfully Championing ABC

Successfully implementing ABC systems requires more than an understanding of the technical details. ABC implementation often represents a significant change in the costing system and, as the chapter indicates, it requires a manager to make major choices with respect to the definition of activities and the level of detail. What then are some of the behavioral issues that the management accountant must be sensitive to?

1. **Gaining support of top management and creating a sense of urgency for the ABC effort.** This requires management accountants to lay out the vision for the ABC project and to clearly communicate its strategic benefits (for example, the resulting improvements in product and process design). It also requires selling the idea to end users and working with members of other departments as business partners of the managers in the various areas affected by the ABC project. For example, at USAA Federal Savings Bank, project managers demonstrated how the information gained from ABC would provide insights into the efficiency of bank operations, which was previously unavailable. Now the finance area communicates regularly with operations about new reports and proposed changes to the financial reporting package that managers receive.

2. **Creating a guiding coalition of managers throughout the value chain for the ABC effort.** ABC systems measure how the resources of an organization are used. Managers responsible for these resources have the best knowledge about activities and cost drivers. Getting managers to cooperate and take the initiative for implementing ABC is essential for gaining the required expertise, the proper credibility, and the necessary leadership.

   Gaining wider participation among managers has other benefits. Managers who feel more involved in the process are likely to commit more time to and be less skeptical of the ABC effort. Engaging managers throughout the value chain also creates greater opportunities for coordination and cooperation across the different functions, for example, design and manufacturing.

3. **Educating and training employees in ABC as a basis for employee empowerment.** Disseminating information about ABC throughout an organization allows workers in all areas of a business to use their knowledge of ABC to make improvements. For example, WS Industries, an Indian manufacturer of insulators, not only shared ABC information with its workers but also established an incentive plan that gave employees a percentage of the cost savings. The results were dramatic because employees were empowered and motivated to implement numerous cost-saving projects.

4. **Seeking small short-run successes as proof that the ABC implementation is yielding results.** Too often, managers and management accountants seek big results and major changes far too quickly. In many situations, achieving a significant change overnight is difficult. However, showing how ABC information has helped improve a process and save costs, even if only in small ways, motivates the team to stay on course and build momentum. The credibility gained from small victories leads to additional and bigger improvements involving larger numbers of people and different parts of the organization. Eventually ABC and ABM become rooted in the culture of the organization. Sharing short-term successes may also help motivate employees to be innovative. At USAA Federal Savings Bank, managers created a "process improvement" mailbox in Microsoft Outlook to facilitate the sharing of process improvement ideas.

5. **Recognizing that ABC information is not perfect because it balances the need for better information against the costs of creating a complex system that few managers and employees can understand.** The management accountant must help managers recognize both the value and the limitations of ABC and not oversell it. Open and honest communication about ABC ensures that managers use ABC thoughtfully to make good decisions. Critical judgments can then be made without being adversarial, and tough questions can be asked to help drive better decisions about the system.

material-handling costs, because data on degree of difficulty and distance of moves are difficult to obtain. When erroneous cost-allocation bases are used, activity-cost information can be misleading. For example, if the cost per load moved decreases, a company may conclude that it has become more efficient in its materials-handling operations. In fact, the lower cost per load move may have resulted solely from moving many lighter loads over shorter distances.

Many companies, such as Kanthal, the Swedish manufacturer of heating elements, have found the strategic and operational benefits of a less-detailed ABC system to be good enough to not warrant incurring the costs and challenges of operating a more-detailed system. Other organizations, such as Hewlett-Packard, implement ABC in chosen divisions or functions. As improvements in information technology and accompanying declines in measurement costs continue, more-detailed ABC systems have become a practical alternative in many companies. As such trends persist, more detailed ABC systems will be better able to pass the cost–benefit test.

Global surveys of company practice suggest that ABC implementation varies among companies. Nevertheless, its framework and ideas provide a standard for judging whether any simple costing system is good enough for a particular management's purposes. Any contemplated changes in a simple costing system will inevitably be improved by ABC thinking. The Concepts in Action box on page 155 describes some of the behavioral issues that management accountants must be sensitive to as they seek to immerse an organization in ABC thinking.

Decision Point ▶

What should managers consider when deciding to implement ABC systems?

Learning Objective 7

Explain how activity-based costing systems are used in activity-based management

. . . such as pricing decisions, product-mix decisions, and cost reduction

Using ABC Systems for Improving Cost Management and Profitability

The emphasis of this chapter so far has been on the role of ABC systems in obtaining better product costs. However, Plastim's managers must now use this information to make decisions (Step 4 of the 5-step decision process, p. 145) and to implement the decision, evaluate performance, and learn (Step 5, p. 145). **Activity-based management (ABM)** is a method of management decision making that uses activity-based costing information to improve customer satisfaction and profitability. We define ABM broadly to include decisions about pricing and product mix, cost reduction, process improvement, and product and process design.

Pricing and Product-Mix Decisions

An ABC system gives managers information about the costs of making and selling diverse products. With this information, managers can make pricing and product-mix decisions. For example, the ABC system indicates that Plastim can match its competitor's price of $53 for the S3 lens and still make a profit because the ABC cost of S3 is $49.98 (see Exhibit 5-5).

Plastim's managers offer Giovanni Motors a price of $52 for the S3 lens. Plastim's managers are confident that they can use the deeper understanding of costs that the ABC system provides to improve efficiency and further reduce the cost of the S3 lens. Without information from the ABC system, Plastim managers might have erroneously concluded that they would incur an operating loss on the S3 lens at a price of $53. This incorrect conclusion would have probably caused Plastim to reduce its business in simple lenses and focus instead on complex lenses, where its single indirect-cost-pool system indicated it is very profitable.

Focusing on complex lenses would have been a mistake. The ABC system indicates that the cost of making the complex lens is much higher—$132.07 versus $97 indicated by the direct manufacturing labor-hour-based costing system Plastim had been using. As Plastim's operations staff had thought all along, Plastim has no competitive advantage in making CL5 lenses. At a price of $137 per lens for CL5, the profit margin is very small ($137.00 – $132.07 = $4.93). As Plastim reduces its prices on simple lenses, it would need to negotiate a higher price for complex lenses with Giovanni Motors.

Cost Reduction and Process Improvement Decisions

Manufacturing and distribution personnel use ABC systems to focus on how and where to reduce costs. Managers set cost reduction targets in terms of reducing the cost per unit of the cost-allocation base in different activity areas. For example, the supervisor of the distribution activity area at Plastim could have a performance target of decreasing distribution cost per cubic foot of products delivered from $5.80 to $5.40 by reducing distribution labor and warehouse rental costs. The goal is to reduce these costs by improving the way work is done without compromising customer service or the actual or perceived value (usefulness) customers obtain from the product or service. That is, Plastim will attempt to take out only those costs that are *nonvalue added*. Controlling physical cost drivers, such as setup-hours or cubic feet delivered, is another fundamental way that operating personnel manage costs. For example, Plastim can decrease distribution costs by packing the lenses in a way that reduces the bulkiness of the packages delivered.

The following table shows the reduction in distribution costs of the S3 and CL5 lenses as a result of actions that lower cost per cubic foot delivered (from $5.80 to $5.40) and total cubic feet of deliveries (from 45,000 to 40,000 for S3 and 22,500 to 20,000 for CL5).

	60,000 (S3) Lenses		15,000 (CL5) Lenses	
	Total (1)	per Unit (2) = (1) ÷ 60,000	Total (3)	per Unit (4) = (3) ÷ 15,000
Distribution costs (from Exhibit 5-5)				
S3, 45,000 cubic feet × $5.80/cubic foot	$261,000	$4.35		
CL5, 22,500 cubic feet × $5.80/cubic foot			$130,500	$8.70
Distribution costs as a result of process improvements				
S3, 40,000 cubic feet × $5.40/cubic foot	216,000	3.60		
CL5, 20,000 cubic feet × $5.40/cubic foot			108,000	7.20
Savings in distribution costs from process improvements	$ 45,000	$0.75	$ 22,500	$1.50

In the long run, total distribution costs will decrease from $391,500 ($261,000 + $130,500) to $324,000 ($216,000 + $108,000). In the short run, however, distribution costs may be fixed and may not decrease. Suppose all $391,500 of distribution costs are fixed costs in the short run. The efficiency improvements (using less distribution labor and space) mean that the same $391,500 of distribution costs can now be used to distribute $72,500 \left(\dfrac{\$391,500}{\$5.40 \text{ per cubic foot}} \right)$ cubic feet of lenses. In this case, how should costs be allocated to the S3 and CL5 lenses?

ABC systems distinguish *costs incurred* from *resources used* to design, manufacture, and deliver products and services. For the distribution activity, after process improvements,

Costs incurred = $391,500

Resources used = $216,000 (for S3 lens) + $108,000 (for CL5 lens) = $324,000

On the basis of the resources used by each product, Plastim's ABC system allocates $216,000 to S3 and $108,000 to CL5 for a total of $324,000. The difference of $67,500 ($391,500 − $324,000) is shown as costs of unused but available distribution capacity. Plastim's ABC system does not allocate the costs of unused capacity to products so as not to burden the product costs of S3 and CL5 with the cost of resources not used by these products. Instead, the system highlights the amount of unused capacity as a separate line item to signal to managers the need to reduce these costs, such as by redeploying labor to other uses or laying off workers. Chapter 9 discusses issues related to unused capacity in more detail.

Design Decisions

Management can evaluate how its current product and process designs affect activities and costs as a way of identifying new designs to reduce costs. For example, design decisions that decrease complexity of the mold reduce costs of design, materials, labor, machine setups, machine operations, and mold cleaning and maintenance. Plastim's customers may be willing to give up some features of the lens in exchange for a lower price. Note that Plastim's previous costing system, which used direct manufacturing labor-hours as the cost-allocation base for all indirect costs, would have mistakenly signaled that Plastim choose those designs that most reduce direct manufacturing labor-hours when, in fact, there is a weak cause-and-effect relationship between direct manufacturing labor-hours and indirect costs.

Planning and Managing Activities

Many companies implementing ABC systems for the first time analyze actual costs to identify activity-cost pools and activity-cost rates. To be useful for planning, making decisions, and managing activities, companies calculate a budgeted cost rate for each activity and use these budgeted cost rates to cost products as we saw in the Plastim example. At year-end, budgeted costs and actual costs are compared to provide feedback on how well activities were managed and to make adjustments for underallocated or overallocated indirect costs for each activity using methods described in Chapter 4. As activities and processes are changed, new activity-cost rates are calculated.

We will return to activity-based management in later chapters. Management decisions that use activity-based costing information are described in Chapter 6, in which we discuss activity-based budgeting; Chapter 11, in which we discuss outsourcing and adding or dropping business segments; in Chapter 12, in which we evaluate alternative design choices to improve efficiency and reduce nonvalue-added costs; in Chapter 13, in which we cover reengineering and downsizing; in Chapter 14, in which we explore managing customer profitability; in Chapter 19, in which we explain quality improvements; and in Chapter 20, in which we describe how to evaluate suppliers.

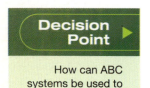

Decision Point

How can ABC systems be used to manage better?

Activity-Based Costing and Department Costing Systems

Companies often use costing systems that have features of ABC systems—such as multiple cost pools and multiple cost-allocation bases—but that do not emphasize individual activities. Many companies have evolved their costing systems from using a single indirect cost rate system to using separate indirect cost rates for each department (such as design, manufacturing, distribution, and so on) or each subdepartment (such as machining and assembly departments within manufacturing) that can be thought of as representing broad tasks. ABC systems, with its focus on specific activities, are a further refinement of department costing systems. In this section, we compare ABC systems and department costing systems.

Plastim uses the design department indirect cost rate to cost its design activity. Plastim calculates the design activity rate by dividing total design department costs by total parts-square feet, a measure of the complexity of the mold and the driver of design department costs. Plastim does not find it worthwhile to calculate separate activity rates within the design department for the different design activities, such as designing products, making temporary molds, and designing processes. Why? Because complexity of a mold is an appropriate cost-allocation base for costs incurred in each design activity. Design department costs are homogeneous with respect to this cost-allocation base.

In contrast, the manufacturing department identifies two activity cost pools—a setup cost pool and a machine operations cost pool—instead of a single manufacturing department overhead cost pool. It identifies these activity cost pools for two reasons. First, each of these activities within manufacturing incurs significant costs and has a different cost driver, setup-hours for the setup cost pool and machine-hours for the machine operations cost pool. Second, the S3 and CL5 lenses do not use resources from these two activity areas in the same proportion. For example, CL5 uses 75% (1,500 ÷ 2,000) of the setup-hours but only 29.4% (3,750 ÷ 12,750) of the machine-hours. Using only machine-hours, say, to allocate all manufacturing department costs at Plastim would result in CL5 being undercosted because it would not be charged for the significant amounts of setup resources it actually uses.

Based on what we just explained, using department indirect cost rates to allocate costs to products results in similar information as activity cost rates if (1) a single activity accounts for a sizable proportion of the department's costs; or (2) significant costs are incurred on different activities within a department, but each activity has the same cost driver and hence cost-allocation base (as was the case in Plastim's design department). From a purely product costing standpoint, department and activity indirect cost rates

Learning Objective 8

Compare activity-based costing systems and department costing systems

. . . activity-based costing systems are a refinement of department costing systems into more-focused and homogenous cost pools

will also result in the same product costs if (1) significant costs are incurred for different activities with different cost-allocation bases within a department but (2) different products use resources from the different activity areas in the same proportions (for example, if CL5 had used 65%, say, of the setup-hours and 65% of the machine-hours). In this case, though, not identifying activities and cost drivers within departments conceals activity cost information that would be valuable for cost management and design and process improvements.

We close this section with a note of caution. Do not assume that because department costing systems require the creation of multiple indirect cost pools that they properly recognize the drivers of costs within departments as well as how resources are used by products. As we have indicated, in many situations, department costing systems can be refined using ABC. Emphasizing activities leads to more-focused and homogeneous cost pools, aids in identifying cost-allocation bases for activities that have a better cause-and-effect relationship with the costs in activity cost pools, and leads to better design and process decisions. But these benefits of an ABC system would need to be balanced against its costs and limitations.

> **Decision Point**
>
> When can department costing systems be used instead of ABC systems?

ABC in Service and Merchandising Companies

Although many of the early examples of ABC originated in manufacturing, ABC has many applications in service and merchandising companies. In addition to manufacturing activities, the Plastim example includes the application of ABC to a service activity—design—and to a merchandising activity—distribution. Companies such as the Cooperative Bank, Braintree Hospital, BCTel in the telecommunications industry, and Union Pacific in the railroad industry have implemented some form of ABC system to identify profitable product mixes, improve efficiency, and satisfy customers. Similarly, many retail and wholesale companies—for example, Supervalu, a retailer and distributor of grocery store products, and Owens and Minor, a medical supplies distributor—have used ABC systems. Finally, as we describe in Chapter 14, a large number of financial services companies (as well as other companies) employ variations of ABC systems to analyze and improve the profitability of their customer interactions.

The widespread use of ABC systems in service and merchandising companies reinforces the idea that ABC systems are used by managers for strategic decisions rather than for inventory valuation. (Inventory valuation is fairly straightforward in merchandising companies and not needed in service companies.) Service companies, in particular, find great value from ABC because a vast majority of their cost structure comprises indirect costs. After all, there are few direct costs when a bank makes a loan, or when a representative answers a phone call at a call center. As we have seen, a major benefit of ABC is its ability to assign indirect costs to cost objects by identifying activities and cost drivers. As a result, ABC systems provide greater insight than traditional systems into the management of these indirect costs. The general approach to ABC in service and merchandising companies is similar to the ABC approach in manufacturing.

The Cooperative Bank followed the approach described in this chapter when it implemented ABC in its retail banking operations. It calculated the costs of various activities, such as performing ATM transactions, opening and closing accounts, administering mortgages, and processing Visa transactions. It then used the activity cost rates to calculate costs of various products, such as checking accounts, mortgages, and Visa cards and the costs of supporting different customers. ABC information helped the Cooperative Bank to improve its processes and to identify profitable products and customer segments. The Concepts in Action feature on page 160 describes how Charles Schwab has similarly benefited from using ABC analysis.

Activity-based costing raises some interesting issues when it is applied to a public service institution such as the U.S. Postal Service. The costs of delivering mail to remote locations are far greater than the costs of delivering mail within urban areas. However, for fairness and community-building reasons, the Postal Service cannot charge higher prices to customers in remote areas. In this case, activity-based costing is valuable for understanding, managing, and reducing costs but not for pricing decisions.

Concepts in Action — Time-Driven Activity-Based Costing at Charles Schwab

Time-driven activity-based costing ("TDABC") helps Charles Schwab, the leading stock brokerage, with strategic-analysis, measurement, and management of its stock trading activity across multiple channels such as branches, call centers, and the Internet. Because the costs for each channel are different, TDABC helps answer questions such as the following: What are the total costs of branch transactions versus online transactions? Which channels help reduce overall costs? How can Charles Schwab price its services to drive changes in customer behavior?

TDABC assigns all of the company's resource costs to cost objects using a framework that requires two sets of estimates. TDABC first calculates the cost of supplying resource capacity, such as broker time. The total cost of resources including personnel, management, occupancy, technology, and supplies is divided by the available capacity—the time available for brokers to do the work—to obtain the capacity cost rate. Next, TDABC uses the capacity cost rate to drive resource costs to cost objects, such as stock trades executed through brokers at a branch, by estimating the demand for resource capacity (time) that the cost object requires.

Realizing that trades executed online cost much less than trades completed through brokers, Charles Schwab developed a fee structure for trading of mutual funds to stimulate the use of cheaper channels. Charles Schwab also used TDABC information to lower process costs by several hundred million dollars annually and to better align product pricing and account management to the company's diverse client segments. The company is working on other opportunities, including priority-call routing and email marketing, to further reduce costs while maintaining or enhancing Charles Schwab's already top-rated customer service.

Sources: Kaplan, R. S. and S. R., Anderson. 2007. The innovation of time-driven activity-based costing. *Cost Management,* March–April: 5–15; Kaplan R. S. and S.R. Anderson. 2007. *Time-driven activity-based costing.* Boston, MA: Harvard Business School Press; Martinez-Jerez, F. Asis. 2007. Understanding customer profitability at Charles Schwab. Harvard Business School Case Study No. 9-106-102, January.

Problem for Self-Study

Family Supermarkets (FS) has decided to increase the size of its Memphis store. It wants information about the profitability of individual product lines: soft drinks, fresh produce, and packaged food. FS provides the following data for 2011 for each product line:

	Soft Drinks	Fresh Produce	Packaged Food
Revenues	$317,400	$840,240	$483,960
Cost of goods sold	$240,000	$600,000	$360,000
Cost of bottles returned	$ 4,800	$ 0	$ 0
Number of purchase orders placed	144	336	144
Number of deliveries received	120	876	264
Hours of shelf-stocking time	216	2,160	1,080
Items sold	50,400	441,600	122,400

FS also provides the following information for 2011:

Activity (1)	Description of Activity (2)	Total Support Costs (3)	Cost-Allocation Base (4)
1. Bottle returns	Returning of empty bottles to store	$ 4,800	Direct tracing to soft-drink line
2. Ordering	Placing of orders for purchases	$ 62,400	624 purchase orders
3. Delivery	Physical delivery and receipt of merchandise	$100,800	1,260 deliveries
4. Shelf-stocking	Stocking of merchandise on store shelves and ongoing restocking	$ 69,120	3,456 hours of shelf-stocking time
5. Customer support	Assistance provided to customers, including checkout and bagging	$122,880	614,400 items sold
Total		$360,000	

Required

1. Family Supermarkets currently allocates store support costs (all costs other than cost of goods sold) to product lines on the basis of cost of goods sold of each product line. Calculate the operating income and operating income as a percentage of revenues for each product line.
2. If Family Supermarkets allocates store support costs (all costs other than cost of goods sold) to product lines using an ABC system, calculate the operating income and operating income as a percentage of revenues for each product line.
3. Comment on your answers in requirements 1 and 2.

Solution

1. The following table shows the operating income and operating income as a percentage of revenues for each product line. All store support costs (all costs other than cost of goods sold) are allocated to product lines using cost of goods sold of each product line as the cost-allocation base. Total store support costs equal $360,000 (cost of bottles returned, $4,800 + cost of purchase orders, $62,400 + cost of deliveries, $100,800 + cost of shelf-stocking, $69,120 + cost of customer support, $122,880). The allocation rate for store support costs = $360,000 ÷ $1,200,000 (soft drinks $240,000 + fresh produce $600,000 + packaged food, $360,000) = 30% of cost of goods sold. To allocate support costs to each product line, FS multiplies the cost of goods sold of each product line by 0.30.

	Soft Drinks	Fresh Produce	Packaged Food	Total
Revenues	$317,400	$840,240	$483,960	$1,641,600
Cost of goods sold	240,000	600,000	360,000	1,200,000
Store support cost				
($240,000; $600,000; $360,000) × 0.30	72,000	180,000	108,000	360,000
Total costs	312,000	780,000	468,000	1,560,000
Operating income	$ 5,400	$ 60,240	$ 15,960	$ 81,600
Operating income ÷ Revenues	1.70%	7.17%	3.30%	4.97%

2. Under an ABC system, FS identifies bottle-return costs as a direct cost because these costs can be traced to the soft drink product line. FS then calculates cost-allocation rates for each activity area (as in Step 5 of the seven-step costing system, described in the chapter, p. 152). The activity rates are as follows:

Activity (1)	Cost Hierarchy (2)	Total Costs (3)	Quantity of Cost-Allocation Base (4)	Overhead Allocation Rate (5) = (3) ÷ (4)
Ordering	Batch-level	$ 62,400	624 purchase orders	$100 per purchase order
Delivery	Batch-level	$100,800	1,260 deliveries	$80 per delivery
Shelf-stocking	Output unit-level	$ 69,120	3,456 shelf-stocking-hours	$20 per stocking-hour
Customer support	Output unit-level	$122,880	614,400 items sold	$0.20 per item sold

Store support costs for each product line by activity are obtained by multiplying the total quantity of the cost-allocation base for each product line by the activity cost rate. Operating income and operating income as a percentage of revenues for each product line are as follows:

	Soft Drinks	Fresh Produce	Packaged Food	Total
Revenues	$317,400	$840,240	$483,960	$1,641,600
Cost of goods sold	240,000	600,000	360,000	1,200,000
Bottle-return costs	4,800	0	0	4,800
Ordering costs				
(144; 336; 144) purchase orders × $100	14,400	33,600	14,400	62,400
Delivery costs				
(120; 876; 264) deliveries × $80	9,600	70,080	21,120	100,800
Shelf-stocking costs				
(216; 2,160; 1,080) stocking-hours × $20	4,320	43,200	21,600	69,120
Customer-support costs				
(50,400; 441,600; 122,400) items sold × $0.20	10,080	88,320	24,480	122,880
Total costs	283,200	835,200	441,600	1,560,000
Operating income	$ 34,200	$ 5,040	$ 42,360	$ 81,600
Operating income ÷ Revenues	10.78%	0.60%	8.75%	4.97%

3. Managers believe the ABC system is more credible than the simple costing system. The ABC system distinguishes the different types of activities at FS more precisely. It also tracks more accurately how individual product lines use resources. Rankings of relative profitability—operating income as a percentage of revenues—of the three product lines under the simple costing system and under the ABC system are as follows:

Simple Costing System		ABC System	
1. Fresh produce	7.17%	1. Soft drinks	10.78%
2. Packaged food	3.30%	2. Packaged food	8.75%
3. Soft drinks	1.70%	3. Fresh produce	0.60%

The percentage of revenues, cost of goods sold, and activity costs for each product line are as follows:

	Soft Drinks	Fresh Produce	Packaged Food
Revenues	19.34%	51.18%	29.48%
Cost of goods sold	20.00	50.00	30.00
Bottle returns	100.00	0	0
Activity areas:			
Ordering	23.08	53.84	23.08
Delivery	9.53	69.52	20.95
Shelf-stocking	6.25	62.50	31.25
Customer-support	8.20	71.88	19.92

Soft drinks have fewer deliveries and require less shelf-stocking time and customer support than either fresh produce or packaged food. Most major soft-drink suppliers deliver merchandise to the store shelves and stock the shelves themselves. In contrast, the fresh produce area has the most deliveries and consumes a large percentage of shelf-stocking time. It also has the highest number of individual sales items and so requires the most customer support. The simple costing system assumed that each product line used the resources in each activity area in the same ratio as their respective individual cost of goods sold to total cost of goods sold. Clearly, this assumption is incorrect. Relative to cost of goods sold, soft drinks and packaged food use fewer resources while fresh produce uses more resources. As a result, the ABC system reduces the costs assigned to soft drinks and packaged food and increases the costs assigned to fresh produce. The simple costing system is an example of averaging that is too broad.

FS managers can use the ABC information to guide decisions such as how to allocate a planned increase in floor space. An increase in the percentage of space allocated to soft drinks is warranted. Note, however, that ABC information should be but one input into decisions about shelf-space allocation. FS may have minimum limits on the shelf space allocated to fresh produce because of shoppers' expectations that supermarkets will carry products from this product line. In many situations, companies cannot make product decisions in isolation but must consider the effect that dropping or deemphasizing a product might have on customer demand for other products.

Pricing decisions can also be made in a more informed way with ABC information. For example, suppose a competitor announces a 5% reduction in soft-drink prices. Given the 10.78% margin FS currently earns on its soft-drink product line, it has flexibility to reduce prices and still make a profit on this product line. In contrast, the simple costing system erroneously implied that soft drinks only had a 1.70% margin, leaving little room to counter a competitor's pricing initiatives.

Decision Points

The following question-and-answer format summarizes the chapter's learning objectives. Each decision presents a key question related to a learning objective. The guidelines are the answer to that question.

Decision	Guidelines
1. When does product undercosting or overcosting occur?	Product undercosting (overcosting) occurs when a product or service consumes a high (low) level of resources but is reported to have a low (high) cost. Broad averaging, or peanut-butter costing, a common cause of undercosting or overcosting, is the result of using broad averages that uniformly assign, or spread, the cost of resources to products when the individual products use those resources in a nonuniform way. Product-cost cross-subsidization exists when one undercosted (overcosted) product results in at least one other product being overcosted (undercosted).
2. How do managers refine a costing system?	Refining a costing system means making changes that result in cost numbers that better measure the way different cost objects, such as products, use different amounts of resources of the company. These changes can require additional direct-cost tracing, the choice of more-homogeneous indirect cost pools, or the use of cost drivers as cost-allocation bases.
3. What is the difference between the design of a simple costing system and an activity-based costing (ABC) system?	The ABC system differs from the simple system by its fundamental focus on activities. The ABC system typically has more-homogeneous indirect-cost pools than the simple system, and more cost drivers are used as cost-allocation bases.

4. What is a cost hierarchy?

A cost hierarchy categorizes costs into different cost pools on the basis of the different types of cost-allocation bases or different degrees of difficulty in determining cause-and-effect (or benefits-received) relationships. A four-part hierarchy to cost products consists of output unit-level costs, batch-level costs, product-sustaining or service-sustaining costs, and facility-sustaining costs.

5. How do managers cost products or services using ABC systems?

In ABC, costs of activities are used to assign costs to other cost objects such as products or services based on the activities the products or services consume.

6. What should managers consider when deciding to implement ABC systems?

ABC systems are likely to yield the most decision-making benefits when indirect costs are a high percentage of total costs or when products and services make diverse demands on indirect resources. The main costs of ABC systems are the difficulties of the measurements necessary to implement and update the systems.

7. How can ABC systems be used to manage better?

Activity-based management (ABM) is a management method of decision making that uses ABC information to satisfy customers and improve profits. ABC systems are used for such management decisions as pricing, product-mix, cost reduction, process improvement, product and process redesign, and planning and managing activities.

8. When can department costing systems be used instead of ABC systems?

Activity-based costing systems are a refinement of department costing systems into more-focused and homogeneous cost pools. Cost information in department costing systems approximates cost information in ABC systems only when each department has a single activity (or a single activity accounts for a significant proportion of department costs), a single cost driver for different activities, or when different products use the different activities of the department in the same proportions.

Terms to Learn

This chapter and the Glossary at the end of this book contain definitions of the following important terms:

activity (**p. 146**)
activity-based costing (ABC) (**p. 146**)
activity-based management (ABM)
 (**p. 156**)
batch-level costs (**p. 149**)

cost hierarchy (**p. 149**)
facility-sustaining costs (**p. 149**)
output unit-level costs (**p. 149**)
product-cost cross-subsidization
 (**p. 140**)

product overcosting (**p. 140**)
product-sustaining costs (**p. 149**)
product undercosting (**p. 140**)
refined costing system (**p. 145**)
service-sustaining costs (**p. 149**)

Assignment Material

MyAccountingLab

Questions

5-1 What is broad averaging and what consequences can it have on costs?
5-2 Why should managers worry about product overcosting or undercosting?
5-3 What is costing system refinement? Describe three guidelines for refinement.
5-4 What is an activity-based approach to designing a costing system?
5-5 Describe four levels of a cost hierarchy.
5-6 Why is it important to classify costs into a cost hierarchy?
5-7 What are the key reasons for product cost differences between simple costing systems and ABC systems?
5-8 Describe four decisions for which ABC information is useful.
5-9 "Department indirect-cost rates are never activity-cost rates." Do you agree? Explain.
5-10 Describe four signs that help indicate when ABC systems are likely to provide the most benefits.

5-11 What are the main costs and limitations of implementing ABC systems?

5-12 "ABC systems only apply to manufacturing companies." Do you agree? Explain.

5-13 "Activity-based costing is the wave of the present and the future. All companies should adopt it." Do you agree? Explain.

5-14 "Increasing the number of indirect-cost pools is guaranteed to sizably increase the accuracy of product or service costs." Do you agree? Why?

5-15 The controller of a retail company has just had a $50,000 request to implement an ABC system quickly turned down. A senior vice president, in rejecting the request, noted, "Given a choice, I will always prefer a $50,000 investment in improving things a customer sees or experiences, such as our shelves or our store layout. How does a customer benefit by our spending $50,000 on a supposedly better accounting system?" How should the controller respond?

Exercises

5-16 **Cost hierarchy.** Hamilton, Inc., manufactures boom boxes (music systems with radio, cassette, and compact disc players) for several well-known companies. The boom boxes differ significantly in their complexity and their manufacturing batch sizes. The following costs were incurred in 2011:

a. Indirect manufacturing labor costs such as supervision that supports direct manufacturing labor, $1,450,000

b. Procurement costs of placing purchase orders, receiving materials, and paying suppliers related to the number of purchase orders placed, $850,000

c. Cost of indirect materials, $275,000

d. Costs incurred to set up machines each time a different product needs to be manufactured, $630,000

e. Designing processes, drawing process charts, making engineering process changes for products, $775,000

f. Machine-related overhead costs such as depreciation, maintenance, production engineering, $1,500,000 (These resources relate to the activity of running the machines.)

g. Plant management, plant rent, and plant insurance, $925,000

1. Classify each of the preceding costs as output unit-level, batch-level, product-sustaining, or facility-sustaining. Explain each answer. ● **Required**

2. Consider two types of boom boxes made by Hamilton, Inc. One boom box is complex to make and is produced in many batches. The other boom box is simple to make and is produced in few batches. Suppose that Hamilton needs the same number of machine-hours to make each type of boom box and that Hamilton allocates all overhead costs using machine-hours as the only allocation base. How, if at all, would the boom boxes be miscosted? Briefly explain why.

3. How is the cost hierarchy helpful to Hamilton in managing its business?

5-17 **ABC, cost hierarchy, service.** (CMA, adapted) Vineyard Test Laboratories does heat testing (HT) and stress testing (ST) on materials and operates at capacity. Under its current simple costing system, Vineyard aggregates all operating costs of $1,190,000 into a single overhead cost pool. Vineyard calculates a rate per test-hour of $17 ($1,190,000 ÷ 70,000 total test-hours). HT uses 40,000 test-hours, and ST uses 30,000 test-hours. Gary Celeste, Vineyard's controller, believes that there is enough variation in test procedures and cost structures to establish separate costing and billing rates for HT and ST. The market for test services is becoming competitive. Without this information, any miscosting and mispricing of its services could cause Vineyard to lose business. Celeste divides Vineyard's costs into four activity-cost categories.

a. Direct-labor costs, $146,000. These costs can be directly traced to HT, $100,000, and ST, $46,000.

b. Equipment-related costs (rent, maintenance, energy, and so on), $350,000. These costs are allocated to HT and ST on the basis of test-hours.

c. Setup costs, $430,000. These costs are allocated to HT and ST on the basis of the number of setup-hours required. HT requires 13,600 setup-hours, and ST requires 3,600 setup-hours.

d. Costs of designing tests, $264,000. These costs are allocated to HT and ST on the basis of the time required for designing the tests. HT requires 3,000 hours, and ST requires 1,400 hours.

1. Classify each activity cost as output unit-level, batch-level, product- or service-sustaining, or facility-sustaining. Explain each answer. ● **Required**

2. Calculate the cost per test-hour for HT and ST. Explain briefly the reasons why these numbers differ from the $17 per test-hour that Vineyard calculated using its simple costing system.

3. Explain the accuracy of the product costs calculated using the simple costing system and the ABC system. How might Vineyard's management use the cost hierarchy and ABC information to better manage its business?

5-18 Alternative allocation bases for a professional services firm. The Walliston Group (WG) provides tax advice to multinational firms. WG charges clients for (a) direct professional time (at an hourly rate) and (b) support services (at 30% of the direct professional costs billed). The three professionals in WG and their rates per professional hour are as follows:

Professional	Billing Rate per Hour
Max Walliston	$640
Alexa Boutin	220
Jacob Abbington	100

WG has just prepared the May 2011 bills for two clients. The hours of professional time spent on each client are as follows:

Professional	Hours per Client	
	San Antonio Dominion	Amsterdam Enterprises
Walliston	26	4
Boutin	5	14
Abbington	39	52
Total	70	70

Required

1. What amounts did WG bill to San Antonio Dominion and Amsterdam Enterprises for May 2011?
2. Suppose support services were billed at $75 per professional labor-hour (instead of 30% of professional labor costs). How would this change affect the amounts WG billed to the two clients for May 2011? Comment on the differences between the amounts billed in requirements 1 and 2.
3. How would you determine whether professional labor costs or professional labor-hours is the more appropriate allocation base for WG's support services?

5-19 Plant-wide, department, and ABC indirect cost rates. Automotive Products (AP) designs and produces automotive parts. In 2011, actual variable manufacturing overhead is $308,600. AP's simple costing system allocates variable manufacturing overhead to its three customers based on machine-hours and prices its contracts based on full costs. One of its customers has regularly complained of being charged noncompetitive prices, so AP's controller Devon Smith realizes that it is time to examine the consumption of overhead resources more closely. He knows that there are three main departments that consume overhead resources: design, production, and engineering. Interviews with the department personnel and examination of time records yield the following detailed information:

	Home	Insert	Page Layout	Formulas	Data	Review	View	

	A	B	C	D	E	F
1			Variable Manufacturing Overhead in 2011	Usage of Cost Drivers by Customer Contract		
2	Department	Cost Driver		United Motors	Holden Motors	Leland Vehicle
3	Design	CAD-design-hours	$ 39,000	110	200	80
4	Production	Engineering-hours	29,600	70	60	240
5	Engineering	Machine-hours	240,000	120	2,800	1,080
6	Total		$308,600			

Required

1. Compute the variable manufacturing overhead allocated to each customer in 2011 using the simple costing system that uses machine-hours as the allocation base.
2. Compute the variable manufacturing overhead allocated to each customer in 2011 using department-based variable manufacturing overhead rates.
3. Comment on your answers in requirements 1 and 2. Which customer do you think was complaining about being overcharged in the simple system? If the new department-based rates are used to price contracts, which customer(s) will be unhappy? How would you respond to these concerns?

4. How else might AP use the information available from its department-by-department analysis of variable manufacturing overhead costs?

5. AP's managers are wondering if they should further refine the department-by-department costing system into an ABC system by identifying different activities within each department. Under what conditions would it not be worthwhile to further refine the department costing system into an ABC system?

5-20 Plant-wide, department, and activity-cost rates. Tarquin's Trophies makes trophies and plaques and operates at capacity. Tarquin does large custom orders, such as the participant trophies for the Mishawaka Little League. The controller has asked you to compare plant-wide, department, and activity-based cost allocation.

Tarquin's Trophies
Budgeted Information
For the Year Ended November 30, 2011

Forming Department	Trophies	Plaques	Total
Direct materials	$13,000	$11,250	$24,250
Direct labor	15,600	9,000	24,600
Overhead Costs			
Setup			12,000
Supervision			10,386

Assembly Department	Trophies	Plaques	Total
Direct materials	$ 2,600	$ 9,375	$11,975
Direct labor	7,800	10,500	18,300
Overhead costs			
Setup			23,000
Supervision			10,960

Other information follows:

Setup costs vary with the number of batches processed in each department. The budgeted number of batches for each product line in each department is as follows:

	Trophies	Plaques
Forming department	40	116
Assembly department	43	103

Supervision costs vary with direct labor costs in each department.

Required

1. Calculate the budgeted cost of trophies and plaques based on a single plant-wide overhead rate, if total overhead is allocated based on total direct costs.
2. Calculate the budgeted cost of trophies and plaques based on departmental overhead rates, where forming department overhead costs are allocated based on direct labor costs of the forming department, and assembly department overhead costs are allocated based on total direct costs of the assembly department.
3. Calculate the budgeted cost of trophies and plaques if Tarquin allocates overhead costs in each department using activity-based costing.
4. Explain how the disaggregation of information could improve or reduce decision quality.

5-21 ABC, process costing. Parker Company produces mathematical and financial calculators and operates at capacity. Data related to the two products are presented here:

	Mathematical	Financial
Annual production in units	50,000	100,000
Direct material costs	$150,000	$300,000
Direct manufacturing labor costs	$ 50,000	$100,000
Direct manufacturing labor-hours	2,500	5,000
Machine-hours	25,000	50,000
Number of production runs	50	50
Inspection hours	1,000	500

Total manufacturing overhead costs are as follows:

	Total
Machining costs	$375,000
Setup costs	120,000
Inspection costs	105,000

Required

1. Choose a cost driver for each overhead cost pool and calculate the manufacturing overhead cost per unit for each product.

2. Compute the manufacturing cost per unit for each product.

5-22 Activity-based costing, service company. Quikprint Corporation owns a small printing press that prints leaflets, brochures, and advertising materials. Quikprint classifies its various printing jobs as standard jobs or special jobs. Quikprint's simple job-costing system has two direct-cost categories (direct materials and direct labor) and a single indirect-cost pool. Quikprint operates at capacity and allocates all indirect costs using printing machine-hours as the allocation base.

Quikprint is concerned about the accuracy of the costs assigned to standard and special jobs and therefore is planning to implement an activity-based costing system. Quickprint's ABC system would have the same direct-cost categories as its simple costing system. However, instead of a single indirect-cost pool there would now be six categories for assigning indirect costs: design, purchasing, setup, printing machine operations, marketing, and administration. To see how activity-based costing would affect the costs of standard and special jobs, Quikprint collects the following information for the fiscal year 2011 that just ended.

| | Home | Insert | Page Layout | Formulas | Data | Review | View | | |

	A	B	C	D	E	F	G	H
1		Standard Job	Special Job	Total	Cause-and-Effect Relationship Between Allocation Base and Activity Cost			
2	Number of printing jobs	400	200					
3	Price per job	$1,200	$ 1,500					
4	Cost of supplies per job	$ 200	$ 250					
5	Direct labor costs per job	$ 180	$ 200					
6	Printing machine-hours per job	10	10					
7	Cost of printing machine operations			$150,000	Indirect costs of operating printing machines			
8					increase with printing machine hours			
9	Setup-hours per job	4	7					
10	Setup costs			$ 90,000	Indirect setup costs increase with setup hours			
11	Total number of purchase orders	400	500					
12	Purchase order costs			$ 36,000	Indirect purchase order costs increase with			
13					number of purchase orders			
14	Design costs	$8,000	$32,000	$ 40,000	Design costs are allocated to standard and special			
15					jobs based on a special study of the design department			
16	Marketing costs as a percentage of revenues	5%	5%	$ 39,000				
17	Administration costs			$ 48,000	Demand for administrative resources increases with direct labor costs			

Required

1. Calculate the cost of a standard job and a special job under the simple costing system.
2. Calculate the cost of a standard job and a special job under the activity-based costing system.
3. Compare the costs of a standard job and a special job in requirements 1 and 2. Why do the simple and activity-based costing systems differ in the cost of a standard job and a special job?
4. How might Quikprint use the new cost information from its activity-based costing system to better manage its business?

5-23 Activity-based costing, manufacturing. Open Doors, Inc., produces two types of doors, interior and exterior. The company's simple costing system has two direct cost categories (materials and labor) and one indirect cost pool. The simple costing system allocates indirect costs on the basis of machine-hours. Recently, the owners of Open Doors have been concerned about a decline in the market share for their interior doors, usually their biggest seller. Information related to Open Doors production for the most recent year follows:

	Interior	Exterior
Units sold	3,200	1,800
Selling price	$ 125	$ 200
Direct material cost per unit	$ 30	$ 45
Direct manufacturing labor cost per hour	$ 16	$ 16
Direct manufacturing labor-hours per unit	1.50	2.25
Production runs	40	85
Material moves	72	168
Machine setups	45	155
Machine-hours	5,500	4,500
Number of inspections	250	150

The owners have heard of other companies in the industry that are now using an activity-based costing system and are curious how an ABC system would affect their product costing decisions. After analyzing the indirect cost pool for Open Doors, six activities were identified as generating indirect costs: production scheduling, material handling, machine setup, assembly, inspection, and marketing. Open Doors collected the following data related to the indirect cost activities:

Activity	Activity Cost	Activity Cost Driver
Production scheduling	$95,000	Production runs
Material handling	$45,000	Material moves
Machine setup	$25,000	Machine setups
Assembly	$60,000	Machine-hours
Inspection	$ 8,000	Number of inspections

Marketing costs were determined to be 3% of the sales revenue for each type of door.

Required

1. Calculate the cost of an interior door and an exterior door under the existing simple costing system.
2. Calculate the cost of an interior door and an exterior door under an activity-based costing system.
3. Compare the costs of the doors in requirements 1 and 2. Why do the simple and activity-based costing systems differ in the cost of an interior and exterior door?
4. How might Open Door, Inc., use the new cost information from its activity-based costing system to address the declining market share for interior doors?

5-24 ABC, retail product-line profitability. Family Supermarkets (FS) operates at capacity and decides to apply ABC analysis to three product lines: baked goods, milk and fruit juice, and frozen foods. It identifies four activities and their activity cost rates as follows:

Ordering	$100 per purchase order
Delivery and receipt of merchandise	$ 80 per delivery
Shelf-stocking	$ 20 per hour
Customer support and assistance	$ 0.20 per item sold

The revenues, cost of goods sold, store support costs, the activities that account for the store support costs, and activity-area usage of the three product lines are as follows:

	Baked Goods	Milk and Fruit Juice	Frozen Products
Financial data			
Revenues	$57,000	$63,000	$52,000
Cost of goods sold	$38,000	$47,000	$35,000
Store support	$11,400	$14,100	$10,500
Activity-area usage (cost-allocation base)			
Ordering (purchase orders)	30	25	13
Delivery (deliveries)	98	36	28
Shelf-stocking (hours)	183	166	24
Customer support (items sold)	15,500	20,500	7,900

Under its simple costing system, FS allocated support costs to products at the rate of 30% of cost of goods sold.

1. Use the simple costing system to prepare a product-line profitability report for FS.
2. Use the ABC system to prepare a product-line profitability report for FS.
3. What new insights does the ABC system in requirement 2 provide to FS managers?

5-25 ABC, wholesale, customer profitability. Ramirez Wholesalers operates at capacity and sells furniture items to four department-store chains (customers). Mr. Ramirez commented, "We apply ABC to determine product-line profitability. The same ideas apply to customer profitability, and we should find out our customer profitability as well." Ramirez Wholesalers sends catalogs to corporate purchasing departments on a monthly basis. The customers are entitled to return unsold merchandise within a six-month period from the purchase date and receive a full purchase price refund. The following data were collected from last year's operations:

	Chain			
	1	**2**	**3**	**4**
Gross sales	$55,000	$25,000	$100,000	$75,000
Sales returns:				
Number of items	101	25	65	35
Amount	$11,000	$ 3,500	$ 7,000	$ 6,500
Number of orders:				
Regular	45	175	52	75
Rush	11	48	11	32

Ramirez has calculated the following activity rates:

Activity	Cost-Driver Rate
Regular order processing	$25 per regular order
Rush order processing	$125 per rush order
Returned items processing	$15 per item
Catalogs and customer support	$1,100 per customer

Customers pay the transportation costs. The cost of goods sold averages 70% of sales.

Determine the contribution to profit from each chain last year. Comment on your solution.

5-26 ABC, activity area cost-driver rates, product cross-subsidization. Idaho Potatoes (IP) operates at capacity and processes potatoes into potato cuts at its highly automated Pocatello plant. It sells potatoes to the retail consumer market and to the institutional market, which includes hospitals, cafeterias, and university dormitories.

IP's simple costing system, which does not distinguish between potato cuts processed for retail and institutional markets, has a single direct-cost category (direct materials, i.e. raw potatoes) and a single indirect-cost pool (production support). Support costs, which include packaging materials, are allocated on the basis of pounds of potato cuts processed. The company uses 1,200,000 pounds of raw potatoes to process 1,000,000 pounds of potato cuts. At the end of 2011, IP unsuccessfully bid for a large institutional contract. Its bid was reported to be 30% above the winning bid. This feedback came as a shock because IP included only a minimum profit margin on its bid and the Pocatello plant was acknowledged as the most efficient in the industry.

As a result of its review process of the lost contract bid, IP decided to explore ways to refine its costing system. The company determined that 90% of the direct materials (raw potatoes) related to the retail market and 10% to the institutional market. In addition, the company identified that packaging materials could be directly traced to individual jobs ($180,000 for retail and $8,000 for institutional). Also, the company used ABC to identify three main activity areas that generated support costs: cleaning, cutting, and packaging.

- **Cleaning Activity Area**—The cost-allocation base is pounds of raw potatoes cleaned.

- **Cutting Activity Area**—The production line produces (a) 250 pounds of retail potato cuts per cutting-hour and (b) 400 pounds of institutional potato cuts per cutting-hour. The cost-allocation base is cutting-hours on the production line.

- **Packaging Activity Area**—The packaging line packages (a) 25 pounds of retail potato cuts per packaging-hour and (b) 100 pounds of institutional potato cuts per packaging-hour. The cost-allocation base is packaging-hours on the production line.

The following table summarizes the actual costs for 2011 before and after the preceding cost analysis:

	Before the cost analysis	After the cost analysis Production Support	Retail	Institutional	Total
Direct materials used					
Potatoes	$ 150,000		$135,000	$15,000	$ 150,000
Packaging			180,000	8,000	188,000
Production support	983,000				
Cleaning		$120,000			120,000
Cutting		231,000			231,000
Packaging		444,000			444,000
Total	$1,133,000	$795,000	$315,000	$23,000	$1,133,000

1. Using the simple costing system, what is the cost per pound of potato cuts produced by IP?
2. Calculate the cost rate per unit of the cost driver in the (a) cleaning, (b) cutting, and (c) packaging activity areas.
3. Suppose IP uses information from its activity cost rates to calculate costs incurred on retail potato cuts and institutional potato cuts. Using the ABC system, what is the cost per pound of (a) retail potato cuts and (b) institutional potato cuts?
4. Comment on the cost differences between the two costing systems in requirements 1 and 3. How might IP use the information in requirement 3 to make better decisions?

Required

5-27 Activity-based costing. The job costing system at Smith's Custom Framing has five indirect cost pools (purchasing, material handling, machine maintenance, product inspection, and packaging). The company is in the process of bidding on two jobs; Job 215, an order of 15 intricate personalized frames, and Job 325, an order of 6 standard personalized frames. The controller wants you to compare overhead allocated under the current simple job-costing system and a newly-designed activity-based job-costing system. Total budgeted costs in each indirect cost pool and the budgeted quantity of activity driver are as follows:

	Budgeted Overhead	Activity Driver	Budgeted Quantity of Activity Driver
Purchasing	$ 70,000	Purchase orders processed	2,000
Material handling	87,500	Material moves	5,000
Machine maintenance	237,300	Machine-hours	10,500
Product inspection	18,900	Inspections	1,200
Packaging	39,900	Units produced	3,800
	$453,600		

Information related to Job 215 and Job 325 follows. Job 215 incurs more batch-level costs because it uses more types of materials that need to be purchased, moved, and inspected relative to Job 325.

	Job 215	Job 325
Number of purchase orders	25	8
Number of material moves	10	4
Machine-hours	40	60
Number of inspections	9	3
Units produced	15	6

1. Compute the total overhead allocated to each job under a simple costing system, where overhead is allocated based on machine-hours.
2. Compute the total overhead allocated to each job under an activity-based costing system using the appropriate activity drivers.
3. Explain why Smith's Custom Framing might favor the ABC job-costing system over the simple job-costing system, especially in its bidding process.

5-28 ABC, product costing at banks, cross-subsidization. National Savings Bank (NSB) is examining the profitability of its Premier Account, a combined savings and checking account. Depositors receive a 7% annual interest rate on their average deposit. NSB earns an interest rate spread of 3% (the difference between the rate at which it lends money and the rate it pays depositors) by lending money for home loan purposes at 10%. Thus, NSB would gain $60 on the interest spread if a depositor had an average Premier Account balance of $2,000 in 2011 ($2,000 × 3% = $60).

The Premier Account allows depositors unlimited use of services such as deposits, withdrawals, checking accounts, and foreign currency drafts. Depositors with Premier Account balances of $1,000 or more receive unlimited free use of services. Depositors with minimum balances of less than $1,000 pay a $22-a-month service fee for their Premier Account.

NSB recently conducted an activity-based costing study of its services. It assessed the following costs for six individual services. The use of these services in 2011 by three customers is as follows:

	Activity-Based Cost per "Transaction"	Account Usage		
		Holt	Turner	Graham
Deposit/withdrawal with teller	$ 2.30	42	48	5
Deposit/withdrawal with automatic teller machine (ATM)	0.70	7	19	17
Deposit/withdrawal on prearranged monthly basis	0.40	0	13	62
Bank checks written	8.40	11	1	3
Foreign currency drafts	12.40	4	2	6
Inquiries about account balance	1.40	12	20	9
Average Premier Account balance for 2011		$1,100	$700	$24,600

Assume Holt and Graham always maintain a balance above $1,000, whereas Turner always has a balance below $1,000.

Required

1. Compute the 2011 profitability of the Holt, Turner, and Graham Premier Accounts at NSB.
2. Why might NSB worry about the profitability of individual customers if the Premier Account product offering is profitable as a whole?
3. What changes would you recommend for NSB's Premier Account?

MyAccountingLab

Problems

5-29 Job costing with single direct-cost category, single indirect-cost pool, law firm. Wigan Associates is a recently formed law partnership. Ellery Hanley, the managing partner of Wigan Associates, has just finished a tense phone call with Martin Offiah, president of Widnes Coal. Offiah strongly complained about the price Wigan charged for some legal work done for Widnes Coal.

Hanley also received a phone call from its only other client (St. Helen's Glass), which was very pleased with both the quality of the work and the price charged on its most recent job.

Wigan Associates operates at capacity and uses a cost-based approach to pricing (billing) each job. Currently it uses a simple costing system with a single direct-cost category (professional labor-hours) and a single indirect-cost pool (general support). Indirect costs are allocated to cases on the basis of professional labor-hours per case. The job files show the following:

	Widnes Coal	St. Helen's Glass
Professional labor	104 hours	96 hours

Professional labor costs at Wigan Associates are $70 an hour. Indirect costs are allocated to cases at $105 an hour. Total indirect costs in the most recent period were $21,000.

Required

1. Why is it important for Wigan Associates to understand the costs associated with individual jobs?
2. Compute the costs of the Widnes Coal and St. Helen's Glass jobs using Wigan's simple costing system.

5-30 Job costing with multiple direct-cost categories, single indirect-cost pool, law firm (continuation of 5-29). Hanley asks his assistant to collect details on those costs included in the $21,000 indirect-cost pool that can be traced to each individual job. After analysis, Wigan is able to reclassify $14,000 of the $21,000 as direct costs:

Other Direct Costs	Widnes Coal	St. Helen's Glass
Research support labor	$1,600	$ 3,400
Computer time	500	1,300
Travel and allowances	600	4,400
Telephones/faxes	200	1,000
Photocopying	250	750
Total	$3,150	$10,850

Hanley decides to calculate the costs of each job as if Wigan had used six direct cost-pools and a single indirect-cost pool. The single indirect-cost pool would have $7,000 of costs and would be allocated to each case using the professional labor-hours base.

1. What is the revised indirect-cost allocation rate per professional labor-hour for Wigan Associates when total indirect costs are $7,000? **Required**

2. Compute the costs of the Widnes and St. Helen's jobs if Wigan Associates had used its refined costing system with multiple direct-cost categories and one indirect-cost pool.

3. Compare the costs of Widnes and St. Helen's jobs in requirement 2 with those in requirement 2 of Problem 5-29. Comment on the results.

5-31 Job costing with multiple direct-cost categories, multiple indirect-cost pools, law firm (continuation of 5-29 and 5-30). Wigan has two classifications of professional staff: partners and associates. Hanley asks his assistant to examine the relative use of partners and associates on the recent Widnes Coal and St. Helen's jobs. The Widnes job used 24 partner-hours and 80 associate-hours. The St. Helen's job used 56 partner-hours and 40 associate-hours. Therefore, totals of the two jobs together were 80 partner-hours and 120 associate-hours. Hanley decides to examine how using separate direct-cost rates for partners and associates and using separate indirect-cost pools for partners and associates would have affected the costs of the Widnes and St. Helen's jobs. Indirect costs in each indirect-cost pool would be allocated on the basis of total hours of that category of professional labor. From the total indirect cost-pool of $7,000, $4,600 is attributable to the activities of partners, and $2,400 is attributable to the activities of associates.

The rates per category of professional labor are as follows:

Category of Professional Labor	Direct Cost per Hour	Indirect Cost per Hour
Partner	$100.00	$4,600 ÷ 80 hours = $57.50
Associate	50.00	$2,400 ÷ 120 hours = $20.00

1. Compute the costs of the Widnes and St. Helen's cases using Wigan's further refined system, with multiple direct-cost categories and multiple indirect-cost pools. **Required**

2. For what decisions might Wigan Associates find it more useful to use this job-costing approach rather than the approaches in Problem 5-29 or 5-30?

5-32 Plant-wide, department, and activity-cost rates. Allen's Aero Toys makes two models of toy airplanes, fighter jets, and cargo planes. The fighter jets are more detailed and require smaller batch sizes. The controller has asked you to compare plant-wide, department, and activity-based cost allocations.

Allen's Aero Toys
Budgeted Information per unit
For the Year Ended 30 November 2010

Assembly Department	Fighters	Cargo	Total
Direct materials	$2.50	$3.75	$ 6.25
Direct manufacturing labor	3.50	2.00	5.50
Total direct cost per unit	$6.00	$5.75	$11.75

Painting Department	Fighters	Cargo	
Direct materials	$0.50	$1.00	$ 1.50
Direct manufacturing labor	2.25	1.50	3.75
Total direct cost per unit	$2.75	$2.50	$ 5.25

Number of units produced	800	740	

The budgeted overhead cost for each department is as follows:

	Assembly Department	Painting Department	Total
Materials handling	$1,700	$ 900	$ 2,600
Quality inspection	2,750	1,150	3,900
Utilities	2,580	2,100	4,680
	$7,030	$4,150	$11,180

Other information follows:

Materials handling and quality inspection costs vary with the number of batches processed in each department. The budgeted number of batches for each product line in each department is as follows:

	Fighters	Cargo	Total
Assembly department	150	48	198
Painting department	100	32	132
Total	250	80	330

Utilities costs vary with direct manufacturing labor cost in each department.

Required

1. Calculate the budgeted cost per unit for fighter jets and cargo planes based on a single plant-wide overhead rate, if total overhead is allocated based on total direct costs.
2. Calculate the budgeted cost per unit for fighter jets and cargo planes based on departmental overhead rates, where assembly department overhead costs are allocated based on direct manufacturing labor costs of the assembly department and painting department overhead costs are allocated based on total direct costs of the painting department.
3. Calculate the budgeted cost per unit for fighter jets and cargo planes if Allen's Aero Toys allocates overhead costs using activity-based costing.
4. Explain how activity-based costing could improve or reduce decision quality.

5-33 Department and activity-cost rates, service sector. Roxbury's Radiology Center (RRC) performs X-rays, ultrasounds, CT scans, and MRIs. RRC has developed a reputation as a top Radiology Center in the state. RRC has achieved this status because it constantly reexamines its processes and procedures. RRC has been using a single, facility-wide overhead allocation rate. The VP of Finance believes that RRC can make better process improvements if it uses more disaggregated cost information. She says, "We have state of the art medical imaging technology. Can't we have state of the art accounting technology?"

Roxbury's Radiology Center
Budgeted Information
For the Year Ended May 30, 2011

	X-rays	Ultrasound	CT scan	MRI	Total
Technician labor	$ 64,000	$104,000	$119,000	$106,000	$ 393,000
Depreciation	136,800	231,000	400,200	792,000	1560,000
Materials	22,400	16,500	23,900	30,800	93,600
Administration					19,000
Maintenance					260,000
Sanitation					267,900
Utilities					121,200
	$223,200	$351,500	$543,100	$928,800	$2,714,700
Number of procedures	2,555	4,760	3,290	2,695	
Minutes to clean after each procedure	10	10	20	40	
Minutes for each procedure	5	20	15	40	

RRC operates at capacity. The proposed allocation bases for overhead are as follows:

Administration	Number of procedures
Maintenance (including parts)	Capital cost of the equipment (use Depreciation)
Sanitation	Total cleaning minutes
Utilities	Total procedure minutes

Required

1. Calculate the budgeted cost per service for X-rays, Ultrasounds, CT scans, and MRIs using direct technician labor costs as the allocation basis.
2. Calculate the budgeted cost per service of X-rays, Ultrasounds, CT scans, and MRIs if RRC allocated overhead costs using activity-based costing.
3. Explain how the disaggregation of information could be helpful to RRC's intention to continuously improve its services.

5-34 Choosing cost drivers, activity-based costing, activity-based management. Annie Warbucks runs a dance studio with childcare and adult fitness classes. Annie's budget for the upcoming year is as follows:

Annie Warbuck's Dance Studio
Budgeted Costs and Activities
For the Year Ended June 30, 2010

Dance teacher salaries	$62,100	
Child care teacher salaries	24,300	
Fitness instructor salaries	39,060	
Total salaries		$125,460
Supplies (art, dance accessories, fitness)		21,984
Rent, maintenance, and utilities		97,511
Administration salaries		50,075
Marketing expenses		21,000
Total		$316,030

Other budget information follows:

	Dance	Childcare	Fitness	Total
Square footage	6,000	3,150	2,500	11,650
Number of participants	1,485	450	270	2,205
Teachers per hour	3	3	1	7
Number of advertisements	26	24	20	70

Required

1. Determine which costs are direct costs and which costs are indirect costs of different programs.
2. Choose a cost driver for the indirect costs and calculate the budgeted cost per unit of the cost driver. Explain briefly your choice of cost driver.
3. Calculate the budgeted costs of each program.
4. How can Annie use this information for pricing? What other factors should she consider?

5-35 Activity-based costing, merchandising. Pharmacare, Inc., a distributor of special pharmaceutical products, operates at capacity and has three main market segments:

a. General supermarket chains
b. Drugstore chains
c. Mom-and-Pop single-store pharmacies

Rick Flair, the new controller of Pharmacare, reported the following data for 2011:

	A	B	C	D	E
1					
2	Pharmacare, 2011	General			
3		Supermarket	Drugstore	Mom-and-Pop	
4		Chains	Chains	Single Stores	Pharmacare
5	Revenues	$3,708,000	$3,150,000	$1,980,000	$8,838,000
6	Cost of goods sold	3,600,000	3,000,000	1,800,000	8,400,000
7	Gross margin	$ 108,000	$ 150,000	$ 180,000	438,000
8	Other operating costs				301,080
9	Operating income				$ 136,920

For many years, Pharmacare has used gross margin percentage [(Revenue − Cost of goods sold) ÷ Revenue] to evaluate the relative profitability of its market segments. But, Flair recently attended a seminar on activity-based costing and is considering using it at Pharmacare to analyze and allocate "other operating costs." He meets with all the key managers and several of his operations and sales staff and they agree that there are five key activities that drive other operating costs at Pharmacare:

Activity Area	Cost Driver
Order processing	Number of customer purchase orders
Line-item processing	Number of line items ordered by customers
Delivering to stores	Number of store deliveries
Cartons shipped to store	Number of cartons shipped
Stocking of customer store shelves	Hours of shelf-stocking

Each customer order consists of one or more line items. A line item represents a single product (such as Extra-Strength Tylenol Tablets). Each product line item is delivered in one or more separate cartons. Each store delivery entails the delivery of one or more cartons of products to a customer. Pharmacare's staff stacks cartons directly onto display shelves in customers' stores. Currently, there is no additional charge to the customer for shelf-stocking and not all customers use Pharmacare for this activity. The level of each activity in the three market segments and the total cost incurred for each activity in 2011 is as follows:

	Home	Insert	Page Layout	Formulas	Data	Review	View	
	A		B		C		D	E
13								
14	Activity-based Cost Data				Activity Level			
15	Pharmacare 2011		General					Total Cost
16			Supermarket		Drugstore		Mom-and-Pop	of Activity
17	Activity		Chains		Chains		Single Stores	in 2011
18	Orders processed (number)		140		360		1,500	$ 80,000
19	Line-items ordered (number)		1,960		4,320		15,000	63,840
20	Store deliveries made (number)		120		360		1,000	71,000
21	Cartons shipped to stores (number)		36,000		24,000		16,000	76,000
22	Shelf stocking (hours)		360		180		100	10,240
23								$301,080

Required

1. Compute the 2011 gross-margin percentage for each of Pharmacare's three market segments.
2. Compute the cost driver rates for each of the five activity areas.
3. Use the activity-based costing information to allocate the $301,080 of "other operating costs" to each of the market segments. Compute the operating income for each market segment.
4. Comment on the results. What new insights are available with the activity-based costing information?

5-36 Choosing cost drivers, activity-based costing, activity-based management. Pumpkin Bags (PB) is a designer of high quality backpacks and purses. Each design is made in small batches. Each spring, PB comes out with new designs for the backpack and for the purse. The company uses these designs for a year, and then moves on to the next trend. The bags are all made on the same fabrication equipment that is expected to operate at capacity. The equipment must be switched over to a new design and set up to prepare for the production of each new batch of products. When completed, each batch of products is immediately shipped to a wholesaler. Shipping costs vary with the number of shipments. Budgeted information for the year is as follows:

Pumpkin Bags
Budget for costs and Activities
For the Year Ended February 28, 2011

Direct materials—purses	$ 379,290
Direct materials—backpacks	412,920
Direct manufacturing labor—purses	98,000
Direct manufacturing labor—backpacks	120,000
Setup	65,930
Shipping	73,910
Design	166,000
Plant utilities and administration	243,000
Total	$1,559,050

Other budget information follows:

	Backpacks	Purses	Total
Number of bags	6,050	3,350	9,400
Hours of production	1,450	2,600	4,050
Number of batches	130	60	190
Number of designs	2	2	4

Required

1. Identify the cost hierarchy level for each cost category.
2. Identify the most appropriate cost driver for each cost category. Explain briefly your choice of cost driver.
3. Calculate the budgeted cost per unit of cost driver for each cost category.
4. Calculate the budgeted total costs and cost per unit for each product line.
5. Explain how you could use the information in requirement 4 to reduce costs.

5-37 ABC, health care. Uppervale Health Center runs two programs: drug addict rehabilitation and aftercare (counseling and support of patients after release from a mental hospital). The center's budget for 2010 follows:

Professional salaries:		
4 physicians × $150,000	$600,000	
12 psychologists × $75,000	900,000	
16 nurses × $30,000	480,000	$1,980,000
Medical supplies		220,000
Rent and clinic maintenance		126,000
Administrative costs to manage patient charts, food, laundry		440,000
Laboratory services		84,000
Total		$2,850,000

Muriel Clayton, the director of the center, is keen on determining the cost of each program. Clayton compiled the following data describing employee allocations to individual programs:

	Drug	Aftercare	Total Employees
Physicians	4		4
Psychologists	4	8	12
Nurses	6	10	16

Clayton has recently become aware of activity-based costing as a method to refine costing systems. She asks her accountant, Huey Deluth, how she should apply this technique. Deluth obtains the following budgeted information for 2010:

	Drug	Aftercare	Total
Square feet of space occupied by each program	9,000	12,000	21,000
Patient-years of service	50	60	110
Number of laboratory tests	1,400	700	2,100

Required

1. **a.** Selecting cost-allocation bases that you believe are the most appropriate for allocating indirect costs to programs, calculate the budgeted indirect cost rates for medical supplies; rent and clinic maintenance; administrative costs for patient charts, food, and laundry; and laboratory services.
   b. Using an activity-based costing approach to cost analysis, calculate the budgeted cost of each program and the budgeted cost per patient-year of the drug program.
   c. What benefits can Uppervale Health Center obtain by implementing the ABC system?
2. What factors, other than cost, do you think Uppervale Health Center should consider in allocating resources to its programs?

5-38 Unused capacity, activity-based costing, activity-based management. Nivag's Netballs is a manufacturer of high quality basketballs and volleyballs. Setup costs are driven by the number of batches. Equipment and maintenance costs increase with the number of machine-hours, and lease rent is paid per square foot. Capacity of the facility is 12,000 square feet and Nivag is using only 70% of this capacity. Nivag records the cost of unused capacity as a separate line item, and not as a product cost. The following is the budgeted information for Nivag:

Nivag's Netballs
Budgeted Costs and Activities
For the Year Ended August 31, 2012

Direct materials—basketballs	$ 209,750
Direct materials—volleyballs	358,290
Direct manufacturing labor—basketballs	107,333
Direct manufacturing labor—volleyballs	102,969
Setup	143,500
Equipment and maintenance costs	109,900
Lease rent	216,000
Total	$1,247,742

Other budget information follows:

	Basketballs	Volleyballs
Number of balls	66,000	100,000
Machine-hours	11,000	12,500
Number of batches	300	400
Square footage of production space used	3,360	5,040

Required

1. Calculate the budgeted cost per unit of cost driver for each indirect cost pool.
2. What is the budgeted cost of unused capacity?
3. What is the budgeted total cost and the cost per unit of resources used to produce (a) basketballs and (b) volleyballs?
4. What factors should Nivag consider if it has the opportunity to manufacture a new line of footballs?

5-39 Activity-based job costing, unit-cost comparisons. The Tracy Corporation has a machining facility specializing in jobs for the aircraft-components market. Tracy's previous simple job-costing system had two direct-cost categories (direct materials and direct manufacturing labor) and a single indirect-cost pool (manufacturing overhead, allocated using direct manufacturing labor-hours). The indirect cost-allocation rate of the simple system for 2010 would have been $115 per direct manufacturing labor-hour.

Recently a team with members from product design, manufacturing, and accounting used an ABC approach to refine its job-costing system. The two direct-cost categories were retained. The team decided to replace the single indirect-cost pool with five indirect-cost pools. The cost pools represent five activity areas at the plant, each with its own supervisor and budget responsibility. Pertinent data are as follows:

Activity Area	Cost-Allocation Base	Cost-Allocation Rate
Materials handling	Parts	$ 0.40
Lathe work	Lathe turns	0.20
Milling	Machine-hours	20.00
Grinding	Parts	0.80
Testing	Units tested	15.00

Information-gathering technology has advanced to the point at which the data necessary for budgeting in these five activity areas are collected automatically.

Two representative jobs processed under the ABC system at the plant in the most recent period had the following characteristics:

	Job 410	Job 411
Direct material cost per job	$ 9,700	$59,900
Direct manufacturing labor cost per job	$750	$11,250
Number of direct manufacturing labor-hours per job	25	375
Parts per job	500	2,000
Lathe turns per job	20,000	59,250
Machine-hours per job	150	1,050
Units per job (all units are tested)	10	200

Required

1. Compute the manufacturing cost per unit for each job under the previous simple job-costing system.
2. Compute the manufacturing cost per unit for each job under the activity-based costing system.
3. Compare the per-unit cost figures for Jobs 410 and 411 computed in requirements 1 and 2. Why do the simple and the activity-based costing systems differ in the manufacturing cost per unit for each job? Why might these differences be important to Tracy Corporation?
4. How might Tracy Corporation use information from its ABC system to better manage its business?

5-40 ABC, implementation, ethics. (CMA, adapted) Applewood Electronics, a division of Elgin Corporation, manufactures two large-screen television models: the Monarch, which has been produced since 2006 and sells for $900, and the Regal, a newer model introduced in early 2009 that sells for $1,140. Based on the following income statement for the year ended November 30, 2010, senior management at Elgin have decided to concentrate Applewood's marketing resources on the Regal model and to begin to phase out the Monarch model because Regal generates a much bigger operating income per unit.

Applewood Electronics
Income Statement
For the Fiscal Year Ended November 30, 2010

	Monarch	Regal	Total
Revenues	$19,800,000	$4,560,000	$24,360,000
Cost of goods sold	12,540,000	3,192,000	15,732,000
Gross margin	7,260,000	1,368,000	8,628,000
Selling and administrative expense	5,830,000	978,000	6,808,000
Operating income	$ 1,430,000	$ 390,000	$ 1,820,000
Units produced and sold	22,000	4,000	
Operating income per unit sold	$65.00	$97.50	

Details for cost of goods sold for Monarch and Regal are as follows:

	Monarch Total	Monarch Per unit	Regal Total	Regal Per unit
Direct materials	$ 4,576,000	$208	$2,336,000	$584
Direct manufacturing labor[a]	396,000	18	168,000	42
Machine costs[b]	3,168,000	144	288,000	72
Total direct costs	$ 8,140,000	$370	$2,792,000	$698
Manufacturing overhead costs[c]	$ 4,400,000	$200	$ 400,000	$100
Total cost of goods sold	$12,540,000	$570	$3,192,000	$798

[a] Monarch requires 1.5 hours per unit and Regal requires 3.5 hours per unit. The direct manufacturing labor cost is $12 per hour.
[b] Machine costs include lease costs of the machine, repairs, and maintenance. Monarch requires 8 machine-hours per unit and Regal requires 4 machine-hours per unit. The machine hour rate is $18 per hour.
[c] Manufacturing overhead costs are allocated to products based on machine-hours at the rate of $25 per hour.

Applewood's controller, Susan Benzo, is advocating the use of activity-based costing and activity-based management and has gathered the following information about the company's manufacturing overhead costs for the year ended November 30, 2010.

Activity Center (Cost-Allocation Base)	Total Activity Costs	Units of the Cost-Allocation Base Monarch	Regal	Total
Soldering (number of solder points)	$ 942,000	1,185,000	385,000	1,570,000
Shipments (number of shipments)	860,000	16,200	3,800	20,000
Quality control (number of inspections)	1,240,000	56,200	21,300	77,500
Purchase orders (number of orders)	950,400	80,100	109,980	190,080
Machine power (machine-hours)	57,600	176,000	16,000	192,000
Machine setups (number of setups)	750,000	16,000	14,000	30,000
Total manufacturing overhead	$4,800,000			

After completing her analysis, Benzo shows the results to Fred Duval, the Applewood division president. Duval does not like what he sees. "If you show headquarters this analysis, they are going to ask us to phase out the Regal line, which we have just introduced. This whole costing stuff has been a major problem for us. First Monarch was not profitable and now Regal."

"Looking at the ABC analysis, I see two problems. First, we do many more activities than the ones you have listed. If you had included all activities, maybe your conclusions would be different. Second, you used number of setups and number of inspections as allocation bases. The numbers would be different had you used setup-hours and inspection-hours instead. I know that measurement problems precluded you from using these other cost-allocation bases, but I believe you ought to make some adjustments to our current numbers to compensate for these issues. I know you can do better. We can't afford to phase out either product."

Benzo knows that her numbers are fairly accurate. As a quick check, she calculates the profitability of Regal and Monarch using more and different allocation bases. The set of activities and activity rates she had used results in numbers that closely approximate those based on more detailed analyses. She is confident that headquarters, knowing that Regal was introduced only recently, will not ask Applewood to phase it out. She is also aware that a sizable portion of Duval's bonus is based on division revenues. Phasing out either product would adversely affect his bonus. Still, she feels some pressure from Duval to do something.

Required

1. Using activity-based costing, calculate the gross margin per unit of the Regal and Monarch models.
2. Explain briefly why these numbers differ from the gross margin per unit of the Regal and Monarch models calculated using Applewood's existing simple costing system.
3. Comment on Duval's concerns about the accuracy and limitations of ABC.
4. How might Applewood find the ABC information helpful in managing its business?
5. What should Susan Benzo do in response to Duval's comments?

Collaborative Learning Problem

5-41 Activity-based costing, activity-based management, merchandising. Super Bookstore (SB) is a large city bookstore that sells books and music CDs, and has a café. SB operates at capacity and allocates selling, general, and administration (S, G & A) costs to each product line using the cost of merchandise of each product line. SB wants to optimize the pricing and cost management of each product line. SB is wondering if its accounting system is providing it with the best information for making such decisions.

Super Bookstore
Product Line Information
For the Year Ended December 31, 2010

	Books	CDs	Café
Revenues	$3,720,480	$2,315,360	$736,216
Cost of merchandise	$2,656,727	$1,722,311	$556,685
Cost of café cleaning	—	—	$ 18,250
Number of purchase orders placed	2,800	2,500	2,000
Number of deliveries received	1,400	1,700	1,600
Hours of shelf stocking time	15,000	14,000	10,000
Items sold	124,016	115,768	368,108

Super Bookstore incurs the following selling, general, and administration costs:

Super Bookstore
Selling, General, & Administration (S, G & A) Costs
For the Year Ended December 31, 2010

Purchasing department expenses	$ 474,500
Receiving department expenses	432,400
Shelf stocking labor expense	487,500
Customer support expense (cashiers and floor employees)	91,184
	$1,485,584

1. Suppose Super Bookstore uses cost of merchandise to allocate all S, G & A costs. Prepare product line and total company income statements. **Required**
2. Identify an improved method for allocating costs to the three product lines. Explain. Use the method for allocating S, G & A costs that you propose to prepare new product line and total company income statements. Compare your results to the results in requirement 1.
3. Write a memo to Super Bookstore's management describing how the improved system might be useful for managing Super Bookstore.

6 Master Budget and Responsibility Accounting

Amid the recent recession, one of the hottest innovations was the growth of Web sites that enable users to get an aggregate picture of their financial data and to set up budgets to manage their spending and other financial decisions online. (Mint.com, a pioneer in this market, was acquired by Intuit for $170 million in September 2009.)

Budgets play a similar crucial role in businesses. Without budgets, it's difficult for managers and their employees to know whether they're on target for their growth and spending goals. You might think a budget is only for companies that are in financial difficulty (such as Citigroup) or whose profit margins are slim—Wal-Mart, for example. As the following article shows, even companies that sell high-dollar value goods and services adhere to budgets.

"Scrimping" at the Ritz: Master Budgets

"Ladies and gentlemen serving ladies and gentlemen." That's the motto of the Ritz-Carlton. With locations ranging from South Beach (Miami) to South Korea, the grand hotel chain is known for its indulgent luxury and sumptuous surroundings. However, the aura of the chain's old-world elegance stands in contrast to its rather heavy emphasis—behind the scenes, of course—on cost control and budgets. It is this very approach, however, that makes it possible for the Ritz to offer the legendary grandeur its guests expect during their stay.

A Ritz hotel's performance is the responsibility of its general manager and controller at each location worldwide. Local forecasts and budgets are prepared annually and are the basis of subsequent performance evaluations for the hotel and people who work there.

The preparation of a hotel's budget begins with the hotel's sales director, who is responsible for all hotel revenues. Sources of revenue include hotel rooms, conventions, weddings, meeting facilities, merchandise, and food and beverage. The controller then seeks input about costs. Standard costs, based on cost per occupied room, are used to build the budget for guest room stays. Other standard costs are used to calculate costs for meeting rooms and food and beverages. The completed sales budget and annual operating budget are sent to corporate headquarters. From there, the hotel's actual monthly performance is monitored against the approved budget.

The managers of each hotel meet daily to review the hotel's performance to date relative to plan. They have the ability to adjust prices in the reservation system if they so choose. Adjusting prices can be particularly important if a hotel experiences unanticipated changes in occupancy rates.

Each month, the hotel's actual performance is monitored against the approved budget. The controller of each hotel receives a report from corporate headquarters that shows how the hotel performed against budget, as well as against the actual performance of other Ritz hotels. Any ideas for boosting revenues and reducing costs are regularly shared among hotel controllers.

Why does a successful company feel the need to watch its spending so closely? In many profitable companies, a strict budget is actually a key to their success. As the Ritz-Carlton example illustrates, budgeting is a critical function in organizations. Southwest Airlines, for example, uses budgets to monitor and manage fuel costs. Wal-Mart depends on its budget to maintain razor-thin margins as it competes with Target. Gillette uses budgets to plan marketing campaigns for its razors and blades.

Budgeting is a common accounting tool that companies use for implementing strategy. Management uses budgets to communicate directions and goals throughout a company. Budgets turn managers' perspectives forward and aid in planning and controlling the actions managers must undertake to satisfy their customers and succeed in the marketplace. Budgets provide measures of the financial results a company expects from its planned activities and help define objectives and timelines against which progress can be measured. Through budgeting, managers learn to anticipate and avoid potential problems. Interestingly, even when it comes to entrepreneurial activities, business planning has been shown to increase a new venture's probability of survival, as well as its product development and venture organizing activities.[1] As the old adage goes: "If you fail to plan, you plan to fail."

---

[1] For more details, take a look at F. Delmar and S. Shane, "Does Business Planning Facilitate the Development of New Ventures?" *Strategic Management Journal*, December 2003.

Budgets and the Budgeting Cycle

**Learning
Objective** **1**

Describe the master
budget

. . . The master budget
is the initial budget
prepared before the
start of a period

and explain its benefits

. . . benefits include
planning, coordination,
and control

A *budget* is (a) the quantitative expression of a proposed plan of action by management for a specified period and (b) an aid to coordinate what needs to be done to implement that plan. A budget generally includes both financial and nonfinancial aspects of the plan, and it serves as a blueprint for the company to follow in an upcoming period. A financial budget quantifies management's expectations regarding income, cash flows, and financial position. Just as financial statements are prepared for past periods, financial statements can be prepared for future periods—for example, a budgeted income statement, a budgeted statement of cash flows, and a budgeted balance sheet. Underlying these financial budgets are nonfinancial budgets for, say, units manufactured or sold, number of employees, and number of new products being introduced to the marketplace.

Strategic Plans and Operating Plans

Budgeting is most useful when it is integrated with a company's strategy. *Strategy* specifies how an organization matches its own capabilities with the opportunities in the marketplace to accomplish its objectives. In developing successful strategies, managers consider questions such as the following:

- What are our objectives?
- How do we create value for our customers while distinguishing ourselves from our competitors?
- Are the markets for our products local, regional, national, or global? What trends affect our markets? How are we affected by the economy, our industry, and our competitors?
- What organizational and financial structures serve us best?
- What are the risks and opportunities of alternative strategies, and what are our contingency plans if our preferred plan fails?

A company, such as Home Depot, can have a strategy of providing quality products or services at a low price. Another company, such as Pfizer or Porsche, can have a strategy of providing a unique product or service that is priced higher than the products or services of competitors. Exhibit 6-1 shows that strategic plans are expressed through long-run budgets and operating plans are expressed via short-run budgets. But there is more to the story! The exhibit shows arrows pointing backward as well as forward. The backward arrows are a way of graphically indicating that budgets can lead to changes in plans and strategies. Budgets help managers assess strategic risks and opportunities by providing them with feedback about the likely effects of their strategies and plans. Sometimes the feedback signals to managers that they need to revise their plans and possibly their strategies.

Boeing's experience with the 747-8 program illustrates how budgets can help managers rework their operating plans. Boeing viewed updating its 747 jumbo jet by sharing design synergies with the ongoing 787 Dreamliner program as a relatively inexpensive way to take sales from Airbus' A380 superjumbo jet. However, continued cost overruns and delays have undermined that strategy: The 747-8 program is already $2 billion over budget and a year behind schedule. The company recently revealed that it expects to earn no profit on virtually any of the 105 747-8 planes on its order books. With the budget for 2010 revealing higher-than-expected costs in design, rework, and production, Boeing has postponed plans to accelerate the jumbo's production to 2013. Some aerospace experts are urging Boeing to consider more dramatic steps, including discontinuing the passenger aircraft version of the 747-8 program.

Exhibit 6-1

Strategy, Planning, and
Budgets

Budgeting Cycle and Master Budget

Well-managed companies usually cycle through the following budgeting steps during the course of the fiscal year:

1. Working together, managers and management accountants plan the performance of the company as a whole and the performance of its subunits (such as departments or divisions). Taking into account past performance and anticipated changes in the future, managers at all levels reach a common understanding on what is expected.

2. Senior managers give subordinate managers a frame of reference, a set of specific financial or nonfinancial expectations against which actual results will be compared.

3. Management accountants help managers investigate variations from plans, such as an unexpected decline in sales. If necessary, corrective action follows, such as a reduction in price to boost sales or cutting of costs to maintain profitability.

4. Managers and management accountants take into account market feedback, changed conditions, and their own experiences as they begin to make plans for the next period. For example, a decline in sales may cause managers to make changes in product features for the next period.

The preceding four steps describe the ongoing budget process. The working document at the core of this process is called the *master budget*. The **master budget** expresses management's operating and financial plans for a specified period (usually a fiscal year), and it includes a set of budgeted financial statements. The master budget is the initial plan of what the company intends to accomplish in the budget period. The master budget evolves from both operating and financing decisions made by managers.

- Operating decisions deal with how to best use the limited resources of an organization.
- Financing decisions deal with how to obtain the funds to acquire those resources.

The terminology used to describe budgets varies among companies. For example, budgeted financial statements are sometimes called **pro forma statements**. Some companies, such as Hewlett-Packard, refer to budgeting as *targeting*. And many companies, such as Nissan Motor Company and Owens Corning, refer to the budget as a *profit plan*. Microsoft refers to goals as *commitments* and distributes firm-level goals across the company, connecting them to organizational, team, and ultimately individual commitments.

This book's focus centers on how management accounting helps managers make operating decisions, which is why this chapter emphasizes operating budgets. Managers spend a significant part of their time preparing and analyzing budgets. The many advantages of budgeting make spending time on the budgeting process a worthwhile investment of managers' energies.

◄ Decision Point

What is the master budget and why is it useful?

Advantages of Budgets

Budgets are an integral part of management control systems. When administered thoughtfully by managers, budgets do the following:

- Promote coordination and communication among subunits within the company
- Provide a framework for judging performance and facilitating learning
- Motivate managers and other employees

Learning Objective 2

Describe the advantages of budgets

. . . advantages include coordination, communication, performance evaluation, and managerial motivation

Coordination and Communication

Coordination is meshing and balancing all aspects of production or service and all departments in a company in the best way for the company to meet its goals. *Communication* is making sure those goals are understood by all employees.

Coordination forces executives to think of relationships among individual departments within the company, as well as between the company and its supply chain partners. Consider budgeting at Pace, a United Kingdom-based manufacturer of electronic products. A key product is Pace's digital set-top box for decoding satellite broadcasts. The production manager can achieve more timely production by coordinating and communicating with the company's marketing team to understand when set-top boxes will be needed. In turn, the marketing team can make better predictions of future demand for set-top boxes by coordinating and communicating with Pace's customers.

Suppose BSkyB, one of Pace's largest customers, is planning to launch a new high-definition personal video recorder service. If Pace's marketing group is able to obtain information about the launch date for the service, it can share this information with Pace's manufacturing group. The manufacturing group must then coordinate and communicate with Pace's materials-procurement group, and so on. The point to understand is that Pace is more likely to have satisfied customers (by having personal video recorders in the demanded quantities at the times demanded) if Pace coordinates and communicates both within its business functions and with its suppliers and customers during the budgeting process as well as during the production process.

Framework for Judging Performance and Facilitating Learning

Budgets enable a company's managers to measure actual performance against predicted performance. Budgets can overcome two limitations of using past performance as a basis for judging actual results. One limitation is that past results often incorporate past miscues and substandard performance. Consider a cellular telephone company (Mobile Communications) examining the current-year (2012) performance of its sales force. Suppose the performance for 2011 incorporated the efforts of many salespeople who have since left Mobile because they did not have a good understanding of the marketplace. (The president of Mobile said, "They could not sell ice cream in a heat wave.") Using the sales record of those departed employees would set the performance bar for 2012 much too low.

The other limitation of using past performance is that future conditions can be expected to differ from the past. Consider again Mobile Communications. Suppose, in 2012, Mobile had a 20% revenue increase, compared with a 10% revenue increase in 2011. Does this increase indicate outstanding sales performance? Before you say yes, consider the following facts. In November 2011, an industry trade association forecasts that the 2012 growth rate in industry revenues will be 40%, which also turned out to be the actual growth rate. As a result, Mobile's 20% actual revenue gain in 2012 takes on a negative connotation, even though it exceeded the 2011 actual growth rate of 10%. Using the 40% budgeted sales growth rate provides a better measure of the 2012 sales performance than using the 2011 actual growth rate of 10%.

It is important to remember that a company's budget should not be the only benchmark used to evaluate performance. Many companies also consider performance relative to peers as well as improvement over prior years. The problem with evaluating performance relative only to a budget is it creates an incentive for subordinates to set a target that is relatively easy to achieve.[2] Of course, managers at all levels recognize this incentive, and therefore work to make the budget more challenging to achieve for the individuals who report to them. Negotiations occur among managers at each of these levels to understand what is possible and what is not. The budget is the end product of these negotiations.

One of the most valuable benefits of budgeting is that it helps managers gather relevant information for improving future performance. When actual outcomes fall short of budgeted or planned results, it prompts thoughtful senior managers to ask questions about what happened and why, and how this knowledge can be used to ensure that such shortfalls do not occur again. This probing and learning is one of the most important reasons why budgeting helps improve performance.

Motivating Managers and Other Employees

Research shows that challenging budgets improve employee performance because employees view falling short of budgeted numbers as a failure. Most employees are motivated to work more intensely to avoid failure than to achieve success. As employees get

---

[2] For several examples, see J. Hope and R. Fraser, *Beyond Budgeting* (Boston, MA: Harvard Business School Press, 2003). The authors also criticize the tendency for managers to administer budgets rigidly even when changing market conditions have rendered the budget obsolete.

closer to a goal, they work harder to achieve it. Therefore, many executives like to set demanding but achievable goals for their subordinate managers and employees.[3] Creating a little anxiety improves performance, but overly ambitious and unachievable budgets increase anxiety without motivation because employees see little chance of avoiding failure. General Electric's former CEO, Jack Welch, describes challenging, yet achievable, budgets as energizing, motivating, and satisfying for managers and other employees, and capable of unleashing out-of-the-box and creative thinking.

Challenges in Administering Budgets

The budgeting process involves all levels of management. Top managers want lower-level managers to participate in the budgeting process because lower-level managers have more specialized knowledge and first-hand experience with day-to-day aspects of running the business. Participation creates greater commitment and accountability toward the budget among lower-level managers. This is the bottom-up aspect of the budgeting process.

The budgeting process, however, is a time-consuming one. It has been estimated that senior managers spend about 10% to 20% of their time on budgeting, and finance planning departments spend as much as 50% of their time on it.[4] For most organizations, the annual budget process is a months-long exercise that consumes a tremendous amount of resources. Despite his admiration for setting challenging targets, Jack Welch has also referred to the budgeting process as "the most ineffective process in management," and as "the bane of corporate America."

The widespread prevalence of budgets in companies ranging from major multinational corporations to small local businesses indicates that the advantages of budgeting systems outweigh the costs. To gain the benefits of budgeting, management at all levels of a company should understand and support the budget and all aspects of the management control system. This is critical for obtaining lower-level management's participation in the formulation of budgets and for successful administration of budgets. Lower-level managers who feel that top management does not "believe" in a budget are unlikely to be active participants in a budget process.

Budgets should not be administered rigidly. Attaining the budget is not an end in itself, especially when conditions change dramatically. A manager may commit to a budget, but if a situation arises in which some unplanned repairs or an unplanned advertising program would serve the long-run interests of the company, the manager should undertake the additional spending. On the flip side, the dramatic decline in consumer demand during the recent recession led designers such as Gucci to slash their ad budgets and put on hold planned new boutiques. Macy's and other retailers, stuck with shelves of merchandise ordered before the financial crisis, had no recourse but to slash prices and cut their workforce. JCPenney eventually missed its sales projections for 2008–09 by $2 billion. However, its aggressive actions during the year enabled it to survive the recession and emerge with sophisticated new inventory management plans to profit from the next holiday season.

Developing an Operating Budget

Budgets are typically developed for a set period, such as a month, quarter, year, and so on. The set period can itself be broken into subperiods. For example, a 12-month cash budget may be broken into 12 monthly periods so that cash inflows and outflows can be better coordinated.

Time Coverage of Budgets

The motive for creating a budget should guide a manager in choosing the period for the budget. For example, consider budgeting for a new Harley-Davidson 500-cc motorcycle. If the purpose is to budget for the total profitability of this new model, a five-year period (or more) may be suitable and long enough to cover the product from design through to manufacture, sales, and after-sales support. In contrast, consider budgeting for a school

> **◀ Decision Point**
>
> When should a company prepare budgets? What are the advantages of preparing budgets?

> **Learning Objective 3**
>
> Prepare the operating budget
>
> . . . the budgeted income statement
>
> and its supporting schedules
>
> . . . such as cost of goods sold and nonmanufacturing costs

---

[3] For a detailed discussion and several examples of the merits of setting specific hard goals, see G. Latham, "The Motivational Benefits of Goal-Setting," *Academy of Management Executive* 18, no. 4, (2004).

[4] See P. Horvath and R. Sauter, "Why Budgeting Fails: One Management System is Not Enough," Balanced Scorecard Report, (September 2004).

Exhibit 6-2

Overview of the Master
Budget for Stylistic
Furniture

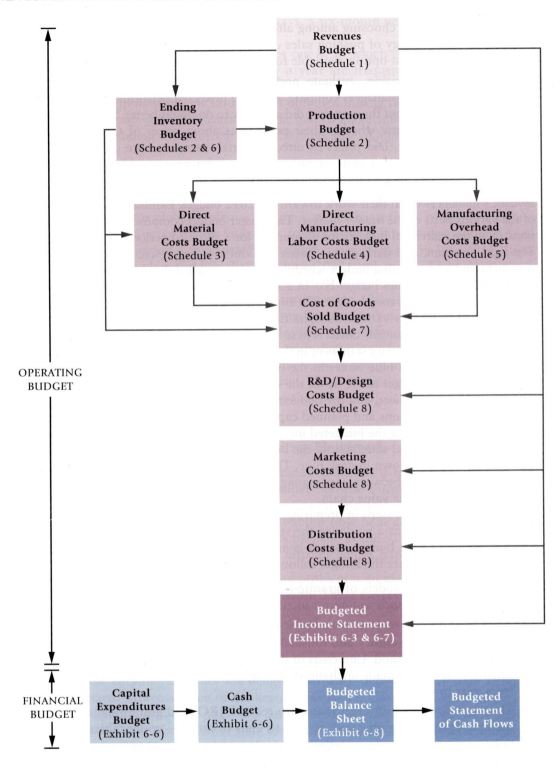

OPERATING
BUDGET

FINANCIAL
BUDGET

■ Nonmanufacturing costs consist of product design, marketing, and distribution costs.
All product design costs are fixed costs for 2012. The variable component of marketing costs equals the 6.5% sales commission on revenues paid to salespeople. The variable portion of distribution costs varies with cubic feet of tables moved.

The following data are available for the 2012 budget:

Direct materials	
Red Oak	$ 7 per board foot (b.f.) (same as in 2011)
Granite	$10 per square foot (sq. ft.) (same as in 2011)
Direct manufacturing labor	$20 per hour

Content of Each Product Unit

	Product	
	Casual Granite Table	**Deluxe Granite Table**
Red Oak	12 board feet	12 board feet
Granite	6 square feet	8 square feet
Direct manufacturing labor	4 hours	6 hours

	Product	
	Casual Granite Table	**Deluxe Granite Table**
Expected sales in units	50,000	10,000
Selling price	$ 600	$ 800
Target ending inventory in units	11,000	500
Beginning inventory in units	1,000	500
Beginning inventory in dollars	$384,000	$262,000

	Direct Materials	
	Red Oak	**Granite**
Beginning inventory	70,000 b.f.	60,000 sq. ft.
Target ending inventory	80,000 b.f.	20,000 sq. ft.

Stylistic bases its budgeted cost information on the costs it predicts it will incur to support its revenue budget, taking into account the efficiency improvements it expects to make in 2012. Recall from Step 3 in the decision-making process (p. 188) that efficiency improvements are critical to offset anticipated increases in the cost of inputs and to maintain Stylistic's 12% operating margin. Some companies rely heavily on past results when developing budgeted amounts; others rely on detailed engineering studies. Companies differ in how they compute their budgeted amounts.

Most companies have a budget manual that contains a company's particular instructions and relevant information for preparing its budgets. Although the details differ among companies, the following basic steps are common for developing the operating budget for a manufacturing company. Beginning with the revenues budget, each of the other budgets follows step-by-step in logical fashion.

Step 1: Prepare the Revenues Budget. A revenues budget, calculated in Schedule 1, is the usual starting point for the operating budget. That's because the production level and the inventory level—and therefore manufacturing costs—as well as nonmanufacturing costs, generally depend on the forecasted level of unit sales or revenues. Many factors influence the sales forecast, including the sales volume in recent periods, general economic and industry conditions, market research studies, pricing policies, advertising and sales promotions, competition, and regulatory policies. In Stylistic's case, the revenues budget for 2012 reflects Stylistic's strategy to grow revenues by increasing sales of Deluxe tables from 8,000 tables in 2011 to 10,000 tables in 2012.

Schedule 1: Revenues Budget
For the Year Ending December 31, 2012

	Units	Selling Price	Total Revenues
Casual	50,000	$600	$30,000,000
Deluxe	10,000	800	8,000,000
Total			$38,000,000

The $38,000,000 is the amount of revenues in the budgeted income statement. The revenues budget is often the result of elaborate information gathering and discussions among sales managers and sales representatives who have a detailed understanding of customer needs, market potential, and competitors' products. This information is often gathered through a customer response management (CRM) or sales management system. Statistical approaches such as regression and trend analysis can also help in sales forecasting. These techniques use indicators of economic activity and past sales data to forecast future sales. Managers should use statistical analysis only as one input to forecast sales. In the final analysis, the sales forecast should represent the collective experience and judgment of managers.

The usual starting point for Step 1 is to base revenues on expected demand. Occasionally, a factor other than demand limits budgeted revenues. For example, when demand is greater than available production capacity or a manufacturing input is in short supply, the revenues budget would be based on the maximum units that could be produced. Why? Because sales would be limited by the amount produced.

Step 2:   Prepare the Production Budget (in Units). After revenues are budgeted, the manufacturing manager prepares the production budget, which is calculated in Schedule 2. The total finished goods units to be produced depend on budgeted unit sales and expected changes in units of inventory levels:

$$
\begin{array}{c}
\text{Budget} \\
\text{production} \\
\text{(units)}
\end{array}
=
\begin{array}{c}
\text{Budget} \\
\text{sales} \\
\text{(units)}
\end{array}
+
\begin{array}{c}
\text{Target ending} \\
\text{finished goods} \\
\text{inventory} \\
\text{(units)}
\end{array}
-
\begin{array}{c}
\text{Beginning} \\
\text{finished goods} \\
\text{inventory} \\
\text{(units)}
\end{array}
$$

Schedule 2: Production Budget (in Units)
For the Year Ending December 31, 2012

	Product	
	Casual	**Deluxe**
Budgeted unit sales (Schedule 1)	50,000	10,000
Add target ending finished goods inventory	11,000	500
Total required units	61,000	10,500
Deduct beginning finished goods inventory	1,000	500
Units of finished goods to be produced	60,000	10,000

Step 3:   Prepare the Direct Material Usage Budget and Direct Material Purchases Budget. The number of units to be produced, calculated in Schedule 2, is the key to computing the usage of direct materials in quantities and in dollars. The direct material quantities used depend on the efficiency with which materials are consumed to produce a table. In determining budgets, managers are constantly anticipating ways to make process improvements that increase quality and reduce waste, thereby reducing direct material usage and costs.

Like many companies, Stylistic has a *bill of materials*, stored and updated in its computer systems. This document identifies how each product is manufactured, specifying all materials (and components), the sequence in which the materials are used, the quantity of materials in each finished unit, and the work centers where the operations are performed. For example, the bill of materials would indicate that 12 board feet of red oak and 6 square feet of granite are needed to produce each Casual coffee table, and 12 board feet of red oak and 8 square feet of granite to produce each Deluxe coffee table. This information is then used to calculate the amounts in Schedule 3A.

Schedule 3A: Direct Material Usage Budget in Quantity and Dollars
For the Year Ending December 31, 2012

	Material		Total
	Red Oak	**Granite**	
Physical Units Budget			
Direct materials required for Casual tables	720,000 b.f.	360,000 sq. ft.	
(60,000 units × 12 b.f. and 6 sq. ft.)			
Direct materials required for Deluxe tables	120,000 b.f.	80,000 sq. ft.	
(10,000 units × 12 b.f. and 8 sq. ft.)			
Total quantity of direct materials to be used	840,000 b.f.	440,000 sq. ft.	
Cost Budget			
Available from beginning direct materials inventory			
(under a FIFO cost-flow assumption)			
Red Oak: 70,000 b.f. × $7 per b.f.	$ 490,000		
Granite: 60,000 sq. ft. × $10 per sq. ft.		$ 600,000	
To be purchased this period			
Red Oak: (840,000 − 70,000) b.f. × $7 per b.f.	5,390,000		
Granite: (440,000 − 60,000) sq. ft. × $10 per sq. ft.		3,800,000	
Direct materials to be used this period	$5,880,000	$4,400,000	$10,280,000

The purchasing manager prepares the budget for direct material purchases, calculated in Schedule 3B, based on the budgeted direct materials to be used, the beginning inventory of direct materials, and the target ending inventory of direct materials:

$$\begin{array}{ccc} \text{Purchases} & \text{Direct} & \text{Target ending} & \text{Beginning} \\ \text{of direct} = & \text{materials} + \text{inventory} - \text{inventory} \\ \text{materials} & \text{used in} & \text{of direct} & \text{of direct} \\ & \text{production} & \text{materials} & \text{materials} \end{array}$$

Schedule 3B: Direct Material Purchases Budget
For the Year Ending December 31, 2012

	Material		
	Red Oak	**Granite**	**Total**
Physical Units Budget			
To be used in production (from Schedule 3A)	840,000 b.f.	440,000 sq. ft.	
Add target ending inventory	80,000 b.f.	20,000 sq. ft.	
Total requirements	920,000 b.f.	460,000 sq. ft.	
Deduct beginning inventory	70,000 b.f.	60,000 sq. ft.	
Purchases to be made	850,000 b.f.	400,000 sq. ft.	
Cost Budget			
Red Oak: 850,000 b.f. × $7 per b.f.	$5,950,000		
Granite: 400,000 sq. ft. × $10 per sq. ft.		$4,000,000	
Purchases	$5,950,000	$4,000,000	$9,950,000

Step 4: Prepare the Direct Manufacturing Labor Costs Budget. In this step, manufacturing managers use *labor standards*, the time allowed per unit of output, to calculate the direct manufacturing labor costs budget in Schedule 4. These costs depend on wage rates, production methods, process and efficiency improvements, and hiring plans.

Schedule 4: Direct Manufacturing Labor Costs Budget
For the Year Ending December 31, 2012

	Output Units Produced (Schedule 2)	Direct Manufacturing Labor-Hours per Unit	Total Hours	Hourly Wage Rate	Total
Casual	60,000	4	240,000	$20	$4,800,000
Deluxe	10,000	6	60,000	20	1,200,000
Total			300,000		$6,000,000

Step 5: Prepare the Manufacturing Overhead Costs Budget. As we described earlier, direct manufacturing labor-hours is the cost driver for the variable portion of manufacturing operations overhead and setup labor-hours is the cost driver for the variable portion of machine setup overhead costs. The use of activity-based cost drivers such as these gives rise to *activity-based budgeting*. **Activity-based budgeting (ABB)** focuses on the budgeted cost of the activities necessary to produce and sell products and services.

For the 300,000 direct manufacturing labor-hours, Stylistic's manufacturing managers estimate various line items of overhead costs that constitute manufacturing operations overhead (that is, all costs for which direct manufacturing labor-hours is the cost driver). Managers identify opportunities for process improvements and determine budgeted manufacturing operations overhead costs in the operating department. They also determine the resources that they will need from the two support departments—kilowatt hours of energy from the power department and hours of maintenance service from the maintenance department. The support department managers, in turn, plan the costs of personnel and supplies that they will need in order to provide the operating department with the support services it requires. The costs of the support departments are then allocated (first-stage cost allocation) as part of manufacturing operations overhead. Chapter 15 describes how the allocation of support department costs to operating departments is done when support departments provide services to each other and to operating departments. The upper half of Schedule 5 shows the various line items of costs that constitute manufacturing operations overhead costs—that is, all overhead costs that are caused by the 300,000 direct manufacturing labor-hours (the cost driver).

Stylistic's managers determine how setups should be done for the Casual and Deluxe line of tables, taking into account past experiences and potential improvements in setup efficiency. For example, managers consider the following:

- Increasing the length of the production run per batch so that fewer batches (and therefore fewer setups) are needed for the budgeted production of tables
- Decreasing the setup time per batch
- Reducing the supervisory time needed, for instance by increasing the skill base of workers

Stylistic's managers forecast the following setup information for the Casual and Deluxe tables:

	Casual Tables	Deluxe Tables	Total
1. Quantity of tables to be produced	60,000 tables	10,000 tables	
2. Number of tables to be produced per batch	50 tables/batch	40 tables/batch	
3. Number of batches (1) ÷ (2)	1,200 batches	250 batches	
4. Setup time per batch	10 hours/batch	12 hours/batch	
5. Total setup-hours (3) × (4)	12,000 hours	3,000 hours	15,000 hours
6. Setup-hours per table (5) ÷ (1)	0.2 hour	0.3 hour	

Using an approach similar to the one described for manufacturing operations overhead costs, Stylistic's managers estimate various line items of costs that comprise machine setup overhead costs—that is, all costs that are caused by the 15,000 setup labor-hours (the cost driver). Note how using activity-based cost drivers provide additional and detailed information that improves decision making compared with budgeting based solely on output-based cost drivers. Of course, managers must always evaluate whether the expected benefit of adding more cost drivers exceeds the expected cost.[5] The bottom half of Schedule 5 summarizes these costs.

Schedule 5: Manufacturing Overhead Costs Budget
For the Year Ending December 31, 2012
Manufacturing Operations Overhead Costs

Variable costs		
Supplies	$1,500,000	
Indirect manufacturing labor	1,680,000	
Power (support department costs)	2,100,000	
Maintenance (support department costs)	1,200,000	$6,480,000
Fixed costs (to support capacity of 300,000 direct manufacturing labor-hours)		
Depreciation	1,020,000	
Supervision	390,000	
Power (support department costs)	630,000	
Maintenance (support department costs)	480,000	2,520,000
Total manufacturing operations overhead costs		$9,000,000

Machine Setup Overhead Costs

Variable costs		
Supplies	$ 390,000	
Indirect manufacturing labor	840,000	
Power (support department costs)	90,000	$ 1,320,000
Fixed costs (to support capacity of 15,000 setup labor-hours)		
Depreciation	603,000	
Supervision	1,050,000	
Power (support department costs)	27,000	1,680,000
Total machine setup overhead costs		$ 3,000,000
Total manufacturing operations overhead costs		$12,000,000

[5] The Stylistic example illustrates ABB using setup costs included in Stylistic's manufacturing overhead costs budget. ABB implementations in practice include costs in many parts of the value chain. For an example, see S. Borjesson, "A Case Study on Activity-Based Budgeting," *Journal of Cost Management* 10, no. 4: 7–18.

Step 6: Prepare the Ending Inventories Budget. The management accountant prepares the ending inventories budget, calculated in Schedules 6A and 6B. In accordance with generally accepted accounting principles, Stylistic treats both variable and fixed manufacturing overhead as inventoriable (product) costs. Stylistic is budgeted to operate at capacity. Manufacturing operations overhead costs are allocated to finished goods inventory at the budgeted rate of $30 per direct manufacturing labor-hour (total budgeted manufacturing operations overhead, $9,000,000 ÷ 300,000 budgeted direct manufacturing labor-hours). Machine setup overhead costs are allocated to finished goods inventory at the budgeted rate of $200 per setup-hour (total budgeted machine setup overhead, $3,000,000 ÷ 15,000 budgeted setup labor-hours). Schedule 6A shows the computation of the unit cost of coffee tables started and completed in 2012.

Schedule 6A: Unit Costs of Ending Finished Goods Inventory
December 31, 2012

| | | Product | | | |
| | | Casual Tables | | Deluxe Tables | |
	Cost per Unit of Input	Input per Unit of Output	Total	Input per Unit of Output	Total
Red Oak	$ 7	12 b.f.	$ 84	12 b.f.	$ 84
Granite	10	6 sq. ft.	60	8 sq. ft.	80
Direct manufacturing labor	20	4 hrs.	80	6 hrs.	120
Manufacturing overhead	30	4 hrs.	120	6 hrs.	180
Machine setup overhead	200	0.2 hrs.	40	0.3 hrs.	60
Total			$384		$524

Under the FIFO method, this unit cost is used to calculate the cost of target ending inventories of finished goods in Schedule 6B.

Schedule 6B: Ending Inventories Budget
December 31, 2012

	Quantity	Cost per Unit		Total
Direct materials				
Red Oak	80,000*	$ 7	$ 560,000	
Granite	20,000*	10	200,000	$ 760,000
Finished goods				
Casual	11,000**	$384***	$4,224,000	
Deluxe	500**	524***	262,000	4,486,000
Total ending inventory				$5,246,000

*Data are from page 191. **Data are from page 191 ***From Schedule 6A, this is based on 2012 costs of manufacturing finished goods because under the FIFO costing method, the units in finished goods ending inventory consists of units that are produced during 2012.

Step 7: Prepare the Cost of Goods Sold Budget. The manufacturing and purchase managers, together with the management accountant, use information from Schedules 3 through 6 to prepare Schedule 7.

Schedule 7: Cost of Goods Sold Budget
For the Year Ending December 31, 2012

	From Schedule		Total
Beginning finished goods inventory, January 1, 2012	Given*		$ 646,000
Direct materials used	3A	$10,280,000	
Direct manufacturing labor	4	6,000,000	
Manufacturing overhead	5	12,000,000	
Cost of goods manufactured			28,280,000
Cost of goods available for sale			28,926,000
Deduct ending finished goods inventory, December 31, 2012	6B		4,486,000
Cost of goods sold			$24,440,000

*Given in the description of basic data and requirements (Casual, $384,000, Deluxe $262,000).

Step 8: Prepare the Nonmanufacturing Costs Budget. Schedules 2 through 7 cover budgeting for Stylistic's production function of the value chain. For brevity, other parts of the value chain—product design, marketing, and distribution—are combined into a single schedule. Just as in the case of manufacturing costs, managers in other functions of the value chain build in process and efficiency improvements and prepare nonmanufacturing cost budgets on the basis of the quantities of cost drivers planned for 2012.

Product design costs are fixed costs, determined on the basis of the product design work anticipated for 2012. The variable component of budgeted marketing costs is the commissions paid to sales people equal to 6.5% of revenues. The fixed component of budgeted marketing costs equal to $1,330,000 is tied to the marketing capacity for 2012. The cost driver of the variable component of budgeted distribution costs is cubic feet of tables moved (Casual: 18 cubic feet × 50,000 tables + Deluxe: 24 cubic feet × 10,000 tables = 1,140,000 cubic feet). Variable distribution costs equal $2 per cubic foot. The fixed component of budgeted distribution costs equals $1,596,000 and is tied to the distribution capacity for 2012. Schedule 8 shows the product design, marketing, and distribution costs budget for 2012.

Schedule 8: Nonmanufacturing Costs Budget
For the Year Ending December 31, 2012

Business Function	Variable Costs	Fixed Costs	Total Costs
Product design	—	$1,024,000	$1,024,000
Marketing (Variable cost: $38,000,000 × 0.065)	$2,470,000	1,330,000	3,800,000
Distribution (Variable cost: $2 × 1,140,000 cu. ft.)	2,280,000	1,596,000	3,876,000
	$4,750,000	$3,950,000	$8,700,000

Step 9: Prepare the Budgeted Income Statement. The CEO and managers of various business functions, with help from the management accountant, use information in Schedules 1, 7, and 8 to finalize the budgeted income statement, shown in Exhibit 6-3. The style used in Exhibit 6-3 is typical, but more details could be included in the income statement; the more details that are put in the income statement, the fewer supporting schedules that are needed for the income statement.

Budgeting is a cross-functional activity. Top management's strategies for achieving revenue and operating income goals influence the costs planned for the different business functions of the value chain. For example, a budgeted increase in sales based on spending more for marketing must be matched with higher production costs to ensure that there is an adequate supply of tables and with higher distribution costs to ensure timely delivery of tables to customers.

Rex Jordan, the CEO of Stylistic Furniture, is very pleased with the 2012 budget. It calls for a 10% increase in operating income compared with 2011. The keys to achieving a higher operating income are a significant increase in sales of Deluxe tables, and process improvements and efficiency gains throughout the value chain. As Rex studies the budget

Exhibit 6-3

Budgeted Income Statement for Stylistic Furniture

	A	B	C	D
	Home Insert Page Layout Formulas Data Review View			
1	Budgeted Income Statement for Stylistic Furniture			
2	For the Year Ending December 31, 2012			
3	Revenues	Schedule 1		$38,000,000
4	Cost of goods sold	Schedule 7		24,440,000
5	Gross margin			13,560,000
6	Operating costs			
7	Product design costs	Schedule 8	$1,024,000	
8	Marketing costs	Schedule 8	3,800,000	
9	Distribution costs	Schedule 8	3,876,000	8,700,000
10	Operating income			$ 4,860,000

more carefully, however, he is struck by two comments appended to the budget: First, to achieve the budgeted number of tables sold, Stylistic may need to reduce its selling prices by 3% to $582 for Casual tables and to $776 for Deluxe tables. Second, a supply shortage in direct materials may result in a 5% increase in the prices of direct materials (red oak and granite) above the material prices anticipated in the 2012 budget. If direct materials prices increase, however, no reduction in selling prices is anticipated. He asks Tina Larsen, the management accountant, to use Stylistic's financial planning model to evaluate how these outcomes will affect budgeted operating income.

Decision Point ◀

What is the operating budget and what are its components?

Financial Planning Models and Sensitivity Analysis

Financial planning models are mathematical representations of the relationships among operating activities, financing activities, and other factors that affect the master budget. Companies can use computer-based systems, such as Enterprise Resource Planning (ERP) systems, to perform calculations for these planning models. Companies that use ERP systems, and other such budgeting tools, find that these systems simplify budgeting and reduce the computational burden and time required to prepare budgets. The Concepts in Action box on page 198 provides an example of one such company. ERP systems store vast quantities of information about the materials, machines and equipment, labor, power, maintenance, and setups needed to manufacture different products. Once sales quantities for different products have been identified, the software can quickly compute the budgeted costs for manufacturing these products.

Software packages typically have a module on sensitivity analysis to assist managers in their planning and budgeting activities. *Sensitivity analysis* is a "what-if" technique that examines how a result will change if the original predicted data are not achieved or if an underlying assumption changes.

To see how sensitivity analysis works, we consider two scenarios identified as possibly affecting Stylistic Furniture's budget model for 2012.

> **Scenario 1:** A 3% decrease in the selling price of the Casual table and a 3% decrease in the selling price of the Deluxe table.

> **Scenario 2:** A 5% increase in the price per board foot of red oak and a 5% increase in the price per square foot of granite.

Exhibit 6-4 presents the budgeted operating income for the two scenarios.

Note that under Scenario 1, a change in selling prices per table affects revenues (Schedule 1) as well as variable marketing costs (sales commissions, Schedule 8). The Problem for Self-Study at the end of the chapter shows the revised schedules for Scenario 1. Similarly, a change in the price of direct materials affects the direct material usage budget (Schedule 3A), the unit cost of ending finished goods inventory (Schedule 6A), the ending

Learning Objective 4

Use computer-based financial planning models in sensitivity analysis

. . . for example, understand the effects of changes in selling prices and direct material prices on budgeted income

Exhibit 6-4 Effect of Changes in Budget Assumptions on Budgeted Operating Income for Stylistic Furniture

	A	B	C	D	E	F	G	H	I
		Home	Insert	Page Layout	Formulas	Data	Review	View	
1		**Key Assumptions**							
2		**Units Sold**		**Selling Price**		**Direct Material Cost**		**Budgeted Operating Income**	
3	**What-If Scenario**	Casual	Deluxe	Casual	Deluxe	Red Oak	Granite	Dollars	**Change from Master Budget**
4	Master budget	50,000	10,000	$600	$800	$7.00	$10.00	$4,860,000	
5	Scenario 1	50,000	10,000	582	776	$7.00	$10.00	3,794,100	22% decrease
6	Scenario 2	50,000	10,000	600	800	$7.35	$10.50	4,483,800	8% decrease

Concepts in Action

Web-Enabled Budgeting and Hendrick Motorsports

In recent years, an increasing number of companies have implemented comprehensive software packages that manage budgeting and forecasting functions across the organization. One such option is Microsoft Forecaster, which was originally designed by FRx Software for businesses looking to gain control over their budgeting and forecasting process within a fully integrated Web-based environment.

Among the more unique companies implementing Web-enabled budgeting is Hendrick Motorsports. Featuring champion drivers Jeff Gordon and Jimmie Johnson, Hendrick is the premier NASCAR Sprint Cup stock car racing organization. According to Forbes magazine, Hendrick is NASCAR's most valuable team, with an estimated value of $350 million. Headquartered on a 12 building, 600,000-square-foot campus near Charlotte, North Carolina, Hendrick operates four full-time teams in the Sprint Cup series, which runs annually from February through November and features 36 races at 22 speedways across the United States. The Hendrick organization has annual revenues of close to $195 million and more than 500 employees, with tasks ranging from accounting and marketing to engine building and racecar driving. Such an environment features multiple functional areas and units, varied worksites, and ever-changing circumstances. Patrick Perkins, director of marketing, noted, "Racing is a fast business. It's just as fast off the track as it is on it. With the work that we put into development of our teams and technologies, and having to respond to change as well as anticipate change, I like to think of us in this business as change experts."

Microsoft Forecaster, Hendrick's Web-enabled budgeting package, has allowed Hendrick's financial managers to seamlessly manage the planning and budgeting process. Authorized users from each functional area or team sign on to the application through the corporate intranet. Security on the system is tight: Access is limited to only the accounts that a manager is authorized to budget. (For example, Jeff Gordon's crew chief is not able to see what Jimmie Johnson's team members are doing.) Forecaster also allows users at the racetrack to access the application remotely, which allows mangers to receive or update real-time "actuals" from the system. This way, team managers know their allotted expenses for each race. Forecaster also provides users with additional features, including seamless links with general ledger accounts and the option to perform what-if (sensitivity) analyses. Scott Lampe, chief financial officer, said, "Forecaster allows us to change our forecasts to respond to changes, either rule changes [such as changes in the series' points system] or technology changes [such as pilot testing NASCAR's new, safer "Car of Tomorrow"] throughout the racing season."

Hendrick's Web-enabled budgeting system frees the finance department so it can work on strategy, analysis, and decision making. It also allows Hendrick to complete its annual budgeting process in only six weeks, a 50% reduction in the time spent budgeting and planning, which is critical given NASCAR's extremely short off-season. Patrick Pearson from Hendrick Motorsports believes the system gives the organization a competitive advantage: "In racing, the team that wins is not only the team with the fastest car, but the team that is the most disciplined and prepared week in and week out. Forecaster allows us to respond to that changing landscape."

Sources: Gage, Jack. 2009. Nascar's most valuable teams. Forbes.com, June 3. http://www.forbes.com/2009/06/03/nascar-most-valuable-teams-business-sports-nascar.html; Goff, John. 2004. In the fast lane. *CFO Magazine*, December 1; Hendrick Motorsports. 2010. About Hendrick Motorsports. Hendrick Motorsports Web site, May 28. www.hendrickmotorsports.com; Lampe, Scott. 2003. NASCAR racing team stays on track with FRx Software's comprehensive budget planning solution. *DM Review*, July 1; Microsoft Corporation. 2009. Microsoft Forecaster: Hendrick Motorsports customer video. October 8. http://www.microsoft.com/BusinessSolutions/frx_hendrick_video.mspx; Ryan, Nate. 2006. Hendrick empire strikes back with three contenders in chase for the Nextel Cup. *USA Today*, September 17.

finished goods inventories budget (in Schedule 6B) and the cost of goods sold budget (Schedule 7). Sensitivity analysis is especially useful in incorporating such interrelationships into budgeting decisions by managers.

Exhibit 6-4 shows a substantial decrease in operating income as a result of decreases in selling prices but a smaller decline in operating income if direct material prices increase by 5%. The sensitivity analysis prompts Stylistic's managers to put in place contingency plans. For example, should selling prices decline in 2012, Stylistic may choose to postpone some product development programs that it had included in its 2012 budget but that could be deferred to a later year. More generally, when the success or viability of a venture is highly dependent on attaining one or more targets, managers should frequently update their budgets as uncertainty is resolved. These updated budgets can help managers to adjust expenditure levels as circumstances change.

Instructors and students who, at this point, want to explore the cash budget and the budgeted balance sheet for the Stylistic Furniture example can skip ahead to the appendix on page 206.

Decision Point

How can managers plan for changes in the assumptions underlying the budget?

Budgeting and Responsibility Accounting

To attain the goals described in the master budget, a company must coordinate the efforts of all its employees—from the top executive through all levels of management to every supervised worker. Coordinating the company's efforts means assigning responsibility to managers who are accountable for their actions in planning and controlling human and other resources. How each company structures its own organization significantly shapes how the company's efforts will be coordinated.

Learning Objective 5

Describe responsibility centers

. . . a part of an organization that a manager is accountable for

and responsibility accounting

. . . measurement of plans and actual results that a manager is accountable for

Organization Structure and Responsibility

Organization structure is an arrangement of lines of responsibility within the organization. A company such as ExxonMobil is organized by business function—exploration, refining, marketing, and so on—with the president of each business-line company having decision-making authority over his or her function. Another company, such as Procter & Gamble, the household-products giant, is organized primarily by product line or brand. The managers of the individual divisions (toothpaste, soap, and so on) would each have decision-making authority concerning all the business functions (manufacturing, marketing, and so on) within that division.

Each manager, regardless of level, is in charge of a responsibility center. A **responsibility center** is a part, segment, or subunit of an organization whose manager is accountable for a specified set of activities. The higher the manager's level, the broader the responsibility center and the larger the number of his or her subordinates. **Responsibility accounting** is a system that measures the plans, budgets, actions, and actual results of each responsibility center. Four types of responsibility centers are as follows:

1. **Cost center**—the manager is accountable for costs only.
2. **Revenue center**—the manager is accountable for revenues only.
3. **Profit center**—the manager is accountable for revenues and costs.
4. **Investment center**—the manager is accountable for investments, revenues, and costs.

The maintenance department of a Marriott hotel is a cost center because the maintenance manager is responsible only for costs, so this budget is based on costs. The sales department is a revenue center because the sales manager is responsible primarily for revenues, so this budget is based on revenues. The hotel manager is in charge of a profit center because the manager is accountable for both revenues and costs, so this budget is based on revenues and costs. The regional manager responsible for determining the amount to be invested in new hotel projects and for revenues and costs generated from these investments is in charge of an investment center, so this budget is based on revenues, costs, and the investment base.

A responsibility center can be structured to promote better alignment of individual and company goals. For example, until recently, OPD, an office products distributor, operated its sales department as a revenue center. Each salesperson received a commission of 3% of the revenues per order, regardless of its size, the cost of processing it, or the cost of delivering the office products. An analysis of customer profitability at OPD found that many customers were unprofitable. The main reason was the high ordering and delivery costs of small orders. OPD's managers decided to make the sales department a profit center, accountable for revenues and costs, and to change the incentive system for salespeople to 15% of the monthly profits per customer. The costs for each customer included the ordering and delivery costs. The effect of this change was immediate. The sales department began charging customers for ordering and delivery, and salespeople at OPD actively encouraged customers to consolidate their purchases into fewer orders. As a result, each order began producing larger revenues. Customer profitability increased because of a 40% reduction in ordering and delivery costs in one year.

Feedback

Budgets coupled with responsibility accounting provide feedback to top management about the performance relative to the budget of different responsibility center managers.

Differences between actual results and budgeted amounts—called *variances*—if properly used, can help managers implement and evaluate strategies in three ways:

1. *Early warning.* Variances alert managers early to events not easily or immediately evident. Managers can then take corrective actions or exploit the available opportunities. For example, after observing a small decline in sales this period, managers may want to investigate if this is an indication of an even steeper decline to follow later in the year.

2. *Performance evaluation.* Variances prompt managers to probe how well the company has performed in implementing its strategies. Were materials and labor used efficiently? Was R&D spending increased as planned? Did product warranty costs decrease as planned?

3. *Evaluating strategy.* Variances sometimes signal to managers that their strategies are ineffective. For example, a company seeking to compete by reducing costs and improving quality may find that it is achieving these goals but that it is having little effect on sales and profits. Top management may then want to reevaluate the strategy.

Responsibility and Controllability

Controllability is the degree of influence that a specific manager has over costs, revenues, or related items for which he or she is responsible. A **controllable cost** is any cost that is primarily subject to the influence of a given *responsibility center manager* for a given *period*. A responsibility accounting system could either exclude all uncontrollable costs from a manager's performance report or segregate such costs from the controllable costs. For example, a machining supervisor's performance report might be confined to direct materials, direct manufacturing labor, power, and machine maintenance costs and might exclude costs such as rent and taxes paid on the plant.

In practice, controllability is difficult to pinpoint for at least two reasons:

1. Few costs are clearly under the sole influence of one manager. For example, prices of direct materials may be influenced by a purchasing manager, but these prices also depend on market conditions beyond the manager's control. Quantities used may be influenced by a production manager, but quantities used also depend on the quality of materials purchased. Moreover, managers often work in teams. Think about how difficult it is to evaluate individual responsibility in a team situation.

2. With a long enough time span, all costs will come under somebody's control. However, most performance reports focus on periods of a year or less. A current manager may benefit from a predecessor's accomplishments or may inherit a predecessor's problems and inefficiencies. For example, present managers may have to work under undesirable contracts with suppliers or labor unions that were negotiated by their predecessors. How can we separate what the current manager actually controls from the results of decisions made by others? Exactly what is the current manager accountable for? Answers may not be clear-cut.

Executives differ in how they embrace the controllability notion when evaluating those reporting to them. Some CEOs regard the budget as a firm commitment that subordinates must meet. Failure to meet the budget is viewed unfavorably. Other CEOs believe a more risk-sharing approach with managers is preferable, in which noncontrollable factors and performance relative to competitors are taken into account when judging the performance of managers who fail to meet their budgets.

Managers should avoid overemphasizing controllability. Responsibility accounting is more far-reaching. It focuses on gaining *information and knowledge*, not only on control. *Responsibility accounting helps managers to first focus on whom they should ask to obtain information and not on whom they should blame.* For example, if actual revenues at a Marriott hotel are less than budgeted revenues, the managers of the hotel may be tempted to blame the sales manager for the poor performance. The fundamental purpose of responsibility accounting, however, is not to fix blame but to gather information to enable future improvement.

Managers want to know who can tell them the most about the specific item in question, regardless of that person's ability to exert personal control over that item. For instance, purchasing managers may be held accountable for total purchase costs, not because of their ability to control market prices, but because of their ability to predict uncontrollable prices and to explain uncontrollable price changes. Similarly, managers at a Pizza Hut unit may be held responsible for operating income of their units, even though they (a) do not fully control selling prices or the costs of many food items and (b) have minimal flexibility about what items to sell or the ingredients in the items they sell. They are, however, in the best position to explain differences between their actual operating incomes and their budgeted operating incomes.

Performance reports for responsibility centers are sometimes designed to change managers' behavior in the direction top management desires. A cost-center manager may emphasize efficiency and deemphasize the pleas of sales personnel for faster service and rush orders. When evaluated as a profit center, the manager will more likely consider ways to influence activities that affect sales and weigh the impact of decisions on costs and revenues rather than on costs alone. To induce that change, some companies have changed the accountability of a cost center to a profit center. Call centers are an interesting example of this trend. As firms continue to differentiate on customer service while attempting to control operating expenses, driving efficiency wherever possible in the call centers has become a critical issue—as has driving revenue through this unique channel. There is increasing pressure for customer service representatives to promote new offers through upsell and cross-sell tactics. Microsoft, Oracle, and others offer software platforms that seek to evolve the call center from cost center to profit center. The new adage is, "Every service call is a sales call."

Decision Point

How do companies use responsibility centers? Should performance reports of responsibility center managers include only costs the manager can control?

Human Aspects of Budgeting

Why did we discuss the two major topics, the master budget and responsibility accounting, in the same chapter? Primarily to emphasize that human factors are crucial in budgeting. Too often, budgeting is thought of as a mechanical tool as the budgeting techniques themselves are free of emotion. However, the administration of budgeting requires education, persuasion, and intelligent interpretation.

Learning Objective 6

Recognize the human aspects of budgeting

. . . to engage subordinate managers in the budgeting process

Budgetary Slack

As we discussed earlier in this chapter, budgeting is most effective when lower-level managers actively participate and meaningfully engage in the budgeting process. Participation adds credibility to the budgeting process and creates greater commitment and accountability toward the budget. But participation requires "honest" communication about the business from subordinates and lower-level managers to their bosses.

At times, subordinates may try to "play games" and build in *budgetary slack*. **Budgetary slack** describes the practice of underestimating budgeted revenues, or overestimating budgeted costs, to make budgeted targets more easily achievable. It frequently occurs when budget variances (the differences between actual results and budgeted amounts) are used to evaluate performance. Line managers are also unlikely to be fully honest in their budget communications if top management mechanically institutes across-the-board cost reductions (say, a 10% reduction in all areas) in the face of projected revenue reductions.

Budgetary slack provides managers with a hedge against unexpected adverse circumstances. But budgetary slack also misleads top management about the true profit potential

Exhibit 6-6   Cash Budget for Stylistic Furniture for the Year Ending December 31, 2012

	Home	Insert	Page Layout	Formulas	Data	Review	View		
		A		B	C	D	E	F	

	A	1	2	3	4	Year as a Whole
1			Stylistic Furniture			
2			Cash Budget			
3			For Year Ending December 31, 2012			
4				Quarters		Year as a
5		1	2	3	4	Whole
6	Cash balance, beginning	$ 300,000	$ 350,715	$ 350,657	$ 350,070	$ 300,000
7	Add receipts					
8	Collections from customers	9,136,600	10,122,000	10,263,200	8,561,200	38,083,000
9	Total cash available for needs (x)	9,436,600	10,472,715	10,613,857	8,911,270	38,383,000
10	Deduct disbursements					
11	Direct materials	2,947,605	2,714,612	2,157,963	2,155,356	9,975,536
12	Payroll	3,604,512	2,671,742	2,320,946	2,562,800	11,160,000
13	Manufacturing overhead costs	2,109,018	1,530,964	1,313,568	1,463,450	6,417,000
14	Nonmanufacturing costs	1,847,750	1,979,000	1,968,250	1,705,000	7,500,000
15	Machinery purchase			758,000		758,000
16	Income taxes	725,000	400,000	400,000	400,000	1,925,000
17	Total disbursements (y)	11,233,885	9,296,318	8,918,727	8,286,606	37,735,536
18	Minimum cash balance desired	350,000	350,000	350,000	350,000	350,000
19	Total cash needed	11,583,885	9,646,318	9,268,727	8,636,606	38,085,536
20	Cash excess (deficiency)*	$ (2,147,285)	$ 826,397	$ 1,345,130	$ 274,664	$ 297,464
21	Financing					
22	Borrowing (at beginning)	$ 2,148,000	$ 0	$ 0	$ 0	$ 2,148,000
23	Repayment (at end)	0	(779,000)	(1,234,000)	(135,000)	(2,148,000)
24	Interest (at 12% per year)**	0	(46,740)	(111,060)	(16,200)	(174,000)
25	Total effects of financing (z)	$ 2,148,000	$ (825,740)	$ (1,345,060)	$ (151,200)	$ (174,000)
26	Cash balance, ending***	$ 350,715	$ 350,657	$ 350,070	$ 473,464	$ 473,464
27	*Excess of total cash available for needs − Total cash needed before financing.					
28	**Note that the short-term interest payments pertain only to the amount of principal being repaid at the end of a quarter. The specific computations regarding interest are $779,000 × 0.12 × 0.5 = $46,740; $1,234,000 × 0.12 × 0.75 = $111,060; $135,000 × 0.12 = $16,200. Also note that *depreciation does not require a cash outlay.*					
29	***Ending cash balance = Total cash available for needs (x) − Total disbursements (y) + Total effects of financing (z)					

ii. *Direct labor and other wage and salary outlays.* All payroll-related costs are paid in the month in which the labor effort occurs.

iii. *Other costs.* These depend on timing and credit terms. (In the Stylistic case, all other costs are paid in the month in which the cost is incurred.) *Note, depreciation does not require a cash outlay.*

iv. *Other disbursements.* These include outlays for property, plant, equipment, and other long-term investments.

v. Income tax payments.

c. **Financing effects.** Short-term financing requirements depend on how the total cash available for needs [keyed as (x) in Exhibit 6-6] compares with the total cash disbursements [keyed as (y)], plus the minimum ending cash balance desired. The financing plans will depend on the relationship between total cash available for needs and total cash needed. If there is a deficiency of cash, loans will be obtained. If there is excess cash, any outstanding loans will be repaid.

d. **Ending cash balance.** The cash budget in Exhibit 6-6 shows the pattern of short-term "self-liquidating" cash loans. In quarter 1, Stylistic budgets a $2,147,285 cash deficiency. Hence, it undertakes short-term borrowing of $2,148,000 that it pays off over the course of the year. Seasonal peaks of production or sales often result in heavy cash disbursements for purchases, payroll, and other operating outlays as the products are produced and sold. Cash receipts from customers typically lag behind sales. The loan is *self-liquidating* in the sense that the borrowed money is used to acquire resources that are used to produce and sell finished goods, and the proceeds from sales are used to repay the loan. This self-liquidating cycle is the movement from cash to inventories to receivables and back to cash.

2. The budgeted income statement is presented in Exhibit 6-7. It is merely the budgeted operating income statement in Exhibit 6-3 (p. 196) expanded to include interest expense and income taxes.

3. The budgeted balance sheet is presented in Exhibit 6-8. Each item is projected in light of the details of the business plan as expressed in all the previous budget schedules. For example, the ending balance of accounts receivable of $1,628,000 is computed by adding the budgeted revenues of $38,000,000 (from Schedule 1 on page 191) to the beginning balance of accounts receivable of $1,711,000 (from Exhibit 6-5) and subtracting cash receipts of $38,083,000 (from Exhibit 6-6).

For simplicity, the cash receipts and disbursements were given explicitly in this illustration. Usually, the receipts and disbursements are calculated based on the lags between the items reported on the accrual basis of accounting in an income statement and balance sheet and their related cash receipts and disbursements. Consider accounts receivable. In the first three quarters, Stylistic estimates that 80% of all sales made in a quarter are collected in the same quarter and 20% are collected in the following quarter. Estimated collections from customers each quarter are calculated in the following table (assuming sales by quarter of $9,282,000; $10,332,000; $10,246,000; and $8,140,000 that equal 2012 budgeted sales of $38,000,000).

Schedule of Cash Collections

	Quarters			
	1	2	3	4
Accounts receivable balance on 1-1-2012 (p. 207)				
(Fourth quarter sales from prior year collected in first quarter of 2012)	$1,711,000			
From first-quarter 2012 sales (9,282,000 × 0.80; 9,282,000 × 0.20)	7,425,600	$ 1,856,400		
From second-quarter 2012 sales (10,332,000 × 0.80; 10,332,000 × 0.20)		8,265,600	$ 2,066,400	
From third-quarter 2012 sales (10,246,000 × 0.80; 10,246,000 × 0.20)			8,196,800	$2,049,200
From fourth-quarter 2012 sales (8,140,000 × 0.80)				6,512,000
Total collections	$9,136,600	$10,122,000	$10,263,200	$8,561,200

Note that the quarterly cash collections from customers calculated in this schedule equal the cash collections by quarter shown on page 206. Furthermore, the difference between fourth-quarter sales and the cash collected from fourth-quarter sales, $8,140,000 − $6,512,000 = $1,628,000 appears as accounts receivable in the budgeted balance sheet as of December 31, 2012 (see Exhibit 6-8).

	A	B	C	D
1	Stylistic Furniture			
2	Budgeted Income Statement			
3	For the Year Ending December 31, 2012			
4	Revenues	Schedule 1		$38,000,000
5	Cost of goods sold	Schedule 7		24,440,000
6	Gross margin			13,560,000
7	Operating costs			
8	Product design costs	Schedule 8	$1,024,000	
9	Marketing costs	Schedule 8	3,800,000	
10	Distribution costs	Schedule 8	3,876,000	8,700,000
11	Operating income			4,860,000
12	Interest expense	Exhibit 6-6		174,000
13	Income before income taxes			4,686,000
14	Income taxes (at 40%)			1,874,400
15	Net income			$ 2,811,600

Exhibit 6-7

Budgeted Income Statement for Stylistic Furniture for the Year Ending December 31, 2012

Exhibit 6-8 Budgeted Balance Sheet for Stylistic Furniture, December 31, 2012

Home	Insert	Page Layout	Formulas	Data	Review	View

	A	B	C	D
1	Stylistic Furniture			
2	Budgeted Balance Sheet			
3	December 31, 2012			
4	Assets			
5	Current assets			
6	Cash (from Exhibit 6-6)		$ 473,464	
7	Accounts receivable (1)		1,628,000	
8	Direct materials inventory (2)		760,000	
9	Finished goods inventory (2)		4,486,000	$ 7,347,464
10	Property, plant, and equipment			
11	Land (3)		2,000,000	
12	Building and equipment (4)	$22,758,000		
13	Accumulated depreciation (5)	(8,523,000)	14,235,000	16,235,000
14	Total			$23,582,464
15	Liabilities and Stockholders' Equity			
16	Current liabilities			
17	Accounts payable (6)		$ 878,464	
18	Income taxes payable (7)		274,400	$ 1,152,864
19	Stockholders' equity			
20	Common stock, no-par, 25,000 shares outstanding (8)		3,500,000	
21	Retained earnings (9)		18,929,600	22,429,600
22	Total			$23,582,464
23				
24	Notes:			
25	Beginning balances are used as the starting point for most of the following computations:			
26	(1) $1,711,000 + $38,000,000 revenues − $38,083,000 receipts (Exhibit 6-6) = $1,628,000			
27	(2) From Schedule 6B, p. 195			
28	(3) From beginning balance sheet, p. 207			
29	(4) $22,000,000 + $758,000 purchases = $22,758,0000			
30	(5) $6,900,000 + $1,020,000 + $603,000 depreciation from Schedule 5, p. 194			
31	(6) $904,000 + $9,950,000 (Schedule 3B) − $9,975,536 (Exhibit 6-6) = $878,464			
32	There are no other current liabilities. Cash flows for payroll, manufacturing overhead and nonmanufacturing costs totaling $25,077,000 on the cash budget (Exhibit 6-6) consists of direct manufacturing labor costs of $6,000,000 from Schedule 4 + cash manufacturing overhead costs of $10,377,000 ($12,000,000 − depreciation of $1,623,000) from Schedule 5 + cash nonmanufacturing costs of $8,700,000 from Schedule 8.			
33	(7) $325,000 + $1,874,400 current year − $1,925,0000 payment = $274,400.			
34	(8) From beginning balance sheet.			
35	(9) $16,118,000 + $2,811,600 net income per Exhibit 6-7 = $18,929,600			

Sensitivity Analysis and Cash Flows

Exhibit 6-4 (p. 197) shows how differing assumptions about selling prices of coffee tables and direct material prices led to differing amounts for budgeted operating income for Stylistic Furniture. A key use of sensitivity analysis is to budget cash flow. Exhibit 6-9 outlines the short-term borrowing implications of the two combinations examined in Exhibit 6-4. Scenario 1, with the lower selling prices per table ($582 for the Casual table and $776 for the Deluxe table), requires $2,352,000 of short-term borrowing in quarter 1 that cannot be fully repaid as of December 31, 2012. Scenario 2, with the 5% higher direct material costs, requires $2,250,000 borrowing by Stylistic Furniture that also cannot be repaid by December 31, 2012. Sensitivity analysis helps managers anticipate such outcomes and take steps to minimize the effects of expected reductions in cash flows from operations.

Exhibit 6-9 Sensitivity Analysis: Effects of Key Budget Assumptions in Exhibit 6-4 on 2012 Short-Term Borrowing for Stylistic Furniture

	Home	Insert	Page Layout	Formulas	Data	Review	View			
	A	B	C	D	E	F	G	H	I	J
1				Direct Material			Short-Term Borrowing and Repayment by Quarter			
2		Selling Price		Purchase Costs		Budgeted	Quarters			
3	Scenario	Casual	Deluxe	Red Oak	Granite	Operating Income	1	2	3	4
4	1	$582	$776	$7.00	$10.00	$3,794,100	$2,352,000	($511,000)	($ 969,000)	($ 30,000)
5	2	$600	$800	7.35	10.50	4,483,800	2,250,000	(651,000)	(1,134,000)	(149,000)

Terms to Learn

The chapter and the Glossary at the end of the book contain definitions of the following important terms:

activity-based budgeting (ABB) (**p. 193**)

budgetary slack (**p. 201**)

cash budget (**p. 207**)

continuous budget (**p. 188**)

controllability (**p. 200**)

controllable cost (**p. 200**)

cost center (**p. 199**)

financial budget (**p. 189**)

financial planning models (**p. 197**)

investment center (**p. 199**)

kaizen budgeting (**p. 203**)

master budget (**p. 185**)

operating budget (**p. 189**)

organization structure (**p. 199**)

pro forma statements (**p. 185**)

profit center (**p. 199**)

responsibility accounting (**p. 199**)

responsibility center (**p. 199**)

revenue center (**p. 199**)

rolling budget (**p. 188**)

Assignment Material

Questions

6-1 What are the four elements of the budgeting cycle?

6-2 Define master budget.

6-3 "Strategy, plans, and budgets are unrelated to one another." Do you agree? Explain.

6-4 "Budgeted performance is a better criterion than past performance for judging managers." Do you agree? Explain.

6-5 "Production managers and marketing managers are like oil and water. They just don't mix." How can a budget assist in reducing battles between these two areas?

6-6 "Budgets meet the cost-benefit test. They force managers to act differently." Do you agree? Explain.

6-7 Define rolling budget. Give an example.

6-8 Outline the steps in preparing an operating budget.

6-9 "The sales forecast is the cornerstone for budgeting." Why?

6-10 How can sensitivity analysis be used to increase the benefits of budgeting?

6-11 Define kaizen budgeting.

6-12 Describe how nonoutput-based cost drivers can be incorporated into budgeting.

6-13 Explain how the choice of the type of responsibility center (cost, revenue, profit, or investment) affects behavior.

6-14 What are some additional considerations that arise when budgeting in multinational companies?

6-15 "Cash budgets must be prepared before the operating income budget." Do you agree? Explain.

Exercises

6-16 Sales budget, service setting. In 2011, Rouse & Sons, a small environmental-testing firm, performed 12,200 radon tests for $290 each and 16,400 lead tests for $240 each. Because newer homes are being built with lead-free pipes, lead-testing volume is expected to decrease by 10% next year. However, awareness of radon-related health hazards is expected to result in a 6% increase in radon-test volume each year in the near future. Jim Rouse feels that if he lowers his price for lead testing to $230 per test, he will have to face only a 7% decline in lead-test sales in 2012.

Required

1. Prepare a 2012 sales budget for Rouse & Sons assuming that Rouse holds prices at 2011 levels.
2. Prepare a 2012 sales budget for Rouse & Sons assuming that Rouse lowers the price of a lead test to $230. Should Rouse lower the price of a lead test in 2012 if its goal is to maximize sales revenue?

6-17 Sales and production budget. The Mendez Company expects sales in 2012 of 200,000 units of serving trays. Mendez's beginning inventory for 2012 is 15,000 trays and its target ending inventory is 25,000 trays. Compute the number of trays budgeted for production in 2012.

6-18 Direct material budget. Inglenook Co. produces wine. The company expects to produce 2,500,000 two-liter bottles of Chablis in 2012. Inglenook purchases empty glass bottles from an outside vendor. Its target ending inventory of such bottles is 80,000; its beginning inventory is 50,000. For simplicity, ignore breakage. Compute the number of bottles to be purchased in 2012.

6-19 Budgeting material purchases. The Mahoney Company has prepared a sales budget of 45,000 finished units for a three-month period. The company has an inventory of 16,000 units of finished goods on hand at December 31 and has a target finished goods inventory of 18,000 units at the end of the succeeding quarter.

It takes three gallons of direct materials to make one unit of finished product. The company has an inventory of 60,000 gallons of direct materials at December 31 and has a target ending inventory of 50,000 gallons at the end of the succeeding quarter. How many gallons of direct materials should be purchased during the three months ending March 31?

6-20 Revenues and production budget. Purity, Inc., bottles and distributes mineral water from the company's natural springs in northern Oregon. Purity markets two products: twelve-ounce disposable plastic bottles and four-gallon reusable plastic containers.

Required

1. For 2012, Purity marketing managers project monthly sales of 400,000 twelve-ounce bottles and 100,000 four-gallon containers. Average selling prices are estimated at $0.25 per twelve-ounce bottle and $1.50 per four-gallon container. Prepare a revenues budget for Purity, Inc., for the year ending December 31, 2012.
2. Purity begins 2012 with 900,000 twelve-ounce bottles in inventory. The vice president of operations requests that twelve-ounce bottles ending inventory on December 31, 2012, be no less than 600,000 bottles. Based on sales projections as budgeted previously, what is the minimum number of twelve-ounce bottles Purity must produce during 2012?
3. The VP of operations requests that ending inventory of four-gallon containers on December 31, 2012, be 200,000 units. If the production budget calls for Purity to produce 1,300,000 four-gallon containers during 2012, what is the beginning inventory of four-gallon containers on January 1, 2012?

6-21 Budgeting; direct material usage, manufacturing cost and gross margin. Xerxes Manufacturing Company manufactures blue rugs, using wool and dye as direct materials. One rug is budgeted to use 36 skeins of wool at a cost of $2 per skein and 0.8 gallons of dye at a cost of $6 per gallon. All other materials are indirect. At the beginning of the year Xerxes has an inventory of 458,000 skeins of wool at a cost of $961,800 and 4,000 gallons of dye at a cost of $23,680. Target ending inventory of wool and dye is zero. Xerxes uses the FIFO inventory cost flow method.

Xerxes blue rugs are very popular and demand is high, but because of capacity constraints the firm will produce only 200,000 blue rugs per year. The budgeted selling price is $2,000 each. There are no rugs in beginning inventory. Target ending inventory of rugs is also zero.

Xerxes makes rugs by hand, but uses a machine to dye the wool. Thus, overhead costs are accumulated in two cost pools—one for weaving and the other for dyeing. Weaving overhead is allocated to products based on direct manufacturing labor-hours (DMLH). Dyeing overhead is allocated to products based on machine-hours (MH).

There is no direct manufacturing labor cost for dyeing. Xerxes budgets 62 direct manufacturing labor-hours to weave a rug at a budgeted rate of $13 per hour. It budgets 0.2 machine-hours to dye each skein in the dyeing process.

The following table presents the budgeted overhead costs for the dyeing and weaving cost pools:

	Dyeing (based on 1,440,000 MH)	Weaving (based on 12,400,000 DMLH)
Variable costs		
Indirect materials	$ 0	$15,400,000
Maintenance	6,560,000	5,540,000
Utilities	7,550,000	2,890,000
Fixed costs		
Indirect labor	347,000	1,700,000
Depreciation	2,100,000	274,000
Other	723,000	5,816,000
Total budgeted costs	$17,280,000	$31,620,000

Required

1. Prepare a direct material usage budget in both units and dollars.

2. Calculate the budgeted overhead allocation rates for weaving and dyeing.

3. Calculate the budgeted unit cost of a blue rug for the year.

4. Prepare a revenue budget for blue rugs for the year, assuming Xerxes sells (a) 200,000 or (b) 185,000 blue rugs (that is, at two different sales levels).

5. Calculate the budgeted cost of goods sold for blue rugs under each sales assumption.

6. Find the budgeted gross margin for blue rugs under each sales assumption.

6-22 Revenues, production, and purchases budgets. The Suzuki Co. in Japan has a division that manufactures two-wheel motorcycles. Its budgeted sales for Model G in 2013 is 900,000 units. Suzuki's target ending inventory is 80,000 units, and its beginning inventory is 100,000 units. The company's budgeted selling price to its distributors and dealers is 400,000 yen (¥) per motorcycle.

Suzuki buys all its wheels from an outside supplier. No defective wheels are accepted. (Suzuki's needs for extra wheels for replacement parts are ordered by a separate division of the company.) The company's target ending inventory is 60,000 wheels, and its beginning inventory is 50,000 wheels. The budgeted purchase price is 16,000 yen (¥) per wheel.

1. Compute the budgeted revenues in yen.

2. Compute the number of motorcycles to be produced.

3. Compute the budgeted purchases of wheels in units and in yen.

Required

6-23 Budgets for production and direct manufacturing labor. (CMA, adapted) Roletter Company makes and sells artistic frames for pictures of weddings, graduations, and other special events. Bob Anderson, the controller, is responsible for preparing Roletter's master budget and has accumulated the following information for 2013:

	2013				
	January	**February**	**March**	**April**	**May**
Estimated sales in units	10,000	12,000	8,000	9,000	9,000
Selling price	$54.00	$51.50	$51.50	$51.50	$51.50
Direct manufacturing labor-hours per unit	2.0	2.0	1.5	1.5	1.5
Wage per direct manufacturing labor-hour	$10.00	$10.00	$10.00	$11.00	$11.00

In addition to wages, direct manufacturing labor-related costs include pension contributions of $0.50 per hour, worker's compensation insurance of $0.15 per hour, employee medical insurance of $0.40 per hour, and Social Security taxes. Assume that as of January 1, 2013, the Social Security tax rates are 7.5% for employers and 7.5% for employees. The cost of employee benefits paid by Roletter on its employees is treated as a direct manufacturing labor cost.

Roletter has a labor contract that calls for a wage increase to $11 per hour on April 1, 2013. New labor-saving machinery has been installed and will be fully operational by March 1, 2013. Roletter expects to have 16,000 frames on hand at December 31, 2012, and it has a policy of carrying an end-of-month inventory of 100% of the following month's sales plus 50% of the second following month's sales.

Prepare a production budget and a direct manufacturing labor budget for Roletter Company by month and for the first quarter of 2013. Both budgets may be combined in one schedule. The direct manufacturing labor budget should include labor-hours, and show the details for each labor cost category.

Required

6-24 Activity-based budgeting. The Chelsea store of Family Supermarket (FS), a chain of small neighborhood grocery stores, is preparing its activity-based budget for January 2011. FS has three product categories: soft drinks, fresh produce, and packaged food. The following table shows the four activities that consume indirect resources at the Chelsea store, the cost drivers and their rates, and the cost-driver amount budgeted to be consumed by each activity in January 2011.

	Home	Insert	Page Layout	Formulas	Data	Review	View	

	A	B	C	D	E	F
1			**January 2011**	**January 2011 Budgeted**		
2			**Budgeted**	**Amount of Cost Driver Used**		
3	**Activity**	**Cost Driver**	**Cost-Driver Rate**	**Soft Drinks**	**Fresh Produce**	**Packaged Food**
4	Ordering	Number of purchase orders	$90	14	24	14
5	Delivery	Number of deliveries	$82	12	62	19
6	Shelf stocking	Hours of stocking time	$21	16	172	94
7	Customer support	Number of items sold	$ 0.18	4,600	34,200	10,750

1. What is the total budgeted indirect cost at the Chelsea store in January 2011? What is the total budgeted cost of each activity at the Chelsea store for January 2011? What is the budgeted indirect cost of each product category for January 2011?
2. Which product category has the largest fraction of total budgeted indirect costs?
3. Given your answer in requirement 2, what advantage does FS gain by using an activity-based approach to budgeting over, say, allocating indirect costs to products based on cost of goods sold?

6-25 Kaizen approach to activity-based budgeting (continuation of 6-24). Family Supermarkets (FS) has a kaizen (continuous improvement) approach to budgeting monthly activity costs for each month of 2011. Each successive month, the budgeted cost-driver rate decreases by 0.4% relative to the preceding month. So, for example, February's budgeted cost-driver rate is 0.996 times January's budgeted cost-driver rate, and March's budgeted cost-driver rate is 0.996 times the budgeted February 2011 rate. FS assumes that the budgeted amount of cost-driver usage remains the same each month.

1. What is the total budgeted cost for each activity and the total budgeted indirect cost for March 2011?
2. What are the benefits of using a kaizen approach to budgeting? What are the limitations of this approach, and how might FS management overcome them?

6-26 Responsibility and controllability. Consider each of the following independent situations for Anderson Forklifts. Anderson manufactures and sells forklifts. The company also contracts to service both its own and other brands of forklifts. Anderson has a manufacturing plant, a supply warehouse that supplies both the manufacturing plant and the service technicians (who often need parts to repair forklifts) and 10 service vans. The service technicians drive to customer sites to service the forklifts. Anderson owns the vans, pays for the gas, and supplies forklift parts, but the technicians own their own tools.

1. In the manufacturing plant the production manager is not happy with the engines that the purchasing manager has been purchasing. In May the production manager stops requesting engines from the supply warehouse, and starts purchasing them directly from a different engine manufacturer. Actual materials costs in May are higher than budgeted.
2. Overhead costs in the manufacturing plant for June are much higher than budgeted. Investigation reveals a utility rate hike in effect that was not figured into the budget.
3. Gasoline costs for each van are budgeted based on the service area of the van and the amount of driving expected for the month. The driver of van 3 routinely has monthly gasoline costs exceeding the budget for van 3. After investigating, the service manager finds that the driver has been driving the van for personal use.
4. At Bigstore Warehouse, one of Anderson's forklift service customers, the service people are only called in for emergencies and not for routine maintenance. Thus, the materials and labor costs for these service calls exceeds the monthly budgeted costs for a contract customer.
5. Anderson's service technicians are paid an hourly wage, with overtime pay if they exceed 40 hours per week, excluding driving time. Fred Snert, one of the technicians, frequently exceeds 40 hours per week. Service customers are happy with Fred's work, but the service manager talks to him constantly about working more quickly. Fred's overtime causes the actual costs of service to exceed the budget almost every month.
6. The cost of gasoline has increased by 50% this year, which caused the actual gasoline costs to greatly exceed the budgeted costs for the service vans.

For each situation described, determine where (that is, with whom) (a) responsibility and (b) controllability lie. Suggest what might be done to solve the problem or to improve the situation.

6-27 Cash flow analysis, sensitivity analysis. Game Guys is a retail store selling video games. Sales are uniform for most of the year, but pick up in June and December, both because new releases come out and because games are purchased in anticipation of summer or winter holidays. Game Guys also sells and repairs game systems. The forecast of sales and service revenue for the second quarter of 2012 is as follows:

Sales and Service Revenue Budget
Second Quarter, 2012

Month	Expected Sales Revenue	Expected Service Revenue	Total Revenue
April	$ 5,500	$1,000	$ 6,500
May	6,200	1,400	7,600
June	9,700	2,600	12,300
Total	$21,400	$5,000	$26,400

Almost all the service revenue is paid for by bank credit card, so Game Guys budgets this as 100% bank card revenue. The bank cards charge an average fee of 3% of the total. Half of the sales revenue is also paid for by bank credit card, for which the fee is also 3% on average. About 10% of the sales are paid in cash, and the rest (the remaining 40%) are carried on a store account. Although the store tries to give store credit only to the best customers, it still averages about 2% for uncollectible accounts; 90% of store accounts are paid in the month following the purchase, and 8% are paid two months after purchase.

1. Calculate the cash that Game Guys expects to collect in May and in June of 2012. Show calculations for each month.
2. Game Guys has budgeted expenditures for May of $4,350 for the purchase of games and game systems, $1,400 for rent and utilities and other costs, and $1,000 in wages for the two part time employees.
   a. Given your answer to requirement 1, will Game Guys be able to cover its payments for May?
   b. The projections for May are a budget. Assume (independently for each situation) that May revenues might also be 5% less and 10% less, and that costs might be 8% higher. Under each of those three scenarios show the total net cash for May and the amount Game Guys would have to borrow if cash receipts are less than cash payments. Assume the beginning cash balance for May is $100.
3. Suppose the costs for May are as described in requirement 2, but the expected cash receipts for May are $6,200 and beginning cash balance is $100. Game Guys has the opportunity to purchase the games and game systems on account in May, but the supplier offers the company credit terms of 2/10 net 30, which means if Game Guys pays within 10 days (in May) it will get a 2% discount on the price of the merchandise. Game Guys can borrow money at a rate of 24%. Should Game Guys take the purchase discount?

Problems

6-28 Budget schedules for a manufacturer. Logo Specialties manufactures, among other things, woolen blankets for the athletic teams of the two local high schools. The company sews the blankets from fabric and sews on a logo patch purchased from the licensed logo store site. The teams are as follows:

- Knights, with red blankets and the Knights logo
- Raiders, with black blankets and the Raider logo

Also, the black blankets are slightly larger than the red blankets.

The budgeted direct-cost inputs for each product in 2012 are as follows:

	Knights Blanket	Raiders Blanket
Red wool fabric	3 yards	0
Black wool fabric	0	3.3 yards
Knight logo patches	1	0
Raider logo patches	0	1
Direct manufacturing labor	1.5 hours	2 hours

Unit data pertaining to the direct materials for March 2012 are as follows:

Actual Beginning Direct Materials Inventory (3/1/2012)

	Knights Blanket	Raiders Blanket
Red wool fabric	30 yards	0
Black wool fabric	0	10 yards
Knight logo patches	40	0
Raider logo patches	0	55

Target Ending Direct Materials Inventory (3/31/2012)

	Knights Blanket	Raiders Blanket
Red wool fabric	20 yards	0
Black wool fabric	0	20 yards
Knight logo patches	20	0
Raider logo patches	0	20

Unit cost data for direct-cost inputs pertaining to February 2012 and March 2012 are as follows:

	February 2012 (actual)	March 2012 (budgeted)
Red wool fabric (per yard)	$8	$9
Black wool fabric (per yard)	10	9
Knight logo patches (per patch)	6	6
Raider logo patches (per patch)	5	7
Manufacturing labor cost per hour	25	26

Manufacturing overhead (both variable and fixed) is allocated to each blanket on the basis of budgeted direct manufacturing labor-hours per blanket. The budgeted variable manufacturing overhead rate for March 2012 is $15 per direct manufacturing labor-hour. The budgeted fixed manufacturing overhead for March 2012 is $9,200. Both variable and fixed manufacturing overhead costs are allocated to each unit of finished goods.

Data relating to finished goods inventory for March 2012 are as follows:

	Knights Blankets	Raiders Blankets
Beginning inventory in units	10	15
Beginning inventory in dollars (cost)	$1,210	$2,235
Target ending inventory in units	20	25

Budgeted sales for March 2012 are 120 units of the Knights blankets and 180 units of the Raiders blankets. The budgeted selling prices per unit in March 2012 are $150 for the Knights blankets and $175 for the Raiders blankets. Assume the following in your answer:

■ Work-in-process inventories are negligible and ignored.

■ Direct materials inventory and finished goods inventory are costed using the FIFO method.

■ Unit costs of direct materials purchased and finished goods are constant in March 2012.

Required

1. Prepare the following budgets for March 2012:
   a. Revenues budget
   b. Production budget in units
   c. Direct material usage budget and direct material purchases budget
   d. Direct manufacturing labor budget
   e. Manufacturing overhead budget
   f. Ending inventories budget (direct materials and finished goods)
   g. Cost of goods sold budget

2. Suppose Logo Specialties decides to incorporate continuous improvement into its budgeting process. Describe two areas where it could incorporate continuous improvement into the budget schedules in requirement 1.

6-29 Budgeted costs; kaizen improvements. DryPool T-Shirt Factory manufactures plain white and solid colored T-shirts. Inputs include the following:

	Price	Quantity	Cost per unit of output
Fabric	$ 6 per yard	1 yard per unit	$6 per unit
Labor	$12 per DMLH	0.25 DMLH per unit	$3 per unit

Additionally, the colored T-shirts require 3 ounces of dye per shirt at a cost of $0.20 per ounce. The shirts sell for $15 each for white and $20 each for colors. The company expects to sell 12,000 white T-shirts and 60,000 colored T-shirts uniformly over the year.

DryPool has the opportunity to switch from using the dye it currently uses to using an environmentally friendly dye that costs $1.00 per ounce. The company would still need three ounces of dye per shirt. DryPool is reluctant to change because of the increase in costs (and decrease in profit) but the Environmental Protection Agency has threatened to fine them $102,000 if they continue to use the harmful but less expensive dye.

Required

1. Given the preceding information, would DryPool be better off financially by switching to the environmentally friendly dye? (Assume all other costs would remain the same.)

2. Assume DryPool chooses to be environmentally responsible regardless of cost, and it switchs to the new dye. The production manager suggests trying Kaizen costing. If DryPool can reduce fabric and labor costs each by 1% per month, how close will it be at the end of 12 months to the gross profit it would have earned before switching to the more expensive dye? (Round to the nearest dollar for calculating cost reductions)

3. Refer to requirement 2. How could the reduction in material and labor costs be accomplished? Are there any problems with this plan?

6-30 Revenue and production budgets. (CPA, adapted) The Scarborough Corporation manufactures and sells two products: Thingone and Thingtwo. In July 2011, Scarborough's budget department gathered the following data to prepare budgets for 2012:

2012 Projected Sales

Product	Units	Price
Thingone	60,000	$165
Thingtwo	40,000	$250

2012 Inventories in Units

	Expected Target	
Product	January 1, 2012	December 31, 2012
Thingone	20,000	25,000
Thingtwo	8,000	9,000

The following direct materials are used in the two products:

		Amount Used per Unit	
Direct Material	Unit	Thingone	Thingtwo
A	pound	4	5
B	pound	2	3
C	each	0	1

Projected data for 2012 with respect to direct materials are as follows:

Direct Material	Anticipated Purchase Price	Expected Inventories January 1, 2012	Target Inventories December 31, 2012
A	$12	32,000 lb.	36,000 lb.
B	5	29,000 lb.	32,000 lb.
C	3	6,000 units	7,000 units

Projected direct manufacturing labor requirements and rates for 2012 are as follows:

Product	Hours per Unit	Rate per Hour
Thingone	2	$12
Thingtwo	3	16

Manufacturing overhead is allocated at the rate of $20 per direct manufacturing labor-hour.

Based on the preceding projections and budget requirements for Thingone and Thingtwo, prepare the following budgets for 2012:

Required

1. Revenues budget (in dollars)
2. Production budget (in units)
3. Direct material purchases budget (in quantities)
4. Direct material purchases budget (in dollars)
5. Direct manufacturing labor budget (in dollars)
6. Budgeted finished goods inventory at December 31, 2012 (in dollars)

6-31 Budgeted income statement. (CMA, adapted) Easecom Company is a manufacturer of videoconferencing products. Regular units are manufactured to meet marketing projections, and specialized units are made after an order is received. Maintaining the videoconferencing equipment is an important area of customer satisfaction. With the recent downturn in the computer industry, the videoconferencing equipment segment has suffered, leading to a decline in Easecom's financial performance. The following income statement shows results for 2011:

Easecom Company
Income Statement
For the Year Ended December 31, 2011 (in thousands)

Revenues:		
Equipment	$6,000	
Maintenance contracts	1,800	
Total revenues		$7,800
Cost of goods sold		4,600
Gross margin		3,200
Operating costs		
Marketing	600	
Distribution	150	
Customer maintenance	1,000	
Administration	900	
Total operating costs		2,650
Operating income		$ 550

Easecom's management team is in the process of preparing the 2012 budget and is studying the following information:

1. Selling prices of equipment are expected to increase by 10% as the economic recovery begins. The selling price of each maintenance contract is expected to remain unchanged from 2011.
2. Equipment sales in units are expected to increase by 6%, with a corresponding 6% growth in units of maintenance contracts.
3. Cost of each unit sold is expected to increase by 3% to pay for the necessary technology and quality improvements.
4. Marketing costs are expected to increase by $250,000, but administration costs are expected to remain at 2011 levels.
5. Distribution costs vary in proportion to the number of units of equipment sold.
6. Two maintenance technicians are to be hired at a total cost of $130,000, which covers wages and related travel costs. The objective is to improve customer service and shorten response time.
7. There is no beginning or ending inventory of equipment.

Required

Prepare a budgeted income statement for the year ending December 31, 2012.

6-32 **Responsibility in a restaurant.** Barney Briggs owns a restaurant franchise that is part of a chain of "southern homestyle" restaurants. One of the chain's popular breakfast items is biscuits and gravy. Central Warehouse makes and freezes the biscuit dough, which is then sold to the franchise stores; there, it is thawed and baked in the individual stores by the cook. Each franchise also has a purchasing agent who orders the biscuits (and other items) based on expected demand. In March, 2012, one of the freezers in Central Warehouse breaks down and biscuit production is reduced by 25% for three days. During those three days, Barney's franchise runs out of biscuits but demand does not slow down. Barney's franchise cook, Janet Trible, sends one of the kitchen helpers to the local grocery store to buy refrigerated ready-to-bake biscuits. Although the customers are kept happy, the refrigerated biscuits cost Barney's franchise three times the cost of the Central Warehouse frozen biscuits, and the franchise loses money on this item for those three days. Barney is angry with the purchasing agent for not ordering enough biscuits to avoid running out of stock, and with Janet for spending too much money on the replacement biscuits.

Required

Who is responsible for the cost of the biscuits? At what level is the cost controllable? Do you agree that Barney should be angry with the purchasing agent? With Janet? Why or why not?

6-33 **Comprehensive problem with ABC costing.** Pet Luggage Company makes two pet carriers, the Cat-allac and the Dog-eriffic. They are both made of plastic with metal doors, but the Cat-allac is smaller. Information for the two products for the month of April is given in the following tables:

Input Prices

Direct materials	
Plastic	$ 4 per pound
Metal	$ 3 per pound
Direct manufacturing labor	$14 per direct manufacturing labor-hour

Input Quantities per Unit of Output

	Cat-allac	Dog-eriffic
Direct materials		
Plastic	3 pounds	5 pounds
Metal	0.5 pounds	1 pound
Direct manufacturing labor-hours (DMLH)	3 hours	5 hours
Machine-hours (MH)	13 MH	20 MH

Inventory Information, Direct Materials

	Plastic	Metal
Beginning inventory	230 pounds	70 pounds
Target ending inventory	400 pounds	65 pounds
Cost of beginning inventory	$874	$224

Pet Luggage accounts for direct materials using a FIFO cost flow assumption.

Sales and Inventory Information, Finished Goods

	Cat-allac	Dog-eriffic
Expected sales in units	580	240
Selling price	$ 190	$ 275
Target ending inventory in units	45	25
Beginning inventory in units	25	40
Beginning inventory in dollars	$2,500	$7,440

Pet Luggage uses a FIFO cost flow assumption for finished goods inventory.

Pet Luggage uses an activity-based costing system and classifies overhead into three activity pools: Setup, Processing, and Inspection. Activity rates for these activities are $130 per setup-hour, $5 per machine-hour, and $20 per inspection-hour, respectively. Other information follows:

Cost Driver Information

	Cat-allac	Dog-eriffic
Number of units per batch	25	13
Setup time per batch	1.25 hours	2.00 hours
Inspection time per batch	0.5 hour	0.6 hour

Nonmanufacturing fixed costs for March equal $32,000, of which half are salaries. Salaries are expected to increase 5% in April. The only variable nonmanufacturing cost is sales commission, equal to 1% of sales revenue.

Prepare the following for April:

Required

1. Revenues budget
2. Production budget in units
3. Direct material usage budget and direct material purchases budget
4. Direct manufacturing labor cost budget
5. Manufacturing overhead cost budgets for each of the three activities
6. Budgeted unit cost of ending finished goods inventory and ending inventories budget
7. Cost of goods sold budget
8. Nonmanufacturing costs budget
9. Budgeted income statement (ignore income taxes)

6-34 Cash budget (continuation of 6-33). Refer to the information in Problem 6-33.

Assume the following: Pet Luggage (PL) does not make any sales on credit. PL sells only to the public, and accepts cash and credit cards; 90% of its sales are to customers using credit cards, for which PL gets the cash right away less a 2% transaction fee.

Purchases of materials are on account. PL pays for half the purchases in the period of the purchase, and the other half in the following period. At the end of March, PL owes suppliers $8,400.

PL plans to replace a machine in April at a net cash cost of $13,800.

Labor, other manufacturing costs, and nonmanufacturing costs are paid in cash in the month incurred except of course, depreciation, which is not a cash flow. $22,500 of the manufacturing cost and $12,500 of the nonmanufacturing cost for April is depreciation.

PL currently has a $2,600 loan at an annual interest rate of 24%. The interest is paid at the end of each month. If PL has more than $10,000 cash at the end of April it will pay back the loan. PL owes $5,400 in income taxes that need to be remitted in April. PL has cash of $5,200 on hand at the end of March.

Prepare a cash budget for April for Pet Luggage.

Required

6-35 Comprehensive operating budget, budgeted balance sheet. Slopes, Inc., manufactures and sells snowboards. Slopes manufactures a single model, the Pipex. In the summer of 2011, Slopes' management accountant gathered the following data to prepare budgets for 2012:

Materials and Labor Requirements
Direct materials
    Wood   5 board feet (b.f.) per snowboard
    Fiberglass   6 yards per snowboard
Direct manufacturing labor   5 hours per snowboard

Slopes' CEO expects to sell 1,000 snowboards during 2012 at an estimated retail price of $450 per board. Further, the CEO expects 2012 beginning inventory of 100 snowboards and would like to end 2012 with 200 snowboards in stock.

Direct Materials Inventories

	Beginning Inventory 1/1/2012	Ending Inventory 12/31/2012
Wood	2,000 b.f.	1,500 b.f.
Fiberglass	1,000 yards	2,000 yards

Variable manufacturing overhead is $7 per direct manufacturing labor-hour. There are also $66,000 in fixed manufacturing overhead costs budgeted for 2012. Slopes combines both variable and fixed manufacturing overhead into a single rate based on direct manufacturing labor-hours. Variable marketing costs are allocated at the rate of $250 per sales visit. The marketing plan calls for 30 sales visits during 2012. Finally, there are $30,000 in fixed nonmanufacturing costs budgeted for 2012.

Other data include the following:

	2011 Unit Price	2012 Unit Price
Wood	$28.00 per b.f.	$30.00 per b.f.
Fiberglass	$ 4.80 per yard	$ 5.00 per yard
Direct manufacturing labor	$24.00 per hour	$25.00 per hour

The inventoriable unit cost for ending finished goods inventory on December 31, 2011, is $374.80. Assume Slopes uses a FIFO inventory method for both direct materials and finished goods. Ignore work in process in your calculations.

Budgeted balances at December 31, 2012, in the selected accounts are as follows:

Cash	$ 10,000
Property, plant, and equipment (net)	850,000
Current liabilities	17,000
Long-term liabilities	178,000
Stockholders' equity	800,000

Required

1. Prepare the 2012 revenues budget (in dollars).
2. Prepare the 2012 production budget (in units).
3. Prepare the direct material usage and purchases budgets for 2012.
4. Prepare a direct manufacturing labor budget for 2012.
5. Prepare a manufacturing overhead budget for 2012.
6. What is the budgeted manufacturing overhead rate for 2012?
7. What is the budgeted manufacturing overhead cost per output unit in 2012?
8. Calculate the cost of a snowboard manufactured in 2012.
9. Prepare an ending inventory budget for both direct materials and finished goods for 2012.
10. Prepare a cost of goods sold budget for 2012.
11. Prepare the budgeted income statement for Slopes, Inc., for the year ending December 31, 2012.
12. Prepare the budgeted balance sheet for Slopes, Inc., as of December 31, 2012.

6-36 Cash budgeting. Retail outlets purchase snowboards from Slopes, Inc., throughout the year. However, in anticipation of late summer and early fall purchases, outlets ramp up inventories from May through August. Outlets are billed when boards are ordered. Invoices are payable within 60 days. From past experience, Slopes' accountant projects 20% of invoices will be paid in the month invoiced, 50% will be paid in the following month, and 30% of invoices will be paid two months after the month of invoice. The average selling price per snowboard is $450.

To meet demand, Slopes increases production from April through July, because the snowboards are produced a month prior to their projected sale. Direct materials are purchased in the month of production and are paid for during the following month (terms are payment in full within 30 days of the invoice date). During this period there is no production for inventory, and no materials are purchased for inventory.

Direct manufacturing labor and manufacturing overhead are paid monthly. Variable manufacturing overhead is incurred at the rate of $7 per direct manufacturing labor-hour. Variable marketing costs are driven by the number of sales visits. However, there are no sales visits during the months studied. Slopes, Inc., also incurs fixed manufacturing overhead costs of $5,500 per month and fixed nonmanufacturing overhead costs of $2,500 per month.

Projected Sales	
May 80 units	August 100 units
June 120 units	September 60 units
July 200 units	October 40 units

Direct Materials and Direct Manufacturing Labor Utilization and Cost

	Units per Board	Price per Unit	Unit
Wood	5	$30	board feet
Fiberglass	6	5	yard
Direct manufacturing labor	5	25	hour

The beginning cash balance for July 1, 2012, is $10,000. On October 1, 2011, Slopes had a cash crunch and borrowed $30,000 on a 6% one-year note with interest payable monthly. The note is due October 1, 2012. Using the information provided, you will need to determine whether Slopes will be in a position to pay off this short-term debt on October 1, 2012.

Required

1. Prepare a cash budget for the months of July through September 2012. Show supporting schedules for the calculation of receivables and payables.
2. Will Slopes be in a position to pay off the $30,000 one-year note that is due on October 1, 2012? If not, what actions would you recommend to Slopes' management?
3. Suppose Slopes is interested in maintaining a minimum cash balance of $10,000. Will the company be able to maintain such a balance during all three months analyzed? If not, suggest a suitable cash management strategy.

6-37 **Cash budgeting.** On December 1, 2011, the Itami Wholesale Co. is attempting to project cash receipts and disbursements through January 31, 2012. On this latter date, a note will be payable in the amount of $100,000. This amount was borrowed in September to carry the company through the seasonal peak in November and December.

Selected general ledger balances on December 1 are as follows:

Cash	$ 88,000	
Inventory	65,200	
Accounts payable		136,000

Sales terms call for a 3% discount if payment is made within the first 10 days of the month after sale, with the balance due by the end of the month after sale. Experience has shown that 50% of the billings will be collected within the discount period, 30% by the end of the month after purchase, and 14% in the following month. The remaining 6% will be uncollectible. There are no cash sales.

The average selling price of the company's products is $100 per unit. Actual and projected sales are as follows:

October actual	$ 280,000
November actual	320,000
December estimated	330,000
January estimated	250,000
February estimated	240,000
Total estimated for year ending June 30, 2012	$2,400,000

All purchases are payable within 15 days. Approximately 60% of the purchases in a month are paid that month, and the rest the following month. The average unit purchase cost is $80. Target ending inventories are 500 units plus 10% of the next month's unit sales.

Total budgeted marketing, distribution, and customer-service costs for the year are $600,000. Of this amount, $120,000 are considered fixed (and include depreciation of $30,000). The remainder varies with sales. Both fixed and variable marketing, distribution, and customer-service costs are paid as incurred.

Required

Prepare a cash budget for December 2011 and January 2012. Supply supporting schedules for collections of receivables; payments for merchandise; and marketing, distribution, and customer-service costs.

6-38 **Comprehensive problem; ABC manufacturing, two products.** Follete Inc. operates at capacity and makes plastic combs and hairbrushes. Although the combs and brushes are a matching set, they are sold individually and so the sales mix is not 1:1. Follette Inc. is planning its annual budget for fiscal year 2011. Information for 2011 follows:

Input Prices
Direct materials
    Plastic $ 0.20 per ounce
    Bristles $ 0.50 per bunch
Direct manufacturing labor $12 per direct manufacturing labor-hour

Input Quantities per Unit of Output

	Combs	Brushes
Direct materials		
Plastic	5 ounces	8 ounces
Bristles	—	16 bunches
Direct manufacturing labor	0.05 hours	0.2 hours
Machine-hours (MH)	0.025 MH	0.1 MH

Inventory Information, Direct Materials

	Plastic	Bristles
Beginning inventory	1,600 ounces	1,820 bunches
Target ending inventory	1,766 ounces	2,272 bunches
Cost of beginning inventory	$304	$946

Folette Inc. accounts for direct materials using a FIFO cost flow.

Sales and Inventory Information, Finished Goods

	Combs	Brushes
Expected sales in units	12,000	14,000
Selling price	$ 6	$ 20
Target ending inventory in units	1,200	1,400
Beginning inventory in units	600	1,200
Beginning inventory in dollars	$ 1,800	$18,120

Folette Inc. uses a FIFO cost flow assumption for finished goods inventory.

Combs are manufactured in batches of 200, and brushes are manufactured in batches of 100. It takes 20 minutes to set up for a batch of combs, and one hour to set up for a batch of brushes.

Folette Inc. uses activity-based costing and has classified all overhead costs as shown in the following table:

Cost Type	Budgeted Variable	Budgeted Fixed	Cost Driver/Allocation Base
Manufacturing:			
Materials handling	$11,490	$15,000	Number of ounces of plastic used
Setup	6,830	11,100	Setup-hours
Processing	7,760	20,000	Machine-hours
Inspection	7,000	1,040	Number of units produced
Nonmanufacturing:			
Marketing	14,100	60,000	Sales revenue
Distribution	0	780	Number of deliveries

Delivery trucks transport units sold in delivery sizes of 1,000 combs or 1,000 brushes.

Required Do the following for the year 2011:

1. Prepare the revenues budget.
2. Use the revenue budget to
   a. find the budgeted allocation rate for marketing costs.
   b. find the budgeted number of deliveries and allocation rate for distribution costs.
3. Prepare the production budget in units.
4. Use the production budget to
   a. find the budgeted number of setups, setup-hours, and the allocation rate for setup costs.
   b. find the budgeted total machine-hours and the allocation rate for processing costs.
   c. find the budgeted total units produced and the allocation rate for inspection costs.
5. Prepare the direct material usage budget and the direct material purchases budgets in both units and dollars; round to whole dollars.
6. Use the direct material usage budget to find the budgeted allocation rate for materials handling costs.
7. Prepare the direct manufacturing labor cost budget.
8. Prepare the manufacturing overhead cost budget for materials handling, setup, and processing.
9. Prepare the budgeted unit cost of ending finished goods inventory and ending inventories budget.

10. Prepare the cost of goods sold budget.
11. Prepare the nonmanufacturing overhead costs budget for marketing and distribution.
12. Prepare a budgeted income statement (ignore income taxes).

6-39 Budgeting and ethics. Delma Company manufactures a variety of products in a variety of departments, and evaluates departments and departmental managers by comparing actual cost and output relative to the budget. Departmental managers help create the budgets, and usually provide information about input quantities for materials, labor, and overhead costs.

Wert Mimble is the manager of the department that produces product Z. Wert has estimated these inputs for product Z:

Input	Budget Quantity per Unit of Output
Direct material	4 pounds
Direct manufacturing labor	15 minutes
Machine time	12 minutes

The department produces about 100 units of product Z each day. Wert's department always gets excellent evaluations, sometimes exceeding budgeted production quantities. Each 100 units of product Z uses, on average, about 24 hours of direct manufacturing labor (four people working six hours each), 395 pounds of material, and 19.75 machine-hours.

Top management of Delma Company has decided to implement budget standards that will challenge the workers in each department, and it has asked Wert to design more challenging input standards for product Z. Wert provides top management with the following input quantities:

Input	Budget Quantity per Unit of Output
Direct material	3.95 pounds
Direct manufacturing labor	14.5 minutes
Machine time	11.8 minutes

Discuss the following:

Required

1. Are these standards challenging standards for the department that produces product Z?
2. Why do you suppose Wert picked these particular standards?
3. What steps can Delma Company's top management take to make sure Wert's standards really meet the goals of the firm?

6-40 Human Aspects of Budgeting in a Service Firm. Jag Meerkat owns three upscale hair salons: Hair Suite I, II, and III. Each of the salons has a manager and 10 stylists who rent space in the salons as independent contractors and who pay a fee of 10% of each week's revenue to the salon as rent. In exchange they get to use the facility and utilities, but must bring their own equipment.

The manager of each salon schedules each customer appointment to last an hour, and then allows the stylist 10 minutes between appointments to clean up, rest, and prepare for the next appointment. The salons are open from 10 A.M. to 6 P.M., so each stylist can serve seven customers per day. Stylists each work five days a week on a staggered schedule, so the salon is open seven days a week. Everyone works on Saturdays, but some stylists have Sunday and Monday off, some have Tuesday and Wednesday off, and some have Thursday and Friday off.

Jag Meerkat knows that utility costs are rising. Jag wants to increase revenues to cover at least some part of rising utility costs, so Jag tells each of the managers to find a way to increase productivity in the salons so that the stylists will pay more to the salons. Jag does not want to increase the rental fee above 10% of revenue for fear the stylists will leave, and each salon has only 10 stations, so he feels each salon cannot hire more than 10 full-time stylists.

The manager of Hair Suite I attacks the problem by simply telling the stylists that, from now on, customers will be scheduled for 40 minute appointments and breaks will be five minutes. This will allow each stylist to add one more customer per day.

The manager of Hair Suite II asks the stylists on a voluntary basis to work one extra hour per day, from 10 A.M. to 7 P.M., to add an additional customer per stylist per day.

The manager of Hair Suite III sits down with the stylists and discusses the issue. After considering shortening the appointment and break times, or lengthening the hours of operation, one of the stylists says, "I know we rent stations in your store, but I am willing to share my station. You could hire an eleventh stylist, who will simply work at whatever station is vacant during our days off. Since we use our own equipment, this will not be a problem for me as long as there is a secure place I can leave my equipment on my days off." Most of the other stylists agree that this is a good solution.

Required

1. Which manager's style do you think is most effective? Why?
2. How do you think the stylists will react to the managers of salons I and II? What can they do to indicate their displeasure, assuming they are displeased?
3. In Hair Suite III, if the stylists did not want to share their stations with another party, how else could they find a way to increase revenues?
4. Refer again to the action that the manager of Hair Suite I has chosen. How does this relate to the concept of stretch targets?

Collaborative Learning Problem

6-41 **Comprehensive budgeting problem; activity based costing, operating and financial budgets.** Borkenstick makes a very popular undyed cloth sandal in one style, but in Regular and Deluxe. The Regular sandals have cloth soles and the Deluxe sandals have cloth covered wooden soles. Borkenstick is preparing its budget for June 2012, and has estimated sales based on past experience.

Other information for the month of June follows:

Input Prices

Direct materials	
Cloth	$3.50 per yard
Wood	$5.00 per board foot
Direct manufacturing labor	$10 per direct manufacturing labor-hour

Input Quantities per Unit of Output (per pair of sandals)

	Regular	Deluxe
Direct materials		
Cloth	1.3 yards	1.5 yards
Wood	0	2 b.f.
Direct manufacturing labor-hours (DMLH)	5 hours	7 hours
Setup-hours per batch	2 hours	3 hours

Inventory Information, Direct Materials

	Cloth	Wood
Beginning inventory	610 yards	800 b.f.
Target ending inventory	386 yards	295 b.f.
Cost of beginning inventory	$2,146	$4,040

Borkenstick accounts for direct materials using a FIFO cost flow assumption.

Sales and Inventory Information, Finished Goods

	Regular	Deluxe
Expected sales in units (pairs of sandals)	2,000	3,000
Selling price	$ 80	$ 130
Target ending inventory in units	400	600
Beginning inventory in units	250	650
Beginning inventory in dollars	$15,500	$61,750

Borkenstick uses a FIFO cost flow assumption for finished goods inventory.

All the sandals are made in batches of 50 pairs of sandals. Borkenstick incurs manufacturing overhead costs, marketing and general administration, and shipping costs. Besides materials and labor, manufacturing costs include setup, processing, and inspection costs. Borkenstick ships 40 pairs of sandals per shipment. Borkenstick uses activity-based costing and has classified all overhead costs for the month of June as shown in the following chart:

Cost type	Denominator Activity	Rate
Manufacturing:		
Setup	Setup-hours	$12 per setup-hour
Processing	Direct manufacturing labor-hours	$1.20 per DMLH
Inspection	Number of pairs of sandals	$0.90 per pair
Nonmanufacturing:		
Marketing and general administration	Sales revenue	8%
Shipping	Number of shipments	$10 per shipment

1. Prepare each of the following for June:
   a. Revenues budget
   b. Production budget in units
   c. Direct material usage budget and direct material purchases budget in both units and dollars; round to dollars
   d. Direct manufacturing labor cost budget
   e. Manufacturing overhead cost budgets for processing and setup activities
   f. Budgeted unit cost of ending finished goods inventory and ending inventories budget
   g. Cost of goods sold budget
   h. Marketing and general administration costs budget

2. Borkenstick's balance sheet for May 31 follows. Use it and the following information to prepare a cash budget for Borkenstick for June. Round to dollars.
   ■ All sales are on account; 60% are collected in the month of the sale, 38% are collected the following month, and 2% are never collected and written off as bad debts.
   ■ All purchases of materials are on account. Borkenstick pays for 80% of purchases in the month of purchase and 20% in the following month.
   ■ All other costs are paid in the month incurred, including the declaration and payment of a $10,000 cash dividend in June.
   ■ Borkenstick is making monthly interest payments of 0.5% (6% per year) on a $100,000 long term loan.
   ■ Borkenstick plans to pay the $7,200 of taxes owed as of May 31 in the month of June. Income tax expense for June is zero.
   ■ 30% of processing and setup costs, and 10% of marketing and general administration costs are depreciation.

Borkenstick
Balance Sheet
as of May 31

Assets

Cash		$ 6,290
Accounts receivable	$216,000	
Less: Allowance for bad debts	10,800	205,200
Inventories		
Direct materials		6,186
Finished goods		77,250
Fixed assets	$580,000	
Less: Accumulated depreciation	90,890	489,110
Total assets		$784,036

Liabilities and Equity

Accounts payable	$ 10,400
Taxes payable	7,200
Interest payable	500
Long-term debt	100,000
Common stock	200,000
Retained earnings	465,936
Total liabilities and equity	$784,036

3. Prepare a budgeted income statement for June and a budgeted balance sheet for Borkenstick as of June 30.

7 Flexible Budgets, Direct-Cost Variances, and Management Control

Professional sports leagues thrive on providing excitement for their fans.

It seems that no expense is spared to entertain spectators and keep them occupied before, during, and after games. Professional basketball has been at the forefront of this trend, popularizing such crowd-pleasing distractions as pregame pyrotechnics, pumped-in noise, fire-shooting scoreboards, and T-shirt-shooting cheerleaders carrying air guns. What is the goal of investing millions in such "game presentation" activities? Such showcasing attracts and maintains the loyalty of younger fans. But eventually, every organization, regardless of its growth, has to step back and take a hard look at the wisdom of its spending choices. And when customers are affected by a recession, the need for an organization to employ budgeting and variance analysis tools for cost control becomes especially critical, as the following article shows.

The NBA: Where Frugal Happens[1]

For more than 20 years, the National Basketball Association (NBA) flew nearly as high as one of LeBron James's slam dunks. The league expanded from 24 to 30 teams, negotiated lucrative TV contracts, and made star players like Kobe Bryant and Dwayne Wade household names and multimillionaires. The NBA was even advertised as "where amazing happens." While costs for brand new arenas and player contracts increased, fans continued to pay escalating ticket prices to see their favorite team. But when the economy nosedived in 2008, the situation changed dramatically.

In the season that followed (2008–2009), more than half of the NBA's franchises lost money. Fans stopped buying tickets and many companies could no longer afford pricy luxury suites. NBA commissioner David Stern announced that overall league revenue for the 2009–2010 season was expected to fall by an additional 5% over the previous disappointing campaign. With revenues dwindling and operating profits tougher to achieve, NBA teams began to heavily emphasize cost control and operating-variance reduction for the first time since the 1980s.

Some of the changes were merely cosmetic. The Charlotte Bobcats stopped paying for halftime entertainment, which cost up to

---

[1] Sources: Arnold, Gregory. 2009. NBA teams cut rosters, assistants, scouts to reduce costs. The Oregonian, October 26; Biderman, David. 2009. The NBA: Where frugal happens. Wall Street Journal, October 27.

$15,000 per game, while the Cleveland Cavaliers saved $40,000 by switching from paper holiday cards to electronic ones. Many other teams—including the Dallas Mavericks, Indiana Pacers, and Miami Heat—reduced labor costs by laying off front-office staff.

Other changes, however, affected play on the court. While NBA teams were allowed to have 15 players on their respective rosters, 10 teams chose to save money by employing fewer players. For example, the Memphis Grizzlies eliminated its entire scouting department, which provided important information on upcoming opponents and potential future players, while the New Jersey Nets traded away most of its high-priced superstars and chose to play with lower-salaried younger players. Each team cutting costs experienced different results. The Grizzlies were a playoff contender, but the Nets were on pace for one of the worst seasons in NBA history.

Just as companies like General Electric and Bank of America have to manage costs and analyze variances for long-term sustainability, so, too, do sports teams. "The NBA is a business just like any other business," Sacramento Kings co-owner Joe Maloof said. "We have to watch our costs and expenses, especially during this trying economic period. It's better to be safe and watch your expenses and make sure you keep your franchise financially strong."

In Chapter 6, you saw how budgets help managers with their planning function. We now explain how budgets, specifically flexible budgets, are used to compute variances, which assist managers in their control function. Flexible budgets and variances enable managers to make meaningful comparisons of actual results with planned performance, and to obtain insights into why actual results differ from planned performance. They form the critical final function in the five-step decision-making process, by making it possible for managers to *evaluate performance and learn* after decisions are implemented. In this chapter and the next, we explain how.

Static Budgets and Variances

A **variance** is the difference between actual results and expected performance. The expected performance is also called **budgeted performance**, which is a point of reference for making comparisons.

The Use of Variances

Variances lie at the point where the planning and control functions of management come together. They assist managers in implementing their strategies by enabling **management by exception**. This is the practice of focusing management attention on areas that are not

Learning Objective 1

Understand static budgets

. . . the master budget based on output planned at start of period

and static-budget variances

. . . the difference between the actual result and the corresponding budgeted amount in the static budget

operating as expected (such as a large shortfall in sales of a product) and devoting less time to areas operating as expected. In other words, by highlighting the areas that have deviated most from expectations, variances enable managers to focus their efforts on the most critical areas. Consider scrap and rework costs at a Maytag appliances plant. If actual costs are much higher than budgeted, the variances will guide managers to seek explanations and to take early corrective action, ensuring that future operations result in less scrap and rework. Sometimes a large positive variance may occur, such as a significant decrease in manufacturing costs of a product. Managers will try to understand the reasons for this decrease (better operator training or changes in manufacturing methods for example), so these practices can be appropriately continued and transferred to other divisions within the organization.

Variances are also used in performance evaluation and to motivate managers. Production-line managers at Maytag may have quarterly efficiency incentives linked to achieving a budgeted amount of operating costs.

Sometimes variances suggest that the company should consider a change in strategy. For example, large negative variances caused by excessive defect rates for a new product may suggest a flawed product design. Managers may then want to investigate the product design and potentially change the mix of products being offered.

Variance analysis contributes in many ways to making the five-step decision-making process more effective. It allows managers to evaluate performance and learn by providing a framework for correctly assessing current performance. In turn, managers take corrective actions to ensure that decisions are implemented correctly and that previously budgeted results are attained. Variances also enable managers to generate more informed predictions about the future, and thereby improve the quality of the five-step decision-making process.

The benefits of variance analysis are not restricted to companies. In today's difficult economic environment, public officials have realized that the ability to make timely tactical alterations based on variance information guards against having to make more draconian adjustments later. For example, the city of Scottsdale, Arizona, monitors its tax and fee performance against expenditures monthly. Why? One of the city's goals is to keep its water usage rates stable. By monitoring the extent to which water revenues are meeting current expenses and obligations, while simultaneously building up funds for future infrastructure projects, the city can avoid rate spikes and achieve long-run rate stability.[2]

How important is variance analysis? A survey by the United Kingdom's Chartered Institute of Management Accountants in July 2009 found that variance analysis was easily the most popular costing tool in practice, and retained that distinction across organizations of all sizes.

Static Budgets and Static-Budget Variances

We will take a closer look at variances by examining one company's accounting system. Note as you study the exhibits in this chapter that "level" followed by a number denotes the amount of detail shown by a variance analysis. Level 1 reports the least detail; level 2 offers more information; and so on.

Consider Webb Company, a firm that manufactures and sells jackets. The jackets require tailoring and many other hand operations. Webb sells exclusively to distributors, who in turn sell to independent clothing stores and retail chains. For simplicity, we assume that Webb's only costs are in the manufacturing function; Webb incurs no costs in other value-chain functions, such as marketing and distribution. We also assume that all units manufactured in April 2011 are sold in April 2011. Therefore, all direct materials are purchased and used in the same budget period, and there is no direct materials inventory at either the beginning or the end of the period. No work-in-process or finished goods inventories exist at either the beginning or the end of the period.

---

[2] For an excellent discussion and other related examples from governmental settings, see S. Kavanagh and C. Swanson, "Tactical Financial Management: Cash Flow and Budgetary Variance Analysis," *Government Finance Review* (October 1, 2009).

Webb has three variable-cost categories. The budgeted variable cost per jacket for each category is as follows:

Cost Category	Variable Cost per Jacket
Direct material costs	$60
Direct manufacturing labor costs	16
Variable manufacturing overhead costs	12
Total variable costs	$88

The *number of units manufactured* is the cost driver for direct materials, direct manufacturing labor, and variable manufacturing overhead. The relevant range for the cost driver is from 0 to 12,000 jackets. Budgeted and actual data for April 2011 follow:

Budgeted fixed costs for production between 0 and 12,000 jackets	$276,000
Budgeted selling price	$ 120 per jacket
Budgeted production and sales	12,000 jackets
Actual production and sales	10,000 jackets

The **static budget**, or master budget, is based on the level of output planned at the start of the budget period. The master budget is called a static budget because the budget for the period is developed around a single (static) planned output level. Exhibit 7-1, column 3, presents the static budget for Webb Company for April 2011 that was prepared at the end of 2010. For each line item in the income statement, Exhibit 7-1, column 1, displays data for the actual April results. For example, actual revenues are $1,250,000, and the actual selling price is $1,250,000 ÷ 10,000 jackets = $125 per jacket—compared with the budgeted selling price of $120 per jacket. Similarly, actual direct material costs are $621,600, and the direct material cost per jacket is $621,600 ÷ 10,000 = $62.16 per jacket—compared with the budgeted direct material cost per jacket of $60. We describe potential reasons and explanations for these differences as we discuss different variances throughout the chapter.

The **static-budget variance** (see Exhibit 7-1, column 2) is the difference between the actual result and the corresponding budgeted amount in the static budget.

A **favorable variance**—denoted F in this book—has the effect, when considered in isolation, of increasing operating income relative to the budgeted amount. For revenue

Level 1 Analysis

	Actual Results (1)	Static-Budget Variances (2) = (1) – (3)	Static Budget (3)
Units sold	10,000	2,000 U	12,000
Revenues	$ 1,250,000	$190,000 U	$1,440,000
Variable costs			
Direct materials	621,600	98,400 F	720,000
Direct manufacturing labor	198,000	6,000 U	192,000
Variable manufacturing overhead	130,500	13,500 F	144,000
Total variable costs	950,100	105,900 F	1,056,000
Contribution margin	299,900	84,100 U	384,000
Fixed costs	285,000	9,000 U	276,000
Operating income	$ 14,900	$ 93,100 U	$ 108,000

$ 93,100 U

Static-budget variance

items, F means actual revenues exceed budgeted revenues. For cost items, F means actual costs are less than budgeted costs. An **unfavorable variance**—denoted U in this book—has the effect, when viewed in isolation, of decreasing operating income relative to the budgeted amount. Unfavorable variances are also called *adverse variances* in some countries, such as the United Kingdom.

The unfavorable static-budget variance for operating income of $93,100 in Exhibit 7-1 is calculated by subtracting static-budget operating income of $108,000 from actual operating income of $14,900:

$$\begin{array}{c}\text{Static-budget}\\ \text{variance for}\\ \text{operating income}\end{array} = \begin{array}{c}\text{Actual}\\ \text{result}\end{array} - \begin{array}{c}\text{Static-budget}\\ \text{amount}\end{array}$$

$$= \$14,900 - \$108,000$$

$$= \$93,100 \text{ U.}$$

The analysis in Exhibit 7-1 provides managers with additional information on the static-budget variance for operating income of $93,100 U. The more detailed breakdown indicates how the line items that comprise operating income—revenues, individual variable costs, and fixed costs—add up to the static-budget variance of $93,100.

Remember, Webb produced and sold only 10,000 jackets, although managers anticipated an output of 12,000 jackets in the static budget. *Managers want to know how much of the static-budget variance is because of inaccurate forecasting of output units sold and how much is due to Webb's performance in manufacturing and selling 10,000 jackets.* Managers, therefore, create a flexible budget, which enables a more in-depth understanding of deviations from the static budget.

Decision Point ▶

What are static budgets and static-budget variances?

Flexible Budgets

Learning Objective 2

Examine the concept of a flexible budget

. . . the budget that is adjusted (flexed) to recognize the actual output level

and learn how to develop it

. . . proportionately increase variable costs; keep fixed costs the same

A **flexible budget** calculates budgeted revenues and budgeted costs based on *the actual output in the budget period.* The flexible budget is prepared at the end of the period (April 2011), after the actual output of 10,000 jackets is known. The flexible budget is the *hypothetical* budget that Webb would have prepared at the start of the budget period if it had correctly forecast the actual output of 10,000 jackets. In other words, the flexible budget is not the plan Webb initially had in mind for April 2011 (remember Webb planned for an output of 12,000 jackets instead). Rather, it is the budget Webb *would have* put together for April if it knew in advance that the output for the month would be 10,000 jackets. In preparing the flexible budget, note that:

- The budgeted selling price is the same $120 per jacket used in preparing the static budget.
- The budgeted unit variable cost is the same $88 per jacket used in the static budget.
- The budgeted *total* fixed costs are the same static-budget amount of $276,000. Why? Because the 10,000 jackets produced falls within the relevant range of 0 to 12,000 jackets. Therefore, Webb would have budgeted the same amount of fixed costs, $276,000, whether it anticipated making 10,000 or 12,000 jackets.

The *only* difference between the static budget and the flexible budget is that the static budget is prepared for the planned output of 12,000 jackets, whereas the flexible budget is based on the actual output of 10,000 jackets. The static budget is being "flexed," or adjusted, from 12,000 jackets to 10,000 jackets.[3] The flexible budget for 10,000 jackets assumes that all costs are either completely variable or completely fixed with respect to the number of jackets produced.

Webb develops its flexible budget in three steps.

Step 1: Identify the Actual Quantity of Output. In April 2011, Webb produced and sold 10,000 jackets.

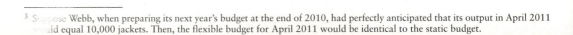

[3] Suppose Webb, when preparing its next year's budget at the end of 2010, had perfectly anticipated that its output in April 2011 would equal 10,000 jackets. Then, the flexible budget for April 2011 would be identical to the static budget.

Step 2: Calculate the Flexible Budget for Revenues Based on Budgeted Selling Price and Actual Quantity of Output.

$$\text{Flexible-budget revenues} = \$120 \text{ per jacket} \times 10,000 \text{ jackets}$$

$$= \$1,200,000$$

Step 3: Calculate the Flexible Budget for Costs Based on Budgeted Variable Cost per Output Unit, Actual Quantity of Output, and Budgeted Fixed Costs.

Flexible-budget variable costs	
Direct materials, $60 per jacket × 10,000 jackets	$ 600,000
Direct manufacturing labor, $16 per jacket × 10,000 jackets	160,000
Variable manufacturing overhead, $12 per jacket × 10,000 jackets	120,000
Total flexible-budget variable costs	880,000
Flexible-budget fixed costs	276,000
Flexible-budget total costs	$1,156,000

These three steps enable Webb to prepare a flexible budget, as shown in Exhibit 7-2, column 3. The flexible budget allows for a more detailed analysis of the $93,100 unfavorable static-budget variance for operating income.

Flexible-Budget Variances and Sales-Volume Variances

Exhibit 7-2 shows the flexible-budget-based variance analysis for Webb, which subdivides the $93,100 unfavorable static-budget variance for operating income into two parts: a flexible-budget variance of $29,100 U and a sales-volume variance of $64,000 U. The **sales-volume variance** is the difference between a flexible-budget amount and the corresponding static-budget amount. The **flexible-budget variance** is the difference between an actual result and the corresponding flexible-budget amount.

> **Decision Point**
>
> How can managers develop a flexible budget and why is it useful to do so?

Exhibit 7-2   Level 2 Flexible-Budget-Based Variance Analysis for Webb Company for April 2011[a]

Level 2 Analysis

	Actual Results (1)	Flexible-Budget Variances (2) = (1) − (3)	Flexible Budget (3)	Sales-Volume Variances (4) = (3) − (5)	Static Budget (5)
Units sold	10,000	0	10,000	2,000 U	12,000
Revenues	$1,250,000	$50,000 F	$1,200,000	$240,000 U	$1,440,000
Variable costs					
Direct materials	621,600	21,600 U	600,000	120,000 F	720,000
Direct manufacturing labor	198,000	38,000 U	160,000	32,000 F	192,000
Variable manufacturing overhead	130,500	10,500 U	120,000	24,000 F	144,000
Total variable costs	950,100	70,100 U	880,000	176,000 F	1,056,000
Contribution margin	299,900	20,100 U	320,000	64,000 U	384,000
Fixed manufacturing costs	285,000	9,000 U	276,000	0	276,000
Operating income	$ 14,900	$29,100 U	$ 44,000	$ 64,000 U	$ 108,000

Level 2	$29,100 U	$ 64,000 U
	Flexible-budget variance	Sales-volume variance

Level 1	$93,100 U
	Static-budget variance

[a]F = favorable effect on operating income; U = unfavorable effect on operating income.

Sales-Volume Variances

Learning Objective 3

Calculate flexible-budget variances

. . . each flexible-budget variance is the difference between an actual result and a flexible-budget amount

and sales-volume variances

. . . each sales-volume variance is the difference between a flexible-budget amount and a static-budget amount

Keep in mind that the flexible-budget amounts in column 3 of Exhibit 7-2 and the static-budget amounts in column 5 are both computed using budgeted selling prices, budgeted variable cost per jacket, and budgeted fixed costs. The difference between the static-budget and the flexible-budget amounts is called the sales-volume variance because it arises *solely* from the difference between the 10,000 actual quantity (or volume) of jackets sold and the 12,000 quantity of jackets expected to be sold in the static budget.

$$\text{Sales-volume variance for operating income} = \text{Flexible-budget amount} - \text{Static-budget amount}$$

$$= \$44,000 - \$108,000$$

$$= \$64,000 \text{ U}$$

The sales-volume variance in operating income for Webb measures the change in budgeted contribution margin because Webb sold only 10,000 jackets rather than the budgeted 12,000.

$$\text{Sales-volume variance for operating income} = \left(\begin{array}{c}\text{Budgeted contribution} \\ \text{margin per unit}\end{array}\right) \times \left(\begin{array}{c}\text{Actual units} \\ \text{sold}\end{array} - \begin{array}{c}\text{Static-budget} \\ \text{units sold}\end{array}\right)$$

$$= \left(\begin{array}{c}\text{Budgeted selling} \\ \text{price}\end{array} - \begin{array}{c}\text{Budgeted variable} \\ \text{cost per unit}\end{array}\right) \times \left(\begin{array}{c}\text{Actual units} \\ \text{sold}\end{array} - \begin{array}{c}\text{Static-budget} \\ \text{units sold}\end{array}\right)$$

$$= (\$120 \text{ per jacket} - \$88 \text{ per jacket}) \times (10,000 \text{ jackets} - 12,000 \text{ jackets})$$

$$= \$32 \text{ per jacket} \times (-2,000 \text{ jackets})$$

$$= \$64,000 \text{ U}$$

Exhibit 7-2, column 4, shows the components of this overall variance by identifying the sales-volume variance for each of the line items in the income statement. Webb's managers determine that the unfavorable sales-volume variance in operating income could be because of one or more of the following reasons:

1. The overall demand for jackets is not growing at the rate that was anticipated.
2. Competitors are taking away market share from Webb.
3. Webb did not adapt quickly to changes in customer preferences and tastes.
4. Budgeted sales targets were set without careful analysis of market conditions.
5. Quality problems developed that led to customer dissatisfaction with Webb's jackets.

How Webb responds to the unfavorable sales-volume variance will be influenced by what management believes to be the cause of the variance. For example, if Webb's managers believe the unfavorable sales-volume variance was caused by market-related reasons (reasons 1, 2, 3, or 4), the sales manager would be in the best position to explain what happened and to suggest corrective actions that may be needed, such as sales promotions or market studies. If, however, managers believe the unfavorable sales-volume variance was caused by quality problems (reason 5), the production manager would be in the best position to analyze the causes and to suggest strategies for improvement, such as changes in the manufacturing process or investments in new machines. The appendix shows how to further analyze the sales volume variance to identify the reasons behind the unfavorable outcome.

The static-budget variances compared actual revenues and costs for 10,000 jackets against budgeted revenues and costs for 12,000 jackets. A portion of this difference, the sales-volume variance, reflects the effects of inaccurate forecasting of output units sold.

By removing this component from the static-budget variance, managers can compare actual revenues earned and costs incurred for April 2011 against the flexible budget—the revenues and costs Webb would have budgeted for the 10,000 jackets actually produced and sold. *These flexible-budget variances are a better measure of operating performance than static-budget variances because they compare actual revenues to budgeted revenues and actual costs to budgeted costs for the same 10,000 jackets of output.*

Flexible-Budget Variances

The first three columns of Exhibit 7-2 compare actual results with flexible-budget amounts. Flexible-budget variances are in column 2 for each line item in the income statement:

$$\text{Flexible-budget variance} = \text{Actual result} - \text{Flexible-budget amount}$$

The operating income line in Exhibit 7-2 shows the flexible-budget variance is $29,100 U ($14,900 − $44,000). The $29,100 U arises because actual selling price, actual variable cost per unit, and actual fixed costs differ from their budgeted amounts. The actual results and budgeted amounts for the selling price and variable cost per unit are as follows:

	Actual Result	**Budgeted Amount**
Selling price	$125.00 ($1,250,000 ÷ 10,000 jackets)	$120.00 ($1,200,000 ÷ 10,000 jackets)
Variable cost per jacket	$ 95.01 ($ 950,100 ÷ 10,000 jackets)	$ 88.00 ($ 880,000 ÷ 10,000 jackets)

The flexible-budget variance for revenues is called the **selling-price variance** because it arises solely from the difference between the actual selling price and the budgeted selling price:

$$\text{Selling-price variance} = \left(\text{Actual selling price} - \text{Budgeted selling price} \right) \times \text{Actual units sold}$$

$$= (\$125 \text{ per jacket} - \$120 \text{ per jacket}) \times 10,000 \text{ jackets}$$

$$= \$50,000 \text{ F}$$

Webb has a favorable selling-price variance because the $125 actual selling price exceeds the $120 budgeted amount, which increases operating income. Marketing managers are generally in the best position to understand and explain the reason for this selling price difference. For example, was the difference due to better quality? Or was it due to an overall increase in market prices? Webb's managers concluded it was due to a general increase in prices.

The flexible-budget variance for total variable costs is unfavorable ($70,100 U) for the actual output of 10,000 jackets. It's unfavorable because of one or both of the following:

■ Webb used greater quantities of inputs (such as direct manufacturing labor-hours) compared to the budgeted quantities of inputs.

■ Webb incurred higher prices per unit for the inputs (such as the wage rate per direct manufacturing labor-hour) compared to the budgeted prices per unit of the inputs.

Higher input quantities and/or higher input prices relative to the budgeted amounts could be the result of Webb deciding to produce a better product than what was planned or the result of inefficiencies in Webb's manufacturing and purchasing, or both. *You should always think of variance analysis as providing suggestions for further investigation rather than as establishing conclusive evidence of good or bad performance.*

The actual fixed costs of $285,000 are $9,000 more than the budgeted amount of $276,000. This unfavorable flexible-budget variance reflects unexpected increases in the cost of fixed indirect resources, such as factory rent or supervisory salaries.

In the rest of this chapter, we will focus on variable direct-cost input variances. Chapter 8 emphasizes indirect (overhead) cost variances.

Decision Point

How are flexible-budget and sales-volume variances calculated?

Price Variances and Efficiency Variances for Direct-Cost Inputs

To gain further insight, almost all companies subdivide the flexible-budget variance for direct-cost inputs into two more-detailed variances:

1. A price variance that reflects the difference between an actual input price and a budgeted input price

2. An efficiency variance that reflects the difference between an actual input quantity and a budgeted input quantity

The information available from these variances (which we call level 3 variances) helps managers to better understand past performance and take corrective actions to implement superior strategies in the future. Managers generally have more control over efficiency variances than price variances because the quantity of inputs used is primarily affected by factors inside the company (such as the efficiency with which operations are performed), while changes in the price of materials or in wage rates may be largely dictated by market forces outside the company (see the Concepts in Action feature on p. 237).

Obtaining Budgeted Input Prices and Budgeted Input Quantities

To calculate price and efficiency variances, Webb needs to obtain budgeted input prices and budgeted input quantities. Webb's three main sources for this information are past data, data from similar companies, and standards.

1. **Actual input data from past periods.** Most companies have past data on actual input prices and actual input quantities. These historical data could be analyzed for trends or patterns (using some of the techniques we will discuss in Chapter 10) to obtain estimates of budgeted prices and quantities. The advantage of past data is that they represent quantities and prices that are real rather than hypothetical and can serve as benchmarks for continuous improvement. Another advantage is that past data are typically available at low cost. However, there are limitations to using past data. Past data can include inefficiencies such as wastage of direct materials. They also do not incorporate any changes expected for the budget period.

2. **Data from other companies that have similar processes.** The benefit of using data from peer firms is that the budget numbers represent competitive benchmarks from other companies. For example, Baptist Healthcare System in Louisville, Kentucky, maintains detailed flexible budgets and benchmarks its labor performance against hospitals that provide similar types of services and volumes and are in the upper quartile of a national benchmark. The main difficulty of using this source is that input-price and input quantity data from other companies are often not available or may not be comparable to a particular company's situation. Consider American Apparel, which makes over 1 million articles of clothing a week. At its sole factory, in Los Angeles, workers receive hourly wages, piece rates, and medical benefits well in excess of those paid by its competitors, virtually all of whom are offshore. Moreover, because sourcing organic cotton from overseas results in too high of a carbon footprint, American Apparel purchases more expensive domestic cotton in keeping with its sustainability programs.

3. **Standards developed by Webb.** A **standard** is a carefully determined price, cost, or quantity that is used as a benchmark for judging performance. Standards are usually expressed on a per-unit basis. Consider how Webb determines its direct manufacturing labor standards. Webb conducts engineering studies to obtain a detailed breakdown of the steps required to make a jacket. Each step is assigned a standard time based on work performed by a *skilled* worker using equipment operating in an *efficient* manner. There are two advantages of using standard times: (i) They aim to exclude past inefficiencies and (ii) they aim to take into account changes expected to occur in the budget period. An example of (ii) is the decision by Webb, for strategic reasons, to lease new

sewing machines that operate at a faster speed and enable output to be produced with lower defect rates. Similarly, Webb determines the standard quantity of square yards of cloth required by a skilled operator to make each jacket.

The term "standard" refers to many different things. Always clarify its meaning and how it is being used. A **standard input** is a carefully determined quantity of input—such as square yards of cloth or direct manufacturing labor-hours—required for one unit of output, such as a jacket. A **standard price** is a carefully determined price that a company expects to pay for a unit of input. In the Webb example, the standard wage rate that Webb expects to pay its operators is an example of a standard price of a direct manufacturing labor-hour. A **standard cost** is a carefully determined cost of a unit of output—for example, the standard direct manufacturing labor cost of a jacket at Webb.

$$\text{Standard cost per output unit for each variable direct-cost input} = \text{Standard input allowed for one output unit} \times \text{Standard price per input unit}$$

Standard direct material cost per jacket: 2 square yards of cloth input allowed per output unit (jacket) manufactured, at $30 standard price per square yard

Standard direct material cost per jacket = 2 square yards × $30 per square yard = $60

Standard direct manufacturing labor cost per jacket: 0.8 manufacturing labor-hour of input allowed per output unit manufactured, at $20 standard price per hour

Standard direct manufacturing labor cost per jacket = 0.8 labor-hour × $20 per labor-hour = $16

How are the words "budget" and "standard" related? Budget is the broader term. To clarify, budgeted input prices, input quantities, and costs need *not* be based on standards. As we saw previously, they could be based on past data or competitive benchmarks, for example. However, when standards *are* used to obtain budgeted input quantities and prices, the terms "standard" and "budget" are used interchangeably. The standard cost of each input required for one unit of output is determined by the standard quantity of the input required for one unit of output and the standard price per input unit. See how the standard-cost computations shown previously for direct materials and direct manufacturing labor result in the budgeted direct material cost per jacket of $60 and the budgeted direct manufacturing labor cost of $16 referred to earlier (p. 229).

In its standard costing system, Webb uses standards that are attainable through efficient operations but that allow for normal disruptions. An alternative is to set more-challenging standards that are more difficult to attain. As we discussed in Chapter 6, setting challenging standards can increase motivation and performance. If, however, standards are regarded by workers as essentially unachievable, it can increase frustration and hurt performance.

Data for Calculating Webb's Price Variances and Efficiency Variances

Consider Webb's two direct-cost categories. The actual cost for each of these categories for the 10,000 jackets manufactured and sold in April 2011 is as follows:

Direct Materials Purchased and Used[4]
1. Square yards of cloth input purchased and used	22,200
2. Actual price incurred per square yard	$ 28
3. Direct material costs (22,200 × $28) [shown in Exhibit 7-2, column 1]	$621,600

Direct Manufacturing Labor
1. Direct manufacturing labor-hours	9,000
2. Actual price incurred per direct manufacturing labor-hour	$ 22
3. Direct manufacturing labor costs (9,000 × $22) [shown in Exhibit 7-2, column 1]	$198,000

Decision Point

What is a standard cost and what are its purposes?

Learning Objective 5

Compute price variances

. . . each price variance is the difference between an actual input price and a budgeted input price

and efficiency variances

. . . each efficiency variance is the difference between an actual input quantity and a budgeted input quantity for actual output

for direct-cost categories

---

[4] The Problem for Self-Study (pp. 246–247) relaxes the assumption that the quantity of direct materials used equals the quantity of direct materials purchased.

Let's use the Webb Company data to illustrate the price variance and the efficiency variance for direct-cost inputs.

A **price variance** is the difference between actual price and budgeted price, multiplied by actual input quantity, such as direct materials purchased or used. A price variance is sometimes called an **input-price variance** or **rate variance**, especially when referring to a price variance for direct manufacturing labor. An **efficiency variance** is the difference between actual input quantity used—such as square yards of cloth of direct materials—and budgeted input quantity allowed for actual output, multiplied by budgeted price. An efficiency variance is sometimes called a **usage variance**. Let's explore price and efficiency variances in greater detail so we can see how managers use these variances to improve their future performance.

Price Variances

The formula for computing the price variance is as follows:

$$\text{Price variance} = \left(\begin{array}{c} \text{Actual price} \\ \text{of input} \end{array} - \begin{array}{c} \text{Budgeted price} \\ \text{of input} \end{array} \right) \times \begin{array}{c} \text{Actual quantity} \\ \text{of input} \end{array}$$

Price variances for Webb's two direct-cost categories are as follows:

Direct-Cost Category	$\left(\begin{array}{c}\text{Actual price} \\ \text{of input} \end{array} - \begin{array}{c}\text{Budgeted price} \\ \text{of input} \end{array} \right) \times$	Actual quantity of input	Price = Variance
Direct materials	($28 per sq. yard – $30 per sq. yard) ×	22,200 square yards	= $44,400 F
Direct manufacturing labor	($22 per hour – $20 per hour) ×	9,000 hours	= $18,000 U

The direct materials price variance is favorable because actual price of cloth is less than budgeted price, resulting in an increase in operating income. The direct manufacturing labor price variance is unfavorable because actual wage rate paid to labor is more than the budgeted rate, resulting in a decrease in operating income.

Always consider a broad range of possible causes for a price variance. For example, Webb's favorable direct materials price variance could be due to one or more of the following:

- Webb's purchasing manager negotiated the direct materials prices more skillfully than was planned for in the budget.
- The purchasing manager changed to a lower-price supplier.
- Webb's purchasing manager ordered larger quantities than the quantities budgeted, thereby obtaining quantity discounts.
- Direct material prices decreased unexpectedly because of, say, industry oversupply.
- Budgeted purchase prices of direct materials were set too high without careful analysis of market conditions.
- The purchasing manager received favorable prices because he was willing to accept unfavorable terms on factors other than prices (such as lower-quality material).

Webb's response to a direct materials price variance depends on what is believed to be the cause of the variance. Assume Webb's managers attribute the favorable price variance to the purchasing manager ordering in larger quantities than budgeted, thereby receiving quantity discounts. Webb could examine if purchasing in these larger quantities resulted in higher storage costs. If the increase in storage and inventory holding costs exceeds the quantity discounts, purchasing in larger quantities is not beneficial. Some companies have reduced their materials storage areas to prevent their purchasing managers from ordering in larger quantities.

Efficiency Variance

For any actual level of output, the efficiency variance is the difference between actual quantity of input used and the budgeted quantity of input allowed for that output level, multiplied by the budgeted input price:

$$\text{Efficiency Variance} = \left(\begin{array}{c} \text{Actual} \\ \text{quantity of} \\ \text{input used} \end{array} - \begin{array}{c} \text{Budgeted quantity} \\ \text{of input allowed} \\ \text{for actual output} \end{array} \right) \times \begin{array}{c} \text{Budgeted price} \\ \text{of input} \end{array}$$

Concepts in Action

Starbucks Reduces Direct-Cost Variances to Brew a Turnaround

Along with coffee, Starbucks brewed profitable growth for many years. From Seattle to Singapore, customers lined up to buy $4 lattes and Frappuccinos. Walking around with a coffee drink from Starbucks became an affordable-luxury status symbol. But when consumers tightened their purse strings amid the recession, the company was in serious trouble. With customers cutting back and lower-priced competition—from Dunkin' Donuts and McDonald's among others—increasing, Starbucks' profit margins were under attack.

For Starbucks, profitability depends on making each high-quality beverage at the lowest possible costs. As a result, an intricate understanding of direct costs is critical. Variance analysis helps managers assess and maintain profitability at desired levels. In each Starbucks store, the two key direct costs are materials and labor.

Materials costs at Starbucks include coffee beans, milk, flavoring syrups, pastries, paper cups, and lids. To reduce budgeted costs for materials, Starbucks focused on two key inputs: coffee and milk. For coffee, Starbucks sought to avoid waste and spoilage by no longer brewing decaffeinated and darker coffee blends in the afternoon and evening, when store traffic is slower. Instead, baristas were instructed to brew a pot only when a customer ordered it. With milk prices rising (and making up around 10% of Starbucks' cost of sales), the company switched to 2% milk, which is healthier and costs less, and redoubled efforts to reduce milk-related spoilage.

Labor costs at Starbucks, which cost 24% of company revenue annually, were another area of variance focus. Many stores employed fewer baristas. In other stores, Starbucks adopted many "lean" production techniques. With 30% of baristas' time involved in walking around behind the counter, reaching for items, and blending drinks, Starbucks sought to make its drink-making processes more efficient. While the changes seem small—keeping bins of coffee beans on top of the counter so baristas don't have to bend over, moving bottles of flavored syrups closer to where drinks are made, and using colored tape to quickly differentiate between pitchers of soy, nonfat, and low-fat milk—some stores experienced a 10% increase in transactions using the same number of workers or fewer.

The company took additional steps to align labor costs with its pricing. Starbucks cut prices on easier-to-make drinks like drip coffee, while lifting prices by as much as 30 cents for larger and more complex drinks, such as a venti caramel macchiato.

Starbucks' focus on reducing year-over-year variances paid off. In fiscal year 2009, the company reduced its store operating expenses by $320 million, or 8.5%. Continued focus on direct-cost variances will be critical to the company's future success in any economic climate.

Sources: Adamy, Janet. 2009. Starbucks brews up new cost cuts by putting lid on afternoon decaf. *Wall Street Journal*, January 28; Adamy, Janet. 2008. New Starbucks brew attracts customers, flak. *Wall Street Journal*, July 1; Harris, Craig. 2007. Starbucks slips; lattes rise. *Seattle Post Intelligencer*, July 23; Jargon, Julie. 2010. Starbucks growth revives, perked by Via. *Wall Street Journal*, January 21; Jargon, Julie. 2009. Latest Starbucks buzzword: 'Lean' Japanese techniques. *Wall Street Journal*, August 4; Kesmodel, David. 2009. Starbucks sees demand stirring again. *Wall Street Journal*, November 6.

The idea here is that a company is inefficient if it uses a larger quantity of input than the budgeted quantity for its actual level of output; the company is efficient if it uses a smaller quantity of input than was budgeted for that output level.

The efficiency variances for each of Webb's direct-cost categories are as follows:

Direct-Cost Category	$\begin{pmatrix} \text{Actual} & \text{Budgeted quantity} \\ \text{quantity of} & - & \text{of input allowed} \\ \text{input used} & & \text{for actual output} \end{pmatrix}$	$\times$ Budgeted price of input	= Efficiency Variance
Direct materials	[22,200 sq. yds. − (10,000 units × 2 sq. yds./unit)]	× $30 per sq. yard	
	= (22,200 sq. yds. − 20,000 sq. yds.)	× $30 per sq. yard	= $66,000 U
Direct manufacturing labor	[9,000 hours − (10,000 units × 0.8 hour/unit)]	× $20 per hour	
	= (9,000 hours − 8,000 hours)	× $20 per hour	= 20,000 U

The two manufacturing efficiency variances—direct materials efficiency variance and direct manufacturing labor efficiency variance—are each unfavorable because more input was used than was budgeted for the actual output, resulting in a decrease in operating income.

As with price variances, there is a broad range of possible causes for these efficiency variances. For example, Webb's unfavorable efficiency variance for direct manufacturing labor could be because of one or more of the following:

■ Webb's personnel manager hired underskilled workers.

■ Webb's production scheduler inefficiently scheduled work, resulting in more manufacturing labor time than budgeted being used per jacket.

■ Webb's maintenance department did not properly maintain machines, resulting in more manufacturing labor time than budgeted being used per jacket.

■ Budgeted time standards were set too tight without careful analysis of the operating conditions and the employees' skills.

Decision Point

Why should a company calculate price and efficiency variances?

Suppose Webb's managers determine that the unfavorable variance is due to poor machine maintenance. Webb may then establish a team consisting of plant engineers and machine operators to develop a maintenance schedule that will reduce future breakdowns and thereby prevent adverse effects on labor time and product quality.

Exhibit 7-3 provides an alternative way to calculate price and efficiency variances. It also illustrates how the price variance and the efficiency variance subdivide the flexible-budget variance. Consider direct materials. The direct materials flexible-budget variance of $21,600 U is the difference between actual costs incurred (actual input quantity × actual price) of $621,600 shown in column 1 and the flexible budget (budgeted input quantity allowed for actual output × budgeted price) of $600,000 shown in column 3. Column 2 (actual input quantity × budgeted price) is inserted between column 1 and column 3. The difference between columns 1 and 2 is the price variance of $44,400 F. This price variance occurs because the same actual input quantity (22,200 sq. yds.) is multiplied by *actual price* ($28) in column 1 and *budgeted price* ($30) in column 2. The difference between columns 2 and 3 is the efficiency variance of $66,000 U because the same budgeted price ($30) is multiplied by *actual input quantity* (22,200 sq. yds) in column 2

Exhibit 7-3 Columnar Presentation of Variance Analysis: Direct Costs for Webb Company for April 2011[a]

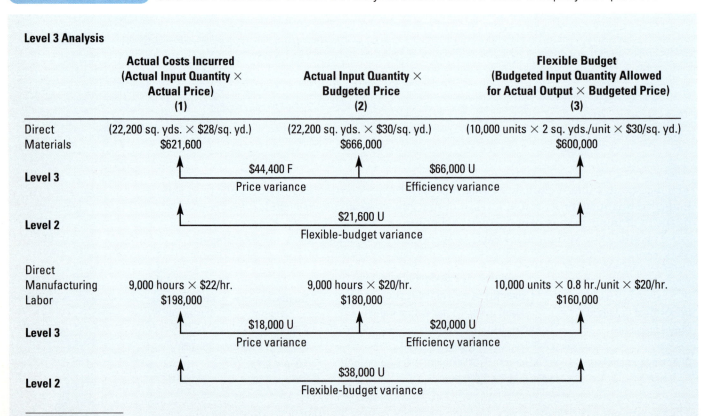

Level 3 Analysis

	Actual Costs Incurred (Actual Input Quantity × Actual Price) (1)	Actual Input Quantity × Budgeted Price (2)	Flexible Budget (Budgeted Input Quantity Allowed for Actual Output × Budgeted Price) (3)
Direct Materials	(22,200 sq. yds. × $28/sq. yd.) $621,600	(22,200 sq. yds. × $30/sq. yd.) $666,000	(10,000 units × 2 sq. yds./unit × $30/sq. yd.) $600,000

Level 3 → $44,400 F Price variance ← → $66,000 U Efficiency variance ←

Level 2 → $21,600 U Flexible-budget variance ←

| Direct Manufacturing Labor | 9,000 hours × $22/hr. $198,000 | 9,000 hours × $20/hr. $180,000 | 10,000 units × 0.8 hr./unit × $20/hr. $160,000 |

Level 3 → $18,000 U Price variance ← → $20,000 U Efficiency variance ←

Level 2 → $38,000 U Flexible-budget variance ←

[a]F = favorable effect on operating income; U = unfavorable effect on operating income.

and *budgeted input quantity allowed for actual output* (20,000 sq. yds.) in column 3. The sum of the direct materials price variance, $44,400 F, and the direct materials efficiency variance, $66,000 U, equals the direct materials flexible budget variance, $21,600 U.

Summary of Variances

Exhibit 7-4 provides a summary of the different variances. Note how the variances at each higher level provide disaggregated and more detailed information for evaluating performance.

The following computations show why actual operating income is $14,900 when the static-budget operating income is $108,000. The numbers in the computations can be found in Exhibits 7-2 and 7-3.

Static-budget operating income			$108,000
Unfavorable sales-volume variance for operating income			(64,000)
Flexible-budget operating income			44,000
Flexible-budget variances for operating income:			
Favorable selling-price variance		$50,000	
Direct materials variances:			
Favorable direct materials price variance	$ 44,400		
Unfavorable direct materials efficiency variance	(66,000)		
Unfavorable direct materials variance		(21,600)	
Direct manufacturing labor variances:			
Unfavorable direct manufacturing labor price variance	(18,000)		
Unfavorable direct manufacturing labor efficiency variance	(20,000)		
Unfavorable direct manufacturing labor variance		(38,000)	
Unfavorable variable manufacturing overhead variance		(10,500)	
Unfavorable fixed manufacturing overhead variance		(9,000)	
Unfavorable flexible-budget variance for operating income			(29,100)
Actual operating income			$ 14,900

The summary of variances highlights three main effects:

1. Webb sold 2,000 fewer units than budgeted, resulting in an unfavorable sales volume variance of $64,000. Sales declined because of quality problems and new styles of jackets introduced by Webb's competitors.

2. Webb sold units at a higher price than budgeted, resulting in a favorable selling-price variance of $50,000. Webb's prices, however, were lower than the prices charged by Webb's competitors.

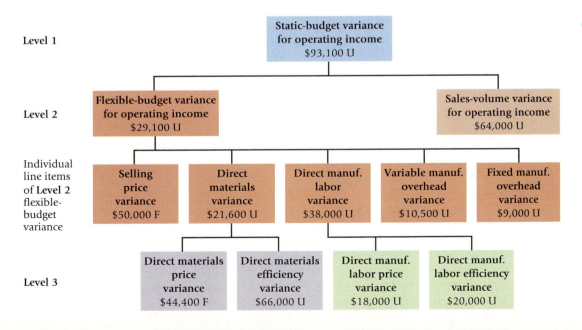

Exhibit 7-4

Summary of Level 1, 2, and 3 Variance Analyses

Level 1

Level 2

Individual line items of Level 2 flexible-budget variance

Level 3

3. Manufacturing costs for the actual output produced were higher than budgeted—direct materials by $21,600, direct manufacturing labor by $38,000, variable manufacturing overhead by $10,500, and fixed overhead by $9,000 because of poor quality of cloth, poor maintenance of machines, and underskilled workers.

We now present Webb's journal entries under its standard costing system.

Journal Entries Using Standard Costs

Chapter 4 illustrated journal entries when normal costing is used. We will now illustrate journal entries for Webb Company using standard costs. Our focus is on direct materials and direct manufacturing labor. All the numbers included in the following journal entries are found in Exhibit 7-3.

Note: In each of the following entries, unfavorable variances are always debits (they decrease operating income), and favorable variances are always credits (they increase operating income).

JOURNAL ENTRY 1A: Isolate the direct materials price variance at the time of purchase by increasing (debiting) Direct Materials Control at standard prices. This is the earliest time possible to isolate this variance.

1a.	Direct Materials Control		
	(22,200 square yards × $30 per square yard)	666,000	
	Direct Materials Price Variance		
	(22,200 square yards × $2 per square yard)		44,400
	Accounts Payable Control		
	(22,200 square yards × $28 per square yard)		621,600
	To record direct materials purchased.		

JOURNAL ENTRY 1B: Isolate the direct materials efficiency variance at the time the direct materials are used by increasing (debiting) Work-in-Process Control at standard quantities allowed for actual output units manufactured times standard prices.

1b.	Work-in-Process Control		
	(10,000 jackets × 2 yards per jacket × $30 per square yard)	600,000	
	Direct Materials Efficiency Variance		
	(2,200 square yards × $30 per square yard)	66,000	
	Direct Materials Control		
	(22,200 square yards × $30 per square yard)		666,000
	To record direct materials used.		

JOURNAL ENTRY 2: Isolate the direct manufacturing labor price variance and efficiency variance at the time this labor is used by increasing (debiting) Work-in-Process Control at standard quantities allowed for actual output units manufactured at standard prices. Note that Wages Payable Control measures the actual amounts payable to workers based on actual hours worked and actual wage rates.

2.	Work-in-Process Control		
	(10,000 jackets × 0.80 hour per jacket × $20 per hour)	160,000	
	Direct Manufacturing Labor Price Variance		
	(9,000 hours × $2 per hour)	18,000	
	Direct Manufacturing Labor Efficiency Variance		
	(1,000 hours × $20 per hour)	20,000	
	Wages Payable Control		
	(9,000 hours × $22 per hour)		198,000
	To record liability for direct manufacturing labor costs.		

We have seen how standard costing and variance analysis help to focus management attention on areas not operating as expected. The journal entries here point to another advantage of standard costing systems—that is, standard costs simplify product costing. As each unit is manufactured, costs are assigned to it using the standard cost of direct materials, the standard cost of direct manufacturing labor and, as you will see in Chapter 8, standard manufacturing overhead cost.

From the perspective of control, all variances are isolated at the earliest possible time. For example, by isolating the direct materials price variance at the time of purchase, corrective actions—such as seeking cost reductions from the current supplier or obtaining price quotes from other potential suppliers—can be taken immediately when a large unfavorable variance is first known rather than waiting until after the materials are used in production.

At the end of the fiscal year, the variance accounts are written off to cost of goods sold if they are immaterial in amount. For simplicity, we assume that the balances in the different direct cost variance accounts as of April 2011 are also the balances at the end of 2011 and therefore immaterial in total. Webb would record the following journal entry to write off the direct cost variance accounts to Cost of Goods Sold.

Cost of Goods Sold	59,600	
Direct Materials Price Variance	44,400	
Direct Materials Efficiency Variance		66,000
Direct Manufacturing Labor Price Variance		18,000
Direct Manufacturing Labor Efficiency Variance		20,000

Alternatively, assuming Webb has inventories at the end of the fiscal year, and the variances are material in their amounts, the variance accounts are prorated between cost of goods sold and various inventory accounts using the methods described in Chapter 4 (pp. 117–122). For example, Direct Materials Price Variance is prorated among Materials Control, Work-in-Process Control, Finished Goods Control and Cost of Goods Sold on the basis of the standard costs of direct materials in each account's ending balance. Direct Materials Efficiency Variance is prorated among Work-in-Process Control, Finished Goods Control, and Cost of Goods Sold on the basis of the direct material costs in each account's ending balance (after proration of the direct materials price variance).

Many accountants, industrial engineers, and managers maintain that to the extent that variances measure inefficiency or abnormal efficiency during the year, they should be written off instead of being prorated among inventories and cost of goods sold. This reasoning argues for applying a combination of the write-off and proration methods for each individual variance. Consider the efficiency variance. The portion of the efficiency variance that is due to inefficiency and could have been avoided should be written off to cost of goods sold while the portion that is unavoidable should be prorated. If another variance, such as the direct materials price variance, is considered unavoidable because it is entirely caused by general market conditions, it should be prorated. Unlike full proration, this approach avoids carrying the costs of inefficiency as part of inventoriable costs.

Implementing Standard Costing

Standard costing provides valuable information for the management and control of materials, labor, and other activities related to production.

Standard Costing and Information Technology

Modern information technology promotes the increased use of standard costing systems for product costing and control. Companies such as Dell and Sandoz store standard prices and standard quantities in their computer systems. A bar code scanner records the receipt of materials, immediately costing each material using its stored standard price. The receipt of materials is then matched with the purchase order to record accounts payable and to isolate the direct materials price variance.

The direct materials efficiency variance is calculated as output is completed by comparing the standard quantity of direct materials that should have been used with the computerized request for direct materials submitted by an operator on the production floor. Labor variances are calculated as employees log into production-floor terminals and punch in their employee numbers, start and end times, and the quantity of product they helped produce. Managers use this instantaneous feedback from variances to initiate immediate corrective action, as needed.

c. Price and efficiency variances for the following:
- Direct materials: frames
- Direct materials: lenses
- Direct manufacturing labor

2. Give three possible explanations for each of the three price and efficiency variances at Styles in requirement 1c.

7-33 **Possible causes for price and efficiency variances.** You are a student preparing for a job interview with a *Fortune* 100 consumer products manufacturer. You are applying for a job in the finance department. This company is known for its rigorous case-based interview process. One of the students who successfully obtained a job with them upon graduation last year advised you to "know your variances cold!" When you inquired further, she told you that she had been asked to pretend that she was investigating wage and materials variances. Per her advice, you have been studying the causes and consequences of variances. You are excited when you walk in and find that the first case deals with variance analysis. You are given the following data for May for a detergent bottling plant located in Mexico:

Actual

Bottles filled	340,000
Direct materials used in production	6,150,000 oz.
Actual direct material cost	2,275,500 pesos
Actual direct manufacturing labor-hours	26,000 hours
Actual direct labor cost	784,420 pesos

Standards

Purchase price of direct materials	0.36 pesos/oz
Bottle size	15 oz.
Wage rate	29.25 pesos/hour
Bottles per minute	0.50

Required

Please respond to the following questions as if you were in an interview situation:

1. Calculate the materials efficiency and price variance, and the wage and labor efficiency variances for the month of May.
2. You are given the following context: "Union organizers are targeting our detergent bottling plant in Puebla, Mexico, for a union." Can you provide a better explanation for the variances that you have calculated on the basis of this information?

7-34 **Material cost variances, use of variances for performance evaluation.** Katharine Stanley is the owner of Better Bikes, a company that produces high quality cross-country bicycles. Better Bikes participates in a supply chain that consists of suppliers, manufacturers, distributors, and elite bicycle shops. For several years Better Bikes has purchased titanium from suppliers in the supply chain. Better Bikes uses titanium for the bicycle frames because it is stronger and lighter than other metals and therefore increases the quality of the bicycle. Earlier this year, Better Bikes hired Michael Scott, a recent graduate from State University, as purchasing manager. Michael believed that he could reduce costs if he purchased titanium from an online marketplace at a lower price.

Better Bikes established the following standards based upon the company's experience with previous suppliers. The standards are as follows:

Cost of titanium	$22 per pound
Titanium used per bicycle	8 lb.

Actual results for the first month using the online supplier of titanium are as follows:

Bicycles produced	800
Titanium purchased	8,400 lb. for $159,600
Titanium used in production	7,900 lb.

Required

1. Compute the direct materials price and efficiency variances.
2. What factors can explain the variances identified in requirement 1? Could any other variances be affected?
3. Was switching suppliers a good idea for Better Bikes? Explain why or why not.
4. Should Michael Scott's performance evaluation be based solely on price variances? Should the production manager's evaluation be based solely on efficiency variances? Why it is important for Katharine Stanley to understand the causes of a variance before she evaluates performance?
5. Other than performance evaluation, what reasons are there for calculating variances?
6. What future problems could result from Better Bikes' decision to buy a lower quality of titanium from the online marketplace?

7-35 Direct manufacturing labor and direct materials variances, missing data. (CMA, heavily adapted) Morro Bay Surfboards manufactures fiberglass surfboards. The standard cost of direct materials and direct manufacturing labor is $225 per board. This includes 30 pounds of direct materials, at the budgeted price of $3 per pound, and 9 hours of direct manufacturing labor, at the budgeted rate of $15 per hour. Following are additional data for the month of July:

Units completed	5,500 units
Direct material purchases	190,000 pounds
Cost of direct material purchases	$579,500
Actual direct manufacturing labor-hours	49,000 hours
Actual direct labor cost	$739,900
Direct materials efficiency variance	$ 1,500 F

There were no beginning inventories.

Required

1. Compute direct manufacturing labor variances for July.
2. Compute the actual pounds of direct materials used in production in July.
3. Calculate the actual price per pound of direct materials purchased.
4. Calculate the direct materials price variance.

7-36 Direct materials and manufacturing labor variances, solving unknowns. (CPA, adapted) On May 1, 2012, Bovar Company began the manufacture of a new paging machine known as Dandy. The company installed a standard costing system to account for manufacturing costs. The standard costs for a unit of Dandy follow:

Direct materials (3 lb. at $5 per lb.)	$15.00
Direct manufacturing labor (1/2 hour at $20 per hour)	10.00
Manufacturing overhead (75% of direct manufacturing labor costs)	7.50
	$32.50

The following data were obtained from Bovar's records for the month of May:

	Debit	Credit
Revenues		$125,000
Accounts payable control (for May's purchases of direct materials)		68,250
Direct materials price variance	$3,250	
Direct materials efficiency variance	2,500	
Direct manufacturing labor price variance	1,900	
Direct manufacturing labor efficiency variance		2,000

Actual production in May was 4,000 units of Dandy, and actual sales in May were 2,500 units.

The amount shown for direct materials price variance applies to materials purchased during May. There was no beginning inventory of materials on May 1, 2012.

Compute each of the following items for Bovar for the month of May. Show your computations.

Required

1. Standard direct manufacturing labor-hours allowed for actual output produced
2. Actual direct manufacturing labor-hours worked
3. Actual direct manufacturing labor wage rate
4. Standard quantity of direct materials allowed (in pounds)
5. Actual quantity of direct materials used (in pounds)
6. Actual quantity of direct materials purchased (in pounds)
7. Actual direct materials price per pound

7-37 Direct materials and manufacturing labor variances, journal entries. Shayna's Smart Shawls, Inc., is a small business that Shayna developed while in college. She began hand-knitting shawls for her dorm friends to wear while studying. As demand grew, she hired some workers and began to manage the operation. Shayna's shawls require wool and labor. She experiments with the type of wool that she uses, and she has great variety in the shawls she produces. Shayna has bimodal turnover in her labor. She has some employees who have been with her for a very long time and others who are new and inexperienced.

Shayna uses standard costing for her shawls. She expects that a typical shawl should take 4 hours to produce, and the standard wage rate is $10.00 per hour. An average shawl uses 12 skeins of wool. Shayna shops around for good deals, and expects to pay $3.50 per skein.

Shayna uses a just-in-time inventory system, as she has clients tell her what type and color of wool they would like her to use.

For the month of April, Shayna's workers produced 235 shawls using 925 hours and 3,040 skeins of wool. Shayna bought wool for $10,336 (and used the entire quantity), and incurred labor costs of $9,620.

Required

1. Calculate the price and efficiency variances for the wool, and the price and efficiency variances for direct manufacturing labor.
2. Record the journal entries for the variances incurred.
3. Discuss logical explanations for the combination of variances that Shayna experienced.

7-38 Use of materials and manufacturing labor variances for benchmarking. You are a new junior accountant at Clearview Corporation, maker of lenses for eyeglasses. Your company sells generic-quality lenses for a moderate price. Your boss, the Controller, has given you the latest month's report for the lens trade association. This report includes information related to operations for your firm and three of your competitors within the trade association. The report also includes information related to the industry benchmark for each line item in the report. You do not know which firm is which, except that you know you are Firm A.

Unit Variable Costs
Member Firms
For the Month Ended September 30, 2012

	Firm A	Firm B	Firm C	Firm D	Industry Benchmark
Materials input	2.00	1.95	2.15	2.50	2.0 oz. of glass
Materials price	$ 4.90	$ 5.60	$ 5.00	$ 4.50	$ 5.00 per oz.
Labor-hours used	1.10	1.15	0.95	1.00	1.00 hours
Wage rate	$15.00	$15.50	$16.50	$15.90	$13.00 per DLH
Variable overhead rate	$ 9.00	$13.50	$ 7.50	$11.25	$12.00 per DLH

Required

1. Calculate the total variable cost per unit for each firm in the trade association. Compute the percent of total for the material, labor, and variable overhead components.
2. Using the trade association's industry benchmark, calculate direct materials and direct manufacturing labor price and efficiency variances for the four firms. Calculate the percent over standard for each firm and each variance.
3. Write a brief memo to your boss outlining the advantages and disadvantages of belonging to this trade association for benchmarking purposes. Include a few ideas to improve productivity that you want your boss to take to the department heads' meeting.

7-39 Comprehensive variance analysis review. Sonnet, Inc., has the following budgeted standards for the month of March 2011:

Average selling price per diskette	$ 6.00
Total direct material cost per diskette	$ 1.50
Direct manufacturing labor	
Direct manufacturing labor cost per hour	$ 12.00
Average labor productivity rate (diskettes per hour)	300
Direct marketing cost per unit	$ 0.30
Fixed overhead	$ 800,000

Sales of 1,500,000 units are budgeted for March. The expected total market for this product was 7,500,000 diskettes. Actual March results are as follows:

■ Unit sales and production totaled 95% of plan.
■ Actual average selling price increased to $6.10.
■ Productivity dropped to 250 diskettes per hour.
■ Actual direct manufacturing labor cost is $12.20 per hour.
■ Actual total direct material cost per unit increased to $1.60.
■ Actual direct marketing costs were $0.25 per unit.
■ Fixed overhead costs were $10,000 above plan.
■ Actual market size was 8,906,250 diskettes.

Required Calculate the following:

1. Static-budget and actual operating income
2. Static-budget variance for operating income
3. Flexible-budget operating income
4. Flexible-budget variance for operating income
5. Sales-volume variance for operating income
6. Market share and market size variances
7. Price and efficiency variances for direct manufacturing labor
8. Flexible-budget variance for direct manufacturing labor

7-40 Comprehensive variance analysis. (CMA) Iceland, Inc., is a fast-growing ice-cream maker. The company's new ice-cream flavor, Cherry Star, sells for $9 per pound. The standard monthly production level is 300,000 pounds, and the standard inputs and costs are as follows:

	Home	Insert	Page Layout	Formulas	Data	Review	
	A		B	C	D	E	
1			**Quantity per**		**Standard**		
2	**Cost Item**		**Pound of Ice Cream**		**Unit Costs**		
3	Direct materials						
4	Cream		12	oz.	$ 0.03	/oz.	
5	Vanilla extract		4	oz.	0.12	/oz.	
6	Cherry		1	oz.	0.45	/oz.	
7							
8	Direct manufacturing labor[a]						
9	Preparing		1.2	min.	14.40	/hr.	
10	Stirring		1.8	min.	18.00	/hr.	
11							
12	Variable overhead[b]		3	min.	32.40	/hr.	
13							
14	[a] Direct manufacturing labor rates include employee benefits.						
15	[b] Allocated on the basis of direct manufacturing labor-hours.						

Molly Cates, the CFO, is disappointed with the results for May 2011, prepared based on these standard costs.

	Home	Insert	Page Layout	Formulas	Data	Review	View		
	A		B	C	D	E	F	G
17			**Performance Report, May 2011**					
18			**Actual**		**Budget**		**Variance**	
19	Units (pounds)		275,000		300,000		25,000	U
20	Revenues		$2,502,500		$2,700,000		$197,500	U
21	Direct materials		432,500		387,000		45,500	U
22	Direct manufacturing labor		174,000		248,400		74,400	F

Cates notes that despite a sizable increase in the pounds of ice cream sold in May, Cherry Star's contribution to the company's overall profitability has been lower than expected. Cates gathers the following information to help analyze the situation:

	Home	Insert	Page Layout	Formulas	Data	Review	
	A		B	C	D	
25			**Usage Report, May 2011**			
26	**Cost Item**		**Quantity**		**Actual Cost**	
27	Direct materials					
28	Cream		3,120,000	oz.	$124,800	
29	Vanilla extract		1,230,000	oz.	184,500	
30	Cherry		325,000	oz.	133,250	
31						
32	Direct manufacturing labor					
33	Preparing		310,000	min.	77,500	
34	Stirring		515,000	min.	154,500	

Required Compute the following variances. Comment on the variances, with particular attention to the variances that may be related to each other and the controllability of each variance:

1. Selling-price variance
2. Direct materials price variance
3. Direct materials efficiency variance
4. Direct manufacturing labor efficiency variance

7-41 Price and efficiency variances, problems in standard-setting, and benchmarking. Stuckey, Inc., manufactures industrial 55 gallon drums for storing chemicals used in the mining industry. The body of the drums is made from aluminum and the lid is made of chemical resistant plastic. Andy Jorgenson, the controller, is becoming increasingly disenchanted with Stuckey's standard costing system. The budgeted information for direct materials and direct manufacturing labor for June 2011 were as follows:

	Budget
Drums and lids produced	5,200
Direct materials price per sq. ft.	
Aluminum	$ 3.00
Plastic	$ 1.50
Direct materials per unit	
Aluminum (sq. ft.)	20
Plastic (sq. ft.)	7
Direct labor-hours per unit	2.3
Direct labor cost per hour	$12.00

The actual number of drums and lids produced was 4,920. The actual cost of aluminum and plastic was $283,023 (95,940 sq. ft.) and $50,184 (33,456 sq. ft.), respectively. The actual direct labor cost incurred was $118,572 (9,840 hours). There were no beginning or ending inventories of materials.

Standard costs are based on a study of the operations conducted by an independent consultant six months earlier. Jorgenson observes that since that study he has rarely seen an unfavorable variance of any magnitude. He notes that even at their current output levels, the workers seem to have a lot of time for sitting around and gossiping. Jorgenson is concerned that the production manager, Charlie Fenton, is aware of this but does not want to tighten up the standards because the lax standards make his performance look good.

Required

1. Compute the price and efficiency variances of Stuckey, Inc., for each direct material and direct manufacturing labor in June 2011.
2. Describe the types of actions the employees at Stuckey, Inc., may have taken to reduce the accuracy of the standards set by the independent consultant. Why would employees take those actions? Is this behavior ethical?
3. If Jorgenson does nothing about the standard costs, will his behavior violate any of the Standards of Ethical Conduct for Management Accountants described in Exhibit 1-7 on page 16?
4. What actions should Jorgenson take?
5. Jorgenson can obtain benchmarking information about the estimated costs of Stuckey's major competitors from Benchmarking Clearing House (BCH). Discuss the pros and cons of using the BCH information to compute the variances in requirement 1.

Collaborative Learning Problem

7-42 Comprehensive variance analysis. Sol Electronics, a fast-growing electronic device producer, uses a standard costing system, with standards set at the beginning of each year.

In the second quarter of 2011, Sol faced two challenges: It had to negotiate and sign a new short-term labor agreement with its workers' union, and it also had to pay a higher rate to its suppliers for direct materials. The new labor contract raised the cost of direct manufacturing labor relative to the company's 2011 standards. Similarly, the new rate for direct materials exceeded the company's 2011 standards. However, the materials were of better quality than expected, so Sol's management was confident that there would be less waste and less rework in the manufacturing process. Management also speculated that the per-unit direct manufacturing labor cost might decline as a result of the materials' improved quality.

At the end of the second quarter, Sol's CFO, Terence Shaw, reviewed the following results:

	Home	Insert	Page Layout	Formulas	Data	Review	View											
	A	B	C	D	E	F	G	H	I	J	K	L	M	N	O	P	Q	R	S
1		Variable Costs Per Unit																	
2	Per Unit Variable Costs	Standard						First Quarter 2011 Actual Results						Second Quarter 2011 Actual Results					
3	Direct materials	2.2	lb.	at	$5.70	per lb.	$12.54	2.3	lb.	at	$5.80	per lb.	$13.34	2.0	lb.	at	$6.00	per lb.	$12.00
4	Direct manufacturing labor	0.5	hrs.	at	$12	per hr.	$6.00	0.52	hrs.	at	$12	per hr.	$6.24	0.45	hrs.	at	$14	per hr.	$6.30
5	Other variable costs						$10.00						$10.00						$9.85
6							$28.54						$29.58						$28.15

	Home	Insert	Page Layout	Formulas	Data	Review	View
	U	V	W	X
1				
2		Static Budget for Each Quarter Based on 2011	First Quarter 2011 Results	Second Quarter 2011 Results
3	Units	4,000	4,400	4,800
4	Selling price	$ 70	$ 72	$ 71.50
5	Sales	$280,000	$316,800	$343,200
6	Variable costs			
7	Direct materials	50,160	58,696	57,600
8	Direct manufacturing labor	24,000	27,456	30,240
9	Other variable costs	40,000	44,000	47,280
10	Total variable costs	114,160	130,152	135,120
11	Contribution margin	165,840	186,648	208,080
12	Fixed costs	68,000	66,000	68,400
13	Operating income	$ 97,840	$120,648	$139,680

Shaw was relieved to see that the anticipated savings in material waste and rework seemed to have materialized. But, he was concerned that the union would press hard for higher wages given that actual unit costs came in below standard unit costs and operating income continued to climb.

Required

1. Prepare a detailed variance analysis of the second quarter results relative to the static budget. Show how much of the improvement in operating income arose due to changes in sales volume and how much arose for other reasons. Calculate variances that isolate the effects of price and usage changes in direct materials and direct manufacturing labor.
2. Use the results of requirement 1 to prepare a rebuttal to the union's anticipated demands in light of the second quarter results.
3. Terence Shaw thinks that the company can negotiate better if it changes the standards. Without performing any calculations, discuss the pros and cons of immediately changing the standards.

8 Flexible Budgets, Overhead Cost Variances, and Management Control

What do this week's weather forecast and organization performance have in common?

Most of the time, reality doesn't match expectations. Cloudy skies that cancel a little league game may suddenly let the sun shine through just as the vans are packed. Jubilant business owners may change their tune when they tally their monthly bills and discover that skyrocketing operation costs have significantly reduced their profits. Differences, or variances, are all around us.

For organizations, variances are of great value because they highlight the areas where performance most lags expectations. By using this information to make corrective adjustments, companies can achieve significant savings, as the following article shows.

Overhead Cost Variances Force Macy's to Shop for Changes in Strategy[1]

Managers frequently review the differences, or variances, in overhead costs and make changes in the operations of a business. Sometimes staffing levels are increased or decreased, while at other times managers identify ways to use fewer resources like, say, office supplies and travel for business meetings that don't add value to the products and services that customers buy.

At the department-store chain Macy's, however, managers analyzed overhead cost variances and changed the way the company purchased the products it sells. In 2005, when Federated Department Stores and the May Department Store Company merged, Macy's operated seven buying offices across the United States. Each of these offices was responsible for purchasing some of the clothes, cosmetics, jewelry, and many other items Macy's sells. But overlapping responsibilities, seasonal buying patterns (clothes are generally purchased in the spring and fall) and regional differences in costs and salaries (for example, it costs more for employees and rent in San Francisco than Cincinnati) led to frequent and significant variances in overhead costs.

These overhead costs weighed on the company as the retailer struggled with disappointing sales after the merger. As a result, Macy's leaders felt pressured to reduce its costs that were not directly related to selling merchandise in stores and online.

---

[1] *Sources*: Boyle, Matthew. 2009. A leaner Macy's tries to cater to local tastes. *BusinessWeek.com*, September 3; Kapner, Suzanne. 2009. Macy's looking to cut costs. *Fortune*, January 14. http://money.cnn.com/2009/01/14/news/companies/macys_consolidation.fortune/; *Macy's 2009 Corporate Fact Book*. 2009. Cincinnati: Macy's, Inc., 7.

In early 2009, the company announced plans to consolidate its network of seven buying offices into one location in New York. With all centralized buying and merchandise planning in one location, Macy's buying structure and overhead costs were in line with how many other large chains operate, including JCPenney and Kohl's. All told, the move to centralized buying would generate $100 million in annualized cost savings for the company.

While centralized buying was applauded by industry experts and shareholders, Macy's CEO Terry Lundgren was concerned about keeping a "localized flavor" in his stores. To ensure that nationwide buying accommodated local tastes, a new team of merchants was formed in each Macy's market to gauge local buying habits. That way, the company could reduce its overhead costs while ensuring that Macy's stores near water parks had extra swimsuits.

Companies such as DuPont, International Paper, and U.S. Steel, which invest heavily in capital equipment, or Amazon.com and Yahoo!, which invest large amounts in software, have high overhead costs. As the Macy's example suggests, understanding the behavior of overhead costs, planning for them, performing variance analysis, and acting appropriately on the results are critical for a company.

In this chapter, we will examine how flexible budgets and variance analysis can help managers plan and control overhead costs. Chapter 7 emphasized the direct-cost categories of direct materials and direct manufacturing labor. In this chapter, we focus on the indirect-cost categories of variable manufacturing overhead and fixed manufacturing overhead. Finally, we explain why managers should be careful when interpreting variances based on overhead-cost concepts developed primarily for financial reporting purposes.

Learning Objective 1

Explain the similarities and differences in planning variable overhead costs and fixed overhead costs

. . . for both, plan only essential activities and be efficient; fixed overhead costs are usually determined well before the budget period begins

Planning of Variable and Fixed Overhead Costs

We'll use the Webb Company example again to illustrate the planning and control of variable and fixed overhead costs. Recall that Webb manufactures jackets that are sold to distributors who in turn sell to independent clothing stores and retail chains. For simplicity, we assume Webb's only costs are *manufacturing* costs. For ease of exposition, we use the term overhead costs instead of manufacturing overhead costs. Variable (manufacturing) overhead costs for Webb include energy, machine maintenance, engineering support, and indirect materials. Fixed (manufacturing) overhead costs include plant leasing costs, depreciation on plant equipment, and the salaries of the plant managers.

Planning Variable Overhead Costs

To effectively plan variable overhead costs for a product or service, managers must focus attention on the activities that create a superior product or service for their customers and eliminate activities that do not add value. Webb's managers examine how each of their variable overhead costs relates to delivering a superior product or service to customers. For example, customers expect Webb's jackets to last, so managers at Webb consider sewing to be an essential activity. Therefore, maintenance activities for sewing machines—included in Webb's variable overhead costs—are also essential activities for which management must plan. In addition, such maintenance should be done in a cost-effective way, such as by scheduling periodic equipment maintenance rather than waiting for sewing machines to break down. For many companies today, it is critical to plan for ways to become more efficient in the use of energy, a rapidly growing component of variable overhead costs. Webb installs smart meters in order to monitor energy use in real time and steer production operations away from peak consumption periods.

Planning Fixed Overhead Costs

Effective planning of fixed overhead costs is similar to effective planning for variable overhead costs—planning to undertake only essential activities and then planning to be efficient in that undertaking. But in planning fixed overhead costs, there is one more strategic issue that managers must take into consideration: choosing the appropriate level of capacity or investment that will benefit the company in the long run. Consider Webb's leasing of sewing machines, each having a fixed cost per year. Leasing more machines than necessary—if Webb overestimates demand—will result in additional fixed leasing costs on machines not fully used during the year. Leasing insufficient machine capacity—say, because Webb underestimates demand or because of limited space in the plant—will result in an inability to meet demand, lost sales of jackets, and unhappy customers. Consider the example of AT&T, which did not foresee the iPhone's appeal or the proliferation of "apps" and did not upgrade its network sufficiently to handle the resulting data traffic. AT&T has since had to impose limits on how customers can use the iPhone (such as by curtailing tethering and the streaming of Webcasts). In December 2009, AT&T had the lowest customer satisfaction ratings among all major carriers.

The planning of fixed overhead costs differs from the planning of variable overhead costs in one important respect: timing. At the start of a budget period, management will have made most of the decisions that determine the level of fixed overhead costs to be incurred. But, it's the day-to-day, ongoing operating decisions that mainly determine the level of variable overhead costs incurred in that period. In health care settings, for example, variable overhead, which includes disposable supplies, unit doses of medication, suture packets, and medical waste disposal costs, is a function of the number and nature of procedures carried out, as well as the practice patterns of the physicians. However, the majority of the cost of providing hospital service is related to buildings, equipment, and salaried labor, which are fixed overhead items, unrelated to the volume of activity.[2]

Decision Point ►

How do managers plan variable overhead costs and fixed overhead costs?

Standard Costing at Webb Company

Learning Objective 2

Develop budgeted variable overhead cost rates

. . . budgeted variable costs divided by quantity of cost-allocation base

and budgeted fixed overhead cost rates

. . . budgeted fixed costs divided by quantity of cost-allocation base

Webb uses standard costing. The development of standards for Webb's direct manufacturing costs was described in Chapter 7. This chapter discusses the development of standards for Webb's manufacturing overhead costs. **Standard costing** is a costing system that (a) traces direct costs to output produced by multiplying the standard prices or rates by the standard quantities of inputs allowed for actual outputs produced and (b) allocates overhead costs on the basis of the standard overhead-cost rates times the standard quantities of the allocation bases allowed for the actual outputs produced.

---

[2] Related to this, free-standing surgery centers have thrived because they have an economic advantage of lower fixed overhead when compared to a traditional hospital. For an enlightening summary of costing issues in health care, see A. Macario, "What Does One Minute of Operating Room Time Cost?" Stanford University School of Medicine (2009).

The standard cost of Webb's jackets can be computed at the start of the budget period. This feature of standard costing simplifies record keeping because no record is needed of the actual overhead costs or of the actual quantities of the cost-allocation bases used for making the jackets. What is needed are the standard overhead cost rates for variable and fixed overhead. Webb's management accountants calculate these cost rates based on the planned amounts of variable and fixed overhead and the standard quantities of the allocation bases. We describe these computations next. Note that once standards have been set, the costs of using standard costing are low relative to the costs of using actual costing or normal costing.

Developing Budgeted Variable Overhead Rates

Budgeted variable overhead cost-allocation rates can be developed in four steps. We use the Webb example to illustrate these steps. Throughout the chapter, we use the broader term "budgeted rate" rather than "standard rate" to be consistent with the term used in describing normal costing in earlier chapters. In standard costing, the budgeted rates are standard rates.

Step 1: Choose the Period to Be Used for the Budget. Webb uses a 12-month budget period. Chapter 4 (p. 103) provides two reasons for using annual overhead rates rather than, say, monthly rates. The first relates to the numerator (such as reducing the influence of seasonality on the cost structure) and the second to the denominator (such as reducing the effect of varying output and number of days in a month). In addition, setting overhead rates once a year saves management the time it would need 12 times during the year if budget rates had to be set monthly.

Step 2: Select the Cost-Allocation Bases to Use in Allocating Variable Overhead Costs to Output Produced. Webb's operating managers select machine-hours as the cost-allocation base because they believe that machine-hours is the only cost driver of variable overhead. Based on an engineering study, Webb estimates it will take 0.40 of a machine-hour per actual output unit. For its budgeted output of 144,000 jackets in 2011, Webb budgets 57,600 (0.40 × 144,000) machine-hours.

Step 3: Identify the Variable Overhead Costs Associated with Each Cost-Allocation Base. Webb groups all of its variable overhead costs, including costs of energy, machine maintenance, engineering support, indirect materials, and indirect manufacturing labor in a single cost pool. Webb's total budgeted variable overhead costs for 2011 are $1,728,000.

Step 4: Compute the Rate per Unit of Each Cost-Allocation Base Used to Allocate Variable Overhead Costs to Output Produced. Dividing the amount in Step 3 ($1,728,000) by the amount in Step 2 (57,600 machine-hours), Webb estimates a rate of $30 per standard machine-hour for allocating its variable overhead costs.

In standard costing, the variable overhead rate per unit of the cost-allocation base ($30 per machine-hour for Webb) is generally expressed as a standard rate per output unit. Webb calculates the budgeted variable overhead cost rate per output unit as follows:

$$
\begin{array}{c}
\text{Budgeted variable} \\
\text{overhead cost rate} \\
\text{per output unit}
\end{array}
=
\begin{array}{c}
\text{Budgeted input} \\
\text{allowed per} \\
\text{output unit}
\end{array}
\times
\begin{array}{c}
\text{Budgeted variable} \\
\text{overhead cost rate} \\
\text{per input unit}
\end{array}
$$

$$= 0.40 \text{ hour per jacket} \times \$30 \text{ per hour}$$

$$= \$12 \text{ per jacket}$$

Webb uses $12 per jacket as the budgeted variable overhead cost rate in both its static budget for 2011 and in the monthly performance reports it prepares during 2011.

The $12 per jacket represents the amount by which Webb's variable overhead costs are expected to change with respect to output units for planning and control purposes. Accordingly, as the number of jackets manufactured increases, variable overhead costs are allocated to output units (for the inventory costing purpose) at the same rate of $12 per jacket. Of course, this presents an overall picture of total variable overhead costs, which in reality consist of many items, including energy, repairs, indirect labor, and so on. Managers help control variable overhead costs by budgeting each line item and then investigating possible causes for any significant variances.

Developing Budgeted Fixed Overhead Rates

Fixed overhead costs are, by definition, a lump sum of costs that remains unchanged in total for a given period, despite wide changes in the level of total activity or volume related to those overhead costs. Fixed costs are included in flexible budgets, but they remain the same total amount within the relevant range of activity regardless of the output level chosen to "flex" the variable costs and revenues. Recall from Exhibit 7-2, page 231 and the steps in developing a flexible budget, that the fixed-cost amount is the same $276,000 in the static budget and in the flexible budget. Do not assume, however, that fixed overhead costs can never be changed. Managers can reduce fixed overhead costs by selling equipment or by laying off employees. But they are fixed in the sense that, unlike variable costs such as direct material costs, fixed costs do not *automatically* increase or decrease with the level of activity within the relevant range.

The process of developing the budgeted fixed overhead rate is the same as that detailed earlier for calculating the budgeted variable overhead rate. The four steps are as follows:

Step 1:   Choose the Period to Use for the Budget. As with variable overhead costs, the budget period for fixed overhead costs is typically 12 months to help smooth out seasonal effects.

Step 2:   Select the Cost-Allocation Bases to Use in Allocating Fixed Overhead Costs to Output Produced. Webb uses machine-hours as the only cost-allocation base for fixed overhead costs. Why? Because Webb's managers believe that, in the long run, fixed overhead costs will increase or decrease to the levels needed to support the amount of machine-hours. Therefore, in the long run, the amount of machine-hours used is the only cost driver of fixed overhead costs. The number of machine-hours is the denominator in the budgeted fixed overhead rate computation and is called the **denominator level** or, in manufacturing settings, the **production-denominator level**. For simplicity, we assume Webb expects to operate at capacity in fiscal year 2011—with a budgeted usage of 57,600 machine-hours for a budgeted output of 144,000 jackets.[3]

Step 3:   Identify the Fixed Overhead Costs Associated with Each Cost-Allocation Base. Because Webb identifies only a single cost-allocation base—machine-hours—to allocate fixed overhead costs, it groups all such costs into a single cost pool. Costs in this pool include depreciation on plant and equipment, plant and equipment leasing costs, and the plant manager's salary. Webb's fixed overhead budget for 2011 is $3,312,000.

Step 4:   Compute the Rate per Unit of Each Cost-Allocation Base Used to Allocate Fixed Overhead Costs to Output Produced. Dividing the $3,312,000 from Step 3 by the 57,600 machine-hours from Step 2, Webb estimates a fixed overhead cost rate of $57.50 per machine-hour:

$$\frac{\text{Budgeted fixed overhead cost per unit of cost-allocation base}} = \frac{\text{Budgeted total costs in fixed overhead cost pool}}{\text{Budgeted total quantity of cost-allocation base}} = \frac{\$3,312,000}{57,600} = \$57.50 \text{ per machine-hour}$$

In standard costing, the $57.50 fixed overhead cost per machine-hour is usually expressed as a standard cost per output unit. Recall that Webb's engineering study estimates that it will take 0.40 machine-hour per output unit. Webb can now calculate the budgeted fixed overhead cost per output unit as follows:

$$\text{Budgeted fixed overhead cost per output unit} = \text{Budgeted quantity of cost-allocation base allowed per output unit} \times \text{Budgeted fixed overhead cost per unit of cost-allocation base}$$

$$= 0.40 \text{ of a machine-hour per jacket} \times \$57.50 \text{ per machine-hour}$$

$$= \$23.00 \text{ per jacket}$$

---

[3] Because Webb plans its capacity over multiple periods, anticipated demand in 2011 could be such that budgeted output for 2011 is less than capacity. Companies vary in the denominator levels they choose; some may choose budgeted output and others may choose capacity. In either case, the basic approach and analysis presented in this chapter is unchanged. Chapter 9 discusses choosing a denominator level and its implications in more detail.

When preparing monthly budgets for 2011, Webb divides the $3,312,000 annual total fixed costs into 12 equal monthly amounts of $276,000.

Variable Overhead Cost Variances

Decision Point

How are budgeted variable overhead and fixed overhead cost rates calculated?

We now illustrate how the budgeted variable overhead rate is used in computing Webb's variable overhead cost variances. The following data are for April 2011, when Webb produced and sold 10,000 jackets:

	Actual Result	Flexible-Budget Amount
1. Output units (jackets)	10,000	10,000
2. Machine-hours per output unit	0.45	0.40
3. Machine-hours (1 × 2)	4,500	4,000
4. Variable overhead costs	$130,500	$120,000
5. Variable overhead costs per machine-hour (4 ÷ 3)	$ 29.00	$ 30.00
6. Variable overhead costs per output unit (4 ÷ 1)	$ 13.05	$ 12.00

As we saw in Chapter 7, the flexible budget enables Webb to highlight the differences between actual costs and actual quantities versus budgeted costs and budgeted quantities for the actual output level of 10,000 jackets.

Flexible-Budget Analysis

The **variable overhead flexible-budget variance** measures the difference between actual variable overhead costs incurred and flexible-budget variable overhead amounts.

$$\begin{array}{c}\text{Variable overhead} \\ \text{flexible-budget variance}\end{array} = \begin{array}{c}\text{Actual costs} \\ \text{incurred}\end{array} - \begin{array}{c}\text{Flexible-budget} \\ \text{amount}\end{array}$$

$$= \$130,500 - \$120,000$$

$$= \$10,500 \text{ U}$$

This $10,500 unfavorable flexible-budget variance means Webb's actual variable overhead exceeded the flexible-budget amount by $10,500 for the 10,000 jackets actually produced and sold. Webb's managers would want to know why actual costs exceeded the flexible-budget amount. Did Webb use more machine-hours than planned to produce the 10,000 jackets? If so, was it because workers were less skilled than expected in using machines? Or did Webb spend more on variable overhead costs, such as maintenance?

Just as we illustrated in Chapter 7 with the flexible-budget variance for direct-cost items, Webb's managers can get further insight into the reason for the $10,500 unfavorable variance by subdividing it into the efficiency variance and spending variance.

Variable Overhead Efficiency Variance

The **variable overhead efficiency variance** is the difference between actual quantity of the cost-allocation base used and budgeted quantity of the cost-allocation base that should have been used to produce actual output, multiplied by budgeted variable overhead cost per unit of the cost-allocation base.

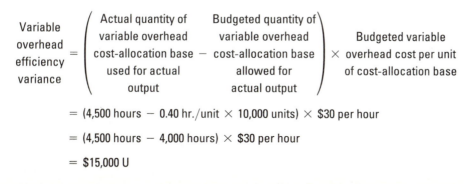

$$= (4,500 \text{ hours} - 0.40 \text{ hr./unit} \times 10,000 \text{ units}) \times \$30 \text{ per hour}$$

$$= (4,500 \text{ hours} - 4,000 \text{ hours}) \times \$30 \text{ per hour}$$

$$= \$15,000 \text{ U}$$

Learning Objective 3

Compute the variable overhead flexible-budget variance,

. . . difference between actual variable overhead costs and flexible-budget variable overhead amounts

the variable overhead efficiency variance,

. . . difference between actual quantity of cost-allocation base and budgeted quantity of cost-allocation base

and the variable overhead spending variance

. . . difference between actual variable overhead cost rate and budgeted variable overhead cost rate

Columns 2 and 3 of Exhibit 8-1 depict the variable overhead efficiency variance. Note the variance arises solely because of the difference between actual quantity (4,500 hours) and budgeted quantity (4,000 hours) of the cost-allocation base. The variable overhead efficiency variance is computed the same way the efficiency variance for direct-cost items is (Chapter 7, pp. 236–239). However, the interpretation of the variance is quite different. Efficiency variances for direct-cost items are based on differences between actual inputs used and budgeted inputs allowed for actual output produced. For example, a forensic laboratory (the kind popularized by television shows such as *CSI* and *Dexter*) would calculate a direct labor efficiency variance based on whether the lab used more or fewer hours than the standard hours allowed for the actual number of DNA tests. In contrast, the efficiency variance for variable overhead cost is based on the efficiency with which *the cost-allocation base* is used. Webb's unfavorable variable overhead efficiency variance of $15,000 means that the actual machine-hours (the cost-allocation base) of 4,500 hours turned out to be higher than the budgeted machine-hours of 4,000 hours allowed to manufacture 10,000 jackets.

The following table shows possible causes for Webb's actual machine-hours exceeding budgeted machine-hours and management's potential responses to each of these causes.

Possible Causes for Exceeding Budget	Potential Management Responses
1. Workers were less skilled than expected in using machines.	1. Encourage the human resources department to implement better employee-hiring practices and training procedures.
2. Production scheduler inefficiently scheduled jobs, resulting in more machine-hours used than budgeted.	2. Improve plant operations by installing production scheduling software.
3. Machines were not maintained in good operating condition.	3. Ensure preventive maintenance is done on all machines.
4. Webb's sales staff promised a distributor a rush delivery, which resulted in more machine-hours used than budgeted.	4. Coordinate production schedules with sales staff and distributors and share information with them.
5. Budgeted machine time standards were set too tight.	5. Commit more resources to develop appropriate standards.

Management would assess the cause(s) of the $15,000 U variance in April 2011 and respond accordingly. Note how, depending on the cause(s) of the variance, corrective actions may need to be taken not just in manufacturing but also in other business functions of the value chain, such as sales and distribution.

Exhibit 8-1   Columnar Presentation of Variable Overhead Variance Analysis: Webb Company for April 2011[a]

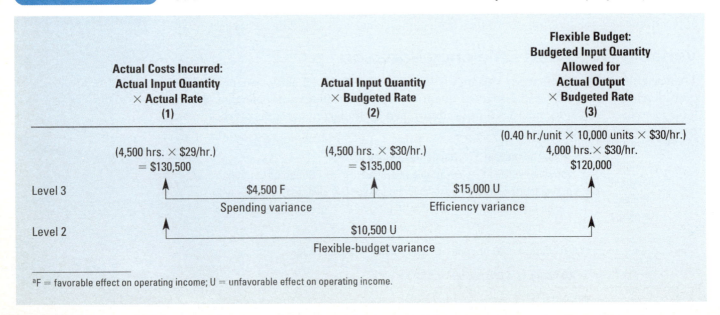

Actual Costs Incurred: Actual Input Quantity × Actual Rate (1)		Actual Input Quantity × Budgeted Rate (2)		Flexible Budget: Budgeted Input Quantity Allowed for Actual Output × Budgeted Rate (3)
(4,500 hrs. × $29/hr.) = $130,500		(4,500 hrs. × $30/hr.) = $135,000		(0.40 hr./unit × 10,000 units × $30/hr.) 4,000 hrs.× $30/hr. $120,000
Level 3	↑ $4,500 F Spending variance	↑	$15,000 U Efficiency variance	↑
Level 2	↑	$10,500 U Flexible-budget variance		↑

[a]F = favorable effect on operating income; U = unfavorable effect on operating income.

Webb's managers discovered that one reason the machines operated below budgeted efficiency levels in April 2011 was insufficient maintenance performed in the prior two months. A former plant manager delayed maintenance in a presumed attempt to meet monthly budget cost targets. As we discussed in Chapter 6, managers should not be focused on meeting short-run budget targets if they are likely to result in harmful long-run consequences. Webb is now strengthening its internal maintenance procedures so that failure to do monthly maintenance as needed will raise a "red flag" that must be immediately explained to management. Another reason for actual machine-hours exceeding budgeted machine-hours was the use of underskilled workers. As a result, Webb is initiating steps to improve hiring and training practices.

Variable Overhead Spending Variance

The **variable overhead spending variance** is the difference between actual variable overhead cost per unit of the cost-allocation base and budgeted variable overhead cost per unit of the cost-allocation base, multiplied by the actual quantity of variable overhead cost-allocation base used for actual output.

$$
\begin{pmatrix} \text{Variable} \\ \text{overhead} \\ \text{spending} \\ \text{variance} \end{pmatrix} = \begin{pmatrix} \text{Actual variable} \\ \text{overhead cost per unit} \\ \text{of cost-allocation base} \end{pmatrix} - \begin{pmatrix} \text{Budgeted variable} \\ \text{overhead cost per unit} \\ \text{of cost-allocation base} \end{pmatrix} \times \begin{pmatrix} \text{Actual quantity of} \\ \text{variable overhead} \\ \text{cost-allocation base} \\ \text{used for actual output} \end{pmatrix}
$$

$$= (\$29 \text{ per machine-hour} - \$30 \text{ per machine-hour}) \times 4{,}500 \text{ machine-hours}$$

$$= (-\$1 \text{ per machine-hour}) \times 4{,}500 \text{ machine-hours}$$

$$= \$4{,}500 \text{ F}$$

Since Webb operated in April 2011 with a lower-than-budgeted variable overhead cost per machine-hour, there is a favorable variable overhead spending variance. Columns 1 and 2 in Exhibit 8-1 depict this variance.

To understand the favorable variable overhead spending variance and its implications, Webb's managers need to recognize why *actual* variable overhead cost per unit of the cost-allocation base ($29 per machine-hour) is *lower* than the *budgeted* variable overhead cost per unit of the cost-allocation base ($30 per machine-hour). Overall, Webb used 4,500 machine-hours, which is 12.5% greater than the flexible-budget amount of 4,000 machine hours. However, actual variable overhead costs of $130,500 are only 8.75% greater than the flexible-budget amount of $120,000. Thus, relative to the flexible budget, the percentage increase in actual variable overhead costs is *less* than the percentage increase in machine-hours. Consequently, actual variable overhead cost per machine-hour is lower than the budgeted amount, resulting in a favorable variable overhead spending variance.

Recall that variable overhead costs include costs of energy, machine maintenance, indirect materials, and indirect labor. Two possible reasons why the percentage increase in actual variable overhead costs is less than the percentage increase in machine-hours are as follows:

1. Actual prices of individual inputs included in variable overhead costs, such as the price of energy, indirect materials, or indirect labor, are lower than budgeted prices of these inputs. For example, the actual price of electricity may only be $0.09 per kilowatt-hour, compared with a price of $0.10 per kilowatt-hour in the flexible budget.

2. Relative to the flexible budget, the percentage increase in the actual usage of individual items in the variable overhead-cost pool is less than the percentage increase in machine-hours. Compared with the flexible-budget amount of 30,000 kilowatt-hours, suppose actual energy used is 32,400 kilowatt-hours, or 8% higher. The fact that this is a smaller percentage increase than the 12.5% increase in machine-hours (4,500 actual machine-hours versus a flexible budget of 4,000 machine hours) will lead to a favorable variable overhead spending variance. The favorable spending variance can be partially or completely traced to the efficient use of energy and other variable overhead items.

As part of the last stage of the five-step decision-making process, Webb's managers will need to examine the signals provided by the variable overhead variances to *evaluate performance and learn*. By understanding the reasons for these variances, Webb can take appropriate actions and make more precise predictions in order to achieve improved results in future periods.

For example, Webb's managers must examine why actual prices of variable overhead cost items are different from budgeted prices. The price effects could be the result of skillful negotiation on the part of the purchasing manager, oversupply in the market, or lower quality of inputs such as indirect materials. Webb's response depends on what is believed to be the cause of the variance. If the concerns are about quality, for instance, Webb may want to put in place new quality management systems.

Similarly, Webb's managers should understand the possible causes for the efficiency with which variable overhead resources are used. These causes include skill levels of workers, maintenance of machines, and the efficiency of the manufacturing process. Webb's managers discovered that Webb used fewer supervision resources per machine-hour because of manufacturing process improvements. As a result, they began organizing crossfunctional teams to see if more process improvements could be achieved.

We emphasize that a favorable variable overhead spending variance is not always desirable. For example, the variable overhead spending variance would be favorable if Webb's managers purchased lower-priced, poor-quality indirect materials, hired less-talented supervisors, or performed less machine maintenance. These decisions, however, are likely to hurt product quality and harm the long-run prospects of the business.

To clarify the concepts of variable overhead efficiency variance and variable overhead spending variance, consider the following example. Suppose that (a) energy is the only item of variable overhead cost and machine-hours is the cost-allocation base; (b) actual machine-hours used equals the number of machine hours under the flexible budget; and (c) the actual price of energy equals the budgeted price. From (a) and (b), it follows that there is no efficiency variance — the company has been efficient with respect to the number of machine-hours (the cost-allocation base) used to produce the actual output. However, and despite (c), there could still be a spending variance. Why? Because even though the company used the correct number of machine hours, the energy consumed *per machine hour* could be higher than budgeted (for example, because the machines have not been maintained correctly). The cost of this higher energy usage would be reflected in an unfavorable spending variance.

Journal Entries for Variable Overhead Costs and Variances

We now prepare journal entries for Variable Overhead Control and the contra account Variable Overhead Allocated.

Entries for variable overhead for April 2011 (data from Exhibit 8-1) are as follows:

1. Variable Overhead Control   130,500
      Accounts Payable and various other accounts   130,500
     To record actual variable overhead costs incurred.
2. Work-in-Process Control   120,000
      Variable Overhead Allocated   120,000
     To record variable overhead cost allocated
       (0.40 machine-hour/unit × 10,000 units × $30/machine-hour). (The costs accumulated in Work-in-Process Control are transferred to Finished Goods Control when production is completed and to Cost of Goods Sold when the products are sold.)
3. Variable Overhead Allocated   120,000
     Variable Overhead Efficiency Variance   15,000
       Variable Overhead Control   130,500
       Variable Overhead Spending Variance   4,500
     To record variances for the accounting period.

These variances are the underallocated or overallocated variable overhead costs. At the end of the fiscal year, the variance accounts are written off to cost of goods sold if immaterial in amount. If the variances are material in amount, they are prorated among Work-in-Process Control, Finished Goods Control, and Cost of Goods Sold on the basis of the variable overhead allocated to these accounts, as described in Chapter 4, pages 117–122. As we discussed in Chapter 7, only unavoidable costs are prorated. Any part of the variances attributable to avoidable inefficiency are written off in the period. Assume that the balances in the variable overhead variance accounts as of April 2011 are also the balances at the end of the 2011 fiscal year and are immaterial in amount. The following journal entry records the write-off of the variance accounts to cost of goods sold:

Cost of Goods Sold	10,500	
Variable Overhead Spending Variance	4,500	
Variable Overhead Efficiency Variance		15,000

Decision Point

What variances can be calculated for variable overhead costs?

We next consider fixed overhead cost variances.

Fixed Overhead Cost Variances

The flexible-budget amount for a fixed-cost item is also the amount included in the static budget prepared at the start of the period. No adjustment is required for differences between actual output and budgeted output for fixed costs, because fixed costs are unaffected by changes in the output level within the relevant range. At the start of 2011, Webb budgeted fixed overhead costs to be $276,000 per month. The actual amount for April 2011 turned out to be $285,000. The **fixed overhead flexible-budget variance** is the difference between actual fixed overhead costs and fixed overhead costs in the flexible budget:

$$\frac{\text{Fixed overhead}}{\text{flexible-budget variance}} = \frac{\text{Actual costs}}{\text{incurred}} - \frac{\text{Flexible-budget}}{\text{amount}}$$

$$= \$285,000 - \$276,000$$

$$= \$9,000 \text{ U}$$

The variance is unfavorable because $285,000 actual fixed overhead costs exceed the $276,000 budgeted for April 2011, which decreases that month's operating income by $9,000.

The variable overhead flexible-budget variance described earlier in this chapter was subdivided into a spending variance and an efficiency variance. There is not an efficiency variance for fixed overhead costs. That's because a given lump sum of fixed overhead costs will be unaffected by how efficiently machine-hours are used to produce output in a given budget period. As we will see later on, this does not mean that a company cannot be efficient or inefficient in its use of fixed-overhead-cost resources. As Exhibit 8-2 shows, because there is no efficiency variance, the **fixed overhead spending variance** is the same amount as the fixed overhead flexible-budget variance:

$$\frac{\text{Fixed overhead}}{\text{spending variance}} = \frac{\text{Actual costs}}{\text{incurred}} - \frac{\text{Flexible-budget}}{\text{amount}}$$

$$= \$285,000 - \$276,000$$

$$= \$9,000 \text{ U}$$

Reasons for the unfavorable spending variance could be higher plant-leasing costs, higher depreciation on plant and equipment, or higher administrative costs, such as a higher-than-budgeted salary paid to the plant manager. Webb investigated this variance and found that there was a $9,000 per month unexpected increase in its equipment-leasing costs. However, management concluded that the new lease rates were competitive with lease rates available elsewhere. If this were not the case, management would look to lease equipment from other suppliers.

Exhibit 8-2   Columnar Presentation of Fixed Overhead Variance Analysis: Webb Company for April 2011[a]

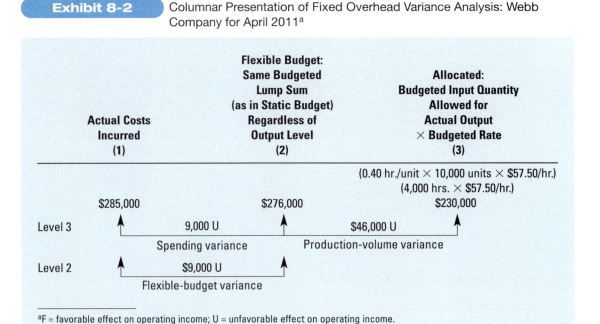

[a]F = favorable effect on operating income; U = unfavorable effect on operating income.

Production-Volume Variance

We now examine a variance—the production-volume variance—that arises only for fixed costs. Recall that at the start of the year, Webb calculated a budgeted fixed overhead rate of $57.50 per machine hour. Under standard costing, Webb's budgeted fixed overhead costs are allocated to actual output produced during the period at the rate of $57.50 per standard machine-hour, equivalent to a rate of $23 per jacket (0.40 machine-hour per jacket × $57.50 per machine-hour). If Webb produces 1,000 jackets, $23,000 ($23 per jacket × 1,000 jackets) out of April's budgeted fixed overhead costs of $276,000 will be allocated to the jackets. If Webb produces 10,000 jackets, $230,000 ($23 per jacket × 10,000 jackets) will be allocated. Only if Webb produces 12,000 jackets (that is, operates at capacity), will all $276,000 ($23 per jacket × 12,000 jackets) of the budgeted fixed overhead cost be allocated to the jacket output. The key point here is that even though Webb budgets fixed overhead costs to be $276,000, it does not necessarily allocate all these costs to output. The reason is that Webb budgets $276,000 of fixed costs to support its planned production of 12,000 jackets. If Webb produces fewer than 12,000 jackets, it only allocates the budgeted cost of capacity actually needed and used to produce the jackets.

The **production-volume variance**, also referred to as the **denominator-level variance**, is the difference between budgeted fixed overhead and fixed overhead allocated on the basis of actual output produced. The allocated fixed overhead can be expressed in terms of allocation-base units (machine-hours for Webb) or in terms of the budgeted fixed cost per unit:

$$\begin{aligned} \text{Production} \atop \text{volume variance} &= \text{Budgeted} \atop \text{fixed overhead} - \text{Fixed overhead allocated} \atop \text{for actual output units produced} \\ &= \$276,000 - (0.40 \text{ hour per jacket} \times \$57.50 \text{ per hour} \times 10,000 \text{ jackets}) \\ &= \$276,000 - (\$23 \text{ per jacket} \times 10,000 \text{ jackets}) \\ &= \$276,000 - \$230,000 \\ &= \$46,000 \text{ U} \end{aligned}$$

As shown in Exhibit 8-2, the budgeted fixed overhead ($276,000) will be the lump sum shown in the static budget and also in any flexible budget within the relevant range. Fixed overhead allocated ($230,000) is the amount of fixed overhead costs allocated; it is calculated by multiplying the number of output units produced during the budget period (10,000 units) by the budgeted cost per output unit ($23). The $46,000 U production-volume variance can also be thought of as \$23 per jacket × 2,000 jackets that were *not* produced (12,000 jackets planned – 10,000 jackets produced). We will explore possible causes for the unfavorable production-volume variance and its management implications in the following section.

Exhibit 8-3 is a graphic presentation of the production-volume variance. Exhibit 8-3 shows that for planning and control purposes, fixed (manufacturing) overhead costs do not change in the 0- to 12,000-unit relevant range. Contrast this behavior of fixed costs with how these costs are depicted for the inventory costing purpose in Exhibit 8-3. Under generally accepted accounting principles, fixed (manufacturing) overhead costs are allocated as an inventoriable cost to the output units produced. Every output unit that Webb manufactures will increase the fixed overhead allocated to products by \$23. That is, for purposes of allocating fixed overhead costs to jackets, these costs are viewed *as if* they had a variable-cost behavior pattern. As the graph in Exhibit 8-3 shows, the difference between the fixed overhead costs budgeted of \$276,000 and the \$230,000 of costs allocated is the \$46,000 unfavorable production-volume variance.

Managers should always be careful to distinguish the true behavior of fixed costs from the manner in which fixed costs are assigned to products. In particular, while fixed costs are unitized and allocated for inventory costing purposes in a certain way, as described previously, managers should be wary of using the same unitized fixed overhead costs for planning and control purposes. When forecasting fixed costs, managers should concentrate on total lump-sum costs. Similarly, when managers are looking to assign costs for control purposes or identify the best way to use capacity resources that are fixed in the short run, we will see in Chapters 9 and Chapter 11 that the use of unitized fixed costs often leads to incorrect decisions.

Interpreting the Production-Volume Variance

Lump-sum fixed costs represent costs of acquiring capacity that do not decrease automatically if the resources needed turn out to be less than the resources acquired. Sometimes costs are fixed for a specific time period for contractual reasons, such as an annual lease contract for a plant. At other times, costs are fixed because capacity has to be acquired or disposed of in fixed increments, or lumps. For example, suppose that acquiring a sewing machine gives Webb the ability to produce 1,000 jackets. Then, if it is not possible to buy or lease a fraction of a machine, Webb can add capacity only in increments of 1,000 jackets. That is, Webb may choose capacity levels of 10,000; 11,000; or 12,000 jackets, but nothing in between.

Webb's management would want to analyze why this overcapacity occurred. Is demand weak? Should Webb reevaluate its product and marketing strategies? Is there a quality problem? Or did Webb make a strategic mistake by acquiring too much capacity? The causes of the \$46,000 unfavorable production-volume variance will drive the actions Webb's managers will take in response to this variance.

In contrast, a favorable production-volume variance indicates an overallocation of fixed overhead costs. That is, the overhead costs allocated to the actual output produced exceed the budgeted fixed overhead costs of \$276,000. The favorable production-volume variance comprises the fixed costs recorded in excess of \$276,000.

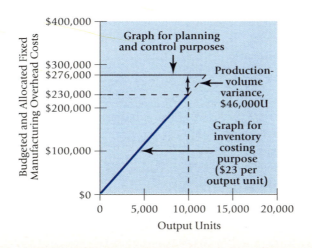

Exhibit 8-3

Behavior of Fixed Manufacturing Overhead Costs: Budgeted for Planning and Control Purposes and Allocated for Inventory Costing Purposes for Webb Company for April 2011

Be careful when drawing conclusions regarding a company's decisions about capacity planning and usage from the type (that is, favorable, F, or unfavorable, U) or the magnitude associated with a production-volume variance. To interpret the $46,000 unfavorable variance, Webb should consider why it sold only 10,000 jackets in April. Suppose a new competitor had gained market share by pricing below Webb's selling price. To sell the budgeted 12,000 jackets, Webb might have had to reduce its own selling price on all 12,000 jackets. Suppose it decided that selling 10,000 jackets at a higher price yielded higher operating income than selling 12,000 jackets at a lower price. The production-volume variance does not take into account such information. The failure of the production-volume variance to consider such information is why Webb should not interpret the $46,000 U amount as the total economic cost of selling 2,000 jackets fewer than the 12,000 jackets budgeted. If, however, Webb's managers anticipate they will not need capacity beyond 10,000 jackets, they may reduce the excess capacity, say, by canceling the lease on some of the machines.

Companies plan their plant capacity strategically on the basis of market information about how much capacity will be needed over some future time horizon. For 2011, Webb's budgeted quantity of output is equal to the maximum capacity of the plant for that budget period. Actual demand (and quantity produced) turned out to be below the budgeted quantity of output, so Webb reports an unfavorable production-volume variance for April 2011. However, it would be incorrect to conclude that Webb's management made a poor planning decision regarding plant capacity. Demand for Webb's jackets might be highly uncertain. Given this uncertainty and the cost of not having sufficient capacity to meet sudden demand surges (including lost contribution margins as well as reduced repeat business), Webb's management may have made a wise choice in planning 2011 plant capacity. Of course, if demand is unlikely to pick up again, Webb's managers may look to cancel the lease on some of the machines or to sublease the machines to other parties with the goal of reducing the unfavorable production-volume variance.

Managers must always explore the why of a variance before concluding that the label unfavorable or favorable necessarily indicates, respectively, poor or good management performance. Understanding the reasons for a variance also helps managers decide on future courses of action. Should Webb's managers try to reduce capacity, increase sales, or do nothing? Based on their analysis of the situation, Webb's managers decided to reduce some capacity but continued to maintain some excess capacity to accommodate unexpected surges in demand. Chapter 9 and Chapter 13 examine these issues in more detail. The Concepts in Action feature on page 280 highlights another example of managers using variances, and the reasons behind them, to help guide their decisions.

Next we describe the journal entries Webb would make to record fixed overhead costs using standard costing.

Journal Entries for Fixed Overhead Costs and Variances

We illustrate journal entries for fixed overhead costs for April 2011 using Fixed Overhead Control and the contra account Fixed Overhead Allocated (data from Exhibit 8-2).

1.	Fixed Overhead Control	285,000	
	Salaries Payable, Accumulated Depreciation, and various other accounts		285,000
	To record actual fixed overhead costs incurred.		
2.	Work-in-Process Control	230,000	
	Fixed Overhead Allocated		230,000
	To record fixed overhead costs allocated		
	(0.40 machine-hour/unit × 10,000 units × $57.50/machine-hour). (The costs accumulated in Work-in-Process Control are transferred to Finished Goods Control when production is completed and to Cost of Goods Sold when the products are sold.)		
3.	Fixed Overhead Allocated	230,000	
	Fixed Overhead Spending Variance	9,000	
	Fixed Overhead Production-Volume Variance	46,000	
	Fixed Overhead Control		285,000
	To record variances for the accounting period.		

Overall, $285,000 of fixed overhead costs were incurred during April, but only $230,000 were allocated to jackets. The difference of $55,000 is precisely the underallocated fixed overhead costs that we introduced when studying normal costing in Chapter 4. The third entry illustrates how the fixed overhead spending variance of $9,000 and the fixed overhead production-volume variance of $46,000 together record this amount in a standard costing system.

At the end of the fiscal year, the fixed overhead spending variance is written off to cost of goods sold if it is immaterial in amount, or prorated among Work-in-Process Control, Finished Goods Control, and Cost of Goods Sold on the basis of the fixed overhead allocated to these accounts as described in Chapter 4, pages 117–122. Some companies combine the write-off and proration methods—that is, they write off the portion of the variance that is due to inefficiency and could have been avoided and prorate the portion of the variance that is unavoidable. Assume that the balance in the Fixed Overhead Spending Variance account as of April 2011 is also the balance at the end of 2011 and is immaterial in amount. The following journal entry records the write-off to Cost of Goods Sold.

Cost of Goods Sold	9,000	
Fixed Overhead Spending Variance		9,000

We now consider the production-volume variance. Assume that the balance in Fixed Overhead Production-Volume Variance as of April 2011 is also the balance at the end of 2011. Also assume that some of the jackets manufactured during 2011 are in work-in-process and finished goods inventory at the end of the year. Many management accountants make a strong argument for writing off to Cost of Goods Sold and not prorating an unfavorable production-volume variance. Proponents of this argument contend that the unfavorable production-volume variance of $46,000 measures the cost of resources expended for 2,000 jackets that were not produced ($23 per jacket × 2,000 jackets = $46,000). Prorating these costs would inappropriately allocate fixed overhead costs incurred for the 2,000 jackets that were not produced to the jackets that were produced. The jackets produced already bear their representative share of fixed overhead costs of $23 per jacket. Therefore, this argument favors charging the unfavorable production-volume variance against the year's revenues so that fixed costs of unused capacity are not carried in work-in-process inventory and finished goods inventory.

There is, however, an alternative view. This view regards the denominator level chosen as a "soft" rather than a "hard" measure of the fixed resources required and needed to produce each jacket. Suppose that either because of the design of the jacket or the functioning of the machines, it took more machine-hours than previously thought to manufacture each jacket. Consequently, Webb could make only 10,000 jackets rather than the planned 12,000 in April. In this case, the $276,000 of budgeted fixed overhead costs support the production of the 10,000 jackets manufactured. Under this reasoning, prorating the fixed overhead production-volume variance would appropriately spread fixed overhead costs among Work-in-Process Control, Finished Goods Control, and Cost of Goods Sold.

What about a favorable production-volume variance? Suppose Webb manufactured 13,800 jackets in April 2011.

$$\text{Production-volume variance} = \begin{matrix}\text{Budgeted} \\ \text{fixed} \\ \text{overhead}\end{matrix} - \begin{matrix}\text{Fixed overhead allocated using} \\ \text{budgeted cost per output unit overhead} \\ \text{allowed for actual output produced}\end{matrix}$$

$$= \$276{,}000 - (\$23 \text{ per jacket} \times 13{,}800 \text{ jackets})$$

$$= \$276{,}000 - \$317{,}400 = \$41{,}400 \text{ F}$$

Because actual production exceeded the planned capacity level, clearly the fixed overhead costs of $276,000 supported production of, and so should be allocated to, all 13,800 jackets. Prorating the favorable production-volume variance achieves this outcome and reduces the amounts in Work-in-Process Control, Finished Goods Control, and Cost of Goods Sold. Proration is also the more conservative approach in the sense that it results in a lower operating income than if the entire favorable production-volume variance were credited to Cost of Goods Sold.

One more point is relevant to the discussion of whether to prorate the production-volume variance or to write it off to cost of goods sold. If variances are always written off to cost of goods sold, a company could set its standards to either increase (for financial reporting purposes) or decrease (for tax purposes) operating income. In other words, always writing off variances invites gaming behavior. For example, Webb could generate a favorable (unfavorable) production-volume variance by setting the denominator level used to allocate fixed overhead costs low (high) and thereby increase (decrease) operating income. The proration method has the effect of approximating the allocation of fixed costs based on actual costs and actual output so it is not susceptible to the manipulation of operating income via the choice of the denominator level.

There is no clear-cut or preferred approach for closing out the production-volume variance. The appropriate accounting procedure is a matter of judgment and depends on the circumstances of each case. Variations of the proration method may be desirable. For example, a company may choose to write off a portion of the production-volume variance and prorate the rest. The goal is to write off that part of the production-volume variance that represents the cost of capacity not used to support the production of output during the period. The rest of the production-volume variance is prorated to Work-in-Process Control, Finished Goods Control, and Cost of Goods Sold.

If Webb were to write off the production-volume variance to cost of goods sold, it would make the following journal entry.

Cost of Goods Sold	46,000	
Fixed Overhead Production-Volume Variance		46,000

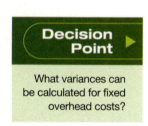

Decision Point ▶

What variances can be calculated for fixed overhead costs?

Learning Objective 5

Show how the 4-variance analysis approach reconciles the actual overhead incurred with the overhead amounts allocated during the period

. . . the 4-variance analysis approach identifies spending and efficiency variances for variable overhead costs and spending and production-volume variances for fixed overhead costs

Integrated Analysis of Overhead Cost Variances

As our discussion indicates, the variance calculations for variable overhead and fixed overhead differ:

- Variable overhead has no production-volume variance.
- Fixed overhead has no efficiency variance.

Exhibit 8-4 presents an integrated summary of the variable overhead variances and the fixed overhead variances computed using standard costs for April 2011. Panel A shows the variances for variable overhead, while Panel B contains the fixed overhead variances. As you study Exhibit 8-4, note how the columns in Panels A and B are aligned to measure the different variances. In both Panels A and B,

- the difference between columns 1 and 2 measures the spending variance.
- the difference between columns 2 and 3 measures the efficiency variance (if applicable).
- the difference between columns 3 and 4 measures the production-volume variance (if applicable).

Panel A contains an efficiency variance; Panel B has no efficiency variance for fixed overhead. As discussed earlier, a lump-sum amount of fixed costs will be unaffected by the degree of operating efficiency in a given budget period.

Panel A does not have a production-volume variance, because the amount of variable overhead allocated is always the same as the flexible-budget amount. Variable costs never have any unused capacity. When production and sales decline from 12,000 jackets to 10,000 jackets, budgeted variable overhead costs proportionately decline. Fixed costs are different. Panel B has a production-volume variance (see Exhibit 8-3) because Webb had to acquire the fixed manufacturing overhead resources it had committed to when it planned production of 12,000 jackets, even though it produced only 10,000 jackets and did not use some of its capacity.

| **Exhibit 8-4** | Columnar Presentation of Integrated Variance Analysis: Webb Company for April 2011[a] |

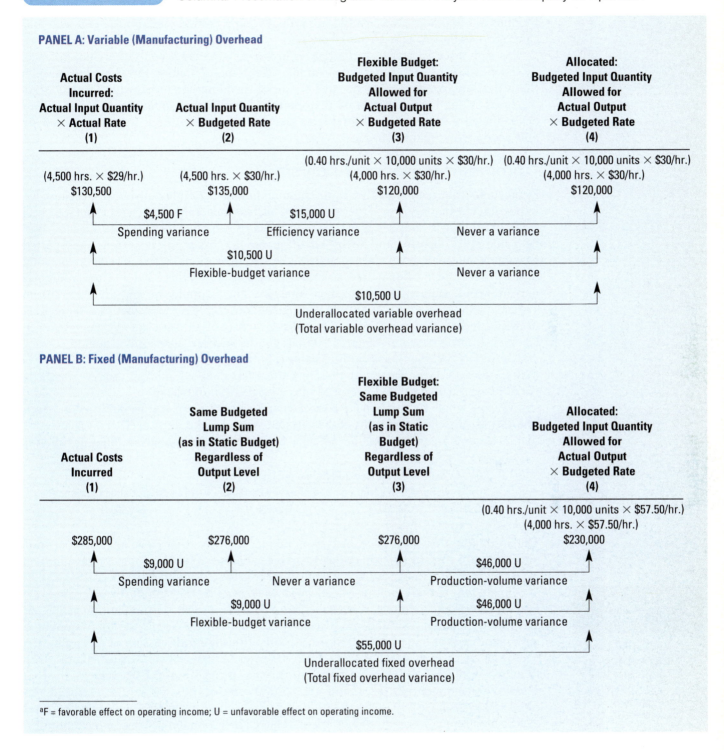

PANEL A: Variable (Manufacturing) Overhead

PANEL B: Fixed (Manufacturing) Overhead

[a]F = favorable effect on operating income; U = unfavorable effect on operating income.

4-Variance Analysis

When all of the overhead variances are presented together as in Exhibit 8-4, we refer to it as a 4-variance analysis:

	4-Variance Analysis		
	Spending Variance	**Efficiency Variance**	**Production-Volume Variance**
Variable overhead	$4,500 F	$15,000 U	Never a variance
Fixed overhead	$9,000 U	Never a variance	$46,000 U

Note that the 4-variance analysis provides the same level of information as the variance analysis carried out earlier for variable overhead and fixed overhead separately (in Exhibits 8-1 and 8-2, respectively), but it does so in a unified presentation that also indicates those variances that are never present.

As with other variances, the variances in Webb's 4-variance analysis are not necessarily independent of each other. For example, Webb may purchase lower-quality machine fluids (leading to a favorable variable overhead spending variance), which results in the machines taking longer to operate than budgeted (causing an unfavorable variable overhead efficiency variance), and producing less than budgeted output (causing an unfavorable production-volume variance).

Combined Variance Analysis

Detailed 4-variance analyses are most common in large, complex businesses, because it is impossible for managers at large companies, such as General Electric and Disney, to keep track of all that is happening within their areas of responsibility. The detailed analyses help managers identify and focus attention on the areas not operating as expected. Managers of small businesses understand their operations better based on personal observations and nonfinancial measures. They find less value in doing the additional measurements required for 4-variance analyses. For example, to simplify their costing systems, small companies may not distinguish variable overhead incurred from fixed overhead incurred because making this distinction is often not clear-cut. As we saw in Chapter 2 and will see in Chapter 10, many costs such as supervision, quality control, and materials handling have both variable- and fixed-cost components that may not be easy to separate. Managers may therefore use a less detailed analysis that *combines* the variable overhead and fixed overhead into a single total overhead.

When a single total overhead cost category is used, it can still be analyzed in depth. The variances are now the sums of the variable overhead and fixed overhead variances for that level, as computed in Exhibit 8-4. The combined variance analysis looks as follows:

	Combined 3-Variance Analysis		
	Spending Variance	**Efficiency Variance**	**Production-Volume Variance**
Total overhead	$4,500 U	$15,000 U	$46,000 U

The accounting for 3-variance analysis is simpler than for 4-variance analysis, but some information is lost. In particular, the 3-variance analysis combines the variable and fixed overhead spending variances into a single total overhead spending variance.

Finally, the overall **total-overhead variance** is given by the sum of the preceding variances. In the Webb example, this equals $65,500 U. Note that this amount, which aggregates the flexible-budget and production-volume variances, equals the total amount of underallocated (or underapplied) overhead costs. (Recall our discussion of underallocated overhead costs in normal costing from Chapter 4, page 118.) Using figures from Exhibit 8-4, the $65,500 U total-overhead variance is the difference between (a) the total actual overhead incurred ($130,500 + $285,000 = $415,500) and (b) the overhead allocated ($120,000 + $230,000 = $350,000) to the actual output produced. If the total-overhead variance were favorable, it would have corresponded instead to the amount of overapplied overhead costs.

Decision Point ▶

What is the most detailed way for a company to reconcile actual overhead incurred with the amount allocated during a period?

Production-Volume Variance and Sales-Volume Variance

As we complete our study of variance analysis for Webb Company, it is helpful to step back to see the "big picture" and to link the accounting and performance evaluation functions of standard costing. Exhibit 7-2, page 231, subdivided the static-budget variance of $93,100 U into a flexible-budget variance of $29,100 U and a sales-volume variance of $64,000 U. In both Chapter 7 and this chapter, we presented more detailed variances that subdivided, whenever possible, individual flexible-budget variances for selling price, direct materials, direct manufacturing labor, variable overhead, and fixed overhead. Here is a summary:

Selling price	$50,000 F
Direct materials (Price, $44,400 F + Efficiency, $66,000 U)	21,600 U
Direct manufacturing labor (Price, $18,000 U + Efficiency, $20,000 U)	38,000 U
Variable overhead (Spending, $4,500 F + Efficiency, $15,000 U)	10,500 U
Fixed overhead (Spending, $9,000 U)	9,000 U
Total flexible budget variance	$29,100 U

Learning Objective 6

Explain the relationship between the sales-volume variance and the production-volume variance

. . . the production-volume and operating-income volume variances together comprise the sales-volume variance

We also calculated one other variance in this chapter, the production-volume variance, which is not part of the flexible-budget variance. Where does the production-volume variance fit into the "big picture"? As we shall see, the production-volume variance is a component of the sales-volume variance.

Under our assumption of actual production and sales of 10,000 jackets, Webb's costing system debits to Work-in-Process Control the standard costs of the 10,000 jackets produced. These amounts are then transferred to Finished Goods and finally to Cost of Goods Sold:

Direct materials (Chapter 7, p. 240, entry 1b)	
($60 per jacket × 10,000 jackets)	$ 600,000
Direct manufacturing labor (Chapter 7, p. 240, entry 2)	
($16 per jacket × 10,000 jackets)	160,000
Variable overhead (Chapter 8, p. 270, entry 2)	
($12 per jacket × 10,000 jackets)	120,000
Fixed overhead (Chapter 8, p. 274, entry 2)	
($23 per jacket × 10,000 jackets)	230,000
Cost of goods sold at standard cost	
($111 per jacket × 10,000 jackets)	$1,110,000

Webb's costing system also records the revenues from the 10,000 jackets sold at the budgeted selling price of $120 per jacket. The net effect of these entries on Webb's budgeted operating income is as follows:

Revenues at budgeted selling price	
($120 per jacket × 10,000 jackets)	$1,200,000
Cost of goods sold at standard cost	
($111 per jacket × 10,000 jackets)	1,110,000
Operating income based on budgeted profit per jacket	
($9 per jacket × 10,000 jackets)	$ 90,000

A crucial point to keep in mind is that in standard costing, fixed overhead cost is treated as if it is a variable cost. That is, in determining the budgeted operating income of $90,000, only $230,000 ($23 per jacket × 10,000 jackets) of fixed overhead is considered, whereas the budgeted fixed overhead costs are $276,000. Webb's accountants then record the $46,000 unfavorable production-volume variance (the difference between budgeted fixed overhead costs, $276,000, and allocated fixed overhead costs, $230,000, p. 274, entry 2), as well as the various flexible-budget variances (including the fixed overhead spending variance) that total $29,100 unfavorable (see Exhibit 7-2, p. 231). This results in actual operating income of $14,900 as follows:

Operating income based on budgeted profit per jacket	
($9 per jacket × 10,000 jackets)	$ 90,000
Unfavorable production-volume variance	(46,000)
Flexible-budget operating income (Exhibit 7-2)	44,000
Unfavorable flexible-budget variance for operating income (Exhibit 7-2)	(29,100)
Actual operating income (Exhibit 7-2)	$ 14,900

Concepts in Action

Variance Analysis and Standard Costing Help Sandoz Manage Its Overhead Costs

In the United States, the importance of generic pharmaceuticals is growing dramatically. In recent years, Wal-Mart has been selling hundreds of generic drugs for $4 per prescription, a price many competitors have since matched. Moreover, with recent legislation extending health insurance coverage to 32 million previously uninsured Americans, the growing use of generic drugs is certain to accelerate, a trend rooted both in demographics—the aging U.S. population takes more drugs each year—and in the push to cut health care costs.

Sandoz US, a $7.5 billion subsidiary of Swiss-based Novartis AG, is one of the largest developers of generic pharmaceutical substitutes for market-leading therapeutic drugs. Market pricing pressure means that Sandoz, Teva Pharmaceutical, and other generic manufacturers operate on razor-thin margins. As a result, along with an intricate analysis of direct-cost variances, firms like Sandoz must also tackle the challenge of accounting for overhead costs. Sandoz uses standard costing and variance analysis to manage its overhead costs.

Each year, Sandoz prepares an overhead budget based on a detailed production plan, planned overhead spending, and other factors, including inflation, efficiency initiatives, and anticipated capital expenditures and depreciation. Sandoz then uses activity-based costing techniques to assign budgeted overhead costs to different work centers (for example, mixing, blending, tableting, testing, and packaging). Finally, overhead costs are assigned to products based on the activity levels required by each product at each work center. The resulting standard product cost is used in product profitability analysis and as a basis for making pricing decisions. The two main focal points in Sandoz's performance analyses are overhead absorption analysis and manufacturing overhead variance analysis.

Each month, Sandoz uses absorption analysis to compare actual production and actual costs to the standard costs of processed inventory. The monthly analysis evaluates two key trends:

1. Are costs in line with the budget? If not, the reasons are examined and the accountable managers are notified.
2. Are production volume and product mix conforming to plan? If not, Sandoz reviews and adjusts machine capacities and the absorption trend is deemed to be permanent. Plant management uses absorption analysis as a compass to determine if it is on budget and has an appropriate capacity level to efficiently satisfy the needs of its customers.

Manufacturing overhead variances are examined at the work center level. These variances help determine when equipment is not running as expected, which leads to repair or replacement. Variances also help in identifying inefficiencies in processing and setup and cleaning times, which leads to more efficient ways to use equipment. Sometimes, manufacturing overhead variance analysis leads to the review and improvement of the standards themselves—a critical element in planning the level of plant capacity. Management reviews current and future capacity use on a monthly basis, using standard hours entered into the plan's enterprise resource planning system. The standards are a useful tool in identifying capacity constraints and future capital needs.

As the plant controller remarked, "Standard costing at Sandoz produces costs that are not only understood by management accountants and industrial engineers, but by decision makers in marketing and on the production floor. Management accountants at Sandoz achieve this by having a high degree of process understanding and involvement. The result is better pricing and product mix decisions, lower waste, process improvements, and efficient capacity choices—all contributing to overall profitability."

Source: Booming US Generic Drug Market. Delhi, India: RNCOS Ltd, 2010; Conversations with, and documents prepared by, Eric Evans and Erich Erchr (of Sandoz US), 2004; Day, Kathleen. 2006. Wal-Mart sets $4 price for many generic drugs. *Washington Post*, September 22; Halpern, Steven. 2010. Teva: Generic gains from health care reform. *AOL Inc.* "Blogging Stocks" blog, May 13. http://www.bloggingstocks.com/2010/05/13/teva-teva-generic-gains-from-healthcare-reform/

In contrast, the static-budget operating income of $108,000 (p. 229) is not entered in Webb's costing system, because standard costing records budgeted revenues, standard costs, and variances only for the 10,000 jackets actually produced and sold, not for the 12,000 jackets that were *planned* to be produced and sold. As a result, the sales-volume variance of $64,000 U, which is the difference between static-budget operating income,

$108,000, and flexible-budget operating income, $44,000 (Exhibit 7-2, p. 231), is never actually recorded in standard costing. Nevertheless, the sales-volume variance is useful because it helps managers understand the lost contribution margin from selling 2,000 fewer jackets (the sales-volume variance assumes fixed costs remain at the budgeted level of $276,000).

The sales-volume variance has two components. They are as follows:

1. A difference between the static-budget operating income of $108,000 for 12,000 jackets and budgeted operating income of $90,000 for 10,000 jackets. This is the **operating-income volume variance** of $18,000 U ($108,000 – $90,000), and reflects the fact that Webb produced and sold 2,000 fewer units than budgeted.

2. A difference between the budgeted operating income of $90,000 and the flexible budget operating income of $44,000 (Exhibit 7-2, p. 231) for the 10,000 actual units. This difference arises because Webb's costing system treats fixed costs as if they behave in a variable manner and so assumes fixed costs equal the allocated amount of $230,000, rather than the budgeted fixed costs of $276,000. Of course, the difference between the allocated and budgeted fixed costs is precisely the production-volume variance of $46,000 U.

In summary, we have the following:

	Operating-income volume variance	$18,000 U
(+)	Production-volume variance	46,000 U
Equals	Sales-volume variance	$64,000 U

That is, the sales-volume variance is comprised of operating-income volume and production-volume variances.

Level 2	Sales-volume variance $64,000 U
Level 3	Production-volume variance $46,000 U — Operating-income volume variance $18,000 U

Decision Point

What is the relationship between the sales-volume variance and the production-volume variance?

Variance Analysis and Activity-Based Costing

Activity-based costing (ABC) systems focus on individual activities as the fundamental cost objects. ABC systems classify the costs of various activities into a cost hierarchy— output unit-level costs, batch-level costs, product-sustaining costs, and facility-sustaining costs (see p. 149). In this section, we show how a company that has an ABC system and batch-level costs can benefit from variance analysis. Batch-level costs are the costs of activities related to a group of units of products or services rather than to each individual unit of product or service. We illustrate variance analysis for variable batch-level direct costs and fixed batch-level setup overhead costs.[4]

Consider Lyco Brass Works, which manufactures many different types of faucets and brass fittings. Because of the wide range of products it produces, Lyco uses an activity-based costing system. In contrast, Webb uses a simple costing system because it makes only one type of jacket. One of Lyco's products is Elegance, a decorative brass faucet for home spas. Lyco produces Elegance in batches.

For each product Lyco makes, it uses dedicated materials-handling labor to bring materials to the production floor, transport work in process from one work center to the next, and take the finished goods to the shipping area. Therefore, materials-handling labor costs for Elegance are direct costs of Elegance. Because the materials for a batch are moved together, materials-handling labor costs vary with number of batches rather than with number of units in a batch. Materials-handling labor costs are variable direct batch-level costs.

Learning Objective 7

Calculate variances in activity-based costing

. . . compare budgeted and actual overhead costs of activities

---

[4] The techniques we demonstrate can be applied to analyze variable batch-level overhead costs as well.

To manufacture a batch of Elegance, Lyco must set up the machines and molds. Setting up the machines and molds requires highly trained skills. Hence, a separate setup department is responsible for setting up machines and molds for different batches of products. Setup costs are overhead costs of products. For simplicity, assume that setup costs are fixed with respect to the number of setup-hours. They consist of salaries paid to engineers and supervisors and costs of leasing setup equipment.

Information regarding Elegance for 2012 follows:

	Actual Result	Static-Budget Amount
1. Units of Elegance produced and sold	151,200	180,000
2. Batch size (units per batch)	140	150
3. Number of batches (Line 1 ÷ Line 2)	1,080	1,200
4. Materials-handling labor-hours per batch	5.25	5
5. Total materials-handling labor-hours (Line 3 × Line 4)	5,670	6,000
6. Cost per materials-handling labor-hour	$ 14.50	$ 14
7. Total materials-handling labor costs (Line 5 × Line 6)	$ 82,215	$ 84,000
8. Setup-hours per batch	6.25	6
9. Total setup-hours (Line 3 × Line 8)	6,750	7,200
10. Total fixed setup overhead costs	$220,000	$216,000

Flexible Budget and Variance Analysis for Direct Labor Costs

To prepare the flexible budget for materials-handling labor costs, Lyco starts with the actual units of output produced, 151,200 units, and proceeds with the following steps.

Step 1: Using Budgeted Batch Size, Calculate the Number of Batches that Should Have Been Used to Produce Actual Output. At the budgeted batch size of 150 units per batch, Lyco should have produced the 151,200 units of output in 1,008 batches (151,200 units ÷ 150 units per batch).

Step 2: Using Budgeted Materials-Handling Labor-Hours per Batch, Calculate the Number of Materials-Handling Labor-Hours that Should Have Been Used. At the budgeted quantity of 5 hours per batch, 1,008 batches should have required 5,040 materials-handling labor-hours (1,008 batches × 5 hours per batch).

Step 3: Using Budgeted Cost per Materials-Handling Labor-Hour, Calculate the Flexible-Budget Amount for Materials-Handling Labor-Hours. The flexible-budget amount is 5,040 materials-handling labor-hours × $14 budgeted cost per materials-handling labor-hour = $70,560.

Note how the flexible-budget calculations for materials-handling labor costs focus on batch-level quantities (materials-handling labor-hours per batch rather than per unit). Flexible-budget quantity computations focus at the appropriate level of the cost hierarchy. For example, because materials handling is a batch-level cost, the flexible-budget quantity calculations are made at the batch level—the quantity of materials-handling labor-hours that Lyco should have used based on the number of batches it should have used to produce the actual quantity of 151,200 units. If a cost had been a product-sustaining cost—such as product design cost—the flexible-budget quantity computations would focus at the product-sustaining level, for example, by evaluating the actual complexity of product design relative to the budget.

The flexible-budget variance for materials-handling labor costs can now be calculated as follows:

$$\text{Flexible-budget variance} = \text{Actual costs} - \text{Flexible-budget costs}$$

$$= (5,670 \text{ hours} \times \$14.50 \text{ per hour}) - (5,040 \text{ hours} \times \$14 \text{ per hour})$$

$$= \$82,215 - \$70,560$$

$$= \$11,655 \text{ U}$$

The unfavorable variance indicates that materials-handling labor costs were $11,655 higher than the flexible-budget target. We can get some insight into the possible reasons for this unfavorable outcome by examining the price and efficiency components of the flexible-budget variance. Exhibit 8-5 presents the variances in columnar form.

$$\begin{array}{c} \text{Price} \\ \text{variance} \end{array} = \left(\begin{array}{c} \text{Actual price} \\ \text{of input} \end{array} - \begin{array}{c} \text{Budgeted price} \\ \text{of input} \end{array} \right) \times \begin{array}{c} \text{Actual quantity} \\ \text{of input} \end{array}$$

$$= (\$14.50 \text{ per hour} - \$14 \text{ per hour}) \times 5{,}670 \text{ hours}$$

$$= \$0.50 \text{ per hour} \times 5{,}670 \text{ hours}$$

$$= \$2{,}835 \text{ U}$$

The unfavorable price variance for materials-handling labor indicates that the $14.50 actual cost per materials-handling labor-hour exceeds the $14.00 budgeted cost per materials-handling labor-hour. This variance could be the result of Lyco's human resources manager negotiating wage rates less skillfully or of wage rates increasing unexpectedly due to scarcity of labor.

$$\begin{array}{c} \text{Efficiency} \\ \text{variance} \end{array} = \left(\begin{array}{c} \text{Actual} \\ \text{quantity of} \\ \text{input used} \end{array} - \begin{array}{c} \text{Budgeted quantity} \\ \text{of input allowed} \\ \text{for actual output} \end{array} \right) \times \begin{array}{c} \text{Budgeted price} \\ \text{of input} \end{array}$$

$$= (5{,}670 \text{ hours} - 5{,}040 \text{ hours}) \times \$14 \text{ per hour}$$

$$= 630 \text{ hours} \times \$14 \text{ per hour}$$

$$= \$8{,}820 \text{ U}$$

The unfavorable efficiency variance indicates that the 5,670 actual materials-handling labor-hours exceeded the 5,040 budgeted materials-handling labor-hours for actual output. Possible reasons for the unfavorable efficiency variance are as follows:

- Smaller actual batch sizes of 140 units, instead of the budgeted batch sizes of 150 units, resulting in Lyco producing the 151,200 units in 1,080 batches instead of 1,008 (151,200 ÷ 150) batches
- Higher actual materials-handling labor-hours per batch of 5.25 hours instead of budgeted materials-handling labor-hours of 5 hours

Reasons for smaller-than-budgeted batch sizes could include quality problems when batch sizes exceed 140 faucets and high costs of carrying inventory.

Exhibit 8-5 Columnar Presentation of Variance Analysis for Direct Materials-Handling Labor Costs: Lyco Brass Works for 2012[a]

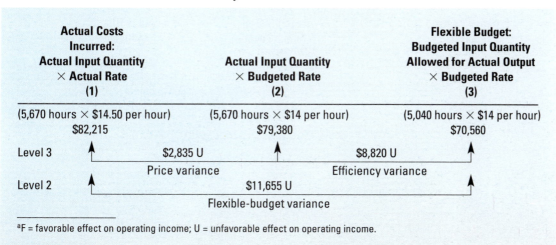

Actual Costs Incurred: Actual Input Quantity × Actual Rate (1)	Actual Input Quantity × Budgeted Rate (2)	Flexible Budget: Budgeted Input Quantity Allowed for Actual Output × Budgeted Rate (3)
(5,670 hours × $14.50 per hour) $82,215	(5,670 hours × $14 per hour) $79,380	(5,040 hours × $14 per hour) $70,560
Level 3	$2,835 U Price variance	$8,820 U Efficiency variance
Level 2	$11,655 U Flexible-budget variance	

[a]F = favorable effect on operating income; U = unfavorable effect on operating income.

Possible reasons for larger actual materials-handling labor-hours per batch are as follows:

- Inefficient layout of the Elegance production line
- Materials-handling labor having to wait at work centers before picking up or delivering materials
- Unmotivated, inexperienced, and underskilled employees
- Very tight standards for materials-handling time

Identifying the reasons for the efficiency variance helps Lyco's managers develop a plan for improving materials-handling labor efficiency and to take corrective action that will be incorporated into future budgets.

We now consider fixed setup overhead costs.

Flexible Budget and Variance Analysis for Fixed Setup Overhead Costs

Exhibit 8-6 presents the variances for fixed setup overhead costs in columnar form. Lyco's fixed setup overhead flexible-budget variance is calculated as follows:

$$\begin{array}{c}\text{Fixed-setup}\\\text{overhead}\\\text{flexible-budget}\\\text{variance}\end{array} = \begin{array}{c}\text{Actual costs}\\\text{incurred}\end{array} - \begin{array}{c}\text{Flexible-budget}\\\text{costs}\end{array}$$

$$= \$220,000 - \$216,000$$

$$= \$4,000 \text{ U}$$

Note that the flexible-budget amount for fixed setup overhead costs equals the static-budget amount of $216,000. That's because there is no "flexing" of fixed costs. Moreover, because fixed overhead costs have no efficiency variance, the fixed setup overhead spending variance is the same as the fixed overhead flexible-budget variance. The spending variance could be unfavorable because of higher leasing costs of new setup equipment or higher salaries paid to engineers and supervisors. Lyco may have incurred these costs to alleviate some of the difficulties it was having in setting up machines.

Exhibit 8-6 Columnar Presentation of Fixed Setup Overhead Variance Analysis: Lyco Brass Works for 2012[a]

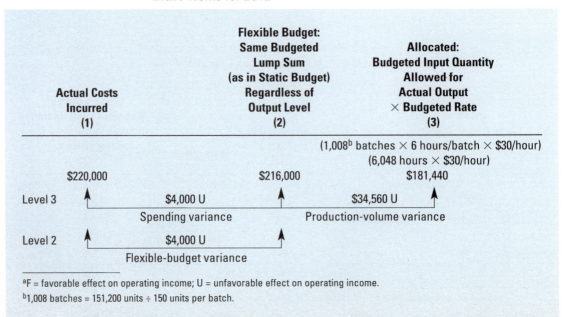

[a]F = favorable effect on operating income; U = unfavorable effect on operating income.
[b]1,008 batches = 151,200 units ÷ 150 units per batch.

To calculate the production-volume variance, Lyco first computes the budgeted cost-allocation rate for fixed setup overhead costs using the same four-step approach described on page 266.

Step 1: Choose the Period to Use for the Budget. Lyco uses a period of 12 months (the year 2012).

Step 2: Select the Cost-Allocation Base to Use in Allocating Fixed Overhead Costs to Output Produced. Lyco uses budgeted setup-hours as the cost-allocation base for fixed setup overhead costs. Budgeted setup-hours in the static budget for 2012 are 7,200 hours.

Step 3: Identify the Fixed Overhead Costs Associated with the Cost-Allocation Base. Lyco's fixed setup overhead cost budget for 2012 is $216,000.

Step 4: Compute the Rate per Unit of the Cost-Allocation Base Used to Allocate Fixed Overhead Costs to Output Produced. Dividing the $216,000 from Step 3 by the 7,200 setup-hours from Step 2, Lyco estimates a fixed setup overhead cost rate of $30 per setup-hour:

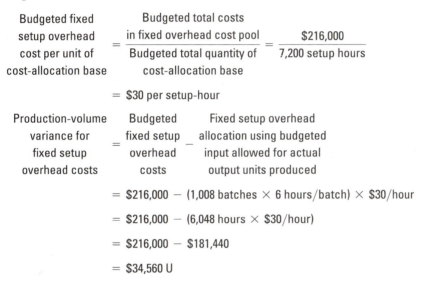

$$\begin{array}{l}\text{Budgeted fixed setup overhead cost per unit of cost-allocation base} = \dfrac{\text{Budgeted total costs in fixed overhead cost pool}}{\text{Budgeted total quantity of cost-allocation base}} = \dfrac{\$216,000}{7,200 \text{ setup hours}}\end{array}$$

$$= \$30 \text{ per setup-hour}$$

$$\begin{array}{l}\text{Production-volume variance for fixed setup overhead costs}\end{array} = \begin{array}{l}\text{Budgeted fixed setup overhead costs}\end{array} - \begin{array}{l}\text{Fixed setup overhead allocation using budgeted input allowed for actual output units produced}\end{array}$$

$$= \$216,000 - (1,008 \text{ batches} \times 6 \text{ hours/batch}) \times \$30/\text{hour}$$

$$= \$216,000 - (6,048 \text{ hours} \times \$30/\text{hour})$$

$$= \$216,000 - \$181,440$$

$$= \$34,560 \text{ U}$$

During 2012, Lyco planned to produce 180,000 units of Elegance but actually produced 151,200 units. The unfavorable production-volume variance measures the amount of extra fixed setup costs that Lyco incurred for setup capacity it had but did not use. One interpretation is that the unfavorable $34,560 production-volume variance represents inefficient use of setup capacity. However, Lyco may have earned higher operating income by selling 151,200 units at a higher price than 180,000 units at a lower price. As a result, Lyco's managers should interpret the production-volume variance cautiously because it does not consider effects on selling prices and operating income.

Overhead Variances in Nonmanufacturing Settings

Our Webb Company example examines variable manufacturing overhead costs and fixed manufacturing overhead costs. Should the overhead costs of the nonmanufacturing areas of the company be examined using the variance analysis framework discussed in this chapter? Companies often use variable-cost information pertaining to nonmanufacturing, as well as manufacturing, costs in pricing and product mix decisions. Managers consider variance analysis of all variable overhead costs when making such decisions and when managing costs. For example, managers in industries in which distribution costs are high, such as automobiles, consumer durables, and cement and steel, may use standard costing to give reliable and timely information on variable distribution overhead spending variances and efficiency variances.

Consider service-sector companies such as airlines, hospitals, hotels, and railroads. The measures of output commonly used in these companies are passenger-miles flown,

Decision Point

How can variance analysis be used in an activity-based costing system?

Learning Objective 8

Examine the use of overhead variances in nonmanufacturing settings

. . . analyze nonmanufacturing variable overhead costs for decision making and cost management; fixed overhead variances are especially important in service settings

patient days provided, room-days occupied, and ton-miles of freight hauled, respectively. Few costs can be traced to these outputs in a cost-effective way. The majority of costs are fixed overhead costs, such as the costs of equipment, buildings, and staff. Using capacity effectively is the key to profitability, and fixed overhead variances can help managers in this task. Retail businesses, such as Kmart, also have high capacity-related fixed costs (lease and occupancy costs). In the case of Kmart, sales declines resulted in unused capacity and unfavorable fixed-cost variances. Kmart reduced fixed costs by closing some of its stores, but it also had to file for Chapter 11 bankruptcy in January 2002.

Consider the following data for the mainline operations of United Airlines for selected years from the past decade. Available seat miles (ASMs) are the actual seats in an airplane multiplied by the distance traveled.

Year	Total ASMs (Millions) (1)	Operating Revenue per ASM (2)	Operating Cost per ASM (3)	Operating Income per ASM (4) = (2) − (3)
2000	175,485	11.0 cents	10.6 cents	0.4 cents
2003	136,630	9.6 cents	10.5 cents	−0.9 cents
2006	143,095	11.5 cents	11.2 cents	0.3 cents
2008	135,861	12.6 cents	15.7 cents	−3.1 cents

After September 11, 2001, as air travel declined, United's revenues decreased but a majority of its costs comprising fixed costs of airport facilities, equipment, and personnel did not. United had a large unfavorable production-volume variance as its capacity was underutilized. As column 1 of the table indicates, United responded by reducing its capacity substantially over the next few years. Available seat miles declined from 175,485 million in 2000 to 136,630 million in 2003. Yet, United was unable to fill even the planes it had retained, so revenue per ASM declined (column 2) and cost per ASM stayed roughly the same (column 3). United filed for Chapter 11 bankruptcy in December 2002 and began seeking government guarantees to obtain the loans it needed. Subsequently, strong demand for airline travel, as well as yield improvements gained by more efficient use of resources and networks, led to increased traffic and higher average ticket prices. By maintaining a disciplined approach to capacity and tight control over growth, United saw close to a 20% increase in its revenue per ASM between 2003 and 2006. The improvement in performance allowed United to come out of bankruptcy on February 1, 2006. In the past year, however, the severe global recession and soaring jet fuel prices have had a significant negative impact on United's performance (and that of its competitor airlines), as reflected in the negative operating income for 2008.

Financial and Nonfinancial Performance Measures

The overhead variances discussed in this chapter are examples of financial performance measures. As the preceding examples illustrate, nonfinancial measures such as those related to capacity utilization and physical measures of input usage also provide useful information. Returning to the Webb example one final time, we can see that nonfinancial measures that managers of Webb would likely find helpful in planning and controlling its overhead costs include the following:

1. Quantity of actual indirect materials used per machine-hour, relative to quantity of budgeted indirect materials used per machine-hour

2. Actual energy used per machine-hour, relative to budgeted energy used per machine-hour

3. Actual machine-hours per jacket, relative to budgeted machine-hours per jacket

These performance measures, like the financial variances discussed in this chapter and Chapter 7, can be described as signals to direct managers' attention to problems. These nonfinancial performance measures probably would be reported daily or hourly on the production floor. The overhead variances we discussed in this chapter capture the financial effects of items such as the three factors listed, which in many cases first appear as nonfinancial performance measures. An especially interesting example along these lines comes from Japan, where some companies have introduced budgeted-to-actual variance analysis and internal trading systems among group units as a means to rein in their CO_2 emissions. The goal is to raise employee awareness of emissions reduction in preparation for the anticipated future costs of greenhouse-gas reduction plans being drawn up by the new Japanese government.

Finally, both financial and nonfinancial performance measures are used to evaluate the performance of managers. Exclusive reliance on either is always too simplistic because each gives a different perspective on performance. Nonfinancial measures (such as those described previously) provide feedback on individual aspects of a manager's performance, whereas financial measures evaluate the overall effect of and the tradeoffs among different nonfinancial performance measures. We provide further discussion of these issues in Chapters 13, 19, and 23.

> **Decision Point**
>
> How are overhead variances useful in nonmanufacturing settings?

Problem for Self-Study

Nina Garcia is the newly appointed president of Laser Products. She is examining the May 2012 results for the Aerospace Products Division. This division manufactures wing parts for satellites. Garcia's current concern is with manufacturing overhead costs at the Aerospace Products Division. Both variable and fixed overhead costs are allocated to the wing parts on the basis of laser-cutting-hours. The following budget information is available:

Budgeted variable overhead rate	$200 per hour
Budgeted fixed overhead rate	$240 per hour
Budgeted laser-cutting time per wing part	1.5 hours
Budgeted production and sales for May 2012	5,000 wing parts
Budgeted fixed overhead costs for May 2012	$1,800,000

Actual results for May 2012 are as follows:

Wing parts produced and sold	4,800 units
Laser-cutting-hours used	8,400 hours
Variable overhead costs	$1,478,400
Fixed overhead costs	$1,832,200

1. Compute the spending variance and the efficiency variance for variable overhead.
2. Compute the spending variance and the production-volume variance for fixed overhead.
3. Give two explanations for each of the variances calculated in requirements 1 and 2.

Required

Solution

1 and 2. See Exhibit 8-7.
3. a. Variable overhead spending variance, $201,600 F. One possible reason for this variance is that the actual prices of individual items included in variable overhead (such as cutting fluids) are lower than budgeted prices. A second possible reason is that the percentage increase in the actual quantity usage of individual items in the variable overhead cost pool is less than the percentage increase in laser-cutting-hours compared to the flexible budget.
   b. Variable overhead efficiency variance, $240,000 U. One possible reason for this variance is inadequate maintenance of laser machines, causing them to take more laser-cutting time per wing part. A second possible reason is use of undermotivated, inexperienced, or underskilled workers with the laser-cutting machines, resulting in more laser-cutting time per wing part.

Exhibit 8-7 Columnar Presentation of Integrated Variance Analysis: Laser Products for May 2012[a]

PANEL A: Variable (Manufacturing) Overhead

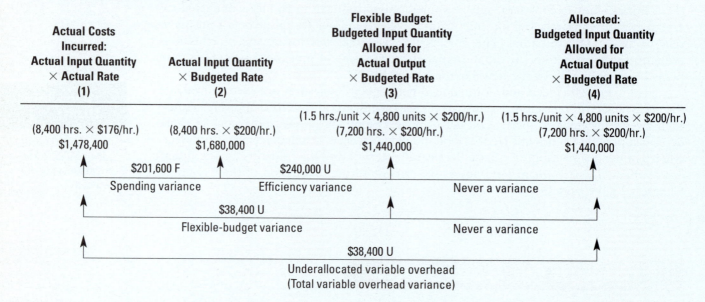

PANEL B: Fixed (Manufacturing) Overhead

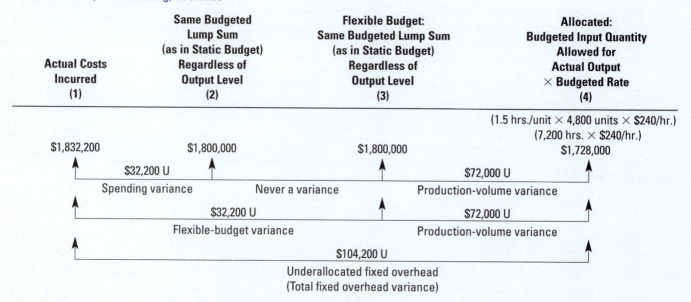

[a]F = favorable effect on operating income; U = unfavorable effect on operating income.

Source: Strategic finance by Paul Sherman. Copyright 2003 by INSTITUTE OF MANAGEMENT ACCOUNTANTS. Reproduced with permission of INSTITUTE OF MANAGEMENT ACCOUNTANTS in the format Other book via Copyright Clearance Center.

c. Fixed overhead spending variance, $32,200 U. One possible reason for this variance is that the actual prices of individual items in the fixed-cost pool unexpectedly increased from the prices budgeted (such as an unexpected increase in machine leasing costs). A second possible reason is misclassification of items as fixed that are in fact variable.

d. Production-volume variance, $72,000 U. Actual production of wing parts is 4,800 units, compared with 5,000 units budgeted. One possible reason for this variance is demand factors, such as a decline in an aerospace program that led to a decline in demand for aircraft parts. A second possible reason is supply factors, such as a production stoppage due to labor problems or machine breakdowns.

Decision Points

The following question-and-answer format summarizes the chapter's learning objectives. Each decision presents a key question related to a learning objective. The guidelines are the answer to that question.

Decision	Guidelines
1. How do managers plan variable overhead costs and fixed overhead costs?	Planning of both variable and fixed overhead costs involves undertaking only activities that add value and then being efficient in that undertaking. The key difference is that for variable-cost planning, ongoing decisions during the budget period play a much larger role; whereas for fixed-cost planning, most key decisions are made before the start of the period.
2. How are budgeted variable overhead and fixed overhead cost rates calculated?	The budgeted variable (fixed) overhead cost rate is calculated by dividing the budgeted variable (fixed) overhead costs by the denominator level of the cost-allocation base.
3. What variances can be calculated for variable overhead costs?	When the flexible budget for variable overhead is developed, an overhead efficiency variance and an overhead spending variance can be computed. The variable overhead efficiency variance focuses on the difference between the actual quantity of the cost-allocation base used relative to the budgeted quantity of the cost-allocation base. The variable overhead spending variance focuses on the difference between the actual variable overhead cost per unit of the cost-allocation base relative to the budgeted variable overhead cost per unit of the cost-allocation base.
4. What variances can be calculated for fixed overhead costs?	For fixed overhead, the static and flexible budgets coincide. The difference between the budgeted and actual amount of fixed overhead is the flexible-budget variance, also referred to as the spending variance. The production-volume variance measures the difference between budgeted fixed overhead and fixed overhead allocated on the basis of actual output produced.
5. What is the most detailed way for a company to reconcile actual overhead incurred with the amount allocated during a period?	A 4-variance analysis presents spending and efficiency variances for variable overhead costs and spending and production-volume variances for fixed overhead costs. By analyzing these four variances together, managers can reconcile the actual overhead costs with the amount of overhead allocated to output produced during a period.
6. What is the relationship between the sales-volume variance and the production-volume variance?	The production-volume variance is a component of the sales-volume variance. The production-volume and operating-income volume variances together comprise the sales-volume variance.
7. How can variance analysis be used in an activity-based costing system?	Flexible budgets in ABC systems give insight into why actual activity costs differ from budgeted activity costs. Using output and input measures for an activity, a 4-variance analysis can be conducted.
8. How are overhead variances useful in nonmanufacturing settings?	Managers consider variance analysis of all variable overhead costs, including those outside the manufacturing function, when making pricing and product mix decisions and when managing costs. Fixed overhead variances are especially important in service settings, where using capacity effectively is the key to profitability. In all cases, the information provided by variances can be supplemented by the use of suitable nonfinancial metrics.

Terms to Learn

The chapter and the Glossary at the end of the book contain definitions of the following important terms:

denominator level (**p. 266**)

denominator-level variance (**p. 272**)

fixed overhead flexible-budget variance (**p. 271**)

fixed overhead spending variance (**p. 271**)

operating-income volume variance (**p. 281**)

production-denominator level (**p. 266**)

production-volume variance (**p. 272**)

standard costing (**p. 264**)

total-overhead variance (**p. 278**)

variable overhead efficiency variance (**p. 267**)

variable overhead flexible-budget variance (**p. 267**)

variable overhead spending variance (**p. 269**)

Assignment Material

Questions

8-1 How do managers plan for variable overhead costs?

8-2 How does the planning of fixed overhead costs differ from the planning of variable overhead costs?

8-3 How does standard costing differ from actual costing?

8-4 What are the steps in developing a budgeted variable overhead cost-allocation rate?

8-5 What are the factors that affect the spending variance for variable manufacturing overhead?

8-6 Assume variable manufacturing overhead is allocated using machine-hours. Give three possible reasons for a favorable variable overhead efficiency variance.

8-7 Describe the difference between a direct materials efficiency variance and a variable manufacturing overhead efficiency variance.

8-8 What are the steps in developing a budgeted fixed overhead rate?

8-9 Why is the flexible-budget variance the same amount as the spending variance for fixed manufacturing overhead?

8-10 Explain how the analysis of fixed manufacturing overhead costs differs for (a) planning and control and (b) inventory costing for financial reporting.

8-11 Provide one caveat that will affect whether a production-volume variance is a good measure of the economic cost of unused capacity.

8-12 "The production-volume variance should always be written off to Cost of Goods Sold." Do you agree? Explain.

8-13 What are the variances in a 4-variance analysis?

8-14 "Overhead variances should be viewed as interdependent rather than independent." Give an example.

8-15 Describe how flexible-budget variance analysis can be used in the control of costs of activity areas.

Exercises

8-16 Variable manufacturing overhead, variance analysis. Esquire Clothing is a manufacturer of designer suits. The cost of each suit is the sum of three variable costs (direct material costs, direct manufacturing labor costs, and manufacturing overhead costs) and one fixed-cost category (manufacturing overhead costs). Variable manufacturing overhead cost is allocated to each suit on the basis of budgeted direct manufacturing labor-hours per suit. For June 2012 each suit is budgeted to take four labor-hours. Budgeted variable manufacturing overhead cost per labor-hour is $12. The budgeted number of suits to be manufactured in June 2012 is 1,040.

Actual variable manufacturing costs in June 2012 were $52,164 for 1,080 suits started and completed. There were no beginning or ending inventories of suits. Actual direct manufacturing labor-hours for June were 4,536.

Required

1. Compute the flexible-budget variance, the spending variance, and the efficiency variance for variable manufacturing overhead.
2. Comment on the results.

8-17 Fixed manufacturing overhead, variance analysis (continuation of 8-16). Esquire Clothing allocates fixed manufacturing overhead to each suit using budgeted direct manufacturing labor-hours per suit. Data pertaining to fixed manufacturing overhead costs for June 2012 are budgeted, $62,400, and actual, $63,916.

Required

1. Compute the spending variance for fixed manufacturing overhead. Comment on the results.
2. Compute the production-volume variance for June 2012. What inferences can Esquire Clothing draw from this variance?

8-18 **Variable manufacturing overhead variance analysis.** The French Bread Company bakes baguettes for distribution to upscale grocery stores. The company has two direct-cost categories: direct materials and direct manufacturing labor. Variable manufacturing overhead is allocated to products on the basis of standard direct manufacturing labor-hours. Following is some budget data for the French Bread Company:

Direct manufacturing labor use	0.02 hours per baguette
Variable manufacturing overhead	$10.00 per direct manufacturing labor-hour

The French Bread Company provides the following additional data for the year ended December 31, 2012:

Planned (budgeted) output	3,200,000 baguettes
Actual production	2,800,000 baguettes
Direct manufacturing labor	50,400 hours
Actual variable manufacturing overhead	$680,400

Required

1. What is the denominator level used for allocating variable manufacturing overhead? (That is, for how many direct manufacturing labor-hours is French Bread budgeting?)
2. Prepare a variance analysis of variable manufacturing overhead. Use Exhibit 8-4 (p. 277) for reference.
3. Discuss the variances you have calculated and give possible explanations for them.

8-19 **Fixed manufacturing overhead variance analysis (continuation of 8-18).** The French Bread Company also allocates fixed manufacturing overhead to products on the basis of standard direct manufacturing labor-hours. For 2012, fixed manufacturing overhead was budgeted at $4.00 per direct manufacturing labor-hour. Actual fixed manufacturing overhead incurred during the year was $272,000.

Required

1. Prepare a variance analysis of fixed manufacturing overhead cost. Use Exhibit 8-4 (p. 277) as a guide.
2. Is fixed overhead underallocated or overallocated? By what amount?
3. Comment on your results. Discuss the variances and explain what may be driving them.

8-20 **Manufacturing overhead, variance analysis.** The Solutions Corporation is a manufacturer of centrifuges. Fixed and variable manufacturing overheads are allocated to each centrifuge using budgeted assembly-hours. Budgeted assembly time is two hours per unit. The following table shows the budgeted amounts and actual results related to overhead for June 2012.

	Home	Insert	Page Layout	Formulas	Data	Review	View	
	A	B	C	D	E		F	G
1			The Solutions Corporation (June 2012)				Actual Results	Static Budget
2	Number of centrifuges assembled and sold						216	200
3	Hours of assembly time						411	
4	Variable manufacturing overhead cost per hour of assembly time							$30.00
5	Variable manufacturing overhead costs						$12,741	
6	Fixed manufacturing overhead costs						$20,550	$19,200

Required

1. Prepare an analysis of all variable manufacturing overhead and fixed manufacturing overhead variances using the columnar approach in Exhibit 8-4 (p. 277).
2. Prepare journal entries for Solutions' June 2012 variable and fixed manufacturing overhead costs and variances; write off these variances to cost of goods sold for the quarter ending June 30, 2012.
3. How does the planning and control of variable manufacturing overhead costs differ from the planning and control of fixed manufacturing overhead costs?

8-21 **4-variance analysis, fill in the blanks.** Rozema, Inc., produces chemicals for large biotech companies. It has the following data for manufacturing overhead costs during August 2013:

	Variable	Fixed
Actual costs incurred	$31,000	$18,000
Costs allocated to products	33,000	14,600
Flexible budget	———	13,400
Actual input × budgeted rate	30,800	———

Use F for favorable and U for unfavorable:

	Variable	Fixed
(1) Spending variance	$_____	$_____
(2) Efficiency variance	_____	_____
(3) Production-volume variance	_____	_____
(4) Flexible-budget variance	_____	_____
(5) Underallocated (overallocated) manufacturing overhead	_____	_____

8-22 Straightforward 4-variance overhead analysis. The Lopez Company uses standard costing in its manufacturing plant for auto parts. The standard cost of a particular auto part, based on a denominator level of 4,000 output units per year, included 6 machine-hours of variable manufacturing overhead at $8 per hour and 6 machine-hours of fixed manufacturing overhead at $15 per hour. Actual output produced was 4,400 units. Variable manufacturing overhead incurred was $245,000. Fixed manufacturing overhead incurred was $373,000. Actual machine-hours were 28,400.

Required

1. Prepare an analysis of all variable manufacturing overhead and fixed manufacturing overhead variances, using the 4-variance analysis in Exhibit 8-4 (p. 277).
2. Prepare journal entries using the 4-variance analysis.
3. Describe how individual fixed manufacturing overhead items are controlled from day to day.
4. Discuss possible causes of the fixed manufacturing overhead variances.

8-23 Straightforward coverage of manufacturing overhead, standard-costing system. The Singapore division of a Canadian telecommunications company uses standard costing for its machine-paced production of telephone equipment. Data regarding production during June are as follows:

Variable manufacturing overhead costs incurred	$618,840
Variable manufacturing overhead cost rate	$8 per standard machine-hour
Fixed manufacturing overhead costs incurred	$145,790
Fixed manufacturing overhead costs budgeted	$144,000
Denominator level in machine-hours	72,000
Standard machine-hour allowed per unit of output	1.2
Units of output	65,500
Actual machine-hours used	76,400
Ending work-in-process inventory	0

Required

1. Prepare an analysis of all manufacturing overhead variances. Use the 4-variance analysis framework illustrated in Exhibit 8-4 (p. 277).
2. Prepare journal entries for manufacturing overhead costs and their variances.
3. Describe how individual variable manufacturing overhead items are controlled from day to day.
4. Discuss possible causes of the variable manufacturing overhead variances.

8-24 Overhead variances, service sector. Meals on Wheels (MOW) operates a meal home-delivery service. It has agreements with 20 restaurants to pick up and deliver meals to customers who phone or fax orders to MOW. MOW allocates variable and fixed overhead costs on the basis of delivery time. MOW's owner, Josh Carter, obtains the following information for May 2012 overhead costs:

	Home	Insert	Page Layout	Formulas	Data	Review
	A				B	C
1	**Meals on Wheels (May 2012)**				**Actual Results**	**Static Budget**
2	Output units (number of deliveries)				8,800	10,000
3	Hours per delivery					0.70
4	Hours of delivery time				5,720	
5	Variable overhead cost per hour of delivery time					$ 1.50
6	Variable overhead costs				$10,296	
7	Fixed overhead costs				$38,600	$35,000

Required

1. Compute spending and efficiency variances for MOW's variable overhead in May 2012.
2. Compute the spending variance and production-volume variance for MOW's fixed overhead in May 2012.
3. Comment on MOW's overhead variances and suggest how Josh Carter might manage MOW's variable overhead differently from its fixed overhead costs.

8-25 Total overhead, 3-variance analysis. Furniture, Inc., specializes in the production of futons. It uses standard costing and flexible budgets to account for the production of a new line of futons. For 2011, budgeted variable overhead at a level of 3,600 standard monthly direct labor-hours was $43,200; budgeted total overhead at 4,000 standard monthly direct labor-hours was $103,400. The standard cost allocated to each output included a total overhead rate of 120% of standard direct labor costs. For October, Furniture, Inc., incurred total overhead of $120,700 and direct labor costs of $128,512. The direct labor price variance was $512 unfavorable. The direct labor flexible-budget variance was $3,512 unfavorable. The standard labor price was $25 per hour. The production-volume variance was $34,600 favorable.

Required

1. Compute the direct labor efficiency variance and the spending and efficiency variances for overhead. Also, compute the denominator level.
2. Describe how individual variable overhead items are controlled from day to day. Also, describe how individual fixed overhead items are controlled.

8-26 Overhead variances, missing information. Dvent budgets 18,000 machine-hours for the production of computer chips in August 2011. The budgeted variable overhead rate is $6 per machine-hour. At the end of August, there is a $375 favorable spending variance for variable overhead and a $1,575 unfavorable spending variance for fixed overhead. For the computer chips produced, 14,850 machine-hours are budgeted and 15,000 machine-hours are actually used. Total actual overhead costs are $120,000.

Required

1. Compute efficiency and flexible-budget variances for Dvent's variable overhead in August 2011. Will variable overhead be over- or underallocated? By how much?
2. Compute production-volume and flexible-budget variances for Dvent's fixed overhead in August 2011. Will fixed overhead be over- or underallocated? By how much?

8-27 Identifying favorable and unfavorable variances. Purdue, Inc., manufactures tires for large auto companies. It uses standard costing and allocates variable and fixed manufacturing overhead based on machine-hours. For each independent scenario given, indicate whether each of the manufacturing variances will be favorable or unfavorable or, in case of insufficient information, indicate "CBD" (cannot be determined).

Scenario	Variable Overhead Spending Variance	Variable Overhead Efficiency Variance	Fixed Overhead Spending Variance	Fixed Overhead Production-Volume Variance
Production output is 4% less than budgeted, and actual fixed manufacturing overhead costs are 5% more than budgeted				
Production output is 12% less than budgeted; actual machine-hours are 7% more than budgeted				
Production output is 9% more than budgeted				
Actual machine-hours are 20% less than flexible-budget machine-hours				
Relative to the flexible budget, actual machine-hours are 12% less, and actual variable manufacturing overhead costs are 20% greater				

8-28 **Flexible-budget variances, review of Chapters 7 and 8.** David James is a cost accountant and business analyst for Doorknob Design Company (DDC), which manufactures expensive brass doorknobs. DDC uses two direct cost categories: direct materials and direct manufacturing labor. James feels that manufacturing overhead is most closely related to material usage. Therefore, DDC allocates manufacturing overhead to production based upon pounds of materials used.

At the beginning of 2012, DDC budgeted annual production of 400,000 doorknobs and adopted the following standards for each doorknob:

	Input	Cost/Doorknob
Direct materials (brass)	0.3 lb. @ $10/lb.	$ 3.00
Direct manufacturing labor	1.2 hours @ $20/hour	24.00
Manufacturing overhead:		
Variable	$6/lb. × 0.3 lb.	1.80
Fixed	$15/lb. × 0.3 lb.	4.50
Standard cost per doorknob		$33.30

Actual results for April 2012 were as follows:

Production	35,000 doorknobs
Direct materials purchased	12,000 lb. at $11/lb.
Direct materials used	10,450 lb.
Direct manufacturing labor	38,500 hours for $808,500
Variable manufacturing overhead	$64,150
Fixed manufacturing overhead	$152,000

Required

1. For the month of April, compute the following variances, indicating whether each is favorable (F) or unfavorable (U):
   a. Direct materials price variance (based on purchases)
   b. Direct materials efficiency variance
   c. Direct manufacturing labor price variance
   d. Direct manufacturing labor efficiency variance
   e. Variable manufacturing overhead spending variance
   f. Variable manufacturing overhead efficiency variance
   g. Production-volume variance
   h. Fixed manufacturing overhead spending variance
2. Can James use any of the variances to help explain any of the other variances? Give examples.

MyAccountingLab | **Problems**

8-29 **Comprehensive variance analysis.** Kitchen Whiz manufactures premium food processors. The following is some manufacturing overhead data for Kitchen Whiz for the year ended December 31, 2012:

Manufacturing Overhead	Actual Results	Flexible Budget	Allocated Amount
Variable	$ 76,608	$ 76,800	$ 76,800
Fixed	350,208	348,096	376,320

Budgeted number of output units: 888

Planned allocation rate: 2 machine-hours per unit

Actual number of machine-hours used: 1,824

Static-budget variable manufacturing overhead costs: $71,040

Required

Compute the following quantities (you should be able to do so in the prescribed order):

1. Budgeted number of machine-hours planned
2. Budgeted fixed manufacturing overhead costs per machine-hour
3. Budgeted variable manufacturing overhead costs per machine-hour
4. Budgeted number of machine-hours allowed for actual output produced
5. Actual number of output units
6. Actual number of machine-hours used per output unit

8-30 Journal entries (continuation of 8-29).

1. Prepare journal entries for variable and fixed manufacturing overhead (you will need to calculate the various variances to accomplish this).
2. Overhead variances are written off to the Cost of Goods Sold (COGS) account at the end of the fiscal year. Show how COGS is adjusted through journal entries.

Required

8-31 Graphs and overhead variances. Best Around, Inc., is a manufacturer of vacuums and uses standard costing. Manufacturing overhead (both variable and fixed) is allocated to products on the basis of budgeted machine-hours. In 2012, budgeted fixed manufacturing overhead cost was $17,000,000. Budgeted variable manufacturing overhead was $10 per machine-hour. The denominator level was 1,000,000 machine-hours.

1. Prepare a graph for fixed manufacturing overhead. The graph should display how Best Around, Inc.'s fixed manufacturing overhead costs will be depicted for the purposes of (a) planning and control and (b) inventory costing.
2. Suppose that 1,125,000 machine-hours were allowed for actual output produced in 2012, but 1,150,000 actual machine-hours were used. Actual manufacturing overhead was $12,075,000, variable, and $17,100,000, fixed. Compute (a) the variable manufacturing overhead spending and efficiency variances and (b) the fixed manufacturing overhead spending and production-volume variances. Use the columnar presentation illustrated in Exhibit 8-4 (p. 277).
3. What is the amount of the under- or overallocated variable manufacturing overhead and the under- or overallocated fixed manufacturing overhead? Why are the flexible-budget variance and the under- or overallocated overhead amount always the same for variable manufacturing overhead but rarely the same for fixed manufacturing overhead?
4. Suppose the denominator level was 1,360,000 rather than 1,000,000 machine-hours. What variances in requirement 2 would be affected? Recompute them.

Required

8-32 4-variance analysis, find the unknowns. Consider the following two situations—cases A and B— independently. Data refer to operations for April 2012. For each situation, assume standard costing. Also assume the use of a flexible budget for control of variable and fixed manufacturing overhead based on machine-hours.

	Cases	
	A	B
(1) Fixed manufacturing overhead incurred	$ 84,920	$23,180
(2) Variable manufacturing overhead incurred	$120,000	—
(3) Denominator level in machine-hours	—	1,000
(4) Standard machine-hours allowed for actual output achieved	6,200	—
(5) Fixed manufacturing overhead (per standard machine-hour)	—	—
Flexible-Budget Data:		
(6) Variable manufacturing overhead (per standard machine-hour)	—	$ 42.00
(7) Budgeted fixed manufacturing overhead	$ 88,200	$20,000
(8) Budgeted variable manufacturing overhead[a]	—	—
(9) Total budgeted manufacturing overhead[a]	—	—
Additional Data:		
(10) Standard variable manufacturing overhead allocated	$124,000	—
(11) Standard fixed manufacturing overhead allocated	$ 86,800	—
(12) Production-volume variance	—	$ 4,000 F
(13) Variable manufacturing overhead spending variance	$ 4,600 F	$ 2,282 F
(14) Variable manufacturing overhead efficiency variance	—	$ 2,478 F
(15) Fixed manufacturing overhead spending variance	—	—
(16) Actual machine-hours used	—	—

[a]For standard machine-hours allowed for actual output produced.

Fill in the blanks under each case. [*Hint:* Prepare a worksheet similar to that in Exhibit 8-4 (p. 277). Fill in the knowns and then solve for the unknowns.]

Required

8-33 Flexible budgets, 4-variance analysis. (CMA, adapted) Nolton Products uses standard costing. It allocates manufacturing overhead (both variable and fixed) to products on the basis of standard direct manufacturing labor-hours (DLH). Nolton develops its manufacturing overhead rate from the current annual budget. The manufacturing overhead budget for 2012 is based on budgeted output of 720,000 units, requiring 3,600,000 DLH. The company is able to schedule production uniformly throughout the year.

A total of 66,000 output units requiring 315,000 DLH was produced during May 2012. Manufacturing overhead (MOH) costs incurred for May amounted to $375,000. The actual costs, compared with the annual budget and 1/12 of the annual budget, are as follows:

Annual Manufacturing Overhead Budget 2012

	Total Amount	Per Output Unit	Per DLH Input Unit	Monthly MOH Budget May 2012	Actual MOH Costs for May 2012
Variable MOH					
Indirect manufacturing labor	$ 900,000	$1.25	$0.25	$ 75,000	$ 75,000
Supplies	1,224,000	1.70	0.34	102,000	111,000
Fixed MOH					
Supervision	648,000	0.90	0.18	54,000	51,000
Utilities	540,000	0.75	0.15	45,000	54,000
Depreciation	1,008,000	1.40	0.28	84,000	84,000
Total	$4,320,000	$6.00	$1.20	$360,000	$375,000

Required

Calculate the following amounts for Nolton Products for May 2012:

1. Total manufacturing overhead costs allocated
2. Variable manufacturing overhead spending variance
3. Fixed manufacturing overhead spending variance
4. Variable manufacturing overhead efficiency variance
5. Production-volume variance

Be sure to identify each variance as favorable (F) or unfavorable (U).

8-34 Direct Manufacturing Labor and Variable Manufacturing Overhead Variances. Sarah Beth's Art Supply Company produces various types of paints. Actual direct manufacturing labor hours in the factory that produces paint have been higher than budgeted hours for the last few months and the owner, Sarah B. Jones, is concerned about the effect this has had on the company's cost overruns. Because variable manufacturing overhead is allocated to units produced using direct manufacturing labor hours, Sarah feels that the mismanagement of labor will have a twofold effect on company profitability. Following are the relevant budgeted and actual results for the second quarter of 2011.

	Budget Information	Actual Results
Paint set production	25,000	29,000
Direct manuf. labor hours per paint set	2 hours	2.3 hours
Direct manufacturing labor rate	$10/hour	$10.40/hour
Variable manufacturing overhead rate	$20/hour	$18.95/hour

Required

1. Calculate the direct manufacturing labor price and efficiency variances and indicate whether each is favorable (F) or unfavorable (U).
2. Calculate the variable manufacturing overhead spending and efficiency variances and indicate whether each is favorable (F) or unfavorable (U).
3. For both direct manufacturing labor and variable manufacturing overhead, do the price/spending variances help Sarah explain the efficiency variances?
4. Is Sarah correct in her assertion that the mismanagement of labor has a twofold effect on cost overruns? Why might the variable manufacturing overhead efficiency variance not be an accurate representation of the effect of labor overruns on variable manufacturing overhead costs?

8-35 Activity-based costing, batch-level variance analysis. Pointe's Fleet Feet, Inc., produces dance shoes for stores all over the world. While the pairs of shoes are boxed individually, they are crated and shipped in batches. The shipping department records both variable direct batch-level costs and fixed batch-level overhead costs. The following information pertains to shipping department costs for 2011.

	Static-Budget Amounts	Actual Results
Pairs of shoes shipped	250,000	175,000
Average number of pairs of shoes per crate	10	8
Packing hours per crate	1.1 hours	0.9 hour
Variable direct cost per hour	$22	$24
Fixed overhead cost	$55,000	$52,500

1. What is the static budget number of crates for 2011?
2. What is the flexible budget number of crates for 2011?
3. What is the actual number of crates shipped in 2011?
4. Assuming fixed overhead is allocated using crate-packing hours, what is the predetermined fixed overhead allocation rate?
5. For variable direct batch-level costs, compute the price and efficiency variances.
6. For fixed overhead costs, compute the spending and the production-volume variances.

8-36 **Activity-based costing, batch-level variance analysis.** Jo Nathan Publishing Company specializes in printing specialty textbooks for a small but profitable college market. Due to the high setup costs for each batch printed, Jo Nathan holds the book requests until demand for a book is approximately 500. At that point Jo Nathan will schedule the setup and production of the book. For rush orders, Jo Nathan will produce smaller batches for an additional charge of $400 per setup.

Budgeted and actual costs for the printing process for 2012 were as follows:

	Static-Budget Amounts	Actual Results
Number of books produced	300,000	324,000
Average number of books per setup	500	480
Hours to set up printers	8 hours	8.2 hours
Direct variable cost per setup-hour	$40	$39
Total fixed setup overhead costs	$105,600	$119,000

1. What is the static budget number of setups for 2012?
2. What is the flexible budget number of setups for 2012?
3. What is the actual number of setups in 2012?
4. Assuming fixed setup overhead costs are allocated using setup-hours, what is the predetermined fixed setup overhead allocation rate?
5. Does Jo Nathan's charge of $400 cover the budgeted direct variable cost of an order? The budgeted total cost?
6. For direct variable setup costs, compute the price and efficiency variances.
7. For fixed setup overhead costs, compute the spending and the production-volume variances.
8. What qualitative factors should Jo Nathan consider before accepting or rejecting a special order?

8-37 **Production-Volume Variance Analysis and Sales Volume Variance.** Dawn Floral Creations, Inc., makes jewelry in the shape of flowers. Each piece is hand-made and takes an average of 1.5 hours to produce because of the intricate design and scrollwork. Dawn uses direct labor hours to allocate the overhead cost to production. Fixed overhead costs, including rent, depreciation, supervisory salaries, and other production expenses, are budgeted at $9,000 per month. These costs are incurred for a facility large enough to produce 1,000 pieces of jewelry a month.

During the month of February, Dawn produced 600 pieces of jewelry and actual fixed costs were $9,200.

1. Calculate the fixed overhead spending variance and indicate whether it is favorable (F) or unfavorable (U).
2. If Dawn uses direct labor hours available at capacity to calculate the budgeted fixed overhead rate, what is the production-volume variance? Indicate whether it is favorable (F) or unfavorable (U).
3. An unfavorable production-volume variance is a measure of the under-allocation of fixed overhead cost caused by production levels at less than capacity. It therefore could be interpreted as the economic cost of unused capacity. Why would Dawn be willing to incur this cost? Your answer should separately consider the following two unrelated factors:
   a. Demand could vary from month to month while available capacity remains constant.
   b. Dawn would not want to produce at capacity unless it could sell all the units produced. What does Dawn need to do to raise demand and what effect would this have on profit?
4. Dawn's budgeted variable cost per unit is $25 and it expects to sell its jewelry for $55 apiece. Compute the sales-volume variance and reconcile it with the production-volume variance calculated in requirement 2. What does each concept measure?

8-38 **Comprehensive review of Chapters 7 and 8, working backward from given variances.** The Mancusco Company uses a flexible budget and standard costs to aid planning and control of its machining manufacturing operations. Its costing system for manufacturing has two direct-cost categories (direct materials and direct manufacturing labor—both variable) and two overhead-cost categories (variable manufacturing overhead and fixed manufacturing overhead, both allocated using direct manufacturing labor-hours).

At the 40,000 budgeted direct manufacturing labor-hour level for August, budgeted direct manufacturing labor is $800,000, budgeted variable manufacturing overhead is $480,000, and budgeted fixed manufacturing overhead is $640,000.

The following actual results are for August:

Direct materials price variance (based on purchases)	$176,000 F
Direct materials efficiency variance	69,000 U
Direct manufacturing labor costs incurred	522,750
Variable manufacturing overhead flexible-budget variance	10,350 U
Variable manufacturing overhead efficiency variance	18,000 U
Fixed manufacturing overhead incurred	597,460
Fixed manufacturing overhead spending variance	42,540 F

The standard cost per pound of direct materials is $11.50. The standard allowance is three pounds of direct materials for each unit of product. During August, 30,000 units of product were produced. There was no beginning inventory of direct materials. There was no beginning or ending work in process. In August, the direct materials price variance was $1.10 per pound.

In July, labor unrest caused a major slowdown in the pace of production, resulting in an unfavorable direct manufacturing labor efficiency variance of $45,000. There was no direct manufacturing labor price variance. Labor unrest persisted into August. Some workers quit. Their replacements had to be hired at higher wage rates, which had to be extended to all workers. The actual average wage rate in August exceeded the standard average wage rate by $0.50 per hour.

Required

1. Compute the following for August:
   a. Total pounds of direct materials purchased
   b. Total number of pounds of excess direct materials used
   c. Variable manufacturing overhead spending variance
   d. Total number of actual direct manufacturing labor-hours used
   e. Total number of standard direct manufacturing labor-hours allowed for the units produced
   f. Production-volume variance
2. Describe how Mancusco's control of variable manufacturing overhead items differs from its control of fixed manufacturing overhead items.

8-39 Review of Chapters 7 and 8, 3-variance analysis. (CPA, adapted) The Beal Manufacturing Company's costing system has two direct-cost categories: direct materials and direct manufacturing labor. Manufacturing overhead (both variable and fixed) is allocated to products on the basis of standard direct manufacturing labor-hours (DLH). At the beginning of 2012, Beal adopted the following standards for its manufacturing costs:

	Input	Cost per Output Unit
Direct materials	3 lb. at $5 per lb.	$ 15.00
Direct manufacturing labor	5 hrs. at $15 per hr.	75.00
Manufacturing overhead:		
Variable	$6 per DLH	30.00
Fixed	$8 per DLH	40.00
Standard manufacturing cost per output unit		$160.00

The denominator level for total manufacturing overhead per month in 2012 is 40,000 direct manufacturing labor-hours. Beal's flexible budget for January 2012 was based on this denominator level. The records for January indicated the following:

Direct materials purchased	25,000 lb. at $5.20 per lb.
Direct materials used	23,100 lb.
Direct manufacturing labor	40,100 hrs. at $14.60 per hr.
Total actual manufacturing overhead (variable and fixed)	$600,000
Actual production	7,800 output units

Required

1. Prepare a schedule of total standard manufacturing costs for the 7,800 output units in January 2012.
2. For the month of January 2012, compute the following variances, indicating whether each is favorable (F) or unfavorable (U):
   a. Direct materials price variance, based on purchases
   b. Direct materials efficiency variance
   c. Direct manufacturing labor price variance
   d. Direct manufacturing labor efficiency variance
   e. Total manufacturing overhead spending variance
   f. Variable manufacturing overhead efficiency variance
   g. Production-volume variance

8-40 Non-financial variances. Supreme Canine Products produces high quality dog food distributed only through veterinary offices. To ensure that the food is of the highest quality and has taste appeal, Supreme has a rigorous inspection process. For quality control purposes, Supreme has a standard based on the pounds of food inspected per hour and the number of pounds that pass or fail the inspection.

Supreme expects that for every 15,000 pounds of food produced, 1,500 pounds of food will be inspected. Inspection of 1,500 pounds of dog food should take 1 hour. Supreme also expects that 6% of the food inspected will fail the inspection. During the month of May, Supreme produced 3,000,000 pounds of food and inspected 277,500 pounds of food in 215 hours. Of the 277,500 pounds of food inspected, 15,650 pounds of food failed to pass the inspection.

Required

1. Compute two variances that help determine whether the time spent on inspections was more or less than expected. (Follow a format similar to the one used for the variable overhead spending and efficiency variances, but without prices.)
2. Compute two variances that can be used to evaluate the percentage of the food that fails the inspection.

8-41 Overhead variances and sales volume variance. Eco-Green Company manufactures cloth shopping bags that it plans to sell for $5 each. Budgeted production and sales for these bags for 2011 is 800,000 bags, with a standard of 400,000 machine hours for the whole year. Budgeted fixed overhead costs are $470,000, and variable overhead cost is $1.60 per machine hour.

Because of increased demand, actual production and sales of the bags for 2010 are 900,000 bags using 440,000 actual machine hours. Actual variable overhead costs are $699,600 and actual fixed overhead is $501,900. Actual selling price is $6 per bag.

Direct materials and direct labor actual costs were the same as standard costs, which were $1.20 per unit and $1.80 per unit, respectively.

Required

1. Calculate the variable overhead and fixed overhead variances (spending, efficiency, spending and volume).
2. Create a chart like that in Exhibit 7-2 showing Flexible Budget Variances and Sales Volume Variances for revenues, costs, contribution margin, and operating income.
3. Calculate the operating income based on budgeted profit per shopping bag.
4. Reconcile the budgeted operating income from requirement 3 to the actual operating income from your chart in requirement 2.
5. Calculate the operating income volume variance and show how the sales volume variance is comprised of the production volume variance and the operating income volume variance.

Collaborative Learning Problem

8-42 Overhead variances, ethics. Zeller Company uses standard costing. The company has two manufacturing plants, one in Nevada and the other in Ohio. For the Nevada plant, Zeller has budgeted annual output of 4,000,000 units. Standard labor hours per unit are 0.25, and the variable overhead rate for the Nevada plant is $3.25 per direct labor hour. Fixed overhead for the Nevada plant is budgeted at $2,500,000 for the year.

For the Ohio plant, Zeller has budgeted annual output of 4,200,000 units with standard labor hours also 0.25 per unit. However, the variable overhead rate for the Ohio plant is $3 per hour, and the budgeted fixed overhead for the year is only $2,310,000.

Firm management has always used variance analysis as a performance measure for the two plants, and has compared the results of the two plants.

Jack Jones has just been hired as a new controller for Zeller. Jack is good friends with the Ohio plant manager and wants him to get a favorable review. Jack suggests allocating the firm's budgeted common fixed costs of $3,150,000 to the two plants, but on the basis of one-third to the Ohio plant and two-thirds to the Nevada plant. His explanation for this allocation base is that Nevada is a more expensive state than Ohio.

At the end of the year, the Nevada plant reported the following actual results: output of 3,900,000 using 1,014,000 labor hours in total, at a cost of $3,244,800 in variable overhead and $2,520,000 in fixed overhead. Actual results for the Ohio plant are an output of 4,350,000 units using 1,218,000 labor hours with a variable cost of $3,775,800 and fixed overhead cost of $2,400,000. The actual common fixed costs for the year were $3,126,000.

Required

1. Compute the budgeted fixed cost per labor hour for the fixed overhead separately for each plant:
   a. Excluding allocated common fixed costs
   b. Including allocated common fixed costs
2. Compute the variable overhead spending variance and the variable overhead efficiency variance separately for each plant.
3. Compute the fixed overhead spending and volume variances for each plant:
   a. Excluding allocated common fixed costs
   b. Including allocated common fixed costs
4. Did Jack Jones's attempt to make the Ohio plant look better than the Nevada plant by allocating common fixed costs work? Why or why not?
5. Should common fixed costs be allocated in general when variances are used as performance measures? Why or why not?
6. What do you think of Jack Jones's behavior overall?

Inventory Costing and Capacity Analysis

Few numbers capture the attention of managers and shareholders more than operating profits.

In industries that require significant upfront investments in capacity, the decisions made regarding the level of such fixed investments, and the extent to which the capacity is eventually utilized to meet customer demand, have a substantial impact on corporate profits. Unfortunately, the choice of compensation and reward systems, as well as the choice of inventory-costing methods, may induce managerial decisions that benefit short-term earnings at the expense of a firm's long-term health. It may take a substantial external shock, like a sharp economic slowdown, to motivate firms to make the right capacity and inventory choices, as the following article illustrates.

Lean Manufacturing Helps Companies Reduce Inventory and Survive the Recession[1]

Can changing the way a mattress is pieced together save a company during an economic downturn? For Sealy, the world's largest mattress manufacturer, the answer is a resounding "yes!"

Sealy is among thousands of manufacturers that have remained profitable during the recession by using lean manufacturing to become more cost-efficient. Lean manufacturing involves producing output in an uninterrupted flow, rather than as part of unfinished batches, and producing only what customers order. Driving this lean movement is an urgent need to pare inventory, which reduces inventory costs.

Before the adoption of lean practices, the company used to manufacture units at peak capacity. That is, it made as many mattresses as its resources allowed. Sealy employees were also paid based on the number of mattresses produced each day. While factories operated at peak capacity, inventory often piled up, which cost the company millions of dollars each year.

While Sealy launched its lean strategy in 2004, its efforts intensified during the recession. Old processes were reconfigured to be more efficient. As a result, each bed is now completed in 4 hours, down from 21. Median delivery times have been cut to 60 hours from 72, and plants have cut their raw-material inventories by 50%.

Additionally, the company now adheres to a precise production schedule that reflects orders from retailers such as Mattress Discounters

[1] *Source*: Paul Davidson. 2009. Lean manufacturing helps companies survive recession. *USA Today*, November 2; Sealy Corporation. 2009. Annual Report. Trinity, NC: Sealy Corporation, 2010. http://ccbn.10kwizard.com/xml/download.php?repo=tenk&ipage=6709696&format=PDF

and Macy's. While factories no longer run at full capacity, no mattress is made now until a customer orders it.

Sealy's manufacturing and inventory strategy has been key to its survival during the recession. While 2009 sales were 14% less than 2008 sales, earnings rose more than $16 million. Moreover, a large part of the earnings increase was due to reductions in inventory costs, which were lower by 12%, or nearly $8 million, in 2009.

Managers in industries with high fixed costs, like manufacturing, must manage capacity levels and make decisions about the use of available capacity. Managers must also decide on a production and inventory policy (as Sealy did). These decisions and the accounting choices managers make affect the operating incomes of manufacturing companies. This chapter focuses on two types of cost accounting choices:

1. *The inventory-costing choice* determines which manufacturing costs are treated as inventoriable costs. Recall from Chapter 2 (p. 37), *inventoriable costs* are all costs of a product that are regarded as assets when they are incurred and expensed as cost of goods sold when the product is sold. There are three types of inventory costing methods: absorption costing, variable costing, and throughput costing.

2. *The denominator-level capacity choice* focuses on the cost allocation base used to set budgeted fixed manufacturing cost rates. There are four possible choices of capacity levels: theoretical capacity, practical capacity, normal capacity utilization, and master-budget capacity utilization.

Variable and Absorption Costing

The two most common methods of costing inventories in manufacturing companies are *variable costing* and *absorption costing*. We describe each next and then discuss them in detail, using a hypothetical lens-manufacturing company as an example.

Variable Costing

Variable costing is a method of inventory costing in which all variable manufacturing costs (direct and indirect) are included as inventoriable costs. All fixed manufacturing costs are excluded from inventoriable costs and are instead treated as costs of the period in which they are incurred. Note that *variable costing* is a less-than-perfect term to

Learning Objective 1

Identify what distinguishes variable costing

. . . fixed manufacturing costs excluded from inventoriable costs

from absorption costing

. . . fixed manufacturing costs included in inventoriable costs describe this inventory-costing method, because only variable manufacturing costs are inventoried; variable nonmanufacturing costs are still treated as period costs and are expensed. Another common term used to describe this method is **direct costing**. This is also a misnomer because variable costing considers variable manufacturing overhead (an indirect cost) as inventoriable, while excluding direct marketing costs, for example.

Absorption Costing

Absorption costing is a method of inventory costing in which all variable manufacturing costs and all fixed manufacturing costs are included as inventoriable costs. That is, inventory "absorbs" all manufacturing costs. The job costing system you studied in Chapter 4 is an example of absorption costing.

Under both variable costing and absorption costing, all variable manufacturing costs are inventoriable costs and all nonmanufacturing costs in the value chain (such as research and development and marketing), whether variable or fixed, are period costs and are recorded as expenses when incurred.

Comparing Variable and Absoption Costing

The easiest way to understand the difference between variable costing and absorption costing is with an example. We will study Stassen Company, an optical consumer-products manufacturer, in this chapter. We focus in particular on its product line of high-end telescopes for aspiring astronomers.

Stassen uses standard costing:

- Direct costs are traced to products using standard prices and standard inputs allowed for actual outputs produced.

- Indirect (overhead) manufacturing costs are allocated using standard indirect rates times standard inputs allowed for actual outputs produced.

Stassen's management wants to prepare an income statement for 2012 (the fiscal year just ended) to evaluate the performance of the telescope product line. The operating information for the year is as follows:

	Home	Insert	Page Layout	Formulas	Data	
		A				B
1						**Units**
2	Beginning inventory					0
3	Production					8,000
4	Sales					6,000
5	Ending inventory					2,000

Actual price and cost data for 2012 are as follows:

	Home	Insert	Page Layout	Formulas	Data	Review	
		A					B
10	Selling price						$ 1,000
11	Variable manufacturing cost per unit						
12	Direct material cost per unit						$ 110
13	Direct manufacturing labor cost per unit						40
14	Manufacturing overhead cost per unit						50
15	Total variable manufacturing cost per unit						$ 200
16	Variable marketing cost per unit sold						$ 185
17	Fixed manufacturing costs (all indirect)						$1,080,000
18	Fixed marketing costs (all indirect)						$1,380,000

For simplicity and to focus on the main ideas, we assume the following about Stassen:

- Stassen incurs manufacturing and marketing costs only. The cost driver for all variable manufacturing costs is units produced; the cost driver for variable marketing costs is units sold. There are no batch-level costs and no product-sustaining costs.

- There are no price variances, efficiency variances, or spending variances. Therefore, the *budgeted* (standard) price and cost data for 2012 are the same as the *actual* price and cost data.

- Work-in-process inventory is zero.

- Stassen budgeted production of 8,000 units for 2012. This was used to calculate the budgeted fixed manufacturing cost per unit of $135 ($1,080,000/8,000 units).

- Stassen budgeted sales of 6,000 units for 2012, which is the same as the actual sales for 2012.

- The actual production for 2012 is 8,000 units. As a result, there is no production-volume variance for manufacturing costs in 2012. Later examples, based on data for 2013 and 2014, do include production-volume variances. However, even in those cases, the income statements contain no variances other than the production-volume variance.

- All variances are written off to cost of goods sold in the period (year) in which they occur.

Based on the preceding information, Stassen's inventoriable costs per unit produced in 2012 under the two inventory costing methods are as follows:

	Variable Costing		Absorption Costing	
Variable manufacturing cost per unit produced:				
Direct materials	$110		$110	
Direct manufacturing labor	40		40	
Manufacturing overhead	50	$200	50	$200
Fixed manufacturing cost per unit produced		—		135
Total inventoriable cost per unit produced		$200		$335

To summarize, the main difference between variable costing and absorption costing is the accounting for fixed manufacturing costs:

- Under variable costing, fixed manufacturing costs are not inventoried; they are treated as an expense of the period.

- Under absorption costing, fixed manufacturing costs are inventoriable costs. In our example, the standard fixed manufacturing cost is $135 per unit ($1,080,000 ÷ 8,000 units) produced.

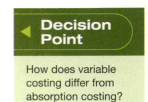

Decision Point

How does variable costing differ from absorption costing?

Variable vs. Absorption Costing: Operating Income and Income Statements

When comparing variable and absorption costing, we must also take into account whether we are looking at short- or long-term numbers. How does the data for a one-year period differ from that of a three-year period under variable and absorption costing?

Comparing Income Statements for One Year

What will Stassen's operating income be if it uses variable costing or absorption costing? The differences between these methods are apparent in Exhibit 9-1. Panel A shows the variable costing income statement and Panel B the absorption-costing income statement for Stassen's telescope product line for 2012. The variable-costing income statement uses the contribution-margin format introduced in Chapter 3. The absorption-costing income statement uses the gross-margin format introduced in Chapter 2. Why these differences in format? The distinction between variable costs and fixed costs is central to variable

| Exhibit 9-1 | | Comparison of Variable Costing and Absorption Costing for Stassen Company: Telescope Product-Line Income Statements for 2012 |

	A	B	C	D	E	F	G
1	**Panel A: VARIABLE COSTING**				**Panel B: ABSORPTION COSTING**		
2	Revenues: $1,000 × 6,000 units		$6,000,000		Revenues: $1,000 × 6,000 units		$6,000,000
3	Variable cost of goods sold:				Cost of goods sold:		
4	Beginning inventory	$ 0			Beginning inventory	$ 0	
5	Variable manufacturing costs: $200 × 8,000 units	1,600,000			Variable manufacturing costs: $200 × 8,000 unit	1,600,000	
6					Allocated fixed manufacturing costs: $135 × 8,000 units	1,080,000	
7	Cost of goods available for sale	1,600,000			Cost of goods available for sale	2,680,000	
8	Deduct ending inventory: $200 × 2,000 units	(400,000)			Deduct ending inventory: $335 × 2,000 units	(670,000)	
9	Variable cost of goods sold		1,200,000		Cost of goods sold		2,010,000
10	Variable marketing costs: $185 × 6,000 units sold		1,110,000				
11	Contribution margin		3,690,000		Gross Margin		3,990,000
12	Fixed manufacturing costs		1,080,000		Variable marketing costs: $185 × 6,000 units sold		1,110,000
13	Fixed marketing cost		1,380,000		Fixed marketing costs		1,380,000
14	Operating income		$1,230,000		Operating Income		$1,500,000
15							
16	Manufacturing costs expensed in Panel A:				Manufacturing costs expensed in Panel B:		
17	Variable cost of goods sold		$1,200,000				
18	Fixed manufacturing costs		1,080,000				
19	Total		$2,280,000		Cost of goods sold		$2,010,000

Learning Objective 2

Compute income under absorption costing

. . . using the gross-margin format

and variable costing,

. . . using the contribution-margin format

and explain the difference in income

. . . affected by the unit level of production and sales under absorption costing, but only the unit level of sales under variable costing

costing, and it is highlighted by the contribution-margin format. Similarly, the distinction between manufacturing and nonmanufacturing costs is central to absorption costing, and it is highlighted by the gross-margin format.

Absorption-costing income statements need not differentiate between variable and fixed costs. However, we will make this distinction between variable and fixed costs in the Stassen example to show how individual line items are classified differently under variable costing and absorption costing. In Exhibit 9-1, Panel B, note that inventoriable cost is $335 per unit under absorption costing: allocated fixed manufacturing costs of $135 per unit plus variable manufacturing costs of $200 per unit.

Notice how the fixed manufacturing costs of $1,080,000 are accounted for under variable costing and absorption costing in Exhibit 9-1. The income statement under variable costing deducts the $1,080,000 lump sum as an expense for 2012. In contrast, under absorption costing, the $1,080,000 ($135 per unit × 8,000 units) is initially treated as an inventoriable cost in 2012. Of this $1,080,000, $810,000 ($135 per unit × 6,000 units sold) subsequently becomes a part of cost of goods sold in 2012, and $270,000 ($135 per unit × 2,000 units) remains an asset—part of ending finished goods inventory on December 31, 2012.

Operating income is $270,000 higher under absorption costing compared with variable costing, because only $810,000 of fixed manufacturing costs are expensed under absorption costing, whereas all $1,080,000 of fixed manufacturing costs are expensed under variable costing. Note that the variable manufacturing cost of $200 per unit is accounted for the same way in both income statements in Exhibit 9-1.

These points can be summarized as follows:

	Variable Costing	Absorption Costing
Variable manufacturing costs: $200 per telescope produced	Inventoriable	Inventoriable
Fixed manufacturing costs: $1,080,000 per year	Deducted as an expense of the period	Inventoriable at $135 per telescope produced using budgeted denominator level of 8,000 units produced per year ($1,080,000 ÷ 8,000 units = $135 per unit)

The basis of the difference between variable costing and absorption costing is how fixed manufacturing costs are accounted for. If inventory levels change, operating income will differ between the two methods because of the difference in accounting for fixed manufacturing costs. To see this difference, let's compare telescope sales of 6,000; 7,000; and 8,000 units by Stassen in 2012, when 8,000 units were produced. Of the $1,080,000 total fixed manufacturing costs, the amount expensed in the 2012 income statement under each of these scenarios would be as follows:

	Home	Insert	Page Layout	Formulas	Data	Review	View		
	A	B	C	D	E		G	H	
1			**Variable Costing**				**Absorption Costing**		
2							**Fixed Manufacturing Costs**		
3	**Units**	**Ending**	**Fixed Manufacturing Costs**				**Included in Inventory**	**Amount Expensed**	
4	**Sold**	**Inventory**	**Included in Inventory**	**Amount Expensed**			**=$135 × Ending Inv.**	**=$135 × Units Sold**	
5	6,000	2,000	$0	$1,080,000			$270,000	$ 810,000	
6	7,000	1,000	$0	$1,080,000			$135,000	$ 945,000	
7	8,000	0	$0	$1,080,000			$ 0	$1,080,000	

In the last scenario, where 8,000 units are produced and sold, both variable and absorption costing report the same net income because inventory levels are unchanged. This chapter's appendix describes how the choice of variable costing or absorption costing affects the breakeven quantity of sales when inventory levels are allowed to vary.

Comparing Income Statements for Three Years

To get a more comprehensive view of the effects of variable costing and absorption costing, Stassen's management accountants prepare income statements for three years of operations, starting with 2012. In both 2013 and 2014, Stassen has a production-volume variance, because actual telescope production differs from the budgeted level of production of 8,000 units per year used to calculate budgeted fixed manufacturing cost per unit. The actual quantities sold for 2013 and 2014 are the same as the sales quantities budgeted for these respective years, which are given in units in the following table:

	Home	Insert	Page Layout	Formulas	Data
	E	F	G	H	
1		**2012**	**2013**	**2014**	
2	Budgeted production	8,000	8,000	8,000	
3	Beginning inventory	0	2,000	500	
4	Actual production	8,000	5,000	10,000	
5	Sales	6,000	6,500	7,500	
6	Ending inventory	2,000	500	3,000	

All other 2012 data given earlier for Stassen also apply for 2013 and 2014.

Exhibit 9-2 presents the income statement under variable costing in Panel A and the income statement under absorption costing in Panel B for 2012, 2013, and 2014. As you study Exhibit 9-2, note that the 2012 columns in both Panels A and B show the same figures as Exhibit 9-1. The 2013 and 2014 columns are similar to 2012 *except for the production-volume variance line item under absorption costing in Panel B*. Keep in mind the following points about absorption costing as you study Panel B of Exhibit 9-2:

1. The $135 fixed manufacturing cost rate is based on the budgeted denominator capacity level of 8,000 units in 2012, 2013, and 2014 ($1,080,000 ÷ 8,000 units = $135 per unit). Whenever production (the quantity produced, not the quantity sold) deviates from the denominator level, there will be a production-volume variance. The amount of Stassen's production-volume variance is determined by multiplying $135 per unit by the difference between the actual level of production and the denominator level.

Exhibit 9-2	Comparison of Variable Costing and Absorption Costing for Stassen Company: Telescope Product-Line Income Statements for 2012, 2013, and 2014

	Home	Insert	Page Layout	Formulas	Data	Review	View					
	A					B	C	D	E	F	G
1	Panel A: VARIABLE COSTING										
2							2012		2013		2014
3	Revenues: $1,000 × 6,000; 6,500; 7,500 units						$6,000,000		$6,500,000		$7,500,000
4	Variable cost of goods sold:										
5	Beginning inventory: $200 × 0; 2,000; 500 units					$ 0		$ 400,000		$ 100,000	
6	Variable manufacturing costs: $200 × 8,000; 5,000; 10,000 units					1,600,000		1,000,000		2,000,000	
7	Cost of goods available for sale					1,600,000		1,400,000		2,100,000	
8	Deduct ending inventory: $200 × 2,000; 500; 3,000 units					(400,000)		(100,000)		(600,000)	
9	Variable cost of goods sold						1,200,000		1,300,000		1,500,000
10	Variable marketing costs: $185 × 6,000; 6,500; 7,500 units						1,110,000		1,202,500		1,387,500
11	Contribution margin						3,690,000		3,997,500		4,612,500
12	Fixed manufacturing costs						1,080,000		1,080,000		1,080,000
13	Fixed marketing costs						1,380,000		1,380,000		1,380,000
14	Operating income						$1,230,000		$1,537,500		$2,152,500
15											
16	Panel B: ABSORPTION COSTING										
17							2012		2013		2014
18	Revenues: $1,000 × 6,000; 6,500; 7,500 units						$6,000,000		$6,500,000		$7,500,000
19	Cost of goods sold:										
20	Beginning inventory: $335 × 0; 2,000; 500 units					$ 0		$ 670,000		$ 167,500	
21	Variable manufacturing costs: $200 × 8,000; 5,000; 10,000 units					1,600,000		1,000,000		2,000,000	
22	Allocated fixed manufacturing costs: $135 × 8,000; 5,000; 10,000 units					1,080,000		675,000		1,350,000	
23	Cost of goods available for sale					2,680,000		2,345,000		3,517,500	
24	Deduct ending inventory: $335 × 2,000; 500; 3,000 units					(670,000)		(167,500)		(1,005,000)	
25	Adjustment for production-volume variance[a]					0		405,000 U		(270,000) F	
26	Cost of goods sold						2,010,000		2,582,500		2,242,500
27	Gross Margin						3,990,000		3,917,500		5,257,500
28	Variable marketing costs: $185 × 6,000; 6,500; 7,500 units						1,110,000		1,202,500		1,387,500
29	Fixed marketing costs						1,380,000		1,380,000		1,380,000
30	Operating Income						$1,500,000		$1,335,000		$2,490,000
31											
32	[a]Production-volume variance = Budgeted fixed manufacturing costs − Fixed manufacturing overhead allocated using budgeted cost per output unit allowed for actual output produced (Panel B, line 22)										
33	2012: $1,080,000 − ($135 × 8,000) = $1,080,000 − $1,080,000 = $0										
34	2013: $1,080,000 − ($135 × 5,000) = $1,080,000 − $675,000 = $405,000 U										
35	2014: $1,080,000 − ($135 × 10,000) = $1,080,000 − $1,350,000 = ($270,000) F										
36											
37	Production volume variance can also be calculated as follows:										
38	Fixed manufacturing cost per unit × (Denominator level − Actual output units produced)										
39	2012: $135 × (8,000 − 8,000) units = $135 × 0 = $0										
40	2013: $135 × (8,000 − 5,000) units = $135 × 3,000 = $405,000 U										
41	2014: $135 × (8,000 − 10,000) units = $135 × (2,000) = ($270,000) F										

In 2013, production was 5,000 units, 3,000 lower than the denominator level of 8,000 units. The result is an unfavorable production-volume variance of $405,000 ($135 per unit × 3,000 units). The year 2014 has a favorable production-volume variance of $270,000 ($135 per unit × 2,000 units), due to production of 10,000 units, which exceeds the denominator level of 8,000 units.

Recall how standard costing works under absorption costing. Each time a unit is manufactured, $135 of fixed manufacturing costs is included in the cost of goods manufactured and available for sale. In 2013, when 5,000 units are manufactured, $675,000 ($135 per unit × 5,000 units) of fixed manufacturing costs is included in the cost of goods available for sale (see Exhibit 9-2, Panel B, line 22). Total fixed manufacturing costs for 2013 are $1,080,000. The production-volume variance of $405,000 U equals the difference between $1,080,000 and $675,000. In Panel B, note how, for each year, the fixed manufacturing costs included in the cost of goods available for sale plus the production-volume variance always equals $1,080,000.

2. The production-volume variance, which relates only to fixed manufacturing overhead, exists under absorption costing but not under variable costing. Under variable costing, fixed manufacturing costs of $1,080,000 are always treated as an expense of the period, regardless of the level of production (and sales).

Here's a summary (using information from Exhibit 9-2) of the operating-income differences for Stassen Company during the 2012 to 2014 period:

	2012	2013	2014
1. Absorption-costing operating income	$1,500,000	$1,335,000	$2,490,000
2. Variable-costing operating income	$1,230,000	$1,537,500	$2,152,500
3. Difference: (1) – (2)	$ 270,000	$ (202,500)	$ 337,500

The sizeable differences in the preceding table illustrate why managers whose performance is measured by reported income are concerned about the choice between variable costing and absorption costing.

Why do variable costing and absorption costing usually report different operating income numbers? In general, if inventory increases during an accounting period, less operating income will be reported under variable costing than absorption costing. Conversely, if inventory decreases, more operating income will be reported under variable costing than absorption costing. The difference in reported operating income is due solely to (a) moving fixed manufacturing costs into inventories as inventories increase and (b) moving fixed manufacturing costs out of inventories as inventories decrease.

The difference between operating income under absorption costing and variable costing can be computed by formula 1, which focuses on fixed manufacturing costs in beginning inventory and ending inventory:

Home	Insert	Page Layout	Formulas	Data	Review	View		
A	B	C	D	E	F	G	H	
1 Formula 1								
2					Fixed manufacturing		Fixed manufacturing	
3	Absorption-costing	–	Variable-costing	=	costs in ending inventory	–	costs in beginning inventory	
4	operating income		operation income		under absorption costing		under absorption costing	
5 2012	$1,500,000	–	$1,230,000	=	($135 × 2,000 units)	–	($135 × 0 units)	
6			$ 270,000	=	$270,000			
7								
8 2013	$1,335,000	–	$1,537,500	=	($135 × 500 units)	–	($135 × 2,000 units)	
9			($ 202,500)		($202,500)			
10								
11 2014	$2,490,000	–	$2,152,500	=	($135 × 3,000 units)	–	($135 × 500 units)	
12			$ 337,500	=	$337,500			

Fixed manufacturing costs in ending inventory are deferred to a future period under absorption costing. For example, $270,000 of fixed manufacturing overhead is deferred to 2013 at December 31, 2012. Under variable costing, all $1,080,000 of fixed manufacturing costs are treated as an expense of 2012.

Recall that,

$$\frac{\text{Beginning}}{\text{inventory}} + \frac{\text{Cost of goods}}{\text{manufactured}} = \frac{\text{Cost of goods}}{\text{sold}} + \frac{\text{Ending}}{\text{Inventory}}$$

Therefore, instead of focusing on fixed manufacturing costs in ending and beginning inventory (as in formula 1), we could alternatively look at fixed manufacturing costs in units produced and units sold. The latter approach (see formula 2) highlights how fixed manufacturing costs move between units produced and units sold during the fiscal year.

	Home	Insert	Page Layout	Formulas	Data	Review	View		
	A	B	C	D	E	F	G	H
16	Formula 2							
17						Fixed manufacturing costs		Fixed manufacturing costs
18		Absorption-costing	–	Variable-costing	=	inventoried in units produced	–	in cost of goods sold
19		operating income		operation income		under absorption costing		under absorption costing
20	2012	$1,500,000	–	$1,230,000	=	($135 × 8,000 units)	–	($135 × 6,000 units)
21				$ 270,000	=	$270,000		
22								
23	2013	$1,335,000	–	$1,537,500	=	($135 × 5,000 units)	–	($135 × 6,500 units)
24				($ 202,500)	=	($202,500)		
25								
26	2014	$2,490,000	–	$2,152,500	=	($135 × 10,000 units)	–	($135 × 7,500 units)
27				$ 337,500	=	$337,500		

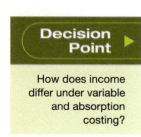

Decision Point ▶

How does income differ under variable and absorption costing?

Managers face increasing pressure to reduce inventory levels. Some companies are achieving steep reductions in inventory levels using policies such as just-in-time production—a production system under which products are manufactured only when needed. Formula 1 illustrates that, as Stassen reduces its inventory levels, operating income differences between absorption costing and variable costing become immaterial. Consider, for example, the formula for 2012. If instead of 2,000 units in ending inventory, Stassen had only 2 units in ending inventory, the difference between absorption-costing operating income and variable-costing operating income would drop from $270,000 to just $270.

Variable Costing and the Effect of Sales and Production on Operating Income

Given a constant contribution margin per unit and constant fixed costs, the period-to-period change in operating income under variable costing is *driven solely by changes in the quantity of units actually sold.* Consider the variable-costing operating income of Stassen in (a) 2013 versus 2012 and (b) 2014 versus 2013. Recall the following:

$$\frac{\text{Contribution}}{\text{margin per unit}} = \text{Selling price} - \frac{\text{Variable manufacturing}}{\text{cost per unit}} - \frac{\text{Variable marketing}}{\text{cost per unit}}$$

$$= \$1{,}000 \text{ per unit} - \$200 \text{ per unit} - \$185 \text{ per unit}$$

$$= \$615 \text{ per unit}$$

$$\frac{\text{Change in}}{\substack{\text{variable-costing} \\ \text{operating income}}} = \frac{\text{Contribution}}{\substack{\text{margin} \\ \text{per unit}}} \times \frac{\text{Change in quantity}}{\text{of units sold}}$$

(a) 2013 vs. 2012: $1,537,500 − $1,230,000 = $615 per unit × (6,500 unit − 6,000 units)

$$\$307{,}500 = \$307{,}500$$

(b) 2014 vs. 2013: $2,152,500 − $1,537,500 = $615 per unit × (7,500 units − 6,500 units)

$$\$615{,}000 = \$615{,}000$$

Under variable costing, Stassen managers cannot increase operating income by "producing for inventory." Why not? Because, as you can see from the preceding computations, when using variable costing, only the quantity of units sold drives operating income. We'll explain later in this chapter that absorption costing enables managers to increase operating income by increasing the unit level of sales, as well as by producing more units. Before you proceed to the next section, make sure that you examine Exhibit 9-3 for a detailed comparison of the differences between variable costing and absorption costing.

| Exhibit 9-3 | Comparative Income Effects of Variable Costing and Absorption Costing |

Question	Variable Costing	Absorption Costing	Comment
Are fixed manufacturing costs inventoried?	No	Yes	Basic theoretical question of when these costs should be expensed
Is there a production-volume variance?	No	Yes	Choice of denominator level affects measurement of operating income under absorption costing only
Are classifications between variable and fixed costs routinely made?	Yes	Infrequently	Absorption costing can be easily modified to obtain subclassifications for variable and fixed costs, if desired (for example, see Exhibit 9-1, Panel B)
How do changes in unit inventory levels affect operating income?[a]			Differences are attributable to the timing of when fixed manufacturing costs are expensed
Production = sales	Equal	Equal	
Production > sales	Lower[b]	Higher[c]	
Production < sales	Higher	Lower	
What are the effects on cost-volume-profit relationship (for a given level of fixed costs and a given contribution margin per unit)?	Driven by unit level of sales	Driven by (a) unit level of sales, (b) unit level of production, and (c) chosen denominator level	Management control benefit: Effects of changes in production level on operating income are easier to understand under variable costing

[a]Assuming that all manufacturing variances are written off as period costs, that no change occurs in work-in-process inventory, and no change occurs in the budgeted fixed manufacturing cost rate between accounting periods.

[b]That is, lower operating income than under absorption costing.

[c]That is, higher operating income than under variable costing.

Absorption Costing and Performance Measurement

Absorption costing is the required inventory method for external reporting in most countries. Many companies use absorption costing for internal accounting as well. Why? Because it is cost-effective and less confusing to managers to use one common method of inventory costing for both external and internal reporting and performance evaluation. A common method of inventory costing can also help prevent managers from taking actions that make their performance measure look good but that hurt the income they report to shareholders. Another advantage of absorption costing is that it measures the cost of all manufacturing resources, whether variable or fixed, necessary to produce inventory. Many companies use inventory costing information for long-run decisions, such as pricing and choosing a product mix. For these long-run decisions, inventory costs should include both variable *and* fixed costs.

One problem with absorption costing is that it enables a manager to increase operating income in a specific period by increasing production—even if there is no customer demand for the additional production! By producing more ending inventory, the firm's margins and income can be made higher. Stassen's managers may be tempted to do this to get higher bonuses based on absorption-costing operating income. Generally, higher operating income also has a positive effect on stock price, which increases managers' stock-based compensation.

To reduce the undesirable incentives to build up inventories that absorption costing can create, a number of companies use variable costing for internal reporting. Variable costing focuses attention on distinguishing variable manufacturing costs from fixed manufacturing costs. This distinction is important for short-run decision making (as in cost-volume-profit analysis in Chapter 3 and in planning and control in Chapters 6, 7, and 8).

Learning Objective **3**

Understand how absorption costing can provide undesirable incentives for managers to build up inventory

. . . producing more units for inventory absorbs fixed manufacturing costs and increases operating income

Companies that use both methods for internal reporting—variable costing for short-run decisions and performance evaluation and absorption costing for long-run decisions—benefit from the different advantages of both. In the next section, we explore in more detail the challenges that arise from absorption costing.

Undesirable Buildup of Inventories

Recall that one motivation for an undesirable buildup of inventories could be because a manager's bonus is based on reported absorption-costing operating income. Assume that Stassen's managers have such a bonus plan. Exhibit 9-4 shows how Stassen's absorption costing operating income for 2013 changes as the production level changes. This exhibit assumes that the production-volume variance is written off to cost of goods sold at the end of each year. Beginning inventory of 2,000 units and sales of 6,500 units for 2013 are unchanged from the case shown in Exhibit 9-2. *As you review Exhibit 9-4, keep in mind that the computations are basically the same as those in Exhibit 9-2.*

Exhibit 9-4 shows that production of 4,500 units meets the 2013 sales budget of 6,500 units (2,000 units from beginning inventory + 4,500 units produced). Operating income at this production level is $1,267,500. By producing more than 4,500 units, commonly referred to as *producing for inventory*, Stassen increases absorption-costing operating income. Each additional unit in 2013 ending inventory will increase operating income by $135. For example, if 9,000 units are produced (the last column in Exhibit 9-4), ending inventory will be 4,500 units and operating income increases to $1,875,000. This amount is $607,500 more than the operating income with zero ending inventory ($1,875,000 − $1,267,500, or 4,500 units × $135 per unit = $607,500). Under absorption costing, the company, by producing 4,500 units for inventory, includes $607,500 of fixed manufacturing costs in finished goods inventory, so those costs are not expensed in 2013.

Can top management implement checks and balances that limit managers from producing for inventory under absorption costing? While the answer is yes, as we will see in

---

Exhibit 9-4	Effect on Absorption-Costing Operating Income of Different Production Levels for Stassen Company: Telescope Product-Line Income Statement for 2013 at Sales of 6,500 Units

	A	B	C	D	E	F	G	H	I	J	K
1	**Unit Data**										
2	Beginning inventory	2,000		2,000		2,000		2,000		2,000	
3	Production	4,500		5,000		6,500		8,000		9,000	
4	Goods available for sale	6,500		7,000		8,500		10,000		11,000	
5	Sales	6,500		6,500		6,500		6,500		6,500	
6	Ending inventory	0		500		2,000		3,500		4,500	
7											
8	**Income Statement**										
9	Revenues	$6,500,000		$6,500,000		$6,500,000		$6,500,000		$6,500,000	
10	Cost of goods sold:										
11	Beginning inventory ($335 × 2,000)	670,000		670,000		670,000		670,000		670,000	
12	Variable manufacturing costs: $200 × production	900,000		1,000,000		1,300,000		1,600,000		1,800,000	
13	Allocated fixed manufacturing costs: $135 × production	607,500		675,000		877,500		1,080,000		1,215,000	
14	Cost of goods available for sale	2,177,500		2,345,000		2,847,500		3,350,000		3,685,000	
15	Deduct ending inventory: $335 × ending inventory	0		(167,500)		(670,000)		(1,172,500)		(1,507,500)	
16	Adjustment for production-volume variance[a]	472,500	U	405,000	U	202,500	U	0		(135,000)	F
17	Cost of goods sold	2,650,000		2,582,500		2,380,000		2,177,500		2,042,500	
18	Gross Margin	3,850,000		3,917,500		4,120,000		4,322,500		4,457,500	
19	Marketing costs: ($1,380,000 + $185 per unit × 6,500 units sold)	2,582,500		2,582,500		2,582,500		2,582,500		2,582,500	
20	Operating Income	$1,267,500		$1,335,000		$1,537,500		$1,740,000		$1,875,000	
21											
22	[a]Production-volume variance = Budgeted fixed manufacturing costs − Allocated fixed manufacturing costs (Income Statement, line 13)										
23	At production of 4,500 units: $1,080,000 − $607,500 = $472,500 U										
24	At production of 5,000 units: $1,080,000 − $675,000 = $405,000 U										
25	At production of 6,500 units: $1,080,000 − $877,500 = $202,500 U										
26	At production of 8,000 units: $1,080,000 − $1,080,000 = $0										
27	At production of 9,000 units: $1,080,000 − $1,215,000 = ($135,000) F										

the next section, producing for inventory cannot completely be prevented. There are many subtle ways a manager can produce for inventory that, if done to a limited extent, may not be easy to detect. For example, consider the following:

- A plant manager may switch to manufacturing products that absorb the highest amount of fixed manufacturing costs, regardless of the customer demand for these products (called "cherry picking" the production line). Production of items that absorb the least or lower fixed manufacturing costs may be delayed, resulting in failure to meet promised customer delivery dates (which, over time, can result in unhappy customers).

- A plant manager may accept a particular order to increase production, even though another plant in the same company is better suited to handle that order.

- To increase production, a manager may defer maintenance beyond the current period. Although operating income in this period may increase as a result, future operating income could decrease by a larger amount if repair costs increase and equipment becomes less efficient.

The example in Exhibit 9-4 focuses on only one year (2013). A Stassen manager who built up ending inventories of telescopes to 4,500 units in 2013 would have to further increase ending inventories in 2014 to increase that year's operating income by producing for inventory. There are limits to how much inventory levels can be increased over time (because of physical constraints on storage space and management supervision and controls). Such limits reduce the likelihood of incurring some of absorption costing's undesirable effects.

Proposals for Revising Performance Evaluation

Top management, with help from the controller and management accountants, can take several steps to reduce the undesirable effects of absorption costing.

- Focus on careful budgeting and inventory planning to reduce management's freedom to build up excess inventory. For example, the budgeted monthly balance sheets have estimates of the dollar amount of inventories. If actual inventories exceed these dollar amounts, top management can investigate the inventory buildups.

- Incorporate a carrying charge for inventory in the internal accounting system. For example, the company could assess an inventory carrying charge of 1% per month on the investment tied up in inventory and for spoilage and obsolescence when it evaluates a manager's performance. An increasing number of companies are beginning to adopt this inventory carrying charge.

- Change the period used to evaluate performance. Critics of absorption costing give examples in which managers take actions that maximize quarterly or annual income at the potential expense of long-run income. When their performance is evaluated over a three- to five-year period, managers will be less tempted to produce for inventory.

- Include nonfinancial as well as financial variables in the measures used to evaluate performance. Examples of nonfinancial measures that can be used to monitor the performance of Stassen's managers in 2014 (see data on p. 305) are as follows:

$$\text{(a)} \quad \frac{\text{Ending inventory in units in 2014}}{\text{Beginning inventory in units in 2014}} = \frac{3{,}000}{500} = 6$$

$$\text{(b)} \quad \frac{\text{Units produced in 2014}}{\text{Units sold in 2014}} = \frac{10{,}000}{7{,}500} = 1.33$$

Decision Point

Why might managers build up finished goods inventory if they use absorption costing?

Top management would want to see production equal to sales and relatively stable levels of inventory. Companies that manufacture or sell several products could report these two measures for each of the products they manufacture and sell.

Comparing Inventory Costing Methods

Learning Objective 4

Differentiate throughput costing

. . . direct material costs inventoried

from variable costing

. . . variable manufacturing costs inventoried

and absorption costing

. . . variable and fixed manufacturing costs inventoried

Before we begin our discussion of capacity, we will look at *throughput costing*, a variation of variable costing, and compare the various costing methods.

Throughput Costing

Some managers maintain that even variable costing promotes an excessive amount of costs being inventoried. They argue that only direct materials are "truly variable" in output. **Throughput costing**, which also is called **super-variable costing**, is an extreme form of variable costing in which only direct material costs are included as inventoriable costs. All other costs are costs of the period in which they are incurred. In particular, variable direct manufacturing labor costs and variable manufacturing overhead costs are regarded as period costs and are deducted as expenses of the period.

Exhibit 9-5 is the throughput-costing income statement for Stassen Company for 2012, 2013, and 2014. *Throughput margin* equals revenues minus all direct material cost of the goods sold. Compare the operating income amounts reported in Exhibit 9-5 with those for absorption costing and variable costing:

	2012	2013	2014
Absorption-costing operating income	$1,500,000	$1,335,000	$2,490,000
Variable-costing operating income	$1,230,000	$1,537,500	$2,152,500
Throughput-costing operating income	$1,050,000	$1,672,500	$1,927,500

Decision Point ▶

How does throughput costing differ from variable costing and absorption costing?

Only the $110 direct material cost per unit is inventoriable under throughput costing, compared with $335 per unit for absorption costing and $200 per unit for variable costing. When the production quantity exceeds sales as in 2012 and 2014, throughput costing results in the largest amount of expenses in the current period's income statement. Advocates of throughput costing say it provides less incentive to produce for inventory than either variable costing or, especially, absorption costing. Throughput costing is a more recent phenomenon in comparison with variable costing and absorption costing and has avid supporters, but so far it has not been widely adopted.[2]

Exhibit 9-5

Throughput Costing for Stassen Company: Telescope Product-Line Income Statements for 2012, 2013, and 2014

	A	B	C	D
1		2012	2013	2014
2	Revenues: $1,000 × 6,000; 6,500; 7,500 units	$6,000,000	$6,500,000	$7,500,000
3	Direct material cost of goods sold			
4	Beginning inventory: $110 × 0; 2,000; 500 units	0	220,000	55,000
5	Direct materials: $110 × 8,000; 5,000; 10,000 units	880,000	550,000	1,100,000
6	Cost of goods available for sale	880,000	770,000	1,155,000
7	Deduct ending inventory: $110 × 2,000; 500; 3,000 units	(220,000)	(55,000)	(330,000)
8	Direct material cost of goods sold	660,000	715,000	825,000
9	Throughput margin[a]	5,340,000	5,785,000	6,675,000
10	Manufacturing costs (other than direct materials)[b]	1,800,000	1,530,000	1,980,000
11	Marketing costs[c]	2,490,000	2,582,500	2,767,500
12	Operating income	$1,050,000	$1,672,500	$1,927,500
13				
14	[a]Throughput margin equals revenues minus all direct material cost of goods sold			
15	[b]Fixed manuf. costs + [(variable manuf. labor cost per unit + variable manuf. overhead cost per unit)			
16	× units produced]; $1,080,000 + [($40 + $50) × 8,000; 5,000; 10,000 units]			
17	[c]Fixed marketing costs + (variable marketing cost per unit × units sold);			
18	$1,380,000 + ($185 × 6,000; 6,500; 7,500 units)			

Home   Insert   Page Layout   Formulas   Data   Review   View

---

[2] See E. Goldratt, *The Theory of Constraints* (New York: North River Press, 1990); E. Noreen, D. Smith, and J. Mackey, *The Theory of Constraints and Its Implications for Management Accounting* (New York: North River Press, 1995).

A Comparison of Alternative Inventory-Costing Methods

Variable costing and absorption costing (as well as throughput costing) may be combined with actual, normal, or standard costing. Exhibit 9-6 compares product costing under six alternative inventory-costing systems.

Variable Costing	Absorption Costing
Actual costing	Actual costing
Standard costing	Standard costing
Normal costing	Normal costing

Variable costing has been controversial among accountants, not because of disagreement about the need to delineate between variable and fixed costs for internal planning and control, but as it pertains to *external reporting*. Accountants who favor variable costing for external reporting maintain that the fixed portion of manufacturing costs is more closely related to the capacity to produce than to the actual production of specific units. Hence, fixed costs should be expensed, not inventoried.

Accountants who support absorption costing for *external reporting* maintain that inventories should carry a fixed-manufacturing-cost component. Why? Because both variable manufacturing costs and fixed manufacturing costs are necessary to produce goods. Therefore, both types of costs should be inventoried in order to match all manufacturing costs to revenues, regardless of their different behavior patterns. For external reporting to shareholders, companies around the globe tend to follow the generally accepted accounting principle that all manufacturing costs are inventoriable.

Similarly, for tax reporting in the United States, direct production costs, as well as fixed and variable indirect production costs, must be taken into account in the computation of inventoriable costs in accordance with the "full absorption" method of inventory costing. Indirect production costs include items such as rent, utilities, maintenance, repair expenses, indirect materials, and indirect labor. For other indirect cost categories (including depreciation, insurance, taxes, officers' salaries, factory administrative expenses, and strike-related costs), the portion of the cost that is "incident to and necessary for production or manufacturing operations or processes" is inventoriable for tax

Exhibit 9-6 Comparison of Alternative Inventory-Costing Systems

			Actual Costing	Normal Costing	Standard Costing
Absorption Costing	Variable Costing	**Variable Direct Manufacturing Cost**	Actual prices × Actual quantity of inputs used	Actual prices × Actual quantity of inputs used	Standard prices × Standard quantity of inputs allowed for actual output achieved
		Variable Manufacturing Overhead Costs	Actual variable overhead rates × Actual quantity of cost-allocation bases used	Budgeted variable overhead rates × Actual quantity of cost-allocation bases used	Standard variable overhead rates × Standard quantity of cost-allocation bases allowed for actual output achieved
		Fixed Direct Manufacturing Costs	Actual prices × Actual quantity of inputs used	Actual prices × Actual quantity of inputs used	Standard prices × Standard quantity of inputs allowed for actual output achieved
		Fixed Manufacturing Overhead Costs	Actual fixed overhead rates × Actual quantity of cost-allocation bases used	Budgeted fixed overhead rates × Actual quantity of cost-allocation bases used	Standard fixed overhead rates × Standard quantity of cost-allocation bases allowed for actual output achieved

purposes if (and only if) it is treated as inventoriable for the purposes of financial reporting. Accordingly, costs must often be allocated between those portions related to manufacturing activities and those not related to manufacturing.[3]

Denominator-Level Capacity Concepts and Fixed-Cost Capacity Analysis

We have seen that the difference between variable and absorption costing methods arises solely from the treatment of fixed manufacturing costs. Spending on fixed manufacturing costs enables firms to obtain the scale or capacity needed to satisfy the expected demand from customers. Determining the "right" amount of spending, or the appropriate level of capacity, is one of the most strategic and most difficult decisions managers face. Having too much capacity to produce relative to that needed to meet market demand means incurring some costs of unused capacity. Having too little capacity to produce means that demand from some customers may be unfilled. These customers may go to other sources of supply and never return. Therefore, both managers and accountants should have a clear understanding of the issues that arise with capacity costs.

We start by analyzing a key question in absorption costing: Given a level of spending on fixed manufacturing costs, what capacity level should be used to compute the fixed manufacturing cost per unit produced? We then study the broader question of how a firm should decide on its level of capacity investment.

Absorption Costing and Alternative Denominator-Level Capacity Concepts

Earlier chapters, especially Chapters 4, 5, and 8, have highlighted how normal costing and standard costing report costs in an ongoing timely manner throughout a fiscal year. The choice of the capacity level used to allocate budgeted fixed manufacturing costs to products can greatly affect the operating income reported under normal costing or standard costing and the product-cost information available to managers.

Consider the Stassen Company example again. Recall that the annual fixed manufacturing costs of the production facility are $1,080,000. Stassen currently uses absorption costing with standard costs for external reporting purposes, and it calculates its budgeted fixed manufacturing rate on a per unit basis. We will now examine four different capacity levels used as the denominator to compute the budgeted fixed manufacturing cost rate: theoretical capacity, practical capacity, normal capacity utilization, and master-budget capacity utilization.

Theoretical Capacity and Practical Capacity

In business and accounting, capacity ordinarily means a "constraint," an "upper limit." **Theoretical capacity** is the level of capacity based on producing at full efficiency all the time. Stassen can produce 25 units per shift when the production lines are operating at maximum speed. If we assume 360 days per year, the theoretical annual capacity for 2 shifts per day is as follows:

$$25 \text{ units per shift} \times 2 \text{ shifts per day} \times 360 \text{ days} = 18,000 \text{ units}$$

Theoretical capacity is theoretical in the sense that it does not allow for any plant maintenance, shutdown periods, interruptions because of downtime on the assembly lines, or any other factors. Theoretical capacity represents an ideal goal of capacity utilization. Theoretical capacity levels are unattainable in the real world but they provide a target to which a company can aspire.

---

[3] Details regarding tax rules can be found in Section 1.471-11 of the U.S. Internal Revenue Code: Inventories of Manufacturers (see http://ecfr.gpoaccess.gov). Recall from Chapter 2 that costs not related to production, such as marketing, distribution, or research expenses, are treated as period expenses for financial reporting. Under U.S. tax rules, a firm can still consider these costs as inventoriable for tax purposes provided that it does so consistently.

Practical capacity is the level of capacity that reduces theoretical capacity by considering unavoidable operating interruptions, such as scheduled maintenance time, shutdowns for holidays, and so on. Assume that practical capacity is the practical production rate of 20 units per shift (as opposed to 25 units per shift under theoretical capacity) for 2 shifts per day for 300 days a year (as distinguished from 360 days a year under theoretical capacity). The practical annual capacity is as follows:

$$20 \text{ units per shift} \times 2 \text{ shifts per day} \times 300 \text{ days} = 12{,}000 \text{ units}$$

Engineering and human resource factors are both important when estimating theoretical or practical capacity. Engineers at the Stassen facility can provide input on the technical capabilities of machines for cutting and polishing lenses. Human-safety factors, such as increased injury risk when the line operates at faster speeds, are also necessary considerations in estimating practical capacity. With difficulty, practical capacity is attainable.

Normal Capacity Utilization and Master-Budget Capacity Utilization

Both theoretical capacity and practical capacity measure capacity levels in terms of what a plant can *supply*—available capacity. In contrast, normal capacity utilization and master-budget capacity utilization measure capacity levels in terms of *demand* for the output of the plant, that is, the amount of available capacity the plant expects to use based on the demand for its products. In many cases, budgeted demand is well below production capacity available.

Normal capacity utilization is the level of capacity utilization that satisfies average customer demand over a period (say, two to three years) that includes seasonal, cyclical, and trend factors. **Master-budget capacity utilization** is the level of capacity utilization that managers expect for the current budget period, which is typically one year. These two capacity-utilization levels can differ—for example, when an industry, such as automobiles or semiconductors, has cyclical periods of high and low demand or when management believes that budgeted production for the coming period is not representative of long-run demand.

Consider Stassen's master budget for 2012, based on production of 8,000 telescopes per year. Despite using this master-budget capacity-utilization level of 8,000 telescopes for 2012, top management believes that over the next three years the normal (average) annual production level will be 10,000 telescopes. It views 2012's budgeted production level of 8,000 telescopes to be "abnormally" low because a major competitor has been sharply reducing its selling price and spending large amounts on advertising. Stassen expects that the competitor's lower price and advertising blitz will not be a long-run phenomenon and that, by 2014 and beyond, Stassen's production and sales will be higher.

Effect on Budgeted Fixed Manufacturing Cost Rate

We now illustrate how each of these four denominator levels affects the budgeted fixed manufacturing cost rate. Stassen has budgeted (standard) fixed manufacturing overhead costs of $1,080,000 for 2012. This lump-sum is incurred to provide the capacity to produce telescopes. The amount includes, among other costs, leasing costs for the facility and the compensation of the facility managers. The budgeted fixed manufacturing cost rates for 2012 for each of the four capacity-level concepts are as follows:

	Home	Insert	Page Layout	Formulas	Data	Review	View	

	A	B	C	D
1		**Budgeted Fixed**	**Budget**	**Budgeted Fixed**
2	**Denominator-Level**	**Manufacturing**	**Capacity Level**	**Manufacturing**
3	**Capacity Concept**	**Costs per Year**	**(in units)**	**Cost per Unit**
4	(1)	(2)	(3)	(4) = (2) / (3)
5	Theoretical capacity	$1,080,000	18,000	$ 60
6	Practical capacity	$1,080,000	12,000	$ 90
7	Normal capacity utilization	$1,080,000	10,000	$108
8	Master-budget capacity utilization	$1,080,000	8,000	$135

The significant difference in cost rates (from $60 to $135) arises because of large differences in budgeted capacity levels under the different capacity concepts.

Budgeted (standard) variable manufacturing cost is $200 per unit. The total budgeted (standard) manufacturing cost per unit for alternative capacity-level concepts is as follows:

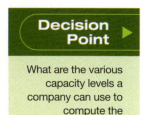

	A	B	C	D
1		Budgeted Variable	Budgeted Fixed	Budgeted Total
2	Denominator-Level	Manufacturing	Manufacturing	Manufacturing
3	Capacity Concept	Cost per Unit	Cost per Unit	Cost per Unit
4	(1)	(2)	(3)	(4) = (2) + (3)
5	Theoretical capacity	$200	$ 60	$260
6	Practical capacity	$200	$ 90	$290
7	Normal capacity utilization	$200	$108	$308
8	Master-budget capacity utilization	$200	$135	$335

Because different denominator-level capacity concepts yield different budgeted fixed manufacturing costs per unit, Stassen must decide which capacity level to use. Stassen is not required to use the same capacity-level concept, say, for management planning and control, external reporting to shareholders, and income tax purposes.

Choosing a Capacity Level

As we just saw, at the start of each fiscal year, managers determine different denominator levels for the different capacity concepts and calculate different budgeted fixed manufacturing costs per unit. We now discuss the problems with and effects of different denominator-level choices for different purposes, including (a) product costing and capacity management, (b) pricing, (c) performance evaluation, (d) external reporting, and (e) tax requirements.

Product Costing and Capacity Management

Data from normal costing or standard costing are often used in pricing or product-mix decisions. As the Stassen example illustrates, use of theoretical capacity results in an unrealistically small fixed manufacturing cost per unit because it is based on an idealistic and unattainable level of capacity. Theoretical capacity is rarely used to calculate budgeted fixed manufacturing cost per unit because it departs significantly from the real capacity available to a company.

Many companies favor practical capacity as the denominator to calculate budgeted fixed manufacturing cost per unit. Practical capacity in the Stassen example represents the maximum number of units (12,000) that Stassen can reasonably expect to produce per year for the $1,080,000 it will spend annually on capacity. If Stassen had consistently planned to produce fewer units, say 6,000 telescopes each year, it would have built a smaller plant and incurred lower costs.

Stassen budgets $90 in fixed manufacturing cost per unit based on the $1,080,000 it costs to acquire the capacity to produce 12,000 units. This level of plant capacity is an important strategic decision that managers make well before Stassen uses the capacity and even before Stassen knows how much of the capacity it will actually use. That is, budgeted fixed manufacturing cost of $90 per unit measures the *cost per unit of supplying the capacity*.

Demand for Stassen's telescopes in 2012 is expected to be 8,000 units, which is 4,000 units lower than the practical capacity of 12,000 units. However, it costs Stassen $1,080,000 per year to acquire the capacity to make 12,000 units, so the cost of *supplying* the capacity needed to make 12,000 units is still $90 per unit. The capacity and its cost are fixed *in the short run*; unlike variable costs, the capacity supplied does not automatically reduce to match the capacity needed in 2012. As a result, not all of the capacity supplied at $90 per unit will be needed or used in 2012. Using practical capacity as the denominator level, managers can subdivide the cost of resources supplied into used and unused components. At the supply cost of $90 per unit, the manufacturing resources that Stassen will use equal $720,000 ($90 per unit × 8,000 units). Manufacturing resources that Stassen will not use are $360,000 [$90 per unit × (12,000 – 8,000) units].

Using practical capacity as the denominator level sets the cost of capacity at the cost of supplying the capacity, regardless of the demand for the capacity. Highlighting the cost of capacity acquired but not used directs managers' attention toward managing unused capacity, perhaps by designing new products to fill unused capacity, by leasing unused capacity to others, or by eliminating unused capacity. In contrast, using either of the capacity levels based on the demand for Stassen's telescopes—master-budget capacity utilization or normal capacity utilization—hides the amount of unused capacity. If Stassen had used master-budget capacity utilization as the capacity level, it would have calculated budgeted fixed manufacturing cost per unit as $135 ($1,080,000 ÷ 8,000 units). This calculation does not use data about practical capacity, so it does not separately identify the cost of unused capacity. Note, however, that the cost of $135 per unit includes a charge for unused capacity: It comprises the $90 fixed manufacturing resource that would be used to produce each unit at practical capacity plus the cost of unused capacity allocated to each unit, $45 per unit ($360,000 ÷ 8,000 units).

From the perspective of long-run product costing, which cost of capacity should Stassen use for pricing purposes or for benchmarking its product cost structure against competitors: $90 per unit based on practical capacity or $135 per unit based on master-budget capacity utilization? Probably the $90 per unit based on practical capacity. Why? Because $90 per unit represents the budgeted cost per unit of only the capacity used to produce the product, and it explicitly excludes the cost of any unused capacity. Stassen's customers will be willing to pay a price that covers the cost of the capacity actually used but will not want to pay for unused capacity that provides no other benefits to them. Customers expect Stassen to manage its unused capacity or to bear the cost of unused capacity, not pass it along to them. Moreover, if Stassen's competitors manage unused capacity more effectively, the cost of capacity in the competitors' cost structures (which guides competitors' pricing decisions) is likely to approach $90. In the next section we show how the use of normal capacity utilization or master-budget capacity utilization can result in setting selling prices that are not competitive.

Pricing Decisions and the Downward Demand Spiral

The **downward demand spiral** for a company is the continuing reduction in the demand for its products that occurs when competitor prices are not met; as demand drops further, higher and higher unit costs result in greater reluctance to meet competitors' prices.

The easiest way to understand the downward demand spiral is via an example. Assume Stassen uses master-budget capacity utilization of 8,000 units for product costing in 2012. The resulting manufacturing cost is $335 per unit ($200 variable manufacturing cost per unit + $135 fixed manufacturing cost per unit). Assume that in December 2011, a competitor offers to supply a major customer of Stassen (a customer who was expected to purchase 2,000 units in 2012) telescopes at $300 per unit. The Stassen manager, not wanting to show a loss on the account and wanting to recoup all costs in the long run, declines to match the competitor's price. The account is lost. The loss means budgeted fixed manufacturing costs of $1,080,000 will be spread over the remaining master-budget volume of 6,000 units at a rate of $180 per unit ($1,080,000 ÷ 6,000 units).

Suppose yet another Stassen customer, who also accounts for 2,000 units of budgeted volume, receives a bid from a competitor at a price of $350 per unit. The Stassen manager compares this bid with his revised unit cost of $380 ($200 + $180), declines to match the competition, and the account is lost. Planned output would shrink further to 4,000 units. Budgeted fixed manufacturing cost per unit for the remaining 4,000 telescopes would now be $270 ($1,080,000 ÷ 4,000 units). The following table shows the effect of spreading fixed manufacturing costs over a shrinking amount of master-budget capacity utilization:

	A	B	C	D
	Home Insert Page Layout Formulas Data Review View			
1	Master-Budget		Budgeted Fixed	
2	Capacity Utilization	Budgeted Variable	Manufacturing	Budgeted Total
3	Denominator Level	Manufacturing Cost	Cost per Unit	Manufacturing
4	(Units)	per Unit	[$1,080,000 ÷ (1)]	Cost per Unit
5	(1)	(2)	(3)	(4) = (2) + (3)
6	8,000	$200	$135	$335
7	6,000	$200	$180	$380
8	4,000	$200	$270	$470
9	3,000	$200	$360	$560

Practical capacity, by contrast, is a stable measure. The use of practical capacity as the denominator to calculate budgeted fixed manufacturing cost per unit avoids the recalculation of unit costs when expected demand levels change, because the fixed cost rate is calculated based on *capacity available* rather than *capacity used to meet demand*. Managers who use reported unit costs in a mechanical way to set prices are less likely to promote a downward demand spiral when they use practical capacity than when they use normal capacity utilization or master-budget capacity utilization.

Using practical capacity as the denominator level also gives the manager a more accurate idea of the resources needed and used to produce a unit by excluding the cost of unused capacity. As discussed earlier, the cost of manufacturing resources supplied to produce a telescope is $290 ($200 variable manufacturing cost per unit plus $90 fixed manufacturing cost per unit). This cost is lower than the prices offered by Stassen's competitors and would have correctly led the manager to match the prices and retain the accounts (assuming for purposes of this discussion that Stassen has no other costs). If, however, the prices offered by competitors were lower than $290 per unit, the Stassen manager would not recover the cost of resources used to supply telescopes. This would signal to the manager that Stassen was noncompetitive even if it had no unused capacity. The only way then for Stassen to be profitable and retain customers in the long run would be to reduce its manufacturing cost per unit. The Concepts in Action feature on page 319 highlights the downward spiral currently at work in the traditional landline phone industry.

Performance Evaluation

Consider how the choice among normal capacity utilization, master-budget capacity utilization, and practical capacity affects the evaluation of a marketing manager. Normal capacity utilization is often used as a basis for long-run plans. Normal capacity utilization depends on the time span selected and the forecasts made for each year. *However, normal capacity utilization is an average that provides no meaningful feedback to the marketing manager for a particular year.* Using normal capacity utilization as a reference for judging current performance of a marketing manager is an example of misusing a long-run measure for a short-run purpose. Master-budget capacity utilization, rather than normal capacity utilization or practical capacity, should be used to evaluate a marketing manager's performance in the current year, because the master budget is the principal short-run planning and control tool. Managers feel more obligated to reach the levels specified in the master budget, which should have been carefully set in relation to the maximum opportunities for sales in the current year.

When large differences exist between practical capacity and master-budget capacity utilization, several companies (such as Texas Instruments, Polysar, and Sandoz) classify the difference as *planned unused capacity*. One reason for this approach is performance

Concepts in Action

The "Death Spiral" and the End of Landline Telephone Service

Can you imagine a future without traditional landline telephone service? Verizon and AT&T, the two largest telephone service providers in the United States, are already working to make that future a reality. Recently, both companies announced plans to reduce their focus on providing copper-wire telephone service to homes and businesses. According to AT&T, with the rise of mobile phones and Internet communications such as voice over Internet Protocol (VoIP), less than 20% of Americans now rely exclusively on landlines for voice service and another 25% have abandoned them altogether.

But why would telephone companies abandon landlines if 75% of Americans still use them? Continued reduced service demand is leading to higher unit costs, or a downward demand spiral. As AT&T recently told the U.S. Federal Communications Commission, "The business model for legacy phone services is in a death spiral. With an outdated product, falling revenues, and rising costs, the plain-old telephone service business is unsustainable for the long run."

Marketplace statistics support AT&T's claim. From 2000 to 2008, total long-distance access minutes fell by 42%. As a result, revenue from traditional landline phone service decreased by 27% between 2000 and 2007. In 2008 alone, AT&T lost 12% of its landline customers, while Verizon lost 10%. Industry observers estimate that customers are permanently disconnecting 700,000 landline phones every month.

As all these companies lose landline customers and revenue, the costs of maintaining the phone wires strung on poles and dug through trenches is not falling nearly as quickly. It now costs phone companies an average of $52 per year to maintain a copper phone line, up from $43 in 2003, largely because of the declining number of landlines. These costs do not include other expenses required to maintain landline phone service including local support offices, call centers, and garages.

New competitors are taking advantage of this situation. Vonage, the leading Internet phone company, offers its services for as little as $18 per month. Without relying on wires to transmit calls, its direct costs of providing telephone service come to $6.67 a month for each subscriber. And the largest part of that is not true cost, but subsidies to rural phone carriers for connecting long distance calls. As Vonage attracts more customers, its economies of scale will increase while its costs of providing service will decrease for each additional subscriber.

Hamstrung by increasing unit costs, legacy carriers like Verizon and AT&T are unable to compete with Vonage on price. As such, their traditional landline businesses are in permanent decline. So what are these companies doing about it? Verizon is reducing its landline operations by selling large parts of its copper-wire business to smaller companies at a significant discount. AT&T recently petitioned the U.S. government to waive a requirement that it and other carriers maintain their costly landline networks. As the landline phone service "death spiral" continues, the future of telecommunications will include more wireless, fiber optics, and VoIP with less of Alexander Graham Bell's original vision of telephones connected by copper wires.

Source: *Comments of AT&T Inc. on the Transition from the Legacy Circuit-switched Network to Broadband*. Washington, DC: AT&T Inc., December 21, 2009. http://fjallfoss.fcc.gov/ecfs/document/view?id=7020354032; Hansell, Saul. 2009. Verizon boss hangs up on landline phone business. *New York Times*, September 17; Hansell, Saul. 2009. Will the phone industry need a bailout, too? *New York Times*, May 8.

---

evaluation. Consider our Stassen telescope example. The managers in charge of capacity planning usually do not make pricing decisions. Top management decided to build a production facility with 12,000 units of practical capacity, focusing on demand over the next five years. But Stassen's marketing managers, who are mid-level managers, make the pricing decisions. These marketing managers believe they should be held accountable only for the manufacturing overhead costs related to their potential customer base in 2012. The master-budget capacity utilization suggests a customer base in 2012 of 8,000 units (2/3 of the 12,000 practical capacity). Using responsibility accounting principles (see Chapter 6, pp. 199–201), only 2/3 of the budgeted total fixed manufacturing costs ($1,080,000 × 2/3 = $720,000) would be attributed to the fixed capacity costs of meeting 2012 demand. The remaining 1/3 of the numerator ($1,080,000 × 1/3 = $360,000) would be separately shown as the capacity cost of meeting increases in long-run demand expected to occur beyond 2012.[4]

External Reporting

The magnitude of the favorable/unfavorable production-volume variance under absorption costing is affected by the choice of the denominator level used to calculate the budgeted fixed manufacturing cost per unit. Assume the following actual operating information for Stassen in 2012:

	A	B	C
1	Beginning inventory	0	
2	Production	8,000	units
3	Sales	6,000	units
4	Ending inventory	2,000	units
5	Selling price	$ 1,000	per unit
6	Variable manufacturing cost	$ 200	per unit
7	Fixed manufacturing costs	$ 1,080,000	
8	Variable marketing cost	$ 185	per unit sold
9	Fixed marketing costs	$ 1,380,000	

Note that this is the same data used to calculate the income under variable and absorption costing for Stassen in Exhibit 9-1. As before, we assume that there are no price, spending, or efficiency variances in manufacturing costs.

Recall from Chapter 8 the equation used to calculate the production-volume variance:

$$\text{Production-volume variance} = \left(\begin{array}{c}\text{Budgeted} \\ \text{fixed} \\ \text{manufacturing} \\ \text{overhead}\end{array}\right) - \left(\begin{array}{c}\text{Fixed manufacturing overhead allocated using} \\ \text{budgeted cost per output unit} \\ \text{allowed for actual output produced}\end{array}\right)$$

The four different capacity-level concepts result in four different budgeted fixed manufacturing overhead cost rates per unit. The different rates will result in different amounts of fixed manufacturing overhead costs allocated to the 8,000 units actually produced and different amounts of production-volume variance. Using the budgeted fixed manufacturing costs of $1,080,000 (equal to actual fixed manufacturing costs) and the rates calculated on page 315 for different denominator levels, the production-volume variance computations are as follows:

Production-volume variance (theoretical capacity) = $1,080,000 − (8,000 units × $60 per unit)

= $1,080,000 − 480,000

= 600,000 U

Production-volume variance (practical capacity) = $1,080,000 − (8,000 units × $90 per unit)

= $1,080,000 − 720,000

= 360,000 U

Production-volume variance (normal capacity utilization) = $1,080,000 − (8,000 units × $108 per unit)

= $1,080,000 − 864,000

= 216,000 U

---

[4] For further discussion, see T. Klammer, *Capacity Measurement and Improvement* (Chicago: Irwin, 1996). This research was facilitated by CAM-I, an organization promoting innovative cost management practices. CAM-I's research on capacity costs explores ways in which companies can identify types of capacity costs that can be reduced (or eliminated) without affecting the required output to meet customer demand. An example is improving processes to successfully eliminate the costs of capacity held in anticipation of handling difficulties due to imperfect coordination with suppliers and customers.

Production-volume variance (master-budget capacity utilization) $= \$1,080,000 - (8,000 \text{ units} \times \$135 \text{ per unit})$

$= \$1,080,000 - 1,080,000$

$= 0$

How Stassen disposes of its production-volume variance at the end of the fiscal year will determine the effect this variance has on the company's operating income. We now discuss the three alternative approaches Stassen can use to dispose of the production-volume variance. These approaches were first discussed in Chapter 4 (pp. 117–122).

1. **Adjusted allocation-rate approach.** This approach restates all amounts in the general and subsidiary ledgers by using actual rather than budgeted cost rates. Given that actual fixed manufacturing costs are $1,080,000 and actual production is 8,000 units, the recalculated fixed manufacturing cost is $135 per unit ($1,080,000 ÷ 8,000 actual units). Under the adjusted allocation-rate approach, the choice of the capacity level used to calculate the budgeted fixed manufacturing cost per unit has no effect on year-end financial statements. In effect, actual costing is adopted at the end of the fiscal year.

2. **Proration approach.** The underallocated or overallocated overhead is spread among ending balances in Work-in-Process Control, Finished Goods Control, and Cost of Goods Sold. The proration restates the ending balances in these accounts to what they would have been if actual cost rates had been used rather than budgeted cost rates. The proration approach also results in the choice of the capacity level used to calculate the budgeted fixed manufacturing cost per unit having no effect on year-end financial statements.

3. **Write-off variances to cost of goods sold approach.** Exhibit 9-7 shows how use of this approach affects Stassen's operating income for 2012. Recall that Stassen had no beginning inventory, and it had production of 8,000 units and sales of 6,000 units. Therefore, the ending inventory on December 31, 2012, is 2,000 units. Using master-budget capacity utilization as the denominator-level results in assigning the highest amount of fixed manufacturing cost per unit to the 2,000 units in ending inventory (see the line item "deduct ending inventory" in Exhibit 9-7). Accordingly, operating income is highest using master-budget capacity utilization. The differences in operating income for the four denominator-level concepts in Exhibit 9-7 are due to different amounts of fixed manufacturing overhead being inventoried at the end of 2012:

**Fixed Manufacturing Overhead
In December 31, 2012, Inventory**

Theoretical capacity	2,000 units × $60 per unit = $120,000
Practical capacity	2,000 units × $90 per unit = $180,000
Normal capacity utilization	2,000 units × $108 per unit = $216,000
Master-budget capacity utilization	2,000 units × $135 per unit = $270,000

In Exhibit 9-7, for example, the $54,000 difference ($1,500,000 – $1,446,000) in operating income between master-budget capacity utilization and normal capacity utilization is due to the difference in fixed manufacturing overhead inventoried ($270,000 – $216,000).

What is the common reason and explanation for the increasing operating-income numbers in Exhibit 9-4 (p. 310) and Exhibit 9-7? It is the amount of fixed manufacturing costs incurred that is included in ending inventory at the end of the year. As this amount increases, so does operating income. The amount of fixed manufacturing costs inventoried depends on two factors: the number of units in ending inventory and the rate at which fixed manufacturing costs are allocated to each unit. Exhibit 9-4 shows the effect on operating income of increasing the number of units in ending inventory (by increasing production). Exhibit 9-7 shows the effect on operating income of increasing the fixed manufacturing cost allocated per unit (by decreasing the denominator level used to calculate the rate).

Chapter 8 (pp. 275–276) discusses the various issues managers and management accountants must consider when deciding whether to prorate the production-volume

Exhibit 9-7 Income-Statement Effects of Using Alternative Capacity-Level Concepts: Stassen Company for 2012

	A	B	C	D	E	F	G	H	I
1		**Theoretical Capacity**		**Practical Capacity**		**Normal Capacity Utilization**		**Master-Budget Capacity Utilization**	
2	Denominator level in cases	18,000		12,000		10,000		8,000	
3	Revenues[a]	$6,000,000		$6,000,000		$6,000,000		$6,000,000	
4	Cost of goods sold								
5	Beginning inventory	0		0		0		0	
6	Variable manufacturing costs[b]	1,600,000		1,600,000		1,600,000		1,600,000	
7	Fixed manufacturing costs[c]	480,000		720,000		864,000		1,080,000	
8	Cost of goods available for sale	2,080,000		2,320,000		2,464,000		2,680,000	
9	Deduct ending inventory[d]	(520,000)		(580,000)		(616,000)		(670,000)	
10	Cost of goods sold (at standard cost)	1,560,000		1,740,000		1,848,000		2,010,000	
11	Adjustment for production-volume variance	600,000	U	360,000	U	216,000	U	0	
12	Cost of goods sold	2,160,000		2,100,000		2,064,000		2,010,000	
13	Gross margin	3,840,000		3,900,000		3,936,000		3,990,000	
14	Marketing costs[e]	2,490,000		2,490,000		2,490,000		2,490,000	
15	Operating income	$1,350,000		$1,410,000		$1,446,000		$1,500,000	
16									
17	[a]$1,000 × 6,000 units = $6,000,000			[d]Ending inventory costs:					
18	[b]$200 × 8,000 units = $1,600,000			($200 + $60)　 × 2,000 units = $520,000					
19	[c]Fixed manufacturing overhead costs:			($200 + $90)　 × 2,000 units = $580,000					
20	$60 ×　8,000 units = $　480,000			($200 + $108) × 2,000 units = $616,000					
21	$90 ×　8,000 units = $　720,000			($200 + $135) × 2,000 units = $670,000					
22	$108 × 8,000 units = $　864,000			[e]Marketing costs:					
23	$135 × 8,000 units = $1,080,000			$1,380,000 + $185 × 6,000 units = $2,490,000					

variance among inventories and cost of goods sold or to simply write off the variance to cost of goods sold. The objective is to write off the portion of the production-volume variance that represents the cost of capacity not used to support the production of output during the period. Determining this amount is almost always a matter of judgment.

Tax Requirements

Decision Point ▶

What are the major factors managers consider in choosing the capacity level to compute the budgeted fixed manufacturing cost rate?

For tax reporting purposes in the United States, the Internal Revenue Service (IRS) requires companies to assign inventoriable indirect production costs by a "method of allocation which fairly apportions such costs among the various items produced." Approaches that involve the use of either overhead rates (which the IRS terms the "manufacturing burden rate method") or standard costs are viewed as acceptable. Under either approach, U.S. tax reporting requires end-of-period reconciliation between actual and applied indirect costs using the adjusted allocation-rate method or the proration method.[5] More interestingly, under either approach, the IRS permits the use of practical capacity to calculate budgeted fixed manufacturing cost per unit. Further, the production-volume variance thus generated can be deducted for tax purposes in the year in which the cost is incurred. The tax benefits from this policy are evident from Exhibit 9-7. Note that the operating income when the

---

[5] For example, Section 1.471-11 of the U.S. Internal Revenue Code states, "The proper use of the standard cost method . . . requires that a taxpayer must reallocate to the goods in ending inventory a pro rata portion of any net negative or net positive overhead variances." Of course, if the variances are not material in amount, they can be expensed (i.e., written off to cost of goods sold), provided the same treatment is carried out in the firm's financial reports.

denominator is set to practical capacity (column D, where the production volume variance of $360,000 is written off to cost of goods sold) is lower than those under normal capacity utilization (column F) or master-budget capacity utilization (column H).

Planning and Control of Capacity Costs

In addition to the issues previously discussed, managers must take a variety of other factors into account when planning capacity levels and in deciding how best to control and assign capacity costs. These include the level of uncertainty regarding both the expected costs and the expected demand for the installed capacity, the presence of capacity-related issues in nonmanufacturing settings, and the potential use of activity-based costing techniques in allocating capacity costs.

Difficulties in Forecasting Chosen Denominator-Level Concept

Practical capacity measures the available supply of capacity. Managers can usually use engineering studies and human-resource considerations (such as worker safety) to obtain a reliable estimate of this denominator level for the budget period. It is more difficult to obtain reliable estimates of demand-side denominator-level concepts, especially longer-term normal capacity utilization figures. For example, many U.S. steel companies in the 1980s believed they were in the downturn of a demand cycle that would have an upturn within two or three years. After all, steel had been a cyclical business in which upturns followed downturns, making the notion of normal capacity utilization appear reasonable. Unfortunately, the steel cycle in the 1980s did not turn up; some companies and numerous plants closed. More recently, the global economic slowdown has made a mockery of demand projections. Consider that in 2006, the forecast for the Indian automotive market was that annual demand for cars and passenger vehicles would hit 1.92 million in the year 2009–2010. In early 2009, the forecast for the same period was revised downward to 1.37 million vehicles. Even ignoring the vagaries of economic cycles, another problem is that marketing managers of firms are often prone to overestimate their ability to regain lost sales and market share. Their estimate of "normal" demand for their product may consequently reflect an overly optimistic outlook. Master-budget capacity utilization focuses only on the expected demand for the next year. Therefore, master-budget capacity utilization can be more reliably estimated than normal capacity utilization. However, it is still just a forecast, and the true demand realization can be either higher or lower than this estimate.

It is important to understand that costing systems, such as normal costing or standard costing, do not recognize uncertainty the way managers recognize it. A single amount, rather than a range of possible amounts, is used as the denominator level when calculating the budgeted fixed manufacturing cost per unit in absorption costing. Consider Stassen's facility, which has an estimated practical capacity of 12,000 units. The estimated master-budget capacity utilization for 2012 is 8,000 units. However, there is still substantial doubt regarding the actual number of units Stassen will have to manufacture in 2012 and in future years. Managers recognize uncertainty in their capacity-planning decisions. Stassen built its current plant with a 12,000 unit practical capacity in part to provide the capability to meet possible demand surges. Even if such surges do not occur in a given period, do not conclude that capacity unused in a given period is wasted resources. The gains from meeting sudden demand surges may well require having unused capacity in some periods.

Difficulties in Forecasting Fixed Manufacturing Costs

The fixed manufacturing cost rate is based on a numerator (budgeted fixed manufacturing costs) and a denominator (some measure of capacity or capacity utilization). Our discussion so far has emphasized issues concerning the choice of the denominator. Challenging issues also arise in measuring the numerator. For example, deregulation of the U.S. electric utility industry has resulted in many electric utilities becoming unprofitable. This situation has led to write-downs in the values of the utilities' plants and equipment. The

Learning Objective **7**

Understand other issues that play an important role in capacity planning and control

. . . uncertainty regarding the expected spending on capacity costs and the demand for installed capacity, the role of capacity-related issues in nonmanufacturing areas, and the possible use of activity-based costing techniques in allocating capacity costs

write-downs reduce the numerator because there is less depreciation expense included in the calculation of fixed capacity cost per kilowatt-hour of electricity produced. The difficulty that managers face in this situation is that the amount of write-downs is not clear-cut but, rather, a matter of judgment.

Nonmanufacturing Costs

Capacity costs also arise in nonmanufacturing parts of the value chain. Stassen may acquire a fleet of vehicles capable of distributing the practical capacity of its production facility. When actual production is below practical capacity, there will be unused-capacity cost issues with the distribution function, as well as with the manufacturing function.

As you saw in Chapter 8, capacity cost issues are prominent in many service-sector companies, such as airlines, hospitals, and railroads—even though these companies carry no inventory and so have no inventory costing problems. For example, in calculating the fixed overhead cost per patient-day in its obstetrics and gynecology department, a hospital must decide which denominator level to use: practical capacity, normal capacity utilization, or master-budget capacity utilization. Its decision may have implications for capacity management, as well as pricing and performance evaluation.

Activity-Based Costing

> **Decision Point** ▶
>
> What issues must managers take into account when planning capacity levels and for assigning capacity costs?

To maintain simplicity and the focus on choosing a denominator to calculate a budgeted fixed manufacturing cost rate, our Stassen example assumed that all fixed manufacturing costs had a single cost driver: telescope units produced. As you saw in Chapter 5, activity-based costing systems have multiple overhead cost pools at the output-unit, batch, product-sustaining, and facility-sustaining levels—each with its own cost driver. In calculating activity cost rates (for fixed costs of setups and material handling, say), management must choose a capacity level for the quantity of the cost driver (setup-hours or loads moved). Should management use practical capacity, normal capacity utilization, or master-budget capacity utilization? For all the reasons described in this chapter (such as pricing and capacity management), most proponents of activity-based costing argue that practical capacity should be used as the denominator level to calculate activity cost rates.

Problem for Self-Study

Assume Stassen Company on January 1, 2012, decides to contract with another company to preassemble a large percentage of the components of its telescopes. The revised manufacturing cost structure during the 2012–2014 period is as follows:

Variable manufacturing cost per unit produced		
Direct materials	$	250
Direct manufacturing labor		20
Manufacturing overhead		5
Total variable manufacturing cost per unit produced	$	275
Fixed manufacturing costs		$480,000

Under the revised cost structure, a larger percentage of Stassen's manufacturing costs are variable with respect to units produced. The denominator level of production used to calculate budgeted fixed manufacturing cost per unit in 2012, 2013, and 2014 is 8,000 units. Assume no other change from the data underlying Exhibits 9-1 and 9-2. Summary information pertaining to absorption-costing operating income and variable-costing operating income with this revised cost structure is as follows:

	2012	2013	2014
Absorption-costing operating income	$1,500,000	$1,560,000	$2,340,000
Variable-costing operating income	1,380,000	1,650,000	2,190,000
Difference	$ 120,000	$ (90,000)	$ 150,000

Required

1. Compute the budgeted fixed manufacturing cost per unit in 2012, 2013, and 2014.
2. Explain the difference between absorption-costing operating income and variable-costing operating income in 2012, 2013, and 2014, focusing on fixed manufacturing costs in beginning and ending inventory.
3. Why are these differences smaller than the differences in Exhibit 9-2?
4. Assume the same preceding information, except that for 2012, the master-budget capacity utilization is 10,000 units instead of 8,000. How would Stassen's absorption-costing income for 2012 differ from the $1,500,000 shown previously? Show your computations.

Solution

1.
$$\text{Budgeted fixed manufacturing cost per unit} = \frac{\text{Budgeted fixed manufacturing costs}}{\text{Budgeted production units}}$$

$$= \frac{\$480,000}{8,000 \text{ units}}$$

$$= \$60 \text{ per unit}$$

2.
$$\begin{array}{l} \text{Absorption-costing} \\ \text{operating} \\ \text{income} \end{array} - \begin{array}{l} \text{Variable-costing} \\ \text{operating} \\ \text{income} \end{array} = \begin{array}{l} \text{Fixed manufacturing} \\ \text{costs in ending inventory} \\ \text{under absorption costing} \end{array} - \begin{array}{l} \text{Fixed manufacturing costs} \\ \text{in beginning inventory} \\ \text{under absorption costing} \end{array}$$

2012: $1,500,000 − $1,380,000 = ($60 per unit × 2,000 units) − ($600 per unit × 0 units)

$120,000 = $120,000

2013: $1,560,000 − $1,650,000 = ($60 per unit × 500 units) − ($60 per unit × 2,000 units)

−$90,000 = −$90,000

2014: $2,340,000 − $2,190,000 = ($60 per unit × 3,000 units) − ($60 per unit × 500 units)

$150,000 = $150,000

3. Subcontracting a large part of manufacturing has greatly reduced the magnitude of fixed manufacturing costs. This reduction, in turn, means differences between absorption costing and variable costing are much smaller than in Exhibit 9-2.

4. Given the higher master-budget capacity utilization level of 10,000 units, the budgeted fixed manufacturing cost rate for 2012 is now as follows:

$$\frac{\$480,000}{10,000 \text{ units}} = \$48 \text{ per unit}$$

The manufacturing cost per unit is $323 ($275 + $48). So, the production-volume variance for 2012 is

(10,000 units − 8,000 units) × $48 per unit = $96,000 U

The absorption-costing income statement for 2012 is as follows:

Revenues: $1,000 per unit × 6,000 units	$6,000,000
Cost of goods sold:	
Beginning inventory	0
Variable manufacturing costs: $275 per unit × 8,000 units	2,200,000
Fixed manufacturing costs: $48 per unit × 8,000 units	384,000
Cost of goods available for sale	2,584,000
Deduct ending inventory: $323 per unit × 2,000 units	(646,000)
Cost of goods sold (at standard costs)	1,938,000
Adjustment for production-volume variance	96,000 U
Cost of goods sold	2,034,000
Gross margin	3,966,000
Marketing costs: $1,380,000 fixed + ($185 per unit) × (6,000 units sold)	2,490,000
Operating income	$1,476,000

The higher denominator level used to calculate the budgeted fixed manufacturing cost per unit means that fewer fixed manufacturing costs are inventoried ($48 per unit × 2,000 units = $96,000) than when the master-budget capacity utilization was 8,000 units ($60 per unit × 2,000 units = $120,000). This difference of $24,000 ($120,000 – $96,000) results in operating income being lower by $24,000 relative to the prior calculated income level of $1,500,000.

Decision Points

The following question-and-answer format summarizes the chapter's learning objectives. Each decision presents a key question related to a learning objective. The guidelines are the answer to that question.

Decision	Guidelines
1. How does variable costing differ from absorption costing?	Variable costing and absorption costing differ in only one respect: how to account for fixed manufacturing costs. Under variable costing, fixed manufacturing costs are excluded from inventoriable costs and are a cost of the period in which they are incurred. Under absorption costing, fixed manufacturing costs are inventoriable and become a part of cost of goods sold in the period when sales occur.
2. How does income differ under variable and absorption costing?	The variable-costing income statement is based on the contribution-margin format. Under it, operating income is driven by the unit level of sales. Under absorption costing, the income statement follows the gross-margin format. Operating income is driven by the unit level of production, the unit level of sales, and the denominator level used for assigning fixed costs.
3. Why might managers build up finished goods inventory if they use absorption costing?	When absorption costing is used, managers can increase current operating income by producing more units for inventory. Producing for inventory absorbs more fixed manufacturing costs into inventory and reduces costs expensed in the period. Critics of absorption costing label this manipulation of income as the major negative consequence of treating fixed manufacturing costs as inventoriable costs.
4. How does throughput costing differ from variable costing and absorption costing?	Throughput costing treats all costs except direct materials as costs of the period in which they are incurred. Throughput costing results in a lower amount of manufacturing costs being inventoried than either variable or absorption costing.
5. What are the various capacity levels a company can use to compute the budgeted fixed manufacturing cost rate?	Capacity levels can be measured in terms of capacity supplied—theoretical capacity or practical capacity. Capacity can also be measured in terms of output demanded—normal capacity utilization or master-budget capacity utilization.
6. What are the major factors managers consider in choosing the capacity level to compute the budgeted fixed manufacturing cost rate?	The major factors managers consider in choosing the capacity level to compute the budgeted fixed manufacturing cost rate are (a) effect on product costing and capacity management, (b) effect on pricing decisions, (c) effect on performance evaluation, (d) effect on financial statements, and (e) regulatory requirements.
7. What issues must managers take into account when planning capacity levels and for assigning capacity costs?	Critical factors in this regard include the uncertainty about the expected spending on capacity costs and the demand for the installed capacity, the role of capacity-related issues in nonmanufacturing areas, and the possible use of activity-based costing techniques in allocating capacity costs.

Appendix

Breakeven Points in Variable Costing and Absorption Costing

Chapter 3 introduced cost-volume-profit analysis. If variable costing is used, the breakeven point (that's where operating income is $0) is computed in the usual manner. There is only one breakeven point in this case, and it depends on (1) fixed (manufacturing and operating) costs and (2) contribution margin per unit.

The formula for computing the breakeven point under variable costing is a special case of the more general target operating income formula from Chapter 3 (p. 70):

$$\text{Let } Q = \text{Number of units sold to earn the target operating income}$$

$$\text{Then } Q = \frac{\text{Total fixed costs} + \text{Target operating income}}{\text{Contribution margin per unit}}$$

Breakeven occurs when the target operating income is $0. In our Stassen illustration for 2012 (see Exhibit 9-1, p. 304):

$$Q = \frac{(\$1,080,000 + \$1,380,000) + \$0}{(\$1,000 - (\$200 + \$185))} = \frac{\$2,460,000}{\$615}$$

$$= 4,000 \text{ units}$$

We now verify that Stassen will achieve breakeven under variable costing by selling 4,000 units:

Revenues, $1,000 × 4,000 units	$4,000,000
Variable costs, $385 × 4,000 units	1,540,000
Contribution margin, $615 × 4,000 units	2,460,000
Fixed costs	2,460,000
Operating income	$ 0

If absorption costing is used, the required number of units to be sold to earn a specific target operating income is not unique because of the number of variables involved. The following formula shows the factors that will affect the target operating income under absorption costing:

$$Q = \frac{\begin{array}{c}\text{Total} \\ \text{fixed} \\ \text{costs}\end{array} + \begin{array}{c}\text{Target} \\ \text{operating} \\ \text{income}\end{array} + \left[\begin{array}{c}\text{Fixed} \\ \text{manufacturing} \\ \text{cost rate}\end{array} \times \left(\begin{array}{c}\text{Breakeven} \\ \text{sales} \\ \text{in units}\end{array} - \begin{array}{c}\text{Units} \\ \text{produced}\end{array}\right)\right]}{\text{Contribution margin per unit}}$$

In this formula, the numerator is the sum of three terms (from the perspective of the two "+" signs), compared with two terms in the numerator of the variable-costing formula stated earlier. The additional term in the numerator under absorption costing is as follows:

$$\left[\begin{array}{c}\text{Fixed manufacturing} \\ \text{cost rate}\end{array} \times \left(\begin{array}{c}\text{Breakeven sales} \\ \text{in units}\end{array} - \begin{array}{c}\text{Units} \\ \text{produced}\end{array}\right)\right]$$

This term reduces the fixed costs that need to be recovered when units produced exceed the breakeven sales quantity. When production exceeds the breakeven sales quantity, some of the fixed manufacturing costs that are expensed under variable costing are not expensed under absorption costing; they are instead included in finished goods inventory.[6]

For Stassen Company in 2012, suppose that actual production is 5,280 units. Then, one breakeven point, Q, under absorption costing is as follows:

$$Q = \frac{(\$1,080,000 + \$1,380,000) + \$0 + [\$135 \times (Q - 5,280)]}{(\$1,000 - (\$200 + \$185))}$$

$$= \frac{(\$2,460,000 + \$135Q - \$712,800)}{\$615}$$

$$\$615Q = \$1,747,200 + \$135Q$$

$$\$480Q = \$1,747,200$$

$$Q = 3,640$$

---

[6] The reverse situation, where production is lower than the breakeven sales quantity, is not possible unless the firm has opening inventory. In that case, provided the variable manufacturing cost per unit and the fixed manufacturing cost rate are constant over time, the breakeven formula given is still valid.

We next verify that production of 5,280 units and sales of 3,640 units will lead Stassen to breakeven under absorption costing:

Revenues, $1,000 × 3,640 units		$3,640,000
Cost of goods sold:		
Cost of goods sold at standard cost, $335 × 3,640 units	$1,219,400	
Production-volume variance, $135 × (8,000 – 5,280) units	367,200 U	1,586,600
Gross margin		2,053,400
Marketing costs:		
Variable marketing costs, $185 × 3,640 units	673,400	
Fixed marketing costs	1,380,000	2,053,400
Operating income		$ 0

The breakeven point under absorption costing depends on (1) fixed manufacturing costs, (2) fixed operating (marketing) costs, (3) contribution margin per unit, (4) unit level of production, and (5) the capacity level chosen as the denominator to set the fixed manufacturing cost rate. For Stassen in 2012, a combination of 3,640 units sold, fixed manufacturing costs of $1,080,000, fixed marketing costs of $1,380,000, contribution margin per unit of $615, an 8,000-unit denominator level, and production of 5,280 units would result in an operating income of $0. *Note, however, that there are many combinations of these five factors that would give an operating income of $0.* For example, holding all other factors constant, a combination of 6,240 units produced and 3,370 units sold also results in an operating income of $0 under absorption costing. We provide verification of this alternative breakeven point next:

Revenues, $1,000 × 3,370 units		$3,370,000
Cost of goods sold:		
Cost of goods sold at standard cost, $335 × 3,370 units	$1,128,950	
Production-volume variance, $135 × (8,000 – 6,240) units	237,600 U	1,366,550
Gross margin		2,003,450
Marketing costs:		
Variable marketing costs, $185 × 3,370 units	623,450	
Fixed marketing costs	1,380,000	2,003,450
Operating income		$ 0

Suppose actual production in 2012 was equal to the denominator level, 8,000 units, and there were no units sold and no fixed marketing costs. All the units produced would be placed in inventory, so all the fixed manufacturing costs would be included in inventory. There would be no production-volume variance. Under these conditions, the company could break even under absorption costing with no sales whatsoever! In contrast, under variable costing, the operating loss would be equal to the fixed manufacturing costs of $1,080,000.

Terms to Learn

This chapter and the Glossary at the end of the book contain definitions of the following important terms:

absorption costing (**p. 302**)

direct costing (**p. 302**)

downward demand spiral (**p. 317**)

master-budget capacity utilization (**p. 315**)

normal capacity utilization (**p. 315**)

practical capacity (**p. 315**)

super-variable costing (**p. 312**)

theoretical capacity (**p. 314**)

throughput costing (**p. 312**)

variable costing (**p. 301**)

Assignment Material

MyAccountingLab

Questions

9-1 Differences in operating income between variable costing and absorption costing are due solely to accounting for fixed costs. Do you agree? Explain.

9-2 Why is the term *direct costing* a misnomer?

9-3 Do companies in either the service sector or the merchandising sector make choices about absorption costing versus variable costing?

9-4 Explain the main conceptual issue under variable costing and absorption costing regarding the timing for the release of fixed manufacturing overhead as expense.

9-5 "Companies that make no variable-cost/fixed-cost distinctions must use absorption costing, and those that do make variable-cost/fixed-cost distinctions must use variable costing." Do you agree? Explain.

9-6 The main trouble with variable costing is that it ignores the increasing importance of fixed costs in manufacturing companies. Do you agree? Why?

9-7 Give an example of how, under absorption costing, operating income could fall even though the unit sales level rises.

9-8 What are the factors that affect the breakeven point under (a) variable costing and (b) absorption costing?

9-9 Critics of absorption costing have increasingly emphasized its potential for leading to undesirable incentives for managers. Give an example.

9-10 What are two ways of reducing the negative aspects associated with using absorption costing to evaluate the performance of a plant manager?

9-11 What denominator-level capacity concepts emphasize the output a plant can supply? What denominator-level capacity concepts emphasize the output customers demand for products produced by a plant?

9-12 Describe the downward demand spiral and its implications for pricing decisions.

9-13 Will the financial statements of a company always differ when different choices at the start of the accounting period are made regarding the denominator-level capacity concept?

9-14 What is the IRS's requirement for tax reporting regarding the choice of a denominator-level capacity concept?

9-15 "The difference between practical capacity and master-budget capacity utilization is the best measure of management's ability to balance the costs of having too much capacity and having too little capacity." Do you agree? Explain.

Exercises

9-16 **Variable and absorption costing, explaining operating-income differences.** Nascar Motors assembles and sells motor vehicles and uses standard costing. Actual data relating to April and May 2011 are as follows:

	Home	Insert	Page Layout	Formulas	Data	Review	
	A				B	C	D
1					April		May
2	Unit data						
3	Beginning inventory				0		150
4	Production				500		400
5	Sales				350		520
6	Variable costs						
7	Manufacturing cost per unit produced				$ 10,000		$ 10,000
8	Operating (marketing) cost per unit sold				3,000		3,000
9	Fixed costs						
10	Manufacturing costs				$2,000,000		$2,000,000
11	Operating (marketing) costs				600,000		600,000

The selling price per vehicle is $24,000. The budgeted level of production used to calculate the budgeted fixed manufacturing cost per unit is 500 units. There are no price, efficiency, or spending variances. Any production-volume variance is written off to cost of goods sold in the month in which it occurs.

1. Prepare April and May 2011 income statements for Nascar Motors under (a) variable costing and (b) absorption costing.   **Required**
2. Prepare a numerical reconciliation and explanation of the difference between operating income for each month under variable costing and absorption costing.

9-17 **Throughput costing (continuation of 9-16).** The variable manufacturing costs per unit of Nascar Motors are as follows:

	Home	Insert	Page Layout	Formulas	Data	Review
	A				B	C
1					April	May
7	Direct material cost per unit				$6,700	$6,700
8	Direct manufacturing labor cost per unit				1,500	1,500
9	Manufacturing overhead cost per unit				1,800	1,800

Required

1. Prepare income statements based on variable costing for each of the two years.
2. Prepare income statements based on absorption costing for each of the two years.
3. Prepare a numerical reconciliation and explanation of the difference between operating income for each year under absorption costing and variable costing.
4. Critics have claimed that a widely used accounting system has led to undesirable buildups of inventory levels. (a) Is variable costing or absorption costing more likely to lead to such buildups? Why? (b) What can be done to counteract undesirable inventory buildups?

9-24 Variable and absorption costing, sales, and operating-income changes. Helmetsmart, a three-year-old company, has been producing and selling a single type of bicycle helmet. Helmetsmart uses standard costing. After reviewing the income statements for the first three years, Stuart Weil, president of Helmetsmart, commented, "I was told by our accountants—and in fact, I have memorized—that our breakeven volume is 49,000 units. I was happy that we reached that sales goal in each of our first two years. But, here's the strange thing: In our first year, we sold 49,000 units and indeed we broke even. Then, in our second year we sold the same volume and had a positive operating income. I didn't complain, of course . . . but here's the bad part. In our third year, we *sold 20% more* helmets, but our *operating income fell by more than 80%* relative to the second year! We didn't change our selling price or cost structure over the past three years and have no price, efficiency, or spending variances . . . so what's going on?!"

	Home	Insert	Page Layout	Formulas	Data	Review	View
	A				B	C	D
1	**Absorption Costing**						
2					**2011**	**2012**	**2013**
3	Sales (units)				49,000	49,000	58,800
4	Revenues				$1,960,000	$1,960,000	$2,352,000
5	Cost of goods sold						
6	Beginning inventory				0	0	352,800
7	Production				1,764,000	2,116,800	1,764,000
8	Available for sale				1,764,000	2,116,800	2,116,800
9	Deduct ending inventory				0	(352,800)	0
10	Adjustment for production-volume variance				0	(215,600)	0
11	Cost of goods sold				1,764,000	1,548,400	2,116,800
12	Gross margin				196,000	411,600	235,200
13	Selling and administrative expenses (all fixed)				196,000	196,000	196,000
14	Operating income				$ 0	$ 215,600	$ 39,200
15							
16	Beginning inventory				0	0	9,800
17	Production (units)				49,000	58,800	49,000
18	Sales (units)				49,000	49,000	58,800
19	Ending inventory				0	9,800	0
20	Variable manufacturing cost per unit				$ 14	$ 14	$ 14
21	Fixed manufacturing overhead costs				$1,078,000	$1,078,000	$1,078,000
22	Fixed manuf. costs allocated per unit produced				$ 22	$ 22	$ 22

Required

1. What denominator level is Helmetsmart using to allocate fixed manufacturing costs to the bicycle helmets? How is Helmetsmart disposing of any favorable or unfavorable production-volume variance at the end of the year? Explain your answer briefly.
2. How did Helmetsmart's accountants arrive at the breakeven volume of 49,000 units?
3. Prepare a variable costing-based income statement for each year. Explain the variation in variable costing operating income for each year based on contribution margin per unit and sales volume.
4. Reconcile the operating incomes under variable costing and absorption costing for each year, and use this information to explain to Stuart Weil the positive operating income in 2012 and the drop in operating income in 2013.

9-25 **Capacity management, denominator-level capacity concepts.** Match each of the following items with one or more of the denominator-level capacity concepts by putting the appropriate letter(s) by each item:

a. Theoretical capacity
b. Practical capacity
c. Normal capacity utilization
d. Master-budget capacity utilization

1. Measures the denominator level in terms of what a plant can supply
2. Is based on producing at full efficiency all the time
3. Represents the expected level of capacity utilization for the next budget period
4. Measures the denominator level in terms of demand for the output of the plant
5. Takes into account seasonal, cyclical, and trend factors
6. Should be used for performance evaluation in the current year
7. Represents an ideal benchmark
8. Highlights the cost of capacity acquired but not used
9. Should be used for long-term pricing purposes
10. Hides the cost of capacity acquired but not used
11. If used as the denominator-level concept, would avoid the restatement of unit costs when expected demand levels change

9-26 **Denominator-level problem.** Thunder Bolt, Inc., is a manufacturer of the very popular G36 motorcycles. The management at Thunder Bolt has recently adopted absorption costing and is debating which denominator-level concept to use. The G36 motorcycles sell for an average price of $8,200. Budgeted fixed manufacturing overhead costs for 2012 are estimated at $6,480,000. Thunder Bolt, Inc., uses subassembly operators that provide component parts. The following are the denominator-level options that management has been considering:

a. Theoretical capacity—based on three shifts, completion of five motorcycles per shift, and a 360-day year—$3 \times 5 \times 360 = 5,400$.
b. Practical capacity—theoretical capacity adjusted for unavoidable interruptions, breakdowns, and so forth—$3 \times 4 \times 320 = 3,840$.
c. Normal capacity utilization—estimated at 3,240 units.
d. Master-budget capacity utilization—the strengthening stock market and the growing popularity of motorcycles have prompted the marketing department to issue an estimate for 2012 of 3,600 units.

1. Calculate the budgeted fixed manufacturing overhead cost rates under the four denominator-level concepts.   `Required`
2. What are the benefits to Thunder Bolt, Inc., of using either theoretical capacity or practical capacity?
3. Under a cost-based pricing system, what are the negative aspects of a master-budget denominator level? What are the positive aspects?

9-27 **Variable and absorption costing and breakeven points.** Mega-Air, Inc., manufactures a specialized snowboard made for the advanced snowboarder. Mega-Air began 2011 with an inventory of 240 snowboards. During the year, it produced 900 boards and sold 995 for $750 each. Fixed production costs were $280,000 and variable production costs were $335 per unit. Fixed advertising, marketing, and other general and administrative expenses were $112,000 and variable shipping costs were $15 per board. Assume that the cost of each unit in beginning inventory is equal to 2011 inventory cost.

1. Prepare an income statement assuming Mega-Air uses variable costing.   `Required`
2. Prepare an income statement assuming Mega-Air uses absorption costing. Mega-Air uses a denominator level of 1,000 units. Production-volume variances are written off to cost of goods sold.
3. Compute the breakeven point in units sold assuming Mega-Air uses the following:
  a. Variable costing
  b. Absorption costing (Production = 900 boards)
4. Provide proof of your preceding breakeven calculations.
5. Assume that $20,000 of fixed administrative costs were reclassified as fixed production costs. Would this change affect breakeven point using variable costing? What if absorption costing were used? Explain.
6. The company that supplies Mega-Air with its specialized impact-resistant material has announced a price increase of $25 for each board. What effect would this have on the breakeven points previously calculated?

Problems

9-28 Variable costing versus absorption costing. The Mavis Company uses an absorption-costing system based on standard costs. Total variable manufacturing cost, including direct material cost, is $3 per unit; the standard production rate is 10 units per machine-hour. Total budgeted and actual fixed manufacturing overhead costs are $420,000. Fixed manufacturing overhead is allocated at $7 per machine-hour ($420,000 ÷ 60,000 machine-hours of denominator level). Selling price is $5 per unit. Variable operating (nonmanufacturing) cost, which is driven by units sold, is $1 per unit. Fixed operating (nonmanufacturing) costs are $120,000. Beginning inventory in 2012 is 30,000 units; ending inventory is 40,000 units. Sales in 2012 are 540,000 units. The same standard unit costs persisted throughout 2011 and 2012. For simplicity, assume that there are no price, spending, or efficiency variances.

Required

1. Prepare an income statement for 2012 assuming that the production-volume variance is written off at year-end as an adjustment to cost of goods sold.
2. The president has heard about variable costing. She asks you to recast the 2012 statement as it would appear under variable costing.
3. Explain the difference in operating income as calculated in requirements 1 and 2.
4. Graph how fixed manufacturing overhead is accounted for under absorption costing. That is, there will be two lines: one for the budgeted fixed manufacturing overhead (which is equal to the actual fixed manufacturing overhead in this case) and one for the fixed manufacturing overhead allocated. Show how the production-volume variance might be indicated in the graph.
5. Critics have claimed that a widely used accounting system has led to undesirable buildups of inventory levels. (a) Is variable costing or absorption costing more likely to lead to such buildups? Why? (b) What can be done to counteract undesirable inventory buildups?

9-29 Variable costing and absorption costing, the All-Fixed Company. (R. Marple, adapted) It is the end of 2011. The All-Fixed Company began operations in January 2010. The company is so named because it has no variable costs. All its costs are fixed; they do not vary with output.

The All-Fixed Company is located on the bank of a river and has its own hydroelectric plant to supply power, light, and heat. The company manufactures a synthetic fertilizer from air and river water and sells its product at a price that is not expected to change. It has a small staff of employees, all paid fixed annual salaries. The output of the plant can be increased or decreased by adjusting a few dials on a control panel.

The following budgeted and actual data are for the operations of the All-Fixed Company. All-Fixed uses budgeted production as the denominator level and writes off any production-volume variance to cost of goods sold.

	2010	2011[a]
Sales	20,000 tons	20,000 tons
Production	40,000 tons	0 tons
Selling price	$ 20 per ton	$ 20 per ton
Costs (all fixed):		
Manufacturing	$320,000	$320,000
Operating (nonmanufacturing)	$ 60,000	$ 60,000

[a] Management adopted the policy, effective January 1, 2011, of producing only as much product as needed to fill sales orders. During 2011, sales were the same as for 2010 and were filled entirely from inventory at the start of 2011.

Required

1. Prepare income statements with one column for 2010, one column for 2011, and one column for the two years together, using (a) variable costing and (b) absorption costing.
2. What is the breakeven point under (a) variable costing and (b) absorption costing?
3. What inventory costs would be carried in the balance sheet on December 31, 2010 and 2011, under each method?
4. Assume that the performance of the top manager of the company is evaluated and rewarded largely on the basis of reported operating income. Which costing method would the manager prefer? Why?

9-30 **Comparison of variable costing and absorption costing.** Hinkle Company uses standard costing. Tim Bartina, the new president of Hinkle Company, is presented with the following data for 2012:

	A	B	C
		Home Insert Page Layout Formulas Data Review View	
1	Hinkle Company		
2	Income Statements for the Year Ended December 31, 2012		
3		**Variable**	**Absorption**
4		**Costing**	**Costing**
5	Revenues	$9,000,000	$9,000,000
6	Cost of goods sold (at standard costs)	4,680,000	5,860,000
7	Fixed manufacturing overhead (budgeted)	1,200,000	-
8	Fixed manufacturing overhead variances (all unfavorable):		
9	Spending	100,000	100,000
10	Production volume	-	400,000
11	Total marketing and administrative costs (all fixed)	1,500,000	1,500,000
12	Total costs	7,480,000	7,860,000
13	Operating income	$1,520,000	$1,140,000
14			
15	Inventories (at standard costs)		
16	December 31, 2011	$1,200,000	$1,720,000
17	December 31, 2012	66,000	206,000

Required

1. At what percentage of denominator level was the plant operating during 2012?
2. How much fixed manufacturing overhead was included in the 2011 and the 2012 ending inventory under absorption costing?
3. Reconcile and explain the difference in 2012 operating incomes under variable and absorption costing.
4. Tim Bartina is concerned: He notes that despite an increase in sales over 2011, 2012 operating income has actually declined under absorption costing. Explain how this occurred.

9-31 **Effects of differing production levels on absorption costing income: Metrics to minimize inventory buildups.** University Press produces textbooks for college courses. The company recently hired a new editor, Leslie White, to handle production and sales of books for an introduction to accounting course. Leslie's compensation depends on the gross margin associated with sales of this book. Leslie needs to decide how many copies of the book to produce. The following information is available for the fall semester 2011:

Estimated sales	20,000 books
Beginning inventory	0 books
Average selling price	$80 per book
Variable production costs	$50 per book
Fixed production costs	$400,000 per semester

The fixed cost allocation rate is based on expected sales and is therefore equal to $400,000/20,000 books = $20 per book

Leslie has decided to produce either 20,000, 24,000, or 30,000 books.

Required

1. Calculate expected gross margin if Leslie produces 20,000, 24,000, or 30,000 books. (Make sure you include the production-volume variance as part of cost of goods sold.)
2. Calculate ending inventory in units and in dollars for each production level.

3. Managers who are paid a bonus that is a function of gross margin may be inspired to produce a product in excess of demand to maximize their own bonus. The chapter suggested metrics to discourage managers from producing products in excess of demand. Do you think the following metrics will accomplish this objective? Show your work.

   a. Incorporate a charge of 10% of the cost of the ending inventory as an expense for evaluating the manager.

   b. Include nonfinancial measures (such as the ones recommended on p. 311) when evaluating management and rewarding performance.

9-32 Alternative denominator-level capacity concepts, effect on operating income. Lucky Lager has just purchased the Austin Brewery. The brewery is two years old and uses absorption costing. It will "sell" its product to Lucky Lager at $45 per barrel. Paul Brandon, Lucky Lager's controller, obtains the following information about Austin Brewery's capacity and budgeted fixed manufacturing costs for 2012:

	Home	Insert	Page Layout	Formulas	Data	Review	View	
	A		B	C	D	E		
1			Budgeted Fixed	Days of	Hours of			
2	Denominator-Level		Manufacturing	Production	Production	Barrels		
3	Capacity Concept		Overhead per Period	per Period	per Day	per Hour		
4	Theoretical capacity		$28,000,000	360	24	540		
5	Practical capacity		$28,000,000	350	20	500		
6	Normal capacity utilization		$28,000,000	350	20	400		
7	Master-budget capacity for each half year							
8	(a) January–June 2012		$14,000,000	175	20	320		
9	(b) July–December 2012		$14,000,000	175	20	480		

Required

1. Compute the budgeted fixed manufacturing overhead rate per barrel for each of the denominator-level capacity concepts. Explain why they are different.
2. In 2012, the Austin Brewery reported these production results:

	Home	Insert	Page Layout	Formulas	Data	
	A				B	
12	Beginning inventory in barrels, 1-1-2012				0	
13	Production in barrels				2,600,000	
14	Ending inventory in barrels, 12-31-2012				200,000	
15	Actual variable manufacturing costs				$78,520,000	
16	Actual fixed manufacturing overhead costs				$27,088,000	

There are no variable cost variances. Fixed manufacturing overhead cost variances are written off to cost of goods sold in the period in which they occur. Compute the Austin Brewery's operating income when the denominator-level capacity is (a) theoretical capacity, (b) practical capacity, and (c) normal capacity utilization.

9-33 Motivational considerations in denominator-level capacity selection (continuation of 9-32).

Required

1. If the plant manager of the Austin Brewery gets a bonus based on operating income, which denominator-level capacity concept would he prefer to use? Explain.
2. What denominator-level capacity concept would Lucky Lager prefer to use for U.S. income-tax reporting? Explain.
3. How might the IRS limit the flexibility of an absorption-costing company like Lucky Lager attempting to minimize its taxable income?

9-34 Denominator-level choices, changes in inventory levels, effect on operating income. Koshu Corporation is a manufacturer of computer accessories. It uses absorption costing based on standard costs and reports the following data for 2011:

	A	B	C
1	Theoretical capacity	280,000	units
2	Practical capacity	224,000	units
3	Normal capacity utilization	200,000	units
4	Selling price	$ 40	per unit
5	Beginning inventory	20,000	units
6	Production	220,000	units
7	Sales volume	230,000	units
8	Variable budgeted manufacturing cost	$ 5	per unit
9	Total budgeted fixed manufacturing costs	$2,800,000	
10	Total budgeted operating (nonmanuf.) costs (all fixed)	$ 900,000	

There are no price, spending, or efficiency variances. Actual operating costs equal budgeted operating costs. The production-volume variance is written off to cost of goods sold. For each choice of denominator level, the budgeted production cost per unit is also the cost per unit of beginning inventory.

Required

1. What is the production-volume variance in 2011 when the denominator level is (a) theoretical capacity, (b) practical capacity, and (c) normal capacity utilization?
2. Prepare absorption costing–based income statements for Koshu Corporation using theoretical capacity, practical capacity, and normal capacity utilization as the denominator levels.
3. Why is the operating income under normal capacity utilization lower than the other two scenarios?
4. Reconcile the difference in operating income based on theoretical capacity and practical capacity with the difference in fixed manufacturing overhead included in inventory.

9-35 Effects of denominator-level choice. Carlisle Company is a manufacturer of precision surgical tools. It initiated standard costing and a flexible budget on January 1, 2011. The company president, Monica Carlisle, has been pondering how fixed manufacturing overhead should be allocated to products. Machine-hours have been chosen as the allocation base. Her remaining uncertainty is the denominator level for machine-hours. She decides to wait for the first month's results before making a final choice of what denominator level should be used from that day forward.

During January 2011, the actual units of output had a standard of 37,680 machine-hours allowed. The fixed manufacturing overhead spending variance was $6,000, favorable. If the company used practical capacity as the denominator level, the production-volume variance would be $12,200, unfavorable. If the company used normal capacity utilization as the denominator level, the production-volume variance would be $2,400, unfavorable. Budgeted fixed manufacturing overhead was $96,600 for the month.

Required

1. Compute the denominator level, assuming that the normal-capacity-utilization concept is chosen.
2. Compute the denominator level, assuming that the practical-capacity concept is chosen.
3. Suppose you are the executive vice president. You want to maximize your 2011 bonus, which depends on 2011 operating income. Assume that the production-volume variance is written off to cost of goods sold at year-end, and assume that the company expects inventories to increase during the year. Which denominator level would you favor? Why?

9-36 Downward demand spiral. Spirelli Company is about to enter the highly competitive personal electronics market with a new optical reader. In anticipation of future growth, the company has leased a large manufacturing facility, and has purchased several expensive pieces of equipment. In 2011, the company's first year, Spirelli budgets for production and sales of 25,000 units, compared with its practical capacity of 50,000. The company's cost data follow:

	A	B
1	Variable manufacturing costs per unit:	
2	Direct materials	$ 24
3	Direct manufacturing labor	36
4	Manufacturing overhead	12
5	Fixed manufacturing overhead	$700,000

Exhibit 10-4

Plot of Weekly Indirect
Manufacturing Labor
Costs and Machine-
Hours for Elegant Rugs

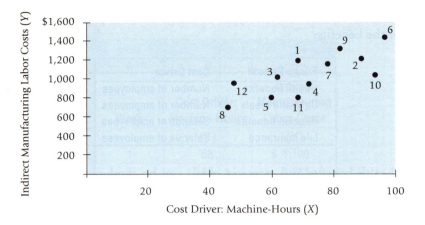

Step 6: Evaluate the cost driver of the estimated cost function. In this step, we describe criteria for evaluating the cost driver of the estimated cost function. We do this after illustrating the high-low method and regression analysis.

High-Low Method

The simplest form of quantitative analysis to "fit" a line to data points is the **high-low method**. It uses only the highest and lowest observed values of the cost driver within the relevant range and their respective costs to estimate the slope coefficient and the constant of the cost function. It provides a first cut at understanding the relationship between a cost driver and costs. We illustrate the high-low method using data from Exhibit 10-3.

	Cost Driver: Machine-Hours (X)	Indirect Manufacturing Labor Costs (Y)
Highest observation of cost driver (week 6)	96	$1,456
Lowest observation of cost driver (week 8)	46	710
Difference	50	$ 746

The slope coefficient, b, is calculated as follows:

$$\text{Slope coefficient} = \frac{\text{Difference between costs associated with highest and lowest observations of the cost driver}}{\text{Difference between highest and lowest observations of the cost driver}}$$

$$= \$746 \div 50 \text{ machine-hours} = \$14.92 \text{ per machine-hour}$$

To compute the constant, we can use either the highest or the lowest observation of the cost driver. Both calculations yield the same answer because the solution technique solves two linear equations with two unknowns, the slope coefficient and the constant. Because

$$y = a + bX$$
$$a = y - bX$$

At the highest observation of the cost driver, the constant, a, is calculated as follows:

$$\text{Constant} = \$1,456 - (\$14.92 \text{ per machine-hour} \times 96 \text{ machine-hours}) = \$23.68$$

And at the lowest observation of the cost driver,

$$\text{Constant} = \$710 - (\$14.92 \text{ per machine-hour} \times 46 \text{ machine-hours}) = \$23.68$$

Thus, the high-low estimate of the cost function is as follows:

$$y = a + bX$$
$$y = \$23.68 + (\$14.92 \text{ per machine-hour} \times \text{Number of machine-hours})$$

The purple line in Exhibit 10-5 shows the estimated cost function using the high-low method (based on the data in Exhibit 10-3). The estimated cost function is a straight line joining the observations with the highest and lowest values of the cost driver (number of machine-hours). Note how this simple high-low line falls "in-between" the data points with three observations on the line, four above it and five below it. The intercept (a = $23.68), the point where the dashed extension of the purple line meets the y-axis, is the constant component of the equation that provides the best linear approximation of how a cost behaves *within the relevant range* of 46 to 96 machine-hours. The intercept should *not* be interpreted as an estimate of the fixed costs of Elegant Rugs if no machines were run. That's because running no machines and shutting down the plant—that is, using zero machine-hours—is *outside the relevant range*.

Suppose indirect manufacturing labor costs in week 6 were $1,280, instead of $1,456, while 96 machine-hours were used. In this case, the highest observation of the cost driver (96 machine-hours in week 6) will not coincide with the newer highest observation of the costs ($1,316 in week 9). How would this change affect our high-low calculation? Given that the cause-and-effect relationship runs *from* the cost driver *to* the costs in a cost function, we choose the highest and lowest observations of the cost driver (the factor that causes the costs to change). The high-low method would still estimate the new cost function using data from weeks 6 (high) and 8 (low).

There is a danger of relying on only two observations to estimate a cost function. Suppose that because a labor contract guarantees certain minimum payments in week 8, indirect manufacturing labor costs in week 8 were $1,000, instead of $710, when only 46 machine-hours were used. The blue line in Exhibit 10-5 shows the cost function that would be estimated by the high-low method using this revised cost. Other than the two points used to draw the line, all other data lie on or below the line! In this case, choosing the highest and lowest observations for machine-hours would result in an estimated cost function that poorly describes the underlying linear cost relationship between number of machine-hours and indirect manufacturing labor costs. In such situations, the high-low method can be modified so that the two observations chosen to estimate the cost function are a *representative high* and a *representative low*. By using this adjustment, managers can avoid having extreme observations, which arise from abnormal events, influence the estimate of the cost function. The modification allows managers to estimate a cost function that is representative of the relationship between the cost driver and costs and, therefore, is more useful for making decisions (such as pricing and performance evaluation).

The advantage of the high-low method is that it is simple to compute and easy to understand; it gives a quick, initial insight into how the cost driver—number of machine-hours—affects indirect manufacturing labor costs. The disadvantage is that it ignores information from all but two observations when estimating the cost function. We next describe the regression analysis method of quantitative analysis that uses all available data to estimate the cost function.

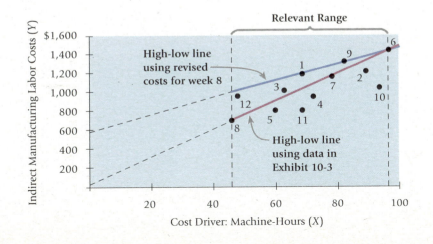

Exhibit 10-5

High-Low Method for Weekly Indirect Manufacturing Labor Costs and Machine-Hours for Elegant Rugs

Regression Analysis Method

Regression analysis is a statistical method that measures the average amount of change in the dependent variable associated with a unit change in one or more independent variables. In the Elegant Rugs example, the dependent variable is total indirect manufacturing labor costs. The independent variable, or cost driver, is number of machine-hours. **Simple regression** analysis estimates the relationship between the dependent variable and *one* independent variable. **Multiple regression** analysis estimates the relationship between the dependent variable and *two or more* independent variables. Multiple regression analysis for Elegant Rugs might use as the independent variables, or cost drivers, number of machine-hours and number of batches. The appendix to this chapter will explore simple regression and multiple regression in more detail.

In later sections, we will illustrate how Excel performs the calculations associated with regression analysis. The following discussion emphasizes how managers interpret and use the output from Excel to make critical strategic decisions. Exhibit 10-6 shows the line developed using regression analysis that best fits the data in columns B and C of Exhibit 10-3. Excel estimates the cost function to be

$$y = \$300.98 + \$10.31X$$

The regression line in Exhibit 10-6 is derived using the least-squares technique. The least-squares technique determines the regression line by minimizing the sum of the squared vertical differences from the data points (the various points in the graph) to the regression line. The vertical difference, called the **residual term**, measures the distance between actual cost and estimated cost for each observation of the cost driver. Exhibit 10-6 shows the residual term for the week 1 data. The line from the observation to the regression line is drawn perpendicular to the horizontal axis, or *x*-axis. The smaller the residual terms, the better the fit between actual cost observations and estimated costs. *Goodness of fit* indicates the strength of the relationship between the cost driver and costs. The regression line in Exhibit 10-6 rises from left to right. The positive slope of this line and small residual terms indicate that, on average, indirect manufacturing labor costs increase as the number of machine-hours increases. The vertical dashed lines in Exhibit 10-6 indicate the relevant range, the range within which the cost function applies.

Instructors and students who want to explore the technical details of estimating the least-squares regression line, can go to the appendix, pages 367–371 and return to this point without any loss of continuity.

The estimate of the slope coefficient, *b*, indicates that indirect manufacturing labor costs vary at the average amount of $10.31 for every machine-hour used within the relevant range. Management can use the regression equation when budgeting for future indirect manufacturing labor costs. For instance, if 90 machine-hours are budgeted for the upcoming week, the predicted indirect manufacturing labor costs would be

$$y = \$300.98 + (\$10.31 \text{ per machine-hour} \times 90 \text{ machine-hours}) = \$1,228.88$$

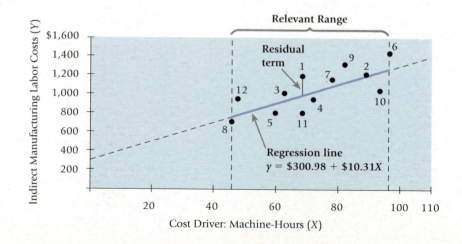

Exhibit 10-6

Regression Model for Weekly Indirect Manufacturing Labor Costs and Machine-Hours for Elegant Rugs

As we have already mentioned, the regression method is more accurate than the high-low method because the regression equation estimates costs using information from all observations, whereas the high-low equation uses information from only two observations. The inaccuracies of the high-low method can mislead managers. Consider the high-low method equation in the preceding section, y = \$23.68 + \$14.92 per machine-hour × Number of machine-hours. For 90 machine-hours, the predicted weekly cost based on the high-low method equation is \$23.68 + (\$14.92 per machine-hour × 90 machine-hours) = \$1,366.48. Suppose that for 7 weeks over the next 12-week period, Elegant Rugs runs its machines for 90 hours each week. Assume average indirect manufacturing labor costs for those 7 weeks are \$1,300. Based on the high-low method prediction of \$1,366.48, Elegant Rugs would conclude it has performed well because actual costs are less than predicted costs. But comparing the \$1,300 performance with the more-accurate \$1,228.88 prediction of the regression model tells a much different story and would probably prompt Elegant Rugs to search for ways to improve its cost performance.

Accurate cost estimation helps managers predict future costs and evaluate the success of cost-reduction initiatives. Suppose the manager at Elegant Rugs is interested in evaluating whether recent strategic decisions that led to changes in the production process and resulted in the data in Exhibit 10-3 have reduced indirect manufacturing labor costs, such as supervision, maintenance, and quality control. Using data on number of machine-hours used and indirect manufacturing labor costs of the previous process (not shown here), the manager estimates the regression equation,

$$y = \$546.26 + (\$15.86 \text{ per machine-hour} \times \text{Number of machine-hours})$$

The constant (\$300.98 versus \$545.26) and the slope coefficient (\$10.31 versus \$15.86) are both smaller for the new process relative to the old process. It appears that the new process has decreased indirect manufacturing labor costs.

Evaluating Cost Drivers of the Estimated Cost Function

How does a company determine the best cost driver when estimating a cost function? In many cases, the choice of a cost driver is aided substantially by understanding both operations and cost accounting.

To see why the understanding of operations is needed, consider the costs to maintain and repair metal-cutting machines at Helix Corporation, a manufacturer of treadmills. Helix schedules repairs and maintenance at a time when production is at a low level to avoid having to take machines out of service when they are needed most. An analysis of the monthly data will then show high repair costs in months of low production and low repair costs in months of high production. Someone unfamiliar with operations might conclude that there is an inverse relationship between production and repair costs. The engineering link between units produced and repair costs, however, is usually clear-cut. Over time, there is a cause-and-effect relationship: the higher the level of production, the higher the repair costs. To estimate the relationship correctly, operating managers and analysts will recognize that repair costs will tend to lag behind periods of high production, and hence, they will use production of prior periods as the cost driver.

In other cases, choosing a cost driver is more subtle and difficult. Consider again indirect manufacturing labor costs at Elegant Rugs. Management believes that both the number of machine-hours and the number of direct manufacturing labor-hours are plausible cost drivers of indirect manufacturing labor costs. However, management is not sure which is the better cost driver. Exhibit 10-7 presents weekly data (in Excel) on indirect manufacturing labor costs and number of machine-hours for the most recent 12-week period from Exhibit 10-3, together with data on the number of direct manufacturing labor-hours for the same period.

◄ Decision Point

What are the steps to estimate a cost function using quantitative analysis?

Learning Objective 5

Describe three criteria used to evaluate and choose cost drivers

. . . economically plausible relationships, goodness of fit, and significant effect of the cost driver on costs

Exhibit 10-7

Weekly Indirect
Manufacturing Labor
Costs, Machine-Hours,
and Direct
Manufacturing Labor-
Hours for Elegant Rugs

	Home	Insert	Page Layout	Formulas	Data	Review
	A	B	C	D		
1	Week	Original Cost Driver: Machine-Hours	Alternate Cost Driver: Direct Manufacturing Labor-Hours (X)	Indirect Manufacturing Labor Costs (Y)		
2	1	68	30	$ 1,190		
3	2	88	35	1,211		
4	3	62	36	1,004		
5	4	72	20	917		
6	5	60	47	770		
7	6	96	45	1,456		
8	7	78	44	1,180		
9	8	46	38	710		
10	9	82	70	1,316		
11	10	94	30	1,032		
12	11	68	29	752		
13	12	48	38	963		
14	Total	862	462	$12,501		
15						

Choosing Among Cost Drivers

What guidance do the different cost-estimation methods provide for choosing among cost drivers? The industrial engineering method relies on analyzing physical relationships between cost drivers and costs, relationships that are difficult to specify in this case. The conference method and the account analysis method use subjective assessments to choose a cost driver and to estimate the fixed and variable components of the cost function. In these cases, managers must rely on their best judgment. Managers cannot use these methods to test and try alternative cost drivers. The major advantages of quantitative methods are that they are objective—a given data set and estimation method result in a unique estimated cost function—and managers can use them to evaluate different cost drivers. We use the regression analysis approach to illustrate how to evaluate different cost drivers.

First, the cost analyst at Elegant Rugs enters data in columns C and D of Exhibit 10-7 in Excel and estimates the following regression equation of indirect manufacturing labor costs based on number of direct manufacturing labor-hours:

$$y = \$744.67 + \$7.72X$$

Exhibit 10-8 shows the plot of the data points for number of direct manufacturing labor-hours and indirect manufacturing labor costs, and the regression line that best fits the data. Recall that Exhibit 10-6 shows the corresponding graph when number of machine-hours is the cost driver. To decide which of the two cost drivers Elegant Rugs should choose, the analyst compares the machine-hour regression equation and the direct manufacturing labor-hour regression equation. There are three criteria used to make this evaluation.

1. **Economic plausibility.** Both cost drivers are economically plausible. However, in the state-of-the-art, highly automated production environment at Elegant Rugs, managers familiar with the operations believe that costs such as machine maintenance are likely to be more closely related to number of machine-hours used than to number of direct manufacturing labor-hours used.

2. **Goodness of fit.** Compare Exhibits 10-6 and 10-8. The vertical differences between actual costs and predicted costs are much smaller for the machine-hours regression than for the direct manufacturing labor-hours regression. Number of machine-hours used, therefore, has a stronger relationship—or goodness of fit—with indirect manufacturing labor costs.

Exhibit 10-8

Regression Model for
Weekly Indirect
Manufacturing Labor
Costs and Direct
Manufacturing Labor-
Hours for Elegant Rugs

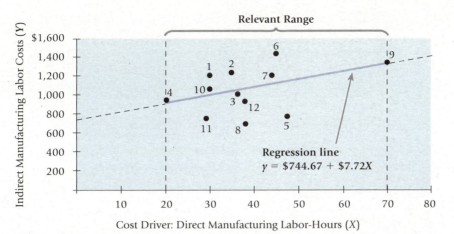

3. **Significance of independent variable.** Again compare Exhibits 10-6 and 10-8 (both of which have been drawn to roughly the same scale). The machine-hours regression line has a steep slope relative to the slope of the direct manufacturing labor-hours regression line. *For the same (or more) scatter of observations about the line (goodness of fit), a flat, or slightly sloped regression line indicates a weak relationship between the cost driver and costs.* In our example, changes in direct manufacturing labor-hours appear to have a small influence or effect on indirect manufacturing labor costs.

Based on this evaluation, managers at Elegant Rugs select number of machine-hours as the cost driver and use the cost function $y = \$300.98 + (\$10.31$ per machine-hour $\times$ Number of machine-hours) to predict future indirect manufacturing labor costs.

Instructors and students who want to explore how regression analysis techniques can be used to choose among different cost drivers can go to the appendix, pages 371–374 and return to this point without any loss of continuity.

Why is choosing the correct cost driver to estimate indirect manufacturing labor costs important? Because identifying the wrong drivers or misestimating cost functions can lead management to incorrect (and costly) decisions along a variety of dimensions. Consider the following strategic decision that management at Elegant Rugs must make. The company is thinking of introducing a new style of carpet that, from a manufacturing standpoint, is similar to the carpets it has manufactured in the past. Prices are set by the market and sales of 650 square yards of this carpet are expected each week. Management estimates 72 machine-hours and 21 direct manufacturing labor-hours would be required per week to produce the 650 square yards of carpet needed. Using the machine-hour regression equation, Elegant Rugs would predict indirect manufacturing labor costs of $y = \$300.98 + (\$10.31$ per machine-hour $\times$ 72 machine-hours) = $1,043.30. If it used direct manufacturing labor-hours as the cost driver, it would incorrectly predict costs of $744.67 + ($7.72 per labor-hour $\times$ 21 labor-hours) = $906.79. If Elegant Rugs chose similarly incorrect cost drivers for other indirect costs as well and systematically underestimated costs, it would conclude that the costs of manufacturing the new style of carpet would be low and basically fixed (fixed because the regression line is nearly flat). But the actual costs driven by number of machine-hours used and other correct cost drivers would be higher. By failing to identify the proper cost drivers, management would be misled into believing the new style of carpet would be more profitable than it actually is. It might decide to introduce the new style of carpet, whereas if Elegant identifies the correct cost driver it might decide not to introduce the new carpet.

Incorrectly estimating the cost function would also have repercussions for cost management and cost control. Suppose number of direct manufacturing labor-hours were used as the cost driver, and actual indirect manufacturing labor costs for the new carpet were $970. Actual costs would then be higher than the predicted costs of $906.79. Management would feel compelled to find ways to cut costs. In fact, on the basis of the preferred machine-hour cost driver, the plant would have actual costs lower than the $1,043.30 predicted costs—a performance that management should seek to replicate, not change!

Concepts in Action

Activity-Based Costing: Identifying Cost and Revenue Drivers

Many cost estimation methods presented in this chapter are essential to service, manufacturing, and retail-sector implementations of activity-based costing across the globe. To determine the cost of an activity in the banking industry, ABC systems often rely on expert analyses and opinions gathered from operating personnel (the conference method). For example, the loan department staff at the Co-operative Bank in the United Kingdom subjectively estimate the costs of the loan processing activity and the quantity of the related cost driver—the number of loans processed, a batch-level cost driver, as distinguished from the amount of the loans, an output unit-level cost driver—to derive the cost of processing a loan.

Elsewhere in the United Kingdom, the City of London police force uses input-output relationships (the industrial engineering method) to identify cost drivers and the cost of an activity. Using a surveying methodology, officials can determine the total costs associated with responding to house robberies, dealing with burglaries, and filling out police reports. In the United States, the Boeing Commercial Airplane Group's Wichita Division used detailed analyses of its commercial airplane-manufacturing methods to support make/buy decisions for complex parts required in airplane assembly. The industrial engineering method is also used by U.S. government agencies such as the U.S. Postal Service to determine the cost of each post office transaction and the U.S. Patent and Trademark Office to identify the costs of each patent examination.

Regression analysis is another helpful tool for determining the cost drivers of activities. Consider how fuel service retailers (that is, gas stations with convenience stores) identify the principal cost driver for labor within their operations. Two possible cost drivers are gasoline sales and convenience store sales. Gasoline sales are batch-level activities because payment transactions occur only once for each gasoline purchase, regardless of the volume of gasoline purchased; whereas convenience store sales are output unit-level activities that vary based on the amount of food, drink, and other products sold. Fuel service retailers generally use convenience store sales as the basis for assigning labor costs because multiple regression analyses confirm that convenience store sales, not gasoline sales, are the major cost driver of labor within their operations.

While popular, these are not the only methods used to evaluate cost drivers. If you recall from chapter five, Charles Schwab is one of the growing number of companies using time-driven activity based costing, which uses time as the cost driver. At Citigroup, the company's internal technology infrastructure group uses time to better manage the labor capacity required to provide reliable, secure, and cost effective technology services to about 60 Citigroup business units around the world.

The trend of using activity-based costing to identify cost and revenue drivers also extends into emerging areas. For example, the U.S. government allocated $19 billion in 2009 to support the adoption of electronic health records. Using the input-output method, many health clinics and doctor's offices are leveraging activity-based costing to identify the cost of adopting this new health information technology tool.

Sources: Barton, T., and J. MacArthur. 2003. Activity-based costing and predatory pricing: The case of the retail industry. *Management Accounting Quarterly* (Spring); Carter, T., A. Sedaghat, and T. Williams. 1998. How ABC changed the post office. *Management Accounting,* (February); The Cooperative Bank. Harvard Business School. Case No. N9-195-196; Federowicz, M., M. Grossman, B. Hayes, and J. Riggs. 2010. A tutorial on activity-based costing of electronic health records. *Quality Management in Health Care* (January–March); Kaplan, Robert, and Steven Anderson. 2008. *Time-driven activity-based costing: A simpler and more powerful path to higher profits.* Boston: Harvard Business School Publishing; Leapman, B. 2006. Police spend £500m filling in forms. *The Daily Telegraph,* January 22; Paduano, Rocco, and Joel Cutcher-Gershenfeld. 2001. Boeing Commercial Airplane Group Wichita Division (Boeing Co.). MIT Labor Aerospace Research Agenda Case Study. Cambridge, MA: MIT; Peckenpaugh, J. 2002. Teaching the ABCs. *Government Executive,* April 1; The United Kingdom Home Office. 2007. *The police service national ABC model: Manual of guidance.* London: Her Majesty's Stationary Office.

Cost Drivers and Activity-Based Costing

Activity-based costing (ABC) systems focus on individual activities—such as product design, machine setup, materials handling, distribution, and customer service—as the fundamental cost objects. To implement ABC systems, managers must identify a cost driver for each activity. For example, using methods described in this chapter, the manager must decide whether the number of loads moved or the weight of loads moved is the cost driver of materials-handling costs.

To choose the cost driver and use it to estimate the cost function in our materials-handling example, the manager collects data on materials-handling costs and the quantities of the two competing cost drivers over a reasonably long period. Why a long period? Because in the short run, materials-handling costs may be fixed and, therefore, will not vary with changes in the level of the cost driver. In the long run, however, there is a clear cause-and-effect relationship between materials-handling costs and the cost driver. Suppose number of loads moved is the cost driver of materials-handling costs. Increases in the number of loads moved will require more materials-handling labor and equipment; decreases will result in equipment being sold and labor being reassigned to other tasks.

ABC systems have a great number and variety of cost drivers and cost pools. That means ABC systems require many cost relationships to be estimated. In estimating the cost function for each cost pool, the manager must pay careful attention to the cost hierarchy. For example, if a cost is a batch-level cost such as setup cost, the manager must only consider batch-level cost drivers like number of setup-hours. In some cases, the costs in a cost pool may have more than one cost driver from different levels of the cost hierarchy. In the Elegant Rugs example, the cost drivers for indirect manufacturing labor costs could be machine-hours and number of production batches of carpet manufactured. Furthermore, it may be difficult to subdivide the indirect manufacturing labor costs into two cost pools and to measure the costs associated with each cost driver. In these cases, companies use multiple regression to estimate costs based on more than one independent variable. The appendix to this chapter discusses multiple regression in more detail.

As the Concepts in Action feature (p. 356) illustrates, managers implementing ABC systems use a variety of methods—industrial engineering, conference, and regression analysis—to estimate slope coefficients. In making these choices, managers trade off level of detail, accuracy, feasibility, and costs of estimating cost functions.

Nonlinear Cost Functions

In practice, cost functions are not always linear. A **nonlinear cost function** is a cost function for which the graph of total costs (based on the level of a single activity) is not a straight line within the relevant range. To see what a nonlinear cost function looks like, return to Exhibit 10-2 (p. 344). The relevant range is currently set at 20,000 to 65,000 snowboards. But if we extend the relevant range to encompass the region from 0 to 80,000 snowboards produced, it is evident that the cost function over this expanded range is graphically represented by a line that is not straight.

Consider another example. Economies of scale in advertising may enable an advertising agency to produce double the number of advertisements for less than double the costs. Even direct material costs are not always linear variable costs because of quantity discounts on direct material purchases. As shown in Exhibit 10-9 (p. 358), Panel A, total direct material costs rise as the units of direct materials purchased increase. But, because of quantity discounts, these costs rise more slowly (as indicated by the slope coefficient) as the units of direct materials purchased increase. This cost function has b = $25 per unit for 1–1,000 units purchased, b = $15 per unit for 1,001–2,000 units purchased, and b = $10 per unit for 2,001–3,000 units purchased. The direct material cost per unit falls at each price break—that is, the cost per unit decreases with larger purchase orders. If managers are interested in understanding cost behavior over the relevant range from 1 to 3,000 units, the cost function is nonlinear—not a straight line. If, however, managers are only interested in understanding cost behavior over a more narrow relevant range (for example, from 1 to 1,000 units), the cost function is linear.

Step cost functions are also examples of nonlinear cost functions. A **step cost function** is a cost function in which the cost remains the same over various ranges of the level of activity, but the cost increases by discrete amounts—that is, increases in steps—as the level of activity increases from one range to the next. Panel B in Exhibit 10-9 shows a *step variable-cost function*, a step cost function in which cost remains the same over *narrow* ranges of the level of activity in each relevant range. Panel B presents the relationship between units of production and setup costs. The pattern is a step cost function because, as we described in Chapter 5 on activity-based costing, setup costs are

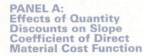

Examples of Nonlinear Cost Functions

PANEL A:
Effects of Quantity Discounts on Slope Coefficient of Direct Material Cost Function

PANEL B:
Step Variable-Cost Function

PANEL C:
Step Fixed-Cost Function

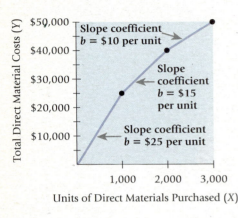

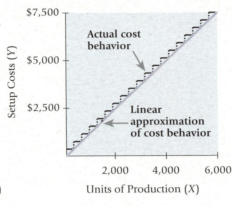

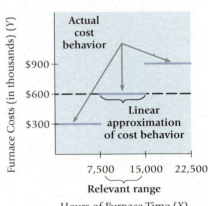

related to each production batch started. If the relevant range is considered to be from 0 to 6,000 production units, the cost function is nonlinear. However, as shown by the blue line in Panel B, managers often approximate step variable costs with a continuously-variable cost function. This type of step cost pattern also occurs when production inputs such as materials-handling labor, supervision, and process engineering labor are acquired in discrete quantities but used in fractional quantities.

Panel C in Exhibit 10-9 shows a *step fixed-cost function* for Crofton Steel, a company that operates large heat-treatment furnaces to harden steel parts. Looking at Panel C and Panel B, you can see that the main difference between a step variable-cost function and a step fixed-cost function is that the cost in a step fixed-cost function remains the same over *wide* ranges of the activity in each relevant range. The ranges indicate the number of furnaces being used (each furnace costs $300,000). The cost increases from one range to the next higher range when the hours of furnace time needed require the use of another furnace. The relevant range of 7,500 to 15,000 hours of furnace time indicates that the company expects to operate with two furnaces at a cost of $600,000. Management considers the cost of operating furnaces as a fixed cost within this relevant range of operation. However, if the relevant range is considered to be from 0 to 22,500 hours, the cost function is nonlinear: The graph in Panel C is not a single straight line; it is three broken lines.

Learning Curves

Nonlinear cost functions also result from learning curves. A **learning curve** is a function that measures how labor-hours per unit decline as units of production increase because workers are learning and becoming better at their jobs. Managers use learning curves to predict how labor-hours, or labor costs, will increase as more units are produced.

The aircraft-assembly industry first documented the effect that learning has on efficiency. In general, as workers become more familiar with their tasks, their efficiency improves. Managers learn how to improve the scheduling of work shifts and how to operate the plant more efficiently. As a result of improved efficiency, unit costs decrease as productivity increases, and the unit-cost function behaves nonlinearly. These nonlinearities must be considered when estimating and predicting unit costs.

Managers have extended the learning-curve notion to other business functions in the value chain, such as marketing, distribution, and customer service, and to costs other than labor costs. The term *experience curve* describes this broader application of the learning curve. An **experience curve** is a function that measures the decline in cost per unit in various business functions of the value chain—marketing, distribution, and so on—as the amount of these activities increases. For companies such as Dell Computer, Wal-Mart, and McDonald's, learning curves and experience curves are key elements of their strategies. These companies use learning curves and experience curves to reduce costs and increase customer satisfaction, market share, and profitability.

We now describe two learning-curve models: the cumulative average-time learning model and the incremental unit-time learning model.

Cumulative Average-Time Learning Model

In the **cumulative average-time learning model**, cumulative average time per unit declines by a constant percentage each time the cumulative quantity of units produced doubles. Consider Rayburn Corporation, a radar systems manufacturer. Rayburn has an 80% learning curve. The 80% means that when the quantity of units produced is doubled from X to 2X, cumulative average time *per unit* for 2X units is 80% of cumulative average time *per unit* for X units. Average time per unit has dropped by 20% (100% – 80%). Exhibit 10-10 is an Excel spreadsheet showing the calculations for the cumulative average-time learning model for Rayburn Corporation. Note that as the number of units produced doubles from 1 to 2 in column A, cumulative average time per unit declines from 100 hours to 80% of 100 hours (0.80 × 100 hours = 80 hours) in column B. As the number of units doubles from 2 to 4, cumulative average time per unit declines to 80% of 80 hours = 64 hours, and so on. To obtain the cumulative total time in column D, multiply cumulative average time per unit by the cumulative number of units produced. For example, to produce 4 cumulative units would require 256 labor-hours (4 units × 64 cumulative average labor-hours per unit).

Exhibit 10-10 Cumulative Average-Time Learning Model for Rayburn Corporation

	A	B	C	D	E
1	Cumulative Average-Time Learning Model for Rayburn Corporation				
3		80% Learning Curve			
5-7	Cumulative Number of Units (X)	Cumulative Average Time per Unit (y)*: Labor-Hours		Cumulative Total Time: Labor-Hours	Individual Unit Time for Xth Unit: Labor-Hours
9				D = Col A × Col B	
11	1	100.00		100.00	100.00
12	2	80.00	= (100 × 0.8)	160.00	60.00
13	3	70.21		210.63	50.63
14	4	64.00	= (80 × 0.8)	256.00	45.37
15	5	59.56		297.82	41.82
16	6	56.17		337.01	39.19
17	7	53.45		374.14	37.13
18	8	51.20	= (64 × 0.8)	409.60	35.46
19	9	49.29		443.65	34.05
20	10	47.65		476.51	32.86
21	11	46.21		508.32	31.81
22	12	44.93		539.22	30.89
23	13	43.79		569.29	30.07
24	14	42.76		598.63	29.34
25	15	41.82		627.30	28.67
26	16	40.96	= (51.2 × 0.8)	655.36	28.06

E13 = D13 – D12 = 210.63 – 160.00

*The mathematical relationship underlying the cumulative average-time learning model is as follows:

$$y = aX^b$$

where y = Cumulative average time (labor-hours) per unit
  X = Cumulative number of units produced
  a = Time (labor-hours) required to produce the first unit
  b = Factor used to calculate cumulative average time to produce units

The value of b is calculated as

$$\frac{\ln (\text{learning-curve \% in decimal form})}{\ln 2}$$

For an 80% learning curve, $b = \ln 0.8/\ln 2 = -0.2231/0.6931 = -0.3219$
For example, when X = 3, a = 100, b = –0.3219,

$$y = 100 \times 3^{-0.3219} = 70.21 \text{ labor-hours}$$

The cumulative total time when X = 3 is 70.21 × 3 = 210.63 labor-hours. Numbers in table may not be exact because of rounding.

Incremental Unit-Time Learning Model

In the **incremental unit-time learning model**, incremental time needed to produce the last unit declines by a constant percentage each time the cumulative quantity of units produced doubles. Again, consider Rayburn Corporation and an 80% learning curve. The 80% here means that when the quantity of units produced is doubled from X to $2X$, the time needed to produce the last unit when $2X$ total units are produced is 80% of the time needed to produce the last unit when X total units are produced. Exhibit 10-11 is an Excel spreadsheet showing the calculations for the incremental unit-time learning model for Rayburn Corporation based on an 80% learning curve. Note how when units produced double from 2 to 4 in column A, the time to produce unit 4 (the last unit when 4 units are produced) is 64 hours in column B, which is 80% of the 80 hours needed to produce unit 2 (the last unit when 2 units are produced). We obtain the cumulative total time in column D by summing individual unit times in column B. For example, to produce 4 cumulative units would require 314.21 labor-hours (100.00 + 80.00 + 70.21 + 64.00).

Exhibit 10-12 presents graphs using Excel for the cumulative average-time learning model (using data from Exhibit 10-10) and the incremental unit-time learning model (using data from Exhibit 10-11). Panel A graphically illustrates cumulative average time per unit as a function of cumulative units produced for each model (column A in Exhibit 10-10 or 10-11). The curve for the cumulative average-time learning model is plotted using the data from Exhibit 10-10, column B, while the curve for the incremental unit-time learning model is plotted using the data from Exhibit 10-11, column E. Panel B graphically illustrates cumulative total labor-hours, again as a function of cumulative units produced for each model. The curve for the cumulative average-time learning model is plotted using the data from Exhibit 10-10, column D, while that for the incremental unit-time learning model is plotted using the data from Exhibit 10-11, column D.

Exhibit 10-11	Incremental Unit-Time Learning Model for Rayburn Corporation

	A	B	C	D	E	F	G	H	I
1	Incremental Unit-Time Learning Model for Rayburn Corporation								
2									
3		80% Learning Curve							
4									
5	Cumulative	Individual Unit Time		Cumulative	Cumulative				
6	Number	for Xth Unit (y)*:		Total Time:	Average Time				
7	of Units (X)	Labor-Hours		Labor-Hours	per Unit:				
8					Labor-Hours				
9									
10					E = Col D ÷ Col A				
11									
12	1	100.00		100.00	100.00				
13	2	80.00	= (100 × 0.8)	180.00	90.00				
14	3	70.21		250.21	83.40				
15	4	64.00	= (80 × 0.8)	314.21	78.55				
16	5	59.56		373.77	74.75				
17	6	56.17		429.94	71.66				
18	7	53.45		483.39	69.06				
19	8	51.20	= (64 × 0.8)	534.59	66.82				
20	9	49.29		583.89	64.88				
21	10	47.65		631.54	63.15				
22	11	46.21		677.75	61.61				
23	12	44.93		722.68	60.22				
24	13	43.79		766.47	58.96				
25	14	42.76		809.23	57.80				
26	15	41.82		851.05	56.74				
27	16	40.96	= (51.2 × 0.8)	892.01	55.75				
28									

D14 = D13 + B14
= 180.00 + 70.21

*The mathematical relationship underlying the incremental unit-time learning model is as follows:

$$y = aX^b$$

where y = Time (labor-hours) taken to produce the last single unit
X = Cumulative number of units produced
a = Time (labor-hours) required to produce the first unit
b = Factor used to calculate incremental unit time to produce units

$$= \frac{\ln (\text{learning-curve \% in decimal form})}{\ln 2}$$

For an 80% learning curve, $b = \ln 0.8 \div \ln 2 = -0.2231 \div 0.6931 = -0.3219$
For example, when $X = 3$, $a = 100$, $b = -0.3219$,
$$y = 100 \times 3^{-0.3219} = 70.21 \text{ labor-hours}$$
The cumulative total time when $X = 3$ is $100 + 80 + 70.21 = 250.21$ labor-hours. Numbers in the table may not be exact because of rounding.

Exhibit 10-12   Plots for Cumulative Average-Time Learning Model and Incremental Unit-Time Learning Model for Rayburn Corporation

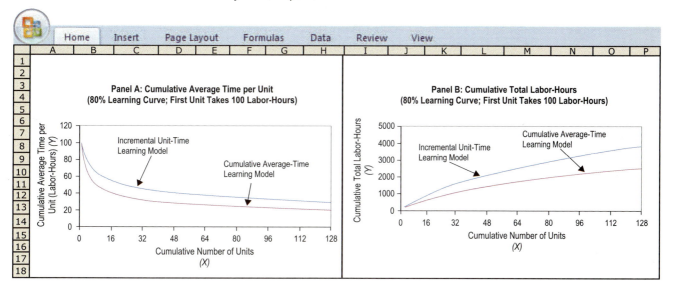

The incremental unit-time learning model predicts a higher cumulative total time to produce 2 or more units than the cumulative average-time learning model, assuming the same learning rate for both models. That is, in Exhibit 10-12, Panel B, the graph for the 80% incremental unit-time learning model lies above the graph for the 80% cumulative average-time learning model. If we compare the results in Exhibit 10-10 (column D) with the results in Exhibit 10-11 (column D), to produce 4 cumulative units, the 80% incremental unit-time learning model predicts 314.21 labor-hours versus 256.00 labor-hours predicted by the 80% cumulative average-time learning model. That's because under the cumulative average-time learning model *average labor-hours needed to produce all 4 units* is 64 hours; the labor-hour amount needed to produce unit 4 is much less than 64 hours—it is 45.37 hours (see Exhibit 10-10). Under the incremental unit-time learning model, the labor-hour amount needed to produce unit 4 is 64 hours, and the labor-hours needed to produce the first 3 units are more than 64 hours, so average time needed to produce all 4 units is more than 64 hours.

How do managers choose which model and what percent learning curve to use? It is important to recognize that managers make their choices on a case-by-case basis. For example, if the behavior of manufacturing labor-hour usage as production levels increase follows a pattern like the one predicted by the 80% learning curve cumulative average-time learning model, then the 80% learning curve cumulative average-time learning model should be used. Engineers, plant managers, and workers are good sources of information on the amount and type of learning actually occurring as production increases. Plotting this information and estimating the model that best fits the data is helpful in selecting the appropriate model.[2]

Incorporating Learning-Curve Effects into Prices and Standards

How do companies use learning curves? Consider the data in Exhibit 10-10 for the cumulative average-time learning model at Rayburn Corporation. Suppose variable costs subject to learning effects consist of direct manufacturing labor, at $20 per hour, and related overhead, at $30 per direct manufacturing labor-hour. Managers should predict the costs shown in Exhibit 10-13.

These data show that the effects of the learning curve could have a major influence on decisions. For example, managers at Rayburn Corporation might set an extremely low selling price on its radar systems to generate high demand. As its production increases to meet this growing demand, cost per unit drops. Rayburn "rides the product down the

[2] For details, see C. Bailey, "Learning Curve Estimation of Production Costs and Labor-Hours Using a Free Excel Add-In," *Management Accounting Quarterly,* (Summer 2000: 25–31). Free software for estimating learning curves is available at Dr. Bailey's Web site, www.profbailey.com.

Exhibit 10-13

Predicting Costs Using
Learning Curves at
Rayburn Corporation

	A	B	C	D	E	F
1		Cumulative				
2	Cumulative	Average Time	Cumulative	Cumulative Costs		Additions to
3	Number of	per Unit:	Total Time:	at $50 per		Cumulative
4	Units	Labor-Hours[a]	Labor-Hours[a]	Labor-Hour		Costs
5	1	100.00	100.00	$ 5,000	(100.00 × $50)	$ 5,000
6	2	80.00	160.00	8,000	(160.00 × $50)	3,000
7	4	64.00	256.00	12,800	(256.00 × $50)	4,800
8	8	51.20	409.60	20,480	(409.60 × $50)	7,680
9	16	40.96	655.36	32,768	(655.36 × $50)	12,288
10						
11	[a]Based on the cumulative average-time learning model. See Exhibit 10-10 for the computations					
12	of these amounts.					

**Decision
Point** ▶

What is a nonlinear
cost function and in
what ways do
learning curves give
rise to nonlinearities?

learning curve" as it establishes a larger market share. Although it may have earned little operating income on its first unit sold—it may actually have lost money on that unit—Rayburn earns more operating income per unit as output increases.

Alternatively, subject to legal and other considerations, Rayburn's managers might set a low price on just the final 8 units. After all, the total labor and related overhead costs per unit for these final 8 units are predicted to be only $12,288 ($32,768 – $20,480). On these final 8 units, the $1,536 cost per unit ($12,288 ÷ 8 units) is much lower than the $5,000 cost per unit of the first unit produced.

Many companies, such as Pizza Hut and Home Depot, incorporate learning-curve effects when evaluating performance. The Nissan Motor Company expects its workers to learn and improve on the job and evaluates performance accordingly. It sets assembly-labor efficiency standards for new models of cars after taking into account the learning that will occur as more units are produced.

The learning-curve models examined in Exhibits 10-10 to 10-13 assume that learning is driven by a single variable (production output). Other models of learning have been developed (by companies such as Analog Devices and Hewlett-Packard) that focus on how quality—rather than manufacturing labor-hours—will change over time, regardless of whether more units are produced. Studies indicate that factors other than production output, such as job rotation and organizing workers into teams, contribute to learning that improves quality.

Data Collection and Adjustment Issues

**Learning
Objective** **7**

Be aware of data
problems encountered
in estimating cost
functions

. . . for example,
unreliable data and poor
record keeping, extreme
observations, treating
fixed costs as if they are
variable, and a changing
relationship between a
cost driver and cost

The ideal database for estimating cost functions quantitatively has two characteristics:

1. **The database should contain numerous reliably measured observations of the cost driver (the independent variable) and the related costs (the dependent variable).** Errors in measuring the costs and the cost driver are serious. They result in inaccurate estimates of the effect of the cost driver on costs.

2. **The database should consider many values spanning a wide range for the cost driver.** Using only a few values of the cost driver that are grouped closely considers too small a segment of the relevant range and reduces the confidence in the estimates obtained.

Unfortunately, cost analysts typically do not have the advantage of working with a database having both characteristics. This section outlines some frequently encountered data problems and steps the cost analyst can take to overcome these problems.

1. The time period for measuring the dependent variable (for example, machine-lubricant costs) does not properly match the period for measuring the cost driver. This problem often arises when accounting records are not kept on the accrual basis. Consider a cost function with machine-lubricant costs as the dependent variable and number of machine-hours as the cost driver. Assume that the lubricant is purchased sporadically

and stored for later use. Records maintained on the basis of lubricants purchased will indicate little lubricant costs in many months and large lubricant costs in other months. These records present an obviously inaccurate picture of what is actually taking place. The analyst should use accrual accounting to measure cost of lubricants consumed to better match costs with the machine-hours cost driver in this example.

2. Fixed costs are allocated as if they are variable. For example, costs such as depreciation, insurance, or rent may be allocated to products to calculate cost per unit of output. *The danger is to regard these costs as variable rather than as fixed. They seem to be variable because of the allocation methods used.* To avoid this problem, the analyst should carefully distinguish fixed costs from variable costs and not treat allocated fixed cost per unit as a variable cost.

3. Data are either not available for all observations or are not uniformly reliable. Missing cost observations often arise from a failure to record a cost or from classifying a cost incorrectly. For example, marketing costs may be understated because costs of sales visits to customers may be incorrectly recorded as customer-service costs. Recording data manually rather than electronically tends to result in a higher percentage of missing observations and erroneously entered observations. Errors also arise when data on cost drivers originate outside the internal accounting system. For example, the accounting department may obtain data on testing-hours for medical instruments from the company's manufacturing department and data on number of items shipped to customers from the distribution department. One or both of these departments might not keep accurate records. To minimize these problems, the cost analyst should design data collection reports that regularly and routinely obtain the required data and should follow up immediately whenever data are missing.

4. Extreme values of observations occur from errors in recording costs (for example, a misplaced decimal point), from nonrepresentative periods (for example, from a period in which a major machine breakdown occurred or from a period in which a delay in delivery of materials from an international supplier curtailed production), or from observations outside the relevant range. Analysts should adjust or eliminate unusual observations before estimating a cost relationship.

5. There is no homogeneous relationship between the cost driver and the individual cost items in the dependent variable-cost pool. A homogeneous relationship exists when each activity whose costs are included in the dependent variable has the same cost driver. In this case, a single cost function can be estimated. As discussed in Step 2 for estimating a cost function using quantitative analysis (p. 348), when the cost driver for each activity is different, separate cost functions (each with its own cost driver) should be estimated for each activity. Alternatively, as discussed on pages 372–374, the cost function should be estimated with more than one independent variable using multiple regression.

6. The relationship between the cost driver and the cost is not stationary. That is, the underlying process that generated the observations has not remained stable over time. For example, the relationship between number of machine-hours and manufacturing overhead costs is unlikely to be stationary when the data cover a period in which new technology was introduced. One way to see if the relationship is stationary is to split the sample into two parts and estimate separate cost relationships—one for the period before the technology was introduced and one for the period after the technology was introduced. Then, if the estimated coefficients for the two periods are similar, the analyst can pool the data to estimate a single cost relationship. When feasible, pooling data provides a larger data set for the estimation, which increases confidence in the cost predictions being made.

7. Inflation has affected costs, the cost driver, or both. For example, inflation may cause costs to change even when there is no change in the level of the cost driver. To study the underlying cause-and-effect relationship between the level of the cost driver and costs, the analyst should remove purely inflationary price effects from the data by dividing each cost by the price index on the date the cost was incurred.

In many cases, a cost analyst must expend considerable effort to reduce the effect of these problems before estimating a cost function on the basis of past data.

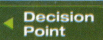

Decision Point

What are the common data problems a company must watch for when estimating costs?

Problem for Self-Study

The Helicopter Division of GLD, Inc., is examining helicopter assembly costs at its Indiana plant. It has received an initial order for eight of its new land-surveying helicopters. GLD can adopt one of two methods of assembling the helicopters:

	A	B	C	D	E
			Labor-Intensive Assembly Method	**Machine-Intensive Assembly Method**	
1			**Labor-Intensive Assembly Method**	**Machine-Intensive Assembly Method**	
2	Direct material cost per helicopter		$ 40,000	$36,000	
3	Direct-assembly labor time for first helicopter		2,000 labor-hours	800 labor-hours	
4	Learning curve for assembly labor time per helicopter		85% cumulative average time*	90% incremental unit time**	
5	Direct-assembly labor cost		$ 30 per hour	$ 30 per hour	
6	Equipment-related indirect manufacturing cost		$ 12 per direct-assembly labor-hour	$ 45 per direct-assembly labor-hour	
7	Material-handling-related indirect manufacturing cost		50% of direct material cost	50% of direct material cost	
8					
9					
10	*Using the formula (p. 359), for an 85% learning curve, $b = \dfrac{\ln 0.85}{\ln 2} = \dfrac{-0.162519}{0.693147} = -0.234465$				
11					
12					
13					
14					
15	**Using the formula (p. 360), for a 90% learning curve, $b = \dfrac{\ln 0.90}{\ln 2} = \dfrac{-0.105361}{0.693147} = -0.152004$				
16					
17					

Required

1. How many direct-assembly labor-hours are required to assemble the first eight helicopters under (a) the labor-intensive method and (b) the machine-intensive method?
2. What is the total cost of assembling the first eight helicopters under (a) the labor-intensive method and (b) the machine-intensive method?

Solution

1. a. The following calculations show the labor-intensive assembly method based on an 85% cumulative average-time learning model (using Excel):

	G	H	I	J	K
1	**Cumulative**	**Cumulative**		**Cumulative**	**Individual**
2	**Number**	**Average Time**		**Total Time:**	**time for**
3	**of Units**	**per Unit (y):**		**Labor-Hours**	**Xth unit:**
4		**Labor-Hours**			**Labor-Hours**
5				Col J = Col G × Col H	
6	1	2,000		2,000	2,000
7	2	1,700	(2,000 × 0.85)	3,400	1,400
8	3	1,546		4,637	1,237
9	4	1,445	(1,700 × 0.85)	5,780	1,143
10	5	1,371		6,857	1,077
11	6	1,314		7,884	1,027
12	7	1,267		8,871	987
13	8	1,228.25	(1,445 × 0.85)	9,826	955
14					

Cumulative average-time per unit for the Xth unit in column H is calculated as $y = aX^b$; see Exhibit 10-10 (p. 359). For example, when $X = 3$, $y = 2{,}000 \times 3^{-0.234465} = 1{,}546$ labor-hours.

b. The following calculations show the machine-intensive assembly method based on a 90% incremental unit-time learning model:

	G	H	I	J	K
1	Cumulative	Individual		Cumulative	Cumulative
2	Number	Unit Time		Total Time:	Average Time
3	of Units	for Xth Unit (y):		Labor-Hours	Per Unit:
4		Labor-Hours			Labor-Hours
5					Col K = Col J ÷ Col G
6	1	800		800	800
7	2	720	(800 × 0.9)	1,520	760
8	3	677		2,197	732
9	4	648	(720 × 0.9)	2,845	711
10	5	626		3,471	694
11	6	609		4,081	680
12	7	595		4,676	668
13	8	583	(648 × 0.9)	5,258	657

Individual unit time for the Xth unit in column H is calculated as $y = aX^b$; see Exhibit 10-11 (p. 360). For example, when $X = 3$, $y = 800 \times 3^{-0.152004} = 677$ labor-hours.

2. Total costs of assembling the first eight helicopters are as follows:

	O	P	Q
1		Labor-Intensive	Machine-Intensive
2		Assembly Method	Assembly Method
3		(using data from part 1a)	(using data from part 1b)
4	Direct materials:		
5	8 helicopters × $40,000; $36,000 per helicopter	$320,000	$288,000
6	Direct-assembly labor:		
7	9,826 hrs.; 5,258 hrs. × $30/hr.	294,780	157,740
8	Indirect manufacturing costs		
9	Equipment related		
10	9,826 hrs. × $12/hr.; 5,258 hrs. × $45/hr.	117,912	236,610
11	Materials-handling related		
12	0.50 × $320,000; $288,000	160,000	144,000
13	Total assembly costs	$892,692	$826,350

The machine-intensive method's assembly costs are $66,342 lower than the labor-intensive method ($892,692 – $826,350).

Decision Points

The following question-and-answer format summarizes the chapter's learning objectives. Each decision presents a key question related to a learning objective. The guidelines are the answer to that question.

Decision	Guidelines
1. What is a linear cost function and what types of cost behavior can it represent?	A linear cost function is a cost function in which, within the relevant range, the graph of total costs based on the level of a single activity is a straight line. Linear cost functions can be described by a constant, a, which represents the estimate of the total cost component that, within the relevant range, does not vary with changes in the level of the activity; and a slope coefficient, b, which represents the estimate of the amount by which total costs change for each unit change in the level of the activity within the relevant range. Three types of linear cost functions are variable, fixed, and mixed (or semivariable).
2. What is the most important issue in estimating a cost function?	The most important issue in estimating a cost function is determining whether a cause-and-effect relationship exists between the level of an activity and the costs related to that level of activity. Only a cause-and-effect relationship—not merely correlation—establishes an economically plausible relationship between the level of an activity and its costs.
3. What are the different methods that can be used to estimate a cost function?	Four methods for estimating cost functions are the industrial engineering method, the conference method, the account analysis method, and the quantitative analysis method (which includes the high-low method and the regression analysis method). If possible, the cost analyst should apply more than one method. Each method is a check on the others.
4. What are the steps to estimate a cost function using quantitative analysis?	There are six steps to estimate a cost function using quantitative analysis: (a) Choose the dependent variable; (b) identify the cost driver; (c) collect data on the dependent variable and the cost driver; (d) plot the data; (e) estimate the cost function; and (f) evaluate the cost driver of the estimated cost function. In most situations, working closely with operations managers, the cost analyst will cycle through these steps several times before identifying an acceptable cost function.
5. How should a company evaluate and choose cost drivers?	Three criteria for evaluating and choosing cost drivers are (a) economic plausibility, (b) goodness of fit, and (c) significance of independent variable.
6. What is a nonlinear cost function and in what ways do learning curves give rise to nonlinearities?	A nonlinear cost function is one in which the graph of total costs based on the level of a single activity is not a straight line within the relevant range. Nonlinear costs can arise because of quantity discounts, step cost functions, and learning-curve effects. With learning curves, labor-hours per unit decline as units of production increase. In the cumulative average-time learning model, cumulative average-time per unit declines by a constant percentage each time the cumulative quantity of units produced doubles. In the incremental unit-time learning model, the time needed to produce the last unit declines by a constant percentage each time the cumulative quantity of units produced doubles.
7. What are the common data problems a company must watch for when estimating costs?	The most difficult task in cost estimation is collecting high-quality, reliably measured data on the costs and the cost driver. Common problems include missing data, extreme values of observations, changes in technology, and distortions resulting from inflation.

Appendix

Regression Analysis

This appendix describes estimation of the regression equation, several commonly used regression statistics, and how to choose among cost functions that have been estimated by regression analysis. We use the data for Elegant Rugs presented in Exhibit 10-3 (p. 348) and displayed here again for easy reference.

Week	Cost Driver: Machine-Hours (X)	Indirect Manufacturing Labor Costs (Y)
1	68	$ 1,190
2	88	1,211
3	62	1,004
4	72	917
5	60	770
6	96	1,456
7	78	1,180
8	46	710
9	82	1,316
10	94	1,032
11	68	752
12	48	963
Total	862	$12,501

Estimating the Regression Line

The least-squares technique for estimating the regression line minimizes the sum of the squares of the vertical deviations from the data points to the estimated regression line (also called *residual term* in Exhibit 10-6, p. 352). The objective is to find the values of a and b in the linear cost function $y = a + bX$, where y is the *predicted* cost value as distinguished from the *observed* cost value, which we denote by Y. We wish to find the numerical values of a and b that minimize $\Sigma(Y - y)^2$, the sum of the squares of the vertical deviations between Y and y. Generally, these computations are done using software packages such as Excel. For the data in our example,[3] a = $300.98 and b = $10.31, so that the equation of the regression line is y = $300.98 + $10.31X.

Goodness of Fit

Goodness of fit measures how well the predicted values, y, based on the cost driver, X, match actual cost observations, Y. The regression analysis method computes a measure of goodness of fit, called the **coefficient of determination**. The coefficient of determination (r^2) measures the percentage of variation in Y explained by X (the independent variable).

---

[3] The formulae for a and b are as follows:

$$a = \frac{(\Sigma Y)(\Sigma X^2) - (\Sigma X)(\Sigma XY)}{n(\Sigma X^2) - (\Sigma X)(\Sigma X)} \quad \text{and } b = \frac{n(\Sigma XY) - (\Sigma X)(\Sigma Y)}{n(\Sigma X^2) - (\Sigma X)(\Sigma X)}$$

where for the Elegant Rugs data in Exhibit 10-3,

n = number of data points = 12

ΣX = sum of the given X values = 68 + 88 + ... + 48 = 862

ΣX^2 = sum of squares of the X values = $(68)^2 + (88)^2 + ... + (48)^2 + 4,624 + 7,744 + ... + 2,304$ = 64,900

ΣY = sum of given Y values = 1,190 + 1,211 + ... + 963 = 12,501

ΣXY = sum of the amounts obtained by multiplying each of the given X values by the associated observed
Y value = (68) (1,190) + (88) (1,211) + ... + (48) (963)
= 80,920 + 106,568 + ... + 46,224 = 928,716

$$a = \frac{(12,501)(64,900) - (862)(928,716)}{12(64,900) - (862)(862)} = \$300.98$$

$$b = \frac{12(928,716) - (862)(12,501)}{12(64,900) - (862)(862)} = \$10.31$$

It is more convenient to express the coefficient of determination as 1 minus the proportion of total variance that is *not* explained by the independent variable—that is, 1 minus the ratio of unexplained variation to total variation. The unexplained variance arises because of differences between the actual values, Y, and the predicted values, y, which in the Elegant Rugs example is given by[4]

$$r^2 = 1 - \frac{\text{Unexplained variation}}{\text{Total variation}} = 1 - \frac{\Sigma(Y - y)^2}{\Sigma(Y - \bar{Y})^2} = 1 - \frac{290{,}824}{607{,}699} = 0.52$$

The calculations indicate that r^2 increases as the predicted values, y, more closely approximate the actual observations, Y. The range of r^2 is from 0 (implying no explanatory power) to 1 (implying perfect explanatory power). Generally, an r^2 of 0.30 or higher passes the goodness-of-fit test. However, do not rely exclusively on goodness of fit. It can lead to the indiscriminate inclusion of independent variables that increase r^2 but have no economic plausibility as cost drivers. *Goodness of fit has meaning only if the relationship between the cost drivers and costs is economically plausible.*

An alternative and related way to evaluate goodness of fit is to calculate the *standard error of the regression*. The **standard error of the regression** is the variance of the residuals. It is equal to

$$S = \sqrt{\frac{\Sigma(Y - y)^2}{\text{Degrees of freedom}}} = \sqrt{\frac{\Sigma(Y - y)^2}{n - 2}} = \sqrt{\frac{290{,}824}{12 - 2}} = \$170.54$$

Degrees of freedom equal the number of observations, 12, *minus* the number of coefficients estimated in the regression (in this case two, a and b). On average, actual Y and the predicted value, y, differ by \$170.54. For comparison, $\bar{Y}$, the average value of Y, is \$1,041.75. The smaller the standard error of the regression, the better the fit and the better the predictions for different values of X.

Significance of Independent Variables

Do changes in the economically plausible independent variable result in significant changes in the dependent variable? Or alternatively stated, is the slope coefficient, b = \$10.31, of the regression line statistically significant (that is, different from \$0)? Recall, for example, that in the regression of number of machine-hours and indirect manufacturing labor costs in the Elegant Rugs illustration, b is estimated from a sample of 12 weekly observations. The estimate, b, is subject to random factors, as are all sample statistics. That is, a different sample of 12 data points would undoubtedly give a different estimate of b. The **standard error of the estimated coefficient** indicates how much the estimated value, b, is likely to be affected by random factors. The t-value of the b coefficient measures how large the value of the estimated coefficient is relative to its standard error.

The cutoff t-value for making inferences about the b coefficient is a function of the number of degrees of freedom, the significance level, and whether it is a one-sided or two-sided test. A 5% level of significance indicates that there is less than a 5% probability that random factors could have affected the coefficient b. A two-sided test assumes that random factors could have caused the coefficient to be either greater than \$10.31 or less than \$10.31 with equal probability. At a 5% level of significance, this means that there is less than a 2.5% (5% ÷ 2) probability that random factors could have caused the coefficient to be greater than \$10.31 and less than 2.5% probability that random factors could have caused the coefficient to be less than \$10.31. Under the expectation that the coefficient of b is positive, a one-sided test at the 5% level of significance assumes that there is less than 5% probability that random factors would have caused the coefficient to be less than \$10.31. The cutoff t-value at the 5% significance level and 10 degrees of freedom for a two-sided test is 2.228. If there were more observations and 60 degrees of freedom, the cutoff t-value would be 2.00 at a 5% significance level for a two-sided test.

The t-value (called t Stat in the Excel output) for the slope coefficient b is the value of the estimated coefficient, \$10.31 ÷ the standard error of the estimated coefficient \$3.12 = 3.30, which exceeds the cutoff t-value of 2.228. In other words, a relationship exists between the independent variable, machine-hours, and the dependent variable that cannot be attributed to random chance alone. Exhibit 10-14 shows a convenient format (in Excel) for summarizing the regression results for number of machine-hours and indirect manufacturing labor costs.

---

[4] From footnote 3, ΣY = 12,501 and $\bar{Y}$ = 12,501 ÷ 12 = 1,041.75

$$\Sigma(Y - \bar{Y})^2 = (1{,}190 - 1{,}041.75)^2 + (1{,}211 - 1{,}041.75)^2 + \ldots + (963 - 1{,}041.75)^2 = 607{,}699$$

Each value of X generates a predicted value of y. For example, in week 1, y = \$300.98 + (\$10.31 × 68) = \$1002.06; in week 2, y = \$300.98 + (\$10.31 × 88) = \$1,208.26; and in week 12, y = \$300.98 + (\$10.31 × 48) = \$795.86. Comparing the predicted and actual values,

$$\Sigma(Y - y)^2 = (1{,}190 - 1{,}002.06)^2 + (1{,}211 - 1208.26)^2 + \ldots + (963 - 795.86)^2 = 290{,}824.$$

Exhibit 10-14	Simple Regression Results with Indirect Manufacturing Labor Costs as Dependent Variable and Machine-Hours as Independent Variable (Cost Driver) for Elegant Rugs

	A	B	C	D	E	F
1		**Coefficients**	**Standard Error**	**t Stat**		= Coefficient/Standard Error
2		**(1)**	**(2)**	**(3) = (1) ÷ (2)**		= B3/C3
3	Intercept	$300.98	$229.75	1.31 ——→		= 300.98/229.75
4	Independent Variable: Machine-Hours (X)	$ 10.31	$ 3.12	3.30		
5						
6	**Regression Statistics**					
7	R Square	0.52				
8	Durbin-Watson Statistic	2.05				

An alternative way to test that the coefficient b is significantly different from zero is in terms of a *confidence interval*: There is less than a 5% chance that the true value of the machine-hours coefficient lies outside the range $10.31 ± (2.228 × $3.12), or $10.31 ± $6.95, or from $3.36 to $17.26. Because 0 does not appear in the confidence interval, we can conclude that changes in the number of machine-hours do affect indirect manufacturing labor costs. Similarly, using data from Exhibit 10-14, the *t*-value for the constant term a is $300.98 ÷ $229.75 = 1.31, which is less than 2.228. This *t*-value indicates that, within the relevant range, the constant term is *not* significantly different from zero. The Durbin-Watson statistic in Exhibit 10-14 will be discussed in the following section.

Specification Analysis of Estimation Assumptions

Specification analysis is the testing of the assumptions of regression analysis. If the assumptions of (1) linearity within the relevant range, (2) constant variance of residuals, (3) independence of residuals, and (4) normality of residuals all hold, then the simple regression procedures give reliable estimates of coefficient values. This section provides a brief overview of specification analysis. When these assumptions are not satisfied, more-complex regression procedures are necessary to obtain the best estimates.[5]

1. **Linearity within the relevant range.** A common assumption—and one that appears to be reasonable in many business applications—is that a linear relationship exists between the independent variable X and the dependent variable Y within the relevant range. If a linear regression model is used to estimate a nonlinear relationship, however, the coefficient estimates obtained will be inaccurate.

   When there is only one independent variable, the easiest way to check for linearity is to study the data plotted in a scatter diagram, a step that often is unwisely skipped. Exhibit 10-6 (p. 352) presents a scatter diagram for the indirect manufacturing labor costs and machine-hours variables of Elegant Rugs shown in Exhibit 10-3 (p. 348). The scatter diagram reveals that linearity appears to be a reasonable assumption for these data.

   The learning-curve models discussed in this chapter (pp. 358–361) are examples of nonlinear cost functions. Costs increase when the level of production increases, but by lesser amounts than would occur with a linear cost function. In this case, the analyst should estimate a nonlinear cost function that incorporates learning effects.

2. **Constant variance of residuals.** The vertical deviation of the observed value Y from the regression line estimate y is called the *residual term, disturbance term,* or *error term,* $u = Y - y$. The assumption of constant variance implies that the residual terms are unaffected by the level of the cost driver. The assumption also implies that there is a uniform scatter, or dispersion, of the data points about the regression line as in Exhibit 10-15, Panel A. This assumption is likely to be violated, for example, in cross-sectional estimation of costs in operations of different sizes. For example, suppose Elegant Rugs has production areas of varying sizes. The company collects data from these different production areas to estimate the relationship between machine-hours and indirect manufacturing labor costs. It is very possible that the residual terms in this regression will be larger for the larger production

---

[5] For details see, for example, W. H. Greene, *Econometric Analysis*, 6th ed. (Upper Saddle River, NJ: Prentice Hall, 2007).

Exhibit 10-15   Constant Variance of Residuals Assumption

PANEL A:
Constant Variance
(Uniform Scatter of Data
Points Around Regression Line)

PANEL B:
Nonconstant Variance
(Higher Outputs Have
Larger Residuals)

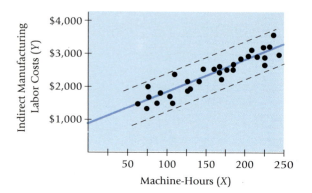

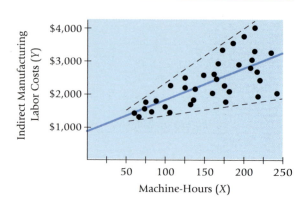

areas that have higher machine-hours and higher indirect manufacturing labor costs. There would not be a uniform scatter of data points about the regression line (see Exhibit 10-15, Panel B). Constant variance is also known as *homoscedasticity*. Violation of this assumption is called *heteroscedasticity*.

Heteroscedasticity does not affect the accuracy of the regression estimates *a* and *b*. It does, however, reduce the reliability of the estimates of the standard errors and thus affects the precision with which inferences about the population parameters can be drawn from the regression estimates.

3. **Independence of residuals.** The assumption of independence of residuals is that the residual term for any one observation is not related to the residual term for any other observation. The problem of *serial correlation* (also called *autocorrelation*) in the residuals arises when there is a systematic pattern in the sequence of residuals such that the residual in observation *n* conveys information about the residuals in observations *n* + 1, *n* + 2, and so on. Consider another production cell at Elegant Rugs that has, over a 20-week period, seen an increase in production and hence machine-hours. Exhibit 10-16 Panel B is a scatter diagram of machine-hours and indirect manufacturing labor costs. Observe the systematic pattern of the residuals in Panel B—positive residuals for extreme (high and low) quantities of machine-hours and negative residuals for moderate quantities of machine-hours. One reason for this observed pattern at low values of the cost driver is the "stickiness" of costs. When machine-hours are below 50 hours, indirect manufacturing labor costs do not decline. When machine-hours increase over time as production is ramped up, indirect manufacturing labor costs increase more as managers at Elegant Rugs struggle

Exhibit 10-16   Independence of Residuals Assumption

PANEL B:
Serial Correlation in Residuals
(A Pattern of Positive Residuals for
Extreme Machine-Hours Used;
Negative Residuals for Moderate
Machine-Hours Used)

PANEL A:
Independence of Residuals
(No Pattern in Residuals)

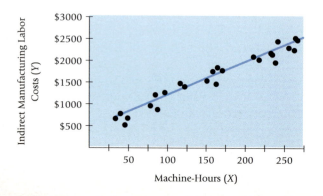

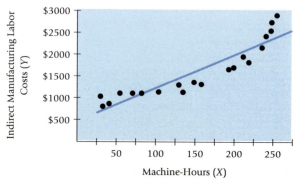

to manage the higher volume. How would the plot of residuals look if there were no auto-correlation? Like the plot in Exhibit 10-16, Panel A that shows no pattern in the residuals.

Like nonconstant variance of residuals, serial correlation does not affect the accuracy of the regression estimates a and b. It does, however, affect the standard errors of the coefficients, which in turn affect the precision with which inferences about the population parameters can be drawn from the regression estimates.

The Durbin-Watson statistic is one measure of serial correlation in the estimated residuals. For samples of 10 to 20 observations, a Durbin-Watson statistic in the 1.10–2.90 range indicates that the residuals are independent. The Durbin-Watson statistic for the regression results of Elegant Rugs in Exhibit 10-14 is 2.05. Therefore, an assumption of independence in the estimated residuals is reasonable for this regression model.

4. **Normality of residuals.** The normality of residuals assumption means that the residuals are distributed normally around the regression line. The normality of residuals assumption is frequently satisfied when using regression analysis on real cost data. Even when the assumption does not hold, accountants can still generate accurate estimates based on the regression equation, but the resulting confidence interval around these estimates is likely to be inaccurate.

Using Regression Output to Choose Cost Drivers of Cost Functions

Consider the two choices of cost drivers we described earlier in this chapter for indirect manufacturing labor costs (y):

$$y = a + (b \times \text{Number of machine-hours})$$

$$y = a + (b \times \text{Number of direct manufacturing labor-hours})$$

Exhibits 10-6 and 10-8 show plots of the data for the two regressions. Exhibit 10-14 reports regression results for the cost function using number of machine-hours as the independent variable. Exhibit 10-17 presents comparable regression results (in Excel) for the cost function using number of direct manufacturing labor-hours as the independent variable.

On the basis of the material presented in this appendix, which regression is better? Exhibit 10-18 compares these two cost functions in a systematic way. For several criteria, the cost function based on machine-hours is preferable to the cost function based on direct manufacturing labor-hours. The economic plausibility criterion is especially important.

Do not always assume that any one cost function will perfectly satisfy all the criteria in Exhibit 10-18. A cost analyst must often make a choice among "imperfect" cost functions, in the sense that the data of any particular cost function will not perfectly meet one or more of the assumptions underlying regression analysis. For example, both of the cost functions in Exhibit 10-18 are imperfect because, as stated in the section on specification analysis of estimation assumptions, inferences drawn from only 12 observations are not reliable.

Exhibit 10-17   Simple Regression Results with Indirect Manufacturing Labor Costs as Dependent Variable and Direct Manufacturing Labor-Hours as Independent Variable (Cost Driver) for Elegant Rugs

	A	B	C	D	E	F	G	H
1		**Coefficients**	**Standard Error**	***t* Stat**				
2		(1)	(2)	(3) = (1) ÷ (2)				
3	Intercept	$744.67	$217.61	3.42				
4	Independent Variable: Direct Manufacturing Labor-Hours (X)	$ 7.72	$ 5.40	1.43		= Coefficient/Standard Error = B4/C4 = 7.72/5.40		
5								
6	**Regression Statistics**							
7	R Square	0.17						
8	Durbin-Watson Statistic	2.26						

Exhibit 10-18   Comparison of Alternative Cost Functions for Indirect Manufacturing Labor Costs Estimated with Simple Regression for Elegant Rugs

Criterion	Cost Function 1: Machine-Hours as Independent Variable	Cost Function 2: Direct Manufacturing Labor-Hours as Independent Variable
Economic plausibility	A positive relationship between indirect manufacturing labor costs (technical support labor) and machine-hours is economically plausible in Elegant Rugs' highly automated plant	A positive relationship between indirect manufacturing labor costs and direct manufacturing labor-hours is economically plausible, but less so than machine-hours in Elegant Rugs' highly automated plant on a week-to-week basis.
Goodness of fit[a]	$r^2 = 0.52$; standard error of regression = $170.50. Excellent goodness of fit.	$r^2 = 0.17$; standard error of regression = $224.60. Poor goodness of fit.
Significance of independent variable(s)	The t-value of 3.30 is significant at the 0.05 level.	The t-value of 1.43 is not significant at the 0.05 level.
Specification analysis of estimation assumptions	Plot of the data indicates that assumptions of linearity, constant variance, independence of residuals (Durbin-Watson statistic = 2.05), and normality of residuals hold, but inferences drawn from only 12 observations are not reliable.	Plot of the data indicates that assumptions of linearity, constant variance, independence of residuals (Durbin-Watson statistic = 2.26), and normality of residuals hold, but inferences drawn from only 12 observations are not reliable.

[a]If the number of observations available to estimate the machine-hours regression differs from the number of observations available to estimate the direct manufacturing labor-hours regression, an *adjusted* r^2 can be calculated to take this difference (in degrees of freedom) into account. Programs such as Excel calculate and present *adjusted* r^2.

Multiple Regression and Cost Hierarchies

In some cases, a satisfactory estimation of a cost function may be based on only one independent variable, such as number of machine-hours. In many cases, however, basing the estimation on more than one independent variable (that is, *multiple regression*) is more economically plausible and improves accuracy. The most widely used equations to express relationships between two or more independent variables and a dependent variable are linear in the form

$$y = a + b_1 X_1 + b_2 X_2 + \ldots + u$$

where,

$$y = \text{Cost to be predicted}$$
$$X_1, X_2, \ldots = \text{Independent variables on which the prediction is to be based}$$
$$a, b_1, b_2, \ldots = \text{Estimated coefficients of the regression model}$$
$$u = \text{Residual term that includes the net effect of other factors not in the model as well as measurement errors in the dependent and independent variables}$$

Example: Consider the Elegant Rugs data in Exhibit 10-19. The company's ABC analysis indicates that indirect manufacturing labor costs include large amounts incurred for setup and changeover costs when a new batch of carpets is started. Management believes that in addition to number of machine-hours (an output unit-level cost driver), indirect manufacturing labor costs are also affected by the number of batches of carpet produced during each week (a batch-level driver). Elegant Rugs estimates the relationship between two independent variables, number of machine-hours and number of production batches of carpet manufactured during the week, and indirect manufacturing labor costs.

Exhibit 10-19

Weekly Indirect
Manufacturing Labor
Costs, Machine-Hours,
Direct Manufacturing
Labor-Hours, and
Number of Production
Batches for
Elegant Rugs

	Home	Insert	Page Layout	Formulas	Data	Review	View	
	A	B	C	D	E			
1	Week	Machine-Hours (X_1)	Number of Production Batches (X_2)	Direct Manufacturing Labor-Hours	Indirect Manufacturing Labor Costs (Y)			
2	1	68	12	30	$ 1,190			
3	2	88	15	35	1,211			
4	3	62	13	36	1,004			
5	4	72	11	20	917			
6	5	60	10	47	770			
7	6	96	12	45	1,456			
8	7	78	17	44	1,180			
9	8	46	7	38	710			
10	9	82	14	70	1,316			
11	10	94	12	30	1,032			
12	11	68	7	29	752			
13	12	48	14	38	963			
14	Total	862	144	462	$12,501			
15								

Exhibit 10-20 presents results (in Excel) for the following multiple regression model, using data in columns B, C, and E of Exhibit 10-19:

$$y = \$42.58 + \$7.60X_1 + \$37.77X_2$$

where X_1 is the number of machine-hours and X_2 is the number of production batches. It is economically plausible that both number of machine-hours and number of production batches would help explain variations in indirect manufacturing labor costs at Elegant Rugs. The r^2 of 0.52 for the simple regression using number of machine-hours (Exhibit 10-14) increases to 0.72 with the multiple regression in Exhibit 10-20. The t-values suggest that the independent variable coefficients of both number of machine-hours ($\$7.60$) and number of production batches ($\$37.77$) are significantly different from zero ($t = 2.74$ is the t-value for number of machine-hours, and $t = 2.48$ is the t-value for number of production batches compared to the cut-off t-value of 2.26). The multiple regression model in Exhibit 10-20 satisfies both economic plausibility and statistical criteria, and it explains much greater variation (that

Exhibit 10-20 Multiple Regression Results with Indirect Manufacturing Labor Costs and Two Independent Variables of Cost Drivers (Machine-Hours and Production Batches) for Elegant Rugs

	Home	Insert	Page Layout	Formulas	Data	Review	View	
	A	B	C	D	E	F		
1		Coefficients	Standard Error	t Stat				
2		(1)	(2)	(3) = (1) ÷ (2)				
3	Intercept	$42.58	$213.91	0.20				
4	Independent Variable 1: Machine-Hours ($X1$)	$ 7.60	$ 2.77	2.74		= Coefficient/Standard Error = B4/C4 = 7.60/2.77		
5	Independent Variable 2: Number of Production Batches ($X2$)	$37.77	$ 15.25	2.48				
6								
7	**Regression Statistics**							
8	R Square	0.72						
9	Durbin-Watson Statistic	2.49						

is, r^2 of 0.72 versus r^2 of 0.52) in indirect manufacturing labor costs than the simple regression model using only number of machine-hours as the independent variable.[6] The standard error of the regression equation that includes number of batches as an independent variable is

$$\sqrt{\frac{\Sigma(Y - y)^2}{n - 3}} = \sqrt{\frac{170,156}{9}} = \$137.50$$

which is lower than the standard error of the regression with only machine-hours as the independent variable, $170.50. That is, even though adding a variable reduces the degrees of freedom in the denominator, it substantially improves fit so that the numerator, $\Sigma(Y - y)^2$, decreases even more. Number of machine-hours and number of production batches are both important cost drivers of indirect manufacturing labor costs at Elegant Rugs.

In Exhibit 10-20, the slope coefficients—$7.60 for number of machine-hours and $37.77 for number of production batches—measure the change in indirect manufacturing labor costs associated with a unit change in an independent variable (assuming that the other independent variable is held constant). For example, indirect manufacturing labor costs increase by $37.77 when one more production batch is added, assuming that the number of machine-hours is held constant.

An alternative approach would create two separate cost pools for indirect manufacturing labor costs: one for costs related to number of machine-hours and another for costs related to number of production batches. Elegant Rugs would then estimate the relationship between the cost driver and the costs in each cost pool. The difficult task under this approach is to properly subdivide the indirect manufacturing labor costs into the two cost pools.

Multicollinearity

A major concern that arises with multiple regression is multicollinearity. **Multicollinearity** exists when two or more independent variables are highly correlated with each other. Generally, users of regression analysis believe that a *coefficient of correlation* between independent variables greater than 0.70 indicates multicollinearity. Multicollinearity increases the standard errors of the coefficients of the individual variables. That is, variables that are economically and statistically significant will appear not to be significantly different from zero.

The matrix of correlation coefficients of the different variables described in Exhibit 10-19 are as follows:

	Indirect Manufacturing Labor Costs	Machine-Hours	Number of Production Batches	Direct Manufacturing Labor-Hours
Indirect manufacturing labor costs	1			
Machine-hours	0.72	1		
Number of production batches	0.69	0.4	1	
Direct manufacturing labor-hours	0.41	0.12	0.31	1

These results indicate that multiple regressions using any pair of the independent variables in Exhibit 10-19 are not likely to encounter multicollinearity problems.

When multicollinearity exists, try to obtain new data that do not suffer from multicollinearity problems. Do not drop an independent variable (cost driver) that should be included in a model because it is correlated with another independent variable. Omitting such a variable will cause the estimated coefficient of the independent variable included in the model to be biased away from its true value.

---

[6] Adding another variable always increases r^2. The question is whether adding another variable increases r^2 sufficiently. One way to get insight into this question is to calculate an adjusted r^2 as follows:

Adjusted $r^2 = 1 - (1 - r^2)\dfrac{n - 1}{n - p - 1}$, where n is the number of observations and p is the number of coefficients estimated. In the model with only machine-hours as the independent variable, adjusted $r^2 = 1 - (1 - 0.52)\dfrac{12 - 1}{12 - 2 - 1} = 0.41$. In the model with both machine-hours and number of batches as independent variables, adjusted $r^2 = 1 - (1 - 0.72)\dfrac{12 - 1}{12 - 3 - 1} = 0.62$. Adjusted r^2 does not have the same interpretation as r^2 but the increase in adjusted r^2 when number of batches is added as an independent variable suggests that adding this variable significantly improves the fit of the model in a way that more than compensates for the degree of freedom lost by estimating another coefficient.

Terms to Learn

This chapter and the Glossary at the end of this book contain definitions of the following important terms:

account analysis method (**p. 347**)
coefficient of determination (r^2) (**p. 367**)
conference method (**p. 346**)
constant (**p. 343**)
cost estimation (**p. 344**)
cost function (**p. 341**)
cost predictions (**p. 344**)
cumulative average-time learning
  model (**p. 359**)
dependent variable (**p. 348**)
experience curve (**p. 358**)
high-low method (**p. 350**)

incremental unit-time learning model
  (**p. 360**)
independent variable (**p. 348**)
industrial engineering method (**p. 346**)
intercept (**p. 343**)
learning curve (**p. 358**)
linear cost function (**p. 342**)
mixed cost (**p. 343**)
multicollinearity (**p. 374**)
multiple regression (**p. 352**)
nonlinear cost function (**p. 357**)
regression analysis (**p. 352**)

residual term (**p. 352**)
semivariable cost (**p. 343**)
simple regression (**p. 352**)
slope coefficient (**p. 342**)
specification analysis (**p. 369**)
standard error of the estimated
  coefficient (**p. 368**)
standard error of the regression
  (**p. 368**)
step cost function (**p. 357**)
work-measurement method (**p. 346**)

Assignment Material

Questions

10-1 What two assumptions are frequently made when estimating a cost function?

10-2 Describe three alternative linear cost functions.

10-3 What is the difference between a linear and a nonlinear cost function? Give an example of each type of cost function.

10-4 "High correlation between two variables means that one is the cause and the other is the effect." Do you agree? Explain.

10-5 Name four approaches to estimating a cost function.

10-6 Describe the conference method for estimating a cost function. What are two advantages of this method?

10-7 Describe the account analysis method for estimating a cost function.

10-8 List the six steps in estimating a cost function on the basis of an analysis of a past cost relationship. Which step is typically the most difficult for the cost analyst?

10-9 When using the high-low method, should you base the high and low observations on the dependent variable or on the cost driver?

10-10 Describe three criteria for evaluating cost functions and choosing cost drivers.

10-11 Define learning curve. Outline two models that can be used when incorporating learning into the estimation of cost functions.

10-12 Discuss four frequently encountered problems when collecting cost data on variables included in a cost function.

10-13 What are the four key assumptions examined in specification analysis in the case of simple regression?

10-14 "All the independent variables in a cost function estimated with regression analysis are cost drivers." Do you agree? Explain.

10-15 "Multicollinearity exists when the dependent variable and the independent variable are highly correlated." Do you agree? Explain.

Exercises

10-16 Estimating a cost function. The controller of the Ijiri Company wants you to estimate a cost function from the following two observations in a general ledger account called Maintenance:

Month	Machine-Hours	Maintenance Costs Incurred
January	6,000	$4,000
February	10,000	5,400

Required

1. Estimate the cost function for maintenance.
2. Can the constant in the cost function be used as an estimate of fixed maintenance cost per month? Explain.

10-17 Identifying variable-, fixed-, and mixed-cost functions. The Pacific Corporation operates car rental agencies at more than 20 airports. Customers can choose from one of three contracts for car rentals of one day or less:

- Contract 1: $50 for the day
- Contract 2: $30 for the day plus $0.20 per mile traveled
- Contract 3: $1 per mile traveled

Required

1. Plot separate graphs for each of the three contracts, with costs on the vertical axis and miles traveled on the horizontal axis.
2. Express each contract as a linear cost function of the form $y = a + bX$.
3. Identify each contract as a variable-, fixed-, or mixed-cost function.

10-18 Various cost-behavior patterns. (CPA, adapted) Select the graph that matches the numbered manufacturing cost data (requirements 1–9). Indicate by letter which graph best fits the situation or item described.

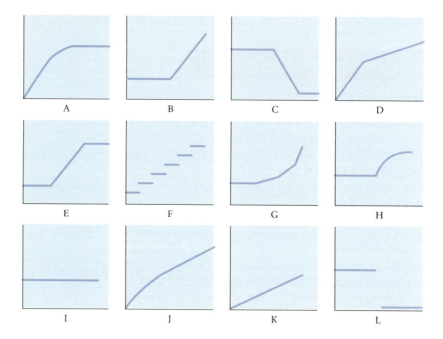

The vertical axes of the graphs represent total cost, and the horizontal axes represent units produced during a calendar year. In each case, the zero point of dollars and production is at the intersection of the two axes. The graphs may be used more than once.

Required

1. Annual depreciation of equipment, where the amount of depreciation charged is computed by the machine-hours method.
2. Electricity bill—a flat fixed charge, plus a variable cost after a certain number of kilowatt-hours are used, in which the quantity of kilowatt-hours used varies proportionately with quantity of units produced.
3. City water bill, which is computed as follows:

First 1,000,000 gallons or less	$1,000 flat fee
Next 10,000 gallons	$0.003 per gallon used
Next 10,000 gallons	$0.006 per gallon used
Next 10,000 gallons	$0.009 per gallon used
and so on	and so on

The gallons of water used vary proportionately with the quantity of production output.

4. Cost of direct materials, where direct material cost per unit produced decreases with each pound of material used (for example, if 1 pound is used, the cost is $10; if 2 pounds are used, the cost is $19.98; if 3 pounds are used, the cost is $29.94), with a minimum cost per unit of $9.20.

5. Annual depreciation of equipment, where the amount is computed by the straight-line method. When the depreciation schedule was prepared, it was anticipated that the obsolescence factor would be greater than the wear-and-tear factor.
6. Rent on a manufacturing plant donated by the city, where the agreement calls for a fixed-fee payment unless 200,000 labor-hours are worked, in which case no rent is paid.
7. Salaries of repair personnel, where one person is needed for every 1,000 machine-hours or less (that is, 0 to 1,000 hours requires one person, 1,001 to 2,000 hours requires two people, and so on).
8. Cost of direct materials used (assume no quantity discounts).
9. Rent on a manufacturing plant donated by the county, where the agreement calls for rent of $100,000 to be reduced by $1 for each direct manufacturing labor-hour worked in excess of 200,000 hours, but a minimum rental fee of $20,000 must be paid.

10-19 Matching graphs with descriptions of cost and revenue behavior. (D. Green, adapted) Given here are a number of graphs.

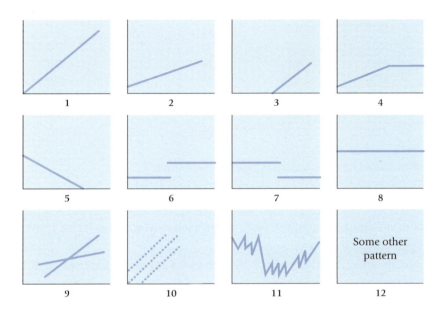

The horizontal axis represents the units produced over the year and the vertical axis represents total cost or revenues. Indicate by number which graph best fits the situation or item described (a–h). Some graphs may be used more than once; some may not apply to any of the situations.

a. Direct material costs
b. Supervisors' salaries for one shift and two shifts
c. A cost-volume-profit graph
d. Mixed costs—for example, car rental fixed charge plus a rate per mile driven
e. Depreciation of plant, computed on a straight-line basis
f. Data supporting the use of a variable-cost rate, such as manufacturing labor cost of $14 per unit produced
g. Incentive bonus plan that pays managers $0.10 for every unit produced above some level of production
h. Interest expense on $2 million borrowed at a fixed rate of interest

10-20 Account analysis method. Lorenzo operates a car wash. Incoming cars are put on an automatic conveyor belt. Cars are washed as the conveyor belt carries them from the start station to the finish station. After a car moves off the conveyor belt, it is dried manually. Workers then clean and vacuum the inside of the car. Lorenzo serviced 80,000 cars in 2012. Lorenzo reports the following costs for 2012:

Account Description	Costs
Car wash labor	$260,000
Soap, cloth, and supplies	42,000
Water	38,000
Electric power to move conveyor belt	72,000
Depreciation	64,000
Salaries	46,000

Required

1. Classify each account as variable or fixed with respect to the number of cars washed. Explain.
2. Suppose Lorenzo washed 90,000 cars in 2012. Use the cost classification you developed in requirement 1 to estimate Lorenzo's total costs in 2012. Depreciation is computed on a straight-line basis.

10-21 Account analysis, high-low. Java Joe Coffees wants to find an equation to estimate monthly utility costs. Java Joe's has been in business for one year and has collected the following cost data for utilities:

Month	Electricity Bill	Kilowatt Hours Used	Telephone Bill	Telephone Minutes Used	Water Bill	Gallons of Water Used
January	$360	1,200	$92.00	1,100	$60	30,560
February	$420	1,400	$91.20	1,060	$60	26,800
March	$549	1,830	$94.80	1,240	$60	31,450
April	$405	1,350	$89.60	980	$60	29,965
May	$588	1,960	$98.00	1,400	$60	30,568
June	$624	2,080	$98.80	1,440	$60	25,540
July	$522	1,740	$93.40	1,170	$60	32,690
August	$597	1,990	$96.20	1,310	$60	31,222
September	$630	2,100	$95.60	1,280	$60	33,540
October	$615	2,050	$93.80	1,190	$60	31,970
November	$594	1,980	$91.00	1,050	$60	28,600
December	$633	2,110	$97.00	1,350	$60	34,100

Required

1. Which of the preceding costs is variable? Fixed? Mixed? Explain.
2. Using the high-low method, determine the cost function for each cost.
3. Combine the preceding information to get a monthly utility cost function for Java Joe's.
4. Next month, Java Joe's expects to use 2,200 kilowatt hours of electricity, make 1,500 minutes of telephone calls, and use 32,000 gallons of water. Estimate total cost of utilities for the month.

10-22 Account analysis method. Gower, Inc., a manufacturer of plastic products, reports the following manufacturing costs and account analysis classification for the year ended December 31, 2012.

Account	Classification	Amount
Direct materials	All variable	$300,000
Direct manufacturing labor	All variable	225,000
Power	All variable	37,500
Supervision labor	20% variable	56,250
Materials-handling labor	50% variable	60,000
Maintenance labor	40% variable	75,000
Depreciation	0% variable	95,000
Rent, property taxes, and administration	0% variable	100,000

Gower, Inc., produced 75,000 units of product in 2012. Gower's management is estimating costs for 2013 on the basis of 2012 numbers. The following additional information is available for 2013.

a. Direct materials prices in 2013 are expected to increase by 5% compared with 2012.
b. Under the terms of the labor contract, direct manufacturing labor wage rates are expected to increase by 10% in 2013 compared with 2012.
c. Power rates and wage rates for supervision, materials handling, and maintenance are not expected to change from 2012 to 2013.
d. Depreciation costs are expected to increase by 5%, and rent, property taxes, and administration costs are expected to increase by 7%.
e. Gower expects to manufacture and sell 80,000 units in 2013.

Required

1. Prepare a schedule of variable, fixed, and total manufacturing costs for each account category in 2013. Estimate total manufacturing costs for 2013.
2. Calculate Gower's total manufacturing cost per unit in 2012, and estimate total manufacturing cost per unit in 2013.
3. How can you obtain better estimates of fixed and variable costs? Why would these better estimates be useful to Gower?

10-23 **Estimating a cost function, high-low method.** Reisen Travel offers helicopter service from suburban towns to John F. Kennedy International Airport in New York City. Each of its 10 helicopters makes between 1,000 and 2,000 round-trips per year. The records indicate that a helicopter that has made 1,000 round-trips in the year incurs an average operating cost of $350 per round-trip, and one that has made 2,000 round-trips in the year incurs an average operating cost of $300 per round-trip.

Required

1. Using the high-low method, estimate the linear relationship $y = a + bX$, where y is the total annual operating cost of a helicopter and X is the number of round-trips it makes to JFK airport during the year.
2. Give examples of costs that would be included in a and in b.
3. If Reisen Travel expects each helicopter to make, on average, 1,200 round-trips in the coming year, what should its estimated operating budget for the helicopter fleet be?

10-24 **Estimating a cost function, high-low method.** Laurie Daley is examining customer-service costs in the southern region of Capitol Products. Capitol Products has more than 200 separate electrical products that are sold with a six-month guarantee of full repair or replacement with a new product. When a product is returned by a customer, a service report is prepared. This service report includes details of the problem and the time and cost of resolving the problem. Weekly data for the most recent 8-week period are as follows:

Week	Customer-Service Department Costs	Number of Service Reports
1	$13,700	190
2	20,900	275
3	13,000	115
4	18,800	395
5	14,000	265
6	21,500	455
7	16,900	340
8	21,000	305

Required

1. Plot the relationship between customer-service costs and number of service reports. Is the relationship economically plausible?
2. Use the high-low method to compute the cost function, relating customer-service costs to the number of service reports.
3. What variables, in addition to number of service reports, might be cost drivers of weekly customer-service costs of Capitol Products?

10-25 **Linear cost approximation.** Terry Lawler, managing director of the Chicago Reviewers Group, is examining how overhead costs behave with changes in monthly professional labor-hours billed to clients. Assume the following historical data:

Total Overhead Costs	Professional Labor-Hours Billed to Clients
$335,000	2,000
400,000	3,000
430,000	4,000
472,000	5,000
533,000	6,500
582,000	7,500

Required

1. Compute the linear cost function, relating total overhead costs to professional labor-hours, using the representative observations of 3,000 and 6,500 hours. Plot the linear cost function. Does the constant component of the cost function represent the fixed overhead costs of the Chicago Reviewers Group? Why?
2. What would be the predicted total overhead costs for (a) 4,000 hours and (b) 7,500 hours using the cost function estimated in requirement 1? Plot the predicted costs and actual costs for 4,000 and 7,500 hours.
3. Lawler had a chance to accept a special job that would have boosted professional labor-hours from 3,000 to 4,000 hours. Suppose Lawler, guided by the linear cost function, rejected this job because it would have brought a total increase in contribution margin of $35,000, before deducting the predicted increase in total overhead cost, $38,000. What is the total contribution margin actually forgone?

10-26 Cost-volume-profit and regression analysis. Goldstein Corporation manufactures a children's bicycle, model CT8. Goldstein currently manufactures the bicycle frame. During 2012, Goldstein made 32,000 frames at a total cost of $1,056,000. Ryan Corporation has offered to supply as many frames as Goldstein wants at a cost of $32.50 per frame. Goldstein anticipates needing 35,000 frames each year for the next few years.

Required

1. **a.** What is the average cost of manufacturing a bicycle frame in 2012? How does it compare to Ryan's offer?
   b. Can Goldstein use the answer in requirement 1a to determine the cost of manufacturing 35,000 bicycle frames? Explain.
2. Goldstein's cost analyst uses annual data from past years to estimate the following regression equation with total manufacturing costs of the bicycle frame as the dependent variable and bicycle frames produced as the independent variable:

$$y = \$435{,}000 + \$19X$$

During the years used to estimate the regression equation, the production of bicycle frames varied from 31,000 to 35,000. Using this equation, estimate how much it would cost Goldstein to manufacture 35,000 bicycle frames. How much more or less costly is it to manufacture the frames rather than to acquire them from Ryan?
3. What other information would you need to be confident that the equation in requirement 2 accurately predicts the cost of manufacturing bicycle frames?

10-27 Regression analysis, service company. (CMA, adapted) Bob Jones owns a catering company that prepares food and beverages for banquets and parties. For a standard party the cost on a per-person basis is as follows:

Food and beverages	$15
Labor (0.5 hour × $10 per hour)	5
Overhead (0.5 hour × $14 per hour)	7
Total cost per person	$27

Jones is quite certain about his estimates of the food, beverages, and labor costs but is not as comfortable with the overhead estimate. The overhead estimate was based on the actual data for the past 12 months, which are presented here. These data indicate that overhead costs vary with the direct labor-hours used. The $14 estimate was determined by dividing total overhead costs for the 12 months by total labor-hours.

Month	Labor-Hours	Overhead Costs
January	2,500	$ 55,000
February	2,700	59,000
March	3,000	60,000
April	4,200	64,000
May	7,500	77,000
June	5,500	71,000
July	6,500	74,000
August	4,500	67,000
September	7,000	75,000
October	4,500	68,000
November	3,100	62,000
December	6,500	73,000
Total	57,500	$805,000

Jones has recently become aware of regression analysis. He estimated the following regression equation with overhead costs as the dependent variable and labor-hours as the independent variable:

$$y = \$48{,}271 + \$3.93X$$

Required

1. Plot the relationship between overhead costs and labor-hours. Draw the regression line and evaluate it using the criteria of economic plausibility, goodness of fit, and slope of the regression line.
2. Using data from the regression analysis, what is the variable cost per person for a standard party?
3. Bob Jones has been asked to prepare a bid for a 200-person standard party to be given next month. Determine the minimum bid price that Jones would be willing to submit to recoup variable costs.

10-28 High-low, regression. Melissa Crupp is the new manager of the materials storeroom for Canton Manufacturing. Melissa has been asked to estimate future monthly purchase costs for part #4599, used in two of Canton's products. Melissa has purchase cost and quantity data for the past nine months as follows:

Month	Cost of Purchase	Quantity Purchased
January	$10,390	2,250 parts
February	10,550	2,350
March	14,400	3,390
April	13,180	3,120
May	10,970	2,490
June	11,580	2,680
July	12,690	3,030
August	8,560	1,930
September	12,450	2,960

Estimated monthly purchases for this part based on expected demand of the two products for the rest of the year are as follows:

Month	Purchase Quantity Expected
October	2,800 parts
November	3,100
December	2,500

Required

1. The computer in Melissa's office is down and Melissa has been asked to immediately provide an equation to estimate the future purchase cost for part # 4599. Melissa grabs a calculator and uses the high-low method to estimate a cost equation. What equation does she get?
2. Using the equation from requirement 1, calculate the future expected purchase costs for each of the last three months of the year.
3. After a few hours Melissa's computer is fixed. Melissa uses the first nine months of data and regression analysis to estimate the relationship between the quantity purchased and purchase costs of part #4599. The regression line Melissa obtains is as follows:

$$y = \$1,779.6 + 3.67X$$

Evaluate the regression line using the criteria of economic plausibility, goodness of fit, and significance of the independent variable. Compare the regression equation to the equation based on the high-low method. Which is a better fit? Why?

4. Use the regression results to calculate the expected purchase costs for October, November, and December. Compare the expected purchase costs to the expected purchase costs calculated using the high-low method in requirement 2. Comment on your results.

10-29 Learning curve, cumulative average-time learning model. Global Defense manufactures radar systems. It has just completed the manufacture of its first newly designed system, RS-32. Manufacturing data for the RS-32 follow:

	Home	Insert	Page Layout	Formulas	Data	Review	View	
	A					B	C	
1	Direct material cost					$160,000	per unit of RS-32
2	Direct manufacturing labor time for first unit					6,000	direct manufacturing labor-hours
3	Learning curve for manufacturing labor time per radar system					85%	cumulative average time[a]
4	Direct manufacturing labor cost					$ 30	per direct manufacturing labor-hour
5	Variable manufacturing overhead cost					$ 20	per direct manufacturing labor-hour
6							
7	[a]Using the formula (p. 359), for a 85% learning curve, $b = \dfrac{\ln 0.85}{\ln 2} = \dfrac{-0.162519}{0.693147} = -0.234465$						
8							

Required   Calculate the total variable costs of producing 2, 4, and 8 units.

10-30 **Learning curve, incremental unit-time learning model.** Assume the same information for Global Defense as in Exercise 10-29, except that Global Defense uses an 85% incremental unit-time learning model as a basis for predicting direct manufacturing labor-hours. (An 85% learning curve means $b = -0.234465$.)

Required
1. Calculate the total variable costs of producing 2, 3, and 4 units.
2. If you solved Exercise 10-29, compare your cost predictions in the two exercises for 2 and 4 units. Why are the predictions different? How should Global Defense decide which model it should use?

MyAccountingLab

Problems

10-31 **High-low method.** Ken Howard, financial analyst at KMW Corporation, is examining the behavior of quarterly maintenance costs for budgeting purposes. Howard collects the following data on machine-hours worked and maintenance costs for the past 12 quarters:

Quarter	Machine-Hours	Maintenance Costs
1	100,000	$205,000
2	120,000	240,000
3	110,000	220,000
4	130,000	260,000
5	95,000	190,000
6	115,000	235,000
7	105,000	215,000
8	125,000	255,000
9	105,000	210,000
10	125,000	245,000
11	115,000	200,000
12	140,000	280,000

Required
1. Estimate the cost function for the quarterly data using the high-low method.
2. Plot and comment on the estimated cost function.
3. Howard anticipates that KMW will operate machines for 100,000 hours in quarter 13. Calculate the predicted maintenance costs in quarter 13 using the cost function estimated in requirement 1.

10-32 **High-low method and regression analysis.** Local Harvest, a cooperative of organic family-owned farms outside of Columbus, Ohio, has recently started a fresh produce club to provide support to the group's member farms, and to promote the benefits of eating organic, locally-produced food to the nearby suburban community. Families pay a seasonal membership fee of $50, and place their orders a week in advance for a price of $40 per week. In turn, Local Harvest delivers fresh-picked seasonal local produce to several neighborhood distribution points. Eight hundred families joined the club for the first season, but the number of orders varied from week to week.

Harvey Hendricks has run the produce club for the first 10-week season. Before becoming a farmer, Harvey had been a business major in college, and he remembers a few things about cost analysis. In planning for next year, he wants to know how many orders will be needed each week for the club to break even, but first he must estimate the club's fixed and variable costs. He has collected the following data over the club's first 10 weeks of operation:

Week	Number of Orders per Week	Weekly Total Costs
1	351	$18,795
2	385	21,597
3	410	22,800
4	453	22,600
5	425	21,900
6	486	24,600
7	455	23,900
8	467	22,900
9	525	25,305
10	510	24,500

1. Plot the relationship between number of orders per week and weekly total costs.
2. Estimate the cost equation using the high-low method, and draw this line on your graph.
3. Harvey uses his computer to calculate the following regression formula:

$$\text{Total weekly costs} = \$8,631 + (\$31.92 \times \text{Number of weekly orders})$$

Draw the regression line on your graph. Use your graph to evaluate the regression line using the criteria of economic plausibility, goodness of fit, and significance of the independent variable. Is the cost function estimated using the high-low method a close approximation of the cost function estimated using the regression method? Explain briefly.
4. Did Fresh Harvest break even this season? Remember that each of the families paid a seasonal membership fee of $50.
5. Assume that 900 families join the club next year, and that prices and costs do not change. How many orders, on average, must Fresh Harvest receive each week to break even?

10-33 High-low method; regression analysis. (CIMA, adapted) Anna Martinez, the financial manager at the Casa Real restaurant, is checking to see if there is any relationship between newspaper advertising and sales revenues at the restaurant. She obtains the following data for the past 10 months:

Month	Revenues	Advertising Costs
March	$50,000	$2,000
April	70,000	3,000
May	55,000	1,500
June	65,000	3,500
July	55,000	1,000
August	65,000	2,000
September	45,000	1,500
October	80,000	4,000
November	55,000	2,500
December	60,000	2,500

She estimates the following regression equation:

$$\text{Monthly revenues} = \$39,502 + (\$8.723 \times \text{Advertising costs})$$

1. Plot the relationship between advertising costs and revenues.
2. Draw the regression line and evaluate it using the criteria of economic plausibility, goodness of fit, and slope of the regression line.
3. Use the high-low method to compute the function, relating advertising costs and revenues.
4. Using (a) the regression equation and (b) the high-low equation, what is the increase in revenues for each $1,000 spent on advertising within the relevant range? Which method should Martinez use to predict the effect of advertising costs on revenues? Explain briefly.

10-34 Regression, activity-based costing, choosing cost drivers. Fitzgerald Manufacturing has been using activity-based costing to determine the cost of product X-678. One of the activities, "Inspection," occurs just before the product is finished. Fitzgerald inspects every 10th unit, and has been using "number of units inspected" as the cost driver for inspection costs. A significant component of inspection costs is the cost of the test-kit used in each inspection.

Neela McFeen, the line manager, is wondering if inspection labor-hours might be a better cost driver for inspection costs. Neela gathers information for weekly inspection costs, units inspected, and inspection labor-hours as follows:

Week	Units Inspected	Inspection Labor-Hours	Inspection Costs
1	1,400	190	$3,700
2	400	70	1,800
3	1,700	230	4,500
4	2,400	240	5,900
5	2,100	210	5,300
6	700	90	2,400
7	900	110	2,900

Neela runs regressions on each of the possible cost drivers and estimates these cost functions:

$$\text{Inspection Costs} = \$977 + (\$2.05 \times \text{Number of units inspected})$$
$$\text{Inspection Costs} = \$478 + (\$20.31 \times \text{Inspection labor-hours})$$

Required

1. Explain why number of units inspected and inspection labor-hours are plausible cost drivers of inspection costs.
2. Plot the data and regression line for units inspected and inspection costs. Plot the data and regression line for inspection labor-hours and inspection costs. Which cost driver of inspection costs would you choose? Explain.
3. Neela expects inspectors to work 140 hours next period and to inspect 1,100 units. Using the cost driver you chose in requirement 2, what amount of inspection costs should Neela budget? Explain any implications of Neela choosing the cost driver you did not choose in requirement 2 to budget inspection costs.

10-35 Interpreting regression results, matching time periods. Brickman Apparel produces equipment for the extreme-sports market. It has four peak periods, each lasting two months, for manufacturing the merchandise suited for spring, summer, fall, and winter. In the off-peak periods, Brickman schedules equipment maintenance. Brickman's controller, Sascha Green, wants to understand the drivers of equipment maintenance costs. The data collected is shown in the table as follows:

Month	Machine-Hours	Maintenance Costs
January	5,000	$ 1,300
February	5,600	2,200
March	1,500	12,850
April	6,500	1,665
May	5,820	2,770
June	1,730	15,250
July	7,230	1,880
August	5,990	2,740
September	2,040	15,350
October	6,170	1,620
November	5,900	2,770
December	1,500	14,700

A regression analysis of one year of monthly data yields the following relationships:

$$\text{Maintenance costs} = \$18,552 - (\$2.683 \times \text{Number of machine-hours})$$

Upon examining the results, Green comments, "So, all I have to do to reduce maintenance costs is run my machines longer?! This is hard to believe, but numbers don't lie! I would have guessed just the opposite."

Required

1. Explain why Green made this comment. What is wrong with her analysis?
2. Upon further reflection, Sascha Green reanalyzes the data, this time comparing quarterly machine-hours with quarterly maintenance expenditures. This time, the results are very different. The regression yields the following formula:

$$\text{Maintenance costs} = \$2,622.80 + (\$1.175 \times \text{Number of machine-hours})$$

What caused the formula to change, in light of the fact that the data was the same?

10-36 Cost estimation, cumulative average-time learning curve. The Nautilus Company, which is under contract to the U.S. Navy, assembles troop deployment boats. As part of its research program, it completes the assembly of the first of a new model (PT109) of deployment boats. The Navy is impressed with the PT109. It requests that Nautilus submit a proposal on the cost of producing another six PT109s.

Nautilus reports the following cost information for the first PT109 assembled and uses a 90% cumulative average-time learning model as a basis for forecasting direct manufacturing labor-hours for the next six PT109s. (A 90% learning curve means $b = -0.152004$.)

	Home	Insert	Page Layout	Formulas	Data	Review	View	
	A					B		C
1	Direct material					$200,000		
2	Direct manufacturing labor time for first boat					15,000	labor-hours	
3	Direct manufacturing labor rate					$ 40	per direct manufacturing labor-hour	
4	Variable manufacturing overhead cost					$ 25	per direct manufacturing labor-hour	
5	Other manufacturing overhead					20%	of direct manufacturing labor costs	
6	Tooling costs[a]					$280,000		
7	Learning curve for manufacturing labor time per boat					90%	cumulative average time[b]	
8								
9	[a]Tooling can be reused at no extra cost because all of its cost has been assigned to the first deployment boat.							
10								
11	[b]Using the formula (p. 359), for a 90% learning curve, $b = \dfrac{\ln 0.9}{\ln 2} = \dfrac{-0.105361}{0.693147} = -0.152004$							
12								

Required

1. Calculate predicted total costs of producing the six PT109s for the Navy. (Nautilus will keep the first deployment boat assembled, costed at $1,575,000, as a demonstration model for potential customers.)
2. What is the dollar amount of the difference between (a) the predicted total costs for producing the six PT109s in requirement 1, and (b) the predicted total costs for producing the six PT109s, assuming that there is no learning curve for direct manufacturing labor? That is, for (b) assume a linear function for units produced and direct manufacturing labor-hours.

10-37 Cost estimation, incremental unit-time learning model. Assume the same information for the Nautilus Company as in Problem 10-36 with one exception. This exception is that Nautilus uses a 90% incremental unit-time learning model as a basis for predicting direct manufacturing labor-hours in its assembling operations. (A 90% learning curve means $b = -0.152004$.)

Required

1. Prepare a prediction of the total costs for producing the six PT109s for the Navy.
2. If you solved requirement 1 of Problem 10-36, compare your cost prediction there with the one you made here. Why are the predictions different? How should Nautilus decide which model it should use?

10-38 Regression; choosing among models. Tilbert Toys (TT) makes the popular Floppin' Freddy Frog and Jumpin' Jill Junebug dolls in batches. TT has recently adopted activity-based costing. TT incurs setup costs for each batch of dolls that it produces. TT uses "number of setups" as the cost driver for setup costs.

TT has just hired Bebe Williams, an accountant. Bebe thinks that "number of setup-hours" might be a better cost driver because the setup time for each product is different. Bebe collects the following data.

	Home	Insert	Page Layout	Formulas	Data	Review	View
	A	B		C		D	
1	Month	Number of Setups		Number of Setup Hours		Setup Costs	
2	1	300		1,840		$104,600	
3	2	410		2,680		126,700	
4	3	150		1,160		57,480	
5	4	480		3,800		236,840	
6	5	310		3,680		178,880	
7	6	460		3,900		213,760	
8	7	420		2,980		209,620	
9	8	300		1,200		90,080	
10	9	270		3,280		221,040	

1. Estimate the regression equation for (a) setup costs and number of setups and (b) setup costs and number of setup-hours. You should obtain the following results:

Regression 1: Setup costs = $a + (b \times$ Number of setups)

Variable	Coefficient	Standard Error	t-Value
Constant	$12,890	$61,365	0.21
Independent variable 1: No. of setups	$ 426.77	$ 171	2.49

$r^2 = 0.47$; Durbin-Watson statistic = 1.65

Regression 2: Setup costs = $a + (b \times$ Number of setup-hours)

Variable	Coefficient	Standard Error	t-Value
Constant	$6,573	$ 25,908	0.25
Independent variable 1: No. of setup-hours	$ 56.27	$ 8.90	6.32

$r^2 = 0.85$; Durbin-Watson statistic = 1.50

2. On two different graphs plot the data and the regression lines for each of the following cost functions:
   a. Setup costs = $a + (b \times$ Number of setups)
   b. Setup costs = $a + (b \times$ Number of setup-hours)
3. Evaluate the regression models for "Number of setups" and "Number of setup-hours" as the cost driver according to the format of Exhibit 10-18 (p. 372).
4. Based on your analysis, which cost driver should Tilbert Toys use for setup costs, and why?

10-39 Multiple regression (continuation of 10-38). Bebe Williams wonders if she should run a multiple regression with both number of setups and number of setup-hours, as cost drivers.

1. Run a multiple regression to estimate the regression equation for setup costs using both number of setups and number of setup-hours as independent variables. You should obtain the following result:

Regression 3: Setup costs = $a (b_1 \times$ No. of setups) + $(b_2 \times$ No. of setup-hours)

Variable	Coefficient	Standard Error	t-Value
Constant	-$2,807	$34,850	-0.08
Independent variable 1: No. of setups	$ 58.62	$ 133.42	0.44
Independent variable 2: No. of setup-hours	$ 52.31	$ 13.08	4.00

$r^2 = 0.86$; Durbin-Watson statistic = 1.38

2. Evaluate the multiple regression output using the criteria of economic plausibility goodness of fit, significance of independent variables, and specification of estimation assumptions. (Assume linearity, constant variance, and normality of residuals.)
3. What difficulties do not arise in simple regression analysis that may arise in multiple regression analysis? Is there evidence of such difficulties in the multiple regression presented in this problem? Explain.
4. Which of the regression models from Problems 10-38 and 10-39 would you recommend Bebe Williams use? Explain.

10-40 Purchasing department cost drivers, activity-based costing, simple regression analysis. Fashion Bling operates a chain of 10 retail department stores. Each department store makes its own purchasing decisions. Barry Lee, assistant to the president of Fashion Bling, is interested in better understanding the drivers of purchasing department costs. For many years, Fashion Bling has allocated purchasing department costs to products on the basis of the dollar value of merchandise purchased. A $100 item is allocated 10 times as many overhead costs associated with the purchasing department as a $10 item.

Lee recently attended a seminar titled "Cost Drivers in the Retail Industry." In a presentation at the seminar, Couture Fabrics, a leading competitor that has implemented activity-based costing, reported number of purchase orders and number of suppliers to be the two most important cost drivers of purchasing department costs. The dollar value of merchandise purchased in each purchase order was not found to be a significant cost driver. Lee interviewed several members of the purchasing department at the Fashion Bling store in Miami. They believed that Couture Fabrics' conclusions also applied to their purchasing department.

Lee collects the following data for the most recent year for Fashion Bling's 10 retail department stores:

	Home	Insert	Page Layout	Formulas	Data	Review	View
	A		B	C	D	E	
1	Department Store		Purchasing Department Costs (PDC)	Dollar Value of Merchandise Purchased (MP$)	Number of Purchase Orders (No. of POs)	Number of Suppliers (No. of Ss)	
2	Baltimore		$1,522,000	$ 68,307,000	4,345	125	
3	Chicago		1,095,000	33,463,000	2,548	230	
4	Los Angeles		542,000	121,800,000	1,420	8	
5	Miami		2,053,000	119,450,000	5,935	188	
6	New York		1,068,000	33,575,000	2,786	21	
7	Phoenix		517,000	29,836,000	1,334	29	
8	Seattle		1,544,000	102,840,000	7,581	101	
9	St. Louis		1,761,000	38,725,000	3,623	127	
10	Toronto		1,605,000	139,300,000	1,712	202	
11	Vancouver		1,263,000	130,110,000	4,736	196	

Lee decides to use simple regression analysis to examine whether one or more of three variables (the last three columns in the table) are cost drivers of purchasing department costs. Summary results for these regressions are as follows:

Regression 1: PDC = $a + (b \times$ MP$)

Variable	Coefficient	Standard Error	t-Value
Constant	$1,041,421	$346,709	3.00
Independent variable 1: MP$	0.0031	0.0038	0.83

$r^2 = 0.08$; Durbin-Watson statistic = 2.41

Regression 2: PDC = $a (b \times$ No. of POs)

Variable	Coefficient	Standard Error	t-Value
Constant	$722,538	$265,835	2.72
Independent variable 1: No. of POs	$ 159.48	$ 64.84	2.46

$r^2 = 0.43$; Durbin-Watson statistic = 1.97

Regression 3: PDC = $a + (b \times$ No. of Ss)

Variable	Coefficient	Standard Error	t-Value
Constant	$828,814	$246,570	3.36
Independent variable 1: No. of Ss	$ 3,816	$ 1,698	2.25

$r^2 = 0.39$; Durbin-Watson statistic = 2.01

Required

1. Compare and evaluate the three simple regression models estimated by Lee. Graph each one. Also, use the format employed in Exhibit 10-18 (p. 372) to evaluate the information.
2. Do the regression results support the Couture Fabrics' presentation about the purchasing department's cost drivers? Which of these cost drivers would you recommend in designing an ABC system?
3. How might Lee gain additional evidence on drivers of purchasing department costs at each of Fashion Bling's stores?

10-41 Purchasing department cost drivers, multiple regression analysis (continuation of 10-40). Barry Lee decides that the simple regression analysis used in Problem 10-40 could be extended to a multiple regression analysis. He finds the following results for two multiple regression analyses:

Regression 4: PDC = $a + (b_1 \times$ No. of POs$) + (b_2 \times$ No. of Ss$)$

Variable	Coefficient	Standard Error	t-Value
Constant	$484,522	$256,684	1.89
Independent variable 1: No. of POs	$ 126.66	$ 57.80	2.19
Independent variable 2: No. of Ss	$ 2,903	$ 1,459	1.99

$r^2 = 0.64$; Durbin-Watson statistic = 1.91

Regression 5: PDC = $a + (b_1 \times$ No. of POs$) + (b_2 \times$ No. of Ss$) + (b_3 \times$ MP$)$

Variable	Coefficient	Standard Error	t-Value
Constant	$483,560	$312,554	1.55
Independent variable 1: No. of POs	$ 126.58	$ 63.75	1.99
Independent variable 2: No. of Ss	$ 2,901	$ 1,622	1.79
Independent variable 3: MP$	0.00002	0.0029	0.01

$r^2 = 0.64$; Durbin-Watson statistic = 1.91

The coefficients of correlation between combinations of pairs of the variables are as follows:

	PDC	MP$	No. of POs
MP$	0.28		
No. of POs	0.66	0.27	
No. of Ss	0.62	0.30	0.29

Required

1. Evaluate regression 4 using the criteria of economic plausibility, goodness of fit, significance of independent variables and specification analysis. Compare regression 4 with regressions 2 and 3 in Problem 10-40. Which one of these models would you recommend that Lee use? Why?
2. Compare regression 5 with regression 4. Which one of these models would you recommend that Lee use? Why?
3. Lee estimates the following data for the Baltimore store for next year: dollar value of merchandise purchased, $78,000,000; number of purchase orders, 4,000; number of suppliers, 95. How much should Lee budget for purchasing department costs for the Baltimore store for next year?
4. What difficulties do not arise in simple regression analysis that may arise in multiple regression analysis? Is there evidence of such difficulties in either of the multiple regressions presented in this problem? Explain.
5. Give two examples of decisions in which the regression results reported here (and in Problem 10-40) could be informative.

Collaborative Learning Problem

10-42 Interpreting regression results, matching time periods, ethics. Jayne Barbour is working as a summer intern at Mode, a trendy store specializing in clothing for twenty-somethings. Jayne has been working closely with her cousin, Gail Hubbard, who plans promotions for Mode. The store has only been in business for 10 months, and Valerie Parker, the store's owner, has been unsure of the effectiveness of the store's advertising. Wanting to impress Valerie with the regression analysis skills she acquired in a cost accounting course the previous semester, Jayne decides to prepare an analysis of the effect of advertising on revenues. She collects the following data:

	Home	Insert	Page Layout	Formulas
	A	B		C
1	Month	Advertising Expense		Revenue
2	October	4,560		$35,400
3	November	3,285		44,255
4	December	1,200		56,300
5	January	4,099		28,764
6	February	3,452		49,532
7	March	1,075		43,200
8	April	4,768		30,600
9	May	4,775		52,137
10	June	1,845		49,640
11	July	1,430		29,542

Jayne performs a regression analysis, comparing each month's advertising expense with that month's revenue, and obtains the following formula:

$$\text{Revenue} = \$47,801 - (1.92 \times \text{Advertising expense})$$

Variable	Coefficient	Standard Error	t-Value
Constant	$47,801.72	7,628.39	6.27
Independent variable: Advertising expense	−1.92	2.26	−0.85

$r^2 = 0.43$; Standard error = 10,340.18

1. Plot the preceding data on a graph and draw the regression line. What does the cost formula indicate about the relationship between monthly advertising expense and monthly revenues? Is the relationship economically plausible? **Required**

2. Jayne worries that if she makes her presentation to the owner as planned, it will reflect poorly on her cousin Gail's performance. Is she ethically obligated to make the presentation?

3. Jayne thinks further about her analysis, and discovers a significant flaw in her approach. She realizes that advertising done in a given month should be expected to influence the following month's sales, not necessarily the current month's. She modifies her analysis by comparing, for example, October advertising expense with November sales revenue. The modified regression yields the following:

$$\text{Revenue} = \$23,538 + (5.92 \times \text{Advertising expense})$$

Variable	Coefficient	Standard Error	t-Value
Constant	$23,538.45	4,996.60	4.71
Independent variable: Previous month's advertising expense	5.92	1.42	4.18

$r^2 = 0.71$; Standard error = 6,015.67

What does the revised cost formula indicate? Plot the revised data on a graph. (You will need to discard October revenue and July advertising expense from the data set.) Is this relationship economically plausible?

4. Can Jayne conclude that there is a cause and effect relationship between advertising expense and sales revenue? Why or why not?

How many decisions have you made today?

Maybe you made a big one, such as accepting a job offer. Or maybe your decision was as simple as settling on your plans for the weekend or choosing a restaurant for dinner. Regardless of whether decisions are significant or routine, most people follow a simple, logical process when making them. This process involves gathering information, making predictions, making a choice, acting on the choice, and evaluating results. It also includes deciding what costs and benefits each choice affords. Some costs are irrelevant. For example, once a coffee maker is purchased, its cost is irrelevant when deciding how much money a person saves each time he or she brews coffee at home versus buying it at Starbucks. The cost of the coffee maker was incurred in the past, and the money is spent and can't be recouped. This chapter will explain which costs and benefits are relevant and which are not—and how you should think of them when choosing among alternatives.

Relevant Costs, JetBlue, and Twitter[1]

What does it cost JetBlue to fly a customer on a round-trip flight from New York City to Nantucket? The incremental cost is very small, around $5 for beverages, because the other costs (the plane, pilots, ticket agents, fuel, airport landing fees, and baggage handlers) are fixed. Because most costs are fixed, would it be worthwhile for JetBlue to fill a seat provided it earns at least $5 for that seat? The answer depends on whether the flight is full.

Suppose JetBlue normally charges $330 for this round-trip ticket. If the flight is full, JetBlue would not sell the ticket for anything less than $330, because there are still customers willing to pay this fare for the flight. What if there are empty seats? Selling a ticket for something more than $5 is better than leaving the seat empty and earning nothing.

If a customer uses the Internet to purchase the ticket a month in advance, JetBlue will likely quote $330 because it expects the flight to be full. If, on the Monday before the scheduled Friday departure, JetBlue finds that the plane will not be full, the airline may be willing to lower its prices dramatically in hopes of attracting more customers and earning a profit on the unfilled seats.

---

[1] *Source*: Jones, Charisse. 2009. JetBlue and United give twitter a try to sell airline seats fast. *USA Today*, August 2. www.usatoday.com/travel/flights/2009-08-02-jetblue-united-twitter-airfares_N.htm

Enter Twitter. Like the e-mails that Jet Blue has sent out to customers for years, the widespread messaging service allows JetBlue to quickly connect with customers and fill seats on flights that might otherwise take off less than full. When JetBlue began promoting last-minute fare sales on Twitter in 2009 and Twitter-recipients learned that $330 round-trip tickets from New York City to Nantucket were available for just $18, the flights filled up quickly. JetBlue's Twitter fare

sales usually last only eight hours, or until all available seats are sold. To use such a pricing strategy requires a deep understanding of costs in different decision situations.

Just like JetBlue, managers in corporations around the world use a decision process to help them make decisions. Managers at JPMorgan Chase gather information about financial markets, consumer preferences, and economic trends before determining whether to offer new services to customers. Macy's managers examine all the relevant information related to domestic and international clothing manufacturing before selecting vendors. Managers at Porsche gather cost information to decide whether to manufacture a component part or purchase it from a supplier. The decision process may not always be easy, but as Napoleon Bonaparte said, "Nothing is more difficult, and therefore more precious, than to be able to decide."

Information and the Decision Process

Managers usually follow a *decision model* for choosing among different courses of action. A **decision model** is a formal method of making a choice that often involves both quantitative and qualitative analyses. Management accountants analyze and present relevant data to guide managers' decisions.

Consider a strategic decision facing management at Precision Sporting Goods, a manufacturer of golf clubs: Should it reorganize its manufacturing operations to reduce manufacturing labor costs? Precision Sporting Goods has only two alternatives: Do not reorganize or reorganize.

Reorganization will eliminate all manual handling of materials. Current manufacturing labor consists of 20 workers—15 workers operate machines, and 5 workers handle materials. The 5 materials-handling workers have been hired on contracts that

Exhibit 11-1

Five-Step Decision-
Making Process
for Precision
Sporting Goods

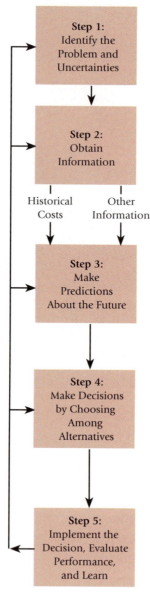

Step 1:
Identify the
Problem and
Uncertainties

Should Precision Sporting Goods reorganize its manufacturing operations to reduce manufacturing labor costs? An important uncertainty is how the reorganization will affect employee morale.

Step 2:
Obtain
Information

Historical hourly wage rates are $14 per hour. However, a recently negotiated increase in employee benefits of $2 per hour will increase wages to $16 per hour. The reorganization of manufacturing operations is expected to reduce the number of workers from 20 to 15 by eliminating all 5 workers who handle materials. The reorganization is likely to have negative effects on employee morale.

Historical
Costs

Other
Information

Step 3:
Make
Predictions
About the Future

Managers use information from Step 2 as a basis for predicting future manufacturing labor costs. Under the existing do-not-reorganize alternative, costs are predicted to be $640,000 (20 workers × 2,000 hours per worker per year × $16 per hour), and under the reorganize alternative, costs are predicted to be $480,000 (15 workers × 2,000 hours per worker per year × $16 per hour). Recall, the reorganization is predicted to cost $90,000 per year.

Step 4:
Make Decisions
by Choosing
Among
Alternatives

Managers compare the predicted benefits calculated in Step 3 ($640,000 − $480,000 = $160,000—that is, savings from eliminating materials-handling labor costs, 5 workers × 2,000 hours per worker per year × $16 per hour = $160,000) against the cost of the reorganization ($90,000) along with other considerations (such as likely negative effects on employee morale). Management chooses the reorganize alternative because the financial benefits are significant and the effects on employee morale are expected to be temporary and relatively small.

Step 5:
Implement the
Decision, Evaluate
Performance,
and Learn

Evaluating performance after the decision is implemented provides critical feedback for managers, and the five-step sequence is then repeated in whole or in part. Managers learn from actual results that the new manufacturing labor costs are $540,000, rather than the predicted $480,000, because of lower-than-expected manufacturing labor productivity. This (now) historical information can help managers make better subsequent predictions that allow for more learning time. Alternatively, managers may improve implementation via employee training and better supervision.

**Decision
Point** ▶

What is the five-step
process that
managers can use to
make decisions?

permit layoffs without additional payments. Each worker works 2,000 hours annually. Reorganization is predicted to cost $90,000 each year (mostly for new equipment leases). Production output of 25,000 units as well as the selling price of $250, the direct material cost per unit of $50, manufacturing overhead of $750,000, and marketing costs of $2,000,000 will be unaffected by the reorganization.

Managers use the five-step decision-making process presented in Exhibit 11-1 and first introduced in Chapter 1 to make this decision. Study the sequence of steps in this exhibit and note how Step 5 evaluates performance to provide feedback about actions taken in the previous steps. This feedback might affect future predictions, the prediction methods used, the way choices are made, or the implementation of the decision.

The Concept of Relevance

Much of this chapter focuses on Step 4 in Exhibit 11-1 and on the concepts of relevant costs and relevant revenues when choosing among alternatives.

Relevant Costs and Relevant Revenues

Relevant costs are *expected future costs*, and **relevant revenues** are *expected future revenues* that differ among the alternative courses of action being considered. Revenues and costs that are *not relevant* are said to be *irrelevant*. It is important to recognize that to be relevant costs and relevant revenues they *must*:

Learning Objective **2**

Distinguish relevant from irrelevant information in decision situations

. . . only costs and revenues that are expected to occur in the future and differ among alternative courses of action are relevant

- **Occur in the future**—every decision deals with selecting a course of action based on its expected future results.

- **Differ among the alternative courses of action**—costs and revenues that do not differ will not matter and, hence, will have no bearing on the decision being made.

The question is always, "What difference will an action make?"

Exhibit 11-2 presents the financial data underlying the choice between the do-not-reorganize and reorganize alternatives for Precision Sporting Goods. There are two ways to analyze the data. The first considers "All revenues and costs," while the second considers only "Relevant revenues and costs."

The first two columns describe the first way and present *all data*. The last two columns describe the second way and present *only relevant costs*—the $640,000 and $480,000 expected future manufacturing labor costs and the $90,000 expected future reorganization costs that differ between the two alternatives. The revenues, direct materials, manufacturing overhead, and marketing items can be ignored because they will remain the same whether or not Precision Sporting Goods reorganizes. They do not differ between the alternatives and, therefore, are irrelevant.

Note, the past (historical) manufacturing hourly wage rate of $14 and total past (historical) manufacturing labor costs of $560,000 (20 workers × 2,000 hours per worker per year × $14 per hour) do not appear in Exhibit 11-2. *Although they may be a useful basis for making informed predictions of the expected future manufacturing labor costs of $640,000 and $480,000, historical costs themselves are past costs that, therefore, are irrelevant to decision making.* Past costs are also called **sunk costs** because they are unavoidable and cannot be changed no matter what action is taken.

The analysis in Exhibit 11-2 indicates that reorganizing the manufacturing operations will increase predicted operating income by $70,000 each year. Note that the managers at Precision Sporting Goods reach the same conclusion whether they use all data or include only relevant data in the analysis. By confining the analysis to only the relevant data, managers

---

Exhibit 11-2   Determining Relevant Revenues and Relevant Costs for Precision Sporting Goods

	All Revenues and Costs		Relevant Revenues and Costs	
	Alternative 1: Do Not Reorganize	**Alternative 2: Reorganize**	**Alternative 1: Do Not Reorganize**	**Alternative 2: Reorganize**
Revenues[a]	$6,250,000	$6,250,000	—	—
Costs:				
Direct materials[b]	1,250,000	1,250,000	—	—
Manufacturing labor	640,000[c]	480,000[d]	$ 640,000[c]	$ 480,000[d]
Manufacturing overhead	750,000	750,000	—	—
Marketing	2,000,000	2,000,000	—	—
Reorganization costs	—	90,000	—	90,000
Total costs	4,640,000	4,570,000	640,000	570,000
Operating income	$1,610,000	$1,680,000	$(640,000)	$(570,000)

                     $70,000 Difference $70,000 Difference

[a]25,000 units × $250 per unit = $6,250,000   [c]20 workers × 2,000 hours per worker × $16 per hour = $640,000
[b]25,000 units × $50 per unit = $1,250,000   [d]15 workers × 2,000 hours per worker × $16 per hour = $480,000

| Exhibit 11-3 | Key Features of Relevant Information |

- Past (historical) costs may be helpful as a basis for making *predictions*. However, past costs themselves are always irrelevant when making *decisions*.
- Different alternatives can be compared by examining differences in expected total future revenues and expected total future costs.
- Not all expected future revenues and expected future costs are relevant. Expected future revenues and expected future costs that do not differ among alternatives are irrelevant and, hence, can be eliminated from the analysis. The key question is always, "What difference will an action make?"
- Appropriate weight must be given to qualitative factors and quantitative nonfinancial factors.

can clear away the clutter of potentially confusing irrelevant data. Focusing on the relevant data is especially helpful when all the information needed to prepare a detailed income statement is unavailable. Understanding which costs are relevant and which are irrelevant helps the decision maker concentrate on obtaining only the pertinent data and is more efficient.

Qualitative and Quantitative Relevant Information

Managers divide the outcomes of decisions into two broad categories: *quantitative* and *qualitative*. **Quantitative factors** are outcomes that are measured in numerical terms. Some quantitative factors are financial; they can be expressed in monetary terms. Examples include the cost of direct materials, direct manufacturing labor, and marketing. Other quantitative factors are nonfinancial; they can be measured numerically, but they are not expressed in monetary terms. Reduction in new product-development time and the percentage of on-time flight arrivals are examples of quantitative nonfinancial factors. **Qualitative factors** are outcomes that are difficult to measure accurately in numerical terms. Employee morale is an example.

Relevant-cost analysis generally emphasizes quantitative factors that can be expressed in financial terms. *But just because qualitative factors and quantitative nonfinancial factors cannot be measured easily in financial terms does not make them unimportant.* In fact, managers must wisely weigh these factors. In the Precision Sporting Goods example, managers carefully considered the negative effect on employee morale of laying-off materials-handling workers, a qualitative factor, before choosing the reorganize alternative. Comparing and trading off nonfinancial and financial considerations is seldom easy.

Exhibit 11-3 summarizes the key features of relevant information.

An Illustration of Relevance: Choosing Output Levels

The concept of relevance applies to all decision situations. In this and the following several sections of this chapter, we present some of these decision situations. Later chapters describe other decision situations that require application of the relevance concept, such as Chapter 12 on pricing, Chapter 16 on joint costs, Chapter 19 on quality and timeliness, Chapter 20 on inventory management and supplier evaluation, Chapter 21 on capital investment, and Chapter 22 on transfer pricing. We start by considering decisions that affect output levels such as whether to introduce a new product or to try to sell more units of an existing product.

One-Time-Only Special Orders

One type of decision that affects output levels is accepting or rejecting special orders when there is idle production capacity and the special orders have no long-run implications. We use the term **one-time-only special order** to describe these conditions.

Example 1: Surf Gear manufactures quality beach towels at its highly automated Burlington, North Carolina, plant. The plant has a production capacity of 48,000 towels each month. Current monthly production is 30,000 towels. Retail department stores account for all existing sales. Expected results for the coming month (August) are shown in Exhibit 11-4. (These amounts are predictions based on past costs.) We assume all costs can be classified as either fixed or variable with respect to a single cost driver (units of output).

As a result of a strike at its existing towel supplier, Azelia, a luxury hotel chain, has offered to buy 5,000 towels from Surf Gear in August at $11 per towel. No subsequent sales to Azelia are anticipated. Fixed manufacturing costs are based on the 48,000-towel production capacity. That is, fixed manufacturing costs relate to the production capacity available and not the actual capacity used. If Surf Gear accepts the special order, it will use existing idle capacity to produce the 5,000 towels, and fixed manufacturing costs will not change. No marketing costs will be necessary for the 5,000-unit one-time-only special order. Accepting this special order is not expected to affect the selling price or the quantity of towels sold to regular customers. Should Surf Gear accept Azelia's offer?

Exhibit 11-4 presents data for this example on an absorption-costing basis (that is, both variable and fixed manufacturing costs are included in inventoriable costs and cost of goods sold). In this exhibit, the manufacturing cost of $12 per unit and the marketing cost of $7 per unit include both variable and fixed costs. The sum of all costs (variable and fixed) in a particular business function of the value chain, such as manufacturing costs or marketing costs, are called **business function costs. Full costs of the product,** in this case $19 per unit, are the sum of all variable and fixed costs in all business functions of the value chain (R&D, design, production, marketing, distribution, and customer service). For Surf Gear, full costs of the product consist of costs in manufacturing and marketing because these are the only business functions. No marketing costs are necessary for the special order, so the manager of Surf Gear will focus

	A	B	C	D
		Total	**Per Unit**	
1				
2	Units sold	30,000		
3				
4	Revenues	$600,000	$20.00	
5	Cost of goods sold (manufacturing costs)			
6	Variable manufacturing costs	225,000	7.50[b]	
7	Fixed manufacturing costs	135,000	4.50[c]	
8	Total cost of goods sold	360,000	12.00	
9	Marketing costs			
10	Variable marketing costs	150,000	5.00	
11	Fixed marketing costs	60,000	2.00	
12	Total marketing costs	210,000	7.00	
13	Full costs of the product	570,000	19.00	
14	Operating income	$ 30,000	$ 1.00	
15				
16	[a]Surf Gear incurs no R&D, product-design, distribution, or customer-service costs			
17	[b]Variable manufacturing _ Direct material , Variable direct manufacturing , Variable manufacturing			
18	cost per unit ⁼ cost per unit ⁺ labor cost per unit ⁺ overhead cost per unit			
19	= $6.00 + $0.50 + $1.00 = $7.50			
20	[c]Fixed manufacturing _ Fixed direct manufacturing , Fixed manufacturing			
21	cost per unit ⁼ labor cost per unit ⁺ overhead cost per unit			
22	= $1.50 + $3.00 = $4.50			

Home   Insert   Page Layout   Formulas   Data   Review   View

Exhibit 11-4

Budgeted Income Statement for August, Absorption-Costing Format for Surf Gear[a]

only on manufacturing costs. Based on the manufacturing cost per unit of $12—which is greater than the $11-per-unit price offered by Azelia—the manager might decide to reject the offer.

Exhibit 11-5 separates manufacturing and marketing costs into their variable- and fixed-cost components and presents data in the format of a contribution income statement. The relevant revenues and costs are the expected future revenues and costs that differ as a result of accepting the special offer—revenues of $55,000 ($11 per unit × 5,000 units) and variable manufacturing costs of $37,500 ($7.50 per unit × 5,000 units). The fixed manufacturing costs and all marketing costs (*including variable marketing costs*) are irrelevant in this case because these costs will not change in total whether the special order is accepted or rejected. Surf Gear would gain an additional $17,500 (relevant revenues, $55,000 – relevant costs, $37,500) in operating income by accepting the special order. In this example, comparing total amounts for 30,000 units versus 35,000 units or focusing only on the relevant amounts in the difference column in Exhibit 11-5 avoids a misleading implication—the implication that would result from comparing the $11-per-unit selling price against the manufacturing cost per unit of $12 (Exhibit 11-4), which includes both variable and fixed manufacturing costs.

The assumption of no long-run or strategic implications is crucial to management's analysis of the one-time-only special-order decision. Suppose Surf Gear concludes that the retail department stores (its regular customers) will demand a lower price if it sells towels at $11 apiece to Azelia. In this case, revenues from regular customers will be relevant. Why? Because the future revenues from regular customers will differ depending on whether the special order is accepted or rejected. The relevant-revenue and relevant-cost analysis of the Azelia order would have to be modified to consider both the short-run benefits from accepting the order and the long-run consequences on profitability if prices were lowered to all regular customers.

Exhibit 11-5

One-Time-Only Special-Order Decision for Surf Gear: Comparative Contribution Income Statements

		Home	Insert	Page Layout	Formulas	Data	Review	View	
		A	B	C	D	E	F	G	H
1			Without the Special Order				With the Special Order		Difference: Relevant Amounts
2			30,000				35,000		for the
3			Units to be Sold				Units to be Sold		5,000
4			Per Unit		Total		Total		Units Special Order
5			(1)		(2) = (1) × 30,000		(3)		(4) = (3) – (2)
6	Revenues		$20.00		$600,000		$655,000		$55,000[a]
7	Variable costs:								
8	Manufacturing		7.50		225,000		262,500		37,500[b]
9	Marketing		5.00		150,000		150,000		0[c]
10	Total variable costs		12.50		375,000		412,500		37,500
11	Contribution margin		7.50		225,000		242,500		17,500
12	Fixed costs:								
13	Manufacturing		4.50		135,000		135,000		0[d]
14	Marketing		2.00		60,000		60,000		0[d]
15	Total fixed costs		6.50		195,000		195,000		0
16	Operating income		$ 1.00		$ 30,000		$ 47,500		$17,500
17									
18	[a]5,000 units × $11.00 per unit = $55,000.								
19	[b]5,000 units × $7.50 per unit = $37,500.								
20	[c]No variable marketing costs would be incurred for the 5,000-unit one-time-only special order.								
21	[d]Fixed manufacturing costs and fixed marketing costs would be unaffected by the special order.								

Potential Problems in Relevant-Cost Analysis

Managers should avoid two potential problems in relevant-cost analysis. First, they must watch for incorrect general assumptions, such as all variable costs are relevant and all fixed costs are irrelevant. In the Surf Gear example, the variable marketing cost of $5 per unit is irrelevant because Surf Gear will incur no extra marketing costs by accepting the special order. But fixed manufacturing costs could be relevant. The extra production of 5,000 towels per month does not affect fixed manufacturing costs because we assumed that the relevant range is from 30,000 to 48,000 towels per month. In some cases, however, producing the extra 5,000 towels might increase fixed manufacturing costs. Suppose Surf Gear would need to run three shifts of 16,000 towels per shift to achieve full capacity of 48,000 towels per month. Increasing the monthly production from 30,000 to 35,000 would require a partial third shift because two shifts could produce only 32,000 towels. The extra shift would increase fixed manufacturing costs, thereby making these additional fixed manufacturing costs relevant for this decision.

Second, unit-cost data can potentially mislead decision makers in two ways:

1. **When irrelevant costs are included.** Consider the $4.50 of fixed manufacturing cost per unit (direct manufacturing labor, $1.50 per unit, plus manufacturing overhead, $3.00 per unit) included in the $12-per-unit manufacturing cost in the one-time-only special-order decision (see Exhibits 11-4 and 11-5). This $4.50-per-unit cost is irrelevant, given the assumptions in our example, so it should be excluded.

2. **When the same unit costs are used at different output levels.** Generally, managers use total costs rather than unit costs because total costs are easier to work with and reduce the chance for erroneous conclusions. Then, if desired, the total costs can be unitized. In the Surf Gear example, total fixed manufacturing costs remain at $135,000 even if Surf Gear accepts the special order and produces 35,000 towels. Including the fixed manufacturing cost per unit of $4.50 as a cost of the special order would lead to the erroneous conclusion that total fixed manufacturing costs would increase to $157,500 ($4.50 per towel × 35,000 towels).

The best way for managers to avoid these two potential problems is to keep focusing on (1) total revenues and total costs (rather than unit revenue and unit cost) and (2) the relevance concept. Managers should always require all items included in an analysis to be expected total future revenues and expected total future costs that differ among the alternatives.

Insourcing-versus-Outsourcing and Make-versus-Buy Decisions

We now apply the concept of relevance to another strategic decision: whether a company should make a component part or buy it from a supplier. We again assume idle capacity.

Outsourcing and Idle Facilities

Outsourcing is purchasing goods and services from outside vendors rather than producing the same goods or providing the same services within the organization, which is **insourcing**. For example, Kodak prefers to manufacture its own film (insourcing) but has IBM do its data processing (outsourcing). Honda relies on outside vendors to supply some component parts but chooses to manufacture other parts internally.

Decisions about whether a producer of goods or services will insource or outsource are also called **make-or-buy decisions.** Surveys of companies indicate that managers consider quality, dependability of suppliers, and costs as the most important factors in the make-or-buy decision. Sometimes, however, qualitative factors dominate management's make-or-buy decision. For example, Dell Computer buys the Pentium chip for its personal computers from Intel because Dell does not have the know-how and technology to make

> ◄ **Decision Point**
>
> When is a revenue or cost item relevant for a particular decision and what potential problems should be avoided in relevant cost analysis?

> **Learning Objective 3**
>
> Explain the opportunity-cost concept and why it is used in decision making
>
> . . . in all decisions, it is important to consider the contribution to income forgone by choosing a particular alternative and rejecting others

the chip itself. In contrast, to maintain the secrecy of its formula, Coca-Cola does not outsource the manufacture of its concentrate.

Example 2: The Soho Company manufactures a two-in-one video system consisting of a DVD player and a digital media receiver (that downloads movies and video from internet sites such as NetFlix). Columns 1 and 2 of the following table show the expected total and per-unit costs for manufacturing the DVD-player of the video system. Soho plans to manufacture the 250,000 units in 2,000 batches of 125 units each. Variable batch-level costs of $625 per batch vary with the number of batches, not the total number of units produced.

	Expected Total Costs of Producing 250,000 Units in 2,000 Batches Next Year (1)	Expected Cost per Unit (2) = (1) ÷ 250,000
Direct materials ($36 per unit × 250,000 units)	$ 9,000,000	$36.00
Direct manufacturing labor ($10 per unit × 250,000 units)	2,500,000	10.00
Variable manufacturing overhead costs of power and utilities ($6 per unit × 250,000 units)	1,500,000	6.00
Mixed (variable and fixed) batch-level manufacturing overhead costs of materials handling and setup [$750,000 + ($625 per batch × 2,000 batches)]	2,000,000	8.00
Fixed manufacturing overhead costs of plant lease, insurance, and administration	3,000,000	12.00
Total manufacturing cost	$18,000,000	$72.00

Broadfield, Inc., a manufacturer of DVD players, offers to sell Soho 250,000 DVD players next year for $64 per unit on Soho's preferred delivery schedule. Assume that financial factors will be the basis of this make-or-buy decision. Should Soho make or buy the DVD player?

Columns 1 and 2 of the preceding table indicate the expected total costs and expected cost per unit of producing 250,000 DVD players next year. The expected manufacturing cost per unit for next year is $72. At first glance, it appears that the company should buy DVD players because the expected $72-per-unit cost of making the DVD player is more than the $64 per unit to buy it. But a make-or-buy decision is rarely obvious. To make a decision, management needs to answer the question, "What is the difference in relevant costs between the alternatives?"

For the moment, suppose (a) the capacity now used to make the DVD players will become idle next year if the DVD players are purchased and (b) the $3,000,000 of fixed manufacturing overhead will continue to be incurred next year regardless of the decision made. Assume the $750,000 in fixed salaries to support materials handling and setup will not be incurred if the manufacture of DVD players is completely shut down.

Exhibit 11-6 presents the relevant-cost computations. Note that Soho will *save* $1,000,000 by making DVD players rather than buying them from Broadfield. Making DVD players is the preferred alternative.

Note how the key concepts of relevance presented in Exhibit 11-3 apply here:

- Exhibit 11-6 compares differences in expected total future revenues and expected total future costs. Past costs are always irrelevant when making decisions.
- Exhibit 11-6 shows $2,000,000 of future materials-handling and setup costs under the make alternative but not under the buy alternative. Why? Because buying DVD players and not manufacturing them will save $2,000,000 in future variable costs per batch and avoidable fixed costs. The $2,000,000 represents future costs that differ between the alternatives and so is relevant to the make-or-buy decision.

Relevant Items	Total Relevant Costs		Relevant Cost Per Unit	
	Make	Buy	Make	Buy
Outside purchase of parts ($64 × 250,000 units)		$16,000,000		$64
Direct materials	$ 9,000,000		$36	
Direct manufacturing labor	2,500,000		10	
Variable manufacturing overhead	1,500,000		6	
Mixed (variable and fixed) materials-handling and setup overhead	2,000,000		8	
Total relevant costs[a]	$15,000,000	$16,000,000	$58	$64
Difference in favor of making DVD players	$1,000,000		$4	

[a]The $3,000,000 of plant-lease, plant-insurance, and plant-administration costs could be included under both alternatives. Conceptually, they do not belong in a listing of relevant costs because these costs are irrelevant to the decision. Practically, some managers may want to include them in order to list all costs that will be incurred under each alternative.

■ Exhibit 11-6 excludes the $3,000,000 of plant-lease, insurance, and administration costs under both alternatives. Why? Because these future costs will not differ between the alternatives, so they are irrelevant.

A common term in decision making is *incremental cost*. An **incremental cost** is the additional total cost incurred for an activity. In Exhibit 11-6, the incremental cost of making DVD players is the additional total cost of $15,000,000 that Soho will incur if it decides to make DVD players. The $3,000,000 of fixed manufacturing overhead is not an incremental cost because Soho will incur these costs whether or not it makes DVD players. Similarly, the incremental cost of buying DVD players from Broadfield is the additional total cost of $16,000,000 that Soho will incur if it decides to buy DVD players. A **differential cost** is the difference in total cost between two alternatives. In Exhibit 11-6, the differential cost between the make-DVD-players and buy-DVD-players alternatives is $1,000,000 ($16,000,000 − $15,000,000). Note that *incremental cost* and *differential cost* are sometimes used interchangeably in practice. When faced with these terms, always be sure to clarify what they mean.

We define *incremental revenue* and *differential revenue* similarly to incremental cost and differential cost. **Incremental revenue** is the additional total revenue from an activity. **Differential revenue** is the difference in total revenue between two alternatives.

Strategic and Qualitative Factors

Strategic and qualitative factors affect outsourcing decisions. For example, Soho may prefer to manufacture DVD players in-house to retain control over the design, quality, reliability, and delivery schedules of the DVD players it uses in its video-systems. Conversely, despite the cost advantages documented in Exhibit 11-6, Soho may prefer to outsource, become a leaner organization, and focus on areas of its core competencies—the manufacture and sale of video systems. As an example of focus, advertising companies, such as J. Walter Thompson, only do the creative and planning aspects of advertising (their core competencies), and outsource production activities, such as film, photographs, and illustrations.

Outsourcing is not without risks. As a company's dependence on its suppliers increases, suppliers could increase prices and let quality and delivery performance slip. To minimize these risks, companies generally enter into long-run contracts specifying costs, quality, and delivery schedules with their suppliers. Intelligent managers build close partnerships or alliances with a few key suppliers. Toyota goes so far as to send its own engineers to improve suppliers' processes. Suppliers of companies such as Ford, Hyundai, Panasonic, and Sony have researched and developed innovative products, met demands for increased quantities, maintained quality and on-time delivery, and lowered costs—actions that the companies themselves would not have had the competencies to achieve.

Concepts in Action

Pringles Prints and the Offshoring of Innovation

According to a recent survey, 67% of U.S. companies are engaged in the rapidly-evolving process of "offshoring," which is the outsourcing of business processes and jobs to other countries. Offshoring was initially popular with companies because it yielded immediate labor-cost savings for activities such as software development, call centers, and technical support.

While the practice remains popular today, offshoring has transformed from lowering costs on back-office processes to accessing global talent for innovation. With global markets expanding and domestic talent scarce, companies are now hiring qualified engineers, scientists, inventors, and analysts all over the world for research and development (R&D), new product development (NPD), engineering, and knowledge services.

Innovation Offshoring Services

R&D	NPD	Engineering	Knowledge Services
■ Programming	■ Prototype design	■ Testing	■ Market analysis
■ Code development	■ Product development	■ Reengineering	■ Credit analysis
■ New technologies	■ Systems design	■ Drafting/modeling	■ Data mining
■ New materials/ process research	■ Support services	■ Embedded systems development	■ Forecasting
			■ Risk management

By utilizing offshoring innovation, companies not only continue to reduce labor costs, but cut back-office costs as well. Companies also obtain local market knowledge and access to global best practices in many important areas.

Some companies are leveraging offshore resources by creating global innovation networks. Procter & Gamble (P&G), for instance, established "Connect and Develop," a multi-national effort to create and leverage innovative ideas for product development. When the company wanted to create a new line of Pringles potato chips with pictures and words—trivia questions, animal facts, and jokes—printed on each chip, the company turned to offshore innovation.

Rather than trying to invent the technology required to print images on potato chips in-house, Procter & Gamble created a technology brief that defined the problems it needed to solve, and circulated it throughout the company's global innovation network for possible solutions. As a result, P&G discovered a small bakery in Bologna, Italy, run by a university professor who also manufactured baking equipment. He had invented an ink-jet method for printing edible images on cakes and cookies, which the company quickly adapted for potato chips.

As a result, Pringles Prints were developed in less than a year—as opposed to a more traditional two year process—and immediately led to double-digit product growth.

Sources: Cuoto, Vinay, Mahadeva Mani, Vikas Sehgal, Arie Lewin, Stephan Manning, and Jeff Russell. 2007. *Offshoring 2.0: Contracting knowledge and innovation to expand global capabilities*. Duke University Offshoring Research Network: Durham, NC. Heijmen, Ton, Arie Lewin, Stephan Manning, Nidthida Prem-Ajchariyawong, and Jeff Russell. 2008. *Offshoring reaches the c-suite*. Duke University Offshoring Research Network: Durham, NC. Huston, Larry and Nabil Sakkab. 2006. Connect and develop: Inside Procter & Gamble's new model for innovation. *Harvard Business Review*, March.

Outsourcing decisions invariably have a long-run horizon in which the financial costs and benefits of outsourcing become more uncertain. Almost always, strategic and qualitative factors such as the ones described here become important determinants of the outsourcing decision. Weighing all these factors requires the exercise of considerable management judgment and care.

International Outsourcing

What additional factors would Soho have to consider if the supplier of DVD players was based in Mexico? The most important would be exchange-rate risk. Suppose the Mexican supplier offers to sell Soho 250,000 DVD players for 192,000,000 Pesos. Should Soho make or buy? The answer depends on the exchange rate that Soho expects next year. If Soho forecasts an exchange rate of 12 Pesos per $1, Soho's expected purchase cost equals

$16,000,000 (192,000,000 Pesos/12 Pesos per $) greater than the $15,000,000 relevant costs for making the DVD players in Exhibit 11-6, so Soho would prefer to make DVD players rather than buy them. If, however, Soho anticipates an exchange rate of 13.50 Pesos per $1, Soho's expected purchase cost equals $14,222,222 (192,000,000 Pesos/13.50 Pesos per $), which is less than the $15,000,000 relevant costs for making the DVD players, so Soho would prefer to buy rather than make the DVD players.

Another option is for Soho to enter into a forward contract to purchase 192,000,000 Pesos. A forward contract allows Soho to contract today to purchase pesos next year at a predetermined, fixed cost, thereby protecting itself against exchange rate risk. If Soho decides to go this route, it would make (buy) DVD players if the cost of the contract is greater (less) than $15,000,000. International outsourcing requires companies to evaluate exchange rate risks and to implement strategies and costs for managing them. The Concepts in Action feature (p. 400) describes *offshoring*—the practice of outsourcing services to lower-cost countries.

Opportunity Costs and Outsourcing

In the simple make-or-buy decision in Exhibit 11-6, we assumed that the capacity currently used to make DVD players will remain idle if Soho purchases the parts from Broadfield. Often, however, the released capacity can be used for other, profitable purposes. In this case, the choice Soho's managers are faced with is not whether to make or buy; the choice now centers on how best to use available production capacity.

Example 3: Suppose that if Soho decides to buy DVD players for its video systems from Broadfield, then Soho's best use of the capacity that becomes available is to produce 100,000 Digiteks, a portable, stand-alone DVD player. From a manufacturing standpoint, Digiteks are similar to DVD players made for the video system. With help from operating managers, Soho's management accountant estimates the following future revenues and costs if Soho decides to manufacture and sell Digiteks:

Incremental future revenues		$8,000,000
Incremental future costs		
Direct materials	$3,400,000	
Direct manufacturing labor	1,000,000	
Variable overhead (such as power, utilities)	600,000	
Materials-handling and setup overheads	500,000	
Total incremental future costs		5,500,000
Incremental future operating income		$2,500,000

Because of capacity constraints, Soho can make either DVD players for its video-system unit or Digiteks, but not both. Which of the following two alternatives should Soho choose?

1. Make video-system DVD players and do not make Digiteks
2. Buy video-system DVD players and make Digiteks

Exhibit 11-7, Panel A, summarizes the "total-alternatives" approach—the future costs and revenues for *all* products. Alternative 2, buying video-system DVD players and using the available capacity to make and sell Digiteks, is the preferred alternative. The future incremental costs of buying video-system DVD players from an outside supplier ($16,000,000) exceed the future incremental costs of making video-system DVD players in-house ($15,000,000). Soho can use the capacity freed up by buying video-system DVD players to gain $2,500,000 in operating income (incremental future revenues of $8,000,000 minus total incremental future costs of $5,500,000) by making and selling Digiteks. The *net relevant* costs of buying video-system DVD players and making and selling Digiteks are $16,000,000 – $2,500,000 = $13,500,000.

Exhibit 11-7	Total-Alternatives Approach and Opportunity-Cost Approach to Make-or-Buy Decisions for Soho Company

	Alternatives for Soho	
Relevant Items	**1. Make Video-System DVD Players and Do Not Make Digitek**	**2. Buy Video-System DVD Players and Make Digitek**
PANEL A Total-Alternatives Approach to Make-or-Buy Decisions		
Total incremental future costs of making/buying video-system DVD players (from Exhibit 11-6)	$15,000,000	$16,000,000
Deduct excess of future revenues over future costs from Digitek	0	(2,500,000)
Total relevant costs under total-alternatives approach	$15,000,000	$13,500,000
	1. Make Video-System DVD Players	**2. Buy Video-System DVD Players**
PANEL B Opportunity-Cost Approach to Make-or-Buy Decisions		
Total incremental future costs of making/buying video-system DVD players (from Exhibit 11-6)	$15,000,000	$16,000,000
Opportunity cost: Profit contribution forgone because capacity will not be used to make Digitek, the next-best alternative	2,500,000	0
Total relevant costs under opportunity-cost approach	$17,500,000	$16,000,000

Note that the differences in costs across the columns in Panels A and B are the same: The cost of alternative 3 is $1,500,000 less than the cost of alternative 1, and $2,500,000 less than the cost of alternative 2.

The Opportunity-Cost Approach

Deciding to use a resource in a particular way causes a manager to forgo the opportunity to use the resource in alternative ways. This lost opportunity is a cost that the manager must consider when making a decision. **Opportunity cost** is the contribution to operating income that is forgone by not using a limited resource in its next-best alternative use. For example, the (relevant) cost of going to school for an MBA degree is not only the cost of tuition, books, lodging, and food, but also the income sacrificed (opportunity cost) by not working. Presumably, the estimated future benefits of obtaining an MBA (for example, a higher-paying career) will exceed these costs.

Exhibit 11-7, Panel B, displays the opportunity-cost approach for analyzing the alternatives faced by Soho. *Note that the alternatives are defined differently in the total alternatives approach (1. Make Video-System DVD Players and Do Not Make Digiteks and 2. Buy Video-System DVD Players and Make Digiteks) and the opportunity cost approach (1. Make Video-System DVD Players and 2. Buy Video-System DVD Players), which does not reference Digiteks. Under the opportunity-cost approach, the cost of each alternative includes (1) the incremental costs and (2) the opportunity cost, the profit forgone from not making Digiteks. This opportunity cost arises because Digitek is excluded from formal consideration in the alternatives.*

Consider alternative 1, making video-system DVD players. What are all the costs of making video-system DVD players? Certainly Soho will incur $15,000,000 of incremental costs to make video-system DVD players, but is this the entire cost? No, because by deciding to use limited manufacturing resources to make video-system DVD players, Soho will give up the opportunity to earn $2,500,000 by not using these resources to make Digiteks. Therefore, the relevant costs of making video-system DVD players are the incremental costs of $15,000,000 plus the opportunity cost of $2,500,000.

Next, consider alternative 2, buy video-system DVD players. The incremental cost of buying video-system DVD players will be $16,000,000. The opportunity cost is zero.

Why? Because by choosing this alternative, Soho will not forgo the profit it can earn from making and selling Digiteks.

Panel B leads management to the same conclusion as Panel A: buying video-system DVD players and making Digiteks is the preferred alternative.

Panels A and B of Exhibit 11-7 describe two consistent approaches to decision making with capacity constraints. The total-alternatives approach in Panel A includes all future incremental costs and revenues. For example, under alternative 2, the additional future operating income from *using capacity to make and sell Digiteks* ($2,500,000) is subtracted from the future incremental cost of buying video-system DVD players ($16,000,000). The opportunity-cost analysis in Panel B takes the opposite approach. It focuses only on video-system DVD players. *Whenever capacity is not going to be used to make and sell Digiteks* the future forgone operating income is added as an opportunity cost of making video-system DVD players, as in alternative 1. (Note that when Digiteks are made, as in alternative 2, there is no "opportunity cost of not making Digiteks.") Therefore, whereas Panel A *subtracts* $2,500,000 under alternative 2, Panel B *adds* $2,500,000 under alternative 1. *Panel B highlights the idea that when capacity is constrained, the relevant revenues and costs of any alternative equal (1) the incremental future revenues and costs plus (2) the opportunity cost.* However, when more than two alternatives are being considered simultaneously, it is generally easier to use the total-alternatives approach.

Opportunity costs are not recorded in financial accounting systems. Why? Because historical record keeping is limited to transactions involving alternatives that were *actually selected*, rather than alternatives that were rejected. Rejected alternatives do not produce transactions and so they are not recorded. If Soho makes video-system DVD players, it will not make Digiteks, and it will not record any accounting entries for Digiteks. Yet the opportunity cost of making video-system DVD players, which equals the operating income that Soho forgoes by not making Digiteks, is a crucial input into the make-or-buy decision. Consider again Exhibit 11-7, Panel B. On the basis of only the incremental costs that are systematically recorded in accounting systems, it is less costly for Soho to make rather than buy video-system DVD players. Recognizing the opportunity cost of $2,500,000 leads to a different conclusion: Buying video-system DVD players is preferable.

Suppose Soho has sufficient capacity to make Digiteks even if it makes video-system DVD players. In this case, the opportunity cost of making video-system DVD players is $0 because Soho does not give up the $2,500,000 operating income from making Digiteks even if it chooses to make video-system DVD players. The relevant costs are $15,000,000 (incremental costs of $15,000,000 plus opportunity cost of $0). Under these conditions, Soho would prefer to make video-system DVD players, rather than buy them, and also make Digiteks.

Besides quantitative considerations, the make-or-buy decision should also consider strategic and qualitative factors. If Soho decides to buy video-system DVD players from an outside supplier, it should consider factors such as the supplier's reputation for quality and timely delivery. Soho would also want to consider the strategic consequences of selling Digiteks. For example, will selling Digiteks take Soho's focus away from its video-system business?

Carrying Costs of Inventory

To see another example of an opportunity cost, consider the following data for Soho:

Annual estimated video-system DVD player requirements for next year	250,000 units
Cost per unit when each purchase is equal to 2,500 units	$64.00
Cost per unit when each purchase is equal to or greater than 125,000 units; $64 minus 1% discount	$63.36
Cost of a purchase order	$500

Alternatives under consideration:

    A. Make 100 purchases of 2,500 units each during next year

    B. Make 2 purchases of 125,000 units during the year

Solution

1. The following table considers all cost items when comparing future costs of workstations and networked PCs:

	Three Years Together		
	Workstations	Networked PCs	Difference
All Items	(1)	(2)	(3) = (1) − (2)
Revenues	$3,000,000	$3,000,000	—
Operating costs			
Noncomputer-related operating costs	2,640,000	2,640,000	—
Computer-related cash operating costs	120,000	30,000	$ 90,000
Workstations' book value			
Periodic write-off as depreciation or	180,000	—	—
Lump-sum write-off	—	180,000 }	
Current disposal value of workstations	—	(95,000)	95,000
Networked PCs, written off periodically as depreciation	—	135,000	(135,000)
Total operating costs	2,940,000	2,890,000	50,000
Operating income	$ 60,000	$ 110,000	$ (50,000)

Alternatively, the analysis could focus on only those items in the preceding table that differ between the alternatives.

	Three Years Together		
Relevant Items	Workstations	Networked PCs	Difference
Computer-related cash operating costs	$120,000	$ 30,000	$90,000
Current disposal value of workstations	—	(95,000)	95,000
Networked PCs, written off periodically as depreciation	—	135,000	(135,000)
Total relevant costs	$120,000	$ 70,000	$ 50,000

The analysis suggests that it is cost-effective to replace the workstations with the networked PCs.

2. The accrual-accounting operating incomes *for the first year* under the keep workstations versus the buy networked PCs alternatives are as follows:

	Keep Workstations		Buy Networked PCs	
Revenues		$1,000,000		$1,000,000
Operating costs				
Noncomputer-related operating costs	$880,000		$880,000	
Computer-related cash operating costs	40,000		10,000	
Depreciation	60,000		45,000	
Loss on disposal of workstations	—		85,000[a]	
Total operating costs		980,000		1,020,000
Operating income (loss)		$ 20,000		$ (20,000)

[a] $85,000 = Book value of workstations, $180,000 − Current disposal value, $95,000.

Lewis would be less happy with the expected operating loss of $20,000 if the networked PCs are purchased than he would be with the expected operating income of $20,000 if the workstations are kept. Buying the networked PCs would eliminate the component of his bonus based on operating income. He might also perceive the $20,000 operating loss as reducing his chances of being promoted to a group vice president.

Decision Points

The following question-and-answer format summarizes the chapter's learning objectives. Each decision presents a key question related to a learning objective. The guidelines are the answer to that question.

Decision

Guidelines

1. What is the five-step process that managers can use to make decisions?

The five-step decision-making process is (a) identify the problem and uncertainties, (b) obtain information, (c) make predictions about the future, (d) make decisions by choosing among alternatives, and (e) implement the decision, evaluate performance, and learn.

2. When is a revenue or cost item relevant for a particular decision and what potential problems should be avoided in relevant-cost analysis?

To be relevant for a particular decision, a revenue or cost item must meet two criteria: (a) It must be an expected future revenue or expected future cost, and (b) it must differ among alternative courses of action. The outcomes of alternative actions can be quantitative and qualitative. Quantitative outcomes are measured in numerical terms. Some quantitative outcomes can be expressed in financial terms, others cannot. Qualitative factors, such as employee morale, are difficult to measure accurately in numerical terms. Consideration must be given to relevant quantitative and qualitative factors in making decisions.

Two potential problems to avoid in relevant-cost analysis are (a) making incorrect general assumptions—such as all variable costs are relevant and all fixed costs are irrelevant—and (b) losing sight of total amounts, focusing instead on unit amounts.

3. What is an opportunity cost and why should it be included when making decisions?

Opportunity cost is the contribution to income that is forgone by not using a limited resource in its next-best alternative use. Opportunity cost is included in decision making because the relevant cost of any decision is (1) the incremental cost of the decision plus (2) the opportunity cost of the profit forgone from making that decision.

4. When resources are constrained, how should managers choose which of multiple products to produce and sell?

When resources are constrained, managers should select the product that yields the highest contribution margin per unit of the constraining or limiting resource (factor). In this way, total contribution margin will be maximized.

5. In deciding to add or drop customers or to add or discontinue branch offices or segments, what should managers focus on and how should they take into account allocated overhead costs?

When making decisions about adding or dropping customers or adding or discontinuing branch offices and segments, managers should focus on only those costs that will change and any opportunity costs. Managers should ignore allocated overhead costs.

6. Is book value of existing equipment relevant in equipment-replacement decisions?

Book value of existing equipment is a past (historical or sunk) cost and, therefore, is irrelevant in equipment-replacement decisions.

7. How can conflicts arise between the decision model used by a manager and the performance-evaluation model used to evaluate that manager?

Top management faces a persistent challenge: making sure that the performance-evaluation model of lower-level managers is consistent with the decision model. A common inconsistency is to tell these managers to take a multiple-year view in their decision making but then to judge their performance only on the basis of the current year's operating income.

Appendix

Linear Programming

In this chapter's Power Recreation example (pp. 405–406), suppose both the snowmobile and boat engines must be tested on a very expensive machine before they are shipped to customers. The available machine-hours for testing are limited. Production data are as follows:

Department	Available Daily Capacity in Hours	Use of Capacity in Hours per Unit of Product		Daily Maximum Production in Units	
		Snowmobile Engine	Boat Engine	Snowmobile Engine	Boat Engine
Assembly	600 machine-hours	2.0 machine-hours	5.0 machine-hours	300[a] snow engines	120 boat engines
Testing	120 testing-hours	1.0 machine-hour	0.5 machine-hour	120 snow engines	240 boat engines

[a] For example, 600 machine-hours ÷ 2.0 machine-hours per snowmobile engine = 300, the maximum number of snowmobile engines that the assembly department can make if it works exclusively on snowmobile engines.

Exhibit 11-13 summarizes these and other relevant data. In addition, as a result of material shortages for boat engines, Power Recreation cannot produce more than 110 boat engines per day. How many engines of each type should Power Recreation produce and sell daily to maximize operating income?

Because there are multiple constraints, a technique called *linear programming* or *LP* can be used to determine the number of each type of engine Power Recreation should produce. LP models typically assume that all costs are either variable or fixed with respect to a single cost driver (units of output). As we shall see, LP models also require certain other linear assumptions to hold. When these assumptions fail, other decision models should be considered.[3]

Steps in Solving an LP Problem

We use the data in Exhibit 11-13 to illustrate the three steps in solving an LP problem. Throughout this discussion, S equals the number of units of snowmobile engines produced and sold, and B equals the number of units of boat engines produced and sold.

Step 1: Determine the objective function. The **objective function** of a linear program expresses the objective or goal to be maximized (say, operating income) or minimized (say, operating costs). In our example, the objective is to find the combination of snowmobile engines and boat engines that maximizes total contribution margin. Fixed costs remain the same regardless of the product-mix decision and are irrelevant. The linear function expressing the objective for the total contribution margin (TCM) is as follows:

$$TCM = \$240S + \$375B$$

Step 2: Specify the constraints. A **constraint** is a mathematical inequality or equality that must be satisfied by the variables in a mathematical model. The following linear inequalities express the relationships in our example:

Assembly department constraint	$2S + 5B \leq 600$
Testing department constraint	$1S + 0.5B \leq 120$
Materials-shortage constraint for boat engines	$B \leq 110$
Negative production is impossible	$S \geq 0$ and $B \geq 0$

Exhibit 11-13   Operating Data for Power Recreation

	Department Capacity (per Day) In Product Units		Selling Price	Variable Cost per Unit	Contribution Margin per Unit
	Assembly	Testing			
Only snowmobile engines	300	120	$ 800	$560	$240
Only boat engines	120	240	$1,000	$625	$375

---

[3] Other decision models are described in J. Moore and L. Weatherford, *Decision Modeling with Microsoft Excel*, 6th ed. (Upper Saddle River, NJ: Prentice Hall, 2001); and S. Nahmias, *Production and Operations Analysis*, 6th ed. (New York: McGraw-Hill/Irwin, 2008).

The three solid lines on the graph in Exhibit 11-14 show the existing constraints for assembly and testing and the materials-shortage constraint.[4] The feasible or technically possible alternatives are those combinations of quantities of snowmobile engines and boat engines that satisfy all the constraining resources or factors. The shaded "area of feasible solutions" in Exhibit 11-14 shows the boundaries of those product combinations that are feasible.

Step 3: Compute the optimal solution. Linear programming (LP) is an optimization technique used to maximize the *objective function* when there are multiple *constraints*. We present two approaches for finding the optimal solution using LP: trial-and-error approach and graphic approach. These approaches are easy to use in our example because there are only two variables in the objective function and a small number of constraints. Understanding these approaches provides insight into LP. In most real-world LP applications, managers use computer software packages to calculate the optimal solution.[5]

Trial-and-Error Approach

The optimal solution can be found by trial and error, by working with coordinates of the corners of the area of feasible solutions.

First, select any set of corner points and compute the total contribution margin. Five corner points appear in Exhibit 11-14. It is helpful to use simultaneous equations to obtain the exact coordinates in the graph. To illustrate, the corner point ($S = 75$, $B = 90$) can be derived by solving the two pertinent constraint inequalities as simultaneous equations:

$$2S + 5B = 600 \quad (1)$$

$$1S + 0.5B = 120 \quad (2)$$

Multiplying (2) by 2: $\quad 2S + B = 240 \quad (3)$

Subtracting (3) from (1): $\quad 4B = 360$

Therefore, $\quad B = 360 \div 4 = 90$

Substituting for B in (2): $1S + 0.5(90) = 120$

$$S = 120 - 45 = 75$$

Given $S = 75$ snowmobile engines and $B = 90$ boat engines, TCM = ($240 per snowmobile engine × 75 snowmobile engines) + ($375 per boat engine × 90 boat engines) = $51,750.

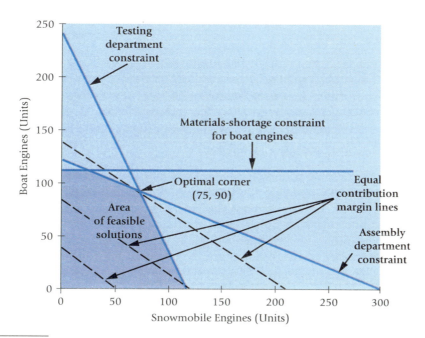

Exhibit 11-14

Linear Programming:
Graphic Solution for
Power Recreation

---

[4] As an example of how the lines are plotted in Exhibit 11-14, use equal signs instead of inequality signs and assume for the assembly department that $B = 0$; then $S = 300$ (600 machine-hours ÷ 2 machine-hours per snowmobile engine). Assume that $S = 0$; then $B = 120$ (600 machine-hours ÷ 5 machine-hours per boat engine). Connect those two points with a straight line.

[5] Standard computer software packages rely on the simplex method. The *simplex method* is an iterative step-by-step procedure for determining the optimal solution to an LP problem. It starts with a specific feasible solution and then tests it by substitution to see whether the result can be improved. These substitutions continue until no further improvement is possible and the optimal solution is obtained.

Second, move from corner point to corner point and compute the total contribution margin at each corner point.

Trial	Corner Point (S, B)	Snowmobile Engines (S)	Boat Engines (B)	Total Contribution Margin
1	(0, 0)	0	0	$240(0) + $375(0) = $0
2	(0, 110)	0	110	$240(0) + $375(110) = $41,250
3	(25,110)	25	110	$240(25) + $375(110) = $47,250
4	(75, 90)	75	90	$240(75) + $375(90) = $51,750[a]
5	(120, 0)	120	0	$240(120) + $375(0) = $28,800

[a] The optimal solution.

The optimal product mix is the mix that yields the highest total contribution: 75 snowmobile engines and 90 boat engines. To understand the solution, consider what happens when moving from the point (25,110) to (75,90). Power Recreation gives up $7,500 [$375 × (110 − 90)] in contribution margin from boat engines while gaining $12,000 [$240 × (75 − 25)] in contribution margin from snowmobile engines. This results in a net increase in contribution margin of $4,500 ($12,000 − $7,500), from $47,250 to $51,750.

Graphic Approach

Consider all possible combinations that will produce the same total contribution margin of, say, $12,000. That is,

$$\$240S + \$375B = \$12,000$$

This set of $12,000 contribution margins is a straight dashed line through [S = 50 ($12,000 ÷ $240); B = 0)] and [S = 0, B = 32 ($12,000 ÷ $375)] in Exhibit 11-14. Other equal total contribution margins can be represented by lines parallel to this one. In Exhibit 11-14, we show three dashed lines. Lines drawn farther from the origin represent more sales of both products and higher amounts of equal contribution margins.

The optimal line is the one farthest from the origin but still passing through a point in the area of feasible solutions. This line represents the highest total contribution margin. The optimal solution—the number of snowmobile engines and boat engines that will maximize the objective function, total contribution margin—is the corner point (S = 75, B = 90). This solution will become apparent if you put a straight-edge ruler on the graph and move it outward from the origin and parallel with the $12,000 contribution margin line. Move the ruler as far away from the origin as possible—that is, increase the total contribution margin—without leaving the area of feasible solutions. In general, the optimal solution in a maximization problem lies at the corner where the dashed line intersects an extreme point of the area of feasible solutions. Moving the ruler out any farther puts it outside the area of feasible solutions.

Sensitivity Analysis

What are the implications of uncertainty about the accounting or technical coefficients used in the objective function (such as the contribution margin per unit of snowmobile engines or boat engines) or the constraints (such as the number of machine-hours it takes to make a snowmobile engine or a boat engine)? Consider how a change in the contribution margin of snowmobile engines from $240 to $300 per unit would affect the optimal solution. Assume the contribution margin for boat engines remains unchanged at $375 per unit. The revised objective function will be as follows:

$$TCM = \$300S + \$375B$$

Using the trial-and-error approach to calculate the total contribution margin for each of the five corner points described in the previous table, the optimal solution is still (S = 75, B = 90). What if the contribution margin of snowmobile engines falls to $160 per unit? The optimal solution remains the same (S = 75, B = 90). Thus, big changes in the contribution margin per unit of snowmobile engines have no effect on the optimal solution in this case. That's because, although the slopes of the equal contribution margin lines in Exhibit 11-14 change as the contribution margin of snowmobile engines changes from $240 to $300 to $160 per unit, the farthest point at which the equal contribution margin lines intersect the area of feasible solutions is still (S = 75, B = 90).

Terms to Learn

This chapter and the Glossary at the end of the book contain definitions of the following important terms:

book value (**p. 410**)

business function costs (**p. 395**)

constraint (**p. 416**)

decision model (**p. 391**)

differential cost (**p. 399**)

differential revenue (**p. 399**)

full costs of the product (**p. 395**)

incremental cost (**p. 399**)

incremental revenue (**p. 399**)

insourcing (**p. 397**)

linear programming (LP) (**p. 417**)

make-or-buy decisions (**p. 397**)

objective function (**p. 416**)

one-time-only special order (**p. 394**)

opportunity cost (**p. 402**)

outsourcing (**p. 397**)

product-mix decisions (**p. 405**)

qualitative factors (**p. 394**)

quantitative factors (**p. 394**)

relevant costs (**p. 393**)

relevant revenues (**p. 393**)

sunk costs (**p. 393**)

Assignment Material

Questions

11-1 Outline the five-step sequence in a decision process.

11-2 Define relevant costs. Why are historical costs irrelevant?

11-3 "All future costs are relevant." Do you agree? Why?

11-4 Distinguish between quantitative and qualitative factors in decision making.

11-5 Describe two potential problems that should be avoided in relevant-cost analysis.

11-6 "Variable costs are always relevant, and fixed costs are always irrelevant." Do you agree? Why?

11-7 "A component part should be purchased whenever the purchase price is less than its total manufacturing cost per unit." Do you agree? Why?

11-8 Define opportunity cost.

11-9 "Managers should always buy inventory in quantities that result in the lowest purchase cost per unit." Do you agree? Why?

11-10 "Management should always maximize sales of the product with the highest contribution margin per unit." Do you agree? Why?

11-11 "A branch office or business segment that shows negative operating income should be shut down." Do you agree? Explain briefly.

11-12 "Cost written off as depreciation on equipment already purchased is always irrelevant." Do you agree? Why?

11-13 "Managers will always choose the alternative that maximizes operating income or minimizes costs in the decision model." Do you agree? Why?

11-14 Describe the three steps in solving a linear programming problem.

11-15 How might the optimal solution of a linear programming problem be determined?

Exercises

11-16 Disposal of assets. Answer the following questions.

1. A company has an inventory of 1,100 assorted parts for a line of missiles that has been discontinued. The inventory cost is $78,000. The parts can be either (a) remachined at total additional costs of $24,500 and then sold for $33,000 or (b) sold as scrap for $6,500. Which action is more profitable? Show your calculations.

2. A truck, costing $101,000 and uninsured, is wrecked its first day in use. It can be either (a) disposed of for $17,500 cash and replaced with a similar truck costing $103,500 or (b) rebuilt for $89,500, and thus be brand-new as far as operating characteristics and looks are concerned. Which action is less costly? Show your calculations.

11-17 Relevant and irrelevant costs. Answer the following questions.

1. DeCesare Computers makes 5,200 units of a circuit board, CB76 at a cost of $280 each. Variable cost per unit is $190 and fixed cost per unit is $90. Peach Electronics offers to supply 5,200 units of CB76 for $260. If DeCesare buys from Peach it will be able to save $10 per unit in fixed costs but continue to incur the remaining $80 per unit. Should DeCesare accept Peach's offer? Explain.

2. LN Manufacturing is deciding whether to keep or replace an old machine. It obtains the following information:

	Old Machine	New Machine
Original cost	$10,700	$9,000
Useful life	10 years	3 years
Current age	7 years	0 years
Remaining useful life	3 years	3 years
Accumulated depreciation	$7,490	Not acquired yet
Book value	$3,210	Not acquired yet
Current disposal value (in cash)	$2,200	Not acquired yet
Terminal disposal value (3 years from now)	$0	$0
Annual cash operating costs	$17,500	$15,500

LN Manufacturing uses straight-line depreciation. Ignore the time value of money and income taxes. Should LN Manufacturing replace the old machine? Explain.

11-18 Multiple choice. (CPA) Choose the best answer.

1. The Woody Company manufactures slippers and sells them at $10 a pair. Variable manufacturing cost is $4.50 a pair, and allocated fixed manufacturing cost is $1.50 a pair. It has enough idle capacity available to accept a one-time-only special order of 20,000 pairs of slippers at $6 a pair. Woody will not incur any marketing costs as a result of the special order. What would the effect on operating income be if the special order could be accepted without affecting normal sales: (a) $0, (b) $30,000 increase, (c) $90,000 increase, or (d) $120,000 increase? Show your calculations.

2. The Reno Company manufactures Part No. 498 for use in its production line. The manufacturing cost per unit for 20,000 units of Part No. 498 is as follows:

Direct materials	$ 6
Direct manufacturing labor	30
Variable manufacturing overhead	12
Fixed manufacturing overhead allocated	16
Total manufacturing cost per unit	$64

The Tray Company has offered to sell 20,000 units of Part No. 498 to Reno for $60 per unit. Reno will make the decision to buy the part from Tray if there is an overall savings of at least $25,000 for Reno. If Reno accepts Tray's offer, $9 per unit of the fixed overhead allocated would be eliminated. Furthermore, Reno has determined that the released facilities could be used to save relevant costs in the manufacture of Part No. 575. For Reno to achieve an overall savings of $25,000, the amount of relevant costs that would have to be saved by using the released facilities in the manufacture of Part No. 575 would be which of the following: (a) $80,000, (b) $85,000, (c) $125,000, or (d) $140,000? Show your calculations.

11-19 Special order, activity-based costing. (CMA, adapted) The Award Plus Company manufactures medals for winners of athletic events and other contests. Its manufacturing plant has the capacity to produce 10,000 medals each month. Current production and sales are 7,500 medals per month. The company normally charges $150 per medal. Cost information for the current activity level is as follows:

Variable costs that vary with number of units produced	
Direct materials	$ 262,500
Direct manufacturing labor	300,000
Variable costs (for setups, materials handling, quality control, and so on)	75,000
that vary with number of batches, 150 batches × $500 per batch	
Fixed manufacturing costs	275,000
Fixed marketing costs	175,000
Total costs	$1,087,500

Award Plus has just received a special one-time-only order for 2,500 medals at $100 per medal. Accepting the special order would not affect the company's regular business. Award Plus makes medals for its existing customers in batch sizes of 50 medals (150 batches × 50 medals per batch = 7,500 medals). The special order requires Award Plus to make the medals in 25 batches of 100 each.

Required

1. Should Award Plus accept this special order? Show your calculations.
2. Suppose plant capacity were only 9,000 medals instead of 10,000 medals each month. The special order must either be taken in full or be rejected completely. Should Award Plus accept the special order? Show your calculations.
3. As in requirement 1, assume that monthly capacity is 10,000 medals. Award Plus is concerned that if it accepts the special order, its existing customers will immediately demand a price discount of $10 in the month in which the special order is being filled. They would argue that Award Plus's capacity costs are now being spread over more units and that existing customers should get the benefit of these lower costs. Should Award Plus accept the special order under these conditions? Show your calculations.

11-20 Make versus buy, activity-based costing. The Svenson Corporation manufactures cellular modems. It manufactures its own cellular modem circuit boards (CMCB), an important part of the cellular modem. It reports the following cost information about the costs of making CMCBs in 2011 and the expected costs in 2012:

	Current Costs in 2011	Expected Costs in 2012
Variable manufacturing costs		
Direct material cost per CMCB	$ 180	$ 170
Direct manufacturing labor cost per CMCB	50	45
Variable manufacturing cost per batch for setups, materials handling, and quality control	1,600	1,500
Fixed manufacturing cost		
Fixed manufacturing overhead costs that can be avoided if CMCBs are not made	320,000	320,000
Fixed manufacturing overhead costs of plant depreciation, insurance, and administration that cannot be avoided even if CMCBs are not made	800,000	800,000

Svenson manufactured 8,000 CMCBs in 2011 in 40 batches of 200 each. In 2012, Svenson anticipates needing 10,000 CMCBs. The CMCBs would be produced in 80 batches of 125 each.

The Minton Corporation has approached Svenson about supplying CMCBs to Svenson in 2012 at $300 per CMCB on whatever delivery schedule Svenson wants.

Required

1. Calculate the total expected manufacturing cost per unit of making CMCBs in 2012.
2. Suppose the capacity currently used to make CMCBs will become idle if Svenson purchases CMCBs from Minton. On the basis of financial considerations alone, should Svenson make CMCBs or buy them from Minton? Show your calculations.
3. Now suppose that if Svenson purchases CMCBs from Minton, its best alternative use of the capacity currently used for CMCBs is to make and sell special circuit boards (CB3s) to the Essex Corporation. Svenson estimates the following incremental revenues and costs from CB3s:

Total expected incremental future revenues	$2,000,000
Total expected incremental future costs	$2,150,000

On the basis of financial considerations alone, should Svenson make CMCBs or buy them from Minton? Show your calculations.

11-21 Inventory decision, opportunity costs. Lawn World, a manufacturer of lawn mowers, predicts that it will purchase 264,000 spark plugs next year. Lawn World estimates that 22,000 spark plugs will be required each month. A supplier quotes a price of $7 per spark plug. The supplier also offers a special discount option: If all 264,000 spark plugs are purchased at the start of the year, a discount of 2% off the $7 price will be given. Lawn World can invest its cash at 10% per year. It costs Lawn World $260 to place each purchase order.

Required

1. What is the opportunity cost of interest forgone from purchasing all 264,000 units at the start of the year instead of in 12 monthly purchases of 22,000 units per order?
2. Would this opportunity cost be recorded in the accounting system? Why?
3. Should Lawn World purchase 264,000 units at the start of the year or 22,000 units each month? Show your calculations.

11-22 Relevant costs, contribution margin, product emphasis. The Seashore Stand is a take-out food store at a popular beach resort. Susan Sexton, owner of the Seashore Stand, is deciding how much refrigerator space to devote to four different drinks. Pertinent data on these four drinks are as follows:

	Cola	Lemonade	Punch	Natural Orange Juice
Selling price per case	$18.75	$20.50	$27.75	$39.30
Variable cost per case	$13.75	$15.60	$20.70	$30.40
Cases sold per foot of shelf space per day	22	12	6	13

Sexton has a maximum front shelf space of 12 feet to devote to the four drinks. She wants a minimum of 1 foot and a maximum of 6 feet of front shelf space for each drink.

Required

1. Calculate the contribution margin per case of each type of drink.
2. A coworker of Sexton's recommends that she maximize the shelf space devoted to those drinks with the highest contribution margin per case. Evaluate this recommendation.
3. What shelf-space allocation for the four drinks would you recommend for the Seashore Stand? Show your calculations.

11-23 Selection of most profitable product. Body-Builders, Inc., produces two basic types of weight-lifting equipment, Model 9 and Model 14. Pertinent data are as follows:

	A	B	C
		Per Unit	
1		Model 9	Model 14
2			
3	Selling price	$100.00	$70.00
4	Costs		
5	Direct material	28.00	13.00
6	Direct manufacturing labor	15.00	25.00
7	Variable manufacturing overhead*	25.00	12.50
8	Fixed manufacturing overhead*	10.00	5.00
9	Marketing (all variable)	14.00	10.00
10	Total cost	92.00	65.50
11	Operating income	$ 8.00	$ 4.50
12			
13	*Allocated on the basis of machine-hours		

The weight-lifting craze is such that enough of either Model 9 or Model 14 can be sold to keep the plant operating at full capacity. Both products are processed through the same production departments.

Required Which products should be produced? Briefly explain your answer.

11-24 Which center to close, relevant-cost analysis, opportunity costs. Fair Lakes Hospital Corporation has been operating ambulatory surgery centers in Groveton and Stockdale, two small communities each about an hour away from its main hospital. As a cost control measure the hospital has decided that it needs only one of those two centers permanently, so one must be shut down. The decision regarding which center to close will be made on financial considerations alone. The following information is available:

a. The Groveton center was built 15 years ago at a cost of $5 million on land leased from the City of Groveton at a cost of $40,000 per year. The land and buildings will immediately revert back to the city if the center is closed. The center has annual operating costs of $2.5 million, all of which will be saved if the center is closed. In addition, Fair Lakes allocates $800,000 of common administrative costs to the Groveton center. If the center is closed, these costs would be reallocated to other ambulatory centers. If the center is kept open, Fair Lakes plans to invest $1 million in a fixed income note, which will earn the $40,000 that Fair Lakes needs for the lease payments.

b. The Stockdale center was built 20 years ago at a cost of $4.8 million, of which Fair Lakes and the City of Stockdale each paid half, on land donated by a hospital benefactor. Two years ago, Fair Lakes spent $2 million to renovate the facility. If the center is closed, the property will be sold to developers for $7 million. The operating costs of the center are $3 million per year, all of which will be saved if the center is closed. Fair Lakes allocates $1 million of common administrative costs to the Stockdale center. If the center is closed, these costs would be reallocated to other ambulatory centers.

c. Fair Lakes estimates that the operating costs of whichever center remains open will be $3.5 million per year.

Required The City Council of Stockdale has petitioned Fair Lakes to close the Groveton facility, thus sparing the Stockdale center. The Council argues that otherwise the $2 million spent on recent renovations would be wasted. Do you agree with the Stockdale City Council's arguments and conclusions? In your answer, identify and explain all costs that you consider relevant and all costs that you consider irrelevant for the center-closing decision.

11-25 Closing and opening stores. Sanchez Corporation runs two convenience stores, one in Connecticut and one in Rhode Island. Operating income for each store in 2012 is as follows:

	Connecticut Store	Rhode Island Store
Revenues	$1,070,000	$860,000
Operating costs		
Cost of goods sold	750,000	660,000
Lease rent (renewable each year)	90,000	75,000
Labor costs (paid on an hourly basis)	42,000	42,000
Depreciation of equipment	25,000	22,000
Utilities (electricity, heating)	43,000	46,000
Allocated corporate overhead	50,000	40,000
Total operating costs	1,000,000	885,000
Operating income (loss)	$ 70,000	$ (25,000)

The equipment has a zero disposal value. In a senior management meeting, Maria Lopez, the management accountant at Sanchez Corporation, makes the following comment, "Sanchez can increase its profitability by closing down the Rhode Island store or by adding another store like it."

Required

1. By closing down the Rhode Island store, Sanchez can reduce overall corporate overhead costs by $44,000. Calculate Sanchez's operating income if it closes the Rhode Island store. Is Maria Lopez's statement about the effect of closing the Rhode Island store correct? Explain.
2. Calculate Sanchez's operating income if it keeps the Rhode Island store open and opens another store with revenues and costs identical to the Rhode Island store (including a cost of $22,000 to acquire equipment with a one-year useful life and zero disposal value). Opening this store will increase corporate overhead costs by $4,000. Is Maria Lopez's statement about the effect of adding another store like the Rhode Island store correct? Explain.

11-26 Choosing customers. Broadway Printers operates a printing press with a monthly capacity of 2,000 machine-hours. Broadway has two main customers: Taylor Corporation and Kelly Corporation. Data on each customer for January follows:

	Taylor Corporation	Kelly Corporation	Total
Revenues	$120,000	$80,000	$200,000
Variable costs	42,000	48,000	90,000
Contribution margin	78,000	32,000	110,000
Fixed costs (allocated)	60,000	40,000	100,000
Operating income	$ 18,000	$ (8,000)	$ 10,000
Machine-hours required	1,500 hours	500 hours	2,000 hours

Kelly Corporation indicates that it wants Broadway to do an *additional* $80,000 worth of printing jobs during February. These jobs are identical to the existing business Broadway did for Kelly in January in terms of variable costs and machine-hours required. Broadway anticipates that the business from Taylor Corporation in February will be the same as that in January. Broadway can choose to accept as much of the Taylor and Kelly business for February as its capacity allows. Assume that total machine-hours and fixed costs for February will be the same as in January.

What action should Broadway take to maximize its operating income? Show your calculations.

Required

11-27 Relevance of equipment costs. The Auto Wash Company has just today paid for and installed a special machine for polishing cars at one of its several outlets. It is the first day of the company's fiscal year. The machine costs $20,000. Its annual cash operating costs total $15,000. The machine will have a four-year useful life and a zero terminal disposal value.

After the machine has been used for only one day, a salesperson offers a different machine that promises to do the same job at annual cash operating costs of $9,000. The new machine will cost $24,000 cash, installed. The "old" machine is unique and can be sold outright for only $10,000, minus $2,000 removal cost. The new machine, like the old one, will have a four-year useful life and zero terminal disposal value.

Revenues, all in cash, will be $150,000 annually, and other cash costs will be $110,000 annually, regardless of this decision.

For simplicity, ignore income taxes and the time value of money.

Required

1. a. Prepare a statement of cash receipts and disbursements for each of the four years under each alternative. What is the cumulative difference in cash flow for the four years taken together?

b. Prepare income statements for each of the four years under each alternative. Assume straight-line depreciation. What is the cumulative difference in operating income for the four years taken together?

c. What are the irrelevant items in your presentations in requirements a and b? Why are they irrelevant?

2. Suppose the cost of the "old" machine was $1 million rather than $20,000. Nevertheless, the old machine can be sold outright for only $10,000, minus $2,000 removal cost. Would the net differences in requirements 1a and 1b change? Explain.

3. Is there any conflict between the decision model and the incentives of the manager who has just purchased the "old" machine and is considering replacing it a day later?

11-28 Equipment upgrade versus replacement. (A. Spero, adapted) The TechGuide Company produces and sells 7,500 modular computer desks per year at a selling price of $750 each. Its current production equipment, purchased for $1,800,000 and with a five-year useful life, is only two years old. It has a terminal disposal value of $0 and is depreciated on a straight-line basis. The equipment has a current disposal price of $450,000. However, the emergence of a new molding technology has led TechGuide to consider either upgrading or replacing the production equipment. The following table presents data for the two alternatives:

	Home	Insert	Page Layout	Formulas	Data	Review	
		A			B	C	
1					Upgrade	Replace	
2	One-time equipment costs				$3,000,000	$4,800,000	
3	Variable manufacturing cost per desk				$ 150	$ 75	
4	Remaining useful life of equipment (years)				3	3	
5	Terminal disposal value of equipment				$ 0	$ 0	

All equipment costs will continue to be depreciated on a straight-line basis. For simplicity, ignore income taxes and the time value of money.

Required

1. Should TechGuide upgrade its production line or replace it? Show your calculations.

2. Now suppose the one-time equipment cost to replace the production equipment is somewhat negotiable. All other data are as given previously. What is the maximum one-time equipment cost that TechGuide would be willing to pay to replace the old equipment rather than upgrade it?

3. Assume that the capital expenditures to replace and upgrade the production equipment are as given in the original exercise, but that the production and sales quantity is not known. For what production and sales quantity would TechGuide (i) upgrade the equipment or (ii) replace the equipment?

4. Assume that all data are as given in the original exercise. Dan Doria is TechGuide's manager, and his bonus is based on operating income. Because he is likely to relocate after about a year, his current bonus is his primary concern. Which alternative would Doria choose? Explain.

MyAccountingLab

Problems

11-29 Special Order. Louisville Corporation produces baseball bats for kids that it sells for $32 each. At capacity, the company can produce 50,000 bats a year. The costs of producing and selling 50,000 bats are as follows:

	Cost per Bat	Total Costs
Direct materials	$12	$ 600,000
Direct manufacturing labor	3	150,000
Variable manufacturing overhead	1	50,000
Fixed manufacturing overhead	5	250,000
Variable selling expenses	2	100,000
Fixed selling expenses	4	200,000
Total costs	$27	$1,350,000

Required

1. Suppose Louisville is currently producing and selling 40,000 bats. At this level of production and sales, its fixed costs are the same as given in the preceding table. Ripkin Corporation wants to place a one-time special order for 10,000 bats at $25 each. Louisville will incur no variable selling costs for this special order. Should Louisville accept this one-time special order? Show your calculations.

2. Now suppose Louisville is currently producing and selling 50,000 bats. If Louisville accepts Ripkin's offer it will have to sell 10,000 fewer bats to its regular customers. (a) On financial considerations alone, should Louisville accept this one-time special order? Show your calculations. (b) On financial considerations alone, at what price would Louisville be indifferent between accepting the special order and continuing to sell to its regular customers at $32 per bat. (c) What other factors should Louisville consider in deciding whether to accept the one-time special order?

11-30 International outsourcing. Bernie's Bears, Inc., manufactures plush toys in a facility in Cleveland, Ohio. Recently, the company designed a group of collectible resin figurines to go with the plush toy line. Management is trying to decide whether to manufacture the figurines themselves in existing space in the Cleveland facility or to accept an offer from a manufacturing company in Indonesia. Data concerning the decision follows:

Expected annual sales of figurines (in units)	400,000
Average selling price of a figurine	$5
Price quoted by Indonesian company, in Indonesian Rupiah (IDR), for each figurine	27,300 IDR
Current exchange rate	9,100 IDR = $1
Variable manufacturing costs	$2.85 per unit
Incremental annual fixed manufacturing costs associated with the new product line	$200,000
Variable selling and distribution costs[a]	$0.50 per unit
Annual fixed selling and distribution costs[a]	$285,000

[a] Selling and distribution costs are the same regardless of whether the figurines are manufactured in Cleveland or imported.

Required

1. Should Bernie's Bears manufacture the 400,000 figurines in the Cleveland facility or purchase them from the Indonesian supplier? Explain.
2. Bernie's Bears believes that the US dollar may weaken in the coming months against the Indonesian Rupiah and does not want to face any currency risk. Assume that Bernie's Bears can enter into a forward contract today to purchase 27,300 IDRs for $3.40. Should Bernie's Bears manufacture the 400,000 figurines in the Cleveland facility or purchase them from the Indonesian supplier? Explain.
3. What are some of the qualitative factors that Bernie's Bears should consider when deciding whether to outsource the figurine manufacturing to Indonesia?

11-31 Relevant costs, opportunity costs. Larry Miller, the general manager of Basil Software, must decide when to release the new version of Basil's spreadsheet package, Easyspread 2.0. Development of Easyspread 2.0 is complete; however, the diskettes, compact discs, and user manuals have not yet been produced. The product can be shipped starting July 1, 2011.

The major problem is that Basil has overstocked the previous version of its spreadsheet package, Easyspread 1.0. Miller knows that once Easyspread 2.0 is introduced, Basil will not be able to sell any more units of Easyspread 1.0. Rather than just throwing away the inventory of Easyspread 1.0, Miller is wondering if it might be better to continue to sell Easyspread 1.0 for the next three months and introduce Easyspread 2.0 on October 1, 2011, when the inventory of Easyspread 1.0 will be sold out.

The following information is available:

	Easyspread 1.0	Easyspread 2.0
Selling price	$160	$195
Variable cost per unit of diskettes, compact discs, user manuals	25	30
Development cost per unit	70	100
Marketing and administrative cost per unit	35	40
Total cost per unit	130	170
Operating income per unit	$ 30	$ 25

Development cost per unit for each product equals the total costs of developing the software product divided by the anticipated unit sales over the life of the product. Marketing and administrative costs are fixed costs in 2011, incurred to support all marketing and administrative activities of Basil Software. Marketing and administrative costs are allocated to products on the basis of the budgeted revenues of each product. The preceding unit costs assume Easyspread 2.0 will be introduced on October 1, 2011.

Required

1. On the basis of financial considerations alone, should Miller introduce Easyspread 2.0 on July 1, 2011, or wait until October 1, 2011? Show your calculations, clearly identifying relevant and irrelevant revenues and costs.
2. What other factors might Larry Miller consider in making a decision?

11-32 Opportunity costs. (H. Schaefer) The Wild Boar Corporation is working at full production capacity producing 13,000 units of a unique product, Rosebo. Manufacturing cost per unit for Rosebo is as follows:

Direct materials	$ 5
Direct manufacturing labor	1
Manufacturing overhead	7
Total manufacturing cost	$13

Manufacturing overhead cost per unit is based on variable cost per unit of $4 and fixed costs of $39,000 (at full capacity of 13,000 units). Marketing cost per unit, all variable, is $2, and the selling price is $26.

A customer, the Miami Company, has asked Wild Boar to produce 3,500 units of Orangebo, a modification of Rosebo. Orangebo would require the same manufacturing processes as Rosebo. Miami has offered to pay Wild Boar $20 for a unit of Orangebo and share half of the marketing cost per unit.

Required

1. What is the opportunity cost to Wild Boar of producing the 3,500 units of Orangebo? (Assume that no overtime is worked.)
2. The Buckeye Corporation has offered to produce 3,500 units of Rosebo for Wolverine so that Wild Boar may accept the Miami offer. That is, if Wild Boar accepts the Buckeye offer, Wild Boar would manufacture 9,500 units of Rosebo and 3,500 units of Orangebo and purchase 3,500 units of Rosebo from Buckeye. Buckeye would charge Wild Boar $18 per unit to manufacture Rosebo. On the basis of financial considerations alone, should Wild Boar accept the Buckeye offer? Show your calculations.
3. Suppose Wild Boar had been working at less than full capacity, producing 9,500 units of Rosebo at the time the Miami offer was made. Calculate the minimum price Wild Boar should accept for Orangebo under these conditions. (Ignore the previous $20 selling price.)

11-33 Product mix, special order. (N. Melumad, adapted) Pendleton Engineering makes cutting tools for metalworking operations. It makes two types of tools: R3, a regular cutting tool, and HP6, a high-precision cutting tool. R3 is manufactured on a regular machine, but HP6 must be manufactured on both the regular machine and a high-precision machine. The following information is available.

	R3	HP6
Selling price	$ 100	$ 150
Variable manufacturing cost per unit	$ 60	$ 100
Variable marketing cost per unit	$ 15	$ 35
Budgeted total fixed overhead costs	$350,000	$550,000
Hours required to produce one unit on the regular machine	1.0	0.5

Additional information includes the following:

a. Pendleton faces a capacity constraint on the regular machine of 50,000 hours per year.
b. The capacity of the high-precision machine is not a constraint.
c. Of the $550,000 budgeted fixed overhead costs of HP6, $300,000 are lease payments for the high-precision machine. This cost is charged entirely to HP6 because Pendleton uses the machine exclusively to produce HP6. The lease agreement for the high-precision machine can be canceled at any time without penalties.
d. All other overhead costs are fixed and cannot be changed.

Required

1. What product mix—that is, how many units of R3 and HP6—will maximize Pendleton's operating income? Show your calculations.
2. Suppose Pendleton can increase the annual capacity of its regular machines by 15,000 machine-hours at a cost of $150,000. Should Pendleton increase the capacity of the regular machines by 15,000 machine-hours? By how much will Pendleton's operating income increase? Show your calculations.
3. Suppose that the capacity of the regular machines has been increased to 65,000 hours. Pendleton has been approached by Carter Corporation to supply 20,000 units of another cutting tool, S3, for $120 per unit. Pendleton must either accept the order for all 20,000 units or reject it totally. S3 is exactly like R3 except that its variable manufacturing cost is $70 per unit. (It takes one hour to produce one unit of S3 on the regular machine, and variable marketing cost equals $15 per unit.) What product mix should Pendleton choose to maximize operating income? Show your calculations.

11-34 Dropping a product line, selling more units. The Northern Division of Grossman Corporation makes and sells tables and beds. The following estimated revenue and cost information from the division's activity-based costing system is available for 2011.

	4,000 Tables	5,000 Beds	Total
Revenues ($125 × 4,000; $200 × 5,000)	$500,000	$1,000,000	$1,500,000
Variable direct materials and direct manufacturing labor costs ($75 × 4,000; $105 × 5,000)	300,000	525,000	825,000
Depreciation on equipment used exclusively by each product line	42,000	58,000	100,000
Marketing and distribution costs $40,000 (fixed) + ($750 per shipment × 40 shipments) $60,000 (fixed) + ($750 per shipment × 100 shipments)	70,000	135,000 }	205,000
Fixed general-administration costs of the division allocated to product lines on the basis of revenue	110,000	220,000	330,000
Corporate-office costs allocated to product lines on the basis of revenues	50,000	100,000	150,000
Total costs	572,000	1,038,000	1,610,000
Operating income (loss)	$(72,000)	$ (38,000)	$ (110,000)

Additional information includes the following:

a. On January 1, 2011, the equipment has a book value of $100,000, a one-year useful life, and zero disposal value. Any equipment not used will remain idle.
b. Fixed marketing and distribution costs of a product line can be avoided if the line is discontinued.
c. Fixed general-administration costs of the division and corporate-office costs will not change if sales of individual product lines are increased or decreased or if product lines are added or dropped.

Required

1. On the basis of financial considerations alone, should the Northern Division discontinue the tables product line for the year, assuming the released facilities remain idle? Show your calculations.
2. What would be the effect on the Northern Division's operating income if it were to sell 4,000 more tables? Assume that to do so the division would have to acquire additional equipment costing $42,000 with a one-year useful life and zero terminal disposal value. Assume further that the fixed marketing and distribution costs would not change but that the number of shipments would double. Show your calculations.
3. Given the Northern Division's expected operating loss of $110,000, should Grossman Corporation shut it down for the year? Assume that shutting down the Northern Division will have no effect on corporate-office costs but will lead to savings of all general-administration costs of the division. Show your calculations.
4. Suppose Grossman Corporation has the opportunity to open another division, the Southern Division, whose revenues and costs are expected to be identical to the Northern Division's revenues and costs (including a cost of $100,000 to acquire equipment with a one-year useful life and zero terminal disposal value). Opening the new division will have no effect on corporate-office costs. Should Grossman open the Southern Division? Show your calculations.

11-35 Make or buy, unknown level of volume. (A. Atkinson) Oxford Engineering manufactures small engines. The engines are sold to manufacturers who install them in such products as lawn mowers. The company currently manufactures all the parts used in these engines but is considering a proposal from an external supplier who wishes to supply the starter assemblies used in these engines.

The starter assemblies are currently manufactured in Division 3 of Oxford Engineering. The costs relating to the starter assemblies for the past 12 months were as follows:

Direct materials	$200,000
Direct manufacturing labor	150,000
Manufacturing overhead	400,000
Total	$750,000

Over the past year, Division 3 manufactured 150,000 starter assemblies. The average cost for each starter assembly is $5 ($750,000 ÷ 150,000).

Further analysis of manufacturing overhead revealed the following information. Of the total manufacturing overhead, only 25% is considered variable. Of the fixed portion, $150,000 is an allocation of general overhead that will remain unchanged for the company as a whole if production of the starter assemblies is discontinued. A further $100,000 of the fixed overhead is avoidable if production of the starter assemblies is discontinued. The balance of the current fixed overhead, $50,000, is the division manager's salary. If production of the starter assemblies is discontinued, the manager of Division 3 will be transferred to Division 2 at the same salary. This move will allow the company to save the $40,000 salary that would otherwise be paid to attract an outsider to this position.

Required
1. Tidnish Electronics, a reliable supplier, has offered to supply starter-assembly units at $4 per unit. Because this price is less than the current average cost of $5 per unit, the vice president of manufacturing is eager to accept this offer. On the basis of financial considerations alone, should the outside offer be accepted? Show your calculations. (*Hint:* Production output in the coming year may be different from production output in the past year.)
2. How, if at all, would your response to requirement 1 change if the company could use the vacated plant space for storage and, in so doing, avoid $50,000 of outside storage charges currently incurred? Why is this information relevant or irrelevant?

11-36 **Make versus buy, activity-based costing, opportunity costs.** The Weaver Company produces gas grills. This year's expected production is 20,000 units. Currently, Weaver makes the side burners for its grills. Each grill includes two side burners. Weaver's management accountant reports the following costs for making the 40,000 burners:

	Cost per Unit	Costs for 40,000 Units
Direct materials	$5.00	$200,000
Direct manufacturing labor	2.50	100,000
Variable manufacturing overhead	1.25	50,000
Inspection, setup, materials handling		4,000
Machine rent		8,000
Allocated fixed costs of plant administration, taxes, and insurance		50,000
Total costs		$412,000

Weaver has received an offer from an outside vendor to supply any number of burners Weaver requires at $9.25 per burner. The following additional information is available:

a. Inspection, setup, and materials-handling costs vary with the number of batches in which the burners are produced. Weaver produces burners in batch sizes of 1,000 units. Weaver will produce the 40,000 units in 40 batches.
b. Weaver rents the machine used to make the burners. If Weaver buys all of its burners from the outside vendor, it does not need to pay rent on this machine.

Required
1. Assume that if Weaver purchases the burners from the outside vendor, the facility where the burners are currently made will remain idle. On the basis of financial considerations alone, should Weaver accept the outside vendor's offer at the anticipated volume of 40,000 burners? Show your calculations.
2. For this question, assume that if the burners are purchased outside, the facilities where the burners are currently made will be used to upgrade the grills by adding a rotisserie attachment. (Note: Each grill contains two burners and one rotisserie attachment.) As a consequence, the selling price of grills will be raised by $30. The variable cost per unit of the upgrade would be $24, and additional tooling costs of $100,000 per year would be incurred. On the basis of financial considerations alone, should Weaver make or buy the burners, assuming that 20,000 grills are produced (and sold)? Show your calculations.
3. The sales manager at Weaver is concerned that the estimate of 20,000 grills may be high and believes that only 16,000 grills will be sold. Production will be cut back, freeing up work space. This space can be used to add the rotisserie attachments whether Weaver buys the burners or makes them in-house. At this lower output, Weaver will produce the burners in 32 batches of 1,000 units each. On the basis of financial considerations alone, should Weaver purchase the burners from the outside vendor? Show your calculations.

11-37 **Multiple choice, comprehensive problem on relevant costs.** The following are the Class Company's unit costs of manufacturing and marketing a high-style pen at an output level of 20,000 units per month:

Manufacturing cost	
Direct materials	$1.00
Direct manufacturing labor	1.20
Variable manufacturing overhead cost	0.80
Fixed manufacturing overhead cost	0.50
Marketing cost	
Variable	1.50
Fixed	0.90

Required
The following situations refer only to the preceding data; there is *no connection* between the situations. Unless stated otherwise, assume a regular selling price of $6 per unit. Choose the best answer to each question. Show your calculations.
1. For an inventory of 10,000 units of the high-style pen presented in the balance sheet, the appropriate unit cost to use is (a) $3.00, (b) $3.50, (c) $5.00, (d) $2.20, or (e) $5.90.

2. The pen is usually produced and sold at the rate of 240,000 units per year (an average of 20,000 per month). The selling price is $6 per unit, which yields total annual revenues of $1,440,000. Total costs are $1,416,000, and operating income is $24,000, or $0.10 per unit. Market research estimates that unit sales could be increased by 10% if prices were cut to $5.80. Assuming the implied cost-behavior patterns continue, this action, if taken, would

   a. decrease operating income by $7,200.

   b. decrease operating income by $0.20 per unit ($48,000) but increase operating income by 10% of revenues ($144,000), for a net increase of $96,000.

   c. decrease fixed cost per unit by 10%, or $0.14, per unit, and thus decrease operating income by $0.06 ($0.20 − $0.14) per unit.

   d. increase unit sales to 264,000 units, which at the $5.80 price would give total revenues of $1,531,200 and lead to costs of $5.90 per unit for 264,000 units, which would equal $1,557,600, and result in an operating loss of $26,400.

   e. None of these

3. A contract with the government for 5,000 units of the pens calls for the reimbursement of all manufacturing costs plus a fixed fee of $1,000. No variable marketing costs are incurred on the government contract. You are asked to compare the following two alternatives:

Sales Each Month to	Alternative A	Alternative B
Regular customers	15,000 units	15,000 units
Government	0 units	5,000 units

   Operating income under alternative B is greater than that under alternative A by (a) $1,000, (b) $2,500, (c) $3,500, (d) $300, or (e) none of these.

4. Assume the same data with respect to the government contract as in requirement 3 except that the two alternatives to be compared are as follows:

Sales Each Month to	Alternative A	Alternative B
Regular customers	20,000 units	15,000 units
Government	0 units	5,000 units

   Operating income under alternative B relative to that under alternative A is (a) $4,000 less, (b) $3,000 greater, (c) $6,500 less, (d) $500 greater, or (e) none of these.

5. The company wants to enter a foreign market in which price competition is keen. The company seeks a one-time-only special order for 10,000 units on a minimum-unit-price basis. It expects that shipping costs for this order will amount to only $0.75 per unit, but the fixed costs of obtaining the contract will be $4,000. The company incurs no variable marketing costs other than shipping costs. Domestic business will be unaffected. The selling price to break even is (a) $3.50, (b) $4.15, (c) $4.25, (d) $3.00, or (e) $5.00.

6. The company has an inventory of 1,000 units of pens that must be sold immediately at reduced prices. Otherwise, the inventory will become worthless. The unit cost that is relevant for establishing the minimum selling price is (a) $4.50, (b) $4.00, (c) $3.00, (d) $5.90, or (e) $1.50.

7. A proposal is received from an outside supplier who will make and ship the high-style pens directly to the Class Company's customers as sales orders are forwarded from Class's sales staff. Class's fixed marketing costs will be unaffected, but its variable marketing costs will be slashed by 20%. Class's plant will be idle, but its fixed manufacturing overhead will continue at 50% of present levels. How much per unit would the company be able to pay the supplier without decreasing operating income? (a) $4.75, (b) $3.95, (c) $2.95, (d) $5.35, or (e) none of these.

11-38 **Closing down divisions.** Belmont Corporation has four operating divisions. The budgeted revenues and expenses for each division for 2011 follows:

	Division			
	A	**B**	**C**	**D**
Sales	$630,000	$ 632,000	$960,000	$1,240,000
Cost of goods sold	550,000	620,000	765,000	925,000
Selling, general, and administrative expenses	120,000	135,000	144,000	210,000
Operating income/loss	$ (40,000)	$(123,000)	$ 51,000	$ 105,000

Further analysis of costs reveals the following percentages of variable costs in each division:

Cost of goods sold	90%	80%	90%	85%
Selling, general, and administrative expenses	50%	50%	60%	60%

Closing down any division would result in savings of 40% of the fixed costs of that division.

Top management is very concerned about the unprofitable divisions (A and B) and is considering closing them for the year.

Required
1. Calculate the increase or decrease in operating income if Belmont closes division A.
2. Calculate the increase or decrease in operating income if Belmont closes division B.
3. What other factors should the top management of Belmont consider before making a decision?

11-39 Product mix, constrained resource. Westford Company produces three products, A110, B382, and C657. Unit data for the three products follows:

	Product		
	A110	**B382**	**C657**
Selling price	$84	$56	70
Variable costs			
Direct materials	24	15	9
Labor and other costs	28	27	40
Quantity of Bistide per unit	8 lb.	5 lb.	3 lb.

All three products use the same direct material, Bistide. The demand for the products far exceeds the direct materials available to produce the products. Bistide costs $3 per pound and a maximum of 5,000 pounds is available each month. Westford must produce a minimum of 200 units of each product.

Required
1. How many units of product A110, B382, and C657 should Westford produce?
2. What is the maximum amount Westford would be willing to pay for another 1,000 pounds of Bistide?

11-40 Optimal product mix. (CMA adapted) Della Simpson, Inc., sells two popular brands of cookies: Della's Delight and Bonny's Bourbon. Della's Delight goes through the Mixing and Baking departments, and Bonny's Bourbon, a filled cookie, goes through the Mixing, Filling, and Baking departments.

Michael Shirra, vice president for sales, believes that at the current price, Della Simpson can sell all of its daily production of Della's Delight and Bonny's Bourbon. Both cookies are made in batches of 3,000. In each department, the time required per batch and the total time available each day are as follows:

	Home	Insert	Page Layout	Formulas	Data	Review
	A			B	C	D
1				**Department Minutes**		
2				**Mixing**	**Filling**	**Baking**
3	Della's Delight			30	0	10
4	Bonny's Bourbon			15	15	15
5	Total available per day			660	270	300

Revenue and cost data for each type of cookie are as follows:

	Home	Insert	Page Layout	Formulas	Data
	A			B	C
7				Della's	Bonny's
8				Delight	Bourbon
9	Revenue per batch			$ 475	$ 375
10	Variable cost per batch			175	125
11	Contribution margin per batch			$ 300	$ 250
12	Monthly fixed costs				
13	(allocated to each product)			$18,650	$22,350

1. Using *D* to represent the batches of Della's Delight and *B* to represent the batches of Bonny's Bourbon made and sold each day, formulate Shirra's decision as an LP model.
2. Compute the optimal number of batches of each type of cookie that Della Simpson, Inc., should make and sell each day to maximize operating income.

11-41 Dropping a customer, activity-based costing, ethics. Jack Arnoldson is the management accountant for Valley Restaurant Supply (VRS). Bob Gardner, the VRS sales manager, and Jack are meeting to discuss the profitability of one of the customers, Franco's Pizza. Jack hands Bob the following analysis of Franco's activity during the last quarter, taken from Valley's activity-based costing system:

Sales	$15,600
Cost of goods sold (all variable)	9,350
Order processing (25 orders processed at $200 per order)	5,000
Delivery (2,500 miles driven at $0.50 per mile)	1,250
Rush orders (3 rush orders at $110 per rush order)	330
Sales calls (3 sales calls at $100 per call)	300
Profits	($ 630)

Bob looks at the report and remarks, "I'm glad to see all my hard work is paying off with Franco's. Sales have gone up 10% over the previous quarter!"

Jack replies, "Increased sales are great, but I'm worried about Franco's margin, Bob. We were showing a profit with Franco's at the lower sales level, but now we're showing a loss. Gross margin percentage this quarter was 40%, down five percentage points from the prior quarter. I'm afraid that corporate will push hard to drop them as a customer if things don't turn around."

"That's crazy," Bob responds. "A lot of that overhead for things like order processing, deliveries, and sales calls would just be allocated to other customers if we dropped Franco's. This report makes it look like we're losing money on Franco's when we're not. In any case, I am sure you can do something to make its profitability look closer to what we think it is. No one doubts that Franco is a very good customer."

1. Assume that Bob is partly correct in his assessment of the report. Upon further investigation, it is determined that 10% of the order processing costs and 20% of the delivery costs would not be avoidable if VRS were to drop Franco's. Would VRS benefit from dropping Franco's? Show your calculations.
2. Bob's bonus is based on meeting sales targets. Based on the preceding information regarding gross margin percentage, what might Bob have done last quarter to meet his target and receive his bonus? How might VRS revise its bonus system to address this?
3. Should Jack rework the numbers? How should he respond to Bob's comments about making Franco look more profitable?

Collaborative Learning Problem

11-42 Equipment replacement decisions and performance evaluation. Bob Moody manages the Knoxville plant of George Manufacturing. He has been approached by a representative of Darda Engineering regarding the possible replacement of a large piece of manufacturing equipment that George uses in its process with a more efficient model. While the representative made some compelling arguments in favor of replacing the 3-year old equipment, Moody is hesitant. Moody is hoping to be promoted next year to manager of the larger Chicago plant, and he knows that the accrual-basis net operating income of the Knoxville plant will be evaluated closely as part of the promotion decision. The following information is available concerning the equipment replacement decision:

- The historic cost of the old machine is $300,000. It has a current book value of $120,000, two remaining years of useful life, and a market value of $72,000. Annual depreciation expense is $60,000. It is expected to have a salvage value of $0 at the end of its useful life.

- The new equipment will cost $180,000. It will have a two-year useful life and a $0 salvage value. George uses straight-line depreciation on all equipment.

- The new equipment will reduce electricity costs by $35,000 per year, and will reduce direct manufacturing labor costs by $30,000 per year.

For simplicity, ignore income taxes and the time value of money.

1. Assume that Moody's priority is to receive the promotion, and he makes the equipment replacement decision based on next year's accrual-based net operating income. Which alternative would he choose? Show your calculations.
2. What are the relevant factors in the decision? Which alternative is in the best interest of the company over the next two years? Show your calculations.
3. At what cost of the new equipment would Moody be willing to purchase it? Explain.

Most companies make a tremendous effort to analyze their costs and prices.

They know if the price is too high, customers will look elsewhere, too low, and the firm won't be able to cover the cost of making the product. Some companies, however, understand that it is possible to charge a low price to stimulate demand and meet customer needs while relentlessly managing costs to earn a profit. Tata Motors is one such company.

Target Pricing and Tata Motors' $2,500 Car[1]

Despite India's rapid economic growth and growing market for consumer goods, transportation options in the world's most populous country remain limited. Historically, Indians relied on public transportation, bicycles, and motorcycles to get around. Less than 1% owned cars, with most foreign models ill-suited to India's unique traffic conditions. Most cars had unnecessary product features and were priced too high for the vast majority of Indians.

But Ratan Tata, chairman of India's Tata Motors, saw India's dearth of cars as an opportunity. In 2003, after seeing a family riding dangerously on a two-wheel scooter, Mr. Tata set a challenge for his company to build a 'people's car' for the Indian market with three requirements: It should (1) adhere to existing regulatory requirements, (2) achieve certain performance targets for fuel efficiency and acceleration, and (3) cost only $2,500, about the price of the optional DVD player in a new Lexus sport utility vehicle sold in the United States.

The task was daunting: $2,500 was about half the price of the cheapest Indian car. One of Tata's suppliers said, "It's basically throwing out everything the auto industry has thought about cost structures in the past and taking a clean sheet of paper and asking, 'What's possible?'" Mr. Tata and his managers responded with what some analysts have described as "Gandhian engineering"

---

[1] *Sources*: Giridharadas, Anand. 2008. Four wheels for the masses: The $2,500 car. *New York Times*, January 8. http://www.nytimes.com/2008/01/08/business/worldbusiness/08indiacar.html Kripalani, Manjeet. 2008. Inside the Tata Nano Factory. *BusinessWeek*, May 9. http://www.businessweek.com/print/innovate/content/may2008/id2008059_312111.htm

principles: deep frugality with a willingness to challenge conventional wisdom.

At a fundamental level, Tata Motors' engineers created a new category of car by doing more with less. Extracting costs from traditional car development, Tata eschewed traditional long-term supplier relationships, and instead forced suppliers to compete for its business using Internet-based auctions. Engineering innovations led to a hollowed-out steering-wheel shaft, a smaller diameter drive shaft, a trunk with space for a briefcase, one windshield wiper instead of two, and a rear-mounted engine not much more powerful than a high-end riding lawnmower. Moreover, Tata's car has no radio, no power steering, no power windows, and no air conditioning—features standard on most vehicles.

But when Tata Motors introduced the "Nano" in 2008, the company had successfully built a $2,500 entry-level car that is fuel efficient, 50 miles to the gallon; reaches 65 miles per hour; and meets all current Indian emission, pollution, and safety standards. While revolutionizing the Indian automotive marketplace, the "Nano" is also changing staid global automakers. Already, the French-Japanese alliance Renault-Nissan and the Indian-Japanese joint venture Maruti Suzuki are trying to make ultra-cheap cars for India, while Ford recently made India the manufacturing hub for all of its low-cost cars.

Just like Ratan Tata, managers at many innovative companies are taking a fresh look at their strategic pricing decisions. This chapter describes how managers evaluate demand at different prices and manage costs across the value chain and over a product's life cycle to achieve profitability.

Major Influences on Pricing Decisions

Learning Objective **1**

Discuss the three major influences on pricing decisions

. . . customers, competitors, and costs

Consider for a moment how managers at Adidas might price their newest line of sneakers, or how decision makers at Microsoft would determine how much to charge for a monthly subscription of MSN Internet service. How companies price a product or a service ultimately depends on the demand and supply for it. Three influences on demand and supply are customers, competitors, and costs.

Customers, Competitors, and Costs

Customers

Customers influence price through their effect on the demand for a product or service, based on factors such as the features of a product and its quality. As the Tata Motors example illustrates, companies must always examine pricing decisions through the eyes of their customers and then manage costs to earn a profit.

Competitors

No business operates in a vacuum. Companies must always be aware of the actions of their competitors. At one extreme, alternative or substitute products of competitors hurt demand and force a company to lower prices. At the other extreme, a company without a competitor is free to set higher prices. When there are competitors, companies try to learn about competitors' technologies, plant capacities, and operating strategies to estimate competitors' costs—valuable information when setting prices.

Because competition spans international borders, fluctuations in exchange rates between different countries' currencies affect costs and pricing decisions. For example, if the yen weakens against the U.S. dollar, Japanese products become cheaper for American consumers and, consequently, more competitive in U.S. markets.

Costs

Costs influence prices because they affect supply. The lower the cost of producing a product, the greater the quantity of product the company is willing to supply. Generally, as companies increase supply, the cost of producing an additional unit initially declines but eventually increases. Companies supply products as long as the revenue from selling additional units exceeds the cost of producing them. Managers who understand the cost of producing products set prices that make the products attractive to customers while maximizing operating income.

Weighing Customers, Competitors, and Costs

Surveys indicate that companies weigh customers, competitors, and costs differently when making pricing decisions. At one extreme, companies operating in a perfectly competitive market sell very similar commodity-type products, such as wheat, rice, steel, and aluminum. These companies have no control over setting prices and must accept the price determined by a market consisting of many participants. Cost information is only helpful in deciding the quantity of output to produce to maximize operating income.

In less-competitive markets, such as those for cameras, televisions, and cellular phones, products are differentiated, and all three factors affect prices: The value customers place on a product and the prices charged for competing products affect demand, and the costs of producing and delivering the product influence supply.

As competition lessens even more, the key factor affecting pricing decisions is the customer's willingness to pay based on the value that customers place on the product or service, not costs or competitors. In the extreme, there are monopolies. A monopolist has no competitors and has much more leeway to set high prices. Nevertheless, there are limits. The higher the price a monopolist sets, the lower the demand for the monopolist's product as customers seek substitute products.

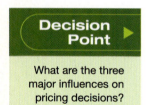

Decision Point ▶

What are the three major influences on pricing decisions?

Costing and Pricing for the Short Run

Short-run pricing decisions typically have a time horizon of less than a year and include decisions such as (a) pricing a *one-time-only special order* with no long-run implications and (b) adjusting product mix and output volume in a competitive market. Long-run pricing decisions have a time horizon of a year or longer and include pricing a product in a market where there is some leeway in setting price.

Consider a short-run pricing decision facing the management team at Astel Computers. Astel manufactures two brands of personal computers (PCs)—Deskpoint, Astel's top-of-the-line product, and Provalue, a less-powerful Pentium chip-based machine. Datatech Corporation has asked Astel to bid on supplying 5,000 Provalue computers over the last three months of 2010. After this three-month period, Datatech is unlikely to place any future sales orders with Astel. Datatech will sell Provalue computers under its own brand name in regions and markets where Astel does not sell Provalue. Whether Astel accepts or rejects this order will not affect Astel's revenues—neither the units sold nor the selling price—from existing sales channels.

Relevant Costs for Short-Run Pricing Decisions

Before Astel can bid on Datatech's offer, Astel's managers must estimate how much it will cost to supply the 5,000 computers. Similar to the Surf Gear example in Chapter 11, the relevant costs Astel's managers must focus on include all direct and indirect costs throughout the value chain that will change in total by accepting the one-time-only special order from Datatech. Astel's managers outline the relevant costs as follows:

Direct materials ($460 per computer × 5,000 computers)	$2,300,000
Direct manufacturing labor ($64 per computer × 5,000 computers)	320,000
Fixed costs of additional capacity to manufacture Provalue	250,000
Total costs	$2,870,000*

*No additional costs will be required for R&D, design, marketing, distribution, or customer service.

The relevant cost per computer is $574 ($2,870,000 ÷ 5,000). Therefore, any selling price above $574 will improve Astel's profitability in the short run. What price should Astel's managers bid for the 5,000-computer order?

Strategic and Other Factors in Short-Run Pricing

Based on its market intelligence, Astel believes that competing bids will be between $596 and $610 per computer, so Astel makes a bid of $595 per computer. If it wins this bid, operating income will increase by $105,000 (relevant revenues, $595 × 5,000 = $2,975,000 minus relevant costs, $2,870,000). In light of the extra capacity and strong competition, management's strategy is to bid as high above $574 as possible while remaining lower than competitors' bids.

What if Astel were the only supplier and Datatech could undercut Astel's selling price in Astel's current markets? The relevant cost of the bidding decision would then include the contribution margin lost on sales to existing customers. What if there were many parties eager to bid and win the Datatech contract? In this case, the contribution margin lost on sales to existing customers would be irrelevant to the decision because the existing business would be undercut by Datatech regardless of whether Astel wins the contract.

In contrast to the Astel case, in some short-run situations, a company may experience strong demand for its products or have limited capacity. In these circumstances, a company will strategically increase prices in the short run to as much as the market will bear. We observe high short-run prices in the case of new products or new models of older products, such as microprocessors, computer chips, cellular telephones, and software.

Effect of Time Horizon on Short-Run Pricing Decisions

Two key factors affect short-run pricing.

1. Many costs are irrelevant in short-run pricing decisions. In the Astel example, most of Astel's costs in R&D, design, manufacturing, marketing, distribution, and customer service are irrelevant for the short-run pricing decision, because these costs will not

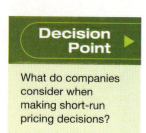

Decision Point ▶

What do companies consider when making short-run pricing decisions?

change whether Astel wins or does not win the Datatech business. These costs will change in the long run and therefore will be relevant.

2. Short-run pricing is opportunistic. Prices are decreased when demand is weak and competition is strong and increased when demand is strong and competition is weak. As we will see, long-run prices need to be set to earn a reasonable return on investment.

Learning Objective 3

Understand how companies make long-run pricing decisions

Consider all future variable and fixed costs as relevant and earn a target return on investment

Costing and Pricing for the Long Run

Long-run pricing is a strategic decision designed to build long-run relationships with customers based on stable and predictable prices. A stable price reduces the need for continuous monitoring of prices, improves planning, and builds long-run buyer–seller relationships. But to charge a stable price and earn the target long-run return, a company must, over the long run, know and manage its costs of supplying products to customers. As we will see, relevant costs for long-run pricing decisions include *all* future fixed and variable costs.

Calculating Product Costs for Long-Run Pricing Decisions

Let's return to the Astel example. However, this time consider the long-run pricing decision for Provalue.

We start by reviewing data for the year just ended, 2011. Astel has no beginning or ending inventory of Provalue and manufactures and sells 150,000 units during the year. Astel uses activity-based costing (ABC) to calculate the manufacturing cost of Provalue. Astel has three direct manufacturing costs, direct materials, direct manufacturing labor, and direct machining costs, and three manufacturing overhead cost pools, ordering and receiving components, testing and inspection of final products, and rework (correcting and fixing errors and defects), in its accounting system. Astel treats machining costs as a direct cost of Provalue because Provalue is manufactured on machines that only make Provalue.[2]

Astel uses a long-run time horizon to price Provalue. Over this horizon, Astel's managers observe the following:

- Direct material costs vary with number of units of Provalue produced.

- Direct manufacturing labor costs vary with number of direct manufacturing labor-hours used.

- Direct machining costs are fixed costs of leasing 300,000 machine-hours of capacity over multiple years. These costs do not vary with the number of machine-hours used each year. Each unit of Provalue requires 2 machine-hours. In 2011, Astel uses the entire machining capacity to manufacture Provalue (2 machine-hours per unit × 150,000 units = 300,000 machine-hours).

- Ordering and receiving, testing and inspection, and rework costs vary with the quantity of their respective cost drivers. For example, ordering and receiving costs vary with the number of orders. In the long run, staff members responsible for placing orders can be reassigned or laid off if fewer orders need to be placed, or increased if more orders need to be processed.

The following Excel spreadsheet summarizes manufacturing cost information to produce 150,000 units of Provalue in 2011.

---

[2] Recall that Astel makes two types of PCs: Deskpoint and Provalue. If Deskpoint and Provalue had shared the same machines, Astel would have allocated machining costs on the basis of the budgeted machine-hours used to manufacture the two products and would have treated these costs as fixed overhead costs.

	Home	Insert	Page Layout		Formulas	Data	Review	View		
	A	B	C	D	E	F		G	H	
1				Manufacturing Cost Information						
2				to Produce 150,000 Units of Provalue						
3	Cost Category	Cost Driver		Details of Cost Driver Quantities				Total Quantity of Cost Driver	Cost per Unit of Cost Driver	
4	(1)	(2)		(3)		(4)		(5) = (3) × (4)	(6)	
5	Direct Manufacturing Costs									
6	Direct materials	No. of kits	1	kit per unit	150,000	units		150,000	$460	
7	Direct manufacturing labor (DML)	DML hours	3.2	DML hours per unit	150,000	units		480,000	$ 20	
8	Direct machining (fixed)	Machine-hours						300,000	$ 38	
9	Manufacturing Overhead Costs									
10	Ordering and receiving	No. of orders	50	orders per component	450	components		22,500	$ 80	
11	Testing and inspection	Testing-hours	30	testing-hours per unit	150,000	units		4,500,000	$ 2	
12	Rework				8%	defect rate				
13		Rework-hours	2.5	rework-hours per defective unit	12,000[a]	defective units		30,000	$ 40	
14										
15	[a]8% defect rate × 150,000 units = 12,000 defective units									

Exhibit 12-1 indicates that the total cost of manufacturing Provalue in 2011 is $102 million, and the manufacturing cost per unit is $680. Manufacturing, however, is just one business function in the value chain. To set long-run prices, Astel's managers must calculate the *full cost* of producing and selling Provalue.

For each nonmanufacturing business function, Astel's managers trace direct costs to products and allocate indirect costs using cost pools and cost drivers that measure cause-and-effect relationships (supporting calculations not shown). Exhibit 12-2 summarizes Provalue's 2011 operating income and shows that Astel earned $15 million from Provalue, or $100 per unit sold in 2011.

Alternative Long-Run Pricing Approaches

How should managers at Astel use product cost information to price Provalue in 2012? Two different approaches for pricing decisions are as follows:

1. Market-based
2. Cost-based, which is also called cost-plus

The market-based approach to pricing starts by asking, "Given what our customers want and how our competitors will react to what we do, what price should we charge?" Based on this price, managers control costs to earn a target return on investment. The cost-based approach to pricing starts by asking, "Given what it costs us to make this product, what price should we charge that will recoup our costs and achieve a target return on investment?"

Exhibit 12-1   Manufacturing Costs of Provalue for 2011 Using Activity-Based Costing

	A	B	C
		Total Manufacturing	
1		Costs for	Manufacturing
2		150,000 Units	Cost per Unit
3		(1)	(2) = (1) ÷ 150,000
4			
5	Direct manufacturing costs		
6	Direct material costs		
7	(150,000 kits × $460 per kit)	$ 69,000,000	$460
8	Direct manufacturing labor costs		
9	(480,000 DML-hours × $20 per hour)	9,600,000	64
10	Direct machining costs		
11	(300,000 machine-hours × $38 per machine-hour)	11,400,000	76
12	Direct manufacturing costs	90,000,000	600
13			
14	Manufacturing overhead costs		
15	Ordering and receiving costs		
16	(22,500 orders × $80 per order)	1,800,000	12
17	Testing and inspection costs		
18	(4,500,000 testing-hours × $2 per hour)	9,000,000	60
19	Rework costs		
20	(30,000 rework-hours × $40 per hour)	1,200,000	8
21	Manufacturing overhead cost	12,000,000	80
22	Total manufacturing costs	$102,000,000	$680

Exhibit 12-2   Product Profitability of Provalue for 2011 Using Value-Chain Activity-Based Costing

	A	B	C
		Total Amounts	
1		for 150,000 Units	Per Unit
2		(1)	(2) = (1) ÷ 150,000
3			
4	Revenues	$150,000,000	$1,000
5	Costs of goods sold[a] (from Exhibit 12-1)	102,000,000	680
6	Operating costs[b]		
7	R&D costs	5,400,000	36
8	Design cost of product and process	6,000,000	40
9	Marketing costs	15,000,000	100
10	Distribution costs	3,600,000	24
11	Customer-service costs	3,000,000	20
12	Operating costs	33,000,000	220
13	Full cost of the product	135,000,000	900
14	Operating income	$ 15,000,000	$ 100
15			
16	[a]Cost of goods sold = Total manufacturing costs because there is no beginning or ending inventory		
17	of Provalue in 2011		
18	[b]Numbers for operating cost line-items are assumed without supporting calculations		

Companies operating in *competitive* markets (for example, commodities such as steel, oil, and natural gas) use the market-based approach. The items produced or services provided by one company are very similar to items produced or services provided by others. Companies in these markets must accept the prices set by the market.

Companies operating in *less competitive* markets offer products or services that differ from each other (for example, automobiles, computers, management consulting, and legal services), can use either the market-based or cost-based approach as the starting point for pricing decisions. Some companies first look at costs because cost information is more easily available and then consider customers or competitors: the cost-based approach. Others start by considering customers and competitors and then look at costs: the market-based approach. Both approaches consider customers, competitors, and costs. Only their starting points differ. Management must always keep in mind market forces, regardless of which pricing approach it uses. For example, building contractors often bid on a cost-plus basis but then reduce their prices during negotiations to respond to other lower-cost bids.

Companies operating in markets that are *not competitive* favor cost-based approaches. That's because these companies do not need to respond or react to competitors' prices. The margin they add to costs to determine price depends on the value customers place on the product or service.

We consider first the market-based approach.

Decision Point

How do companies make long-run pricing decisions?

Target Costing for Target Pricing

Market-based pricing starts with a target price. A **target price** is the estimated price for a product or service that potential customers are willing to pay. This estimate is based on an understanding of customers' perceived value for a product or service and how competitors will price competing products or services. This understanding of customers and competitors is becoming increasingly important for three reasons:

1. Competition from lower-cost producers is continually restraining prices.
2. Products are on the market for shorter periods of time, leaving less time and opportunity to recover from pricing mistakes, loss of market share, and loss of profitability.
3. Customers are becoming more knowledgeable and incessantly demanding products of higher and higher quality at lower and lower prices.

Learning Objective 4

Price products using the target-costing approach

. . . target costing identifies an estimated price customers are willing to pay and then computes a target cost to earn the desired profit

Understanding Customers' Perceived Value

A company's sales and marketing organization, through close contact and interaction with customers, identifies customer needs and perceptions of product value. Companies such as Apple also conduct market research on features that customers want and the prices they are willing to pay for those features for products such as the iPhone and the Macintosh computer.

Doing Competitor Analysis

To gauge how competitors might react to a prospective price, a company must understand competitors' technologies, products or services, costs, and financial conditions. In general, the more distinctive its product or service, the higher the price a company can charge. Where do companies like Ford Motors or PPG Industries obtain information about their competitors? Usually from former customers, suppliers, and employees of competitors. Another source of information is *reverse engineering*—that is, disassembling and analyzing competitors' products to determine product designs and materials and to become acquainted with the technologies competitors use. At no time should a company resort to illegal or unethical means to obtain information about competitors. For example, a company should never pay off current employees or pose as a supplier or customer in order to obtain competitor information.

Implementing Target Pricing and Target Costing

There are five steps in developing target prices and target costs. We illustrate these steps using our Provalue example.

Step 1:   Develop a product that satisfies the needs of potential customers. Customer requirements and competitors' products dictate the product features and design modifications for Provalue for 2012. Astel's market research indicates that customers do not value Provalue's extra features, such as special audio features and designs that accommodate upgrades to make the PC run faster. They want Astel to redesign Provalue into a no-frills but reliable PC and to sell it at a much lower price.

Step 2:   Choose a target price. Astel expects its competitors to lower the prices of PCs that compete with Provalue to $850. Astel's management wants to respond aggressively, reducing Provalue's price by 20%, from $1,000 to $800 per unit. At this lower price, Astel's marketing manager forecasts an increase in annual sales from 150,000 to 200,000 units.

Step 3:   Derive a target cost per unit by subtracting target operating income per unit from the target price. Target operating income per unit is the operating income that a company aims to earn per unit of a product or service sold. **Target cost per unit** is the estimated long-run cost per unit of a product or service that enables the company to achieve its target operating income per unit when selling at the target price.[3] *Target cost per unit* is the target price minus *target operating income per unit* and is often lower than the existing *full cost of the product*. Target cost per unit is really just that—a target—something the company must commit to achieve.

To attain the target return on the capital invested in the business, Astel's management needs to earn 10% target operating income on target revenues.

Total target revenues	= $800 per unit × 200,000 units = $160,000,000
Total target operating income	= 10% × $160,000,000 = $16,000,000
Target operating income per unit	= $16,000,000 ÷ 200,000 units = $80 per unit
Target cost per unit	= Target price – Target operating income per unit
	= $800 per unit – $80 per unit = $720 per unit
Total current full costs of Provalue	= $135,000,000 (from Exhibit 12-2)
Current full cost per unit of Provalue	= $135,000,000 ÷ 150,000 units = $900 per unit

Provalue's $720 target cost per unit is $180 below its existing $900 unit cost. Astel must reduce costs in all parts of the value chain—from R&D to customer service—including achieving lower prices on materials and components, while maintaining quality.

Target costs include *all* future costs, variable costs and costs that are fixed in the short run, because in the long run, a company's prices and revenues must recover all its costs if it is to remain in business. Contrast relevant costs for long-run pricing decisions (all variable and fixed costs) with relevant costs for short-run pricing decisions (costs that change in the short run, mostly but not exclusively variable costs).

Step 4:   Perform cost analysis. This step analyzes the specific aspects of a product or service to target for cost reduction. Astel's managers focus on the following elements of Provalue:

- The functions performed by and the current costs of different component parts, such as the motherboard, disc drives, and the graphics and video cards.

- The importance that customers place on different product features. For example, Provalue's customers value reliability more than video quality.

- The relationship and tradeoffs across product features and component parts. For example, choosing a simpler mother board enhances reliability but is unable to support the top-of-the-line video card.

---

[3] For a more-detailed discussion of target costing, see S. Ansari, J. Bell, and The CAM-I Target Cost Core Group, *Target Costing: The Next Frontier in Strategic Cost Management* (Martinsville, IN: Mountain Valley Publishing, 2009). For implementation information, see S. Ansari, L. D. Swenson, and J. Bell, "A Template for Implementing Target Costing," *Cost Management* (September–October 2006): 20–27.

Concepts in Action

Extreme Target Pricing and Cost Management at IKEA

Around the world, IKEA has exploded into a furniture-retailing-industry phenomenon. Known for products named after small Swedish towns, modern design, flat packaging, and do-it-yourself instructions, IKEA has grown from humble beginnings to become the world's largest furniture retailer with 301 stores in 38 countries. How did this happen? Through aggressive target pricing, coupled with relentless cost management. IKEA's prices typically run 30%–50% below its competitors' prices. Moreover, while the prices of other companies' products rise over time, IKEA says it has reduced its retail prices by about 20% over the last four years.

During the conceptualization phase, product developers identify gaps in IKEA's current product portfolio. For example, they might identify the need to create a new flat-screen-television stand. "When we decide about a product, we always start with the consumer need" IKEA Product Developer June Deboehmler said. Second, product developers and their teams survey competitors to determine how much they charge for similar items, if offered, and then select a target price that is 30%–50% less than the competitor's price. With a product and price established, product developers then determine what materials will be used and what manufacturer will do the assembly work—all before the new item is fully designed. For example, a brief describing a new couch's target cost and basic specifications like color and style is submitted for bidding among IKEA's over 1,800 suppliers in more than 50 countries. Suppliers vie to offer the most attractive bid based on price, function, and materials to be used. This value-engineering process promotes volume-based cost efficiencies throughout the design and production process.

Aggressive cost management does not stop there. All IKEA products are designed to be shipped unassembled in flat packages. The company estimates that shipping costs would be at least six times greater if all products were assembled before shipping. To ensure that shipping costs remain low, packaging and shipping technicians work with product developers throughout the product development process. When IKEA recently designed its Lillberg chair, a packaging technician made a small tweak in the angle of the chair's arm. This change allowed more chairs to fit into a single shipping container, which meant a lower cost to the consumer.

What about products that have already been developed? IKEA applies the same cost management techniques to those products, too. For example, one of IKEA's best selling products is the Lack bedside table, which has retailed for the same low price since 1981. How is this possible, you may ask. Since hitting store shelves, more than 100 technical development projects have been performed on the Lack table. Despite the steady increase in the cost of raw materials and wages, IKEA has aggressively sought to reduce product and distribution costs to maintain the Lack table's initial retail price without jeopardizing the company's profit on the product.

As founder Ingvar Kamprad once summarized, "Waste of resources is a mortal sin at IKEA. Expensive solutions are a sign of mediocrity, and an idea without a price tag is never acceptable."

Sources: Baraldi, Enrico and Torkel Strömsten. 2009. Managing product development the IKEA way. Using target costing in inter-organizational networks. Working Paper, December. Margonelli, Lisa. 2002. How IKEA designs its sexy price tags. *Business 2.0*, October. Terdiman, Daniel. 2008. Anatomy of an IKEA product. CNET News.com, April 19.

Step 5: Perform value engineering to achieve target cost. Value engineering is a systematic evaluation of all aspects of the value chain, with the objective of reducing costs and achieving a quality level that satisfies customers. As we describe next, value engineering encompasses improvements in product designs, changes in materials specifications, and modifications in process methods. (See the Concepts in Action feature to learn about IKEA's approach to target pricing and target costing.)

◀ **Decision Point**

How do companies determine target costs?

Value Engineering, Cost Incurrence, and Locked-In Costs

To implement value engineering, managers distinguish value-added activities and costs from nonvalue-added activities and costs. A **value-added cost** is a cost that, if eliminated, would reduce the actual or perceived value or utility (usefulness) customers experience from using the product or service. Examples are costs of specific product features and attributes desired by customers, such as reliability, adequate memory, preloaded software, clear images, and, in the case of Provalue, prompt customer service.

A **nonvalue-added cost** is a cost that, if eliminated, would not reduce the actual or perceived value or utility (usefulness) customers gain from using the product or service. It is a cost that the customer is unwilling to pay for. Examples of nonvalue-added costs are costs of producing defective products and cost of machine breakdowns. Successful companies keep nonvalue-added costs to a minimum.

Activities and their costs do not always fall neatly into value-added or nonvalue-added categories. Some costs, such as supervision and production control, fall in a gray area because they include mostly value-added but also some nonvalue-added components. Despite these troublesome gray areas, attempts to distinguish value-added from nonvalue-added costs provide a useful overall framework for value engineering.

In the Provalue example, direct materials, direct manufacturing labor, and direct machining costs are value-added costs. Ordering, receiving, testing, and inspection costs fall in the gray area. Rework costs are nonvalue-added costs.

Through value engineering, Astel's managers plan to reduce, and possibly eliminate, nonvalue-added costs and increase the efficiency of value-added activities. They start by distinguishing cost incurrence from locked-in costs. **Cost incurrence** describes when a resource is consumed (or benefit forgone) to meet a specific objective. Costing systems measure cost incurrence. Astel, for example, recognizes direct material costs of Provalue as each unit of Provalue is assembled and sold. But Provalue's direct material cost per unit is *locked in*, or *designed in*, much earlier, when product designers choose Provalue's components. **Locked-in costs**, or **designed-in costs**, are costs that have not yet been incurred but, based on decisions that have already been made, will be incurred in the future.

To manage costs well, a company must identify how design choices lock in costs *before* the costs are incurred. For example, scrap and rework costs incurred during manufacturing are often locked in much earlier by faulty design. Similarly, in the software industry, costly and difficult-to-fix errors that appear during coding and testing are frequently locked in by bad software design and analysis.

Exhibit 12-3 illustrates the locked-in cost curve and the cost-incurrence curve for Provalue. The bottom curve uses information from Exhibit 12-2 to plot the cumulative cost per unit incurred across different business functions of the value chain. The top curve plots how cumulative costs are locked in. (The specific numbers underlying this curve are not presented.) Total cumulative cost per unit for both curves is $900. *Observe, however, the wide divergence between when costs are locked in and when they are incurred.* For example, product design decisions lock in more than 86% ($780 ÷ $900) of the unit cost of Provalue (for example, direct materials, ordering, testing, rework, distribution, and customer service), when only about 8% ($76 ÷ $900) of the unit cost is actually incurred!

Value-Chain Analysis and Cross-Functional Teams

A cross-functional value-engineering team consisting of marketing managers, product designers, manufacturing engineers, purchasing managers, suppliers, dealers, and management accountants redesign Provalue to reduce costs while retaining features that customers value. Some of the team's ideas are as follows:

- Use a simpler, more-reliable motherboard without complex features to reduce manufacturing and repair costs.
- Snap-fit rather than solder parts together to decrease direct manufacturing labor-hours and related costs.

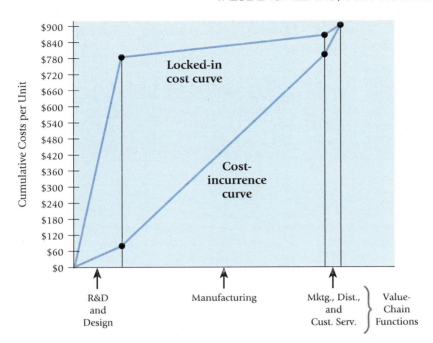

Exhibit 12-3

Pattern of Cost
Incurrence and
Locked-In Costs for
Provalue

- Use fewer components to decrease ordering, receiving, testing, and inspection costs.
- Make Provalue lighter and smaller to reduce distribution and packaging costs.

Management accountants use their understanding of the value chain to estimate cost savings. Not all costs are locked in at the design stage. Managers always have opportunities to reduce costs by improving operating efficiency and productivity. *Kaizen*, or *continuous improvement*, seeks to reduce the time it takes to do a task and to eliminate waste during production and delivery of products.

In summary, the key steps in value-engineering are as follows:

1. Understanding customer requirements, value-added and nonvalue-added costs

2. Anticipating how costs are locked in before they are incurred

3. Using cross-functional teams to redesign products and processes to reduce costs while meeting customer needs

Achieving the Target Cost per Unit for Provalue

Exhibit 12-4 uses an activity-based approach to compare cost-driver quantities and rates for the 150,000 units of Provalue manufactured and sold in 2011 and the 200,000 units of Provalue II budgeted for 2012. Value engineering decreases both value-added costs (by designing Provalue II to reduce direct materials and component costs, direct manufacturing labor-hours, and testing-hours) and nonvalue-added costs (by simplifying Provalue II's design to reduce rework). Value engineering also reduces the machine-hours required to make Provalue II to 1.5 hours per unit. Astel can now use the 300,000 machine-hours of capacity to make 200,000 units of Provalue II (versus 150,000 units for Provalue) reducing machining cost per unit. For simplicity, we assume that value engineering will not reduce the $20 cost per direct manufacturing labor-hour, the $80 cost per order, the $2 cost per testing-hour, or the $40 cost per rework-hour. (The Problem for Self-Study, p. 452, explores how value engineering can also reduce these cost-driver rates.)

Exhibit 12-5 presents the target manufacturing costs of Provalue II, using cost driver and cost-driver rate data from Exhibit 12-4. For comparison, Exhibit 12-5 also shows the actual 2011 manufacturing cost per unit of Provalue from Exhibit 12-1. Astel's managers expect the new design to reduce total manufacturing cost per unit by $140 (from $680 to $540) and cost per unit in other business functions from $220 (Exhibit 12-2) to $180 (calculations not shown) at the budgeted sales quantity of 200,000 units. The budgeted full unit cost of Provalue II is $720 ($540 + $180), the target cost per unit. At the end of 2012,

Exhibit 12-4 Cost-Driver Quantities and Rates for Provalue in 2011 and Provalue II for 2012 Using Activity-Based Costing

			Manufacturing Cost Information for 150,000 Units of Provalue in 2011				Manufacturing Cost Information for 200,000 Units of Provalue II for 2012		
Cost Category	Cost Driver	Details of Actual Cost Driver Quantities		Actual Total Quantity of Cost Driver	Actual Cost per Unit of Cost Driver (p.437)	Details of Budgeted Cost Driver Quantities		Budgeted Total Quantity of Cost Driver	Budgeted Cost per Unit of Cost Driver (Given)
(1)	(2)	(3)	(4)	(5)=(3)×(4)	(6)	(7)	(8)	(9)=(7)×(8)	(10)
Direct Manufacturing Costs									
Direct materials	No. of kits	1 kit per unit	150,000 units	150,000	$460	1 kit per unit	200,000 units	200,000	$385
Direct manuf. labor (DML)	DML hours	3.2 DML hours per unit	150,000 units	480,000	$20	2.65 DML hours per unit	200,000 units	530,000	$20
Direct machining (fixed)	Machine-hours			300,000	$38			300,000	$38
Manufacturing Overhead Costs									
Ordering and receiving	No. of orders	50 orders per component	450 components	22,500	$80	50 orders per component	425 components	21,250	$80
Testing and inspection	Testing-hours	30 testing-hours per unit	150,000 units	4,500,000	$2	15 testing hours per unit	200,000 units	3,000,000	$2
Rework			8% defect rate				6.5% defect rate		
	Rework-hours	2.5 rework-hours per defective unit	12,000[a] defective units	30,000	$40	2.5 rework-hours per defective unit	13,000[b] defective units	32,500	$40

[a] 8% defect rate × 150,000 units = 12,000 defective units

[b] 6.5% defect rate × 200,000 units = 13,000 defective units

Astel's managers will compare actual costs and target costs to gain insight about improvements that can be made in subsequent target-costing efforts.

Unless managed properly, value engineering and target costing can have undesirable effects:

- Employees may feel frustrated if they fail to attain targets.
- The cross-functional team may add too many features just to accommodate the different wishes of team members.
- A product may be in development for a long time as alternative designs are evaluated repeatedly.
- Organizational conflicts may develop as the burden of cutting costs falls unequally on different business functions in the company's value chain, for example, more on manufacturing than on marketing.

Exhibit 12-5 Target Manufacturing Costs of Provalue II for 2012

		Home	Insert	Page Layout	Formulas	Data	Review	View	

	A	B	C	D	E	F
1		PROVALUE II				PROVALUE
2		Budgeted		Budgeted		Actual Manufacturing
3		Manufacturing Costs		Manufacturing		Cost per Unit
4		for 200,000 Units		Cost per Unit		(Exhibit 12-1)
5		(1)		(2) = (1) ÷ 200,000		(3)
6	Direct manufacturing costs					
7	Direct material costs					
8	(200,000 kits × $385 per kit)	$ 77,000,000		$385.00		$460.00
9	Direct manufacturing labor costs					
10	(530,000 DML-hours × $20 per hour)	10,600,000		53.00		64.00
11	Direct machining costs					
12	(300,000 machine-hours × $38 per machine-hour)	11,400,000		57.00		76.00
13	Direct manufacturing costs	99,000,000		495.00		600.00
14	Manufacturing overhead costs					
15	Ordering and receiving costs					
16	(21,250 orders × $80 per order)	1,700,000		8.50		12.00
17	Testing and inspection costs					
18	(3,000,000 testing-hours × $2 per hour)	6,000,000		30.00		60.00
19	Rework costs					
20	(32,500 rework-hours × $40 per hour)	1,300,000		6.50		8.00
21	Manufacturing overhead costs	9,000,000		45.00		80.00
22	Total manufaturing costs	$108,000,000		$540.00		$ 680.00

To avoid these pitfalls, target-costing efforts should always (a) encourage employee participation and celebrate small improvements toward achieving the target, (b) focus on the customer, (c) pay attention to schedules, and (d) set cost-cutting targets for all value-chain functions to encourage a culture of teamwork and cooperation.

> ◀ **Decision Point**
>
> Why is it important to distinguish cost incurrence from locked-in costs?

Cost-Plus Pricing

Instead of using the market-based approach for long-run pricing decisions, managers sometimes use a cost-based approach. The general formula for setting a cost-based price adds a markup component to the cost base to determine a prospective selling price. Because a markup is added, cost-based pricing is often called cost-plus pricing, with the plus referring to the markup component. Managers use the cost-plus pricing formula as a starting point. The markup component is rarely a rigid number. Instead, it is flexible, depending on the behavior of customers and competitors. The markup component is ultimately determined by the market.[4]

> **Learning Objective 6**
>
> Price products using the cost-plus approach
>
> . . . cost-plus pricing is based on some measure of cost plus a markup

Cost-Plus Target Rate of Return on Investment

We illustrate a cost-plus pricing formula for Provalue II assuming Astel uses a 12% markup on the full unit cost of the product when computing the selling price.

Cost base (full unit cost of Provalue II)	$720.00
Markup component of 12% (0.12 × $720)	86.40
Prospective selling price	$806.40

---

[4] Exceptions are pricing of electricity and natural gas in many countries, where prices are set by the government on the basis of costs plus a return on invested capital. Chapter 15 discusses the use of costs to set prices in the defense-contracting industry. In these situations, products are not subject to competitive forces and cost accounting techniques substitute for markets as the basis for setting prices.

How is the markup percentage of 12% determined? One way is to choose a markup to earn a *target rate of return on investment*. The **target rate of return on investment** is the target annual operating income divided by invested capital. Invested capital can be defined in many ways. In this chapter, we define it as total assets—that is, long-term assets plus current assets. Suppose Astel's (pretax) target rate of return on investment is 18% and Provalue II's capital investment is $96 million. The target annual operating income for Provalue II is as follows:

Invested capital	$96,000,000
Target rate of return on investment	18%
Target annual operating income (0.18 × $96,000,000)	$17,280,000
Target operating income per unit of Provalue II ($17,280,000 ÷ 200,000 units)	$ 86.40

This calculation indicates that Astel needs to earn a target operating income of $86.40 on each unit of Provalue II. The markup ($86.40) expressed as a percentage of the full unit cost of the product ($720) equals 12% ($86.40 ÷ $720).

Do not confuse the 18% target rate of return on investment with the 12% markup percentage.

- The 18% target rate of return on investment expresses Astel's expected annual operating income as a percentage of investment.

- The 12% markup expresses operating income per unit as a percentage of the full product cost per unit.

Astel uses the target rate of return on investment to calculate the markup percentage.

Alternative Cost-Plus Methods

Computing the specific amount of capital invested in a product is seldom easy because it requires difficult and arbitrary allocations of investments in equipment and buildings to individual products. The following table uses alternative cost bases (without supporting calculations) and assumed markup percentages to set prospective selling prices for Provalue II without explicitly calculating invested capital to set prices.

Cost Base	Estimated Cost per Unit (1)	Markup Percentage (2)	Markup Component (3) = (1) × (2)	Prospective Selling Price (4) = (1) + (3)
Variable manufacturing cost	$475.00	65%	$308.75	$783.75
Variable cost of the product	547.00	45	246.15	793.15
Manufacturing cost	540.00	50	270.00	810.00
Full cost of the product	720.00	12	86.40	806.40

The different cost bases and markup percentages give four prospective selling prices that are close to each other. In practice, a company chooses a reliable cost base and markup percentage to recover its costs and earn a target return on investment. For example, consulting companies often choose the full cost of a client engagement as their cost base because it is difficult to distinguish variable costs from fixed costs.

The markup percentages in the preceding table vary a great deal, from a high of 65% on variable manufacturing cost to a low of 12% on full cost of the product. Why the wide variation? When determining a prospective selling price, a cost base such as variable manufacturing cost (that includes fewer costs) requires a higher markup percentage because the price needs to be set to earn a profit margin *and* to recover costs that have been excluded from the base.

Surveys indicate that most managers use the full cost of the product for cost-based pricing decisions—that is, they include both fixed and variable costs when calculating the cost per unit. Managers include fixed cost per unit in the cost base for several reasons:

1. **Full recovery of all costs of the product.** In the long run, the price of a product must exceed the full cost of the product if a company is to remain in business. Using just the variable cost as a base may tempt managers to cut prices as long as prices are

above variable cost and generate a positive contribution margin. As the experience in the airline industry has shown, variable cost pricing may cause companies to lose money because revenues are too low to recover the full cost of the product.

2. **Price stability.** Managers believe that using the full cost of the product as the basis for pricing decisions promotes price stability, because it limits the ability and temptations of salespersons to cut prices. Stable prices facilitate more-accurate forecasting and planning.

3. **Simplicity.** A full-cost formula for pricing does not require a detailed analysis of cost-behavior patterns to separate product costs into fixed and variable components. Variable and fixed cost components are difficult to identify for many costs such as testing, inspection, and setups.

Including fixed cost per unit in the cost base for pricing is not without problems. Allocating fixed costs to products can be arbitrary. Also, calculating fixed cost per unit requires a denominator level that is based on an estimate of capacity or expected units of future sales. Errors in these estimates will cause actual full cost per unit of the product to differ from the estimated amount.

Cost-Plus Pricing and Target Pricing

The selling prices computed under cost-plus pricing are *prospective* prices. Suppose Astel's initial product design results in a $750 full cost for Provalue II. Assuming a 12% markup, Astel sets a prospective price of $840 [$750 + (0.12 × $750)]. In the competitive personal computer market, customer and competitor reactions to this price may force Astel to reduce the markup percentage and lower the price to, say, $800. Astel may then want to redesign Provalue II to reduce the full cost to $720 per unit, as in our example, and achieve a markup close to 12% while keeping the price at $800. The eventual design and cost-plus price must trade-off cost, markup, and customer reactions.

The target-pricing approach reduces the need to go back and forth among prospective cost-plus prices, customer reactions, and design modifications. In contrast to cost-plus pricing, target pricing first determines product characteristics and target price on the basis of customer preferences and expected competitor responses, and then computes a target cost.

Suppliers who provide unique products and services, such as accountants and management consultants, usually use cost-plus pricing. Professional service firms set prices based on hourly cost-plus billing rates of partners, managers, and associates. These prices are, however, lowered in competitive situations. Professional service firms also take a multiple-year client perspective when deciding prices. Certified public accountants, for example, sometimes charge a client a low price initially and a higher price later.

Service companies such as home repair services, automobile repair services, and architectural firms use a cost-plus pricing method called the *time-and-materials method*. Individual jobs are priced based on materials and labor time. The price charged for materials equals the cost of materials plus a markup. The price charged for labor represents the cost of labor plus a markup. That is, the price charged for each direct cost item includes its own markup. The markups are chosen to recover overhead costs and to earn a profit.

Decision Point

How do companies price products using the cost-plus approach?

Life-Cycle Product Budgeting and Costing

Companies sometimes need to consider target prices and target costs over a multiple-year product life cycle. The **product life cycle** spans the time from initial R&D on a product to when customer service and support is no longer offered for that product. For automobile companies such as DaimlerChrysler, Ford, and Nissan, the product life cycle is 12 to 15 years to design, introduce, and sell different car models. For pharmaceutical products, the life cycle at companies such as Pfizer, Merck, and Glaxo Smith Kline may be 15 to 20 years. For banks such as Wachovia and Chase Manhattan Bank, a product such as a newly designed savings account with specific privileges can have a life cycle of 10 to 20 years. Personal computers have a shorter life-cycle of 3 to 5 years, because rapid

Learning Objective 7

Use life-cycle budgeting and costing when making pricing decisions

. . . accumulate all costs of a product from initial R&D to final customer service for each year of the product's life

innovations in the computing power and speed of microprocessors that run the computers make older models obsolete.

In **life-cycle budgeting**, managers estimate the revenues and business function costs across the entire value chain from a product's initial R&D to its final customer service and support. **Life-cycle costing** tracks and accumulates business function costs across the entire value chain from a product's initial R&D to its final customer service and support. Life-cycle budgeting and life-cycle costing span several years.

Life-Cycle Budgeting and Pricing Decisions

Budgeted life-cycle costs provide useful information for strategically evaluating pricing decisions. Consider Insight, Inc., a computer software company, which is developing a new accounting package, "General Ledger." Assume the following budgeted amounts for General Ledger over a six-year product life cycle:

Years 1 and 2

	Total Fixed Costs
R&D costs	$240,000
Design costs	160,000

Years 3 to 6

	Total Fixed Costs	Variable Cost per Package
Production costs	$100,000	$25
Marketing costs	70,000	24
Distribution costs	50,000	16
Customer-service costs	80,000	30

Exhibit 12-6 presents the six-year life-cycle budget for General Ledger for three alternative selling-price/sales-quantity combinations.

Several features make life-cycle budgeting particularly important:

1. **The development period for R&D and design is long and costly.** When a high percentage of total life-cycle costs are incurred before any production begins and any revenues are received, as in the General Ledger example, the company needs to evaluate revenues and costs over the life-cycle of the product in order to decide whether to begin the costly R&D and design activities.

2. **Many costs are locked in at R&D and design stages, even if R&D and design costs themselves are small.** In our General Ledger example, a poorly designed accounting software package, which is difficult to install and use, would result in higher marketing, distribution, and customer-service costs in several subsequent years. These costs would be even higher if the product failed to meet promised quality-performance levels. A life-cycle revenue-and-cost budget prevents Insight's managers from overlooking these multiple-year relationships among business-function costs. Life-cycle budgeting highlights costs throughout the product's life cycle and, in doing so, facilitates target pricing, target costing, and value engineering at the design stage before costs are locked in. The amounts presented in Exhibit 12-6 are the outcome of value engineering.

Insight decides to sell the General Ledger package for $480 per package because this price maximizes life-cycle operating income. Insight's managers compare actual costs to life-cycle budgets to obtain feedback and to learn about how to estimate costs better for subsequent products. Exhibit 12-6 assumes that the selling price per package is the same over the entire life cycle. For strategic reasons, however, Insight may decide to skim the market by charging higher prices to eager customers when General Ledger is first introduced and then lowering prices later as the product matures. In these later stages, Insight may even add new features to differentiate the product to maintain prices and sales. The life-cycle budget must then incorporate the revenues and costs of these strategies.

Exhibit 12-6	Budgeting Life-Cycle Revenues and Costs for "General Ledger" Software Package of Insight, Inc.[a]

| | Alternative Selling-Price/ Sales-Quantity Combinations | | |
	A	B	C
Selling price per package	$400	$480	$600
Sales quantity in units	5,000	4,000	2,500
Life-cycle revenues			
($400 × 5,000; $480 × 4,000; $600 × 2,500)	$2,000,000	$1,920,000	$1,500,000
Life-cycle costs			
R&D costs	240,000	240,000	240,000
Design costs of product/process	160,000	160,000	160,000
Production costs			
$100,000 + ($25 × 5,000); $100,000 +			
($25 × 4,000); $100,000 + ($25 × 2,500)	225,000	200,000	162,500
Marketing costs			
$70,000 + ($24 × 5,000); $70,000 +			
($24 × 4,000); $70,000 + ($24 × 2,500)	190,000	166,000	130,000
Distribution costs			
$50,000 + ($16 × 5,000); $50,000 +			
($16 × 4,000); $50,000 + ($16 × 2,500)	130,000	114,000	90,000
Customer-service costs			
$80,000 + ($30 × 5,000); $80,000 +			
($30 × 4,000); $80,000 + ($30 × 2,500)	230,000	200,000	155,000
Total life-cycle costs	1,175,000	1,080,000	937,500
Life-cycle operating income	$ 825,000	$ 840,000	$ 562,500

[a]This exhibit does not take into consideration the time value of money when computing life-cycle revenues or life-cycle costs. Chapter 21 outlines how this important factor can be incorporated into such calculations.

Management of environmental costs provides another example of life-cycle costing and value engineering. Environmental laws like the U.S. Clean Air Act and the U.S. Superfund Amendment and Reauthorization Act have introduced tougher environmental standards, imposed stringent cleanup requirements, and introduced severe penalties for polluting the air and contaminating subsurface soil and groundwater. Environmental costs that are incurred over several years of the product's life-cycle are often locked in at the product- and process-design stage. To avoid environmental liabilities, companies in industries such as oil refining, chemical processing, and automobiles practice value engineering; they design products and processes to prevent and reduce pollution over the product's life cycle. For example, laptop computer manufacturers like Hewlett Packard and Apple have introduced costly recycling programs to ensure that chemicals from nickel-cadmium batteries do not leak hazardous chemicals into the soil.

Customer Life-Cycle Costing

A different notion of life-cycle costs is *customer life-cycle costs*. **Customer life-cycle costs** focus on the total costs incurred by a customer to acquire, use, maintain, and dispose of a product or service. Customer life-cycle costs influence the prices a company can charge for its products. For example, Ford can charge a higher price and/or gain market share if its cars require minimal maintenance for 100,000 miles. Similarly, Maytag charges higher prices for appliances that save electricity and have low maintenance costs. Boeing Corporation justifies a higher price for the Boeing 777 because the plane's design allows mechanics easier access to different areas of the plane to perform routine maintenance, reduces the time and cost of maintenance, and significantly decreases the life-cycle cost of owning the plane.

Decision Point

Describe life-cycle budgeting and life-cycle costing and when companies should use these techniques.

Additional Considerations for Pricing Decisions

**Learning
Objective 8**

Describe two pricing
practices in which
noncost factors are
important when setting
prices

. . . price
discrimination—
charging different
customers different
prices for the same
product—and peak-
load pricing—charging
higher prices when
demand approaches
capacity limits

In some cases, cost is *not* a major factor in setting prices. We explore some of the ways that market structures and laws and regulations influence price setting outside of cost.

Price Discrimination

Consider the prices airlines charge for a round-trip flight from Boston to San Francisco. A coach-class ticket for a flight with seven-day advance purchase is $450 if the passenger stays in San Francisco over a Saturday night. It is $1,000 if the passenger returns without staying over a Saturday night. Can this price difference be explained by the difference in the cost to the airline of these round-trip flights? No; it costs the same amount to transport the passenger from Boston to San Francisco and back, regardless of whether the passenger stays in San Francisco over a Saturday night. This difference in price is due to *price discrimination*.

Price discrimination is the practice of charging different customers different prices for the same product or service. How does price discrimination work in the airline example? The demand for airline tickets comes from two main sources: business travelers and pleasure travelers. Business travelers must travel to conduct business for their organizations, so their demand for air travel is relatively insensitive to price. Airlines can earn higher operating incomes by charging business travelers higher prices. Insensitivity of demand to price changes is called *demand inelasticity*. Also, business travelers generally go to their destinations, complete their work, and return home without staying over a Saturday night. Pleasure travelers, in contrast, usually don't need to return home during the week, and prefer to spend weekends at their destinations. Because they pay for their tickets themselves, pleasure travelers' demand is price-elastic, lowering prices stimulates demand. Airlines can earn higher operating incomes by charging pleasure travelers lower prices.

How can airlines keep fares high for business travelers while, at the same time, keeping fares low for pleasure travelers? Requiring a Saturday night stay discriminates between the two customer segments. The airlines price-discriminate to take advantage of different sensitivities to prices exhibited by business travelers and pleasure travelers. Prices differ even though there is no difference in cost in serving the two customer segments.

What if economic conditions weaken such that business travelers become more sensitive to price? The airlines may then need to lower the prices they charge to business travelers. Following the events of September 11, 2001, airlines started offering discounted fares on certain routes without requiring a Saturday night stay to stimulate business travel. Business travel picked up and airlines started filling more seats than they otherwise would have. Unfortunately, travel did not pick up enough, and the airline industry as a whole suffered severe losses over the next few years.

Peak-Load Pricing

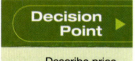

**Decision
Point**

Describe price
discrimination and
peak-load pricing.

In addition to price discrimination, other noncost factors such as capacity constraints affect pricing decisions. **Peak-load pricing** is the practice of charging a higher price for the same product or service when the demand for the product or service approaches the physical limit of the capacity to produce that product or service. When demand is high and production capacity is limited, customers are willing to pay more to get the product or service. In contrast, slack or excess capacity leads companies to lower prices in order to stimulate demand and utilize capacity. Peak-load pricing occurs in the telephone, telecommunications, hotel, car rental, and electric-utility industries. During the 2008 Summer Olympics in Beijing, for example, hotels charged very high rates and required multiple-night stays. Airlines charged high fares for flights into and out of many cities in the region for roughly a month around the time of the games. Demand far exceeded capacity and the hospitality industry and airlines employed peak-load pricing to increase their profits.

International Considerations

Another example of factors other than costs affecting prices occurs when the same product is sold in different countries. Consider software, books, and medicines produced in one country and sold globally. The prices charged in each country vary much more than the costs of delivering the product to each country. These price differences arise because of differences in the purchasing power of consumers in different countries (a form of price discrimination) and government restrictions that may limit the prices that can be charged.

Antitrust Laws

Legal considerations also affect pricing decisions. Companies are not always free to charge whatever price they like. For example, under the U.S. Robinson-Patman Act, a manufacturer cannot price-discriminate between two customers if the intent is to lessen or prevent competition for customers. Two key features of price-discrimination laws are as follows:

1. Price discrimination is permissible if differences in prices can be justified by differences in costs.

2. Price discrimination is illegal only if the intent is to lessen or prevent competition.

The price discrimination by airline companies described earlier is legal because their practices do not hinder competition.

Predatory Pricing

To comply with U.S. antitrust laws, such as the Sherman Act, the Clayton Act, the Federal Trade Commission Act, and the Robinson-Patman Act, pricing must not be predatory.[5] A company engages in **predatory pricing** when it deliberately prices below its costs in an effort to drive competitors out of the market and restrict supply, and then raises prices rather than enlarge demand.[6]

The U.S. Supreme Court established the following conditions to prove that predatory pricing has occurred:

- The predator company charges a price below an appropriate measure of its costs.
- The predator company has a reasonable prospect of recovering in the future, through larger market share or higher prices, the money it lost by pricing below cost.

The Supreme Court has not specified the "appropriate measure of costs."[7]

Most courts in the United States have defined the "appropriate measure of costs" as the short-run marginal or average variable costs.[8] In *Adjustor's Replace-a-Car* v. *Agency Rent-a-Car*, Adjustor's (the plaintiff) claimed that it was forced to withdraw from the Austin and San Antonio, Texas, markets because Agency had engaged in predatory pricing.[9] To prove predatory pricing, Adjustor pointed to "the net loss from operations" in Agency's income statement, calculated after allocating Agency's headquarters overhead. The judge, however, ruled that Agency had not engaged in predatory

Learning Objective 9

Explain the effects of antitrust laws on pricing

. . . antitrust laws attempt to counteract pricing below costs to drive out competitors or fixing prices artificially high to harm consumers

---

[5] Discussion of the Sherman Act and the Clayton Act is in A. Barkman and J. Jolley, "Cost Defenses for Antitrust Cases," *Management Accounting* 67 (no. 10): 37–40.

[6] For more details, see W. Viscusi, J. Harrington, and J. Vernon, *Economics of Regulation and Antitrust*, 4th ed. (Cambridge, MA: MIT Press, 2006); and J. L. Goldstein, "Single Firm Predatory Pricing in Antitrust Law: The Rose Acre Recoupment Test and the Search for an Appropriate Judicial Standard," *Columbia Law Review* 91 (1991): 1557–1592.

[7] *Brooke Group* v. *Brown & Williamson Tobacco*, 113 S. Ct. (1993); T. J. Trujillo, "Predatory Pricing Standards Under Recent Supreme Court Decisions and Their Failure to Recognize Strategic Behavior as a Barrier to Entry," *Iowa Journal of Corporation Law* (Summer 1994): 809–831.

[8] An exception is *McGahee* v. *Northern Propane Gas Co.* [858 F, 2d 1487 (1988)], in which the Eleventh Circuit Court held that prices below average total cost constitute evidence of predatory intent. For more discussion, see P. Areeda and D. Turner, "Predatory Pricing and Related Practices under Section 2 of Sherman Act," *Harvard Law Review* 88 (1975): 697–733. For an overview of case law, see W. Viscusi, J. Harrington, and J. Vernon, *Economics of Regulation and Antitrust*, 4th ed. (Cambridge, MA: MIT Press, 2006). See also the "Legal Developments" section of the *Journal of Marketing* for summaries of court cases.

[9] *Adjustor's Replace-a-Car, Inc.* v. *Agency Rent-a-Car*, 735 2d 884 (1984).

pricing because the price it charged for a rental car never dropped below its average variable costs.

The Supreme Court decision in *Brooke Group v. Brown & Williamson Tobacco* (*BWT*) increased the difficulty of proving predatory pricing. The Court ruled that pricing below average variable costs is not predatory if the company does not have a reasonable chance of later increasing prices or market share to recover its losses.[10] The defendant, BWT, a cigarette manufacturer, sold brand-name cigarettes and had 12% of the cigarette market. The introduction of generic cigarettes threatened BWT's market share. BWT responded by introducing its own version of generics priced below average variable cost, thereby making it difficult for generic manufacturers to continue in business. The Supreme Court ruled that BWT's action was a competitive response and not predatory pricing. That's because, given BWT's small 12% market share and the existing competition within the industry, it would be unable to later charge a monopoly price to recoup its losses.

Dumping

Closely related to predatory pricing is dumping. Under U.S. laws, **dumping** occurs when a non-U.S. company sells a product in the United States at a price below the market value in the country where it is produced, and this lower price materially injures or threatens to materially injure an industry in the United States. If dumping is proven, an antidumping duty can be imposed under U.S. tariff laws equal to the amount by which the foreign price exceeds the U.S. price. Cases related to dumping have occurred in the cement, computer, lumber, paper, semiconductor, steel, sweater, and tire industries. In September 2009, the U.S. Commerce Department said it would place import duties of 25%–35% on imports of automobile and light-truck tires from China.[11] China challenged the decision to the dispute settlement panel of the World Trade Organization (WTO), an international institution created with the goal of promoting and regulating trade practices among countries.

Collusive Pricing

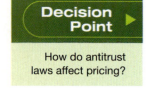

Decision Point ▶

How do antitrust laws affect pricing?

Another violation of antitrust laws is collusive pricing. **Collusive pricing** occurs when companies in an industry conspire in their pricing and production decisions to achieve a price above the competitive price and so restrain trade. In 2008, for example, LG agreed to pay $400 million and Sharp $120 million for colluding to fix prices of LCD picture tubes in the United States.

---

[10] *Brooke Group v. Brown & Williamson Tobacco*, 113 S. Ct. (1993).
[11] Edmund Andrews, "U.S. Adds Tariffs on Chinese Tires," *New York Times* (September 11, 2009).

Problem for Self-Study

Reconsider the Astel Computer example (pp. 436–437). Astel's marketing manager realizes that a further reduction in price is necessary to sell 200,000 units of Provalue II. To maintain a target profitability of $16 million, or $80 per unit, Astel will need to reduce costs of Provalue II by $6 million, or $30 per unit. Astel targets a reduction of $4 million, or $20 per unit, in manufacturing costs, and $2 million, or $10 per unit, in marketing, distribution, and customer-service costs. The cross-functional team assigned to this task proposes the following changes to manufacture a different version of Provalue, called Provalue III:

1. Reduce direct materials and ordering costs by purchasing subassembled components rather than individual components.

2. Reengineer ordering and receiving to reduce ordering and receiving costs per order.

3. Reduce testing time and the labor and power required per hour of testing.

4. Develop new rework procedures to reduce rework costs per hour.

No changes are proposed in direct manufacturing labor cost per unit and in total machining costs.

The following table summarizes the cost-driver quantities and the cost per unit of each cost driver for Provalue III compared with Provalue II.

	Home	Insert		Page Layout		Formulas		Data		Review		View		

	A	B	C	D	E	F	G	H	I	J	K	L	M	N
1				Manufacturing Cost Information						Manufacturing Cost Information				
2				for 200,000 Units of Provalue II for 2012						for 200,000 Units of Provalue III for 2012				
3	Cost Category	Cost Driver		Details of Budgeted Cost Driver Quantities			Budgeted Total Quantity of Cost Driver	Budgeted Cost per Unit of Cost Driver		Details of Budgeted Cost Driver Quantities			Budgeted Total Quantity of Cost Driver	Budgeted Cost per Unit of Cost Driver
4	(1)	(2)		(3)	(4)		(5)=(3)×(4)	(6)		(7)	(8)		(9)=(7)×(8)	(10)
5	Direct materials	No. of kits	1	kit per unit	200,000	units	200,000	$385	1	kit per unit	200,000	units	200,000	$375
6	Direct manuf. labor (DML)	DML hours	2.65	DML hours per unit	200,000	units	530,000	$ 20	2.65	DML hours per unit	200,000	units	530,000	$ 20
7	Direct machining (fixed)	Machine-hours					300,000	$ 38					300,000	$ 38
8	Ordering and receiving	No. of orders	50	orders per component	425	compo-nents	21,250	$ 80	50	orders per component	400	compo-nents	20,000	$ 60
9	Test and inspection	Testing-hours	15	testing-hours per unit	200,000	units	3,000,000	$ 2	14	testing-hours per unit	200,000	units	2,800,000	$ 1.70
10	Rework				6.5%	defect rate					6.5%	defect rate		
11		Rework-hours	2.5	rework-hours per defective unit	13,000ᵃ	defec-tive units	32,500	$ 40	2.5	rework-hours per defective unit	13,000ᵃ	defec-tive units	32,500	$ 32
12														
13	ᵃ6.5% defect rate × 200,000 units = 13,000 defective units													

Required

Will the proposed changes achieve Astel's targeted reduction of $4 million, or $20 per unit, in manufacturing costs for Provalue III? Show your computations.

Solution

Exhibit 12-7 presents the manufacturing costs for Provalue III based on the proposed changes. Manufacturing costs will decline from $108 million, or $540 per unit (Exhibit 12-5), to $104 million, or $520 per unit (Exhibit 12-7), and will achieve the target reduction of $4 million, or $20 per unit.

Exhibit 12-7 Target Manufacturing Costs of Provalue III for 2012 Based on Proposed Changes

	A	B	C	D
		Home Insert Page Layout Formulas Data Review View		
1		**Budgeted**		**Budgeted**
2		**Manufacturing Costs**		**Manufacturing**
3		**for 200,000 Units**		**Cost per Unit**
4		**(1)**		**(2) = (1) ÷ 200,000**
5	Direct manufacturing costs			
6	Direct material costs			
7	(200,000 kits × $375 per kit)	$ 75,000,000		$375.00
8	Direct manufacturing labor costs			
9	(530,000 DML-hours × $20 per hour)	10,600,000		53.00
10	Direct machining costs			
11	(300,000 machine-hours × $38 per machine-hour)	11,400,000		57.00
12	Direct manufacturing costs	97,000,000		485.00
13				
14	Manufacturing overhead costs			
15	Ordering and receiving costs			
16	(20,000 orders × $60 per order)	1,200,000		6.00
17	Testing and inspection costs			
18	(2,800,000 testing-hours × $1.70 per hour)	4,760,000		23.80
19	Rework costs			
20	(32,500 rework-hours × $32 per hour)	1,040,000		5.20
21	Manufacturing overhead costs	7,000,000		35.00
22	Total manufacturing costs	$104,000,000		$520.00

Decision Points

The following question-and-answer format summarizes the chapter's learning objectives. Each decision presents a key question related to a learning objective. The guidelines are the answers to that question.

Decision	Guidelines
1. What are the three major influences on pricing decisions?	Customers, competitors, and costs influence prices through their effects on demand and supply; customers and competitors affect demand, and costs affect supply.
2. What do companies consider when making short-run pricing decisions?	When making short-run pricing decisions companies only consider those (relevant) costs that will change in total as a result of the decision. Pricing is done opportunistically based on demand and competition.
3. How do companies make long-run pricing decisions?	Companies consider all future variable and fixed costs as relevant and use a market-based or a cost-based pricing approach to earn a target return on investment.
4. How do companies determine target costs?	One approach to long-run pricing is to use a target price. Target price is the estimated price that potential customers are willing to pay for a product or service. Target operating income per unit is subtracted from the target price to determine target cost per unit. Target cost per unit is the estimated long-run cost of a product or service that when sold enables the company to achieve target operating income per unit. The challenge for the company is to make the cost improvements necessary through value-engineering methods to achieve the target cost.

5. Why is it important to distinguish cost incurrence from locked-in costs?

Cost incurrence describes when a resource is sacrificed. Locked-in costs are costs that have not yet been incurred but, based on decisions that have already been made, will be incurred in the future. To reduce costs, techniques such as value engineering are most effective *before* costs are locked in.

6. How do companies price products using the cost-plus approach?

The cost-plus approach to pricing adds a markup component to a cost base as the starting point for pricing decisions. Many different costs, such as full cost of the product or manufacturing cost, can serve as the cost base in applying the cost-plus formula. Prices are then modified on the basis of customers' reactions and competitors' responses. Therefore, the size of the "plus" is determined by the marketplace.

7. Describe life-cycle budgeting and life-cycle costing and when companies should use these techniques.

Life-cycle budgeting estimates and life-cycle costing tracks and accumulates the costs (and revenues) attributable to a product from its initial R&D to its final customer service and support. These life-cycle techniques are particularly important when (a) a high percentage of total life-cycle costs are incurred before production begins and revenues are earned over several years, and (b) a high fraction of the life-cycle costs are locked in at the R&D and design stages.

8. Describe price discrimination and peak-load pricing.

Price discrimination is charging some customers a higher price for a given product or service than other customers. Peak-load pricing is charging a higher price for the same product or service when demand approaches physical-capacity limits. Under price discrimination and peak-load pricing, prices differ among market segments and across time periods even though the cost of providing the product or service is approximately the same.

9. How do antitrust laws affect pricing?

To comply with antitrust laws, a company must not engage in predatory pricing, dumping, or collusive pricing, which lessens competition; puts another company at an unfair competitive disadvantage; or harms consumers.

Terms to Learn

The chapter and the Glossary at the end of the book contain definitions of the following important terms:

collusive pricing (**p. 452**)
cost incurrence (**p. 442**)
customer life-cycle costs (**p. 449**)
designed-in costs (**p. 442**)
dumping (**p. 452**)
life-cycle budgeting (**p. 448**)
life-cycle costing (**p. 448**)

locked-in costs (**p. 442**)
nonvalue-added cost (**p. 442**)
peak-load pricing (**p. 450**)
predatory pricing (**p. 451**)
price discrimination (**p. 450**)
product life cycle (**p. 447**)
target cost per unit (**p. 440**)

target operating income per unit (**p. 440**)
target price (**p. 439**)
target rate of return on investment (**p. 446**)
value-added cost (**p. 442**)
value engineering (**p. 441**)

Assignment Material

Questions

12-1 What are the three major influences on pricing decisions?

12-2 "Relevant costs for pricing decisions are full costs of the product." Do you agree? Explain.

12-3 Give two examples of pricing decisions with a short-run focus.

12-4 How is activity-based costing useful for pricing decisions?

12-5 Describe two alternative approaches to long-run pricing decisions.

12-6 What is a target cost per unit?

12-7 Describe value engineering and its role in target costing.

12-8 Give two examples of a value-added cost and two examples of a nonvalue-added cost.

12-9 "It is not important for a company to distinguish between cost incurrence and locked-in costs." Do you agree? Explain.

12-10 What is cost-plus pricing?

12-11 Describe three alternative cost-plus pricing methods.

12-12 Give two examples in which the difference in the costs of two products or services is much smaller than the difference in their prices.

12-13 What is life-cycle budgeting?

12-14 What are three benefits of using a product life-cycle reporting format?

12-15 Define predatory pricing, dumping, and collusive pricing.

MyAccountingLab

Exercises

12-16 **Relevant-cost approach to pricing decisions, special order.** The following financial data apply to the DVD production plant of the Dill Company for October 2011:

	Budgeted Manufacturing Cost per DVD Pack
Direct materials	$1.60
Direct manufacturing labor	0.90
Variable manufacturing overhead	0.70
Fixed manufacturing overhead	1.00
Total manufacturing cost	$4.20

Variable manufacturing overhead varies with the number of DVD packs produced. Fixed manufacturing overhead of $1 per pack is based on budgeted fixed manufacturing overhead of $150,000 per month and budgeted production of 150,000 packs per month. The Dill Company sells each pack for $5.

Marketing costs have two components:

■ Variable marketing costs (sales commissions) of 5% of revenues

■ Fixed monthly costs of $65,000

During October 2011, Lyn Randell, a Dill Company salesperson, asked the president for permission to sell 1,000 packs at $4.00 per pack to a customer not in Dill's normal marketing channels. The president refused this special order because the selling price was below the total budgeted manufacturing cost.

Required

1. What would have been the effect on monthly operating income of accepting the special order?
2. Comment on the president's "below manufacturing costs" reasoning for rejecting the special order.
3. What other factors should the president consider before accepting or rejecting the special order?

12-17 **Relevant-cost approach to short-run pricing decisions.** The San Carlos Company is an electronics business with eight product lines. Income data for one of the products (XT-107) for June 2011 are as follows:

Revenues, 200,000 units at average price of $100 each		$20,000,000
Variable costs		
Direct materials at $35 per unit	$7,000,000	
Direct manufacturing labor at $10 per unit	2,000,000	
Variable manufacturing overhead at $6 per unit	1,200,000	
Sales commissions at 15% of revenues	3,000,000	
Other variable costs at $5 per unit	1,000,000	
Total variable costs		14,200,000
Contribution margin		5,800,000
Fixed costs		5,000,000
Operating income		$ 800,000

Abrams, Inc., an instruments company, has a problem with its preferred supplier of XT-107. This supplier has had a three-week labor strike. Abrams approaches the San Carlos sales representative, Sarah Holtz, about providing 3,000 units of XT-107 at a price of $75 per unit. Holtz informs the XT-107 product manager, Jim McMahon, that she would accept a flat commission of $8,000 rather than the usual 15% of revenues if this special order were accepted. San Carlos has the capacity to produce 300,000 units of XT-107 each month, but demand has not exceeded 200,000 units in any month in the past year.

Required

1. If the 3,000-unit order from Abrams is accepted, how much will operating income increase or decrease? (Assume the same cost structure as in June 2011.)

2. McMahon ponders whether to accept the 3,000-unit special order. He is afraid of the precedent that might be set by cutting the price. He says, "The price is below our full cost of $96 per unit. I think we should quote a full price, or Abrams will expect favored treatment again and again if we continue to do business with it." Do you agree with McMahon? Explain.

12-18 Short-run pricing, capacity constraints. Colorado Mountains Dairy, maker of specialty cheeses, produces a soft cheese from the milk of Holstein cows raised on a special corn-based diet. One kilogram of soft cheese, which has a contribution margin of $10, requires 4 liters of milk. A well-known gourmet restaurant has asked Colorado Mountains to produce 2,600 kilograms of a hard cheese from the same milk of Holstein cows. Knowing that the dairy has sufficient unused capacity, Elise Princiotti, owner of Colorado Mountains, calculates the costs of making one kilogram of the desired hard cheese:

Milk (8 liters × $2.00 per liter)	$16
Variable direct manufacturing labor	5
Variable manufacturing overhead	4
Fixed manufacturing cost allocated	6
Total manufacturing cost	$31

Required

1. Suppose Colorado Mountains can acquire all the Holstein milk that it needs. What is the minimum price per kilogram it should charge for the hard cheese?
2. Now suppose that the Holstein milk is in short supply. Every kilogram of hard cheese produced by Colorado Mountains will reduce the quantity of soft cheese that it can make and sell. What is the minimum price per kilogram it should charge to produce the hard cheese?

12-19 Value-added, nonvalue-added costs. The Marino Repair Shop repairs and services machine tools. A summary of its costs (by activity) for 2011 is as follows:

a.	Materials and labor for servicing machine tools	$800,000
b.	Rework costs	75,000
c.	Expediting costs caused by work delays	60,000
d.	Materials-handling costs	50,000
e.	Materials-procurement and inspection costs	35,000
f.	Preventive maintenance of equipment	15,000
g.	Breakdown maintenance of equipment	55,000

Required

1. Classify each cost as value-added, nonvalue-added, or in the gray area between.
2. For any cost classified in the gray area, assume 65% is value-added and 35% is nonvalue-added. How much of the total of all seven costs is value-added and how much is nonvalue-added?
3. Marino is considering the following changes: (a) introducing quality-improvement programs whose net effect will be to reduce rework and expediting costs by 75% and materials and labor costs for servicing machine tools by 5%; (b) working with suppliers to reduce materials-procurement and inspection costs by 20% and materials-handling costs by 25%; and (c) increasing preventive-maintenance costs by 50% to reduce breakdown-maintenance costs by 40%. Calculate the effect of programs (a), (b), and (c) on value-added costs, nonvalue-added costs, and total costs. Comment briefly.

12-20 Target operating income, value-added costs, service company. Calvert Associates prepares architectural drawings to conform to local structural-safety codes. Its income statement for 2012 is as follows:

Revenues	$701,250
Salaries of professional staff (7,500 hours × $52 per hour)	390,000
Travel	15,000
Administrative and support costs	171,600
Total costs	576,600
Operating income	$124,650

Following is the percentage of time spent by professional staff on various activities:

Making calculations and preparing drawings for clients	77%
Checking calculations and drawings	3
Correcting errors found in drawings (not billed to clients)	8
Making changes in response to client requests (billed to clients)	5
Correcting own errors regarding building codes (not billed to clients)	7
Total	100%

Assume administrative and support costs vary with professional-labor costs.

Consider each requirement independently.

Required

1. How much of the total costs in 2012 are value-added, nonvalue-added, or in the gray area between? Explain your answers briefly. What actions can Calvert take to reduce its costs?
2. Suppose Calvert could eliminate all errors so that it did not need to spend any time making corrections and, as a result, could proportionately reduce professional-labor costs. Calculate Calvert's operating income for 2012.
3. Now suppose Calvert could take on as much business as it could complete, but it could not add more professional staff. Assume Calvert could eliminate all errors so that it does not need to spend any time correcting errors. Assume Calvert could use the time saved to increase revenues proportionately. Assume travel costs will remain at $15,000. Calculate Calvert's operating income for 2012.

12-21 **Target prices, target costs, activity-based costing.** Snappy Tiles is a small distributor of marble tiles. Snappy identifies its three major activities and cost pools as ordering, receiving and storage, and shipping, and it reports the following details for 2011:

Activity	Cost Driver	Quantity of Cost Driver	Cost per Unit of Cost Driver
1. Placing and paying for orders of marble tiles	Number of orders	500	$50 per order
2. Receiving and storage	Loads moved	4,000	$30 per load
3. Shipping of marble tiles to retailers	Number of shipments	1,500	$40 per shipment

For 2011, Snappy buys 250,000 marble tiles at an average cost of $3 per tile and sells them to retailers at an average price of $4 per tile. Assume Snappy has no fixed costs and no inventories.

Required

1. Calculate Snappy's operating income for 2011.
2. For 2012, retailers are demanding a 5% discount off the 2011 price. Snappy's suppliers are only willing to give a 4% discount. Snappy expects to sell the same quantity of marble tiles in 2012 as in 2011. If all other costs and cost-driver information remain the same, calculate Snappy's operating income for 2012.
3. Suppose further that Snappy decides to make changes in its ordering and receiving-and-storing practices. By placing long-run orders with its key suppliers, Snappy expects to reduce the number of orders to 200 and the cost per order to $25 per order. By redesigning the layout of the warehouse and reconfiguring the crates in which the marble tiles are moved, Snappy expects to reduce the number of loads moved to 3,125 and the cost per load moved to $28. Will Snappy achieve its target operating income of $0.30 per tile in 2012? Show your calculations.

12-22 **Target costs, effect of product-design changes on product costs.** Medical Instruments uses a manufacturing costing system with one direct-cost category (direct materials) and three indirect-cost categories:

a. Setup, production order, and materials-handling costs that vary with the number of batches
b. Manufacturing-operations costs that vary with machine-hours
c. Costs of engineering changes that vary with the number of engineering changes made

In response to competitive pressures at the end of 2010, Medical Instruments used value-engineering techniques to reduce manufacturing costs. Actual information for 2010 and 2011 is as follows:

	2010	2011
Setup, production-order, and materials-handling costs per batch	$ 8,000	$ 7,500
Total manufacturing-operations cost per machine-hour	$ 55	$ 50
Cost per engineering change	$12,000	$10,000

The management of Medical Instruments wants to evaluate whether value engineering has succeeded in reducing the target manufacturing cost per unit of one of its products, HJ6, by 10%.

Actual results for 2010 and 2011 for HJ6 are as follows:

	Actual Results for 2010	Actual Results for 2011
Units of HJ6 produced	3,500	4,000
Direct material cost per unit of HJ6	$ 1,200	$ 1,100
Total number of batches required to produce HJ6	70	80
Total machine-hours required to produce HJ6	21,000	22,000
Number of engineering changes made	14	10

Required

1. Calculate the manufacturing cost per unit of HJ6 in 2010.
2. Calculate the manufacturing cost per unit of HJ6 in 2011.

3. Did Medical Instruments achieve the target manufacturing cost per unit for HJ6 in 2011? Explain.
4. Explain how Medical Instruments reduced the manufacturing cost per unit of HJ6 in 2011.

12-23 Cost-plus target return on investment pricing. John Blodgett is the managing partner of a business that has just finished building a 60-room motel. Blodgett anticipates that he will rent these rooms for 15,000 nights next year (or 15,000 room-nights). All rooms are similar and will rent for the same price. Blodgett estimates the following operating costs for next year:

Variable operating costs	$5 per room-night
Fixed costs	
Salaries and wages	$173,000
Maintenance of building and pool	52,000
Other operating and administration costs	150,000
Total fixed costs	$375,000

The capital invested in the motel is $900,000. The partnership's target return on investment is 25%. Blodgett expects demand for rooms to be uniform throughout the year. He plans to price the rooms at full cost plus a markup on full cost to earn the target return on investment.

Required

1. What price should Blodgett charge for a room-night? What is the markup as a percentage of the full cost of a room-night?
2. Blodgett's market research indicates that if the price of a room-night determined in requirement 1 is reduced by 10%, the expected number of room-nights Blodgett could rent would increase by 10%. Should Blodgett reduce prices by 10%? Show your calculations.

12-24 Cost-plus, target pricing, working backward. Road Warrior manufactures and sells a model of motorcycle, XR500. In 2011, it reported the following:

Units produced and sold	1,500
Investment	$8,400,000
Markup percentage on full cost	9%
Rate of return on investment	18%
Variable cost per unit	$8,450

Required

1. What was Road Warrior's operating income on XR500 in 2011? What was the full cost per unit? What was the selling price? What was the percentage markup on variable cost?
2. Road Warrior is considering increasing the annual spending on advertising for the XR500 by $500,000. The company believes that the investment will translate into a 10% increase in unit sales. Should the investment be made? Show your calculations.
3. Refer back to the original data. In 2012, Road Warrior believes that it will only be able to sell 1,400 units at the price calculated in requirement 1. Management has identified $125,000 in fixed cost that can be eliminated. If Road Warrior wants to maintain a 9% markup on full cost, what is the target variable cost per unit?

12-25 Life cycle product costing. Gadzooks, Inc., develops and manufactures toys that it then sells through infomercials. Currently, the company is designing a toy robot that it intends to begin manufacturing and marketing next year. Because of the rapidly changing nature of the toy industry, Gadzooks management projects that the robot will be produced and sold for only three years. At the end of the product's life cycle, Gadzooks plans to sell the rights to the robot to an overseas company for $250,000. Cost information concerning the robot follows:

		Total Fixed Costs over Four Years	Variable Cost per Unit
Year 1	Design costs	$ 650,000	—
Years 2–4	Production costs	$3,560,000	$20 per unit
	Marketing and distribution costs	$2,225,000	$5 per unit

For simplicity, ignore the time value of money.

Required

1. Suppose the managers at Gadzooks price the robot at $50 per unit. How many units do they need to sell to break even?
2. The managers at Gadzooks are thinking of two alternative pricing strategies.
   a. Sell the robot at $50 each from the outset. At this price they expect to sell 500,000 units over its life-cycle.
   b. Boost the selling price of the robot in year 2 when it first comes out to $70 per unit. At this price they expect to sell 100,000 units in year 2. In years 3 and 4 drop the price to $40 per unit. The managers expect to sell 300,000 units each year in years 3 and 4. Which pricing strategy would you recommend? Explain.

Problems

12-26 Relevant-cost approach to pricing decisions. Burst, Inc., cans peaches for sale to food distributors. All costs are classified as either manufacturing or marketing. Burst prepares monthly budgets. The March 2012 budgeted absorption-costing income statement is as follows:

Revenues (1,000 crates × $117 a crate)	$117,000
Cost of goods sold	65,000
Gross margin	52,000
Marketing costs	30,000
Operating income	$ 22,000

Gross margin markup percentage: $52,000 ÷ $65,000
= 80% of cost of goods sold (full manufacturing cost)

Monthly costs are classified as fixed or variable (with respect to the number of crates produced for manufacturing costs and with respect to the number of crates sold for marketing costs):

	Fixed	Variable
Manufacturing	$30,000	$35,000
Marketing	13,000	17,000

Burst has the capacity to can 2,000 crates per month. The relevant range in which monthly fixed manufacturing costs will be "fixed" is from 500 to 2,000 crates per month.

Required

1. Calculate the markup percentage based on total variable costs.
2. Assume that a new customer approaches Burst to buy 200 crates at $55 per crate for cash. The customer does not require any marketing effort. Additional manufacturing costs of $3,000 (for special packaging) will be required. Burst believes that this is a one-time-only special order because the customer is discontinuing business in six weeks' time. Burst is reluctant to accept this 200-crate special order because the $55-per-crate price is below the $65-per-crate full manufacturing cost. Do you agree with this reasoning? Explain.
3. Assume that the new customer decides to remain in business. How would this longevity affect your willingness to accept the $55-per-crate offer? Explain.

12-27 Considerations other than cost in pricing decisions. Executive Suites operates a 100-suite hotel in a busy business park. During April, a 30-day month, Executive Suites experienced a 90% occupancy rate from Monday evening through Thursday evening (weeknights), with business travelers making up virtually all of its guests. On Friday through Sunday evenings (weekend nights), however, occupancy dwindled to 20%. Guests on these nights were all leisure travelers. (There were 18 weeknights and 12 weekend nights in April.) Executive Suites charges $68 per night for a suite. Fran Jackson has recently been hired to manage the hotel, and is trying to devise a way to increase the hotel's profitability. The following information relates to Executive Suites' costs:

	Fixed Cost	Variable Cost
Depreciation	$20,000 per month	
Administrative costs	$35,000 per month	
Housekeeping and supplies	$12,000 per month	$25 per room night
Breakfast	$ 5,000 per month	$5 per breakfast served

Executive Suites offers free breakfast to guests. In April, there were an average of 1.0 breakfasts served per room night on weeknights and 2.5 breakfasts served per room night on weekend nights.

Required

1. Calculate the average cost per guest night for April. What was Executive Suites' operating income or loss for the month?
2. Fran Jackson estimates that if Executive Suites increases the nightly rates to $80, weeknight occupancy will only decline to 85%. She also estimates that if the hotel reduces the nightly rate on weekend nights to $50, occupancy on those nights will increase to 50%. Would this be a good move for Executive Suites? Show your calculations.
3. Why would the $30 price difference per night be tolerated by the weeknight guests?
4. A discount travel clearing-house has approached Executive Suites with a proposal to offer last-minute deals on empty rooms on both weeknights and weekend nights. Assuming that there will be an average of two breakfasts served per night per room, what is the minimum price that Executive Suites could accept on the last-minute rooms?

12-28 Cost-plus, target pricing, working backward. The new CEO of Radco Manufacturing has asked for a variety of information about the operations of the firm from last year. The CEO is given the following information, but with some data missing:

Total sales revenue	?
Number of units produced and sold	500,000 units
Selling price	?
Operating income	$195,000
Total investment in assets	$2,000,000
Variable cost per unit	$3.75
Fixed costs for the year	$3,000,000

1. Find (a) total sales revenue, (b) selling price, (c) rate of return on investment, and (d) markup percentage on full cost for this product.   **Required**
2. The new CEO has a plan to reduce fixed costs by $200,000 and variable costs by $0.60 per unit while continuing to produce and sell 500,000 units. Using the same markup percentage as in requirement 1, calculate the new selling price.
3. Assume the CEO institutes the changes in requirement 2 including the new selling price. However, the reduction in variable cost has resulted in lower product quality resulting in 10% fewer units being sold compared to before the change. Calculate operating income (loss).

12-29 Target prices, target costs, value engineering, cost incurrence, locked-in costs, activity-based costing. Cutler Electronics makes an MP3 player, CE100, which has 80 components. Cutler sells 7,000 units each month for $70 each. The costs of manufacturing CE100 are $45 per unit, or $315,000 per month. Monthly manufacturing costs are as follows:

Direct material costs	$182,000
Direct manufacturing labor costs	28,000
Machining costs (fixed)	31,500
Testing costs	35,000
Rework costs	14,000
Ordering costs	3,360
Engineering costs (fixed)	21,140
Total manufacturing costs	$315,000

Cutler's management identifies the activity cost pools, the cost driver for each activity, and the cost per unit of the cost driver for each overhead cost pool as follows:

Manufacturing Activity	Description of Activity	Cost Driver	Cost per Unit of Cost Driver
1. Machining costs	Machining components	Machine-hour capacity	$4.50 per machine-hour
2. Testing costs	Testing components and final product (Each unit of CE100 is tested individually.)	Testing-hours	$2 per testing-hour
3. Rework costs	Correcting and fixing errors and defects	Units of CE100 reworked	$20 per unit
4. Ordering costs	Ordering of components	Number of orders	$21 per order
5. Engineering costs	Designing and managing of products and processes	Engineering-hour capacity	$35 per engineering-hour

Cutler's management views direct material costs and direct manufacturing labor costs as variable with respect to the units of CE100 manufactured. Over a long-run horizon, each of the overhead costs described in the preceding table varies, as described, with the chosen cost drivers.

The following additional information describes the existing design:

a. Testing time per unit is 2.5 hours.
b. 10% of the CE100s manufactured are reworked.
c. Cutler places two orders with each component supplier each month. Each component is supplied by a different supplier.
d. It currently takes one hour to manufacture each unit of CE100.

In response to competitive pressures, Cutler must reduce its price to $62 per unit and its costs by $8 per unit. No additional sales are anticipated at this lower price. However, Cutler stands to lose significant sales if it does not reduce its price. Manufacturing has been asked to reduce its costs by $6 per unit. Improvements in manufacturing efficiency are expected to yield a net savings of $1.50 per MP3 player, but that is not enough. The chief engineer has proposed a new modular design that reduces the number of components to 50 and also simplifies testing. The newly designed MP3 player, called "New CE100" will replace CE100.

The expected effects of the new design are as follows:

a. Direct material cost for the New CE100 is expected to be lower by $2.20 per unit.
b. Direct manufacturing labor cost for the New CE100 is expected to be lower by $0.50 per unit.
c. Machining time required to manufacture the New CE100 is expected to be 20% less, but machine-hour capacity will not be reduced.
d. Time required for testing the New CE100 is expected to be lower by 20%.
e. Rework is expected to decline to 4% of New CE100s manufactured.
f. Engineering-hours capacity will remain the same.

Assume that the cost per unit of each cost driver for CE100 continues to apply to New CE100.

Required

1. Calculate Cutler's manufacturing cost per unit of New CE100.
2. Will the new design achieve the per-unit cost-reduction targets that have been set for the manufacturing costs of New CE100? Show your calculations.
3. The problem describes two strategies to reduce costs: (a) improving manufacturing efficiency and (b) modifying product design. Which strategy has more impact on Cutler's costs? Why? Explain briefly.

12-30 Cost-plus, target return on investment pricing. Vend-o-licious makes candy bars for vending machines and sells them to vendors in cases of 30 bars. Although Vend-o-licious makes a variety of candy, the cost differences are insignificant, and the cases all sell for the same price.

Vend-o-licious has a total capital investment of $13,000,000. It expects to produce and sell 500,000 cases of candy next year. Vend-o-licious requires a 10% target return on investment.

Expected costs for next year are as follows:

Variable production costs	$3.50 per case
Variable marketing and distribution costs	$1.50 per case
Fixed production costs	$1,000,000
Fixed marketing and distribution costs	$700,000
Other fixed costs	$500,000

Vend-o-licious prices the cases of candy at full cost plus markup to generate profits equal to the target return on capital.

Required

1. What is the target operating income?
2. What is the selling price Vend-o-licious needs to charge to earn the target operating income? Calculate the markup percentage on full cost.
3. Vend-o-licious's closest competitor has just increased its candy case price to $15, although it sells 36 candy bars per case. Vend-o-licious is considering increasing its selling price to $14 per case. Assuming production and sales decrease by 5%, calculate Vend-o-licious' return on investment. Is increasing the selling price a good idea?

12-31 Cost-plus, time and materials, ethics. R & C Mechanical sells and services plumbing, heating, and air conditioning systems. R & C's cost accounting system tracks two cost categories: direct labor and direct materials. R & C uses a time-and-materials pricing system, with direct labor marked up 100% and direct materials marked up 60% to recover indirect costs of support staff, support materials, and shared equipment and tools, and to earn a profit.

R & C technician Greg Garrison is called to the home of Ashley Briggs on a particularly hot summer day to investigate her broken central air conditioning system. He considers two options: replace the compressor or repair it. The cost information available to Garrison follows:

	Labor	Materials
Repair option	5 hrs.	$100
Replace option	2 hrs.	$200
Labor rate	$30 per hour	

Required

1. If Garrison presents Briggs with the replace or repair options, what price would he quote for each?
2. If the two options were equally effective for the three years that Briggs intends to live in the home, which option would she choose?
3. If Garrison's objective is to maximize profits, which option would he recommend to Briggs? What would be the ethical course of action?

12-32 Cost-plus and market-based pricing. Florida Temps, a large labor contractor, supplies contract labor to building-construction companies. For 2012, Florida Temps has budgeted to supply 84,000 hours of contract labor. Its variable costs are $13 per hour, and its fixed costs are $168,000. Roger Mason, the general manager, has proposed a cost-plus approach for pricing labor at full cost plus 20%.

1. Calculate the price per hour that Florida Temps should charge based on Mason's proposal. **Required**
2. The marketing manager supplies the following information on demand levels at different prices:

Price per Hour	Demand (Hours)
$16	124,000
17	104,000
18	84,000
19	74,000
20	61,000

   Florida Temps can meet any of these demand levels. Fixed costs will remain unchanged for all the demand levels. On the basis of this additional information, calculate the price per hour that Florida Temps should charge to maximize operating income.
3. Comment on your answers to requirements 1 and 2. Why are they the same or different?

12-33 Cost-plus and market-based pricing. (CMA, adapted) Best Test Laboratories evaluates the reaction of materials to extreme increases in temperature. Much of the company's early growth was attributable to government contracts, but recent growth has come from expansion into commercial markets. Two types of testing at Best Test are Heat Testing (HTT) and Arctic-condition Testing (ACT). Currently, all of the budgeted operating costs are collected in a single overhead pool. All of the estimated testing-hours are also collected in a single pool. One rate per test-hour is used for both types of testing. This hourly rate is marked up by 45% to recover administrative costs and taxes, and to earn a profit.

Rick Shaw, Best Test's controller, believes that there is enough variation in the test procedures and cost structure to establish separate costing rates and billing rates at a 45% mark up. He also believes that the inflexible rate structure currently being used is inadequate in today's competitive environment. After analyzing the company data, he has divided operating costs into the following three cost pools:

Labor and supervision	$ 491,840
Setup and facility costs	402,620
Utilities	368,000
Total budgeted costs for the period	$1,262,460

Rick Shaw budgets 106,000 total test-hours for the coming period. This is also the cost driver for labor and supervision. The budgeted quantity of cost driver for setup and facility costs is 800 setup hours. The budgeted quantity of cost driver for utilities is 10,000 machine-hours.

Rick has estimated that HTT uses 60% of the testing hours, 25% of the setup hours, and half the machine-hours.

1. Find the single rate for operating costs based on test-hours and the hourly billing rate for HTT and ACT. **Required**
2. Find the three activity-based rates for operating costs.
3. What will the billing rate for HTT and ACT be based on the activity-based costing structure? State the rates in terms of testing hours. Referring to both requirements 1 and 2, which rates make more sense for Best Test?
4. If Best Test's competition all charge $20 per hour for arctic testing, what can Best Test do to stay competitive?

12-34 Life-cycle costing. New Life Metal Recycling and Salvage has just been given the opportunity to salvage scrap metal and other materials from an old industrial site. The current owners of the site will sign over the site to New Life at no cost. New Life intends to extract scrap metal at the site for 24 months, and then will clean up the site, return the land to useable condition, and sell it to a developer. Projected costs associated with the project follow:

		Fixed	Variable
Months 1–24	Metal extraction and processing	$4,000 per month	$100 per ton
Months 1–27	Rent on temporary buildings	$2,000 per month	—
	Administration	$5,000 per month	—
Months 25–27	Clean-up	$30,000 per month	—
	Land restoration	$475,000 total	—
	Cost of selling land	$150,000 total	—

Ignore time value of money.

1. Assuming that New Life expects to salvage 50,000 tons of metal from the site, what is the total project life cycle cost?
2. Suppose New Life can sell the metal for $150 per ton and wants to earn a profit (before taxes) of $40 per ton. At what price must New Life sell the land at the end of the project to achieve its target profit per ton?
3. Now suppose New Life can only sell the metal for $140 per ton and the land at $100,000 less than what you calculated in requirement 2. If New Life wanted to maintain the same mark-up percentage on total project life-cycle cost as in requirement 2, by how much would it have to reduce its total project life-cycle cost?

12-35 **Airline pricing, considerations other than cost in pricing.** Air Eagle is about to introduce a daily round-trip flight from New York to Los Angeles and is determining how it should price its round-trip tickets.

The market research group at Air Eagle segments the market into business and pleasure travelers. It provides the following information on the effects of two different prices on the number of seats expected to be sold and the variable cost per ticket, including the commission paid to travel agents:

		Number of Seats Expected to Be Sold	
Price Charged	Variable Cost per Ticket	Business	Pleasure
$ 500	$ 65	200	100
2,100	175	180	20

Pleasure travelers start their travel during one week, spend at least one weekend at their destination, and return the following week or thereafter. Business travelers usually start and complete their travel within the same work week. They do not stay over weekends.

Assume that round-trip fuel costs are fixed costs of $24,000 and that fixed costs allocated to the round-trip flight for airplane-lease costs, ground services, and flight-crew salaries total $188,000.

1. If you could charge different prices to business travelers and pleasure travelers, would you? Show your computations.
2. Explain the key factor (or factors) for your answer in requirement 1.
3. How might Air Eagle implement price discrimination? That is, what plan could the airline formulate so that business travelers and pleasure travelers each pay the price desired by the airline?

12-36 **Ethics and pricing.** Apex Art has been requested to prepare a bid on 500 pieces of framed artwork for a new hotel. Winning the bid would be a big boost for sales representative Jason Grant, who works entirely on commission. Sonja Gomes, the cost accountant for Apex, prepares the bid based on the following cost information:

Direct costs		
Artwork		$30,000
Framing materials		40,000
Direct manufacturing labor		20,000
Delivery and installation		7,500
Overhead costs		
Production order	2,000	
Setup	4,000	
Materials handling	5,500	
General and administration	12,000	
Total overhead costs		23,500
Full product costs		$121,000

Based on the company policy of pricing at 125% of full cost, Gomes gives Grant a figure of $151,250 to submit for the job. Grant is very concerned. He tells Gomes that at that price, Apex has no chance of winning the job. He confides in her that he spent $500 of company funds to take the hotel's purchasing agent to a basketball playoff game where the purchasing agent disclosed that a bid of $145,000 would win the job. He hadn't planned to tell Gomes because he was confident that the bid she developed would be below that amount. Gomes reasons that the $500 he spent will be wasted if Apex doesn't capitalize on this valuable information. In any case, the company will still make money if it wins the bid at $145,000 because it is higher than the full cost of $121,000.

1. Is the $500 spent on the basketball tickets relevant to the bid decision? Why or why not?
2. Gomes suggests that if Grant is willing to use cheaper materials for the frame, he can achieve a bid of $145,000. The artwork has already been selected and cannot be changed, so the entire amount of reduction in cost will need to come from framing materials. What is the target cost of framing materials that will allow Grant to submit a bid of $145 assuming a target markup of 25% of full cost?
3. Evaluate whether Gomes' suggestion to Grant to use the purchasing agent's tip is unethical. Would it be unethical for Grant to redo the project's design to arrive at a lower bid? What steps should Grant and Gomes take to resolve this situation?

Collaborative Learning Problem

12-37 Value engineering, target pricing, and locked-in costs. Pacific Décor, Inc., designs, manufactures, and sells contemporary wood furniture. Ling Li is a furniture designer for Pacific. Li has spent much of the past month working on the design of a high-end dining room table. The design has been well-received by Jose Alvarez, the product development manager. However, Alvarez wants to make sure that the table can be priced competitively. Amy Hoover, Pacific's cost accountant, presents Alvarez with the following cost data for the expected production of 200 tables:

Design cost	$ 5,000
Direct materials	120,000
Direct manufacturing labor	142,000
Variable manufacturing overhead	64,000
Fixed manufacturing overhead	46,500
Marketing	15,000

1. Alvarez thinks that Pacific can successfully market the table for $2,000. The company's target operating income is 10% of revenue. Calculate the target full cost of producing the 200 tables. Does the cost estimate developed by Hoover meet Pacific's requirements? Is value engineering needed?
2. Alvarez discovers that Li has designed the table two inches wider than the standard size of wood normally used by Pacific. Reducing the table's size by two inches will lower the cost of direct materials by 40%. However, the redesign will require an additional $6,000 of design cost, and the table will be sold for $1,950. Will this design change allow the table to meet its target cost? Are the costs of materials a locked-in cost?
3. Li insists that the two inches are an absolute necessity in terms of the table's design. She believes that spending an additional $7,000 on better marketing will allow Pacific to sell the tables for $2,200. If this is the case, will the table's target cost be achieved without any value engineering?
4. Compare the total operating income on the 200 tables for requirements 2 and 3. What do you recommend Pacific do, based solely on your calculations? Explain briefly.

13

Strategy, Balanced Scorecard, and Strategic Profitability Analysis

Olive Garden wants to know.

So do Barnes and Noble, PepsiCo, and L.L.Bean. Even your local car dealer and transit authority are curious. They all want to know how well they are doing and how they score against the measures they strive to meet. The balanced scorecard can help them answer this question by evaluating key performance measures. Many companies have successfully used the balanced scorecard approach. Infosys Technologies, one of India's leading information technology companies, is one of them.

Balanced Scorecard Helps Infosys Transform into a Leading Consultancy[1]

In the early 2000s, Infosys Technologies was a company in transition. The Bangalore-based company was a market leader in information technology outsourcing, but needed to expand to meet increased client demand. Infosys invested in many new areas including business process outsourcing, project management, and management consulting. This put Infosys in direct competition with established consulting firms, such as IBM and Accenture.

Led by CEO Kris Gopalakrishnan, the company developed an integrated management structure that would help align these new, diverse initiatives. Infosys turned to the balanced scorecard to provide a framework the company could use to formulate and monitor its strategy. The balanced scorecard measures corporate performance along four dimensions—financial, customer, internal business process, and learning and growth.

The balanced scorecard immediately played a role in the transformation of Infosys. The executive team used the scorecard to guide discussion during its meetings. The continual process of adaptation, execution, and management that the scorecard fostered helped the team respond to, and even anticipate, its clients' evolving needs. Eventually, use of the scorecard for performance measurement spread to the rest of the organization, with monetary incentives linked to the company's performance along the different dimensions.

Over time, the balanced scorecard became part of the Infosys culture. In recent years, Infosys has begun using the balanced

---

[1] *Source*: Asis Martinez-Jerez, F., Robert S. Kaplan, and Katherine Miller. 2011. Infosys's relationship scorecard: Measuring transformational partnerships. Harvard Business School Case No. 9-109-006. Boston: Harvard Business School Publishing.

scorecard concept to create "relationship scorecards" for many of its largest clients. Using the scorecard framework, Infosys began measuring its performance for key clients not only on project management and client satisfaction, but also on repeat business and anticipating clients' future strategic needs.

The balanced scorecard helped successfully steer the transformation of Infosys from a technology outsourcer to a leading business consultancy. From 1999 to 2007, the company had a compound annual growth rate of 50%, with sales growing from $120 million in 1999 to more than $3 billion in 2007. Infosys was recognized for its achievements by making the *Wired* 40, *BusinessWeek* IT 100, and *BusinessWeek* Most Innovative Companies lists.

This chapter focuses on how management accounting information helps companies such as Infosys, Merck, Verizon, and Volkswagen implement and evaluate their strategies. Strategy drives the operations of a company and guides managers' short-run and long-run decisions. We describe the balanced scorecard approach to implementing strategy and methods to analyze operating income to evaluate the success of a strategy. We also show how management accounting information helps strategic initiatives, such as productivity improvement, reengineering, and downsizing.

What Is Strategy?

Strategy specifies how an organization matches its own capabilities with the opportunities in the marketplace to accomplish its objectives. In other words, strategy describes how an organization can create value for its customers while differentiating itself from its competitors. For example, Wal-Mart, the retail giant, creates value for its customers by locating stores in suburban and rural areas, and by offering low prices, a wide range of product categories, and few choices within each product category. Consistent with its strategy, Wal-Mart has developed the capability to keep costs down by aggressively negotiating low prices with its suppliers in exchange for high volumes and by maintaining a no-frills, cost-conscious environment.

In formulating its strategy, an organization must first thoroughly understand its industry. Industry analysis focuses on five forces: (1) competitors, (2) potential entrants into the market, (3) equivalent products, (4) bargaining power of customers, and (5) bargaining power of input suppliers.[2] The collective effect of these forces shapes an organization's profit potential. In general, profit potential decreases with greater competition, stronger potential entrants, products that are similar, and more-demanding customers and suppliers. We illustrate these five forces for Chipset, Inc., maker of linear integrated circuit

Learning Objective 1

Recognize which of two generic strategies a company is using

. . . product differentiation or cost leadership

---

[2] M. Porter, *Competitive Strategy* (New York: Free Press, 1980); M. Porter, *Competitive Advantage* (New York: Free Press, 1985); and M. Porter, "What Is Strategy?" *Harvard Business Review* (November–December 1996): 61–78.

devices (LICDs) used in modems and communication networks. Chipset produces a single specialized product, CX1, a standard, high-performance microchip, which can be used in multiple applications. Chipset designed CX1 with extensive input from customers.

1. **Competitors.** The CX1 model faces severe competition with respect to price, timely delivery, and quality. Companies in the industry have high fixed costs, and persistent pressures to reduce selling prices and utilize capacity fully. Price reductions spur growth because it makes LICDs a cost-effective option in new applications such as digital subscriber lines (DSLs).

2. **Potential entrants into the market.** The small profit margins and high capital costs discourage new entrants. Moreover, incumbent companies such as Chipset are further down the learning curve with respect to lowering costs and building close relationships with customers and suppliers.

3. **Equivalent products.** Chipset tailors CX1 to customer needs and lowers prices by continuously improving CX1's design and processes to reduce production costs. This reduces the risk of equivalent products or new technologies replacing CX1.

4. **Bargaining power of customers.** Customers, such as EarthLink and Verizon, negotiate aggressively with Chipset and its competitors to keep prices down because they buy large quantities of product.

5. **Bargaining power of input suppliers.** To produce CX1, Chipset requires high-quality materials (such as silicon wafers, pins for connectivity, and plastic or ceramic packaging) and skilled engineers, technicians, and manufacturing labor. The skill-sets suppliers and employees bring gives them bargaining power to demand higher prices and wages.

In summary, strong competition and the bargaining powers of customers and suppliers put significant pressure on Chipset's selling prices. To respond to these challenges, Chipset must choose one of two basic strategies: *differentiating its product* or *achieving cost leadership*.

Product differentiation is an organization's ability to offer products or services perceived by its customers to be superior and unique relative to the products or services of its competitors. Apple Inc. has successfully differentiated its products in the consumer electronics industry, as have Johnson & Johnson in the pharmaceutical industry and Coca-Cola in the soft drink industry. These companies have achieved differentiation through innovative product R&D, careful development and promotion of their brands, and the rapid push of products to market. Differentiation increases brand loyalty and the willingness of customers to pay higher prices.

Cost leadership is an organization's ability to achieve lower costs relative to competitors through productivity and efficiency improvements, elimination of waste, and tight cost control. Cost leaders in their respective industries include Wal-Mart (consumer retailing), Home Depot and Lowe's (building products), Texas Instruments (consumer electronics), and Emerson Electric (electric motors). These companies provide products and services that are similar to—not differentiated from—their competitors, but at a lower cost to the customer. Lower selling prices, rather than unique products or services, provide a competitive advantage for these cost leaders.

What strategy should Chipset follow? To help it decide, Chipset develops the customer preference map shown in Exhibit 13-1. The y-axis describes various attributes of the product desired by customers. The x-axis describes how well Chipset and Visilog, a competitor of Chipset that follows a product-differentiation strategy, do along the various attributes desired by customers from 1 (poor) to 5 (very good). The map highlights the trade-offs in any strategy. It shows the advantages CX1 enjoys in terms of price, scalability (the CX1 technology allows Chispet's customer to achieve different performance levels by simply altering the number of CX1 units in their product), and customer service. Visilog's chips, however, are faster and more powerful, and are customized for various applications such as different types of modems and communication networks.

CX1 is somewhat differentiated from competing products. Differentiating CX1 further would be costly, but Chipset may be able to charge a higher price. Conversely, reducing the cost of manufacturing CX1 would allow Chipset to lower price, spur growth, and increase market share. The scalability of CX1 makes it an effective solution for meeting

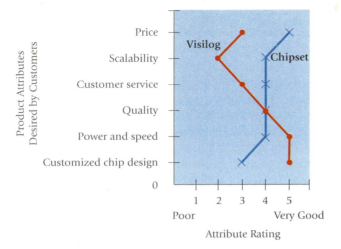

Exhibit 13-1

Customer Preference
Map for LICDs

varying customer needs. Also, Chipset's current engineering staff is more skilled at making product and process improvements than at creatively designing new products and technologies. Chipset decides to follow a cost-leadership strategy.

To achieve its cost-leadership strategy, Chipset must improve its own internal capabilities. It must enhance quality and reengineer processes to downsize and eliminate excess capacity. At the same time, Chipset's management team does not want to make cuts in personnel that would hurt company morale and hinder future growth.

Building Internal Capabilities: Quality Improvement and Reengineering at Chipset

To improve product quality—that is, to reduce defect rates and improve yields in its manufacturing process—Chipset must maintain process parameters within tight ranges based on real-time data about manufacturing-process parameters, such as temperature and pressure. Chipset must also train its workers in quality-management techniques to help them identify the root causes of defects and ways to prevent them and empower them to take actions to improve quality.

A second element of Chipset's strategy is reengineering its order-delivery process. Some of Chipset's customers have complained about the lengthening time span between ordering products and receiving them. **Reengineering** is the fundamental rethinking and redesign of business processes to achieve improvements in critical measures of performance, such as cost, quality, service, speed, and customer satisfaction.[3] To illustrate reengineering, consider the order-delivery system at Chipset in 2010. When Chipset received an order from a customer, a copy was sent to manufacturing, where a production scheduler began planning the manufacturing of the ordered products. Frequently, a considerable amount of time elapsed before production began on the ordered product. After manufacturing was complete, CX1 chips moved to the shipping department, which matched the quantities of CX1 to be shipped against customer orders. Often, completed CX1 chips stayed in inventory until a truck became available for shipment. If the quantity to be shipped was less than the number of chips requested by the customer, a special shipment was made for the balance of the chips. Shipping documents moved to the billing department for issuing invoices. Special staff in the accounting department followed up with customers for payments.

The many transfers of CX1 chips and information across departments (sales, manufacturing, shipping, billing, and accounting) to satisfy a customer's order created delays. Furthermore, no single individual was responsible for fulfilling a customer order. To respond to these challenges, Chipset formed a cross-functional team in late 2010 and implemented a reengineered order-delivery process in 2011.

Decision Point

What are two generic strategies a company can use?

Learning Objective 2

Understand what comprises reengineering

. . . redesigning business processes to improve performance by reducing cost and improving quality

---

[3] See M. Hammer and J. Champy, *Reengineering the Corporation: A Manifesto for Business Revolution* (New York: Harper, 1993); E. Ruhli, C. Treichler, and S. Schmidt, "From Business Reengineering to Management Reengineering—A European Study," *Management International Review* (1995): 361–371; and K. Sandberg, "Reengineering Tries a Comeback—This Time for Growth, Not Just for Cost Savings," *Harvard Management Update* (November 2001).

Under the new system, a customer-relationship manager is responsible for each customer and negotiates long-term contracts specifying quantities and prices. The customer-relationship manager works closely with the customer and with manufacturing to specify delivery schedules for CX1 one month in advance of shipment. The schedule of customer orders and delivery dates is sent electronically to manufacturing. Completed chips are shipped directly from the manufacturing plant to customer sites. Each shipment automatically triggers an electronic invoice and customers electronically transfer funds to Chipset's bank.

Companies, such as AT&T, Banca di America e di Italia, Cigna Insurance, Cisco, PepsiCo, and Siemens Nixdorf, have realized significant benefits by reengineering their processes across design, production, and marketing (just as in the Chipset example). Reengineering has only limited benefits when reengineering efforts focus on only a single activity such as shipping or invoicing rather than the entire order-delivery process. To be successful, reengineering efforts must focus on changing roles and responsibilities, eliminating unnecessary activities and tasks, using information technology, and developing employee skills.

Take another look at Exhibit 13-1 and note the interrelatedness and consistency in Chipset's strategy. To help meet customer preferences for price, quality, and customer service, Chipset decides on a cost-leadership strategy. And to achieve cost leadership, Chipset builds internal capabilities by reengineering its processes. Chipset's next challenge is to effectively implement its strategy

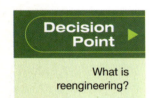

Decision Point

What is reengineering?

Learning Objective 3

Understand the four perspectives of the balanced scorecard

. . . financial, customer, internal business process, and learning and growth

Strategy Implementation and the Balanced Scorecard

Many organizations, such as Allstate Insurance, Bank of Montreal, BP, and Dow Chemical, have introduced a *balanced scorecard* approach to track progress and manage the implementation of their strategies.

The Balanced Scorecard

The **balanced scorecard** translates an organization's mission and strategy into a set of performance measures that provides the framework for implementing its strategy.[4] The balanced scorecard does not focus solely on achieving short-run financial objectives. It also highlights the nonfinancial objectives that an organization must achieve to meet and sustain its financial objectives. The scorecard measures an organization's performance from four perspectives: (1) financial, the profits and value created for shareholders; (2) customer, the success of the company in its target market; (3) internal business processes, the internal operations that create value for customers; and (4) learning and growth, the people and system capabilities that support operations. A company's strategy influences the measures it uses to track performance in each of these perspectives.

Why is this tool called a balanced scorecard? Because it balances the use of financial and nonfinancial performance measures to evaluate short-run and long-run performance in a single report. The balanced scorecard reduces managers' emphasis on short-run financial performance, such as quarterly earnings, because the key strategic nonfinancial and operational indicators, such as product quality and customer satisfaction, measure changes that a company is making for the long run. The financial benefits of these long-run changes may not show up immediately in short-run earnings; however, strong improvement in nonfinancial measures usually indicates the creation of future economic value. For example, an increase in customer satisfaction, as measured by customer surveys and repeat purchases, signals a strong likelihood of higher sales and income in the future. By balancing the mix of financial and nonfinancial measures, the balanced scorecard

---

4 See R. S. Kaplan and D. P. Norton, *The Balanced Scorecard* (Boston: Harvard Business School Press, 1996); R. S. Kaplan and D. P. Norton, *The Strategy-Focused Organization: How Balanced Scorecard Companies Thrive in the New Business Environment* (Boston: Harvard Business School Press, 2001); R. S. Kaplan and D. P. Norton, *Strategy Maps: Converting Intangible Assets into Tangible Outcomes* (Boston: Harvard Business School Press, 2004); and R. S. Kaplan and D. P. Norton, *Alignment: Using the Balanced Scorecard to Create Corporate Synergies* (Boston: Harvard Business School Press, 2006).
For simplicity, this chapter, and much of the literature, emphasizes long-run financial objectives as the primary goal of for-profit companies. For-profit companies interested in long-run financial, environmental, and social objectives adapt the balanced scorecard to implement all three objectives.

broadens management's attention to short-run *and* long-run performance. *Never lose sight of the key point. In for-profit companies, the primary goal of the balanced scorecard is to sustain long-run financial performance. Nonfinancial measures simply serve as leading indicators for the hard-to-measure long-run financial performance.*

Strategy Maps and the Balanced Scorecard

We use the Chipset example to develop strategy maps and the four perspectives of the balanced scorecard. The objectives and measures Chipset's managers choose for each perspective relates to the action plans for furthering Chipset's cost leadership strategy: *improving quality* and *reengineering processes.*

Strategy Maps

A useful first step in designing a balanced scorecard is a *strategy map*. A **strategy map** is a diagram that describes how an organization creates value by connecting strategic objectives in explicit cause-and-effect relationships with each other in the financial, customer, internal business process, and learning and growth perspectives. Exhibit 13-2 presents Chipset's strategy map. Follow the arrows to see how a strategic objective affects other strategic objectives. For example, empowering the workforce helps align employee and organization goals and improves processes. Employee and organizational alignment also helps improve processes that improve manufacturing quality and productivity, reduce customer delivery time, meet specified delivery dates, and improve post-sales service, all of which increase customer satisfaction. Improving manufacturing quality and productivity

Exhibit 13-2   Strategy Map for Chipset, Inc., for 2011

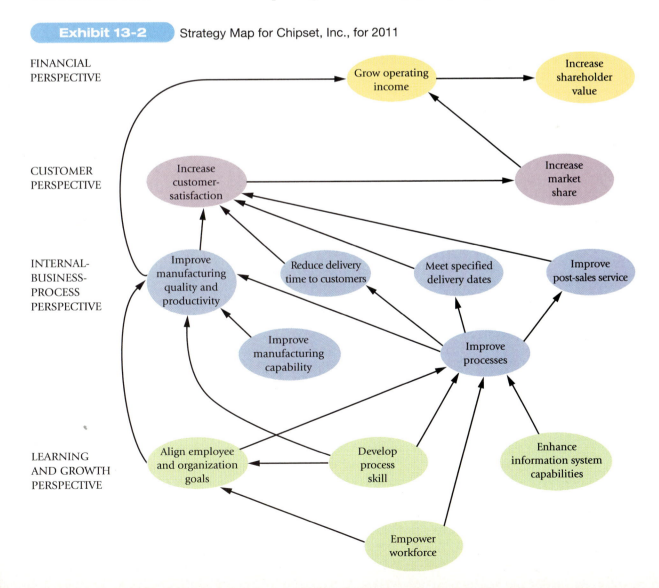

grows operating income and increases customer satisfaction that, in turn, increases market share, operating income, and shareholder value.

Chipset operates in a knowledge-intensive business. To compete successfully, Chipset invests in its employees, implements new technology and process controls, improves quality, and reengineers processes. Doing these activities well enables Chipset to build capabilities and intangible assets, which are not recorded as assets in its financial books. The strategy map helps Chipset evaluate whether these intangible assets are generating financial returns.

Chipset could include many other cause-and-effect relationships in the strategy map in Exhibit 13-2. But, Chipset, like other companies implementing the balanced scorecard, focuses on only those relationships that it believes to be the most significant.

Chipset uses the strategy map from Exhibit 13-2 to build the balanced scorecard presented in Exhibit 13-3. The scorecard highlights the four perspectives of performance: financial, customer, internal business process, and learning and growth. The first column presents the strategic objectives from the strategy map in Exhibit 13-2. At the beginning of 2011, the company's managers specify the strategic objectives, measures, initiatives (the actions necessary to achieve the objectives), and target performance (the first four columns of Exhibit 13-3).

Chipset wants to use the balanced scorecard targets to drive the organization to higher levels of performance. Managers therefore set targets at a level of performance that is achievable, yet distinctly better than competitors. Chipset's managers complete the fifth column, reporting actual performance at the end of 2011. This column compares Chipset's performance relative to target.

Four Perspectives of the Balanced Scorecard

We next describe the perspectives in general terms and illustrate each perspective using the measures chosen by Chipset in the context of its strategy.

1. **Financial perspective.** This perspective evaluates the profitability of the strategy and the creation of shareholder value. Because Chipset's key strategic initiatives are cost reduction relative to competitors' costs and sales growth, the financial perspective focuses on how much operating income results from reducing costs and selling more units of CX1.

2. **Customer perspective.** This perspective identifies targeted customer and market segments and measures the company's success in these segments. To monitor its customer objectives, Chipset uses measures such as market share in the communication-networks segment, number of new customers, and customer-satisfaction ratings.

3. **Internal-business-process perspective.** This perspective focuses on internal operations that create value for customers that, in turn, help achieve financial performance. Chipset determines internal-business-process improvement targets after benchmarking against its main competitors using information from published financial statements, prevailing prices, customers, suppliers, former employees, industry experts, and financial analysts. The internal-business-process perspective comprises three subprocesses:
   - **Innovation process:** Creating products, services, and processes that will meet the needs of customers. This is a very important process for companies that follow a product-differentiation strategy and must constantly design and develop innovative new products to remain competitive in the marketplace. Chipset's innovation focuses on improving its manufacturing capability and process controls to lower costs and improve quality. Chipset measures innovation by the number of improvements in manufacturing processes and percentage of processes with advanced controls.
   - **Operations process:** Producing and delivering existing products and services that will meet the needs of customers. Chipset's strategic initiatives are (a) improving manufacturing quality, (b) reducing delivery time to customers, and (c) meeting specified delivery dates so it measures yield, order-delivery time, and on-time deliveries.
   - **Postsales-service process:** Providing service and support to the customer after the sale of a product or service. Chipset monitors how quickly and accurately it is responding to customer-service requests.

| Exhibit 13-3 | The Balanced Scorecard for Chipset, Inc., for 2011 |

Strategic Objectives	Measures	Initiatives	Target Performance	Actual Performance
Financial Perspective				
Grow operating income	Operating income from productivity gain	Manage costs and unused capacity	$1,850,000	$1,912,500
Increase shareholder value	Operating income from growth	Build strong customer relationships	$2,500,000	$2,820,000
	Revenue growth		9%	10%[a]
Customer Perspective				
Increase market share	Market share in communication-networks segment	Identify future needs of customers	6%	7%
Increase customer satisfaction	Number of new customers	Identify new target-customer segments	1	1[b]
	Customer-satisfaction ratings	Increase customer focus of sales organization	90% of customers give top two ratings	87% of customers give top two ratings
Internal-Business-Process Perspective				
Improve postsales service	Service response time	Improve customer-service process	Within 4 hours	Within 3 hours
Improve manufacturing quality and productivity	Yield	Identify root causes of problems and improve quality	78%	79.3%
Reduce delivery time to customers	Order-delivery time	Reengineer order-delivery process	30 days	30 days
Meet specified delivery dates	On-time delivery	Reengineer order-delivery process	92%	90%
Improve processes	Number of major improvements in manufacturing and business processes	Organize teams from manufacturing and sales to modify processes	5	5
Improve manufacturing capability	Percentage of processes with advanced controls	Organize R&D/manufacturing teams to implement advanced controls	75%	75%
Learning-and-Growth Perspective				
Align employee and organization goals	Employee-satisfaction ratings	Employee participation and suggestions program to build teamwork	80% of employees give top two ratings	88% of employees give top two ratings
Empower workforce	Percentage of line workers empowered to manage processes	Have supervisors act as coaches rather than decision makers	85%	90%
Develop process skill	Percentage of employees trained in process and quality management	Employee training programs	90%	92%
Enhance information-system capabilities	Percentage of manufacturing processes with real-time feedback	Improve online and offline data gathering	80%	80%

[a](Revenues in 2011 − Revenues in 2010) ÷ Revenues in 2010 = ($25,300,000 − $23,000,000) ÷ $23,000,000 = 10%.
[b]Number of customers increased from seven to eight in 2011.

4. **Learning-and-growth perspective.** This perspective identifies the capabilities the organization must excel at to achieve superior internal processes that in turn create value for customers and shareholders. Chipset's learning and growth perspective emphasizes three capabilities: (1) information-system capabilities, measured by the percentage of manufacturing processes with real-time feedback; (2) employee capabilities, measured by the percentage of employees trained in process and quality management; and (3) motivation, measured by employee satisfaction and the percentage of manufacturing and sales employees (line employees) empowered to manage processes.

The arrows in Exhibit 13-3 indicate the *broad* cause-and-effect linkages: how gains in the learning-and-growth perspective lead to improvements in internal business processes, which lead to higher customer satisfaction and market share, and finally lead to superior financial performance. Note how the scorecard describes elements of Chipset's strategy implementation. Worker training and empowerment improve employee satisfaction and lead to manufacturing and business-process improvements that improve quality and reduce delivery time. The result is increased customer satisfaction and higher market share. These initiatives have been successful from a financial perspective. Chipset has earned significant operating income from its cost leadership strategy, and that strategy has also led to growth.

A major benefit of the balanced scorecard is that it promotes causal thinking. Think of the balanced scorecard as a *linked scorecard* or a *causal scorecard*. Managers must search for empirical evidence (rather than rely on faith alone) to test the validity and strength of the various connections. A causal scorecard enables a company to focus on the key drivers that steer the implementation of the strategy. Without convincing links, the scorecard loses much of its value.

Implementing a Balanced Scorecard

To successfully implement a balanced scorecard requires commitment and leadership from top management. At Chipset, the team building the balanced scorecard (headed by the vice president of strategic planning) conducted interviews with senior managers, probed executives about customers, competitors, and technological developments, and sought proposals for balanced scorecard objectives across the four perspectives. The team then met to discuss the responses and to build a prioritized list of objectives.

In a meeting with all senior managers, the team sought to achieve consensus on the scorecard objectives. Senior management was then divided into four groups, with each group responsible for one of the perspectives. In addition, each group broadened the base of inputs by including representatives from the next-lower levels of management and key functional managers. The groups identified measures for each objective and the sources of information for each measure. The groups then met to finalize scorecard objectives, measures, targets, and the initiatives to achieve the targets. Management accountants played an important role in the design and implementation of the balanced scorecard, particularly in determining measures to represent the realities of the business. This required management accountants to understand the economic environment of the industry, Chipset's customers and competitors, and internal business issues such as human resources, operations, and distribution.

Managers made sure that employees understood the scorecard and the scorecard process. The final balanced scorecard was communicated to all employees. Sharing the scorecard allowed engineers and operating personnel, for example, to understand the reasons for customer satisfaction and dissatisfaction and to make suggestions for improving internal processes directly aimed at satisfying customers and implementing Chipset's strategy. Too often, scorecards are seen by only a select group of managers. By limiting the scorecard's exposure, an organization loses the opportunity for widespread organization engagement and alignment.

Chipset (like Cigna Property, Casualty Insurance, and Wells Fargo) also encourages each department to develop its own scorecard that ties into Chipset's main scorecard described in Exhibit 13-3. For example, the quality control department's scorecard has measures that its department managers use to improve yield—number of quality circles, statistical process control charts, Pareto diagrams, and root-cause analyses (see

Chapter 19, pp. 675–677 for more details). Department scorecards help align the actions of each department to implement Chipset's strategy.

Companies frequently use balanced scorecards to evaluate and reward managerial performance and to influence managerial behavior. Using the balanced scorecard for performance evaluation widens the performance management lens and motivates managers to give greater attention to nonfinancial drivers of performance. Surveys indicate, however, that companies continue to assign more weight to the financial perspective (55%) than to the other perspectives—customer (19%), internal business process (12%), and learning and growth (14%). Companies cite several reasons for the relatively smaller weight on nonfinancial measures: difficulty evaluating the relative importance of nonfinancial measures; challenges in measuring and quantifying qualitative, nonfinancial data; and difficulty in compensating managers despite poor financial performance (see Chapter 23 for a more detailed discussion of performance evaluation). Many companies, however, are giving greater weight to nonfinancial measures in promotion decisions because they believe that nonfinancial measures (such as customer satisfaction, process improvements, and employee motivation) better assess a manager's potential to succeed at senior levels of management. For the balanced scorecard to be effective, managers must view it as fairly assessing and rewarding all important aspects of a manager's performance and promotion prospects.

Aligning the Balanced Scorecard to Strategy

Different strategies call for different scorecards. Recall Chipset's competitor Visilog, which follows a product-differentiation strategy by designing custom chips for modems and communication networks. Visilog designs its balanced scorecard to fit its strategy. For example, in the financial perspective, Visilog evaluates how much of its operating income comes from charging premium prices for its products. In the customer perspective, Visilog measures the percentage of its revenues from new products and new customers. In the internal-business-process perspective, Visilog measures the number of new products introduced and new product development time. In the learning-and-growth perspective, Visilog measures the development of advanced manufacturing capabilities to produce custom chips. Visilog also uses some of the measures described in Chipset's balanced scorecard in Exhibit 13-3. For example, revenue growth, customer satisfaction ratings, order-delivery time, on-time delivery, percentage of frontline workers empowered to manage processes, and employee-satisfaction ratings are also important measures under the product-differentiation strategy. The goal is to align the balanced scorecard with company strategy.[5] Exhibit 13-4 presents some common measures found on company scorecards in the service, retail, and manufacturing sectors.

Features of a Good Balanced Scorecard

A well-designed balanced scorecard has several features:

1. It tells the story of a company's strategy, articulating a sequence of cause-and-effect relationships—the links among the various perspectives that align implementation of the strategy. In for-profit companies, each measure in the scorecard is part of a cause-and-effect chain leading to financial outcomes. Not-for-profit organizations design the cause-and-effect chain to achieve their strategic service objectives—for example, number of people no longer in poverty, or number of children still in school.

2. The balanced scorecard helps to communicate the strategy to all members of the organization by translating the strategy into a coherent and linked set of understandable and measurable operational targets. Guided by the scorecard, managers and employees take actions and make decisions to achieve the company's strategy. Companies that have distinct strategic business units (SBUs)—such as consumer

---

[5] For simplicity, we have presented the balanced scorecard in the context of companies that have followed either a cost-leadership or a product-differentiation strategy. Of course, a company may have some products for which cost leadership is critical and other products for which product differentiation is important. The company will then develop separate scorecards to implement the different product strategies. In still other contexts, product differentiation may be of primary importance, but some cost leadership must also be achieved. The balanced scorecard measures would then be linked in a cause-and-effect way to this strategy.

Exhibit 13-4

Frequently Cited
Balanced Scorecard
Measures

Financial Perspective
Income measures: Operating income, gross margin percentage
Revenue and cost measures: Revenue growth, revenues from new products, cost reductions in key areas
Income and investment measures: Economic value added [a](EVA®), return on investment
Customer Perspective
Market share, customer satisfaction, customer-retention percentage, time taken to fulfill customers' requests, number of customer complaints
Internal-Business-Process Perspective
Innovation Process: Operating capabilities, number of new products or services, new-product development times, and number of new patents
Operations Process: Yield, defect rates, time taken to deliver product to customers, percentage of on-time deliveries, average time taken to respond to orders, setup time, manufacturing downtime
Postsales Service Process: Time taken to replace or repair defective products, hours of customer training for using the product
Learning-and-Growth Perspective
Employee measures: Employee education and skill levels, employee-satisfaction ratings, employee turnover rates, percentage of employee suggestions implemented, percentage of compensation based on individual and team incentives
Technology measures: Information system availability, percentage of processes with advanced controls

[a]This measure is described in Chapter 23.

products and pharmaceuticals at Johnson & Johnson—develop their balanced scorecards at the SBU level. Each SBU has its own unique strategy and implementation goals; building separate scorecards allows each SBU to choose measures that help implement its distinctive strategy.

3. In for-profit companies, the balanced scorecard must motivate managers to take actions that eventually result in improvements in financial performance. Managers sometimes tend to focus too much on innovation, quality, and customer satisfaction as ends in themselves. For example, Xerox spent heavily to increase customer satisfaction without a resulting financial payoff because higher levels of satisfaction did not increase customer loyalty. Some companies use statistical methods, such as regression analysis, to test the anticipated cause-and-effect relationships among nonfinancial measures and financial performance. The data for this analysis can come from either time series data (collected over time) or cross-sectional data (collected, for example, across multiple stores of a retail chain). In the Chipset example, improvements in nonfinancial factors have, in fact, already led to improvements in financial factors.

4. The balanced scorecard limits the number of measures, identifying only the most critical ones. Chipset's scorecard, for example, has 16 measures, between 3 and 6 measures for each perspective. Limiting the number of measures focuses managers' attention on those that most affect strategy implementation. Using too many measures makes it difficult for managers to process relevant information.

5. The balanced scorecard highlights less-than-optimal trade-offs that managers may make when they fail to consider operational and financial measures together. For example, a company whose strategy is innovation and product differentiation could achieve superior short-run financial performance by reducing spending on R&D. A good balanced scorecard would signal that the short-run financial performance might have been achieved by taking actions that hurt future financial performance because a leading indicator of that performance, R&D spending and R&D output, has declined.

Pitfalls in Implementing a Balanced Scorecard

Pitfalls to avoid in implementing a balanced scorecard include the following:

1. Managers should not assume the cause-and-effect linkages are precise. They are merely hypotheses. Over time, a company must gather evidence of the strength and timing of the linkages among the nonfinancial and financial measures. With experience,

organizations should alter their scorecards to include those nonfinancial strategic objectives and measures that are the best leading indicators (the causes) of financial performance (a lagging indicator or the effect). Understanding that the scorecard evolves over time helps managers avoid unproductively spending time and money trying to design the "perfect" scorecard at the outset. Furthermore, as the business environment and strategy change over time, the measures in the scorecard also need to change.

2. Managers should not seek improvements across all of the measures all of the time. For example, strive for quality and on-time performance but not beyond the point at which further improvement in these objectives is so costly that it is inconsistent with long-run profit maximization. Cost-benefit considerations should always be central when designing a balanced scorecard.

3. Managers should not use only objective measures in the balanced scorecard. Chipset's balanced scorecard includes both objective measures (such as operating income from cost leadership, market share, and manufacturing yield) and subjective measures (such as customer- and employee-satisfaction ratings). When using subjective measures, though, managers must be careful that the benefits of this potentially rich information are not lost by using measures that are inaccurate or that can be easily manipulated.

4. Despite challenges of measurement, top management should not ignore nonfinancial measures when evaluating managers and other employees. Managers tend to focus on the measures used to reward their performance. Excluding nonfinancial measures when evaluating performance will reduce the significance and importance that managers give to nonfinancial measures.

Evaluating the Success of Strategy and Implementation

Decision Point

How can an organization translate its strategy into a set of performance measures?

To evaluate how successful Chipset's strategy and its implementation have been, its management compares the target- and actual-performance columns in the balanced scorecard (Exhibit 13-3). Chipset met most targets set on the basis of competitor benchmarks in 2011 itself. That's because, in the Chipset context, improvements in the learning and growth perspective quickly ripple through to the financial perspective. Chipset will continue to seek improvements on the targets it did not achieve, but meeting most targets suggests that the strategic initiatives that Chipset identified and measured for learning and growth resulted in improvements in internal business processes, customer measures, and financial performance.

How would Chipset know if it had problems in strategy implementation? If it did not meet its targets on the two perspectives that are more internally focused: learning and growth and internal business processes.

What if Chipset performed well on learning and growth and internal business processes, but customer measures and financial performance in this year and the next did not improve? Chipset's managers would then conclude that Chipset did a good job of implementation (the various internal nonfinancial measures it targeted improved) but that its strategy was faulty (there was no effect on customers or on long-run financial performance and value creation). Management failed to identify the correct causal links. It implemented the wrong strategy well! Management would then reevaluate the strategy and the factors that drive it.

Now what if Chipset performed well on its various nonfinancial measures, and operating income over this year and the next also increased? Chipset's managers might be tempted to declare the strategy a success because operating income increased. Unfortunately, management still cannot conclude with any confidence that Chipset successfully formulated and implemented its strategy. Why? Because operating income can increase simply because entire markets are expanding, not because a company's strategy has been successful. Also, changes in operating income might occur because of factors outside the strategy. For example, a company such as Chipset that has chosen a cost-leadership strategy may find that its operating-income increase actually resulted from, say, some degree of product differentiation. *To evaluate the success of a strategy, managers and management accountants need to link strategy to the sources of operating-income increases.*

For Chipset to conclude that it was successful in implementing its strategy, it must demonstrate that improvements in its financial performance and operating income over time resulted from achieving targeted cost savings and growth in market share. Fortunately, the top two rows of Chipset's balanced scorecard in Exhibit 13-3 show that operating-income gains from productivity ($1,912,500) and growth ($2,820,000) exceeded targets. The next section of this chapter describes how these numbers were calculated. Because its strategy has been successful, Chipset's management can be more confident that the gains will be sustained in subsequent years.

Chipset's management accountants subdivide changes in operating income into components that can be identified with product differentiation, cost leadership, and growth. Why growth? Because successful product differentiation or cost leadership generally increases market share and helps a company to grow. Subdividing the change in operating income to evaluate the success of a strategy is conceptually similar to the variance analysis discussed in Chapters 7 and 8. One difference, however, is that management accountants compare actual operating performance over two different periods, not actual to budgeted numbers in the same time period as in variance analysis.[6]

Strategic Analysis of Operating Income

Learning Objective **4**

Analyze changes in operating income to evaluate strategy

. . . growth, price recovery, and productivity

The following illustration explains how to subdivide the change in operating income from one period to *any* future period. The individual components describe company performance with regard to product differentiation, cost leadership, and growth.[7] We illustrate the analysis using data from 2010 and 2011 because Chipset implemented key elements of its strategy in late 2010 and early 2011 and expects the financial consequences of these strategies to occur in 2011. Suppose the financial consequences of these strategies had been expected to affect operating income in only 2012. Then we could just as easily have compared 2010 to 2012. If necessary, we could also have compared 2010 to 2011 and 2012 taken together.

Chipset's data for 2010 and 2011 follow:

	2010	2011
1. Units of CX1 produced and sold	1,000,000	1,150,000
2. Selling price	$23	$22
3. Direct materials (square centimeters of silicon wafers)	3,000,000	2,900,000
4. Direct material cost per square centimeter	$1.40	$1.50
5. Manufacturing processing capacity (in square centimeters of silicon wafer)	3,750,000	3,500,000
6. Conversion costs (all manufacturing costs other than direct material costs)	$16,050,000	$15,225,000
7. Conversion cost per unit of capacity (row 6 ÷ row 5)	$4.28	$4.35

Chipset provides the following additional information:

1. Conversion costs (labor and overhead costs) for each year depend on production processing capacity defined in terms of the quantity of square centimeters of silicon wafers that Chipset can process. These costs do not vary with the actual quantity of silicon wafers processed.

2. Chipset incurs no R&D costs. Its marketing, sales, and customer-service costs are small relative to the other costs. Chipset has fewer than 10 customers, each purchasing roughly the same quantities of CX1. Because of the highly technical nature of the product, Chipset uses a cross-functional team for its marketing, sales, and customer-service activities. This cross-functional approach ensures that, although marketing, sales, and customer-service costs are small, the entire Chipset organization, including manufacturing engineers, remains focused on increasing customer satisfaction and

---

[6] Other examples of focusing on actual performance over two periods rather than comparisons of actuals with budgets can be found in J. Hope and R. Fraser, *Beyond Budgeting* (Boston, MA: Harvard Business School Press, 2003).

[7] For other details, see R. Banker, S. Datar, and R. Kaplan, "Productivity Measurement and Management Accounting," *Journal of Accounting, Auditing and Finance* (1989): 528–554; and A. Hayzen and J. Reeve, "Examining the Relationships in Productivity Accounting," *Management Accounting Quarterly* (2000): 32–39.

market share. (The Problem for Self-Study at the end of this chapter describes a situation in which marketing, sales, and customer-service costs are significant.)

3. Chipset's asset structure is very similar in 2010 and 2011.

4. Operating income for each year is as follows:

	2010	2011
Revenues		
($23 per unit × 1,000,000 units; $22 per unit × 1,150,000 units)	$23,000,000	$25,300,000
Costs		
Direct material costs		
($1.40/sq. cm. × 3,000,000 sq. cm.; $1.50/sq. cm. × 2,900,000 sq. cm.)	4,200,000	4,350,000
Conversion costs		
($4.28/sq. cm. × 3,750,000 sq. cm.; $4.35/sq. cm. × 3,500,000 sq. cm.)	16,050,000	15,225,000
Total costs	20,250,000	19,575,000
Operating income	$ 2,750,000	$ 5,725,000
Change in operating income	$2,975,000 F	

The goal of Chipset's managers is to evaluate how much of the $2,975,000 increase in operating income was caused by the successful implementation of the company's cost-leadership strategy. To do this, management accountants start by analyzing three main factors: growth, price recovery, and productivity.

The **growth component** measures the change in operating income attributable solely to the change in the quantity of output sold between 2010 and 2011.

The **price-recovery component** measures the change in operating income attributable solely to changes in Chipset's prices of inputs and outputs between 2010 and 2011. The price-recovery component measures change in output price compared with changes in input prices. A company that has successfully pursued a strategy of product differentiation will be able to increase its output price faster than the increase in its input prices, boosting profit margins and operating income: It will show a large positive price-recovery component.

The **productivity component** measures the change in costs attributable to a change in the quantity of inputs used in 2011 relative to the quantity of inputs that would have been used in 2010 to produce the 2011 output. The productivity component measures the amount by which operating income increases by using inputs efficiently to lower costs. A company that has successfully pursued a strategy of cost leadership will be able to produce a given quantity of output with a lower cost of inputs: It will show a large positive productivity component. Given Chipset's strategy of cost leadership, we expect the increase in operating income to be attributable to the productivity and growth components, not to price recovery. We now examine these three components in detail.

Growth Component of Change in Operating Income

The growth component of the change in operating income measures the increase in revenues minus the increase in costs from selling more units of CX1 in 2011 (1,150,000 units) than in 2010 (1,000,000 units), *assuming nothing else has changed*.

Revenue Effect of Growth

$$\begin{array}{l} \text{Revenue effect} \\ \text{of growth} \end{array} = \left(\begin{array}{c} \text{Actual units of} \\ \text{output sold} \\ \text{in 2011} \end{array} - \begin{array}{c} \text{Actual units of} \\ \text{output sold} \\ \text{in 2010} \end{array} \right) \times \begin{array}{c} \text{Selling} \\ \text{price} \\ \text{in 2010} \end{array}$$

$$= (1,150,000 \text{ units} - 1,000,000 \text{ units}) \times \$23 \text{ per unit}$$

$$= \$3,450,000 \text{ F}$$

This component is favorable (F) because the increase in output sold in 2011 increases operating income. Components that decrease operating income are unfavorable (U).

Note that Chipset uses the 2010 price of CX1 and focuses only on the increase in units sold between 2010 and 2011, because the revenue effect of growth component measures how much revenues would have changed in 2010 if Chipset had sold 1,150,000 units instead of 1,000,000 units.

Cost Effect of Growth

The cost effect of growth measures how much costs would have changed in 2010 if Chipset had produced 1,150,000 units of CX1 instead of 1,000,000 units. To measure the cost effect of growth, Chipset's managers distinguish variable costs such as direct material costs from fixed costs such as conversion costs, because as units produced (and sold) increase, variable costs increase proportionately but fixed costs, generally, do not change.

$$\begin{pmatrix} \text{Cost effect of} \\ \text{growth for} \\ \text{variable costs} \end{pmatrix} = \begin{pmatrix} \text{Units of input} & \text{Actual units of} \\ \text{required to} & \text{input used} \\ \text{produce 2011} - \text{to produce} \\ \text{output in 2010} & \text{2010 output} \end{pmatrix} \times \begin{matrix} \text{Input} \\ \text{price} \\ \text{in 2010} \end{matrix}$$

$$\begin{matrix} \text{Cost effect of} \\ \text{growth for} \\ \text{direct materials} \end{matrix} = \left(3{,}000{,}000 \text{ sq. cm.} \times \frac{1{,}150{,}000 \text{ units}}{1{,}000{,}000 \text{ units}} - 3{,}000{,}000 \text{ sq. cm.} \right) \times \$1.40 \text{ per sq. cm.}$$

$$= (3{,}450{,}000 \text{ sq. cm.} - 3{,}000{,}000 \text{ sq. cm.}) \times \$1.40 \text{ per sq. cm.} = \$630{,}000 \text{ U}$$

The units of input required to produce 2011 output in 2010 can also be calculated as follows:

$$\text{Units of input per unit of output in 2010} = \frac{3{,}000{,}000 \text{ sq. cm.}}{1{,}000{,}000 \text{ units}} = 3 \text{ sq. cm./unit}$$

Units of input required to produce 2011 output of 1,150,000 units in 2010 = 3 sq. cm. per unit × 1,150,000 units = 3,450,000 sq. cm.

$$\begin{matrix} \text{Cost effect of} \\ \text{growth for} \\ \text{fixed costs} \end{matrix} = \begin{pmatrix} \text{Actual units of capacity in} & \text{Actual units} \\ \text{2010 because adequate capacity} - \text{of capacity} \\ \text{exists to produce 2011 output in 2010} & \text{in 2010} \end{pmatrix} \times \begin{matrix} \text{Price per} \\ \text{unit of} \\ \text{capacity} \\ \text{in 2010} \end{matrix}$$

$$\begin{matrix} \text{Cost effect of} \\ \text{growth for} \\ \text{conversion costs} \end{matrix} = (3{,}750{,}000 \text{ sq. cm.} - 3{,}750{,}000 \text{ sq. cm.}) \times \$4.28 \text{ per sq. cm.} = \$0$$

Conversion costs are fixed costs at a given level of capacity. Chipset has manufacturing capacity to process 3,750,000 square centimeters of silicon wafers in 2010 at a cost of $4.28 per square centimeter (rows 5, and 7 of data on p. 478). To produce 1,150,000 units of output in 2010, Chipset needs to process 3,450,000 square centimeters of direct materials, which is less than the available capacity of 3,750,000 sq. cm. Throughout this chapter, we assume adequate capacity exists in the current year (2010) to produce next year's (2011) output. Under this assumption, the cost effect of growth for capacity-related fixed costs is, by definition, $0. Had 2010 capacity been inadequate to produce 2011 output in 2010, we would need to calculate the additional capacity required to produce 2011 output in 2010. These calculations are beyond the scope of the book.

In summary, the net increase in operating income attributable to growth equals the following:

Revenue effect of growth		$3,450,000 F
Cost effect of growth		
Direct material costs	$630,000 U	
Conversion costs	0	630,000 U
Change in operating income due to growth		$2,820,000 F

Price-Recovery Component of Change in Operating Income

Assuming that the 2010 relationship between inputs and outputs continued in 2011, the price-recovery component of the change in operating income measures solely the effect of price changes on revenues and costs to produce and sell the 1,150,000 units of CX1 in 2011.

Revenue Effect of Price Recovery

$$\text{Revenue effect of price recovery} = \left(\begin{array}{c}\text{Selling price} \\ \text{in 2011}\end{array} - \begin{array}{c}\text{Selling price} \\ \text{in 2010}\end{array}\right) \times \begin{array}{c}\text{Actual units} \\ \text{of output} \\ \text{sold in 2011}\end{array}$$

$$= (\$22 \text{ per unit} - \$23 \text{ per unit}) \times 1{,}150{,}000 \text{ units}$$

$$= \$1{,}150{,}000 \text{ U}$$

Note that the calculation focuses on revenue changes caused by changes in the selling price of CX1 between 2010 and 2011.

Cost Effect of Price Recovery

Chipset's management accountants calculate the cost effects of price recovery separately for variable costs and for fixed costs, just as they did when calculating the cost effect of growth.

$$\begin{array}{c}\text{Cost effect of} \\ \text{price recovery for} \\ \text{variable costs}\end{array} = \left(\begin{array}{c}\text{Input price} \\ \text{in 2011}\end{array} - \begin{array}{c}\text{Input price} \\ \text{in 2010}\end{array}\right) \times \begin{array}{c}\text{Units of input} \\ \text{required to} \\ \text{produce 2011} \\ \text{output in 2010}\end{array}$$

$$\begin{array}{c}\text{Cost effect of} \\ \text{price recovery for} \\ \text{direct materials}\end{array} = (\$1.50 \text{ per sq.cm.} - \$1.40 \text{ per sq.cm.}) \times 3{,}450{,}000 \text{ sq.} = \$345{,}000 \text{ U}$$

Recall that the direct materials of 3,450,000 square centimeters required to produce 2011 output in 2010 had already been calculated when computing the cost effect of growth (p. 480).

$$\begin{array}{c}\text{Cost effect of} \\ \text{price recovery for} \\ \text{fixed costs}\end{array} = \left(\begin{array}{c}\text{Price per} \\ \text{unit of} \\ \text{capacity} \\ \text{in 2011}\end{array} - \begin{array}{c}\text{Price per} \\ \text{unit of} \\ \text{capacity} \\ \text{in 2010}\end{array}\right) \times \begin{array}{c}\text{Actual units of capacity in} \\ \text{2010 (because adequate} \\ \text{capacity exists to produce} \\ \text{2011 output in 2010)}\end{array}$$

Cost effect of price recovery for fixed costs is as follows:

Conversion costs: $(\$4.35 \text{ per sq. cm.} - \$4.28 \text{ per sq. cm.}) \times 3{,}750{,}000 \text{ sq. cm.} = \$262{,}500 \text{ U}$

Note that the detailed analyses of capacities were presented when computing the cost effect of growth (p. 480).

In summary, the net decrease in operating income attributable to price recovery equals the following:

Revenue effect of price recovery		$1,150,000 U
Cost effect of price recovery		
Direct material costs	$345,000 U	
Conversion costs	262,500 U	607,500 U
Change in operating income due to price recovery		$1,757,500 U

The price-recovery analysis indicates that, even as the prices of its inputs increased, the selling prices of CX1 decreased and Chipset could not pass on input-price increases to its customers.

Productivity Component of Change in Operating Income

The productivity component of the change in operating income uses 2011 input prices to measure how costs have decreased as a result of using fewer inputs, a better mix of inputs, and/or less capacity to produce 2011 output, compared with the inputs and capacity that would have been used to produce this output in 2010.

The productivity-component calculations use 2011 prices and output. That's because the productivity component isolates the change in costs between 2010 and 2011 caused solely by the change in the quantities, mix, and/or capacities of inputs.[8]

$$
\begin{array}{l}
\text{Cost effect of} \\
\text{productivity for} = \\
\text{variable costs}
\end{array}
\left(
\begin{array}{l}
\text{Actual units of} \\
\text{input used} \\
\text{to produce} \\
\text{2011 output}
\end{array}
-
\begin{array}{l}
\text{Units of input} \\
\text{required to} \\
\text{produce 2011} \\
\text{output in 2010}
\end{array}
\right)
\times
\begin{array}{l}
\text{Input} \\
\text{price} \\
\text{in 2011}
\end{array}
$$

Using the 2011 data given on page 478 and the calculation of units of input required to produce 2011 output in 2010 when discussing the cost effects of growth (p. 480),

$$
\begin{array}{l}
\text{Cost effect of} \\
\text{productivity for} = (2,900,000 \text{ sq. cm.} - 3,450,000 \text{ sq. cm.}) \times \$1.50 \text{ per sq. cm} \\
\text{direct materials}
\end{array}
$$

$$
= 550,000 \text{ sq. cm.} \times \$1.50 \text{ per sq. cm.} = \$825,000 \text{ F}
$$

Chipset's quality and yield improvements reduced the quantity of direct materials needed to produce output in 2011 relative to 2010.

$$
\begin{array}{l}
\text{Cost effect of} \\
\text{productivity for} = \\
\text{fixed costs}
\end{array}
\left(
\begin{array}{l}
\text{Actual units of} \\
\text{capacity} \\
\text{in 2011}
\end{array}
-
\begin{array}{l}
\text{Actual units of capacity in} \\
\text{2010 because adequate} \\
\text{capacity exists to produce} \\
\text{2011 output in 2010}
\end{array}
\right)
\times
\begin{array}{l}
\text{Price per} \\
\text{unit of} \\
\text{capacity} \\
\text{in 2011}
\end{array}
$$

To calculate the cost effect of productivity for fixed costs, we use the 2011 data given on page 478, and the analyses of capacity required to produce 2011 output in 2010 when discussing the cost effect of growth (p. 480).

Cost effects of productivity for fixed costs are

Conversion costs: $(3,500,000 \text{ sq. cm} - 3,750,000 \text{ sq. cm.}) \times \$4.35 \text{ per sq. cm.} = \$1,087,500 \text{ F}$

Chipset's managers decreased manufacturing capacity in 2011 to 3,500,000 square centimeters by selling off old equipment and laying off workers.

In summary, the net increase in operating income attributable to productivity equals,

Cost effect of productivity	
Direct material costs	$ 825,000 F
Conversion costs	1,087,500 F
Change in operating income due to productivity	1,912,500 F

The productivity component indicates that Chipset was able to increase operating income by improving quality and productivity and eliminating capacity to reduce costs. The appendix to this chapter examines partial and total factor productivity changes between 2010 and 2011 and describes how the management accountant can obtain a deeper understanding of Chipset's cost-leadership strategy. Note that the productivity component focuses exclusively on costs, so there is no revenue effect for this component.

Exhibit 13-5 summarizes the growth, price-recovery, and productivity components of the changes in operating income. Generally, companies that have been successful at cost leadership will show favorable productivity and growth components. Companies that

---

[8] Note that the productivity-component calculation uses actual 2011 input prices, whereas its counterpart, the efficiency variance in Chapters 7 and 8, uses budgeted prices. (In effect, the budgeted prices correspond to 2010 prices). Year 2011 prices are used in the productivity calculation because Chipset wants its managers to choose input quantities to minimize costs in 2011 based on currently prevailing prices. If 2010 prices had been used in the productivity calculation, managers would choose input quantities based on irrelevant input prices that prevailed a year ago! Why does using budgeted prices in Chapters 7 and 8 not pose a similar problem? Because, unlike 2010 prices that describe what happened a year ago, budgeted prices represent prices that are expected to prevail in the current period. Moreover, budgeted prices can be changed, if necessary, to bring them in line with actual current-period prices.

| | **Exhibit 13-5** | Strategic Analysis of Profitability |

	Income Statement Amounts in 2010 (1)	Revenue and Cost Effects of Growth Component in 2011 (2)	Revenue and Cost Effects of Price-Recovery Component in 2011 (3)	Cost Effect of Productivity Component in 2011 (4)	Income Statement Amounts in 2011 (5) = (1) + (2) + (3) + (4)
Revenues	$23,000,000	$3,450,000 F	$1,150,000 U	—	$25,300,000
Costs	20,250,000	630,000 U	607,500 U	$1,912,000 F	19,575,000
Operating income	$ 2,750,000	$2,820,000 F	$1,757,500 U	$1,912,500 F	$ 5,725,000
			$2,975,000 F		

Change in operating income

have successfully differentiated their products will show favorable price-recovery and growth components. In Chipset's case, consistent with its strategy and its implementation, productivity contributed $1,912,500 to the increase in operating income, and growth contributed $2,820,000. Price-recovery contributed a $1,757,500 decrease in operating income, however, because, even as input prices increased, the selling price of CX1 decreased. Had Chipset been able to differentiate its product and charge a higher price, the price-recovery effects might have been less unfavorable or perhaps even favorable. As a result, Chipset's managers plan to evaluate some modest changes in product features that might help differentiate CX1 somewhat more from competing products.

Further Analysis of Growth, Price-Recovery, and Productivity Components

As in all variance and profit analysis, Chipset's managers want to more closely analyze the change in operating income. Chipset's growth might have been helped, for example, by an increase in industry market size. Therefore, at least part of the increase in operating income may be attributable to favorable economic conditions in the industry rather than to any successful implementation of strategy. Some of the growth might relate to the management decision to decrease selling price, made possible by the productivity gains. In this case, the increase in operating income from cost leadership must include operating income from productivity-related growth in market share in addition to the productivity gain.

We illustrate these ideas, using the Chipset example and the following additional information. *Instructors who do not wish to cover these detailed calculations can go to the next section on "Applying the Five-Step Decision-Making Framework to Strategy" without any loss of continuity.*

- The market growth rate in the industry is 8% in 2011. Of the 150,000 (1,150,000 – 1,000,000) units of increased sales of CX1 between 2010 and 2011, 80,000 (0.08 × 1,000,000) units are due to an increase in industry market size (which Chipset should have benefited from regardless of its productivity gains), and the remaining 70,000 units are due to an increase in market share.

- During 2011, Chipset could have maintained the price of CX1 at the 2010 price of $23 per unit. But management decided to take advantage of the productivity gains to reduce the price of CX1 by $1 to grow market share leading to the 70,000-unit increase in sales.

The effect of the industry-market-size factor on operating income (not any specific strategic action) is as follows:

Change in operating income due to growth in industry market size

$$\$2,820,000 \text{ (Exhibit 13-5, column 2)} \times \frac{80,000 \text{ units}}{150,000 \text{ units}} = \$1,504,000 \text{ F}$$

Concepts in Action

The Growth Versus Profitability Choice at Facebook

Competitive advantage comes from product differentiation or cost leadership. Successful implementation of these strategies helps a company to be profitable and to grow. Many Internet start-ups pursue a strategy of short-run growth to build a customer base, with the goal of later benefiting from such growth by either charging user fees or sustaining a free service for users supported by advertisers. However, during the 1990s dot-com boom (and subsequent bust), the most spectacular failures occurred in dot-com companies that followed the "get big fast" model but then failed to differentiate their products or reduce their costs.

Today, many social networking companies (Web-based communities that connect friends, colleagues, and groups with shared interests) face this same challenge. At Facebook, the most notable of the social networking sites, users can create personal profiles that allow them to interact with friends through messaging, chat, sharing Web site links, video clips, and more. Additionally, Facebook encourages other companies to build third-party programs, including games and surveys, for its Web site and mobile applications on the iPhone and BlackBerry devices. From 2007 to 2010, Facebook grew from 12 million users to more than 400 million users uploading photos, sharing updates, planning events, and playing games in the Facebook ecosystem.

During this phenomenal growth, the company wrestled with one key question: How could Facebook become profitable? In 2009, experts estimate that Facebook had revenues of $635 million, mostly through advertising and the sale of virtual gifts (as a private company, Facebook does not publicly disclose its financial information). But the company still did not turn a profit. Why not? To keep its global Web site and mobile applications operating, Facebook requires a massive amount of electricity, Internet bandwidth, and storage servers for digital files. In 2009, the company earmarked $100 million to buy 50,000 new servers, along with a new $2 million network storage system per week.

The cost structure of Facebook means that the company must generate tens of millions a month in revenue to sustain its operations over the long term. But how? Facebook has implemented the following popular methods of online revenue generation:

- **Additional advertising:** To grow its already significant advertising revenue, Facebook recently introduced "Fan Pages" for brands and companies seeking to communicate directly with its users. The company is also working on a tool that will let users share information about their physical whereabouts via the site, which will allow Facebook to sell targeted advertisements for nearby businesses.

- **Transactions:** Facebook is also testing a feature that would expand Facebook Credits, its transactions platform that allows users to purchase games and gifts, into an Internet-wide "virtual currency," that could be accepted by any Web site integrating the Facebook Connect online identity management platform. Facebook currently gets a 30% cut of all transactions conducted through Facebook Credits.

Despite rampant rumors, Facebook has rejected the idea of charging monthly subscription fees for access to its Web site or for advanced features and premium content.

With increased growth around the world, Facebook anticipates 2010 revenues to exceed $1 billion. Despite the opportunity to become the "world's richest twenty-something," Facebook's 25-year-old CEO Mark Zuckerberg has thus far resisted taking the company public through an initial public offering (IPO). "A lot of companies can go off course because of corporate pressures," says Mr. Zuckerberg. "I don't know what we are going to be building five years from now." With his company's focus on facilitating people's ability to share almost any- and everything with anyone, at any time, via the Internet, mobile phones, and even videogames, Facebook expects to offer users a highly personal and differentiated online experience in the years ahead and expects that this product differentiation will drive its future growth and profitability.

Sources: Vascellaro, Jessica E. 2010. Facebook CEO in no rush to 'friend' wall street. *Wall Street Journal*, March 3. http://online.wsj.com/article/ SB10001424052748703787304575075942803630712.html; Eldon, Eric. 2010. Facebook revenues up to $700 million in 2009, on track towards $1.1 billion in 2010. *Inside Facebook*. Blog, March 2. http://www.insidefacebook.com/2010/03/02/facebook-made-up-to-700-million-in-2009-on-track-towards-1-1-billion-in-2010/; Arrington, Michael. 2010. Facebook may be growing too fast. And hitting the capital markets again. *Tech Crunch*. Blog, October 31. http://techcrunch.com/2010/10/31/facebooks-growing-problem/

Lacking a differentiated product, Chipset could have maintained the price of CX1 at $23 per unit even while the prices of its inputs increased.

The effect of product differentiation on operating income is as follows:

Change in prices of inputs (cost effect of price recovery)	607,500 U
Change in operating income due to product differentiation	$607,500 U

To exercise cost and price leadership, Chipset made the strategic decision to cut the price of CX1 by $1. This decision resulted in an increase in market share and 70,000 units of additional sales.

The effect of cost leadership on operating income is as follows:

Productivity component	$1,912,500 F
Effect of strategic decision to reduce price ($1/unit × 1,150,000 units)	1,150,000 U
Growth in market share due to productivity improvement and strategic decision to reduce prices	
$2,820,000 (Exhibit 13-5, column 2) × $\dfrac{70,000 \text{ units}}{150,000 \text{ units}}$	1,316,000 F
Change in operating income due to cost leadership	$2,078,500 F

A summary of the change in operating income between 2010 and 2011 follows.

Change due to industry market size	$1,504,000 F
Change due to product differentiation	607,500 U
Change due to cost leadership	2,078,500 F
Change in operating income	$2,975,000 F

Consistent with its cost-leadership strategy, the productivity gains of $1,912,500 in 2011 were a big part of the increase in operating income from 2010 to 2011. Chipset took advantage of these productivity gains to decrease price by $1 per unit at a cost of $1,150,000 to gain $1,316,000 in operating income by selling 70,000 additional units. The Problem for Self-Study on page 488 describes the analysis of the growth, price-recovery, and productivity components for a company following a product-differentiation strategy. The Concepts in Action feature (p. 484) describes the unique challenges that dot-com companies face in choosing a profitable strategy.

Under different assumptions about the change in selling price, the analysis will attribute different amounts to the different strategies.

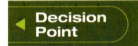

Decision Point

How can a company analyze changes in operating income to evaluate the success of its strategy?

Applying the Five-Step Decision-Making Framework to Strategy

We next briefly describe how the five-step decision-making framework, introduced in Chapter 1, is also useful in making decisions about strategy.

1. *Identify the problem and uncertainties.* Chipset's strategy choice depends on resolving two uncertainties—whether Chipset can add value to its customers that its competitors cannot emulate, and whether Chipset can develop the necessary internal capabilities to add this value.

2. *Obtain information.* Chipset's managers develop customer preference maps to identify various product attributes desired by customers and the competitive advantage or disadvantage it has on each attribute relative to competitors. The managers also gather data on Chipset's internal capabilities. How good is Chipset in designing and developing innovative new products? How good are its process and marketing capabilities?

3. *Make predictions about the future.* Chipset's managers conclude that they will not be able to develop innovative new products in a cost-effective way. They believe that Chipset's strength lies in improving quality, reengineering processes, reducing costs, and delivering products faster to customers.

Decision Point ▶

How can a company identify and manage unused capacity?

$1,087,500 ($4.35 per sq. cm. × 250,000 sq. cm.). It retains some extra capacity for future growth. By avoiding greater reductions in capacity, it also maintains the morale of its skilled and capable workforce. The success of this strategy will depend on Chipset achieving the future growth it has projected.

Because identifying unused capacity for discretionary costs, such as R&D costs, is difficult, downsizing or otherwise managing this unused capacity is also difficult. Management must exercise considerable judgment in deciding the level of R&D costs that would generate the needed product and process improvements. Unlike engineered costs, there is no clear-cut way to know whether management is spending too much (or too little) on R&D.

Problem for Self-Study

Following a strategy of product differentiation, Westwood Corporation makes a high-end kitchen range hood, KE8. Westwood's data for 2010 and 2011 follow:

		2010	2011
1.	Units of KE8 produced and sold	40,000	42,000
2.	Selling price	$100	$110
3.	Direct materials (square feet)	120,000	123,000
4.	Direct material cost per square foot	$10	$11
5.	Manufacturing capacity for KE8	50,000 units	50,000 units
6.	Conversion costs	$1,000,000	$1,100,000
7.	Conversion cost per unit of capacity (row 6 ÷ row 5)	$20	$22
8.	Selling and customer-service capacity	30 customers	29 customers
9.	Selling and customer-service costs	$720,000	$725,000
10.	Cost per customer of selling and customer-service capacity (row 9 ÷ row 8)	$24,000	$25,000

In 2011, Westwood produced no defective units and reduced direct material usage per unit of KE8. Conversion costs in each year are tied to manufacturing capacity. Selling and customer service costs are related to the number of customers that the selling and service functions are designed to support. Westwood has 23 customers (wholesalers) in 2010 and 25 customers in 2011.

Required

1. Describe briefly the elements you would include in Westwood's balanced scorecard.
2. Calculate the growth, price-recovery, and productivity components that explain the change in operating income from 2010 to 2011.
3. Suppose during 2011, the market size for high-end kitchen range hoods grew 3% in terms of number of units and all increases in market share (that is, increases in the number of units sold greater than 3%) are due to Westwood's product-differentiation strategy. Calculate how much of the change in operating income from 2010 to 2011 is due to the industry-market-size factor, cost leadership, and product differentiation.
4. How successful has Westwood been in implementing its strategy? Explain.

Solution

1. The balanced scorecard should describe Westwood's product-differentiation strategy. Elements that should be included in its balanced scorecard are as follows:
   - **Financial perspective.** Increase in operating income from higher margins on KE8 and from growth
   - **Customer perspective.** Customer satisfaction and market share in the high-end market
   - **Internal business process perspective.** New product features, development time for new products, improvements in manufacturing processes, manufacturing quality, order-delivery time, and on-time delivery
   - **Learning-and-growth perspective.** Percentage of employees trained in process and quality management and employee satisfaction ratings

2. Operating income for each year is as follows:

	2010	2011
Revenues		
($100 per unit × 40,000 units; $110 per unit × 42,000 units)	$4,000,000	$4,620,000
Costs		
Direct material costs		
($10 per sq. ft. × 120,000 sq. ft.; $11 per sq. ft. × 123,000 sq. ft.)	1,200,000	1,353,000
Conversion costs		
($20 per unit × 50,000 units; $22 per unit × 50,000 units)	1,000,000	1,100,000
Selling and customer-service cost		
($24,000 per customer × 30 customers;		
$25,000 per customer × 29 customers)	720,000	725,000
Total costs	2,920,000	3,178,000
Operating income	$1,080,000	$1,442,000
Change in operating income		$362,000 F

Growth Component of Operating Income Change

$$\text{Revenue effect of growth} = \left(\begin{array}{c} \text{Actual units of} \\ \text{output sold} \\ \text{in 2011} \end{array} - \begin{array}{c} \text{Actual units of} \\ \text{output sold} \\ \text{in 2010} \end{array} \right) \times \begin{array}{c} \text{Selling} \\ \text{price} \\ \text{in 2010} \end{array}$$

$$= (42{,}000 \text{ units} - 40{,}000 \text{ units}) \times \$100 \text{ per unit} = \$200{,}000 \text{ F}$$

$$\text{Cost effect of growth for variable costs} = \left(\begin{array}{c} \text{Units of input} \\ \text{required to produce} \\ \text{2011 output in 2010} \end{array} - \begin{array}{c} \text{Actual units of input} \\ \text{used to produce} \\ \text{2010 output} \end{array} \right) \times \begin{array}{c} \text{Input} \\ \text{price} \\ \text{in 2010} \end{array}$$

$$\text{Cost effect of growth for direct materials} = \left(120{,}000 \text{ sq. ft.} \times \frac{42{,}000 \text{ units}}{40{,}000 \text{ units}} - 120{,}000 \text{ sq. ft.} \right) \times \$10 \text{ per sq. ft.}$$

$$= (126{,}000 \text{ sq. ft.} - 120{,}000 \text{ sq. ft.}) \times \$10 \text{ per sq. ft.} = \$60{,}000 \text{ U}$$

$$\text{Cost effect of growth for fixed costs} = \left(\begin{array}{c} \text{Actual units of capacity in} \\ \text{2010, because adequate capacity} \\ \text{exists to produce 2011 output in 2010} \end{array} - \begin{array}{c} \text{Actual units} \\ \text{of capacity} \\ \text{in 2010} \end{array} \right) \times \begin{array}{c} \text{Price per} \\ \text{unit of} \\ \text{capacity} \\ \text{in 2010} \end{array}$$

Cost effects of growth for fixed costs are as follows:

$$\text{Conversion costs: } (50{,}000 \text{ units} - 50{,}000 \text{ units}) \times \$20 \text{ per unit} = \$0$$

$$\text{Selling and customer-service costs: } (30 \text{ customers} - 30 \text{ customers}) \times \$24{,}000 \text{ per customer} = \$0$$

In summary, the net increase in operating income attributable to growth equals the following:

Revenue effect of growth		$200,000 F
Cost effect of growth		
Direct material costs	$60,000 U	
Conversion costs	0	
Selling and customer-service costs	0	60,000 U
Change in operating income due to growth		$140,000 F

Price-Recovery Component of Operating-Income Change

$$\begin{matrix} \text{Revenue effect of} \\ \text{price recovery} \end{matrix} = \left(\begin{matrix} \text{Selling price} \\ \text{in 2011} \end{matrix} - \begin{matrix} \text{Selling price} \\ \text{in 2010} \end{matrix} \right) \times \begin{matrix} \text{Actual units} \\ \text{of output} \\ \text{sold in 2011} \end{matrix}$$

$$= (\$110 \text{ per unit} - \$100 \text{ per unit}) \times 42{,}000 \text{ units} = \$420{,}000 \text{ F}$$

$$\begin{matrix} \text{Cost effect of} \\ \text{price recovery} \\ \text{for variable costs} \end{matrix} = \left(\begin{matrix} \text{Input} \\ \text{price} \\ \text{in 2011} \end{matrix} - \begin{matrix} \text{Input} \\ \text{price} \\ \text{in 2010} \end{matrix} \right) \times \begin{matrix} \text{Units of input} \\ \text{required to produce} \\ \text{2011 output in 2010} \end{matrix}$$

Direct material costs: ($11 per sq. ft. − $10 per sq. ft.) × 126,000 sq. ft. = $126,000 U

$$\begin{matrix} \text{Cost effect of} \\ \text{price recovery} \\ \text{for fixed costs} \end{matrix} = \left(\begin{matrix} \text{Price per} \\ \text{unit of} \\ \text{capacity} \\ \text{in 2011} \end{matrix} - \begin{matrix} \text{Price per} \\ \text{unit of} \\ \text{capacity} \\ \text{in 2010} \end{matrix} \right) \times \begin{matrix} \text{Actual units of capacity in} \\ \text{2010, because adequate capacity} \\ \text{exists to produce 2011 output in 2010} \end{matrix}$$

Cost effects of price recovery for fixed costs are as follows:

Conversion costs: ($22 per unit − 20 per unit) × 50,000 units = $100,000 U

Selling and cust.-service costs: ($25,000 per cust. − $24,000 per cust.) × 30 customers = $30,000 U

In summary, the net increase in operating income attributable to price recovery equals the following:

Revenue effect of price recovery		$420,000 F
Cost effect of price recovery		
Direct material costs	$126,000 U	
Conversion costs	100,000 U	
Selling and customer-service costs	30,000 U	256,000 U
Change in operating income due to price recovery		$164,000 F

Productivity Component of Operating-Income Change

$$\begin{matrix} \text{Cost effect of} \\ \text{productivity for} \\ \text{variable costs} \end{matrix} = \left(\begin{matrix} \text{Actual units of} \\ \text{input used to produce} \\ \text{2011 output} \end{matrix} - \begin{matrix} \text{Units of input} \\ \text{required to produce} \\ \text{2011 output in 2010} \end{matrix} \right) \times \begin{matrix} \text{Input} \\ \text{price in} \\ \text{2011} \end{matrix}$$

$$\begin{matrix} \text{Cost effect of} \\ \text{productivity for} \\ \text{direct materials} \end{matrix} = (123{,}000 \text{ sq. ft.} - 126{,}000 \text{ sq. ft.}) \times \$11 \text{ per sq. ft.} = \$33{,}000 \text{ F}$$

$$\begin{matrix} \text{Cost effect of} \\ \text{productivity for} \\ \text{fixed costs} \end{matrix} = \left(\begin{matrix} \text{Actual units} \\ \text{of capacity} \\ \text{in 2011} \end{matrix} - \begin{matrix} \text{Actual units of capacity in} \\ \text{2010, because adequate} \\ \text{capacity exists to produce} \\ \text{2011 output in 2010} \end{matrix} \right) \times \begin{matrix} \text{Price per} \\ \text{unit of} \\ \text{capacity} \\ \text{in 2011} \end{matrix}$$

Cost effects of productivity for fixed costs are as follows:

Conversion costs: (50,000 units − 50,000 units) × $22 per unit = $0

Selling and customer-service costs: (29 customers − 30 customers) × $25,000/customer = $25,000 F

In summary, the net increase in operating income attributable to productivity equals the following:

Cost effect of productivity:	
Direct material costs	$33,000 F
Conversion costs	0
Selling and customer-service costs	25,000 F
Change in operating income due to productivity	$58,000 F

A summary of the change in operating income between 2010 and 2011 follows:

	Income Statement Amounts in 2010 (1)	Revenue and Cost Effects of Growth Component in 2011 (2)	Revenue and Cost Effects of Price-Recovery Component in 2011 (3)	Cost Effect of Productivity Component in 2011 (4)	Income Statement Amounts in 2011 (5) = (1) + (2) + (3) + (4)
Revenue	$4,000,000	$200,000 F	$420,000 F	—	$4,620,000
Costs	2,920,000	60,000 U	256,000 U	$58,000 F	3,178,000
Operating income	$1,080,000	$140,000 F	$164,000 F	$58,000 F	$1,442,000
			362,000 F		

Change in operating income

3. **Effect of the Industry-Market-Size Factor on Operating Income**
   Of the increase in sales from 40,000 to 42,000 units, 3%, or 1,200 units ($0.03 \times$ 40,000), is due to growth in market size, and 800 units (2,000 – 1,200) are due to an increase in market share. The change in Westwood's operating income from the industry-market-size factor rather than specific strategic actions is as follows:

$$\$140,000 \text{ (column 2 of preceding table)} \times \frac{1,200 \text{ units}}{2,000 \text{ units}} \qquad \$84,000 \text{ F}$$

Effect of Product Differentiation on Operating Income

Increase in the selling price of KE8 (revenue effect of the price-recovery component)	$420,000 F
Increase in prices of inputs (cost effect of the price-recovery component)	256,000 U
Growth in market share due to product differentiation	
$\$140,000 \text{ (column 2 of preceding table)} \times \dfrac{800 \text{ units}}{2,000 \text{ units}}$	56,000 F
Change in operating income due to product differentiation	$220,000 F

Effect of Cost Leadership on Operating Income

Productivity component	$ 58,000 F

A summary of the net increase in operating income from 2010 to 2011 follows:

Change due to the industry-market-size factor	$ 84,000 F
Change due to product differentiation	220,000 F
Change due to cost leadership	58,000 F
Change in operating income	$362,000 F

4. The analysis of operating income indicates that a significant amount of the increase in operating income resulted from Westwood's successful implementation of its product-differentiation strategy. The company was able to continue to charge a premium price for KE8 while increasing market share. Westwood was also able to earn additional operating income from improving its productivity.

Decision Points

The following question-and-answer format summarizes the chapter's learning objectives. Each decision presents a key question related to a learning objective. The guidelines are the answer to that question.

Decision	Guidelines
1. What are two generic strategies a company can use?	Two generic strategies are product differentiation and cost leadership. Product differentiation is offering products and services that are perceived by customers as being superior and unique. Cost leadership is achieving low costs relative to competitors. A company chooses its strategy based on an understanding of customer preferences and its own internal capabilities, while differentiating itself from its competitors.
2. What is reengineering?	Reengineering is the rethinking of business processes, such as the order-delivery process, to improve critical performance measures such as cost, quality, and customer satisfaction.
3. How can an organization translate its strategy into a set of performance measures?	An organization can develop a balanced scorecard that provides the framework for a strategic measurement and management system. The balanced scorecard measures performance from four perspectives: (1) financial, (2) customer, (3) internal business processes, and (4) learning and growth. To build their balanced scorecards, organizations often create strategy maps to represent the cause-and-effect relationships across various strategic objectives.
4. How can a company analyze changes in operating income to evaluate the success of its strategy?	To evaluate the success of its strategy, a company can subdivide the change in operating income into growth, price-recovery, and productivity components. The growth component measures the change in revenues and costs from selling more or less units, assuming nothing else has changed. The price-recovery component measures changes in revenues and costs solely as a result of changes in the prices of outputs and inputs. The productivity component measures the decrease in costs from using fewer inputs, a better mix of inputs, and reducing capacity. If a company is successful in implementing its strategy, changes in components of operating income align closely with strategy.
5. How can a company identify and manage unused capacity?	A company must first distinguish engineered costs from discretionary costs. Engineered costs result from a cause-and-effect relationship between output and the resources needed to produce that output. Discretionary costs arise from periodic (usually annual) management decisions regarding the amount of cost to be incurred. Discretionary costs are not tied to a cause-and-effect relationship between inputs and outputs. Identifying unused capacity is easier for engineered costs and more difficult for discretionary costs. Downsizing is an approach to managing unused capacity that matches costs to the activities that need to be performed to operate effectively.

Appendix

Productivity Measurement

Productivity measures the relationship between actual inputs used (both quantities and costs) and actual outputs produced. The lower the inputs for a given quantity of outputs or the higher the outputs for a given quantity of inputs, the higher the productivity. Measuring productivity improvements over time highlights the specific input-output relationships that contribute to cost leadership.

Partial Productivity Measures

Partial productivity, the most frequently used productivity measure, compares the quantity of output produced with the quantity of an individual input used. In its most common form, partial productivity is expressed as a ratio:

$$\text{Partial productivity} = \frac{\text{Quantity of output produced}}{\text{Quantity of input used}}$$

The higher the ratio, the greater the productivity.

Consider direct materials productivity at Chipset in 2011.

$$\frac{\text{Direct materials}}{\text{partial productivity}} = \frac{\text{Quantity of CX1 units produced during 2011}}{\text{Quantity of direct materials used to produce CX1 in 2011}}$$

$$= \frac{\text{1,150,000 units of CX1}}{\text{2,900,000 sq. cm. of direct materials}}$$

$$= 0.397 \text{ units of CX1 per sq. cm. of direct materials}$$

Note direct materials partial productivity ignores Chipset's other input, manufacturing conversion capacity. Partial-productivity measures become more meaningful when comparisons are made that examine productivity changes over time, either across different facilities or relative to a benchmark. Exhibit 13-6 presents partial-productivity measures for Chipset's inputs for 2011 and the comparable 2010 inputs that would have been used to produce 2011 output, using information from the productivity-component calculations on page 482. These measures compare actual inputs used in 2011 to produce 1,150,000 units of CX1 with inputs that would have been used in 2011 had the input–output relationship from 2010 continued in 2011.

Evaluating Changes in Partial Productivities

Note how the partial-productivity measures differ for variable-cost and fixed-cost components. For variable-cost elements, such as direct materials, productivity improvements measure the reduction in input resources used to produce output (3,450,000 square centimeters of silicon wafers to 2,900,000 square centimeters). For fixed-cost elements such as manufacturing conversion capacity, partial productivity measures the reduction in overall capacity from 2010 to 2011 (3,750,000 square centimeters of silicon wafers to 3,500,000 square centimeters) regardless of the amount of capacity actually used in each period.

An advantage of partial-productivity measures is that they focus on a single input. As a result, they are simple to calculate and easily understood by operations personnel. Managers and operators examine these numbers and try to understand the reasons for the productivity changes—such as, better training of workers, lower labor turnover, better incentives, improved methods, or substitution of materials for labor. Isolating the relevant factors helps Chipset implement and sustain these practices in the future.

For all their advantages, partial-productivity measures also have serious drawbacks. Because partial productivity focuses on only one input at a time rather than on all inputs simultaneously, managers cannot evaluate the effect on overall productivity, if (say) manufacturing-conversion-capacity partial productivity increases while direct materials partial productivity decreases. Total factor productivity (TFP), or total productivity, is a measure of productivity that considers all inputs simultaneously.

| Exhibit 13-6 | Comparing Chipset's Partial Productivities in 2010 and 2011 |

Input (1)	Partial Productivity in 2011 (2)	Comparable Partial Productivity Based on 2010 Input–Output Relationships (3)	Percentage Change from 2010 to 2011 (4)
Direct materials	$\frac{1,150,000}{2,900,000} = 0.397$	$\frac{1,150,000}{3,450,000} = 0.333$	$\frac{0.397 - 0.333}{0.333} = 19.2\%$
Manufacturing conversion capacity	$\frac{1,150,000}{3,500,000} = 0.329$	$\frac{1,150,000}{3,750,000} = 0.307$	$\frac{0.329 - 0.307}{0.307} = 7.2\%$

3. Draw a strategy map as in Exhibit 13-2 with two strategic objectives you would expect to see under each balanced scorecard perspective.

4. For each strategic objective indicate a measure you would expect to see in Ridgecrest's balanced scorecard for 2012.

13-17 Analysis of growth, price-recovery, and productivity components (continuation of 13-16). An analysis of Ridgecrest's operating-income changes between 2011 and 2012 shows the following:

Operating income for 2011	$1,850,000
Add growth component	85,000
Deduct price-recovery component	(72,000)
Add productivity component	150,000
Operating income for 2011	$2,013,000

The industry market size for corrugated cardboard boxes did not grow in 2012, input prices did not change, and Ridgecrest reduced the prices of its boxes.

Required

1. Was Ridgecrest's gain in operating income in 2012 consistent with the strategy you identified in requirement 1 of Exercise 13-16?

2. Explain the productivity component. In general, does it represent savings in only variable costs, only fixed costs, or both variable and fixed costs?

13-18 Strategy, balanced scorecard, merchandising operation. Roberto & Sons buys T-shirts in bulk, applies its own trendsetting silk-screen designs, and then sells the T-shirts to a number of retailers. Roberto wants to be known for its trendsetting designs, and it wants every teenager to be seen in a distinctive Roberto T-shirt. Roberto presents the following data for its first two years of operations, 2010 and 2011.

		2010	2011
1	Number of T-shirts purchased	200,000	250,000
2	Number of T-shirts discarded	2,000	3,300
3	Number of T-shirts sold (row 1 – row 2)	198,000	246,700
4	Average selling price	$25.00	$26.00
5	Average cost per T-shirt	$10.00	$8.50
6	Administrative capacity (number of customers)	4,000	3,750
7	Administrative costs	$1,200,000	$1,162,500
8	Administrative cost per customer (row 8 ÷ row 7)	$300	$310

Administrative costs depend on the number of customers that Roberto has created capacity to support, not on the actual number of customers served. Roberto had 3,600 customers in 2010 and 3,500 customers in 2011.

Required

1. Is Roberto 's strategy one of product differentiation or cost leadership? Explain briefly.

2. Describe briefly the key measures Roberto should include in its balanced scorecard and the reasons it should do so.

13-19 Strategic analysis of operating income (continuation of 13-18). Refer to Exercise 13-18.

Required

1. Calculate Roberto's operating income in both 2010 and 2011.

2. Calculate the growth, price-recovery, and productivity components that explain the change in operating income from 2010 to 2011.

3. Comment on your answers in requirement 2. What does each of these components indicate?

13-20 Analysis of growth, price-recovery, and productivity components (continuation of 13-19). Refer to Exercise 13-19. Suppose that the market for silk-screened T-shirts grew by 10% during 2011. All increases in sales greater than 10% are the result of Roberto's strategic actions.

Required

Calculate the change in operating income from 2010 to 2011 due to growth in market size, product differentiation, and cost leadership. How successful has Roberto been in implementing its strategy? Explain.

13-21 Identifying and managing unused capacity (continuation of 13-18). Refer to Exercise 13-18.

Required

1. Calculate the amount and cost of unused administrative capacity at the beginning of 2011, based on the actual number of customers Roberto served in 2011.

2. Suppose Roberto can only add or reduce administrative capacity in increments of 250 customers. What is the maximum amount of costs that Roberto can save in 2011 by downsizing administrative capacity?

3. What factors, other than cost, should Roberto consider before it downsizes administrative capacity?

13-22 Strategy, balanced scorecard. Stanmore Corporation makes a special-purpose machine, D4H, used in the textile industry. Stanmore has designed the D4H machine for 2011 to be distinct from its competitors. It has been generally regarded as a superior machine. Stanmore presents the following data for 2010 and 2011.

	2010	**2011**
1. Units of D4H produced and sold	200	210
2. Selling price	$40,000	$42,000
3. Direct materials (kilograms)	300,000	310,000
4. Direct material cost per kilogram	$8	$8.50
5. Manufacturing capacity in units of D4H	250	250
6. Total conversion costs	$2,000,000	$2,025,000
7. Conversion cost per unit of capacity (row 6 ÷ row 5)	$8,000	$8,100
8. Selling and customer-service capacity	100 customers	95 customers
9. Total selling and customer-service costs	$1,000,000	$940,500
10. Selling and customer-service capacity cost per customer (row 9 ÷ row 8)	$10,000	$9,900

Stanmore produces no defective machines, but it wants to reduce direct materials usage per D4H machine in 2011. Conversion costs in each year depend on production capacity defined in terms of D4H units that can be produced, not the actual units produced. Selling and customer-service costs depend on the number of customers that Stanmore can support, not the actual number of customers it serves. Stanmore has 75 customers in 2010 and 80 customers in 2011.

1. Is Stanmore's strategy one of product differentiation or cost leadership? Explain briefly. **Required**
2. Describe briefly key measures that you would include in Stanmore's balanced scorecard and the reasons for doing so.

13-23 Strategic analysis of operating income (continuation of 13-22). Refer to Exercise 13-22.

1. Calculate the operating income of Stanmore Corporation in 2010 and 2011. **Required**
2. Calculate the growth, price-recovery, and productivity components that explain the change in operating income from 2010 to 2011.
3. Comment on your answer in requirement 2. What do these components indicate?

13-24 Analysis of growth, price-recovery, and productivity components (continuation of 13-23). Suppose that during 2011, the market for Stanmore's special-purpose machines grew by 3%. All increases in market share (that is, sales increases greater than 3%) are the result of Stanmore's strategic actions.

Calculate how much of the change in operating income from 2010 to 2011 is due to the industry-market-size **Required** factor, product differentiation, and cost leadership. How successful has Stanmore been in implementing its strategy? Explain.

13-25 Identifying and managing unused capacity (continuation of 13-22). Refer to Exercise 13-22.

1. Calculate the amount and cost of (a) unused manufacturing capacity and (b) unused selling and **Required** customer-service capacity at the beginning of 2011 based on actual production and actual number of customers served in 2011.
2. Suppose Stanmore can add or reduce its manufacturing capacity in increments of 30 units. What is the maximum amount of costs that Stanmore could save in 2011 by downsizing manufacturing capacity?
3. Stanmore, in fact, does not eliminate any of its unused manufacturing capacity. Why might Stanmore not downsize?

13-26 Strategy, balanced scorecard, service company. Westlake Corporation is a small information-systems consulting firm that specializes in helping companies implement standard sales-management software. The market for Westlake's services is very competitive. To compete successfully, Westlake must deliver quality service at a low cost. Westlake presents the following data for 2010 and 2011.

	2010	**2011**
1. Number of jobs billed	60	70
2. Selling price per job	$50,000	$48,000
3. Software-implementation labor-hours	30,000	32,000
4. Cost per software-implementation labor-hour	$60	$63
5. Software-implementation support capacity (number of jobs it can do)	90	90
6. Total cost of software-implementation support	$360,000	$369,000
7. Software-implementation support-capacity cost per job (row 6 ÷ row 5)	$4,000	$4,100

Software-implementation labor-hour costs are variable costs. Software-implementation support costs for each year depend on the software-implementation support capacity Westlake chooses to maintain each year (that is the number of jobs it can do each year). It does not vary with the actual number of jobs done that year.

Required

1. Is Westlake Corporation's strategy one of product differentiation or cost leadership? Explain briefly.
2. Describe key measures you would include in Westlake's balanced scorecard and your reasons for doing so.

13-27 Strategic analysis of operating income (continuation of 13-26). Refer to Exercise 13-26.

Required

1. Calculate the operating income of Westlake Corporation in 2010 and 2011.
2. Calculate the growth, price-recovery, and productivity components that explain the change in operating income from 2010 to 2011.
3. Comment on your answer in requirement 2. What do these components indicate?

13-28 Analysis of growth, price-recovery, and productivity components (continuation of 13-27). Suppose that during 2011 the market for implementing sales-management software increases by 5%. Assume that any decrease in selling price and any increase in market share more than 5% are the result of strategic choices by Westlake's management to implement its strategy.

Required

Calculate how much of the change in operating income from 2010 to 2011 is due to the industry-market-size factor, product differentiation, and cost leadership. How successful has Westlake been in implementing its strategy? Explain.

13-29 Identifying and managing unused capacity (continuation of 13-26). Refer to Exercise 13-26.

Required

1. Calculate the amount and cost of unused software-implementation support capacity at the beginning of 2011, based on the number of jobs actually done in 2011.
2. Suppose Westlake can add or reduce its software-implementation support capacity in increments of 15 units. What is the maximum amount of costs that Westlake could save in 2011 by downsizing software-implementation support capacity?
3. Westlake, in fact, does not eliminate any of its unused software-implementation support capacity. Why might Westlake not downsize?

MyAccountingLab

Problems

13-30 Balanced scorecard and strategy. Music Master Company manufactures an MP3 player called the Mini. The company sells the player to discount stores throughout the country. This player is significantly less expensive than similar products sold by Music Master's competitors, but the Mini offers just four gigabytes of space, compared with eight offered by competitor Vantage Manufacturing. Furthermore, the Mini has experienced production problems that have resulted in significant rework costs. Vantage's model has an excellent reputation for quality, but is considerably more expensive.

Required

1. Draw a simple customer preference map for Music Master and Vantage using the attributes of price, quality, and storage capacity. Use the format of Exhibit 13-1.
2. Is Music Master's current strategy that of product differentiation or cost leadership?
3. Music Master would like to improve quality and decrease costs by improving processes and training workers to reduce rework. Music Master's managers believe the increased quality will increase sales. Draw a strategy map as in Exhibit 13-2 describing the cause-and-effect relationships among the strategic objectives you would expect to see in Music Master's balanced scorecard.
4. For each strategic objective suggest a measure you would recommend in Music Master's balanced scorecard.

13-31 Strategic analysis of operating income (continuation of 13-30). Refer to Problem 13-30. As a result of the actions taken, quality has significantly improved in 2011 while rework and unit costs of the Mini have decreased. Music Master has reduced manufacturing capacity because capacity is no longer needed to support rework. Music Master has also lowered the Mini's selling price to gain market share and unit sales have increased. Information about the current period (2011) and last period (2010) follows:

	2010	2011
1. Units of Mini produced and sold	8,000	9,000
2. Selling price	$45	$43
3. Ounces of direct materials used	32,000	33,000
4. Direct material cost per ounce	$3.50	$3.50
5. Manufacturing capacity in units	12,000	11,000
6. Total conversion costs	$156,000	$143,000
7. Conversion cost per unit of capacity (row 6 ÷ row 5)	$13	$13
8. Selling and customer-service capacity	90 customers	90 customers
9. Total selling and customer-service costs	$45,000	$49,500
10. Selling and customer-service capacity cost per customer (row 9 ÷ row 8)	$500	$550

Conversion costs in each year depend on production capacity defined in terms of units of Mini that can be produced, not the actual units produced. Selling and customer-service costs depend on the number of customers that Music Master can support, not the actual number of customers it serves. Music Master has 70 customers in 2010 and 80 customers in 2011.

1. Calculate operating income of Music Master Company for 2010 and 2011.
2. Calculate the growth, price-recovery, and productivity components that explain the change in operating income from 2010 to 2011.
3. Comment on your answer in requirement 2. What do these components indicate?

Required

13-32 Analysis of growth, price-recovery, and productivity components (continuation of 13-31). Suppose that during 2011, the market for MP3 players grew 3%. All decreases in the selling price of the Mini and increases in market share (that is, sales increases greater than 3%) are the result of Music Master's strategic actions.

Calculate how much of the change in operating income from 2010 to 2011 is due to the industry-market-size factor, product differentiation, and cost leadership. How does this relate to Music Master's strategy and its success in implementation? Explain.

Required

13-33 Identifying and managing unused capacity (continuation of 13-31) Refer to the information for Music Master Company in 13-31.

1. Calculate the amount and cost of (a) unused manufacturing capacity and (b) unused selling and customer-service capacity at the beginning of 2011 based on actual production and actual number of customers served in 2011.
2. Suppose Music Master can add or reduce its selling and customer-service capacity in increments of five customers. What is the maximum amount of costs that Music Master could save in 2011 by downsizing selling and customer-service capacity?
3. Music Master, in fact, does not eliminate any of its unused selling and customer-service capacity. Why might Music Master not downsize?

Required

13-34 Balanced scorecard. Following is a random-order listing of perspectives, strategic objectives, and performance measures for the balanced scorecard.

Perspectives	Performance Measures
Internal business process	Percentage of defective-product units
Customer	Return on assets
Learning and growth	Number of patents
Financial	Employee turnover rate
Strategic Objectives	Net income
Acquire new customers	Customer profitability
Increase shareholder value	Percentage of processes with real-time feedback
Retain customers	Return on sales
Improve manufacturing quality	Average job-related training-hours per employee
Develop profitable customers	Return on equity
Increase proprietary products	Percentage of on-time deliveries by suppliers
Increase information-system capabilities	Product cost per unit
Enhance employee skills	Profit per salesperson
On-time delivery by suppliers	Percentage of error-free invoices
Increase profit generated by each salesperson	Customer cost per unit
Introduce new products	Earnings per share
Minimize invoice-error rate	Number of new customers
	Percentage of customers retained

For each perspective, select those strategic objectives from the list that best relate to it. For each strategic objective, select the most appropriate performance measure(s) from the list.

Required

13-35 Balanced scorecard. (R. Kaplan, adapted) Caltex, Inc., refines gasoline and sells it through its own Caltex Gas Stations. On the basis of market research, Caltex determines that 60% of the overall gasoline market consists of "service-oriented customers," medium- to high-income individuals who are willing to pay a higher price for gas if the gas stations can provide excellent customer service, such as a clean facility, a convenience store, friendly employees, a quick turnaround, the ability to pay by credit card, and high-octane premium gasoline. The remaining 40% of the overall market are "price shoppers" who look to buy the cheapest gasoline available. Caltex's strategy is to focus on the 60% of service-oriented customers. Caltex's balanced scorecard for 2011 follows. For brevity, the initiatives taken under each objective are omitted.

Objectives	Measures	Target Performance	Actual Performance
Financial Perspective			
Increase shareholder value	Operating-income changes from price recovery	$90,000,000	$95,000,000
	Operating-income changes from growth	$65,000,000	$67,000,000
Customer Perspective			
Increase market share	Market share of overall gasoline market	10%	9.8%
Internal-Business-Process Perspective			
Improve gasoline quality	Quality index	94 points	95 points
Improve refinery performance	Refinery-reliability index (%)	91%	91%
Ensure gasoline availability	Product-availability index (%)	99%	100%
Learning-and-Growth Perspective			
Increase refinery process capability	Percentage of refinery processes with advanced controls	88%	90%

Required

1. Was Caltex successful in implementing its strategy in 2011? Explain your answer.
2. Would you have included some measure of employee satisfaction and employee training in the learning-and-growth perspective? Are these objectives critical to Caltex for implementing its strategy? Why or why not? Explain briefly.
3. Explain how Caltex did not achieve its target market share in the total gasoline market but still exceeded its financial targets. Is "market share of overall gasoline market" the correct measure of market share? Explain briefly.
4. Is there a cause-and-effect linkage between improvements in the measures in the internal business-process perspective and the measure in the customer perspective? That is, would you add other measures to the internal-business-process perspective or the customer perspective? Why or why not? Explain briefly.
5. Do you agree with Caltex's decision not to include measures of changes in operating income from productivity improvements under the financial perspective of the balanced scorecard? Explain briefly.

13-36 Balanced scorecard. Lee Corporation manufactures various types of color laser printers in a highly automated facility with high fixed costs. The market for laser printers is competitive. The various color laser printers on the market are comparable in terms of features and price. Lee believes that satisfying customers with products of high quality at low costs is key to achieving its target profitability. For 2011, Lee plans to achieve higher quality and lower costs by improving yields and reducing defects in its manufacturing operations. Lee will train workers and encourage and empower them to take the necessary actions. Currently, a significant amount of Lee's capacity is used to produce products that are defective and cannot be sold. Lee expects that higher yields will reduce the capacity that Lee needs to manufacture products. Lee does not anticipate that improving manufacturing will automatically lead to lower costs because Lee has high fixed costs. To reduce fixed costs per unit, Lee could lay off employees and sell equipment, or it could use the capacity to produce and sell more of its current products or improved models of its current products.

Lee's balanced scorecard (initiatives omitted) for the just-completed fiscal year 2011 follows:

Objectives	Measures	Target Performance	Actual Performance
Financial Perspective			
Increase shareholder value	Operating-income changes from productivity improvements	$1,000,000	$400,000
	Operating-income changes from growth	$1,500,000	$600,000
Customer Perspective			
Increase market share	Market share in color laser printers	5%	4.6%
Internal-Business-Process Perspective			
Improve manufacturing quality	Yield	82%	85%
Reduce delivery time to customers	Order-delivery time	25 days	22 days
Learning-and-Growth Perspective			
Develop process skills	Percentage of employees trained in process and quality management	90%	92%
Enhance information-system capabilities	Percentage of manufacturing processes with real-time feedback	85%	87%

Required

1. Was Lee successful in implementing its strategy in 2011? Explain.
2. Is Lee's balanced scorecard useful in helping the company understand why it did not reach its target market share in 2011? If it is, explain why. If it is not, explain what other measures you might want to add under the customer perspective and why.
3. Would you have included some measure of employee satisfaction in the learning-and-growth perspective and new-product development in the internal-business-process perspective? That is, do you think employee satisfaction and development of new products are critical for Lee to implement its strategy? Why or why not? Explain briefly.
4. What problems, if any, do you see in Lee improving quality and significantly downsizing to eliminate unused capacity?

13-37 Partial productivity measurement. Gerhart Company manufactures wallets from fabric. In 2011, Gerhart made 2,520,000 wallets using 2,000,000 yards of fabric. In 2011, Gerhart has capacity to make 3,307,500 wallets and incurs a cost of $9,922,500 for this capacity. In 2012, Gerhart plans to make 2,646,000 wallets, make fabric use more efficient, and reduce capacity.

Suppose that in 2012 Gerhart makes 2,646,000 wallets, uses 1,764,000 yards of fabric, and reduces capacity to 2,700,000 wallets, incurring a cost of $8,370,000 for this capacity.

Required

1. Calculate the partial-productivity ratios for materials and conversion (capacity costs) for 2012, and compare them to a benchmark for 2011 calculated based on 2012 output.
2. How can Gerhart Company use the information from the partial-productivity calculations?

13-38 Total factor productivity (continuation of 13-37). Refer to the data for Problem 13-37. Assume the fabric costs $3.70 per yard in 2012 and $3.85 per yard in 2011.

Required

1. Compute Gerhart Company's total factor productivity (TFP) for 2012.
2. Compare TFP for 2012 with a benchmark TFP for 2011 inputs based on 2012 prices and output.
3. What additional information does TFP provide that partial productivity measures do not?

Collaborative Learning Problem

13-39 Strategic analysis of operating income. Halsey Company sells women's clothing. Halsey's strategy is to offer a wide selection of clothes and excellent customer service and to charge a premium price. Halsey presents the following data for 2010 and 2011. For simplicity, assume that each customer purchases one piece of clothing.

	2010	2011
1. Pieces of clothing purchased and sold	40,000	40,000
2. Average selling price	$60	$59
3. Average cost per piece of clothing	$40	$41
4. Selling and customer-service capacity	51,000 customers	43,000 customers
5. Selling and customer-service costs	$357,000	$296,700
6. Selling and customer-service capacity cost per customer (row 5 ÷ row 4)	$7 per customer	$6.90 per customer
7. Purchasing and administrative capacity	980 designs	850 designs
8. Purchasing and administrative costs	$245,000	$204,000
9. Purchasing and administrative capacity cost per distinct design (row 8 ÷ row 7)	$250 per design	$240 per design

Total selling and customer-service costs depend on the number of customers that Halsey has created capacity to support, not the actual number of customers that Halsey serves. Total purchasing and administrative costs depend on purchasing and administrative capacity that Halsey has created (defined in terms of the number of distinct clothing designs that Halsey can purchase and administer). Purchasing and administrative costs do not depend on the actual number of distinct clothing designs purchased. Halsey purchased 930 distinct designs in 2010 and 820 distinct designs in 2011.

At the start of 2010, Halsey planned to increase operating income by 10% over operating income in 2011.

Required

1. Is Halsey's strategy one of product differentiation or cost leadership? Explain.
2. Calculate Halsey's operating income in 2010 and 2011.
3. Calculate the growth, price-recovery, and productivity components of changes in operating income between 2010 and 2011.
4. Does the strategic analysis of operating income indicate Halsey was successful in implementing its strategy in 2011? Explain.

Purpose	Examples
1. To provide information for economic decisions	To decide whether to add a new airline flight To decide whether to manufacture a component part of a television set or to purchase it from another manufacturer To decide on the selling price for a customized product or service To evaluate the cost of available capacity used to support different products
2. To motivate managers and other employees	To encourage the design of products that are simpler to manufacture or less costly to service To encourage sales representatives to emphasize high-margin products or services
3. To justify costs or compute reimbursement amounts	To cost products at a "fair" price, often required by law and government defense contracts To compute reimbursement for a consulting firm based on a percentage of the cost savings resulting from the implementation of its recommendations
4. To measure income and assets	To cost inventories for reporting to external parties To cost inventories for reporting to tax authorities

For the motivation purpose, costs from more than one but not all business functions are often included to emphasize to decision makers how costs in different functions are related to one another. For example, to estimate product costs, product designers at companies such as Hitachi and Toshiba include costs of production, distribution, and customer service. The goal is to focus designers' attention on how different product-design alternatives affect total costs.

For the cost-reimbursement purpose, a particular contract will often stipulate what costs will be reimbursed. For instance, cost-reimbursement rules for U.S. government contracts explicitly exclude marketing costs.

For the purpose of income and asset measurement for reporting to external parties under GAAP, only manufacturing costs, and in some cases product-design costs, are inventoriable and allocated to products. In the United States, R&D costs in most industries, marketing, distribution, and customer-service costs are period costs that are expensed as they are incurred. Under International Financial Reporting Standards (IFRS), research costs must be expensed as incurred but development costs must be capitalized if a product/process has reached technical feasibility and the firm has the intention and ability to use or sell the future asset.

Decision Point

What are four purposes for allocating costs to cost objects?

Learning Objective 2

Understand criteria to guide cost-allocation decisions

. . . such as identifying factors that cause resources to be consumed

Criteria to Guide Cost-Allocation Decisions

After identifying the purposes of cost allocation, managers and management accountants must decide how to allocate costs.

Exhibit 14-2 presents four criteria used to guide cost-allocation decisions. These decisions affect both the number of indirect-cost pools and the cost-allocation base for each indirect-cost pool. We emphasize the superiority of the cause-and-effect and the benefits-received criteria, especially when the purpose of cost allocation is to provide information for economic decisions or to motivate managers and employees.[2] Cause and effect is the primary criterion used in activity-based costing (ABC) applications. ABC systems use the concept of a cost hierarchy to identify the cost drivers that best demonstrate the cause-and-effect relationship between each activity and the costs in the related cost pool. The cost drivers are then chosen as cost-allocation bases.

Fairness and ability-to-bear are less-frequently-used and more problematic criteria than cause-and-effect or benefits-received. Fairness is a difficult criterion on which to

---

[2] The Federal Accounting Standards Advisory Board (which sets standards for management accounting for U.S. government departments and agencies) recommends the following: "Cost assignments should be performed by: (a) directly tracing costs whenever feasible and economically practicable, (b) assigning costs on a cause-and-effect basis, and (c) allocating costs on a reasonable and consistent basis" (FASAB, 1995, p. 12).

Exhibit 14-2

Criteria for Cost-Allocation Decisions

1. **Cause and Effect.** Using this criterion, managers identify the variables that cause resources to be consumed. For example, managers may use hours of testing as the variable when allocating the costs of a quality-testing area to products. Cost allocations based on the cause-and-effect criterion are likely to be the most credible to operating personnel.

2. **Benefits Received.** Using this criterion, managers identify the beneficiaries of the outputs of the cost object. The costs of the cost object are allocated among the beneficiaries in proportion to the benefits each receives. Consider a corporatewide advertising program that promotes the general image of the corporation rather than any individual product. The costs of this program may be allocated on the basis of division revenues; the higher the revenues, the higher the division's allocated cost of the advertising program. The rationale behind this allocation is that divisions with higher revenues apparently benefited from the advertising more than divisions with lower revenues and, therefore, ought to be allocated more of the advertising costs.

3. **Fairness or Equity.** This criterion is often cited in government contracts when cost allocations are the basis for establishing a price satisfactory to the government and its suppliers. Cost allocation here is viewed as a "reasonable" or "fair" means of establishing a selling price in the minds of the contracting parties. For most allocation decisions, fairness is a matter of judgment rather than an operational criterion.

4. **Ability to Bear**. This criterion advocates allocating costs in proportion to the cost object's ability to bear costs allocated to it. An example is the allocation of corporate executive salaries on the basis of division operating income. The presumption is that the more-profitable divisions have a greater ability to absorb corporate headquarters' costs.

obtain agreement. What one party views as fair, another party may view as unfair.[3] For example, a university may view allocating a share of general administrative costs to government contracts as fair because general administrative costs are incurred to support all activities of the university. The government may view the allocation of such costs as unfair because the general administrative costs would have been incurred by the university regardless of whether the government contract existed. Perhaps the fairest way to resolve this issue is to understand, as well as possible, the cause-and-effect relationship between the government contract activity and general administrative costs. In other words, fairness is more a matter of judgment than an easily implementable choice criterion.

To get a sense of the issues that arise when using the ability-to-bear criterion, consider a product that consumes a large amount of indirect costs and currently sells for a price below its direct costs. This product has no ability to bear any of the indirect costs it uses. However, if the indirect costs it consumes are allocated to other products, these other products are subsidizing the product that is losing money. An integrated airline, for example, might allocate fewer costs to its activities in a highly contested market such as freight transportation, thereby subsidizing it via passenger transport. Some airports cross-subsidize costs associated with serving airline passengers through sales of duty-free goods. Such practices provide a distorted view of relative product and service profitability, and have the potential to invite both regulatory scrutiny as well as competitors attempting to undercut artificially higher-priced services.

Most importantly, companies must weigh the costs and benefits when designing and implementing their cost allocations. Companies incur costs not only in collecting data but also in taking the time to educate managers about cost allocations. In general, the more complex the cost allocations, the higher these education costs.

The costs of designing and implementing complex cost allocations are highly visible. Unfortunately, the benefits from using well-designed cost allocations, such as enabling managers to make better-informed sourcing decisions, pricing decisions, cost-control decisions, and so on, are difficult to measure. Nevertheless, when making cost allocations, managers should consider the benefits as well as the costs. As costs of collecting and processing information decrease, companies are building more-detailed cost allocations.

◄ **Decision Point**

What criteria should managers use to guide cost-allocation decisions?

---

[3] Kaplow and Shavell, in a review of the legal literature, note that "notions of fairness are many and varied. They are analyzed and rationalized by different writers in different way, and they also typically depend upon the circumstances under consideration. Accordingly, it is not possible to identify and consensus view on these notions..." See L. Kaplow and S. Shavell, "Fairness Versus Welfare," *Harvard Law Review* (February 2001); and L. Kaplow and S. Shavell, *Fairness Versus Welfare* (Boston: Harvard University Press, 2002).

Cost Allocation Decisions

In this section, we focus on the first purpose of cost allocation: to provide information for economic decisions, such as pricing, by measuring the full costs of delivering products based on an ABC system.

Chapter 5 described how ABC systems define indirect-cost pools for different activities and use cost drivers as allocation bases to assign costs of indirect-cost pools to products (the second stage of cost allocation). In this section, we focus on the first stage of cost allocation, the assignment of costs to indirect-cost pools.

We will use Consumer Appliances, Inc. (CAI), to illustrate how costs incurred in different parts of a company can be assigned, and then reassigned, for costing products, services, customers, or contracts. CAI has two divisions; each has its own manufacturing plant. The refrigerator division has a plant in Minneapolis, and the clothes dryer division has a plant in St. Paul. CAI's headquarters is in a separate location in Minneapolis. Each division manufactures and sells multiple products that differ in size and complexity.

CAI's management team collects costs at the following levels:

- **Corporate costs**—There are three major categories of corporate costs:
  1. **Treasury costs**—$900,000 of costs incurred for financing the construction of new assembly equipment in the two divisions. The cost of new assembly equipment is $5,200,000 in the refrigerator division and $3,800,000 in the clothes dryer division.
  2. **Human resource management costs**—recruitment and ongoing employee training and development, $1,600,000.
  3. **Corporate administration costs**—executive salaries, rent, and general administration costs, $5,400,000.

- **Division costs**—Each division has two direct-cost categories (direct materials and direct manufacturing labor) and seven indirect-cost pools—one cost pool each for the five activities (design, setup, manufacturing, distribution, and administration), one cost pool to accumulate facility costs, and one cost pool for the allocated corporate treasury costs. Exhibit 14-3 presents data for six of the division indirect-cost pools and cost-allocation bases. (In a later section, we describe how corporate treasury

Exhibit 14-3 Division Indirect-Cost Pools and Cost-Allocation Bases, CAI, for Refrigerator Division (R) and Clothes Dryer Division (CD)

Division Indirect-Cost Pools	Example of Costs		Total Indirect Costs	Cost Hierarchy Category	Cost-Allocation Base	Cause-and-Effect Relationship That Motivates Management's Choice of Allocation Base
Design	Design engineering salaries	(R) (CD)	$6,000,000 4,250,000	Product sustaining	Parts times cubic feet	Complex products (more parts and larger size) require greater design resources.
Setup of machines	Setup labor and equipment cost	(R) (CD)	$3,000,000 2,400,000	Batch level	Setup-hours	Overhead costs of the setup activity increase as setup-hours increase.
Manufacturing operations	Plant and equipment, energy	(R) (CD)	$25,000,000 18,750,000	Output unit level	Machine-hours	Manufacturing-operations overhead costs support machines and, hence, increase with machine usage.
Distribution	Shipping labor and equipment	(R) (CD)	$8,000,000 5,500,000	Output unit level	Cubic feet	Distribution-overhead costs increase with cubic feet of product shipped.
Administration	Division executive salaries	(R) (CD)	$1,000,000 800,000	Facility sustaining	Revenues	Weak relationship between division executive salaries and revenues, but justified by CAI on a benefits-received basis.
Facility	Annual building and space costs	(R) (CD)	$4,500,000 3,500,000	All	Square feet	Facility costs increase with square feet of space.

costs are allocated to each division to create the seventh division indirect-cost pool.) CAI identifies the cost hierarchy category for each cost pool: output-unit level, batch level, product sustaining level, and facility-sustaining level (as described in Chapter 5, p. 149).

Exhibit 14-4 presents an overview diagram of the allocation of corporate and division indirect costs to products of the refrigerator division. Note: The clothes dryer division has its own seven indirect-cost pools used to allocate costs to products. These cost pools and cost-allocation bases parallel the indirect-cost pools and allocation bases for the refrigerator division.

Look first at the middle row of the exhibit, where you see "Division Indirect-Cost Pools," and scan the lower half. It is similar to Exhibit 5-3 (p. 150), which illustrates ABC

Exhibit 14-4 Overview Diagram of Allocation of Corporate and Division Indirect Costs to Products of the Refrigerator Division, CAI

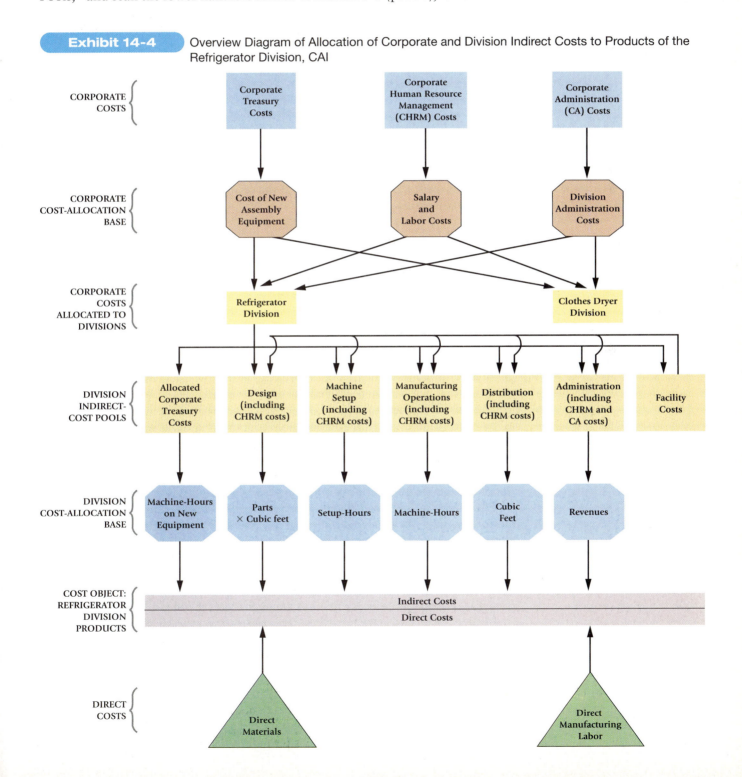

systems using indirect-cost pools and cost drivers for different activities. A major difference in the lower half of Exhibit 14-4 is the cost pool called Facility Costs (far right, middle row), which accumulates all annual costs of buildings and furnishings (such as depreciation) incurred in the division. The arrows in Exhibit 14-4 indicate that CAI allocates facility costs to the five activity-cost pools. Recall from Exhibit 14-3 that CAI uses square feet area required for various activities (design, setup, manufacturing, distribution, and administration) to allocate these facility costs. These activity-cost pools then include the costs of the building and facilities needed to perform the various activities.

The costs in the six remaining indirect-cost pools (that is, after costs of the facility cost pool have been allocated to other cost pools) are allocated to products on the basis of cost drivers described in Exhibit 14-3. These cost drivers are chosen as the cost-allocation bases because there is a cause-and-effect relationship between the cost drivers and the costs in the indirect-cost pool. A cost rate per unit is calculated for each cost-allocation base. Indirect costs are allocated to products on the basis of the total quantity of the cost allocation base for each activity used by the product.

Next focus on the upper half of Exhibit 14-4: how corporate costs are allocated to divisions and then to indirect-cost pools.

Before getting into the details of the allocations, let's first consider some broader choices that CAI faces regarding the allocation of corporate costs.

Allocating Corporate Costs to Divisions and Products

CAI's management team has several choices to make when accumulating and allocating corporate costs to divisions.

1. Which corporate-cost categories should CAI allocate as indirect costs of the divisions? Should CAI allocate all corporate costs or only some of them?
   - Some companies allocate all corporate costs to divisions because corporate costs are incurred to support division activities. Allocating all corporate costs motivates division managers to examine how corporate costs are planned and controlled. Also, companies that want to calculate the full cost of products must allocate all corporate costs to indirect-cost pools of divisions.
   - Other companies do not allocate corporate costs to divisions because these costs are not controllable by division managers.
   - Still other companies allocate only those corporate costs, such as corporate human resources, that are widely perceived as causally related to division activities or that provide explicit benefits to divisions. These companies exclude corporate costs such as corporate donations to charitable foundations because division managers often have no say in making these decisions and because the benefits to the divisions are less evident or too remote. If a company decides not to allocate some or all corporate costs, this results in total company profitability being less than the sum of individual division or product profitabilities.

     For some decision purposes, allocating some but not all corporate costs to divisions may be the preferred alternative. Consider the performance evaluation of division managers. The controllability notion (see p. 200) is frequently used to justify excluding some corporate costs from division reports. For example, salaries of the top management at corporate headquarters are often excluded from responsibility accounting reports of division managers. Although divisions tend to benefit from these corporate costs, division managers argue they have no say in ("are not responsible for") how much of these corporate resources they use or how much they cost. The contrary argument is that full allocation is justified because the divisions receive benefits from all corporate costs.

2. When allocating corporate costs to divisions, should CAI allocate only costs that vary with division activity or should the company assign fixed costs as well? Companies allocate both variable and fixed costs to divisions and then to products, because the resulting product costs are useful for making long-run strategic decisions, such as which products to sell and at what price. To make good long-run decisions, managers

need to know the cost of all resources (whether variable or fixed) required to produce products. Why? Because in the long run, firms can manage the levels of virtually all of their costs; very few costs are truly fixed. Moreover, to survive and prosper in the long run, firms must ensure that the prices charged for products exceed the total resources consumed to produce them, regardless of whether these costs are variable or fixed in the short run.

Companies that allocate corporate costs to divisions must carefully identify relevant costs for specific decisions. Suppose a division is profitable before any corporate costs are allocated but "unprofitable" after allocation of corporate costs. Should the division be closed down? The relevant corporate costs in this case are not the allocated corporate costs but those corporate costs that will be saved if the division is closed. If division profits exceed the relevant corporate costs, the division should not be closed.

3. If CAI allocates corporate costs to divisions, how many cost pools should it use? One extreme is to aggregate all corporate costs into a single cost pool. The other extreme is to have numerous individual corporate cost pools. As discussed in Chapter 5, a major consideration is to construct **homogeneous cost pools** so that all of the costs in the cost pool have the same or a similar cause-and-effect or benefits-received relationship with the cost-allocation base.

For example, when allocating corporate costs to divisions, CAI can combine corporate administration costs and corporate human-resource-management costs into a single cost pool if both cost categories have the same or similar cause-and-effect relationship with the same cost-allocation base (such as the number of employees in each division). If, however, each cost category has a cause-and-effect relationship with a different cost-allocation base (for example, number of employees in each division affects corporate human-resource-management costs, whereas revenues of each division affect corporate administration costs), CAI will prefer to maintain separate cost pools for each of these costs. Determining homogeneous cost pools requires judgment and should be revisited on a regular basis.

The benefit of using a multiple cost-pool system must be balanced against the costs of implementing it. Advances in information-gathering technology make it more likely that multiple cost-pool systems will pass the cost-benefit test.

Implementing Corporate Cost Allocations

After much discussion and debate, CAI's management team chooses to allocate all corporate costs to divisions. We now illustrate the allocation of corporate costs to divisions in CAI's ABC system.

The demands for corporate resources by the refrigerator division and the clothes dryer division depend on the demands that each division's products place on these resources. The top half of Exhibit 14-4 graphically represents the allocations.

1. CAI allocates treasury costs to each division on the basis of the cost of new assembly equipment installed in each division (the cost driver of treasury costs). It allocates the $900,000 of treasury costs as follows (using information from p. 506):

$$\text{Refrigerator Division: } \$900,000 \times \frac{\$5,200,000}{\$5,200,000 + \$3,800,000} = \$520,000$$

$$\text{Clothes Dryer Division: } \$900,000 \times \frac{\$3,800,000}{\$5,200,000 + \$3,800,000} = \$380,000$$

Each division then creates a *separate cost pool* consisting of the allocated corporate treasury costs and reallocates these costs to products on the basis of machine-hours used on the new equipment. Treasury costs are an output unit-level cost because they represent resources used on activities performed on each individual unit of a product.

2. CAI's analysis indicates that the demand for corporate human resource management (CHRM) costs for recruitment and training varies with total salary and labor costs in

each division. Suppose salary and labor costs are $44,000,000 in the refrigerator division and $36,000,000 in the clothes dryer division. Then CHRM costs are allocated to the divisions as follows:

$$\text{Refrigerator Division: } \$1,600,000 \times \frac{\$44,000,000}{\$44,000,000 + \$36,000,000} = \$880,000$$

$$\text{Clothes Dryer Division: } \$1,600,000 \times \frac{\$36,000,000}{\$44,000,000 + \$36,000,000} = \$720,000$$

Each division reallocates the CHRM costs allocated to it to the indirect-cost pools—design, machine setup, manufacturing operations, distribution, and division administration (the allocated-corporate-treasury cost pool and the facility costs pool have no salary and labor costs, so no CHRM costs are allocated to them)—on the basis of total salary and labor costs of each indirect-cost pool. CHRM costs that are added to division indirect-cost pools are then allocated to products using the cost driver for the respective cost pool. Therefore, CHRM costs are product-sustaining costs (for the portion of CHRM costs allocated to the design cost pool), batch-level costs (for the portion of CHRM costs allocated to the machine-setup cost pool), output unit-level costs (for the portions of CHRM costs allocated to the manufacturing-operations and distribution cost pools), and facility-sustaining costs (for the portion of CHRM costs allocated to the division-administration cost pool).

3. CAI allocates corporate administration costs to each division on the basis of division-administration costs (Exhibit 14-3 shows the amounts of division-administration costs) because corporate administration's main role is to support division administration.

$$\text{Refrigerator Division: } \$5,400,000 \times \frac{\$1,000,000}{\$1,000,000 + \$800,000} = \$3,000,000$$

$$\text{Clothes Dryer Division: } \$5,400,000 \times \frac{\$800,000}{\$1,000,000 + \$800,000} = \$2,400,000$$

Each division adds the allocated corporate-administration costs to the division-administration cost pool. The costs in this cost pool are facility-sustaining costs and do not have a cause-and-effect relationship with individual products produced and sold by each division. CAI's policy, however, is to allocate all costs to products so that CAI's division managers become aware of all costs incurred at CAI in their pricing and other decisions. It allocates the division-administration costs (including allocated corporate-administration costs) to products on the basis of product revenues (a benefits-received criterion).

The issues discussed in this section regarding divisions and products apply nearly identically to customers, as we shall show next. *Instructors and students who, at this point, want to explore more-detailed issues in cost allocation rather than focusing on how activity-based costing extends to customer profitability can skip ahead to Chapter 15.*

Customer-Profitability Analysis

Customer-profitability analysis is the reporting and assessment of revenues earned from customers and the costs incurred to earn those revenues. An analysis of customer differences in revenues and costs can provide insight into why differences exist in the operating income earned from different customers. Managers use this information to ensure that customers making large contributions to the operating income of a company receive a high level of attention from the company.

Consider Spring Distribution Company, which sells bottled water. It has two distribution channels: (1) a wholesale distribution channel, in which the wholesaler sells to supermarkets, drugstores, and other stores, and (2) a retail distribution channel for a small number of business customers. We focus mainly on customer-profitability analysis in Spring's retail distribution channel. The list selling price in this channel is $14.40 per case

---

Decision Point

What are two key decisions managers must make when collecting costs in indirect-cost pools?

Learning Objective 4

Discuss why a company's revenues and costs can differ across customers

. . . revenues can differ because of differences in the quantity purchased and the price discounts given, while costs can differ because different customers place different demands on a company's resources

(24 bottles). The full cost to Spring is $12 per case. If every case is sold at list price in this distribution channel, Spring would earn a gross margin of $2.40 per case.

Customer-Revenue Analysis

Consider revenues from 4 of Spring's 10 retail customers in June 2012:

	Home	Insert	Page Layout	Formulas	Data	Review	View
	A		B	C	D	E
1			**CUSTOMER**			
2			A	B	G	J
3	Cases sold		42,000	33,000	2,900	2,500
4	List selling price		$ 14.40	$ 14.40	$ 14.40	$ 14.40
5	Price discount		$ 0.96	$ 0.24	$ 1.20	$ 0.00
6	Invoice price		$ 13.44	$ 14.16	$ 13.20	$ 14.40
7	Revenues (Row 3 × Row 6)		$564,480	$467,280	$38,280	$36,000

Two variables explain revenue differences across these four customers: (1) the number of cases they purchased and (2) the magnitude of price discounting. A **price discount** is the reduction in selling price below list selling price to encourage customers to purchase more. Companies that record only the final invoice price in their information system cannot readily track the magnitude of their price discounting.[4]

Price discounts are a function of multiple factors, including the volume of product purchased (higher-volume customers receive higher discounts) and the desire to sell to a customer who might help promote sales to other customers. Discounts could also be because of poor negotiating by a salesperson or the unwanted effect of an incentive plan based only on revenues. At no time should price discounts run afoul of the law by way of price discrimination, predatory pricing, or collusive pricing (pp. 451–452).

Tracking price discounts by customer and by salesperson helps improve customer profitability. For example, Spring Distribution may decide to strictly enforce its volume-based price discounting policy. It may also require its salespeople to obtain approval for giving large discounts to customers who do not normally qualify for such discounts. In addition, the company could track the future sales of customers who its salespeople have given sizable price discounts to because of their "high growth potential." For example, Spring should track future sales to customer G to see if the $1.20-per-case discount translates into higher future sales.

Customer revenues are one element of customer profitability. The other element that is equally important to understand is the cost of acquiring, serving, and retaining customers. We study this topic next.

Customer-Cost Analysis

We apply to customers the cost hierarchy discussed in the previous section and in Chapter 5 (page 149). A **customer-cost hierarchy** categorizes costs related to customers into different cost pools on the basis of different types of cost drivers, or cost-allocation bases, or different degrees of difficulty in determining cause-and-effect or benefits-received relationships. Spring's ABC system focuses on customers rather than products. It has one direct cost, the cost of bottled water, and multiple indirect-cost pools. Spring identifies five categories of indirect costs in its customer-cost hierarchy:

1. **Customer output unit-level costs**—costs of activities to sell each unit (case) to a customer. An example is product-handling costs of each case sold.

---

[4] Further analysis of customer revenues could distinguish gross revenues from net revenues. This approach highlights differences across customers in sales returns. Additional discussion of ways to analyze revenue differences across customers is in R. S. Kaplan and R. Cooper, *Cost and Effect* (Boston, MA: Harvard Business School Press, 1998, Chapter 10); and G. Cokins, *Activity-Based Cost Management: An Executive's Guide* (New York: John Wiley & Sons, 2001, Chapter 3).

2. **Customer batch-level costs**—costs of activities related to a group of units (cases) sold to a customer. Examples are costs incurred to process orders or to make deliveries.

3. **Customer-sustaining costs**—costs of activities to support individual customers, regardless of the number of units or batches of product delivered to the customer. Examples are costs of visits to customers or costs of displays at customer sites.

4. **Distribution-channel costs**—costs of activities related to a particular distribution channel rather than to each unit of product, each batch of product, or specific customers. An example is the salary of the manager of Spring's retail distribution channel.

5. **Corporate-sustaining costs**—costs of activities that cannot be traced to individual customers or distribution channels. Examples are top-management and general-administration costs.

Note from these descriptions that four of the five levels of Spring's cost hierarchy closely parallel the cost hierarchy described in Chapter 5, except that Spring focuses on *customers* whereas the cost hierarchy in Chapter 5 focused on *products*. Spring has one additional cost hierarchy category, distribution-channel costs, for the costs it incurs to support its wholesale and retail distribution channels.

Customer-Level Costs

Spring is particularly interested in analyzing *customer-level indirect costs*—costs incurred in the first three categories of the customer-cost hierarchy: customer output-unit-level costs, customer batch-level costs, and customer-sustaining costs. Spring wants to work with customers to reduce these costs. It believes customer actions will have less impact on distribution-channel and corporate-sustaining costs. The following table shows five activities (in addition to cost of goods sold) that Spring identifies as resulting in customer-level costs. The table indicates the cost drivers and cost-driver rates for each activity, as well as the cost-hierarchy category for each activity.

	G	H	I	J
1	**Activity Area**	**Cost Driver and Rate**		**Cost-Hierarchy Category**
2	Product handling	$0.50	per case sold	Customer output-unit-level costs
3	Order taking	$ 100	per purchase order	Customer batch-level costs
4	Delivery vehicles	$ 2	per delivery mile traveled	Customer batch-level costs
5	Rush deliveries	$ 300	per expedited delivery	Customer batch-level costs
6	Visits to customers	$ 80	per sales visit	Customer-sustaining costs

Information on the quantity of cost drivers used by each of four customers is as follows:

	A	B	C	D	E
10		**CUSTOMER**			
11		**A**	**B**	**G**	**J**
12	Number of purchase orders	30	25	15	10
13	Number of deliveries	60	30	20	15
14	Miles traveled per delivery	5	12	20	6
15	Number of rush deliveries	1	0	2	0
16	Number of visits to customers	6	5	4	3

Exhibit 14-5 shows a customer-profitability analysis for the four retail customers using information on customer revenues previously presented (p. 511) and customer-level costs from the ABC system.

Spring Distribution can use the information in Exhibit 14-5 to work with customers to reduce the quantity of activities needed to support them. Consider a comparison of customer G and customer A. Customer G purchases only 7% of the cases that customer A purchases (2,900 versus 42,000). Yet, compared with customer A, customer G uses one-half as many purchase orders, two-thirds as many visits to customers, one-third as many deliveries, and twice as many rush deliveries. By implementing charges for each of these services, Spring might be able to induce customer G to make fewer but larger purchase orders, and require fewer customer visits, deliveries, and rush deliveries while looking to increase sales in the future.

Consider Owens and Minor, a distributor of medical supplies to hospitals. It strategically prices each of its services separately. For example, if a hospital wants a rush delivery or special packaging, Owens and Minor charges the hospital an additional price for each particular service. How have Owens and Minor's customers reacted? Hospitals that value these services continue to demand and pay for them while hospitals that do not value these services stop asking for them, saving Owens and Minor some costs. Owens and Minor's pricing strategy influences customer behavior in a way that increases its revenues or decreases its costs.

The ABC system also highlights a second opportunity for cost reduction. Spring can seek to reduce the costs of each activity. For example, improving the efficiency of the ordering process (such as by having customers order electronically) can reduce costs even if customers place the same number of orders.

Exhibit 14-6 shows a monthly operating income statement for Spring Distribution. The customer-level operating income of customers A and B in Exhibit 14-5 are shown in columns 8 and 9 of Exhibit 14-6. The format of Exhibit 14-6 is based on Spring's cost hierarchy. All costs incurred to serve customers are not included in customer-level costs and therefore are not allocated to customers in Exhibit 14-6. For example, distribution-channel costs such as the salary of the manager of the retail distribution channel are not included in customer-level costs and are not allocated to customers. Instead, these costs are identified as costs of the retail channel as a whole, because Spring's management believes that changes in customer behavior will not affect distribution-channel costs. These costs will be affected only by decisions pertaining to the whole channel, such as a decision to discontinue retail distribution. Another reason Spring does not allocate distribution-channel costs to customers is motivation. Spring's managers contend that

| Exhibit 14-5 | Customer-Profitability Analysis for Four Retail Channel Customers of Spring Distribution for June 2012 |

	Home	Insert	Page Layout	Formulas	Data	Review	View		
	A						B	C	D	E
1							CUSTOMER			
2							A	B	G	J
3	Revenues at list price: $14.40 × 42,000; 33,000; 2,900; 2,500						$604,800	$475,200	$41,760	$36,000
4	Price discount: $0.96 x 42,000; $0.24 × 33,000; $1.20 × 2,900; $0 × 2,500						40,320	7,920	3,480	0
5	Revenues (at actual price)						564,480	467,280	38,280	36,000
6	Cost of goods sold: $12 × 42,000; 33,000; 2,900; 2,500						504,000	396,000	34,800	30,000
7	Gross margin						60,480	71,280	3,480	6,000
8	Customer-level operating costs									
9	Product handling $0.50 × 42,000; 33,000; 2,900; 2,500						21,000	16,500	1,450	1,250
10	Order taking $100 × 30; 25; 15; 10						3,000	2,500	1,500	1,000
11	Delivery vehicles $2 × (5 × 60); (12 × 30); (20 × 20); (6 × 15)						600	720	800	180
12	Rush deliveries $300 × 1; 0; 2; 0						300	0	600	0
13	Visits to customers $80 × 6; 5; 4; 3						480	400	320	240
14	Total customer-level operating costs						25,380	20,120	4,670	2,670
15	Customer-level operating income						$ 35,100	$ 51,160	$ (1,190)	$ 3,330

Exhibit 14-6   Income Statement of Spring Distribution for June 2012

	Home	Insert	Page Layout	Formulas	Data	Review	View						

	A	B	C	D	E	F G H	I	J	K	L M
1				CUSTOMER DISTRIBUTION CHANNELS						
2			Wholesale Customers				Retail Customers			
3		Total	Total	A1	A2	A3 ☐	Total	A^a	B^a	C ☐
4		(1) = (2) + (7)	(2)	(3)	(4)	(5) (6)	(7)	(8)	(9)	(10) (11)
5	Revenues (at actual prices)	$12,138,120	$10,107,720	$1,946,000	$1,476,000	☐ ☐	$2,030,400	$564,480	$467,280	☐ ☐
6	Customer-level costs	11,633,760	9,737,280	1,868,000	1,416,000	☐ ☐	1,896,480	529,380^b	416,120^b	☐ ☐
7	Customer-level operating income	504,360	370,440	$ 78,000	$ 60,000	☐ ☐	133,920	$ 35,100	$ 51,160	☐ ☐
8	Distribution-channel costs	160,500	102,500				58,000			
9	Distribution-channel-level operating income	343,860	$ 267,940				$ 75,920			
10	Corporate-sustaining costs	263,000								
11	Operating income	$ 80,860								
12										
13	^{a}Full details are presented in Exhibit 14-5.									
14	^{b}Cost of goods sold + Total customer-level operating costs from Exhibit 14-5.									

salespersons responsible for managing individual customer accounts would lose motivation if their bonuses were affected by the allocation to customers of distribution-channel costs over which they had minimal influence.

Next, consider corporate-sustaining costs such as top-management and general-administration costs. Spring's managers have concluded that there is no cause-and-effect or benefits-received relationship between any cost-allocation base and corporate-sustaining costs. Consequently, allocation of corporate-sustaining costs serves no useful purpose in decision making, performance evaluation, or motivation. For example, suppose Spring allocated the $263,000 of corporate-sustaining costs to its distribution channels: $173,000 to the wholesale channel and $90,000 to the retail channel. Using information from Exhibit 14-6, the retail channel would then show a loss of $14,080 ($75,920 – $90,000).

If this same situation persisted in subsequent months, should Spring shut down the retail distribution channel? No, because if retail distribution were discontinued, corporate-sustaining costs would be unaffected. Allocating corporate-sustaining costs to distribution channels could give the misleading impression that the potential cost savings from discontinuing a distribution channel would be greater than the likely amount.

Some managers and management accountants advocate fully allocating all costs to customers and distribution channels so that (1) the sum of operating incomes of all customers in a distribution channel (segment) equals the operating income of the distribution channel and (2) the sum of the distribution-channel operating incomes equals company-wide operating income. These managers and management accountants argue that customers and products must eventually be profitable on a full-cost basis. In the previous example, CAI allocated all corporate and division-level costs to its refrigerator and clothes dryer products (see pp. 509–510). For some decisions, such as pricing, allocating all costs ensures that long-run prices are set at a level to cover the cost of all resources used to produce and sell products. Nevertheless, the value of the hierarchical format in Exhibit 14-6 is that it distinguishes among various degrees of objectivity when allocating costs, and it dovetails with the different levels at which decisions are made and performance is evaluated. The issue of when and what costs to allocate is another example of the "different costs for different purposes" theme emphasized throughout this book.

> **Decision Point** ▶
>
> How can a company's revenues and costs differ across customers?

> **Learning Objective 5**
>
> Identify the importance of customer-profitability profiles
>
> . . . highlight that a small percentage of customers contributes a large percentage of operating income.

Customer-Profitability Profiles

Customer-profitability profiles provide a useful tool for managers. Exhibit 14-7 ranks Spring's 10 retail customers based on customer-level operating income. (Four of these customers are analyzed in Exhibit 14-5.)

Column 4, computed by adding the individual amounts in column 1, shows the cumulative customer-level operating income. For example, customer C has a cumulative

Exhibit 14-7 Customer-Profitability Analysis for Retail Channel Customers: Spring Distribution, June 2012

	Home	Insert	Page Layout	Formulas	Data	Review	View
	A	B	C	D	E	F

	A	B	C	D	E	F
1	**Customers Ranked on Customer-Level Operating Income**					
2						**Cumulative**
3						**Customer-Level**
4						**Operating Income**
5				**Customer-Level**	**Cumulative**	**as a % of Total**
6	**Retail**	**Customer-Level**	**Customer**	**Operating Income**	**Customer-Level**	**Customer-Level**
7	**Customer**	**Operating Income**	**Revenue**	**Divided by Revenue**	**Operating Income**	**Operating Income**
8	**Code**	**(1)**	**(2)**	**(3) = (1) ÷ (2)**	**(4)**	**(5) = (4) ÷ $133,920**
9	B	$ 51,160	$ 467,280	10.9%	$ 51,160	38%
10	A	35,100	564,480	6.2%	86,260	64%
11	C	27,070	295,640	9.2%	113,330	85%
12	D	20,580	277,000	7.4%	133,910	100%
13	F	12,504	143,500	8.7%	146,414	109%
14	J	3,330	41,000	8.1%	149,744	112%
15	E	176	123,000	0.1%	149,920	112%
16	G	−1,190	38,280	−3.1%	148,730	111%
17	H	−5,690	38,220	−14.9%	143,040	107%
18	I	−9,120	42,000	−21.7%	133,920	100%
19		$133,920	$2,030,400			
20						

income of $113,330 in column 4. This $113,330 is the sum of $51,160 for customer B, $35,100 for customer A, and $27,070 for customer C.

Column 5 shows what percentage the $113,330 *cumulative* total for customers B, A, and C is of the total customer-level operating income of $133,920 earned in the retail distribution channel from all 10 customers. The three most profitable customers contribute 85% of total customer-level operating income. These customers deserve the highest service and priority. Companies try to keep their best customers happy in a number of ways: special phone numbers and upgrade privileges for elite-level frequent flyers, free usage of luxury hotel suites and big credit limits for high-rollers at casinos, and so on. In many companies, it is common for a small number of customers to contribute a high percentage of operating income. Microsoft uses the phrase "not all revenue dollars are endowed equally in profitability" to stress this point.

Column 3 shows the profitability per dollar of revenue by customer. This measure of customer profitability indicates that, although customer A contributes the second-highest operating income, the profitability per dollar of revenue is lower because of high price discounts. Spring's goal is to increase profit margins for customer A by decreasing the price discounts or saving customer-level costs while maintaining or increasing sales. Customer J has a higher profit margin but has lower total sales. Spring's challenge with customer J is to maintain margins while increasing sales.

Presenting Profitability Analysis

There are two common ways of presenting the results of customer-profitability analysis. Managers often find the bar chart presentation in Exhibit 14-8, Panel A, to be an intuitive way to visualize customer profitability. The highly profitable customers clearly stand out. Moreover, the number of "unprofitable" customers and the magnitude of their losses are apparent. A popular alternative way to express customer profitability is

Exhibit 14-8

Panel A: Bar Chart of Customer-Level Operating Income for Spring Distribution's Retail Channel Customers in June 2012

Panel B: The Whale Curve of Cumulative Profitability for Spring Distribution's Retail Channel Customers in June 2012

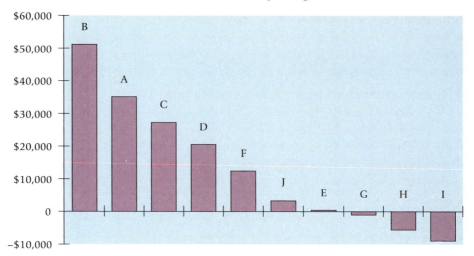

Customer-Level Operating Income

Retail Channel Customers

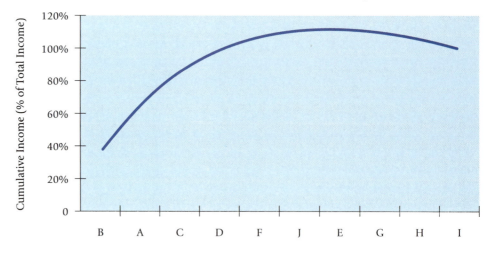

The Whale Curve of Cumulative Profitability for Spring Distribution's Retail Channel Customers in June 2012

by plotting the contents of column 5 of Exhibit 14-7. This chart is called the **whale curve** since it is backward bending at the point where customers start to become unprofitable, and thus resembles a humpback whale.[5]

Spring's managers must explore ways to make unprofitable customers profitable. Exhibits 14-5 to 14-8 emphasize short-run customer profitability. Other factors managers should consider in deciding how to allocate resources among customers include the following:

- **Likelihood of customer retention.** The more likely a customer will continue to do business with a company, the more valuable the customer. Customers differ in their loyalty and their willingness to frequently "shop their business."

- **Potential for sales growth.** The higher the likely growth of the customer's industry and the customer's sales, the more valuable the customer. Customers to whom a company can cross-sell other products are more desirable.

- **Long-run customer profitability.** This factor will be influenced by the first two factors specified and the cost of customer-support staff and special services required to retain customer accounts.

---

[5] In practice, the curve of the chart can be quite steep. The whale curve for cumulative profitability usually reveals that the most profitable 20% of customers generate between 150% and 300% of total profits, the middle 70% of customers break even, and the least profitable 10% of customers lose from 50% to 200% of total profits (see Robert Kaplan and V.G. Narayanan, Measuring and Managing Customer Profitability, Journal of Cost Management, Sept/Oct 2001, pp. 1–11).

- **Increases in overall demand from having well-known customers.** Customers with established reputations help generate sales from other customers through product endorsements.
- **Ability to learn from customers.** Customers who provide ideas about new products or ways to improve existing products are especially valuable.

Managers should be cautious when deciding to discontinue customers. In Exhibit 14-7, the current unprofitability of customer G, for example, may provide misleading signals about G's profitability in the long-run. Moreover, as in any ABC-based system, the costs assigned to customer G are not all variable. In the short run, it may well have been efficient for Spring to use its spare capacity to serve G on a contribution-margin basis. Discontinuing customer G will not eliminate all the costs assigned to that customer, and will leave the firm worse off than before.

Of course, particular customers might be chronically unprofitable and hold limited future prospects. Or they might fall outside a firm's target market or require unsustainably high levels of service relative to the firm's strategies and capabilities. In such cases, organizations are becoming increasingly aggressive in severing customer relationships. For example, ING Direct, the largest direct lender and fastest growing financial services organization in the United States, asks 10,000 "high maintenance" customers to close their accounts each month.[6] The Concepts in Action feature on page 518 provides an example of a company that is struggling with the question of how to manage its resources and profitability without affecting the satisfaction of its customers.

Using the Five-Step Decision-Making Process to Manage Customer Profitability

The different types of customer analyses that we have just covered provide companies with key information to guide the allocation of resources across customers. Use the five-step decision-making process, introduced in Chapter 1, to think about how managers use these analyses to make customer-management decisions.

1. *Identify the problem and uncertainties.* The problem is how to manage and allocate resources across customers.

2. *Obtain information.* Managers identify past revenues generated by each customer and customer-level costs incurred in the past to support each customer.

3. *Make predictions about the future.* Managers estimate the revenues they expect from each customer and the customer-level costs they will incur in the future. In making these predictions, managers consider the effects that future price discounts will have on revenues, the effect that pricing for different services (such as rush deliveries) will have on the demand for these services by customers, and ways to reduce the cost of providing services. For example, Deluxe, Corp., a leading check printer, initiated process reductions to rein in its cost to serve customers by opening an electronic channel to shift customers from paper to automated ordering.

4. *Make decisions by choosing among alternatives.* Managers use the customer-profitability profiles to identify the small set of customers who deserve the highest service and priority. They also identify ways to make less-profitable customers (such as Spring's customer G) more profitable. Banks, for example, often impose minimum balance requirements on customers. Distribution firms may require minimum order quantities or levy a surcharge for smaller or customized orders. In making resource-allocation decisions, managers also consider long-term effects, such as the potential for future sales growth and the opportunity to leverage a particular customer account to make sales to other customers.

5. *Implement the decision, evaluate performance, and learn.* After the decision is implemented, managers compare actual results to predicted outcomes to evaluate the decision they made, its implementation, and ways in which they might improve profitability.

Decision Point

How do customer-profitability profiles help managers?

---

[6] See, for example, "The New Math of Customer Relationships" at http://hbswk.hbs.edu/item/5884.html.

Concepts in Action

iPhone "Apps" Challenge Customer Profitability at AT&T

AT&T is the second largest wireless provider in the United States. The company provides mobile telephone and data access to more than 85 million individuals, businesses, and government agencies. AT&T uses cost accounting to price its various wireless service plans and calculate overall profitability for its customers, including more than 10 million owners of Apple's iPhone. AT&T is the exclusive wireless provider for the popular iPhone smart phone.

Traditionally, the cost of serving different wireless customers varied. Most business customers, for example, required reliable service during business hours and large amounts of data bandwidth for e-mail and Internet access. In contrast, many individuals use their wireless devices extensively on nights and weekends and use features such as text messages and music ringtones. Accordingly, wireless providers considered the costs for these services when developing pricing plans and calculating customer profitability. Therefore, individuals using their phone service sparingly could select a less-expensive plan with fewer minutes, for use mostly at night and on weekends, whereas more-demanding individuals and lucrative business customers chose plans with more telephone minutes, large amounts of wireless data bandwidth, and guaranteed reliability . . . for a higher price.

When AT&T began selling the iPhone in mid-2007, cost accountants projected the profitability for its new customers, and new plans were designed accordingly. Similar to traditional wireless plans, iPhone buyers were offered subscription options with different amounts of telephone minutes at different price points. For example, 450 telephone minutes cost $59.99, while 1,350 minutes were $99.99. However, to showcase the iPhone's wireless and Internet capabilities, Apple insisted that AT&T offer only one data package, an unlimited plan.

While the unlimited data package proved initially lucrative, technology developments added significant costs to AT&T. When Apple introduced the iPhone 3G in 2008, the third-generation data capabilities encouraged software developers to build new programs for the iPhone platform. Within two years, nearly 140,000 applications, ranging from Pandora's mobile music player to Mint's on-the-go budgeting program, were downloaded more than 3 billion times by iPhone users. Each of the applications, however, uses a lot of data bandwidth.

Recall that AT&T does not charge iPhone subscribers for marginal bandwidth use. As a result, subscribers who download and use many iPhone applications quickly became unprofitable for the company. With each 100MB of bandwidth costing AT&T $1, the company is currently considering cost-reducing options, such as limiting data access and changing its all-you-can-eat data subscription plan, but it is very concerned about alienating its customers.

iPhone application usage has also created a bigger cost problem for the company. With data bandwidth on the AT&T wireless network increasing by 5,000% between 2006 and 2009, the company's network is showing signs of strain and poor performance. To act on these concerns, AT&T will spend $18–19 billion making improvements to its data network in 2010, and more in the years to come. As a result, AT&T will need to balance customer satisfaction with ensuring that its iPhone customers remain profitable for the carrier.

Sources: AT&T Inc. and Apple Inc. 2007. AT&T and Apple announce simple, affordable service plans for iPhone. AT&T Inc. and Apple Inc. Press Release, June 26. http://www.apple.com/pr/library/2007/06/26plans.html; Fazard, Roben. 2010. AT&T's iPhone mess. *BusinessWeek*, February 3; Sheth, Niraj. 2010. AT&T, boosted and stressed by iPhone, lays out network plans. *Wall Street Journal*, January 29; Sheth, Niraj. 2010. For wireless carriers, iPad signals further loss of clout. *Wall Street Journal*, January 28.

Sales Variances

The customer-profitability analysis in the previous section focused on the actual profitability of individual customers within a distribution channel (retail, for example) and their effect on Spring Distribution's profitability for June 2012. At a more-strategic level, however, recall that Spring operates in two different markets: wholesale and retail. The operating margins in the retail market are much higher than the operating margins in the wholesale market. In June 2012, Spring had budgeted to sell 80% of its cases to wholesalers and 20% to retailers. It sold more cases in total than it had budgeted, but its actual sales mix (in cases) was 84% to wholesalers and 16% to retailers. Regardless of the profitability of sales to individual customers within each of the retail and wholesale channels, Spring's actual operating income, relative to the master budget, is likely to be positively affected by the higher sales of cases and negatively affected by the shift in mix away from the more-profitable retail customers. Sales-quantity and sales-mix variances can identify the effect of each of these factors on Spring's profitability. Companies such as Cisco, GE, and Hewlett-Packard perform similar analyses because they sell their products through multiple distribution channels like the Internet, over the telephone, and retail stores.

Spring classifies all customer-level costs as variable costs and distribution-channel and corporate-sustaining costs as fixed costs. To simplify the sales-variances analysis and calculations, we assume that all of the variable costs are variable with respect to units (cases) sold. (This means that average batch sizes remain the same as the total cases sold vary.) Without this assumption, the analysis would become more complex and would have to be done using the ABC-variance analysis approach described in Chapter 8, page 281–285. The basic insights, however, would not change.

Budgeted and actual operating data for June 2012 are as follows:

Budget Data for June 2012

	Selling Price (1)	Variable Cost per Unit (2)	Contribution Margin per Unit (3) = (1) − (2)	Sales Volume in Units (4)	Sales Mix (Based on Units) (5)	Contribution Margin (6) = (3) × (4)
Wholesale channel	$13.37	$12.88	$0.49	712,000	80%[a]	$348,880
Retail channel	14.10	13.12	0.98	178,000	20%	174,440
Total				890,000	100%	$523,320

[a] Percentage of unit sales to wholesale channel = 712,000 units ÷ 890,000 total unit = 80%.

Actual Results for June 2012

	Selling Price (1)	Variable Cost per Unit (2)	Contribution Margin per Unit (3) = (1) − (2)	Sales Volume in Units (4)	Sales Mix (Based on Units) (5)	Contribution Margin (6) = (3) × (4)
Wholesale channel	$13.37	$12.88	$0.49	756,000	84%[a]	$370,440
Retail channel	14.10	13.17	0.93	144,000	16%	133,920
Total				900,000	100%	$504,360

[a] Percentage of unit sales to wholesale channel = 756,000 units ÷ 900,000 total unit = 84%.

The budgeted and actual fixed distribution-channel costs and corporate-sustaining costs are $160,500 and $263,000, respectively (see Exhibit 14-6, p. 514).

Recall that the levels of detail introduced in Chapter 7 (pages 230–233) included the static-budget variance (level 1), the flexible-budget variance (level 2), and the sales-volume variance (level 2). The sales-quantity and sales-mix variances are level 3 variances that subdivide the sales-volume variance.[7]

[7] The presentation of the variances in this chapter and the appendix draws on teaching notes prepared by J. K. Harris.

Static-Budget Variance

The *static-budget variance* is the difference between an actual result and the corresponding budgeted amount in the static budget. Our analysis focuses on the difference between actual and budgeted contribution margins (column 6 in the preceding tables). The total static-budget variance is $18,960 U (actual contribution margin of $504,360 – budgeted contribution margin of $523,320). Exhibit 14-9 (columns 1 and 3) uses the columnar format introduced in Chapter 7 to show detailed calculations of the static-budget variance. Managers can gain more insight about the static-budget variance by subdividing it into the flexible-budget variance and the sales-volume variance.

Flexible-Budget Variance and Sales-Volume Variance

The *flexible-budget variance* is the difference between an actual result and the corresponding flexible-budget amount based on actual output level in the budget period. The flexible budget contribution margin is equal to budgeted contribution margin per unit times actual units sold of each product. Exhibit 14-9, column 2, shows the flexible-budget calculations. The flexible budget measures the contribution margin that Spring would have budgeted for the actual quantities of cases sold. The flexible-budget variance is the difference between columns 1 and 2 in Exhibit 14-9. The only difference between columns 1 and 2 is that actual units sold of each product is multiplied by actual contribution margin per unit in column 1 and budgeted contribution margin per unit in column 2. The $7,200 U flexible-budget variance arises because actual contribution margin on retail sales of $0.93 per case is lower than the budgeted amount of $0.98 per case. Spring's management is aware that this difference of $0.05 per case resulted from excessive price discounts, and it has put in place action plans to reduce discounts in the future.

The *sales-volume variance* is the difference between a flexible-budget amount and the corresponding static-budget amount. In Exhibit 14-9, the sales-volume variance shows the effect on budgeted contribution margin of the difference between actual quantity of units sold and budgeted quantity of units sold. The sales-volume variance of $11,760 U is the difference between columns 2 and 3 in Exhibit 14-9. In this case, it is unfavorable overall because while wholesale unit sales were higher than budgeted, retail sales, which are expected to be twice as profitable on a per unit basis, were below budget. Spring's

Exhibit 14-9   Flexible-Budget and Sales-Volume Variance Analysis of Spring Distribution for June 2012

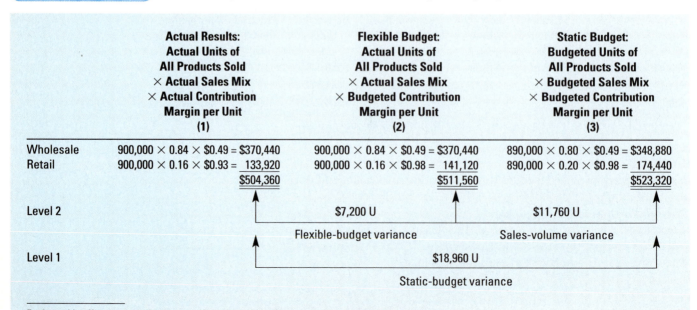

F = favorable effect on operating income; U = unfavorable effect on operating income.

managers can gain substantial insight into the sales-volume variance by subdividing it into the sales-mix variance and the sales-quantity variance.

Sales-Mix Variance

The **sales-mix variance** is the difference between (1) budgeted contribution margin for the *actual sales mix* and (2) budgeted contribution margin for the *budgeted sales mix*. The formula and computations (using data from p. 519) are as follows:

	Actual Units of All Products Sold	×	(Actual Sales - Mix Percentage − Budgeted Sales - Mix Percentage)	×	Budgeted Contribution Margin per Unit	=	Sales-Mix Variance
Wholesale	900,000 units	×	(0.84 − 0.80)	×	$0.49 per unit	=	$17,640 F
Retail	900,000 units	×	(0.16 − 0.20)	×	$0.98 per unit	=	35,280 U
Total sales-mix variance							$17,640 U

A favorable sales-mix variance arises for the wholesale channel because the 84% actual sales-mix percentage exceeds the 80% budgeted sales-mix percentage. In contrast, the retail channel has an unfavorable variance because the 16% actual sales-mix percentage is less than the 20% budgeted sales-mix percentage. The sales-mix variance is unfavorable because actual sales mix shifted toward the less-profitable wholesale channel relative to budgeted sales mix.

The concept underlying the sales-mix variance is best explained in terms of composite units. A **composite unit** is a hypothetical unit with weights based on the mix of individual units. Given the budgeted sales for June 2012, the composite unit consists of 0.80 units of sales to the wholesale channel and 0.20 units of sales to the retail channel. Therefore, the budgeted contribution margin per composite unit for the budgeted sales mix is as follows:

$$(0.80) \times (\$0.49) + (0.20) \times (\$0.98) = \$0.5880.[8]$$

Similarly, for the actual sales mix, the composite unit consists of 0.84 units of sales to the wholesale channel and 0.16 units of sales to the retail channel. The budgeted contribution margin per composite unit for the actual sales mix is therefore as follows:

$$(0.84) \times (\$0.49) + (0.16) \times (\$0.98) = \$0.5684.$$

The impact of the shift in sales mix is now evident. Spring obtains a lower budgeted contribution margin per composite unit of $0.0196 ($0.5880 − $0.5684). For the 900,000 units actually sold, this decrease translates to a $17,640 U sales-mix variance ($0.0196 per unit × 900,000 units).

Managers should probe why the $17,640 U sales-mix variance occurred in June 2012. Is the shift in sales mix because, as the analysis in the previous section showed, profitable retail customers proved to be more difficult to find? Is it because of a competitor in the retail channel providing better service at a lower price? Or is it because the initial sales-volume estimates were made without adequate analysis of the potential market?

Exhibit 14-10 uses the columnar format to calculate the sales-mix variance and the sales-quantity variances.

Sales-Quantity Variance

The **sales-quantity variance** is the difference between (1) budgeted contribution margin based on *actual units sold of all products* at the budgeted mix and (2) contribution margin in the static budget (which is based on *budgeted units of all products to*

---

[8] Budgeted contribution margin per composite unit can be computed in another way by dividing total budgeted contribution margin of $523,320 by total budgeted units of 890,000 (p. 519): $523,320 ÷ 890,000 units = $0.5880 per unit.

| Exhibit 14-10 | Sales-Mix and Sales-Quantity Variance Analysis of Spring Distribution for June 2012 |

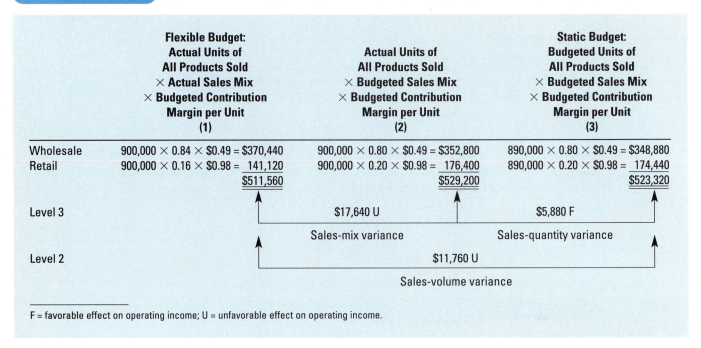

be sold at budgeted mix). The formula and computations (using data from p. 519) are as follows:

			×	Budgeted Sales-Mix Percentages	×	Budgeted Contribution Margin per Unit	=	Sales-Quantity Variance
Wholesale	(900,000 units – 890,000 units)		×	0.80	×	$0.49 per unit	=	$3,920 F
Retail	(900,000 units – 890,000 units)		×	0.20	×	$0.98 per unit	=	1,960 F
Total sales-quantity variance								$5,880 F

This variance is favorable when actual units of all products sold exceed budgeted units of all products sold. Spring sold 10,000 more cases than were budgeted, resulting in a $5,880 F sales-quantity variance (also equal to budgeted contribution margin per composite unit for the budgeted sales mix times additional cases sold, $0.5880 × 10,000). Managers would want to probe the reasons for the increase in sales. Did higher sales come as a result of a competitor's distribution problems? Better customer service? Or growth in the overall market? Additional insight into the causes of the sales-quantity variance can be gained by analyzing changes in Spring's share of the total industry market and in the size of that market. The sales-quantity variance can be decomposed into market-share and market-size variances, as illustrated in the appendix to Chapter 7.[9]

Exhibit 14-11 presents an overview of the sales-mix and sales-quantity variances for the Spring example. The sales-mix variance and sales-quantity variance can also be calculated in a multiproduct company, in which each individual product has a different contribution margin per unit. The Problem for Self-Study takes you through such a setting, and also demonstrates the link between these sales variances and the market-share and market-size variances studied earlier. The appendix to this chapter describes mix and quantity variances for production inputs.

Decision Point

What are the two components of the sales-volume variance?

---

[9] Recall that the market-share and market-size variances in the appendix to Chapter 7 (pp. 248–249) were computed for Webb Company, which sold a single product (jackets) using a single distribution channel. The calculation of these variances is virtually unaffected when multiple distribution channels exist, as in the Spring example. The only change required is to replace the phrase "Budgeted Contribution Margin per Unit" in the market-share and market-size variance formulas with "Budgeted Contribution Margin per Composite Unit for Budgeted Sales Mix" (which equals $0.5880 in the Spring example). For additional details and an illustration, see the Problem for Self-Study for this chapter.

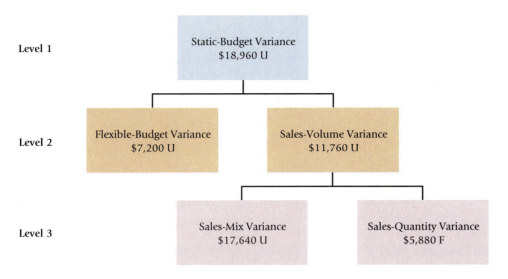

F = favorable effect on operating income; U = unfavorable effect on operating income

Problem for Self-Study

The Payne Company manufactures two types of vinyl flooring. Budgeted and actual operating data for 2012 are as follows:

	Static Budget			Actual Results		
	Commercial	**Residential**	**Total**	**Commercial**	**Residential**	**Total**
Unit sales in rolls	20,000	60,000	80,000	25,200	58,800	84,000
Contribution margin	$10,000,000	$24,000,000	$34,000,000	$11,970,000	$24,696,000	$36,666,000

In late 2011, a marketing research firm estimated industry volume for commercial and residential vinyl flooring for 2012 at 800,000 rolls. Actual industry volume for 2012 was 700,000 rolls.

1. Compute the sales-mix variance and the sales-quantity variance by type of vinyl flooring and in total. (Compute all variances in terms of contribution margins.)
2. Compute the market-share variance and the market-size variance (see Chapter 7, pp. 248–249).
3. What insights do the variances calculated in requirements 1 and 2 provide about Payne Company's performance in 2012?

Required

Solution

1. Actual sales-mix percentage:

$$\text{Commercial} = 25{,}200 \div 84{,}000 = 0.30, \text{ or } 30\%$$

$$\text{Residential} = 58{,}800 \div 84{,}000 = 0.70, \text{ or } 70\%$$

Budgeted sales-mix percentage:

$$\text{Commercial} = 20{,}000 \div 80{,}000 = 0.25, \text{ or } 25\%$$

$$\text{Residential} = 60{,}000 \div 80{,}000 = 0.75, \text{ or } 75\%$$

Budgeted contribution margin per unit:

$$\text{Commercial} = \$10{,}000{,}000 \div 20{,}000 \text{ units} = \$500 \text{ per unit}$$

$$\text{Residential} = \$24{,}000{,}000 \div 60{,}000 \text{ units} = \$400 \text{ per unit}$$

	Actual Units of All Products Sold	×	$\left(\begin{array}{c}\text{Actual Sales-Mix Percentage}\end{array} - \begin{array}{c}\text{Budgeted Sales-Mix Percentage}\end{array}\right)$	×	Budgeted Contribution Margin per Unit	=	Sales-Mix Variance
Commercial	84,000 units	×	(0.30 − 0.25)	×	$500 per unit	=	$2,100,000 F
Residential	84,000 units	×	(0.70 − 0.75)	×	$400 per unit	=	1,680,000 U
Total sales-mix variance							$ 420,000 F

	$\left(\begin{array}{c}\text{Actual Units of All Products Sold}\end{array} - \begin{array}{c}\text{Budgeted Units of All Products Sold}\end{array}\right)$	×	Budgeted Sales-Mix Percentage	×	Budgeted Contribution Margin per Unit	=	Sales-Quantity Variance
Commercial	(84,000 units − 80,000 units)	×	0.25	×	$500 per unit	=	$ 500,000 F
Residential	(84,000 units − 80,000 units)	×	0.75	×	$400 per unit	=	1,200,000 F
Total sales-quantity variance							$1,700,000 F

2. Actual market share = 84,000 ÷ 700,000 = 0.12, or 12%
    Budgeted market share = 80,000 ÷ 800,000 units = 0.10, or 10%

$$\begin{array}{l}\text{Budgeted contribution margin}\\ \quad\text{per composite unit} \\ \quad\text{of budgeted mix}\end{array} = \$34,000,000 \div 80,000 \text{ units} = \$425 \text{ per unit}$$

Budgeted contribution margin per composite unit of budgeted mix can also be calculated as follows:

Commercial: $500 per unit × 0.25	=	$125
Residential: $400 per unit × 0.75	=	300
Budgeted contribution margin per composite unit	=	$425

$$\begin{array}{l}\text{Market-share}\\ \text{variance}\end{array} = \begin{array}{c}\text{Actual}\\ \text{market size}\\ \text{in units}\end{array} \times \left(\begin{array}{c}\text{Actual}\\ \text{market}\\ \text{share}\end{array} - \begin{array}{c}\text{Budgeted}\\ \text{market}\\ \text{share}\end{array}\right) \times \begin{array}{c}\text{Budgeted}\\ \text{contribution margin}\\ \text{per composite unit}\\ \text{for budgeted mix}\end{array}$$

$$= 700,000 \text{ units} \times (0.12 - 0.10) \times \$425 \text{ per unit}$$

$$= \$5,950,000 \text{ F}$$

$$\begin{array}{l}\text{Market-size}\\ \text{variance}\end{array} = \left(\begin{array}{c}\text{Actual}\\ \text{market size}\\ \text{in units}\end{array} - \begin{array}{c}\text{Budgeted}\\ \text{market size}\\ \text{in units}\end{array}\right) \times \begin{array}{c}\text{Budgeted}\\ \text{market}\\ \text{share}\end{array} \times \begin{array}{c}\text{Budgeted}\\ \text{contribution margin}\\ \text{per composite unit}\\ \text{for budgeted mix}\end{array}$$

$$= (700,000 \text{ units} - 800,000 \text{ units}) \times 0.10 \times \$425 \text{ per unit}$$

$$= \$4,250,000 \text{ U}$$

Note that the algebraic sum of the market-share variance and the market-size variance is equal to the sales-quantity variance: $5,950,000 F + $4,250,000 U = $1,700,000 F.

3. Both the total sales-mix variance and the total sales-quantity variance are favorable. The favorable sales-mix variance occurred because the actual mix comprised more of the higher-margin commercial vinyl flooring. The favorable total sales-quantity variance occurred because the actual total quantity of rolls sold exceeded the budgeted amount.

    The company's large favorable market-share variance is due to a 12% actual market share compared with a 10% budgeted market share. The market-size variance is unfavorable because the actual market size was 100,000 rolls less than the budgeted market size. Payne's performance in 2012 appears to be very good. Although overall market size declined, the company sold more units than budgeted and gained market share.

Decision Points

The following question-and-answer format summarizes the chapter's learning objectives. Each decision presents a key question related to a learning objective. The guidelines are the answer to that question.

Decision	Guidelines
1. What are four purposes for allocating costs to cost objects?	Four purposes of cost allocation are (a) to provide information for economic decisions, (b) to motivate managers and other employees, (c) to justify costs or compute reimbursement amounts, and (d) to measure income and assets for reporting to external parties. Different cost allocations are appropriate for different purposes.
2. What criteria should managers use to guide cost-allocation decisions?	Managers should use the cause-and-effect and the benefits-received criteria to guide most cost-allocation decisions. Other criteria are fairness or equity and ability to bear.
3. What are two key decisions managers must make when collecting costs in indirect-cost pools?	Two key decisions related to indirect-cost pools are the number of indirect-cost pools to form and the individual cost items to be included in each cost pool to make homogeneous cost pools.
4. How can a company's revenues and costs differ across customers?	Revenues can differ because of differences in the quantity purchased and price discounts given from the list selling price. Costs can differ as different customers place different demands on a company's resources in terms of processing purchase orders, making deliveries, and customer support.
5. How do customer-profitability profiles help managers?	Companies should be aware of and devote sufficient resources to maintaining and expanding relationships with customers who contribute significantly to profitability. Customer-profitability profiles often highlight that a small percentage of customers contributes a large percentage of operating income.
6. What are the two components of the sales-volume variance?	The two components of sales-volume variance are (a) the difference between actual sales mix and budgeted sales mix (the sales-mix variance) and (b) the difference between actual unit sales and budgeted unit sales (the sales-quantity variance).

Appendix

Mix and Yield Variances for Substitutable Inputs

The framework for calculating the sales-mix variance and the sales-quantity variance can also be used to analyze production-input variances in cases in which managers have some leeway in combining and substituting inputs. For example, Del Monte can combine material inputs (such as pineapples, cherries, and grapes) in varying proportions for its cans of fruit cocktail. Within limits, these individual fruits are *substitutable inputs* in making the fruit cocktail.

We illustrate how the efficiency variance discussed in Chapter 7 (pp. 236–237) can be subdivided into variances that highlight the financial impact of input mix and input yield when inputs are substitutable. Consider Delpino Corporation, which makes tomato ketchup. Our example focuses on direct material inputs and substitution among three of these inputs. The same approach can also be used to examine substitutable direct manufacturing labor inputs.

To produce ketchup of a specified consistency, color, and taste, Delpino mixes three types of tomatoes grown in different regions: Latin American tomatoes (Latoms), California tomatoes (Caltoms), and Florida tomatoes

(Flotoms). Delpino's production standards require 1.60 tons of tomatoes to produce 1 ton of ketchup; 50% of the tomatoes are budgeted to be Latoms, 30% Caltoms, and 20% Flotoms. The direct material inputs budgeted to produce 1 ton of ketchup are as follows:

0.80 (50% of 1.6) ton of Latoms at $70 per ton	$ 56.00
0.48 (30% of 1.6) ton of Caltoms at $80 per ton	38.40
0.32 (20% of 1.6) ton of Flotoms at $90 per ton	28.80
Total budgeted cost of 1.6 tons of tomatoes	$123.20

Budgeted average cost per ton of tomatoes is $123.20 ÷ 1.60 tons = $77 per ton.

Because Delpino uses fresh tomatoes to make ketchup, no inventories of tomatoes are kept. Purchases are made as needed, so all price variances relate to tomatoes purchased and used. Actual results for June 2012 show that a total of 6,500 tons of tomatoes were used to produce 4,000 tons of ketchup:

3,250 tons of Latoms at actual cost of $70 per ton	$227,500
2,275 tons of Caltoms at actual cost of $82 per ton	186,550
975 tons of Flotoms at actual cost of $96 per ton	93,600
6,500 tons of tomatoes	507,650
Budgeted cost of 4,000 tons of ketchup at $123.20 per ton	492,800
Flexible-budget variance for direct materials	$ 14,850 U

Given the standard ratio of 1.60 tons of tomatoes to 1 ton of ketchup, 6,400 tons of tomatoes should be used to produce 4,000 tons of ketchup. At standard mix, quantities of each type of tomato required are as follows:

Latoms:	0.50 × 6,400 = 3,200 tons
Caltoms:	0.30 × 6,400 = 1,920 tons
Flotoms:	0.20 × 6,400 = 1,280 tons

Direct Materials Price and Efficiency Variances

Exhibit 14-12 presents in columnar format the analysis of the flexible-budget variance for direct materials discussed in Chapter 7. The materials price and efficiency variances are calculated separately for each input material and then added together. The variance analysis prompts Delpino to investigate the unfavorable price and efficiency variances. Why did it pay more for tomatoes and use greater quantities than it had budgeted? Were actual market prices of tomatoes higher, in general, or could the purchasing department have negotiated lower prices? Did the inefficiencies result from inferior tomatoes or from problems in processing?

Exhibit 14-12   Direct Materials Price and Efficiency Variances for the Delpino Corporation June 2012

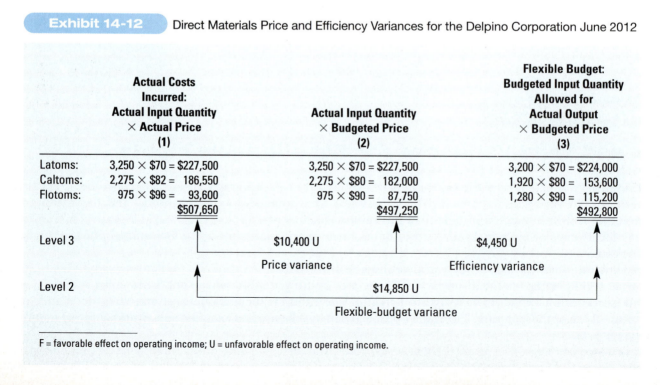

	Actual Costs Incurred: Actual Input Quantity × Actual Price (1)	Actual Input Quantity × Budgeted Price (2)	Flexible Budget: Budgeted Input Quantity Allowed for Actual Output × Budgeted Price (3)
Latoms:	3,250 × $70 = $227,500	3,250 × $70 = $227,500	3,200 × $70 = $224,000
Caltoms:	2,275 × $82 = 186,550	2,275 × $80 = 182,000	1,920 × $80 = 153,600
Flotoms:	975 × $96 = 93,600	975 × $90 = 87,750	1,280 × $90 = 115,200
	$507,650	$497,250	$492,800

Level 3 $10,400 U   Price variance $4,450 U   Efficiency variance

Level 2 $14,850 U   Flexible-budget variance

F = favorable effect on operating income; U = unfavorable effect on operating income.

Direct Materials Mix and Direct Materials Yield Variances

Managers sometimes have discretion to substitute one material for another. The manager of Delpino's ketchup plant has some leeway in combining Latoms, Caltoms, and Flotoms without affecting the ketchup's quality. We will assume that to maintain quality, mix percentages of each type of tomato can only vary up to 5% from standard mix. For example, the percentage of Caltoms in the mix can vary between 25% and 35% (30% ± 5%). When inputs are substitutable, direct materials efficiency improvement relative to budgeted costs can come from two sources: (1) using a cheaper mix to produce a given quantity of output, measured by the direct materials mix variance, and (2) using less input to achieve a given quantity of output, measured by the direct materials yield variance.

Holding actual total quantity of all direct materials inputs used constant, the total **direct materials mix variance** is the difference between (1) budgeted cost for actual mix of actual total quantity of direct materials used and (2) budgeted cost of budgeted mix of actual total quantity of direct materials used. Holding budgeted input mix constant, the **direct materials yield variance** is the difference between (1) budgeted cost of direct materials based on actual total quantity of direct materials used and (2) flexible-budget cost of direct materials based on budgeted total quantity of direct materials allowed for actual output produced. Exhibit 14-13 presents the direct materials mix and yield variances for the Delpino Corporation.

Direct Materials Mix Variance

The total direct materials mix variance is the sum of the direct materials mix variances for each input:

$$\begin{pmatrix} \text{Direct} \\ \text{materials} \\ \text{mix variance} \\ \text{for each input} \end{pmatrix} = \begin{pmatrix} \text{Actual total} \\ \text{quantity of all} \\ \text{direct materials} \\ \text{inputs used} \end{pmatrix} \times \begin{pmatrix} \text{Actual} \\ \text{direct materials} \\ \text{input mix} \\ \text{percentage} - \begin{matrix} \text{Budgeted} \\ \text{direct materials} \\ \text{input mix} \\ \text{percentage} \end{matrix} \end{pmatrix} \times \begin{pmatrix} \text{Budgeted} \\ \text{price of} \\ \text{direct materials} \\ \text{input} \end{pmatrix}$$

The direct materials mix variances are as follows:

Latoms:	6,500 tons × (0.50 − 0.50) × $70 per ton = 6,500 × 0.00 × $70	= $ 0
Caltoms:	6,500 tons × (0.35 − 0.30) × $80 per ton = 6,500 × 0.05 × $80	= 26,000 U
Flotoms:	6,500 tons × (0.15 − 0.20) × $90 per ton = 6,500 × −0.05 × $90	= 29,250 F
Total direct materials mix variance		$ 3,250 F

The total direct materials mix variance is favorable because relative to the budgeted mix, Delpino substitutes 5% of the cheaper Caltoms for 5% of the more-expensive Flotoms.

Exhibit 14-13   Total Direct Materials Yield and Mix Variances for the Delpino Corporation for June 2012

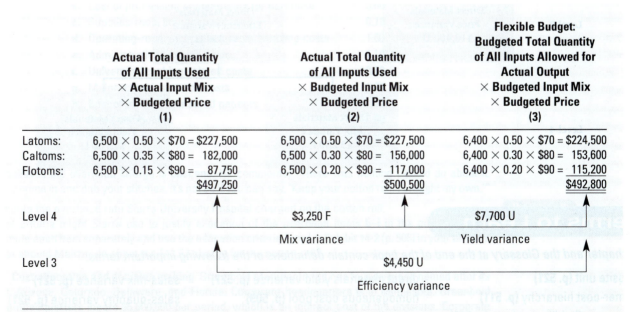

	Actual Total Quantity of All Inputs Used × Actual Input Mix × Budgeted Price (1)	Actual Total Quantity of All Inputs Used × Budgeted Input Mix × Budgeted Price (2)	Flexible Budget: Budgeted Total Quantity of All Inputs Allowed for Actual Output × Budgeted Input Mix × Budgeted Price (3)
Latoms:	6,500 × 0.50 × $70 = $227,500	6,500 × 0.50 × $70 = $227,500	6,400 × 0.50 × $70 = $224,500
Caltoms:	6,500 × 0.35 × $80 = 182,000	6,500 × 0.30 × $80 = 156,000	6,400 × 0.30 × $80 = 153,600
Flotoms:	6,500 × 0.15 × $90 = 87,750	6,500 × 0.20 × $90 = 117,000	6,400 × 0.20 × $90 = 115,200
	$497,250	$500,500	$492,800

Level 4 $3,250 F $7,700 U

                                            Mix variance   Yield variance

Level 3 $4,450 U

                                                       Efficiency variance

F = favorable effect on operating income; U = unfavorable effect on operating income.

14-24 **Variance analysis, working backward.** The Jinwa Corporation sells two brands of wine glasses: Plain and Chic. Jinwa provides the following information for sales in the month of June 2011:

Static-budget total contribution margin	$11,000
Budgeted units to be sold of all glasses	2,000 units
Budgeted contribution margin per unit of Plain	$4 per unit
Budgeted contribution margin per unit of Chic	$10 per unit
Total sales-quantity variance	$2,200 U
Actual sales-mix percentage of Plain	60%

All variances are to be computed in contribution-margin terms.

Required

1. Calculate the sales-quantity variances for each product for June 2011.
2. Calculate the individual-product and total sales-mix variances for June 2011. Calculate the individual-product and total sales-volume variances for June 2011.
3. Briefly describe the conclusions you can draw from the variances.

14-25 **Variance analysis, multiple products.** Soda-King manufactures and sells three soft drinks: Kola, Limor, and Orlem. Budgeted and actual results for 2011 are as follows:

	Budget for 2011			Actual for 2011		
Product	Selling Price	Variable Cost per Carton	Cartons Sold	Selling Price	Variable Cost per Carton	Cartons Sold
Kola	$8.00	$5.00	480,000	$8.20	$5.50	467,500
Limor	$6.00	$3.80	720,000	$5.75	$3.75	852,500
Orlem	$7.50	$5.50	1,200,000	$7.80	$5.60	1,430,000

Required

1. Compute the total sales-volume variance, the total sales-mix variance, and the total sales-quantity variance. (Calculate all variances in terms of contribution margin.) Show results for each product in your computations.
2. What inferences can you draw from the variances computed in requirement 1?

14-26 **Market-share and market-size variances (continuation of 14-25).** Soda-King prepared the budget for 2011 assuming a 12% market share based on total sales in the western region of the United States. The total soft drinks market was estimated to reach sales of 20 million cartons in the region. However, actual total sales volume in the western region was 27.5 million cartons.

Required

Calculate the market-share and market-size variances for Soda-King in 2011. (Calculate all variances in terms of contribution margin.) Comment on the results.

MyAccountingLab

Problems

14-27 **Allocation of corporate costs to divisions.** Dusty Rhodes, controller of Richfield Oil Company, is preparing a presentation to senior executives about the performance of its four divisions. Summary data (dollar amounts in millions) related to the four divisions for the most recent year are as follows:

	Home	Insert	Page Layout	Formulas	Data	Review	View

	A	B	C	D	E	F
1				DIVISIONS		
2		Oil & Gas Upstream	Oil & Gas Downstream	Chemical Products	Copper Mining	Total
3	Revenues	$ 8,000	$16,000	$4,800	$3,200	$32,000
4	Operating Costs	3,000	15,000	3,800	3,500	25,300
5	Operating Income	$ 5,000	$ 1,000	$1,000	$ (300)	$ 6,700
6						
7	Identifiable assets	$14,000	$ 6,000	$3,000	$2,000	$25,000
8	Number of employees	9,000	12,000	6,000	3,000	30,000

Under the existing accounting system, costs incurred at corporate headquarters are collected in a single cost pool ($3,228 million in the most recent year) and allocated to each division on the basis of its actual revenues. The top managers in each division share in a division-income bonus pool. Division income is defined as operating income less allocated corporate costs.

Rhodes has analyzed the components of corporate costs and proposes that corporate costs be collected in four cost pools. The components of corporate costs for the most recent year (dollar amounts in millions) and Rhodes' suggested cost pools and allocation bases are as follows:

	Home	Insert	Page Layout	Formulas	Data	Review	View	
	A		B	C	D	E		F
11	Corporate Cost Category		Amount	Suggested Cost Pool	Suggested Allocation Base			
12	Interest on debt		$2,000	Cost Pool 1	Identifiable assets			
13	Corporate salaries		150	Cost Pool 2				
14	Accounting and control		110	Cost Pool 2				
15	General marketing		200	Cost Pool 2	Division revenues			
16	Legal		140	Cost Pool 2				
17	Research and development		200	Cost Pool 2				
18	Public affairs		203	Cost Pool 3	Positive operating income*			
19	Personnel and payroll		225	Cost Pool 4	Number of employees			
20	Total		$3,228					
21								
22	*Since public affairs cost includes the cost of public relations staff, lobbyists, and donations to							
23	environmental charities, Rhodes proposes that this cost be allocated using operating income (if positive)							
24	of divisions, with only divisions with positive operating income included in the allocation base.							

Required

1. Discuss two reasons why Richfield Oil should allocate corporate costs to each division.
2. Calculate the operating income of each division when all corporate costs are allocated based on revenues of each division.
3. Calculate the operating income of each division when all corporate costs are allocated using the four cost pools.
4. How do you think the new proposal will be received by the division managers? What are the strengths and weaknesses of Rhodes' proposal relative to the existing single-cost-pool method?

14-28 Cost allocation to divisions. Forber Bakery makes baked goods for grocery stores, and has three divisions: bread, cake, and doughnuts. Each division is run and evaluated separately, but the main headquarters incurs costs that are indirect costs for the divisions. Costs incurred in the main headquarters are as follows:

Human resources (HR) costs	$1,900,000
Accounting department costs	1,400,000
Rent and depreciation	1,200,000
Other	600,000
Total costs	$5,100,000

The Forber upper management currently allocates this cost to the divisions equally. One of the division managers has done some research on activity-based costing and proposes the use of different allocation bases for the different indirect costs—number of employees for HR costs, total revenues for accounting department costs, square feet of space for rent and depreciation costs, and equal allocation among the divisions of "other" costs. Information about the three divisions follows:

	Bread	Cake	Doughnuts
Total revenues	$20,900,000	$4,500,000	$13,400,000
Direct costs	14,500,000	3,200,000	7,250,000
Segment margin	$ 6,400,000	$1,300,000	$ 6,150,000
Number of employees	400	100	300
Square feet of space	10,000	4,000	6,000

Required

1. Allocate the indirect costs of Forber to each division equally. Calculate division operating income after allocation of headquarter costs.

2. Allocate headquarter costs to the individual divisions using the proposed allocation bases. Calculate the division operating income after allocation. Comment on the allocation bases used to allocate headquarter costs.
3. Which division manager do you think suggested this new allocation. Explain briefly. Which allocation do you think is "better?"

14-29 Customer profitability. Ring Delights is a new company that manufactures custom jewelry. Ring Delights currently has six customers referenced by customer number: 01, 02, 03, 04, 05, and 06. Besides the costs of making the jewelry, the company has the following activities:

1. Customer orders. The salespeople, designers, and jewelry makers spend time with the customer. The cost driver rate is $40 per hour spent with a customer.
2. Customer fittings. Before the jewelry piece is completed the customer may come in to make sure it looks right and fits properly. Cost driver rate is $25 per hour.
3. Rush orders. Some customers want their jewelry quickly. The cost driver rate is $100 per rush order.
4. Number of customer return visits. Customers may return jewelry up to 30 days after the pickup of the jewelry to have something refitted or repaired at no charge. The cost driver rate is $30 per return visit.

Information about the six customers follows. Some customers purchased multiple items. The cost of the jewelry is 70% of the selling price.

Customer number	01	02	03	04	05	06
Sales revenue	$600	$4,200	$300	$2,500	$4,900	$700
Cost of item(s)	$420	$2,940	$210	$1,750	$3,430	$490
Hours spent on customer order	2	7	1	5	20	3
Hours on fittings	1	2	0	0	4	1
Number of rush orders	0	0	1	1	3	0
Number of returns visits	0	1	0	1	5	1

Required

1. Calculate the customer-level operating income for each customer. Rank the customers in order of most to least profitable and prepare a customer-profitability analysis, as in Exhibit 14-7.
2. Are any customers unprofitable? What is causing this? What should Ring Delights do with respect to these customers?

14-30 Customer profitability, distribution. Spring Distribution has decided to analyze the profitability of five new customers (see pp. 510–517). It buys bottled water at $12 per case and sells to retail customers at a list price of $14.40 per case. Data pertaining to the five customers are as follows:

	Customer				
	P	Q	R	S	T
Cases sold	2,080	8,750	60,800	31,800	3,900
List selling price	$14.40	$14.40	$14.40	$14.40	$14.40
Actual selling price	$14.40	$14.16	$13.20	$13.92	$12.96
Number of purchase orders	15	25	30	25	30
Number of customer visits	2	3	6	2	3
Number of deliveries	10	30	60	40	20
Miles traveled per delivery	14	4	3	8	40
Number of expedited deliveries	0	0	0	0	1

Its five activities and their cost drivers are as follows:

Activity	Cost Driver Rate
Order taking	$100 per purchase order
Customer visits	$80 per customer visit
Deliveries	$2 per delivery mile traveled
Product handling	$0.50 per case sold
Expedited deliveries	$300 per expedited delivery

Required

1. Compute the customer-level operating income of each of the five retail customers now being examined (P, Q, R, S, and T). Comment on the results.

2. What insights are gained by reporting both the list selling price and the actual selling price for each customer?

3. What factors should Spring Distribution consider in deciding whether to drop one or more of the five customers?

14-31 Customer profitability in a manufacturing firm. Bizzan Manufacturing makes a component called P14-31. This component is manufactured only when ordered by a customer, so Bizzan keeps no inventory of P14-31. The list price is $100 per unit, but customers who place "large" orders receive a 10% discount on price. Currently, the salespeople decide whether an order is large enough to qualify for the discount. When the product is finished, it is packed in cases of 10. When a customer order is not a multiple of 10, Bizzan uses a full case to pack the partial amount left over (e.g., if customer C orders 25 units, three cases will be required). Customers pick up the order so Bizzan incurs costs of holding the product in the warehouse until customer pick up. The customers are manufacturing firms; if the component needs to be exchanged or repaired, customers can come back within 10 days for free exchange or repair.

The full cost of manufacturing a unit of P14-31 is $80. In addition, Bizzan incurs customer-level costs. Customer-level cost-driver rates are as follows:

Order taking	$390 per order
Product handling	$10 per case
Warehousing (holding finished product)	$55 per day
Rush order processing	$540 per rush order
Exchange and repair costs	$45 per unit

Information about Bizzan's five biggest customers follows:

	A	B	C	D	E
Number of units purchased	6,000	2,500	1,300	4,200	7,800
Discounts given	10%	0	10%	0	10% on half the units
Number of orders	10	12	52	18	12
Number of cases	600	250	120	420	780
Days in warehouse (total for all orders)	14	18	0	12	140
Number of rush orders	0	3	0	0	6
Number of units exchanged/repaired	0	25	4	25	80

The salesperson gave customer C a price discount because, although customer C ordered only 1,300 units in total, 52 orders (one per week) were placed. The salesperson wanted to reward customer C for repeat business. All customers except E ordered units in the same order size. Customer E's order quantity varied, so E got a discount part of the time but not all the time.

1. Calculate the customer-level operating income for these five customers. Use the format in Exhibit 14-5. Prepare a customer-profitability analysis by ranking the customers from most to least profitable, as in Exhibit 14-7 **[Required]**

2. Discuss the results of your customer-profitability analysis. Does Bizzan have unprofitable customers? Is there anything Bizzan should do differently with its five customers?

14-32 Variance analysis, sales-mix and sales-quantity variances. Chicago Infonautics, Inc., produces handheld Windows CE™-compatible organizers. Chicago Infonautics markets three different handheld models: PalmPro is a souped-up version for the executive on the go, PalmCE is a consumer-oriented version, and PalmKid is a stripped-down version for the young adult market. You are Chicago Infonautics' senior vice president of marketing. The CEO has discovered that the total contribution margin came in lower than budgeted, and it is your responsibility to explain to him why actual results are different from the budget. Budgeted and actual operating data for the company's third quarter of 2012 are as follows:

Budgeted Operating Data, Third Quarter 2012

	Selling Price	Variable Cost per Unit	Contribution Margin per Unit	Sales Volume in Units
PalmPro	$374	$185	$189	13,580
PalmCE	272	96	176	35,890
PalmKid	144	66	78	47,530
				97,000

is allocated the additional cost that arises from two users instead of only the primary user. The third-ranked user is the *second-incremental user* (*second-incremental party*) and is allocated the additional cost that arises from three users instead of two users, and so on.

To see how this method works, consider again Jason Stevens and his $1,500 airfare cost. Assume the Albany employer is viewed as the primary party. Stevens' rationale is that he had already committed to go to Albany before accepting the invitation to interview in Chicago. The cost allocations would be as follows:

Party	Costs Allocated	Cumulative Costs Allocated
Albany (primary)	$1,200	$1,200
Chicago (incremental)	300 ($1,500 − $1,200)	$1,500
Total	$1,500	

The Albany employer is allocated the full Seattle–Albany airfare. The unallocated part of the total airfare is then allocated to the Chicago employer. If the Chicago employer had been chosen as the primary party, the cost allocations would have been Chicago $800 (the stand-alone round-trip Seattle–Chicago airfare) and Albany $700 ($1,500 – $800). When there are more than two parties, this method requires them to be ranked from first to last (such as by the date on which each employer invited the candidate to interview).

Under the incremental method, the primary party typically receives the highest allocation of the common costs. If the incremental users are newly formed companies or subunits, such as a new product line or a new sales territory, the incremental method may enhance their chances for short-run survival by assigning them a low allocation of the common costs. The difficulty with the method is that, particularly if a large common cost is involved, every user would prefer to be viewed as the incremental party!

One approach to sidestep disputes in such situations is to use the stand-alone cost-allocation method. Another approach is to use the *Shapley value*, which considers each party as first the primary party and then the incremental party. From the calculations shown earlier, the Albany employer is allocated $1,200 as the primary party and $700 as the incremental party, for an average of $950 [($1,200 + $700) ÷ 2]. The Chicago employer is allocated $800 as the primary party and $300 as the incremental party, for an average of $550 [($800 + 300) ÷ 2]. The Shapley value method allocates, to each employer, the average of the costs allocated as the primary party and as the incremental party: $950 to the Albany employer and $550 to the Chicago employer.[8]

As our discussion suggests, allocating common costs is not clear-cut and can generate disputes. Whenever feasible, the rules for such allocations should be agreed on in advance. If this is not done, then, rather than blindly follow one method or another, managers should exercise judgment when allocating common costs. For instance, Stevens must choose an allocation method for his airfare cost that is acceptable to each prospective employer. He cannot, for example, exceed the maximum reimbursable amount of airfare for either firm. The next section discusses the role of cost data in various types of contracts, another area where disputes about cost allocation frequently arise.

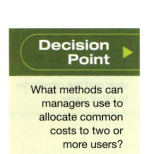

Decision Point ▶

What methods can managers use to allocate common costs to two or more users?

Cost Allocations and Contract Disputes

Learning Objective 5

Explain the importance of explicit agreement between contracting parties when the reimbursement amount is based on costs incurred

. . . to avoid disputes regarding allowable cost items and how indirect costs should be allocated

Many commercial contracts include clauses based on cost accounting information. Examples include the following:

■ A contract between the Department of Defense and a company designing and assembling a new fighter plane specifies that the price paid for the plane is to be based on the contractor's direct and overhead costs plus a fixed fee.

■ A contract between an energy-consulting firm and a hospital specifies that the consulting firm receive a fixed fee plus a share of the energy-cost savings that arise from implementing the consulting firm's recommendations.

[8] For further discussion of the Shapley value, see J. Demski, "Cost Allocation Games," in *Joint Cost Allocations*, ed. S. Moriarity (University of Oklahoma Center for Economic and Management Research, 1981); L. Kruz and P. Bronisz, "Cooperative Game Solution Concepts to a Cost Allocation Problem," *European Journal of Operations Research* 122 (2000): 258–271.

Contract disputes often arise with respect to cost allocation. The areas of dispute between the contracting parties can be reduced by making the "rules of the game" explicit and in writing at the time the contract is signed. Such rules of the game include the definition of allowable cost items; the definitions of terms used, such as what constitutes direct labor; the permissible cost-allocation bases; and how to account for differences between budgeted and actual costs.

Contracting with the U.S. Government

The U.S. government reimburses most contractors in one of two main ways:

1. **The contractor is paid a set price without analysis of actual contract cost data.** This approach is used, for example, when there is competitive bidding, when there is adequate price competition, or when there is an established catalog with prices quoted for items sold in substantial quantities to the general public.

2. **The contractor is paid after analysis of actual contract cost data.** In some cases, the contract will explicitly state that the reimbursement amount is based on actual allowable costs plus a fixed fee.[9] This arrangement is called a *cost-plus contract*.

All contracts with U.S. government agencies must comply with cost accounting standards issued by the **Cost Accounting Standards Board** (**CASB**). For government contracts, the CASB has the exclusive authority to make, put into effect, amend, and rescind cost accounting standards and interpretations. The standards are designed to achieve *uniformity and consistency* in regard to measurement, assignment, and allocation of costs to government contracts within the United States.[10]

In government contracting, there is a complex interplay of political considerations and accounting principles. Terms such as "fairness" and "equity," as well as cause and effect and benefits received, are often used in government contracts.

Fairness of Pricing

In many defense contracts, there is great uncertainty about the final cost to produce a new weapon or equipment. Such contracts are rarely subject to competitive bidding. The reason is that no contractor is willing to assume all the risk of receiving a fixed price for the contract and subsequently incurring high costs to fulfill it. Hence, setting a market-based fixed price for the contract fails to attract contractors, or requires a contract price that is too high from the government's standpoint. To address this issue, the government typically assumes a major share of the risk of the potentially high costs of completing the contract. Rather than relying on selling prices as ordinarily set by suppliers in the marketplace, the government negotiates contracts on the basis of *costs plus a fixed fee*. In costs-plus-fixed-fee contracts, which often involve billions of dollars, the allocation of a specific cost may be difficult to defend on the basis of any cause-and-effect reasoning. Nonetheless, the contracting parties may still view it as a "reasonable" or "fair" means to help establish a contract amount.

Some costs are "allowable;" others are "unallowable." An **allowable cost** is a cost that the contract parties agree to include in the costs to be reimbursed. Some contracts specify how allowable costs are to be determined. For example, only economy-class airfares are allowable in many U.S. government contracts. Other contracts identify cost categories that are unallowable. For example, the costs of lobbying activities and alcoholic beverages are not allowable costs in U.S. government contracts. However, the set of allowable costs is not always clear-cut. Contract disputes and allegations about overcharging the government arise from time to time (see Concepts in Action, p. 560).

Decision Point

How can contract disputes over reimbursement amounts based on costs be reduced?

---

[9] The Federal Acquisition Regulation (FAR), issued in March 2005 (see https://www.acquisition.gov/far/current/pdf/FAR.pdf) includes the following definition of "allocability" (in FAR 31.201-4): "A cost is allocable if it is assignable or chargeable to one or more cost objectives on the basis of relative benefits received or other equitable relationship. Subject to the foregoing, a cost is allocable to a Government contract if it:
(a) Is incurred specifically for the contract;
(b) Benefits both the contract and other work, and can be distributed to them in reasonable proportion to the benefits received; or
(c) Is necessary to the overall operation of the business, although a direct relationship to any particular cost objective cannot be shown."

[10] Details on the Cost Accounting Standards Board are available at www.whitehouse.gov/omb/procurement/casb.html. The CASB is part of the Office of Federal Procurement Policy, U.S. Office of Management and Budget.

Concepts in Action

Contract Disputes over Reimbursable Costs for the U.S. Department of Defense

For 2011, United States combat activities in Afghanistan are budgeted to cost $159 billion. As in prior years, a portion of this money is allocated to private companies to carry out specific contracted services for the U.S. Department of Defense. In recent years, the U.S. government has pursued cases against several contractors for overcharging for services provided in the combat zone. The following four examples are from cases pursued by the U.S. Department of Justice's Civil Division, who did so on behalf of the federal government. These recent examples illustrate several types of cost disputes that arise in practice.

1. Eagle Global Logistics agreed to pay $4 million to settle allegations of allegedly inflating invoices for military cargo shipments to Iraq. The complaint alleged that a company executive added an extra 50 cents per kilogram "war risk surcharge" to invoices for flights between Dubai and Iraq. This bogus surcharge, which was not part of Eagle's U.S. Department of Defense contract, was applied 379 times between 2003 and 2004.

2. In another shipping case, APL Limited paid the federal government $26.3 million to resolve claims of knowingly overcharging and double-billing the U.S. Department of Defense to transport thousands of containers to destinations in Afghanistan and Iraq. APL was accused of inflating invoices in several ways: marking up electricity costs for containers with perishable cargo, billing in excess of the contractual rate to maintain the operation of refrigerated containers in the port of Karachi, Pakistan, and billing for non-reimbursable services performed by an APL subcontractor at a Kuwaiti port.

3. L-3 communications, a leading defense contractor, paid $4 million to settle a complaint that it overbilled for hours worked by the firm's employees on a contract supporting military operations by the United States in Iraq. The company allegedly submitted false time records and inflated claims for personnel hours as part of an ongoing contract with the U.S. Army to provide helicopter maintenance services at Camp Taji, Iraq.

4. In late 2009, Public Warehousing Company—a principal food supplier for the U.S. military in Iraq, Kuwait, and Jordan since 2003—was sued by the U.S. government for presenting false claims for payment under the company's multibillion dollar contract with the Defense Logistics Agency. The complaint alleged that the company overcharged the U.S. for locally available fresh fruits and vegetables and failed to disclose pass through rebates and discounts it obtained from U.S.-based suppliers, as required by its contracts.

Source: Press releases from the United States Department of Justice, Civil Division (2006–2009).

Learning Objective 6

Understand how bundling of products

. . . two or more products sold for a single-price

gives rise to revenue allocation issues

. . . allocating revenues to each product in the bundle to evaluate managers of individual products

and the methods for doing so

. . . using the stand-alone method or the incremental method

Bundled Products and Revenue Allocation Methods

Allocation issues can also arise when revenues from multiple products (for example, different software programs or cable and internet packages) are bundled together and sold at a single price. The methods for revenue allocation parallel those described for common-cost allocations.

Bundling and Revenue Allocation

Revenues are inflows of assets (almost always cash or accounts receivable) received for products or services provided to customers. Similar to cost allocation, **revenue allocation** occurs when revenues are related to a particular *revenue object* but cannot be traced to it in an economically feasible (cost-effective) way. A **revenue object** is anything for which a separate measurement of revenue is desired. Examples of revenue objects include products, customers, and divisions. We illustrate revenue-allocation issues for Dynamic Software Corporation, which develops, sells, and supports three software programs:

1. WordMaster, a word-processing program, released 36 months ago
2. DataMaster, a spreadsheet program, released 18 months ago
3. FinanceMaster, a budgeting and cash-management program, released six months ago with a lot of favorable media attention

Dynamic Software sells these three products individually as well as together as bundled products.

A **bundled product** is a package of two or more products (or services) that is sold for a single price but whose individual components may be sold as separate items at their own "stand-alone" prices. The price of a bundled product is typically less than the sum of the prices of the individual products sold separately. For example, banks often provide individual customers with a bundle of services from different departments (checking, safety-deposit box, and investment advisory) for a single fee. A resort hotel may offer, for a single amount per customer, a weekend package that includes services from its lodging (the room), food (the restaurant), and recreational (golf and tennis) departments. When department managers have revenue or profit responsibilities for individual products, the bundled revenue must be allocated among the individual products in the bundle.

Dynamic Software allocates revenues from its bundled product sales (called "suite sales") to individual products. Individual-product profitability is used to compensate software engineers, outside developers, and product managers responsible for developing and managing each product.

How should Dynamic Software allocate suite revenues to individual products? Consider information pertaining to the three "stand-alone" and "suite" products in 2012:

	Selling Price	Manufacturing Cost per Unit
Stand-alone		
WordMaster	$125	$18
DataMaster	150	20
FinanceMaster	225	25
Suite		
Word + Data	$220	
Word + Finance	280	
Finance + Data	305	
Word + Finance + Data	380	

Just as we saw in the section on common-cost allocations, the two main revenue-allocation methods are the stand-alone method and the incremental method.

Stand-Alone Revenue-Allocation Method

The **stand-alone revenue-allocation method** uses product-specific information on the products in the bundle as weights for allocating the bundled revenues to the individual products. The term *stand-alone* refers to the product as a separate (nonsuite) item. Consider the Word + Finance suite, which sells for $280. Three types of weights for the stand-alone method are as follows:

1. **Selling prices.** Using the individual selling prices of $125 for WordMaster and $225 for FinanceMaster, the weights for allocating the $280 suite revenues between the products are as follows:

$$\text{WordMaster: } \frac{\$125}{\$125 + \$225} \times \$280 = 0.357 \times \$280 = \$100$$

$$\text{FinanceMaster: } \frac{\$225}{\$125 + \$225} \times \$280 = 0.643 \times \$280 = \$180$$

2. **Unit costs.** This method uses the costs of the individual products (in this case, manufacturing cost per unit) to determine the weights for the revenue allocations.

$$\text{WordMaster: } \frac{\$18}{\$18 + \$25} \times \$280 = 0.419 \times \$280 = \$117$$

$$\text{FinanceMaster: } \frac{\$25}{\$18 + \$25} \times \$280 = 0.581 \times \$280 = \$163$$

3. **Physical units.** This method gives each product unit in the suite the same weight when allocating suite revenue to individual products. Therefore, with two products in the Word + Finance suite, each product is allocated 50% of the suite revenues.

$$\text{WordMaster: } \frac{1}{1+1} \times \$280 = 0.50 \times \$280 = \$140$$

$$\text{FinanceMaster: } \frac{1}{1+1} \times \$280 = 0.50 \times \$280 = \$140$$

These three approaches to determining weights for the stand-alone method result in very different revenue allocations to the individual products:

Revenue-Allocation Weights	WordMaster	FinanceMaster
Selling prices	$100	$180
Unit costs	117	163
Physical units	140	140

Which method is preferred? The selling prices method is best, because the weights explicitly consider the prices customers are willing to pay for the individual products. Weighting approaches that use revenue information better capture "benefits received" by customers than unit costs or physical units.[11] The physical-units revenue-allocation method is used when any of the other methods cannot be used (such as when selling prices are unstable or unit costs are difficult to calculate for individual products).

Incremental Revenue-Allocation Method

The **incremental revenue-allocation method** ranks individual products in a bundle according to criteria determined by management—such as the product in the bundle with the most sales—and then uses this ranking to allocate bundled revenues to individual products. The first-ranked product is the *primary product* in the bundle. The second-ranked product is the *first-incremental product*, the third-ranked product is the *second-incremental product*, and so on.

How do companies decide on product rankings under the incremental revenue-allocation method? Some organizations survey customers about the importance of each of the individual products to their purchase decision. Others use data on the recent stand-alone sales performance of the individual products in the bundle. A third approach is for top managers to use their knowledge or intuition to decide the rankings.

Consider again the Word + Finance suite. Assume WordMaster is designated as the primary product. If the suite selling price exceeds the stand-alone price of the primary product, the primary product is allocated 100% of its *stand-alone* revenue. Because the suite price of $280 exceeds the stand-alone price of $125 for WordMaster, WordMaster is allocated revenues of $125, with the remaining revenue of $155 ($280 – $125) allocated to FinanceMaster:

Product	Revenue Allocated	Cumulative Revenue Allocated
WordMaster	$125	$125
FinanceMaster	155 ($280 – $125)	$280
Total	$280	

If the suite price is less than or equal to the stand-alone price of the primary product, the primary product is allocated 100% of the *suite* revenue. All other products in the suite receive no allocation of revenue.

---

[11] Revenue-allocation issues also arise in external reporting. The AICPA's Statement of Position 97-2 (Software Revenue Recognition) states that with bundled products, revenue allocation "based on vendor-specific objective evidence (VSOE) of fair value" is required. The "price charged when the element is sold separately" is said to be "objective evidence of fair value" (see "Statement of Position 97-2," Jersey City, NJ: AICPA, 1998). In September 2009, the FASB ratified Emerging Issues Task Force (EITF) Issue 08-1, specifying that with no VSOE or third-party evidence of selling price for all units of accounting in an arrangement, the consideration received for the arrangement should be allocated to the separate units based upon their relative selling prices.

Now suppose FinanceMaster is designated as the primary product and WordMaster as the first-incremental product. Then, the incremental revenue-allocation method allocates revenues of the Word + Finance suite as follows:

Product	Revenue Allocated	Cumulative Revenue Allocated
FinanceMaster	$225	$225
WordMaster	55 ($280 – $225)	$280
Total	$280	

If Dynamic Software sells equal quantities of WordMaster and FinanceMaster, then the Shapley value method allocates to each product the average of the revenues allocated as the primary and first-incremental products:

$$\text{WordMaster:} \qquad (\$125 + \$55) \div 2 = \$180 \div 2 = \$\ 90$$
$$\text{FinanceMaster:} \qquad (\$225 + \$155) \div 2 = \$380 \div 2 = \underline{\ 190}$$
$$\text{Total} \qquad\qquad\qquad\qquad\qquad\qquad\qquad \underline{\$280}$$

But what if, in the most recent quarter, the firm sells 80,000 units of WordMaster and 20,000 units of FinanceMaster. Because Dynamic Software sells four times as many units of WordMaster, its managers believe that the sales of the Word + Finance suite are four times more likely to be driven by WordMaster as the primary product. The *weighted Shapley value method* takes this fact into account. It assigns four times as much weight to the revenue allocations when WordMaster is the primary product as when FinanceMaster is the primary product, resulting in the following allocations:

$$\text{WordMaster:} \qquad (\$125 \times 4 + \$55 \times 1) \div (4 + 1) = \$555 \div 5 = \$111$$
$$\text{FinanceMaster:} \qquad (\$225 \times 1 + \$155 \times 4) \div (4 + 1) = \$845 \div 5 = \underline{\ 169}$$
$$\text{Total} \qquad\qquad\qquad\qquad\qquad\qquad\qquad\qquad\qquad\qquad \underline{\$280}$$

When there are more than two products in the suite, the incremental revenue-allocation method allocates suite revenues sequentially. Assume WordMaster is the primary product in Dynamic Software's three-product suite (Word + Finance + Data). FinanceMaster is the first-incremental product, and DataMaster is the second-incremental product. This suite sells for $380. The allocation of the $380 suite revenues proceeds as follows:

Product	Revenue Allocated	Cumulative Revenue Allocated
WordMaster	$125	$125
FinanceMaster	155 ($280 – $125)	$280 (price of Word + Finance suite)
DataMaster	100 ($380 – $280)	$380 (price of Word + Finance + Data suite)
Total	$380	

Now suppose WordMaster is the primary product, DataMaster is the first-incremental product, and FinanceMaster is the second-incremental product.

Product	Revenue Allocated	Cumulative Revenue Allocated
WordMaster	$125	$125
DataMaster	95 ($220 – $125)	$220 (price of Word + Data suite)
FinanceMaster	160 ($380 – $220)	$380 (price of Word + Data + Finance suite)
Total	$380	

The ranking of the individual products in the suite determines the revenues allocated to them. Product managers at Dynamic Software likely would differ on how they believe their individual products contribute to sales of the suite products. In fact, each product manager would claim to be responsible for the primary product in the Word + Finance + Data suite![12]

Decision Point

What is product bundling and how can managers allocate revenues of a bundled product to individual products in the package?

---

[12] Calculating the Shapley value mitigates this problem because each product is considered as a primary, first-incremental, and second-incremental product. Assuming equal weights on all products, the revenue allocated to each product is an average of the revenues calculated for the product under these different assumptions. In the preceding example, the interested reader can verify that this will result in the following revenue assignments: FinanceMaster, $180; WordMaster, $87.50; and DataMaster, $112.50.

Because the stand-alone revenue-allocation method does not require rankings of individual products in the suite, this method is less likely to cause debates among product managers.

Problem for Self-Study

This problem illustrates how costs of two corporate support departments are allocated to operating divisions using the dual-rate method. Fixed costs are allocated using budgeted costs and budgeted hours used by other departments. Variable costs are allocated using actual costs and actual hours used by other departments.

Computer Horizons budgets the following amounts for its two central corporate support departments (legal and personnel) in supporting each other and the two manufacturing divisions, the laptop division (LTD) and the work station division (WSD):

	Home Insert Page Layout Formulas Data Review View						
	A	B	C	D	E	F	G
1		SUPPORT			OPERATING		
2		Legal Department	Personnel Department		LTD	WSD	Total
3	**BUDGETED USAGE**						
4	Legal (hours)	—	250		1,500	750	2,500
5	(Percentages)	—	10%		60%	30%	100%
6	Personnel (hours)	2,500	—		22,500	25,000	50,000
7	(Percentages)	5%	—		45%	50%	100%
8							
9	**ACTUAL USAGE**						
10	Legal (hours)	—	400		400	1,200	2,000
11	(Percentages)	—	20%		20%	60%	100%
12	Personnel (hours)	2,000	—		26,600	11,400	40,000
13	(Percentages)	5%	—		66.50%	28.5%	100%
14	Budgeted fixed overhead costs before any						
15	interdepartment cost allocations	$360,000	$475,000		—	—	$835,000
16	Actual variable overhead costs before any						
17	interdepartment cost allocations	$200,000	$600,000		—	—	$800,000

Required What amount of support-department costs for legal and personnel will be allocated to LTD and WSD using (a) the direct method, (b) the step-down method (allocating the legal department costs first), and (c) the reciprocal method using linear equations?

Solution

Exhibit 15-7 presents the computations for allocating the fixed and variable support-department costs. A summary of these costs follows:

	Laptop Division (LTD)	Work Station Division (WSD)
(a) Direct Method		
Fixed costs	$465,000	$370,000
Variable costs	470,000	330,000
	$935,000	$700,000
(b) Step-Down Method		
Fixed costs	$458,053	$376,947
Variable costs	488,000	312,000
	$946,053	$688,947
(c) Reciprocal Method		
Fixed costs	$462,513	$372,487
Variable costs	476,364	323,636
	$938,877	$696,123

Exhibit 15-7 Alternative Methods of Allocating Corporate Support-Department Costs to Operating Divisions of Computer Horizons: Dual-Rate Method

	Home	Insert	Page Layout	Formulas	Data	Review	View

	A	B	C	D	E	F	G
20		CORPORATE SUPPORT DEPARTMENTS			OPERATING DIVISIONS		
21	**Allocation Method**	Legal Department	Personnel Department		LTD	WSD	Total
22	**A. DIRECT METHOD**						
23	Fixed costs	$360,000	$475,000				
24	Legal (1,500 ÷ 2,250; 750 ÷ 2,250)	(360,000)			$240,000	$120,000	
25	Personnel (22,500 ÷ 47,500; 25,000 ÷ 47,500)		(475,000)		225,000	250,000	
26	Fixed support dept. cost allocated to operating divisions	$ 0	0		$465,000	$370,000	$835,000
27	Variable costs	$200,000	$600,000				
28	Legal (400 ÷ 1,600; 1,200 ÷ 1,600)	(200,000)			$ 50,000	$150,000	
29	Personnel (26,600 ÷ 38,000; 11,400 ÷ 38,000)		(600,000)		420,000	180,000	
30	Variable support dept. cost allocated to operating divisions	$ 0	0		$470,000	$330,000	$800,000
31	**B. STEP-DOWN METHOD**						
32	(Legal department first)						
33	Fixed costs	$360,000	$475,000				
34	Legal (250 ÷ 2,500; 1,500 ÷ 2,500; 750 ÷ 2,500)	(360,000)	36,000		$216,000	$108,000	
35	Personnel (22,500 ÷ 47,500; 25,000 ÷ 47,500)		(511,000)		242,053	268,947	
36	Fixed support dept. cost allocated to operating divisions	$ 0	0		$458,053	$376,947	$835,000
37	Variable costs	$200,000	$600,000				
38	Legal (400 ÷ 2,000; 400 ÷ 2,000; 1,200 ÷ 2,000)	(200,000)	40,000		$ 40,000	$120,000	
39	Personnel (26,600 ÷ 38,000; 11,400 ÷ 38,000)		(640,000)		448,000	192,000	
40	Variable support dept. cost allocated to operating divisions	$ 0	0		$488,000	$312,000	$800,000
41	**C. RECIPROCAL METHOD**						
42	Fixed costs	$360,000	$475,000				
43	Legal (250 ÷ 2,500; 1,500 ÷ 2,500; 750 ÷ 2,500)	(385,678)[a]	38,568		$231,407	$115,703	
44	Personnel (2,500 ÷ 50,000; 22,500 ÷ 50,000; 25,000 ÷ 50,000)	25,678	(513,568)[a]		231,106	256,784	
45	Fixed support dept. cost allocated to operating divisions	$ 0	$ 0		$462,513	$372,487	$835,000
46	Variable costs	$200,000	$600,000				
47	Legal (400 ÷ 2,000; 400 ÷ 2,000; 1,200 ÷ 2,000)	(232,323)[b]	46,465		$ 46,465	$139,393	
48	Personnel (2,000 ÷ 40,000; 26,600 ÷ 40,000; 11,400 ÷ 40,000)	32,323	(646,465)[b]		429,899	184,243	
49	Variable support dept. cost allocated to operating divisions	$ 0	$ 0		$476,364	$323,636	$800,000
50							
51	[a] FIXED COSTS	[b] VARIABLE COSTS					
52	Letting LF = Legal department fixed costs, and PF = Personnel department fixed costs, the simultaneous equations for the reciprocal method for fixed costs are	Letting LF = Legal department variable costs, and PV = Personnel department variable costs, the simultaneous equations for the reciprocal method for variable costs are					
53	$LF = \$360{,}000 + 0.05\ PF$	$LV = \$200{,}000 + 0.05\ PV$					
54	$PF = \$475{,}000 + 0.10\ LF$	$PV = \$600{,}000 + 0.20\ LV$					
55	$LF = \$360{,}000 + 0.05\ (\$475{,}000 + 0.10\ LF)$	$LV = \$200{,}000 + 0.05\ (\$600{,}000 + 0.20\ LV)$					
56	$LF = \$385{,}678$	$LV = \$232{,}323$					
57	$PF = \$475{,}000 + 0.10\ (\$385{,}678) = \$513{,}568$	$PV = \$600{,}000 + 0.20\ (\$232{,}323) = \$646{,}465$					

Decision Points

The following question-and-answer format summarizes the chapter's learning objectives. Each decision presents a key question related to a learning objective. The guidelines are the answer to that question.

Decision	Guidelines
1. When should managers use the dual-rate method over the single-rate method?	The single-rate method aggregates fixed and variable costs and allocates them to objects using a single allocation base and rate. Under the dual-rate method, costs are grouped into separate variable cost and fixed cost pools; each pool uses a different cost-allocation base and rate. If costs can be easily separated into variable and fixed costs, the dual-rate method should be used because it provides better information for making decisions.
2. What factors should managers consider when deciding between allocation based on budgeted and actual rates, and budgeted and actual usage?	The use of budgeted rates enables managers of user departments to have certainty about the costs allocated to them, and insulates users from inefficiencies in the supplier department. Charging budgeted variable cost rates to users based on actual usage is causally appropriate and promotes control of resource consumption. Charging fixed cost rates on the basis of budgeted usage helps user divisions with planning, and leads to goal congruence when considering outsourcing decisions.
3. What methods can managers use to allocate costs of multiple support departments to operating departments?	The three methods managers can use are the direct, the step-down, and the reciprocal methods. The direct method allocates each support department's costs to operating departments without allocating a support department's costs to other support departments. The step-down method allocates support-department costs to other support departments and to operating departments in a sequential manner that partially recognizes the mutual services provided among all support departments. The reciprocal method fully recognizes mutual services provided among all support departments.
4. What methods can managers use to allocate common costs to two or more users?	Common costs are the costs of a cost object (such as operating a facility or performing an activity) that are shared by two or more users. The stand-alone cost-allocation method uses information pertaining to each user of the cost object to determine cost-allocation weights. The incremental cost-allocation method ranks individual users of the cost object and allocates common costs first to the primary user and then to the other incremental users. The Shapley value method considers each user, in turn, as the primary and the incremental user.
5. How can contract disputes over reimbursement amounts based on costs be reduced?	Disputes can be reduced by making the cost-allocation rules as explicit as possible and in writing at the time the contract is signed. These rules should include details such as the allowable cost items, the acceptable cost-allocation bases, and how differences between budgeted and actual costs are to be accounted for.
6. What is product bundling and how can managers allocate revenues of a bundled product to individual products in the package?	Bundling occurs when a package of two or more products (or services) is sold for a single price. Revenue allocation of the bundled price is required when managers of the individual products in the bundle are evaluated on product revenue or product operating income. Revenues can be allocated for a bundled product using the stand-alone method, the incremental method, or the Shapley value method.

Terms to Learn

This chapter and the Glossary at the end of the book contain definitions of the following important terms:

allowable cost (**p. 559**)

artificial costs (**p. 554**)

bundled product (**p. 561**)

common cost (**p. 557**)

complete reciprocated costs (**p. 554**)

Cost Accounting Standards Board (CASB) (**p. 559**)

direct method (**p. 550**)

Assignment Material

Questions

15-1 Distinguish between the single-rate and the dual-rate methods.

15-2 Describe how the dual-rate method is useful to division managers in decision making.

15-3 How do budgeted cost rates motivate the support-department manager to improve efficiency?

15-4 Give examples of allocation bases used to allocate support-department cost pools to operating departments.

15-5 Why might a manager prefer that budgeted rather than actual cost-allocation rates be used for costs being allocated to his or her department from another department?

15-6 "To ensure unbiased cost allocations, fixed costs should be allocated on the basis of estimated long-run use by user-department managers." Do you agree? Why?

15-7 Distinguish among the three methods of allocating the costs of support departments to operating departments.

15-8 What is conceptually the most defensible method for allocating support-department costs? Why?

15-9 Distinguish between two methods of allocating common costs.

15-10 What role does the Cost Accounting Standards Board play when companies contract with the U.S. government?

15-11 What is one key way to reduce cost-allocation disputes that arise with government contracts?

15-12 Describe how companies are increasingly facing revenue-allocation decisions.

15-13 Distinguish between the stand-alone and the incremental revenue-allocation methods.

15-14 Identify and discuss arguments that individual product managers may put forward to support their preferred revenue-allocation method.

15-15 How might a dispute over the allocation of revenues of a bundled product be resolved?

Exercises

15-16 Single-rate versus dual-rate methods, support department. The Chicago power plant that services all manufacturing departments of MidWest Engineering has a budget for the coming year. This budget has been expressed in the following monthly terms:

Manufacturing Department	Needed at Practical Capacity Production Level (Kilowatt-Hours)	Average Expected Monthly Usage (Kilowatt-Hours)
Rockford	10,000	8,000
Peoria	20,000	9,000
Hammond	12,000	7,000
Kankakee	8,000	6,000
Total	50,000	30,000

The expected monthly costs for operating the power plant during the budget year are $15,000: $6,000 variable and $9,000 fixed.

Required

1. Assume that a single cost pool is used for the power plant costs. What budgeted amounts will be allocated to each manufacturing department if (a) the rate is calculated based on practical capacity and costs are allocated based on practical capacity, and (b) the rate is calculated based on expected monthly usage and costs are allocated based on expected monthly usage?

2. Assume the dual-rate method is used with separate cost pools for the variable and fixed costs. Variable costs are allocated on the basis of expected monthly usage. Fixed costs are allocated on the basis of practical capacity. What budgeted amounts will be allocated to each manufacturing department? Why might you prefer the dual-rate method?

15-17 Single-rate method, budgeted versus actual costs and quantities. Chocolat Inc. is a producer of premium chocolate based in Palo Alto. The company has a separate division for each of its two products: dark chocolate and milk chocolate. Chocolat purchases ingredients from Wisconsin for its dark chocolate division and from Louisiana for its milk chocolate division. Both locations are the same distance from Chocolat's Palo Alto plant.

Chocolat Inc. operates a fleet of trucks as a cost center that charges the divisions for variable costs (drivers and fuel) and fixed costs (vehicle depreciation, insurance, and registration fees) of operating the fleet. Each division is evaluated on the basis of its operating income. For 2012, the trucking fleet had a practical capacity of 50 round-trips between the Palo Alto plant and the two suppliers. It recorded the following information:

	Home	Insert	Page Layout	Formulas	Data	Review	View
	A				B	C	
1					**Budgeted**	**Actual**	
2	Costs of truck fleet				$115,000	$96,750	
3	Number of round-trips for dark chocolate division (Palo Alto plant—Wisconsin)				30	30	
4	Number of round-trips for milk chocolate division (Palo Alto plant—Louisiana)				20	15	

Required

1. Using the single-rate method, allocate costs to the dark chocolate division and the milk chocolate division in these three ways.
   a. Calculate the budgeted rate per round-trip and allocate costs based on round-trips budgeted for each division.
   b. Calculate the budgeted rate per round-trip and allocate costs based on actual round-trips used by each division.
   c. Calculate the actual rate per round-trip and allocate costs based on actual round-trips used by each division.
2. Describe the advantages and disadvantages of using each of the three methods in requirement 1. Would you encourage Chocolat Inc. to use one of these methods? Explain and indicate any assumptions you made.

15-18 Dual-rate method, budgeted versus actual costs and quantities (continuation of 15-17). Chocolat Inc. decides to examine the effect of using the dual-rate method for allocating truck costs to each round-trip. At the start of 2012, the budgeted costs were as follows:

Variable cost per round-trip	$ 1,350
Fixed costs	$47,500

The actual results for the 45 round-trips made in 2012 were as follows:

Variable costs	$58,500
Fixed costs	38,250
	$96,750

Assume all other information to be the same as in Exercise 15-17.

Required

1. Using the dual-rate method, what are the costs allocated to the dark chocolate division and the milk chocolate division when (a) variable costs are allocated using the budgeted rate per round-trip and actual round-trips used by each division and when (b) fixed costs are allocated based on the budgeted rate per round-trip and round-trips budgeted for each division?
2. From the viewpoint of the dark chocolate division, what are the effects of using the dual-rate method rather than the single-rate methods?

15-19 Support-department cost allocation; direct and step-down methods. Phoenix Partners provides management consulting services to government and corporate clients. Phoenix has two support departments—administrative services (AS) and information systems (IS)—and two operating departments—government consulting (GOVT) and corporate consulting (CORP). For the first quarter of 2012, Phoenix's cost records indicate the following:

	A	B	C	D	E	F	G
	Home	Insert	Page Layout	Formulas	Data	Review	View
1		SUPPORT			OPERATING		
2		AS	IS		GOVT	CORP	Total
3	Budgeted overhead costs before any						
4	interdepartment cost allocations	$600,000	$2,400,000		$8,756,000	$12,452,000	$24,208,000
5	Support work supplied by AS (budgeted head count)	—	25%		40%	35%	100%
6	Support work supplied by IS (budgeted computer time)	10%	—		30%	60%	100%

1. Allocate the two support departments' costs to the two operating departments using the following methods: **Required**
   a. Direct method
   b. Step-down method (allocate AS first)
   c. Step-down method (allocate IS first)
2. Compare and explain differences in the support-department costs allocated to each operating department.
3. What approaches might be used to decide the sequence in which to allocate support departments when using the step-down method?

15-20 Support-department cost allocation, reciprocal method (continuation of 15-19). Refer to the data given in Exercise 15-19.

1. Allocate the two support departments' costs to the two operating departments using the reciprocal   **Required**
   method. Use (a) linear equations and (b) repeated iterations.
2. Compare and explain differences in requirement 1 with those in requirement 1 of Exercise 15-19. Which method do you prefer? Why?

15-21 Direct and step-down allocation. E-books, an online book retailer, has two operating departments—corporate sales and consumer sales—and two support departments—human resources and information systems. Each sales department conducts merchandising and marketing operations independently. E-books uses number of employees to allocate human resources costs and processing time to allocate information systems costs. The following data are available for September 2012:

	A	B	C	D	E	F
	Home	Insert	Page Layout	Formulas	Data	Review	View
1		SUPPORT DEPARTMENTS			OPERATING DEPARTMENTS	
2		Human Resources	Information Systems		Corporate Sales	Consumer Sales
3	Budgeted costs incurred before any					
4	interdepartment cost allocations	$72,700	$234,400		$998,270	$489,860
5	Support work supplied by human resources department					
6	Budgeted number of employees	—	21		42	28
7	Support work supplied by information systems department					
8	Budgeted processing time (in minutes)	320	—		1,920	1,600

1. Allocate the support departments' costs to the operating departments using the direct method.   **Required**
2. Rank the support departments based on the percentage of their services provided to other support departments. Use this ranking to allocate the support departments' costs to the operating departments based on the step-down method.
3. How could you have ranked the support departments differently?

15-22 Reciprocal cost allocation (continuation of 15-21). Consider E-books again. The controller of E-books reads a widely used textbook that states that "the reciprocal method is conceptually the most defensible." He seeks your assistance.

Required
1. Describe the key features of the reciprocal method.
2. Allocate the support departments' costs (human resources and information systems) to the two operating departments using the reciprocal method.
3. In the case presented in this exercise, which method (direct, step-down, or reciprocal) would you recommend? Why?

15-23 Allocation of common costs. Ben and Gary are students at Berkeley College. They share an apartment that is owned by Gary. Gary is considering subscribing to an Internet provider that has the following packages available:

Package	Per Month
A. Internet access	$60
B. Phone services	15
C. Internet access + phone services	65

Ben spends most of his time on the Internet ("everything can be found online now"). Gary prefers to spend his time talking on the phone rather than using the Internet ("going online is a waste of time"). They agree that the purchase of the $65 total package is a "win–win" situation.

Required
1. Allocate the $65 between Ben and Gary using (a) the stand-alone cost-allocation method, (b) the incremental cost-allocation method, and (c) the Shapley value method.
2. Which method would you recommend they use and why?

15-24 Allocation of common costs. Sunny Gunn, a self-employed consultant near Sacramento, received an invitation to visit a prospective client in Baltimore. A few days later, she received an invitation to make a presentation to a prospective client in Chicago. She decided to combine her visits, traveling from Sacramento to Baltimore, Baltimore to Chicago, and Chicago to Sacramento.

Gunn received offers for her consulting services from both companies. Upon her return, she decided to accept the engagement in Chicago. She is puzzled over how to allocate her travel costs between the two clients. She has collected the following data for regular round-trip fares with no stopovers:

Sacramento to Baltimore	$1,200
Sacramento to Chicago	$ 800

Gunn paid $1,600 for her three-leg flight (Sacramento–Baltimore, Baltimore–Chicago, Chicago–Sacramento). In addition, she paid $40 each way for limousines from her home to Sacramento Airport and back when she returned.

Required
1. How should Gunn allocate the $1,600 airfare between the clients in Baltimore and Chicago using (a) the stand-alone cost-allocation method, (b) the incremental cost-allocation method, and (c) the Shapley value method?
2. Which method would you recommend Gunn use and why?
3. How should Gunn allocate the $80 limousine charges between the clients in Baltimore and Chicago?

15-25 Revenue allocation, bundled products. Yves Parfum Company blends and sells designer fragrances. It has a Men's Fragrances Division and a Women's Fragrances Division, each with different sales strategies, distribution channels, and product offerings. Yves is now considering the sale of a bundled product consisting of a men's cologne and a women's perfume. For the most recent year, Yves reported the following:

	Home	Insert	Page Layout	Formulas
		A		B
1		**Product**		**Retail Price**
2	Monaco (men's cologne)			$ 48
3	Innocence (women's perfume)			112
4	L'Amour (Monaco + Innocence)			130

Required
1. Allocate revenue from the sale of each unit of L'Amour to Monaco and Innocence using the following:
   a. The stand-alone revenue-allocation method based on selling price of each product
   b. The incremental revenue-allocation method, with Monaco ranked as the primary product
   c. The incremental revenue-allocation method, with Innocence ranked as the primary product
   d. The Shapley value method, assuming equal unit sales of Monaco and Innocence
2. Of the four methods in requirement 1, which one would you recommend for allocating L'Amour's revenues to Monaco and Innocence? Explain.

15-26 Allocation of common costs. Jim Dandy Auto Sales uses all types of media to advertise its products (television, radio, newspaper, etc.). At the end of 2011, the company president, Jim Dandridge, decided that all advertising costs would be incurred by corporate headquarters and allocated to each of the company's three sales locations based on number of vehicles sold. Jim was confident that his corporate purchasing manager could negotiate better advertising contracts on a corporate-wide basis than each of the sales managers could on their own. Dandridge budgeted total advertising cost for 2012 to be $1.8 million. He introduced the new plan to his sales managers just before the New Year.

The manager of the east sales location, Tony Snider, was not happy. He complained that the new allocation method was unfair and would increase his advertising costs significantly over the prior year. The east location sold high volumes of low-priced used cars and most of the corporate advertising budget was related to new car sales.

Following Tony's complaint, Jim decided to take another hard look at what each of the divisions were paying for advertising before the new allocation plan. The results were as follows:

Sales Location	Actual Number of Cars Sold in 2011	Actual Advertising Cost Incurred in 2011
East	3,150	$ 324,000
West	1,080	432,000
North	2,250	648,000
South	2,520	756,000
	9,000	$2,160,000

1. Using 2011 data as the cost bases, show the amount of the 2012 advertising cost ($1,800,000) that would be allocated to each of the divisions under the following criteria:
   a. Dandridge's allocation method based on number of cars sold
   b. The stand-alone method
   c. The incremental-allocation method, with divisions ranked on the basis of dollars spent on advertising in 2011
2. Which method do you think is most equitable to the divisional sales managers? What other options might President Jim Dandridge have for allocating the advertising costs?

Problems

MyAccountingLab

15-27 Single-rate, dual-rate, and practical capacity allocation. Perfection Department Store has a new promotional program that offers a free gift-wrapping service for its customers. Perfection's customer-service department has practical capacity to wrap 7,000 gifts at a budgeted fixed cost of $6,650 each month. The budgeted variable cost to gift wrap an item is $0.40. Although the service is free to customers, a gift-wrapping service cost allocation is made to the department where the item was purchased. The customer-service department reported the following for the most recent month:

	A	B	C	D
	Home Insert Page Layout Formulas Data Review View			
1	Department	Actual Number of Gifts Wrapped	Budgeted Number of Gifts to Be Wrapped	Practical Capacity Available for Gift-Wrapping
2	Women's face wash	2,020	2,470	2,640
3	Men's face wash	730	825	945
4	Fragrances	1,560	1,805	1,970
5	Body wash	545	430	650
6	Hair products	1,495	1,120	795
7	Total	6,350	6,650	7,000

1. Using the single-rate method, allocate gift-wrapping costs to different departments in these three ways.
   a. Calculate the budgeted rate based on the budgeted number of gifts to be wrapped and allocate costs based on the budgeted use (of gift-wrapping services).
   b. Calculate the budgeted rate based on the budgeted number of gifts to be wrapped and allocate costs based on actual usage.
   c. Calculate the budgeted rate based on the practical gift-wrapping capacity available and allocate costs based on actual usage.

2. Using the dual-rate method, compute the amount allocated to each department when (a) the fixed-cost rate is calculated using budgeted costs and the practical gift-wrapping capacity, (b) fixed costs are allocated based on budgeted usage of gift-wrapping services, and (c) variable costs are allocated using the budgeted variable-cost rate and actual usage.

3. Comment on your results in requirements 1 and 2. Discuss the advantages of the dual-rate method.

15-28 Revenue allocation. Lee Shu-yu Inc. produces and sells DVDs to business people and students who are planning extended stays in China. It has been very successful with two DVDs: Beginning Mandarin and Conversational Mandarin. It is introducing a third DVD, Reading Chinese Characters. It has decided to market its new DVD in two different packages grouping the Reading Chinese Characters DVD with each of the other two language DVDs. Information about the separate DVDs and the packages follow.

DVD	Selling Price
Beginning Mandarin (BegM)	$ 50
Conversational Mandarin (ConM)	$ 90
Reading Chinese Characters (RCC)	$ 30
BegM + RCC	$ 60
ConM + RCC	$100

Required

1. Using the selling prices, allocate revenues from the BegM + RCC package to each DVD in that package using **(a)** the stand-alone method; **(b)** the incremental method, in either order; and **(c)** the Shapley value method.

2. Using the selling prices, allocate revenues from the ConM + RCC package to each DVD in that package using **(a)** the stand-alone method; **(b)** the incremental method, in either order; and **(c)** the Shapley value method.

3. Which method is most appropriate for allocating revenues among the DVDs? Why?

15-29 Fixed cost allocation. State University completed construction of its newest administrative building at the end of 2011. The University's first employees moved into the building on January 1, 2012. The building consists of office space, common meeting rooms (including a conference center), a cafeteria and even a workout room for its exercise enthusiasts. The total 2012 building space of 125,000 square feet was utilized as follows:

Usage of Space	% of Total Building Space
Office space (occupied)	52%
Vacant office space	8%
Common meeting space	25%
Workout room	5%
Cafeteria	10%

The new building cost the university $30 million and was depreciated using the straight-line method over 20 years. At the end of 2012 three departments occupied the building: executive offices of the president, accounting, and human resources. Each department's usage of its assigned space was as follows:

Department	Actual Office Space Used (sq. ft.)	Planned Office Space Used (sq. ft.)	Practical Capacity Office Space (sq. ft.)
Executive	16,250	12,400	18,000
Accounting	26,000	26,040	33,000
Human resources	22,750	23,560	24,000

Required

1. How much of the total building cost will be allocated in 2012 to each of the departments, if allocated on the basis of the following?
   a. Actual usage
   b. Planned usage
   c. Practical capacity

2. Assume that State University allocates the total annual building cost in the following manner:
   a. All vacant office space is absorbed by the university and is not allocated to the departments.
   b. All occupied office space costs are allocated on the basis of actual square footage used.
   c. All common costs are allocated on the basis of a department's practical capacity.
   Calculate the cost allocated to each department in 2012 under this plan. Do you think the allocation method used here is appropriate? Explain.

15-30 Allocating costs of support departments; step-down and direct methods. The Central Valley Company has prepared department overhead budgets for budgeted-volume levels before allocations as follows:

Support departments:		
Building and grounds	$10,000	
Personnel	1,000	
General plant administration	26,090	
Cafeteria: operating loss	1,640	
Storeroom	2,670	$ 41,400
Operating departments:		
Machining	$34,700	
Assembly	48,900	83,600
Total for support and operating departments		$125,000

Management has decided that the most appropriate inventory costs are achieved by using individual-department overhead rates. These rates are developed after support-department costs are allocated to operating departments.

Bases for allocation are to be selected from the following:

Department	Direct Manufacturing Labor-Hours	Number of Employees	Square Feet of Floor Space Occupied	Manufacturing Labor-Hours	Number of Requisitions
Building and grounds	0	0	0	0	0
Personnel[a]	0	0	2,000	0	0
General plant administration	0	35	7,000	0	0
Cafeteria: operating loss	0	10	4,000	1,000	0
Storeroom	0	5	7,000	1,000	0
Machining	5,000	50	30,000	8,000	2,000
Assembly	15,000	100	50,000	17,000	1,000
Total	20,000	200	100,000	27,000	3,000

[a]Basis used is number of employees.

Required

1. Using the step-down method, allocate support-department costs. Develop overhead rates per direct manufacturing labor-hour for machining and assembly. Allocate the costs of the support departments in the order given in this problem. Use the allocation base for each support department you think is most appropriate.
2. Using the direct method, rework requirement 1.
3. Based on the following information about two jobs, determine the total overhead costs for each job by using rates developed in (a) requirement 1 and (b) requirement 2.

	Direct Manufacturing Labor-Hours	
	Machining	**Assembly**
Job 88	18	2
Job 89	3	17

4. The company evaluates the performance of the operating department managers on the basis of how well they managed their total costs, including allocated costs. As the manager of the machining department, which allocation method would you prefer from the results obtained in requirements 1 and 2? Explain.

15-31 Support-department cost allocations; single-department cost pools; direct, step-down, and reciprocal methods. The Manes Company has two products. Product 1 is manufactured entirely in department X. Product 2 is manufactured entirely in department Y. To produce these two products, the Manes Company has two support departments: A (a materials-handling department) and B (a power-generating department).

An analysis of the work done by departments A and B in a typical period follows:

	Used By			
Supplied By	**A**	**B**	**X**	**Y**
A	—	100	250	150
B	500	—	100	400

16 Cost Allocation: Joint Products and Byproducts

Many companies, such as petroleum refiners, produce and sell two or more products simultaneously.

Similarly, some companies, such as health care providers, sell or provide multiple services. The question is, "How should these companies allocate costs to 'joint' products and services?" Knowing how to allocate joint product costs isn't something that only companies need to understand. It's something that farmers have to deal with, too, especially when it comes to the lucrative production of corn to make billions of gallons of ethanol fuel.

Joint Cost Allocation and the Production of Ethanol Fuel[1]

The increased global demand for oil has driven prices higher and forced countries to look for environmentally-sustainable alternatives. In the United States, the largest source of alternative fuel comes from corn-based ethanol. In 2009, the U.S. produced 10.75 billion gallons of ethanol, or 55% of the world's production, up from 1.7 billion gallons per year in 2001.

Producing ethanol requires a significant amount of corn. In 2011, the U.S. Department of Agriculture predicts that more than one-third of U.S. domestic corn production will be used to create ethanol fuel. But not all of that corn winds up in the ethanol that gets blended into gasoline and sold at service station.

Most biotechnology operations, such as making ethanol, produce two or more products. While distilling corn into ethanol, cell mass from the process—such as antibiotic and yeast fermentations—separates from the liquid and becomes a separate product, which is often sold as animal feed. This separation point, where outputs become distinctly identifiable, is called the splitoff point. Similarly, the residues from corn processing plants create secondary products including distillers' dried grains and gluten.

Accountants refer to these secondary products as byproducts. Ethanol byproducts like animal feed and gluten are accounted for by deducting the income from selling these products from the cost of ethanol fuel, the major product. With ethanol production costing

[1] *Sources:* Hacking, Andrew. 1987. *Economic aspects of biotechnology*. Cambridge, United Kingdom: Cambridge University Press; Leber, Jessica. 2010. Economics improve for first commercial cellulosic ethanol plants. *New York Times*, February 16; *USDA Agricultural Predictions to 2019*. 2010. Washington, DC: Government Printing Office; PBS. 2006. Glut of ethanol byproducts coming. *The Environmental Report*, Spring; *Entrepreneur*. 2007. Edible ethanol byproduct is source of novel foods. August.

around $2 per gallon and byproducts selling for a few cents per pound, most of the costs of production are allocated to the ethanol fuel itself, the main product. Since manufacturers would otherwise have to pay to dispose of their ethanol byproducts, most just try to "break even" on byproduct revenue.

In the coming years, however, this may change. With ethanol production growing, corn-based animal feed byproducts are becoming more plentiful. Some ethanol manufacturers are working together to create a market for ethanol feed, which is cheaper and higher in protein than plain corn. This allows ranchers' animals to gain weight faster and at a lower cost per pound. Additionally, scientists are trying to create an edible byproduct from distillers' dry grains, which could become a low-calorie, low-carbohydrate substitute in foods like breads and pastas.

Accounting concerns similar to those in the ethanol example also arise when traditional energy companies like ExxonMobil simultaneously produce crude oil, natural gas, and raw liquefied petroleum gas (LPS) from petroleum, in a single process. This chapter examines methods for allocating costs to joint products. We also examine how cost numbers appropriate for one purpose, such as external reporting, may not be appropriate for other purposes, such as decisions about the further processing of joint products.

Joint-Cost Basics

Joint costs are the costs of a production process that yields multiple products simultaneously. Consider the distillation of coal, which yields coke, natural gas, and other products. The costs of this distillation are joint costs. The **splitoff point** is the juncture in a joint production process when two or more products become separately identifiable. An example is the point at which coal becomes coke, natural gas, and other products. **Separable costs** are all costs—manufacturing, marketing, distribution, and so on—incurred beyond the splitoff point that are assignable to each of the specific products identified at the splitoff point. At or beyond the splitoff point, decisions relating to the sale or further processing of each identifiable product can be made independently of decisions about the other products.

Industries abound in which a production process simultaneously yields two or more products, either at the splitoff point or after further processing. Exhibit 16-1 presents examples of joint-cost situations in diverse industries. In each of these examples, no individual product can be produced without the accompanying products appearing, although in some cases the proportions can be varied. The focus of joint costing is on allocating costs to individual products at the splitoff point.

The outputs of a joint production process can be classified into two general categories: outputs with a positive sales value and outputs with a zero sales value.[2] For

Learning Objective 1

Identify the splitoff point in a joint-cost situation

. . . the point at which two or more products become separately identifiable

and distinguish joint products

. . . products with high sales values

from byproducts

. . . products with low sales values

---

[2] Some outputs of a joint production process have "negative" revenue when their disposal costs (such as the costs of handling nonsalable toxic substances that require special disposal procedures) are considered. These disposal costs should be added to the joint production costs that are allocated to joint or main products.

Exhibit 16-1

Examples of Joint-Cost
Situations

Industry	Separable Products at the Splitoff Point
Agriculture and Food Processing Industries	
Cocoa beans	Cocoa butter, cocoa powder, cocoa drink mix, tanning cream
Lambs	Lamb cuts, tripe, hides, bones, fat
Hogs	Bacon, ham, spare ribs, pork roast
Raw milk	Cream, liquid skim
Lumber	Lumber of varying grades and shapes
Turkeys	Breast, wings, thighs, drumsticks, digest, feather meal, and poultry meal
Extractive Industries	
Coal	Coke, gas, benzol, tar, ammonia
Copper ore	Copper, silver, lead, zinc
Petroleum	Crude oil, natural gas
Salt	Hydrogen, chlorine, caustic soda
Chemical Industries	
Raw LPG (liquefied petroleum gas)	Butane, ethane, propane
Crude oil	Gasoline, kerosene, benzene, naphtha
Semiconductor Industry	
Fabrication of silicon-wafer chips	Memory chips of different quality (as to capacity), speed, life expectancy, and temperature tolerance

example, offshore processing of hydrocarbons yields oil and natural gas, which have positive sales value, and it also yields water, which has zero sales value and is recycled back into the ocean. The term **product** describes any output that has a positive total sales value (or an output that enables a company to avoid incurring costs, such as an intermediate chemical product used as input in another process). The total sales value can be high or low.

When a joint production process yields one product with a high total sales value, compared with total sales values of other products of the process, that product is called a **main product.** When a joint production process yields two or more products with high total sales values compared with the total sales values of other products, if any, those products are called **joint products.** The products of a joint production process that have low total sales values compared with the total sales value of the main product or of joint products are called **byproducts.**

Consider some examples. If timber (logs) is processed into standard lumber and wood chips, standard lumber is a main product and wood chips are the byproduct, because standard lumber has a high total sales value compared with wood chips. If, however, logs are processed into fine-grade lumber, standard lumber, and wood chips, fine-grade lumber and standard lumber are joint products, and wood chips are the byproduct. That's because both fine-grade lumber and standard lumber have high total sales values when compared with wood chips.

Distinctions among main products, joint products, and byproducts are not so definite in practice. For example, some companies may classify kerosene obtained when refining crude oil as a byproduct because they believe kerosene has a low total sales value relative to the total sales values of gasoline and other products. Other companies may classify kerosene as a joint product because they believe kerosene has a high total sales value relative to the total sales values of gasoline and other products. Moreover, the classification of products—main, joint, or byproduct—can change over time, especially for products such as lower-grade semiconductor chips, whose market prices may increase or decrease by 30% or more in a year. When prices of lower-grade chips are high, they are considered joint products together with higher-grade chips; when prices of lower-grade chips fall considerably, they are considered byproducts. In practice, it is important to understand how a specific company chooses to classify its products.

Decision Point ▶

What do the terms joint cost and splitoff point mean, and how do joint products differ from byproducts?

Allocating Joint Costs

Before a manager is able to allocate joint costs, she must first look at the context for doing so. There are several contexts in which joint costs are required to be allocated to individual products or services. These include the following:

Learning Objective 2

Explain why joint costs are allocated to individual products

. . . to calculate cost of goods sold and inventory, and for reimbursements under cost-plus contracts and other types of claims

- Computation of inventoriable costs and cost of goods sold. Recall from Chapter 9 that absorption costing is required for financial accounting and tax reporting purposes. This necessitates the allocation of joint manufacturing or processing costs to products for calculating ending inventory values.

- Computation of inventoriable costs and cost of goods sold for internal reporting purposes. Many firms use internal accounting data based on joint cost allocations for the purpose of analyzing divisional profitability and in order to evaluate division managers' performance.

- Cost reimbursement for companies that have a few, but not all, of their products or services reimbursed under cost-plus contracts with, say, a government agency. In this case, stringent rules typically specify the manner in which joint costs are assigned to the products or services covered by the cost-plus agreement. That said, fraud in defense contracting, which is often done via cost-plus contracts, remains one of the most active areas of false claim litigation under the Federal False Claims Act. A common practice is "cross-charging," where a contractor shifts joint costs from "fixed-price" defense contracts to those that are done on a cost-plus basis. Defense contractors have also attempted to secure contracts from private businesses or foreign governments by allocating an improper share of joint costs onto the cost-plus agreements they have with the United States government.[3]

- Rate or price regulation for one or more of the jointly produced products or services. This issue is conceptually related to the previous point, and is of great importance in the extractive and energy industries where output prices are regulated to yield a fixed return on a cost basis that includes joint cost allocations. In telecommunications, for example, it is often the case that a firm with significant market power has some products subject to price regulation (e.g., interconnection) and other activities that are unregulated (such as end-user equipment rentals). In this case, it is critical in allocating joint costs to ensure that costs are not transferred from unregulated services to regulated ones.[4]

Decision Point

Why are joint costs allocated to individual products?

- Insurance-settlement computations for damage claims made on the basis of cost information of jointly produced products. In this case, the joint cost allocations are essential in order to provide a cost-based analysis of the loss in value.

- More generally, any commercial litigation situation in which costs of joint products or services are key inputs requires the allocation of joint costs.

Approaches to Allocating Joint Costs

Two approaches are used to allocate joint costs.

- **Approach 1.** Allocate joint costs using *market-based* data such as revenues. This chapter illustrates three methods that use this approach:
  1. Sales value at splitoff method
  2. Net realizable value (NRV) method
  3. Constant gross-margin percentage NRV method
- **Approach 2.** Allocate joint costs using *physical measures*, such as the weight, quantity (physical units), or volume of the joint products.

Learning Objective 3

Allocate joint costs using four methods

. . . sales value at splitoff, physical measure, net realizable value (NRV), and constant gross-margin percentage NRV

In preceding chapters, we used the cause-and-effect and benefits-received criteria for guiding cost-allocation decisions (see Exhibit 14-2, p. 505). Joint costs do not have a cause-and-effect relationship with individual products because the production process simultaneously yields multiple products. Using the benefits-received criterion leads to a preference for methods under approach 1 because revenues are, in general, a better

---

[3] See, for example, www.dodig.mil/iginformation/IGInformationReleases/3eSettlementPR.pdf
[4] For details, see the International Telecommunication Union's ICT Regulation Toolkit at www.ictregulationtoolkit.org/en/Section.3497.html.

indicator of benefits received than physical measures. Mining companies, for example, receive more benefits from 1 ton of gold than they do from 10 tons of coal.

In the simplest joint production process, the joint products are sold at the splitoff point without further processing. Example 1 illustrates the two methods that apply in this case: the sales value at splitoff method and the physical-measure method. Then we introduce joint production processes that yield products that require further processing beyond the splitoff point. Example 2 illustrates the NRV method and the constant-gross margin percentage NRV method. To help you focus on key concepts, we use numbers and amounts that are smaller than the numbers that are typically found in practice.

The exhibits in this chapter use the following symbols to distinguish a joint or main product from a byproduct:

Joint Product or Main Product   Byproduct

To compare methods, we report gross-margin percentages for individual products under each method.

> Example 1: Farmers' Dairy purchases raw milk from individual farms and processes it until the splitoff point, when two products—cream and liquid skim—emerge. These two products are sold to an independent company, which markets and distributes them to supermarkets and other retail outlets.
>
> In May 2012, Farmers' Dairy processes 110,000 gallons of raw milk. During processing, 10,000 gallons are lost due to evaporation and spillage, yielding 25,000 gallons of cream and 75,000 gallons of liquid skim. Summary data follow:

	Home	Insert	Page Layout	Formulas	Data	Review
		A			B	C
1					**Joint Costs**	
2	Joint costs (costs of 110,000 gallons raw milk and processing to splitoff point)				$400,000	
3						
4					**Cream**	**Liquid Skim**
5	Beginnning inventory (gallons)				0	0
6	Production (gallons)				25,000	75,000
7	Sales (gallons)				20,000	30,000
8	Ending inventory (gallons)				5,000	45,000
9	Selling price per gallon				$ 8	$ 4

Exhibit 16-2 depicts the basic relationships in this example.

How much of the $400,000 joint costs should be allocated to the cost of goods sold of 20,000 gallons of cream and 30,000 gallons of liquid skim, and how much should be allocated to the ending inventory of 5,000 gallons of cream and 45,000 gallons of liquid skim? We begin by illustrating the two methods that use the properties of the products at the splitoff point, the sales value at splitoff method and the physical-measure method.

Sales Value at Splitoff Method

The **sales value at splitoff method** allocates joint costs to joint products produced during the accounting period on the basis of the relative total sales value at the splitoff point. Using this method for Example 1, Exhibit 16-3, Panel A, shows how joint costs

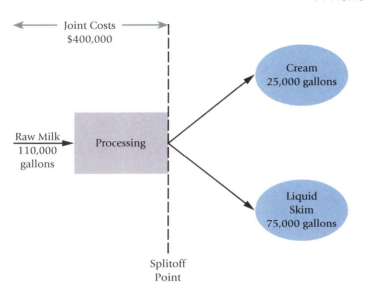

Exhibit 16-2

Example 1: Overview of
Farmers' Dairy

are allocated to individual products to calculate cost per gallon of cream and liquid skim for valuing ending inventory. This method uses the sales value of the *entire production of the accounting period* (25,000 gallons of cream and 75,000 gallons of liquid skim), not just the quantity sold (20,000 gallons of cream and 30,000 gallons of liquid skim). The reason this method does not rely solely on the quantity sold is that the joint costs were incurred on all units produced, not just the portion sold during the current period. Exhibit 16-3, Panel B, presents the product-line income statement using the sales value at splitoff method. Note that the gross-margin percentage for each product is 20%, because the sales value at splitoff method allocates joint costs to each product in proportion to the sales value of total production (cream: $160,000 ÷ $200,000 = 80%; liquid skim: $240,000 ÷ $300,000 = 80%). Therefore, the gross-margin percentage for each product manufactured in May 2012 is the same: 20%.[5]

Note how the sales value at splitoff method follows the benefits-received criterion of cost allocation: Costs are allocated to products in proportion to their revenue-generating

Exhibit 16-3 Joint-Cost Allocation and Product-Line Income Statement Using Sales Value at Splitoff Method: Farmers' Dairy for May 2012

	A	B	C	D
		Cream	**Liquid Skim**	**Total**
1	**PANEL A: Allocation of Joint Costs Using Sales Value at Splitoff Method**	Cream	Liquid Skim	Total
2	Sales value of total production at splitoff point			
3	(25,000 gallons × $8 per gallon; 75,000 gallons × $4 per gallon)	$200,000	$300,000	$500,000
4	Weighting ($200,000 ÷ $500,000; $300,000 ÷ 500,000)	0.40	0.60	
5	Joint costs allocated (0.40 × $400,000; 0.60 × $400,000)	$160,000	$240,000	$400,000
6	Joint production cost per gallon			
7	($160,000 ÷ 25,000 gallons; $240,000 ÷ 75,000 gallons)	$ 6.40	$ 3.20	
8				
9	**PANEL B: Product-Line Income Statement Using Sales Value at Splitoff Method for May 2012**	Cream	Liquid Skim	Total
10	Revenues (20,000 gallons × $8 per gallon; 30,000 gallons × $4 per gallon)	$160,000	$120,000	$280,000
11	Cost of goods sold (joint costs)			
12	Production costs (0.40 × $400,000; 0.60 × $400,000)	160,000	240,000	400,000
13	Deduct ending inventory (5,000 gallons × $6.40 per gallon; 45,000 gallons × $3.20 per gallon)	32,000	144,000	176,000
14	Cost of goods sold (joint costs)	128,000	96,000	224,000
15	Gross margin	$ 32,000	$ 24,000	$ 56,000
16	Gross margin percentage ($32,000 ÷ $160,000; $24,000 ÷ $120,000; $56,000 ÷ $280,000)	20%	20%	20%

[5] Suppose Farmers' Dairy has beginning inventory of cream and liquid milk in May 2012 and when this inventory is sold, Farmers' earns a gross margin different from 20%. Then the gross-margin percentage for cream and liquid skim will not be the same. The relative gross-margin percentages will depend on how much of the sales of each product came from beginning inventory and how much came from current-period production.

power (their expected revenues). The cost-allocation base (total sales value at splitoff) is expressed in terms of a common denominator (the amount of revenues) that is systematically recorded in the accounting system. To use this method, selling prices must exist for all products at the splitoff point.

Physical-Measure Method

The **physical-measure method** allocates joint costs to joint products produced during the accounting period on the basis of a *comparable* physical measure, such as the relative weight, quantity, or volume at the splitoff point. In Example 1, the $400,000 joint costs produced 25,000 gallons of cream and 75,000 gallons of liquid skim. Using the number of gallons produced as the physical measure, Exhibit 16-4, Panel A, shows how joint costs are allocated to individual products to calculate the cost per gallon of cream and liquid skim.

Because the physical-measure method allocates joint costs on the basis of the number of gallons, cost per gallon is the same for both products. Exhibit 16-4, Panel B, presents the product-line income statement using the physical-measure method. The gross-margin percentages are 50% for cream and 0% for liquid skim.

Under the benefits-received criterion, the physical-measure method is much less desirable than the sales value at splitoff method, because the physical measure of the individual products may have no relationship to their respective revenue-generating abilities. Consider a gold mine that extracts ore containing gold, silver, and lead. Use of a common physical measure (tons) would result in almost all costs being allocated to lead, the product that weighs the most but has the lowest revenue-generating power. In the case of metals, the method of cost allocation is inconsistent with the main reason that the mining company is incurring mining costs—to earn revenues from gold and silver, not lead. When a company uses the physical-measure method in a product-line income statement, products that have a high sales value per ton, like gold and silver, would show a large "profit," and products that have a low sales value per ton, like lead, would show sizable losses.

Obtaining comparable physical measures for all products is not always straightforward. Consider the joint costs of producing oil and natural gas; oil is a liquid and gas is a vapor. To use a physical measure, the oil and gas need to be converted to the energy equivalent for oil and gas, British thermal units (BTUs). Using some physical measures to allocate joint costs may require assistance from technical personnel outside of accounting.

Determining which products of a joint process to include in a physical-measure computation can greatly affect the allocations to those products. Outputs with no sales value

---

Exhibit 16-4 Joint-Cost Allocation and Product-Line Income Statement Using Physical-Measure Method: Farmers' Dairy for May 2012

	A	B	C	D
		Home Insert Page Layout Formulas Data Review View		
1	**PANEL A: Allocation of Joint Costs Using Physical-Measure Method**	**Cream**	**Liquid Skim**	**Total**
2	Physical measure of total production (gallons)	25,000	75,000	100,000
3	Weighting (25,000 gallons ÷ 100,000 gallons; 75,000 gallons ÷ 100,000 gallons)	0.25	0.75	
4	Joint costs allocated (0.25 × $400,000; 0.75 × $400,000)	$100,000	$300,000	$400,000
5	Joint production cost per gallon ($100,000 ÷ 25,000 gallons; $300,000 ÷ 75,000 gallons)	$ 4.00	$ 4.00	
6				
7	**PANEL B: Product-Line Income Statement Using Physical-Measure Method for May 2012**	**Cream**	**Liquid Skim**	**Total**
8	Revenues (20,000 gallons × $8 per gallon; 30,000 gallons × $4 per gallon)	$160,000	$120,000	$280,000
9	Cost of goods sold (joint costs)			
10	Production costs (0.25 × $400,000; 0.75 × $400,000)	100,000	300,000	400,000
11	Deduct ending inventory (5,000 gallons × $4 per gallon; 45,000 gallons × $4 per gallon)	20,000	180,000	200,000
12	Cost of goods sold (joint costs)	80,000	120,000	200,000
13	Gross margin	$ 80,000	$ 0	$ 80,000
14	Gross margin percentage ($80,000 ÷ $160,000; $0 ÷ $120,000; $80,000 ÷ $280,000)	50%	0%	28.6%

(such as dirt in gold mining) are always excluded. Although many more tons of dirt than gold are produced, costs are not incurred to produce outputs that have zero sales value. Byproducts are also often excluded from the denominator used in the physical-measure method because of their low sales values relative to the joint products or the main product. The general guideline for the physical-measure method is to include only the joint-product outputs in the weighting computations.

Net Realizable Value Method

In many cases, products are processed beyond the splitoff point to bring them to a marketable form or to increase their value above their selling price at the splitoff point. For example, when crude oil is refined, the gasoline, kerosene, benzene, and naphtha must be processed further before they can be sold. To illustrate, let's extend the Farmers' Dairy example.

Example 2: Assume the same data as in Example 1 except that both cream and liquid skim can be processed further:

- Cream → Buttercream: 25,000 gallons of cream are further processed to yield 20,000 gallons of buttercream at additional processing costs of $280,000. Buttercream, which sells for $25 per gallon, is used in the manufacture of butter-based products.

- Liquid Skim → Condensed Milk: 75,000 gallons of liquid skim are further processed to yield 50,000 gallons of condensed milk at additional processing costs of $520,000. Condensed milk sells for $22 per gallon.

- Sales during May 2012 are 12,000 gallons of buttercream and 45,000 gallons of condensed milk.

Exhibit 16-5, Panel A, depicts how (a) raw milk is converted into cream and liquid skim in the joint production process, and (b) how cream is separately processed into buttercream and liquid skim is separately processed into condensed milk. Panel B shows the data for Example 2.

The **net realizable value (NRV) method** allocates joint costs to joint products produced during the accounting period on the basis of their relative NRV—final sales value minus separable costs. The NRV method is typically used in preference to the sales value at splitoff method only when selling prices for one or more products at splitoff do not exist. Using this method for Example 2, Exhibit 16-6, Panel A, shows how joint costs are allocated to individual products to calculate cost per gallon of buttercream and condensed milk.

Exhibit 16-6, Panel B presents the product-line income statement using the NRV method. Gross-margin percentages are 22.0% for buttercream and 26.4% for condensed milk.

The NRV method is often implemented using simplifying assumptions. For example, even when selling prices of joint products vary frequently, companies implement the

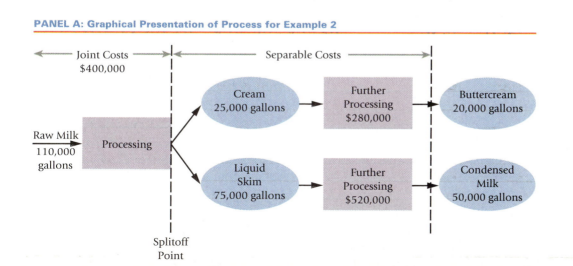

PANEL A: Graphical Presentation of Process for Example 2

Exhibit 16-5

Example 2: Overview of Farmers' Dairy

Joint Costs $400,000 | Separable Costs

Raw Milk 110,000 gallons → Processing → Cream 25,000 gallons → Further Processing $280,000 → Buttercream 20,000 gallons

Liquid Skim 75,000 gallons → Further Processing $520,000 → Condensed Milk 50,000 gallons

Splitoff Point

Exhibit 16-5 Example 2: Overview of Farmers' Dairy (*continued*)

PANEL B: Data for Example 2

	A	B	C	D	E
			Joint Costs	**Buttercream**	**Condensed Milk**
1					
2	Joint costs (costs of 110,000 gallons raw milk and processing to splitoff point)		$400,000		
3	Separable cost of processing 25,000 gallons cream into 20,000 gallons buttercream			$280,000	
4	Separable cost of processing 75,000 gallons liquid skim into 50,000 gallons condensed milk				$520,000
5					
6		**Cream**	**Liquid Skim**	**Buttercream**	**Condensed Milk**
7	Beginning inventory (gallons)	0	0	0	0
8	Production (gallons)	25,000	75,000	20,000	50,000
9	Transfer for further processing (gallons)	25,000	75,000		
10	Sales (gallons)			12,000	45,000
11	Ending inventory (gallons)	0	0	8,000	5,000
12	Selling price per gallon	$ 8	$ 4	$ 25	$ 22

Exhibit 16-6 Joint-Cost Allocation and Product-Line Income Statement Using NRV Method: Farmers' Dairy for May 2012

	A	B	C	D
		Buttercream	**Condensed Milk**	**Total**
1	PANEL A: Allocation of Joint Costs Using Net Realizable Value Method			
2	Final sales value of total production during accounting period			
3	(20,000 gallons × $25 per gallon; 50,000 gallons × $22 per gallon)	$500,000	$1,100,000	$1,600,000
4	Deduct separable costs	280,000	520,000	800,000
5	Net realizable value at splitoff point	$220,000	$ 580,000	$ 800,000
6	Weighting ($220,000 ÷ $800,000; $580,000 ÷ $800,000)	0.275	0.725	
7	Joint costs allocated (0.275 × $400,000; 0.725 × $400,000)	$110,000	$ 290,000	$ 400,000
8	Production cost per gallon			
9	([$110,000 + $280,000] ÷ 20,000 gallons; [$290,000 + $520,000] ÷ 50,000 gallons)	$ 19.50	$ 16.20	
10				
11	PANEL B: Product-Line Income Statement Using Net Realizable Value Method for May 2012	**Buttercream**	**Condensed Milk**	**Total**
12	Revenues (12,000 gallons × $25 per gallon; 45,000 gallons × $22 per gallon)	$300,000	$ 990,000	$1,290,000
13	Cost of goods sold			
14	Joint costs (0.275 × $400,000; 0.725 × $400,000)	110,000	290,000	400,000
15	Separable costs	280,000	520,000	800,000
16	Production costs	390,000	810,000	1,200,000
17	Deduct ending inventory (8,000 gallons × $19.50 per gallon; 5,000 gallons × $16.20 per gallon)	156,000	81,000	237,000
18	Cost of goods sold	234,000	729,000	963,000
19	Gross margin	$ 66,000	$ 261,000	$ 327,000
20	Gross margin percentage ($66,000 ÷ $300,000; $261,000 ÷ $990,000; $327,000 ÷ $1,290,000)	22.0%	26.4%	25.3%

NRV method using a given set of selling prices throughout the accounting period. Similarly, even though companies may occasionally change the number or sequence of processing steps beyond the splitoff point in order to adjust to variations in input quality or local conditions, they assume a specific constant set of such steps when implementing the NRV method.

Constant Gross-Margin Percentage NRV Method

The **constant gross-margin percentage NRV method** allocates joint costs to joint products produced during the accounting period in such a way that each individual product achieves an identical gross-margin percentage. The method works backward in that the overall gross margin is computed first. Then, for each product, this gross-margin percentage and any separable costs are deducted from the final sales value of production in order to back into the joint cost allocation for that product. The method can be broken down into three discrete steps. Exhibit 16-7, Panel A, shows these steps for allocating the $400,000 joint costs between buttercream and condensed milk in the Farmers' Dairy example. As we describe each step, refer to Exhibit 16-7, Panel A, for an illustration of the step.

Step 1: Compute overall gross margin percentage. The overall gross-margin percentage for all joint products together is calculated first. This is based on the final sales value of *total production* during the accounting period, not the *total revenues* of the period. Note, Exhibit 16-7, Panel A, uses $1,600,000, the final expected sales value of the entire output of buttercream and condensed milk, not the $1,290,000 in actual sales revenue for the month of May.

Step 2: Compute total production costs for each product. The gross margin (in dollars) for each product is computed by multiplying the overall gross-margin percentage by the product's final sales value of total production. The difference between the final sales value of total production and the gross margin then yields the total production costs that the product must bear.

Step 3: Compute allocated joint costs. As the final step, the separable costs for each product are deducted from the total production costs that the product must bear to obtain the joint-cost allocation for that product.

Exhibit 16-7, Panel B, presents the product-line income statement for the constant gross-margin percentage NRV method.

Exhibit 16-7 Joint-Cost Allocation and Product-Line Income Statement Using Constant Gross-Margin Percentage NRV Method: Farmers' Dairy for May 2012

	A	B	C	D
1	**PANEL A: Allocation of Joint Costs Using Constant Gross-Margin Percentage NRV Method**			
2	**Step 1**			
3	Final sales value of total production during accounting period: (20,000 gallons × $25 per gallon) + (50,000 gallons × $22 per gallon)	$1,600,000		
4	Deduct joint and separable costs ($400,000 + $280,000 + $520,000)	1,200,000		
5	Gross margin	$ 400,000		
6	Gross margin percentage ($400,000 ÷ $1,600,000)	25%		
7		**Buttercream**	**Condensed Milk**	**Total**
8	**Step 2**			
9	Final sales value of total production during accounting period: (20,000 gallons × $25 per gallon; 50,000 gallons × $22 per gallon)	$ 500,000	$1,100,000	$1,600,000
10	Deduct gross margin, using overall gross-margin percentage (25% × $500,000; 25% × $1,100,000)	125,000	275,000	400,000
11	Total production costs	375,000	825,000	1,200,000
12	**Step 3**			
13	Deduct separable costs	280,000	520,000	800,000
14	Joint costs allocated	$ 95,000	$ 305,000	$ 400,000
15				
16	**PANEL B: Product-Line Income Statement Using Constant Gross-Margin Percentage NRV Method for May 2012**	**Buttercream**	**Condensed Milk**	**Total**
17	Revenues (12,000 gallons × $25 per gallon; 45,000 gallons × $22 per gallon)	$ 300,000	$ 990,000	$1,290,000
18	Cost of goods sold			
19	Joint costs (from Panel A)	95,000	305,000	400,000
20	Separable costs	280,000	520,000	800,000
21	Production costs	375,000	825,000	1,200,000
22	Deduct ending inventory			
23	(8,000 gallons × $18.75 per gallon[a]; 5,000 gallons × $16.50 per gallon[b])	150,000	82,500	232,500
24	Cost of goods sold	225,000	742,500	967,500
25	Gross margin	$ 75,000	$ 247,500	$ 322,500
26	Gross margin percentage ($75,000 ÷ 300,000; $247,500 ÷ $990,000; $322,500 ÷ $1,290,000)	25%	25%	25%
27				
28	[a]Total production costs of buttercream ÷ Total production of buttercream = $375,000 ÷ 20,000 gallons = $18.75 per gallon.			
29	[b]Total production costs of condensed milk ÷ Total production of condensed milk = $825,000 ÷ 50,000 gallons = $16.50 per gallon.			

Decision Point ▶

What methods can be used to allocate joint costs to individual products?

The constant gross-margin percentage NRV method is the only method of allocating joint costs under which products may receive negative allocations. This may be required in order to bring the gross-margin percentages of relatively unprofitable products up to the overall average. The constant gross-margin percentage NRV method also differs from the other two market-based joint-cost-allocation methods described earlier in another fundamental way. Neither the sales value at splitoff method nor the NRV method takes account of profits earned either before or after the splitoff point when allocating the joint costs. In contrast, the constant gross-margin percentage NRV method allocates both joint costs and profits: Gross margin is allocated to the joint products in order to determine the joint-cost allocations so that the resulting gross-margin percentage for each product is the same.

Choosing an Allocation Method

Learning Objective 4

Explain when the sales value at splitoff method is preferred when allocating joint costs

. . . because it objectively measures the benefits received by each product

Which method of allocating joint costs should be used? The sales value at splitoff method is preferable when selling-price data exist at splitoff (even if further processing is done). Reasons for using the sales value at splitoff method include the following:

1. **Measurement of the value of the joint products at the splitoff point.** Sales value at splitoff is the best measure of the benefits received as a result of joint processing relative to all other methods of allocating joint costs. It is a meaningful basis for allocating joint costs because generating revenues is the reason why a company incurs joint costs in the first place. It is also sometimes possible to vary the physical mix of final output and thereby produce more or less market value by incurring more joint costs. In such cases, there is a clear causal link between total cost and total output value, thereby further validating the use of the sales value at splitoff method.[6]

2. **No anticipation of subsequent management decisions.** The sales value at splitoff method does not require information on the processing steps after splitoff if there is further processing. In contrast, the NRV and constant gross-margin percentage NRV methods require information on (a) the specific sequence of further processing decisions, (b) the separable costs of further processing, and (c) the point at which individual products will be sold.

3. **Availability of a common basis to allocate joint costs to products.** The sales value at splitoff method (as well as other market-based methods) has a common basis to allocate joint costs to products, which is revenue. In contrast, the physical-measure at splitoff method may lack an easily identifiable common basis to allocate joint costs to individual products.

4. **Simplicity.** The sales value at splitoff method is simple. In contrast, the NRV and constant gross-margin percentage NRV methods can be complex for processing operations having multiple products and multiple splitoff points. This complexity increases when management makes frequent changes in the specific sequence of post-splitoff processing decisions or in the point at which individual products are sold.

When selling prices of all products at the splitoff point are unavailable, the NRV method is commonly used because it attempts to approximate sales value at splitoff by subtracting from selling prices separable costs incurred after the splitoff point. The NRV method assumes that all the markup or profit margin is attributable to the joint process and none of the markup is attributable to the separable costs. Profit, however, is attributable to all phases of production and marketing, not just the joint process. More of the profit may be attributable to the joint process if the separable process is relatively routine, whereas more of the profit may be attributable to the separable process if the separable process uses a special patented technology. Despite its complexities, the NRV method is used when selling prices at splitoff are not available as it provides a better measure of benefits received compared with the constant gross-margin percentage NRV method or the physical-measure method.

---

[6] In the semiconductor industry, for example, the use of cleaner facilities, higher quality silicon wafers, and more sophisticated equipment (all of which require higher joint costs) shifts the distribution of output to higher-quality memory devices with more market value. For details, see J. F. Gatti and D. J. Grinnell, "Joint Cost Allocations: Measuring and Promoting Productivity and Quality Improvements," *Journal of Cost Management* (2000). The authors also demonstrate that joint cost allocations based on market value are preferable for promoting quality and productivity improvements.

The constant gross-margin percentage NRV method makes the simplifying assumption of treating the joint products as though they comprise a single product. This method calculates the aggregate gross-margin percentage, applies this gross-margin percentage to each product, and views the residual after separable costs are accounted for as the implicit amount of joint costs assigned to each product. An advantage of this method is that it avoids the complexities inherent in the NRV method to measure the benefits received by each of the joint products at the splitoff point. The main issue with the constant gross-margin percentage NRV method is the assumption that all products have the same ratio of cost to sales value. Recall from our discussion of activity-based costing (ABC) in Chapter 5 that such a situation is very uncommon when companies offer a diverse set of products.

Although there are difficulties in using the physical-measure method—such as lack of congruence with the benefits-received criterion—there are instances when it may be preferred. Consider rate or price regulation. Market-based measures are difficult to use in this context because using selling prices as a basis for setting prices (rates) and at the same time using selling prices to allocate the costs on which prices (rates) are based leads to circular reasoning. To avoid this dilemma, the physical-measure method is useful in rate regulation.

Not Allocating Joint Costs

Some companies choose to not allocate joint costs to products. The usual rationale given by these firms is the complexity of their production or extraction processes and the difficulty of gathering sufficient data for carrying out the allocations correctly. For example, a recent survey of nine sawmills in Norway revealed that none of them allocated joint costs. The study's authors noted that the "interviewed sawmills considered the joint cost problem very interesting, but pointed out that the problem is not easily solved. For example, there is clearly a shortcoming in management systems designed for handling joint cost allocation."[7]

In the absence of joint cost allocation, some firms simply subtract the joint costs directly from total revenues in the management accounts. If substantial inventories exist, then firms that do not allocate joint costs often carry their product inventories at NRV. Industries that use variations of this approach include meatpacking, canning, and mining. Accountants do not ordinarily record inventories at NRV because this practice results in recognizing income on each product at the time production is completed and *before* sales are made. In response, some companies using this no-allocation approach carry their inventories at NRV minus an estimated operating income margin. When any end-of-period inventories are sold in the next period, the cost of goods sold then equals this carrying value. This approach is akin to the "production method" of accounting for byproducts, which we describe in detail later in this chapter.

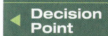

Decision Point

When is the sales value at splitoff method considered preferable for allocating joint costs to individual products and why?

Irrelevance of Joint Costs for Decision Making

Chapter 11 introduced the concepts of *relevant revenues*, expected future revenues that differ among alternative courses of action, and *relevant costs*, expected future costs that differ among alternative courses of action. These concepts can be applied to decisions on whether a joint product or main product should be sold at the splitoff point or processed further.

Learning Objective 5

Explain why joint costs are irrelevant in a sell-or-process-further decision

. . . because joint costs are the same whether or not further processing occurs

Sell-or-Process-Further Decisions

Consider Farmers' Dairy's decision to either sell the joint products, cream and liquid skim, at the splitoff point or to further process them into buttercream and condensed milk. The decision to incur additional costs for further processing should be based on the incremental operating income attainable beyond the splitoff point. Example 2 assumed it was profitable for both cream and liquid skim to be further processed into buttercream

---

[7] For further details, see T. Tunes, A. Nyrud, and B. Eikenes, "Cost and Performance Management in the Sawmill Industry," *Scandinavian Forest Economics* (2006).

and condensed milk, respectively. The incremental analysis for the decision to process further is as follows:

Further Processing Cream into Buttercream

Incremental revenues	
($25/gallon × 20,000 gallons) − ($8/gallon × 25,000 gallons)	$300,000
Deduct incremental processing costs	280,000
Increase in operating income from buttercream	$ 20,000

Further Processing Liquid Skim into Condensed Milk

Incremental revenues	
($22/gallon × 50,000 gallons) − ($4/gallon × 75,000 gallons)	$800,000
Deduct incremental processing costs	520,000
Increase in operating income from condensed milk	$280,000

In this example, operating income increases for both products, so the manager decides to process cream into buttercream and liquid skim into condensed milk. *The $400,000 joint costs incurred before the splitoff point are irrelevant in deciding whether to process further.* Why? Because the joint costs of $400,000 are the same whether the products are sold at the splitoff point or processed further.

Incremental costs are the additional costs incurred for an activity, such as further processing. *Do not assume all separable costs in joint-cost allocations are always incremental costs.* Some separable costs may be fixed costs, such as lease costs on buildings where the further processing is done; some separable costs may be sunk costs, such as depreciation on the equipment that converts cream into buttercream; and some separable costs may be allocated costs, such as corporate costs allocated to the condensed milk operations. None of these costs will differ between the alternatives of selling products at the splitoff point or processing further; therefore, they are irrelevant.

Joint-Cost Allocation and Performance Evaluation

The potential conflict between cost concepts used for decision making and cost concepts used for evaluating the performance of managers could also arise in sell-or-process-further decisions. To see how, let us continue with Example 2. Suppose *allocated* fixed corporate and administrative costs of further processing cream into buttercream equal $30,000 and that these costs will be allocated only to buttercream and to the manager's product-line income statement if buttercream is produced. How might this policy affect the decision to process further?

As we have seen, on the basis of incremental revenues and incremental costs, Farmers' operating income will increase by $20,000 if it processes cream into buttercream. However, producing the buttercream also results in an additional charge for allocated fixed costs of $30,000. If the manager is evaluated on a full-cost basis (that is, after allocating all costs), processing cream into buttercream will lower the manager's performance-evaluation measure by $10,000 (incremental operating income, $20,000 − allocated fixed costs, $30,000). Therefore, the manager may be tempted to sell cream at splitoff and not process it into buttercream.

A similar conflict can also arise with respect to production of joint products. Consider again Example 1. Suppose Farmers' Dairy has the option of selling raw milk at a profit of $20,000. From a decision-making standpoint, Farmers' would maximize operating income by processing raw milk into cream and liquid skim because the total revenues from selling both joint products ($500,000, see Exhibit 16-3, p. 581) exceed the joint costs ($400,000, p. 580) by $100,000. (This amount is greater than the $20,000 Farmers' Dairy would make if it sold the raw milk instead of processing it.) Suppose, however, the cream and liquid-skim product lines are managed by different managers, each of whom is evaluated based on a product-line income statement. If the physical-measure method of joint-cost allocation is used and the selling price per gallon of liquid skim falls below $4.00 per gallon, the liquid-skim product line will show a loss (from Exhibit 16-4, p. 582, revenues will be less than $120,000, but cost of goods sold will be unchanged at $120,000). The manager of the liquid-skim line will prefer, from his or her performance-evaluation standpoint, to not produce liquid skim but rather to sell the raw milk.

This conflict between decision making and performance evaluation is less severe if Farmers' Dairy uses any of the market-based methods of joint-cost allocations—sales value at splitoff, NRV, or constant gross-margin percentage NRV—because each of these methods allocates costs using revenues, which generally leads to a positive income for each joint product.

Pricing Decisions

Firms should be wary of using the full cost of a joint product (that is, the cost after joint costs are allocated) as the basis for making pricing decisions. Why? Because in many situations, there is no direct cause-and-effect relationship that identifies the resources demanded by each joint product that can then be used as a basis for pricing. In fact, the use of the sales value at splitoff or the net realizable value method to allocate joint costs results in a reverse effect—selling prices of joint products drive joint-cost allocations, rather than cost allocations serving as the basis for the pricing of joint products! Of course, the principles of pricing covered in Chapter 12 apply to the joint process taken as a whole. Even if the firm cannot alter the mix of products generated by the joint process, it must ensure that the joint products generate sufficient combined revenue in the long run to cover the joint costs of processing.

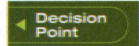

Decision Point

Are joint costs relevant in a sell-or-process-further decision?

Accounting for Byproducts

Joint production processes may yield not only joint products and main products but also byproducts. Although byproducts have relatively low total sales values, the presence of byproducts in a joint production process can affect the allocation of joint costs. Let's consider a two-product example consisting of a main product and a byproduct (also see the Concepts in Action feature on p. 590).

Learning Objective 6

Account for byproducts using two methods

. . . recognize in financial statements at time of production or at time of sale

> Example 3: The Westlake Corporation processes timber into fine-grade lumber and wood chips that are used as mulch in gardens and lawns. Information about these products follows:
>
> ■ Fine-Grade lumber (the main product)—sells for $6 per board foot (b.f.)
>
> ■ Wood chips (the byproduct)—sells for $1 per cubic foot (c.f.)
>
> Data for July 2012 are as follows:

	Beginning Inventory	Production	Sales	Ending Inventory
Fine-Grade lumber (b.f.)	0	50,000	40,000	10,000
Wood chips (c.f.)	0	4,000	1,200	2,800

Joint manufacturing costs for these products in July 2012 are $250,000, comprising $150,000 for direct materials and $100,000 for conversion costs. Both products are sold at the splitoff point without further processing, as Exhibit 16-8 shows.

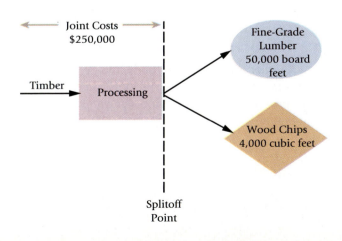

Exhibit 16-8

Example 3: Overview of Westlake Corporation

Concepts in Action

Byproduct Costing Keeps Wendy's Chili Profitable . . . and on the Menu

There are many examples in which joint and byproduct costing issues arise, including coal mining, semiconductor manufacturing, and Wendy's chili. You may be asking yourself, "chili from Wendy's?" Yes! The primary ingredient in chili at Wendy's, one of the largest fast-food chains in the United States, is a byproduct of overcooked, unsellable hamburger patties.

The most important product that Wendy's offers its customers is an "old-fashioned" hamburger, which is a hamburger served from the grill in accordance with individual customer orders. Operationally, the only way to serve hamburgers this way is to anticipate customer demand and have a sufficient supply of hamburgers already cooking when the customers arrive at the restaurant. The problem with this approach, however, is the fate of the extra hamburgers that become too well done whenever the cooks overestimate customer demand. Throwing them away would be too costly and wasteful, but serving them as "old-fashioned" hamburgers would likely result in considerable customer dissatisfaction.

For Wendy's, the solution to this dilemma involved finding a product that was unique to the fast-food industry and required ground beef as one of the major ingredients. Thus, Wendy's "rich and meaty" chili became one of its original menu items. For each batch of chili, which is prepared daily in each restaurant, Wendy's needs 48 quarter-pound cooked ground-beef patties along with crushed tomatoes, tomato juice, red beans, and seasoning. Only 10% of the time is it necessary for Wendy's to cook meat specifically for use in making chili.

Several years ago, Wendy's management considered eliminating some of its traditional menu items. Chili, composing only about 5% of total restaurant sales, was targeted for possible elimination, and at $0.99 for an eight-ounce serving, it brought in far less revenue than a product like a single hamburger, which sold for $1.89. When Wendy's compared the cost of making chili to its sale price, however, the product remained on the menu. How? The beef in Wendy's chili recipe was a byproduct of hamburger patties, its main product, which affected the allocation of joint costs.

Excluding ground beef, the costs to produce Wendy's chili are around $0.37 per eight-ounce serving, which includes labor. When Wendy's has to cook meat for its chili, again only 10% of the time, the recipe calls for ground beef that costs around $0.73 per serving. Under those circumstances, the chili costs Wendy's $1.10 to make, and each $.99 serving sells at a $0.11 loss. However, the 90% of the time Wendy's uses precooked ground beef for its chili, most of those costs have already been allocated to hamburgers, the primary product. As a result, each eight-ounce serving of chili Wendy's sells using precooked ground beef is sold at a significant profit. With a lucrative profit margin for each serving sold, customers are likely to find chili on the Wendy's menu for a long time to come.

Source: Brownlee, E. Richard. 2005. Wendy's chili: A costing conundrum. The University of Virginia Darden School of Business Case No. UVA-C-2206. Charlottesville, VA: Darden Business Publishing.

We present two byproduct accounting methods: the production method and the sales method. The production method recognizes byproducts in the financial statements at the time production is completed. The sales method delays recognition of byproducts until the time of sale.[8] Exhibit 16-9 presents the income statement of Westlake Corporation under both methods.

---

[8] For a discussion of joint cost allocation and byproduct accounting methods, see P. D. Marshall and R. F. Dombrowski, "A Small Business Review of Accounting for Primary Products, Byproducts and Scrap," *The National Public Accountant* (February/March 2003): 10–13.

	Production Method	Sales Method
Revenues		
Main product: Fine-grade lumber (40,000 b.f. × $6 per b.f.)	$240,000	$240,000
Byproduct: Wood chips (1,200 c.f. × $1 per c.f.)	—	1,200
Total revenues	240,000	241,200
Cost of goods sold		
Total manufacturing costs	250,000	250,000
Deduct byproduct revenue (4,000 c.f. × $1 per c.f.)	(4,000)	—
Net manufacturing costs	246,000	250,000
Deduct main-product inventory	(49,200)[a]	(50,000)[b]
Cost of goods sold	196,800	200,000
Gross margin	$ 43,200	$ 41,200
Gross-margin percentage ($43,200 ÷ $240,000; $41,200 ÷ $241,200)	18.00%	17.08%
Inventoriable costs (end of period):		
Main product: Fine-grade lumber	$ 49,200	$ 50,000
Byproduct: Wood chips (2,800 c.f. × $1 per c.f.)[c]	2,800	0

Exhibit 16-9

Income Statements of Westlake Corporation for July 2012 Using the Production and Sales Methods for Byproduct Accounting

[a](10,000 ÷ 50,000) × net manufacturing cost = (10,000 ÷ 50,000) × $246,000 = $49,200.
[b](10,000 ÷ 50,000) × total manufacturing cost = (10,000 ÷ 50,000) × $250,000 = $50,000.
[c]Recorded at selling prices.

Production Method: Byproducts Recognized at Time Production Is Completed

This method recognizes the byproduct in the financial statements—the 4,000 cubic feet of wood chips—in the month it is produced, July 2012. The NRV from the byproduct produced is offset against the costs of the main product. The following journal entries illustrate the production method:

1. Work in Process	150,000	
Accounts Payable		150,000
To record direct materials purchased and used in production during July.		
2. Work in Process	100,000	
Various accounts such as Wages Payable and Accumulated Depreciation		100,000
To record conversion costs in the production process during July; examples include energy, manufacturing supplies, all manufacturing labor, and plant depreciation.		
3. Byproduct Inventory—Wood Chips (4,000 c.f. × $1 per c.f.)	4,000	
Finished Goods—Fine-Grade Lumber ($250,000 − $4,000)	246,000	
Work in Process ($150,000 + $100,000)		250,000
To record cost of goods completed during July.		
4a. Cost of Goods Sold [(40,000 b.f. ÷ 50,000 b.f.) × $246,000]	196,800	
Finished Goods—Fine-Grade Lumber		196,800
To record the cost of the main product sold during July.		
4b. Cash or Accounts Receivable (40,000 b.f. × $6 per b.f.)	240,000	
Revenues—Fine-Grade Lumber		240,000
To record the sales of the main product during July.		
5. Cash or Accounts Receivable (1,200 c.f. × $1 per c.f.)	1,200	
Byproduct Inventory—Wood Chips		1,200
To record the sales of the byproduct during July.		

The production method reports the byproduct inventory of wood chips in the balance sheet at its $1 per cubic foot selling price [(4,000 cubic feet − 1,200 cubic feet) × $1 per cubic foot = $2,800].

One variation of this method would be to report byproduct inventory at its NRV reduced by a normal profit margin ($2,800 − 20% × $2,800 = $2,240, assuming a normal profit margin of 20%).[9] When byproduct inventory is sold in a subsequent period, the income statement will match the selling price, $2,800, with the "cost" reported for the byproduct inventory, $2,240, resulting in a byproduct operating income of $560 ($2,800 − $2,240).

Sales Method: Byproducts Recognized at Time of Sale

This method makes no journal entries for byproducts until they are sold. Revenues of the byproduct are reported as a revenue item in the income statement at the time of sale. These revenues are either grouped with other sales, included as other income, or are deducted from cost of goods sold. In the Westlake Corporation example, byproduct revenues in July 2012 are $1,200 (1,200 cubic feet × $1 per cubic foot) because only 1,200 cubic feet of wood chips are sold in July (of the 4,000 cubic feet produced). The journal entries are as follows:

1. and 2.	*Same as for the production method.*		
	Work in Process	150,000	
	Accounts Payable		150,000
	Work in Process	100,000	
	Various accounts such as Wages Payable and Accumulated Depreciation		100,000
3.	Finished Goods—Fine-Grade Lumber	250,000	
	Work in Process		250,000
	To record cost of main product completed during July.		
4a.	Cost of Goods Sold [(40,000 b.f. ÷ 50,000 b.f.) × $250,000]	200,000	
	Finished Goods—Fine-Grade Lumber		200,000
	To record the cost of the main product sold during July.		
4b.	Same as for the production method.		
	Cash or Accounts Receivable (40,000 b.f. × $6 per b.f.)	240,000	
	Revenues—Fine-Grade Lumber		240,000
5.	Cash or Accounts Receivable	1,200	
	Revenues—Wood Chips		1,200
	To record the sales of the byproduct during July.		

Decision Point

What methods can be used to account for byproducts and which of them is preferable?

Which method should a company use? The production method is conceptually correct in that it is consistent with the matching principle. This method recognizes byproduct inventory in the accounting period in which it is produced and simultaneously reduces the cost of manufacturing the main or joint products, thereby better matching the revenues and expenses from selling the main product. However, the sales method is simpler and is often used in practice, primarily on the grounds that the dollar amounts of byproducts are immaterial. Then again, the sales method permits managers to "manage" reported earnings by timing when they sell byproducts. Managers may store byproducts for several periods and give revenues and income a "small boost" by selling byproducts accumulated over several periods when revenues and profits from the main product or joint products are low.

Problem for Self-Study

Inorganic Chemicals (IC) processes salt into various industrial products. In July 2012, IC incurred joint costs of $100,000 to purchase salt and convert it into two products: caustic soda and chlorine. Although there is an active outside market for chlorine, IC processes all 800 tons of chlorine it produces into 500 tons of PVC (polyvinyl chloride), which is

---

[9] One way to make this calculation is to assume all products have the same "normal" profit margin like the constant gross-margin percentage NRV method. Alternatively, the company might allow products to have different profit margins based on an analysis of the margins earned by other companies that sell these products individually.

then sold. There were no beginning or ending inventories of salt, caustic soda, chlorine, or PVC in July. Information for July 2012 production and sales follows:

	A	B	C	D
1		**Joint Costs**		**PVC**
2	Joint costs (costs of salt and processing to splitoff point)	$100,000		
3	Separable cost of processing 800 tons chlorine into 500 tons PVC			$20,000
4				
5		**Caustic Soda**	**Chlorine**	**PVC**
6	Beginning inventory (tons)	0	0	0
7	Production (tons)	1,200	800	500
8	Transfer for further processing (tons)		800	
9	Sales (tons)	1,200		500
10	Ending inventory (tons)	0	0	0
11	Selling price per ton in active outside market (for products not actually sold)		$ 75	
12	Selling price per ton for products sold	$ 50		$ 200

Required

1. Allocate the joint costs of $100,000 between caustic soda and PVC under (a) the sales value at splitoff method and (b) the physical-measure method.
2. Allocate the joint costs of $100,000 between caustic soda and PVC under the NRV method.
3. Under the three allocation methods in requirements 1 and 2, what is the gross-margin percentage of (a) caustic soda and (b) PVC?
4. Lifetime Swimming Pool Products offers to purchase 800 tons of chlorine in August 2012 at $75 per ton. Assume all other production and sales data are the same for August as they were for July. This sale of chlorine to Lifetime would mean that no PVC would be produced by IC in August. How would accepting this offer affect IC's August 2012 operating income?

Solution

The following picture provides a visual illustration of the main facts in this problem.

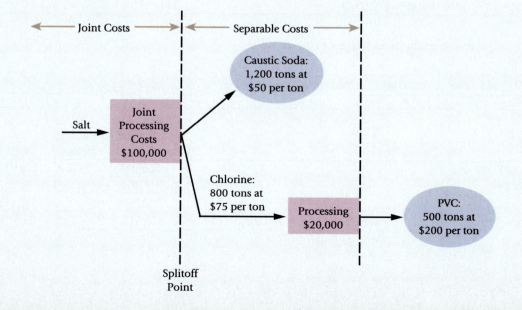

Note that caustic soda is sold as is while chlorine, despite having a market value at split-off, is sold only in processed form as PVC. The goal is to allocate the joint costs of $100,000 to the final products—caustic soda and PVC. However, since PVC exists only in the form of chlorine at the splitoff point, we use chlorine's sales value and physical measure as the basis for allocating joint costs to PVC under the sales value at splitoff and physical measure at splitoff methods. Detailed calculations are shown next.

1a. Sales value at splitoff method

	A	B	C	D
	Home Insert Page Layout Formulas Data Review View			
	A	B	C	D
1	**Allocation of Joint Costs Using Sales Value at Splitoff Method**	**Caustic Soda**	**PVC / Chlorine**	**Total**
2	Sales value of total production at splitoff point			
3	(1,200 tons × $50 per ton; 800 × $75 per ton)	$60,000	$60,000	$120,000
4	Weighting ($60,000 ÷ $120,000; $60,000 ÷ $120,000)	0.50	0.50	
5	Joint costs allocated (0.50 × $100,000; 0.50 × $100,000)	$50,000	$50,000	$100,000

1b. Physical-measure method

	A	B	C	D
	Home Insert Page Layout Formulas Data Review View			
	A	B	C	D
8	**Allocation of Joint Costs Using Physical-Measure Method**	**Caustic Soda**	**PVC / Chlorine**	**Total**
9	Physical measure of total production (tons)	1,200	800	2,000
10	Weighting (1,200 tons ÷ 2,000 tons; 800 tons ÷ 2,000 tons)	0.60	0.40	
11	Joint cost allocated (0.60 × $100,000; 0.40 × $100,000)	$60,000	$40,000	$100,000

2. Net realizable value (NRV) method

	A	B	C	D
	Home Insert Page Layout Formulas Data Review View			
	A	B	C	D
14	**Allocation of Joint Costs Using Net Realizable Value Method**	**Caustic Soda**	**PVC**	**Total**
15	Final sales value of total production during accounting period			
16	(1,200 tons × $50 per ton; 500 tons × $200 per ton)	$60,000	$100,000	$160,000
17	Deduct separable costs to complete and sell	0	20,000	20,000
18	Net realizable value at splitoff point	$60,000	$ 80,000	$140,000
19	Weighting ($60,000 ÷ $140,000; $80,000 ÷ $140,000)	3/7	4/7	
20	Joint costs allocated (3/7 × $100,000; 4/7 × $100,000)	$42,857	$ 57,143	$100,000

3a. Gross-margin percentage of caustic soda

	A	B	C	D
	Home Insert Page Layout Formulas Data Review View			
	A	Sales Value at Splitoff Point	Physical Measure	NRV
23	**Caustic Soda**			
24	Revenues (1,200 tons × $50 per ton)	$60,000	$60,000	$60,000
25	Cost of goods sold (joint costs)	50,000	60,000	42,857
26	Gross margin	$10,000	$ 0	$17,143
27	Gross margin percentage ($10,000 ÷ $60,000; $0 ÷ $60,000; $17,143 ÷ $60,000)	16.67%	0.00%	28.57%

3b. Gross-margin percentage of PVC

PVC	Sales Value at Splitoff Point	Physical Measure	NRV
31 Revenues (500 tons × $200 per ton)	$100,000	$100,000	$100,000
32 Cost of goods sold			
33 Joint costs	50,000	40,000	57,143
34 Separable costs	20,000	20,000	20,000
35 Cost of goods sold	70,000	60,000	77,143
36 Gross margin	$ 30,000	$ 40,000	$ 22,857
37 Gross margin percentage ($30,000 ÷ $100,000; $40,000 ÷ $100,000; $22,857 ÷ $100,000)	30.00%	40.00%	22.86%

4. Sale of chlorine versus processing into PVC

	A	B
40	Incremental revenue from processing 800 tons of chlorine into 500 tons of PVC	
41	(500 tons × $200 per ton) – (800 tons × $75 per ton)	$40,000
42	Incremental cost of processing 800 tons of chlorine into 500 tons of PVC	20,000
43	Incremental operating income from further processing	$ 20,000

If IC sells 800 tons of chlorine to Lifetime Swimming Pool Products instead of further processing it into PVC, its August 2012 operating income will be reduced by $20,000.

Decision Points

The following question-and-answer format summarizes the chapter's learning objectives. Each decision presents a key question related to a learning objective. The guidelines are the answer to that question.

Decision

1. What do the terms joint cost and splitoff point mean, and how do joint products differ from byproducts?

2. Why are joint costs allocated to individual products?

3. What methods can be used to allocate joint costs to individual products?

Guidelines

A joint cost is the cost of a single production process that yields multiple products simultaneously. The splitoff point is the juncture in a joint production process when the products become separately identifiable. Joint products have high total sales values at the splitoff point. A byproduct has a low total sales value at the splitoff point compared with the total sales value of a joint or main product.

The purposes for allocating joint costs to products include inventory costing for financial accounting and internal reporting, cost reimbursement, insurance settlements, rate regulation, and product-cost litigation.

The methods to allocate joint costs to products are the sales value at splitoff, NRV, constant gross-margin percentage NRV, and physical-measure methods.

4. **When is the sales value at splitoff method considered preferable for allocating joint costs to individual products and why?**

The sales value at splitoff method is preferable when market prices exist at splitoff because using revenues is consistent with the benefits-received criterion; further, the method does not anticipate subsequent management decisions on further processing, and is simple.

5. **Are joint costs relevant in a sell-or-process-further decision?**

No, joint costs and how they are allocated are irrelevant in deciding whether to process further because joint costs are the same regardless of whether further processing occurs.

6. **What methods can be used to account for byproducts and which of them is preferable?**

The production method recognizes byproducts in financial statements at the time of production, whereas the sales method recognizes byproducts in financial statements at the time of sale. The production method is conceptually superior, but the sales method is often used in practice because dollar amounts of byproducts are immaterial.

Terms to Learn

This chapter and the Glossary at the end of the book contain definitions of the following important terms:

byproducts **(p. 578)**

constant gross-margin percentage NRV method **(p. 584)**

joint costs **(p. 577)**

joint products **(p. 578)**

main product **(p. 578)**

net realizable value (NRV) method **(p. 583)**

physical-measure method **(p. 582)**

product **(p. 578)**

sales value at splitoff method **(p. 580)**

separable costs **(p. 577)**

splitoff point **(p. 577)**

Assignment Material

Questions

16-1 Give two examples of industries in which joint costs are found. For each example, what are the individual products at the splitoff point?

16-2 What is a joint cost? What is a separable cost?

16-3 Distinguish between a joint product and a byproduct.

16-4 Why might the number of products in a joint-cost situation differ from the number of outputs? Give an example.

16-5 Provide three reasons for allocating joint costs to individual products or services.

16-6 Why does the sales value at splitoff method use the sales value of the total production in the accounting period and not just the revenues from the products sold?

16-7 Describe a situation in which the sales value at splitoff method cannot be used but the NRV method can be used for joint-cost allocation.

16-8 Distinguish between the sales value at splitoff method and the NRV method.

16-9 Give two limitations of the physical-measure method of joint-cost allocation.

16-10 How might a company simplify its use of the NRV method when final selling prices can vary sizably in an accounting period and management frequently changes the point at which it sells individual products?

16-11 Why is the constant gross-margin percentage NRV method sometimes called a "joint-cost-allocation and a profit-allocation" method?

16-12 "Managers must decide whether a product should be sold at splitoff or processed further. The sales value at splitoff method of joint-cost allocation is the best method for generating the information managers need for this decision." Do you agree? Explain.

16-13 "Managers should consider only additional revenues and separable costs when making decisions about selling at splitoff or processing further." Do you agree? Explain.

16-14 Describe two major methods to account for byproducts.

16-15 Why might managers seeking a monthly bonus based on attaining a target operating income prefer the sales method of accounting for byproducts rather than the production method?

Exercises

16-16 **Joint-cost allocation, insurance settlement.** Quality Chicken grows and processes chickens. Each chicken is disassembled into five main parts. Information pertaining to production in July 2012 is as follows:

Parts	Pounds of Product	Wholesale Selling Price per Pound When Production Is Complete
Breasts	100	$0.55
Wings	20	0.20
Thighs	40	0.35
Bones	80	0.10
Feathers	10	0.05

Joint cost of production in July 2012 was $50.

A special shipment of 40 pounds of breasts and 15 pounds of wings has been destroyed in a fire. Quality Chicken's insurance policy provides reimbursement for the cost of the items destroyed. The insurance company permits Quality Chicken to use a joint-cost-allocation method. The splitoff point is assumed to be at the end of the production process.

Required

1. Compute the cost of the special shipment destroyed using the following:
   a. Sales value at splitoff method
   b. Physical-measure method (pounds of finished product)
2. What joint-cost-allocation method would you recommend Quality Chicken use? Explain.

16-17 Joint products and byproducts (continuation of 16-16). Quality Chicken is computing the ending inventory values for its July 31, 2012, balance sheet. Ending inventory amounts on July 31 are 15 pounds of breasts, 4 pounds of wings, 6 pounds of thighs, 5 pounds of bones, and 2 pounds of feathers.

Quality Chicken's management wants to use the sales value at splitoff method. However, management wants you to explore the effect on ending inventory values of classifying one or more products as a byproduct rather than a joint product.

Required

1. Assume Quality Chicken classifies all five products as joint products. What are the ending inventory values of each product on July 31, 2012?
2. Assume Quality Chicken uses the production method of accounting for byproducts. What are the ending inventory values for each joint product on July 31, 2012, assuming breasts and thighs are the joint products and wings, bones, and feathers are byproducts?
3. Comment on differences in the results in requirements 1 and 2.

16-18 Net realizable value method. Convad Company is one of the world's leading corn refiners. It produces two joint products—corn syrup and corn starch—using a common production process. In July 2012, Convad reported the following production and selling-price information:

	Home	Insert	Page Layout	Formulas	Data	Review	View			
	A							B	C	D
1								**Corn Syrup**	**Corn Starch**	**Joint Costs**
2	Joint costs (costs of processing corn to splitoff point)									$325,000
3	Separable cost of processing beyond splitoff point							$375,000	$93,750	
4	Beginning inventory (cases)							0	0	
5	Production and Sales (cases)							12,500	6,250	
6	Ending inventory (cases)							0	0	
7	Selling price per case							50	$ 25	

Allocate the $325,000 joint costs using the NRV method.

Required

16-19 Alternative joint-cost-allocation methods, further-process decision. The Wood Spirits Company produces two products—turpentine and methanol (wood alcohol)—by a joint process. Joint costs amount to $120,000 per batch of output. Each batch totals 10,000 gallons: 25% methanol and 75% turpentine. Both products are processed further without gain or loss in volume. Separable processing costs are methanol, $3 per gallon; turpentine, $2 per gallon. Methanol sells for $21 per gallon. Turpentine sells for $14 per gallon.

Required

1. How much of the joint costs per batch will be allocated to turpentine and to methanol, assuming that joint costs are allocated based on the number of gallons at splitoff point?
2. If joint costs are allocated on an NRV basis, how much of the joint costs will be allocated to turpentine and to methanol?
3. Prepare product-line income statements per batch for requirements 1 and 2. Assume no beginning or ending inventories.
4. The company has discovered an additional process by which the methanol (wood alcohol) can be made into a pleasant-tasting alcoholic beverage. The selling price of this beverage would be $60 a gallon. Additional processing would increase separable costs $9 per gallon (in addition to the $3 per gallon separable cost

required to yield methanol). The company would have to pay excise taxes of 20% on the selling price of the beverage. Assuming no other changes in cost, what is the joint cost applicable to the wood alcohol (using the NRV method)? Should the company produce the alcoholic beverage? Show your computations.

16-20 Alternative methods of joint-cost allocation, ending inventories. The Evrett Company operates a simple chemical process to convert a single material into three separate items, referred to here as X, Y, and Z. All three end products are separated simultaneously at a single splitoff point.

Products X and Y are ready for sale immediately upon splitoff without further processing or any other additional costs. Product Z, however, is processed further before being sold. There is no available market price for Z at the splitoff point.

The selling prices quoted here are expected to remain the same in the coming year. During 2012, the selling prices of the items and the total amounts sold were as follows:

- X—75 tons sold for $1,800 per ton
- Y—225 tons sold for $1,300 per ton
- Z—280 tons sold for $800 per ton

The total joint manufacturing costs for the year were $328,000. Evrett spent an additional $120,000 to finish product Z.

There were no beginning inventories of X, Y, or Z. At the end of the year, the following inventories of completed units were on hand: X, 175 tons; Y, 75 tons; Z, 70 tons. There was no beginning or ending work in process.

Required

1. Compute the cost of inventories of X, Y, and Z for balance sheet purposes and the cost of goods sold for income statement purposes as of December 31, 2012, using the following joint cost allocation methods:
   a. NRV method
   b. Constant gross-margin percentage NRV method
2. Compare the gross-margin percentages for X, Y, and Z using the two methods given in requirement 1.

16-21 Joint-cost allocation, process further. Sinclair Oil & Gas, a large energy conglomerate, jointly processes purchased hydrocarbons to generate three nonsaleable intermediate products: ICR8, ING4, and XGE3. These intermediate products are further processed separately to produce crude oil, natural gas liquids (NGL), and natural gas (measured in liquid equivalents). An overview of the process and results for August 2012 are shown here. (Note: The numbers are small to keep the focus on key concepts.)

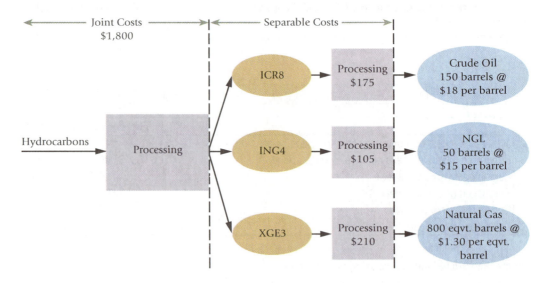

A new federal law has recently been passed that taxes crude oil at 30% of operating income. No new tax is to be paid on natural gas liquid or natural gas. Starting August 2012, Sinclair Oil & Gas must report a separate product-line income statement for crude oil. One challenge facing Sinclair Oil & Gas is how to allocate the joint cost of producing the three separate saleable outputs. Assume no beginning or ending inventory.

Required

1. Allocate the August 2012 joint cost among the three products using the following:
   a. Physical-measure method
   b. NRV method
2. Show the operating income for each product using the methods in requirement 1.
3. Discuss the pros and cons of the two methods to Sinclair Oil & Gas for making decisions about product emphasis (pricing, sell-or-process-further decisions, and so on).
4. Draft a letter to the taxation authorities on behalf of Sinclair Oil & Gas that justifies the joint-cost-allocation method you recommend Sinclair use.

16-22 **Joint-cost allocation, sales value, physical measure, NRV methods.** Instant Foods produces two types of microwavable products—beef-flavored ramen and shrimp-flavored ramen. The two products share common inputs such as noodle and spices. The production of ramen results in a waste product referred to as stock, which Instant dumps at negligible costs in a local drainage area. In June 2012, the following data were reported for the production and sales of beef-flavored and shrimp-flavored ramen:

	A	B	C
1		**Joint Costs**	
2	Joint costs (costs of noodles, spices, and other inputs and processing to splitoff point)	$240,000	
3			
4		**Beef Ramen**	**Shrimp Ramen**
5	Beginning inventory (tons)	0	0
6	Production (tons)	10,000	20,000
7	Sales (tons)	10,000	20,000
8	Selling price per ton	$ 10	$ 15

Due to the popularity of its microwavable products, Instant decides to add a new line of products that targets dieters. These new products are produced by adding a special ingredient to dilute the original ramen and are to be sold under the names Special B and Special S, respectively. The following is the monthly data for all the products:

	A	B	C	D	E
11		**Joint Costs**		**Special B**	**Special S**
12	Joint costs (costs of noodles, spices, and other inputs and processing to splitoff point)	$240,000			
13	Separable costs of processing 10,000 tons of Beef Ramen into 12,000 tons of Special B			$48,000	
14	Separable cost of processing 20,000 tons of Shrimp Ramen into 24,000 tons of Special S				$168,000
15					
16		**Beef Ramen**	**Shrimp Ramen**	**Special B**	**Special S**
17	Beginning inventory (tons)	0	0	0	0
18	Production (tons)	10,000	20,000	12,000	24,000
19	Transfer for further processing (tons)	10,000	20,000		
20	Sales (tons)			12,000	24,000
21	Selling price per ton	$ 10	$ 15	$ 18	$ 25

Required

1. Calculate Instant's gross-margin percentage for Special B and Special S when joint costs are allocated using the following:
   a. Sales value at splitoff method
   b. Physical-measure method
   c. Net realizable value method
2. Recently, Instant discovered that the stock it is dumping can be sold to cattle ranchers at $5 per ton. In a typical month with the production levels shown, 4,000 tons of stock are produced and can be sold by incurring marketing costs of $10,800. Sherrie Dong, a management accountant, points out that treating the stock as a joint product and using the sales value at splitoff method, the stock product would lose about $2,228 each month, so it should not be sold. How did Dong arrive at that final number, and what do you think of her analysis? Should Instant sell the stock?

16-23 Joint cost allocation: sell immediately or process further. Iowa Soy Products (ISP) buys soy beans and processes them into other soy products. Each ton of soy beans that ISP purchases for $300 can be converted for an additional $200 into 500 pounds of soy meal and 100 gallons of soy oil. A pound of soy meal can be sold at splitoff for $1 and soy oil can be sold in bulk for $4 per gallon.

ISP can process the 500 pounds of soy meal into 600 pounds of soy cookies at an additional cost of $300. Each pound of soy cookies can be sold for $2 per pound. The 100 gallons of soy oil can be packaged at a cost of $200 and made into 400 quarts of Soyola. Each quart of Soyola can be sold for $1.25.

Required

1. Allocate the joint cost to the cookies and the Soyola using the following:
   a. Sales value at splitoff method
   b. NRV method
2. Should ISP have processed each of the products further? What effect does the allocation method have on this decision?

16-24 Accounting for a main product and a byproduct. (Cheatham and Green, adapted) Tasty, Inc., is a producer of potato chips. A single production process at Tasty, Inc., yields potato chips as the main product and a byproduct that can also be sold as a snack. Both products are fully processed by the splitoff point, and there are no separable costs.

For September 2012, the cost of operations is $500,000. Production and sales data are as follows:

	Production (in pounds)	Sales (in pounds)	Selling Price per Pound
Main Product:			
Potato Chips	52,000	42,640	$16
Byproduct	8,500	6,500	$10

There were no beginning inventories on September 1, 2012.
1. What is the gross margin for Tasty, Inc., under the production method and the sales method of byproduct accounting?
2. What are the inventory costs reported in the balance sheet on September 30, 2012, for the main product and byproduct under the two methods of byproduct accounting in requirement 1?

16-25 Joint costs and byproducts. (W. Crum adapted) Royston, Inc., is a large food processing company. It processes 150,000 pounds of peanuts in the peanuts department at a cost of $180,000 to yield 12,000 pounds of product A, 65,000 pounds of product B, and 16,000 pounds of product C.

■ Product A is processed further in the salting department to yield 12,000 pounds of salted peanuts at a cost of $27,000 and sold for $12 per pound.
■ Product B (raw peanuts) is sold without further processing at $3 per pound.
■ Product C is considered a byproduct and is processed further in the paste department to yield 16,000 pounds of peanut butter at a cost of $12,000 and sold for $6 per pound.

The company wants to make a gross margin of 10% of revenues on product C and needs to allow 20% of revenues for marketing costs on product C. An overview of operations follows:

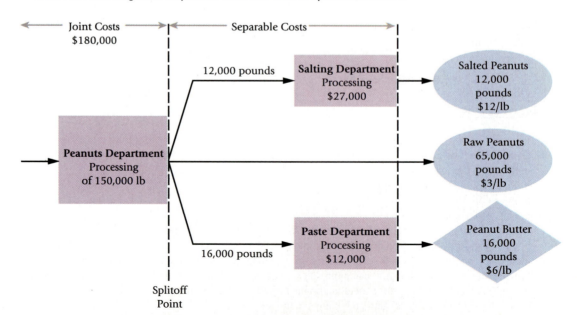

1. Compute unit costs per pound for products A, B, and C, treating C as a byproduct. Use the NRV method for allocating joint costs. Deduct the NRV of the byproduct produced from the joint cost of products A and B.
2. Compute unit costs per pound for products A, B, and C, treating all three as joint products and allocating joint costs by the NRV method.

Problems

16-26 Accounting for a byproduct. Sunny Day Juice Company produces oranges from various organic growers in Florida. The juice is extracted from the oranges and the pulp and peel remain. Sunny Day considers the pulp and peel byproducts of its juice production and can sell them to a local farmer for $2.00 per pound. During the most recent month, Sunny Day purchased 4,000 pounds of oranges and produced 1,500 gallons of juice and 900 pounds of pulp and peel at a joint cost of $7,200. The selling price for a half-gallon of orange juice is $2.50. Sunny Day sold 2,800 half-gallons of juice and 860 pounds of pulp and peel during the most recent month. The company had no beginning inventories.

1. Assuming Sunny Day accounts for the byproduct using the production method, what is the inventoriable cost for each product and Sunny Day's gross margin?
2. Assuming Sunny Day accounts for the byproduct using the sales method, what is the inventoriable cost for each product and Sunny Day's gross margin?
3. Discuss the difference between the two methods of accounting for byproducts.

16-27 Alternative methods of joint-cost allocation, product-mix decisions. The Southern Oil Company buys crude vegetable oil. Refining this oil results in four products at the splitoff point: A, B, C, and D. Product C is fully processed by the splitoff point. Products A, B, and D can individually be further refined into Super A, Super B, and Super D. In the most recent month (December), the output at the splitoff point was as follows:

- Product A, 322,400 gallons
- Product B, 119,600 gallons
- Product C, 52,000 gallons
- Product D, 26,000 gallons

The joint costs of purchasing and processing the crude vegetable oil were $96,000. Southern had no beginning or ending inventories. Sales of product C in December were $24,000. Products A, B, and D were further refined and then sold. Data related to December are as follows:

	Separable Processing Costs to Make Super Products	Revenues
Super A	$249,600	$300,000
Super B	102,400	160,000
Super D	152,000	160,000

Southern had the option of selling products A, B, and D at the splitoff point. This alternative would have yielded the following revenues for the December production:

- Product A, $84,000
- Product B, $72,000
- Product D, $60,000

1. Compute the gross-margin percentage for each product sold in December, using the following methods for allocating the $96,000 joint costs:
   a. Sales value at splitoff
   b. Physical-measure
   c. NRV
2. Could Southern have increased its December operating income by making different decisions about the further processing of products A, B, or D? Show the effect on operating income of any changes you recommend.

16-28 Comparison of alternative joint-cost-allocation methods, further-processing decision, chocolate products. The Chocolate Factory manufactures and distributes chocolate products. It purchases cocoa beans and processes them into two intermediate products: chocolate-powder liquor base and milk-chocolate liquor base. These two intermediate products become separately identifiable at a single splitoff point. Every 1,500 pounds of cocoa beans yields 60 gallons of chocolate-powder liquor base and 90 gallons of milk-chocolate liquor base.

The chocolate-powder liquor base is further processed into chocolate powder. Every 60 gallons of chocolate-powder liquor base yield 600 pounds of chocolate powder. The milk-chocolate liquor base is further processed into milk chocolate. Every 90 gallons of milk-chocolate liquor base yield 1,020 pounds of milk chocolate.

Production and sales data for August 2012 are as follows (assume no beginning inventory):

■ Cocoa beans processed, 15,000 pounds
■ Costs of processing cocoa beans to splitoff point (including purchase of beans), $30,000

	Production	Sales	Selling Price	Separable Processing Costs
Chocolate powder	6,000 pounds	6,000 pounds	$4 per pound	$12,750
Milk chocolate	10,200 pounds	10,200 pounds	$5 per pound	$26,250

Chocolate Factory fully processes both of its intermediate products into chocolate powder or milk chocolate. There is an active market for these intermediate products. In August 2012, Chocolate Factory could have sold the chocolate-powder liquor base for $21 a gallon and the milk-chocolate liquor base for $26 a gallon.

Required

1. Calculate how the joint costs of $30,000 would be allocated between chocolate powder and milk chocolate under the following methods:
   a. Sales value at splitoff
   b. Physical-measure (gallons)
   c. NRV
   d. Constant gross-margin percentage NRV
2. What are the gross-margin percentages of chocolate powder and milk chocolate under each of the methods in requirement 1?
3. Could Chocolate Factory have increased its operating income by a change in its decision to fully process both of its intermediate products? Show your computations.

16-29 Joint-cost allocation, process further or sell. (CMA, adapted) Sonimad Sawmill, Inc., (SSI) purchases logs from independent timber contractors and processes the logs into three types of lumber products:

■ Studs for residential buildings (walls, ceilings)
■ Decorative pieces (fireplace mantels, beams for cathedral ceilings)
■ Posts used as support braces (mine support braces, braces for exterior fences on ranch properties)

These products are the result of a joint sawmill process that involves removal of bark from the logs, cutting the logs into a workable size (ranging from 8 to 16 feet in length), and then cutting the individual products from the logs.

The joint process results in the following costs of products for a typical month:

Direct materials (rough timber logs)	$ 500,000
Debarking (labor and overhead)	50,000
Sizing (labor and overhead)	200,000
Product cutting (labor and overhead)	250,000
Total joint costs	$1,000,000

Product yields and average sales values on a per-unit basis from the joint process are as follows:

Product	Monthly Output of Materials at Splitoff Point	Fully Processed Selling Price
Studs	75,000 units	$ 8
Decorative pieces	5,000 units	100
Posts	20,000 units	20

The studs are sold as rough-cut lumber after emerging from the sawmill operation without further processing by SSI. Also, the posts require no further processing beyond the splitoff point. The decorative pieces must be planed and further sized after emerging from the sawmill. This additional processing costs $100,000 per month and normally results in a loss of 10% of the units entering the process. Without this planing and sizing process, there is still an active intermediate market for the unfinished decorative pieces in which the selling price averages $60 per unit.

Required

1. Based on the information given for Sonimad Sawmill, allocate the joint processing costs of $1,000,000 to the three products using:
   a. Sales value at splitoff method
   b. Physical-measure method (volume in units)
   c. NRV method
2. Prepare an analysis for Sonimad Sawmill that compares processing the decorative pieces further, as it currently does, with selling them as a rough-cut product immediately at splitoff.

3. Assume Sonimad Sawmill announced that in six months it will sell the unfinished decorative pieces at splitoff due to increasing competitive pressure. Identify at least three types of likely behavior that will be demonstrated by the skilled labor in the planing-and-sizing process as a result of this announcement. Include in your discussion how this behavior could be influenced by management.

16-30 Joint-cost allocation. Elsie Dairy Products Corp. buys one input, full-cream milk, and refines it in a churning process. From each gallon of milk Elsie produces three cups of butter and nine cups of buttermilk. During May 2010, Elsie bought 12,000 gallons of milk for $22,250. Elsie spent another $9,430 on the churning process to separate the milk into butter and buttermilk. Butter could be sold immediately for $2.20 per pound and buttermilk could be sold immediately for $1.20 per quart (note: two cups = one pound; four cups = one quart).

Elsie chooses to process the butter further into spreadable butter by mixing it with canola oil, incurring an additional cost of $1.60 per pound. This process results in two tubs of spreadable butter for each pound of butter processed. Each tub of spreadable butter sells for $2.30.

1. Allocate the $31,680 joint cost to the spreadable butter and the buttermilk using the following:
   a. Physical-measure method (using cups) of joint cost allocation
   b. Sales value at splitoff method of joint cost allocation
   c. NRV method of joint cost allocation
   d. Constant gross margin percentage NRV method of joint cost allocation
2. Each of these measures has advantages and disadvantages; what are they?
3. Some claim that the sales value at split off method is the best method to use. Discuss the logic behind this claim.

Required

16-31 Further processing decision (continuation of 16-30). Elsie has decided that buttermilk may sell better if it was marketed for baking and sold in pints. This would involve additional packaging at an incremental cost of $0.35 per pint. Each pint could be sold for $0.75 (note: one quart = two pints).
1. If Elsie uses the sales value at splitoff method, what combination of products should Elsie sell to maximize profits?
2. If Elsie uses the physical-measure method, what combination of products should Elsie sell to maximize profits?
3. Explain the effect that the different cost allocation methods have on the decision to sell the products at split off or to process them further.

16-32 Joint-cost allocation with a byproduct. Mat Place purchases old tires and recycles them to produce rubber floor mats and car mats. The company washes, shreds, and molds the recycled tires into sheets. The floor and car mats are cut from these sheets. A small amount of rubber shred remains after the mats are cut. The rubber shreds can be sold to use as cover for paths and playgrounds. The company can produce 25 floor mats, 75 car mats, and 40 pounds of rubber shreds from 100 old tires.

In May, Mat Place, which had no beginning inventory, processed 125,000 tires and had joint production costs of $600,000. Mat Place sold 25,000 floor mats, 85,000 car mats, and 43,000 pounds of rubber shreds. The company sells each floor mat for $12 and each car mat for $6. The company treats the rubber shreds as a byproduct that can be sold for $0.70 per pound.

1. Assume that Mat Place allocates the joint costs to floor mats and car mats using the sales value at splitoff method and accounts for the byproduct using the production method. What is the ending inventory cost for each product and gross margin for Mat Place?
2. Assume that Mat Place allocates the joint costs to floor mats and car mats using the sales value at splitoff method and accounts for the byproduct using the sales method. What is the ending inventory cost for each product and gross margin for Mat Place?
3. Discuss the difference between the two methods of accounting for byproducts, focusing on what conditions are necessary to use each method.

Required

16-33 Byproduct-costing journal entries (continuation of 16-32). The Mat Place's accountant needs to record the information about the joint and byproducts in the general journal, but is not sure what the entries should be. The company has hired you as a consultant to help its accountant.
1. Show journal entries at the time of production and at the time of sale assuming the Mat Place accounts for the byproduct using the production method.
2. Show journal entries at the time of production and at the time of sale assuming the Mat Place accounts for the byproduct using the sales method.

Required

16-34 Process further or sell, byproduct. (CMA, adapted) Rochester Mining Company (RMC) mines coal, puts it through a one-step crushing process, and loads the bulk raw coal onto river barges for shipment to customers.

RMC's management is currently evaluating the possibility of further processing the raw coal by sizing and cleaning it and selling it to an expanded set of customers at higher prices. The option of building a new sizing and cleaning plant is ruled out as being financially infeasible. Instead, Amy Kimbell, a mining engineer, is asked to explore outside-contracting arrangements for the cleaning and sizing process. Kimbell puts together the following summary:

	A	B	C
1	Selling price of raw coal	$ 27	per ton
2	Cost of producing raw coal	$ 21	per ton
3	Selling price of sized and cleaned coal	$ 35	per ton
4	Annual raw coal output	9,800,000	tons
5	Percentage of material weight loss in sizing/cleaning coal	10%	
6			
7		**Incremental Costs of Sizing & Cleaning Processes**	
8	Direct labor	$ 820,000	per year
9	Supervisory personnel	$ 225,000	per year
10	Heavy equipment: rental, operating, maintenance costs	$ 15,000	per month
11	Contract sizing and cleaning	$ 3.60	per ton of raw coal
12	Outbound rail freight	$ 210	per 60-ton rail car
13			
14	Percentage of sizing/cleaning waste that can be salvaged for coal fines	75%	
15	Range of costs per ton for preparing coal fine for sale	$2	$4
16	Range of coal fine selling prices (per ton)	$16	$27

Kimbell also learns that 75% of the material loss that occurs in the cleaning and sizing process can be salvaged as coal fines, which can be sold to steel manufacturers for their furnaces. The sale of coal fines is erratic and RMC may need to stockpile it in a protected area for up to one year. The selling price of coal fine ranges from $16 to $27 per ton and costs of preparing coal fines for sale range from $2 to $4 per ton.

Required

1. Prepare an analysis to show whether it is more profitable for RMC to continue selling raw bulk coal or to process it further through sizing and cleaning. (Ignore coal fines in your analysis.)
2. How would your analysis be affected if the cost of producing raw coal could be held down to $17 per ton?
3. Now consider the potential value of the coal fines and prepare an addendum that shows how their value affects the results of your analysis prepared in requirement 1.

16-35 Joint Cost Allocation. Memory Manufacturing Company (MMC) produces memory modules in a two-step process: chip fabrication and module assembly.

In chip fabrication, each batch of raw silicon wafers yields 400 *standard* chips and 600 *deluxe* chips. Chips are classified as standard or deluxe on the basis of their density (the number of memory bits on each chip). Standard chips have 500 memory bits per chip, and deluxe chips have 1,000 memory bits per chip. Joint costs to process each batch are $28,900.

In module assembly, each batch of standard chips is converted into standard memory modules at a separately identified cost of $1,050 and then sold for $14,000. Each batch of deluxe chips is converted into deluxe memory modules at a separately identified cost of $2,450 and then sold for $26,500.

Required

1. Allocate joint costs of each batch to deluxe modules and standard modules using (a) the NRV method, (b) the constant gross-margin percentage NRV method, and (c) the physical-measure method, based on the number of memory bits. Which method should MMC use?
2. MMC can process each batch of 400 standard memory modules to yield 350 DRAM modules at an additional cost of $1,600. The selling price per DRAM module would be $46. Assume MMC uses the physical-measure method. Should MMC sell the standard memory modules or the DRAM modules?

16-36 Joint cost allocation, ending work in process inventories. Tastee Freez, Inc., produces two specialty ice cream mix flavors for soft serve ice cream machines. The two flavors, Extreme Chocolate and Very Strawberry, both start with a vanilla base. The vanilla base can be sold for $2 per gallon. The company did not have any beginning inventories but produced 8,000 gallons of the vanilla base during the most recent month at a cost of $5,200. The 8,000 gallons of base was used to begin production of 5,000 gallons of Extreme Chocolate and 3,000 gallons of Very Strawberry.

At the end of the month, the company had some of its ice cream mix still in process. There were 1,200 gallons of Extreme Chocolate 30% complete and 200 gallons of Very Strawberry 80% complete. Processing costs during the month for Extreme Chocolate and Very Strawberry were $9,152 and $8,880, respectively. The selling prices for Extreme Chocolate and Very Strawberry are $4 and $5, respectively.

1. Allocate the joint costs to Extreme Chocolate and Very Strawberry under the following methods: **Required**
   a. Sales value at splitoff
   b. Net realizable value
   c. Constant gross margin percentage NRV
2. Compute the gross margin percentages for Extreme Chocolate and Very Strawberry under each of the methods in requirement 1.

Collaborative Learning Problem

16-37 Joint Cost Allocation, processing further and ethics. Unified Chemical Company has a joint production process that converts Zeta into two chemicals: Alpha and Beta. The company purchases Zeta for $12 per pound and incurs a cost of $30 per pound to process it into Alpha and Beta. For every 10 pounds of Zeta, the company can produce 8 pounds of Alpha and 2 pounds of Beta. The selling price for Alpha and Beta are $76.50 and $144.00, respectively.

Unified Chemical generally processes Alpha and Beta further in separable processes to produce more refined products. Alpha is processed separately into Alphalite at a cost of $25.05 per pound. Beta is processed separately into Betalite at a cost of $112.80 per pound. Alphalite and Betalite sell for $105 and $285 per pound, respectively. In the most recent month, Unified Chemical purchased 15,000 pounds of Zeta. The company had no beginning or ending inventory of Zeta.

1. Allocate the joint costs to Alphalite and Betalite under the following methods: **Required**
   a. Sales value at splitoff
   b. Physical measure (pounds)
   c. Net realizable value
   d. Constant gross margin percentage NRV
2. Unified Chemical is considering an opportunity to process Betalite further into a new product called Ultra-Betalite. The separable processing will cost $85 per pound and expects an additional $15 per pound packaging cost for Ultra-Betalite. The expected selling price would be $360 per pound. Should Unified Chemical sell Betalite or Ultra-Betalite? What selling price for Ultra-Betalite would make Unified Chemical indifferent between selling Betalite and Ultra-Betalite?
3. Independent of your answer to requirement (2), suppose Danny Dugard, the assistant controller, has completed an analysis that shows Ultra-Betalite should not be produced. Before presenting his results to top management, he received a visit from Sally Kemper. Sally had been personally responsible for developing Ultra-Betalite and was upset to learn that it would not be manufactured.

   Sally: The company is making a big mistake by passing up this opportunity. Ultra-Betalite will be a big seller and will get us into new markets.
   Danny: But the analysis shows that we would be losing money on every pound of Ultra-Betalite we manufacture.
   Sally: But that is a temporary problem. Eventually the cost of processing will be reduced.
   Danny: Do you have any estimates on the cost reductions you expect?
   Sally: There is no way of knowing that right now. Can't you just fudge the numbers a little to help me get approval to produce Ultra-Betalite. I am confident that cost reductions will follow.

   Comment on the ethical issues in this scenario. What should Danny do?

Companies that produce identical or similar units of a product or service (for example, an oil-refining company) often use process costing.

A key part of process costing is valuing inventory, which entails determining how many units of the product the firm has on hand at the end of an accounting reporting period, evaluating the units' stages of completion, and assigning costs to the units. There are different methods for doing this, each of which can result in different profits. At times, variations in international rules and customs make it difficult to compare inventory costs across competitors. In the case of ExxonMobil, differences in accounting rules between the United States and Europe also reduce the company's profits and tax liability.

ExxonMobil and Accounting Differences in the Oil Patch[1]

In 2010, ExxonMobil was number two on the *Fortune* 500 annual ranking of the largest U.S. companies. In 2009, the company had $284 billion dollars in revenue with more than $19 billion in profits. Believe it or not, however, by one measure ExxonMobil's profits are *understated*.

ExxonMobil, like most U.S. energy companies, uses last-in, first-out (LIFO) accounting. Under this treatment, ExxonMobil records its cost of inventory at the latest price paid for crude oil in the open market, even though it is often selling oil produced at a much lower cost. This increases the company's cost of goods sold, which in turn reduces profit. The benefit of using LIFO accounting for financial reporting is that ExxonMobil is then permitted to use LIFO for tax purposes as well, thereby lowering its payments to the tax authorities.

In contrast, International Financial Reporting Standards (IFRS) do not permit the use of LIFO accounting. European oil companies such as Royal Dutch Shell and British Petroleum use the first-in, first-out (FIFO) methodology instead when accounting for inventory. Under FIFO, oil companies use the cost of the oldest crude in their inventory to calculate the cost of barrels of oil sold. This reduces costs on the income statement, therefore increasing gross margins.

Assigning costs to inventory is a critical part of process costing, and a company's choice of method can result in substantially different

---

[1] *Source:* Exxon Mobil Corporation. 2010. 2009 Annual Report. Irving, TX: Exxon Mobil Corporation; Kaminska, Izabella. 2010. Shell, BP, and the increasing cost of inventory. *Financial Times.* "FT Alphaville" blog, April 29; Reilly, David. 2006. Big oil's accounting methods fuel criticism. *Wall Street Journal*, August 8.

profits. For instance, ExxonMobil's 2009 net income would have been $7.1 billion higher under FIFO. Moreover, at the end of fiscal 2009, the cumulative difference—or "LIFO Reserve"—between the value of inventory ExxonMobil was carrying on its balance sheet based on the initial cost versus the current replacement cost of that inventory was $17.1 billion. This number takes on special relevance in the context of current efforts to achieve convergence between U.S. GAAP and IFRS. Should that happen, and if U.S. firms are forced to adopt FIFO for financial and tax reporting, they would have to pay additional taxes on the cumulative savings to date from showing a higher cost of goods sold in LIFO. As an approximation, applying a marginal tax rate of 35% to ExxonMobil's LIFO Reserve of $17.1 billion suggests an incremental tax burden of almost $6 billion.

Companies such as ExxonMobil, Coca-Cola, and Novartis produce many identical or similar units of a product using mass-production techniques. The focus of these companies on individual production processes gives rise to process costing. This chapter describes how companies use process costing methods to determine the costs of products or services and to value inventory and cost of goods sold (using methods like FIFO).

Illustrating Process Costing

Before we examine process costing in more detail, let's briefly compare job costing and process costing. Job-costing and process-costing systems are best viewed as ends of a continuum:

Learning Objective 1

Identify the situations in which process-costing systems are appropriate

. . . when masses of identical or similar units are produced

Job-costing system	Process-costing system
Distinct, identifiable units of a product or service (for example, custom-made machines and houses)	Masses of identical or similar units of a product or service (for example, food or chemical processing)

In a *process-costing system*, the unit cost of a product or service is obtained by assigning total costs to many identical or similar units of output. In other words, unit costs are calculated by dividing total costs incurred by the number of units of output from the production process. In a manufacturing process-costing setting, each unit receives the same or similar amounts of direct material costs, direct manufacturing labor costs, and indirect manufacturing costs (manufacturing overhead).

The main difference between process costing and job costing is the *extent of averaging* used to compute unit costs of products or services. In a job-costing system, individual jobs use different quantities of production resources, so it would be incorrect to cost each job at the same average production cost. In contrast, when identical or similar units of products or services are mass-produced, not processed as individual jobs, process costing is used to calculate an average production cost for all units produced. Some processes such as clothes manufacturing have aspects of both process costing (cost per unit of each operation, such as cutting or sewing, is identical) and job costing (different materials are used in different batches of clothing, say, wool versus cotton). The final section in this chapter describes "hybrid" costing systems that combine elements of both job and process costing.

Consider the following illustration of process costing: Suppose that Pacific Electronics manufactures a variety of cell phone models. These models are assembled in the assembly department. Upon completion, units are transferred to the testing department. We focus on the assembly department process for one model, SG-40. All units of SG-40 are identical and must meet a set of demanding performance specifications. The process-costing system for SG-40 in the assembly department has a single direct-cost category—direct materials— and a single indirect-cost category—conversion costs. Conversion costs are all manufacturing costs other than direct material costs, including manufacturing labor, energy, plant depreciation, and so on. Direct materials are added at the beginning of the assembly process. Conversion costs are added evenly during assembly.

The following graphic represents these facts:

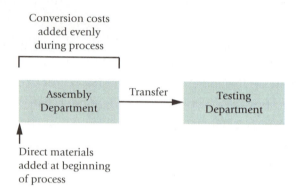

Process-costing systems separate costs into cost categories according to *when costs are introduced into the process*. Often, as in our Pacific Electronics example, only two cost classifications—direct materials and conversion costs—are necessary to assign costs to products. Why only two? Because *all* direct materials are added to the process at one time and all conversion costs generally are added to the process evenly through time. If, however, two different direct materials were added to the process at different times, two different direct-materials categories would be needed to assign these costs to products. Similarly, if manufacturing labor costs were added to the process at a different time from when the other conversion costs were added, an additional cost category—direct manufacturing labor costs—would be needed to separately assign these costs to products.

We will use the production of the SG-40 component in the assembly department to illustrate process costing in three cases, starting with the simplest case and introducing additional complexities in subsequent cases:

■ **Case 1**—Process costing with zero beginning and zero ending work-in-process inventory of SG-40. (That is, all units are started and fully completed within the accounting period.) *This case presents the most basic concepts of process costing and illustrates the feature of averaging of costs.*

■ **Case 2**—Process costing with zero beginning work-in-process inventory and some ending work-in-process inventory of SG-40. (That is, some units of SG-40 started during the accounting period are incomplete at the end of the period.) *This case introduces the five steps of process costing and the concept of equivalent units.*

■ **Case 3**—Process costing with both some beginning and some ending work-in-process inventory of SG-40. *This case adds more complexity and illustrates the effect of weighted-average and first-in, first-out (FIFO) cost flow assumptions on cost of units completed and cost of work-in-process inventory.*

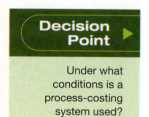

Under what conditions is a process-costing system used?

Case 1: Process Costing with No Beginning or Ending Work-in-Process Inventory

On January 1, 2012, there was no beginning inventory of SG-40 units in the assembly department. During the month of January, Pacific Electronics started, completely assembled, and transferred out to the testing department 400 units.

Data for the assembly department for January 2012 are as follows:

Physical Units for January 2012

Work in process, beginning inventory (January 1)	0 units
Started during January	400 units
Completed and transferred out during January	400 units
Work in process, ending inventory (January 31)	0 units

Physical units refer to the number of output units, whether complete or incomplete. In January 2012, all 400 physical units started were completed.

Total Costs for January 2012

Direct material costs added during January	$32,000
Conversion costs added during January	24,000
Total assembly department costs added during January	$56,000

Pacific Electronics records direct material costs and conversion costs in the assembly department as these costs are incurred. By averaging, assembly cost of SG-40 is $56,000 ÷ 400 units = $140 per unit, itemized as follows:

Direct material cost per unit ($32,000 ÷ 400 units)	$ 80
Conversion cost per unit ($24,000 ÷ 400 units)	60
Assembly department cost per unit	$140

Case 1 shows that in a process-costing system, average unit costs are calculated by dividing total costs in a given accounting period by total units produced in that period. Because each unit is identical, we assume all units receive the same amount of direct material costs and conversion costs. Case 1 applies whenever a company produces a homogeneous product or service but has no incomplete units when each accounting period ends, which is a common situation in service-sector organizations. For example, a bank can adopt this process-costing approach to compute the unit cost of processing 100,000 customer deposits, each similar to the other, made in a month.

Case 2: Process Costing with Zero Beginning and Some Ending Work-in-Process Inventory

In February 2012, Pacific Electronics places another 400 units of SG-40 into production. Because all units placed into production in January were completely assembled, there is no beginning inventory of partially completed units in the assembly department on February 1. Some customers order late, so not all units started in February are completed by the end of the month. Only 175 units are completed and transferred to the testing department.

Data for the assembly department for February 2012 are as follows:

	Physical Units (SG-40s) (1)	Direct Materials (2)	Conversion Costs (3)	Total Costs (4) = (2) + (3)
2 Work in process, beginning inventory (February 1)	0			
3 Started during February	400			
4 Completed and transferred out during February	175			
5 Work in process, ending inventory (February 29)	225			
6 Degree of completion of ending work in process		100%	60%	
7 Total costs added during February		$32,000	$18,600	$50,600

The 225 partially assembled units as of February 29, 2012, are fully processed with respect to direct materials, because all direct materials in the assembly department are added at the beginning of the assembly process. Conversion costs, however, are added evenly during assembly. Based on the work completed relative to the total work required

to complete the SG-40 units still in process at the end of February, an assembly depart-ment supervisor estimates that the partially assembled units are, on average, 60% com-plete with respect to conversion costs.

The accuracy of the completion estimate of conversion costs depends on the care, skill, and experience of the estimator and the nature of the conversion process. Estimating the degree of completion is usually easier for direct material costs than for conversion costs, because the quantity of direct materials needed for a completed unit and the quantity of direct materials in a partially completed unit can be measured more accurately. In contrast, the conversion sequence usually consists of a number of operations, each for a specified period of time, at various steps in the production process.[2] The degree of completion for conversion costs depends on the proportion of the total conversion costs needed to com-plete one unit (or a batch of production) that has already been incurred on the units still in process. It is a challenge for management accountants to make this estimate accurately.

Because of these uncertainties, department supervisors and line managers—individuals most familiar with the process—often make conversion cost estimates. Still, in some industries, such as semiconductor manufacturing, no exact estimate is possible; in other settings, such as the textile industry, vast quantities in process make the task of estimation too costly. In these cases, it is necessary to assume that all work in process in a department is complete to some preset degree with respect to conversion costs (for example, one-third, one-half, or two-thirds complete).

The point to understand here is that a partially assembled unit is not the same as a fully assembled unit. Faced with some fully assembled units and some partially assembled units, we require a common metric that will enable us to compare the work done in each category and, more important, obtain a total measure of work done. The concept we will use in this regard is that of *equivalent units*. We will explain this notion in greater detail next as part of the set of five steps required to calculate (1) the cost of fully assembled units in February 2012 and (2) the cost of partially assembled units still in process at the end of that month, for Pacific Electronics. The five steps of process costing are as follows:

Step 1:   Summarize the flow of physical units of output.
Step 2:   Compute output in terms of equivalent units.
Step 3:   Summarize total costs to account for.
Step 4:   Compute cost per equivalent unit.
Step 5:   Assign total costs to units completed and to units in ending work in process.

Physical Units and Equivalent Units (Steps 1 and 2)

Step 1 tracks physical units of output. Recall that physical units are the number of out-put units, whether complete or incomplete. Where did physical units come from? Where did they go? The physical-units column of Exhibit 17-1 tracks where the physical units came from (400 units started) and where they went (175 units completed and transferred out, and 225 units in ending inventory). Remember, when there is no opening inventory, units started must equal the sum of units transferred out and ending inventory.

Because not all 400 physical units are fully completed, output in **Step 2** is computed in *equivalent units*, not in *physical units*. To see what we mean by equivalent units, let's say that during a month, 50 physical units were started but not completed by the end of the month. These 50 units in ending inventory are estimated to be 70% complete with respect to conversion costs. Let's examine those units from the perspective of the conversion costs already incurred to get the units to be 70% complete. Suppose we put all the conversion costs represented in the 70% into making fully completed units. How many units could have been 100% complete by the end of the month? The answer is 35 units. Why? Because 70% of conversion costs incurred on 50 incomplete units could have been incurred to make 35 (0.70×50) complete units by the end of the month. That is, if all the conversion-cost input in the 50 units in inventory had been used to make completed output units, the com-pany would have produced 35 completed units (also called *equivalent units*) of output.

---

[2] For example, consider the conventional tanning process for converting hide to leather. Obtaining 250–300 kg of leather requires putting one metric ton of raw hide through as many as 15 steps: from soaking, liming, and pickling to tanning, dye-ing, and fatliquoring, the step in which oils are introduced into the skin before the leather is dried.

Exhibit 17-1

Steps 1 and 2:
Summarize Output in
Physical Units and
Compute Output in
Equivalent Units for
Assembly Department
of Pacific Electronics
for February 2012

	A	B	C	D
		(Step 1)	(Step 2)	
1			Equivalent Units	
2				
3	**Flow of Production**	**Physical Units**	**Direct Materials**	**Conversion Costs**
4	Work in process, beginning	0		
5	Started during current period	400		
6	To account for	400		
7	Completed and transferred out during current period	175	175	175
8	Work in process, ending[a]	225		
9	(225 × 100%; 225 × 60%)		225	135
10	Accounted for	400		
11	Equivalent units of work done in current period		400	310
12				
13	[a]Degree of completion in this department; direct materials, 100%; conversion costs, 60%.			

Equivalent units is a derived amount of output units that (1) takes the quantity of each input (factor of production) in units completed and in incomplete units of work in process and (2) converts the quantity of input into the amount of completed output units that could be produced with that quantity of input. Note that equivalent units are calculated separately for each input (such as direct materials and conversion costs). Moreover, every completed unit, by definition, is composed of one equivalent unit of each input required to make it. This chapter focuses on equivalent-unit calculations in manufacturing settings. Equivalent-unit concepts are also found in nonmanufacturing settings. For example, universities convert their part-time student enrollments into "full-time student equivalents."

When calculating equivalent units in Step 2, focus on quantities. Disregard dollar amounts until after equivalent units are computed. In the Pacific Electronics example, all 400 physical units—the 175 fully assembled units and the 225 partially assembled units— are 100% complete with respect to direct materials because all direct materials are added in the assembly department at the start of the process. Therefore, Exhibit 17-1 shows output as 400 *equivalent units* for direct materials: 175 equivalent units for the 175 physical units assembled and transferred out, and 225 equivalent units for the 225 physical units in ending work-in-process inventory.

The 175 fully assembled units are also completely processed with respect to conversion costs. The partially assembled units in ending work in process are 60% complete (on average). Therefore, conversion costs in the 225 partially assembled units are *equivalent* to conversion costs in 135 (60% of 225) fully assembled units. Hence, Exhibit 17-1 shows output as 310 *equivalent units* with respect to conversion costs: 175 equivalent units for the 175 physical units assembled and transferred out and 135 equivalent units for the 225 physical units in ending work-in-process inventory.

Calculation of Product Costs (Steps 3, 4, and 5)

Exhibit 17-2 shows Steps 3, 4, and 5. Together, they are called the *production cost worksheet*.

Step 3 summarizes total costs to account for. Because the beginning balance of work-in-process inventory is zero on February 1, total costs to account for (that is, the total charges or debits to the Work in Process—Assembly account) consist only of costs added during February: direct materials of $32,000 and conversion costs of $18,600, for a total of $50,600.

Step 4 in Exhibit 17-2 calculates cost per equivalent unit separately for direct materials and for conversion costs by dividing direct material costs and conversion costs added during February by the related quantity of equivalent units of work done in February (as calculated in Exhibit 17-1).

To see the importance of using equivalent units in unit-cost calculations, compare conversion costs for January and February 2012. Total conversion costs of $18,600 for the 400 units worked on during February are lower than the conversion costs of

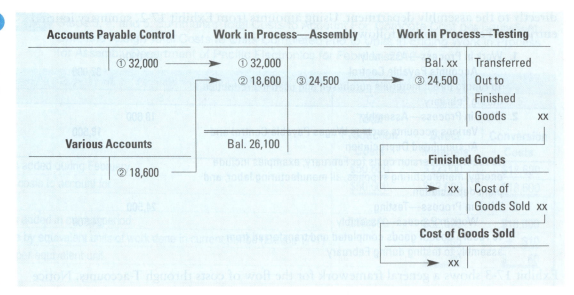

Weighted-Average Method

The **weighted-average process-costing method** calculates cost per equivalent unit of all *work done to date* (regardless of the accounting period in which it was done) and assigns this cost to equivalent units completed and transferred out of the process and to equivalent units in ending work-in-process inventory. The weighted-average cost is the total of all costs entering the Work in Process account (whether the costs are from beginning work in process or from work started during the current period) divided by total equivalent units of work done to date. We now describe the weighted-average method using the five-step procedure introduced on page 610.

Step 1: Summarize the Flow of Physical Units of Output. The physical-units column of Exhibit 17-4 shows where the units came from—225 units from beginning inventory and 275 units started during the current period—and where they went—400 units completed and transferred out and 100 units in ending inventory.

Step 2: Compute Output in Terms of Equivalent Units. The weighted-average cost of inventory is calculated by merging together the costs of beginning inventory and the manufacturing costs of a period and dividing by the total number of units in beginning inventory and units produced during the accounting period. We apply the same concept here

	Home Insert Page Layout Formulas Data Review View			
	A	B	C	D
1		(Step 1)	(Step 2)	
2			Equivalent Units	
3	**Flow of Production**	Physical Units	Direct Materials	Conversion Costs
4	Work in process, beginning (given, p. 613)	225		
5	Started during current period (given, p. 613)	275		
6	To account for	500		
7	Completed and transferred out during current period	400	400	400
8	Work in process, ending[a] (given, p. 613)	100		
9	(100 × 100%; 100 × 50%)		100	50
10	Accounted for	500		
11	Equivalent units of work done to date		500	450
12				
13	[a]Degree of completion in this department; direct materials, 100%; conversion costs, 50%.			

except that calculating the units—in this case equivalent units—is done differently. We use the relationship shown in the following equation:

$$\begin{array}{c}\text{Equivalent units}\\\text{in beginning work}\\\text{in process}\end{array} + \begin{array}{c}\text{Equivalent units}\\\text{of work done in}\\\text{current period}\end{array} = \begin{array}{c}\text{Equivalent units}\\\text{completed and transferred}\\\text{out in current period}\end{array} + \begin{array}{c}\text{Equivalent units}\\\text{in ending work}\\\text{in process}\end{array}$$

Although we are interested in calculating the left-hand side of the preceding equation, it is easier to calculate this sum using the equation's right-hand side: (1) equivalent units completed and transferred out in the current period plus (2) equivalent units in ending work in process. *Note that the stage of completion of the current-period beginning work in process is not used in this computation.*

The equivalent-units columns in Exhibit 17-4 show equivalent units of work done to date: 500 equivalent units of direct materials and 450 equivalent units of conversion costs. All completed and transferred-out units are 100% complete as to both direct materials and conversion costs. Partially completed units in ending work in process are 100% complete as to direct materials because direct materials are introduced at the beginning of the process, and 50% complete as to conversion costs, based on estimates made by the assembly department manager.

Step 3: Summarize Total Costs to Account For. Exhibit 17-5 presents Step 3. Total costs to account for in March 2012 are described in the example data on page 615: beginning work in process, $26,100 (direct materials, $18,000, plus conversion costs, $8,100), plus costs added during March, $36,180 (direct materials, $19,800, plus conversion costs, $16,380). The total of these costs is $62,280.

Step 4: Compute Cost per Equivalent Unit. Exhibit 17-5, Step 4, shows the computation of weighted-average cost per equivalent unit for direct materials and conversion costs. Weighted-average cost per equivalent unit is obtained by dividing the sum of costs for beginning work in process plus costs for work done in the current period by total

---

Exhibit 17-5 Steps 3, 4, and 5: Summarize Total Costs to Account For, Compute Cost per Equivalent Unit, and Assign Total Costs to Units Completed and to Units in Ending Work in Process Using Weighted-Average Method of Process Costing for Assembly Department of Pacific Electronics for March 2012

	A	B	C	D	E
			Total Production Costs	Direct Materials	Conversion Costs
1					
2	(Step 3)	Work in process, beginning (given, p. 613)	$26,100	$18,000	$ 8,100
3		Costs added in current period (given, p. 613)	36,180	19,800	16,380
4		Total costs to account for	$62,280	$37,800	$24,480
5					
6	(Step 4)	Costs incurred to date		$37,800	$24,480
7		Divide by equivalent units of work done to date (Exhibit 17-4)		÷ 500	÷ 450
8		Cost per equivalent unit of work done to date		$ 75.60	$ 54.40
9					
10	(Step 5)	Assignment of costs:			
11		Completed and transferred out (400 units)	$52,000	(400[a] × $75.60)	+(400[a] × $54.40)
12		Work in process, ending (100 units):	10,280	(100[b] × $75.60)	+ (50[b] × $54.40)
13		Total costs accounted for	$62,280	$37,800	+ $24,480
14					
15	[a]Equivalent units completed and transferred out from Exhibit 17-4, Step 2.				
16	[b]Equivalent units in ending work in process from Exhibit 17-4, Step 2.				

equivalent units of work done to date. When calculating weighted-average conversion cost per equivalent unit in Exhibit 17-5, for example, we divide total conversion costs, $24,480 (beginning work in process, $8,100, plus work done in current period, $16,380), by total equivalent units of work done to date, 450 (equivalent units of conversion costs in beginning work in process and in work done in current period), to obtain weighted-average cost per equivalent unit of $54.40.

Step 5: Assign Total Costs to Units Completed and to Units in Ending Work in Process.
Step 5 in Exhibit 17-5 takes the equivalent units completed and transferred out and equivalent units in ending work in process calculated in Exhibit 17-4, Step 2, and assigns dollar amounts to them using the weighted-average cost per equivalent unit for direct materials and conversion costs calculated in Step 4. For example, total costs of the 100 physical units in ending work in process are as follows:

Direct materials:	
100 equivalent units × weighted-average cost per equivalent unit of $75.60	$ 7,560
Conversion costs:	
50 equivalent units × weighted-average cost per equivalent unit of $54.40	2,720
Total costs of ending work in process	$10,280

The following table summarizes total costs to account for ($62,280) and how they are accounted for in Exhibit 17-5. The arrows indicate that the costs of units completed and transferred out and units in ending work in process are calculated using weighted-average total costs obtained after merging costs of beginning work in process and costs added in the current period.

Costs to Account For		Costs Accounted for Calculated on a Weighted-Average Basis	
Beginning work in process	$26,100	Completed and transferred out	$52,000
Costs added in current period	36,180	Ending work in process	10,280
Total costs to account for	$62,280	Total costs accounted for	$62,280

Before proceeding, review Exhibits 17-4 and 17-5 to check your understanding of the weighted-average method. Note: Exhibit 17-4 deals with only physical and equivalent units, not costs. Exhibit 17-5 shows the cost amounts.

Using amounts from Exhibit 17-5, the summary journal entries under the weighted-average method for March 2012 at Pacific Electronics are as follows:

1. Work in Process—Assembly	19,800	
Accounts Payable Control		19,800
To record direct materials purchased and used in production during March.		
2. Work in Process—Assembly	16,380	
Various accounts such as Wages Payable Control and Accumulated Depreciation		16,380
To record conversion costs for March; examples include energy, manufacturing supplies, all manufacturing labor, and plant depreciation.		
3. Work in Process—Testing	52,000	
Work in Process—Assembly		52,000
To record cost of goods completed and transferred from assembly to testing during March.		

The T-account Work in Process—Assembly, under the weighted-average method, is as follows:

Work in Process—Assembly

Beginning inventory, March 1	26,100	③ Completed and transferred	52,000
① Direct materials	19,800	out to Work in Process—	
② Conversion costs	16,380	Testing	
Ending inventory, March 31	10,280		

First-In, First-Out Method

The **first-in, first-out (FIFO) process-costing method** (1) assigns the cost of the previous accounting period's equivalent units in beginning work-in-process inventory to the first units completed and transferred out of the process, and (2) assigns the cost of equivalent units worked on during the *current* period first to complete beginning inventory, next to start and complete new units, and finally to units in ending work-in-process inventory. The FIFO method assumes that the earliest equivalent units in work in process are completed first.

A distinctive feature of the FIFO process-costing method is that work done on beginning inventory before the current period is kept separate from work done in the current period. Costs incurred and units produced in the current period are used to calculate cost per equivalent unit of work done in the current period. In contrast, equivalent-unit and cost-per-equivalent-unit calculations under the weighted-average method *merge* units and costs in beginning inventory with units and costs of work done in the current period.

We now describe the FIFO method using the five-step procedure introduced on page 610.

Step 1: Summarize the Flow of Physical Units of Output. Exhibit 17-6, Step 1, traces the flow of physical units of production. The following observations help explain the calculation of physical units under the FIFO method for Pacific Electronics.

- The first physical units assumed to be completed and transferred out during the period are 225 units from beginning work-in-process inventory.

- The March data on page 613 indicate that 400 physical units were completed during March. The FIFO method assumes that of these 400 units, 175 units (400 units − 225 units from beginning work-in-process inventory) must have been started and completed during March.

- Ending work-in-process inventory consists of 100 physical units—the 275 physical units started minus the 175 units that were started and completed.

- The physical units "to account for" equal the physical units "accounted for" (500 units).

Step 2: Compute Output in Terms of Equivalent Units. Exhibit 17-6 also presents the computations for Step 2 under the FIFO method. *The equivalent-unit calculations for each cost category focus on equivalent units of work done in the current period (March) only.*

Under the FIFO method, equivalent units of work done in March on the beginning work-in-process inventory equal 225 physical units times *the percentage of work remaining to be done in March to complete these units*: 0% for direct materials, because beginning work in process is 100% complete with respect to direct materials, and 40% for conversion costs, because beginning work in process is 60% complete with respect to conversion costs. The results are 0 (0% × 225) equivalent units of work for direct materials and 90 (40% × 225) equivalent units of work for conversion costs.

The equivalent units of work done on the 175 physical units started and completed equals 175 units times 100% for both direct materials and conversion costs, because all work on these units is done in the current period.

The equivalent units of work done on the 100 units of ending work in process equal 100 physical units times 100% for direct materials (because all direct materials for these units are added in the current period) and 50% for conversion costs (because 50% of the conversion-costs work on these units is done in the current period).

Step 3: Summarize Total Costs to Account For. Exhibit 17-7 presents Step 3 and summarizes total costs to account for in March 2012 (beginning work in process and costs added in the current period) of $62,280, as described in the example data (p. 613).

Step 4: Compute Cost per Equivalent Unit. Exhibit 17-7 shows the Step 4 computation of cost per equivalent unit for *work done in the current period only* for direct materials and conversion costs. For example, conversion cost per equivalent unit of $52 is obtained by dividing current-period conversion costs of $16,380 by current-period conversion-costs equivalent units of 315.

Step 5: Assign Total Costs to Units Completed and to Units in Ending Work in Process. Exhibit 17-7 shows the assignment of costs under the FIFO method. Costs of work done in the current period are assigned (1) first to the additional work done to complete the beginning

Exhibit 17-6

Steps 1 and 2:
Summarize Output in
Physical Units and
Compute Output in
Equivalent Units Using
FIFO Method of
Process Costing for
Assembly Department
of Pacific Electronics
for March 2012

	A	B	C	D
		(Step 1)	**(Step 2)**	
			Equivalent Units	
	Flow of Production	**Physical Units**	**Direct Materials**	**Conversion Costs**
4	Work in process, beginning (given, p. 613)	225	(work done before current period)	
5	Started during current period (given, p. 613)	275		
6	To account for	500		
7	Completed and transferred out during current period:			
8	From beginning work in process[a]	225		
9	[225 × (100% − 100%); 225 × (100% − 60%)]		0	90
10	Started and completed	175[b]		
11	(175 × 100%; 175 × 100%)		175	175
12	Work in process, ending[c] (given, p. 613)	100		
13	(100 × 100%; 100 × 50%)		100	50
14	Accounted for	500		
15	Equivalent units of work done in current period		275	315
16				
17	[a]Degree of completion in this department; direct materials, 100%; conversion costs, 60%.			
18	[b]400 physical units completed and transferred out minus 225 physical units completed and			
19	transferred out from beginning work-in-process inventory.			
20	[c]Degree of completion in this department: direct materials, 100%; conversion costs, 50%.			

work in process, then (2) to work done on units started and completed during the current period, and finally (3) to ending work in process. *Step 5 takes each quantity of equivalent units calculated in Exhibit 17-6, Step 2, and assigns dollar amounts to them (using the cost-per-equivalent-unit calculations in Step 4).* The goal is to use the cost of work done in the current period to determine total costs of all units completed from beginning inventory and from work started and completed in the current period, and costs of ending work in process.

Of the 400 completed units, 225 units are from beginning inventory and 175 units are started and completed during March. The FIFO method starts by assigning the costs of beginning work-in-process inventory of $26,100 to the first units completed and transferred out. As we saw in Step 2, an additional 90 equivalent units of conversion costs are needed to complete these units in the current period. Current-period conversion cost per equivalent unit is $52, so $4,680 (90 equivalent units × $52 per equivalent unit) of additional costs are incurred to complete beginning inventory. Total production costs for units in beginning inventory are $26,100 + $4,680 = $30,780. The 175 units started and completed in the current period consist of 175 equivalent units of direct materials and 175 equivalent units of conversion costs. These units are costed at the cost per equivalent unit in the current period (direct materials, $72, and conversion costs, $52) for a total production cost of $21,700 [175 × ($72 + $52)].

Under FIFO, ending work-in-process inventory comes from units that were started but not fully completed during the current period. Total costs of the 100 partially assembled physical units in ending work in process are as follows:

Direct materials:		
100 equivalent units × $72 cost per equivalent unit in March		$7,200
Conversion costs:		
50 equivalent units × $52 cost per equivalent unit in March		2,600
Total cost of work in process on March 31		$9,800

The following table summarizes total costs to account for and costs accounted for of $62,280 in Exhibit 17-7. Notice how under the FIFO method, the layers of beginning work in process and costs added in the current period are kept separate. The arrows

Exhibit 17-7	Steps 3, 4, and 5: Summarize Total Costs to Account For, Compute Cost per Equivalent Unit, and Assign Total Costs to Units Completed and to Units in Ending Work in Process Using FIFO Method of Process Costing for Assembly Department of Pacific Electronics for March 2012

	A	B	C	D	E
1			Total Production Costs	Direct Material	Conversion Costs
2	(Step 3)	Work in process, beginning (given, p. 613)	$26,100	$18,000	$ 8,100
3		Costs added in current period (given, p. 613)	36,180	19,800	16,380
4		Total costs to account for	$62,280	$37,800	$24,480
5					
6	(Step 4)	Costs added in current period		$19,800	$16,380
7		Divide by equivalent units of work done in current period (Exhibit 17-6)		÷ 275	÷ 315
8		Cost per equivalent unit of work done in current period		$ 72	$ 52
9					
10	(Step 5)	Assignment of costs:			
11		Completed and transferred out (400 units):			
12		Work in process, beginning (225 units)	$26,100	$18,000 + $8,100	
13		Costs added to beginning work in process in current period	4,680	$(0^a \times \$72) + (90^a \times \$52)$	
14		Total from beginning inventory	30,780		
15		Started and completed (175 units)	21,700	$(175^b \times \$72) + (175^b \times \$52)$	
16		Total costs of units completed and transferred out	52,480		
17		Work in process, ending (100 units):	9,800	$(100^c \times \$72) + (50^c \times \$52)$	
18		Total costs accounted for	$62,280	$37,800 + $24,480	
19					
20	[a]Equivalent units used to complete beginning work in process from Exhibit 17-6, Step 2.				
21	[b]Equivalent units started and completed from Exhibit 17-6, Step 2.				
22	[c]Equivalent units in ending work in process from Exhibit 17-6, Step 2.				

indicate where the costs in each layer go—that is, to units completed and transferred out or to ending work in process. Be sure to include costs of beginning work in process ($26,100) when calculating costs of units completed from beginning inventory.

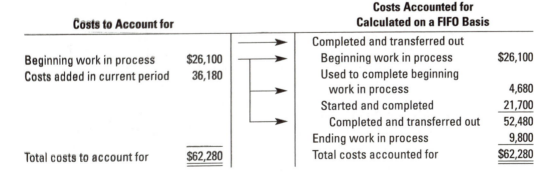

Before proceeding, review Exhibits 17-6 and 17-7 to check your understanding of the FIFO method. Note: Exhibit 17-6 deals with only physical and equivalent units, not costs. Exhibit 17-7 shows the cost amounts.

The journal entries under the FIFO method are identical to the journal entries under the weighted-average method except for one difference. The entry to record the cost of goods completed and transferred out would be $52,480 under the FIFO method instead of $52,000 under the weighted-average method.

Keep in mind that FIFO is applied within each department to compile the cost of units *transferred out*. As a practical matter, however, units *transferred in* during a given period usually are carried at a single average unit cost. For example, the assembly department uses FIFO in the preceding example to distinguish between monthly batches of production. The resulting average cost of units transferred out of the assembly department is $52,480 ÷ 400 units = $131.20 per SG-40 unit. The succeeding department, testing, however, costs these units (which consist of costs incurred in both February and March) at one average unit cost ($131.20 in this illustration). If this averaging were not done, the attempt to track costs on a pure FIFO basis throughout a series of processes would be cumbersome. As a result, the FIFO method should really be called a *modified* or *department* FIFO method.

Comparison of Weighted-Average and FIFO Methods

Consider the summary of the costs assigned to units completed and to units still in process under the weighted-average and FIFO process-costing methods in our example for March 2012:

	Weighted Average (from Exhibit 17-5)	FIFO (from Exhibit 17-7)	Difference
Cost of units completed and transferred out	$52,000	$52,480	+ $480
Work in process, ending	10,280	9,800	− $480
Total costs accounted for	$62,280	$62,280	

The weighted-average ending inventory is higher than the FIFO ending inventory by $480, or 4.9% ($480 ÷ $9,800 = 0.049, or 4.9%). This would be a significant difference when aggregated over the many thousands of products that Pacific Electronics makes. When completed units are sold, the weighted-average method in our example leads to a lower cost of goods sold and, therefore, higher operating income and higher income taxes than the FIFO method. To see why the weighted-average method yields a lower cost of units completed, recall the data on page 613. Direct material cost per equivalent unit in beginning work-in-process inventory is $80, and conversion cost per equivalent unit in beginning work-in-process inventory is $60. These costs are greater, respectively, than the $72 direct materials cost and the $52 conversion cost per equivalent unit of work done during the current period. The current-period costs could be lower due to a decline in the prices of direct materials and conversion-cost inputs, or as a result of Pacific Electronics becoming more efficient in its processes by using smaller quantities of inputs per unit of output, or both.

For the assembly department, FIFO assumes that (1) all the higher-cost units from the previous period in beginning work in process are the first to be completed and transferred out of the process and (2) ending work in process consists of only the lower-cost current-period units. The weighted-average method, however, smooths out cost per equivalent unit by assuming that (1) more of the lower-cost units are completed and transferred out and (2) some of the higher-cost units are placed in ending work in process. The decline in the current-period cost per equivalent unit results in a lower cost of units completed and transferred out and a higher ending work-in-process inventory under the weighted-average method compared with FIFO.

Cost of units completed and, hence, operating income can differ materially between the weighted-average and FIFO methods when (1) direct material or conversion cost per equivalent unit varies significantly from period to period and (2) physical-inventory levels of work in process are large in relation to the total number of units transferred out of the process. As companies move toward long-term procurement contracts that reduce differences in unit costs from period to period and reduce inventory levels, the difference in cost of units completed under the weighted-average and FIFO methods will decrease.[3]

---

[3] For example, suppose beginning work-in-process inventory for March were 125 physical units (instead of 225), and suppose costs per equivalent unit of work done in the current period (March) were direct materials, $75, and conversion costs, $55. Assume that all other data for March are the same as in our example. In this case, the cost of units completed and transferred out would be $52,833 under the weighted-average method and $53,000 under the FIFO method. The work-in-process ending inventory would be $10,417 under the weighted-average method and $10,250 under the FIFO method (calculations not shown). These differences are much smaller than in the chapter example. The weighted-average ending inventory is higher than the FIFO ending inventory by only $167 ($10,417 − $10,250), or 1.6% ($167 ÷ $10,250 = 0.016, or 1.6%), compared with 4.9% higher in the chapter example.

Managers use information from process-costing systems to aid them in pricing and product-mix decisions and to provide them with feedback about their performance. FIFO provides managers with information about changes in costs per unit from one period to the next. Managers can use this information to adjust selling prices based on current conditions (for example, based on the $72 direct material cost and $52 conversion cost in March). They can also more easily evaluate performance in the current period compared with a budget or relative to performance in the previous period (for example, recognizing the decline in both unit direct material and conversion costs relative to the prior period). By focusing on work done and costs of work done during the current period, the FIFO method provides useful information for these planning and control purposes.

The weighted-average method merges unit costs from different accounting periods, obscuring period-to-period comparisons. For example, the weighted-average method would lead managers at Pacific Electronics to make decisions based on the $75.60 direct materials and $54.40 conversion costs, rather than the costs of $72 and $52 prevailing in the current period. Advantages of the weighted-average method, however, are its relative computational simplicity and its reporting of a more-representative average unit cost when input prices fluctuate markedly from month to month.

Activity-based costing plays a significant role in our study of job costing, but how is activity-based costing related to process costing? Each process—assembly, testing, and so on—can be considered a different (production) activity. However, no additional activities need to be identified within each process. That's because products are homogeneous and use resources of each process in a uniform way. The bottom line is that activity-based costing has less applicability in process-costing environments. *The appendix illustrates the use of the standard costing method for the assembly department.*

Decision Point

What are the weighted-average and first-in, first-out (FIFO) methods of process costing? Under what conditions will they yield different levels of operating income?

Transferred-In Costs in Process Costing

Many process-costing systems have two or more departments or processes in the production cycle. As units move from department to department, the related costs are also transferred by monthly journal entries. **Transferred-in costs** (also called **previous-department costs**) are costs incurred in previous departments that are carried forward as the product's cost when it moves to a subsequent process in the production cycle.

We now extend our Pacific Electronics example to the testing department. As the assembly process is completed, the assembly department of Pacific Electronics immediately transfers SG-40 units to the testing department. Conversion costs are added evenly during the testing department's process. At the *end of the process* in testing, units receive additional direct materials, including crating and other packing materials to prepare units for shipment. As units are completed in testing, they are immediately transferred to Finished Goods. Computation of testing department costs consists of transferred-in costs, as well as direct materials and conversion costs that are added in testing.

The following diagram represents these facts:

Learning Objective 5

Apply process-costing methods to situations with transferred-in costs

. . . using weighted-average and FIFO methods

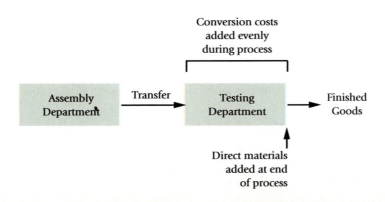

Data for the testing department for March 2012 are as follows:

	Home	Insert	Page Layout	Formulas	Data	Review	View	

	A	B	C	D	E
1		Physical Units (SG-40s)	Transferred-In Costs	Direct Materials	Conversion Costs
2	Work in process, beginning inventory (March 1)	240	$33,600	$ 0	$18,000
3	Degree of completion of beginning work in process		100%	0%	62.5%
4	Transferred in during March	400			
5	Completed and transferred out during March	440			
6	Work in process, ending inventory (March 31)	200			
7	Degree of completion of ending work in process		100%	0%	80%
8	Total costs added during March				
9	Direct materials and conversion costs			$13,200	$48,600
10	Transferred in (Weighted-average from Exhibit 17-5)[a]		$52,000		
11	Transferred in (FIFO from Exhibit 17-7)[a]		$52,480		
12					
13	[a]The transferred-in costs during March are different under the weighted-average method (Exhibit 17-5) and the FIFO method (Exhibit 17-7). In our example, beginning work-in-process inventory, $51,600 ($33,600 + $0 + $18,000) is the same under both the weighted-average and FIFO inventory methods because we assume costs per equivalent unit to be the same in both January and February. If costs per equivalent unit had been different in the two months, work-in-process inventory at the end of February (beginning of March) would be costed differently under the weighted-average and FIFO methods. The basic approach to process costing with transferred-in costs, however, would still be the same as what we describe in this section.				

Transferred-in costs are treated as if they are a separate type of direct material added at the beginning of the process. That is, transferred-in costs are always 100% complete as of the beginning of the process in the new department. When successive departments are involved, transferred units from one department become all or a part of the direct materials of the next department; however, they are called transferred-in costs, not direct material costs.

Transferred-In Costs and the Weighted-Average Method

To examine the weighted-average process-costing method with transferred-in costs, we use the five-step procedure described earlier (p. 610) to assign costs of the testing department to units completed and transferred out and to units in ending work in process.

Exhibit 17-8 shows Steps 1 and 2. The computations are similar to the calculations of equivalent units under the weighted-average method for the assembly department in Exhibit 17-4. The one difference here is that we have transferred-in costs as an additional input. All units, whether completed and transferred out during the period or in ending work in process, are always fully complete with respect to transferred-in costs. The reason is that the transferred-in costs refer to costs incurred in the assembly department, and any units received in the testing department must have first been completed in the assembly department. However, direct material costs have a zero degree of completion in both beginning and ending work-in-process inventories because, in testing, direct materials are introduced at the *end* of the process.

Exhibit 17-9 describes Steps 3, 4, and 5 for the weighted-average method. Beginning work in process and work done in the current period are combined for purposes of computing cost per equivalent unit for transferred-in costs, direct material costs, and conversion costs.

The journal entry for the transfer from testing to Finished Goods (see Exhibit 17-9) is as follows:

Finished Goods Control	120,890	
Work in Process—Testing		120,890
To record cost of goods completed and transferred from testing to Finished Goods.		

Entries in the Work in Process—Testing account (see Exhibit 17-9) are as follows:

Work in Process—Testing

Beginning inventory, March 1	51,600	Transferred out	120,890
Transferred-in costs	52,000		
Direct materials	13,200		
Conversion costs	48,600		
Ending inventory, March 31	44,510		

Exhibit 17-8 Steps 1 and 2: Summarize Output in Physical Units and Compute Output in Equivalent Units Using Weighted-Average Method of Process Costing for Testing Department of Pacific Electronics for March 2012

	Home	Insert	Page Layout	Formulas	Data	Review	View		
	A				B	C	D	E	
1					(Step 1)		(Step 2)		
2							Equivalent Units		
3		Flow of Production			Physical Units	Transferred-In Costs	Direct Materials	Conversion Costs	
4	Work in process, beginning (given, p. 622)				240				
5	Transferred in during current period (given, p. 622)				400				
6	To account for				640				
7	Completed and transferred out during current period				440	440	440	440	
8	Work in process, ending[a] (given, p. 622)				200				
9	(200 × 100%; 200 × 0%; 200 × 80%)					200	0	160	
10	Accounted for				640				
11	Equivalent units of work done to date					640	440	600	
12									
13	[a]Degree of completion in this department; transferred-in costs, 100%; direct materials, 0%; conversion costs, 80%.								

Exhibit 17-9 Steps 3, 4, and 5: Summarize Total Costs to Account For, Compute Cost per Equivalent Unit, and Assign Total Costs to Units Completed and to Units in Ending Work in Process Using Weighted-Average Method of Process Costing for Testing Department of Pacific Electronics for March 2012

	Home	Insert	Page Layout	Formulas	Data	Review	View		
	A	B			C	D	E	F	
1					Total Production Costs	Transferred-In Costs	Direct Materials	Conversion Costs	
2	(Step 3)	Work in process, beginning (given, p. 622)			$ 51,600	$33,600	$ 0	$18,000	
3		Costs added in current period (given, p. 622)			113,800	52,000	13,200	48,600	
4		Total costs to account for			$165,400	$85,600	$13,200	$66,600	
5									
6	(Step 4)	Costs incurred to date				$85,600	$13,200	$66,600	
7		Divide by equivalent units of work done to date (Exhibit 17-8)				÷ 640	÷ 440	÷ 600	
8		Cost per equivalent unit of work done to date				$133.75	$ 30.00	$111.00	
9									
10	(Step 5)	Assignment of costs:							
11		Completed and transferred out (440 units)			$120,890	(440[a] × $133.75) +	(440[a] × $30) +	(440[a] × $111)	
12		Work in process, ending (200 units):			44,510	(200[b] × $133.75) +	(0[b] × $30) +	(160[b] × $111)	
13		Total costs accounted for			$165,400	$85,600 +	$13,200 +	$66,600	
14									
15	[a]Equivalent units completed and transferred out from Exhibit 17-8, Step 2.								
16	[b]Equivalent units in ending work in process from Exhibit 17-8, Step 2.								

Transferred-In Costs and the FIFO Method

To examine the FIFO process-costing method with transferred-in costs, we again use the five-step procedure. Exhibit 17-10 shows Steps 1 and 2. Other than considering transferred-in costs, computations of equivalent units are the same as under the FIFO method for the assembly department shown in Exhibit 17-6.

Exhibit 17-11 describes Steps 3, 4, and 5. In Step 3, total costs to account for of $165,880 under the FIFO method differs from the corresponding amount under the weighted-average method of $165,400. The reason is the difference in cost of completed units transferred in from the assembly department under the two methods—$52,480 under FIFO and $52,000 under weighted average. Cost per equivalent unit for the current period in Step 4 is calculated on the basis of costs transferred in and work done in the current period only. Step 5 then accounts for the total costs of $165,880 by assigning them to the units transferred out and those in ending work in process. Again, other than considering transferred-in costs, the calculations mirror those under the FIFO method for the assembly department shown in Exhibit 17-7.

Remember that in a series of interdepartmental transfers, each department is regarded as separate and distinct for accounting purposes. The journal entry for the transfer from testing to Finished Goods (see Exhibit 17-11) is as follows:

Finished Goods Control	122,360	
Work in Process—Testing		122,360
To record cost of goods completed and transferred from testing to Finished Goods.		

Exhibit 17-10   Steps 1 and 2: Summarize Output in Physical Units and Compute Output in Equivalent Units Using FIFO Method of Process Costing for Testing Department of Pacific Electronics for March 2012

	Home	Insert	Page Layout	Formulas	Data	Review	View		

	A	B	C	D	E
1		**(Step 1)**		**(Step 2)**	
2				**Equivalent Units**	
3	**Flow of Production**	**Physical Units**	**Transferred-In Costs**	**Direct Materials**	**Conversion Costs**
4	Work in process, beginning (given, p. 622)	240	(work done before current period)		
5	Transferred in during current period (given, p. 622)	400			
6	To account for	640			
7	Completed and transferred out during current period:				
8	From beginning work in process[a]	240			
9	[240 × (100% − 100%); 240 × (100% − 0%); 240 × (100% − 62.5%)]		0	240	90
10	Started and completed	200[b]			
11	(200 × 100%; 200 × 100%; 200 × 100%)		200	200	200
12	Work in process, ending[c] (given, p. 000)	200			
13	(200 × 100%; 200 × 0%; 200 × 80%)		200	0	160
14	Accounted for	640			
15	Equivalent units of work done in current period		400	440	450
16					
17	[a]Degree of completion in this department: transferred-in costs, 100%; direct materials, 0%; conversion costs, 62.5%.				
18	[b]440 physical units completed and transferred out minus 240 physical units completed and transferred out from beginning				
19	work-in-process inventory.				
20	[c]Degree of completion in this department: transferred-in costs, 100%; direct materials, 0%; conversion costs, 80%.				

Exhibit 17-11   Steps 3, 4, and 5: Summarize Total Costs to Account For, Compute Cost per Equivalent Unit, and Assign Total Costs to Units Completed and to Units in Ending Work in Process Using FIFO Method of Process Costing for Testing Department of Pacific Electronics for March 2012

	Home	Insert	Page Layout	Formulas	Data	Review	View			
	A	B				C	D	E	F	
1						Total Production Costs	Transferred-In Cost	Direct Material	Conversion Costs	
2	(Step 3)	Work in process, beginning (given, p. 622)				$ 51,600	$33,600	$ 0	$18,000	
3		Costs added in current period (given, p. 622)				114,280	52,480	13,200	48,600	
4		Total costs to account for				$165,880	$86,080	$13,200	$66,600	
5										
6	(Step 4)	Costs added in current period					$52,480	$13,200	$48,600	
7		Divide by equivalent units of work done in current period (Exhibit 17-10)					÷ 400	÷ 440	÷ 450	
8		Cost per equivalent unit of work done in current period					$131.20	$ 30	$ 108	
9										
10	(Step 5)	Assignment of costs:								
11		Completed and transferred out (440 units)								
12		Work in process, beginning (240 units)				$ 51,600	$33,600 +	$0 +	$18,000	
13		Costs added to beginning work in process in current period				16,920	(0ᵃ × $131.20) +	(240ᵃ × $30) +	(90ᵃ × $108)	
14		Total from beginning inventory				68,520				
15		Started and completed (200 units)				53,840	(200ᵇ × $131.20) +	(200ᵇ × $30) +	(200ᵇ × $108)	
16		Total costs of units completed and transferred out				122,360				
17		Work in process, ending (200 units):				43,520	(200ᶜ × $131.20) +	(0ᶜ × $30) +	(160ᶜ × $108)	
18		Total costs accounted for				$165,880	$86,080 +	$13,200 +	$66,600	
19										
20	ᵃEquivalent units used to complete beginning work in process from Exhibit 17-10, Step 2.									
21	ᵇEquivalent units started and completed from Exhibit 17-10, Step 2.									
22	ᶜEquivalent units in ending work in process from Exhibit 17-10, Step 2.									

Entries in the Work in Process—Testing account (see Exhibit 17-11) are as follows:

Work in Process—Testing

Beginning inventory, March 1	51,600	Transferred out	122,360
Transferred-in costs	52,480		
Direct materials	13,200		
Conversion costs	48,600		
Ending inventory, March 31	43,520		

Points to Remember About Transferred-In Costs

Some points to remember when accounting for transferred-in costs are as follows:

1. Be sure to include transferred-in costs from previous departments in your calculations.

2. In calculating costs to be transferred on a FIFO basis, do not overlook costs assigned in the previous period to units that were in process at the beginning of the current period but are now included in the units transferred. For example, do not overlook the $51,600 in Exhibit 17-11.

3. Unit costs may fluctuate between periods. Therefore, transferred units may contain batches accumulated at different unit costs. For example, the 400 units transferred in

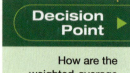

Decision Point ▶

How are the weighted-average and FIFO process-costing methods applied to transferred-in costs?

at \$52,480 in Exhibit 17-11 using the FIFO method consist of units that have different unit costs of direct materials and conversion costs when these units were worked on in the assembly department (see Exhibit 17-7). Remember, however, that when these units are transferred to the testing department, they are costed at *one average unit cost* of \$131.20 (\$52,480 ÷ 400 units), as in Exhibit 17-11.

4. Units may be measured in different denominations in different departments. Consider each department separately. For example, unit costs could be based on kilograms in the first department and liters in the second department. Accordingly, as units are received in the second department, their measurements must be converted to liters.

Hybrid Costing Systems

Learning Objective 6

Understand the need for hybrid-costing systems such as operation-costing

. . . when product-costing does not fall into job-costing or process-costing categories

Product-costing systems do not always fall neatly into either job-costing or process-costing categories. Consider Ford Motor Company. Automobiles may be manufactured in a continuous flow (suited to process costing), but individual units may be customized with a special combination of engine size, transmission, music system, and so on (which requires job costing). A **hybrid-costing system** blends characteristics from both job-costing and process-costing systems. Product-costing systems often must be designed to fit the particular characteristics of different production systems. Many production systems are a hybrid: They have some features of custom-order manufacturing and other features of mass-production manufacturing. Manufacturers of a relatively wide variety of closely related standardized products (for example, televisions, dishwashers, and washing machines) tend to use hybrid-costing systems. The Concepts in Action feature (p. 627) describes a hybrid-costing system at Adidas. The next section explains *operation costing*, a common type of hybrid-costing system.

Overview of Operation-Costing Systems

An **operation** is a standardized method or technique that is performed repetitively, often on different materials, resulting in different finished goods. Multiple operations are usually conducted within a department. For instance, a suit maker may have a cutting operation and a hemming operation within a single department. The term *operation*, however, is often used loosely. It may be a synonym for a department or process. For example, some companies may call their finishing department a finishing process or a finishing operation.

An **operation-costing system** is a hybrid-costing system applied to batches of similar, but not identical, products. Each batch of products is often a variation of a single design, and it proceeds through a sequence of operations. Within each operation, all product units are treated exactly alike, using identical amounts of the operation's resources. A key point in the operation system is that each batch does not necessarily move through the same operations as other batches. Batches are also called production runs.

In a company that makes suits, management may select a single basic design for every suit to be made, but depending on specifications, each batch of suits varies somewhat from other batches. Batches may vary with respect to the material used or the type of stitching. Semiconductors, textiles, and shoes are also manufactured in batches and may have similar variations from batch to batch.

An operation-costing system uses work orders that specify the needed direct materials and step-by-step operations. Product costs are compiled for each work order. Direct materials that are unique to different work orders are specifically identified with the appropriate work order, as in job costing. However, each unit is assumed to use an identical amount of conversion costs for a given operation, as in process costing. A single average conversion cost per unit is calculated for each operation, by dividing total conversion costs for that operation by the number of units that pass through it. This average cost is then assigned to each unit passing through the operation. Units that do not pass through an operation are not allocated any costs of that

Concepts in Action

Hybrid Costing for Customized Shoes at Adidas

Adidas has been designing and manufacturing athletic footwear for nearly 90 years. Although shoemakers have long individually crafted shoes for professional athletes like Reggie Bush of the New Orleans Saints, Adidas took this concept a step further when it initiated the *mi adidas* program. *Mi adidas* gives customers the opportunity to create shoes to their exact personal specifications for function, fit, and aesthetics. *Mi adidas* is available in retail stores around the world, and in special *mi adidas* "Performance Stores" in cities such as New York, Chicago, and San Francisco.

The process works as follows: The customer goes to a *mi adidas* station, where a salesperson develops an in-depth customer profile, a 3-D computer scanner develops a scan of the customer's feet, and the customer selects from among 90 to 100 different styles and colors for his or her modularly designed shoe. During the three-step, 30-minute high-tech process, *mi adidas* experts take customers through the "mi fit," "mi performance," and "mi design" phases, resulting in a customized shoe to fit their needs. The resulting data are transferred to an Adidas plant, where small, multiskilled teams produce the customized shoe. The measuring and fitting process is free, but purchasing your own specially made shoes costs between $40 and $65 on top of the normal retail price, depending on the style.

Historically, costs associated with individually customized products have fallen into the domain of job costing. Adidas, however, uses a hybrid-costing system—job costing for the material and customizable components that customers choose and process costing to account for the conversion costs of production. The cost of making each pair of shoes is calculated by accumulating all production costs and dividing by the number of shoes made. In other words, even though each pair of shoes is different, the conversion cost of each pair is assumed to be the same.

The combination of customization with certain features of mass production is called mass customization. It is the consequence of being able to digitize information that individual customers indicate is important to them. Various products that companies are now able to customize within a mass-production setting (for example, personal computers, blue jeans, bicycles) still require job costing of materials and considerable human intervention. However, as manufacturing systems become flexible, companies are also using process costing to account for the standardized conversion costs.

Sources: Adidas. 2010. New Orleans Saints running back Reggie Bush designs custom Adidas shoes to aid in Haiti relief efforts. AG press release. Portland, OR: February 5; Kamenev, Marina. 2006. Adidas' high tech footwear. *Business Week.com*, November 3; Seifert, Ralf. 2003. The "mi adidas" mass customization initiative. IMD No. 159. Lausanne, Switzerland: International Institute for Management Development.

operation. Our examples assume only two cost categories—direct materials and conversion costs—but operation costing can have more than two cost categories. Costs in each category are identified with specific work orders using job-costing or process-costing methods as appropriate.

Managers find operation costing useful in cost management because operation costing focuses on control of physical processes, or operations, of a given production system. For example, in clothing manufacturing, managers are concerned with fabric waste, how many fabric layers that can be cut at one time, and so on. Operation costing measures, in financial terms, how well managers have controlled physical processes.

Illustration of an Operation-Costing System

The Baltimore Clothing Company, a clothing manufacturer, produces two lines of blazers for department stores: those made of wool and those made of polyester. Wool blazers use better-quality materials and undergo more operations than polyester blazers do.

Operations information on work order 423 for 50 wool blazers and work order 424 for 100 polyester blazers is as follows:

	Work Order 423	**Work Order 424**
Direct materials	Wool	Polyester
	Satin full lining	Rayon partial lining
	Bone buttons	Plastic buttons
Operations		
1. Cutting cloth	Use	Use
2. Checking edges	Use	Do not use
3. Sewing body	Use	Use
4. Checking seams	Use	Do not use
5. Machine sewing of collars and lapels	Do not use	Use
6. Hand sewing of collars and lapels	Use	Do not use

Cost data for these work orders, started and completed in March 2012, are as follows:

	Work Order 423	**Work Order 424**
Number of blazers	50	100
Direct material costs	$ 6,000	$3,000
Conversion costs allocated:		
Operation 1	580	1,160
Operation 2	400	—
Operation 3	1,900	3,800
Operation 4	500	—
Operation 5	—	875
Operation 6	700	—
Total manufacturing costs	$10,080	$8,835

As in process costing, all product units in any work order are assumed to consume identical amounts of conversion costs of a particular operation. Baltimore's operation-costing system uses a budgeted rate to calculate the conversion costs of each operation. The budgeted rate for Operation 1 (amounts assumed) is as follows:

$$\frac{\text{Operation 1 budgeted}}{\text{conversion-cost rate for 2012}} = \frac{\text{Operation 1 budgeted conversion costs for 2012}}{\text{Operation 1 budgeted product units for 2012}}$$

$$= \frac{\$232,000}{20,000 \text{ units}}$$

$$= \$11.60 \text{ per unit}$$

Budgeted conversion costs of Operation 1 include labor, power, repairs, supplies, depreciation, and other overhead of this operation. If some units have not been completed (so all units in Operation 1 have not received the same amounts of conversion costs), the conversion-cost rate is computed by dividing budgeted conversion costs by *equivalent units* of conversion costs, as in process costing.

As goods are manufactured, conversion costs are allocated to the work orders processed in Operation 1 by multiplying the $11.60 conversion cost per unit by the number of units processed. Conversion costs of Operation 1 for 50 wool blazers (work order 423) are $11.60 per blazer × 50 blazers = $580, and for 100 polyester blazers (work order 424) are $11.60 per blazer × 100 blazers = $1,160. When equivalent units are used to calculate the conversion-cost rate, costs are allocated to work orders by multiplying conversion cost per equivalent unit by number of equivalent units in the work order. Direct material costs of $6,000 for the 50 wool blazers (work order 423) and $3,000 for the 100 polyester blazers (work order 424) are specifically identified with each order, as in job costing. Remember the basic point in operation costing: Operation unit costs are assumed to be the same regardless of the work order, but direct material costs vary across orders when the materials for each work order vary.

Journal Entries

Actual conversion costs for Operation 1 in March 2012—assumed to be $24,400, including actual costs incurred for work order 423 and work order 424—are entered into a Conversion Costs Control account:

1.	Conversion Costs Control	24,400	
	Various accounts (such as Wages Payable Control and Accumulated Depreciation)		24,400

Summary journal entries for assigning costs to polyester blazers (work order 424) follow. Entries for wool blazers would be similar. Of the $3,000 of direct materials for work order 424, $2,975 are used in Operation 1, and the remaining $25 of materials are used in another operation. The journal entry to record direct materials used for the 100 polyester blazers in March 2012 is as follows:

2.	Work in Process, Operation 1	2,975	
	Materials Inventory Control		2,975

The journal entry to record the allocation of conversion costs to products uses the budgeted rate of $11.60 per blazer times the 100 polyester blazers processed, or $1,160:

3.	Work in Process, Operation 1	1,160	
	Conversion Costs Allocated		1,160

The journal entry to record the transfer of the 100 polyester blazers (at a cost of $2,975 + $1,160) from Operation 1 to Operation 3 (polyester blazers do not go through Operation 2) is as follows:

4.	Work in Process, Operation 3	4,135	
	Work in Process, Operation 1		4,135

After posting these entries, the Work in Process, Operation 1, account appears as follows:

Work in Process, Operation 1

② Direct materials	2,975	④ Transferred to Operation 3	4,135
③ Conversion costs allocated	1,160		
Ending inventory, March 31	0		

Costs of the blazers are transferred through the operations in which blazers are worked on and then to finished goods in the usual manner. Costs are added throughout the fiscal year in the Conversion Costs Control account and the Conversion Costs Allocated account. Any overallocation or underallocation of conversion costs is disposed of in the same way as overallocated or underallocated manufacturing overhead in a job-costing system (see pp. 117–122).

Decision Point

What is an operation-costing system and when is it a better approach to product-costing?

4. What are the weighted-average and first-in, first-out methods of process costing? Under what conditions will they yield different levels of operating income?

The weighted-average method computes unit costs by dividing total costs in the Work in Process account by total equivalent units completed to date, and assigns this average cost to units completed and to units in ending work-in-process inventory.

The first-in, first-out (FIFO) method computes unit costs based on costs incurred during the current period and equivalent units of work done in the current period.

Operating income can differ materially between the two methods when (1) direct material or conversion cost per equivalent unit varies significantly from period to period and (2) physical-inventory levels of work in process are large in relation to the total number of units transferred out of the process.

5. How are the weighted-average and FIFO process-costing methods applied to transferred-in costs?

The weighted-average method computes transferred-in costs per unit by dividing total transferred-in costs to date by total equivalent transferred-in units completed to date, and assigns this average cost to units completed and to units in ending work-in-process inventory. The FIFO method computes transferred-in costs per unit based on costs transferred in during the current period and equivalent units of transferred-in costs of work done in the current period. The FIFO method assigns transferred-in costs in beginning work in process to units completed and costs transferred in during the current period first to complete beginning inventory, next to start and complete new units, and finally to units in ending work-in-process inventory.

6. What is an operation-costing system and when is it a better approach to product-costing?

Operation-costing is a hybrid-costing system that blends characteristics from both job-costing and process-costing systems. It is a better approach to product-costing when production systems share some features of custom-order manufacturing and other features of mass-production manufacturing.

Appendix

Standard-Costing Method of Process Costing

Chapter 7 described accounting in a standard-costing system. Recall that this involves making entries using standard costs and then isolating variances from these standards in order to support management control. This appendix describes how the principles of standard costing can be employed in process-costing systems.

Benefits of Standard Costing

Companies that use process-costing systems produce masses of identical or similar units of output. In such companies, it is fairly easy to set standards for quantities of inputs needed to produce output. Standard cost per input unit can then be multiplied by input quantity standards to develop standard cost per output unit.

The weighted-average and FIFO methods become very complicated when used in process industries that produce a wide variety of similar products. For example, a steel-rolling mill uses various steel alloys and produces sheets of various sizes and finishes. The different types of direct materials used and the operations performed are few, but used in various combinations, they yield a wide variety of products. Similarly, complex conditions are frequently found, for example, in plants that manufacture rubber products, textiles, ceramics, paints, and packaged food products. In each of these cases, if the broad averaging procedure of *actual* process costing were used, the result would be inaccurate costs for each product. Therefore, the standard-costing method of process costing is widely used in these industries.

Under the standard-costing method, teams of design and process engineers, operations personnel, and management accountants work together to determine *separate* standard costs per equivalent unit on the basis of different technical processing specifications for each product. Identifying standard costs for each product overcomes the disadvantage of costing all products at a single average amount, as under actual costing.

Computations Under Standard Costing

We return to the assembly department of Pacific Electronics, but this time we use standard costs. Assume the same standard costs apply in February and March of 2012. Data for the assembly department are as follows:

A	Physical Units (SG-40s) (1)	Direct Materials (2)	Conversion Costs (3)	Total Costs (4) = (2) + (3)
2 Standard cost per unit		$ 74	$ 54	
3 Work in process, beginning inventory (March 1)	225			
4 Degree of completion of beginning work in process		100%	60%	
5 Beginning work in process inventory at standard costs		$16,650[a]	$ 7,290[a]	$23,940
6 Started during March	275			
7 Completed and transferred out during March	400			
8 Work in process, ending inventory (March 31)	100			
9 Degree of completion of ending work in process		100%	50%	
10 Actual total costs added during March		$19,800	$16,380	$36,180
11				
12 [a]Work in process, beginning inventory at standard costs				
13 Direct materials: 225 physical units × 100% completed × $74 per unit = $16,650				
14 Conversion costs: 225 physical units × 60% completed × $54 per unit = $7,290				

We illustrate the standard-costing method of process costing using the five-step procedure introduced earlier (p. 610).

Exhibit 17-12 presents Steps 1 and 2. These steps are identical to the steps described for the FIFO method in Exhibit 17-6 because, as in FIFO, the standard-costing method also assumes that the earliest equivalent units in beginning work in process are completed first. Work done in the current period for direct materials is 275 equivalent units. Work done in the current period for conversion costs is 315 equivalent units.

Exhibit 17-13 describes Steps 3, 4, and 5. In Step 3, total costs to account for (that is, the total debits to Work in Process—Assembly) differ from total debits to Work in Process—Assembly under the actual-cost-based weighted-average

Exhibit 17-12

Steps 1 and 2: Summarize Output in Physical Units and Compute Output in Equivalent Units Using Standard-Costing Method of Process Costing for Assembly Department of Pacific Electronics for March 2012

Flow of Production	(Step 1) Physical Units	(Step 2) Equivalent Units Direct Materials	Conversion Costs
4 Work in process, beginning (given, p. 633)	225		
5 Started during current period (given, p. 633)	275		
6 To account for	500		
7 Completed and transferred out during current period:			
8 From beginning work in process[a]	225		
9 [225 × (100% − 100%); 225 × (100% − 60%)]		0	90
10 Started and completed	175[b]		
11 (175 × 100%; 175 × 100%)		175	175
12 Work in process, ending[c] (given, p. 633)	100		
13 (100 × 100%; 100 × 50%)		100	50
14 Accounted for	500		
15 Equivalent units of work done in current period		275	315
17 [a]Degree of completion in this department: direct materials, 100%; conversion costs, 60%.			
18 [b]400 physical units completed and transferred out minus 225 physical units completed and transferred out from beginning work-in-process inventory.			
19 [c]Degree of completion in this department: direct materials, 100%; conversion costs, 50%.			

Exhibit 17-13 Steps 3, 4, and 5: Summarize Total Costs to Account For, Compute Cost per Equivalent Unit, and Assign Total Costs to Units Completed and to Units in Ending Work in Process Using Standard-Costing Method of Process Costing for Assembly Department of Pacific Electronics for March 2012

	Home	Insert	Page Layout	Formulas	Data	Review	View			

	A	B	C	D	E	F	G
1			Total Production Costs	Direct Materials		Conversion Costs	
2	(Step 3)	Work in process, beginning (given, p. 633)					
3		Direct materials, 225 × $74; Conversion costs, 135 × $54	$23,940	$16,650		$ 7,290	
4		Costs added in current period at standard costs					
5		Direct materials, 275 × $74; Conversion costs, 315 × $54	37,360	20,350		17,010	
6		Total costs to account for	$61,300	$37,000		$24,300	
7							
8	(Step 4)	Standard cost per equivalent unit (given, p. 633)		$ 74		$ 54	
9							
10	(Step 5)	Assignment of costs at standard costs:					
11		Completed and transferred out (400 units):					
12		Work in process, beginning (225 units)	$23,940	$16,650	+	$ 7,290	
13		Costs added to beginning work in process in current period	4,860	(0[a] × $74)	+	(90[a] × $54)	
14		Total from beginning inventory	28,800				
15		Started and completed (175 units)	22,400	(175[b] × $74)	+	(175[b] × $54)	
16		Total costs of units completed and transferred out	51,200				
17		Work in process, ending (100 units):	10,100	(100[c] × $74)	+	(50[c] × $54)	
18		Total costs accounted for	$61,300	$37,000	+	$24,300	
19							
20		Summary of variances for current performance:					
21		Costs added in current period at standard costs (see step 3)		$20,350		$17,010	
22		Actual costs incurred (given, p. 633)		$19,800		$16,380	
23		Variance		$ 550	F	$ 630	F
24							
25		[a]Equivalent units used to complete beginning work in process from Exhibit 17-12, Step 2.					
26		[b]Equivalent units started and completed from Exhibit 17-12, Step 2.					
27		[c]Equivalent units in ending work in process from Exhibit 17-12, Step 2.					

and FIFO methods. That's because, as in all standard-costing systems, the debits to the Work in Process account are at standard costs, rather than actual costs. These standard costs total $61,300 in Exhibit 17-13. In Step 4, costs per equivalent unit are standard costs: direct materials, $74, and conversion costs, $54. *Therefore, costs per equivalent unit do not have to be computed as they were for the weighted-average and FIFO methods.*

Exhibit 17-13, Step 5, assigns total costs to units completed and transferred out and to units in ending work-in-process inventory, as in the FIFO method. Step 5 assigns amounts of standard costs to equivalent units calculated in Exhibit 17-12. These costs are assigned (1) first to complete beginning work-in-process inventory, (2) next to start and complete new units, and (3) finally to start new units that are in ending work-in-process inventory. Note how the $61,300 total costs accounted for in Step 5 of Exhibit 17-13 equal total costs to account for.

Accounting for Variances

Process-costing systems using standard costs record actual direct material costs in Direct Materials Control and actual conversion costs in Conversion Costs Control (similar to Variable and Fixed Overhead Control in Chapter 8). In the journal entries that follow, the first two record these *actual costs*. In entries 3 and 4a, the Work-in-Process—Assembly account accumulates direct material costs and conversion costs at *standard costs*. Entries 3 and 4b isolate total variances. The final entry transfers out completed goods at standard costs.

1. Assembly Department Direct Materials Control (at actual costs) — 19,800
   Accounts Payable Control — 19,800
   To record direct materials purchased and used in production during March. This cost control account is debited with actual costs.

2. Assembly Department Conversion Costs Control (at actual costs)   16,380

      Various accounts such as Wages Payable Control and Accumulated Depreciation   16,380

    To record assembly department conversion costs for March. This cost control account is debited with actual costs.

Entries 3, 4, and 5 use standard cost amounts from Exhibit 17-13.

3. Work in Process—Assembly (at standard costs)   20,350

      Direct Materials Variances   550

      Assembly Department Direct Materials Control   19,800

    To record standard costs of direct materials assigned to units worked on and total direct materials variances.

4a. Work in Process—Assembly (at standard costs)   17,010

      Assembly Department Conversion Costs Allocated   17,010

    To record conversion costs allocated at standard rates to the units worked on during March.

4b. Assembly Department Conversion Costs Allocated   17,010

      Conversion Costs Variances   630

      Assembly Department Conversion Costs Control   16,380

    To record total conversion costs variances.

5. Work in Process—Testing (at standard costs)   51,200

      Work in Process—Assembly (at standard costs)   51,200

    To record standard costs of units completed and transferred out from assembly to testing.

Variances arise under standard costing, as in entries 3 and 4b. That's because the standard costs assigned to products on the basis of work done in the current period do not equal actual costs incurred in the current period. Recall that variances that result in higher income than expected are termed favorable, while those that reduce income are unfavorable. From an accounting standpoint, favorable cost variances are credit entries, while unfavorable ones are debits. In the preceding example, both direct materials and conversion cost variances are favorable. This is also reflected in the "F" designations for both variances in Exhibit 17-13.

Variances can be analyzed in little or great detail for planning and control purposes, as described in Chapters 7 and 8. Sometimes direct materials price variances are isolated at the time direct materials are purchased and only efficiency variances are computed in entry 3. Exhibit 17-14 shows how the costs flow through the general-ledger accounts under standard costing.

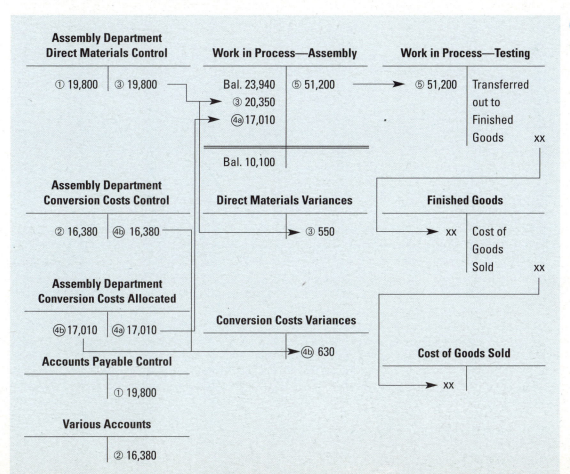

Exhibit 17-14

Flow of Standard Costs in a Process-Costing System for Assembly Department of Pacific Electronics for March 2012

Terms to Learn

This chapter and the Glossary at the end of the book contain definitions of the following important terms:

equivalent units **(p. 611)**

first-in, first-out (FIFO) process-costing
  method **(p. 617)**

hybrid-costing system **(p. 626)**

operation **(p. 626)**

operation-costing system **(p. 626)**

previous-department costs **(p. 621)**

transferred-in costs **(p. 621)**

weighted-average process-costing
  method **(p. 614)**

Assignment Material

Questions

17-1 Give three examples of industries that use process-costing systems.

17-2 In process costing, why are costs often divided into two main classifications?

17-3 Explain equivalent units. Why are equivalent-unit calculations necessary in process costing?

17-4 What problems might arise in estimating the degree of completion of semiconductor chips in a semiconductor plant?

17-5 Name the five steps in process costing when equivalent units are computed.

17-6 Name the three inventory methods commonly associated with process costing.

17-7 Describe the distinctive characteristic of weighted-average computations in assigning costs to units completed and to units in ending work in process.

17-8 Describe the distinctive characteristic of FIFO computations in assigning costs to units completed and to units in ending work in process.

17-9 Why should the FIFO method be called a modified or department FIFO method?

17-10 Identify a major advantage of the FIFO method for purposes of planning and control.

17-11 Identify the main difference between journal entries in process costing and job costing.

17-12 "The standard-costing method is particularly applicable to process-costing situations." Do you agree? Why?

17-13 Why should the accountant distinguish between transferred-in costs and additional direct material costs for each subsequent department in a process-costing system?

17-14 "Transferred-in costs are those costs incurred in the preceding accounting period." Do you agree? Explain.

17-15 "There's no reason for me to get excited about the choice between the weighted-average and FIFO methods in my process-costing system. I have long-term contracts with my materials suppliers at fixed prices." Do you agree with this statement made by a plant controller? Explain.

Exercises

17-16 Equivalent units, zero beginning inventory. Nihon, Inc., is a manufacturer of digital cameras. It has two departments: assembly and testing. In January 2012, the company incurred $750,000 on direct materials and $798,000 on conversion costs, for a total manufacturing cost of $1,548,000.

Required

1. Assume there was no beginning inventory of any kind on January 1, 2012. During January, 10,000 cameras were placed into production and all 10,000 were fully completed at the end of the month. What is the unit cost of an assembled camera in January?

2. Assume that during February 10,000 cameras are placed into production. Further assume the same total assembly costs for January are also incurred in February, but only 9,000 cameras are fully completed at the end of the month. All direct materials have been added to the remaining 1,000 cameras. However, on average, these remaining 1,000 cameras are only 50% complete as to conversion costs. (a) What are the equivalent units for direct materials and conversion costs and their respective costs per equivalent unit for February? (b) What is the unit cost of an assembled camera in February 2012?

3. Explain the difference in your answers to requirements 1 and 2.

17-17 **Journal entries (continuation of 17-16).** Refer to requirement 2 of Exercise 17-16.

Required

Prepare summary journal entries for the use of direct materials and incurrence of conversion costs. Also prepare a journal entry to transfer out the cost of goods completed. Show the postings to the Work in Process account.

17-18 **Zero beginning inventory, materials introduced in middle of process.** Roary Chemicals has a mixing department and a refining department. Its process-costing system in the mixing department has two direct materials cost categories (chemical P and chemical Q) and one conversion costs pool. The following data pertain to the mixing department for July 2012:

Units	
Work in process, July 1	0
Units started	50,000
Completed and transferred to refining department	35,000
Costs	
Chemical P	$250,000
Chemical Q	70,000
Conversion costs	135,000

Chemical P is introduced at the start of operations in the mixing department, and chemical Q is added when the product is three-fourths completed in the mixing department. Conversion costs are added evenly during the process. The ending work in process in the mixing department is two-thirds complete.

Required

1. Compute the equivalent units in the mixing department for July 2012 for each cost category.
2. Compute (a) the cost of goods completed and transferred to the refining department during July and (b) the cost of work in process as of July 31, 2012.

17-19 **Weighted-average method, equivalent units.** Consider the following data for the assembly division of Fenton Watches, Inc.:

The assembly division uses the weighted-average method of process costing.

	Physical Units (Watches)	Direct Materials	Conversion Costs
Beginning work in process (May 1)[a]	80	$ 493,360	$ 91,040
Started in May 2012	500		
Completed during May 2012	460		
Ending work in process (May 31)[b]	120		
Total costs added during May 2012		$3,220,000	$1,392,000

[a]Degree of completion: direct materials, 90%; conversion costs, 40%.
[b]Degree of completion: direct materials, 60%; conversion costs, 30%.

Required

Compute equivalent units for direct materials and conversion costs. Show physical units in the first column of your schedule.

17-20 **Weighted-average method, assigning costs (continuation of 17-19).**

Required

For the data in Exercise 17-19, summarize total costs to account for, calculate cost per equivalent unit for direct materials and conversion costs, and assign total costs to units completed (and transferred out) and to units in ending work in process.

17-21 **FIFO method, equivalent units.** Refer to the information in Exercise 17-19. Suppose the assembly division at Fenton Watches, Inc., uses the FIFO method of process costing instead of the weighted-average method.

Required

Compute equivalent units for direct materials and conversion costs. Show physical units in the first column of your schedule.

17-22 **FIFO method, assigning costs (continuation of 17-21).**

Required

For the data in Exercise 17-19, use the FIFO method to summarize total costs to account for, calculate cost per equivalent unit for direct materials and conversion costs, and assign total costs to units completed (and transferred out) and to units in ending work in process.

17-23 **Operation Costing.** Whole Goodness Bakery needs to determine the cost of two work orders for the month of June. Work order 215 is for 1,200 packages of dinner rolls and work order 216 is for 1,400 loaves of multigrain bread. Dinner rolls are mixed and cut into individual rolls before being baked and then packaged. Multigrain loaves are mixed and shaped before being baked, sliced, and packaged. The following information applies to work order 215 and work order 216:

	Work Order 215	Work Order 216
Quantity (packages)	1,200	1,400
Operations		
1. Mix	Use	Use
2. Shape loaves	Do not use	Use
3. Cut rolls	Use	Do not use
4. Bake	Use	Use
5. Slice loaves	Do not use	Use
6. Package	Use	Use

Selected budget information for June follows:

	Dinner Rolls	Multigrain Loaves	Total
Packages	4,800	6,500	11,300
Direct material costs	$2,640	$5,850	$ 8,490

Budgeted conversion costs for each operation for June follow:

Mixing	$9,040
Shaping	1,625
Cutting	720
Baking	7,345
Slicing	650
Packaging	8,475

Required

1. Using budgeted number of packages as the denominator, calculate the budgeted conversion-cost rates for each operation.
2. Using the information in requirement 1, calculate the budgeted cost of goods manufactured for the two June work orders.
3. Calculate the cost per package of dinner rolls and multigrain loaves for work order 215 and 216.

17-24 Weighted-average method, assigning costs. Bio Doc Corporation is a biotech company based in Milpitas. It makes a cancer-treatment drug in a single processing department. Direct materials are added at the start of the process. Conversion costs are added evenly during the process. Bio Doc uses the weighted-average method of process costing. The following information for July 2011 is available.

		Equivalent Units	
	Physical Units	Direct Materials	Conversion Costs
Work in process, July 1	8,500[a]	8,500	1,700
Started during July	35,000		
Completed and transferred out during July	33,000	33,000	33,000
Work in process, July 31	10,500[b]	10,500	6,300

[a]Degree of completion: direct materials, 100%; conversion costs, 20%.
[b]Degree of completion: direct materials, 100%; conversion costs, 60%.

Total Costs for July 2008		
Work in process, beginning		
Direct materials	$63,100	
Conversion costs	45,510	$108,610
Direct materials added during July		284,900
Conversion costs added during July		485,040
Total costs to account for		$878,550

Required

1. Calculate cost per equivalent unit for direct materials and conversion costs.
2. Summarize total costs to account for, and assign total costs to units completed (and transferred out) and to units in ending work in process.

17-25 FIFO method, assigning costs.

Do Exercise 17-24 using the FIFO method. Note that you first need to calculate the equivalent units of work done in the current period (for direct materials and conversion costs) to complete beginning work in process, to start and complete new units, and to produce ending work in process. **Required**

17-26 Standard-costing method, assigning costs. Refer to the information in Exercise 17-24. Suppose Bio Doc determines standard costs of $8.25 per equivalent unit for direct materials and $12.70 per equivalent unit for conversion costs for both beginning work in process and work done in the current period.

1. Do Exercise 17-24 using the standard-costing method. Note that you first need to calculate the equivalent units of work done in the current period (for direct materials and conversion costs) to complete beginning work in process, to start and complete new units, and to produce ending work in process. **Required**
2. Compute the total direct materials and conversion costs variances for July 2011.

17-27 Transferred-in costs, weighted-average method. Asaya Clothing, Inc., is a manufacturer of winter clothes. It has a knitting department and a finishing department. This exercise focuses on the finishing department. Direct materials are added at the end of the process. Conversion costs are added evenly during the process. Asaya uses the weighted-average method of process costing. The following information for June 2012 is available.

	Home	Insert	Page Layout	Formulas	Data	Review	View	
	A				B	C	D	E
1					Physical Units (tons)	Transferred-In Costs	Direct Materials	Conversion Costs
2	Work in process, beginning inventory (June 1)				75	$ 75,000	$ 0	$30,000
3	Degree of completion, beginning work in process					100%	0%	60%
4	Transferred in during June				135			
5	Completed and transferred out during June				150			
6	Work in process, ending inventory (June 30)				60			
7	Degree of completion, ending work in process					100%	0%	75%
8	Total costs added during June					$142,500	$37,500	$78,000

1. Calculate equivalent units of transferred-in costs, direct materials, and conversion costs. **Required**
2. Summarize total costs to account for, and calculate the cost per equivalent unit for transferred-in costs, direct materials, and conversion costs.
3. Assign total costs to units completed (and transferred out) and to units in ending work in process.

17-28 Transferred-in costs, FIFO method. Refer to the information in Exercise 17-27. Suppose that Asaya uses the FIFO method instead of the weighted-average method in all of its departments. The only changes to Exercise 17-27 under the FIFO method are that total transferred-in costs of beginning work in process on June 1 are $60,000 (instead of $75,000) and total transferred-in costs added during June are $130,800 (instead of $142,500).

Do Exercise 17-27 using the FIFO method. Note that you first need to calculate equivalent units of work done in the current period (for transferred-in costs, direct materials, and conversion costs) to complete beginning work in process, to start and complete new units, and to produce ending work in process. **Required**

17-29 Operation Costing. UB Healthy Company manufactures three different types of vitamins: vitamin A, vitamin B, and a multivitamin. The company uses four operations to manufacture the vitamins: mixing, tableting, encapsulating, and bottling. Vitamins A and B are produced in tablet form (in the tableting department) and the multivitamin is produced in capsule form (in the encapsulating department). Each bottle contains 200 vitamins, regardless of the product.

Conversion costs are applied based on the number of bottles in the tableting and encapsulating departments. Conversion costs are applied based on labor hours in the mixing department. It takes 1.5 minutes to mix the ingredients for a 200-unit bottle for each product. Conversion costs are applied based on machine hours in the bottling department. It takes 1 minute of machine time to fill a 200-unit bottle, regardless of the product.

UB Healthy is planning to complete one batch of each type of vitamin in July. The budgeted number of bottles and expected direct material cost for each type of vitamin is as follows:

	Vitamin A	Vitamin B	Multivitamin
Number of 200 unit bottles	12,000	9,000	18,000
Direct material cost	$23,040	$21,600	$47,520

The budgeted conversion costs for each department for July are as follows:

Department	Budgeted Conversion Cost
Mixing	$ 8,190
Tableting	24,150
Encapsulating	25,200
Bottling	3,510

Required

1. Calculate the conversion cost rates for each department.
2. Calculate the budgeted cost of goods manufactured for vitamin A, vitamin B, and the multivitamin for the month of July.
3. Calculate the cost per 200-unit bottle for each type of vitamin for the month of July.

MyAccountingLab

Problems

17-30 Weighted-average method. Larsen Company manufactures car seats in its San Antonio plant. Each car seat passes through the assembly department and the testing department. This problem focuses on the assembly department. The process-costing system at Larsen Company has a single direct-cost category (direct materials) and a single indirect-cost category (conversion costs). Direct materials are added at the beginning of the process. Conversion costs are added evenly during the process. When the assembly department finishes work on each car seat, it is immediately transferred to testing.

Larsen Company uses the weighted-average method of process costing. Data for the assembly department for October 2012 are as follows:

	Physical Units (Car Seats)	Direct Materials	Conversion Costs
Work in process, October 1[a]	5,000	$1,250,000	$ 402,750
Started during October 2012	20,000		
Completed during October 2012	22,500		
Work in process, October 31[b]	2,500		
Total costs added during October 2012		$4,500,000	$2,337,500

[a]Degree of completion: direct materials, ?%; conversion costs, 60%.
[b]Degree of completion: direct materials, ?%; conversion costs, 70%.

Required

1. For each cost category, compute equivalent units in the assembly department. Show physical units in the first column of your schedule.
2. For each cost category, summarize total assembly department costs for October 2012 and calculate the cost per equivalent unit.
3. Assign total costs to units completed and transferred out and to units in ending work in process.

17-31 Journal entries (continuation of 17-30).

Required

Prepare a set of summarized journal entries for all October 2012 transactions affecting Work in Process—Assembly. Set up a T-account for Work in Process—Assembly and post your entries to it.

17-32 FIFO method (continuation of 17-30).

Required

Do Problem 17-30 using the FIFO method of process costing. Explain any difference between the cost per equivalent unit in the assembly department under the weighted-average method and the FIFO method.

17-33 Transferred-in costs, weighted-average method (related to 17-30 to 17-32). Larsen Company, as you know, is a manufacturer of car seats. Each car seat passes through the assembly department and testing department. This problem focuses on the testing department. Direct materials are added when the testing department process is 90% complete. Conversion costs are added evenly during the testing department's process. As work in assembly is completed, each unit is immediately transferred to testing. As each unit is completed in testing, it is immediately transferred to Finished Goods.

Larsen Company uses the weighted-average method of process costing. Data for the testing department for October 2012 are as follows:

	Physical Units (Car Seats)	Transferred-In Costs	Direct Materials	Conversion Costs
Work in process, October 1[a]	7,500	$2,932,500	$ 0	$ 835,460
Transferred in during October 2012	?			
Completed during October 2012	26,300			
Work in process, October 31[b]	3,700			
Total costs added during October 2012		$7,717,500	$9,704,700	$3,955,900

[a]Degree of completion: transferred-in costs, ?%; direct materials, ?%; conversion costs, 70%.
[b]Degree of completion: transferred-in costs, ?%; direct materials, ?%; conversion costs, 60%.

Required

1. What is the percentage of completion for (a) transferred-in costs and direct materials in beginning work-in-process inventory, and (b) transferred-in costs and direct materials in ending work-in-process inventory?
2. For each cost category, compute equivalent units in the testing department. Show physical units in the first column of your schedule.
3. For each cost category, summarize total testing department costs for October 2012, calculate the cost per equivalent unit, and assign total costs to units completed (and transferred out) and to units in ending work in process.
4. Prepare journal entries for October transfers from the assembly department to the testing department and from the testing department to Finished Goods.

17-34 Transferred-in costs, FIFO method (continuation of 17-33). Refer to the information in Problem 17-33. Suppose that Larsen Company uses the FIFO method instead of the weighted-average method in all of its departments. The only changes to Problem 17-33 under the FIFO method are that total transferred-in costs of beginning work in process on October 1 are $2,881,875 (instead of $2,932,500) and that total transferred-in costs added during October are $7,735,250 (instead of $7,717,500).

Using the FIFO process-costing method, complete Problem 17-33.

Required

17-35 Weighted-average method. Ashworth Handcraft is a manufacturer of picture frames for large retailers. Every picture frame passes through two departments: the assembly department and the finishing department. This problem focuses on the assembly department. The process-costing system at Ashworth has a single direct-cost category (direct materials) and a single indirect-cost category (conversion costs). Direct materials are added when the assembly department process is 10% complete. Conversion costs are added evenly during the assembly department's process.

Ashworth uses the weighted-average method of process costing. Consider the following data for the assembly department in April 2012:

	Physical Unit (Frames)	Direct Materials	Conversion Costs
Work in process, April 1[a]	95	$ 1,665	$ 988
Started during April 2012	490		
Completed during April 2012	455		
Work in process, April 30[b]	130		
Total costs added during April 2012		$17,640	$11,856

[a]Degree of completion: direct materials, 100%; conversion costs, 40%.
[b]Degree of completion: direct materials, 100%; conversion costs, 30%.

Summarize total assembly department costs for April 2012, and assign total costs to units completed (and transferred out) and to units in ending work in process.

Required

17-36 Journal entries (continuation of 17-35).

Prepare a set of summarized journal entries for all April transactions affecting Work in Process—Assembly. Set up a T-account for Work in Process—Assembly and post your entries to it.

Required

17-37 FIFO method (continuation of 17-35).

Do Problem 17-35 using the FIFO method of process costing. If you did Problem 17-35, explain any difference between the cost of work completed and transferred out and the cost of ending work in process in the assembly department under the weighted-average method and the FIFO method.

Required

17-38 Transferred-in costs, weighted-average method. Bookworm, Inc., has two departments: printing and binding. Each department has one direct-cost category (direct materials) and one indirect-cost category (conversion costs). This problem focuses on the binding department. Books that have undergone the printing process are immediately transferred to the binding department. Direct material is added when the binding process is 80% complete. Conversion costs are added evenly during binding operations. When those operations are done, the books are immediately transferred to Finished Goods. Bookworm, Inc., uses the weighted-average method of process costing. The following is a summary of the April 2012 operations of the binding department.

	Home	Insert	Page Layout	Formulas	Data	Review	View		
	A				B	C	D	E
1					Physical Units (books)	Transferred-In Costs	Direct Materials	Conversion Costs
2	Beginning work in process				1,050	$ 32,550	$ 0	$13,650
3	Degree of completion, beginning work in process					100%	0%	50%
4	Transferred in during April 2012				2,400			
5	Completed and transferred out during April				2,700			
6	Ending work in process (April 30)				750			
7	Degree of completion, ending work in process					100%	0%	70%
8	Total costs added during April					$129,600	$23,490	$70,200

Required

1. Summarize total binding department costs for April 2012, and assign these costs to units completed (and transferred out) and to units in ending work in process.
2. Prepare journal entries for April transfers from the printing department to the binding department and from the binding department to Finished Goods.

17-39 Transferred-in costs, FIFO method. Refer to the information in Problem 17-38. Suppose that Bookworm, Inc., uses the FIFO method instead of the weighted-average method in all of its departments. The only changes to Problem 17-38 under the FIFO method are that total transferred-in costs of beginning work in process on April 1 are $36,750 (instead of $32,550) and that total transferred-in costs added during April are $124,800 (instead of $129,600).

Required

1. Using the FIFO process-costing method, complete Problem 17-38.
2. If you did Problem 17-38, explain any difference between the cost of work completed and transferred out and the cost of ending work in process in the binding department under the weighted-average method and the FIFO method.

17-40 Transferred-in costs, weighted-average and FIFO methods. Frito-Lay, Inc., manufactures convenience foods, including potato chips and corn chips. Production of corn chips occurs in four departments: cleaning, mixing, cooking, and drying and packaging. Consider the drying and packaging department, where direct materials (packaging) are added at the end of the process. Conversion costs are added evenly during the process. The accounting records of a Frito-Lay plant provide the following information for corn chips in its drying and packaging department during a weekly period (week 37):

	Physical Units (Cases)	Transferred-In Costs	Direct Materials	Conversion Costs
Beginning work in process[a]	1,200	$26,750	$ 0	$ 4,020
Transferred in during week 37 from cooking department	4,200			
Completed during week 37	4,000			
Ending work in process, week 37[b]	1,400			
Total costs added during week 37		$91,510	$23,000	$27,940

[a]Degree of completion: transferred-in costs, 100%; direct materials, ?%; conversion costs, 25%.
[b]Degree of completion: transferred-in costs, 100%; direct materials, ?%; conversion costs, 50%.

Required

1. Using the weighted-average method, summarize the total drying and packaging department costs for week 37, and assign total costs to units completed (and transferred out) and to units in ending work in process.
2. Assume that the FIFO method is used for the drying and packaging department. Under FIFO, the transferred-in costs for work-in-process beginning inventory in week 37 are $28,920 (instead of $26,750 under the weighted-average method), and the transferred-in costs during week 37 from the cooking department are $93,660 (instead of $91,510 under the weighted-average method). All other data are unchanged. Summarize the total drying and packaging department costs for week 37, and assign total costs to units completed and transferred out and to units in ending work in process using the FIFO method.

17-41 **Standard-costing with beginning and ending work in process.** Penelope's Pearls Company (PPC) is a manufacturer of knock off jewelry. Penelope attends Fashion Week in New York City every September and February to gauge the latest fashion trends in jewelry. She then makes trendy jewelry at a fraction of the cost of those designers who participate in Fashion Week. This Fall's biggest item is triple-stranded pearl necklaces. Because of her large volume, Penelope uses process costing to account for her production. In October, she had started some of the triple strands. She continued to work on those in November. Costs and output figures are as follows:

Penelope's Pearls Company
Process Costing
For the Month Ended November 30, 2012

	Units	Direct Materials	Conversion Costs
Standard cost per unit		$3.00	$10.50
Work in process, beginning inventory (Nov. 1)	24,000	$72,000	$176,400
Degree of completion of beginning work in process		100%	70%
Started during November	124,400		
Completed and transferred out	123,000		
Work in process, ending inventory (Nov. 30)	25,400		
Degree of completion of ending work in process		100%	50%
Total costs added during November		$329,000	$1,217,000

Required

1. Compute equivalent units for direct materials and conversion costs. Show physical units in the first column of your schedule.
2. Compute the total standard costs of pearls transferred out in November and the total standard costs of the November 30 inventory of work in process.
3. Compute the total November variances for direct materials and conversion costs.

Collaborative Learning Problem

17-42 **Standard-costing method.** Ozumo's Gardening makes several different kinds of mulch. Its busy period is in the summer months. In August, the controller suddenly quit due to a stress-related disorder. He took with him the standard costing results for RoseBark, Ozumo's highest quality mulch. The controller had already completed the assignment of costs to finished goods and work in process, but Ozumo does not know standard costs or the completion levels of inventory. The following information is available:

Physical and Equivalent Units for RoseBark
For the Month Ended August 31, 2012

	Physical Units (Yards of Mulch)	Equivalent Units (yards) Direct Materials	Equivalent Units (yards) Conversion Costs
Completion of beginning work in process	965,000	—	434,250
Started and completed	845,000	845,000	845,000
Work on ending work in process	1,817,000	1,817,000	1,090,200
		2,662,000	2,369,450
Units to account for	3,627,000		

	Costs
Cost of units completed from beginning work in process	$ 7,671,750
Cost of new units started and completed	6,717,750
Cost of units completed in August	14,389,500
Cost of ending work in process	12,192,070
Total costs accounted for	$26,581,570

Required

1. Calculate the completion percentages of beginning work in process with respect to the two inputs.
2. Calculate the completion percentages of ending work in process with respect to the two inputs.
3. What are the standard costs per unit for the two inputs?
4. What is the total cost of work-in-process inventory as of August 1, 2012?

18 Spoilage, Rework, and Scrap

▶ Learning Objectives

1. Understand the definitions of spoilage, rework, and scrap

2. Identify the differences between normal and abnormal spoilage

3. Account for spoilage in process costing using the weighted-average method and the first-in, first-out (FIFO) method

4. Account for spoilage at various stages of completion in process costing

5. Account for spoilage in job costing

6. Account for rework in job costing

7. Account for scrap

When a product doesn't meet specification but is subsequently repaired and sold, it is called rework.

Firms try to minimize rework, as well as spoilage and scrap, during production. Why? Because higher-than-normal levels of spoilage and scrap can have a significant negative effect on a company's profits. Rework can also cause substantial production delays, as the following article about Boeing shows.

Rework Delays the Boeing Dreamliner by Three Years[1]

In 2007, Boeing was scheduled to introduce its newest airplane, the Dreamliner 787. Engineered to be the most fuel-efficient commercial plane, the Dreamliner received nearly 600 customer orders, making it the fastest selling commercial airplane in history.

By 2010, however, the first Dreamliner still had not rolled off the production line. The design and assembly process was riddled with production snafus, parts shortages, and supply-chain bottlenecks. The Dreamliner was Boeing's first major attempt at giving suppliers and partners far-ranging responsibility for designing and building the wings, fuselage, and other critical components to be shipped to Boeing for final assembly. The approach did not work as planned, with many of the 787's components delivered unfinished, with flaws, and lacking parts.

As a result, the Boeing Dreamliner aircraft required significant rework. The company's engineers had to redesign structural flaws in the airplane's wings, repair cracks in the composite materials used to construct the airplane, and fix faulty software among many other problems. In 2009, one of Boeing's unions calculated that half of its members' time was spent doing rework.

This rework led to costly delays for Boeing. Many of its customers, including Virgin Atlantic and Japan's All Nippon Airways, asked the company to compensate them for keeping less fuel-efficient planes in the air. Other customers cancelled their orders. Australia's Quantas Airways and a Dubai-based aircraft leasing firm each cancelled its

---

[1] *Sources:* Lunsford, J. Lynn. 2009. Dubai firm cancels 16 of Boeing's Dreamliners. *Wall Street Journal*, February 5; Matlack, Carol. 2009. More Boeing 787 woes as Quantas drops order. *Business Week*, June 26; Sanders, Peter. 2009. At Boeing, Dreamliner fix turns up new glitch. *Wall Street Journal*, November 13; West, Karen. 2009. Boeing has much to prove with 787. *MSNBC.com*, December 16; Wilhelm, Steve. 2009. Boeing engineers seek credit for fixing goofs. *Puget Sound Business Journal*, August 17.

orders for 15 airplanes, which cost Boeing at least $4.5 billion. The company also took a $2.5 billion charge in 2009 related to development costs on the Dreamliner program.

Like Boeing, companies are increasingly focused on improving the quality of, and reducing defects in, their products, services, and activities. A rate of defects regarded as normal in the past is no longer tolerable. In this chapter, we focus on three types of costs that arise as a result of defects—spoilage, rework, and scrap—and ways to account for them. We also describe how to determine (1) cost of products, (2) cost of goods sold, and (3) inventory values when spoilage, rework, and scrap occur.

Defining Spoilage, Rework and Scrap

While the terms used in this chapter may seem familiar, be sure you understand them in the context of management accounting.

Spoilage is units of production—whether fully or partially completed—that do not meet the specifications required by customers for good units and that are discarded or sold at reduced prices. Some examples of spoilage are defective shirts, jeans, shoes, and carpeting sold as "seconds," or defective aluminum cans sold to aluminum manufacturers for remelting to produce other aluminum products.

Rework is units of production that do not meet the specifications required by customers but that are subsequently repaired and sold as good finished units. For example, defective units of products (such as pagers, computers, and telephones) detected during or after the production process but before units are shipped to customers can sometimes be reworked and sold as good products.

Scrap is residual material that results from manufacturing a product. Examples are short lengths from woodworking operations, edges from plastic molding operations, and frayed cloth and end cuts from suit-making operations. Scrap can sometimes be sold for relatively small amounts. In that sense, scrap is similar to byproducts, which we studied in Chapter 16. The difference is that scrap arises as a residual from the manufacturing process, and is not a product targeted for manufacture or sale by the firm.

Some amounts of spoilage, rework, or scrap are inherent in many production processes. For example, semiconductor manufacturing is so complex and delicate that some spoiled units are commonly produced; usually, the spoiled units cannot be reworked. In the manufacture of high-precision machine tools, spoiled units can be reworked to meet standards, but only at a considerable cost. And in the mining industry, companies process ore that contains varying amounts of valuable metals and rock. Some amount of rock, which is scrap, is inevitable.

Two Types of Spoilage

Accounting for spoilage aims to determine the magnitude of spoilage costs and to distinguish between costs of normal and abnormal spoilage.[2] To manage, control, and reduce spoilage costs, companies need to highlight them, not bury them as an unidentified part of the costs of good units manufactured.

To illustrate normal and abnormal spoilage, consider Mendoza Plastics, which makes casings for the iMac computer using plastic injection molding. In January 2012, Mendoza incurs costs of $615,000 to produce 20,500 units. Of these 20,500 units, 20,000 are good units and 500 are spoiled units. Mendoza has no beginning inventory and no ending inventory that month. Of the 500 spoiled units, 400 units are spoiled because the injection molding machines are unable to manufacture good casings 100% of the time. That is, these units are spoiled even though the machines were run carefully and efficiently. The remaining 100 units are spoiled because of machine breakdowns and operator errors.

Normal Spoilage

Normal spoilage is spoilage inherent in a particular production process. In particular, it arises even when the process is operated in an efficient manner. The costs of normal spoilage are typically included as a component of the costs of good units manufactured, because good units cannot be made without also making some units that are spoiled. There is a tradeoff between the speed of production and the normal spoilage rate. Management makes a conscious decision about how many units to produce per hour with the understanding that, at the rate decided on, a certain level of spoilage is almost unavoidable. For this reason, the cost of normal spoilage is included in the cost of the good units completed. At Mendoza Plastics, the 400 units spoiled because of the limitations of injection molding machines and despite efficient operating conditions are considered normal spoilage. The calculations are as follows:

Manufacturing cost per unit, $615,000 ÷ 20,500 units = $30

Manufacturing costs of good units alone, $30 per unit × 20,000 units	$600,000
Normal spoilage costs, $30 per unit × 400 units	12,000
Manufacturing costs of good units completed (includes normal spoilage)	$612,000

$$\text{Manufacturing cost per good unit} = \frac{\$612,000}{20,000 \text{ units}} = \$30.60$$

Because normal spoilage is the spoilage related to the good units produced, normal spoilage rates are computed by dividing units of normal spoilage by total *good units completed*, not total *actual units started* in production. At Mendoza Plastics, the normal spoilage rate is therefore computed as 400 ÷ 20,000 = 2%.

Abnormal Spoilage

Abnormal spoilage is spoilage that is not inherent in a particular production process and would not arise under efficient operating conditions. If a firm has 100% good units as its goal, then any spoilage would be considered abnormal. At Mendoza, the 100 units spoiled due to machine breakdowns and operator errors are abnormal spoilage. Abnormal spoilage is usually regarded as avoidable and controllable. Line operators and other plant personnel generally can decrease or eliminate abnormal spoilage by identifying the reasons for machine breakdowns, operator errors, etc., and by taking steps to prevent their recurrence. To highlight the effect of abnormal spoilage costs, companies calculate the units of abnormal spoilage and record the cost in the Loss from Abnormal Spoilage account, which appears as a separate line item in the income statement. At Mendoza, the loss from abnormal spoilage is $3,000 ($30 per unit × 100 units).

Issues about accounting for spoilage arise in both process-costing and job-costing systems. We discuss both instances next, beginning with spoilage in process-costing.

---

[2] The helpful suggestions of Samuel Laimon, University of Saskatchewan, are gratefully acknowledged.

Spoilage in Process Costing Using Weighted-Average and FIFO

How do process-costing systems account for spoiled units? We have already said that units of abnormal spoilage should be counted and recorded separately in a Loss from Abnormal Spoilage account. But what about units of normal spoilage? The correct method is to count these units when computing output units—physical or equivalent—in a process-costing system. The following example and discussion illustrate this approach.

Learning Objective 3

Account for spoilage in process costing using the weighted-average method

. . . spoilage cost based on total costs and equivalent units completed to date

and the first-in, first-out (FIFO) method

. . . spoilage cost based on costs of current period and equivalent units of work done in current period

Count All Spoilage

Example 1: Chipmakers, Inc., manufactures computer chips for television sets. All direct materials are added at the beginning of the production process. To highlight issues that arise with normal spoilage, we assume no beginning inventory and focus only on direct material costs. The following data are available for May 2012.

Home | Insert | Page Layout | Formulas | Data | Review | View

	A	B	C
1		Physical Units	Direct Materials
2	Work in process, beginning inventory (May 1)	0	
3	Started during May	10,000	
4	Good units completed and transferred out during May	5,000	
5	Units spoiled (all normal spoilage)	1,000	
6	Work in process, ending inventory (May 31)	4,000	
7	Direct material costs added in May		$270,000

Spoilage is detected upon completion of the process and has zero net disposal value.

An **inspection point** is the stage of the production process at which products are examined to determine whether they are acceptable or unacceptable units. Spoilage is typically assumed to occur at the stage of completion where inspection takes place. As a result, the spoiled units in our example are assumed to be 100% complete with respect to direct materials.

Exhibit 18-1 calculates and assigns cost per unit of direct materials. Overall, Chipmakers generated 10,000 equivalent units of output: 5,000 equivalent units in good units completed (5,000 physical units × 100%), 4,000 units in ending work in process

Exhibit 18-1

Effect of Recognizing Equivalent Units in Spoilage for Direct Material Costs for Chipmakers, Inc., for May 2012

Home | Insert | Page Layout | Formulas | Data | Review | View

	A	B
1		Approach Counting Spoiled Units When Computing Output in Equivalent Units
2	Costs to account for	$270,000
3	Divide by equivalent units of output	÷ 10,000
4	Cost per equivalent unit of output	$ 27
5	Assignment of costs:	
6	Good units completed (5,000 units × $27 per unit)	$135,000
7	Add normal spoilage (1,000 units × $27 per unit)	27,000
8	Total costs of good units completed and transferred out	162,000
9	Work in process, ending (4,000 units × $27 per unit)	108,000
10	Costs accounted for	$270,000

(4,000 physical units × 100%), and 1,000 equivalent units in normal spoilage (1,000 physical units × 100%). Given total direct material costs of $270,000 in May, this yields an equivalent-unit cost of $27. The total cost of good units completed and transferred out, which includes the cost of normal spoilage, is then $162,000 (6,000 equivalent units × $27), while the ending work in process is assigned a cost of $108,000 (4,000 equivalent units × $27).

There are two noteworthy features of this approach. First, the 4,000 units in ending work in process are not assigned any of the costs of normal spoilage. This is appropriate because the units have not yet been inspected. While the units in ending work in process undoubtedly include some that will be detected as spoiled when inspected, these units will only be identified when the units are completed in the subsequent accounting period. At that time, costs of normal spoilage will be assigned to the good units completed in that period. Second, the approach used in Exhibit 18-1 delineates the cost of normal spoilage as $27,000. By highlighting the magnitude of this cost, the approach helps to focus management's attention on the potential economic benefits of reducing spoilage.

Five-Step Procedure for Process Costing with Spoilage

Example 2: Anzio Company manufactures a recycling container in its forming department. Direct materials are added at the beginning of the production process. Conversion costs are added evenly during the production process. Some units of this product are spoiled as a result of defects, which are detectable only upon inspection of finished units. Normally, spoiled units are 10% of the finished output of good units. That is, for every 10 good units produced, there is 1 unit of normal spoilage. Summary data for July 2012 are as follows:

	A	Physical Units (1)	Direct Materials (2)	Conversion Costs (3)	Total Costs (4) = (2) + (3)
2	Work in process, beginning inventory (July 1)	1,500	$12,000	$ 9,000	$ 21,000
3	Degree of completion of beginning work in process		100%	60%	
4	Started during July	8,500			
5	Good units completed and transferred out during July	7,000			
6	Work in process, ending inventory (July 31)	2,000			
7	Degree of completion of ending work in process		100%	50%	
8	Total costs added during July		$76,500	$89,100	$165,600
9	Normal spoilage as a percentage of good units	10%			
10	Degree of completion of normal spoilage	·	100%	100%	
11	Degree of completion of abnormal spoilage		100%	100%	

The five-step procedure for process costing used in Chapter 17 needs only slight modification to accommodate spoilage.

Step 1: Summarize the Flow of Physical Units of Output. Identify the number of units of both normal and abnormal spoilage.

$$\text{Total Spoilage} = \left(\begin{array}{c} \text{Units in beginning} \\ \text{work-in-process inventory} \end{array} + \begin{array}{c} \text{Units} \\ \text{started} \end{array} \right) - \left(\begin{array}{c} \text{Good units} \\ \text{completed and} \\ \text{transferred out} \end{array} + \begin{array}{c} \text{Units in ending} \\ \text{work-in-process inventory} \end{array} \right)$$

$$= (1,500 + 8,500) - (7,000 + 2,000)$$

$$= 10,000 - 9,000$$

$$= 1,000 \text{ units}$$

Recall that normal spoilage is 10% of good output at Anzio Company. Therefore, normal spoilage = 10% of the 7,000 units of *good* output = 700 units.

$$\text{Abnormal spoilage} = \text{Total spoilage} - \text{Normal spoilage}$$

$$= 1,000 \text{ units} - 700 \text{ units}$$

$$= 300 \text{ units}$$

Step 2: Compute Output in Terms of Equivalent Units. Compute equivalent units for spoilage in the same way we compute equivalent units for good units. As illustrated previously, all spoiled units are included in the computation of output units. Because Anzio's inspection point is at the completion of production, the same amount of work will have been done on each spoiled and each completed good unit.

Step 3: Summarize Total Costs to Account For. The total costs to account for are all the costs debited to Work in Process. The details for this step are similar to Step 3 in Chapter 17.

Step 4: Compute Cost per Equivalent Unit. This step is similar to Step 4 in Chapter 17.

Step 5: Assign Total Costs to Units Completed, to Spoiled Units, and to Units in Ending Work in Process. This step now includes computation of the cost of spoiled units and the cost of good units.

We illustrate these five steps of process costing for the weighted-average and FIFO methods next. *The standard-costing method is illustrated in the appendix to this chapter.*

Weighted-Average Method and Spoilage

Exhibit 18-2, Panel A, presents Steps 1 and 2 to calculate equivalent units of work done to date and includes calculations of equivalent units of normal and abnormal spoilage. Exhibit 18-2, Panel B, presents Steps 3, 4, and 5 (together called the production-cost worksheet).

Step 3 summarizes total costs to account for. Step 4 presents cost-per-equivalent-unit calculations using the weighted-average method. Note how, for each cost category, costs of beginning work in process and costs of work done in the current period are totaled and divided by equivalent units of all work done to date to calculate the weighted-average cost per equivalent unit. Step 5 assigns total costs to completed units, normal and abnormal spoiled units, and ending inventory by multiplying the equivalent units calculated in Step 2 by the cost per equivalent unit calculated in Step 4. Also note that the $13,825 costs of normal spoilage are added to the costs of the related good units completed and transferred out.

$$\begin{array}{c} \text{Cost per good unit} \\ \text{completed and transferred} \\ \text{out of the process} \end{array} = \frac{\text{Total costs transferred out (including normal spoilage)}}{\text{Number of good units produced}}$$

$$= \$152,075 \div 7,000 \text{ good units} = \$21.725 \text{ per good unit}$$

This amount is not equal to $19.75 per good unit, the sum of the $8.85 cost per equivalent unit of direct materials plus the $10.90 cost per equivalent unit of conversion costs. That's because the cost per good unit equals the sum of the direct material and conversion costs per equivalent unit, $19.75, plus a share of normal spoilage, $1.975 ($13,825 ÷ 7,000 good units), for a total of $21.725 per good unit. The $5,925 costs of abnormal spoilage are charged to the Loss from Abnormal Spoilage account and do not appear in the costs of good units.[3]

FIFO Method and Spoilage

Exhibit 18-3, Panel A, presents Steps 1 and 2 using the FIFO method, which focuses on equivalent units of work done in the current period. Exhibit 18-3, Panel B, presents Steps 3, 4, and 5. Note how when assigning costs, the FIFO method keeps the costs of

---

[3] The actual costs of spoilage (and rework) are often greater than the costs recorded in the accounting system because the opportunity costs of disruption of the production line, storage, and lost contribution margins are not recorded in accounting systems. Chapter 19 discusses these opportunity costs from the perspective of cost management.

Exhibit 18-2	Weighted-Average Method of Process Costing with Spoilage for Forming Department of the Anzio Company for July 2012

PANEL A: Steps 1 and 2—Summarize Output in Physical Units and Compute Equivalent Units

	A	B	C	D	E
	Home	Insert Page Layout Formulas Data Review View			
1			(Step 1)	(Step 2)	
2				Equivalent Units	
3		Flow of Production	Physical Units	Direct Materials	Conversion Costs
4		Work in process, beginning (given, p. 648)	1,500		
5		Started during current period (given, p. 648)	8,500		
6		To account for	10,000		
7		Good units completed and transferred out during current period	7,000	7,000	7,000
8		Normal spoilage[a]	700		
9		(700 × 100%; 700 × 100%)		700	700
10		Abnormal spoilage[b]	300		
11		(300 × 100%; 300 × 100%)		300	300
12		Work in process, ending[c] (given, p. 648)	2,000		
13		(2,000 × 100%; 2,000 × 50%)		2,000	1,000
14		Accounted for	10,000		
15		Equivalent units of work done to date		10,000	9,000
16					
17		[a]Normal spoilage is 10% of good units transferred out: 10% × 7,000 = 700 units. Degree of completion of normal spoilage			
18		in this department: direct materials, 100%; conversion costs, 100%.			
19		[b]Abnormal spoilage = Total spoilage – Normal spoilage = 1,000 – 700 = 300 units. Degree of completion of abnormal spoilage			
20		in this department: direct materials, 100%; conversion costs, 100%.			
21		[c]Degree of completion in this department: direct materials, 100%; conversion costs, 50%.			

PANEL B: Steps 3, 4, and 5—Summarize Total Costs to Account For, Compute Cost per Equivalent Unit, and Assign Total Costs to Units Completed, to Spoiled Units, and to Units in Ending Work Process

			Total Production Costs	Direct Materials	Conversion Costs
23					
24	(Step 3)	Work in process, beginning (given, p. 648)	$ 21,000	$12,000	$ 9,000
25		Costs added in current period (given, p. 648)	165,600	76,500	89,100
26		Total costs to account for	$186,600	$88,500	$98,100
27	(Step 4)	Costs incurred to date		$88,500	$98,100
28		Divide by equivalent units of work done to date (Panel A)		÷10,000	÷ 9,000
29		Cost per equivalent unit		$ 8.85	$ 10.90
30	(Step 5)	Assignment of costs:			
31		Good units completed and transferred out (7,000 units)			
32		Costs before adding normal spoilage	$138,250	(7,000[d] × $8.85) + (7,000[d] × $10.90)	
33		Normal spoilage (700 units)	13,825	(700[d] × $8.85) + (700[d] × $10.90)	
34	(A)	Total costs of good units completed and transferred out	152,075		
35	(B)	Abnormal spoilage (300 units)	5,925	(300[d] × $8.85) + (300[d] × $10.90)	
36	(C)	Work in process, ending (2,000 units)	28,600	(2,000[d] × $8.85) + (1,000[d] × $10.90)	
37	(A)+(B)+(C)	Total costs accounted for	$186,600	$88,500 + $98,100	
38					
39		[d]Equivalent units of direct materials and conversion costs calculated in Step 2 in Panel A.			

PANEL A: Steps 1 and 2—Summarize Output in Physical Units and Compute Equivalent Units

Exhibit 18-3

First-In, First-Out (FIFO) Method of Process Costing with Spoilage for Forming Department of the Anzio Company for July 2012

		Home Insert Page Layout Formulas Data Review View			
	A	B	C	D	E
1			(Step 1)	(Step 2)	
2				Equivalent Units	
3		Flow of Production	Physical Units	Direct Materials	Conversion Costs
4		Work in process, beginning (given, p. 648)	1,500		
5		Started during current period (given, p. 648)	8,500		
6		To account for	10,000		
7		Good units completed and transferred out during current period:			
8		From beginning work in process[a]	1,500		
9		[1,500 × (100% −100%); 1,500 × (100% −60%)]		0	600
10		Started and completed	5,500[b]		
11		(5,500 × 100%; 5,500 × 100%)		5,500	5,500
12		Normal spoilage[c]	700		
13		(700 × 100%; 700 × 100%)		700	700
14		Abnormal spoilage[d]	300		
15		(300 × 100%; 300 × 100%)		300	300
16		Work in process, ending[e] (given, p. 648)	2,000		
17		(2,000 × 100%; 2,000 × 50%)		2,000	1,000
18		Accounted for	10,000		
19		Equivalent units of work done in current period		8,500	8,100
20					
21		[a]Degree of completion in this department: direct materials, 100%; conversion costs, 60%.			
22		[b]7,000 physical units completed and transferred out minus 1,500 physical units completed and transferred out from beginning			
23		work-in-process inventory.			
24		[c]Normal spoilage is 10% of good units transferred out: 10% × 7,000 = 700 units. Degree of completion of normal spoilage			
25		in this department: direct materials, 100%; conversion costs, 100%.			
26		[d]Abnormal spoilage = Actual spoilage − Normal spoilage = 1,000 − 700 = 300 units. Degree of completion of abnormal spoilage			
27		in this department: direct materials, 100%; conversion costs, 100%.			
28		[e]Degree of completion in this department: direct materials, 100%; conversion costs, 50%.			

PANEL B: Steps 3, 4, and 5—Summarize Total Costs to Account for, Compute Cost per Equivalent Unit, and Assign Total Costs to Units Completed, to Spoiled Units, and to Units in Ending Work in Process

			Total Production Costs	Direct Materials	Conversion Costs
30					
31	(Step 3)	Work in process, beginning (given, p. 648)	$ 21,000	$12,000	$ 9,000
32		Costs added in current period (given, p. 648)	165,600	76,500	89,100
33		Total costs to account for	$186,600	$88,500	$98,100
34	(Step 4)	Costs added in current period		$76,500	$89,100
35		Divide by equivalent units of work done in current period (Panel A)		÷ 8,500	÷ 8,100
36		Cost per equivalent unit		$ 9.00	$ 11.00
37	(Step 5)	Assignment of costs:			
38		Good units completed and transferred out (7,000 units)			
39		Work in process, beginning (1,500 units)	$ 21,000	$12,000 +	$9,000
40		Costs added to beginning work in process in current period	6,600	(0[f] × $9) +	(600[f] × $11)
41		Total from beginning inventory before normal spoilage	27,600		
42		Started and completed before normal spoilage (5,500 units)	110,000	(5,500[f] × $9) +	(5,500[f] × $11)
43		Normal spoilage (700 units)	14,000	(700[f] × $9) +	(700[f] × $11)
44	(A)	Total costs of good units completed and transferred out	151,600		
45	(B)	Abnormal spoilage (300 units)	6,000	(300[f] × $9) +	(300[f] × $11)
46	(C)	Work in process, ending (2,000 units)	29,000	(2,000[f] × $9) +	(1,000[f] × $11)
47	(A)+(B)+(C)	Total costs accounted for	$186,600	$88,500 +	$98,100
48					
49					
50					
51		[f]Equivalent units of direct materials and conversion costs calculated in Step 2 in Panel A.			

the beginning work in process separate and distinct from the costs of work done in the current period. All spoilage costs are assumed to be related to units completed during this period, using the unit costs of the current period.[4]

Journal Entries

The information from Panel B in Exhibits 18-2 and 18-3 supports the following journal entries to transfer good units completed to finished goods and to recognize the loss from abnormal spoilage.

Decision Point ▶

How do the weighted-average and FIFO methods of process costing calculate the costs of good units and spoilage?

	Weighted Average		FIFO	
Finished Goods	152,075		151,600	
Work in Process—Forming		152,075		151,600
To record transfer of good units completed in July.				
Loss from Abnormal Spoilage	5,925		6,000	
Work in Process—Forming		5,925		6,000
To record abnormal spoilage detected in July.				

Inspection Points and Allocating Costs of Normal Spoilage

Learning Objective 4

Account for spoilage at various stages of completion in process costing

. . . spoilage costs vary based on the point at which inspection is carried out

Our Anzio Company example assumes inspection occurs upon completion of the units. Although spoilage is typically detected only at one or more inspection points, it might actually occur at various stages of a production process. The cost of spoiled units is assumed to equal all costs incurred in producing spoiled units up to the point of inspection. When spoiled goods have a disposal value (for example, carpeting sold as "seconds"), the net cost of spoilage is computed by deducting the disposal value from the costs of the spoiled goods that have been accumulated up to the inspection point.

The unit costs of normal and abnormal spoilage are the same when the two are detected at the same inspection point. However, situations may arise when abnormal spoilage is detected at a different point from normal spoilage. Consider shirt manufacturing. Normal spoilage in the form of defective shirts is identified upon inspection at the end of the production process. Now suppose a faulty machine causes many defective shirts to be produced at the halfway point of the production process. These defective shirts are abnormal spoilage and occur at a different point in the production process from normal spoilage. In such cases, the unit cost of abnormal spoilage, which is based on costs incurred up to the halfway point of the production process, differs from the unit cost of normal spoilage, which is based on costs incurred through the end of the production process.

Costs of abnormal spoilage are separately accounted for as losses of the accounting period in which they are detected. However, recall that normal spoilage costs are added to the costs of good units, which raises an additional issue: Should normal spoilage costs be allocated between completed units and ending work-in-process inventory? *The common approach is to presume that normal spoilage occurs at the inspection point in the production cycle and to allocate its cost over all units that have passed that point during the accounting period.*

In the Anzio Company example, spoilage is assumed to occur when units are inspected at the end of the production process, so no costs of normal spoilage are allocated to ending work in process. If the units in ending work in process have passed the inspection point, however, the costs of normal spoilage are allocated to units in ending work in process as well as to completed units. For example, if the inspection point is at the halfway point of production, then any ending work in process that is at least 50% complete would be allocated a full measure of normal spoilage costs, and those spoilage costs would be calculated on the basis of all costs incurred up to the inspection point. If ending work in process is less than 50% complete, however, no normal spoilage costs would be allocated to it.

To better understand these issues, let us now assume that inspection at Anzio Company occurs at various stages in the production process. How does this affect the

---

[4] To simplify calculations under FIFO, spoiled units are accounted for as if they were started in the current period. Although some of the beginning work in process probably did spoil, all spoilage is treated as if it came from current production.

amount of normal and abnormal spoilage? As before, consider the forming department, and recall that direct materials are added at the start of production, while conversion costs are added evenly during the process.

Consider three different cases: Inspection occurs at (1) the 20%, (2) the 55%, or (3) the 100% completion stage. The last option is the one we have analyzed so far (see Exhibit 18-2). Assume that normal spoilage is 10% of the good units passing inspection. A total of 1,000 units are spoiled in all three cases. Normal spoilage is computed on the basis of the number of *good units* that pass the inspection point *during the current period*. The following data are for July 2012. Note how the number of units of normal and abnormal spoilage changes, depending on when inspection occurs.

	Home Insert Page Layout Formulas Data Review View			
	A	B	C	D
1		**Physical Units: Stage of Completion at Which Inspection Occurs**		
2	**Flow of Production**	**20%**	**55%**	**100%**
3	Work in process, beginning[a]	1,500	1,500	1,500
4	Started during July	8,500	8,500	8,500
5	To account for	10,000	10,000	10,000
6	Good units completed and transferred out			
7	(10,000 – 1,000 spoiled – 2,000 ending)	7,000	7,000	7,000
8	Normal spoilage	750[c]	550[d]	700[e]
9	Abnormal spoilage (1,000 – normal spoilage)	250	450	300
10	Work in process, ending[b]	2,000	2,000	2,000
11	Accounted for	10,000	10,000	10,000
12				
13	[a]Degree of completion in this department: direct materials, 100%; conversion costs, 60%.			
14	[b]Degree of completion in this department: direct materials, 100%; conversion costs, 50%.			
15	[c]10% × (8,500 units started – 1,000 units spoiled), because only the units started passed the 20% completion			
16	inspection point in the current period. Beginning work in process is excluded from this calculation because,			
17	being 60% complete at the start of the period, it passed the inspection point in the previous period.			
18	[d]10% × (8,500 units started – 1,000 units spoiled – 2,000 units in ending work in process). Both beginning and			
19	ending work in process are excluded since neither was inspected this period.			
20	[e]10% × 7,000, because 7,000 units are fully completed and inspected in the current period.			

The following diagram shows the flow of physical units for July and illustrates the normal spoilage numbers in the table. Note that 7,000 good units are completed and transferred out—1,500 from beginning work in process and 5,500 started and completed during the period—while 2,000 units are in ending work in process.

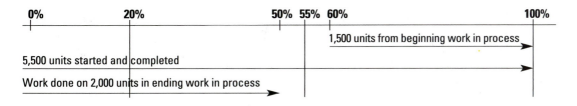

To see the number of units passing each inspection point, consider in the diagram the vertical lines at the 20%, 55%, and 100% inspection points. Note that the vertical line at 20% crosses two horizontal lines—5,500 good units started and completed and 2,000 units in ending work in process—for a total of 7,500 good units. (The 20% vertical line does not cross the line representing work done on the 1,500 good units completed from beginning work in process, because these units are already 60% complete at the start of the period and, hence, are not inspected this period.) Normal spoilage equals 10% of 7,500 = 750 units. On the other hand, the vertical line at the 55% point crosses just the second horizontal line, indicating that only 5,500 good units pass this point. Normal spoilage in this case is 10% of 5,500 = 550 units. At the 100% point, normal spoilage = 10% of 7,000 (1,500 + 5,500) good units = 700 units.

Exhibit 18-4 shows the computation of equivalent units under the weighted-average method, assuming inspection at the 20% completion stage. The calculations depend on the direct materials and conversion costs incurred to get the units to this inspection point. The spoiled units have a full measure of direct materials and a 20% measure of conversion costs. Calculations of costs per equivalent unit and the assignment of total costs to units completed and to ending work in process are similar to calculations in previous illustrations in this chapter. Because ending work in process has passed the inspection point, these units bear normal spoilage costs, just like the units that have been completed and transferred out. For example, conversion costs for units completed and transferred out include conversion costs for 7,000 good units produced plus 20% × (10% × 5,500) = 110 equivalent units of normal spoilage. *We multiply by 20% to obtain equivalent units of normal spoilage because conversion costs are only 20% complete at the inspection point.* Conversion costs of ending work in process include conversion costs of 50% of 2,000 = 1,000 equivalent good units plus 20% × (10% × 2,000) = 40 equivalent units of normal spoilage. Thus, the equivalent units of normal spoilage accounted for are 110 equivalent units related to units completed and transferred out plus 40 equivalent units related to units in ending work in process, for a total of 150 equivalent units, as shown in Exhibit 18-4.

Early inspections can help prevent any further direct materials and conversion costs being wasted on units that are already spoiled. For example, if inspection can occur when units are 70% (rather than 100%) complete as to conversion costs and spoilage occurs prior to the 70% point, a company can avoid incurring the final 30% of conversion costs on the spoiled units. The downside to conducting inspections at too early a stage is that spoilage that happens at later stages of the process may go undetected. It is for these reasons that firms often conduct multiple inspections and also empower workers to identify and resolve defects on a timely basis.

Decision Point

How does inspection at various stages of completion affect the amount of normal and abnormal spoilage?

Exhibit 18-4

Computing Equivalent Units with Spoilage Using Weighted-Average Method of Process Costing with Inspection at 20% of Completion for Forming Department of Anzio Company for July 2012

	A	B	C	D
		(Step 1)	**(Step 2)**	
			Equivalent Units	
	Flow of Production	**Physical Units**	**Direct Materials**	**Conversion Costs**
4	Work in process, beginning[a]	1,500		
5	Started during current period	8,500		
6	To account for	10,000		
7	Good units completed and transferred out:	7,000	7,000	7,000
8	Normal spoilage	750		
9	(750 × 100%; 750 × 20%)		750	150
10	Abnormal spoilage	250		
11	(250 × 100%; 250 × 20%)		250	50
12	Work in process, ending[b]	2,000		
13	(2,000 × 100%; 2,000 × 50%)		2,000	1,000
14	Accounted for	10,000		
15	Equivalent units of work done to date		10,000	8,200
16				
17	[a]Degree of completion: direct materials, 100%; conversion costs, 60%.			
18	[b]Degree of completion: direct materials, 100%; conversion costs, 50%.			

Job Costing and Spoilage

The concepts of normal and abnormal spoilage also apply to job-costing systems. Abnormal spoilage is separately identified so companies can work to eliminate it altogether. Costs of abnormal spoilage are not considered to be inventoriable costs and are written off as costs of the accounting period in which the abnormal spoilage is detected. Normal spoilage costs in job-costing systems—as in process-costing systems—are inventoriable costs, although increasingly companies are tolerating only small amounts of spoilage as normal. When assigning costs, job-costing systems generally distinguish *normal spoilage attributable to a specific job from normal spoilage common to all jobs.*

We describe accounting for spoilage in job costing using the following example.

> Example 3: In the Hull Machine Shop, 5 aircraft parts out of a job lot of 50 aircraft parts are spoiled. Costs assigned prior to the inspection point are $2,000 per part. When the spoilage is detected, the spoiled goods are inventoried at $600 per part, the net disposal value.

Learning Objective 5

Account for spoilage in job costing

. . . normal spoilage assigned directly or indirectly to job; abnormal spoilage written off as a loss of the period

Our presentation here and in subsequent sections focuses on how the $2,000 cost per part is accounted for.

Normal Spoilage Attributable to a Specific Job

When normal spoilage occurs because of the specifications of a particular job, that job bears the cost of the spoilage minus the disposal value of the spoilage. The journal entry to recognize disposal value (items in parentheses indicate subsidiary ledger postings) is as follows:

Materials Control (spoiled goods at current net disposal value): 5 units × $600 per unit	3,000	
Work-in-Process Control (specific job): 5 units × $600 per unit		3,000

Note, the Work-in-Process Control (specific job) has already been debited (charged) $10,000 for the spoiled parts (5 spoiled parts × $2,000 per part). The net cost of normal spoilage = $7,000 ($10,000 − $3,000), which is an additional cost of the 45 (50 − 5) good units produced. Therefore, total cost of the 45 good units is $97,000: $90,000 (45 units × $2,000 per unit) incurred to produce the good units plus the $7,000 net cost of normal spoilage. Cost per good unit is $2,155.56 ($97,000 ÷ 45 good units).

Normal Spoilage Common to All Jobs

In some cases, spoilage may be considered a normal characteristic of the production process. The spoilage inherent in production will, of course, occur when a specific job is being worked on. But the spoilage is not attributable to, and hence is not charged directly to, the specific job. Instead, the spoilage is allocated indirectly to the job as manufacturing overhead because the spoilage is common to all jobs. The journal entry is as follows:

Materials Control (spoiled goods at current disposal value): 5 units × $600 per unit	3,000	
Manufacturing Overhead Control (normal spoilage): ($10,000 − $3,000)	7,000	
Work-in-Process Control (specific job): 5 units × $2,000 per unit		10,000

When normal spoilage is common to all jobs, the budgeted manufacturing overhead rate includes a provision for normal spoilage cost. Normal spoilage cost is spread, through overhead allocation, over all jobs rather than allocated to a specific job.[5] For example, if Hull produced 140 good units from all jobs in a given month, the $7,000 of normal spoilage overhead costs would be allocated at the rate of $50 per good unit ($7,000 ÷ 140 good units). Normal spoilage overhead costs allocated to the 45 good units in the job would be $2,250 ($50 × 45 good units). Total cost of the 45 good units is $92,250: $90,000 (45 units × $2,000 per unit) incurred to produce the good units plus $2,250 of normal spoilage overhead costs. Cost per good unit is $2,050 ($92,250 ÷ 45 good units).

---

[5] Note that costs already assigned to products are charged back to Manufacturing Overhead Control, which generally accumulates only costs incurred, not both costs incurred and costs already assigned.

Abnormal Spoilage

If the spoilage is abnormal, the net loss is charged to the Loss from Abnormal Spoilage account. Unlike normal spoilage costs, abnormal spoilage costs are not included as a part of the cost of good units produced. Total cost of the 45 good units is $90,000 (45 units × $2,000 per unit). Cost per good unit is $2,000 ($90,000 ÷ 45 good units).

Materials Control (spoiled goods at current disposal value): 5 units × $600 per unit	3,000	
Loss from Abnormal Spoilage ($10,000 − $3,000)	7,000	
Work-in-Process Control (specific job): 5 units × $2,000 per unit		10,000

Even though, for external reporting purposes, abnormal spoilage costs are written off in the accounting period and are not linked to specific jobs or units, companies often identify the particular reasons for abnormal spoilage, and, when appropriate, link abnormal spoilage with specific jobs or units for cost management purposes.

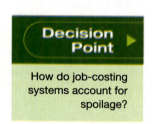

Decision Point

How do job-costing systems account for spoilage?

Learning Objective 6

Account for rework in job costing

. . . normal rework assigned directly or indirectly to job; abnormal rework written off as a loss of the period

Job Costing and Rework

Rework is units of production that are inspected, determined to be unacceptable, repaired, and sold as acceptable finished goods. We again distinguish (1) normal rework attributable to a specific job, (2) normal rework common to all jobs, and (3) abnormal rework.

Consider the Hull Machine Shop data in Example 3 on page 655. Assume the five spoiled parts are reworked. The journal entry for the $10,000 of total costs (the details of these costs are assumed) assigned to the five spoiled units before considering rework costs is as follows:

Work-in-Process Control (specific job)	10,000	
Materials Control		4,000
Wages Payable Control		4,000
Manufacturing Overhead Allocated		2,000

Assume the rework costs equal $3,800 (comprising $800 direct materials, $2,000 direct manufacturing labor, and $1,000 manufacturing overhead).

Normal Rework Attributable to a Specific Job

If the rework is normal but occurs because of the requirements of a specific job, the rework costs are charged to that job. The journal entry is as follows:

Work-in-Process Control (specific job)	3,800	
Materials Control		800
Wages Payable Control		2,000
Manufacturing Overhead Allocated		1,000

Normal Rework Common to All Jobs

When rework is normal and not attributable to a specific job, the costs of rework are charged to manufacturing overhead and are spread, through overhead allocation, over all jobs.

Manufacturing Overhead Control (rework costs)	3,800	
Materials Control		800
Wages Payable Control		2,000
Manufacturing Overhead Allocated		1,000

Abnormal Rework

If the rework is abnormal, it is recorded by charging abnormal rework to a loss account.

Loss from Abnormal Rework	3,800	
Materials Control		800
Wages Payable Control		2,000
Manufacturing Overhead Allocated		1,000

Accounting for rework in a process-costing system also requires abnormal rework to be distinguished from normal rework. Process costing accounts for abnormal rework in the same way as job costing. Accounting for normal rework follows the accounting described for normal rework common to all jobs (units) because masses of identical or similar units are being manufactured.

Costing rework focuses managers' attention on the resources wasted on activities that would not have to be undertaken if the product had been made correctly. The cost of rework prompts managers to seek ways to reduce rework, for example, by designing new products or processes, training workers, or investing in new machines. To eliminate rework and to simplify the accounting, some companies set a standard of zero rework. All rework is then treated as abnormal and is written off as a cost of the current period.

Decision Point

How do job-costing systems account for rework?

Accounting for Scrap

Scrap is residual material that results from manufacturing a product; it has low total sales value compared with the total sales value of the product. No distinction is made between normal and abnormal scrap because no cost is assigned to scrap. The only distinction made is between scrap attributable to a specific job and scrap common to all jobs.

There are two aspects of accounting for scrap:

1. Planning and control, including physical tracking
2. Inventory costing, including when and how scrap affects operating income

Learning Objective 7

Account for scrap

. . . reduces cost of job either at time of sale or at time of production

Initial entries to scrap records are commonly expressed in physical terms. In various industries, companies quantify items such as stamped-out metal sheets or edges of molded plastic parts by weighing, counting, or some other measure. Scrap records not only help measure efficiency, but also help keep track of scrap, and so reduce the chances of theft. Companies use scrap records to prepare periodic summaries of the amounts of actual scrap compared with budgeted or standard amounts. Scrap is either sold or disposed of quickly or it is stored for later sale, disposal, or reuse.

Careful tracking of scrap often extends into the accounting records. Many companies maintain a distinct account for scrap costs somewhere in their accounting system. The issues here are similar to the issues in Chapter 16 regarding the accounting for byproducts:

- When should the value of scrap be recognized in the accounting records—at the time scrap is produced or at the time scrap is sold?
- How should revenues from scrap be accounted for?

To illustrate, we extend our Hull example. Assume the manufacture of aircraft parts generates scrap and that the scrap from a job has a net sales value of $900.

Recognizing Scrap at the Time of Its Sale

When the dollar amount of scrap is immaterial, the simplest accounting is to record the physical quantity of scrap returned to the storeroom and to regard scrap sales as a separate line item in the income statement. In this case, the only journal entry is as follows:

Sale of scrap:	Cash or Accounts Receivable	900	
	Scrap Revenues		900

When the dollar amount of scrap is material and the scrap is sold quickly after it is produced, the accounting depends on whether the scrap is attributable to a specific job or is common to all jobs.

Scrap Attributable to a Specific Job

Job-costing systems sometimes trace scrap revenues to the jobs that yielded the scrap. This method is used only when the tracing can be done in an economically feasible way. For example, the Hull Machine Shop and its customers, such as the U.S. Department of Defense, may reach an agreement that provides for charging specific jobs with all rework or spoilage costs and then crediting these jobs with all scrap revenues that arise from the jobs. The journal entry is as follows:

Scrap returned to storeroom:	No journal entry. [Notation of quantity received and related job entered in the inventory record]		
Sale of scrap:	Cash or Accounts Receivable	900	
	Work-in-Process Control		900
	Posting made to specific job cost record.		

Unlike spoilage and rework, there is no cost assigned to the scrap, so no distinction is made between normal and abnormal scrap. All scrap revenues, whatever the amount, are credited to the specific job. Scrap revenues reduce the costs of the job.

Scrap common to all jobs

The journal entry in this case is as follows:

Scrap returned to storeroom:	No journal entry. [Notation of quantity received and related job entered in the inventory record]		
Sale of scrap:	Cash or Accounts Receivable	900	
	Manufacturing Overhead Control		900
	Posting made to subsidiary ledger—"Sales of Scrap" column on department cost record.		

Scrap is not linked with any particular job or product. Instead, all products bear production costs without any credit for scrap revenues except in an indirect manner: Expected scrap revenues are considered when setting the budgeted manufacturing overhead rate. Thus, the budgeted overhead rate is lower than it would be if the overhead budget had not been reduced by expected scrap revenues. This method of accounting for scrap is also used in process costing when the dollar amount of scrap is immaterial, because the scrap in process costing is common to the manufacture of all the identical or similar units produced (and cannot be identified with specific units).

Recognizing Scrap at the Time of Its Production

Our preceding illustrations assume that scrap returned to the storeroom is sold quickly, so it is not assigned an inventory cost figure. Sometimes, as in the case with edges of molded plastic parts, the value of scrap is not immaterial, and the time between storing it and selling or reusing it can be long and unpredictable. In these situations, the company assigns an inventory cost to scrap at a conservative estimate of its net realizable value so that production costs and related scrap revenues are recognized in the same accounting period. Some companies tend to delay sales of scrap until its market price is considered attractive. Volatile price fluctuations are typical for scrap metal. In these cases, it's not easy to determine some "reasonable inventory value."

Scrap Attributable to a Specific Job

The journal entry in the Hull example is as follows:

Scrap returned to storeroom:	Materials Control	900	
	Work-in-Process Control		900

Scrap Common to All Jobs

The journal entry in this case is as follows:

Scrap returned to storeroom:	Materials Control	900	
	Manufacturing Overhead Control		900

Observe that the Materials Control account is debited in place of Cash or Accounts Receivable. When the scrap is sold, the journal entry is as follows:

Sale of scrap:	Cash or Accounts Receivable	900	
	Materials Control		900

Concepts in Action

Managing Waste and Environmental Costs at KB Home

KB Home is one of the largest home builders in the United States. In recent years, public awareness of environmental issues and interest in environmentally-friendly products and services has led to increased demand for sustainable home construction. KB Home has responded by increasing the sustainability of its homebuilding operations, which includes reducing its waste and environmental costs.

Through its "My Home. My Earth." program, launched in 2007, KB Home has established environmental sustainability as top-priority management issue. It developed core principles to guide its efforts including using "innovation and our process-driven approach to reduce waste and natural resource usage throughout our organization." Much of that focus involves reducing scrap, the residual materials that result from its homebuilding processes. These materials pose additional problems for companies like KB Home, because many federal and state environmental laws dictate that scrap materials be deposed of in an environmentally friendly way; therefore, they add to the cost of generating waste.

To reduce these costs during the homebuilding process, all new homes are built with pre-engineered roof trusses, while 90% also use preconstructed panels. These preconstructed materials are cut offsite for greater precision, which reduces wood waste. Further, these precut materials are made of engineered wood products, which reduce the use of long solid boards that require larger trees to be cut. Beyond scrap reduction, these trusses and panels also eliminate the need for costly job-site rework, or the repair of defective materials during construction.

Similarly, all new homes use oriented strand board, which is made from wood chip rather than plywood. Wood chip is both cheaper and more environmentally sustainable than traditional construction materials. These sustainable practices helped KB Home reduce the cost, exclusive of land, of each home manufactured in 2009 by nearly 39% over the previous year, while increasing profit margins by 13% despite the broader U.S. housing market collapse.

Beyond the construction process, KB Home also includes earth-friendly standard features in all of its homes, at no cost to homebuyers, including energy-efficient windows, recyclable carpets, programmable thermostats, and faucets that reduce water usage. Beyond cutting costs, KB Home's efforts to effectively manage waste and environmental costs have helped the company partially stabilize revenues in a difficult real-estate market. Chief executive Jeffrey Mazger said, "Less than 2% of customers a few years ago were asking about energy-efficient options. Since we introduced 'My Home. My Earth.' in April 2007, it's gone up to 75%." This has helped KB Home differentiate itself within a very competitive market for homebuilders.

Sources: KB Home. 2010. 2009 annual report. Los Angeles: KB Home; KB Home. 2010. 2009 sustainability report. Los Angeles: KB Home; Tischler, Linda. 2008. The green housing boom. *Fast Company*, June 23.

Scrap is sometimes reused as direct material rather than sold as scrap. In this case, Materials Control is debited at its estimated net realizable value and then credited when the scrap is reused. For example, the entries when the scrap is common to all jobs are as follows:

Scrap returned to storeroom:	Materials Control	900	
	Manufacturing Overhead Control		900
Reuse of scrap:	Work-in-Process Control	900	
	Materials Control		900

Accounting for scrap under process costing is similar to accounting under job costing when scrap is common to all jobs. That's because the scrap in process costing is common to the manufacture of masses of identical or similar units.

Managers focus their attention on ways to reduce scrap and to use it more profitably, especially when the cost of scrap is high (see Concepts in Action on p. 659). For example, General Motors has redesigned its plastic injection molding processes to reduce the scrap plastic that must be broken away from its molded products. General Motors also regrinds and reuses the plastic scrap as direct material, saving substantial input costs.

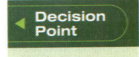

Decision Point

How is scrap accounted for?

Problem for Self-Study

Burlington Textiles has some spoiled goods that had an assigned cost of $40,000 and zero net disposal value.

Required Prepare a journal entry for each of the following conditions under (a) process costing (department A) and (b) job costing:

1. Abnormal spoilage of $40,000
2. Normal spoilage of $40,000 regarded as common to all operations
3. Normal spoilage of $40,000 regarded as attributable to specifications of a particular job

Solution

	(a) Process Costing			(b) Job Costing		
1.	Loss from Abnormal Spoilage	40,000		Loss from Abnormal Spoilage	40,000	
	Work in Process—Dept. A		40,000	Work-in-Process Control (specific job)		40,000
2.	No entry until units are completed and transferred out. Then the normal spoilage costs are transferred as part of the cost of good units.			Manufacturing Overhead Control	40,000	
				Work-in-Process Control (specific job)		40,000
	Work in Process—Dept. B	40,000				
	Work in Process—Dept. A		40,000			
3.	Not applicable			No entry. Normal spoilage cost remains in Work-in-Process Control (specific job)		

Decision Points

The following question-and-answer format summarizes the chapter's learning objectives. Each decision presents a key question related to a learning objective. The guidelines are the answer to that question.

Decision	Guidelines
1. What are spoilage, rework, and scrap?	Spoilage is units of production that do not meet the specifications required by customers for good units and that are discarded or sold at reduced prices. Spoilage is generally divided into normal spoilage, which is inherent to a particular production process, and abnormal spoilage, which arises because of inefficiency in operations. Rework is unacceptable units that are subsequently repaired and sold as acceptable finished goods. Scrap is residual material that results from manufacturing a product; it has low total sales value compared with the total sales value of the product.
2. What is the distinction between normal and abnormal spoilage?	Normal spoilage is inherent in a particular production process and arises when the process is operated in an efficient manner. Abnormal spoilage on the other hand is not inherent in a particular production process and would not arise under efficient operating conditions. Abnormal spoilage is usually regarded as avoidable and controllable.
3. How do the weighted-average and FIFO methods of process costing calculate the costs of good units and spoilage?	The weighted-average method combines costs in beginning inventory with costs of the current period when determining the costs of good units, which include normal spoilage, and the costs of abnormal spoilage, which are written off as a loss of the accounting period.

The FIFO method keeps separate the costs in beginning inventory from the costs of the current period when determining the costs of good units (which include normal spoilage) and the costs of abnormal spoilage, which are written off as a loss of the accounting period.

4. How does inspection at various stages of completion affect the amount of normal and abnormal spoilage?

The cost of spoiled units is assumed to equal all costs incurred in producing spoiled units up to the point of inspection. Spoilage costs therefore vary based on different inspection points.

5. How do job-costing systems account for spoilage?

Normal spoilage specific to a job is assigned to that job, or when common to all jobs, is allocated as part of manufacturing overhead. Cost of abnormal spoilage is written off as a loss of the accounting period.

6. How do job-costing systems account for rework?

Completed reworked units should be indistinguishable from non-reworked good units. Normal rework specific to a job is assigned to that job, or when common to all jobs, is allocated as part of manufacturing overhead. Cost of abnormal rework is written off as a loss of the accounting period.

7. How is scrap accounted for?

Scrap is recognized in the accounting records either at the time of its sale or at the time of its production. Sale of scrap, if immaterial, is often recognized as other revenue. If not immaterial, sale of scrap or its net realizable value reduces the cost of a specific job or, when common to all jobs, reduces Manufacturing Overhead Control.

Appendix

Standard-Costing Method and Spoilage

The standard-costing method simplifies the computations for normal and abnormal spoilage. To illustrate, we return to the Anzio Company example in the chapter. Suppose Anzio develops the following standard costs per unit for work done in the forming department in July 2012:

Direct materials	$ 8.50
Conversion costs	10.50
Total manufacturing cost	$19.00

Assume the same standard costs per unit also apply to the beginning inventory: 1,500 (1,500 × 100%) equivalent units of direct materials and 900 (1,500 × 60%) equivalent units of conversion costs. Hence, the beginning inventory at standard costs is as follows:

Direct materials, 1,500 units × $8.50 per unit	$12,750
Conversion costs, 900 units × $10.50 per unit	9,450
Total manufacturing costs	$22,200

Exhibit 18-5, Panel A, presents Steps 1 and 2 for calculating physical and equivalent units. These steps are the same as for the FIFO method described in Exhibit 18-3. Exhibit 18-5, Panel B, presents Steps 3, 4, and 5.

The costs to account for in Step 3 are at standard costs and, hence, they differ from the costs to account for under the weighted-average and FIFO methods, which are at actual costs. In Step 4, cost per equivalent unit is simply the standard cost: $8.50 per unit for direct materials and $10.50 per unit for conversion costs. The standard-costing method makes calculating equivalent-unit costs unnecessary, so it simplifies process costing. Step 5 assigns standard costs to units completed (including normal spoilage), to abnormal spoilage, and to ending work-in-process inventory by multiplying the equivalent units calculated in Step 2 by the standard costs per equivalent unit presented in Step 4. Variances can then be measured and analyzed in the manner described in the appendix to Chapter 17 (pp. 634–635).[6]

---

[6] For example, from Exhibit 18-5, Panel B, the standard costs for July are direct materials used, 8,500 × $8.50 = $72,250, and conversion costs, 8,100 × $10.50 = $85,050. From page 648, the actual costs added during July are direct materials, $76,500, and conversion costs, $89,100, resulting in a direct materials variance of $72,250 − $76,500 = $4,250 U and a conversion costs variance of $85,050 − $89,100 = $4,050 U. These variances could then be subdivided further as in Chapters 7 and 8; the abnormal spoilage would be part of the efficiency variance.

Exhibit 18-5	Standard-Costing Method of Process Costing with Spoilage for Forming Department of the Anzio Company for July 2012

PANEL A: Steps 1 and 2—Summarize Output in Physical Units and Compute Equivalent Units

	Home	Insert	Page Layout	Formulas	Data	Review	View	

	A	B	C	D	E
1			(Step 1)	(Step 2)	
2				Equivalent Units	
3		Flow of Production	Physical Units	Direct Materials	Conversion Costs
4		Work in process, beginning (given, p. 648)	1,500		
5		Started during current period (given, p. 648)	8,500		
6		To account for	10,000		
7		Good units completed and transferred out during current period:			
8		From beginning work in process[a]	1,500		
9		[1,500 × (100% −100%); 1,500 × (100% −60%)]		0	600
10		Started and completed	5,500[b]		
11		(5,500 × 100%; 5,500 × 100%)		5,500	5,500
12		Normal spoilage[c]	700		
13		(700 × 100%; 700 × 100%)		700	700
14		Abnormal spoilage[d]	300		
15		(300 × 100%; 300 × 100%)		300	300
16		Work in process, ending[e] (given, p. 648)	2,000		
17		(2,000 × 100%; 2,000 × 50%)		2,000	1,000
18		Accounted for	10,000		
19		Equivalent units of work done in current period		8,500	8,100
20					
21	[a]Degree of completion in this department: direct materials, 100%; conversion costs, 60%.				
22	[b]7,000 physical units completed and transferred out minus 1,500 physical units completed and transferred out from beginning				
23	work-in-process inventory.				
24	[c]Normal spoilage is 10% of good units transferred out: 10% × 7,000 = 700 units. Degree of completion of normal spoilage in this				
25	department: direct materials, 100%; conversion costs, 100%.				
26	[d]Abnormal spoilage = Actual spoilage − Normal spoilage = 1,000 − 700 = 300 units. Degree of completion of abnormal spoilage in this				
27	department: direct materials, 100%; conversion costs, 100%.				
28	[e]Degree of completion in this department: direct materials, 100%; conversion costs, 50%.				

PANEL B: Steps 3, 4, and 5—Summarize Total Costs to Account for, Compute Cost per Equivalent Unit, and Assign Total Costs to Units Completed, to Spoiled Units, and to Units in Ending Work in Process

	A	B	C	D	E
30			Total Production Costs	Direct Materials	Conversion Costs
31	(Step 3)	Work in process, beginning (given, p. 661)	$ 22,200	(1,500 × $8.50)	(900 × $10.50)
32		Costs added in current period at standard prices	157,300	(8,500 × $8.50)	(8,100 × $10.50)
33		Total costs to account for	$179,500	$85,000	$94,500
34	(Step 4)	Standard costs per equivalent unit (given, p. 661)	$ 19.00	$ 8.50	$ 10.50
35	(Step 5)	Assignment of costs at standard costs:			
36		Good units completed and transferred out (7,000 units)			
37		Work in process, beginning (1,500 units)	$ 22,200	(1,500 × $8.50) +	(900 × $10.50)
38		Costs added to beginning work in process in current period	6,300	(0[f] × $8.50) +	(600[f] × $10.50)
39		Total from beginning inventory before normal spoilage	28,500		
40		Started and completed before normal spoilage (5,500 units)	104,500	(5,500[f] × $8.50) +	(5,500[f] × $10.50)
41		Normal spoilage (700 units)	13,300	(700[f] × $8.50) +	(700[f] × $10.50)
42	(A)	Total costs of good units completed and transferred out	146,300		
43	(B)	Abnormal spoilage (300 units)	5,700	(300[f] × $8.50) +	(300[f] × $10.50)
44	(C)	Work in process, ending (2,000 units)	27,500	(2,000[f] × $8.50) +	(1,000[f] × $10.50)
45	(A)+(B)+(C)	Total costs accounted for	$179,500	$85,000 +	$94,500
46					
47	[f]Equivalent units of direct materials and conversion costs calculated in Step 2 in Panel A.				

Finally, note that the journal entries corresponding to the amounts calculated in Step 5 are as follows:

Finished Goods	146,300	
Work in Process—Forming		146,300
To record transfer of good units completed in July.		
Loss from Abnormal Spoilage	5,700	
Work in Process—Forming		5,700
To record abnormal spoilage detected in July.		

Terms to Learn

This chapter and the Glossary at the end of the book contain definitions of the following important terms:

abnormal spoilage (**p. 646**)   normal spoilage (**p. 646**)   scrap (**p. 645**)

inspection point (**p. 647**)   rework (**p. 645**)   spoilage (**p. 645**)

Assignment Material

Questions

18-1 Why is there an unmistakable trend in manufacturing to improve quality?

18-2 Distinguish among spoilage, rework, and scrap.

18-3 "Normal spoilage is planned spoilage." Discuss.

18-4 "Costs of abnormal spoilage are losses." Explain.

18-5 "What has been regarded as normal spoilage in the past is not necessarily acceptable as normal spoilage in the present or future." Explain.

18-6 "Units of abnormal spoilage are inferred rather than identified." Explain.

18-7 "In accounting for spoiled units, we are dealing with cost assignment rather than cost incurrence." Explain.

18-8 "Total input includes abnormal as well as normal spoilage and is, therefore, inappropriate as a basis for computing normal spoilage." Do you agree? Explain.

18-9 "The inspection point is the key to the allocation of spoilage costs." Do you agree? Explain.

18-10 "The unit cost of normal spoilage is the same as the unit cost of abnormal spoilage." Do you agree? Explain.

18-11 "In job costing, the costs of normal spoilage that occur while a specific job is being done are charged to the specific job." Do you agree? Explain.

18-12 "The costs of rework are always charged to the specific jobs in which the defects were originally discovered." Do you agree? Explain.

18-13 "Abnormal rework costs should be charged to a loss account, not to manufacturing overhead." Do you agree? Explain.

18-14 When is a company justified in inventorying scrap?

18-15 How do managers use information about scrap?

Exercises

18-16 Normal and abnormal spoilage in units. The following data, in physical units, describe a grinding process for January:

Work in process, beginning	19,000
Started during current period	150,000
To account for	169,000
Spoiled units	12,000
Good units completed and transferred out	132,000
Work in process, ending	25,000
Accounted for	169,000

Inspection occurs at the 100% completion stage. Normal spoilage is 5% of the good units passing inspection.

1. Compute the normal and abnormal spoilage in units.
2. Assume that the equivalent-unit cost of a spoiled unit is $10. Compute the amount of potential savings if all spoilage were eliminated, assuming that all other costs would be unaffected. Comment on your answer.

 Required

18-17 Weighted-average method, spoilage, equivalent units. (CMA, adapted) Consider the following data for November 2012 from Gray Manufacturing Company, which makes silk pennants and uses a process-costing system. All direct materials are added at the beginning of the process, and conversion costs are added evenly during the process. Spoilage is detected upon inspection at the completion of the process. Spoiled units are disposed of at zero net disposal value. Gray Manufacturing Company uses the weighted-average method of process costing.

	Physical Units (Pennants)	Direct Materials	Conversion Costs
Work in process, November 1[a]	1,000	$ 1,423	$ 1,110
Started in November 2012	?		
Good units completed and transferred out during November 2012	9,000		
Normal spoilage	100		
Abnormal spoilage	50		
Work in process, November 30[b]	2,000		
Total costs added during November 2012		$12,180	$27,750

[a]Degree of completion: direct materials, 100%; conversion costs, 50%.
[b]Degree of completion: direct materials, 100%; conversion costs, 30%.

Required

Compute equivalent units for direct materials and conversion costs. Show physical units in the first column of your schedule.

18-18 Weighted-average method, assigning costs (continuation of 18-17).

Required

For the data in Exercise 18-17, summarize total costs to account for; calculate the cost per equivalent unit for direct materials and conversion costs; and assign total costs to units completed and transferred out (including normal spoilage), to abnormal spoilage, and to units in ending work in process.

18-19 FIFO method, spoilage, equivalent units. Refer to the information in Exercise 18-17. Suppose Gray Manufacturing Company uses the FIFO method of process costing instead of the weighted-average method.

Required

Compute equivalent units for direct materials and conversion costs. Show physical units in the first column of your schedule.

18-20 FIFO method, assigning costs (continuation of 18-19).

Required

For the data in Exercise 18-17, use the FIFO method to summarize total costs to account for; calculate the cost per equivalent unit for direct materials and conversion costs; and assign total costs to units completed and transferred out (including normal spoilage), to abnormal spoilage, and to units in ending work in process.

18-21 Weighted-average method, spoilage. Appleton Company makes wooden toys in its forming department, and it uses the weighted-average method of process costing. All direct materials are added at the beginning of the process, and conversion costs are added evenly during the process. Spoiled units are detected upon inspection at the end of the process and are disposed of at zero net disposal value. Summary data for August 2012 are as follows:

	A	B	C	D
1		Physical Units	Direct Materials	Conversion Costs
2	Work in process, beginning inventory (August 1)	2,000	$17,700	$10,900
3	Degree of completion of beginning work in process		100%	50%
4	Started during August	10,000		
5	Good units completed and transferred out during August	9,000		
6	Work in process, ending inventory (August 31)	1,800		
7	Degree of completion of ending work in process		100%	75%
8	Total costs added during August		$81,300	$93,000
9	Normal spoilage as a percentage of good units	10%		
10	Degree of completion of normal spoilage		100%	100%
11	Degree of completion of abnormal spoilage		100%	100%

Required

1. For each cost category, calculate equivalent units. Show physical units in the first column of your schedule.
2. Summarize total costs to account for; calculate cost per equivalent unit for each cost category; and assign total costs to units completed and transferred out (including normal spoilage), to abnormal spoilage, and to units in ending work in process.

18-22 Standard costing method, spoilage, journal entries. Jordan, Inc., is a manufacturer of vents for water heaters. The company uses a process-costing system to account for its work-in-process inventories. When Job 512 was being processed in the machining department, a piece of sheet metal was off center in the bending machine and two vents were spoiled. Because this problem occurs periodically, it is considered normal spoilage and is consequently recorded as an overhead cost. Because this step comes first in the procedure for making the vents, the only costs incurred were $475 for direct materials. Assume the sheet metal cannot be sold, and its cost has been recorded in work-in-process inventory.

Prepare the journal entries to record the spoilage incurred.

Required

18-23 Recognition of loss from spoilage. Arokia Electronics manufactures cell phone models in its Walnut Creek plant. Suppose the company provides you with the following information regarding operations for September 2011:

Total cell phones manufactured	8,000
Phones rejected as spoiled units	300
Total manufacturing cost	$320,000

Assume the spoiled units have no disposal value.

Required

1. What is the unit cost of making the 8,000 cell phones?
2. What is the total cost of the 300 spoiled units?
3. If the spoilage is considered normal, what is the increase in the unit cost of good phones manufactured as a result of the spoilage?
4. If the spoilage is considered abnormal, prepare the journal entries for the spoilage incurred.

18-24 Weighted-average method, spoilage. Chipcity is a fast-growing manufacturer of computer chips. Direct materials are added at the start of the production process. Conversion costs are added evenly during the process. Some units of this product are spoiled as a result of defects not detectable before inspection of finished goods. Spoiled units are disposed of at zero net disposal value. Chipcity uses the weighted-average method of process costing.

   Summary data for September 2011 are as follows:

	Home	Insert	Page Layout	Formulas	Data	Review	View			
	A						B	C	D
1							**Physical Units (Computer Chips)**	**Direct Materials**	**Conversion Costs**
2	Work in process, beginning inventory (September 1)						600	$ 96,000	$ 15,300
3	Degree of completion of beginning work in process							100%	30%
4	Started during September						2,550		
5	Good units completed and transferred out during September						2,100		
6	Work in process, ending inventory (September 30)						450		
7	Degree of completion of ending work in process							100%	40%
8	Total costs added during September							$567,000	$230,400
9	Normal spoilage as a percentage of good units						15%		
10	Degree of completion of normal spoilage							100%	100%
11	Degree of completion of abnormal spoilage							100%	100%

Required

1. For each cost category, compute equivalent units. Show physical units in the first column of your schedule.
2. Summarize total costs to account for; calculate cost per equivalent unit for each cost category; and assign total costs to units completed and transferred out (including normal spoilage), to abnormal spoilage, and to units in ending work in process.

18-25 FIFO method, spoilage. Refer to the information in Exercise 18-24.

Required Do Exercise 18-24 using the FIFO method of process costing.

18-26 Standard-costing method, spoilage. Refer to the information in Exercise 18-24. Suppose Chipcity determines standard costs of $200 per equivalent unit for direct materials and $75 per equivalent unit for conversion costs for both beginning work in process and work done in the current period.

Required Do Exercise 18-24 using the standard-costing method.

18-27 Spoilage and job costing. (L. Bamber) Barrett Kitchens produces a variety of items in accordance with special job orders from hospitals, plant cafeterias, and university dormitories. An order for 2,100 cases of mixed vegetables costs $9 per case: direct materials, $4; direct manufacturing labor, $3; and manufacturing overhead allocated, $2. The manufacturing overhead rate includes a provision for normal spoilage. Consider each requirement independently.

Required
1. Assume that a laborer dropped 420 cases. Suppose part of the 420 cases could be sold to a nearby prison for $420 cash. Prepare a journal entry to record this event. Calculate and explain briefly the unit cost of the remaining 1,680 cases.
2. Refer to the original data. Tasters at the company reject 420 of the 2,100 cases. The 420 cases are disposed of for $840. Assume that this rejection rate is considered normal. Prepare a journal entry to record this event, and do the following:
   a. Calculate the unit cost if the rejection is attributable to exacting specifications of this particular job.
   b. Calculate the unit cost if the rejection is characteristic of the production process and is not attributable to this specific job.
   c. Are unit costs the same in requirements 2a and 2b? Explain your reasoning briefly.
3. Refer to the original data. Tasters rejected 420 cases that had insufficient salt. The product can be placed in a vat, salt can be added, and the product can be reprocessed into jars. This operation, which is considered normal, will cost $420. Prepare a journal entry to record this event and do the following:
   a. Calculate the unit cost of all the cases if this additional cost was incurred because of the exacting specifications of this particular job.
   b. Calculate the unit cost of all the cases if this additional cost occurs regularly because of difficulty in seasoning.
   c. Are unit costs the same in requirements 3a and 3b? Explain your reasoning briefly.

18-28 Reworked units, costs of rework. White Goods assembles washing machines at its Auburn plant. In February 2012, 60 tumbler units that cost $44 each (from a new supplier who subsequently went bankrupt) were defective and had to be disposed of at zero net disposal value. White Goods was able to rework all 60 washing machines by substituting new tumbler units purchased from one of its existing suppliers. Each replacement tumbler cost $50.

Required
1. What alternative approaches are there to account for the material cost of reworked units?
2. Should White Goods use the $44 tumbler or the $50 tumbler to calculate the cost of materials reworked? Explain.
3. What other costs might White Goods include in its analysis of the total costs of rework due to the tumbler units purchased from the (now) bankrupt supplier?

18-29 Scrap, job costing. The Morgan Company has an extensive job-costing facility that uses a variety of metals. Consider each requirement independently.

Required
1. Job 372 uses a particular metal alloy that is not used for any other job. Assume that scrap is material in amount and sold for $520 quickly after it is produced. Prepare the journal entry.
2. The scrap from Job 372 consists of a metal used by many other jobs. No record is maintained of the scrap generated by individual jobs. Assume that scrap is accounted for at the time of its sale. Scrap totaling $4,400 is sold. Prepare two alternative journal entries that could be used to account for the sale of scrap.
3. Suppose the scrap generated in requirement 2 is returned to the storeroom for future use, and a journal entry is made to record the scrap. A month later, the scrap is reused as direct material on a subsequent job. Prepare the journal entries to record these transactions.

MyAccountingLab

Problems

18-30 Weighted-average method, spoilage. The Boston Company is a food-processing company based in San Francisco. It operates under the weighted-average method of process costing and has two departments: cleaning and packaging. For the cleaning department, conversion costs are added evenly during the process, and direct materials are added at the beginning of the process. Spoiled units are detected upon inspection at the end of the process and are disposed of at zero net disposal value. All completed work is transferred to the packaging department. Summary data for May follow:

Home	Insert	Page Layout	Formulas	Data	Review	View		

	A	B	C	D
1	**The Boston Company: Cleaning Department**	**Physical Units**	**Direct Materials**	**Conversion Costs**
2	Work in process, beginning inventory (May 1)	3,000	$ 4,500	$ 2,700
3	Degree of completion of beginning work in process		100%	60%
4	Started during May	25,000		
5	Good units completed and transferred out during May	20,500		
6	Work in process, ending inventory (May 31)	4,200		
7	Degree of completion of ending work in process		100%	30%
8	Total costs added during May		$46,250	$37,216
9	Normal spoilage as a percentage of good units	10%		
10	Degree of completion of normal spoilage		100%	100%
11	Degree of completion of abnormal spoilage		100%	100%

Required

For the cleaning department, summarize total costs to account for and assign total costs to units completed and transferred out (including normal spoilage), to abnormal spoilage, and to units in ending work in process. Carry unit-cost calculations to four decimal places when necessary. Calculate final totals to the nearest dollar. (Problem 18-32 explores additional facets of this problem.)

18-31 FIFO method, spoilage. Refer to the information in Problem 18-30.

Required

Do Problem 18-30 using the FIFO method of process costing. (Problem 18-33 explores additional facets of this problem.)

18-32 Weighted-average method, packaging department (continuation of 18-30). In Boston Company's packaging department, conversion costs are added evenly during the process, and direct materials are added at the end of the process. Spoiled units are detected upon inspection at the end of the process and are disposed of at zero net disposal value. All completed work is transferred to the next department. The transferred-in costs for May equal the total cost of good units completed and transferred out in May from the cleaning department, which were calculated in Problem 18-30 using the weighted-average method of process costing. Summary data for May follow.

Home	Insert	Page Layout	Formulas	Data	Review	View			

	A	B	C	D	E
1	**The Boston Company: Packaging Department**	**Physical Units**	**Transferred-In Costs**	**Direct Materials**	**Conversion Costs**
2	Work in process, beginning inventory (May 1)	10,500	$39,460	$ 0	$14,700
3	Degree of completion of beginning work in process		100%	0%	70%
4	Started during May	20,500			
5	Good units completed and transferred out during May	22,000			
6	Work in process, ending inventory (May 31)	7,000			
7	Degree of completion of ending work in process		100%	0%	40%
8	Total costs added during May		?	$4,800	$38,900
9	Normal spoilage as a percentage of good units	8%			
10	Degree of completion of normal spoilage			100%	100%
11	Degree of completion of abnormal spoilage			100%	100%

Required

For the packaging department, use the weighted-average method to summarize total costs to account for and assign total costs to units completed and transferred out (including normal spoilage), to abnormal spoilage, and to units in ending work in process.

18-33 FIFO method, packaging department (continuation of 18-31). Refer to the information in Problem 18-32 except for the transferred-in costs for May, which equal the total cost of good units completed and transferred out in May from the cleaning department, which were calculated in Problem 18-31 using the FIFO method of process costing.

Required

For the packaging department, use the FIFO method to summarize total costs to account for and assign total costs to units completed and transferred out (including normal spoilage), to abnormal spoilage, and to units in ending work in process.

18-34 Job-costing spoilage and scrap. MetalWorks, Inc., manufactures various metal parts in batches as ordered by customers, and accounts for them using job costing. Job 2346-8, a large job for customer X, incurred $240,000 of direct materials costs and $620,000 of direct labor costs. MetalWorks applies overhead at a rate of 150% of direct labor cost. MetalWorks quoted customer X a fixed price for the job of $2,000,000. The job consisted of 90,000 good units and 10,000 spoiled units with no rework or disposal value. The job also created 200 pounds of scrap which can be sold for $3 per pound.

1. Calculate the gross margin MetalWorks will earn for this job, assuming the scrap sale is treated as material, and
   a. all spoilage is considered abnormal.
   b. normal spoilage is 8% of good units.
   c. normal spoilage is 12% of good units.
2. How would your answer to number 1 differ if the scrap sale is treated as immaterial?

18-35 Spoilage in job costing. Crystal Clear Machine Shop is a manufacturer of motorized carts for vacation resorts.

Peter Cruz, the plant manager of Crystal Clear, obtains the following information for Job #10 in August 2010. A total of 32 units were started, and 7 spoiled units were detected and rejected at final inspection, yielding 25 good units. The spoiled units were considered to be normal spoilage. Costs assigned prior to the inspection point are $1,450 per unit. The current disposal price of the spoiled units is $230 per unit. When the spoilage is detected, the spoiled goods are inventoried at $230 per unit.

Required

1. What is the normal spoilage rate?
2. Prepare the journal entries to record the normal spoilage, assuming the following:
   a. The spoilage is related to a specific job.
   b. The spoilage is common to all jobs.
   c. The spoilage is considered to be abnormal spoilage.

18-36 Rework in job costing, journal entry (continuation of 18-35). Assume that the 7 spoiled units of Whitefish Machine Shop's Job #10 can be reworked for a total cost of $1,700. A total cost of $10,150 associated with these units has already been assigned to Job #10 before the rework.

Required

Prepare the journal entries for the rework, assuming the following:

a. The rework is related to a specific job.
b. The rework is common to all jobs.
c. The rework is considered to be abnormal.

18-37 Scrap at time of sale or at time of production, journal entries (continuation of 18-35). Assume that Job #10 of Crystal Clear Machine Shop generates normal scrap with a total sales value of $650 (it is assumed that the scrap returned to the storeroom is sold quickly).

Required

Prepare the journal entries for the recognition of scrap, assuming the following:

a. The value of scrap is immaterial and scrap is recognized at the time of sale.
b. The value of scrap is material, is related to a specific job, and is recognized at the time of sale.
c. The value of scrap is material, is common to all jobs, and is recognized at the time of sale.
d. The value of scrap is material, and scrap is recognized as inventory at the time of production and is recorded at its net realizable value.

18-38 Physical units, inspection at various stages of completion. Fantastic Furniture manufactures plastic lawn furniture in a continuous process. The company pours molten plastic into molds and then cools the plastic. Materials are added at the beginning of the process, and conversion is considered uniform through the period. Occasionally, the plastic does not completely fill a mold because of air pockets, and the chair is then considered spoiled. Normal spoilage is 6% of the good units that pass inspection. The following information pertains to March, 2011:

Beginning inventory	1,400 units (100% complete for materials; 20% complete for conversion costs)
Units started	12,000
Units in ending work in process	1,100 (100% complete for materials; 70% complete for conversion costs)
Fantastic Furniture had 1,000 spoiled units in March, 2011.	

Required

Using the format on page 653, compute the normal and abnormal spoilage in units, assuming the inspection point is at (a) the 15% stage of completion, (b) the 40% stage of completion, and (c) the 100% stage of completion.

18-39 Weighted-average method, inspection at 80% completion. (A. Atkinson) The Kim Company is a furniture manufacturer with two departments: molding and finishing. The company uses the weighted-average method of process costing. In August, the following data were recorded for the finishing department:

Units of beginning work in process inventory	12,500
Percentage completion of beginning work in process units	25%
Cost of direct materials in beginning work in process	$0
Units started	87,500
Units completed	62,500
Units in ending inventory	25,000
Percentage completion of ending work in process units	95%
Spoiled units	12,500
Total costs added during current period:	
Direct materials	$819,000
Direct manufacturing labor	$794,500
Manufacturing overhead	$770,000
Work in process, beginning:	
Transferred-in costs	$103,625
Conversion costs	$52,500
Cost of units transferred in during current period	$809,375

Conversion costs are added evenly during the process. Direct material costs are added when production is 90% complete. The inspection point is at the 80% stage of production. Normal spoilage is 10% of all good units that pass inspection. Spoiled units are disposed of at zero net disposal value.

Required

For August, summarize total costs to account for and assign these costs to units completed and transferred out (including normal spoilage), to abnormal spoilage, and to units in ending work in process.

18-40 Job costing, rework. Riposte Corporation manufactures a computer chip called XD1. Manufacturing costs of one XD1 chip, excluding rework costs, are direct materials, $60; direct manufacturing labor, $12; and manufacturing overhead, $38. At the inspection point, defective units are sent back for rework. Rework costs per XD1 chip are direct materials, $12; direct manufacturing labor, $9; and manufacturing overhead, $15.

In August 2011, Riposte manufactured 1,000 XD1 chips, 80 of which required rework. Of these 80 chips, 50 were considered normal rework common to all jobs and the other 30 were considered abnormal rework.

Required

1. Prepare journal entries to record the accounting for both the normal and abnormal rework.
2. What were the total rework costs of XD1 chips in August 2011?
3. Now assume instead that the normal rework is attributable entirely to job #3879, for 200 units of XD1. In this case, what would be the total and unit cost of the good units produced for that job in August 2011? Prepare journal entries for the manufacture of the 200 units, as well as the normal rework costs.

Collaborative Learning Problem

18-41 Physical units, inspection at various levels of completion, weighted-average process costing report. Lester Company makes metal products and has a forging department. In this department, materials are added at the beginning of the process and conversion takes place uniformly. At the start of November 2011, the forging department had 20,000 units in beginning work in process, which are 100% complete for materials and 40% complete for conversion costs. An additional 100,000 units are started in the department in November, and 30,000 units remain in work in process at the end of the month. These unfinished units are 100% complete for materials and 70% complete for conversion costs.

The forging department had 15,000 spoiled units in November. Normal spoilage is 12% of good units. The department's costs for the month of November are as follows:

	Beginning WIP	Costs Incurred During Period
Direct materials costs	$ 64,000	$ 200,000
Conversion costs	102,500	1,000,000

Required

1. Using the format on page 653, compute the normal and abnormal spoilage in units for November, assuming the inspection point is at (a) the 30% stage of completion, (b) the 60% stage of completion, and (c) the 100% stage of completion.
2. Refer to your answer in requirement 1. Why are there different amounts of normal and abnormal spoilage at different inspection points?
3. Now assume that the forging department inspects at the 60% stage of completion. Using the weighted-average method, calculate the cost of units transferred out, the cost of abnormal spoilage, and the cost of ending inventory for the forging department in November.

19 Balanced Scorecard: Quality, Time, and the Theory of Constraints

To satisfy ever-increasing customer expectations, managers need to find cost-effective ways to continuously improve the quality of their products and services and shorten response times.

This requires trading off the costs of achieving these improvements and the benefits from higher performance on these dimensions. When companies do not meet customer expectations, the losses can be substantial, as the following article about Toyota Motor Corporation shows.

Toyota Plans Changes After Millions of Defective Cars Are Recalled[1]

Toyota Motor Corporation, the Japanese automaker, built its reputation on manufacturing reliable cars. In 2002, Toyota executives set an ambitious goal to gain 15% of the global auto industry by 2010, meaning it would surpass General Motors as the world's largest carmaker. In the subsequent years, Toyota grew sales by 50% and managed to win bragging rights as the world's biggest car company. But the company's focus on rapid growth appears to have come at a cost to its reputation for quality.

Between November 2009 and January 2010, Toyota was forced to recall 9 million vehicles worldwide because gas pedals began to stick and were causing unwanted acceleration on eight Toyota models. After months of disagreements with government safety officials, the company ultimately recalled 12 models and suspended the production and sales of eight new Toyota and Lexus models, including its popular Camry and Corolla sedans. While most cars were quickly returned to the sales floor, some industry analysts estimated that the loss of revenue to Toyota could have been as much as $500 million each week.

Beyond lost revenue, Toyota's once-vaunted image took a serious hit. As the crisis unfolded, Toyota was slow to take responsibility for manufacturing problems. The company then faced the long and difficult task of restoring its credibility and assuring

---
[1] *Sources*: Kaufman, Wendy. 2010. Can Toyota recover its reputation for quality? Morning Edition, National Public Radio, February 9. http://www.npr.org/templates/story/story.php?storyId=123519027&ps=rs; Linebaugh, Kate and Norihiko Shirouzu. 2010. Toyota heir faces crisis at the wheel. *Wall Street Journal*, January 27. http://online .wsj.com/article/SB10001424052748704094304575029493222357402.html; Maynard, Micheline and Hiroko Tabuchi. 2010. Rapid growth has its perils, Toyota learns. *New York Times*, January 27. http://www .nytimes.com/2010/01/28/business/28toyota.html; Kageyama, Yuri. 2010. Toyota holds quality meeting to help repair reputation; promises quicker complaint response. *Associated Press*, March 29. http://abcnews .go.com/International/wireStory?id=10238266

owners and new-car shoppers that it had fixed the problems.

It established a quality committee led by Akio Toyoda, the company's chief executive; announced plans to add a brake override system to all new models; added four new quality training facilities; and promised faster decisions on future recall situations. "Listening to consumer voices is most important in regaining credibility from our customers," Mr. Toyoda said.

The Toyota example vividly illustrates the importance of quality. But improving quality is hard work. This chapter describes how a balanced scorecard approach helps managers and management accountants improve quality, customer-response time, and throughput.

This chapter covers three topics. The first topic addresses quality as a competitive tool, looking at quality from the financial perspective, the customer perspective, the internal business process perspective, and the learning-and-growth perspective before discussing the evaluation of quality performance. The second topic addresses time as a competitive tool and focuses on customer response time, on-time performance, time drivers, and the cost of time. The third topic looks closely at the theory of constraints and throughput-margin analysis, covering the management of bottlenecks and nonfinancial measures of time. The presentation is modular so you can omit a topic or explore it in any order.

Quality as a Competitive Tool

The American Society for Quality defines **quality** as the total features and characteristics of a product or a service made or performed according to specifications to satisfy customers at the time of purchase and during use. Many companies throughout the world—like Cisco Systems and Motorola in the United States and Canada, British Telecom in the United Kingdom, Fujitsu and Honda in Japan, Crysel in Mexico, and Samsung in South Korea—emphasize quality as an important strategic initiative. These companies have found that focusing on the quality of a product or service generally builds expertise in producing it, lowers the costs of providing it, creates higher satisfaction for customers using it, and generates higher future revenues for the company selling it. Several high-profile awards, such as the Malcolm Baldrige National Quality Award in the United States, the Deming Prize in Japan, and the Premio Nacional de Calidad in Mexico, are given to companies that have produced high-quality products and services.

International quality standards have also emerged. ISO 9000, developed by the International Organization for Standardization, is a set of five international standards for quality management adopted by more than 85 countries. ISO 9000 enables companies to effectively document and certify the elements of their production processes that lead to quality. To ensure that their suppliers deliver high-quality products at competitive costs, companies such as DuPont and General Electric require their suppliers to obtain ISO 9000 certification. Documenting evidence of quality through ISO 9000 has become a necessary condition for competing in the global marketplace.

As corporations' responsibilities toward the environment grow, managers are applying the quality management and measurement practices discussed in this chapter to find cost-effective ways to reduce the environmental and economic costs of air pollution, wastewater, oil spills, and hazardous waste disposal. An environmental management standard, ISO 14000, encourages organizations to pursue environmental goals vigorously by developing (1) environmental management systems to reduce environmental costs and (2) environmental auditing and performance-evaluation systems to review and provide feedback on environmental goals. Nowhere has the issue of quality and the environment come together in a bigger way than at the British Petroleum (BP) Deepwater Horizon oil rig in the Gulf of Mexico. An explosion on the oil-drilling platform in April of 2010 resulted in millions of gallons of oil spilling out in the Gulf, causing environmental damage over thousands of square miles and resulting in billions of dollars of clean up costs for BP.

We focus on two basic aspects of quality: design quality and conformance quality. **Design quality** refers to how closely the characteristics of a product or service meet the needs and wants of customers. **Conformance quality** is the performance of a product or service relative to its design and product specifications. Apple Inc. has built a reputation for design quality by developing many innovative products such as the iPod, iPhone, and iPad that have uniquely met customers' music, telephone, entertainment, and business needs. Apple's products have also had excellent conformance quality; the products did what they were supposed to do. In the case of the iPhone 4, however, many customers complained about very weak signal receptions on their phones. The enthusiastic customer response to the iPhone 4 when it was launched in the summer of 2010 indicates good design quality, as customers liked what the iPhone 4 had to offer. The problem with its antenna that caused signals not to be received is a problem of conformance quality, because the phone did not do what it was designed to do. The following diagram illustrates that actual performance can fall short of customer satisfaction because of design-quality failure and because of conformance-quality failure.

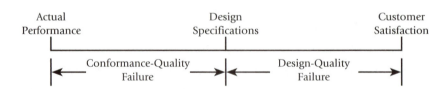

We illustrate the issues in managing quality—computing the costs of quality, identifying quality problems, and taking actions to improve quality—using Photon Corporation. While Photon makes many products, we will focus only on Photon's photocopying machines, which earned an operating income of $24 million on revenues of $300 million (from sales of 20,000 copiers) in 2011.

Quality has both financial and nonfinancial components relating to customer satisfaction, improving internal quality processes, reducing defects, and the training and empowering of workers. To provide some structure, we discuss quality from the four perspectives of the balanced scorecard: financial, customer, internal business process, and learning and growth.

The Financial Perspective: Costs of Quality

The financial perspective of Photon's balanced scorecard includes measures such as revenue growth and operating income, financial measures that are impacted by quality. The most direct financial measure of quality, however, is *costs of quality*. **Costs of quality (COQ)**

Learning Objective **1**

Explain the four cost categories in a costs-of-quality program

. . . prevention, appraisal, internal failure, and external failure costs are the costs incurred to prevent, or the costs arising as a result of, the production of a low-quality product. Costs of quality are classified into four categories; examples for each category are listed in Exhibit 19-1.

1. **Prevention costs**—costs incurred to preclude the production of products that do not conform to specifications

2. **Appraisal costs**—costs incurred to detect which of the individual units of products do not conform to specifications

3. **Internal failure costs**—costs incurred on defective products *before* they are shipped to customers

4. **External failure costs**—costs incurred on defective products *after* they have been shipped to customers

The items in Exhibit 19-1 come from all business functions of the value chain, and they are broader than the internal failure costs of spoilage, rework, and scrap described in Chapter 18.

An important role for management accountants is preparing COQ reports for managers. Photon determines the COQ of its photocopying machines by adapting the seven-step activity-based costing approach described in Chapter 5.

Step 1: Identify the Chosen Cost Object. The cost object is the quality of the photocopying machine that Photon made and sold in 2011. Photon's goal is to calculate the total costs of quality of these 20,000 machines.

Step 2: Identify the Direct Costs of Quality of the Product. The photocopying machines have no direct costs of quality because there are no resources such as inspection or repair workers dedicated to managing the quality of the photocopying machines.

Step 3: Select the Activities and Cost-Allocation Bases to Use for Allocating Indirect Costs of Quality to the Product. Column 1 of Exhibit 19-2, Panel A, classifies the activities that result in prevention, appraisal, and internal and external failure costs of quality at Photon Corporation and the business functions of the value chain in which these costs occur. For example, the quality-inspection activity results in appraisal costs and occurs in the manufacturing function. Photon identifies the total number of inspection-hours (across all products) as the cost-allocation base for the inspection activity. (To avoid details not needed to explain the concepts here, we do not show the total quantities of each cost-allocation base.)

Step 4: Identify the Indirect Costs of Quality Associated with Each Cost-Allocation Base. These are the total costs (variable and fixed) incurred for each of the costs-of-quality activities, such as inspections, across all of Photon's products. (To avoid details not needed to understand the points described here, we do not present these total costs.)

Step 5: Compute the Rate per Unit of Each Cost-Allocation Base. For each activity, total costs (identified in Step 4) are divided by total quantity of the cost-allocation base (calculated in Step 3) to compute the rate per unit of each cost-allocation base. Column 2 of Exhibit 19-2, Panel A, shows these rates (without supporting calculations).

Prevention Costs	Appraisal Costs	Internal Failure Costs	External Failure Costs
Design engineering	Inspection	Spoilage	Customer support
Process engineering	Online product	Rework	Manufacturing/
Supplier evaluations	manufacturing	Scrap	process
Preventive equipment	and process	Machine repairs	engineering
maintenance	inspection	Manufacturing/	for external
Quality training	Product testing	process	failures
Testing of new		engineering on	Warranty repair
materials		internal failures	costs
			Liability claims

Exhibit 19-1

Items Pertaining to Costs-of-Quality Reports

Exhibit 19-2	Analysis of Activity-Based Costs of Quality (COQ) for Photocopying Machines at Photon Corporation

| Home | Insert | Page Layout | Formulas | Data | Review | View |

	A	B	C	D	E	F	G
1	**PANEL A: ACCOUNTING COQ REPORT**						**Percentage of**
2		**Cost Allocation**		**Quantity of Cost**		**Total**	**Revenues**
3	**Cost of Quality and Value-Chain Category**	**Rate**[a]		**Allocation Base**		**Costs**	**(5) = (4) ÷**
4	**(1)**	**(2)**		**(3)**		**(4) = (2) x (3)**	**$300,000,000**
5	Prevention costs						
6	Design engineering (R&D/Design)	$ 80	per hour	40,000	hours	$ 3,200,000	1.1%
7	Process engineering (R&D/Design)	$ 60	per hour	45,000	hours	2,700,000	0.9%
8	Total prevention costs					5,900,000	2.0%
9	Appraisal costs						
10	Inspection (Manufacturing)	$ 40	per hour	240,000	hours	9,600,000	3.2%
11	Total appraisal costs					9,600,000	3.2%
12	Internal failure costs						
13	Rework (Manufacturing)	$100	per hour	100,000	hours	10,000,000	3.3%
14	Total internal failure costs					10,000,000	3.3%
15	External failure costs						
16	Customer support (Marketing)	$ 50	per hour	12,000	hours	600,000	0.2%
17	Transportation (Distribution)	$240	per load	3,000	loads	720,000	0.2%
18	Warranty repair (Customer service)	$110	per hour	120,000	hours	13,200,000	4.4%
19	Total external failure costs					14,520,000	4.8%
20	Total costs of quality					$40,020,000	13.3%
21							
22	[a]Calculations not shown.						
23							
24	**PANEL B: OPPORTUNITY COST ANALYSIS**						
25						**Total Estimated**	**Percentage**
26						**Contribution**	**of Revenues**
27	**Cost of Quality Category**					**Margin Lost**	**(3) = (2) ÷**
28	**(1)**					**(2)**	**$300,000,000**
29	External failure costs						
30	Estimated forgone contribution margin						
31	and income on lost sales					$12,000,000[b]	4.0%
32	Total external failure costs					$12,000,000	4.0%
33							
34	[b]Calculated as total revenues minus all variable costs (whether output-unit, batch, product-sustaining, or facility-sustaining) on						
35	lost sales in 2011. If poor quality causes Photon to lose sales in subsequent years as well, the opportunity costs will be						
36	even greater.						

Step 6: Compute the Indirect Costs of Quality Allocated to the Product. The indirect costs of quality of the photocopying machines, shown in Exhibit 19-2, Panel A, column 4, equal the cost-allocation rate from Step 5 (column 2) multiplied by the total quantity of the cost-allocation base used by the photocopying machines for each activity (column 3). For example, inspection costs for assuring the quality of the photocopying machines are $9,600,000 ($40 per hour × 240,000 inspection-hours).

Step 7: Compute the Total Costs of Quality by Adding All Direct and Indirect Costs of Quality Assigned to the Product. Photon's total costs of quality in the COQ report for photocopying machines is $40.02 million (Exhibit 19-2, Panel A, column 4) or 13.3% of current revenues (column 5).

As we have seen in Chapter 11, opportunity costs are not recorded in financial accounting systems. Yet, a very significant component of costs of quality is the opportunity cost of the contribution margin and income forgone from lost sales, lost production, and lower prices resulting from poor design and conformance quality. Photon's market research department estimates that design and conformance quality problems experienced by some customers resulted in lost sales of 2,000 photocopying machines in 2011 and forgone contribution margin and operating income of $12 million (Exhibit 19-2, Panel B). Total costs of quality, including opportunity costs, equal $52.02 million ($40.02 million recorded in the accounting system and shown in Panel A + $12 million of opportunity costs shown in Panel B), or 17.3% of current revenues. Opportunity costs account for 23.1% ($12 million ÷ $52.02 million) of Photon's total costs of quality.

We turn next to the leading indicators of the costs of quality, the nonfinancial measures of customer satisfaction about the quality of Photon's photocopiers.

The Customer Perspective: Nonfinancial Measures of Customer Satisfaction

Similar to Unilever, Federal Express, and TiVo, Photon tracks the following measures of customer satisfaction:

- Market research information on customer preferences for and customer satisfaction with specific product features (to measure design quality)
- Market share
- Percentage of highly satisfied customers
- Number of defective units shipped to customers as a percentage of total units shipped
- Number of customer complaints (Companies estimate that for every customer who actually complains, there are 10–20 others who have had bad experiences with the product or service but did not complain.)
- Percentage of products that fail soon after delivery
- Average delivery delays (difference between the scheduled delivery date and the date requested by the customer)
- On-time delivery rate (percentage of shipments made on or before the scheduled delivery date)

Photon's management monitors whether these numbers improve or deteriorate over time. Higher customer satisfaction should lead to lower costs of quality and higher future revenues from greater customer retention, loyalty, and positive word-of-mouth advertising. Lower customer-satisfaction indicates that costs of quality will likely increase in the future. We next turn to the driver of customer satisfaction, the internal business processes to identify and analyze quality problems and to improve quality.

The Internal-Business-Process Perspective: Analyzing Quality Problems and Improving Quality

We present three techniques for identifying and analyzing quality problems: control charts, Pareto diagrams, and cause-and-effect diagrams.

Control Charts

Statistical quality control (SQC), also called statistical process control (SPC), is a formal means of distinguishing between random and nonrandom variations in an operating process. Random variations occur, for example, when chance fluctuations in the speed of equipment cause defective products to be produced such as copiers that produce fuzzy and unclear copies or copies that are too light or too dark. Nonrandom variations occur when defective products are produced as a result of a systematic problem such as an incorrect speed setting, a flawed part design, or mishandling of a component part. A **control chart**, an important tool in SQC, is a graph of a series of successive observations of a particular step, procedure, or operation taken at regular intervals of time. Each observation is plotted relative to specified ranges that represent the limits within which

Decision Point

What are the four cost categories of a costs-of-quality program?

Learning Objective 2

Develop nonfinancial measures

. . . customer satisfaction measures such as number of customer complaints, internal-business process measures such as percentage of defective and reworked products, and learning and growth measures such as employee empowerment and training

and methods to improve quality

. . . control charts, Pareto diagrams, and cause-and-effect diagrams

observations are expected to fall. Only those observations outside the control limits are ordinarily regarded as nonrandom and worth investigating.

Exhibit 19-3 presents control charts for the daily defect rates (defective copiers divided by the total number of copiers produced) observed at Photon's three photocopying-machine production lines. Defect rates in the prior 60 days for each production line were assumed to provide a good basis from which to calculate the distribution of daily defect rates. The arithmetic mean (μ, read as mu) and standard deviation (σ, read as sigma, how much an observation deviates from the mean) are the two parameters of the distribution that are used in the control charts in Exhibit 19-3. On the basis of experience, the company decides that any observation outside the $\mu \pm 2\sigma$ range should be investigated.

For production line A, all observations are within the range of $\mu \pm 2\sigma$, so management believes no investigation is necessary. For production line B, the last two observations signal that a much higher percentage of copiers are not performing as they should, indicating that the problem is probably because of a nonrandom, out-of-control occurrence such as an incorrect speed setting or mishandling of a component part. Given the $\pm 2\sigma$ rule, both observations would be investigated. Production line C illustrates a process that would not prompt an investigation under the $\pm 2\sigma$ rule but that may well be out of control, because the last eight observations show a clear direction, and over the last six days, the percentage of defective copiers are increasing and getting further and further away from the mean. The pattern of observations moving away from the mean could be due, for example, to the tooling on a machine beginning to wear out, resulting in poorly machined parts. As the tooling deteriorates further, the trend in producing defective copiers is likely to persist until the production line is no longer in statistical control. Statistical procedures have been developed using the trend as well as the variation to evaluate whether a process is out of control.

Pareto Diagrams

Observations outside control limits serve as inputs for Pareto diagrams. A **Pareto diagram** is a chart that indicates how frequently each type of defect occurs, ordered from the most frequent to the least frequent. Exhibit 19-4 presents a Pareto diagram of quality problems for all observations outside the control limits at the final inspection point in 2011. Fuzzy and unclear copies are the most frequently recurring problem. Fuzzy and unclear copies result in high rework costs. Sometimes fuzzy and unclear copies occur at customer sites and result in high warranty and repair costs and low customer satisfaction.

Cause-and-Effect Diagrams

The most frequently recurring and costly problems identified by the Pareto diagram are analyzed using cause-and-effect diagrams. A **cause-and-effect diagram** identifies potential causes of defects using a diagram that resembles the bone structure of a fish (hence, cause-and-effect diagrams are also called *fishbone diagrams*).[2] Exhibit 19-5 presents the

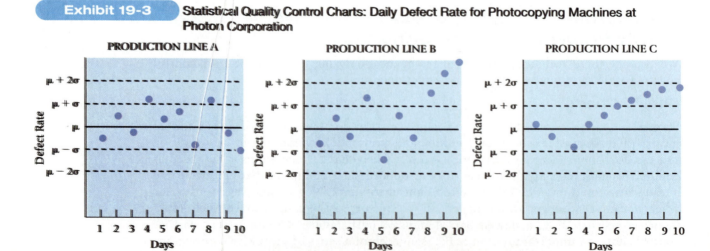

Exhibit 19-3 Statistical Quality Control Charts: Daily Defect Rate for Photocopying Machines at Photon Corporation

2 See P. Clark, "Getting the Most from Cause-and-Effect Diagrams," *Quality Progress* (June 2000).

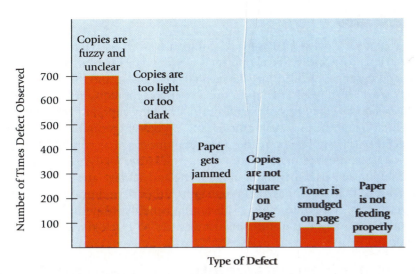

cause-and-effect diagram describing potential reasons for fuzzy and unclear copies. The "backbone" of the diagram represents the problem being examined. The large "bones" coming off the backbone represent the main categories of potential causes of failure. The exhibit identifies four of these: human factors, methods and design factors, machine-related factors, and materials and components factors. Photon's engineers identify the materials and components factor as an important reason for the fuzzy and unclear copies. Additional arrows or bones are added to provide more-detailed reasons for each higher-level cause. For example, the engineers determine that two potential causes of material and component problems are variation in purchased components and incorrect component specification. They quickly settle on variation in purchased components as the likely cause and focus on the use of multiple suppliers and mishandling of purchased parts as the root causes of variation in purchased components. Further analysis leads them to conclude that mishandling of the steel frame that holds in place various components of the copier such as drums, mirrors, and lenses results in the misalignment of these components, causing fuzzy and unclear copies.

The analysis of quality problems is aided by automated equipment and computers that record the number and types of defects and the operating conditions that existed at the time the defects occurred. Using these inputs, computer programs simultaneously and iteratively prepare control charts, Pareto diagrams, and cause-and-effect diagrams with the goal of continuously reducing the mean defect rate, μ, and the standard deviation, σ.

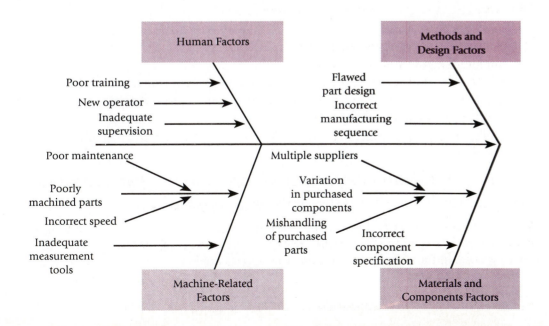

Six Sigma Quality

The ultimate goal of quality programs at companies such as Motorola, Honeywell, and General Electric is to achieve Six Sigma quality.[3] This means that the process is so well-understood and tightly controlled that the mean defect rate, μ, and the standard deviation, σ, are both very small. As a result, the upper and lower control limits in Exhibit 19-3 can be set at a distance of 6σ (six sigma) from the mean (μ). The implication of controlling a process at a Six Sigma level is that the process produces only 3.4 defects per million products produced.

To implement Six Sigma, companies use techniques such as control charts, Pareto diagrams, and cause-and-effect diagrams to define, measure, analyze, improve, and control processes to minimize variability in manufacturing and achieve almost zero defects. Critics of Six Sigma argue that it emphasizes incremental rather than dramatic or disruptive innovation. Nevertheless, companies report substantial benefits from Six Sigma initiatives.

Companies routinely use nonfinancial measures to track the quality improvements they are making.

Nonfinancial Measures of Internal-Business-Process Quality

Photon uses the following measures of internal-business-process quality:

- Percentage of defective products
- Percentage of reworked products
- Number of different types of defects analyzed using control charts, Pareto diagrams, and cause-and-effect diagrams
- Number of design and process changes made to improve design quality or reduce costs of quality

Photon's managers believe that improving these measures will lead to greater customer satisfaction, lower costs of quality, and better financial performance.

The Learning-and-Growth Perspective: Quality Improvements

What are the drivers of internal-business-process quality? Photon believes that recruiting outstanding design engineers, providing more employee training, and lowering employee turnover as a result of greater employee empowerment and satisfaction will reduce the number of defective products and increase customer satisfaction, leading to better financial performance. Photon measures the following factors in the learning-and-growth perspective in the balanced scorecard:

- Experience and qualifications of design engineers
- Employee turnover (ratio of number of employees who leave the company to the average total number of employees)
- Employee empowerment (ratio of the number of processes in which employees have the right to make decisions without consulting supervisors to the total number of processes)
- Employee satisfaction (ratio of employees indicating high satisfaction ratings to the total number of employees surveyed)
- Employee training (percentage of employees trained in different quality-enhancing methods)

> **Decision Point** ►
>
> What nonfinancial measures and methods can managers use to improve quality?

Making Decisions and Evaluating Quality Performance

Relevant Costs and Benefits of Quality Improvement

When making decisions and evaluating performance, companies combine financial and nonfinancial information. We use the Photon example to illustrate relevant revenues and relevant costs in the context of decisions to improve quality.

---

[3] Six Sigma is a registered trademark of Motorola Inc.

Recall that Photon's cause-and-effect diagram reveals that the steel frame (or chassis) of the copier is often mishandled as it travels from a supplier's warehouse to Photon's plant. The frame must meet very precise specifications or else copier components (such as drums, mirrors, and lenses) will not fit exactly on the frame. Mishandling frames during transport causes misalignment and results in fuzzy and unclear copies.

A team of engineers offers two solutions: (1) inspect the frames immediately on delivery or (2) redesign and strengthen the frames and their shipping containers to withstand mishandling during transportation. The cost structure for 2012 is expected to be the same as the cost structure for 2011 presented in Exhibit 19-2.

To evaluate each alternative versus the status quo, management identifies the relevant costs and benefits for each solution by focusing on *how total costs and total revenues will change under each alternative*. As explained in Chapter 11, relevant-cost and relevant-revenue analysis ignores allocated amounts.

Photon uses only a one-year time horizon (2012) for the analysis because it plans to introduce a completely new line of copiers at the end of 2012. The new line is so different that the choice of either the inspection or the redesign alternative will have no effect on the sales of copiers in future years.

Exhibit 19-6 shows the relevant costs and benefits for each alternative.

Learning Objective 3

Combine financial and nonfinancial measures to make decisions and evaluate quality performance

. . . Identify relevant incremental and opportunity costs to evaluate tradeoffs across costs of quality and nonfinancial measures to identify problem areas and to highlight leading indicators of future performance

1. **Estimated incremental costs:** $400,000 for the inspection alternative; $460,000 for the redesign alternative.

2. **Cost savings from less rework, customer support, and repairs:** Exhibit 19-6, line 10, shows that reducing rework results in savings of $40 per hour. Exhibit 19-2, Panel A, column 2, line 13, shows total rework cost per hour of $100. Why the difference? Because as it improves quality, Photon will only save the $40 variable cost per rework-hour, not the $60 fixed cost per rework-hour. Exhibit 19-6, line 10, shows total savings of $960,000 ($40 per hour × 24,000 rework-hours saved) if it inspects the frames and $1,280,000 ($40 per rework-hour × 32,000 rework-hours saved) if it redesigns the frames. Exhibit 19-6 also shows expected variable-cost savings in customer support, transportation, and warranty repair for the two alternatives.

3. **Increased contribution margin from higher sales as a result of building a reputation for quality and performance (Exhibit 19-6, line 14):** $1,500,000 for 250 copiers under the inspection alternative and $1,800,000 for 300 copiers under the redesign alternative. Management should always look for opportunities to generate higher revenues, not just cost reductions, from quality improvements.

Exhibit 19-6 Estimated Effects of Quality-Improvement Actions on Costs of Quality for Photocopying Machines at Photon Corporation

	A	B	C	D	E	F	G	H	I	J
1						Relevant Costs and Benefits of				
2				Further Inspecting Incoming Frames				Redesigning Frames		
3	Relevant Items	Relevant Benefit per Unit		Quantity		Total Benefits		Quantity		Total Benefits
4	(1)	(2)		(3)		(4)		(5)		(6)
5	Additional inspection and testing costs					$ (400,000)				
6	Additional process engineering costs									$ (300,000)
7	Additional design engineering costs									(160,000)
8										
9						(2) × (3)				(2) × (5)
10	Savings in rework costs	$ 40	per hour	24,000	hours	$ 960,000		32,000	hours	$1,280,000
11	Savings in customer-support costs	$ 20	per hour	2,000	hours	40,000		2,800	hours	56,000
12	Savings in transportation costs for repair parts	$ 180	per load	500	loads	90,000		700	loads	126,000
13	Savings in warranty repair costs	$ 45	per hour	20,000	hours	900,000		28,000	hours	1,260,000
14	Total contribution margin from additional sales	$6,000	per copier	250	copiers	1,500,000		300	copiers	1,800,000
15										
16	Net cost savings and additional contribution margin					$3,090,000				$4,062,000
17										
18	Difference in favor of redesigning frames (J16) – (F16)						$972,000			

Exhibit 19-6 shows that both the inspection and the redesign alternatives yield net benefits relative to the status quo. However, the net benefits from the redesign alternative are expected to be $972,000 greater.

Note how making improvements in internal business processes affects the COQ numbers reported in the financial perspective. In our example, redesigning the frame increases prevention costs (design and process engineering), decreases internal failure costs (rework), and decreases external failure costs (customer support and warranty repairs). COQ reports provide more insight about quality improvements when managers compare trends over time. In successful quality programs, companies decrease costs of quality and, in particular, internal and external failure costs, as a percentage of revenues. Many companies, such as Hewlett-Packard, go further and believe they should eliminate all failure costs and have zero defects.

How should Photon use financial and nonfinancial measures to evaluate quality performance? They should utilize both types of measures because financial (COQ) and nonfinancial measures of quality have different advantages.

Advantages of COQ Measures

- Consistent with the attention-directing role of management accounting, COQ measures focus managers' attention on the costs of poor quality.

- Total COQ provides a measure of quality performance for evaluating trade-offs among prevention costs, appraisal costs, internal failure costs, and external failure costs.

- COQ measures assist in problem solving by comparing costs and benefits of different quality-improvement programs and setting priorities for cost reduction.

Advantages of Nonfinancial Measures of Quality

- Nonfinancial measures of quality are often easy to quantify and understand.

- Nonfinancial measures direct attention to physical processes and hence help managers identify the precise problem areas that need improvement.

- Nonfinancial measures, such as number of defects, provide immediate short-run feedback on whether quality-improvement efforts are succeeding.

- Nonfinancial measures such as measures of customer satisfaction and employee satisfaction are useful indicators of long-run performance.

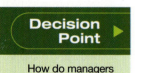

Decision Point ▶

How do managers identify the relevant costs and benefits of quality improvement programs and use financial and nonfinancial measures to evaluate quality?

COQ measures and nonfinancial measures complement each other. Without financial quality measures, companies could be spending more money on improving nonfinancial quality measures than it is worth. Without nonfinancial quality measures, quality problems might not be identified until it is too late. Most organizations use both types of measures to gauge quality performance. McDonald's, for example, evaluates employees and individual franchisees on multiple measures of quality and customer satisfaction. A mystery shopper, an outside party contracted by McDonald's to evaluate restaurant performance, scores individual restaurants on quality, cleanliness, service, and value. A restaurant's performance on these dimensions is evaluated over time and against other restaurants. In its balanced scorecard, Photon evaluates whether improvements in various nonfinancial quality measures eventually lead to improvements in financial measures.

Time as a Competitive Tool

Companies increasingly view time as a driver of strategy.[4] For example, CapitalOne has increased business on its Web site by promising home-loan approval decisions in 30 minutes or less. Companies such as AT&T, General Electric, and Wal-Mart attribute not only higher revenues but also lower costs to doing things faster and on time. They cite, for example, the need to carry less inventory due to their ability to respond rapidly to customer demands.

---

[4] See K. Eisenhardt and S. Brown, "Time Pacing: Competing in Strategic Markets That Won't Stand Still," *Harvard Business Review* (March–April 1998); and T. Willis and A. Jurkus, "Product Development: An Essential Ingredient of Time-Based Competition," *Review of Business* (2001).

Companies need to measure time to manage it properly. In this section, we focus on two *operational measures of time*: *customer-response time*, which reveals how quickly companies respond to customers' demands for their products and services, and *on-time performance*, which indicates how reliably they meet scheduled delivery dates. We also show how companies measure the causes and costs of delays.

Customer-Response Time and On-Time Performance

Customer-response time is how long it takes from the time a customer places an order for a product or service to the time the product or service is delivered to the customer. Fast responses to customers are of strategic importance in industries such as construction, banking, car rental, and fast food. Some companies, such as Airbus, have to pay penalties to compensate their customers (airline companies) for lost revenues and profits (from being unable to operate flights) as a result of delays in delivering aircraft to them.

Exhibit 19-7 describes the components of customer-response time. *Receipt time* is how long it takes the marketing department to specify to the manufacturing department the exact requirements in the customer's order. **Manufacturing cycle time** (also called **manufacturing lead time**) is how long it takes from the time an order is received by manufacturing to the time a finished good is produced. Manufacturing cycle time is the sum of waiting time and manufacturing time for an order. For example, an aircraft order received by Airbus may need to wait before the equipment required to process it becomes available. *Delivery time* is how long it takes to deliver a completed order to a customer.

Some companies evaluate their response time improvement efforts using a measure called **manufacturing cycle efficiency (MCE):**

$$\text{MCE} = (\text{Value-added manufacturing time} \div \text{Manufacturing cycle time})$$

As discussed in Chapter 12, value-added manufacturing activities are activities that customers perceive as adding value or utility to a product. The time actually spent assembling the product is value-added manufacturing time. The rest of manufacturing cycle time, such as the time the product spends waiting for parts or for the next stage in the production process, and being repaired, represents nonvalue-added manufacturing time. Identifying and minimizing the sources of nonvalue-added manufacturing time increases customer responsiveness and reduces costs.

Similar measures apply to service-sector companies. Consider a 40-minute doctor's office visit, of which 9 minutes is spent on administrative tasks such as filling out forms, 20 minutes is spent waiting in the reception area and examination room, and 11 minutes is spent with a nurse or doctor. The service cycle efficiency for this visit equals $11 \div 40$, or 0.275. In other words, only 27.5% of the time in the office added value to the customer. Minimizing nonvalue-added service time in their medical delivery processes has allowed hospitals such as Alle-Kiski Medical Center in Pennsylvania to treat more patients in less time.

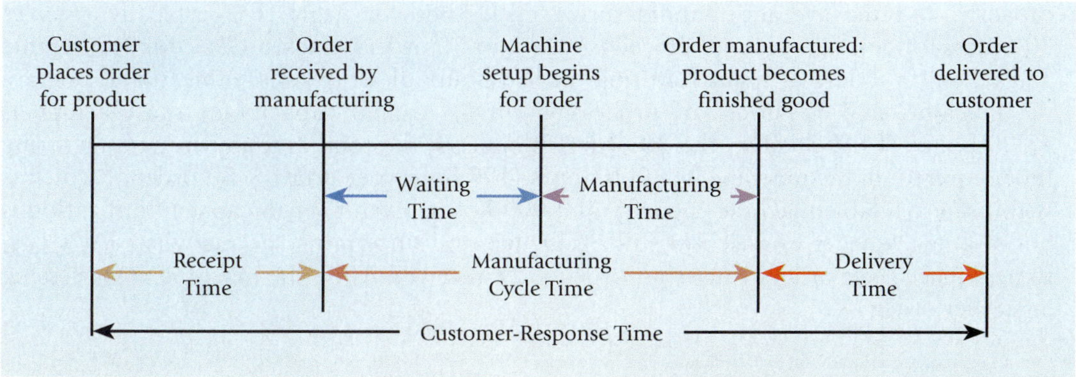

Learning Objective 4

Describe customer-response time

. . . time between receipt of customer order and product delivery

and explain why delays happen and their costs

. . . uncertainty about the timing of customer orders and limited capacity lead to lower revenues and higher inventory carrying costs

Exhibit 19-7

Components of Customer-Response Time

On-time performance is delivery of a product or service by the time it is scheduled to be delivered. Consider Federal Express, which specifies a price per package and a next-day delivery time of 10:30 A.M. for its overnight courier service. Federal Express measures on-time performance by how often it meets its stated delivery time of 10:30 A.M. On-time performance increases customer satisfaction. For example, commercial airlines gain loyal passengers as a result of consistent on-time service. But there is a trade-off between a customer's desire for shorter customer-response time and better on-time performance. Scheduling longer customer-response times, such as airlines lengthening scheduled arrival times, displeases customers on the one hand but increases customer satisfaction on the other hand by improving on-time performance.

Bottlenecks and Time Drivers

Managing customer-response time and on-time performance requires understanding the causes and costs of delays that occur, for example, at a machine in a manufacturing plant or at a checkout counter in a store.

A **time driver** is any factor that causes a change in the speed of an activity when the factor changes. Two time drivers are as follows:

1. **Uncertainty about when customers will order products or services.** For example, the more randomly Airbus receives orders for its airplanes, the more likely queues will form and delays will occur.

2. **Bottlenecks due to limited capacity.** A **bottleneck** occurs in an operation when the work to be performed approaches or exceeds the capacity available to do it. For example, a bottleneck results and causes delays when products that must be processed at a particular machine arrive while the machine is being used to process other products. Bottlenecks also occur on the Internet, for example, when many users try to operate wireless mobile devices at the same time (see Concepts in Action, p. 684). Many banks, such as Bank of China; grocery stores, such as Krogers; and entertainment parks, such as Disneyland, actively work to reduce queues and delays to better serve their customers.

Consider Falcon Works (FW), which uses one turning machine to convert steel bars into a special gear for planes. FW makes this gear, which is its sole product, only after customers have ordered it. To focus on manufacturing cycle time, we assume FW's receipt time and delivery time are minimal. FW's strategy is to differentiate itself from competitors by offering faster delivery. The company's manager is examining opportunities to sell other products to increase profits without sacrificing the competitive advantage provided by short customer-response times. The manager examines these opportunities using the five-step decision-making process introduced in Chapter 1.

Step 1: Identify the problem and uncertainties. FW's manager is considering introducing a second product, a piston for pumps. The primary uncertainty is how the introduction of a second product will affect manufacturing cycle times for gears.

Step 2: Obtain information. The manager gathers data on the number of orders for gears FW has received in the past, the time it takes to manufacture gears, the available capacity, and the average manufacturing cycle time for gears. FW typically receives 30 orders for gears, but it could receive 10, 30, or 50 orders. Each order is for 1,000 units and takes 100 hours of manufacturing time (8 hours of setup time to clean and prepare the machine, and 92 hours of processing time). Annual capacity of the machine is 4,000 hours. If FW receives the 30 orders it expects, the total amount of manufacturing time required on the machine is 3,000 hours (100 hours per order × 30 orders), which is within the available machine capacity of 4,000 hours. Even though capacity utilization is not strained, queues and delays still occur, because uncertainty about when FW's customers place their orders causes an order to be received while the machine is processing an earlier order.

Average waiting time, the average amount of time that an order waits in line before the machine is set up and the order is processed, equals,[5]

$$\frac{\begin{array}{c}\text{Annual average} \\ \text{number of} \\ \text{orders for gears}\end{array} \times \left(\begin{array}{c}\text{Manufacturing} \\ \text{time per order} \\ \text{for gears}\end{array}\right)^2}{2 \times \left[\begin{array}{c}\text{Annual machine} \\ \text{capacity}\end{array} - \left(\begin{array}{c}\text{Annual average number} \\ \text{of orders for gears}\end{array} \times \begin{array}{c}\text{Manufacturing} \\ \text{time per order for gears}\end{array}\right)\right]}$$

$$= \frac{30 \times (100)^2}{2 \times [4{,}000 - (30 \times 100)]} = \frac{30 \times 10{,}000}{2 \times (4{,}000 - 3{,}000)} = \frac{300{,}000}{2 \times 1{,}000} = \frac{300{,}000}{2{,}000} = 150 \text{ hours per order (for gears)}$$

Therefore, the average manufacturing cycle time for an order is 250 hours (150 hours of average waiting time + 100 hours of manufacturing time). Note that manufacturing time per order is a squared term in the numerator. It indicates the disproportionately large impact manufacturing time has on waiting time. As the manufacturing time lengthens, there is a much greater chance that the machine will be in use when an order arrives, leading to longer delays. The denominator in this formula is a measure of the unused capacity, or cushion. As the unused capacity becomes smaller, the chance that the machine is processing an earlier order becomes more likely, leading to greater delays.

The formula describes only the *average* waiting time. A particular order might arrive when the machine is free, in which case manufacturing will start immediately. In another situation, FW may receive an order while two other orders are waiting to be processed, which means the delay will be longer than 150 hours.

Step 3: Make predictions about the future. The manager makes the following predictions about pistons: FW expects to receive 10 orders for pistons, each order for 800 units, in the coming year. Each order will take 50 hours of manufacturing time, comprising 3 hours for setup and 47 hours of processing. Expected demand for FW's gears will be unaffected by whether FW introduces pistons.

Average waiting time *before* machine setup begins is expected to be (the formula is an extension of the preceding formula for the single-product case) as follows:

$$\frac{\left[\begin{array}{c}\text{Annual average number} \\ \text{of orders for gears}\end{array} \times \left(\begin{array}{c}\text{Manufacturing} \\ \text{time per order} \\ \text{for gears}\end{array}\right)^2\right] + \left[\begin{array}{c}\text{Annual average number} \\ \text{of orders for pistons}\end{array} \times \left(\begin{array}{c}\text{Manufacturing} \\ \text{time per order} \\ \text{for pistons}\end{array}\right)^2\right]}{2 \times \left[\begin{array}{c}\text{Annual machine} \\ \text{capacity}\end{array} - \left(\begin{array}{c}\text{Annual average number} \\ \text{of orders for gears}\end{array} \times \begin{array}{c}\text{Manufacturing} \\ \text{time per order} \\ \text{for gears}\end{array}\right) - \left(\begin{array}{c}\text{Annual average number} \\ \text{of orders for pistons}\end{array} \times \begin{array}{c}\text{Manufacturing} \\ \text{time per order} \\ \text{for pistons}\end{array}\right)\right]}$$

$$= \frac{[30 \times (100)^2] + [10 \times (50)^2]}{2 \times [4{,}000 - (30 \times 100) - (10 \times 50)]} = \frac{(30 \times 10{,}000) + (10 \times 2{,}500)}{2 \times (4{,}000 - 3{,}000 - 500)}$$

$$= \frac{300{,}000 + 25{,}000}{2 \times 500} = \frac{325{,}000}{1{,}000} = 325 \text{ hours per order (for gears } and \text{ pistons)}$$

Introducing pistons will cause average waiting time for an order to more than double, from 150 hours to 325 hours. Waiting time increases because introducing pistons will cause unused capacity to shrink, increasing the probability that new orders will arrive while current orders are being manufactured or waiting to be manufactured. Average waiting time is very sensitive to the shrinking of unused capacity.

If the manager decides to make pistons, average manufacturing cycle time will be 425 hours for a gear order (325 hours of average waiting time + 100 hours of manufacturing time), and 375 hours for a piston order (325 hours of average waiting time + 50 hours

---

[5] The technical assumptions are (a) that customer orders for the product follow a Poisson distribution with a mean equal to the expected number of orders (30 in our example), and (b) that orders are processed on a first-in, first-out (FIFO) basis. The Poisson arrival pattern for customer orders has been found to be reasonable in many real-world settings. The FIFO assumption can be modified. Under the modified assumptions, the basic queuing and delay effects will still occur, but the precise formulas will be different.

Concepts in Action   Overcoming Wireless Data Bottlenecks

The wired world is quickly going wireless. In 2010, sales of smartphones—such as the Apple iPhone and BlackBerry—in the United States were predicted to be 53 million units. In addition to the smartphone boom, emerging devices including e-book readers and machine-to-machine appliances (the so-called "Internet of things") will add to rapidly growing data traffic.

With every new device that lets users browse the Internet, and every new business that taps into the convenience and speed of the wireless world, the invisible information superhighway gets a little more crowded. Cisco recently forecast that data traffic will grow at a compound rate of 108% from 90,000 terabytes per month in 2009 to 3.6 million terabytes per month by 2014.

This astronomical growth already causes many users to suffer from mobile bottlenecks caused by too many users trying to transfer mobile data at the same time in a given area. These bottlenecks are most harmful to companies buying and selling products and services over the mobile Internet. Without access, Amazon.com Kindle owners cannot download new e-books and mobile brokerage users cannot buy and sell stocks "on the go."

To relieve mobile bottlenecks, wireless providers and other high-tech companies are working on more efficient mobile broadband networks, such as LTE, that make use of complementary technologies to automatically choose the best available wireless network to increase capacity. Technology providers are also deploying Wi-Fi direct, which allows mobile users to freely transfer video, digital music, and photos between mobile devices without choking up valuable bandwidth. Companies and government agencies around the world are also trying to increase the wireless broadband spectrum. In the United States, for example, current holders of spectrum—such as radio stations—are being encouraged to sell their excess capacity to wireless providers in exchange for a share of the profits.

Sources: Edwards, Cliff. 2010. Wi-fi direct seen as way to alleviate network congestion. *BusinessWeek,* January 7. www.businessweek.com/technology/content/jan2010/tc2010017_884186.htm; Morris, John. 2010. CTIA: More spectrum, and other ways to break the wireless data bottleneck. *ZDNet.* "Laptops & Desktops," blog March 24. http://www.zdnet.com/blog/computers/ctia-more-spectrum-and-other-ways-to-break-the-wireless-data-bottleneck/1877; Pyle, George. 2010. Wireless growth leading to bottlenecks. *Buffalo News,* May 9. www.buffalonews.com/2010/05/09/1044893/wireless-growth-leading-to-bottlenecks.html.

of manufacturing time). A gear order will spend 76.5% (325 hours ÷ 425 hours) of its manufacturing cycle time just waiting for manufacturing to start!

Step 4: Make decisions by choosing among alternatives. Given the anticipated effects on manufacturing cycle time of adding pistons, should FW's manager introduce pistons? To help the manager make a decision, the management accountant identifies and analyzes the relevant revenues and relevant costs of adding the piston product and, in particular, the cost of delays on all products. The rest of this section focuses on Step 4. While we do not cover Step 5 in this example, we discuss later in the chapter how the balanced scorecard can be a useful tool to evaluate and learn about time-based performance.

Relevant Revenues and Relevant Costs of Time

To determine the relevant revenues and costs of adding pistons under Step 4, the management accountant prepares the following additional information:

Product	Annual Average Number of Orders	Average Selling Price per Order If Average Manufacturing Cycle Time per Order Is		Direct Material Cost per Order	Inventory Carrying Cost per Order per Hour
		Less Than 300 Hours	More Than 300 Hours		
Gears	30	$22,000	$21,500	$16,000	$1.00
Pistons	10	10,000	9,600	8,000	0.50

Manufacturing cycle times affect both revenues and costs. Revenues are affected because customers are willing to pay a higher price for faster delivery. On the cost side, direct material costs and inventory carrying costs are the only relevant costs of introducing pistons (all other costs are unaffected and hence irrelevant). Inventory carrying costs equal the opportunity costs of investment tied up in inventory (see Chapter 11, pp. 403–405) and the relevant costs of storage, such as space rental, spoilage, deterioration, and materials handling. Usually, companies calculate inventory carrying costs on a per-unit, per-year basis. To simplify calculations, the management accountant calculates inventory carrying costs on a per-order, per-hour basis. Also, FW acquires direct materials at the time the order is received by manufacturing and, therefore, calculates inventory carrying costs for the duration of the manufacturing cycle time.

Exhibit 19-8 presents relevant revenues and relevant costs for the "introduce pistons" and "do not introduce pistons" alternatives. Based on the analysis, FW's managers decide not to introduce pistons, even though pistons have a positive contribution margin of $1,600 ($9,600 − $8,000) per order and FW has the capacity to process pistons. If it produces pistons, FW will, on average, use only 3,500 (Gears: 100 hours per order × 30 orders + Pistons: 50 hours per order × 10 orders) of the available 4,000 machine-hours. So why is FW better off not introducing pistons? *Because of the negative effects that producing pistons will have on the existing product, gears.* The following table presents the *costs of time,* the expected loss in revenues and expected increase in carrying costs as a result of delays caused by using machine capacity to manufacture pistons.

| | **Effect of Increasing Average Manufacturing Cycle Time** | | **Expected Loss in Revenues Plus** |
| | **Expected Loss in Revenues for Gears** | **Expected Increase in Carrying Costs for All Products** | **Expected Increase in Carrying Costs of Introducing Pistons** |
Product	**(1)**	**(2)**	**(3) = (1) + (2)**
Gears	$15,000[a]	$5,250[b]	$20,250
Pistons	—	1,875[c]	1,875
Total	$15,000	$7,125	$22,125

[a]($22,000 − $21,500) per order × 30 expected orders = $15,000.
[b](425 − 250) hours per order × $1.00 per hour × 30 expected orders = $5,250.
[c](375 − 0) hours per order × $0.50 per hour × 10 expected orders = $1,875.

Introducing pistons causes the average manufacturing cycle time of gears to increase from 250 hours to 425 hours. Longer manufacturing cycle times increases inventory carrying costs of gears and decreases gear revenues (average manufacturing cycle time for gears exceeds 300 hours so the average selling price per order decreases from $22,000 to $21,500). Together

Exhibit 19-8

Determining Expected Relevant Revenues and Relevant Costs for Falcon Works' Decision to Introduce Pistons

Relevant Items	Alternative 1: Introduce Pistons (1)	Alternative 2: Do Not Introduce Pistons (2)	Difference (3) = (1) − (2)
Expected revenues	741,000[a]	$660,000[b]	$ 81,000
Expected variable costs	560,000[c]	480,000[d]	(80,000)
Expected inventory carrying costs	14,625[e]	7,500[f]	(7,125)
Expected total costs	574,625	487,500	(87,125)
Expected revenues minus expected costs	$166,375	$172,500	$ (6,125)

[a]($21,500 × 30) + ($9,600 × 10) = $741,000; average manufacturing cycle time will be more than 300 hours.
[b]($22,000 × 30) = $660,000; average manufacturing cycle time will be less than 300 hours.
[c]($16,000 × 30) + ($8,000 × 10) = $560,000.
[d]$16,000 × 30 = $480,000.
[e](Average manufacturing cycle time for gears × Unit carrying cost per order for gears × Expected number of orders for gears) + (Average manufacturing cycle time for pistons × Unit carrying cost per order for pistons × Expected number of orders for pistons) = (425 × $1.00 × 30) + (375 × $0.50 × 10) = $12,750 + $1,875 = $14,625.
[f]Average manufacturing cycle time for gears × Unit carrying cost per order for gears × Expected number of orders for gears = 250 × $1.00 × 30 = $7,500.

Decision Point ▶

What is customer-response time? What are the reasons for and the costs of delays?

with the inventory carrying cost of pistons, the expected costs of introducing pistons, $22,125, exceeds the expected contribution margin of $16,000 ($1,600 per order × 10 expected orders) from selling pistons by $6,125 (the difference calculated in Exhibit 19-8).

This simple example illustrates that when demand uncertainty is high, some unused capacity is desirable.[6] Increasing the capacity of a bottleneck resource reduces manufacturing cycle times and delays. One way to increase capacity is to reduce the time required for setups and processing via more-efficient setups and processing. Another way to increase capacity is to invest in new equipment, such as flexible manufacturing systems that can be programmed to switch quickly from producing one product to producing another. Delays can also be reduced through careful scheduling of orders on machines, such as by batching similar jobs together for processing.

Theory of Constraints and Throughput-Margin Analysis

In this section, we consider products that are made from multiple parts and processed on multiple machines. With multiple parts and machines, dependencies arise among operations—that is, some operations cannot be started until parts from the preceding operation are available. Furthermore, some operations are bottlenecks (have limited capacity), and others are not.

Managing Bottlenecks

Learning Objective 5

Explain how to manage bottlenecks

. . . keep bottlenecks busy and increase their efficiency and capacity by increasing throughput margin

The **theory of constraints** (TOC) describes methods to maximize operating income when faced with some bottleneck and some nonbottleneck operations.[7] The TOC defines three measures as follows:

1. **Throughput margin** equals revenues minus the direct material costs of the goods sold.
2. *Investments* equal the sum of material costs in direct materials, work-in-process, and finished goods inventories; R&D costs; and costs of equipment and buildings.
3. *Operating costs* equal all costs of operations (other than direct materials) incurred to earn throughput margin. Operating costs include salaries and wages, rent, utilities, depreciation, and the like.

The objective of the TOC is to increase throughput margin while decreasing investments and operating costs. *The TOC considers a short-run time horizon and assumes operating costs are fixed.* It focuses on managing bottleneck operations as explained in the following steps:

Step 1: Recognize that the bottleneck operation determines throughput margin of the entire system.

Step 2: Identify the bottleneck operation by identifying operations with large quantities of inventory waiting to be worked on.

Step 3: Keep the bottleneck operation busy and subordinate all nonbottleneck operations to the bottleneck operation. That is, the needs of the bottleneck operation determine the production schedule of the nonbottleneck operations.

Step 3 represents one of the key concepts described in Chapter 11: To maximize operating income, the manager must maximize contribution margin (in this case, throughput margin) of the constrained or bottleneck resource (see pp. 405–406). The bottleneck machine must always be kept running; it should not be waiting for jobs. To achieve this objective, companies often maintain a small buffer inventory of jobs at the bottleneck machine. The bottleneck machine sets the pace for all nonbottleneck machines. Workers at nonbottleneck machines do not produce more output than can be

---

[6] Other complexities, such as analyzing a network of machines, priority scheduling, and allowing for uncertainty in processing times, are beyond the scope of this book. In these cases, the basic queuing and delay effects persist, but the precise formulas are more complex.

[7] See E. Goldratt and J. Cox, *The Goal* (New York: North River Press, 1986); E. Goldratt, *The Theory of Constraints* (New York: North River Press, 1990); E. Noreen, D. Smith, and J. Mackey, *The Theory of Constraints and Its Implications for Management Accounting* (New York: North River Press, 1995); and M. Woeppel, *Manufacturers' Guide to Implementing the Theory of Constraints* (Boca Raton, FL: Lewis Publishing, 2000).

processed by the bottleneck machine, because producing more nonbottleneck output only creates excess inventory; it does not increase throughput margin.

Step 4: Take actions to increase the efficiency and capacity of the bottleneck operation as long as throughput margin exceeds the incremental costs of increasing efficiency and capacity.

We illustrate Step 4 using data from Cardinal Industries (CI). CI manufactures car doors in two operations: stamping and pressing.

	Stamping	Pressing
Capacity per hour	20 units	15 units
Annual capacity (6,000 hours of capacity available in each operation)		
6,000 hours × 20 units/hour; 6,000 hours × 15 units/hour)	120,000 units	90,000 units
Annual production and sales	90,000 units	90,000 units
Other fixed operating costs (excluding direct materials)	$720,000	$1,080,000
Other fixed operating costs per unit produced		
($720,000 ÷ 90,000 units; $1,080,000 ÷ 90,000 units)	$8 per unit	$12 per unit

Each door sells for $100 and has a direct material cost of $40. Variable costs in other functions of the value chain—design of products and processes, marketing, distribution, and customer service—are negligible. CI's output is constrained by the capacity of 90,000 units in the pressing operation. What can CI do to relieve the bottleneck constraint of the pressing operation?

Desirable actions include the following:

1. **Eliminate idle time at the bottleneck operation (time when the pressing machine is neither being set up to process products nor actually processing products).** CI's manager is evaluating permanently positioning two workers at the pressing operation to unload finished units as soon as one batch of units is processed and to set up the machine to begin processing the next batch. This action will cost $48,000 and bottleneck output will increase by 1,000 doors per year. Should CI incur the additional costs? Yes, because CI's throughput margin will increase by $60,000 [(selling price per door, $100 − direct material cost per door, $40) × 1,000 doors], which is greater than the incremental cost of $48,000. All other costs are irrelevant.

2. **Process only those parts or products that increase throughput margin, not parts or products that will be placed in finished goods or spare parts inventories.** Making products that remain in inventory will not increase throughput margin.

3. **Shift products that do not have to be made on the bottleneck machine to nonbottleneck machines or to outside processing facilities.** Suppose Spartan Corporation, an outside contractor, offers to press 1,500 doors at $15 per door from stamped parts that CI supplies. Spartan's quoted price is greater than CI's own operating costs in the pressing department of $12 per door. Should CI accept the offer? Yes, because pressing is the bottleneck operation. Getting additional doors pressed by Spartan will increase throughput margin by $90,000 [($100 − $40) per door × 1,500 doors], while the relevant cost of increasing capacity will be $22,500 ($15 per door × 1,500 doors). The fact that CI's unit cost is less than Spartan's quoted price is irrelevant.

   Suppose Gemini Industries, another outside contractor, offers to stamp 2,000 doors from direct materials that CI supplies at $6 per door. Gemini's price is lower than CI's operating cost of $8 per door in the stamping department. Should CI accept the offer? No, because other operating costs are fixed costs. CI will not save any costs by subcontracting the stamping operations. Instead, its costs will increase by $12,000 ($6 per door × 2,000 doors) with no increase in throughput margin, which is constrained by pressing capacity.

4. **Reduce setup time and processing time at bottleneck operations (for example, by simplifying the design or reducing the number of parts in the product).** Suppose CI can press 2,500 more doors at a cost of $55,000 a year by reducing setup time at the pressing operation. Should CI incur this cost? Yes, because throughput margin will increase by $150,000 [($100 − $40) per door × 2,500 doors], which is greater than

the incremental costs of $55,000. Will CI find it worthwhile to incur costs to reduce machining time at the nonbottleneck stamping operation? No. Other operating costs will increase, while throughput margin will remain unchanged because bottleneck capacity of the pressing operation will not increase.

5. **Improve the quality of parts or products manufactured at the bottleneck operation.** Poor quality is more costly at a bottleneck operation than at a nonbottleneck operation. The cost of poor quality at a nonbottleneck operation is the cost of materials wasted. If CI produces 1,000 defective doors at the stamping operation, the cost of poor quality is $40,000 (direct material cost per door, $40, × 1,000 doors). No throughput margin is forgone because stamping has unused capacity. Despite the defective production, stamping can produce and transfer 90,000 good-quality doors to the pressing operation. At a bottleneck operation, the cost of poor quality is the cost of materials wasted *plus* the opportunity cost of lost throughput margin. Bottleneck capacity not wasted in producing defective units could be used to generate additional throughput margin. If CI produces 1,000 defective units at the pressing operation, the cost of poor quality is the lost revenue of $100,000, or alternatively stated, direct material costs of $40,000 (direct material cost per door, $40, × 1,000 doors) plus forgone throughput margin of $60,000 [($100 − $40) per door × 1,000 doors].

The high cost of poor quality at the bottleneck operation means that bottleneck time should not be wasted processing units that are defective. That is, parts should be inspected before the bottleneck operation to ensure that only good-quality parts are processed at the bottleneck operation. Furthermore, quality-improvement programs should place special emphasis on minimizing defects at bottleneck machines.

If successful, the actions in Step 4 will increase the capacity of the pressing operation until it eventually exceeds the capacity of the stamping operation. The bottleneck will then shift to the stamping operation. CI would then focus continuous-improvement actions on increasing stamping efficiency and capacity. For example, the contract with Gemini Industries to stamp 2,000 doors at $6 per door from direct material supplied by CI will become attractive because throughput margin will increase by ($100 − $40) per door × 2,000 doors = $120,000, which is greater than the incremental costs of $12,000 ($6 per door × 2,000 doors).

The theory of constraints emphasizes management of bottleneck operations as the key to improving performance of production operations as a whole. It focuses on short-run maximization of throughput margin, revenues minus direct material costs of goods sold. Because TOC regards operating costs as difficult to change in the short run, it does not identify individual activities and drivers of costs. TOC is, therefore, less useful for the long-run management of costs. In contrast, activity-based costing (ABC) systems take a long-run perspective and focus on improving processes by eliminating nonvalue-added activities and reducing the costs of performing value-added activities. ABC systems, therefore, are more useful for long-run pricing, cost control, and capacity management. The short-run TOC emphasis on maximizing throughput margin by managing bottlenecks complements the long-run strategic-cost-management focus of ABC.[8]

Balanced Scorecard and Time-Related Measures

In this section, we focus on the final step of the five-step decision-making process by tracking changes in time-based measures, evaluating and learning whether these changes affect financial performance, and modifying decisions and plans to achieve the company's goals. We use the structure of the balanced scorecard perspectives—financial, customer, internal business processes, and learning and growth—to summarize how financial and nonfinancial measures of time relate to one another, reduce delays, and increase output of bottleneck operations.

Financial measures
Revenue losses or price discounts attributable to delays
Carrying cost of inventories
Throughput margin minus operating costs

---

[8] For an excellent evaluation of TOC, operations management, cost accounting, and the relationship between TOC and activity-based costing, see A. Atkinson, "Cost Accounting, the Theory of Constraints, and Costing," (Issue Paper, CMA Canada, December 2000).

Customer measures

Customer-response time (the time it takes to fulfill a customer order)

On-time performance (delivering a product or service by the scheduled time)

Internal-business-process measures

Average manufacturing time for key products

Manufacturing cycle efficiency for key processes

Idle time at bottleneck operations

Defective units produced at bottleneck operations

Average reduction in setup time and processing time at bottleneck operations

Learning-and-growth measures

Employee satisfaction

Number of employees trained in managing bottleneck operations

To see the cause-and-effect linkages across these balanced scorecard perspectives, consider the example of the Bell Group, a designer and manufacturer of equipment for the jewelry industry. Based on TOC analysis, the company determined that a key financial measure was improving throughput margin by 18% for a specific product line. In the customer perspective, the company set a goal of a two-day turn-around time on all orders for the product. To achieve this goal, the internal-business-process measure was the amount of time a bottleneck machine operated, with a goal of running 22 hours per day, six days a week. Finally, in the learning perspective, the company focused on training new employees to carry out nonbottleneck operations in order to free experienced employees to operate the bottleneck machine. The Bell Group's emphasis on time-related measures in its balanced scorecard has allowed the company to substantially increase manufacturing throughput and slash response times, leading to higher revenues and increased profits.[9]

Decision Point

What are the steps managers can take to manage bottlenecks?

Problem for Self-Study

The Sloan Moving Corporation transports household goods from one city to another within the continental United States. It measures quality of service in terms of (a) time required to transport goods, (b) on-time delivery (within two days of agreed-upon delivery date), and (c) number of lost or damaged items. Sloan is considering investing in a new scheduling-and-tracking system costing $160,000 per year, which should help it improve performance with respect to items (b) and (c). The following information describes Sloan's current performance and the expected performance if the new system is implemented:

	Current Performance	Expected Future Performance
On-time delivery performance	85%	95%
Variable cost per carton lost or damaged	$60	$60
Fixed cost per carton lost or damaged	$40	$40
Number of cartons lost or damaged per year	3,000 cartons	1,000 cartons

Sloan expects each percentage point increase in on-time performance to increase revenue by $20,000 per year. Sloan's contribution margin percentage is 45%.

Required

1. Should Sloan acquire the new system? Show your calculations.
2. Sloan is very confident about the cost savings from fewer lost or damaged cartons as a result of introducing the new system but unsure about the increase in revenues. Calculate the minimum amount of increase in revenues needed to make it worthwhile for Sloan to invest in the new system.

---

[9] Management Roundtable, "The Bell Group Uses the Balanced Scorecard with the Theory of Constraints to Keep Strategic Focus," FastTrack.roundtable.com, fasttrack.roundtable.com/app/content/knowledgesource/item/197 (accessed May 15, 2007).

Solution

1. Additional costs of the new scheduling-and-tracking system are $160,000 per year. Additional annual benefits of the new scheduling-and-tracking system are as follows:

Additional annual revenues from a 10% improvement in on-time performance, from 85% to 95%, $20,000 per 1% × 10 percentage points	$200,000
45% contribution margin from additional annual revenues (0.45 × $200,000)	$ 90,000
Decrease in costs per year from fewer cartons lost or damaged (only variable costs are relevant)[$60 per carton × (3,000 − 1,000) cartons]	120,000
Total additional benefits	$210,000

Because the benefits of $210,000 exceed the costs of $160,000, Sloan should invest in the new system.

2. As long as Sloan earns a contribution margin of $40,000 (to cover incremental costs of $160,000 minus relevant variable-cost savings of $120,000) from additional annual revenues, investing in the new system is beneficial. This contribution margin corresponds to additional revenues of $40,000 ÷ 0.45 = $88,889.

Decision Points

The following question-and-answer format summarizes the chapter's learning objectives. Each decision presents a key question related to a learning objective. The guidelines are the answer to that question.

Decision	Guidelines
1. What are the four cost categories of a costs-of-quality program?	Four cost categories in a costs-of-quality program are prevention costs (costs incurred to preclude the production of products that do not conform to specifications), appraisal costs (costs incurred to detect which of the individual units of products do not conform to specifications), internal failure costs (costs incurred on defective products before they are shipped to customers), and external failure costs (costs incurred on defective products after they are shipped to customers).
2. What nonfinancial measures and methods can managers use to improve quality?	Nonfinancial quality measures managers can use include customer satisfaction measures such as number of customer complaints and percentage of defective units shipped to customers; internal-business process measures such as percentage of defective and reworked products; and learning and growth measures such as percentage of employees trained in and empowered to use quality principles. Three methods to identify quality problems and to improve quality are (a) control charts, to distinguish random from nonrandom variations in an operating process; (b) Pareto diagrams, to indicate how frequently each type of failure occurs; and (c) cause-and-effect diagrams, to identify and respond to potential causes of failure.
3. How do managers identify the relevant costs and benefits of quality improvement programs and use financial and nonfinancial measures to evaluate quality?	The relevant costs of quality improvement programs are the expected incremental costs to implement the program. The relevant benefits are the cost savings and the estimated increase in contribution margin from the higher revenues expected from quality improvements. Financial measures are helpful to evaluate trade-offs among prevention costs, appraisal costs, and failure costs. Nonfinancial measures identify problem areas that need improvement and serve as indicators of future long-run performance.

4. What is customer-response time? What are the reasons for and the costs of delays?

Customer-response time is how long it takes from the time a customer places an order for a product or service to the time the product or service is delivered to the customer. Delays occur because of (a) uncertainty about when customers will order products or services and (b) bottlenecks due to limited capacity. Bottlenecks are operations at which the work to be performed approaches or exceeds available capacity. Costs of delays include lower revenues and increased inventory carrying costs.

5. What are the steps managers can take to manage bottlenecks?

The four steps in managing bottlenecks are (1) recognize that the bottleneck operation determines throughput margin, (2) identify the bottleneck, (3) keep the bottleneck busy and subordinate all nonbottleneck operations to the bottleneck operation, and (4) increase bottleneck efficiency and capacity.

Terms to Learn

This chapter and the Glossary at the end of the book contain definitions of the following important terms:

appraisal costs (**p. 673**)
average waiting time (**p. 683**)
bottleneck (**p. 682**)
cause-and-effect diagram (**p. 676**)
conformance quality (**p. 672**)
control chart (**p. 675**)
costs of quality (COQ) (**p. 672**)
customer-response time (**p. 681**)

design quality (**p. 672**)
external failure costs (**p. 673**)
internal failure costs (**p. 673**)
manufacturing cycle efficiency (MCE) (**p. 681**)
manufacturing cycle time (**p. 681**)
manufacturing lead time (**p. 681**)

on-time performance (**p. 682**)
Pareto diagram (**p. 676**)
prevention costs (**p. 673**)
quality (**p. 671**)
theory of constraints (TOC) (**p. 686**)
throughput margin (**p. 686**)
time driver (**p. 682**)

Assignment Material

Questions

19-1 Describe two benefits of improving quality.
19-2 How does conformance quality differ from design quality? Explain.
19-3 Name two items classified as prevention costs.
19-4 Distinguish between internal failure costs and external failure costs.
19-5 Describe three methods that companies use to identify quality problems.
19-6 "Companies should focus on financial measures of quality because these are the only measures of quality that can be linked to bottom-line performance." Do you agree? Explain.
19-7 Give two examples of nonfinancial measures of customer satisfaction relating to quality.
19-8 Give two examples of nonfinancial measures of internal-business-process quality.
19-9 Distinguish between customer-response time and manufacturing cycle time.
19-10 "There is no trade-off between customer-response time and on-time performance." Do you agree? Explain.
19-11 Give two reasons why delays occur.
19-12 "Companies should always make and sell all products whose selling prices exceed variable costs." Assuming fixed costs are irrelevant, do you agree? Explain.
19-13 Describe the three main measures used in the theory of constraints.
19-14 Describe the four key steps in managing bottleneck operations.
19-15 Describe three ways to improve the performance of a bottleneck operation.

Exercises

19-16 **Costs of quality.** (CMA, adapted) Costen, Inc., produces cell phone equipment. Jessica Tolmy, Costen's president, decided to devote more resources to the improvement of product quality after learning that her company had been ranked fourth in product quality in a 2009 survey of cell phone users. Costen's quality-improvement program has now been in operation for two years, and the cost report shown here has recently been issued.

8,000 hours of warranty repairs, and (5) sell an additional 140 printing presses, for a total contribution margin of $1,680,000. SpeedPrint believes that even as it improves quality, it will not be able to save any of the fixed costs of rework or repair. SpeedPrint uses a one-year time horizon for this decision because it plans to introduce a new press at the end of the year.

Required

1. Should SpeedPrint change to the new component? Show your calculations.
2. Suppose the estimate of 140 additional printing presses sold is uncertain. What is the minimum number of additional printing presses that SpeedPrint needs to sell to justify adopting the new component?

19-21 Quality improvement, relevant costs, relevant revenues. Flagstar Conference Center and Catering is a conference center and restaurant facility that hosts over 300 national and international events each year attended by 50,000 professionals. Due to increased competition and soaring customer expectations, the company has been forced to revisit its quality standards. In the company's 25 year history, customer demand has never been greater for high quality products and services. Flagstar has the following budgeted fixed and variable costs for 2011:

	Total Conference Center Fixed Cost	Variable Cost per Conference Attendee
Building and facilities	$3,600,000	
Management salaries	$1,400,000	
Customer support and service personnel		$ 55
Food and drink		$100
Conference materials		$ 35
Incidental products and services		$ 15

The company's budgeted operating income is $3,500,000.

After conducting a survey of 3,000 conference attendees, the company has learned that its customers would most like to see the following changes in the quality of the company's products and services: 1) more menu options and faster service, 2) more incidental products and services (wireless access in all meeting rooms, computer stations for internet use, free local calling, etc.), and 3) upscale and cleaner meeting facilities. To satisfy these customer demands, the company would be required to increase fixed costs by 50% per year and increase variable costs by $10 per attendee as follows:

	Additional Variable Cost per Conference Attendee
Customer support and service personnel	$3
Food and drink	$5
Conference materials	$0
Incidental products and services	$2

Flagstar believes that the preceding improvements in product and service quality would increase overall conference attendance by 40%.

Required

1. What is the budgeted revenue per conference attendee?
2. Assuming budgeted revenue per conference attendee is unchanged, should Flagstar implement the proposed changes?
3. Assuming budgeted revenue per conference attendee is unchanged, what is the variable cost per conference attendee at which Flagstar would be indifferent between implementing and not implementing the proposed changes?

19-22 Waiting time, service industry. The registration advisors at a small midwestern university (SMU) help 4,200 students develop each of their class schedules and register for classes each semester. Each advisor works for 10 hours a day during the registration period. SMU currently has 10 advisors. While advising an individual student can take anywhere from 2 to 30 minutes, it takes an average of 12 minutes per student. During the registration period, the 10 advisors see an average of 300 students a day on a first-come, first-served basis.

Required

1. Using the formula on page 683, calculate how long the average student will have to wait in the advisor's office before being advised.

2. The head of the registration advisors would like to increase the number of students seen each day, because at 300 students a day it would take 14 working days to see all of the students. This is a problem because the registration period lasts for only two weeks (10 working days). If the advisors could advise 420 students a day, it would take only two weeks (10 days). However, the head advisor wants to make sure that the waiting time is not excessive. What would be the average waiting time if 420 students were seen each day?

3. SMU wants to know the effect of reducing the average advising time on the average wait time. If SMU can reduce the average advising time to 10 minutes, what would be the average waiting time if 420 students were seen each day?

19-23 Waiting time, cost considerations, customer satisfaction. Refer to the information presented in Exercise 19-22. The head of the registration advisors at SMU has decided that the advisors must finish their advising in two weeks and therefore must advise 420 students a day. However, the average waiting time given a 12-minute advising period will result in student complaints, as will reducing the average advising time to 10 minutes. SMU is considering two alternatives:

A. Hire two more advisors for the two-week (10-working day) advising period. This will increase the available number of advisors to 12 and therefore lower the average waiting time.

B. Increase the number of days that the advisors will work during the two-week registration period to six days a week. If SMU increases the number of days worked to six per week, then the 10 advisors need only see 350 students a day to advise all of the students in two weeks.

1. What would the average wait time be under alternative A and under alternative B?

2. If advisors earn $100 per day, which alternative would be cheaper for SMU (assume that if advisors work six days in a given work week, they will be paid time and a half for the sixth day)?

3. From a student satisfaction point of view, which of the two alternatives would be preferred? Why?

Required

19-24 Nonfinancial measures of quality, manufacturing cycle efficiency. (CMA, adapted) Torrance Manufacturing evaluates the performance of its production managers based on a variety of factors, including cost, quality, and cycle time. The following are nonfinancial measures for quality and time for 2010 and 2011 for its only product:

Nonfinancial Quality Measures	2010	2011
Number of returned goods	385	462
Number of defective units reworked	1,122	834
Annual hours spent on quality training per employee	32	36
Number of units delivered on time	12,438	14,990

Annual Totals	2010	2011
Units of finished goods shipped	14,240	16,834
Average total hours worked per employee	2,000	2,000

The following information relates to the average amount of time needed to complete an order:

Time to Complete an Order	2010	2011
Wait time		
From order being placed to start of production	8	6
From start of production to completion	6	7
Inspection time	2	1
Process time	4	4
Move time	2	2

1. Compute the manufacturing cycle efficiency for an order for 2010 and 2011.

2. For each year 2010 and 2011, calculate the following:
   a. Percentage of goods returned
   b. Defective units reworked as a percentage of units shipped
   c. Percentage of on-time deliveries
   d. Percentage of hours spent by each employee on quality training

3. Evaluate management's performance on quality and timeliness over the two years.

Required

19-25 Theory of constraints, throughput margin, relevant costs. The Mayfield Corporation manufactures filing cabinets in two operations: machining and finishing. It provides the following information:

	Machining	Finishing
Annual capacity	100,000 units	80,000 units
Annual production	80,000 units	80,000 units
Fixed operating costs (excluding direct materials)	$640,000	$400,000
Fixed operating costs per unit produced ($640,000 ÷ 80,000; $400,000 ÷ 80,000)	$8 per unit	$5 per unit

Each cabinet sells for $72 and has direct material costs of $32 incurred at the start of the machining operation. Mayfield has no other variable costs. Mayfield can sell whatever output it produces. The following requirements refer only to the preceding data. There is no connection between the requirements.

Required

1. Mayfield is considering using some modern jigs and tools in the finishing operation that would increase annual finishing output by 1,000 units. The annual cost of these jigs and tools is $30,000. Should Mayfield acquire these tools? Show your calculations.
2. The production manager of the machining department has submitted a proposal to do faster setups that would increase the annual capacity of the machining department by 10,000 units and would cost $5,000 per year. Should Mayfield implement the change? Show your calculations.
3. An outside contractor offers to do the finishing operation for 12,000 units at $10 per unit, double the $5 per unit that it costs Mayfield to do the finishing in-house. Should Mayfield accept the subcontractor's offer? Show your calculations.
4. The Hunt Corporation offers to machine 4,000 units at $4 per unit, half the $8 per unit that it costs Mayfield to do the machining in-house. Should Mayfield accept Hunt's offer? Show your calculations.

19-26 Theory of constraints, throughput margin, quality. Refer to the information in Exercise 19-25 in answering the following requirements. There is no connection between the requirements.

Required

1. Mayfield produces 2,000 defective units at the machining operation. What is the cost to Mayfield of the defective items produced? Explain your answer briefly.
2. Mayfield produces 2,000 defective units at the finishing operation. What is the cost to Mayfield of the defective items produced? Explain your answer briefly.

MyAccountingLab

Problems

19-27 Quality improvement, relevant costs, and relevant revenues. The Thomas Corporation sells 300,000 V262 valves to the automobile and truck industry. Thomas has a capacity of 110,000 machine-hours and can produce 3 valves per machine-hour. V262's contribution margin per unit is $8. Thomas sells only 300,000 valves because 30,000 valves (10% of the good valves) need to be reworked. It takes one machine-hour to rework 3 valves, so 10,000 hours of capacity are used in the rework process. Thomas's rework costs are $210,000. Rework costs consist of the following:

■ Direct materials and direct rework labor (variable costs): $3 per unit
■ Fixed costs of equipment, rent, and overhead allocation: $4 per unit

Thomas's process designers have developed a modification that would maintain the speed of the process and ensure 100% quality and no rework. The new process would cost $315,000 per year. The following additional information is available:

■ The demand for Thomas's V262 valves is 370,000 per year.
■ The Jackson Corporation has asked Thomas to supply 22,000 T971 valves (another product) if Thomas implements the new design. The contribution margin per T971 valve is $10. Thomas can make two T971 valves per machine-hour with 100% quality and no rework.

Required

1. Suppose Thomas's designers implement the new design. Should Thomas accept Jackson's order for 22,000 T971 valves? Show your calculations.
2. Should Thomas implement the new design? Show your calculations.
3. What nonfinancial and qualitative factors should Thomas consider in deciding whether to implement the new design?

19-28 Quality improvement, relevant costs, and relevant revenues. The Tan Corporation uses multicolor molding to make plastic lamps. The molding operation has a capacity of 200,000 units per year. The demand for lamps is very strong. Tan will be able to sell whatever output quantities it can produce at $40 per lamp.

Tan can start only 200,000 units into production in the molding department because of capacity constraints on the molding machines. If a defective unit is produced at the molding operation, it must be scrapped at a net disposal value of zero. Of the 200,000 units started at the molding operation, 30,000 defective units (15%) are produced. The cost of a defective unit, based on total (fixed and variable) manufacturing costs incurred up to the molding operation, equals $25 per unit, as follows:

Direct materials (variable)	$16 per unit
Direct manufacturing labor, setup labor, and materials-handling labor (variable)	3 per unit
Equipment, rent, and other allocated overhead, including inspection and testing costs on scrapped parts (fixed)	6 per unit
Total	$25 per unit

Tan's designers have determined that adding a different type of material to the existing direct materials would result in no defective units being produced, but it would increase the variable costs by $4 per lamp in the molding department.

Required

1. Should Tan use the new material? Show your calculations.
2. What nonfinancial and qualitative factors should Tan consider in making the decision?

19-29 Statistical quality control. Keltrex Cereals produces a wide variety of breakfast products. The company's three best selling breakfast cereals are Double Bran Bits, Honey Wheat Squares, and Sugar King Pops. Each box of a particular type of cereal is required to meet pre-determined weight specifications, so that no single box contains more or less cereal than another. The company measures the mean weight per production run to determine if there are variances over or under the company's specified upper and lower level control limits. A production run that falls outside of the specified control limit does not meet quality standards and is investigated further by management to determine the cause of the variance. The three Keltrex breakfast cereals had the following weight standards and production run data for the month of March:

Quality Standard: Mean Weight per Production Run

Double Bran Bits	Honey Wheat Squares	Sugar King Pops
17.97 ounces	14 ounces	16.02 ounces

Actual Mean Weight per Production Run (Ounces)

Production Run	Double Bran Bits	Honey Wheat Squares	Sugar King Pops
1	18.23	14.11	15.83
2	18.14	14.13	16.11
3	18.22	13.98	16.24
4	18.30	13.89	15.69
5	18.10	13.91	15.95
6	18.05	14.01	15.50
7	17.84	13.94	15.86
8	17.66	13.99	16.23
9	17.60	14.03	16.15
10	17.52	13.97	16.60
Standard Deviation	0.28	0.16	0.21

Required

1. Using the $\pm 2\sigma$ rule, what variance investigation decisions would be made?
2. Present control charts for each of the three breakfast cereals for March. What inferences can you draw from the charts?
3. What are the costs of quality in this example? How could Keltrex employ Six Sigma programs to improve quality?

19-30 Compensation linked with profitability, waiting time, and quality measures. East Coast Healthcare operates two medical groups, one in Philadelphia and one in Baltimore. The semi-annual bonus plan for each medical group's president has three components:

a. Profitability performance. Add 0.75% of operating income.
b. Average patient waiting time. Add $40,000 if the average waiting time for a patient to see a doctor after the scheduled appointment time is less than 10 minutes. If average patient waiting time is more than 10 minutes, add nothing.
c. Patient satisfaction performance. Deduct $40,000 if patient satisfaction (measured using a survey asking patients about their satisfaction with their doctor and their overall satisfaction with East Coast Healthcare) falls below 65 on a scale from 0 (lowest) to 100 (highest). No additional bonus is awarded for satisfaction scores of 65 or more.

Semi-annual data for 2011 for the Philadelphia and Baltimore groups are as follows:

	January–June	July–December
Philadelphia		
Operating income	$11,150,000	$10,500,000
Average waiting time	13 minutes	12 minutes
Patient satisfaction	74	72
Baltimore		
Operating income	$ 9,500,000	$ 5,875,000
Average waiting time	12 minutes	9.5 minutes
Patient satisfaction	59	68

Required

1. Compute the bonuses paid in each half year of 2011 to the Philadelphia and Baltimore medical group presidents.
2. Discuss the validity of the components of the bonus plan as measures of profitability, waiting time performance, and patient satisfaction. Suggest one shortcoming of each measure and how it might be overcome (by redesign of the plan or by another measure).
3. Why do you think East Coast Healthcare includes measures of both operating income and waiting time in its bonus plan for group presidents? Give one example of what might happen if waiting time was dropped as a performance measure.

19-31 Waiting times, manufacturing cycle times. The Seawall Corporation uses an injection molding machine to make a plastic product, Z39, after receiving firm orders from its customers. Seawall estimates that it will receive 50 orders for Z39 during the coming year. Each order of Z39 will take 80 hours of machine time. The annual machine capacity is 5,000 hours.

Required

1. Calculate (a) the average amount of time that an order for Z39 will wait in line before it is processed and (b) the average manufacturing cycle time per order for Z39.
2. Seawall is considering introducing a new product, Y28. The company expects it will receive 25 orders of Y28 in the coming year. Each order of Y28 will take 20 hours of machine time. Assuming the demand for Z39 will not be affected by the introduction of Y28, calculate (a) the average waiting time for an order received and (b) the average manufacturing cycle time per order for each product, if Seawall introduces Y28.

19-32 Waiting times, relevant revenues, and relevant costs (continuation of 19-31). Seawall is still debating whether it should introduce Y28. The following table provides information on selling prices, variable costs, and inventory carrying costs for Z39 and Y28:

Product	Annual Average Number of Orders	Selling Price per Order if Average Manufacturing Cycle Time per Order Is Less Than 320 Hours	Selling Price per Order if Average Manufacturing Cycle Time per Order Is More Than 320 Hours	Variable Cost per Order	Inventory Carrying Cost per Order per Hour
Z39	50	$27,000	$26,500	$15,000	$0.75
Y28	25	8,400	8,000	5,000	0.25

Required

1. Using the average manufacturing cycle times calculated in Problem 19-31, requirement 2, should Seawall manufacture and sell Y28? Show your calculations.
2. Should Seawall manufacture and sell Y28 if the data are changed as follows:

Product	Annual Average Number of Orders	Selling Price per Order if Average Manufacturing Cycle Time per Order Is Less Than 320 Hours	Selling Price per Order if Average Manufacturing Cycle Time per Order Is More Than 320 Hours	Variable Cost per Order	Inventory Carrying Cost per Order per Hour
Z39	50	$27,000	$26,500	$15,000	$0.75
Y28	25	6,400	6,000	5,000	0.25

19-33 Manufacturing cycle times, relevant revenues, and relevant costs. The Brandt Corporation makes wire harnesses for the aircraft industry only upon receiving firm orders form its customers. Brandt has recently purchased a new machine to make two types of wire harnesses, one for Boeing airplanes (B7) and the other for Airbus Industries airplanes (A3). The annual capacity of the new machine is 6,000 hours. The following information is available for next year:

Customer	Annual Average Number of Orders	Manufacturing Time Required	Selling Price per Order if Average Manufacturing Cycle Time per Order Is		Variable Cost per Order	Inventory Carrying Cost per Order per Hour
			Less Than 200 Hours	More Than 200 Hours		
B7	125	40 hours	$15,000	$14,400	$10,000	$0.50
A3	10	50 hours	13,500	12,960	9,000	0.45

Required

1. Calculate the average manufacturing cycle times per order (a) if Brandt manufactures only B7 and (b) if Brandt manufactures both B7 and A3.
2. Even though A3 has a positive contribution margin, Brandt's managers are evaluating whether Brandt should (a) make and sell only B7 or (b) make and sell both B7 and A3. Which alternative will maximize Brandt's operating income? Show your calculations.
3. What other factors should Brandt consider in choosing between the alternatives in requirement 2?

19-34 Theory of constraints, throughput margin, and relevant costs. Nevada Industries manufactures electronic testing equipment. Nevada also installs the equipment at customers' sites and ensures that it functions smoothly. Additional information on the manufacturing and installation departments is as follows (capacities are expressed in terms of the number of units of electronic testing equipment):

	Equipment Manufactured	Equipment Installed
Annual capacity	400 units per year	250 units per year
Equipment manufactured and installed	250 units per year	250 units per year

Nevada manufactures only 250 units per year because the installation department has only enough capacity to install 250 units. The equipment sells for $60,000 per unit (installed) and has direct material costs of $35,000. All costs other than direct material costs are fixed. The following requirements refer only to the preceding data. There is no connection between the requirements.

Required

1. Nevada's engineers have found a way to reduce equipment manufacturing time. The new method would cost an additional $60 per unit and would allow Nevada to manufacture 20 additional units a year. Should Nevada implement the new method? Show your calculations.
2. Nevada's designers have proposed a change in direct materials that would increase direct material costs by $3,000 per unit. This change would enable Nevada to install 280 units of equipment each year. If Nevada makes the change, it will implement the new design on all equipment sold. Should Nevada use the new design? Show your calculations.
3. A new installation technique has been developed that will enable Nevada's engineers to install 7 additional units of equipment a year. The new method will increase installation costs by $45,000 each year. Should Nevada implement the new technique? Show your calculations.
4. Nevada is considering how to motivate workers to improve their productivity (output per hour). One proposal is to evaluate and compensate workers in the manufacturing and installation departments on the basis of their productivities. Do you think the new proposal is a good idea? Explain briefly.

19-35 Theory of constraints, throughput margin, quality, and relevant costs. Aardee Industries manufactures pharmaceutical products in two departments: mixing and tablet making. Additional information on the two departments follows. Each tablet contains 0.5 gram of direct materials.

	Mixing	Tablet Making
Capacity per hour	150 grams	200 tablets
Monthly capacity (2,000 hours available in each department)	300,000 grams	400,000 tablets
Monthly production	200,000 grams	390,000 tablets
Fixed operating costs (excluding direct materials)	$16,000	$39,000
Fixed operating cost per unit ($16,000 ÷ 200,000 grams; $39,000 ÷ 390,000 tablets)	$0.08 per gram	$0.10 per tablet

The mixing department makes 200,000 grams of direct materials mixture (enough to make 400,000 tablets) because the tablet-making department has only enough capacity to process 400,000 tablets. All direct material costs of $156,000 are incurred in the mixing department. The tablet-making department manufactures only 390,000 tablets from the 200,000 grams of mixture processed; 2.5% of the direct materials mixture is lost in the tablet-making process. Each tablet sells for $1. All costs other than direct material costs are fixed costs. The following requirements refer only to the preceding data. There is no connection between the requirements.

Required

1. An outside contractor makes the following offer: If Aardee will supply the contractor with 10,000 grams of mixture, the contractor will manufacture 19,500 tablets for Aardee (allowing for the normal 2.5% loss of the mixture during the tablet-making process) at $0.12 per tablet. Should Aardee accept the contractor's offer? Show your calculations.

2. Another company offers to prepare 20,000 grams of mixture a month from direct materials Aardee supplies. The company will charge $0.07 per gram of mixture. Should Aardee accept the company's offer? Show your calculations.

3. Aardee's engineers have devised a method that would improve quality in the tablet-making department. They estimate that the 10,000 tablets currently being lost would be saved. The modification would cost $7,000 a month. Should Aardee implement the new method? Show your calculations.

4. Suppose that Aardee also loses 10,000 grams of mixture in its mixing department. These losses can be reduced to zero if the company is willing to spend $9,000 per month in quality-improvement methods. Should Aardee adopt the quality-improvement method? Show your calculations.

5. What are the benefits of improving quality in the mixing department compared with improving quality in the tablet-making department?

19-36 Theory of constraints, contribution margin, sensitivity analysis. Fun Time Toys (FTT) produces dolls in two processes: molding and assembly. FTT is currently producing two models: Chatty Chelsey and Talking Tanya. Production in the molding department is limited by the amount of materials available. Production in the assembly department is limited by the amount of trained labor available. The only variable costs are materials in the molding department and labor in the assembly department. Following are the requirements and limitations by doll model and department:

	Molding Materials	**Assembly Time**	**Selling Price**
Chatty Chelsey	1.5 pounds per doll	20 minutes per doll	$39 per doll
Talking Tanya	2 pounds per doll	30 minutes per doll	$51 per doll
Materials/Labor Available	30,000 pounds	8,500 hours	
Cost	$12 per pound	$18 per hour	

Required

1. If there were enough demand for either doll, which doll would FTT produce? How many of these dolls would it make and sell?

2. If FTT sells two Chatty Chelseys for each Talking Tanya, how many dolls of each type would it produce and sell? What would be the total contribution margin?

3. If FTT sells two Chatty Chelseys for each Talking Tanya, how much would production and contribution margin increase if the molding department could buy 15 more pounds of materials for $12 per pound?

4. If FTT sells two Chatty Chelseys for each Talking Tanya, how much would production and contribution margin increase if the assembly department could get 10 more labor hours at $18 per hour?

19-37 Quality improvement, Pareto diagram, cause-and-effect diagram. Pauli's Pizza has recently begun collecting data on the quality of its customer order processing and delivery. Pauli's made 1,800 deliveries during the first quarter of 2012. The following quality data pertains to first quarter deliveries:

Type of Quality Failure	Quality Failure Incidents First Quarter 2012
Late delivery	50
Damaged or spoiled product delivered	5
Incorrect order delivered	12
Service complaints by customer of delivery personnel	8
Failure to deliver incidental items with order (drinks, side items, etc.)	18

Required

1. Draw a Pareto diagram of the quality failures experienced by Pauli's Pizza.
2. Give examples of prevention activities that could reduce the failures experienced by Pauli's.
3. Draw a cause-and-effect diagram of possible causes for late deliveries.

19-38 Ethics and quality. Wainwright Corporation manufactures auto parts for two leading Japanese automakers. Nancy Evans is the management accountant for one of Wainwright's largest manufacturing plants. The plant's General Manager, Chris Sheldon, has just returned from a meeting at corporate headquarters where quality expectations were outlined for 2012. Chris calls Nancy into his office to relay the corporate quality objective that total quality costs will not exceed 10% of total revenues by plant under any circumstances. Chris asks Nancy to provide him with a list of options for meeting corporate headquarter's quality objective. The plant's initial budgeted revenues and quality costs for 2012 are as follows:

Revenue	3,400,000
Quality Costs:	
Testing of purchased materials	32,000
Quality control training for production staff	5,000
Warranty repairs	82,000
Quality design engineering	48,000
Customer support	37,000
Materials scrap	12,000
Product inspection	102,000
Engineering redesign of failed parts	21,000
Rework of failed parts	18,000

Prior to receiving the new corporate quality objective, Nancy had collected information for all of the plant's possible options for improving both product quality and costs of quality. She was planning to introduce the idea of reengineering the manufacturing process at a one-time cost of $75,000, which would decrease product inspection costs by approximately 25% per year and was expected to reduce warranty repairs and customer support by an estimated 40% per year. After seeing the new corporate objective, Nancy is reconsidering the reengineering idea.

Nancy returns to her office and crunches the numbers again to look for other alternatives. She concludes that by increasing the cost of quality control training for production staff by $15,000 per year, the company would reduce inspection costs by 10% annually and reduce warranty repairs and customer support costs by 20% per year, as well. She is leaning toward only presenting this latter option to Chris, the general manager, since this is the only option that meets the new corporate quality objective.

Required

1. Calculate the ratio of each costs-of-quality category (prevention, appraisal, internal failure, and external failure) to revenues for 2012. Are the total costs of quality as a percentage of revenues currently less than 10%?
2. Which of the two quality options should Nancy propose to the general manager, Chris Sheldon? Show the two-year outcome for each option: (a) reengineer the manufacturing process for $75,000 and (b) increase quality training expenditure by $15,000 per year.
3. Suppose Nancy decides not to present the reengineering option to Chris. Is Nancy's action unethical? Explain.

Collaborative Learning Problem

19-39 Quality improvement, theory of constraints. The Wellesley Corporation makes printed cloth in two departments: weaving and printing. Currently, all product first moves through the weaving department and then through the printing department before it is sold to retail distributors for $1,250 per roll. Wellesley provides the following information:

	Weaving	Printing
Monthly capacity	10,000 rolls	15,000 rolls
Monthly production	9,500 rolls	8,550 rolls
Direct material cost per roll of cloth processed at each operation	$500	$100
Fixed operating costs	$2,850,000	$427,500

Wellesley can start only 10,000 rolls of cloth in the weaving department because of capacity constraints of the weaving machines. Of the 10,000 rolls of cloth started in the weaving department, 500 (5%) defective rolls are scrapped at zero net disposal value. The good rolls from the weaving department (called gray cloth) are sent to the printing department. Of the 9,500 good rolls started at the printing operation, 950 (10%) defective rolls are scrapped at zero net disposal value. The Wellesley Corporation's total monthly sales of printed cloth equal the printing department's output.

Required

1. The printing department is considering buying 5,000 additional rolls of gray cloth from an outside supplier at $900 per roll, which is much higher than Wellesley's cost to manufacture the roll. The printing department expects that 10% of the rolls obtained from the outside supplier will result in defective products. Should the printing department buy the gray cloth from the outside supplier? Show your calculations.
2. Wellesley's engineers have developed a method that would lower the printing department's rate of defective products to 6% at the printing operation. Implementing the new method would cost $350,000 per month. Should Wellesley implement the change? Show your calculations.
3. The design engineering team has proposed a modification that would lower the weaving department's rate of defective products to 3%. The modification would cost the company $175,000 per month. Should Wellesley implement the change? Show your calculations.

Suppose you could receive a large quantity discount for a product that you regularly use, but the discount requires you to buy a year's supply and necessitates a large up-front expenditure.

Would you take the quantity discount? Companies face similar decisions because firms pay a price for tying up money in inventory sitting on their shelves or elsewhere. Money tied up in inventory is a particularly serious problem when times are tough. When faced with these circumstances, companies like Costco work very hard to better manage their inventories.

Costco Aggressively Manages Inventory to Thrive in Tough Times[1]

When consumers reduced their spending in 2008, traditional stalwarts like Circuit City and Linens 'n Things wilted under the weight of their own massive inventories. They could not turn their inventories quickly enough to pay suppliers and were forced to close their doors when cash ran out.

At the same time, Costco continued to thrive! How? By intentionally stocking *fewer* items than its competitors—and employing inventory management practices that successfully reduced costs throughout its operations. While the average grocery store carries around 40,000 items, Costco limits its offerings to about 4,000 products, or 90% less! Limiting the number of products on its shelves reduces Costco's costs of carrying inventory.

Costco also employs a just-in-time inventory management system, which includes sharing data directly with many of its largest suppliers. Companies like Kimberly-Clark calculate re-order points in real time and send new inventory, as needed, to replenish store shelves. Costco also works to redesign product packaging to squeeze more bulky goods onto trucks and shelves, reducing the number of orders Costco needs to place with suppliers.

Occasionally, the company leverages its 75 million square feet of warehouse space to reduce purchasing costs. For example, when Procter & Gamble recently announced a 6% price increase for its paper goods, Costco bought 258 truckloads of paper towels at the old rate and stored them using available capacity in its distribution centers and warehouses.

---

[1] *Source*: McGregor, Jena. 2008. Costco's artful discounts. *Business Week*, October 20.

These inventory management techniques have allowed Costco to succeed in tough times while others have failed. Costco turns its inventory nearly 12 times a year, far more often than other retailers. With many suppliers agreeing to be paid 30 days after delivery, Costco often sells many of its goods before it even has to pay for them!

Inventory management is important because materials costs often account for more than 40% of total costs of manufacturing companies and more than 70% of total costs in merchandising companies. In this chapter, we describe the components of inventory costs, relevant costs for different inventory-related decisions, and planning and control systems for managing inventory.

Inventory Management in Retail Organizations

Inventory management includes planning, coordinating, and controlling activities related to the flow of inventory into, through, and out of an organization. Consider this breakdown of operations for three major retailers for which cost of goods sold constitutes their largest cost item.

	Kroger	Costco	Wal-Mart
Revenues	100.0%	100.0%	100.0%
Deduct costs:			
Cost of goods sold	76.8%	87.2%	74.7%
Selling and administration costs	21.7%	10.2%	19.5%
Other costs, interest, and taxes	1.4%	1.1%	2.3%
Total costs	99.9%	98.5%	96.5%
Net income	0.1%	1.5%	3.5%

The low percentages of net income to revenues mean that improving the purchase and management of goods for sale can cause dramatic percentage increases in net income.

Costs Associated with Goods for Sale

Managing inventories to increase net income requires companies to effectively manage costs that fall into the following six categories:

1. **Purchasing costs** are the cost of goods acquired from suppliers, including incoming freight costs. These costs usually make up the largest cost category of goods for sale. Discounts for various purchase-order sizes and supplier payment terms affect purchasing costs.

Learning Objective 1

Identify six categories of costs associated with goods for sale

. . . purchasing, ordering, carrying, stockout, quality, and shrinkage

2. **Ordering costs** arise in preparing and issuing purchase orders, receiving and inspecting the items included in the orders, and matching invoices received, purchase orders, and delivery records to make payments. Ordering costs include the cost of obtaining purchase approvals, as well as other special processing costs.

3. **Carrying costs** arise while holding an inventory of goods for sale. Carrying costs include the opportunity cost of the investment tied up in inventory (see Chapter 11, pp. 403–405) and the costs associated with storage, such as space rental, insurance, obsolescence, and spoilage.

4. **Stockout costs** arise when a company runs out of a particular item for which there is customer demand, a *stockout*. The company must act quickly to replenish inventory to meet that demand or suffer the costs of not meeting it. A company may respond to a stockout by expediting an order from a supplier, which can be expensive because of additional ordering costs plus any associated transportation costs. Or the company may lose sales due to the stockout. In this case, the opportunity cost of the stockout includes lost contribution margin on the sale not made plus any contribution margin lost on future sales due to customer ill will.

5. **Costs of quality** result when features and characteristics of a product or service are not in conformance with customer specifications. There are four categories of quality costs (prevention costs, appraisal costs, internal failure costs, and external failure costs), as described in Chapter 19.

6. **Shrinkage costs** result from theft by outsiders, embezzlement by employees, misclassifications, and clerical errors. Shrinkage is measured by the difference between (a) the cost of the inventory recorded on the books in the absence of theft and other incidents just mentioned, and (b) the cost of inventory when physically counted. Shrinkage can often be an important measure of management performance. Consider, for example, the grocery business, where operating income percentages hover around 2%. With such small margins, it is easy to see why one of a store manager's prime responsibilities is controlling inventory shrinkage. A $1,000 increase in shrinkage will erase the operating income from sales of $50,000 (2% × $50,000 = $1,000).

Note that not all inventory costs are available in financial accounting systems. For example, opportunity costs are not recorded in these systems and are a significant component in several of these cost categories.

Information-gathering technology increases the reliability and timeliness of inventory information and reduces costs in the six cost categories. For example, barcoding technology allows a scanner to record purchases and sales of individual units. As soon as a unit is scanned, an instantaneous record of inventory movements is created that helps in the management of purchasing, carrying, and stockout costs. In the next several sections, we consider how relevant costs are computed for different inventory-related decisions in merchandising companies.

Economic-Order-Quantity Decision Model

The first decision in managing goods for sale is *how much to order* of a given product. The **economic order quantity** (EOQ) is a decision model that, under a given set of assumptions, calculates the optimal quantity of inventory to order.

- The simplest version of an EOQ model assumes there are only ordering and carrying costs.

- The same quantity is ordered at each reorder point.

- Demand, ordering costs, and carrying costs are known with certainty. The **purchase-order lead time**, the time between placing an order and its delivery, is also known with certainty.

- Purchasing cost per unit is unaffected by the order quantity. This assumption makes purchasing costs irrelevant to determining EOQ, because the purchase price is the same, whatever the order size.

Decision Point

What are the six categories of costs associated with goods for sale?

Learning Objective 2

Balance ordering costs with carrying costs using the economic-order-quantity (EOQ) decision model

. . . choose the inventory quantity per order to minimize these costs

- No stockouts occur. The basis for this assumption is that the costs of stockouts are so high that managers maintain adequate inventory to prevent them.
- In deciding on the size of a purchase order, managers consider costs of quality and shrinkage costs only to the extent that these costs affect ordering or carrying costs.

Given these assumptions, EOQ analysis ignores purchasing costs, stockout costs, costs of quality, and shrinkage costs. EOQ is the order quantity that minimizes the relevant ordering and carrying costs (that is, the ordering and carrying costs affected by the quantity of inventory ordered):

$$\text{Relevant total costs} = \text{Relevant ordering costs} + \text{Relevant carrying costs}$$

We use the following notations:

D = Demand in units for a specified period (one year in this example)

Q = Size of each order (order quantity)

$$\text{Number of purchase orders per period (one year)} = \frac{\text{Demand in units for a period (one year)}}{\text{Size of each order (order quantity)}} = \frac{D}{Q}$$

Average inventory in units = $\frac{Q}{2}$, because each time the inventory goes down to 0, an order for Q units is received. The inventory varies from Q to 0 so the average inventory is $\frac{0 + Q}{2}$.

P = Relevant ordering cost per purchase order

C = Relevant carrying cost of one unit in stock for the time period used for D (one year)

For any order quantity, Q,

$$\text{Annual relevant ordering costs} = \left(\begin{array}{c}\text{Number of} \\ \text{purchase orders} \times \\ \text{per year}\end{array}\begin{array}{c}\text{Relevant ordering} \\ \text{cost per} \\ \text{purchase order}\end{array}\right) = \left(\frac{D}{Q} \times P\right)$$

$$\text{Annual relevant carrying costs} = \left(\begin{array}{c}\text{Average inventory} \\ \text{in units}\end{array} \times \begin{array}{c}\text{Annual} \\ \text{relevant carrying} \\ \text{cost per unit}\end{array}\right) = \left(\frac{Q}{2} \times C\right)$$

$$\text{Annual relevant total costs} = \begin{array}{c}\text{Annual} \\ \text{relevant ordering} \\ \text{costs}\end{array} + \begin{array}{c}\text{Annual} \\ \text{relevant carrying} \\ \text{costs}\end{array} = \left(\frac{D}{Q} \times P\right) + \left(\frac{Q}{2} \times C\right)$$

The order quantity that minimizes annual relevant total costs is

$$EOQ = \sqrt{\frac{2DP}{C}}$$

The EOQ model is solved using calculus but the key intuition is that relevant total costs are minimized when relevant ordering costs equal relevant carrying costs. If carrying costs are less (greater) than ordering costs, total costs can be reduced by increasing (decreasing) the order quantity. To solve for EOQ, we set

$$\left(\frac{Q}{2} \times C\right) = \left(\frac{D}{Q} \times P\right)$$

Multiplying both sides by $\frac{2Q}{C}$, we get $Q^2 = \frac{2DP}{C}$

$$Q = \sqrt{\frac{2DP}{C}}$$

The formula indicates that EOQ increases with higher demand and/or higher ordering costs and decreases with higher carrying costs.

Let's consider an example to see how EOQ analysis works. CD World is an independent electronics store that sells blank compact disks. CD World purchases the CDs from

Sontek at $14 a package (each package contains 20 disks). Sontek pays for all incoming freight. No inspection is necessary at CD World because Sontek supplies quality merchandise. CD World's annual demand is 13,000 packages, at a rate of 250 packages per week. CD World requires a 15% annual rate of return on investment. The purchase-order lead time is two weeks. Relevant ordering cost per purchase order is $200.

Relevant carrying cost per package per year is as follows:

Required annual return on investment, 0.15 × $14	$2.10
Relevant costs of insurance, materials handling, breakage, shrinkage, and so on, per year	3.10
Total	$5.20

What is the EOQ of packages of disks?

Substituting D = 13,000 packages per year, P = $200 per order, and C = $5.20 per package per year, in the EOQ formula, we get,

$$EOQ = \sqrt{\frac{2 \times 13{,}000 \times \$200}{\$5.20}} = \sqrt{1{,}000{,}000} = 1{,}000 \text{ packages}$$

Purchasing 1,000 packages per order minimizes total relevant ordering and carrying costs. Therefore, the number of deliveries each period (one year in this example) is as follows:

$$\frac{D}{EOQ} = \frac{13{,}000}{1{,}000} = 13 \text{ deliveries}$$

Recall the annual relevant total costs (RTC) = $\left(\dfrac{D}{Q} \times P\right) + \left(\dfrac{Q}{2} \times C\right)$
For Q = 1,000 units,

$$RTC = \frac{13{,}000 \times \$200}{1{,}000} + \frac{1{,}000 \times \$5.20}{2}$$

$$= \$2{,}600 + \$2{,}600 = \$5{,}200$$

Exhibit 20-1 graphs the annual relevant total costs of ordering (DP/Q) and carrying inventory ($QC/2$) under various order sizes (Q), and it illustrates the trade-off between these two types of costs. The larger the order quantity, the lower the annual relevant ordering costs, but the higher the annual relevant carrying costs. *Annual relevant total costs are at a minimum at the EOQ at which the relevant ordering and carrying costs are equal.*

Exhibit 20-1　Graphic Analysis of Ordering Costs and Carrying Costs for Compact Disks at CD World

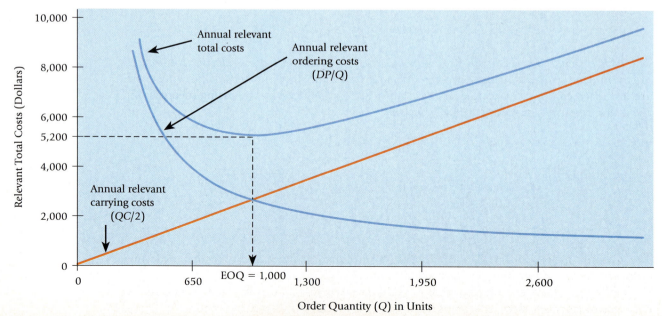

When to Order, Assuming Certainty

The second decision in managing goods for sale is *when to order* a given product. The **reorder point** is the quantity level of inventory on hand that triggers a new purchase order. The reorder point is simplest to compute when both demand and purchase-order lead time are known with certainty:

$$\text{Reorder point} = \frac{\text{Number of units sold}}{\text{per time period}} \times \frac{\text{Purchase-order}}{\text{lead time}}$$

In our CD World example, we choose one week as the time period in the reorder-point formula:

Economic order quantity	1,000 packages
Number of units sold per week	250 packages per week (13,000 packages ÷ 52 weeks)
Purchase-order lead time	2 weeks

$$\text{Reorder point} = 250 \text{ packages per week} \times 2 \text{ weeks} = 500 \text{ packages}$$

CD World will order 1,000 packages each time inventory stock falls to 500 packages.[2] The graph in Exhibit 20-2 shows the behavior of the inventory level of compact disk packages, assuming demand occurs uniformly during each week. If purchase-order lead time is two weeks, a new order will be placed when the inventory level falls to 500 packages, so the 1,000 packages ordered will be received at the precise time that inventory reaches zero.

Safety Stock

We have assumed that demand and purchase-order lead time are known with certainty. Retailers who are uncertain about demand, lead time, or the quantity that suppliers can provide, hold safety stock. **Safety stock** is inventory held at all times regardless of the quantity of inventory ordered using the EOQ model. Safety stock is used as a buffer against unexpected increases in demand, uncertainty about lead time, and unavailability of stock from suppliers. Suppose that in the CD World example, the only uncertainty is about demand. CD World's managers will have some notion (usually based on experience) of the range of weekly demand. CD World's managers expect demand to be 250 packages per week, but they feel that a maximum demand of 400 packages per week

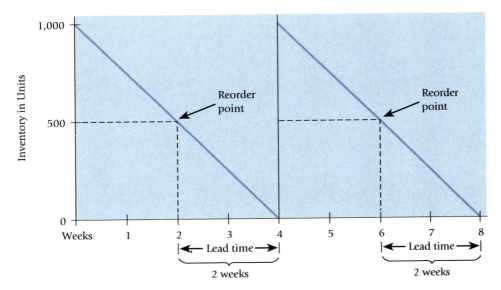

Exhibit 20-2

Inventory Level of
Compact Disks at
CD World[a]

[a] This exhibit assumes that demand and purchase-order lead time are certain:
Demand = 250 CD packages per week
Purchase-order lead time = 2 weeks

---

[2] This handy but special formula does not apply when receipt of the order fails to increase inventory to the reorder-point quantity (for example, when lead time is three weeks and the order is a one-week supply). In these cases, orders will overlap.

may occur. If stockout costs are very high, CD World will hold a safety stock of 300 packages and incur higher carrying costs. The 300 packages equal the maximum excess demand of 150 (400 – 250) packages per week times the two weeks of purchase-order lead time. If stockout costs are minimal, CD World will hold no safety stocks and avoid incurring the additional carrying costs.

A frequency distribution based on prior daily or weekly levels of demand forms the basis for computing safety-stock levels. Assume that one of the following levels of demand will occur over the two-week purchase-order lead time at CD World.

Total Demand for 2 Weeks	200 Units	300 Units	400 Units	500 Units	600 Units	700 Units	800 Units
Probability (sums to 1.00)	0.06	0.09	0.20	0.30	0.20	0.09	0.06

We see that 500 units is the most likely level of demand for two weeks because it has the highest probability of occurrence. We see also a 0.35 probability that demand will be 600, 700, or 800 packages (0.20 + 0.09 + 0.06 = 0.35).

If a customer wants to buy compact disks and the store has none in stock, CD World can "rush" them to the customer at an additional cost to CD World of $4 per package. The relevant stockout costs in this case are $4 per package. The optimal safety-stock level is the quantity of safety stock that minimizes the sum of annual relevant stockout and carrying costs. Note that CD World will place 13 orders per year and will incur the same ordering costs whatever level of safety stock it chooses. Therefore, ordering costs are irrelevant for the safety-stock decision. Recall that the relevant carrying cost for CD World is $5.20 per package per year.

Exhibit 20-3 tabulates annual relevant total stockout and carrying costs when the reorder point is 500 units. Over the two-week purchase-order lead time, stockouts can occur if demand is 600, 700, or 800 units because these levels of demand exceed the 500 units in stock at the time CD World places the purchase orders. Consequently, CD World only evaluates safety stock levels of 0, 100, 200, and 300 units. If safety stock is 0 units, CD World will

Exhibit 20-3   Computation of Safety Stock for CD World When Reorder Point Is 500 Units

	Safety Stock Level in Units (1)	Demand Levels Resulting in Stockouts (2)	Stockout in Units[a] (3) = (2) – 500 – (1)	Probability of Stockout (4)	Relevant Stockout Costs[b] (5) = (3) × $4	Number of Orders per Year[c] (6)	Expected Stockout Costs[d] (7) = (4) × (5) × (6)	Relevant Carrying Costs[e] (8) = (1) × $5.20	Relevant Total Costs (9) = (7) + (8)
6	0	600	100	0.20	$ 400	13	$1,040		
7		700	200	0.09	800	13	936		
8		800	300	0.06	1,200	13	936		
9							$2,912	$ 0	$2,912
10	100	700	100	0.09	400	13	$ 468		
11		800	200	0.06	800	13	624		
12							$1,092	$ 520	$1,612
13	200	800	100	0.06	400	13	$ 312	$1,040	$1,352
14	300	-	-	-	-	-	$ 0[f]	$1,560	$1,560

[a] Demand level resulting in stockouts – Inventory available during lead time (excluding safety stock), 500 units – Safety stock.
[b] Stockout in units × Relevant stockout costs of $4.00 per unit.
[c] Annual demand, 13,000 ÷ 1,000 EOQ = 13 orders per year.
[d] Probability of stockout × Relevant stockout costs × Number of orders per year.
[e] Safety stock × Annual relevant carrying costs of $5.20 per unit (assumes that safety stock is on hand at all times and that there is no overstocking caused by decreases in expected usage).
[f] At a safety stock level of 300 units, no stockout will occur and, hence, expected stockout costs = $0.

incur stockout costs if demand is 600, 700, or 800 units but will have no additional carrying costs. At the other extreme, if safety stock is 300 units, CD World will never incur stockout costs but will have higher carrying costs. As Exhibit 20-3 shows, annual relevant total stockout and carrying costs would be the lowest ($1,352) when a safety stock of 200 packages is maintained. Therefore, 200 units is the optimal safety-stock level. Consider the 200 units of safety stock as extra stock that CD World maintains. For example, CD World's total inventory of compact disks at the time of reordering its EOQ of 1,000 units would be 700 units (the reorder point of 500 units plus safety stock of 200 units).

Decision Point

What does the EOQ decision model help managers do and how do managers decide on the level of safety stocks?

Estimating Inventory-Related Relevant Costs and Their Effects

Just as we did in earlier chapters, we need to determine which costs are relevant when making and evaluating inventory management decisions. We next describe the estimates that need to be made to calculate the annual relevant carrying costs of inventory, stockout costs, and ordering costs.

Learning Objective 3

Identify the effect of errors that can arise when using the EOQ decision model

. . . errors in predicting parameters have a small effect on costs

and ways to reduce conflicts between the EOQ model and models used for performance evaluation

. . . by making the two models congruent

Considerations in Obtaining Estimates of Relevant Costs

Relevant inventory carrying costs consist of the *relevant incremental costs* plus the *relevant opportunity cost of capital*.

What are the *relevant incremental costs* of carrying inventory? Only those costs of the purchasing company, such as warehouse rent, warehouse workers' salaries, costs of obsolescence, costs of shrinkage, and costs of breakage, that change with the quantity of inventory held. Salaries paid to clerks, stock keepers, and materials handlers are irrelevant if they are unaffected by changes in inventory levels. Suppose, however, that as inventories increase (decrease), total salary costs increase (decrease) as clerks, stock keepers, and materials handlers are added (transferred to other activities or laid off). In this case, salaries paid are relevant costs of carrying inventory. Similarly, costs of storage space owned that cannot be used for other profitable purposes when inventories decrease are irrelevant. But if the space has other profitable uses, or if total rental cost is tied to the amount of space occupied, storage costs are relevant costs of carrying inventory.

What is the *relevant opportunity cost of capital*? It is the return forgone by investing capital in inventory rather than elsewhere. It is calculated as the required rate of return multiplied by the per-unit costs such as the purchase price of units, incoming freight, and incoming inspection. Opportunity costs are not computed on investments (say, in buildings) if these investments are unaffected by changes in inventory levels.

In the case of stockouts, the relevant incremental cost is the cost of expediting an order from a supplier. The relevant opportunity cost is (1) the lost contribution margin on sales forgone because of the stockout and (2) lost contribution margin on future sales forgone as a result of customer ill will.

Relevant ordering costs are only those ordering costs that change with the number of orders placed (for example, costs of preparing and issuing purchase orders and receiving and inspecting materials).

Cost of a Prediction Error

Predicting relevant costs is difficult and seldom flawless, which raises the question, "What is the cost when actual relevant costs differ from the estimated relevant costs used for decision making?"

Let's revisit the CD World example. Suppose relevant ordering costs per purchase order are $100, while the manager predicts them to be $200 at the time of calculating the order quantity. We can calculate the cost of this "prediction" error using a three-step approach.

Step 1: Compute the Monetary Outcome from the Best Action That Could Be Taken, Given the *Actual* Amount of the Cost Input (Cost per Purchase Order). This is the benchmark, the decision the manager would have made if the manager had known the correct ordering cost against which actual performance can be measured. Using $D = 13,000$ packages per year, $P = \$100$, and $C = \$5.20$ per package per year,

$$EOQ = \sqrt{\frac{2DP}{C}}$$

$$= \sqrt{\frac{2 \times 13,000 \times \$100}{\$5.20}} = \sqrt{500,000}$$

$$= 707 \text{ packages (rounded)}$$

Annual relevant total costs when EOQ = 707 packages are as follows:

$$RTC = \frac{DP}{Q} + \frac{QC}{2}$$

$$= \frac{13,000 \times \$100}{707} + \frac{707 \times \$5.20}{2}$$

$$= \$1,839 + \$1,838 = \$3,677$$

Step 2: Compute the Monetary Outcome from the Best Action Based on the Incorrect *Predicted* Amount of the Cost Input (Cost per Purchase Order). In this step, the manager calculates the order quantity based on the prediction (that later proves to be wrong) that the ordering cost is $200. If the relevant ordering cost per purchase order is predicted to be $200, the best action is to purchase 1,000 packages in each order (p. 706). The actual cost of the purchase order turns out to be $100 so the actual annual relevant total costs when $D = 13,000$ packages per year, $Q = 1,000$ packages, $P = \$100$, and $C = \$5.20$ per package per year are as follows:

$$RTC = \frac{13,000 \times \$100}{1,000} + \frac{1,000 \times \$5.20}{2}$$

$$= \$1,300 + \$2,600 = \$3,900$$

Step 3: Compute the Difference Between the Monetary Outcomes from Step 1 and Step 2.

	Monetary Outcome
Step 1	$3,677
Step 2	3,900
Difference	$ (223)

The cost of the prediction error, $223, is less than 7% of the relevant total costs of $3,677. Note that the annual relevant-total-costs curve in Exhibit 20-1 is somewhat flat over the range of order quantities from 650 to 1,300 units. *The square root in the EOQ model dampens the effect of errors in predicting parameters because taking square roots results in the incorrect numbers becoming smaller.*

In the next section, we consider a planning-and-control and performance-evaluation issue that frequently arises when managing inventory.

Decision Point ▶

What is the effect on costs of errors in predicting parameters of the EOQ model? How can companies reduce the conflict between the EOQ decision model and models used for performance evaluation?

Conflict Between the EOQ Decision Model and Managers' Performance Evaluation

What happens if the order quantity calculated based on the EOQ decision model differs from the order quantity that managers making inventory management decisions would choose to make their own performance look best? For example, because there are no opportunity costs recorded in financial accounting systems, conflicts may arise between the EOQ model's optimal order quantity and the order quantity that purchasing managers (who are evaluated on financial accounting numbers) will regard as optimal. As a result of ignoring some carrying costs (the opportunity costs), managers will be inclined to purchase larger lot sizes of materials than the lot sizes calculated according to the EOQ model. To achieve congruence between the EOQ decision model and managers' performance evaluations, companies such as Wal-Mart design performance-evaluation models that charge managers responsible for managing inventory levels with carrying costs that include a required return on investment.

Just-in-Time Purchasing

Just-in-time (JIT) purchasing is the purchase of materials (or goods) so that they are delivered just as needed for production (or sales). Consider JIT purchasing for Hewlett-Packard's (HP's) manufacture of computer printers. HP has long-term agreements with suppliers for the major components of its printers. Each supplier is required to make frequent deliveries of small orders directly to the production floor, based on the production schedule that HP gives its suppliers. Suppliers work hard to keep their commitments because failure to deliver components on time, or to meet agreed-upon quality standards, can cause an HP assembly plant not to meet its own scheduled deliveries for printers.

Learning Objective 4

Describe why companies are using just-in-time purchasing

. . . high carrying costs, low ordering costs, high-quality suppliers, and reliable supply chains

JIT Purchasing and EOQ Model Parameters

Companies moving toward JIT purchasing to reduce their costs of carrying inventories (parameter C in the EOQ model) say that, in the past, carrying costs have actually been much greater than estimated because costs of warehousing, handling, shrinkage, and investment have not been fully identified. At the same time, the cost of placing a purchase order (parameter P in the EOQ model) is decreasing because of the following:

■ Companies are establishing long-term purchasing agreements that define price and quality terms over an extended period. Individual purchase orders covered by those agreements require no additional negotiation regarding price or quality.

■ Companies are using electronic links to place purchase orders at a cost that is estimated to be a small fraction of the cost of placing orders by telephone or by mail.

■ Companies are using purchase-order cards (similar to consumer credit cards such as VISA and MasterCard). As long as purchasing personnel stay within preset total and individual-transaction dollar limits, traditional labor-intensive procurement-approval procedures are not required.

Exhibit 20-4 tabulates the sensitivity of CD World's EOQ (p. 705) to changes in carrying and ordering costs. Exhibit 20-4 supports JIT purchasing because, as relevant carrying costs increase and relevant ordering costs per purchase order decrease, EOQ decreases and ordering frequency increases.

Relevant Costs of JIT Purchasing

JIT purchasing is not guided solely by the EOQ model. The EOQ model is designed only to emphasize the trade-off between relevant carrying and ordering costs. However, inventory management also includes purchasing costs, stockout costs, costs of quality, and shrinkage costs. We next present the calculation of relevant costs in a JIT purchasing decision.

Exhibit 20-4

Sensitivity of EOQ to Variations in Relevant Ordering and Carrying Costs for CD World

	Home	Insert	Page Layout	Formulas	Data	Review	View
	A	B	C	D	E	F	G
1				**Economic Order Quantity in Units**			
2				**At Different Ordering and Carrying Costs**			
3	**Annual Demand (D) =**	**13,000**	**units**				
4							
5	**Relevant Carrying Costs**			**Relevant Ordering Costs per Purchase Order (P)**			
6	**Per Package per Year (C)**			**$ 200**	**$150**	**$100**	**$ 30**
7	$ 5.20			1,000	866	707	387
8	7.00			862	746	609	334
9	10.00			721	624	510	279
10	15.00			589	510	416	228

Exhibit 20-5   Annual Relevant Costs of Current Purchasing Policy and JIT Purchasing Policy for CD World

| Home | Insert | Page Layout | Formulas | Data | Review | View | | | | |

	A	B	C	D	E	F	G	H	I	J
1					Relevant Costs Under					
2			Current Purchasing Policy					JIT Purchasing Policy		
3	Relevant Items	Relevant Cost Per Unit		Quantity Per Year	Total Costs		Relevant Cost Per Unit		Quantity Per Year	Total Costs
4	(1)	(2)		(3)	(4) = (2) × (3)		(5)		(6)	(7) = (5) × (6)
5	Purchasing costs	$14.00	per unit	13,000	$182,000		$14.02	per unit	13,000	$182,260
6	Ordering costs	2.00	per order	13	26		2.00	per order	130	260
7	Opportunity carrying costs	2.10[a]	per unit of average inventory per year	500[b]	1,050		2.10[a]	per unit of average inventory per year	50[c]	105
8	Other carrying costs (insurance, materials handling, and so on)	3.10	per unit of average inventory per year	500[b]	1,550		3.10	per unit of average inventory per year	50[c]	155
9	Stockout costs	4.00	per unit	0	0		4.00	per unit	150	600
10	Total annual relevant costs				$184,626					$183,380
11	Annual difference in favor of JIT purchasing					$1,246				
12										
13	[a]Purchasing cost per unit × 0.15 per year									
14	[b]Order quantity ÷ 2 = 1,000 ÷ 2 = 500 units									
15	[c]Order quantity ÷ 2 = 100 ÷ 2 = 50 units									

CD World has recently established an Internet business-to-business purchase-order link with Sontek. CD World triggers a purchase order for compact disks by a single computer entry. Payments are made electronically for batches of deliveries, rather than for each individual delivery. These changes reduce the ordering cost from $200 to only $2 per purchase order! CD World will use the Internet purchase-order link whether or not it shifts to JIT purchasing. CD World is negotiating to have Sontek deliver 100 packages of disks 130 times per year (5 times every 2 weeks), instead of delivering 1,000 packages 13 times per year, as shown in Exhibit 20-1. Sontek is willing to make these frequent deliveries, but it would add $0.02 to the price per package. As before, CD World's required rate of return on investment is 15% and the annual relevant carrying cost of insurance, materials handling, shrinkage, breakage, and the like is $3.10 per package per year.

Also assume that CD World incurs no stockout costs under its *current* purchasing policy, because demand and purchase-order lead times during each four-week period are known with certainty. CD World is concerned that lower inventory levels from implementing JIT purchasing will lead to more stockouts, because demand variations and delays in supplying disks are more likely in the short time intervals between orders delivered under JIT purchasing. Sontek has flexible manufacturing processes that enable it to respond rapidly to changing demand patterns. Nevertheless, CD World expects to incur stockout costs on 150 compact disk packages per year under the JIT purchasing policy. When a stockout occurs, CD World must rush-order compact disk packages from another supplier at an additional cost of $4 per package. Should CD World implement the JIT purchasing option of 130 deliveries per year? Exhibit 20-5 compares CD World's relevant total costs under the current purchasing policy and the JIT policy, and it shows net cost savings of $1,246 per year by shifting to a JIT purchasing policy.

Supplier Evaluation and Relevant Costs of Quality and Timely Deliveries

Companies that implement JIT purchasing choose their suppliers carefully and develop long-term supplier relationships. Some suppliers are better positioned than others to support JIT purchasing. For example, Frito-Lay, a supplier of potato chips and other snack foods, has a corporate strategy that emphasizes service, consistency, freshness, and quality of the delivered products. As a result, the company makes deliveries to retail outlets more frequently than many of its competitors.

| Exhibit 20-6 | Annual Relevant Costs of Purchasing from Sontek and Denton |

| | Home | Insert | Page Layout | Formulas | Data | Review | View |

	A	B	C	D	E	F	G	H	I	J
1					Relevant Cost of Purchasing From					
2			Sontek					Denton		
3	Relevant Items	Relevant Cost Per Unit		Quantity Per Year	Total Costs		Relevant Cost Per Unit		Quantity Per Year	Total Costs
4	(1)	(2)		(3)	(4) = (2) × (3)		(5)		(6)	(7) = (5) × (6)
5	Purchasing costs	$14.02	per unit	13,000	$182,260		$13.80	per unit	13,000	$179,400
6	Ordering costs	2.00	per order	130	260		2.00	per order	130	260
7	Inspection costs	0.05	per unit	0	0		0.05	per unit	13,000	650
8	Opportunity carrying costs	2.10[a]	per unit of average inventory per year	50[b]	105		2.07[a]	per unit of average inventory per year	50[b]	103
9	Other carrying costs (insurance, materials handling, and so on)	3.10	per unit of average inventory per year	50[b]	155		3.00	per unit of average inventory per year	50[b]	150
10	Customer return costs	10.00	per unit returned	0	0		10.00	per unit returned	325[c]	3,250
11	Stockout costs	4.00	per unit	150	600		4.00	per unit	360	1,440
12	Total annual relevant costs				$183,380					$185,253
13	Annual difference in favor of Sontek					$1,873				
14										
15	[a]Purchasing cost per unit × 0.15 per year									
16	[b]Order quantity ÷ 2 = 100 ÷ 2 = 50 units									
17	[c]2.5% of units returned × 13,000 units									

What are the relevant total costs when choosing suppliers? Consider again CD World. Denton Corporation, another supplier of disks, offers to supply all of CD World's compact disk needs at a price of $13.80 per package, less than Sontek's price of $14.02, under the same JIT delivery terms that Sontek offers. Denton proposes an Internet purchase-order link identical to Sontek's link, making CD World's ordering cost $2 per purchase order. CD World's relevant cost of insurance, materials handling, breakage, and the like would be $3.00 per package per year if it purchases from Denton, versus $3.10 if it purchases from Sontek. Should CD World buy from Denton? To answer this, we need to consider the relevant costs of quality and delivery performance.

CD World has used Sontek in the past and knows that Sontek will deliver quality disks on time. In fact, CD World does not even inspect the compact disk packages that Sontek supplies and therefore incurs zero inspection costs. Denton, however, does not enjoy such a sterling reputation for quality. CD World anticipates the following negative aspects of using Denton:

- Inspection cost of $0.05 per package.
- Average stockouts of 360 packages per year requiring rush orders at an additional cost of $4 per package.
- Product returns of 2.5% of all packages sold due to poor compact disk quality. CD World estimates an additional cost of $10 to handle each returned package.

Exhibit 20-6 shows the relevant total costs of purchasing from Sontek and Denton. Even though Denton is offering a lower price per package, there is a net cost savings of $1,873 per year by purchasing disks from Sontek. Selling Sontek's high-quality compact disks also enhances CD World's reputation and increases customer goodwill, which could lead to higher sales and profitability in the future.

JIT Purchasing, Planning and Control, and Supply-Chain Analysis

The levels of inventories held by retailers are influenced by the demand patterns of their customers and supply relationships with their distributors and manufacturers, the suppliers to their manufacturers, and so on. The *supply chain* describes the flow of goods, services, and information from the initial sources of materials and services to the delivery of products to consumers, regardless of whether those activities occur in the same company or in other companies. Retailers can purchase inventories on a JIT basis only if activities throughout the supply chain are properly planned, coordinated, and controlled.

Procter and Gamble's (P&G's) experience with its Pampers product illustrates the gains from supply-chain coordination. Retailers selling Pampers encountered variability in weekly demand because families purchased disposable diapers randomly. Anticipating even more demand variability and lacking information about available inventory with P&G, retailers' orders to P&G became more variable that, in turn, increased variability of orders at P&G's suppliers, resulting in high levels of inventory at all stages in the supply chain.

How did P&G respond to these problems? By sharing information and planning and coordinating activities throughout the supply chain among retailers, P&G, and P&G's suppliers. Sharing sales information reduced the level of uncertainty that P&G and its suppliers had about retail demand for Pampers and led to (1) fewer stockouts at the retail level, (2) reduced manufacture of Pampers not immediately needed by retailers, (3) fewer manufacturing orders that had to be "rushed" or "expedited," and (4) lower inventories held by each company in the supply chain. The benefits of supply chain coordination at P&G have been so great that retailers such as Wal-Mart have contracted with P&G to manage Wal-Mart's retail inventories on a just-in-time basis. This practice is called *supplier- or vendor-managed inventory*. Supply-chain management, however, has challenges in sharing accurate, timely, and relevant information about sales, inventory, and sales forecasts caused by problems of communication, trust, incompatible information systems, and limited people and financial resources.

Inventory Management, MRP and JIT Production

We now turn our attention away from purchasing to managing production inventories in manufacturing companies. Managers at manufacturing companies have developed numerous systems to plan and implement inventory activities within their plants. We consider two widely used types of systems: materials requirements planning (MRP) and just-in-time (JIT) production.

Materials Requirements Planning

Materials requirements planning (MRP) is a "push-through" system that manufactures finished goods for inventory on the basis of demand forecasts. To determine outputs at each stage of production, MRP uses (1) demand forecasts for final products; (2) a bill of materials detailing the materials, components, and subassemblies for each final product; and (3) available inventories of materials, components, and products. Taking into account the lead time required to purchase materials and to manufacture components and finished products, a master production schedule specifies the quantity and timing of each item to be produced. Once production starts as scheduled, the output of each department is pushed through the production line. This "push through" can sometimes result in an accumulation of inventory when workstations receive work they are not yet ready to process.

Maintaining accurate inventory records and costs is critical in an MRP system. For example, after becoming aware of the full costs of carrying finished goods inventory in its MRP system, National Semiconductor contracted with Federal Express to airfreight its microchips from a central location in Singapore to customer sites worldwide, instead of storing products at geographically dispersed warehouses. This change enabled National to move products from plant to customer in 4 days rather than 45 days and to reduce distribution costs from 2.6% to 1.9% of revenues. These benefits subsequently led National to outsource all its shipping activities to Federal Express.

MRP is a push-through approach. We now consider JIT production, a "demand-pull" approach, which is used by companies such as Toyota in the automobile industry, Dell in the computer industry, and Braun in the appliance industry.

JIT Production

Just-in-time (JIT) production, which is also called **lean production**, is a "demand-pull" manufacturing system that manufactures each component in a production line as soon as, and only when, needed by the next step in the production line. In a JIT production line, manufacturing activity at any particular workstation is prompted by the need for that workstation's output at the following workstation. Demand triggers each step of the production process, starting with customer demand for a finished product at the end of the process and working all the way back to the demand for direct materials at the beginning of the process. In this way, demand pulls an order through the production line. The demand-pull feature of JIT production systems achieves close coordination among workstations. It smooths the flow of goods, despite low quantities of inventory. JIT production systems aim to simultaneously (1) meet customer demand in a timely manner (2) with high-quality products and (3) at the lowest possible total cost.

Decision Point

How do materials requirements planning (MRP) systems differ from just-in-time (JIT) production systems?

Features of JIT Production Systems

A JIT production system has these features:

- Production is organized in **manufacturing cells**, groupings of all the different types of equipment used to make a given product. Materials move from one machine to another, and various operations are performed in sequence, minimizing materials-handling costs.

- Workers are hired and trained to be multiskilled and capable of performing a variety of operations and tasks, including minor repairs and routine equipment maintenance.

- Defects are aggressively eliminated. Because of the tight links between workstations in the production line and the minimal inventories at each workstation, defects arising at one workstation quickly affect other workstations in the line. JIT creates an urgency for solving problems immediately and eliminating the root causes of defects as quickly as possible. Low levels of inventories allow workers to trace problems to and solve problems at earlier workstations in the production process, where the problems likely originated.

- *Setup time*, the time required to get equipment, tools, and materials ready to start the production of a component or product, and *manufacturing cycle time*, the time from when an order is received by manufacturing until it becomes a finished good, are reduced. Setup costs correspond to the ordering costs P in the EOQ model. Reducing setup time and costs makes production in smaller batches economical, which in turn reduces inventory levels. Reducing manufacturing cycle time enables a company to respond faster to changes in customer demand (see also Concepts in Action, p. 717).

- Suppliers are selected on the basis of their ability to deliver quality materials in a timely manner. Most companies implementing *JIT production* also implement *JIT purchasing*. JIT plants expect JIT suppliers to make timely deliveries of high-quality goods directly to the production floor.

We next present a relevant-cost analysis for deciding whether to implement a JIT production system.

Learning Objective 6

Identify the features and benefits of a just-in-time production system

. . . for example, organizing work in manufacturing cells, improving quality, and reducing manufacturing lead time to reduce costs and earn higher margins

Financial Benefits of JIT and Relevant Costs

Early advocates saw the benefit of JIT production as lower carrying costs of inventory. But there are other benefits of lower inventories: heightened emphasis on improving quality by eliminating the specific causes of rework, scrap, and waste, and lower manufacturing cycle times. In computing the relevant benefits and costs of reducing inventories in JIT production systems, the cost analyst should take into account all benefits and all costs.

Consider Hudson Corporation, a manufacturer of brass fittings. Hudson is considering implementing a JIT production system. To implement JIT production, Hudson must incur $100,000 in annual tooling costs to reduce setup times. Hudson expects that JIT will reduce average inventory by $500,000 and that relevant costs of insurance, storage, materials handling, and setup will decline by $30,000 per year. The company's required rate of return on inventory investments is 10% per year. Should Hudson implement a JIT production system? On the basis of the information provided, we would be tempted to say "no," because annual relevant total cost savings amount to $80,000 [(10% of $500,000) + $30,000)], which is less than the additional annual tooling costs of $100,000.

Our analysis, however, is incomplete. We have not considered the other benefits of lower inventories in JIT production. Hudson estimates that implementing JIT will improve quality and reduce rework on 500 units each year, resulting in savings of $50 per unit. Also, better quality and faster delivery will allow Hudson to charge $2 more per unit on the 20,000 units that it sells each year.

The annual relevant benefits and costs from implementing JIT equal the following:

Incremental savings in insurance, storage, materials handling, and set up	$ 30,000
Incremental savings in inventory carrying costs (10% × $500,000)	50,000
Incremental savings from reduced rework ($50 per unit × 500 units)	25,000
Additional contribution margin from better quality and faster delivery ($2 per unit × 20,000 units)	40,000
Incremental annual tooling costs	(100,000)
Net incremental benefit	$ 45,000

Therefore, Hudson *should* implement a JIT production system.

JIT in Service Industries

JIT purchasing and production methods can be applied in service industries as well. For example, inventories and supplies, and the associated labor costs to manage them, represent more than a third of the costs in most hospitals. By implementing a JIT purchasing and distribution system, Eisenhower Memorial Hospital in Palm Springs, California, reduced its inventories and supplies by 90% in 18 months. McDonald's has adapted JIT production practices to making hamburgers.[3] Before, McDonald's precooked a batch of hamburgers that were placed under heat lamps to stay warm until ordered. If the hamburgers didn't sell within a specified period of time, they were discarded resulting in high inventory holding costs and spoilage costs. Moreover, the quality of hamburgers deteriorated the longer they sat under the heat lamps. Finally, customers placing a special order for a hamburger (such as a hamburger with no cheese) had to wait for the hamburger to be cooked. Today, the use of new technology (including an innovative bun toaster) and JIT production practices allow McDonald's to cook hamburgers only when they are ordered, significantly reducing inventory holding and spoilage costs. More importantly, JIT has improved customer satisfaction by increasing the quality of hamburgers and reducing the time needed for special orders.

We next turn our attention to planning and control in JIT production systems.

Enterprise Resource Planning (ERP) Systems[4]

The success of a JIT production system hinges on the speed of information flows from customers to manufacturers to suppliers. Information flows are a problem for large companies that have fragmented information systems spread over dozens of unlinked computer systems. Enterprise Resource Planning (ERP) systems improve these information flows. An ERP system is an integrated set of software modules covering accounting, distribution, manufacturing, purchasing, human resources, and other functions. ERP uses a single database to collect and feed data into all software applications, allowing integrated, real-time information sharing and providing visibility to the company's business processes as a whole. For example, using an ERP system, a salesperson can

---

[3] Charles Atkinson, "McDonald's, A Guide to the Benefits of JIT," *Inventory Management Review*, www.inventorymanagementreview.org/2005/11/mcdonalds_a_gui.html (accessed May 2, 2007).
[4] For an excellent discussion, see T. H. Davenport, "Putting the Enterprise into the Enterprise System," *Harvard Business Review*, (July–August 1998); also see A. Cagilo, "Enterprise Resource Planning Systems and Accountants: Towards Hybridization?" *European Accounting Review*, (May 2003).

Concepts in Action

After the Encore: Just-in-Time Live Concert Recordings

Each year, millions of music fans flock to concerts to see artists ranging from Lady Gaga to rock-band O.A.R. Although many of them stop by the merchandise stand to pick up a t-shirt or poster after the show ends, they increasingly have another option: buying a professional recording of the concert they just saw! Just-in-time production, enabled by recent advances in audio and computer technology, now allows fans to relive the live concert experience just a few minutes after the final chord is played.

Live concert recordings have long been hampered by production and distribution difficulties. Traditionally, fans could only hear these recordings via unofficial "bootleg" cassettes or CDs. Occasionally, artists would release official live albums between studio releases. Further, live albums typically sold few copies, and retail outlets that profit from volume-driven merchandise turnover, like Best Buy, were somewhat reluctant to carry them.

Enter instant concert recordings. Organizations such as Adreea, Concert Live, and Live Nation employ microphones, recording and audio mixing hardware and software, and an army of high-speed computers to produce concert recordings during the show. As soon as each song is complete, engineers burn that track onto hundreds of CDs or USB drives. At the end of the show, they have to burn only one last song. Once completed, the CDs or USB drives are packaged and rushed to merchandise stands throughout the venue for instant sale.

There are, of course, some limitations to this technology. With such a quick turnaround time, engineers cannot edit or remaster any aspect of the show. Also, although just-in-time live recordings work successfully in smaller venues, the logistics for arenas, amphitheatres, and stadiums are much more difficult. Despite these concerns, the benefits of this new technology include sound-quality assurance, near-immediate production turnaround, and low finished-goods carrying costs. These recordings can also be distributed through Apple's iTunes platform and artist Web sites, making live recordings more accessible than ever. With such opportunities, it's no wonder that bands like O.A.R. augment their existing CD sales with just-in-time recordings.

Sources: Buskirk, Eliot Van. 2009. Apple unveils 'live music' in iTunes. *Wired.* "Epicenter," blog November 24. www.wired.com/epicenter/2009/11/apple-unveils-live-music-in-itunes/ Chartrand, Sabra. 2004. How to take the concert home. *New York Times,* May 3. www.nytimes.com/2004/05/03/technology/03patent.html *Daily Telegraph.* 2009. Online exclusive: How Concert Live co-founders overcame barriers. February 3. www.telegraph.co.uk/sponsored/business/businesstruth/diary_of_a/4448290/Online-Exclusive-How-Concert-Live-co-founders-overcame-barriers.html Humphries, Stephen. 2003. Get your official 'bootleg' here. *Christian Science Monitor,* November 21. www.csmonitor.com/2003/1121/p16s01-almp.html *Websites:* Live O.A.R. http://liveoar.com/store/first_index.php Aderra. www.aderra.net/ Concert Live. www.concertlive.co.uk/

generate a contract for a customer in Germany, verify the customer's credit limits, and place a production order. The system then uses this same information to schedule manufacturing in, say, Brazil, requisition materials from inventory, order components from suppliers, and schedule shipments. At the same time, it credits sales commissions to the salesperson and records all the costing and financial accounting information.

ERP systems give lower-level managers, workers, customers, and suppliers access to detailed and timely operating information. This benefit, coupled with tight coordination across business functions of the value chain, enables ERP systems to shift manufacturing and distribution plans rapidly in response to changes in supply and demand. Companies believe that an ERP system is essential to support JIT initiatives because of the effect it has on lead times. Using an ERP system, Autodesk, a maker of computer-aided design software, reduced order lead time from two weeks to one day; and Fujitsu reduced lead time from 18 days to 1.5 days.

ERP systems are large and unwieldy. Because of its complexity, suppliers of ERP systems such as SAP and Oracle provide software packages that are standard but that can be customized, although at considerable cost. Without some customization, unique and distinctive features that confer strategic advantage will not be available. The challenge when implementing ERP systems is to strike the proper balance between the lower cost of standardized systems and the strategic benefits that accrue from customization.

Performance Measures and Control in JIT Production

In addition to personal observation, managers use financial and nonfinancial measures to evaluate and control JIT production. We describe these measures and indicate the effect that JIT systems are expected to have on these measures.

1. Financial performance measures, such as inventory turnover ratio (Cost of goods sold ÷ Average inventory), which is expected to increase

2. Nonfinancial performance measures of inventory, quality, and time such as the following:
   - Number of days of inventory on hand, expected to decrease
   - Units produced per hour, expected to increase
   - $\dfrac{\text{Number of units scrapped or requiring rework}}{\text{Total number of units started and completed}}$, expected to decrease
   - Manufacturing cycle time, expected to decrease
   - $\dfrac{\text{Total setup time for machines}}{\text{Total manufacturing time}}$, expected to decrease

Personal observation and nonfinancial performance measures provide the most timely, intuitive, and easy to understand measures of manufacturing performance. Rapid, meaningful feedback is critical because the lack of inventories in a demand-pull system makes it urgent to detect and solve problems quickly. JIT measures can also be incorporated into the four perspectives of the balanced scorecard (financial, customer, internal business process, and learning and growth). The logic is as follows: Multiskilled, and well-trained employees (learning and growth measures) improve internal business processes measured by the preceding inventory, quality, and time measures. As operational performance improves, customer satisfaction also increases because of greater flexibility, responsiveness, and quality resulting in better financial performance from lower purchasing, inventory holding, and quality costs, and higher revenues.

Effect of JIT Systems on Product Costing

Decision Point

What are the features and benefits of a JIT production system?

By reducing materials handling, warehousing, and inspection, JIT systems reduce overhead costs. JIT systems also aid in direct tracing of some costs usually classified as indirect. For example, the use of manufacturing cells makes it cost-effective to trace materials handling and machine operating costs to specific products or product families made in these cells. These costs then become direct costs of those products. Also, the use of multi-skilled workers in these cells allows the costs of setup, maintenance, and quality inspection to be traced as direct costs. These changes have prompted some companies using JIT to adopt simplified product costing methods that dovetail with JIT production and that are less costly to operate than the traditional costing systems described in Chapters 4, 7, 8, and 17. We examine two of these methods next: backflush costing and lean accounting.

Backflush Costing

Learning Objective 7

Describe different ways backflush costing can simplify traditional inventory-costing systems

. . . for example, by not recording journal entries for work in process, purchase of materials, or production of finished goods

Organizing manufacturing in cells, reducing defects and manufacturing cycle time, and ensuring timely delivery of materials enables purchasing, production, and sales to occur in quick succession with minimal inventories. The absence of inventories makes choices about cost-flow assumptions (such as weighted average or first-in, first-out) or inventory-costing methods (such as absorption or variable costing) unimportant: All manufacturing costs of the accounting period flow directly into cost of goods sold. The rapid conversion of direct materials into finished goods that are immediately sold greatly simplifies the costing system.

Simplified Normal or Standard Costing Systems

Traditional normal or standard-costing systems (Chapters 4, 7, 8, and 17) use **sequential tracking**, which is a costing system in which recording of the journal entries occurs in the same order as actual purchases and progress in production. Costs are tracked sequentially as products pass through each of the following four stages:

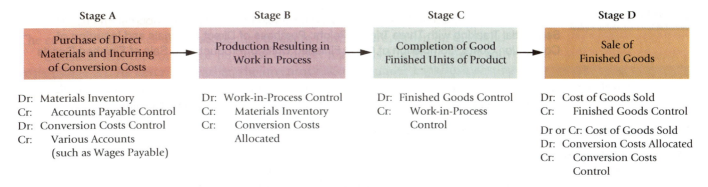

Stage A	Stage B	Stage C	Stage D
Purchase of Direct Materials and Incurring of Conversion Costs	**Production Resulting in Work in Process**	**Completion of Good Finished Units of Product**	**Sale of Finished Goods**

Stage A:
Dr: Materials Inventory
Cr: Accounts Payable Control
Dr: Conversion Costs Control
Cr: Various Accounts (such as Wages Payable)

Stage B:
Dr: Work-in-Process Control
Cr: Materials Inventory
Cr: Conversion Costs Allocated

Stage C:
Dr: Finished Goods Control
Cr: Work-in-Process Control

Stage D:
Dr: Cost of Goods Sold
Cr: Finished Goods Control

Dr or Cr: Cost of Goods Sold
Dr: Conversion Costs Allocated
Cr: Conversion Costs Control

A sequential-tracking costing system has four *trigger points*, corresponding to Stages A, B, C, and D. A **trigger point** is a stage in the cycle, from purchase of direct materials and incurring of conversion costs (Stage A) to sale of finished goods (Stage D), at which journal entries are made in the accounting system. The journal entries (with Dr. representing debits and Cr. representing credits) for each stage are displayed below the box for that stage (as described in Chapter 4).

An alternative approach to sequential tracking is backflush costing. **Backflush costing** is a costing system that omits recording some of the journal entries relating to the stages from purchase of direct materials to the sale of finished goods. When journal entries for one or more stages are omitted, the journal entries for a subsequent stage use normal or standard costs to work backward to "flush out" the costs in the cycle for which journal entries were *not* made. When inventories are minimal, as in JIT production systems, backflush costing simplifies costing systems without losing much information.

Consider the following data for the month of April for Silicon Valley Computer (SVC), which produces keyboards for personal computers.

- There are no beginning inventories of direct materials and no beginning or ending work-in-process inventories.

- SVC has only one direct manufacturing cost category (direct materials) and one indirect manufacturing cost category (conversion costs). All manufacturing labor costs are included in conversion costs.

- From its bill of materials and an operations list (description of operations to be undergone), SVC determines that the standard direct material cost per keyboard unit is $19 and the standard conversion cost is $12.

- SVC purchases $1,950,000 of direct materials. To focus on the basic concepts, we assume SVC has no direct materials variances. Actual conversion costs equal $1,260,000. SVC produces 100,000 good keyboard units and sells 99,000 units.

- Any underallocated or overallocated conversion costs are written off to cost of goods sold at the end of April.

We use three examples to illustrate backflush costing. *They differ in the number and placement of trigger points.*

Example 1: The three trigger points for journal entries are Purchase of direct materials and incurring of conversion costs (Stage A), Completion of good finished units of product (Stage C), and Sale of finished goods (Stage D).

Note that there is no journal entry for Production resulting in work in process (Stage B) because JIT production has minimal work in process.

SVC records two inventory accounts:

Type	Account Title
Combined materials inventory and materials in work in process	Materials and In-Process Inventory Control
Finished goods	Finished Goods Control

Exhibit 20-7, Panel A, summarizes the journal entries for Example 1 with three trigger points: Purchase of direct materials and incurring of conversion costs, Completion of good

The purchasing lead time is 2 weeks. The Denim World is open 250 days a year (50 weeks for 5 days a week).

Required

1. Calculate the EOQ for denim cloth.
2. Calculate the number of orders that will be placed each year.
3. Calculate the reorder point for denim cloth.

20-19 EOQ for manufacturer. Lakeland Company produces lawn mowers and purchases 18,000 units of a rotor blade part each year at a cost of $60 per unit. Lakeland requires a 15% annual rate of return on investment. In addition, the relevant carrying cost (for insurance, materials handling, breakage, and so on) is $6 per unit per year. The relevant ordering cost per purchase order is $150.

Required

1. Calculate Lakeland's EOQ for the rotor blade part.
2. Calculate Lakeland's annual relevant ordering costs for the EOQ calculated in requirement 1.
3. Calculate Lakeland's annual relevant carrying costs for the EOQ calculated in requirement 1.
4. Assume that demand is uniform throughout the year and known with certainty so that there is no need for safety stocks. The purchase-order lead time is half a month. Calculate Lakeland's reorder point for the rotor blade part.

20-20 Sensitivity of EOQ to changes in relevant ordering and carrying costs, cost of prediction error. Alpha Company's annual demand for its only product, XT-590, is 10,000 units. Alpha is currently analyzing possible combinations of relevant carrying cost per unit per year and relevant ordering cost per purchase order, depending on the company's choice of supplier and average levels of inventory. This table presents three possible combinations of carrying and ordering costs.

Relevant Carrying Cost per Unit per Year	Relevant Ordering Cost per Purchase Order
$10	$400
$20	$200
$40	$100

Required

1. For each of the relevant ordering and carrying-cost alternatives, determine (a) EOQ and (b) annual relevant total costs.
2. How does your answer to requirement 1 give insight into the impact of changes in relevant ordering and carrying costs on EOQ and annual relevant total costs? Explain briefly.
3. Suppose the relevant carrying cost per unit per year was $20 and the relevant ordering cost per purchase order was $200. Suppose further that Alpha calculates EOQ after incorrectly estimating relevant carrying cost per unit per year to be $10 and relevant ordering cost per purchase order to be $400. Calculate the actual annual relevant total costs of Alpha's EOQ decision. Compare this cost to the annual relevant total costs that Alpha would have incurred if it had correctly estimated the relevant carrying cost per unit per year of $20 and the relevant ordering cost per purchase order of $200 that you have already calculated in requirement 1. Calculate and comment on the cost of the prediction error.

20-21 Inventory management and the balanced scorecard. Devin Sports Cars (DSC) has implemented a balanced scorecard to measure and support its just-in-time production system. In the learning and growth category, DSC measures the percentage of employees who are cross-trained to perform a wide variety of production tasks. Internal business process measures are inventory turns and on-time delivery. The customer perspective is measured using a customer satisfaction measure and financial performance using operating income. DSC estimates that if it can increase the percentage of cross-trained employees by 5%, the resulting increase in labor productivity will reduce inventory-related costs by $100,000 per year and shorten delivery times by 10%. The 10% reduction in delivery times, in turn, is expected to increase customer satisfaction by 5%, and each 1% increase in customer satisfaction is expected to increase revenues by 2% due to higher prices.

Required

1. Assume that budgeted revenues in the coming year are $5,000,000. Ignoring the costs of training, what is the expected increase in operating income in the coming year if the number of cross-trained employees is increased by 5%?
2. What is the most DSC would be willing to pay to increase the percentage of cross-trained employees if it is only interested in maximizing operating income in the coming year?
3. What factors other than short-term profits should DSC consider when assessing the benefits from employee cross-training?

20-22 JIT production, relevant benefits, relevant costs. The Champion Hardware Company manufactures specialty brass door handles at its Lynchburg plant. Champion is considering implementing a JIT production system. The following are the estimated costs and benefits of JIT production:

a. Annual additional tooling costs would be $100,000.
b. Average inventory would decline by 80% from the current level of $1,000,000.

c. Insurance, space, materials-handling, and setup costs, which currently total $300,000 annually, would decline by 25%.

d. The emphasis on quality inherent in JIT production would reduce rework costs by 30%. Champion currently incurs $200,000 in annual rework costs.

e. Improved product quality under JIT production would enable Champion to raise the price of its product by $4 per unit. Champion sells 40,000 units each year.

Champion's required rate of return on inventory investment is 15% per year.

Required

1. Calculate the net benefit or cost to Champion if it adopts JIT production at the Lynchburg plant.
2. What nonfinancial and qualitative factors should Champion consider when making the decision to adopt JIT production?
3. Suppose Champion implements JIT production at its Lynchburg plant. Give examples of performance measures Champion could use to evaluate and control JIT production. What would be the benefit of Champion implementing an enterprise resource planning (ERP) system?

20-23 Backflush costing and JIT production. Road Warrior Corporation assembles handheld computers that have scaled-down capabilities of laptop computers. Each handheld computer takes six hours to assemble. Road Warrior uses a JIT production system and a backflush costing system with three trigger points:

- Purchase of direct materials and incurring of conversion costs
- Completion of good finished units of product
- Sale of finished goods

There are no beginning inventories of materials or finished goods and no beginning or ending work-in-process inventories. The following data are for August 2011:

Direct materials purchased	$2,754,000	Conversion costs incurred	$723,600
Direct materials used	$2,733,600	Conversion costs allocated	$750,400

Road Warrior records direct materials purchased and conversion costs incurred at actual costs. It has no direct materials variances. When finished goods are sold, the backflush costing system "pulls through" standard direct material cost ($102 per unit) and standard conversion cost ($28 per unit). Road Warrior produced 26,800 finished units in August 2011 and sold 26,400 units. The actual direct material cost per unit in August 2011 was $102, and the actual conversion cost per unit was $27.

Required

1. Prepare summary journal entries for August 2011 (without disposing of under- or overallocated conversion costs).
2. Post the entries in requirement 1 to T-accounts for applicable Materials and In-Process Inventory Control, Finished Goods Control, Conversion Costs Control, Conversion Costs Allocated, and Cost of Goods Sold.
3. Under an ideal JIT production system, how would the amounts in your journal entries differ from those in requirement 1?

20-24 Backflush costing, two trigger points, materials purchase and sale (continuation of 20-23). Assume the same facts as in Exercise 20-23, except that Road Warrior now uses a backflush costing system with the following two trigger points:

- Purchase of direct materials and incurring of conversion costs
- Sale of finished goods

The Inventory Control account will include direct materials purchased but not yet in production, materials in work in process, and materials in finished goods but not sold. No conversion costs are inventoried. Any under- or overallocated conversion costs are written off monthly to Cost of Goods Sold.

Required

1. Prepare summary journal entries for August, including the disposition of under- or overallocated conversion costs.
2. Post the entries in requirement 1 to T-accounts for Inventory Control, Conversion Costs Control, Conversion Costs Allocated, and Cost of Goods Sold.

20-25 Backflush costing, two trigger points, completion of production and sale (continuation of 20-23). Assume the same facts as in Exercise 20-23, except now Road Warrior uses only two trigger points, Completion of good finished units of product and Sale of finished goods. Any under- or overallocated conversion costs are written off monthly to Cost of Goods Sold.

Required

1. Prepare summary journal entries for August, including the disposition of under- or overallocated conversion costs.
2. Post the entries in requirement 1 to T-accounts for Finished Goods Control, Conversion Costs Control, Conversion Costs Allocated, and Cost of Goods Sold.

Problems

20-26 Effect of different order quantities on ordering costs and carrying costs, EOQ. Soothing Meadow, a retailer of bed and bath linen, sells 380,000 packages of Mona Lisa designer sheets each year. Soothing Meadow incurs an ordering cost of $57 per purchase order placed with Mona Lisa Enterprises and an annual carrying cost of $12.00 per package. Liv Carrol, purchasing manager at Soothing Meadow, seeks your help: She wants to understand how ordering and carrying costs vary with order quantity.

	Scenario				
	1	**2**	**3**	**4**	**5**
Annual demand (packages)	380,000	380,000	380,000	380,000	380,000
Cost per purchase order	$ 57	$ 57	$ 57	$ 57	$ 57
Carrying cost per package per year	$ 12.00	$ 12.00	$ 12.00	$ 12.00	$ 12.00
Quantity (packages) per purchase order	760	1,000	1,900	3,800	4,750
Number of purchase orders per year					
Annual relevant ordering costs					
Annual relevant carrying costs					
Annual relevant total costs of ordering and carrying inventory					

Required

1. Complete the table for Liv Carrol. What is the EOQ? Comment on your results.
2. Mona Lisa is about to introduce a Web-based ordering system for its customers. Liv Carrol estimates that Soothing Meadow's ordering costs will reduce to $30 per purchase order. Calculate the new EOQ and the new annual relevant costs of ordering and carrying inventory.
3. Liv Carrol estimates that Soothing Meadow will incur a cost of $2,150 to train its two purchasing assistants to use the new Mona Lisa system. Will Soothing Meadow recoup its training costs within the first year of adoption?

20-27 EOQ, uncertainty, safety stock, reorder point. Chadwick Shoe Co. produces and sells an excellent quality walking shoe. After production, the shoes are distributed to 20 warehouses around the country. Each warehouse services approximately 100 stores in its region. Chadwick uses an EOQ model to determine the number of pairs of shoes to order for each warehouse from the factory. Annual demand for Warehouse OR2 is approximately 120,000 pairs of shoes. The ordering cost is $250 per order. The annual carrying cost of a pair of shoes is $2.40 per pair.

Required

1. Use the EOQ model to determine the optimal number of pairs of shoes per order.
2. Assume each month consists of approximately 4 weeks. If it takes 1 week to receive an order, at what point should warehouse OR2 reorder shoes?
3. Although OR2's average weekly demand is 2,500 pairs of shoes (120,000 ÷ 12 months ÷ 4 weeks), demand each week may vary with the following probability distribution:

Total demand for 1 week	2,000 pairs	2,250 pairs	2,500 pairs	2,750 pairs	3,000 pairs
Probability (sums to 1.00)	0.04	0.20	0.52	0.20	0.04

If a store wants shoes and OR2 has none in stock, OR2 can "rush" them to the store at an additional cost of $2 per pair. How much safety stock should Warehouse OR2 hold? How will this affect the reorder point and reorder quantity?

20-28 MRP, EOQ, and JIT. Global Tunes Corp. produces J-Pods, music players that can download thousands of songs. Global Tunes forecasts that demand in 2011 will be 48,000 J-Pods. The variable production cost of each J-Pod is $54. Due to the large $10,000 cost per setup, Global Tunes plans to produce J-Pods once a month in batches of 4,000 each. The carrying cost of a unit in inventory is $17 per year.

Required

1. Using an MRP system, what is the annual cost of producing and carrying J-Pods in inventory? (Assume that, on average, half of the units produced in a month are in inventory.)
2. A new manager at Global Tunes has suggested that the company use the EOQ model to determine the optimal batch size to produce. (To use the EOQ model, Global Tunes needs to treat the setup cost in the same way it would treat ordering cost in a traditional EOQ model.) Determine the optimal batch size and number of batches. Round up the number of batches to the nearest whole number. What would be the annual cost of producing and carrying J-Pods in inventory if it uses the optimal batch size? Compare this cost to the cost calculated in requirement 1. Comment briefly.
3. Global Tunes is also considering switching from an MRP system to a JIT system. This will result in producing J-Pods in batch sizes of 600 J-Pods and will reduce obsolescence, improve quality, and result in a higher selling price. The frequency of production batches will force Global Tunes to reduce setup

time and will result in a reduction in setup cost. The new setup cost will be $500 per setup. What is the annual cost of producing and carrying J-Pods in inventory under the JIT system?

4. Compare the models analyzed in the previous parts of the problem. What are the advantages and disadvantages of each?

20-29 Effect of management evaluation criteria on EOQ model. Computers 4 U purchases one model of computer at a wholesale cost of $200 per unit and resells it to end consumers. The annual demand for the company's product is 500,000 units. Ordering costs are $800 per order and carrying costs are $50 per computer, including $20 in the opportunity cost of holding inventory.

Required

1. Compute the optimal order quantity using the EOQ model.
2. Compute a) the number of orders per year and b) the annual relevant total cost of ordering and carrying inventory.
3. Assume that when evaluating the manager, the company excludes the opportunity cost of carrying inventory. If the manager makes the EOQ decision excluding the opportunity cost of carrying inventory, the relevant carrying cost would be $30 not $50. How would this affect the EOQ amount and the actual annual relevant cost of ordering and carrying inventory?
4. What is the cost impact on the company of excluding the opportunity cost of carrying inventory when making EOQ decisions? Why do you think the company currently excludes the opportunity costs of carrying inventory when evaluating the manager's performance? What could the company do to encourage the manager to make decisions more congruent with the goal of reducing total inventory costs?

20-30 JIT purchasing, relevant benefits, relevant costs. (CMA, adapted) The Margro Corporation is an automotive supplier that uses automatic turning machines to manufacture precision parts from steel bars. Margro's inventory of raw steel averages $600,000. John Oates, president of Margro, and Helen Gorman, Margro's controller, are concerned about the costs of carrying inventory. The steel supplier is willing to supply steel in smaller lots at no additional charge. Gorman identifies the following effects of adopting a JIT inventory program to virtually eliminate steel inventory:

■ Without scheduling any overtime, lost sales due to stockouts would increase by 35,000 units per year. However, by incurring overtime premiums of $40,000 per year, the increase in lost sales could be reduced to 20,000 units per year. This would be the maximum amount of overtime that would be feasible for Margro.

■ Two warehouses currently used for steel bar storage would no longer be needed. Margro rents one warehouse from another company under a cancelable leasing arrangement at an annual cost of $60,000. The other warehouse is owned by Margro and contains 12,000 square feet. Three-fourths of the space in the owned warehouse could be rented for $1.50 per square foot per year. Insurance and property tax costs totaling $14,000 per year would be eliminated.

Margro's required rate of return on investment is 20% per year. Margro's budgeted income statement for the year ending December 31, 2011 (in thousands) is as follows:

Revenues (900,000 units)		$10,800
Cost of goods sold		
Variable costs	$4,050	
Fixed costs	1,450	
Total costs of goods sold		5,500
Gross margin		5,300
Marketing and distribution costs		
Variable costs	$ 900	
Fixed costs	1,500	
Total marketing and distribution costs		2,400
Operating income		$ 2,900

Required

1. Calculate the estimated dollar savings (loss) for the Margro Corporation that would result in 2011 from the adoption of JIT purchasing.
2. Identify and explain other factors that Margro should consider before deciding whether to adopt JIT purchasing.

20-31 Supply chain effects on total relevant inventory cost. Cow Spot Computer Co. outsources the production of motherboards for its computers. It is currently deciding which of two suppliers to use: Maji or Induk. Due to differences in the product failure rates across the two companies, 5% of motherboards purchased from Maji will be inspected and 25% of motherboards purchased from Induk will be inspected. The following data refers to costs associated with Maji and Induk.

	Maji	Induk
Number of orders per year	50	50
Annual motherboards demanded	10,000	10,000
Price per motherboard	$93	$90
Ordering cost per order	$10	$8
Inspection cost per unit	$5	$5
Average inventory level	100 units	100 units
Expected number of stockouts	100	300
Stockout cost (cost of rush order) per stockout	$5	$8
Units returned by customers for replacing motherboards	50	500
Cost of replacing each motherboard	$25	$25
Required annual return on investment	10%	10%
Other carrying cost per unit per year	$2.50	$2.50

Required

1. What is the relevant cost of purchasing from Maji and Induk?
2. What factors other than cost should Cow Spot consider?

20-32 Backflush costing and JIT production. The Rippel Corporation manufactures electrical meters. For August, there were no beginning inventories of direct materials and no beginning or ending work in process. Rippel uses a JIT production system and backflush costing with three trigger points for making entries in the accounting system:

- Purchase of direct materials and incurring of conversion costs
- Completion of good finished units of product
- Sale of finished goods

Rippel's August standard cost per meter is direct material, $26, and conversion cost, $19. Rippel has no direct materials variances. The following data apply to August manufacturing:

Direct materials purchased	$546,000	Number of finished units manufactured	20,000
Conversion costs incurred	$399,000	Number of finished units sold	19,000

Required

1. Prepare summary journal entries for August (without disposing of under- or overallocated conversion costs). Assume no direct materials variances.
2. Post the entries in requirement 1 to T-accounts for Materials and In-Process Inventory Control, Finished Goods Control, Conversion Costs Control, Conversion Costs Allocated, and Cost of Goods Sold.

20-33 Backflush, two trigger points, materials purchase and sale (continuation of 20-32). Assume that the second trigger point for Rippel Corporation is the sale—rather than the completion—of finished goods. Also, the inventory account is confined solely to direct materials, whether these materials are in a storeroom, in work in process, or in finished goods. No conversion costs are inventoried. They are allocated to the units sold at standard costs. Any under- or overallocated conversion costs are written off monthly to Cost of Goods Sold.

Required

1. Prepare summary journal entries for August, including the disposition of under- or overallocated conversion costs. Assume no direct materials variances.
2. Post the entries in requirement 1 to T-accounts for Inventory Control, Conversion Costs Control, Conversion Costs Allocated, and Cost of Goods Sold.

20-34 Backflush, two trigger points, completion of production and sale (continuation of 20-32). Assume the same facts as in Problem 20-32 except now there are only two trigger points: Completion of good finished units of product and Sale of finished goods.

Required

1. Prepare summary journal entries for August, including the disposition of under- or overallocated conversion costs. Assume no direct materials variances.
2. Post the entries in requirement 1 to T-accounts for Finished Goods Control, Conversion Costs Control, Conversion Costs Allocated, and Cost of Goods Sold.

20-35 Lean Accounting. Flexible Security Devices (FSD) has introduced a just-in-time production process and is considering the adoption of lean accounting principles to support its new production philosophy. The company has two product lines: Mechanical Devices and Electronic Devices. Two individual products are made in each line. Product-line manufacturing overhead costs are traced directly to product lines, and then allocated to the two individual products in each line. The company's traditional cost accounting system allocates all plant-level facility costs and some corporate overhead costs to individual products. The latest accounting report using traditional cost accounting methods included the following information (in thousands of dollars).

	Mechanical Devices		Electronic Devices	
	Product A	Product B	Product C	Product D
Sales	$700	$500	$900	$450
Direct material (based on quantity used)	200	100	250	75
Direct manufacturing labor	150	75	200	60
Manufacturing overhead (equipment lease, supervision, production control)	90	120	200	95
Allocated plant-level facility costs	50	40	80	30
Design and marketing costs	95	50	105	42
Allocated corporate overhead costs	15	10	20	8
Operating income	$100	$105	$ 45	$140

FSD has determined that each of the two product lines represents a distinct value stream. It has also determined that out of the $200,000 ($50,000 + $40,000 + $80,000 + $30,000) plant-level facility costs, product A occupies 22% of the plant's square footage, product B occupies 18%, product C occupies 36%, and product D occupies 14%. The remaining 10% of square footage is not being used. Finally, FSD has decided that direct material should be expensed in the period it is purchased, rather than when the material is used. According to purchasing records, direct material purchase costs during the period were as follows:

	Mechanical Devices		Electronic Devices	
	Product A	Product B	Product C	Product D
Direct material (purchases)	$210	$120	$250	$90

Required

1. What are the cost objects in FSD's lean accounting system?
2. Compute operating income for the cost objects identified in requirement 1 using lean accounting principles. Why does operating income differ from the operating income computed using traditional cost accounting methods? Comment on your results.

Collaborative Learning Problem

20-36 JIT production, relevant benefits, relevant costs, ethics. Parson Container Corporation is considering implementing a JIT production system. The new system would reduce current average inventory levels of $2,000,000 by 75%, but would require a much greater dependency on the company's core suppliers for on-time deliveries and high quality inputs. The company's operations manager, Jim Ingram, is opposed to the idea of a new JIT system. He is concerned that the new system will be too costly to manage; will result in too many stockouts; and will lead to the layoff of his employees, several of whom are currently managing inventory. He believes that these layoffs will affect the morale of his entire production department. The plant controller, Sue Winston is in favor of the new system, due to the likely cost savings. Jim wants Sue to rework the numbers because he is concerned that top management will give more weight to financial factors and not give due consideration to nonfinancial factors such as employee morale. In addition to the reduction in inventory described previously, Sue has gathered the following information for the upcoming year regarding the JIT system:

- Annual insurance and warehousing costs for inventory would be reduced by 60% of current budgeted level of $350,000.
- Payroll expenses for current inventory management staff would be reduced by 15% of the budgeted total of $600,000.
- Additional annual costs for JIT system implementation and management, including personnel costs, would equal $220,000.
- The additional number of stockouts under the new JIT system is estimated to be 5% of the total number of shipments annually. 10,000 shipments are budgeted for the upcoming year. Each stockout would result in an average additional cost of $250.
- Parson's required rate of return on inventory investment is 10% per year.

Required

1. From a financial perspective should Parson adopt the new JIT system?
2. Should Sue Winston rework the numbers?
3. How should she manage Jim Ingram's concerns?

The two DCF methods we describe are the net present value (NPV) method and the internal rate-of-return (IRR) method. Both DCF methods use what is called the **required rate of return (RRR)**, the minimum acceptable annual rate of return on an investment. The RRR is internally set, usually by upper management, and typically reflects the return that an organization could expect to receive elsewhere for an investment of comparable risk. The RRR is also called the **discount rate, hurdle rate, cost of capital,** or **opportunity cost of capital.** Suppose the CFO at Top-Spin has set the required rate of return for the firm's investments at 8% per year.

Net Present Value Method

The **net present value (NPV) method** calculates the expected monetary gain or loss from a project by discounting all expected future cash inflows and outflows back to the present point in time using the required rate of return. To use the NPV method, apply the following three steps:

Step 1: Draw a Sketch of Relevant Cash Inflows and Outflows. The right side of Exhibit 21-2 shows arrows that depict the cash flows of the new carbon-fiber machine. The sketch helps the decision maker visualize and organize the data in a systematic way. *Note that parentheses denote relevant cash outflows throughout all exhibits in Chapter 21.* Exhibit 21-2 includes the outflow for the acquisition of the new machine at the start of year 1 (also referred to as end of year 0), and the inflows over the subsequent five years. The NPV method specifies cash flows regardless of the source of the cash flows, such as from operations, purchase or sale of equipment, or investment in or recovery of working capital. However, accrual-accounting concepts such as sales made on credit or noncash expenses are not included since the focus is on *cash* inflows and outflows.

Exhibit 21-2   Net Present Value Method: Top-Spin's Carbon-Fiber Machine

	A	B	C	D	E	F	G	H	I
			Home Insert Page Layout Formulas Data Review View						
1			Net initial investment	$379,100					
2			Useful life	5 years					
3			Annual cash inflow	$100,000					
4			Required rate of return	8%					
5									
6		Present Value	Present Value of	Sketch of Relevant Cash Flows at End of Each Year					
7		of Cash Flow	$1 Discounted at 8%	0	1	2	3	4	5
8	Approach 1: Discounting Each Year's Cash Flow Separately[a]								
9	Net initial investment	$(379,100) ←	1.000 ←	$(379,100)					
10		92,600 ←	0.926 ←		$100,000				
11		85,700 ←	0.857 ←			$100,000			
12	Annual cash inflow	79,400 ←	0.794 ←				$100,000		
13		73,500 ←	0.735 ←					$100,000	
14		68,100 ←	0.681 ←						$100,000
15	NPV if new machine purchased	$ 20,200							
16									
17	Approach 2: Using Annuity Table[b]								
18	Net initial investment	$(379,100) ←	1.000 ←	$(379,100)					
19					$100,000	$100,000	$100,000	$100,000	$100,000
20									
21	Annual cash inflow	399,300 ←	3.993 ←						
22	NPV if new machine purchased	$ 20,200							
23									
24	Note: Parentheses denote relevant cash outflows throughout all exhibits in Chapter 21.								
25	[a] Present values from Table 2, Appendix A at the end of the book. For example, $0.857 = 1 \div (1.08)^2$.								
26	[b] Annuity present value from Table 4, Appendix A. The annuity value of 3.993 is the sum of the individual discount rates 0.926 + 0.857 + 0.794 + 0.735 + 0.681.								

Step 2: Discount the Cash Flows Using the Correct Compound Interest Table from Appendix A and Sum Them. In the Top-Spin example, we can discount each year's cash flow separately using Table 2, or we can compute the present value of an annuity, a series of equal cash flows at equal time intervals, using Table 4. (Both tables are in Appendix A.) If we use Table 2, we find the discount factors for periods 1–5 under the 8% column. Approach 1 in Exhibit 21-2 uses the five discount factors. To obtain the present value amount, multiply each discount factor by the corresponding amount represented by the arrow on the right in Exhibit 21-2 (− $379,100 × 1.000; $100,000 × 0.926; and so on to $100,000 × 0.681). Because the investment in the new machine produces an annuity, we may also use Table 4. Under Approach 2, we find that the annuity factor for five periods under the 8% column is 3.993, which is the sum of the five discount factors used in Approach 1. We multiply the uniform annual cash inflow by this factor to obtain the present value of the inflows ($399,300 = $100,000 × 3.993). Subtracting the initial investment then reveals the NPV of the project as $20,200 ($20,200 = $399,300 − $379,100).

Step 3: Make the Project Decision on the Basis of the Calculated NPV. If NPV is zero or positive, financial considerations suggest that the project should be accepted; its expected rate of return equals or exceeds the required rate of return. If NPV is negative, the project should be rejected; its expected rate of return is below the required rate of return.

Exhibit 21-2 calculates an NPV of $20,200 at the required rate of return of 8% per year. The project is acceptable based on financial information. The cash flows from the project are adequate (1) to recover the net initial investment in the project and (2) to earn a return greater than 8% per year on the investment tied up in the project over its useful life.

Managers must also weigh nonfinancial factors such as the effect that purchasing the machine will have on Top-Spin's brand. This is a nonfinancial factor because the financial benefits that accrue from Top-Spin's brand are very difficult to estimate. Nevertheless, managers must consider brand effects before reaching a final decision. Suppose, for example, that the NPV of the carbon-fiber machine is negative. Management may still decide to buy the machine if it maintains Top-Spin's technological image and helps sell other Top-Spin products.

Pause here. Do not proceed until you understand what you see in Exhibit 21-2. Compare Approach 1 with Approach 2 in Exhibit 21-2 to see how Table 4 in Appendix A merely aggregates the present value factors of Table 2. That is, the fundamental table is Table 2. Table 4 simply reduces calculations when there is an annuity.

Internal Rate-of-Return Method

The **internal rate-of-return (IRR) method** calculates the discount rate at which an investment's present value of all expected cash inflows equals the present value of its expected cash outflows. That is, the IRR is the discount rate that makes NPV = $0. Exhibit 21-3 presents the cash flows and shows the calculation of NPV using a 10% annual discount rate for Top-Spin's carbon-fiber project. At a 10% discount rate, the NPV of the project is $0. Therefore, IRR is 10% per year.

How do managers determine the discount rate that yields NPV = $0? In most cases, managers or analysts solving capital budgeting problems use a calculator or computer program to provide the internal rate of return. The following trial-and-error approach can also provide the answer.

Step 1: Use a discount rate and calculate the project's NPV.

Step 2: If the calculated NPV is less than zero, use a lower discount rate. (A *lower* discount rate will *increase* NPV. Remember that we are trying to find a discount rate for which NPV = $0.) If NPV is greater than zero, use a higher discount rate to lower NPV. Keep adjusting the discount rate until NPV = $0. In the Top-Spin example, a discount rate of 8% yields an NPV of + $20,200 (see Exhibit 21-2). A discount rate of 12% yields an NPV of − $18,600 (3.605, the present value annuity factor from Table 4, × $100,000 minus $379,100). Therefore, the discount rate that makes NPV = $0 must lie between 8% and 12%. We use 10% and get NPV = $0. Hence, the IRR is 10% per year.

Exhibit 21-3 Internal Rate-of-Return Method: Top-Spin's Carbon-Fiber Machine[a]

	A	B	C	D	E	F	G	H	I
				Home Insert Page Layout Formulas Data Review View					
1			Net initial investment	$379,100					
2			Useful life	5 years					
3			Annual cash inflow	$100,000					
4			Annual discount rate	10%					
5									
6		Present Value	Present Value of	Sketch of Relevant Cash Flows at End of Each Year					
7		of Cash Flow	$1 Discounted at 10%	0	1	2	3	4	5
8	Approach 1: Discounting Each Year's Cash Flow Separately[b]								
9	Net initial investment	$(379,100)◄	1.000 ◄	$(379,100)					
10		90,900 ◄	0.909 ◄		$100,000				
11		82,600 ◄	0.826 ◄			$100,000			
12	Annual cash inflow	75,100 ◄	0.751 ◄				$100,000		
13		68,300 ◄	0.683 ◄					$100,000	
14		62,100 ◄	0.621 ◄						$100,000
15	NPV if new machine purchased[c]	$ 0							
16	(the zero difference proves that								
17	the internal rate of return is 10%)								
18									
19	Approach 2: Using Annuity Table								
20	Net initial investment	$(379,100)◄	1.000 ◄	$(379,100)					
21					$100,000	$100,000	$100,000	$100,000	$100,000
22									
23	Annual cash inflow	379,100 ◄	3.791[d] ◄						
24	NPV if new machine purchased	$ 0							
25									
26	Note: Parentheses denote relevant cash outflows throughout all exhibits in Chapter 21.								
27	[a]The internal rate of return is computed by methods explained on pp. 743–744.								
28	[b]Present values from Table 2, Appendix A at the end of the book.								
29	[c]Sum is $(100) due to rounding. We round to $0.								
30	[d]Annuity present value from Table 4, Appendix A. The annuity table value of 3.791 is the sum of the individual discount rates								
31	0.909 + 0.826 + 0.751 + 0.683 + 0.621, subject to rounding.								

The step-by-step computations of internal rate of return are easier when the cash inflows are constant, as in our Top-Spin example. Information from Exhibit 21-3 can be expressed as follows:

$379,100 = Present value of annuity of $100,000 at X% per year for five years

Or, what factor F in Table 4 (in Appendix A) will satisfy this equation?

$379,100 = $100,000F

$$F = \$379,100 \div \$100,000 = 3.791$$

On the five-period line of Table 4, find the percentage column that is closest to 3.791. It is exactly 10%. If the factor (F) falls between the factors in two columns, straight-line interpolation is used to approximate IRR. This interpolation is illustrated in the Problem for Self-Study (pp. 759–760).

A project is accepted only if IRR equals or exceeds required rate of return (RRR). In the Top-Spin example, the carbon-fiber machine has an IRR of 10%, which is greater than the RRR of 8%. On the basis of financial factors, Top-Spin should invest in the new machine. In general, the NPV and IRR decision rules result in consistent project acceptance or rejection decisions. If IRR exceeds RRR, then the project has a positive NPV (favoring acceptance). If IRR equals RRR, NPV = $0, so project acceptance and rejection yield the same value. If IRR is less than RRR, NPV is negative (favoring rejection). Obviously, managers prefer projects with higher IRRs to projects with lower IRRs, if all other things are equal. The IRR of 10% means the cash inflows from the project are adequate to (1) recover the net initial investment in the project and (2) earn a return of exactly 10% on the investment tied up in the project over its useful life.

Comparison of Net Present Value and Internal Rate-of-Return Methods

The NPV method is generally regarded as the preferred method for project selection decisions. The reason is that choosing projects using the NPV criterion leads to shareholder value maximization. At an intuitive level, this occurs because the NPV measure for a project captures the value, in today's dollars, of the surplus the project generates for the firm's shareholders, over and above the required rate of return.[2] Next, we highlight some of the limitations of the IRR method relative to the NPV technique.

One advantage of the NPV method is that it expresses computations in dollars, not in percentages. Therefore, we can sum NPVs of individual projects to calculate an NPV of a combination or portfolio of projects. In contrast, IRRs of individual projects cannot be added or averaged to represent the IRR of a combination of projects.

A second advantage is that the NPV of a project can always be computed and expressed as a unique number. From the sign and magnitude of this number, the firm can then make an accurate assessment of the financial consequences of accepting or rejecting the project. Under the IRR method, it is possible that more than one IRR may exist for a given project. In other words, there may be multiple discount rates that equate the NPV of a set of cash flows to zero. This is especially true when the signs of the cash flows switch over time; that is, when there are outflows, followed by inflows, followed by additional outflows and so forth. In such cases, it is difficult to know which of the IRR estimates should be compared to the firm's required rate of return.

A third advantage of the NPV method is that it can be used when the RRR varies over the life of a project. Suppose Top-Spin's management sets an RRR of 9% per year in years 1 and 2 and 12% per year in years 3, 4, and 5. Total present value of the cash inflows can be calculated as $378,100 (computations not shown). It is not possible to use the IRR method in this case. That's because different RRRs in different years mean there is no single RRR that the IRR (a single figure) can be compared against to decide if the project should be accepted or rejected.

Finally, there are specific settings in which the IRR method is prone to indicating erroneous decisions, such as when comparing mutually exclusive projects with unequal lives or unequal levels of initial investment. The reason is that the IRR method implicitly assumes that project cash flows can be reinvested at the *project's* rate of return. The NPV method, in contrast, accurately assumes that project cash flows can only be reinvested at the *company's* required rate of return.

Despite its limitations, surveys report widespread use of the IRR method.[3] Why? Probably because managers find the percentage return computed under the IRR method easy to understand and compare. Moreover, in most instances where a single project is being evaluated, their decisions would likely be unaffected by using IRR or NPV.

Sensitivity Analysis

To present the basics of the NPV and IRR methods, we have assumed that the expected values of cash flows will occur *for certain*. In reality, there is substantial uncertainty associated with the prediction of future cash flows. To examine how a result will change if the predicted financial outcomes are not achieved or if an underlying assumption changes, managers use *sensitivity analysis*, a "what-if" technique introduced in Chapter 3.

A common way to apply sensitivity analysis in capital budgeting decisions is to vary each of the inputs to the NPV calculation by a certain percentage and assess the effect of the change on the project's NPV. Sensitivity analysis can take on other forms as well. Suppose the manager at Top-Spin believes forecasted cash flows are difficult to predict.

---

[2] More detailed explanations of the preeminence of the NPV criterion can be found in corporate finance texts.
[3] In a recent survey, John Graham and Campbell Harvey found that 75.7% of CFOs always or almost always used IRR for capital budgeting decisions, while a slightly smaller number, 74.9%, always or almost always used the NPV criterion.

more effective use of associates' time. The cash savings occur uniformly throughout each year, but are not uniform across years.

Year	Cash Savings	Cumulative Cash Savings	Net Initial Investment Unrecovered at End of Year
0	—	—	$150,000
1	$50,000	$ 50,000	100,000
2	55,000	105,000	45,000
3	60,000	165,000	—
4	85,000	250,000	—
5	90,000	340,000	—

It is clear from the chart that payback occurs during the third year. Straight-line interpolation within the third year reveals that the final $45,000 needed to recover the $150,000 investment (that is, $150,000 − $105,000 recovered by the end of year 2) will be achieved three-quarters of the way through year 3 (in which $60,000 of cash savings occur):

$$\text{Payback period} = 2 \text{ years} + \left(\frac{\$45,000}{\$60,000} \times 1 \text{ year} \right) = 2.75 \text{ years}$$

It is relatively simple to adjust the payback method to incorporate the time value of money by using a similar cumulative approach. The **discounted payback method** calculates the amount of time required for the discounted expected future cash flows to recoup the net initial investment in a project. For the videoconferencing example, we can modify the preceding chart by discounting the cash flows at the 8% required rate of return.

Year (1)	Cash Savings (2)	Present Value of $1 Discounted at 8% (3)	Discounted Cash Savings (4) = (2) × (3)	Cumulative Discounted Cash Savings (5)	Net Initial Investment Unrecovered at End of Year (6)
0	—	1.000	—	—	$150,000
1	$50,000	0.926	$46,300	$ 46,300	103,700
2	55,000	0.857	47,135	93,435	56,565
3	60,000	0.794	47,640	141,075	8,925
4	85,000	0.735	62,475	203,550	—
5	90,000	0.681	61,290	264,840	—

The fourth column represents the present values of the future cash savings. It is evident from the chart that discounted payback occurs between years 3 and 4. At the end of the third year, $8,925 of the initial investment is still unrecovered. Comparing this to the $62,475 in present value of savings achieved in the fourth year, straight-line interpolation then reveals that the discounted payback period is exactly one-seventh of the way into the fourth year:

$$\text{Discounted payback period} = 3 \text{ years} + \left(\frac{\$8,925}{\$62,475} \times 1 \text{ year} \right) = 3.14 \text{ years}$$

While discounted payback does incorporate the time value of money, it is still subject to the other criticism of the payback method—cash flows beyond the discounted payback period are ignored, resulting in a bias toward shorter-term projects. Companies such as Hewlett-Packard value the discounted payback method (HP refers to it as "breakeven time") because they view longer-term cash flows as inherently unpredictable in high-growth industries.

Finally, the videoconferencing example has a single cash outflow of $150,000 in year 0. When a project has multiple cash outflows occurring at different points in time, these outflows are first aggregated to obtain a total cash-outflow figure for the project. For computing the payback period, the cash flows are simply added, with no adjustment for the time value of money. For calculating the discounted payback period, the present values of the outflows are added instead.

Decision Point ▶

What are the payback and discounted payback methods? What are their main weaknesses?

Accrual Accounting Rate-of-Return Method

Learning Objective 4

Use and evaluate the accrual accounting rate-of-return (AARR) method

. . . after-tax operating income divided by investment

We now consider a fourth method for analyzing the financial aspects of capital budgeting projects. The **accrual accounting rate of return (AARR) method** divides the average annual (accrual accounting) income of a project by a measure of the investment in it. We illustrate AARR for the Top-Spin example using the project's net initial investment as the amount in the denominator:

$$\text{Accrual accounting rate of return} = \frac{\text{Increase in expected average annual after-tax operating income}}{\text{Net initial investment}}$$

If Top-Spin purchases the new carbon-fiber machine, its net initial investment is $379,100. The increase in expected average annual after-tax operating cash inflows is $98,200. This amount is the expected after-tax total operating cash inflows of $491,000 ($100,000 for four years and $91,000 in year 5), divided by the time horizon of five years. Suppose that the new machine results in additional depreciation deductions of $70,000 per year ($78,000 in annual depreciation for the new machine, relative to $8,000 per year on the existing machine).[5] The increase in expected average annual after-tax income is therefore $28,200 (the difference between the cash flow increase of $98,200 and the depreciation increase of $70,000). The AARR on net initial investment is computed as follows:

$$AARR = \frac{\$98,200 - \$70,000}{\$379,100} = \frac{\$28,200 \text{ per year}}{\$379,100} = 0.074, \text{ or } 7.4\% \text{ per year}$$

The 7.4% figure for AARR indicates the average rate at which a dollar of investment generates after-tax operating income. The new carbon-fiber machine has a low AARR for two reasons: (1) the use of net initial investment as the denominator, and (2) the use of income as the numerator, which necessitates deducting depreciation charges from the annual operating cash flows. To mitigate the first issue, many companies calculate AARR using an average level of investment. This alternative procedure recognizes that the book value of the investment declines over time. In its simplest form, average investment for Top-Spin is calculated as the arithmetic mean of the net initial investment of $379,100 and the net terminal cash flow of $9,000 (terminal disposal value of machine of $0, plus the terminal recovery of working capital of $9,000):

$$\text{Average investment over five years} = \frac{\text{Net initial investment} + \text{Net terminal cash flow}}{2}$$

$$= \frac{\$379,100 + \$9,000}{2} = \$194,050$$

The AARR on average investment is then calculated as follows:

$$AARR = \frac{\$28,200}{\$194,050} = 0.145, \text{ or } 14.5\% \text{ per year}$$

Our point here is that companies vary in how they calculate AARR. There is no uniformly preferred approach. Be sure you understand how AARR is defined in each individual situation. Projects whose AARR exceeds a specified hurdle required rate of return are regarded as acceptable (the higher the AARR, the better the project is considered to be).

The AARR method is similar to the IRR method in that both methods calculate a rate-of-return percentage. The AARR method calculates return using operating-income numbers after considering accruals and taxes, whereas the IRR method calculates return on the basis of after-tax cash flows and the time value of money. Because cash flows and time value of money are central to capital budgeting decisions, the IRR method is regarded as better than the AARR method.

AARR computations are easy to understand, and they use numbers reported in the financial statements. AARR gives managers an idea of how the accounting numbers they will report in the future will be affected if a project is accepted. Unlike the payback method,

---

[5] We provide further details on these numbers in the next section; see p. 750.

Decision Point ▶

What are the strengths and weaknesses of the accrual accounting rate-of-return (AARR) method for evaluating long-term projects?

which ignores cash flows after the payback period, the AARR method considers income earned *throughout* a project's expected useful life. Unlike the NPV method, the AARR method uses accrual accounting income numbers, it does not track cash flows, and it ignores the time value of money. Critics cite these arguments as drawbacks of the AARR method.

Overall, keep in mind that companies frequently use multiple methods for evaluating capital investment decisions. When different methods lead to different rankings of projects, finance theory suggests that more weight be given to the NPV method because the assumptions made by the NPV method are most consistent with making decisions that maximize company value.

Relevant Cash Flows in Discounted Cash Flow Analysis

Learning Objective 5

Identify relevant cash inflows and outflows for capital budgeting decisions

. . . the differences in expected future cash flows resulting from the investment

So far, we have examined methods for evaluating long-term projects in settings where the expected future cash flows of interest were assumed to be known. One of the biggest challenges in capital budgeting, particularly DCF analysis, however, is determining which cash flows are relevant in making an investment selection. Relevant cash flows are the differences in expected future cash flows as a result of making the investment. In the Top-Spin example, the relevant cash flows are the differences in expected future cash flows between continuing to use the old technology and updating its technology with the purchase of a new machine. *When reading this section, focus on identifying expected future cash flows and the differences in expected future cash flows.*

To illustrate relevant cash flow analysis, consider a more complex version of the Top-Spin example with these additional assumptions:

- Top-Spin is a profitable company. The income tax rate is 40% of operating income each year.

- The before-tax additional operating cash inflows from the carbon-fiber machine are $120,000 in years 1 through 4 and $105,000 in year 5.

- For tax purposes, Top-Spin uses the straight-line depreciation method and assumes no terminal disposal value.

- Gains or losses on the sale of depreciable assets are taxed at the same rate as ordinary income.

- The tax effects of cash inflows and outflows occur at the same time that the cash inflows and outflows occur.

- Top-Spin uses an 8% required rate of return for discounting after-tax cash flows.

Summary data for the machines follow:

	Old Graphite Machine	New Carbon-Fiber Machine
Purchase price	—	$390,000
Current book value	$40,000	—
Current disposal value	6,500	Not applicable
Terminal disposal value five years from now	0	0
Annual depreciation	8,000[a]	78,000[b]
Working capital required	6,000	15,000

[a]$40,000 ÷ 5 years = $8,000 annual depreciation.
[b]$390,000 ÷ 5 years = $78,000 annual depreciation.

Relevant After-Tax Flows

We use the concepts of differential cost and differential revenue introduced in Chapter 11. We compare (1) the after-tax cash outflows as a result of replacing the old machine with (2) the additional after-tax cash inflows generated from using the new machine rather than the old machine.

As Benjamin Franklin said, "Two things in life are certain: death and taxes." Income taxes are a fact of life for most corporations and individuals. It is important first to understand how income taxes affect cash flows in each year. Exhibit 21-5 shows how investing in the new machine will affect Top-Spin's cash flow from operations and its income taxes in year 1. Recall that Top-Spin will generate $120,000 in before-tax additional operating cash inflows by investing in the new machine (p. 750), but it will record additional depreciation of $70,000 ($78,000 − $8,000) for tax purposes.

Panel A shows that the year 1 cash flow from operations, net of income taxes, equals $100,000, using two methods based on the income statement. The first method focuses on cash items only, the $120,000 operating cash inflows minus income taxes of $20,000. The second method starts with the $30,000 increase in net income (calculated after subtracting the $70,000 additional depreciation deductions for income tax purposes) and adds back that $70,000, because depreciation is an operating cost that reduces net income but is a noncash item itself.

Panel B of Exhibit 21-5 describes a third method that we will use frequently to compute cash flow from operations, net of income taxes. The easiest way to interpret the third method is to think of the government as a 40% (equal to the tax rate) partner in Top-Spin. Each time Top-Spin obtains operating cash inflows, C, its income is higher by C, so it will pay 40% of the operating cash inflows ($0.40C$) in taxes. This results in additional after-tax cash operating flows of $C − 0.40C$, which in this example is $120,000 − (0.40 \times $120,000) = $72,000$, or $120,000 \times (1 − 0.40) = $72,000$.

To achieve the higher operating cash inflows, C, Top-Spin incurs higher depreciation charges, D, from investing in the new machine. Depreciation costs do not directly affect cash flows because depreciation is a noncash cost, but higher depreciation cost *lowers* Top-Spin's taxable income by D, saving income tax cash outflows of $0.40D$, which in this example is $0.40 \times $70,000 = $28,000$.

Letting t = tax rate, cash flow from operations, net of income taxes, in this example equals the operating cash inflows, C, minus the tax payments on these inflows, $t \times C$, plus the tax savings on depreciation deductions, $t \times D$: $120,000 − (0.40 \times $120,000) + (0.40 \times $70,000) = $120,000 − $48,000 + $28,000 = $100,000$.

By the same logic, each time Top-Spin has a gain on the sale of assets, G, it will show tax outflows, $t \times G$; and each time Top-Spin has a loss on the sale of assets, L, it will show tax benefits or savings of $t \times L$.

PANEL A: Two Methods Based on the Income Statement

C	Operating cash inflows from investment in machine	$120,000
D	Additional depreciation deduction	70,000
OI	Increase in operating income	50,000
T	Income taxes (Income tax rate $t \times OI$) =	
	40% × $50,000	20,000
NI	Increase in net income	$ 30,000
	Increase in cash flow from operations, net of income taxes	
	Method 1: $C − T$ = $120,000 − $20,000 = $100,000 or	
	Method 2: $NI + D$ = $30,000 + $70,000 = $100,000	

PANEL B: Item-by-Item Method

	Effect of cash operating flows	
C	Operating cash inflows from investment in machine	$120,000
$t \times C$	Deduct income tax cash outflow at 40%	48,000
$C − (t \times C)$	After-tax cash flow from operations	72,000
$= (1 − t) \times C$	(excluding the depreciation effect)	
	Effect of depreciation	
D	Additional depreciation deduction, $70,000	
$t \times D$	Income tax cash savings from additional depreciation	
	deduction at 40% × $70,000	28,000
$(1 − t) \times C + (t \times D)$	Cash flow from operations, net of income taxes	$100,000
$= C − (t \times C) + (t \times D)$		

Exhibit 21-5

Effect on Cash Flow from Operations, Net of Income Taxes, in Year 1 for Top-Spin's Investment in the New Carbon-Fiber Machine

Categories of Cash Flows

A capital investment project typically has three categories of cash flows: (1) net initial investment in the project, which includes the acquisition of assets and any associated additions to working capital, minus the after-tax cash flow from the disposal of existing assets; (2) after-tax cash flow from operations (including income tax cash savings from annual depreciation deductions); and (3) after-tax cash flow from terminal disposal of an asset and recovery of working capital. We use the Top-Spin example to discuss these three categories.

As you work through the cash flows in each category, refer to Exhibit 21-6. This exhibit sketches the relevant cash flows for Top-Spin's decision to purchase the new machine as described in items 1 through 3 here. Note that the total relevant cash flows for each year equal the relevant cash flows used in Exhibits 21-2 and 21-3 to illustrate the NPV and IRR methods.

1. **Net Initial Investment.** Three components of net-initial-investment cash flows are (a) cash outflow to purchase the machine, (b) cash outflow for working capital, and (c) after-tax cash inflow from current disposal of the old machine.

   1a. *Initial machine investment.* These outflows, made for purchasing plant and equipment, occur at the beginning of the project's life and include cash outflows for transporting and installing the equipment. In the Top-Spin example, the $390,000 cost (including transportation and installation) of the carbon-fiber machine is an outflow in year 0. These cash flows are relevant to the capital budgeting decision because they will be incurred only if Top-Spin decides to purchase the new machine.

   1b. *Initial working-capital investment.* Initial investments in plant and equipment are usually accompanied by additional investments in working capital. These additional investments take the form of current assets, such as accounts receivable and inventories, minus current liabilities, such as accounts payable. Working-capital investments are similar to plant and equipment investments in that they require cash. The magnitude of the investment generally increases as a function of the level of additional sales generated by the project. However, the exact relationship varies based on the nature of the project and the operating cycle of the industry.

Exhibit 21-6	Relevant Cash Inflows and Outflows for Top-Spin's Carbon-Fiber Machine

| Home | Insert | Page Layout | Formulas | Data | Review | View |

	A	B	C	D	E	F	G	H
1			Sketch of Relevant Cash Flows at End of Year					
2			0	1	2	3	4	5
3	1a.	Initial machine investment	$(390,000)					
4	1b.	Initial working-capital investment	(9,000)					
5	1c.	After-tax cash flow from current disposal						
6		of old machine	19,900					
7	Net initial investment		(379,100)					
8	2a.	Annual after-tax cash flow from operations						
9		(excluding the depreciation effect)		$ 72,000	$ 72,000	$ 72,000	$ 72,000	$ 63,000
10	2b.	Income tax cash savings from annual						
11		depreciation deductions		28,000	28,000	28,000	28,000	28,000
12	3a.	After-tax cash flow from terminal disposal						
13		of machine						0
14	3b.	After-tax cash flow from recovery of						
15		working capital						9,000
16	Total relevant cash flows,							
17	as shown in Exhibits 21-2 and 21-3		$(379,100)	$ 100,000	$100,000	$100,000	$100,000	$100,000
18								

For a given dollar of sales, a maker of heavy equipment, for example, would require more working capital support than Top-Spin, which in turn has to invest more in working capital than a retail grocery store.

The Top-Spin example assumes a $9,000 additional investment in working capital (for supplies and spare-parts inventory) if the new machine is acquired. The additional working-capital investment is the difference between working capital required to operate the new machine ($15,000) and working capital required to operate the old machine ($6,000). The $9,000 additional investment in working capital is a cash outflow in year 0 and is returned, that is, becomes a cash inflow, at the end of year 5.

1c. *After-tax cash flow from current disposal of old machine.* Any cash received from disposal of the old machine is a relevant cash inflow (in year 0). That's because it is an expected future cash flow that differs between the alternatives of investing and not investing in the new machine. Top-Spin will dispose of the old machine for $6,500 only if it invests in the new carbon-fiber machine. Recall from Chapter 11 (p. 414) that the book value (which is original cost minus accumulated depreciation) of the old equipment is generally irrelevant to the decision since it is a past, or sunk, cost. However, when tax considerations are included, book value does play a role. The reason is that the book value determines the gain or loss on sale of the machine and, therefore, the taxes paid (or saved) on the transaction.

Consider the tax consequences of disposing of the old machine. We first have to compute the gain or loss on disposal:

Current disposal value of old machine (given, p. 750)	$ 6,500
Deduct current book value of old machine (given, p. 750)	40,000
Loss on disposal of machine	$(33,500)

Any loss on the sale of assets lowers taxable income and results in tax savings. The after-tax cash flow from disposal of the old machine is as follows:

Current disposal value of old machine	$ 6,500
Tax savings on loss (0.40 × $33,500)	13,400
After-tax cash inflow from current disposal of old machine	$19,900

The sum of items **1a**, **1b**, and **1c** appears in Exhibit 21-6 as the year 0 net initial investment for the new carbon-fiber machine equal to $379,100 (initial machine investment, $390,000, plus additional working-capital investment, $9,000, minus after-tax cash inflow from current disposal of the old machine, $19,900).[6]

2. **Cash Flow from Operations.** This category includes the difference between each year's cash flow from operations under the two alternatives. Organizations make capital investments to generate future cash inflows. These inflows may result from savings in operating costs, or, as for Top-Spin, from producing and selling additional goods. Annual cash flow from operations can be net outflows in some years. Chevron makes periodic upgrades to its oil extraction equipment, and in years of upgrades, cash flow from operations tends to be negative for the site being upgraded, although in the long-run such upgrades are NPV positive. Always focus on cash flow from operations, not on revenues and expenses under accrual accounting.

Top-Spin's additional operating cash inflows—$120,000 in each of the first four years and $105,000 in the fifth year—are relevant because they are expected future cash flows that will differ between the alternatives of investing and not investing in the new machine. The after-tax effects of these cash flows follow.

2a. *Annual after-tax cash flow from operations (excluding the depreciation effect).* The 40% tax rate reduces the benefit of the $120,000 additional operating cash

---

[6] To illustrate the case when there is a gain on disposal, suppose that the old machine could be sold now for $50,000 instead. Then, the firm would record a gain on disposal of $10,000 ($50,000 less the book value of $40,000), resulting in additional tax payments of $4,000 (0.40 tax rate × $10,000 gain). The after-tax cash inflow from current disposal would therefore equal $46,000 (the disposal value of $50,000, less the tax payment of $4,000).

malls or manufacturing plants. The building projects are more complex, so monitoring and controlling the investment schedules and budgets are critical to successfully completing the investment activity. This leads to the second dimension of stage 5 in the capital budgeting process: evaluate performance and learn.

Post-Investment Audits

A post-investment audit provides management with feedback about the performance of a project, so management can compare actual results to the costs and benefits expected at the time the project was selected. Suppose actual outcomes (such as additional operating cash flows from the new carbon-fiber machine in the Top-Spin example) are much lower than expected. Management must then investigate to determine if this result occurred because the original estimates were overly optimistic or because of implementation problems. Either of these explanations is a concern.

Optimistic estimates may result in the acceptance of a project that should have been rejected. To discourage optimistic estimates, companies such as DuPont maintain records comparing actual results to the estimates made by individual managers when seeking approval for capital investments. Post-investment audits punish inaccurate estimates, and therefore discourage unrealistic forecasts. This prevents managers from overstating project cash inflows and accepting projects that should never have been undertaken. Implementation problems, such as weak project management, poor quality control, or inadequate marketing are also a concern. Post-investment audits help to alert senior management to these problems so that they can be quickly corrected.

However, post-investment audits require thoughtfulness and care. They should be done only after project outcomes have stabilized because performing audits too early may yield misleading feedback. Obtaining actual results to compare against estimates is often not easy. For example, additional revenues from the new carbon-fiber technology may not be comparable to the estimated revenues because in any particular season, the rise or decline of a tennis star can greatly affect the popularity of the sport and the subsequent demand for racquets. A better evaluation would look at the average revenues across a couple of seasons.

Performance Evaluation

As the preceding discussion suggests, ideally one should evaluate managers on a project-by-project basis and look at how well managers achieve the amounts and timing of forecasted cash flows. In practice, however, managers are often evaluated based on aggregate information, especially when multiple projects are underway at any point in time. It is important then to ensure that the method of evaluation does not conflict with the use of the NPV method for making capital budgeting decisions. For example, suppose that Top-Spin uses the accrual accounting rate of return generated in each period to assess managerial performance. We know from the NPV method that the manager of the racquet production plant should purchase the carbon-fiber machine because it has a positive NPV of $20,200. Despite that, the project may be rejected if the AARR of 7.4% on the net initial investment is lower than the minimum accounting rate of return the manager is required to achieve.

There is an inconsistency between using the NPV method as best for capital budgeting decisions and then using a different method to evaluate performance. This inconsistency means managers are tempted to make capital budgeting decisions on the basis of the method by which they are being evaluated. Such temptations become more pronounced if managers are frequently transferred (or promoted), or if their bonuses are affected by the level of year-to-year accrual income.

Other conflicts between decision making and performance evaluation persist even if a company uses similar measures for both purposes. If the AARR on the carbon-fiber machine exceeds the minimum required AARR but is below the current AARR of the production plant, the manager may still be tempted to reject purchase of the carbon-fiber machine because the lower AARR of the carbon-fiber machine will reduce the AARR of the entire plant and hurt the manager's reported performance. Or, consider an example where the cash inflows from the carbon-fiber machine occur mostly in the later years of the project. Then, even if the AARR on the project exceeds the current AARR of the plant

Decision Point ▶

What conflicts can arise between using DCF methods for capital budgeting decisions and accrual accounting for performance evaluation? How can these conflicts be reduced?

(as well as the minimum required return), the manager may still reject the purchase since it will have a negative effect on the realized accrual accounting rate of return for the first few years. In Chapter 23, we study these conflicts in greater depth and describe how performance evaluation models such as economic value added (EVA®) help achieve greater congruency with decision-making models.

Strategic Considerations in Capital Budgeting

A company's strategy is the source of its strategic capital budgeting decisions. Strategic decisions by United Airlines, Westin Hotels, Federal Express, and Pizza Hut to expand in Europe and Asia required capital investments to be made in several countries (see also Concepts in Action feature, p. 758). The strategic decision by Barnes & Noble to support book sales over the Internet required capital investments creating barnesandnoble.com and an Internet infrastructure. News Corp.'s decision to enlarge its online presence resulted in a large investment to purchase MySpace, and additional supporting investments to integrate MySpace with the firm's pre-existing assets. Pfizer's decision to develop its cholesterol-reducing drug Lipitor led to major investments in R&D and marketing. Toyota's decision to offer a line of hybrids across both its Toyota and Lexus platforms required start-up investments to form a hybrid division and ongoing investments to fund the division's continuing research efforts.

Capital investment decisions that are strategic in nature require managers to consider a broad range of factors that may be difficult to estimate. Consider some of the difficulties of justifying investments made by companies such as Mitsubishi, Sony, and Audi in computer-integrated manufacturing (CIM) technology. In CIM, computers give instructions that quickly and automatically set up and run equipment to manufacture many different products. Quantifying these benefits requires some notion of how quickly consumer-demand will change in the future. CIM technology also increases worker knowledge of, and experience with automation; however, the benefit of this knowledge and experience is difficult to measure. Managers must develop judgment and intuition to make these decisions.

Investment in Research and Development

Companies such as GlaxoSmithKline, in the pharmaceutical industry, and Intel, in the semiconductor industry, regard research and development (R&D) projects as important strategic investments. The distant payoffs from R&D investments, however, are more uncertain than other investments such as new equipment. On the positive side, R&D investments are often staged: As time unfolds, companies can increase or decrease the resources committed to a project based on how successful it has been up to that point. This option feature of R&D investments, called real options, is an important aspect of R&D investments and increases the NPV of these investments, because a company can limit its losses when things are going badly and take advantage of new opportunities when things are going well.

Customer Value and Capital Budgeting

Finally, note that the framework described in this chapter to evaluate investment projects can also be used to make strategic decisions regarding which customers to invest in. Consider Potato Supreme, which makes potato products for sale to retail outlets. It is currently analyzing two of its customers: Shine Stores and Always Open. Potato Supreme predicts the following cash flow from operations, net of income taxes (in thousands), from each customer account for the next five years:

	2011	2012	2013	2014	2015
Shine Stores	$1,450	$1,305	$1,175	$1,058	$ 950
Always Open	690	1,160	1,900	2,950	4,160

Which customer is more valuable to Potato Supreme? Looking at only the current period, 2011, Shine Stores provides more than double the cash flow compared to Always Open ($1,450 versus $690). A different picture emerges, however, when looking over the entire

> **Learning Objective 7**
>
> Identify strategic considerations in capital budgeting decisions
>
> . . . critical investments whose benefits are uncertain or difficult to estimate

Part B

Assume that Top-Spin is subject to income tax at a 40% rate. All other information from Part A is unchanged. Compute the NPV of the new carbon-fiber machine project.

Solution

To save space, Exhibit 21-7 shows the calculations using a format slightly different from the format used in this chapter. Item **2a** is where the new $130,000 cash flow assumption affects the NPV analysis (compared to Exhibit 21-6). All other amounts in Exhibit 21-7 are identical to the corresponding amounts in Exhibit 21-6. For years 1 through 4, after-tax cash flow (excluding the depreciation effect) is as follows:

Annual cash flow from operations with new machine	$130,000
Deduct income tax payments (0.40 × $130,000)	52,000
Annual after-tax cash flow from operations	$ 78,000

For year 5, after-tax cash flow (excluding the depreciation effect) is as follows:

Annual cash flow from operations with new machine	$121,000
Deduct income tax payments (0.40 × $121,000)	48,400
Annual after-tax cash flow from operations	$ 72,600

NPV in Exhibit 21-7 is $46,610. As computed in Part A, NPV when there are no income taxes is $126,590. The difference in these two NPVs illustrates the impact of income taxes in capital budgeting analysis.

Exhibit 21-7 Net Present Value Method Incorporating Income Taxes: Top-Spin's Carbon-Fiber Machine with Revised Annual Cash Flow from Operations

	A	B	C	D	E	F	G	H	I	J
			Present	Present Value of						
1			Value of	$1 Discounted at		Sketch of Relevant Cash Flows at End of Year				
2			Cash Flow	8%	0	1	2	3	4	5
3										
4	1a.	Initial machine investment	$(390,000)	← 1.000 ←	$(390,000)					
5										
6	1b.	Initial working-capital investment	(9,000)	← 1.000 ←	$ (9,000)					
7	1c.	After-tax cash flow from current								
8		disposal of old machine	19,900	← 1.000 ←	$ 19,900					
9	Net initial investment		(379,100)							
10	2a.	Annual after-tax cash flow from								
11		operations (excluding the depreciation effect)								
12		Year 1	72,228	← 0.926 ←		$78,000				
13		Year 2	66,846	← 0.857 ←			$78,000			
14		Year 3	61,932	← 0.794 ←				$78,000		
15		Year 4	57,330	← 0.735 ←					$78,000	
16		Year 5	49,441	← 0.681 ←						$72,600
17	2b.	Income tax cash savings from annual								
18		depreciation deductions								
19		Year 1	25,928	← 0.926 ←		$28,000				
20		Year 2	23,996	← 0.857 ←			$28,000			
21		Year 3	22,232	← 0.794 ←				$28,000		
22		Year 4	20,580	← 0.735 ←					$28,000	
23		Year 5	19,068	← 0.681 ←						$28,000
24	3.	After-tax cash flow from								
25		a. Terminal disposal of machine	0	← 0.681 ←						$ 0
26		b. Recovery of working capital	6,129	← 0.681 ←						$ 9,000
27	NPV if new machine purchased		$ 46,610							
28										

Decision Points

The following question-and-answer format summarizes the chapter's learning objectives. Each decision presents a key question related to a learning objective. The guidelines are the answer to that question.

Decision	Guidelines
1. What are the five stages of capital budgeting?	Capital budgeting is long-run planning for proposed investment projects. The five stages of capital budgeting are as follows: 1) Identify projects: Identify potential capital investments that agree with the organization's strategy; 2) Obtain information: Gather information from all parts of the value chain to evaluate alternative projects; 3) Make predictions: Forecast all potential cash flows attributable to the alternative projects; 4) Make decisions by choosing among alternatives: Determine which investment yields the greatest benefit and the least cost to the organization; and 5) Implement the decision, evaluate performance, and learn: Obtain funding and make the investments selected in stage 4; track realized cash flows, compare against estimated numbers, and revise plans if necessary.
2. What are the two primary discounted cash flow (DCF) methods for project evaluation?	The two main DCF methods are the net present value (NPV) method and the internal rate-of-return (IRR) method. The NPV method calculates the expected net monetary gain or loss from a project by discounting to the present all expected future cash inflows and outflows, using the required rate of return. A project is acceptable in financial terms if it has a positive NPV. The IRR method computes the rate of return (also called the discount rate) at which the present value of expected cash inflows from a project equals the present value of expected cash outflows from the project. A project is acceptable in financial terms if its IRR exceeds the required rate of return. DCF is the best approach to capital budgeting. It explicitly includes all project cash flows and recognizes the time value of money. The NPV method is the preferred DCF method.
3. What are the payback and discounted payback methods? What are their main weaknesses?	The payback method measures the time it will take to recoup, in the form of cash inflows, the total cash amount invested in a project. The payback method neglects the time value of money and ignores cash flows beyond the payback period. The discounted payback method measures the time taken for the present value of cash inflows to equal the present value of outflows. It adjusts for the time value of money but overlooks cash flows after the discounted payback period.
4. What are the strengths and weaknesses of the accrual accounting rate-of-return (AARR) method for evaluating long-term projects?	The accrual accounting rate of return (AARR) divides an accrual accounting measure of average annual income from a project by an accrual accounting measure of its investment. AARR gives managers an idea of the effect of accepting a project on their future reported accounting profitability. However, AARR uses accrual accounting income numbers, does not track cash flows, and ignores the time value of money.
5. What are the relevant cash inflows and outflows for capital budgeting decisions? How should accrual accounting concepts be considered?	Relevant cash inflows and outflows in DCF analysis are the differences in expected future cash flows as a result of making the investment. Only cash inflows and outflows matter; accrual accounting concepts are irrelevant for DCF methods. For example, the income taxes saved as a result of depreciation deductions are relevant because they decrease cash outflows, but the depreciation itself is a noncash item.
6. What conflicts can arise between using DCF methods for capital budgeting decisions and accrual accounting for performance evaluation? How can these conflicts be reduced?	Using accrual accounting to evaluate the performance of a manager may create conflicts with using DCF methods for capital budgeting. Frequently, the decision made using a DCF method will not report good "operating income" results in the project's early years under accrual accounting. For this reason, managers are tempted to not use DCF methods even though the decisions based on them would be in the best interests of the company as a whole over the long run. This conflict can be reduced by evaluating managers on a project-by-project basis and by looking at their ability to achieve the amounts and timing of forecasted cash flows.

(excluding the depreciation effect), and income tax cash savings from annual depreciation deductions. The NPV is $202,513 and, based on financial considerations alone, Network Communications should purchase the equipment.

Terms to Learn

This chapter and the Glossary at the end of the book contain definitions of the following important terms:

accrual accounting rate of return (AARR) method **(p. 749)**

capital budgeting **(p. 739)**

cost of capital **(p. 742)**

discount rate **(p. 742)**

discounted cash flow (DCF) methods **(p. 741)**

discounted payback method **(p. 748)**

hurdle rate **(p. 742)**

inflation **(p. 762)**

internal rate-of-return (IRR) method **(p. 743)**

net present value (NPV) method **(p. 742)**

nominal rate of return **(p. 762)**

opportunity cost of capital **(p. 742)**

payback method **(p. 746)**

real rate of return **(p. 762)**

required rate of return (RRR) **(p. 742)**

time value of money **(p. 741)**

Assignment Material

Questions

21-1 "Capital budgeting has the same focus as accrual accounting." Do you agree? Explain.

21-2 List and briefly describe each of the five stages in capital budgeting.

21-3 What is the essence of the discounted cash flow methods?

21-4 "Only quantitative outcomes are relevant in capital budgeting analyses." Do you agree? Explain.

21-5 How can sensitivity analysis be incorporated in DCF analysis?

21-6 What is the payback method? What are its main strengths and weaknesses?

21-7 Describe the accrual accounting rate-of-return method. What are its main strengths and weaknesses?

21-8 "The trouble with discounted cash flow methods is that they ignore depreciation." Do you agree? Explain.

21-9 "Let's be more practical. DCF is not the gospel. Managers should not become so enchanted with DCF that strategic considerations are overlooked." Do you agree? Explain.

21-10 "All overhead costs are relevant in NPV analysis." Do you agree? Explain.

21-11 Bill Watts, president of Western Publications, accepts a capital budgeting project proposed by division X. This is the division in which the president spent his first 10 years with the company. On the same day, the president rejects a capital budgeting project proposal from division Y. The manager of division Y is incensed. She believes that the division Y project has an internal rate of return at least 10 percentage points higher than the division X project. She comments, "What is the point of all our detailed DCF analysis? If Watts is panting over a project, he can arrange to have the proponents of that project massage the numbers so that it looks like a winner." What advice would you give the manager of division Y?

21-12 Distinguish different categories of cash flows to be considered in an equipment-replacement decision by a taxpaying company.

21-13 Describe three ways income taxes can affect the cash inflows or outflows in a motor-vehicle-replacement decision by a taxpaying company.

21-14 How can capital budgeting tools assist in evaluating a manager who is responsible for retaining customers of a cellular telephone company?

21-15 Distinguish the nominal rate of return from the real rate of return.

Exercises

21-16 Exercises in compound interest, no income taxes. To be sure that you understand how to use the tables in Appendix A at the end of this book, solve the following exercises. Ignore income tax considerations. The correct answers, rounded to the nearest dollar, appear on pages 772–773.

Required

1. You have just won $10,000. How much money will you accumulate at the end of 10 years if you invest it at 8% compounded annually? At 10%?

2. Ten years from now, the unpaid principal of the mortgage on your house will be $154,900. How much do you need to invest today at 4% interest compounded annually to accumulate the $154,900 in 10 years?

3. If the unpaid mortgage on your house in 10 years will be $154,900, how much money do you need to invest at the end of each year at 10% to accumulate exactly this amount at the end of the 10th year?

4. You plan to save $7,500 of your earnings at the end of each year for the next 10 years. How much money will you accumulate at the end of the 10th year if you invest your savings compounded at 8% per year?

5. You have just turned 65 and an endowment insurance policy has paid you a lump sum of $250,000. If you invest the sum at 8%, how much money can you withdraw from your account in equal amounts at the end of each year so that at the end of 10 years (age 75) there will be nothing left?

6. You have estimated that for the first 10 years after you retire you will need a cash inflow of $65,000 at the end of each year. How much money do you need to invest at 8% at your retirement age to obtain this annual cash inflow? At 12%?

7. The following table shows two schedules of prospective operating cash inflows, each of which requires the same net initial investment of $10,000 now:

	Annual Cash Inflows	
Year	**Plan A**	**Plan B**
1	$ 3,000	$ 1,000
2	5,000	2,000
3	2,000	3,000
4	3,000	4,000
5	2,000	5,000
Total	$15,000	$15,000

The required rate of return is 8% compounded annually. All cash inflows occur at the end of each year. In terms of net present value, which plan is more desirable? Show your computations.

21-17 Capital budgeting methods, no income taxes. Riverbend Company runs hardware stores in a tri-state area. Riverbend's management estimates that if it invests $250,000 in a new computer system, it can save $67,000 in annual cash operating costs. The system has an expected useful life of eight years and no terminal disposal value. The required rate of return is 8%. Ignore income tax issues in your answers. Assume all cash flows occur at year-end except for initial investment amounts.

1. Calculate the following for the new computer system: **Required**
   a. Net present value
   b. Payback period
   c. Discounted payback period
   d. Internal rate of return (using the interpolation method)
   e. Accrual accounting rate of return based on the net initial investment (assume straight-line depreciation)
2. What other factors should Riverbend consider in deciding whether to purchase the new computer system?

21-18 Capital budgeting methods, no income taxes. City Hospital, a non-profit organization, estimates that it can save $28,000 a year in cash operating costs for the next 10 years if it buys a special-purpose eye-testing machine at a cost of $110,000. No terminal disposal value is expected. City Hospital's required rate of return is 14%. Assume all cash flows occur at year-end except for initial investment amounts. City Hospital uses straight-line depreciation.

1. Calculate the following for the special-purpose eye-testing machine: **Required**
   a. Net present value
   b. Payback period
   c. Internal rate of return
   d. Accrual accounting rate of return based on net initial investment
   e. Accrual accounting rate of return based on average investment
2. What other factors should City Hospital consider in deciding whether to purchase the special-purpose eye-testing machine?

21-19 Capital budgeting, income taxes. Assume the same facts as in Exercise 21-18 except that City Hospital is a taxpaying entity. The income tax rate is 30% for all transactions that affect income taxes.

1. Do requirement 1 of Exercise 21-18.   **Required**
2. How would your computations in requirement 1 be affected if the special-purpose machine had a $10,000 terminal disposal value at the end of 10 years? Assume depreciation deductions are based on the $110,000 purchase cost and zero terminal disposal value using the straight-line method. Answer briefly in words without further calculations.

21-20 Capital budgeting with uneven cash flows, no income taxes. Southern Cola is considering the purchase of a special-purpose bottling machine for $23,000. It is expected to have a useful life of four years with no terminal disposal value. The plant manager estimates the following savings in cash operating costs:

Year	Amount
1	$10,000
2	8,000
3	6,000
4	5,000
Total	$29,000

Southern Cola uses a required rate of return of 16% in its capital budgeting decisions. Ignore income taxes in your analysis. Assume all cash flows occur at year-end except for initial investment amounts.

Required

Calculate the following for the special-purpose bottling machine:
1. Net present value
2. Payback period
3. Discounted payback period
4. Internal rate of return (using the interpolation method)
5. Accrual accounting rate of return based on net initial investment (Assume straight-line depreciation. Use the average annual savings in cash operating costs when computing the numerator of the accrual accounting rate of return.)

21-21 Comparison of projects, no income taxes. (CMA, adapted) New Bio Corporation is a rapidly growing biotech company that has a required rate of return of 10%. It plans to build a new facility in Santa Clara County. The building will take two years to complete. The building contractor offered New Bio a choice of three payment plans, as follows:

- **Plan I** Payment of $100,000 at the time of signing the contract and $4,575,000 upon completion of the building. The end of the second year is the completion date.
- **Plan II** Payment of $1,550,000 at the time of signing the contract and $1,550,000 at the end of each of the two succeeding years.
- **Plan III** Payment of $200,000 at the time of signing the contract and $1,475,000 at the end of each of the three succeeding years.

Required

1. Using the net present value method, calculate the comparative cost of each of the three payment plans being considered by New Bio.
2. Which payment plan should New Bio choose? Explain.
3. Discuss the financial factors, other than the cost of the plan, and the nonfinancial factors that should be considered in selecting an appropriate payment plan.

21-22 Payback and NPV methods, no income taxes. (CMA, adapted) Andrews Construction is analyzing its capital expenditure proposals for the purchase of equipment in the coming year. The capital budget is limited to $6,000,000 for the year. Lori Bart, staff analyst at Andrews, is preparing an analysis of the three projects under consideration by Corey Andrews, the company's owner.

	Home	Insert	Page Layout	Formulas	Data	Review	View
	A			B	C	D	
1				**Project A**	**Project B**	**Project C**	
2	**Projected cash outflow**						
3	Net initial investment			$3,000,000	$1,500,000	$4,000,000	
4							
5	**Projected cash inflows**						
6	Year 1			$1,000,000	$ 400,000	$2,000,000	
7	Year 2			1,000,000	900,000	2,000,000	
8	Year 3			1,000,000	800,000	200,000	
9	Year 4			1,000,000		100,000	
10							
11	Required rate of return			10%	10%	10%	

Required

1. Because the company's cash is limited, Andrews thinks the payback method should be used to choose between the capital budgeting projects.
   a. What are the benefits and limitations of using the payback method to choose between projects?

b. Calculate the payback period for each of the three projects. Ignore income taxes. Using the payback method, which projects should Andrews choose?

2. Bart thinks that projects should be selected based on their NPVs. Assume all cash flows occur at the end of the year except for initial investment amounts. Calculate the NPV for each project. Ignore income taxes.

3. Which projects, if any, would you recommend funding? Briefly explain why.

21-23 DCF, accrual accounting rate of return, working capital, evaluation of performance, no income taxes. Century Lab plans to purchase a new centrifuge machine for its New Hampshire facility. The machine costs $137,500 and is expected to have a useful life of eight years, with a terminal disposal value of $37,500. Savings in cash operating costs are expected to be $31,250 per year. However, additional working capital is needed to keep the machine running efficiently. The working capital must continually be replaced, so an investment of $10,000 needs to be maintained at all times, but this investment is fully recoverable (will be "cashed in") at the end of the useful life. Century Lab's required rate of return is 14%. Ignore income taxes in your analysis. Assume all cash flows occur at year-end except for initial investment amounts. Century Lab uses straight-line depreciation for its machines.

Required

1. Calculate net present value.
2. Calculate internal rate of return.
3. Calculate accrual accounting rate of return based on net initial investment.
4. Calculate accrual accounting rate of return based on average investment.
5. You have the authority to make the purchase decision. Why might you be reluctant to base your decision on the DCF methods?

21-24 New equipment purchase, income taxes. Anna's Bakery plans to purchase a new oven for its store. The oven has an estimated useful life of four years. The estimated pretax cash flows for the oven are as shown in the table that follows, with no anticipated change in working capital. Anna's Bakery has a 12% after-tax required rate of return and a 40% income tax rate. Assume depreciation is calculated on a straight-line basis for tax purposes using the initial oven investment and estimated terminal disposal value of the oven. Assume all cash flows occur at year-end except for initial investment amounts.

	Home	Insert	Page Layout	Formulas	Data	Review	View		
	A		B	C	D	E	F		
1			Relevant Cash Flows at End of Each Year						
2			0	1	2	3	4		
3	Initial machine investment		$(88,000)						
4	Annual cash flow from operations (excluding the depreciation effect)			$36,000	$36,000	$36,000	$36,000		
5	Cash flow from terminal disposal of machine						$ 8,000		

Required

1. Calculate (a) net present value, (b) payback period, and (c) internal rate of return.
2. Calculate accrual accounting rate of return based on net initial investment.

21-25 New equipment purchase, income taxes. Innovation, Inc., is considering the purchase of a new industrial electric motor to improve efficiency at its Fremont plant. The motor has an estimated useful life of five years. The estimated pretax cash flows for the motor are shown in the table that follows, with no anticipated change in working capital. Innovation has a 10% after-tax required rate of return and a 35% income tax rate. Assume depreciation is calculated on a straight-line basis for tax purposes. Assume all cash flows occur at year-end except for initial investment amounts.

	Home	Insert	Page Layout	Formulas	Data	Review	View		
	A		B	C	D	E	F	G	
1			Relevant Cash Flows at End of Each Year						
2			0	1	2	3	4	5	
3	Initial motor investment		$(75,000)						
4	Annual cash flow from operations (excluding the depreciation effect)			$25,000	$25,000	$25,000	$25,000	$25,000	
5	Cash flow from terminal disposal of motor							$ 0	

Required

1. Calculate (a) net present value, (b) payback period, (c) discounted payback period, and (d) internal rate of return.
2. Compare and contrast the capital budgeting methods in requirement 1.

21-26 Selling a plant, income taxes. (CMA, adapted) The Crossroad Company is an international clothing manufacturer. Its Santa Monica plant will become idle on December 31, 2011. Peter Laney, the corporate controller, has been asked to look at three options regarding the plant.

- ■ Option 1: The plant, which has been fully depreciated for tax purposes, can be sold immediately for $450,000.
- ■ Option 2: The plant can be leased to the Austin Corporation, one of Crossroad's suppliers, for four years. Under the lease terms, Austin would pay Crossroad $110,000 rent per year (payable at year-end) and would grant Crossroad a $20,000 annual discount off the normal price of fabric purchased by Crossroad. (Assume that the discount is received at year-end for each of the four years.) Austin would bear all of the plant's ownership costs. Crossroad expects to sell this plant for $75,000 at the end of the four-year lease.
- ■ Option 3: The plant could be used for four years to make souvenir jackets for the Olympics. Fixed overhead costs (a cash outflow) before any equipment upgrades are estimated to be $10,000 annually for the four-year period. The jackets are expected to sell for $55 each. Variable cost per unit is expected to be $43. The following production and sales of jackets are expected: 2012, 9,000 units; 2013, 13,000 units; 2014, 15,000 units; 2015, 5,000 units. In order to manufacture the jackets, some of the plant equipment would need to be upgraded at an immediate cost of $80,000. The equipment would be depreciated using the straight-line depreciation method and zero terminal disposal value over the four years it would be in use. Because of the equipment upgrades, Crossroad could sell the plant for $135,000 at the end of four years. No change in working capital would be required.

Crossroad treats all cash flows as if they occur at the end of the year, and it uses an after-tax required rate of return of 10%. Crossroad is subject to a 35% tax rate on all income, including capital gains.

Required

1. Calculate net present value of each of the options and determine which option Crossroad should select using the NPV criterion.
2. What nonfinancial factors should Crossroad consider before making its choice?

MyAccountingLab

Problems

21-27 Equipment replacement, no income taxes. Pro Chips is a manufacturer of prototype chips based in Dublin, Ireland. Next year, in 2012, Pro Chips expects to deliver 552 prototype chips at an average price of $80,000. Pro Chips' marketing vice president forecasts growth of 60 prototype chips per year through 2018. That is, demand will be 552 in 2012, 612 in 2013, 672 in 2014, and so on.

The plant cannot produce more than 540 prototype chips annually. To meet future demand, Pro Chips must either modernize the plant or replace it. The old equipment is fully depreciated and can be sold for $3,600,000 if the plant is replaced. If the plant is modernized, the costs to modernize it are to be capitalized and depreciated over the useful life of the updated plant. The old equipment is retained as part of the modernize alternative. The following data on the two options are available:

	Modernize	Replace
Initial investment in 2012	$33,600,000	$58,800,000
Terminal disposal value in 2018	$6,000,000	$14,400,000
Useful life	7 years	7 years
Total annual cash operating costs per prototype chip	$62,000	$56,000

Pro Chips uses straight-line depreciation, assuming zero terminal disposal value. For simplicity, we assume no change in prices or costs in future years. The investment will be made at the beginning of 2012, and all transactions thereafter occur on the last day of the year. Pro Chips' required rate of return is 12%.

There is no difference between the modernize and replace alternatives in terms of required working capital. Pro Chips has a special waiver on income taxes until 2018.

Required

1. Sketch the cash inflows and outflows of the modernize and replace alternatives over the 2012–2018 period.
2. Calculate payback period for the modernize and replace alternatives.
3. Calculate net present value of the modernize and replace alternatives.
4. What factors should Pro Chips consider in choosing between the alternatives?

21-28 Equipment replacement, income taxes (continuation of 21-27). Assume the same facts as in Problem 21-27, except that the plant is located in Austin, Texas. Pro Chips has no special waiver on income taxes. It pays a 30% tax rate on all income. Proceeds from sales of equipment above book value are taxed at the same 30% rate.

1. Sketch the after-tax cash inflows and outflows of the modernize and replace alternatives over the 2012–2018 period.
2. Calculate net present value of the modernize and replace alternatives.
3. Suppose Pro Chips is planning to build several more plants. It wants to have the most advantageous tax position possible. Pro Chips has been approached by Spain, Malaysia, and Australia to construct plants in their countries. Use the data in Problem 21-27 and this problem to briefly describe in qualitative terms the income tax features that would be advantageous to Pro Chips.

21-29 DCF, sensitivity analysis, no income taxes. (CMA, adapted) Whimsical Corporation is an international manufacturer of fragrances for women. Management at Whimsical is considering expanding the product line to men's fragrances. From the best estimates of the marketing and production managers, annual sales (all for cash) for this new line is 900,000 units at $100 per unit; cash variable cost is $50 per unit; and cash fixed costs is $9,000,000 per year. The investment project requires $120,000,000 of cash outflow and has a project life of seven years.

At the end of the seven-year useful life, there will be no terminal disposal value. Assume all cash flows occur at year-end except for initial investment amounts.

Men's fragrance is a new market for Whimsical, and management is concerned about the reliability of the estimates. The controller has proposed applying sensitivity analysis to selected factors. Ignore income taxes in your computations. Whimsical's required rate of return on this project is 10%.

1. Calculate the net present value of this investment proposal.
2. Calculate the effect on the net present value of the following two changes in assumptions. (Treat each item independently of the other.)
   a. 20% reduction in the selling price
   b. 20% increase in the variable cost per unit
3. Discuss how management would use the data developed in requirements 1 and 2 in its consideration of the proposed capital investment.

21-30 NPV, IRR, and sensitivity analysis. Crumbly Cookie Company is considering expanding by buying a new (additional) machine that costs $62,000, has zero terminal disposal value, and has a 10-year useful life. It expects the annual increase in cash revenues from the expansion to be $28,000 per year. It expects additional annual cash costs to be $18,000 per year. Its cost of capital is 8%. Ignore taxes.

1. Calculate the net present value and internal rate of return for this investment.
2. Assume the finance manager of Crumbly Cookie Company is not sure about the cash revenues and costs. The revenues could be anywhere from 10% higher to 10% lower than predicted. Assume cash costs are still $18,000 per year. What are NPV and IRR at the high and low points for revenue?
3. The finance manager thinks that costs will vary with revenues, and if the revenues are 10% higher, the costs will be 7% higher. If the revenues are 10% lower, the costs will be 10% lower. Recalculate the NPV and IRR at the high and low revenue points with this new cost information.
4. The finance manager has decided that the company should earn 2% more than the cost of capital on any project. Recalculate the original NPV in requirement 1 using the new discount rate and evaluate the investment opportunity.
5. Discuss how the changes in assumptions have affected the decision to expand.

21-31 Payback methods, even and uneven cash flows. You have the opportunity to expand your business by purchasing new equipment for $159,000. The equipment has a useful life of nine years. You expect to incur cash fixed costs of $96,000 per year to use this new equipment, and you expect to incur cash variable costs in the amount of 10% of cash revenues. Your cost of capital is 12%.

1. Calculate the payback period and the discounted payback period for this investment, assuming you will generate $140,000 in cash revenues every year.
2. Assume instead that you expect the following cash revenue stream for this investment:

Year 1	$ 90,000
Year 2	115,000
Year 3	130,000
Year 4	155,000
Year 5	170,000
Year 6	180,000
Year 7	140,000
Year 8	125,000
Year 9	110,000

Based on this estimated revenue stream, what are the payback and discounted payback periods for this investment?

21-32 Replacement of a machine, income taxes, sensitivity. (CMA, adapted) The Smacker Company is a family-owned business that produces fruit jam. The company has a grinding machine that has been in use for three years. On January 1, 2011, Smacker is considering the purchase of a new grinding machine. Smacker has two options: (1) continue using the old machine or (2) sell the old machine and purchase a new machine. The seller of the new machine isn't offering a trade-in. The following information has been obtained:

	A	B	C
	Home Insert Page Layout Formulas Data Review View		
		Old Machine	**New Machine**
1		Old Machine	New Machine
2	Initial purchase cost of machines	$150,000	$190,000
3	Useful life from acquisition date (years)	8	5
4	Terminal disposal value at the end of useful life on Dec. 31, 2015, assumed for depreciation purposes	$ 20,000	$ 25,000
5	Expected annual cash operating costs:		
6	Variable cost per can of jam	$ 0.25	$ 0.19
7	Total fixed costs	$ 25,000	$ 24,000
8	Depreciation method for tax purposes	Straight line	Straight line
9	Estimated disposal value of machines:		
10	January 1, 2011	$ 68,000	$190,000
11	December 31, 2015	$ 12,000	$ 22,000
12	Expected cans of jam made and sold each year	475,000	475,000

Smacker is subject to a 36% income tax rate. Assume that any gain or loss on the sale of machines is treated as an ordinary tax item and will affect the taxes paid by Smacker in the year in which it occurs. Smacker's after-tax required rate of return is 14%. Assume all cash flows occur at year-end except for initial investment amounts.

Required

1. You have been asked whether Smacker should buy the new machine. To help in your analysis, calculate the following:
   a. One-time after-tax cash effect of disposing of the old machine on January 1, 2011
   b. Annual recurring after-tax cash operating savings from using the new machine (variable and fixed)
   c. Cash tax savings due to differences in annual depreciation of the old machine and the new machine
   d. Difference in after-tax cash flow from terminal disposal of new machine and old machine
2. Use your calculations in requirement 1 and the net present value method to determine whether Smacker should use the old machine or acquire the new machine.
3. How much more or less would the recurring after-tax cash operating savings of the new machine need to be for Smacker to earn exactly the 14% after-tax required rate of return? Assume that all other data about the investment do not change.

21-33 NPV and AARR, goal-congruence issues. Jack Garrett, a manager of the plate division for the Marble Top Manufacturing company, has the opportunity to expand the division by investing in additional machinery costing $420,000. He would depreciate the equipment using the straight-line method, and expects it to have no residual value. It has a useful life of seven years. The firm mandates a required after-tax rate of return of 14% on investments. Jack estimates annual net cash inflows for this investment of $125,000 before taxes, and an investment in working capital of $2,500. Tax rate is 35%.

Required

1. Calculate the net present value of this investment.
2. Calculate the accrual accounting rate of return on initial investment for this project.
3. Should Jack accept the project? Will Jack accept the project if his bonus depends on achieving an accrual accounting rate of return of 14%? How can this conflict be resolved?

21-34 Recognizing cash flows for capital investment projects. Ludmilla Quagg owns a fitness center and is thinking of replacing the old Fit-O-Matic machine with a brand new Flab-Buster 3000. The old Fit-O-Matic has a historical cost of $50,000 and accumulated depreciation of $46,000, but has a trade-in value of $5,000. It currently costs $1,200 per month in utilities and another $10,000 a year in maintenance to run the Fit-O-Matic. Ludmilla feels that the Fit-O-Matic can be used for another 10 years, after which it would have no salvage value.

The Flab-Buster 3000 would reduce the utilities costs by 30% and cut the maintenance cost in half. The Flab-Buster 3000 costs $98,000, has a 10-year life, and an expected disposal value of $10,000 at the end of its useful life.

Ludmilla charges customers $10 per hour to use the fitness center. Replacing the fitness machine will not affect the price of service or the number of customers she can serve.

1. Ludmilla wants to evaluate the Flab-Buster 3000 project using capital budgeting techniques, but does not know how to begin. To help her, read through the problem and separate the cash flows into four groups: (1) net initial investment cash flows, (2) cash flow savings from operations, (3) cash flows from terminal disposal of investment, and (4) cash flows not relevant to the capital budgeting problem.
2. Assuming a tax rate of 40%, a required rate of return of 8%, and straight-line depreciation over remaining useful life of machines, should Ludmilla buy the Flab-Buster 3000?

21-35 Recognizing cash flows for capital investment projects, NPV. Unbreakable Manufacturing manufactures over 20,000 different products made from metal, including building materials, tools, and furniture parts. The manager of the furniture parts division has proposed that his division expand into bicycle parts as well. The furniture parts division currently generates cash revenues of $5,000,000 and incurs cash costs of $3,550,000, with an investment in assets of $12,050,000. One-fourth of the cash costs are direct labor.

The manager estimates that the expansion of the business will require an investment in working capital of $25,000. Because the company already has a facility, there would be no additional rent or purchase costs for a building, but the project would generate an additional $390,000 in annual cash overhead. Moreover, the manager expects annual materials cash costs for bicycle parts to be $1,300,000, and labor for the bicycle parts to be about the same as the labor cash costs for furniture parts.

The controller of Unbreakable, working with various managers, estimates that the expansion would require the purchase of equipment with a $2,575,000 cost and an expected disposal value of $370,000 at the end of its seven-year useful life. Depreciation would occur on a straight-line basis.

The CFO of Unbreakable determines the firm's cost of capital as 14%. The CFO's salary is $150,000 per year. Adding another division will not change that. The CEO asks for a report on expected revenues for the project, and is told by the marketing department that it might be able to achieve cash revenues of $3,372,500 annually from bicycle parts. Unbreakable Manufacturing has a tax rate of 35%.

1. Separate the cash flows into four groups: (1) net initial investment cash flows, (2) cash flows from operations, (3) cash flows from terminal disposal of investment, and (4) cash flows not relevant to the capital budgeting problem.
2. Calculate the NPV of the expansion project and comment on your analysis.

21-36 NPV, inflation and taxes. Best-Cost Foods is considering replacing all 10 of its old cash registers with new ones. The old registers are fully depreciated and have no disposal value. The new registers cost $749,700 (in total). Because the new registers are more efficient than the old registers, Best-Cost will have annual incremental cash savings from using the new registers in the amount of $160,000 per year. The registers have a seven-year useful life and no terminal disposal value, and are depreciated using the straight-line method. Best-Cost requires an 8% real rate of return.

1. Given the preceding information, what is the net present value of the project? Ignore taxes.
2. Assume the $160,000 cost savings are in current real dollars, and the inflation rate is 5.5%. Recalculate the NPV of the project.
3. Based on your answers to requirements 1 and 2, should Best-Cost buy the new cash registers?
4. Now assume that the company's tax rate is 30%. Calculate the NPV of the project assuming no inflation.
5. Again assuming that the company faces a 30% tax rate, calculate the NPV of the project under an inflation rate of 5.5%.
6. Based on your answers to requirements 4 and 5, should Best-Cost buy the new cash registers?

21-37 Net present value, Internal Rate of Return, Sensitivity Analysis. Sally wants to purchase a Burgers-N-Fries franchise. She can buy one for $500,000. Burgers-N-Fries headquarters provides the following information:

Estimated annual cash revenues	$280,000
Typical annual cash operating expenses	$165,000

Sally will also have to pay Burgers-N-Fries a franchise fee of 10% of her revenues each year. Sally wants to earn at least 10% on the investment because she has to borrow the $500,000 at a cost of 6%. Use a 10-year window, and ignore taxes.

1. Find the NPV and IRR of Sally's investment.
2. Sally is nervous about the revenue estimate provided by Burgers-N-Fries headquarters. Calculate the NPV and IRR under alternative annual revenue estimates of $260,000 and $240,000.
3. Sally estimates that if her revenues are lower, her costs will be lower as well. For each revised level of revenue used in requirement 2, recalculate NPV and IRR with a proportional decrease in annual operating expenses.

4. Suppose Sally also negotiates a lower franchise and has to pay Burgers-N-Fries only 8% of annual revenues. Redo the calculations in requirement 3.

5. Discuss how the sensitivity analysis will affect Sally's decision to buy the franchise.

Collaborative Learning Problem

21-38 NPV, Relevant costs, Income taxes. Phish Corporation is the largest manufacturer and distributor of novelty ice creams across the East Coast. The company's products, because of their perishable nature, require careful packaging and transportation. Phish uses a special material called ICI that insulates the core of its boxes, thereby preserving the quality and freshness of the ice creams.

Patrick Scott, the newly appointed COO, believed that the company could save money by closing the internal Packaging department and outsourcing the manufacture of boxes to an outside vendor. He requested a report outlining Phish Corporation's current costs of manufacturing boxes from the company's controller, Reesa Morris. After conducting some of his own research, he approached a firm that specialized in packaging, Containers Inc., and obtained a quote for the insulated boxes. Containers Inc. quoted a rate of $700,000 for 7,000 boxes annually. The contract would run for five years and if there was a greater demand for boxes the cost would increase proportionately. Patrick compared these numbers to those on the cost report prepared by Reesa. Her analysis of the packaging department's annual costs is as follows:

Direct material (ICI)	$ 80,000
Other direct material	120,000
Direct labor	220,000
Department manager's salary	85,000
Depreciation of machinery	60,000
Department overhead	65,000
Rent	15,000
Allocation of general administrative overhead	70,000

After consulting with Reesa, Patrick gathers the following additional information:

i. The machinery used for production was purchased two years ago for $430,000 and was expected to last for seven years, with a terminal disposal value of $10,000. Its current salvage value is $280,000.

ii. Phish uses 20 tons of ICI each year. Three years ago, Phish purchased 100 tons of ICI for $400,000. ICI has since gone up in value and new purchases would cost $4,500 a ton. If Phish were to discontinue manufacture of boxes, it could dispose of its stock of ICI for a net amount of $3,800 per ton, after handling and transportation expenses.

iii. Phish has no inventory of other direct materials; it purchases them on an as-needed basis.

iv. The rent charge represents an allocation based on the packaging department's share of the building's floor space. Phish is currently renting a secondary warehouse for $27,000; this space would no longer be needed if the contract is signed with Containers Inc.

v. If the manufacture of boxes is outsourced, the packaging department's overhead costs would be avoided. The department manager would be moved to a similar position in another group that the company has been looking to fill with an external hire.

vi. Phish has a marginal tax rate of 40% and an after-tax required rate of return of 10%.

Required

1. Sketch the cash inflows and outflows of the two alternatives over a five-year time period.

2. Using the NPV criterion, which option should Phish Corporation select?

3. What other factors should Phish Corporation consider in choosing between the alternatives?

Answers to Exercises in Compound Interest (Exercise 21-16)

The general approach to these exercises centers on a key question: Which of the four basic tables in Appendix A should be used? No computations should be made until this basic question has been answered with confidence.

1. From Table 1. The $10,000 is the present value P of your winnings. Their future value S in 10 years will be as follows:

$$S = P(1 + r)^n$$

The conversion factor, $(1 + r)^n$, is on line 10 of Table 1.

Substituting at 8%: $S = \$10,000(2.159) = \$21,590$

Substituting at 10%: $S = \$10,000(2.594) = \$25,940$

2. **From Table 2.** The $154,900 is a future value. You want the present value of that amount. $P = S \div (1 + r)^n$. The conversion factor, $1 \div (1 + r)^n$, is on line 10 of Table 2. Substituting,

$$P = \$154,900(.676) = \$104,712.40$$

3. **From Table 3.** The $154,900 is a future value. You are seeking the uniform amount (annuity) to set aside annually. Note that $1 invested each year for 10 years at 10% has a future value of $15.937 after 10 years, from line 10 of Table 3.

$$\$154,900 / 15.937 = \$9719.52$$

4. **From Table 3.** You need to find the future value of an annuity of $7,500 per year. Note that $1 invested each year for 10 years at 8% has a future value of $14.487 after 10 years.

$$\$7,500 \,(14.487) = \$108,652.50$$

5. **From Table 4.** When you reach age 65, you will get $250,000, a present value at that time. You need to find the annuity that will exactly exhaust the invested principal in 10 years. To pay yourself $1 each year for 10 years when the interest rate is 6% requires you to have $6.710 today, from line 10 of Table 4.

$$\$250,000 / 6.710 = \$37,257.82$$

6. **From Table 4.** You need to find the present value of an annuity for 10 years at 8% and at 12%:

$$8\%: \$65,000 \,(6.710) = \$436,150.00$$

$$12\%: \$65,000 \,(5.650) = \$367,250.00$$

7. Plan A is preferable. The NPV of plan A exceeds that of plan B by $851.

		Plan A		Plan B	
Year	PV Factor at 8%	Cash Inflows	PV of Cash Inflows	Cash Inflows	PV of Cash Inflows
0	1.000	$(10,000)	$ (10,000)	$(10,000)	$ (10,000)
1	0.926	3,000	2,778.00	1,000	926.00
2	0.857	5,000	4285.00	2,000	1,714.00
3	0.794	2,000	1,588.00	3,000	2,382.00
4	0.735	3,000	2,205.00	4,000	2,940.00
5	0.681	2,000	1,362.00	5,000	3,405.00
			$2,218.00		$1,367.00

Even though plans A and B have the same total cash inflows over the five years, plan A is preferred because it has greater cash inflows occurring earlier.

management accounting system, which provides information regarding costs, revenues, and income; the human resources systems, which provide information on recruiting, training, absenteeism, and accidents; and the quality systems, which provide information on yield, defective products, and late deliveries to customers.

The informal management control system includes shared values, loyalties, and mutual commitments among members of the organization, company culture, and the unwritten norms about acceptable behavior for managers and other employees. Examples of company slogans that reinforce values and loyalties are "At Ford, Quality Is Job 1," and "At Home Depot, Low Prices Are Just the Beginning."

Effective Management Control

To be effective, management control systems should be closely aligned with the organization's strategies and goals. Two examples of strategies at ExxonMobil are (1) providing innovative products and services to increase market share in key customer segments (by targeting customers who are willing to pay more for faster service, better facilities, and well-stocked convenience stores) and (2) reducing costs and targeting price-sensitive customers. Suppose ExxonMobil decides to pursue the former strategy. The management control system must then reinforce this goal, and ExxonMobil should tie managers' rewards to achieving the targeted measures.

Management control systems should also be designed to support the organizational responsibilities of individual managers. Different levels of management at ExxonMobil need different kinds of information to perform their tasks. For example, top management needs stock-price information to evaluate how much shareholder value the company has created. Stock price, however, is less important for line managers supervising individual refineries. They are more concerned with obtaining information about on-time delivery of gasoline, equipment downtime, product quality, number of days lost to accidents and environmental problems, cost per gallon of gasoline, and employee satisfaction. Similarly, marketing managers are more concerned with information about service at gas stations, customer satisfaction, and market share.

Effective management control systems should also motivate managers and other employees. **Motivation** is the desire to attain a selected goal (the *goal-congruence* aspect) combined with the resulting pursuit of that goal (the *effort* aspect).

Goal congruence exists when individuals and groups work toward achieving the organization's goals—that is, managers working in their own best interest take actions that align with the overall goals of top management. Suppose the goal of ExxonMobil's top management is to maximize operating income. If the management control system evaluates the refinery manager *only* on the basis of costs, the manager may be tempted to make decisions that minimize cost but overlook product quality or timely delivery to retail stations. This oversight is unlikely to maximize operating income of the company as a whole. In this case, the management control system will not achieve goal congruence.

Effort is the extent to which managers strive or endeavor in order to achieve a goal. Effort goes beyond physical exertion, such as a worker producing at a faster rate, to include mental actions as well. For example, effort includes the diligence or acumen with which a manager gathers and analyzes data before authorizing a new investment. It is impossible to directly observe or reward effort. As a result, management control systems motivate employees to exert effort by rewarding them for the achievement of observable goals, such as profit targets or stock returns. This induces managers to exert effort because higher levels of effort increase the likelihood that the goals are achieved. The rewards can be monetary (such as cash, shares of company stock, use of a company car, or membership in a club) or nonmonetary (such as a better title, greater responsibility, or authority over a larger number of employees).

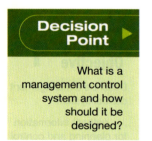

Decision Point

What is a management control system and how should it be designed?

Decentralization

Management control systems must fit an organization's structure. An organization whose structure is decentralized has additional issues to consider for its management control system to be effective.

Decentralization is the freedom for managers at lower levels of the organization to make decisions. **Autonomy** is the degree of freedom to make decisions. The greater the freedom, the greater the autonomy. As we discuss the issues of decentralization and autonomy, we use the term "subunit" to refer to any part of an organization. A subunit may be a large division, such as the refining division of ExxonMobil, or a small group, such as a two-person advertising department of a local clothing chain.

Until the mid-twentieth century, many firms were organized in a centralized, hierarchical fashion. Power was concentrated at the top and there was relatively little freedom for managers at the lower levels to make decisions. Perhaps the most famous example of a highly centralized structure is the Soviet Union, prior to its collapse in the late 1980s. Today, organizations are far more decentralized and many companies have pushed decision-making authority down to subunit managers. Examples of firms with decentralized structures include Nucor, the U.S. steel giant, which allows substantial operational autonomy to the general managers of its plants, and Tesco, Britain's largest retailer, which offers great latitude to its store managers. Of course, no firm is completely decentralized. At Nucor headquarters management still retains responsibility for overall strategic planning, company financing, setting base salary levels and bonus targets, purchase of steel scrap, etc. How much decentralization is optimal? Companies try to choose the degree of decentralization that maximizes benefits over costs. From a practical standpoint, top management can seldom quantify either the benefits or the costs of decentralization. Still, the cost-benefit approach helps management focus on the key issues.

Learning Objective 2

Describe the benefits of decentralization

. . . responsiveness to customers, faster decision making, management development

and the costs of decentralization

. . . loss of control, duplication of activities

Benefits of Decentralization

Supporters of decentralizing decision making and granting responsibilities to managers of subunits advocate the following benefits:

1. **Creates greater responsiveness to needs of a subunit's customers, suppliers, and employees.** Good decisions cannot be made without good information. Compared with top managers, subunit managers are better informed about their customers, competitors, suppliers, and employees, as well as about local factors that affect performance, such as ways to decrease costs, improve quality, and be responsive to customers. Eastman Kodak reports that two advantages of decentralization are an "increase in the company's knowledge of the marketplace and improved service to customers."

2. **Leads to gains from faster decision making by subunit managers.** Decentralization speeds decision making, creating a competitive advantage over centralized organizations. Centralization slows decision making as responsibility for decisions creeps upward through layer after layer of management. Interlake, a manufacturer of materials handling equipment, cites this benefit of decentralization: "We have distributed decision-making powers more broadly to the cutting edge of product and market opportunity." Interlake's materials-handling equipment must often be customized to fit customers' needs. Delegating decision making to the sales force allows Interlake to respond faster to changing customer requirements.

3. **Increases motivation of subunit managers.** Subunit managers are more motivated and committed when they can exercise initiative. Hawei & Hawei, a highly decentralized company, maintains that "Decentralization = Creativity = Productivity."

4. **Assists management development and learning.** Giving managers more responsibility helps develop an experienced pool of management talent to fill higher-level management positions. The company also learns which people are unlikely to be successful top managers. According to Tektronix, an electronics instruments company, "Decentralized units provide a training ground for general managers and a visible field of combat where product champions can fight for their ideas."

5. **Sharpens the focus of subunit managers, broadens the reach of top management.** In a decentralized setting, the manager of a subunit has a concentrated focus. The head of Yahoo Japan, for example, can develop country-specific knowledge and expertise (local advertising trends, cultural norms, payment forms, etc.) and focus attention on maximizing Yahoo's profits in Japan. At the same time, this relieves Yahoo's top

Decision Point ▶

What are the benefits and costs of decentralization?

A common misconception is that *profit center*—and, in some cases, *investment center*—is a synonym for a decentralized subunit, and *cost center* is a synonym for a centralized subunit. *Profit centers can be coupled with a highly centralized organization, and cost centers can be coupled with a highly decentralized organization.* For example, managers in a division organized as a profit center may have little freedom in making decisions. They may need to obtain approval from corporate headquarters for introducing new products and services, or to make expenditures over some preset limit. When Michael Eisner ran Walt Disney Co., the giant media and entertainment conglomerate, the strategic-planning division applied so much scrutiny to business proposals that managers were reluctant to even pitch new ideas.[4] In other companies, divisions such as Information Technology may be organized as cost centers, but their managers may have great latitude with regard to capital expenditures and the purchase of materials and services. In short, the labels "profit center" and "cost center" are independent of the degree of centralization or decentralization in a company.

Transfer Pricing

Learning Objective 3

Explain transfer prices

. . . price one subunit charges another for product

and four criteria used to evaluate alternative transfer-pricing methods

. . . goal congruence, management effort, subunit performance evaluation, and subunit autonomy

In decentralized organizations, much of the decision-making power resides in its individual subunits. In these cases, the management control system often uses *transfer prices* to coordinate the actions of the subunits and to evaluate their performance.

As you may recall from the opener, a **transfer price** is the price one subunit (department or division) charges for a product or service supplied to another subunit of the same organization. If, for example, a car manufacturer has a separate division that manufactures engines, the transfer price is the price the engine division charges when it transfers engines to the car assembly division. The transfer price creates revenues for the selling subunit (the engine division in our example) and purchase costs for the buying subunit (the assembly division in our example), affecting each subunit's operating income. These operating incomes can be used to evaluate subunits' performances and to motivate their managers. The product or service transferred between subunits of an organization is called an **intermediate product**. This product may either be further worked on by the receiving subunit (as in the engine example) or, if transferred from production to marketing, sold to an external customer.

In one sense, transfer pricing is a curious phenomenon. Activities within an organization are clearly nonmarket in nature; products and services are not bought and sold as they are in open-market transactions. Yet, establishing prices for transfers among subunits of a company has a distinctly market flavor. The rationale for transfer prices is that subunit managers (such as the manager of the engine division), when making decisions, need only focus on how their decisions will affect their subunit's performance without evaluating their impact on company-wide performance. In this sense, transfer prices ease the subunit managers' information-processing and decision-making tasks. In a well-designed transfer-pricing system, a manager focuses on optimizing subunit performance (the performance of the engine division) and in so doing optimizes the performance of the company as a whole.

Criteria for Evaluating Transfer Prices

As in all management control systems, transfer prices should help achieve a company's strategies and goals and fit its organization structure. We describe four criteria to evaluate transfer pricing: (1) Transfer prices should promote goal congruence. (2) They should induce managers to exert a high level of effort. Subunits selling a product or service should be motivated to hold down their costs; subunits buying the product or service should be motivated to acquire and use inputs efficiently. (3) The transfer price should help top management evaluate the performance of individual subunits. (4) If top management favors a high degree of decentralization, transfer prices should preserve a high degree of subunit autonomy in decision making. That is, a subunit manager seeking to maximize the operating income of the subunit should have the freedom to transact with other subunits of the company (on the basis of transfer prices) or to transact with external parties.

---

[4] When Robert Iger replaced Eisner as CEO in 2005, one of his first acts was to disassemble the strategic-planning division, thereby giving more authority to Disney's business units (parks and resorts, consumer products, and media networks).

Calculating Transfer Prices

There are three broad categories of methods for determining transfer prices. They are as follows:

1. **Market-based transfer prices.** Top management may choose to use the price of a similar product or service publicly listed in, say, a trade association Web site. Also, top management may select, for the internal price, the external price that a subunit charges to outside customers.

2. **Cost-based transfer prices.** Top management may choose a transfer price based on the cost of producing the product in question. Examples include variable production cost, variable and fixed production costs, and full cost of the product. Full cost of the product includes all production costs plus costs from other business functions (R&D, design, marketing, distribution, and customer service). The cost used in cost-based transfer prices can be actual cost or budgeted cost. Sometimes, the cost-based transfer price includes a markup or profit margin that represents a return on subunit investment.

3. **Hybrid transfer prices.** Hybrid transfer prices take into account both cost and market information. Top management may administer such prices, for example by specifying a transfer price that is an average of the cost of producing and transporting the product internally and the market price for comparable products. At other times, a hybrid transfer price may take the form where the revenue recognized by the selling unit is different from the cost recognized by the buying unit. The most common form of hybrid prices arise via negotiation—the subunits of a company are asked to negotiate the transfer price between them and to decide whether to buy and sell internally or deal with external parties. The eventual transfer price is then the outcome of a bargaining process between selling and buying subunits. Even though there is no requirement that the chosen transfer price bear any specific relationship to cost or market-price data, information regarding costs and prices plays a critical role in the negotiation process. Negotiated transfer prices are often employed when market prices are volatile and change constantly.

To see how each of the three transfer-pricing methods works and to see the differences among them, we examine transfer pricing at Horizon Petroleum against the four criteria of promoting goal congruence, motivating management effort, evaluating subunit performance, and preserving subunit autonomy (if desired).

An Illustration of Transfer Pricing

Horizon Petroleum has two divisions, each operating as a profit center. The transportation division purchases crude oil in Matamoros, Mexico, and transports it from Matamoros to Houston, Texas. The refining division processes crude oil into gasoline. For simplicity, we assume gasoline is the only salable product the Houston refinery makes and that it takes two barrels of crude oil to yield one barrel of gasoline.

Variable costs in each division are variable with respect to a single cost driver: barrels of crude oil transported by the transportation division, and barrels of gasoline produced by the refining division. The fixed cost per unit is based on the budgeted annual fixed costs and practical capacity of crude oil that can be transported by the transportation division, and the budgeted fixed costs and practical capacity of gasoline that can be produced by the refining division. Horizon Petroleum reports all costs and revenues of its non-U.S. operations in U.S. dollars using the prevailing exchange rate.

- The transportation division has obtained rights to certain oil fields in the Matamoros area. It has a long-term contract to purchase crude oil produced from these fields at $72 per barrel. The division transports the oil to Houston and then "sells" it to the refining division. The pipeline from Matamoros to Houston has the capacity to carry 40,000 barrels of crude oil per day.

- The refining division has been operating at capacity (30,000 barrels of crude oil a day), using oil supplied by Horizon's transportation division (an average of 10,000 barrels per day) and oil bought from another producer and delivered to the Houston refinery (an average of 20,000 barrels per day at $85 per barrel).

- The refining division sells the gasoline it produces to outside parties at $190 per barrel.

Exhibit 22-1 summarizes Horizon Petroleum's variable and fixed costs per barrel of crude oil in the transportation division and variable and fixed costs per barrel of gasoline in the refining division, the external market prices of buying crude oil, and the external market price of selling gasoline. What's missing in the exhibit is the actual transfer price from the transportation division to the refining division. This transfer price will vary depending on the transfer-pricing method used. Transfer prices from the transportation division to the refining division under each of the three methods are as follows:

1. Market-based transfer price of $85 per barrel of crude oil based on the competitive market price in Houston.

2. Cost-based transfer prices at, say, 105% of full cost, where full cost is the cost of the crude oil purchased in Matamoros plus the transportation division's own variable and fixed costs (from Exhibit 22-1): $1.05 \times (\$72 + \$1 + \$3) = \$79.80$.

3. Hybrid transfer price of, say, $82 per barrel of crude oil, which is between the market-based and cost-based transfer prices. We describe later in this section the various ways in which hybrid prices can be determined.

Exhibit 22-2 presents division operating incomes per 100 barrels of crude oil purchased under each transfer-pricing method. Transfer prices create income for the selling division and corresponding costs for the buying division that cancel out when division results are consolidated for the company as a whole. The exhibit assumes all three transfer-pricing methods yield transfer prices that are in a range that does not cause division managers to change the business relationships shown in Exhibit 22-1. That is, Horizon Petroleum's total operating income from purchasing, transporting, and refining the 100 barrels of crude oil and selling the 50 barrels of gasoline is the same, $1,200, *regardless of the internal transfer prices used.*

$$\text{Operating income} = \text{Revenues} - \begin{array}{c}\text{Cost of crude}\\\text{oil purchases}\\\text{in Matamoros}\end{array} - \begin{array}{c}\text{Transportation}\\\text{Division}\\\text{costs}\end{array} - \begin{array}{c}\text{Refining}\\\text{Division}\\\text{costs}\end{array}$$

$$= (\$190 \times 50 \text{ barrels of gasoline}) - (\$72 \times 100 \text{ barrels of crude oil})$$

$$- (\$4 \times 100 \text{ barrels of crude oil}) - (\$14 \times 50 \text{ barrels of gasoline})$$

$$= \$9,500 - \$7,200 - \$400 - \$700 = \$1,200$$

Note further that under all three methods, summing the two division operating incomes equals Horizon Petroleum's total operating income of $1,200. By keeping total operating

---

Exhibit 22-1 Operating Data for Horizon Petroleum

	A	B	C	D	E	F	G	H
1								
2				**Transportation Division**				
3	Contract price per barrel of crude oil supplied in Matamoros			Variable cost per barrel of crude oil	$1			
4		= $72	→	Fixed cost per barrel of crude oil	3			
5				Full cost per barrel of crude oil	$4			
6								
7								
8				Barrels of crude oil transferred				
9								
10								
11				**Refining Division**				
12	Market price per barrel of crude oil supplied to Houston refinery			Variable cost per barrel of gasoline	$ 8		Market price per barrel of gasoline sold to external parties	= $190
13		= $85	→	Fixed cost per barrel of gasoline	6	→		
14				Full cost per barrel of gasoline	$14			
15								

Exhibit 22-2   Division Operating Income of Horizon Petroleum for 100 Barrels of Crude Oil Under Alternative Transfer-Pricing Methods

	A	B	C	D	E	F	G	H
		Home Insert Page Layout Formulas Data Review View						
1		Production and Sales Data						
2		Barrels of crude oil transferred = 100						
3		Barrels of gasoline sold = 50						
4								
5		Internal Transfers at			Internal Transfers at			
6		Market Price =			105% of Full Cost =		Hybrid Price =	
7		$85 per Barrel			$79.80 per Barrel		$82 per Barrel	
8	Transportation Division							
9	Revenues, $85, $79.80, $82 × 100 barrels of crude oil	$8,500			$7,980		$8,200	
10	Costs							
11	Crude oil purchase costs, $72 × 100 barrels of crude oil	7,200			7,200		7,200	
12	Division variable costs, $1 × 100 barrels of crude oil	100			100		100	
13	Division fixed costs, $3 × 100 barrels of crude oil	300			300		300	
14	Total division costs	7,600			7,600		7,600	
15	Division operating income	$ 900			$ 380		$ 600	
16								
17	Refining Division							
18	Revenues, $190 × 50 barrels of gasoline	$9,500			$9,500		$9,500	
19	Costs							
20	Transferred-in costs, $85, $79.80, $82							
21	× 100 barrels of crude oil	8,500			7,980		8,200	
22	Division variable costs, $8 × 50 barrels of gasoline	400			400		400	
23	Division fixed costs, $6 × 50 barrels of gasoline	300			300		300	
24	Total division costs	9,200			8,680		8,900	
25	Division operating income	$ 300			$ 820		$ 600	
26	Operating income of both divisions together	$1,200			$1,200		$1,200	

income the same, we focus attention on the effects of different transfer-pricing methods on the operating income of each division. Subsequent sections of this chapter show that different transfer-pricing methods can cause managers to take different actions leading to different total operating incomes.

Consider the two methods in the first two columns of Exhibit 22-2. The operating income of the transportation division is $520 more ($900 − $380) if transfer prices are based on market prices rather than on 105% of full cost. The operating income of the refining division is $520 more ($820 − $300) if transfer prices are based on 105% of full cost rather than market prices. If the transportation division's sole criterion were to maximize its own division operating income, it would favor transfer prices at market prices. In contrast, the refining division would prefer transfer prices at 105% of full cost to maximize its own division operating income. The hybrid transfer price of $82 is between the 105% of full cost and market-based transfer prices. It splits the $1,200 of operating income equally between the divisions, and could arise as a result of negotiations between the transportation and refining division managers.

It's not surprising that subunit managers, especially those whose compensation or promotion directly depends on subunit operating income, take considerable interest in setting transfer prices. To reduce the excessive focus of subunit managers on their own subunits, many companies compensate subunit managers on the basis of both subunit and company-wide operating incomes.

We next examine market-based, cost-based, and hybrid transfer prices in more detail. We show how the choice of transfer-pricing method combined with managers' sourcing decisions can determine the size of the company-wide operating-income pie itself.

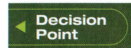

Decision Point

What are alternative ways of calculating transfer prices, and what criteria should be used to evaluate them?

Market-Based Transfer Prices

Learning Objective 4

Illustrate how market-based transfer prices promote goal congruence in perfectly competitive markets

. . . division managers transacting internally are motivated to take the same actions as if they were transacting externally

Transferring products or services at market prices generally leads to optimal decisions when three conditions are satisfied: (1) The market for the intermediate product is perfectly competitive, (2) interdependencies of subunits are minimal, and (3) there are no additional costs or benefits to the company as a whole from buying or selling in the external market instead of transacting internally.

Perfectly-Competitive-Market Case

A **perfectly competitive market** exists when there is a homogeneous product with buying prices equal to selling prices and no individual buyers or sellers can affect those prices by their own actions. By using market-based transfer prices in perfectly competitive markets, a company can (1) promote goal congruence, (2) motivate management effort, (3) evaluate subunit performance, and (4) preserve subunit autonomy.

Consider Horizon Petroleum again. Assume there is a perfectly competitive market for crude oil in the Houston area. As a result, the transportation division can sell and the refining division can buy as much crude oil as each wants at $85 per barrel. Horizon would prefer its managers to buy or sell crude oil internally. Think about the decisions that Horizon's division managers would make if each had the autonomy to sell or buy crude oil externally. If the transfer price between Horizon's transportation and refining divisions is set below $85, the manager of the transportation division will be motivated to sell all crude oil to external buyers in the Houston area at $85 per barrel. If the transfer price is set above $85, the manager of the refining division will be motivated to purchase all crude oil requirements from external suppliers. Only an $85 transfer price will motivate the transportation division and the refining division to buy and sell internally. That's because neither division profits by buying or selling in the external market.

Suppose Horizon evaluates division managers on the basis of their individual division's operating income. The transportation division will sell, either internally or externally, as much crude oil as it can profitably transport, and the refining division will buy, either internally or externally, as much crude oil as it can profitably refine. An $85-per-barrel transfer price achieves goal congruence—the actions that maximize each division's operating income are also the actions that maximize operating income of Horizon Petroleum as a whole. Furthermore, because the transfer price is not based on costs, it motivates each division manager to exert management effort to maximize his or her own division's operating income. Market prices also serve to evaluate the economic viability and profitability of each division individually. For example, Koch Industries, the second-largest private company in the United States, uses market-based pricing for all internal transfers. As their CFO, Steve Feilmeier, notes, "We believe that the alternative for any given asset should always be considered in order to best optimize the profitability of the asset. If you simply transfer price between two different divisions at cost, then you may be subsidizing your whole operation and not know it." Returning to our Horizon example, suppose that under market-based transfer prices, the refining division consistently shows small or negative profits. Then, Horizon may consider shutting down the refining division and simply transport and sell the oil to other refineries in the Houston area.

Distress Prices

When supply outstrips demand, market prices may drop well below their historical averages. If the drop in prices is expected to be temporary, these low market prices are sometimes called "distress prices." Deciding whether a current market price is a distress price is often difficult. Prior to the worldwide spike in commodity prices in the 2006–2008 period, the market prices of several mineral and agricultural commodities, including nickel, uranium, and wheat, stayed for many years at what people initially believed were temporary distress levels!

Which transfer price should be used for judging performance if distress prices prevail? Some companies use the distress prices themselves, but others use long-run average prices, or "normal" market prices. In the short run, the manager of the selling subunit should supply the product or service at the distress price as long as it exceeds the *incremental costs* of supplying the product or service. If the distress price is used as the transfer price, the selling division will show a loss because the distress price will not exceed the *full cost* of the division. If the long-run average market price is used, forcing the manager to buy internally at a price above the current market price will hurt the buying division's short-run operating income. But the long-run average market price will provide a better measure of the long-run profitability and viability of the supplier division. Of course, if the price remains low in the long run, the company should use the low market price as the transfer price. If this price is lower than the variable and fixed costs that can be saved if manufacturing facilities are shut down, the production facilities of the selling subunit should be sold, and the buying subunit should purchase the product from an external supplier.

Imperfect Competition

If markets are not perfectly competitive, selling prices affect the quantity of product sold. If the selling division sells its product in the external market, the selling division manager would choose a price and quantity combination that would maximize the division's operating income. If the transfer price is set at this selling price, the buying division may find that acquiring the product is too costly and results in a loss. It may decide not to purchase the product. Yet, from the point of view of the company as a whole, it may well be that profits are maximized if the selling division transfers the product to the buying division for further processing and sale. For this reason, when the market for the intermediate good is imperfectly competitive, the transfer price must generally be set below the external market price (but above the selling division's variable cost) in order to induce efficient transfers.[5]

Decision Point

Under what market conditions do market-based transfer prices promote goal congruence?

Cost-Based Transfer Prices

Cost-based transfer prices are helpful when market prices are unavailable, inappropriate, or too costly to obtain, such as when markets are not perfectly competitive, when the product is specialized, or when the internal product is different from the products available externally in terms of quality and customer service.

Learning Objective 5

Understand how to avoid making suboptimal decisions when transfer prices are based on full cost plus a markup

. . . in situations when buying divisions regard the fixed costs and the markup as variable costs

Full-Cost Bases

In practice, many companies use transfer prices based on full cost. To approximate market prices, cost-based transfer prices are sometimes set at full cost plus a margin. These transfer prices, however, can lead to suboptimal decisions. Suppose Horizon Petroleum makes internal transfers at 105% of full cost. Recall that the refining division purchases, on average, 20,000 barrels of crude oil per day from a local Houston supplier, who delivers the crude oil to the refinery at a price of $85 per barrel. To reduce crude oil costs, the refining division has located an independent producer in Matamoros—Gulfmex Corporation— that is willing to sell 20,000 barrels of crude oil per day at $79 per barrel, delivered to Horizon's pipeline in Matamoros. Given Horizon's organization structure, the transportation division would purchase the 20,000 barrels of crude oil in Matamoros from Gulfmex, transport it to Houston, and then sell it to the refining division. The pipeline has unused capacity and can ship the 20,000 barrels per day at its variable cost of $1 per barrel without affecting the shipment of the 10,000 barrels of crude oil per day acquired under its existing long-term contract arrangement. Will Horizon Petroleum incur lower costs by

---

[5] Consider a firm where division S produces the intermediate product. S has a capacity of 15 units and a variable cost per unit of $2. The imperfect competition is reflected in a downward-sloping demand curve for the intermediate product—if S wants to sell Q units, it has to lower the market price to P = 20 − Q. The division's profit function is therefore given by Q × (20 − Q) − 2Q = 18Q − Q². Simple calculus reveals that it is optimal for S to sell 9 units of the intermediate product at a price of $11, thereby making a profit of $81. Now, suppose that division B in the same firm can take the intermediate product, incur an additional variable cost of $4 and sell it in the external market for $12. Since S has surplus capacity (it only uses 9 of its 15 units of capacity), it is clearly in the firm's interest to have S make additional units and transfer them to B. The firm makes an incremental profit of $12 − $2 − $4 = $6 for each transferred unit. However, if the transfer price for the intermediate product were set equal to the market price of $11, B would reject the transaction since it would lose money on it ($12 − $11 − $4 = − $3 per unit).

To resolve this conflict, the transfer price should be set at a suitable *discount* to the external price in order to induce the buying division to seek internal transfers. In our example, the selling price must be greater than S's variable cost of $2, but less than B's contribution margin of $8. That is, the transfer price has to be discounted relative to the market price ($11) by a minimum of $3. We explore the issue of feasible transfer pricing ranges further in the section on hybrid transfer prices.

A General Guideline for Transfer-Pricing Situations

Learning Objective 7

Apply a general guideline for determining a minimum transfer price

. . . incremental cost plus opportunity cost of supplying division

Exhibit 22-3 summarizes the properties of market-based, cost-based, and negotiated transfer-pricing methods using the criteria described in this chapter. As the exhibit indicates, it is difficult for a transfer-pricing method to meet all criteria. Market conditions, the goal of the transfer-pricing system, and the criteria of promoting goal congruence, motivating management effort, evaluating subunit performance, and preserving subunit autonomy (if desired) must all be considered simultaneously. The transfer price a company will eventually choose depends on the economic circumstances and the decision at hand. Surveys of company practice indicate that the full-cost-based transfer price is generally the most frequently used transfer-pricing method around the world, followed by market-based transfer price and negotiated transfer price.

Our discussion thus far highlight that, barring settings in which a perfectly competitive market exists for the intermediate product, there is generally a range of possible transfer prices that would induce goal congruence. We now provide a general guideline for determining the minimum price in that range. The following formula is a helpful first step in setting the minimum transfer price in many situations:

$$\text{Minimum transfer price} = \begin{matrix} \text{Incremental cost} \\ \text{per unit} \\ \text{incurred up} \\ \text{to the point of transfer} \end{matrix} + \begin{matrix} \text{Opportunity cost} \\ \text{per unit} \\ \text{to the selling subunit} \end{matrix}$$

Incremental cost in this context means the additional cost of producing and transferring the product or service. Opportunity cost here is the maximum contribution margin forgone by the selling subunit if the product or service is transferred internally. For example, if the selling subunit is operating at capacity, the opportunity cost of transferring a unit internally rather than selling it externally is equal to the market price minus variable cost. That's because by transferring a unit internally, the subunit forgoes the contribution margin it could have obtained by selling the unit in the external market. We distinguish incremental cost from opportunity cost because financial accounting systems record incremental cost but do not record opportunity cost. The guideline measures a *minimum* transfer price because it represents the selling unit's cost of transferring the product. We illustrate the general guideline in some specific situations using data from Horizon Petroleum.

1. **A perfectly competitive market for the intermediate product exists, and the selling division has no unused capacity.** If the market for crude oil in Houston is perfectly

Exhibit 22-3

Comparison of Different Transfer-Pricing Methods

Criteria	Market-Based	Cost-Based	Negotiated
Achieves goal congruence	Yes, when markets are competitive	Often, but not always	Yes
Motivates management effort	Yes	Yes, when based on budgeted costs; less incentive to control costs if transfers are based on actual costs	Yes
Useful for evaluating subunit performance	Yes, when markets are competitive	Difficult unless transfer price exceeds full cost and even then is somewhat arbitrary	Yes, but transfer prices are affected by bargaining strengths of the buying and selling divisions
Preserves subunit autonomy	Yes, when markets are competitive	No, because it is rule-based	Yes, because it is based on negotiations between subunits
Other factors	Market may not exist, or markets may be imperfect or in distress	Useful for determining full cost of products and services; easy to implement	Bargaining and negotiations take time and may need to be reviewed repeatedly as conditions change

competitive, the transportation division can sell all the crude oil it transports to the external market at $85 per barrel, and it will have no unused capacity. The transportation division's incremental cost (as shown in Exhibit 22-1, p. 782) is $73 per barrel (purchase cost of $72 per barrel plus variable transportation cost of $1 per barrel) for oil purchased under the long-term contract or $80 per barrel (purchase cost of $79 plus variable transportation cost of $1) for oil purchased at current market prices from Gulfmex. The transportation division's opportunity cost per barrel of transferring the oil internally is the contribution margin per barrel forgone by not selling the crude oil in the external market: $12 for oil purchased under the long-term contract (market price, $85, minus variable cost, $73) and $5 for oil purchased from Gulfmex (market price, $85, minus variable cost, $80). In either case,

$$\begin{array}{c}\text{Minimum transfer price} \\ \text{per barrel}\end{array} = \begin{array}{c}\text{Incremental cost} \\ \text{per barrel}\end{array} + \begin{array}{c}\text{Opportunity cost} \\ \text{per barrel}\end{array}$$

$$= \$73 + \$12 = \$85$$
$$\text{or}$$
$$= \$80 + \$5 = \$85$$

2. **An intermediate market exists that is not perfectly competitive, and the selling division has unused capacity.** In markets that are not perfectly competitive, capacity utilization can only be increased by decreasing prices. Unused capacity exists because decreasing prices is often not worthwhile—it decreases operating income.

    If the transportation division has unused capacity, its opportunity cost of transferring the oil internally is zero because the division does not forgo any external sales or contribution margin from internal transfers. In this case,

$$\begin{array}{c}\text{Minimum transfer price} \\ \text{per barrel}\end{array} = \begin{array}{c}\text{Incremental cost} \\ \text{per barrel}\end{array} = \begin{array}{c}\$73 \text{ per barrel for oil purchased under the} \\ \text{long-term contract or } \$80 \text{ per barrel for} \\ \text{oil purchased from Gulfmex in Matamoros}\end{array}$$

In general, when markets are not perfectly competitive, the potential to influence demand and operating income through prices complicates the measurement of opportunity costs. The transfer price depends on constantly changing levels of supply and demand. There is not just one transfer price. Rather, the transfer prices for various quantities supplied and demanded depend on the incremental costs and opportunity costs of the units transferred.

3. **No market exists for the intermediate product.** This situation would occur for the Horizon Petroleum case if the crude oil transported by the transportation division could be used only by the Houston refinery (due to, say, its high tar content) and would not be wanted by external parties. Here, the opportunity cost of supplying crude oil internally is zero because the inability to sell crude oil externally means no contribution margin is forgone. For the transportation division of Horizon Petroleum, the minimum transfer price under the general guideline is the incremental cost per barrel (either $73 or $80). As in the previous case, any transfer price between the incremental cost and $85 will achieve goal congruence.

Decision Point

What is the general guideline for determining a minimum transfer price?

Multinational Transfer Pricing and Tax Considerations

Transfer pricing is an important accounting priority for managers around the world. A 2007 Ernst & Young survey of multinational enterprises in 24 countries found that 74% of parent firms and 81% of subsidiary respondents believed that transfer pricing was "absolutely critical" or "very important" to their organizations. The reason is that parent companies identify transfer pricing as the single most important tax issue they face. The sums of money involved are often staggering. Google, for example, has a 90% market share of UK internet searches and earned £1.6 billion in advertising revenues last year in Britain; yet, Google UK reported a pretax loss of £26 million. The reason is that revenues from customers in Britain are transferred to Google's European headquarters in Dublin. By paying the low Irish corporate tax rate of 12.5%, Google saved £450 million in UK taxes in 2009 alone. Transfer prices affect not just income taxes, but

Learning Objective 8

Incorporate income tax considerations in multinational transfer pricing

. . . set transfer prices to minimize tax payments to the extent permitted by tax authorities

The general guideline that was introduced in the chapter (p. 790) as a first step in setting a transfer price can be used to highlight the alternatives:

	Home	Insert	Page Layout		Formulas	Data	Review	View	
	A	B	C		D	E	F	G
1	Case	Incremental Cost per Unit Incurred to Point of Transfer	+		Opportunity Cost per Unit to the Supplying Division	=	Transfer Price	External Market Price
2	a	$190	+		$0	=	$190.00	$200
3	b	$190	+		$14.50ᵃ	=	$204.50	$200
4	c	$190	+		$0	=	$190.00	$185
5								
6	ᵃOpportunity cost per unit	=	Total opportunity costs	÷	Number of crankshafts	= $29,000 ÷ 2,000 = $14.50		
7								

Comparing transfer price to external-market price, the tractor division will maximize annual operating income of Pillercat Corporation as a whole by purchasing from the machining division in case **a** and by purchasing from the external supplier in cases **b** and **c**.

2. Pillercat Corporation is a highly decentralized company. If no forced transfer were made, the tractor division would use an external supplier, a decision that would be in the best interest of the company as a whole in cases **b** and **c** of requirement 1 but not in case **a**.

Suppose in case **a**, the machining division refuses to meet the price of $200. This decision means that the company will be $20,000 worse off in the short run. Should top management interfere and force a transfer at $200? This interference would undercut the philosophy of decentralization. Many top managers would not interfere because they would view the $20,000 as an inevitable cost of a suboptimal decision that can occur under decentralization. But how high must this cost be before the temptation to interfere would be irresistible? $30,000? $40,000?

Any top management interference with lower-level decision making weakens decentralization. Of course, Pillercat's management may occasionally interfere to prevent costly mistakes. But recurring interference and constraints would hurt Pillercat's attempts to operate as a decentralized company.

Decision Points

The following question-and-answer format summarizes the chapter's learning objectives. Each decision presents a key question related to a learning objective. The guidelines are the answer to that question.

Decision	Guidelines
1. What is a management control system and how should it be designed?	A management control system is a means of gathering and using information to aid and coordinate the planning and control decisions throughout the organization and to guide the behavior of managers and other employees. Effective management control systems (a) are closely aligned to the organization's strategy, (b) support the organizational responsibilities of individual managers, and (c) motivate managers and other employees to give effort to achieve the organization's goals.

2. **What are the benefits and costs of decentralization?**

The benefits of decentralization include (a) greater responsiveness to local needs, (b) gains from faster decision making, (c) increased motivation of subunit managers, (d) greater management development and learning, and (e) sharpened focus of subunit managers. The costs of decentralization include (a) suboptimal decision making, (b) excessive focus on the subunit rather than the company as a whole, (c) increased costs of information gathering, and (d) duplication of activities.

3. **What are alternative ways of calculating transfer prices, and what criteria should be used to evaluate them?**

A transfer price is the price one subunit charges for a product or service supplied to another subunit of the same organization. Transfer prices can be (a) market-based, (b) cost-based, or (c) hybrid. Different transfer-pricing methods produce different revenues and costs for individual subunits, and hence, different operating incomes for the subunits. Transfer prices seek to (a) promote goal congruence, (b) motivate management effort, (c) help evaluate subunit performance, and (d) preserve subunit autonomy (if desired).

4. **Under what market conditions do market-based transfer prices promote goal congruence?**

In perfectly competitive markets, there is no unused capacity, and division managers can buy and sell as much of a product or service as they want at the market price. In such settings, using the market price as the transfer price motivates division managers to transact internally and to take exactly the same actions as they would if they were transacting in the external market.

5. **What problems can arise when full cost plus a markup is used as the transfer price?**

A transfer price based on full cost plus a markup may lead to suboptimal decisions because it leads the buying division to regard the fixed costs and the markup of the selling division as a variable cost. The buying division may then purchase products from an external supplier expecting savings in costs that, in fact, will not occur.

6. **Within a range of feasible transfer prices, what are alternative ways for firms to arrive at the eventual price?**

When there is unused capacity, the transfer-price range lies between the minimum price at which the selling division is willing to sell (its variable cost per unit) and the maximum price the buying division is willing to pay (the lower of its contribution or price at which the product is available from external suppliers). Methods for arriving at a price in this range include proration (such as splitting the difference equally or on the basis of relative variable costs), negotiation between divisions, and dual pricing.

7. **What is the general guideline for determining a minimum transfer price?**

The general guideline states that the minimum transfer price equals the incremental cost per unit incurred up to the point of transfer plus the opportunity cost per unit to the selling division resulting from transferring products or services internally.

8. **How do income tax considerations affect transfer pricing in multinationals?**

Transfer prices can reduce income tax payments by reporting more income in low-tax-rate countries and less income in high-tax-rate countries. However, tax regulations of different countries restrict the transfer prices that companies can use.

Terms to Learn

This chapter and the Glossary at the end of the book contain definitions of the following important terms:

autonomy (**p. 777**)

decentralization (**p. 777**)

dual pricing (**p. 789**)

dysfunctional decision making (**p. 778**)

effort (**p. 776**)

goal congruence (**p. 776**)

incongruent decision making (**p. 778**)

intermediate product (**p. 780**)

management control system (**p. 775**)

motivation (**p. 776**)

perfectly competitive market (**p. 784**)

suboptimal decision making (**p. 778**)

transfer price (**p. 780**)

Assignment Material

Questions

MyAccountingLab

22-1 What is a management control system?

22-2 Describe three criteria you would use to evaluate whether a management control system is effective.

22-3 What is the relationship among motivation, goal congruence, and effort?

22-4 Name three benefits and two costs of decentralization.

22-5 "Organizations typically adopt a consistent decentralization or centralization philosophy across all their business functions." Do you agree? Explain.

22-6 "Transfer pricing is confined to profit centers." Do you agree? Explain.

22-7 What are the three methods for determining transfer prices?

22-8 What properties should transfer-pricing systems have?

22-9 "All transfer-pricing methods give the same division operating income." Do you agree? Explain.

22-10 Under what conditions is a market-based transfer price optimal?

22-11 What is one potential limitation of full-cost-based transfer prices?

22-12 Give two reasons why the dual-pricing system of transfer pricing is not widely used.

22-13 "Cost and price information play no role in negotiated transfer prices." Do you agree? Explain.

22-14 "Under the general guideline for transfer pricing, the minimum transfer price will vary depending on whether the supplying division has unused capacity or not." Do you agree? Explain.

22-15 How should managers consider income tax issues when choosing a transfer-pricing method?

MyAccountingLab

Exercises

22-16 Evaluating management control systems, balanced scorecard. Adventure Parks Inc. (API) operates ten theme parks throughout the United States. The company's slogan is "Name Your Adventure," and its mission is to offer an exciting theme park experience to visitors of all ages. API's corporate strategy supports this mission by stressing the importance of sparkling clean surroundings, efficient crowd management and, above all, cheerful employees. Of course, improved shareholder value drives this strategy.

Required

1. Assuming that API uses a balanced scorecard approach (see Chapter 13) to formulating its management control system. List three measures that API might use to evaluate each of the four balanced scorecard perspectives: financial perspective, customer perspective, internal-business-process perspective, and learning-and-growth perspective.
2. How would the management controls related to financial and customer perspectives at API differ between the following three managers: a souvenir shop manager, a park general manager, and the corporation's CEO?

22-17 Cost centers, profit centers, decentralization, transfer prices. Fenster Corporation manufactures windows with wood and metal frames. Fenster has three departments: glass, wood, and metal. The glass department makes the window glass and sends it to either the wood or metal department where the glass is framed. The window is then sold. Upper management sets the production schedules for the three departments and evaluates them on output quantity, cost variances, and product quality.

Required

1. Are the three departments cost centers, revenue centers, or profit centers?
2. Are the three departments centralized or decentralized?
3. Can a centralized department be a profit center? Why or why not?
4. Suppose the upper management of Fenster Corporation decides to let the three departments set their own production schedules, buy and sell products in the external market, and have the wood and metal departments negotiate with the glass department for the glass panes using a transfer price.
   a. Will this change your answers to requirements 1 and 2?
   b. How would you recommend upper management evaluate the three departments if this change is made?

22-18 Benefits and costs of decentralization. Jackson Markets, a chain of traditional supermarkets, is interested in gaining access to the organic and health food retail market by acquiring a regional company in that sector. Jackson intends to operate the newly-acquired stores independently from its supermarkets.

One of the prospects is Health Source, a chain of twenty stores in the mid-Atlantic. Buying for all twenty stores is done by the company's central office. Store managers must follow strict guidelines for all aspects of store management in an attempt to maintain consistency among stores. Store managers are evaluated on the basis of achieving profit goals developed by the central office.

The other prospect is Harvest Moon, a chain of thirty stores in the Northeast. Harvest Moon managers are given significant flexibility in product offerings, allowing them to negotiate purchases with local organic farmers. Store managers are rewarded for exceeding self-developed return on investment goals with company stock options. Some managers have become significant shareholders in the company, and have even decided on their own to open additional store locations to improve market penetration. However, the increased autonomy has led to competition and price cutting among Harvest Moon stores within the same geographic market, resulting in lower margins.

Required

1. Would you describe Health Source as having a centralized or a decentralized structure? Explain.
2. Would you describe Harvest Moon as having a centralized or a decentralized structure? Discuss some of the benefits and costs of that type of structure.

3. Would stores in each chain be considered cost centers, revenue centers, profit centers, or investment centers? How does that tie into the evaluation of store managers?

4. Assume that Jackson chooses to acquire Harvest Moon. What steps can Jackson take to improve goal congruence between store managers and the larger company?

22-19 Multinational transfer pricing, effect of alternative transfer-pricing methods, global income tax minimization. Tech Friendly Computer, Inc., with headquarters in San Francisco, manufactures and sells a desktop computer. Tech Friendly has three divisions, each of which is located in a different country:

a. China division—manufactures memory devices and keyboards

b. South Korea division—assembles desktop computers using locally manufactured parts, along with memory devices and keyboards from the China division

c. U.S. division—packages and distributes desktop computers

Each division is run as a profit center. The costs for the work done in each division for a single desktop computer are as follows:

$$\text{China division:} \quad \text{Variable cost} = 900 \text{ yuan}$$

$$\text{Fixed cost} = 1{,}980 \text{ yuan}$$

$$\text{South Korea division:} \quad \text{Variable cost} = 350{,}000 \text{ won}$$

$$\text{Fixed cost} = 470{,}000 \text{ won}$$

$$\text{U.S. division:} \quad \text{Variable cost} = \$125$$

$$\text{Fixed cost} = \$325$$

■ Chinese income tax rate on the China division's operating income: 40%
■ South Korean income tax rate on the South Korea division's operating income: 20%
■ U.S. income tax rate on the U.S. division's operating income: 30%

Each desktop computer is sold to retail outlets in the United States for $3,800. Assume that the current foreign exchange rates are as follows:

$$9 \text{ yuan} = \$1 \text{ U.S.}$$

$$1{,}000 \text{ won} = \$1 \text{ U.S.}$$

Both the China and the South Korea divisions sell part of their production under a private label. The China division sells the comparable memory/keyboard package used in each Tech Friendly desktop computer to a Chinese manufacturer for 4,500 yuan. The South Korea division sells the comparable desktop computer to a South Korean distributor for 1,340,000 won.

Required

1. Calculate the after-tax operating income per unit earned by each division under the following transfer-pricing methods: (a) market price, (b) 200% of full cost, and (c) 350% of variable cost. (Income taxes are not included in the computation of the cost-based transfer prices.)

2. Which transfer-pricing method(s) will maximize the after-tax operating income per unit of Tech Friendly Computer?

22-20 Transfer-pricing methods, goal congruence. British Columbia Lumber has a raw lumber division and a finished lumber division. The variable costs are as follows:

■ Raw lumber division: $100 per 100 board-feet of raw lumber
■ Finished lumber division: $125 per 100 board-feet of finished lumber

Assume that there is no board-feet loss in processing raw lumber into finished lumber. Raw lumber can be sold at $200 per 100 board-feet. Finished lumber can be sold at $275 per 100 board-feet.

Required

1. Should British Columbia Lumber process raw lumber into its finished form? Show your calculations.

2. Assume that internal transfers are made at 110% of variable cost. Will each division maximize its division operating-income contribution by adopting the action that is in the best interest of British Columbia Lumber as a whole? Explain.

3. Assume that internal transfers are made at market prices. Will each division maximize its division operating-income contribution by adopting the action that is in the best interest of British Columbia Lumber as a whole? Explain.

22-21 Effect of alternative transfer-pricing methods on division operating income. (CMA, adapted) Ajax Corporation has two divisions. The mining division makes toldine, which is then transferred to the metals division. The toldine is further processed by the metals division and is sold to customers at a price of $150 per unit. The mining division is currently required by Ajax to transfer its total yearly output of

200,000 units of toldine to the metals division at 110% of full manufacturing cost. Unlimited quantities of toldine can be purchased and sold on the outside market at $90 per unit.

The following table gives the manufacturing cost per unit in the mining and metals divisions for 2012:

	Mining Division	**Metals Division**
Direct material cost	$12	$ 6
Direct manufacturing labor cost	16	20
Manufacturing overhead cost	32[a]	25[b]
Total manufacturing cost per unit	$60	$51

[a]Manufacturing overhead costs in the mining division are 25% fixed and 75% variable.
[b]Manufacturing overhead costs in the metals division are 60% fixed and 40% variable.

Required

1. Calculate the operating incomes for the mining and metals divisions for the 200,000 units of toldine transferred under the following transfer-pricing methods: (a) market price and (b) 110% of full manufacturing cost.
2. Suppose Ajax rewards each division manager with a bonus, calculated as 1% of division operating income (if positive). What is the amount of bonus that will be paid to each division manager under the transfer-pricing methods in requirement 1? Which transfer-pricing method will each division manager prefer to use?
3. What arguments would Brian Jones, manager of the mining division, make to support the transfer-pricing method that he prefers?

22-22 Transfer pricing, general guideline, goal congruence. (CMA, adapted). Quest Motors, Inc., operates as a decentralized multidivision company. The Vivo division of Quest Motors purchases most of its airbags from the airbag division. The airbag division's incremental cost for manufacturing the airbags is $90 per unit. The airbag division is currently working at 80% of capacity. The current market price of the airbags is $125 per unit.

Required

1. Using the general guideline presented in the chapter, what is the minimum price at which the airbag division would sell airbags to the Vivo division?
2. Suppose that Quest Motors requires that whenever divisions with unused capacity sell products internally, they must do so at the incremental cost. Evaluate this transfer-pricing policy using the criteria of goal congruence, evaluating division performance, motivating management effort, and preserving division autonomy.
3. If the two divisions were to negotiate a transfer price, what is the range of possible transfer prices? Evaluate this negotiated transfer-pricing policy using the criteria of goal congruence, evaluating division performance, motivating management effort, and preserving division autonomy.
4. Instead of allowing negotiation, suppose that Quest specifies a hybrid transfer price that "splits the difference" between the minimum and maximum prices from the divisions' standpoint. What would be the resulting transfer price for airbags?

22-23 Multinational transfer pricing, global tax minimization. The Mornay Company manufactures telecommunications equipment at its plant in Toledo, Ohio. The company has marketing divisions throughout the world. A Mornay marketing division in Vienna, Austria, imports 10,000 units of Product 4A36 from the United States. The following information is available:

U.S. income tax rate on the U.S. division's operating income	35%
Austrian income tax rate on the Austrian division's operating income	40%
Austrian import duty	15%
Variable manufacturing cost per unit of Product 4A36	$ 550
Full manufacturing cost per unit of Product 4A36	$ 800
Selling price (net of marketing and distribution costs) in Austria	$1,150

Suppose the United States and Austrian tax authorities only allow transfer prices that are between the full manufacturing cost per unit of $800 and a market price of $950, based on comparable imports into Austria. The Austrian import duty is charged on the price at which the product is transferred into Austria. Any import duty paid to the Austrian authorities is a deductible expense for calculating Austrian income taxes due.

Required

1. Calculate the after-tax operating income earned by the United States and Austrian divisions from transferring 10,000 units of Product 4A36 (a) at full manufacturing cost per unit and (b) at market price of comparable imports. (Income taxes are not included in the computation of the cost-based transfer prices.)
2. Which transfer price should the Mornay Company select to minimize the total of company import duties and income taxes? Remember that the transfer price must be between the full manufacturing cost per unit of $800 and the market price of $950 of comparable imports into Austria. Explain your reasoning.

22-24 Multinational transfer pricing, goal congruence (continuation of 22-23). Suppose that the U.S. division could sell as many units of Product 4A36 as it makes at $900 per unit in the U.S. market, net of all marketing and distribution costs.

Required

1. From the viewpoint of the Mornay Company as a whole, would after-tax operating income be maximized if it sold the 10,000 units of Product 4A36 in the United States or in Austria? Show your computations.
2. Suppose division managers act autonomously to maximize their division's after-tax operating income. Will the transfer price calculated in requirement 2 of Exercise 22-23 result in the U.S. division manager taking the actions determined to be optimal in requirement 1 of this exercise? Explain.
3. What is the minimum transfer price that the U.S. division manager would agree to? Does this transfer price result in the Mornay Company as a whole paying more import duty and taxes than the answer to requirement 2 of Exercise 22-23? If so, by how much?

22-25 Transfer-pricing dispute. The Allison-Chambers Corporation, manufacturer of tractors and other heavy farm equipment, is organized along decentralized product lines, with each manufacturing division operating as a separate profit center. Each division manager has been delegated full authority on all decisions involving the sale of that division's output both to outsiders and to other divisions of Allison-Chambers. Division C has in the past always purchased its requirement of a particular tractor-engine component from division A. However, when informed that division A is increasing its selling price to $150, division C's manager decides to purchase the engine component from external suppliers.

Division C can purchase the component for $135 per unit in the open market. Division A insists that, because of the recent installation of some highly specialized equipment and the resulting high depreciation charges, it will not be able to earn an adequate return on its investment unless it raises its price. Division A's manager appeals to top management of Allison-Chambers for support in the dispute with division C and supplies the following operating data:

C's annual purchases of the tractor-engine component	1,000 units
A's variable cost per unit of the tractor-engine component	$120
A's fixed cost per unit of the tractor-engine component	$ 20

Required

1. Assume that there are no alternative uses for internal facilities of division A. Determine whether the company as a whole will benefit if division C purchases the component from external suppliers for $135 per unit. What should the transfer price for the component be set at so that division managers acting in their own divisions' best interests take actions that are also in the best interest of the company as a whole?
2. Assume that internal facilities of division A would not otherwise be idle. By not producing the 1,000 units for division C, division A's equipment and other facilities would be used for other production operations that would result in annual cash-operating savings of $18,000. Should division C purchase from external suppliers? Show your computations.
3. Assume that there are no alternative uses for division A's internal facilities and that the price from outsiders drops $20. Should division C purchase from external suppliers? What should the transfer price for the component be set at so that division managers acting in their own divisions' best interests take actions that are also in the best interest of the company as a whole?

22-26 Transfer-pricing problem (continuation of 22-25). Refer to Exercise 22-25. Assume that division A can sell the 1,000 units to other customers at $155 per unit, with variable marketing cost of $5 per unit.

Determine whether Allison-Chambers will benefit if division C purchases the 1,000 units from external suppliers at $135 per unit. Show your computations.

Required

Problems

22-27 General guideline, transfer pricing. The Slate Company manufactures and sells television sets. Its assembly division (AD) buys television screens from the screen division (SD) and assembles the TV sets. The SD, which is operating at capacity, incurs an incremental manufacturing cost of $65 per screen. The SD can sell all its output to the outside market at a price of $100 per screen, after incurring a variable marketing and distribution cost of $8 per screen. If the AD purchases screens from outside suppliers at a price of $100 per screen, it will incur a variable purchasing cost of $7 per screen. Slate's division managers can act autonomously to maximize their own division's operating income.

Required

1. What is the minimum transfer price at which the SD manager would be willing to sell screens to the AD?
2. What is the maximum transfer price at which the AD manager would be willing to purchase screens from the SD?
3. Now suppose that the SD can sell only 70% of its output capacity of 20,000 screens per month on the open market. Capacity cannot be reduced in the short run. The AD can assemble and sell more than 20,000 TV sets per month.
   a. What is the minimum transfer price at which the SD manager would be willing to sell screens to the AD?

b. From the point of view of Slate's management, how much of the SD output should be transferred to the AD?

c. If Slate mandates the SD and AD managers to "split the difference" on the minimum and maximum transfer prices they would be willing to negotiate over, what would be the resulting transfer price? Does this price achieve the outcome desired in requirement 3b?

22-28 Pertinent transfer price. Europa, Inc., has two divisions, A and B, that manufacture expensive bicycles. Division A produces the bicycle frame, and division B assembles the rest of the bicycle onto the frame. There is a market for both the subassembly and the final product. Each division has been designated as a profit center. The transfer price for the subassembly has been set at the long-run average market price. The following data are available for each division:

Selling price for final product	$300
Long-run average selling price for intermediate product	200
Incremental cost per unit for completion in division B	150
Incremental cost per unit in division A	120

The manager of division B has made the following calculation:

Selling price for final product		$300
Transferred-in cost per unit (market)	$200	
Incremental cost per unit for completion	150	350
Contribution (loss) on product		$(50)

Required

1. Should transfers be made to division B if there is no unused capacity in division A? Is the market price the correct transfer price? Show your computations.
2. Assume that division A's maximum capacity for this product is 1,000 units per month and sales to the intermediate market are now 800 units. Should 200 units be transferred to division B? At what transfer price? Assume that for a variety of reasons, division A will maintain the $200 selling price indefinitely. That is, division A is not considering lowering the price to outsiders even if idle capacity exists.
3. Suppose division A quoted a transfer price of $150 for up to 200 units. What would be the contribution to the company as a whole if a transfer were made? As manager of division B, would you be inclined to buy at $150? Explain.

22-29 Pricing in imperfect markets (continuation of 22-28). Refer to Problem 22-28.

Required

1. Suppose the manager of division A has the option of (a) cutting the external price to $195, with the certainty that sales will rise to 1,000 units or (b) maintaining the external price of $200 for the 800 units and transferring the 200 units to division B at a price that would produce the same operating income for division A. What transfer price would produce the same operating income for division A? Is that price consistent with that recommended by the general guideline in the chapter so that the resulting decision would be desirable for the company as a whole?
2. Suppose that if the selling price for the intermediate product were dropped to $195, sales to external parties could be increased to 900 units. Division B wants to acquire as many as 200 units if the transfer price is acceptable. For simplicity, assume that there is no external market for the final 100 units of division A's capacity.
   a. Using the general guideline, what is (are) the minimum transfer price(s) that should lead to the correct economic decision? Ignore performance-evaluation considerations.
   b. Compare the total contributions under the alternatives to show why the transfer price(s) recommended lead(s) to the optimal economic decision.

22-30 Effect of alternative transfer-pricing methods on division operating income. Crango Products is a cranberry cooperative that operates two divisions, a harvesting division and a processing division. Currently, all of harvesting's output is converted into cranberry juice by the processing division, and the juice is sold to large beverage companies that produce cranberry juice blends. The processing division has a yield of 500 gallons of juice per 1,000 pounds of cranberries. Cost and market price data for the two divisions are as follows:

	Home	Insert	Page Layout	Formulas	Data	Review	View	

	A	B	C	D	E
1	**Harvesting Division**			**Processing Division**	
2	Variable cost per pound of cranberries	$0.10		Variable processing cost per gallon of juice produced	$0.20
3	Fixed cost per pound of cranberries	$0.25		Fixed cost per gallon of juice produced	$0.40
4	Selling price per pound of cranberries in outside market	$0.60		Selling price per gallon of juice	$2.10

1. Compute Crango's operating income from harvesting 400,000 pounds of cranberries during June 2012 and processing them into juice.
2. Crango rewards its division managers with a bonus equal to 5% of operating income. Compute the bonus earned by each division manager in June 2012 for each of the following transfer pricing methods:
   a. 200% of full cost
   b. Market price
3. Which transfer-pricing method will each division manager prefer? How might Crango resolve any conflicts that may arise on the issue of transfer pricing?

Required

22-31 Goal-congruence problems with cost-plus transfer-pricing methods, dual-pricing system (continuation of 22-30). Assume that Pat Borges, CEO of Crango, had mandated a transfer price equal to 200% of full cost. Now he decides to decentralize some management decisions and sends around a memo that states the following: "Effective immediately, each division of Crango is free to make its own decisions regarding the purchase of direct materials and the sale of finished products."

1. Give an example of a goal-congruence problem that will arise if Crango continues to use a transfer price of 200% of full cost and Borges's decentralization policy is adopted.
2. Borges feels that a dual transfer-pricing policy will improve goal congruence. He suggests that transfers out of the harvesting division be made at 200% of full cost and transfers into the processing division be made at market price. Compute the operating income of each division under this dual transfer pricing method when 400,000 pounds of cranberries are harvested during June 2012 and processed into juice.
3. Why is the sum of the division operating incomes computed in requirement 2 different from Crango's operating income from harvesting and processing 400,000 pounds of cranberries?
4. Suggest two problems that may arise if Crango implements the dual transfer prices described in requirement 2.

Required

22-32 Multinational transfer pricing, global tax minimization. Industrial Diamonds, Inc., based in Los Angeles, has two divisions:

- South African mining division, which mines a rich diamond vein in South Africa
- U.S. processing division, which polishes raw diamonds for use in industrial cutting tools

The processing division's yield is 50%: It takes 2 pounds of raw diamonds to produce 1 pound of top-quality polished industrial diamonds. Although all of the mining division's output of 8,000 pounds of raw diamonds is sent for processing in the United States, there is also an active market for raw diamonds in South Africa. The foreign exchange rate is 6 ZAR (South African Rand) = $1 U.S. The following information is known about the two divisions:

	A	B	C	D	F	G
1	**South African Mining Division**					
2	Variable cost per pound of raw diamonds				600	ZAR
3	Fixed cost per pound of raw diamonds				1,200	ZAR
4	Market price per pound of raw diamonds				3,600	ZAR
5	Tax rate				25%	
6						
7	**U.S. Processing Division**					
8	Variable cost per pound of polished diamonds				220	U.S. dollars
9	Fixed cost per pound of polished diamonds				850	U.S. dollars
10	Market price per pound of polished diamonds				3,500	U.S. dollars
11	Tax rate				40%	

Required

1. Compute the annual pretax operating income, in U.S. dollars, of each division under the following transfer-pricing methods: (a) 250% of full cost and (b) market price.
2. Compute the after-tax operating income, in U.S. dollars, for each division under the transfer-pricing methods in requirement 1. (Income taxes are not included in the computation of cost-based transfer price, and Industrial Diamonds does not pay U.S. income tax on income already taxed in South Africa.)
3. If the two division managers are compensated based on after-tax division operating income, which transfer-pricing method will each prefer? Which transfer-pricing method will maximize the total after-tax operating income of Industrial Diamonds?
4. In addition to tax minimization, what other factors might Industrial Diamonds consider in choosing a transfer-pricing method?

22-33 International transfer pricing, taxes, goal congruence. Argone division of Gemini Corporation is located in the United States. Its effective income tax rate is 30%. Another division of Gemini, Calcia, is located in Canada, where the income tax rate is 42%. Calcia manufactures, among other things, an intermediate product for Argone called IP-2007. Calcia operates at capacity and makes 15,000 units of IP-2007 for Argone each period, at a variable cost of $60 per unit. Assume that there are no outside customers for IP-2007. Because the IP-2007 must be shipped from Canada to the United States, it costs Calcia an additional $4 per unit to ship the IP-2007 to Argone. There are no direct fixed costs for IP-2007. Calcia also manufactures other products.

A product similar to IP-2007 that Argone could use as a substitute is available in the United States for $75 per unit.

Required

1. What is the minimum and maximum transfer price that would be acceptable to Argone and Calcia for IP-2007, and why?
2. What transfer price would minimize income taxes for Gemini Corporation as a whole? Would Calcia and Argone want to be evaluated on operating income using this transfer price?
3. Suppose Gemini uses the transfer price from requirement 2, and each division is evaluated on its own after-tax division operating income. Now suppose Calcia has an opportunity to sell 8,000 units of IP-2007 to an outside customer for $68 each. Calcia will not incur shipping costs because the customer is nearby and offers to pay for shipping. Assume that if Calcia accepts the special order, Argone will have to buy 8,000 units of the substitute product in the United States at $75 per unit.
   a. Will accepting the special order maximize after-tax operating income for Gemini Corporation as a whole?
   b. Will Argone want Calcia to accept this special order? Why or why not?
   c. Will Calcia want to accept this special order? Explain.
   d. Suppose Gemini Corporation wants to operate in a decentralized manner. What transfer price should Gemini set for IP-2007 so that each division acting in its own best interest takes actions with respect to the special order that are in the best interests of Gemini Corporation as a whole?

22-34 Transfer pricing, goal congruence. The Bosh Corporation makes and sells 20,000 multisystem music players each year. Its assembly division purchases components from other divisions of Bosh or from external suppliers and assembles the multisystem music players. In particular, the assembly division can purchase the CD player from the compact disc division of Bosh or from Hawei Corporation. Hawei agrees to meet all of Bosh's quality requirements and is currently negotiating with the assembly division to supply 20,000 CD players at a price between $44 and $52 per CD player.

A critical component of the CD player is the head mechanism that reads the disc. To ensure the quality of its multisystem music players, Bosh requires that if Hawei wins the contract to supply CD players, it must purchase the head mechanism from Bosh's compact disc division for $24 each.

The compact disc division can manufacture at most 22,000 CD players annually. It also manufactures as many additional head mechanisms as can be sold. The incremental cost of manufacturing the head mechanism is $18 per unit. The incremental cost of manufacturing a CD player (including the cost of the head mechanism) is $30 per unit, and any number of CD players can be sold for $45 each in the external market.

Required

1. What are the incremental costs minus revenues from sale to external buyers for the company as a whole if the compact disc division transfers 20,000 CD players to the assembly division and sells the remaining 2,000 CD players on the external market?
2. What are the incremental costs minus revenues from sales to external buyers for the company as a whole if the compact disc division sells 22,000 CD players on the external market and the assembly division accepts Hawei's offer at (a) $44 per CD player or (b) $52 per CD player?
3. What is the minimum transfer price per CD player at which the compact disc division would be willing to transfer 20,000 CD players to the assembly division?
4. Suppose that the transfer price is set to the minimum computed in requirement 3 plus $2, and the division managers at Bosh are free to make their own profit-maximizing sourcing and selling decisions. Now, Hawei offers 20,000 CD players for $52 each.
   a. What decisions will the managers of the compact disc division and assembly division make?
   b. Are these decisions optimal for Bosh as a whole?
   c. Based on this exercise, at what price would you recommend the transfer price be set?

22-35 Transfer pricing, goal congruence, ethics. Jeremiah Industries manufactures high-grade aluminum luggage made from recycled metal. The company operates two divisions: metal recycling and luggage fabrication. Each division operates as a decentralized entity. The metal recycling division is free to sell sheet aluminum to outside buyers, and the luggage fabrication division is free to purchase recycled sheet aluminum from other sources. Currently, however, the recycling division sells all of its output to the fabrication division, and the fabrication division does not purchase materials from any outside suppliers.

Aluminum is transferred from the recycling division to the fabrication division at 110% of full cost. The recycling division purchases recyclable aluminum for $0.50 per pound. The division's other variable costs equal $2.80 per pound, and fixed costs at a monthly production level of 50,000 pounds are $1.50 per pound.

During the most recent month, 50,000 pounds of aluminum were transferred between the two divisions. The recycling division's capacity is 70,000 pounds.

Due to increased demand, the fabrication division expects to use 60,000 pounds of aluminum next month. Metalife Corporation has offered to sell 10,000 pounds of recycled aluminum next month to the fabrication division for $5.00 per pound.

Required

1. Calculate the transfer price per pound of recycled aluminum. Assuming that each division is considered a profit center, would the fabrication manager choose to purchase 10,000 pounds next month from Metalife?
2. Is the purchase in the best interest of Jeremiah Industries? Show your calculations. What is the cause of this goal incongruence?
3. The fabrication division manager suggests that $5.00 is now the market price for recycled sheet aluminum, and that this should be the new transfer price. Jeremiah's corporate management tends to agree. The metal recycling manager is suspicious. Metalife's prices have always been considerably higher than $5.00 per pound. Why the sudden price cut? After further investigation by the recycling division manager, it is revealed that the $5.00 per pound price was a one-time-only offer made to the fabrication division due to excess inventory at Metalife. Future orders would be priced at $5.50 per pound. Comment on the validity of the $5.00 per pound market price and the ethics of the fabrication manager. Would changing the transfer price to $5.00 matter to Jeremiah Industries?

Collaborative Learning Problem

22-36 Transfer pricing, utilization of capacity. (J. Patell, adapted) The California Instrument Company (CIC) consists of the semiconductor division and the process-control division, each of which operates as an independent profit center. The semiconductor division employs craftsmen who produce two different electronic components: the new high-performance Super-chip and an older product called Okay-chip. These two products have the following cost characteristics:

	Super-chip	Okay-chip
Direct materials	$ 5	$ 2
Direct manufacturing labor, 3 hours × $20; 1 hour × $20	60	20

Due to the high skill level necessary for the craftsmen, the semiconductor division's capacity is set at 45,000 hours per year.

Maximum demand for the Super-chip is 15,000 units annually, at a price of $80 per chip. There is unlimited demand for the Okay-chip at $26 per chip.

The process-control division produces only one product, a process-control unit, with the following cost structure:

■ Direct materials (circuit board): $70
■ Direct manufacturing labor (3 hours × $15): $45

The current market price for the control unit is $132 per unit.

A joint research project has just revealed that a single Super-chip could be substituted for the circuit board currently used to make the process-control unit. Direct labor cost of the process-control unit would be unchanged. The improved process-control unit could be sold for $145.

Required

1. Calculate the contribution margin per direct-labor hour of selling Super-chip and Okay-chip. If no transfers of Super-chip are made to the process-control division, how many Super-chips and Okay-chips should the semiconductor division manufacture and sell? What would be the division's annual contribution margin? Show your computations.
2. The process-control division expects to sell 5,000 process-control units this year. From the viewpoint of California Instruments as a whole, should 5,000 Super-chips be transferred to the process-control division to replace circuit boards? Show your computations.
3. What transfer price, or range of prices, would ensure goal congruence among the division managers? Show your calculations.
4. If labor capacity in the semiconductor division were 60,000 hours instead of 45,000, would your answer to requirement 3 differ? Show your calculations.

Performance Measurement, Compensation, and Multinational Considerations

At the end of this school term, you're going to receive a grade that represents a measure of your performance in this course.

Your grade will likely consist of four elements—homework, quizzes, exams, and class participation. Do some of these elements better reflect your knowledge of the material than others? Would the relative weights placed on the various elements when determining your final grade influence how much effort you expend to improve performance on the different elements? Would it be fair if you received a good grade regardless of your performance? The following article about former AIG chief executive Martin Sullivan examines that very situation in a corporate context. Sullivan continued to receive performance bonuses despite pushing AIG to the brink of bankruptcy. By failing to link pay to performance, the AIG board of directors rewarded behavior that led to a government takeover of the firm.

Misalignment Between CEO Compensation and Performance at AIG[1]

After the September 2008 collapse of AIG, many shareholders and observers focused on the company's executive compensation. Many believed that the incentive structures for executives helped fuel the real estate bubble. Though people were placing long-term bets on mortgage-backed securities, much of their compensation was in the form of short-term bonuses. This encouraged excessive risk without the fear of significant repercussions.

Executive compensation at AIG had been under fire for many years. The Corporate Library, an independent research firm specializing in corporate governance, called the company "a serial offender in the category of outrageous CEO compensation."

Judging solely by company financial measures, AIG's 2007 results were a failure. Driven by the write-down of $11.1 billion in fixed income guarantees, the company's revenue was down 56% from 2006 results. AIG also reported $5 billion in losses in the final quarter of 2007 and warned of possible future losses due to ill-advised investments. Despite this, AIG chief executive Martin Sullivan earned $14.3 million in salary, bonus, stock options, and other long-term

---

[1] *Source:* Blair, Nathan. 2009. AIG – Blame for the bailout. Stanford Graduate School of Business No. A-203, Stanford, CA: Stanford Graduate School of Business; Son, Hugh. 2008. AIG chief Sullivan's compensation fell 32 percent. *Bloomberg.com*, April 4; Son, Hugh and Erik Holm. 2008. AIG's former chief Sullivan gets $47 million package. *Bloomberg.com*, July 1.

incentives. Sullivan's compensation was in the 90th percentile for CEOs of S&P 500 firms for 2007.

On June 15, 2008, AIG replaced Sullivan as CEO. By then, AIG reported cumulative losses totaling $20 billion. During Sullivan's three-year tenure at the helm, AIG lost 46% of its market value. At the time of his dismissal, the AIG board of directors agreed to give the ousted CEO about $47 million in severance pay, bonus, and long-term compensation.

Two months later, on the verge of bankruptcy, the U.S. government nationalized AIG. At a Congressional hearing in the aftermath of AIG's failure, one witness testified on Sullivan's compensation stating, "I think it is fair to say by any standard of measurement that this pay plan is as uncorrelated to performance as it is possible to be."

Companies measure reward and performance to motivate managers to achieve company strategies and goals. As the AIG example illustrates, however, if the measures are inappropriate or not connected to sustained performance, managers may improve their performance evaluations and increase compensation without achieving company goals. This chapter discusses the general design, implementation, and uses of performance measures, part of the final step in the decision-making process.

Financial and Nonfinancial Performance Measures

Many organizations are increasingly presenting financial and nonfinancial performance measures for their subunits in a single report called the *balanced scorecard* (Chapter 13). Different organizations stress different measures in their scorecards, but the measures are always derived from a company's strategy. Consider the case of Hospitality Inns, a chain of hotels. Hospitality Inns' strategy is to provide excellent customer service and to charge a higher room rate than its competitors. Hospitality Inns uses the following measures in its balanced scorecard:

1. **Financial perspective**—stock price, net income, return on sales, return on investment, and economic value added
2. **Customer perspective**—market share in different geographic locations, customer satisfaction, and average number of repeat visits
3. **Internal-business-process perspective**—customer-service time for making reservations, for check-in, and in restaurants; cleanliness of hotel and room, quality of room service; time taken to clean rooms; quality of restaurant experience; number of new services provided to customers (fax, wireless Internet, video games); time taken to plan and build new hotels

Learning Objective 1

Select financial performance measures

. . . such as return on investment, residual income

and nonfinancial performance measures to use in a balanced scorecard

. . . such as customer-satisfaction, number of defects

Economic Value Added[3]

Economic value added is a specific type of RI calculation that is used by many companies. **Economic value added (EVA®)** equals after-tax operating income *minus* the (after-tax) weighted-average cost of capital *multiplied* by total assets minus current liabilities.

$$\text{Economic value added (EVA)} = \text{After-tax operating income} - \left[\begin{array}{c} \text{Weighted-average cost of capital} \end{array} \times \left(\begin{array}{c} \text{Total assets} - \text{Current liabilities} \end{array} \right) \right]$$

EVA substitutes the following numbers in the RI calculations: (1) income equal to after-tax operating income, (2) required rate of return equal to the (after-tax) weighted-average cost of capital, and (3) investment equal to total assets minus current liabilities.[4]

We use the Hospitality Inns data in Exhibit 23-1 to illustrate the basic EVA calculations. The weighted-average cost of capital (WACC) equals the *after-tax* average cost of all the long-term funds used by Hospitality Inns. The company has two sources of long-term funds: (a) long-term debt with a market value and book value of $4.5 million issued at an interest rate of 10%, and (b) equity capital that also has a market value of $4.5 million (but a book value of $1 million).[5] Because interest costs are tax-deductible and the income tax rate is 30%, the after-tax cost of debt financing is $0.10 \times (1 - \text{Tax rate}) = 0.10 \times (1 - 0.30) = 0.10 \times 0.70 = 0.07$, or 7%. The cost of equity capital is the opportunity cost to investors of not investing their capital in another investment that is similar in risk to Hospitality Inns. Hospitality Inns' cost of equity capital is 14%.[6] The WACC computation, which uses market values of debt and equity, is as follows:

$$WACC = \frac{(7\% \times \text{Market value of debt}) + (14\% \times \text{Market value of equity})}{\text{Market value of debt} + \text{Market value of equity}}$$

$$= \frac{(0.07 \times \$4,500,000) + (0.14 \times \$4,500,000)}{\$4,500,000 + \$4,500,000}$$

$$= \frac{\$945,000}{\$9,000,000} = 0.105, \text{ or } 10.5\%$$

The company applies the same WACC to all its hotels because each hotel faces similar risks. Total assets minus current liabilities (see Exhibit 23-1) can also be computed as follows:

$$\text{Total assets} - \text{Current liabilities} = \text{Long-term assets} + \text{Current assets} - \text{Current liabilities}$$

$$= \text{Long-term assets} + \text{Working capital}$$

where

$$\text{Working capital} = \text{Current assets} - \text{Current liabilities}$$

After-tax hotel operating income is:

$$\text{Hotel operating income} \times (1 - \text{Tax rate}) = \text{Hotel operating income} \times (1 - 0.30) = \text{Hotel operating income} \times 0.70$$

[3] S. O'Byrne and D. Young, *EVA and Value-Based Management: A Practical Guide to Implementation* (New York: McGraw-Hill, 2000); J. Stein, J. Shiely, and I. Ross, *The EVA Challenge: Implementing Value Added Change in an Organization* (New York: John Wiley and Sons, 2001).

[4] When implementing EVA, companies make several adjustments to the operating income and asset numbers reported under generally accepted accounting principles (GAAP). For example, when calculating EVA, costs such as R&D, restructuring costs, and leases that have long-run benefits are recorded as assets (which are then amortized), rather than as current operating costs. The goal of these adjustments is to obtain a better representation of the economic assets, particularly intangible assets, used to earn income. Of course, the specific adjustments applicable to a company will depend on its individual circumstances.

[5] The market value of Hospitality Inns' equity exceeds book value because book value, based on historical cost, does not measure the current value of the company's assets and because various intangible assets, such as the company's brand name, are not shown at current value in the balance sheet under GAAP.

[6] In practice, the most common method of calculating the cost of equity capital is by applying the capital asset pricing model (CAPM). For details, see J. Berk and P. DeMarzo, *Corporate Finance*, 2nd ed. (Upper Saddle River, NJ: Prentice Hall, 2010).

EVA calculations for Hospitality Inns are as follows:

Hotel	After-Tax Operating Income	−	WACC ×	Total Assets − Current Liabilities	=	EVA
San Francisco	$240,000 × 0.70	−	[10.50% ×	($1,000,000 − $ 50,000)]	=	$68,250
Chicago	$300,000 × 0.70	−	[10.50% ×	($2,000,000 − $150,000)]	=	$15,750
New Orleans	$510,000 × 0.70	−	[10.50% ×	($3,000,000 − $300,000)]	=	$73,500

The New Orleans hotel has the highest EVA. Economic value added, like residual income, charges managers for the cost of their investments in long-term assets and working capital. Value is created only if after-tax operating income exceeds the cost of investing the capital. To improve EVA, managers can, for example, (a) earn more after-tax operating income with the same capital, (b) use less capital to earn the same after-tax operating income, or (c) invest capital in high-return projects.[7]

Managers in companies such as Briggs and Stratton, Coca-Cola, CSX, Equifax, and FMC use the estimated impact on EVA to guide their decisions. Division managers find EVA helpful because it allows them to incorporate the cost of capital, which is generally only available at the company-wide level, into decisions at the division level. Comparing the actual EVA achieved to the estimated EVA is useful for evaluating performance and providing feedback to managers about performance. CSX, a railroad company, credits EVA for decisions such as to run trains with three locomotives instead of four and to schedule arrivals just in time for unloading rather than having trains arrive at their destination several hours in advance. The result? Higher income because of lower fuel costs and lower capital investments in locomotives.

Return on Sales

The income-to-revenues ratio (or sales ratio), often called *return on sales* (ROS), is a frequently used financial performance measure. As we have seen, ROS is one component of ROI in the DuPont method of profitability analysis. To calculate ROS for each of Hospitality's hotels, we divide operating income by revenues:

Hotel	Operating Income	÷	Revenues (Sales)	=	ROS
San Francisco	$240,000	÷	$1,200,000	=	20.0%
Chicago	$300,000	÷	$1,400,000	=	21.4%
New Orleans	$510,000	÷	$3,185,000	=	16.0%

The Chicago hotel has the highest ROS, but its performance is rated worse than the other hotels using measures such as ROI, RI, and EVA.

Comparing Performance Measures

The following table summarizes the performance of each hotel and ranks it (in parentheses) under each of the four performance measures:

Hotel	ROI	RI	EVA	ROS
San Francisco	24% (1)	$120,000 (2)	$68,250 (2)	20.0% (2)
Chicago	15% (3)	$ 60,000 (3)	$15,750 (3)	21.4% (1)
New Orleans	17% (2)	$150,000 (1)	$73,500 (1)	16.0% (3)

The RI and EVA rankings are the same. They differ from the ROI and ROS rankings. Consider the ROI and RI rankings for the San Francisco and New Orleans hotels. The New Orleans hotel has a smaller ROI. Although its operating income is only slightly more than

[7] Observe that the sum of the divisional after-tax operating incomes used in the EVA calculation, ($240,000 + $300,000 + $510,000) × 0.7 = $735,000, exceeds the firm's net income of $420,000. The difference is due to the firm's after-tax interest expense on its long-term debt, which amounts to $450,000 × 0.7 = $315,000. Because the EVA measure includes a charge for the weighted average cost of capital, which includes the after-tax cost of debt, the income figure used in computing EVA should reflect the after-tax profit before interest payments on debt are considered. After-tax operating income (often referred to in practice as NOPAT, or net operating profit after taxes) is thus the relevant measure of divisional profit for EVA calculations.

EVA calculations for Hospitality Inns are as follows:

Hotel	After-Tax Operating Income	−	[WACC ×	(Total Assets − Current Liabilities)]	=	EVA
San Francisco	$240,000 × 0.70	−	[10.50% ×	($1,000,000 − $ 50,000)]	=	$68,250
Chicago	$300,000 × 0.70	−	[10.50% ×	($2,000,000 − $150,000)]	=	$15,750
New Orleans	$510,000 × 0.70	−	[10.50% ×	($3,000,000 − $300,000)]	=	$73,500

The New Orleans hotel has the highest EVA. Economic value added, like residual income, charges managers for the cost of their investments in long-term assets and working capital. Value is created only if after-tax operating income exceeds the cost of investing the capital. To improve EVA, managers can, for example, (a) earn more after-tax operating income with the same capital, (b) use less capital to earn the same after-tax operating income, or (c) invest capital in high-return projects.[7]

Managers in companies such as Briggs and Stratton, Coca-Cola, CSX, Equifax, and FMC use the estimated impact on EVA to guide their decisions. Division managers find EVA helpful because it allows them to incorporate the cost of capital, which is generally only available at the company-wide level, into decisions at the division level. Comparing the actual EVA achieved to the estimated EVA is useful for evaluating performance and providing feedback to managers about performance. CSX, a railroad company, credits EVA for decisions such as to run trains with three locomotives instead of four and to schedule arrivals just in time for unloading rather than having trains arrive at their destination several hours in advance. The result? Higher income because of lower fuel costs and lower capital investments in locomotives.

Return on Sales

The income-to-revenues ratio (or sales ratio), often called *return on sales* (ROS), is a frequently used financial performance measure. As we have seen, ROS is one component of ROI in the DuPont method of profitability analysis. To calculate ROS for each of Hospitality's hotels, we divide operating income by revenues:

Hotel	Operating Income	÷	Revenues (Sales)	=	ROS
San Francisco	$240,000	÷	$1,200,000	=	20.0%
Chicago	$300,000	÷	$1,400,000	=	21.4%
New Orleans	$510,000	÷	$3,185,000	=	16.0%

The Chicago hotel has the highest ROS, but its performance is rated worse than the other hotels using measures such as ROI, RI, and EVA.

Comparing Performance Measures

The following table summarizes the performance of each hotel and ranks it (in parentheses) under each of the four performance measures:

Hotel	ROI	RI	EVA	ROS
San Francisco	24% (1)	$120,000 (2)	$68,250 (2)	20.0% (2)
Chicago	15% (3)	$ 60,000 (3)	$15,750 (3)	21.4% (1)
New Orleans	17% (2)	$150,000 (1)	$73,500 (1)	16.0% (3)

The RI and EVA rankings are the same. They differ from the ROI and ROS rankings. Consider the ROI and RI rankings for the San Francisco and New Orleans hotels. The New Orleans hotel has a smaller ROI. Although its operating income is only slightly more than

---

[7] Observe that the sum of the divisional after-tax operating incomes used in the EVA calculation, ($240,000 + $300,000 + $510,000) × 0.7 = $735,000, exceeds the firm's net income of $420,000. The difference is due to the firm's after-tax interest expense on its long-term debt, which amounts to $450,000 × 0.7 = $315,000. Because the EVA measure includes a charge for the weighted average cost of capital, which includes the after-tax cost of debt, the income figure used in computing EVA should reflect the after-tax profit before interest payments on debt are considered. After-tax operating income (often referred to in practice as NOPAT, or net operating profit after taxes) is thus the relevant measure of divisional profit for EVA calculations.

twice the operating income of the San Francisco hotel—$510,000 versus $240,000—its total assets are three times as large—$3 million versus $1 million. The New Orleans hotel has a higher RI because it earns a higher income after covering the required rate of return on investment of 12%. The high ROI of the San Francisco hotel indicates that its assets are being used efficiently. Even though each dollar invested in the New Orleans hotel does not give the same return as the San Francisco hotel, this large investment creates considerable value because its return exceeds the required rate of return. The Chicago hotel has the highest ROS but the lowest ROI. The high ROS indicates that the Chicago hotel has the lowest cost structure per dollar of revenues of all of Hospitality Inns' hotels. The reason for Chicago's low ROI is that it generates very low revenues per dollar of assets invested. Is any method better than the others for measuring performance? No, because each evaluates a different aspect of performance.

ROS measures how effectively costs are managed. To evaluate overall aggregate performance, ROI, RI, or EVA measures are more appropriate than ROS because they consider both income and investment. ROI indicates which investment yields the highest return. RI and EVA measures overcome some of the goal-congruence problems of ROI. Some managers favor EVA because of the accounting adjustments related to the capitalization of investments in intangibles. Other managers favor RI because it is easier to calculate and because, in most cases, it leads to the same conclusions as EVA. Generally, companies use multiple financial measures to evaluate performance.

Choosing the Details of the Performance Measures

It is not sufficient for a company to identify the set of performance measures it wishes to use. The company has to make several choices regarding the specific details of how the measures are computed. These range from decisions regarding the time frame over which the measures are computed, to the definition of key terms such as "investment" and the calculation of particular components of each performance measure.

Alternative Time Horizons

An important element in designing accounting-based performance measures is choosing the time horizon of the performance measures. The ROI, RI, EVA, and ROS calculations represent the results for a single period, one year in our example. Managers could take actions that cause short-run increases in these measures but that conflict with the long-run interest of the company. For example, managers may curtail R&D and plant maintenance in the last three months of a fiscal year to achieve a target level of annual operating income. For this reason, many companies evaluate subunits on the basis of ROI, RI, EVA, and ROS over multiple years.

Another reason to evaluate subunits over multiple years is that the benefits of actions taken in the current period may not show up in short-run performance measures, such as the current year's ROI or RI. For example, an investment in a new hotel may adversely affect ROI and RI in the short run but benefit ROI and RI in the long run.

A multiyear analysis highlights another advantage of the RI measure: Net present value of all cash flows over the life of an investment equals net present value of the RIs.[8]

---

[8] This equivalence, often referred to as the "Conservation Property" of residual income, was originally articulated by Gabriel Preinreich in 1938. To see the equivalence, suppose the $400,000 investment in the San Francisco hotel increases operating income by $70,000 per year as follows: Increase in operating cash flows of $150,000 each year for 5 years minus depreciation of $80,000 ($400,000 ÷ 5) per year, assuming straight-line depreciation and $0 terminal disposal value. Depreciation reduces the investment amount by $80,000 each year. Assuming a required rate of return of 12%, net present values of cash flows and residual incomes are as follows:

Year		0	1	2	3	4	5	Net Present Value
(1)	Cash flow	–$400,000	$150,000	$150,000	$150,000	$150,000	$150,000	
(2)	Present value of $1 discounted at 12%	1	0.89286	0.79719	0.71178	0.63552	0.56743	
(3)	Present value: (1) × (2)	–$400,000	$133,929	$119,578	$106,767	$ 95,328	$ 85,114	$140,716
(4)	Operating income		$ 70,000	$ 70,000	$ 70,000	$ 70,000	$ 70,000	
(5)	Assets at start of year		$400,000	$320,000	$240,000	$160,000	$ 80,000	
(6)	Capital charge: (5) × 12%		$ 48,000	$ 38,400	$ 28,800	$ 19,200	$ 9,600	
(7)	Residual income: (4) − (6)		$ 22,000	$ 31,600	$ 41,200	$ 50,800	$ 60,400	
(8)	Present value of RI: (7) × (2)		$ 19,643	$ 25,191	$ 29,325	$ 32,284	$ 34,273	$140,716

Decision Point

What are the relative merits of return on investment (ROI), residual income (RI), and economic value added (EVA) as performance measures for subunit managers?

Learning Objective 3

Analyze the key measurement choices in the design of each performance measure

. . . choice of time horizon, alternative definitions, and measurement of assets

This characteristic means that if managers use the net present value method to make investment decisions (as advocated in Chapter 21), then using multiyear RI to evaluate managers' performances achieves goal congruence.

Another way to motivate managers to take a long-run perspective is by compensating them on the basis of changes in the market price of the company's stock, because stock prices incorporate the expected future effects of current decisions.

Alternative Definitions of Investment

Companies use a variety of definitions for measuring investment in divisions. Four common alternative definitions used in the construction of accounting-based performance measures are as follows:

1. **Total assets available**—includes all assets, regardless of their intended purpose.
2. **Total assets employed**—total assets available minus the sum of idle assets and assets purchased for future expansion. For example, if the New Orleans hotel in Exhibit 23-1 has unused land set aside for potential expansion, total assets employed by the hotel would exclude the cost of that land.
3. **Total assets employed minus current liabilities**—total assets employed, excluding assets financed by short-term creditors. One negative feature of defining investment in this way is that it may encourage subunit managers to use an excessive amount of short-term debt because short-term debt reduces the amount of investment.
4. **Stockholders' equity**—calculated by assigning liabilities among subunits and deducting these amounts from the total assets of each subunit. One drawback of this method is that it combines operating decisions made by hotel managers with financing decisions made by top management.

Companies that use ROI or RI generally define investment as the total assets available. When top management directs a subunit manager to carry extra or idle assets, total assets employed can be more informative than total assets available. Companies that adopt EVA define investment as total assets employed minus current liabilities. The most common rationale for using total assets employed minus current liabilities is that the subunit manager often influences decisions on current liabilities of the subunit.

Alternative Asset Measurements

To design accounting-based performance measures, we must consider different ways to measure assets included in the investment calculations. Should assets be measured at historical cost or current cost? Should gross book value (that is, original cost) or net book value (original cost minus accumulated depreciation) be used for depreciable assets?

Current Cost

Current cost is the cost of purchasing an asset today identical to the one currently held, or the cost of purchasing an asset that provides services like the one currently held if an identical asset cannot be purchased. Of course, measuring assets at current costs will result in different ROIs than the ROIs calculated on the basis of historical costs.

We illustrate the current-cost ROI calculations using the data for Hospitality Inns (Exhibit 23-1) and then compare current-cost-based ROIs and historical-cost-based ROIs. Assume the following information about the long-term assets of each hotel:

	San Francisco	Chicago	New Orleans
Age of facility in years (at end of 2012)	8	4	2
Gross book value (original cost)	$1,400,000	$2,100,000	$2,730,000
Accumulated depreciation	$ 800,000	$ 600,000	$ 390,000
Net book value (at end of 2012)	$ 600,000	$1,500,000	$2,340,000
Depreciation for 2012	$ 100,000	$ 150,000	$ 195,000

Hospitality Inns assumes a 14-year estimated useful life, zero terminal disposal value for the physical facilities, and straight-line depreciation.

An index of construction costs indicating how the cost of construction has changed over the eight-year period that Hospitality Inns has been operating (2004 year-end = 100) is as follows:

Year	2005	2006	2007	2008	2009	2010	2011	2012
Construction cost index	110	122	136	144	152	160	174	180

Earlier in this chapter, we computed an ROI of 24% for San Francisco, 15% for Chicago, and 17% for New Orleans (p. 809). One possible explanation of the high ROI for the San Francisco hotel is that its long-term assets are expressed in 2004 construction-price levels—prices that prevailed eight years ago—and the long-term assets for the Chicago and New Orleans hotels are expressed in terms of higher, more-recent construction-price levels, which depress ROIs for these two hotels.

Exhibit 23-2 illustrates a step-by-step approach for incorporating current-cost estimates of long-term assets and depreciation expense into the ROI calculation. We make these calculations to approximate what it would cost today to obtain assets that would produce the same expected operating income that the subunits currently earn. (Similar adjustments to represent the current costs of capital employed and depreciation expense can also be made in the RI and EVA calculations.) The current-cost adjustment reduces the ROI of the San Francisco hotel by more than half.

	Historical-Cost ROI	Current-Cost ROI
San Francisco	24%	10.8%
Chicago	15%	11.1%
New Orleans	17%	14.7%

Adjusting assets to recognize current costs negates differences in the investment base caused solely by differences in construction-price levels. Compared with historical-cost ROI, current-cost ROI better measures the current economic returns from the investment. If Hospitality Inns were to invest in a new hotel today, investing in one like the New Orleans hotel offers the best ROI.

Current cost estimates may be difficult to obtain for some assets. Why? Because the estimate requires a company to consider, in addition to increases in price levels, technological advances and processes that could reduce the current cost of assets needed to earn today's operating income.

Long-Term Assets: Gross or Net Book Value?

Historical cost of assets is often used to calculate ROI. There has been much discussion about whether gross book value or net book value of assets should be used. Using the data in Exhibit 23-1 (p. 809), we calculate ROI using net and gross book values of plant and equipment as follows:

	Operating Income (from Exhibit 23-1) (1)	Net Book Value of Total Assets (from Exhibit 23-1) (2)	Accumulated Depreciation (from p. 815) (3)	Gross Book Value of Total Assets (4) = (2) + (3)	2012 ROI Using Net Book Value of Total Assets (calculated earlier) (5) = (1) ÷ (2)	2012 ROI Using Gross Book Value of Total Assets (6) = (1) ÷ (4)
San Francisco	$240,000	$1,000,000	$800,000	$1,800,000	24%	13.3%
Chicago	$300,000	$2,000,000	$600,000	$2,600,000	15%	11.5%
New Orleans	$510,000	$3,000,000	$390,000	$3,390,000	17%	15.0%

Using gross book value, the 13.3% ROI of the older San Francisco hotel is lower than the 15.0% ROI of the newer New Orleans hotel. Those who favor using gross book value claim it enables more accurate comparisons of ROI across subunits. For example, using

Exhibit 23-2 ROI for Hospitality Inns: Computed Using Current-Cost Estimates as of the End of 2012 for Depreciation Expense and Long-Term Assets

	A	B	C	D	E	F	G	H	I	J
1	**Step 1:** Restate long-term assets from gross book value at historical cost to gross book value at current cost as of the end of 2012.									
2		**Gross book value of long-term assets at historical cost**	×	**Construction cost index in 2012**	÷	**Construction cost index in year of construction**	=	**Gross book value of long-term assets at current cost at end of 2012**		
3	San Francisco	$1,400,000	×	(180	÷	100)	=	$2,520,000		
4	Chicago	$2,100,000	×	(180	÷	144)	=	$2,625,000		
5	New Orleans	$2,730,000	×	(180	÷	160)	=	$3,071,250		
6										
7	**Step 2:** Derive net book value of long-term assets at current cost as of the end of 2012. (Assume estimated useful life of each hotel is 14 years.)									
8		**Gross book value of long-term assets at current cost at end of 2012**	×	**Estimated remaining useful life**	÷	**Estimated total useful life**	=	**Net book value of long-term assets at current cost at end of 2012**		
9	San Francisco	$2,520,000	×	(6	÷	14)	=	$1,080,000		
10	Chicago	$2,625,000	×	(10	÷	14)	=	$1,875,000		
11	New Orleans	$3,071,250	×	(12	÷	14)	=	$2,632,500		
12										
13	**Step 3:** Compute current cost of total assets in 2012. (Assume current assets of each hotel are expressed in 2012 dollars.)									
14		**Current assets at end of 2012 (from Exhibit 23-1)**	+	**Long-term assets from Step 2**	=	**Current cost of total assets at end of 2012**				
15	San Francisco	$400,000	+	$1,080,000	=	$1,480,000				
16	Chicago	$500,000	+	$1,875,000	=	$2,375,000				
17	New Orleans	$660,000	+	$2,632,500	=	$3,292,500				
18										
19	**Step 4:** Compute current-cost depreciation expense in 2012 dollars.									
20		**Gross book value of long-term assets at current cost at end of 2012 (from Step 1)**	÷	**Estimated total useful life**	=	**Current-cost depreciation expense in 2012 dollars**				
21	San Francisco	$2,520,000	÷	14	=	$180,000				
22	Chicago	$2,625,000	÷	14	=	$187,500				
23	New Orleans	$3,071,250	÷	14	=	$219,375				
24										
25	**Step 5:** Compute 2012 operating income using 2012 current-cost depreciation expense.									
26		**Historical-cost operating income**	−	**Current-cost depreciation expense in 2012 dollars (from Step 4)**	−	**Historical-cost depreciation expense**	=	**Operating income for 2012 using current-cost depreciation expense in 2012 dollars**		
27	San Francisco	$240,000	−	($180,000	−	$100,000)	=	$160,000		
28	Chicago	$300,000	−	($187,500	−	$150,000)	=	$262,500		
29	New Orleans	$510,000	−	($219,375	−	$195,000)	=	$485,625		
30										
31	**Step 6:** Compute ROI using current-cost estimates for long-term assets and depreciation expense.									
32		**Operating income for 2012 using current-cost depreciation expense in 2012 dollars (from Step 5)**	÷	**Current cost of total assets at end of 2012 (from Step 3)**	=	**ROI using current-cost estimate**				
33	San Francisco	$160,000	÷	$1,480,000	=	10.8%				
34	Chicago	$262,500	÷	$2,375,000	=	11.1%				
35	New Orleans	$485,625	÷	$3,292,500	=	14.7%				

Decision Point ▶

Over what time frame should companies measure performance, and what are the alternative choices for calculating the components of each performance measure?

gross-book-value calculations, the return on the original plant-and-equipment investment is higher for the newer New Orleans hotel than for the older San Francisco hotel. This difference probably reflects the decline in earning power of the San Francisco hotel. Using the net book value masks this decline in earning power because the constantly decreasing investment base results in a higher ROI for the San Francisco hotel—24% in this example. This higher rate may mislead decision makers into thinking that the earning power of the San Francisco hotel has not decreased.

The proponents of using net book value as an investment base maintain that it is less confusing because (1) it is consistent with the amount of total assets shown in the conventional balance sheet, and (2) it is consistent with income computations that include deductions for depreciation expense. Surveys report net book value to be the dominant measure of assets used by companies for internal performance evaluation.

Target Levels of Performance and Feedback

Now that we have covered the different types of measures and how to choose them, let us turn our attention to how mangers set and measure target levels of performance.

Choosing Target Levels of Performance

Learning Objective 4

Study the choice of performance targets and design of feedback mechanisms

. . . carefully crafted budgets and sufficient feedback for timely corrective action

We next consider target-setting for accounting-based measures of performance against which actual performance can be compared. Historical-cost-based accounting measures are usually inadequate for evaluating economic returns on new investments, and in some cases, they create disincentives for expansion. Despite these problems, historical-cost ROIs can be used to evaluate current performance by establishing *target* ROIs. For Hospitality Inns, we need to recognize that the hotels were built in different years, which means they were built at different construction-price levels. Top management could adjust the target historical-cost-based ROIs accordingly, say, by setting San Francisco's ROI at 26%, Chicago's at 18%, and New Orleans' at 19%.

This useful alternative of comparing actual results with target or budgeted performance is frequently overlooked. The budget should be carefully negotiated with full knowledge of historical-cost accounting pitfalls. *Companies should tailor a budget to a particular subunit, a particular accounting system, and a particular performance measure.* For example, many problems of asset valuation and income measurement can be resolved if top management can get subunit managers to focus on what is attainable in the forthcoming budget period—whether ROI, RI, or EVA is used and whether the financial measures are based on historical cost or some other measure, such as current cost.

A popular way to establish targets is to set continuous improvement targets. If a company is using EVA as a performance measure, top management can evaluate operations on year-to-year changes in EVA, rather than on absolute measures of EVA. Evaluating performance on the basis of *improvements* in EVA makes the initial method of calculating EVA less important.

In establishing targets for financial performance measures, companies using the balanced scorecard simultaneously determine targets in the customer, internal-business-process, and learning-and-growth perspectives. For example, Hospitality Inns will establish targets for employee training and employee satisfaction, customer-service time for reservations and check-in, quality of room service, and customer satisfaction that each hotel must reach to achieve its ROI and EVA targets.

Choosing the Timing of Feedback

A final critical step in designing accounting-based performance measures is the timing of feedback. Timing of feedback depends largely on (a) how critical the information is for the success of the organization, (b) the specific level of management receiving the feedback, and (c) the sophistication of the organization's information technology. For example, hotel managers responsible for room sales want information on the number of rooms sold (rented) on a daily or weekly basis, because a large percentage of hotel costs are fixed costs. Achieving high room sales and taking quick action to reverse any declining sales trends are critical to the financial success of each hotel. Supplying managers with daily information about room sales is much easier if Hospitality Inns has a computerized room-reservation and check-in system. Top management, however, may look at information about daily room sales only on a monthly basis. In some instances, for example, because of concern about the low sales-to-total-assets ratio of the Chicago hotel, management may want the information weekly.

The timing of feedback for measures in the balanced scorecard varies. For example, human resources managers at each hotel measure employee satisfaction annually because satisfaction is best measured over a longer horizon. However, housekeeping department managers measure the quality of room service over much shorter time horizons, such as a week, because poor levels of performance in these areas for even a short period of time can harm a hotel's reputation for a long period. Moreover, housekeeping problems can be detected and resolved over a short time period.

Performance Measurement in Multinational Companies

Our discussion so far has focused on performance evaluation of different divisions of a company operating within a single country. We next discuss the additional difficulties created when the performance of divisions of a company operating in different countries is compared. Several issues arise.[9]

- The economic, legal, political, social, and cultural environments differ significantly across countries.

- Governments in some countries may limit selling prices of, and impose controls on, a company's products. For example, some countries in Asia, Latin America, and Eastern Europe impose tariffs and custom duties to restrict imports of certain goods.

- Availability of materials and skilled labor, as well as costs of materials, labor, and infrastructure (power, transportation, and communication), may also differ significantly across countries.

- Divisions operating in different countries account for their performance in different currencies. Issues of inflation and fluctuations in foreign-currency exchange rates affect performance measures.

As a result of these differences, adjustments need to be made to compare performance measures across countries.

Calculating the Foreign Division's ROI in the Foreign Currency

Suppose Hospitality Inns invests in a hotel in Mexico City. The investment consists mainly of the costs of buildings and furnishings. Also assume the following:

- The exchange rate at the time of Hospitality's investment on December 31, 2011, is 10 pesos = \$1.

- During 2012, the Mexican peso suffers a steady decline in its value. The exchange rate on December 31, 2012, is 15 pesos = \$1.

- The average exchange rate during 2012 is $[(10 + 15) \div 2] = 12.5$ pesos = \$1.

- The investment (total assets) in the Mexico City hotel is 30,000,000 pesos.

- The operating income of the Mexico City hotel in 2012 is 6,000,000 pesos.

What is the historical-cost-based ROI for the Mexico City hotel in 2012?

To answer this question, Hospitality Inns' managers first have to determine if they should calculate the ROI in pesos or in dollars. If they calculate the ROI in dollars, what exchange rate should they use? The managers may also be interested in how the

---

[9] See M. Z. Iqbal, *International Accounting—A Global Perspective* (Cincinnati: South-Western College Publishing, 2002).

Table 1

Compound Amount of $1.00 (The Future Value of $1.00)

$S = P(1 + r)^n$. In this table $P = \$1.00$

Periods	2%	4%	6%	8%	10%	12%	14%	16%	18%	20%	22%	24%	26%	28%	30%	32%	40%	Periods
1	1.020	1.040	1.060	1.080	1.100	1.120	1.140	1.160	1.180	1.200	1.220	1.240	1.260	1.280	1.300	1.320	1.400	1
2	1.040	1.082	1.124	1.166	1.210	1.254	1.300	1.346	1.392	1.440	1.488	1.538	1.588	1.638	1.690	1.742	1.960	2
3	1.061	1.125	1.191	1.260	1.331	1.405	1.482	1.561	1.643	1.728	1.816	1.907	2.000	2.097	2.197	2.300	2.744	3
4	1.082	1.170	1.262	1.360	1.464	1.574	1.689	1.811	1.939	2.074	2.215	2.364	2.520	2.684	2.856	3.036	3.842	4
5	1.104	1.217	1.338	1.469	1.611	1.762	1.925	2.100	2.288	2.488	2.703	2.932	3.176	3.436	3.713	4.007	5.378	5
6	1.126	1.265	1.419	1.587	1.772	1.974	2.195	2.436	2.700	2.986	3.297	3.635	4.002	4.398	4.827	5.290	7.530	6
7	1.149	1.316	1.504	1.714	1.949	2.211	2.502	2.826	3.185	3.583	4.023	4.508	5.042	5.629	6.275	6.983	10.541	7
8	1.172	1.369	1.594	1.851	2.144	2.476	2.853	3.278	3.759	4.300	4.908	5.590	6.353	7.206	8.157	9.217	14.758	8
9	1.195	1.423	1.689	1.999	2.358	2.773	3.252	3.803	4.435	5.160	5.987	6.931	8.005	9.223	10.604	12.166	20.661	9
10	1.219	1.480	1.791	2.159	2.594	3.106	3.707	4.411	5.234	6.192	7.305	8.594	10.086	11.806	13.786	16.060	28.925	10
11	1.243	1.539	1.898	2.332	2.853	3.479	4.226	5.117	6.176	7.430	8.912	10.657	12.708	15.112	17.922	21.199	40.496	11
12	1.268	1.601	2.012	2.518	3.138	3.896	4.818	5.936	7.288	8.916	10.872	13.215	16.012	19.343	23.298	27.983	56.694	12
13	1.294	1.665	2.133	2.720	3.452	4.363	5.492	6.886	8.599	10.699	13.264	16.386	20.175	24.759	30.288	36.937	79.371	13
14	1.319	1.732	2.261	2.937	3.797	4.887	6.261	7.988	10.147	12.839	16.182	20.319	25.421	31.691	39.374	48.757	111.120	14
15	1.346	1.801	2.397	3.172	4.177	5.474	7.138	9.266	11.974	15.407	19.742	25.196	32.030	40.565	51.186	64.359	155.568	15
16	1.373	1.873	2.540	3.426	4.595	6.130	8.137	10.748	14.129	18.488	24.086	31.243	40.358	51.923	66.542	84.954	217.795	16
17	1.400	1.948	2.693	3.700	5.054	6.866	9.276	12.468	16.672	22.186	29.384	38.741	50.851	66.461	86.504	112.139	304.913	17
18	1.428	2.026	2.854	3.996	5.560	7.690	10.575	14.463	19.673	26.623	35.849	48.039	64.072	85.071	112.455	148.024	426.879	18
19	1.457	2.107	3.026	4.316	6.116	8.613	12.056	16.777	23.214	31.948	43.736	59.568	80.731	108.890	146.192	195.391	597.630	19
20	1.486	2.191	3.207	4.661	6.727	9.646	13.743	19.461	27.393	38.338	53.358	73.864	101.721	139.380	190.050	257.916	836.683	20
21	1.516	2.279	3.400	5.034	7.400	10.804	15.668	22.574	32.324	46.005	65.096	91.592	128.169	178.406	247.065	340.449	1171.356	21
22	1.546	2.370	3.604	5.437	8.140	12.100	17.861	26.186	38.142	55.206	79.418	113.574	161.492	228.360	321.184	449.393	1639.898	22
23	1.577	2.465	3.820	5.871	8.954	13.552	20.362	30.376	45.008	66.247	96.889	140.831	203.480	292.300	417.539	593.199	2295.857	23
24	1.608	2.563	4.049	6.341	9.850	15.179	23.212	35.236	53.109	79.497	118.205	174.631	256.385	374.144	542.801	783.023	3214.200	24
25	1.641	2.666	4.292	6.848	10.835	17.000	26.462	40.874	62.669	95.396	144.210	216.542	323.045	478.905	705.641	1033.590	4499.880	25
26	1.673	2.772	4.549	7.396	11.918	19.040	30.167	47.414	73.949	114.475	175.936	268.512	407.037	612.998	917.333	1364.339	6299.831	26
27	1.707	2.883	4.822	7.988	13.110	21.325	34.390	55.000	87.260	137.371	214.642	332.955	512.867	784.638	1192.533	1800.927	8819.764	27
28	1.741	2.999	5.112	8.627	14.421	23.884	39.204	63.800	102.967	164.845	261.864	412.864	646.212	1004.336	1550.293	2377.224	12347.670	28
29	1.776	3.119	5.418	9.317	15.863	26.750	44.693	74.009	121.501	197.814	319.474	511.952	814.228	1285.550	2015.381	3137.935	17286.737	29
30	1.811	3.243	5.743	10.063	17.449	29.960	50.950	85.850	143.371	237.376	389.758	634.820	1025.927	1645.505	2619.996	4142.075	24201.432	30
35	2.000	3.946	7.686	14.785	28.102	52.800	98.100	180.314	327.997	590.668	1053.402	1861.054	3258.135	5653.911	9727.860	16599.217	130161.112	35
40	2.208	4.801	10.286	21.725	45.259	93.051	188.884	378.721	750.378	1469.772	2847.038	5455.913	10347.175	19426.689	36118.865	66520.767	700037.697	40

Table 2 (Place a clip on this page for easy reference.)

Present Value of $1.00

$$P = \frac{S}{(1 + r)^n}. \text{ In this table } S = \$1.00.$$

Periods	2%	4%	6%	8%	10%	12%	14%	16%	18%	20%	22%	24%	26%	28%	30%	32%	40%	Periods
1	0.980	0.962	0.943	0.926	0.909	0.893	0.877	0.862	0.847	0.833	0.820	0.806	0.794	0.781	0.769	0.758	0.714	1
2	0.961	0.925	0.890	0.857	0.826	0.797	0.769	0.743	0.718	0.694	0.672	0.650	0.630	0.610	0.592	0.574	0.510	2
3	0.942	0.889	0.840	0.794	0.751	0.712	0.675	0.641	0.609	0.579	0.551	0.524	0.500	0.477	0.455	0.435	0.364	3
4	0.924	0.855	0.792	0.735	0.683	0.636	0.592	0.552	0.516	0.482	0.451	0.423	0.397	0.373	0.350	0.329	0.260	4
5	0.906	0.822	0.747	0.681	0.621	0.567	0.519	0.476	0.437	0.402	0.370	0.341	0.315	0.291	0.269	0.250	0.186	5
6	0.888	0.790	0.705	0.630	0.564	0.507	0.456	0.410	0.370	0.335	0.303	0.275	0.250	0.227	0.207	0.189	0.133	6
7	0.871	0.760	0.665	0.583	0.513	0.452	0.400	0.354	0.314	0.279	0.249	0.222	0.198	0.178	0.159	0.143	0.095	7
8	0.853	0.731	0.627	0.540	0.467	0.404	0.351	0.305	0.266	0.233	0.204	0.179	0.157	0.139	0.123	0.108	0.068	8
9	0.837	0.703	0.592	0.500	0.424	0.361	0.308	0.263	0.225	0.194	0.167	0.144	0.125	0.108	0.094	0.082	0.048	9
10	0.820	0.676	0.558	0.463	0.386	0.322	0.270	0.227	0.191	0.162	0.137	0.116	0.099	0.085	0.073	0.062	0.035	10
11	0.804	0.650	0.527	0.429	0.350	0.287	0.237	0.195	0.162	0.135	0.112	0.094	0.079	0.066	0.056	0.047	0.025	11
12	0.788	0.625	0.497	0.397	0.319	0.257	0.208	0.168	0.137	0.112	0.092	0.076	0.062	0.052	0.043	0.036	0.018	12
13	0.773	0.601	0.469	0.368	0.290	0.229	0.182	0.145	0.116	0.093	0.075	0.061	0.050	0.040	0.033	0.027	0.013	13
14	0.758	0.577	0.442	0.340	0.263	0.205	0.160	0.125	0.099	0.078	0.062	0.049	0.039	0.032	0.025	0.021	0.009	14
15	0.743	0.555	0.417	0.315	0.239	0.183	0.140	0.108	0.084	0.065	0.051	0.040	0.031	0.025	0.020	0.016	0.006	15
16	0.728	0.534	0.394	0.292	0.218	0.163	0.123	0.093	0.071	0.054	0.042	0.032	0.025	0.019	0.015	0.012	0.005	16
17	0.714	0.513	0.371	0.270	0.198	0.146	0.108	0.080	0.060	0.045	0.034	0.026	0.020	0.015	0.012	0.009	0.003	17
18	0.700	0.494	0.350	0.250	0.180	0.130	0.095	0.069	0.051	0.038	0.028	0.021	0.016	0.012	0.009	0.007	0.002	18
19	0.686	0.475	0.331	0.232	0.164	0.116	0.083	0.060	0.043	0.031	0.023	0.017	0.012	0.009	0.007	0.005	0.002	19
20	0.673	0.456	0.312	0.215	0.149	0.104	0.073	0.051	0.037	0.026	0.019	0.014	0.010	0.007	0.005	0.004	0.001	20
21	0.660	0.439	0.294	0.199	0.135	0.093	0.064	0.044	0.031	0.022	0.015	0.011	0.008	0.006	0.004	0.003	0.001	21
22	0.647	0.422	0.278	0.184	0.123	0.083	0.056	0.038	0.026	0.018	0.013	0.009	0.006	0.004	0.003	0.002	0.001	22
23	0.634	0.406	0.262	0.170	0.112	0.074	0.049	0.033	0.022	0.015	0.010	0.007	0.005	0.003	0.002	0.002	0.000	23
24	0.622	0.390	0.247	0.158	0.102	0.066	0.043	0.028	0.019	0.013	0.008	0.006	0.004	0.003	0.002	0.001	0.000	24
25	0.610	0.375	0.233	0.146	0.092	0.059	0.038	0.024	0.016	0.010	0.007	0.005	0.003	0.002	0.001	0.001	0.000	25
26	0.598	0.361	0.220	0.135	0.084	0.053	0.033	0.021	0.014	0.009	0.006	0.004	0.002	0.002	0.001	0.001	0.000	26
27	0.586	0.347	0.207	0.125	0.076	0.047	0.029	0.018	0.011	0.007	0.005	0.003	0.002	0.001	0.001	0.001	0.000	27
28	0.574	0.333	0.196	0.116	0.069	0.042	0.026	0.016	0.010	0.006	0.004	0.002	0.002	0.001	0.001	0.000	0.000	28
29	0.563	0.321	0.185	0.107	0.063	0.037	0.022	0.014	0.008	0.005	0.003	0.002	0.001	0.001	0.000	0.000	0.000	29
30	0.552	0.308	0.174	0.099	0.057	0.033	0.020	0.012	0.007	0.004	0.003	0.002	0.001	0.001	0.000	0.000	0.000	30
35	0.500	0.253	0.130	0.068	0.036	0.019	0.010	0.006	0.003	0.002	0.001	0.001	0.000	0.000	0.000	0.000	0.000	35
40	0.453	0.208	0.097	0.046	0.022	0.011	0.005	0.003	0.001	0.001	0.000	0.000	0.000	0.000	0.000	0.000	0.000	40

Table 3
Compound Amount of Annuity of $1.00 in Arrears* (Future Value of Annuity)

$$S_n = \frac{(1 + r)^n - 1}{r}$$

Periods	2%	4%	6%	8%	10%	12%	14%	16%	18%	20%	22%	24%	26%	28%	30%	32%	40%	Periods
1	1.000	1.000	1.000	1.000	1.000	1.000	1.000	1.000	1.000	1.000	1.000	1.000	1.000	1.000	1.000	1.000	1.000	1
2	2.020	2.040	2.060	2.080	2.100	2.120	2.140	2.160	2.180	2.200	2.220	2.240	2.260	2.280	2.300	2.320	2.400	2
3	3.060	3.122	3.184	3.246	3.310	3.374	3.440	3.506	3.572	3.640	3.708	3.778	3.848	3.918	3.990	4.062	4.360	3
4	4.122	4.246	4.375	4.506	4.641	4.779	4.921	5.066	5.215	5.368	5.524	5.684	5.848	6.016	6.187	6.362	7.104	4
5	5.204	5.416	5.637	5.867	6.105	6.353	6.610	6.877	7.154	7.442	7.740	8.048	8.368	8.700	9.043	9.398	10.946	5
6	6.308	6.633	6.975	7.336	7.716	8.115	8.536	8.977	9.442	9.930	10.442	10.980	11.544	12.136	12.756	13.406	16.324	6
7	7.434	7.898	8.394	8.923	9.487	10.089	10.730	11.414	12.142	12.916	13.740	14.615	15.546	16.534	17.583	18.696	23.853	7
8	8.583	9.214	9.897	10.637	11.436	12.300	13.233	14.240	15.327	16.499	17.762	19.123	20.588	22.163	23.858	25.678	34.395	8
9	9.755	10.583	11.491	12.488	13.579	14.776	16.085	17.519	19.086	20.799	22.670	24.712	26.940	29.369	32.015	34.895	49.153	9
10	10.950	12.006	13.181	14.487	15.937	17.549	19.337	21.321	23.521	25.959	28.657	31.643	34.945	38.593	42.619	47.062	69.814	10
11	12.169	13.486	14.972	16.645	18.531	20.655	23.045	25.733	28.755	32.150	35.962	40.238	45.031	50.398	56.405	63.122	98.739	11
12	13.412	15.026	16.870	18.977	21.384	24.133	27.271	30.850	34.931	39.581	44.874	50.895	57.739	65.510	74.327	84.320	139.235	12
13	14.680	16.627	18.882	21.495	24.523	28.029	32.089	36.786	42.219	48.497	55.746	64.110	73.751	84.853	97.625	112.303	195.929	13
14	15.974	18.292	21.015	24.215	27.975	32.393	37.581	43.672	50.818	59.196	69.010	80.496	93.926	109.612	127.913	149.240	275.300	14
15	17.293	20.024	23.276	27.152	31.772	37.280	43.842	51.660	60.965	72.035	85.192	100.815	119.347	141.303	167.286	197.997	386.420	15
16	18.639	21.825	25.673	30.324	35.950	42.753	50.980	60.925	72.939	87.442	104.935	126.011	151.377	181.868	218.472	262.356	541.988	16
17	20.012	23.698	28.213	33.750	40.545	48.884	59.118	71.673	87.068	105.931	129.020	157.253	191.735	233.791	285.014	347.309	759.784	17
18	21.412	25.645	30.906	37.450	45.599	55.750	68.394	84.141	103.740	128.117	158.405	195.994	242.585	300.252	371.518	459.449	1064.697	18
19	22.841	27.671	33.760	41.446	51.159	63.440	78.969	98.603	123.414	154.740	194.254	244.033	306.658	385.323	483.973	607.472	1491.576	19
20	24.297	29.778	36.786	45.762	57.275	72.052	91.025	115.380	146.628	186.688	237.989	303.601	387.389	494.213	630.165	802.863	2089.206	20
21	25.783	31.969	39.993	50.423	64.002	81.699	104.768	134.841	174.021	225.026	291.347	377.465	489.110	633.593	820.215	1060.779	2925.889	21
22	27.299	34.248	43.392	55.457	71.403	92.503	120.436	157.415	206.345	271.031	356.443	469.056	617.278	811.999	1067.280	1401.229	4097.245	22
23	28.845	36.618	46.996	60.893	79.543	104.603	138.297	183.601	244.487	326.237	435.861	582.630	778.771	1040.358	1388.464	1850.622	5737.142	23
24	30.422	39.083	50.816	66.765	88.497	118.155	158.659	213.978	289.494	392.484	532.750	723.461	982.251	1332.659	1806.003	2443.821	8032.999	24
25	32.030	41.646	54.865	73.106	98.347	133.334	181.871	249.214	342.603	471.981	650.955	898.092	1238.636	1706.803	2348.803	3226.844	11247.199	25
26	33.671	44.312	59.156	79.954	109.182	150.334	208.333	290.088	405.272	567.377	795.165	1114.634	1561.682	2185.708	3054.444	4260.434	15747.079	26
27	35.344	47.084	63.706	87.351	121.100	169.374	238.499	337.502	479.221	681.853	971.102	1383.146	1968.719	2798.706	3971.778	5624.772	22046.910	27
28	37.051	49.968	68.528	95.339	134.210	190.699	272.889	392.503	566.481	819.223	1185.744	1716.101	2481.586	3583.344	5164.311	7425.699	30866.674	28
29	38.792	52.966	73.640	103.966	148.631	214.583	312.094	456.303	669.447	984.068	1447.608	2128.965	3127.798	4587.680	6714.604	9802.923	43214.343	29
30	40.568	56.085	79.058	113.263	164.494	241.333	356.787	530.312	790.948	1181.882	1767.081	2640.916	3942.026	5873.231	8729.985	12940.859	60501.081	30
35	49.994	73.652	111.435	172.317	271.024	431.663	693.573	1120.713	1816.652	2948.341	4783.645	7750.225	12527.442	20188.966	32422.868	51869.427	325400.279	35
40	60.402	95.026	154.762	259.057	442.593	767.091	1342.025	2360.757	4163.213	7343.858	12936.535	22728.803	39792.982	69377.460	120392.883	207874.272	1750091.741	40

*Payments (or receipts) at the end of each period.

Table 4 (*Place a clip on this page for easy reference.*)

Present Value of Annuity $1.00 in Arrears*

$$P_n = \frac{1}{r}\left[1 - \frac{1}{(1+r)^n}\right]$$

Periods	2%	4%	6%	8%	10%	12%	14%	16%	18%	20%	22%	24%	26%	28%	30%	32%	40%	Periods
1	0.980	0.962	0.943	0.926	0.909	0.893	0.877	0.862	0.847	0.833	0.820	0.806	0.794	0.781	0.769	0.758	0.714	1
2	1.942	1.886	1.833	1.783	1.736	1.690	1.647	1.605	1.566	1.528	1.492	1.457	1.424	1.392	1.361	1.331	1.224	2
3	2.884	2.775	2.673	2.577	2.487	2.402	2.322	2.246	2.174	2.106	2.042	1.981	1.923	1.868	1.816	1.766	1.589	3
4	3.808	3.630	3.465	3.312	3.170	3.037	2.914	2.798	2.690	2.589	2.494	2.404	2.320	2.241	2.166	2.096	1.849	4
5	4.713	4.452	4.212	3.993	3.791	3.605	3.433	3.274	3.127	2.991	2.864	2.745	2.635	2.532	2.436	2.345	2.035	5
6	5.601	5.242	4.917	4.623	4.355	4.111	3.889	3.685	3.498	3.326	3.167	3.020	2.885	2.759	2.643	2.534	2.168	6
7	6.472	6.002	5.582	5.206	4.868	4.564	4.288	4.039	3.812	3.605	3.416	3.242	3.083	2.937	2.802	2.677	2.263	7
8	7.325	6.733	6.210	5.747	5.335	4.968	4.639	4.344	4.078	3.837	3.619	3.421	3.241	3.076	2.925	2.786	2.331	8
9	8.162	7.435	6.802	6.247	5.759	5.328	4.946	4.607	4.303	4.031	3.786	3.566	3.366	3.184	3.019	2.868	2.379	9
10	8.983	8.111	7.360	6.710	6.145	5.650	5.216	4.833	4.494	4.192	3.923	3.682	3.465	3.269	3.092	2.930	2.414	10
11	9.787	8.760	7.887	7.139	6.495	5.938	5.453	5.029	4.656	4.327	4.035	3.776	3.543	3.335	3.147	2.978	2.438	11
12	10.575	9.385	8.384	7.536	6.814	6.194	5.660	5.197	4.793	4.439	4.127	3.851	3.606	3.387	3.190	3.013	2.456	12
13	11.348	9.986	8.853	7.904	7.103	6.424	5.842	5.342	4.910	4.533	4.203	3.912	3.656	3.427	3.223	3.040	2.469	13
14	12.106	10.563	9.295	8.244	7.367	6.628	6.002	5.468	5.008	4.611	4.265	3.962	3.695	3.459	3.249	3.061	2.478	14
15	12.849	11.118	9.712	8.559	7.606	6.811	6.142	5.575	5.092	4.675	4.315	4.001	3.726	3.483	3.268	3.076	2.484	15
16	13.578	11.652	10.106	8.851	7.824	6.974	6.265	5.668	5.162	4.730	4.357	4.033	3.751	3.503	3.283	3.088	2.489	16
17	14.292	12.166	10.477	9.122	8.022	7.120	6.373	5.749	5.222	4.775	4.391	4.059	3.771	3.518	3.295	3.097	2.492	17
18	14.992	12.659	10.828	9.372	8.201	7.250	6.467	5.818	5.273	4.812	4.419	4.080	3.786	3.529	3.304	3.104	2.494	18
19	15.678	13.134	11.158	9.604	8.365	7.366	6.550	5.877	5.316	4.843	4.442	4.097	3.799	3.539	3.311	3.109	2.496	19
20	16.351	13.590	11.470	9.818	8.514	7.469	6.623	5.929	5.353	4.870	4.460	4.110	3.808	3.546	3.316	3.113	2.497	20
21	17.011	14.029	11.764	10.017	8.649	7.562	6.687	5.973	5.384	4.891	4.476	4.121	3.816	3.551	3.320	3.116	2.498	21
22	17.658	14.451	12.042	10.201	8.772	7.645	6.743	6.011	5.410	4.909	4.488	4.130	3.822	3.556	3.323	3.118	2.498	22
23	18.292	14.857	12.303	10.371	8.883	7.718	6.792	6.044	5.432	4.925	4.499	4.137	3.827	3.559	3.325	3.120	2.499	23
24	18.914	15.247	12.550	10.529	8.985	7.784	6.835	6.073	5.451	4.937	4.507	4.143	3.831	3.562	3.327	3.121	2.499	24
25	19.523	15.622	12.783	10.675	9.077	7.843	6.873	6.097	5.467	4.948	4.514	4.147	3.834	3.564	3.329	3.122	2.499	25
26	20.121	15.983	13.003	10.810	9.161	7.896	6.906	6.118	5.480	4.956	4.520	4.151	3.837	3.566	3.330	3.123	2.500	26
27	20.707	16.330	13.211	10.935	9.237	7.943	6.935	6.136	5.492	4.964	4.524	4.154	3.839	3.567	3.331	3.123	2.500	27
28	21.281	16.663	13.406	11.051	9.307	7.984	6.961	6.152	5.502	4.970	4.528	4.157	3.840	3.568	3.331	3.124	2.500	28
29	21.844	16.984	13.591	11.158	9.370	8.022	6.983	6.166	5.510	4.975	4.531	4.159	3.841	3.569	3.332	3.124	2.500	29
30	22.396	17.292	13.765	11.258	9.427	8.055	7.003	6.177	5.517	4.979	4.534	4.160	3.842	3.569	3.332	3.124	2.500	30
35	24.999	18.665	14.498	11.655	9.644	8.176	7.070	6.215	5.539	4.992	4.541	4.164	3.845	3.571	3.333	3.125	2.500	35
40	27.355	19.793	15.046	11.925	9.779	8.244	7.105	6.233	5.548	4.997	4.544	4.166	3.846	3.571	3.333	3.125	2.500	40

*Payments (or receipts) at the end of each period.

Glossary

Abnormal spoilage. Spoilage that would not arise under efficient operating conditions; it is not inherent in a particular production process. (646)

Absorption costing. Method of inventory costing in which all variable manufacturing costs and all fixed manufacturing costs are included as inventoriable costs. (302)

Account analysis method. Approach to cost function estimation that classifies various cost accounts as variable, fixed, or mixed with respect to the identified level of activity. Typically, qualitative rather than quantitative analysis is used when making these cost-classification decisions. (347)

Accrual accounting rate of return (AARR) method. Capital budgeting method that divides an accrual accounting measure of average annual income of a project by an accrual accounting measure of its investment. See also *return on investment (ROI)*. (749)

Activity. An event, task, or unit of work with a specified purpose. (146)

Activity-based budgeting (ABB). Budgeting approach that focuses on the budgeted cost of the activities necessary to produce and sell products and services. (193)

Activity-based costing (ABC). Approach to costing that focuses on individual activities as the fundamental cost objects. It uses the costs of these activities as the basis for assigning costs to other cost objects such as products or services. (146)

Activity-based management (ABM). Method of management decision-making that uses activity-based costing information to improve customer satisfaction and profitability. (156)

Actual cost. Cost incurred (a historical or past cost), as distinguished from a budgeted or forecasted cost. (27)

Actual costing. A costing system that traces direct costs to a cost object by using the actual direct-cost rates times the actual quantities of the direct-cost inputs and allocates indirect costs based on the actual indirect-cost rates times the actual quantities of the cost allocation bases. (102)

Actual indirect-cost rate. Actual total indirect costs in a cost pool divided by the actual total quantity of the cost-allocation base for that cost pool. (110)

Adjusted allocation-rate approach. Restates all overhead entries in the general ledger and subsidiary ledgers using actual cost rates rather than budgeted cost rates. (118)

Allowable cost. Cost that the contract parties agree to include in the costs to be reimbursed. (559)

Appraisal costs. Costs incurred to detect which of the individual units of products do not conform to specifications. (673)

Artificial costs. See *complete reciprocated costs*. (554)

Autonomy. The degree of freedom to make decisions. (777)

Average cost. See *unit cost*. (35)

Average waiting time. The average amount of time that an order will wait in line before the machine is set up and the order is processed. (683)

Backflush costing. Costing system that omits recording some of the journal entries relating to the stages from purchase of direct material to the sale of finished goods. (719)

Balanced scorecard. A framework for implementing strategy that translates an organization's mission and strategy into a set of performance measures. (470)

Batch-level costs. The costs of activities related to a group of units of products or services rather than to each individual unit of product or service. (149)

Belief systems. Lever of control that articulates the mission, purpose, norms of behaviors, and core values of a company intended to inspire managers and other employees to do their best. (827)

Benchmarking. The continuous process of comparing the levels of performance in producing products and services and executing activities against the best levels of performance in competing companies or in companies having similar processes. (244)

Book value. The original cost minus accumulated depreciation of an asset. (410)

Bottleneck. An operation where the work to be performed approaches or exceeds the capacity available to do it. (682)

Boundary systems. Lever of control that describes standards of behavior and codes of conduct expected of all employees, especially actions that are off-limits. (826)

Breakeven point (BEP). Quantity of output sold at which total revenues equal total costs, that is where the operating income is zero. (68)

Budget. Quantitative expression of a proposed plan of action by management for a specified period and an aid to coordinating what needs to be done to implement that plan. (10)

Budgetary slack. The practice of underestimating budgeted revenues, or overestimating budgeted costs, to make budgeted targets more easily achievable. (201)

Budgeted cost. Predicted or forecasted cost (future cost) as distinguished from an actual or historical cost. (27)

Budgeted indirect-cost rate. Budgeted annual indirect costs in a cost pool divided by the budgeted annual quantity of the cost allocation base. (104)

Budgeted performance. Expected performance or a point of reference to compare actual results. (227)

Bundled product. A package of two or more products (or services) that is sold for a single price, but whose individual components may be sold as separate items at their own "stand-alone" prices. (561)

Business function costs. The sum of all costs (variable and fixed) in a particular business function of the value chain. (395)

Byproducts. Products from a joint production process that have low total sales values compared with the total sales value of the main product or of joint products. (578)

Capital budgeting. The making of long-run planning decisions for investments in projects. (739)

Carrying costs. Costs that arise while holding inventory of goods for sale. (704)

Cash budget. Schedule of expected cash receipts and disbursements. (207)

Cause-and-effect diagram. Diagram that identifies potential causes of defects. Four categories of potential causes of failure are human factors, methods and design factors, machine-related factors, and materials and components factors. Also called a *fishbone diagram*. (676)

Chief financial officer (CFO). Executive responsible for overseeing the financial operations of an organization. Also called *finance director*. (13)

Choice criterion. Objective that can be quantified in a decision model. (84)

Coefficient of determination (r^2). Measures the percentage of variation in a dependent variable explained by one or more independent variables. (367)

Collusive pricing. Companies in an industry conspire in their pricing and production decisions to achieve a price above the competitive price and so restrain trade. (452)

Common cost. Cost of operating a facility, activity, or like cost object that is shared by two or more users. (557)

Complete reciprocated costs. The support department's own costs plus any interdepartmental cost allocations. Also called the *artificial costs* of the support department. (554)

Composite unit. Hypothetical unit with weights based on the mix of individual units. (521)

Conference method. Approach to cost function estimation on the basis of analysis and opinions about costs and their drivers gathered from various departments of a company (purchasing, process engineering, manufacturing, employee relations, and so on). (346)

Conformance quality. Refers to the performance of a product or service relative to its design and product specifications. (672)

Constant. The component of total cost that, within the relevant range, does not vary with changes in the level of the activity. Also called *intercept*. (343)

Constant gross-margin percentage NRV method. Method that allocates joint costs to joint products in such a way that the overall gross-margin percentage is identical for the individual products. (584)

Constraint. A mathematical inequality or equality that must be satisfied by the variables in a mathematical model. (416)

Continuous budget. See *rolling budget*. (188)

Contribution income statement. Income statement that groups costs into variable costs and fixed costs to highlight the contribution margin. (65)

Contribution margin. Total revenues minus total variable costs. (64)

Contribution margin per unit. Selling price minus the variable cost per unit. (65)

Contribution margin percentage. Contribution margin per unit divided by selling price. Also called *contribution margin ratio*. (65)

Contribution margin ratio. See *contribution margin percentage*. (65)

Control. Taking actions that implement the planning decisions, deciding how to evaluate performance, and providing feedback and learning that will help future decision making. (10)

Control chart. Graph of a series of successive observations of a particular step, procedure, or operation taken at regular intervals of time. Each observation is plotted relative to specified ranges that represent the limits within which observations are expected to fall. (675)

Controllability. Degree of influence that a specific manager has over costs, revenues, or related items for which he or she is responsible. (200)

Controllable cost. Any cost that is primarily subject to the influence of a given responsibility center manager for a given period. (200)

Controller. The financial executive primarily responsible for management accounting and financial accounting. Also called *chief accounting officer*. (13)

Conversion costs. All manufacturing costs other than direct material costs. (43)

Cost. Resource sacrificed or forgone to achieve a specific objective. (27)

Cost accounting. Measures, analyzes, and reports financial and nonfinancial information relating to the costs of acquiring or using resources in an organization. It provides information for both management accounting and financial accounting. (4)

Cost Accounting Standards Board (CASB). Government agency that has the exclusive authority to make, put into effect, amend, and rescind cost accounting standards and interpretations thereof designed to achieve uniformity and consistency in regard to measurement, assignment, and allocation of costs to government contracts within the United States. (559)

Cost accumulation. Collection of cost data in some organized way by means of an accounting system. (28)

Cost allocation. Assignment of indirect costs to a particular cost object. (29)

Cost-allocation base. A factor that links in a systematic way an indirect cost or group of indirect costs to a cost object. (100)

Cost-application base. Cost-allocation base when the cost object is a job, product, or customer. (100)

Cost assignment. General term that encompasses both (1) tracing accumulated costs that have a direct relationship to a cost object and (2) allocating accumulated costs that have an indirect relationship to a cost object. (29)

Cost-benefit approach. Approach to decision-making and resource allocation based on a comparison of the expected benefits from attaining company goals and the expected costs. (12)

Cost center. Responsibility center where the manager is accountable for costs only. (199)

Cost driver. A variable, such as the level of activity or volume, that causally affects costs over a given time span. (32)

Cost estimation. The attempt to measure a past relationship based on data from past costs and the related level of an activity. (344)

Cost function. Mathematical description of how a cost changes with changes in the level of an activity relating to that cost. (341)

Cost hierarchy. Categorization of indirect costs into different cost pools on the basis of the different types of cost drivers, or cost-allocation bases, or different degrees of difficulty in determining cause-and-effect (or benefits received) relationships. (149)

Cost incurrence. Describes when a resource is consumed (or benefit forgone) to meet a specific objective. (442)

Cost leadership. Organization's ability to achieve lower costs relative to competitors through productivity and efficiency improvements, elimination of waste, and tight cost control. (468)

Cost management. The approaches and activities of managers to use resources to increase value to customers and to achieve organizational goals. (4)

Cost object. Anything for which a measurement of costs is desired. (27)

Cost of capital. See *required rate of return (RRR)*. (742)

Cost of goods manufactured. Cost of goods brought to completion, whether they were started before or during the current accounting period. (41)

Cost pool. A grouping of individual cost items. (100)

Cost predictions. Forecasts about future costs. (344)

Cost tracing. Describes the assignment of direct costs to a particular cost object. (28)

Costs of quality (COQ). Costs incurred to prevent, or the costs arising as a result of, the production of a low-quality product. (672)

Cost-volume-profit (CVP) analysis. Examines the behavior of total revenues, total costs, and operating income as changes occur in the units sold, the selling price, the variable cost per unit, or the fixed costs of a product. (63)

Cumulative average-time learning model. Learning curve model in which the cumulative average time per unit declines by a constant percentage each time the cumulative quantity of units produced doubles. (359)

Current cost. Asset measure based on the cost of purchasing an asset today identical to the one currently held, or the cost of purchasing an asset that provides services like the one currently held if an identical asset cannot be purchased. (815)

Customer-cost hierarchy. Hierarchy that categorizes costs related to customers into different cost pools on the basis of different types of cost drivers, or cost-allocation bases, or different degrees of difficulty in determining cause-and-effect or benefits-received relationships. (511)

Customer life-cycle costs. Focuses on the total costs incurred by a customer to acquire, use, maintain, and dispose of a product or service. (449)

Customer-profitability analysis. The reporting and analysis of revenues earned from customers and the costs incurred to earn those revenues. (510)

Customer-response time. Duration from the time a customer places an order for a product or service to the time the product or service is delivered to the customer. (681)

Customer service. Providing after-sale support to customers. (6)

Decentralization. The freedom for managers at lower levels of the organization to make decisions. (777)

Decision model. Formal method for making a choice, often involving both quantitative and qualitative analyses. (391)

Decision table. Summary of the alternative actions, events, outcomes, and probabilities of events in a decision model. (85)

Degree of operating leverage. Contribution margin divided by operating income at any given level of sales. (76)

Denominator level. The denominator in the budgeted fixed overhead rate computation. (266)

Denominator-level variance. See *production-volume variance*. (272)

Dependent variable. The cost to be predicted. (348)

Design of products and processes. The detailed planning and engineering of products and processes. (6)

Design quality. Refers to how closely the characteristics of a product or service meet the needs and wants of customers. (672)

Designed-in costs. See *locked-in costs*. (442)

Diagnostic control systems. Lever of control that monitors critical performance variables that help managers track progress toward achieving a company's strategic goals. Managers are held accountable for meeting these goals. (826)

Differential cost. Difference in total cost between two alternatives. (399)

Differential revenue. Difference in total revenue between two alternatives. (399)

Direct costing. See *variable costing*. (302)

Direct costs of a cost object. Costs related to the particular cost object that can be traced to that object in an economically feasible (cost-effective) way. (28)

Direct manufacturing labor costs. Include the compensation of all manufacturing labor that can be traced to the cost object (work in process and then finished goods) in an economically feasible way. (37)

Direct material costs. Acquisition costs of all materials that eventually become part of the cost object (work in process and then finished goods), and that can be traced to the cost object in an economically feasible way. (37)

Direct materials inventory. Direct materials in stock and awaiting use in the manufacturing process. (37)

Direct materials mix variance. The difference between (1) budgeted cost for actual mix of the actual total quantity of direct materials used and (2) budgeted cost of budgeted mix of the actual total quantity of direct materials used. (527)

Direct materials yield variance. The difference between (1) budgeted cost of direct materials based on the actual total quantity of direct materials used and (2) flexible-budget cost of direct materials based on the budgeted total quantity of direct materials allowed for the actual output produced. (527)

Direct method. Cost allocation method that allocates each support department's costs to operating departments only. (550)

Discount rate. See *required rate of return (RRR)*. (742)

Discounted cash flow (DCF) methods. Capital budgeting methods that measure all expected future cash inflows and outflows of a project as if they occurred at the present point in time. (741)

Discounted payback method. Capital budgeting method that calculates the amount of time required for the discounted expected future cash flows to recoup the net initial investment in a project. (748)

Discretionary costs. Arise from periodic (usually annual) decisions regarding the maximum amount to be incurred and have no measurable cause-and-effect relationship between output and resources used. (486)

Distribution. Delivering products or services to customers. (6)

Downsizing. An integrated approach of configuring processes, products, and people to match costs to the activities that need to be performed to operate effectively and efficiently in the present and future. Also called *rightsizing*. (487)

Downward demand spiral. Pricing context where prices are raised to spread capacity costs over a smaller number of output units. Continuing reduction in the demand for products that occurs when the prices of competitors' products are not met and, as demand drops further, higher and higher unit costs result in more and more reluctance to meet competitors' prices. (317)

Dual pricing. Approach to transfer pricing using two separate transfer-pricing methods to price each transfer from one subunit to another. (789)

Dual-rate method. Allocation method that classifies costs in each cost pool into two pools (a variable-cost pool and a fixed-cost pool) with each pool using a different cost-allocation base. (544)

Dumping. Under U.S. laws, it occurs when a non-U.S. company sells a product in the United States at a price below the market value in the country where it is produced, and this lower price materially injures or threatens to materially injure an industry in the United States. (452)

Dysfunctional decision making. See *suboptimal decision making*. (778)

Economic order quantity (EOQ). Decision model that calculates the optimal quantity of inventory to order under a set of assumptions. (704)

Economic value added (EVA®). After-tax operating income minus the (after-tax) weighted-average cost of capital multiplied by total assets minus current liabilities. (812)

Effectiveness. The degree to which a predetermined objective or target is met. (243)

Efficiency. The relative amount of inputs used to achieve a given output level. (243)

Efficiency variance. The difference between actual input quantity used and budgeted input quantity allowed for actual output, multiplied by budgeted price. Also called *usage variance*. (236)

Effort. Exertion toward achieving a goal. (776)

Engineered costs. Costs that result from a cause-and-effect relationship between the cost driver, output, and the (direct or indirect) resources used to produce that output. (486)

Equivalent units. Derived amount of output units that (a) takes the quantity of each input (factor of production) in units completed and in incomplete units of work in process and (b) converts the quantity of input into the amount of completed output units that could be produced with that quantity of input. (611)

Event. A possible relevant occurrence in a decision model. (84)

Expected monetary value. See *expected value*. (85)

Expected value. Weighted average of the outcomes of a decision with the probability of each outcome serving as the weight. Also called *expected monetary value*. (85)

Experience curve. Function that measures the decline in cost per unit in various business functions of the value chain, such as manufacturing, marketing, distribution, and so on, as the amount of these activities increases. (358)

External failure costs. Costs incurred on defective products after they are shipped to customers. (673)

Facility-sustaining costs. The costs of activities that cannot be traced to individual products or services but support the organization as a whole. (149)

Factory overhead costs. See *indirect manufacturing costs*. (37)

Favorable variance. Variance that has the effect of increasing operating income relative to the budgeted amount. Denoted F. (229)

Finance director. See *chief financial officer (CFO)*. (13)

Financial accounting. Measures and records business transactions and provides financial statements that are based on generally accepted accounting principles. It focuses on reporting to external parties such as investors and banks. (3)

Financial budget. Part of the master budget that focuses on how operations and planned capital outlays affect cash. It is made up of the capital expenditures budget, the cash budget, the budgeted balance sheet, and the budgeted statement of cash flows. (189)

Financial planning models. Mathematical representations of the relationships among operating activities, financial activities, and other factors that affect the master budget. (197)

Finished goods inventory. Goods completed but not yet sold. (37)

First-in, first-out (FIFO) process-costing method. Method of process costing that assigns the cost of the previous accounting period's equivalent units in beginning work-in-process inventory to the first units completed and transferred out of the process, and assigns the cost of equivalent units worked on during the current period first to complete beginning inventory, next to start and complete new units, and finally to units in ending work-in-process inventory. (617)

Fixed cost. Cost that remains unchanged in total for a given time period, despite wide changes in the related level of total activity or volume. (30)

Fixed overhead flexible-budget variance. The difference between actual fixed overhead costs and fixed overhead costs in the flexible budget. (271)

Fixed overhead spending variance. Same as the fixed overhead flexible-budget variance. The difference between actual fixed overhead costs and fixed overhead costs in the flexible budget. (271)

Flexible budget. Budget developed using budgeted revenues and budgeted costs based on the actual output in the budget period. (230)

Flexible-budget variance. The difference between an actual result and the corresponding flexible-budget amount based on the actual output level in the budget period. (231)

Full costs of the product. The sum of all variable and fixed costs in all business functions of the value chain (R&D, design, production, marketing, distribution, and customer service). (395)

Goal congruence. Exists when individuals and groups work toward achieving the organization's goals. Managers working in their own best interest take actions that align with the overall goals of top management. (776)

Gross margin percentage. Gross margin divided by revenues. (82)

Growth component. Change in operating income attributable solely to the change in the quantity of output sold between one period and the next. (479)

High-low method. Method used to estimate a cost function that uses only the highest and lowest observed values of the cost driver within the relevant range and their respective costs. (350)

Homogeneous cost pool. Cost pool in which all the costs have the same or a similar cause-and-effect or benefits-received relationship with the cost-allocation base. (509)

Hurdle rate. See *required rate of return (RRR)*. (742)

Hybrid-costing system. Costing system that blends characteristics from both job-costing systems and process-costing systems. (626)

Idle time. Wages paid for unproductive time caused by lack of orders, machine breakdowns, material shortages, poor scheduling, and the like. (45)

Imputed costs. Costs recognized in particular situations but not incorporated in financial accounting records. (810)

Incongruent decision making. See *suboptimal decision making*. (778)

Incremental cost. Additional total cost incurred for an activity. (399)

Incremental cost-allocation method. Method that ranks the individual users of a cost object in the order of users most responsible for the common cost and then uses this ranking to allocate cost among those users. (557)

Incremental revenue. Additional total revenue from an activity. (399)

Incremental revenue-allocation method. Method that ranks individual products in a bundle according to criteria determined by management (for example, sales), and then uses this ranking to allocate bundled revenues to the individual products. (562)

Incremental unit-time learning model. Learning curve model in which the incremental time needed to produce the last unit declines by a constant percentage each time the cumulative quantity of units produced doubles. (360)

Independent variable. Level of activity or cost driver used to predict the dependent variable (costs) in a cost estimation or prediction model. (348)

Indirect costs of a cost object. Costs related to the particular cost object that cannot be traced to that object in an economically feasible (cost-effective) way. (28)

Indirect manufacturing costs. All manufacturing costs that are related to the cost object (work in process and then finished goods) but that cannot be traced to that cost object in an economically feasible way. Also called *manufacturing overhead costs* and *factory overhead costs*. (37)

Industrial engineering method. Approach to cost function estimation that analyzes the relationship between inputs and outputs in physical terms. Also called *work measurement method*. (346)

Inflation. The decline in the general purchasing power of the monetary unit, such as dollars. (762)

Input-price variance. See *price variance*. (236)

Insourcing. Process of producing goods or providing services within the organization rather than purchasing those same goods or services from outside vendors. (397)

Inspection point. Stage of the production process at which products are examined to determine whether they are acceptable or unacceptable units. (647)

Interactive control systems. Formal information systems that managers use to focus organization attention and learning on key strategic issues. (827)

Intercept. See *constant*. (343)

Intermediate product. Product transferred from one subunit to another subunit of an organization. This product may either be further worked on by the receiving subunit or sold to an external customer. (780)

Internal failure costs. Costs incurred on defective products before they are shipped to customers. (673)

Internal rate-of-return (IRR) method. Capital budgeting discounted cash flow (DCF) method that calculates the discount rate at which the present value of expected cash inflows from a project equals the present value of its expected cash outflows. (743)

Inventoriable costs. All costs of a product that are considered as assets in the balance sheet when they are incurred and that become cost of goods sold only when the product is sold. (37)

Inventory management. Planning, coordinating, and controlling activities related to the flow of inventory into, through, and out of an organization. (703)

Investment. Resources or assets used to generate income. (808)

Investment center. Responsibility center where the manager is accountable for investments, revenues, and costs. (199)

Job. A unit or multiple units of a distinct product or service. (100)

Job-cost record. Source document that records and accumulates all the costs assigned to a specific job, starting when work begins. Also called *job-cost sheet*. (104)

Job-cost sheet. See *job-cost record*. (104)

Job-costing system. Costing system in which the cost object is a unit or multiple units of a distinct product or service called a job. (100)

Joint costs. Costs of a production process that yields multiple products simultaneously. (577)

Joint products. Two or more products that have high total sales values compared with the total sales values of other products yielded by a joint production process. (578)

Just-in-time (JIT) production. Demand-pull manufacturing system in which each component in a production line is produced as soon as, and only when, needed by the next step in the production line. Also called *lean production*. (715)

Just-in-time (JIT) purchasing. The purchase of materials (or goods) so that they are delivered just as needed for production (or sales). (711)

Kaizen budgeting. Budgetary approach that explicitly incorporates continuous improvement anticipated during the budget period into the budget numbers. (203)

Labor-time sheet. Source document that contains information about the amount of labor time used for a specific job in a specific department. (106)

Lean accounting. Costing method that supports creating value for the customer by costing the entire value stream, not individual products or departments, thereby eliminating waste in the accounting process. (727)

Lean production. See *just-in-time (JIT) production*. (715)

Learning. Involves managers examining past performance and systematically exploring alternative ways to make better-informed decisions and plans in the future. (10)

Learning curve. Function that measures how labor-hours per unit decline as units of production increase because workers are learning and becoming better at their jobs. (358)

Life-cycle budgeting. Budget that estimates the revenues and business function costs of the value chain attributable to each product from initial R&D to final customer service and support. (448)

Life-cycle costing. System that tracks and accumulates business function costs of the value chain attributable to each product from initial R&D to final customer service and support. (448)

Line management. Managers (for example, in production, marketing, or distribution) who are directly responsible for attaining the goals of the organization. (13)

Linear cost function. Cost function in which the graph of total costs versus the level of a single activity related to that cost is a straight line within the relevant range. (342)

Linear programming (LP). Optimization technique used to maximize an objective function (for example, contribution margin of a mix of products), when there are multiple constraints. (417)

Locked-in costs. Costs that have not yet been incurred but, based on decisions that have already been made, will be incurred in the future. Also called *designed-in costs*. (442)

Main product. Product from a joint production process that has a high total sales value compared with the total sales values of all other products of the joint production process. (578)

Make-or-buy decisions. Decisions about whether a producer of goods or services will insource (produce goods or services within the firm) or outsource (purchase them from outside vendors). (397)

Management accounting. Measures, analyzes, and reports financial and nonfinancial information that helps managers make decisions to fulfill the goals of an organization. It focuses on internal reporting. (4)

Management by exception. Practice of focusing management attention on areas not operating as expected and giving less attention to areas operating as expected. (227)

Management control system. Means of gathering and using information to aid and coordinate the planning and control decisions throughout an organization and to guide the behavior of its managers and employees. (775)

Manufacturing cells. Grouping of all the different types of equipment used to make a given product. (715)

Manufacturing cycle efficiency (MCE). Value-added manufacturing time divided by manufacturing cycle time. (681)

Manufacturing cycle time. See *manufacturing lead time*. (681)

Manufacturing lead time. Duration between the time an order is received by manufacturing to the time a finished good is produced. Also called *manufacturing cycle time*. (681)

Manufacturing overhead allocated. Amount of manufacturing overhead costs allocated to individual jobs, products, or services based on the budgeted rate multiplied by the actual quantity used of the cost-allocation base. Also called *manufacturing overhead applied*. (113)

Manufacturing overhead applied. See *manufacturing overhead allocated*. (113)

Manufacturing overhead costs. See *indirect manufacturing costs*. (37)

Manufacturing-sector companies. Companies that purchase materials and components and convert them into various finished goods. (36)

Margin of safety. Amount by which budgeted (or actual) revenues exceed breakeven revenues. (74)

Marketing. Promoting and selling products or services to customers or prospective customers. (6)

Market-share variance. The difference in budgeted contribution margin for actual market size in units caused solely by actual market share being different from budgeted market share. (249)

Market-size variance. The difference in budgeted contribution margin at the budgeted market share caused solely by actual market size in units being different from budgeted market size in units. (249)

Master budget. Expression of management's operating and financial plans for a specified period (usually a fiscal year) including a set of budgeted financial statements. Also called *pro forma statements*. (185)

Master-budget capacity utilization. The expected level of capacity utilization for the current budget period (typically one year). (315)

Materials requirements planning (MRP). Push-through system that manufactures finished goods for inventory on the basis of demand forecasts. (714)

Materials-requisition record. Source document that contains information about the cost of direct materials used on a specific job and in a specific department. (105)

Matrix method. See *reciprocal method*. (554)

Merchandising-sector companies. Companies that purchase and then sell tangible products without changing their basic form. (36)

Mixed cost. A cost that has both fixed and variable elements. Also called a *semivariable cost*. (343)

Moral hazard. Describes situations in which an employee prefers to exert less effort (or to report distorted information) compared with the effort (or accurate information) desired by the owner because the employee's effort (or validity of the reported information) cannot be accurately monitored and enforced. (822)

Motivation. The desire to attain a selected goal (the goal-congruence aspect) combined with the resulting pursuit of that goal (the effort aspect). (776)

Multicollinearity. Exists when two or more independent variables in a multiple regression model are highly correlated with each other. (374)

Multiple regression. Regression model that estimates the relationship between the dependent variable and two or more independent variables. (352)

Net income. Operating income plus nonoperating revenues (such as interest revenue) minus nonoperating costs (such as interest cost) minus income taxes. (70)

Net present value (NPV) method. Capital budgeting discounted cash flow (DCF) method that calculates the expected monetary gain or loss from a project by discounting all expected future cash inflows and outflows to the present point in time, using the required rate of return. (742)

Net realizable value (NRV) method. Method that allocates joint costs to joint products on the basis of final sales value minus separable costs of total production of the joint products during the accounting period. (583)

Nominal rate of return. Made up of three elements: (a) a risk-free element when there is no expected inflation, (b) a business-risk element, and (c) an inflation element. (762)

Nonlinear cost function. Cost function in which the graph of total costs based on the level of a single activity is not a straight line within the relevant range. (357)

Nonvalue-added cost. A cost that, if eliminated, would not reduce the actual or perceived value or utility (usefulness) customers obtain from using the product or service. (442)

Normal capacity utilization. The level of capacity utilization that satisfies average customer demand over a period (say, two to three years) that includes seasonal, cyclical, and trend factors. (315)

Normal costing. A costing system that traces direct costs to a cost object by using the actual direct-cost rates times the actual quantities of the direct-cost inputs and that allocates indirect costs based on the budgeted indirect-cost rates times the actual quantities of the cost-allocation bases. (104)

Normal spoilage. Spoilage inherent in a particular production process that arises even under efficient operating conditions. (646)

Objective function. Expresses the objective to be maximized (for example, operating income) or minimized (for example, operating costs) in a decision model (for example, a linear programming model). (416)

On-time performance. Delivering a product or service by the time it is scheduled to be delivered. (682)

One-time-only special order. Orders that have no long-run implications. (394)

Operating budget. Budgeted income statement and its supporting budget schedules. (189)

Operating department. Department that directly adds value to a product or service. Also called a *production department* in manufacturing companies. (543)

Operating income. Total revenues from operations minus cost of goods sold and operating costs (excluding interest expense and income taxes). (42)

Operating-income volume variance. The difference between static-budget operating income and the operating income based on budgeted profit per unit and actual units of output. (281)

Operating leverage. Effects that fixed costs have on changes in operating income as changes occur in units sold and hence in contribution margin. (76)

Operation. A standardized method or technique that is performed repetitively, often on different materials, resulting in different finished goods. (626)

Operation-costing system. Hybrid-costing system applied to batches of similar, but not identical, products. Each batch of products is often a variation of a single design, and it proceeds through a sequence of operations, but each batch does not necessarily move through the same operations as other batches. Within each operation, all product units use identical amounts of the operation's resources. (626)

Opportunity cost. The contribution to operating income that is forgone or rejected by not using a limited resource in its next-best alternative use. (402)

Opportunity cost of capital. See *required rate of return (RRR)*. (742)

Ordering costs. Costs of preparing, issuing, and paying purchase orders, plus receiving and inspecting the items included in the orders. (704)

Organization structure. Arrangement of lines of responsibility within the organization. (199)

Outcomes. Predicted economic results of the various possible combinations of actions and events in a decision model. (85)

Output unit-level costs. The costs of activities performed on each individual unit of a product or service. (149)

Outsourcing. Process of purchasing goods and services from outside vendors rather than producing the same goods or providing the same services within the organization. (397)

Overabsorbed indirect costs. See *overallocated indirect costs*. (118)

Overallocated indirect costs. Allocated amount of indirect costs in an accounting period is greater than the actual (incurred) amount in that period. Also called *overapplied indirect costs* and *overabsorbed indirect costs*. (118)

Overapplied indirect costs. See *overallocated indirect costs*. (118)

Overtime premium. Wage rate paid to workers (for both direct labor and indirect labor) in excess of their straight-time wage rates. (44)

Pareto diagram. Chart that indicates how frequently each type of defect occurs, ordered from the most frequent to the least frequent. (676)

Partial productivity. Measures the quantity of output produced divided by the quantity of an individual input used. (493)

Payback method. Capital budgeting method that measures the time it will take to recoup, in the form of expected future cash flows, the net initial investment in a project. (746)

Peak-load pricing. Practice of charging a higher price for the same product or service when the demand for it approaches the physical limit of the capacity to produce that product or service. (450)

Perfectly competitive market. Exists when there is a homogeneous product with buying prices equal to selling prices and no individual buyers or sellers can affect those prices by their own actions. (784)

Period costs. All costs in the income statement other than cost of goods sold. (38)

Physical-measure method. Method that allocates joint costs to joint products on the basis of the relative weight, volume, or other physical measure at the splitoff point of total production of these products during the accounting period. (582)

Planning. Selecting organization goals, predicting results under various alternative ways of achieving those goals, deciding how to attain the desired goals, and communicating the goals and how to attain them to the entire organization. (10)

Practical capacity. The level of capacity that reduces theoretical capacity by unavoidable operating interruptions such as scheduled maintenance time, shutdowns for holidays, and so on. (315)

Predatory pricing. Company deliberately prices below its costs in an effort to drive out competitors and restrict supply and then raises prices rather than enlarge demand. (451)

Prevention costs. Costs incurred to preclude the production of products that do not conform to specifications. (673)

Previous-department costs. See *transferred-in costs*. (621)

Price discount. Reduction in selling price below list selling price to encourage increases in customer purchases. (511)

Price discrimination. Practice of charging different customers different prices for the same product or service. (450)

Price-recovery component. Change in operating income attributable solely to changes in prices of inputs and outputs between one period and the next. (479)

Price variance. The difference between actual price and budgeted price multiplied by actual quantity of input. Also called *input-price variance* or *rate variance*. (236)

Prime costs. All direct manufacturing costs. (43)

Pro forma statements. Budgeted financial statements. (185)

Probability. Likelihood or chance that an event will occur. (84)

Probability distribution. Describes the likelihood (or the probability) that each of the mutually exclusive and collectively exhaustive set of events will occur. (84)

Process-costing system. Costing system in which the cost object is masses of identical or similar units of a product or service. (101)

Product. Any output that has a positive total sales value (or an output that enables an organization to avoid incurring costs). (578)

Product cost. Sum of the costs assigned to a product for a specific purpose. (45)

Product-cost cross-subsidization. Costing outcome where one undercosted (overcosted) product results in at least one other product being overcosted (undercosted). (140)

Product differentiation. Organization's ability to offer products or services perceived by its customers to be superior and unique relative to the products or services of its competitors. (468)

Product life cycle. Spans the time from initial R&D on a product to when customer service and support is no longer offered for that product. (447)

Product-mix decisions. Decisions about which products to sell and in what quantities. (405)

Product overcosting. A product consumes a low level of resources but is reported to have a high cost per unit. (140)

Product-sustaining costs. The costs of activities undertaken to support individual products regardless of the number of units or batches in which the units are produced. (149)

Product undercosting. A product consumes a high level of resources but is reported to have a low cost per unit. (140)

Production. Acquiring, coordinating, and assembling resources to produce a product or deliver a service. (6)

Production-denominator level. The denominator in the budgeted manufacturing fixed overhead rate computation. (266)

Production department. See *operating department*. (543)

Production-volume variance. The difference between budgeted fixed overhead and fixed overhead allocated on the basis of actual output produced. Also called *denominator-level variance*. (272)

Productivity. Measures the relationship between actual inputs used (both quantities and costs) and actual outputs produced; the lower the inputs for a given quantity of outputs or the higher the outputs for a given quantity of inputs, the higher the productivity. (492)

Productivity component. Change in costs attributable to a change in the quantity of inputs used in the current period relative to the quantity of inputs that would have been used in the prior period to produce the quantity of current period output. (479)

Profit center. Responsibility center where the manager is accountable for revenues and costs. (199)

Proration. The spreading of underallocated manufacturing overhead or overallocated manufacturing overhead among ending work in process, finished goods, and cost of goods sold. (119)

Purchase-order lead time. The time between placing an order and its delivery. (704)

Purchasing costs. Cost of goods acquired from suppliers including incoming freight or transportation costs. (703)

PV graph. Shows how changes in the quantity of units sold affect operating income. (70)

Qualitative factors. Outcomes that are difficult to measure accurately in numerical terms. (394)

Quality. The total features and characteristics of a product made or a service performed according to specifications to satisfy customers at the time of purchase and during use. (671)

Quantitative factors. Outcomes that are measured in numerical terms. (394)

Rate variance. See *price variance*. (236)

Real rate of return. The rate of return demanded to cover investment risk (with no inflation). It has a risk-free element and a business-risk element. (762)

Reciprocal method. Cost allocation method that fully recognizes the mutual services provided among all support departments. Also called *matrix method*. (553)

Reengineering. The fundamental rethinking and redesign of business processes to achieve improvements in critical measures of performance, such as cost, quality, service, speed, and customer satisfaction. (469)

Refined costing system. Costing system that reduces the use of broad averages for assigning the cost of resources to cost objects (jobs, products, services) and provides better measurement of the costs of indirect resources used by different cost objects—no matter how differently various cost objects use indirect resources. (145)

Regression analysis. Statistical method that measures the average amount of change in the dependent variable associated with a unit change in one or more independent variables. (352)

Relevant costs. Expected future costs that differ among alternative courses of action being considered. (393)

Relevant range. Band of normal activity level or volume in which there is a specific relationship between the level of activity or volume and the cost in question. (33)

Relevant revenues. Expected future revenues that differ among alternative courses of action being considered. (393)

Reorder point. The quantity level of inventory on hand that triggers a new purchase order. (707)

Required rate of return (RRR). The minimum acceptable annual rate of return on an investment. Also called the *discount rate*, *hurdle rate*, *cost of capital*, or *opportunity cost of capital*. (742)

Research and development. Generating and experimenting with ideas related to new products, services, or processes. (6)

Residual income (RI). Accounting measure of income minus a dollar amount for required return on an accounting measure of investment. (810)

Residual term. The vertical difference or distance between actual cost and estimated cost for each observation in a regression model. (352)

Responsibility accounting. System that measures the plans, budgets, actions, and actual results of each responsibility center. (199)

Responsibility center. Part, segment, or subunit of an organization whose manager is accountable for a specified set of activities. (199)

Return on investment (ROI). An accounting measure of income divided by an accounting measure of investment. See also *accrual accounting rate of return method*. (809)

Revenue allocation. The allocation of revenues that are related to a particular revenue object but cannot be traced to it in an economically feasible (cost-effective) way. (561)

Revenue center. Responsibility center where the manager is accountable for revenues only. (199)

Revenue driver. A variable, such as volume, that causally affects revenues. (68)

Revenue object. Anything for which a separate measurement of revenue is desired. (561)

Revenues. Inflows of assets (usually cash or accounts receivable) received for products or services provided to customers. (38)

Rework. Units of production that do not meet the specifications required by customers for finished units that are subsequently repaired and sold as good finished units. (645)

Rightsizing. See *downsizing*. (487)

Rolling budget. Budget or plan that is always available for a specified future period by adding a period (month, quarter, or year) to the period that just ended. Also called *continuous budget*. (188)

Safety stock. Inventory held at all times regardless of the quantity of inventory ordered using the EOQ model. (707)

Sales mix. Quantities of various products or services that constitute total unit sales. (77)

Sales-mix variance. The difference between (1) budgeted contribution margin for the actual sales mix, and (2) budgeted contribution margin for the budgeted sales mix. (521)

Sales-quantity variance. The difference between (1) budgeted contribution margin based on actual units sold of all products at the budgeted mix and (2) contribution margin in the static budget (which is based on the budgeted units of all products to be sold at the budgeted mix). (521)

Sales value at splitoff method. Method that allocates joint costs to joint products on the basis of the relative total sales value at the splitoff point of the total production of these products during the accounting period. (580)

Sales-volume variance. The difference between a flexible-budget amount and the corresponding static-budget amount. (231)

Scrap. Residual material left over when making a product. (645)

Selling-price variance. The difference between the actual selling price and the budgeted selling price multiplied by the actual units sold. (233)

Semivariable cost. See *mixed cost*. (343)

Sensitivity analysis. A what-if technique that managers use to calculate how an outcome will change if the original predicted data are not achieved or if an underlying assumption changes. (73)

Separable costs. All costs (manufacturing, marketing, distribution, and so on) incurred beyond the splitoff point that are assignable to each of the specific products identified at the splitoff point. (577)

Sequential allocation method. See *step-down method*. (552)

Sequential tracking. Approach in a product-costing system in which recording of the journal entries occurs in the same order as actual purchases and progress in production. (718)

Service department. See *support department*. (543)

Service-sector companies. Companies that provide services or intangible products to their customers. (36)

Service-sustaining costs. The costs of activities undertaken to support individual services. (149)

Shrinkage costs. Costs that result from theft by outsiders, embezzlement by employees, misclassifications, and clerical errors. (704)

Simple regression. Regression model that estimates the relationship between the dependent variable and one independent variable. (352)

Single-rate method. Allocation method that allocates costs in each cost pool to cost objects using the same rate per unit of a single allocation base. (544)

Slope coefficient. Coefficient term in a cost estimation model that indicates the amount by which total cost changes when a one-unit change occurs in the level of activity within the relevant range. (342)

Source document. An original record that supports journal entries in an accounting system. (104)

Specification analysis. Testing of the assumptions of regression analysis. (369)

Splitoff point. The juncture in a joint-production process when two or more products become separately identifiable. (577)

Spoilage. Units of production that do not meet the specifications required by customers for good units and that are discarded or sold at reduced prices. (645)

Staff management. Staff (such as management accountants and human resources managers) who provide advice and assistance to line management. (13)

Stand-alone cost-allocation method. Method that uses information pertaining to each user of a cost object as a separate entity to determine the cost-allocation weights. (557)

Stand-alone revenue-allocation method. Method that uses product-specific information on the products in the bundle as weights for allocating the bundled revenues to the individual products. (561)

Standard. A carefully determined price, cost, or quantity that is used as a benchmark for judging performance. It is usually expressed on a per unit basis. (234)

Standard cost. A carefully determined cost of a unit of output. (235)

Standard costing. Costing system that traces direct costs to output produced by multiplying the standard prices or rates by the standard quantities of inputs allowed for actual outputs produced and allocates overhead costs on the basis of the standard overhead-cost rates times the standard quantities of the allocation bases allowed for the actual outputs produced. (264)

Standard error of the estimated coefficient. Regression statistic that indicates how much the estimated value of the coefficient is likely to be affected by random factors. (368)

Standard error of the regression. Statistic that measures the variance of residuals in a regression analysis. (368)

Standard input. A carefully determined quantity of input required for one unit of output. (235)

Standard price. A carefully determined price that a company expects to pay for a unit of input. (235)

Static budget. Budget based on the level of output planned at the start of the budget period. (229)

Static-budget variance. Difference between an actual result and the corresponding budgeted amount in the static budget. (229)

Step cost function. A cost function in which the cost remains the same over various ranges of the level of activity, but the cost increases by discrete amounts (that is, increases in steps) as the level of activity changes from one range to the next. (357)

Step-down method. Cost allocation method that partially recognizes the mutual services provided among all support departments. Also called *sequential allocation method*. (552)

Stockout costs. Costs that result when a company runs out of a particular item for which there is customer demand. The company must act to meet that demand or suffer the costs of not meeting it. (704)

Strategic cost management. Describes cost management that specifically focuses on strategic issues. (5)

Strategy. Specifies how an organization matches its own capabilities with the opportunities in the marketplace to accomplish its objectives. (5)

Strategy map. A diagram that describes how an organization creates value by connecting strategic objectives in explicit cause-and-effect relationships with each other in the financial, customer, internal business process, and learning and growth perspectives. (471)

Suboptimal decision making. Decisions in which the benefit to one subunit is more than offset by the costs or loss of benefits to the organization as a whole. Also called *incongruent decision making* or *dysfunctional decision making*. (778)

Sunk costs. Past costs that are unavoidable because they cannot be changed no matter what action is taken. (393)

Super-variable costing. See *throughput costing*. (312)

Supply chain. Describes the flow of goods, services, and information from the initial sources of materials and services to the delivery of products to consumers, regardless of whether those activities occur in the same organization or in other organizations. (7)

Support department. Department that provides the services that assist other internal departments (operating departments and other support departments) in the company. Also called a *service department*. (543)

Target cost per unit. Estimated long-run cost per unit of a product or service that enables the company to achieve its target operating income per unit when selling at the target price. Target cost per unit is derived by subtracting the target operating income per unit from the target price. (440)

Target operating income per unit. Operating income that a company aims to earn per unit of a product or service sold. (440)

Target price. Estimated price for a product or service that potential customers will pay. (439)

Target rate of return on investment. The target annual operating income that an organization aims to achieve divided by invested capital. (446)

Theoretical capacity. The level of capacity based on producing at full efficiency all the time. (314)

Theory of constraints (TOC). Describes methods to maximize operating income when faced with some bottleneck and some nonbottleneck operations. (686)

Throughput costing. Method of inventory costing in which only variable direct material costs are included as inventoriable costs. Also called *super-variable costing*. (312)

Throughput margin. Revenues minus the direct material costs of the goods sold. (686)

Subject